16 edition

Fundamental Accounting Principles

Kermit D. Larson
University of Texas at Austin

John J. Wild
University of Wisconsin at Madison

Barbara Chiappetta
Nassau Community College

McGraw-Hill Irwin

Boston   Burr Ridge, IL   Dubuque, IA   Madison, WI   New York
San Francisco   St. Louis   Bangkok   Bogotá   Caracas   Kuala   Lumpur
Lisbon   London   Madrid   Mexico City   Milan   Montreal   New   Delhi
Santiago   Seoul   Singapore   Sydney   Taipei   Toronto

To my wife **Nancy.**

To my wife **Gail** and children, **Kimberly, Jonathan, Stephanie,** and **Trevor.**

To my husband **Bob,** my sons **Michael** and **David,** and my **mother.**

McGraw-Hill Higher Education

*A Division of The **McGraw-Hill** Companies*

FUNDAMENTAL ACCOUNTING PRINCIPLES

Published by McGraw-Hill/Irwin, an imprint of The McGraw-Hill Companies, Inc. 1221 Avenue of the Americas, New York, NY, 10020. Copyright © 2002, 1999, 1996, 1993, 1990, 1987, 1984, 1981, 1978, 1975, 1972, 1969, 1966, 1963, 1959, 1955, by The McGraw-Hill Companies, Inc. All rights reserved. No part of this publication may be reproduced or distributed in any form or by any means, or stored in a database or retrieval system, without the prior written consent of The McGraw-Hill Companies, Inc., including, but not limited to, in any network or other electronic storage or transmission, or broadcast for distance learning.

Some ancillaries, including electronic and print components, may not be available to customers outside the United States.

This book is printed on acid-free paper.

domestic   1 2 3 4 5 6 7 8 9 0 VNH/VNH 0 9 8 7 6 5 4 3 2 1
international   1 2 3 4 5 6 7 8 9 0 VNH/VNH 0 9 8 7 6 5 4 3 2 1

ISBN 0-07-242339-0 (complete text)
ISBN 0-07-246466-6 (Volume 1)
ISBN 0-07-246467-4 (Volume 2)
ISBN 0-07-246495-X (Volume 1, Instructor's Edition)
ISBN 0-07-246468-2 (Financial Chapters, Chapters 1–18)

Publisher: *Brent Gordon*
Sponsoring editor: *Melody Marcus*
Developmental editors: *Tracey Douglas/Kristin Leahy/Jackie Scruggs*
Editorial assistant: *Kelly Odom*
Marketing manager: *Rich Kolasa*
Senior project manager: *Kimberly D. Hooker*
Senior production supervisor: *Michael McCormick*
Senior designer: *Jennifer McQueen*
Photo research coordinator: *Judy Kausal*
Photo researcher: *Charlotte Goldman*
Lead supplement coordinator: *Becky Szura*
Media technology producers: *Edward Przyzycki/Todd Labak*
Cover illustration: *Tom Nemoda/Asylum Studios*
Compositor: **TECH**BOOKS
Typeface: *10.5/12 Times Roman*
Printer: *Von Hoffman Press, Inc.*

Library of Congress Cataloging-in-Publication Data

Larson, Kermit D.
    Fundamental accounting principles / Kermit D. Larson, John J. Wild, Barbara Chiappetta.—16th ed.
        p. cm.
    Includes bibliographical references and index.
    ISBN 0-07-242339-0 (alk. paper)
    1. Accounting. I. Wild, John J. II. Chiappetta, Barbara. III. Title.
HF5635.P975 2002
657—dc21   2001030128

INTERNATIONAL EDITION ISBN 0-07-112222-2

Copyright © 2002. Exclusive rights by The McGraw-Hill Companies, Inc. for manufacture and export. This book cannot be re-exported from the country to which it is sold by McGraw-Hill. The International Edition is not available in North America.

ABOUT THE AUTHORS

KERMIT D. LARSON is the Arthur Andersen & Co. Alumni Professor of Accounting Emeritus at the University of Texas at Austin. He served as chairman of the University of Texas, Department of Accounting and was visiting associate professor at Tulane University. His scholarly articles have been published in a variety of journals, including *The Accounting Review, Journal of Accountancy,* and *Abacus.* He is the author of several books, including *Financial Accounting* and *Fundamentals of Financial and Managerial Accounting,* both published by McGraw-Hill/Irwin.

Professor Larson is a member of the American Accounting Association, the Texas Society of CPAs, and the American Institute of CPAs. His positions with the AAA have included vice president, southwest regional vice president, and chairperson of several committees, including the Committee of Concepts and Standards. He was a member of the committee that planned the first AAA doctoral consortium and served as its director.

Professor Larson served as president of the Richard D. Irwin Foundation. He also served on the Accounting Accreditation Committee and on the Accounting Standards Committee of the AACSB. He was a member of the Constitutional Drafting Committee of the Federation of Schools of Accountancy and a member of the Commission on Professional Accounting Education. He has been an expert witness on cases involving mergers, antitrust litigation, consolidation criteria, franchise taxes, and expropriation of assets by foreign governments. Professor Larson served on the Board of Directors and Executive Committee of Tekcon, Inc., and on the National Accountants Advisory Board of Safe-Guard Business Systems. In his leisure time, he enjoys skiing and is an avid sailor and golfer.

JOHN J. WILD is a professor of business and the Vilas Research Scholar at the University of Wisconsin at Madison. He has previously held appointments at Michigan State University and the University of Manchester in England. He received his BBA, MS, and PhD from the University of Wisconsin.

Professor Wild teaches courses at both the undergraduate and graduate levels. He has received the Mabel W. Chipman Excellence-in-Teaching Award and the departmental Excellence-in-Teaching Award at the University of Wisconsin. He also received the Beta Alpha Psi and Roland F. Salmonson Excellence-in Teaching Award from Michigan State University. Professor Wild is a past KPMG Peat Marwick National Fellow and is a recipient of fellowships from the American Accounting Association and the Ernst and Young Foundation.

Professor Wild is an active member of the American Accounting Association and its sections. He has served on several notable committees of these organizations, including the Outstanding Accounting Educator Award, National Program Advisory, Publications, and Research Committees. Professor Wild is author of *Financial Statement Analysis* and *Financial Accounting: Information for Decisions,* both published by McGraw-Hill/Irwin. His research publications appear in *The Accounting Review, Journal of Accounting Research, Journal of Accounting and Economics, Contemporary Accounting Research, Journal of Accounting, Auditing and Finance, Journal of Accounting and Public Policy,* and other business periodicals. He is associate editor of *Contemporary Accounting Research* and has served on several editorial boards including *The Accounting Review.*

Professor Wild, his wife, and four children enjoy travel, music, sports, and community activities.

BARBARA CHIAPPETTA received her BBA in Accountancy and MS in Education from Hofstra University and is a tenured full professor at Nassau Community College. For the past 20 years, she has been an active executive board member of the Teachers of Accounting at Two-Year Colleges (TACTYC), serving 10 years as vice president and 5 years as president. As an active member of the American Accounting Association, she has served on the Northeast Regional Steering Committee, chaired the Curriculum Revision Committee of the Two-Year Section, and participated in numerous national committees. In April 1998, Professor Chiappetta was inducted into the American Accounting Association Hall of Fame for the Northeast Region. She received the Nassau Community College dean of instruction's Faculty Distinguished Achievement Award in the spring of 1995. Professor Chiappetta was honored with the State University of New York Chancellor's Award for Teaching Excellence in 1997. As a confirmed believer in the benefits of the active learning pedagogy, Professor Chiappetta has authored *Student Learning Tools,* an active learning workbook for a first-year accounting course, published by McGraw-Hill/Irwin.

In her leisure time, Professor Chiappetta enjoys tennis and participates on a U.S.T.A. team. She also enjoys the challenge of bridge. Her husband, Robert, is an entrepreneur in the leisure sport industry. She has two sons—Michael, a lawyer, currently practicing in New York City, and David, formerly lead guitarist in the rock band Blindman's Sun and currently pursuing a career in film scoring.

PUTTING THE STUDENT
ON A PEDESTAL

(handwritten notes) Read Chapter 4
Q 4-1 4-2
4-3 4-4

A WORD TO THE STUDENT

WHEN we set about revising FAP, we spoke to hundreds of educators throughout the country, listening to their thoughts about what worked in previous editions and what they felt could be improved. The experience they brought to us was born of countless hours of teaching, of helping students just like you to master what can be a challenging subject. They had a great deal to tell us and we listened.

(handwritten notes) Chapter 7
QS 7-5
7-10
7-6
Ex 7-5 A
7-6 A
7-9
Prob 7-5 A
7-6 A

NOW, after nearly two years of work, we present to you the **SIXTEENTH EDITION** of **FAP**. It is the result of a simple, guiding principle: **THE STUDENT COMES FIRST**. Every change to this edition, from the **ENTREPRENEURIAL FLAVOR** to the extensive use of helpful **STUDY AIDS**, is designed to make the principles of accounting easier for you to learn—and more fun too! You will encounter chapter-opening vignettes and "Did You Know" boxes containing names like eBay, FUBU, Birdhouse, NetLedger, Freeplay and Red Hat, **YOUNG COMPANIES** helping to shape the **NEW ECONOMY** in which you will soon **COMPETE FOR WORK**. You'll also notice a boxed feature entitled "You Make the Call" that challenges you to apply your understanding to a real-world situation.

(handwritten notes) Chapter 12
QS 12-3
12-4
12-7
Ex 12-7
12-8
Prob 12-5A
12-R

And we haven't stopped with the text. A new, 2-volume CD-ROM called **FAP Partner** offers additional help for the most challenging topics in the principles course while **NetTutor** gives you free, real-time access to an accounting expert ready to help you with any questions you have.

There's a great deal more to this edition of **FAP** as you'll discover when you read the following pages. We hope you'll agree that **Fundamental Accounting Principles** by **Larson, Wild, and Chiappetta** provides you with everything you need to master the principles of accounting.

Sincerely,

The McGraw-Hill/Irwin FAP Team

TECHNOLOGY SOLUTIONS
TO MEET EVERY NEED

TODAY, nearly **200,000** college instructors use the **INTERNET** in their respective courses. Some are just getting started, while others are **READY TO EMBRACE** the very latest advances in educational **CONTENT DELIVERY** and **COURSE MANAGEMENT**

That's why we at McGraw-Hill/Irwin offer you a complete range of digital solutions. Your students can use **FAP**'s complete Online Learning Center (OLC), NetTutor, and PowerWeb on their own or we can help you create your own course Web site using McGraw-Hill's PageOut. We can even help you achieve dot-com nirvana with your entire principles course online.

In addition to Web-based assets, **FAP** boasts CDs for students and instructors alike. Students in particular will be grateful for **FAP Partner,** the two-volume CD-ROM that offers special assistance for the most demanding principles of accounting topics. Instructors have access to nearly every crucial supplement, from the Instructor's Resource Manual to the PowerPoint slides, on both CD and the Internet.

McGraw-Hill is a leader in bringing helpful technology into the classroom. And with **FAP,** your class gets all the benefits of the digital age.

Concept 1-1

ONLINE LEARNING CENTER (OLC)

www.mhhe.com/FAP16e

More and more students are studying online. That's why we offer an **Online Learning Center (OLC)** that follows FAP chapter by chapter. It doesn't require any building or maintenance on your part.

It's ready to go the moment you and your students type in the address.

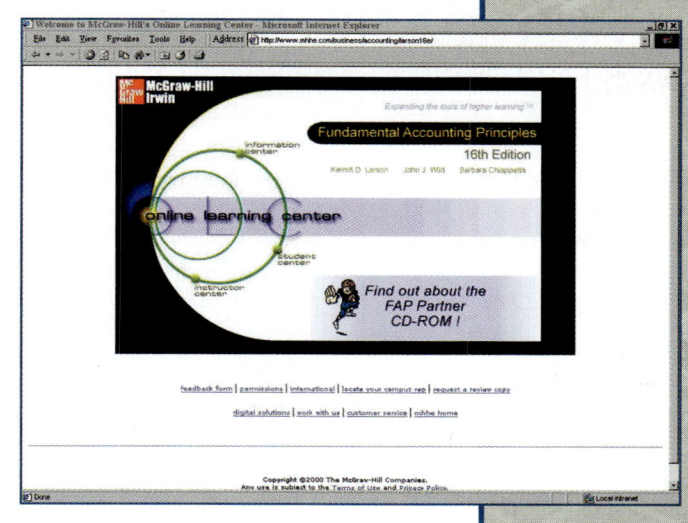

As your students study, they can refer to the OLC Web site for such benefits as:

- Internet-based activities
- self-grading quizzes
- links to text references
- links to professional resources on the Web and job opportunity information
- learning objectives
- chapter overviews

A secured Instructor Resource Center stores your essential course materials to save you prep time before class. The Instructor's Manual, Solutions, PowerPoint, and sample syllabi are now just a couple of clicks away. You will also find useful packaging information and transition notes.

The OLC Web site also serves as a doorway to other technology solutions like PageOut, NetTutor and PowerWeb which are free to **FAP** adopters.

COURSE MANAGEMENT

PAGEOUT

McGraw-Hill's Course Management System

PageOut is the easiest way to create a Web site for your accounting course.

There's no need for HTML coding, graphic design, or a thick how-to book. Just fill in a series of boxes with plain English and click on one of our professional designs. In no time, your course is online!

Should you need assistance in preparing your Web site, we can help you. In addition to many pre-built course Web sites, we offer a team of product specialists ready to help. Just send them your course materials, and after a brief phone consultation, they will build your PageOut Web site from scratch. (For information on how to do this, see "Superior Service" on the next page.)

PageOut is free when you adopt **FAP**! To learn more, please visit **http://www.pageout.net**.

THIRD-PARTY COURSE MANAGEMENT SYSTEMS

For the ambitious instructor, we offer **FAP** content for complete online courses. To make this possible, we have joined forces with the most popular delivery platforms currently available. These platforms are designed for instructors who want complete control over course content and how it is presented to students. You can customize the **FAP** Online Learning Center content and author your own course materials. It's entirely up to you.

Products like WebCT, Blackboard, eCollege, and TopClass (a product of WBT) all expand the reach of your course. Online discussion and message boards will now complement your office hours. Thanks to a sophisticated tracking system, you will know which students need more attention – even if they don't ask for help. That's because online testing scores are recorded and automatically placed in your grade book, and if a student is struggling with coursework, a special alert message lets you know.

Remember, **FAP**'s content is flexible enough to use with any platform currently available. If your department or school is already using a platform, we can help. For information on McGraw-Hill/Irwin's course management services, including Instructor Advantage and Knowledge Gateway, see "Superior Service" on the next page.

SUPERIOR SERVICE

No matter which online course solution you choose, you can count on the highest level of service. That's what sets McGraw-Hill apart. Once you choose FAP, our specialists offer free training and answer any question you have through the life of your adoption.

PAGEOUT

Now you can put your course online without knowing a word of HTML, using either our OLC content or your own content.

If you want a custom site but don't have time to build it yourself, we offer a team of specialists ready to help. Just call 1-800-541-7145, and ask to speak with a **PageOut** specialist. You will be asked to send in your course materials and then participate in a brief telephone consultation. Once we have your information, we build your Web site for you, from scratch.

INSTRUCTOR ADVANTAGE and
INSTRUCTOR ADVANTAGE PLUS

Instructor Advantage is a special level of service McGraw-Hill offers in conjunction with WebCT and Blackboard. A team of platform specialists is always available, either by toll-free phone or e-mail, to ensure everything runs smoothly through the life of your adoption. Instructor Advantage is available free to all McGraw-Hill customers.

Instructor Advantage Plus is available to qualifying McGraw-Hill adopters (see your representative for details). **IA Plus** guarantees you a full day of on-site training by a Blackboard or WebCT specialist, for yourself and up to nine colleagues. Thereafter, you will enjoy the benefits of unlimited telephone and e-mail support throughout the life of your adoption. **IA Plus** users also have the opportunity to access the **McGraw-Hill Knowledge Gateway** (see below).

KNOWLEDGE GATEWAY

Developed with the help of our partner Eduprise, the **McGraw-Hill Knowledge Gateway** is an all-purpose service and resource center for instructors teaching online.

The First Level of **Knowledge Gateway** is available to all professors browsing the McGraw-Hill Higher Education Website, and consists of an introduction to OLC content, access to the first level of the Resource Library, technical support, and information on Instructional Design Services available through Eduprise.

The Second Level is password-protected and provides access to the expanded Resource Library, technical and pedagogical support for WebCT, Blackboard, and TopClass, the online Instructional Design helpdesk and an online discussion forum for users. The **Knowledge Gateway** provides a considerable advantage for teaching online—and it's only available through McGraw-Hill.

To see how these platforms can assist your online course, visit **www.mhhe.com/solutions**.

NɛTUTOR

NetTutor allows students and tutors to communicate with each other in a variety of ways:

- The **Live Tutor Center** via NetTutor's WWWhiteboard enables a tutor to hold an interactive online tutorial with several students whose questions are placed in a queue and answered sequentially.

- The **Q&A Center** allows students to submit questions at any time and retrieve answers within 24 hours.

- The **Message Center*** is where students will be able to send questions, messages, and comments to other students and teachers.

- The **Archive Center** allows students to browse for answers to previously asked questions. They can also search for questions pertinent to a particular topic. If they encounter an answer they do not understand, they can ask a follow-up question.

- The **Management Center*** will make it easy to create, update, and delete groups and members as well as to customize the site to suit the needs of the group.

Students are issued 10 hours of free **NetTutor** time when they purchase a new copy of **FAP**. Additional time may be purchased in 5-hour increments. Live tutor availability will vary throughout the course of the term with a peak availability of around 60 hours a week.

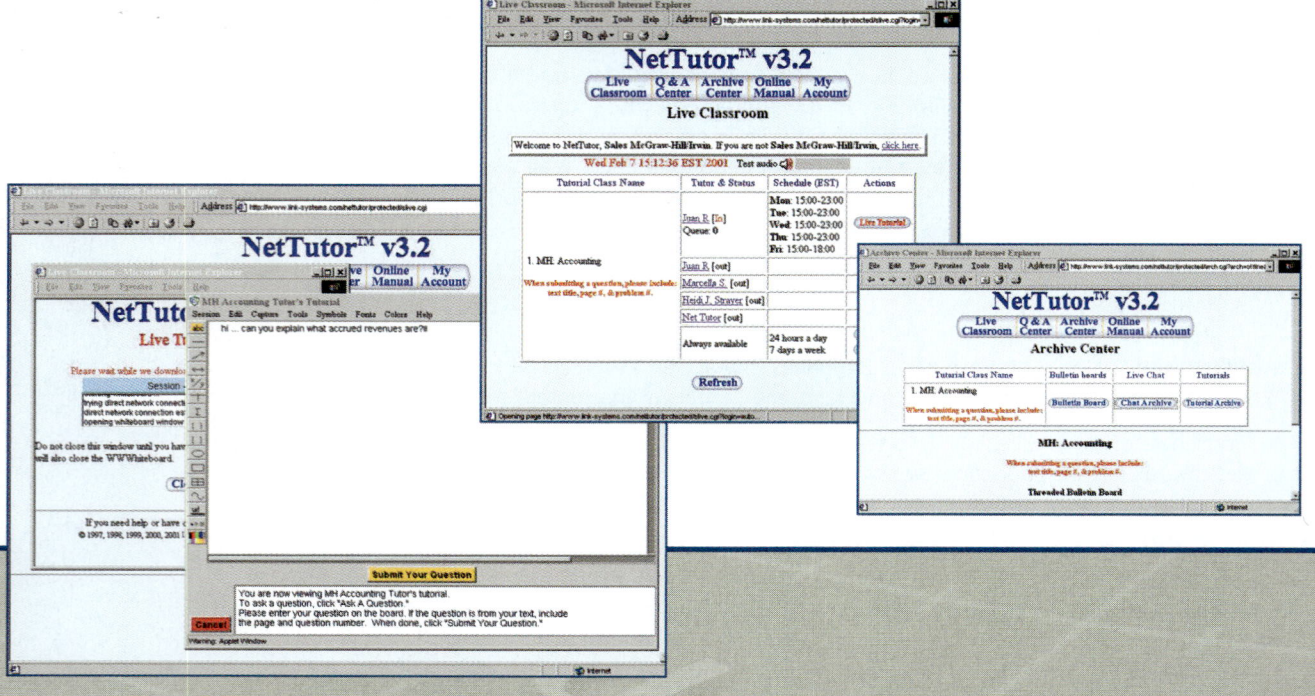

*Note: Certain **NetTutor** features marked by an asterisk (*) may not be available at the time of the book's initial publication.

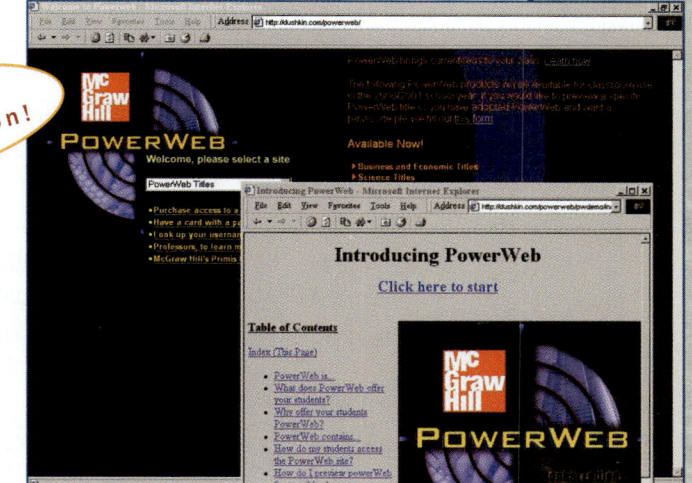

FREE
With Adoption!

POWERWEB

Keeping your course current can be a job
in itself and now McGraw-Hill does that job
for you. **PowerWeb** extends the learning
experience beyond the core textbook by offering all of the latest news and developments
pertinent to your course, brought to you via
the Internet without all the clutter and dead
links of a typical online search.

PowerWeb offers current articles related to principles of accounting, weekly
updates with assessment tools, informative and timely world news culled by an
accounting principles expert, refereed Web links, and more.

In addition, **PowerWeb** provides a trove of helpful learning aids, including self-
grading quizzes and interactive glossaries and exercises. Students may also access
study tips, conduct online research, and learn about different career paths.

Visit the **PowerWeb** site at **http://www.dushkin.com/powerweb**
and see firsthand what **PowerWeb** can mean to your course.

SOLID ACCOUNTING COVERAGE...

WE LISTENED! **IN ADDITION** to a number of reviewers, we held focus groups in cities around the country to learn what **INSTRUCTORS LIKE YOU** are thinking about in the principles of accounting course and the materials you use to teach it. John Wild attended every session to listen and ask questions. We got **FANTASTIC FEEDBACK** and our authors have integrated that feedback into this new edition of the text. We think you'll like what you see.

THROUGHOUT THE TEXT:

Increased coverage of e-business, the Web, and entrepreneurship as related to accounting is integrated throughout the text as appropriate. Following are *some* content revisions:

Chapter 1

JobDirect **NEW opener**

New, early introduction to financial statements

Revised motivation on the relevance of accounting

Revised section on accounting and related careers

New table on compensation in accounting careers

Chapter 2

Simplified transaction analysis with accounting equation

Early introduction to statement of cash flows

Revised Nintendo financials

Top 10 list of key entrepreneurial qualities

Chapter 3

Creative Assets **NEW opener**

Streamlined section on using T-Accounts

Shortened section on posting of transactions

New discussion of using entries to analyze transactions

Chapter 4

CrossWorlds **NEW opener**

Revised presentation on accounting adjustments

Streamlined discussion of the adjusting process

Chapter 5

Red Hat **NEW opener**

Shortened section on closing entries

New Excel screen captures with acetates for work sheet

Streamlined section on account numbering system

Chapter 6

Wooden Ships of Hoboken **NEW opener**

Simplified presentation of income statement formats

Streamlined section on merchandising cash flows

Chapter 7

FUBU **NEW opener**

Streamlined presentation of gross profit method

Toys "R" Us **Updated**

Chapter 8

NetLedger **NEW opener**

More discussion on Web-based accounting

New simplified visuals for special journals (using PeachTree screen captures)

Revised special journals using perpetual inventory system

Streamlined coverage of special journals

New analysis of Harley-Davidson segments

Chapter 9

eBay **NEW opener**

New feature on cyber fraud

Shortened discussion of voucher system of control

Chapter 10

Tarina Tarantino **NEW opener**

Streamlined discussion on full disclosure principle

Dell and Apple **Updated**

Chapter 11

Papa John's **NEW opener**

Streamlined discussion of partial-year depreciation

Shortened and simplified section on "Revenue and Capital Expenditures"

Deleted section on exchange of dissimilar assets

Coors and Anheuser-Busch **Updated**

Chapter 12

Sector 9 **NEW opener**

New section on employee bonus plans

Shortened section on "Income Tax Liabilities"

Best Buy **Updated**

Revised appendix on payroll records

Chapter 13

AltiTUNES **NEW opener**

Expanded discussion of limited liability companies

New section on partnership return on equity

Boston Celtics revised feature

Chapter 14

World Wrestling Federation **NEW opener**

Deleted section on "Issuing Stock through Subscriptions"

Streamlined section on participating and nonparticipating preferred stock dividends

Deleted the Dividends Declared account to streamline journal entries for cash (and stock) dividends

Deleted the section on "Liquidating Cash Dividends"

Shortened section on "Discontinued Segments"

Simplified section on "Changes in Accounting Principles"

Streamlined section on diluted earnings per share

Shortened sections on book value per share and dividend yield

Chapter 15

David Bowie Bonds **NEW opener**

Streamlined Appendix on "Present Values of Bonds and Notes"

New Appendix 15B on "Leases and Pensions"

Chapter 16

Freeplay **NEW opener**

New illustrations on adjustments for unrealized gains and losses on securities

Chapter 17

Interactive Sports **NEW opener**

Simplified preparation of the statement of cash flows

Shortened section on "Analyzing Cash Sources and Uses"

Chapter 18

Nike vs. Reebok **Updated**

Revised discussion on comparative analysis (benchmarking)

Streamlined section on "Working Capital and Current Ratio"

Chapter 19

American Paper Optics **NEW opener**

New section on "Lean Business Model"

Shortened discussion on manufacturing management principles

Expanded discussion of service businesses

New presentation of manufacturing statement

Chapter 20

i-FRONTIER **NEW opener**

Moved manufacturing statement to Chapter 19

Simplified section on "Overapplied and Underapplied Overhead"

Deleted section on "Multiple Overhead Allocation Rates"

New section on costing and pricing for service businesses

Moved Appendix 20A on General Accounting System to the Web

Chapter 21

INCA **NEW opener**

New footnote illustration of process costing using weighted-average method

Deleted section on "Spoiled Units of Production"

New section on "Hybrid Costing"

Chapter 22

Kate Spade **NEW opener**

Simplified discussion of "Activity-Based Costing"

Streamlined sections on "Departmental Accounting"

Chapter 23

Latham Entertainment **NEW opener**

Streamlined section on "Assumptions of CVP Analysis"

Chapter 24

Birdhouse **NEW opener**

Deleted section on "Zero-Based Budgeting"

Streamlined section on the budgeted balance sheet

New section on "Activity-Based Budgeting"

Chapter 25

Toes on the Noes **NEW opener**

New discussion of service applications

Chapter 26

Leading Edge Aviation Services **NEW opener**

New applications to service businesses

...SET IN A MODERN FRAMEWORK

An Entrepreneurial Icon calls out all relevant material within the chapters, whether an opening vignette, box, or end-of-chapter assignment.

ENTREPRENEURIAL CHAPTER-OPENERS

These opening vignettes focus on young entrepreneurs and the relevance of accounting in their business decisions. We highlight companies like eBay, FUBU, Red Hat, NetLedger, JobDirect, Sector 9, Kate Spade, INCA, Birdhouse, Freeplay, and WWF—names that students will recognize from magazines, newspapers, television, and the Internet. The openers discuss how accounting information and an understanding of it aided these start-ups in successfully launching and running their operations. They serve as excellent motivators—showing the importance of accounting in business.

ENTREPRENEURIAL FLAVOR — NEW

Today's students live in a world where start-up companies have redefined traditional notions of success in business. To reflect this shift, **FAP** integrates ideas and practices followed by today's entrepreneurs, speaking more directly to students and better preparing them for the workforce they will enter. **This approach is distinctive in the accounting principles market**.

FAP weaves the entrepreneurial flavor throughout the text in a variety of ways.

9

Cash and Internal Control

"I hope to make it easier to conduct business with strangers over the Net."—Pierre Omidyar

A Look Back

Chapter 8 focused on accounting information systems. We explained the fundamental principles and components of information systems, the use of special journals and subsidiary ledgers, and technology-based systems. We also discussed the analysis of segment data.

A Look at This Chapter

This chapter extends our study of accounting to the area of internal control and accounting for cash. We describe procedures that are good for internal control. We also explain the control of and accounting for cash.

A Look Ahead

Chapter 10 focuses on receivables and short-term investments. These items are the most liquid assets other than cash. We explain how to account and report for these assets.

ENTREPRENEURIAL DECISION PROBLEM

A new Entrepreneurial Decision problem is included at the end of each chapter (in the "Beyond the Numbers" assignment section). These problems focus on small businesses and the relevance of accounting in helping solve business problems or guide business strategy. No other text offers such assignments specifically directed at small businesses.

350   Chapter 8   Accounting Information Systems

Entrepreneurial Decision
P1

BTN 8-8   Dakota Rice has operated a local gift shop for two years. Initially, she handled all aspects of the store's accounting manually. Over the past year, she has focused on upgrading the store to a computerized system and has successfully installed software to handle billing, purchasing, and payroll. Dakota hopes this year to move from a periodic inventory system to a perpetual one. She is thinking of investing in a bar code labeler and scanner system to help manage inventory.

Required

1. What are the cost-benefit considerations of a bar code system?
2. How would a bar code system work with the accounting information system to accomplish perpetual inventory accounting?

Part Three

Learning Objectives

Conceptual

C1 Define internal control and its purpose.

C2 Identify principles of internal control.

C3 Define cash and cash equivalents and explain how to report them.

C4 Identify control features of banking activities.

Analytical

A1 Compute the days' sales uncollected ratio and use it to analyze liquidity.

Procedural

P1 Apply internal control to cash receipts.

P2 Apply the voucher system to control cash disbursements.

P3 Explain and record petty cash fund transactions.

P4 Apply the net method to control purchase discounts.

P5 Prepare a bank reconciliation.

ENTREPRENEURIAL BOXES

A selected number of new *Did You Know?* and *You Make The Call* boxes focus on entrepreneurial issues and decisions. The *Did You Know?* boxes provide current and informative observations relevant to business start-ups. The *You Make the Call* boxes engage students to apply accounting to decisions confronting entrepreneurs. These boxes are especially effective at engaging students interested in small business and start-up possibilities.

Flea Market in Cyberspace

SAN JOSE, CA—Who ever thought a flea market could be worth $12 billion? Paris-born entrepreneur Pierre Omidyar started his Net auction service, **eBay** (a combination of the words *electronic* and *Bay Area*), five years ago to help his girlfriend collect Pez candy dispensers (**eBay.com**). Omidyar, then 27, saw a need for a Web site where people could buy and sell all kinds of items such as computers, antiques, toys, and music. eBay is now the largest person-to-person auction site on the Web. It creates the marketplace, but buyers and sellers do their own work. eBay never touches the goods or the money. Its earnings derive from commissions, between 1 and 5%, depending on the item's value.

Omidyar calls eBay an experiment in e-commerce. But how does he persuade strangers to trust one another enough to hand over merchandise or cash? "Most people are honest, trustworthy people," says Omidyar. Still, he set up basic controls to establish responsibilities of each party to a trade and to monitor and record transactions. When complications still arose between buyers and sellers, Omidyar had to install a better control system.

Omidyar's response was fourfold. First, he devised a control system whereby buyers and sellers rate their experiences with the other party. This *Feedback Forum* is a public record of past eBay dealings of buyers and sellers. Omidyar says, "It's become a kind of virtuous cycle that's encouraged good behavior." Second, he brought in escrow services to assist traders in making deals. Buyers can have their goods delivered to an escrow service before their money is sent to the seller. Likewise, sellers can require that a buyer send money to the escrow service before sending the goods. Third, he gave traders free i[...] up SafeHarbo[...] dependent re[...]

Omidyar is [...] creating an o[...] hope to make[...] Omidyar's cu[...] $3 billion fron[...] [Sources: Busi[...] Web Site, Dec[...]

Did You Know?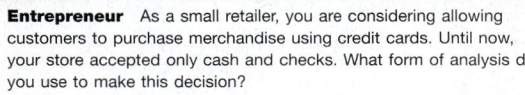

Entrepreneurial Giving   Many entrepreneurs donate 10% or more of their pretax income to charities. Consultants cite evidence that socially conscious behavior brings tangible financial rewards. A recent survey found 76% of respondents saying they'd switch from their current store to one with a good cause if price and quality are equal.

You Make the Call

Entrepreneur   As a small retailer, you are considering allowing customers to purchase merchandise using credit cards. Until now, your store accepted only cash and checks. What form of analysis do you use to make this decision?

Answer—p. 421

The CAP Model

The Conceptual/Analytical/Procedural (CAP) Model allows courses to be specially designed to meet instructional and learning needs. This model identifies learning objectives, textual material, assignments, and test material by C, A, or P, allowing different instructors to teach from the same materials, yet easily customizes their courses toward a conceptual, analytical, or procedural approach (or a combination thereof) based on personal preferences.

Quick Check

These short question/answer features reinforce the material immediately preceding them. They allow the reader to pause and reflect on the topics described, then receive immediate feedback before going on to new topics. Answers are provided at the end of each chapter.

Marginal Student Annotations-NEW

These annotations provide students with additional hints, tips, and examples to help them more fully understand the concepts and retain what they have learned. They also include notes on global implications for accounting.

Did You Know?

These relevant, topical items are useful for preparing, analyzing and using accounting information. Strategically placed throughout the text, these items help students understand and effectively apply accounting.

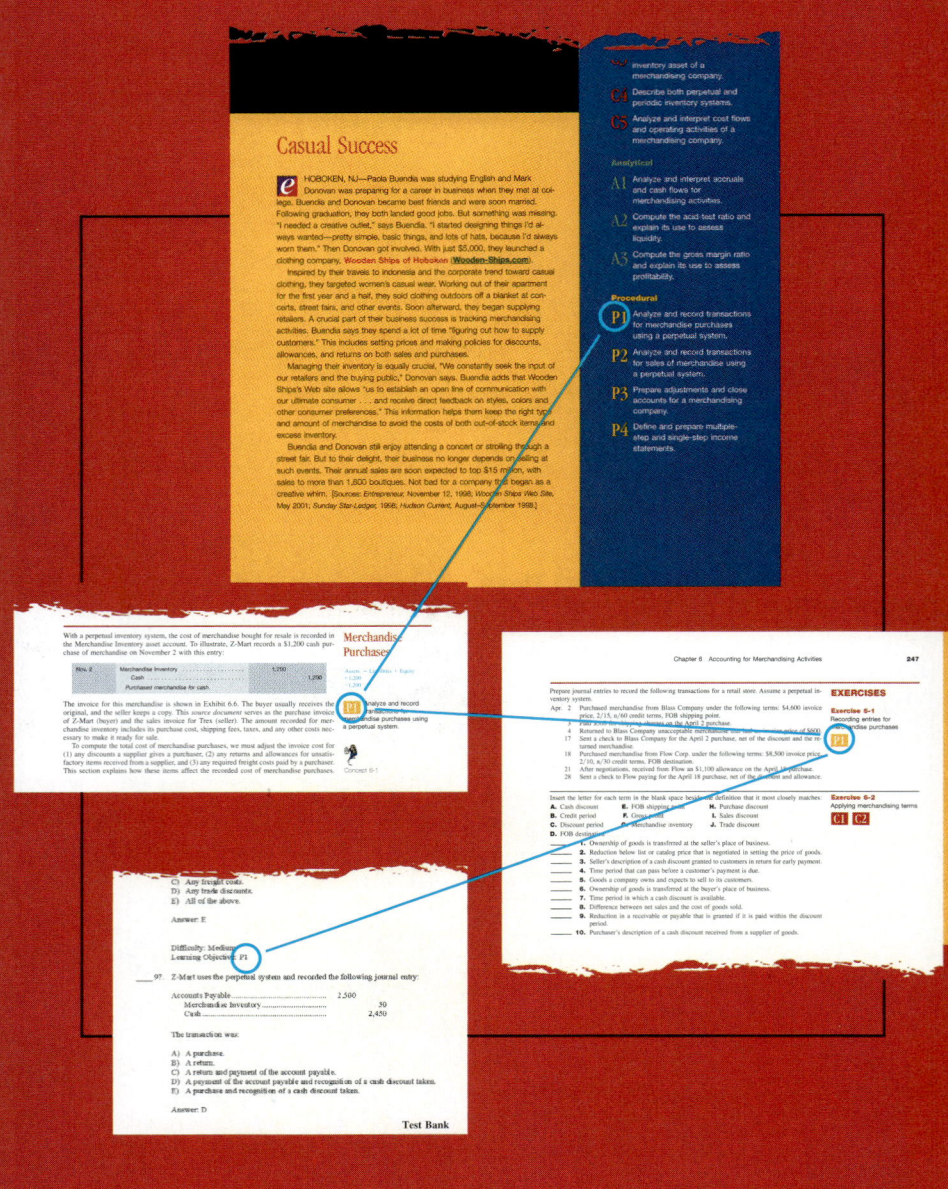

Using the Information   Profit Margin

A2 Compute profit margin and describe its use in analyzing company performance.

Business decision makers want financial statements to reflect relevant information about a company's financial performance and condition. A useful measure of a company's operating results is the ratio of its net income to net sales (revenues). This ratio is called **profit margin**, or *return on sales*, and is computed as shown in Exhibit 4.23.

Exhibit 4.23
Profit Margin

$$\text{Profit margin} = \frac{\text{Net income}}{\text{Net sales}}$$

This ratio is interpreted as reflecting the percent of profit in each dollar of sales. To illustrate how we compute and use profit margin, let's look at the results of **Ben & Jerry's Homemade Ice Cream** in Exhibit 4.24. Profit margin is one measure we can use to help evaluate Ben & Jerry's performance during the past four years.

Exhibit 4.24
Ben & Jerry's Profit Margin

	1999	1998	1997	1996
Net income (in mil.)	$ 3.4	$ 6.2	$ 3.9	$ 3.9
Net sales (in mil.)	$237.0	$209.2	$174.2	$167.2
Profit margin	1.4%	3.0%	2.2%	2.3%
Industry profit margin	2.2%	1.6%	2.0%	2.1%

Ben & Jerry's average profit margin is 2.2% over this period. Year 1999 especially stands out as poor. This is mainly due to special charges tied to the discontinuance of a manufacturing plant. The profit margin is expected to increase in subsequent years. Also note the

3. Present journal entries to record the adjustments entered on the six-column table. Assume BeGone's adjusted balance for Merchandise Inventory matches the year-end physical count.
4. Prepare a single-step income statement, a statement of changes in owner's equity, and a classified balance sheet.

Check Net income, $23,370. Total assets, $98,271

Beyond the Numbers

BTN 12-1 Refer to the financial statements for **Nike** in Appendix A to respond to the following:
1. Compute times interest earned for the years ended May 31, 2000, 1999, and 1998. Comment on Nike's ability to cover its interest expense for this period.
2. What evidence can you identify for an indication that Nike has temporary differences between income reported on its income statement and income reported on its tax return?

Reporting in Action
C3 A1
NIKE

Swoosh Ahead
3. Access Nike's annual report for fiscal years ending after May 31, 2000, at its Web site [www.nike.com] or the SEC's EDGAR database [www.sec.gov]. Compute Nike's times interest earned for years ending after May 31, 2000, that you have access to.

BTN 12-2 Key comparative figures ($ millions) for both **Nike** and **Reebok** follow:

Key Figures	NIKE			Reebok		
	Current Year	One Year Prior	Two Years Prior	Current Year	One Year Prior	Two Years Prior
Net income	$579.1	$451.4	$399.6	$11.0	$23.9	$135.1
Income taxes	340.1	294.7	253.4	10.1	11.9	12.5
Interest expense	45.0	44.1	60.0	49.7	60.7	64.4

Comparative Analysis
A1
NIKE
Reebok

Required
1. Compute times interest earned for the three years' data shown for each company.
2. Comment on which company appears stronger in its ability to pay interest obligations if income should decline.

BTN 12-3 Mike Gates is a sales manager for an automobile dealership. He earns a bonus each year based on revenue from the number of autos sold in the year less related warranty expenses. Actual warranty expenses have varied over the prior 10 years from a low of 3% of an automobile's selling price to a high of 10%. In the past, Mike has tended to estimate warranty expenses on the high end to be conservative. He must work with the dealership's accountant at year-end to arrive at the warranty expense accrual for cars sold this year.
1. Does the warranty accrual decision create any ethical dilemma for Gates?
2. Since warranty expenses vary, what percent do you think Gates should choose for this year? Justify your response.

Ethics Challenge
P4

BTN 12-4 Matthew Stafford is the accounting and finance manager for a manufacturer. At year-end, he must determine how to account for the company's contingencies. His manager, John Harris, objects to Matthew's proposal to recognize an expense and a liability for warranty service on units of a new product introduced in the fourth quarter. John comments, "There's no way we can estimate this warranty cost. We don't owe anyone anything until a product breaks and is returned. Let's report an expense if and when we do repairs."

Communicating in Practice
C3

Required
Prepare a one-page memorandum for Matthew to send to John defending his proposal.

INSTRUCTOR SUPPLEMENTS

Instructor's Resource CD-ROM
007246500X

This is your all-in-one resource. It allows you to create custom presentations from your own materials or from the following text-specific materials provided in the CD's asset library:

- Instructor's Resource Manual
- Solutions Manual
- Test Bank
- Ready Shows (PowerPoint® Slides)—Ready Shows is a multimedia, lecture slide package using Microsoft® PowerPoint 7.0 to illustrate chapter concepts and procedures. It allows revision of lecture slides and includes a viewer, allowing screens to be shown with or without the software.
- General Ledger Applications Software (GLAS)
- Spreadsheet Applications Template Software (SPATS)
- Tutorial Software
- Link to PageOut
- Video Clips

Ready Show Slides
Volume 1: 0072468408
Volume 2: 0072468432

Prepared by Jon A. Booker, Charles W. Caldwell, Susan C. Galbreath and Richard S. Rand of Tennessee Technological University

An overhead presentation package including color teaching transparencies selected from the Ready Shows (PowerPoint®) slides, as well as a booklet of black and white masters for all of the Ready Show slides.

Financial and Managerial Accounting Video Library
Financial Videos: 0072376163
Managerial Videos: 0072376171

See next page for more information

Instructor's Resource Manual
Volume 1: 0072464836
Volume 2: 0072465034

Written by Barbara Chiappetta.

These manuals contain (for each chapter) a Lecture Outline, a chart linking all assignment materials to Learning Objectives, a list of relevant active learning activities, and additional visuals with transparency masters.

Instructor's Manual for *Student Learning Tools*
0256256470

Textbook Options
The textbook is published in several variations, including (1) Complete Edition—Chapters 1–26 (2) Volume 1—Chapters 1–13, (3) Volume 2—Chapters 13–26, (4) Financial Chapters 1–18, (5) Volume 1 w/Working Papers (paperback), and (6) Volume 2 w/Working Papers (paperback).

Solutions Manual
Volume 1: 0072464852
(Solutions Transparencies 0072464895**)**
Volume 2: 0072465042
(Solutions Transparencies 0072465069**)**

Written by John J. Wild, Suresh Kalagnanam, Jo Lynne Koehn, and Marilyn Sagrillo

Test Bank
Volume 1: 0072464909
Volume 2: 0072465050

Written by Marilyn Sagrillo and John J. Wild

Brownstone Test Bank
0072464925

Available for Windows only.

Instructor Booklet for Student Software CD-ROM
0072465204

This contains the solutions to the SPATS and PeachTree problems.

Practice Sets
Manual Practice Sets

	Instructor	Student
Cogg Hill Camping Equipment	007246450X	0072464577
Republic Lighting Company	0072464496	0072464550
Freewheel Corporation, Inc. *Prepared by Christie W. Johnson, Montana State University*	0072464526	0072464615
Understanding Corporate Annual Reports *Prepared by William R. Pasewark, University of Houston*	0072387165	0072387149

Computerized Practice Sets
Prepared by Leland Mansuetti and Keith Weidkamp, Sierra College

	Instructor	Student
Granite Bay Jet Ski, Level 1	0072426896	0072426942
Granite Bay Jet Ski, Inc., Level 2	0072426209	0072426950
Wheels Exquisite, Inc., Level 1	0072427531	0072428457
Thunder Mountain Snowmobile	0072341157	0072341149
Gold Run Snowmobile, Inc.	0072341092	0072341076
Ramblewood Manufacturing, Inc.	0072346426	0072348151

STUDENT SUPPLEMENTS

FAP Partner (Topic Tackler and Mastering the Accounting Cycle)

Topic Tackler developed by Jeannie M. Folk, College of DuPage

Mastering the Accounting Cycle developed by Carol Yacht (content) and Rick Birney, Arizona State University (shell)

See inside front cover for a complete description.

Student Software CD

0072463422

GLAS, SPATS, and PeachTree templates prepared by Jack E. Terry, ComSource Associates, Inc.

Tutorial software prepared by Leland Mansuetti and Keith Weidkamp, Sierra College

Not to be confused with **FAP Partner**, this CD contains four separate software applications:

- General Ledger Applications Software (GLAS)
- Spreadsheet Applications Template Software (SPATS)
- PeachTree Templates
- Tutorial Software

GLAS, SPATS, and PeachTree allow students to use various software programs to help solve selected text assignments. The Tutorial Software gives students a chance to review each chapter's material using journal entries, glossary review, true/false questions, multiple choice questions, and fill-in-the-blank exercises.

Study Guide

Volume 1: 0072464860
Volume 2: 0072465107
Chapters 1-18: 0072465158

Prepared by Barbara Chiappetta, Nassau Community College and Linda J. Schain, Hofstra University

Covers each chapter and appendix with reviews of the learning objectives, outlines of the chapters, summaries of chapter materials, and additional problems with solutions.

Working Papers

Volume 1: 007246481X
Volume 2: 0072464992
Chapters 1-18: 0072465166

Written by John J. Wild

Working Papers are available to help direct students in solving all assignments. In addition, each chapter contains one set of papers that can be used for either the A or B series of problems.

Ready Notes

Volume 1: 0072464941
Volume 2: 0072465085

Telecourse Guide

Volume 1: 0072464933
Volume 2: 0072465077

Student Learning Tools

0256255776

Prepared by Barbara Chiappetta

This workbook helps students develop and use critical thinking and learning-to-learn skills in a collaborative team environment. It contains class activities, writing assignments, and team presentation assignments.

Building an E-Business: From the Ground Up

0072426365

Written by Elizabeth Reding

Steeped in hands-on experience, this book was written specifically for those who want to develop Web skills and business plans for use in starting an e-business.

VIDEOS

Financial and Managerial Accounting Video Library

These short, action-oriented videos, developed by Dallas County Community College for the *Accounting in Action* distance-learning course, provide an impetus for lively classroom discussion. Tied closely to **FAP**'s pedagogical framework, these videos avoid talking-head footage in favor of dynamic, documentary-style explorations of how businesses use accounting information. For a complete listing of topics covered in this library, visit the FAP Web site at **www.mhhe.com/FAP16e**.

Video Telecourse

To acquire the complete telecourse, call Dallas TeleLearning at 972-669-6666, send them a FAX at 972-669-6668, or visit their Web site at **http://www.lecroy.dcccd.edu./prodsvcs/catalog/courseList/aia.htm**.

FOCUS GROUP PARTICIPANTS

FOCUS GROUP PARTICIPANTS

We are thankful for the suggestions, comments, and counsel of the following:

Thomas Badley, Baker College

Edward Banas, Northern Virginia Community College/Woodbridge

Scott Barhight, Northampton Community College

Daniel A. Bayak, Northampton Community College

Shifei Chung, Rowan University

Anthony Cioffi, Lorain County Community College

James L. Cosby, John Tyler Community College

Sid Davidson, Foothill College

Victoria Doby, Villa Julie College

Roger Dufresne, Northern Essex Community College

James Forcier, Las Positas College

J. Thomas Franco, Wayne County Community College

James S. Gale, Northern Virginia Community College/Alexandria

Shirley Glass, Macomb Community College

John J. Godfrey, Springfield Technical Community College

Jennifer Gregorski, Bristol Community College

Gloria Halpern, Montgomery College

Robert J. Hardin, Henry Ford Community College

Richard Howden, Delta College

Jill Kolody, Anne Arundel Community College

Lawrence Kreiser, Cleveland State University

Christopher Kwak, Ohlone College

Phillip Landers, Pennsylvania College of Technology

Betty Lipford, Community College of Baltimore County

Paul Lospennato, North Shore Community College

Andrea M. Murowski, Brookdale Community College

Christopher Myers, Yuba College

Ramesh Narasimhan, Montclair State University

Leah O'Goley, Holyoke Community College

Rochelle Olive, College of Alameda

Douglas R. Pfister, Lansing Community College

George M. Roy, Concordia College

Alphonse Ruggiero, Suffolk County Community College

Jill Russell, Camden County College

Steve Schaefer, Contra Costa College

Linda Schain, Hofstra University

Sara Seyedin, Foothill College

Charles A. Spector, SUNY Oswego

Mary Ston, Oakland Community College

Joseph Tabet, North Shore Community College

Steven Teeter, Utah Valley State College

Leslie Thysell, Richard Bland College

John C. VanSantvoord, New Hampshire College

Jan Williams, Morgan State University

Orville Wright, Morgan State University

REVIEWERS

We also thank the following for their valuable comments and suggestions:

Vernon Allen, Central Florida Community College

Abdul Baten, Northern Virginia Community College/Manassas

Peggy A. Boerman, Madison Area Technical College

Bob Coburn, Franklin Pierce College

Ellen Goldberg, Northern Virginia Community College/Loudoun

Susan Hamlen, SUNY—Buffalo

Jerry C.Y. Han, SUNY—Buffalo

Sara Harris, Arapahoe Community College

Frank Heflin, Purdue University

Yvonne Phang-Hatami, Borough of Manhattan Community College

Barbara Houchen, Anne Arundel Community College

Stephen Kerr, Hendrix College

Tom Kimberling, Ventura College

Shirly Kleiner, Johnson County Community College

Eddy McClelland, Roanoke College

William Mundy, Columbus State Community College

Lynn Pape, Northern Virginia Community College/Alexandria

Susan Pope, University of Akron

Delta Heath-Simpson, Lewis Clark State College

Daniel Small, J. Sargeant Reynolds Community College

K.R. Subramanyam, University of Southern California

Thomas Thompson, Madison Area Technical College

Theron Ray Wurzburger, New River Community College

In addition to the helpful and generous colleagues listed above, we would like to thank the entire McGraw-Hill/Irwin FAP team, including Melody Marcus, Tracey Douglas, Kristin Leahy, Jackie Scruggs, Edward Przyzycki, Kimberly Hooker, Michael McCormick, Jennifer McQueen, Judy Kausal, Becky Szura, and Kelly Odom. We also owe thanks to a great marketing and sales support staff, including Kurt Strand, Rich Kolasa, and Melissa Larmon. We would also like to thank our accuracy checkers, Barbara Schnathorst, CPA, of The Write Solution Inc., and Beth Woods, CPA, of Accuracy Counts. In addition, many talented educators and professionals worked hard to create the supplements for this book, and for their efforts we're grateful to Rick Birney, Jon A. Booker, Charles W. Caldwell, Jeannie M. Folk, Susan C. Galbreath, Suresh Kalagnanam, Jo Lynne Koehn, Leland Mansuetti, Richard S. Rand, Marilyn Sagrillo, Jack E. Terry, Keith Weidkamp and Carol Yacht. Finally, many more people we either did not meet or whose efforts we did not personally witness nevertheless helped to make this book everything that it is, and we thank them all.

ABOUT THE CONTRIBUTORS

Jo Lynne Koehn is an associate professor at Central Missouri State University. She received her PhD and Master's of Accountancy from the University of Wisconsin—Madison. Her scholarly articles have been published in a variety of journals including *Issues in Accounting Education, The CPA Journal, The Tax Advisor,* and *Accounting Enquiries*. Professor Koehn is a member of the American Accounting Association and the American Institute of CPAs. She also holds a Certified Financial Planning license and is active in promoting a financial planning curriculum at Central Missouri State University. In her leisure time, Professor Koehn indulges her passion for golf and participates in the Executive Women's Golf Association of Kansas City. Professor Koehn also enjoys reading, traveling, and visiting bookstores.

Suresh Kalagnanam is an associate professor of accounting at the University of Saskatchewan. He received his B.Eng. from the University of Madras, MBA from Gujarat University (both in India), MBA and MSc in Accounting from the University of Saskatchewan, and PhD from the University of Wisconsin at Madison. His scholarly articles have been published in *Accounting, Organizations and Society, The Journal of Cost Management,* and *Management Accounting*. He has also written a teaching case which has been published by the Institute of Management Accountants. Dr. Kalagnaman is a member of the American Accounting Association, American Society for Quality, Canadian Academic Accounting Association, and the Institute of Management Accountants, and is an associate member of the Society of Management Accountants of Saskatchewan. Dr. Kalagnaman has two children, Pallavi and Siddharth. His wife, Viji, is a homemaker and a part-time university student.

Marilyn Sagrillo is an associate professor at the University of Wisconsin – Green Bay. She received her BA and MS in Accounting from Northern Illinois University and her PhD from the University of Wisconsin – Madison. Her scholarly articles have been published in *Accounting Enquiries*, *Journal of Accounting Case Research*, and the *Missouri Society of CPAs Casebook*. She is a member of the American Accounting Association and the Institute of Management Accountants. In 1989 she received the UWGB Founder's Association Faculty Award for Excellence in Teaching. Professor Sagrillo is an active volunteer for the Midwest Renewable Energy Association, an organization devoted to promoting renewable energy and energy conservation. She also enjoys reading, traveling, and hiking.

Jeannie M. Folk teaches financial and managerial accounting at College of DuPage and mentors accounting students working in cooperative education positions. In addition, she is active in the area of online, distance education. Professor Folk serves on the Scholarship Committee of TACTYC (Teachers of Accounting at Two-Year Colleges) and the Illinois CPA Society's Outstanding Educator Award Committee. She is also a member of the American Accounting Association and the American Institute of Certified Public Accountants. She was honored with the Illinois CPA Society Outstanding Educator Award and was a recipient of the Women in Management, Inc., Charlotte Danstrom Woman of Achievement Award. Before entering academe, Professor Folk was a general practice auditor with Coopers & Lybrand (now PriceWaterhouseCoopers). She received her BBA from Loyola University Chicago and MAS in Accountancy from Northern Illinois University. Professor Folk enjoys travel, camping, hiking and community activities with her three children.

Carol Yacht received her MA in business and Economic Education from California State University, Los Angeles and BS in Business Education from the University of New Mexico. She is the author of McGraw-Hill/Irwin's *Computer Accounting with PeachTree for Microsoft Windows* books, and is a recognized expert in payroll accounting and reporting. She has worked as an educational consultant for IBM corporation, an accounting instructor at Yavapai College, and a business education department chair at Beverly Hills High School in California. She chairs the Distance Learning Committee of the Computer Education Task Force, National Business Education Association. Professor Yacht's son, Matthew, is completing his accounting degree at Northern Arizona University. Her husband, Brice Wood, is an artist and part owner of a fine arts gallery. She is active in community activities and chairs the Planning and Zoning Commission of her town.

CrossWords Tanna Japanese Designs

Papa John's i-FRONTER

Netledger Freeplay INCA Tours Toes on the Nose

Kate Spade

FUBU eBay WWF JobDirect Sector 9

AltiTUNES Red Hat Birdhouse

Wooden Ships of H

Brief Contents

Preface v

Part I **Financial Reporting and the Accounting Cycle**

1 Accounting in the Information Age 2
2 Financial Statements and Business Transactions 34
3 Analyzing and Recording Transactions 78
4 Accrual Accounting and Financial Statements 124
5 Completing the Accounting Cycle 168

Part II **Accounting for Operating Activities**

6 Accounting for Merchandising Activities 212
7 Merchandise Inventories and Cost of Sales 260
8 Accounting Information Systems 300

Part III **Accounting for Investing and Financing Activities**

9 Cash and Internal Control 352
10 Receivables and Short-Term Investments 394
11 Plant Assets, Natural Resources, and Intangibles 436
12 Current Liabilities 480

Part IV **Accounting for Partnerships and Corporations**

13 Partnerships 526
14 Equity Transactions and Corporate Reporting 554
15 Long-Term Liabilities 614
16 Long-Term Investments and International Transactions 660

Part V **Analysis of Accounting Information**

17 Reporting and Analyzing Cash Flows 690
18 Analysis of Financial Statements 740

Part VI **Managerial Accounting and Product Costing**

19 Managerial Accounting Concepts and Principles 784
20 Job Order Cost Accounting 826
21 Process Cost Accounting 864
22 Cost Allocation and Performance Measurement 906

Part VII **Cost Planning and Control**

23 Cost-Volume-Profit Analysis 946
24 Master Budgets and Planning 978
25 Flexible Budgets and Standard Costs 1016

Part VIII **Strategic Analysis in Managerial and Cost Accounting**

26 Capital Budgeting and Managerial Decisions 1060
A Financial Statement Information A-1
   Nike A-2
   Reebok A-11
   Gap A-15
B Present and Future Values B-1
   Credits CR-1
   Index IND-1
   Chart of Accounts C-1

Contents

Preface   v

1 Accounting in the Information Age   2

Information Age   4
- *Influence of Accounting   4*
- *Business and Investment   4*
- *Focus on Accounting   6*
- *Setting Accounting Rules   7*
- *Accounting and Technology   7*

Forms of Organization   7
- *Business Organization   8*
- *Nonbusiness Organization   9*

Activities in Organizations   10
- *Planning   10*
- *Financing   10*
- *Investing   10*
- *Operating   11*

Financial Statements   11
- *Balance Sheet   12*
- *Income Statement   12*
- *Statement of Changes in Owner's Equity   12*
- *Statement of Cash Flows   12*

Users of Accounting Information   13
- *External Information Users   13*
- *Internal Information Users   14*

Ethics and Social Responsibility   16
- *Understanding Ethics   16*
- *Social Responsibility   17*

Opportunities in Practice   18
- *Financial Accounting   18*
- *Managerial Accounting   19*
- *Tax Accounting   19*
- *Accounting Specialization   19*
- *Accounting-Related Opportunities   20*

Using the Information—Return on Investment   21

2 Financial Statements and Business Transactions   34

Communicating with Financial Statements   36
- *Previewing Financial Statements   36*
- *Financial Statements and Organizational Form   40*

Generally Accepted Accounting Principles   41
- *Financial Reporting Environment   41*
- *Setting Accounting Principles   42*
- *International Accounting Principles   43*
- *Principles of Accounting   43*

Transactions and the Accounting Equation   46
- *Transaction Analysis—Part I   46*
- *Transaction Analysis—Part II   49*
- *Summary of Transactions   51*

Financial Statements   52
- *Income Statement   52*
- *Statement of Changes in Owner's Equity   53*
- *Balance Sheet   53*
- *Statement of Cash Flows   53*

Using the Information—Return on Equity   56

3 Analyzing and Recording Transactions   78

Transactions and Documents   80
- *Transactions and Events   80*
- *Source Documents   80*

Accounts and Double-Entry Accounting   81
- *The Account   81*
- *Asset Accounts   82*
- *Liability Accounts   83*
- *Equity Accounts   84*
- *Ledger and Chart of Accounts   85*
- *Debits and Credits   86*
- *Double-Entry Accounting   87*

Processing Transactions   88
- *Journalizing Transactions   89*
- *Balance Column Accounts   89*
- *Posting Journal Entries   90*

Analyzing Transactions   92
- *Accounting Equation Analysis   96*
- *Financial Statement Links   97*

Trial Balance   97
- *Preparing a Trial Balance   97*
- *Using a Trial Balance   97*
- *Searching for Errors   98*
- *Correcting Errors   100*
- *Presentation Issues   100*

Using the Information—Debt Ratio   101

4   Accrual Accounting and Financial Statements   124

Timing and Reporting   126
  The Accounting Period   126
  Purpose of Adjusting   127
  Recognizing Revenues and Expenses   127
  Accrual Basis versus Cash Basis   128
Adjusting Accounts   129
  Framework for Adjustments   129
  Adjusting Prepaid Expenses   130
  Adjusting for Depreciation   131
  Adjusting Unearned Revenues   133
  Adjusting Accrued Expenses   134
  Adjusting Accrued Revenues   136
  Links to Financial Statements   137
  Adjusted Trial Balance   138
  Accrual Reversals in Future Periods   138
Preparing Financial Statements   140
Using the Information—Profit Margin   142
Appendix 4A Alternative Accounting for Prepaids   144

5   Completing the Accounting Cycle   168

Closing Process   170
  Temporary and Permanent Accounts   170
  Recording Closing Entries   170
  Post-Closing Trial Balance   174
Work Sheet as a Tool   174
  Benefits of a Work Sheet   176
  Using a Work Sheet   176
  Statement of Cash Flows   180
  Reviewing the Accounting Cycle   181
Classified Balance Sheet   182
  Classification Structure   182
  Classification Categories   183
Using the Information—Current Ratio   185
Appendix 5A Reversing Entries   188

6   Accounting for Merchandising Activities   212

Merchandising Activities   214
  Reporting Financial Performance   214
  Reporting Financial Condition   215
  Operating Cycle   215
  Inventory Systems   216
Merchandise Purchases   217
  Trade Discounts   218
  Purchase Discounts   218
  Managing Discounts   219
  Purchase Returns and Allowances   220
  Discounts and Returns   221
  Transportation Costs   221
  Transfer of Ownership   221
  Recording Purchases Information   222
Merchandise Sales   223
  Sales Transactions   223
  Sales Discounts   224
  Sales Returns and Allowances   225
Additional Merchandising Issues   226
  Cost and Price Adjustments   226
  Adjusting Entries   227
  Closing Entries   228
  Merchandising Cost Flows   229
  Merchandising Cost Accounts   229
Income Statement Formats   230
  Multiple-Step Income Statement   230
  Single-Step Income Statement   230
  Merchandising Cash Flows   231
Using the Information—Acid-Test and Gross Margin   232
Appendix 6A Comparing Periodic and Perpetual Inventory Systems   237

7   Merchandise Inventories and Cost of Sales   260

Assigning Costs to Inventory   262
  Specific Identification   263
  First-In, First-Out   264
  Last-In, First-Out   265
  Weighted Average   265
  Inventory Costing and Technology   265
Inventory Analysis and Effects   266
  Financial Reporting   266
  Tax Reporting   267
  Consistency in Reporting   268
  Errors in Reporting Inventory   268
Inventory Items and Costs   270
  Items in Merchandise Inventory   270
  Costs of Merchandise Inventory   271
  Physical Count of Merchandise Inventory   271
  Subsidiary Inventory Records   272
Other Inventory Valuations   273
  Lower of Cost or Market   273
  Retail Inventory Method   274
  Gross Profit Method   275
Using the Information—Inventory Turnover and Days' Sales in Inventory   277
Appendix 7A Assigning Costs to Inventory—Periodic System   283

8　Accounting Information Systems　300

Fundamental System Principles　302
  Control Principle　302
  Relevance Principle　302
  Compatibility Principle　302
  Flexibility Principle　302
  Cost-Benefit Principle　303
Components of Accounting Systems　303
  Source Documents　303
  Input Devices　303
  Information Processor　304
  Information Storage　304
  Output Devices　304
Special Journals in Accounting　305
  Basics of Special Journals　305
  Subsidiary Ledgers　306
  Sales Journal　307
  Cash Receipts Journal　311
  Purchases Journal　313
  Cash Disbursements Journal　315
  General Journal Transactions　316
Technology-Based Accounting Systems　316
  Computer Technology in Accounting　317
  Data Processing in Accounting　317
  Computer Networks in Accounting　318
  Enterprise Resource Planning Software　318
Using the Information—Business Segments　319
Appendix 8A Special Journals under a Periodic System　324

9　Cash and Internal Control　352

Internal Control　354
  Purpose of Internal Control　354
  Principles of Internal Control　354
  Technology and Internal Control　356
  Limitations of Internal Control　357
Control of Cash　358
  Cash, Cash Equivalents, and Liquidity　358
  Control of Cash Receipts　359
  Control of Cash Disbursements　361
Banking Activities as Controls　366
  Basic Bank Services　366
  Electronic Funds Transfer　367
  Bank Statement　367
  Bank Reconciliation　369
Using the Information—Days' Sales Uncollected　373
Appendix 9A Document Flow in a Voucher System　375

10　Receivables and Short-Term Investments　394

Accounts Receivable　396
  Recognizing Accounts Receivable　396
  Valuing Accounts Receivable　399
  Direct Write-Off Method　400
  Allowance Method　401
  Estimating Bad Debts Expense　403
  Installment Accounts Receivable　407
Notes Receivable　407
  Computations for Notes　408
  Receipt of a Note　409
  Honoring and Dishonoring a Note　409
  End-of-Period Interest Adjustment　410
Converting Receivables to Cash before Maturity　411
  Selling Accounts Receivable　411
  Pledging Accounts Receivable　411
  Discounting Notes Receivable　411
Short-Term Investments　413
  Accounting for Short-Term Investments　413
  Valuing and Reporting Short-Term Investments　414
Using the Information—Accounts Receivable Turnover　416

11　Plant Assets, Natural Resources, and Intangibles　436

SECTION 1—PLANT ASSETS　438
Cost of Plant Assets　439
  Land　439
  Land Improvements　440
  Buildings　440
  Machinery and Equipment　440
  Lump-Sum Purchase　440
Depreciation　441
  Factors in Computing Depreciation　441
  Depreciation Methods　442
  Partial Year Depreciation　447
  Revising Depreciation　447
  Reporting Depreciation　448
Revenue and Capital Expenditures　449
  Ordinary Repairs　449
  Betterments and Extraordinary Repairs　450
Disposals of Plant Assets　450
  Discarding Plant Assets　451
  Selling Plant Assets　451
  Exchanging Plant Assets　452

SECTION 2—NATURAL RESOURCES   454
  Acquisition and Depletion   454
  Plant Assets Used in Extracting Resources   455
SECTION 3—INTANGIBLE ASSETS   455
  Accounting for Intangible Assets   455
  Patents   456
  Copyrights   456
  Leaseholds   456
  Leasehold Improvements   457
  Franchises and Licenses   457
  Goodwill   457
  Trademarks and Trade Names   459
Cash Flow Impacts of Long-Term Assets   459
Using the Information—Total Asset Turnover   459

12   Current Liabilities   480

Characteristics of Liabilities   482
  Defining Liabilities   482
  Classifying Liabilities   482
  Uncertainty in Liabilities   483
Known (Determinable) Liabilities   484
  Accounts Payable   484
  Sales Taxes Payable   484
  Unearned Revenues   484
  Short-Term Notes Payable   485
  Payroll Liabilities   489
Estimated Liabilities   492
  Health and Pension Benefits   492
  Vacation Pay   493
  Bonus Plans   493
  Warranty Liabilities   493
  Income Tax Liabilities   494
  Deferred Income Tax Liabilities   495
Contingent Liabilities   496
  Accounting for Contingent Liabilities   496
  Reasonably Possible Contingent Liabilities   496
Long-Term Liabilities   497
  Known Long-Term Liabilities   497
  Estimated Long-Term Liabilities   498
  Contingent Long-Term Liabilities   498
Using the Information—Times Interest Earned   498
Appendix 12A Payroll Reports, Records, and
Procedures   502

13   Partnerships   526

Partnership Form of Organization   528
  Characteristics of Partnerships   528
  Organizations with Partnership
  Characteristics   529
  Choosing a Business Form   530
Basic Partnership Accounting   531
  Organizing a Partnership   531
  Dividing Income or Loss   532
  Partnership Financial Statements   534
Admission and Withdrawal of Partners   535
  Admission of a Partner   535
  Withdrawal of a Partner   536
  Death of Partner   538
Liquidation of a Partnership   538
  No Capital Deficiency   538
  Capital Deficiency   539
Using the Information—Partner Return on
Equity   540

**14   Equity Transactions and Corporate
Reporting   554**

Corporate Form of Organization   556
  Characteristics of Corporations   556
  Organizing and Managing a Corporation   557
Stock of a Corporation   558
  Basics of Capital Stock   559
Common Stock   562
  Issuing Par Value Stock   562
  Issuing No-Par Value Stock   563
  Issuing Stated Value Stock   563
  Issuing Stock for Noncash Assets   563
Preferred Stock   564
  Issuing Preferred Stock   565
  Dividend Preference   565
  Convertible Preferred Stock   567
  Callable Preferred Stock   567
  Motivation for Preferred Stock   567
Dividends   568
  Cash Dividends   568
  Stock Dividends   570
  Stock Splits   572
Treasury Stock   573
  Purchasing Treasury Stock   573
  Reissuing Treasury Stock   574
  Retiring Stock   575
Reporting Income Information   576
  Continuing Operations   576
  Discontinued Segments   576
  Extraordinary Items   576

Changes in Accounting Principles   578

Earnings per Share   579

Stock Options   581

Retained Earnings   581

Restricted Retained Earnings   582

Appropriated Retained Earnings   582

Prior Period Adjustments   582

Changes in Accounting Estimates   583

Statement of Changes in Stockholders' Equity   583

Using the Information—Book Value per Share, Dividend Yield, and Price-Earnings Ratio   583

15   Long-Term Liabilities   614

Basics of Bonds   616

Bond Financing   616

Types of Bonds   617

Bond Trading   618

Bond-Issuing Procedures   619

Bond Issuances   619

Issuing Bonds at Par   619

Bond Discount or Premium   620

Issuing Bonds at a Discount   621

Amortizing a Bond Discount   621

Issuing Bonds at a Premium   624

Amortizing a Bond Premium   625

Issuing Bonds between Interest Dates   627

Accruing Bond Interest Expense   628

Bond Pricing   629

Bond Retirement   630

Bond Retirement at Maturity   630

Bond Retirement before Maturity   630

Bond Retirement by Conversion   631

Long-Term Notes Payable   631

Interest-Bearing Notes   632

Noninterest-Bearing Notes   633

Installment Notes   634

Mortgage Notes   637

Using the Information—Pledged Assets to Secured Liabilities   638

Appendix 15A   Present Values of Bonds and Notes   641

Appendix 15B   Leases and Pensions   644

16   Long-Term Investments and International Transactions   660

Classifying Investments   662

Short-Term versus Long-Term Investments   662

Classes of Long-Term Investments   662

Long-Term Investments in Securities   663

Held-to-Maturity Securities   663

Available-for-Sale Securities   664

Investment in Equity Securities with Significant Influence   666

Investment in Equity Securities with Controlling Influence   668

Accounting Summary for Investments in Securities   669

Investments in International Operations   669

Exchange Rates between Currencies   669

Sales and Purchases Listed in a Foreign Currency   670

Consolidated Statements with International Subsidiaries   671

Comprehensive Income   671

Using the Information—Components of Return on Total Assets   672

17   Reporting and Analyzing Cash Flows   690

Basics of Cash Flow Reporting   692

Purpose of the Statement of Cash Flows   692

Importance of Cash Flows   692

Measuring Cash Flows   693

Classifying Cash Flows   693

Noncash Investing and Financing   694

Format of the Statement of Cash Flows   696

Preparing the Statement of Cash Flows   696

Cash Flows from Operating   699

Reporting Operating Cash Flows   699

Direct Method of Reporting   701

Indirect Method of Reporting   706

Cash Flows from Investing   712

Analysis of Noncurrent Assets   712

Analysis of Other Assets   713

Cash Flows from Financing   714

Analysis of Noncurrent Liabilities   714

Analysis of Equity   715

Proving Cash Balances   716

Using the Information—Cash Flow Analysis   716

Appendix 17A   Spreadsheet Preparation of the Statement of Cash Flows   721

18   Analysis of Financial Statements   740

Basics of Analysis   742

Purpose of Analysis   742

Building Blocks of Analysis   742

Information for Analysis   743
Standards for Comparison   744
Tools for Analysis   744
Horizontal Analysis   745
Comparative Statements   745
Trend Analysis   748
Vertical Analysis   749
Common-Size Statements   750
Common-Size Graphics   750
Ratio Analysis   754
Liquidity and Efficiency   754
Solvency   758
Profitability   760
Market Prospects   761
Summary of Ratios   762
Using the Information—Analysis
Reporting   764

**19   Managerial Accounting Concepts and
Principles   784**

Introduction to Managerial Accounting   786
Purpose of Managerial Accounting   786
Nature of Managerial Accounting   787
Decision-Making Focus   789
*Increased Relevance of Managerial
Accounting*   789
Cost Accounting Concepts   791
Classification by Behavior   791
Classification by Traceability   791
Classification by Controllability   792
Classification by Relevance   792
Classification by Function   792
Identifying Cost Classification   793
Cost Concepts for Service Companies   794
Reporting Manufacturing Activities   794
Manufacturer's Balance Sheet   794
Manufacturer's Income Statement   796
Flow of Manufacturing Activities   799
Manufacturing Statement   800
Using the Information—Unit Contribution
Margin   802

20   Job Order Cost Accounting   826

The Inventory System and Accounting for Costs   828
General Accounting System   828
Cost Accounting System   828
Job Order Cost Accounting   828
Job Order Manufacturing   828
Job Order Cost Sheet   830

Materials Cost Flows and Documents   831
Labor Cost Flows and Documents   833
Overhead Cost Flows and Documents   835
Summary of Manufacturing Cost Flows   836
Adjusting Overapplied and Underapplied
Overhead   839
Underapplied Overhead   840
Overapplied Overhead   840
Using the Information—Pricing for Services   840

21   Process Cost Accounting   864

Process Operations   866
Comparing Job Order and Process Operations   866
Organization of Process Operations   867
GenX Company—An Illustration   867
Process Cost Accounting   869
Direct and Indirect Costs   869
Accounting for Materials Costs   870
Accounting for Labor Costs   871
Accounting for Factory Overhead   871
Equivalent Units of Production   873
Accounting for Goods in Process   873
*Differences between Equivalent Units for
Materials and for Labor and Overhead*   874
Accounting for First (Grinding) Department   874
Physical Flow of Units   875
Equivalent Units of Production   875
Cost per Equivalent Unit   877
Cost Reconciliation   877
Process Cost Summary   878
Transfers between Departments   879
Accounting for Second (Mixing) Department   881
Equivalent Units of Production   881
Process Cost Summary   883
Transfers to Finished Goods Inventory and Cost of
Goods Sold   883
Summary of Cost Flows   884
*Lean Business Model and Process
Operations*   884
Using the Information—Hybrid Costing
System   885

**22   Cost Allocation and Performance
Measurement   906**

Overhead Cost Allocation Methods   908
Two-Stage Cost Allocation   908
Activity-Based Costing   909
Departmental Accounting   913
Motivation for Departmentalization   913

Departmental Evaluation   914

Departmental Reporting and Analysis   914

Departmental Expense Allocation   915

Direct and Indirect Expenses   915

Allocation of Indirect Expenses   916

Departmental Income Statements   917

Departmental Contribution to Overhead   920

Responsibility Accounting   921

Controllable versus Direct Costs   922

Responsibility Accounting System   922

Joint Costs   924

Using the Information—Return on Total Assets by Investment Centers   926

23   Cost-Volume-Profit Analysis   946

Identifying Cost Behavior   948

Fixed Costs   948

Variable Costs   949

Mixed Costs   949

Step-Wise Costs   949

Curvilinear Costs   950

Measuring Cost Behavior   951

Scatter Diagrams   951

High-Low Method   952

Least-Squares Regression   952

Comparing Cost Estimation Methods   953

Break-Even Analysis   953

Computing Break-Even Point   953

Preparing a Cost-Volume-Profit Chart   955

Assumptions of Cost-Volume-Profit Analysis   956

Applying Cost-Volume-Profit Analysis   957

Computing Income from Sales and Costs   957

Computing Sales for a Target Income   958

Computing the Margin of Safety   959

Sensitivity Analysis   959

Computing Multiproduct Break-Even Point   960

Using the Information—Operating Leverage   962

24   Master Budgets and Planning   978

Budgeting Process   980

Analysis and Future Focus   980

Basis for Evaluation   980

Employee Motivation   980

Coordination of Activities   981

Communication of Plans   981

Budget Administration   981

Budget Committee   981

Budget Reporting   982

Budget Timing   983

Master Budget   984

Master Budget Components   984

Operating Budgets   986

Capital Expenditures Budget   989

Financial Budgets   990

Using the Information—Activity-Based Budgeting   994

Appendix 24A Production and Manufacturing Budgets   999

25   Flexible Budgets and Standard Costs   1016

SECTION 1—FLEXIBLE BUDGETS   1018

Budgetary Process   1018

Budgetary Control and Reporting   1018

Fixed Budget Performance Report   1018

Budget Reports for Evaluation   1019

Flexible Budget Reports   1020

Purpose of Flexible Budgets   1020

Preparing Flexible Budgets   1020

Flexible Budget Performance Report   1022

SECTION 2—STANDARD COSTS   1023

Materials and Labor Standards   1023

Identifying Standard Costs   1023

Setting Standard Costs   1024

Cost Variances   1024

Cost Variance Analysis   1025

Computing Cost Variances   1025

Materials and Labor Variances   1026

Overhead Standards and Variances   1028

Setting Overhead Standards   1028

Overhead Cost Variance Analysis   1030

Computing Overhead Cost Variances   1031

Extending Standard Costs   1034

Standard Costs for Control   1034

Standard Costs for Services   1034

Standard Cost Accounting System   1034

Using the Information—Sales Variances   1036

26   Capital Budgeting and Managerial Decisions   1060

SECTION 1—CAPITAL BUDGETING   1062

Methods Not Using Time Value of Money   1062

Payback Period   1062

Accounting Rate of Return   1065

Methods Using Time Value of Money   1066

Net Present Value   1066

Internal Rate of Return   1069

Comparing Capital Budgeting Methods   1071

SECTION 2—MANAGERIAL DECISIONS   1072
Decisions and Information   1072
   Decision Making   1072
   Relevant Costs   1072
Managerial Decision Tasks   1073
   Additional Business   1073
   Make or Buy   1075
   Scrap or Rework   1075
   Sell or Process   1076
   Selecting Sales Mix   1077
   Eliminating a Segment   1078
   Qualitative Decision Factors   1079
Using the Information—Break-Even Time   1080

Appendix A Financial Statement Information   A-1
   Nike A-2
   Reebok A-11
   Gap A-15

Appendix B Present and Future Values   B-1

Credits   CR-1

Index   IND-1

Chart of Accounts   C-1

Fundamental
Accounting
Principles

1

Accounting in the Information Age

"Take the high road; do not sacrifice your goal or ethics," Rachel Bell (left) and Sara Sutton.

A Look at This Chapter

Accounting plays a crucial role in the information age. In this chapter, we discuss the importance of accounting to different types of organizations and describe its many users and uses. We see that ethics and social responsibility are crucial to accounting, and that the information age provides many new accounting opportunities.

A Look Ahead

Chapter 2 explains financial statements and the principles underlying them. It also describes and analyzes business transactions. More generally, Chapters 2 through 5 focus on the accounting cycle and show how financial statements reflect transactions and events.

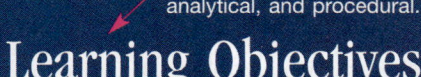

Learning Objectives

Conceptual

C1 Explain the aim and influence of accounting in the information age.

C2 Identify forms of organizations and their characteristics.

C3 Identify and describe the three major activities in organizations.

C4 Identify users and uses of accounting.

C5 Explain why ethics and social responsibility are crucial to accounting.

C6 Identify opportunities in accounting and related fields.

Analytical

A1 Describe income and its two major components.

A2 Explain the relation between return and risk.

A3 Explain and interpret the accounting equation.

A4 Compute and interpret return on investment.

Procedural

P1 Identify and prepare basic financial statements.

Have Résumés, Will Travel

e STAMFORD, CT—Four years ago, 21-year-old college students Rachel Bell and Sara Sutton were in a Boston taxi "stressing" about finding jobs. Sutton was frustrated by her fruitless searches on the Net for openings. Bell remembered her father's advice: "You don't have to work for a company. You can start one yourself." Their idea was a Web-based service for job seekers. "We were so fired up and excited about the concept," Sutton recalls. "We could reach out to students like us, and we could help our friends."

Bell and Sutton's plans led to the launch of **JobDirect** (**www.JobDirect.com**). First, they raised $60,000 in financing from family and friends as start-up money. Then, Bell and Sutton invested in a school bus and hired graffiti artists to paint it to look like their Web site. They equipped the bus with 15 laptops for students to type in résumés and drove off on their first promotional tour of campuses. Forty-three campuses later, their database contained the résumés of 5,000 job seekers. "We knew it would work. There was just no way it couldn't," says Bell.

JobDirect's revenues exceeded $1.3 million for its first full year of service, all from fees paid by employers to use the service. Over 500 clients currently subscribe, including IBM, Charles Schwab, and Chase Manhattan. Students use JobDirect for free. It now has three graffiti-decorated buses, and they travel with the summer's H.O.R.D.E. music festival, where Blues Traveler fans can launch job searches. JobDirect was recently acquired by Korn/Ferry International, the world's largest executive recruitment firm.

Bell and Sutton marvel at the direction their careers have taken. "Rachel and I didn't expect to go into business," says Sutton. "We weren't techies." Yet they formed a company, managed business activities, and prepared, analyzed, and used accounting reports. Bell and Sutton admit it sometimes takes starting a company to see the importance of accounting in business. [Sources: *Business Week,* May 1998; *JobDirect Web Site,* March 2001.]

Chapter Preview

Accounting in the information age is about people like Rachel Bell and Sara Sutton from the opening vignette. Today's world is one of information—its preparation, communication, analysis, and use. Accounting is at the heart of this information age. Knowledge of accounting gives us opportunities. It also gives us the insight to benefit from these opportunities. By studying this book, you will learn about concepts, procedures, and analyses that are useful in our everyday activities. This knowledge will help us make better financial decisions throughout our lives. In this chapter we describe accounting, the users and uses of accounting information, the forms and activities of organizations, and the importance of ethics and social responsibility. We also explain several important accounting principles. This chapter provides a foundation for those who have little or no understanding of business. Chapter 2 will build on this foundation when we consider business transactions.

A **Preview** opens each chapter with a summary of topics covered.

Information Age

Key **terms** are printed in bold and defined again in the end-of-chapter **glossary**.

Check out this book's Web site created especially for you.

Concept 1-1

C1 Explain the aim and influence of accounting in the information age.

We live in an **information age**—a time of communication, data, news, facts, access, and commentary. The information age encourages timeliness, independence, and freedom of expression. Access to and understanding of information affect how we live, whom we associate with, and the opportunities we have. We use information to pick and choose among products and services. Examples are product rankings (*Consumer Reports*), medical advice (*American Medical Association*), and credit ratings (*Standard & Poor's*).

Communication with others and access to data make up much of the *information superhighway*. The information superhighway has redefined communication, especially business communication. Global computer networks and telecommunications equipment allow us quick access to all types of business information. To fully benefit from this information, we need knowledge of the information system. An information system involves the collecting, processing, and reporting of information to decision makers. Knowledge of the information system means personal opportunities and real increases in pay. Studies show that two-year degree graduates with this knowledge can make upward of 30 to 40% more than high school graduates, and bachelor degree graduates can make at least 50 to 75% more than high school graduates. This added pay is for an ability to understand and process information.

Understanding and processing information is the core of accounting. To get the most from our education and opportunities in life, we must know accounting. Your instructor will provide you with many assignments from this book and related materials to help you master accounting. We also encourage you to join us on the information superhighway to explore the opportunities. For your help, we devote an entire Web site solely for your use with this book [**www.mhhe.com/FAP16e**].

Influence of Accounting

One of the most important roles of the information superhighway is the reporting of business activities. Providing information about what businesses own, what they owe, and how they perform is the aim of accounting. **Accounting** is an information and measurement system that identifies, records, and communicates relevant, reliable, and comparable information about an organization's business activities. It helps us make better decisions, including assessing opportunities, products, investments, and social and community responsibilities.

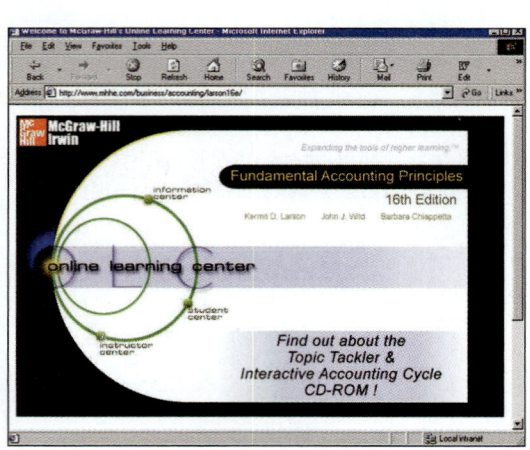

Completing this course will help you apply information in a way you can use in your everyday life. The use of information is not limited to accountants or even to people in business. Often the greatest benefits from understanding accounting come to those outside of accounting and business. We can use accounting to get better terms for a loan, to start a business, and to make better investment decisions. We will use accounting knowledge in whatever career we choose.

Business and Investment

A **business** is one or more individuals selling products or services for profit. Products such as athletic apparel (**Nike, Reebok, Converse**), computers

(**Intel, Cisco, Apple**) and clothing (**Levis, Limited, Gap**) are part of our lives. Services such as information communication (**Yahoo!, Microsoft**), dining (**McDonald's, Wendy's**), and car rental (**Hertz, Budget, Alamo**) make our lives easier. A business can be as small as an at-home-Web service provider or as massive as **Wal-Mart.** Nearly 1 million new businesses are started in the United States each year, no different than **JobDirect** in the opening vignette. Most of these are started by people who want freedom from ordinary jobs, a new challenge in life, or the advantage of extra money.

Business Income

A common feature of all businesses is the desire for income. **Income,** also called **net income, profit** or **earnings,** is the amount a business earns after subtracting expenses from its sales. **Sales,** also called **revenues,** are the amounts earned from selling products and services. **Expenses** are the costs incurred with producing sales. For **JobDirect,** income is the amount earned from client fees less expenses such as travel, salaries, advertising, and promotion. Not all businesses make income. A **loss** arises when expenses are more than sales. Many new businesses incur losses in their first several months or years of business. **Amazon.com** is one example. No business can continually have losses, however, and survive.

Nike's income breakdown is in Exhibit 1.1. If we pay $100 for a pair of Nike athletic footwear, $6.44 is income to Nike. The rest goes to cover expenses such as materials and labor ($60.08) and advertising ($10.87). Nike also pays $3.78 in total taxes. One question confronting our society today is what is the "right" amount of profit. Also, should business pay more for charitable giving or community services? Are taxes too high or too low? For us to seriously consider important questions like these, we must understand accounting.

Return and Risk

Income is often linked to **return.** The term return derives from the idea of getting something back from an investment, referred to as a return on investment. **Return on investment** is commonly stated in ratio form as income divided by amount invested. For example, banks or savings and loans often report our return on investment from a savings account in the form of an interest return. For example, we might have a 4% savings account or invest our college money in an 8% money market fund.

We can invest our money in many ways. If we invest it in a savings account or in U.S. government treasury bills, we get a return of around 3% to 7%. We could also invest in a company's stock, or even start our own business. How do we decide among these investment options? The answer depends on our trade-off between return and risk.

Risk is the uncertainty about the return we expect to earn. All business decisions involve risk, but some decisions involve more than others. The lower the risk of an investment, the lower is our expected return. The reason that savings accounts pay such a low return is the low risk of our not being repaid with interest (the government guarantees most savings accounts from default). Similarly, U.S. government bonds pay a low return because of the low risk that the U.S. government will default on its

A1 Describe income and its two major components.

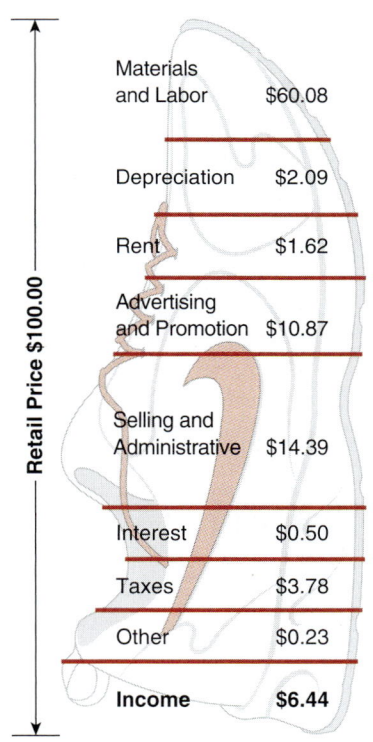

Materials and Labor	$60.08
Depreciation	$2.09
Rent	$1.62
Advertising and Promotion	$10.87
Selling and Administrative	$14.39
Interest	$0.50
Taxes	$3.78
Other	$0.23
Income	**$6.44**

Retail Price $100.00

Exhibit 1.1

Where Our Money Goes When We Buy a Pair of Nikes

Did You Know? is a feature that highlights relevant items from practice.

Did You Know?

Celebrity Investment How do fame and fortune translate into return and risk? A poll asked people which celebrity is the best investment. Similar to business investments, people named performers with years of earning power ahead—see listing to the right.

Oprah Winfrey	27%
Steven Spielberg	19
Tiger Woods	15
Michael Jordan	14
Tom Cruise	8
Rosie O'Donnell	5
Jerry Seinfeld	4
Madonna	2

A2 Explain the relation between return and risk.

payments. If we buy a share of **Nike** or any other company we might obtain a large return, however, we have no guarantee of any return. There is even the risk of loss.

The bar graph in Exhibit 1.2 shows recent returns for bonds with different risks. **Bonds** are written promises by organizations to repay amounts loaned with interest. U.S. treasury bonds provide us a low expected return, but they also offer low risk since they are backed by the U.S. government. High-risk corporate bonds offer a much larger expected return but with much higher risk.

Exhibit 1.2
Returns for Bonds with Different Risks

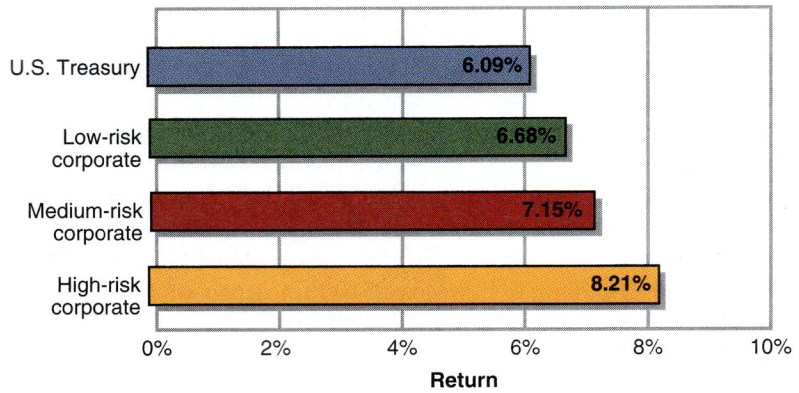

Source: *The Wall Street Journal.*

You Make the Call are role-playing exercises that stress the relevance of accounting for people in and outside of business.

You Make the Call

Programmer   You are considering two job offers. Both require your computer programming skills. One is with a new start-up Internet provider at an annual salary of $41,000; the other is with an established insurance company for $34,500 a year. Which offer do you accept? [*Answers are at the end of each chapter.*]

Answer—p. 23

Exhibit 1.3
Accounting Activities

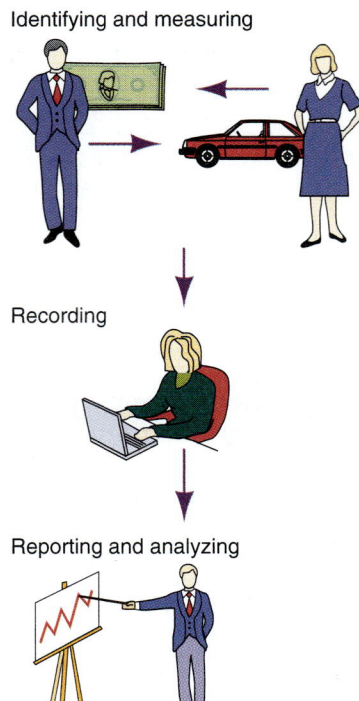

Identifying and measuring

Recording

Reporting and analyzing

The trade-off between return and risk is a normal part of business. Higher risk implies higher, but riskier, expected returns. To help us make better decisions, we use accounting information to measure both return and risk.

Focus of Accounting

We need to guard against a narrow view of accounting. The most common contact with accounting is through credit approvals, checking accounts, tax forms, and payroll. These experiences are limited and tend to focus on the recordkeeping parts of accounting. **Recordkeeping,** or **bookkeeping,** is the recording of financial transactions and events, either manually or electronically. While recordkeeping is essential to data reliability, accounting is this and much more.

The primary objective of accounting is to provide useful information for decision making as shown in Exhibit 1.3. Accounting activities include identifying, measuring, recording, reporting, and analyzing business transactions and events. *Transactions* are exchanges between businesses. Examples are product sales, money lending, and payment of expenses. *Events* are incidents affecting a business's financial position. Examples are bankruptcies, labor strikes, and casualties. Accounting also involves interpreting information and designing information systems to provide useful reports that monitor and control a company's activities.

We benefit our careers by understanding how accounting information is prepared and used. To gain this understanding, we need to learn certain recordkeeping skills. This book provides these skills and the skills for us to read and interpret financial data.

Setting Accounting Rules

There are rules for reporting on a business's performance and financial condition. These rules increase the usefulness of reports, including their reliability and comparability. The rules are determined by many individuals and groups and are referred to as **generally accepted accounting principles,** or **GAAP.** Since accounting is a service activity, these rules reflect our society's needs, and not those of accountants or any other single constituency. Congress has charged the **Securities and Exchange Commission (SEC)** with the authority to set accounting rules for companies that issue stock to the public. For the most part, the SEC has passed authority to set accounting rules to the **Financial Accounting Standards Board (FASB).** Many interested groups and individuals lobby the FASB in their self-interests. They include unions, investors, government agencies, lenders, and politicians.

Accounting and Technology

Technology is a key part of modern business and plays a major role in accounting. Computing technology reduces the time, effort, and cost of recordkeeping while improving clerical accuracy. Some smaller organizations continue to perform various accounting tasks manually, but they are still impacted by information technology.

As technology has changed the way we store, process, and summarize large masses of data, accounting has been freed to expand its field. Consulting, planning, and other financial services are now part of accounting. These services require sorting through masses of data, interpreting their meaning, identifying key factors, and analyzing their implications. Technology is increasingly important in accounting information systems, and is encouraged by advances in computer technology, networks, and enterprise-application software.

Global: Another important group in setting GAAP is the International Organization of Securities Commissions (IOSCO), a group of regulators representing about 90% of global financial markets.

Margin notes further enhance the textual material.

Point: Computing technology is only as good as the accounting data available, and users' decisions are only as good as their understanding of accounting. The best software and recordkeeping cannot make up for lack of accounting knowledge.

Quick Check

1. What is the purpose of accounting?
2. Describe income, sales, and expenses.
3. Explain the trade-off between return and risk.
4. What is the relation between accounting and recordkeeping?
5. Who sets accounting rules?
6. Identify some advantages of technology for accounting.

Quick Checks offer a chance to stop and reflect on key points.

Answers—p. 23

Organizations can be classified as either business or nonbusiness as shown in Exhibit 1.4. Typically, businesses are organized for profit; nonbusinesses serve us in ways not always measured by profit.

Forms of Organization

C2 Identify forms of organization and their characteristics.

Exhibit 1.4

Forms of Organizations

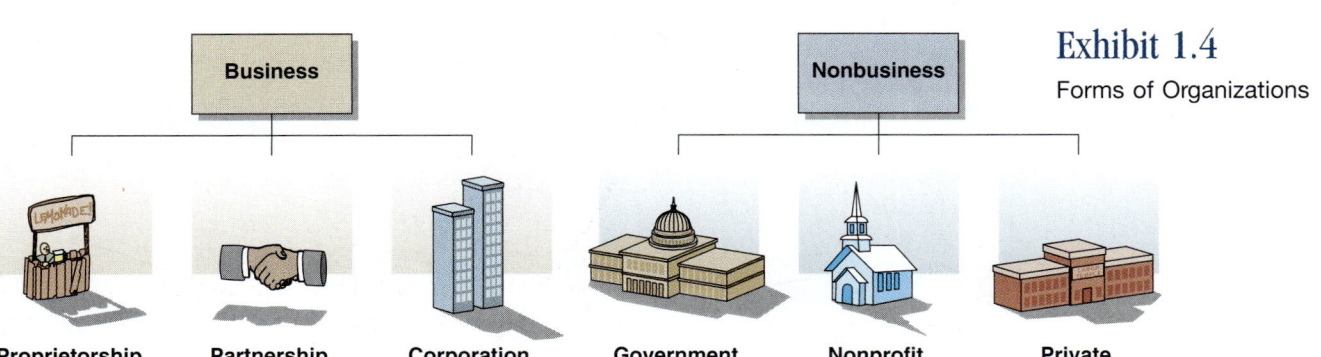

Business			Nonbusiness		
Proprietorship	Partnership	Corporation	Government	Nonprofit	Private

Nearly all organizations engage in some types of business activities. These can include the usual business activities of purchasing materials and labor and of selling products and services. They can also involve nonbusiness activities such as collecting money through taxes, dues, contributions, investments, or borrowings, and providing free services. A common feature in all organizations is the influence and use of accounting.

Business Organization

A business is organized and operated to make a profit. It can take one of three legal forms: *sole proprietorship, partnership,* or *corporation.* Exhibit 1.5 shows the proportion of these different forms in business today.

Sole Proprietorship

A **sole proprietorship,** or simply **proprietorship,** is a business owned by one person. No special legal requirements must be met to start a proprietorship. It is a separate entity for accounting purposes, but it is *not* a separate legal entity from its owner. This means, for example, that a court can order an owner to sell personal belongings to pay a proprietorship's debt. An owner is even responsible for debts that exceed an owner's net investment in the proprietorship. This *unlimited liability* of a proprietorship is sometimes a disadvantage.

Tax authorities do not separate a proprietorship from its owner. This means the income of a proprietorship is not subject to a business income tax but is reported and taxed on the owner's personal income tax return. The rate of tax on a proprietorship's income depends on the level of total income from all sources that the owner had for the year. Proprietorships are by far the most common form of business organization in our society. Its characteristics are summarized in Exhibit 1.6.

Partnership

A **partnership** is a business owned by two or more people, called *partners.* Like a proprietorship, no special legal requirements must be met in starting a partnership. The only requirement is an agreement between partners to run a business together. The agreement can be either oral or written and usually indicates how income and losses are shared. A written agreement is preferred because it can help partners avoid or resolve disputes. A partnership, like a proprietorship, is *not* legally separate from its owners. This means that each partner's share of profits is reported and taxed on that partner's tax return. It also means *unlimited liability* for its partners.

Two types of partnerships limit liability. A *limited partnership* includes a general partner(s) with unlimited liability and a limited partner(s) with liability restricted to the amount invested. A *limited liability partnership* restricts partners' liabilities to their own acts and the acts of individuals under their control. This protects an innocent partner from the neg-

Exhibit 1.5

Different Forms of Businesses

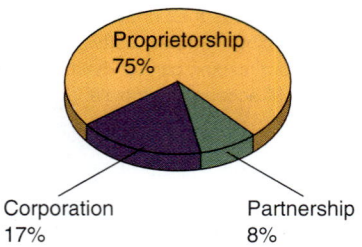

Proprietorship 75%

Corporation 17%

Partnership 8%

Source: *Statistical Abstract of the United States.*

Point: Boston Celtics Limited Partnership (BCLP) directs Celtic basketball. It has 2,703,664 ownership units. Based on recent transactions, each unit is worth about $11 to $12.

Point: Sole proprietorships and partnerships are usually managed on a regular basis by their owners. In a corporation, the owners (shareholders) elect a board of directors who appoint managers to run the business.

Exhibit 1.6

Characteristics of Businesses

Characteristic	Proprietorship	Partnership	Corporation
Business entity	yes	yes	yes
Legal entity	no	no	yes
Limited liability	no	no	yes
Unlimited life	no	no	yes
Business taxed	no	no	yes
One owner allowed	yes	no	yes

ligence of another partner. Yet all partners remain responsible for partnership debts.[1] **Nike** began as an entrepreneurial partnership and was originally called **Blue Ribbon Sports**. The partners, Philip Knight and Bill Bowerman, each contributed $500 and shipped shoes out of Knight's basement. They represent one of many entrepreneurial success stories.

Corporation

A **corporation** is a business legally separate from its owners, meaning it is responsible for its own acts and its own debts. It can enter into contracts, and it can buy, own, and sell property. It can also sue and be sued. Separate legal status means that a corporation can conduct business with the rights, duties, and responsibilities of a person. A corporation acts through its managers, who are its legal agents. Separate legal status also means that its owners, who are called **shareholders** (or **stockholders**), are not personally liable for corporate acts and debts. Shareholders are legally distinct from the business, and their loss is limited to their net investment in purchased shares. This limited liability lowers shareholder risk and is a key reason that corporations can raise resources from shareholders. It also encourages riskier investment with higher expected returns.

A corporation is legally chartered (*incorporated*) under state or federal law. Separate legal status results in a corporation having unlimited life. Ownership, or *equity,* of all corporations is divided into units called **shares** or **stock.** A shareholder can sell or transfer shares to another person without affecting the operations of a corporation. When a corporation issues only one class of stock, we call it **common stock** (or *capital stock*).

A corporation is subject to *double taxation*. This means that it is taxed on its net income, and any distribution of corporate income to its owners (through dividends) is also taxed as part of their personal income. An exception to this is an *S corporation*, a corporation with certain characteristics that give it special tax status. This special tax status removes its double taxation. Shareholders of S corporations report their share of corporate income or loss as part of their personal income.

Real company documents are often shown to enhance learning.

Nonbusiness Organization

Nonbusiness organizations plan and operate for goals other than profit. These goals include security, health, education, transportation, judicial, religious, cultural, and social. A list of nonbusiness organizations often includes museums, libraries, fraternities, utilities, roadways, hospitals, shelters, prisons, churches, parks, schools, transportation, security, and airports. Roughly one-third of U.S. business activity is done by nonbusiness organizations. Some of these organizations, such as hospitals, can operate as private, nonprofit, or government operations.

Nonbusiness organizations lack an identifiable owner. Still, the demand for accounting information in nonbusiness organizations is high because they are accountable to their sponsors. Sponsors include taxpayers, donors, lenders, legislators, regulators, or other constituents. Accounting for these organizations usually follows a *fund-based* system, but the basic principles are similar to accounting for business organizations. In all of these organizations, accounting captures and reports key information about their activities.

You Make the Call—Ethics are role-playing exercises that stress ethics in accounting and business.

You Make the Call—Ethics

Entrepreneur You and a friend develop a new design for in-line skates that improves speed and performance by 25% to 40%. You plan to form a business to manufacture and market these skates. You and your friend want to minimize taxes, but your prime concern is potential lawsuits from individuals who might be injured on these skates. What form of organization do you set up?

Answer—p. 23

---

[1] **Limited liability companies (LLCs)** are usually organized as a form of partnership (they can also be set up for a proprietorship). LLCs represent the fastest growing form of business organization, which has led to a renewed interest in accounting for partnerships. LLCs offer the limited liability of a corporation and the tax treatment of a partnership (or proprietorship). Chapter 13 describes LLCs in more detail.

Activities in Organizations

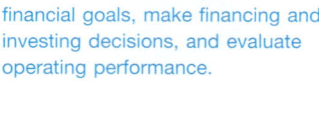

Identify and describe the three major activities in organizations.

Real company names are printed in red when referred to in the text.

Explain and interpret the accounting equation.

Organizations carry out their activities in many different ways. These differences extend to their products, services, goals, organization form, management style, worker compensation, and community giving, yet the major activities of organizations are similar. We discuss the three major types of business activities: financing, investing, and operating. Each of these activities requires planning, and it is discussed first.

Planning

All organizations begin with planning. **Planning** involves defining an organization's ideas, goals, and actions. Strategies and tactics must be laid out. Employees must be informed and motivated. Managers must be credible and display leadership and vision. All of these tasks are part of planning and are the duties of *executive management*. Executive management sets the organization's strategic goals and policies that are captured in an *organization plan*. The owner(s) leads executive management in most organizations. This responsibility often carries with it the title of president, chief executive officer, or chairman of the board of directors. In nonprofit organizations the title for the top manager often is executive director.

External parties benefit from knowledge of an organization's plans. They look for clues on tactics, market demands, competitors, promotion, pricing, innovations, and projections. Much of this information appears in accounting reports. Most public corporations use the *Management Discussion and Analysis* section in their annual reports for this purpose. For example, **Nike** declares in its annual report that "management believes there is tremendous opportunity for growth in markets outside the United States. The Company continues to invest in infrastructure and local marketing and advertising to capitalize on these opportunities." Planning also involves change and reaction to it. It is not cast in stone. This adds *risk* to both the setting of an organization's plans and analysis of them. Accounting information can reduce this risk with more informed analysis and decision making.

Financing

An organization requires financing to begin and operate according to its plans. **Financing activities** are the means organizations use to pay for resources such as land, buildings, and equipment to carry out plans. Organizations are careful in acquiring and managing financing activities because of their potential to determine success or failure.

The two main sources of financing are owner and nonowner. *Owner financing* refers to resources contributed by the owner along with any income the owner chooses to leave in the organization. *Nonowner* (or *creditor*) *financing* refers to resources contributed by creditors (lenders). Creditors often include banks, savings and loans, and other financial institutions. *Financial management* is the task of planning how to obtain these resources and to set the right mix between the amounts of owner and creditor financing. **Nike**'s total financing at May 31, 2000, equaled $5,856.9 million. It comprised $3,136.0 million in owner financing and $2,720.9 million in creditor financing.

Investing

Investing activities are the acquiring and disposing of resources (assets) that an organization uses to acquire and sell its products or services. **Assets** are resources that are expected to possess current and future benefits and are funded by an organization's financing. Assets include land, buildings, equipment, inventories, supplies, cash, and all investments needed for operating an organization. **Nike**'s assets, at May 31, 2000, totaled $5,856.9 million. Organizations differ on the amount and makeup of their assets. Some organizations require land and factories to operate. Others might need only an office. Determining the amount and type of assets for operations is called *asset management*.

The concept that an organization's investing and financing totals are *always* equal is important. Invested amounts are referred to as *assets,* and financing is made up of creditor and owner financing. This implies creditors and owners hold claims on assets. Creditors' claims are called **liabilities** and the owner's claim is called **owner's equity** (or simply *equity*). This equality can be written as follows:

$$\text{Assets} = \text{Liabilities} + \text{Equity}$$

This equality is called the **accounting equation.** At May 31, 2000, **Nike**'s assets of $5,856.9 equal its liabilities of $2,720.9 plus its equity of $3,136.0 (in millions):

$$\text{Assets} = \text{Liabilities} + \text{Equity}$$
$$\$5,856.9 = \$2,720.9 + \$3,136.0$$

The accounting equation works for all organizations at all times. It is an important part of accounting. We will return to and use the accounting equation in our analysis of transactions throughout the book.

Operating

An organization's main purpose is to carry out operating activities. **Operating activities** involve using resources to research, develop, purchase, produce, distribute, and market products and services. They also include management activities such as worker supervision and compliance with laws. Sales are the inflow of assets from selling products and services. Costs and expenses are the outflow of assets to support operating activities. Examples of costs and expenses are salaries, rent, electricity, and supplies. *Strategic management* is the process of determining the right mix of operating activities for the type of organization, its plans, and its market. How well an organization carries out its operating activities determines its success and return.

Exhibit 1.7 summarizes these activities. Planning is part of each activity, and gives the activities meaning and focus. Investing (assets) and financing (liabilities and equity) are set opposite each other to stress their balance. Operating activities are shown below investing and financing activities to emphasize that operating activities are the result of investing and financing.

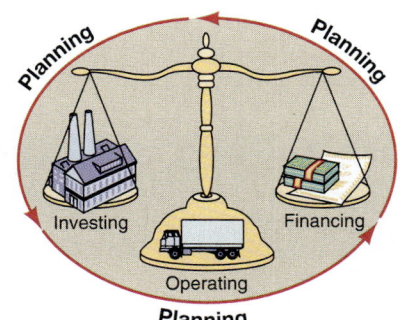

Exhibit 1.7
Activities in Organizations

Infographics reinforce key concepts through visual learning.

Quick Check

7. What are the three basic forms of business organization?
8. What are examples of nonbusiness organizations?
9. What are the three major activities in organizations?

Answers—p. 23

Four basic financial statements report on an organization's activities: balance sheet, income statement, statement of changes in owner's (or shareholders') equity, and statement of cash flows. This section introduces us to each of these statements using **Nike**'s data. We cover details of each statement in later chapters.

Financial Statements

P1   Identify and prepare basic financial statements.

Concept 1-2

Balance Sheet

A balance sheet reports on investing and financing. It lists amounts for assets, liabilities, and equity at a *point in time*. The balance sheet for **Nike** is shown in Exhibit 1.8. Its accounting (fiscal) year ends on May 31. Nike's numbers are all in millions, meaning we must multiply its numbers by 1 million to get actual amounts. Nike's assets total $5,856.9 and is the amount invested. Its liabilities are $2,720.9, and its equity is $3,136.0—their sum equals total financing.

Exhibit 1.8

Balance Sheet

NIKE Balance Sheet (in millions) May 31, 2000			
Assets	$5,856.9	Liabilities	$2,720.9
. . . .		Equity	3,136.0
Total assets	$5,856.9	Total liabilities and equity	$5,856.9

Exhibit 1.9

Income Statement

NIKE Income Statement (in millions) For Year Ended May 31, 2000	
Revenues	$8,995.1
Costs and expenses	8,416.0
Net income	$ 579.1

Income Statement

An income statement reports on operating activities. It lists amounts for sales (revenues) less all costs and expenses over a *period of time*. This yields the "bottom line" net income amount. **Nike**'s income statement is shown in Exhibit 1.9. Net income is $579.1 and is computed as revenues of $8,995.1 less its costs and expenses of $8,416.0 (in millions).

Statement of Changes in Owner's Equity

Exhibit 1.10

Statement of Changes in Owner's (Shareholders') Equity

NIKE Statement of Changes in Owner's (Shareholders') Equity (in millions) For Year Ended May 31, 2000	
Equity, May 31, 1999	$3,334.6
Add: Net income	579.1
Less: Withdrawals (dividends) . . .	(131.5)
Other changes	(646.2)
Equity, May 31, 2000	$3,136.0

A statement of changes in owner's equity reports changes in the owner's claim on the business's assets over a *period of time*. This includes changes due to income and any owner contributions and withdrawals. Since **Nike** is a corporation, its owners are called *shareholders*. The statement of changes in shareholders' equity for Nike is shown in Exhibit 1.10. Two major items affecting Nike's equity are its net income of $579.1 and withdrawals (dividends) of $131.5.

Statement of Cash Flows

Exhibit 1.11

Statement of Cash Flows

NIKE Statement of Cash Flows (in millions) For Year Ended May 31, 2000	
Cash from operating activities	$759.9
Cash from investing activities	(440.0)
Cash from financing activities	(263.7)
Net increase in cash	$ 56.2

The statement of cash flows reports on cash flows for operating, investing, and financing activities over a *period of time*. **Nike**'s statement of cash flows is shown in Exhibit 1.11. Its cash balance increased by $56.2. Of this increase in cash, Nike's operating activities provided $759.9 in cash, its investing activities used $440.0, and its financing activities (including exchange rate changes) used $263.7.

Organizations set up accounting information systems to help them and others make better decisions. Every organization uses some type of information system to report on its activities. Exhibit 1.12 shows that the accounting information system serves many kinds of users including managers, lenders, suppliers, customers, directors, auditors, employees, and current and potential investors.

Users of Accounting Information

 Identify users and uses of accounting.

External Information Users

External users of accounting information are *not* directly involved in running the organization. They include shareholders, lenders, directors, customers, suppliers, regulators, lawyers, brokers, and the press. External users rely on accounting information to make better decisions. For example, lenders are less likely to make bad loans and shareholders bad investments when they know the current and past income of a business.

Internal users

- Managers
- Officers
- Internal auditors
- Sales staff
- Budget officers
- Controllers

External users

- Lenders
- Shareholders
- Governments
- Labor unions
- External auditors
- Customers

Exhibit 1.12

Users of Accounting Information

Financial accounting is the area of accounting aimed at serving external users. Its main objective is to provide financial statements to help users analyze an organization's activities. External users have limited access to an organization's information. Their success depends on financial statements that are reliable, relevant, and comparable. Some governmental and regulatory agencies have the power to require statements in specific forms, but most external users must rely on *general-purpose financial statements*. The phrase *general-purpose* refers to the broad range of purposes for which external users rely on these statements.

Each external user has special information needs depending on the types of decisions to be made. These decisions involve getting answers to key questions, answers that are often available in accounting reports. This section describes several external users and questions they ask.

Point: EDGAR is a database of documents that public companies file electronically with the SEC. Several Web sites offer easy-to-use interfaces (most are free), making it a snap to find most public info on a company—see www.freeedgar.com, www.edgar-online.com, or edgarscan.tc.pw.com.

Lenders (Creditors)

Lenders loan money or other resources to an organization. They include banks, savings and loans, co-ops, and mortgage and finance companies. Lenders look for information to help them assess whether an organization is likely to repay its loans with interest. Financial statements help them answer questions about an organization such as:

- Has it promptly paid past loans?
- What are its current risks?
- Can it repay current loans?
- What is its income outlook?

The questions can also change for short- and long-term lending decisions. The more long-term a loan, the more a lender's questions look like those of an owner.

Shareholders (Owners)

Shareholders have legal control over part or all of a corporation. They are its owners and in many cases are not part of management. Owners are exposed to the greatest return and risk. Risk is high because there is no promise of either repayment or a return on investment. They

Point: The World Wrestling
Federation has 56,667,000 shares of
Class B common stock and
11,500,000 shares of Class A
common stock outstanding.

Real company logos often
accompany references to actual
financial data.

can lose their entire investment. On the upside, owners have a claim on assets after a business pays its debts. Many businesses do not return income to owners but instead invests it in company growth. Financial statements aim to help answer shareholder (owner) questions such as these:

- What is current and past income?
- Are assets adequate to meet plans?
- Do expenses seem reasonable?
- Do customers pay bills promptly?
- Do loan amounts seem too high?

Shareholders typically elect a board of directors to oversee their interests in an organization. Since directors are responsible to shareholders, their questions are similar.

External Auditors

External (independent) auditors examine financial statements and provide an opinion on whether the statements are prepared according to generally accepted accounting principles. Auditors use financial statements of competing organizations to help assess the reasonableness of a client's statements. **Nike**'s auditor is **PricewaterhouseCoopers LLP**.

Employees

Employees have a special interest in an organization. They are interested in judging the fairness of wages and in assessing future job prospects. Financial statements provide information useful in addressing these interests. They are also used in bargaining for better wages when an organization is successful.

Regulators

Global: In some countries, financial
reporting is based on tax reports.
Companies in these countries have
incentives to reduce reported
income.

Regulators often have legal authority or significant influence over the activities of organizations. The Internal Revenue Service (IRS) and other tax authorities require organizations to use specific reports in computing taxes. These taxes include income, unemployment, sales, and social security. Tax reports usually require special forms and supporting records. Examples of other regulators include utility boards that use accounting information to set utility rates and securities regulators that require special filings for businesses with publicly traded securities.

Other Important External Users

Point: Microsoft's income levels
encouraged recent antitrust actions
against it.

Accounting serves the needs of many other important external users. Voters, legislators, and elected officials use accounting information to monitor and evaluate a government's receipts and expenses. Contributors to nonprofit organizations use accounting information to evaluate the use and impact of their donations. Suppliers use accounting information to judge the soundness of a customer before making sales on credit. Customers use financial reports to assess the staying power of potential suppliers.

Point: The "top 5" greatest
investors of the 20th century, as
compiled in a recent survey:
1. Warren Buffett,
   Berkshire Hathaway
2. Peter Lynch,
   Fidelity Funds
3. John Templeton,
   Templeton Group
4. Benjamin Graham &
   David Dodd, professors
5. George Soros,
   Soros Fund

Internal Information Users

Internal users of accounting information are individuals directly involved in managing and operating an organization. The internal role of accounting is to provide information to help improve the efficiency and effectiveness of an organization in delivering products and services.

   Managerial accounting is the area of accounting aimed at serving the decision-making needs of internal users. It provides internal reports to help internal users improve an organization's activities. Internal reports are not subject to the same rules as external reports because decisions of internal users are not constrained by the need to keep certain information private due to competitive concerns. Costs to prepare internal reports usually represent the only constraint on internal reporting. Internal reports aim to answer questions such as these:

- What are costs per product?
- What service mix is most profitable?
- Are sales sufficient to break even?
- Which activities are most profitable?
- What costs vary with sales?

Information to help answer these questions is important for success.

Exhibit 1.13 shows seven internal operating functions common to most organizations: research and development, purchasing, human resources, production, distribution, marketing, and servicing. Accounting is essential to the operation of each function. Each unit often has its own internal user (manager) who makes decisions. Depending on the type of business, not all of these functions may be necessary (or some may be combined). For example, publishing companies usually do not require separate research and development units, and banks do not require production units. We briefly describe the information needs of each function:

Exhibit 1.13
Internal Operating Functions

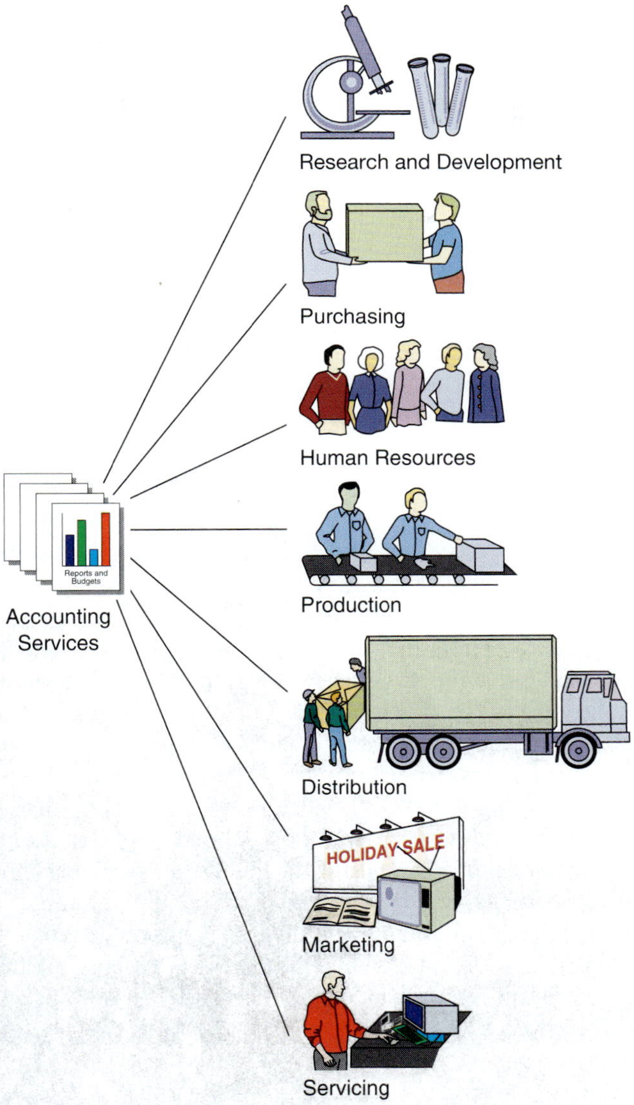

- **Research and development** Research and development seeks to create or improve products and services. Managers need information about current and projected costs and sales.
- **Purchasing** Purchasing involves acquiring and managing materials for operations. Managers need to know what, when, and how much to purchase.
- **Human resources** Human resources management locates, screens, hires, trains, compensates, promotes, and counsels employees. Managers need information about current and potential employees, payroll, benefits, performance, and compensation.
- **Production** Production is the mix of activities to produce products and services. Good production methods depend on information to monitor costs and ensure quality.
- **Distribution** Distribution involves timely and accurate delivery of products and services. Information is often key to quality, low-cost distribution.
- **Marketing** Marketing promotes and advertises products and services. Marketing managers use reports about sales and costs to target consumers, set prices, and monitor consumer needs, tastes, and price concerns.

Point: There are 3 different types of businesses: (1) Services—provide services for profit, (2) Merchandisers—buy products and sell them for profit, and (3) Manufacturers—create products and sell them for profit.

■ **Servicing**   Servicing customers after selling products and services is often key to success. It includes training, assistance, installation, warranties, and maintenance. Information is needed on both the costs and benefits of servicing.

Both internal and external users rely on internal controls to monitor and control these functions. Internal controls are procedures set up to protect assets, ensure reliable accounting reports, promote efficiency, and encourage adherence to company policies.

Ethics and Social Responsibility

C5 Explain why ethics and social responsibility are crucial to accounting.

Ethics and ethical behavior are important. We are reminded of this when we run across stories in the media about cheating, harassment, misconduct, bribery, or when we witness wrongful actions. This section explains ethics and their effect on organizations. We consider ethics early in our study because of their importance to accounting. The goal of accounting is to provide useful information for decisions. For information to be useful, it must be trusted. This demands ethics in accounting. This section also discusses social responsibility for organizations.

Understanding Ethics

Ethics are beliefs that distinguish right from wrong. They are accepted standards of good and bad behavior. Ethics and laws often coincide, with the result that many unethical actions (such as theft and physical violence) are also illegal. Yet other actions are legal but are considered unethical, such as not helping people in need. Because of differences between laws and ethics, we cannot look to laws to always keep people ethical.

Identifying the ethical path is sometimes difficult. The preferred path is a course of action that avoids casting doubt on our decision. For example, accounting users are less likely to trust an auditor's report if the auditor's pay depends on the success of the client. To avoid such concerns, ethics rules are often set. For example, auditors are banned from direct investment in their client. Auditors also cannot accept pay that depends on figures in the client's reports. Exhibit 1.14 gives guidelines for making ethical decisions. A commitment to ethical behavior requires us to think carefully before we act to be certain we are making ethical decisions.

Point: AICPAs *Code of Professional Conduct* is available at www.AICPA.org.

Exhibit 1.14

Guidelines for Ethical Decision Making

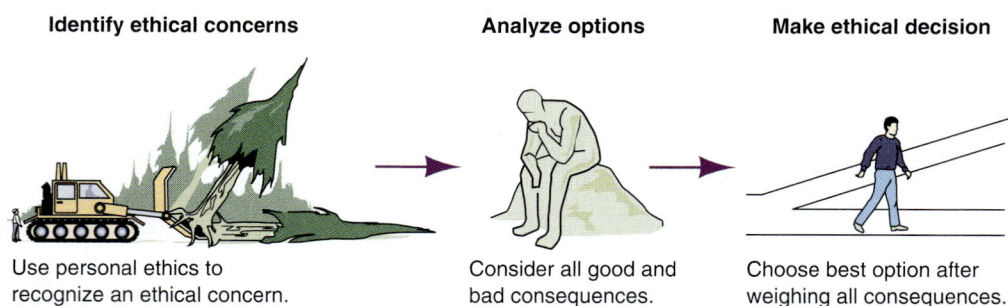

| **Identify ethical concerns** | **Analyze options** | **Make ethical decision** |
| Use personal ethics to recognize an ethical concern. | Consider all good and bad consequences. | Choose best option after weighing all consequences. |

Organizational Ethics

Organizational ethics are likely learned through example and leadership. Companies such as **McDonald's, Marriott,** and **IBM** work hard to instill ethics in employees, yet we still hear people express concern about what they see as poor ethics in organizations. One survey of executives, educators, and legislators showed that 9 of 10 participants believe organizations are troubled by ethical problems. Yet this survey also revealed that the vast majority of participants believe organizations that are successful over the long run follow high ethical standards. This finding confirms an old saying: *Good ethics are good business*. Ethical practices build trust, which promotes loyalty and long-term relationships with customers, suppliers, and employees. Because of this and the public interest in ethics, many organizations have their own code of ethics. These codes set standards for internal activities and external relationships.

Accounting Ethics

Ethics are crucial in accounting. Providers of accounting information often face ethical choices as they prepare financial reports. Their choices can affect both the use and receipt of money, including taxes owed and the money dispersed to owners. They can affect the price a buyer pays and the wages paid to workers. They can even affect the success of products, services, and divisions. Misleading information can lead to a wrongful closing of a division that harms workers, customers, and suppliers. Accordingly, codes of accounting ethics are set up and enforced. These codes include those of the American Institute of Certified Public Accountants and the Institute of Management Accountants. These codes can help when confronted with ethical dilemmas. For example, organizations often pay managers bonuses based on the amount of income reported. Managers can benefit from applying accounting in ways to increase their pay. This can reduce the money available for employee wages, training programs, and community giving. Ethics codes also can help in dealing with confidential information. For example, auditors have access to an organization's confidential salaries and strategies. Organizations can be harmed if auditors pass this information to others. To prevent this, auditors' ethics codes require them to keep this information confidential. Internal accountants also are not to use confidential information for personal gain.

Social Responsibility

Social responsibility refers to a concern for the impact of actions on society. Organizations are increasingly concerned with their social responsibility. **Reebok** proclaims in its annual report: "We have a deep-felt commitment to operate in a socially responsible way and we stand for human rights throughout the world." Society has increased the pressure on organizations to act responsibly, and they have responded to this challenge.

An organization's social responsibility can include donations to hospitals, colleges, community programs, and law enforcement. It also can include programs to reduce pollution, increase product safety, improve worker conditions, support continuing education, and better use our natural resources. Yet most organizations are more likely to invest in their own social programs. For example, **Nike** invests in its *P.L.A.Y.* (*Participate in the Lives of America's Youth*) program that provides facilities for kids to pursue fitness and fun. **Xerox** offers its workers up to a one-year leave to work for a nonprofit organization. During their leaves, the workers receive full salary and benefits. We are aware of well over 1,000 businesses that offer social programs to their employees to pursue community service activities. These programs are not limited to large companies. For example, many independently owned theaters and sports businesses offer discounts to students and senior citizens. Still others help sponsor events such as the Special Olympics and summer reading programs with the local library.

Graphical displays are often used to illustrate key points.

Did You Know?

Returns on Social Responsibility Virtue is not always its own reward. Compare the **S&P 500,** which includes companies selling weapons, alcohol, and tobacco, with the **Domini Social Index (DSI),** which covers 400 companies that have especially good records of social responsibility. Notice that returns for companies with socially responsible behavior are at least as high if not higher than those of the S&P 500.

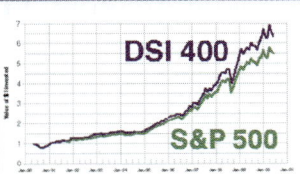

Point: Paul Newman donates all income from sale of his *Newman's Own* products to charity.

Support for social programs by organizations is not universal. Some argue that an organization's interests might be different from those of its workers and customers. It is sometimes argued that an organization should instead increase pay to its workers so that they can contribute to their own community's concerns. While debate about the charitable giving of organizations will continue, social responsibility is part of modern business.

Quick Check

10. Who are the internal and external users of accounting information?
11. Identify seven internal operating functions in organizations.
12. Why are internal controls important?
13. What are the guidelines in helping us make ethical decisions?
14. Why are ethics and social responsibility valuable to organizations?
15. Why are ethics crucial in accounting?

Answers—p. 23

Opportunities in Practice

C6 Identify opportunities in accounting and related fields.

Accounting information affects many aspects of our lives. When we earn money, pay taxes, invest savings, budget earnings, and plan for the future, we are influenced by accounting. Accounting knowledge helps us better perform and compete in society. This section discusses four areas of opportunities in accounting: financial, managerial, taxation, and accounting-related. Exhibit 1.15 lists selected opportunities in each area. These areas employ millions of individuals in accounting or accounting-related careers.

Exhibit 1.15

Opportunities in Practice

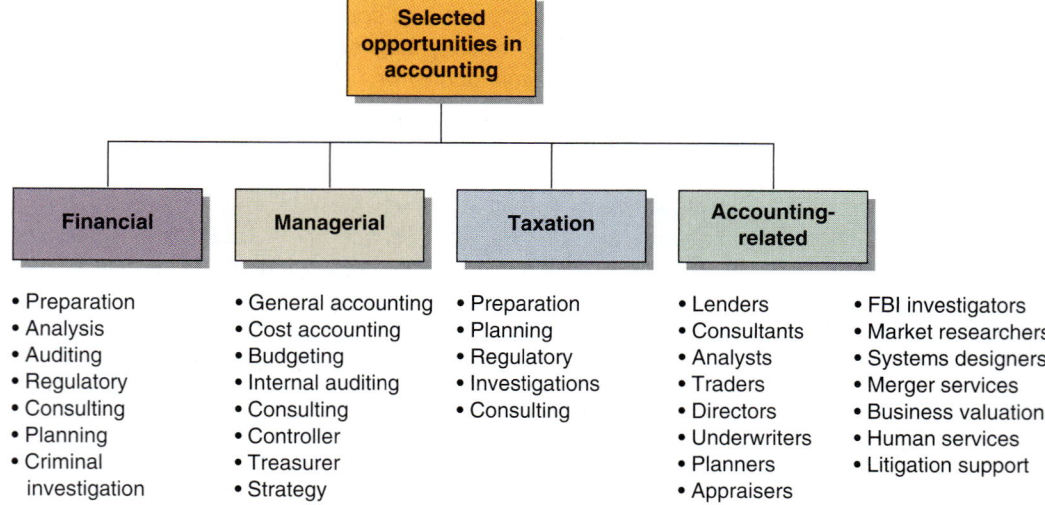

Financial Accounting

Financial accounting provides information to decision makers that are external to an organization. This information is normally in the form of general-purpose financial statements. The process of preparing financial statements demands the input of many individuals within and outside accounting. There is also a demand for auditing in financial accounting. An **audit** is a check of an organization's accounting systems and records using various tests. It increases the credibility of financial statements. When an audit is complete, an auditor writes an *audit report* expressing a professional *opinion* about whether the financial statements are fairly presented. It is an opinion because an auditor does not verify every transaction and event. **Nike**'s audit report is in Appendix A.

Managerial Accounting

Managerial accounting provides information to an organization's internal decision makers. Managerial accounting activities generally fall within one of five areas:

1. *General accounting* refers to the recording of transactions, the processing of data, and the preparing of reports for internal use. It is supervised by a chief accounting officer called a *controller*.
2. *Cost accounting* is a process of accumulating the information managers need to identify, measure, and control costs. It involves accounting for the costs of products and services and is useful for evaluating managerial performance.
3. *Budgeting* is the development of formal plans for an organization's future activities. It provides a basis for evaluating actual performance.
4. *Internal auditing* adds credibility to reports that are produced and used within the organization. Internal auditors assess the effectiveness and efficiency of established operating procedures.
5. *Management consulting* helps organizations design and install new accounting and control systems, develop budgeting procedures, and set up employee benefit plans.

Point: Accounting offers many career opportunities that are both challenging and rewarding and that require strong interpersonal and communication skills.

Tax Accounting

Taxes raised by federal, state, and local governments include those based on income reported by taxpayers. *Tax accounting* helps taxpayers comply with the law by preparing tax returns. It also plans future transactions to minimize taxes. The Internal Revenue Service is a major employer of tax services. It is responsible for collecting federal taxes and enforcing tax law.

Point: The Internal Revenue Code is complex. As a result, it is often less costly for small companies to pay accountants to do their tax work than to develop the necessary expertise among their employees.

Accounting Specialization

The majority of accounting professionals work in **private accounting** as shown in Exhibit 1.16. A large company can employ 100 or more accounting professionals, but most have fewer. Another large number of accounting professionals are employed in **public accounting** whose services are available to the public. Many in public accounting are self-employed; others work for public accounting firms whose employees number from few to several thousand. Another large number of accounting professionals work in nonbusiness organizations, with many of these in federal, state, or local government. *Government accountants* perform accounting services for government units, including business regulation and investigation of law violations.

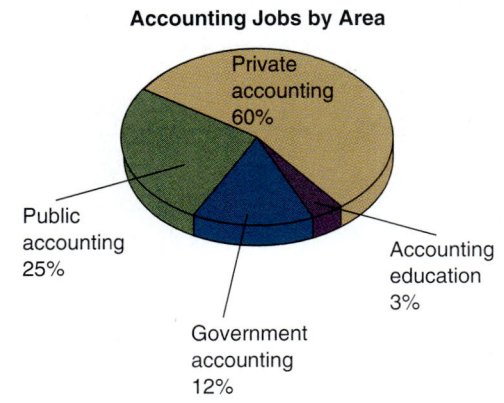

Accounting Jobs by Area

Exhibit 1.16

Accounting Jobs by Area

Accounting specialists are highly regarded. Their professional standing often is denoted by a certificate. Certified Public Accountants (CPAs) must meet education and experience requirements, pass the CPA examination, and exhibit ethical character. Most states require a college degree with the equivalent of a major in accounting. The CPA examination covers topics in financial and managerial accounting, taxation, auditing, and business law. Many accounting specialists hold certificates in addition to or instead of the CPA license. Two of the most common are the Certificate in Management Accounting (CMA) and the Certified Internal Auditor (CIA). Holders of these certificates must meet examination, education, and experience requirements similar to those of a CPA. The CMA is awarded by the Institute of Management Accountants and the CIA is granted by the Institute of Internal Auditors. Another prestigious certificate is the Chartered Financial Analyst (CFA) awarded by the Association for Investment Management and

Point: Many states accept graduate study in accounting as a substitute for experience in meeting CPA requirements.

Research (AIMR). Employers also look for specialists with designations such as certified bookkeeper (CB), certified payroll professional (CPP), and personal financial specialist (PFS).

Accounting-Related Opportunities

Accounting-related opportunities are vast. Accounting is the common language of modern business communications. It spans professions, continents, and economies. Exhibit 1.15 listed several accounting-related opportunities, including lenders, consultants, analysts, and planners. Less traditional ones include community activist, political consultant, reporter, salesperson, union official, entrepreneur, programmer, and engineer.

Outlook and Compensation

Point: The firm of Ernst & Young gives its interns a vacation at Disney World.

Employers are desperately seeking to hire individuals with accounting knowledge. Beyond the usual accounting work, however, employers want these individuals to help with financial analysis, strategic planning, e-commerce, product feasibility, information technology, and financial management. Demand is so great that many employers are offering signing bonuses along with stock options, profit sharing, and performance bonuses. Benefit packages often include flexible work schedules, telecommuting options, career path options, casual work environments, extended vacation time, and child and elder care. Employers are also offering options to full-time work, including temporary employment and project work.

Point: For updated salary information, check out
www.accountemps.com
www.aicpa.org
www.abbott-langer.com
www.experienceondemand.com
www.mamag.com/strategicfinance

Intense demand for accounting specialists led the American Institute of Certified Public Accountants (AICPA) to send career information to thousands of high schools. Demand for accounting specialists is also boosting salaries. Exhibit 1.17 reports average starting salaries for several accounting positions. Note that for each position, salary variation depends on location, company size, professional designation, expertise, experience, and other factors. For example, salaries for chief financial officers range from under $75,000 to more than $500,000 per year. Likewise, salaries for bookkeepers range from under $28,000 to more than $45,000.

Exhibit 1.17
Accounting Salaries

Title (experience)	2000 Salary	2005 Estimate*
Public Accounting		
Partner	$121,000	$155,000
Manager	66,500	82,000
Senior	45,500	59,000
Staff (1–3 years)	39,000	48,000
Entry (0–1 years)	34,000	43,500
Private Accounting		
CFO/Treasurer	149,000	185,500
Controller	111,000	144,000
Asst. treasurer/Controller	70,000	87,500
Manager	64,000	80,000
Senior	46,000	60,000
Staff (1–3 years)	39,000	49,000
Entry (0–1 years)	33,500	42,500
Bookkeeping		
Full-charge bookkeeper	38,000	47,500
Payroll manager	35,000	44,500
Accounts manager	34,500	44,000
Assistant bookkeeper	30,500	38,500
Accounting clerk	26,500	34,500

* Estimates assume a 5% compounded annual increase over current levels; these estimates are likely low since the National Association of Colleges and Employers reported an 8.8% increase in starting pay of accounting graduates for 2000 alone.

Using The Information (a section at the end of each chapter) introduces and explains important ratios and tools helpful in decision making. It illustrates these using real company data.

Return on Investment

We introduced return on investment in assessing return and risk earlier in the chapter. Return on investment is also useful in evaluating management, analyzing and forecasting profits, and planning activities. **Dell Computer** has its marketing department compute return on investment for *every* mailing. Dell's chief financial officer says it spent over a year teaching its workers how to apply return on investment. This section describes return on investment and how it can help us with financial analysis. **Return on investment (ROI),** also called *return on assets (ROA),* is viewed as an indicator of operating efficiency and is defined in Exhibit 1.18.

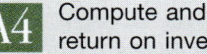 Compute and interpret return on investment.

$$\text{Return on investment} = \frac{\text{Net income}}{\text{Average total assets}}$$

Exhibit 1.18

Return on Investment

Net income is usually taken from the annual income statement.[2] The average total assets figure is usually computed by adding the beginning and ending amounts of total assets for that same period and dividing by 2. To illustrate, let's look at Nike. Nike reports net income of $579.1 million in 2000. At the beginning of 2000, its total assets are $5,247.7 million and at the end of 2000 they total $5,856.9 million. Nike's return on investment for 2000 is:

$$\text{Return on investment} = \frac{\$579.1 \text{ mil.}}{(\$5,247.7 \text{ mil.} + \$5,856.9 \text{ mil.})/2} = 10.4\%$$

Is a 10.4% return on investment good or bad for Nike? To help answer this question and others like it, we can compare (benchmark) Nike's return on investment with its prior performance, the returns of similar companies (such as **Reebok, Converse, Skechers,** and **Vans**), and the returns from alternative investments. Nike's return on investment for each of the prior five years is reported in the second column of Exhibit 1.19, which ranges from 7.4% to 17.1%. These returns suggest a recent decline with Nike's efficiency in using its assets. We can also compare Nike to a similar company such as Reebok, whose return on investment is shown in the third column of Exhibit 1.19. In four of the five years shown, Nike's return exceeds Reebok's, and its average return is higher for this period. We can also

	Return on Investment		
Fiscal Year	**Nike**	**Reebok**	**Industry**
2000	10.4%	0.7%	1.4%
1999	8.5	1.4	1.8
1998	7.4	7.7	3.7
1997	17.1	8.1	5.9
1996	15.6	10.0	8.6

Exhibit 1.19

Nike, Reebok, and Industry Returns

---

[2] For a noncorporation, the owner's effort on its behalf is not a recordable expense. This is because a noncorporation is not legally separate from its owner(s). Therefore, for a noncorporation, we compute a *modified return on investment* ratio that reduces net income by the value of the owner's effort (if any) as follows:

$$\text{Modified return on investment} = \frac{\text{Net income} - \text{Value of owner's effort}}{\text{Average total assets}}$$

You Make the Call concludes each *Using the Information* section with a role-playing scenario to show the usefulness of the ratio.

You Make the Call   *e*

Entrepreneur   You own a small winter ski resort that earns a 21% return on its investment. An opportunity to purchase a winter ski equipment manufacturer is offered to you. This manufacturer earns a 19% return on its investment. The industry return for this manufacturer is 14%. Do you purchase this manufacturer?

Answer—p. 23

compare Nike's return to the normal return for manufacturers of athletic footwear. Industry averages are available from services such as **Dun & Bradstreet**'s (D&B) *Industry Norms and Key Ratios* and **Robert Morris Associates**' (RMA) *Annual Statement Studies*. When compared to its competitors, Nike performs well.[3] Another useful analysis is to compare Nike's returns to those of companies outside its industry.

A **Summary** organized by learning objectives concludes each chapter.

Summary

C1   Explain the aim and influence of accounting in the information age. Accounting is an information and measurement system that aims to identify, record, and communicate relevant, reliable, and comparable information about business activities. It helps assess opportunities, products, investments, and social and community responsibilities.

C2   Identify forms of organization and their characteristics. Organizations can be classified as either businesses or nonbusinesses. Businesses are organized for profit; nonbusinesses serve us in ways not always measured by profit. Businesses take one of three basic forms: sole proprietorship, partnership, or corporation. These forms of organization have characteristics that hold important implications for legal liability, taxation, continuity, number of owners, and legal status.

C3   Identify and describe the three major activities in organizations. Organizations carry out three major activities: financing, investing, and operating. Financing is the means used to pay for resources such as land, buildings, and machines. Investing refers to the buying and selling of resources used in acquiring and selling products and services. Operating activities are those necessary for carrying out the organization's plans.

C4   Identify users and uses of accounting. Users of accounting are both internal and external. Some users and uses of accounting include (a) managers in controlling, monitoring, and planning; (b) lenders for measuring the risk and return of loans; (c) shareholders for assessing the return and risk of stock; (d) directors for overseeing management; and (e) employees for judging employment opportunities.

C5   Explain why ethics and social responsibility are crucial to accounting. The goal of accounting is to provide useful information for decision making. For information to be useful, it must be trusted. This demands ethics and socially responsible behavior in accounting.

C6   Identify opportunities in accounting and related fields. Opportunities in accounting include financial, managerial, and tax accounting. They also include accounting-related fields such as lending, consulting, managing, and planning. Many other opportunities with accounting knowledge also exist.

A1   Describe income and its two major components. Income (also called profit or earnings) is the amount a business earns after subtracting all expenses necessary for its sales (Sales − Expenses = Income). Sales (also called revenues) are the amounts earned from selling products and services. Expenses are the costs incurred with generating sales. A loss arises when expenses are more than sales.

A2   Explain the relation between return and risk. *Return* refers to income, and *risk* is the uncertainty about the return we hope to make. All business decisions involve risk. The lower the risk of an investment, the lower is its expected return. Higher risk implies higher, but riskier, expected return.

A3   Explain and interpret the accounting equation. Investing activities are funded by financing activities. An organization cannot have more or less assets than its financing and, similarly, it cannot have more or less nonowner (liabilities) and owner (equity) financing than its assets. This relation yields the accounting equation: Assets = Liabilities + Equity.

A4   Compute and interpret return on investment. Return on investment is computed as net income divided by the average amount invested. For example, if we have an average balance of $100 in a savings account and it earns $5 interest for the year, the return on investment is $5/$100, or 5%.

P1   Identify and prepare basic financial statements. Four basic financial statements report on an organization's activities: balance sheet, income statement, statement of changes in owner's equity, and statement of cash flows.

---

[3] The industry ratio, shown in the fourth column of Exhibit 1.19, is the median value computed from 10 competitors, including Fila, Converse, Stride Rite, K-Swiss, Skechers, and Vans among others.

Guidance Answers to **You Make the Call**

Programmer As the computer programmer, you confront a trade-off between return (salary) and risk (dependable employment). The start-up company has an uncertain future and is willing to increase your pay to balance the added risk you take in working for it (it could fail). The established company pays less, but you are reasonably assured of employment. If you or others depend on your salary, the risk of the start-up company might be too high. Yet if you depend less on your salary, the increased pay might be worth the risk.

Entrepreneur You should probably form the business as a corporation if potential lawsuits are of prime concern. The corporate form of organization protects your personal property from lawsuits directed at the business and would place only the corporation's resources at risk. A downside of the corporate form is double taxation—the corporation must pay taxes on its income, and you must

pay taxes on any money distributed to you from the business (even though the corporation already paid taxes on this money). You should also examine the ethical and socially responsible aspects of starting a business in which you anticipate injuries to others. (Chapter 13 describes LLCs as another reasonable form.)

Entrepreneur The 19% return on investment for the manufacturer exceeds the 14% industry return (and many others). This is a positive factor for a potential purchase. Also, the purchase of this manufacturer is an opportunity to spread your risk over two businesses as opposed to one. Still, you should hesitate to purchase a business whose return of 19% is lower than your current resort's return of 21%. You are probably better off directing efforts to increase investment in your resort, assuming you can continue to earn a 21% return.

Guidance Answers to **Quick Checks**

1. Accounting is an information and measurement system that identifies, records, and communicates relevant information to help people make better decisions. These decisions can involve opportunities, products, investments, and social and community activities.

2. Income is what a business earns after paying for all expenses necessary for its sales. Sales are the amounts earned from providing products and services. Expenses are the costs incurred with generating sales.

3. The lower the risk of an investment, the lower is the expected return. Similarly, higher expected return offsets higher risk (*actual* return usually differs from *expected* return). Higher risk implies higher, but riskier, expected returns.

4. Recordkeeping, also called *bookkeeping,* is the recording of financial transactions and events, either manually or electronically. Recordkeeping is essential to data reliability; accounting is this and much more. Accounting includes identifying, measuring, recording, reporting, and analyzing business events and transactions.

5. Many individuals and groups determine accounting rules that reflect society's needs, not those of accountants or any other single constituency. Major participants in setting rules include the Securities and Exchange Commission (SEC) and the Financial Accounting Standards Board (FASB).

6. Technology offers increased accuracy, speed, efficiency, and convenience in accounting.

7. The three basic forms of business organizations are sole proprietorships, partnerships, and corporations.

8. Nonbusiness organizations include airports, libraries, museums, churches, cities, police, colleges, bus lines, utilities, highways, fraternities, shelters, parks, hospitals, and schools.

9. Organizations pursue financing, investing, and operating activities. These three major activities all require planning.

10. External users of accounting include lenders, shareholders, directors, customers, suppliers, regulators, lawyers, brokers, and the press. Internal users of accounting include managers, officers, and other internal decision makers involved with strategic and operating decisions.

11. Internal operating functions include research and development, purchasing, human resources, production, distribution, marketing, and servicing.

12. Internal controls are procedures set up to protect assets, ensure reliable accounting reports, promote efficiency, and encourage adherence to company policies. Internal controls are crucial for relevant and reliable information.

13. Ethical guidelines are threefold: (1) identify ethical concerns using personal ethics, (2) analyze options considering all good and bad consequences, and (3) make ethical decision after weighing all consequences.

14. Ethics and social responsibility often translate into higher profits and a better working environment.

15. For accounting to provide useful information for decisions, it must be trusted. Trust demands ethics in accounting.

Glossary

Accounting an information and measurement system that identifies, records, and communicates relevant information about a company's business activities. (p. 4).

Accounting equation the equality where Assets = Liabilities + Equity. (p. 11).

Assets resources expected to produce current and future benefits. (p. 10).

Audit an analysis and report of an organization's accounting system and its records using various tests. (p. 18).

A **Glossary** of key terms concludes each chapter (a complete glossary is on the book's Web site).

Bonds written promises to repay amounts loaned with interest. (p. 6).

Bookkeeping part of accounting that involves recording transactions and events, either electronically or manually (also called *recordkeeping*). (p. 6).

Business one or more individuals selling products and/or services for profit. (p. 4).

Common stock a corporation's basic ownership share (also called *capital stock*). (p. 9).

Corporation a business that is a separate legal entity under state or federal laws with owners called *shareholders* or *stockholders*. (p. 9).

Earnings (see *income*). (p. 5).

Ethics codes of conduct by which actions are judged as right or wrong, fair or unfair, honest or dishonest. (p. 16).

Expenses the costs incurred to earn sales. (p. 5).

External users persons using accounting information who are not directly involved in running the organization. (p. 13).

Financial accounting area of accounting aimed at serving external users. (p. 13).

Financial Accounting Standards Board (FASB) independent group of seven full-time members who are responsible for setting accounting rules. (p. 7).

Financing activities means organizations use to pay for their resources such as land, buildings, and machinery. (p. 10).

Generally accepted accounting principles (GAAP) rules that specify acceptable accounting practice. (p. 7).

Income (see *net income*). (p. 5).

Information age a time period that emphasizes communication, data, news, facts, access, and commentary. (p. 4).

Internal users persons using accounting information who are directly involved in managing the organization. (p. 14).

Investing activities the buying and selling of resources that an organization controls. (p. 10).

Liabilities creditors' claims on an organization's assets. (p. 11).

Loss arises when expenses are more than sales. (p. 5).

Managerial accounting area of accounting aimed at serving the decision-making needs of internal users. (p. 14).

Net income amount earned after subtracting all expenses necessary for sales (also called *income, profit* or *earnings*). (p. 5).

Operating activities use of assets to carry out an organization's plans in the areas of research, development, purchasing, production, distribution, and marketing. (p. 11).

Owner's equity owner's claim on an organization's assets (also called *equity*). (p. 11).

Partnership a business owned by two or more people that is not organized as a corporation. (p. 8).

Planning term for an organization's ideas, goals, and strategic actions. (p. 10).

Private accounting accounting services provided for an employer other than the government. (p. 19).

Profit (see *income*). (p. 5).

Public accounting accounting services provided to many different clients. (p. 19).

Recordkeeping part of accounting that involves recording transactions and events, either manually or electronically (also called *bookkeeping*). (p. 6).

Return the income from an investment. (p. 5).

Return on investment a ratio serving as an indicator of operating efficiency; defined as net income divided by average total assets. (p. 5).

Revenues amounts earned from selling products or services (also called *sales*). (p. 5).

Risk the amount of uncertainty about an expected return. (p. 5).

Sales amounts earned from selling products or services (also called *revenues*). (p. 5).

Securities and Exchange Commission (SEC) federal agency charged by Congress to set reporting rules for organizations that sell ownership shares to the public. (p. 7).

Shareholders owners of a corporation (also called *stockholders*). (p. 9).

Shares equity of a corporation divided into units (also called *stock*). (p. 9).

Social responsibility being accountable for the impact one's actions might have on society. (p. 17).

Sole proprietorship business owned by one person that is not organized as a corporation (also called *proprietorship*). (p. 8).

Stock (see *shares*). (p. 9).

Stockholders (see *shareholders*). (p. 9).

Questions

1. What is the purpose of accounting in society?
2. What is the relation between accounting and the information superhighway?
3. Identify three businesses that offer services and three businesses that offer products.
4. Explain business income and its computation.
5. Explain return and risk. Discuss the trade-off between them.
6. Why do organizations license and monitor accounting and accounting-related professionals?
7. Technology is increasingly used to process accounting data. Why then do we need to study and understand accounting?
8. Describe the three basic forms of business organization and their characteristics.

9. Identify three types of organizations that can be formed as either profit-oriented businesses, government units, or non-profit establishments.
10. Describe the three major activities in organizations.
11. Explain why investing (assets) and financing (liabilities and equity) totals are always equal.
12. Identify four external users and their uses of accounting information.
13. What are at least three questions business owners might be able to answer by looking at accounting information?
14. Identify at least four managerial accounting tasks performed by both private and government accountants.
15. Describe the internal role of accounting for organizations.

16. What type of accounting information might be useful to those who carry out the marketing activities of a business?

17. What ethical issues might accounting professionals face in dealing with confidential information?

18. Identify three types of services typically offered by accounting professionals.

19. Why is accounting described as a service activity?

20. Identify at least three tasks performed by government accounting professionals.

21. What work do tax accounting professionals perform in addition to preparing tax returns?

22. Define and explain *return on investment* (return on assets).

23. This chapter introduced **Nike**'s financial statements. Nike

was initially organized as a partnership. Identify important characteristics of partnerships and their implications.

24. Access the SEC's EDGAR database [**www.sec.gov**] and retrieve **Nike**'s 10-K for fiscal year 2000. Identify Nike's chief financial officer. How many directors does Nike have?

25. Identify the dollar amounts of **Reebok**'s 1999 assets, liabilities, and equity shown in its statements in Appendix A near the end of the book.

26. Access the SEC EDGAR database [**www.sec.gov**] and retrieve **Gap**'s 10-K for year 2000. Identify its audit firm. What responsibility does its independent auditor claim regarding Gap's financial statements?

Quick Study exercises give readers a brief test of key elements.

QUICK STUDY

Identify the meaning of each of the following accounting and business abbreviations: GAAP, SEC, FASB, IOSCO, and AICPA.

QS 1-1
Identifying accounting abbreviations
C1

Accounting provides information about an organization's business transactions and events. Identify at least two examples of both (*a*) business transactions and (*b*) business events.

QS 1-2
Identifying transactions and events
C3

Identify at least three responsibilities in the *executive management* (planning) activity of an organization.

QS 1-3
Identifying planning activities
C3

An important responsibility of many accounting professionals is to design and implement internal control procedures for organizations. Explain the purpose of internal control procedures.

QS 1-4
Explaining internal control
C4

Identify at least three main areas of opportunities for accounting professionals. For each area, identify at least three accounting-related work opportunities in practice.

QS 1-5
Accounting opportunities
C6

Accounting professionals must sometimes choose between two or more acceptable methods of accounting for business transactions and events. Explain why these situations can involve difficult matters of ethical concern.

QS 1-6
Identifying ethical concerns
C5

---

a. Total assets of Keller Financial Co. equal $50,000 and its equity is $20,000. What is the amount of its liabilities?

b. Total assets of Echo Valley Co. equal $25,000 and its liabilities and equity amounts are equal. What is the amount of its liabilities? What is the amount of its equity?

QS 1-7
Applying the accounting equation

QS 1-8
Applying the accounting equation

Use the accounting equation to compute the missing financial statement amounts.

Assets	=	Liabilities	+	Equity
$ 40,000		$ (a)		$10,000
$ (b)		$60,000		$20,000
$110,000		$20,000		$ (c)

QS 1-9
Identifying and computing assets, liabilities, and equity

Use **Gap**'s January 2000 annual report, printed in Appendix A near the end of the book, to answer the following:

a. Identify the dollar amounts of Gap's 2000 (1) assets, (2) liabilities, and (3) equity.

b. Using Gap's amounts from part (a), verify that: Assets = Liabilities + Equity.

QS 1-10
Identifying items in financial statements

Indicate in which financial statement each item would most likely appear: income statement (I), balance sheet (B), statement of changes in owner's equity (OE), or statement of cash flows (CF).

a. Assets   **d.** Liabilities   **g.** Total liabilities and equity

b. Revenues   **e.** Withdrawal   **h.** Cash from operating activities

c. Equity   **f.** Costs and expenses   **i.** Net decrease (or increase) in cash

---

EXERCISES

Exercise 1-1
Distinguishing business organizations

The following describe several different business organizations. Determine whether the description refers to a sole proprietorship, partnership, or corporation.

a. Ownership of Cola Company is divided into 1,000 shares of stock.

b. Trimark is owned by Sarah Gates, who is personally liable for the debts of the business.

c. Jerry Staley and Susan Morris own Financial Services, a financial services provider. Neither Staley nor Morris has personal responsibility for the debts of Financial Services.

d. Nancy Case and Frank Pruitt own Get-It-There, a courier service. Both are personally liable for the debts of the business.

e. WSP Consulting Services does not have separate legal existence apart from the one person who owns it.

f. BioLife Enterprises does not pay taxes and has one owner.

g. Tampa Trade pays its own taxes and has two owners.

Exercise 1-2
Identifying business activities

Match each task to a major type of organization activity: financing activities (F), investing activities (I), or operating activities (O).

a. _____ An owner contributes resources to the business.

b. _____ An organization purchases equipment.

c. _____ An organization advertises a new product.

d. _____ The organization borrows money from a bank.

e. _____ An organization sells some of its assets.

Exercise 1-3
Describing accounting responsibilities

Many accounting professionals work in one of the following three areas:

A. Financial accounting   **B.** Managerial accounting   **C.** Tax accounting

Identify the area of accounting that is most involved in each of the following responsibilities:

_____ **1.** Auditing financial statements.

_____ **2.** Planning transactions to minimize taxes.

_____ **3.** Cost accounting.

_____ **4.** Preparing external financial statements.

_____ **5.** Reviewing reports for SEC compliance.

_____ **6.** Budgeting.

_____ **7.** Internal auditing.

_____ **8.** Investigating violations of tax laws.

Identify at least three external users of accounting information and indicate some questions they might seek to answer through their use of accounting information.

Exercise 1-4
Identifying accounting users and uses

Select the internal operating function from the two choices provided that is most likely to regularly use the information described. The information is likely used in both functions, but it is most relevant to one.

a. Which internal operating function is more likely to use payroll information: marketing or human resources?

b. Which internal operating function is more likely to use sales report information: marketing or research and development?

c. Which internal operating function is more likely to use inventory information: purchasing or human resources?

d. Which internal operating function is more likely to use budget and cost information: production or distribution?

e. Which internal operating function is more likely to use product quality information: human resources or production?

Exercise 1-5
Determining accounting use in internal operating functions

Assume the following role and describe a situation in which ethical considerations play an important part in guiding your action:

a. You are a student in an accounting principles course.

b. You are a manager with responsibility for several employees.

c. You are an accounting professional preparing tax returns for clients.

d. You are an accounting professional with audit clients that are competitors in business.

Exercise 1-6
Identifying ethical concerns

Indicate which term best fits each of the following descriptions:

A. Audit   **C.** Cost accounting   **E.** Ethics   **G.** Budgeting
B. Controller   **D.** GAAP   **F.** General accounting   **H.** Tax accounting

_____ **1.** An accounting area that includes planning future transactions to minimize taxes paid.

_____ **2.** A managerial accounting system designed to help managers identify, measure, and control operating costs.

_____ **3.** Principles that determine whether an action is right or wrong.

_____ **4.** An examination of an organization's accounting system and its records that adds credibility to financial statements.

_____ **5.** The task of recording transactions, processing recorded data, and preparing reports and financial statements.

_____ **6.** The chief accounting officer of an organization.

Exercise 1-7
Learning the language of business

Indicate which term best fits each of the following descriptions:

A. Government accountants   **C.** IRS   **E.** CIA   **G.** Risk   **I.** AICPA
B. Internal auditing   **D.** SEC   **F.** Income   **H.** Public accountants   **J.** CMA

_____ **1.** Process of examining an organization's recordkeeping, assessing whether managers are following established procedures, and appraising the efficiency of operating techniques.

_____ **2.** Amount of uncertainty associated with an expected return.

_____ **3.** Amount a business earns after paying all expenses and costs associated with its sales.

_____ **4.** Federal agency responsible for collecting federal taxes and enforcing tax law.

_____ **5.** Accounting professionals who provide services to many different clients.

_____ **6.** Accounting professionals employed by federal, state, or local branches of government.

Exercise 1-8
Learning the language of business

Exercise 1-9
Using the accounting equation

Answer the following questions. (*Hint:* Use the accounting equation.)

a. Wes Knight's medical supplies business has assets equal to $119,000 and liabilities equal to $47,000 at the end of the year. What is the total equity for Knight's business at the end of the year?

b. At the beginning of the year, Amber Company's assets are $300,000 and its equity is $100,000. During the year, assets increase $80,000 and liabilities increase $50,000. What is the equity at the end of the year?

c. At the beginning of the year, New Navy Company's liabilities equal $70,000. During the year, assets increase by $60,000, and at year-end they equal $190,000. Liabilities decrease $5,000 during the year. What are the beginning and ending amounts of equity?

Exercise 1-10
Using the accounting equation

Determine the amount missing from each accounting equation below.

	Assets	=	Liabilities	+	Equity
a.	?	=	$20,000	+	$45,000
b.	$100,000	=	$34,000	+	?
c.	$154,000	=	?	+	$40,000

Exercise 1-11
Return on investment

Fineva Group reports net income of $30,000 for 2002. At the beginning of 2002, Fineva Group had $110,000 in assets. By the end of 2002, assets had grown to $150,000. What is Fineva Group's return on investment?

A **Problem Set B** located at the end of **Problem Set A** is provided for *each* problem to reinforce the learning process.

PROBLEM SET A

Problem 1-1A
Computing and interpreting return on investment

Check (1) PepsiCo return, 11.68%

Coca-Cola and PepsiCo both produce and market beverages that are direct competitors. Key financial figures (in $ millions) for these businesses over the past year follow:

Key Figures	Coca-Cola	PepsiCo
Sales	$19,805	$20,237
Net income	2,431	2,050
Average invested (assets)	21,623	17,551

Required

1. Compute return on investment for (*a*) Coca-Cola and (*b*) PepsiCo.

2. Which company is more successful in its amount of sales to consumers?

3. Which company is more successful in returning net income from its amount invested?

Analysis Component

4. Write a one-paragraph memorandum explaining which company you would invest your money in and why.

Problem 1-2A
Identifying risk and return

All business decisions involve risk and return.

Required

Identify the risk and return in each of the following activities:

1. Investing $2,000 in a 5% savings account.

2. Placing a $2,500 bet on your favorite sports team.

3. Investing $10,000 in Yahoo! stock.

4. Taking out a $7,500 college loan to study accounting.

Quadcomm manufactures, markets, and sells cellular telephones. The average amount invested, or average total assets, in Quadcomm is $250,000. In its most recent year, Quadcomm reported net income of $65,000 on sales of $475,000.

Required

1. What is Quadcomm's return on investment?

2. Does return on investment seem satisfactory for Quadcomm given that its competitors average a 12% return on investment?

3. What are total expenses for Quadcomm in its most recent year?

4. What is the average total amount of financing (liabilities plus equity) for Quadcomm?

Problem 1-3A
Determining profits, sales, costs, and returns

Check (3) $410,000

A new startup company often engages in the following transactions in its first year of operations. Classify these transactions in one of the three major categories of an organization's business activities.

A. Financing   **B.** Investing   **C.** Operating

_____ **1.** Contributing land to the business.

_____ **2.** Purchasing a building.

_____ **3.** Purchasing land.

_____ **4.** Borrowing cash from a bank.

_____ **5.** Purchasing equipment.

_____ **6.** Selling and distributing products.

_____ **7.** Conducting advertising.

_____ **8.** Paying employee wages.

Problem 1-4A
Describing organizational activities

Identify an organization's three major business activities, including descriptions for each.

Problem 1-5A
Describing organizational activities

The following is selected financial information for Vasero Energy for the year ended December 31, 2002: Revenues, $55,000; costs and expenses, $40,000; net income, $15,000.

Required

Prepare the 2002 annual income statement for Vasero Energy.

Problem 1-6A
Preparing an income statement

The following is selected financial information for Sumoco as of December 31, 2002: Liabilities, $44,000; equity, $46,000; assets, $90,000.

Required

Prepare the balance sheet for Sumoco as of December 31, 2002.

Problem 1-7A
Preparing a balance sheet

The following is selected financial information for ComCast for the year ended December 31, 2002:

Cash used by investing activities	$(2,000)
Net increase in cash	1,200
Cash used by financing activities	(2,800)
Cash from operating activities	6,000

Required

Prepare the 2002 annual statement of cash flows for ComCast.

Problem 1-8A
Preparing a statement of cash flows

The following is selected financial information for Boardwalk for the year ended December 31, 2002:

Equity, Dec. 31, 2002	$14,000	Withdrawals	$1,000
Net income	8,000	Equity, Dec. 31, 2001	7,000

Required

Prepare the 2002 annual statement of changes in owner's equity for Boardwalk.

Problem 1-9A
Preparing a statement of changes in owner's equity

PROBLEM SET B

Problem 1-1B
Computing and interpreting return on investment

AT&T and GTE produce and market telecommunications products and are competitors. Key financial figures (in $ millions) for these businesses over the past year follow:

Key Figures	AT&T	GTE
Sales	$ 62,391	$25,336
Net income	5,450	4,033
Average invested (assets) ..	130,973	50,832

Required

Check (1) GTE return, 7.9%

1. Compute return on investment for (*a*) AT&T and (*b*) GTE.
2. Which company is more successful in the amount of sales to consumers?
3. Which company is more successful in returning net income from its amount invested?

Analysis Component

4. Write a one-paragraph memorandum explaining which company you would invest your money in.

Problem 1-2B
Identifying risk and return

All business decisions involve risk and return.

Required

Identify the risk and return in each of the following activities:

1. Stashing $500 under your mattress.
2. Placing a $250 bet on a horse running in the Kentucky Derby.
3. Investing $20,000 in Nike stock.
4. Investing $25,000 in U.S. Savings Bonds.

Problem 1-3B
Determining profits, sales, costs, and returns

Kasper Company manufactures, markets, and sells snowmobile equipment. The average amount invested, or average total assets, in Kasper Company is $3,000,000. In its most recent year, Kasper reported net income of $200,000 on sales of $1,400,000.

Required

1. What is Kasper Company's return on investment?
2. Does return on investment seem satisfactory for Kasper given that its competitors average a 9.5% return on investment?

Check (3) $1,200,000

3. What are the total expenses for Kasper Company in its most recent year?
4. What is the average total amount of financing (liabilities plus equity) for Kasper Company?

Problem 1-4B
Describing organizational activities

A new start-up company often engages in the following activities during its first year of operations. Classify each of the following activities into one of the three major activities of an organization:

A. Financing   **B.** Investing   **C.** Operating

_____ **1.** Providing services.   _____ **5.** Supervising workers.
_____ **2.** Obtaining a bank loan.   _____ **6.** Contributing savings to the business.
_____ **3.** Purchasing machinery.   _____ **7.** Renting office space.
_____ **4.** Researching products.   _____ **8.** Paying utilities expenses.

Problem 1-5B
Describing organizational activities

Identify in outline format the three major business activities of an organization. For each activity, identify at least two specific actions normally undertaken by its owners or managers.

The following is selected financial information for Pricenet for the year ended December 31, 2002:

Problem 1-6B
Preparing an income statement

Revenues $68,000	Costs and expenses $40,000	Net income $28,000

Required

Use the information provided to prepare the 2002 annual income statement for Pricenet.

The following is selected financial information for MicroUS as of December 31, 2002:

Problem 1-7B
Preparing a balance sheet

Liabilities $64,000	Equity $50,000	Assets $114,000

Required

Use the information provided to prepare the balance sheet for MicroUS as of December 31, 2002.

The following is selected financial information of Intertec for the year ended December 31, 2002:

Problem 1-8B
Preparing a statement of cash flows

Cash from investing activities	$1,600
Net increase in cash	400
Cash from financing activities	1,800
Cash used by operating activities	(3,000)

Required

Use this information to prepare the 2002 annual statement of cash flows for Intertec.

The following is selected financial information of CountryUS for the year ended December 31, 2002:

Problem 1-9B
Preparing a statement of changes in owner's equity

Equity, Dec. 31, 2002	$47,000	Withdrawals	$ 7,000
Net income	5,000	Equity, Dec. 31, 2001	49,000

Required

Prepare the 2002 annual statement of changes in owner's equity for CountryUS.

Beyond the Numbers is a special problem section aimed to refine communication, conceptual analysis, and research skills. It includes many activities helpful in developing an active learning environment.

Beyond the Numbers

BTN 1-1 Key financial figures for **Nike**'s fiscal year ended May 31, 2000, follow:

Reporting in Action

Key Figure	In Millions
Financing (liabilities + equity)	$5,856.9
Net income (profit)	579.1
Revenues (sales)	8,995.1

Required

1. What is the total amount of assets invested in Nike?
2. What is Nike's return on investment? Nike's assets at May 31, 1999, equal $5,247.7 (in millions).
3. How much are total expenses for Nike?
4. Does Nike's return on investment seem satisfactory if competitors average a 2% return?

Swoosh Ahead

5. Obtain Nike's annual report(s) (Form 10-K) for fiscal years ending after May 31, 2000, from its Web site (**www.nike.com**) or from the SEC Web site (**www.sec.gov**). Compute Nike's return on investment using this current annual report information. Compare the May 31, 2000, fiscal year-end return on investment to any subsequent years' returns you are able to compute.

Comparative Analysis

BTN 1-2   Key comparative figures ($ millions) for both **Nike** and **Reebok** follow:

Key Figure	Nike	Reebok
Financing (liabilities + equity)	$5,856.9	$1,564.1
Net income (profit)	579.1	11.0
Revenues (sales)	8,995.1	2,899.9

Required

1. What is the total amount of assets invested in (*a*) Nike and (*b*) Reebok?

2. What is the return on investment for (*a*) Nike and (*b*) Reebok? Nike's beginning-year assets equal $5,247.7 (in millions) and Reebok's beginning-year assets equal $1,684.6 (in millions).

3. How much are expenses for (*a*) Nike and (*b*) Reebok?

4. Is return on investment satisfactory for (*a*) Nike and (*b*) Reebok [assume competitors average a 2% return]?

5. What can you conclude about Nike and Reebok from these computations?

Ethics Challenge

C5

BTN 1-3   Julian Brown works in a public accounting firm and hopes to eventually be a partner. The management of Vianet Company invites Brown to prepare a bid to audit Vianet's financial statements. In discussing the audit's fee, Vianet's management suggests a fee range in which the amount depends on the reported profit of Vianet. The higher its profit, the higher will be the audit fee paid to Brown's firm.

Required

1. Identify the parties potentially affected by this situation.

2. What are the ethical factors in this situation? Explain.

3. Would you recommend that Brown accept this audit fee arrangement? Why or why not?

4. Describe some ethical considerations guiding your recommendation.

Communicating in Practice

A2   **C2**

BTN 1-4   Refer to this chapter's opening vignette about **JobDirect**. Assume that before establishing the business, Bell and Sutton met with a loan officer of a Pittsburgh bank to discuss a loan.

Required

1. Prepare a one-half-page report outlining the information you would request from Bell and Sutton if you were the loan officer.

2. Indicate whether the information you request and your loan decision are affected by the form of business organization for **JobDirect**.

Taking It to the Net

  C4

BTN 1-5   In 1999, the **Worldwide Wrestling Federation** began selling stock to the public. A company's first sale of stock to investors outside the company is termed an *initial public offering* (*IPO*). Access Edgar Online at www.edgar-online.com. Click on the IPO Headlines link. Next Search IPOs by Worldwide Wrestling Federation's ticker symbol WWFE. You should see a link to information regarding WWFE's recent initial public offering. Search links at this page and determine the initial opening stock offering price for the Worldwide Wrestling Federation.

BTN 1-6 Teamwork is important in today's business world. Successful teams schedule convenient meetings, maintain regular communications, and cooperate with and support team members. This assignment aims to establish accounting principles' support teams, initiate discussions, and set meeting times.

Teamwork in Action

Required

1. Form teams and open a team discussion to determine a regular time and place for your team to meet between each scheduled class meeting. Notify your instructor via a memorandum or e-mail message as to when and where your team will hold regularly scheduled meetings.

2. Develop a list of telephone numbers and/or e-mail addresses of your teammates.

BTN 1-7 *Business Week* publishes a ranking of the top 1,000 companies based on several performance measures. This issue is called the **BUSINESS WEEK GLOBAL 1000.** Obtain the July 10, 2000 (or more recent) publication of this issue—this book's Web site maintains free access to this article.

Business Week Activity

Book's Web site provides free and easy access to all articles for every Business Week Activity.

Required

1. What are the top 10 companies on the basis of market value?

2. Which companies are ranked in the top 10 in both 1999 and 2000 for market value?

3. How many of the top 10 on market capitalization are not U.S. companies?

BTN 1-8 Shanda Lowry is preparing to launch her new business, Your Boards (YB). YB would be a small retail store located on the Pacific coast that buys and sells skateboards, surfboards, snowboards, and related accessories.

Entrepreneurial Decision

Required

1. As what organization form should YB be set up? Explain.

2. YB obtains a $25,000 bank loan and Lowry contributes $28,000 of her own assets to the business.

    a. What is YB's total amount of financing?

    b. What is YB's total amount of assets?

2

Financial Statements and Business Transactions

A Look Back

Chapter 1 considered the role of accounting in the information age. We described accounting for different organizations and identified users and uses of accounting.

A Look at This Chapter

In this chapter, we describe financial statements and key accounting principles guiding their preparation. An important part of this chapter is transaction analysis using the accounting equation. We prepare and analyze financial statements based on transaction analysis.

A Look Ahead

Chapter 3 explains the recording of transactions. We introduce the double-entry accounting system and show how T-accounts are helpful in analyzing transactions. Journals and trial balances are also explained.

"I use accounting in all my business decisions,"—Chuck Taylor.

Shoes on Trial

e **LOS ANGELES**—Tucked along an oceanside street, **FastForward** could be another trendy sports shop. But its small back lot, where Chuck Taylor runs up grassy mounds, in sand pits, and through mud, makes clear this is something far different. These obstacles are product research tools. FastForward consults on athletic footwear. In just one year, Taylor has become a consultant sought after by sports clubs, schools, and amateur athletes.

FastForward's story is the envy of every entrepreneur. Taylor, 29, loved sports—but hated his shoes. He never had the right shoes for the right conditions. Independent tests of shoe performance were either nonexistent or outdated. So this past year, Taylor had an idea. He went out and purchased 21 pairs of the best off-road training shoes on the market. He ran the shoes through a battery of tests under many different conditions. His results were striking. Many medium-priced, lesser-known shoes performed on par with or better than many big-ticket, big-name shoes. He carried his findings to sports clubs and amateur athletes, and got a welcome reception and payment for his services.

Taylor recently quit his job to devote full time to his new business. "I instantly needed accounting skills to keep track of receipts, bills, everything," says Taylor. "When I applied for a loan, the bank couldn't believe my poor accounting records. But what'd you expect from a sports junkie!"

Taylor eventually shaped up his accounting and got the loan. To boost growth, FastForward is now moving into testing of soccer, track, cross-trainer, adventure, and skateboarding shoes. "We are meeting a market need and satisfying people," says Taylor. And you can count Taylor as one of the satisfied. [Source: Adapted from *Californian*, September 2001; *Sporting Trends*, July 4, 2001.]

Learning Objectives

Conceptual

C1 Identify and explain the content and reporting aims of financial statements.

C2 Describe differences in financial statements across forms of business organization.

C3 Explain the financial reporting environment.

C4 Identify those responsible for setting accounting and auditing principles.

C5 Identify, explain, and apply accounting principles.

Analytical

A1 Analyze business transactions using the accounting equation.

A2 Compute return on equity and use it to analyze company performance.

Procedural

P1 Prepare financial statements from business transactions.

Chapter Preview

Financial statements report on the financial performance and condition of an organization. They are some of the most important products of accounting and are useful to both internal and external decision makers. Chuck Taylor of **FastForward** recognized the importance of accounting reports in running his own business and in applying for a loan. Financial statements are the way businesspeople communicate. Knowledge of their preparation, organization, and analysis is important. In this chapter, we describe the type of information reflected in financial statements. We also discuss the principles and assumptions guiding their preparation. This discussion includes those that regulate and influence accounting. An important goal of this chapter is to illustrate how transactions are reflected in financial statements and how they impact our analysis. Special attention is devoted to a discussion of FastForward, whose first month's transactions are a main focus of our analysis.

Communicating with Financial Statements

In Chapter 1, we discussed how accounting provides information to help people make better decisions. Many organizations report their accounting information to internal and external users in the form of financial statements. These statements are useful in revealing an organization's financial health and performance in a summarized and easy-to-read format. They give an overall view of an organization's financing, investing, and operating activities.

Previewing Financial Statements

C1 Identify and explain the content and reporting aims of financial statements.

Concept 2-1

The four major **financial statements** are income statement, balance sheet, statement of changes in owner's equity, and statement of cash flows. We begin our study of these statements with a brief description of each.

How these statements are linked in time is illustrated in Exhibit 2.1. A balance sheet reports on an organization's financial position at a *point in time*. The income statement, statement of changes in owner's equity, and statement of cash flows report on financial performance over a *period of time*. The three statements in the middle column of Exhibit 2.1 link balance sheets from the beginning to the end of a reporting period. They explain how the financial position of an organization changes from one point to another.

Preparers and users (including regulatory agencies) determine the length of the reporting period. A one-year, or annual, reporting period is common, as are semiannual, quarterly, and monthly periods. The one-year reporting period is known as the *accounting,* or *fiscal, year.* Businesses whose accounting year begins on January 1 and ends on December 31 are known as *calendar-year* companies. Many companies choose a fiscal year ending on a date other than December 31. **Nike** is a *noncalendar-year* company as reflected in the headings of its

Point: A statement's heading lists the 3 W's: **W**ho—name of organization, **W**hat—name of statement, **W**hen—statement's point in time or period of time.

Exhibit 2.1

Link between Financial Statements

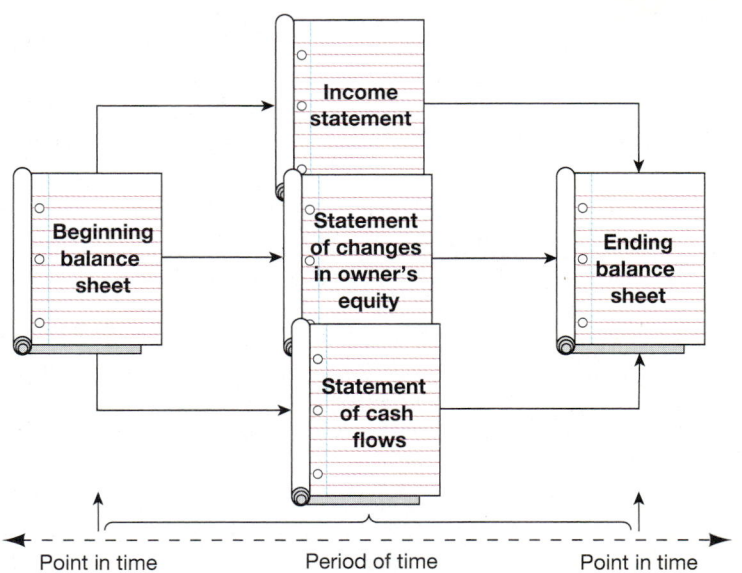

36

May 31 year-end financial statements in Appendix A. Some companies choose a fiscal year-end when sales and inventory are low. For example, **GAP**'s fiscal year-end is always near February 1, after the busy holiday season.

Income Statement

An **income statement** reports the revenues earned less the expenses incurred by a business over a period of time. **Net income** occurs when revenues exceed expenses. A **net loss,** or simply *loss,* occurs when expenses exceed revenues.

The income statement for FastForward's first month of operations is shown in Exhibit 2.2 (FastForward is a sole proprietorship).[1] An income statement does not simply report net income or net loss. It lists the types and amounts of important revenues and expenses. This is crucial information for users because it helps in understanding and predicting company performance. For example, **Walt Disney** classifies its revenues and expenses in three categories: theme parks, filmed entertainment, and consumer products. **Midway Games** separates its revenues into two groups: company-operated video and home video.

Exhibit 2.2

Income Statement

FASTFORWARD Income Statement For Month Ended December 31, 2001		
Revenues		
Consulting revenue . .	$5,800	
Rental revenue	300	
Total revenues		$6,100
Expenses		
Rent expense	1,000	
Salaries expense	700	
Total expenses		1,700
Net income		$4,400

Revenues

Revenues are inflows of assets in exchange for products and services provided to customers as part of a company's operations. Assets include items such as cash, land, equipment, and buildings. The income statement in Exhibit 2.2 shows that FastForward earned total revenues of $6,100 during December from both consulting and rental revenue.

Point: An income statement is also referred to as an *earnings statement, a statement of operations,* or a *P&L* (Profit and Loss) *statement.*

Expenses

Expenses are outflows or the using up of assets in providing products and services to customers. The income statement in Exhibit 2.2 shows FastForward used $1,000 of its assets in paying for rented store space. FastForward also paid $700 for an employee's salary.

The income statement heading identifies the company, the type of statement, and the time period covered. Knowledge of the time period is important in judging whether a company's performance is satisfactory. In assessing whether FastForward's $4,400 net income is satisfactory, we must remember it earned this amount during a one-month period.

Example: How would the income statement in Exhibit 2.2 change if FastForward paid $3,000 for rent? How would this change impact net income? *Answer:* Total operating expenses increase to $3,700 and net income decreases to $2,400.

You Make the Call

Web Designer You are working as a Web Designer at a local Internet Consulting Company and feel your wages are too low. You decide to ask the owner for a raise. How can you use the company's income statement to help in your request?

Answer—p. 58

Statement of Changes in Owner's Equity

Equity refers to the owner's claim on assets. The **statement of changes in owner's equity** (SCOE) reports on changes in equity over the reporting period. This statement starts with beginning equity and adjusts it for transactions and events that (1) increase it—investments by the owner and net income and (2) decrease it—net loss and owner withdrawals.

Point: While all revenues earned increase equity and expenses incurred decrease equity, the amounts are not reported in detail in the SCOE. Instead, the net effect of revenues and expenses is summarized in net income.

---

[1] For simplicity, FastForward's financial statements in this chapter do not reflect *all* of its December transactions. Its other December transactions are introduced in Chapter 3 and 4.

The statement of changes in owner's equity for FastForward's first month of operations is shown in Exhibit 2.3. This statement describes events that changed owner's equity during the month. It reports Taylor's initial equity investment of $30,000. It also reports $4,400 of net income earned during the month, and Taylor's $600 withdrawal. Taylor's equity balance at the end of the month is $33,800.[2]

Exhibit 2.3
Statement of Changes in Owner's Equity

FASTFORWARD Statement of Changes in Owner's Equity For Month Ended December 31, 2001		
C.Taylor, Capital, December 1, 2001		$ 0
Add: Investments by owner	$30,000	
Net income	4,400	34,400
		$34,400
Less: Withdrawals by owner		(600)
C.Taylor, Capital, December 31, 2001		$33,800

Balance Sheet

The **balance sheet** (also called the *statement of financial position*) reports the financial position of a company at a point in time, usually at the end of a month, quarter, or year. The balance sheet describes financial position by listing the types and dollar amounts of important assets, liabilities, and equity. Exhibit 2.4 shows the balance sheet for FastForward as of December 31. The balance sheet heading lists the company, the statement, and the date on which assets, liabilities, and equity are identified and measured. The amounts in the balance sheet are measured as of the close of business on that date.

Exhibit 2.4
Balance Sheet

FASTFORWARD Balance Sheet December 31, 2001				
Assets			**Liabilities**	
Cash	$ 4,400		Accounts payable	$ 6,200
Supplies	9,600		Total liabilities	$ 6,200
Equipment	26,000			
			Equity	
			C.Taylor, Capital	$33,800
Total assets	$40,000		Total liabilities and equity	$40,000

Example: How would the balance sheet in Exhibit 2.4 change if FastForward pays off $4,000 of its payable on December 31 using its Cash account? What would be the new amount of total assets? Would the balance sheet still balance? *Answers:* Cash would be $400, accounts payable would be $2,200, total assets (and liabilities) would be $36,000, and the balance sheet would still balance.

The balance sheet for FastForward shows it owns three different assets at the close of business on December 31: cash, supplies, and equipment. The total dollar amount for these assets is $40,000. The balance sheet also shows total liabilities of $6,200. Owner's equity is $33,800. Consistent with the accounting equation, the total amounts on each side of the balance sheet are equal (Assets = Liabilities + Equity). This equality is the reason the statement is named a *balance sheet*. This name also reflects the reporting of asset, liability, and equity *balances* in the statement.

---

[2] The beginning capital balance in the statement of changes in owner's equity is rarely zero. An exception is for the first period of a company's operations. Since FastForward began operations in December, its beginning capital balance for the month of December is zero. The beginning capital balance in January 2002 for FastForward is $33,800 (this is December's ending balance).

Assets

Assets are resources owned or controlled by a company that provide expected future benefits to the company. Assets are of many types. A familiar asset is cash. Another is accounts receivable. An **account receivable** is an asset created by selling products or services on credit. It reflects amounts owed to a company by its credit customers. These customers and other individuals and organizations who owe a company are called its **debtors.** Other common assets include merchandise held for sale, supplies, equipment, buildings, and land. Assets also can include intangible rights such as those granted by a patent, copyright, or license.

Liabilities

Liabilities are obligations of a company that reflect the claims of others against assets. A common characteristic of liabilities is their potential for reducing future assets or requiring future services or products. Liabilities take many forms. An **account payable** is a liability created by buying products or services on credit. It reflects amounts owed to others. A **note payable** is a liability expressed by a written promise to make a future payment at a specific time. Other familiar liabilities are salaries and wages owed to employees and interest payable.

   Individuals and organizations that own the right to receive payments from a company are called its **creditors.** One entity's payable is another entity's receivable. If a company fails to pay its obligations, the law gives creditors a right to force the sale of this company's assets to obtain the money to meet creditors' claims. When assets are sold under these conditions, creditors are paid first, but only up to the amount of their claims. Any remaining money, the residual, goes to the owner of the company. Creditors often use a balance sheet to help decide whether to loan money to a company. They compare the amounts of liabilities and assets. A loan is less risky if liabilities are small in comparison to assets because there are more resources than claims on resources.

Equity

Equity is the owner's claim on the assets of a business. It is the owner's *residual interest* in the assets of a business after deducting liabilities. Equity is also called **net assets.** Owner investments and revenues increase owner's equity. It is decreased by owner withdrawals and by expenses. Exhibit 2.5 shows these important relations. Owner investments are assets the owner put into the business. Owner withdrawals are assets the owner takes from the business. These changes in equity are reported in the statement of changes in owner's equity and yield the ending equity balance called *capital*. This ending balance is also reported in the balance sheet.

Point: Review these concepts by preparing your own personal balance sheet.

Statement of Cash Flows

The **statement of cash flows** describes the sources (inflows) and uses (outflows) of cash for a reporting period. It also reports the amount of cash at both the beginning and end of

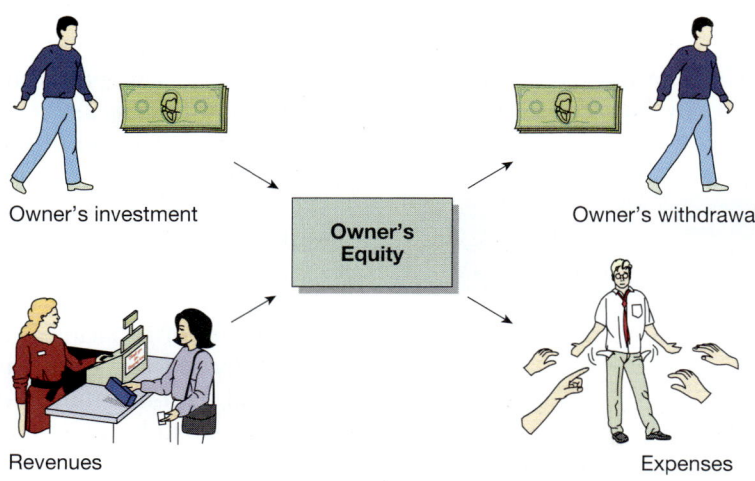

Owner's investment

Owner's withdrawal

Revenues

Expenses

Exhibit 2.5

Flows in and out of Owner's Equity

a period. The statement of cash flows is organized according to a company's major activities: operating, investing, and financing. A company must carefully manage cash if it is to survive and prosper.

FastForward's statement of cash flows for December is in Exhibit 2.6. The first section shows that net cash flows from operating activities equal $1,000. This is the result of $6,100 of cash received from customers less $5,100 paid for supplies, rent, and salaries. The second section reports on investing activities and shows a $26,000 cash outflow for buying equipment. The third section reports a $29,400 net cash inflow from financing activities that include an investment and a withdrawal by the owner.

Exhibit 2.6

Statement of Cash Flows

FASTFORWARD Statement of Cash Flows For Month Ended December 31, 2001		
Cash flows from operating activities:		
Cash received from clients	$ 6,100	
Cash paid for supplies	(3,400)	
Cash paid for rent	(1,000)	
Cash paid to employee	(700)	
Net cash provided by operating activities		$ 1,000
Cash flows from investing activities:		
Purchase of equipment	(26,000)	
Net cash used by investing activities		(26,000)
Cash flows from financing activities:		
Investments by owner	30,000	
Withdrawals by owner	(600)	
Net cash provided by financing activities		29,400
Net increase in cash		$ 4,400
Cash balance, December 1, 2001		0
Cash balance, December 31, 2001		$ 4,400

C2 Describe differences in financial statements across forms of business organization.

Financial Statements and Organizational Form

Chapter 1 described three different forms of business organization: proprietorship, partnership, and corporation. Financial statements for these organizations are very similar. The most visible *difference* is in the equity section of the balance sheet. A proprietorship's balance sheet lists the equity balance beside the owner's name as in Exhibit 2.4. A partnership's balance sheet uses the same approach, unless it has too many owners to fit their names in the available space. For example, if Chuck Taylor is part of an equal partnership with his sister Jane, the equity section would appear as in Exhibit 2.7.

A corporation's balance sheet does not list the names of its shareholders. Instead, equity is divided into **contributed capital** (also called **paid-in capital**) and **retained earnings.** Contributed capital reflects shareholders' investments. Retained earn-

Exhibit 2.7

Equity Section of a Partnership Balance Sheet

FASTFORWARD Partial Balance Sheet December 31, 2001	
Partners' Equity	
Chuck Taylor, Capital	$16,900
Jane Taylor, Capital	16,900
Total partners' equity	$33,800

ings equals a corporation's accumulated net income (loss) for all prior periods that has not been distributed to shareholders. To illustrate, assume Chuck Taylor had set up FastForward as a corporation in which he was the sole shareholder. If he is issued common stock equal to his $30,000 investment, the equity section of the balance sheet would look like the one in Exhibit 2.8. FastForward earned $4,400 in its first (and only) period, of which $600 is distributed to Taylor, leaving $3,800 in retained earnings.

Exhibit 2.8

Equity Section of a Corporation Balance Sheet

FASTFORWARD Partial Balance Sheet December 31, 2001	
Shareholders' Equity	
Contributed capital:	
Common stock	$30,000
Retained earnings	3,800
Total shareholders' equity	$33,800

When an owner of a proprietorship or a partnership takes cash or other assets from a company, the distributions are called **withdrawals.** When an owner of a corporation receives cash or other assets from a company, the distributions are called **dividends.** Withdrawals and dividends are not reported as part of the income statement because they are *not* expenses incurred to generate revenues. Also, when the owner of a proprietorship is its manager, no salary expense is reported on the income statement for this service. The same is true for a partnership. But since a corporation is a separate legal entity, salaries paid to its managers are reported as expenses on its income statement. This different treatment of owners' salaries requires special consideration when analyzing an income statement. We explain one special adjustment for return on equity near the end of this chapter.

The emphasis in the early chapters of this book is on sole proprietorships. This allows us to focus on important measurement and reporting issues in accounting without getting caught up in the complexities of different organizational forms. We do discuss forms of organization and provide examples when appropriate. Chapters 13 and 14 return to this topic and provide details about the financial statements of both partnerships and corporations.

Global: Global markets present challenges in terminology. For example, U.S. users refer to equity shares as *stock,* while U.K. users refer to inventory as *stock.*

Quick Check

1. What are the four major financial statements?
2. Describe revenues and expenses.
3. Explain assets, liabilities, and equity.
4. What are three differences in financial statements for the three different organizational forms?

Answer—p. 58

Generally Accepted Accounting Principles

We explained in Chapter 1 how financial accounting practice is governed by rules called *generally accepted accounting principles,* or *GAAP.* To use and interpret financial statements effectively, we need to understand these principles. A main purpose of GAAP is to make information in financial statements relevant, reliable, and comparable. *Relevant information* affects the decisions of its users. *Reliable information* is trusted by users. *Comparable information* is helpful in comparing organizations. This section describes the process for setting GAAP and identifies several crucial accounting principles.

Financial Reporting Environment

Accounting principles are developed in response to users' needs. Exhibit 2.9 shows how accounting principles, auditing standards, and various parties interact in the financial reporting environment. Accounting principles are applied in preparing financial statements. Preparers use preferred procedures in accounting for business transactions and events. Audits are performed in accordance with **generally accepted auditing standards (GAAS),** which are the accepted rules for conducting audits of financial statements. Both accounting and auditing help assure users that financial statements include relevant, reliable, and comparable information. An audit report tells whether or not the statements are prepared using

C3 Explain the financial reporting environment.

Point: An audit does *not* attest to the absolute accuracy of financial statements.

C4 Identify those responsible for setting accounting and auditing principles.

accepted accounting principles. **Ernst and Young** states in its audit report of **Harley-Davidson:** "In our opinion, the consolidated financial statements . . . present fairly, in all material respects . . . in conformity with generally accepted accounting principles."

Setting Accounting Principles

Accounting principles were historically developed through common usage. A principle was acceptable if most professionals permitted it. This history is reflected in the phrase *generally accepted*. As business transactions became more complex, users were less satisfied with the lack of more concrete guidance. Many of these users desired more uniformity in practice. Authority for developing accepted principles was eventually assigned to a select group of professionals.

Exhibit 2.9 shows the primary authoritative sources of GAAP and GAAS. The Financial Accounting Standards Board (FASB) is the primary authoritative source of GAAP. The Board seeks advice from all users and often holds public hearings. Its goal is to improve financial reporting and balance the interests of all users. The FASB communicates its decisions in various publications. Most notable are **Statements of Financial Accounting Standards (SFAS).** These statements set generally accepted standards in the United States and often affect international practices.[3]

Exhibit 2.9

Financial Reporting Environment

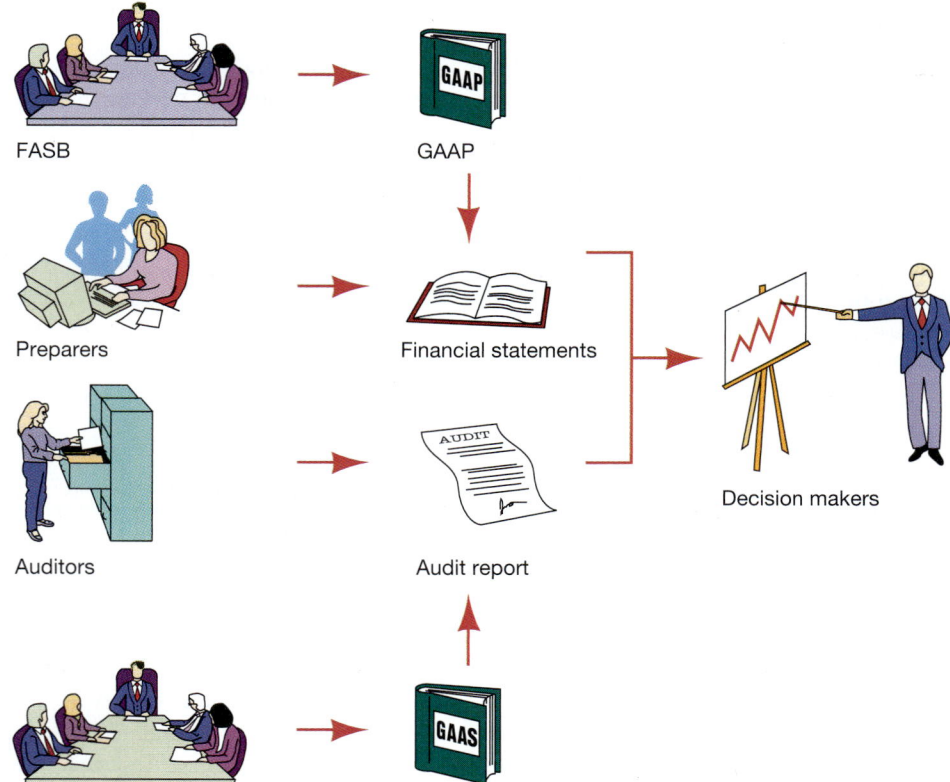

FASB   GAAP

Preparers   Financial statements

Auditors   Audit report   Decision makers

ASB   GAAS

Point: The five largest international accounting firms are Arthur Andersen, Deloitte & Touche, Ernst & Young, KPMG Peat Marwick, and PricewaterhouseCoopers.

Global: Both U.S. and the U.K. accounting principles are developed in the private sector. This is likely tied to both countries' legal systems based on English common law, in which professionals tend to make the rules. In contrast, government sets accounting principles in most continental European countries. This is likely tied to their legal systems that tend to be based on codified law.

The FASB draws its authority from two major sources. The first is the Securities and Exchange Commission (SEC), which Congress created to regulate securities markets, including the flow of information from companies to the public. The SEC designates the FASB as its primary authority for setting GAAP. It can overrule the FASB but rarely does so. The second source of authority comes from state boards that license CPAs. State ethics codes

---

[3] Predecessors to the FASB were the Accounting Principles Board (APB) and the Committee on Accounting Procedure (CAP).

require CPAs who audit financial statements to disclose areas where they fail to comply with FASB rules. If CPAs fail to report noncompliance, they can lose their licenses to practice. Also, the AICPA's Code of Professional Conduct states that a member can be expelled for not objecting to financial statements that fail to comply with FASB rules.[4] Authority for generally accepted auditing standards (GAAS) belongs to the *Auditing Standards Board (ASB),* a special committee of the AICPA with unpaid volunteer members.

International Accounting Principles

In today's global economy, companies in different countries increasingly do business with each other. For example, **Coca-Cola** does business with numerous companies located in nearly 200 countries across the world. **Nike** says the following about its global operations: "The Company currently markets its products in approximately 110 countries . . . through independent distributors, licensees, subsidiaries and branch offices . . . Non-U.S. sales accounted for 43 percent of total revenues . . ."

Despite this global economy, most countries continue to maintain a unique set of accounting practices. Consider a Canadian company selling stock to foreign investors. Should it prepare financial statements that comply with Canadian standards or with the standards of another country? Should it prepare different sets of reports to gain access to financial markets in more countries? This is a difficult and pressing problem.

One response has been to create an **International Accounting Standards Committee (IASC).** The IASC issues *International Accounting Standards* that identify preferred accounting practices. By narrowing the range of alternative practices, the IASC hopes to create more harmony among accounting practices

Did You Know?

Global Prospects   Nearly one-third of mutual fund investors now hold international securities. A survey of investors shows that investments in **Europe, the Pacific Basin,** and **China** are all expected to do well, whereas investments in **Africa** and the **Middle East** are expected to fare the worst.

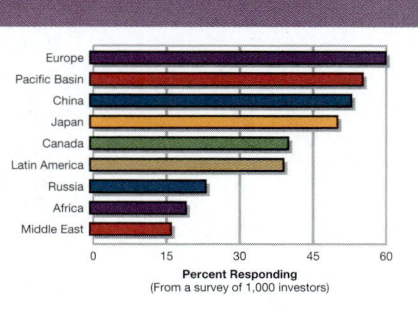

of different countries. If standards are harmonized, one company can use a single set of financial statements in all financial markets. Many countries' standard setters support the IASC, yet it does not have authority to impose its standards on companies. While interest in moving U.S. GAAP toward the IASC's preferred practices is growing, authority to make such changes rests with the FASB and the SEC.

Global: The IASC has its own set of accounting concepts to help guide the setting of international accounting principles.

Global: IASC standards are frequently adopted by newly industrialized countries such as Malaysia and Singapore, and by developing countries such as Nigeria.

Quick Check

5. What organization sets U.S. GAAP? From where does it draw authority?

6. What is GAAS? What organization sets GAAS?

7. How are U.S. companies affected by international accounting standards?

Answers—p. 58

Principles of Accounting

Accounting principles are both general and specific. *General principles* are the basic assumptions, concepts, and guidelines for preparing financial statements. *Specific principles* are detailed rules used in reporting business transactions and events. General principles stem from long-used accounting practices. Specific principles arise more often from the rulings of authoritative groups.

C5 Identify, explain, and apply accounting principles.

---

[4] Many other professional organizations support the FASB, including the American Accounting Association (AAA), Financial Executives Institute (FEI), Institute of Management Accountants (IMA), Association for Investment Management and Research (AIMR), and Securities Industry Association (SIA). They increase the Board's credibility by participating in its process for setting GAAP. Working alongside the FASB is the Governmental Accounting Standards Board (GASB), which identifies special accounting principles to be applied in preparing financial statements for state and local governments.

We need to understand both general and specific principles to effectively use accounting information. Since general principles are especially crucial in using accounting information, we emphasize them in the early chapters of this book. The general principles described in this chapter include business entity, objectivity, cost, going-concern, monetary unit, and revenue recognition. General principles described in later chapters include time period, matching, materiality, full disclosure, consistency, and conservatism. General principles are portrayed as building blocks for the *House of GAAP* in Exhibit 2.10. The specific principles are especially important to understanding individual items in financial statements. They are described as we encounter them.

Exhibit 2.10

Building Blocks for the House of GAAP

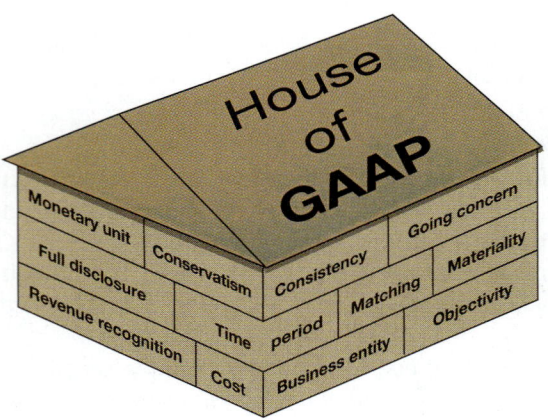

Business Entity Principle

The **business entity principle** means that a business is accounted for separately from its owner(s). It also means we account separately for each business that is controlled by the same owner. The reason for this principle is that separate information about each business is necessary for good decisions. To illustrate, suppose Chuck Taylor, the owner, wants to know how well FastForward is doing. For financial statements to serve his need, FastForward's transactions must be separate from his personal transactions. For example, Taylor's personal expenses (such as entertainment and clothes) must not be subtracted from FastForward's revenues on its income statement because they are not part of its business. A company's statements must reflect only the transactions and events of its *own business*. For reports and decision making to be effective, businesses must apply the entity principle.

Sham-Barter Transactions   Abuse of the objectivity and cost principles brought down executives at **Itex Corp** who bartered assets of little or no value and then reported them at grossly inflated values—recognizing fictitious gains and assets. The barter deals involved difficult-to-value assets such as artwork and stamp collections.

Objectivity Principle

The **objectivity principle** means that financial statement information is supported by independent, unbiased evidence. It demands more than one person's opinion. Information is not reliable if it is based only on what a preparer thinks might be true. A preparer can be too optimistic or pessimistic. An unethical preparer might try to mislead users by misrepresenting the truth. The objectivity principle is intended to make financial statements useful by ensuring they report reliable and verifiable information.

Global: Accounting principles are set by *directives* in the European Union.

Point: The cost principle is also called the *historical cost principle.*

Cost Principle

The **cost principle** means financial statements are based on actual costs incurred in business transactions. Cost is measured on a cash or equal-to-cash basis. This means if cash is given for an asset or service, its cost is measured as the amount of cash paid. If something besides cash is exchanged (such as a car traded for a truck), cost is measured as the cash equal to what is given up or received. The cost principle emphasizes reliability and relevance. It is also consistent with *objectivity* in that information based on cost is considered objective. For example, reporting purchases of assets and services at cost is more objective than reporting a manager's estimate of their current value. To illustrate this principle, suppose FastForward pays $5,000 for equipment. The cost principle requires that this purchase be recorded at a cost of $5,000. It makes no difference if Chuck Taylor thinks this equipment is really worth $7,000.

Going-Concern Principle

The **going-concern principle** means financial statements reflect an assumption that the business will continue operating instead of being closed or sold. This means a balance sheet reports items at cost instead of, say, liquidation values that assume closure. If a company is expected to fail or be liquidated, neither the going-concern principle nor the cost principle is appropriate. Instead, market values are then relevant.

Monetary Unit Principle

The **monetary unit principle** means we can express transactions and events in monetary, or money, units. Money is the common denominator in business. Expressing transactions and events in monetary units is crucial to the use of financial statements for business communications. Examples of monetary units are the dollar in the United States, Canada, Australia, and Singapore; the pound sterling in the United Kingdom; and the peso in Mexico, the Philippines, and Chile. An *exchange rate* expresses the value of one currency relative to another. Exchange rates change frequently and are tied to many economic and political factors. The following chart lists recent exchange rates in terms of U.S. dollars:

Country	U.S. $ Equivalent	Country	U.S. $ Equivalent
Canada (dollar)	0.68	United Kingdom (pound)	1.50
Taiwan (dollar)	0.03	Mexico (peso)	0.11
Germany (mark)	0.47	Europe (Euro)	0.91

The monetary unit an organization uses in its reports usually depends on the country where it operates, but more companies are expressing financial statements in more than one monetary unit. Exhibit 2.11 shows that **Nintendo** reports its financial statements in *both* yen and dollars.

NINTENDO'S FINANCIAL HIGHLIGHTS Year Ended March 31, 1999	Yen (¥) in Millions	U.S. $ in Millions
Total revenues	¥598,417	$4,946
Net income	85,817	709
Total assets	893,374	7,383
Total equity	700,292	5,788

Exhibit 2.11

Nintendo's Financial Highlights in both Dollars and Yen

Accounting generally assumes a *stable* monetary unit. This means the value of a currency is not expected to change. The more changes in the monetary unit, the more difficult it is to use and interpret financial statements, especially across time.

Quick Check

8. Why is the business entity principle important?

9. How are the objectivity and cost principles related?

Answers—p. 58

Point: There are exceptions to the cost principle. For example, investments in some securities are reported at market values. We cover this when we study investments.

Point: For currency conversion, check out *CNNfn* at cnnfn.com/markets/currencies.

Example: Cadbury, a leading chocolate producer, recently reported sales of **£5,115 million.** What is the U.S. $ equivalent of these sales using the exchange rate from the preceding chart? *Answer:* $7,673 million (5,115 × 1.50)

Transactions and the Accounting Equation

Financial statements reflect a company's business activities. We know many of these activities, such as purchases and sales, involve transactions. To understand information in financial statements, we need to know how an accounting system captures relevant data about transactions, classifies and records data, and reports data in financial statements. This section starts us on this important path.

The basic tool of modern accounting systems is the **accounting equation:**

$$\textbf{Assets = Liabilities + Equity}$$

The accounting equation is also called the **balance sheet equation** because of its link to the balance sheet. Like any mathematical equation, the accounting equation can be modified by rearranging terms. Moving liabilities to the left side of the equality, for example, gives us an equation for equity in terms of assets and liabilities:

Point: To apply these concepts, work QS 2-1 or QS 2-2.

$$\textbf{Assets} - \textbf{Liabilities = Equity}$$

The accounting equation helps track changes in a company's assets, liabilities, and equity to provide useful information and to help with interpretation.

Transaction Analysis—Part I

A1 Analyze business transactions using the accounting equation.

Concept 2-2

A **business transaction** is an exchange of economic consideration between two parties. Examples of economic consideration include products, services, money, and rights to collect money. A transaction affects one or more components of the accounting equation. Remember that each transaction leaves the equation in balance. Assets *always* equal the sum of liabilities and equity. We show how this equality is preserved by looking at 11 transactions for FastForward in its first month of operations.

Transaction 1: Investment by Owner

On December 1, Chuck Taylor forms an athletic shoe consulting business. He sets it up as a proprietorship. Taylor owns and manages the business. The marketing plan for the business is to focus primarily on consulting with schools, sports clubs, amateur athletes, and others who place orders of athletic shoes with manufacturers. Taylor personally invests $30,000 cash in the new company and deposits it in a bank account opened under the name of **FastForward.** After this transaction, the cash (an asset) and the owner's equity (called *C. Taylor, Capital*) each equal $30,000. The effect of this transaction on FastForward as reflected in the accounting equation follows:

	Assets	=	Liabilities	+	Equity
	Cash	=			C.Taylor, Capital
(1)	+$30,000	=			+$30,000 Investment

This transaction analysis reveals that FastForward has one asset, cash, equal to $30,000. It reveals no liabilities and an owner's equity of $30,000. The source of increase in equity is identified as an owner investment. Notice that the accounting equation is in balance.

Transaction 2: Purchase Supplies for Cash

FastForward uses $2,500 of its cash to buy supplies of brand name athletic shoes for testing over the next few months. This transaction is an exchange of cash, an asset, for another kind of asset, supplies. It merely changes the form of assets from cash to supplies. The decrease in cash is exactly equal to the increase in supplies. These supplies of athletic shoes are assets because of the expected future benefits from the test results of their performance. This transaction is reflected in the accounting equation as follows:

	Assets		=	Liabilities	+	Equity
	Cash	+ Supplies	=			C.Taylor, Capital
Old Bal.	$30,000		=			$30,000
(2)	−2,500	+ $2,500				
New Bal.	$27,500	+ $2,500	=			$30,000
	$30,000				$30,000	

Transaction 3: Purchase Equipment for Cash

FastForward spends $26,000 to acquire equipment for testing athletic shoes. Like transaction 2, transaction 3 is an exchange of one asset, cash, for another asset, equipment. The equipment is an asset because of the expected future benefits from using it to test athletic shoes. This purchase changes the makeup of assets but does not change the asset total. The equation remains in balance.

	Assets				=	Liabilities	+	Equity
	Cash	+	Supplies	+ Equipment	=			C.Taylor, Capital
Old Bal.	$27,500	+	$2,500		=			$30,000
(3)	−26,000			+$26,000				
New Bal.	$1,500	+	$2,500	+ $26,000	=			$30,000
	$30,000					$30,000		

Transaction 4: Purchase Supplies on Credit

Taylor decides he needs more supplies of athletic shoes. These supplies total $7,100, but as we see from the accounting equation in transaction 3, FastForward has only $1,500 in cash. Taylor arranges to purchase them on credit from CalTech Supply Company. Thus, FastForward acquires supplies in exchange for a promise to pay for them later. This yields a liability to CalTech Supply of $7,100. The effects of this purchase on the accounting equation are as follows:

	Assets					=	Liabilities	+	Equity
	Cash	+	Supplies	+	Equipment	=	Accounts Payable	+	C.Taylor, Capital
Old Bal.	$1,500	+	$2,500	+	$26,000	=			$30,000
(4)		+	7,100				+$7,100		
New Bal.	$1,500	+	$9,600	+	$26,000	=	$7,100	+	$30,000
			$37,100				$37,100		

This purchase increases assets by $7,100 in supplies while liabilities (called *accounts payable*) increase by the same amount.

Transaction 5: Services Rendered for Cash

A main business objective is to increase its owner's wealth. This goal is met when a business produces sufficient *net income*. Net income is reflected in the accounting equation as an increase in equity. FastForward earns revenues by consulting with clients about test results on athletic shoes. FastForward earns net income only if its revenues are greater than

Example: If FastForward pays $500 in cash in transaction 4, how does this cash payment affect the liability to CalTech? What would be FastForward's cash balance? *Answers:* The liability to CalTech would be reduced to $6,600 and the cash balance would be reduced to $1,000.

its expenses incurred in earning them. In one of its first jobs FastForward provides consulting services to an athletic club and immediately collects $4,200 cash. The accounting equation reflects an increase in cash of $4,200 and in equity of $4,200. This increase in equity is identified in the far right column as a revenue because it is earned by providing services. These identifications are useful in later preparing and interpreting both the statement of changes in owner's equity and the income statement.

	Assets				=	Liabilities	+	Equity	
	Cash	+	Supplies	+	Equipment	=	Accounts Payable	+	C.Taylor, Capital	
Old Bal.	$1,500	+	$9,600	+	$26,000	=	$7,100	+	$30,000	
(5)	+ 4,200							+	4,200	Consulting Revenue
New Bal.	$5,700	+	$9,600	+	$26,000	=	$7,100	+	$34,200	
			$41,300					$41,300		

Transactions 6 and 7: Payment of Expenses in Cash

FastForward pays $1,000 rent to the landlord of the building where its store is located. Paying this amount allows FastForward to occupy the space for the month of December. The effects of this payment as reflected in the accounting equation follow as transaction 6. FastForward also pays the biweekly $700 salary of the company's only employee. This is reflected in the accounting equation as transaction 7.

	Assets				=	Liabilities	+	Equity	
	Cash	+	Supplies	+	Equipment	=	Accounts Payable	+	C.Taylor, Capital	
Old Bal.	$5,700	+	$9,600	+	$26,000	=	$7,100	+	$34,200	
(6)	-1,000								- 1,000	Rent Expense
Bal.	$4,700	+	$9,600	+	$26,000	=	$7,100	+	$33,200	
(7)	- 700								- 700	Salary Expense
New Bal.	$4,000	+	$9,600	+	$26,000	=	$7,100	+	$32,500	
			$39,600					$39,600		

Both transactions 6 and 7 are December expenses for FastForward. The costs of both rent and salary are expenses, as opposed to assets, because their benefits are used in December (they have no future benefits after December). These transactions use up an asset (cash) as part of FastForward's operations. The accounting equation shows both transactions reduce cash and equity. The far right column identifies these decreases as expenses.

Summary of Part I Transactions

FastForward has net income when its revenues exceed its expenses. Net income increases equity. If expenses exceed revenues, a net loss occurs and decreases equity. Net income (and loss) is not affected by transactions between a business and its owner. This means Taylor's initial investment of $30,000 is not income to FastForward, although it increased equity. To stress that revenues and expenses yield changes in equity, we have added revenues directly to equity and subtracted expenses directly from equity in this chapter. In practice and in later chapters, information about revenues and expenses is compiled separately during the accounting period. These amounts are then added to or subtracted from equity at the *end* of the period. We describe this process in Chapters 3, 4, and 5.

Point: To apply these concepts, work Exercises 2-1 and 2-3.

Revenue Recognition Principle

We briefly interrupt the analysis of FastForward's transactions to describe the revenue recognition principle. Companies need guidance in deciding when to recognize revenue. *Recognize* means to record a transaction or event for purposes of reporting its effects in financial statements. If revenue is recognized too early, the income statement reports revenue sooner than it should, and the business looks more profitable than it is. If revenue is recognized too late, the income statement shows lower revenue and net income than it should, and the business looks less profitable than it is. In both cases, the income statement does not provide decision makers with the most useful information about company success.

The **revenue recognition principle** provides guidance on when to recognize revenue on the income statement. The recognition principle includes three important guidelines:

1. *Revenue is recognized when earned.* Preparing for services, finding customers, and promoting sales all contribute to revenue. Yet, we usually cannot reliably determine revenue earned until services or products are delivered. This means revenue is usually not recognized until the earnings process is complete. The earnings process is normally complete when services are rendered or the seller transfers ownership of products to the buyer. To illustrate, suppose a customer pays in advance of taking delivery of a product or service. The seller must not recognize revenue because the earnings process is not complete. This practice is called the *sales basis* of revenue recognition.

Did You Know?

Revenues for the New York Yankees baseball team include ticket sales, television and cable broadcasts, radio rights, concessions, and advertising. Revenues from ticket sales are recognized when the Yankees play each game. Advance ticket sales are not revenues; instead, they represent a liability for the Yankees to play a baseball game at a later specified date.

2. *Assets received from selling products and services need not be in cash.* A common noncash asset received by a seller in a revenue transaction is a customer's promise to pay at a future date. The seller views the customer's promise as an account receivable. These transactions are called *credit sales*. If evidence shows the seller has the right to collect from a customer, this seller recognizes an asset (account receivable) and records revenue. When cash is later collected, no additional revenue is recognized. It merely changes the makeup of assets from a receivable to cash.

Example: When a bookstore sells a textbook on credit is its earnings process complete? *Answer:* The bookstore can record sales for these book sales minus an amount expected for returns.

3. *Revenue recognized is measured by the cash received plus the cash equivalent (market) value of any other assets received.* This means, for example, if a revenue transaction creates an account receivable, the seller recognizes revenue equal to the value of the receivable, which usually is the amount of cash expected to be collected.

Financial statements include an explanation of the revenue recognition method used. **General Motors,** for instance, reports in its annual report that "sales are generally recorded by the Corporation when products are shipped to independent dealers."

Transaction Analysis—Part II

To show how revenue recognition works, let's return to FastForward's transactions.

Transaction 8: Services and Facilities Rendered for Credit

FastForward provides consulting services of $1,600 and rented its test facilities to an amateur sports team for $300. The rental involved allowing team members to try recommended shoes at FastForward's testing grounds. The sports team is billed for the $1,900 total. This transaction results in a new asset, account receivable, from this client. It also yields an increase in equity from the two revenue components identified in the far right column of the accounting equation:

	Cash	+	Accounts Receivable	+	Supplies	+	Equipment	=	Accounts Payable	+	C.Taylor, Capital	
	Assets							=	**Liabilities**	+	**Equity**	
Old Bal.	$4,000	+			+ $9,600	+	$26,000	=	$7,100	+	$32,500	
(8)			+ $1,900							+	1,600	Consulting Revenue
										+	300	Rental Revenue
New Bal.	$4,000	+	$1,900		+ $9,600	+	$26,000	=	$7,100	+	$34,400	
			$41,500							$41,500		

Transaction 9: Receipt of Cash from Accounts Receivable

Point: Note that receipt of cash is not necessarily a revenue.

The client (amateur sports team) pays $1,900 10 days after it is billed for consulting services in transaction 8. This transaction 9 does not change the total amount of assets and does not affect liabilities or equity. It converts the receivable (an asset) to cash (another asset). It does not create new revenue. Revenue was recognized when FastForward rendered the services (transaction 8), not when the cash is now collected. This emphasis on the earnings process instead of cash flows is a goal of the revenue recognition principle and yields useful information to users. The new balances follow:

	Cash	+	Accounts Receivable	+	Supplies	+	Equipment	=	Accounts Payable	+	C.Taylor, Capital
					Assets			=	**Liabilities**	+	**Equity**
Old Bal.	$4,000	+	$1,900	+	$9,600	+	$26,000	=	$7,100	+	$34,400
(9)	+ 1,900		−1,900								
New Bal.	$5,900	+	$ 0	+	$9,600	+	$26,000	=	$7,100	+	$34,400
			$41,500							$41,500	

Transaction 10: Payment of Accounts Payable

FastForward pays $900 to CalTech Supply as partial payment for its earlier $7,100 purchase of supplies (transaction 4), leaving $6,200 unpaid. The accounting equation shows this transaction decreases FastForward's cash by $900 and decreases its liability to CalTech Supply by $900. Equity does not change. This event does not create an expense even though cash flows out of FastForward (the expense is recorded when FastForward derives the benefits from these supplies—Chapter 3 will explain this concept in detail).

	Cash	+	Accounts Receivable	+	Supplies	+	Equipment	=	Accounts Payable	+	C.Taylor, Capital
					Assets			=	**Liabilities**	+	**Equity**
Old Bal.	$5,900	+	$ 0	+	$9,600	+	$26,000	=	$7,100	+	$34,400
(10)	− 900								− 900		
New Bal.	$5,000	+	$ 0	+	$9,600	+	$26,000	=	$6,200	+	$34,400
			$40,600							$40,600	

Transaction 11: Withdrawal of Cash by Owner

Taylor withdraws $600 in cash from FastForward for personal living expenses. A proprietorship's distribution of cash, or other assets, to its owner is called a *withdrawal*. Withdrawals (decreases in equity) are not expenses because they are not part of the company's earnings process. Since withdrawals are not expenses, they are not used in computing net income.

	Assets							=	Liabilities	+	Equity	
	Cash	+	Accounts Receivable	+	Supplies	+	Equipment	=	Accounts Payable	+	C.Taylor, Capital	
Old Bal.	$5,000	+	$ 0	+	$9,600	+	$26,000	=	$6,200	+	$34,400	
(11)	− 600										− 600	Withdrawal
New Bal.	$4,400	+	$ 0	+	$9,600	+	$26,000	=	$6,200	+	$33,800	
			$40,000								$40,000	

Summary of Transactions

FastForward engaged in transactions with five major entities: the owner, its suppliers, an employee, its customers, and the landlord. We identify the transactions by number with the specific entity in Exhibit 2.12. We also summarize in Exhibit 2.13 the effects of these 11 transactions of FastForward using the accounting equation. Three points should be noted. First, the accounting equation remains in balance after each transaction. Second, transactions can be analyzed by their effects on components of the accounting equation. For example, in transactions 2, 3, and 9, one asset increased while another decreased by equal amounts. Third, the equality of effects in the accounting equation is crucial to the double-entry accounting system. We discuss this system in the next chapter.

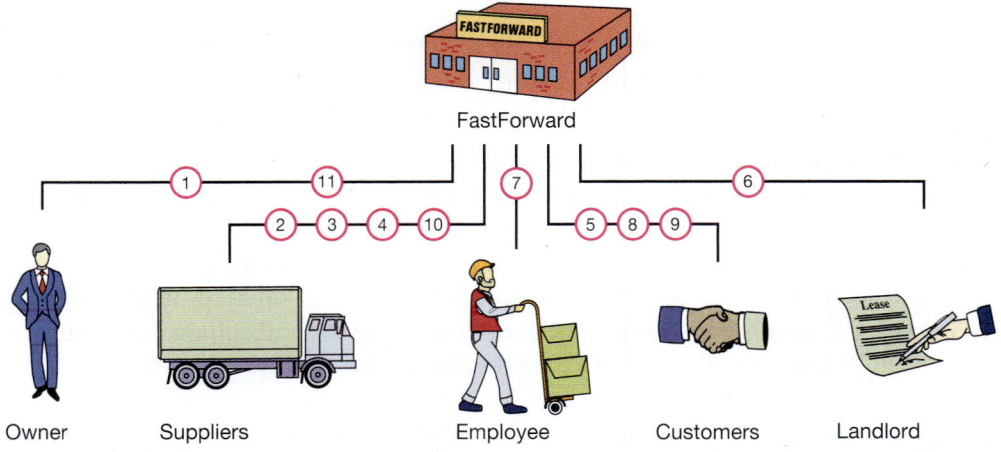

Exhibit 2.12

FastForward's Transactions Grouped by Entities

Quick Check

12. Why is the revenue recognition principle important?

13. Identify a transaction decreasing both assets and liabilities.

14. When is the accounting equation in balance, and what does that mean?

Answer—p. 58

Exhibit 2.13

Summary of Transactions Using the Accounting Equation

			Assets			= Liabilities +	Equity	
		Cash	+ Accounts Receivable	+ Supplies	+ Equipment =	Accounts Payable	+ C.Taylor, Capital	
(1)		$30,000					$30,000	Investment
(2)		−2,500		+$2,500				
Bal.		27,500		2,500			30,000	
(3)		−26,000			+$26,000			
Bal.		1,500		2,500	26,000		30,000	
(4)				+7,100		+$7,100		
Bal.		1,500		9,600	26,000	7,100	30,000	
(5)		+4,200					+4,200	Consulting Revenue
Bal.		5,700		9,600	26,000	7,100	34,200	
(6)		−1,000					−1,000	Rent Expense
Bal.		4,700		9,600	26,000	7,100	33,200	
(7)		− 700					− 700	Salary Expense
Bal.		4,000		9,600	26,000	7,100	32,500	
(8)			+$1,900				+1,600	Consulting Revenue
							+ 300	Rental Revenue
Bal.		4,000	1,900	9,600	26,000	7,100	34,400	
(9)		+1,900	−1,900					
Bal.		5,900	0	9,600	26,000	7,100	34,400	
(10)		− 900				− 900		
Bal.		5,000	0	9,600	26,000	6,200	34,400	
(11)		− 600					− 600	Withdrawal
Bal.		$4,400 +	$ 0 +	$9,600 +	$26,000 =	$6,200 +	$33,800	

Financial Statements

P1 Prepare financial statements from business transactions.

This section shows how the four major financial statements are prepared from business transactions. Recall that the four major financial statements and their purposes are:

1. *Income statement*—describes a company's revenues and expenses along with the resulting net income or loss over a period of time. It explains how equity changes during a period due to earnings activities.
2. *Statement of changes in owner's equity*—explains changes in equity from net income (or loss) and the owner's investments and withdrawals over a period of time.
3. *Statement of cash flows*—identifies cash inflows (receipts) and outflows (payments) over a period of time. It explains how the cash balance on the balance sheet changes from the beginning to the end of a period.
4. *Balance sheet*—describes a company's financial position (types and amounts of assets, liabilities, and equity) at a point in time.

We prepare these financial statements using the first 11 transactions of FastForward.

Income Statement

FastForward's income statement for December is shown at the top of Exhibit 2.15. Information about revenues and expenses is conveniently taken from the equity column of Exhibit 2.13. Revenues are reported first on the income statement. They include consulting revenues of $5,800 from transactions 5 and 8, and rental revenue of $300 from transaction 8. Expenses

Point: Knowing how financial statements are prepared improves our analysis of them. We develop the skills for analysis of financial statements throughout the book. Chapter 18 focuses on financial statement analysis.

are reported after revenues. We can list revenues and expenses in different ways. For convenience in this chapter, we list larger amounts first. Rent and salary expenses are from transactions 6 and 7. Expenses reflect the costs to generate the revenues reported. Net income (or loss) is reported at the bottom of the statement and is the amount earned in December. Owner's investments and withdrawals are *not* part of income. Pie charts shown in Exhibit 2.14 are helpful in analyzing the makeup of revenues and expenses.

Revenue sources for FastForward

Consulting

Rental

Expense sources for FastForward

Rent

Salary

Exhibit 2.14

Pie Chart Analysis

Statement of Changes in Owner's Equity

The statement of changes in owner's equity reports information about how equity changes over the reporting period. This statement shows beginning equity, events that increase it (investments by owner and net income), and events that decrease it (withdrawals and net loss). Ending equity is computed in this statement and is carried over and reported on the balance sheet. FastForward's statement of changes in owner's equity is the second report in Exhibit 2.15. The beginning balance of equity is measured as of the start of business on December 1. It is zero because FastForward did not exist before then. An existing business reports the beginning balance as of the end of the prior reporting period (such as from November 30). FastForward's statement shows that Taylor's initial investment created $30,000 of equity. It also shows the $4,400 of net income earned during the month. This links the income statement to the statement of changes in owner's equity. The statement also reports Taylor's $600 withdrawal and FastForward's $33,800 end-of-month equity balance.

Example: If Taylor purchased $3,000 of additional equipment with personal funds and invested it, how would the financial statement in Exhibit 2.15 change? *Answer:* The statement of changes in owner's equity would show owner's investments of $33,000 and an ending balance of $36,800. The balance sheet would show equipment with a cost of $29,000, total assets of $43,000, equity of $36,800, and total liabilities and equity of $43,000.

Balance Sheet

FastForward's balance sheet is the third report in Exhibit 2.15. This statement refers to FastForward's financial condition at the close of business on December 31. The left side of the balance sheet lists FastForward's assets: cash, supplies, and equipment. The upper right side of the balance sheet shows FastForward owes $6,200 to creditors. All other liabilities (such as a bank loan) would be listed here. The equity section shows an ending balance of $33,800. Note the link between the ending balance of the statement of changes in owner's equity and the equity balance here. (This presentation of the balance sheet is called the *account form*—assets on the left and liabilities and equity on the right. Another presentation is the *report form*—assets on top, followed by liabilities and then equity. Either presentation is acceptable.)

You Make the Call

Entrepreneur You open a wholesale business selling entertainment equipment to retail outlets. You find that most of your customers demand to buy on credit. How can you use the balance sheets of these customers to decide which ones to extend credit to?

Answer—p. 58

Statement of Cash Flows

FastForward's statement of cash flows is the final report in Exhibit 2.15. This statement describes where FastForward's cash came from and where it went during December. It also shows the amount of cash at the beginning of the period and the amount left at the end. This information is important because a company must carefully manage cash if it is to succeed. **Amazon.com** must do a better job of managing its cash flows if it is to prosper.

Exhibit 2.15

Financial Statements and
Their Links

FASTFORWARD
Income Statement
For Month Ended December 31, 2001

Revenues:

Consulting revenue ($4,200 + $1,600)	$5,800	
Rental revenue	300	
Total revenues		$6,100

Expenses:

Rent expense	1,000	
Salaries expense	700	
Total expenses		1,700
Net income		**$4,400** ◄

FASTFORWARD
Statement of Changes in Owner's Equity
For Month Ended December 31, 2001

C.Taylor, Capital, December 1, 2001		$ 0
Plus: Investments by owner	$30,000	
Net income	4,400	34,400
		$34,400
Less: Withdrawals by owner		(600)
C.Taylor, Capital, December 31, 2001		**$33,800** ◄

FASTFORWARD
Balance Sheet
December 31, 2001

Assets		**Liabilities**	
► Cash	$ 4,400	Accounts payable	$ 6,200
Supplies	9,600	Total liabilities	$ 6,200
Equipment	26,000		
		Equity	
		C.Taylor, Capital.	**$33,800** ◄
Total assets	$40,000	Total liabilities and equity .	$40,000

FASTFORWARD
Statement of Cash Flows
For Month Ended December 31, 2001

Cash flows from operating activities:

Cash received from clients ($4,200 + $1,900) . .	$ 6,100	
Cash paid for supplies ($2,500 + $900)	(3,400)	
Cash paid for rent	(1,000)	
Cash paid to employee	(700)	
Net cash provided by operating activities		$ 1,000

Cash flows from investing activities:

Purchase of equipment	(26,000)	
Net cash used by investing activities		(26,000)

Cash flows from financing activities:

Investments by owner	30,000	
Withdrawals by owner	(600)	
Net cash provided by financing activities		29,400
Net increase in cash		$ 4,400
Cash balance, December 1, 2001		0
► Cash balance, December 31, 2001		**$ 4,400**

Point: Arrow lines show how the
statements are linked.

Point: Final totals are double
underlined. Negative amounts are
often in parentheses.

The first section reports cash flows from *operating activities*. The $6,100 of cash received from clients equals total revenue on the income statement because FastForward collected all revenues in cash. If some credit sales are not collected, or if credit sales from a prior period are collected this period, the amount of cash received from customers will not equal the revenues reported on the income statement for this period. This section also lists cash paid for supplies, rent, and employee salaries. These cash flows are from

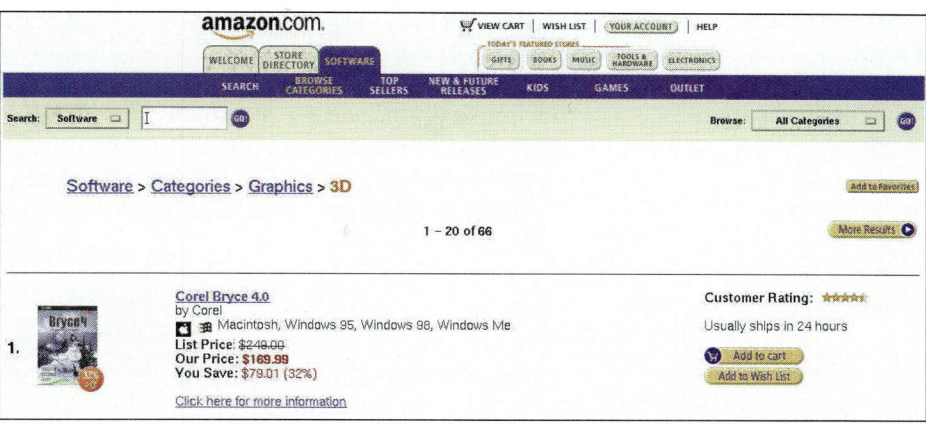

transactions 2, 6, and 7. We put these amounts in parentheses to indicate they are subtracted. Amounts for rent and salaries equal the expenses on FastForward's income statement because it paid these expenses in cash. The payment for supplies is an operating activity because they are expected to be used up in short-term operations (their benefits are not long term). Net cash provided by operating activities for December is $1,000. If cash paid exceeded cash received, we would call it "cash used by operating activities." Decision makers are especially interested in the operating section of the statement of cash flows as it helps assess how much income is in the form of cash.

The second section of the statement of cash flows describes *investing activities*. Investing activities involve buying and selling assets such as land and equipment that are held for *long-term use* in the business. FastForward's only investing activity is the $26,000 purchase of equipment in transaction 3. Decision makers are interested in this section of the statement because it describes how a company is preparing for its future. If it is spending cash on productive assets, it should be able to grow and increase net income. A user is also concerned that a company does not overly spend on productive assets and face a cash shortage. If a company is selling its productive assets, it is downsizing its operations.

Point: Investing activities refer to long-term asset investments in the company, *not* to owner investments.

The third section shows cash flows related to *financing activities*. Financing activities include *long-term* borrowing and repaying cash from lenders, and the owner's cash investments and withdrawals. The statement of cash flows in Exhibit 2.15 shows FastForward received $30,000 from Chuck Taylor's initial investment in transaction 1. If the business had borrowed cash, that amount would appear here as an increase in cash. The financing section also shows the $600 owner withdrawal in transaction 11. The total effect of financing activities is a $29,400 net inflow of cash. The financing section shows us why FastForward did not run out of cash even though it spent $26,000 on equipment and generated only $1,000 from operating activities: it used the owner's cash investment. Decision makers are interested in the financing section because excessive borrowing can burden a company and reduce its potential for growth.

Example: How would the cash flow statement in Exhibit 2.15 change if FastForward had paid $27,000 cash for the equipment and had borrowed $5,000 from a bank to help finance future operations? *Answer:* The investing section would show the $27,000 paid for equipment; the financing section would report the $5,000 loan as additional cash provided; and the net increase in cash and ending cash balance would be increased from $4,400 to $8,400.

The final part of the statement of cash flows is the net increase or decrease in cash. It shows FastForward increased its cash balance to $4,400 in December. Because it started with no cash, the ending balance is also $4,400. This ending amount is the link from the statement of cash flows to the balance sheet. We give a more detailed explanation of the statement of cash flows in Chapters 5 and 17.

Quick Check

15. Explain the link between the income statement and the statement of changes in owner's equity.

16. Describe the link between the balance sheet and the statement of changes in owner's equity.

17. Discuss the three major sections of the statement of cash flows.

Answers—p. 58

A2 Compute return on equity and use it to analyze company performance.

An important reason for recording information about assets, liabilities, equity, and income is to help an owner judge the company's success compared to other business or personal opportunities. One measure of success is the **return on equity** ratio. This ratio is computed by taking net income and dividing it by average equity for the period as shown in Exhibit 2.16.

Exhibit 2.16

Return on Equity

$$\text{Return on equity} = \frac{\text{Net income}}{\text{Average equity}}$$

FastForward's return on equity for the month of December is computed as[5]

$$\frac{\$4,400}{[\$30,000 + \$33,800]/2} = 13.8\%$$

Taylor's return for December is high compared to many investments, especially for the first month of operations, but we must remember that net income for a proprietorship does not include an expense for the effort exerted by the owner to manage its operations. To consider this, we can compute a **modified return on equity** for proprietorships and partnerships. This modified return on equity reduces net income by the value of the owner's efforts and is computed as shown in Exhibit 2.17.

Exhibit 2.17

Modified Return on Equity

$$\text{Modified return on equity} = \frac{\text{Net income} - \text{Value of owner's efforts}}{\text{Average equity}}$$

Other employment opportunities suggest that Taylor's efforts are valued at $3,800 per month. FastForward's modified return on equity is then computed as

$$\frac{\$4,400 - \$3,800}{[\$30,000 + \$33,800]/2} = 1.9\%$$

This modified return of 1.9% per month is quite different from the 13.8%. Taylor would then compare this return with other opportunities to determine whether it is adequate. Examples of other opportunities are savings accounts, company stock, and different jobs.

Exhibit 2.18

Return on Equity for Selected Industries

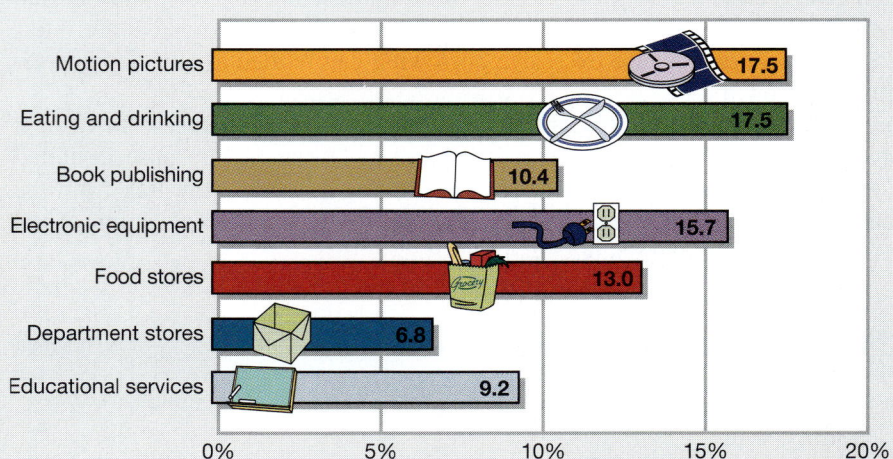

---

[5] A simple average is computed as the sum of the beginning and ending balances divided by 2. For a company's first period of operations, the owner's initial investment is commonly used as the beginning balance.

Taylor likely will continue to operate FastForward because 1.9% per month is more than 20% per year.[6] For further comparison, Exhibit 2.18 shows the return on equity for different industries. FastForward's return exceeds these.

Three additional points are important. First, an evaluation of returns should recognize risk. Risk can differ considerably across investment alternatives. Second, income can vary from month to month. Income variation is related to risk. Third, because of company, business, and economic fluctuations, a better measure of return is obtained by computing it over a longer period such as one year.

You Make the Call

Engineer You are considering launching a proprietorship to manufacture custom-fit athletic shoes. Your current salary is $2,500 per month. You estimate the new business will yield a net income of $4,500 per month and require an average equity balance of $400,000. Do you pursue this opportunity?

Answer—p. 58

Summary

C1 **Identify and explain the content and reporting aims of financial statements.** The major financial statements are income statement, balance sheet, statement of changes in owner's equity, and statement of cash flows. An income statement shows a company's profitability, including revenues, expenses, and net income (loss). A balance sheet reports a company's financial position, including assets, liabilities, and equity. A statement of changes in owner's equity explains how equity changes from the beginning to the end of a period, and the statement of cash flows identifies all cash inflows and outflows for the period.

C2 **Describe differences in financial statements across forms of business organization.** One important difference is in the equity section of the balance sheet. Proprietorship and partnership balance sheets list the equity balance beside the owner's name. Names of a corporation's shareholders are not listed. Another difference is in the way assets are taken. When an owner of a proprietorship or a partnership takes them from the company, they are called *withdrawals*. When owners of a corporation receive assets from the company, they are called *dividends*. Another difference is that no salary expense is recorded when the owner of a proprietorship or partnership is its manager.

C3 **Explain the financial reporting environment.** Accounting professionals prepare financial statements, independent auditors often examine them and prepare an audit report, and users rely on them to make important decisions. Preparers use GAAP, and auditors are guided by GAAS. Applying both GAAP and GAAS helps ensure that financial statements include relevant, reliable, and comparable information.

C4 **Identify those responsible for setting accounting and auditing principles.** The FASB is the primary authoritative source of GAAP. The FASB draws its authority from two major sources: the SEC and state boards that license CPAs. Authority for GAAS belongs to the ASB. The SEC is an important source of the ASB's authority.

C5 **Identify, explain, and apply accounting principles.** Accounting principles aid in producing relevant, reliable, and comparable information. The business entity principle means that a business is accounted for separately from its owner(s). The objectivity principle means independent, objective evidence supports the information. The cost principle means financial statements are based on actual costs incurred. The monetary unit principle assumes transactions can be captured in money terms. The going-concern principle means financial statements assume the business will continue. The revenue recognition principle means revenue is recognized when earned.

A1 **Analyze business transactions using the accounting equation.** A transaction is an exchange of economic consideration between two parties. Examples include exchanges of products, services, money, and rights to collect money. Business transactions always have at least two effects on one or more components of the accounting equation. The accounting equation is: Assets = Liabilities + Equity. This equation is always in balance.

A2 **Compute return on equity and use it to analyze company performance.** Return on equity is computed as net income divided by average equity. A modified return on equity for proprietorships and partnerships is computed as net income less the value of the owner's efforts, and then this quantity is divided by average equity.

P1 **Prepare financial statements from business transactions.** Business transactions can be summarized using the accounting equation from which we can prepare financial statements. The balance sheet uses the ending balances in the accounting equation. The statement of changes in owner's equity and the income statement use data from the Equity column for the period. The statement of cash flows uses data from the Cash column.

---

[6] The annual rate is approximated by taking the 1.9% monthly rate and multiplying by the 12 months in a year, or 22.8%.

Guidance Answers to **You Make the Call**

Web Designer   A designer's efforts are reflected in the income statement. The income statement reports information on the revenues and expenses associated with operating activities. If operating activities are successful and you can point to specific contributions such as increased sales or reduced expenses, you are more likely to get a wage increase.

Entrepreneur   We can use the accounting equation to help us identify risky customers to whom we would likely not want to extend credit. The accounting equation is: Assets = Liabilities + Equity. A balance sheet provides amounts for each of these key components. The lower equity is relative to liabilities, the less likely you would extend credit. A low equity means the business has little value that does not already have creditor claims to it.

Engineer   The modified return on equity is relevant for your decision. This return equals 0.5%, computed as [\$4,500 − \$2,500]/\$400,000. This is about 6% per year, approximated as 0.5% × 12 months. You would not likely quit your current job and salary and take the risk of a new business for an expected return of 6% per year.

Guidance Answers to **Quick Checks**

1. The four major financial statements are income statment, balance sheet, statement of changes in owner's (or shareholders') equity, and statement of cash flows.

2. Revenues are inflows of assets in exchange for products or services provided to customers as part of the main operations of a business. Expenses are outflows or the using up of assets that result from providing products or services to customers.

3. Assets are the resources a business owns or controls that carry expected future benefits. Liabilities are the obligations of a business, representing the claims of others against the assets of a business. Equity is the owner's claim on the assets of the business after deducting liabilities.

4. Note three differences: (*a*) A proprietorship's balance sheet lists the equity balance beside the owner's name. Partnerships do the same unless they have too many owners to list. Names of a corporation's owners are not listed in the balance sheet. (*b*) Distributions of cash or other assets to owners of a proprietorship or partnership are called *withdrawals*. Distributions of cash or other assets to owners of a corporation are called *dividends*. (*c*) When the owner of a proprietorship is also its manager, no salary expense is reported on the income statement. The same is true for a partnership, but salaries paid to a corporation's owners are reported as expenses on its income statement.

5. The FASB is the primary organization that sets GAAP. Its decisions are reflected in *Statements of Financial Accounting Standards*. The FASB draws authority from two main sources: the SEC and state boards that license CPAs.

6. *GAAS* refer to generally accepted auditing standards and are the guidelines for performing audits of financial statements. GAAS are set by the Auditing Standards Board (ASB).

7. U.S. companies are not directly affected by international accounting standards. International standards are put forth as preferred accounting practices. However, stock exchanges and other parties are increasing the pressure to narrow differences in worldwide accounting practices. International accounting standards are playing an important role in that process.

8. Users desire information about the performance of a specific entity. If information is mixed between two or more entities, its usefulness decreases.

9. The objectivity and cost principles are related in that most users consider information based on cost as objective. Information prepared using both principles is considered highly reliable and often relevant.

10. A transaction that changes the makeup of assets would not affect liability and equity accounts. Both transactions 2 and 3 are examples. Each exchanges one asset for another.

11. Earning revenue by performing services, such as in transaction 5, increases equity (and assets). Incurring expenses while servicing clients, such as in transactions 6 and 7, decreases equity (and assets). Other examples include owner investments that increase equity and withdrawals that decrease equity.

12. The revenue recognition principle gives preparers guidelines on when to recognize (record) revenue. This is important; for example, if revenue is recognized too early, the income statement reports revenue sooner than it should and the business looks more profitable than it is.

13. Paying a liability with an asset reduces both asset and liability totals. One example is transaction 10 of FastForward, where a payable is reduced by paying cash.

14. The accounting equation is: Assets = Liabilities + Equity. This equation is always in balance, both before and after every transaction.

15. An income statement presents a company's revenues and expenses along with the resulting net income or loss. A statement of changes in owner's equity shows changes in equity, including that from net income or loss. Both statements report transactions occurring over a period of time.

16. The balance sheet describes a company's financial position (assets, liabilities, and equity) at a point in time. The equity account in the balance sheet is obtained from the statement of changes in owner's equity.

17. Cash flows from operating activities report cash receipts and payments from the primary business the company is engaged in. Cash flows from investing activities involve cash transactions from buying and selling long-term assets. Cash flows from financing activities include long-term cash borrowings and repayments from lenders and the cash investments and withdrawals of the owner.

After several months of planning, Sylvia Workman started a haircutting business, Expressions. The following events occurred during its first month:

a. On August 1, Workman put $3,000 cash into a checking account in the name of Expressions. She also invested $15,000 of equipment that she already owned.

b. On August 2, Workman paid $600 cash for furniture for the shop.

c. On August 3, Workman paid $500 cash to rent space in a strip mall for August.

d. On August 4, Workman purchased some new equipment for the shop that she bought on credit (using a note payable) for $1,200.

e. On August 5, Expressions opened for business. Cash received from services provided in the first week and a half of business (ended August 15) is $825.

f. On August 15, Workman provided haircutting services on account for $100.

g. On August 17, Workman received a $100 check for services previously rendered on account.

h. On August 17, Workman paid $125 to an assistant for working during the grand opening.

i. Cash received from services provided during the second half of August is $930.

j. On August 31, Workman paid a $400 installment on the note payable entered into on August 4.

k. On August 31, Workman withdrew $900 cash for her personal use.

Required

1. Arrange the following asset, liability, and equity titles in a table similar to the one in Exhibit 2.13: Cash, Accounts Receivable, Furniture, Store Equipment, Note Payable, and Sylvia Workman, Capital. Show the effects of each transaction on the equation. Add explanations for each of the changes in equity.

2. Prepare an income statement for August.

3. Prepare a statement of changes in owner's equity for August.

4. Prepare a balance sheet as of August 31.

5. Prepare a statement of cash flows for August.

6. Determine the return on equity ratio for August.

7. Determine the modified return on equity ratio for August, assuming Workman's management efforts were worth $1,000.

Planning the Solution

- Set up a table with the appropriate columns, including a final column for describing the transactions that affect equity.

- Analyze each transaction and show its effects as increases or decreases in the appropriate columns. Be sure the accounting equation remains in balance after each transaction.

- To prepare the income statement, find revenues and expenses in the last column. List those items on the statement, compute the difference, and label the result as *net income* or *net loss*.

- Use information in the explanations column to prepare the statement of changes in owner's equity.

- Use information in the last row of the table to prepare the balance sheet.

- To prepare the statement of cash flows, include all events listed in the Cash column of the table. Classify each cash flow as operating, investing, or financing.

- Calculate return on equity by dividing net income by average equity. Calculate the modified return by subtracting the $1,000 value of Workman's efforts from net income, and then dividing the difference by average equity.

Demonstration Problem

*The **Demonstration Problem** is a review of key chapter materials. The Planning the Solution offers strategies in solving the problem.*

Solution to Demonstration Problem

1.

	Assets				= Liabilities +		Equity	
	Cash	+ Accounts Receivable	+ Furni- ture	+ Store Equip- ment	= Note Payable	+ Sylvia Workman, Capital	Explanation of Change
a.	$3,000			$15,000		$18,000	Investment
b.	− 600		+$600				
Bal.	2,400		600	15,000		18,000	
c.	− 500					− 500	Rent Expense
Bal.	1,900		600	15,000		17,500	
d.				+ 1,200	+$1,200		
Bal.	1,900		600	16,200	1,200	17,500	
e.	+ 825					+ 825	Haircutting Services Revenue
Bal.	2,725		600	16,200	1,200	18,325	
f.		+$100				+ 100	Haircutting Services Revenue
Bal.	2,725	100	600	16,200	1,200	18,425	
g.	+ 100	− 100					
Bal.	2,825	0	600	16,200	1,200	18,425	
h.	− 125					− 125	Wages Expense
Bal.	2,700		600	16,200	1,200	18,300	
i.	+ 930					+ 930	Haircutting Services Revenue
Bal.	3,630		600	16,200	1,200	19,230	
j.	− 400				− 400		
Bal.	3,230		600	16,200	800	19,230	
k.	− 900					− 900	Withdrawal
Bal.	$2,330 +		$600 +	$16,200 =	$800	+ $18,330	

2.

EXPRESSIONS Income Statement For Month Ended August 31		
Revenues:		
Haircutting services revenue		$1,855
Operating expenses:		
Rent expense	$500	
Wages expense	125	
Total operating expenses		625
Net Income		$1,230

3.

EXPRESSIONS		
Statement of Changes in Owner's Equity		
For Month Ended August 31		
S. Workman, Capital, August 1		$ 0
Plus: Investments by owner	$18,000	
Net income	1,230	19,230
		$19,230
Less: Withdrawals by owner		(900)
S. Workman, Capital, August 31		$18,330

4.

EXPRESSIONS			
Balance Sheet			
August 31			
Assets		**Liabilities**	
Cash	$ 2,330	Note payable	$ 800
Furniture	600	**Equity**	
Store equipment	16,200	S. Workman, Capital	18,330
Total assets	$19,130	Total liabilities and equity	$19,130

5.

EXPRESSIONS		
Statement of Cash Flows		
For Month Ended August 31		
Cash flows from operating activities:		
Cash received from customers	$1,855	
Cash paid for rent	(500)	
Cash paid for wages	(125)	
Net cash provided by operating activities		$1,230
Cash flows from investing activities:		
Cash paid for furniture		(600)
Cash flows from financing activities:		
Cash received from owner	3,000	
Cash paid to owner	(900)	
Partial repayment of note payable	(400)	
Net cash provided by financing activities		1,700
Net increase in cash		$2,330
Cash balance, August 1		0
Cash balance, August 31		$2,330

6. $\text{Return on equity} = \dfrac{\text{Net income}}{\text{Average equity}} = \dfrac{\$1,230}{(\$18,000 + \$18,330)/2} = \dfrac{\$1,230}{\$18,165} = \underline{\underline{6.77\%}}$

7. $\text{Modified return on equity} = \dfrac{\text{Net income} - \text{Owner's efforts}}{\text{Average equity}}$

$= \dfrac{\$1,230 - \$1,000}{(\$18,000 + \$18,330)/2} = \dfrac{\$230}{\$18,165} = \underline{\underline{1.27\%}}$

Glossary

Accounting equation relation between a company's assets, liabilities, and equity; expressed as Assets = Liabilities + Equity; also called *balance sheet equation*. (p. 46).

Account payable liability created by buying goods or services on credit. (p. 39).

Account receivable asset created by selling products or services on credit. (p. 39).

Assets resources a business owns or controls that are expected to provide future benefits to the business. (p. 39).

Balance sheet financial statement that lists the types and dollar amounts of assets, liabilities, and equity at a specific date; also called *statement of financial position*. (p. 38).

Balance sheet equation (see *accounting equation*). (p. 46).

Business entity principle the principle that requires a business to be accounted for separately from its owner(s). (p. 44).

Business transaction an exchange of economic consideration (such as goods, services, money, or rights to collect money) between two parties. (p. 46).

Contributed capital the category of equity created by shareholders' investments; also called *paid-in capital*. (p. 40).

Cost principle the accounting principle that requires financial statement information to be based on actual costs incurred in business transactions. (p. 44).

Creditors individuals or organizations entitled to receive payments from a company. (p. 39).

Debtors individuals or organizations that owe money to a business. (p. 39).

Dividends a corporation's distributions of assets to its owners. (p. 41).

Equity owner's claim on the assets of a business; equals the residual interest in an entity's assets after deducting liabilities; also called *net assets*. (p. 39).

Expenses outflows or the using up of assets as part of operations of a business to generate sales. (p. 37).

Financial statements includes the balance sheet, income statement, statement of changes in owner's equity, and statement of cash flows. (p. 36).

Generally accepted auditing standards (GAAS) rules adopted for conducting audits of financial statements. (p. 41).

Going-concern principle a principle that requires financial statements to reflect the assumption that the business will continue operating; also called *continuing-concern principle*. (p. 45).

Income statement financial statement that subtracts expenses from revenues to yield a net income or loss over a specified period of time. (p. 37).

International Accounting Standards Committee (IASC) a committee that identifies preferred accounting practices and encourages their worldwide acceptance. (p. 43).

Liabilities claims by others that will reduce the future assets of a business or require services or products. (p. 39).

Modified return on equity ratio of net income minus the value of owner's effort divided by average equity. (p. 56).

Monetary unit principle a principle that assumes transactions and events can be expressed in money units. (p. 45).

Net assets (see *equity*). (p. 39).

Net income the excess of revenues over expenses for a period. (p. 37).

Net loss the excess of expenses over revenues for a period (p. 37).

Note payable a liability expressed by a written promise to make a future payment at a specific time. (p. 39).

Objectivity principle a principle that requires financial statement information to be supported by independent, unbiased evidence. (p. 44).

Paid-in capital (see *contributed capital*). (p. 40).

Retained earnings a corporation's accumulated net income and losses that have not been distributed to shareholders. (p. 40).

Return on equity ratio of net income to average equity. (p. 56).

Revenue recognition principle the principle that revenue is recognized when earned. (p. 49).

Revenues inflows of assets received in exchange for goods or services provided to customers as part of operations. (p. 37).

Statement of cash flows a financial statement that lists cash inflows (receipts) and cash outflows (payments) during a period; arranged by operating, investing, and financing. (p. 39).

Statement of changes in owner's equity a report of changes in equity over a period; adjusted for increases (owner investment and net income) and for decreases (withdrawals and net loss). (p. 37).

Statements of Financial Accounting Standards (SFAS) FASB publications that establish U.S. GAAP. (p. 42).

Withdrawal a payment of cash or other assets from a proprietorship or partnership to its owner or owners. (p. 41).

Questions

1. Identify the four main financial statements of a business.
2. What information is reported in an income statement?
3. What do accountants mean by the term *revenue?*
4. Why does the user of an income statement need to know the time period that it covers?
5. Give two examples of expenses a business might incur.
6. Which financial statement is sometimes called the *statement of financial position?*
7. What information is reported in a balance sheet?
8. Define (*a*) assets, (*b*) liabilities, (*c*) equity, and (*d*) net assets.
9. The statement of cash flows reports on what major activities?
10. Contrast the equity sections of the balance sheet for a sole proprietorship, partnership, and corporation.
11. What FASB pronouncements make up generally accepted accounting principles?
12. Identify two categories of accounting principles.
13. What does the objectivity principle require for information reported in financial statements? Why?
14. A business reports its own office stationery on the balance sheet at its $430 cost, although it cannot be sold for more than $10 as scrap paper. Which accounting principle justifies this treatment?

15. Why is the revenue recognition principle needed? What does it require?
16. What events or transactions change owner's equity?
17. To what should a company's return on equity ratio be compared with to determine whether the owner has made a good investment?
18. Refer to the financial statements of **Nike** in Appendix A. To what level of significance are the dollar amounts rounded? What time period does the income statement cover? **NIKE**
19. Review the balance sheet of **Reebok** in **Reebok** Appendix A. What amount of total assets is reported at December 31, 1999? Prove the accounting equation for Reebok at December 31, 1999.
20. Refer to **Gap**'s income statement in Appendix A. How does the name of this statement differ **GAP** from FastForward's income statement? How does Gap's 2000 net income compare to its previous year?
21. Refer to FastForward's financial statements in the chapter for the month ended December 31, 2001. (*a*) Review the balance sheet and identify the business form Chuck Taylor used to organize his business. (*b*) How much net cash did FastForward generate from the total of its operating, investing, and financing activities in December 2001?

Instructions: In this book's assignments, assume no income taxes unless explicitly mentioned.

Determine the missing amount for each of the following separate cases:

	Assets	=	Liabilities	+	Equity
a.	$ 80,000	=	$ 42,500	+	?
b.	$500,000	=	?	+	$225,000
c.	?	=	$193,000	+	$ 47,000

QUICK STUDY

QS 2-1
Applying the accounting equation

A1

Use the accounting equation in the following separate cases to determine the:
a. Equity in a business that has $195,000 of assets and $23,000 of liabilities.
b. Liabilities of a business having $162,400 of assets and $122,900 of equity.
c. Assets of a business having $32,890 of liabilities and $134,655 of equity.

QS 2-2
Applying the accounting equation

A1

Identify the financial statement(s) where each of the following items appears:
a. Service fees earned
b. Owner cash withdrawals
c. Office equipment
d. Accounts payable
e. Cash repaid on bank loan
f. Utilities expenses
g. Office supplies
h. Cash received from prior period credit sale

QS 2-3
Identifying financial statement items

C1

QS 2-4

Computing return on equity

In a recent year's financial statements, **Boeing Company,** which is the largest aerospace company in the United States, reported the following:

Sales	$57,993 million
Net income	2,309 million
Total assets	36,147 million
Total beginning-of-year equity	12,316 million
Total end-of-year equity	11,462 million

Calculate Boeing's return on equity for that year.

QS 2-5

Identifying accounting principles

Identify which general accounting principle best describes each of the following practices:

a. Le Ann Welch owns both Sailing Passions and Dockside Supplies, both of which are sole proprietorships. In preparing financial statements for Dockside Supplies, Welch makes sure that the expense transactions of Sailing Passions are kept separate from Dockside's statements.

b. In December, 2001, Renew-A-Floor received a customer's order to install carpet in a new house that would not be ready for installation until March 2002. Renew-A-Floor should record the revenue for the order in March 2002, not in December 2001.

c. If $40,000 cash is paid to buy land, the land is reported on the buyer's balance sheet at $40,000.

EXERCISES

Exercise 2-1

Analysis using the accounting equation

Sarah Wells began a new consulting firm on January 5. The accounting equation showed the following balances after each of the company's first five transactions. Analyze the accounting equation for each transaction and describe each of the five transactions with their amounts.

					Assets				=	Liabilities	+	Equity
Trans-action	Cash	+	Accounts Receivable	+	Office Supplies	+	Office Furniture	=	Accounts Payable	+	S. Wells, Capital
a.	$20,000		$ 0		$ 0		$ 0		$ 0		$20,000
b.	19,000		0		1,500		0		500		20,000
c.	11,000		0		1,500		8,000		500		20,000
d.	11,000		3,000		1,500		8,000		500		23,000
e.	11,500		3,000		1,500		8,000		500		23,500

Exercise 2-2

Identifying effects of transactions on the accounting equation

The following changes in items of the accounting equation are described in the separate cases *a* through *g*. Provide an example of a transaction that creates the described effects for each case.

a. Decreases an asset and decreases equity.

b. Increases an asset and increases a liability.

c. Decreases a liability and increases a liability.

d. Increases an asset and decreases an asset.

e. Decreases an asset and decreases a liability.

f. Increases a liability and decreases equity.

g. Increases an asset and increases equity.

Exercise 2-3

Identifying effects of transactions on accounting equation

The following table shows the effects of five transactions (*a* through *e*) on the assets, liabilities, and equity of Benton Boutique. Write short descriptions of the probable nature of each transaction.

	Assets				=	Liabilities	+	Equity
	Cash +	Accounts Receivable +	Office Supplies +	Land =		Accounts Payable +		C. Benton, Capital
	$10,500		$1,500	$ 9,500				$21,500
a.	− 2,000			+ 2,000				
	8,500		1,500	11,500				21,500
b.			+ 500			+$500		
	8,500		2,000	11,500		500		21,500
c.		+$950						+ 950
	8,500	950	2,000	11,500		500		22,450
d.	− 500					− 500		
	8,000	950	2,000	11,500		0		22,450
e.	+ 950	−950						
	$ 8,950 +	$ 0 +	$2,000 +	$11,500 =		$ 0 +		$22,450

A sole proprietorship had the following assets and liabilities at the beginning and end of a recent year:

Exercise 2-4
Computing net income

	Assets	Liabilities
Beginning of the year	$ 60,000	$20,000
End of the year	105,000	36,000

Determine the net income earned or net loss incurred by the business during the year under each of the following separate assumptions:

a. Owner made no investments in the business and withdrew no assets during the year.

b. Owner made no investments in the business during the year but withdrew $1,250 per month to pay personal expenses.

c. Owner withdrew no assets during the year but invested an additional $55,000 cash.

d. Owner withdrew $1,250 per month to pay personal expenses and invested an additional $35,000 cash.

Mary Campion began a professional practice on June 1 and plans to prepare financial statements at the end of each month. During June, Campion completed these transactions:

a. Invested $60,000 cash along with equipment that had an $8,000 market value.

b. Paid $1,500 cash for rent of office space for the month.

c. Purchased $15,000 of additional equipment on credit.

d. Completed work for a client and immediately collected the $1,000 cash earned.

e. Completed work for a client and sent a bill for $6,000 to be paid within 30 days.

f. Purchased additional equipment for $5,000 cash.

g. Paid an assistant $2,700 cash as wages for the month.

h. Collected $4,000 cash on the amount owed by the client described in transaction *e*.

i. Paid cash for the equipment purchased in transaction *c*.

j. Withdrew $900 cash for personal use.

Exercise 2-5
Identifying effects of transactions on the accounting equation and computing return on equity

Required

Create a table like the one in Exhibit 2.13, using the following headings for columns: Cash; Accounts Receivable; Equipment; Accounts Payable; and M. Campion, Capital. Then use additions and subtractions to show the effects of the transactions on individual items of the accounting equation. Show new balances after each transaction. Determine the modified return on equity for Campion assuming that her management efforts during June have a value of $4,000.

Check Net income, $2,800

Exercise 2-6

Identifying accounting principles

Match each of the following numbered descriptions with the principle it best reflects. Indicate your answer by writing the letter for the appropriate principle in the blank space next to each description.

A. General accounting principle   **E.** Specific accounting principle

B. Cost principle   **F.** Objectivity principle

C. Business entity principle   **G.** Going-concern principle

D. Revenue recognition principle

_____ **1.** Usually created by a pronouncement from an authoritative body.

_____ **2.** Requires financial statements to reflect the assumption that the business will continue operating.

_____ **3.** Derived from long-used and generally accepted accounting practices.

_____ **4.** Requires financial statement information to be supported by evidence other than some-one's opinion or belief.

_____ **5.** Requires every business to be accounted for separately from its owner or owners.

_____ **6.** Requires revenue to be recorded only when the earnings process is complete.

_____ **7.** Requires information to be based on costs incurred in transactions.

Exercise 2-7

Reporting financial statement items

Match each of the following numbered items with the financial statement or statements on which it should be reported. Indicate your answer by writing the letter or letters for the correct statement in the blank space next to each item.

A. Income statement

B. Statement of changes in owner's equity

C. Balance sheet

D. Statement of cash flows

_____ **1.** Office supplies

_____ **2.** Cash received from customers

_____ **3.** Consulting fees earned and received in cash

_____ **4.** Rent expense incurred and paid in cash

_____ **5.** Investments of cash by owner

_____ **6.** Accounts payable

_____ **7.** Cash withdrawals by owner

_____ **8.** Accounts receivable

Exercise 2-8

Preparing a statement of changes in owner's equity

Compute the amount of the missing item in each of the following separate cases *a* through *d*:

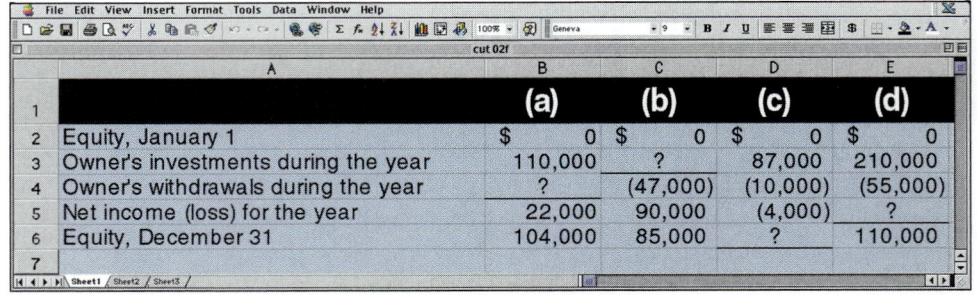

	(a)	(b)	(c)	(d)
Equity, January 1	$ 0	$ 0	$ 0	$ 0
Owner's investments during the year	110,000	?	87,000	210,000
Owner's withdrawals during the year	?	(47,000)	(10,000)	(55,000)
Net income (loss) for the year	22,000	90,000	(4,000)	?
Equity, December 31	104,000	85,000	?	110,000

Exercise 2-9

Identifying sections of statement of cash flows

Indicate the section where each of the following cash flows would appear on the statement of cash flows.

A. Cash flow from operating activity   **C.** Cash flow from financing activity

B. Cash flow from investing activity

_____ **1.** Cash paid for wages   _____ **5.** Cash paid on a payable

_____ **2.** Cash withdrawal by owner   _____ **6.** Cash investment by owner

_____ **3.** Cash purchase of equipment   _____ **7.** Cash received from clients

_____ **4.** Cash paid for advertising   _____ **8.** Cash paid for rent

On October 1, Bernice Haddox organized a new consulting firm called Tech Answers. On October 31, the company's records show the following items and amounts. Use this information to prepare an October income statement for the business.

Cash	$11,000	Owner's withdrawals	$ 2,360
Accounts receivable	14,000	Consulting fees earned	14,000
Office supplies	3,250	Rent expense	3,550
Automobiles	46,000	Salaries expense	7,000
Office equipment	18,000	Telephone expense	760
Accounts payable	8,500	Miscellaneous expenses	580
Owner's investments	84,000		

Exercise 2-10
Preparing an income statement

Check Net income, $2,110

Use the information in Exercise 2-10 to prepare an October statement of changes in owner's equity for Tech Answers.

Exercise 2-11
Preparing a statement of changes in owner's equity

Use the information in Exercise 2-10 (if completed, you can also use your solution to Exercise 2-11) to prepare an October 31 balance sheet for Tech Answers.

Exercise 2-12
Preparing a balance sheet

Use the information in Exercise 2-10 to prepare an October 31 statement of cash flows for Tech Answers. Also assume the following:

- The owner's initial investment consists of $38,000 cash and $46,000 in automobiles.
- The $18,000 equipment purchase is paid in cash.
- The accounts payable balance of $8,500 consists of the $3,250 office supplies purchase and $5,250 in employee salaries yet to be paid.
- The rent, telephone, and miscellaneous expenses are paid in cash.
- No cash has yet been collected for consulting services provided.

Exercise 2-13
Preparing a statement of cash flows

Use information from each of the following separate cases *a* through *d* to calculate the company's return on equity and its modified return on equity:

Exercise 2-14
Calculating return on equity

	File Edit View Insert Format Tools Data Window Help				
	A	B	C	D	E
1		**(a)**	**(b)**	**(c)**	**(d)**
2	Average equity	$100,000	$900,000	$250,000	$633,000
3	Net income	20,000	210,000	110,000	178,000
4	Value of owner's efforts	6,000	80,000	54,000	125,000
5					

PROBLEM SET A

The following financial statement information is known about five separate proprietorships:

Problem 2-1A

Calculating missing information using accounting knowledge

	Company A	Company B	Company C	Company D	Company E
December 31, 2001:					
Assets	$55,000	$34,000	$24,000	$60,000	$119,000
Liabilities	24,500	21,500	9,000	40,000	?
December 31, 2002:					
Assets	58,000	40,000	?	85,000	113,000
Liabilities	?	26,500	29,000	24,000	70,000
During year 2002:					
Owner investments	6,000	1,400	9,750	?	6,500
Net income	8,500	?	8,000	14,000	20,000
Owner withdrawals	3,500	2,000	5,875	0	11,000

Required

1. Answer the following questions about Company A:
   a. What is the equity amount on December 31, 2001?
   b. What is the equity amount on December 31, 2002?
   c. What is the amount of liabilities on December 31, 2002?

2. Answer the following questions about Company B:
   a. What is the equity amount on December 31, 2001?
   b. What is the equity amount on December 31, 2002?
   c. What is net income for year 2002?

Check   Co. C, Dec. 31, 2002, Assets, $55,875

3. Calculate the amount of assets for Company C on December 31, 2002.

4. Calculate the amount of owner investments in Company D during year 2002.

5. Calculate the amount of liabilities for Company E on December 31, 2001.

Problem 2-2A

Identifying effects of transactions on financial statements

Identify how each of the following separate transactions affects financial statements. For the balance sheet, identify how each transaction affects total assets, total liabilities, and equity. For the income statement, identify how each transaction affects net income. For the statement of cash flows, identify how each transaction affects cash flows from operating activities, cash flows from financing activities, and cash flows from investing activities. For increases, place a "+" in the column or columns. For decreases, place a "−" in the column or columns. If both an increase and a decrease occur, place a "+/−" in the column or columns. The first transaction is completed as an example.

		Balance Sheet			Income Statement	Statement of Cash Flows		
	Transaction	**Total Assets**	**Total Liab.**	**Equity**	**Net Income**	**Operating Activities**	**Financing Activities**	**Investing Activities**
1	Owner invests cash	+		+			+	
2	Performs services for cash							
3	Pays wages incurred with cash							
4	Pays for services received on credit							
5	Borrows cash by signing note payable							
6	Owner withdraws cash							
7	Buys land by signing note payable							
8	Performs services on credit							
9	Buys office equipment for cash							
10	Collects cash on receivable from (8)							

A new start-up business, Copy This, has the following beginning cash balance and cash flows for the month of December:

Cash balance, December 1	$ 0
Cash withdrawal by owner	600
Cash received from customers	5,000
Cash payment of long-term liabilities	1,200
Cash paid for store supplies	2,800
Cash purchase of equipment	23,000
Cash paid for rent	1,000
Cash paid to employee	570
Cash investment by owner	38,000

Problem 2-3A

Preparing a statement of cash flows

Required

Prepare a statement of cash flows for Copy This for the month of December.

Check   Cash bal.,
Dec. 31, $13,830

John Elfrink started a new business called Elfrink Enterprises and it completed the following transactions during its first six months of operations:

a. Elfrink invests $50,000 cash and office equipment valued at $25,000 in the business.

b. Paid $200,000 for a building to be used as an office. Elfrink paid $40,000 in cash and signed a note payable promising to pay the balance over the next four years.

c. Purchased office supplies for $5,000 cash.

d. Purchased $27,000 of office equipment on credit.

e. Performed services and billed the client $5,000 to be received later.

f. Paid a local newspaper $800 cash for an advertisement of the new business.

g. Performed services for a client and collected $22,000 cash.

h. Made a $3,000 cash payment on the equipment purchased in transaction *d*.

i. Received $4,000 cash from the client described in transaction *e*.

j. Paid $2,000 cash for the office secretary's wages.

k. Elfrink withdrew $2,400 cash from the company bank account for personal living expenses.

Problem 2-4A

Analyzing effects of transactions and computing return on equity

Required

Preparation Component

1. Create a table like the one in Exhibit 2.13, using the following headings for the columns: Cash; Accounts Receivable; Office Supplies; Office Equipment; Building; Accounts Payable; Note Payable; and J. Elfrink, Capital. Leave space for an Explanation column to the right of the Capital column. Identify revenues and expenses by name in the Explanation column.

2. Use additions and subtractions to show the transactions' effects on individual items of the accounting equation. Show new balances after each transaction. Indicate next to each change in equity whether it was caused by an investment, a revenue, an expense, or a withdrawal.

3. Once you have completed the table, determine the company's net income.

Check   Net income, $24,200

Analysis Component

4. Determine the return on equity for Elfrink Enterprises (use the $75,000 initial investment as the beginning balance of equity). Assuming Elfrink could have earned $5,000 for the period from another job, determine the modified return on equity for the period. State whether you think the business is a good use of Elfrink's money if an alternative investment would have returned 8% for the same period.

JD Simpson started a new business called The Simpson Co. that began operations on May 1. Simpson completed the following transactions during the month:

May	1	Simpson invested $40,000 cash in the business.
	1	Rented a furnished office and paid $2,200 cash for May's rent.
	3	Purchased office equipment for $1,890 on credit.
	5	Paid $750 cash for this month's cleaning services.
	8	Provided consulting services for a client and immediately collected $5,400 cash.

Problem 2-5A

Preparing a balance sheet, an income statement, a statement of changes in owner's equity, and a statement of cash flows

12	Provided $2,500 of consulting services for a client on credit.
15	Paid $750 cash for an assistant's salary for the first half of this month.
20	Received cash payment in full for the services provided on May 12.
22	Provided $3,200 of consulting services on credit.
28	Received full cash payment for the services provided on May 22.
29	Paid cash for the office equipment purchased on May 3.
30	Purchased $80 of advertising in this month's local paper on credit; cash payment is due June 1.
30	Paid $300 cash for this month's telephone bill.
30	Paid $280 cash for this month's utilities.
30	Paid $750 cash for an assistant's salary for the second half of this month.
30	Simpson withdrew $1,400 cash from the business for personal use.

Required

1. Arrange the following asset, liability, and equity titles in a table like Exhibit 2.13: Cash; Accounts Receivable; Office Equipment; Accounts Payable; and JD Simpson, Capital. Include an Explanation column for changes in equity.

2. Show effects of the transactions on the items of the accounting equation by recording increases and decreases in the appropriate columns. Do not determine new account balances after each transaction. Next to each change in equity, state whether it was caused by an investment, a revenue, an expense, or a withdrawal. Determine the final total for each item and verify that the equation is in balance.

Check Net income, $5,990

3. Prepare an income statement for May, a statement of changes in owner's equity for May, a May 31 balance sheet, and a statement of cash flows for May.

Problem 2-6A
Computing net income, preparing a balance sheet, and calculating return on equity

The accounting records of Sarasota Shipping Services show the following assets and liabilities as of December 31, 2001, and 2002:

	December 31	
	2001	**2002**
Cash	$ 64,300	$ 15,640
Accounts receivable	26,240	19,390
Office supplies	3,160	1,960
Office equipment	148,000	157,000
Trucks	44,000	44,000
Building	0	80,000
Land	0	60,000
Accounts payable	3,500	33,500
Note payable	0	40,000

Late in December 2002, Trey Davis, the owner, purchased a small office building and moved the business from rented quarters to the new building. The building and the land it occupies cost $140,000. The business paid $100,000 cash toward the purchase and a $40,000 note payable was signed for the balance. Davis had to invest $35,000 cash in the business to enable it to pay the $100,000. Davis also withdraws $3,000 cash per month from his proprietorship for personal expenses.

Required

1. Prepare balance sheets for the business as of December 31, 2001, and 2002. (Remember that equity equals the difference between assets and liabilities.)

Check Net income, $23,290

2. By comparing equity amounts from the balance sheets and using the additional information presented in this problem, prepare a calculation to show how much net income was earned by the business during 2002.

Check Modified return on equity, 1.1%

3. Calculate the year 2002 return on equity for the business. Also calculate the modified return on equity assuming that Davis's efforts are worth $20,000 for the year.

Curtis Hamilton started a new business and completed these transactions during December:

Dec. 1   Curtis Hamilton transferred $65,000 cash from a personal savings account to a checking account in the name of Hamilton Electric.
      1   Rented office space and paid $1,000 cash for the December rent.
      3   Purchased electrical equipment from an electrician who was going out of business for $13,000 by paying $4,800 cash and agreeing to pay the balance in six months.
      5   Purchased office supplies by paying $800 cash.
      6   Completed electrical work and immediately collected $1,200 cash for the work.
      8   Purchased $2,530 of office equipment on credit.
     15   Completed electrical work on credit in the amount of $5,000.
     18   Purchased $350 of office supplies on credit.
     20   Paid cash for the office equipment purchased on December 8.
     24   Billed a client $900 for electrical work completed; the balance is due in 30 days.
     28   Received $5,000 cash for the work completed on December 15.
     30   Paid the assistant's salary of $1,400 cash for this month.
     30   Paid $540 cash for this month's utility bill.
     30   Hamilton withdrew $950 cash from the business for personal use.

Required

Preparation Component

1. Arrange the following asset, liability, and equity titles in a table like Exhibit 2.13: Cash; Accounts Receivable; Office Supplies; Office Equipment; Electrical Equipment; Accounts Payable; and Curtis Hamilton, Capital. Leave space for an Explanation column to the right of Curtis Hamilton, Capital.

2. Use additions and subtractions to show the effects of each transaction on the items in the accounting equation. Show new balances after each transaction. Next to each change in equity, state whether the change was caused by an investment, a revenue, an expense, or a withdrawal.

3. Use the increases and decreases in the last column of the table from part 2 to prepare an income statement and a statement of changes in owner's equity for the month. Also prepare a balance sheet as of the end of the month.

4. Calculate the return on equity for the month, using the $65,000 initial investment as the beginning balance of equity.

Analysis Component

5. Assume the investment transaction on December 1 was $49,000 instead of $65,000 and that Hamilton obtained the $16,000 difference by borrowing it from a bank. Explain the effect of this change on total assets, total liabilities, equity, and return on equity.

Problem 2-7A

Analyzing transactions, preparing financial statements, and calculating return on equity

Check   Ending owner's equity, $68,210

The following financial statement information is known about five separate proprietorships:

PROBLEM SET B

Computing Problem 2-1B
Computing missing information using accounting knowledge

	Company V	Company W	Company X	Company Y	Company Z
December 31, 2001:					
Assets	$54,000	$80,000	$141,500	$92,500	$144,000
Liabilities	25,000	60,000	68,500	51,500	?
December 31, 2002:					
Assets	59,000	100,000	186,500	?	170,000
Liabilities	36,000	?	65,800	42,000	42,000
During year 2002:					
Owner investments	5,000	20,000	?	48,100	60,000
Net income	?	40,000	18,500	24,000	32,000
Owner withdrawals	5,500	2,000	0	20,000	8,000

Required

1. Answer the following questions about Company V:
   a. What is the amount of equity on December 31, 2001?
   b. What is the amount of equity on December 31, 2002?
   c. What is net income for year 2002?
2. Answer the following questions about Company W:
   a. What is the amount of equity on December 31, 2001?
   b. What is the amount of equity on December 31, 2002?
   c. What is the amount of liabilities on December 31, 2002?
3. Calculate the amount of owner investments in Company X during 2002.
4. Calculate the amount of assets for Company Y on December 31, 2002.
5. Calculate the amount of liabilities for Company Z on December 31, 2001.

Check Co. Y, Dec. 31, 2002
Assets, $135,100

Problem 2-2B
Identifying effects of transactions on financial statements

Identify how each of the following separate transactions affects the company's financial statements. For the balance sheet, identify how each transaction affects total assets, total liabilities, and equity. For the income statement, identify how each transaction affects net income. For the statement of cash flows, identify how each transaction affects cash flows from operating activities, cash flows from financing activities, and cash flows from investing activities. For increases, place a "+" in the column or columns. For decreases, place a "−" in the column or columns. If both an increase and a decrease occur, place "+/−" in the column or columns. The first transaction is completed as an example.

	Transaction	Total Assets	Total Liab.	Equity	Net Income	Operating Activities	Financing Activities	Investing Activities
		Balance Sheet			**Income Stmt.**	**Statement of Cash Flows**		
1	Owner invests cash	+		+			+	
2	Borrows cash by signing note payable							
3	Pays wages incurred with cash							
4	Performs services for cash							
5	Pays rent incurred with cash							
6	Pays for services received on credit							
7	Buys store equipment for cash							
8	Owner withdraws cash							
9	Performs services on credit							
10	Collects cash on receivable from (9)							

Problem 2-3B
Preparing a statement of cash flows

A new business, AllNet, has the following cash balance and cash flows for the month of December:

Cash balance, December 1	$ 0
Cash withdrawal by owner	2,000
Cash received from customers	12,400
Cash payment of long-term liabilities	1,500
Cash paid for store supplies	3,200
Cash purchase of equipment	39,000
Cash paid for rent	1,750
Cash paid to employee	2,000
Cash investment by owner	57,000

Check Cash Bal., Dec. 31,
$19,950

Required

Prepare a statement of cash flows for AllNet for the month of December.

Fiona Dare started a new business called Midwest Consulting and it completed the following transactions during its first year of operations:

a. Dare invests $70,000 cash and office equipment valued at $10,000 in the business.

b. Paid $150,000 for a building to use as an office. Dare paid $20,000 in cash and signed a note payable promising to pay the balance over the next ten years.

c. Purchased office equipment for $15,000 cash.

d. Purchased $1,200 of office supplies and $1,700 of office equipment on credit.

e. Paid a local newspaper $500 cash for an announcement of the office's opening.

f. Completed a financial plan on credit and billed the client $2,800 for the service.

g. Designed a financial plan for another client and collected a $4,000 cash fee.

h. Dare withdrew $3,275 cash from the company bank account to pay personal expenses.

i. Received $1,800 cash from the client described in transaction *f*.

j. Made a $700 cash payment on the equipment purchased in transaction *d*.

k. Paid $1,800 cash for the office secretary's wages.

Required

Preparation Component

1. Create a table like the one in Exhibit 2.13, using the following headings for the columns: Cash; Accounts Receivable; Office Supplies; Office Equipment; Building; Accounts Payable; Note Payable; and Fiona Dare, Capital. Leave space for an Explanation column to the right of the Capital column. Identify revenues and expenses by name in the Explanation column.

2. Use additions and subtractions to show the effects of these transactions on individual items of the accounting equation. Show new balances after each transaction. Indicate next to each change in equity whether it was caused by an investment, a revenue, an expense, or a withdrawal.

3. Once you have completed the table, determine the company's net income.

Analysis Component

4. Determine the return on equity for Midwest Consulting (use the $80,000 initial investment as the beginning balance of equity). Assuming that Dare could have earned $3,000 for the period from another job, determine the modified return on equity for the period. State whether you think the business is a good use of Dare's money if an alternative investment would have returned 10% for the same period.

Ken Stone launched a new business called Ken's Maintenance Co. that began operations on June 1. The following transactions were completed during the month:

June 1 Stone invested $130,000 cash in the business.

  1 Rented a furnished office of a maintenance company that was going out of business and paid $6,000 cash for June's rent.

  4 Purchased tools for $2,400 on credit.

  6 Paid $1,150 cash for advertising the opening of the business.

  8 Completed maintenance services for a customer and immediately collected $850 cash.

  14 Completed $7,500 of maintenance services for First Union Center on credit.

  16 Paid $800 cash for an assistant's salary for the first half of the month.

  20 Received cash payment in full for services completed for First Union Center on June 14.

  21 Completed $7,900 of maintenance services for Skyway Co. on credit.

  24 Completed $675 of maintenance services for Comfort Motel on credit.

  29 Received full cash payment from Skyway Co. for the work completed on June 21.

  29 Made a payment of $2,400 cash for the tools purchased on June 4.

  30 Paid $150 cash for this month's telephone bill.

  30 Paid $890 cash for this month's utilities.

  30 Paid $800 cash for an assistant's salary for the second half of this month.

  30 Stone withdrew $4,000 cash from the business for personal use.

Required

1. Arrange the following asset, liability, and equity titles in a table like Exhibit 2.13: Cash; Accounts Receivable; Tools; Accounts Payable; Ken Stone, Capital. Include an Explanation column for changes in equity.

2. Show the effects of the transactions on the items of the accounting equation by recording increases and decreases in the appropriate columns. Do not determine new account balances after each transaction. Next to each change in equity, state whether it was caused by an investment, a revenue, an expense, or a withdrawal. Determine the final total for each item and verify that the equation is in balance.

Check Ending owner's equity, $133,135

3. Prepare a June income statement, a June statement of changes in owner's equity, a June 30 balance sheet, and a June statement of cash flows.

Problem 2-6B

Calculating net income, preparing a balance sheet, and calculating return on equity

The accounting records of Affleck Co. show the following assets and liabilities as of December 31, 2001, and 2002:

	December 31	
	2001	**2002**
Cash	$20,000	$ 5,000
Accounts receivable	35,000	25,000
Office supplies	8,000	13,500
Office equipment	40,000	40,000
Machinery	28,500	28,500
Building	0	250,000
Land	0	50,000
Accounts payable	4,000	12,000
Note payable	0	250,000

Late in December 2002, Wes Affleck, the owner, purchased a small office building and moved the business to it from rented quarters. The building and the land it occupies cost $300,000. The business paid $50,000 cash toward the purchase and a $250,000 note payable was signed for the balance. Affleck had to invest an additional $15,000 cash to enable it to pay the $50,000. Affleck also withdraws $250 cash per month from his proprietorship for personal use.

Required

1. Prepare balance sheets for the business as of December 31, 2001, and 2002. (Remember that equity equals the difference between assets and liabilities.)

Check Net income, $10,500

2. By comparing equity amounts from the balance sheets and using the additional information presented in the problem, prepare a calculation to show how much net income was earned by the business during 2002.

Check Modified return on equity, −6.85%

3. Calculate the year 2002 return on equity for the business. Also, calculate the modified return on equity assuming that Affleck's efforts are worth $20,000 for the year.

Problem 2-7B

Analyzing transactions, preparing financial statements, and calculating return on equity

Swender Excavating Co., owned by Patrick Swender, began operations in July and completed these transactions during the month:

July 1 Swender invested $80,000 cash in the business.
    1 Rented office space and paid $700 cash for the July rent.
    1 Purchased excavating equipment for $5,000 by paying $1,000 cash and agreeing to pay the balance in six months.
    6 Purchased office supplies by paying $600 cash.
    8 Completed work for a customer and immediately collected $7,600 cash for the work.
  10 Purchased $2,300 of office equipment on credit.
  15 Completed work for a customer on credit in the amount of $8,200.
  17 Purchased $3,100 of office supplies on credit.
  23 Paid cash for the office equipment purchased on July 10.
  25 Billed a customer $5,000 for completed work; the balance is due in 30 days.
  28 Received $8,200 cash for the work completed on July 15.
  31 Paid an assistant's salary of $1,560 cash for this month.
  31 Paid $295 cash for this month's utility bill.
  31 Swender withdrew $1,800 cash from the business to pay personal expenses.

Required

Preparation Component

1. Arrange the following asset, liability, and equity titles in a table like Exhibit 2.13: Cash; Accounts Receivable; Office Supplies; Office Equipment; Excavating Equipment; Accounts Payable; and Patrick Swender, Capital. Leave space for an Explanation column to the right of the Patrick Swender, Capital column.

2. Use additions and subtractions to show the effects of each transaction on the items in the accounting equation. Show new balances after each transaction. Next to each change in equity, state whether the change was caused by an investment, a revenue, an expense, or a withdrawal.

3. Use the increases and decreases in the last column of the table from part 2 to prepare an income statement and a statement of changes in owner's equity for the month. Also prepare a balance sheet as of the end of the month.

Check   Ending owner's equity, $96,445

4. Calculate return on equity for the month, using the $80,000 initial investment as the beginning balance of equity.

Analysis Component

5. Assume that Swender's $5,000 purchase of excavating equipment on July 1 was financed from his personal investment of another $5,000 cash in the business (instead of the purchase conditions described in the transaction). Explain the effect of this change on total assets, total liabilities, equity, and return on equity.

Beyond the Numbers

BTN 2-1   Refer to **Nike**'s annual report in Appendix A to answer the following questions:

Reporting in Action

C1   A2

NIKE

Required

1. Examine Nike's consolidated balance sheet. To what level are its dollar amounts rounded?
2. What is the reporting date of Nike's most recent annual reporting period?
3. What amount of net income did Nike earn for the fiscal year ended May 31, 2000?
4. How much cash (and equivalents) did Nike hold at fiscal year-end May 31, 2000?
5. What was the net amount of cash provided by its operating activities for the fiscal year ended May 31, 2000?
6. Did its investing activities for fiscal year ended May 31, 2000, create a net cash inflow or outflow? What was the amount of this net cash flow?
7. Compare fiscal year 2000's results to 1999's results to determine whether revenues increased or decreased. What was the amount of the increase or decrease?
8. What is the change in net income between fiscal years 2000 and 1999?
9. What amount is reported as total assets at fiscal year-end 2000?
10. Calculate return on equity for fiscal year ended May 31, 2000.

Swoosh Ahead

11. Obtain Nike's annual report for a fiscal year ending after May 31, 2000, from its Web site [**www.nike.com**] or the SEC's EDGAR database [**www.sec.gov**]. Recompute Nike's return on equity with the updated annual report information. Compare the May 31, 2000, fiscal year-end return on equity to any subsequent year's return you are able to calculate. Also compare how Nike's total assets, total revenues, and net income have changed since May 31, 2000.

BTN 2-2   Key comparative figures ($ millions) for both **Nike** and **Reebok** follow:

Comparative Analysis

A2

Key Figures	Nike	Reebok
Beginning equity	$3,334.6	$524.4
Ending equity	3,136.0	528.8
Net income	579.1	11.05

Required

1. What is the return on equity for (*a*) Nike and (*b*) Reebok?
2. Is return on equity satisfactory for (*a*) Nike and (*b*) Reebok if competitors average a 10% return?
3. Would it be appropriate to calculate the modified return on equity for either Reebok or Nike?

Ethics Challenge
C5

BTN 2-3   Damara Crist is an entry-level accountant for a mail-order company that specializes in supplying skateboards and accessories. At the end of its fiscal period, Damara is advised by a supervisor to include as revenue for the period any orders that have been charged by phone but not yet shipped. Damara is also advised to include as revenue any orders received by mail with checks enclosed that are also pending shipment.

Required

1. Identify the most relevant accounting principle in assessing the supervisor's instructions.
2. What are the ethical factors in this situation?
3. Would you recommend that Damara follow the supervisor's directions?
4. What alternatives might be available to Damara other than following the supervisor's directions?

Communicating in Practice
C1

BTN 2-4   Rochelle Roither is an aspiring entrepreneur and your friend. She is having difficulty understanding the purposes of financial statements and how they fit together across time.

Required

Write a one-page memorandum to Rochelle Roither explaining the purposes of the four major financial statements and how they are linked in time.

Taking It to the Net
C1 C5

BTN 2-5   Visit the Edgar database online at www.edgar-online.com. Alphabetically search for **Fogdog Sports** (ticker FOGD). Fogdog Sports is an online retailer of sports clothing and equipment. View Fogdog's March 20, 2000, 10-K405 report filed with the SEC. Using the full filing feature of Edgar, search Fogdog's 10-K until you find the annual income statement that reports results for 1999, 1998, and 1997.

Required

1. What is the net income trend (level and direction) for Fogdog during its most recent 3 years?
2. What expense reported on the income statement provides a clue that Fogdog is an Internet-based company?

Teamwork in Action
C5 A1

BTN 2-6   The accounting equation can be used to reveal useful information on changes in a company's assets, liabilities, and equity.

Required

1. Form *learning teams* of four (or more) members. Each team member must select one of the following four categories (each team must have at least one expert in each category): (*a*) assets, (*b*) liabilities, (*c*) equity—investments and withdrawals, and (*d*) equity—revenues and expenses.
2. Form *expert teams* from individuals who have selected the same category in (*1*). Expert teams are to discuss and draft a report that each expert will present to his/her learning team addressing the following:
   a. Description of a transaction, with amounts, that increases its category.
   b. Using the transaction and amounts in (*a*), verify the equality of the accounting equation.
   c. Description of a transaction, with amounts, that decreases its category.
   d. Using the transaction and amounts in (*c*), verify the equality of the accounting equation.
3. Each expert should return to his/her learning team. In rotation, each member presents his/her expert team's report to the learning team. Team discussion is encouraged.

BTN 2-7   *Business Week* periodically publishes a ranking of "Hot Growth Companies." It contains tables of selected accounting measures. Obtain the most recent issue on hot growth companies. (*Note:* May 29, 2000, was one such issue.)

Business Week Activity

Required

1. What company is ranked number 1 using return on equity (also called return on capital)?

2. What is the return on equity (capital) for the number 1 company?

3. Refer to the return on equity (capital) table and consider the relation between return and risk. Identify and discuss common risk characteristics for the top five companies.

BTN 2-8   On weekends, Richard Hepperly is the organizer and member of a rock band. Hepperly is considering pursuing his rock band full-time. To help in this decision, he has made the following annual financial estimates: Average equity investment required, $250,000; Revenues, $310,000; and Expenses, $189,000.

Entrepreneurial Decision

Required

1. Compute an estimated return on equity for R. Hepperly.

2. Compute an estimated modified return on equity for R. Hepperly knowing that he will be giving up $50,000 in annual wages from his current job.

3. Should R. Hepperly pursue his rock band full-time?

3

Analyzing and Recording Transactions

A Look Back

We explained the value of accounting in the information age. We showed how financial statements, prepared according to accounting principles, communicate useful information. We also analyzed and prepared simple financial statements from transactions.

A Look at This Chapter

This chapter focuses on the accounting process. We describe transactions and source documents as inputs for analysis. We explain analysis and recording of transactions for preparing financial statements. T-accounts, postings, ledgers, and trial balances are shown as useful tools in carrying out these steps.

A Look Ahead

Chapter 4 extends our focus on processing information. We explain the importance of adjusting accounts and the procedures in preparing financial statements.

"The only thing that sets you apart from your competitors is people"— Kristin Knight

Creative Assets

e SEATTLE—When 22-year-old Kristin Knight quit her job at Microsoft to pursue her dream of starting a company, she didn't get much encouragement, "Most people thought I was crazy to leave," says Knight.

Crazy like a fox. Knight now runs **Creative Assets**, a company offering its clients access to some of the best freelance talent around [**Creative Assets.com**]. "We represent freelance creative talent in the digital media area and match them up with companies," explains Knight. About two-thirds of her creative people are graphic designers or production artists, and a growing number are writers. Projects typically last from 3 to 9 months. Last year, its revenues exceeded $5 million. This year that figure is expected to hit $20 million. Entrepreneur Magazine recently listed Knight among its "entrepreneurial superstars under 40."

Yet, while a great idea is key, Knight asserts that a successful business depends on accurate accounting information. When Creative Assets added its first branch office, Knight confesses it "didn't have the [accounting] systems in place to support the growth that came with it, especially on the financial side." She adds, "I overlooked the vital role . . . of accounting, technology, and database systems."

Mistakes in the recording and analyzing of business transactions proved costly for the company, but taught Knight a valuable lesson. "It was an expensive . . . lesson, but now I realize the importance of setting up [accounting] systems." Creative Assets continues to astound observers with its rapid growth. But this entrepreneurial venture, like most others, would not have achieved what it has without effective accounting systems. [Sources: *Creative Assets Web Site*, May 2001; *Pugent Sound Business Journal*, March 16, 1998; *Seattle Times,* July 14, 1998]

Learning Objectives

Conceptual

C1 Explain the steps in processing transactions.

C2 Describe source documents and their purpose.

C3 Describe an account and its use in recording information about transactions.

C4 Describe a ledger and a chart of accounts.

C5 Define debits and credits and explain their role in double-entry accounting.

Analytical

A1 Analyze the impact of transactions on accounts and financial statements.

A2 Compute the debt ratio and describe its use in analyzing company performance.

Procedural

P1 Record transactions in a journal and post entries to a ledger.

P2 Prepare and explain the use of a trial balance.

The accounting process is crucial to producing useful financial information. We explained in Chapter 2 how the accounting equation (Assets = Liabilities + Equity) helps us understand and analyze transactions and events. In this chapter we further describe processing transactions and recording their effects in accounts. All accounting systems use procedures similar to those described here. These procedures are important steps leading to financial statements. We begin by describing how source documents provide crucial information about transactions. We then describe accounts and explain their purpose. Debits and credits are introduced and identified as valuable tools in helping us understand and process transactions. This background enables us to describe the process of recording events in a journal and how they are posted to a ledger. We return to transactions of **FastForward**, first introduced in Chapter 2, to illustrate these procedures. We conclude the chapter by describing how to use a company's debt ratio to assess its risk.

Transactions and Documents

C1 Explain the steps in processing transactions.

We explained in Chapter 1 how accounting provides information to help people make better decisions. This information is the result of an accounting process that reflects business transactions and events, analyzes and records their effects, and summarizes and prepares information in reports and financial statements. These reports and statements are used for making investing, lending, and other business decisions. We illustrate the steps in the accounting process in Exhibit 3.1.

Exhibit 3.1

Accounting Process

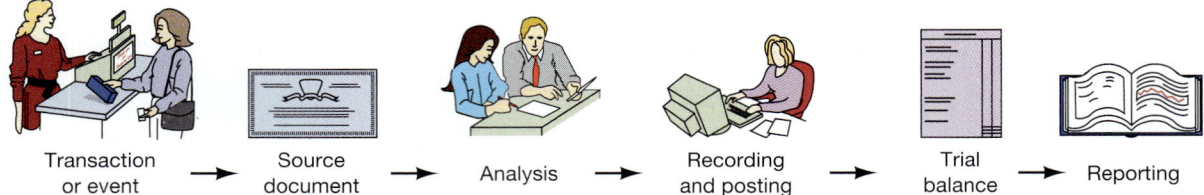

| Transaction or event | → | Source document | → | Analysis | → | Recording and posting | → | Trial balance | → | Reporting |

Transactions and events are the starting points in the accounting process. Relying on source documents, we analyze transactions and events using the accounting equation to understand how they affect company performance and financial position. These effects are recorded in accounting records, informally referred to as the *accounting books,* or simply the *books.* Additional processing steps such as posting and preparing a trial balance help us summarize and classify the effects of transactions and events. A final step in the accounting process is to provide information in useful reports or financial statements to decision makers. We begin our overview of the accounting process with a discussion of transactions and events. Later sections explain the remaining steps.

Transactions and Events

Business activities can be described in terms of transactions and events. **External transactions** are exchanges of economic consideration between two separate entities. External transactions yield changes in the accounting equation. **Internal transactions** are exchanges within an entity; they can also affect the accounting equation. One example is a company using supplies in its operating activities. As supplies are used, their costs are reported as expenses.

Events are happenings that both affect an entity's financial position and can be reliably measured. These include financial events such as changes in the market value of certain assets and liabilities and natural events such as floods and fires that destroy assets and create losses.

Source Documents

C2 Describe source documents and their purpose.

Companies use various documents when doing business. **Source documents,** or *business papers,* identify and describe transactions and events entering the accounting process. They are the sources of accounting information and can be in either hard copy or electronic form.

Examples are sales tickets, checks, purchase orders, charges to customers, bills from suppliers, employee earnings records, and bank statements.

For example, when we buy an item on credit, the store usually prepares at least two copies of a sales invoice. One copy is given to us. Another gives rise to an entry in the store's information system to record a sale. This copy is often sent electronically. Also, for both cash and credit sales, the item is usually entered into a register that records the amount of each sale. Many registers record this information for each sale on a tape or electronic file locked inside the register. Total sales for a day, or for any time period, can be obtained immediately from these registers. This record can be used as a source document for recording sales in the accounting records. These accounting procedures are also part of an information system designed to ensure that accounting records include all transactions. They also help prevent mistakes and theft. To encourage employees to follow procedures such as these, stores often give discounts or free goods if a customer is not provided a receipt. This is part of good internal control. Both buyers and sellers use sales invoices as source documents. Sellers use them for recording sales and for control. Buyers use them for recording purchases and for monitoring purchasing activity. In both cases, a copy of the invoice is a source document.

Point: To ensure that all sales are rung up on the register, it helps to require customers to have their receipts to exchange or return purchased items.

You Make the Call—Ethics

Cashier   When you were hired as a cashier, the manager explained the policy of immediately entering each sale. Recently, lunch hour traffic has increased and the assistant manager asks you to avoid delays by taking customers' cash and making change without entering sales. The assistant manager says she will add up cash and enter sales after lunch. She says that in this way, the register will always match the cash amount when the manager arrives at three o'clock. What do you do?

Answer—p. 106

Source documents, especially if obtained from outside the organization, provide objective and reliable evidence about transactions and events and their amounts. Many accounting systems still require manual (pencil and paper) recording and processing of transaction data. These are mostly limited to small businesses. In today's information age, computers assist us in recording and processing data, yet they are only part of the process, and modern technology still demands human insight and understanding of transactions. In our discussion of the steps making up the accounting process, we often refer to a *manual system* for simplicity in presentation, but the fundamental concepts of the manual system are identical to those of a computerized information system.

Quick Check

1. Describe external and internal transactions.
2. Identify examples of accounting source documents.
3. Explain the importance of source documents.

Answers—p. 106

Accounts and Double-Entry Accounting

This section explains what an *account* is and its importance to accounting and business. We also describe several crucial elements and tools that support an accounting system. These include ledgers, T-accounts, debits and credits, and double-entry accounting.

The Account

An **account** is a detailed record of increases and decreases in a specific asset, liability, equity, revenue, or expense. Information is taken from an account, then analyzed, summarized, and presented in reports and financial statements. A separate account is kept for each asset, liability, equity, revenue, and expense item important to business decisions. Changes in owner withdrawals and contributions are also kept in separate accounts.

A **ledger** is a record containing all accounts used by a company. This is often in electronic form and is what we mean when we refer to the *books*. While most companies' ledgers contain similar accounts, several accounts are often unique to a company because of its type

C3   Describe an account and its use in recording information about transactions.

of operations. Accounts are arranged into three general categories (based on the accounting equation) as shown in Exhibit 3.2.

| Asset Accounts | = | Liability Accounts | + | Equity Accounts |

The remainder of this section describes accounts common to most organizations.

Asset Accounts

Assets are resources owned or controlled by a company that have expected future benefits. Most accounting systems include separate accounts for the assets described here.

Cash

A *Cash* account reflects the cash balance, and increases and decreases in cash are recorded in it. A Cash account includes money and any medium of exchange that a bank accepts for deposit (coins, currency, checks, money orders, and checking account balances).

Accounts Receivable

Products and services are often sold to customers in return for promises to pay in the future. These transactions are often called *credit sales* or *sales on account*. Promises of payment from buyers are called *accounts receivable* to sellers. Accounts receivable are increased by credit sales and are decreased by customer payments. A company needs to know the amount currently due from each customer to send bills. A separate record for each customer's purchases and payments is necessary for this purpose. We describe the system for maintaining these records in Chapters 6 and 10. For now, we use the simpler practice of recording all increases and decreases in receivables in a single account called *Accounts Receivable*. The importance of accounts receivable to a company, like many other accounts, depends on its type of business. For example, **Florida Panthers**' accounts receivable amount to less than 3% of its assets. In comparison, **Nike**'s accounts receivable amount to more than 30% of its assets.

Note Receivable

A **note receivable,** or **promissory note,** is a written promise to pay a definite sum of money on a specified future date(s). A company holding a promissory note signed by another party has an asset that is recorded in a Note (or Notes) Receivable account.

Prepaid Expenses

Prepaid expenses are assets because they represent prepayments of future expenses (*not* current expenses). In the future, when the expenses are incurred, the amounts in prepaid expenses are transferred to expense accounts. Common examples of prepaid expenses include prepaid insurance, prepaid rent, and prepaid services (such as club memberships). Prepaid expenses expire with the passage of time (such as with rent) or through use (such as with prepaid meal tickets). When financial statements are prepared, prepaid expenses are adjusted so that (1) all expired and used prepaid expenses are recorded as regular expenses and (2) all unexpired and unused prepaid expenses are recorded as assets (reflecting future use in future periods). An exception exists for prepaid expenses that will expire or be used before the end of the current accounting period when financial statements will be prepared. In this case, the prepayments *can* be recorded immediately as expenses.

For example, if FastForward pays $1,000 for December rent at the beginning of the month, it can record this prepaid rent as rent expense since its benefit will be fully expired when the statements are prepared on December 31. As another example consider prepaid insurance, one of the most common prepaid expenses. Insurance contracts provide us protection against losses caused by fire, theft, accidents, and other events. An insurance policy often requires the fee, called a *premium,* to be paid in advance. Protection can be purchased for almost any time period, including a month, year, or several years. When an insurance premium is paid in advance, the cost is typically recorded in an asset account called *Prepaid Insurance.* Over time, the expiring portion of the insurance cost is removed from this asset account and reported in expenses on the income statement. Any unexpired portion remains in Prepaid Insurance and is reported on the balance sheet as an asset.

Point: Prepaid expenses that apply to current *and* future periods are assets. These assets are adjusted at the end of each period to reflect only those amounts that have not yet expired, and to record as expenses those amounts that have expired.

Office Supplies

All companies use office supplies such as stationery, computer paper and toner, and pens. These supplies are assets until they are used. When they are used up, their costs are then reported as expenses. The costs of unused supplies are recorded in an *Office Supplies* asset account.

Store Supplies

Many stores keep supplies for circumstances such as wrapping and packaging purchases for customers. These include plastic and paper bags, gift boxes, cartons, and ribbons. The costs of these unused supplies are recorded in a *Store Supplies* asset account. When supplies are used, their costs are transferred from the supplies asset account to the supplies expense account.

Equipment

Most organizations own computers, printers, desks, chairs, and other office equipment. Costs incurred to buy this equipment are recorded in an *Office Equipment* asset account. The costs of assets used in a store such as counters, showcases, forklifts, hoists, and cash registers are recorded in a *Store Equipment* asset account.

Point: Some assets are described as *intangible* because they do not have physical existence or their benefits are highly uncertain. A recent balance sheet for Coca-Cola Company shows $1.96 billion in intangible assets.

Buildings

Buildings owned by an organization can provide space for a store, an office, a warehouse, and a factory. Buildings are assets because they provide expected future benefits. Their costs are recorded in a *Buildings* asset account. When several buildings are owned, separate accounts are sometimes kept for each of them.

Land

A *Land* account records the cost of land owned by a business. The cost of land is separated from the cost of buildings located on the land to provide more useful information in financial statements.

Did You Know?				e
Wish List Entrepreneurs were asked whom they would want—if they could have anyone—to help run their businesses for a week. Bill Gates led with 24%, followed by Donald Trump and Warren Buffet—see selected survey results.		Bill Gates	24%	
		Donald Trump	6.8	
		Warren Buffet	5.8	
		Lee Iacocca	5.2	
		Ross Perot	3.1	
		Hillary Clinton	1.4	

Liability Accounts

Liabilities are obligations to transfer assets or provide products or services to other entities. An organization often has several different liabilities, each represented by a separate account. The more common liability accounts are described here.

Accounts Payable

Purchases of merchandise, supplies, equipment, or services made by an oral or implied promise to pay later create liabilities called *Payables.* Accounting systems keep separate records about purchases from and payments to each creditor. We describe these individual records in Chapter 6. For now, we use the simpler practice of recording all increases and decreases in such payables in a single account called *Accounts Payable.*

Point: Accounts Payable are also called Trade Payables.

Note Payable

When an organization formally recognizes a promise to pay a future amount by signing a **promissory note,** the resulting liability is a **Note Payable.** It is recorded in either a Short-Term

Note Payable account or a Long-Term Note Payable account depending on when it must be repaid. We explain details of short- and long-term classification in Chapter 5.

Unearned Revenue

Chapter 2 explained that the *revenue recognition principle* requires that revenues be reported on the income statement when earned. This principle means that when customers pay in advance for products or services (before revenue is earned), the seller considers this pay as unearned revenues. **Unearned Revenue** is a liability account that is settled in the future when products or services are delivered. Examples of unearned revenue include magazine subscriptions collected in advance by a publisher, sales of gift certificates by stores, and season ticket sales by sports teams. The seller would record these in liability accounts such as Unearned Subscriptions, Unearned Store Sales, and Unearned Ticket Revenue. When products and services are delivered, the earned portion of the unearned revenues is transferred to revenue accounts such as Subscription Fees, Store Sales, and Ticket Sales.[1]

> **Did You Know?**
>
> **MLB Accounting** The **Cleveland Indians** report *Unearned Revenues* of nearly $50 million that consist of advance ticket sales. When the Indians play their regular season home games, they settle this liability to their customers (fans) and transfer the amount to *Ticket Revenues*.

Accrued Liabilities

Common accrued liabilities include wages payable, taxes payable, and interest payable. Each represents amounts owed that are not yet paid. These are often recorded in separate liability account by the same title. If they are not large in amount, one or more of them may be added and reported as a single amount on the balance sheet. For example, the liabilities section of **Harley-Davidson**'s balance sheet reports accrued liabilities of more than $160 million.

Point: Many companies offer warranties on their products and must report a liability by estimating future warranty costs.

Equity Accounts

Chapter 2, described the four types of transactions that affect owner's equity. They are (1) investments by the owner, (2) withdrawals by the owner, (3) revenues, and (4) expenses. We entered all equity transactions in a single column under the owner's name in Chapter 2. When we later prepared the income statement and the statement of changes in owner's equity, we reviewed the items in that column to properly classify them in financial statements. To better track these items, four separate account categories are used: Owner's Capital, Owner's Withdrawals, Revenues, and Expenses. We show this visually in Exhibit 3.3 by expanding the accounting equation.

Exhibit 3.3

Expanded Accounting Equation

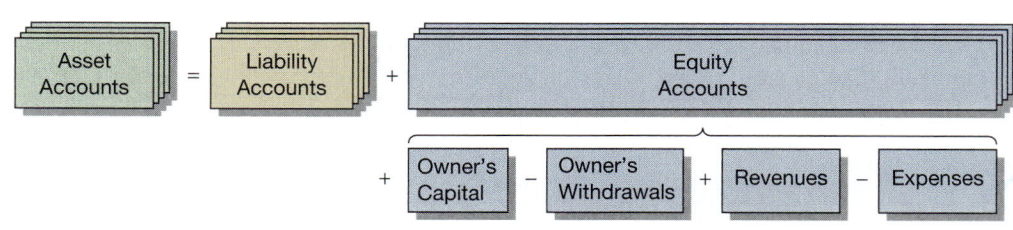

---

[1] In practice, account titles vary. As one example, Subscription Fees is sometimes called Subscription Fees Revenue, Subscription Fees Earned, or Earned Subscription Fees. As another example, Rent Earned is sometimes called Rent Revenue, Rental Revenue, or Earned Rent Revenue. We must use our good judgment when reading financial statements, since titles can differ even within the same industry. For example, product sales are called *revenues* at **Nike** and **K. Swiss**, but *net sales* at **Reebok** and **Converse**. The term *revenues* or *fees* is more commonly used with service businesses, and *net sales* or *sales* with product businesses.

Information in these separate categories is then readily used to prepare financial statements. We describe these four types of accounts in this section.

Owner's Capital

When a person invests in a proprietorship or partnership, the invested amount is recorded in an account identified by the owner's name and the title Capital. An account called *Chuck Taylor, Capital,* is used to record Taylor's investment in FastForward. Any further investments by the owner also are recorded in this capital account.

Owner's Withdrawals

Equity increases when a company earns income. The owner can leave this equity intact or can withdraw assets from the business. When the owner withdraws assets, perhaps to cover personal expenses, the withdrawal decreases both the company's assets and its equity. Owners of proprietorships commonly withdraw weekly or monthly amounts of cash. Owners of proprietorships cannot receive salaries because they are not legally separate from their companies and cannot enter into salary (or any other) contracts with themselves. Withdrawals are neither income to the owners nor expenses of the business. They are simply the opposite of investments by owners. Most accounting systems use an account with the name of the owner and the word *withdrawals* in recording withdrawals by the owner. An account called *Chuck Taylor, Withdrawals,* is used to record Taylor's withdrawals from FastForward.

Point: The Owner's Withdrawals account (also called *Drawing* or *Personal* account) is sometimes referred to as a contra equity account because it reduces the normal balance of equity.

Point: Withdrawals in a partnership are treated similarly to those of a proprietorship.

Revenues and Expenses

Decision makers often want information about revenues earned and expenses incurred for a period. Various revenue and expense accounts are used to report this information. Different companies have different kinds of revenue and expense accounts reflecting their own unique activities. Examples of revenue accounts are Sales, Commissions Earned, Professional Fees Earned, Rent Earned, and Interest Earned. Examples of expense accounts are Advertising Expense, Store Supplies Expense, Office Salaries Expense, Office Supplies Expense, Rent Expense, Utilities Expense, and Insurance Expense. We can get an idea of the variety of revenues and expenses by looking at the *chart of accounts* which follows the index at the back of this book. It lists accounts needed to solve some of the assignments in the book.[2]

Did You Know?

NBA Accounting   The **Boston Celtics** report the following major revenue and expense accounts:

Revenues	Expenses
Basketball ticket sales	Team salaries
TV and radio broadcast fees	Game costs
Advertising revenues	NBA franchise costs

Ledger and Chart of Accounts

The actual recording of accounts can differ depending on the system. Computerized systems store accounts in files on electronic storage devices. Manual systems often record accounts on separate pages in a file. The collection of all accounts for an information system is called a *ledger*. If accounts are in files on a

---

Did You Know?

Ledger Bytes   What does technology mean for accounting information processing? Using computing technology, **Sears** shrank its annual financial plan from 100 square-foot flow charts with more than 300 steps to 25 steps on *one* $8^{1}/_{2}$-by-11-inch sheet of paper! Technology also allows Sears' execs to analyze budgets and financial plans on their PCs. Sears says it slashed $100 million in recordkeeping costs.

---

[2] Different companies sometimes use different account titles than those in this book's chart of accounts. For example, a company might use Interest Revenue instead of Interest Earned, or Rental Expense instead of Rent Expense. It is important only that an account title describe the item it represents.

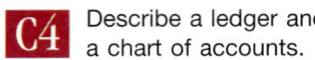

Describe a ledger and a chart of accounts.

hard drive, the sum of those files is the ledger. If the accounts are pages in a file, that file is the ledger.

A company's size and diversity of operations affect the number of accounts needed in its accounting system. A small company may get by with as few as 20 or 30 accounts; a large company may need several thousand. The **chart of accounts** is a list of all accounts a company uses. The chart includes an identification number assigned to each account. A small business might use the following numbering system for its accounts:

101–199	Asset accounts
201–299	Liability accounts
301–399	Equity accounts
401–499	Revenue accounts
501–699	Expense accounts

These numbers provide a three-digit code that is useful in recordkeeping. In this case, the first digit assigned to asset accounts is a 1, the first digit assigned to liability accounts is a 2, and so on. The second and third digits also relate to the accounts' subcategories. A partial chart of accounts is shown in Exhibit 3.4 for FastForward.

Exhibit 3.4

Partial Chart of Accounts

Account Number	Account Name	Account Number	Account Name
101	Cash	301	C. Taylor, Capital
106	Accounts receivable	302	C. Taylor, Withdrawals
126	Supplies	403	Consulting revenue
128	Prepaid insurance	406	Rental revenue
167	Equipment	622	Salaries expense
201	Accounts payable	637	Insurance expense
236	Unearned consulting revenue	640	Rent expense
		652	Supplies expense
		690	Utilities expense

Debits and Credits

Define *debits* and *credits* and explain their role in double-entry accounting.

Point: Think of *debit* and *credit* as accounting directions for left and right.

The left side of an account is called the **debit** side, often abbreviated *Dr*. The right side is called the **credit** side, abbreviated *Cr*.[3] To enter amounts on the left side of an account is to *debit* the account. To enter amounts on the right side is to *credit* the account. We must guard against the error of thinking that the terms *debit* and *credit* mean increase or decrease. Whether a debit is an increase or decrease depends on the account. Similarly, whether a credit is an increase or decrease depends on the account. In each account, however, a debit and a credit have opposite effects. In an account where a debit is an increase, the credit is a decrease; in an account where a debit is a decrease, the credit is an increase. Identifying the account is the key to understanding the effects of debits and credits. The difference between total debits and total credits for an account is the **account balance.** When the sum of debits exceeds the sum of credits, the account has a *debit balance*. It has a *credit balance* when the sum of credits exceeds the sum of debits. When the sum of debits equals the sum of credits, the account has a *zero balance*.

A **T-account** is a helpful tool in analyzing the effects of transactions and events on individual accounts. Its name comes from its shape like the letter **T.** The T-account is shown in Exhibit 3.5.

---

[3] These abbreviations are remnants of 18th-century English recordkeeping practices where the terms *debitor* and *creditor* were used instead of *debit* and *credit*. The abbreviations use the first and last letters of these terms, just as we still do for Saint (St.) and Doctor (Dr.).

The format of a T-account is (1) the account title on top, (2) a left, or debit side, and (3) a right, or credit, side. One side is for recording increases in the account and the other side is for decreases. Whether increases are recorded on the right or the left side depends on the type of account.

Account Title	
(Left side) **Debit**	(Right side) **Credit**

Exhibit 3.5
The T-Account

Point: Debits and credits do not mean favorable or unfavorable. A debit to an asset increases it, as does a debit to an expense. A credit to a liability increases it, as does a credit to a revenue.

To determine the account's balance, we start with the beginning balance and then (1) compute the total increases shown on one side, (2) compute the total decreases shown on the other side, and (3) subtract the sum of the decreases from the sum of the increases. The T-account for FastForward's Cash account, reflecting the transactions from Chapter 2 (Exhibit 2.13), is shown in Exhibit 3.6. The total increases in its Cash account are $36,100, the total decreases are $31,700, and the account balance is $4,400.

Cash			
Investment by owner	30,000	Purchase of supplies	2,500
Consulting services revenue earned	4,200	Purchase of equipment	26,000
Collection of account receivable	1,900	Payment of rent	1,000
		Payment of salary	700
		Payment of note payable	900
		Withdrawal by owner	600
Total increases	**36,100**	Total decreases	**31,700**
Less decreases	−31,700		
Balance	**4,400**		

Exhibit 3.6
Computing the Balance for a T-Account

Point: The ending balance is on the side with the largest dollar amount.

Quick Check

4. Identify each of the following accounts as either an asset, liability, or equity: (a) Prepaid Rent, (b) Unearned Fees, (c) Building, (d) Wages Payable, and (e) Office Supplies.
5. What is an account? What is a ledger?
6. What determines the number and types of accounts a company uses?
7. Does *debit* always mean increase and *credit* always mean decrease?

Answers—p. 106

Double-Entry Accounting

Double-entry accounting requires that each transaction affect, and be recorded in, at least two accounts. It also means the *total amount debited must equal the total amount credited* for each transaction. Accordingly, the sum of the debits for all entries must equal the sum of the credits for all entries, and the sum of debit account balances in the ledger must equal the sum of credit account balances.

The system for recording debits and credits follows from the usual accounting equation—see Exhibit 3.7. Assets are on the left side of this equation. Liabilities and equity are on the right side. Two points are important here. First, like any simple mathematical relation, net increases or decreases on one side have equal net effects on the other side. For example, a net increase in assets must be accompanied by an identical net increase in the liabilities and equity side. Also recall that some transactions affect only one side of the equation, meaning that two or more accounts on one side are affected, but their net effect on this one side is zero. Second, we treat the left side as the *normal balance* side for assets, and the right side as the *normal balance* for liabilities and equity. This matches their layout in the accounting equation.

"Total debits equal total credits for each entry."

Point: Luca Pacioli is considered a pioneer in accounting and the first to devise double-entry accounting.

Exhibit 3.7

Debits and Credits in the
Accounting Equation

Three important rules for recording transactions in a double-entry accounting system follow from Exhibit 3.7:

1. Increases in assets are debits to asset accounts. Decreases in assets are credits to asset accounts.
2. Increases in liabilities are credits to liability accounts. Decreases in liabilities are debits to liability accounts.
3. Increases in equity are credits to equity accounts. Decreases in equity are debits to equity accounts.

We showed in Chapter 2 how equity increases from owner's investments and revenues and how it decreases from expenses and withdrawals. These important equity relations are conveyed by expanding the accounting equation to include debits and credits in double-entry form as shown in Exhibit 3.8.

Exhibit 3.8

Debit and Credit Effects for
Component Accounts

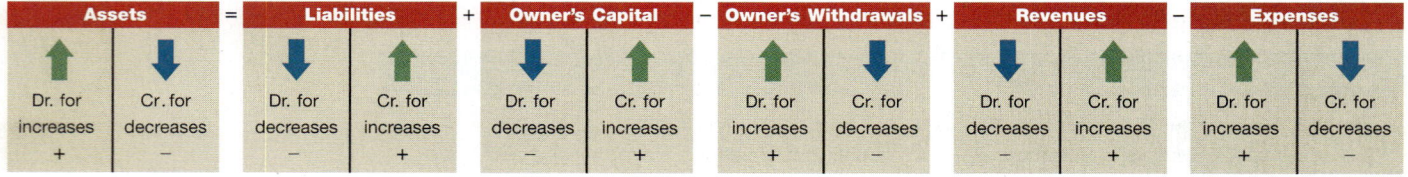

Point: Consider mnemonic aids: *DAWE*–<u>D</u>ebit <u>A</u>ssets, <u>W</u>ithdrawals, <u>E</u>xpenses. *CRIL*–<u>C</u>redit <u>R</u>evenues, <u>I</u>nvestments, <u>L</u>iabilities.

Increases (credits) to capital or revenues *increase* owner's equity; increases (debits) to withdrawals or expenses *decrease* owner's equity. These relations are reflected in the following important rules:

1. Investments are credited to owner's capital because they increase equity.
2. Withdrawals are debited to owner's withdrawals because they decrease equity.
3. Revenues are credited to revenue accounts because they increase equity.
4. Expenses are debited to expense accounts because they decrease equity.

You Make the Call

Marketing Manager   You are a marketing manager and you want to know your company's revenues for this period. Financial statements are not yet available. Where do you search for this information? Would source documents or the ledger be more useful?

Answer—p. 106

Our understanding of these diagrams and rules is especially helpful in analyzing and recording transactions. It also helps us prepare, analyze, and interpret financial statements.

Processing Transactions

P1   Record transactions in a journal and post entries to a ledger.

Processing transactions is a crucial part of accounting. The four main steps of this process are depicted in Exhibit 3.9. Steps 1 and 2—involving transaction analysis and double-entry accounting—were introduced in the prior section. This section extends that discussion and focuses on steps 3 and 4 of the accounting process. Step 3 is to record each transaction in a journal. A **journal** gives us a complete record of each transaction in one place. It also shows debits and credits for each transaction. The process of recording transactions in a journal is called **journalizing.** Step 4 is to transfer (or **post**) entries from the journal to the ledger. The process of transferring journal entry information to the ledger is called **posting.** This section describes both journalizing and posting transactions.

Journalizing Transactions

The process of journalizing transactions requires an understanding of a journal. While companies can use various journals, every company uses a **general journal,** which shows the debits and credits of each transaction. It can be used to record any transaction. A general journal entry includes the following information about each transaction: (1) date of transaction, (2) titles of affected accounts, (3) dollar amount of each debit and credit, and (4) explanation of the transaction. Exhibit 3.10 shows how the first two transactions of FastForward are recorded in a general journal. This process is similar for manual and computerized systems. Computerized journals are often designed to look like a manual journal page as in Exhibit 3.10. Computerized systems typically include error-checking routines that ensure debits equal credits for each entry. Shortcuts often allow recordkeepers to enter account numbers instead of names and to enter account names and numbers with pull-down menus.

Recording entries in a general journal follow standard procedures. It is helpful to refer to the entries in Exhibit 3.10 when reviewing these steps.

1. Date the transaction: Enter the year at the top of the first column and the month on the first line of the journal entry. Enter the day of the transaction in the second column on the first line of each entry.
2. Enter titles of accounts debited. Account titles are taken from the chart of accounts and are aligned with the left margin of the Account Titles and Explanation column. Enter debit amounts in the Debit column on the same line as the accounts debited.
3. Enter titles of accounts credited. Account titles are taken from the chart of accounts and are indented from the left margin of the Account Titles and Explanation column to distinguish them from debited accounts. Enter credit amounts in the Credit column on the same line as the accounts credited.
4. Enter a brief explanation of the transaction on the line below the entry (it often references a source document). This explanation is indented about half as far as the credited account titles to avoid confusing it with accounts. We italicize explanations.
5. Skip a line between each journal entry for clarity.

The **posting reference (PR) column** is left blank when a transaction is initially recorded. Individual account numbers are later entered into the PR column when entries are posted to the ledger.

Balance Column Account

T-accounts are simple and direct means to show how the accounting process works. Accounting systems in practice need more structure and use **balance column accounts** as in Exhibit 3.11.

Exhibit 3.9

Steps in Processing Transactions

Step 1: Analyze transactions and source documents.

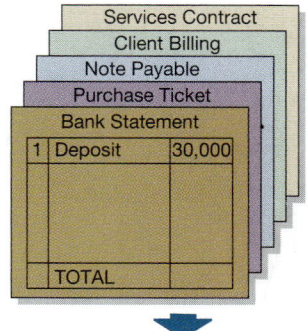

Step 2: Apply double-entry accounting.

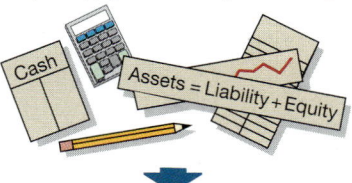

Step 3: Record journal entry.

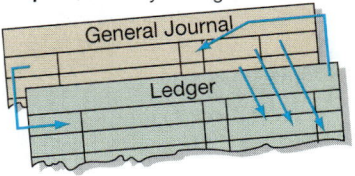

Step 4: Post entry to ledger.

Exhibit 3.10

Partial General Journal for FastForward

Concept 3-2

General Journal					Page 1
Date		Account Titles and Explanation	PR	Debit	Credit
2001 Dec.	1	Cash		30,000	
		C. Taylor, Capital			30,000
		Investment by owner.			
	2	Supplies		2,500	
		Cash			2,500
		Purchased store supplies for cash.			

Exhibit 3.11

Cash Account in Balance
Column Format

Cash					Account No. 101	
Date		**Explanation**	**PR**	**Debit**	**Credit**	**Balance**
2001 Dec	1		G1	30,000		30,000
	2		G1		2,500	27,500
	3		G1		26,000	1,500
	10		G1	4,200		5,700

The balance column account format is similar to a T-account in having columns for debits and credits. It is different by including transaction date and explanation columns. It also has a column with the balance of the account after each entry is recorded. For example, FastForward's Cash account in Exhibit 3.11 is debited on December 1 for the $30,000 investment by Taylor, yielding a $30,000 debit balance. The account is credited on December 2 for $2,500, yielding a $27,500 debit balance. On December 3, it is credited again, this time for $26,000, and its debit balance is reduced to $1,500. The Cash account is debited for $4,200 on December 10, and its debit balance increases to $5,700.

Point: A journal is often referred to as the *book of original entry.*

When a balance column account is used, the heading of the Balance column does not show whether it is a debit or credit balance. An account is assumed to have a *normal balance.* The normal balance of each account (asset, liability, equity, revenue, or expense) refers to the left or right (debit or credit) side where *increases* are recorded. Exhibit 3.12 shows normal balances for accounts.

Exhibit 3.12

Normal Balances for Accounts

Assets		=	**Liabilities**		+	**Owner's Capital**		−	**Owner's Withdrawals**		+	**Revenues**		−	**Expenses**	
Dr. for increases	Cr. for decreases		Dr. for decreases	Cr. for increases		Dr. for decreases	Cr. for increases		Dr. for increases	Cr. for decreases		Dr. for decreases	Cr. for increases		Dr. for increases	Cr. for decreases
+	−		−	+		−	+		+	−		−	+		+	−
Normal				**Normal**			**Normal**		**Normal**				**Normal**		**Normal**	

Point: The ledger is referred to as the *book of final entry* because financial statements are prepared from it.

Unusual events can sometimes temporarily give an account an abnormal balance. An *abnormal balance* refers to a balance on the side where decreases are recorded. For example, a customer might mistakenly overpay a bill. This gives that customer's account receivable an abnormal (credit) balance. An abnormal balance is often identified by circling it or by entering it in red or some other unusual color. Computerized systems often provide a code beside a balance such as *dr.* or *cr.* to identify its balance. A zero balance for an account is usually shown by writing zeros or a dash in the Balance column. This practice avoids confusion between a zero balance and one omitted in error.

Posting Journal Entries

Step 4 of processing transactions is to post journal entries to ledger accounts (see Exhibit 3.9). To ensure that the ledger is up to date, entries are posted as soon as possible. This might be daily, weekly, or when time permits. All entries

Did You Know?

New Accountant What are duties of accounting professionals? A recent article indicates they include long-term planning, revenue strategy, using technology, and interpreting information. This suggests accounting professionals require more analytical and conceptual skills than in the past.

must be posted to the ledger by the end of a reporting period. This is necessary so account balances are current when financial statements are prepared. When entries are posted to the ledger, the debits in journal entries are copied into ledger accounts as debits, and credits are copied into ledger accounts as credits. The usual process is to post debits first and then credits. Exhibit 3.13 shows the four steps to post a journal entry. First, identify the ledger account that is debited in the entry. In the ledger, enter the date of the entry, the journal and page in the PR column[4], the debit amount from the journal, and the new balance of the ledger account. Second, enter the ledger account number in the PR column of the journal next to the entry. Next, repeat these two steps for credit entries and amounts.

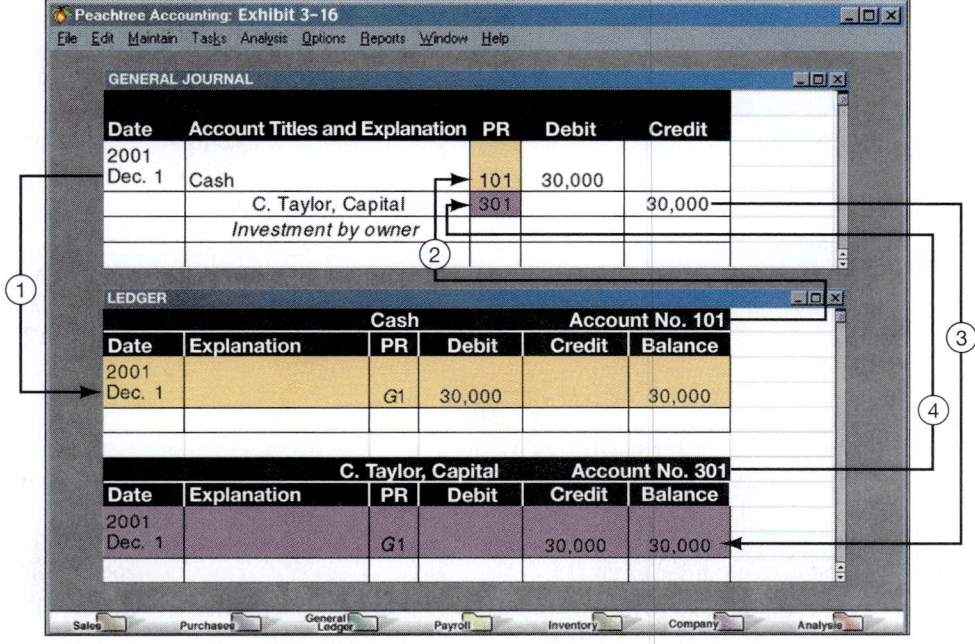

Exhibit 3.13

Posting an Entry to the Ledger

Key:
1. Identify debit account in Ledger: enter date, journal page, amount, and balance.
2. Enter the debit account number from the Ledger in the PR column of the journal.
3. Identify credit account in Ledger: enter date, journal page, amount, and balance.
4. Enter the credit account number from the Ledger in the PR column of the journal.

The posting process creates a link between the ledger and the journal entry. This link is a useful cross-reference for tracing an amount from one record to another. It also shows the stage of completion in the posting process. This permits you to easily start and stop the posting process. Computerized systems require no added effort to post journal entries to the ledger. These systems automatically transfer debit and credit entries from the journal to the ledger. Many systems have programs testing the reasonableness of a journal entry and the account balance when recorded. For example, the payroll program might alert a preparer to hourly wage rates exceeding $500.

Point: Explanations are typically only included in ledger accounts for unusual transactions or events.

---

[4] The letter *G* shows it came from the General Journal. Other journals are identified by their own letters. We discuss other journals in Chapter 8.

Analyzing Transactions

A1 Analyze the impact of transactions on accounts and financial statements.

Concept 3-1

We return to the activities of **FastForward** to show how double-entry accounting is useful in analyzing and processing transactions. We analyze each of FastForward's transactions in four stages. First, we review the transaction and any source documents. Second, we analyze the transaction using the accounting equation. Third, we use double-entry accounting to record the transaction, in both the required journal entry form and the optional T-account form (the T-accounts can be viewed as simple ledger accounts). Fourth, we show how each transaction affects (links to) the financial statements. Exhibit 3.15 (on page 99) eventually summarizes these links.

We should study each transaction thoroughly before proceeding to the next transaction. The first 11 transactions are familiar to us from Chapter 2. We expand our analysis of these transactions and consider five other FastForward December transactions (numbered 12 through 16) that were omitted from Chapter 2.

1. Investment by Owner

Cash	101
(1) 30,000	

C.Taylor, Capital	301
	(1) 30,000

Transaction: Chuck Taylor invests $30,000 cash in FastForward on December 1.

Analysis:

Assets	=	Liabilities	+	Equity
+30,000	=	0	+	30,000

Double entry:

(1)	Cash	101	30,000	
	C.Taylor, Capital	301		30,000

Statements affected:[5] BS, SCF, and SCOE

2. Purchase Supplies for Cash

Supplies	126
(2) 2,500	

Cash	101
(1) 30,000	(2) 2,500

Transaction: FastForward pays $2,500 cash for supplies.

Analysis:

Assets	=	Liabilities	+	Equity
+2,500 $\Big\}$ −2,500	=	0	+	0

Changes the composition of assets but not their total.

Double entry:

(2)	Supplies	126	2,500	
	Cash	101		2,500

Statements affected: BS and SCF

3. Purchase Equipment for Cash

Equipment	167
(3) 26,000	

Cash	101
(1) 30,000	(2) 2,500
	(3) 26,000

Transaction: FastForward pays $26,000 cash for equipment.

Analysis:

Assets	=	Liabilities	+	Equity
+26,000 $\Big\}$ −26,000	=	0	+	0

Changes the composition of assets but not their total.

Double entry:

(3)	Equipment	167	26,000	
	Cash	101		26,000

Statements affected: BS and SCF

4. Purchase Supplies on Credit

Supplies	126
(2) 2,500	
(4) 7,100	

Accounts Payable	201
	(4) 7,100

Transaction: FastForward purchases $7,100 of supplies on credit.

Analysis:

Assets	=	Liabilities	+	Equity
+7,100	=	+7,100	+	0

Double entry:

(4)	Supplies	126	7,100	
	Accounts Payable	201		7,100

Statements affected: BS

---

[5] We use abbreviations for the statements: income statement (IS), balance sheet (BS), statement of cash flows (SCF), and statement of changes in owner's equity (SCOE).

5. Provide Services for Cash

Cash			101
(1)	30,000	(2)	2,500
(5)	4,200	(3)	26,000

Consulting Revenue			403
		(5)	4,200

Transaction: FastForward provides consulting services and immediately collects $4,200 cash.

Analysis:

Assets	=	Liabilities	+	Equity
+4,200	=	0	+	4,200

Double entry:

(5)	Cash	101	4,200	
	Consulting Revenue	403		4,200

Statements affected: BS, IS, SCF, and SCOE

6. Payment of Expense in Cash

Rent Expense			640
(6)	1,000		

Cash			101
(1)	30,000	(2)	2,500
(5)	4,200	(3)	26,000
		(6)	1,000

Transaction: FastForward pays $1,000 cash for December rent.

Analysis:

Assets	=	Liabilities	+	Equity
−1,000	=	0	+	−1,000

Double entry:

(6)	Rent Expense	640	1,000	
	Cash	101		1,000

Statements affected: BS, IS, SCF, and SCOE

7. Payment of Expense in Cash

Salaries Expense			622
(7)	700		

Cash			101
(1)	30,000	(2)	2,500
(5)	4,200	(3)	26,000
		(6)	1,000
		(7)	700

Transaction: FastForward pays $700 cash in employee wages.

Analysis:

Assets	=	Liabilities	+	Equity
−700	=	0	+	−700

Double entry:

(7)	Salaries Expense	622	700	
	Cash	101		700

Statements affected: BS, IS, SCF, and SCOE

Point: *Salary* usually refers to compensation for an employee who receives a fixed amount for a given time period, whereas *wages* usually refers to compensation based on time worked.

8. Provide Consulting and Rental Services on Credit

Accounts Receivable			106
(8)	1,900		

Consulting Revenue			403
		(5)	4,200
		(8)	1,600

Rental Revenue			406
		(8)	300

Transaction: FastForward provides consulting services of $1,600 and rents its test facilities for $300. The customer is billed $1,900 for these services.

Analysis:

Assets	=	Liabilities	+	Equity
+1,900	=	0	+	+1,600
				+ 300

Double entry:

(8)	Accounts Receivable	106	1,900	
	Consulting Revenue	403		1,600
	Rental Revenue	406		300

Statements affected: BS, IS, and SCOE

Point: Transaction 8 is a **compound journal entry.** A compound journal entry affects three or more accounts.

9. Receipt of Cash on Account

Cash			101
(1)	30,000	(2)	2,500
(5)	4,200	(3)	26,000
(9)	1,900	(6)	1,000
		(7)	700

Accounts Receivable			106
(8)	1,900	(9)	1,900

Transaction: FastForward receives $1,900 cash from the client billed in transaction 8.

Analysis:

Assets	=	Liabilities	+	Equity
+1,900				
−1,900	=	0	+	0

Double entry:

(9)	Cash	101	1,900	
	Accounts Receivable	106		1,900

Statements affected: BS and SCF

Point: The *revenue recognition principle* requires revenue to be recognized when earned, which is when the company provides products or services to a customer. This is not necessarily the same time that the customer pays. A customer can pay before or after the product or service is provided.

10. Partial Payment of Accounts Payable

Accounts Payable 201			
(10)	900	(4)	7,100

Cash			101
(1)	30,000	(2)	2,500
(5)	4,200	(3)	26,000
(9)	1,900	(6)	1,000
		(7)	700
		(10)	900

Transaction: FastForward pays CalTech Supply $900 cash toward the payable of transaction 4.

Analysis: Assets   = Liabilities + Equity
             −900   =   −900   +   0

Double entry:

(10)	Accounts Payable	201	900	
	Cash	101		900

Statements affected: BS and SCF

11. Withdrawal of Cash by Owner

C.Taylor, Withdrawals			302
(11)	600		

Cash			101
(1)	30,000	(2)	2,500
(5)	4,200	(3)	26,000
(9)	1,900	(6)	1,000
		(7)	700
		(10)	900
		(11)	600

Transaction: Chuck Taylor withdraws $600 cash from FastForward for personal expenses.

Analysis: Assets   = Liabilities + Equity
             −600   =   0   +   −600

Double entry:

(11)	C.Taylor, Withdrawals	302	600	
	Cash	101		600

Statements affected: BS, SCF, and SCOE

12. Receipt of Cash for Future Services

Cash			101
(1)	30,000	(2)	2,500
(5)	4,200	(3)	26,000
(9)	1,900	(6)	1,000
(12)	3,000	(7)	700
		(10)	900
		(11)	600

Unearned Consulting Revenue			236
		(12)	3,000

Transaction: FastForward receives $3,000 cash in advance of providing consulting services to a customer.

Analysis: Assets   = Liabilities + Equity
             +3,000   =   +3,000   +   0

Accepting $3,000 cash obligates FastForward to perform future services and is a liability. No revenue is earned until services are provided.

Double entry:

(12)	Cash	101	3,000	
	Unearned Consulting Revenue	236		3,000

Statements affected: BS and SCF

13. Pay Cash for Future Insurance Coverage

Prepaid Insurance 128			
(13)	2,400		

Cash			101
(1)	30,000	(2)	2,500
(5)	4,200	(3)	26,000
(9)	1,900	(6)	1,000
(12)	3,000	(7)	700
		(10)	900
		(11)	600
		(13)	2,400

Transaction: FastForward pays $2,400 cash (premium) for a 2-year insurance policy. Coverage begins on December 1.

Analysis: Assets   = Liabilities + Equity
             +2,400}
             −2,400} =   0   +   0

Changes the composition of assets from cash to prepaid insurance. Expense is incurred as insurance coverage expires.

Double entry:

(13)	Prepaid Insurance	128	2,400	
	Cash	101		2,400

Statements affected: BS and SCF

14. Purchase Supplies for Cash

Supplies		126
(2)	2,500	
(4)	7,100	
(14)	**120**	

Cash		101
(1)	30,000	(2)	2,500
(5)	4,200	(3)	26,000
(9)	1,900	(6)	1,000
(12)	3,000	(7)	700
		(10)	900
		(11)	600
		(13)	2,400
		(14)	**120**

Transaction: FastForward pays $120 cash for supplies.

Analysis:

Assets	= Liabilities	+ Equity
+120		
−120	= 0	+ 0

Double entry:

(14)	Supplies	126	120	
	Cash	101		120

Statements affected: BS and SCF

15. Payment of Expense in Cash

Utilities Expense		690
(15)	**230**	

Cash		101
(1)	30,000	(2)	2,500
(5)	4,200	(3)	26,000
(9)	1,900	(6)	1,000
(12)	3,000	(7)	700
		(10)	900
		(11)	600
		(13)	2,400
		(14)	120
		(15)	**230**

Transaction: FastForward pays $230 cash for December utilities.

Analysis:

Assets	= Liabilities	+ Equity
−230	= 0	+ −230

Double entry:

(15)	Utilities Expense	690	230	
	Cash	101		230

Statements affected: BS, IS, SCF, and SCOE

16. Payment of Expense in Cash

Salaries Expense		622
(7)	700	
(16)	**700**	

Cash		101
(1)	30,000	(2)	2,500
(5)	4,200	(3)	26,000
(9)	1,900	(6)	1,000
(12)	3,000	(7)	700
		(10)	900
		(11)	600
		(13)	2,400
		(14)	120
		(15)	230
		(16)	**700**

Transaction: FastForward pays $700 cash in employee wages.

Analysis:

Assets	= Liabilities	+ Equity
−700	= 0	+ −700

Double entry:

(16)	Salaries Expense	622	700	
	Cash	101		700

Statements affected: BS, IS, SCE, and SCOE

Point: We could merge transactions 14–16 into one *compound entry*.

Point: Some small businesses use an outside recordkeeping service to make entries once each month.

Point: Technology does not provide the judgment required to analyze most business transactions. Analysis requires the expertise of skilled and ethical professionals.

Accounting Equation Analysis

Exhibit 3.14 shows the accounts of FastForward after all 16 transactions have been recorded and the balances computed. The accounts are grouped into three major columns corresponding to the accounting equation: assets, liabilities, and equity. Note several important points. First, as with each transaction, the totals for the three columns must obey the accounting equation. Specifically, assets equal \$42,070 (\$3,950 + \$0 + \$9,720 + \$2,400 + \$26,000); liabilities equal \$9,200 (\$6,200 + \$3,000); and equity equals \$32,870 (\$30,000 − \$600 + \$5,800 + \$300 − \$1,400 − \$1,000 − \$230). These numbers obey the accounting equation: \$42,070 = \$9,200 + \$32,870. Second, the capital, withdrawals, revenue, and expense accounts reflect the transactions that change equity. Their balances make up the statement of changes in owner's equity. Third, the revenue and expense account balances will be summarized and reported in the income statement. Fourth, components of the cash account make up the elements reported in the statement of cash flows.

Exhibit 3.14

Ledger for FastForward
(in T-account Form)

Assets			=	Liabilities			+	Equity		
Cash		**101**		**Accounts Payable**		**201**		**C. Taylor, Capital**		**301**
(1)	30,000	(2) 2,500		(10) 900	(4)	7,100			(1)	30,000
(5)	4,200	(3) 26,000			Balance	6,200				
(9)	1,900	(6) 1,000						**C. Taylor, Withdrawals**		**302**
(12)	3,000	(7) 700						(11) 600		
		(10) 900		**Unearned Consulting Revenue 236**						
		(11) 600			(12)	3,000		**Consulting Revenue**		**403**
		(13) 2,400							(5)	4,200
		(14) 120							(8)	1,600
		(15) 230							Balance	5,800
		(16) 700								
Balance	3,950							**Rental Revenue**		**406**
									(8)	300
Accounts Receivable		**106**								
(8)	1,900	(9) 1,900						**Salaries Expense**		**622**
Balance	0							(7) 700		
								(16) 700		
Supplies		**126**						Balance 1,400		
(2)	2,500									
(4)	7,100							**Rent Expense**		**640**
(14)	120							(6) 1,000		
Balance	9,720									
								Utilities Expense		**690**
Prepaid Insurance		**128**						(15) 230		
(13)	2,400									
								Accounts in this white area reflect those reported on the income statement.		
Equipment		**167**								
(3)	26,000									
$42,070			**=**	**$9,200**			**+**	**$32,870**		

Financial Statement Links

Exhibit 3.15 extends the analysis and summarizes how **FastForward**'s transactions impact all financial statements. Some transactions such as purchasing supplies on credit (No. 4) impact only one statement. Others such as receiving cash for services performed (No. 5) impact all of the statements. We should review this exhibit and understand how transactions link to financial statements. We return to explain the details of these links in Chapter 4, including the adjusting and closing processes.

Quick Check

8. What types of transactions increase equity? What types decrease equity?

9. Why are accounting systems called *double entry?*

10. For each transaction, double-entry accounting requires: (a) Debits to asset accounts must create credits to liability or equity accounts, (b) A debit to a liability account must create a credit to an asset account, or (c) Total debits must equal total credits.

11. An owner invests $15,000 cash and equipment having a market value of $23,000 in a proprietorship. Prepare the journal entry to record this owner's investment.

12. Explain what a compound journal entry is.

13. Why are posting reference numbers entered in the journal when entries are posted to ledger accounts?

Answers—p. 106

Trial Balance

Double-entry accounting requires the sum of debit account balances to equal the sum of credit account balances. A trial balance is used to verify this. A **trial balance** is a list of accounts and their balances at a point in time. Account balances are reported in the debit or credit column of a trial balance. Exhibit 3.16 shows the trial balance for FastForward after its 16 entries have been posted to the ledger.

P2 Prepare and explain the use of a trial balance.

Preparing a Trial Balance

Preparing a trial balance involves three steps:

1. List each account title and its amount (from the ledger) in the trial balance.[6]
2. Compute the total of debit balances and the total of credit balances.
3. Verify (*prove*) total debit balances equal total credit balances.

The total of debit balances equals the total of credit balances for the trial balance in Exhibit 3.16. If these two totals were not equal, then one or more errors exist. However, equality of these two totals does not guarantee that no errors were made.

Point: The ordering of accounts in a trial balance typically follows their identification number from the chart of accounts.

Point: A trial balance is *not* a financial statement but a mechanism for checking equality of debits and credits in the ledger. Financial statements do not have debit and credit columns.

Using a Trial Balance

One or more errors exist when a trial balance does not balance (when its columns are not equal). When errors exist, they often occur in one of the following steps in the accounting process: (1) preparing journal entries, (2) posting entries to the ledger, (3) computing account balances, (4) entering account balances on the trial balance, or (5) totaling the trial balance columns. When a trial balance does balance, the accounts are likely free of the kinds of errors that create unequal debits and credits, yet errors can still exist. One example is when a debit or credit of a correct amount is made to a wrong account. This can occur when either journalizing or posting. This error would produce incorrect balances in two accounts, but the trial balance would balance. Another error is to record equal debits and credits of an incorrect amount. This error produces incorrect balances in two accounts, but again the

---

[6] If an account has a zero balance, it can be listed in the trial balance with a zero in its normal balance column.

		Balance Sheet (BS)									
Transactions		**Assets**					**=**	**Liabilities**		**+**	**Equity**
No.	**Description**	**Cash**	**+ Accts. Rec.**	**+ Prepaid Insur.**	**+ Supplies**	**+ Equip.**	**= Accts. Pay.**	**+ Unearned Revenue**		**+**	**Taylor Capital**
1	Owner investment	30,000					=			+	30,000
2	Purch. supp.	(2,500)			2,500		=			+	
3	Purch. equip.	(26,000)				26,000	=			+	
4	Credit purch.				7,100		= 7,100			+	
5	Services for cash	4,200					=			+	4,200
6	Rent exp.	(1,000)					=			+	(1,000)
7	Salary exp.	(700)					=			+	(700)
8	Services for credit		1,900				=			+	1,600 300
9	Cash rec'd. on Acct. Rec.	1,900	(1,900)				=			+	
10	Payment of Acct. Pay.	(900)					= (900)			+	
11	Owner Withdrawal	(600)					=			+	(600)
12	Cash for future service	3,000					=		3,000	+	
13	Payment of future insur.	(2,400)		2,400			=			+	
14	Purch. supp.	(120)			120		=			+	
15	Utility exp.	(230)					=			+	(230)
16	Salary exp.	(700)					=			+	(700)
	Totals	3,950	0	2,400	9,720	26,000	= 6,200		3,000	+	32,870

Example: If a credit to Unearned Consulting Revenue were incorrectly posted from the journal as a credit to the Consulting Revenue ledger account, would the ledger still balance? Would the financial statements be correct? *Answers:* The ledger would still balance, but the financial statements would be incorrect. Liabilities would be understated, equity would be overstated, and net income would be overstated as a result of overstated revenues.

debits and credits are equal. These examples show that when a trial balance does balance, it does not prove that all entries have been recorded and posted correctly.

Searching for Errors

If the trial balance does not balance, the error (or errors) must be found and corrected before preparing financial statements. Searching for the error is more efficient if we check the journalizing, posting, and trial balance preparation process in *reverse order*. While methods vary, we suggest the following sequence of steps. Step 1 is to verify that the trial balance columns are correctly added. If step 1 fails to find the error, then step 2 is to verify that account balances are accurately entered from the ledger. Step 3 is to see whether a debit (or credit) balance is mistakenly listed in the trial balance as a credit (or debit). A clue to this kind of error is when the difference between total debits and total credits in the trial balance equals twice the amount of the incorrect account balance. If the error is still undiscovered, Step 4 is to recompute each account balance in the ledger. Step 5 is to verify that each journal entry is properly posted to ledger accounts. Step 6 is to verify that the original journal entry has equal debits and credits. At this point, all errors should be uncovered.[7]

---

[7] *Transposition* occurs when two digits are switched, or transposed, within a number. If transposition is the only error, it yields a difference between the two trial balance totals that is evenly divisible by 9. For example, assume that a $691 debit in an entry is incorrectly posted to the ledger as $619. Total credits in the trial balance are then larger than total debits by $72 ($691 − $619). The $72 error is *evenly* divisible by 9 (72/9 = 8). The first digit

Income Statement (IS)			Statement of Cash Flows (SCF)				Transactions		
Rev.	− Exp. =	Net Inc.	Oper. + Cash Flow	Inv. + Cash Flow	Fin. = Cash Flow	Net Cash Flow	No.	Description	
	− =				30,000 =	30,000	1	Owner investment	
	− =		(2,500)		=	(2,500)	2	Purch. supp.	
	− =			(26,000)	=	(26,000)	3	Purch. equip.	
	− =				=		4	Credit purch.	
4,200	− =	4,200	4,200		=	4,200	5	Services for cash	
	− 1,000 =	(1,000)	(1,000)		=	(1,000)	6	Rent exp.	
	− 700 =	(700)	(700)		=	(700)	7	Salary exp.	
1,600	− =	1,600					8	Services	
300	− =	300						for credit	
	− =		1,900		=	1,900	9	Cash rec'd. on Acct. Rec.	
	− =		(900)		=	(900)	10	Payment of Acct. Pay.	
	− =				(600) =	(600)	11	Owner Withdrawal	
	− =		3,000		=	3,000	12	Cash for future service	
	− =		(2,400)		=	(2,400)	13	Payment of future insur.	
	− =		(120)		=	(120)	14	Purch. supp.	
	− 230 =	(230)	(230)		=	(230)	15	Utilities exp.	
	− 700 =	(700)	(700)		=	(700)	16	Salary exp.	
6,100	− 2,630 =	3,470	550 +	(26,000) +	29,400 =	3,950		Totals	

Exhibit 3.15

Financial Statement Links to Transactions

Exhibit 3.16

Trial Balance

Peachtree Accounting: Exercise 3-18

File Edit Maintain Tasks Analysis Options Reports Window Help

FAST FORWARD
Trial Balance
December 31, 2001

	Debit	Credit
Cash	$ 3,950	
Accounts Receivable	0	
Supplies	9,720	
Prepaid insurance	2,400	
Equipment	26,000	
Accounts payable		$ 6,200
Unearned consulting revenue		3,000
C. Taylor, Capital		30,000
C. Taylor, Withdrawals	600	
Consulting revenue		5,800
Rental revenue		300
Salaries expense	1,400	
Rent expense	1,000	
Utilities expense	230	
Totals	$ 45,300	$ 45,300

Sales   Purchases   General Ledger   Payroll   Inventory   Company   Analysis

of the quotient (in our example it is 8) equals the difference between the digits of the two transposed numbers (the 9 and the 1). The number of digits in the quotient also tells the location of the transposition, starting from the right. The quotient in our example had only one digit (8), so it tells us the transposition is in the first digit. Consider another example where a transposition error involves posting $961 instead of the correct $691. The difference in these numbers in $270, and its quotient is 30 (270/9). The quotient has two digits, so it tells us to check the second digit from the right for a transposition of two numbers that have a difference of 3.

Correcting Errors

If errors are discovered in either the journal or the ledger, they must be corrected. Our approach to correcting errors depends on the type of error and when it is discovered.

In one case, if an error in a journal entry is discovered before the error is posted, it can be corrected in a manual system by drawing a line through the incorrect information. The correct information is written above it to create a record of change for the auditor. Many computerized systems allow the operator to replace the incorrect information directly. If a correct amount in the journal is posted incorrectly to the ledger, we can correct it the same way.

Another case occurs when an error in a journal entry is not discovered until after it has been posted. We usually do not strike through both erroneous entries in the journal and ledger. Instead, the usual practice is to correct the error in the original journal entry by creating *another* journal entry. This *correcting entry* removes the amount from the wrong account and records it to the correct account. As an example, suppose we recorded a purchase of office supplies in the journal with an incorrect debit to Office Equipment:

Assets = Liabilities + Equity
+1,600
−1,600

Oct. 14	Office Equipment	1,600	
(Incorrect	Cash		1,600
Entry)	*To record the purchase of office supplies.*		

We then post this incorrect entry to the ledger. The Office Supplies ledger account balance is understated by $1,600, and the Office Equipment ledger account balance is overstated by $1,600. When we discover the error three days later, we make the following correcting entry:

Assets = Liabilities + Equity
+1,600
−1,600

Oct. 17	Office Supplies	1,600	
(Correcting	Office Equipment		1,600
Entry)	*To correct Oct. 14 entry that incorrectly debited Office Equipment.*		

Did You Know?

Window on Accounting   Computerized systems perform many routine tasks in accounting. They also allow regular updating (batch-time) or continuous (real-time) processing of information. Many programs point out errors such as unequal debits and credits. Computerized systems have freed accounting professionals to spend more time and effort on analyzing and interpreting information.

The credit in the correcting entry removes the error from the first entry. The debit correctly records the office supplies. The explanation reports exactly what happened. Computerized systems often use similar correcting entries. The exact procedure depends on the system used and management policy. Nearly all systems include controls to show when and where a correction is made.

Presentation Issues

Dollar signs are not used in journals and ledgers. They do appear in financial statements and other reports such as trial balances. The usual practice is to put a dollar sign beside the first amount in each column of numbers, and beside the first amount appearing after a ruled line. The financial statements in Exhibit 2.15 demonstrate this. Another practice is to put dollar signs beside only the first and last numbers in a column. **Nike**'s financial statements in Appendix A show this. When amounts are entered in a journal, ledger, or trial balance, commas are optional to indicate thousands, millions, and so forth. However, commas are always used in financial statements. Companies also commonly round amounts to the nearest dollar, or even to a higher level. Nike is typical of many companies in that it rounds its financial statement amounts to the nearest one-tenth of a million. This decision is based on the perceived impact of rounding for users' business decisions.

Quick Check

14. Describe a chart of accounts.

15. Where are dollar signs typically entered in financial statements?

16. If a $4,000 debit to Equipment in a journal entry is incorrectly posted to the ledger as a $4,000 credit, and the ledger account has a resulting debit balance of $20,000, what is the effect of this error on the trial balance column totals?

Answers—p. 106

| Debt Ratio | Using the Information |

Accounting records are designed to provide useful information to users of financial statements. One important objective for many users is gathering information to help them assess a company's risk of failing to pay its debts when they are due. This section describes the debt ratio and how it can help in this task.

Most companies finance a portion of their assets with liabilities and the remaining portion with equity. A company that finances a relatively large portion of its assets with liabilities is said to have a high degree of *financial leverage*. Higher financial leverage involves greater risk because liabilities must be repaid and often require regular interest payments (equity financing does not). The risk that a company might not be able to meet required payments is higher if it has more liabilities (is more highly leveraged).

One way to assess the risk associated with a company's use of liabilities is to compute and analyze the debt ratio. The **debt ratio** reflects the relation between a company's liabilities and its assets and is defined in Exhibit 3.17.

A2 Compute the debt ratio and describe its use in analyzing company performance.

$$\text{Debt ratio} = \frac{\text{Total liabilities}}{\text{Total assets}}$$

Exhibit 3.17

Debt Ratio

To see how we apply the debt ratio, let's look at **Stride Rite**'s liabilities and assets—it makes Keds, Pro-Keds, and other footwear. Exhibit 3.18 computes and reports the debt ratio for Stride Rite at the end of each of the past five years.

	1999	1998	1997	1996	1995
Total liabilities (in mil.)	$ 96	$ 91	$102	$103	$ 99
Total assets (in mil.)	$346	$335	$344	$364	$367
Debt ratio	**.277**	**.272**	**.297**	**.283**	**.270**
Industry debt ratio*	.46	.52	.59	.64	.47

Exhibit 3.18

Computation and Analysis of Debt Ratio

* Industry debt ratio is the median value from ten competitors.

Note that Stride Rite's debt ratio is stable over recent years, ranging from a low of .270 to a high of .297. This ratio is low for Stride Rite and most other companies as evidenced by comparisons with its industry ratio. Stride Rite also reports that it carries no long-term debt, which is also unusual. This analysis implies a low risk from financial leverage for Stride Rite. Still, evaluating a company's debt ratio depends on several factors, such as the nature of its operations, its ability to generate cash flows, its

You Make the Call

Investor You consider buying stock in **Converse**. As part of your analysis, you compute its debt ratio for 1997, 1998, and 1999: 1.20, 1.35, and 1.74, respectively.* Based on the debt ratio, is Converse a low-risk investment? Has the risk of buying Converse stock changed over this period?

*Converse's equity balance is negative for these years because of losses.

Answer—p. 106

industry, and its economic conditions. Saying that a specific debt ratio is good or bad for a company is not possible. Instead, we need to compare performance over time and across companies both inside and outside the industry. In simplest terms, we need to compare the company's return on the money it has borrowed to the rate it is paying creditors. If the company's return is higher, it is successfully borrowing money to make more money. We must be aware that company returns change over time due to many factors. Accordingly, a company's success with making money from borrowed money can quickly turn unprofitable if its own return declines.

Demonstration Problem

(*Note: This demonstration problem is based on the same facts as the demonstration problem at the end of Chapter 2.*) The following events occurred during the first month of Sylvia Workman's new haircutting business called Expressions:

a. On August 1, Workman put $3,000 cash into a checking account in the name of Expressions. She also invested $15,000 of equipment that she already owned.

b. On August 2, Workman paid $600 cash for furniture for the shop.

c. On August 3, Workman paid $500 cash to rent space in a strip mall for August.

d. On August 4, Workman purchased some new equipment for the shop that she bought on credit (using a note payable) for $1,200.

e. On August 5, Expressions opened for business. Cash receipts from haircutting services provided in the first week and a half of business (ended August 15) are $825.

f. On August 15, Workman provided haircutting services on account for $100.

g. On August 17, Workman received a $100 check for services previously rendered on account.

h. On August 17, Workman paid $125 cash to an assistant for working during the grand opening.

i. Cash received from services provided during the second half of August is $930.

j. On August 31, Workman paid a $400 cash installment on the note payable from part (*d*).

k. On August 31, Workman withdrew $900 cash for her personal use.

Required

1. Prepare general journal entries for the preceding transactions.

2. Open the following accounts (account numbers are in parentheses): Cash (101); Accounts Receivable (102); Furniture (161); Store Equipment (165); Note Payable (240); Sylvia Workman, Capital (301); Sylvia Workman, Withdrawals (302); Haircutting Services Revenue (403); Wages Expense (623); and Rent Expense (640).

3. Post the journal entries from (1) to the ledger accounts from part (2).

4. Prepare a trial balance as of August 31.

Extended Analysis

5. In the coming months, Expressions will experience an even greater variety of business transactions. Identify which accounts are debited and which are credited for the following transactions. (*Hint:* You may have to use some accounts not listed in part (2).)

   a. Purchase supplies with cash.

   b. Pay cash for future insurance coverage.

   c. Receive cash for services to be provided in the future.

   d. Purchase supplies on account.

Planning the Solution

• Analyze each transaction to identify the accounts affected and the amount of each effect.

• Use the debit and credit rules to prepare a journal entry for each transaction.

• Post each debit and each credit in journal entries to their ledger accounts and cross-reference each amount in the Posting Reference columns of the journal and ledger.

• Calculate each account balance and list the accounts with their balances on a trial balance.

• Verify that total debits in the trial balance equal total credits.

• Analyze the future transactions to identify the accounts affected and apply debit and credit rules.

Solution to Demonstration Problem

1. General journal entries:

Date	Account Titles and Explanations	PR	Debit	Credit
Aug. 1	Cash	101	3,000	
	Store Equipment	165	15,000	
	Sylvia Workman, Capital	301		18,000
	Owner's initial investment.			
2	Furniture	161	600	
	Cash	101		600
	Purchased furniture for cash.			
3	Rent Expense	640	500	
	Cash	101		500
	Paid rent for August.			
4	Store Equipment	165	1,200	
	Note Payable	240		1,200
	Purchased additional equipment on credit.			
15	Cash	101	825	
	Haircutting Services Revenue	403		825
	Cash receipts from 10 days of operations.			
15	Accounts Receivable	102	100	
	Haircutting Services Revenue	403		100
	To record revenue for services provided on account.			
17	Cash	101	100	
	Accounts Receivable	102		100
	To record cash received as payment on account.			
17	Wages Expense	623	125	
	Cash	101		125
	Paid wages to assistant.			
31	Cash	101	930	
	Haircutting Services Revenue	403		930
	Cash receipts from second half of August.			
31	Note Payable	240	400	
	Cash	101		400
	Paid an installment on the note payable.			
31	Sylvia Workman, Withdrawals	302	900	
	Cash	101		900
	Owner withdrew cash from the business.			

2. & 3. Open ledger accounts and post journal entries from (1):

		Cash			Account No. 101	
Date		Explanation	PR	Debit	Credit	Balance
Aug.	1		G1	3,000		3,000
	2		G1		600	2,400
	3		G1		500	1,900
	15		G1	825		2,725
	17		G1	100		2,825
	17		G1		125	2,700
	31		G1	930		3,630
	31		G1		400	3,230
	31		G1		900	2,330

		Accounts Receivable			Account No. 102	
Date		Explanation	PR	Debit	Credit	Balance
Aug.	15		G1	100		100
	17		G1		100	0

		Furniture			Account No. 161	
Date		Explanation	PR	Debit	Credit	Balance
Aug.	2		G1	600		600

		Store Equipment			Account No. 165	
Date		Explanation	PR	Debit	Credit	Balance
Aug.	1		G1	15,000		15,000
	4		G1	1,200		16,200

		Note Payable			Account No. 240	
Date		Explanation	PR	Debit	Credit	Balance
Aug.	4		G1		1,200	1,200
	31		G1	400		800

		Sylvia Workman, Capital			Account No. 301	
Date		Explanation	PR	Debit	Credit	Balance
Aug.	1		G1		18,000	18,000

		Sylvia Workman, Withdrawals			Account No. 302	
Date		Explanation	PR	Debit	Credit	Balance
Aug.	31		G1	900		900

		Haircutting Services Revenue			Account No. 403	
Date		Explanation	PR	Debit	Credit	Balance
Aug.	15		G1		825	825
	15		G1		100	925
	31		G1		930	1,855

		Wages Expense			Account No. 623	
Date		Explanation	PR	Debit	Credit	Balance
Aug.	17		G1	125		125

		Rent Expense			Account No. 640	
Date		Explanation	PR	Debit	Credit	Balance
Aug.	3		G1	500		500

4. Prepare trial balance from ledger:

EXPRESSIONS Trial Balance August 31		
	Debit	**Credit**
Cash	$ 2,330	
Accounts receivable	0	
Furniture	600	
Store equipment	16,200	
Note payable		$ 800
Sylvia Workman, Capital		18,000
Sylvia Workman, Withdrawals	900	
Haircutting services revenue		1,855
Wages expense	125	
Rent expense	500	
Totals	$20,655	$20,655

5a. Supplies debited
    Cash credited

5b. Prepaid Insurance debited
    Cash credited

5c. Cash debited
    Unearned Services Revenue credited

5d. Supplies debited
    Accounts Payable credited

Summary

C1 **Explain the steps in processing transactions.** The accounting process captures business transactions and events, analyzes and records their effects, and summarizes and prepares information useful in making decisions. Transactions and events are the starting points in the accounting process. Source documents help in their analysis. The effects of transactions and events are recorded in journals. Posting along with a trial balance helps summarize and classify these effects.

C2 **Describe source documents and their purpose.** Source documents identify and describe transactions and events. Examples are sales tickets, checks, purchase orders, bills, and bank statements. Source documents provide objective and reliable evidence, making information more useful.

C3 **Describe an account and its use in recording information about transactions.** An account is a detailed record of increases and decreases in a specific asset, liability, equity, revenue, or expense item. Information is taken from accounts and then analyzed, summarized, and presented in reports and financial statements for decision makers to use.

C4 **Describe a ledger and a chart of accounts.** A ledger is a record containing all accounts used by a company and their balances. This is referred to as the *books*. The chart of accounts is a list of all accounts and usually includes an identification number assigned to each account.

C5 **Define debits and credits and explain their role in double-entry accounting.** *Debit* refers to left, and *credit* refers to right. Debits increase assets, withdrawals, and expenses, while credits decrease them. Credits increase liabilities, capital, and revenues; debits decrease them. Double-entry accounting means each transaction affects at least two accounts and has at least one debit and one credit. The system for recording debits and credits follows from the accounting equation. The left side of an account is the normal balance for assets and expenses, and the right side is the normal balance for liabilities, equity, and revenues.

A1 **Analyze the impact of transactions on accounts and financial statements.** We analyze transactions using concepts of double-entry accounting. This analysis is performed by determining a transaction's effects on accounts. These effects are recorded in journals and posted to ledgers.

A2 **Compute the debt ratio and describe its use in analyzing company performance.** A company's debt ratio is computed as total liabilities divided by total assets. It tells us how much of the assets are financed by creditor (nonowner) financing. The higher this ratio, the more risk a company faces because liabilities must be repaid at specific dates.

P1 **Record transactions in a journal and post entries to a ledger.** Transactions are recorded in a journal. Each entry in a journal is posted to the accounts in the ledger. This provides information for accounts that is used to produce financial statements. Balance column accounts are widely used and include columns for debits, credits, and the account balance.

P2 **Prepare and explain the use of a trial balance.** A trial balance is a list of accounts from the ledger showing their debit or credit balances in separate columns. The trial balance is a convenient summary of the ledger's contents and is useful in preparing financial statements and in revealing errors.

Guidance Answers to **You Make the Call**

Cashier The advantages to the process proposed by the assistant manager include improved customer service, fewer delays, and less work for you. However, you should have serious concerns about internal control and the potential for fraud. In particular, the assistant manager could steal cash and simply enter fewer sales to match the remaining cash. You should reject her suggestion without the manager's approval. Moreover, you should have an ethical concern about the assistant manager's suggestion to ignore store policy.

Marketing Manager You direct your search to the accounting information system. Source documents contain all revenue information you desire but you must go through all documents, identify revenues, and compute the total. The ledger also contains the information you desire and is a preferred source because it keeps a running balance of each account and directly answers your question.

Investor The debt ratio suggests the stock of **Converse** is of higher risk than normal and that this risk is rising. Industry ratios reported in Exhibit 3.18 further support this conclusion. The debt ratio for Converse is now more than triple the industry norm of 0.46. Also, a debt ratio larger than 1.0 indicates negative equity. Excessive cumulative losses for Converse led to its negative equity.

Guidance Answers to **Quick Checks**

1. External transactions are exchanges of economic consideration between an organization and some other entity. Internal transactions are exchanges within an organization, for example, a company using equipment in its operations.

2. Examples of source documents are sales tickets, checks, purchase orders, charges to customers, bills from suppliers, employee earnings records, and bank statements.

3. Source documents serve many purposes, including record-keeping and internal control. Source documents, especially if obtained from outside the organization, provide objective and reliable evidence about transactions and their amounts.

4.

Assets	Liabilities	Equity
a,c,e	b,d	—

5. An account is a record in an accounting system that records and stores the increases and decreases in a specific asset, liability, equity, revenue, or expense. A ledger is a collection of all the accounts of a company.

6. A company's size and diversity affect the number of accounts in its accounting system. The types of accounts used depend on information the company needs to both effectively operate and report its activities in financial statements.

7. No. Debit and credit both can mean increase or decrease. The particular meaning in a circumstance depends on the *type of account*. For example, a debit increases the balance of asset and expense accounts, but it decreases the balance of liability, equity, and revenue accounts.

8. Equity is increased by revenues and by an owner's investments. Equity is decreased by expenses and by withdrawals.

9. The name *double entry* is used because all transactions affect at least two accounts. There must be at least one debit in one account and at least one credit in another account.

10. Answer is (c).

11.

Cash	15,000	
Equipment	23,000	
"Owner", Capital		38,000
Investment by owner of cash and equipment.		

12. A compound journal entry affects three or more accounts.

13. Posting reference numbers are entered in the journal when posting to the ledger as a cross-reference that allows the recordkeeper or auditor to trace debits and credits from one record to another. They also create a "marker" in case the posting process is interrupted.

14. A chart of accounts is a list of all of a company's accounts and their identification numbers.

15. At a minimum, dollar signs are placed beside the first and last numbers in a column. It is also common to place dollar signs beside any amount that appears after a ruled line to indicate that an addition or subtraction has occurred.

16. The Equipment account balance is incorrectly reported at $20,000—it should be $28,000. The effect of this error understates the trial balance's Debit column total by $8,000. This results in an $8,000 difference between the two columns' totals.

Glossary

Account a record within an accounting system where increases and decreases in a specific asset, liability, equity, revenue, or expense are entered and stored. (p. 81).

Account balance the difference between total debits and total credits (including the beginning balance) for an account. (p. 86).

Balance column account an account with debit and credit columns for recording entries and another column for showing the balance of the account after each entry. (p. 89).

Chart of accounts a list of accounts used by a company; includes an identification number for each account. (p. 86).

Compound journal entry a journal entry that affects at least three accounts. (p. 93).

Credit recorded on the right side; an entry that decreases asset and expense accounts, and increases liability, equity, and revenue accounts; abbreviated Cr. (p. 86).

Debit recorded on the left side; an entry that increases asset and expense accounts, and decreases liability, equity, and revenue accounts; abbreviated Dr. (p. 86).

Debt ratio the ratio of total liabilities to total assets; used to reflect risk associated with a company's debts. (p. 101).

Double-entry accounting an accounting system in which each transaction affects at least two accounts and has at least one debit and one credit. (p. 87).

Events happenings that both affect an organization's financial position and can be reliably measured. (p. 80).

External transactions exchanges of economic consideration between one entity and another entity. (p. 80).

General journal a record of the debits and credits of transactions and events. (p. 89).

Internal transactions activities within an organization that can affect the accounting equation. (p. 80).

Journal a record where transactions are recorded before they are posted to ledger accounts; also called *book of original entry*. (p. 88).

Journalizing process of recording transactions in a journal. (p. 89).

Ledger record containing all accounts (with amounts) for a business. (p. 81).

Note payable written promise to pay a definite sum of money on demand or on a specific future date(s); also called *promissory note*. (p. 83).

Posting process of transferring journal entry information to the ledger. (p. 89).

Posting reference (PR) column a column in journals where individual account num-

bers are entered when entries are posted to ledger accounts. (p. 89).

Promissory note see *note payable* or *note receivable*. (p. 82).

Source documents the source of information for accounting entries and can be in either paper or electronic form; also called *business papers*. (p. 80).

T-account an account form used as a tool to show the effects of transactions and events on individual accounts. (p. 86).

Trial balance list of accounts and their balances at a point in time; total debit balances equal total credit balances. (p. 97).

Unearned revenue a liability created when customers pay in advance for products or services; earned when the products or services are delivered in the future. (p. 84).

Questions

1. What is the difference between a note payable and an account payable?
2. Provide the names of two (a) asset accounts, (b) liability accounts, and (c) equity accounts.
3. Discuss the steps in processing business transactions.
4. Are debits or credits listed first in general journal entries? Are the debits or the credits indented?
5. What kinds of transactions can be recorded in a general journal?
6. Should a transaction be recorded first in a journal or the ledger? Why?
7. If assets are valuable resources and asset accounts have debit balances, why do expense accounts have debit balances?

8. Why does the recordkeeper prepare a trial balance?
9. Review the **Nike** balance sheet in Appendix A. Identify three accounts on the balance sheet that carry debit balances and three accounts on the balance sheet that carry credit balances.
10. Review the **Reebok** balance sheet in Appendix A. Identify three different liability accounts that include the word *payable* in the account title.
11. Locate **Gap**'s income statement in Appendix A. What is the name of its revenue account?
12. If a wrong amount is journalized and posted to the accounts, how should the error be corrected?

Indicate whether a debit or credit *decreases* the normal balance of each of the following accounts:

a. Office Supplies
b. Repair Services Revenue
c. Interest Payable
d. Accounts Receivable
e. Salaries Expense
f. Owner, Capital
g. Prepaid Insurance
h. Buildings
i. Interest Revenue
j. Owner, Withdrawals

QUICK STUDY

QS 3-1
Linking debit or credit with normal balance C5

Identify whether a debit or credit yields the indicated change for each of the following accounts:

a. To increase Store Equipment
b. To increase Owner, Withdrawals
c. To decrease Cash
d. To increase Utilities Expense
e. To increase Fees Earned
f. To decrease Unearned Revenue
g. To decrease Prepaid Insurance
h. To increase Notes Payable
i. To decrease Accounts Receivable
j. To increase Owner, Capital

QS 3-2
Analyzing debit or credit by account C5

QS 3-3
Identifying source documents

Select items from the following list that are likely to serve as source documents:

a. Bank statement   **e.** Telephone bill

b. Sales ticket   **f.** Invoice from supplier

c. Income statement   **g.** Owner's withdrawals account

d. Trial balance   **h.** Balance sheet

QS 3-4
Classifying accounts in
financial statements

Indicate the financial statement on which each of the following accounts appears. Use IS for income statement, SCOE for statement of changes in owner's equity, and BS for balance sheet:

a. Office Supplies   **f.** Equipment

b. Services Revenue   **g.** Prepaid Insurance

c. Interest Payable   **h.** Buildings

d. Accounts Receivable   **i.** Interest Revenue

e. Salaries Expense   **j.** Owner, Withdrawals

QS 3-5
Identifying a posting error

A trial balance has total debits of $20,000 and total credits of $24,500. Which one of the following errors would create this imbalance? Explain.

a. A $2,250 debit to Rent Expense in a journal entry is incorrectly posted to the ledger as a $2,250 credit, leaving the Rent Expense account with a $3,000 debit balance.

b. A $4,500 debit to Salaries Expense in a journal entry is incorrectly posted to the ledger as a $4,500 credit, leaving the Salaries Expense account with a $750 debit balance.

c. A $2,250 credit to Consulting Fees Earned in a journal entry is incorrectly posted to the ledger as a $2,250 debit, leaving the Consulting Fees Earned account with a $6,300 credit balance.

QS 3-6
Preparing journal entries

Prepare journal entries for each of the following selected transactions:

a. On January 13, Bella Woods opens a landscaping business called Showcase Yards by investing $70,000 cash along with equipment having a $30,000 value.

b. On January 21, Showcase Yards purchases office supplies on credit for $280.

c. On January 29, Showcase Yards receives $7,800 cash for performing landscaping services.

EXERCISES

Exercise 3-1
Analyzing effects of
transactions on accounts

Lori Fitterling recently notified a client that it would have to pay a $62,000 fee for services. Unfortunately, the client did not have enough cash to pay the entire bill. Fitterling agreed to accept the following items in full payment: (1) $10,000 cash, (2) computer equipment worth $80,000, and (3) assumed responsibility for a $28,000 note payable related to the computer equipment. The entry Fitterling makes to record this transaction includes which one or more of the following items?

a. $28,000 increase in a liability account.   **d.** $62,000 increase in L. Fitterling, Capital account.

b. $10,000 increase in the Cash account.   **e.** $62,000 increase in a revenue account.

c. $10,000 increase in a revenue account.

Exercise 3-2
Recording effects of
transactions in T-accounts

Open the following T-accounts: Cash; Accounts Receivable; Office Supplies; Office Equipment; Accounts Payable; Robert Dejonge, Capital; Robert Dejonge, Withdrawals; Fees Earned; and Rent Expense. Record the transactions of Dejonge Company by recording the debit and credit entries directly in T-accounts. Use the letters beside each transaction to identify entries. Determine the ending balance of each T-account.

a. Robert Dejonge invested $13,325 cash in the business.

b. Purchased office supplies for $475 cash.

c. Purchased $6,235 of office equipment on credit.

d. Received $2,000 cash as fees for services provided to a customer.

e. Paid cash to settle the payable for the office equipment purchased in transaction c.

f. Billed a customer $3,300 as fees for services provided.

g. Paid the monthly rent with $775 cash.

h. Collected $2,300 cash toward the account receivable created in transaction f.

i. Robert Dejonge withdrew $800 cash from the business for personal use.

After recording the transactions of Exercise 3-2 in T-accounts and calculating the balance of each account, prepare a trial balance. Use May 31, 2002, as its date.

Exercise 3-3
Preparing a trial balance

Complete the following table by (1) identifying the type of account as an asset, liability, equity, revenue, or expense, (2) entering *debit (Dr.)* or *credit (Cr.)* to identify the kind of entry that would increase or decrease the account balance, and (3) identifying the normal balance of the account.

Exercise 3-4
Identifying increases, decreases, and normal balances of accounts

	Account	Type of Account	Increase (Dr. or Cr.)	Decrease (Dr. or Cr.)	Normal Balance
a.	Unearned revenue				
b.	Accounts payable				
c.	Postage expense				
d.	Prepaid insurance				
e.	Land				
f.	P. Maben, Capital				
g.	Accounts receivable				
h.	P. Maben, Withdrawals				
i.	Cash				
j.	Equipment				
k.	Fees earned				
l.	Wages expense				

Seven transactions *a* through *g* are posted to the following T-accounts. Provide a short description of each transaction. Include the amounts in your descriptions.

Exercise 3-5
Describing transactions from T-accounts

Cash			
(a)	6,000	(b)	4,800
(e)	4,500	(c)	900
		(f)	1,600
		(g)	820

Office Supplies	
(c)	900
(d)	300

Prepaid Insurance	
(b)	4,800

Equipment	
(a)	7,600
(d)	9,700

Automobiles	
(a)	12,000

Accounts Payable			
(f)	1,600	(d)	10,000

David Joy, Capital			
		(a)	25,600

Delivery Services Revenue			
		(e)	4,500

Gas and Oil Expense	
(g)	820

Use information from the T-accounts in Exercise 3-5 to prepare general journal entries for the seven transaction *a* through *g*.

Exercise 3-6
Preparing general journal entries

Exercise 3-7

Analyzing account entries and balances

Use the information in each of the following separate cases to calculate the unknown amount:

1. During October, Rightlane Company had $102,500 of cash receipts and $103,150 of cash disbursements. The October 31 Cash balance was $18,600. Determine how much cash the company had at the close of business on September 30.

2. On September 30, Rightlane had a $102,500 balance in Accounts Receivable. During October, the company collected $102,890 from its credit customers. The October 31 balance in Accounts Receivable was $89,000. Determine the amount of sales on account that occurred in October.

3. Rightlane had $152,000 of accounts payable on September 30 and $132,500 on October 31. Total purchases on account during October were $281,000. Determine how much cash was paid on accounts payable during October.

Exercise 3-8

Preparing general journal entries

Prepare general journal entries for the following transactions of a new business called Click and Shoot.

Aug. 1   Hannah Hicks, the owner, invested $6,500 cash and $33,500 of photography equipment.
      1   Paid $2,100 cash for an insurance policy covering the next two years.
      5   Purchased office supplies for $880 cash.
      20 Received $3,331 cash in photography fees earned.
      31 Paid $675 cash for August utilities.

Exercise 3-9

Preparing T-accounts and the trial balance

Use the information provided in Exercise 3-8 to prepare an August 31 trial balance for Click and Shoot. Open these T-accounts: Cash; Office Supplies; Prepaid Insurance; Photography Equipment; Hannah Hicks, Capital; Photography Fees Earned; and Utilities Expense. Post the general journal entries to the T-accounts, and prepare a trial balance.

Exercise 3-10

Analyzing and journalizing revenue transactions

Examine the following transactions and identify those that create revenues for Stout Services, a sole proprietorship owned by David Stout. Prepare general journal entries to record those transactions and explain why the other transactions did not create revenues.

a. David Stout invests $39,350 cash in the business.

b. Provided $2,300 of services on credit.

c. Provided services to a client and received $875 cash.

d. Received $10,200 cash from a client in payment for services to be provided next year.

e. Received $3,500 cash from a client in partial payment of an account receivable.

f. Borrowed $120,000 cash from the bank by signing a promissory note.

Exercise 3-11

Analyzing and journalizing expense transactions

Examine the following transactions and identify those that create expenses for Stout Services. Prepare general journal entries to record those transactions and explain why the other transactions did not create expenses.

a. Paid $12,200 cash for office supplies purchased 13 months previously.

b. Paid $1,233 cash for the two-week salary of the receptionist.

c. Paid $39,200 cash for equipment.

d. Paid utility bill with $870 cash.

e. Owner withdrew $4,500 cash from the business for personal use.

Exercise 3-12

Preparing a corrected trial balance

On January 1, Megan Taylor started a new business called The Right Stuff. Because she lacked accounting knowledge, Taylor made a number of mistakes in preparing the year-end trial balance shown here.

An analysis of the situation reveals the following:

a. The sum of the debits in the Cash ledger account is $38,125 and the sum of its credits is $31,490.

b. A $425 payment from a credit customer is posted to Cash but is not posted to Accounts Receivable.

THE RIGHT STUFF		
Trial Balance		
December 31, 2002		
	Debit	**Credit**
Cash	$ 5,500	
Accounts receivable . .		$ 7,900
Office supplies	2,650	
Office equipment	20,500	
Accounts payable . . .		9,465
Megan Taylor, Capital .	16,745	
Services revenue		22,350
Wages expense		6,000
Rent expense		4,800
Advertising expense . .		1,400
Totals	$45,395	$51,985

c. A credit purchase of office supplies for $500 is completely unrecorded.

d. A transposition error occurred in copying the balance of the Services Revenue account to the trial balance. The correct amount is $23,250.

e. Errors are also made in assigning account balances (all with normal balances) to the Debit and Credit columns of the trial balance and in computing totals of the columns.

Use this information to prepare a correct trial balance.

Posting errors are identified in the following table. In column (1), enter the amount of the difference between the two (debit and credit) trial balance columns due to the error. In column (2), identify the trial balance column (debit or credit) with the larger amount if they are not equal. In column (3), identify the account(s) affected by the error. In column (4), indicate the amount by which the account(s) in column (3) is (are) under- or overstated. Answers for the first error are given.

Exercise 3-13

Identifying effects of posting errors on the trial balance

	Description of Posting Error	**(1)** Difference between Debit and Credit Columns	**(2)** Column with the Larger Total	**(3)** Identify Account(s) Incorrectly Stated	**(4)** Amount that Account(s) is Over- or Understated
a.	$3,600 debit to Rent Expense is posted as a $1,340 debit.	$2,260	Credit	Rent Expense	Rent Expense understated $2,260
b.	$6,500 credit to Cash is posted twice as two credits to Cash.				
c.	$10,900 debit to the owner's withdrawals account is debited to owner's capital.				
d.	$2,050 debit to Prepaid Insurance is posted as a debit to Insurance Expense.				
e.	$38,000 debit to Machinery is posted as a debit to Accounts Payable.				
f.	$5,850 credit to Services Revenue is posted as a $585 credit.				
g.	$1,390 debit to Store Supplies is not posted.				

1. Calculate the debt ratio for each of the following six separate cases:

Exercise 3-14

Computing and interpreting the debt ratio

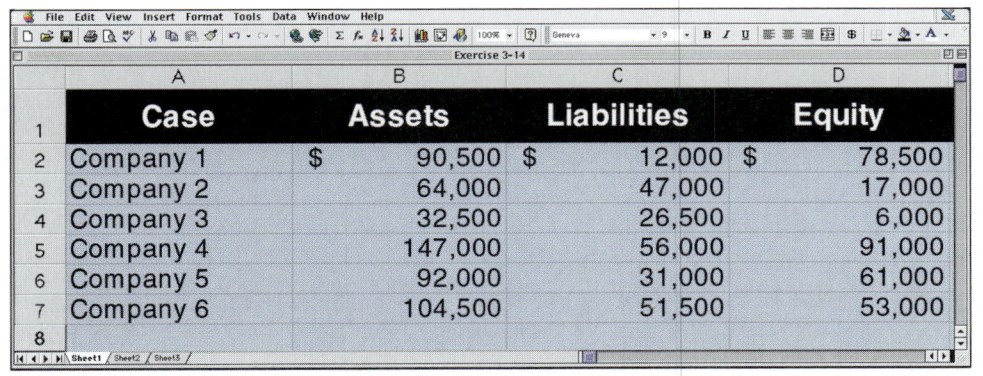

	Case	Assets	Liabilities	Equity
2	Company 1	$ 90,500	$ 12,000	$ 78,500
3	Company 2	64,000	47,000	17,000
4	Company 3	32,500	26,500	6,000
5	Company 4	147,000	56,000	91,000
6	Company 5	92,000	31,000	61,000
7	Company 6	104,500	51,500	53,000

2. Of the six cases, which business relies most heavily on creditor (non-owner) financing?

3. Of the six cases, which business relies most heavily on equity (owner) financing?

4. Which two companies indicate the greatest risk?

Exercise 3-15

Analyzing a trial balance error

You are told the column totals in a trial balance are not equal. After careful analysis, you discover only one error. Specifically, the balance of the Office Equipment account has a debit balance of $37,100 on the trial balance. However, you find that a correctly journalized credit purchase of a computer for $18,950 is posted from the journal to the ledger with an $18,950 debit to Office Equipment and another $18,950 debit to Accounts Payable. Answer each of the following questions and compute the dollar amount of any misstatement:

a. Is the debit column total of the trial balance overstated, understated, or correctly stated?

b. Is the credit column total of the trial balance overstated, understated, or correctly stated?

c. Is the balance of the Office Equipment account overstated, understated, or correctly stated in the trial balance?

d. Is the balance of the Accounts Payable account overstated, understated, or correctly stated in the trial balance?

e. If the debit column total of the trial balance is $360,000 before correcting the error, what is the total of the credit column before correction?

PROBLEM SET A

Problem 3-1A

Preparing and posting general journal entries; preparing a trial balance

Roberto Ricci opens a computer consulting business called Financial Consultants and completes the following transactions in April:

April	1	Ricci invests $80,000 cash along with office equipment valued at $26,000.
	1	Prepaid $9,000 cash for three months' rent for office space. (*Hint:* Debit Prepaid Rent for $9,000.)
	2	Made credit purchases of office equipment for $8,000 and office supplies for $3,600.
	6	Completed services for a client and immediately received $4,000 cash.
	9	Completed a $6,000 project for a client, who will pay within 30 days.
	10	Paid the account payable created on April 2 in cash.
	19	Paid $2,400 cash for the premium on a 12-month insurance policy.
	22	Received $4,400 cash as partial payment for the work completed on April 9.
	25	Completed work for another client for $2,890 on credit.
	30	Ricci withdrew $5,500 cash from the business for personal use.
	30	Purchased $600 of additional office supplies on credit.
	30	Paid $435 cash for this month's utility bill.

Required

1. Prepare general journal entries to record these transactions (use account titles listed in part 2).

2. Open the following ledger accounts (use the balance column format): Cash (101); Accounts Receivable (106); Office Supplies (124); Prepaid Insurance (128); Prepaid Rent (131); Office Equipment (163); Accounts Payable (201); Roberto Ricci, Capital (301); Roberto Ricci, Withdrawals (302); Services Revenue (403); and Utilities Expense (690). Post journal entries from part *1* to the ledger accounts and enter the balance after each posting.

3. Prepare a trial balance as of the end of this month's operations.

Check   Cash Bal., $59,465

Problem 3-2A

Recording transactions in T-accounts; preparing a trial balance

Business transactions completed by Steven Woolery during the month of September are as follows:

a. Steven Woolery invested $60,000 cash along with office equipment valued at $25,000 in a new sole proprietorship named SW Consulting.

b. Purchased land and a small office building. The land is worth $40,000, and the building is worth $160,000. The purchase price is paid with $30,000 cash and a long-term note payable for $170,000.

c. Purchased $2,000 of office supplies on credit.

d. Steven Woolery invested his personal automobile in the business. The automobile has a value of $16,500 and is to be used exclusively in the business.

e. Purchased $5,600 of additional office equipment on credit.

f. Paid $1,800 cash salary to an assistant.

g. Provided services to a client and collected $8,000 cash.

h. Paid $635 cash for this month's utilities.

i. Paid cash to settle the account payable created in transaction *c*.

j. Purchased $30,000 of new office equipment by paying $20,300 cash and trading in old equipment with a recorded net cost of $9,700.

k. Completed $6,250 of services for a client. This amount is to be received within 30 days.

l. Paid $1,800 cash salary to an assistant.

m. Received $4,000 cash on the receivable created in transaction *k*.

n. Woolery withdrew $2,800 cash from the business for personal use.

Required

1. Open the following T-accounts: Cash; Accounts Receivable; Office Supplies; Automobiles; Office Equipment; Building; Land; Accounts Payable; Long-Term Notes Payable; Steven Woolery, Capital; Steven Woolery, Withdrawals; Fees Earned; Salaries Expense; and Utilities Expense.

2. Record the preceding transactions by entering debits and credits directly in T-accounts. Use the transaction letters to identify each debit and credit entry.

3. Determine the balance of each account and prepare a trial balance as of September 30.

Check   Trial balance totals, $291,350

Shelton Engineering, a sole proprietorship, completed the following transactions in the month of June.

a. Sandra Shelton, the owner, invested $100,000 cash, office equipment with a value of $5,000, and $60,000 of drafting equipment to launch the business.

b. Purchased land for an office. The land is worth $49,000, and is paid with $6,300 cash and a long-term note payable for $42,700.

c. Purchased a portable building with $55,000 cash and moved it onto the business's land.

d. Paid $3,000 cash for the premium on a two-year insurance policy.

e. Completed and delivered a set of plans for a client and collected $6,200 cash.

f. Purchased additional drafting equipment for $20,000. Paid $9,500 cash and signed a long-term note payable for the $10,500 balance.

g. Completed $14,000 of engineering services for a client. This amount is to be received in 30 days.

h. Purchased $1,150 of additional office equipment on credit.

i. Completed engineering services for $22,000 on credit.

j. Received a bill for rent of equipment that was used on a recently completed job. The $1,333 rent must be paid within 30 days.

k. Collected $7,000 cash from the client described in transaction *g*.

l. Paid $1,200 cash wages to a drafting assistant.

m. Paid cash to settle the account payable created in transaction *h*.

n. Paid $925 cash for some repairs to an item of drafting equipment.

o. Sandra Shelton withdrew $9,480 cash from the business for personal use.

p. Paid $1,200 cash wages to a drafting assistant.

q. Paid $2,500 cash for advertisements in the local newspaper during June.

Problem 3-3A
Recording transactions in T-accounts, preparing a trial balance, and computing a debt ratio

Required

1. Open the following T-accounts: Cash; Accounts Receivable; Prepaid Insurance; Office Equipment; Drafting Equipment; Building; Land; Accounts Payable; Long-Term Notes Payable; Sandra Shelton, Capital; Sandra Shelton, Withdrawals; Engineering Fees Earned; Wages Expense; Equipment Rental Expense; Advertising Expense; and Repairs Expense.

2. Record the transactions by entering debits and credits directly in T-accounts. Use the transaction letters to identify each debit and credit. Prepare a trial balance as of June 30.

3. Calculate the company's debt ratio. Use $245,095 as the total assets. Are the company's assets financed more by debt or equity?

Check   Trial balance totals, $261,733

Problem 3-4A

Preparing and posting general journal entries; preparing a trial balance

Stuart Birch opens a Web consulting business called Show-Me-the-Money Consultants and completes the following transactions in March:

March	1	Birch invested $150,000 cash along with $22,000 of office equipment.
	1	Prepaid $6,000 cash for three months' rent for an office. (*Hint:* Debit Prepaid Rent for $6,000.)
	2	Made credit purchases of office equipment for $3,000 and office supplies for $1,200.
	6	Completed services for a client and immediately received $4,000 cash.
	9	Completed a $7,500 project for a client, who will pay within 30 days.
	10	Paid cash to settle the account payable created on March 2.
	19	Paid $5,000 cash for the premium on a 12-month insurance policy.
	22	Received $3,500 cash as partial payment for the work completed on March 9.
	25	Completed work for another client for $3,820 on credit.
	31	Birch withdrew $5,100 cash from the business for personal use.
	31	Purchased $600 of additional office supplies on credit.
	31	Paid $500 cash for this month's utility bill.

Required

1. Prepare general journal entries to record these transactions (use the account titles listed in part 2).

2. Open the following accounts (use the balance column format): Cash (101); Accounts Receivable (106); Office Supplies (124); Prepaid Insurance (128); Prepaid Rent (131); Office Equipment (163); Accounts Payable (201); Stuart Birch, Capital (301); Stuart Birch, Withdrawals (302); Services Revenue (403); and Utilities Expense (690). Post journal entries to the accounts and enter the balance after each posting.

Check   Cash bal. $136,700

3. Prepare a trial balance as of the end of this month's operations.

Problem 3-5A

Classifying accounts in financial statements

Loretta Pacey operates a surveying company. For the first few months of the company's life (through February 28), the accounting records were maintained by an outside accounting service. According to those records, the L. Pacey, Capital account balance is $65,000 as of February 28. To save on expenses, Pacey decides to keep the records herself. She manages to record March's transactions properly, but she has problems classifying accounts in financial statements. Her versions of the balance sheet and income statement follow. Using the information contained in these financial statements, prepare revised statements, including a statement of changes in owner's equity for the month of March.

PACEY SURVEYING		
Income Statement		
For Month Ended March 31, 2002		
Revenue		
Investments by owner	$4,000	
Unearned surveying fees	8,000	
Total revenues		$12,000
Expenses		
Rent expense	4,100	
Telephone expense	700	
Surveying equipment	6,400	
Advertising expense	4,200	
Utilities expense	400	
Insurance expense	1,000	
Withdrawals by owner	3,000	
Total expenses		19,800
Net income (loss)		$(7,800)

PACEY SURVEYING
Balance Sheet
March 31, 2002

Assets		Liabilities	
Cash	$ 4,900	Accounts payable	$ 3,400
Accounts receivable	3,700	Surveying fees earned	20,000
Prepaid insurance	2,800	Short-term notes payable	55,400
Prepaid rent	3,200	Total liabilities	$ 78,800
Office supplies	400		
Buildings	71,000		
Land	46,000	**Equity**	
Salaries expense	4,000	Loretta Pacey, Capital	$ 57,200
Total assets	$136,000	Total liabilities and equity	$136,000

Check L. Pacey, Capital, March 31, 2002, $71,600

Mark Bauman started a business called Bauman Movers and began operations in June. He correctly recorded the following journal entries during June:

Problem 3-6A

Interpreting journals; posting; correcting a trial balance

June 1	Cash		50,000	
	Trucks		34,000	
	Mark Bauman, Capital			84,000
2	Office Supplies		1,393	
	Cash			1,393
4	Moving Equipment		11,500	
	Accounts Payable			11,500
8	Cash		1,000	
	Accounts Receivable		12,000	
	Moving Fees Earned			13,000
12	Cash		2,200	
	Moving Fees Earned			2,200
15	Prepaid Insurance		3,400	
	Cash			3,400
21	Cash		12,000	
	Accounts Receivable			12,000
23	Accounts Payable		11,500	
	Cash			11,500
25	Office Equipment		17,800	
	Mark Bauman, Capital			17,800
29	Office Supplies		3,105	
	Accounts Payable			3,105
30	Mark Bauman, Withdrawals		5,913	
	Cash			5,913
30	Wages Expense		7,384	
	Cash			7,384

Based on these entries, Bauman prepared the trial balance shown on the top of the next page.

Preparation Component

1. Bauman remembers something about trial balances and realizes that he has at least one error. To help him find the error(s), set up the following balance column accounts and post his entries to them: Cash (101); Accounts Receivable (106); Office Supplies (124); Prepaid Insurance (128); Trucks (153); Office Equipment (163); Moving Equipment (167); Accounts Payable (201); Mark Bauman, Capital (301); Mark Bauman, Withdrawals (302); Moving Fees Earned (401); and Wages Expense (623).

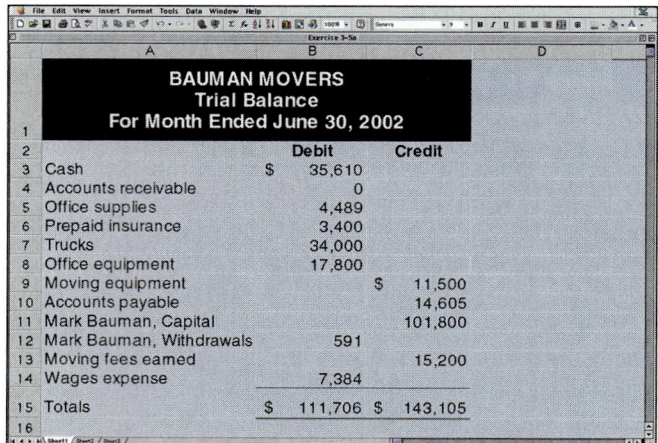

Analysis Components

2. Although Bauman's journal entries are correct, he forgot to provide explanations. Analyze each entry and present a reasonable explanation of what happened for each one.

3. Prepare a correct trial balance and describe the errors that Bauman made.

Problem 3-7A
Analyzing account balances and reconstructing transactions

Juan Mayetta started an engineering firm called Mayetta Engineering. He began operations and completed seven transactions in May, which included his initial investment of $18,000 cash. After these transactions, the ledger included the following accounts with normal balances:

Cash	$37,641
Office supplies	890
Prepaid insurance	4,600
Office equipment	12,900
Accounts payable	12,900
Juan Mayetta, Capital	18,000
Juan Mayetta, Withdrawals	3,329
Engineering fees earned	36,000
Rent expense	7,540

Required

Preparation Component

1. Prepare a trial balance for this business at the end of May.

Analysis Components

2. Analyze the accounts and their balances and prepare a list that describes each of the seven most likely transactions and their amounts.

3. Prepare a schedule of cash received and cash paid showing how the seven transactions in part (2) yield the $37,641 ending Cash balance.

PROBLEM SET B

Problem 3-1B
Preparing and posting general journal entries; preparing a trial balance

Lummus Management Services opens for business and completes these transactions in September:

Sept. 1 Rhonda Lummus, the owner, invests $38,000 cash along with office equipment valued at $15,000.

2 Prepaid $9,000 cash for three months' rent for office space. (*Hint:* Debit Prepaid Rent for $9,000.)

4 Made credit purchases of office equipment for $8,000 and office supplies for $2,400.

8 Completed work for a client and immediately received $3,280 cash.

12 Completed a $15,400 project for a client, who will pay within 30 days.

13 Paid the account payable created on September 4 in cash.

19 Paid $1,900 cash for the premium on an 18-month insurance policy.

22 Received $7,700 cash as partial payment for the work completed on September 12.

24 Completed work for another client for $2,100 on credit.

28 Rhonda Lummus withdrew $5,300 cash from the business for personal use.

29 Purchased $550 of additional office supplies on credit.

30 Paid $860 cash for this month's utility bill.

Required

1. Prepare general journal entries to record these transactions (use account titles listed in part 2).
2. Open the following ledger accounts (use the balance column format): Cash (101); Accounts Receivable (106); Office Supplies (124); Prepaid Insurance (128); Prepaid Rent (131); Office Equipment (163); Accounts Payable (201); Rhonda Lummus, Capital (301); Rhonda Lummus, Withdrawals (302); Service Fees Earned (401); and Utilities Expense (690). Post journal entries from part *1* to the ledger accounts and enter the balance after each posting.
3. Prepare a trial balance as of the end of this month's operations.

Check   Cash Bal., $21,520

North Consulting completed the following transactions during June:

a. Nick North, the sole proprietor, invested $35,000 cash along with office equipment valued at $11,000 in the new business.
b. Purchased land and a small office building. The land is worth $7,500, and the building is worth $40,000. The purchase price is paid with $15,000 cash and a long-term note payable for $32,500.
c. Purchased $500 of office supplies on credit.
d. Nick North invested his personal automobile in the business. The automobile has a value of $8,000 and is to be used exclusively in the business.
e. Purchased $1,200 of additional office equipment on credit.
f. Paid $1,000 cash salary to an assistant.
g. Provided services to a client and collected $3,200 cash.
h. Paid $540 cash for this month's utilities.
i. Paid cash to settle the account payable created in transaction *c*.
j. Purchased $5,000 of new office equipment by paying $3,400 cash and trading in old equipment with a recorded net cost of $1,600.
k. Completed $4,200 of services for a client. This amount is to be received within 30 days.
l. Paid $1,000 cash salary to an assistant.
m. Received $2,200 cash on the receivable created in transaction *k*.
n. North withdrew $1,100 cash from the business for personal use.

Problem 3-2B
Recording transactions in T-accounts; preparing a trial balance

Required

1. Open the following T-accounts: Cash; Accounts Receivable; Office Supplies; Automobiles; Office Equipment; Building; Land; Accounts Payable; Long-Term Notes Payable; Nick North, Capital; Nick North, Withdrawals; Fees Earned; Salaries Expense; and Utilities Expense.
2. Record the preceding transactions by entering debits and credits directly in T-accounts. Use the transaction letters to identify each debit and credit entry.
3. Determine the balance of each account and prepare a trial balance as of June 30.

Check   Trial balance totals, $95,100

At the beginning of April, Brooke Wilson launched a custom computer programming company called Softways. The company had the following transactions during April:

a. Brooke Wilson invested $65,000 cash, office equipment with a value of $5,750, and $30,000 of computer equipment.
b. Purchased land for an office. The land is worth $22,000 and is paid for with $5,000 cash and a long-term note payable for $17,000.
c. Purchased a portable building with $34,500 cash and moved it onto the business's land.
d. Paid $5,000 cash for the premium on a two-year insurance policy.
e. Provided services to a client and collected $4,600 cash.
f. Purchased additional computer equipment for $4,500. Paid $800 cash and signed a long-term note payable for the $3,700 balance.
g. Completed $4,250 of services for a client. This amount is to be received within 30 days.
h. Purchased $950 of additional office equipment on credit.

Problem 3-3B
Recording transactions in T-accounts; preparing a trial balance; computing a debt ratio

i. Completed client services for $10,200 on credit.

j. Received a bill for rent of a computer testing device that was used on a recently completed job. The $580 rent must be paid within 30 days.

k. Collected $5,100 cash from the client described in transaction *i*.

l. Paid $1,800 cash wages to an assistant.

m. Paid cash to settle the account payable created in transaction *h*.

n. Paid $608 cash for some repairs to an item of computer equipment.

o. Brooke Wilson withdrew $6,230 cash from the business for personal use.

p. Paid $1,800 cash wages to an assistant.

q. Paid $750 cash for advertisements in the local newspaper during April.

Required

1. Open the following T-accounts: Cash; Accounts Receivable; Prepaid Insurance; Office Equipment; Computer Equipment; Building; Land; Accounts Payable; Long-Term Notes Payable; Brooke Wilson, Capital; Brooke Wilson, Withdrawals; Fees Earned; Wages Expense; Computer Rental Expense; Advertising Expense; and Repairs Expense.

Check Trial balance totals, $141,080

2. Record the transactions by entering debits and credits directly in T-accounts. Use the transaction letters to identify each debit and credit. Prepare a trial balance as of April 30.

3. Calculate the company's debt ratio. Use $129,312 as its total assets. Are the company's assets financed more by debt or equity?

Problem 3-4B

Preparing and posting general journal entries; preparing a trial balance

Shaw Management Services opens for business and completes these transactions in November:

Nov. 1   Ken Shaw, the owner, invested $30,000 cash along with $15,000 of office equipment.

     2   Prepaid $4,500 cash for three months' rent for an office (*Hint:* Debit Prepaid Rent for $4,500.)

     4   Made credit purchases of office equipment for $2,500 and of office supplies for $600.

     8   Completed work for a client and immediately received $3,400 cash.

     12   Completed a $10,200 project for a client, who will pay within 30 days.

     13   Paid cash to settle the account payable created on November 4.

     19   Paid $1,800 cash for the premium on a 24-month insurance policy.

     22   Received $5,200 cash as partial payment for the work completed on November 12.

     24   Completed work for another client for $1,750 on credit.

     28   Ken Shaw withdrew $5,300 cash from the business for personal use.

     29   Purchased $249 of additional office supplies on credit.

     30   Paid $831 cash for this month's utility bill.

Required

1. Prepare general journal entries to record these transactions (use account titles listed in part 2).

2. Open the following accounts (use the balance column format): Cash (101); Accounts Receivable (106); Office Supplies (124); Prepaid Insurance (128); Prepaid Rent (131); Office Equipment (163); Accounts Payable (201); Ken Shaw, Capital (301); Ken Shaw, Withdrawals (302); Services Revenue (403); and Utilities Expense (690). Post journal entries to the accounts and enter the balance after each posting.

Check Cash bal., $23,069

3. Prepare a trial balance as of the end of this month's operations.

Problem 3-5B

Classifying accounts in financial statements

Christina Savery operates a computer programming company specializing in html programming and Web site construction. For the first few months of the company's life (through April 30), the accounting records were maintained by an outside accounting service. According to those records, C. Savery, Capital account balance is $13,500 as of April 30. To save on expenses, Savery decides to keep the records herself. She manages to record May's transactions properly, but she has problems classifying accounts in financial statements. Her versions of the balance sheet and income statement follow. Using the information contained in these financial statements, prepare revised statements, including a statement of changes in owner's equity for the month of May.

R2D2 CONSULTING
Income Statement
May 31

Revenue		
Investments by owner	$5,000	
Unearned programming fees	7,000	
Total revenues		$12,000
Expenses		
Rent expense	3,100	
Telephone expense	800	
Office equipment	5,500	
Advertising expense	2,200	
Utilities expense	580	
Insurance expense	900	
Withdrawals by owner	6,555	
Total expenses		19,635
Net income (loss)		$(7,635)

R2D2 CONSULTING
Balance Sheet
For Month Ended May 31

Assets		Liabilities	
Cash	$ 5,900	Accounts payable	$ 2,000
Accounts receivable	3,600	Programming fees earned	40,000
Prepaid insurance	1,800	Short-term notes payable	3,135
Prepaid rent	5,100	Total liabilities	$45,135
Office supplies	600		
Computer equipment	30,000	**Equity**	
Salaries expense	4,000	Christina Savery, Capital	5,865
Total assets	$51,000	Total liabilities and equity	$51,000

Check   Savery, Capital, May 31,
$40,365

Chuck Naylor started a business called All Board on April 1 and completed several transactions in April. The following are the journal entries that he correctly recorded during April:

Problem 3-6B

Interpreting journals; posting; correcting a trial balance

April 1	Cash	12,000	
	Store Equipment	8,000	
	Chuck Naylor, Capital		20,000
2	Prepaid Insurance	600	
	Cash		600
6	Accounts Receivable	2,000	
	Fees Earned		2,000
9	Office Supplies	400	
	Office Equipment	4,100	
	Accounts Payable		4,500
11	Cash	1,100	
	Fees Earned		1,100
14	Accounts Payable	200	
	Office Supplies		200
20	Cash	1,750	
	Accounts Receivable		1,750
21	Accounts Payable	4,300	
	Cash		4,300
23	Automobile	9,000	
	Chuck Naylor, Capital		9,000
28	Chuck Naylor, Withdrawals	800	
	Cash		800
29	Salaries Expense	1,200	
	Cash		1,200
30	Office Supplies	490	
	Accounts Payable		490

Based on these entries, Naylor prepared this trial balance:

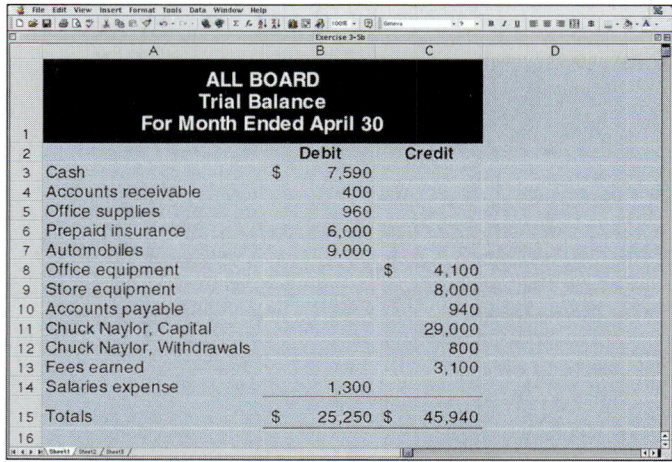

ALL BOARD Trial Balance For Month Ended April 30		
	Debit	Credit
Cash	$ 7,590	
Accounts receivable	400	
Office supplies	960	
Prepaid insurance	6,000	
Automobiles	9,000	
Office equipment		$ 4,100
Store equipment		8,000
Accounts payable		940
Chuck Naylor, Capital		29,000
Chuck Naylor, Withdrawals		800
Fees earned		3,100
Salaries expense	1,300	
Totals	$ 25,250	$ 45,940

Required

Preparation Component

1. Naylor remembers something about trial balances and realizes that he has at least one error. To help him find the error(s), set up the following balance column accounts and post his entries to them: Cash (101); Accounts Receivable (106); Office Supplies (124); Prepaid Insurance (128); Automobiles (151); Office Equipment (163); Store Equipment (165); Accounts Payable (201); Chuck Naylor, Capital (301); Chuck Naylor, Withdrawals (302); Fees Earned (401); and Salaries Expense (622).

Analysis Component

2. Although Naylor's journal entries are correct, he forgot to provide explanations. Analyze each entry and present a reasonable explanation of what happened for each one.

Check Trial balance total, $32,590

3. Prepare a correct trial balance and describe the errors that Naylor made.

Problem 3-7B
Analyzing account balances and reconstructing transactions

Cassandra Todd started a Web consulting firm called Todd Solutions. She began operations and completed seven transactions in April that resulted in the following accounts, which all have normal balances:

Cash	$19,982
Office supplies	760
Prepaid rent	1,800
Office equipment	12,250
Accounts payable	12,250
Cassandra Todd, Capital	15,000
Cassandra Todd, Withdrawals	5,200
Consulting fees earned	20,400
Operating expenses	7,658

Required

Preparation Component

Check Trial balance total, $47,650

1. Prepare a trial balance for this business at the end of April.

Analysis Component

2. Analyze the accounts and their balances and prepare a list that describes each of the seven most likely transactions and their amounts.

3. Present a schedule that shows how the seven transactions in part (2) yield the $19,982 Cash balance.

(This comprehensive problem starts in this chapter and continues in Chapters 4 and 5. Because of its length, it is most readily solved if you use the Working Papers that accompany this textbook.)

On October 1, 2002, Sela Solstise launched a computer services company called **Sierra Systems**, which is organized as a sole proprietorship and provides consulting services, computer system installations, and custom program development. Solstise adopts the calendar year for reporting purposes and expects to prepare the company's first set of financial statements on December 31, 2002. The initial chart of accounts for its accounting system includes these items:

Account	No.	Account	No.
Cash	101	Sela Solstise, Capital	301
Accounts Receivable	106	Sela Solstise, Withdrawals	302
Computer Supplies	126	Computer Services Revenue	403
Prepaid Insurance	128	Wages Expense	623
Prepaid Rent	131	Advertising Expense	655
Office Equipment	163	Mileage Expense	676
Computer Equipment	167	Miscellaneous Expenses	677
Accounts Payable	201	Repairs Expense, Computer	684

Required

1. Prepare journal entries to record each of the following transactions for Sierra Systems.

Oct. 1 Sela Solstise invested $55,000 cash, a $20,000 computer system, and $8,000 of office equipment in the business.

2 Paid $3,300 cash for four months' rent. (*Hint:* Debit Prepaid Rent for $3,300.)

3 Purchased computer supplies on credit for $1,420 from Appier Office Products.

5 Paid $2,220 cash for one year's premium on a property and liability insurance policy. (*Hint:* Debit Prepaid Insurance for $2,220.)

6 Billed Prime Leasing $4,800 for services performed in installing a new Web server.

8 Paid cash for the computer supplies purchased from Appier Office Products on Oct. 3.

10 Hired Suzie Smith as a part-time assistant for $125 per day, as needed.

12 Billed Prime Leasing another $1,400 for services performed.

15 Received $4,800 cash from Prime Leasing on its account.

17 Paid $805 cash to repair computer equipment damaged when moving it.

20 Paid $1,940 cash for an advertisement in the local newspaper.

22 Received $1,400 cash from Prime Leasing on its account.

28 Billed Dade Company $5,208 for services performed.

31 Paid Suzie Smith's wages in cash for seven days' work.

31 Solstise withdrew $3,600 cash from the business for personal use.

Nov. 1 Reimbursed Solstise in cash for business automobile mileage allowance (Solstise logged 1,000 miles at $0.32 per mile).

2 Received $4,633 cash from Elan Corporation for computer services performed.

5 Purchased computer supplies for $1,125 cash from Appier Office Products.

8 Billed Foster Co. $5,668 for services performed.

13 Received notification from Antonio's Engineering Co. that Sierra's bid of $3,950 for an upcoming project is accepted.

18 Received $2,208 cash from Dade Company as partial payment of the bill dated October 28.

22 Donated $250 cash to the United Way in the company's name.

24 Completed work for Antonio's Engineering Co. and sent it a bill for $3,950.

25 Sent another bill to Dade Company for the past-due amount of $3,000.

28 Reimbursed Solstise in cash for business automobile mileage (1,200 miles at $0.32 per mile).

30 Paid Suzie Smith's wages in cash for 14 days' work.

30 Solstise withdrew $2,000 cash from the business for personal use.

2. Open balance column ledger accounts and post the journal entries from part *1* to them.

Beyond the Numbers

Reporting in Action

BTN 3-1   Refer to **Nike**'s financial statements in Appendix A to answer the following questions.

Required

1. How many revenue categories does Nike report on its consolidated statement of income?
2. What current assets are reported on Nike's consolidated balance sheet?
3. What current liabilities are reported on its balance sheet?
4. For the year ended May 31, 2000, how much cash is paid in dividends?
5. What is Nike's debt ratio at May 31, 2000? (*Hint:* Use Liabilities = Assets − Shareholders' Equity.) How does this compare to its ratio at May, 31 1999?

Swoosh Ahead

6. Assess Nike's annual report for a fiscal year ending after May 31, 2000, from its Web site [**www.nike.com**] or through the SEC's EDGAR database [**www.sec.gov**]. Recompute Nike's debt ratio with the updated annual report information. Compare the May 31, 2000, fiscal year-end debt ratio to any subsequent year's debt ratio that you are able to calculate.

Comparative Analysis

BTN 3-2   Key comparative figures ($ millions) for both **Nike** and **Reebok** follow:

Key Figures	Nike	Reebok
Total liabilities	$2,720.9	$1,035.3
Total equity	3,136.0	528.8

Required

Use the information in the preceding table to answer the following questions:

1. What are total assets for (*a*) Nike and (*b*) Reebok?
2. What is the debt ratio for (*a*) Nike and (*b*) Reebok?
3. Which of the two companies has the higher degree of financial leverage? What does this imply?

Ethics Challenge

BTN 3-3   Review the *You Make the Call—Ethics* case from the first part of this chapter involving the cashier. The guidance answer suggests that you should not comply with the assistant manager's request.

Required

Propose and evaluate two other courses of action you might consider, and explain why.

Communicating in Practice

BTN 3-4   The class should be divided into teams. Each team is to select an industry, and each team member is to select a different company in that industry. Each team member is to acquire the annual report of the company selected. Annual reports can be obtained in many ways, including accessing the SEC's EDGAR database [**www.sec.gov**].

Required

1. Each team member should use the annual report to compute the debt ratio.
2. Communicate with teammates via a meeting, e-mail, or telephone. The team must prepare a single memorandum reporting (*a*) the meaning of the debt ratio, (*b*) how different companies compare to each other, and (*c*) the industry norm. Identify any conclusions or consensus of opinion reached during the team's discussion. The memo is to be copied and distributed to the instructor and all classmates.

BTN 3-5   Access EDGAR online [www.edgar-online.com] and locate the 10-K report of **Amazon.com** (ticker AMZN) filed on March 29, 2000. Review its cash flow statements reported for fiscal years ended 1997, 1998, and 1999 to answer the following questions:

1. What are the amounts of its net losses reported for each of these three years?
2. Does Amazon's operations provide cash or use cash for each of these three years?
3. If Amazon has a net loss and a use of cash provided by operations in 1999, how is it possible that the cash balance at December 31, 1999, shows an increase relative to the balance at January 1, 1999?

Taking It to the Net

A1

BTN 3-6   The expanded accounting equation consisting of assets, liabilities, owner's capital, owner's withdrawals, revenues, and expenses can give us useful information on changes in a company's financial position.

Required

1. Form *learning teams* of six (or more) members. Each team member must select one of the six components and each team must have at least one expert on each component: (*a*) assets, (*b*) liabilities, (*c*) owner's capital, (*d*) owner's withdrawals, (*e*) revenues, and (*f*) expenses.
2. Form *expert teams* of individuals who selected the same component in (*1*). Expert teams are to draft a report that each expert will present to his/her learning team addressing the following:
   a. Identify for its component the (i) increase and decrease side of the account and (ii) normal balance side of the account.
   b. Describe a transaction, with amounts, that increases its component.
   c. Using the transaction and amounts in (*b*), verify the equality of the accounting equation and then explain any effects on the income statement and statement of cash flows.
   d. Describe a transaction, with amounts, that decreases its component.
   e. Using the transaction and amounts in (*d*), verify the equality of the accounting equation and then explain any effects on the income statement and statement of cash flows.
3. Each expert should return to his/her learning team. In rotation, each member presents his/her expert team's report to the learning team. Team discussion is encouraged.

Teamwork in Action

C3   A1

BTN 3-7   Read the article "Can Amazon Make It?" in the July 10, 2000, issue of *Business Week*. You may access this article online at the book's Web site.

Required

1. As of July 2000, why were analysts and investors skeptical about **Amazon**'s future?
2. In the article, how does CEO Jeff Bezos respond to the critics?
3. What five strategies for Amazon's survival does the article suggest?

Business Week Activity

C3   A1

BTN 3-8   Liang Lu is a young entrepreneur who operates Lu Music Services, offering singing lessons and instruction on musical instruments. Lu wishes to expand but needs a loan. The bank requests Lu to prepare a balance sheet and key financial ratios. Lu has not kept formal records but is able to provide the following accounts and their amounts as of December 31, 2002:

Entrepreneurial Decision

 A1   A2

Cash	$ 1,800	Accounts Receivable . . .	$4,800	Prepaid Insurance . .	$ 750
Prepaid Rent	4,700	Store Supplies	3,300	Equipment	25,000
Accounts Payable . .	1,100	Unearned Lesson Fees . .	7,800	L. Lu, Capital*	31,450
Annual net income . .	20,000				

* Capital account reflects all revenues, expenses, and withdrawals through Dec. 31, 2002.

Required

1. Prepare a balance sheet as of December 31, 2002, for Lu Music Services.
2. Compute Lu's debt ratio, return on equity (from Chapter 2), and return on assets (from Chapter 1). Assume average equity and average assets equal their respective ending balances.
3. Do you think the prospects of a $15,000 bank loan are good? Why or why not?

4

Accrual Accounting and Financial Statements

"I think you have to go with your gut and stay on course"—Katrina Garnett

A Look Back

Chapter 3 explained the analysis and recording of transactions. We showed how to work with source documents, T-accounts, double-entry accounting, ledgers, postings, and trial balances.

A Look at This Chapter

This chapter explains the timing of reports and the need to adjust accounts. Adjusting accounts is important for recognizing revenues and expenses in the proper period. We also describe the adjusted trial balance and how it is used to prepare financial statements.

A Look Ahead

Chapter 5 highlights the completion of the accounting cycle. We explain the important final steps in the accounting process. These include closing procedures, the post-closing trial balance, and reversing entries.

CrossWorlds of Accounting

e BURLINGAME, CA—Although ads for her company show her in black eveningwear, Australian-born Katrina Garnett is much more than a pretty face. "In Silicon Valley, the first question you get as a woman is 'How technical are you?'" says Garnett. With degrees in both business and engineering and experience in product management, she certainly meets the threshold. But Garnett is not your stereotypical nerd from Silicon Valley. Her captivating charm and keen business sense set her apart. Her two-year-old company, **CrossWorlds** (**CrossWorlds.com**) has set itself apart in making *Fortune*'s list of *Cool Companies*.

CrossWorlds pioneers new software known as *processware*. Processware integrates the business activities of a company, including its accounting processes. However, getting quality output from processware requires quality accounting data recorded from business transactions. It also requires the user to understand the accounting process.

Unfortunately, "integration [of business and accounting processes] has been a runaway expense" for most companies, explains Garnett. CrossWorlds offers a new way to control those expenses. The secret of CrossWorlds' success is its innovative software that links business transactions, accounting reports, and decision making. For integration to work, however, decision makers must understand the concept of accounting adjustments, the system of accounting entries and reports, and the difference between accrual and cash numbers.

CrossWorlds' processware has attracted the attention of such clients as Hewlett-Packard and digital TV provider PRIMESTAR. Its sales are expected to approach $20 million this year. The total processware market is about $2 billion per year and growing. "It's an open opportunity for everyone," says Garnett. This means "being aggressive and pursuing it and networking like a fiend." But success with processware (and business) requires an understanding of accounting processes and reports—without it you don't stand a chance. [Sources: *Entrepreneur*, November 12, 1998; *CrossWorlds Web Site*, May, 2001; *Sydney Morning Herald*, May 26, 1998.]

Learning Objectives

Conceptual

C1 Explain the importance of periodic reporting and the time period principle.

C2 Describe the purpose of adjusting accounts at the end of a period.

C3 Explain accrual accounting and how it makes financial statements more useful.

C4 Identify the types of adjustments and their purpose.

Analytical

A1 Explain how accounting adjustments link to financial statements.

A2 Compute profit margin and describe its use in analyzing company performance.

Procedural

P1 Prepare and explain adjusting entries.

P2 Explain and prepare an adjusted trial balance.

P3 Prepare financial statements from an adjusted trial balance.

Chapter Preview

Financial statements reflect revenues when earned and expenses when incurred. This is known as *accrual accounting*. Accrual accounting requires several steps. We described many of these steps in Chapter 3. We showed how companies use accounting systems to collect information about *external* transactions and events. We also explained how journals, ledgers, and other procedures are useful in preparing financial statements. This chapter describes the accounting process for producing useful information involving *internal* transactions and events. An important part of this process is adjusting the account balances, which are then reported in financial statements. Adjusting accounts is necessary so that financial statements at the end of a reporting period reflect the effects of all transactions. We also define and explain a company's profit margin.

Timing and Reporting

Regular, or periodic, reporting is an important part of the accounting process. This section describes the impact on the accounting process of the point in time or the period of time that a report refers to.

The Accounting Period

C1 Explain the importance of periodic reporting and the time period principle.

The value of information is often linked to its timeliness. Useful information must reach decision makers frequently and promptly. To provide timely information, accounting systems prepare reports at regular intervals. This results in an accounting process impacted by the time period (or periodicity) principle. The **time period principle** assumes that an organization's activities can be divided into specific time periods such as a month, a three-month quarter, or a year as shown in Exhibit 4.1. Time periods covered by statements are called **accounting,** or *reporting,* **periods.** Most organizations use a year as their primary accounting period. Reports covering a one-year period are known as **annual financial statements.** Many organizations also prepare **interim financial statements** covering one, three, or six months of activity.

"Nike releases its earnings per share of . . ."

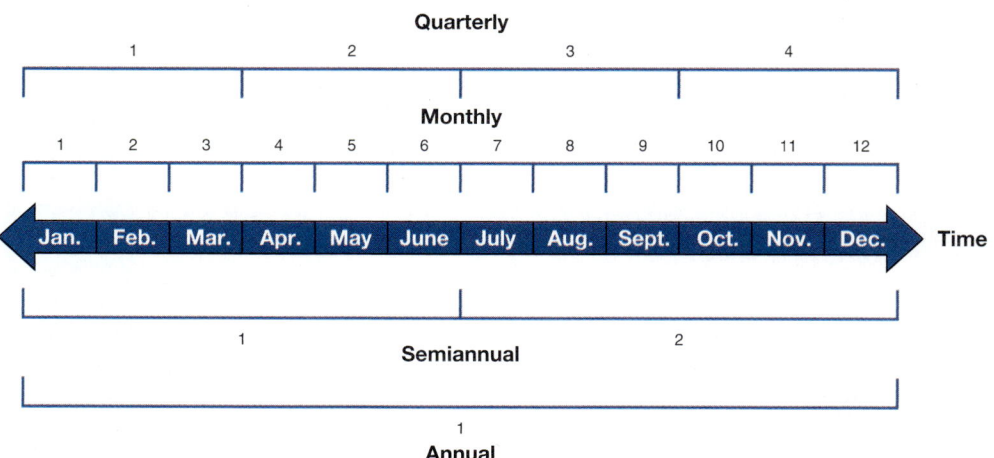

Exhibit 4.1

Accounting Periods

The annual reporting period is not always a calendar year ending on December 31. An organization can adopt a **fiscal year** consisting of any 12 consecutive months. It is also acceptable to adopt an annual reporting period of 52 weeks. For example, **GAP**'s fiscal year consistently ends the final week of January or the first week of February each year.

Companies with little seasonal variation in sales during the year often choose the calendar year as their fiscal year. For example, the financial statements of **Alcoa** reflect a fiscal year that ends on December 31. Companies experiencing seasonal variations in sales often choose a fiscal year corresponding to their natural business year. The **natural business year** ends when sales activities are at their lowest point during the year. The natural business year for retailers ends around January 31, after the holiday season. Examples of these companies include **Wal-Mart**, **Kmart**, **Dell**, and **FUBU**. Most start their annual accounting periods on or near February 1.

Purpose of Adjusting

The usual accounting process is to record external transactions and events (with outside parties) during an accounting period. After external transactions have been recorded, several accounts in the ledger need adjustments before their balances appear in financial statements. This need arises because internal transactions and events remain unrecorded.

An example is the cost of certain assets that expire as time passes. The Prepaid Insurance account of **FastForward** is one of these. FastForward's trial balance (in Exhibit 3.16) shows Prepaid Insurance (asset) with a balance of $2,400. This amount is the premium for *two years* of insurance benefits beginning on December 1. By December 31, one month's coverage is used up. Because these benefits cost an average of $100 per month ($2,400/24 months), the Prepaid Insurance account balance must be reduced by one month's cost. The December income statement must report a $100 cost as insurance expense. Moreover, at December 31, the Prepaid Insurance asset account is adjusted to a balance of $2,300. This adjusted balance reflects the remaining 23 months of insurance benefits.

Another example is FastForward's $9,720 balance in Supplies. This balance includes the costs of all supplies that FastForward purchased in December. At December 31, many of these supplies have been used up. The costs of supplies used must be reported as an expense on the December income statement. Also, the Supplies asset account balance must be adjusted to include the costs of only the remaining unused supplies. Other accounts also require adjustments to prepare financial statements. We explain in the next section how this adjusting process is carried out.

C2 Describe the purpose of adjusting accounts at the end of a period.

Concept 4-1

Point: Many companies record adjusting entries only at the end of each year because of the time and cost necessary. For interim financial statements, adjustments sometimes are omitted.

Recognizing Revenues and Expenses

We use the time period principle to divide a company's activities into specific time periods, but not all activities are complete when financial statements are prepared. This means we must make some adjustments in reporting to avoid misleading decision makers.

We rely on two principles in the adjusting process: revenue recognition and matching. Chapter 2 explained that the *revenue recognition principle* requires that revenue be recorded when earned, not before and not after. Most companies earn revenue when they provide services and products to customers. If FastForward provides consulting to a client in December, the revenue is earned in December. This means it must be reported on the December income statement, even if the client paid for the services in a month other than December. A major goal of the adjusting process is to have revenue recognized (reported) in the time period when it is earned.

The **matching principle** aims to record expenses in the same accounting period as the revenues that are earned as a result of these expenses. This matching of costs (expenses) with benefits (revenues) is a major part of the adjusting process. One example is FastForward, which earns monthly revenues while operating in rented store space. The earning of revenues required rented space. The matching principle tells us that rent must be reported on the income statement for December, even if rent is paid in a month either before or after December. This ensures that rent expense for December is matched with December's revenues.

Point: IBM's revenues from services to customers is recorded when services are performed. Its revenues from product sales are recorded when products are shipped.

> ### Did You Know?
>
> **Doing Accounting Time**   **Centennial Technology**, like many companies, recognizes revenue when it ships products. What is not common is that Centennial's CEO shipped products to the warehouses of friends and reported it as revenue. In another case, **Informix**, a database software maker, records revenue when products are passed to distributors. It admits now that there were "errors in the way revenues had been recorded," and its CEO is in jail. These and other risky revenue recognition practices are often revealed by a large increase in the accounts receivable to sales ratio.

Global: Some countries allow *income smoothing*. This means balance sheet reserves can be set up by reducing income in good years and drawing down those reserves in bad years to increase income.

C3 Explain accrual accounting and how it makes financial statements more useful.

Point: Cash basis accounting is generally used for tax returns.

Exhibit 4.2
Accrual Basis Accounting for Prepaid Insurance

Matching expenses with revenues often requires us to predict certain events. When we use financial statements, we must understand that they require estimates. This means they include measures that are not precise. **Walt Disney**'s annual report explains that its film and television production costs from shows such as *Dinosaur* and *The Kid* are matched to revenues based on a ratio of current revenues from the show divided by its predicted total revenues.

Accrual Basis versus Cash Basis

Accrual basis accounting uses the adjusting process to recognize revenues when earned and to match expenses with revenues. This means that the economic effects of revenues and expenses are recorded when earned or incurred, not when cash is received or paid.

Cash basis accounting means that revenues are recognized when cash is received and expenses are recorded when cash is paid. For example, if a business provides services in December but does not receive cash from clients until January, then cash basis accounting reports this revenue in January. This means that cash basis net income for a period is the difference between cash receipts and cash payments (disbursements). Cash basis accounting for the income statement, balance sheet, and statement of changes in owner's equity is not consistent with accepted accounting principles. It is commonly held that accrual accounting better indicates business performance than information about cash receipts and payments. Accrual accounting also increases the *comparability* of financial statements from one period to another. Yet many companies and users of statements still find cash basis accounting useful for several internal reports and business decisions. While accrual basis accounting is generally accepted for external reporting, information about cash flows is also useful and is the reason companies must report a statement of cash flows.

To see the impact of these different accounting systems, let's consider FastForward's Prepaid Insurance account. FastForward paid $2,400 for two years of insurance coverage beginning on December 1, 2001. Accrual accounting says that $100 of insurance expense is reported on December's income statement. Another $1,200 of expense is reported in year 2002, and the remaining $1,100 is reported as expense in the first 11 months of 2003. Exhibit 4.2 illustrates this allocation of insurance cost across these three years.

Transaction: Purchase 24 months' insurance beginning December 2001	Insurance Expense 2001				Insurance Expense 2002				Insurance Expense 2003			
	Jan $0	Feb $0	Mar $0	Apr $0	Jan $100	Feb $100	Mar $100	Apr $100	Jan $100	Feb $100	Mar $100	Apr $100
	May $0	June $0	July $0	Aug $0	May $100	June $100	July $100	Aug $100	May $100	June $100	July $100	Aug $100
	Sept $0	Oct $0	Nov $0	Dec $100	Sept $100	Oct $100	Nov $100	Dec $100	Sept $100	Oct $100	Nov $100	Dec $0

Exhibit 4.3
Cash Basis Accounting for Prepaid Insurance

A cash basis income statement for December 2001 reports insurance expense of $2,400 as shown in Exhibit 4.3. The cash basis income statements for years 2002 and 2003 report no insurance expense from this policy.

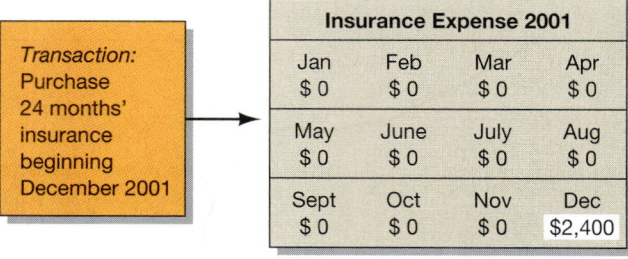

Transaction: Purchase 24 months' insurance beginning December 2001	Insurance Expense 2001				Insurance Expense 2002				Insurance Expense 2003			
	Jan $0	Feb $0	Mar $0	Apr $0	Jan $0	Feb $0	Mar $0	Apr $0	Jan $0	Feb $0	Mar $0	Apr $0
	May $0	June $0	July $0	Aug $0	May $0	June $0	July $0	Aug $0	May $0	June $0	July $0	Aug $0
	Sept $0	Oct $0	Nov $0	Dec $2,400	Sept $0	Oct $0	Nov $0	Dec $0	Sept $0	Oct $0	Nov $0	Dec $0

The accrual basis balance sheet reports the remaining unexpired premium as a Prepaid Insurance asset. The cash basis never reports this asset. The cash basis information is less useful for most business decisions because reported income for 2001–2003 fails to match the cost of insurance with the insurance benefits received for those years.

Quick Check

1. Describe a company's annual reporting period.
2. Why do companies prepare interim financial statements?
3. What accounting principles most directly drive the adjusting process?
4. Is cash basis accounting consistent with the matching principle? Why or why not?
5. If your company pays a $4,800 premium on April 1, 2002, for two years' insurance coverage, how much insurance expense is reported in 2003 using cash basis accounting?

Answers—p. 147

The process of adjusting accounts involves analyzing each account balance, and the transactions and events that affect it, to determine any needed adjustments. An **adjusting entry** is recorded to bring an asset or liability account balance to its proper amount when an adjustment is needed. This entry also updates the related expense or revenue account. This section explains why adjusting entries are needed to provide useful information. It also shows the mechanics of adjusting entries and their links to financial statements.

Adjusting Accounts

C4 Identify the types of adjustments and their purpose.

Framework for Adjustments

Adjustments are necessary for transactions and events that extend over more than one period. It is helpful to group adjustments by the timing of cash receipt or cash payment in relation to the recognition of the related revenues or expenses. Exhibit 4.4 identifies four types of adjustments that involve both expenses and revenues.

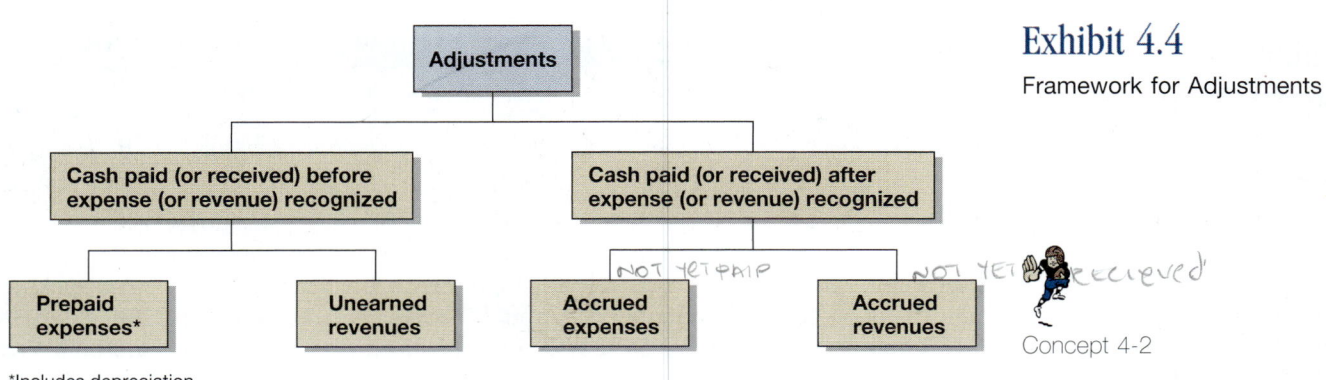

*Includes depreciation.

Exhibit 4.4

Framework for Adjustments

Concept 4-2

Both prepaid expenses (including depreciation) and unearned revenues reflect transactions when cash is paid or received *before* a related expense or revenue is recognized. (Prepaids are also called *deferrals* because the recognition of an expense (or revenue) is *deferred* until after the related cash is paid (or received).) Accrued expenses and accrued revenues reflect transactions when cash is paid or received *after* a related expense or revenue is recognized. Adjusting entries are necessary for each of these so that revenues, expenses, assets, and liabilities are correctly reported. It is helpful to remember that each adjusting entry affects one or more income statement accounts *and* one or more balance sheet accounts. An adjusting entry *never* involves the Cash account.

Point: Source documents provide information for daily transactions, and in many businesses the recordkeepers record them. Adjustments often require more knowledge and are usually handled by more senior accounting professionals.

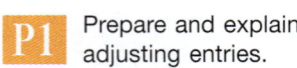

Prepare and explain
adjusting entries.

"Here is the first 24 months'
insurance in advance."

Adjusting Prepaid Expenses

Prepaid expenses refer to items *paid for* in advance of receiving their benefits. Prepaid expenses are assets. When these assets are used, their costs become expenses. Adjusting entries for prepaids involve increasing (debiting) expenses and decreasing (crediting) assets as shown in the T-accounts of Exhibit 4.5. Adjustments are made to reflect transactions and events that impact the amount of prepaid expenses (including passage of time). To illustrate the accounting for prepaid expenses, this section focuses on prepaid insurance, supplies, and depreciation.

Prepaid Insurance

We illustrate prepaid insurance using **FastForward**'s payment of $2,400 for 24 months of insurance benefits beginning on December 1, 2001. With the passage of time, the benefits of the insurance gradually expire and a portion of the Prepaid Insurance asset becomes expense. For instance, one month's insurance coverage expires by December 31, 2001. This expense is $100, or 1/24 of $2,400. Our adjusting entry to record this expense and reduce the asset follows:

Exhibit 4.5

Adjusting for Prepaid
Expenses

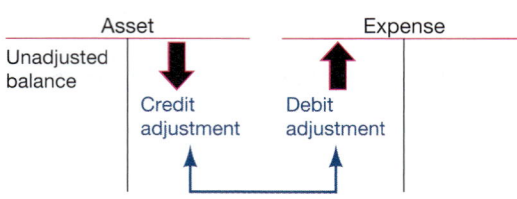

Assets = Liabilities + Equity
  −100   −100

	Adjustment (a)		
Dec. 31	Insurance Expense	100	
	Prepaid Insurance		100
	To record first month's expired insurance.		

Posting this adjusting entry affects the accounts as shown in Exhibit 4.6.

Exhibit 4.6

Insurance Accounts after
Adjusting for Prepaids

Prepaid Insurance			128
Dec. 26	2,400	**Dec. 31**	**100**
Balance	2,300		

Insurance Expense			637
Dec. 31	**100**		

Point: An alternative method to
record prepaids is to initially debit
expense for the total amount. The
adjusted financial statement
information is identical under either
method. We discuss this alternative
in the appendix to this chapter.

After adjusting and posting, the $100 balance in Insurance Expense and the $2,300 balance in Prepaid Insurance are ready for reporting in financial statements. *Not* making the adjustment on or before December 31 would (1) understate expenses by $100 and overstate net income by $100 for the December income statement and (2) overstate both Prepaid Insurance (assets) and equity (because of net income) by $100 in the December 31 balance sheet. It is also evident from Exhibit 4.2 that year 2002's adjustments must transfer a total of $1,200 from Prepaid Insurance to Insurance Expense, and year 2003's adjustments must transfer the remaining $1,100 to Insurance Expense.

Supplies

Supplies are another prepaid expense often requiring adjustment. FastForward purchased $9,720 of supplies in December and used some of them during that month. Use of supplies creates expenses equal to their cost. Daily usage of supplies is not recorded in FastForward's accounts because this information is not needed. Also, making only one adjusting entry when financial statements are prepared can reduce recordkeeping costs. Because the income statement is for December, the cost of supplies used during December must be recognized as an expense. FastForward computes (takes inventory of) its remaining unused supplies. The amount of these remaining supplies is then deducted from the total unadjusted amount of supplies to obtain the amount used. FastForward has $8,670 of supplies remaining of the $9,720 total supplies in December. The $1,050 difference between these two amounts is the cost of the supplies used. This amount is December's supplies expense. Our adjusting entry to record this expense and reduce the Supplies asset account follows:

Point: Some assets, liabilities, revenues, and expenses are so small in amount they do not affect analyses of financial statements. For example, office supplies are sometimes immaterial and immediately recorded as expenses. Management still sets up controls over their use.

Adjustment (b)		
Dec. 31	Supplies Expense	1,050
	Supplies	1,050
	To record supplies used.	

Assets = Liabilities + Equity
−1,050   −1,050

Posting this adjusting entry affects the accounts as shown in Exhibit 4.7. The balance of the Supplies account is $8,670 after posting—equaling the cost of remaining supplies. *Not* making the adjustment on or before December 31 would (1) understate expenses by $1,050 and overstate net income by $1,050 for the December income statement and (2) overstate both Supplies and equity (because of net income) by $1,050 in the December 31 balance sheet.

Supplies			126
Dec. 2	2,500	Dec. 31	1,050
6	7,100		
26	120		
Balance	8,670		

Supplies Expense			652
Dec. 31	1,050		

Exhibit 4.7

Supplies Accounts after Adjusting for Prepaids

Other Prepaid Expenses

Other prepaid expenses, such as Prepaid Rent, are accounted for exactly as Insurance and Supplies are. We should also note that some prepaid expenses are both paid for and fully used up within a single accounting period. One example is when a company pays monthly rent on the first day of each month. This payment creates a prepaid expense on the first day of each month that fully expires by the end of the month. In these special cases, we can record the cash paid with a debit to the expense account instead of an asset account. This practice is described more completely later in the chapter.

You Make the Call

Appraiser A small publishing company signs a well-known athlete to write a book. The company pays the athlete $500,000 to sign, plus future book royalties. A note to the company's financial statement says "prepaid expenses include $500,000 in author signing fees to be matched against future expected sales." Is this accounting for the signing bonus acceptable? How does it affect your appraisal?

Answer—p. 147

Adjusting for Depreciation

A special category of prepaid expenses is that of plant and equipment. **Plant and equipment** refers to long-term tangible assets used to produce and sell products and services. These assets are expected to provide benefits for more than one period. Examples of plant and equipment are buildings, machines, vehicles, and fixtures. All plant and equipment assets, with a general exception for land, eventually wear out or decline in usefulness. The costs of these assets are deferred but are gradually reported as expenses in the income statement over the assets' useful lives (benefit periods). **Depreciation** is the process of allocating the cost of these assets over their expected useful lives. Depreciation expense is recorded with an adjusting entry similar to that for other prepaid expenses.

Recall **FastForward** purchased equipment for $26,000 in early December to use in earning revenue. This equipment's cost must be depreciated. Chuck Taylor expects this

Point: Depreciation does not necessarily measure the decline in market value.

Point: We use straight-line depreciation in the early chapters of the book when necessary to explain accounting for plant and equipment.

equipment to have a useful life (benefit period) of four years. He expects to sell the equipment for about $8,000 at the end of four years. This means the *net* cost of this equipment over its useful life is $18,000 ($26,000 − $8,000). We can use several methods to allocate this $18,000 net cost to expense. FastForward uses a method called *straight-line depreciation.* (Depreciation methods are explained in Chapter 11, but we briefly describe the straight-line method to help explain the adjusting process). **Straight-line depreciation** allocates equal amounts of an asset's net cost to depreciation during its useful life. Dividing the $18,000 net cost by the 48 months in the asset's useful life gives an average monthly cost of $375 ($18,000/48). Our adjusting entry to record monthly depreciation expense follows:

Assets = Liabilities + Equity
−375   −375

Adjustment (c)		
Dec. 31	Depreciation Expense	375	
	Accumulated Depreciation—Equipment ...		375
	To record monthly equipment depreciation.		

Posting this adjusting entry affects the accounts as shown in Exhibit 4.8. After posting the adjustment, the Equipment account ($26,000) less its Accumulated Depreciation ($375) account equals the $25,625 net cost of the 47 remaining months in the benefit period. The $375 balance in the Depreciation Expense account is reported in the December income statement. *Not* making the adjustment at December 31 would (1) understate expenses by $375 and overstate net income by $375 for the December income statement and (2) overstate both assets and equity (because of income) by $375 in the December 31 balance sheet.

Exhibit 4.8

Accounts after Depreciation Adjustments

Equipment 167				Accumulated Depreciation — Equipment 168				Depreciation Expense — Equipment 612	
Dec. 3	26,000				Dec. 31	375	Dec. 31	375	

Decreases in an asset account are commonly recorded with a credit to the account, but this procedure is *not* followed when recording depreciation. Instead, depreciation is recorded in a separate contra account. A **contra account** is an account linked with another account and having an opposite normal balance. It is reported as a subtraction from the other account's balance. For instance, FastForward's contra account of Accumulated Depreciation—Equipment is subtracted from the Equipment account in the balance sheet (see Exhibit 4.22).

Use of a contra account allows balance sheet readers to know both the full cost of an asset and the total amount of depreciation charged to expense. By knowing both these amounts, decision makers can better assess a company's capacity and its need to replace an asset. For example, FastForward's balance sheet shows both the $26,000 original cost of equipment and the $375 balance in the accumulated depreciation contra account. This information reveals that the equipment is close to new. If FastForward reports equipment only at its net amount of $25,625, users cannot assess the equipment's age or its need for replacement.

The title of this contra account, *Accumulated Depreciation,* indicates that the account includes total depreciation expense for all prior periods for which the asset was used. For instance, FastForward's Equipment and Accumulated Depreciation accounts appear as shown in Exhibit 4.9 on February 28, 2002, after three months of adjusting entries.

You Make the Call

Entrepreneur You are preparing an offer to purchase a family-run restaurant. The depreciation schedule for the restaurant's building and equipment shows costs of $175,000 and accumulated depreciation of $155,000. This leaves a net for building and equipment of $20,000. Is this information useful in deciding on a purchase offer?

Answer—p. 147

Point: The cost principle requires an asset to be initially recorded at original cost. Depreciation causes the asset's book value to decline over time.

Equipment		167
Dec. 3	26,000	

Accumulated Depreciation – Equipment		168
	Dec. 31	375
	Jan. 31	375
	Feb. 28	375
	Balance	**1,125**

Exhibit 4.9

Accounts after Three Months of Depreciation Adjustments

These account balances would be reported in the assets section of the February 28 balance sheet as shown in Exhibit 4.10. The net amount is called *book value*. **Book value** equals the asset's original costs less its accumulated depreciation.

Assets		
Cash		$ _____
⋮		
Equipment	$26,000	
Less accumulated depreciation	(1,125)	24,875
Total Assets		$ _____

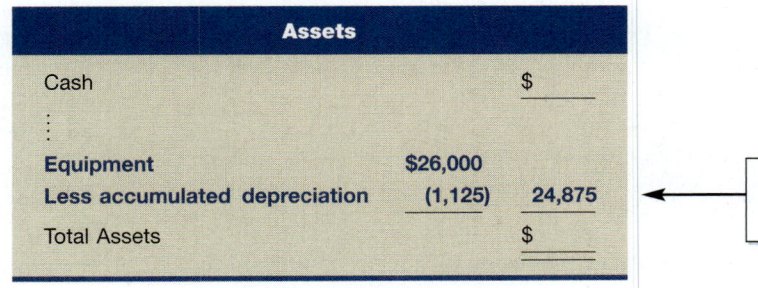

Commonly titled *Equipment, net*

Exhibit 4.10

Equipment and Accumulated Depreciation in the February 28th Balance Sheet

Adjusting Unearned Revenues

Unearned revenues refer to cash *received* in advance of providing products and services. Unearned revenues, also known as *deferred revenues,* are liabilities. When cash is accepted, an obligation to provide products or services is accepted. As products or services are provided, the unearned revenues become *earned* revenues. Adjusting entries for unearned revenues involve increasing (crediting) revenues and decreasing (debiting) unearned revenues as shown in Exhibit 4.11. These adjustments reflect transactions and events that impact unearned revenues (including passage of time).

An example of unearned revenues is from **The New York Times**, which reports unexpired (unearned) subscriptions of more than $80 million: "Proceeds from subscriptions . . . are deferred at the time

Point: *To defer* is to postpone. We postpone reporting amounts received as revenues until they are earned.

Liability		Revenue	
↓	Unadjusted balance		↑
Debit adjustment		Credit adjustment	

Exhibit 4.11

Adjusting for Unearned Revenues

of sale and are included in . . . income on a pro rata basis over the terms of the subscription." Unearned revenues are more than 10% of total current liabilities for the Times. Another example comes from the **Boston Celtics**. When the Celtics receive cash from advance ticket sales and broadcast fees, they record it in an unearned revenue account called *Deferred Game Revenues.* The Celtics recognize this unearned revenue with adjusting entries on a game-by-game basis. Because the NBA regular season begins in October and ends in April, revenue recognition is mainly limited to this period. For a recent season, the Celtics' quarterly revenues (in millions) were $0 for July–September; $25 for October–December; $40 for January–March; and $11 for April–June.

FastForward also has unearned revenues. It agreed on December 26 to provide consulting services to a client for a fixed fee of $1,500 for 30 days. On that same day, this client paid the first 60 days' fees in advance, covering the period December 27 to February 24. The entry to record the cash received in advance is

Assets = Liabilities + Equity
+3,000　　+3,000

Dec. 26	Cash	3,000	
	Unearned Consulting Revenue		3,000
	Received advance payment for services over the next 60 days.		

This advance payment increases cash and creates an obligation to do consulting work over the next 60 days. As time passes, FastForward will earn this payment through consulting. By December 31, it has provided five days' service and earns one-twelfth of the $3,000 unearned revenue. This amounts to $250 ($3,000 × 5/60). The *revenue recognition principle* implies that $250 of unearned revenue must be reported as revenue on the December income statement. The adjusting entry to reduce the liability account and recognize earned revenue is

Assets = Liabilities + Equity
　　　　−250　　+250

	Adjustment (d)		
Dec. 31	Unearned Consulting Revenue	250	
	Consulting Revenue		250
	To record earned revenue that was received in advance ($3,000 × 5/60).		

After posting the adjusting entry, the accounts appear as in Exhibit 4.12. The adjusting entry transfers $250 from unearned revenue (a liability account) to a revenue account. *Not* making the adjustment (1) understates revenue and net income by $250 in the December income statement and (2) overstates unearned revenue and understates equity by $250 on the December 31 balance sheet.

Exhibit 4.12

Revenue Accounts after Adjusting for Prepaids

Unearned Consulting Revenue		236	
Dec. 31	**250**	Dec. 26	3,000
		Balance	2,750

Consulting Revenue		403
	Dec. 10	4,200
	12	1,600
	31	250
	Balance	6,050

Adjusting Accrued Expenses

Accrued expenses refer to costs that are incurred in a period but are both unpaid and unrecorded. Accrued expenses must be reported on the income statement of the period when incurred. Adjusting entries for recording accrued expenses involves increasing (debiting) expenses and increasing (crediting) liabilities as shown in Exhibit 4.13. This adjustment recognizes expenses incurred in a period but not yet paid. Common examples of accrued expenses are salaries, interest, rent, and taxes. We use salaries and interest to show how to adjust accounts for accrued expenses.

Exhibit 4.13

Adjusting for Accrued Expenses

Accrued Salaries Expense

FastForward's employee earns $70 per day, or $350 for a five-day workweek beginning on Monday and ending on Friday. This employee is paid every two weeks on Friday. On December 12 and 26, the wages are paid, recorded in the journal, and posted to the ledger.

However, the calendar in Exhibit 4.14 shows three working days after the December 26 payday (29, 30, and 31). This means the employee has earned three days' salary by the close of business on Wednesday, December 31, yet this salary cost is not paid or recorded.

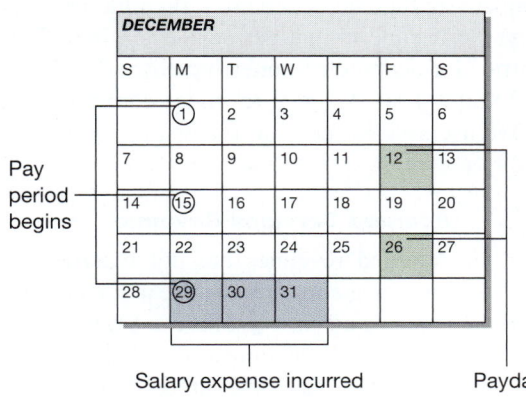

 is part of the Exhibit below.

DECEMBER								JANUARY						
S	M	T	W	T	F	S		S	M	T	W	T	F	S
	①	2	3	4	5	6						1	2	3
7	8	9	10	11	12	13		4	5	6	7	8	9	10
14	⑮	16	17	18	19	20		11	12	13	14	15	16	17
21	22	23	24	25	26	27		18	19	20	21	22	23	24
28	㉙	30	31					25	26	27	28	29	30	31

Pay period begins

Salary expense incurred   Payday   Payday

Exhibit 4.14
Salary Accrual and Paydays

Point: Assume: (1) the last payday for the year is December 19, (2) the next payday is January 2, and (3) December 25 is a paid holiday. Record the December 31 adjusting entry. *Answer:* We must accrue pay for eight working days instead of three:
Salaries Expense . . . 560
  Salaries Payable 560

The financial statements would be incomplete if FastForward fails to report the added expense and liability to the employee for unpaid salary from December 29–31. The adjusting entry to account for accrued salaries is

	Adjustment (e)		
Dec. 31	Salaries Expense	210	
	Salaries Payable		210
	To record three days' accrued salary (3 × $70).		

Assets = Liabilities + Equity
        +210   −210

After the adjusting entry is posted, the expense and liability accounts appear as shown in Exhibit 4.15:

Salaries Expense	**622**	**Salaries Payable**	**209**
Dec. 12	700		Dec. 31	210
26	700		
31	210		
Balance	1,610		

Exhibit 4.15
Salary Accounts after Accrual Adjustments

This means that $1,610 of salaries expense is reported on the income statement and a $210 salaries payable (liability) is reported in the balance sheet. *Not* making the adjustment (1) understates Salaries Expense and overstates net income by $210 in the December income statement and (2) understates Salaries Payable (liabilities) and overstates equity by $210 on the December 31 balance sheet.

Point: An employer records salaries expense and vacation pay liability when employees earn vacation pay.

Accrued Interest Expense

Companies commonly have accrued interest expense on notes payable and other long-term liabilities at the end of a period. Interest expense is incurred with the passage of time. Unless interest is paid on the last day of an accounting period, we need to adjust accounts for interest expense incurred but not yet paid. This means we must accrue interest cost from the most recent payment date up to the end of the period. (The formula for computing accrued interest is: *Payable amount owed × Annual interest rate × Fraction of year since last payment date.*) The adjusting entry is similar to the one for accruing unpaid salary, with a debit to Interest Expense and a credit to Interest Payable (liability).

Adjusting Accrued Revenues

Accrued revenues refer to revenues earned in a period that are both unrecorded and not yet received in cash (or other assets). Accrued revenues are earned revenues that must be reported on the income statement. An example is a technician who bills customers only when the job is done. If one-third of a job is complete by the end of a period, then the technician must record one-third of the expected billing as revenue in that period—even though there is no billing or collection. The adjusting entries for accrued revenues increase (debit) assets and increase (credit) revenues as shown in Exhibit 4.16. Accrued revenues commonly arise from services, products, interest, and rent. We use service fees and interest to show how to adjust accounts for accrued revenues.

Exhibit 4.16

Adjusting for Accrued Revenues

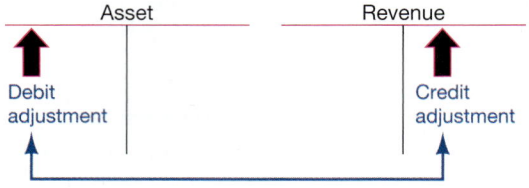

Accrued Services Revenue

Accrued revenues are not recorded until adjusting entries are made at the end of the accounting period. These accrued revenues are earned but unrecorded because either the buyer has not yet paid for them or the seller has not yet billed the buyer.

FastForward provides an example. In the second week of December, it agreed to provide 30 days of consulting services to a local sports club for a fixed fee of $2,700. The terms of the initial agreement call for FastForward to provide services from December 12, 2001, through January 10, 2002, or 30 days of service. The club agrees to pay FastForward $2,700 on January 10, 2002, when the service period is complete. At December 31, 2001, 20 days of services have already been provided. Since the contracted services are not yet entirely provided, FastForward has neither billed the club yet nor recorded the services already provided. Still, FastForward has earned two-thirds of the 30-day fee, or $1,800 ($2,700 × 20/30). The *revenue recognition principle* implies we must report the $1,800 on the December income statement because it was earned in December. The balance sheet also must report that the club owes FastForward $1,800. The year-end adjusting entry to account for accrued services revenue is

Assets = Liabilities + Equity
+1,800   +1,800

	Adjustment (f)		
Dec. 31	Accounts Receivable	1,800	
	Consulting Revenue		1,800
	To record 20 days' accrued revenue.		

The debit to accounts receivable reflects the amount the club owes FastForward for consulting services already provided. After the adjusting entry is posted, the affected accounts appear as shown in Exhibit 4.17.

Exhibit 4.17

Receivable and Revenue Accounts after Accrual Adjustments

Accounts Receivable			106
Dec. 12	1,900	Dec. 22	1,900
31	1,800		
Balance	1,800		

Consulting Revenue			403
		Dec. 10	4,200
		12	1,600
		31	250
		31	1,800
		Balance	7,850

Point: What is the adjusting entry if the 30-day consulting period began on December 22? *Answer:* One-third of the fee is earned:
Accounts Receivable . . . 900
  Consulting Revenue . . . 900

Accounts receivable are reported on the balance sheet at $1,800, and $7,850 of consulting revenue is reported on the income statement. *Not* making the adjustment would understate (1) both Consulting Revenue and net income by $1,800 in the December income statement and (b) both Accounts Receivable (assets) and equity by $1,800 on the December 31 balance sheet.

Accrued Interest Revenue

In addition to the accrued interest expense we described earlier, interest can yield an accrued revenue when a debtor owes money (or other assets) to a company. If a company is holding notes or accounts receivable that produce interest revenue, we must adjust the accounts to record any earned and yet uncollected interest revenue. The adjusting entry is similar to the one for accruing services revenue. Specifically, we debit Interest Receivable (asset) and credit Interest Revenue.

Links to Financial Statements

The process of adjusting accounts is intended to bring an asset or liability account balance to its correct amount. The adjusting entry also updates a related expense or revenue account. These adjustments are necessary for transactions and events that extend over more than one period. Adjusting entries are posted like any other entry.

Exhibit 4.18 lists the four types of transactions requiring adjustment. Adjusting entries are necessary for each. Understanding this exhibit is important to understanding the adjusting process and its importance to financial statements. Remember that each adjusting entry affects one or more income statement accounts *and* one or more balance sheet accounts. An adjusting entry never affects cash.

Exhibit 4.19 summarizes the adjusting entries of FastForward on December 31. The post-

> ### You Make the Call
>
> **Loan Officer** You are the loan officer when the owner of an electronics store applies for a business loan. The store's financial statements reveal large increases in current year's revenues and profits. Analysis shows these increases are due to a promotion that lets consumers buy now and pay nothing until January 1 of next year. The store records these sales as accrued revenue. Does your analysis raise any concerns?
>
> Answer—p. 147

> ### You Make the Call—Ethics
>
> **Financial Officer** At year-end, the president instructs you, the financial officer, to not record accrued expenses until next year because they will not be paid until then. The president also asks about a recent purchase order from a major customer that requires merchandise to be delivered two weeks after the year-end. The president points out that the order has been received, that your company is ready to make delivery, and that you are to record this sale in the current year. Your company would report a net income instead of a net loss if you carry out these orders. What do you do?
>
> Answer—p. 147

A1 Explain how accounting adjustments link to financial statements.

Category	Before Adjusting		Adjusting Entry
	Balance Sheet	**Income Statement**	
Prepaid expense	Asset overstated	Expense understated	Dr. Expense Cr. Asset*
Unearned revenues	Liability overstated	Revenue understated	Dr. Liability Cr. Revenue
Accrued expenses	Liability understated	Expense understated	Dr. Expense Cr. Liability
Accrued revenues	Asset understated	Revenue understated	Dr. Asset Cr. Revenue

* For depreciation, the credit is to Accumulated Depreciation (contra asset).

Exhibit 4.18

Summary of Adjustments and Financial Statement Links

ing of each adjusting entry to ledger accounts was shown when we described each transaction and is not repeated here. Adjusting entries are often set apart from other journal entries with the caption Adjusting Entries as shown.

Exhibit 4.19

Journalizing Adjusting Entries

GENERAL JOURNAL				Page #	
Date	**Account Titles and Explanation**	**PR**	**Debit**	**Credit**	
2001	Adjusting Entries				
(a) Dec. 31	Insurance Expense		100		
	Prepaid Insurance			100	
	To record expired insurance.				
(b) 31	Supplies Expense		1,050		
	Supplies			1,050	
	To record supplies used.				
(c) 31	Depreciation Expense—Equipment		375		
	Accumulated Depreciation—Equipment			375	
	To record monthly depreciation on equipment.				
(d) 31	Unearned Consulting Revenue		250		
	Consulting Revenue			250	
	To record earned revenue received in advance.				
(e) 31	Salaries Expense		210		
	Salaries Payable			210	
	To record three days' accrued salary.				
(f) 31	Accounts Receivable		1,800		
	Consulting Revenue			1,800	
	To record 20 days' accrued revenue.				

Quick Check

6. If you omit an adjusting entry for accrued revenues of $200 at year-end, what is this error's effect on the year-end income statement and balance sheet?

7. What is a contra account? Explain.

8. What is an accrued expense? Give an example.

9. Describe how an unearned revenue arises. Give an example.

Answers—p. 147

Adjusted Trial Balance

P2 Explain and prepare an adjusted trial balance.

An **unadjusted trial balance** is a list of accounts and balances prepared *before* adjustments are recorded. An **adjusted trial balance** is a list of accounts and balances prepared *after* adjusting entries have been recorded and posted to the ledger. Exhibit 4.20 shows both the unadjusted and the adjusted trial balances for **FastForward** at December 31, 2001. Several new accounts arise from the adjusting entries. The order of accounts in the trial balance is usually set up to match the order in the chart of accounts.

Exhibit 4.20 shows all the accounts, their adjustments, and their final adjusted balances. Each adjustment is identified by a letter in parentheses that links it to an adjusting entry shown earlier (see Exhibit 4.19 for a summary). Each amount in the Adjusted Trial Balance columns is computed by taking that account's amount from the Unadjusted Trial Balance columns and adding or subtracting its adjustment(s). To illustrate, Supplies has a $9,720 Dr. balance in the unadjusted columns. Subtracting the $1,050 Cr. amount shown in the adjustments columns yields an adjusted $8,670 Dr. balance for Supplies. An account can have more than one adjustment, such as for Consulting Revenue. Also, some accounts might not require adjusting, such as Accounts Payable for this period.

Accrual Reversals in Future Periods

The adjusting entries for both accrued expenses and accrued revenues foretell cash transactions in future periods. For example, accrued expenses at the end of one accounting period usually result in cash *payments* in the *next* period. Also, accrued revenues at the end of one

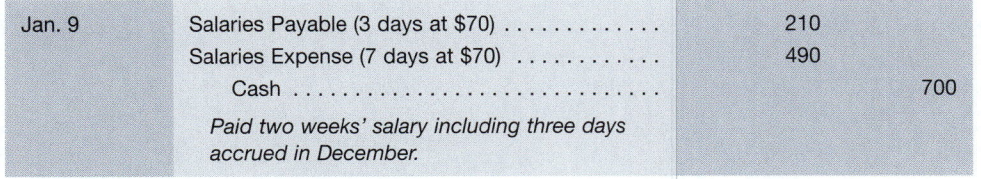

Exhibit 4.20

Unadjusted and Adjusted Trial Balances

FASTFORWARD
Trial Balance
December 31, 2001

	Unadjusted Trial Balance		Adjustments		Adjusted Trial Balance	
	Dr.	Cr.	Dr.	Cr.	Dr.	Cr.
Cash	$ 3,950				$ 3,950	
Accounts receivable	0		(f) 1,800		1,800	
Supplies	9,720			(b) 1,050	8,670	
Prepaid insurance	2,400			(a) 100	2,300	
Equipment	26,000				26,000	
Accumulated depreciation—Equip.		$ 0		(c) 375		$ 375
Accounts payable		6,200				6,200
Salaries payable		0		(e) 210		210
Unearned consulting revenue		3,000	(d) 250			2,750
Chuck Taylor, Capital		30,000				30,000
Chuck Taylor, Withdrawals	600				600	
Consulting revenue		5,800		(d) 250		7,850
				(f) 1,800		
Rental revenue		300				300
Depreciation expense—Equip.	0		(c) 375		375	
Salaries expense	1,400		(e) 210		1,610	
Insurance expense	0		(a) 100		100	
Rent expense	1,000				1,000	
Supplies expense	0		(b) 1,050		1,050	
Utilities expense	230				230	
Totals	$ 45,300	$ 45,300	$ 3,785	$ 3,785	$ 47,685	$ 47,685

accounting period usually result in cash *receipts* in the *next* period. This section explains how we account for these cash payments and cash receipts in future periods.

Paying Accrued Expenses

Recall that FastForward recorded accrued salaries with this adjusting entry:

(e) Dec. 31	Salaries Expense	210	
	Salaries Payable		210
	To record three days' accrued salary (3 × $70).		

Assets = Liabilities + Equity
       +210   −210

On Friday, January 9, the first payday of the next period, the following entry settles the accrued liability (salaries payable) and records additional salaries expense for seven days of work in January:

Jan. 9	Salaries Payable (3 days at $70)	210	
	Salaries Expense (7 days at $70)	490	
	Cash		700
	Paid two weeks' salary including three days accrued in December.		

Assets = Liabilities + Equity
−700   −210   −490

The first debit in the January 9 entry records the payment of the liability for the three days' salary accrued on December 31. The second debit records the salary for January's first seven working days (including the New Year's Day holiday) as an expense of the new accounting period. The credit records the total amount of cash paid to the employee.

Receiving Accrued Revenues

Recall that **FastForward** made the following adjusting entry to record 20 days' accrued revenue earned from its consulting contract:

(f) Dec. 31	Accounts Receivable	1,800	
	Consulting Revenue		1,800
	To record 20 days' accrued revenue.		

Assets = Liabilities + Equity
+1,800   +1,800

When FastForward receives the first month's fee on January 10, it makes the following entry to remove the accrued asset (accounts receivable) and recognize the additional revenue earned in January:

Assets = Liabilities + Equity
+2,700   +900
−1,800

Jan. 10	Cash	2,700	
	Accounts Receivable		1,800
	Consulting Revenue		900
	Received cash for accrued asset and recorded earned consulting revenue.		

The debit reflects the cash received. The first credit reflects the removal of the receivable, and the second credit records the revenue earned in January.

Preparing Financial Statements

P3 Prepare financial statements from an adjusted trial balance.

Exhibit 4.21

Preparing the Income Statement and Statement of Changes in Owner's Equity from the Adjusted Trial Balance

We can prepare financial statements directly from information in the *adjusted* trial balance. An adjusted trial balance (see the right-most columns in Exhibit 4.20) includes all balances appearing in financial statements. A trial balance summarizes information in the ledger by listing accounts and their balances, and is easier to work from than the entire ledger when preparing financial statements.

Exhibit 4.21 shows how **FastForward**'s revenue and expense balances are transferred from the adjusted trial balance to (1) the income statement and (2) the statement of changes in owner's equity. Notice that we use the net income and withdrawals account to prepare the statement of changes in owner's equity.

Exhibit 4.22 shows how FastForward's asset and liability balances on the adjusted trial balance are transferred to the balance sheet. The ending owner's equity is determined on the statement of changes in owner's equity and is transferred to the balance sheet. The balance sheet in Exhibit 4.22 is in report form. The **report form balance sheet** lists assets, liabilities, and

From Exhibit 4.20

FastForward
Adjusted Trial Balance
December 31, 2001

Acct. No.	Account Title	Debit	Credit
101	Cash	$ 3,950	
106	Accounts receivable	1,800	
126	Supplies	8,670	
128	Prepaid insurance	2,300	
167	Equipment	26,000	
168	Accumulated depreciation-Equip.		$ 375
201	Accounts payable		6,200
209	Salaries payable		210
236	Unearned consulting revenue		2,750
301	C. Taylor, Capital		30,000
302	C. Taylor, Withdrawals	600	
403	Consulting revenue		7,850
406	Rental revenue		300
612	Depreciation expense-Equip.	375	
622	Salaries expense	1,610	
637	Insurance expense	100	
640	Rent expense	1,000	
652	Supplies expense	1,050	
690	Utilities expense	230	
	Totals	$47,685	$47,685

Step 1 Prepare income statement

FastForward
Income Statement
For Month Ended December 31, 2001

Revenues:		
Consulting revenue	$7,850	
Rental revenue	300	
Total revenues		$8,150
Expenses:		
Depreciation expense—Equip.	$ 375	
Salaries expense............................	1,610	
Insurance expense.........................	100	
Rent expense.................................	1,000	
Supplies expense...........................	1,050	
Utilities expense.............................	230	
Total expenses...............................		4,365
Net income......................................		$3,785

Step 2 Prepare statement of changes in owner's equity

FastForward
Statement of Changes in Owner's Equity
For Month Ended December 31, 2001

C. Taylor, Capital, December 1.......		$ 0
Plus: Investments by owner	$30,000	
Net income	3,785	
		33,785
		$33,785
Less: Withdrawals by owner		600
C. Taylor, Capital, December 31		$33,185

From Exhibit 4.20

Step Three Prepare balance sheet

Exhibit 4.22

Preparing the
Balance Sheet
from the Adjusted
Trial Balance

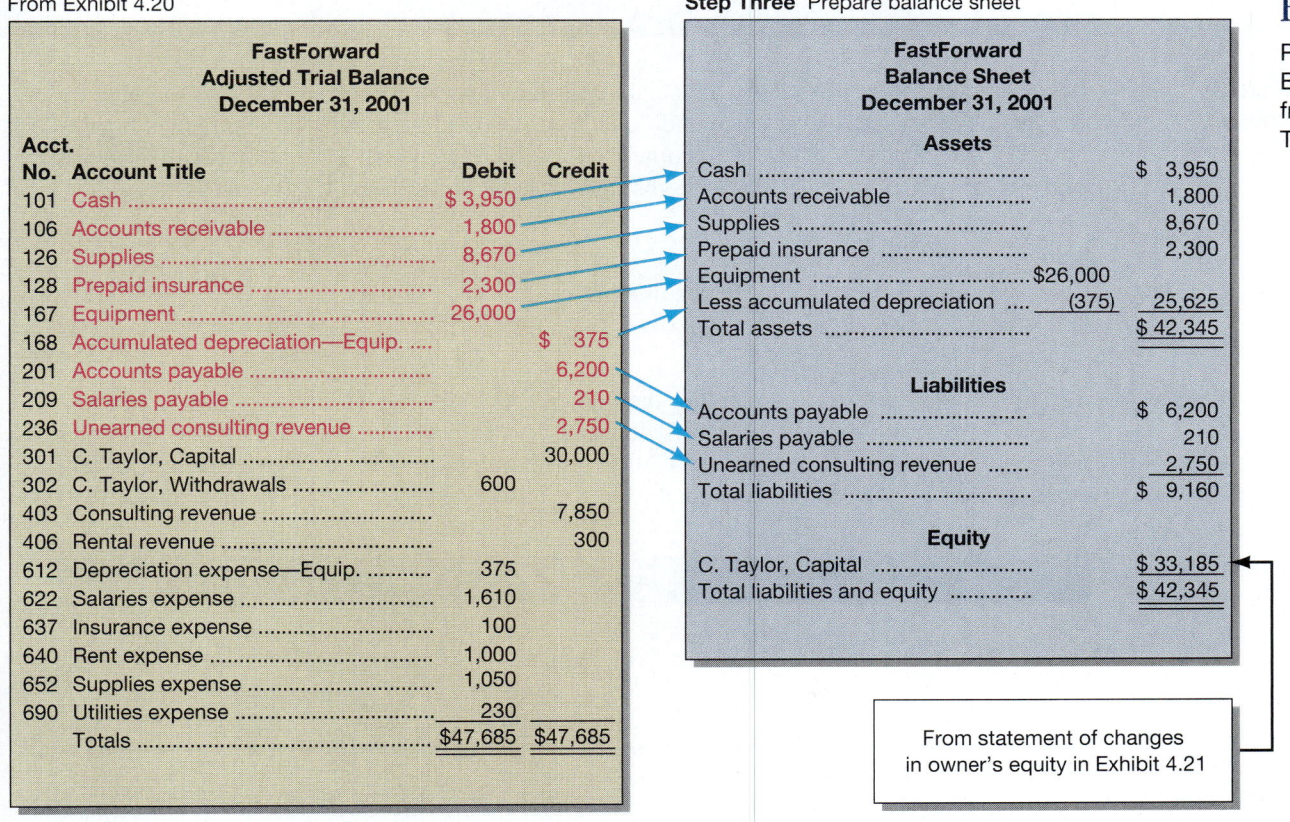

FastForward
Adjusted Trial Balance
December 31, 2001

Acct. No.	Account Title	Debit	Credit
101	Cash	$ 3,950	
106	Accounts receivable	1,800	
126	Supplies	8,670	
128	Prepaid insurance	2,300	
167	Equipment	26,000	
168	Accumulated depreciation—Equip.		$ 375
201	Accounts payable		6,200
209	Salaries payable		210
236	Unearned consulting revenue		2,750
301	C. Taylor, Capital		30,000
302	C. Taylor, Withdrawals	600	
403	Consulting revenue		7,850
406	Rental revenue		300
612	Depreciation expense—Equip.	375	
622	Salaries expense	1,610	
637	Insurance expense	100	
640	Rent expense	1,000	
652	Supplies expense	1,050	
690	Utilities expense	230	
	Totals	$47,685	$47,685

FastForward
Balance Sheet
December 31, 2001

Assets

Cash		$ 3,950
Accounts receivable		1,800
Supplies		8,670
Prepaid insurance		2,300
Equipment	$26,000	
Less accumulated depreciation	(375)	25,625
Total assets		$ 42,345

Liabilities

Accounts payable	$ 6,200
Salaries payable	210
Unearned consulting revenue	2,750
Total liabilities	$ 9,160

Equity

C. Taylor, Capital	$ 33,185
Total liabilities and equity	$ 42,345

From statement of changes
in owner's equity in Exhibit 4.21

equity in vertical order. **Nike** uses a report form. The **account form balance sheet** lists assets on the left and liabilities and equity on the right side. Its name comes from its link to the accounting equation, Assets = Liabilities + Equity. The balance sheet in Exhibit 2.15 is in account form. Both forms are widely used and are considered equally helpful to users.

We usually prepare financial statements in the following order: income statement, statement of changes in owner's equity, and balance sheet. This order makes sense since the balance sheet uses information from the statement of changes in owner's equity, which in turn uses information from the income statement. We describe the preparation of the statement of cash flows in Chapters 5 and 17.

Quick Check

10. Music-Mart records $1,000 of accrued salaries on December 31. Five days later, on January 5 (the next payday), salaries of $7,000 are paid. What is the January 5 entry?

11. Jordan Air has the following information in its unadjusted and adjusted trial balances:

	Unadjusted		Adjusted	
	Debit	Credit	Debit	Credit
Prepaid insurance	$6,200		$5,900	
Salaries payable		$ 0		$1,400

What are the adjusting entries that Jordan Air likely recorded?

12. What accounts are taken from the adjusted trial balance to prepare an income statement?

13. In preparing financial statements from an adjusted trial balance, what statement is usually prepared second?

Using the Information	**Profit Margin**

A2 Compute profit margin and describe its use in analyzing company performance.

Business decision makers want financial statements to reflect relevant information about a company's financial performance and condition. A useful measure of a company's operating results is the ratio of its net income to net sales (revenues). This ratio is called **profit margin,** or *return on sales,* and is computed as shown in Exhibit 4.23.

Exhibit 4.23

Profit Margin

$$\text{Profit margin} = \frac{\text{Net income}}{\text{Net sales}}$$

This ratio is interpreted as reflecting the percent of profit in each dollar of sales. To illustrate how we compute and use profit margin, let's look at the results of **Ben & Jerry's Homemade Ice Cream** in Exhibit 4.24. Profit margin is one measure we can use to help evaluate Ben & Jerry's performance during the past four years.

Exhibit 4.24

Ben & Jerry's Profit Margin

	1999	1998	1997	1996
Net income (in mil.)	$ 3.4	$ 6.2	$ 3.9	$ 3.9
Net sales (in mil.)	$237.0	$209.2	$174.2	$167.2
Profit margin	1.4%	3.0%	2.2%	2.3%
Industry profit margin	2.2%	1.6%	2.0%	2.1%

Ben & Jerry's average profit margin is 2.2% over this period. Year 1999 especially stands out as poor. This is mainly due to special charges tied to the discontinuance of a manufacturing plant. The profit margin is expected to increase in subsequent years. Also note the steady increase in Ben & Jerry's sales, from less than $170 million in 1996 to more than $237 million in 1999. This analysis can also benefit from a comparison of profit margins across competitors (see last row of Exhibit 4.24). Ben & Jerry's is a relatively small competitor in the super-premium ice cream industry, but its historical profit margins tend to be at or better than those of its competitors. Still, competition from larger super-premium companies keeps Ben & Jerry's from enjoying a higher margin, and played a part in its recent purchase by **Unilever**.

It is important when we evaluate the profit margin of a sole proprietorship that we modify the profit margin ratio by subtracting the value of the owner's efforts from net income. To illustrate this for **FastForward**, assume that other job opportunities indicate that the efforts of Chuck Taylor, the owner, are worth $3,500 per month. FastForward's profit margin for December 2001 is then computed as shown in Exhibit 4.25.

Point: Because sole proprietorships and partnerships are not separate legal entities, salaries to owners are not expenses. This leads to their use of the modified profit margin.

Exhibit 4.25

Modified Profit Margin

$$\text{Modified profit margin} = \frac{\text{Net income} - \text{Value of owner's efforts}}{\text{Net sales}}$$
$$= \frac{(\$3,785 - \$3,500)}{\$8,150} = 3.5\%$$

Demonstration Problem

The following information relates to Fanning's Electronics on December 31, 2002. The company, which uses the calendar year as its annual reporting period, initially records prepaid and unearned items in balance sheet accounts (assets and liabilities, respectively).

a. The company's weekly payroll is 8,750, paid every Friday for a five-day workweek. December 31, 2002, falls on a Monday, but the employees will not be paid their wages until Friday, January 4, 2003.

b. Eighteen months earlier, on July 1, 2001, the company purchased equipment that cost $20,000 and had no salvage value. Its useful life is predicted to be five years.

c. On October 1, 2002, the company agreed to work on a new housing development. For installing alarm systems in 24 new homes, the company is paid $120,000 in advance on October 1. That amount was credited to the Unearned Services Revenue account. Between October 1 and December 31, work on 20 homes was completed.

d. On September 1, 2002, the company purchased a 12-month insurance policy for $1,800. The transaction was recorded with an $1,800 debit to Prepaid Insurance.

e. On December 29, 2002, the company performed a $7,000 service that has not been billed as of December 31, 2002.

Required

1. Prepare adjusting entries needed on December 31, 2002, to record the previously unrecorded effects of these transactions and events.

2. Prepare T-accounts for accounts affected by adjusting entries. Post adjusting entries to T-accounts. Determine the adjusted balances for the Unearned Revenue and the Prepaid Insurance accounts.

3. Complete the following table describing the amounts and effects of your adjusting entries on the year 2002 income statement and the December 31, 2002, balance sheet. Use up (down) arrows to indicate an increase (decrease) in the Effect columns.

Entry	Amount in the Entry	Effect on Net Income	Effect on Total Assets	Effect on Total Liabilities	Effect on Equity

Planning the Solution

- Analyze information for each situation to determine which accounts need to be updated with an adjustment.
- Calculate the amount of each adjustment and prepare the necessary journal entries.
- Show the amount entered by each adjustment in the designated accounts, determine the adjusted balance, and then determine the balance sheet classification that the account falls within.
- Determine each entry's effect on net income for the year and on total assets, total liabilities, and equity at the end of the year.

Solution to Demonstration Problem

1. Adjusting journal entries.

(a) Dec. 31	Wages Expense	1,750	
	Wages Payable		1,750
	To accrue wages for the last day of the year ($8,750 × 1/5).		
(b) Dec. 31	Depreciation Expense—Equipment	4,000	
	Accumulated Depreciation—Equipment ...		4,000
	To record depreciation expense for the year ($20,000/5 years = $4,000 per year).		
(c) Dec. 31	Unearned Services Revenue	100,000	
	Services Revenue		100,000
	To recognize services revenue earned ($120,000 × 20/24).		
(d) Dec. 31	Insurance Expense	600	
	Prepaid Insurance		600
	To adjust for expired portion of insurance ($1,800 × 4/12).		
(e) Dec. 31	Accounts Receivable	7,000	
	Services Revenue		7,000
	To record services revenue earned.		

2. T-accounts for adjusting journal entries *a* through *e*.

Wages Expense				Wages Payable	
(a)	1,750			(a)	1,750

Depreciation Expense – Equipment				Accumulated Depreciation – Equipment	
(b)	4,000			(b)	4,000

Unearned Revenue				Services Revenue	
		Beg. Bal.	120,000	(c)	100,000
(c)	100,000			(e)	7,000
		End Bal.	20,000	Adj. Bal.	107,000

Insurance Expense				Prepaid Insurance	
(d)	600		Beg. Bal	1,800	
				(d)	600

Accounts Receivable				
(e)	7,000	End. Bal.	1,200	

3. Financial statement effects of adjusting journal entries.

Entry	Amount in the Entry	Effect on Net Income	Effect on Total Assets	Effect on Total Liabilities	Effect on Equity
a	$ 1,750	$ 1,750 ↓	No effect	$ 1,750 ↑	$ 1,750 ↓
b	4,000	4,000 ↓	$4,000 ↓	No effect	4,000 ↓
c	100,000	100,000 ↑	No effect	$100,000 ↓	100,000 ↑
d	600	600 ↓	$ 600 ↓	No effect	600 ↓
e	7,000	7,000 ↑	$7,000 ↑	No effect	7,000 ↑

APPENDIX

4A Alternative Accounting for Prepaids

This section explains an alternative in accounting for prepaid expenses and for unearned (prepaid) revenues.

Recording Prepaid Expenses in Expense Accounts

P4 Identify and explain an alternative in accounting for prepaids.

An alternative method is to record *all* prepaid expenses with debits to expense accounts. If any prepaids remain unused or unexpired at the end of an accounting period, then adjusting entries must transfer the cost of the unused portions from expense accounts to prepaid expense (asset) accounts. This alternative method is acceptable. The financial statements are identical under either method, but the adjusting entries are different. To illustrate the accounting differences between these two methods, let's look at **FastForward**'s cash payment of December 26 for 24 months of insurance coverage beginning on December 1. FastForward recorded that payment with a debit to an asset account, but it could have recorded a debit to an expense account. These alternatives are shown in Exhibit 4A.1.

			Payment Recorded as Asset	Payment Recorded as Expense
Dec. 26	Prepaid Insurance	2,400		
	Cash		2,400	
Dec. 26	Insurance Expense			2,400
	Cash			2,400

Exhibit 4A.1

Alternative Initial Entries for Prepaid Expenses

At the end of its accounting period on December 31, insurance protection for one month has expired. This means $100 ($2,400/24) of the insurance coverage expires and becomes an expense for December. The adjusting entry depends on how the original payment was recorded. This is shown in Exhibit 4A.2.

			Payment Recorded as Asset	Payment Recorded as Expense
Dec. 31	Insurance Expense	100		
	Prepaid Insurance		100	
Dec. 31	Prepaid Insurance			2,300
	Insurance Expense			2,300

Exhibit 4A.2

Adjusting Entry for Prepaid Expenses for the Two Alternatives

When these entries are posted to the accounts in the ledger, we can see that these two methods give identical results. The December 31 adjusted account balances in Exhibit 4A.3 show Prepaid Insurance of $2,300 and Insurance Expense of $100 for both methods.

Payment Recorded as Asset				Payment Recorded as Expense			
Prepaid Insurance			128	**Prepaid Insurance**			128
Dec. 26	2,400	Dec. 31	100	Dec. 31	2,300		
Balance	2,300						

Insurance Expense			637	Insurance Expense			637
Dec. 31	100			Dec. 26	2,400	Dec. 31	2,300
				Balance	100		

Exhibit 4A.3

Account Balances under Two Alternatives for Recording Prepaid Expenses

Recording Unearned Revenues in Revenue Accounts

As with prepaid expenses, an alternative method is to record *all* unearned revenues with credits to revenue accounts. If any revenues are unearned at the end of an accounting period, then adjusting entries must transfer the unearned portions from revenue accounts to unearned revenue (liability) accounts. This alternative method is acceptable. While the adjusting entries are different for these two alternatives, the financial statements are identical. To illustrate the accounting differences between these two methods, let's look at FastForward's December 26 receipt of $3,000 for consulting services covering the period December 27 to February 24. FastForward recorded this transaction with a credit to a liability account. The alternative is to record it with a credit to a revenue account as shown in Exhibit 4A.4.

			Receipt Recorded as Liability	Receipt Recorded as Revenue
Dec. 26	Cash	3,000		
	Unearned Consulting Revenue		3,000	
Dec. 26	Cash			3,000
	Consulting Revenue			3,000

Exhibit 4A.4

Alternative Initial Entries for Unearned Revenues

By the end of its accounting period on December 31, FastForward has earned $250 of this revenue. This means $250 of the liability has been satisfied. Depending on how the initial receipt is recorded, the adjusting entry is as shown in Exhibit 4A.5.

Exhibit 4A.5

Adjusting Entry for Unearned Revenues for the Two Alternatives

		Receipt Recorded as Liability	Receipt Recorded as Revenue
Dec. 31	Unearned Consulting Revenue	250	
	Consulting Revenue		250	
Dec. 31	Consulting Revenue		2,750
	Unearned Consulting Revenue			2,750

After adjusting entries are posted, the two alternatives give identical results. The December 31 adjusted account balances in Exhibit 4A.6 show unearned consulting revenue of $2,750 and consulting revenue of $250 for both methods.

Exhibit 4A.6

Account Balances under Two Alternatives for Recording Unearned Revenues

Receipt Recorded as Liability

Unearned Consulting Revenue 236			
Dec. 31	250	Dec. 26	3,000
		Balance	2,750

Consulting Revenue 403		
	Dec. 31	250

Receipt Recorded as Revenue

Unearned Consulting Revenue 236	
	Dec. 31	2,750

Consulting Revenue 403			
Dec. 31	2,750	Dec. 26	3,000
		Balance	250

Summary

C1 Explain the importance of periodic reporting and the time period principle. The value of information is often linked to its timeliness. To provide timely information, accounting systems prepare periodic reports at regular intervals. The time period principle assumes that an organization's activities can be divided into specific time periods for periodic reporting.

C2 Describe the purpose of adjusting accounts at the end of a period. After recording external transactions and events, several accounts often need adjusting for correct balances in financial statements. This need arises because internal transactions and events remain unrecorded. The purpose of adjusting accounts at the end of a period is to properly recognize revenues earned and expenses incurred for the period.

C3 Explain accrual accounting and how it enhances financial statements. Accrual accounting recognizes revenue when earned and expenses when incurred—not necessarily when cash inflows and outflows occur. This information is valuable in assessing a company's financial position and performance.

C4 Identify the types of adjustments and their purpose. Adjustments can be grouped according to the timing of cash receipts and payments relative to when they are recognized as revenues or expenses as follows: prepaid expenses, unearned revenues, accrued expenses, and accrued revenues. Adjusting entries are necessary so that revenues, expenses, assets, and liabilities are correctly reported.

A1 Explain how accounting adjustments link to financial statements. Accounting adjustments bring an asset or liability account balance to its correct amount. They also update related expense or revenue accounts. Every adjusting entry affects one or more income statement accounts *and* one or more balance sheet accounts. An adjusting entry never affects cash.

A2 Compute profit margin and describe its use in analyzing company performance. *Profit margin* is defined as the reporting period's net income divided by net sales for the same period. Profit margin reflects on a company's earnings activities by showing how much profit is in each dollar of sales.

P1 Prepare and explain adjusting entries. *Prepaid expenses* refer to items paid for in advance of receiving their benefits. Prepaid expenses are assets. Adjusting entries for prepaids involve increasing (debiting) expenses and decreasing (crediting) assets. *Unearned (or prepaid) revenues* refer to cash received in advance of providing products and services. Unearned revenues are liabilities. Adjusting entries for unearned revenues involves increasing (crediting) revenues and decreasing (debiting) unearned revenues. *Accrued expenses* refer to costs incurred in a period that are both unpaid and unrecorded. Adjusting entries for recording accrued expenses involves increasing (debiting) expenses and increasing (crediting) liabilities. *Accrued revenues* refer to revenues earned in a period that are both unrecorded and not yet received in cash. Adjusting entries for recording accrued revenues involves increasing (debiting) assets and increasing (crediting) revenues.

P2 **Explain and prepare an adjusted trial balance.** An adjusted trial balance is a list of accounts and balances prepared after recording and posting adjusting entries. Financial statements are often prepared from the adjusted trial balance.

P3 **Prepare financial statements from an adjusted trial balance.** Revenue and expense balances are transferred to the income statement and statement of changes in owner's equity. Asset, liability, and equity balances are transferred to the balance sheet. We usually prepare statements in the following order:

income statement, statement of changes in owner's equity, balance sheet, and statement of cash flows.

P4 **Identify and explain alternatives in accounting for prepaids.** Charging all prepaid expenses to expense accounts when they are purchased is acceptable. When this is done, adjusting entries must transfer any unexpired amounts from expense accounts to asset accounts. Crediting all unearned revenues to revenue accounts when cash is received is also acceptable. In this case, the adjusting entries must transfer any unearned amounts from revenue accounts to unearned revenue accounts.

Guidance Answers to **You Make the Call**

Appraiser   Prepaid expenses are items paid for in advance of receiving their benefits. They are assets and are expensed as they are used up. The publishing company's treatment of the signing bonus is acceptable provided future book sales can at least match the $500,000 expense. As an appraiser, you are concerned about the risk of future book sales. The riskier the likelihood of future book sales is, the more likely your analysis is to treat the $500,000, or a portion of it, as an expense, not a prepaid expense (asset).

Entrepreneur   Depreciation is a process of cost allocation, not asset valuation. Knowing the depreciation schedule is not especially useful in your estimation of what the building and equipment are currently worth. Your own assessment of the age, quality, and usefulness of the building and equipment is more important.

Loan Officer   Your concern in lending to this store arises from analysis of current-year sales. While increased revenues and profits

are fine, your concern is with the collectibility of these promotional sales. If the owner sold products to customers with poor records of paying bills, then probable collectibility of these sales is low. Your analysis must assess this possibility and recognize any expected losses.

Financial Officer   Omitting accrued expenses and recognizing revenue early can mislead financial statement users (including managers, owners, and lenders). One action is to request a second meeting with the president so you can explain that accruing expenses when incurred and recognizing revenue when earned are required practices. You should also mention the ethical implications of not complying with accepted practice. If the president persists, you might discuss the situation with legal counsel and any auditors involved. Your ethical action might cost you this job, but the potential pitfalls for falsification of statements, reputation loss, personal integrity, and other costs are too great.

Guidance Answers to **Quick Checks**

1. An annual reporting (or accounting) period covers one year and refers to the preparation of annual financial statements. The annual reporting period is not always a calendar year that ends on December 31. An organization can adopt a fiscal year consisting of any consecutive 12 months or 52 weeks.

2. Interim (less than one year) financial statements are prepared to provide decision makers information frequently and promptly.

3. The revenue recognition principle and the matching principle lead most directly to the adjusting process.

4. No. Cash basis accounting is not consistent with the matching principle because it reports expenses when paid, not in the period when revenue is earned as a result of those expenses.

5. No expense is reported in 2003. Under cash basis accounting the entire $4,800 is reported as expense in April 2002 when the premium is paid.

6. If the accrued revenues adjustment of $200 is not made, then both revenues and net income are understated by $200 on the

current year's income statement, and both assets and equity are understated by $200 on the balance sheet.

7. A contra account is an account that is subtracted from the balance of a related account. Use of a contra account provides more information than simply reporting a net amount.

8. An accrued expense is a cost incurred in a period that is both unpaid and unrecorded prior to adjusting entries. One example is salaries earned but not yet paid at period-end.

9. An unearned revenue arises when a firm receives cash (or other assets) from a customer before providing the services or products to the customer. A magazine subscription paid in advance is one example, season ticket sales is another.

10.

Salaries Payable	1,000	
Salaries Expense	6,000	
Cash		7,000

Paid salary including accrual from December.

11. The probable adjusting entries of Jordan Air are

Insurance Expense ....:.....	300	
Prepaid Insurance		300
To record insurance expired.		
Salaries Expense	1,400	
Salaries Payable		1,400
To record accrued salaries.		

12. Revenue accounts and expense accounts.

13. Statement of changes in owner's equity.

Glossary

Account form balance sheet balance sheet that lists assets on the left side and liabilities and equity on the right. (p. 141).

Accounting period length of time covered by financial statements; also called *reporting period*. (p. 126).

Accrual basis accounting accounting system that recognizes revenues when earned and expenses when incurred; the basis for GAAP. (p. 128).

Accrued expenses costs incurred in a period that are both unpaid and unrecorded; adjusting entries for recording accrued expenses involve increasing (debiting) expenses and increasing (crediting) liabilities. (p. 134).

Accrued revenues revenues earned in a period that are both unrecorded and not yet received in cash (or other assets); adjusting entries for recording accrued revenues involve increasing (debiting) assets and increasing (crediting) revenues. (p. 136).

Adjusted trial balance list of accounts and balances prepared after adjustments are recorded and posted. (p. 138).

Adjusting entry journal entry at the end of an accounting period to bring an asset or liability account to its proper amount and update the related expense or revenue account. (p. 129).

Annual financial statements financial statements covering a one-year period; often based on a calendar year, but any consecutive 12-month (or 52-week) period is acceptable. (p. 126).

Book value equals the asset's original costs less its accumulated depreciation. (p. 133).

Cash basis accounting accounting system that recognizes revenues when cash is received and records expenses when cash is paid. (p. 128).

Contra account account linked with another account and having an opposite normal balance; reported as a subtraction from the other account's balance. (p. 132).

Depreciation expense created by allocating the cost of plant and equipment to periods in which they are used; represents the expense of using the asset. (p. 131).

Fiscal year consecutive 12 months (or 52 weeks) chosen as the organization's annual accounting period. (p. 126).

Interim financial statements financial statements covering periods of less than one year; usually based on one-, three-, or six-month periods. (p. 126).

Matching principle requires expenses to be reported in the same period as the revenues that were earned as a result of the expenses. (p. 127).

Natural business year 12-month period that ends when a company's sales activities are at their lowest point. (p. 127).

Plant and equipment tangible long-lived assets used to produce or sell products and services; also called *fixed assets*. (p. 131).

Prepaid expenses items paid for in advance of receiving their benefits; classified as assets. (p. 130).

Profit margin ratio of a company's net income to its net sales; the percent of profit in each dollar of revenue. (p. 142).

Report form balance sheet balance sheet that lists accounts vertically in the order of assets, liabilities, and equity. (p. 140).

Straight-line depreciation method allocates equal amounts of an asset's cost (less any salvage value) to depreciation expense during its useful life. (p. 132).

Time period principle assumes an organization's activities can be divided into specific time periods such as months, quarters, or years. (p. 126).

Unadjusted trial balance list of accounts and balances prepared before adjustments are recorded and posted. (p. 138).

Unearned revenues cash (or other assets) received in advance of providing products or services; a liability. (p. 133).

[Superscript letter ᴬ denotes assignments based on Appendix 4A.]

Questions

1. What is the difference between the cash and accrual bases of accounting?

2. Why is the accrual basis of accounting generally preferred over the cash basis?

3. What type of business is most likely to select a fiscal year that corresponds to the natural business year instead of the calendar year?

4. Where is a prepaid expense reported in the financial statements?

5. What type of asset(s) requires adjusting entries to record depreciation?

6. What contra account is used when recording and reporting the effects of depreciation? Why is it used?

7. Where is unearned revenue reported in financial statements?

8. What is an accrued revenue? Give an example.

9. Why does a sole proprietorship require special procedures in calculating the profit margin?

10.^A If a company initially records prepaid expenses with debits to expense accounts, what type of account is debited in the adjusting entries for prepaid expenses?

11. Review the balance sheet of **Nike** in Appendix A. Identify two asset accounts that require adjustment before annual financial statements can be prepared.

What would be the effect on the income statement if these two asset accounts were not adjusted?

12. Review the balance sheet of **Reebok** in Appendix A. In addition to prepaid expenses and property and equipment, identify two accounts (either assets or liabilities) requiring adjusting entries.

13. Refer to **Gap**'s balance sheet in Appendix A. Identify three types of property and equipment that it must depreciate.

---

a. On July 1, 2002, McCay Company paid $1,200 for six months of insurance coverage. No adjustments have been made to the Prepaid Insurance account and it is now December 31, 2002. Prepare the journal entry to show the expiration of the insurance as of December 31, 2002.

b. Taylor Company has a supplies balance of $500 on January 1, 2002. During 2002, it purchased $2,000 of supplies. As of December 31, 2002, a supplies inventory shows $800 of supplies available. Prepare the adjusting journal entry to correctly state the balance of the Supplies account and Supplies Expense account as of December 31, 2002.

---

a. Decker Company purchases $20,000 of equipment on January 1, 2002. The equipment is expected to last five years and be worth $2,000 at the end of that time. Prepare the entry to record one year's depreciation expense for Decker's equipment as of December 31, 2002.

b. Decker Company purchases $10,000 of land on January 1, 2002. The land is expected to last indefinitely. What depreciation adjustment, if any, should Decker Company make with respect to the Land account as of December 31, 2002?

---

a. William Nelson has a client that paid $10,000 cash in advance for legal fee. He will work on this client's case over a four-month period. William receives the cash advance on October 1, 2002, and records it by debiting Cash and crediting Unearned Revenue for $10,000. It is now December 31, 2002, and William has worked as planned on the client's case. What adjusting entry should William make to account for the work performed from October 1 through December 31, 2002?

b. Patty Tidwell has started a new publication called *Contest News*. Her subscribers pay $24 to receive 12 issues of the magazine. With every new subscriber, Patty debits Cash and credits Unearned Subscription Revenue for the amounts received. Patty has 100 subscribers as of July 1, 2002. She sends *Contest News* to each subscriber every month from July through December. Assuming no changes in subscribers, prepare the journal entry that Patty must make as of December 31, 2002, to adjust the Subscription Revenue account and the Unearned Subscription Revenue account.

Robin Fischer employs three college students every summer in her coffee shop. The students work the five weekdays and are paid on Friday one week after their pay period ends. (For example, a student who works Monday through Friday, June 1 through June 5, is paid for that work on Friday, June 12.) Robin adjusts her books monthly, if needed, to show salaries earned but unpaid at month-end. All three students work the last week of July—Friday is August 1. If each student earns $100 per day, what adjusting entry must Robin make to correctly record salaries expense for July?

Classify the following adjusting entries as involving prepaid expenses (PE), depreciation (D), unearned revenues (UR), accrued expenses (AE), or accrued revenues (AR).

a. _____ Entry to show revenue earned that was previously received as cash in advance.

b. _____ Entry to record annual depreciation expense.

c. _____ Entry to show wages earned but not yet paid (recorded).

d. _____ Entry to show revenue earned but not yet billed (recorded).

e. _____ Entry to show expiration of prepaid insurance.

QS 4-6
Recording and analyzing
adjusting entries

Adjusting entries affect at least one balance sheet account and at least one income statement account. For the following entries, identify the account to be debited and the account to be credited. Indicate which of the accounts is the income statement account and which is the balance sheet account.

a. Entry to record revenue earned that was previously received as cash in advance.

b. Entry to record annual depreciation expense.

c. Entry to record wages earned but not yet paid (recorded).

d. Entry to record revenue earned but not yet billed (recorded).

e. Entry to record expiration of prepaid insurance.

QS 4-7
Using accrual and
cash accounting

In its first year of operations, Heyer Co. earned $42,000 in revenues and received $37,000 cash from customers. The company incurred expenses of $25,500 but had not paid $5,250 of them at year-end. In addition, Heyer prepaid $6,750 cash for expenses that would be incurred the next year. Calculate the first year's net income under both the cash basis and the accrual basis of accounting.

QS 4-8
Preparing adjusting entries

During the year, Stone Co. records prepayments of expenses in asset accounts and receipts of unearned revenues in liability accounts. At the end of its annual accounting period, the company must make three adjusting entries: (1) accrue salaries expense, (2) adjust the Unearned Services Revenue account to recognize earned revenue, and (3) record the earning of services revenue for which cash will be received the following period. For each of these adjusting entries (1), (2), and (3), use the letters assigned to the following accounts to indicate the account to be debited and the account to be credited.

a. Accounts Receivable   **e.** Unearned Services Revenue

b. Prepaid Salaries   **f.** Salaries Expense

c. Cash   **g.** Services Revenue

d. Salaries Payable

QS 4-9
Determining effects of
adjusting entries

In making adjusting entries at the end of its accounting period, Malson Consulting Agency failed to record $1,600 of insurance premiums that had expired. This cost had been initially debited to the Prepaid Insurance account. The company also failed to record accrued salaries payable of $1,000. As a result of these two oversights, the financial statements for the reporting period will [choose one] (1) understate assets by $1,600; (2) understate expenses by $2,600; (3) understate net income by $1,000; or (4) overstate liabilities by $1,000.

QS 4-10
Interpreting adjusting entries

The following information is taken from Case Company's unadjusted and adjusted trial balances:

	Unadjusted		Adjusted	
	Debit	Credit	Debit	Credit
Prepaid insurance	$4,100		$3,700	
Interest payable		$ 0		$800

Given this information, which of the following items must be included among its adjusting entries?

a. A $400 credit to Prepaid Insurance and an $800 debit to Interest Payable.

b. A $400 debit to Insurance Expense and an $800 debit to Interest Payable.

c. A $400 debit to Insurance Expense and an $800 debit to Interest Expense.

QS 4-11
Analyzing profit margin

Hao Company had net income of $48,152 and net sales of $425,000 for the year ended December 31, 2002. Calculate Hao's profit margin. Interpret the profit margin calculation.

QS 4-12^A
Preparing adjusting entries

Bergez Consulting Company initially records prepaid and unearned items in income statement accounts. Given Bergez Consulting Company's accounting practices, which of the following applies to the preparation of adjusting entries at the end of the company's first accounting period?

a. Earned but unbilled (and unrecorded) consulting fees will be recorded with a debit to Unearned Consulting Fees and a credit to Consulting Fees Earned.

b. Unpaid salaries will be recorded with a debit to Prepaid Salaries and a credit to Salaries Expense.

c. The cost of unused office supplies will be recorded with a debit to Supplies Expense and a credit to Office Supplies.

d. Unearned fees (on which cash was received in advance earlier in the period) will be recorded with a debit to Consulting Fees Earned and a credit to Unearned Consulting Fees.

For each of the following separate cases, prepare adjusting entries required for financial statements for the year (or date) ended December 31, 2002. (Assume prepaid expenses are initially recorded in asset accounts and that fees collected in advance of work are initially recorded as liabilities.)

a. One-third of the work related to $15,000 cash received in advance is performed this period.

b. Wages of $8,000 are earned by workers but not paid as of December 31, 2002.

c. Depreciation on the company's equipment for 2002 is $18,534.

d. The Office Supplies account had a $240 debit balance on January 1, 2002. During the year, $5,239 of office supplies are purchased. A physical count of supplies at December 31, 2002, shows $487 of supplies available.

e. The Prepaid Insurance account had a $4,000 balance on January 1, 2002. An analysis of the company's insurance policies shows that $1,200 of unexpired insurance benefits remain at December 31, 2002.

f. The company has earned (but not recorded) $1,000 of interest from investments in CDs as of December 31, 2002. The interest earned will be received on January 10, 2003.

g. The company has a bank loan and has incurred (but not recorded) interest expenses of $2,500 as of December 31, 2002. The company must pay the interest on January 2, 2003.

EXERCISES

Exercise 4-1
Preparing adjusting entries

Prepare adjusting journal entries for the year ended December 31, 2002, for each of these independent situations. Assume prepaid expenses are initially recorded in asset accounts. Also assume fees collected in advance of work are initially recorded as liabilities.

a. Depreciation on the company's equipment for 2002 is computed to be $18,000.

b. The Prepaid Insurance account had a $6,000 debit balance at December 31, 2002, before adjusting for the costs of any expired coverage. An analysis of the company's insurance policies showed that $1,100 of unexpired insurance remained in effect.

c. The Office Supplies account had a $700 debit balance on January 1, 2002; $3,480 of office supplies were purchased during the year; and the December 31, 2002, physical count showed $298 of supplies available.

d. One-half of the work related to $15,000 cash received in advance was performed this period.

e. The Prepaid Insurance account had a $6,800 debit balance at December 31, 2002 before adjusting for the costs of any expired coverage. An analysis of the company's insurance policies showed that $5,800 of coverage had expired.

f. Wages of $3,200 have been earned by workers but not paid as of December 31, 2002.

Exercise 4-2
Preparing adjusting entries

Asset Management has five part-time employees, each of whom earns $250 per day. They are normally paid on Fridays for work completed Monday through Friday of the same week. They were paid in full on Friday, December 28, 2002. The next week, the five employees worked only four days because New Year's Day was an unpaid holiday. Show the adjusting entry that would be recorded on Monday, December 31, 2002, and the journal entry that would be made to record paying the employees' wages on Friday, January 4, 2003.

Exercise 4-3
Adjusting and paying accrued wages

In the blank space beside each adjusting entry, enter the letter of the explanation *a* through *f* that most closely describes the entry:

a. To record this period's depreciation expense.

b. To record accrued salaries expense.

c. To record this period's use of a prepaid expense.

d. To record accrued interest income.

e. To record accrued interest expense.

f. To record the earning of previously unearned income.

Exercise 4-4
Classifying adjusting entry

_____ 1.	Salaries Expense	13,280	
	Salaries Payable		13,280
_____ 2.	Interest Expense	2,208	
	Interest Payable		2,208
_____ 3.	Insurance Expense	3,180	
	Prepaid Insurance		3,180
_____ 4.	Unearned Professional Fees	19,250	
	Professional Fees Earned		19,250
_____ 5.	Interest Receivable	3,300	
	Interest Revenue		3,300
_____ 6.	Depreciation Expense	38,217	
	Accumulated Depreciation		38,217

Exercise 4-5

Determining cost flows through accounts

Determine the missing amounts in each of these four separate situations *a* through *d*:

	a	b	c	d
Supplies available—January 1	$ 400	$1,200	$1,260	?
Supplies purchased during the year	2,800	6,500	8,490	$3,000
Supplies available—December 31	650	?	1,350	700
Supplies expense for the year	?	1,200	8,400	4,588

Exercise 4-6

Adjusting and paying accrued expenses

The following three situations require adjusting journal entries to prepare financial statements as of April 30. For each situation, present both the adjusting entry and the entry to record the payment of the accrued liability during May.

a. On April 1, the company retained an attorney at a flat monthly fee of $3,500. This amount is payable on the 12th of the following month.

b. An $800,000 note payable requires 1.0% interest to be paid every 30 days. The interest was last paid on April 20 and the next payment is due on May 20.   10 days

c. Total weekly salaries expense for all employees is $10,000. This amount is paid at the end of the day on Friday of each 5-day workweek. April 30 falls on Tuesday of this year, which means that the employees had worked two days since the last payday. The next payday is May 3.

Exercise 4-7

Determining assets and expenses for accrual and cash accounting

On March 1, 2001, a company paid an $18,000 premium on a three-year insurance policy for coverage beginning on that date. Refer to that policy and fill in the blanks in the following table:

	Balance Sheet Asset under the			Insurance Expense under the	
	Accrual Basis	Cash Basis		Accrual Basis	Cash Basis
Dec. 31, 2001	$_____	$_____	2001	$_____	$_____
Dec. 31, 2002	_____	_____	2002	_____	_____
Dec. 31, 2003	_____	_____	2003	_____	_____
Dec. 31, 2004	_____	_____	2004	_____	_____
			Total	$_____	$_____

Exercise 4-8

Computing and interpreting profit margin

Use the following information to compute profit margin for each separate company *a* through *e*:

	Net Income	Net Sales		Net Income	Net Sales
a.	$ 4,390	$ 44,830	**d.**	$65,234	$1,458,999
b.	97,644	398,954	**e.**	80,158	435,925
c.	111,385	257,082			

Which of the five companies is the most profitable according to the profit margin ratio? Interpret that company's profit margin ratio.

Following are two income statements for Clark Co. for the year ended December 31. The left column is prepared before any adjusting entries are recorded, and the right column includes the effects of adjusting entries. The company records cash receipts and disbursements related to unearned and prepaid items in balance sheet accounts. Analyze the statements and prepare the eight adjusting entries that must have been recorded. (*Note:* 30% of the $7,000 adjustment for Fees Earned has been earned but not billed, and the other 70% has been earned by performing services that were paid for in advance.)

Exercise 4-9
Analyzing and preparing adjusting entries

CLARK CO. Income Statements For Year Ended December 31	Before Adjustments	After Adjustments
Revenues		
Fees earned	$18,000	$25,000
Commissions earned	36,500	36,500
Total revenues	$54,500	$61,500
Expenses		
Depreciation expense—Computers	0	1,600
Depreciation expense—Office furniture	0	1,850
Salaries expense	13,500	15,750
Insurance expense	0	1,400
Rent expense	3,800	3,800
Office supplies expense	0	580
Advertising expense	2,500	2,500
Utilities expense	1,245	1,335
Total expenses	$21,045	$28,815
Net income	$33,455	$32,685

Tri-Mark Construction began operations on December 1. In setting up its accounting procedures, the company decided to debit expense accounts when it prepays its expenses and to credit revenue accounts when customers pay for services in advance. Prepare journal entries for (a) through (d) and the adjusting entries as of December 31 for items (e) through (g).

a. Supplies are purchased on December 1 for $2,000 cash.

b. The company prepaid its insurance premiums for $1,540 cash on December 2.

c. On December 15, the company receives an advance payment of $13,000 cash from a customer for remodeling work.

d. On December 28, the company receives $3,700 cash from another customer for remodeling work to be performed in January.

e. A physical count on December 31, indicates that Tri-Mark has $1,840 of supplies available.

f. An analysis of the insurance policies in effect on December 31 shows that $340 of insurance coverage had expired.

g. As of December 31, only one project has been completed. The $5,570 fee for this project had been received in advance.

Exercise 4-10^A
Adjusting for prepaids recorded as expense and unearned revenues recorded as revenue

Globus Company experienced the following events and transactions during July:

July 1   Received $3,000 cash in advance of performing work for Nicole Renker.
      6   Received $7,500 cash in advance of performing work for Lisa Gardner.
   12   Completed the job for Nicole Renker.
   18   Received $8,500 cash in advance of performing work for Drew Hanson.
   27   Completed the job for Lisa Gardner.
   31   None of the work for Drew Hanson has been performed.

Exercise 4-11^A
Recording and reporting revenues received in advance

a. Prepare journal entries (including any adjusting entry as of the end of the month) to record these events using the procedure of initially crediting the Unearned Fees account when payment is received from a customer in advance of performing services.

b. Prepare journal entries (including any adjusting entry as of the end of the month) to record these events using the procedure of initially crediting the Fees Earned account when payment is received from a customer in advance of performing services.

c. Under each method, determine the amount of earned fees reported on the income statement for July and the amount of unearned fees reported on the balance sheet as of July 31.

PROBLEM SET A

Problem 4-1A

Identifying adjusting entries with explanations

For each of the following entries, enter the letter of the explanation that most closely describes it in the space beside each entry. (You can use letters more than once.)

a. To record receipt of unearned revenue.

b. To record this period's earning of prior unearned revenue.

c. To record payment of an accrued expense.

d. To record receipt of an accrued revenue.

e. To record an accrued expense.

f. To record an accrued revenue.

g. To record this period's use of a prepaid expense.

h. To record payment of a prepaid expense.

i. To record this period's depreciation expense.

_____	1.	Rent Expense	2,000	
		Prepaid Rent		2,000
_____	2.	Interest Expense	1,000	
		Interest Payable		1,000
_____	3.	Depreciation Expense	4,000	
		Accumulated Depreciation		4,000
_____	4.	Unearned Professional Fees	3,000	
		Professional Fees Earned		3,000
_____	5.	Insurance Expense	4,200	
		Prepaid Insurance		4,200
_____	6.	Salaries Payable	1,400	
		Cash		1,400
_____	7.	Prepaid Rent	4,500	
		Cash		4,500
_____	8.	Salaries Expense	6,000	
		Salaries Payable		6,000
_____	9.	Interest Receivable	5,000	
		Interest Revenue		5,000
_____	10.	Cash	9,000	
		Accounts Receivable		9,000
_____	11.	Cash	7,500	
		Unearned Professional Fees		7,500
_____	12.	Cash	2,000	
		Interest Receivable		2,000

Problem 4-2A

Preparing adjusting and subsequent journal entries

Feinman Co. follows the practice of recording prepaid expenses and unearned revenues in balance sheet accounts. Feinman's annual accounting period ends on December 31, 2003. The following information concerns the adjusting entries to be recorded as of that date:

a. The Office Supplies account started the year with a $4,000 balance. During 2003, the company purchased supplies for $13,400, which was added to the Office Supplies account. The inventory of supplies available at December 31 totaled $2,554.

b. An analysis of the company's insurance policies provided these facts:

Policy	Date of Purchase	Years of Coverage	Cost
A	April 1, 2002	2	$14,400
B	April 1, 2003	3	12,960
C	August 1, 2003	1	2,400

The total premium for each policy was paid in full (for all years) at the purchase date, and the Prepaid Insurance account was debited for the full cost.

c. The company has 14 employees who earn a total of $1,960 in salaries every working day. They are paid each Monday for their work in the five-day workweek ending on the previous Friday. December 31, 2003, falls on Tuesday, and all 14 employees worked the first two days of that week. Because New Year's Day is a paid holiday, they will be paid salaries for five full days on Monday, January 6, 2004.

d. The company purchased a building on January 1, 2003. It cost $960,000 and is expected to have a $45,000 salvage value at the end of its predicted 30-year life.

e. Since the company is not large enough to occupy the entire building, it rented some space to a tenant at $3,000 per month, starting on November 1, 2003. The rent was paid on time on November 1, and the amount received was credited to the Rent Earned account. However, the tenant has not paid the December rent. The company has worked out an agreement with the tenant, who has promised to pay both December and January rent in full on January 15. The tenant has agreed not to fall behind again.

f. On November 1, the company rented space to another tenant for $2,800 per month. The tenant paid five months' rent in advance on that date. The payment was recorded with a credit to the Unearned Rent account.

Required

1. Use the information to prepare adjusting entries as of December 31, 2003.

2. Prepare journal entries to record the first subsequent cash transaction for both parts (c) and (e).

Check Insurance expense, $11,440

Thomas Technical Institute, a school owned by Joshua Thomas, provides training to individuals who pay tuition directly to the school. The school also offers training to groups in off-site locations. The school's unadjusted trial balance as of December 31, 2002, follows. Thomas Technical Institute initially records prepaid expenses and unearned revenues in balance sheet accounts. Items that require adjusting entries on December 31, 2002, are described after the trial balance.

Problem 4-3A
Making adjusting entries, preparing financial statements, and calculating profit margin

THOMAS TECHNICAL INSTITUTE
Unadjusted Trial Balance
December 31, 2002

Cash	$ 34,000	
Accounts receivable	0	
Teaching supplies	8,000	
Prepaid insurance	12,000	
Prepaid rent	3,000	
Professional library	35,000	
Accumulated depreciation—Professional library		$ 10,000
Equipment	80,000	
Accumulated depreciation—Equipment		15,000
Accounts payable		26,000
Salaries payable		0
Unearned training fees		12,500
J. Thomas, Capital		70,000
J. Thomas, Withdrawals	30,000	
Tuition fees earned		123,900
Training fees earned		40,000
Depreciation expense—Professional library	0	
Depreciation expense—Equipment	0	
Salaries expense	50,000	
Insurance expense	0	
Rent expense	33,000	
Teaching supplies expense	0	
Advertising expense	6,000	
Utilities expense	6,400	
Totals	$ 297,400	$ 297,400

Additional Items

a. An analysis of the company's insurance policies shows that $2,400 of coverage has expired.

b. An inventory shows that teaching supplies costing $2,800 are available at year-end.

c. Annual depreciation on the equipment is $13,200.

d. Annual depreciation on the professional library is $7,200.

e. On November 1, the company agreed to do a special six-month course for a client. The contract calls for a monthly fee of $2,500, and the client paid the first five months' fees in advance. When the cash was received, the Unearned Training Fees account was credited. The fee for the sixth month will be recorded when it is collected in 2003.

f. On October 15, the school agreed to teach a four-month class for an individual for $3,000 tuition per month payable at the end of the class. The services are being provided as agreed, and no payment has been received. (*Hint:* The class began on October 15.)

g. The school's two employees are paid weekly. As of the end of the year, two days' wages have accrued at the rate of $100 per day for each employee.

h. The balance in the Prepaid Rent account represents rent for December.

Required

1. Prepare T-accounts with the balances from the unadjusted trial balance.

2. Prepare adjusting journal entries for items (a) through (h) and post them to the T-accounts. Assume adjusting entries are made only at year-end.

3. Update balances in the T-accounts for the adjusting entries and prepare an adjusted trial balance.

Check   Ending owner's equity, $89,600

4. Prepare Thomas Technical Institute's income statement and statement of changes in owner's equity for the year 2002 and prepare its balance sheet as of December 31, 2002.

5. Calculate the company's profit margin for the year. The owner does not work in the company.

Problem 4-4A

Interpreting unadjusted and adjusted trial balances, preparing financial statements, and calculating profit margin

A six-column table for JLK Company follows. The first two columns contain the unadjusted trial balance for the company as of July 31, 2002. The last two columns contain the adjusted trial balance as of the same date.

	Unadjusted Trial Balance		Adjustments		Adjusted Trial Balance	
Cash	$ 34,000				$ 34,000	
Accounts receivable	14,000				22,000	
Office supplies	16,000				2,000	
Prepaid insurance	8,540				2,960	
Office equipment	84,000				84,000	
Accum. depreciation— Office equip.		$ 14,000				$ 20,000
Accounts payable		9,100				10,000
Interest payable		0				1,000
Salaries payable		0				7,000
Unearned consulting fees .		18,000				15,000
Long-term notes payable ..		52,000				52,000
J.L. Kane, Capital		40,000				40,000
J.L. Kane, Withdrawals ...	5,000				5,000	
Consulting fees earned ...		123,240				134,240
Depreciation expense— Office equip.	0				6,000	
Salaries expense	67,000				74,000	
Interest expense	1,200				2,200	
Insurance expense	0				5,580	
Rent expense	14,500				14,500	
Office supplies expense ...	0				14,000	
Advertising expense	12,100				13,000	
Totals	$256,340	$256,340			$279,240	$279,240

Required

Preparation Component

1. Prepare the company's income statement and its statement of changes in owner's equity for the year ended July 31, 2002.

2. Prepare the company's balance sheet as of July 31, 2002.

3. Calculate the company's profit margin for the year ended July 31, 2002.

Check   Profit margin, 3.7%

Analysis Component

4. Analyze the differences between the unadjusted and adjusted trial balances to determine the adjustments that must have been made. Show the results of your analysis by inserting amounts from this company's adjusting journal entries in the table's two middle columns. Label each adjustment with a letter and provide a short description of it.

The adjusted trial balance for Callahay Company as of December 31, 2002, follows:

Problem 4-5A
Preparing financial statements from the adjusted trial balance and calculating profit margin

	Debit	Credit
Cash.	$ 30,000	
Accounts receivable.	52,000	
Interest receivable	18,000	
Notes receivable (due in 90 days)	168,000	
Office supplies.	16,000	
Automobiles	168,000	
Accumulated depreciation—Automobiles.		$ 50,000
Equipment.	138,000	
Accumulated depreciation—Equipment		18,000
Land.	78,000	
Accounts payable		96,000
Interest payable.		20,000
Salaries payable.		19,000
Unearned fees.		30,000
Long-term notes payable		138,000
J. Callahay, Capital.		255,800
J. Callahay, Withdrawals.	46,000	
Fees earned		484,000
Interest earned.		24,000
Depreciation expense—Automobiles	26,000	
Depreciation expense—Equipment	18,000	
Salaries expense	188,000	
Wages expense.	40,000	
Interest expense	32,000	
Office supplies expense	34,000	
Advertising expense.	58,000	
Repairs expense—Automobiles.	24,800	
Totals	$1,134,800	$1,134,800

Required

1. Use the information in the adjusted trial balance to prepare (a) the income statement for the year ended December 31, 2002; (b) the statement of changes in owner's equity for the year ended December 31, 2002; and (c) the balance sheet as of December 31, 2002.

Check   Total assets, $600,000

2. Assume that J. Callahay's services to the business are valued at $40,000 for the year. Calculate the modified profit margin for year 2002.

Problem 4-6A

Computing accrual income
from cash income

The records for Turf's Up Landscape Co. are kept on the cash basis instead of the accrual basis. The company is now applying for a loan and the bank wants to know what its net income for year 2002 is under the accrual basis. Its income statement for year 2002 under the cash basis follows:

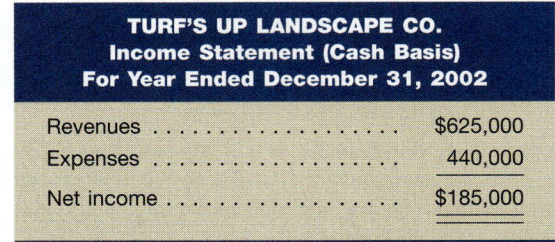

TURF'S UP LANDSCAPE CO.
Income Statement (Cash Basis)
For Year Ended December 31, 2002

Revenues	$625,000
Expenses	440,000
Net income	$185,000

Additional information was gathered to help convert the income statement to the accrual basis:

Hint

Cash inflows 2002
+ Accrued revenues 2002
+ Unearned revenues 2001
– Accrued revenues 2001
– Unearned revenues 2002
Accrual revenues 2002

	As of 12/31/2001	As of 12/31/2002
Accrued revenues	$13,000	$17,500
Unearned revenues	67,000	22,000
Accrued expenses	15,700	10,000
Prepaid expenses	28,000	21,700

All prepaid expenses from the beginning of the year have been used or expired, all unearned revenues from the beginning of the year have been earned, and all accrued expenses and accrued revenues from the beginning of the year have been paid or collected.

Required

Check   Net income, $233,900

Prepare the accrual basis income statement for year 2002. Provide schedules that explain how you converted from cash revenues and cash expenses to accrual revenues and accrual expenses.

Problem 4-7A[A]

Recording prepaid expenses
and unearned revenues

Quisp Co. had the following transactions in the last two months of its year ended December 31:

Nov. 1   Paid $1,800 cash for future newspaper advertising.
      1   Paid $2,460 cash for 12 months of insurance through October 31 of the following year.
      30   Received $3,600 cash for future services to be provided to a customer.
Dec. 1   Paid $3,000 cash for a consultant's services to be received over the next three months.
      15   Received $7,950 cash for future services to be provided to a customer.
      31   Of the advertising paid for on November 1, $1,200 worth is yet to be used.
      31   A portion of the insurance paid for on November 1 has expired.
      31   Services worth $1,500 are not yet provided to the customer who paid on November 30.
      31   One-third of the consulting services paid for on December 1 have been received.
      31   The company has performed $3,300 of services that the customer paid for on December 15.

Required

Preparation Component

1. Prepare entries for these transactions under the method that records prepaid expenses as assets and records unearned revenues as liabilities. Also prepare adjusting entries at the end of the year.

2. Prepare entries for these transactions under the method that records prepaid expenses as expenses and records unearned revenues as revenues. Also prepare adjusting entries at the end of the year.

Analysis Component

3. Explain why the alternative sets of entries in requirements (1) and (2) do not result in different financial statement amounts.

PROBLEM SET B

Problem 4-1B

Identifying adjusting
entries with
explanations

For each of the following entries, enter the letter of the explanation that most closely describes it in the space beside each entry. (You can use letters more than once.)

a. To record receipt of accrued revenue.

b. To record payment of an accrued expense.

c. To record payment of a prepaid expense.

d. To record this period's depreciation expense.

e. To record this period's earning of prior unearned revenue.

f. To record this period's use of a prepaid expense.

g. To record an accrued revenue.

h. To record receipt of unearned revenue.

i. To record an accrued expense.

_____	**1.**	Unearned Professional Fees	6,000	
		Professional Fees Earned		6,000
_____	**2.**	Interest Receivable	3,500	
		Interest Revenue		3,500
_____	**3.**	Salaries Payable	9,000	
		Cash		9,000
_____	**4.**	Depreciation Expense	8,000	
		Accumulated Depreciation		8,000
_____	**5.**	Cash	9,000	
		Unearned Professional Fees		9,000
_____	**6.**	Insurance Expense	4,000	
		Prepaid Insurance		4,000
_____	**7.**	Interest Expense	5,000	
		Interest Payable		5,000
_____	**8.**	Cash	1,500	
		Accounts Receivable		1,500
_____	**9.**	Salaries Expense	7,000	
		Salaries Payable		7,000
_____	**10.**	Cash	1,000	
		Interest Receivable		1,000
_____	**11.**	Prepaid Rent	3,000	
		Cash		3,000
_____	**12.**	Rent Expense	7,500	
		Prepaid Rent		7,500

Sanuk Co. follows the practice of recording prepaid expenses and unearned revenues in balance sheet accounts. Sanuk's annual accounting period ends on October 31, 2003. The following information concerns the adjusting entries that need to be recorded as of that date:

Problem 4-2B
Preparing adjusting and subsequent journal entries

a. The Office Supplies account started the fiscal year with a $600 balance. During the fiscal year, the company purchased supplies for $4,570, which was added to the Office Supplies account. The supplies available at October 31 totaled $800.

b. An analysis of the company's insurance policies provided these facts:

Policy	Date of Purchase	Years of Coverage	Cost
A	April 1, 2002	2	$6,000
B	April 1, 2003	3	7,200
C	August 1, 2003	1	1,320

The total premium for each policy was paid in full (for all years) at the purchase date, and the Prepaid Insurance account was debited for the full cost.

c. The company has five employees who earn a total of $1,000 for every work day. They are paid each Monday for their work in the five-day workweek ending on the previous Friday. October 31, 2003, falls on Monday, and all five employees worked the first day of that week. They will be paid salaries for five full days on Monday, November 7, 2003.

d. The company purchased a building on November 1, 2002, that cost $175,000 and is expected to have a $40,000 salvage value at the end of its predicted 25-year life.

e. Since the company is not large enough to occupy the entire building, it rented some space to a tenant at $1,000 per month, starting on September 1, 2003. The rent was paid on time on September 1, and the amount received was credited to the Rent Earned account. However, the October rent has not been paid. The company has worked out an agreement with the tenant, who has promised to pay both October and November rent in full on November 15. The tenant has agreed not to fall behind again.

f. On September 1, the company rented space to another tenant for $725 per month. The tenant paid five months' rent in advance on that date. The payment was recorded with a credit to the Unearned Rent account.

Required

Check   Insurance expense, $4,730

1. Use the information to prepare adjusting entries as of October 31, 2003.

2. Prepare journal entries to record the first subsequent cash transaction for both parts (c) and (e).

Problem 4-3B

Preparing adjusting entries, preparing financial statements, and calculating profit margin

Following is the unadjusted trial balance for Triangle Institute as of December 31, 2002, which initially records prepaid expenses and unearned revenues in balance sheet accounts. The institute provides one-on-one training to individuals who pay tuition directly to the business and offers extension training to groups in off-site locations. Shown after the trial balance are items that require adjusting entries as of December 31, 2002.

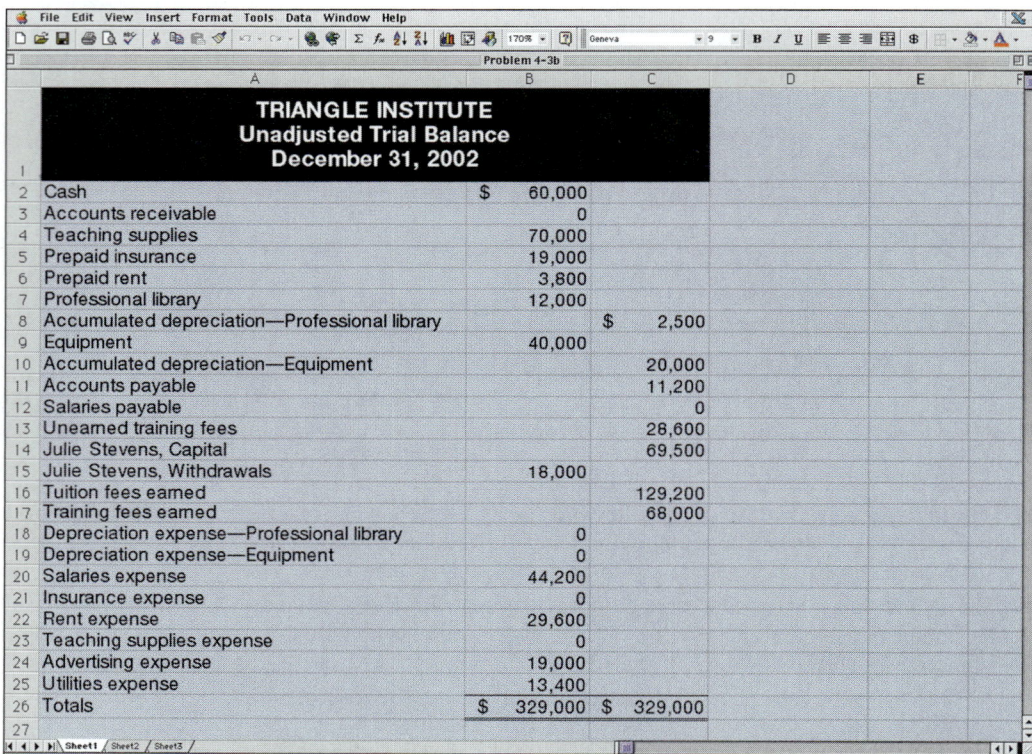

TRIANGLE INSTITUTE
Unadjusted Trial Balance
December 31, 2002

Cash	$ 60,000	
Accounts receivable	0	
Teaching supplies	70,000	
Prepaid insurance	19,000	
Prepaid rent	3,800	
Professional library	12,000	
Accumulated depreciation—Professional library		$ 2,500
Equipment	40,000	
Accumulated depreciation—Equipment		20,000
Accounts payable		11,200
Salaries payable		0
Unearned training fees		28,600
Julie Stevens, Capital		69,500
Julie Stevens, Withdrawals	18,000	
Tuition fees earned		129,200
Training fees earned		68,000
Depreciation expense—Professional library	0	
Depreciation expense—Equipment	0	
Salaries expense	44,200	
Insurance expense	0	
Rent expense	29,600	
Teaching supplies expense	0	
Advertising expense	19,000	
Utilities expense	13,400	
Totals	$ 329,000	$ 329,000

Additional Items

a. An analysis of the institute's insurance policies shows that $9,500 of coverage has expired.

b. An inventory shows that teaching supplies costing $20,000 are available at the end of the year.

c. Annual depreciation on the equipment is $5,000.

d. Annual depreciation on the professional library is $2,400.

e. On November 1, the institute agreed to do a special four-month course for a client. The contract calls for a $5,600 monthly fee, and the client paid the first two months' fees in advance. When the cash was received, the Unearned Training Fees account was credited. The last two months' fees will be recorded when collected in 2003.

f. On October 15, the institute agreed to teach a four-month class to an individual for $2,300 tuition per month payable at the end of the class. The class started on October 15, but no payment has been received.

g. The institute's only employee is paid weekly. As of the end of the year, three days' wages have accrued at the rate of $150 per day.

h. The balance in the Prepaid Rent account represents rent for December.

Required

1. Prepare T-accounts with the balances from the unadjusted trial balance.

2. Prepare adjusting journal entries for items (a) through (h) and post them to the T-accounts.

3. Update balances in the T-accounts for the adjusting entries and prepare an adjusted trial balance.

4. Prepare Triangle Institute's income statement and the statement of changes in owner's equity for the year 2002, and prepare its balance sheet as of December 31, 2002.

5. Compute the company's profit margin for the year. The owner does not work for the company.

Check Ending owner's equity, $88,300

A six-column table for Daxu Consulting Company follows. The first two columns contain the unadjusted trial balance for the company as of December 31, 2002, and the last two columns contain the adjusted trial balance as of the same date.

Problem 4-4B

Interpreting unadjusted and adjusted trial balances, preparing financial statements, and calculating profit margin

	Unadjusted Trial Balance		Adjustments		Adjusted Trial Balance	
Cash	$ 45,000				$ 45,000	
Accounts receivable	60,000				66,660	
Office supplies	40,000				17,000	
Prepaid insurance	8,200				3,600	
Office equipment	120,000				120,000	
Accumulated depreciation— Office equip.		$ 20,000				$ 30,000
Accounts payable		26,000				32,000
Interest payable		0				2,150
Salaries payable		0				16,000
Unearned consulting fees		40,000				27,800
Long-term notes payable		75,000				75,000
Daxu Chen, Capital		80,200				80,200
Daxu Chen, Withdrawals	20,000				20,000	
Consulting fees earned		234,600				253,460
Depreciation expense— Office equip.	0				10,000	
Salaries expense	112,000				128,000	
Interest expense	8,600				10,750	
Insurance expense	0				4,600	
Rent expense	20,000				20,000	
Office supplies expense	0				23,000	
Advertising expense	42,000				48,000	
Totals	$475,800	$475,800			$516,610	$516,610

Required

Preparation Component

1. Prepare this company's income statement and its statement of changes in owner's equity for the year ended December 31, 2002.

2. Prepare the company's balance sheet as of December 31, 2002.

3. Calculate the company's modified profit margin for the year ended December 31, 2002, assuming the value of the owner's services to the business during the year is $30,000.

Check Modified profit margin, −8.2%

Analysis Component

4. Analyze the differences between the unadjusted and adjusted trial balances to determine the adjustments that must have been made. Show the results of your analysis by inserting amounts from this company's adjusting journal entries in the table's two middle columns. Label each adjustment with a letter and provide a short description of it.

Problem 4-5B

Preparing financial statements from the adjusted trial balance and calculating profit margin

The adjusted trial balance for Lightning Courier as of December 31, 2002, follows:

	Debit	Credit
Cash	$ 58,000	
Accounts receivable	120,000	
Interest receivable	7,000	
Notes receivable (due in 90 days)	210,000	
Office supplies	22,000	
Trucks	134,000	
Accumulated depreciation—Trucks		$ 58,000
Equipment	270,000	
Accumulated depreciation—Equipment		200,000
Land	100,000	
Accounts payable		134,000
Interest payable		20,000
Salaries payable		28,000
Unearned delivery fees		120,000
Long-term notes payable		200,000
J. Hallam, Capital		125,000
J. Hallam, Withdrawals	50,000	
Delivery fees earned		611,800
Interest earned		34,000
Depreciation expense—Trucks	29,000	
Depreciation expense—Equipment	48,000	
Salaries expense	74,000	
Wages expense	300,000	
Interest expense	15,000	
Office supplies expense	31,000	
Advertising expense	27,200	
Repairs expense—Trucks	35,600	
Totals	$1,530,800	$1,530,800

Required

Check   Total assets, $663,000

1. Use the information in the adjusted trial balance to prepare (a) the income statement for the year ended December 31, 2002, (b) the statement of changes in owner's equity for the year ended December 31, 2002, and (c) the balance sheet as of December 31, 2002.

2. Assume the services of the owner to the business during year 2002 are valued at $30,000. Calculate the modified profit margin for year 2002.

Problem 4-6B

Computing accrual income from cash income

The records for Web Products are kept on the cash basis instead of the accrual basis. The company is now applying for a loan and the bank wants to know what its net income for year 2002 is under the accrual basis. Its income statement for year 2002 under the cash basis follows:

WEB PRODUCTS Income Statement (Cash Basis) For Year Ended December 31, 2002	
Revenues	$185,000
Expenses	86,000
Net income	$ 99,000

Additional information was gathered to help convert the income statement to the accrual basis:

	As of 12/31/2001	As of 12/31/2002
Accrued revenues	$13,100	$ 5,600
Unearned revenues	9,050	9,800
Accrued expenses	6,800	13,400
Prepaid expenses	8,300	5,300

Hint
Cash outflows 2002
+ Accrued expenses 2002
+ Prepaid expenses 2001
− Accrued expenses 2001
− Prepaid expenses 2002
Accrual expenses 2002

All prepaid expenses from the beginning of the year are used or expired, all unearned revenues from the beginning of the year are earned, and all accrued expenses and accrued revenues from the beginning of the year are paid or collected.

Required

Prepare the accrual basis income statement for year 2002. Provide schedules that explain how you converted from cash revenues and cash expenses to accrual revenues and accrual expenses.

Check Net income, $81,150

Quake Company had the following transactions in the last two months of its fiscal year ended May 31:

Apr. 1 Paid $2,450 cash for future consulting services.
1 Paid $3,600 cash for 12 months of insurance through March 31 of the following year.
30 Received $8,500 cash for future services to be provided to a customer.
May 1 Paid $4,450 cash for future newspaper advertising.
23 Received $10,450 cash for future services to be provided to a customer.
31 Of the consulting services paid for on April 1, $2,000 worth has been received.
31 A portion of the insurance paid for on April 1 has expired. No adjustment was made in April to Prepaid Insurance.
31 Services worth $4,600 are not yet provided to the customer who paid on April 30.
31 Of the advertising paid for on May 1, $2,050 worth is not yet used.
31 The company has performed $5,500 of services that the customer paid for on May 23.

Problem 4-7B[A]
Recording prepaid expenses and unearned revenues

Required

Preparation Component

1. Prepare entries for these transactions under the method that records prepaid expenses and unearned revenues in balance sheet accounts. Also prepare adjusting entries at the end of the year.

2. Prepare entries for these transactions under the method that records prepaid expenses and unearned revenues in income statement accounts. Also prepare adjusting entries at the end of the year.

Analysis Component

3. Explain why the alternative sets of entries in parts (1) and (2) do not result in different financial statement amounts.

---

*(This serial problem involving **Sierra Systems** was introduced in Chapter 3 and continues in Chapters 5 and 6. If the Chapter 3 segment has not been completed, the assignment can begin at this point. You need to use the facts for the serial problem at the end of Chapter 3. Because of its length, this problem is best solved if you use the Working Papers that accompany this book.)*

SERIAL PROBLEM

Sierra Systems

After the success of its first two months, Sela Solstise decides to continue operating Sierra Systems. (Transactions that occurred in these first two months are described in Chapter 3.) On December 1, Solstise adds these new accounts to its chart of accounts:

Account	No.
Accumulated Depreciation—Office equipment	164
Accumulated Depreciation—Computer equipment	168
Wages Payable	210
Unearned Computer Services Revenue	236
Depreciation Expense—Office equipment	612

[continued on next page]

[continued from previous page]

Account	No.
Depreciation Expense—Computer equipment	613
Insurance Expense	637
Rent Expense	640
Computer Supplies Expense	652
Income Summary	901

Sierra Systems had the following transactions and events in December 2002:

Dec. 2   Paid $1,025 cash to Hilldale Mall for Sierra Systems' share of mall advertising costs.
       3   Paid $500 cash to repair the company's computer.
       4   Received $3,950 cash from Antonio's Engineering Co. for the receivable from November.
      10   Paid Suzie Smith cash for six days of work at the rate of $125 per day.
      14   Notified by Antonio's Engineering Co. that Sierra's bid of $7,000 on a proposed project
           has been accepted. Antonio's paid an advance of $1,500 cash.
      15   Purchased $1,100 of computer supplies on credit from Appier Office Products.
      16   Sent a reminder to Foster Co. to pay the fee for services recorded on November 8.
      20   Completed project for Elan Corporation and received $5,625 cash.
   22–26   Took the week off for the holidays.
      28   Received $3,000 cash from Foster Co. on its receivable.
      29   Reimbursed Solstise's business automobile mileage (600 miles at $0.32 per mile).
      31   Solstise withdrew $1,500 cash from the business.

The following additional facts are collected for use in making adjusting entries prior to preparing financial statements for the company's first three months:

a. The December 31 inventory of computer supplies is $580.

b. Three months have passed since the annual insurance premium was paid.

c. As of December 31, Suzie Smith has not been paid for four days of work at $125 per day.

d. The company's computer is expected to have a four-year life with no salvage value.

e. The office equipment is expected to have a five-year life with no salvage value.

f. Prepaid rent for three of the four months has expired.

Required

1. Prepare journal entries to record each of the December transactions and events for Sierra Systems. Post entries to the accounts in the ledger.

2. Prepare all necessary adjusting entries. Post these entries to the accounts in the ledger.

Check Adjusted trial balance totals, $119,034

3. Prepare an adjusted trial balance as of December 31, 2002.

4. Prepare an income statement for the three months ended December 31, 2002.

5. Prepare a statement of changes in owner's equity for the three months ended December 31, 2002.

6. Prepare a balance sheet as of December 31, 2002.

Beyond the Numbers

Reporting in Action

BTN 4-1   Refer to the financial statements for **Nike** in Appendix A to answer the following questions:

1. What are the major items making up Nike's prepaid expenses listed in its balance sheet?

2. When does Nike recognize its prepaid advertising costs as expenses?

3. What is Nike's profit margin for 2000 and 1999?

Swoosh Ahead

4. Access Nike's annual report for fiscal years ending after May 31, 2000, at its Web site **[www.nike.com]** or the SEC's EDGAR database **[www.sec.gov].** Compare the May 31, 2000, fiscal year profit margin to any subsequent year's profit margin that you are able to calculate. Also compare the change in Nike's net amount of property, plant, and equipment since May 31, 2000.

BTN 4-2   Key comparative figures ($ millions) for both **Nike** and **Reebok** follow:

Key Figures	Nike		Reebok	
	Current Year	Prior Year	Current Year	Prior Year
Net income ..	$ 579	$ 451	$ 11	$ 24
Net sales ...	8,995	8,777	2,900	3,225

Comparative Analysis

A2

Required

1. Compute profit margins for (a) Nike and (b) Reebok for the two years of data shown.
2. Which company is more successful on the basis of profit margin?
3. Is it appropriate to calculate the modified profit margin for Nike and/or Reebok?

BTN 4-3   Jackie Houston works for Seitzer Co. She and Bob Welch, her manager, are preparing adjusting entries for annual financial statements. Jackie computes depreciation and records it as

Ethics Challenge

A1

Depreciation Expense—Equipment	123,000	
Accumulated Depreciation—Equipment		123,000

Bob agrees with her computation but says the credit entry should be directly to the Equipment account. He argues that while accumulated depreciation is technically correct, "it is less hassle not to use a contra account and just credit the Equipment account directly. And besides, the balance sheet shows the same amount for total assets under either method."

Required

1. How should depreciation be recorded? Do you support Jackie or Bob?
2. Evaluate the strengths and weaknesses of Bob's reasons for preferring his method.
3. Indicate whether the situation Jackie faces is an ethical problem.

BTN 4-4   Failure to properly apply accounting principles can influence reported profits as well as the success or failure of a business. Read the article, "Anatomy of the Kurzweil Fraud," in the September 1996 issue of *Business Week*. Write a summary that includes the following:

Communicating in Practice

C1 C2 A1

1. Identification of the specific accounting principle that this article discusses and an explanation of what this principle requires and prohibits.
2. A description of the accounting practice for Kurzweil that the article questions.
3. Identification of stakeholders and possible consequences of the questioned accounting practice.
4. An explanation of how this article relates to the material in the chapter.

BTN 4-5   Access the **Cannondale** promotional Web site at **www.cannondale.com.**

Taking It to the Net

1. What is the primary product that Cannondale sells?
2. Review its 10-K, the annual report required by the SEC. You can access this from the Edgar system [**www.sec.gov**]. You must scroll down the form to find the statements.
3. What is Cannondale's fiscal year-end?
4. What are Cannondale's net sales for the annual period ended July 3, 1999?
5. What is Cannondale's net income for the annual period ended July 3, 1999?
6. Compute Cannondale's profit margin ratio for the annual period ended July 3, 1999.
7. Do you think its decision to use a year-end of late June or early July relates to its natural business year?

Teamwork in Action

BTN 4-6   Five types of adjustments are described in the chapter: (1) prepaid expenses, (2) depreciation (part of prepaid), (3) unearned revenues, (4) accrued expenses, and (5) accrued revenues.

Required

1. Form *learning teams* of five (or more) members. Each team member must select one of the five adjustments as an area of expertise (each team must have at least one expert in each area).
2. Form *expert teams* from the individuals who have selected the same area of expertise. Expert teams are to discuss and write a report that each expert will present to his/her learning team addressing the following:
   a. Description of the adjustment and why it's necessary.
   b. Example of a transaction or event, with dates and amounts, that requires adjustment.
   c. Adjusting entry(ies) for the example in requirement (b).
   d. Status of the affected account(s) before and after the adjustment in requirement (c).
   e. Effects on financial statements of not making the adjustment.
3. Each expert should return to his/her learning team. In rotation, each member should present his/her expert team's report to the learning team. Team discussion is encouraged.

Business Week Activity

BTN 4-7   Read the article, "Gaping Holes at the Gap," in the April 24, 2000, issue of *Business Week*.

Required

1. Identify the three different chains owned by **Gap**.
2. What are some of the challenges facing its CEO?
3. Is the sales trend for the **Old Navy** stores positive or negative? What factors are driving the trend you identified?
4. Do the new stores opened in 2000 grow faster or slower than the new stores opened in 1999?
5. Who are Gap's retail competitors cited in the article?

Entrepreneurial Decision

BTN 4-8   Robin Drucker operates a collection agency. For a 50% commission, she collects on accounts receivables from her clients' customers who are delinquent in their payments. For example, a company turns over a $100 accounts receivable to Robin. If she can collect the $100 from the customer, then she keeps $50 and remits the other $50 to her client. Robin has more than 100 clients. As her client list has grown, manually accounting for her business activities is becoming increasingly challenging.

Required

1. Why would a company hire a collection agency to pursue its accounts?
2. Robin is trying to decide whether to buy preprogrammed collection software from a major vendor in her industry or hire a programmer to write specialized software tailored exactly to her needs. Identify advantages and disadvantages of packaged versus proprietary software.

5

Completing the Accounting Cycle

"The revolution is over, and the revolutionaries won."—Bob Young.

A Look Back

Chapter 4 explained the timing of reports. We described why adjusting accounts is important for recognizing revenues and expenses in the proper period. We explained how to prepare an adjusted trial balance and use it in preparing financial statements.

A Look at This Chapter

This chapter emphasizes the final steps in the accounting process and reviews the entire accounting cycle. We explain the closing process, including accounting procedures and the use of a post-closing trial balance. We show how a work sheet aids in preparing financial statements. A classified balance sheet and its use in analyzing information are explained.

A Look Ahead

Chapter 6 looks at accounting for merchandising activities. We describe the sale and purchase of merchandise and their implications for preparing and analyzing financial statements.

Red Hat Trick

e DURHAM, NC–Bill Gates, watch your back. Here comes Bob Young. In just four years, the former newsletter publisher has made his company, **Red Hat** [**RedHat.com**], the hot name in the growing Linux movement. Linux is *open source* software, meaning it's developed and refined by thousands of individuals in a desire to advance accounting and information services. And, best of all, its free. But unlike Windows or Macintosh systems, Linux doesn't hide computing from the user. That means friendly interfaces and prompts are typically absent. Enter Red Hat. It pastes friendly, easy-to-use interfaces on Linux accounting and other software. While abhorrent to Linux geeks, such improvements are great for entrepreneurs. Especially, according to Young, those interested in "higher-quality, better-priced" accounting software–extending from accounting transaction analysis and recording to financial statement preparation and e-commerce applications.

Still, Young claims he is not out to compete with mighty Microsoft. Instead, he says Red Hat reflects "a revolution" in the accounting software model in favor of users. But you would never guess it from the attention he is getting from the software giant. In confidential memos, Microsoft researchers warned Chairman Bill Gates that Red Hat poses a serious threat. Microsoft lawyers even hoisted a copy of Red Hat's latest release during Microsoft's antitrust trial as proof that it faces plenty of competition. Young does, however, concede a battle between proprietary and open source accounting software. "It is a David and Goliath battle," says Young. "But we are Goliath and Microsoft is David."

Make no mistake, Red Hat is red-hot these days. Young's unwavering brand evangelism, delivered with an aw-shucks twang, and savvy marketing maneuvers has made his company's trademark red fedora synonymous with Linux. As evidence of success, Young's net worth is now reported to exceed $2 billion. Moreover, his company's revenues are projected to exceed $50 million this year. While many challenges remain, many are betting that Red Hat will stay red hot. [Sources: *Business Week*, 10 January 2000, *Linux World*, 24 March 2000 and 25 May 1999; *Red Hat Web site*, May 2001]

Learning Objectives

Conceptual

C1 Explain why temporary accounts are closed each period.

C2 Identify steps in the accounting cycle.

C3 Explain and prepare a classified balance sheet.

Analytical

A1 Compute the current ratio and describe what it reveals about a company's financial condition.

Procedural

P1 Describe and prepare closing entries.

P2 Explain and prepare a post-closing trial balance.

P3 Prepare a work sheet and explain its usefulness.

Financial statement preparation is a major purpose of accounting. Many of the important steps leading to financial statements were explained in earlier chapters. We described how transactions and events are analyzed, journalized, and posted. We also described important adjustments that are often necessary to properly reflect both revenues when earned and expenses when incurred. This chapter describes the final steps in the accounting process. It explains the closing process that readies revenue, expense, and withdrawal accounts for the next reporting period and updates the capital account. A work sheet is shown as a useful tool in preparing financial statements. We explain how accounts are classified on a balance sheet to increase their usefulness to decision makers. We also describe the current ratio and explain how it is used to assess a company's ability to pay its liabilities in the near future.

Closing Process

C1 Explain why temporary accounts are closed each period.

Temporary Accounts

Temporary Accounts
Revenues
Expenses
Withdrawals
Income Summary

Permanent Accounts

Permanent Accounts
Assets
Liabilities
Capital

P1 Describe and prepare closing entries.

Concept 5-1

Point: To understand the closing process, it can help to focus on its *outcomes—updating* the capital account balance to its proper ending balance, and getting *temporary accounts* to show *zero balances* for purposes of accumulating data for the next period.

The **closing process** is an important step at the end of an accounting period *after* financial statements have been completed. It prepares accounts for recording the transactions and the events of the *next* period. In the closing process we must (1) Identify accounts for closing, (2) Record and post the closing entries, (3) Prepare a post-closing trial balance. The purpose of the closing process is twofold. First, it resets revenue, expense, and withdrawal account balances to zero at the end of each period. This is done so that these accounts can properly measure income and withdrawal amounts for the next period. Second, it helps in summarizing a period's revenues and expenses. This section explains the closing process.

Temporary and Permanent Accounts

Temporary (or *nominal*) **accounts** accumulate data related to one accounting period. They include all income statement accounts, withdrawal accounts, and Income Summary. They are temporary because the accounts are opened at the beginning of a period, used to record events for that period, and then closed at the end of the period. *The closing process applies only to temporary accounts.* **Permanent** (or *real*) **accounts** report on activities related to one or more future accounting periods. They carry their ending balances into the next period and include all balance sheet accounts. Asset, liability, and capital accounts are not closed as long as a company continues to own the assets, owe the liabilities, and have equity.

Recording Closing Entries

To record and post **closing entries** is to transfer the end-of-period balances in revenue, expense, and withdrawal accounts to the permanent owner's capital account. Closing entries are necessary at the end of each period after financial statements are prepared because

■ Revenue, expense, and withdrawal accounts must begin each period with zero balances.

■ The owner's capital account must reflect (1) increases from revenues and (2) decreases from both expenses and withdrawals.

An income statement aims to report revenues earned and expenses incurred for a specific accounting period. It is prepared from information recorded in revenue and expense accounts. The statement of changes in owner's equity aims to report changes in the owner's capital account for a specific period. It uses information on revenues and expense along with amounts in the withdrawals account. Because revenue, expense, and withdrawal accounts accumulate information for only one period, they must start each period with zero balances.

To close revenue and expense accounts, we transfer their balances first to an account called *Income Summary*. **Income Summary** is a temporary account that contains a credit for the sum of all revenues and a debit for the sum of all expenses. Its balance equals net income or net loss and is transferred to the owner's capital account. We then transfer the withdrawals account balance to the owner's capital account. After these closing entries are posted, the revenue, expense, Income Summary, and withdrawals accounts have zero balances. These accounts are then said to be *closed* or *cleared*. This process is illustrated in Exhibit 5.1.

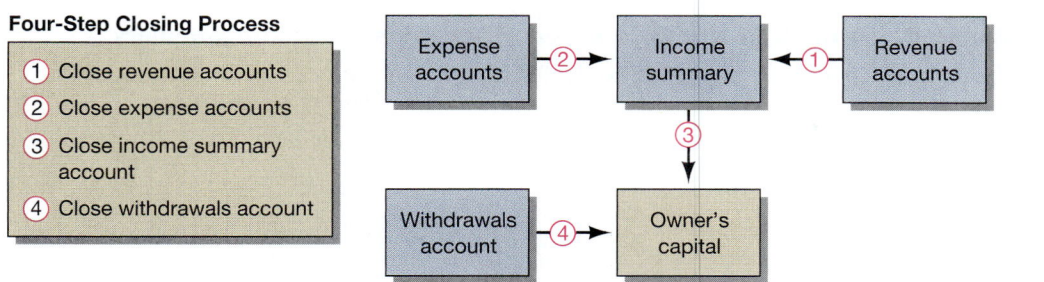

Exhibit 5.1
Closing Process

Exhibit 5.2 uses the adjusted account balances of **FastForward** from Exhibit 4.20 (repeated on the left side of Exhibit 5.3) to show the four steps necessary to close its revenue, expense, Income Summary, and withdrawals accounts. We explain each of these four steps.

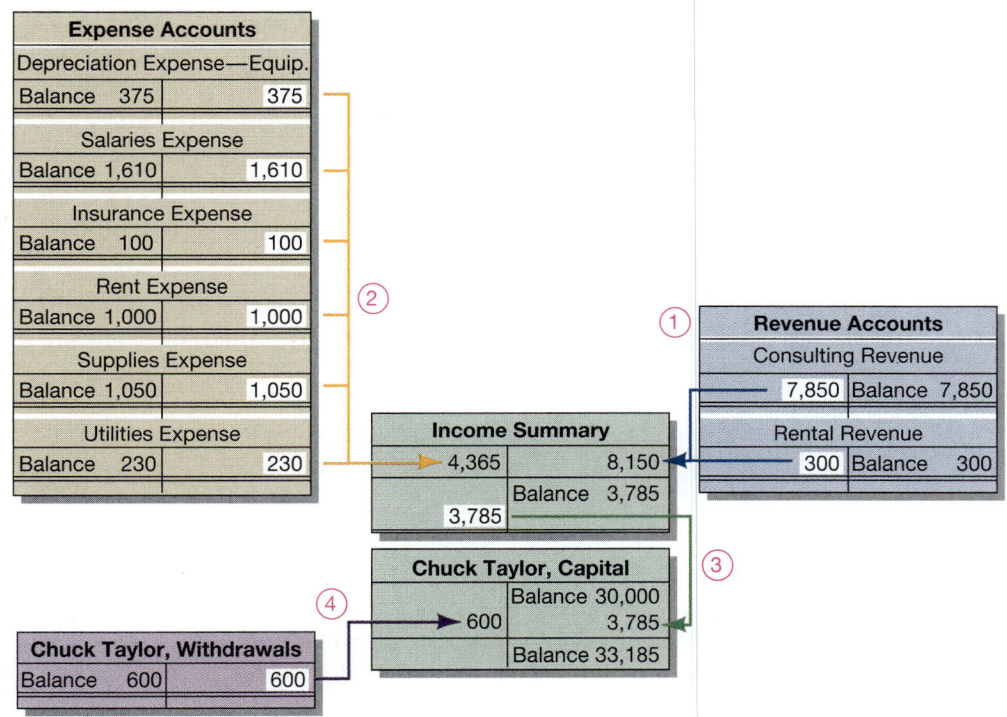

Exhibit 5.2
Closing Entries for FastForward

Step 1: Close Credit Balances in Revenue Accounts to Income Summary

The first closing entry transfers credit balances in revenue accounts to the Income Summary account. We bring accounts with credit balances to zero by debiting them. For FastForward, this journal entry is

Dec. 31	Consulting Revenue	7,850	
	Rental Revenue	300	
	Income Summary		8,150
	To close revenue accounts.		

This entry closes revenue accounts and leaves them with zero balances. They are now ready to record revenues for the next period. The Income Summary account is created and used *only* for the closing process. The current $8,150 credit balance in Income Summary equals total revenues for the period.

Step 2: Close Debit Balances in Expense Accounts to Income Summary

The second closing entry transfers debit balances in expense accounts to the Income Summary account. We bring expense accounts' debit balances to zero by crediting them. With a balance of zero, these accounts are ready to accumulate a record of expenses for the next period. This second closing entry for FastForward is

Dec. 31	Income Summary	4,365	
	Depreciation Expense—Equipment		375
	Salaries Expense		1,610
	Insurance Expense		100
	Rent Expense		1,000
	Supplies Expense		1,050
	Utilities Expense		230
	To close expense accounts.		

Exhibit 5.2 shows that posting this entry gives each expense account a zero balance. The entry also makes the balance of Income Summary equal to December's net income of $3,785. All debit and credit balances related to expense and revenue accounts are now collected in the Income Summary account.

Step 3: Close Income Summary to Owner's Capital

The third closing entry transfers the balance of the Income Summary account to the owner's capital account. This entry closes the Income Summary account and adds the company's net income to the owner's capital account:

Dec. 31	Income Summary	3,785	
	Chuck Taylor, Capital		3,785
	To close the Income Summary account.		

The Income Summary account has a zero balance after posting this entry. It continues to have a zero balance until the closing process occurs at the end of the next period. The owner's capital account has now been increased by the amount of net income. Increases to owner's capital from net income are credits.

Point: The Income Summary is used only for closing entries.

Step 4: Close Withdrawals Account to Owner's Capital

The fourth closing entry transfers any debit balance in the withdrawals account to the owner's capital account. This entry for FastForward is

Dec. 31	Chuck Taylor, Capital	600	
	Chuck Taylor, Withdrawals		600
	To close the withdrawals account.		

This entry gives the withdrawals account a zero balance, and the account is ready to accumulate next period's withdrawals. This entry also reduces the capital account balance to the $33,185 amount reported on the balance sheet in Exhibit 4.22.

Sources of Closing Entry Information

We select the accounts and amounts needing to be closed by identifying individual revenue, expense, and withdrawals accounts in the ledger. If we prepare an adjusted trial balance after the adjusting process, the information for closing entries is readily taken from it. This is illustrated in Exhibit 5.3 where we show how to prepare closing entries using only the adjusted trial balance.

Exhibit 5.3

Preparing Closing Entries from an Adjusted Trial Balance

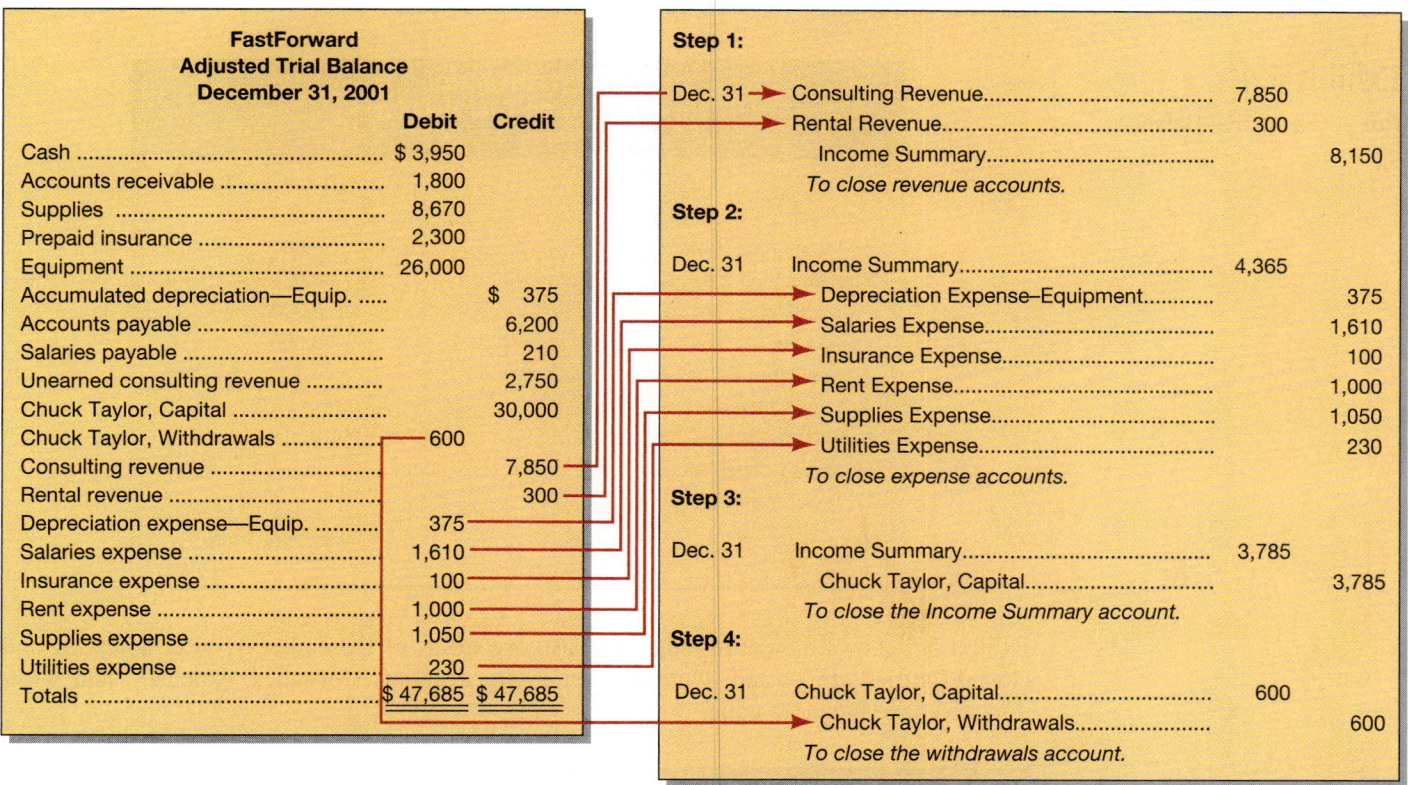

A company is usually not able to make all adjusting and closing entries on the last day of each period. Information about some transactions and events that require adjusting is not always available until several days or even weeks later. This means some adjusting and closing entries are recorded later than, but dated as of, the last day of the period. One example is a company that receives a utility bill on January 14 for costs incurred for the month of December. When it receives the bill, the company records the expense and the payable as of December 31. Other examples include long-distance phone usage and costs of many Web billings. The December income statement reflects these additional expenses incurred, and

Did You Know?

Virtual Financial Statements
Leading-edge companies venturing into the information age are seeing changes in the accounting process. Quantum leaps in computing technology are increasing the importance of accounting analysis and interpretation. We are moving toward what Clark Johnson, chief financial officer of **Johnson & Johnson**, calls the "virtual financial statement." This means we can get up-to-date financials with a click of a mouse.

the December 31 balance sheet includes these payables, although the amounts were not actually known on December 31.[1]

Post-Closing Trial Balance

P2 Explain and prepare a post-closing trial balance.

A **post-closing trial balance** is a list of permanent accounts and their balances from the ledger after all closing entries have been journalized and posted. It lists the balances for all accounts not closed. These accounts are a company's assets, liabilities, and equity, and they are identical to those in the balance sheet. The aim of a post-closing trial balance is to verify that (1) total debits equal total credits for permanent accounts and (2) all temporary accounts have zero balances. **FastForward**'s post-closing trial balance is shown in Exhibit 5.4. The post-closing trial balance is the last step in the accounting process. Like the unadjusted and adjusted trial balances, the post-closing trial balance does not necessarily tell us that all transactions are recorded or the ledger is correct.

Exhibit 5.4

Post-Closing Trial Balance

FASTFORWARD **Post-Closing Trial Balance** **December 31, 2001**		
	Debit	**Credit**
Cash	$ 3,950	
Accounts receivable	1,800	
Supplies	8,670	
Prepaid insurance	2,300	
Equipment	26,000	
Accumulated depreciation—Equipment		$ 375
Accounts payable		6,200
Salaries payable		210
Unearned consulting revenue		2,750
C. Taylor, Capital		33,185
Totals	$42,720	$42,720

Exhibit 5.5 shows the entire ledger of FastForward as of December 31 after adjusting and closing entries are posted. Note the temporary accounts (revenues, expenses, and withdrawals) have balances equal to zero.

Quick Check

1. What are the four major steps in preparing closing entries?

2. Why are revenue and expense accounts called *temporary*? Are there other temporary accounts?

3. What accounts are listed on the post-closing trial balance?

Answers—p. 191

Work Sheet as a Tool

Accountants use various analyses and internal documents when organizing information for reports to internal and external decision makers. Internal documents are important and are often called **working papers.** One widely used working paper is the **work sheet** which is a useful tool for preparers in working with accounting information. It is usually not available to external decision makers.

---

[1] The closing process has focused on proprietorships. It is identical for partnerships with the exception that each owner has separate capital and withdrawals accounts (for steps 3 and 4). The closing process for a corporation is identical with the exception that it uses a Retained Earnings account instead of a capital account (for step 3) and a withdrawals account (for step 4).

Exhibit 5.5

Ledger after the Closing
Process for FastForward

General Ledger

Asset Accounts

Cash — Acct. No. 101

Date	Explan.	PR	Debit	Credit	Balance
2001					
Dec. 1		G1	30,000		30,000
2		G1		2,500	27,500
3		G1		26,000	1,500
10		G1	4,200		5,700
12		G1		1,000	4,700
12		G1		700	4,000
22		G1	1,900		5,900
24		G1		900	5,000
24		G1		600	4,400
26		G1	3,000		7,400
26		G1		2,400	5,000
26		G1		120	4,880
26		G1		230	4,650
26		G1		700	**3,950**

Accounts Receivable — Acct. No. 106

Date	Explan.	PR	Debit	Credit	Balance
2001					
Dec. 12		G1	1,900		1,900
22		G1		1,900	0
31	Adj.	G1	1,800		**1,800**

Supplies — Acct. No. 126

Date	Explan.	PR	Debit	Credit	Balance
2001					
Dec. 2		G1	2,500		2,500
6		G1	7,100		9,600
26		G1	120		9,720
31	Adj.	G1		1,050	**8,670**

Prepaid Insurance — Acct. No. 128

Date	Explan.	PR	Debit	Credit	Balance
2001					
Dec. 26		G1	2,400		2,400
31	Adj.	G1		100	**2,300**

Equipment — Acct. No. 167

Date	Explan.	PR	Debit	Credit	Balance
2001					
Dec. 3		G1	26,000		**26,000**

Accumulated Depreciation— Equipment — Acct. No. 168

Date	Explan.	PR	Debit	Credit	Balance
2001					
Dec. 31	Adj.	G1		375	**375**

Liability and Equity Accounts

Accounts Payable — Acct. No. 201

Date	Explan.	PR	Debit	Credit	Balance
2001					
Dec. 6		G1		7,100	**7,100**
24		G1	900		**6,200**

Salaries Payable — Acct. No. 209

Date	Explan.	PR	Debit	Credit	Balance
2001					
Dec. 31	Adj.	G1		210	**210**

Unearned Consulting Revenue — Acct. No. 236

Date	Explan.	PR	Debit	Credit	Balance
2001					
Dec. 26		G1		3,000	3,000
31	Adj.	G1	250		**2,750**

C. Taylor, Capital — Acct. No. 301

Date	Explan.	PR	Debit	Credit	Balance
2001					
Dec. 1		G1		30,000	30,000
31	Closing	G1		3,785	33,785
31	Closing	G1	600		33,185

C. Taylor, Withdrawals — Acct. No. 302

Date	Explan.	PR	Debit	Credit	Balance
2001					
Dec. 24		G1	600		600
31	Closing	G1		600	0

Revenue and Expense Accounts (including Income Summary)

Consulting Revenue — Acct. No. 403

Date	Explan.	PR	Debit	Credit	Balance
2001					
Dec. 10		G1		4,200	4,200
12		G1		1,600	5,800
31	Adj.	G1		250	6,050
31	Adj.	G1		1,800	7,850
31	Closing	G1	7,850		0

Rental Revenue — Acct. No. 406

Date	Explan.	PR	Debit	Credit	Balance
2001					
Dec. 12		G1		300	300
31	Closing	G1	300		0

Depreciation Expense— Equipment — Acct. No. 612

Date	Explan.	PR	Debit	Credit	Balance
2001					
Dec. 31	Adj.	G1	375		375
31	Closing	G1		375	0

Salaries Expense — Acct. No. 622

Date	Explan.	PR	Debit	Credit	Balance
2001					
Dec. 12		G1	700		700
26		G1	700		1,400
31	Adj.	G1	210		1,610
31	Closing	G1		1,610	0

Insurance Expense — Acct. No. 637

Date	Explan.	PR	Debit	Credit	Balance
2001					
Dec. 31	Adj.	G1	100		100
31	Closing	G1		100	0

Rent Expense — Acct. No. 640

Date	Explan.	PR	Debit	Credit	Balance
2001					
Dec. 12		G1	1,000		1,000
31	Closing	G1		1,000	0

Supplies Expense — Acct. No. 652

Date	Explan.	PR	Debit	Credit	Balance
2001					
Dec. 31	Adj.	G1	1,050		1,050
31	Closing	G1		1,050	0

Utilities Expense — Acct. No. 690

Date	Explan.	PR	Debit	Credit	Balance
2001					
Dec. 26		G1	230		230
31	Closing	G1		230	0

Income Summary — Acct. No. 901

Date	Explan.	PR	Debit	Credit	Balance
2001					
Dec. 31	Closing	G1		8,150	8,150
31	Closing	G1	4,365		3,785
31	Closing	G1	3,785		0

Benefits of a Work Sheet

P3   Prepare a work sheet and explain its usefulness.

A work sheet is *not* a required financial report, yet using a manual or electronic work sheet has several potential benefits: (1) Reduces errors when working with systems involving many accounts and adjustments, (2) Links accounts and adjustments to their impacts in financial statements, (3) Assists in planning and organizing an audit of financial statements—it can be used to reflect any adjustments necessary, (4) Is useful in preparing interim (monthly or quarterly) financial statements when the journalizing and posting of adjusting entries are postponed until the year-end, (5) Is helpful in showing the effects of proposed or "what if" transactions.

Did You Know?

Silicon Accounting   An electronic work sheet using spreadsheet software such as **Excel** allows us to easily change numbers, assess the impact of alternative strategies, and quickly prepare financial statements at lower cost. It can also decrease the time devoted to the accounting process and increase the time for analysis and interpretation.

Using a Work Sheet

Point: A work sheet sometimes has two separate columns for the balance sheet and two separate columns for the statement of changes in owner's equity.

When a work sheet is used to prepare financial statements, it is constructed at the end of a period before the adjusting process. The work sheet includes a listing of the accounts, their balances and adjustments, and their sorting into financial statement columns. Exhibit 5.6 shows the form of a work sheet and the five steps in preparing it. The work sheet provides two columns each for the unadjusted trial balance, the adjustments, the adjusted trial balance, the income statement, and the balance sheet (including the statement of changes in owner's equity).

Exhibit 5.6

Form and Preparation of a Work Sheet

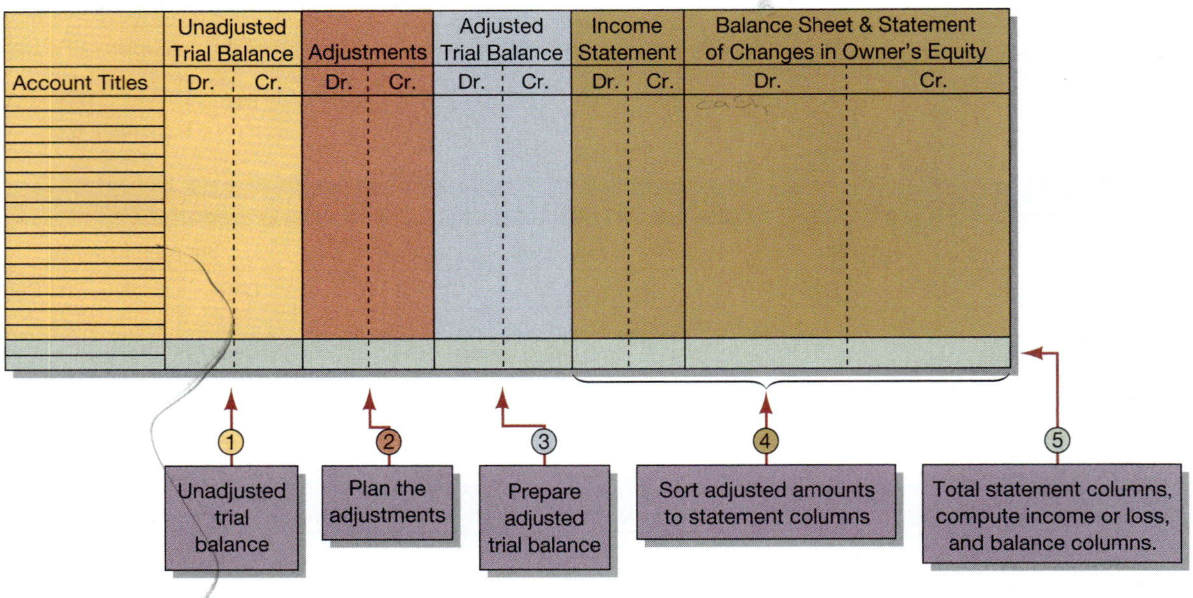

To describe and interpret the work sheet, we use the information from **FastForward**. Preparing the work sheet has five important steps. Each step, 1 through 5, is color-coded and explained with reference to Exhibits 5.7 and 5.8.[2]

---

[2] The *Ready Slides* PowerPoint presentation mimics this acetate overlay.

① Step 1. Enter Unadjusted Trial Balance

Refer to Exhibit 5.7. The first step in preparing a work sheet is to list the title of every account that is expected to appear on the company's financial statements.[3] The unadjusted balance for each account in the ledger is recorded in the appropriate Debit or Credit column of the unadjusted trial balance. The totals of these two columns must be equal. Exhibit 5.7 shows FastForward's work sheet after completing this first step. The unadjusted trial balance reflects the account balances after the December transactions are recorded but *before any adjusting entries are journalized and posted.* Sometimes blank lines are left on the work sheet based on past experience to indicate where lines will be needed for adjustments to certain accounts. Exhibit 5.7 shows Consulting Revenue as one example. An alternative is to squeeze adjustments on one line or to combine the effects of two or more adjustments in one amount.

② Step 2. Enter Adjustments

Refer to Exhibit 5.8a (turn over first transparency). The second step in preparing a work sheet is to enter adjustments in the Adjustments columns, as shown in Exhibit 5.8a. The adjustments shown are the same ones we discussed in Exhibit 4.20. An identifying letter links the debit and credit of each adjusting entry. This is called *keying* the adjustments. After preparing a work sheet, we still must enter adjusting entries in the journal and post them to the ledger.

Point: A recordkeeper often can complete the procedural task of journalizing and posting adjusting entries by using a work sheet and the guidance that *keying* provides.

③ Step 3. Prepare Adjusted Trial Balance

Refer to Exhibit 5.8b (turn over second transparency). The adjusted trial balance is prepared by combining the adjustments with the unadjusted balances for each account. As an example, the Prepaid Insurance account has a $2,400 debit balance in the Unadjusted Trial Balance columns. This $2,400 debit is combined with the $100 credit in the Adjustments columns to give Prepaid Insurance a $2,300 debit in the Adjusted Trial Balance columns. The totals of the Adjusted Trial Balance columns confirm the equality of debits and credits.

Point: To avoid omitting the transfer of an account balance, start with the first line (cash) and continue in account order.

④ Step 4. Sort Adjusted Trial Balance Amounts to Financial Statements

Refer to Exhibit 5.8c (turn over third transparency). This step involves sorting account balances in the adjusted trial balance to their proper financial statement columns. Expenses go to the Income Statement Debit column and revenues to the Income Statement Credit column. Assets and withdrawals go to the Balance Sheet & Statement of Changes in Owner's Equity Debit column. Liabilities and owner's capital go to the Balance Sheet & Statement of Changes in Owner's Equity Credit column.

⑤ Step 5. Total Statement Columns, Compute Income or Loss, and Balance Columns

Refer to Exhibit 5.8d (turn over fourth transparency). Each financial statement column (from Step 4) is totaled. The difference between the totals of the Income Statement columns is net income or net loss. This occurs because revenues are entered in the Credit column and expenses in the Debit column. If the Credit total exceeds the Debit total, there is net income. If the Debit total exceeds the Credit total, there is a net loss. For FastForward, the Credit total exceeds the Debit total, giving a $3,785 net income.

The net income from the Income Statement columns is then entered in the Balance Sheet & Statement of Changes in Owner's Equity Credit column. Adding net income to the last Credit column implies it is to be added to owner's capital. If a loss occurs, it is added to the Debit column. This implies it is to be subtracted from owner's capital. The ending balance of owner's capital does not appear in the last two columns as a single amount, but it is computed as the owner's capital account balance *plus* net income (or minus net loss) and

(continued on p. 180)

---

[3] This includes all accounts in the ledger plus any new ones from adjusting entries. Most adjusting entries—including expenses from salaries, supplies, depreciation, and insurance—are predictable and recurring. In the unusual case when an account is not predicted, we can add a new line for such an account following the *Totals* line for the adjusted trial balance.

Exhibit 5.7
Work Sheet with Unadjusted Trial Balance

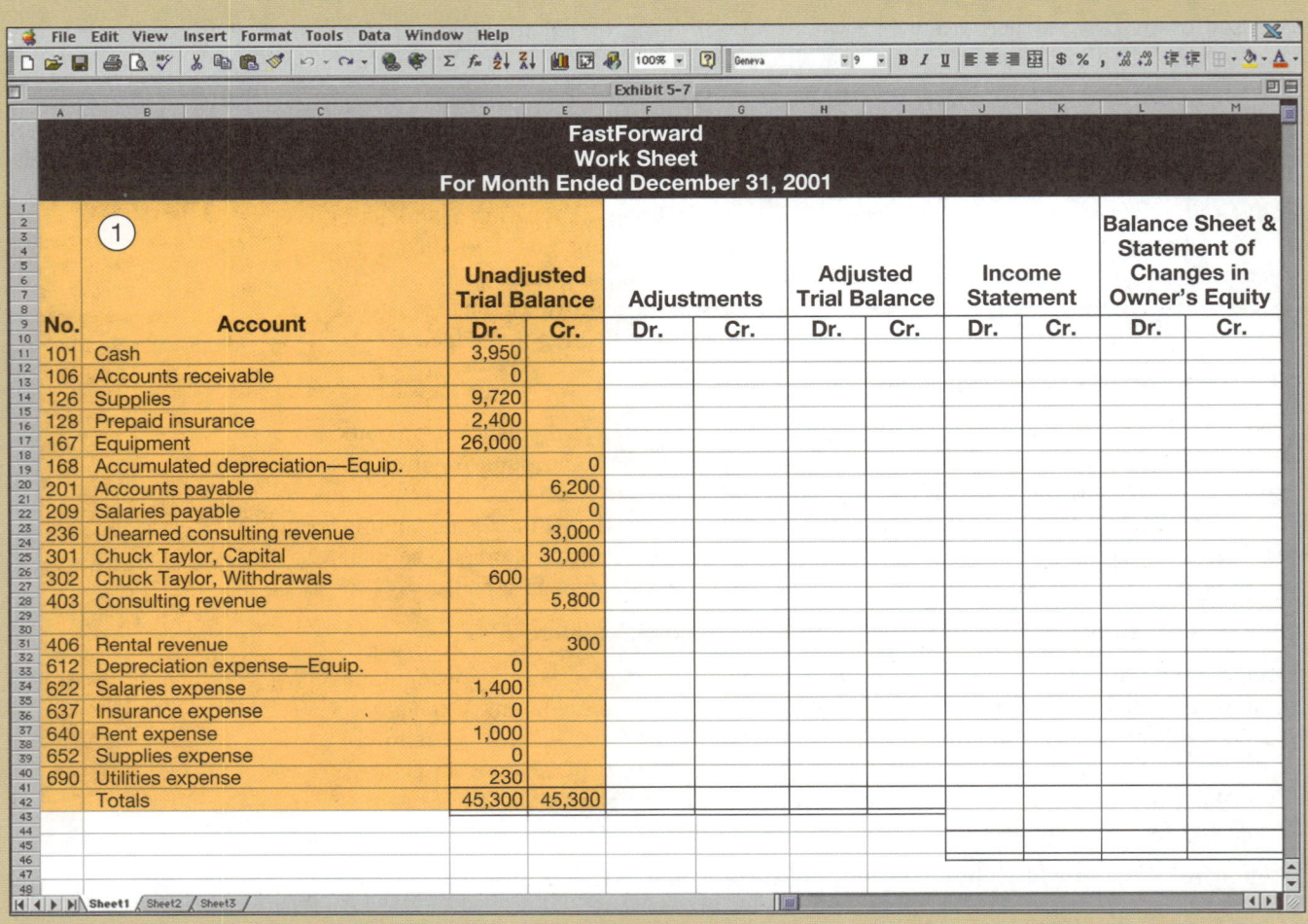

FastForward
Work Sheet
For Month Ended December 31, 2001

No.	Account	Unadjusted Trial Balance Dr.	Cr.	Adjustments Dr.	Cr.	Adjusted Trial Balance Dr.	Cr.	Income Statement Dr.	Cr.	Balance Sheet & Statement of Changes in Owner's Equity Dr.	Cr.
101	Cash	3,950									
106	Accounts receivable	0									
126	Supplies	9,720									
128	Prepaid insurance	2,400									
167	Equipment	26,000									
168	Accumulated depreciation—Equip.		0								
201	Accounts payable		6,200								
209	Salaries payable		0								
236	Unearned consulting revenue		3,000								
301	Chuck Taylor, Capital		30,000								
302	Chuck Taylor, Withdrawals	600									
403	Consulting revenue		5,800								
406	Rental revenue		300								
612	Depreciation expense—Equip.	0									
622	Salaries expense	1,400									
637	Insurance expense	0									
640	Rent expense	1,000									
652	Supplies expense	0									
690	Utilities expense	230									
	Totals	45,300	45,300								

List all accounts from the ledger and those expected to arise from adjusting entries.

Enter all amounts available from ledger accounts. Column totals must be equal.

A worksheet collects and summarizes information used to prepare adjusting entries, financial statements, and closing entries.

Enter adjustment amounts and use letters to cross-reference debit and credit adjustments. Column totals must be equal.

Exhibit 5.8d

Compute and Enter the Net Income or Loss and Complete the Work sheet

Enter two new lines for the net income or loss and for the totals.

Totals for the income statement columns differ by the amount of net income or net loss.

Net income (loss) is extended to the credit (debit) column of these columns.

FASTFORWARD
Income Statement
For Month Ended December 31, 2001

Revenues		
Consulting revenue	$ 7,850	
Rental revenue	300	
Total revenues		$ 8,150
Expenses		
Depreciation expense—Equip.	375	
Salaries expense	1,610	
Insurance expense	100	
Rent expense	1,000	
Supplies expense	1,050	
Utilities expense	230	
Total expenses		4,365
Net income		$ 3,785

FASTFORWARD
Statement of Changes in Owner's Equity
For Month Ended December 31, 2001

C. Taylor, Capital, December 1		$ 0
Add: Investment by owner	$30,000	
Net income	3,785	33,785
		$33,785
Less: Withdrawals by owner		600
C. Taylor, Capital, December 31		$33,185

FASTFORWARD
Balance Sheet
December 31, 2001

Assets		
Cash		$ 3,950
Accounts receivable		1,800
Supplies		8,670
Prepaid insurance		2,300
Equipment	$26,000	
Accumulated depreciation—Equip.	(375)	25,625
Total assets		$42,345
Liabilities		
Accounts payable		$ 6,200
Salaries payable		210
Unearned consulting revenue		2,750
Total liabilities		$ 9,160
Equity		
C. Taylor, Capital		$33,185
Total liabilities and equity		$42,345

Exhibit 5.9

Financial Statements Prepared from the Work Sheet

minus the withdrawals account balance. When net income or net loss is added to the proper Balance Sheet & Statement of Changes in Owner's Equity column, the totals of the last two columns must balance. If they do not, one or more errors have been made. The error can be mathematical or involve sorting one or more amounts to incorrect columns. A balance in the last two columns is not proof of no errors.

Entering adjustments in the Adjustments columns of a work sheet does not adjust the ledger accounts. Adjusting entries still must be entered in the general journal and posted to ledger accounts. The Adjustments columns provide the information for these entries. The adjustments in Exhibit 5.8a match the adjusting entries we described in Exhibit 4.19. Also, all items in the Income Statement columns must be closed to Income Summary. The resulting net income or loss shown in the Income Summary, along with the withdrawals account from the right-most Debit column, must be closed to owner's capital.

You Make the Call 𝑒

Entrepreneur You make a printout of the electronic work sheet used to prepare financial statements. There is no depreciation adjustment, yet you own a large amount of equipment. Does the lack of depreciation adjustment concern you?

Answer—p. 190

Work Sheet Application and Analysis

A work sheet does not substitute for financial statements; it is a tool we can use at the end of an accounting period to help organize data and prepare financial statements. FastForward's financial statements are shown in Exhibit 5.9. Its income statement amounts are taken from the Income Statement columns of the work sheet. Similarly, amounts for its balance sheet and its statement of changes in owner's equity are taken from the Balance Sheet & Statement of Changes in Owner's Equity columns of the work sheet. FastForward's statement of cash flows is prepared from the Cash account and supporting documents.

Work sheets are also useful in analyzing the effects of proposed, or what-if, transactions. This is done by entering financial statement amounts in the Unadjusted (what-if) columns. Proposed transactions are then entered in the Adjustments columns. We then compute "adjusted" amounts from these proposed transactions. The extended amounts in the financial statement columns show the effects of these proposed transactions. These financial statement columns yield **pro forma financial statements** because they show the statements *as if* the proposed transactions occurred.

Quick Check

4. Where do we get the amounts to enter in the Unadjusted Trial Balance columns of a work sheet?

5. What are the advantages of using a work sheet to help prepare adjusting entries?

6. What are the overall benefits of a work sheet?

Answers—p. 191

Statement of Cash Flows

The statement of cash flows is usually the final statement prepared. All of **FastForward**'s cash receipts and cash payments are recorded in its Cash account in the ledger. This Cash account holds information about cash flows from operating, investing, and financing activities and is shown in Exhibit 5.10. It reports individual cash transactions that are keyed to the transactions numbered (1) through (16) from Chapter 3.

To prepare the statement of cash flows, we must determine whether a cash flow reflects an operating, investing, or financing activity. We then report amounts in their proper category on the statement of cash flows. FastForward's statement of cash flows is shown in Exhibit 5.11.

Analysis of the Cash account provides a direct means to prepare the statement of cash flows, but this method has two limitations. First, companies often have so many individual cash receipts and disbursements that it is difficult to review them all. Second, the Cash account often does not contain a description of each cash transaction. Chapter 17 explains how to prepare the statement of cash flows when facing these limitations.

Global: Both U.S. and international standards require that cash flows be classified as operating, investing, or financing.

Cash

Cash			
Investment by owner (1)	30,000	Purchase of supplies (2)	2,500
Consulting revenue (5)	4,200	Purchase of equipment (3)	26,000
Collection of account receivable (9)	1,900	Payment of rent (6)	1,000
Receipts for future services (12)	3,000	Payment of salary (7)	700
		Payment of account payable (10)	900
		Withdrawal by owner (11)	600
		Payment of insurance (13)	2,400
		Purchase of supplies (14)	120
		Payment of utilities (15)	230
		Payment of salary (16)	700
Balance	**3,950**		

Exhibit 5.10

Cash Account of FastForward

FASTFORWARD
Statement of Cash Flows
For Month Ended December 31, 2001

Cash flows from operating activities		
Cash received from clients (5 + 9 + 12)	$ 9,100	
Cash paid for supplies (2 + 10 + 14)	(3,520)	
Cash paid for rent (6)	(1,000)	
Cash paid for insurance (13)	(2,400)	
Cash paid for utilities (15)	(230)	
Cash paid to employee (7 + 16)	(1,400)	
Net cash provided by operating activities		$ 550
Cash flows from investing activities		
Purchase of equipment (3)	(26,000)	
Net cash used by investing activities		(26,000)
Cash flows from financing activities		
Investment by owner (1)	30,000	
Withdrawal by owner (11)	(600)	
Net cash provided by financing activities		29,400
Net increase in cash		$ 3,950
Cash balance, December 1		0
Cash balance, December 31		$ 3,950

Exhibit 5.11

Statement of Cash Flows*

*Transaction numbers from Exhibit 5.10 are shown in parentheses.

Reviewing the Accounting Cycle

The **accounting cycle** refers to the steps in preparing financial statements. It is called a *cycle* because the steps are repeated each reporting period. Exhibit 5.12 shows the 10 steps in the cycle. They are shown in order, beginning with analyzing transactions and ending with a post-closing trial balance or reversing entries. Steps 1 through 3 usually occur regularly as a company enters into transactions. Steps 4 through 9 are done at the end of a period. Reversing entries in step 10 are optional and are explained in Appendix 5A. Detailed descriptions of these steps are in Chapters 3, 4, and 5.

C2 Identify steps in the accounting cycle.

Did You Know?

Data Speedway Five years ago **Sun Microsystems** took almost a month to prepare statements after its year-end. Today, it takes only 24 hours to deliver preliminary figures to key decision makers. What is Sun's secret? Transactions are entered into a network of computers so everyone can share and quickly manage data. This frees its accounting professionals for a more active role in managing and strategizing.

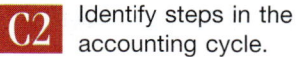

Exhibit 5.12

Steps in the
Accounting Cycle*

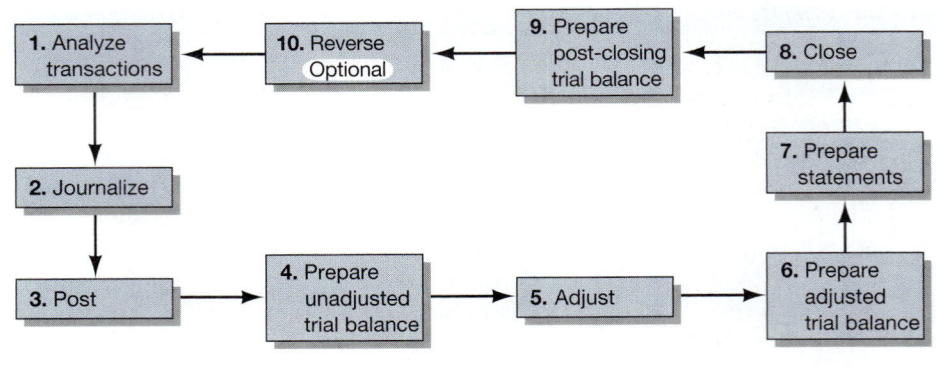

Explanations

1. Analyze transaction	Analyze transactions to prepare for journalizing.
2. Journalize	Record accounts, including debits and credits, in a journal.
3. Post	Transfer debits and credits from the journal to the ledger.
4. Prepare unadjusted trial balance	Summarize unadjusted ledger accounts and amounts.
5. Adjust	Record adjustments to bring account balances up to date; journalize and post adjusting entries.
6. Prepare adjusted trial balance	Summarize adjusted ledger accounts and amounts.
7. Prepare statements	Use adjusted trial balance to prepare statements.
8. Close	Journalize and post entries to close temporary accounts and update the owner's capital account.
9. Prepare post-closing trial balance	Test clerical accuracy of the closing procedures.
10. Reverse (optional)	Reverse certain adjustments in the next period—optional step; see Appendix 5A.

*Steps 4, 6, and 9 can be done on a work sheet. A work sheet is useful in planning adjustments, but adjustments (step 5) must always be journalized and posted.

Classified Balance Sheet

C3 Explain and prepare a classified balance sheet.

Exhibit 5.13

Typical Categories in a Classified Balance Sheet

Concept 5-2

Our discussion to this point has been limited to unclassified financial statements. But companies also prepare classified financial statements. This section focuses on a classified balance sheet. Chapter 6 describes a classified income statement. An **unclassified balance sheet** is one whose items are broadly grouped into assets, liabilities, and equity. One example is FastForward's balance sheet in Exhibit. 5.9. A **classified balance sheet** organizes assets and liabilities into important subgroups. The information in a balance sheet is more useful to decision makers if assets and liabilities are classified into subgroups. One example is information to distinguish liabilities that are due soon from those not due for several years. This information helps us better assess a company's ability to meet liabilities when they come due.

Assets	Liabilities and Equity
Current assets	Current liabilities
Noncurrent assets	Noncurrent liabilities
Long-term investments	Equity
Plant assets	
Intangible assets	

Classification Structure

A classified balance sheet has no required layout. At the very least, it usually contains the categories in Exhibit 5.13. One of the more important classifications is the separation between current and noncurrent items for both assets and liabilities. Current items are those expected to come due (either collected or owed) within the longer of (a) one year or (b) the company's operating cycle. An operating cycle is the length of time between (1) purchases of services or products from suppliers and (2) cash receipts from the sale of services or products to customers. The length of a company's operating cycle depends on its activities. Exhibit 5.14 shows key points in the operating cycle for both a service company and a merchandising company. For a service company, the **operating cycle** is the normal time between (1) paying employees who perform the services and (2)

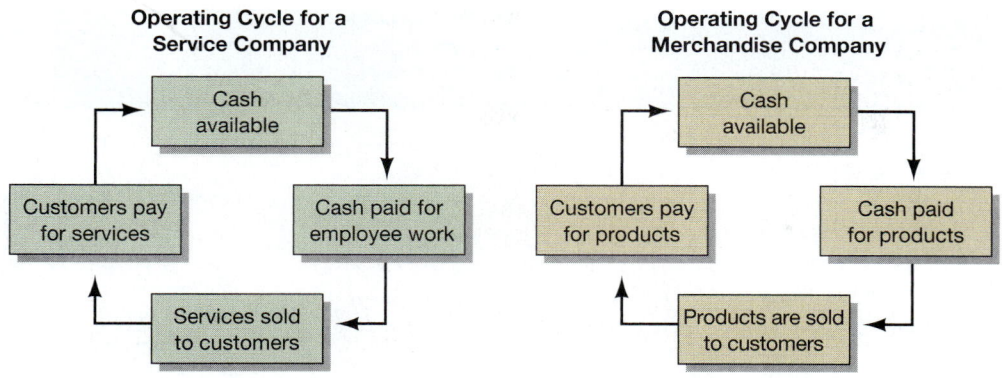

Exhibit 5.14

Operating Cycles for a Service Company and a Merchandise Company

receiving cash from customers. For a merchandiser selling products, the operating cycle is the normal time between (1) paying suppliers for merchandise and (2) receiving cash from customers.

Most operating cycles are less than one year. This means most companies use a one-year period in deciding which assets and liabilities are current. Other companies have an operating cycle longer than one year. For instance, producers of certain beverages (wine) and products (ginseng) that require aging for several years have operating cycles longer than one year. These companies use their multiyear operating cycles in deciding which balance sheet items are current or noncurrent.

A balance sheet usually lists current assets before noncurrent assets and current liabilities before noncurrent liabilities. This consistency in presentation allows users to quickly identify current assets that are most easily converted to cash and current liabilities that are shortly coming due. Items in the current group are usually listed in the order of how quickly they will be converted to, or paid in, cash.

The balance sheet for **Music Components** is shown in Exhibit 5.15. It shows the more typical categories. Its assets are classified as either current or noncurrent. Its noncurrent assets include three main categories: investments, plant assets, and intangible assets. Its liabilities are classified as either current or long term. Not all companies use the same categories of assets and liabilities for their balance sheets. **K2**'s balance sheet lists only three asset classes: current assets; property, plant and equipment; and other assets.

Classification Categories

This section describes the most common categories in a classified balance sheet.

Current Assets

Current assets are cash and other resources that are expected to be sold, collected, or used within the longer of one year or the company's operating cycle. Examples are cash, short-term investments, accounts receivable, short-term notes receivable, goods for sale (called *merchandise* or *inventory*), and prepaid expenses. A company's prepaid expenses are usually small in amount compared to many other assets and are often combined and shown as a single item. The prepaid expenses in Exhibit 5.15 likely include items such as prepaid insurance, prepaid rent, office supplies, and store supplies. Prepaid expenses are usually listed last because they will not be converted to cash (instead, they are used).

Long-Term Investments

A second major balance sheet classification is **long-term** (or *noncurrent*) **investments.** Notes receivable and investments in stocks and bonds are long-term assets when they are expected to be held for more than the longer of one year or the operating cycle. We further explain the differences between short- and long-term investments later in the book.

Point: Current is also called *short term,* and noncurrent is also called *long term.*

Point: Short-term investments maturing within three months are combined with cash on both the balance sheet and cash flow statement. This combination is called *cash and cash equivalents.*

Global: In the U.K. and many countries influenced by U.K. reporting, noncurrent assets are listed first and current assets are listed last.

Exhibit 5.15

Typical Example of a Classified Balance Sheet

MUSIC COMPONENTS
Balance Sheet
January 31, 2002

Assets

Current assets

Cash	$ 6,500	
Short-term investments	2,100	
Accounts receivable	4,400	
Merchandise inventory	27,500	
Prepaid expenses	2,400	
Total current assets		$ 42,900

Long-term investments

Notes receivable	1,500	
Disney common stock	18,000	
Land held for future expansion	48,000	
Total investments		67,500

Plant assets

Store equipment	$ 33,200		
Less accumulated depreciation	8,000	25,200	
Buildings	170,000		
Less accumulated depreciation	45,000	125,000	
Land		73,200	
Total plant assets			223,400
Intangible assets			10,000
Total assets			$343,800

Liabilities

Current liabilities

Accounts payable	$15,300	
Wages payable	3,200	
Notes payable	3,000	
Current portion of long-term liabilities	7,500	
Total current liabilities		$ 29,000
Long-term liabilities (net of current portion)		150,000
Total liabilities		$179,000

Equity

D. Bowie, Capital		164,800
Total liabilities and equity		$343,800

Plant Assets

Point: Plant assets are also called **fixed assets** and **property, plant and equipment.**

Plant assets are tangible long-lived assets used to help produce or sell products and services. Examples are equipment, vehicles, buildings, and land. Items in this category are both *long lived* and *used to produce* or *sell products and services*. For example, land held for future expansion is *not* a plant asset because it is not used to produce or sell products and services. The order of listing plant assets is usually from most liquid to least liquid such as equipment and machinery to buildings and land.

Intangible Assets

Intangible assets are long-term resources used to produce or sell products and services. They usually lack physical form and have uncertain benefits. Examples are patents, trademarks, copyrights, franchises, and goodwill. Their value comes from the privileges or rights granted to or held by the owner. **Outboard Marine** reports intangible assets of $79.3 million, which is nearly 10 percent of its total assets. Its intangibles include trademarks, patents, and its dealer network.

Point: Companies sometimes have intangible assets but because of materiality or cost principles, they are not reported.

Current Liabilities

Current liabilities are obligations due to be paid or settled within the longer of one year or the operating cycle. They are usually settled by paying out current assets such as cash. Current liabilities often include accounts payable, notes payable, wages payable, taxes payable, interest payable, and unearned revenues. Also, any portion of a long-term liability due to be paid within the longer of one year or the operating cycle is a current liability—Exhibit 5.15 shows an example. Unearned revenues are current liabilities when they will be settled by delivering products or services within the longer of the year or the operating cycle. Although practice varies, current liabilities are often reported in the order of those to be settled first.

Point: Many financial ratios are distorted if accounts are not classified correctly. We must be especially careful when analyzing accounts whose balances are separated into short and long term.

Long-Term Liabilities

Long-term liabilities are obligations *not* due within the longer of one year or the operating cycle. Notes payable, mortgages payable, bonds payable, and lease obligations are common long-term liabilities. If a company has both short- and long-term items in one of these accounts, they are commonly separated into two accounts in the ledger.

Point Many companies report two or more categories of long-term liabilities. See the balance sheets in Appendix A for examples.

Equity

Owner's equity is the owner's claim on a proprietorship's assets. It is reported in the equity section with an owner's capital account. For a partnership, the equity section reports a capital account for each partner. For a corporation, the equity section is divided into two main subsections, capital stock and retained earnings. Chapter 2 described these alternative organization forms and their implications for financial reporting.

Quick Check

7. Identify which of the following assets are classified as (1) current assets or (2) plant assets: (a) land used in operations, (b) office supplies, (c) receivables from customers due in 10 months, (d) insurance protection for the next nine months, (e) trucks used to provide services to customers, (f) trademarks.

8. Cite two examples of assets classified as investments on the balance sheet.

9. Explain the operating cycle for a service company.

Answers—p. 191

Current Ratio

Using the Information

An important use of financial statements is to aid in assessing a company's ability to pay its debts in the near future. This type of analysis affects decisions by suppliers when allowing a company to buy on credit. It also affects decisions by creditors when lending money to a company, including loan terms such as interest rate, due date, and collateral requirements. It can also affect a manager's decisions about using cash to pay existing debts when they come due. The **current ratio** is an important measure of a company's ability to pay its short-term obligations. It is defined in Exhibit 5.16 as current assets divided by current liabilities:

A1 Compute the current ratio and describe what it reveals about a company's financial condition.

$$\text{Current ratio} = \frac{\text{Current assets}}{\text{Current liabilities}}$$

Exhibit 5.16

Current Ratio

Using financial information from **Ben & Jerry**'s, we compute its current ratios for a recent four-year period. The results are shown in Exhibit 5.17.

Exhibit 5.17

Ben & Jerry's Current Ratio

($ in Millions)	1999	1998	1997	1996
Total current assets	$87.3	$82.3	$80.1	$68.1
Total current liabilities	$44.5	$33.9	$28.7	$18.1
Current ratio	2.0	2.4	2.8	3.8
Industry current ratio	1.8	2.1	2.3	2.2

Ben & Jerry's current ratio dipped to 2.0 in 1999 compared to higher ratios for prior years. Still, the current ratio for all of these years suggests that its short-term obligations can be covered with its short-term assets. If the ratio moved closer to 1, Ben & Jerry's would expect to face more challenges in covering liabilities. If the ratio were *less* than 1, Ben & Jerry's current liabilities would exceed its current assets, and it would likely face problems in covering current liabilities. However, in this case, Ben & Jerry's current ratio implies that its ability to pay short-term obligations is good.

You Make the Call

Analyst   You are analyzing the financial condition of a fitness club to assess its ability to meet upcoming loan payments. You compute its current ratio as 1.2. You also find that a major portion of accounts receivable is due from one client who has not made any payments in the past 12 months. Removing this receivable from current assets drops the current ratio to 0.7. What do you conclude?

Answer—p. 191

Demonstration Problem

Following is the partial work sheet of Midtown Repair Company at December 31, 2002:

	Adjusted Trial Balance		Income Statement		Balance Sheet and Statement of Changes in Owner's Equity	
	Debit	**Credit**	**Debit**	**Credit**	**Debit**	**Credit**
Cash	95,600					
Notes receivable	50,000					
Prepaid insurance	16,000					
Prepaid rent	4,000					
Equipment	170,000					
Accumulated depreciation—Equipment		57,000				
Accounts payable		52,000				
Long-term notes payable		63,000				
C. Trout, Capital		178,500				
C. Trout, Withdrawals	30,000					
Repair services revenue		180,800				
Interest earned		7,500				
Depreciation expense—Equipment	28,500					
Wages expense	85,000					
Rent expense	48,000					
Insurance expense	6,000					
Interest expense	5,700					
Totals	538,800	538,800				

Required

1. Complete the work sheet by extending the adjusted trial balance totals to the appropriate financial statement columns.

2. Prepare closing entries for Midtown Repair Company.

3. Set up the Income Summary and the C. Trout, Capital account in the general ledger and post the closing entries to these accounts.

4. Determine the balance of the C. Trout, Capital account to be reported on the December 31, 2002 balance sheet.

Planning the Solution

• Extend the adjusted trial balance account balances to the appropriate financial statement columns.

• Prepare entries to close the revenue accounts to Income Summary, to close the expense accounts to Income Summary, to close Income Summary to the capital account, and to close the withdrawals account to the capital account.

• Post the first and second closing entries to the Income Summary account. Examine the balance of income summary and verify that it agrees with the net income shown on the work sheet.

• Post the third and fourth closing entries to the capital account.

Solution to Demonstration Problem

1. Completing the work sheet:

	Adjusted Trial Balance		Income Statement		Balance Sheet and Statement of Changes in Owner's Equity	
	Debit	**Credit**	**Debit**	**Credit**	**Debit**	**Credit**
Cash	95,600				95,600	
Notes receivable	50,000				50,000	
Prepaid insurance	16,000				16,000	
Prepaid rent	4,000				4,000	
Equipment	170,000				170,000	
Accumulated depreciation—Equipment		57,000				57,000
Accounts payable		52,000				52,000
Long-term notes payable		63,000				63,000
C. Trout, Capital		178,500				178,500
C. Trout, Withdrawals	30,000				30,000	
Repair services revenue		180,800		180,800		
Interest earned		7,500		7,500		
Depreciation expense—Equipment	28,500		28,500			
Wages expense	85,000		85,000			
Rent expense	48,000		48,000			
Insurance expense	6,000		6,000			
Interest expense	5,700		5,700			
Totals	538,800	538,800	173,200	188,300	365,600	350,500
Net Income			15,100			15,100
Totals			188,300	188,300	365,600	365,600

2. Closing entries:

Dec. 31	Repair Services Revenue	180,800	
	Interest Earned	7,500	
	Income Summary		188,300
	To close revenue accounts.		

[continued on next page]

[continued from previous page]

Dec. 31	Income Summary		173,200	
	Depreciation Expense—Equipment			28,500
	Wages Expense			85,000
	Rent Expense			48,000
	Insurance Expense			6,000
	Interest Expense			5,700
	To close expense accounts.			
Dec. 31	Income Summary		15,100	
	C. Trout, Capital			15,100
	To close the Income Summary account.			
Dec. 31	C. Trout, Capital		30,000	
	C. Trout, Withdrawals			30,000
	To close the withdrawals account.			

3. Set up the Income Summary and the capital ledger accounts and post the closing entries.

Income Summary					**Account No. 901**
Date	**Explanation**	**PR**	**Debit**	**Credit**	**Balance**
2002					
Jan. 1	Beginning balance				0
Dec. 31	Close revenue accounts			188,300	188,300
31	Close expense accounts		173,200		15,100
31	Close income summary		15,100		0

C. Trout, Capital					**Account No. 301**
Date	**Explanation**	**PR**	**Debit**	**Credit**	**Balance**
2002					
Jan. 1	Beginning balance				178,500
Dec. 31	Close Income Summary			15,100	193,600
31	Close C. Trout, Withdrawals		30,000		163,600

4. The final capital balance of $163,600 [from part (3)] will be reported on the December 31, 2002 balance sheet. The final capital balance reflects the increase due to the net income earned during the year and the decrease for the owner's withdrawals during the year.

APPENDIX

5A   Reversing Entries

This appendix describes the use of reversing entries in accounting.

Reversing Entries

Point: As a general rule, adjusting entries that create new asset or liability accounts are likely candidates for reversing.

Reversing entries are optional. They are linked to accrued assets and liabilities that were created by adjusting entries at the end of a reporting period. The purpose of reversing entries is to simplify a company's recordkeeping. Exhibit 5A.1 shows how reversing entries work for **FastForward**. The top of the exhibit shows the adjusting entry FastForward recorded on December 31 for its employee's earned but unpaid salary. The entry recorded three days' salary of $210, which increased December's total salary expense to $1,610. The entry also recognized a liability of $210. The expense is reported on December's income statement. The expense account is then closed. The ledger on January 1, 2002, shows a $210 liability and a zero balance in the Salaries Expense account. At this point, the choice is made between using or not using reversing entries.

Accounting *without* Reversing Entries

The path down the left side of Exhibit 5A.1 is described in detail in Chapter 4. To summarize here, when the next payday occurs on January 9, we record payment with a compound entry that debits both the expense and liability accounts and credits Cash. Posting that entry creates a $490 balance in

Exhibit 5A.1

Reversing Entries for Accrued Expenses

Accrue salaries expense on December 31, 2001

Salaries Expense 210
    Salaries Payable 210

Salaries Expense

Date	Expl.	Debit	Credit	Balance
2001				
Dec. 12	(7)	700		700
26	(16)	700		1,400
31	(e)	210		1,610

Salaries Payable

Date	Expl.	Debit	Credit	Balance
2001				
Dec. 31	(e)		210	210

 — OR —

No reversing entry recorded on January 1, 2002

NO ENTRY

Salaries Expense

Date	Expl.	Debit	Credit	Balance
2002				

Salaries Payable

Date	Expl.	Debit	Credit	Balance
2001				
Dec. 31	(e)		210	210
2002				

Reversing entry recorded on January 1, 2002

Salaries Payable 210
    Salaries Expense 210

Salaries Expense*

Date	Expl.	Debit	Credit	Balance
2002				
Jan. 1			210	(210)

Salaries Payable

Date	Expl.	Debit	Credit	Balance
2001				
Dec. 31	(e)		210	210
2002				
Jan. 1		210		0

Pay the accrued and current salaries on January 9, the first payday in 2002

Salaries Expense 490
Salaries Payable 210
    Cash 700

Salaries Expense

Date	Expl.	Debit	Credit	Balance
2002				
Jan. 9		490		490

Salaries Payable

Date	Expl.	Debit	Credit	Balance
2001				
Dec. 31	(e)		210	210
2002				
Jan. 9		210		0

Salaries Expense 700
    Cash 700

Salaries Expense*

Date	Expl.	Debit	Credit	Balance
2002				
Jan. 1			210	(210)
Jan. 9		700		490

Salaries Payable

Date	Expl.	Debit	Credit	Balance
2001				
Dec. 31	(e)		210	210
2002				
Jan. 1		210		0

Under both approaches, the expense and liability accounts have identical balances after the cash payment on January 9.

Salaries Expense $490
Salaries Payable .... $ 0

*Circled numbers in the *Balance* column indicate abnormal balances.

the expense account and reduces the liability account balance to zero because the debt has been settled. The disadvantage of this approach is the slightly more complex entry required on January 9. Paying the accrued liability means that this entry differs from the routine entries made on all other paydays. To construct the proper entry on January 9, we must recall the effect of the December 31 adjusting entry. Reversing entries overcome this disadvantage.

Accounting *with* Reversing Entries

P4 Prepare reversing entries and explain their purpose.

The right side of Exhibit 5A.1 shows how a reversing entry on January 1 overcomes the disadvantage of the January 9 entry when not using reversing entries. A reversing entry is the exact opposite of an adjusting entry. For FastForward, the Salaries Payable liability account is debited for $210, meaning that this account now has a zero balance after the entry is posted. The Salaries Payable account temporarily understates the liability, but this is not a problem since financial statements are not prepared before the liability is settled on January 9. The credit to the Salaries Expense account is unusual because it gives the account an *abnormal credit balance*. We highlight an abnormal balance by circling it. Because of the reversing entry, the January 9 entry to record payment is straightforward. This entry debits the Salaries Expense account and credits Cash for the full $700 paid. It is the same as all other entries made to record 10 day's salary for the employee. Notice that after the payment entry is posted, the Salaries Expense account has a $490 balance that reflects seven days' salary of $70 per day, (see the lower right side of Exhibit 5A.1). The zero balance in the Salaries Payable account is now correct.

The lower section of Exhibit 5A.1 shows that the expense and liability accounts have exactly the same balances whether reversing entries are used or not. This means both approaches yield identical results.

Summary

C1 **Explain why temporary accounts are closed each period.** Temporary accounts are closed at the end of each accounting period for two main reasons. First, the closing process updates the owner's capital account to include the effects of all transactions and events recorded for the period. Second, it prepares revenue, expense, and withdrawals accounts for the next reporting period by giving them zero balances.

C2 **Identify steps in the accounting cycle.** The accounting cycle consists of 10 steps: (1) analyze transactions, (2) journalize, (3) post, (4) prepare an unadjusted trial balance, (5) adjust accounts, (6) prepare an adjusted trial balance, (7) prepare statements, (8) close, (9) prepare a post-closing trial balance, and (10) prepare (optional) reversing entries.

C3 **Explain and prepare a classified balance sheet.** Classified balance sheets usually report assets and liabilities in two categories: current and noncurrent. Noncurrent assets often include long-term investments, plant and equipment, and intangible assets. Owner's equity for proprietorships and partners' equity for partnerships report the capital account balances. A corporation separates equity into contributed capital and retained earnings.

A1 **Compute the current ratio and describe what it reveals about a company's financial condition.** A company's current ratio is defined as current assets divided by current liabilities. We use it to evaluate a company's ability to pay its current liabilities out of current assets.

P1 **Describe and prepare closing entries.** Closing entries involve four steps: (1) close credit balances in revenue accounts to income summary, (2) close debit balances in expense accounts to income summary, (3) close income summary to owner's capital, and (4) close withdrawals account to owner's capital.

P2 **Explain and prepare a post-closing trial balance.** A post-closing trial balance is a list of permanent accounts and their balances after all closing entries have been journalized and posted. Its purpose is to verify that (1) total debits equal total credits for permanent accounts and (2) all temporary accounts have zero balances.

P3 **Prepare a work sheet and explain its usefulness.** A work sheet can be a useful tool in preparing and analyzing financial statements. It is helpful at the end of a period in preparing adjusting entries, an adjusted trial balance, and financial statements. A work sheet often contains five pairs of columns: Unadjusted Trial Balance, Adjustments, Adjusted Trial Balance, Income Statement, and Balance Sheet and Statement of Changes in Owner's Equity.

P4 **Prepare reversing entries and explain their purpose.** Reversing entries are an optional step. They are applied to accrued assets and liabilities. The purpose of reversing entries is to simplify subsequent journal entries. Financial statements are unaffected by the choice to use or not use reversing entries.

Guidance Answers to **You Make the Call**

Entrepreneur Yes, you are concerned about the absence of a depreciation adjustment. Equipment does depreciate, and financial statements must recognize this occurrence. Its absence suggests an error or a misrepresentation.

Analyst A current ratio of 1.2 suggests that current assets are sufficient to cover current liabilities—but it implies a minimal buffer in case of errors in measuring current assets or liabilities. Removing tardy receivables reduces the current ratio to 0.7. Your assessment is that the club will have difficulty meeting its loan payments.

Guidance Answers to **Quick Checks**

1. The four major steps in preparing closing entries are to close (1) credit balances in revenue accounts to Income Summary, (2) debit balances in expense accounts to Income Summary, (3) Income Summary to owner's capital, and (4) any withdrawals account to owner's capital.

2. Revenue and expense accounts are called *temporary* because they are opened and closed each period. The Income Summary and owner's withdrawals accounts are also temporary.

3. Permanent accounts make up the post-closing trial balance. These accounts are asset, liability, and equity accounts.

4. Amounts in the Unadjusted Trial Balance columns are taken from account balances in the ledger. The balances for new accounts expected to arise from adjusted entries can be left blank or set at zero.

5. A work sheet offers the advantage of listing on one page all necessary information to make adjusting entries.

6. A worksheet can help in (a) avoiding errors, (b) linking transactions and events to their effects in financial statements, (c) showing adjustments for audit purposes, (d) preparing interim financial statements, and (e) showing effects from proposed, or what-if, transactions.

7. Current assets: (b), (c), (d). Plant assets: (a), (e). Item (f) is an intangible asset.

8. Investment in common stock, investment in bonds, land held for future expansion.

9. For a service company, the operating cycle is the usual time between (1) paying employees who do the services and (2) receiving cash from customers for services provided.

Glossary

Accounting cycle recurring steps performed each accounting period, starting with analyzing transactions and continuing through the post-closing trial balance (or reversing entries). (p. 181).

Classified balance sheet balance sheet that presents assets and liabilities in relevant subgroups. (p. 182).

Closing entries entries recorded at the end of each accounting period to transfer end-of-period balances in revenue, expense, and withdrawals accounts to the owner's capital account (p. 170).

Closing process necessary steps to prepare the accounts for recording the transactions of the next period. (p. 170).

Current assets cash or other assets that are expected to be sold, collected, or used within the longer of one year or the company's operating cycle. (p. 183).

Current liabilities obligations due to be paid or settled within the longer of one year or the operating cycle. (p. 185).

Current ratio ratio used to evaluate a company's ability to pay its short-term obligations, calculated by dividing current assets by current liabilities. (p. 185).

Income Summary temporary account used only in the closing process to which the balances of revenue and expense accounts are transferred; its balance is transferred to the owner's capital account. (p. 170).

Intangible assets long-term assets (resources) used to produce or sell products or services; they usually lack physical form and their benefits are uncertain. (p. 184).

Long-term investments assets such as notes receivable and investments in stocks and bonds that are held for more than the longer of one year or the operating cycle. (p. 183).

Long-term liabilities obligations that are not due to be paid within the longer of one year or the operating cycle. (p. 185).

Nominal accounts (*see temporary account*). (p. 170).

Operating cycle normal time between paying cash for merchandise or employee services and receiving cash from customers. (p. 182).

Owner's equity owner's claim on a company's assets. (p. 185).

Permanent accounts accounts used to report activities related to one or more future periods; balance sheet accounts whose balances are not closed; also called *real accounts*. (p. 170).

Plant assets tangible long-lived assets used to produce or sell products or services; also called *property, plant and equipment* or *fixed assets*. (p. 184).

Post-closing trial balance list of permanent accounts and their balances from the ledger after all closing entries are journalized and posted. (p. 174).

Pro forma financial statements statements that show the effects of proposed transactions as if they had occurred. (p. 180).

Real accounts (*see permanent account*). (p. 170).

Reversing entries optional entries recorded at the beginning of a new period that prepare the accounts for the usual journal entries as if adjusting entries had not occurred. (p. 188).

Temporary accounts accounts used to record revenues, expenses, and withdrawals; they are closed at the end of each period; also called *nominal accounts*. (p. 170).

Unclassified balance sheet balance sheet that broadly groups assets, liabilities, and equity accounts. (p. 182).

Working papers analyses and other informal reports prepared by accountants when organizing information for formal reports and financial statements. (p. 174).

Work sheet spreadsheet used to draft an unadjusted trial balance, adjusting entries, adjusted trial balance, and financial statements; an optional step in the accounting process. (p. 174).

[Superscript letter ^A denotes assignments based on Appendix 5A.]

Questions

1. What accounts are affected by closing entries? What accounts are not affected?
2. What two purposes are accomplished by recording closing entries?
3. What are the basic four closing entries?
4. What is the purpose of the Income Summary account?
5. Explain whether an error has occurred if a post-closing trial balance includes the account Depreciation Expense—Building.
6. What tasks are aided by a work sheet?
7. Why are the debit and credit entries in the Adjustments columns of the work sheet identified with letters?
8. What is a company's operating cycle?
9. What classes of assets and liabilities are shown on a typical classified balance sheet?

10. How is unearned revenue classified on the balance sheet?
11. What are the characteristics of plant assets?
12.^A How do reversing entries simplify a company's recordkeeping?
13.^A If a company accrued unpaid salaries expense of $500 at the end of a fiscal year, what reversing entry could be made? When would it be made?
14. Refer to the balance sheet for **Nike** in Appendix A. What percent of Nike's long-term debt is coming due before May 31, 2001?
15. Refer to **Reebok**'s balance sheet in Appendix A. Identify the accounts listed as current liabilities.
16. Refer to **Gap**'s financial statements in Appendix A. What journal entry was likely recorded as of Jan. 29, 2000, to close the company's Income Summary account?

QUICK STUDY

QS 5-1

Identifying the accounting cycle

List the following steps of the accounting cycle in their proper order:

a. Preparing the post-closing trial balance.
b. Posting the journal entries.
c. Journalizing and posting adjusting entries.
d. Preparing the adjusted trial balance.
e. Journalizing and posting closing entries.
f. Analyzing transactions and events.
g. Preparing the financial statements.
h. Preparing the unadjusted trial balance.
I. Journalizing transactions and events.

QS 5-2

Determining effects of closing entries

Argosy Company began the current period with a $15,000 balance in the Dane Argosy, Capital account. At the end of the period, the company's adjusted account balances include the following temporary accounts with normal balances:

Service fees earned	$36,000	Interest revenue	$4,500
Salaries expense	20,000	Dane Argosy, Withdrawals	7,000
Depreciation expense	5,000	Utilities expense	3,300

After closing revenue and expense accounts, what will be the balance of the Income Summary account? After all closing entries are journalized and posted, what will be the balance of the Dane Argosy Capital account?

QS 5-3

Computing current ratio

Compute Neon Company's current ratio using the following information:

Accounts receivable	$16,000	Long-term notes payable	$21,000
Accounts payable	11,000	Office supplies	2,800
Buildings	43,000	Prepaid insurance	3,500
Cash	7,000	Unearned services revenue	5,000

QS 5-4

Classifying balance sheet items

The following are common categories on a classified balance sheet:

A. Current assets
B. Long-term investments
C. Plant assets
D. Intangible assets
E. Current liabilities
F. Long-term liabilities

For each of the following items, select the letter that identifies the balance sheet category where the item typically would appear.

_____ **1.** Trademarks   _____ **5.** Cash
_____ **2.** Accounts receivable   _____ **6.** Wages payable
_____ **3.** Land not currently used in operations   _____ **7.** Store equipment
_____ **4.** Notes payable (due in three years) _____ **8.** Accounts payable

---

The following information is taken from the work sheet for Hafka Company as of December 31, 2002. Using this information, determine the amount for S. Hafka, Capital, that should be reported on its December 31, 2002, balance sheet.

QS 5-5
Interpreting a work sheet

P3

	Income Statement		Balance Sheet and Statement of Changes in Owner's Equity	
	Dr.	Cr.	Dr.	Cr.
S. Hafka, Capital				72,000
S. Hafka, Withdrawals			39,000	
Totals	122,000	181,000		

In preparing a work sheet, indicate the financial statement debit column to which a normal balance in the following accounts should be extended. Use IS for the Income Statement Debit column and BS for the Balance Sheet and Statement of Changes in Owner's Equity Debit column.

QS 5-6
Applying a work sheet

P3

_____ **a.** Insurance expense   _____ **d.** Depreciation expense—Equipment
_____ **b.** Equipment   _____ **e.** Prepaid rent
_____ **c.** Owner, Withdrawals   _____ **f.** Accounts receivable

---

On December 31, 2002, Yates Co. prepared an adjusting entry for $7,600 of earned but unrecorded management fees. On January 16, 2003, Yates received $25,500 of management fees, which included the accrued fees earned in 2002. Assuming the company uses reversing entries, prepare the reversing entry and the January 16, 2003, entry.

QS 5-7[A]
Reversing entries

P4

Use information from the following T-accounts to prepare closing journal entries and post them to the T-accounts.

EXERCISES

Exercise 5-1
Preparing and posting closing entries

P1

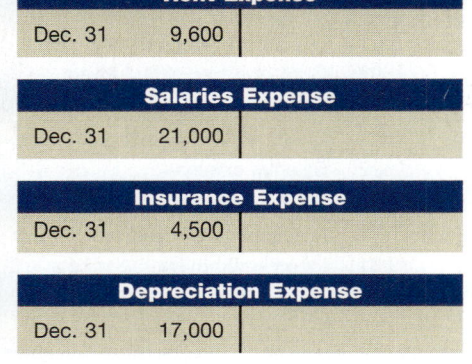

M. Mallon, Capital		
	Dec. 31	42,000

Rent Expense		
Dec. 31	9,600	

M. Mallon, Withdrawals		
Dec. 31	25,000	

Salaries Expense		
Dec. 31	21,000	

Income Summary		

Insurance Expense		
Dec. 31	4,500	

Services Revenue		
	Dec. 31	74,000

Depreciation Expense		
Dec. 31	17,000	

Exercise 5-2
Preparing
closing entries

The following adjusted trial balance contains the accounts and balances of Clover Company as of December 31, 2002, the end of its fiscal year:

No.	Account Title	Debit	Credit
101	Cash	$19,000	
126	Supplies	13,000	
128	Prepaid insurance	3,000	
167	Equipment	24,000	
168	Accumulated depreciation—Equipment		$ 7,500
301	R. Showers, Capital		47,600
302	R. Showers, Withdrawals	7,000	
404	Services revenue		44,000
612	Depreciation expense—Equipment	3,000	
622	Salaries expense	22,000	
637	Insurance expense	2,500	
640	Rent expense	3,400	
652	Supplies expense	2,200	
	Totals	$99,100	$99,100

Prepare closing entries for Clover Company.

Exercise 5-3
Preparing closing entries and
a post-closing trial balance

The adjusted trial balance for Schwepker Marketing Co. follows. Prepare a table with two columns under each of the following headings: Adjusted Trial Balance, Closing Entries, and Post-Closing Trial Balance. Complete the table by providing four closing entries and the post-closing trial balance.

No.	Account Title	Debit	Credit
101	Cash	$ 9,200	
106	Accounts receivable	25,000	
153	Equipment	42,000	
154	Accumulated depreciation—Equipment		$ 17,500
193	Franchise	31,000	
201	Accounts payable		15,000
209	Salaries payable		4,200
233	Unearned fees		3,600
301	C. Schwepker, Capital		68,500
302	C. Schwepker, Withdrawals	15,400	
401	Marketing fees earned		80,000
611	Depreciation expense—Equipment	12,000	
622	Salaries expense	32,500	
640	Rent expense	13,000	
677	Miscellaneous expenses	8,700	
901	Income summary		
	Totals	$188,800	$188,800

The following balances of Retained Earnings and the temporary accounts are from the adjusted trial balance of Rider, Inc.:

Exercise 5-4
Preparing closing entries
for a corporation

Account Title	Debit	Credit
Retained earnings		$34,600
Services revenue		33,000
Interest earned		6,300
Salaries expense	$26,400	
Insurance expense	4,800	
Rental expense	7,400	
Supplies expense	4,100	
Depreciation expense—Trucks	11,600	

Prepare the closing entries, and then determine the amount of retained earnings to be reported on the company's balance sheet.

Use the following adjusted trial balance of Webb Trucking Company to prepare a classified balance sheet as of December 31, 2002.

Account Title	Debit	Credit
Cash	$ 8,000	
Accounts receivable	17,500	
Office supplies	3,000	
Trucks	172,000	
Accumulated depreciation—Trucks		$ 36,000
Land	85,000	
Accounts payable		12,000
Interest payable		4,000
Long-term notes payable		53,000
K. Webb, Capital		175,000
K. Webb, Withdrawals	20,000	
Trucking fees earned		130,000
Depreciation expense—Trucks	23,500	
Salaries expense	61,000	
Office supplies expense	8,000	
Repairs expense—Trucks	12,000	
Total	$410,000	$410,000

Use the information in the adjusted trial balance reported in Exercise 5-5 to compute the current ratio as of the balance sheet date.

Calculate the current ratio in each of the following separate cases:

	Current Assets	Current Liabilities
Case 1	$ 79,000	$ 32,000
Case 2	105,000	76,000
Case 3	45,000	49,000
Case 4	85,500	81,600
Case 5	61,000	100,000

Exercise 5-8

Preparing a 10-column worksheet

The following unadjusted trial balance contains the accounts and balances of the Dalton Delivery Company as of December 31, 2002. Use the following information about the company's adjustments to complete a 10-column worksheet for Delivery.

a. Unrecorded depreciation on the trucks at the end of the year is $40,000.

b. The total amount of incurred but unpaid interest at year-end is $6,000.

c. The cost of unused office supplies still available at the end of the year is $2,000.

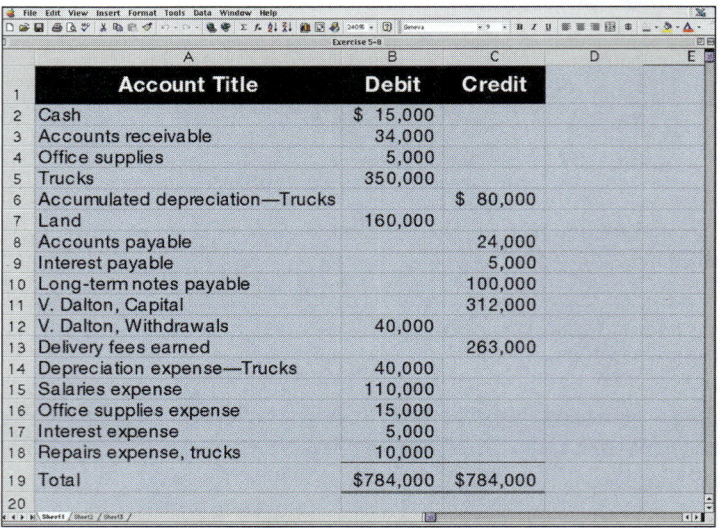

Account Title	Debit	Credit
Cash	$ 15,000	
Accounts receivable	34,000	
Office supplies	5,000	
Trucks	350,000	
Accumulated depreciation—Trucks		$ 80,000
Land	160,000	
Accounts payable		24,000
Interest payable		5,000
Long-term notes payable		100,000
V. Dalton, Capital		312,000
V. Dalton, Withdrawals	40,000	
Delivery fees earned		263,000
Depreciation expense—Trucks	40,000	
Salaries expense	110,000	
Office supplies expense	15,000	
Interest expense	5,000	
Repairs expense, trucks	10,000	
Total	$784,000	$784,000

Exercise 5-9

Preparing adjusting entries from work sheet

Use the following information from the Adjustments columns of a 10-column work sheet to prepare the necessary adjusting journal entries:

No.	Account Title	Adjustments	
		Debit	Credit
109	Interest receivable	(d) $ 880	
124	Office supplies		(b) $ 1,750
128	Prepaid insurance		(a) 900
164	Accumulated depreciation—Office equipment		(c) 2,200
209	Salaries payable		(e) 560
409	Interest revenue		(d) 880
612	Depreciation expense—Office equipment	(c) 2,200	
620	Office salaries expense	(e) 560	
636	Insurance expense, office equipment	(a) 332	
637	Insurance expense, store equipment	(a) 568	
650	Office supplies expense	(b) 1,750	
	Totals	$ 6,290	$ 6,290

Exercise 5-10

Extending adjusted account balances on a work sheet

P3

These 16 accounts are from the Adjusted Trial Balance columns of a company's 10-column work sheet. In the blank space beside each account, write the letter of the appropriate financial statement column (A, B, C, or D) to which a normal account balance is extended.

A. Debit column for the Income Statement columns.

B. Credit column for the Income Statement columns.

C. Debit column for the Balance Sheet and Statement of Changes in Owner's Equity columns.

D. Credit column for the Balance Sheet and Statement of Changes in Owner's Equity columns.

_____ **1.** Office Supplies
_____ **2.** Accounts Payable
_____ **3.** Owner, Capital
_____ **4.** Wages Payable
_____ **5.** Machinery
_____ **6.** Interest Receivable
_____ **7.** Interest Expense
_____ **8.** Owner, Withdrawals

_____ **9.** Service Fees Revenue
_____ **10.** Insurance Expense
_____ **11.** Accumulated Depreciation
_____ **12.** Interest Revenue
_____ **13.** Accounts Receivable
_____ **14.** Rent Expense
_____ **15.** Depreciation Expense
_____ **16.** Cash

The Adjusted Trial Balance columns of a 10-column work sheet for Tara Company follow. Complete the work sheet by extending the account balances into the appropriate financial statement columns and by entering the amount of net income for the reporting period.

Exercise 5-11
Extending accounts in a work sheet

No.	Account Title	Debit	Credit
101	Cash	$ 7,000	
106	Accounts receivable	27,200	
153	Trucks	42,000	
154	Accumulated depreciation—Trucks		$ 17,500
183	Land	32,000	
201	Accounts payable		15,000
209	Salaries payable		4,200
233	Unearned fees		3,600
301	T. Snow, Capital		65,500
302	T. Snow, Withdrawals	15,400	
401	Plumbing fees earned		84,000
611	Depreciation expense—Trucks	6,500	
622	Salaries expense	38,000	
640	Rent expense	13,000	
677	Miscellaneous expenses	8,700	
	Totals	$189,800	$189,800

These partially completed Income Statement columns from a 10-column work sheet are for Red Sail Rental Co. Use the information to determine the amount that should be entered on the net income line of the work sheet. In addition, prepare closing entries for Red Sail Rental. The owner, LeAnn Welch, did not make any withdrawals.

Exercise 5-12
Completing the income statement columns and preparing closing entries

P3

Account Title	Debit	Credit
Rent earned		120,000
Salaries expense	46,300	
Insurance expense	7,400	
Dock rental expense	16,000	
Boat supplies expense	4,200	
Depreciation expense—Boats	20,500	
Totals		
Net income		
Totals		

Exercise 5-13^A

Preparing reversing entries

The following two events occurred for Totten Co. on October 31, 2002, the end of its fiscal year:

a. Totten rents a building from its owner for $2,800 per month. By a prearrangement, the company delayed paying October's rent until November 5. On this date, the company paid the rent for both October and November.

b. Totten rents space in a building it owns to a tenant for $850 per month. By prearrangement, the tenant delayed paying the October rent until November 8. On this date, the tenant paid the rent for both October and November.

Required

1. Prepare adjusting entries that Totten must record for these events as of October 31.

2. Assuming Totten does *not* use reversing entries, prepare journal entries to record Totten's payment of rent on November 5 and the collection of rent on November 8 from Totten's tenant.

3. Assuming that Totten uses reversing entries, prepare reversing entries on November 1 and the journal entries to record Totten's payment of rent on November 5 and the collection of rent on November 8 from Totten's tenant.

Exercise 5-14^A

Preparing reversing entries

Hinson Company records prepaid assets and unearned revenues in balance sheet accounts. The following information was used to prepare adjusting entries for Hinson Company as of August 31, the end of the company's fiscal year:

a. The company has earned $6,000 of unrecorded service fees.

b. The expired portion of prepaid insurance is $2,800.

c. Earned $2,000 of the total balance of the Unearned Service Fees account balance.

d. Depreciation expense for office equipment is $2,100.

e. Employees have earned but have not been paid salaries of $2,570.

Prepare necessary reversing entries assuming that Hinson uses reversing entries in its accounting system.

PROBLEM SET A

Problem 5-1A

Applying the accounting cycle

On April 1, 2002, Jennifer Stafford created a new travel agency, Ambassador Travel. The following transactions occurred during the company's first month:

April	1	Stafford invested $30,000 cash and computer equipment worth $20,000.
	2	Rented furnished office space by paying $1,800 cash for the first month's rent.
	3	Purchased $1,000 of office supplies for cash.
	10	Paid $2,400 cash for the premium on a one-year insurance policy. Coverage began on April 10.
	14	Paid $1,600 cash for two weeks' salaries to employees.
	24	Collected $8,000 cash on commissions from airlines on tickets obtained for customers.
	28	Paid another $1,600 cash for two weeks' salaries.
	29	Paid this month's $750 telephone bill in cash.
	30	Paid $350 cash to repair the company's computer.
	30	Stafford withdrew $1,500 cash from the business for personal use.

The company's chart of accounts included the following:

101 Cash	405 Commissions Earned
106 Accounts Receivable	612 Depreciation Expense—Computer Equip.
124 Office Supplies	622 Salaries Expense
128 Prepaid Insurance	637 Insurance Expense
167 Computer Equipment	640 Rent Expense
168 Accumulated Depreciation—Computer Equip.	650 Office Supplies Expense
209 Salaries Payable	684 Repairs Expense
301 J. Stafford, Capital	688 Telephone Expense
302 J. Stafford, Withdrawals	901 Income Summary

Required

1. Use the balance column format to set up each account listed in its chart of accounts.

2. Prepare journal entries to record the transactions for April and post them to the accounts. The company records prepaid and unearned items in balance sheet accounts.

3. Prepare an unadjusted trial balance as of April 30.

4. Use the following information to journalize and post adjusting entries for the month:

   a. Two-thirds of one month's insurance coverage has expired.

   b. There are $600 of office supplies available at the end of the month.

   c. Depreciation on the computer equipment is $500.

   d. The employees earned $420 of unpaid and unrecorded salaries.

   e. The company earned $1,750 of commissions that are not yet billed.

5. Prepare the income statement, the statement of changes in owner's equity for April, and the balance sheet at April 30, 2002.

Check   Ending capital balance, $50,697; insurance expense, $133

6. Prepare journal entries to close the temporary accounts and then post them to the accounts.

7. Prepare a post-closing trial balance.

Sedona Repairs' adjusted trial balance on December 31, 2002, follows:

Problem 5-2A
Preparing closing entries, financial statements, and current ratio

No.	Account Title	Debit	Credit
	SEDONA REPAIRS **Adjusted Trial Balance** **December 31, 2002**		
101	Cash	$ 14,000	
124	Office supplies	1,300	
128	Prepaid insurance	2,050	
167	Equipment	50,000	
168	Accumulated depreciation—Equipment		$ 5,000
201	Accounts payable		14,000
210	Wages payable		600
301	K. Brown, Capital		33,000
302	K. Brown, Withdrawals	16,000	
401	Repair fees earned		90,950
612	Depreciation expense—Equipment	5,000	
623	Wages expense	37,500	
637	Insurance expense	800	
640	Rent expense	10,600	
650	Office supplies expense	3,600	
690	Utilities expense	2,700	
	Totals	$143,550	$143,550

Required

Preparation Component

1. Prepare an income statement and a statement of changes in owner's equity for the year 2002, and a classified balance sheet at December 31, 2002. There are no owner investments in 2002.

Check   Ending capital balance, $47,750

2. Enter the adjusted trial balance in the first two columns of a six-column table. Use columns three and four for closing entries and the last two columns for a post-closing trial balance. Insert an Income Summary account as the last item in the trial balance.

3. Enter closing entries in the six-column table and prepare journal entries for them.

4. Determine the company's current ratio.

Analysis Component

5. Assume for Sedona Repairs that:

   a. None of the $800 insurance expense expired during the year. Instead, assume it is a prepayment of future insurance protection.

   b. There are no earned and unpaid wages at the end of the year.

Describe the financial statement changes that would result from these two assumptions.

Problem 5-3A

Preparing closing entries, financial statements, and ratios

The adjusted trial balance for Sharp Construction as of December 31, 2002, follows:

SHARP CONSTRUCTION Adjusted Trial Balance December 31, 2002			
No.	Account Title	Debit	Credit
101	Cash	$ 5,000	
104	Short-term investments	23,000	
126	Supplies	8,100	
128	Prepaid insurance	7,000	
167	Equipment	40,000	
168	Accumulated depreciation—Equipment		$ 20,000
173	Building	150,000	
174	Accumulated depreciation—Building		50,000
183	Land	55,000	
201	Accounts payable		16,500
203	Interest payable		2,500
208	Rent payable		3,500
210	Wages payable		2,500
213	Property taxes payable		900
233	Unearned professional fees		7,500
251	Long-term notes payable		67,000
301	J. Sharp, Capital		126,400
302	J. Sharp, Withdrawals	13,000	
401	Professional fees earned		97,000
406	Rent earned		14,000
407	Dividends earned		2,000
409	Interest earned		2,100
606	Depreciation expense—Building	11,000	
612	Depreciation expense—Equipment	6,000	
623	Wages expense	32,000	
633	Interest expense	5,100	
637	Insurance expense	10,000	
640	Rent expense	13,400	
652	Supplies expense	7,400	
682	Postage expense	4,200	
683	Property taxes expense	5,000	
684	Repairs expense	8,900	
688	Telephone expense	3,200	
690	Utilities expense	4,600	
	Totals	$411,900	$411,900

Analysis reveals that Sharp Construction is required to make a $7,000 payment on its long-term note payable during 2003. J. Sharp invested $5,000 cash during year 2002 (the December 31, 2001, balance of the J. Sharp, Capital account was $121,400).

Required

Check   Total assets, $218,100

1. Prepare the income statement and the statement of changes in owner's equity for year 2002, and the classified balance sheet at December 31, 2002.

2. Prepare the necessary closing entries at the end of the year 2002.

3. Use the information in the financial statements to calculate these ratios:

   a. Return on equity.

   b. Modified return on equity, assuming the owner's efforts are valued at $4,000 for the year.

   c. Debt ratio.

   d. Profit margin ratio (use total revenues as the denominator).

   e. Current ratio.

This unadjusted trial balance is for Adams Construction Co. as of the end of its 2002 fiscal year. The June 30, 2001, balance of the owner's capital account was $53,660, and the owner invested $35,000 cash in the company during the 2002 fiscal year.

Problem 5-4A

Preparing work sheet, journal entries, financial statements, and current ratio

No.	Account Title	Debit	Credit
	ADAMS CONSTRUCTION CO.		
	Unadjusted Trial Balance		
	June 30, 2002		
101	Cash	$ 18,500	
126	Supplies	9,900	
128	Prepaid insurance	7,200	
167	Equipment	132,000	
168	Accumulated depreciation—Equipment		$ 26,250
201	Accounts payable		6,800
203	Interest payable		0
208	Rent payable		0
210	Wages payable		0
213	Property taxes payable		0
251	Long-term notes payable		25,000
301	S. Adams, Capital		88,660
302	S. Adams, Withdrawals	33,000	
401	Construction fees earned		132,100
612	Depreciation expense—Equipment	0	
623	Wages expense	46,860	
633	Interest expense	2,750	
637	Insurance expense	0	
640	Rent expense	12,000	
652	Supplies expense	0	
683	Property taxes expense	7,800	
684	Repairs expense	2,910	
690	Utilities expense	5,890	
	Totals	$ 278,810	$ 278,810

Required

Preparation Component

1. Prepare a 10-column work sheet for fiscal year 2002, starting with the unadjusted trial balance and including adjustments based on these additional facts:

   a. The supplies available at the end of fiscal year 2002 had a cost of $3,300.

   b. The cost of expired insurance for the fiscal year is $3,800.

   c. Annual depreciation on equipment is $8,400.

   d. The June utilities expense of $650 is not included in the unadjusted trial balance because the bill arrived after the trial balance was prepared. The $650 amount owed needs to be recorded.

   e. The company's employees have earned $1,800 of accrued wages at fiscal year-end.

   f. The lease for the office requires the company to pay total rent for the year ended June 30 equal to 10% of the company's annual revenues. Rent has been estimated and is being paid to the building owner with monthly payments of $1,000. If the annual rent owed exceeds the total monthly estimated payments, the company must pay the excess before July 31. If the total owed is less than the amount previously paid, the building owner will refund the difference by July 31.

   g. Additional property taxes of $1,000 have been assessed but have not been paid or recorded in the accounts.

   h. The long-term note payable bears interest at 1% per month, which the company is required to pay by the 10th of the following month. The balance of the Interest Expense account equals the amount paid for the first 11 months of the past fiscal year. The interest for June has not yet been paid or recorded. In addition, the company is required to make a $5,000 payment toward the note payable on August 31, 2002.

2. Use the work sheet to enter the adjusting and closing entries; then journalize them.

3. Prepare the income statement and the statement of changes in owner's equity for the year ended June 30, and the classified balance sheet at June 30. Calculate the company's current ratio.

Check Total assets, $122,550; current liabilities, $16,710

Analysis Component

4. Analyze the following separate errors and describe how each would affect the 10-column work sheet. Explain whether the error is likely to be discovered in completing the work sheet and, if not, the effect of the error on the financial statements.

   a. Assume that the adjustment for supplies used had credited Supplies for $3,300 and debited the same amount to Supplies Expense.

   b. When the adjusted trial balance in the work sheet is completed, the $18,500 cash balance is incorrectly entered in the Credit column.

Problem 5-5A

Determining balance sheet classifications

In the blank space beside each numbered balance sheet item, enter the letter of its balance sheet classification. If the item should not appear on the balance sheet, enter a *Z* in the blank.

A. Current assets   **D.** Intangible assets   **G.** Owner's equity
B. Long-term investments   **E.** Current liabilities   **H.** Stockholders' equity
C. Plant assets   **F.** Long-term liabilities

  _C_   **1.** Accumulated depreciation— Trucks
  _A_   **2.** Cash
  _C_   **3.** Buildings
  _H_   **4.** Retained earnings
  _C_   **5.** Office equipment
  _C_   **6.** Land (used in operations)
  ____   **7.** Repairs expense
  _A_   **8.** Prepaid property taxes
  _C_   **9.** Current portion of long-term note payable

  _B_   **10.** Long-term investment in IBM stock
  _g_   **11.** Depreciation expense—Trucks
  _g_   **12.** T. Duncan, Capital
  _C_   **13.** Interest receivable
  _g_   **14.** T. Duncan, Withdrawals
  _C_   **15.** Automobiles
  _F_   **16.** Notes payable (due in 3 years)
  _E_   **17.** Accounts payable
  _A_   **18.** Prepaid insurance
  _B_   **19.** Common stock
  _E_   **20.** Unearned services revenue

Problem 5-6Aᴬ

Making adjusting, reversing, and subsequent entries

This six-column table for Bullseye Ranges includes the unadjusted trial balance as of December 31, 2002.

Account Title	Unadjusted Trial Balance Dr.	Unadjusted Trial Balance Cr.	Adjustments Dr.	Adjustments Cr.	Adjusted Trial Balance Dr.	Adjusted Trial Balance Cr.
BULLSEYE RANGES December 31, 2002						
Cash	$ 14,000					
Accounts receivable	0					
Supplies	6,500					
Equipment	135,000					
Accumulated depreciation— Equipment		$ 30,000				
Interest payable		0				
Salaries payable		0				
Unearned membership fees		15,000				
Notes payable		75,000				
T. Allen, Capital		50,250				
T. Allen, Withdrawals	21,125					
Membership fees earned		42,000				
Depreciation expense— Equipment	0					
Salaries expense	30,000					
Interest expense	5,625					
Supplies expense	0					
Totals	$212,250	$212,250				

Required

1. Complete the six-column table by entering adjustments that reflect the following information:

   a. As of December 31, 2002, employees had earned $1,200 of unpaid and unrecorded salaries. The next payday is January 4, and the total amount of salaries to be paid is $1,500.

   b. The cost of supplies available at December 31, 2002, is $3,000.

   c. The note payable requires an interest payment to be made every three months. The amount of unrecorded accrued interest at December 31, 2002, is $1,875, and the next payment is due on January 15. This payment will be $2,250.

   d. Analysis of the unearned membership fees shows $5,800 remaining unearned at December 31, 2002.

   e. In addition to the membership fees included in the revenue account balance, the company has earned another $9,300 in fees that will be collected on January 21, 2003. The company is also expected to collect $10,000 on the same day for new fees earned during January.

   f. Depreciation expense for the year is $15,000.

2. Prepare journal entries for the adjustments entered in the six-column table for part *1*.

3. Prepare journal entries to reverse the effects of the adjusting entries that involve accruals.

4. Prepare journal entries to record the cash payments and collections described for January.

Check Adjusted trial balance totals, $239,625

On July 1, 2002, Lucinda Fogle created a new self-storage business, SafeStore Co. The following transactions occurred during the company's first month:

July 1	Fogle invested $30,000 cash and buildings worth $150,000.
2	Rented equipment by paying $2,000 rent for the first month.
5	Purchased $2,400 of office supplies for cash.
10	Paid $7,200 for the premium on a one-year insurance policy. Coverage begins on July 10.
14	Paid an employee $1,000 for two weeks' salary.
24	Collected $9,800 of storage fees from customers.
28	Paid another $1,000 for two weeks' salary.
29	Paid the month's $400 telephone bill.
30	Paid $950 cash to repair a leaking roof.
31	Fogle withdrew $2,000 cash from the business for personal use.

The company's chart of accounts included the following accounts.

PROBLEM SET B

Problem 5-1B
Applying the accounting cycle

101	Cash	401	Storage Fees Earned
106	Accounts Receivable	606	Depreciation Expense—Buildings
124	Office Supplies	622	Salaries Expense
128	Prepaid Insurance	637	Insurance Expense
173	Buildings	640	Rent Expense
174	Accumulated Depreciation—Buildings	650	Office Supplies Expense
209	Salaries Payable	684	Repairs Expense
301	Lucinda Fogle, Capital	688	Telephone Expense
302	Lucinda Fogle, Withdrawals	901	Income Summary

Required

1. Use the balance column format to set up each account listed in its chart of accounts.

2. Prepare journal entries to record the transactions for July and post them to the accounts. Record prepaid and unearned items in balance sheet accounts.

3. Prepare an unadjusted trial balance as of July 31.

4. Use the following information to journalize and post adjusting entries for the month:

   a. Two-thirds of one month's insurance coverage has expired.

   b. There are $1,525 of office supplies available at the end of the month.

   c. Depreciation on the buildings is $1,500.

   d. The employee earned $100 of unpaid and unrecorded salary.

   e. The company earned $1,150 of storage fees that are not yet billed.

5. Prepare the income statement, the statement of changes in owner's equity for July, and the balance sheet at July 31, 2002.

6. Prepare journal entries to close the temporary accounts and then post them to the accounts.

7. Prepare a post-closing trial balance.

Problem 5-2B

Preparing closing entries, financial statements, and current ratio

Easy Stride Shoes' adjusted trial balance on December 31, 2002, follows:

No.	Account Title	Debit	Credit
	EASY STRIDE SHOES		
	Adjusted Trial Balance		
	December 31, 2002		
101	Cash	$ 14,450	
125	Store supplies	5,140	
128	Prepaid insurance	1,200	
167	Equipment	31,000	
168	Accumulated depreciation—Equipment		$ 8,000
201	Accounts payable		1,500
210	Wages payable		2,700
301	Paul Holt, Capital		35,650
302	Paul Holt, Withdrawals	15,000	
401	Repair fees earned		54,700
612	Depreciation expense—Equipment	2,000	
623	Wages expense	26,400	
637	Insurance expense	600	
640	Rent expense	3,600	
651	Store supplies expense	1,200	
690	Utilities expense	1,960	
	Totals	$102,550	$102,550

Required

Preparation Component

1. Prepare an income statement and a statement of changes in owner's equity for the year 2002, and a classified balance sheet at December 31, 2002. There are no owner investments in 2002.

2. Enter the adjusted trial balance in the first two columns of a six-column table. Use the middle two columns for closing entries and the last two columns for a post-closing trial balance. Insert an Income Summary account as the last item in the trial balance.

3. Enter closing entries in the six-column table and prepare journal entries for them.

4. Determine the company's current ratio.

Analysis Component

5. Assume for Easy Stride that:

   a. None of the $600 insurance expense expired during the year. Instead, assume it is a prepayment of future insurance protection.

   b. There are no earned and unpaid wages at the end of the year.

   Describe the financial statement changes that would result from these two assumptions.

The adjusted trial balance for Giovanni Co. as of December 31, 2002, follows:

Problem 5-3B

Preparing closing entries, financial statements, and ratios

	GIOVANNI CO. Adjusted Trial Balance December 31, 2002		
No.	**Account Title**	**Debit**	**Credit**
101	Cash	$ 7,400	
104	Short-term investments	11,200	
126	Supplies	4,600	
128	Prepaid insurance	1,000	
167	Equipment	24,000	
168	Accumulated depreciation—Equipment		$ 4,000
173	Building	100,000	
174	Accumulated depreciation—Building		10,000
183	Land	30,500	
201	Accounts payable		3,500
203	Interest payable		1,750
208	Rent payable		400
210	Wages payable		1,280
213	Property taxes payable		3,330
233	Unearned professional fees		750
251	Long-term notes payable		40,000
301	Joe Giovanni, Capital		92,800
302	Joe Giovanni, Withdrawals	8,000	
401	Professional fees earned		59,600
406	Rent earned		4,500
407	Dividends earned		1,000
409	Interest earned		1,320
606	Depreciation expense—Building	2,000	
612	Depreciation expense—Equipment	1,000	
623	Wages expense	18,500	
633	Interest expense	1,550	
637	Insurance expense	1,525	
640	Rent expense	3,600	
652	Supplies expense	1,000	
682	Postage expense	410	
683	Property taxes expense	4,825	
684	Repairs expense	679	
688	Telephone expense	521	
690	Utilities expense	1,920	
	Totals	$224,230	$224,230

Analysis reveals that Giovanni Company is required to make an $8,400 payment on its long-term note payable during 2003. J. Giovanni invested $40,000 cash during year 2002 (the December 31, 2001, balance of the J. Giovanni, Capital account was $52,800).

Required

1. Prepare the income statement and the statement of changes in owner's equity for year 2002, and the classified balance sheet at December 31, 2002.

2. Prepare the necessary closing entries at the end of the year 2002.

3. Use the information in the financial statements to calculate these ratios:

   a. Return on equity.

   b. Modified return on equity, assuming the owner's efforts are valued at $15,000 for the year.

Check Total assets, $164,700

c. Debt ratio.

d. Profit margin ratio (use total revenues as the denominator).

e. Current ratio.

Problem 5-4B

Preparing work sheet, journal entries, financial statements, and current ratio

This unadjusted trial balance is for Smash Demolition Company as of the end of its April 30, 2002, fiscal year. The April 30, 2001, balance of the owner's capital account was $46,900, and the owner invested $40,000 cash in the company during the 2002 fiscal year.

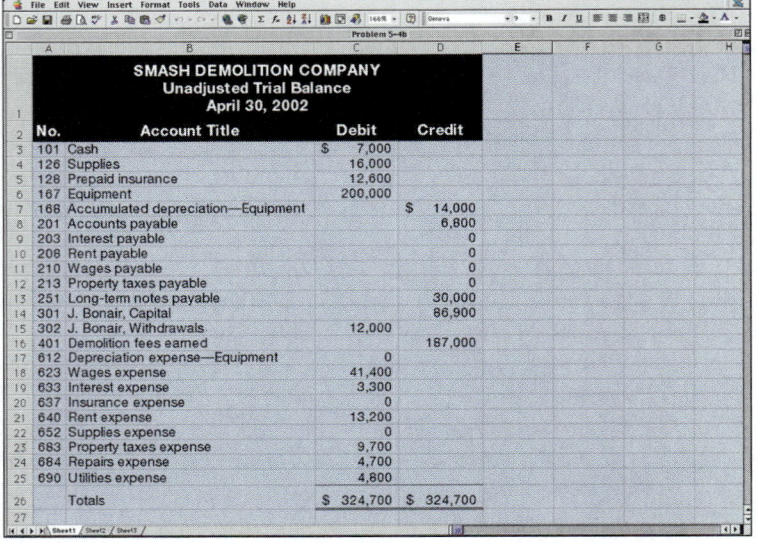

No.	Account Title	Debit	Credit
101	Cash	$ 7,000	
126	Supplies	16,000	
128	Prepaid insurance	12,600	
167	Equipment	200,000	
168	Accumulated depreciation—Equipment		$ 14,000
201	Accounts payable		6,800
203	Interest payable		0
208	Rent payable		0
210	Wages payable		0
213	Property taxes payable		0
251	Long-term notes payable		30,000
301	J. Bonair, Capital		86,900
302	J. Bonair, Withdrawals	12,000	
401	Demolition fees earned		187,000
612	Depreciation expense—Equipment	0	
623	Wages expense	41,400	
633	Interest expense	3,300	
637	Insurance expense	0	
640	Rent expense	13,200	
652	Supplies expense	0	
683	Property taxes expense	9,700	
684	Repairs expense	4,700	
690	Utilities expense	4,800	
	Totals	$ 324,700	$ 324,700

Required

Preparation Component

1. Prepare a 10-column work sheet for fiscal year 2002, starting with the unadjusted trial balance and including these additional facts:

a. The supplies available at the end of fiscal year 2002 had a cost of $7,900.

b. The cost of expired insurance for the fiscal year is $10,600.

c. Annual depreciation on equipment is $7,000.

d. The April utilities expense of $800 is not included in the unadjusted trial balance because the bill arrived after the trial balance was prepared. The $800 amount owed needs to be recorded.

e. The company's employees have earned $2,000 of accrued wages at fiscal year-end.

f. The lease for the office requires the company to pay total rent for each fiscal year equal to 8% of the company's annual revenues. Rent has been estimated and is being paid to the building owner with monthly payments of $1,100. If the annual rent owed exceeds the total monthly estimated payments, the company must pay the excess before May 31. If the total owed is less than the amount previously paid, the building owner will refund the difference by May 31.

g. Additional property taxes of $550 have been assessed but have not been paid or recorded in the accounts.

h. The long-term note payable bears interest at 1% per month, which the company is required to pay by the 10th of the following month. The balance of the Interest Expense account equals the amount paid for the first 11 months of the year. The interest for April has not yet been paid or recorded. In addition, the company is required to make a $10,000 payment toward the note payable on June 30, 2002.

2. Use the work sheet to enter the adjusting and closing entries; then journalize them.

Check   Total assets, $195,900; rent expense, $14,960

3. Prepare the income statement and the statement of changes in owner's equity for the year ended April 30, and the classified balance sheet at April 30. Calculate the company's current ratio.

Analysis Component

4. Analyze the following separate errors and describe how each would affect the 10-column work sheet. Explain whether the error is likely to be discovered in completing the work sheet and, if not, the effect of the error on the financial statements.

a. The adjustment for expiration of the insurance coverage had credited the Prepaid Insurance account for $2,000 and debited the same amount to the Insurance Expense account.

b. When the adjusted trial balance in the work sheet is completed, the $4,700 Repairs Expense account balance is extended to the Debit column for the balance sheet.

In the blank space beside each numbered balance sheet item, enter the letter of its balance sheet classification. If the item should not appear on the balance sheet, enter a Z in the blank.

Problem 5-5B

Determining balance sheet classifications

A. Current assets   **D.** Intangible assets   **G.** Owner's equity
B. Long-term investments   **E.** Current liabilities   **H.** Stockholders' equity
C. Plant assets   **F.** Long-term liabilities

_____ **1.** Buildings	_____ **11.** Office supplies
_____ **2.** Prepaid insurance	_____ **12.** Owner, Capital
_____ **3.** Current portion of long-term note payable	_____ **13.** Common stock
	_____ **14.** Notes receivable (due in 120 days)
_____ **4.** Interest receivable	
_____ **5.** Short-term investments	_____ **15.** Accumulated depreciation—Trucks
_____ **6.** Land (used in operations)	
_____ **7.** Copyrights	_____ **16.** Salaries payable
_____ **8.** Owner, Withdrawals	_____ **17.** Commissions earned
_____ **9.** Depreciation expense—Trucks	_____ **18.** Retained earnings
_____ **10.** Long-term investment in Ford stock	_____ **19.** Office equipment
	_____ **20.** Notes payable (due in 5 years)

This six-column table for Rent-A-Way Co. includes the unadjusted trial balance as of December 31, 2002:

Problem 5-6B[A]

Making adjusting, reversing, and subsequent entries

Account Title	Unadjusted Trial Balance Dr.	Cr.	Adjustments Dr.	Cr.	Adjusted Trial Balance Dr.	Cr.
Cash	$ 10,000					
Accounts receivable	0					
Supplies	7,600					
Machinery	50,000					
Accumulated depreciation—Machinery		$ 20,000				
Interest payable		0				
Salaries payable		0				
Unearned rental fees		7,200				
Notes payable		30,000				
Gary Clay, Capital		14,200				
Gary Clay, Withdrawals	9,500					
Rental fees earned		32,450				
Depreciation expense—Machinery	0					
Salaries expense	24,500					
Interest expense	2,250					
Supplies expense	0					
Totals	$103,850	$103,850				

Required

1. Complete the six-column table by entering adjustments that reflect the following information:

   a. As of December 31, 2002, employees had earned $400 of unpaid and unrecorded wages. The next payday is January 4, and the total wages to be paid are $1,200.

   b. The cost of supplies available at December 31, 2002, is $3,540.

   c. The note payable requires an interest payment to be made every three months. The amount of unrecorded accrued interest at December 31, 2002, is $800, and the next payment is due on January 15. This payment will be $900.

   d. Analysis of the unearned rental fees shows that $3,200 remains unearned at December 31, 2002.

   e. In addition to the machinery rental fees included in the revenue account balance, the company has earned another $2,450 in fees that will be collected on January 21, 2003. The company is also expected to collect $5,400 on the same day for new fees earned during that month.

   f. Depreciation expense for the year is $3,800.

Check Adjusted trial balance totals, $111,300

2. Prepare journal entries for the adjustments entered in the six-column table for part *1*.

3. Prepare journal entries to reverse the effects of the adjusting entries that involve accruals.

4. Prepare journal entries to record the cash payments and collections described for January.

SERIAL PROBLEM

Sierra Systems

[The first two segments of this serial problem were in Chapters 3 and 4, and the final segment is in Chapter 6. If the Chapter 3 and 4 segments have not been completed, the assignment can begin at this point. It is recommended you use the Working Papers that accompany this book because they reflect the account balances that resulted from posting the entries required in Chapters 3 and 4.]
The transactions of Sierra Systems for October through December 2002 have been recorded for the serial problem segments in Chapters 3 and 4, as well as the year-end adjusting entries.

Required

1. Record and post the necessary closing entries for Sierra Systems.

Check Post-closing trial balance totals, $94,898

2. Prepare a post-closing trial balance.

Beyond the Numbers

Reporting in Action

BTN 5-1 Refer to **Nike**'s financial statements in Appendix A to answer the following:

Required

1. For the fiscal year ended May 31, 2000, what amount will be credited to Income Summary to summarize Nike's revenues earned?

2. For the fiscal year ended May 31, 2000, what amount will be debited to Income Summary to summarize Nike's expenses incurred?

3. For the fiscal year ended May 31, 2000, what will be the balance of the Income Summary account before it is closed?

4. In its statement of cash flows for the year ended May 31, 2000, what amount of cash is paid in dividends to common and preferred stockholders?

Swoosh Ahead

5. Access Nike's annual report for fiscal years ending after May 31, 2000, at its Web site [www.nike.com] or the SEC's EDGAR database [www.sec.gov]. How has the amount of net income closed to Income Summary changed in the fiscal years ending after May 31, 2000? How has the amount of cash paid as dividends changed in the fiscal years ending after May 31, 2000?

BTN 5-2   Key figures ($ millions) for the recent two years of both **Nike** and **Reebok** follow:

Key Figures	Nike		Reebok	
	Current Year	Prior Year	Current Year	Prior Year
Current assets	$3,596	$3,265	$1,243	$1,363
Current liabilities	2,140	1,447	624	543

Required

1. Compute the current ratio for both years and both companies.

2. Which has the better ability to pay short-term obligations according to the current ratio?

3. Analyze and comment on each company's current ratios for the past two years.

4. How do Nike's and Reebok's current ratios compare to their industry average ratio of about 1.6?

BTN 5-3   On January 20, 2002, Jennifer Nelson, the accountant for Newby Enterprises, is feeling pressure to complete the annual financial statements. The company president has said he needs up-to-date financial statements to share with the bank on January 21 at a dinner meeting that has been called to discuss Newby's obtaining loan financing for a special building project. Jennifer knows that she will not be able to gather all the needed information in the next 24 hours to prepare the entire set of adjusting entries that must be posted before the financial statements accurately portray the company's performance and financial position for the fiscal period ended December 31, 2001. Jennifer ultimately decides to estimate several expense accruals at the last minute. When deciding on estimates for the expenses, she uses low estimates because she does not want to make the financial statements look worse than they are. Jennifer finishes the financial statements before the deadline and gives them to the president without mentioning that several accounts use estimated balances.

Required

1. Identify several courses of action that Jennifer could have taken instead of the one she took.

2. If you were in Jennifer's situation, what would you have done? Briefly justify your response.

BTN 5-4   Assume that one of your classmates said that the *going-concern principle* states that a company's books should be ongoing and therefore not closed until that business is terminated. This classmate does not understand the objective of the closing process or the meaning of the going-concern principle. Write a one-half page memo to this classmate explaining the concept of the closing process by drawing analogies between (1) a scoreboard for an athletic event and the revenue and expense accounts of a business or (2) a sports team's record book and the capital account. (*Hint:* Think about what would happen if the scoreboard is not cleared before the start of a new game.) Your memo should also clarify the meaning of the going-concern principle.

BTN 5-5   Access **edgar-online.com** and view the April 28, 2000, filing of the 10-K405 report of Dillards, Inc. (Ticker: DDS).

Required

1. Locate Dillards' balance sheet within the 10-K405 report. Compute its current ratio for the years ending January 29, 2000, and January 30, 1999.

2. Analyze and comment on Dillard's current ratio.

Teamwork in Action

BTN 5-6   The unadjusted trial balance and information for the accounting adjustments of Noseworthy Investigators follow. Each team member involved in this project is to assume one of the four responsibilities listed. After completing each of these responsibilities, the team should work together to prove the accounting equation utilizing information from teammates (1 and 4). If your equation does not balance, you are to work as a team to resolve the error. The team's goal is to complete the task as quickly and accurately as possible.

Unadjusted Trial Balance		
Account Title	Debit	Credit
Cash	$15,000	
Supplies	11,000	
Prepaid insurance	2,000	
Equipment	24,000	
Accumulated depreciation—Equipment		$ 6,000
Accounts payable		2,000
D. Noseworthy, Capital		31,000
D. Noseworthy, Withdrawals	5,000	
Investigation fees earned		32,000
Rent expense	14,000	
Totals	$71,000	$71,000

Additional Year-End Information

a. Insurance that expired in the current period amounts to $1,200.

b. Equipment depreciation for the period is $3,000.

c. Unused supplies total $4,000 at period-end.

d. Services in the amount of $500 have been provided but have not been billed or collected.

Responsibilities for Individual Team Members

1. Determine the accounts and adjusted balances to be extended to the balance sheet columns of the work sheet for Noseworthy. Also determine total assets and total liabilities.

2. Determine the adjusted revenue account balance and prepare the entry to close this account.

3. Determine the adjusted account balances for expenses and prepare the entry to close these accounts.

4. Prepare T-accounts for both D. Noseworthy, Capital (reflecting the unadjusted trial balance amount) and Income Summary. Prepare the third and fourth closing entries. Ask teammates assigned to parts (2) and (3) for the postings for Income Summary. Obtain amounts to complete the third closing entry and post both the third and fourth closing entries. Provide the team with the ending capital account balance.

5. The entire team should prove the accounting equation using post-closing balances.

Business Week Activity

BTN 5-7   Read "Computer Learning Centers: School for Scandal?" in the May 4, 1998, issue of *Business Week*.

Required

1. What type of school is CLC?

2. What three revenue accounting issues does the article discuss?

3. Discuss the effects of each of the revenue accounting issues on CLC's financial statements.

BTN 5-8 Identify the entrepreneur of a small business, preferably one you have an interest in. Some possibilities are a musician, singer, consultant, or artist. Call the entrepreneur to set up a time to briefly visit, either in person or over the phone, to answer the following questions.

Entrepreneurial Decision

Required

1. Is the entrepreneur satisfied with his/her accounting for the business? Explain.
2. What is (are) the most difficult aspect(s) of accounting for this business?
3. Does the entrepreneur use accounting software or spreadsheets? If yes, what type?
4. What suggestions for accounting would the entrepreneur offer a person launching a new business?

6

Accounting for Merchandising Activities

A Look Back

Chapter 5 focused on the final steps of the accounting process. We described the closing process, and showed how to prepare financial statements from accounting records.

A Look at This Chapter

This chapter emphasizes merchandising activities. We explain how reporting merchandising activities differs from reporting service activities. Both the perpetual and periodic inventory systems are described. We also analyze and record merchandise purchases and sales transactions and explain the adjustments and closing process for merchandisers.

A Look Ahead

Chapter 7 extends our analysis of merchandising activities and focuses on the valuation of inventory. Topics include the items in inventory, costs assigned, costing methods used, and inventory estimation techniques.

"We constantly seek the input of our retailers and the buying public"—
Mark Donovan

Part Two

Casual Success

e HOBOKEN, NJ—Paola Buendia was studying English and Mark Donovan was preparing for a career in business when they met at college. Buendia and Donovan became best friends and were soon married. Following graduation, they both landed good jobs. But something was missing. "I needed a creative outlet," says Buendia. "I started designing things I'd always wanted—pretty simple, basic things, and lots of hats, because I'd always worn them." Then Donovan got involved. With just $5,000, they launched a clothing company, **Wooden Ships of Hoboken** (**Wooden-Ships.com**).

Inspired by their travels to Indonesia and the corporate trend toward casual clothing, they targeted women's casual wear. Working out of their apartment for the first year and a half, they sold clothing outdoors off a blanket at concerts, street fairs, and other events. Soon afterward, they began supplying retailers. A crucial part of their business success is tracking merchandising activities. Buendia says they spend a lot of time "figuring out how to supply customers." This includes setting prices and making policies for discounts, allowances, and returns on both sales and purchases.

Managing their inventory is equally crucial, "We constantly seek the input of our retailers and the buying public," Donovan says. Buendia adds that Wooden Ships's Web site allows "us to establish an open line of communication with our ultimate consumer . . . and receive direct feedback on styles, colors and other consumer preferences." This information helps them keep the right type and amount of merchandise to avoid the costs of both out-of-stock items and excess inventory.

Buendia and Donovan still enjoy attending a concert or strolling through a street fair. But to their delight, their business no longer depends on selling at such events. Their annual sales are soon expected to top $15 million, with sales to more than 1,800 boutiques. Not bad for a company that began as a creative whim. [Sources: *Entrepreneur,* November 12, 1998; *Wooden Ships Web Site,* May 2001; *Sunday Star-Ledger,* 1998; *Hudson Current,* August–September 1998.]

Learning Objectives

Conceptual

C1 Describe merchandising activities and identify business examples.

C2 Identify and explain the components of income for a merchandising company.

C3 Identify and explain the inventory asset of a merchandising company.

C4 Describe both perpetual and periodic inventory systems.

C5 Analyze and interpret cost flows and operating activities of a merchandising company.

Analytical

A1 Analyze and interpret accruals and cash flows for merchandising activities.

A2 Compute the acid-test ratio and explain its use to assess liquidity.

A3 Compute the gross margin ratio and explain its use to assess profitability.

Procedural

P1 Analyze and record transactions for merchandise purchases using a perpetual system.

P2 Analyze and record transactions for sales of merchandise using a perpetual system.

P3 Prepare adjustments and close accounts for a merchandising company.

P4 Define and prepare multiple-step and single-step income statements.

Merchandising activities are a major part of modern business. Consumers expect a wealth of products, discount prices, inventory on demand, and high quality. This chapter introduces the business and accounting practices used by companies engaged in merchandising activities. These companies buy products and then resell them to customers. We show how financial statements reflect these merchandising activities and explain the new financial statement elements created by merchandising activities. We analyze and record merchandise purchases and sales. We also explain adjustments and the closing process for merchandising companies.

Merchandising Activities

C1 Describe merchandising activities and identify business examples.

Previous chapters emphasized the accounting and reporting activities of service companies such as **JobDirect**, **Creative Assets**, and **CrossWorlds**. In return for services provided to its customers, a service company receives commissions, fares, or fees as revenue. Its net income is the difference between its revenues and the expenses incurred in providing those services.

A merchandising company's activities differ from those of a service company. A **merchandiser** earns net income by buying and selling merchandise. **Merchandise** consists of products, also called *goods,* that a company acquires to resell to customers. Merchandisers are often identified as either wholesalers or retailers. A **wholesaler** is an *intermediary* that buys products from manufacturers or other wholesalers and sells them to retailers or other wholesalers. Wholesalers provide promotion, market information, and financial assistance to retailers. They also provide a sales force, reduced inventory costs, less risk, and market information to manufacturers. Wholesalers include companies such as **Fleming**, **SuperValu**, **McKesson**, and **Sysco**. Another type of intermediary is a **retailer** that buys products from manufacturers or wholesalers and sells them to consumers. Examples of retailers include **Gap**, **Oakley**, **CompUSA**, **Wal-Mart**, and **MusicLand**. Many retailers such as **Best Buy** sell both products and services.

Reporting Financial Performance

C2 Identify and explain the components of income for a merchandising company.

Net income to a merchandiser implies that revenue from selling merchandise exceeds both the cost of merchandise sold to customers and the cost of other expenses for the period (see Exhibit 6.1). The usual accounting term for revenues from selling merchandise is *sales,* and the term used for the cost of buying and preparing the merchandise is *cost of goods sold.*[1] A merchandiser's expenses are often called *operating expenses.*

Exhibit 6.1

Computing Income for a Merchandising Company versus a Service Company

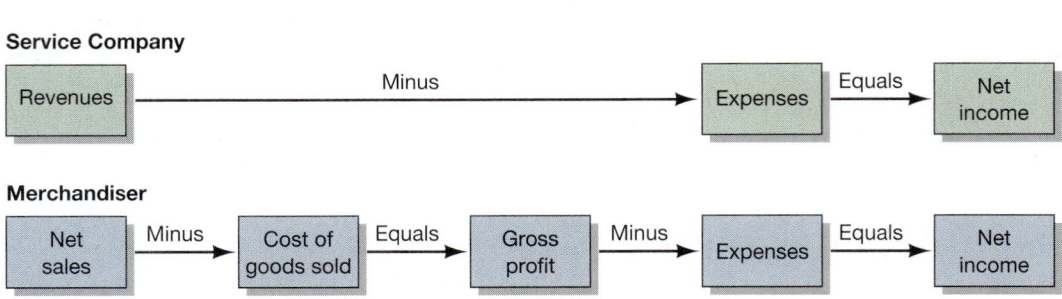

Point: Analysis of gross profit is important to effective business decisions. We describe such analysis later in this chapter.

The condensed income statement for Z-Mart in Exhibit 6.2 shows important components of net income. This statement shows Z-Mart acquired products at a cost of $230,400 and sold them to customers for $314,700. This yields an $84,300 gross profit. **Gross profit,** also called **gross margin,** equals net sales less cost of goods sold. Gross profit is important to merchandisers' profitability. Changes in gross profit often greatly impact a merchandiser's

---

[1] Many service companies use the term *sales* in their income statements to describe revenues. **Marriott** is one example. Cost of goods sold is also called *cost of sales* and is reported as an operating expense.

operations since gross profit must cover all other expenses plus yield a return for the owner. Z-Mart, for instance, used its gross profit to cover $71,400 of other expenses. This left $12,900 in net income.

Reporting Financial Condition

A merchandising company's balance sheet includes a current asset called *merchandise inventory,* an item not on a service company's balance sheet. **Merchandise inventory** refers to products a company owns to sell to customers. Exhibit 6.3 shows the classified balance sheet for Z-Mart, including merchandise inventory of $21,000. The cost of this asset includes the cost incurred to buy the goods, ship them to the store, and make them ready for sale. Many companies simply refer to merchandise inventory as *inventory.*

Exhibit 6.2

Condensed Income Statement for a Merchandiser

Z-MART Condensed Income Statement For Year Ended December 31, 2002	
Net sales	$314,700
Cost of goods sold	(230,400)
Gross profit	$ 84,300
Operating expenses	(71,400)
Net income	$ 12,900

C3 Identify and explain the inventory asset of a merchandising company.

Exhibit 6.3

Classified Balance Sheet for a Merchandiser

Z-MART Balance Sheet December 31, 2002			
Assets			
Current assets			
Cash		$ 8,200	
Accounts receivable		11,200	
Merchandise inventory		**21,000**	
Prepaid expenses		1,100	
Total current assets			$41,500
Plant assets			
Office equipment	$ 4,200		
Less accumulated depreciation	1,400	2,800	
Store equipment	30,000		
Less accumulated depreciation	6,000	24,000	
Total plant assets			26,800
Total assets			$68,300
Liabilities			
Current liabilities			
Accounts payable		$ 6,000	
Salaries payable		800	
Total current liabilities			$ 6,800
Long-term note payable			10,000
Equity			
K. Marty, Capital			$51,500
Total liabilities and equity			$68,300

(handwritten margin notes:) Inventory → products; clothes, food, car, furniture, appliances. Something that you hold for resale.

Operating Cycle

A merchandising company's operating cycle begins by purchasing merchandise and ends by collecting cash from selling the merchandise. An example is a merchandiser who buys products at wholesale and distributes and sells them to consumers at retail. The length of an operating cycle differs across the types of businesses. Department stores such as **The Limited** and **Dayton Hudson** commonly have operating cycles from three to five months.

Operating cycles for grocery merchants such as **Kroger** and **Safeway** usually range from three to eight weeks.

Exhibit 6.4 illustrates an operating cycle for a merchandiser with (1) cash sales and (2) credit sales. The cash sales cycle moves from (a) merchandise purchases to (b) inventory for sale to (c) cash sales. The credit sales cycle moves from (a) merchandise purchases to (b) inventory for sale to (c) credit sales to (d) accounts receivable to (e) cash. Credit sales delay the receipt of cash until the receivable is paid by the customer. Companies try to shorten their operating cycles because assets tied up in inventory or receivables are not productive.

Exhibit 6.4

Operating Cycle of a Merchandiser*

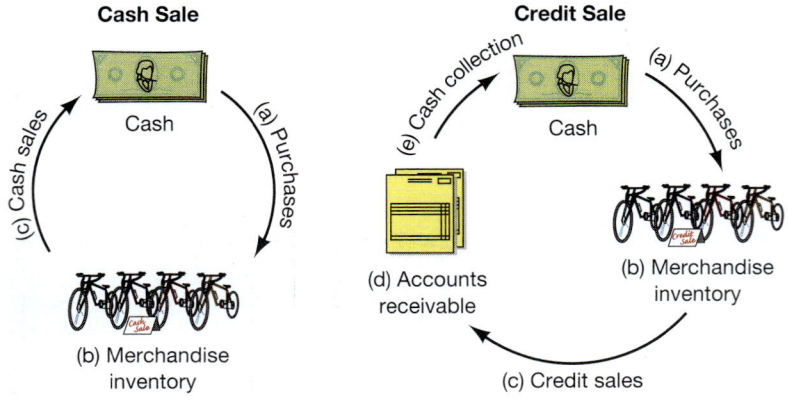

* This exhibit assumes cash purchases. Credit purchases would involve inserting (a) credit purchases, (b) accounts payable, and (c) cash payment in the cycle.

Inventory Systems

We explained that a merchandising company's income statement includes an item called *cost of goods sold* and its balance sheet includes a current asset called *inventory*. **Cost of goods sold** is the cost of merchandise sold to customers during a period. It is often the largest single deduction on a merchandiser's income statement. **Inventory** refers to products a company owns and expects to sell in its normal operations. Inventory items are part of merchandising activities captured in Exhibit 6.5. This exhibit shows that a company's merchandise available for sale is a combination of what it begins with (beginning inventory) and what it purchases (net cost of purchases). The merchandise available is either sold (cost of goods sold) or kept for future sales (ending inventory).

Exhibit 6.5

Merchandising Cost Flow

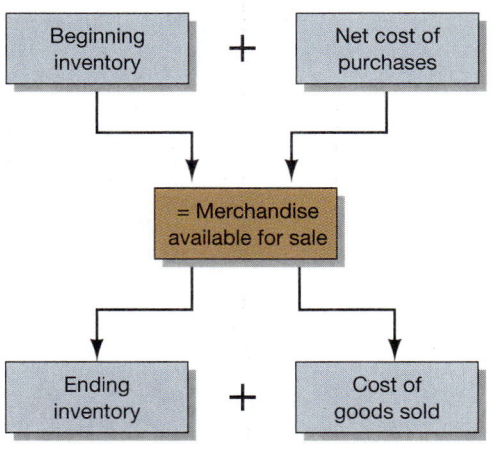

Two alternative inventory accounting systems can be used to collect information about cost of goods sold and cost of inventory available: *periodic system* or *perpetual system*.

Periodic Inventory System

C4 Describe both perpetual and periodic inventory systems.

A **periodic inventory system** requires updating the inventory account only at the *end of a period* to reflect the quantity and cost of goods both available and sold. It does not require continual updating of the inventory account. The cost of merchandise is recorded in a temporary *Purchases* account. When a company sells merchandise, it records revenue but not the cost of the merchandise sold. Instead, when it prepares financial statements, the company takes a *physical count of inventory* by counting the quantities of merchandise available. The cost of merchandise available is computed by linking the quantities counted to the purchase records that show each item's original cost. The cost of merchandise available is then used to compute cost of goods sold. The inventory account is then adjusted to reflect the amount computed from the physical count of inventory. Companies such as hardware, drug, and department stores that sell large quantities of low-value items historically used periodic systems. Without today's computers and scanners, it was not feasible for accounting systems to track numerous, low-cost items such as pens, toothpaste, candy bars, socks, and magazines through inventory and into customers' hands.

Perpetual Inventory System

A **perpetual inventory system** keeps a continual record of the amount of inventory available. A perpetual system accumulates the net cost of merchandise purchases in the inventory account and subtracts the cost of each sale from the same inventory account. When a company sells an item, it records its cost in the *Cost of Goods Sold* account. With a perpetual system we can learn the cost of merchandise available at any time by looking at the balance of the inventory account. We can also learn the current balance of cost of goods sold anytime during a period by looking in the Cost of Goods Sold account.

Point: Growth of super stores such as Price Club and Costco is fed by the efficient use of perpetual inventory techniques and technology.

Before advancements in computing technology, a perpetual system was often limited to businesses making a small number of daily sales such as automobile dealers and major appliance stores. Because transactions were relatively few, a perpetual system was feasible. In today's information age, with widespread use of computing technology, the use of a perpetual system has dramatically increased. A perpetual inventory system gives users more timely information. Accordingly, this chapter emphasizes a perpetual system. However, we analyze and record merchandising transactions using *both* periodic and perpetual inventory systems in the appendix to this chapter.

Did You Know?

Perpetual Info   Technology and perpetual inventory systems are taking the guesswork out of purchasing, slashing inventory cycles, keeping popular items in stock, and cutting return rates. These advances "totally changed the industry from a push industry to a pull industry," says the chairman of **Western Merchandisers**, a supplier of more than 1,000 **Wal-Marts**. A recent study says grocers can cut prices by 11% or more with similar changes.

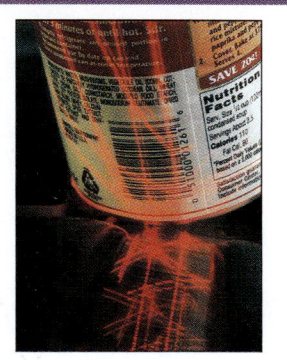

Quick Check

1. Describe a merchandiser's cost of goods sold.
2. What is gross profit for a merchandising company?
3. Explain why use of the perpetual inventory system has dramatically increased.

Answers—p. 244

With a perpetual inventory system, the cost of merchandise bought for resale is recorded in the Merchandise Inventory asset account. To illustrate, Z-Mart records a $1,200 cash purchase of merchandise on November 2 with this entry:

Merchandise Purchases

Nov. 2	Merchandise Inventory	1,200	
	Cash		1,200
	Purchased merchandise for cash.		

Assets = Liabilities + Equity
+1,200
−1,200

The invoice for this merchandise is shown in Exhibit 6.6. The buyer usually receives the original, and the seller keeps a copy. This *source document* serves as the purchase invoice of Z-Mart (buyer) and the sales invoice for Trex (seller). The amount recorded for merchandise inventory includes its purchase cost, shipping fees, taxes, and any other costs necessary to make it ready for sale.

P1 Analyze and record transactions for merchandise purchases using a perpetual system.

To compute the total cost of merchandise purchases, we must adjust the invoice cost for (1) any discounts a supplier gives a purchaser, (2) any returns and allowances for unsatisfactory items received from a supplier, and (3) any required freight costs paid by a purchaser. This section explains how these items affect the recorded cost of merchandise purchases.

Concept 6-1

Exhibit 6.6

Invoice

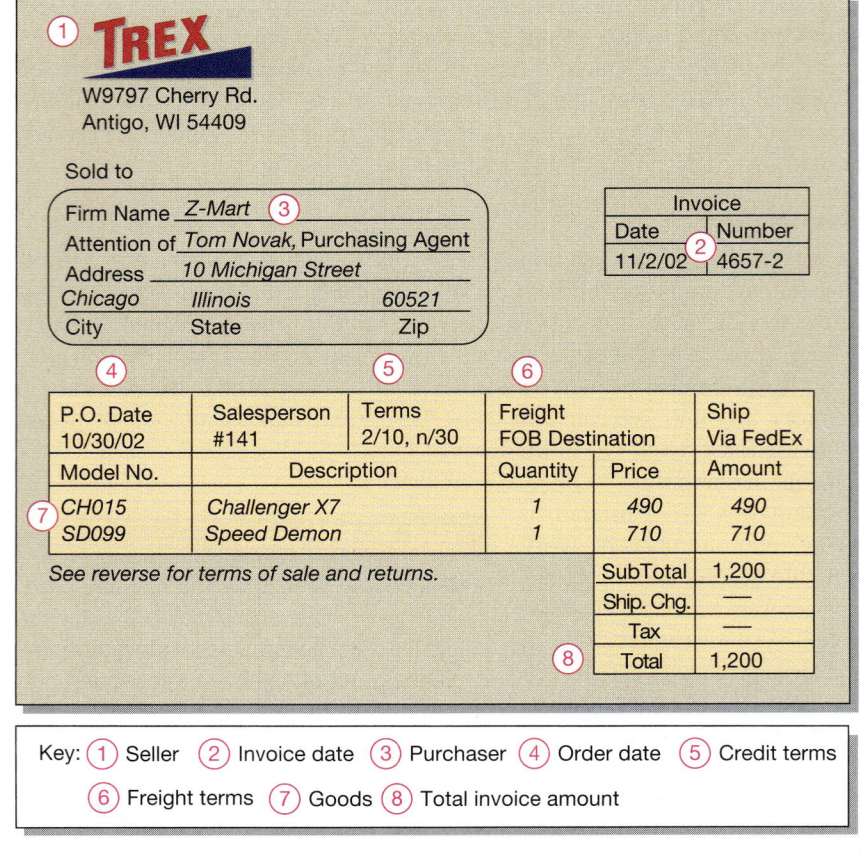

Key: ① Seller   ② Invoice date   ③ Purchaser   ④ Order date   ⑤ Credit terms

⑥ Freight terms   ⑦ Goods   ⑧ Total invoice amount

Point: The Merchandise Inventory account reflects the cost of goods available for resale.

Trade Discounts

When a manufacturer or wholesaler prepares a catalog of items it has for sale, it usually gives each item a **list price,** also called a *catalog price.* List price usually is not the item's intended selling price. Instead, its intended selling price equals list price minus a given percent called a **trade discount.**

The amount of trade discount usually depends on whether a buyer is a wholesaler, retailer, or final consumer. A wholesaler buying in large quantities is often granted a larger discount than a retailer buying in smaller quantities. Manufacturers and wholesalers commonly use trade discounts to change selling prices without republishing their catalogs. When a seller wants to change selling prices, it can notify its customers merely by sending them a new table of trade discounts that they can apply to catalog prices.

A buyer does *not* enter list prices and trade discounts in its accounts. Instead, a buyer records the net amount of list price minus trade discount. For example, in the November 2 purchase of merchandise by Z-Mart, the merchandise was listed in the seller's catalog at $2,000 and Z-Mart received a 40% trade discount. This means that Z-Mart's purchase price is $1,200, computed as $2,000 − (40% × $2,000).

Purchase Discounts

The purchase of goods on credit requires a clear statement of expected amounts and dates of future payments to avoid misunderstandings. **Credit terms** for a purchase include the amounts and timing of payments from a buyer to a seller. Credit terms usually reflect an industry's practices. In some industries, purchasers expect terms requiring payment within 10 days after the end of the month when purchases occur. These credit terms are entered on sales invoices as "n/10 EOM." The **EOM** refers to *end of month.* In other industries, invoices are often due and payable within 30 calendar days after the invoice date. These credit terms are entered as "n/30," expressed as *net 30.* The 30-day period in this case is called the **credit period.** Exhibit 6.7 portrays credit terms.

Point: Since both the buyer and seller know the invoice date, this date is useful in determining the end of the credit period. Alternatively, the date shipped or received is not known by both parties.

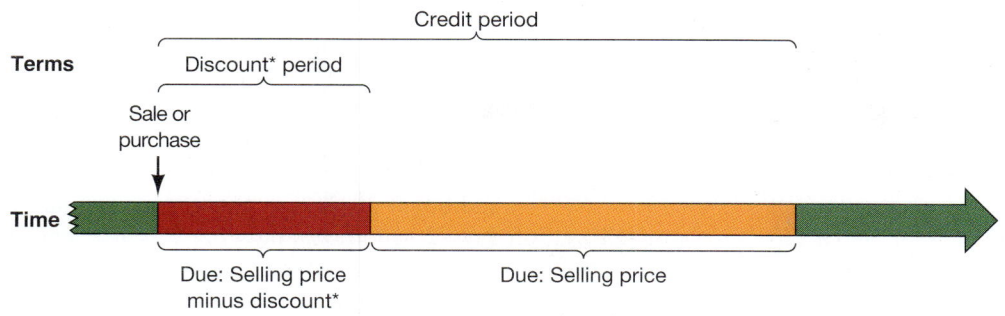

Terms

Credit period

Discount* period

Sale or purchase

Time

Due: Selling price minus discount*

Due: Selling price

*Discount refers to either purchase or sales discounts.

Exhibit 6.7

Credit Terms

Sellers often grant a **cash discount** when the credit period is long and buyers pay within a certain period. A buyer views a cash discount as a **purchase discount.** A seller views a cash discount as a **sales discount.** If cash discounts for early payment exist, they are described as credit terms on the invoice. For example, credit terms of "2/10, n/60" imply that a 60-day credit period occurs before full payment is due. The seller allows the buyer to deduct 2% of the invoice amount if payment is made within 10 days of the invoice date. Sellers do this to encourage early payment. The reduced payment can be made during the **discount period.**

To illustrate how a buyer accounts for a purchase discount, let's assume that Z-Mart's purchase of merchandise for $1,200 is on credit with terms of 2/10, n/30. Z-Mart's entry to record this credit purchase is[2]

(a) Nov. 2	Merchandise Inventory	1,200	
	Accounts Payable		1,200
	Purchased merchandise on credit, invoice dated Nov. 2, terms 2/10, n/30.		

Assets = Liabilities + Equity
+1,200   +1,200

If Z-Mart takes advantage of the discount and pays the amount due on November 12, the entry to record payment is

(b) Nov. 12	Accounts Payable	1,200	
	Merchandise Inventory		24
	Cash		1,176
	Paid for the $1,200 purchase of Nov. 2 less the discount of $24(2% × $1,200).		

Assets = Liabilities + Equity
−24   −1,200
−1,176

Z-Mart's Merchandise Inventory account after this entry reflects the net cost of merchandise purchased. Its Accounts Payable account shows a zero balance, meaning the debt is satisfied. Both accounts, in T-account form, follow here:

Merchandise Inventory				Accounts Payable			
Nov. 2	1,200	Nov. 12	24	Nov. 12	1,200	Nov. 2	1,200
Balance	1,176					Balance	0

Managing Discounts

A buyer's failure to pay within a discount period is often expensive. In the preceding example, if Z-Mart does not pay within the 10-day discount period, it can delay payment by 20 more days. This delay costs Z-Mart an added 2% to the cost of merchandise. Most buyers

---

[2] Appendix 6A repeats journal entries *a* through *f* using a periodic inventory system.

try to take advantage of a purchase discount because of the usually high interest rate implied from not taking it. We can approximate the annual rate of interest attached to not paying within the discount period. For Z-Mart's terms of 2/10, n/30, missing the 2% discount for an additional 20 days is equal to an annual interest rate of 36.5%. This is computed as (365 days/20 additional days) × 2% discount rate.[3]

Most companies set up a system to pay invoices with favorable discounts within the discount period. Careful cash management means that no invoice is paid until the last day of a discount period. One technique to achieve this goal is to file each invoice so that it automatically comes up for payment on the last day of its discount period. A simple filing system uses up to 31 folders, one for each day in a month. After an invoice is recorded, it is placed in the folder matching the last day of its discount period. If the last day of an invoice's discount period is November 12, it is filed in folder 12. This and other invoices in the same folder are removed and paid on November 12.

Purchase Returns and Allowances

Purchase returns refer to merchandise a purchaser receives but then returns to the supplier. A *purchase allowance* is a reduction in the cost of defective or unacceptable merchandise that a purchaser receives from a supplier. Purchasers often keep defective but still marketable merchandise if the supplier grants an acceptable allowance.

The purchaser usually informs the supplier in writing of any returns and allowances, often with a **debit memorandum,** a document the purchaser issues to inform the supplier of a debit made to the supplier's account, including the reason for the return or allowance. Exhibit 6.8 shows a debit memorandum prepared by Z-Mart requesting an allowance from Trex for the defective *SpeedDemon* mountain bike. The November 15 entry by Z-Mart to update the Merchandise Inventory account to reflect the purchase allowance requested in the debit memorandum is

Assets = Liabilities + Equity
−300   −300

(c) Nov. 15	Accounts Payable	300	
	Merchandise Inventory		300
	Allowance for defective merchandise.		

Exhibit 6.8

Debit Memorandum

Case: Z-Mart (buyer) proposes $300 allowance for defective merchandise from Trex (seller)

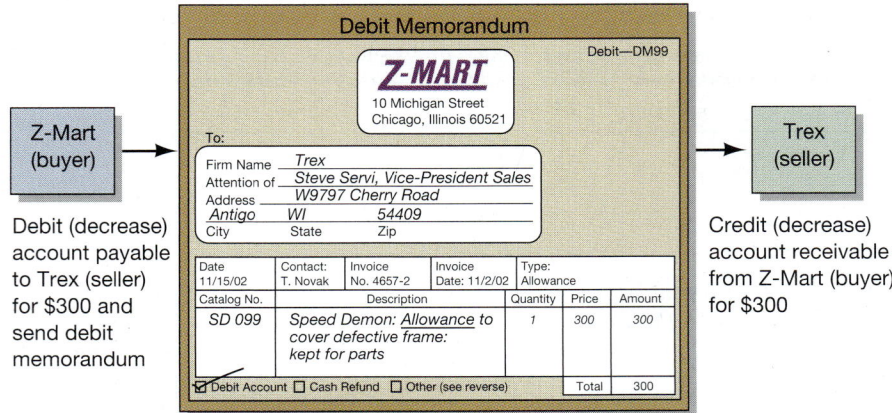

[3] The implied interest rate formula is: (365 days ÷ [Credit period − Discount period]) × Cash discount rate.

If this had been a return, then the total recorded cost of the defective merchandise would have been entered.[4] Z-Mart's agreement with this supplier says the cost of returned and defective merchandise is offset against Z-Mart's next purchase or its current account payable balance. Some agreements with suppliers involve refunding the cost to a buyer. When cash is refunded, the Cash account is debited for $300 instead of Accounts Payable.

Discounts and Returns

When goods are returned within the discount period, a buyer can take the discount on only the remaining balance of the invoice. As an example, suppose Z-Mart purchases $1,000 of merchandise offered with a 2% cash discount. Two days later, Z-Mart returns $100 of goods before paying the invoice. When Z-Mart later pays within the discount period, it can take the 2% discount only on the $900 remaining balance. The discount is $18 (2% × $900), and the cash payment is $882 ($900 − $18).

> ### You Make the Call—Ethics
>
> **Credit Manager** As the new credit manager, you are being trained by the outgoing manager. She explains that the system prepares checks for amounts net of favorable cash discounts, and the checks are dated the last day of the discount period. She also tells you that checks are not mailed until five days later, adding that "the company gets free use of cash for an extra five days, and our department looks better. When a supplier complains, we blame the computer system and the mailroom." Do you continue this payment policy?
>
> Answer—p. 243

Transportation Costs

Depending on terms negotiated with suppliers, a merchandiser is sometimes responsible for paying shipping costs on purchases, often called *transportation-in* or *freight-in* costs. Z-Mart's $1,200 purchase on November 2 is on terms of FOB destination. This means Z-Mart is not responsible for paying transportation costs. When a merchandiser is responsible for paying transportation costs, they are sometimes made to an independent carrier but other times are made directly to the seller. Transportation costs are often included on the invoice when owed to the seller, whereas transportation costs owed to an independent carrier usually are not included on the invoice. The cost principle requires transportation costs be included as part of the cost of purchased merchandise. This means a separate entry is necessary when they are *not* listed on the invoice. For example, Z-Mart's entry to record a $75 freight charge from an independent carrier for merchandise purchased FOB shipping point would be

> **Example:** Suppose Z-Mart pays for $1,000 of merchandise acquired within the discount period and receives a 2% discount. Later, when Z-Mart returns $100 of the original $1,000 merchandise, what amount of cash refund does it receive? How are the return and cash receipt recorded? *Answers:* Cash refund = Net paid for $100 of goods = 98% × $100 = $98. The entry to record this is
>
> | | | |
> |---|---|---|
> | Cash . . . . | 98 | |
> | Merchandise Inventory . | | 98 |

(d) Nov. 24	Merchandise Inventory	75	
	Cash		75
	Paid freight charges on purchased merchandise.		

Assets = Liabilities + Equity
+75
−75

Transportation-in costs differ from the costs of shipping goods to customers. Transportation-in costs are included in the cost of merchandise inventory, but the costs of shipping goods to customers are not. The costs of shipping goods to customers are recorded in a delivery expense account when the merchandiser (seller in this case) is responsible for these costs. Delivery expense, also called *freight-out* or *transportation-out,* is reported as a selling expense in the income statement.

> **Point:** When CompUSA purchases merchandise and then distributes it among its stores, the cost of shipping merchandise to the stores is included in the costs of the store inventories according to the cost principle.

Transfer of Ownership

The buyer and seller must agree on who is responsible for paying any freight costs and who bears the risk of loss during transit for merchandising transactions. This is essentially the same as asking at what point ownership transfers from the seller to the buyer. The point of transfer is called the **FOB** (*free on board*) point. The point when ownership transfers from the seller to the buyer determines who pays transportation costs (and other incidental costs of transit such as insurance).

---

[4] *Recorded cost* is the cost reported in the account minus any discounts.

Exhibit 6.9 identifies two alternative points of transfer. The first is FOB shipping point. *FOB shipping point,* also called *FOB factory,* means the buyer accepts ownership at the seller's place of business. The buyer is then responsible for paying shipping costs and bearing the risk of damage or loss when goods are in transit. The goods are part of the buyer's inventory when they are in transit since ownership has transferred to the buyer. **Midway Games** is a leader in entertainment software and uses FOB shipping point. Midway has released many popular games including Mortal Kombat, Cruis'n USA, Cruis'n World, NBA Jam, Joust, Defender, and Pacman.

Exhibit 6.9

Identifying Transfer of Ownership

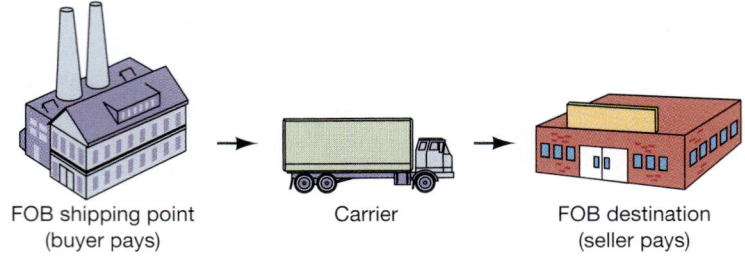

	Ownership Transfers when Goods Passed to	Transportation Costs Paid by
FOB shipping point	Carrier	Buyer
FOB destination	Buyer	Seller

The second means of transfer is *FOB destination,* which means ownership of the goods transfers to the buyer at the buyer's place of business. The seller is responsible for paying shipping charges and bears the risk of damage or loss in transit. The seller does not record revenue from this sale until the goods arrive at the destination because this transaction is not complete before that point. **Compaq Computer** at one time shipped its products FOB shipping point, but it found delivery companies to be unreliable in picking up shipments at scheduled times, causing backups and missing deliveries. This resulted in unhappy consumers. Compaq then changed its agreements to FOB destination, took control of shipping, and eliminated its problems.

In some situations, the party not responsible for shipping costs pays the carrier. In these cases, the party paying these costs either bills the party responsbile or, more commonly, adjusts its account payable or account receivable with the other party. For example, a buyer paying a carrier when terms are FOB destination can decrease its account payable to the seller by the amount of shipping cost. Similarly, a seller who pays a carrier when terms are FOB shipping point can increase its account receivable from the buyer by the amount of shipping cost.

Recording Purchases Information

We explained that purchase discounts, purchase returns and allowances, and transportation-in are included in computing the total cost of merchandise inventory. Purchases are initially recorded as debits to Merchandise Inventory. Any later purchase discounts, returns, and allowances are credited (decreases) to Merchandise Inventory. Transportation-in is debited (added) to Merchandise Inventory. Z-Mart's itemized costs of merchandise purchases for year 2002 are in Exhibit 6.10. The Merchandise Inventory account reflects the net cost of purchased merchandise according to the *cost principle.* Recall that the Merchandise Inventory account is updated after each transaction that affects the cost of goods either purchased or sold. These timely updates of the Merchandise Inventory account reflect a perpetual inventory system.

Exhibit 6.10
Itemized Costs of Merchandise Purchases

Z-MART
Itemized Costs of Merchandise Purchases
For Year Ended December 31, 2002

Invoice cost of merchandise purchases	$235,800
Less: Purchase discounts received	(4,200)
Purchase returns and allowances	(1,500)
Add: Costs of transportation-in	2,300
Total cost of merchandise purchases	**$232,400**

The accounting system described here does not provide separate records for total purchases, total purchase discounts, total purchase returns and allowances, and total transportation-in. Managers usually need this information, however, to evaluate and control each of these cost elements. Nearly all companies collect this information in supplementary records. **Supplementary records,** also called *supplemental records,* refer to information outside the usual accounting records and ledger accounts.

Point: Some companies have separate accounts for purchase discounts, returns and allowances, and transportation-in. Balances of these accounts are then transferred to Merchandise Inventory at the end of each period. This is a hybrid system of perpetual and periodic. That is, Merchandise Inventory is updated on a perpetual basis but only for purchases and cost of goods sold.

Quick Check

4. How long are the credit and discount periods when credit terms are 2/10, n/60?

5. Identify items subtracted from the *list* amount and not recorded when computing purchase price: (a) freight-in; (b) trade discount; (c) purchase discount; (d) purchase return.

6. Explain the meaning of *FOB*. What does *FOB destination* mean?

Answers—p. 244

Merchandise Sales

We explained that companies buying merchandise for resale need to account for purchases, purchase discounts, and purchase returns and allowances. Merchandising companies also must account for sales, sales discounts, sales returns and allowances, and cost of goods sold. A merchandising company such as Z-Mart reports these items in the gross profit section of its income statement as shown in Exhibit 6.11.

Exhibit 6.11
Gross Profit Section of Income Statement

Z-MART
Computation of Gross Profit
For Year Ended December 31, 2002

Sales		$321,000
Less: Sales discounts	$4,300	
Sales returns and allowances	2,000	6,300
Net sales		$314,700
Cost of goods sold		(230,400)
Gross profit		**$ 84,300**

Concept 6-2

This section explains how information in this computation is derived from transactions involving sales, sales discounts, and sales returns and allowances.

Sales Transactions

Each sales transaction for a seller of merchandise involves two parts. One part is the revenue received in the form of an asset from a customer. The second part is the recognition

P2 Analyze and record transactions for sales of merchandise using a perpetual system.

of the cost of merchandise sold to a customer. Accounting for a sales transaction means capturing information about both parts. Moreover, sales transactions of merchandisers usually include both sales for cash and sales on credit. Whether a sale is for cash or on credit, it requires two entries: one for revenue and one for cost. To illustrate, Z-Mart sold $2,400 of merchandise on credit on November 3. The revenue part of this transaction is recorded as

Assets = Liabilities + Equity
+2,400   +2400

(e) Nov. 3	Accounts Receivable	2,400	
	Sales		2,400
	Sold merchandise on credit.		

This entry reflects an increase in Z-Mart's assets in the form of an account receivable. It also shows the revenue (Sales) from the credit sale.[5] If the sale is for cash, the debit is to Cash instead of Accounts Receivable. The cost of the merchandise Z-Mart sold on November 3 is $1,600. (In Chapter 7 we explain the computation of the cost of merchandise.) The entry to record the cost part of this sales transaction (under a perpetual inventory system) is

Assets = Liabilities + Equity
−1,600   −1,600

(e) Nov. 3	Cost of Goods Sold	1,600	
	Merchandise Inventory		1,600
	To record the cost of Nov. 3 sale.		

Since the cost part is recorded each time a sale occurs, the Merchandise Inventory account will reflect the cost of the remaining merchandise available for sale.

Sales Discounts

Selling goods on credit demands that the amounts and dates of future payments be made clear to avoid misunderstandings. We explained earlier in this chapter that credit terms often include a discount to encourage early payment. Companies granting cash discounts to customers refer to these as *sales discounts*. Sales discounts can benefit a seller by decreasing the delay in receiving cash. Prompt payments also reduce future efforts and costs of billing customers.

At the time of a credit sale, a seller does not know whether a customer will pay within the discount period and take advantage of a cash discount. This means the seller usually does not record a sales discount until a customer actually pays within the discount period. To illustrate, Z-Mart completes a credit sale for $1,000 on November 12, subject to terms of 2/10, n/60. The entry to record the revenue part of this sale is

Assets = Liabilities + Equity
+1,000   +1,000

Nov. 12	Accounts Receivable	1,000	
	Sales		1,000
	Sold merchandise under terms of 2/10, n/60.		

This entry records the receivable and the revenue as if the customer will pay the full amount. The customer has two options, however. One is to wait 60 days until January 11 and pay the full $1,000. In this case, Z-Mart records the payment as

Assets = Liabilities + Equity
+1,000
−1,000

Jan. 11	Cash	1,000	
	Accounts Receivable		1,000
	Received payment for Nov. 12 sale.		

The customer's second option is to pay $980 within a 10-day period running through November 22. If the customer pays on or before November 22, Z-Mart records the payment as

---

[5] We describe in Chapter 10 the accounting for sales to customers who use third-party credit cards such as those issued by banks and other organizations.

Nov. 22	Cash	980	
	Sales Discounts	20	
	Accounts Receivable		1,000
	Received payment for Nov. 12 sale less the discount.		

Assets = Liabilities + Equity
+980   −20
−1,000

Sales Discounts is a contra-revenue account. Management monitors Sales Discounts to assess the effectiveness and cost of its discount program. The Sales Discounts account is deducted from the Sales account when computing a company's net sales (see Exhibit 6.11). Information about sales discounts is seldom reported on income statements distributed to external users.

> **Did You Know?**
>
> **Discount Targeting   Catalina Supermarkets** uses bar codes, software, and the Web to help execs keep tabs on who buys what foods, how often, and at what price. Its high-profit customer rate is up because most discounts and services, such as coupons and free delivery, are given almost exclusively to its best customers.

Sales Returns and Allowances

Sales returns refer to merchandise that customers return to the seller after a sale. Many companies allow customers to return merchandise for a full refund. *Sales allowances* refer to reductions in the selling price of merchandise sold to customers. This can occur with damaged merchandise that a customer is willing to purchase with a decrease in selling price. Sales returns and allowances involve dissatisfied customers and the possibility of lost future sales, and managers need information about returns and allowances to monitor these problems. Many accounting systems record returns and allowances in a separate contra-revenue account.

To illustrate, recall Z-Mart's sale of merchandise on November 3 for $2,400 that had cost $1,600. Assume that the customer returns part of the merchandise on November 6, and the returned items sell for $800 and cost $600. The revenue part of this transaction must reflect the decrease in sales from the customer's return of merchandise:

(f) Nov. 6	Sales Returns and Allowances	800	
	Accounts Receivable		800
	Customer returns merchandise of Nov. 3 sale.		

Assets = Liabilities + Equity
−800   −800

Managers monitor the Sales Returns and Allowances contra account for quality purposes. Published income statements usually omit this detail and show only net sales.

If merchandise returned to Z-Mart is not defective and can be resold to another customer, Z-Mart returns these goods to its inventory. The entry necessary to restore the cost of these goods to the Merchandise Inventory account is

> **Did You Know?**
>
> **MegaReturns   Book merchandisers** such as **Barnes & Noble** and **Borders Books** can return unsold books to publishers at purchase price. Publishers say returns of new hardcover books run between 35% and 50%. This compares with 15% to 25% ten years ago.

Nov. 6	Merchandise Inventory	600	
	Cost of Goods Sold		600
	Returned goods to inventory.		

Assets = Liabilities + Equity
+600   +600

But if the merchandise returned is defective, the seller may discard it. In this case, the cost of returned merchandise is not restored to the Merchandise Inventory account but is left in the Cost of Goods Sold account.[6]

---

[6] When managers want to monitor the cost of defective merchandise, a better method is to remove the cost from (credit) Cost of Goods Sold and charge it to (debit) a Loss from Defective Merchandise account.

Another possibility is that $800 of the merchandise Z-Mart sold on November 3 is defective but the customer decides to keep it because Z-Mart offers a $500 price reduction. The only entry Z-Mart must make in this case is to decrease expected revenue and assets:

Assets = Liabilities + Equity
−500   −500

Nov. 6	Sales Returns and Allowances	500	
	Accounts Receivable		500
	To record sales allowance of Nov. 3 sale.		

The seller usually prepares a credit memorandum to confirm a customer's return or allowance. A **credit memorandum** informs a customer of a credit to its Account Receivable account from a sales return or allowance. The information in a credit memorandum is similar to that of a debit memorandum. Z-Mart's credit memorandum issued to the customer for the $500 sales allowance on November 6 is shown in Exhibit 6.12.

Exhibit 6.12

Credit Memorandum

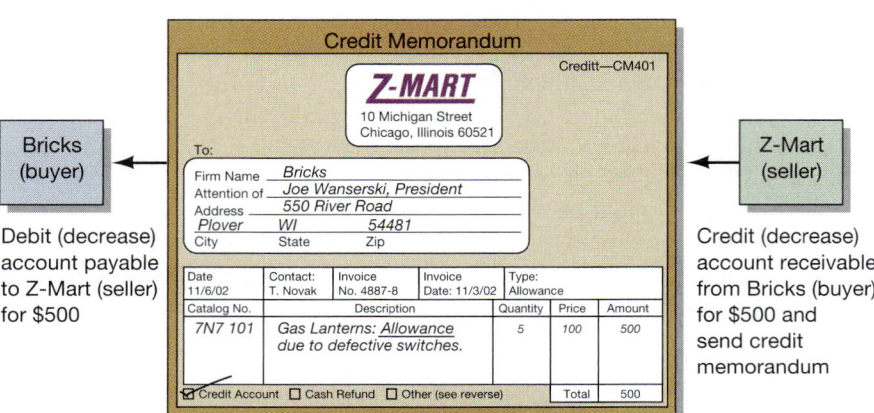

Case: Z-Mart (seller) approves $500 sales allowance to Bricks (buyer)

Quick Check

7. Why are sales discounts and sales returns and allowances recorded in contra-revenue accounts instead of directly in the Sales account?

8. Under what conditions are two entries necessary to record a sales return?

9. When merchandise is sold on credit and the seller notifies the buyer of a price reduction, does the seller send a credit memorandum or a debit memorandum?

Answers—p. 244

Additional Merchandising Issues

This section explains merchandising activities' effect on other accounting processes. We address cost and price adjustments, preparation of adjusting and closing entries, and relations between important accounts.

Cost and Price Adjustments

Buyers and sellers sometimes need to adjust the amount owed between them. Such adjustments can occur when purchased merchandise does not meet specifications, unordered goods are received, quantities different than were ordered and billed are received, or errors occur in billing. The buyer can sometimes adjust the balance without negotiation. For example, when a seller makes an error on an invoice and the buyer discovers it, the buyer can make an adjustment and notify the seller by sending a debit or a credit memorandum. Sometimes adjustments can be made only after negotiations between the buyer and seller, for example, when a buyer claims that some merchandise does not meet specifications. In this case, the amount of allowance given by the seller is usually arrived at only after discussion.

Adjusting Entries

Most adjusting entries are the same for merchandising companies and service companies. In all cases, the adjustments are limited to prepaid expenses (including depreciation), accrued expenses, unearned revenues, and accrued revenues. However, a merchandising company using a perpetual inventory system is usually required to make a special adjustment to update the Merchandise Inventory account to reflect any loss of merchandise. Companies can lose merchandise in several ways, including theft and deterioration. **Shrinkage** is the term used to refer to the loss of inventory.

While a perpetual inventory system tracks all goods as they move in and out of the company, it is unable to directly measure shrinkage. Instead, we compute shrinkage by comparing a physical count of inventory with recorded quantities. A physical count is usually performed at least once annually to verify the Merchandise Inventory account. Most companies record any necessary adjustment due to shrinkage by charging it to Cost of Goods Sold if shrinkage is not abnormally large.

P3 Prepare adjustments and close accounts for a merchandising company.

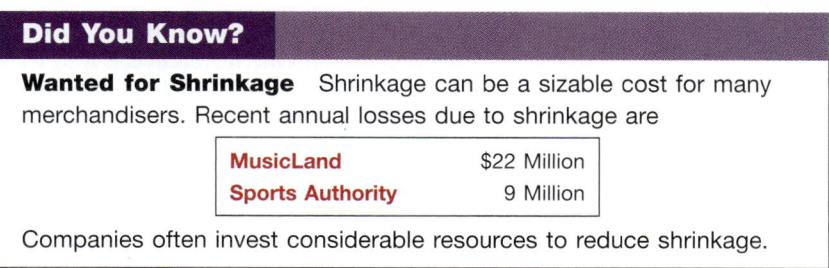

Did You Know?

Wanted for Shrinkage Shrinkage can be a sizable cost for many merchandisers. Recent annual losses due to shrinkage are

MusicLand	$22 Million
Sports Authority	9 Million

Companies often invest considerable resources to reduce shrinkage.

To illustrate, Z-Mart's Merchandise Inventory account at the end of year 2002 has a balance of $21,250. A physical count of inventory reveals only $21,000 of inventory available.

Point: Two-thirds of shoplifting losses are thefts by employees.

Exhibit 6.13

Adjusted Trial Balance for a Merchandiser

Z-MART Adjusted Trial Balance December 31, 2002	Debit	Credit
Cash	$ 8,200	
Accounts receivable	11,200	
Merchandise inventory	21,000	
Office supplies	550	
Store supplies	250	
Prepaid insurance	300	
Office equipment	4,200	
Accumulated depreciation—Office equipment		$ 1,400
Store equipment	30,000	
Accumulated depreciation—Store equipment		6,000
Accounts payable		16,000
Salaries payable		800
K. Marty, Capital		42,600
K. Marty, Withdrawals	4,000	
Sales		321,000
Sales discounts	4,300	
Sales returns and allowances	2,000	
Cost of goods sold	230,400	
Depreciation expense—Store equipment	3,000	
Depreciation expense—Office equipment	700	
Office salaries expense	25,300	
Sales salaries expense	18,500	
Insurance expense	600	
Rent expense, office space	900	
Rent expense, selling space	8,100	
Office supplies expense	1,800	
Store supplies expense	1,200	
Advertising expense	11,300	
Totals	$387,800	$387,800

The adjusting entry to record this $250 shrinkage is

Assets = Liabilities + Equity
−250   −250

Dec. 31	Cost of Goods Sold	250	
	Merchandise Inventory		250
	To adjust for $250 shrinkage revealed by a physical count of inventory.		

Closing Entries

Closing entries are similar for merchandising companies and service companies using a perpetual system. One difference is that we must close additional temporary accounts that arise from merchandising activities. We use Z-Mart's adjusted trial balance in Exhibit 6.13 to show its four-step closing process in Exhibit 6.14.

Exhibit 6.14

Closing Entries for a Merchandiser

Step 1: Close Credit Balances in Temporary Accounts to Income Summary.

Z-Mart has one temporary account with a credit balance; it is closed with this entry:

Dec. 31	**Sales**	**321,000**	
	Income Summary		321,000
	To close credit balances in temporary accounts.		

Step 2: Close Debit Balances in Temporary Accounts to Income Summary.

The second entry closes temporary accounts having debit balances such as Cost of Goods Sold, Sales Discounts, and Sales Returns and Allowances and is shown here:

Dec. 31	Income Summary	308,100	
	Sales Discounts		**4,300**
	Sales Returns and Allowances		**2,000**
	Cost of Goods Sold		**230,400**
	Depreciation Expense—Store Equipment . . .		3,000
	Depreciation Expense—Office Equipment . .		700
	Office Salaries Expense		25,300
	Sales Salaries Expense		18,500
	Insurance Expense		600
	Rent Expense—Office Space		900
	Rent Expense—Selling Space		8,100
	Office Supplies Expense		1,800
	Store Supplies Expense		1,200
	Advertising Expense		11,300
	To close debit balances in temporary accounts.		

Step 3: Close Income Summary to Owner's Capital.

The third closing entry is exactly the same for a merchandising company and a service company. It updates the owner's capital account for income or loss and is shown here:

Dec. 31	Income Summary	12,900	
	K. Marty, Capital		12,900
	To close the Income Summary account.		

The $12,900 amount in the entry is net income reported on the income statement in Exhibit 6.2.

Step 4: Close Withdrawals Account to Owner's Capital.

The fourth closing entry is exactly the same for a merchandising company and a service company. It closes the withdrawals account and adjusts the owner's capital account balance to the amount shown on the balance sheet. This entry for Z-Mart is

Dec. 31	K. Marty, Capital	4,000	
	K. Marty, Withdrawals		4,000
	To close the withdrawals accounts.		

When these entries are posted, all temporary accounts are set to zero and are ready to record events for next year. Also, the capital account now is updated to reflect all prior transactions.

Z-Mart's trial balance includes several accounts unique to merchandising companies: Merchandise Inventory, Sales (of goods), Sales Discounts, Sales Returns and Allowances, and Cost of Goods Sold. Their existence in the ledger means the first two closing entries for a merchandiser are slightly different from the ones described in Chapter 5 for a service company. These differences are bolded in the closing entries of Exhibit 6.14.

Merchandising Cost Flows

Exhibit 6.15 shows the relations between inventory, merchandise purchases, and cost of goods sold across periods. We already explained that the net cost of purchases reflects trade discounts, purchase discounts, and purchase returns and allowances. These items constituting the cost of purchases are recorded in the Merchandise Inventory account under a perpetual system. When each sale occurs, the cost of items sold is transferred from Merchandise Inventory to the Cost of Goods Sold account. Cost of goods sold is reported on the income statement. The ending balance in Merchandise Inventory is reported on the balance sheet.

> **C5** Analyze and interpret cost flows and operating activities of a merchandising company.

The Merchandise Inventory account balance at the end of one period is the amount of beginning inventory for the next period. The cost of each purchase is added to the Merchandise Inventory account, and the cost of each sale is transferred from Merchandise Inventory to Cost of Goods Sold. At the end of the period, the Merchandise Inventory balance is reported on the balance sheet.

Exhibit 6.15

Merchandising Cost Flow Across Periods*

Merchandising Cost Accounts

To explain how merchandising transactions affect the Merchandise Inventory and Cost of Goods Sold accounts, we summarize Z-Mart's merchandising activities for year 2002 using T-accounts in Exhibit 6.16. Most amounts are summary representations of several entries made during the year.

We explained that the perpetual inventory accounting system does not include separate accounts for purchases, purchase discounts, purchase returns and allowances, and transportation-in. But Z-Mart, like most companies, keeps supplementary records of these items. These supplementary records are used to accumulate the information in Exhibit 6.16. Z-Mart also keeps a separate record for the cost of merchandise returned by customers and restored in inventory.

The Cost of Goods Sold ending balance of $230,400 is the amount reported on the income statement in Exhibit 6.2. The Merchandise Inventory ending balance of $21,000 is the amount reported as a current asset on the balance sheet in Exhibit 6.3. These amounts also appear on Z-Mart's adjusted trial balance in Exhibit 6.13.

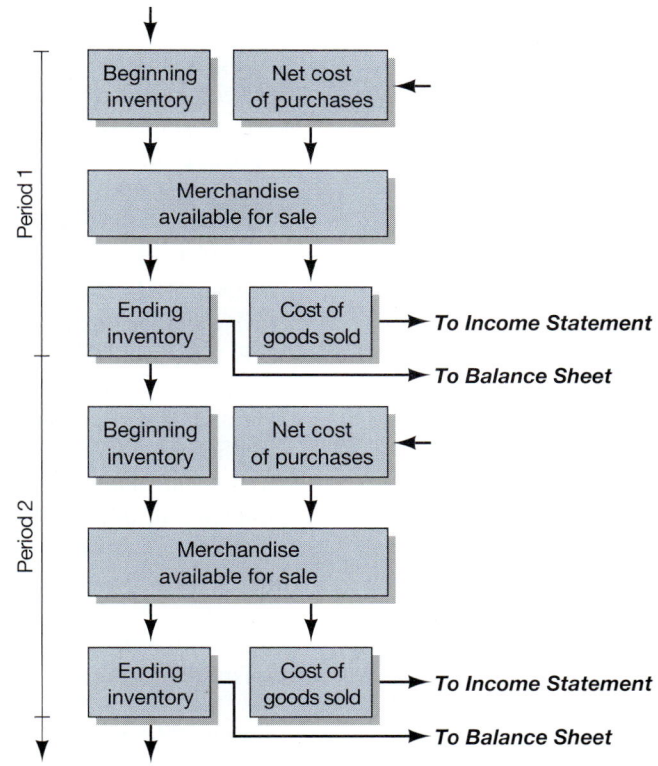

* Cost of goods sold is reported on the income statement. Ending inventory is reported on the balance sheet. One period's ending inventory is the next period's beginning inventory.

Quick Check

10. When a merchandiser uses a perpetual inventory system, why is it sometimes necessary to adjust the Merchandise Inventory balance with an adjusting entry?

11. What temporary accounts do you expect to find in a merchandising business but not in a service business?

12. Describe the closing entries normally made by a merchandising company.

Answers—p. 244

Exhibit 6.16

Merchandising Transactions
Reflected in T-Accounts

Merchandise Inventory			
Jan. 1, balance	19,000		
Purchases of merchandise	235,800	Purchase discounts received	4,200
Merchandise returned by customers		Purchase returns and allowances	1,500
and restored to inventory	1,400		
Transportation-in costs	2,300	Cost of sales to customers	231,550
Dec. 31, unadjusted balance	21,250		
		Dec. 31, shrinkage	250
Dec. 31, adjusted balance	21,000		

Cost of Goods Sold			
Cost of sales	231,550	Merchandise returned by customers	
Inventory shrinkage adjusting entry	250	and restored to inventory	1,400
Dec. 31, balance (before closing)	230,400		

Income Statement Formats

P4 Define and prepare multiple-step and single-step income statements.

Generally accepted accounting principles do not require companies to use any one format for financial statements, and we see many different formats in practice. The main part of this section describes two common income statement formats using Z-Mart's data: multiple step and single step. The final part of this section compares accrual and cash flow measures of gross profit.

Multiple-Step Income Statement

A **multiple-step income statement** contains more detail than simply a list of revenues and expenses. Exhibit 6.17 shows a multiple-step income statement for Z-Mart. This format shows detailed computations of net sales and other costs and expenses, and reports subtotals for various classes of items. Z-Mart's sales section is the same as shown earlier in the chapter. The cost of goods sold section draws on Exhibit 6.16. The difference between net sales and cost of goods sold is Z-Mart's gross profit. Further, its operating expenses are classified into two categories. **Selling expenses** include the expenses of promoting sales by displaying and advertising merchandise, making sales, and delivering goods to customers. **General and administrative expenses** support a company's overall operations and include expenses related to accounting, human resource management, and financial management. Also, expenses are often allocated between categories when they contribute to more than one activity. Exhibit 6.17 shows that Z-Mart allocates rent expense of $9,000 from its store building between two categories: $8,100 to selling expense and $900 to general and administrative expense.

Single-Step Income Statement

A **single-step income statement** is another widely used format, and is shown in Exhibit 6.18 for Z-Mart. It includes cost of goods sold as an operating expense and shows only one subtotal for total expenses. Operating expenses are grouped into very few categories. For example, **Reebok**'s income statement in Appendix A shows a single line item titled *Selling, general and administrative expenses*. Its annual report does, however, include management's discussion and analysis on various details of these expenses. Many companies use formats that combine features of both the single- and multiple-step statements. As long as income statement items are shown sensibly, management can choose the format it wants.[7] Similar options are available for the statement of changes in owner's equity and statement of cash flows.

Point: Many companies report interest expense and interest income in a separate category after income from operations and before subtracting income taxes expense. As one example, see Gap's income statement in Appendix A.

---

[7] In later chapters, we describe some items, such as extraordinary gains and losses, that must be shown in certain locations on the income statement.

Exhibit 6.17

Multiple-Step Income Statement

Z-MART
Income Statement
For Year Ended December 31, 2002

Sales			$321,000
Less: Sales discounts		$ 4,300	
Sales returns and allowances		2,000	6,300
Net sales			$314,700
Cost of goods sold			230,400
Gross profit			$ 84,300
Operating expenses			
Selling expenses			
Depreciation expense—Store equipment	$ 3,000		
Sales salaries expense	18,500		
Rent expense, selling space	8,100		
Store supplies expense	1,200		
Advertising expense	11,300		
Total selling expenses		42,100	
General and administrative expenses			
Depreciation expense—Office equipment	700		
Office salaries expense	25,300		
Insurance expense	600		
Rent expense, office space	900		
Office supplies expense	1,800		
Total general and administrative expenses		29,300	
Total operating expenses			71,400
Net income			$ 12,900

Exhibit 6.18

Single-Step Income Statement

Z-MART
Income Statement
For Year Ended December 31, 2002

Net sales		$314,700
Cost of goods sold	$230,400	
Selling expenses	42,100	
General and administrative expenses	29,300	
Total expenses		301,800
Net income		$ 12,900

Merchandising Cash Flows

A1 Analyze and interpret accruals and cash flows for merchandising activities.

Another aspect of merchandising activities relates to their cash flow impacts. Merchandising sales and costs reported in the income statement usually differ from their cash receipts and payments for a specific period. This is because an income statement is prepared using accrual accounting, not cash flows. Recognition of sales earned rarely equals cash received from customers. Also, recognition of cost of goods sold incurred rarely equals cash paid to suppliers for a given period.

We use Z-Mart's data in Exhibit 6.19 to illustrate this point. Z-Mart's net sales in the income statement total $314,700, yet cash receipts from customers are only $309,200 (shown on the right side of Exhibit 6.19). This difference reflects a $5,500 *increase* in the Accounts Receivable balance during this period for Z-Mart.

Exhibit 6.19

Analysis of Merchandising
Cash Flows

Z-MART For Year Ended December 31, 2002			
Income Statement		**Statement of Cash Flows**	
Net sales	$314,700	Receipts from customers	$309,200
Cost of goods sold	230,400	Payments to suppliers	240,900
Gross profit	$ 84,300	Net cash flows from customers and suppliers . .	$ 68,300

An increase in accounts receivable means both a delay in receipt of cash from customers and that cash received from customers this period is less than net sales. To see this, recall that net sales and cash received are the same if all net sales are cash sales. But when some or all net sales are credit sales, the amounts for net sales and cash likely differ. Since Accounts Receivable increased during the period, we know cash received is less than net sales. But if Accounts Receivable had decreased, then cash received would be greater than net sales.

We apply similar analysis to cost of goods sold. Z-Mart's cost of goods sold reported in its income statement totals $230,400, but cash paid to suppliers is $240,900. The difference between cost of goods sold and cash paid to suppliers reflects *two* items: (1) change in inventory and (2) change in accounts payable.

Buying and selling merchandise is the most important activity for a merchaniser such as Z-Mart. We need to analyze both accrual measures and cash flows of this activity for signs of opportunities or problems. Z-Mart is trying to expand its sales by extending credit to more customers. However, extending credit to customers who do not pay their bills can backfire. For effective decision making, we must always analyze important differences in accrual and cash flow figures and assess their future implications. We analyze the relation between accrual and cash flows in more detail in Chapter 17.

Did You Know?

Entrepreneur Incubators Hundreds of entrepreneur incubators provide startups a space plus services for a fee. Services typically include management advice, office support, and financial, legal, and technical help. Entrepreneurs usually leave an incubator after two to three years. Nearly 90% of entrepreneurs that "hatch" from incubators are still in business six years later, which is more than double the usual success rate.

Using the Information   Acid-Test and Gross Margin

Companies with merchandising activities have at least two major differences from service companies. First, merchandise inventory often makes up a large part of a merchandiser's assets, especially current assets. Second, merchandising activities result in cost of goods sold, which is often the largest cost for these companies. Companies with merchandising activities alter our ratio analysis. This is especially the case with the current ratio and the profit margin ratio (see Chapters 4 and 5). This section describes adjustments to these ratios to help us analyze merchandising companies.

Acid-Test Ratio

A2 Compute the acid-test ratio and explain its use to assess liquidity.

For many merchandising companies, inventory makes up a large portion of current assets. This means a large part of current assets is not readily available for paying liabilities. This happens because inventory must be sold and any resulting accounts receivable must be collected before cash is available. Information about current assets is important since we use it to assess a company's ability to pay its current liabilities. We explained in Chapter 5 that the current ratio, defined as current assets divided by current liabilities, is useful in assessing a company's ability to pay current liabilities. Since it is sometimes unreasonable to assume that inventories are a source of payment for current liabilities, we look to another measure.

One measure to help us assess a company's ability to pay its current liabilities (called *liquidity*) is the acid-test ratio. It differs from the current ratio by excluding less liquid current assets such as inventory. The less liquid assets or liabilities are those that will take longer to be converted to or paid in cash. The **acid-test ratio,** also called *quick ratio,* is defined as *quick assets* (cash, short-term investments, and current receivables) divided by current liabilities—see Exhibit 6.20. This is similar to the current ratio except that the numerator omits inventory and prepaid expenses.

$$\text{Acid-test ratio} = \frac{\text{Cash and equivalents} + \text{Short-term investments} + \text{Short-term receivables}}{\text{Current liabilities}}$$

Exhibit 6.20

Acid-Test (Quick) Ratio

Exhibit 6.21 shows both the acid-test and current ratios of **JCPenney** for 1998 through 2000. Penney's acid-test ratio recently declined. While the industry acid-test ratio also declined, it did not decrease to the extent that Penney's ratio did. Penney's current ratio suggests its short-term obligations can be covered with short-term assets. Still, the acid-test ratio raises some concern. An acid-test ratio less than 1.0 means that Penney's current liabilities exceed its quick assets. A rule of thumb is that the acid-test ratio should have a value of at least 1.0 to conclude that a company is unlikely to face liquidity problems in the near future. A value less than 1.0 suggests a liquidity problem unless a company can generate enough cash from sales or if its accounts payable are not due until late in the next period. Similarly, a value greater than 1.0 can hide a liquidity problem if payables are due shortly and receivables will not be collected until late in the next period. Our analysis of Penney emphasizes that one ratio is seldom enough to reach a conclusion as to strength or weakness. The power of a ratio is often its ability to identify areas for detailed analysis.

Point: Successful use of a just-in-time inventory system can narrow the gap between the acid-test ratio and the current ratio.

You Make the Call

Supplier   A retail store requests to purchase supplies on credit from your company. You have no prior experience with this store. The store's current ratio is 2.1, its acid-test ratio is 0.5, and inventory makes up most of its current assets. Do you extend credit to this store?

Answer—p. 244

($ in millions)	2000	1999	1998
Total quick assets	$2,371	$ 4,779	$ 5,179
Total current assets	$8,472	$11,007	$11,484
Total current liabilities	$4,465	$ 5,912	$ 6,137
Acid-test ratio	0.53	0.81	0.84
Current ratio	1.90	1.86	1.87
Industry acid-test ratio	0.7	0.8	1.0
Industry current ratio	3.0	3.1	3.5

Exhibit 6.21

JCPenney's Acid-Test and Current Ratios

Gross Margin Ratio

Cost of goods sold makes up much of the costs of merchandising companies. This means that success for merchandising companies often depends on the relation between sales and cost of goods sold. Without sufficient gross profit, a merchandising company will likely fail. To help understand this important relation, users often compute the gross margin ratio. It differs from the profit margin ratio in that it excludes all costs except cost of goods sold. The **gross margin ratio** is defined as *gross margin* (net sales minus cost of goods sold) divided by net sales—see Exhibit 6.22.

A3 Compute the gross margin ratio and explain its use to assess profitability.

$$\text{Gross margin ratio} = \frac{\text{Net sales} - \text{Cost of goods sold}}{\text{Net sales}}$$

Exhibit 6.22

Gross Margin Ratio

Exhibit 6.23 shows the gross margin ratio of **JCPenney** for 1998–2000. The ratio reflects the gross margin in each dollar of sales. In the case of JCPenney, each $1 of sales

Exhibit 6.23
JCPenney's Gross
Margin Ratio

($ in millions)	2000	1999	1998
Gross margin	$ 9,136	$ 8,819	$ 9,116
Net sales	$32,510	$30,461	$30,410
Gross margin ratio	28.1%	29.0%	30.0%

in 2000 yielded about 28¢ in gross margin to cover all other expenses and still produce a profit. This 28¢ margin is down from 29¢ in 1999 and from 30¢ in 1998. This decline is an important (and negative) development. Success for merchandisers such as JCPenney depends on maintaining an adequate gross margin. Data in this exhibit reveal that Penney's net sales increase over this period while its gross margin ratio decreases.

You Make the Call

Financial Officer Your merchandising company has a 36% gross margin ratio and a 17% net profit margin ratio. Industry averages are 44% for gross margin and 16% for net profit margin. Do these results concern you?

Answer—p. 244

Demonstration Problem

Use the following adjusted trial balance and additional information to complete the requirements:

KC ANTIQUES
Adjusted Trial Balance
December 31, 2002

	Debit	Credit
Cash	$ 20,000	
Merchandise inventory	60,000	
Store supplies	1,500	
Equipment	45,600	
Accumulated depreciation—Equipment		$ 16,600
Accounts payable		9,000
Salaries payable		2,000
Kyle Carter, Capital		79,000
Kyle Carter, Withdrawals	10,000	
Sales		343,250
Sales discounts	5,000	
Sales returns and allowances	6,000	
Cost of goods sold	159,900	
Depreciation expense—Store equipment	4,100	
Depreciation expense—Office equipment	1,600	
Sales salaries expense	30,000	
Office salaries expense	34,000	
Insurance expense	11,000	
Rent expense (70% is store, 30% is office)	24,000	
Store supplies expense	5,750	
Advertising expense	31,400	
Totals	$449,850	$449,850

KC Antiques' *supplementary records* for 2002 reveal the following itemized costs for merchandising activities:

Invoice cost of merchandise purchases	$150,000
Purchase discounts received	2,500
Purchase returns and allowances	2,700
Cost of transportation-in	5,000

Required

1. Use the supplementary records to compute the total cost of merchandise purchases for 2002.
2. Prepare a 2002 multiple-step income statement. Inventory at December 31, 2001 is $70,100.
3. Prepare a single-step income statement for 2002.
4. Prepare closing entries for KC Antiques at December 31, 2002.
5. Compute the acid-test ratio and the gross margin ratio. Explain the meaning of each ratio and interpret them for KC Antiques.

Planning the Solution

- Compute the total cost of merchandise purchases for 2002.
- To prepare the multiple-step statement, first compute net sales. Then, to compute cost of goods sold, add the net cost of merchandise purchases for the year to beginning inventory and subtract the cost of ending inventory. Subtract cost of goods sold from net sales to get gross profit. Then classify operating expenses as selling expenses or general and administrative expenses.
- To prepare the single-step income statement, begin with net sales. Then list and subtract the operating expenses.
- The first closing entry debits all temporary accounts with credit balances and opens the Income Summary account. The second closing entry credits all temporary accounts with debit balances. The third entry closes the Income Summary account to the owner's capital account, and the fourth closing entry closes the withdrawals account to the capital account.
- Identify the quick assets on the adjusted trial balance. Compute the acid-test ratio by dividing quick assets by the amount of current liabilities. Compute the gross margin ratio by dividing the gross profit from requirement (2) by net sales.

Solution to Demonstration Problem

1.

Invoice cost of merchandise purchases	$150,000
Less: Purchases discounts received	(2,500)
Purchase returns and allowances	(2,700)
Add: Cost of transportation-in	5,000
Total cost of merchandise purchases	$149,800

2. Multiple-step income statement

KC ANTIQUES
Income Statement
Year Ended December 31, 2002

Sales		$343,250
Less: Sales discounts	$ 5,000	
Sales returns and allowances	6,000	11,000
Net sales		$332,250
Cost of goods sold*		159,900
Gross profit		$172,350
Operating expenses		
Selling expenses		
Depreciation expense—Store equipment	$ 4,100	
Sales salaries expense	30,000	
Rent expense—Selling space	16,800	
Store supplies expense	5,750	
Advertising expense	31,400	
Total selling expenses	88,050	

[continued on next page]

[continued from previous page]

General and administrative expenses:			
Depreciation expense—Office equipment	$ 1,600		
Office salaries expense	34,000		
Insurance expense	11,000		
Rent expense—Office space	7,200		
Total general and administrative expenses		53,800	
Total operating expenses			141,850
Net income			$ 30,500

* Cost of goods sold computation:	
Merchandise inventory, December 31, 2001	$ 70,100
Total cost of merchandise purchases (from part *1*)	149,800
Goods available for sale	$219,900
Merchandise inventory, December 31, 2002	60,000
Cost of goods sold	$159,900

3. Single-step income statement

KC ANTIQUES		
Income Statement		
For Year Ended December 31, 2002		
Net sales		$332,250
Cost of goods sold	$159,900	
Selling expenses	88,050	
General and administrative expenses	53,800	301,750
Net income		$ 30,500

4.

Dec. 31	Sales	343,250	
	Income Summary		343,250
	To close credit balances in temporary accounts.		
Dec. 31	Income Summary	312,750	
	Sales Discounts		5,000
	Sales Returns and Allowances		6,000
	Cost of Goods Sold		159,900
	Depreciation Expense—Store Equipment . .		4,100
	Depreciation Expense—Office Equipment . .		1,600
	Sales Salaries Expense		30,000
	Office Salaries Expense		34,000
	Insurance Expense		11,000
	Rent Expense		24,000
	Store Supplies Expense		5,750
	Advertising Expense		31,400
	To close debit balances in temporary accounts.		
Dec. 31	Income Summary	30,500	
	Kyle Carter, Capital		30,500
	To close the Income Summary account.		
Dec. 31	Kyle Carter, Capital	10,000	
	Kyle Carter, Withdrawals		10,000
	To close the withdrawals account.		

5. Acid test ratio = Cash/(Accounts payable + Salaries payable)

$$= \$20,000/(\$9,000 + \$2,000) = \$20,000/\$11,000 = \underline{1.82}$$

Gross margin ratio = Gross profit/Net sales = $172,350/$332,250 = $\underline{0.52}$

KC Antiques has a healthy acid-test ratio of 1.82. This means it has more than $1.80 in liquid assets to satisfy each $1.00 in current liabilities. (With this ratio, neither supplies nor inventory are considered liquid assets readily convertible into cash for use in satisfying short-term obligations.) The gross margin of 0.52 shows that KC Antiques spends 48¢ ($1.00 − $0.52) of every dollar of net sales on the costs of acquiring the merchandise it sells. This leaves 52¢ of every dollar of net sales to cover other expenses incurred in the business and to provide a profit.

APPENDIX

Comparing Periodic and Perpetual Inventory Systems

6A

Recall that under a perpetual system, the Merchandise Inventory account is updated after each purchase and each sale. The Cost of Goods Sold account also is updated after each sale so that during the period its account balance reflects the period's total cost of goods sold to date. Under a periodic inventory system, the Merchandise Inventory account is updated only once each accounting period. This update occurs at the *end* of the period. During the period, the Merchandise Inventory balance remains unchanged. It reflects the beginning inventory balance until it is updated at the end of the period. Similarly, in a periodic inventory system, cost of goods sold is not recorded as each sale occurs. Instead, the total cost of goods sold during the period is computed at the end of the period.

Under a perpetual system, each purchase, purchase return and allowance, purchase discount, and transportation-in transaction is recorded in the Merchandise Inventory account. Under a periodic system, a separate temporary account is set up for *each* of these items. At period-end, each of these temporary accounts is closed and the Merchandise Inventory account is updated. To illustrate the differences, we use parallel columns to show journal entries for the most common transactions using both periodic and perpetual inventory systems (codes (*a*) through (*f*) link these transactions to those in the chapter, and we drop explanations for simplicity).

Recording Merchandise Transactions

P5 Record and compare merchandising transactions using both periodic and perpetual inventory systems.

Purchases

The periodic system uses a temporary *Purchases* account that accumulates the cost of all purchase transactions during the period. Z-Mart purchases merchandise for $1,200 on credit with terms of 2/10, n/30. Z-Mart's entry to record this credit purchase is

(a)

Periodic		
Purchases	1,200	
Accounts Payable . .		1,200

Perpetual		
Merchandise Inventory	1,200	
Accounts Payable		1,200

Purchase Discounts

The periodic system uses a temporary *Purchase Discounts* account that accumulates discounts taken on purchase transactions during the period. If payment in (*a*) is delayed until after the discount period expires, the entry under both methods is to debit Accounts Payable and credit Cash for $1,200 each. However, when Z-Mart pays the supplier for the previous purchase in (*a*) within the discount period, the required payment is $1,176 ($1,200 × 98%) and is recorded as

(b)

	Periodic				Perpetual	
Accounts Payable	1,200			Accounts Payable	1,200	
Purchase Discounts .		24		Merchandise Inventory .		24
Cash		1,176		Cash		1,176

Purchase Returns and Allowances

Z-Mart returns merchandise purchased on November 2 because of defects. In the periodic system, the temporary *Purchase Returns and Allowances* account accumulates the cost of all returns and allowances during a period. If the recorded cost (including discounts) of the defective merchandise is $300, Z-Mart records the return with this entry:

(c)

	Periodic				Perpetual	
Accounts Payable	300			Accounts Payable	300	
Purchase Returns				Merchandise Inventory .		300
and Allowances . .		300				

Transportation-In

Z-Mart paid a $75 freight charge to haul merchandise to its store. In the periodic system, this cost is charged to a temporary *Transportation-In* account.

(d)

	Periodic				Perpetual	
Transportation-In	75			Merchandise Inventory	75	
Cash		75		Cash		75

Sales

Under the periodic system, the cost of goods sold is not recorded at the time of sale. (We later show how to compute total cost of goods sold at the end of a period.) Z-Mart sold $2,400 of merchandise on credit, and its cost of this merchandise is $1,600:

(e)

	Periodic				Perpetual	
Accounts Receivable . . .	2,400			Accounts Receivable	2,400	
Sales		2,400		Sales		2,400
				Cost of Goods Sold	1,600	
				Merchandise Inventory .		1,600

Sales Returns

A customer returns part of the merchandise from the previous transaction in (*e*), where returned items sell for $800 and cost $600. (*Recall:* The periodic system records only the revenue effect, not the cost effect, for sales transactions.) Z-Mart restores the merchandise to inventory and records the return as

(f)

	Periodic				Perpetual	
Sales Returns and				Sales Returns and		
Allowances	800			Allowances	800	
Accounts Receivable		800		Accounts Receivable . .		800
				Merchandise Inventory	600	
				Cost of Goods Sold . . .		600

Adjusting and Closing Entries

The periodic and perpetual inventory systems have slight differences in adjusting and closing entries. Z-Mart's adjusted trial balances (except for shrinkage) under each system are shown in Exhibit 6A.1.

The Merchandise Inventory balance is $19,000 under the periodic system and $21,250 under the perpetual system. Because the periodic system does not revise the Merchandise Inventory balance during the period, the $19,000 amount is the beginning inventory. However, the $21,250 balance un-

Exhibit 6A.1

Comparison of Adjusted Trial Balances (absent shrinkage)—Periodic and Perpetual

Z-MART Adjusted Trial Balance (Periodic System) December 31, 2002	Debit	Credit
Cash	$ 8,200	
Accounts receivable	11,200	
Merchandise inventory	19,000	
Office supplies	550	
Store supplies	250	
Prepaid insurance	300	
Office equipment	4,200	
Accum. depreciation—Office eq.		$ 1,400
Store equipment	30,000	
Accum. depreciation—Store eq.		6,000
Accounts payable		16,000
Salaries payable		800
K. Marty, Capital		42,600
K. Marty, Withdrawals	4,000	
Sales		321,000
Sales discounts	4,300	
Sales returns and allowances	2,000	
Purchases	235,800	
Purchase discounts		4,200
Purchase returns and allowances		1,500
Transportation-in	2,300	
Depreciation expense—Store eq.	3,000	
Depreciation expense—Office eq.	700	
Office salaries expense	25,300	
Sales salaries expense	18,500	
Insurance expense	600	
Rent expense—Office space	900	
Rent expense—Selling space	8,100	
Office supplies expense	1,800	
Store supplies expense	1,200	
Advertising expense	11,300	
Totals	$393,500	$393,500

Z-MART Adjusted Trial Balance (Perpetual System) December 31, 2002	Debit	Credit
Cash	$ 8,200	
Accounts receivable	11,200	
Merchandise inventory	21,250	
Office supplies	550	
Store supplies	250	
Prepaid insurance	300	
Office equipment	4,200	
Accum. depreciation—Office eq.		$ 1,400
Store equipment	30,000	
Accum. depreciation—Store eq.		6,000
Accounts payable		16,000
Salaries payable		800
K. Marty, Capital		42,600
K. Marty, Withdrawals	4,000	
Sales		321,000
Sales discounts	4,300	
Sales returns and allowances	2,000	
Cost of goods sold	230,150	
Depreciation expense—Store eq.	3,000	
Depreciation expense—Office eq.	700	
Office salaries expense	25,300	
Sales salaries expense	18,500	
Insurance expense	600	
Rent expense—Office space	900	
Rent expense—Selling space	8,100	
Office supplies expense	1,800	
Store supplies expense	1,200	
Advertising expense	11,300	
Totals	$387,800	$387,800

der the perpetual system is the recorded ending inventory before adjusting for any inventory shrinkage. A physical count of inventory taken at the end of the period reveals $21,000 of merchandise available. We know then that inventory shrinkage is $21,250 − $21,000 = $250.

The adjusting entry for shrinkage and the closing entries for the two systems are shown in Exhibit 6A.2. The periodic system does not require an adjusting entry to record inventory shrinkage. Instead, it puts the ending inventory of $21,000 in the Merchandise Inventory account (which is net of shrinkage) in the first closing entry and removes the $19,000 beginning inventory balance from the account in the second closing entry.

Exhibit 6A.2

Comparison of Adjusting and
Closing Entries—Periodic and
Perpetual

Periodic		
Adjusting Entry – Shrinkage		
None		

Closing Entries		
(1) Sales	321,000	
Merchandise Inventory	**21,000**	
Purchase Discounts	**4,200**	
Purchase Returns and Allowances	**1,500**	
Income Summary		347,700
(2) Income Summary	334,800	
Sales Discounts		4,300
Sales Returns and Allowances		2,000
Merchandise Inventory		**19,000**
Purchases		**235,800**
Transportation-In		**2,300**
Depreciation Expense—Store eq.		3,000
Depreciation Expense—Office eq.		700
Office Salaries Expense		25,300
Sales Salaries Expense		18,500
Insurance Expense		600
Rent Expense—Office space		900
Rent Expense—Selling space		8,100
Office Supplies Expense		1,800
Store Supplies Expense		1,200
Advertising Expense		11,300
(3) Income Summary	12,900	
K. Marty, Capital		12,900
(4) K. Marty, Capital	4,000	
K. Marty, Withdrawals		4,000

Perpetual		
Adjusting Entry – Shrinkage		
Cost of Goods Sold	250	
Merchandise Inventory		250

Closing Entries		
(1) Sales	321,000	
Income Summary		321,000
(2) Income Summary	308,100	
Sales Discounts		4,300
Sales Returns and Allowances		2,000
Cost of Goods Sold		**230,400**
Depreciation Expense—Store eq.		3,000
Depreciation Expense—Office eq.		700
Office Salaries Expense		25,300
Sales Salaries Expense		18,500
Insurance Expense		600
Rent Expense—Office space		900
Rent Expense—Selling space		8,100
Office Supplies Expense		1,800
Store Supplies Expense		1,200
Advertising Expense		11,300
(3) Income Summary	12,900	
K. Marty, Capital		12,900
(4) K. Marty, Capital	4,000	
K. Marty, Withdrawals		4,000

By updating Merchandise Inventory and closing Purchases, Purchase Discounts, Purchase Returns and Allowances, and Transportation-In, the periodic system transfers the cost of goods sold amount to Income Summary. Review the periodic side of Exhibit 6A.2 and notice that the colored items affect Income Summary as follows:

Credited to Income Summary in the first closing entry	
Merchandise inventory (ending)	$ 21,000
Purchase discounts	4,200
Purchase returns and allowances	1,500
Debited to Income Summary in the second closing entry	
Merchandise inventory (beginning)	(19,000)
Purchases	(235,800)
Transportation-in	(2,300)
Net effect on Income Summary	**$(230,400)**

This $230,400 effect on Income Summary is the cost of goods sold amount. This figure is confirmed as follows:

Beginning inventory		$ 19,000
Purchases	$235,800	
Less purchase discounts	(4,200)	
Less purchase returns and allowances	(1,500)	
Plus transportation-in	2,300	
Net cost of goods purchased		232,400
Cost of goods available for sale		$251,400
Less ending inventory		(21,000)
Cost of goods sold		**$230,400**

This shows that the periodic system transfers cost of goods sold to the Income Summary account but without using a Cost of Goods Sold account. Also, the periodic system does not separately measure shrinkage. Instead, it computes cost of goods available for sale, subtracts the cost of ending inventory, and defines the difference as cost of goods sold. This difference includes shrinkage.

Work Sheet for a Merchandiser

Exhibit 6A.3 shows the work sheet that we could prepare in developing financial statements. It slightly differs from the work sheet in Chapter 5—the differences are bolded. The adjustments in the work sheet reflect the following economic events: (*a*) Expiration of $600 of prepaid insurance. (*b*) Use of $1,200 of store supplies. (*c*) Use of $1,800 of office supplies. (*d*) Depreciation of $3,000 for store

Exhibit 6A.3

Work Sheet for Merchandiser (using a perpetual system)

No.	Account	Unadjusted Trial Balance Dr.	Cr.	Adjustments Dr.	Cr.	Adjusted Trial Balance Dr.	Cr.	Income Statement Dr.	Cr.	Balance Sheet and Statement of Changes in Owner's Equity Dr.	Cr.
101	Cash	8,200				8,200				8,200	
106	Accounts receivable	11,200				11,200				11,200	
119	Merchandise inventory	21,250			(g) 250	21,000				21,000	
124	Office supplies	2,350			(c) 1,800	550				550	
125	Store supplies	1,450			(b) 1,200	250				250	
128	Prepaid insurance	900			(a) 600	300				300	
163	Office equipment	4,200				4,200				4,200	
164	Accum. depr.—office equip.		700		(e) 700		1,400				1,400
165	Store equipment	30,000				30,000				30,000	
166	Accum. depr.—office equip.		3,000		(d) 3,000		6,000				6,000
201	Accounts payable		16,000				16,000				16,000
209	Salaries payable				(f) 800		800				800
301	K. Marty, Capital		42,600				42,600				42,600
302	K. Marty, Withdrawals	4,000				4,000				4,000	
413	Sales		321,000				321,000		321,000		
414	Sales returns and allowances	2,000				2,000		2,000			
415	Sales discounts	4,300				4,300		4,300			
502	Cost of goods sold	230,150		(g) 250		230,400		230,400			
612	Depr. expense—store equip.			(d) 3,000		3,000		3,000			
613	Depr. expense—office equip.			(e) 700		700		700			
620	Office salaries expense	25,000		(f) 300		25,300		25,300			
621	Sales salaries expense	18,000		(f) 500		18,500		18,500			
637	Insurance expense			(a) 600		600		600			
641	Rent expense, office space	900				900		900			
642	Rent expense, selling space	8,100				8,100		8,100			
650	Office supplies expense			(c) 1,800		1,800		1,800			
651	Store supplies expense			(b) 1,200		1,200		1,200			
655	Advertising expense	11,300				11,300		11,300			
	Totals	383,300	383,300	8,350	8,350	387,800	387,800	308,100	321,000	79,700	66,800
	Net income							12,900			12,900
	Totals							321,000	321,000	79,700	79,700

equipment. (*e*) Depreciation of $700 for office equipment. (*f*) Accrual of $300 of unpaid office salaries and $500 of unpaid store salaries. (*g*) Inventory shrinkage of $250. Once the adjusted amounts are extended into the financial statement columns, the information is used to develop financial statements.

Adjusting Entry Method—Periodic System

In our discussion of the periodic system, the change in the Merchandise Inventory account is recorded as part of the closing process. This *closing entry method* is common. An alternative method, called the *adjusting entry method,* also is used. The *adjusting entry method* records the change in the Merchandise Inventory account with adjusting entries. Under this method, the first two closing entries (see Exhibit 6A.2) do not include the Merchandise Inventory account.

Adjusting Entries

Under the adjusting entry method of the periodic system, Z-Mart removes the beginning balance from the Merchandise Inventory account by recording this adjusting entry at the end of the period:

Dec. 31	Income Summary	19,000	
	Merchandise Inventory		19,000
	To remove the beginning balance from the Merchandise Inventory account.		

A second adjusting entry inserts the ending balance in the inventory account:

Dec. 31	Merchandise Inventory	21,000	
	Income Summary		21,000
	To insert the ending balance in the Merchandise Inventory account.		

After these entries are posted, the Merchandise Inventory account appears as follows:

Merchandise Inventory			
Beg. balance	19,000		
		Adjustment	19,000
Adjustment	21,000		
End. balance	21,000		

Closing Entries

If the adjusting entry method for inventory is used, the closing entries do not include the Merchandise Inventory account. In particular, entries (1) and (2) in Exhibit 6A.2 are the same except for removing the Merchandise Inventory account and its balance from both entries (including its amount from Income Summary). Entry (3) to close Income Summary is unchanged. The adjusting entry method took four entries instead of two to get net income of $12,900 into Income Summary.

Quick Check

13. What account is used in a perpetual inventory system but not in a periodic system?

14. Which of the following accounts are temporary accounts under a periodic system? (a) Merchandise Inventory; (b) Purchases; (c) Transportation-In.

15. How is cost of goods sold computed under a periodic inventory system?

16. Do reported amounts of ending inventory and net income differ if the adjusting entry method of recording the change in inventory is used instead of the closing entry method?

Answer—p. 244

Summary

C1 **Describe merchandising activities and identify business examples.** Operations of merchandisers involve buying products and reselling them. Examples of merchandisers include **Wal-Mart**, **Home Depot**, **The Limited**, and **Barnes & Noble**.

C2 **Identify and explain the components of income for a merchandising company.** A merchandiser's costs on an income statement include an amount for cost of goods sold. Gross profit, or gross margin, equals sales minus cost of goods sold.

C3 **Identify and explain the inventory asset of a merchandising company.** The current asset section of a merchandising company's balance sheet includes *merchandise inventory*, which refers to the products a merchandiser sells and are available for sale at the balance sheet date.

C4 **Describe both perpetual and periodic inventory systems.** A perpetual inventory system continuously tracks the cost of goods available for sale and the cost of goods sold. A periodic system accumulates the cost of goods purchased during the period and does not compute the amount of inventory or the cost of goods sold until the end of a period.

C5 **Analyze and interpret cost flows and operating activities of a merchandising company.** Costs of merchandise purchases flow into Merchandise Inventory and from there to Cost of Goods Sold on the income statement. Any remaining Merchandise Inventory is reported as a current asset on the balance sheet.

A1 **Analyze and interpret accruals and cash flows for merchandising activities.** Merchandising sales and costs of sales reported in the income statement usually differ from their corresponding cash receipts and cash payments. Cash received from customers equals net sales less the increase (or plus the decrease) in Accounts Receivable during the period. Cash paid to suppliers equals cost of goods sold less the increase (or plus the decrease) in Accounts Payable and less the decrease (or plus the increase) in Inventory during the period.

A2 **Compute the acid-test ratio and explain its use to assess liquidity.** The acid-test ratio is computed as quick assets (cash, short-term investments, and current receivables) divided by current liabilities. It indicates a company's ability to pay its current liabilities with its existing quick assets. A ratio equal to or greater than 1.0 is often adequate.

A3 **Compute the gross margin ratio and explain its use to assess profitability.** The gross margin ratio is computed as gross margin (net sales minus cost of goods sold) divided by net sales. It indicates a company's profitability before considering operating expenses.

P1 **Analyze and record transactions for merchandise purchases using a perpetual system.** For a perpetual inventory system, purchases of inventory (net of trade discounts) are added (debited) to the Merchandise Inventory account. Purchase discounts and purchase returns and allowances are subtracted (credited) from Merchandise Inventory, and transportation-in costs are added (debited) to Merchandise Inventory.

P2 **Analyze and record transactions for sales of merchandise using a perpetual system.** A merchandiser records sales at list price less any trade discounts. The cost of items sold is transferred from Merchandise Inventory to Cost of Goods Sold. Refunds or credits given to customers for unsatisfactory merchandise are recorded (debited) in Sales Returns and Allowances, a contra account to Sales. If merchandise is returned and restored to inventory, the cost of this merchandise is removed from Cost of Goods Sold and transferred back to Merchandise Inventory. When cash discounts from the sales price are offered and customers pay within the discount period, the seller records (debits) Sales Discounts, a contra account to Sales.

P3 **Prepare adjustments and close accounts for a merchandising company.** With a perpetual system, it is often necessary to make an adjustment for inventory shrinkage. This is computed by comparing a physical count of inventory with the Merchandise Inventory balance. Shrinkage is normally charged to Cost of Goods Sold. Temporary accounts closed to Income Summary for a merchandiser include Sales, Sales Discounts, Sales Returns and Allowances, and Cost of Goods Sold.

P4 **Define and prepare multiple-step and single-step income statements.** Multiple-step income statements include greater detail for sales and expenses than do single-step income statements. They also show details of net sales and report expenses in categories reflecting different activities.

P5 **Record and compare merchandising transactions using both periodic and perpetual inventory systems.** Transactions involving the sale and purchase of merchandise are recorded and analyzed under both the periodic and perpetual inventory systems. Adjusting and closing entries for both inventory systems are illustrated and explained.

Guidance Answers to You Make the Call

Entrepreneur   For terms of 3/10, n/90, missing the 3% discount for an additional 80 days equals an annual interest rate of 13.69% computed as (365 days ÷ 80 days) × 3%. Since you can borrow funds at 11% (assuming no other processing costs), it is better to borrow and pay within the discount period. You save 2.69% (13.69% − 11%) in interest costs by paying early.

Credit Manager—Ethics   Your decision here is whether to comply with prior policy or to create a new policy and not abuse discounts offered by suppliers. Your first step should be to meet with your superior to find out if the late payment policy is the actual policy and, if so, its rationale. If it is the policy to pay late, you must apply your own sense of ethics. One point of view is that the late payment policy is unethical. A deliberate plan to make late payments means the company lies when it pretends to make purchases within the credit terms. The potential is that your company can lose its ability to get future credit. Another view is that the late payment policy is acceptable. In some markets, attempts to take discounts through late payments are accepted as a continued phase of "price negotiation." Also, your company's suppliers can respond by billing your company for the discounts not accepted because of late payments. However, this is a dubious viewpoint, especially since the prior manager proposes you explain late payments as computer or mail problems and given that some suppliers have complained.

Supplier   A current ratio of 2.1 suggests sufficient current assets to cover current liabilities. An acid-test ratio of 0.5 suggests, however, that quick assets can cover only about one-half of current liabilities. This implies the store depends on profits from sales of inventory to pay current liabilities. If sales of inventory decline or profit margins decrease, the likelihood that this store will default

on its payments increases. Your decision is probably not to extend credit to the store. If you do extend credit, you are likely to closely monitor the store's financial condition.

Financial Officer   Your company's net profit margin is about equal to the industry average and suggests typical industry performance. However, gross margin reveals that your company is paying far more in cost of goods sold or receiving far less in sales price than competitors. Your attention must be directed to finding the problem with cost of goods sold, sales, or both. One positive note is that your company's expenses make up 19% of sales ($36\% - 17\%$). This favorably compares with competitors' expenses that make up 28% of sales ($44\% - 16\%$).

Guidance Answers to **Quick Checks**

1. Cost of goods sold is the cost of merchandise purchased from a supplier that is sold to customers during a specific period.
2. Gross profit (or gross margin) is the difference between net sales and cost of goods sold.
3. Widespread use of computing and related technology has dramatically increased the use of the perpetual inventory system.
4. Under credit terms of 2/10, n/60, the credit period is 60 days and the discount period is 10 days.
5. (b)
6. *FOB* means free on board. It is used in identifying the point when ownership transfers from seller to buyer. *FOB destination* means the seller transfers ownership of goods to the buyer when they arrive at the buyer's place of business. It also means the seller is responsible for paying shipping charges and bears the risk of damage or loss during shipment.
7. Recording sales discounts and sales returns and allowances separately from sales gives useful information to managers for internal monitoring and decision making.
8. When a customer returns merchandise *and* the seller restores the merchandise to inventory, two entries are necessary. One entry records the decrease in revenue and credits the cus-

tomer's account. The second entry debits inventory and reduces cost of goods sold.
9. Credit memorandum—seller credits accounts receivable from buyer.
10. Merchandise Inventory may need adjusting to reflect shrinkage.
11. Sales (of goods), Sales Discounts, Sales Returns and Allowances, and Cost of Goods Sold.
12. Four closing entries: (1) close credit balances in temporary accounts to Income Summary, (2) close debit balances in temporary accounts to Income Summary, (3) close Income Summary to owner's capital, and (4) close withdrawals account to owner's capital.
13. Cost of Goods Sold.
14. (b) Purchases and (c) Transportation-In.
15. Under a periodic inventory system, the cost of goods sold is determined at the end of an accounting period by adding the net cost of goods purchased to the beginning inventory and subtracting the ending inventory.
16. Both methods report the same ending inventory and net income.

Glossary

Acid-test ratio ratio used to assess a company's ability to settle its current debts with its most liquid assets; defined as quick assets (cash, short-term investments, and current receivables) over current liabilities. (p. 233).

Cash discount reduction in the price of merchandise granted by a seller to a buyer when payment is made within the *discount period.* (p. 219).

Cost of goods sold cost of inventory sold to customers during a period. (p. 216)

Credit memorandum notification that the sender has credited the recipient's account kept by the sender. (p. 226).

Credit period time period that can pass before a customer's payment is due. (p. 218).

Credit terms description of the amounts and timing of payments that a buyer agrees to make in the future. (p. 218).

Debit memorandum notification that the sender has debited the recipient's account kept by the sender. (p. 220).

Discount period time period in which a cash discount is available and the buyer can make a reduced payment. (p. 219).

EOM abbreviation for *end of month;* used to describe credit terms for some transactions. (p. 218).

FOB abbreviation for *free on board;* the point when ownership of goods passes to the buyer; *FOB shipping point* (or *factory*) means the buyer pays shipping costs and accepts ownership of goods at the seller's place of business; *FOB destination* means the seller pays shipping costs and accepts ownership of goods at the buyer's place of business. (p. 221).

General and administrative expenses expenses that support the operating activities of a business. (p. 230).

Gross margin (see gross profit). (p. 214).

Gross margin ratio gross margin (sales minus cost of goods sold) divided by sales; also called *gross profit ratio*. (p. 233).

Gross profit net sales minus cost of goods sold; also called *gross margin*. (p. 214).

Inventory merchandise a company owns and expects to sell in its normal operations. (p. 216).

List price catalog price of an item before any trade discount is deducted. (p. 218).

Merchandise (see *merchandise inventory*). (p. 214).

Merchandise inventory products that a company owns and expects to sell to customers; also called *merchandise*. (p. 215).

Merchandiser entity that earns net income by buying and selling merchandise. (p. 214).

Multiple-step income statement income statement format that shows subtotals between sales and net income and details of net sales and expenses. (p. 230).

Periodic inventory system method that records the cost of inventory purchased but does not track the quantity available or sold to customers; records are updated at the end of each period to reflect the physical count of goods available. (p. 216).

Perpetual inventory system method that maintains continuous records of the cost of inventory available and the cost of goods sold. (p. 217).

Purchase discount term used by a purchaser to describe a cash discount granted to the purchaser for paying within the discount period. (p. 219).

Retailer intermediary that buys products from manufacturers or wholesalers and sells them to consumers. (p. 214).

Sales discount term used by a seller to describe a cash discount granted to buyers who pay within the discount period. (p. 219).

Selling expenses expenses of promoting sales, such as displaying and advertising merchandise, making sales, and delivering goods to customers. (p. 230).

Shrinkage inventory losses that occur as a result of theft or deterioration. (p. 227).

Single-step income statement income statement format that includes cost of goods sold as an expense and shows only one subtotal for total expenses. (p. 230).

Supplementary records information outside the usual accounting records; also called *supplemental records*. (p. 223).

Trade discount reduction below a list or catalog price that can vary for wholesalers, retailers, and consumers. (p. 218).

Wholesaler intermediary that buys products from manufacturers or other wholesalers and sells them to retailers or other wholesalers. (p. 214).

[The superscript letter [A] denotes assignments based on Appendix 6A.]

Questions

1. In comparing the accounts of a merchandising company with those of a service company, what additional accounts would the merchandising company likely use, assuming it employs a perpetual inventory system?

2. What items appear in financial statements of merchandising companies but not in the statements of service companies?

3. Explain how a business can earn a positive gross profit on its sales and still have a net loss.

4. Why do companies offer a cash discount?

5. How does a company that uses a perpetual inventory system determine the amount of inventory shrinkage?

6. Distinguish between cash discounts and trade discounts. Is the amount of a trade discount on purchased merchandise recorded in the accounts?

7. What is the difference between a sales discount and a purchase discount?

8. Why would a company's manager be concerned about the quantity of its purchase returns if its suppliers allow unlimited returns?

9. Does the sender of a debit memorandum record a debit or a credit in the recipient's account? Which (debit or credit) does the recipient record?

10. What is the difference between single-step and multiple-step income statement formats?

11. Refer to the income statement for **Nike** in Appendix A. What term is used instead of cost of goods sold? Does the company present a detailed calculation of its cost of goods sold?

12. Refer to the balance sheet for **Reebok** in Appendix A. What does Reebok call its inventory account? What alternate name could it use?

13. Refer to the income statement of **Gap** in Appendix A. Does its income statement report a gross profit figure?

14. Companies need to be skillful in negotiating purchase contracts with suppliers. What type of shipping terms should a purchaser attempt to negotiate to minimize freight-in costs?

Prepare journal entries to record each of the following transactions of a merchandising company. Show any supporting calculations. Assume a perpetual inventory system.

Mar. 5   Purchased 600 units of product with a list price of $10 per unit. The purchaser is granted a trade discount of 20%; terms of the sale are 2/10, n/60.

Mar. 7   Returned 25 defective units from the March 5 purchase and received full credit.

Mar. 15   Paid the amount due from the March 5 purchase, less the return on March 7.

QUICK STUDY

QS 6-1

Recording purchases —perpetual system   **P1**

QS 6-2
Recording sales—
perpetual system

Prepare journal entries to record each of the following transactions of a merchandising company. Show any supporting calculations. Assume a perpetual inventory system.

Apr. 1   Sold merchandise for $3,000, granting the customer terms of 2/10, EOM. The cost of the merchandise is $1,800.

Apr. 4   The customer in the April 1 sale returned merchandise and received credit for $600. The merchandise, which had cost $360, is returned to inventory.

Apr. 11   Received payment for the amount due from the April 1 sale less the return on April 4.

QS 6-3ᴬ
Contrasting periodic and
perpetual systems

Identify whether each description best applies to a periodic or a perpetual inventory system.

a. Provides more timely information to managers.

b. Requires an adjusting entry to record inventory shrinkage.

c. Markedly increased in frequency and popularity in business within the past decade.

d. Records cost of goods sold each time a sales transaction occurs.

QS 6-4
Computing and analyzing
gross margin

Compute net sales, gross profit, and the gross margin ratio for each situation (a) through (d):

	a	b	c	d
Sales	$150,000	$550,000	$38,700	$255,700
Sales discounts	5,200	17,500	600	4,200
Sales returns and allowances	20,000	6,000	5,300	900
Cost of goods sold	79,600	329,700	24,300	128,900

Interpret the gross margin ratio for situation (a).

QS 6-5
Acid-test ratio

Use the following information on current assets and current liabilities to compute and interpret the acid-test ratio. Also explain what the acid-test ratio of a company measures.

Cash	$1,500
Accounts receivable	2,800
Inventory	6,000
Prepaid expenses	700
Accounts payable	5,750
Other current liabilities	850

QS 6-6
Contrasting liquidity
ratios

Identify similarities and differences between the acid-test ratio and the current ratio. Compare and describe how the two ratios reflect a company's ability to meet its current obligations.

QS 6-7
Accounting for shrinkage—
perpetual system

Bemis Company's ledger on July 31, its fiscal year-end, includes the following accounts that have normal balances:

Merchandise inventory	$ 37,800	Sales returns and allowances	$ 6,500
T. Bemis, Capital	118,300	Cost of goods sold	105,000
T. Bemis, Withdrawals	7,000	Depreciation expense	10,300
Sales	160,200	Salaries expense	32,500
Sales discounts	4,700	Miscellaneous expenses	5,000

A physical count of its July 31 year-end inventory discloses that the cost of the merchandise available for sale is $35,900. Prepare the entry to record any inventory shrinkage.

QS 6-8
Closing entries

Refer to QS 6-7 and prepare journal entries to close the balances in temporary accounts. Remember to consider the entry that is made to solve QS 6-7.

Prepare journal entries to record the following transactions for a retail store. Assume a perpetual inventory system.

Apr. 2 Purchased merchandise from Blass Company under the following terms: $4,600 invoice price, 2/15, n/60 credit terms, FOB shipping point.

3 Paid $300 for shipping charges on the April 2 purchase.

4 Returned to Blass Company unacceptable merchandise that had an invoice price of $600.

17 Sent a check to Blass Company for the April 2 purchase, net of the discount and the returned merchandise.

18 Purchased merchandise from Flow Corp. under the following terms: $8,500 invoice price, 2/10, n/30 credit terms, FOB destination.

21 After negotiations, received from Flow an $1,100 allowance on the April 18 purchase.

28 Sent a check to Flow paying for the April 18 purchase, net of the discount and allowance.

EXERCISES

Exercise 6-1
Recording entries for
merchandise purchases

Insert the letter for each term in the blank space beside the definition that it most closely matches:

A. Cash discount   **E.** FOB shipping point   **H.** Purchase discount

B. Credit period   **F.** Gross profit   **I.** Sales discount

C. Discount period   **G.** Merchandise inventory   **J.** Trade discount

D. FOB destination

_____ **1.** Ownership of goods is transferred at the seller's place of business.

_____ **2.** Reduction below list or catalog price that is negotiated in setting the price of goods.

_____ **3.** Seller's description of a cash discount granted to customers in return for early payment.

_____ **4.** Time period that can pass before a customer's payment is due.

_____ **5.** Goods a company owns and expects to sell to its customers.

_____ **6.** Ownership of goods is transferred at the buyer's place of business.

_____ **7.** Time period in which a cash discount is available.

_____ **8.** Difference between net sales and the cost of goods sold.

_____ **9.** Reduction in a receivable or payable that is granted if it is paid within the discount period.

_____ **10.** Purchaser's description of a cash discount received from a supplier of goods.

Exercise 6-2
Applying merchandising terms

Sundance Company purchased merchandise for resale from Phoenix with an invoice price of $24,000 and credit terms of 3/10, n/60. The merchandise had cost Phoenix $16,000. Sundance paid within the discount period. Assume that both buyer and seller use a perpetual inventory system.

Required

1. Prepare entries that the buyer should record for the purchase and cash payment.

2. Prepare entries that the seller should record for the sale and cash collection.

3. Assume that the buyer borrowed enough cash to pay the balance on the last day of the discount period at an annual interest rate of 8% and paid it back on the last day of the credit period. Compute how much the buyer saved by following this strategy. (Use a 365-day year.)

Exercise 6-3
Analyzing and recording
merchandise transactions—
both buyer and seller

On May 11, Recovery Co. accepts delivery of $40,000 of merchandise it purchases for resale from Hoak Corporation. With the merchandise is an invoice dated May 11, with terms of 3/10, n/90, FOB factory. The cost of the goods for Hoak is $30,000. When the goods are delivered, Recovery pays $345 to Express Shipping Service for delivery charges on the merchandise. On May 12, Recovery returns $1,400 of goods to Hoak, who receives them one day later and restores them to inventory. The returned goods had cost Hoak $800. On May 20, Recovery mails a check to Hoak Corporation for the amount owed. Hoak receives it the following day.

Required

1. Prepare journal entries that Recovery Co. records for these transactions. Recovery uses a perpetual inventory system.

2. Prepare journal entries that Hoak Corporation records for these transactions. Hoak uses a perpetual inventory system.

Exercise 6-4
Analyzing and recording
merchandise transactions—
both buyer and seller

Exercise 6-5

Calculating expenses and
cost of goods sold

Monk Company's ledger and supplementary records at the end of the period reveal the following:

Sales	$380,000
Sales discounts	6,500
Sales returns	15,000
Merchandise inventory (beginning of period)	31,000
Invoice cost of merchandise purchases	176,000
Purchase discounts received	4,600
Purchase returns and allowances	5,000
Costs of transportation-in	12,000
Gross profit	155,000
Net income	65,000

Required

Compute (1) total operating expenses, (2) cost of goods sold, and (3) merchandise inventory (end of period). (*Hint:* Review Exhibits 6.10 and 6.11.)

Exercise 6-6^A

Determining components of
cost of goods sold

Using the data provided from the general ledger and supplementary records, determine each of the missing numbers in the separate situations (a), (b), and (c):

	a	b	c
Invoice cost of merchandise purchases	$94,000	$40,000	$32,500
Purchase discounts received	5,000	?	800
Purchase returns and allowances	2,000	2,500	1,200
Costs of transportation-in	?	4,500	5,000
Merchandise inventory (beginning of period)	9,000	?	10,000
Total cost of merchandise purchases	91,400	40,500	?
Merchandise inventory (end of period)	5,400	8,500	?
Cost of goods sold	?	42,600	35,130

Exercise 6-7

Recording sales returns and
allowances

A1 Parts is organized on May 1, 2002, and made its first purchase of merchandise on May 3. The purchase is for 2,000 units at a price of $10 per unit. On May 5, A1 Parts sold 600 of the units for $14 per unit to Dean Co. Terms of the sale are 2/10, n/60. Prepare entries for A1 Parts to record the May 5 sale and each of the following separate transactions using a perpetual inventory system.

a. On May 7, Dean returns 200 units because they did not fit the customer's needs. A1 Parts restores the units to its inventory.

b. On May 8, Dean discovers that 200 units are damaged but of some use and, therefore, keeps the units. A1 Parts sends Dean a credit memorandum for $600 to compensate for the damage.

c. On May 15, Dean returns 20 defective units and A1 Parts concludes that these units cannot be resold. As a result, A1 Parts discards them.

Exercise 6-8

Recording purchase
returns and allowances

Refer to Exercise 6-7 and prepare the appropriate journal entries for Dean Co. to record the purchase and each of the three separate transactions. Dean is a retailer that uses a perpetual inventory system and purchases these units for resale.

Fill in the blanks in the following separate income statements *a* through *e*. Identify any negative amount by putting it in parentheses.

Exercise 6-9^A
Calculating revenues, expenses, and income

	a	b	c	d	e
Sales	$62,000	$43,500	$46,000	$?	$25,600
Cost of goods sold					
Merchandise inventory (beginning)	8,000	17,050	7,500	8,000	4,560
Total cost of merchandise purchases	38,000	?	?	32,000	6,600
Merchandise inventory (ending)	?	(2,700)	(9,000)	(6,600)	?
Cost of goods sold	$34,050	$15,900	$?	$?	$ 6,600
Gross profit	$?	$?	$ 3,750	$45,600	$?
Expenses	10,000	10,650	12,150	3,600	6,000
Net income (loss)	$?	$16,950	$(8,400)	$42,000	$?

Briefly explain why a company's manager wants the accounting system to record customers' returns of unsatisfactory goods in the Sales Returns and Allowances account instead of the Sales account. In addition, explain whether this information would be useful for external decision makers.

Exercise 6-10
Sales returns and allowances

A retail company recently completed a physical count of ending merchandise inventory to use in preparing adjusting entries. In determining the cost of the counted inventory, company employees failed to consider that $3,000 of incoming goods had been shipped by a supplier on December 31 under an FOB shipping point agreement. These goods had been recorded in Merchandise Inventory as a purchase, but they were not included in the physical count because they were in transit. Explain how this overlooked fact affects the company's financial statements and the following ratios: return on equity, debt ratio, current ratio, profit margin ratio, and acid-test ratio.

Exercise 6-11
Interpreting physical count error as shrinkage

The following supplementary records summarize Duncan Company's merchandising activities for year 2002. Set up T-accounts for Merchandise Inventory and Cost of Goods Sold. Then record the summarized activities in the T-accounts and compute account balances. (*Hint:* See Exhibit 6.16.)

Exercise 6-12
Recording effects of merchandising activities

Cost of merchandise sold to customers in sales transactions	$196,000
Merchandise inventory, December 31, 2001	25,000
Invoice cost of merchandise purchases	192,500
Shrinkage determined on December 31, 2002	800
Cost of transportation-in	2,900
Cost of merchandise returned by customers and restored to inventory	2,100
Purchase discounts received	1,700
Purchase returns and allowances	4,000

Calculate the current and acid-test ratios for each of the following separate cases:

Exercise 6-13
Computing and analyzing acid-test and current ratios

	Case X	Case Y	Case Z
Cash	$ 900	$ 810	$1,000
Short-term investments	0	0	600
Receivables	0	1,090	700
Inventory	3,000	1,100	4,100
Prepaid expenses	1,300	500	900
Total current assets	$5,200	$3,500	$7,300
Current liabilities	$2,200	$1,200	$3,750

Which company case is in the best position to meet short-term obligations? Explain your choice.

Exercise 6-14
Determining profitability and merchandising cash flows

A1

A company reports the following balances and activities at year-end:

Net sales	$1,010,000
Cost of goods sold	565,000
Increase in accounts receivable for the period	45,000
Cash payments to suppliers of goods	515,000

Required

1. Calculate gross profit.
2. Calculate cash received from customers.
3. Calculate cash flows from customers less cash flows paid to suppliers.

Exercise 6-15^A
Preparing adjusting and closing entries for a merchandiser

P3

The following list includes some permanent accounts and all of the temporary accounts from the December 31, 2002, unadjusted trial balance of Davis Sales, a business owned by Julie Davis. Use these account balances along with the additional information to journalize adjusting and closing entries. Davis Sales uses a perpetual inventory system.

	Debit	Credit
Merchandise inventory	$ 30,000	
Prepaid selling expenses	5,500	
Julie Davis, Withdrawals	2,200	
Sales		$529,000
Sales returns and allowances	17,500	
Sales discounts	5,000	
Cost of goods sold	212,000	
Sales salaries expense	48,000	
Utilities expense	15,000	
Selling expenses	36,000	
Administrative expenses	105,000	

Additional Information

Accrued sales salaries amount to $1,700. Prepaid selling expenses of $3,000 have expired. A physical count of merchandise inventory discloses $28,450 of goods available.

Exercise 6-16^A
Preparing journal entries to contrast the periodic and perpetual systems

Journalize the following merchandising transactions for Texas Systems assuming it uses a (a) periodic system and (b) perpetual system.

1. On November 1, Texas Systems purchases merchandise for $1,500 on credit with terms of 2/5, n/30, FOB shipping point.
2. On November 5, Texas Systems pays cash for the November 1 purchase.
3. On November 7, Texas Systems discovers and returns $200 of defective merchandise purchased on November 1 for a cash refund.
4. On November 10, Texas Systems pays $90 cash for transportation costs with the November 1 purchase.
5. On November 13, Texas Systems sells merchandise for $1,600 on credit. The cost of the merchandise is $800.
6. On November 16, the customer returns merchandise from the November 13 transaction. The returned items sell for $300 and cost $150.

PROBLEM SET A

Problem 6-1A
Preparing journal entries for merchandising activities (perpetual system)

Prepare journal entries to record the following perpetual system merchandising transactions of Heflin Company. (Use a separate account for each receivable and payable; for example, record the purchase on August 1 in Accounts Payable—Chapman Co.)

Aug. 1   Purchased merchandise from Chapman Company for $7,500 under credit terms of 1/10, n/30, FOB destination.

4   At Chapman's request, Heflin paid $200 cash for freight charges on the August 1 purchase, reducing the amount owed to Chapman.

5   Sold merchandise to Griffin Corp. for $5,200 under credit terms of 2/10, n/60, FOB destination. The merchandise had cost $4,000.

8   Purchased merchandise from Follmer Corporation for $5,400 under credit terms of 1/10, n/45, FOB shipping point. The invoice showed that at Heflin's request, Follmer paid the $140 shipping charges and added that amount to the bill.

9   Paid $125 cash for shipping charges related to the August 5 sale to Griffin Corp.

10   Griffin returned merchandise from the August 5 sale that had cost $400 and been sold for $600. The merchandise was restored to inventory.

12   After negotiations with Follmer Corporation concerning problems with the merchandise purchased on August 8, Heflin received a credit memorandum from Follmer granting a price reduction of $700.

15   Received balance due from Griffin Corp. for the August 5 sale less the return on August 10.

18   Paid the amount due Follmer Corporation for the August 8 purchase less the price reduction granted.

Check Aug. 18, Cr. Cash, $4,793

19   Sold merchandise to Trigger for $4,800 under credit terms of 1/10, n/30, FOB shipping point. The merchandise had cost $2,400.

22   Trigger requested a price reduction on the August 19 sale because the merchandise did not meet specifications. Sent Trigger a credit memorandum for $500 to resolve the issue.

29   Received Trigger's cash payment for the amount due from the August 19 purchase.

30   Paid Chapman Company the amount due from the August 1 purchase.

Prepare journal entries to record the following perpetual system merchandising transactions of Beltran Company. (Use a separate account for each receivable and payable; for example, record the purchase on July 1 in Accounts Payable—White Co.)

Problem 6-2A
Preparing journal entries for merchandising activities (perpetual system)

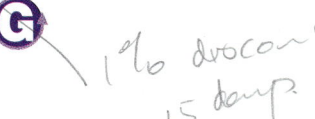

July 1   Purchased merchandise from White Company for $6,000 under credit terms of 1/15, n/30, FOB shipping point.

2   Sold merchandise to Terry Co. for $900 under credit terms of 2/10, n/60, FOB shipping point. The merchandise had cost $500.

3   Paid $125 cash for freight charges on the purchase of July 1.

8   Sold merchandise that cost $1,300 for $1,700 cash.

9   Purchased merchandise from Kane Co. for $2,200 under credit terms of 2/15, n/60, FOB destination.

11   Received a $200 credit memorandum from the return of merchandise purchased on July 9.

12   Received the balance due from Terry Co. for the credit sale dated July 2, net of the discount.

16   Paid the balance due to White Company within the discount period.

19   Sold merchandise that cost $800 to Jolie Co. for $1,200 under credit terms of 2/15, n/60, FOB shipping point.

21   Issued a $150 credit memorandum to Jolie Co. for an allowance on goods sold on July 19.

22   Received a debit memorandum from Jolie Co. for an error that overstated the total sales invoice by $50.

24   Paid Kane Co. the balance due after deducting the discount.

30   Received the balance due from Jolie Co. for the credit sale dated July 19, net of discount.

Check July 30, Dr. Cash, $980

31   Sold merchandise that cost $4,800 to Terry Co. for $7,000 under credit terms of 2/10, n/60, FOB shipping point.

The following unadjusted trial balance is prepared at fiscal year-end for Tioga Company:

Problem 6-3A
Preparing adjusting entries and income statements, and computing gross margin, acid-test, and current ratios

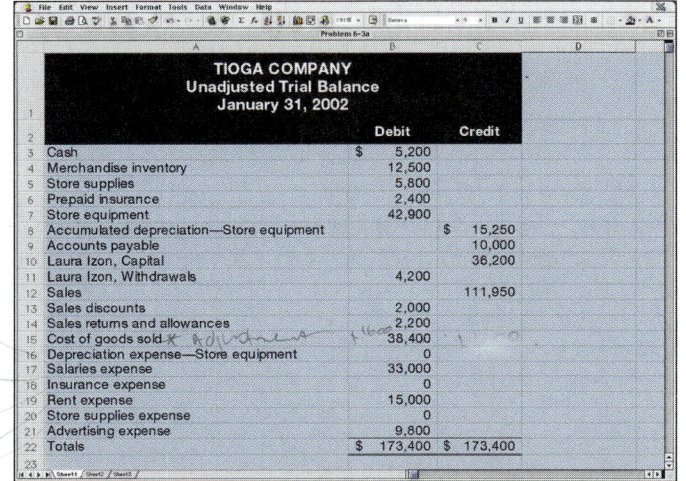

TIOGA COMPANY Unadjusted Trial Balance January 31, 2002	Debit	Credit
Cash	$ 5,200	
Merchandise inventory	12,500	
Store supplies	5,800	
Prepaid insurance	2,400	
Store equipment	42,900	
Accumulated depreciation—Store equipment		$ 15,250
Accounts payable		10,000
Laura Izon, Capital		36,200
Laura Izon, Withdrawals	4,200	
Sales		111,950
Sales discounts	2,000	
Sales returns and allowances	2,200	
Cost of goods sold	38,400	
Depreciation expense—Store equipment	0	
Salaries expense	33,000	
Insurance expense	0	
Rent expense	15,000	
Store supplies expense	0	
Advertising expense	9,800	
Totals	$ 173,400	$ 173,400

Rent and salaries expenses are equally divided between selling activities and the general and administrative activities. Tioga Company uses a perpetual inventory system.

Required

1. Prepare adjusting journal entries for the following:
   a. Store supplies available at fiscal year-end amount to $1,750.
   b. Expired insurance, an administrative expense, for the fiscal year is $1,400.
   c. Depreciation expense on store equipment, a selling expense, is $1,525 for the fiscal year.
   d. To estimate shrinkage, a physical count of ending merchandise inventory is taken. It shows $10,900 of goods are available for sale.
2. Prepare a multiple-step income statement for fiscal year 2002.
3. Prepare a single-step income statement for fiscal year 2002.
4. Compute the company's current ratio, acid-test ratio, and gross margin ratio as of January 31, 2002.

Check   (3) Total expenses, $104,775

Problem 6-4A

Computing and formatting an income statement

Big Star Company's adjusted trial balance on August 31, 2002, its fiscal year-end, follows:

	Debit	Credit
Merchandise inventory	$ 41,000	
Other assets	130,400	
Liabilities		$ 25,000
S. Stone, Capital		110,550
S. Stone, Withdrawals	14,000	
Sales		225,600
Sales discounts	2,250	
Sales returns and allowances	12,000	
Cost of goods sold	74,500	
Sales salaries expense	32,000	
Rent expense, selling space	8,000	
Store supplies expense	1,500	
Advertising expense	13,000	
Office salaries expense	28,500	
Rent expense, office space	3,600	
Office supplies expense	400	
Totals	$361,150	$361,150

On August 31, 2001, merchandise inventory amounted to $26,000. Supplementary records of merchandising activities for the year ended August 31, 2002, reveal the following itemized costs:

Invoice cost of merchandise purchases	$92,000
Purchase discounts received	2,000
Purchase returns and allowances	4,500
Costs of transportation-in	4,000

Required

1. Compute the company's net sales for the year.
2. Compute the company's total cost of merchandise purchased for the year.
3. Prepare a multiple-step income statement that lists the company's net sales, cost of goods sold, and gross profit, as well as the components and amounts of selling expenses and general and administrative expenses.
4. Prepare a single-step income statement that lists these costs: cost of goods sold, selling expenses, and general and administrative expenses.
5. Accounts receivable decreased during the period by $30,000. Compute cash received from customers.

Check   (4) Total expenses, $161,500

Use the data for Big Star Company in Problem 6-4A to complete the following requirements:

Required

Preparation Component

1. Prepare closing entries under the perpetual system as of August 31, 2002.

Analysis Component

2. The company makes all purchases on credit, and its suppliers uniformly offer a 3% sales discount. Does it appear that the company's cash management system is accomplishing the goal of taking all available discounts? Explain.

3. In prior years, the company experienced a 4% return and allowance rate on its sales, which means approximately 4% of its gross sales were eventually returned outright or caused the company to grant allowances to customers. How do this year's results compare to prior years' results?

Problem 6-5A
Preparing closing entries and interpreting information about discounts and returns

Check (1) $49,850 Dr. to close Income Summary

Prepare journal entries to record the following perpetual system merchandising transactions of Whitecap Company. (Use a separate account for each receivable and payable; for example, record the purchase on July 3 in Accounts Payable—MAP Corp.)

PROBLEM SET B

Problem 6-1B
Preparing journal entries for merchandising activities (perpetual system)

July 3   Purchased merchandise from MAP Corp. for $15,000 under credit terms of 1/10, n/30, FOB destination.

4   At MAP's request, Whitecap paid $150 cash for freight charges on the July 3 purchase, reducing the amount owed to MAP.

7   Sold merchandise to Bergez Co. for $11,500 under credit terms of 2/10, n/60, FOB destination. The merchandise had cost $7,750.

10   Purchased merchandise from McFarland Corporation for $14,250 under credit terms of 1/10, n/45, FOB shipping point. The invoice showed that at Whitecap's request, McFarland paid the $500 shipping charges and added that amount to the bill.

11   Paid $300 cash for shipping charges related to the July 7 sale to Bergez Co.

12   Bergez returned merchandise from the July 7 sale that had cost $1,450 and been sold for $1,850. The merchandise was restored to inventory.

14   After negotiations with McFarland Corporation concerning problems with the merchandise purchased on July 10, Whitecap received a credit memorandum from McFarland granting a price reduction of $2,000.

17   Received balance due from Bergez Co. for the July 7 sale less the return on July 12.

20   Paid the amount due McFarland Corporation for the July 10 purchase less the price reduction granted.

21   Sold merchandise to Harden for $11,000 under credit terms of 1/10, n/30, FOB shipping point. The merchandise had cost $7,000.

24   Harden requested a price reduction on the July 21 sale because the merchandise did not meet specifications. Sent Harden a credit memorandum for $1,300 to resolve the issue.

31   Received Harden's cash payment for the amount due from the July 21 purchase.

31   Paid MAP Corp. the amount due from the July 3 purchase.

Check July 20, Cr. Cash, $12,627.5

Prepare journal entries to record the following perpetual system merchandising transactions of Chang Company. (Use a separate account for each receivable and payable; for example, record the purchase on May 2 in Accounts Payable—McManus Co.)

Problem 6-2B
Preparing journal entries for merchandising activities (perpetual system)

May 2   Purchased merchandise from McManus Co. for $10,000 under credit terms of 1/15, n/30, FOB shipping point.

4   Sold merchandise to Four Winds Co. for $11,000 under credit terms of 2/10, n/60, FOB shipping point. The merchandise had cost $5,600.

5   Paid $250 cash for freight charges on the purchase of May 2.

9   Sold merchandise that cost $2,000 for $2,500 cash.

10   Purchased merchandise from Alvarez Co. for $3,650 under credit terms of 2/15, n/60, FOB destination.

12   Received a $400 credit memorandum from the return of merchandise purchased on May 10.

14   Received the balance due from Four Winds Co. for the credit sale dated May 4, net of the discount.

17   Paid the balance due to McManus Co. within the discount period.

20   Sold merchandise that cost $1,450 to Wickham Co. for $2,800 under credit terms of 2/15, n/60, FOB shipping point.

22   Issued a $325 credit memorandum to Wickham Co. for an allowance on goods sold from May 20.

23   Received a debit memorandum from Wickham Co. for an error that overstated the total invoice by $75.

25   Paid Alvarez Co. the balance due after deducting the discount.

30   Received the balance due from Wickham Co. for the credit sale dated May 20, net of discount.

31   Sold merchandise that cost $3,600 to Four Winds Co. for $7,200 under credit terms of 2/10, n/60, FOB shipping point.

Check   May 30, Dr. Cash, $2,352

Problem 6-3B

Preparing adjusting entries and income statements, and computing gross margin, acid-test, and current ratios

The following unadjusted trial balance is prepared at fiscal year-end for Durable Products Co.:

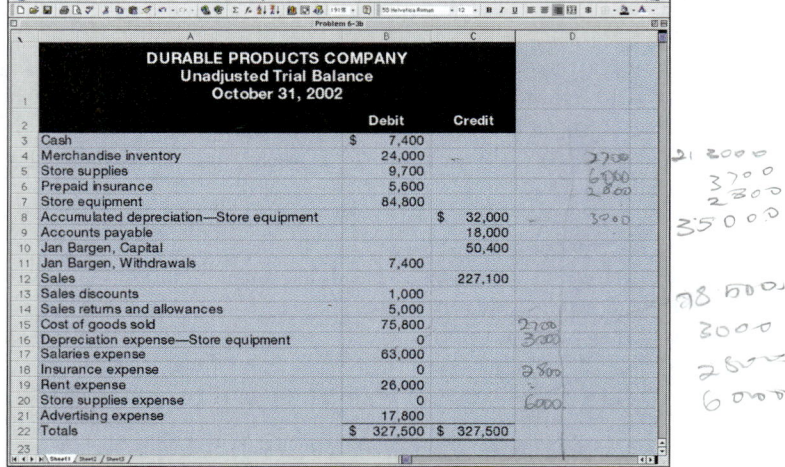

DURABLE PRODUCTS COMPANY
Unadjusted Trial Balance
October 31, 2002

	Debit	Credit
Cash	$ 7,400	
Merchandise inventory	24,000	
Store supplies	9,700	
Prepaid insurance	5,600	
Store equipment	84,800	
Accumulated depreciation—Store equipment		$ 32,000
Accounts payable		18,000
Jan Bargen, Capital		50,400
Jan Bargen, Withdrawals	7,400	
Sales		227,100
Sales discounts	1,000	
Sales returns and allowances	5,000	
Cost of goods sold	75,800	
Depreciation expense—Store equipment	0	
Salaries expense	63,000	
Insurance expense	0	
Rent expense	26,000	
Store supplies expense	0	
Advertising expense	17,800	
Totals	$ 327,500	$ 327,500

Rent and salaries expenses are equally divided between selling activities and the general and administrative activities. Durable Products Company uses a perpetual inventory system.

Required

1. Prepare adjusting journal entries for the following:

   a. Store supplies available at fiscal year-end amount to $3,700.

   b. Expired insurance, an administrative expense, for the fiscal year is $2,800.

   c. Depreciation expense on store equipment, a selling expense, is $3,000 for the fiscal year.

   d. To estimate shrinkage, a physical count of ending merchandise inventory is taken. It shows $21,300 of goods are available for sale.

2. Prepare a multiple-step income statement for fiscal year 2002.

3. Prepare a single-step income statement for fiscal year 2002.

4. Compute the company's current ratio, acid-test ratio, and gross margin ratio as of October 31, 2002.

Check   (3) Total expenses, $197,100

Problem 6-4B

Computing and formatting an income statement

Ryan Company's adjusted trial balance on March 31, 2002, its fiscal year-end, follows:

	Debit	Credit
Merchandise inventory.	$ 56,500	
Other assets.	202,600	
Liabilities		$ 42,500
Cook Ryan, Capital.		175,425
Cook Ryan, Withdrawals	14,000	

[continued on next page]

[continued from previous page]

	Debit	Credit
Sales		332,650
Sales discounts	5,875	
Sales returns and allowances.	20,000	
Cost of goods sold	115,600	
Sales salaries expense	44,500	
Rent expense—Selling space	16,000	
Store supplies expense	3,850	
Advertising expense	26,000	
Office salaries expense	40,750	
Rent expense—Office space	3,800	
Office supplies expense.	1,100	
Totals.	$550,575	$550,575

On March 31, 2001, merchandise inventory amounted to $37,500. Supplementary records of merchandising activities for the year ended March 31, 2002, reveal the following itemized costs:

Invoice cost of merchandise purchases	$138,500
Purchase discounts received	2,950
Purchase returns and allowances	6,700
Costs of transportation-in	5,750

Required

1. Calculate the company's net sales for the year.
2. Calculate the company's total cost of merchandise purchased for the year.
3. Prepare a multiple-step income statement that lists the company's net sales, cost of goods sold, and gross profit, as well as the components and amounts of selling expenses and general and administrative expenses.
4. Prepare a single-step income statement that lists these costs: cost of goods sold, selling expenses, and general and administrative expenses.
5. Accounts receivable increased by $50,000 during the period. Calculate cash received from customers.

Check (4) Total expenses, $251,600

Use the data for Ryan Company in Problem 6-4B to complete the following requirements:

Required

Preparation Component

1. Prepare closing entries under the perpetual system as of March 31, 2002.

Analysis Component

2. The company makes all purchases on credit, and its suppliers uniformly offer a 3% sales discount. Does it appear that the company's cash management system is accomplishing the goal of taking all available discounts? Explain.
3. In prior years, the company experienced a 4% return and allowance rate on its sales, which means approximately 4% of its gross sales were eventually returned outright or caused the company to grant allowances to customers. How do this year's results compare to prior years' results?

Problem 6-5B
Preparing closing entries and interpreting information about discounts and returns

Check (1) $55,175 Dr. to close Income Summary

(The first three segments of this comprehensive problem were presented in Chapters 3, 4, and 5. If those segments have not been completed, the assignment can begin at this point. You should use the Working Papers that accompany this text because they reflect the account balances that resulted from posting the entries required in Chapters 3, 4, and 5.)

Earlier segments of this problem have described how Sela Solstise created Sierra Systems on October 1, 2002. The company has been successful, and its list of customers has grown. To accommodate the growth, the accounting system is modified to set up separate accounts for each customer. The fol-

SERIAL PROBLEM

Sierra Systems

lowing list of customers includes the account number used for each account and any balance as of December 31, 2002. Solstise decided to add a fourth digit with a decimal point to the 106 account number that had been used for the single Accounts Receivable account. This modification allows the company to continue using the existing chart of accounts.

Customer Account	No.	Balance
Antonio's Engineering Co.	106.1	$ 0
Alexander Services	106.2	0
Prime Leasing	106.3	0
Dade Co.	106.4	3,000
Elan Corporation	106.5	0
Foster Co..	106.6	2,668
Olathe Co.	106.7	0
Taos, Inc.	106.8	0
Imagine, Inc..	106.9	0

In response to requests from customers, Solstise has decided to begin selling computer software. The company also will extend credit terms of 1/10, n/30 to all customers who purchase this merchandise. No cash discount will be available on consulting fees. The following additional accounts are added to the general ledger to allow the system to account for the company's new merchandising activities:

Account	No.
Merchandise Inventory	119
Sales.	413
Sales Returns and Allowances	414
Sales Discounts	415
Cost of Goods Sold	502

Sierra Systems does not use reversing entries and, therefore, all revenue and expense accounts have zero balances as of January 1, 2003. Its transactions for January through March follow:

Jan. 4   Paid cash to Suzie Smith for five days' work at the rate of $125 per day. Four of the five days are unpaid days of work from the prior year.

5   Sela Solstise invested an additional $25,000 cash in the business.

7   Purchased $5,800 of merchandise from Jersey Corp. with terms of 1/10, n/30, FOB shipping point.

9   Received $2,668 cash from Foster Co. as final payment on its account.

11   Completed a five-day project for Antonio's Engineering Co. and billed it $5,500, which is the total price of $7,000 less the advance payment of $1,500.

13   Sold merchandise with a retail value of $5,200 and a cost of $3,560 to Elan Corporation with terms of 1/10, n/30, FOB shipping point.

15   Paid $600 cash for freight charges on the merchandise purchased on January 7.

16   Received $4,000 cash from Olathe Co. for computer services provided.

17   Paid Jersey Corp. for the purchase on January 7, net of the discount.

20   Elan Corporation returned $500 of defective merchandise from its purchase on January 13. The returned merchandise, which had a $320 cost, is discarded.

22   Received the balance due from Elan Corporation, net of both the discount and the credit for the returned merchandise.

24   Returned defective merchandise to Jersey Corp. and accepted credit against future purchases. Its cost, net of the discount, was $496.

26   Purchased $9,000 of merchandise from Jersey Corp. with terms of 1/10, n/30, FOB destination.

26   Sold merchandise with a $4,640 cost for $5,800 on credit to Taos, Inc.

29   Received a $496 credit memorandum from Jersey Corp. concerning the merchandise returned on January 24.

31   Paid cash to Suzie Smith for 10 days' work at $125 per day.

Feb. 1   Paid $2,475 cash to Hilldale Mall for another three months' rent in advance.
      3   Paid Jersey Corp. for the balance due, net of the cash discount, less the $496 amount in the credit memorandum.
      5   Paid $600 cash to the local newspaper for an advertising insert in today's paper.
     11   Received the balance due from Antonio's Engineering Co. for fees billed on January 11.
     15   Sela Solstise withdrew $4,800 cash.
     23   Sold merchandise with a $2,660 cost for $3,220 on credit to Olathe Co.
     26   Paid cash to Suzie Smith for eight days' work at $125 per day.
     27   Reimbursed Sela Solstise for business automobile mileage (600 miles at $0.32 per mile).
Mar. 8   Purchased $2,730 of computer supplies from Appier Office Products on credit.
      9   Received the balance due from Olathe Co. for merchandise sold on February 23.
     11   Paid $960 cash to repair the company's computer.
     16   Received $5,260 cash from Imagine, Inc., for computing services provided.
     19   Paid the full amount due to Appier Office Products, including amounts created on December 15 and March 8.
     24   Billed Prime Leasing for $8,900 of computing services provided.
     25   Sold merchandise with a $2,002 cost for $2,800 on credit to Alexander Services.
     30   Sold merchandise with a $1,100 cost for $2,220 on credit to Dade Company.
     31   Reimbursed Sela Solstise for business automobile mileage (400 miles at $0.32 per mile).

The following additional facts are available for preparing adjustments on March 31 prior to financial statement preparation:

a. The March 31 inventory of computer supplies totals $2,005.

b. Three more months have passed since the company purchased its annual insurance policy at a $2,220 cost.

c. Suzie Smith has not been paid for seven days of work.

d. Three months have passed since any prepaid rent has been transferred to expense. The monthly rent is $825.

e. Depreciation on the computer equipment for January 1 through March 31 is $1,250.

f. Depreciation on the office equipment for January 1 through March 31 is $400.

g. The March 31 amount of merchandise inventory totals $704.

Required

1. Prepare journal entries to record each of the January through March transactions.

2. Post the journal entries to the accounts in the company's general ledger. (Begin with the post-closing adjusted balances as of December 31, 2002.)

3. Prepare a partial work sheet consisting of the first six columns (similar to the one shown in Exhibit 6A.3) that includes the unadjusted trial balance, the March 31 adjustments (a) through (g), and the adjusted trial balance. Do not prepare closing entries and do not journalize the adjusting entries or post them to the ledger.

4. Prepare an income statement for the three months ended March 31, 2003. Use a single-step format. List all expenses without differentiating between selling expenses and general and administrative expenses.

5. Prepare a statement of changes in owner's equity for the three months ended March 31, 2003.

6. Prepare a balance sheet as of March 31, 2003.

Beyond the Numbers

BTN 6-1   Refer to **Nike**'s financial statements in Appendix A.

Reporting in Action

A2 C5

NIKE

Required

1. Assume that the amounts reported for inventories and cost of sales reflect items purchased in a form ready for resale. Compute the net cost of goods purchased for the fiscal year ended May 31, 2000.

2. Compute the current and acid-test ratios as of May 31, 2000, and May 31, 1999. Comment on the ratio results.

Swoosh Ahead

3. Access Nike's annual report for fiscal years ending after May 31, 2000, from its Web site [www.nike.com] or the SEC's EDGAR database [www.sec.gov]. Recompute the current and acid-test ratios for fiscal years ending after May 31, 2000.

Comparative Analysis

BTN 6-2   Key comparative figures ($ millions) for both **Nike** and **Reebok** follow:

Key Figures	Nike		Reebok	
	Current Year	Prior Year	Current Year	Prior Year
Revenues (net sales)	$8,995.1	$8,776.9	$2,899.9	$3,224.6
Cost of sales	5,403.8	5,493.5	1,783.9	2,037.5

Required

1. Compute the dollar amount of gross margin and the gross margin ratio for the two years shown for both companies.

2. Which company earns more in gross margin for each dollar of net sales?

3. Did the gross margin ratios improve or decline for these companies?

Ethics Challenge

BTN 6-3   Helen Gaines is a student who plans to attend approximately four professional events a year at her college. Each event requires a new dress and accessories that necessitate a financial outlay of $100–$200 per event. After incurring a major hit to her savings for the first event in her freshman year, Helen developed a different approach. She buys the dress on credit the week before the event, wears it to the event, and returns it the next week to the store for a full refund on her charge card.

Required

1. Comment on the ethics exhibited by Helen and possible consequences of her actions.

2. How does the merchandising company account for the dresses that Helen returns?

Communicating in Practice

BTN 6-4   You are the accountant for **Music and More**, a retailer that sells goods for home entertainment needs. The business owner, Mr. U. Paah, recently reviewed the annual financial statements you prepared and sent you an e-mail stating that he thinks you overstated net income. He explains that although he has invested a great deal in security, he is sure shoplifting and other forms of inventory shrinkage have occurred, but he does not see any deduction for shrinkage on the income statement. The store uses a perpetual inventory system.

Required

Prepare a brief memorandum that responds to the owner's concerns in paper or e-mail format. If the response is made via e-mail, assume that your instructor is the owner instead of Mr. U. Paah.

Taking It to the Net

BTN 6-5   Access **www.edgar-online.com** and obtain the June 2, 2000, 10-K report filed by **eToys.com Inc.** (ticker ETYS). Construct a three-year trend of gross margin ratios for eToys using the net sales and cost of goods sold data on eToys' income statement. Analyze and comment on the trend.

Teamwork in Action

BTN 6-6   **World Brands'** ledger and supplementary records at the end of its current period reveal the following:

Sales	$430,000	Merchandise inventory (beginning of period) . .	$ 49,000
Sales returns	18,000	Invoice cost of merchandise purchases	180,000
Sales discounts	6,600	Purchase discounts received	4,500
Cost of transportation-in	11,000	Purchase returns and allowances	5,500
Operating expenses	20,000	Merchandise inventory (end of period)	42,000

Required

1. *Each* member of the team is to assume responsibility for computing *one* of the following items. You are not to duplicate your teammates' work. Get any necessary amounts to compute your item from the appropriate teammate. Each member is to explain his/her computation to the team in preparation for reporting to the class.

   a. Net sales   **d.** Gross profit
   b. Total cost of merchandise purchases   **e.** Net income
   c. Cost of goods sold

2. Check your net income with the instructor. If correct, proceed to step (3).
3. Assume that a physical inventory finds that actual ending inventory is $38,000. Discuss how this affects previously computed amounts in step (1).

Point: In teams of four, assign the same student (a) and (e). Rotate teams for reporting on a different computation and the analysis in (3).

BTN 6-7   Read the article, "You Can Survive Online Shopping" in the December 6, 1999, issue of *Business Week*.

Business Week Activity

Required

1. How does the 1999 projected dollar volume of online November and December shopping compare to the 1998 figure?
2. Return policies for e-merchants vary widely. Discuss the variety of return policies implemented by online retailers.
3. What account title would you recommend an online retailer use to record goods returned that were purchased online? Would you record these returns in a separate account from goods that were purchased in a store and returned (assuming the retailer operates a "bricks-and-mortar" storefront as well as online retailing)? Explain your answer.

BTN 6-8   Steve Miller is an entrepreneur who buys and sells new and used musical instruments to small retail outlets that offer musical instruments and training to customers. He recently completed his first year of operations. His income statement follows:

Entrepreneurial Decision

MUSICAL INSTRUMENTS **Income Statement** **For Year Ended January 31, 2002**	
Net Sales	$ 250,000
Cost of sales	(175,000)
Expenses	(20,000)
Net income	$ 55,000

To increase income, Miller is proposing to offer sales discounts of 3/10, n/30, and to ship all merchandise FOB shipping point. He presently offers no discounts and ships merchandise FOB destination. The discounts are predicted to increase net sales by 14%; the ratio of cost of sales to net sales is expected to remain unchanged. Since delivery expenses are zero under this proposal, the expenses are predicted to increase by only 10%.

Required

1. Prepare a forecasted income statement for the year ended January 31, 2003, based on Miller's proposal.
2. Do you recommend that Miller implement his proposal given your analysis in part *1*?
3. Identify any concerns you might express to Miller regarding his proposal.

7

Merchandise Inventories and Cost of Sales

A Look Back

Chapter 6 focused on merchandising activities and how they are reported. Both the perpetual and periodic inventory systems were described. We also analyzed and recorded merchandise purchases and sales and explained adjustments and the closing process for merchandising companies.

A Look at This Chapter

This chapter emphasizes accounting for inventory. We describe the methods available for assigning costs to inventory and explain the items and costs making up merchandise inventory. We also analyze the effects of inventory on both financial and tax reporting, and we discuss other methods of estimating and measuring inventory.

A Look Ahead

Chapter 8 emphasizes accounting information systems. We describe fundamental system principles, the system's components, use of special journals and subsidiary ledgers, and technology-based systems. We also discuss segment reports and how to analyze these data.

"Never give up . . . no one believed in us."
—Daymond John.

FUBU The Collection

e NEW YORK—It all began when 22-year-old waiter Daymond John and a friend bought a stocking cap from a street vendor. "It was about $20," recalls John. "And we said to ourselves, 'We can make this, we can sew it at home' because I knew how to sew a little bit from watching my mother hem my pants." The first day John hit the streets, he sold 40 hats and earned himself $800. He was hooked and quickly drew up ideas for shirts and sweatshirts. After enlisting the help of three childhood friends—Carl Brown, J. Alexander Martin, and Keith Perrin—John took a $100,000 mortgage on his home in Queens. He turned one-half of the home into a mini-factory and a new clothing company, dubbed **FUBU**, was born [**www.FUBU.com**].

Within a few short months the "team" had sold hats and T-shirts worth $10,000—FUBU was taking off. Within another 12 months, FUBU had $300,000 worth of orders for hats, shirts, and jeans. But a lack of cash flow and inventory management almost brought FUBU down. "I decided it's either do or die right now," recalls John. "And nobody else really cared about what we were doing or actually believed in us." To ensure inventory to meet the backlog of orders, John bought 10 more sewing machines and hired 4 more employees. "It was a very hard struggle," John says, but he was determined to keep FUBU afloat and overcome inventory problems. He installed better cost management and inventory oversight. The company got a further boost when hometown celebrity, rapper LL Cool J, wore FUBU's clothes in his music videos. FUBU was once again heading for the stars.

Today, just a few short years after its meager beginnings, FUBU The Collection is carried in more than 5,000 stores in the United States alone. They're also sold internationally in Australia, France, Germany, and Japan. Annual sales now top $350 million. From suburban teens to soul and pop musicians, FUBU's authentic quality and street credibility continue to attract new customers. [Sources: *Entrepreneur,* 12 November 1998; *FUBU Web Site,* May 2001; *CNNfn Web Site,* August 10, 1998.]

Learning Objectives

Conceptual

C1 Identify the items making up merchandise inventory.

C2 Identify the costs of merchandise inventory.

Analytical

A1 Analyze the effects of inventory methods for both financial and tax reporting.

A2 Analyze the effects of inventory errors on current and future financial statements.

A3 Assess inventory management using both inventory turnover and days' sales in inventory.

Procedural

P1 Compute inventory in a perpetual system using the methods of specific identification, FIFO, LIFO, and weighted average.

P2 Compute the lower of cost or market amount of inventory.

P3 Apply both the retail inventory and gross profit methods to estimate inventory.

Chapter Preview

Merchandising companies' activities include purchasing and reselling of merchandise. We explained accounting for merchandisers in the last chapter, including the perpetual and periodic inventory systems. In this chapter, we extend the study and analysis of inventory by identifying the items composing it. We also explain the methods used to assign costs to merchandise inventory *and* cost of goods sold. The assigned costs are not always historical cost. Many retailers, wholesalers, and other merchandising companies that purchase products for resale use the principles and methods we describe. These principles and methods affect reported amounts of income, assets, equity, revenues, and expenses. Understanding fundamental concepts of inventory accounting increases our ability to analyze and interpret financial statements. An understanding of these topics also helps people to run their own businesses.

Assigning Costs to Inventory

P1 Compute inventory in a perpetual system using the methods of specific identification, FIFO, LIFO, and weighted average.

Concept 7-1

Point: Inventories are a major current asset for most wholesalers, retailers, and manufacturers. Accounting for inventories is key to determining cost of goods sold on the income statement.

Accounting for inventory affects both the balance sheet and the income statement. A major goal in accounting for inventory is to match relevant costs against revenues. This is important to properly compute income. We use the *matching principle* to decide how much of the cost of the goods available for sale is deducted from sales and how much is carried forward as inventory and matched against future sales. Management must make this decision and several others when accounting for inventory. These decisions include selecting the

- Costing method (specific identification, FIFO, LIFO, or weighted average).
- Inventory system (perpetual or periodic).
- Items included and their costs.
- Use of market values or other estimates.

Decisions on these points affect the reported amounts for inventory, cost of goods sold, gross profit, income, current assets, and other accounts. This chapter discusses all of these important issues and their reporting effects.

One of the most important decisions in accounting for inventory is determining the per unit costs assigned to inventory items. When all units are purchased at the same unit cost, this process is simple. When identical items are purchased at different costs, however, a question arises as to which amounts to record in cost of goods sold when sales occur and which amounts to identify as remaining in inventory. We must record cost of goods sold and reductions in inventory to reflect these sales. How we assign these costs to inventory and cost of goods sold affects the financial statements.

Four methods are commonly used to assign costs to inventory and cost of goods sold: (1) specific identification, (2) first-in, first-out, (3) last-in, first-out, and (4) weighted average. Each method assumes a particular pattern for how costs flow through inventory. Each of these four methods is acceptable whether or not the actual physical flow of goods follows the cost flow assumption.[1] Exhibit 7.1 shows the frequency in the use of these methods.

We use information from **Trekking**, a sporting goods store, to describe the four methods. Among its many products, Trekking carries one type of mountain bike whose sales are directed at biking clubs. Its customers usually purchase in amounts of 10 or more bikes. We use data from Trekking's August 2002 transactions in mountain bikes. Its mountain bike (unit) inventory at the beginning of August and its purchases during August are shown in Exhibit 7.2.

Exhibit 7.1

Frequency in Use of Inventory Methods

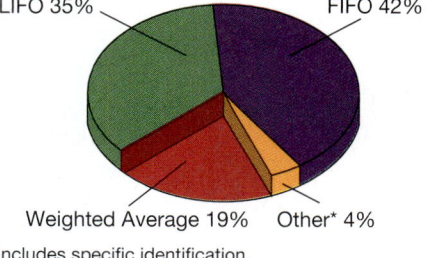

LIFO 35% FIFO 42% Weighted Average 19% Other* 4%

*Includes specific identification.

---

[1] Physical flow of goods depends on the type of product and the way it is stored. Perishable goods such as fresh fruit demand that a business attempt to sell them in a first-in, first-out physical flow pattern. Other products such as lanterns or grills can often be sold in a last-in, first-out physical flow pattern. Physical flow and cost flow need not be the same.

Aug. 1	Beginning inventory	10 units @ $ 91 = $ 910
Aug. 3	Purchases	15 units @ $106 = 1,590
Aug. 17	Purchases	20 units @ $115 = 2,300
Aug. 28	Purchases	10 units @ $119 = 1,190
Totals		**55 units** **$5,990**

Exhibit 7.2

Cost of Goods Available for Sale

Trekking had two large sales of mountain bikes to two different biking clubs in August as shown in Exhibit 7.3. It ends August with 12 bikes remaining in inventory.

Aug. 14	Sales	20 units @ $130 = $2,600
Aug. 31	Sales	23 units @ $150 = 3,450
Totals		**43 units** **$6,050**

Exhibit 7.3

Retail Sales of Goods

Trekking uses the perpetual inventory system. We explained in Chapter 6 that use of the perpetual inventory system is increasing as a result of advances in information and computing technology. Widespread use of electronic scanners and product bar codes encourages a perpetual inventory system. **(In Appendix 7A, we describe the assignment of costs to inventory using a periodic system.)** Regardless of what inventory method or system is used, cost of goods available for sale is allocated between cost of goods sold and ending inventory.

Trekking's use of a perpetual inventory system means that its merchandise inventory account is continually updated to reflect purchases and sales. As described in Chapter 6, the important accounting aspects of a perpetual system are:

■ Each purchase of merchandise for resale increases (debits) inventory.
■ Each sale of merchandise decreases (credits) inventory and increases (debits) costs of goods sold.
■ Necessary costs of merchandise such as transportation-in increase (debit) inventory, and cost reductions such as purchase discounts and purchase returns and allowances decrease (credit) inventory.

Except for any inventory shrinkage, the balance in the Merchandise Inventory account reflects the cost of merchandise available for sale at all times.

Specific Identification

When each item in inventory can be directly identified with a specific purchase and its invoice, we can use **specific identification** (also called *specific invoice inventory pricing*) to assign costs. We also need sales records that identify exactly which items were sold and when. Trekking's internal documents reveal that 12 unsold units were from the August 28 purchase and 6 were from the August 17 purchase. We use this information and the specific identification method to assign costs to the 12 units in ending inventory and to the 43 units sold as shown in Exhibit 7.4. Notice that each unit, whether sold or in inventory, has its own specific cost attached to it.

When using specific identification, Trekking's cost of goods sold reported on the income statement is **$4,586**, the sum of $2,000 and $2,586 from the third column of Exhibit 7.4. Trekking's ending inventory reported on the balance sheet is **$1,404**, which is the final inventory balance from the fourth column of Exhibit 7.4. *The assignment of costs to the goods sold and to inventory using specific identification is the same for both the perpetual and periodic systems.*

Point: Cost of goods sold plus ending inventory equals cost of goods available for sale.

Point: Three key variables determine the dollar value of ending inventory: (1) inventory quantity, (2) costs of inventory, and (3) cost flow assumption.

Point: Companies with expensive, custom-made inventory often use specific identification.

Exhibit 7.4

Specific Identification
Computations

Date	Purchases	Cost of Goods Sold	Inventory Balance
Aug. 1	Beginning balance		10 @ $ 91 = $ 910
Aug. 3	15 @ $106 = $1,590		10 @ $ 91 ⎫ 15 @ $106 ⎭ = $2,500
Aug. 14		8 @ $ 91 = $ 728 ⎫ 12 @ $106 = $1,272 ⎭ = $2,000*	2 @ $ 91 ⎫ 3 @ $106 ⎭ = $ 500
Aug. 17	20 @ $115 = $2,300		2 @ $ 91 ⎫ 3 @ $106 ⎬ = $2,800 20 @ $115 ⎭
Aug. 28	10 @ $119 = $1,190		2 @ $ 91 ⎫ 3 @ $106 ⎬ 20 @ $115 ⎬ = $3,990 10 @ $119 ⎭
Aug. 31		2 @ $ 91 = $ 182 ⎫ 3 @ $106 = $ 318 ⎬ 14 @ $115 = $1,610 ⎬ = $2,586* 4 @ $119 = $ 476 ⎭	6 @ $115 ⎫ 6 @ $119 ⎭ = $1,404

* Identification of the specific items sold (and their costs) is obtained from internal documents that track each unit from its purchase to its sale.

First-In, First-Out

The **first-in, first-out (FIFO)** method of assigning costs to both inventory and cost of goods sold assumes that inventory items are sold in the order acquired. When sales occur, the costs of the earliest units acquired are charged to cost of goods sold. This leaves the costs from the most recent purchases in ending inventory. Use of FIFO for computing the costs of inventory and goods sold is shown in Exhibit 7.5.

Point: Purchases data (column) are identical across all methods. These data are taken from Exhibit 7.2.

Exhibit 7.5

FIFO Computations—
Perpetual System

Date	Purchases	Cost of Goods Sold	Inventory Balance
Aug. 1	Beginning balance		10 @ $ 91 = $ 910
Aug. 3	15 @ $106 = $1,590		10 @ $ 91 ⎫ 15 @ $106 ⎭ = $2,500
Aug. 14		10 @ $ 91 = $ 910 ⎫ 10 @ $106 = $1,060 ⎭ = $1,970	5 @ $106 = $ 530
Aug. 17	20 @ $115 = $2,300		5 @ $106 ⎫ 20 @ $115 ⎭ = $2,830
Aug. 28	10 @ $119 = $1,190		5 @ $106 ⎫ 20 @ $115 ⎬ = $4,020 10 @ $119 ⎭
Aug. 31		5 @ $106 = $ 530 ⎫ 18 @ $115 = $2,070 ⎭ = $2,600	2 @ $115 ⎫ 10 @ $119 ⎭ = $1,420

For the 20 units sold on Aug. 14, the first 10 sold are assigned the earliest cost of $91. The next 10 sold are assigned the next earliest cost of $106.

For the 23 units sold on Aug. 31, the first 5 sold are assigned the earliest available cost of $91 (from Aug. 3 purchase). The next 18 sold are assigned the next earliest cost of $115.

Point: Under FIFO, a unit sold is assigned the earliest (oldest) cost from inventory. This leaves the most recent costs in ending inventory.

Trekking's cost of goods sold reported on the income statement (reflecting the 43 units sold) is **$4,570** ($1,970 + $2,600), and its ending inventory reported on the balance sheet (reflecting the 12 units unsold) is **$1,420**. *The assignment of costs to the goods sold and to inventory using FIFO is the same for both the perpetual and periodic systems.*

Last-In, First-Out

The **last-in, first-out (LIFO)** method of assigning costs assumes that the most recent purchases are sold first. These more recent costs are charged to the goods sold, and the costs of the earliest purchases are assigned to inventory. As with other methods, LIFO is acceptable even when the physical flow of goods does not follow a last-in, first-out pattern. One appeal of LIFO is that by assigning costs from the most recent purchases to cost of goods sold, LIFO comes closest to matching current replacement costs with revenues (compared to FIFO or weighted average). While costs for the most recent purchases are not exactly replacement costs, they usually are close approximations. Exhibit 7.6 shows how LIFO assigns the costs of mountain bikes to the 12 units in inventory and to the 43 units in cost of goods sold.

Point: Under LIFO, a unit sold is assigned the most recent (latest) cost from inventory. This leaves the oldest costs in inventory.

Exhibit 7.6

LIFO Computations—
Perpetual System

Date	Purchases	Cost of Goods Sold	Inventory Balance
Aug. 1	Beginning balance		10 @ $ 91 = $ 910
Aug. 3	15 @ $106 = $1,590		10 @ $ 91 ⎱ = $2,500 15 @ $106 ⎰
Aug. 14		15 @ $106 = $1,590 ⎱ = $2,045 5 @ $ 91 = $ 455 ⎰	5 @ $ 91 = $ 455
Aug. 17	20 @ $115 = $2,300		5 @ $ 91 ⎱ = $2,755 20 @ $115 ⎰
Aug. 28	10 @ $119 = $1,190		5 @ $ 91 ⎱ 20 @ $115 ⎬ = $3,945 10 @ $119 ⎰
Aug. 31		10 @ $119 = $1,190 ⎱ = $2,685 13 @ $115 = $1,495 ⎰	5 @ $ 91 ⎱ = $1,260 7 @ $115 ⎰

For the 20 units sold on Aug. 14, the first 15 sold are assigned the most recent cost of $106. The next 5 sold are assigned the next most recent cost of $91.

For the 23 units sold on Aug. 31, the first 10 sold are assigned the most recent cost of $119. The next 13 sold are assigned the next most recent cost of $115.

Trekking's cost of goods sold reported on the income statement is **$4,730** ($2,045 + $2,685), and its ending inventory reported on the balance sheet is **$1,260**. The assignment of costs to cost of goods sold and to inventory using LIFO usually gives different results, depending on whether a perpetual or periodic system is used. This is so because LIFO under a perpetual system assigns the most recent costs to goods sold at the time of each sale, whereas the periodic system waits to assign costs until the end of a period.

Global: LIFO is mainly used in the U.S. In some countries such as Australia, Ireland, and the United Kingdom, the use of LIFO is rare.

Weighted Average

The **weighted average** (also called **average cost**) method of assigning cost requires that we compute the weighted average cost per unit of inventory at the time of each sale. Weighted average cost per unit at the time of each sale equals the cost of goods available for sale divided by the units available. The results using weighted average for Trekking are shown in Exhibit 7.7.

Trekking's cost of goods sold reported on the income statement (reflecting the 43 units sold) is **$4,622** ($2,000 + $2,622), and its ending inventory reported on the balance sheet (reflecting the 12 units unsold) is **$1,368**. The assignment of costs to cost of goods sold and to inventory using weighted average usually gives different results, depending on whether a perpetual or periodic system is used. This is so because weighted average under a perpetual system recomputes the per unit cost at the time of each sale, whereas under the periodic system, the per unit cost is computed only at the end of a period.

Point: Under weighted average, a unit sold is assigned the average cost of all items currently available for sale.

Inventory Costing and Technology

A perpetual inventory system can be kept in either electronic or manual form. Using a manual form can make a perpetual inventory system too costly for businesses, especially those with many purchases and sales and with many units in inventory. Advances in information

Point: Inventory costing methods need not follow the physical flow of inventory.

Exhibit 7.7

Weighted Average
Computations—
Perpetual System

Date	Purchases	Cost of Goods Sold	Inventory Balance
Aug. 1	Beginning balance		10 @ $ 91 = $ 910
Aug. 3	15 @ $106 = $1,590		10 @ $ 91 ⎫ = $2,500 (or $100 per unit)ᵃ 15 @ $106 ⎭
Aug. 14		20 @ $100 = **$2,000**	5 @ $100 = $ 500 (or $100 per unit)ᵇ
Aug. 17	20 @ $115 = $2,300		5 @ $100 ⎫ = $2,800 (or $112 per unit)ᶜ 20 @ $115 ⎭
Aug. 28	10 @ $119 = $1,190		5 @ $100 ⎫ 20 @ $115 ⎬ = $3,990 (or $114 per unit)ᵈ 10 @ $119 ⎭
Aug. 31		23 @ $114 = **$2,622**	12 @ $114 = **$1,368** (or $114 per unit)ᵉ

ᵃ $100 per unit = [$2,500 inventory balance ÷ 25 units in inventory].

ᵇ $100 per unit = [$ 500 inventory balance ÷ 5 units in inventory].

ᶜ $112 per unit = [$2,800 inventory balance ÷ 25 units in inventory].

ᵈ $114 per unit = [$3,990 inventory balance ÷ 35 units in inventory].

ᵉ $114 per unit = [$1,368 inventory balance ÷ 12 units in inventory].

and computing technology have greatly reduced the cost of a perpetual inventory system. Many companies are now asking whether they can afford *not* to have a perpetual inventory system because timely access to inventory information has become a strategy to gain a competitive advantage. Scanned sales data, for instance, can reveal crucial information on buying patterns. It can also help companies target promotional and advertising activities. These and other applications have greatly increased the use of the perpetual inventory system.

Did You Know?

Battle of Inventory   The Pentagon is applying accounting skills to shrink inventories and speed deliveries. Use of bar codes, laser cards, radio tags, and accounting databases to track supplies speeds delivery from factory to foxhole. "We'll have piles of information instead of piles of stock," says Colonel M.D. Russ.

Inventory Analysis and Effects

This section analyzes and compares the alternative inventory costing methods. We also analyze the tax effects of inventory methods, examine managers' preferences for an inventory method, and consider the effects of inventory errors.

Financial Reporting

A1 Analyze the effects of inventory methods for both financial and tax reporting.

When purchase prices do not change, each inventory costing method assigns the same cost amounts to inventory and to cost of goods sold. When purchase prices are different, however, the methods are likely to assign different cost amounts. We show these differences in Exhibit 7.8 using Trekking's segment income statement for its mountain bike operations. The different inventory costing methods show different results for net income. Because Trekking's purchase prices rose in August, FIFO assigned the least amount to cost of goods sold. This led to the highest gross profit and the highest net income. In contrast, LIFO assigned the highest amount to cost of goods sold. This yielded the lowest gross profit and the lowest net income. As expected, amounts from using the weighted average method fell between FIFO and LIFO.[2] The amounts from using specific identification depend on which units are actually sold.

---

[2] The weighted average amount can be outside the FIFO or LIFO amounts if prices do not steadily increase or decrease but exhibit a cyclical pattern.

TREKKING COMPANY Segment Income Statement—Mountain Bikes For Month Ended August 31				
	Specific Identification	FIFO	LIFO	Weighted Average
Sales	$6,050	$6,050	$6,050	$6,050
Cost of goods sold	**4,586**	**4,570**	**4,730**	**4,622**
Gross profit	$1,464	$1,480	$1,320	$1,428
Operating expenses	450	450	450	450
Income before taxes	$1,014	$1,030	$ 870	$ 978
Income tax expense (30%)	304	309	261	293
Net income	**$ 710**	**$ 721**	**$ 609**	**$ 685**

Exhibit 7.8

Income Statement Effects of
Inventory Costing Methods

All four inventory costing methods are acceptable in practice. Each method offers certain advantages. One advantage of specific identification is that it exactly matches costs and revenues. This is important when each unit has unique features affecting its cost. An advantage of weighted average is that it tends to smooth out changes in costs. An advantage of FIFO is that it assigns an amount to inventory on the balance sheet that closely approximates current replacement cost. An advantage of LIFO is it assigns the most recent costs incurred to cost of goods sold and likely better matches current costs with revenues on the income statement.

The choice of an inventory costing method can greatly impact amounts on financial statements. **Mobil**, for instance, recently changed its inventory method and reported in a news release that this change "will reduce . . . year-to-date, net income by $680 million." Companies must disclose the inventory method used in their financial statements or notes.

Global: Swiss standards require no disclosures related to inventory.

It is important to understand inventory costing for analysis of financial statements. Some companies' financial statements help in our analysis by reporting what the difference would be if another costing method were used. **Kmart**, for instance, reports in a recent annual report that ($ millions): "Inventories valued on LIFO were $360, $407 and $457 lower than amounts that would have been reported using the first-in, first-out (FIFO) method at year end . . . [for the most recent 3 years], respectively."

You Make the Call

Financial Planner One of your clients asks if the inventory account of a company using FIFO needs any "adjustments" for analysis purposes in light of recent inflation. What is your advice? Does your advice depend on changes in the costs of these inventories?

Answer—p. 286

Tax Reporting

Trekking's segment income statement in Exhibit 7.8 reflects the company's formation as a corporation because its income statement includes income tax expense (at a rate of 30%). Because inventory costs affect net income, they have potential tax effects for corporations. Trekking gains a temporary tax advantage by using LIFO. This advantage occurs because LIFO assigns a larger dollar amount to cost of goods sold when purchase prices are increasing as in the case of Trekking. This means less income is reported when LIFO is used and purchase prices are rising. This in turn results in the smallest income tax expense.

Global: Countries allowing LIFO for tax reporting include Germany, Belgium, Japan, Taiwan, and South Korea.

The Internal Revenue Service (IRS) identifies several acceptable methods for inventory costing in reporting taxable income for corporations. It is important to know that companies can and often do use different costing methods for financial reporting and tax reporting. *The only exception is when LIFO is used for tax*

Did You Know?

Entrepreneurial Giving Many entrepreneurs donate 10% or more of their pretax income to charities. Consultants cite evidence that socially conscious behavior brings tangible financial rewards. A recent survey found 76% of respondents saying they'd switch from their current store to one with a good cause if price and quality are equal.

purposes; in this case, the IRS requires it be used in financial statements. Since costs tend to rise, LIFO usually gives a lower taxable income and a tax advantage. Many companies use LIFO for this reason, yet managers often have incentives to report higher net income for reasons such as bonus plans, job security, and reputation. FIFO is sometimes preferred in these cases because it tends to report a higher income when prices are rising.

Consistency in Reporting

Inventory costing methods can affect amounts on financial statements, and some managers might be inclined to choose a method most consistent with their hoped-for results each period. One objective might be to pick the method giving the most favorable financial statement amounts. Managers might also be inclined to pick the method giving them the highest bonus since many management bonus plans are based on net income. If managers were allowed to pick the method each period, users of financial statements would have more difficulty comparing a company's financial statements from one period to the next. If income increased, for instance, a user would need to decide whether it resulted from successful operations or from an accounting method change. The consistency principle is used to avoid this problem.

The **consistency principle** requires a company to use the same accounting methods period after period so that financial statements are comparable across periods. The consistency principle applies to all accounting methods. When a company must choose between alternative methods, consistency requires that the company continue to use the selected method period after period. Users of financial statements can then make comparisons of a company's statements across periods because of the assumption that a company uses the same methods across periods.

The consistency principle does *not* require a company to use one method exclusively. It can use different methods to value different categories of inventory. **Harley-Davidson**, for instance, reports the following: "Inventories located in the United States are valued using the last-in, first-out (LIFO) method. Other inventories . . . are valued at the lower of cost or market using the first-in, first-out (FIFO) method." Also, the consistency principle does not imply that a company can never change from one accounting method to another. Instead it means that a company must argue that the method it is changing to will improve its financial reporting. When an alternative method will improve its reporting, a change is acceptable. The *full-disclosure principle* requires that the notes to the statements report this type of change, its justification, and its effect on net income.

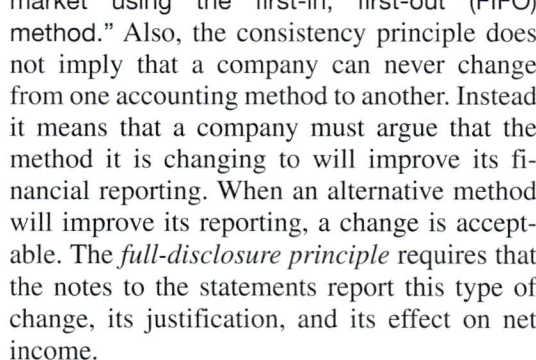

You Make the Call—Ethics

Inventory Manager   Your compensation as inventory manager includes a bonus plan based on gross profit. Your superior asks your opinion on changing the inventory costing method from FIFO to LIFO. Since costs are expected to continue to rise, your superior predicts that LIFO would match higher current costs against sales, thereby lowering taxable income (and gross profit). This proposed change will likely reduce your bonus. What do you recommend?

Answer—p. 286

Errors in Reporting Inventory

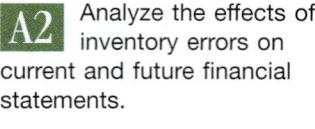 Analyze the effects of inventory errors on current and future financial statements.

Concept 7-2

Companies must take care in both computing and taking a physical count of inventory. An inventory error causes misstatements in cost of goods sold, gross profit, net income, current assets, and equity. It also causes misstatements in the next period's statements because ending inventory of one period is the beginning inventory of the next. An error carried forward causes misstatements in the next period's cost of goods sold, gross profit, and net income. Such misstatements can reduce the usefulness of financial statements.

Income Statement Effects

The income statement effects of an inventory error are evident by reviewing the components of cost of goods sold as shown in Exhibit 7.9—this relation applies to any method under both the perpetual and periodic systems. The effect of an inventory error on cost of goods sold is determined by computing it with the incorrect component amount and comparing it to cost of goods sold when using the correct component amount.

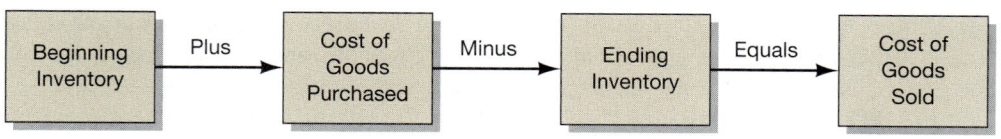

Exhibit 7.9

Cost of Goods Sold
Components

We can see, for example, that understating ending inventory in a physical count overstates cost of goods sold. An overstatement in cost of goods sold yields an understatement in net income. We can do the same analysis with overstating ending inventory and for an error in beginning inventory. Exhibit 7.10 shows the effects of inventory errors on the current period's income statement amounts.

Inventory Error	Cost of Goods Sold	Net Income
Understate ending inventory	Overstated	Understated
Understate beginning inventory	Understated	Overstated
Overstate ending inventory*	Understated	Overstated
Overstate beginning inventory*	Overstated	Understated

Exhibit 7.10

Effects of Inventory Errors
on This Period's
Income Statement

*These errors are unlikely under a perpetual system because they suggest more inventory than is recorded. Accordingly, management will normally follow up and discover and correct these errors before they impact any accounts.

Notice that inventory errors yield opposite effects in cost of goods sold and net income. Inventory errors also carry over to the next period, yielding a reverse effect.

To show these effects, we consider an inventory error for a company with $100,000 in sales for years 2001, 2002, and 2003. If this company maintains a steady $20,000 inventory level during this period and makes $60,000 in purchases in each of these years, its cost of goods sold is $60,000 and its gross profit is $40,000 each year. But what if this company errs in computing its 2001 ending inventory and reports $16,000 instead of the correct amount of $20,000? The effects of this error are shown in Exhibit 7.11. The $4,000 understatement of the year 2001 ending inventory causes a $4,000 overstatement in year 2001 cost of goods sold and a $4,000 understatement in both gross profit and net income for year 2001. Since year 2001 ending inventory becomes year 2002 beginning inventory, this error causes an understatement in 2002 cost of goods sold and a $4,000 overstatement in both gross profit and net income for year 2002. Notice that an inventory error in one period does not affect the third period, year 2003.

If year 2001 ending inventory had been overstated, it would have yielded opposite results. That is, the 2001 net income would have been overstated and the 2002 income understated. An inventory error is said to be *self-correcting* because it always yields an

Example: If year 2001 ending inventory in Exhibit 7.11 is overstated by $3,000, what is the effect on cost of goods sold, gross profit, assets, and equity? *Answer:* Cost of goods sold is understated by $3,000 in 2001 and overstated by $3,000 in 2002. Gross profit and net income are overstated in 2001 and understated in 2002. Assets and equity are overstated in 2001.

Exhibit 7.11

Effects of Inventory Errors
on Three Periods'
Income Statements

	Income Statements		
	2001	**2002**	**2003**
Sales	$100,000	$100,000	$100,000
Cost of goods sold			
Beginning inventory	$20,000	→$16,000*	→$20,000
Cost of goods purchased	60,000	60,000	60,000
Goods available for sale .	$80,000	$76,000	$80,000
Ending inventory	16,000*	20,000	20,000
Cost of goods sold	64,000†	56,000†	60,000
Gross profit	$ 36,000	$ 44,000	$ 40,000
Operating expenses	10,000	10,000	10,000
Net income	$ 26,000	$ 34,000	$ 30,000

* Correct amount is $20,000.   † Correct amount is $60,000.

offsetting error in the next period. This does not make inventory errors less serious. Managers, lenders, owners, and other users make important decisions analysis of changes in net income and cost of goods sold. Therefore, inventory errors must be avoided.

Balance Sheet Effects

Balance sheet effects of an inventory error are evident by considering the components of the accounting equation: Assets = Liabilities + Equity. For example, understating ending inventory understates both current and total assets. An understatement in ending inventory also yields an understatement in equity because of the understatement in net income. Exhibit 7.12 shows the effects of inventory errors on the current period's balance sheet amounts.

Exhibit 7.12

Effects of Inventory Errors on This Period's Balance Sheet

Inventory Error	Assets	Equity
Understate ending inventory	Understated	Understated
Overstate ending inventory	Overstated	Overstated

Errors in *beginning* inventory do not yield misstatements in the end-of-period balance sheet, but they do affect the current period's income statement.

Quick Check

1. Describe one advantage for each of the inventory costing methods: specific identification, FIFO, LIFO, and weighted average.
2. When costs are rising, does LIFO or FIFO report higher net income?
3. When costs are rising, what effect does LIFO have on a balance sheet compared to FIFO?
4. A company takes a physical count of inventory at the end of 2002 and finds that ending inventory is overstated by $10,000. Would this error cause cost of goods sold to be overstated or understated in 2002? In year 2003? If so, by how much?

Answers—pp. 286–287

Inventory Items and Costs

This section identifies the items and costs making up merchandise inventory. This identification is important given the major impact of inventory in financial statements. We also describe the importance of and the method used in taking a physical count of inventory.

Items in Merchandise Inventory

C1 Identify the items making up merchandise inventory.

Merchandise inventory includes all goods that a company owns and holds for sale. This rule holds regardless of where the goods are located when inventory is counted. We must simply see that all items are counted and computations are correct. Certain inventory items require special attention, including goods in transit, goods on consignment, and goods that are damaged or obsolete.

Goods in Transit

Point: Ownership of merchandise held for resale determines whether it is included in inventory. This is consistent with the definition of assets in Chapter 1.

Does a purchaser's inventory include goods in transit from a supplier? The answer is that if ownership has passed to the purchaser, they are included in the purchaser's inventory. Chapter 6 explained how we determine this by reviewing the shipping terms—*FOB destination* or *FOB shipping point*. If the purchaser is responsible for paying freight, ownership passes when goods are loaded on the transport vehicle. If the supplier is responsible for paying freight, owenership passes when goods arrive at their destination.

Goods on Consignment

Goods on consignment are goods shipped by the owner, called the **consignor,** to another party, the **consignee.** A consignee sells goods for the owner. The consignor owns consigned goods and reports them in its inventory. **Score Board**, **Tri Star**, and **Upper Deck**, for instance, pay sports celebrities such as Tiger Woods and Ken Griffey, Jr., to sign memorabilia. These autographed items (footballs, baseballs, jerseys, photos) are offered to shopping networks on consignment and are sold through catalogs and dealers. The consignor must report these items in its inventory until sold.

Goods Damaged or Obsolete

Damaged goods and obsolete (or deteriorated) goods are not counted in inventory if they are unsalable. If these goods are salable at a reduced price, they are included in inventory at a conservative estimate of their **net realizable value.** Net realizable value is sales price minus the cost of making the sale. The period when damage or obsolescence (or deterioration) occurs is the period when the loss in value is reported.

Costs of Merchandise Inventory

Merchandise inventory includes costs of expenditures necessary, directly or indirectly, to bring an item to a salable condition and location. This means the cost of an inventory item includes its invoice price minus any discount, and plus any added or incidental costs necessary to put it in a place and condition for sale. Added or incidental costs can include import duties, transportation-in, storage, insurance, and costs incurred in an aging process (for example, aging wine and cheese).

Accounting principles imply that incidental costs are assigned to the units purchased. The purpose is to properly match all inventory costs against revenue in the period when inventory is sold. Some companies use the *materiality principle* or the *cost-to-benefit constraint* to avoid assigning incidental costs of acquiring merchandise to inventory. These companies argue either that incidental costs are immaterial or that the effort in assigning these costs to inventory outweighs the benefit. Such companies often value inventory using invoice prices only. When this is done, the incidental costs are allocated to cost of goods sold in the period when they are incurred.

> ### Did You Know?
>
> **Inventory Online**   Warehouse clerks can quickly record inventory by scanning bar codes. Thanks to **Motorola**, a wireless portable computer with a two-way radio allows clerks to send and receive data instantly. It gives managers immediate access to up-to-date information on inventory and location.

 **C2** Identify the costs of merchandise inventory.

> ### Did You Know?
>
> **Express Lane Shopping**   Bar codes and readers are common tools for retailers. More retailers are adding bar code readers on shopping carts for customers to swipe the product over the reader, automatically charging it to a credit card. There is no need to stand in a checkout line. Customers simply pass through a gate that verifies that everything in the cart has been scanned.

Physical Count of Merchandise Inventory

The Inventory account under a perpetual system is always up to date, but events can cause the Inventory account balance to be different from the actual inventory available. Such events include theft, loss, damage, and errors. In response, nearly all companies take a *physical count of inventory* at least once each year, sometimes called *taking an inventory.* This often occurs at the end of a fiscal year or when inventory amounts are low. This physical count is used to adjust the Inventory account balance to the actual inventory available.

Concept 7-2

We determine a dollar amount for the physical count of inventory available by (1) counting the units of each product on hand, (2) multiplying the count for each product by its cost per unit, and (3) adding the costs for all products. When taking a count, items are less likely to be counted more than once or omitted by using prenumbered inventory tickets. We show a typical inventory ticket in Exhibit 7.13.

Exhibit 7.13

Inventory Ticket

The process of a physical count of inventory is fairly standard. Before beginning it, we prepare at least one inventory ticket for each product on hand. These tickets are issued to employees doing the count. An employee counts the quantity of a product and obtains information on its purchase date, selling price, and cost. This information is sometimes included with the products but often must be obtained from accounting records or invoices. Once the necessary information has been collected, the employee records it on the inventory ticket and signs the form. The inventory ticket is then attached to the counted inventory. Another employee often recounts and rechecks information on the ticket, signs it, and returns it to the manager. To ensure that no ticket is lost or missed, internal control procedures verify that all prenumbered tickets are returned. The unit and cost data on inventory tickets are aggregated by multiplying the number of units for each product by its unit cost. This gives us the dollar amount for each product in inventory. The sum total of all product costs is the amount reported for inventory on the balance sheet.

Subsidiary Inventory Records

The Merchandise Inventory account is a controlling account for the subsidiary merchandise inventory ledger. The subsidiary ledger contains a separate record for each product, and it can be in electronic or paper form. Subsidiary inventory records assist managers in planning and controlling inventory. A typical subsidiary ledger is shown in Exhibit 7.14. This record shows both the number of units and costs for each purchase and sale of the item, along with the updated balance after each purchase and sale. The record also identifies the item, its catalog number, and its location (at the top). This ledger reveals by its computations that a FIFO cost flow assumption is being used for sports bags.

Exhibit 7.14

Subsidiary Inventory Record

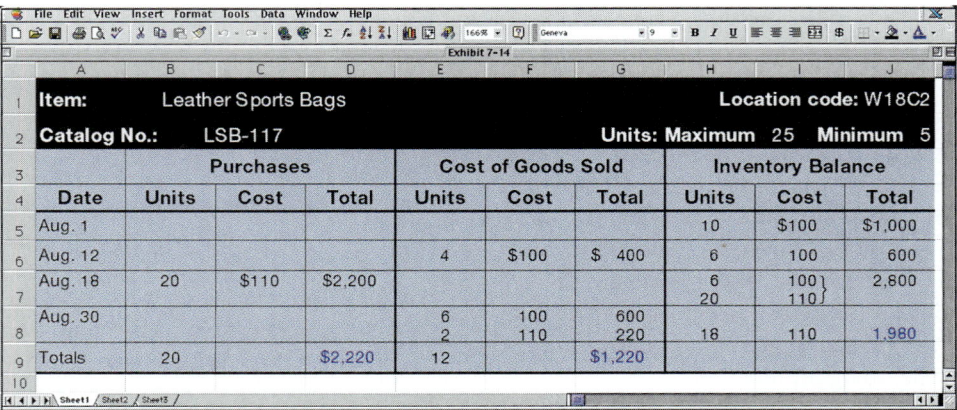

Quick Check

5. What accounting principle most guides the allocation of cost of goods available for sale between ending inventory and cost of goods sold?

6. If **Nike** sells goods to **Target** with terms FOB shipping point, does Nike or Target report these goods in its inventory while they are in transit?

7. An art gallery purchases a painting for $11,400 on terms FOB shipping point. Additional costs in obtaining and offering the artwork for sale include $130 for transportation-in, $150 for import duties, $100 for insurance during shipment, $180 for advertising, $400 for framing, and $800 for office salaries. For computing inventory, what cost is assigned to the painting?

Answers—p. 287

This section describes other methods to value inventory. Knowledge of these methods is important for understanding and analyzing financial statements.

Lower of Cost or Market

We explained how to assign costs to ending inventory and cost of goods sold using one of four costing methods (FIFO, LIFO, weighted average, or specific identification). The cost of inventory, however, is not necessarily the amount always reported on a balance sheet. *Accounting principles require that inventory be reported at the market value (cost) of replacing inventory when market value is lower than cost.* Merchandise inventory is then said to be reported on the balance sheet at the **lower of cost or market (LCM).**

Computing the Lower of Cost or Market

Market in the term LCM is defined as the current market value (cost) of replacing inventory. It is the current cost of purchasing the same inventory items in the usual manner. A decline in market cost reflects a loss of value in inventory because the recorded cost of inventory is higher than the current market cost. When this occurs, a loss is recognized. This is done by recognizing the decline in merchandise inventory from recorded cost to market cost at the end of the current period.

LCM is applied in one of three ways: (1) to each individual item separately, (2) to major categories of items, or (3) to the entire inventory. The less similar the items that make up inventory, the more likely companies are to apply LCM to individual items. Advances in technology further encourage the individual item approach.

To illustrate, we apply LCM to the ending inventory of a motorsports retailer. Inventory data for this retailer and LCM computations are shown in Exhibit 7.15.

Other Inventory Valuations

P2 Compute the lower of cost or market amount of inventory.

Global: In Canada, the Netherlands, and the United Kingdom, the *market* in LCM is defined as "net realizable value" (selling price less costs to complete and sell).

Inventory Items	Units on Hand	Per Unit Cost	Per Unit Market	Total Cost	Total Market	LCM Applied to Items	LCM Applied to Categories	LCM Applied to Whole
Cycles								
Roadster	20	$8,000	$7,000	$160,000	$140,000	$140,000		
Sprint	10	5,000	6,000	50,000	60,000	50,000		
Category subtotal				210,000	200,000		$200,000	
Off-Road								
Trax-4	8	5,000	6,500	40,000	52,000	40,000		
Blazer	5	9,000	7,000	45,000	35,000	35,000		
Category subtotal				85,000	87,000		85,000	
Totals				$295,000	$287,000	**$265,000**	**$285,000**	**$287,000**

Exhibit 7.15

Lower of Cost or Market Computations

When LCM is applied to the *entire* inventory, the market cost is $287,000. Since this market cost is $8,000 lower than the $295,000 recorded cost, it is the amount reported for inventory on the balance sheet. When LCM is applied to the major *categories* of inventory, the market is $285,000. When LCM is applied to individual *items* of inventory, the market cost is $265,000. Since market is again less than the $295,000 recorded cost, market cost is the amount reported for inventory. Any one of these three applications of LCM is acceptable. **Best Buy** follows this method and reports that its "merchandise inventories are recorded at the lower of average cost or market."

The *direct method* is a common way to record inventory at LCM—it substitutes market value (when lower) for cost in the inventory account. Using LCM applied on the entire inventory from Exhibit 7.15, we make the following entry: Cost of Goods Sold, Dr. $8,000; Merchandise Inventory, Cr. $8,000. The Merchandise Inventory account balance is now $287,000, computed as $295,000 minus $8,000.

Conservatism Principle

Accounting rules require recording inventory down to market when market is less than cost, but inventory usually cannot be written up to market when market exceeds cost. If recording inventory down to market is acceptable, why are we not allowed to record inventory up to market? One reason is a concern that the gain from a market increase is not realized until a sales transaction verifies the gain. However, this problem also applies when market is less than cost. The second and primary reason is the **conservatism principle,** which requires the use of the less optimistic amount when more than one estimate of the amount to be received or paid in the future exists and these estimates are about equally likely. LCM is justified with reference to conservatism.

Retail Inventory Method

P3   Apply both the retail inventory and gross profit methods to estimate inventory.

Many companies prepare financial statements on a quarterly or monthly basis, called **interim statements** because they are prepared between the traditional annual statements. The cost of goods sold information needed to prepare interim statements is readily available if a perpetual inventory system is used but requires a physical inventory if the periodic system is used. To avoid the time-consuming and expensive process of taking a physical inventory each month or quarter, some companies use the **retail inventory method** to estimate cost of goods sold and ending inventory. Some companies even use the retail inventory method to prepare the annual statements. **Home Depot**, for instance, says in its recent annual report: "Inventories are stated at the lower of cost (first-in, first-out) or market, as determined by the retail inventory method." Other reasons to estimate inventory are for audit purposes and when inventory is destroyed or damaged.

Computing the Retail Inventory Estimate

The retail inventory method uses a three-step process to estimate ending inventory. We need to know the amount of inventory a company had at the beginning of the period in both *cost* and *retail* amounts. We already explained how to compute the cost of inventory. The retail amount of inventory refers to its dollar amount measured using selling prices of inventory items. We also need to know the net amount of goods purchased (minus returns, allowances, and discounts) in the period, both at cost and at retail. The amount of net sales at retail is also needed. The process is shown in Exhibit 7.16.

The reasoning behind the retail inventory method is if we can get a good estimate of the

Exhibit 7.16

Inventory Estimation Using Retail Inventory Method

cost to retail ratio, we can multiply ending inventory at retail by this ratio to estimate ending inventory at cost. We show in Exhibit 7.17 how these steps are applied to estimate ending inventory for a typical company.

First, we find that $100,000 of goods (at retail selling prices) were available for sale. We see that $70,000 of these goods were sold, leaving $30,000 (retail value) of unsold merchandise in ending inventory. Second, the cost of these goods is 60% of the $100,000 retail

Example: What is the cost of ending inventory in Exhibit 7.17 if the cost of beginning inventory is $22,500 and its retail value is $34,500? *Answer:* $30,000 × 62% = $18,600

	At Cost	At Retail
Goods available for sale		
Beginning inventory	$20,500	$ 34,500
Cost of goods purchased	39,500	65,500
Goods available for sale	$60,000	$100,000
Step 1: Deduct net sales at retail.		70,000
Ending inventory at retail.		$ 30,000

Step 2: Cost to retail ratio: ($60,000 ÷ $100,000) = 60%

Step 3: Estimated ending inventory at cost ($30,000 × 60%) . . . $18,000

Exhibit 7.17

Estimated Ending Inventory Using the Retail Inventory Method

value. Third, since cost for these goods is 60% of retail, the estimated cost of ending inventory is $18,000.

Estimating Physical Inventory at Cost

Items for sale by retailers usually carry price tags listing selling prices. When a retailer takes a physical inventory, it commonly totals inventory using selling prices of items available. It can then reduce the dollar total of this inventory to a cost basis by applying the cost to retail ratio—use of the cost to retail ratio eliminates the need to look up invoice prices of items. To illustrate, assume the company in Exhibit 7.17 estimates its inventory by the retail method and takes a physical inventory using selling prices. If the retail value of this physical inventory is $29,600, we can compute the cost of this inventory by applying its cost to retail ratio as follows: **$29,600 × 60% = $17,760.** The $17,760 cost figure for ending physical inventory is an acceptable number for annual financial statements and for tax reporting.

Estimating Inventory Shortage at Cost

The inventory estimate in Exhibit 7.17 estimates the amount of goods available at the end of the period (at cost). Since it is computed by deducting sales from goods available for sale (at retail), it does not reveal any shrinkage due to breakage, loss, or theft. We can estimate the amount of shrinkage by comparing the inventory computed in Exhibit 7.17 with the amount from taking a physical inventory. In Exhibit 7.17, for example, at retail we estimated ending inventory as $30,000, but a physical inventory revealed only $29,600 of inventory. The company has an inventory shortage (at retail) of $400, computed as $30,000 − $29,600. The inventory shortage (at cost) is $240, computed as $400 × 60%.

Gross Profit Method

The **gross profit method** estimates the cost of ending inventory by applying the gross profit ratio to net sales (at retail). This type of estimate often is needed when inventory is destroyed, lost, or stolen. These cases require an inventory estimate so a company can file a claim with its insurer. Users also apply this method to see whether inventory amounts from a physical count are reasonable. This method uses the historical relation between cost of goods sold and net sales to estimate the proportion of cost of goods sold making up current

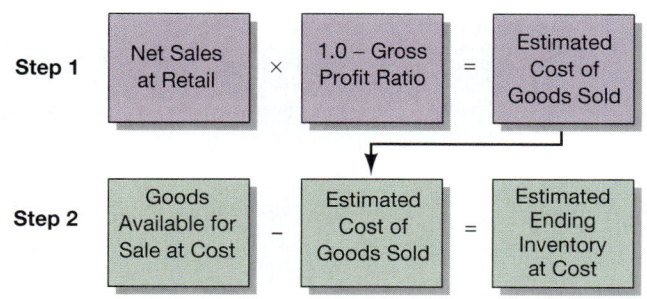

Exhibit 7.18

Ending Inventory Estimated Using the Gross Profit Method

sales. This cost of goods sold estimate is then subtracted from cost of goods available for sale to estimate the ending inventory at cost. These two steps are shown in Exhibit 7.18.

Point: A fire or other catastrophe can result in an insurance claim for lost inventory or income. Backup procedures for financial data and off-site storage of data help ensure coverage for such losses.

We need certain accounting data to apply the gross profit method: the gross profit ratio, beginning inventory (at cost), the net cost of goods purchased, and net sales (at retail). To illustrate, assume that a company's inventory is destroyed by fire in March 2002. This company's normal gross profit ratio is 30% of net sales. When the fire occurs, the company's accounts show the following balances for January through March:

Sales	$31,500
Sales returns	1,500
Inventory, January 1, 2002	12,000
Cost of goods purchased	20,500

Point: Reliability of the gross profit method depends on a good estimate of the gross profit ratio.

We can use the gross profit method to estimate this company's inventory loss. Note that whatever portion of each dollar of net sales is gross profit, the remaining portion is cost of goods sold. If this company's gross profit ratio is 30%, then 30% of each net sales dollar is gross profit and 70% is cost of goods sold. We show in Exhibit 7.19 how this 70% is used to estimate lost inventory of $11,500.

Exhibit 7.19

Estimated Inventory Using the Gross Profit Method

Goods available for sale	
Inventory, January 1, 2002	$12,000
Cost of goods purchased...........................	20,500
Goods available for sale (at cost)	32,500
Net sales at retail ($31,500 − $1,500).....................	$30,000
Step 1: **Estimated cost of goods sold ($30,000 × 70%)**	**(21,000)** ← × 0.70
Step 2: **Estimated March inventory at cost**	**$11,500**

To help understand Exhibit 7.19, think of subtracting ending inventory from goods available for sale to get the cost of goods sold. In Exhibit 7.19 we estimate ending inventory by subtracting cost of goods sold from the goods available for sale.

Quick Check

8. A company's ending inventory includes the following items:

Product	Units	Unit Cost	Unit Market Value
A	20	$ 6	$ 5
B	40	9	8
C	10	12	15

Use LCM applied separately to individual items to compute the amount for inventory.

9. The following data pertain to a company's inventory during its most recent year:

	Cost	Retail
Beginning inventory	$324,000	$530,000
Cost of goods purchased	195,000	335,000
Net sales		320,000

Using the retail method, estimate the cost of ending inventory.

Inventory Turnover and Days' Sales in Inventory	Using the Information

This section describes how we use information about inventory to assess a company's short-term liquidity (ability to pay) and its management of inventory. Two measures useful for these assessments are presented.

<table><tr><td>A3</td><td>Assess inventory management using both inventory turnover and days' sales in inventory.</td></tr></table>

Inventory Turnover

We described in earlier chapters two important ratios useful in evaluating a company's short-term liquidity: current ratio and acid-test ratio. A merchandiser's ability to pay its short-term obligations also depends on how quickly it sells its merchandise inventory. **Inventory turnover,** also called *merchandise inventory turnover,* is one ratio used to assess this. It is computed as shown in Exhibit 7.20.

$$\text{Inventory turnover} = \frac{\text{Cost of goods sold}}{\text{Average inventory}}$$

Exhibit 7.20

Inventory Turnover

This ratio reveals how many *times* a company turns over its inventory during a period. Average inventory is usually computed by adding beginning and ending inventory amounts and dividing the total by two. If a company's inventory greatly varies within a year, it is often better to average inventory amounts from the end of each quarter or month.

Users apply inventory turnover to help analyze short-term liquidity and to assess whether management is doing a good job controlling the amount of inventory available. A low ratio compared to that of competitors suggests inefficient use of assets. The company may be holding more inventory than it needs to support its sales volume. Similarly, a very high ratio compared to that of competitors suggests inventory might be too low. This can cause lost sales because customers must back order merchandise. Inventory turnover has no simple rule except to say *a high ratio is preferable provided inventory is adequate to meet demand.*

We know the inventory costing methods such as FIFO, LIFO, and weighted average affect reported amounts of inventory and cost of goods sold. The inventory costing method also affects computation of inventory turnover. This means that we must take care when we compare turnover ratios across companies that use different costing methods.

Did You Know?

Dell-ocity From its roots in a college dorm room, **Dell** now sells 50 million dollars' worth of computers each day from its Web site. "The Internet," says Michael Dell, "is the ultimate direct model." Web sales now account for nearly one-half of the total PC business. The speed of Web technology has allowed Dell to slash inventories. Dell's operating cycle is less than 15 hours and its days' sales in inventory is 3 days. Michael Dell asserts "Speed is everything in this business."

Days' Sales in Inventory

To better interpret inventory turnover, many users measure the adequacy of inventory to meet sales demand. **Days' sales in inventory,** also called *days' stock on hand,* is a ratio that reveals how much inventory is available in terms of the number of days' sales. It can be interpreted as the number of days one can sell from inventory if no new items are purchased. This ratio is often viewed as a measure of the buffer against out-of-stock inventory and is useful in evaluating liquidity of inventory. Days' sales in inventory is computed as shown in Exhibit 7.21.

$$\text{Days' sales in inventory} = \frac{\text{Ending inventory}}{\text{Cost of goods sold}} \times 365$$

Exhibit 7.21

Days' Sales in Inventory

Days' sales in inventory focuses on ending inventory and it estimates how many days it will take to convert inventory at the end of a period into accounts receivable or cash. Notice that days' sales in inventory focuses on *ending* inventory whereas inventory turnover focuses on *average* inventory.

Analysis of Inventory Management

Inventory management is a major emphasis for most merchandisers. They must both plan and control inventory purchases and sales. **Toys "R" Us** is one of those merchandisers. Its merchandise inventory at January 29, 2000, is $2,027 million. This inventory constitutes 70% of it current assets and 24% of its total assets. We apply the analysis tools in this section to Toys "R" Us as shown in Exhibit 7.22.

Exhibit 7.22

Inventory Turnover and Days' Sales in Inventory for Toys "R" Us

($ in millions)	Jan. 29, 2000	Jan. 30, 1999	Jan. 31, 1998
Cost of goods sold	$8,321	$8,191	$7,710
Ending merchandise inventory	$2,027	$1,902	$2,464
Inventory turnover	**4.24** times	**3.75** times	**3.30** times
Industry inventory turnover.	3.01 times	2.88 times	2.76 times
Days' sales in inventory.	**88.9** days	**84.8** days	**116.6** days
Industry days' sales in inventory.	121.3 days	126.7 days	129.7 days

The 2000 inventory turnover of 4.24 for **Toys "R" Us** is computed as $8,321 ÷ [($2,027 + $1,902) ÷ 2]. This means Toys "R" Us turns over its inventory 4.24 times per year, or once every 86 days (365 days ÷ 4.24). We prefer inventory turnover to be high provided inventory is not out of stock and the company is not losing customers. The 2000 days' sales in inventory of 88.9 for Toys "R" Us helps us assess this likelihood and is computed as ($2,027 ÷ $8,321) × 365. This tells us Toys "R" Us is carrying 88.9 days of sales in its inventory. This inventory buffer seems more than adequate. Toys "R" Us might benefit from further management efforts to increase inventory turnover.

You Make the Call

Entrepreneur   Analysis of your retail store yields an inventory turnover of 5.0 and a days' sales in inventory of 73 days. The industry norm for inventory turnover is 4.4 and for days' sales in inventory is 74 days. Where do you direct your initial review of inventory management?

Answer—p. 286

Demonstration Problem

Mozart Company uses a perpetual inventory system for its one product. Its beginning inventory and purchases during year 2002 follow:

Date			Units	Unit Cost
Jan.	1	Inventory	400	$14
March	10	Purchase	200	15
May	9	Purchase	300	16
Sept.	22	Purchase	250	20
Nov.	28	Purchase	100	21

At December 31, 2002, 550 units are in inventory. Sales in year 2002 are as follows:

Jan. 15	200 units at $30
April 1	200 units at $30
Nov. 1	300 units at $35

Additional unit cost tracking data for use in applying specific identification: (1) January 15 sale—200 units @ $14, (2) April 1 sale—200 units @ $15, and (3) November 1 sale—200 units @ $14 and 100 units @ $20.

Required

1. Calculate the cost of goods available for sale.

2. Apply the four different methods of inventory costing (FIFO, LIFO, weighted average, and specific identification) to calculate ending inventory and cost of goods sold under each method.

3. In preparing financial statements for year 2002, the accountant was instructed to use FIFO but failed to do so and computed cost of goods sold according to LIFO. Determine the impact on year 2002's income from the error. Also determine the effect of this error on year 2003's income. Assume no income taxes.

4. Management wants a report that shows how changing from FIFO to another method would change net income. Prepare a schedule showing (1) the cost of goods sold amount under each of the four methods, (2) the amount by which each cost of goods sold total is different from the FIFO cost of goods sold, and (3) the effect on net income if another method is used instead of FIFO.

Planning the Solution

- Make a schedule showing the calculation of cost of goods available for sale. Multiply the units of beginning inventory and each purchase by the appropriate unit costs to determine the total cost of goods available for sale.

- Prepare a perpetual FIFO schedule showing the composition of beginning inventory and how the composition of inventory changes after each purchase of inventory and after each sale (see Exhibit 7.5).

- Prepare a perpetual LIFO schedule showing the composition of beginning inventory and how the composition of inventory changes after each purchase of inventory and after each sale (see Exhibit 7.6).

- Make a schedule of purchases and sales recalculating the average cost of inventory after each purchase to arrive at the weighted average cost of ending inventory. Total the average costs associated with each sale to determine cost of goods sold (see Exhibit 7.7).

- Prepare a schedule showing the computation of cost of goods sold and ending inventory using the specific identification method. Use the information provided to determine which specific units are sold and which specific units remain in inventory (see Exhibit 7.4).

- Compare the ending year 2002 inventory amounts under FIFO and LIFO to determine the misstatement of year 2002 income that results from using LIFO. The errors for year 2002 and 2003 are equal in amount but opposite in effect.

- Create a schedule showing cost of goods sold under each method and how net income would differ from FIFO net income if an alternate method is adopted.

Solution to Demonstration Problem

1. Cost of goods available for sale (this amount is the same for all methods):

Date			Units	Unit Cost	Total Cost
Jan.	1	Inventory	400	$14	$ 5,600
March 10		Purchase	200	15	3,000
May	9	Purchase	300	16	4,800
Sept.	22	Purchase	250	20	5,000
Nov.	28	Purchase	100	21	2,100
Total cost of goods available for sale					$20,500

2a. FIFO perpetual method:

Date	Purchases	Cost of Goods Sold	Inventory Balance
Jan. 1	Beginning balance		400 @ $14 = $ 5,600
Jan. 15		200 @ $14 = $2,800	200 @ $14 = $ 2,800
Mar. 10	200 @ $15 = $3,000		200 @ $14 200 @ $15 } = $ 5,800
April 1		200 @ $14 = $2,800	200 @ $15 = $ 3,000
May 9	300 @ $16 = $4,800		200 @ $15 300 @ $16 } = $ 7,800
Sept. 22	250 @ $20 = $5,000		200 @ $15 300 @ $16 250 @ $20 } = $12,800
Nov. 1		200 @ $15 = $3,000 100 @ $16 = $1,600	200 @ $16 250 @ $20 } = $ 8,200
Nov. 28	100 @ $21 = $2,100		200 @ $16 250 @ $20 100 @ $21 } = $10,300
Total cost of goods sold		**$10,200**	

Note to students: **In a classroom situation,** once we compute cost of goods available for sale, we can compute the amount for either cost of goods sold or ending inventory—it is a matter of preference. **In practice,** the costs of items sold are identified as sales are made and immediately transferred from the inventory account to the cost of goods sold account. This transfer makes calculating either account balance at the end of a period unnecessary. The previous solution showing the line-by-line approach illustrates actual application in practice. The following alternate solutions illustrate that, once the concepts are understood, other solution approaches are available.

Alternate FIFO Perpetual Solution

[FIFO Alternate No. 1: Computing cost of goods sold first]

Cost of goods available for sale (from part 1)		$20,500
Cost of goods sold		
Jan. 15 Sold (200 @ $14)	$ 2,800	
April 1 Sold (200 @ $14)	2,800	
Nov. 1 Sold (200 @ $15 and 100 @ $16)	4,600	**10,200**
Ending inventory		**$10,300**

[FIFO Alternate No. 2: Computing ending inventory first]

Cost of goods available for sale (from part 1)		$20,500
Ending inventory*		
Nov. 28 Purchase (100 @ $21)	$2,100	
Sept. 22 Purchase (250 @ $20)	5,000	
May 9 Purchase (200 @ $16)	3,200	
Ending inventory		**10,300**
Cost of goods sold		**$10,200**

* Since FIFO assumes that earlier costs relate to items sold, we determine ending inventory by assigning the most recent costs.

2b. LIFO perpetual method:

Date	Purchases	Cost of Goods Sold	Inventory Balance
Jan. 1	Beginning balance		400 @ $14 = $ 5,600
Jan. 15		200 @ $14 = $2,800	200 @ $14 = $ 2,800
Mar. 10	200 @ $15 = $3,000		200 @ $14 200 @ $15 } = $ 5,800
April 1		200 @ $15 = $3,000	200 @ $14 = $ 2,800
May 9	300 @ $16 = $4,800		200 @ $14 300 @ $16 } = $ 7,600
Sept. 22	250 @ $20 = $5,000		200 @ $14 300 @ $16 } = $12,600 250 @ $20
Nov. 1		250 @ $20 = $5,000 50 @ $16 = $ 800	200 @ $14 250 @ $16 } = $ 6,800
Nov. 28	100 @ $21 = $2,100		200 @ $14 250 @ $16 } = **$ 8,900** 100 @ $21
Total cost of goods sold		**$11,600**	

Alternate LIFO Perpetual Solution

[LIFO Alternate No. 1: Computing cost of goods sold first]

Cost of goods available for sale (from part 1)		$20,500
Cost of goods sold with LIFO perpetual		
Jan. 15 200 units @ $14	$2,800	
April 1 200 units @ $15	3,000	
Nov. 1 { 250 units @ $20	5,000	
{ 50 units @ $16	800	
Cost of goods sold		**11,600**
Ending inventory		**$ 8,900**

[LIFO Alternate No. 2: Computing ending inventory first]

Cost of goods available for sale (from part 1)		$20,500
Ending inventory		
Jan. 1 Inventory (200 @ $14)	$2,800	
May 9 Purchase (250 @ $16)	4,000	
Nov. 28 Purchase (100 @ $21)	2,100	
Ending inventory		**8,900**
Cost of goods sold		**$11,600**

2c. Weighted average perpetual method:

Date	Purchases	Cost of Goods Sold	Inventory Balance
Jan. 1	Beginning balance		400 @ $14 = $ 5,600
Jan. 15		200 @ $14 = $2,800	200 @ $14 = $ 2,800
Mar. 10	200 @ $15 = $3,000		200 @ $14 ⎱ = $ 5,800 200 @ $15 ⎰ (avg. cost is $14.5)
April 1		200 @ $14.5 = $2,900	200 @ $14.5 = $ 2,900
May 9	300 @ $16 = $4,800		200 @ $14.5 ⎱ = $ 7,700 300 @ $16 ⎰ (avg. cost is $15.4)
Sept. 22	250 @ $20 = $5,000		200 @ $14.5 ⎱ 300 @ $16 ⎬ = $12,700 250 @ $20 ⎰ (avg. cost is $16.93)
Nov. 1		300 @ $16.93 = $5,079	450 @ $16.93 = $7,618.5
Nov. 28	100 @ $21 = $2,100		450 @ $16.93 ⎱ = $9,718.5 100 @ $21 ⎰
Total cost of goods sold*		**$10,779**	

* The cost of goods sold ($10,779) plus ending inventory ($9,718.5) is $2.5 less than the cost of goods available for sale ($20,500) due to rounding.

2d. Specific identification method:

Date	Purchases	Cost of Goods Sold	Inventory Balance
Jan. 1	Beginning balance		400 @ $14 = $ 5,600
Jan. 15		200 @ $14 = $2,800	200 @ $14 = $ 2,800
Mar. 10	200 @ $15 = $3,000		200 @ $14 ⎱ = $ 5,800 200 @ $15 ⎰
April 1		200 @ $15 = $3,000	200 @ $14 = $ 2,800
May 9	300 @ $16 = $4,800		200 @ $14 ⎱ = $ 7,600 300 @ $16 ⎰
Sept. 22	250 @ $20 = $5,000		200 @ $14 ⎱ 300 @ $16 ⎬ = $12,600 250 @ $20 ⎰
Nov. 1		200 @ $14 = $2,800 100 @ $20 = $2,000	300 @ $16 ⎱ = $ 7,800 150 @ $20 ⎰
Nov. 28	100 @ $21 = $2,100		300 @ $16 ⎱ 150 @ $20 ⎬ = $ 9,900 100 @ $21 ⎰
Total cost of goods sold		**$10,600**	

[Specific Identification Alternate No. 1: Computing cost of goods sold first]

Cost of goods available for sale (from part 1)	$20,500
Cost of goods sold	
Jan. 1 Purchase (400 @ $14) $5,600	
March 10 Purchase (200 @ $15) 3,000	
Nov. 28 Purchase (100 @ $20) 2,000	
Total cost of goods sold	**10,600**
Ending inventory	**$ 9,900**

[Specific Identification Alternate No. 2: Computing ending inventory first]

Cost of goods available for sale (from part 1)	$20,500
Ending inventory	
May 9 Purchase (300 @ $16) $4,800	
Sept. 22 Purchase (150 @ $20) 3,000	
Nov. 28 Purchase (100 @ $21) 2,100	
Total ending inventory	**9,900**
Cost of goods sold	**$10,600**

3. Mistakenly using LIFO when FIFO should have been used overstates cost of goods sold in year 2002 by $1,400, which is the difference between the FIFO and LIFO amounts of ending inventory. It understates income in 2002 by $1,400. In year 2003, income is overstated by $1,400 because of the understatement in beginning inventory.

4. Analysis of the effects of alternative inventory methods:

	Cost of Goods Sold	Difference from FIFO Cost of Goods Sold	Effect on Net Income if Adopted Instead of FIFO
FIFO	$10,200	—	—
LIFO	11,600	+$1,400	$1,400 lower
Weighted average	10,779	+ 579	579 lower
Specific identification	10,600	+ 400	400 lower

APPENDIX

Assigning Costs to Inventory— Periodic System

7A

The aim of the periodic system and the perpetual system is the same: to assign costs to inventory and cost of goods sold. The same four methods are used to assign costs under the periodic system—specific identification; first-in, first-out; last-in, first-out; and weighted average. We use information from **Trekking** to describe how we assign costs using these four methods with a periodic system. Data for sales and purchases are reported in the chapter (see Exhibits 7.2 and 7.3).

P4 Compute inventory in a periodic system using the methods of specific identification, FIFO, LIFO, and weighted average.

Recall that we explained the accounting transactions under a periodic system in Appendix 6A. These are the important accounting aspects of a periodic system:

- Each purchase of merchandise for resale increases (debit) the Purchases account.
- Cost of merchandise sold is *not* recorded at the time of each sale. A physical count of inventory at the end of the period is used to compute cost of goods sold and inventory amounts.
- Necessary costs of merchandise such as transportation-in and cost reductions such as purchase discounts and purchase returns and allowances are recorded in *separate* accounts.

Specific Identification

The amount of costs assigned to inventory and cost of goods sold is the same under the perpetual and periodic systems when using specific identification. This is so because specific identification precisely tracks (identifies) which units are in inventory and which have been sold.

First-In, First-Out

The first-in, first-out (FIFO) method of assigning cost to both inventory and cost of goods sold using the periodic system is shown in Exhibit 7A.1.

Exhibit 7A.1

FIFO Computations—
Periodic System

Total cost of 55 units available for sale		$5,990
Less ending inventory priced using FIFO		
10 units from August 28 purchase at $119 each	$1,190	
2 units from August 17 purchase at $115 each	230	
Ending inventory		1,420
Cost of goods sold		$4,570

Trekking's ending inventory reported on the balance sheet is **$1,420**, and its cost of goods sold reported on the income statement is **$4,570**. These amounts are the same as those computed using the perpetual system. This always occurs because the most recent purchases are in ending inventory under both systems.

Last-In, First-Out

The last-in, first-out (LIFO) method of assigning costs to the 12 remaining units in inventory (and to the 43 units in cost of goods sold) using the periodic system is shown in Exhibit 7A.2.

Exhibit 7A.2

LIFO Computations—
Periodic System

Total cost of 55 units available for sale		$5,990
Less ending inventory priced using LIFO		
10 units in beginning inventory at $ 91 each	$ 910	
2 units from August 3 purchase at $106 each	212	
Ending inventory		1,122
Cost of goods sold		$4,868

Trekking's ending inventory reported on the balance sheet is **$1,122**, and its cost of goods sold reported on the income statement is **$4,868**. When LIFO is used with the periodic system, cost of goods sold is assigned costs from the most recent purchases for the period. With a perpetual system, cost of goods sold is assigned costs from the most recent purchases at the point of *each sale*.

Weighted Average

The weighted average method of assigning cost involves three important steps. The first two steps are shown in Exhibit 7A.3. First, multiply the per unit cost for beginning inventory and each particular purchase by the corresponding number of units. Second, add these amounts and divide by the total number of units available for sale to find the weighted average cost per unit.

Step 1:	10 units @ $ 91 =	$ 910
	15 units @ $106 =	1,590
	20 units @ $115 =	2,300
	10 units @ $119 =	1,190
	55	**$5,990**
Step 2:	$5,990/55 units = **$108.91** weighted average cost per unit	

Exhibit 7A.3

Weighted Average Cost per Unit

Example: In Exhibit 7A.3, if 5 more units had been purchased at $120 each, what would be the weighted average cost per unit?
Answer: $109.83 ($6,590/60)

The third step is to use the weighted average cost per unit to assign costs to inventory and to the units sold as shown in Exhibit 7A.4.

Step 3:	Total cost of 55 units available for sale	$5,990
	Less **ending inventory** priced on a weighted average	
	cost basis: 12 units at $108.91 each (from Exhibit 7A.3)	1,307
	Cost of goods sold	**$4,683**

Exhibit 7A.4

Weighted Average Computations—Periodic

Trekking's ending inventory reported on the balance sheet is **$1,307**, and its cost of goods sold reported on the income statement is **$4,683** when using the weighted average method.

Quick Check

10. A company reports the following beginning inventory and purchases, and it ends the period with 30 units in inventory

Beginning Inventory	100 units at $10 cost per unit
Purchase 1	40 units at $12 cost per unit
Purchase 2	20 units at $14 cost per unit

a. Compute ending inventory using the FIFO periodic system.
b. Compute cost of goods sold using the LIFO periodic system.

Answers—p. 287

Summary

C1 **Identify the items making up merchandise inventory.** Merchandise inventory comprises goods owned by a company and held for resale. Three special cases merit our attention. Goods in transit are reported in inventory of the company that holds ownership rights. Goods on consignment are reported in the consignor's inventory. Goods damaged or obsolete are reported in inventory at their net realizable value.

C2 **Identify the costs of merchandise inventory.** Costs of merchandise inventory comprise expenditures necessary, directly or indirectly, to bring an item to a salable condition and location. This includes its invoice cost minus any discount plus any added or incidental costs necessary to put it in a place and condition for sale.

A1 **Analyze the effects of inventory methods for both financial and tax reporting.** When purchase costs are rising or falling, the inventory costing methods are likely to assign different costs to inventory. Specific identification exactly matches costs and revenues. Weighted average smooths out cost changes. FIFO assigns an amount to inventory closely approximating current replacement cost. LIFO assigns the most recent costs incurred to cost of goods sold and likely better matches current costs with revenues.

A2 **Analyze the effects of inventory errors on current and future financial statements.** An error in the amount of ending inventory affects assets (inventory), net income (cost of goods sold), and equity for that period. Since ending inventory is next period's beginning inventory, an error in ending inventory affects next period's cost of goods sold and net income. Financial statement effects of errors in one period are offset in the next.

A3 **Assess inventory management using both inventory turnover and days' sales in inventory.** We prefer a high inventory turnover provided inventory is not out of stock and customers are not turned away. We use days' sales in inventory to assess the likelihood of inventory being out of stock. We prefer a small number of days' sales in inventory if we can serve customer needs and provide a buffer for uncertainties. Each of these ratios helps assess inventory management and evaluate a company's short-term liquidity.

P1 **Compute inventory in a perpetual system using the methods of specific identification, FIFO, LIFO, and weighted average.** Costs are assigned to the cost of goods sold account *each time* a sale occurs in a perpetual system. Specific identification assigns a cost to each item sold by referring to its actual cost (for example, its net invoice cost). Weighted average assigns a cost to items sold by dividing the current balance in the inventory account by the total items available for sale to determine cost per unit. We then multiply the number of units sold by this cost per unit to get the cost of each sale. FIFO assigns cost to items sold assuming that the earliest units purchased are the first units sold. LIFO assigns cost to items sold assuming that the most recent units purchased are the first units sold.

P2 **Compute the lower of cost or market amount of inventory.** Inventory is reported at market value when market is *lower* than cost, called the *lower of cost or market amount of*

inventory. Market is typically measured as replacement cost. Lower of cost or market can be applied separately to each item, to major categories of items, or to the entire inventory.

P3 **Apply both the retail inventory and gross profit methods to estimate inventory.** The retail inventory method involves three computations: (1) goods available at retail minus net sales at retail equals ending inventory at retail, (2) goods available at cost divided by goods available at retail equals the cost to retail ratio, and (3) ending inventory at retail multiplied by the cost to retail ratio equals estimated ending inventory at cost. The gross profit method involves two computations: (1) net sales at retail multiplied by 1 minus the gross profit ratio equals estimated cost of goods sold, and (2) goods available at cost minus estimated cost of goods sold equals estimated ending inventory at cost.

P4 **Compute inventory in a periodic system using the methods of specific identification, FIFO, LIFO, and weighted average.** Periodic inventory systems allocate the cost of goods available for sale between cost of goods sold and ending inventory *at the end of a period.* Specific identification and FIFO give identical results whether the periodic or perpetual system is used. LIFO assigns costs to cost of goods sold assuming the last units purchased for the period are the first units sold. The weighted average cost per unit is computed by dividing the total cost of beginning inventory and net purchases for the period by the total number of units available. Then, multiply cost per unit by the number of units sold to give cost of goods sold.

Guidance Answers to **You Make the Call**

Financial Planner The FIFO method implies the oldest costs are the first ones assigned to cost of goods sold. This leaves the most recent costs in ending inventory. You report this to your client and note that in most cases, the ending inventory of a company using FIFO is reported at or near its market replacement cost. This means your client need not in most cases adjust the reported value of inventory. Your answer changes only if there are major increases in replacement cost compared to the cost of recent purchases reported in inventory. When major increases in costs occur, your client might wish to adjust inventory (for internal reports) for the difference between the reported cost of inventory and its market replacement cost. (*Note:* Decreases in costs of purchases are recognized under the lower of cost or market adjustment.)

Inventory Manager Your recommendation is difficult. On one hand, it seems your company can save (or at least postpone) taxes by switching to LIFO, but the switch is likely to reduce bonus money

that you think you have earned and deserve. Since the U.S. tax code requires companies that use LIFO for tax reporting also to use it for financial reporting, your options are even further constrained. Your best decision is to tell your superior about the tax savings with LIFO. You also should discuss your bonus plan and how this is likely to hurt you unfairly. You might propose to compute inventory under the LIFO method for reporting purposes but use the FIFO method for your bonus calculations. Another solution is to revise the bonus plan to reflect the company's use of the LIFO method.

Entrepreneur Your inventory turnover is markedly higher than the norm, whereas days' sales in inventory approximates the norm. Since your turnover is already 14% better than average, you are probably best served by directing attention to days' sales in inventory. You should see whether you can reduce the level of inventory while maintaining service to customers. Given your higher turnover, you should be able to hold less inventory.

Guidance Answers to **Quick Checks**

1. Specific identification exactly matches costs and revenues. Weighted average tends to smooth out price changes. FIFO assigns an amount to inventory that closely approximates current replacement cost. LIFO assigns the most recent costs incurred to cost of goods sold and likely better matches current costs with revenues.

2. FIFO—it gives a lower cost of goods sold, a higher gross profit, and a higher net income when prices are rising.

3. LIFO gives a lower inventory figure on the balance sheet as compared to FIFO when costs are rising. FIFO's inventory amount approximates current replacement costs.

4. Cost of goods sold is understated by $10,000 in 2002 and overstated by $10,000 in year 2003.

5. The matching principle.

6. **Target** reports these goods in its inventory.

7. Total cost assigned to the painting is $12,180, computed as $11,400 + $130 + $150 + $100 + $400.

8. The reported LCM inventory amount in $540, computed as $[(20 \times \$5) + (40 \times \$8) + (10 \times \$12)]$.

9. Estimated ending inventory (at cost) is $327,000. It is computed as follows:

Step 1: $(\$530,000 + \$335,000) - \$320,000 = \$545,000$

Step 2: $\dfrac{\$324,000 + \$195,000}{\$530,000 + \$335,000} = 60\%$

Step 3: $\$545,000 \times 60\% = \$327,000$

10. a. FIFO periodic inventory $= (20 \times \$14) + (10 \times \$12)$
$= \$400.$

b. LIFO periodic cost of goods sold
$= (20 \times \$14) + (40 \times \$12) + (70 \times \$10)$
$= \$1,460.$

Glossary

Average cost (see *weighted average cost.*) (p. 265)

Conservatism principle principle that seeks to select the less optimistic estimate when two estimates are about equally likely. (p. 274)

Consignee one who receives and holds goods owned by another for purposes of selling the goods for the owner. (p. 271)

Consignor owner of goods who ships them to another party who will then sell them for the owner. (p. 271)

Consistency principle principle encouraging use of the same accounting methods over time so that financial statements are comparable across periods. (p. 268)

Days' sales in inventory estimate of days needed to convert inventory into receivables or cash; equals ending inventory divided by cost of goods sold and then multiplied by 365; also called *days' stock on hand.* (p. 277)

First-in, first-out (FIFO) method to assign cost to inventory that assumes items are sold in the order acquired, the earliest items purchased are the first items sold. (p. 264)

Gross profit method procedure to estimate inventory when the past gross profit rate is used to estimate cost of goods sold, which is then subtracted from the cost of goods available for sale. (p. 275)

Interim statements financial statements for periods of less than one year. (p. 274)

Inventory turnover number of times a company's average inventory is sold during a period; computed by dividing cost of goods sold by average inventory; also called *merchandise turnover.* (p. 277)

Last-in, first-out (LIFO) method to assign cost to inventory that assumes costs for the most recent items purchased are sold first and charged to cost of goods sold. (p. 265)

Lower of cost or market (LCM) method required to report inventory at market when market is lower than cost; market value is the current replacement cost. (p. 273)

Net realizable value expected selling price of an item minus the cost of making the sale. (p. 271)

Retail inventory method method to estimate ending inventory based on the ratio of the amount of goods for sale at cost to the amount of goods for sale at retail. (p. 274)

Specific identification method to assign cost to inventory when the purchase cost of each item in inventory is identified and used to compute cost of inventory. (p. 263)

Weighted average method to assign cost to inventory that assumes the unit costs of items are weighted by the number of units of each in inventory. The total is then divided by the total number of units available for sale to find the average unit cost of inventory and of the units sold. (p. 265)

[The superscript letter ^{A} denotes assignments based on Appendix 7A.]

Questions

1. Describe the flow of costs for the following methods when applied to inventory: (a) FIFO and (b) LIFO.

2. Where is merchandise inventory disclosed in the financial statements?

3. Why are incidental costs sometimes ignored in inventory costing? Under what principle is this permitted?

4. If costs are falling, will the LIFO or the FIFO method of inventory valuation result in the lower cost of goods sold?

5. What effect does the full-disclosure principle have if a company changes from one acceptable accounting method to another?

6. Can a company change its inventory method each accounting period? Explain.

7. Does the accounting principle of consistency preclude any changes from one accounting method to another?

8. If inventory errors are said to correct themselves, why be concerned when such errors are made?

9. Explain the phrase *inventory errors correct themselves*.

10. What is the meaning of *market* as it is used in determining the lower of cost or market for inventory?

11. What guidance does the principle of conservatism provide?

12. When preparing interim financial statements, what two methods can companies utilize to estimate cost of goods sold and ending inventory?

13. What factors contribute to (or cause) inventory shrinkage?

14. Refer to **Nike**'s financial statements in Appendix A. On May 31, 2000, what percent of current assets are represented by inventory? **NIKE**

15. Refer to **Reebok**'s financial statements in Appendix A. Calculate Reebok's cost of goods available for sale for the year ended December 31, 1999.

16. What percent of **Gap**'s current assets are inventory as of January 29, 2000, and January 30, 1999? **GAP**

17.[A] What accounts are used in a periodic inventory system but not in a perpetual inventory system?

QUICK STUDY

QS 7-1
Assigning costs to inventory

Stein Row starts a merchandising business on December 1 and enters into three inventory purchases:

December 7	10 units @	$7
December 14	20 units @	$8
December 21	15 units @	$10

Stein sells 15 units for $25 each on December 15. Eight of the sold units are from the December 7 purchase and seven are from the December 14 purchase. Stein uses a perpetual inventory system. Determine the December 31 costs assigned to ending inventory when costs are assigned based on (a) FIFO, (b) LIFO, (c) weighted average, and (d) specific identification.

QS 7-2
Inventory costs

A car dealer acquires a used car for $14,000, terms FOB shipping point. Additional costs in obtaining and offering the car for sale include $500 for transportation-in, $900 for import duties, $300 for insurance during shipment, $150 for advertising, and $1,250 for sales staff salaries. For computing inventory, what cost is assigned to the used car?

QS 7-3
Inventory ownership

1. At year-end, Damon Co. had shipped $750 of merchandise FOB destination to Wagner Co. Which company should include the $750 of merchandise in transit as part of its inventory at year-end?

2. Damon Company has shipped $600 of goods to Wagner. Wagner has arranged to sell the goods for Damon. Identify the consignor and the consignee. Which company should include any unsold goods as part of its inventory?

QS 7-4
Inventory ownership

Hobby Crafts, a distributor of handmade gifts, operates out of owner Tina Larsen's house. At the end of the current period, Tina reports she has 1,300 units (products) in her basement, 20 of which were damaged by water and cannot be sold. She also has another 350 units in her van, ready to deliver on a customer order, terms FOB destination, and another 80 units out on consignment to a friend who owns a stationery store. How many units should Tina include in her company's end-of-period inventory?

QS 7-5
Cost of goods available for sale

A company has beginning inventory of 10 units at $60 each. Every week for four weeks it purchases an additional 10 units at respective costs of $61, $62, $65, and $70 per unit for weeks one through four. Calculate the cost of goods available for sale and the units available for sale.

QS 7-6
Contrasting inventory costing methods

Identify the inventory costing method best described by each of the following separate statements. Assume a period of increasing costs.

1. The preferred method when each unit of product has unique features that affect cost.   *specfr*

2. Matches recent costs against net sales.   *LIFO*

3. Provides a tax advantage (deferral) to a corporation.   *LIFO LIFO*

4. Understates the market value of inventory on the balance sheet.   *LIFO*

5. Results in a balance sheet inventory amount similar to replacement cost.   *FIFO*

Bixby & Son, antique dealers, purchased the contents of an estate for $38,500. Terms of the purchase were FOB shipping point, and the cost of transporting the goods to Bixby & Son's warehouse was $1,100. Bixby & Son insured the shipment at a cost of $250. Prior to putting the goods up for sale, they cleaned and refurbished the goods at a cost of $800. Determine the cost of the inventory acquired from the estate.

QS 7-7
Inventory costs

A company had the following beginning inventory and purchases for January. On January 26, 355 units were sold. What is the cost of the 160 units that remain in ending inventory, assuming (a) FIFO, (b) LIFO, and (c) weighted average? (Round unit costs to the nearest cent.)

QS 7-8
Inventory costing methods

	Units	Unit Cost
Beginning inventory on January 1	320	$3.00
Purchase on January 9	85	3.20
Purchase on January 25	110	3.35

Tiffany Trading Co. has the following products in its ending inventory:

QS 7-9
Applying LCM to inventories

Product	Quantity	Cost	Market
Mountain bikes	11	$600	$550
Skateboards	13	350	425
Gliders	26	800	700

Compute lower of cost or market for inventory (a) as a whole and (b) applied separately to each product.

Dell Department Store's inventory is destroyed by a fire on September 5, 2002. The following data for year 2002 are available from the accounting records:

QS 7-10
Estimating inventories

Jan. 1 inventory	$190,000
Jan. 1 through Sept. 5 purchases (net)	$352,000
Jan. 1 through Sept. 5 sales (net)	$685,000
Year 2002 estimated gross profit rate	44%

Estimate the cost of the inventory destroyed by the fire.

In taking a physical inventory at the end of year 2002, Summit Company erroneously forgot to count certain units. Explain how this error affects the following: (a) 2002 cost of goods sold, (b) 2002 gross profit, (c) 2002 net income, (d) 2003 net income, (e) the combined two-year income, and (f) income for years after 2003.

QS 7-11ᴬ
Inventory errors

Mercantile Company begins the year with $150,000 of goods in inventory. At year-end, the amount in inventory has increased to $180,000. Cost of goods sold for the year is $1,200,000. Compute Mercantile's inventory turnover and days' sales in inventory.

QS 7-12
Analyzing inventory

Foor Corporation purchased its salable product in the current year as follows:

EXERCISES

Exercise 7-1
Inventory costing methods—perpetual

Jan. 1	Beginning inventory . .	140 units @ $6.00 =	$ 840
Mar. 7	Purchase	300 units @ $5.60 =	1,680
July 28	Purchase	550 units @ $5.00 =	2,750
Oct. 3	Purchase	350 units @ $4.60 =	1,610
Dec. 19	Purchase	50 units @ $4.10 =	205
	Total	1,390 units	$7,085

Foor Corporation resold its product at $15 per unit on the following dates:

Jan. 10	100 units
Mar. 15	225 units
Oct. 5	700 units
Total	1,025 units

Foor uses a perpetual inventory system. Ending inventory consists of 365 units, 315 from the July 28 purchase and 50 from the December 19 purchase. Determine the cost assigned to ending inventory and to cost of goods sold using (a) specific identification, (b) weighted average, (c) FIFO, and (d) LIFO.

Exercise 7-2
Income effects of inventory methods

Use the data in Exercise 7-1 to prepare comparative income statements for Foor Corporation (calendar year-end 2002) similar to those shown in Exhibit 7.8 for the four inventory methods. Assume operating expenses are $1,250. The applicable income tax rate is 30%.

1. Which method yields the highest net income?
2. Does net income using weighted average fall between that using FIFO and LIFO?
3. If costs are rising instead of falling, which method yields the highest net income?

Exercise 7-3
Inventory costing methods (perpetual)—FIFO and LIFO

Ulsh Company purchased its salable product in the current year as follows:

Jan. 1	Beginning inventory	200 units @ $10	= $ 2,000
Mar. 14	Purchase	350 units @ $15 =	5,250
July 30	Purchase	450 units @ $20 =	9,000
Oct. 26	Purchase	700 units @ $25 =	17,500
	Units available	1,700 units	
	Cost of goods available for sale		$33,750

Ulsh Company resold its product at $40 per unit on the following dates:

Jan. 10	100 units
Mar. 15	150 units
Oct. 5	310 units
Total sales	560 units

Ulsh uses a perpetual inventory system. Determine the costs assigned to ending inventory and to cost of goods sold using (a) FIFO and (b) LIFO. Compute the gross margin for each method.

Exercise 7-4
Specific Identification

Refer to the data in Exercise 7-3. Assume that ending inventory is made up of 100 units from the March 14 purchase, 340 units from the July 30 purchase, and all the units of the October 26 purchase. Using the specific identification method, calculate (a) the costs of goods sold and (b) the gross margin.

Exercise 7-5[A]
Alternative cost flow assumptions—periodic

Rasure & Roney Company purchased its salable product in the current year as follows:

Jan. 1	Beginning inventory	100 units @ $2.00	= $ 200
Mar. 7	Purchase	220 units @ $2.25 =	495
July 28	Purchase	540 units @ $2.50 =	1,350
Oct. 3	Purchase	480 units @ $2.80 =	1,344
Dec. 19	Purchase	160 units @ $2.90 =	464
	Total	1,500 units	$3,853

The company uses a periodic inventory system, and its ending inventory consists of 150 units, 50 from each of the last three purchases. Determine the cost assigned to ending inventory and to cost of goods sold using (a) specific identification, (b) weighted average, (c) FIFO, and (d) LIFO. Which method yields the highest net income?

Erikson Gifts purchased its salable product in the current year as follows:

Exercise 7-6^A
Alternative cost flow
assumptions—periodic

Jan. 1	Beginning inventory	140 units @ $3.00 = $	420
Mar. 7	Purchase	300 units @ $2.80 =	840
July 28	Purchase	400 units @ $2.50 =	1,000
Oct. 3	Purchase	550 units @ $2.30 =	1,265
Dec. 19	Purchase	125 units @ $2.00 =	250
	Total	1,515 units	$3,775

The company uses a periodic inventory system, and its ending inventory consists of 150 units, 50 from each of the last three purchases. Determine the cost assigned to ending inventory and to cost of goods sold using (a) specific identification, (b) weighted average, (c) FIFO, and (d) LIFO. Which method yields the lowest net income?

Legacy Company's ending inventory includes the following items:

Exercise 7-7
Lower of cost or market

Product	Units	Unit Cost	Market Cost per Unit
Helmets	24	$50	$54
Sticks	17	78	72
Skates	38	95	91
Pads	42	36	36

Compute the lower of cost or market for inventory (a) as a whole and (b) applied separately to each product.

Paul Harrison Company had $850,000 of sales in each of three consecutive years 2002–2004, and it purchased merchandise costing $500,000 in each of the years. It also maintained a $250,000 inventory from the beginning to the end of the three-year period. In accounting for inventory, it made an error at the end of year 2002 that caused its year-end 2002 inventory to appear on its statements as $230,000 rather than the correct $250,000.

Exercise 7-8
Analysis of inventory errors

A2

Required

1. Determine the correct amount of the company's gross profit in each of the years 2002–2004.

2. Prepare comparative income statements as in Exhibit 7.11 to show the effect of this error on the company's cost of goods sold and gross profit in years 2002–2004.

On January 1, The Fun Store had $550,000 of inventory at cost. In the first quarter of the year, it purchased $1,690,000 of merchandise, returned $22,200, and paid freight charges of $27,600 on purchased merchandise, terms FOB shipping point. The store's gross profit averages 28%. The store had $2,000,000 of retail sales (net) in the first quarter of the year. Use the gross profit method to estimate its cost of inventory at the end of the first quarter.

Exercise 7-9
Estimating ending inventory—
gross profit method

Exercise 7-10
Estimating ending inventory—retail method

P3

In 2002, Hayden Company had retail sales (net) of $140,000. The following additional information is available from its records at the end of 2002:

	At Cost	At Retail
Beginning inventory	$32,900	$65,200
Cost of goods purchased	58,700	96,600

Use the retail inventory method to estimate Hayden's 2002 ending inventory at cost. (Round the cost to retail ratio to three digits.)

Exercise 7-11
Computing physical inventory at cost—the retail method

P3

Hayden Company of Exercise 7-10 also took a physical inventory using the marked retail prices at the end of 2002. The total of this physical inventory at marked retail prices is $28,200. Compute (a) the amount of this inventory at cost and (b) inventory shrinkage at retail and at cost.

Exercise 7-12
Inventory turnover and days' sales in inventory

A3

Use the following information for Costner Co. to compute inventory turnover for 2003 and 2002 and days' sales in inventory at December 31, 2003 and 2002. (Round answers to one decimal place.)

	2003	2002	2001
Cost of goods sold	$643,825	$426,650	$391,300
Inventory (Dec. 31)	97,400	87,750	92,500

Comment on Costner's efficiency in using its assets to increase sales from 2002 to 2003.

PROBLEM SET A

Problem 7-1A
Alternative cost flows—perpetual

P1

Helton Company's inventory transactions in the fiscal year ended December 31, 2002, follow:

Jan. 1	Beginning inventory	600 units @ $45/unit
Feb. 10	Purchase	350 units @ $42/unit
Mar. 13	Purchase	200 units @ $29/unit
Aug. 21	Purchase	150 units @ $50/unit
Sept. 5	Purchase	545 units @ $48/unit

Helton Company uses a perpetual inventory system. Its inventory had a selling price of $75 per unit, and it entered into the following sales transactions:

Mar. 15	Sales	600 units @ $75/unit
Sept. 10	Sales	100 units @ $75/unit

Required

Preparation Component
1. Compute both cost of goods available for sale and the number of units available for sale.
2. Compute the number of units remaining in ending inventory.
3. Compute the cost assigned to ending inventory using (a) FIFO, (b) LIFO, (c) specific identification (*note:* 600 units from beginning inventory and 100 units from the March 13 purchase are sold), and (d) weighted average.
4. Compute the gross profit earned by the company for each of the costing methods in part *3.*

Analysis Component
5. If Helton Company's manager earns a bonus based on a percent of gross profit, which method of inventory costing will the manager likely prefer?

Check Ending inventory (FIFO), $49,960

Stokeley Company's prior financial statements report the following:

Key Figures		For Year Ended December 31		
		2000	2001	2002
(a)	Cost of goods sold	$ 815,000	$ 957,000	$ 780,000
(b)	Net income	230,000	285,000	241,000
(c)	Total current assets	1,255,000	1,365,000	1,200,000
(d)	Equity	1,387,000	1,530,000	1,242,000

Stokeley recently discovered that in making physical counts of inventory, it had made the following errors: Inventory on December 31, 2000, is understated by $56,000, and inventory on December 31, 2001, is overstated by $20,000.

Required

Preparation Component

1. For each key financial statement figure—(a), (b), (c), and (d)—prepare a schedule similar to the following to show the adjustments necessary to correct the reported amounts.

Figure: _____	2000	2001	2002
Reported amount			
Adjustments: 12/31/2000 error			
12/31/2001 error			
Corrected amount			

Analysis Component

2. What is the error in total net income for the combined three-year period resulting from the inventory errors? Explain.

3. Explain why the understatement of inventory by $56,000 at the end of 2000 results in an understatement of equity by the same amount in that year.

A physical inventory of Rap Unlimited taken at December 31 reveals the following:

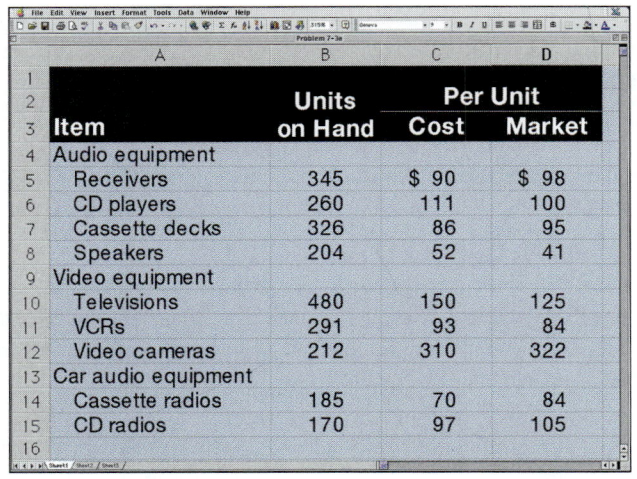

Item	Units on Hand	Per Unit Cost	Per Unit Market
Audio equipment			
Receivers	345	$ 90	$ 98
CD players	260	111	100
Cassette decks	326	86	95
Speakers	204	52	41
Video equipment			
Televisions	480	150	125
VCRs	291	93	84
Video cameras	212	310	322
Car audio equipment			
Cassette radios	185	70	84
CD radios	170	97	105

Required

Calculate the lower of cost or market for the inventory (a) as a whole, (b) by major category, and (c) applied separately to each item.

Problem 7-2A
Analysis of inventory errors

Check   Corrected net income (2002), $261,000

Problem 7-3A
Lower of cost or market

P2

Check   (b) $280,702

Problem 7-4A
Retail inventory method

Check Inventory shortage
at cost, $37,100

The records of Livingston Company provide the following information for the year ended December 31:

	At Cost	At Retail
January 1 beginning inventory	$ 472,450	$ 928,950
Cost of goods purchased	3,376,050	6,381,482
Sales		5,595,800
Sales returns		42,800

Required

1. Use the retail inventory method to estimate the company's year-end inventory. (Round the cost to retail ratio to three digits.)

2. A year-end physical inventory at marked selling prices yields a total inventory of $1,686,900. Prepare a schedule showing the store's loss from shrinkage at cost and at retail.

Problem 7-5A
Gross profit method

Check Estimated ending
inventory, $449,797

Geiger Company wants to prepare interim financial statements for the first quarter. The company wishes to avoid making a physical count of inventory. Geiger's gross profit rate averages 34%. The following information for the first quarter is available from its records:

January 1 beginning inventory	$ 302,580
Cost of goods purchased	941,040
Sales	1,211,160
Sales returns	8,398

Required

Use the gross profit method to estimate the company's first quarter ending inventory.

Problem 7-6A[A]
Alternative cost flows—
periodic

Check Cost of goods
sold (FIFO): $2,027,000

Vandenburg Company began year 2002 with 25,000 units of product in its January 1 inventory costing $15 each. It made successive purchases of its product in year 2002 as follows:

Mar. 7	30,000 units @ $18 each
May 25	32,000 units @ $22 each
Aug. 1	22,000 units @ $24 each
Nov. 10	35,000 units @ $27 each

The company uses a periodic inventory system. On December 31, 2002, a physical count reveals that 40,000 units of its product remain in inventory.

Required

1. Compute the number and total cost of the units available for sale in year 2002.

2. Compute the amounts assigned to the 2002 ending inventory and cost of goods sold using (a) FIFO, (b) LIFO, and (c) weighted average.

Problem 7-7A[A]
Income comparisons and
cost flows—periodic

New Navy Corp. sold 6,500 units of its product at $50 per unit in year 2002 and incurred operating expenses of $5 per unit in selling the units. It began the year with 700 units in inventory and made successive purchases of its product as follows:

Jan. 1	Beginning inventory	700 units @ $18 per unit
Feb. 20	Purchase	1,600 units @ $19 per unit
May 16	Purchase	800 units @ $20 per unit
Oct. 3	Purchase	500 units @ $21 per unit
Dec. 11	Purchase	3,500 units @ $22 per unit
	Total	7,100 units

Required

Preparation Component

1. Prepare comparative income statements for the company similar to Exhibit 7.8 for the three different inventory costing methods of FIFO, LIFO, and weighted average. Include a detailed cost of goods sold section as part of each statement. The company uses a periodic inventory system, and its income tax rate is 28%.

Check   Net income (LIFO), $112,896

Analysis Component

2. How would the financial results from using the three alternative inventory costing methods change if New Navy had been experiencing declining costs in its purchases of inventory?

3. What advantages and disadvantages are offered by using (a) LIFO and (b) FIFO? Assume the continuing trend of increasing costs.

Mercado Company's inventory transactions in the fiscal year ended December 31, 2002, follow:

Jan. 1	Beginning inventory	700 units @ $55/unit
Jan. 10	Purchase	550 units @ $56/unit
Feb. 13	Purchase	220 units @ $57/unit
July 21	Purchase	270 units @ $58/unit
Aug. 5	Purchase	445 units @ $59/unit

Mercado Company uses a perpetual inventory system. Its inventory had a selling price of $100 per unit, and it entered into the following sales transactions:

Feb. 15	Sales	530 units @ $100/unit
Aug. 10	Sales	235 units @ $100/unit

Required

Preparation Component

1. Compute both cost of goods available for sale and the number of units available for sale.

2. Compute the number of units remaining in ending inventory.

3. Compute the cost assigned to ending inventory using (a) FIFO, (b) LIFO, (c) specific identification (*note:* 700 units from beginning inventory and 65 units from the February 13 purchase are sold), and (d) weighted average.

4. Compute the gross profit earned by the company for each of the costing methods in part *3*.

Check   Ending inventory (FIFO), $81,615

Analysis Component

5. If Mercado Company's manager earns a bonus based on a percent of gross profit, which method of inventory costing will the manager likely prefer?

Secado Company's prior financial statements report the following:

	Year Ended December 31		
Key Figures	2000	2001	2002
(a) Cost of goods sold	$207,200	$213,800	$197,060
(b) Net income	175,800	212,270	184,810
(c) Total current assets . . .	276,000	277,500	272,950
(d) Equity	314,000	315,000	346,000

Secado recently discovered that in making physical counts of inventory, it had made the following errors: Inventory on December 31, 2000, is overstated by $18,000, and inventory on December 31, 2001, is understated by $26,000.

PROBLEM SET B

Problem 7-1B
Alternative cost flows—perpetual

Problem 7-2B
Analysis of inventory errors

Required

Preparation Component

1. For each key financial statement figure—(a), (b), (c), and (d)—prepare a schedule similar to the following to show the adjustments necessary to correct the reported amounts.

Figure _____	2000	2001	2002
Reported amount			
Adjustments: 12/31/2000 error			
12/31/2001 error			
Corrected amount			

Analysis Component

2. What is the error in total net income for the combined three-year period resulting from the inventory errors? Explain.

3. Explain why the overstatement of inventory by $18,000 at the end of 2000 results in an overstatement of equity by the same amount in that year.

Problem 7-3B
Lower of cost or market

A physical inventory of Office Outlet taken at December 31 reveals the following:

	A	B	C	D
		Units	**Per Unit**	
1		on Hand	Cost	Market
2	**Item**			
3	Office furniture:			
4	Desks	536	$261	$305
5	Credenzas	395	227	256
6	Chairs	687	49	43
7	Bookshelves	421	93	82
8	Filing cabinets:			
9	Two-drawer	114	81	70
10	Four-drawer	298	135	122
11	Lateral	75	104	118
12	Office equipment:			
13	Fax machines	370	168	200
14	Copiers	475	317	288
15	Telephones	302	125	117
16				

Required

Calculate the lower of cost or market for the inventory (a) as a whole, (b) by major category, and (c) applied separately to each item.

Problem 7-4B
Retail inventory method

The records of R. U. MacBeth Co. provide the following information for the year ended December 31:

	At Cost	At Retail
January 1 beginning inventory	$ 91,770	$ 115,610
Cost of goods purchased	502,250	761,830
Sales		782,300
Sales returns		3,460

Required

1. Use the retail inventory method to estimate the company's year-end inventory. (Round the cost to retail ratio to three digits.)

2. A year-end physical inventory at marked selling prices yields a total inventory of $80,450. Prepare a schedule showing the store's loss from shrinkage at cost and at retail.

Problem 7-5B
Gross profit method

Eck Equipment Co. wants to prepare interim financial statements for the first quarter. The company wishes to avoid making a physical count of inventory. Eck's gross profit rate averages 35%. The following information for the first quarter is available from its records:

January 1 beginning inventory	$ 802,880
Cost of goods purchased	2,209,630
Sales	3,760,250
Sales returns	79,300

Required

Use the gross profit method to estimate the company's first quarter ending inventory.

Blue View Co. began year 2002 with 6,500 units of product in its January 1 inventory costing $35 each. It made successive purchases of its product in year 2002 as follows:

Jan. 4	11,500 units @ $33 each
May 18	13,400 units @ $32 each
July 9	11,000 units @ $29 each
Nov. 21	16,500 units @ $26 each

The company uses a periodic inventory system. On December 31, 2002, a physical count reveals that 18,500 units of its product remain in inventory.

Required

1. Compute the number and total cost of the units available for sale in year 2002.
2. Compute the amounts assigned to the 2002 ending inventory and cost of goods sold using (a) FIFO, (b) LIFO, and (c) weighted average.

Problem 7-6B[A]

Alternative cost flows—periodic

McKray Corp. sold 2,000 units of its product at $108 per unit in year 2002 and incurred operating expenses of $14 per unit in selling the units. It began the year with 840 units in inventory and made successive purchases of its product as follows:

Jan. 1	Beginning inventory	840 units @ $58 per unit
April 2	Purchase	600 units @ $59 per unit
June 14	Purchase	500 units @ $61 per unit
Aug. 29	Purchase	700 units @ $64 per unit
Nov. 18	Purchase	900 units @ $65 per unit
	Total	3,540 units

Problem 7-7B[A]

Income comparisons and cost flows—periodic

Required

Preparation Component

1. Prepare comparative income statements similar to Exhibit 7.8 for the three different inventory costing methods of FIFO, LIFO, and weighted average. Include a detailed cost of goods sold section as part of each statement. The company uses a periodic inventory system, and its income tax rate is 30%.

Analysis Component

2. How would the financial results from using the three alternative inventory costing methods change if McKray had been experiencing decreasing prices in its purchases of inventory?
3. What advantages and disadvantages are offered by using (a) LIFO and (b) FIFO? Assume the continuing trend of increasing costs.

Beyond the Numbers

BTN 7-1   Refer to the financial statements of **Nike** in Appendix A to answer the following:

Required

1. What amount of inventories did Nike hold as a current asset on May 31, 2000? On May 31, 1999?
2. Inventories represent what percent of total assets on May 31, 2000? On May 31, 1999?
3. Comment on the relative size of Nike's inventories compared to its other types of assets.
4. What accounting method did Nike use to compute inventory amounts on its balance sheet?
5. Calculate inventory turnover for fiscal year ended May 31, 2000, and days' sales in inventory as of May 31, 2000. (*Note:* Cost of sales is cost of goods sold.)

Reporting in Action

NIKE

Swoosh Ahead

6. Access Nike's annual report for fiscal years ended after May 31, 2000, at its Web site [**www.nike.com**] or the SEC's EDGAR database [**www.sec.gov**]. Answer questions *1* through *5* using the current Nike information.

Comparative Analysis

A3

NIKE **Reebok**

BTN 7-2   Key comparative figures ($ millions) for both **Nike** and **Reebok** follow:

	Nike			Reebok		
Key Figures	**Current**	**One Year Prior**	**Two Years Prior**	**Current**	**One Year Prior**	**Two Years Prior**
Inventory	$1,446.0	$1,170.6	$1,396.6	$ 414.6	$ 535.1	$ 563.7
Cost of sales . .	5,403.8	5,493.5	6,065.5	1,783.9	2,037.5	2,294.0

Required

1. Calculate inventory turnover for both companies for the most recent two years shown.
2. Calculate days' sales in inventory for both companies for the three years shown.
3. Comment on your findings from parts (1) and (2).

Ethics Challenge

A1

BTN 7-3   U-Golf Corp. is a retail sports store carrying golf apparel and equipment. The store is at the end of its second year of operation and is struggling. Its cost of inventory has increased in the past two years. In the first year of operations, the store assigned inventory costs using LIFO. A loan agreement the store has with its bank, its prime source of financing, requires the store to maintain a certain profit margin and current ratio. The store's owner is currently looking over U-Golf's preliminary annual financial statements. The numbers are not favorable. The only way the store can meet the required financial ratios agreed on with the bank is to change from LIFO to FIFO. The store originally decided on LIFO because of its tax advantages. The owner recalculates ending inventory using FIFO and submits the statements to the loan officer at the bank for the required bank review. The owner thankfully reflects on the available latitude in choosing the inventory costing method.

Required

1. How does U-Golf's use of FIFO improve its net profit margin and current ratio?
2. Is the action by U-Golf's owner ethical? Explain.

Communicating in Practice

A1

BTN 7-4   You are a financial adviser with a client in the wholesale produce business that just completed its first year of operations. Due to weather conditions, the cost of acquiring produce to resell escalated during the later part of this period. Your client, Juana Peabody, mentions that because the business sells perishable goods, she has striven to maintain a FIFO flow of goods. Although sales are good, the increasing cost of inventory has put the business in a tight cash position. Juana has expressed concern regarding the ability of the business to meet income tax obligations.

Required

Point: If an e-mail response is preferred, students need an e-mail address.

Prepare a memorandum or send an e-mail that identifies, explains, and justifies the inventory method you recommend your client Ms. Peabody, adopt. If the response is to be made via e-mail, you can assume that your instructor is your client.

Taking It to the Net

A3

BTN 7-5   Access the March 30, 2000, filing of the 10-K report for **Oakley, Inc.** (Ticker OO), from **www.edgar-online.com**.

Required

1. What product does Oakley sell that is especially popular with college students?
2. What inventory method does Oakley use? (*Hint:* See the notes to its financial statements.)
3. Compute Oakley's gross margin and gross margin ratio for the most current year's data.
4. Compute Oakley's inventory turnover and days' sales in inventory for the most current year's data.

BTN 7-6   Each team member has the responsibility to become an expert on an inventory method. This expertise will be used to facilitate teammates' understanding of the concepts relevant to that method.

1. Each learning team member should select an area for expertise by choosing one of the following inventory methods: specific identification, LIFO, FIFO, or weighted average.

2. Form expert teams made up of students who have selected the same area of expertise. The instructor will identify where each expert team will meet.

3. Using the following data, each expert team must collaborate to develop a presentation that illustrates the relevant concepts and procedures for its inventory method. Each team member must write the presentation in a format that can be shown to the learning team.

Teamwork in Action

Point: Step 1 allows four choices or areas for expertise. Larger teams will have some duplication of choice, but the specific identification method should not be duplicated. Expert teams can use the book and consult with instructor.

Data

Sunmann Corp. uses a perpetual inventory system. It had the following beginning inventory and current year purchases of its product:

Jan.	1	Beginning inventory	50 units @ $10 = $ 500
Jan.	14	Purchase	150 units @ $12 = 1,800
Apr.	30	Purchase	200 units @ $15 = 3,000
Sept.	26	Purchase	300 units @ $20 = 6,000

Sunmann Corp. transacted sales on the following dates at $35 per unit:

Jan. 10	30 units	(specific cost $10)
Feb. 15	100 units	(specific cost $12)
Oct. 5	350 units	(specific cost: 100 @ $15 and 250 @ $20)

Concepts and Procedures to Illustrate in Expert Presentation

a. Identify and compute the costs to assign to the units sold.

b. Identify and compute the costs to assign to the units in ending inventory.

c. How likely is it that this inventory costing method will reflect the actual physical flow of goods? How relevant is that factor in determining whether this is an acceptable method to use?

d. What is the impact of this method versus others in determining net income and income taxes?

e. How closely does ending inventory reflect replacement costs for the units?

4. Re-form learning teams. In rotation, each expert is to present to the team the presentation developed in part (3). Experts are to encourage and respond to questions.

BTN 7-7   Read the article "Yes, Steve, You Fixed It. Congrats! Now What's Act Two?" from the July 31, 2000, issue of *Business Week*.

Business Week Activity

Required

1. What percent of the U.S. home computer market does Apple have? What is Apple's overall worldwide market share? Has Apple's worldwide market share grown or declined from 1993?

2. How many days' worth of parts are in its computer parts inventory? How were efficiencies in the parts' inventory achieved?

3. Do critics think that the days' parts in inventory figure is reliable? Explain.

BTN 7-8   Brad Eldridge is an entrepreneur and owner of Home Security, which designs, sells, and installs home security equipment. The company consistently maintains an inventory level of $50,000, meaning that its average and ending inventory levels are the same. Its cost of sales is $190,000. To cut costs, Brad proposes to slash inventory to a constant level of $25,000 with no impact on cost of sales.

Entrepreneurial Decision

Required

1. Compute the company's inventory turnover and its days' sales in inventory under (a) current conditions and (b) proposed conditions.

2. Evaluate and comment on the merits of Brad's proposal given your analysis in part (1). Identify any concerns you would express about the proposal.

8

Accounting Information Systems

A Look Back

Chapters 6 and 7 focused on merchandising activities and accounting for inventory. We explained both the perpetual and periodic inventory systems, accounting for inventory transactions, and methods for assigning costs to inventory.

A Look at This Chapter

This chapter emphasizes accounting information systems. We describe fundamental system principles, the system's components, use of special journals and subsidiary ledgers, and technology-based systems. We also discuss segment reporting and how to analyze these data.

A Look Ahead

Chapter 9 focuses on internal controls and accounting for cash and cash equivalents. We explain good internal control procedures and their importance for accounting.

"Untapped market—online accounting for small business."—Evan Goldberg.

Learning Objectives

Conceptual

C1 Identify fundamental principles of accounting information systems.

C2 Identify components of accounting information systems.

C3 Explain the goals and uses of special journals.

C4 Describe the use of controlling accounts and subsidiary ledgers.

C5 Explain how technology-based information systems impact accounting.

Analytical

A1 Analyze a company's performance and financial condition by business segments.

Procedural

P1 Journalize and post transactions using special journals.

P2 Prepare and prove the accuracy of subsidiary ledgers.

Do It on the Net

e SAN MATEO, CA—It began with Evan Goldberg's frustration in accounting for his fledgling business. Goldberg was looking for an integrated accounting package that would allow its transaction system to talk to inventory, inventory to talk to payables and receivables, and so on. He also was tired of upgrades and backups. Goldberg's response was to launch **NetLedger** [**NetLedger.com**], a company devoted to an accounting package run entirely on the Web.

NetLedger "eliminates a lot of the hassles" of existing accounting packages for small businesses, says Goldberg. It lets users manage transactions such as receivables, payables, cash disbursements, and cash receipts. It also provides General Ledger capabilities, online sales and order processing, and immediate purchase orders, invoices, and checks. Audit trails exist to track transactions, and security is a top priority. Goldberg says the site features an encryption system more secure than an armored truck. He won't even disclose the location of its data center where customers' electronic "books" are kept.

Goldberg says NetLedger targets companies with fewer than 100 employees. It is a David trying to take on the accounting software giants PeachTree and QuickBooks. Goldberg is hoping NetLedger's price advantage will be the biggest turn-on for customers—less than $5 per month, including a free trial period. The site even lets you convert data directly from QuickBooks.

So far, the 33-year-old Goldberg couldn't be happier. NetLedger is receiving rave reviews, and Larry Ellison, chairman of Oracle, is helping fund Goldberg's start-up. Says Ellison, "NetLedger is creating a new generation of software—one that is never a product but only a service." Goldberg agrees. He adds, "Internet technology has created a new and currently untapped market—online accounting for small business." [Sources: *eWEEK*, August 9, 1999; *NetLedger Web Site*, May 2001; *Business Week*, October 19, 1999]

Accounting for business activities requires collecting and processing information. With increases in the number and complexity of business activities, demands placed on accounting information systems increase. Accounting information systems must meet this challenge in an efficient and effective manner. In this chapter, we learn about fundamental principles guiding information systems, and we study components making up these systems. We also explain procedures that use special journals and subsidiary ledgers to make accounting information systems more efficient. An understanding of the details of accounting reports makes us better decision makers when using financial information, and it improves our ability to analyze and interpret financial statements.

Fundamental System Principles

C1 Identify fundamental principles of accounting information systems.

Accounting information systems collect and process data from transactions and events, organize them in useful forms, and communicate results to decision makers. These systems are crucial to effective decision making for both internal and external users of information. With the increasing complexity of business and the growing need for information, accounting information systems are more important than ever.

Today all decision makers need to have a basic knowledge of how accounting information systems work. This knowledge gives decision makers a competitive edge as they gain a better understanding of information constraints, measurement limitations, and potential applications. It allows them to make more informed decisions and to better balance the risks and returns of different strategies. This section explains five basic principles of accounting information systems as shown in Exhibit 8.1.

Exhibit 8.1

System Principles

Control Principle

Managers need to control and monitor business activities. To this end, the **control principle** requires an accounting information system to have internal controls. *Internal controls* are methods and procedures allowing managers to control and monitor business activities. They include policies to direct operations toward common goals, procedures to ensure reliable financial reports, safeguards to protect company assets, and methods to achieve compliance with laws and regulations.

Relevance Principle

Decision makers need relevant information to make informed decisions. The **relevance principle** requires that an accounting information system report useful, understandable, timely, and pertinent information for effective decision making. This means that an information system is designed to capture data that make a difference in decisions. To ensure this, all decision makers must be considered when identifying relevant information for disclosure.

Compatibility Principle

Accounting information systems must be consistent with the aims of a company. The **compatibility principle** requires that an accounting information system conform with a company's activities, personnel, and structure. It also must adapt to a company's unique characteristics. The system must not be intrusive but must work in harmony with and be driven by company goals. Most start-up entrepreneurs require only a simple information system. **Nike**, on the other hand, demands both a merchandising and a manufacturing information system able to assemble data from its global operations.

Flexibility Principle

Accounting information systems must be able to adjust to changes. The **flexibility principle** requires that an accounting information system be able to adapt to changes in the company, business environment, and needs of decisions makers. Technological advances, competitive pressures, consumer tastes, regulations, and company activities constantly change. A system must be designed to adapt to these changes.

Cost-Benefit Principle

Accounting information systems must balance costs and benefits. The **cost-benefit principle** requires the benefits from an activity in an accounting information system to outweigh the costs of that activity. The costs and benefits of an activity such as reporting certain information impact the decisions of both external and internal users. Decisions regarding other systems principles (control, relevance, compatibility, and flexibility) are also affected by the cost-benefit principle.

Point: A hacker recently stole 300,000 credit card numbers from online music retailer **CDUniverse.**

Accounting information systems consist of people, records, methods, and equipment. The systems are designed to capture information about a company's transactions and to provide output including financial, managerial, and tax reports. All accounting information systems have these same goals, and thus have some basic components. These components apply whether or not a system is heavily computerized, yet the components of computerized systems usually provide more accuracy, speed, efficiency, and convenience.

The five basic components of an accounting information system are source documents, input devices, information processors, information storage, and output devices. Exhibit 8.2 shows these components as a series of steps, yet we know that much two-way communication occurs between many of these components. We briefly describe each of these key components in this section.

Components of Accounting Systems

C2 Identify components of accounting information systems.

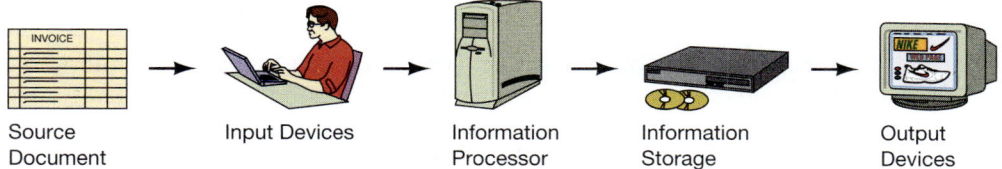

| Source Document | Input Devices | Information Processor | Information Storage | Output Devices |

Exhibit 8.2

Accounting System Components

Source Documents

We described source documents in Chapter 3 and explained their importance for both business transactions and information collection. Source documents provide the basic information processed by an accounting system. Most of us are familiar with source documents such as bank statements and checks received from others. Other examples of source documents include invoices from suppliers, billings to customers, and employee earnings records.

Source documents can be paper based, although they increasingly are taking the form of electronic files and Web communications. A growing number of companies are sending invoices directly from their systems to their customers' and suppliers' systems. The Web is playing a major role in this transformation from paper-based to *paperless* systems.

Accurate source documents are crucial to accounting information systems. Input of faulty or incomplete information seriously impairs the reliability and relevance of the information system. We commonly refer to this as "garbage in, garbage out." Information systems are set up with special attention on control procedures to limit the possibility of entering faulty data in the system.

Input Devices

Input devices capture information from source documents and enable its transfer to the system's information processing component. These

---

Did You Know?

Scan Links Scanners are increasingly embedded in cell phones and other handheld devices to gain access to Web sites equipped with bar code readers. The phones scan the bar codes in, say, magazine or newspaper ads and give the user access to sites that market the products or services.

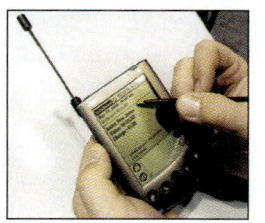

Point: Understanding a manual accounting system is useful in understanding an electronic system.

devices often involve converting data on source documents from written or electronic form to a form usable for the system. Journal entries, both electronic and paper based, are a type of input device. Keyboards, scanners, and modems are some of the most common input devices in practice today. For example, bar code readers capture code numbers and transfer them to the organization's computer for processing. Moreover, a scanner can capture writing samples and other input directly from source documents.

Accounting information systems encourage accuracy by using consistent methods for inputting data. Controls are also used to ensure that only authorized individuals input data to the system. Controls increase the system's reliability and allow false information to be traced back to its source.

Information Processor

An **information processor** is a system that interprets, transforms, and summarizes information for use in analysis and reporting. An important part of an information processor in accounting systems is professional judgment. Accounting principles are never so structured that they limit the need for professional judgment. Other parts of an information processor include journals, ledgers, working papers, and posting procedures. Each assists in transforming raw data to useful information.

Increasingly, computer technology is assisting manual information processors. This assistance is freeing accounting professionals to take on increased analysis, interpretive, and managerial roles. This assistance to information processors includes both computing hardware and software. Web-based application service providers (ASPs) offer another type of information processor.

Information Storage

Point: A financial accounting database can be designed to support a wide range of internal reports for management.

Information storage is the accounting system component that keeps data in a form accessible to information processors. After being input and processed, data are stored for use in future analyses and reports. The database must be accessible to preparers of periodic financial reports. Auditors rely on this database when they audit financial statements and a company's controls. Companies also maintain files of source documents. Technology increasingly assists with information storage. Older systems consisted almost exclusively of paper documents, but most modern systems depend on electronic storage devices. Advances in information storage enable accounting systems to store more detailed data than ever before. This means managers have more data to access and work with in planning and controlling business activities. Information storage can be online, meaning data can be accessed whenever, and from wherever, it is needed. Off-line storage means access often requires assistance and authorization. Information storage is increasingly augmented by Web sources such as SEC databases, benchmarking services, FASB standards, and financial and product markets.

Did You Know?

Geek Chic   Cyberfashion pioneers at **MIT's Media Laboratory** are creating geek chic, a kind of wearable computer. Cyberfashion draws on digital cellular phones, lithium batteries, and miniature monitors. Special thread is woven into clothing to carry low-voltage signals from one part of the system to another, and fabric keyboards are sewn into blue jeans. These creations give new meaning to the term *software*.

Did You Know?

Virtual Output   **Microvision** is developing a screenless computer display. The device, called *virtual retinal display* (VRD), scans rows of pixels directly onto the user's retina by means of a laser, creating images that simulate the experience of viewing a full-size screen. VRDs can also simulate three-dimensional virtual worlds.

Output Devices

Output devices are the means to take information out of an accounting system and make it available to users. Common output devices are printers, monitors, and Web communications. Output devices provide users a variety of items including graphics, analysis reports, bills to customers, checks to suppliers, employee paychecks, financial statements, and internal reports. When requests for output occur, an information processor takes the needed data from a database and prepares the necessary report, which is then sent to an output device.

Information can be output in many forms. For example, one type of output is an electronic fund transfer (EFT) of payroll from the company's bank account to its employees' bank accounts. One output device to accomplish this is an interface that allows a company's accounting system to send payroll data directly to the bank's accounting system. Another EFT output device involves a company recording its payroll data on tape or CD and forwarding it to the bank. The bank then uses this tape or disk to transfer wages earned to employees' accounts.

You Make the Call—Ethics

Accountant Your client requests advice in purchasing new software for its accounting system. You have been offered a 10% commission by a software company for each purchase of its system by one of your clients. Does this commission arrangement affect your evaluation of software? Do you tell your client about the commission arrangement?

Answer—p. 330

Quick Check

1. Identify the five primary components of an accounting information system.
2. What is the aim of the information processor component of an accounting system?
3. How are data in the information storage component of an accounting system used?

Answers—p. 331

Special Journals in Accounting

C3 Explain the goals and uses of special journals.

This section describes the underlying records of accounting information systems. Designed correctly, these records support efficiency in processing transactions and events. They are part of all systems in various forms and are increasingly electronically based. But even in technologically advanced systems, a basic understanding of the records we describe in this section aids in using, interpreting, and applying accounting information. It also improves our knowledge of computer-based systems. We must remember that all accounting systems have common purposes and internal workings whether or not they depend on technology.

This section focuses on special journals and subsidiary ledgers that are an important part of accounting systems. We describe how special journals are used to capture transactions, and we explain how subsidiary ledgers are set up to capture details of accounts. This section uses a *perpetual* inventory system, and the special journals are set up using this system. Appendix 8A describes the slight change in special journals required for a *periodic* system. We also include a note at the bottom of each of the special journals under the perpetual system explaining the minor change required if a company uses a periodic system.

Basics of Special Journals

A general journal is an all-purpose journal in which we can record any transaction. Use of a general journal requires that each debit and each credit entered must be individually posted to its respective ledger account. This requires time and effort in posting individual debits and credits, especially for less technologically advanced systems. The costs of posting accounts can be reduced by organizing transactions into common groups through a special journal. A **special journal** is used to record and post transactions of similar type. Most transactions of a merchandiser, for instance, can be categorized as shown in Exhibit 8.3:

Point: Companies can use as many special journals as necessary given their unique business activities.

Sales Journal	Cash Receipts Journal	Purchases Journal	Cash Disbursement Journal	General Journal
For recording credit sales	For recording cash receipts	For recording credit purchases	For recording cash payments	For transactions not in special journals

Exhibit 8.3

Using Special Journals with a General Journal

sales on credit, purchases on credit, cash receipts, and cash disbursements. This section assumes the use of these four special journals along with the general journal.

The general journal continues to be used for transactions not covered by special journals and for adjusting, closing, and correcting entries. We show in the following discussion that special journals are efficient tools in helping journalize and post transactions. This is done, for instance, by accumulating debits and credits of similar transactions, which allows us to post most amounts as column *totals* rather than as individual amounts. The advantage of this system increases as the number of transactions increases. Special journals also allow an efficient division of labor, which can be an effective control procedure.

Subsidiary Ledgers

C4 Describe the use of controlling accounts and subsidiary ledgers.

Concept 8-1

To understand the details of special journals, it is necessary to understand the workings of a **subsidiary ledger,** which is a list of individual accounts with a common characteristic. A subsidiary ledger supports the general ledger with detailed information on specific accounts, which removes unnecessary details from the general ledger. Accounting information systems often include several subsidiary ledgers. Two of the most important involve the amounts due from customers, called *accounts receivable,* and the amounts owed to creditors, called *accounts payable.* These two subsidiary ledgers are known by these titles:

- *Accounts receivable ledger*—stores transaction data of individual customers.
- *Accounts payable ledger*—stores transaction data of individual suppliers.

Individual accounts in subsidiary ledgers are often arranged alphabetically. We describe accounts receivable and accounts payable ledgers in this section. Our discussion of special journals in the next section uses both of these ledgers.

Accounts Receivable Ledger

When we recorded credit sales in prior chapters, we debited (increased) Accounts Receivable. When a company has more than one credit customer, the accounts receivable records must show how much *each* customer purchased, paid, and has yet to pay. This information is collected by keeping a separate account receivable for each credit customer. A separate account for each customer *could* be kept in the general ledger containing the other financial statement accounts, but this is uncommon. Instead, the general ledger usually has a single Accounts Receivable account and a *subsidiary ledger* is set up to keep a separate account for each customer. This subsidiary ledger is called the **accounts receivable ledger** (also called *accounts receivable subsidiary ledger* or *customers ledger*). Like a general ledger, a subsidiary ledger can exist in electronic or paper form. Customer accounts in a subsidiary ledger are kept separate from the Accounts Receivable account in the general ledger.

Exhibit 8.4 shows the relation between the Accounts Receivable account and its related accounts in the subsidiary ledger. After all items are posted, the balance in the Accounts Receivable account must equal the sum of balances in the customers' accounts. The Accounts Receivable account is said to control the accounts receivable ledger and is called a **controlling account.** Since the accounts receivable ledger is a supplementary record controlled by an account in the general ledger, it is called a *subsidiary ledger.*

Accounts Payable Ledger

There are other controlling accounts and subsidiary ledgers. We know, for example, that many companies buy on credit from several suppliers. This means companies must keep a separate account for each supplier by keeping an Accounts Payable controlling account in the general ledger and a separate account for each supplier (creditor) in an **accounts payable ledger** (also called *accounts payable subsidiary ledger* or *creditors ledger*). The concept of a controlling account and its subsidiary ledger as described with accounts receivable also applies to accounts payable.

Exhibit 8.4

Accounts Receivable
Controlling Account and Its
Subsidiary Ledger

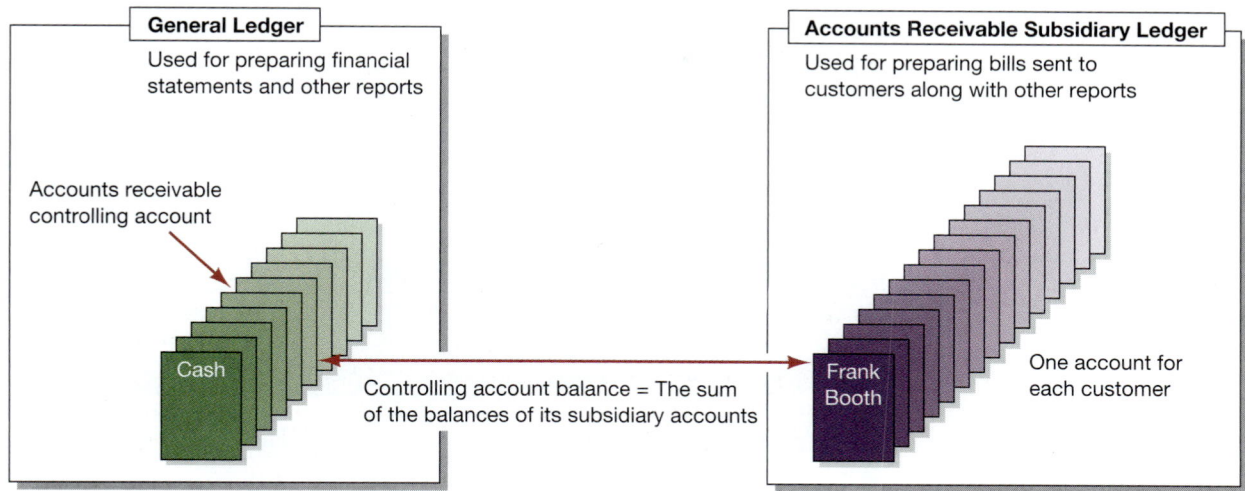

Other Subsidiary Ledgers

Subsidiary ledgers are common for several other accounts. A company with many classes of equipment, for example, might keep only one Equipment account in its general ledger, but its Equipment account would control a subsidiary ledger in which each class of equipment is recorded in a separate account. Similar treatment is common for investments, inventory, and any accounts needing separate detailed records. **Polaris** reports detailed sales information by product line in its annual report. Yet its accounting system most certainly keeps more detailed sales records. Polaris, for instance, sells hundreds of different products and must be able to analyze the sales performance of each of them. This detail can be captured by many different general ledger sales accounts but is more likely captured by using supplementary records that function like subsidiary ledgers. Subsidiary ledgers are applied in many different ways to ensure that the accounting system captures sufficient details to support analyses that decision makers need.

Sales Journal

A **sales journal** is used to record sales of inventory on credit. Sales of inventory for cash are not recorded in a sales journal but in a cash receipts journal. Sales of noninventory assets on credit are recorded in the general journal.

P1 Journalize and post transactions using special journals.

Journalizing

Credit sale transactions are recorded with information about each sale entered separately in a sales journal. This information is often taken from a copy of the sales ticket or invoice prepared at the time of sale. The top portion of Exhibit 8.5 shows a typical sales journal from a merchandiser. It has columns for recording the date, customer's name, invoice number, posting reference, and the retail and cost amounts of each credit sale. The sales journal in this exhibit is called a **columnar journal,** which is any journal with more than one column.

Concept 8-2

Each transaction recorded in the sales journal yields an entry in the Accounts Receivable Dr., Sales Cr. column. We need only one column for these two accounts. An exception is when managers need more information about taxes, returns, and other details of transactions. Each transaction in the sales journal also yields an entry in the Cost of Goods Sold Dr., Inventory Cr. column. This entry reflects the perpetual inventory system of tracking costs with each sale. To illustrate, on February 2, the company sold merchandise on account

Exhibit 8.5

Sales Journal with Posting*

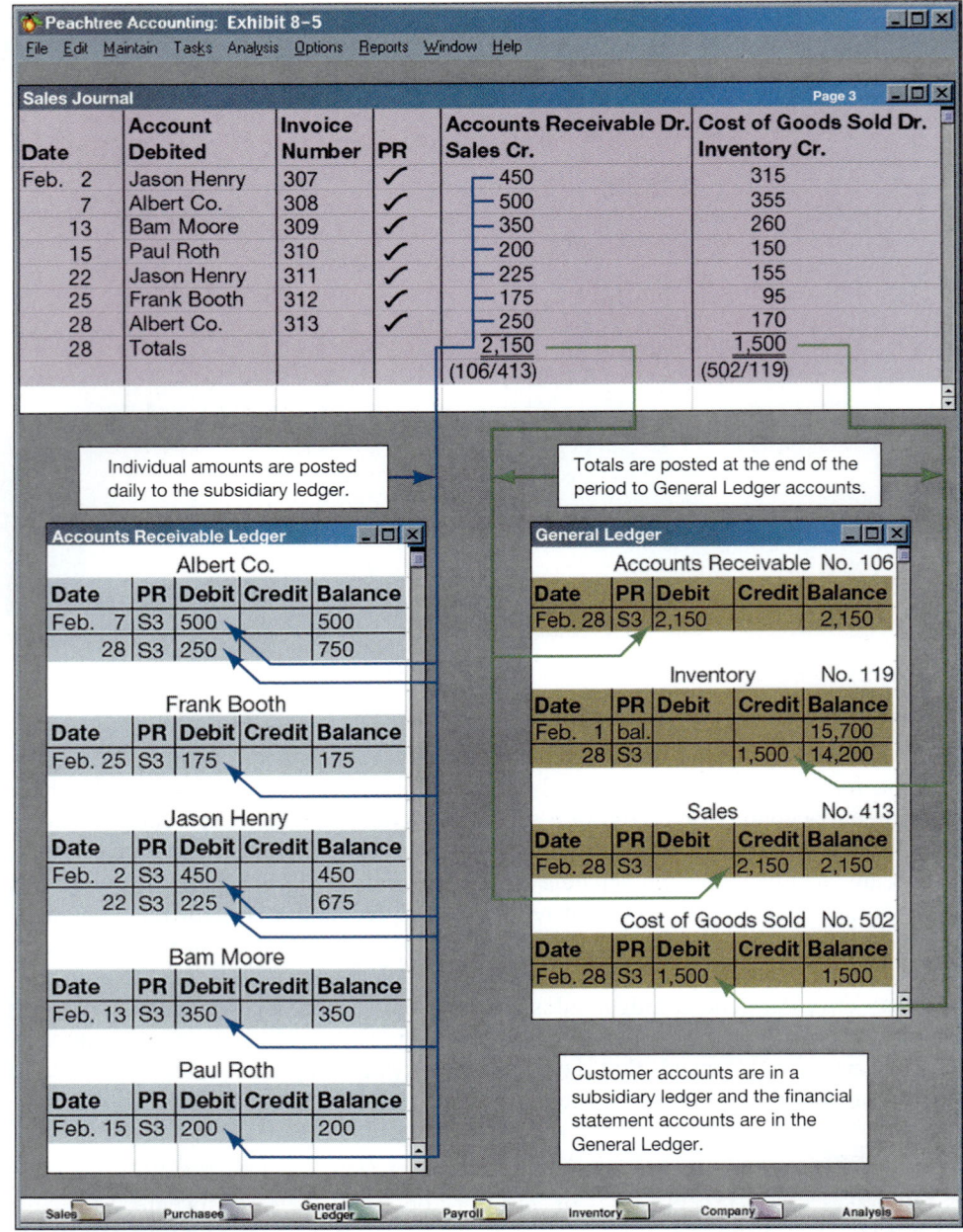

*The Sales Journal in a *periodic* system would exclude the column on the far right titled "Cost of Goods Sold Dr., Inventory Cr." (see Exhibit 8A.1).

to Jason Henry for $450. The invoice number is 307, and the cost of this merchandise is $315. This information is captured on one line in the sales journal. No further explanations or entries are necessary, saving time and effort. Moreover, such a sales journal is consistent with most inventory systems that use bar codes to record both sales and costs with each sale transaction. Note that the Posting Reference (PR) column is not used when entering transactions but is used when posting.

Posting

A sales journal is posted as reflected in the arrow lines of Exhibit 8.5. Two types of posting can be identified: (1) posting to the general ledger and (2) posting to the subsidiary ledger(s).

Point: Continuously updated customer accounts provide timely information for customer inquiries on those accounts. Keeping creditor accounts updated provides timely information on current amounts owed.

Posting to subsidiary ledger. Individual transactions in the sales journal are posted regularly (typically daily) to customer accounts in the accounts receivable ledger. These postings keep customer accounts up to date. This is important for the person granting credit to customers who needs to know the amount owed by credit-seeking customers. If this information in the customer's account is out of date, an incorrect decision can be made. When sales recorded in the sales journal are individually posted to customer accounts in the accounts receivable ledger, check marks are entered in the sales journal's PR column. Check marks are usually used rather than account numbers because customer accounts are not always numbered. Customer accounts usually are arranged alphabetically in the accounts receivable ledger. Note that posting debits to Accounts Receivable twice—once to Accounts Receivable and once to the customer's account—does not violate the accounting equation of debits equal credits. The equality of debits and credits is always maintained in the general ledger. The accounts receivable ledger is a subsidiary record.

Posting to general ledger. The sales journal's dollar amount columns are totaled at the end of each period (the month of February in this case). For the "sales" column, the $2,150 total is debited to Accounts Receivable and credited to Sales in the general ledger (see Exhibit 8.5). The debit records the increase in accounts receivable. The credit records the revenue from sales on account. For the "cost" column, the $1,500 total is debited to Cost of Goods Sold and credited to Inventory in the general ledger (see Exhibit 8.5). When totals are posted to accounts in the general ledger, the account numbers are entered below the column total in the sales journal. For example, we enter (106/413) below the total in the sales column after we post this amount to account number 106 (Accounts Receivable) and account number 413 (Sales). The same rule applies to the cost column total.

A company identifies in the PR column of both ledgers the journal and page number from which an amount is taken. We identify a journal by using an initial. Items posted from the sales journal carry the initial **S** before their journal page numbers in a PR column. Likewise, items from the cash receipts journal carry the initial **R**; items from the cash disbursements journal carry the initial **D**; items from the purchases journal carry the initial **P**; and items from the general journal carry the initial **G**.

Proving the Ledger

Account balances in the general ledger and subsidiary ledgers are proved (or reviewed) for accuracy after posting is complete. We first prepare a trial balance of the general ledger to confirm that debits equal credits (see Chapter 4 for preparing a trial balance). If debits equal credits in the trial balance, the accounts in the general ledger (the controlling accounts) are assumed to be correct. Second, we test the subsidiary ledgers by preparing schedules of individual accounts and amounts. A **schedule of accounts receivable** lists the accounts from the accounts receivable ledger with their balances and the sum of all balances. If this total equals the balance of the Accounts Receivable controlling account, the accounts in the accounts receivable ledger are assumed correct. Exhibit 8.6 shows a schedule of accounts receivable drawn from the accounts receivable ledger of Exhibit 8.5.

P2 Prepare and prove the accuracy of subsidiary ledgers.

Point: In accounting, the word *schedule* generally means a list.

Additional Issues

We consider three additional issues with the sales journal: (1) recording sales taxes, (2) recording sales returns and allowances, and (3) using actual sales invoices as a journal.

Sales taxes

Many cities and states require sellers to collect sales taxes from customers and to periodically send these taxes to the city or state treasurer. When using a columnar sales journal, we can keep a record of taxes collected by adding a Sales Taxes Payable column as shown here:

Schedule of Accounts Receivable February 28	
Frank Booth	$ 175
Jason Henry	675
Bam Moore	350
Paul Roth	200
Albert Co.	750
Total accounts receivable	$2,150

Exhibit 8.6

Schedule of Accounts Receivable

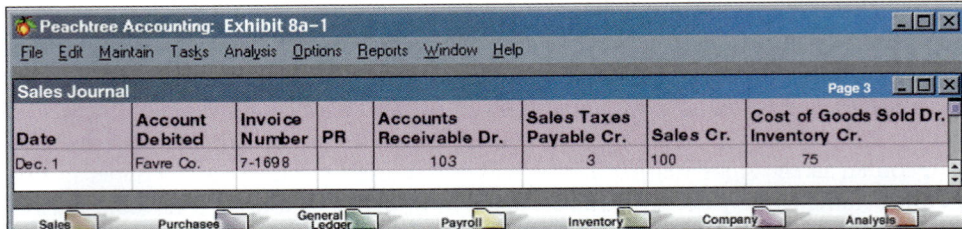

Posting would include crediting the Sales Taxes Payable account for the total of the Sales Taxes Payable column. Individual amounts in the Accounts Receivable column would be posted daily to customer accounts in the accounts receivable ledger. Individual amounts in the Sales Taxes Payable and Sales columns are not posted. A company that collects sales taxes on its cash sales can also use a special Sales Taxes Payable column in its cash receipts journal.

Sales returns and allowances

A company with only a few sales returns and allowances can record them in a general journal with an entry such as this:

May 17	Sales Returns and Allowances	414	175	
	Accounts Receivable—Ray Ball	106/✓		175
	Customer returned merchandise.			

Assets = Liabilities + Equity
−175   −175

The debit in this entry is posted to the Sales Returns and Allowances account (no. 414). The credit is posted to both the Accounts Receivable controlling account (no. 106) and to the customer's account. When we enter the account number and the check mark, 106/✓, in the PR column on the credit line, this means both the Accounts Receivable controlling account in the general ledger and the Ray Ball account in the accounts receivable ledger are credited for $175. Both are credited so that the balance of the controlling account in the general ledger equals the sum of the customer account balances in the subsidiary ledger. A company with a large number of sales returns and allowances can save time by recording them in a special sales returns and allowances journal. More generally, a company will design and use a special journal for any group of similar transactions if it has enough transactions to warrant its use.

Sales invoices as a sales journal

To save costs, some companies avoid using a sales journal for credit sales and instead post each sales invoice amount directly to the customer's account in the subsidiary accounts receivable ledger. Then they put copies of invoices in numerical order in a file. At the end of the period, they total all invoices for that period and make a general journal entry to debit Accounts Receivable and credit Sales for the total amount. The bound invoice copies act as a sales journal. This procedure is called *direct posting of sales invoices*.

Quick Check

4. When special journals are used, where are all cash payments by check recorded?
5. How does a columnar journal save posting time and effort?
6. How do debits and credits remain equal when credit sales to customers are posted twice (once to Accounts Receivable and once to the customer's subsidiary account)?
7. How do we identify the journal from which an amount in a ledger account was posted?
8. How are sales taxes recorded in the context of special journals?
9. What is direct posting of sales invoices?

Answers—p. 331

Cash Receipts Journal

A **cash receipts journal** records all receipts of cash. Exhibit 8.7 shows one common form of the cash receipts journal.

Exhibit 8.7

Cash Receipts Journal with Posting*

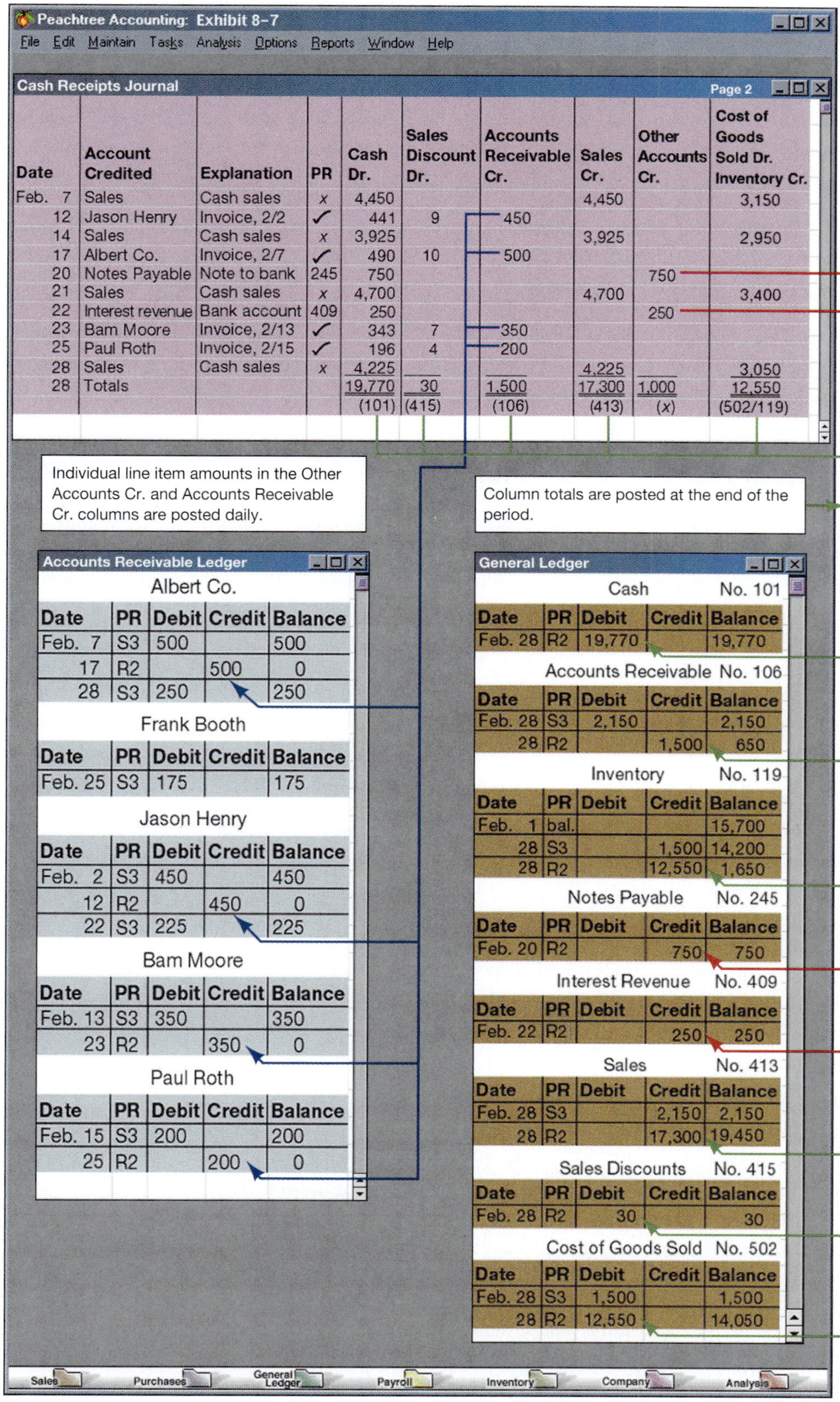

Peachtree Accounting: Exhibit 8–7
File Edit Maintain Tasks Analysis Options Reports Window Help

Cash Receipts Journal — Page 2

Date	Account Credited	Explanation	PR	Cash Dr.	Sales Discount Dr.	Accounts Receivable Cr.	Sales Cr.	Other Accounts Cr.	Cost of Goods Sold Dr. Inventory Cr.
Feb. 7	Sales	Cash sales	x	4,450			4,450		3,150
12	Jason Henry	Invoice, 2/2	✓	441	9	450			
14	Sales	Cash sales	x	3,925			3,925		2,950
17	Albert Co.	Invoice, 2/7	✓	490	10	500			
20	Notes Payable	Note to bank	245	750				750	
21	Sales	Cash sales	x	4,700			4,700		3,400
22	Interest revenue	Bank account	409	250				250	
23	Bam Moore	Invoice, 2/13	✓	343	7	350			
25	Paul Roth	Invoice, 2/15	✓	196	4	200			
28	Sales	Cash sales	x	4,225			4,225		3,050
28	Totals			19,770	30	1,500	17,300	1,000	12,550
				(101)	(415)	(106)	(413)	(x)	(502/119)

Individual line item amounts in the Other Accounts Cr. and Accounts Receivable Cr. columns are posted daily.

Column totals are posted at the end of the period.

Accounts Receivable Ledger

Albert Co.

Date	PR	Debit	Credit	Balance
Feb. 7	S3	500		500
17	R2		500	0
28	S3	250		250

Frank Booth

Date	PR	Debit	Credit	Balance
Feb. 25	S3	175		175

Jason Henry

Date	PR	Debit	Credit	Balance
Feb. 2	S3	450		450
12	R2		450	0
22	S3	225		225

Bam Moore

Date	PR	Debit	Credit	Balance
Feb. 13	S3	350		350
23	R2		350	0

Paul Roth

Date	PR	Debit	Credit	Balance
Feb. 15	S3	200		200
25	R2		200	0

General Ledger

Cash — No. 101

Date	PR	Debit	Credit	Balance
Feb. 28	R2	19,770		19,770

Accounts Receivable — No. 106

Date	PR	Debit	Credit	Balance
Feb. 28	S3	2,150		2,150
28	R2		1,500	650

Inventory — No. 119

Date	PR	Debit	Credit	Balance
Feb. 1	bal.			15,700
28	S3		1,500	14,200
28	R2		12,550	1,650

Notes Payable — No. 245

Date	PR	Debit	Credit	Balance
Feb. 20	R2		750	750

Interest Revenue — No. 409

Date	PR	Debit	Credit	Balance
Feb. 22	R2		250	250

Sales — No. 413

Date	PR	Debit	Credit	Balance
Feb. 28	S3		2,150	2,150
28	R2		17,300	19,450

Sales Discounts — No. 415

Date	PR	Debit	Credit	Balance
Feb. 28	R2	30		30

Cost of Goods Sold — No. 502

Date	PR	Debit	Credit	Balance
Feb. 28	S3	1,500		1,500
28	R2	12,550		14,050

Sales   Purchases   General Ledger   Payroll   Inventory   Company   Analysis

*The Cash Receipts Journal in a *periodic* system would exclude the column on the far right titled "Cost of Goods Sold Dr., Inventory Cr." (see Exhibit 8A.2).

Journalizing and Posting

Cash receipts fall into one of three types: (1) cash from credit customers in payment of their accounts, (2) cash from cash sales, and (3) cash from other sources. The cash receipts journal in Exhibit 8.7 has a separate credit column for each of these three sources. We describe how to journalize transactions for each of these three sources in this section. We then describe how to post them.[1]

Cash from credit customers

Journalizing. To record cash received in payment of a customer's account, the customer's name is first entered in the Account Credited column—see transactions dated February 12, 17, 23, and 25. Then, the amounts debited to both Cash and the Sales Discount (if any) are entered in their respective columns, and the amount credited to the customer's account is entered in the Accounts Receivable Cr. column. The Accounts Receivable Cr. column contains only credits to customer accounts.

Posting. The posting of transactions involving cash from credit customers is twofold. First, individual amounts in the Accounts Receivable Cr. column are posted regularly (daily) to customer accounts in the subsidiary accounts receivable ledger. Second, the $1,500 column total is posted at the end of the period (month) as a credit to the Accounts Receivable controlling account in the general ledger.

Cash sales

Journalizing. When cash sales occur, the debits to Cash are entered in the Cash Debit column and the credits are entered in a separate column titled Sales Cr. The February 7, 14, 21, and 28 transactions are examples of cash sales. (Although cash sales are usually journalized daily (or at point of sale), cash sales are journalized weekly in Exhibit 8.7 for brevity.) Each cash sale also yields an entry to debit Cost of Goods Sold and credit Inventory for the cost of merchandise sold—see the far right column.

Posting. When recording cash sales in the cash receipts journal, we place an *x* in the PR column to indicate that no amount is individually posted from that line of the journal. We post the $17,300 total cash sales for the period in the general ledger as a single amount, taken from the Sales Cr. column. We also post the $12,550 total from the "cost" column to both Cost of Goods Sold and Inventory in the general ledger.

Cash from other sources

Journalizing. Cash from other sources includes money borrowed from a bank, interest received on account, or cash sale of noninventory assets. Examples are the transactions of February 20 and 22. The Other Accounts Cr. column is used for these cash receipt transactions.

Posting. Amounts from these transactions are posted to their general ledger accounts. Postings occur daily, although end-of-period posting of these amounts is acceptable. This journal's PR column is used only for daily postings from the Other Accounts Cr. and the Accounts Receivable Cr. columns. The account numbers in the PR column refer to amounts posted to their respective general ledger accounts.

Footing, Crossfooting, and Posting

To be sure that total debits and credits in a columnar journal are equal, we often crossfoot column totals before posting them. To *foot* a column of numbers is to add it. To *crossfoot* is to add the Debit column totals, then add the Credit column totals, and compare the two sums for equality. Footing and crossfooting of the numbers in Exhibit 8.7 yields the schedule in Exhibit 8.8.

At the end of the period (month), after crossfooting the journal to confirm that debits equal credits, the total amounts from the columns of the cash receipts journal are posted to their general ledger accounts. The Other Accounts Cr. column total is not posted because

Point: Each transaction in the cash receipts journal involves a debit to Cash.

Example: Record the sale of machinery at its cost of $100 using a cash receipts journal. *Answer:* Debit the Cash column for $100, and credit the Other Accounts column for $100 (the account credited is Machinery).

Point: Subsidiary ledgers and their controlling accounts are *in balance* only after all posting is complete.

---

[1] An Explanation column is included in the cash receipts journal to identify the source of each cash receipt.

Debit Columns		Credit Columns	
Cash Dr.	$19,770	Accounts Receivable Cr.	$ 1,500
Sales Discounts Dr.	30	Sales Cr.	17,300
		Other Accounts Cr.	1,000
Total	$19,800	Total	$19,800

Exhibit 8.8

Footing and Crossfooting
Journal Totals

the individual amounts are directly posted to their general ledger accounts. We place an *x* below the Other Accounts Cr. column to indicate that this column total is not posted. The account numbers for the column totals that are posted are entered in parentheses below each column. (*Note:* Posting items daily from the Other Accounts Cr. column with a delayed posting of their offsetting items in the Cash column total causes the general ledger to be out of balance during the period. Posting the Cash Dr. column total at the end of the period corrects this imbalance in the general ledger before the trial balance and financial statements are prepared.)

You Make the Call

Entrepreneur   You want to know how promptly customers are paying their bills. This information can help you decide whether to extend credit and plan your cash payments. Where can you find this information?

Answer—p. 330

Purchases Journal

A **purchases journal** is used to record all purchases on credit. Purchases for cash are recorded in the Cash Disbursements Journal.

Journalizing

The purchases journal in Exhibit 8.9 is a columnar journal in which all credit purchases, including inventory, are recorded. Purchase invoices or other source documents are used to record transactions in the purchases journal. We use the invoice date and terms to compute the date when payment for each purchase is due. The Accounts Payable Cr. column is used to record the amounts owed to each creditor. Inventory purchases are recorded in the Inventory Dr. column. To illustrate, inventory costing $200 is purchased from Ace Manufacturing on February 5. The creditor's name (Ace) is entered in Account column, the invoice date is entered in the Date of Invoice column, and purchase terms are entered in the Terms column. The $200 amount is entered in the Accounts Payable Cr. and the Inventory Dr. columns. When a purchase involves an amount recorded in the Other Accounts Dr. column, we use the Account column to identify the general ledger account debited. For example, the February 28 transaction involves purchases of inventory, office supplies, and store supplies from ITT. The journal has no column for store supplies, so the Other Accounts Dr. column is used. In this case, Store Supplies is entered in the Account column along with the creditor's name (ITT). This purchases journal also includes a separate column for credit purchases of office supplies. A separate column such as this is useful when several transactions involve debits to the same account. Each company uses its own judgment in deciding on the number of separate columns necessary. The Other Accounts Dr. column allows the purchases journal to be used for any purchase transaction on credit.

Point: The number of special journals and the design of each are based on a company's special needs.

Point: Each transaction in the purchases journal involves a credit to Accounts Payable.

Posting

The amounts in the Accounts Payable Cr. column are regularly (daily) posted to individual creditor accounts in the accounts payable subsidiary ledger. Each line of the Account column in Exhibit 8.9 shows the subsidiary ledger account that is posted for amounts in the Accounts Payable Cr. column. Individual amounts in the Other Accounts Dr. column usually are regularly (daily) posted to their general ledger accounts. At the end of the period (month), all column totals except the Other Accounts Dr. column are posted to their general ledger accounts. The balance in the Accounts Payable controlling account must equal the sum of the individual account balances in the accounts payable subsidiary ledger after posting.

Exhibit 8.9

Purchases Journal with Posting*

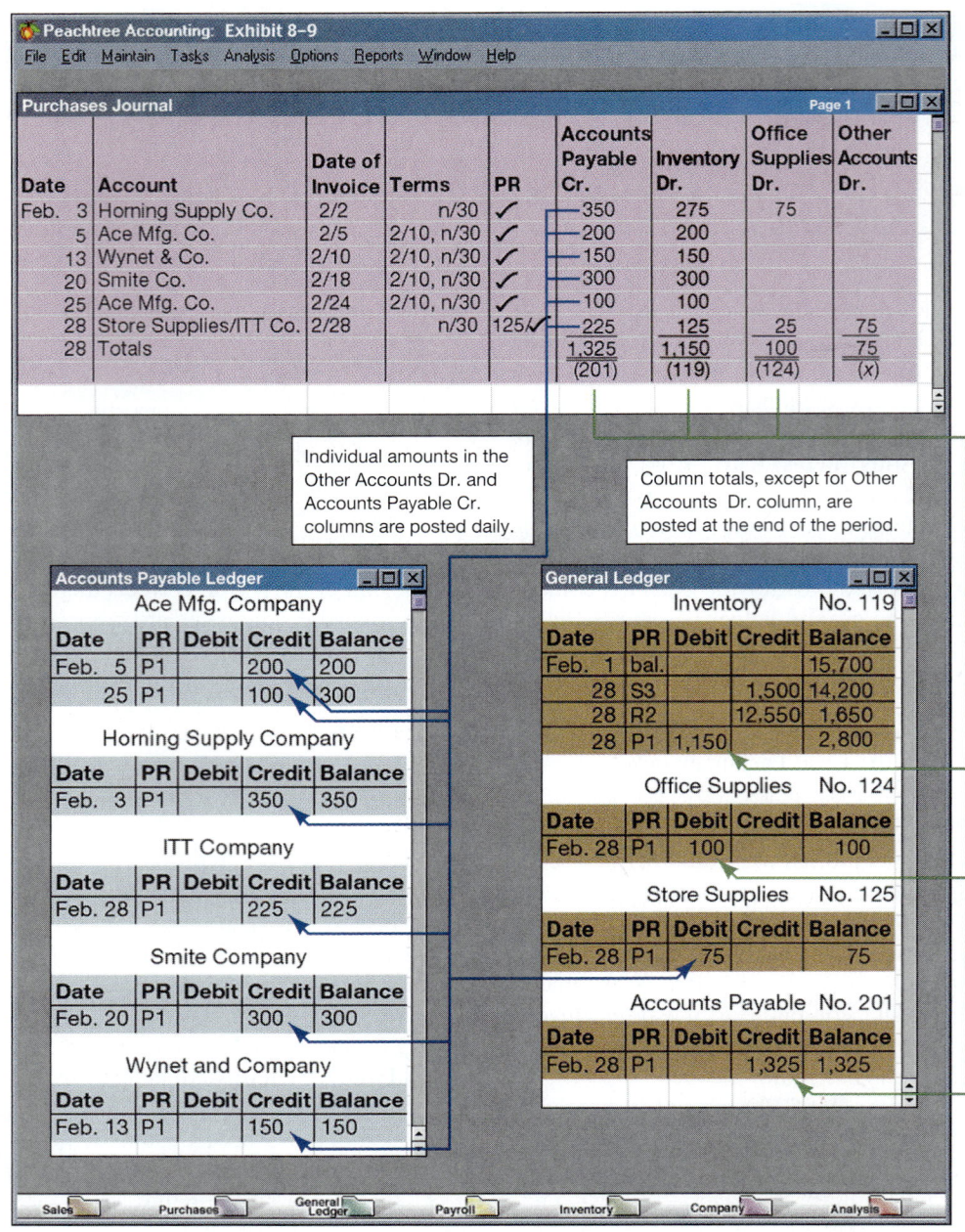

*Purchases Journal in a *periodic* system replaces "Inventory Dr." with "Purchases Dr." (see Exhibit 8A.3).

Exhibit 8.10

Schedule of Accounts Payable

Schedule of Accounts Payable February 28	
Ace Mfg. Company	$ 300
Horning Supply Company	350
ITT Company	225
Smite Company	300
Wynet & Company	150
Total accounts payable	$1,325

Proving the Ledger

Account balances in the general ledger and its subsidiary ledgers are proved for accuracy after posting the purchases journal. Similar to proving the ledger for the sales journal, two steps are necessary. First, we prepare a trial balance of the general ledger to confirm debits equal credits. If debits equal credits in the trial balance, the accounts in the general ledger, including the controlling accounts, are assumed to be correct. Second, we prove the subsidiary ledger by preparing a **schedule of accounts payable,** which is a list of accounts from the accounts payable ledger with their balances and the total. If this total equals the balance of the Accounts Payable controlling account, the accounts in the accounts payable ledger are considered correct. Exhibit 8.10 shows a schedule of accounts payable drawn from the accounts payable ledger of Exhibit 8.9.

Cash Disbursements Journal

A **cash disbursements journal,** also called a *cash payments journal,* is used to record all payments of cash. It is set up as a columnar journal because cash payments are made for several different purposes.

Journalizing

The cash disbursements journal shown in Exhibit 8.11 records repetitive cash payments. Note the repetitive credits to the Cash column of this journal. Also note the frequent credits to Inventory (reflecting purchase discounts) and the debits to Accounts Payable. For

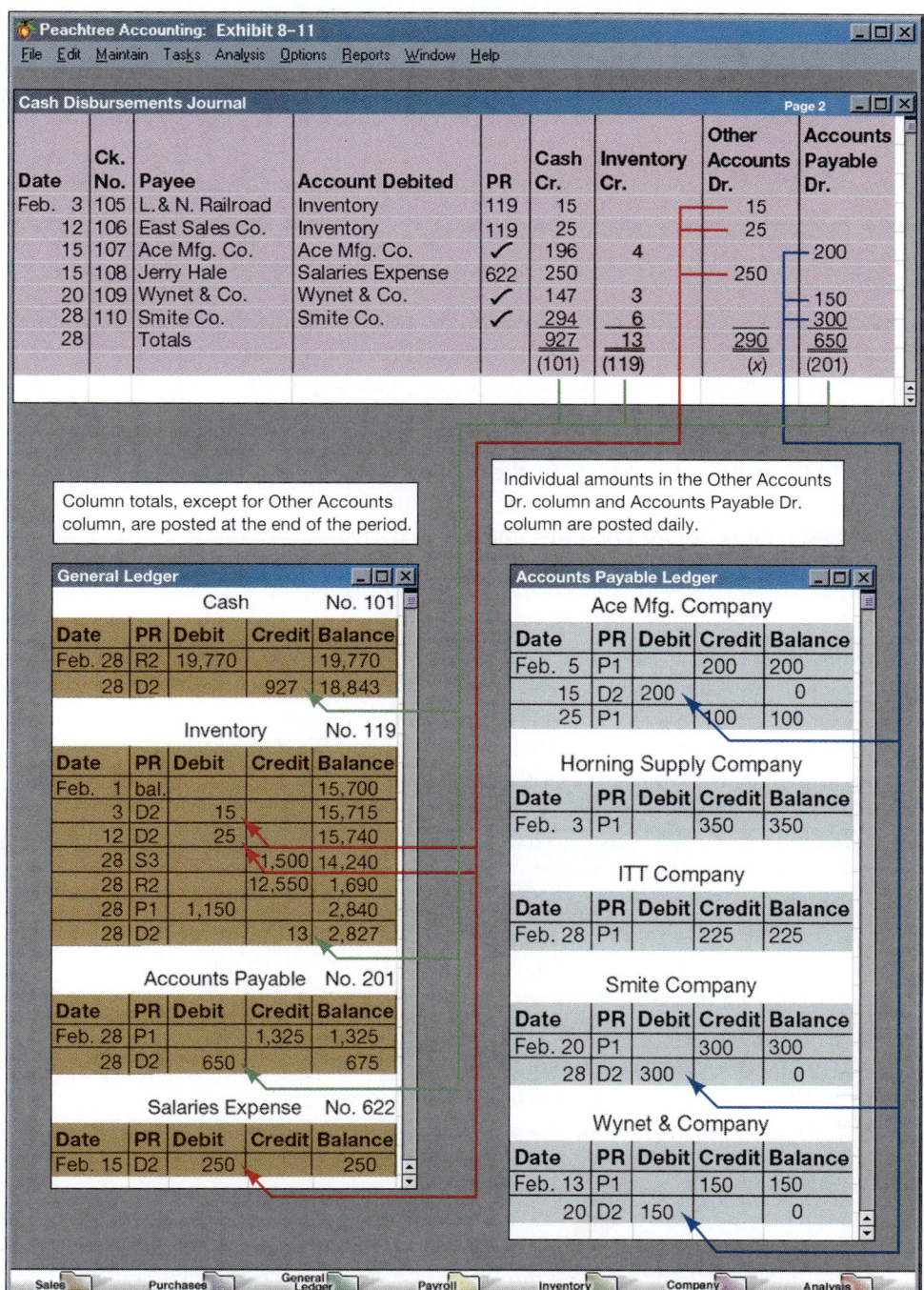

Exhibit 8.11

Cash Disbursements Journal with Posting*

*The Cash Disbursements Journal in a *periodic* system replaces "Inventory Cr." with "Purchases Discounts Cr." (see Exhibit 8A.4).

Point: Each transaction in the cash disbursements journal involves a credit to Cash.

example, on February 15, the company pays Ace on account (credit terms of 2/10, n/30—see February 5 transaction in Exhibit 8.9). Since payment occurs in the discount period, the company pays $196 ($200 invoice less $4 discount). The $4 discount is credited to Inventory. Many companies purchase inventory for cash and, therefore, an Inventory column is not usually included. Instead, the cash purchases of inventory are recorded using the Other Accounts Dr. column and the Cash Cr. column as illustrated in the February 3 and 12 transactions. Generally, the Other Accounts column is used to record cash payments on items for which no column exists. For example, on February 15, the company pays salaries expense of $250. In these cases, the title of the account debited (such as Inventory or Salaries Expense) is entered in the Account Debited column.

The cash disbursements journal has a column titled Ck. No. (check number). For control over cash disbursements, all payments except for those of small amounts are made by check. Checks should be prenumbered and each check's number entered in the journal in numerical order in the column headed Ck. No. This makes it possible to scan the numbers in the column for omitted checks. When a cash disbursements journal has a column for check numbers, it is sometimes called a **check register.**

You Make the Call

Controller   You wish to analyze your company's cash payments to suppliers and its purchases discounts. Where might you find this information?

Answer—p. 330

Posting

Individual amounts in the Other Accounts Dr. column of a cash disbursements journal are posted to their general ledger accounts on a regular (daily) basis. Individual amounts in the Accounts Payable Dr. column are also regularly (daily) posted to creditors' accounts in the subsidiary Accounts Payable ledger. At the end of the period (month), we crossfoot column totals and post the Accounts Payable Dr. column total to the Accounts Payable controlling account. Also at the end of the period, the Inventory Cr. column total is posted to the Inventory account, and the Cash Cr. column total is posted to the Cash account. The Other Accounts Dr. column total is not posted at the end of the period.

General Journal Transactions

When special journals are used, we still need a general journal for adjusting, closing, and correcting entries and for any other transactions not recorded in special journals. Examples of these other transactions include purchases returns and allowances, purchases of plant assets by issuing a note payable, sales returns if a sales returns and allowances journal is not used, and receipt of a note receivable from a customer. We described the recording of transactions in a general journal in Chapters 3 and 4.

Quick Check

10. What are the normal recording and posting procedures when using special journals and controlling accounts with their subsidiary ledgers?

11. What is the rule for posting to a subsidiary ledger and its controlling account?

12. How do we prove the accuracy of account balances in the general ledger and subsidiary ledgers after posting?

13. Why does a company need a general journal when using special journals for sales, purchases, cash receipts, and cash disbursements?

Answers—p. 331

Technology-Based Accounting Systems

Accounting information systems are supported with technology, which can range from simple calculators to state-of-the-art advanced electronic systems. Because technology is increasingly important in accounting information systems, we discuss the impact of computer technology, how data processing works with accounting data, and the role of computer networks.

Computer Technology in Accounting

Computer technology can be separated into two categories, hardware and software. **Computer hardware** is the physical equipment in a computerized accounting information system. The physical equipment includes processing units, hard drives, RAM, modems, CD-ROM drives, monitors, workstations, servers, printers, and scanners. **Computer software**

C5 Explain how technology-based information systems impact accounting.

comprises the programs that direct the operations of computer hardware. A program can be written, for instance, to process customers' merchandise orders. Computer technology provides accuracy, speed, efficiency, and convenience in performing accounting tasks.

> **Did You Know?**
>
> **Middleware** Middleware is software allowing different computer programs in a company or across companies to work together. It allows transfer of purchase orders, invoices, and other electronic documents between accounting systems. It also helps a bank handle a company's electronic payments.

Widespread use of computer technology has increased the range and power of off-the-shelf programs, which include multipurpose software applications for a variety of operations. These include familiar word processing programs such as Word® and WordPerfect®, spreadsheet programs such as Excel®, and database management programs. Other off-the-shelf programs meet the needs of specialized users, including accounting programs such as PeachTree® and QuickBooks®. Off-the-shelf programs are designed to be user friendly and menu driven, and many operate more efficiently as *integrated* systems. In an integrated system, actions taken in one part of the system automatically affect related parts. When a credit sale is recorded in an integrated system, for instance, several parts of the system are automatically updated.

Computer technology can dramatically reduce the time and effort devoted to recordkeeping tasks. Less effort spent on recordkeeping tasks means more time for accounting professionals to concentrate on analysis and managerial decision making. These advances have created a greater demand for accounting professionals who understand financial reports and can draw insights and information from mountains of processed data. Accounting professionals have expertise in determining relevant and reliable information for decision making. They also can assess the effects of transactions and events on a company and its financial statements.

> **Did You Know?**
>
> **Accounting Tools** A new generation of Windows- and Web-based accounting support is available. With the touch of a key, users can create real-time inventory reports showing all payments, charges, and credit limits at any point in the accounting cycle. Many also include "alert signals" notifying the user when, for example, a large order exceeds a customer's credit limit or when purchase orders need to be placed. These tools also support perpetual updating of records.

Knowledge of the accounting described in this book enables us to understand and use accounting output. It also enables us to understand the transactions and events driving the output. In this way—and only in this way—can we expect to reap the full benefits of accounting reports. All the reports available cannot help the external or internal user who fails to understand the accounting principles and methods determining the information.

Data Processing in Accounting

Accounting systems differ as to how input is entered and processed. **Online processing** enters and processes data as soon as source documents are available. This means databases are immediately updated. **Batch processing** accumulates source documents for a period of time and then processes them all at once daily, weekly, or monthly. The advantage of online processing is up-to-date databases. This often requires additional costs related to both software and hardware requirements. Companies such as **NetLedger** are making online processing of accounting data a reality for many businesses. The advantage of batch processing is that it requires only periodic updating of databases. Records used to send bills to customers, for instance, might require updating only once a month. The disadvantage of batch processing is the lack of updated databases for management to use when making business decisions.

Computer Networks in Accounting

Networking, or linking computers with each other, can create information advantages. **Computer networks** are links among computers giving different users and different computers access to common databases and programs. Many college computer labs, for instance, are networked. A small computer network is called a *local area network (LAN)*; it links machines with *hard-wire* hookups. Large computer networks extending over long distances often rely on *modem* or *wireless* communication.

Demand for information sometimes requires advanced networks such as the system **Federal Express** uses to track packages and bill customers and the system **Wal-Mart** uses to monitor inventory levels in its stores. These networks include many computers and satellite communications to gather information and to provide ready access to its databases from all locations.

Answers—p. 331

Quick Check	

14. Identify an advantage of an integrated computer-based accounting system.

15. What advantages do computer systems offer over manual systems?

16. Identify an advantage of computer networks.

Enterprise Resource Planning Software

Enterprise resource planning (or *ERP*) **software** includes the programs that manage a company's vital operations. They extend from order taking to manufacturing to accounting. When working properly, these integrated programs can speed decision making, slash costs, and give managers control over operations with the click of a mouse. For many managers, ERP software is like a lightbulb illuminating the dark recesses of their company's operations. It allows them to scrutinize business, identify where inventories are piling up, and see what plants are most efficient. The software is designed to link every part of a company's operations. This software allowed **Monsanto** to slash production planning from six weeks to three, trim its inventories, and increase its bargaining power with suppliers. Monsanto estimates that this software saves the company $200 million per year.

ERP has six major suppliers. **SAP** leads the market, with **Oracle** a distant second. SAP software runs the back offices of nearly half of the world's 500 largest companies. It links ordering, inventory, production, purchasing, planning, tracking, and human resources. One transaction or event triggers an immediate chain reaction of events throughout the enterprise. It is making companies more efficient and profitable.

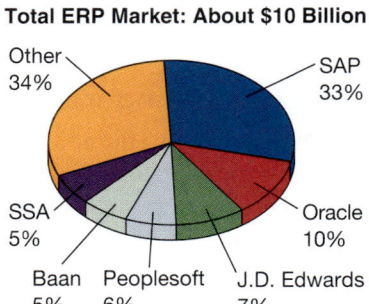

Total ERP Market: About $10 Billion

Other 34%
SAP 33%
Oracle 10%
J.D. Edwards 7%
Peoplesoft 6%
Baan 5%
SSA 5%

ERP is pushing into cyberspace. Now companies can share data with customers and suppliers. Applesauce maker **Mott**'s is using SAP so that distributors can check the status of orders and place them over the Net, and the **Coca-Cola Company** uses it to ship soda on time. ERP is also invading small business. For example, **NetLedger**'s accounting services to small and medium businesses are powered by Oracle's system.

Business Segments

The accounting information system is usually more complex when a company is large and operates in more than one business segment. Special journals and subsidiary ledgers also are usually greater in number and more detailed for these companies. A **business segment** is the part of a company that is separately identified by its products or services or by the geographic market it serves. **Nike**, for instance, reports that it operates in four main geographical markets: United States, Europe, Asia/Pacific, and Latin America/Canada. External users of financial statements are especially interested in segment information to better understand a company's business activities.

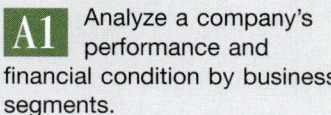
A1 Analyze a company's performance and financial condition by business segments.

Information reported about business segments varies in quality and quantity. The full disclosure principle implies that we ought to see detailed financial statements for each important segment. Full disclosure by segments is rare, however, because of difficulties in separating segments and management's reluctance to release information that can harm its competitive position.

Companies offering their shares to the public in U.S. stock exchanges must disclose segment information under certain conditions. Accounting standards apply the definition of segments to industries, international activities, export sales, and major customers. Companies are required to report certain information for these segments, including sales, operating income, identifiable assets, capital expenditures, depreciation, depletion, and amortization. Exhibit 8.12 shows results from a recent survey on the number of companies with different business segments. Companies often have different rates of profitability, risk, and growth for different segments. Evaluating risk and return is a major goal of decision makers, and segment information is useful in this evaluation.

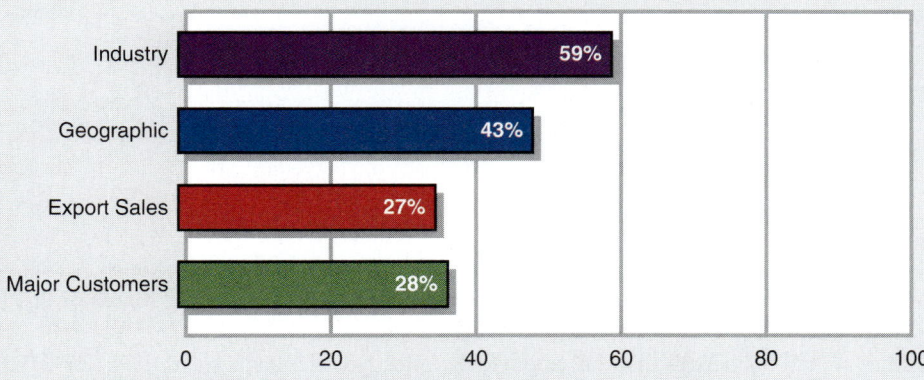

*Total exceeds 100% because companies can report one or more types of segments.

Exhibit 8.12

Percent of Companies
Reporting These Segments*

Analysis of a company's segments is aided by a **segment contribution matrix,** which is a table listing one or more important measures (such as sales) by segments. This list usually includes amounts both in dollars and percents and its growth rate. Such analysis helps answer several questions: What is the contribution of one segment versus another? What is the highest growth segment? And which is the lowest? We prepare a segment contribution matrix for **Harley-Davidson**'s sales in Exhibit 8.13.

The second and third columns in Exhibit 8.13 list sales data by geographical segment. These data are drawn from Harley's annual report. We see that its sales are divided into five major segments: U.S., Canada, Germany, Japan, and Other. Columns four and five of Exhibit 8.13 reveal sales contribution *in percent* by segment. Each number is computed by dividing segment sales by total sales. For example, the 1999 sales contribution in percent for the United States is computed as follows: $1,916 ÷ $2,453 = 0.78, or 78%. The results

Point: Segment information can be used in evaluating a company's decision to spin off a segment.

Point: If a company has two segments, and each sells three products in four geographic regions, how many sales accounts are needed to analyze each product in each region? *Answer:* 2 × 3 × 4 = 24 accounts.

Exhibit 8.13

Segment Contribution Matrix
for Harley-Davidson

Sales ($ in 000s)	Sales Contribution (in $ and %)				One-Year Sales Growth Rate
	1999	1998	1999	1998	
United States	$1,916	$1,567	78%	76%	22%
Canada	80	74	3	4	8
Germany	89	84	4	4	6
Japan	135	102	6	5	32
Other	233	237	9	11	−2
Totals	$2,453	$2,064	100%	100%	19

Point: Software enables us to access electronically stored data and present them in graphical formats such as pie and bar graphs.

show that the United States accounts for nearly 80% of total sales. This shows Harley's sales depend highly on the U.S. market. Analysis of Harley demands special attention to assess future U.S. prospects and the risk of competition in the United States. The far right column of Exhibit 8.13 shows the one-year growth rate in segment sales. A one-year growth rate is computed as follows: (Current period sales ÷ Prior period sales) − 1.0. For example, Harley's one-year growth rate for sales in Japan is computed as follows: ($135 ÷ $102) − 1.0 = 0.32, or 32%. These growth rates reveal that Japan is growing faster than any other segment, followed by the U.S., Canada, and Germany.

We can extend analysis of segment contribution matrixes to other measures such as operating income and assets and to other segments (such as by industry or by Harley vs. Buell motorcycles).

You Make the Call

Banker   A bicycle merchandiser requests a loan from you to expand operations. The owner's financials reveal a solid net income of $220,000, reflecting a 10% increase over the prior year. You ask about any geographic focus. The owner reports that $160,000 of net income is from Cuban operations, reflecting a 60% increase over the prior year. The remaining $60,000 of net income is from U.S. operations, reflecting a 40% decrease. The owner, a Cuban immigrant, tells you of his many business relationships in Cuba. Does this segment information impact your loan decision?

Answer—p. 330

Demonstration Problem— Perpetual System

Pepper Company completes the following transactions and events during March of this year. (Terms of all credit sales are 2/10, n/30.)

Mar. 4   Sold merchandise on credit to Jennifer Nelson, Invoice No. 954, for $16,800 (cost is $12,200).

6   Purchased $1,220 of office supplies on credit from Mack Company. Invoice dated March 3, terms n/30.

6   Sold merchandise on credit to Dennie Hoskins, Invoice No. 955, for $10,200 (cost is $8,100).

11   Received $52,600 of merchandise and an invoice dated March 6, terms 2/10, n/30, from Defore Industries.

12   Borrowed $26,000 cash by giving Commerce Bank a long-term promissory note payable.

14   Received cash payment from Jennifer Nelson for the March 4 sale less the discount.

16   Received a $200 credit memorandum from Defore Industries for unsatisfactory merchandise received on March 11 and returned for credit.

16   Received cash payment from Dennie Hoskins for the March 6 sale less the discount.

18   Purchased $22,850 of store equipment on credit from Schmidt Supply, invoice dated March 15, terms n/30.

20   Sold merchandise on credit to Marjorie Allen, Invoice No. 956, for $5,600 (cost is $3,800).

21   Sent Defore Industries Check No. 516 in payment of its March 6 dated invoice less the returns and the discount.

22   Received $41,625 of merchandise and an invoice dated March 18, terms 2/10, n/30, from Welch Company.

26   Issued a $600 credit memorandum to Marjorie Allen for defective merchandise sold on March 20 and returned for credit.

31   Issued Check No. 517, payable to Payroll, in payment of $15,900 sales salaries for the month. Cashed the check and paid the employees.

31   Cash sales for the month are $134,680 (cost is $67,340). (Cash sales are recorded daily but are recorded only once here to reduce repetitive entries.)

Required

1. Open the following general ledger accounts: Cash (101), Accounts Receivable (106) Inventory (119), Office Supplies (124), Store Equipment (165), Accounts Payable (201), Long-Term Notes Payable (251), Sales (413), Sales Returns and Allowances (414), Sales Discounts (415), Cost of Goods Sold (502), and Sales Salaries Expense (621). Open the following accounts receivable ledger accounts: Marjorie Allen, Dennie Hoskins, and Jennifer Nelson. Open the following accounts payable ledger accounts: Defore Industries, Mack Company, Schmidt Supply, and Welch Company.

2. Enter the transactions using a sales journal, a purchases journal, a cash receipts journal, a cash disbursements journal, and a general journal similar to the ones illustrated in the chapter. Regularly post to the individual customer and creditor accounts. Also, post any amounts that should be posted as individual amounts to general ledger accounts. Foot and crossfoot the journals and make the month-end postings. *Pepper Co. uses the perpetual inventory system.*

3. Prepare a trial balance and prove the accuracy of subsidiary ledgers by preparing schedules of accounts receivable and accounts payable.

Planning the Solution

- Set up the required general ledger, the subsidiary ledger accounts, and the five required journals as illustrated in the chapter.
- Read and analyze each transaction and decide in which special journal (or general journal) the transaction is recorded.
- Record each transaction in the proper journal (and post the appropriate individual amounts).
- Once you have recorded all transactions, total the journal columns. Post from each journal to the appropriate ledger accounts.
- Prepare a trial balance to prove the equality of the debit and credit balances in your general ledger.
- Prepare schedules of accounts receivable and accounts payable. Compare the totals of these schedules to the Accounts Receivable and Accounts Payable controlling account balances, making sure that they agree.

Solution to Demonstration Problem—Perpetual System

Sales Journal					Page 2
Date	Account Debited	Invoice Number	PR	Accts. Rec. Dr. Sales Cr.	Cost of Goods Sold Dr. Inventory Cr.
Mar. 4	Jennifer Nelson....	954	✓	16,800	12,200
6	Dennie Hoskins....	955	✓	10,200	8,100
20	Marjorie Allen	956	✓	5,600	3,800
31	Totals...........			32,600	24,100
				(106/413)	(502/119)

Cash Receipts Journal — Page 3

Date	Account Credited	Explanation	PR	Cash Debit	Sales Discount Debit	Accts. Rec. Credit	Sales Credit	Other Accts. Credit	Cost of Good Sold Dr. Inventory Cr.
Mar. 12	L.T. Notes Payable..	Note to bank	251	26,000				26,000	
14	Jennifer Nelson	Invoice, 3/4	✓	16,464	336	16,800			
16	Dennie Hoskins	Invoice, 3/6	✓	9,996	204	10,200			
31	Sales	Cash sales	x	134,680			134,680		67,340
31	Totals			187,140	540	27,000	134,680	26,000	67,340
				(101)	(415)	(106)	(413)	(x)	(502/119)

Purchases Journal — Page 3

Date	Account	Date of Invoice	Terms	PR	Accts. Payable Credit	Inventory Debit	Office Supplies Debit	Other Accts. Debit
Mar. 6	Office Supplies/Mack Co..............	3/3	n/30	✓	1,220		1,220	
11	Defore Industries...................	3/6	2/10, n/30	✓	52,600	52,600		
18	Store Equipment/Schmidt Supp........	3/15	n/30	165/✓	22,850			22,850
22	Welch Company	3/18	2/10, n/30	✓	41,625	41,625		
31	Totals............................				118,295	94,225	1,220	22,850
					(201)	(119)	(124)	(x)

Cash Disbursements Journal — Page 3

Date	Ck. No.	Payee	Account Debited	PR	Cash Credit	Inventory Credit	Other Accts. Debit	Accts. Payable Debit
Mar. 21	516	Defore Industries......	Defore Industries	✓	51,352	1,048		52,400
31	517	Payroll	Sales Salaries Expense	621	15,900		15,900	
31		Totals			67,252	1,048	15,900	52,400
					(101)	(119)	(x)	(201)

General Journal — Page 2

Mar. 16	Accounts Payable—Defore Industries	201/✓	200	
	Inventory	119		200
	To record credit memorandum received.			
26	Sales Returns and Allowances	414	600	
	Accounts Receivable—Marjorie Allen	106/✓		600
	To record credit memorandum issued.			

Accounts Receivable Ledger

Marjorie Allen

Date	PR	Debit	Credit	Balance
Mar. 20	S2	5,600		5,600
26	G2		600	5,000

Dennie Hoskins

Date	PR	Debit	Credit	Balance
Mar. 6	S2	10,200		10,200
16	R3		10,200	0

Jennifer Nelson

Date	PR	Debit	Credit	Balance
Mar. 4	S2	16,800		16,800
14	R3		16,800	0

Accounts Payable Ledger

Defore Industries

Date	PR	Debit	Credit	Balance
Mar. 11	P3		52,600	52,600
16	G2	200		52,400
21	D3	52,400		0

Mack Company

Date	PR	Debit	Credit	Balance
Mar. 6	P3		1,220	1,220

Schmidt Supply

Date	PR	Debit	Credit	Balance
Mar. 18	P3		22,850	22,850

Welch Company

Date	PR	Debit	Credit	Balance
Mar. 22	P3		41,625	41,625

General Ledger

Cash — Acct. No. 101

Date	PR	Debit	Credit	Balance
Mar. 31	R3	187,140		187,140
31	D4		67,252	119,888

Accounts Receivable — Acct. No. 106

Date	PR	Debit	Credit	Balance
Mar. 26	G2		600	(600)
31	S2	32,600		32,000
31	R3		27,000	5,000

Inventory — Acct. No. 119

Date	PR	Debit	Credit	Balance
Mar. 16	G2		200	(200)
21	D3		1,048	(1,248)
31	P3	94,225		92,977
31	S3		24,100	68,877
31	R3		67,340	1,537

Office Supplies — Acct. No. 124

Date	PR	Debit	Credit	Balance
Mar. 31	P3	1,220		1,220

Store Equipment — Acct. No. 165

Date	PR	Debit	Credit	Balance
Mar. 18	P3	22,850		22,850

Accounts Payable — Acct. No. 201

Date	PR	Debit	Credit	Balance
Mar. 6	G2	200		(200)
31	P3		118,295	118,095
31	D3	52,400		65,695

Long-Term Notes Payable — Acct. No. 251

Date	PR	Debit	Credit	Balance
Mar. 12			26,000	26,000

Sales — Acct. No. 413

Date	PR	Debit	Credit	Balance
Mar. 31	S2		32,600	32,600
31	R3		134,680	167,280

Sales Returns and Allowances — Acct. No. 414

Date	PR	Debit	Credit	Balance
Mar. 26	G2	600		600

Sales Discounts — Acct. No. 415

Date	PR	Debit	Credit	Balance
Mar. 31	R3	540		540

Cost of Good Sold — Acct. No. 502

Date	PR	Debit	Credit	Balance
Mar. 31	R3	67,340		67,340
31	S2	24,100		91,440

Sales Salaries Expense — Acct. No. 621

Date	PR	Debit	Credit	Balance
Mar. 31	D3	15,900		15,900

PEPPER COMPANY
Trial Balance
March 31

	Debit	Credit
Cash	$119,888	
Accounts receivable	5,000	
Inventory	1,537	
Office supplies	1,220	
Store equipment	22,850	
Accounts payable		$ 65,695
Long-term notes payable		26,000
Sales		167,280
Sales returns and allowances	600	
Sales discounts	540	
Cost of goods sold	91,440	
Sales salaries expense	15,900	
Totals	$258,975	$258,975

PEPPER COMPANY
Schedule of Accounts Receivable
March 31

Marjorie Allen	$5,000
Total accounts receivable	$5,000

PEPPER COMPANY
Schedule of Accounts Payable
March 31

Mack Company	$ 1,220
Schmidt Supply	22,850
Welch Company	41,625
Total accounts payable	$65,695

8A
Special Journals under a Periodic System

P3 Journalize and post transactions using special journals in a periodic inventory system.

This appendix describes special journals under a periodic inventory system. Each journal is slightly impacted. The sales journal and the cash receipts journal both require one less column (namely that of Cost of Goods Sold Dr., Inventory Cr.). The Purchases Journal replaces the Inventory Dr. column with a Purchases Dr. column in a periodic system. The cash disbursements journal replaces the Inventory Cr. column with a Purchases Discounts Cr. column in a periodic system. These changes are illustrated.

Sales Journal

The sales journal using the periodic inventory system is shown in Exhibit 8A.1. The difference in the sales journal between the perpetual and periodic system is the exclusion of the column to record cost of goods sold and inventory amounts for each sale. The periodic system does *not* record the increase in cost of goods sold and the decrease in inventory at the time of sale.

Sales Journal				Page 3
Date	**Account Debited**	**Invoice Number**	**PR**	**Accounts Receivable Dr. Sales Cr.**
Feb. 2	Jason Henry	307	✓	450
7	Albert Co.	308	✓	500
13	Bam Moore	309	✓	350
15	Paul Roth	310	✓	200
22	Jason Henry	311	✓	225
25	Frank Booth	312	✓	175
28	Albert Co.	313	✓	250
28	Total			2,150
				(106/413)

Exhibit 8A.1

Sales Journal—
Periodic System

Cash Receipts Journal

The cash receipts journal under the periodic system is shown in Exhibit 8A.2. Note the absence of the column on the far right side to record debits to Cost of Goods Sold and credits to Inventory for the cost of merchandise sold (that we see under the perpetual system). Consistent with the cash receipts journal shown in the chapter, we show only the weekly (summary) cash sale entries.

Exhibit 8A.2

Cash Receipts Journal—
Periodic System

Cash Receipts Journal								Page 2
Date	**Account Credited**	**Explanation**	**PR**	**Cash Dr.**	**Sales Discount Dr.**	**Accounts Receivable Cr.**	**Sales Cr.**	**Other Accounts Cr.**
Feb. 7	Sales	Cash Sales	x	4,450			4,450	
12	Jason Henry	Invoice, 2/2	✓	441	9	450		
14	Sales	Cash sales	x	3,925			3,925	
17	Albert Co.	Invoice, 2/7	✓	490	10	500		
20	Notes Payable	Note to bank	245	750				750
21	Sales	Cash sales	x	4,700			4,700	
22	Interest revenue	Bank account	409	250				250
23	Bam Moore	Invoice, 2/13	✓	343	7	350		
25	Paul Roth	Invoice, 2/15	✓	196	4	200		
28	Sales	Cash sales	x	4,225			4,225	
28	Totals			19,770	30	1,500	17,300	1,000
				(101)	(415)	(106)	(413)	(x)

Purchases Journal

The purchases journal under the periodic system is shown in Exhibit 8A.3. This journal under a perpetual system included an Inventory column where the periodic system now has a Purchases column. All else is identical under the two systems.

Exhibit 8A.3

Purchases Journal—
Periodic System

					Accounts Payable Cr.	Purchases Dr.	Office Supplies Dr.	Other Accounts Dr.
Date	Account	Date of Invoice	Terms	PR				
Feb. 3	Horning Supply Co.	2/2	n/30	✓	350	275	75	
5	Ace Mfg. Co.	2/5	2/10, n/30	✓	200	200		
13	Wynet and Co.	2/10	2/10, n/30	✓	150	150		
20	Smite Co.	2/18	2/10, n/30	✓	300	300		
25	Ace Mfg. Co.	2/24	2/10, n/30	✓	100	100		
28	Store Supplies/ITT Co.	2/28	n/30	125/✓	225	125	25	75
28	Totals				1,325	1,150	100	75
					(201)	(505)	(124)	(x)

Purchases Journal — Page 1

Cash Disbursements Journal

The cash disbursements journal under a periodic system is shown in Exhibit 8A.4. This journal under the perpetual system included an Inventory column where the periodic system now has the Purchases Discounts column. All else is identical under the two systems.

Exhibit 8A.4

Cash Disbursements
Journal—Periodic System

						Purchases Discounts Cr.	Other Accounts Dr.	Accounts Payable Dr.
Date	Ck. No.	Payee	Account Debited	PR	Cash Cr.			
Feb. 3	105	L. and N. Railroad	Purchases	505	15		15	
12	106	East Sales Co.	Purchases	505	25		25	
15	107	Ace Mfg. Co.	Ace Mfg. Co.	✓	196	4		200
15	108	Jerry Hale	Salaries Expense	622	250		250	
20	109	Wynet and Co.	Wynet and Co.	✓	147	3		150
28	110	Smite Co.	Smite Co.	✓	294	6		300
28		Totals			927	13	290	650
					(101)	(507)	(x)	(201)

Cash Disbursements Journal — Page 2

Demonstration Problem—Periodic System

Refer to Pepper Company transactions described under the Demonstration Problem—Perpetual System to fulfill the following requirements.

Required

1. Open the following general ledger accounts: Cash (101), Accounts Receivable (106), Office Supplies (124), Store Equipment (165), Accounts Payable (201), Long-Term Notes Payable (251), Sales (413), Sales Returns and Allowances (414), Sales Discounts (415), Purchases (505), Purchases Returns and Allowances (506), Purchases Discounts (507), and Sales Salaries Expense (621). Open the following accounts receivable ledger accounts: Marjorie Allen, Dennie Hoskins, and Jennifer Nelson. Open the following accounts payable ledger accounts: Defore Industries, Mack Company, Schmidt Supply, and Welch Company.

2. Enter the transactions using a sales journal, a purchases journal, a cash receipts journal, a cash disbursements journal, and a general journal similar to the ones illustrated in Appendix 8A. Regularly post to the individual customer and creditor accounts. Also, post any amounts that should be posted as individual amounts to general ledger accounts. Foot and crossfoot the journals and make the month-end postings. *Pepper Co. uses the periodic inventory system in this problem.*

3. Prepare a trial balance and prove the accuracy of subsidiary ledgers by preparing schedules of accounts receivable and accounts payable.

Solution to Demonstration Problem—Periodic System

Sales Journal				Page 2
Date	Account Debited	Invoice Number	PR	Accts. Rec. Dr. Sales Cr.
Mar. 4	Jennifer Nelson	954	✓	16,800
6	Dennie Hoskins	955	✓	10,200
20	Marjorie Allen	956	✓	5,600
31	Totals			32,600
				(106/413)

Cash Receipts Journal								Page 3
Date	Account Credited	Explanation	PR	Cash Debit	Sales Discount Debit	Accts. Rec. Credit	Sales Credit	Other Accts. Credit
Mar. 12	L.T. Notes Payable	Note to bank	251	26,000				26,000
14	Jennifer Nelson	Invoice, 3/4	✓	16,464	336	16,800		
16	Dennie Hoskins	Invoice, 3/6	✓	9,996	204	10,200		
31	Sales	Cash sales	x	134,680			134,680	
31	Totals			187,140	540	27,000	134,680	26,000
				(101)	(415)	(106)	(413)	(x)

Purchases Journal							Page 3
Date	Account	Date of Invoice	Terms	PR	Accts. Payable Credit	Purchases Debit	Office Supplies Debit	Other Accts. Debit
Mar. 6	Office Supplies/Mack Co	3/3	n/30	✓	1,220		1,220	
11	Defore Industries	3/6	2/10, n/30	✓	52,600	52,600		
18	Store Equipment/Schmidt Supp	3/15	n/30	165/✓	22,850			22,850
22	Welch Company	3/18	2/10, n/30	✓	41,625	41,625		
31	Totals				118,295	94,225	1,220	22,850
					(201)	(505)	(124)	(x)

Cash Disbursements Journal								**Page 3**
Date	**Ck. No.**	**Payee**	**Account Debited**	**PR**	**Cash Credit**	**Purch. Disc. Credit**	**Other. Accts. Debit**	**Accts. Payable Debit**
Mar 21	516	Defore Industries	Defore Industries	✓	51,352	1,048		52,400
31	517	Payroll	Sales Salaries Expense	621	15,900		15,900	
31		Totals			67,252	1,048	15,900	52,400
					(101)	(507)	(x)	(201)

General Journal				**Page 2**
Mar. 16	Accounts Payable—Defore Industries	201/✓	200	
	Purchases Returns and Allowances	506		200
	To record credit memorandum received.			
	Sales Returns and Allowances	414	600	
	Accounts Receivable—Marjorie Allen	106/✓		600
	To record credit memorandum issued.			

Accounts Receivable Ledger

Marjorie Allen

Date	PR	Debit	Credit	Balance
Mar. 20	S2	5,600		5,600
26	G2		600	5,000

Dennie Hoskins

Date	PR	Debit	Credit	Balance
Mar. 6	S2	10,200		10,200
16	R3		10,200	0

Jennifer Nelson

Date	PR	Debit	Credit	Balance
Mar. 4	S2	16,800		16,800
14	R3		16,800	0

Accounts Payable Ledger

Defore Industries

Date	PR	Debit	Credit	Balance
Mar. 11	P3		52,600	52,600
16	G2	200		52,400
21	D3	52,400		0

Mack Company

Date	PR	Debit	Credit	Balance
Mar. 6	P3		1,220	1,220

Schmidt Supply

Date	PR	Debit	Credit	Balance
Mar. 18	P3		22,850	22,850

Welch Company

Date	PR	Debit	Credit	Balance
Mar. 22	P3		41,625	41,625

General Ledger

Cash   Acct. No. 101

Date	PR	Debit	Credit	Balance
Mar. 31	R3	187,140		187,140
31	D4		67,252	119,888

Accounts Receivable   Acct. No. 106

Date	PR	Debit	Credit	Balance
Mar. 26	G2		600	(600)
31	S2	32,600		32,000
31	R3		27,000	5,000

Office Supplies   Acct. No. 124

Date	PR	Debit	Credit	Balance
Mar. 31	P3	1,220		1,220

Store Equipment   Acct. No. 165

Date	PR	Debit	Credit	Balance
Mar. 18	P3	22,850		22,850

Accounts Payable   Acct. No. 201

Date	PR	Debit	Credit	Balance
Mar. 6	G2	200		(200)
31	P3		118,295	118,095
31	D3	52,400		65,695

Long-Term Notes Payable   Acct. No. 251

Date	PR	Debit	Credit	Balance
Mar. 12			26,000	26,000

Sales   Acct. No. 413

Date	PR	Debit	Credit	Balance
Mar. 31	S2		32,600	32,600
31	R3		134,680	167,280

Sales Returns and Allowances   Acct. No. 414

Date	PR	Debit	Credit	Balance
Mar. 26	G2	600		600

Sales Discounts   Acct. No. 415

Date	PR	Debit	Credit	Balance
Mar. 31	R3	540		540

Purchases   Acct. No. 505

Date	PR	Debit	Credit	Balance
Mar. 31	P3	94,225		94,225

Purchases Returns and Allowances   Acct. No. 506

Date	PR	Debit	Credit	Balance
Mar. 6	G2		200	200

Purchases Discounts   Acct. No. 507

Date	PR	Debit	Credit	Balance
Mar. 31	D3		1,048	1,048

Sales Salaries Expense   Acct. No. 621

Date	PR	Debit	Credit	Balance
Mar. 31	D3	15,900		15,900

PEPPER COMPANY
Trial Balance
March 31

	Debit	Credit
Cash	$119,888	
Accounts receivable	5,000	
Office supplies	1,220	
Store equipment	22,850	
Accounts payable		$ 65,695
Long-term notes payable		26,000
Sales		167,280
Sales returns and allowances	600	
Sales discounts	540	
Purchases	94,225	
Purchases returns and allowances		200
Purchases discounts		1,048
Sales salaries expense	15,900	
Totals	$260,223	$260,223

PEPPER COMPANY
Schedule of Accounts Receivable
March 31

Marjorie Allen	$5,000
Total accounts receivable	$5,000

PEPPER COMPANY
Schedule of Accounts Payable
March 31

Mack Company	$ 1,220
Schmidt Supply	22,850
Welch Company	41,625
Total accounts payable	$65,695

Summary

C1 **Identify fundamental principles of accounting information systems.** Accounting information systems are governed by five fundamental principles: control, relevance, compatibility, flexibility, and cost-benefit.

C2 **Identify components of accounting information systems.** The five basic components of an accounting information system are source documents, input devices, information processors, information storage, and output devices.

C3 **Explain the goals and uses of special journals.** Special journals are used for recording transactions of similar type, each meant to cover one kind of transaction. Four of the most common special journals are the sales journal, cash receipts journal, purchases journal, and cash disbursements journal. Special journals are efficient and cost-effective tools in the journalizing and posting processes, and they allow division of labor.

C4 **Describe the use of controlling accounts and subsidiary ledgers.** A general ledger keeps controlling accounts such as Accounts Receivable and Accounts Payable, but details on individual accounts making up the controlling account are kept in subsidiary ledgers (such as an accounts receivable ledger). The balance in a controlling account must equal the sum of its subsidiary account balances after posting is complete.

C5 **Explain how technology-based information systems impact accounting.** Technology-based information systems aim to increase the accuracy, speed, efficiency, and convenience of accounting procedures.

A1 **Analyze a company's performance and financial condition by business segments.** A business segment is a part of a company that is separately identified by its products or services or by the geographic market it serves. Analysis of a company's segments is aided by a segment contribution matrix listing one or more measures such as sales by segments.

P1 **Journalize and post transactions using special journals.** Each special journal is devoted to similar kinds of transactions. Transactions are journalized on one line of a special journal, with columns devoted to specific accounts, dates, names, posting references, explanations, and other necessary information. Posting is threefold: (1) individual amounts in the Other Accounts column are posted to their general ledger accounts on a regular (daily) basis, (2) individual amounts in a column whose total is *not* posted to a controlling account at the end of a period (month) are posted regularly (daily) to their general ledger accounts, and (3) total amounts for all columns except the Other Accounts column are posted at the end of a period (month) to their column's account title in the general ledger.

P2 **Prepare and prove the accuracy of subsidiary ledgers.** Account balances in the general ledger and its subsidiary ledgers are tested for accuracy after posting is complete. This procedure is twofold: (1) prepare a trial balance of the general ledger to confirm that debits equal credits and (2) prepare a schedule to confirm that the controlling account's balance equals the subsidiary ledger's balance.

P3 **Journalize and post transactions using special journals in a periodic inventory system.** Transactions are journalized and posted using special journals in a periodic system. The methods are similar to those in a perpetual system; the primary difference is that both cost of goods sold and inventory are not adjusted at the time of each sale. This usually results in the deletion (or renaming) of one or more columns devoted to these accounts in each special journal.

Guidance Answers to You Make the Call

Accountant   The main issue is whether commissions have an actual or perceived impact on the integrity and objectivity of your advice. You probably should not accept a commission arrangement (the AICPA Code of Ethics prohibits it when you perform the audit or a review). In any event, you should tell the client of your commission arrangement. Also, you need to seriously examine the merits of agreeing to a commission arrangement when you are in a position to exploit it.

Entrepreneur   The accounts receivable ledger has much of the information you need. It lists detailed information for each customer's account, including the amounts, dates for transactions, and dates of payments. It can be reorganized into an "aging schedule" to show how long customers wait before paying their bills. We describe an aging schedule in Chapter 10.

Controller   Much of the information you need is in the accounts payable ledger. It contains information for each supplier, the amounts due, and when payments are made. This subsidiary ledger along with information on credit terms should enable you to conduct your analyses.

Banker   This merchandiser's segment information is likely to greatly impact your loan decision. The risks associated with the company's two sources of net income are quite different. While net income is up by 10%, U.S. operations are performing poorly and Cuban operations are subject to many uncertainties. These uncertainties depend on political events, legal issues, business relationships, Cuban economic conditions, and a host of other risks. Overall, net income results suggested a low-risk loan opportunity, but the segment information reveals a high-risk situation.

Guidance Answers to **Quick Checks**

1. The five components are source documents, input devices, information processors, information storage, and output devices.

2. An information processor interprets, transforms, and summarizes the recorded accounting information so that it can be used in analysis, interpretation, and decision making.

3. Data saved in information storage are used to prepare periodic financial reports and special-purpose internal reports as well as source documentation for auditors.

4. All cash payments by check are recorded in the cash disbursements journal.

5. Columnar journals allow us to accumulate repetitive debits and credits and post them as column totals rather than as individual amounts from each entry.

6. The equality of debits and credits is kept within the general ledger. The subsidiary ledger keeps the customer's individual account and is used only for supplementary information.

7. An initial and the page number of the journal from which the amount was posted are entered in the PR column of the ledger account next to the amount.

8. A separate column for Sales Taxes Payable can be included in both the cash receipts journal and the sales journal.

9. This refers to a procedure of using copies of sales invoices as a sales journal. Each invoice total is posted directly to the customer's account. All invoices are totaled at month-end for posting to the general ledger accounts.

10. The normal recording and posting procedures are threefold. First, transactions are entered in a special journal column if applicable. Second, individual amounts are posted to the subsidiary ledger accounts. Third, column totals are posted to general ledger accounts.

11. Controlling accounts must be debited periodically for an amount or amounts equal to the sum of their respective debits in the subsidiary ledgers, and they must be credited periodically for an amount or amounts equal to the sum of their respective credits in the subsidiary ledgers.

12. Tests for accuracy of account balances in the general ledger and subsidiary ledgers are twofold. First, we prepare a trial balance of the general ledger to confirm that debits equal credits. Second, we prove the subsidiary ledgers by preparing schedules of accounts receivable and accounts payable.

13. The general journal is still needed for adjusting, closing, and correcting entries and for special transactions such as sales returns, purchases returns, and certain asset purchases.

14. Integrated systems can save time and minimize errors. This is so because actions taken in one part of the system automatically affect and update related parts.

15. Computer systems offer increased accuracy, speed, efficiency, and convenience.

16. Computer networks can create advantages by linking computers, giving different users and different computers access to common databases and programs.

Glossary

Accounting information system people, records, and methods that collect and process data from transactions and events, organize them in useful forms, and communicate results to decision makers. (p. 302).

Accounts payable ledger subsidiary ledger listing individual creditor (supplier) accounts. (p. 306).

Accounts receivable ledger subsidiary ledger listing individual customer accounts. (p. 306).

Batch processing approach that accumulates source documents for a period of time and then processes them all at once such as once a day, week, or month. (p. 317).

Business segment part of a company that can be separately identified by the products or services that it provides or by the geographic markets that it serves. (p. 319).

Cash disbursements journal special journal used to record all payments of cash; also called *cash payments journal*. (p. 315).

Cash receipts journal special journal used to record all receipts of cash. (p. 311).

Check register another name for a cash disbursements journal when the journal has a column for check numbers. (p. 316).

Columnar journal journal with more than one column. (p. 307).

Compatibility principle information system principle that requires an accounting system to conform with a company's activities, personnel, and structure. (p. 302).

Computer hardware physical equipment in a computerized accounting information system. (p. 317).

Computer network linkage giving different users and different computers access to common databases and programs. (p. 318).

Computer software programs that direct operations of computer hardware. (p. 317).

Controlling account general ledger account, the balance of which (after posting) equals the sum of the balances in its related subsidiary ledger. (p. 306).

Control principle information system principle that requires an accounting system to aid managers in controlling and monitoring business activities. (p. 302).

Cost-benefit principle information system principle that requires the benefits from an activity in an accounting system to outweigh the costs of that activity. (p. 303).

Enterprise resource planning (ERP) software programs that manage a company's vital operations, which range from order taking to manufacturing to accounting. (p. 318).

Flexibility principle information system principle that requires an accounting system be able to adapt to changes in the company, business, and needs of decision makers. (p. 302).

Information processor component of an accounting system that interprets, transforms, and summarizes information for use in analysis and reporting. (p. 304).

Information storage component of an accounting system that keeps data in a form accessible to information processors. (p. 304).

Input device means of capturing information from source documents that enables its transfer to information processors. (p. 303).

Online processing approach to inputting data from source documents as soon as a document is available. (p. 317).

Output devices means by which information is taken out of the accounting system and made available for use. (p. 304).

Purchases journal journal used to record all purchases on credit. (p. 313).

Relevance principle information system principle requiring that its reports be useful, understandable, timely, and pertinent for decision making. (p. 302).

Sales journal journal used to record sales of merchandise on credit. (p. 307).

Schedule of accounts payable list of the balances of all accounts in the accounts payable ledger and their total. (p. 314).

Schedule of accounts receivable list of balances for all accounts in the accounts receivable ledger and their total. (p. 309).

Segment contribution matrix list of one or more measures (such as sales) by seg-

ment; usually in dollars and percents along with a growth rate. (p. 319).

Special journal any journal used for recording and posting transactions of a similar type. (p. 305).

Subsidiary ledger list of individual accounts with a common characteristic; linked to a controlling account in the general ledger. (p. 306).

[A superscript ^{A} denotes assignments based on Appendix 8A.]

Questions

1. What are the five fundamental principles of accounting information systems?

2. What are five basic components of an accounting system?

3. What are source documents? Give two examples.

4. What is the purpose of an input device? Give examples of input devices for computer systems.

5. What is the difference between data that are stored off-line and data that are stored online?

6. What purpose is served by the output devices of an accounting system?

7. When special journals are used, they are usually used to record each of four different types of transactions. What are these four common types of transactions?

8. What notations are entered into the Posting Reference column of a ledger account?

9. When a general journal entry is used to record a returned credit sale, the credit of the entry must be posted twice. Does this cause the trial balance to be out of balance? Explain.

10. Describe the procedures involving the use of copies of a company's sales invoices as a sales journal.

11. Credits to customer accounts and credits to other Accounts are individually posted from a cash receipts journal such as the one in Exhibit 8.7. Why not put both types of credits in the same column and save journal space?

12. Why should sales to and receipts of cash from credit customers be recorded and posted daily?

13. Locate the note that discusses **Nike**'s operations by major product lines in Appendix A. In what product line does Nike predominantly operate?

14. Does the income statement of **Reebok** in Appendix A indicate the net income earned by Reebok's business segments? If so, list them.

15. Does the balance sheet of **Gap** in Appendix A indicate the identifiable assets owned by Gap's business segments? If so, list them.

QUICK STUDY

QS 8-1

Accounting information
system principles

Place the letter of each systems principle in the blank next to its best description.

A. Control principle   **D.** Flexibility principle

B. Relevance principle   **E.** Cost-benefit principle

C. Compatibility principle

1. _____ The principle requiring the accounting information system to change in response to technological advances and competitive pressures.

2. _____ The principle requiring the accounting information system to help monitor activities.

3. _____ The principle requiring the accounting information system to provide timely information for effective decision making.

4. _____ The principle requiring the accounting information system to adapt to the unique characteristics of the company.

5. _____ The principle that affects all other accounting information system principles.

Fill in the blanks to complete the following descriptions:

1. With _____ processing, source documents are accumulated for a period of time and then processed all at the same time, such as once a day, week, or month.

2. A computer _____ allows different computer users to share access to data and programs.

3. A _____ is an input device that captures writing and other input directly from source documents.

4. _____ _____ _____ software comprises programs that help manage a company's vital operations, from manufacturing to accounting.

QS 8-2
Accounting information system

C2

Identify the most likely role in an accounting system played by each of the lettered items A through L by assigning a number from the list on the left:

1. Source documents
2. Input devices
3. Information processor
4. Information storage
5. Output devices

_____ **A.** Bar code reader
_____ **B.** Filing cabinet
_____ **C.** Bank statement
_____ **D.** Computer scanner
_____ **E.** Computer keyboard
_____ **F.** Zip disc
_____ **G.** Computer monitor
_____ **H.** Invoice from a supplier
_____ **I.** Computer software
_____ **J.** Computer printer
_____ **K.** Digital camera
_____ **L.** MP3 player

QS 8-3
Accounting information system components

C2

Randa Electronics uses a sales journal, a purchases journal, a cash receipts journal, a cash disbursements journal, and a general journal. Randa recently completed the following transactions _a_ through _h_. Identify the journal in which each transaction should be recorded.

a. Paid a creditor.
b. Sold merchandise on credit.
c. Purchased shop supplies on credit.
d. Paid an employee's salary.

e. Borrowed money from the bank.
f. Sold merchandise for cash.
g. Purchased merchandise on credit.
h. Purchased inventory for cash.

QS 8-4
Special journal identification

C3

Buy-The-Book Shop uses a sales journal, a purchases journal, a cash receipts journal, a cash disbursements journal, and a general journal. The following transactions occurred during November. Journalize the November transactions that should be recorded in the general journal.

Nov. 2 Purchased $2,600 of merchandise on credit from the Everly Co., terms 2/10, n/30.
12 The owner, N. Falco, contributed an automobile worth $17,000 to the business.
16 Sold $1,200 of merchandise on credit to G. Paltrow, terms n/30.
19 G. Paltrow returned $175 of merchandise originally purchased on November 16.

QS 8-5
Entries in the general journal

C3

Flex is a company with publicly traded securities that operates in more than one industry. Which of the following items of information about each industry segment must the company report?

1. Operating income.
2. Revenues
3. Operating expenses
4. Net sales

5. Cash flows
6. Capital expenditures
7. Identifiable assets
8. Amortization and depreciation

QS 8-6
Required segment reporting

A1

EXERCISES

Exercise 8-1

Sales journal—perpetual

Weaver Company uses a sales journal, a purchases journal, a cash receipts journal, a cash disbursement journal, and a general journal. The following transactions occur in the month of March:

Mar. 2   Sold merchandise costing $300 to K. Kietzman for $450 cash, invoice no. 5703.
     5   Purchased $2,400 of merchandise on credit from Tent Corp.
     7   Sold merchandise costing $800 to C. Benton for $1,250, terms 2/10, n/30, invoice no. 5704.
     8   Borrowed $9,000 cash by giving a note to the bank.
    12   Sold merchandise costing $200 to R. Laman for $340, terms n/30, invoice no. 5705.
    16   Received $1,225 cash from C. Benton to pay for the purchase of February 7.
    19   Sold $900 of used store equipment to Swender, Inc.
    25   Sold merchandise costing $500 to T. Docking for $750, terms n/30, invoice no. 5706.

Prepare headings for a sales journal like the one in Exhibit 8.5. Journalize the March transactions that should be recorded in this sales journal.

Exercise 8-2^A

Sales journal—periodic

Prepare headings for a sales journal like the one in Exhibit 8A.1. Journalize the March transactions shown in Exercise 8-1 that should be recorded in the sales journal assuming the periodic inventory system is used.

Exercise 8-3

Cash receipts journal—perpetual

True Co. uses a sales journal, a purchases journal, a cash receipts journal, a cash disbursements journal, and a general journal. The following transactions occur in the month of November.

Nov. 3   Purchased $3,200 of merchandise on credit from Passat Co.
     7   Sold merchandise costing $840 on credit to J. Trost for $1,000, subject to a $20 sales discount if paid by the end of the month.
     9   Borrowed $3,750 cash by giving a note to the bank.
    13   J. Atherton, the owner, contributed $5,000 cash to the company.
    18   Sold merchandise costing $250 to B. Baird for $330 cash.
    22   Paid Passat Co. $3,200 cash for the merchandise purchased on November 3.
    27   Received $980 cash from J. Trost in payment of the November 7 purchase.
    30   Paid salaries of $1,650.

Prepare headings for a cash receipts journal like the one in Exhibit 8.7. Journalize the November transactions that should be recorded in the cash receipts journal.

Exercise 8-4^A

Cash receipts journal—periodic

Prepare headings for a cash receipts journal like the one in Exhibit 8A.2. Journalize the November transactions shown in Exercise 8-3 that should be recorded in the cash receipts journal assuming the periodic inventory system is used.

Exercise 8-5

Purchases journal—perpetual

Sweeney Company uses a sales journal, a purchases journal, a cash receipts journal, a cash disbursements journal, and a general journal. The following transactions occur in the month of June.

June 1   Purchased $9,100 of merchandise on credit from Lockett, Inc., terms n/30.
     8   Sold merchandise on credit to R. Jones for $1,400 subject to a $28 sales discount if paid by the end of the month.
    14   Purchased $340 of store supplies from Pak Company on credit, terms n/30.
    17   Purchased $380 of office supplies on credit from Stein Company, terms n/30.
    24   Sold merchandise to L. Leetch for $630 cash.
    28   Purchased store supplies from Quinn's for $90 cash.
    29   Paid Lockett, Inc., $9,100 for the merchandise purchased on July 1.

Prepare headings for a purchases journal like the one in Exhibit 8.9. Journalize the June transactions that should be recorded in the purchases journal.

Exercise 8-6^A

Purchases journal—periodic

Prepare headings for a purchases journal like the one in Exhibit 8A.3. Journalize the June transactions from Exercise 8-5 that should be recorded in the purchases journal assuming the periodic inventory system is used.

Tucker Supply uses a sales journal, a purchases journal, a cash receipts journal, a cash disbursements journal, and a general journal. The following transactions occur in the month of April.

Apr. 3   Purchased merchandise for $2,950 on credit from Strider, Inc., terms 2/10, n/30.
9   Issued check no. 210 to Najima Corp. to buy store supplies for $550.
12   Sold merchandise on credit to C. Kamp for $770, terms n/30.
17   Issued check no. 211 for $1,400 to repay a note payable to City Bank.
20   Purchased merchandise for $4,500 on credit from LeDuc, terms 2/10, n/30.
29   Issued check no. 212 to LeDuc to pay the amount due for the purchase of March 20, less the discount.
31   Paid salary of $1,800 to B. Deal by issuing check no. 213.
31   Issued check no. 214 to Strider, Inc., to pay the amount due for the purchase of March 3.

Prepare headings for a cash disbursements journal like the one in Exhibit 8.11. Journalize the April transactions that should be recorded in the cash disbursements journal.

Exercise 8-7
Cash disbursements journal—perpetual

Prepare headings for a cash disbursements journal like the one in Exhibit 8A.4. Journalize the April transactions from Exercise 8-7 that should be recorded in the cash disbursements journal assuming the periodic inventory system is used.

Exercise 8-8[A]
Cash disbursements journal—periodic

Roscoe Pharmacy uses the following journals: sales journal, purchases journal, cash receipts journal, cash disbursements journal, and general journal. On June 5, Roscoe purchased merchandise priced at $14,000, subject to credit terms of 2/10, n/30. On June 14, the pharmacy paid the net amount due. In journalizing the payment, the pharmacy debited Accounts Payable for $14,000 but failed to record the cash discount on the purchases. Cash was properly credited for the actual amount paid. In what journals would the June 5 and the June 14 transactions be recorded? What procedure is likely to discover the error in journalizing the June 14 transaction?

Exercise 8-9
Special journal transactions and error discovery

At the end of May, the sales journal of Outdoor Horizon appears as follows:

Exercise 8-10
Posting to subsidiary ledger accounts

	Sales Journal				
Date	Account Debited	Invoice Number	PR	Accounts Receivable Dr. Sales Cr.	Cost of Good Sold Dr. Inventory Cr.
May 6	Cameron Smith	190		3,880	3,120
10	Deke Harris	191		2,940	2,325
17	Liz Buck	192		1,850	1,480
25	Deke Harris	193		1,340	1,075
31	Totals			10,010	8,000

Outdoor Horizon also recorded the return of certain merchandise with the following entry:

May 20	Sales Returns and Allowances	350	
	Accounts Receivable—Liz Buck		350
	Customer returned merchandise.		

Required

1. Open an accounts receivable subsidiary ledger that has a T-account for each customer listed in the sales journal. Post to the customer accounts the entries in the sales journal and any portion of the general journal entry that affects a customer's account.

2. Open a general ledger that has T-accounts for Accounts Receivable, Inventory, Sales, Sales Returns and Allowances, and Cost of Goods Sold. Post the sales journal and any portion of the general journal entry that affects these accounts.

3. Prepare a schedule of accounts in the accounts receivable ledger and add their balances to show that the total equals the balance in the Accounts Receivable controlling account.

Exercise 8-11^A

Posting from special journals to general and subsidiary ledgers—periodic

The condensed journals of Tops Trophies follow. The journal column headings are incomplete and do not indicate whether the columns are debit or credit columns.

Sales Journal

Account	
Jack Elfrink	4,700
Dave Joy	9,400
Ken Stone	2,000
Total	16,100

Purchases Journal

Account	
Green Corp.	6,400
Sutter, Inc.	5,500
Alli Company	2,700
Total	14,600

Cash Receipts Journal

Account	Cash	Sales Discounts	Accounts Receivable	Sales	Other Accounts
Jack Elfrink	4,312	88	4,400		
Sales	3,250			3,250	
Notes Payable	6,000				6,000
Sales	825			825	
Dave Joy	9,212	188	9,400		
Store Equipment	500				500
Totals	24,099	276	13,800	4,075	6,500

Cash Disbursements Journal

Account	Cash	Purchases Discounts	Other Accounts	Accounts Payable
Prepaid Insurance	850		850	
Sutter, Inc.	5,335	165		5,500
Green Corp.	5,537	113		5,650
Store Equipment	1,750		1,750	
Totals	13,472	278	2,600	11,150

General Journal

Sales Returns and Allowances		300	
Accounts Receivable—Jack Elfrink			300
Accounts Payable—Green Corp.		750	
Purchases Returns and Allowances			750

Prepare T-accounts for the following general ledger and subsidiary ledger accounts. Separate the accounts of each ledger group as follows:

General Ledger Accounts	Accounts Receivable Ledger Accounts
Cash	
Accounts Receivable	Jack Elfrink
Prepaid Insurance	Dave Joy
Store Equipment	Ken Stone
Accounts Payable	
Notes Payable	Accounts Payable Ledger Accounts
Sales	
Sales Discounts	Green Corp.
Sales Returns and Allowances	Alli Company
Purchases	Sutter, Inc.
Purchase Discounts	
Purchase Returns and Allowances	

Revise and show complete column headings for the special journals, and then post the entries reflected in the journals to their proper T-accounts.

Henderson Company posts its sales invoices directly and then binds them into a Sales Journal. Henderson had the following credit sales to these customers during June:

Exercise 8-12
Accounts receivable ledger

June	2	Jay Hall	$ 4,600
	8	Trey Wiltse	7,100
	10	Tere Bax	14,400
	14	Cindy Smith	21,500
	20	Tere Bax	12,200
	29	Jay Hall	8,300
		Total sales	$68,100

Required

1. Open a subsidiary accounts receivable ledger having a T-account for each customer. Post the invoices to the subsidiary ledger.

2. Open an Accounts Receivable controlling T-account and a Sales T-account. Post the end-of-month total from the sales journal to these accounts.

3. Prepare a schedule of accounts in the accounts receivable subsidiary ledger and add their balances to prove that the total equals the Accounts Receivable controlling balance account.

A company that records credit purchases in a purchases journal and records purchases returns in a general journal made the following errors. Indicate when each error should be discovered:

Exercise 8-13
Purchases journal and error identification

1. Posted a purchases return to the Accounts Payable account and to the creditor's subsidiary account but did not post to the purchases return to the Inventory account.

2. Posted a purchases return to the Inventory account and to the Accounts Payable account but did not post to the creditor's subsidiary account.

3. Correctly recorded a $5,000 purchase in the purchases journal but posted it to the creditor's subsidiary account as a $500 purchase.

4. Made an addition error in determining the balance of a creditor's subsidiary account.

5. Made an addition error in totaling the Office Supplies column of the purchases journal.

Exercise 8-14

Analyzing segment information

Refer to Exhibit 8.13 and complete the segment contribution matrix for DogFog Company. Analyze and interpret the matrix, including identification of segments with the highest and lowest growth rates.

Segment	Sales Contribution (in $mil.)		Sales Contribution (in%)		One-Year Growth Rate Percent
	2002	2001	2002	2001	
Segment					
Skiing Group	$6,235	$3,685			
Skating Group	900	500			
Specialty Footwear	2,200	960			
Other specialty	1,075	425			
Subtotal					
General Merchandise					
South America	3,252	1,739			
United States	887	888			
Europe	549	150			
Subtotal					
Total					

PROBLEM SET A

Problem 8-1A

Special journals, subsidiary ledgers, and schedule of accounts receivable—perpetual

Wellington Company completes these transactions during April of the current year (the terms of all credit sales are 2/10, n/30):

Apr. 2   Purchased $14,300 of merchandise on credit from Duncan Company, invoice dated April 2, terms 2/10, n/60.

     3   Sold merchandise on credit to Joan Schmidt, Invoice No. 760, for $4,000 (cost is $3,000).

     3   Purchased $1,480 of office supplies on credit from Stevens Point, Inc. Invoice dated April 2, terms n/10 EOM.

     4   Issued Check No. 587 to *U.S. Times* for advertising expense, $899.

     5   Sold merchandise on credit to Paul Kane, Invoice No. 761, for $8,000 (cost is $6,500).

     6   Received an $80 credit memorandum from Stevens Point, Inc., for some of the office supplies received on April 3 and returned for credit.

     9   Purchased $12,125 of store equipment on credit from Sarah's Supply, invoice dated April 9, terms n/10 EOM.

     11   Sold merchandise on credit to Janice Griffin, Invoice No. 762, for $10,500 (cost is $7,000).

     12   Issued Check No. 588 to Duncan Company in payment of its April 2 invoice, less the discount.

     13   Received payment from Joan Schmidt for the April 3 sale, less the discount.

     13   Sold $5,100 of merchandise on credit to Joan Schmidt (cost is $3,600), Invoice No. 763.

     14   Received payment from Paul Kane for the April 5 sale, less the discount.

     16   Issued Check No. 589, payable to Payroll, in payment of sales salaries for the first half of the month, $10,750. Cashed the check and paid employees.

     16   Cash sales for the first half of the month are $52,840 (cost is $35,880). (Cash sales are recorded daily from cash register readings but are recorded only twice in this problem to reduce repetitive entries.)

     17   Purchased $13,750 of merchandise on credit from Maben Company, invoice dated April 16, terms 2/10, n/30.

     18   Borrowed $60,000 cash from First State Bank by giving a long-term note payable.

     20   Received payment from Janice Griffin for the April 11 sale, less the discount.

     20   Purchased $830 of store supplies on credit from Sarah's Supply, invoice dated April 19, terms n/10 EOM.

     23   Received a $750 credit memorandum from Maben Company for defective merchandise received on April 17 and returned for credit.

     23   Received payment from Joan Schmidt for the April 13 sale, less the discount.

     25   Purchased $11,375 of merchandise on credit from Duncan Company, invoice dated April 24, terms 2/10, n/60.

     26   Issued Check No. 590 to Maben Company in payment of its April 17 invoice, less the return and the discount.

27   Sold $3,170 of merchandise on credit to Paul Kane, Invoice No. 764 (cost is $2,520).

27   Sold $6,700 of merchandise on credit to Janice Griffin, Invoice No. 765 (cost is $4,305).

30   Issued Check No. 591, payable to Payroll, in payment of the sales salaries for the last half of the month, $10,750.

30   Cash sales for the last half of the month are $73,975 (cost is $58,900).

Required

Preparation Component

1. Prepare a sales journal like Exhibit 8.5 and a cash receipts journal like Exhibit 8.7. Number both journal pages as page 3. Then review the transactions of Wellington Company and enter those that should be journalized in the sales journal and those that should be journalized in the cash receipts journal. Ignore any transactions that should be journalized in a purchases journal, a cash disbursements journal, or a general journal.

2. Open the following general ledger accounts: Cash, Accounts Receivable, Inventory, Long-Term Notes Payable, Cost of Goods Sold, Sales, and Sales Discounts. Enter the March 31 balances for Cash ($85,000), Inventory ($125,000), and Long-Term Notes Payable ($210,000). Also open subsidiary accounts receivable ledger accounts for Paul Kane, Joan Schmidt, and Janice Griffin.

3. Post items that should be posted as individual amounts from the journals. (Such items are posted daily but are posted only once here, because they are few in number.) Foot and crossfoot the journals and make the month-end postings.

4. Prepare a trial balance of the general ledger and prove the accuracy of the subsidiary ledger by preparing a schedule of accounts receivable.

Check Trial balance totals, $434,285

Analysis Component

5. Assume that the sum of account balances for the schedule of Accounts Receivable does not equal the balance of the controlling account in the general ledger. Describe steps you would take to discover the error(s).

Assume that Wellington Co. in Problem 8-1A uses the periodic inventory system.

Required

1. Prepare headings for a sales journal like the one in Exhibit 8A.1. Prepare headings for a cash receipts journal like the one in Exhibit 8A.2. Journalize the April transactions shown in Problem 8-1A that should be recorded in the sales journal and the cash receipts journal assuming the *periodic* inventory system is used.

2. Open the general ledger accounts with balances as shown in Problem 8-1A (do not open a Cost of Goods Sold ledger account). Under the periodic system, an Inventory account exists but is inactive until its balance is updated to the correct inventory balance at year-end. In this problem, the Inventory account remains inactive but must be included to correctly complete the trial balance.

3. Complete parts 3, 4, and 5 of Problem 8-1A using the results of parts 1 and 2 of this problem.

Problem 8-2A^A

Special journals, subsidiary ledgers, and schedule of accounts receivable—periodic

Check Trial balance totals, $434,285

The April transactions of Wellington Company are described in Problem 8-1A.

Required

1. Prepare a general journal, a purchases journal like Exhibit 8.9, and a cash disbursements journal like Exhibit 8.11. Number all journal pages as page 3. Review the April transactions of Wellington Company and enter those transactions that should be journalized in the general journal, the purchases journal, or the cash disbursements journal. Ignore any transactions that should be journalized in a sales journal or cash receipts journal.

2. Open the following general ledger accounts: Cash, Inventory, Office Supplies, Store Supplies, Store Equipment, Accounts Payable, Long-Term Notes Payable, Sales Salaries Expense, and Advertising Expense. Enter the March 31 balances of Cash ($85,000), Inventory ($125,000), and Long-Term Notes Payable ($210,000). Also open accounts payable subsidiary ledger accounts for Sarah's Supply, Duncan Company, Maben Company, and Stevens Point, Inc.

Problem 8-3A

Special journals, subsidiary ledgers, and schedule of accounts payable—perpetual

3. Post items that should be posted as individual amounts from the journals. (Such items are posted daily but are posted only once because they are few in number.) Foot and crossfoot the journals and make the month-end postings.

4. Prepare a trial balance of the general ledger and a schedule of accounts payable.

Problem 8-4A^A

Special journals, subsidiary ledgers, and schedule of accounts payable—periodic

The April transactions of Wellington Co. are described in Problem 8-1A.

Required

1. Prepare a general journal, a purchases journal like Exhibit 8A.3, and a cash disbursements journal like Exhibit 8A.4. Number all journal pages as page 3. Review the April transactions of Wellington Company (Problem 8-1A) and enter those transactions that should be journalized in the general journal, the purchases journal, or the cash disbursements journal. Ignore any transaction that should be journalized in a sales journal or cash receipts journal.

2. Open the following general ledger accounts: Cash, Inventory, Office Supplies, Store Supplies, Store Equipment, Accounts Payable, Long-Term Notes Payable, Purchases, Purchases Returns and Allowances, Purchases Discounts, Sales Salaries Expense, and Advertising Expense. Enter the March 31 balances of Cash ($85,000), Inventory ($125,000), and Long-Term Notes Payable ($210,000). Also open accounts payable subsidiary ledger accounts for Sarah's Supply, Duncan Company, Maben Company, and Stevens Point, Inc.

3. Complete parts 3 and 4 of Problem 8-3A using the results of parts 1 and 2 of this problem.

Problem 8-5A

Special journals, subsidiary ledgers, trial balance—perpetual

(If the Working Papers that accompany this textbook are not being used, omit this problem.)

You have just taken over the accounting for Chanute Enterprises, whose annual accounting period ends December 31. The company's previous accountant journalized its transactions through December 15 and posted all items that required posting as individual amounts (see the journals and ledgers in the Working Papers). The company's transactions beginning on December 16 follow (terms of all credit sales are 2/10, n/30):

Dec. 16 Sold merchandise on credit to Marcia Sayles, Invoice No. 916, for $8,700 (cost is $5,600).

17 Received a $1,040 credit memorandum from Ashley Company for merchandise received on December 15 and returned for credit.

17 Purchased $715 of office supplies on credit from BJ's Supply Company, invoice dated December 16, terms n/10 EOM.

18 Received a $40 credit memorandum from BJ's Supply Company for office supplies received on December 17 and returned for credit.

20 Issued a $500 credit memorandum to Margaret Clark for defective merchandise sold on December 15 and returned for credit.

21 Purchased $7,700 of store equipment on credit from BJ's Supply Company, invoice dated December 21, terms n/10 EOM.

22 Received payment from Marcia Sayles for the December 12 sale less the discount.

23 Issued Check No. 623 to Sonnenschein Company in payment of its December 15 invoice less the discount.

24 Sold merchandise on credit to Trent Smith, Invoice No. 917, for $1,400 (cost is $800).

24 Issued Check No. 624 to Ashley Company in payment of its December 15 invoice less the return and the discount.

25 Received payment from Margaret Clark for the December 15 sale less the return and the discount.

26 Received $8,400 of merchandise and an invoice dated December 25, terms 2/10, n/60, from Sonnenschein Company.

29 Sold a neighboring merchant five boxes of file folders (office supplies) at their cost of $45 cash.

30 Sandra Meade, the owner of Chanute Enterprises, used Check No. 625 to withdraw $3,500 cash from the business for personal use.

31 Issued Check No. 626 to Jamie Sharp, the company's only sales employee, in payment of her $2,222 salary for the last half of December.

31 Issued Check No. 627 to Rural Electric Company in payment of its $810 December electric bill.

31 Cash sales for the last half of the month are $35,800 (cost is $17,400). (Cash sales are recorded daily but are recorded only twice in this problem to reduce repetitive entries.)

Required

1. Record these transactions in the journals provided in the working papers.

2. Post any amounts that should be posted as individual amounts to the general ledger accounts, including posting to the customer and creditor accounts. (Such items are posted daily but are posted only once here because they are few in number.) Foot and crossfoot the journals and make the month-end postings.

3. Prepare a December 31 trial balance and prove the accuracy of the subsidiary ledgers by preparing schedules of both accounts receivable and accounts payable.

Check Trial balance totals, $228,208

Bishop Company completes these transactions and events during March of the current year (terms of all credit sales are 2/10, n/30):

Mar. 1	Received $43,600 of merchandise and an invoice dated March 1, terms 2/15, n/30, from Fox Industries.
2	Sold merchandise on credit to Armand Leon, Invoice No. 854, for $16,800 (cost is $8,400).
3	Purchased $1,230 of office supplies on credit from Hilary Company, invoice dated March 3, terms n/10 EOM.
3	Sold merchandise on credit to Kit Dean, Invoice No. 855, for $10,200 (cost is $5,800).
6	Borrowed $82,000 cash by giving Commerce Bank a long-term note payable.
9	Purchased $21,850 of office equipment on credit from Rose Supply, invoice dated March 9, terms n/10 EOM.
10	Sold merchandise on credit to Taylor Wood, Invoice No. 856, for $5,600 (cost is $2,900).
12	Received payment from Armand Leon for the March 2 sale less the discount.
13	Sent Fox Industries Check No. 416 in payment of the March 1 invoice less the discount.
13	Received payment from Kit Dean for the March 3 sale less the discount.
14	Received $32,625 of merchandise and an invoice dated March 13, terms 2/10, n/30, from the LR Company.
15	Issued Check No. 417, payable to Payroll, in payment of sales salaries for the first half of the month, $18,300. Cashed the check and paid the employees.
15	Cash sales for the first half of the month are $34,680 (cost is $20,210). (Cash sales are recorded daily, but are recorded only twice here to reduce repetitive entries.)
15	Post to the customer and creditor accounts, and post any amounts that should be posted as individual amounts to the general ledger accounts. (Such items are posted daily but are posted only twice here because they are few in number.)
16	Purchased $1,770 of store supplies on credit from Hilary Company, invoice dated March 16, terms n/10 EOM.
17	Received a $2,425 credit memorandum from LR Company for unsatisfactory merchandise received on March 14 and returned for credit.
19	Received a $630 credit memorandum from Rose Supply for office equipment received on March 9 and returned for credit.
20	Received payment from Taylor Wood for the sale of March 10 less the discount.
23	Issued Check No. 418 to LR Company in payment of the invoice of March 13 less the return and the discount.
27	Sold merchandise on credit to Taylor Wood, Invoice No. 857, for $14,910 (cost is $7,220).
28	Sold merchandise on credit to Kit Dean, Invoice No. 858, for $6,315 (cost is $3,280).
31	Issued Check No. 419, payable to Payroll, in payment of sales salaries for the last half of the month, $18,300. Cashed the check and paid the employees.
31	Cash sales for the last half of the month are $30,180 (cost is $16,820).
31	Post to the customer and creditor accounts, and post any amounts that should be posted as individual amounts to the general ledger accounts. Foot and crossfoot the journals and make the month-end postings.

Problem 8-6A
Special journals, subsidiary ledgers, trial balance—perpetual

Required

1. Open the following general ledger accounts: Cash; Accounts Receivable; Inventory (March 1 beg. bal. is $10,000); Office Supplies; Store Supplies; Office Equipment; Accounts Payable; Long-Term Notes Payable; M. Bishop, Capital (March 1 beg. bal. is $10,000); Sales; Sales Discounts; Cost of Goods Sold; and Sales Salaries Expense. Open the following accounts receivable ledger accounts: Taylor Wood, Armand Leon, and Kit Dean. Open the following accounts payable ledger accounts: Hilary Company, Fox Industries, Rose Supply, and LR Company.

2. Enter these transactions in a sales journal like Exhibit 8.5, a purchases journal like Exhibit 8.9, a cash receipts journal like Exhibit 8.7, a cash disbursements journal like Exhibit 8.11, or a general journal. Post when instructed to do so.

3. Prepare a trial balance of the general ledger and prove the accuracy of the subsidiary ledgers by preparing schedules of both accounts receivable and accounts payable.

Check   Trial balance totals, $234,905

Problem 8-7A[A]
Special journals, subsidiary ledgers, trial balance—periodic

Assume that Bishop Co. in Problem 8-6A uses the periodic inventory system.

Required

1. Open the following general ledger accounts: Cash; Accounts Receivable; Inventory (March 1 beg. bal. is $10,000); Office Supplies; Store Supplies; Office Equipment; Accounts Payable; Long-Term Notes Payable; M. Bishop, Capital (March 1 beg. bal. is $10,000); Sales; Sales Discounts; Purchases; Purchases Returns and Allowances; Purchases Discounts; and Sales Salaries Expense. Open the following accounts receivable ledger accounts: Taylor Wood, Armand Leon, and Kit Dean. Open the following Accounts Payable ledger accounts: Hilary Company, Fox Industries, Rose Supply, and LR Company.

2. Enter the transactions from Problem 8-6A in a sales journal like Exhibit 8A.1, a purchases journal like Exhibit 8A.3, a cash receipts journal like Exhibit 8A.2, a cash disbursements journal like Exhibit 8A.4, or a general journal. Post when instructed to do so.

Check   Trial balance totals, $238,806

3. Prepare a trial balance of the general ledger and prove the accuracy of the subsidiary ledgers by preparing schedules of both accounts receivable and accounts payable.

PROBLEM SET B

Problem 8-1B
Special journals, subsidiary ledgers, schedule of accounts receivable—perpetual

Best Industries completes these transactions during July of the current year (the terms of all credit sales are 2/10, n/30):

July 1   Purchased $6,500 of merchandise on credit from Torch Company, invoice dated June 30, terms 2/10, n/30.

3   Issued Check No. 300 to *The Weekly Reader* for advertising expense, $625.

5   Sold merchandise on credit to Kim Jeffries, Invoice No. 918, for $19,200 (cost is $10,500).

6   Sold merchandise on credit to Ruth Nyhus, Invoice No. 919, for $7,500 (cost is $4,300).

7   Purchased $1,250 of store supplies on credit from Prairie, Inc., invoice dated July 7, terms n/10 EOM.

8   Received a $250 credit memorandum from Prairie, Inc., for store supplies received on July 7 and returned for credit.

9   Purchased $38,220 of store equipment on credit from Gardner's Supply, invoice dated July 8, terms n/10 EOM.

10   Issued Check No. 301 to Torch Company in payment of its June 30 invoice, less the discount.

13   Sold merchandise on credit to Stephanie Davis, Invoice No. 920, $8,550 (cost $5,230).

14   Sold merchandise on credit to Kim Jeffries, Invoice No. 921, for $5,100 (cost is $3,800).

15   Received payment from Kim Jeffries for the July 5 sale, less the discount.

15   Issued Check No. 302, payable to Payroll, in payment of sales salaries for the first half of the month, $31,850. Cashed the check and paid employees.

15   Cash sales for the first half of the month are $118,350 (cost is $76,330). (Cash sales are recorded daily from the cash registers but are recorded only twice in this problem to reduce repetitive entries.)

16   Received payment from Ruth Nyhus for the July 6 sale, less the discount.

17   Purchased $7,200 of merchandise on credit from Adams Company, invoice dated July 17, terms 2/10, n/30.

20   Purchased $650 of office supplies on credit from Gardner's Supply, invoice dated July 19, terms n/10 EOM.

21   Borrowed $15,000 cash from College Bank by giving a long-term note payable.

23   Received payment from Stephanie Davis for the July 13 sale, less the discount.

24   Received payment from Kim Jeffries for the July 14 sale, less the discount.

24   Received a $2,400 credit memorandum from Adams Company for defective merchandise received on July 17 and returned for credit.

26 Purchased $9,770 of merchandise on credit from Torch Company, invoice dated July 26, terms 2/10, n/30.

27 Issued Check No. 303 to Adams Company in payment of its July 17 invoice, less the return and the discount.

29 Sold merchandise on credit to Ruth Nyhus, Invoice No. 922, for $17,502 (cost is $10,850).

30 Sold merchandise on credit to Stephanie Davis, Invoice No. 923, for $16,820 (cost is $9,840).

31 Issued Check No. 304, payable to Payroll, in payment of the sales salaries for the last half of the month, $31,850.

31 Cash sales for the last half of the month are $80,244 (cost is $53,855).

Required

Preparation Component

1. Prepare a sales journal like Exhibit 8.5 and a cash receipts journal like Exhibit 8.7. Number both journals as page 3. Then review the transactions of Best Industries and enter those transactions that should be journalized in the sales journal and those that should be journalized in the cash receipts journal. Ignore any transactions that should be journalized in a purchases journal, a cash disbursements journal, or a general journal.

2. Open the following general ledger accounts: Cash, Accounts Receivable, Inventory, Long-Term Notes Payable, Cost of Goods Sold, Sales, and Sales Discounts. Enter the June 30 balances for Cash ($100,000), Inventory ($200,000), and Long-Term Notes Payable ($300,000). Also open subsidiary accounts receivable ledger accounts for Kim Jeffries, Stephanie Davis, and Ruth Nyhus. Post the items that should be posted as individual amounts from the journals. (Such items are posted daily but are posted here only once since they are few in number.) Foot and crossfoot the journals and make the month-end postings.

3. Prepare a trial balance of the general ledger and prove the accuracy of the subsidiary ledger by preparing a schedule of accounts receivable.

Check Trial balance totals, $588,266

Analysis Component

4. Assume that the sum of account balances on the schedule of Accounts Receivable does not equal the balance of the controlling account in the general ledger. Describe steps you would take to discover the error(s).

Assume that Best Industries in Problem 8-1B uses the periodic inventory system.

Problem 8-2B[A]

Special journals, subsidiary ledgers, and schedule of accounts receivable—periodic

Required

1. Prepare headings for a sales journal like the one in Exhibit 8A.1. Prepare headings for a cash receipts journal like the one in Exhibit 8A.2. Journalize the July transactions shown in Problem 8-1B that should be recorded in the sales journal and the cash receipts journal assuming the periodic inventory system is used.

2. Open the general ledger accounts with balances as shown in Problem 8-1B (do not open a Cost of Goods Sold ledger account). Under the periodic system, an Inventory account exists but is inactive until its balance is updated to the correct inventory balance at year-end. In this problem, the Inventory account remains inactive but must be included to correctly complete the trial balance.

Check Trial balance totals, $588,266

3. Complete parts (3, 4, and 5) of Problem 8-1B using the results of parts 1 and 2 of this problem.

The July transactions of Best Industries are described in Problem 8-1B

Problem 8-3B

Special journals, subsidiary ledgers, and schedule of accounts payable—perpetual

Required

1. Prepare a general journal, a purchases journal like Exhibit 8.9, and a cash disbursements journal like Exhibit 8.11. Number all journal pages as page 3. Review the July transactions of Best Industries and enter those transactions that should be journalized in the general journal, the purchases journal, or the cash disbursements journal. Ignore any transactions that should be journalized in a sales journal or cash receipts journal.

2. Open the following general ledger accounts: Cash, Inventory, Office Supplies, Store Supplies, Store Equipment, Accounts Payable, Long-Term Notes Payable, Sales Salaries Expense, and

Advertising Expense. Enter the June 30 balances of Cash ($100,000), Inventory ($200,000), and Long-Term Notes Payable ($300,000). Also open accounts payable subsidiary ledger accounts for Gardner's Supply, Torch Company, Adams Company, and Prairie, Inc.

3. Post items that should be posted as individual amounts from the journals. (Such items are posted daily but are posted here only once since they are few in number.) Foot and crossfoot the journals and make the month-end postings.

Check   Trial balance totals, $349,640

4. Prepare a trial balance of the general ledger and a schedule of accounts payable.

Problem 8-4B^A

Special journals, subsidiary ledgers, and schedule of accounts payable—periodic

Check   Trial balance totals, $352,266

The July transactions of Best Industries are described in Problem 8-1B.

Required

1. Prepare a general journal, a purchases journal like Exhibit 8A.3, and a cash disbursements journal like Exhibit 8A.4. Number all journal pages as page 3. Review the July transactions of Best Company (Problem 8-1B) and enter those transactions that should be journalized in the general journal, the purchases journal, or the cash disbursements journal. Ignore any transaction that should be journalized in a sales journal or cash receipts journal.

2. Open the following general ledger accounts: Cash, Inventory, Office Supplies, Store Supplies, Store Equipment, Accounts Payable, Long-Term Notes Payable, Purchases, Purchases Returns and Allowances, Purchases Discounts, Sales Salaries Expense, and Advertising Expense. Enter the June 30 balances of Cash ($100,000), Inventory ($200,000), and Long-Term Notes Payable ($300,000). Also open accounts payable subsidiary ledger accounts for Torch Company, Prairie, Inc., Gardner's Supply, and Adams Company.

3. Complete parts 3 and 4 of Problem 8-3B using the results of parts 1 and 2 of this problem.

Problem 8-5B

Special journals, subsidiary ledgers, trial balance—perpetual

(If the Working Papers that accompany this textbook are not being used, omit this problem.)

You have just taken over the accounting for EZ Products, whose annual accounting period ends December 31. The company's previous accountant journalized its transactions through December 15 and posted all items that required posting as individual amounts (see the journals and ledgers in the working papers). The company's transactions beginning on December 16 follow (terms of all credit sales are 2/10, n/30):

Dec. 16   Purchased $865 of office supplies on credit from White Supply Company, invoice dated December 16, terms n/10 EOM.

16   Sold merchandise on credit to Brad Farris, Invoice No. 916, for $5,290 (cost is $3,821).

18   Issued a $200 credit memorandum to Leslie Snipes for defective merchandise sold on December 15 and returned for credit.

19   Received a $640 credit memorandum from Muser Company for merchandise received on December 15 and returned for credit.

20   Received a $143 credit memorandum from White Supply Company for office supplies received on December 16 and returned for credit.

20   Purchased $7,850 of store equipment on credit from White Supply Company, invoice dated December 19, terms n/10 EOM.

21   Sold merchandise on credit to Joey Cape, Invoice No. 917, for $6,540 (cost is $4,210).

22   Received payment from Brad Farris for the December 12 sale less the discount.

25   Received payment from Leslie Snipes for the December 15 sale less the return and the discount.

25   Issued Check No. 623 to Muser Company in payment of its December 15 invoice less the return and the discount.

25   Issued Check No. 624 to Cloud Company in payment of its December 15 invoice less a 2% discount.

28   Received $7,030 of merchandise with an invoice dated December 28, terms 2/10, n/60, from Cloud Company.

28   Sold a neighboring merchant a carton of calculator tape (store supplies) at its cost of $68 cash.

29   Berneta Swope, the owner of EZ Products, used Check No. 625 to withdraw $5,000 cash from the business for personal use.

30   Issued Check No. 626 to Truman Electric Company in payment of its $970 December electric bill.

30 Issued Check No. 627 to Jamie Ford, the company's only sales employee, in payment of her $2,620 salary for the last half of December.

31 Cash sales for the last half of the month are $65,130 (cost is $32,850). (Cash sales are recorded daily but are recorded only twice here to reduce repetitive entries.)

Required

1. Record these transactions in the journals provided in the working papers.

2. Post any amounts that should be posted as individual amounts to the general ledger accounts, including posting to the customer and creditor accounts. (Normally, these amounts are posted daily but are posted only once here because they are few in number.) Foot and crossfoot the journals and make the month-end postings.

3. Prepare a December 31 trial balance and prove the accuracy of the subsidiary ledgers by preparing schedules of both accounts receivable and accounts payable.

Check Trial balance totals, $258,095

Randa Company completes these transactions during November of the current year (terms of all credit sales are 2/10, n/30):

Problem 8-6B
Special journals, subsidiary ledgers, trial balance—perpetual

Nov. 1 Purchased $5,058 of office equipment on credit from Ford Supply, invoice dated November 1, terms n/10 EOM.

2 Borrowed $88,500 cash by giving Missouri Bank a long-term note payable.

4 Received $33,500 of merchandise and an invoice dated November 3, terms 2/10, n/30, from ATX Industries.

5 Purchased $1,040 of store supplies on credit from World Company, invoice dated November 5, terms n/10 EOM.

8 Sold merchandise on credit to Seth Farmer, Invoice No. 439, for $6,550 (cost is $3,910).

10 Sold merchandise on credit to Carlos Beltran, Invoice No. 440, for $13,500 (cost is $8,500).

11 Received $2,557 of merchandise and an invoice dated November 10, terms 2/10, n/30, from Chin Company.

12 Sent ATX Industries Check No. 633 in payment of its November 3 invoice less the discount.

15 Issued Check No. 634, payable to Payroll, in payment of sales salaries for the first half of the month, $6,585. Cashed the check and paid the employees.

15 Cash sales for the first half of the month are $18,170 (cost is $9,000). (Cash sales are recorded daily but are recorded only twice in this problem to reduce repetitive entries.)

15 Post to the customer and creditor accounts, and post any amounts that should be posted as individual amounts to the general ledger accounts. (Normally, these items are posted daily but are posted only twice here because they are few in number.)

15 Sold merchandise on credit to Tony Wood, Invoice No. 441, for $5,250 (cost is $2,450).

16 Purchased $459 of office supplies on credit from World Company, invoice dated November 16, terms n/10 EOM.

17 Received a $557 credit memorandum from Chin Company for unsatisfactory merchandise received on November 11 and returned for credit.

18 Received payment from Seth Farmer for the November 8 sale less the discount.

19 Received payment from Carlos Beltran for the November 10 sale less the discount.

19 Issued Check No. 635 to Chin Company in payment of its invoice of November 10 less the return and the discount.

22 Sold merchandise on credit to Carlos Beltran, Invoice No. 442, for $3,695 (cost is $2,060).

24 Sold merchandise on credit to Tony Wood, Invoice No. 443, for $4,280 (cost is $2,130).

25 Received payment from Tony Wood for the sale of November 15 less the discount.

26 Received a $922 credit memorandum from Ford Supply for office equipment received on November 1 and returned for credit.

30 Issued Check No. 636, payable to Payroll, in payment of sales salaries for the last half of the month, $6,585. Cashed the check and paid the employees.

30 Cash sales for the last half of the month are $16,703 (cost is $10,200).

30 Post to the customer and creditor accounts, and post any amounts that should be posted as individual amounts to the general ledger accounts. Foot and crossfoot the journals and make the month-end postings.

Required

1. Open the following general ledger accounts: Cash; Accounts Receivable; Inventory (November 1 beg. bal. is $40,000); Office Supplies; Store Supplies; Office Equipment; Accounts Payable; Long-Term Notes Payable; J. Randa, Capital (November 1 beg. bal. is $40,000); Sales; Sales Discounts; Cost of Goods Sold; and Sales Salaries Expense. Open the following accounts receivable ledger accounts: Carlos Beltran, Tony Wood, and Seth Farmer. Open the following accounts payable ledger accounts: World Company, ATX Industries, Ford Supply, and Chin Company.

2. Enter these transactions in a sales journal like Exhibit 8.5, a purchases journal like Exhibit 8.9, a cash receipts journal like Exhibit 8.7, a cash disbursements journal like Exhibit 8.11, or a general journal. Post when instructed to do so.

Check   Trial balance totals, $202,283

3. Prepare a trial balance of the general ledger and prove the accuracy of the subsidiary ledgers by preparing schedules of both accounts receivable and accounts payable.

Problem 8-7B[A]

Special journals, subsidiary ledgers, trial balance—periodic

Assume that Randa Company in Problem 8-6B uses the periodic inventory system.

Required

1. Open the following general ledger accounts: Cash; Accounts Receivable; Inventory (November 1 beg. bal. is $40,000); Office Supplies; Store Supplies; Office Equipment; Accounts Payable; Long-Term Notes Payable; J. Randa, Capital (November 1 beg. bal. is $40,000); Sales; Sales Discounts; Purchases; Purchases Returns and Allowances; Purchases Discounts; and Sales Salaries Expense. Open the following accounts receivable ledger accounts: Carlos Beltran, Tony Wood, and Seth Farmer. Open the following accounts payable ledger accounts: World Company, ATX Industries, Ford Supply, and Chin Company.

2. Enter the transactions from Problem 8-6B in a sales journal like Exhibit 8A.1, a purchases journal like Exhibit 8A.3, a cash receipts journal like Exhibit 8A.2, a cash disbursements journal like Exhibit 8A.4, or a general journal. Post when instructed to do so.

Check   Trial balance totals, $203,550

3. Prepare a trial balance of the general ledger and prove the accuracy of the subsidiary ledgers by preparing schedules of both accounts receivable and accounts payable.

COMPREHENSIVE PROBLEM— PERPETUAL

Spitz Company

(*If the Working Papers that accompany this text are not available, omit this comprehensive problem.*) Assume it is Monday, May 1, the first business day of the month, and you have just been hired as the accountant for Spitz Company, which operates with monthly accounting periods. All of the company's accounting work is completed through the end of April and its ledgers show April 30 balances. During your first month on the job, the company experiences the following transactions and events (terms of all credit sales are 2/10, n/30):

May 1   Issued Check No. 3410 to J&K Management Co. in payment of the May rent, $3,710. (Use two lines to record the transaction. Charge 80% of the rent to Rent Expense—Selling Space and the balance to Rent Expense—Office Space.)

     2   Sold merchandise on credit to Bowman Company, Invoice No. 8785, for $6,100 (cost is $4,100).

     2   Issued a $175 credit memorandum to Net, Inc., for defective merchandise sold on April 28 and returned for credit. The total selling price (gross) was $4,725.

     3   Received a $798 credit memorandum from Parker Products for merchandise received on April 29 and returned for credit.

     4   Purchased the following on credit from Gates Supply Co.: merchandise, $37,072; store supplies, $574; and office supplies, $83. Invoice dated May 4, terms n/10 EOM.

     5   Received payment from Net, Inc., for the balance from the April 28 sale less the May 2 return and the discount.

     8   Issued Check No. 3411 to Parker Products to pay for the $7,098 of merchandise received on April 29 less the May 3 return and a 2% discount.

     9   Sold store supplies to the merchant next door at their cost of $350 cash.

    10   Purchased $4,074 of office equipment on credit from Gates Supply Co., invoice dated May 10, terms n/10 EOM.

    11   Received payment from Bowman Company for the May 2 sale less the discount.

    11   Received $8,800 of merchandise and an invoice dated May 10, terms 2/10, n/30, from Gatsby, Inc.

    12   Received an $854 credit memorandum from Gates Supply Co. for defective office equipment received on May 10 and returned for credit.

15 Issued Check No. 3412, payable to Payroll, in payment of sales salaries, $5,320, and office salaries, $3,150. Cashed the check and paid the employees.

15 Cash sales for the first half of the month are $59,220 (cost is $38,200). (Cash sales are recorded daily but are recorded only twice here to reduce repetitive entries.)

15 Post to the customer and creditor accounts. Also post individual items that are not included in column totals at the end of the month to the general ledger accounts. (Such items are posted daily but are posted only twice each month because they are few in number.)

16 Sold merchandise on credit to Bowman Company, Invoice No. 8786, for $3,990 (cost is $1,890).

17 Received $13,650 of merchandise and an invoice dated May 14, terms 2/10, n/60, from Joey Corp.

19 Issued Check No. 3413 to Gatsby, Inc., in payment of its May 10 invoice less the discount.

22 Sold merchandise to Karim Services, Invoice No. 8787, for $6,850 (cost is $4,990), terms 2/10, n/60.

23 Issued Check No. 3414 to Joey Corp. in payment of its May 14 invoice less the discount.

24 Purchased the following on credit from Gates Supply Co.: merchandise, $8,120; store supplies, $630; and office supplies, $280. Invoice dated May 24, terms n/10 EOM.

25 Received $3,080 of merchandise and an invoice dated May 23, terms 2/10, n/30, from Parker Products.

26 Sold merchandise on credit to Dexter Corp., Invoice No. 8788, for $14,210 (cost is $8,230).

26 Issued Check No. 3415 to Trinity Power in payment of the April electric bill, $1,283.

29 The owner of Spitz Company, Doug Clinton, used Check No. 3416 to withdraw $7,000 cash from the business for personal use.

30 Received payment from Karim Services for the May 22 sale less the discount.

30 Issued Check No. 3417, payable to Payroll, in payment of sales salaries, $5,320, and office salaries, $3,150. Cashed the check and paid the employees.

31 Cash sales for the last half of the month are $66,052 (cost is $42,500).

31 Post to the customer and creditor accounts. Also post individual items that are not included in column totals at the end of the month to the general ledger accounts. Foot and cross-foot the journals and make the month-end postings.

Required

1. Enter these transactions in a sales journal, a purchases journal, a cash receipts journal, a cash disbursements journal, or a general journal. Post when instructed to do so. Assume a perpetual inventory system.

2. Prepare a trial balance in the Trial Balance columns of the work sheet form provided with the working papers. Complete the work sheet using the following information for accounting adjustments:

   a. Expired insurance, $553.

   b. Ending store supplies inventory, $2,632.

   c. Ending office supplies inventory, $504.

   d. Depreciation of store equipment, $567.

   e. Depreciation of office equipment, $329.

   Prepare and post adjusting and closing entries.

3. Prepare a May 2002 multiple-step income statement, a May 2002 statement of changes in owner's equity, and a May 31, 2002, classified balance sheet.

4. Prepare a post-closing trial balance. Also prove the accuracy of subsidiary ledgers by preparing schedules of both accounts receivable and accounts payable.

Beyond the Numbers

BTN 8-1 Refer to the financial statements for **Nike** in Appendix A to answer the following:

1. Identify the note disclosing Nike's revenues by major product lines.

2. For fiscal year ended May 31, 2000, compute the percent of both total revenue and revenue by product line that Nike earns from each segment. Comment on your findings.

Reporting in Action

A1

Swoosh Ahead

3. Access Nike's annual report for fiscal years ending after May 31, 2000, from its Web site [www.nike.com] or the SEC's EDGAR database [www.sec.gov]. Complete parts *1* and *2* using the latest data available.

Comparative Analysis

A1

NIKE

BTN 8-2 Key comparative figures for both **Nike** and **Reebok** follow ($ millions):

Nike			Reebok		
Revenue by Segment	Current Year	Prior Year	Revenue by Segment	Current Year	Prior Year
United States	$4,732.1	$4,750.7	United States	$1,609.7	$1,858.3
Europe	2,350.9	2,255.8	United Kingdom	545.6	522.4
Asia	955.1	844.5	Europe	476.7	585.7
Americas	550.2	507.1	Other countries	267.9	258.2
Other countries	406.8	418.8			
Total	$8,995.1	$8,776.9	Total	$2,899.9	$3,224.6

Required

1. Compute the percent change in total revenue for each company for the years shown. Comment on your findings.
2. Compute the percent change in revenue by each geographic segment for each company. Comment on your findings.
3. Identify the geographic segment experiencing the largest growth in revenue for each company.

Ethics Challenge

C5

BTN 8-3 Denise Hinson, CPA, is a sole practitioner. She has been practicing as an auditor for 10 years. Recently a long-standing audit client asked Denise to design and implement an integrated computer accounting information system. The fees associated with this additional engagement with the client are very attractive. However, Denise wonders if she can remain objective on subsequent audits in her evaluation of the client's accounting system and its records if she was responsible for its design and implementation. Denise knows that the professional auditing standards require her to remain independent in fact and appearance from her auditing clients.

Required

1. What do you believe auditing standards are concerned with when they require independence in fact? In appearance?
2. Why is it important that auditors remain independent of their clients?
3. Do you think Denise can accept this engagement and remain independent? Justify your response.

Communicating in Practice

C3 C4

BTN 8-4 Your friend, Ivanna B. Sweeter, owns a small retail store that sells candies and nuts. Ivanna acquires her goods from a few select vendors. She generally makes purchase orders by phone and on credit. Sales are primarily for cash. Ivanna keeps her own manual accounting system using a general journal and a general ledger. At the end of each business day, she records one summary entry for cash sales. Ivanna recently began offering goodies in creative gift packages. This has increased sales substantially, and she is now receiving orders from corporate and other clients who order large quantities and prefer to buy on credit. As a result of increased credit transactions in both purchases and sales, keeping the accounting records has become extremely time consuming. Ivanna wants to continue to maintain her own manual system and calls you for advice. Write a memo to her advising how she might modify her current manual accounting system to accommodate the expanded business activities described. Ivanna is accustomed to checking her ledger by using a trial balance. Your memo should explain the advantages of what you propose and of any other verification techniques you recommend.

BTN 8-5   Access the April 14, 2000, filing of the 10-K report for Dell (ticker DELL) at **www.edgar-online.com.** Read the footnote that details Dell's segment information and answer the following:

1. Dell's operations are divided among which three geographic segments?
2. In fiscal year 2000, which geographic area had the largest dollar amount of operating income and identifiable assets?
3. Analyze the net revenue growth for the United States and for foreign countries from 1998 to 1999 and 1999 to 2000. Is Dell growing its revenue faster in domestic markets or foreign markets?
4. For what product groups does Dell provide segment data? What percent of Dell's net revenue is earned by each product group?

Taking It to the Net

BTN 8-6   Each member of the team is to assume responsibility for one of the following tasks:

a. Journalizing in the purchases journal
b. Journalizing in the cash disbursements journal
c. Maintaining and verifying the Accounts Payable ledger
d. Journalizing in the sales and general journal
e. Journalizing in the cash receipts journal
f. Maintaining and verifying the Accounts Receivable ledger

The team should abide by the following procedures in carrying out responsibilities.

Teamwork in Action

Required

1. After tasks (a–f) are assigned, each team member is to quickly read the list of transactions in Problem 8-6A, identifying with initials the journal in which each transaction is to be recorded. Upon completion, the team leader is to read transaction dates, and the appropriate team member is to vocalize responsibility. Any disagreement between teammates must be resolved within the team.
2. Journalize and continually update subsidiary ledgers. Journal recorders should alert teammates assigned to subsidiary ledgers when an entry must be posted to their subsidiary.
3. Team members responsible for tasks (a, b, d, and e) are to summarize and prove journals; members responsible for tasks (c and f) are to prepare both payables and receivables schedules.
4. The team leader is to take charge of the general ledger, rotating team members to obtain amounts to be posted. The person responsible for a journal must complete posting references in the journal. Other team members should verify the accuracy of account balance computations. To avoid any abnormal account balances, post in the following order: P, S, G, R, D. (*Note:* Posting any necessary individual general ledger amounts are also done at this time.)
5. The team leader is to read out general ledger account balances while another team member fills in the trial balance form. Concurrently, one member should keep a running balance of debit account balance totals and another credit account balance totals. Verify the final total of the trial balance and the schedules. If necessary, the team must resolve any errors. Turn in the trial balance and schedules to the instructor.

BTN 8-7   Read the article, "Enterprise Software: A Belated Rush to the Net" in the October 25, 1999, edition of *Business Week*.

Business Week Activity

Required

1. What factor is causing all major enterprise application software makers to substantially revise their software packages?
2. What companies are the major market shareholders in the enterprise application software market?
3. What distinct challenges does each enterprise application software giant face?

Entrepreneurial Decision

BTN 8-8   Dakota Rice has operated a local gift shop for two years. Initially, she handled all aspects of the store's accounting manually. Over the past year, she has focused on upgrading the store to a computerized system and has successfully installed software to handle billing, purchasing, and payroll. Dakota hopes this year to move from a periodic inventory system to a perpetual one. She is thinking of investing in a bar code labeler and scanner system to help manage inventory.

Required

1. What are the cost-benefit considerations of a bar code system?
2. How would a bar code system work with the accounting information system to accomplish perpetual inventory accounting?

Cash and Internal Control

"I hope to make it easier to conduct business with strangers over the Net."—Pierre Omidyar

A Look Back

Chapter 8 focused on accounting information systems. We explained the fundamental principles and components of information systems, the use of special journals and subsidiary ledgers, and technology

A Look at This Chapter

This chapter extends our study of accounting to the area of internal control and accounting for cash. We describe procedures that are good for internal control. We also explain the control of and accounting for cash

A Look Ahead

Chapter 10 focuses on receivables and short-term investments. These items are the most liquid assets other than cash. We explain how to account and report for these assets.

Part Three

Flea Market in Cyberspace

e SAN JOSE, CA—Who ever thought a flea market could be worth $12 billion? Paris-born entrepreneur Pierre Omidyar started his Net auction service, **eBay** (a combination of the words *electronic* and *Bay Area*), five years ago to help his girlfriend collect Pez candy dispensers (**eBay.com**). Omidyar, then 27, saw a need for a Web site where people could buy and sell all kinds of items such as computers, antiques, toys, and music. eBay is now the largest person-to-person auction site on the Web. It creates the marketplace, but buyers and sellers do their own work. eBay never touches the goods or the money. Its earnings derive from commissions, between 1 and 5%, depending on the item's value.

Omidyar calls eBay an experiment in e-commerce. But how does he persuade strangers to trust one another enough to hand over merchandise or cash? "Most people are honest, trustworthy people," says Omidyar. Still, he set up basic controls to establish responsibilities of each party to a trade and to monitor and record transactions. When complications still arose between buyers and sellers, Omidyar had to install a better control system.

Omidyar's response was fourfold. First, he devised a control system whereby buyers and sellers rate their experiences with the other party. This *Feedback Forum* is a public record of past eBay dealings of buyers and sellers. Omidyar says, "It's become a kind of virtuous cycle that's encouraged good behavior." Second, he brought in escrow services to assist traders in making deals. Buyers can have their goods delivered to an escrow service before their money is sent to the seller. Likewise, sellers can require that a buyer send money to the escrow service before sending the goods. Third, he gave traders free insurance against fraud or the mislabeling of goods. Finally, he set up SafeHarbor™, a customer-support team dedicated to providing regular, independent reviews of transactions and users.

Omidyar is confident his new controls will deter fraudulent activities. "By creating an open market that encourages honest dealings," says Omidyar, "I hope to make it easier to conduct business with strangers over the Net." If Omidyar's current record of success is any indication (its said he's made over $3 billion from eBay), he's made Internet *strangers* feel like *bosom buddies!* [Sources: *Business Week*, January 11, 1999; *eBay Web Site*, May 2001; *USA Today Web Site*, December 30, 1998.]

Learning Objectives

Conceptual

C1 Define internal control and its purpose.

C2 Identify principles of internal control.

C3 Define cash and cash equivalents and explain how to report them.

C4 Identify control features of banking activities.

Analytical

A1 Compute the days' sales uncollected ratio and use it to analyze liquidity.

Procedural

P1 Apply internal control to cash receipts.

P2 Apply the voucher system to control cash disbursements.

P3 Explain and record petty cash fund transactions.

P4 Apply the net method to control purchase discounts.

P5 Prepare a bank reconciliation.

Chapter Preview

We all are aware of reports and experiences involving theft and fraud. These occurrences affect us in several ways: we lock doors, chain bikes, review sales receipts, and acquire alarm systems. A company also takes actions to safeguard, control, and manage what it owns. Experience tells us small companies are most vulnerable, usually due to weak internal controls. It is management's responsibility to set up policies and procedures to safeguard a company's assets, especially cash. To do so, management and employees must understand and apply principles of internal control. This chapter describes these principles and how to apply them. We focus special attention on cash because it is easily transferable and often at high risk of loss. Several controls for cash are explained, including a voucher system, petty cash funds, and reconciling bank accounts. This chapter also describes a method to account for purchases that helps us decide whether cash discounts on purchases are being lost and, if so, how much is lost. Our understanding of these controls and procedures makes us more secure in carrying out business activities and in assessing those activities of other companies.

Internal Control

This section describes internal control and its fundamental principles. We also discuss the impact of technology on internal control and the limitations of control procedures.

Purpose of Internal Control

 **C1** Define internal control and its purpose.

Concept 9-1

Managers (or owners) of small businesses often control the entire operation. They supervise workers, participate in all activities, and make major decisions. These managers usually purchase all of the business's assets. They also hire and manage employees, negotiate all contracts, and sign all checks. These managers know from personal contact and observation whether the business is actually receiving the assets and services paid for. Larger companies cannot maintain this close personal supervision. They must delegate responsibilities and rely on formal procedures rather than personal contact in controlling business activities.

Managers use an internal control system to monitor and control business activities. An **internal control system** refers to the policies and procedures managers use to

- Protect assets.
- Ensure reliable accounting.
- Promote efficient operations.
- Urge adherence to company policies.

A properly designed internal control system is a key part of systems design, analysis, and performance. Managers place a high priority on internal control systems because they can prevent avoidable losses, help managers plan operations, and monitor company and employee performance. While internal controls do not provide guarantees, they lower the company's risk of loss from not having internal controls.

Principles of Internal Control

C2 Identify principles of internal control.

Internal control policies and procedures vary from company to company. They depend on factors such as the nature of the business and its size. Certain fundamental internal control principles apply to all companies, however. The **principles of internal control** are to

1. Establish responsibilities.
2. Maintain adequate records.
3. Insure assets and bond key employees.
4. Separate recordkeeping from custody of assets.
5. Divide responsibility for related transactions.
6. Apply technological controls.
7. Perform regular and independent reviews.

Point: When the electronic equipment maker Casio [**Casio.com**] started an e-commerce site last year, 13% of the purchases were fraudulent.

In this section, we explain these seven principles and describe how internal control procedures minimize the risk of fraud and theft. These procedures also increase the reliability and accuracy of accounting records.

Establish Responsibilities

Proper internal control means that responsibility for a task is clearly established and assigned to one person. When responsibility is not identified, determining who is at fault is difficult when a problem occurs. For instance, if two salesclerks share the same cash register, identifying which clerk is at fault if there is a cash shortage is difficult. Neither clerk can prove or disprove the alleged shortage. To prevent this problem, one clerk might be given responsibility for handling all cash sales. Alternately, a company can use a register with separate cash drawers for each clerk. Most of us have waited in line at a retail counter during a change of shift while employees swap cash drawers.

Maintain Adequate Records

Good recordkeeping is part of an internal control system. It helps protect assets and ensures that employees use prescribed procedures. Reliable records are also a source of information that managers use to monitor company activities. When detailed records of equipment are kept, for instance, items are unlikely to be lost or stolen without detection. Similarly, transactions are less likely to be entered in wrong accounts if a chart of accounts is set up and used carefully. Many preprinted forms and internal documents are also designed for use in a good internal control system. When sales slips are properly designed, for instance, sales personnel can record needed information efficiently with less chance of errors or delays to customers. When sales slips are prenumbered and controlled, each one issued is the responsibility of one salesperson, preventing the salesperson from pocketing cash by making a sale and destroying the sales slip. Computerized point-of-sales systems achieve the same control results.

Insure Assets and Bond Key Employees

Good internal control means that assets are adequately insured against casualty and that employees handling cash and negotiable assets are bonded. An employee is *bonded* when a company purchases an insurance policy, or a bond, against losses from theft by that employee. Bonding reduces the risk of loss suffered from theft. It also discourages theft because bonded employees know an independent bonding company will be involved when theft is uncovered and is unlikely to be sympathetic with an employee involved in theft.

Separate Recordkeeping from Custody of Assets

An important principle of internal control is that a person who controls or has access to an asset must not keep that asset's accounting records. This principle reduces the risk of theft or waste of an asset because the person with control over it knows that another person keeps its records. Also, a recordkeeper who does not have access to the asset has no reason to falsify records. This means that two people must both agree to commit a fraud, called *collusion*, to steal an asset and hide the theft from the records. Because collusion is necessary to commit this type of fraud, it is less likely to occur.

Did You Know?

Employee Control   Do you know what lurks behind that spiffy resume you recently reviewed? The Fraud Defense Network's Fraud Tools page [**www.frauddefense.com**] provides links to free search engines to verify Social Security numbers, addresses, and phone numbers. **KnowX.com** lets you check lawsuits and bankruptcies for under $10. **Employeescreen.com** offers full background searches, including employment verification, for under $100. The Association of Certified Fraud Examiners [**www.cfenet.com**] can also help you find a professional examiner.

Did You Know?

High-Tech Threads   Theft and counterfeiting are concerns of most companies. **Tracer Detection Technology** has developed a technique for permanently marking all physical assets. Its technique involves embedding a one-inch-square tag of nylon fibers with different light-absorbing properties. Each pattern of fibers creates a unique optical signature recordable by scanners. It hopes to embed tags in everything from compact disks and credit cards to designer clothes.

Divide Responsibility for Related Transactions

Good internal control divides responsibility for a transaction or a series of related transactions between two or more individuals or departments. This is to ensure that the work of one acts as a check on the other. This principle, often called *separation of duties*, is not a call for duplication of work. Each employee or department should perform unduplicated effort. Examples of transactions with divided responsibility are placing purchase orders, receiving merchandise, and paying vendors. These tasks should not be given to one individual or department. Assigning responsibility for two or more of these tasks to one party increases mistakes and perhaps fraud. Having an independent person, for example, check incoming goods for quality and quantity encourages more care and attention to detail than having the person who placed the order do the checking. Added protection can result from identifying a third person to approve payment of the invoice. We can even designate a fourth person with authority to write checks as another measure of protection.

Apply Technological Controls

Cash registers, check protectors, time clocks, and personal identification scanners are examples of devices that can improve internal control. Technology often improves the effectiveness of controls. A cash register with a locked-in tape or electronic file makes a record of each cash sale. A check protector perforates the amount of a check into its face and makes it difficult to alter the amount. A time clock registers the exact time an employee both arrives at and departs from the job. Mechanical change and currency counters quickly and accurately count amounts, and personal scanners limit access to only authorized individuals. Each of these and other technological controls are an effective part of many internal control systems.

Did You Know?

Face Code   Viisage Technology has licensed a powerful face-recognition program from MIT. It snaps a digital picture of the face and converts key facial features—say, the distance between the eyes—into a series of numerical values. These can be stored on an ID or ATM card as a simple bar code. Welfare agencies in Massachusetts already use the system to identify individuals in fraudulent cases.

Perform Regular and Independent Reviews

No internal control system is perfect. Changes in personnel and technological advances present opportunities for shortcuts and lapses. So does the stress of time pressures. To counter these factors, regular reviews of internal control systems are needed to ensure that procedures are followed. These reviews are preferably done by internal auditors not directly involved in the activities. Their impartial perspective encourages an evaluation of the efficiency as well as the effectiveness of the internal control system. Many companies also pay for audits by independent, external auditors. These external auditors test the company's financial records to give an opinion as to whether its financial statements are presented fairly. Before external auditors decide on how much testing is needed, they evaluate the effectiveness of the internal control system. In the process of their evaluation, they identify and assess internal controls. This information is often helpful to a client.

You Make the Call

Entrepreneur   As owner of a start-up information services company, you hire a systems analyst. One of her first recommendations is to require all employees to take at least one week of vacation per year. Why would she recommend a "forced vacation" policy?

Answer—p. 379

Technology and Internal Control

The fundamental principles of internal control are relevant no matter what the technological state of the accounting system, from purely manual to fully automated systems. Technology impacts an internal control system in several important ways. Perhaps the most obvious is that technology allows us quicker access to databases and information. Used ef-

Point: Information on Internet fraud can be found at these sites:
www.ftc.gov/ftc/consumer.htm
www.sec.gov/consumer/offertip.htm
www.fraud.org

fectively, technology greatly improves managers' abilities to monitor and control business activities. This section describes some technological impacts we must be alert to.

Reduced Processing Errors

Technologically advanced systems reduce the number of errors in processing information. Provided the software and data entry are correct, the risk of mechanical and mathematical errors is nearly eliminated, but erroneous software or data entry does occur and we must be alert to that possibility. Also, less human involvement in data processing also can cause data entry errors to go undiscovered. Similarly, errors in software can produce consistent but erroneous processing of transactions. Continually checking and monitoring all types of systems is important.

> ### Did You Know?
>
> **Shredder or Spy?** That paper shredder in the office could be a high-tech spy tool. A Web site that specializes in gadgets for snooping sold several $5,000 shredders fitted with scanners and wireless transmitters, according to law-enforcement sources. As confidential documents are fed in, they're scanned, and the info is sent to an e-mail address.
>
>

More Extensive Testing of Records

A company's review and audit of electronic records can include more extensive testing when information is easily and rapidly accessed. When accounting records are kept manually, auditors and others likely select only small samples of data to test. When data are accessible with computer technology, however, large samples or even complete data files can be quickly reviewed and analyzed.

Limited Evidence of Processing

Many data processing steps are increasingly done by computer. Accordingly, fewer hard-copy items of documentary evidence are available for review. On the other hand, technologically advanced systems can provide other evidence. They can, for instance, record information such as who made the entries, the date and time, and the source of their entry. Technology can also be designed to require the use of passwords or other identification before access to the system is granted. This means that internal control depends more on the design and operation of the information system and less on the analysis of its resulting documents.

Crucial Separation of Duties

Technological advances in accounting information systems often yield some job eliminations or consolidations. A reduction in workforce carries a risk of losing separation of crucial responsibilities. Companies that use advanced technology also need employees with special skills to operate programs and equipment. The duties of these employees must be controlled and monitored to minimize risk of error and fraud. Better control is maintained if, for instance, the person designing and programming the system does not operate it. The control over programs and files related to cash receipts and disbursements also must be separated. To avoid risk of fraud, the check-writing

> ### Did You Know?
>
> **Accounting Techies**   Most internal control systems rely on information technology. A recent study estimates that 200,000 jobs in information technology are vacant. Demand far outstrips supply, producing a bidding war for digital talent in accounting. The most prized recruits are adept at enterprise software, the Web, intranets, and accounting. A recent survey cited the shortage of accounting techies as one of the greatest barriers to company growth.

activities should not be controlled by a computer operator. Achieving acceptable separation of duties can be especially difficult and costly in small companies with few employees.

Limitations of Internal Control

All internal control policies and procedures have limitations. Probably the most serious limitation is the human element. Internal control policies and procedures are applied by people and often impact other people. This human element creates several potential limitations that we can categorize as either (1) human error or (2) human fraud. *Human error* can occur from negligence, fatigue, misjudgment, or confusion. It is a factor when people carry out internal control policies and procedures. *Human fraud* involves intent by people to defeat internal controls for personal gain. Fraud includes collusion to thwart the separation of duties. The human element highlights the importance of establishing an *internal control environment* to convey management's commitment to internal control policies and procedures.

Another important limitation on internal control is the *cost-benefit principle*. This means the costs of internal controls must not exceed their benefits. Analysis of costs and benefits must consider all factors, including the impact on morale. Most companies, for instance, have a legal right to read employees' e-mail, yet companies seldom exercise that right unless they are confronted with evidence of potential harm to the company. The same holds for drug testing, phone tapping, and hidden camera monitoring. The bottom line is that no internal control system is perfect and that managers must establish internal control policies and procedures with a net benefit to the company.

Quick Check

1. Fundamental principles of internal control suggest which of the following:
   (a) Responsibility for a series of related transactions (such as placing orders, receiving and paying for merchandise) should be assigned to one employee;
   (b) Responsibility for individual tasks should be shared by more than one employee so that one serves as a check on the other; or (c) Employees who handle cash and easily transferable assets should be bonded.
2. What are some impacts of computing technology on internal control?

Answers—p. 380

Control of Cash

Cash is a necessary asset of every company. Most companies include *cash equivalents*, which are similar to cash, as part of cash. Applying principles of internal control to both cash and cash equivalents is important. Cash and cash equivalents are the most liquid of all assets and are easily hidden and moved. An effective system of internal controls protects both cash receipts and cash disbursements and should meet three basic guidelines:

1. Handling cash is separate from recordkeeping of cash.
2. Cash receipts are promptly deposited in a bank.
3. Cash disbursements are made by check.

The first guideline minimizes errors and fraud by separation of duties. As noted earlier, when duties are separated, two or more people must collude to steal cash and conceal this action in the accounting records. The second guideline uses immediate (say, daily) deposits of all cash receipts to produce a timely independent record of the accuracy of the amount of cash received. It also reduces the likelihood of cash theft and loss and the risk that an employee could personally use the money before depositing it. The third guideline uses payments by check to develop an independent bank record of cash disbursements. This guideline also reduces the risk of cash theft and loss.

The exact procedures used to achieve control over cash vary across companies. They depend on factors such as company size, number of employees, volume of cash transactions, and sources of cash. We must therefore view the procedures described in this section as illustrative. This section begins with definitions of cash and cash equivalents. Discussion then focuses on controls and accounting for both cash receipts and disbursements.

Cash, Cash Equivalents, and Liquidity

C3 Define cash and cash equivalents and explain how to report them.

Cash is an important asset for every company and must be managed. Companies also need to carefully control access to cash by employees and others. Good accounting systems both help manage the amount of cash and control who has access to it. The importance of accounting for cash is highlighted by the inclusion of a statement of cash flows in a complete set of financial statements. That statement identifies activities affecting cash.

Point: The most liquid assets are usually reported first on a balance sheet; the least liquid assets are reported last.

Cash and Cash Equivalents Defined

Cash includes currency and coins along with the amounts on deposit in bank accounts, checking accounts (called *demand deposits*), and many savings accounts (called *time deposits*). Cash also includes items that are acceptable for deposit in these accounts such as customers' checks, cashier checks, certified checks, and money orders.

Cash equivalents are short-term, highly liquid investment assets meeting two criteria: (1) readily convertible to a known cash amount and (2) sufficiently close to their maturity date so that their market value is not sensitive to interest rate changes. Only investments purchased within three months of their maturity dates usually satisfy these criteria. Examples of cash equivalents are short-term investments in assets such as U.S. treasury bills, money market funds, and commercial paper (such as short-term corporate notes payable). To increase their return on investment in cash, many companies invest idle cash in cash equivalents. Most companies combine cash equivalents with cash as a single item on the balance sheet. For example, **Mattel** reports a single cash balance and states that "Cash includes cash equivalents, which are highly liquid investments with maturities of three months or less when purchased. Because of the short maturities of these instruments, the carrying amount is a reasonable estimate of fair value."

Cash is the usual means of payment when paying for other assets, services, or liabilities. **Liquidity** refers to a company's ability to pay for its near term obligations. Cash and similar assets are called **liquid assets** because they can be readily used to settle such obligations. A company needs liquid assets to effectively operate.

> ### Did You Know?
>
> **Cash Glut** **I2 Technologies** reports cash and cash equivalents of $455 million in its recent balance sheet. This amount makes up more than one-half of its total assets.

> ### Did You Know?
>
> **Cyber-Sleuths** A team of lawyers at the Federal Trade Commission is on the cutting edge of cybersleuthing. Opportunists in search of easy money on the Internet have been lured to **www.ari.net/NetOpportunities**, where a lurid banner proclaims: "The Internet is a GOLD MINE!!!" It says you can get rich quick—as an "Internet Con$ultant." Take the bait and you get warned—and probably targeted.

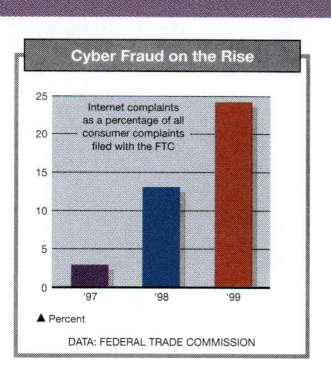

Cyber Fraud on the Rise

Control of Cash Receipts

Internal control of cash receipts ensures that cash received is properly recorded and deposited. Cash receipts arise from transactions such as cash sales, collections of customers' accounts, receipts of interest earned, bank loans, sale of assets, and owner investments. The principles of internal control apply to all cash receipts. This section explains internal control over two important types of cash receipts: over-the-counter and by mail.

P1 Apply internal control to cash receipts.

Over-the-Counter Cash Receipts

For purposes of internal control, over-the-counter cash receipts from sales should be recorded on a cash register at the time of each sale. To help ensure that correct amounts are entered, each register should be located so customers can read the amounts entered. Clerks also should be required to enter each sale before wrapping merchandise and to give the customer a receipt for each sale. The design of each cash register should provide a permanent, locked-in record of each transaction. In many systems, the register is directly linked with computing and accounting services. Less advanced registers simply print a record of each transaction on a paper tape or electronic file locked inside the register.

One principle of internal control states that custody over cash should be separate from its recordkeeping. For over-the-counter cash receipts, this separation begins with the cash sale. The clerk who has access to cash in the register should not have access to its locked-in record. At the end of the clerk's work period, the clerk should count the cash in the register, record the amount, and turn over the cash and a record of its amount to the company's

Register Mammoth With annual sales of about $200 billion, **Wal-Mart** uses a network of information links with its point-of-sale cash registers to coordinate sales, purchases, and distribution. Three of its supercenters, for instance, ring up 15,000 separate sales on heavy days. By using cash register information, it is quick to fix mistakes and to capitalize on sales trends. It is now the largest discounter in the U.S., Canada, and Mexico.

cashier. The cashier, like the clerk, has access to the cash but should not have access to accounting records (or the register tape or file). A third employee compares the record of total register transactions (or the register tape or file) with the cash receipts reported by the cashier. This record (or register tape or file) is the basis for a journal entry recording over-the-counter cash receipts. The third employee has access to the records for cash but not to the actual cash. The clerk and the cashier have access to cash but not to the accounting records. None of them can make a mistake or divert cash without the difference being revealed.

Point: Retailers often require cashiers to restrictively endorse checks immediately on receipt by stamping them "For deposit only."

Cash over and short

Sometimes errors in making change are discovered from differences between the cash in a cash register and the record of the amount of cash receipts. Although a clerk is careful, one or more customers can be given too much or too little change. This means that at the end of a work period, the cash in a cash register might not equal the cash receipts entered. This difference is reported in the **Cash Over and Short** account, which is an income statement account recording the income effects of cash overages and cash shortages. To illustrate, if a cash register shows cash receipts of $550 but the count of cash in the register is $555, the entry to record cash sales and its overage is

Assets = Liabilities + Equity
+555   + 5
                  +550

Cash	555	
Cash Over and Short		**5**
Sales		550
To record cash sales and an overage.		

If a cash register shows cash receipts of $625 but the count of cash in the register is $621, the entry to record cash sales and its shortage is:

Assets = Liabilities + Equity
+621   − 4
                  +625

Cash	621	
Cash Over and Short	**4**	
Sales		625
To record cash sales and a shortage.		

Because customers are more likely to dispute being shortchanged, the Cash Over and Short account usually has a debit balance at the end of an accounting period. This debit balance reflects an expense. It can be shown on the income statement as an item in general and administrative expenses. But since the amount is usually small, it is often combined with other small expenses and reported as part of *miscellaneous expenses*. If Cash Over and Short has a credit balance at the end of the period, it usually is shown on the income statement as part of *miscellaneous revenues*.

Cash Receipts by Mail

Control of cash receipts that arrive through the mail starts with the person who opens the mail. Preferably, two people are assigned the task of, and are present for, opening the mail. In this case, theft of cash receipts by mail requires collusion between these two employees. The person opening the mail enters a list (in triplicate) of money received. This list should contain a record of each sender's name, the amount, and an explanation of why the money is sent. The first copy is sent with the money to the cashier. A second copy is sent to the recordkeeper in the accounting area. A third copy is kept by the clerks who opened the mail. The cashier deposits the money in a bank, and the recordkeeper records the amounts received in the accounting records.

Point: A complete set of financial statements includes a statement of cash flows, which provides useful information about a company's sources and uses of cash and cash equivalents during a period of time.

This process reflects good internal control. First, when the bank balance is reconciled by another person (explained later in the chapter), errors or fraud by the mail clerks, the cashier, or the recordkeeper are revealed. They are revealed because the bank's record of cash deposited must agree with the records from each of the three. Moreover, if the mail clerks do not report all receipts correctly, customers will question their account balances. If the cashier does not deposit all receipts, the bank balance does not agree with the recordkeeper's cash balance. The recordkeeper and the person who reconciles the bank balance do not have access to cash and, therefore, have no opportunity to divert cash to themselves. This system makes errors and fraud highly unlikely. The exception is when employees collude.

> **Did You Know?**
>
> **Entrepreneurs, Head West!**   In a recent survey by the Small Business Survival Foundation [**www.SBSC.org**], 5 of the top 6 states ranked as most entrepreneur friendly are west of the Mississippi. They are (1) South Dakota, (2) Wyoming, (3) Nevada, (4) New Hampshire, (5) Texas, and (6) Washington. The index is based on several factors including taxes, regulations, compensation costs, and crime.

Control of Cash Disbursements

Control of cash disbursements is especially important for companies. Most large thefts occur from payment of fictitious invoices. One key to controlling cash disbursements is to require all expenditures to be made by check. The only exception is small payments made from petty cash. Another key is to deny access to the accounting records to anyone other than the owner who has the authority to sign checks. The owner of a small business often signs checks and knows from personal contact that the items being paid for are actually received. This arrangement is impossible in large businesses. Instead, internal control procedures must be substituted for personal contact. Such procedures are designed to assure the check signer that the obligations recorded are properly incurred and should be paid. This section describes these and other internal control procedures. They include the voucher system, petty cash system, and the management of cash disbursements for purchases.

> **Did You Know?**
>
> **Paper Chase**   Companies are increasingly converting from paper to electronic documents. The basic purposes and features of most paper and electronic documents are the same. But the internal control system must change to reflect different risks and concerns. This includes confidential and competitive-sensitive information that is at greater risk in electronic systems.

Voucher System of Control

A **voucher system** is a set of procedures and approvals designed to control cash disbursements and the acceptance of obligations. The voucher system of control establishes procedures for

P2   Apply the voucher system to control cash disbursements.

■ Verifying, approving, and recording obligations for eventual cash disbursement.
■ Issuing checks for payment of verified, approved, and recorded obligations.

A reliable voucher system follows standard procedures for every transaction. This applies even when multiple purchases are made from the same supplier.

A voucher system's control over cash disbursements begins when a company incurs an obligation that will result in payment of cash. A key factor in this system is that only approved departments and individuals are authorized to incur such obligations. The system often limits the type of obligations that a department or individual can incur. In a large retail store, for instance, only a purchasing department should be authorized to incur obligations for merchandise inventory. Another key factor is that procedures for purchasing, receiving, and paying for merchandise are divided among several departments (or individuals). These departments include the one requesting the purchase, the purchasing department, the receiving department, and the accounting department. To coordinate and control responsibilities of these departments, several different business documents are used. Exhibit 9.1 shows how documents are accumulated in a **voucher,** which is an internal document (or file) used to accumulate information to control cash disbursements and to ensure that a transaction is properly recorded. Appendix 9A describes each document entering and leaving a voucher system. It also describes the internal control objective served by each document.

Exhibit 9.1

Document Flow in a Voucher System

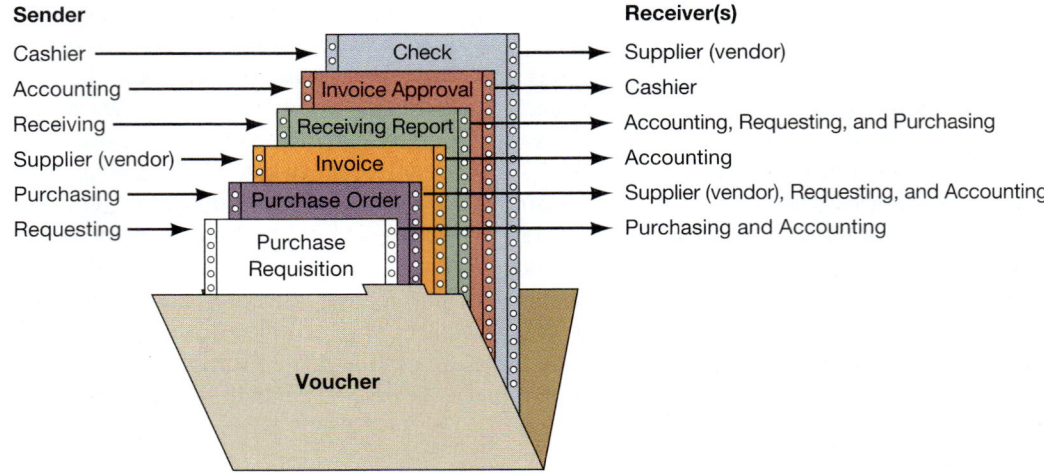

A voucher system should be applied not only to purchases but also to all expenses. To illustrate, when a company receives a monthly telephone bill, the charges should be reviewed and verified. A voucher (file) is prepared and the telephone bill is inserted. This transaction is then recorded with a journal entry. If the amount is due at once, a check is issued. If not, the voucher is filed for payment on its due date.

Vouchers should be prepared for all incurred expenses, whether cash payment occurs now or later. This is so because many invoices or bills are often not received until weeks after work is done. If no expense records exist, verifying the invoice and its amount can be difficult. Also, without records, a dishonest employee could collude with a dishonest supplier to get more than one payment for an obligation, payment for excessive amounts, or payment for goods and services not received. An effective voucher system helps prevent such frauds.

Point: A voucher is an internal document (file).

Quick Check

3. Why must a company own liquid assets?
4. Why does a company own cash equivalent assets in addition to cash?
5. Identify at least two assets that are classified as cash equivalents.
6. Good internal control procedures for cash include which of the following? (a) All cash disbursements, other than those for very small amounts, are made by check; (b) One employee should count cash received from sales and promptly deposit cash receipts; or (c) Cash receipts by mail should be opened by one employee who is then responsible for recording and depositing receipts.
7. Do all companies require a voucher system? At what point in a company's growth would you recommend a voucher system?

Answers—p. 380

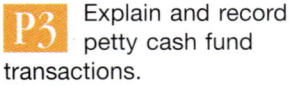 Explain and record petty cash fund transactions.

Petty Cash System of Control

A basic principle for controlling cash disbursements is that all payments must be made by check. An exception to this rule is made for *petty cash disbursements,* which are the small payments required for items such as postage, courier fees, repairs, and low-cost supplies.

Making all small payments by check would require numerous checks for small amounts, and would be both time consuming and expensive. To avoid writing checks for small amounts, a company sets up a petty cash fund and uses the money in this fund to make small payments.

Operating a petty cash fund

Establishing a petty cash fund requires estimating the total amount of small payments likely to be made during a short period such as a week or month. A check is then drawn by the company cashier for an amount slightly in excess of this estimate. This check is recorded with a debit to the Petty Cash account (an asset) and a credit to Cash. The check is cashed, and the currency is given to an employee designated as a *petty cashier,* also called *petty cash custodian.* The petty cashier is responsible for the safekeeping of this cash, making payments from the fund, and its recordkeeping. The petty cashier keeps petty cash and its records in a secure place referred to as the *petty cashbox.*

To illustrate, when each cash disbursement is made, the person receiving payment should sign a *petty cash receipt,* also called *petty cash ticket*—see Exhibit 9.2. The petty cash receipt is then placed in the petty cashbox with the remaining money. Under this system, the sum of all receipts plus the remaining cash equals the total fund amount. A $100 petty cash fund, for instance, contains any combination of cash and petty cash receipts that total $100 (examples are $80 cash plus $20 in receipts, or $10 cash plus $90 in receipts). Each disbursement reduces cash and increases the amount of receipts in the petty cashbox.

Point: A petty cash fund is used only for business expenses.

Petty Cash Receipt		No. 9
Z-Mart		
For _____ Freight charges _____	Date _____ 11/5/02 _____	
Charge to __ Merchandise Inventory __	Amount _____ $6.75 _____	
Approved by __ *Jim Gills* __	Received by __ *Dick Fitch* __	

Exhibit 9.2

Petty Cash Receipt

When the petty cash is nearing zero, it should be reimbursed. The petty cashier first sorts the paid receipts by the type of expense or account and then totals the receipts. The petty cashier presents all paid receipts to the company cashier, who stamps all receipts *paid* so they cannot be reused, files them for recordkeeping, and gives the petty cashier a check for their sum. When this check is cashed and the money placed in the cashbox, the total money in the cashbox is restored to its original amount. The fund is now ready for a new cycle of petty cash payments.

Point: Auditors often find misuse of petty cash when petty cash receipts have either no signature or a forged signature. Companies respond with surprise petty cash counts for verification.

Illustration of a petty cash fund

Z-Mart uses a petty cash fund to avoid writing an excessive number of checks for small amounts. To illustrate, assume that Z-Mart establishes a petty cash fund on November 1. It designates one of its office employees as the petty cashier. A $75 check is drawn, cashed, and the proceeds given to the petty cashier. The entry to record the setup of this petty cash fund is

Nov. 1	Petty Cash	75	
	Cash		75
	To establish a petty cash fund.		

Assets = Liabilities + Equity
+75
−75

This entry transfers $75 from the regular Cash account to the Petty Cash account. After the petty cash fund is established, the Petty Cash account is not debited or credited again unless the size of the total fund is changed. A fund probably should be increased if it is being used and reimbursed too frequently. If the fund is too large, some of its money should be redeposited in the Cash account.

Exhibit 9.3

Petty Cash Payments Report

Z-MART		
Petty Cash Payments Report		
Miscellaneous Expenses		
Nov. 2 Washing windows	$20.00	
Nov. 27 Printer cartridge	26.50	$46.50
Merchandise Inventory (transportation-in)		
Nov. 5 Transport of merchandise purchased	6.75	
Nov. 20 Transport of merchandise purchased	8.30	15.05
Delivery Expense		
Nov. 18 Customer's package delivered		5.00
Office Expense		
Nov. 15 Purchase of office supplies		4.75
Total		**$71.30**

Point: Although individual petty cash disbursements are not evidenced by a check, the initial petty cash fund is evidenced by a check, and later petty cash expenditures are evidenced by a check to replenish them in total.

During November, the petty cashier makes several payments from petty cash. Each person who received payment is required to sign a receipt. On November 27, after making a $26.50 cash payment for a printer cartridge, only $3.70 cash remains in the fund. The petty cashier then summarizes and totals the petty cash receipts as shown in Exhibit 9.3. This summary and all petty cash receipts are given to the company cashier in exchange for a $71.30 check to reimburse the fund. The petty cashier cashes the check and puts the $71.30 cash in the petty cashbox. The company records the check for reimbursement as follows:

Nov. 27	Miscellaneous Expenses	46.50	
	Merchandise Inventory	15.05	
	Delivery Expense	5.00	
	Office Expense	4.75	
	Cash		71.30
	To reimburse petty cash.		

Assets = Liabilities + Equity
−71.30   −46.50
                         −15.05
                         − 5.00
                         − 4.75

Information for this entry is taken from the petty cashier's summary of payments in Exhibit 9.3. The debits in this entry reflect the petty cash payments.

A petty cash fund is often reimbursed at the end of an accounting period even if it is not low on money. This is done to record expenses in the proper period. If the fund is not reimbursed at the end of a period, the financial statements show both an overstated petty cash asset and understated expenses (or assets) that were paid out of petty cash. Some companies do not reimburse the petty cash fund at the end of each period under the assumption that this amount is immaterial to users of financial statements.

Point: To avoid errors in recording petty cash reimbursement, follow these steps: (1) prepare payments report, (2) compute cash needed by subtracting cash remaining from total fund amount, (3) record entry, and (4) check "Dr. = Cr." in entry—any difference is Cash Over and Short.

Increasing or decreasing a petty cash fund

A decision to increase or decrease a petty cash fund is often made when reimbursing it. To illustrate, let's assume Z-Mart decides to *increase* its petty cash fund to $100 on November 27 when it reimburses the fund. The entry to do this is identical to the preceding one except that it includes a (1) debit to Petty Cash for $25 (increasing the fund from $75 to $100) and (2) credit to Cash for $96.30 ($71.30 reimbursement of expenses plus $25 increase in the fund). Alternatively, if Z-Mart *decreases* the petty cash fund from $75 to $55 on November 27, the changes required for the entry on this date

You Make the Call—Ethics

Internal Auditor You are making surprise counts of several $300 petty cash funds. You arrive at one of the petty cashiers when she is on the telephone. She politely asks that you return after lunch so that she can finish her business on the telephone. You agree and return after lunch. In the petty cashbox, you find 14 new $20 bills with consecutive serial numbers plus receipts totaling $20. What is your evaluation?

Answer—p. 380

include a (1) credit to Petty Cash for $20 (decreasing the fund from $75 to $55) and (2) credit to Cash for $51.30 ($71.30 reimbursement of expense minus $20 decrease in the fund).

Cash over and short

Sometimes a petty cashier fails to get a receipt for payment. When this occurs and the fund is later reimbursed, the petty cash payments report plus the cash remaining will not total to the fund balance. This mistake causes the fund to be *short*. If the petty cash fund is short, this shortage is recorded as an expense in the reimbursing entry with a debit to the Cash Over and Short account. (An overage in the petty cash fund is recorded with a credit to Cash Over and Short in the reimbursing entry.)

Example: Prepare the entry to reimburse a $200 petty cash fund when its payments report shows $178 in miscellaneous expenses and $15 cash remains.

Miscel. Expenses	178	
Cash Over & Short	7	
Cash		185

Quick Check

8. Why are some cash payments made from a petty cash fund, and not by check?

9. Why should a petty cash fund be reimbursed at the end of an accounting period?

10. Identify at least two results of reimbursing a petty cash fund.

Answers—p. 380

Control of Purchase Discounts

This section explains how a company can gain more control over cash *disbursements* to take advantage of favorable purchase discounts. Chapter 6 describes the entries to record the receipt and payment of an invoice for a purchase of merchandise. When Z-Mart purchases merchandise at a $1,200 invoice price with terms of 2/10, n/30, it makes this entry:

P4 Apply the net method to control purchase discounts.

Nov. 2	Merchandise Inventory	1,200	
	Accounts Payable		1,200
	Purchased merchandise on credit, invoice		
	dated Nov. 2, terms 2/10, n/30.		

Assets = Liabilities + Equity
+1,200   +1,200

If Z-Mart takes advantage of the discount and pays the amount due on November 12, the entry is

Nov. 12	Accounts Payable	1,200	
	Merchandise Inventory		24
	Cash		1,176
	Paid for the purchase of Nov. 2 less the		
	discount (2% × $1,200).		

Assets = Liabilities + Equity
−24   −1,200
−1,176

These entries reflect the **gross method** of recording purchases, which records the invoice at its *gross* amount of $1,200 *before* recognizing the cash discount. Many companies record invoices in this way.

Another method of recording purchases is the **net method,** which records the invoice at its *net* amount *after* recognizing the cash discount. This method is viewed as providing more useful information to manage cash disbursements. If Z-Mart uses the net method of recording purchases, it deducts the potential $24 cash discount from the gross amount and records the initial purchase at the $1,176 net amount:

Nov. 2	Merchandise Inventory	1,176	
	Accounts Payable		1,176
	Purchased merchandise on credit, invoice		
	dated Nov. 2, terms 2/10, n/30.		

Assets = Liabilities + Equity
+1,176   +1,176

If the invoice for this purchase is paid within the discount period, the entry to record the payment debits Accounts Payable and credits Cash for $1,176. However, if payment is not made within the discount period and the discount is *lost,* the following additional entry must be made either on the date the discount is lost or later when the invoice is paid:

Nov. 13	Discounts Lost	24	
	Accounts Payable		24
	To record the discount lost.		

A check for the full $1,200 invoice amount must be written, recorded, and sent to the creditor.[1] The net method gives management an advantage in controlling and monitoring cash payments involving purchase discounts. When invoices are recorded at *gross* amounts, the amount of any discounts taken is deducted from the balance of the Merchandise Inventory account when cash payment is made. This means that the amount of any discounts lost is not reported in any account or on the income statement. Lost discounts recorded in this way are unlikely to come to the attention of management. However, when purchases are recorded at *net* amounts, a **Discount Lost** expense account is recorded and brought to management's attention as an operating expense. Management can then seek to identify the reason for discounts lost such as oversight, carelessness, or unfavorable terms. This practice gives management better control over persons responsible for paying bills to ensure that they take advantage of favorable discounts.[2]

Banking Activities as Controls

Banks (and other financial institutions) provide many different services. One of their most important services is helping companies control cash and cash transactions. Banks safeguard cash, provide detailed and independent records of cash transactions, and are a source of cash financing. This section describes services and documents provided by banking activities that increase managers' control over cash.

Basic Bank Services

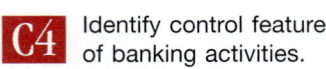

Identify control features of banking activities.

This section explains basic bank services. We include the bank account, the bank deposit, and checking. Each of these services contributes to either or both the control and safeguarding of cash.

Bank Account

A bank account is a record set up by a bank for a customer. It permits a customer to deposit money for safeguarding and helps control withdrawals. To limit access to a bank account, all persons authorized to write checks on the account must sign a **signature card,** which bank employees use to verify signatures on checks. This lowers the risk of loss from forgery. Many companies have more than one bank account to serve different needs and to handle special transactions such as payroll.

Global: If cash is in more than one currency, a company usually translates these amounts into U.S. dollars using the exchange rate as of the balance sheet date.

Bank Deposit

Each bank deposit is supported by a **deposit ticket,** which lists items such as currency, coins, and checks deposited along with their corresponding dollar amounts. The bank gives the customer a copy of the deposit ticket or a deposit receipt as proof of the deposit. Exhibit 9.4 shows one type of deposit ticket.

---

[1] The discount lost can be recorded with the cash payment in a single entry. However, when financial statements are prepared after a discount is lost and before the cash payment is made, an adjusting entry is required to recognize any unrecorded discount lost in the period when incurred.

[2] To help managers assess whether a discount is favorable or not, we compute the *implied interest rate* of not taking the discount: (365 days/[Credit period − Discount period]) × Cash discount percent. For example, if terms are 2/10, n/30, then missing the 2% discount for an additional 20 days implies an annual interest rate of 36.5%, computed as (365 days/[30 days − 10 days]) × 2%. This suggests that if money can be borrowed for less than 36.5%, an entity should take advantage of the discount offered.

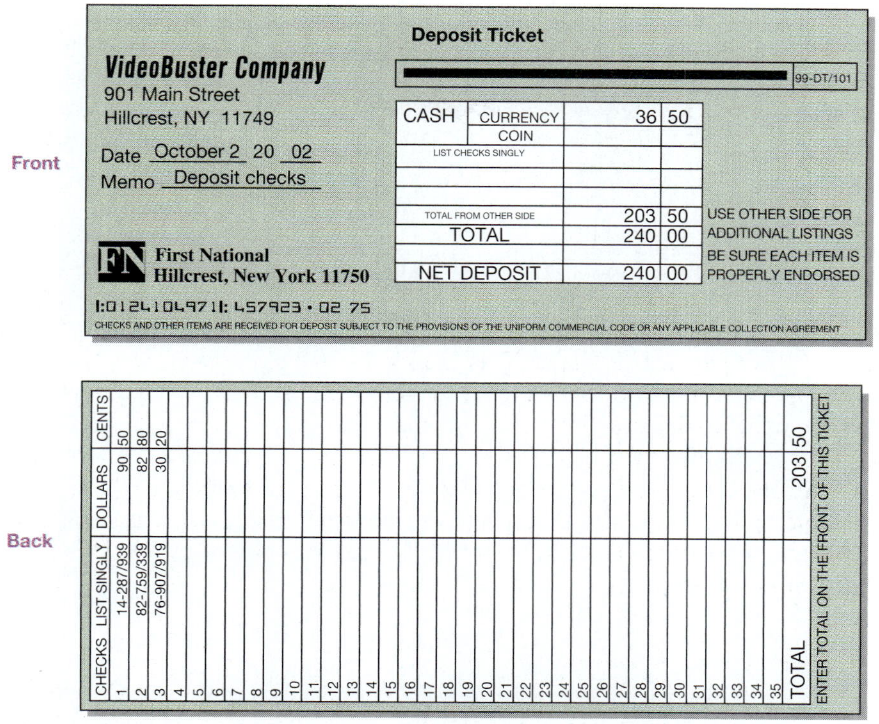

Exhibit 9.4
Deposit Ticket

Bank Check

To withdraw money from an account, the depositor uses a **check,** which is a document signed by the depositor instructing the bank to pay a specified amount of money to a designated recipient. A check involves three parties: a *maker* who signs the check, a *payee* who is the recipient, and a *bank* (or *payer*) on which the check is drawn. The bank provides a depositor the checks that are serially numbered and imprinted with the name and address of both the depositor and bank. Both checks and deposit tickets are imprinted with identification codes in magnetic ink for computer processing. Exhibit 9.5 shows one type of check. It is accompanied with an optional *remittance advice* explaining the payment. When a remittance advice is unavailable, the *memo* line is often used for a brief explanation.

> **Did You Know?**
>
> **Booting Up Your Banker**   Many companies are now balancing checkbooks and paying bills via the Web. The convenience and low cost of banking services anytime, anywhere, are attracting customers. Services include the ability to stop payment on a check, move money between accounts, get up-to-date account balances, and identify checks and deposits that have cleared. Even taxes, suppliers, creditors, and employees can be paid electronically.

Electronic Funds Transfer

Electronic funds transfer (EFT) is electronic communication transfer of cash from one party to another. No paper documents are necessary. Banks simply transfer cash from one account to another with a journal entry. Companies are increasingly using EFT because of its covenience and low cost. For instance, it can cost up to one-half dollar to process a check through the banking system, whereas EFT cost is near zero. We now commonly see items such as payroll, rent, utilities, insurance, and interest payments being handled by EFT. The bank statement lists cash withdrawals by EFT with checks and other deductions. Cash receipts by EFT are listed with deposits and other additions. A bank statement is sometimes a depositor's only notice of an EFT.

Bank Statement

Usually once a month, the bank sends each depositor a bank statement showing the activity in the account during the past month. Different banks use different formats for their bank statements, but all of them include the following items of information:

Exhibit 9.5

Check with Remittance Advice

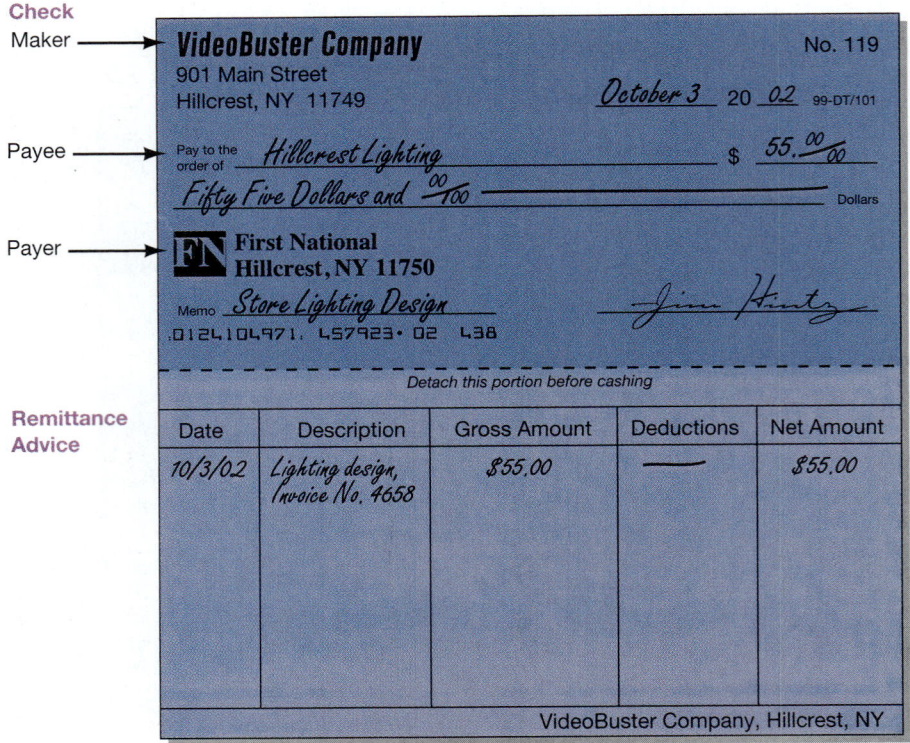

Check Maker → VideoBuster Company

Payee →

Payer →

Remittance Advice

1. Beginning-of-period balance of the depositor's account.
2. Checks and other debits decreasing the account during the period.
3. Deposits and other credits increasing the account during the period.
4. End-of-period balance of the depositor's account.

Point: Good internal control is to deposit all cash receipts daily and make all payments for goods and services by check. This controls access to cash and creates an independent record of all cash activities.

This information reflects the bank's records. Exhibit 9.6 shows one type of bank statement. Identify each of these four items in that statement. Part A of Exhibit 9.6 summarizes changes in the account. Part B lists paid checks along with other debits. Part C lists deposits and credits to the account, and part D shows the daily account balances.

Enclosed with a bank statement is a list of the depositor's canceled checks or the actual canceled checks along with any debit or credit memoranda affecting the account. **Canceled checks** are checks the bank has paid and deducted from the customer's account during the period. Other deductions that can appear on a bank statement include (1) service charges and fees assessed by the bank, (2) checks deposited that are uncollectible, (3) corrections of previous errors, (4) withdrawals through automatic teller machines (ATMs), and (5) periodic payments arranged in advance by a depositor.[3] Except for service charges, the bank notifies the depositor of each deduction with a debit memorandum when the bank reduces the balance. A copy of each debit memorandum is usually sent with the statement.[4]

Transactions also can increase the depositor's account; such as amounts the bank collects on behalf of the depositor and the corrections of previous errors. Credit memoranda notify the depositor of all increases when they are recorded. A copy of each credit memorandum is often sent with the bank statement. Another item sometimes added to the bank balance is interest earned by the depositor. Banks that pay interest on checking accounts often com-

Global: A company must disclose any restrictions on cash accounts located outside the United States.

---

[3] Most business checking accounts do not allow ATM withdrawals because of a desire to make all disbursements by check.

[4] A depositor's account is a liability on the bank's records. This is so because the money belongs to the depositor, not the bank. When a depositor increases the account balance, the bank records it with a *credit* to the account. This means that debit memos from the bank produce *credits* on the depositor's books, and credit memos produce *debits* on the depositor's books.

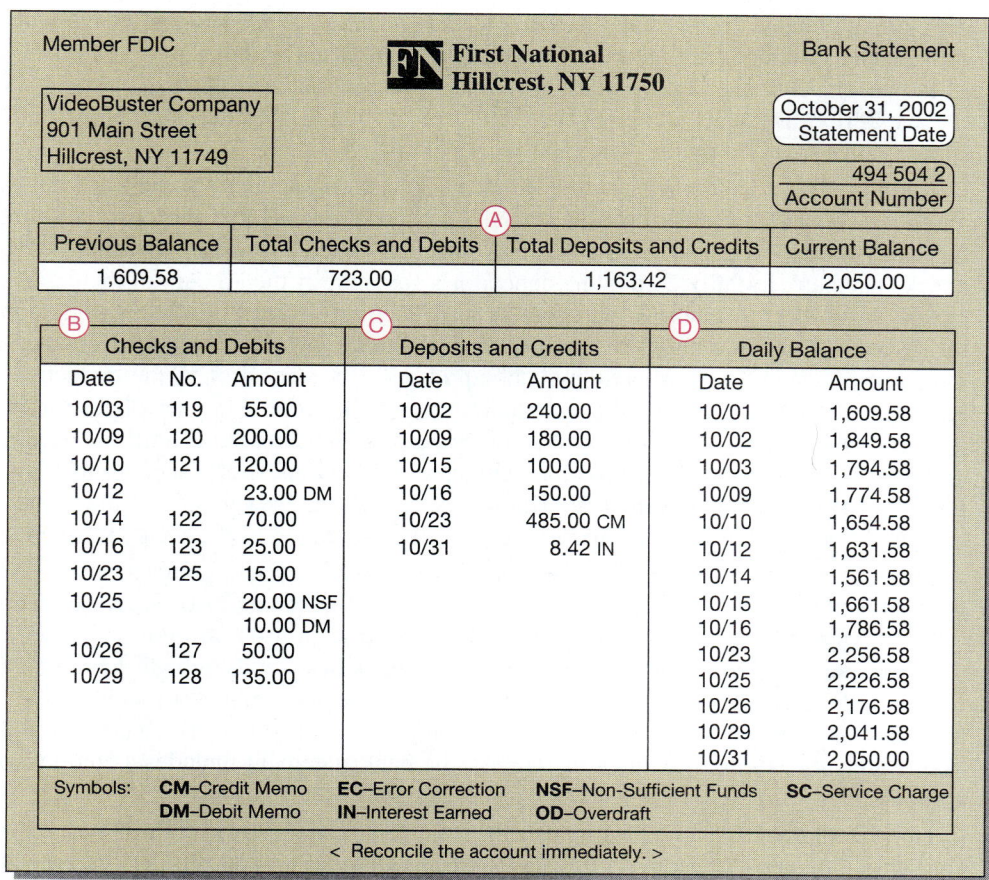

Exhibit 9.6

Bank Statement

pute the amount of interest earned on the average cash balance and credit it to the depositor's account each period. In Exhibit 9.6, the bank credits $8.42 of interest to the account of VideoBuster.

Bank Reconciliation

When a company both deposits all cash receipts and makes all cash payments (except petty cash) by check, it can use the bank statement for proving the accuracy of the depositor's cash records. This is done using a **bank reconciliation**, which is a report explaining any differences between the checking account balance according to the depositor's records and the balance reported on the bank statement.

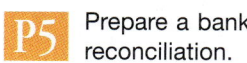

Prepare a bank reconciliation.

Concept 9-2

Purpose of Bank Reconciliation

The balance of a checking account reported on the bank statement rarely equals the balance in the depositor's accounting records. This is usually due to information that one party has that the other does not. We must therefore prove the accuracy of both the depositor's records and those of the bank. This means we must *reconcile* the two balances and explain or account for any differences in these two balances.

Among the factors causing the bank statement balance to differ from the depositor's book balance are these:

1. **Outstanding checks. Outstanding checks** are checks written (or drawn) by the depositor, deducted on the depositor's records, and sent to the payees but not yet received by the bank for payment at the bank statement date.

2. **Deposits in transit** (also called **outstanding deposits**). **Deposits in transit** are deposits made and recorded by the depositor but not yet recorded on the bank statement. For

example, companies often make deposits at the end of a business day after the bank is closed. The bank does not record a deposit in the bank's night depository on the last day of the period until the next business day, and it does not appear on the bank statement for that period. Deposits mailed to the bank near the end of a period also can be in transit and unrecorded when the statement is prepared.

3. **Deductions for uncollectible items and for services.** A company sometimes deposits another's check that is uncollectible (usually meaning the balance in such an account is not large enough to cover the check). This check is called a *non-sufficient funds (NSF)* check. The bank initially credits the depositor's account for the amount of the deposited check. When the bank learns the check is uncollectible, it debits (reduces) the depositor's account for the amount of that check. The bank may also charge the depositor a fee for processing an uncollectible check and notify the depositor of the deduction by sending a debit memorandum. Each deduction should be recorded by the depositor when a debit memorandum is received, but an entry is sometimes not made until the bank reconciliation is prepared. Other possible bank charges to a depositor's account that are reported on a bank statement include printing new checks and service for maintaining the account. Notification of these charges is typically first made in the bank statement.

4. **Additions for collections and for interest.** Banks sometimes act as collection agents for their depositors by collecting notes and other items. Banks can also receive electronic fund transfers to the depositor's account. When a bank collects an item, it is added to the depositor's account, less any service fee. The bank also sends a credit memorandum to notify the depositor of the transaction. When the memorandum is received, the depositor should record it; yet it sometimes remains unrecorded until the bank reconciliation is prepared. If an account earns interest, the bank statement includes a credit for the amount earned.

5. **Errors.** Both banks and depositors can makes errors. Bank errors might not be discovered until the depositor prepares the bank reconciliation. Also, depositor errors are sometimes discovered when the bank balance is reconciled.

Reconciling a Bank Balance

The employee who prepares the bank reconciliation should not be responsible for cash receipts, processing checks, or maintaining cash records. A reconciliation requires this person to

- Compare deposits on the bank statement with deposits in the accounting records. Identify any discrepancies and determine which is correct. List any errors and unrecorded deposits.

- Inspect all credits on the bank statement and determine whether each is recorded. Examples are collections by the bank, correction of previous bank statement errors, and interest earned by the depositor. List any unrecorded credits.

- Compare canceled checks on the bank statement with actual checks returned (if provided) with the statement. For each check, make sure the bank deducts the correct amount and properly charges it to the account. List any discrepancies.

- Compare canceled checks on the bank statement with checks recorded. List any outstanding checks. Inspect and list any canceled checks unrecorded.

- Identify any outstanding checks listed on the previous period's bank reconciliation that are not included in the canceled checks on this period's bank statement. List those checks that still remain outstanding. Send the list to the cashier for follow-up with payees to see if the checks were received.

Point: Small businesses with few employees often allow recordkeepers to both write checks and keep the general ledger. If this is done, it is essential that the owner do the bank reconciliation.

- Inspect all debits on the bank statement and determine whether each is recorded. Examples are bank charges for newly printed checks, NSF checks, and monthly service charges. List any unrecorded debits.

When these tasks are complete, the employee can then prepare the reconciliation.

Illustrating a Bank Reconciliation

We follow nine steps in preparing the bank reconciliation. It is helpful to refer to the bank reconciliation for VideoBuster shown in Exhibit 9.7 when studying steps ① through ⑨.

① Identify the bank balance of the cash account (*balance per bank*).

② Identify and list any unrecorded deposits and any bank errors understating the bank balance. Add them to the bank balance.

③ Identify and list any outstanding checks and any bank errors overstating the bank balance. Deduct them from the bank balance.

④ Compute the *adjusted bank balance,* also called *corrected* or *reconciled balance.*

⑤ Identify the company's book balance of the cash account (*balance per book*).

⑥ Identify and list any unrecorded credit memoranda from the bank, interest earned, and errors understating the book balance. Add them to the book balance.

⑦ Identify and list any unrecorded debit memoranda from the bank, service charges, and errors overstating the book balance. Deduct them from the book balance.

⑧ Compute the *adjusted book balance,* also called *corrected* or *reconciled balance.*

⑨ Verify that the two adjusted balances from steps 4 and 8 are equal. If so, they are reconciled. If not, check for accuracy and missing data to achieve reconciliation.

In reconciling the bank account, VideoBuster gathered the following data:

■ Bank balance shown on the bank statement is $2,050.

■ Book balance shown in the accounting records is $1,404.58.

■ A $145 deposit placed in the bank's night depository on October 31 is not recorded on the bank statement.

■ A comparison of canceled checks with the company's books showed two checks outstanding—No. 124 for $150 and No. 126 for $200.

■ Enclosed with the bank statement is a credit memorandum showing the bank collected a note receivable for the company on October 23. The note's proceeds of $500 (minus a $15 collection fee) are credited to the company's account. The company has not yet recorded this credit memorandum.

■ The bank statement shows a credit of $8.42 for interest earned on the average cash balance. There was no prior notification of this item, and it is not yet recorded.

■ Other debits on the bank statement that are not recorded include (1) a $23 charge for checks printed by the bank and (2) a NSF check for $20 plus a related $10 processing fee. The NSF check is dated October 16 and included in that day's deposit.

The bank reconciliation in Exhibit 9.7 reflects these items. The circled numbers in this reconciliation correspond to the nine steps listed.

Recording Adjusting Entries from a Bank Reconciliation

A bank reconciliation helps identify any errors by both the bank and the depositor. It also identifies unrecorded items that need recording by the company. In VideoBuster's reconciliation, the adjusted balance of $1,845 is the correct balance as of October 31. But the company's accounting records show a $1,404.58 balance. We must prepare journal entries to adjust the book balance to the correct balance. *It is important to remember that only the items reconciling the book balance require adjustment.* A review of Exhibit 9.7 indicates that four entries are required for VideoBuster.

VIDEOBUSTER
Bank Reconciliation
October 31, 2002

①	Bank statement balance		$2,050.00	⑤ Book balance		$1,404.58
②	Add			⑥ Add		
	Deposit of 10/31 in transit		145.00	Collect $500 note less $15 fee . .	$485.00	
			2,195.00	Interest earned	8.42	493.42
③	Deduct					1,898.00
	Outstanding checks			⑦ Deduct		
	No. 124	$150.00		Check printing charge	23.00	
	No. 126	200.00	350.00	NSF check plus service fee	30.00	53.00
④	**Adjusted bank balance**		**$1,845.00**	⑧ **Adjusted book balance . . . .**		**$1,845.00**

⑨ Balances are equal (reconciled)

Exhibit 9.7

Bank Reconciliation

Collection of note

The first entry is to record the proceeds of VideoBuster's note receivable collected by the bank less the expense of having the bank perform that service:

Assets = Liabilities + Equity
+485   −15
−500

Oct. 31	Cash	485	
	Collection Expense	15	
	Notes Receivable		500
	To record the collection fee and proceeds of a note collected by the bank.		

Interest earned

The second entry records the interest credited to VideoBuster's account by the bank:

Assets = Liabilities + Equity
+8.42   +8.42

Oct. 31	Cash	8.42	
	Interest Earned		8.42
	To record interest earned on the cash balance in the checking account.		

Check printing

The third entry debits Miscellaneous Expenses for the check printing charge:

Assets = Liabilities + Equity
−23   −23

Oct. 31	Miscellaneous Expenses	23	
	Cash		23
	Check printing charge.		

NSF check

The fourth entry records the NSF check that is returned as uncollectible. The $20 check was originally received from F. Heflin in payment of his account and then deposited. The bank charged $10 for handling the NSF check and deducted $30 total from VideoBuster's account. This means the entry must reverse the effects of the original entry made when the check was received and also must record the $10 fee:

Assets = Liabilities + Equity
+30
−30

Oct. 31	Accounts Receivable—F. Heflin	30	
	Cash		30
	To charge Heflin's account for $20 NSF check and $10 bank fee.		

not sufficient funds

This entry reflects normal business practice by adding the NSF $10 fee to Heflin's account. The company will try to collect the entire $30 from Heflin. After these four entries are recorded, the book balance of cash is adjusted to the correct amount of $1,845 ($1,404.58 + $485 + $8.42 − $23 − $30).

Quick Check

11. What is a bank statement?

12. What is the meaning of the phrase *to reconcile a bank balance?*

13. Why do we reconcile the bank statement balance of cash and the depositor's book balance of cash?

14. List at least two items affecting the bank side of a bank reconciliation and indicate whether the items are added or subtracted.

15. List at least three items affecting the book side of a bank reconciliation and indicate whether the items are added or subtracted.

Answers—p. 380

Days' Sales Uncollected

Using the Information

Many companies attract customers by selling to them on credit. This means that cash receipts from customers are delayed until accounts receivable are collected. Users of accounting information often want to know how quickly a company can convert its accounts receivable into cash. This is important for evaluating a company's liquidity. One measure of the liquidity of receivables is the **days' sales uncollected,** also called *days' sales in receivables*. This measure is computed by dividing the current balance of receivables by net credit sales over the year just completed and then multiplying by 365 (number of days in a year). Since net credit sales usually are not reported to external users, the net sales (or revenues) figure is commonly used in the computation. This formula for days' sales uncollected is shown in Exhibit 9.8.

A1 Compute the days' sales uncollected ratio and use it to analyze liquidity.

$$\text{Days' sales uncollected} = \frac{\text{Accounts receivable}}{\text{Net sales}} \times 365$$

Exhibit 9.8

Days' Sales Uncollected

We use days' sales uncollected to estimate how much time is likely to pass before the current amount of accounts receivable is received in cash. For evaluation purposes, we need to compare this estimate to that for other companies in the same industry. We also make comparisons between current and prior periods.

To illustrate, we select data from the annual reports of two toy manufacturers, **Hasbro** and **Mattel**. Their days' sales uncollected figures are shown in Exhibit 9.9.

Company	Figure	1999	1998	1997
Hasbro	Accounts receivable	$1,084	$ 959	$ 783
	Net sales	$4,232	$3,304	$3,189
	Days' sales uncollected	**93 days**	**106 days**	**90 days**
Mattel	Accounts receivable	$1,270	$1,150	$1,253
	Net sales	$5,515	$5,621	$5,456
	Days' sales uncollected	**84 days**	**75 days**	**84 days**

Exhibit 9.9

Analysis Using Days' Sales Uncollected ($ millions)

Days' sales uncollected for Hasbro in 1999 is computed as ($1,084/$4,232) × 365 days = 93 days. This means it will take about 93 days to collect cash from ending accounts receivable. This number reflects one or more of the following factors: a company's ability to collect receivables, customer financial health, customer payment strategies, and discount terms. To further assess days' sales uncollected for Hasbro, we compare it to the numbers for two prior years and to those of Mattel. We see that Hasbro's days' sales uncollected varies from 90 to 106 days. In comparison to Mattel, Hasbro takes longer to collect cash from its receivables. Days' sales uncollected for Mattel varies from 75 days to 84 days. This higher liquidity in receivables for Mattel often translates into increased profitability. Running a successful company requires monitoring the liquidity of assets.

You Make the Call

Sales Representative   The sales staff is told to take action to reduce days' sales uncollected. What can you, a salesperson, do to reduce days' sales uncollected?

Answer—p. 380

Demonstration Problem

Prepare a bank reconciliation for Jamboree Enterprises for the month ended November 30, 2002. The following information is available to reconcile Jamboree Enterprises' book balance of cash with its bank statement balance as of November 30, 2002:

a. After all posting is complete on November 30, the company's book balance of Cash has a $16,380 debit balance, but its bank statement shows a $38,520 balance.

b. Checks No. 2024 for $4,810 and No. 2036 for $5,000 are outstanding.

c. In comparing the canceled checks returned by the bank with the entries in the accounting records, it is found that Check No. 2025 in payment of rent is correctly drawn for $1,000 but is erroneously entered in the accounting records as $880.

d. The November 30 deposit of $17,150 was placed in the night depository after banking hours on that date, and this amount does not appear on the bank statement.

e. In reviewing the bank statement, a check belonging to Jumbo Enterprises in the amount of $160 was erroneously drawn against Jamboree's account.

f. A credit memorandum enclosed with the bank statement indicates that the bank collected a $30,000 note and $900 of related interest on Jamboree's behalf. This transaction was not recorded by Jamboree before receiving the statement.

g. A debit memorandum for $1,100 lists a $1,100 NSF check received from a customer, Marilyn Welch. Jamboree had not recorded the return of this check before receiving the statement.

h. Bank service charges for November total $40. These charges were not recorded by Jamboree before receiving the statement.

Planning the Solution

• Set up a bank reconciliation as follows with a bank side and a book side (see Exhibit 9.7). Leave room to both add and deduct items. Each column will result in a reconciled, equal balance.

Bank statement balance	Book balance. . . . .
Add:.	Add:
Deduct:	Deduct:
Adjusted bank balance	Adjusted book balance . . . .

• Examine each item (a) through (h) to determine whether it affects the book or the bank balance and whether it should be added or deducted from the bank or book balance.

• After all items are analyzed, complete the reconciliation and arrive at a reconciled balance between the bank side and the book side.

• For each reconciling item on the book side, prepare an adjusting entry. Additions to the book side require an adjusting entry that debits Cash. Deductions on the book side require an adjusting entry that credits Cash.

Solution to Demonstration Problem

JAMBOREE ENTERPRISES Bank Reconciliation November 30, 2002					
Bank statement balance		$38,520	Book balance		$16,380
Add			Add		
Deposit of Nov. 30. . . .	$17,150		Collection of note . .	$30,000	
Bank error.	160	17,310	Interest earned	900	30,900
		55,830			47,280
Deduct			Deduct		
Outstanding checks		9,810	NSF check	1,100	
			Recording error	120	
			Service charge	40	1,260
Adjusted bank balance		**$46,020**	**Adjusted book balance**		**$46,020**

Required Adjusting Entries for Jamboree

Nov. 30	Cash	30,900	
	Notes Receivable		30,000
	Interest Earned		900
	To record collection of note with interest.		
Nov. 30	Accounts Receivable—M. Welch	1,100	
	Cash		1,100
	To reinstate account due from an NSF check.		
Nov. 30	Rent Expense	120	
	Cash		120
	To correct recording error on check no. 2025.		
Nov. 30	Bank Service Charges	40	
	Cash		40
	To record bank service charges.		

Document Flow in a Voucher System

9A

This appendix describes the important documents in and their flow through a voucher system of control. We explain how this system is useful in controlling cash disbursements.

Purchase Requisition

Department managers are usually not allowed to place orders directly with suppliers. If each manager were allowed to deal directly with suppliers, the merchandise purchased and the resulting lia-

Exhibit 9A.1

Purchase Requisition

Purchase Requisition	No. 917

Z-Mart

From ___ Sporting Goods Department __   **Date** _____ October 28, 2002 _____
To _____ Purchasing Department _____   **Preferred Vendor** ___ Trex _____

Request purchase of the following item(s):

Model No.	Description	Quantity
CH 015	Challenger X7	1
SD 099	SpeedDemon	1

Reason for Request _____ Replenish inventory _____
Approval for Request _____ *J.Z.* _____

For Purchasing Department use only: Order Date _10/30/02_   P.O. No. _____P98____

bilities would not be well-controlled. To gain control over purchases, department managers are usually required to place all orders through a purchasing department. When merchandise is needed, a department manager must inform the purchasing department of its needs by preparing and signing a **purchase requisition,** which lists the merchandise needed and requests that it be purchased—see Exhibit 9A.1. Two copies of the purchase requisition are sent to the purchasing department. The purchasing department then sends one copy to the accounting department. When the accounting department receives a purchase requisition, it creates and maintains a voucher for this transaction. A third copy of the requisition is kept by the requesting department as backup.

Purchase Order

A **purchase order** is a document the purchasing department uses to place an order with a seller (**vendor**). A vendor usually is a manufacturer or wholesaler. A purchase order authorizes a vendor to ship ordered merchandise at the stated price and terms—see Exhibit 9A.2. When the purchasing department receives a purchase requisition, it prepares at least four copies of a purchase order. The copies are distributed as follows: *copy 1* is sent to the vendor as a purchase request and as authority to ship

Exhibit 9A.2

Purchase Order

Purchase Order	No. P98

Z-Mart
10 Michigan Street
Chicago, Illinois 60521

To: Trex
  W9797 Cherry Road
  Antigo, Wisconsin 54409

Date _____ 10/30/02 _____
FOB _____ Destination _____
Ship by _As soon as possible_
Terms _____ 2/15, n/30 _____

Request shipment of the following item(s):

Model No.	Description	Quantity	Price	Amount
CH 015	Challenger X7	1	490	490
SD 099	SpeedDemon	1	710	710

All shipments and invoices must
include purchase order number

Ordered by
_____ *J.W.* _____

merchandise; *copy 2* is sent, along with a copy of the purchase requisition, to the accounting department where it is entered in the voucher and used in approving payment of the invoice; *copy 3* is sent to the requesting department to inform its manager that action is being taken; and *copy 4* is retained on file by the purchasing department.

Invoice

An **invoice** is an itemized statement of goods prepared by the vendor (supplier) listing the customer's name, items sold, sales prices, and terms of sale. An invoice is also a bill sent to the buyer from the supplier. From the vendor's point of view, it is a *sales invoice*. The vendor sends the invoice to a buyer, or **vendee,** who treats it as a *purchase invoice*. When receiving a purchase order, the vendor ships the ordered merchandise to the buyer and includes or mails a copy of the invoice covering the shipment to the buyer. The invoice is sent to the buyer's accounting department where it is placed in the voucher. Exhibit 6.6 shows Z-Mart's purchase invoice.

Receiving Report

Many companies maintain a separate department to receive all merchandise and purchased assets. When each shipment arrives, this receiving department counts the goods and checks them for damage and agreement with the purchase order. It then prepares four or more copies of a **receiving report,** which is used within the company to notify the appropriate persons that ordered goods have been received and to describe the quantities and condition of the goods. One copy is placed in the voucher. Copies are also sent to the requesting department and the purchasing department to notify them that the goods have arrived. The receiving department retains a copy in its files.

Invoice Approval

When a receiving report arrives, the accounting department should have copies of the following documents in the voucher: purchase requisition, purchase order, and invoice. With the information in these documents, the accounting department can record the purchase and approve its payment. In approving an invoice for payment, the department checks and compares information across all documents. To facilitate this checking and to ensure that no step is omitted, the department often uses an **invoice approval,** also called *check authorization*—see Exhibit 9A.3. An invoice approval is a checklist of steps necessary for approving an invoice for recording and payment. It is a separate document either filed in the voucher or preprinted (or stamped) on the voucher.

Point: Recording a purchase is initiated by an invoice approval, not an invoice. An invoice approval verifies that the amount is consistent with that requested, ordered, and received. This controls and verifies purchases and related liabilities.

Invoice Approval			
Document		By	Date
Purchase requisition	917	T.	10/28/02
Purchase order	P98	gw	10/30/02
Receiving report	R85	↓K	11/3/02
Invoice:	4657		11/12/02
Price		C	11/12/02
Calculations		C	11/12/02
Terms		C	11/12/02
Approved for payment		Q	

Exhibit 9A.3

Invoice Approval

As each step in the checklist is approved, the person initials the invoice approval and records the current date. Final approval implies the following steps have occurred:

1. **Requisition check:** Items on invoice are requested per purchase requisition.
2. **Purchase order check:** Items on invoice are ordered per purchase order.
3. **Receiving report check:** Items on invoice are received, per receiving report.
4. **Invoice check: Price:** Invoice prices are as agreed with the vendor.
     Calculations: Invoice has no mathematical errors.
     Terms: Terms are as agreed with the vendor.

Voucher

Once an invoice has been checked and approved, the voucher is complete. A complete voucher is a record summarizing a transaction. Once the voucher certifies a transaction as correct, it authorizes

Exhibit 9A.4

Inside of a Voucher

		Z-Mart Chicago, Illinois		Voucher No. 4657

Date ___ Oct. 28, 2002 _____
Pay to ___ Trex _____
City ____ Antigo _____ State ___ Wisconsin _____

For the following: (attach all invoices and supporting documents)

Date of Invoice	Terms	Invoice Number and Other Details	Terms
Nov. 2, 2002	2/15, n/30	Invoice No. 4657	1,200
		Less discount	24
		Net amount payable	1,176

Payment approved

N. O. Neal

Auditor

recording an obligation. A voucher also contains approval for paying the obligation on an appropriate date. The physical form of a voucher varies across companies. Many are designed so that the invoice and other related source documents are placed inside the voucher, which is often a folder.

Completion of a voucher usually requires a person to enter certain information on both the inside and outside of the voucher. Typical information required on the inside of a voucher is shown in Exhibit 9A.4, and that for the outside is shown in Exhibit 9A.5. This information is taken from the invoice and the supporting documents filed in the voucher. A complete voucher is sent to an authorized individual (often called an *auditor*). This person performs a final review, approves the accounts and amounts for debiting (called the *accounting distribution*), and authorizes recording of the voucher.

After a voucher is approved and recorded, it is filed until its due date, when it is sent to the cashier for payment. The person issuing checks relies on the approved voucher and its signed supporting documents as proof that an obligation has been incurred and must be paid. The purchase requisition and purchase order confirm the purchase was authorized. The receiving report shows items have been received, and the invoice approval form verifies that the invoice has been checked for errors. There is little chance for error and even less chance for fraud without collusion unless all the documents and signatures are forged.

Exhibit 9A.5

Outside of a Voucher

		Voucher No. 4657

Accounting Distribution

Account Debited	Amount
Merch. Inventory	1,200
Store Supplies	
Office Supplies	
Sales Salaries	
Other	
Total Vouch. Pay. Cr.	1,200

Due Date _____ November 12, 2002 _____
Pay to _____ Trex
City _____ Antigo
State _____ Wisconsin

Summary of charges:
     Total charges _____ 1,200
     Discount _____ 24
     Net payment _____ 1,176

Record of payment:
     Paid _____
     Check No. _____

Summary

C1 **Define internal control and its purpose.** An internal control system consists of the policies and procedures managers use to protect assets, ensure reliable accounting, promote efficient operations, and urge adherence to company policies. It can prevent avoidable losses and help managers both plan operations and monitor company and human performance.

C2 **Identify principles of internal control.** Principles of good internal control include establishing responsibilities, maintaining adequate records, insuring assets and bonding employees, separating recordkeeping from custody of assets, dividing responsibilities for related transactions, applying technological controls, and performing regular independent reviews.

C3 **Define cash and cash equivalents and explain how to report them.** Cash includes currency, coins, and amounts on (or acceptable for) deposit in checking and savings accounts. Cash equivalents are short-term, highly liquid investment assets readily convertible to a known cash amount and sufficiently close to their maturity date so that market value is not sensitive to interest rate changes. Cash and cash equivalents are liquid assets because they are readily converted into other assets or can be used to pay for goods, services, or liabilities.

C4 **Identify control features of banking activities.** Banks offer several services that promote the control and safeguarding of cash. A bank account is a record set up by a bank permitting a customer to deposit money for safeguarding and to draw checks on it. A bank deposit is money contributed to the account with a deposit ticket as proof. A check is a document signed by the depositor instructing the bank to pay a specified amount of money to a designated recipient.

A1 **Compute the days' sales uncollected ratio and use it to analyze liquidity.** Many companies attract customers by selling to them on credit. This means that cash flows from customers are delayed until accounts receivable are collected. Users of accounting information often want to know how quickly a company can convert its accounts receivable into cash. This is important for evaluating a company's liquidity. The days' sales uncollected ratio, one measure reflecting liquidity, is computed by dividing the ending balance of receivables by annual net sales, and then multiplying by 365.

P1 **Apply internal control to cash receipts.** Internal control of cash receipts ensures all cash received is properly recorded and deposited. Attention is focused on two important types of cash receipts: over-the-counter and by mail. Good internal control for over-the-counter cash receipts includes use of a cash register, customer review, use of receipts, a permanent transaction record, and separation of the custody of cash from its recordkeeping. Good internal control for cash receipts by mail includes at least two people assigned to open mail and prepare a list with each sender's name, amount, and explanation.

P2 **Apply the voucher system to control cash disbursements.** A voucher system is a set of procedures and approvals designed to control cash disbursements and acceptance of obligations. The voucher system of control relies on several important documents, including the voucher and its supporting files. A key factor in this system is that only approved departments and individuals are authorized to incur certain obligations. To coordinate and control responsibilities, several documents are used.

P3 **Explain and record petty cash fund transactions.** Petty cash disbursements are payments of small amounts for items such as postage, courier fees, repairs, and supplies. A company usually sets up one or more petty cash funds. A petty fund cashier is responsible for safekeeping the cash, making payments from this fund, and keeping receipts and records. A Petty Cash account is debited only when the fund is established or increased in size. The cashier presents all paid receipts to the company cashier for reimbursement. When the fund is replenished, petty cash disbursements are recorded with debits to expense (or asset) accounts and a credit to cash.

P4 **Apply the net method to control purchase discounts.** The net method aids management in monitoring and controlling purchase discounts. When invoices are recorded at gross amounts, the amount of discounts taken is deducted from the balance of the Merchandise Inventory account. This means the amount of any discounts lost is not reported in any account and is unlikely to come to the attention of management. But when purchases are recorded at net amounts, a Discounts Lost account is brought to management's attention as an operating expense. Management can then seek to identify the reason for discounts lost, such as oversight, carelessness, or unfavorable terms.

P5 **Prepare a bank reconciliation.** A bank reconciliation proves the accuracy of the depositor's and the bank's records. The bank statement balance is adjusted for items such as outstanding checks and unrecorded deposits made on or before the bank statement date but not reflected on the statement. The book balance also often requires adjustment for items such as service charges, bank collections for the depositor, and interest earned on the account.

Guidance Answers to **You Make the Call**

Entrepreneur   A forced vacation policy is part of a good system of internal controls. When employees are forced to take vacations, their ability to hide any fraudulent behavior decreases because others must perform the duties of the people on vacation. A replacement employee potentially can uncover fraudulent behavior or falsified records. A forced vacation policy is especially important for employees in more sensitive positions of handling money or in control of easily transferable assets.

Internal Auditor   Your decision is whether to accept the situation or to dig further to see whether the petty cashier is abusing petty cash. Since you were asked to postpone your count, along with the fact the fund consists of 14 new $20 bills, you have legitimate concerns about whether money is being used for personal use. It is possible the most recent reimbursement of the fund was for $280 (14 × $20) or more. In that case, this reimbursement can leave the fund with sequentially numbered $20 bills. But if the most recent reimbursement was for less than $280, the presence of 14 sequentially numbered $20 bills suggests that the new bills were obtained from a bank as replacement for bills that had been removed. Neither situation shows the cashier is stealing money, but the second case indicates the cashier "borrowed" the cash and later replaced it af-ter the auditor showed up. In writing your report, you must not conclude the cashier is unethical unless other evidence supports it. You also might consider additional surprise counts of this petty cashier over the next few weeks.

Sales Representative   A salesperson can take several steps to reduce days' sales uncollected. These include (1) decreasing the proportion of sales on account to total sales by encouraging more cash sales, (2) identifying customers most delayed in their payments and encouraging earlier payments or cash sales, and (3) implementing stricter credit policies to eliminate credit sales to customers that never pay.

Guidance Answers to **Quick Checks**

1. c

2. Technology reduces processing errors. It also allows more extensive testing of records, limits the amount of hard evidence, and highlights the importance of separation of duties.

3. A company owns liquid assets so that it can purchase other assets, buy services, and pay obligations.

4. A company owns cash equivalents because they yield a return greater than what cash earns (and are readily exchanged for cash).

5. Examples of cash equivalents are 90-day U.S. treasury bills, money market funds, and commercial paper (notes).

6. a

7. A voucher system is used when an owner/manager can no longer control purchasing procedures through personal supervision and direct participation.

8. If all cash payments are made by check, numerous checks for small amounts must be written. Because this practice is expensive and time consuming, a petty cash fund is often established for making small cash payments.

9. If the petty cash fund is not reimbursed at the end of an accounting period, the transactions involving petty cash are not yet recorded, and the petty cash asset is overstated.

10. First, when the petty cash fund is reimbursed, the petty cash transactions are recorded. Second, reimbursement provides cash to allow the fund to continue being used. Third, reimbursement identifies any cash shortage or overage in the fund.

11. A bank statement is a report prepared by the bank describing the activities in a depositor's account.

12. To reconcile a bank balance means to explain the difference between the cash balance in the depositor's accounting records and the balance on the bank statement.

13. The purpose of the bank reconciliation is to determine whether the bank or the depositor has made any errors and whether the bank has entered any transactions affecting the account that the depositor has not recorded.

14. Outstanding checks—subtracted
Unrecorded deposits—added

15. Debit memos—subtracted   Interest earned—added
NSF checks—subtracted   Credit memos—added
Bank service charges—subtracted

Glossary

Bank reconciliation report that explains the difference between the book balance of cash and the balance reported on the bank statement. (p. 369).

Canceled checks checks that the bank has paid and deducted from the depositor's account. (p. 368).

Cash includes currency, coins, and amounts on deposit in bank checking or savings accounts. (p. 359).

Cash equivalents short-term, investment assets that are readily convertible to a known cash amount and sufficiently close to their maturity date so that market value is not sensitive to interest rate changes. (p. 359).

Cash Over and Short income statement account used to record cash overages and cash shortages arising from missing petty cash receipts or simple errors. (p. 360).

Check document signed by the depositor instructing the bank to pay a specified amount to a designated recipient. (p. 367).

Days' sales uncollected measure of the liquidity of receivables computed by dividing the current balance of receivables by the annual credit (or net) sales, and then mul-tiplying by 365; also called *days' sales in receivables*. (p. 373).

Deposit in Transit A deposit recorded by the company but not yet by its bank. (p. 369).

Deposit ticket lists items such as currency, coins, and checks deposited and their corresponding dollar amounts. (p. 366).

Discounts Lost expense resulting from a failure to take advantage of cash discounts on purchases. (p. 366).

Electronic funds transfer (EFT) use of electronic communication to transfer cash from one party to another. (p. 367).

Gross method method of recording purchases at the full invoice price without deducting any cash discounts. (p. 365).

Internal control system all policies and procedures used to protect assets, ensure reliable accounting, promote efficient operations, and urge adherence to company policies. (p. 354).

Invoice itemized record of goods prepared by the vendor that lists the customer's name, the items sold, the sales prices, and the terms of sale. (p. 377).

Invoice approval document containing a checklist of steps necessary for approving an invoice for recording and payment; also called *check authorization* (p. 377).

Liquid asset resources such as cash that are easily converted into other assets or used to pay for goods, services, or liabilities. (p. 359).

Liquidity company's ability to pay for its short-term obligations. (p. 359).

Net method method of recording purchases at the full invoice price less any cash discounts. (p. 365).

Outstanding checks checks written and recorded by the depositor but not yet paid by the bank at the bank statement date (p. 369).

Principles of internal control principles requiring management to establish responsibility, maintain records, insure assets, separate recordkeeping from custody of assets, divide responsibility for related transactions, apply technological controls, and perform reviews. (p. 354).

Purchase order document used by the purchasing department to place an order with a seller (vendor). (p. 376).

Purchase requisition document listing merchandise needed by a department and requesting it be purchased. (p. 376).

Receiving report form used to report that ordered goods are received and to describe their quantity and condition. (p. 377).

Signature card includes the signatures of each person authorized to sign checks on the account. (p. 366).

Vendee buyer or purchaser of goods or services. (p. 377).

Vendor seller of goods or services. (p. 376).

Voucher internal file used to store documents and information to control cash disbursements and to ensure that a transaction is properly recorded. (p. 361).

Voucher system procedures and approvals designed to control cash disbursements and acceptance of obligations. (p. 361).

[The Superscript letter ^A denotes assignments based on Appendix 9A.]

Questions

1. List the seven broad principles of internal control.
2. Why should responsibility for related transactions be divided among different departments or individuals?
3. Internal control procedures are important in every business, but at what stage in the development of a business do they become especially critical?
4. Which of the following assets is most liquid? Which is least liquid? Inventory, building, accounts receivable, cash?
5. Why should the person who keeps the records of an asset not be the person responsible for its custody?
6. When a store purchases merchandise, why are individual departments not allowed to directly deal with suppliers?
7. What is a petty cash receipt? Who should sign it?
8. Why should all cash receipts be deposited on the day of receipt?
9. **Nike**'s statement of cash flows in Appendix A describes changes in cash and cash equivalents for the year ended May 31, 2000. What amount is provided (used) by investing activities? What amount is provided (used) by financing activities?
10. **Reebok**'s balance sheet in Appendix A reports cash and cash equivalents as of December 31, 1999 and 1998. Compare and discuss the amount of cash and cash equivalents with the other current assets as of December 31, 1999. Compare and assess the amount of cash and cash equivalents as of December 31, 1999 with its amount at December 31, 1998.
11. Why does **Gap**'s balance sheet in Appendix A not report Accounts Receivable?

---

1. What is the main objective of internal control procedures, and how is it achieved?
2. Why should recordkeeping for assets be separated from custody over the assets?

QUICK STUDY

QS 9-1
Internal control objective

A good system of internal control for cash provides adequate procedures for protecting both cash receipts and cash disbursements. What are three basic guidelines that help achieve this protection?

QS 9-2
Internal control for cash

What is the difference between the terms *liquidity* and *cash equivalent*?

QS 9-3
Terminology C1

QS 9-4
Purchase discounts

Which accounting method uses a Discounts Lost account? What is the advantage of this method?

QS 9-5
Petty cash accounting

1. The petty cash fund of the Roberts Agency is established at $85. At the end of the period, the fund contained $14.80 and had the following receipts: film rentals, $21.30; refreshments for meetings, $30.85 (both expenditures to be classified as Entertainment Expense); postage, $8.95; and printing, $9.10. Prepare journal entries to record (a) establishment of the fund and (b) reimbursement of the fund at the end of the period.

2. Identify the two event(s) that cause a Petty Cash account to be credited in a journal entry.

QS 9-6
Bank reconciliation

1. For each of the following items indicate whether its amount (i) affects the bank or book side of a bank reconciliation and (ii) represents an addition or a subtraction in a bank reconciliation:

(a) Outstanding checks   **(e)** Interest on cash balance

(b) Debit memos   **(f)** Credit memos

(c) NSF checks   **(g)** Bank service charges

(d) Unrecorded deposits

2. Which of the items in part (1) require an adjusting journal entry?

QS 9-7
Days' sales uncollected

The following annual account balances are taken from Daredevil Sports at December 31:

	2002	2001
Accounts receivable	$ 85,692	$ 80,485
Net sales	2,691,855	2,396,858

What is the change in the number of days' sales uncollected between years 2002 and 2001? According to this analysis, is the company's collection of receivables improving? Explain your answer.

EXERCISES

Exercise 9-1
Recommend internal control procedures

What internal control procedures would you recommend in each of the following situations?

1. A concession company has one employee who sells T-shirts and sunglasses at the beach. Each day, the employee is given enough shirts and sunglasses to last through the day and enough cash to make change. The money is kept in a box at the stand.

2. An antique store has one employee who is given cash and sent to garage sales each weekend. The employee pays cash for this merchandise that the antique store resells.

Exercise 9-2
Internal control of cash receipts by mail

Some of O'Hara Co.'s cash receipts from customers are sent to the company with the regular mail. O'Hara's recordkeeper opens these letters and deposits the cash received each day. Identify any internal control problem(s) in this arrangement. What changes do you recommend?

Exercise 9-3
Analyzing internal control

Folkerts Company is a rapidly growing start-up business. Its recordkeeper, who was hired one year ago, left town after the company's manager discovered that a large sum of money had disappeared over the past six months. An audit disclosed that the recordkeeper had written and signed several checks made payable to the recordkeeper's fiancé and then recorded the checks as salaries expense. The fiancé, who cashed the checks but never worked for the company, left town with the recordkeeper. As a result, the company incurred an uninsured loss of $184,000. Evaluate Folkerts's internal control system and indicate which principles of internal control appear to have been ignored.

Exercise 9-4
Petty cash fund with a shortage

Brady Company establishes a $350 petty cash fund on September 9. On September 30, the fund shows $103.25 in cash along with receipts for the following expenditures: transportation-in, $39.85; office supplies, $123.55; and miscellaneous expenses, $80.00. The petty cashier could not account for a $3.35 shortage in the fund. Brady uses the perpetual system in accounting for merchandise inventory. Prepare (1) the September 9 entry to establish the fund and (2) the September 30 entry to reimburse the fund and reduce it to $250.

Eanes Co. establishes a $200 petty cash fund on January 1. One week later, the fund shows $38 in cash along with receipts for the following expenditures: postage, $74; transportation-in, $29; store supplies, $16; and miscellaneous expenses, $43. Eanes uses the perpetual system in accounting for merchandise inventory. Prepare journal entries to (1) establish the fund on January 1, (2) reimburse it on January 8, and (3) reimburse the fund and increase it to $400 on January 8 assuming no entry in part (2).

Exercise 9-5

Petty cash fund

Prepare a table with the following headings for a bank reconciliation dated September 30:

Exercise 9-6

Bank reconciliation and adjusting entries

Bank Balance		Book Balance			Not Shown on the Reconciliation
Add	Deduct	Add	Deduct	Adjust	

For each item following, place an *x* in the appropriate column to indicate whether the item should be added to or deducted from the book or bank balance, or whether it should not appear on the reconciliation. If the book balance is to be adjusted, place a *Dr.* or *Cr.* in the Adjust column to indicate whether the Cash balance should be debited or credited. At the left side of your table, number the items to correspond to the following list.

1. Bank service charge.
2. Checks written and mailed to payees on October 5.
3. Checks written by another depositor but charged against this company's account.
4. Principal and interest collected by the bank but not yet recorded by the company.
5. Special charge for collection of note in part (4) on this company's behalf.
6. Check written against the account and cleared by the bank; erroneously not recorded by the company recordkeeper.
7. Interest earned on the cash balance in the bank.
8. Night deposit made on September 30 after the bank closed.
9. Checks outstanding on August 31 that cleared the bank in September.
10. NSF check from customer returned on September 15 but not yet recorded by this company.
11. Checks written and mailed to payees on September 30.
12. Deposit made on September 5 and processed on September 8.

Ashley Clinic deposits all cash receipts on the day when they are received and makes all cash payments by check. On June 30, 2002, after all posting is complete, its Cash account shows an $11,589 debit balance. Ashley Clinic's June 30 bank statement shows $10,555 on deposit in the bank on that day. Prepare a bank reconciliation for Ashley Clinic using the following information:

a. Outstanding checks total $1,829. *deduction   charging 10m*
b. The bank statement for June included a $16 debit memorandum for bank services.
c. Check No. 919, returned with the canceled checks, was correctly drawn for $467 in payment of a utility bill on June 15. Ashley Clinic mistakenly recorded it with a debit to Utilities Expense and a credit to Cash in the amount of $476.
d. The June 30 cash receipts of $2,856 were placed in the bank's night depository after banking hours and were not recorded on the June 30 bank statement.

Exercise 9-7

Bank reconciliation

476
467
9

Give the adjusting journal entries that Ashley Clinic must record as a result of preparing the bank reconciliation in Exercise 9-7.

Exercise 9-8

Adjusting entries from bank reconciliation

Union Merchandise Co. reported annual net sales for 2001 and 2002 of $665,000 and $747,000, respectively. Also, its year-end balances of accounts receivable were as follows: December 31, 2001, $61,000; and December 31, 2002, $93,000. Calculate the days' sales uncollected at the end of each year and comment on any changes in the liquidity of this company's receivables.

Exercise 9-9

Liquidity of accounts receivable

Exercise 9-10
Record invoices at gross or net amounts

Pelkner's Imports uses the perpetual system in accounting for merchandise inventory and had the following transactions during the month of October. Prepare entries to record these transactions assuming Pelkner's records invoices (a) at gross amounts and (b) at net amounts.

Oct. 2   Received merchandise purchased at a $3,000 invoice price, invoice dated September 29, terms 2/10, n/30.

    10   Received a $500 credit memorandum (at full invoice price) for merchandise received on October 2 and returned for credit.

    17   Received merchandise purchased at a $5,400 invoice price, invoice dated October 16, terms 2/10, n/30.

    26   Paid for the merchandise received on October 17, less the discount.

    28   Paid for the merchandise received on October 2. Payment was delayed because the invoice was mistakenly filed for payment today. This error caused the discount to be lost.

Exercise 9-11ᴬ
Documents in a voucher system

Management uses a voucher system to help control and monitor cash disbursements. Identify at least four key documents that are part of a voucher system of control. Explain each document's purpose, where it originates, and how it flows through the voucher system (including copies).

PROBLEM SET A

Problem 9-1A
Establish, reimburse, and adjust petty cash; accounting adjustments

Roosevelt Co. set up a petty cash fund for payments of small amounts. The following petty cash transactions are reported by the petty cashier as occurring in May (the last month of the company's fiscal year):

May 1   Received a company check for $250 to establish the petty cash fund.

    15   Received a company check to replenish the fund for the following expenditures made since April 1 and to increase the fund to $500.
      a.   Paid $88 for janitorial service.
      b.   Purchased office supplies for $53.68.
      c.   Purchased postage stamps for $53.50.
      d.   Paid $47.15 to *The County Crier* for an advertisement in the newspaper.
      e.   Counted $11.15 remaining in the petty cash box.

    31   The petty cashier reports that $293.39 remains in the fund and decides that the May 15 increase in the fund was too large. A company check is drawn to replenish the fund for the following expenditures made since May 15 and to reduce the fund to $400.
      f.   Purchased office supplies for $147.36.
      g.   Reimbursed office manager for business mileage, $23.50.
      h.   Paid $34.75 courier charges to deliver merchandise to a customer, terms FOB destination.

Required

Preparation Component

1. Prepare journal entries to establish the fund on May 1 and to replenish it on May 15 and on May 31 along with any increase or decrease in the fund balance.

Analysis Component

2. Explain how the company's financial statements are affected if the petty cash fund is not replenished and no entry is made on May 31. (*Hint:* The amount of office supplies that appears on a balance sheet is determined by a physical count of office supplies.)

Check   Cash Cr.: May 15, $488.85; May 31, $106.61

Problem 9-2A
Establish, reimburse, and increase petty cash

Metro Art Gallery had the following petty cash transactions in February of the current year:

Feb. 2   Wrote a $400 check, cashed it, and gave the proceeds and the petty cashbox to Kareena White, the petty cashier.

    5   Purchased paper for the copier, $14.15.

    9   Paid $32.50 COD shipping charges on merchandise purchased for resale, terms FOB shipping point. Metro uses the perpetual system to account for merchandise inventory.

    12   Paid $7.95 postage to express mail a contract to a client.

    14   Reimbursed Liz Walcotte, the manager, $68 for business mileage on her car.

    20   Purchased stationery, $67.77.

    23   Paid a courier $20 to deliver merchandise sold to a customer, terms FOB destination.

25   Paid $13.10 COD shipping charges on merchandise purchased for resale, terms FOB shipping point.

27   Paid $54 for postage stamps.

28   Sorted the petty cash receipts by accounts affected and exchanged them for a check to both reimburse the fund for expenditures and increase the amount of the fund to $500. There was $121.53 cash in the fund.

Required

1. Prepare the journal entry to establish the petty cash fund.

2. Prepare a petty cash payments report for February with these categories: delivery expense, mileage expense, postage expense, merchandise inventory (transportation-in), and office supplies. Sort the payments into the appropriate categories and total the expenditures in each category.

3. Prepare the journal entry to both reimburse and increase the amount in the fund.

Check Feb. 28 entry, Cash, $378.47 Cr.

For each of these five separate cases, identify the principle of internal control that is violated. Recommend what the business should do to ensure adherence to principles of internal control.

1. Heather Hawthorne records all incoming customer cash receipts for her employer and posts the customer payments to their accounts.

2. At Cunningham Company, Jack and Jo alternate lunch hours. Jack is the petty cash custodian, but if someone needs petty cash when he is at lunch, Jo fills in as custodian.

3. Marcia Diamond does all the posting of patient charges and payments at the Provincetown Medical Clinic. Each night Marcia backs up the computerized accounting system to a tape and stores the tape in a locked file at her desk.

4. Bob Magee prides himself on hiring quality workers who require little supervision. As office manager, Bob gives his employees full discretion over their tasks and has seen no reason to perform independent reviews of their work for years.

5. Susan Smith's manager has told her to reduce costs. Susan decides to raise the deductible on the plant's property insurance from $5,000 to $10,000. This cuts the property insurance premium in half. In a related move, she decides that bonding the plant's employees is a waste of money since the company has not experienced any losses due to employee theft. Susan saves the entire amount of the bonding insurance premium by dropping the bonding insurance.

Problem 9-3A
Analyzing internal control

The following information is available to reconcile Colin Company's book balance of cash with its bank statement cash balance as of July 31, 2002:

a. After all posting is complete on July 31, the company's Cash account has a $27,497 debit balance, but its bank statement shows a $27,233 balance.

b. Check No. 3031 for $1,482 and Check No. 3040 for $558 were outstanding on the June 30 bank reconciliation. Check No. 3040 is returned with the July canceled checks, but Check No. 3031 is not. Also, Check No. 3065 for $382 and Check No. 3069 for $2,281, both written in July, are not among the canceled checks returned with the July 31 statement.

c. In comparing the canceled checks returned by the bank with the entries in the accounting records, it is found that Check No. 3056 for July rent was correctly written and drawn for $1,270 but was erroneously entered in the accounting records as $1,250.

d. A credit memorandum enclosed with the bank statement indicates the bank collected an $8,000 noninterest-bearing note for Colin, deducted a $45 collection fee, and credited the remainder to its account. Colin had not recorded this event before receiving the statement.

e. A debit memorandum for $805 lists a $795 NSF check plus a $10 NSF charge. The check had been received from a customer, Jason White. Colin has not yet recorded this check as NSF.

f. Enclosed with the statement is a $25 debit memorandum for bank services. It has not yet been recorded because no previous notification had been received.

g. The July 31 daily cash receipts of $11,514 were placed in the bank's night depository on that date but do not appear on the July 31 bank statement.

Problem 9-4A
Prepare a bank reconciliation and record adjustments

Required

Preparation Component

1. Prepare a bank reconciliation for this company as of July 31, 2002.

Check Reconciled balance, $34,602

2. Prepare the journal entries necessary to bring the company's book balance of cash into conformity with the reconciled cash balance as of July 31, 2002.

Analysis Component

3. Assume that the July 31, 2002, bank reconciliation for this company is prepared and some items are treated incorrectly. For each of the following errors, explain the effect of the error on (i) the adjusted bank statement cash balance and (ii) the adjusted cash account book balance.

    a. The company's unadjusted cash account balance of $27,497 is listed on the reconciliation as $27,947.

    b. The bank's collection of the $8,000 note less the $45 collection fee is added to the bank statement cash balance.

Problem 9-5A

Prepare a bank reconciliation and record adjustments

Clarke Company most recently reconciled its bank statement and book balances of cash on August 31 and it showed two checks outstanding, No. 5888 for $1,028.05 and No. 5893 for $493.95. The following information is available for its September 30, 2002, reconciliation:

From the September 30 Bank Statement

Previous Balance	Total Checks and Debits	Total Deposits and Credits	Current Balance
16,800.45	9,620.05	11,272.85	18,453.25

Checks and Debits			Deposits and Credits		Daily Balance	
Date	No.	Amount	Date	Amount	Date	Amount
09/03	5888	1,028.05	09/05	1,103.75	08/31	16,800.45
09/04	5902	719.90	09/12	2,226.90	09/03	15,772.40
09/07	5901	1,824.25	09/21	4,093.00	09/04	15,052.50
09/17		600.25 NSF	09/25	2,351.70	09/05	16,156.25
09/20	5905	937.00	09/30	12.50 IN	09/07	14,332.00
09/22	5903	399.10	09/30	1,485.00 CM	09/12	16,558.90
09/22	5904	2,090.00			09/17	15,958.65
09/28	5907	213.85			09/20	15,021.65
09/29	5909	1,807.65			09/21	19,114.65
					09/22	16,625.55
					09/25	18,977.25
					09/28	18,763.40
					09/29	16,955.75
					09/30	18,453.25

From Clarke Company's Accounting Records

Cash Receipts Deposited			Cash Disbursements		
Date		Cash Debit	Check No.		Cash Credit
Sept.	5	1,103.75	5901		1,824.25
	12	2,226.90	5902		719.90
	21	4,093.00	5903		399.10
	25	2,351.70	5904		2,060.00
	30	1,682.75	5905		937.00
		11,458.10	5906		982.30
			5907		213.85
			5908		388.00
			5909		1,807.65
					9,332.05

Cash					Acct. No. 101
Date		**Explanation**	**PR**	**Debit**	**Credit**	**Balance**
Aug.	31	Balance				15,278.45
Sept.	30	Total receipts	R12	11,458.10		26,736.55
	30	Total disbursements	D23		9,332.05	17,404.50

Other Information

Check No. 5904 is correctly drawn for $2,090 to pay for computer equipment; however, the record-keeper misread the amount and entered it in the accounting records with a debit to Computer Equipment and a credit to Cash of $2,060. The NSF check shown in the statement was originally received from a customer, S. Nilson, in payment of her account. Its return had not been recorded when the bank first notified the company. The credit memorandum is from the collection of a $1,500 note for Clarke Company by the bank. The bank deducted a $15 collection fee. The collection and fee are not yet recorded.

Required

Preparation Component

1. Prepare the September 30, 2002, bank reconciliation for this company.

2. Prepare the journal entries to adjust the book balance of cash to the reconciled balance.

Analysis Component

3. The bank statement reveals that some of the prenumbered checks in the sequence are missing. Describe three possible situations that could explain this.

Check Reconciled balance, $18,271.75

Cashco Co. establishes a petty cash fund for payments of small amounts. The following transactions involving the petty cash fund occurred in January (the last month of the company's fiscal year).

Jan. 3 A company check for $150 is written and made payable to the petty cashier to establish the petty cash fund.

    14 A company check is written to replenish the fund for the following expenditures made since January 3 and to increase the fund to $200.
  a. Purchased office supplies, $14.29.
  b. Paid $19.60 COD shipping charges on merchandise purchased for resale, terms FOB shipping point. Cashco uses the perpetual system to account for inventory.
  c. Paid $38.57 to All-Tech for minor repairs to a computer.
  d. Paid $12.82 for items classified as miscellaneous expenses.
  e. Counted $62.28 remaining in the petty cash box.

    31 The petty cashier reports that $17.35 remains in the fund and decides that the February 14 increase in the fund was not large enough. A company check is written to replenish the fund for the following expenditures made since January 14 and to increase it to $250.
  f. Paid $50 to *The Smart Saver* for an advertisement in this monthly newsletter.
  g. Paid $48.19 for office supplies.
  h. Paid $78 to *3 Men and a Truck* for delivery of merchandise to a customer, terms FOB destination.

PROBLEM SET B

Problem 9-1B
Establishing, reimbursing, and adjusting petty cash; accounting adjustments

Required

Preparation Component

1. Prepare journal entries to establish the fund on January 3 and to replenish it on January 14 and January 31 along with any increase or decrease in the fund balance.

Check Feb. 28, $232.65 Cr. to Cash

Analysis Component

2. Explain how the company's financial statements are affected if the petty cash fund is not replenished and no entry is made on January 31. (*Hint:* The amount of Office Supplies that appears on a balance sheet is determined by a physical count of office supplies.)

Problem 9-2B

Establish, reimburse, and increase petty cash

Carousel Music Center had the following petty cash transactions in March of the current year:

March 5   Wrote a $250 check, cashed it, and gave the proceeds and the petty cashbox to Claire Mane, the petty cashier.

6   Paid $12.50 COD shipping charges on merchandise purchased for resale, terms FOB shipping point. Carousel uses the perpetual system to account for merchandise inventory.

11   Paid $10.75 delivery charges on merchandise sold to a customer, terms FOB destination.

12   Purchased file folders, $14.13.

14   Reimbursed Trisha Cox, the manager, $11.65 for office supplies purchased.

18   Purchased paper for printer, $20.54.

27   Paid $45.10 COD shipping charges on merchandise purchased for resale, terms FOB shipping point.

28   Purchased postage stamps, $18.

30   Reimbursed Trisha Cox $56.80 for business car mileage.

31   Sorted the petty cash receipts by accounts affected and exchanged them for a check to both reimburse the fund for expenditures and increase the amount of the fund to $300. There was $61.53 cash in the fund.

Required

1. Prepare the general journal entry to establish the petty cash fund.

Check   (2) Total expenses $189.47

2. Prepare a petty cash payments report for March with these categories: delivery expense, mileage expense, postage expense, merchandise inventory (transportation-in), and office supplies. Sort the payments into the appropriate categories and total the expenses in each category.

3. Prepare the general journal entry to both reimburse and increase the amount in the fund.

Problem 9-3B

Analyzing internal control

For each of these five separate cases, identify the principle of internal control that is violated. Recommend what the business should do to ensure adherence to principles of internal control.

1. Sue Stanley is the company's computer specialist and oversees the company's computerized payroll system. Her boss recently asked her to put password protection on all office computers. Sue has put a password in place that allows only the boss access to the file where pay rates are changed and personnel are added or deleted from the payroll.

2. Park Theater has a computerized order-taking system for its tickets. The system is active all week and backed up every Friday night.

3. B2B Company has two employees handling acquisitions of inventory. One employee places purchase orders and pays vendors. The second employee receives the merchandise.

4. The owner of Rite-Aid uses a check protector to perforate checks, making it difficult for anyone to alter the amount of the check. The check protector sits on the owner's desk in an office that contains company checks and is often unlocked.

5. Rison Company is a small organization but has separated the duties of cash receipts and cash disbursements. Also, the employee responsible for cash disbursements reconciles the bank account monthly.

Problem 9-4B

Prepare a bank reconciliation and record adjustments

The following information is available to reconcile Steele Co.'s book balance of cash with its bank statement cash balance as of December 31, 2002:

a. After posting is complete, the December 31 cash balance according to the accounting records is $32,878.30, and the bank statement cash balance for that date is $46,822.40.

b. Check No. 1273 for $4,589.30 and Check No. 1282 for $400.00, both written and entered in the accounting records in December, are not among the canceled checks returned. Two checks, No. 1231 for $2,289.00 and No. 1242 for $410.40, were outstanding on the most recent November 30 reconciliation. Check No. 1231 is returned with the December canceled checks, but Check No. 1242 is not.

c. When the December checks are compared with entries in the accounting records, it is found that Check No. 1267 had been correctly drawn for $3,456 to pay for office supplies but was erroneously entered in the accounting records as $3,465.

d. Two debit memoranda are included with the returned checks and are unrecorded at the time of the reconciliation. One of the debit memoranda is for $762.50 and dealt with an NSF check for $745.00 that had been received from a customer, Tidwell Industries, in payment of its account. The bank assessed a $17.50 fee for processing it. The second debit memorandum is a $99.00 charge for check printing. Steele did not record these transactions before receiving the statement.

e. A credit memorandum indicates that the bank collected a $19,000 note receivable for the company, deducted a $20 collection fee, and credited the balance to the company's cash account. Steele did not record this transaction before receiving the statement.

f. The December 31 daily cash receipts of $9,583.10 were placed in the bank's night depository on that date but do not appear on the December 31 bank statement.

Required

Preparation Component

1. Prepare a bank reconciliation for this company as of December 31, 2002.

2. Prepare the journal entries necessary to bring the company's book balance of cash into conformity with the reconciled cash balance as of December 31, 2002.

Analysis Component

3. Explain the nature of the communications conveyed by a bank when the bank sends the depositor (a) a debit memorandum and (b) a credit memorandum.

Check   Reconciled bal., $51,005.80

Sure Systems most recently reconciled its bank balance on April 30 and showed two checks outstanding at that time, No. 1771 for $781.00 and No. 1780 for $1,425.90. The following information is available for its May 31, 2002, reconciliation:

Problem 9-5B

Prepare a bank reconciliation and record adjustments

P5

From the May 31 Bank Statement

Previous Balance	Total Checks and Debits	Total Deposits and Credits	Current Balance
18,290.70	13,094.80	16,566.80	21,762.70

Checks and Debits			Deposits and Credits		Daily Balance	
Date	No.	Amount	Date	Amount	Date	Amount
05/01	1771	781.00	05/04	2,438.00	04/30	18,290.70
05/02	1783	382.50	05/14	2,898.00	05/01	17,509.70
05/04	1782	1,285.50	05/22	1,801.80	05/02	17,127.20
05/11	1784	1,449.60	05/25	7,350.00 CM	05/04	18,279.70
05/18		431.80 NSF	05/26	2,079.00	05/11	16,830.10
05/25	1787	8,032.50			05/14	19,728.10
05/26	1785	63.90			05/18	19,296.30
05/29	1788	654.00			05/22	21,098.10
05/31		14.00 SC			05/25	20,415.60
					05/26	22,430.70
					05/29	21,776.70
					05/31	21,762.70

From Sure Systems' Accounting Records

Cash Receipts Deposited			Cash Disbursements		
Date		Cash Debit	Check No.		Cash Credit
May 4		2,438.00	1782		1,285.50
14		2,898.00	1783		382.50
22		1,801.80	1784		1,449.60
26		2,079.00	1785		63.90
31		2,727.30	1786		353.10
		11,944.10	1787		8,032.50
			1788		644.00
			1789		639.50
					12,850.60

Cash					Acct. No. 101
Date		**Explanation**	**PR**	**Debit**	**Credit**	**Balance**
Apr.	30	Balance				16,083.80
May	31	Total receipts	R7	11,944.10		28,027.90
	31	Total disbursements	D8		12,850.60	15,177.30

Other Information

Check No. 1788 is correctly drawn for $654 to pay for May utilities; however, the recordkeeper mis-read the amount and entered it in the accounting records with a debit to Utilities Expense and a credit to Cash for $644. The bank paid and deducted the correct amount. The NSF check shown in the statement was originally received from a customer, D. Hunt, in payment of her account. Its return has not yet been recorded. The credit memorandum is from a $7,400 note that the bank collected for the company. The bank deducted a $50 collection fee and deposited the remainder in the company's account. The collection and fee are not yet recorded.

Required

Preparation Component

Check Reconciled balance, $22,071.50

1. Prepare the May 31, 2002, bank reconciliation for Sure Systems.

2. Prepare the journal entries to adjust the book balance of cash to the reconciled balance.

Analysis Component

3. The bank statement reveals that some of the prenumbered checks in the sequence are missing. Describe three possible situations that might explain this.

Beyond the Numbers

Reporting in Action

BTN 9-1   Refer to the financial statements for **Nike** in Appendix A to answer the following:

1. For both fiscal year-end 2000 and 1999, determine the total amount of cash and cash equivalents. Determine the percent this amount represents of total current assets, total current liabilities, total shareholders' equity, and total assets for both years. Comment on any trends.

2. For both fiscal 2000 and 1999, use the information in the statement of cash flows to determine the percent change between the beginning and ending year amounts of cash and cash equivalents.

3. Compute the days' sales uncollected as of May 31, 2000, and May 31, 1999. Has the collection of receivables improved?

Swoosh Ahead

4. Access Nike's annual report for fiscal years ending after May 31, 2000, from its Web site [www.nike.com] or the SEC EDGAR database [www.sec.gov]. Recompute the days' sales uncollected for fiscal years ending after May 31, 2000. Compare this to the days' sales uncollected for 2000 and 1999.

Comparative Analysis

BTN 9-2   Key comparative figures ($ in millions) for both **Nike** and **Reebok** follow:

Key Figures	Nike		Reebok	
	Current Year	**Prior Year**	**Current Year**	**Prior Year**
Accounts receivable	$1,567.2	$1,540.1	$ 417.4	$ 517.8
Net sales	$8,995.1	$8,776.9	$2,899.9	$3,224.6

Required

Compute days' sales uncollected for both companies for the two years shown. Comment on any trends for both companies. Which company has the larger percent change in days' sales uncollected?

BTN 9-3   Susie Martin, Dot Night, and Colleen Walker work for a family physician, Dr. Gillbanks, who is in private practice. Dr. Gillbanks is knowledgeable about office management practices and has segregated the cash receipt duties as follows. Susie opens the mail and prepares a triplicate list of money received. She sends one copy of the list to Dot, the cashier, who deposits the receipts daily in the bank. Colleen, the recordkeeper, receives a copy of the list and posts payments to patients' accounts. About once a month the office clerks have an expensive lunch they pay for as follows. First, Dot endorses a patient's check in Dr. Gillbank's name and cashes it at the bank. Susie then destroys the remittance advice accompanying the check. Finally, Colleen posts payment to the customer's account as a miscellaneous credit. The three justify their actions by their relatively low pay and knowledge that Dr. Gillbanks will likely never miss the money.

Ethics Challenge

C2

Required

1. Who is the best person in Dr. Gillbank's office to reconcile the bank statement?

2. Would a bank reconciliation uncover this office fraud?

3. What are some ways to detect this type of fraud?

4. Suggest additional internal controls that Dr. Gillbanks may want to implement.

BTN 9-4   Assume you are a business consultant. The owner of a company sends you an e-mail expressing concern that the company is not taking advantage of discounts offered by vendors. The company currently uses the gross method of recording purchases. The owner is considering a review of all invoices and payments from the previous period. Due to the volume of purchases, however, the owner recognizes this is time consuming and costly. The owner seeks your advice about monitoring purchase discounts in the future. Provide a response in memorandum form.

Communicating in Practice

P4

BTN 9-5   Visit the Association of Certified Fraud Examiners Web site at **www.cfenet.com.** Research the fraud facts presented at this site and fill in the blanks in the following factual statements.

Taking It to the Net

C1   **C2**

1. Fraud and abuse cost U.S. organizations more than $_____ billion annually.

2. The average organization loses more than $_____ per day per employee to fraud and abuse.

3. The average organization loses about _____% of its total annual revenue to fraud and abuse committed by its own employees.

4. The median fraud loss by males is about $_____; by females, about $_____.

5. Men commit nearly _____% of the offenses.

6. Losses caused by managers are _____ times those caused by employees.

7. Median fraud losses caused by executives are _____ times those of their employees.

8. The most costly abuses occur in organizations with less than _____ employees.

9. The _____ industry experiences the lowest median losses.

10. Occupational fraud and abuse fall into three main categories:_____.

BTN 9-6   Each team must prepare a list of 10 internal controls a consumer could observe in a typical retail department store. When called upon, the team's spokesperson must be prepared to share controls identified by the team that have not been shared by another team's spokesperson.

Teamwork in Action   **C1**   **C2**

BTN 9-7   Read the article "Fraud on the Net" in the April 3, 2000, issue of *Business Week*.

Business Week Activity

C1

Required

1. In 1997, 3% of all consumer complaints were about the Internet. How large is the percent now?

2. What percentage of Nike.com's purchase requests are estimated to be fraudulent?

3. Is the government making progress in detecting Internet fraud? Explain.

4. What are 5 of the top 10 scams on the net?

Entrepreneurial Decision

BTN 9-8   Steffi Kraff is setting up operations for her new carry-out business to sells subs and salads to mainly college students. Customers will order and receive their food at the counter, where a cashier will exchange food for cash. From the counter, customers will be able to see other employees making subs and salads.

Required

Identify the seven principles of internal control along with examples of each that the owner should implement.

10

Receivables and Short-Term Investments

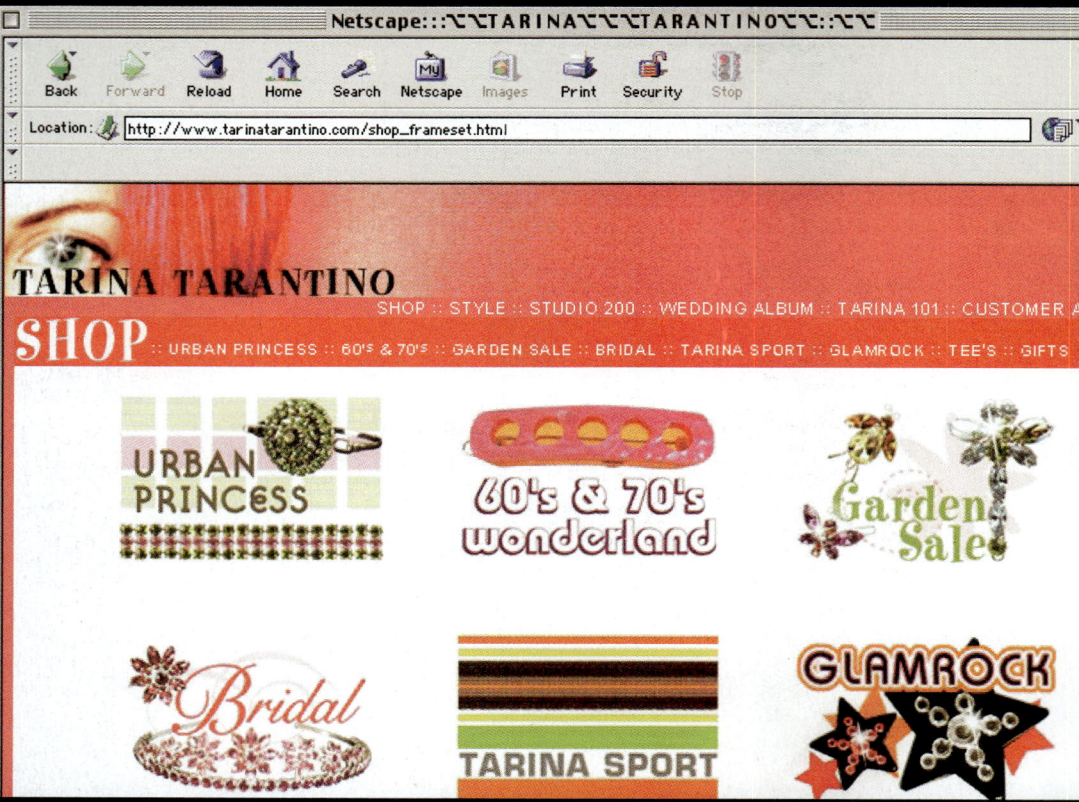

"Everything we make is whimsical and unusual"—Tarina Tarantino.

A Look Back

Chapter 9 focused on internal control and accounting for cash. We described procedures that are good for internal control, and we explained the accounting for and management of cash.

A Look at This Chapter

This chapter emphasizes receivables and short-term investments. We explain that they are liquid assets and describe how companies account for and report them. We also discuss the importance of estimating uncollectibles and the role of market values in analyzing liquid assets.

A Look Ahead

Chapter 11 focuses on plant assets, natural resources, and intangible assets. We explain how to account for, report, and analyze these long-term assets.

Tarina Tarantino

e HOLLYWOOD, CA—Tarina Tarantino had always made jewelry for herself. Having grown up with "artistic hippie parents," Tarantino says she's always been attracted to the bold and offbeat. She and her husband, Alfonso Campos, knew they were unto something when Tarantino would wear her creations to work and return home jewelry-less as customers would buy the jeweled treasures off her hands and head. Campos decided to call some of the best stores and designers in L.A. "I'd tell them all I needed was one minute of their time, and it would be the best minute of their lives," says Campos.

Orders soon flooded in—more than they could handle. **Tarina Tarantino Designs [TarinaTarantino.com]** was launched with $400 in cash and a car that they sold. Not surprisingly, banks scoffed at a loan request. "We had $50,000 worth of orders, and we thought 'Wow! This is going to be it'," says Campos. "They looked at us like '$50,000 is nothing kids. Do you have any collateral?'" Still, they pushed forward, setting up shop in the dining room of their apartment. Both quit jobs to devote all their attention to the business. "Letting go of the security of a paycheck was really the best thing we ever did," says Tarantino.

Tarantino now sells her creations over the Web and in retail stores. "My typical customer is an urban princess," says Tarantino. "She wants something glamorous and funky, something that makes her feel unique." Tarantino also accepts credit cards along with money orders and cashier's checks to encourage sales. Although noncash sales have costs, Tarantino and Campos believe the benefits outweigh them. However, personal checks are not accepted to avoid uncollectible accounts receivable. Tarantino admits entrepreneurship is tough, "It looks easy, but really it's a lot of blood, sweat, and tears." But it has paid off—Tarantino expects sales to exceed $5 million this year. That's a lot of funky jewelry. [Sources: *Tarina Tarantino Web site,* May 2001; *Entrepreneur,* November, 1999; *First Jewelry Web site,* March 2001]

Learning Objectives

Conceptual

C1 Describe accounts receivable and how they occur and are recorded.

C2 Describe a note receivable and the computation of its maturity date and interest.

C3 Explain how receivables can be converted to cash before maturity.

C4 Describe short-term investments in debt and equity securities.

Analytical

A1 Compute accounts receivable turnover and use it to analyze liquidity.

Procedural

P1 Apply the direct write-off and allowance methods to account for accounts receivable.

P2 Estimate uncollectibles using methods based on sales and accounts receivable.

P3 Record the receipt of a note receivable.

P4 Record the honoring and dishonoring of a note and adjustments for interest on a note.

P5 Record short-term investment transactions.

This chapter focuses on accounts receivable, short-term notes receivable, and short-term investments. We describe each of these assets, their uses, and how they are accounted for and reported in financial statements. This knowledge helps us use accounting information to make better decisions. It can also help in predicting future company performance and financial condition.

Accounts Receivable

C1 Describe accounts receivable and how they occur and are recorded.

A *receivable* refers to an amount due from another party. Receivables, cash, cash equivalents, and short-term investments make up the most liquid assets of a company. The two most common receivables are accounts receivable and notes receivable. Other receivables include interest receivable, rent receivable, tax refund receivable, and receivables from officers and employees.

Accounts receivable refer to amounts due from customers for credit sales. This section begins by describing how accounts receivable occur. It includes receivables that occur when customers use credit cards issued by third parties and when a company gives credit directly to customers. When a company does extend credit directly to customers, it must (1) maintain a separate account receivable for each customer and (2) account for bad debts from credit sales.

Recognizing Accounts Receivable

Accounts receivable occur from credit sales to customers. The amount of credit sales has increased in recent years, reflecting several factors including an efficient financial system and a sound economy. Retailers such as **The Limited**, **Chic by H.I.S**, **Best Buy**, and **CompUSA** hold millions of dollars in accounts receivable. Similar amounts are held by wholesalers such as **Nike**, **Reebok**, **SUPERVALU**, **SYSCO**, and **Ace Hardware**. Exhibit 10.1 shows recent dollar amounts of accounts receivable and their percent of total assets for four well-known companies.

Exhibit 10.1

Accounts Receivable for Selected Companies

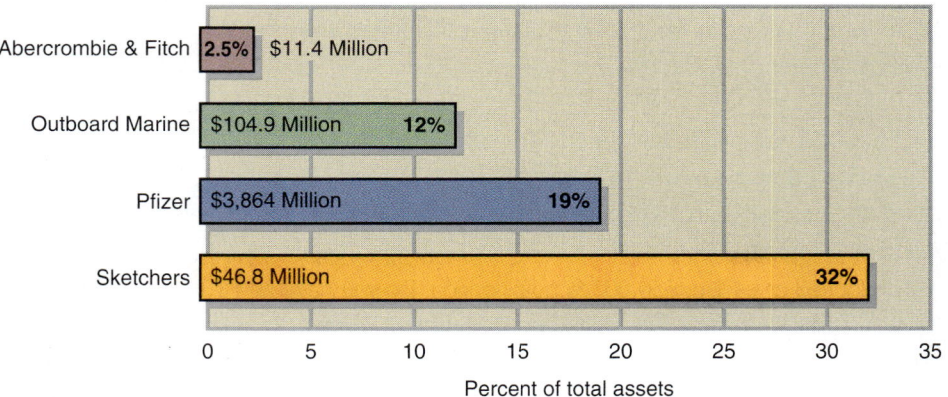

Percent of total assets

Sales on Credit

Credit sales are recorded by increasing (debiting) Accounts Receivable. A company must also maintain a separate account for each customer that tracks how much that customer purchases, has already paid, and still owes. This information provides the basis for sending bills to customers and for other business analyses. To maintain this information, companies that extend credit directly to their customers keep a separate account receivable for each one of them. The general ledger continues to have a single Accounts Receivable account along with the other financial statement accounts, but a supplementary record is created to maintain a separate account for each customer. This supplementary record is called the *accounts receivable ledger*.

Exhibit 10.2 shows the relation between the Accounts Receivable account in the general ledger and its individual customer accounts in the accounts receivable ledger for **TechCom**, a small electronics wholesaler. This exhibit reports a $3,000 ending balance of TechCom's

Exhibit 10.2

General Ledger and the
Accounts Receivable Ledger
(before July 1 transactions)

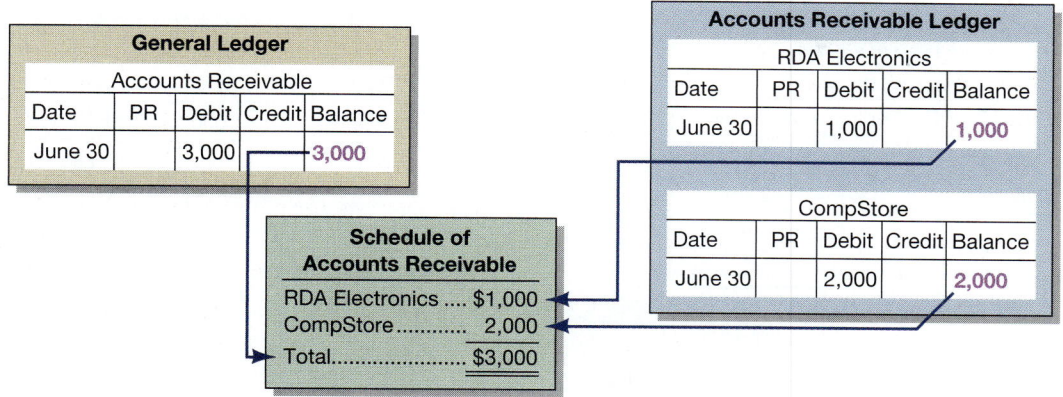

accounts receivable for June 30. TechCom's transactions are mainly in cash, but it has two major credit customers: CompStore and RDA Electronics. Its schedule of accounts receivable shows that the $3,000 balance of the Accounts Receivable account in the general ledger equals the total of its two customers' balances in the accounts receivable ledger.

To see how accounts receivable from credit sales are recognized in the accounting records, we look at two transactions on July 1 between TechCom and its credit customers. The first is a credit sale of $950 to CompStore. A credit sale is posted with both a debit to the Accounts Receivable account in the general ledger and a debit to the customer account in the accounts receivable ledger. The second transaction is a collection of $720 from RDA Electronics from a prior credit sale. Cash receipts from a credit customer are posted with credits to both the Accounts Receivable account in the general ledger and to the customer account in the accounts receivable ledger.[1] Both transactions are journalized in Exhibit 10.3.

July 1	Accounts Receivable—CompStore	950	
	Sales		950
	To record credit sales*		
July 1	Cash	720	
	Accounts Receivable—RDA Electronics . . .		720
	To record collection of credit sales.		

Exhibit 10.3

Accounts Receivable
Transactions

* We omit the entry to Dr. Cost of Sales and Cr. Merchandise Inventory to focus on sales and receivables.

Exhibit 10.4 shows the general ledger and the accounts receivable ledger after recording the two July 1 transactions. The general ledger shows the effects of the sale, the collection, and the resulting balance of $3,230. These events are also reflected in the individual customer accounts: RDA Electronics has an ending balance of $280, and CompStore's ending balance is $2,950. The $3,230 sum of the individual accounts equals the debit balance of the Accounts Receivable account in the general ledger.

Point: New software helps merchants build Web storefronts quickly and easily. Merchants simply enter product details such as names and prices, and out comes a respectable-looking Web site complete with order forms. They also offer security with credit card orders and can track sales and site visits.

[1] Posting debits or credits to Accounts Receivable in two separate ledgers does not violate the requirement that debits equal credits. The equality of debits and credits is maintained in the general ledger. The accounts receivable ledger is a supplementary record providing detailed information on each customer.

Exhibit 10.4

General Ledger and the
Accounts Receivable Ledger
(after July 1 transactions)

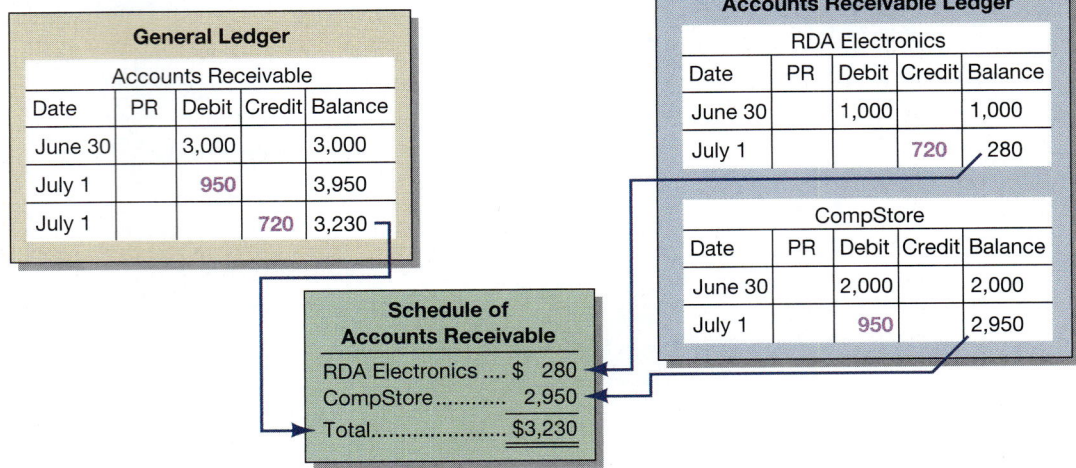

General Ledger

Accounts Receivable

Date	PR	Debit	Credit	Balance
June 30		3,000		3,000
July 1		950		3,950
July 1			720	3,230

Accounts Receivable Ledger

RDA Electronics

Date	PR	Debit	Credit	Balance
June 30		1,000		1,000
July 1			720	280

CompStore

Date	PR	Debit	Credit	Balance
June 30		2,000		2,000
July 1		950		2,950

**Schedule of
Accounts Receivable**

RDA Electronics	$ 280
CompStore............	2,950
Total......................	$3,230

Many large retailers such as **Sears** and **JCPenney** maintain their own credit cards. This allows them to grant credit to approved customers and to earn interest on any balance not paid within a specified period of time. It also allows them to avoid the fee charged by credit card companies. The entries in this case are the same as those for TechCom except for the possibility of added interest revenue. If a customer owes interest on a bill, we debit Interest Receivable and credit Interest Revenue for that amount.

Credit Card Sales

Many companies allow their customers to pay for products and services using credit cards and bankcards such as **Visa**, **MasterCard**, or **American Express**. This practice gives customers the ability to make purchases without cash or checks. Once credit is established with a credit card company or bank, the customer does not have to open an account with each store. Customers using these cards can make single monthly payments instead of several payments to different creditors. They also can defer their payments.

There are several reasons why sellers allow customers to use credit cards and bankcards instead of granting credit directly. First, the seller does not have to evaluate each customer's credit standing or make decisions about who gets credit and how much. Second, the seller avoids the risk of extending credit to customers who cannot or do not pay. This risk is transferred to the card company. Third, the seller typically receives cash from the credit card company and bank sooner than had it granted credit directly to customers. Fourth, a variety of credit options for customers offers a potential increase in sales volume. **Sears** historically offered credit only to customers using a Sears card, but later changed its policy to permit customers to charge purchases to third-party credit card companies in a desire to increase sales. It reported that: "SearsCharge increased its share of Sears retail sales even as the company expanded the payment options available to its customers with the acceptance . . . of VISA, MasterCard, and American Express in addition to the Discover Card."

Did You Know?

Plastic Bust   Web merchants pay twice as much in credit card association fees as other retailers. Why? They suffer 10 times as much fraud. Buyers like credit cards, but sellers are better off with systems such as **PayPal** [**www.paypal.com**]. The safest way? It's not pretty: Get paid with a check, and ship goods after it clears. [*Business Week:* September 11, 2000.]

	Online	Traditional
Transaction costs	3.5% of Sale	1.5% of Sale
Percent of fraudulent transactions .	0.93%	0.06%
Who covers fraud losses .	Merchant Assoc.	Credit Card

There are guidelines in how companies account for credit card and bankcard sales. Some credit cards, but mostly bankcards, credit a seller's Cash account immediately upon deposit. In this case the seller deposits a copy of each credit card sales receipt in its bank account just as it deposits a customer's check. Some other credit cards require the seller to remit a copy (often electronically) of each receipt to the credit card company. Until payment is received, the seller has an account receivable from the credit card company. In both cases, the seller pays a fee for services provided by the card company, often ranging from 2% to 5% of card sales. This charge is deducted from the credit to the seller's account or the cash payment to the seller.

The procedures used in accounting for credit card sales depend on whether cash is received immediately on deposit or cash receipt is delayed until the credit card company makes the payment. To illustrate, if TechCom has $100 of credit card sales with a 4% fee, and its cash is received immediately on deposit, the entry is

July 15	Cash	96	
	Credit Card Expense	4	
	Sales		100
	To record credit card sales less a 4% credit card expense.		

Assets = Liabilities + Equity
+96   −4
                         +100

However, if TechCom must remit copies of the credit card sales receipts to the credit card company and wait for payment, the entry on the date of sale is

July 15	Accounts Receivable—Credit Card Co.	96	
	Credit Card Expense	4	
	Sales		100
	To record credit card sales less 4% credit card expense.		

Assets = Liabilities + Equity
+96   +100
                         −4

When cash is received from the credit card company, the entry to record the receipt is

July 25	Cash	96	
	Accounts Receivable—Credit Card Co.		96
	To record cash receipt.		

Assets = Liabilities + Equity
+96
−96

Some firms report credit card expense in the income statement as a type of discount deducted from sales to get net sales. Other companies classify it as a selling expense or even as an administrative expense. Arguments can be made for each alternative.

You Make the Call

Entrepreneur As a small retailer, you are considering allowing customers to purchase merchandise using credit cards. Until now, your store accepted only cash and checks. What form of analysis do you use to make this decision?

Answer—p. 421

Point: Third-party credit card costs can be large. JCPenney recently reported sales of $32,510 million. Beyond its bad debt expenses, it reported third-party credit costs of nearly $100 million.

Quick Check

1. In recording credit card sales, when do you debit Accounts Receivable and when do you debit Cash?
2. When are credit card expenses recorded when sales receipts are accumulated and remitted to the credit card company for payment? When are these expenses incurred?

Answers—p. 421

Valuing Accounts Receivable

When a company directly grants credit to its customers, some customers do not always pay what they promised. The accounts of these customers are *uncollectible accounts,* commonly called **bad debts.** The total amount of uncollectible accounts is an expense of selling on

P1 Apply the direct write-off and allowance methods to account for accounts receivable.

credit. Why do companies sell on credit if they expect some accounts to be uncollectible? The answer is that companies believe that granting credit will increase sales and net income enough to offset bad debts. They are willing to incur bad debts losses if the net effect is to increase sales and net income. Companies use two methods to account for uncollectible accounts: (1) direct write-off method and (2) allowance method. We describe both.

Direct Write-Off Method

The **direct write-off method** of accounting for bad debts records the loss from an uncollectible account receivable when it is determined to be uncollectible. No attempt is made to predict bad debts expense. Bad debts expense is recorded when specific accounts are written off as uncollectible. To illustrate, if TechCom determines on January 23 that it cannot collect $520 owed to it by its customer Jack Kent, it recognizes the loss using the direct write-off method as follows:

Assets = Liabilities + Equity
−520   −520

Jan. 23	Bad Debts Expense	520	
	Accounts Receivable—J. Kent		520
	To write off an uncollectible account.		

The debit in this entry charges the uncollectible amount directly to the current period's Bad Debts Expense account. The credit removes its balance from the Accounts Receivable account in the general ledger (and its subsidiary ledger).

Sometimes an account written off is later collected. This can be due to factors such as continual collection efforts or customer's good fortune. If the account of Jack Kent that was written off directly to Bad Debts Expense is later collected in full, the following two entries record this recovery:

Assets = Liabilities + Equity
+520   +520

Assets = Liabilities + Equity
+520
−520

Mar. 11	Accounts Receivable—J. Kent	520	
	Bad Debts Expense		520
	To reinstate account previously written off.		
Mar. 11	Cash	520	
	Accounts Receivable—J. Kent		520
	To record full payment of account.		

Companies must weigh at least two accounting principles when considering the use of the direct write-off method: the (1) matching principle and (2) materiality principle.

Matching Principle Applied to Bad Debts

The **matching principle** requires expenses to be reported in the same accounting period as the sales they helped produce. This means that if extending credit to customers helped produce sales, the bad debts expense linked to those sales is matched and reported in the same period. The direct write-off method usually does not best match sales and expenses because bad debts expense is not recorded until an account becomes uncollectible, which often does not occur in the same period as the credit sale. However, applying the matching principle to bad debts presents challenges. Managers realize that some portion of credit sales will be uncollectible, but which credit sales are uncollectible is unknown. If a customer fails to pay within the credit period, most companies send out repeated billings and make other efforts to collect. They do not accept that a customer is not going to pay until they take every reasonable means of collection. This decision point may not be reached until one or more accounting periods after the sale is made. Matching bad debts expense with the sales it produces therefore requires a company to estimate uncollectibles.

Point: Pier 1 Imports reports $4.7 million of bad debts expense is matched against $300.5 million of credit sales in a recent fiscal year.

Materiality Principle Applied to Bad Debts

The **materiality principle** states that an amount can be ignored if its effect on the financial statements is unimportant to users' business decisions. The materiality principle permits the use of the direct write-off method when bad debts expenses are very small in relation to a company's other financial statement items such as sales and net income.

Allowance Method

The **allowance method** of accounting for bad debts matches the *expected* loss from uncollectible accounts receivable against the sales they helped produce. We must use expected losses since management cannot exactly identify the customers who will not pay their bills at the time of sale. This means that at the end of each period, the allowance method requires an estimate of the total bad debts expected to result from that period's sales. An allowance is then recorded for this expected loss. This method has two advantages over the direct write-off method: (1) it charges bad debts expense to the period when it recognizes the related sales and (2) it reports accounts receivable on the balance sheet at the estimated amount of cash to be collected.

Point: Under the direct write-off method, expense is recorded each time an account is written off. Under the allowance method, expense is recorded with an adjusting entry equal to the total estimated uncollectibles for that period's sales.

Concept 10-1

Recording Estimated Bad Debts Expense

The allowance method estimates bad debts expense at the end of each accounting period and records it with an adjusting entry. TechCom, for instance, had credit sales of approximately $300,000 during its first year of operations. At the end of the first year, $20,000 of credit sales remained uncollected. Based on the experience of similar businesses, TechCom estimated that $1,500 of its accounts receivable would be uncollectible. This estimated expense is recorded with the following adjusting entry:

Point: The Office of the Comptroller of the Currency reports that losses from bad debts led to the collapse of 98% of failed banks.

Dec. 31	Bad Debts Expense	1,500	
	Allowance for Doubtful Accounts		1,500
	To record estimated bad debts.		

Assets = Liabilities + Equity
−1,500   −1,500

The estimated Bad Debts Expense of $1,500 from selling on credit is reported on the income statement and matched with the $300,000 credit sales it helped produce. The credit in this entry is to a contra asset account called **Allowance for Doubtful Accounts.** A contra account is used because at the time of the adjusting entry, the company does not know which customers will not pay. Bad Debts Expense often appears on the income statement as an administrative expense rather than a selling expense. The process of evaluating and approving customers for credit is usually not assigned to the selling department because its main goal is to increase sales, and it may approve customers for credit at the expense of increased bad debts. Therefore, responsibility for granting credit is assigned to a separate credit-granting or other administrative department.

Point: Bad Debts Expense is also called *Uncollectible Accounts Expense.* The Allowance for Doubtful Accounts is also called *Allowance for Uncollectible Accounts.*

Bad Debts Related Accounts in Financial Statements

Recall that TechCom has $20,000 of outstanding accounts receivable at the end of its first year of operations. After the bad debts adjusting entry is posted, TechCom's Accounts Receivable and its Allowance for Doubtful Accounts appear as shown in Exhibit 10.5.

Accounts Receivable		Allowance for Doubtful Accounts	
Dec. 31 20,000			Dec. 31 1,500

Exhibit 10.5

General Ledger Balances after Bad Debts Adjusting Entry

The Allowance for Doubtful Accounts credit balance of $1,500 has the effect of reducing accounts receivable (net of the allowance) to its estimated realizable value. **Realizable value** is the expected proceeds from converting an asset into cash. Although credit customers owe $20,000 to TechCom, only $18,500 is expected to be realized in cash collections from these customers. In the balance sheet, the Allowance for Doubtful Accounts is subtracted from Accounts Receivable to show the amount expected to be realized. This information is often reported as shown in Exhibit 10.6.

Exhibit 10.6

Balance Sheet Presentation of the Allowance for Doubtful Accounts

Current assets		
Accounts receivable	**$20,000**	
Less allowance for doubtful accounts	**(1,500)**	**$18,500**

Sometimes the Allowance for Doubtful Accounts is not reported separately. This alternative presentation is shown in Exhibit 10.7.

Exhibit 10.7

Alternative Presentation of the Allowance for Doubtful Accounts

Current assets	
Accounts receivable (net of $1,500 estimated uncollectible accounts)	**$18,500**

Writing Off a Bad Debt

When specific accounts are identified as uncollectible, they are written off against the Allowance for Doubtful Accounts. To illustrate, after spending some time trying to collect from Jack Kent, TechCom decides that Kent's $520 account is uncollectible and makes the following entry to write it off:

Assets = Liabilities + Equity
+520
−520

Jan. 23	Allowance for Doubtful Accounts	520	
	Accounts Receivable—J. Kent		520
	To write off an uncollectible account.		

Posting this write-off entry to the Accounts Receivable account removes the amount of the bad debt from the general ledger. Posting it to Kent's individual account removes the amount of the bad debt from the subsidiary ledger. The general ledger accounts now appear as in Exhibit 10.8 (assuming no other transactions affecting these accounts).

Exhibit 10.8

General Ledger Balances after Write-Off

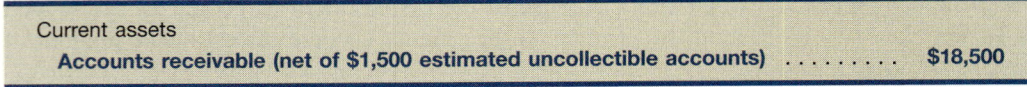

Accounts Receivable				Allowance for Doubtful Accounts			
Dec. 31	20,000					Dec. 31	1,500
		Jan. 23	520	Jan. 23	520		

Point: In posting a write-off of an uncollectible, we use the Explanation column in the ledger to indicate the reason for this credit. Otherwise, this credit might be misinterpreted as payment in full.

Note two points with the write-off entry. First, although bad debts are an expense of selling on credit, the allowance account is debited in the write-off. The expense account is not debited because bad debts expense is previously estimated and recorded with an adjusting entry in the period when the sales occurred. Second, while the write-off removes the uncollectible account receivable from the ledgers, it does not affect the realizable value of TechCom's accounts receivable as shown in Exhibit 10.9. Neither total assets nor net income is affected by the write-off of a specific account. Instead, both assets and net income are affected in the period when bad debts expense is recorded with an adjusting entry.

Exhibit 10.9

Realizable Value before and after Write-Off

	Before Write-Off	After Write-Off
Accounts receivable	$20,000	$19,480
Less allowance for doubtful accounts	1,500	980
Estimated realizable accounts receivable	**$18,500**	**$18,500**

Recovery of a Bad Debt

When a customer fails to pay and the account is written off as uncollectible, his or her credit standing is jeopardized. To help restore credit standing, a customer sometimes chooses to voluntarily pay all or part of the amount owed. A company makes two entries when collecting an account previously written off by the allowance method. The first is to reverse the write-off and reinstate the customer's account. The second entry records the collection of the reinstated account. To illustrate, if on March 11 Kent pays in full his account previously written off, the entries to record this recovery are

Mar. 11	Accounts Receivable—J. Kent	520	
	Allowance for Doubtful Accounts		520
	To reinstate account previously written off.		
Mar. 11	Cash	520	
	Accounts Receivable—J. Kent		520
	To record full payment of account.		

Assets = Liabilities + Equity
+520
−520

Assets = Liabilities + Equity
+520
−520

In this illustration, Kent paid the entire amount previously written off, but sometimes a customer pays only a portion of the amount owed. A question then arises as to whether the entire balance of the account is returned to accounts receivable or just the amount paid. This is a matter of judgment. If we believe this customer will later pay in full, we return the entire amount owed to accounts receivable, but if we expect no further collection, we return only the amount paid.

Example: If TechCom used a collection agency and paid a 35% commission on $520 collected from J. Kent, how is this recorded?
Answer:
Cash 338
Collection Expense 182
    Accts. Recble.—J. Kent . . 520

Quick Check

3. Why must bad debts expense be estimated if possible?

4. What term describes the balance sheet valuation of Accounts Receivable less the Allowance for Doubtful Accounts?

5. Why is estimated bad debts expense credited to a contra account (Allowance for Doubtful Accounts) rather than to the Accounts Receivable account?

Answers—p. 421

Estimating Bad Debts Expense

Companies with direct credit sales must attempt to estimate bad debts expense. They do this to help them manage their receivables and to set credit policies. The allowance method also requires an estimate of bad debts expense to prepare an adjusting entry at the end of each accounting period. There are two common methods to estimate bad debts expense. One is based on the income statement relation between bad debts expense and sales. The second is based on the balance sheet relation between accounts receivable and the allowance for doubtful accounts. Both methods require an analysis of past experience.

P2 Estimate uncollectibles using methods based on sales and accounts receivable.

Percent of Sales Method

The *percent of sales method* uses income statement relations to estimate bad debts. It is based on the idea that a given percent of a company's credit sales for the period are uncollectible.[2] The income statement then reports that percent of sales as the amount of bad debts expense. To illustrate, assume that **MusicLand** has credit sales of $400,000 in year 2002. Based on past experience, MusicLand estimates 0.6% of credit sales to be uncollectible.

Point: When using the percent of sales method for estimating uncollectibles, the amount of the bad debts estimate is the number used in the adjusting entry.

----

[2] The focus is on *credit* sales. Cash sales do not produce bad debts, and they are generally not used in this estimation. If cash sales are small compared to credit sales, there usually is no major impact from including them.

This implies that MusicLand expects $2,400 of bad debts expense from its sales (computed as $400,000 × 0.006 = $2,400). The adjusting entry to record this estimated expense is

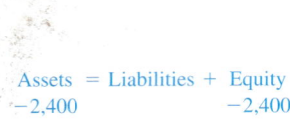
Assets = Liabilities + Equity
−2,400   −2,400

Dec. 31	Bad Debts Expense	2,400	
	Allowance for Doubtful Accounts.		2,400
	To record estimated bad debts.		

This entry does not mean the December 31, 2002, balance in Allowance for Doubtful Accounts will be $2,400. A $2,400 balance occurs only if the account had a zero balance prior to posting the adjusting entry. Unless a company is in its first period of operations, its allowance account has a zero balance only if the prior amounts written off as uncollectible *exactly* equal the prior estimated bad debts expenses. This means the allowance account balance reported on the balance sheet would rarely equal the amount of expense reported on the income statement. Note that expressing bad debts expense as a percent of sales is based on past experience. As new experience is obtained, we often find the percent to be too high or too low. When this happens, we adjust the percent for future periods.

Point: When using an accounts receivable method for estimating uncollectibles, the allowance account balance is adjusted so as to equal the estimate of uncollectibles when recording the adjusting entry.

Accounts Receivable Methods

The *accounts receivable methods* use balance sheet relations to estimate bad debts—mainly the relation between accounts receivable and the allowance amount. These methods focus on some portion of the end-of-period accounts receivable balance that is not collectible. The objective of the bad debts adjusting entry in this case is to make the Allowance for Doubtful Accounts balance equal to the portion of outstanding accounts receivable estimated as uncollectible. To obtain this balance for the Allowance for Doubtful Accounts, we compare its balance before the adjustment with the estimated balance. The estimated balance for the allowance account is obtained in one of two ways: (1) computing the percent uncollectible from the total outstanding accounts receivable or (2) aging accounts receivable.

Percent of accounts receivable method

The *percent of accounts receivable method* assumes a given percent of a company's outstanding receivables to be uncollectible. This percent is based on past experience and is impacted by current conditions such as economic trends and difficulties faced by customers. The total dollar amount of all outstanding receivables is multiplied by this percent to get the estimated dollar amount of uncollectible accounts. This amount is reported in the balance sheet as the Allowance for Doubtful Accounts. To achieve this result, we prepare an adjusting entry debiting Bad Debts Expense and crediting Allowance for Doubtful Accounts. The amount of the adjustment is the amount necessary to yield a balance in the Allowance for Doubtful Accounts that equals the estimated amount of uncollectibles.

Global: In China, government regulation constrains the *percents* used to estimate bad debts.

To illustrate, assume that **MusicLand** has $50,000 of outstanding accounts receivable on December 31, 2002. Past experience suggests 5% of outstanding receivables are uncollectible. This means that after the adjusting entry is posted, we want the Allowance for Doubtful Accounts to show a $2,500 credit balance (computed as 5% of $50,000). Before the adjustment the account appears as follows

Allowance for Doubtful Accounts			
		Dec. 31, 2001, bal.	2,000
Feb. 6	800		
July 10	600		
Nov. 20	400		
		Unadjusted bal.	200

The $2,000 beginning balance is from the December 31, 2001, balance sheet. During 2002, accounts of customers are written off on February 6, July 10, and November 20. The account has a $200 credit balance prior to the December 31, 2002, adjustment. The adjusting entry to give the allowance account the estimated $2,500 balance is

Dec. 31	Bad Debts Expense	2,300	
	Allowance for Doubtful Accounts		2,300
	To record estimated bad debts.		

Assets = Liabilities + Equity
−2,300   −2,300

After this entry the allowance has a $2,500 credit balance as shown in Exhibit 10.10.

Aging of accounts receivable method

Both the percent of sales (income statement) method and the percent of accounts receivable (balance sheet) method use information from *past* experience to estimate the amount of bad debts expense. Another balance sheet method, called the **aging of accounts receivable** method, uses both past and current receivables information to produce a more precise estimate. It reviews *each* account receivable to estimate the amount uncollectible. Each receivable is classified by how long it is past its due date. Then estimates of uncollectible amounts are made assuming that the longer an amount is past due, the more likely it is to be uncollectible. Classifications are often based on 30-day (or one-month) periods. After the amounts are classified (or aged), past experience is used to estimate the percent of each class that is uncollectible. These percents are applied to the amounts in each class to get the estimated balance of the Allowance for Doubtful Accounts. This computation is performed by setting up a schedule such as Exhibit 10.11 for MusicLand.

Allowance for Doubtful Accounts

		Dec. 31, 2001, bal.	2,000
Feb. 6	800		
July 10	600		
Nov. 20	400		
		Unadjusted bal.	200
		Dec. 31 adjustment	**2,300**
		Dec. 31, 2002, bal.	2,500

Exhibit 10.10

Allowance for Doubtful Accounts after Bad Debts Adjusting Entry

Did You Know?

Smart e-Commerce   When you buy online with a credit card, you put your account number at risk. If, however, you slide a smart card into a reader on your PC and enter your password, the merchant never gets your account number but only a code authorizing the sale. Since **American Express** launched the first major U.S. smart card last year, an estimated 2 million consumers have signed up.

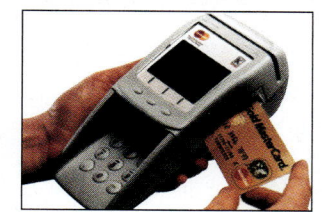

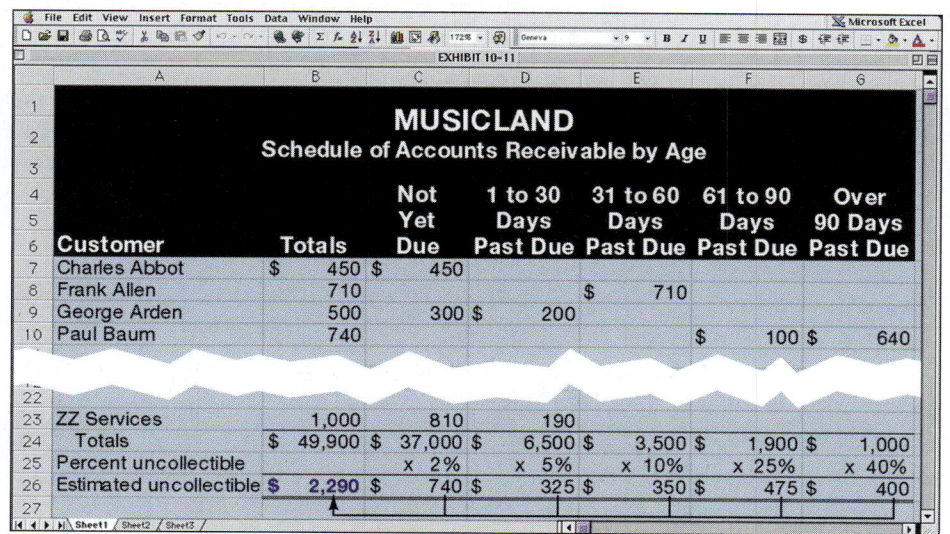

Exhibit 10.11

Aging of Accounts Receivable

MUSICLAND
Schedule of Accounts Receivable by Age

Customer	Totals	Not Yet Due	1 to 30 Days Past Due	31 to 60 Days Past Due	61 to 90 Days Past Due	Over 90 Days Past Due
Charles Abbot	$ 450	$ 450				
Frank Allen	710			$ 710		
George Arden	500	300	$ 200			
Paul Baum	740				$ 100	$ 640
ZZ Services	1,000	810	190			
Totals	$ 49,900	$ 37,000	$ 6,500	$ 3,500	$ 1,900	$ 1,000
Percent uncollectible		x 2%	x 5%	x 10%	x 25%	x 40%
Estimated uncollectible	$ 2,290	$ 740	$ 325	$ 350	$ 475	$ 400

Point: Experience shows the longer a receivable is past due, the lower is the likelihood of collection. An aging schedule exploits this relation and yields useful information to evaluate credit policies.

Exhibit 10.11 lists each customer's total account balance. Then each individual balance is assigned to one of five classes based on its days past due. In computerized systems, this task can be programmed. When all accounts are aged, the amounts in each class are

Point: Spreadsheet software is especially useful for estimating bad debts. Using both current and past data, estimates of bad debts are obtained under different assumptions and economic trends.

Exhibit 10.12

Computation of the Required Adjustment for an Accounts Receivable Method

Assets = Liabilities + Equity
−2,090   −2,090

totaled and multiplied by the estimated percent of uncollectible accounts for each class. The reasonableness of the percents used is regularly reviewed to reflect changes in the company and economy.

To illustrate the aging method, notice that MusicLand has $3,500 in accounts receivable that are 31 to 60 days past due. Its management estimates 10% of the amounts in this age class are not collectible, or a total of $350 (computed as $3,500 × 10%). Similar analysis is done for each of the other four classes. The final total of $2,290 ($740 + $325 + $350 + $475 + $400) shown in the first column is the estimated balance for the Allowance for Doubtful Accounts. Since the allowance account has an unadjusted credit balance of $200, the required adjustment to the Allowance for Doubtful Accounts is $2,090.

Unadjusted balance	$ 200 credit
Estimated balance	2,290 credit
Required adjustment	**$2,090 credit**

This computation is shown in Exhibit 10.12.

To obtain the estimated balance of $2,290, MusicLand prepares the following end-of-period adjusting entry:

Dec. 31	Bad Debts Expense	2,090	
	Allowance for Doubtful Accounts........		2,090
	To record estimated bad debts.		

Alternatively, if the allowance account had an unadjusted *debit* balance of $500 (instead of the $200 credit balance), its required adjustment is computed as follows:

Unadjusted balance	$ 500 debit
Estimated balance	2,290 credit
Required adjustment	**$ 2,790 credit**

The entry to record the end-of-period adjustment for this alternative case is

Assets = Liabilities + Equity
−2,790   −2,790

Dec. 31	Bad Debts Expense	2,790	
	Allowance for Doubtful Accounts........		2,790
	To record estimated bad debts.		

Global: International practices vary as to when receivables should be written off. Some do not write off an account until it is one to two years past due.

To sum up the MusicLand case, when the percent of sales (income statement) method is used, MusicLand's bad debts expense is estimated at $2,400. When the percent of accounts receivable method is used, the expense is $2,300. When the aging of accounts receivable method is used, the expense is $2,090. We expect these amounts to differ since each method gives only an estimate of future payments. The aging of accounts receivable method is a more detailed examination of specific accounts and is usually the most reliable.[3] Exhibit 10.13 summarizes the principles guiding all three estimation methods and their focus of analysis.

Exhibit 10.13

Methods to Estimate Bad Debts

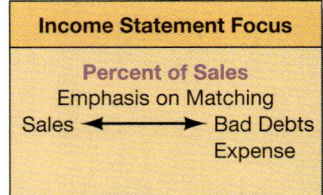

Income Statement Focus	Balance Sheet Focus	Balance Sheet Focus
Percent of Sales	**Percent of Receivables**	**Aging of Receivables**
Emphasis on Matching	Emphasis on Realizable Value	Emphasis on Realizable Value
Sales ⟷ Bad Debts Expense	Accounts ⟷ Allowance Receivable for Doubtful (total) Accounts	Accounts ⟷ Allowance Receivable for Doubtful (individual) Accounts

[3] Aging analysis often is supplemented with information about specific customers, allowing management to decide whether those accounts should be classified as uncollectible. This information usually is supplied by the sales and credit departments.

Installment Accounts Receivable

Many companies allow their credit customers to make periodic payments over several months. For example, **Harley-Davidson** reports more than $400 million in installment receivables. The seller refers to such assets as *installment accounts receivable,* which are amounts owed by customers from credit sales for which payment is required in periodic amounts over an extended time period. Source documents for installment accounts receivable include sales slips or invoices describing the sales transactions. The customer is usually charged interest. Although installment accounts receivable may have credit periods of more than one year, they are classified as current assets if the seller regularly offers customers such terms.

You Make the Call

Labor Union Chief   A week prior to contract negotiations, financial statements are released showing no growth in income. A 10% growth was predicted. In your analysis, you find that the company increased its allowance for uncollectibles from 1.5% to 4.5% of accounts receivable. Without this change, income would show a 9% growth. Does this analysis impact your negotiations?

Answer—p. 421

Notes Receivable

A **promissory note** is a written promise to pay a specified amount of money either on demand or at a definite future date. Promissory notes are used in many transactions, including paying for products and services, lending and borrowing money, and paying for accounts receivable. Sellers sometimes allow customers to sign a note for sales. Sellers also sometimes ask for a note to replace an account receivable when a customer requests additional time to pay a past-due account. Most notes include interest charges. If a seller regularly offers customers this option, such notes are classified as current assets even when their credit period is longer than one year. For legal reasons, sellers generally prefer to receive notes when the credit period is long and when the receivable is for a large amount. If a lawsuit is needed to collect from a customer, a note is the buyer's written acknowledgment of the debt, its amount, and its terms.

Exhibit 10.14 shows a promissory note dated July 10, 2002. For this note, Julia Browne promises to pay TechCom or to its order (according to TechCom's instructions) a specified

C2   Describe a note receivable and the computation of its maturity date and interest.

Concept 10-2

Exhibit 10.14

Promissory Note

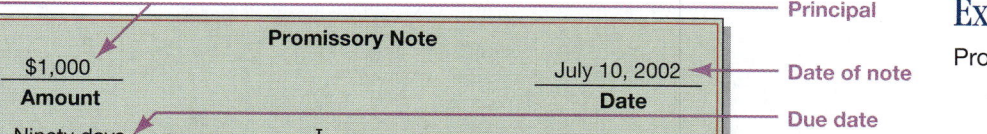

amount of money ($1,000), called the **principal of a note,** at a definite future date (October 8, 2002). As the one who signed the note and promised to pay it at maturity, Browne is the **maker of the note.** As the person to whom the note is payable, TechCom is the **payee of the note.** To Browne, the note is a liability called a *note payable*. To TechCom, the same note is an asset called a *note receivable*. This note bears interest at 12%, as written on the note. **Interest** is the charge for using (not paying) the money until a later date. To a borrower, interest is an expense. To a lender, it is revenue.

Computations for Notes

This section describes key computations for notes including the determination of maturity date, period covered, and interest computation.

Maturity Date and Period

The **maturity date of a note** is the day the note (principal and interest) must be repaid. The *period* of a note is the time from the note's (contract) date to its maturity date. Many notes mature in less than a full year, and the period they cover is often expressed in days. When the time of a note is expressed in days, its maturity date is the specified number of days after the note's date. As an example, a five-day note dated June 15 matures and is due on June 20. A 90-day note dated July 10 matures on October 8. This October 8 due date is computed as shown in Exhibit 10.15.

Exhibit 10.15

Maturity Date Computation

Days in July 31	
Minus the date of the note 10	
Days remaining in July	21
Add days in August	31
Add days in September	30
Days to equal 90 days, or **maturity date of October 8**	8
Period of the note in days	90

The period of a note is sometimes expressed in months or years. When months are used, the note matures and is payable in the month of its maturity on the *same day of the month* as its original date. A nine-month note dated July 10, for instance, is payable on April 10. The same analysis applies when years are used.

Interest Computation

Interest is the cost of borrowing money for the borrower or, alternatively, the profit from lending money for the lender. Unless otherwise stated, the rate of interest on a note is the rate charged for the use of the principal for one year. The formula for computing interest on a note is shown in Exhibit 10.16.

Exhibit 10.16

Computation of Interest Formula

Principal	Annual	Time	
of the	× interest	× expressed	= Interest
note	rate	in years	

To simplify interest computations for notes with periods expressed in days, a year is commonly treated as having 360 days (called the *banker's rule*). **We treat a year as having 360 days in the examples and in the assignments.** Using the promissory note in Exhibit 10.14 where we have a 90-day, 12%, $1,000 note, the total interest is computed as follows:

$$\$1,000 \times 12\% \times \frac{90}{360} = \$1,000 \times .12 \times .25 = \$30$$

Receipt of a Note

Notes receivable are usually recorded in a single Notes Receivable account to simplify recordkeeping. We need only one account because the original notes are kept on file. This means the maker, rate of interest, due date, and other information are available by examining the actual note.[4] To illustrate the recording for the receipt of a note, we use the $1,000, 90-day, 12% promissory note in Exhibit 10.14. TechCom received this note at the time of a product sale to Julia Browne. This transaction is recorded as follows:

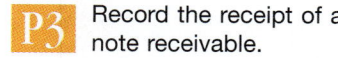

Record the receipt of a note receivable.

July 10	Notes Receivable	1,000	
	Sales		1,000
	Sold goods in exchange for a 90-day, 12% note.		

Assets = Liabilities + Equity
+1,000   +1,000

Companies sometimes accept a note from an overdue customer as a way to grant a time extension on a past-due account receivable. When this occurs, a company might collect part of the past-due balance in cash. This partial payment forces a concession from the customer, reduces the customer's debt (and the seller's risk), and produces a note for a smaller amount. To illustrate, TechCom agreed to accept $232 in cash along with a $600, 60-day, 15% note from Jo Cook to settle her $832 past-due account. TechCom made the following entry to record receipt of this cash and note:

Oct. 5	Cash	232	
	Notes Receivable	600	
	Accounts Receivable—J. Cook		832
	Received cash and note to settle account.		

Assets = Liabilities + Equity
+232
+600
−832

Honoring and Dishonoring a Note

The principal and interest of a note are due on its maturity date. The maker of the note usually *honors* the note and pays it in full. But sometimes a maker *dishonors* the note and does not pay it at maturity.

P4 Record the honoring and dishonoring of a note and adjustments for interest on a note.

Recording an Honored Note

We use the preceding TechCom note transaction to illustrate the honoring of a note. When Cook pays the note on its due date, TechCom records it as follows:

Dec. 4	Cash	615	
	Notes Receivable		600
	Interest Revenue		15
	Collect note with interest of $600 × 15% × 60/360.		

Assets = Liabilities + Equity
+615   +15
−600

Interest Revenue, also called Interest Earned, is reported on the current period's income statement.

Recording a Dishonored Note

When a note's maker is unable or refuses to pay at maturity, the note is dishonored. The act of dishonoring a note does not relieve the maker of the obligation to pay. The payee should use every legitimate means to collect. But how do companies report this event? The balance of the Notes Receivable account should include only those notes that have not matured. When a note is dishonored, we therefore remove the amount of this note from the Notes Receivable account and charge it back to an account receivable from its maker. To illustrate,

Point: When posting a dishonored note to a customer's account, an explanation is included. Otherwise, a later review of the account might misinterpret the debit as a sale on account.

[4] When a company holds a large number of notes, it sometimes sets up a controlling account and a subsidiary ledger for notes. This is similar to the handling of accounts receivable.

TechCom holds an $800, 12%, 60-day note of Greg Hart. At maturity, Hart dishonors the note. TechCom records this dishonoring of the note as follows:

Assets = Liabilities + Equity
+816   +16
−800

Oct. 14	Accounts Receivable—G. Hart	816	
	Interest Revenue		16
	Notes Receivable		800
	To charge account of G. Hart for a dishonored note and interest of $800 × 12% × 60/360.		

Charging a dishonored note back to the account of its maker serves two purposes. First, it removes the amount of the note from the Notes Receivable account and records the dishonored note in the maker's account. Second, and more important, if the maker of the dishonored note applies for credit in the future, his or her account will show all past dealings, including the dishonored note. Restoring the account also reminds the company to continue collection efforts from Hart for both principal and interest. The entry records the full amount, including interest to ensure that it is included in collection efforts.

End-of-Period Interest Adjustment

When notes receivable are outstanding at the end of a period, accrued interest is computed and recorded. This recognizes the interest earned by the note's holder. To illustrate, on December 16, TechCom accepts a $3,000, 60-day, 12% note from a customer in granting an extension on a past-due account. When TechCom's accounting period ends on December 31, $15 of interest has accrued on this note ($3,000 × 12% × 15/360). The following adjusting entry records this revenue:

Assets = Liabilities + Equity
+15   +15

Dec. 31	Interest Receivable	15	
	Interest Revenue		15
	To record accrued interest earned.		

Interest Revenue then appears on the income statement for the period when it is earned, and Interest Receivable appears on the balance sheet as a current asset. When the December 16 note is collected on February 14, TechCom's entry to record the cash receipt is

Assets = Liabilities + Equity
+3,060   +45
  −15
−3,000

Feb. 14	Cash	3,060	
	Interest Revenue		45
	Interest Receivable		15
	Notes Receivable		3,000
	Received payment of note and its interest.		

Total interest earned on the note is $60. The $15 credit to Interest Receivable on February 14 reflects the collection of the interest accrued from the December 31 adjusting entry. The $45 interest earned reflects TechCom's revenue from holding the note from January 1 to February 14 of the current period.

Quick Check

8. Irwin purchases $7,000 of merchandise from Stamford on December 16, 2002. Stamford accepts Irwin's $7,000, 90-day, 12% note as payment. Stamford's accounting period ends on December 31, and it does not make reversing entries. Prepare entries for Stamford on December 16, 2002, and December 31, 2002.

9. Using the information in Quick Check 8, prepare Stamford's March 16, 2003, entry if Irwin dishonors the note.

Answers—p. 422

Sometimes companies convert receivables to cash before they are due. Reasons for this include the need for cash or the desire not to be involved in collection activities. Converting receivables is usually done either by (1) selling them or (2) using them as security for a loan. A recent survey shows that about 20% of large companies obtain cash from either selling of receivables or pledging them as security. In some industries such as textiles and furniture, this is common practice. Recently, this practice has become common for other industries, especially the apparel industry.

Converting Receivables to Cash before Maturity

C3 Explain how receivables can be converted to cash before maturity.

Selling Accounts Receivable

A company can sell all or a portion of its accounts receivable to a finance company or bank. The buyer, called a *factor,* charges the seller a *factoring fee* and then receives cash from the receivables as they come due. By incurring a factoring fee, the seller receives cash earlier and can pass the risk of bad debts to the factor. The seller can also choose to avoid costs of billing and accounting for the receivables. To illustrate, if TechCom sells $20,000 of its accounts receivable and is charged a 4% factoring fee, it records this sale as follows:

Aug. 15	Cash.	19,200	
	Factoring Fee Expense.	800	
	Accounts Receivable		20,000
	Sold accounts receivable for cash, less a		
	4% factoring fee.		

Assets = Liabilities + Equity
+19,200   −800
−20,000

Factoring is a major business today. **CIT Group** is a large factoring firm with annual volume of about $8 billion. Interestingly, about 90% of the factoring industry's business comes from textile, furniture, and apparel businesses.

Global: Companies in export sales increasingly sell their receivables to factors.

Pledging Accounts Receivable

A company can also raise cash by borrowing money and *pledging* its accounts receivable as security for the loan. Pledging receivables does not transfer the risk of bad debts to the lender because the borrower retains ownership of the receivables. If the borrower defaults on the loan, the lender has a right to be paid from the cash receipts of the accounts receivable when collected. To illustrate, when TechCom borrows $35,000 and pledges its receivables as security, it records this transaction as follows:

Point: When accounts receivable are sold, each subsidiary ledger account is credited along with the controlling account for the total.

Aug. 20	Cash.	35,000	
	Notes Payable.		35,000
	Borrowed money with a note secured by		
	pledging accounts receivable.		

Assets = Liabilities + Equity
+35,000   +35,000

Since pledged receivables are committed as security for a specific loan, the borrower's financial statements should disclose the pledging of accounts receivable. TechCom, for instance, includes the following note with its financial statements: *Accounts receivable in the amount of $40,000 are pledged as security for a $35,000 note payable.* Another example is from the notes of **Chock Full O'Nuts**: "Outstanding borrowings . . . are collateralized by, among other things, the trade accounts receivable."

> **Did You Know?**
>
> **Cash Poor?** Both **Zenith** and **Packard Bell** used receivables to get much needed cash. **Zenith** obtained a three-year, $60 million credit agreement by pledging accounts receivable as collateral. **Intel** converted accounts receivable to a note receivable for a customer—widely assumed to be **Packard Bell**.

Discounting Notes Receivable

Notes receivable can be converted to cash before they mature. This can be done by discounting them at a financial institution. To illustrate, TechCom discounts a $3,000, 90-day, 10% note receivable at National Bank. TechCom had held the note for 50 of its 90 days before discounting it. The bank applies a 12% rate in discounting the note, and TechCom receives proceeds of $3,034 from the bank. It recorded the discounting of this note as follows:[5]

Assets = Liabilities + Equity
+3,034   +34
−3,000

Aug. 25	Cash.....................................	3,034	
	Interest Revenue*.......................		34
	Notes Receivable.......................		3,000
	Discounted a note receivable.		

* If the cash proceeds are less than the Note Receivable balance, the difference (a debit) is recorded as Interest Expense.

Notes receivable are discounted without recourse or with recourse. When a note is discounted *without recourse,* the bank assumes the risk of a bad debt loss, and the original payee does not have a contingent liability. A **contingent liability** is an obligation to make a future payment if, and only if, an uncertain future event occurs. Examples are potential tax assessments, debts of others guaranteed by the company, and outstanding lawsuits against the company. A note discounted without recourse is like an outright sale of an asset. If a note is discounted *with recourse* and the original maker of the note fails to pay the bank when it matures, the original payee of the note must pay for it. This means a company discounting a note with recourse has a contingent liability until the bank is paid. A company should disclose contingent liabilities in notes to its financial statements. TechCom included the following note: "The Company is contingently liable for a $3,000 note receivable discounted with recourse." A similar example of a receivables sale with recourse is from the notes of **Tyco**: "The Company entered into an agreement pursuant to which it sold . . . receivables. The Company has retained substantially the same risk of credit loss as if the receivables had not been sold."

The disclosure of contingencies in notes is consistent with the **full disclosure principle,** which requires financial statements (including notes) to report all relevant information about a company's operations and financial position. Relevance is judged by whether a company's disclosure impacts users' business decisions. Besides contingent liabilities, other items often reported to satisfy the full disclosure principle are long-term commitments under contracts (such as long-term leases and the pledging of assets) and the accounting methods used.

Did You Know?

No Place Like Home   Home is where the business is—that according to nearly one-half (49%) of entrepreneurs in a recent survey with annual sales between $50,000 to $500,000. More similarities exist between home-based and not home-based entrepreneurships than commonly assumed. Interestingly, the majority of these companies are set up as proprietorships.

	Home-Based	Not Home-Based
Similarities:		
Years in		
business ...	13.9 yrs.	14.5 yrs.
Checking		
acct. bal.	$ 14,700	$ 15,200
Household		
income	$108,400	$113,200
Differences		
Importance		
of growth ..	11%	21%
Proprietorship .	72%	52%

Point: Notes receivable often are a major part of a company's assets. Likewise, notes payable often are a large part of a company's liabilities.

Point: Much of the information required by the full disclosure principle is in notes to financial statements. This information is critical to financial analysis.

---

[5] Cash proceeds from the bank are computed as follows:

Principal of note	$3,000
+ Interest from note ($3,000 × 10% × 90/360) ...	+ 75
= Maturity value of note	$3,075
− Bank discount ($3,075 × 12% × 40/360)	− (41)
= Cash proceeds	$3,034

The net Interest Revenue ($34) equals the total interest from the note ($75) less the bank's discount ($41). If the bank's discount exceeds the note's total interest, Interest Expense is debited for the difference.

Recall from Chapter 9 that cash equivalents are investments readily converted to known amounts of cash and that mature within three months. Many investments, however, mature between 3 and 12 months. These investments are **short-term investments,** also called *temporary investments,* or *marketable securities.* Specifically, short-term investments are securities that (1) management intends to convert to cash within one year or the operating cycle, whichever is longer, and (2) are readily convertible to cash. Short-term investments are current assets and serve a purpose similar to cash equivalents. Short-term investments can include both debt and equity securities. *Debt securities* reflect a creditor relationship such as investments in notes, bonds, and certificates of deposit. Debt securities are issued by governments, companies, and individuals. *Equity securities* reflect an ownership relationship such as shares of stock issued by companies.

Short-Term Investments

C4 Describe short-term investments in debt and equity securities.

Accounting for Short-Term Investments

This section explains the basics of accounting for short-term investments in both debt and equity securities. Chapter 16 will further explain the accounting for investments.

Debt Securities

Short-term investments in debt (and equity) securities are recorded at cost when purchased. To illustrate, TechCom purchases **Intel** short-term notes payable for $4,000 on January 10. TechCom's entry to record this purchase is

Jan. 10	Short-Term Investments	4,000	
	Cash		4,000
	Bought $4,000 of Intel notes maturing May 10.		

Assets = Liabilities + Equity
+4,000
−4,000

These notes mature on May 10. When the cash proceeds of $4,000 plus the $120 interest ($4,000 $\times$ 9% $\times$ $\frac{120}{360}$) are received at maturity, TechCom records this as:

May 10	Cash.	4,120	
	Short-Term Investments		4,000
	Interest Revenue		120
	Received cash proceeds from matured notes.		

Assets = Liabilities + Equity
+4,120   +120
−4,000

Equity Securities

The cost of a short-term investment in equity securities includes all necessary costs to acquire it, including commissions paid. To illustrate, TechCom purchases 100 shares of Nike common stock as a short-term investment for $50 per share plus $100 in commissions. The entry to record this purchase is

June 2	Short-Term Investments	5,100	
	Cash		5,100
	Bought 100 shares of Nike stock at $50 per share plus $100 commission.		

Example: What is cost per share? *Answer:* Cost per share is the total cost of acquisition, inclusive of fees, divided by number of shares acquired.

Assets = Liabilities + Equity
+5,100
−5,100

The commission is recorded as part of the investment cost. TechCom also receives a $0.40 per share cash dividend on its Nike stock during the current period. This dividend is recorded in a revenue account as follows:

Dec. 12	Cash.	40	
	Dividend Revenue		40
	Received dividend of $0.40 per share on 100 shares of Nike stock.		

Assets = Liabilities + Equity
+40   +40

P5   Record short-term investment transactions.

Valuing and Reporting Short-Term Investments

Companies must value and report most short-term investments at their fair values. *Fair value* of a security is its market value. Accounting requirements vary depending on whether short-term investments are classified as (1) held-to-maturity, (2) trading, or (3) available-for-sale securities. This section describes the financial statement presentation for each of these classifications.

Held-to-Maturity Securities

Point: Only debt securities are classified as *held-to-maturity*. Equity securities have no maturity date.

Held-to-maturity securities are *debt securities* that the company has the intent and ability to hold until they mature. **Dairy Queen**, for instance, in notes to its financial statements, states: "Management determines the appropriate classification of debt securities at the time of purchase and reevaluates such designation as of each balance sheet date. Debt securities are classified as held-to-maturity because the Company has the positive intent and ability to hold such securities to maturity." Held-to-maturity securities are reported in current assets if their maturity dates are within the longer of one year or the operating cycle. Held-to-maturity securities are reported at cost (plus accrued interest).

Trading Securities

Trading securities are *debt and equity securities* that the company intends to actively manage and trade for profit. This means that frequent purchases and sales are made to earn profits on short-term price changes. Trading securities are especially common with financial institutions such as banks and insurance companies.

Valuing and reporting trading securities

Point: The phrase *unrealized* gain or loss refers to a change in an item's market value when the change in value is not yet realized through an actual sale.

Point: Market Adjustment—Trading is a *permanent account*, shown as a deduction or addition to Short-Term Investments—Trading.

The entire portfolio of trading securities is reported at its market (fair) value with a "market adjustment" to the cost of the portfolio. The term *portfolio* refers to a group of securities. Any unrealized gain or loss from a change in the market value of the portfolio of trading securities during a period is reported on the income statement. Most users believe accounting reports are more useful when changes in market value for a portfolio of trading securities are reported in income. To illustrate, TechCom's portfolio of trading securities has a total cost of $11,500 and a market value of $13,000 on December 31, 2002. The difference between the $11,500 cost and the $13,000 market value reflects a $1,500 gain. This gain is an **unrealized gain** because it is not yet confirmed by actual sales of these securities. TechCom records this gain as:

Assets = Liabilities + Equity
+1,500   +1,500

Dec. 31	Market Adjustment—Trading	1,500	
	Unrealized Gain—Income		1,500
	To reflect an unrealized gain in market values of trading securities.		

Point: Unrealized Gain (or Loss)—Income is a *temporary account* that is closed to Income Summary at the end of each period.

Example: If TechCom's portfolio of trading securities has a cost of $14,800 and a market value of $16,100 at December 31, 2003, its adjusting entry is
Unrealized Loss—Income   . 200
  Mkt. Adj.—Trading   200
This entry revises the current balance in the market adjustment account to reflect the market difference from cost ($1,500 Dr. + $200 Cr. = $1,300 Dr.).

The Unrealized Gain (or Loss) is reported in the Other Revenues and Gains (or Expenses and Losses) section on the income statement. After posting this entry, TechCom's investment in trading securities is reported in the current assets section of its balance sheet as shown:

Current Assets		
Short-Term Investments—Trading (at cost)	$11,500	
Market Adjustment—Trading	1,500	
Short-Term Investments—Trading (at market)		$13,000

The total cost of the portfolio of trading securities is maintained in one account and the market adjustment is recorded in a separate account. The market adjustment is revised at the end of each period to equal the difference between the cost and market values.

Selling trading securities

When individual trading securities are sold, the difference between the net proceeds from the sale (sale price less fees) and the cost of the individual trading securities that are sold is recognized as a gain or a loss. To illustrate, when TechCom sells its $5,100 short-term investment in Nike stock on December 15 for net proceeds of $5,400, it recognizes a gain of $300. The entry to record this sale is

Point: The price of a security is sometimes listed in fraction form. For example, an equity security with a price of $22\frac{1}{4}$, is the same as saying its price is $22.25.

Dec. 15	Cash	5,400	
	Gain on Sale of Short-Term Investments		300
	Short-Term Investments		5,100
	To record sale of 100 shares of Nike stock.		

Assets = Liabilities + Equity
+5,400   +300
−5,100

This gain is reported in the Other Revenues and Gains section on the income statement. If a loss is recorded, it is shown in Other Expenses and Losses. When TechCom computes its market adjustment for trading securities at the end of the period, it excludes the cost and market values of the Nike stock since it has been sold.

Available-for-Sale Securities

Available-for-sale securities are *debt and equity securities* not classified as trading or held-to-maturity securities. Available-for-sale securities are purchased to yield interest, dividends, or increases in market value. They are not actively managed like trading securities.

> ## Did You Know?
>
> **Back to the Future**   About 70 years ago banks switched from reporting market values for their short-term investments to reporting them at cost. We now see a return to market value reporting for many short-term investments. This is driven by S&L and other banking failures in disclosing market value changes. Ironically, the Great Depression fueled the conversion from market values to costs out of concern for the lack of reliability of market values.

Valuing and reporting available-for-sale securities

Similar to trading securities, companies adjust the cost of the portfolio of available-for-sale securities to reflect changes in market value. This is done with a market adjustment to its total portfolio cost. However, any unrealized gain or loss for the portfolio of available-for-sale securities is *not* reported on the income statement. Instead, it is reported in the equity section of the balance sheet (and is part of comprehensive income—explained in Chapter 16). Many users believe that since available-for-sale securities are not actively traded, including changes in market value would unnecessarily increase the variability of income and decrease its usefulness. To illustrate, TechCom's portfolio of available-for-sale securities had a total cost of $15,400 and a market value of $14,500 on December 31, 2002. The difference between the $15,400 cost and the $14,500 market value reflects a $900 unrealized loss. TechCom records this loss as:

Dec. 31	Unrealized Loss—Equity	900	
	Market Adjustment—Available-for-Sale		900
	To reflect an unrealized loss in market values		
	of available-for-sale securities.		

Assets = Liabilities + Equity
−900   −900

This is reported in TechCom's current asset and equity sections of its balance sheet as follows:

Current Assets		
Short-Term Investments—Available-for-sale (at cost)	$15,400	
Market Adjustment—Available-for-sale	(900)	
Short-Term Investments—Available-for-sale (at market)		$14,500
Equity		
. . . *usual equity and capital accounts* . . .		
Less: Unrealized loss on available-for-sale securities		$ 900

Selling available-for-sale securities

Accounting for the sale of individual available-for-sale securities is identical to that described for the sale of trading securities. When individual available-for-sale securities are sold, the difference between the cost of the individual securities sold and the net proceeds from the sale (sale price less fees) is recognized as a gain or loss.

Summary of Accounting for Short-Term Investments

Exhibit 10.17 summarizes the accounting for short-term investments in securities.

Exhibit 10.17

Accounting for Short-Term
Investments in Securities

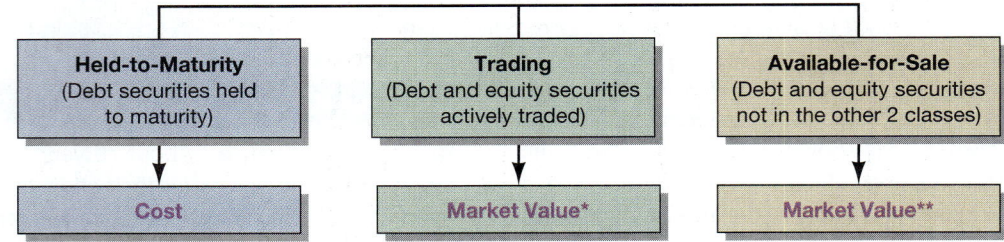

*Unrealized gains or losses reported on income statement.
**Unrealized gains or losses reported in equity section on balance sheet and in comprehensive income.

The balance sheet presentation of short-term investments usually reports the market value for the sum *total* of all three classes of securities instead of each individual class. The cost is also usually reported and the details are sometimes disclosed in the notes. A typical presentation of short-term investments is shown in Exhibit 10.18.

Exhibit 10.18

Statement Presentation of
Short-Term Investments

Current assets	
Short-term investments, at market value (cost is $16,200)	**$14,500**

Although the contra account to Short-Term Investments is not shown, we can determine its balance as $1,700 by comparing the $16,200 cost with the $14,500 market value.

Quick Check

10. How are held-to-maturity securities reported (valued) on the balance sheet?

11. How are trading securities reported (valued) on the balance sheet?

12. Where are unrealized gains and losses on available-for-sale securities reported?

13. Where are unrealized gains and losses on trading securities reported?

14. A company has substantial accounts receivable but needs cash. What alternatives are available for getting cash from its accounts receivable prior to receiving payments from credit customers? Show the entry made for each alternative.

Answers—p. 422

Using the Information   Accounts Receivable Turnover

A1 Compute accounts receivable turnover and use it to analyze liquidity.

For a company selling on credit, we want to assess both the quality and liquidity of its accounts receivable. *Quality* of receivables refers to the likelihood of collection without loss. Experience shows the longer receivables are outstanding beyond their due date, the lower the likelihood of collection. *Liquidity* of receivables refers to the speed of collection. **Accounts receivable turnover** is a measure of both the quality and liquidity of accounts receivable. It indicates how often, on average, receivables are received and collected during the period. The formula for this ratio is shown in Exhibit 10.19.

$$\text{Accounts receivable turnover} = \frac{\text{Net sales}}{\text{Average accounts receivable}}$$

Exhibit 10.19

Accounts Receivable Turnover

We prefer to use net *credit* sales in the numerator because cash sales do not create receivables. Since financial statements rarely report net credit sales, our analysis uses net sales. The denominator is the *average* accounts receivable balance, computed as (Beginning balance + Ending balance) ÷ 2. TechCom has an accounts receivable turnover of 5.1. This indicates its average accounts receivable balance is converted into cash 5.1 times during the period. Exhibit 10.20 shows graphically this turnover activity for TechCom.

5.1 times per year

Jan. Feb. March Apr. May June July Aug. Sept. Oct. Nov. Dec.

Exhibit 10.20

Rate of Accounts Receivable Turnover for TechCom

Accounts receivable turnover also reflects how well management is doing in granting credit to customers in a desire to increase sales. A high turnover in comparison with competitors suggests management should consider using more liberal credit terms to increase sales. A low turnover suggests management should consider stricter credit terms and more aggressive collection efforts to avoid having its resources tied up in accounts receivable.

To illustrate its application, we take data from two competitors: **Dell Computer** and **Apple Computer**. Exhibit 10.21 shows accounts receivable turnover for both companies.

Company	Figure ($ in millions)	1999	1998	1997
Dell	Net sales	$25,265	$18,243	$12,327
	Average accounts receivable	$ 2,351	$ 1,790	$ 1,195
	Accounts receivable turnover	**10.7**	**10.2**	**10.3**
Apple	Net sales	$ 6,134	$ 5,941	$ 7,081
	Average accounts receivable	$ 818	$ 995	$ 1,266
	Accounts receivable turnover	**7.5**	**6.0**	**5.6**

Exhibit 10.21

Analysis Using Accounts Receivable Turnover

Dell's 1999 turnover is computed ($ in millions) as $25,265/$2,351 = 10.7. This means Dell's average accounts receivable balance was converted into cash 10.7 times in 1999. Also, its turnover slightly improved in 1999 (versus its prior two years), and it is superior to Apple. Is Dell's turnover too high? Since sales are markedly growing over this time period, Dell's turnover does not appear to be too high. Instead, its management seems to be doing a good job managing receivables. Similarly, Apple has improved its management of receivables during this period. Turnover for competitors is generally in the range of 6 to 8 for this same period.[6]

> ### You Make the Call
>
> **Family Physician**   Your practice has turned less profitable so you hire a health care analyst to make recommendations. The analyst highlights several points including the following ". . . *accounts receivable turnover is too low. Tighter credit policies are recommended along with discontinuing service to those most delayed in payments.*" How do you interpret these recommendations? What actions do you take?

Answer—p. 421

---

[6] As an approximation of *average days' sales uncollected* (see Chapter 9), we can estimate how many days (*on average*) it takes to collect receivables as follows: 365 days ÷ accounts receivable turnover.

Demonstration Problem

Garden Company completes the following selected transactions during year 2002.

May	8	Purchases 300 shares of Federal Express stock as a short-term investment in available-for-sale securities at a cost of $40 per share plus $975 in broker fees.
July	14	Writes off a $750 account receivable arising from a sale to Briggs Company that dates to 13 months ago. (Garden Company uses the allowance method.)
	30	Garden Company receives a $1,000, 90-day, 10% note from a product sale to Sumrell Company.
Aug.	15	Receives $2,000 cash plus a $10,000 note from a customer in exchange for merchandise that sells for $12,000. The note is dated August 15, bears 12% interest, and matures in 180 days.
Sept.	2	Sells 100 shares of its investment in Federal Express stock at $47 per share and holds the remaining 200 shares. The broker's commission on this sale is $225.
	15	Receives $9,850 cash in exchange for discounting without recourse the $10,000 note (dated August 15) at the local bank.
Oct.	2	Purchases 400 shares of McDonald's stock for $60 per share plus $1,600 in commissions. The stock is held as a short-term investment in available-for-sale securities.
Nov.	1	Completed a $200 credit card sale with a 4% fee. The cash is received immediately from the credit card company.
	5	Completed a $500 credit card sale with a 5% fee. The payment from the credit card company is received on Nov. 7.
	15	Received the full amount of $750 from Briggs Company that was previously written off on July 14. Record the bad debts recovery.
	20	Sumrell Company refuses to pay the note that was due to Garden Company on October 28. Prepare the journal entry to charge the dishonored note plus accrued interest to Sumrell Company's accounts receivable.

Required

1. Prepare journal entries to record these transactions on Garden Company's books.
2. Prepare an adjusting journal entry as of December 31, 2002, assuming the following:
   a. Bad debts expense is estimated by an aging of accounts receivable. The unadjusted balance of the Allowance for Doubtful Accounts is a $1,000 debit, and it is estimated to be a $20,400 credit.
   b. Alternatively, assume that bad debts expense is estimated using the percent of sales method. The Allowance for Doubtful Accounts had a $1,000 debit balance before adjustment, and the company estimates bad debts to be 1% of its credit sales of $2,000,000.
3. Prepare an adjusting journal entry as of December 31, 2002, if the market prices of the equity securities held by Garden Company are $48 per share for Federal Express and $55 per share for McDonald's. (Year 2002 is Garden Co.'s first year of operations.)

Planning the Solution

- Examine each transaction to determine the accounts affected and then record the entries.
- For the year-end adjustment, record the bad debts expense for the two approaches.

Solution to Demonstration Problem

1.

May 8	Short-Term Investments	12,975	
	Cash		12,975
	Purchased 300 shares of Federal Express		
	stock (300 × $40) + $975.		
July 14	Allowance for Doubtful Accounts	750	
	Accounts Receivable—Briggs Co.		750
	Wrote off an uncollectible account.		
July 30	Notes Receivable—Sumrell Co.	1,000	
	Sales		1,000
	Sold merchandise for a 90-day, 10% note.		

Aug. 15	Cash	2,000	
	Notes Receivable...........................	10,000	
	Sales		12,000
	Sold merchandise to customer for $2,000 cash and $10,000 note.		
Sept. 2	Cash	4,475	
	Gain on Sale of Short-term Investment		150
	Short-Term Investments...................		4,325
	Sold 100 shares of Federal Express for $47 per share less a $225 commission. The original cost is ($12,975 × 100/300).		
Sept. 15	Cash	9,850	
	Interest Expense	150	
	Notes Receivable—Sumrell Co............		10,000
	Discounted note receivable dated August 15.		
Oct. 2	Short-Term Investments	25,600	
	Cash		25,600
	Purchased 400 shares of McDonald's for $60 per share plus $1,600 in commissions.		
Nov. 1	Cash	192	
	Credit Card Expense	8	
	Sales		200
	To record credit card sale less a 4% credit card expense.		
Nov. 5	Accounts Receivable—Credit Card Co...........	475	
	Credit Card Expense	25	
	Sales		500
	To record credit card sale less a 5% credit card expense.		
Nov. 7	Cash.......................................	475	
	Accounts Receivable—Credit Card Co........		475
	To record cash receipt.		
Nov. 15	Accounts Receivable—Briggs Co..............	750	
	Allowance for Doubtful Accounts		750
	To reinstate the account of Briggs Company previously written off.		
Nov. 15	Cash.......................................	750	
	Accounts Receivable—Briggs Co.		750
	Cash received in full payment of account.		
Nov. 20	Accounts Receivable—Sumrell Co..............	1,025	
	Interest Revenue......................		25
	Notes Receivable—Sumrell Co.............		1,000
	To charge account of Sumrell Company for a $1,000 dishonored note and interest of $1,000 × 10% × 90/360.		

> Interest Expense of $150 is the *net* of interest revenue from the note *less* the bank discounting charge.

2a. Aging of accounts receivable method:

Dec. 31	Bad Debts Expense........................	21,400	
	Allowance for Doubtful Accounts		21,400
	To adjust allowance account from a $1,000 debit balance to a $20,400 credit balance.		

2b. Percent of sales method:

Dec. 31	Bad Debts Expense	20,000	
	Allowance for Doubtful Accounts		20,000
	To provide for bad debts as 1% × $2,000,000 . . . . . in credit sales.		

(*Note:* For the income statement approach, which requires estimating bad debts as a percent of sales or credit sales, the Allowance account balance is **not** considered when making the adjusting entry.)

3. Computation of unrealized gain or loss:

Short-Term Investments in Available-for-Sale Securities	Shares	Cost per Share	Total Cost	Market Value per Share	Total Market Value	Unrealized Gain (Loss)
Federal Express	200	$43.25	$ 8,650	$ 48.00	$ 9,600	
McDonald's	400	64.00	25,600	55.00	22,000	
Total			$ 34,250		$31,600	$(2,650)

Adjusting entry:

Dec. 31	Unrealized Loss—Equity	2,650	
	Market Adjustment—Available-for-Sale		2,650
	To reflect an unrealized loss in market values of available-for-sale securities.		

Summary

C1 **Describe accounts receivable and how they occur and are recorded.** Accounts receivable are amounts due from customers for credit sales. A subsidiary ledger lists amounts owed by individual customers. Credit sales arise from at least two sources: (1) sales on credit and (2) credit card sales. Sales on credit refer to a company's granting credit directly to customers. Credit card sales involve customers' use of third party credit cards.

C2 **Describe a note receivable and the computation of its maturity date and interest.** A note receivable is a written promise to pay a specified amount of money at a definite future date. The maturity date is the day the note (principal and interest) must be repaid. Interest rates are normally stated in annual terms. The amount of interest on the note is computed by expressing time as a fraction of one year and multiplying the note's principal by this fraction and the annual interest rate.

C3 **Explain how receivables can be converted to cash before maturity.** Receivables can be converted to cash before maturity in three ways. First, a company can sell accounts receivable to a factor, who charges a factoring fee. Second, a company can borrow money by signing a note payable that is se-

cured by pledging the accounts receivable. Third, notes receivable can be discounted at a bank, with or without recourse.

C4 **Describe short-term investments in debt and equity securities.** Short-term investments can include both debt and equity securities. *Debt securities* reflect a creditor relationship and include investments in notes, bonds, and certificates of deposit. *Equity securities* reflect an ownership relationship and include shares of stock issued by other companies.

A1 **Compute accounts receivable turnover and use it to analyze liquidity.** Accounts receivable turnover is a measure of both the quality and liquidity of accounts receivable. The accounts receivable turnover measure indicates how often, on average, receivables are received and collected during the period. Accounts receivable turnover is computed as net sales divided by average accounts receivable.

P1 **Apply the direct write-off and allowance methods to account for accounts receivable.** The direct write-off method charges Bad Debts Expense when accounts are written off as uncollectible. This method is acceptable only when the amount of bad debts expense is immaterial. Under the allowance method, bad debts expense is recorded with an adjustment at the end of each accounting period that debits the Expense account and credits the Allowance for Doubtful Accounts. The uncollectible accounts are later written off with a debit to the Allowance for Doubtful Accounts.

P2 **Estimate uncollectibles using methods based on sales and accounts receivable.** Uncollectibles are estimated by focusing on either (1) the income statement relation between bad debts expense and credit sales or (2) the balance sheet relation between accounts receivable and the allowance for doubtful accounts. The first approach emphasizes the matching principle using the income statement. The second approach emphasizes realizable value of accounts receivable using the balance sheet.

P3 **Record the receipt of a note receivable.** A note received is recorded at its principal amount by debiting the Notes Receivable account. The credit amount is to the asset, product, or service provided in return for the note.

P4 **Record the honoring and dishonoring of a note and adjustments for interest on a note.** When a note is honored,

the payee debits the money received and credits both Notes Receivable and Interest Revenue. Dishonored notes are credited to Notes Receivable and debited to Accounts Receivable (to the account of the maker in an attempt to collect). Interest earned from holding a note is recorded for the amount of time the note is held.

P5 **Record short-term investment transactions.** Short-term investments are initially recorded at cost, and any dividends or interest from these investments is recorded in the income statement. Short-term investments are classified as held-to-maturity securities, trading securities, or available-for-sale securities. Held-to-maturity securities are reported at cost on the balance sheet. Trading securities and available-for-sale securities are reported at their fair (market) values. Unrealized gains and losses on trading securities are reported in income. Unrealized gains and losses on available-for-sale securities are reported in the equity section of the balance sheet. When short-term investments are sold, the difference between the net proceeds from the sale and the cost of the securities is recognized as a gain or loss.

Guidance Answers to **You Make the Call**

Entrepreneur Your analysis of allowing credit card sales should weigh the benefits against the costs. The primary benefit is the potential to increase sales by attracting customers who prefer the convenience of credit cards. The primary cost is the fee charged by the credit card company for providing this service to your store. Your analysis should therefore estimate the expected increase in sales dollars from allowing credit card sales and then subtract (1) the normal costs and expenses and (2) the credit card fees associated with this expected increase in sales dollars. If your analysis shows an increase in profit from allowing credit card sales, your store should probably accept them.

Labor Union Chief Yes, this information is likely to impact your negotiations. The obvious question is why the company increased this allowance to such a large extent. The major increase in this allowance means a substantial increase in bad debts expense *and* a decrease in earnings. Coming immediately prior to labor contract discussions, this change also raises concerns since it reduces

the union's bargaining power for increased compensation. You want to ask management for supporting documentation justifying this increase. You also want data for two or three prior years and similar data from competitors. These data should give you some sense of whether the change in the allowance for uncollectibles is justified.

Family Physician The recommendations are twofold. First, the analyst suggests more stringent screening of patients' credit standing. Second, the analyst suggests dropping patients who are most overdue in payments. You are likely bothered by both suggestions. While they are probably financially wise recommendations, you are troubled by eliminating services to those less able to pay. One alternative is to follow the recommendations while implementing a care program directed at patients less able to pay for services. This allows you to continue services to patients less able to pay and lets you discontinue services to patients able but unwilling to pay.

Guidance Answers to **Quick Checks**

1. If cash is received when credit card sales receipts are deposited in the bank, the company debits Cash at the time of sale. If the company does not receive payment until after it submits receipts to the credit card company, it debits Accounts Receivable at the time of sale (cash is later debited when payment is received from the credit card company).

2. Credit card expenses are usually *recorded* and *incurred* at the time of their related sales; not when cash is received from the credit card company.

3. If possible, bad debts expense must be matched with the sales that gave rise to the accounts receivable. This requires that companies estimate future bad debts at the end of each period before they learn which accounts are uncollectible.

4. Realizable value (also called *net realizable value*).

5. The estimated amount of bad debts expense cannot be credited to the Accounts Receivable account because the specific customer accounts that will prove uncollectible cannot be

identified and removed from the subsidiary Accounts Receivable Ledger. Moreover, if only the Accounts Receivable account is credited its balance would not equal the sum of its subsidiary account balances.

6.

Dec. 31	Bad Debts Expense	5,702	
	Allowance for Doubtful Accounts		5,702

7.

Jan. 10	Allowance for Doubtful Accounts	300	
	Accounts Receivable—Cool Jam		300
Apr. 12	Accounts Receivable—Cool Jam. . . .	300	
	Allowance for Doubtful Accounts.		300
Apr. 12	Cash	300	
	Accounts Receivable—Cool Jam		300

8.

Dec. 16	Note Receivable	7,000	
	Sales		7,000
Dec. 31	Interest Receivable	35	
	Interest Revenue		35
	($7,000 × 12% × 15/360)		

9.

Mar. 16	Accounts Receivable—Irwin	7,210	
	Interest Revenue		175
	Interest Receivable		35
	Notes Receivable		7,000

10. Held-to-maturity securities are reported at cost.

11. Trading securities are reported at fair (market) value.

12. The equity section of the balance sheet (and in comprehensive income).

13. The income statement.

14. Alternatives are (1) selling their accounts receivable to a factor and (2) pledging accounts receivable as loan security. The entries to record these transactions take the following form:

(1) Cash	#	
Factoring Fee Expense	#	
Accounts Receivable		#
(2) Cash	#	
Notes Payable		#

Glossary

Accounts receivable amounts due from customers for credit sales. (p. 396).

Accounts receivable turnover measure of both the quality and liquidity of accounts receivable; indicates how often receivables are received and collected during the period; computed by dividing net sales by average accounts receivable. (p. 416).

Aging of accounts receivable process of classifying accounts receivable by how long they are past due for purposes of estimating uncollectible accounts. (p. 405).

Allowance for Doubtful Accounts contra asset account with a balance approximating uncollectible accounts receivable; also called *Allowance for Uncollectible Accounts*. (p. 401).

Allowance method procedure that (1) estimates and matches bad debts expense with its sales for the period and (2) reports accounts receivable at estimated realizable value. (p. 401).

Available-for-sale securities investments in debt and equity securities that are not classified as trading securities or held-to-maturity securities. (p. 415).

Bad debts accounts of customers who do not pay what they have promised to pay; an expense of selling on credit; also called *uncollectible accounts*. (p. 399).

Contingent liability obligation to make a future payment if, and only if, an uncertain future event occurs. (p. 412).

Direct write-off method method that records the loss from an uncollectible account receivable at the time it is determined to be uncollectible; no attempt is made to estimate bad debts. (p. 400).

Full disclosure principle principle that requires financial statements (including notes) to report all relevant information about an entity's operations and financial condition. (p. 412).

Held-to-maturity securities debt securities that a company has the intent and ability to hold until they mature. (p. 414).

Interest charge for using money (or other assets) until repaid at a future date. (p. 408).

Maker of a note entity who signs a note and promises to pay it at maturity. (p. 408).

Matching principle requires expenses to be reported in the same period as the sales they helped produce. (p. 400).

Materiality principle implies an amount can be ignored if its effect on financial statements is unimportant to users. (p. 401).

Maturity date of a note date when principal and interest of a note are due. (p. 408).

Payee of a note entity to whom a note is made payable. (p. 408).

Principal of a note amount that the signer of a note agrees to pay back when it matures, not including interest. (p. 408).

Promissory note (or **note**) written promise to pay a specified amount either on demand or at a definite future date. (p. 407).

Realizable value expected proceeds from converting an asset into cash. (p. 401).

Short-term investments debt and equity securities that management expects to convert to cash within the next 3 to 12 months (or the operating cycle if longer); also called *temporary investments*. (p. 413).

Trading securities investments in debt and equity securities that the company intends to actively trade for profit. (p. 414).

Unrealized gain (loss) gain (loss) not yet realized by an actual transaction or event such as a sale. (p. 414).

Questions

1. How do sellers benefit from allowing their customers to use credit cards?

2. Why does the direct write-off method of accounting for bad debts usually fail to match revenues and expenses?

3. Explain the accounting principle of materiality.

4. Explain why writing off a bad debt against the Allowance account does not reduce the estimated realizable value of a company's accounts receivable.

5. Why does the Bad Debts Expense account usually not have the same adjusted balance as the Allowance for Doubtful Accounts?

6. Why might a business prefer a note receivable to an account receivable?

7. What does it mean to sell a receivable without recourse?

8. Under what two conditions should investments be classified as current assets?

9. On a balance sheet, what valuation must be reported for short-term investments in trading securities?

10. If a short-term investment in available-for-sale securities costs $6,780 and is sold for $7,500, how should the difference between these two amounts be recorded?

11. Refer to **Nike**'s balance sheet in Appendix A. What percent of accounts receivable at May 31,

2000, has been set aside as an allowance for doubtful accounts? How does this percent compare to the prior year?

12. Refer to the balance sheet of **Reebok** in  Appendix A. Does it use the direct write-off method or allowance method to account for doubtful accounts? What is the realizable value of its accounts receivable as of December 31, 1999? What is another name for the Allowance for Doubtful Accounts?

13. Refer to the balance sheet of **Gap** in Appendix A. Why does it not show any accounts receivable in its current asset section?

Fortune Corp. uses the allowance method to account for uncollectibles. On October 31, it wrote off an $800 account of a customer, Christina Rowland. On December 9, it receives a $300 payment from Rowland.

1. Make the appropriate entry or entries for October 31.
2. Make the appropriate entry or entries for December 9.

QUICK STUDY

QS 10-1
Allowance method for bad debts P1

Blazek Company's year-end unadjusted trial balance shows accounts receivable of $99,000, allowance for doubtful accounts of $600 (credit), and sales of $280,000. Uncollectibles are estimated to be 1.5% of accounts receivable.

1. Prepare the December 31 year-end adjusting entry for uncollectibles.
2. What amount would have been used in the year-end adjustment if the allowance account had a year-end unadjusted debit balance of $300?
3. Assume the same facts as in part (1), except that Blazek estimates uncollectibles as 1% of sales. What amount is used in the year-end adjustment?

QS 10-2
Percent of accounts receivable method

P1

Journalize the following transactions:

1. Sold $20,000 in merchandise on MasterCard credit cards. The net cash receipts from sales are immediately deposited in the seller's bank account. MasterCard charges a 5% fee.
2. Sold $5,000 on an assortment of credit cards. Net cash receipts are received 10 days later, and a 4% fee is charged.

QS 10-3
Credit card sales

C1

On August 2, 2002, PSI Co. receives a $6,000, 90-day, 12% note from customer Tom Cather as payment on his account. Prepare journal entries for August 2 and for the note's maturity date assuming the note is honored by Cather.

QS 10-4
Note receivable P3 P4

Snyder Company's December 31 year-end unadjusted trial balance shows a $10,000 balance in Notes Receivable. This balance is from one 6% note dated December 1, with a period of 45 days. Prepare necessary journal entries for December 31 and for the note's maturity date assuming it is honored.

QS 10-5
Note receivable P3 P4

On April 18, Derek Co. made a short-term investment in 300 shares of Computer Advantage common stock. Their purchase price is $42.5 per share and the broker's fee is $250. The intent is to actively manage these shares. On June 30, Derek Co. receives $1 per share from Computer Advantage in dividends. Prepare the April 18 and June 30 journal entries.

QS 10-6
Short-term equity investments C4

Cooper Co. purchases short-term investments in available-for-sale securities at a cost of $50,000 on November 25, 2002. At December 31, 2002, these securities had a market value of $47,000.

1. Prepare the December 31, 2002 year-end adjusting entry for these securities.
2. For each account in the entry for part (1), explain how it is reported in financial statements.
3. Prepare the April 6, 2003, entry when Cooper sells these securities for $52,000.

QS 10-7
Available-for-Sale Securities C4 P5

The following data are taken from the comparative balance sheets of Fuqua Co.:

	2002	2001
Accounts receivable......	$153,400	$138,500
Net sales.............	854,200	910,600

Compute the accounts receivable turnover for year 2002.

EXERCISES

Exercise 10-1

Accounts receivable
subsidiary ledger

Taku Company recorded the following transactions during November 2002:

Nov. 5	Accounts Receivable—Paint Shop	4,615	
	Sales		4,615
10	Accounts Receivable—Cool Enterprises	1,350	
	Sales		1,350
13	Accounts Receivable—Matt Mahoney	832	
	Sales		832
21	Sales Returns and Allowances	209	
	Accounts Receivable—Matt Mahoney		209
30	Accounts Receivable—Paint Shop	2,713	
	Sales		2,713

1. Open a general ledger having T-accounts for Accounts Receivable, Sales, and Sales Returns and Allowances. Also open a subsidiary accounts receivable ledger having a T-account for each customer. Post these entries to both the general ledger and the accounts receivable ledger.

2. Prepare a schedule of accounts receivable (see Exhibit 10.4) and compare its total with the balance of the Accounts Receivable controlling account as of November 30.

Exercise 10-2

Allowance for doubtful
accounts entries

At year-end, Cayman Company estimates its bad debts as 0.5% of its $975,000 of annual credit sales. On December 31, Cayman adjusts its Allowance for Doubtful Accounts for that amount. On the following February 1, Cayman decides the $580 account of P. Snoop is uncollectible and writes it off as a bad debt. On June 5, Snoop unexpectedly pays the amount previously written off. Prepare the journal entries of Cayman to record these events.

Exercise 10-3

Percent of accounts
receivable method

At year-end, Bayoo Supply Co. uses the percent of accounts receivable method to estimate bad debts. On December 31, 2002, it has outstanding accounts receivable of $55,000, and it estimates that 2% will be uncollectible. Give the entry to record bad debts expense for year 2002 under the assumption that the Allowance for Doubtful Accounts has (1) a $415 credit balance before the adjustment and (2) a $291 debit balance before the adjustment.

Exercise 10-4

Selling and pledging accounts
receivable

On June 30, Koby Co. has $128,700 of accounts receivable. Prepare journal entries to record the following July transactions. Also prepare any footnotes to the July 31 financial statements that result from these transactions.

July 4   Sold $7,245 of merchandise to customers on credit.
      9   Sold $20,000 of accounts receivable to Nations Bank. Nations charges a 4% fee.
      17 Received $5,859 cash from customers in payment on their accounts.
      27 Borrowed $10,000 cash from Nations Bank, pledging $12,500 of accounts receivable as security for the loan.

Busch Company allows customers to use two credit cards in charging purchases. With the NuWay Card, Busch receives an immediate credit when it deposits sales receipts in its checking account. NuWay Card assesses a 4% service charge for credit card sales. The second credit card that Busch accepts is the Continental Bank Card. Busch sends its accumulated receipts to Continental Bank on a weekly basis and is paid by Continental about 10 days later. Continental Bank charges 2.5% of sales for using its card. Prepare journal entries to record the following selected credit card transactions of Busch Company:

Apr. 8   Sold merchandise for $8,400 accepting the customer's NuWay Card. At the end of the day, the NuWay receipts are deposited in Busch's account at the bank.

   12   Sold merchandise for $5,602, accepting the customer's Continental Bank Card. Transferred $5,602 of credit card receipts to Continental Bank, requesting payment.

   20   Received Continental Bank's check for the April 12 billing, less the service charge.

Exercise 10-5
Credit card sales

Prepare journal entries for the following selected transactions of Chandra Company:

2002

Dec. 13   Accepted a $9,600, 60-day, 8% note dated this day in granting Tom Alcox a time extension on his past-due account receivable.

   31   Made an adjusting entry to record the accrued interest on the Alcox note.

   31   Closed the Interest Revenue account to Income Summary.

2003

Feb. 14   Received Alcox's payment for principal and interest on the note dated December 13.

Mar. 2   Accepted a $5,000, 10%, 90-day note dated this day in granting a time extension on the past-due account receivable of BAX Company.

   17   Accepted a $1,800, 30-day, 9% note dated this day in granting Bill Connors a time extension on his past-due account receivable.

Apr. 16   Connors dishonors his note when presented for payment.

May 1   Wrote off the Connors account against the Allowance for Doubtful Accounts.

June 10   Received the BAX payment for principal and interest on the note dated March 2.

Exercise 10-6
Notes receivable transactions and entries

Prepare journal entries to record these selected transactions for Venus Company:

Nov. 1   Accepts a $6,000, 180-day, 8% note dated today from Shelia Denton in granting a time extension on her past-due account receivable.

Dec. 31   Adjusts the accounts for the accrued interest earned on the Denton note.

Apr. 30   Denton honors her note when presented for payment.

Exercise 10-7
Honoring a note

Prepare journal entries to record the following selected transactions of Warren Company:

Mar. 21   Accepts a $2,500, 180-day, 8% note dated today from Tina Adams in granting a time extension on her past-due account receivable.

Sept. 17   Adams dishonors her note when it is presented for payment.

Dec. 31   After exhausting all legal means of collection, Warren Company writes off Adams's account against the Allowance for Doubtful Accounts.

Exercise 10-8
Dishonoring a note

Prepare journal entries to record the following transactions involving the short-term investments of Morford Co., all of which occurred during year 2002:

a. On February 15, paid $120,000 cash to purchase $120,000 of MRI's 90-day short-term debt securities, which are dated February 15 and pay 8% interest.

b. On March 22, bought 700 shares of GRE Company stock at $27.50 plus a $150 brokerage fee.

c. On May 16, received a check from MRI in payment of the principal and 90 days' interest on the debt securities purchased in transaction *a*.

d. On August 1, paid $80,000 cash to purchase $80,000 of Flash Electronics' 10% debt securities, dated July 30, 2002, and maturing January 30, 2003.

e. On September 1, received a $1.00 per share cash dividend on the GRE Company stock purchased in transaction *b*.

Exercise 10-9
Short-term investment transactions

f. On October 8, sold 350 shares of GRE Co. stock for $34 per share, less a $140 brokerage fee.

g. On October 30, received a check from Flash Electronics for 90 days' interest on the debt securities purchased in transaction *d*.

Exercise 10-10
Trading securities

Focus Co. purchases short-term investments in trading securities at a cost of $66,000 on December 27, 2002. At December 31, 2002, these securities had a market value of $72,000.

1. Prepare the December 31, 2002, year-end adjusting entry for these securities.
2. For each account in the entry for part (1), explain how it is reported in financial statements.
3. Prepare the January 3, 2003, entry when Focus sells one-half of these securities for $35,000.

Exercise 10-11
Market values of short-term investments

On December 31, 2002, Quaker Company held the following short-term investments in its securities available-for-sale:

	Cost	Market Value
T.R. Rowe Company common stock	$38,200	$42,100
Valdez Corporation bonds payable	51,400	49,500
Transunion Corporation notes payable	70,600	62,900
Lake Placid Company common stock	86,500	83,100

Quaker had no short-term investments in its prior accounting periods. Prepare the December 31, 2002, adjusting entry to record the market value of these investments.

Exercise 10-12
Accounts receivable turnover

The following information is from the annual financial statements of Whipple Company:

	2003	2002	2001
Net sales	$405,000	$336,000	$388,000
Accounts receivable (December 31)	44,800	41,400	34,800

Compute Whipple's accounts receivable turnover for 2002 and 2003. Compare the two results and give a possible explanation for any major change.

PROBLEM SET A

Problem 10-1A
Estimating bad debts

On December 31, 2002, MidComm's records show the following results for the year:

Cash sales	$1,905,000
Credit sales	5,682,000

In addition, its unadjusted trial balance includes the following items:

Accounts receivable	$1,270,100 debit
Allowance for doubtful accounts	16,580 debit

Required

1. Prepare the adjusting entry for MidComm to recognize bad debts under each of the following independent assumptions:
   a. Bad debts are estimated to be 2% of credit sales.
   b. Bad debts are estimated to be 1% of total sales.
   c. Analysis suggests 5% of accounts receivable at year-end are uncollectible.

2. Show how Accounts Receivable and the Allowance for Doubtful Accounts appear on the December 31, 2002, balance sheet given the facts in part (1a).

3. Show how Accounts Receivable and the Allowance for Doubtful Accounts appear on the December 31, 2002, balance sheet given the facts in part (1c).

Check   (1a) Bad Debts Expense, $113,640 Dr.

Hawkins Company has credit sales of $3.6 million for year 2002. On December 31, 2002, the company's Allowance for Doubtful Accounts has a credit balance of $14,500. Hawkins prepares a schedule of its December 31, 2002, accounts receivable by age. On the basis of past experience, it also estimates the percent of receivables in each age category that will become uncollectible. This information is summarized here:

Problem 10-2A

Aging accounts receivable

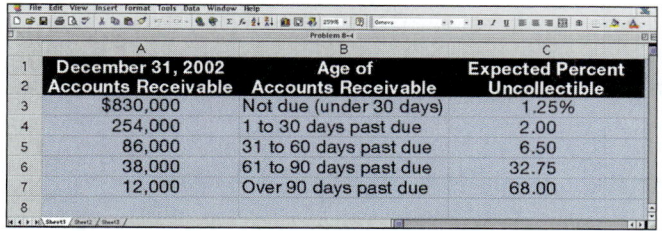

December 31, 2002 Accounts Receivable	Age of Accounts Receivable	Expected Percent Uncollectible
$830,000	Not due (under 30 days)	1.25%
254,000	1 to 30 days past due	2.00
86,000	31 to 60 days past due	6.50
38,000	61 to 90 days past due	32.75
12,000	Over 90 days past due	68.00

Required

Preparation Component

1. Estimate the amount needed in the Allowance for Doubtful Accounts at December 31, 2002, using the aging of accounts receivable method.

2. Prepare the journal entry to record bad debts expense at December 31, 2002.

Check   (2) Bad Debts Expense, $27,150 Dr.

Analysis Component

3. On June 30, 2003, Hawkins Company concludes that a customer's $4,750 receivable (created in 2002) is uncollectible and that the account should be written off. What effect will this action have on Hawkins' 2003 net income? Explain.

Heche Company began operations on January 1, 2002. During its first two years, the company completed a number of transactions involving sales on credit, accounts receivable collections, and bad debts. These transactions are summarized as follows:

Problem 10-3A

Accounts receivable transactions and bad debts adjustments

2002

a. Sold $1,345,400 of merchandise on credit, terms n/30.

b. Wrote off $18,300 of uncollectible accounts receivable.

c. Received $669,200 cash in payment of accounts receivable.

d. In adjusting the accounts on December 31, the company concluded that 1.5% of accounts receivable will be uncollectible.

2003

e. Sold $1,525,600 of merchandise on credit, terms n/30.

f. Wrote off $27,800 of uncollectible accounts receivable.

g. Received $1,204,666 cash in payment of accounts receivable.

h. In adjusting the accounts on December 31, the company concluded that 1.5% of accounts receivable will be uncollectible.

Check   (h) 2003 Bad Debts Expense, $32,197 Dr.

Required

Prepare journal entries to record Heche's 2002 and 2003 summarized transactions and its year-end adjustments to record bad debts expense.

American Co. allows select customers to make purchases on credit. The other customers can use either of two credit cards: Zip Bank or OneCharge. Zip Bank deducts a 3% service charge for sales on its credit card but credits the checking account of American immediately when credit card receipts are deposited. American deposits the Zip Bank credit card receipts at the close of each business day. When customers use OneCharge credit cards, American accumulates the receipts for several days before submitting them to OneCharge for payment. OneCharge deducts a 2% service charge and usually pays within one week of being billed. American completes the following transactions in the month of June. (The terms of all credit sales are 2/15, n/30, and all sales are recorded at the gross price.)

Problem 10-4A

Sales on credit and credit card sales

June 4   Sold $650 of merchandise on credit to Anne Klein.
     5   Sold merchandise for $6,900 to customers who used their Zip Bank credit cards.
     6   Sold merchandise for $5,872 to customers who used their OneCharge credit cards.
     8   Sold merchandise for $4,335 to customers who used their OneCharge credit cards.
    10   Submitted OneCharge card receipts accumulated since June 6 to the credit card company for payment.
    13   Wrote off the account of Mandy Smith against the Allowance for Doubtful Accounts. The $429 balance in Smith's account stemmed from a credit sale in October of last year.
    17   Received the amount due from OneCharge.
    18   Received Klein's check paying for the purchase of June 4.

Check   June 17, Dr. Cash $10,003

Required

Prepare journal entries to record the preceding transactions and events.

Problem 10-5A
Analyzing and journalizing
notes receivable transactions

The following selected transactions are from Van Dyken Company:

2002

Dec. 16   Accepted a $10,800, 60-day, 8% note dated this day in granting Roy Williams a time extension on his past-due account receivable.
    31   Made an adjusting entry to record the accrued interest on the Williams note.
    31   Closed the Interest Revenue account to Income Summary.

2003

Feb. 14   Received Williams' payment for principal and interest on the note dated December 16.
Mar. 2   Accepted a $6,120, 8%, 90-day note dated this day in granting a time extension on the past-due account receivable from DST Company.
    17   Accepted a $2,400, 30-day, 7% note dated this day in granting Penny Kleen a time extension on her past-due account receivable.
Apr. 16   Kleen dishonored her note when presented for payment.
    21   Discounted, with recourse, the DST Company note at BancFirst at a net interest cost of $60 (the $60 is the net of interest from note and the bank discount) receiving cash proceeds of $6,060.
June 2   Received notice from BancFirst that DST Company had dishonored the note due May 31. Paid the bank the principal plus interest due on the note. (*Hint:* Create an account receivable for the maturity value of the note.)
July 17   Received payment from DST Company for the maturity value of its dishonored note plus interest for 46 days beyond maturity at 8%.
Aug. 7   Accepted a $7,450, 90-day, 10% note dated this day in granting a time extension on the past-due account receivable of Mentzer and Oak.
Sept. 3   Accepted a $2,120, 60-day, 10% note dated this day in granting Keva Whitehouse a time extension on her past-due account receivable.
    18   Discounted, without recourse, the Whitehouse note at BancFirst at a net interest cost of $30 (the net of interest from note and the bank discount) receiving cash proceeds of $2,090.
Nov. 5   Received payment of principal plus interest from Mentzer and Oak for the note of August 7.
Dec. 1   Wrote off the Penny Kleen account against Allowance for Doubtful Accounts.

Check   April 21, Dr. Interest Expense $60

Required

Preparation Component

Prepare journal entries to record these transactions and events.

Analysis Component

What reporting is necessary when a business discounts notes receivable with recourse and these notes have not reached maturity by the end of the period? Explain the reason for this requirement and the accounting principle being satisfied.

Problem 10-6A
Short-term investment
transactions and entries

Elliott Company invests its idle cash in trading securities. The following transactions and events are from the company's short-term investment activity with its trading securities:

2002

Jan. 20   Purchased 800 shares of Ford Motor Co. at $26 per share plus a $125 commission.

| Feb. | 9 | Purchased 2,200 shares of Lucent Technology at $44.25 per share plus a $578 commission. |

Feb. 9   Purchased 2,200 shares of Lucent Technology at $44.25 per share plus a $578 commission.
Oct. 12   Purchased 750 shares of Z-Seven at $7.55 per share plus a $200 commission.

2003

Apr. 15   Sold 800 shares of Ford Motor Co. at $29 per share less a $285 commission.
July   5   Sold 750 shares of Z-Seven at $10.25 per share less a $102.50 commission.
      22   Purchased 1,600 shares of Hunt Corp. at $30 per share plus a $444 commission.
Aug. 19   Purchased 1,800 shares of Donna Karan at $8.15 per share plus a $290 commission.

2004

Feb. 27   Purchased 3,400 shares of HCA at $34 per share plus a $420 commission.
Mar.   3   Sold 1,600 shares of Hunt at $25 per share less a $250 commission.
June 21   Sold 2,200 shares of Lucent Technology at $42 per share less a $420 commission.
      30   Purchased 1,200 shares of Black & Decker at $47.50 per share plus a $595 commission.
Nov.   1   Sold 1,800 shares of Donna Karan at $18.25 per share less a $309 commission.

Required

1. Prepare journal entries to record these short-term investment activities for the years shown.

2. On December 31, 2004, prepare the adjusting entry to record the market value of these investments. On December 31, 2004, HCA's share price was $36 and Black & Decker's share price was $43.50.

Check Dr. Market Adjustment—Trading $985

Boca Company had no short-term investments prior to year 2002, but it had the following transactions involving short-term investments in available-for-sale securities during 2002:

Apr. 16   Purchased 4,000 shares of Gem Co. stock at $24.25 per share plus a $180 brokerage fee.
May   1   Paid $100,000 to buy 90-day U.S. Treasury bills (debt securities): $100,000 principal amount, 6% interest, dated May 1.
July   7   Purchased 2,000 shares of PepsiCo stock at $49.25 per share plus a $175 brokerage fee.
      20   Purchased 1,000 shares of Xerox stock at $16.75 per share plus a $205 brokerage fee.
Aug.   3   Received a check for principal and accrued interest on the U.S. Treasury bills that matured on July 29.
      15   Received an $0.85 per share cash dividend on the Gem Co. stock.
      28   Sold 2,000 shares of Gem Co. stock at $30 per share less a $225 brokerage fee.
Oct.   1   Received a $1.90 per share cash dividend on the PepsiCo shares.
Dec. 15   Received a $1.05 per share cash dividend on the remaining Gem Co. stock owned.
      31   Received a $1.30 per share cash dividend on the PepsiCo shares.
      31   Market values per share are Gem Co., $26.50; PepsiCo, $46.50; and Xerox, $13.75.

Problem 10-7A
Short-term investment transactions and entries

C4 P5

G S

Required

Preparation Component

1. Prepare journal entries to record these preceding transactions and events.

2. Prepare a schedule to compare the cost and market values of Boca's short-term investments in available-for-sale securities.

3. Prepare an adjusting entry, if necessary, to record the market adjustment to the short-term investments in available-for-sale securities.

Check (3) Dr. Unrealized Loss—Equity $4,470

Analysis Component

4. Explain the balance sheet presentation of a market adjustment to short-term investments.

5. How do these short-term investments affect Boca's income statement for year 2002 and the equity section of its balance sheet at the end of year 2002?

On December 31, 2002, Sherman Service Co.'s records show the following results for the year:

Cash sales	$1,025,000
Credit sales	1,342,000

PROBLEM SET B

Problem 10-1B
Estimating bad debts

In addition, its unadjusted trial balance includes the following items:

Accounts receivable	$575,000 debit
Allowance for doubtful accounts	7,500 credit

Required

1. Prepare the adjusting entry for Sherman Service Co. to recognize bad debts under each of the following independent assumptions:

    a. Bad debts are estimated to be 2.5% of credit sales.

    b. Bad debts are estimated to be 1.5% of total sales.

    c. Analysis suggests 6% of accounts receivable at year-end are uncollectible.

2. Show how Accounts Receivable and the Allowance for Doubtful Accounts appear on the December 31, 2002, balance sheet given the facts in part (1a).

3. Show how Accounts Receivable and the Allowance for Doubtful Accounts appear on the December 31, 2002, balance sheet given the facts in part (1c).

Check   (1b) Bad debts expense, $35,505

Problem 10-2B

Aging accounts receivable

Quest Company has credit sales of $4.5 million for year 2002. On December 31, 2002, the company's Allowance for Doubtful Accounts has a debit balance of $3,400. Quest prepares a schedule of its December 31, 2002, accounts receivable by age. On the basis of past experience, it also estimates the percent of receivables in each age category that will become uncollectible. This information is summarized here:

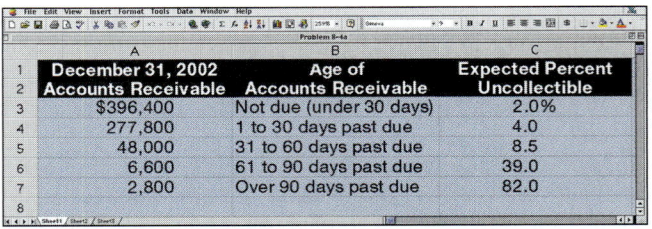

December 31, 2002 Accounts Receivable	Age of Accounts Receivable	Expected Percent Uncollectible
$396,400	Not due (under 30 days)	2.0%
277,800	1 to 30 days past due	4.0
48,000	31 to 60 days past due	8.5
6,600	61 to 90 days past due	39.0
2,800	Over 90 days past due	82.0

Required

Preparation Component

1. Compute the amount needed in the Allowance for Doubtful Accounts at December 31, 2002, using the aging of accounts receivable method.

2. Prepare the journal entry to record bad debts expense at December 31, 2002.

Check   (2) Bad Debts Expense, $31,390 Dr.

Analysis Component

3. On July 31, 2003, Quest concludes that a customer's $3,455 receivable (created in 2002) is uncollectible and that the account should be written off. What effect will this action have on Quest's 2003 net income? Explain.

Problem 10-3B

Accounts receivable transactions and bad debts adjustments

Wergeles Co. began operations on January 1, 2002, and completed several transactions during 2002 and 2003 that involve sales on credit, accounts receivable collections, and bad debts. These transactions are summarized as follows:

2002

    a. Sold $685,320 of merchandise on credit, terms n/30.

    b. Received $482,300 cash in payment of accounts receivable.

    c. Wrote off $9,350 of uncollectible accounts receivable.

    d. In adjusting the accounts on December 31, the company concluded that 1% of accounts receivable will be uncollectible.

2003

    e. Sold $870,200 of merchandise on credit, terms n/30.

    f. Received $990,800 cash in payment of accounts receivable.

g. Wrote off $11,090 of uncollectible accounts receivable.

h. In adjusting the accounts on December 31, the company concludes that 1% of accounts receivable will be uncollectible.

Check (h) 2003 Bad Debts
Expense, $9,773.10 Dr.

Required

Prepare journal entries to record the 2002 and 2003 summarized transactions of Wergeles Co. along with its year-end adjusting entry to record bad debts expense.

King Supply Co. allows select customers to make purchases on credit. The other customers can use either of two credit cards: Commerce Bank or Via. Commerce Bank deducts a 3% service charge for sales on its credit card but immediately credits the checking account of King when credit card receipts are deposited. King deposits the Commerce Bank credit card receipts at the close of each business day. When customers use the Via card, King accumulates the receipts for several days and then submits them to Via for payment. Via deducts a 2% service charge and usually pays within one week of being billed. King completed the following transactions in August (terms of all credit sales are 2/10, n/30; and all sales are recorded at the gross price).

Problem 10-4B

Sales on credit and credit card sales

Aug. 4   Sold $3,700 of merchandise on credit to Tess Wright.
10   Sold merchandise for $5,200 to customers who used their Commerce Bank credit cards.
11   Sold merchandise for $1,250 to customers who used their Via cards.
14   Received Wright's check paying for the purchase of August 4.
15   Sold merchandise for $3,240 to customers who used their Via cards.
18   Submitted Via card receipts accumulated since August 11 to the credit card company for payment.
22   Wrote off the account of Silver City against the Allowance for Doubtful Accounts. The $498 balance in Silver City's account stemmed from a credit sale in November of last year.
25   Received the amount due from Via.

Check Aug. 25, Dr. Cash $4,400

Required

Prepare journal entries to record the preceding transactions and events.

The following selected transactions are from Cruiser Company:

Problem 10-5B

Analyzing and journalizing notes receivable transactions

2002

Nov. 1   Accepted a $4,800, 90-day, 10% note dated this day in granting Terry Mullen a time extension on her past-due account receivable.
Dec. 31   Made an adjusting entry to record the accrued interest on the Mullen note.
31   Closed the Interest Revenue account to Income Summary.

2003

Jan. 30   Received Mullen's payment for principal and interest on the note dated November 1.
Feb. 28   Accepted a $12,600, 8%, 30-day note dated this day in granting a time extension on the past-due account receivable from Coffey Co.
Mar. 1   Accepted a $6,200, 60-day, 12% note dated this day in granting Staci Case a time extension on her past-due account receivable.
23   Discounted, without recourse, the Case note at Firstar Bank at a net interest cost of $60 (the net of interest from note and the bank discount) receiving cash proceeds of $6,140.
30   The Coffey Co. dishonored its note when presented for payment.
June 15   Accepted a $2,000, 60-day, 8% note dated this day in granting a time extension on the past-due account receivable of Sarah Morris.
21   Accepted a $9,500, 90-day, 14% note dated this day in granting Vinnie May a time extension on his past-due account receivable.
July 5   Discounted, with recourse, the V. May note at Firstar Bank at a net interest cost of $200 (the net of interest from note and the bank discount) receiving cash proceeds of $9,300.
Aug. 14   Received payment of principal plus interest from Morris for the note of June 15.
Sept. 25   Received notice from Firstar Bank that the V. May note had been paid.
Nov. 30   Wrote off Coffey Co.'s account against Allowance for Doubtful Accounts.

Check March 23, Dr. Interest Expense $60

Required

Preparation Component

Prepare journal entries to record these transactions and events.

Analysis Component

What reporting is necessary when a business discounts notes receivable with recourse and these notes have not reached maturity by the end of the period? Explain the reason for this requirement and the accounting principle being satisfied.

Problem 10-6B

Short-term investment transactions and entries

Dryfus Enterprises invests its idle cash in trading securities. The following transactions and events relate to the company's short-term investment activity with its trading securities.

2002

Mar. 10	Purchased 2,400 shares of AOL at $59.15 per share plus a $1,545 commission.
May 7	Purchased 5,000 shares of Motorola at $36.25 per share plus a $2,855 commission.
Sept. 1	Purchased 1,200 shares of UPS at $57.25 per share plus a $1,250 commission.

2003

Apr. 26	Sold 5,000 shares of Motorola at $34.50 per share less a $2,050 commission.
27	Sold 1,200 shares of UPS at $60.50 per share less a $1,788 commission.
June 2	Purchased 3,600 shares of SPW Int'l. at $172 per share plus a $3,250 commission.
14	Purchased 900 shares of Wal-Mart at $50.25 per share plus a $1,082 commission.

2004

Jan. 28	Purchased 2,000 shares of PepsiCo at $43 per share plus a $2,890 commission.
31	Sold 3,600 shares of SPW at $168 per share less a $2,040 commission.
Aug. 22	Sold 2,400 shares of AOL at $56.75 per share less a $2,480 commission.
Sept. 3	Purchased 1,500 shares of Vodaphone at $40.50 per share plus a $1,680 commission.
Oct. 9	Sold 900 shares of Wal-Mart at $53.75 per share less a $1,220 commission.

Required

1. Prepare journal entries to record these short-term investment activities for the years shown.

Check Cr. Market Adjustment—
Trading $13,820

2. On December 31, 2004, prepare the adjusting entry to record the market value of these investments. On December 31, 2004 PepsiCo's share price was $41 and Vodaphone's share price was $37.

Problem 10-7B

Short-term investment transactions and entries

Corbin Systems had no short-term investments on December 31, 2001, but it had the following transactions involving short-term investments in available-for-sale securities during 2002.

Feb. 6	Purchased 3,400 shares of Nokia stock at $41.25 per share plus a $3,000 brokerage fee.
15	Paid $20,000 to buy six-month U.S. Treasury bills (debt securities): $20,000 principal amount, 6% interest, dated February 15.
Apr. 7	Purchased 1,200 shares of Dell Co. stock at $39.50 per share plus a $1,255 brokerage fee.
June 2	Purchased 2,500 shares of Merck stock at $72.50 per share plus a $3,890 brokerage fee.
30	Received a $0.19 per share cash dividend on the Nokia shares.
Aug. 11	Sold 850 shares of Nokia stock at $46 per share less a $1,050 brokerage fee.
16	Received a check for principal and accrued interest on the U.S. Treasury bills purchased February 15.
24	Received a $0.10 per share cash dividend on the Dell shares.
Nov. 9	Received a $0.20 per share cash dividend on the remaining Nokia shares.
Dec. 18	Received a $0.15 per share cash dividend on the Dell shares.
31	Market values per share are Nokia, $40.25; Dell, $40.50; and Merck, $59.

Required

Preparation Component

1. Prepare journal entries to record these preceding transactions and events.

2. Prepare a schedule to compare the cost and market values of the short-term investments in available-for-sale securities.

3. Prepare an adjusting entry, if necessary, to record the market adjustment to the short-term investments account in available-for-sale securities.

Analysis Component

4. Explain the balance sheet presentation of a market adjustment to short-term investments.

5. How do these short-term investments affect its income statement for year 2002 and the equity section of its balance sheet at the end of year 2002?

Check (3) Dr. Unrealized Loss—Equity, $42,495

Beyond the Numbers

BTN 10-1   Refer to **Nike**'s financial statements in Appendix A to answer the following:

1. What is the amount of accounts receivable (net) on May 31, 2000?

2. Nike's most liquid assets include "cash and equivalents" and "accounts receivable." Compute its most liquid assets as of May 31, 2000, as a percent of current liabilities. Do the same for May 31, 1999. Comment on the company's ability to satisfy current liabilities at the end of the fiscal year 2000 as compared to the end of fiscal year 1999.

3. What criteria did Nike use to classify items as cash equivalents?

4. Compute Nike's accounts receivable turnover as of May 31, 2000.

Swoosh Ahead

5. Access Nike's annual report for fiscal years ending after May 31, 2000, at its Web site [**www.nike.com**] or the SEC's EDGAR database [**www.sec.gov**]. Recompute parts (2) and (4) and comment on any changes since May 31, 2000.

Reporting in Action

A1

NIKE

BTN 10-2   Key comparative figures ($ in millions) for both **Nike** and **Reebok** follow:

Key Figures	Nike Current Year	Nike One-Year Prior	Nike Two-Years Prior	Reebok Current Year	Reebok One-Year Prior	Reebok Two-Years Prior
Allowance for doubtful accounts	$ 65.4	$ 73.2	$ 71.4	$ 46.2	$ 47.4	$ 44.0
Accounts receivable, net . .	1,567.2	1,540.1	1,674.4	417.4	517.8	561.7
Net sales	8,995.1	8,776.9	9,553.1	2,891.2	3,205.4	3,643.6

Comparative Analysis

A1 P2

NIKE

Required

1. Compute the accounts receivable turnover for both Nike and Reebok for each of the two most recent years using the data shown.

2. Using results from part (1), compute how many days it takes each company, *on average*, to collect receivables.

3. Which company is more efficient in collecting its accounts receivable?

4. Which company estimates a higher percent of uncollectible accounts receivable?

BTN 10-3   Susie Norton is the manager of a medium-size company. A few years ago, Susie persuaded the owner to base a part of her compensation on the net income the company earns each year. Each December Susie estimates year-end financial figures in anticipation of the bonus she will receive. If the bonus is not as high as she would like, she offers several recommendations to the accountant for year-end adjustments. One of her favorite recommendations is for the controller to reduce the estimate of doubtful accounts.

Ethics Challenge

P1 P2

Required

1. What effect does lowering the estimate for doubtful accounts have on the income statement and balance sheet?

2. Do you think Susie's recommendation to adjust the allowance for doubtful accounts is within her right as manager, or do you think this action is an ethics violation? Justify your response.

3. What type of internal control(s) might be useful for this company in overseeing the manager's recommendations for accounting changes?

Communicating in Practice

BTN 10-4   As the accountant for Bel-Air Distributing, you attend a sales managers' meeting devoted to a discussion of credit policies. At the meeting, you report that bad debts expense is estimated to be $59,000 and accounts receivable at year-end amount to $1,750,000 less a $43,000 allowance for doubtful accounts. Stan Waters, a sales manager, expresses confusion over why bad debts expense and the allowance for doubtful accounts are different amounts. Write a one-page memorandum to him explaining why a difference in bad debts expense and the allowance for doubtful accounts is not unusual. The company estimates bad debts expense as 2% of sales.

Taking It to the Net

BTN 10-5   Access the September 28, 1999, 10-K Filing of **Microsoft** (MSFT) at **www.edgar-online.com.** Identify Microsoft's equity and other investments footnote.

Required

1. As of June 30, 1999, did Microsoft's debt securities that were recorded at market show a net unrealized gain or net unrealized loss? What was the amount of this gain or loss?

2. As of June 30, 1999, did Microsoft's equity securities that were recorded at market show a net unrealized gain or net unrealized loss? What was the amount of this gain or loss?

3. Identify two common stocks that Microsoft had in its investment portfolio as of June 30, 1999.

Teamwork in Action

P2

BTN 10-6   Each member of a team is to participate in estimating uncollectibles using the aging schedule and percents shown in Problem 10-2A. The division of labor is up to the team. Your goal is to accurately complete this task as soon as possible. After estimating uncollectibles, check your estimate with the instructor. If the team's estimate is correct, the team then should prepare the adjusting entry and the presentation of net realizable accounts receivable for the December 31, 2002, balance sheet.

Business Week Activity

P1 C1

BTN 10-7   Read the article "For CFS, Bad Debts Are Sweet Profits" in the August 11, 1997, issue of *Business Week*.

Required

1. How does CFS make money by collecting bad debts for others?

2. What was CFS's net margin in 1996? Why is the margin so large?

3. Who are CFS's main competitors?

4. To what does CFS's CEO attribute the company's success?

Entrepreneurial Decision

BTN 10-8   Kimberly Mills operates Musician Memorabilia, a merchandising business that buys and sells souvenirs and mementos linked with contemporary musicians. Mills accepts only cash from buyers. Her monthly cash sales are $25,000, with a net profit margin of 30%. However, buyers are increasingly requesting either to use credit cards with their purchases or to buy on credit. Therefore, Mills has decided to pursue one of two plans (neither plan will impact cash sales nor alter current costs as a percent of sales):

Plan A. *Mills accepts credit cards.* This plan is expected to yield new credit sales equal to 20% of current cash sales. Cost estimates of this plan as a percent of net credit sales are: credit card fee, 4.8%; recordkeeping, 1.2%.

Plan B. *Mills grants credit directly to qualified buyers.* This plan is expected to yield new credit sales equal to 24% of current cash sales. Cost estimates of this plan as a percent of net credit sales are: uncollectibles, 6.7%; collection expenses, 1.3%; recordkeeping, 2.0%.

Required

1. Compute the added monthly net income (loss) expected under (a) Plan A and (b) Plan B.
2. Should Mills pursue either plan? Discuss the financial and nonfinancial factors relevant to this decision.

11

Plant Assets, Natural Resources, and Intangibles

A Look Back

Chapters 9 and 10 focused on short-term assets: cash, cash equivalents, receivables, and short-term investments. We explained why they are known as liquid assets and described how companies account and report for them.

A Look at This Chapter

This chapter introduces us to long-term assets, including plant assets, natural resource assets, and intangible assets. We explain how to record a long-term asset's cost, the allocation of an asset's cost to periods benefiting from it, the recording of additional asset costs after an asset is purchased, and the disposal of an asset.

A Look Ahead

Chapter 12 introduces us to both current and long-term liabilities. We explain how they are computed, recorded, and reported in financial statements. We also explain accounting for payroll.

"What everybody else did was overlook the obvious."—John Schnatter

No Stoppa′ da Papa

e LOUISVILLE, KY—It began with vision, determination, and a sledge-hammer. While running Mick's Tavern, a bar owned by his father in their hometown of Jeffersonville, Ind., 22-year-old John Schnatter knocked down a broom closet with a sledgehammer and installed a pizza oven. As a teenager, he had worked at several pizzerias, learning the art of pizza making. Now it was Schnatter's chance to show everyone he could make a better pizza. His pizza business soon outgrew the tavern. Today, his pizza company, **Papa John's** (**www.PapaJohns.com**), commands 5% of the market, trailing only Pizza Hut and Domino's.

Being a little company among giants, Schnatter had to do more with less. He began with just $1,600 cash and sold 300 to 400 pizzas a week. To save on rent, he slept in the back room of the pizzeria. "You have to keep things simple and focused," says Schnatter. This translates into selling only core products—pizza, breadsticks, cheesesticks, and soft drinks. Schnatter's skill at managing plant assets and intangibles has led to a regular 20 to 40 percent growth in both sales and income. Whereas competitors often earn under $2 in sales per dollar of assets, Papa John's earns about $2.20 in sales per dollar of assets. Schnatter also works at managing two other assets—employees and brand loyalty. His company's mission statements declare that "people are our most important [unrecorded] asset" and that the company "will create superior brand loyalty [intangible asset]." This focus on asset management is a winning recipe for Papa John's.

What's next? Schnatter proclaims, "The stage is set for us to become the No. 1 pizza brand in the world!" To do that, Schnatter must manage plant asset growth, being sure to cover depreciation while not cutting into profits. He must also manage repairs and additions to restaurant equipment and build-ings. With success, annual revenues are likely to approach $1 billion. There aren't many pizzerias with dough that rises like that! [Sources: *Papa John's Web Site,* May 2001; *Time,* October 26, 1998; *Entrepreneur,* November 1997]

Learning Objectives

Conceptual

C1 Describe plant assets and issues in accounting for them.

C2 Explain depreciation and the factors affecting its computation.

C3 Explain depreciation for partial years and changes in estimates.

C4 Identify cash flow impacts of long-term asset transactions.

Analytical

A1 Compare and analyze depreciation for different methods.

A2 Compute total asset turnover and apply it to analyze a company's use of assets.

Procedural

P1 Apply the cost principle to compute the cost of plant assets.

P2 Compute and record depreciation using the straight-line, units-of-production, and declining-balance methods.

P3 Distinguish between revenue and capital expenditures, and account for these expenditures.

P4 Account for asset disposal through discarding, selling, and exchanging an asset.

P5 Account for natural resource assets and their depletion.

P6 Account for intangible assets and their amortization.

Chapter Preview

This chapter focuses on long-term assets used in the operation of a company. These assets can be grouped into plant assets, natural resource assets, and intangible assets. Plant assets are a major investment for most companies. They make up a large part of assets on most balance sheets, and they yield depreciation, often one of the largest expenses on income statements. They also affect the statement of cash flows when cash is paid to acquire plant assets or is received from their sale. When companies acquire or build a plant asset, it is often referred to as a *capital expenditure*. Capital expenditures are important events because they impact both the short- and long-term success of a company. Natural resource assets and intangible assets have similar impacts. Because of these and other reasons, it is important that we understand the accounting for and analysis of these assets. This chapter describes the purchase and use of these assets. We also explain what distinguishes these assets from other types of assets, how to determine their cost, how to allocate their costs to periods benefiting from their use, and how to dispose of them.

Section 1— Plant Assets

C1 Describe plant assets and issues in accounting for them.

Plant assets are tangible assets used in a company's operations that have a useful life of more than one accounting period. Plant assets are also called *plant and equipment; property, plant, and equipment;* and *fixed assets.* For many companies, plant assets make up the single largest asset they own. Exhibit 11.1 shows plant assets as a percent of total assets for several companies. They make up a large percent of these companies' assets, and their dollar values are large. **McDonald's** plant assets, for instance, are reported at more than $16 billion, and **Wal-Mart** reports plant assets of more than $32 billion.

Exhibit 11.1

Plant Assets of Selected Companies

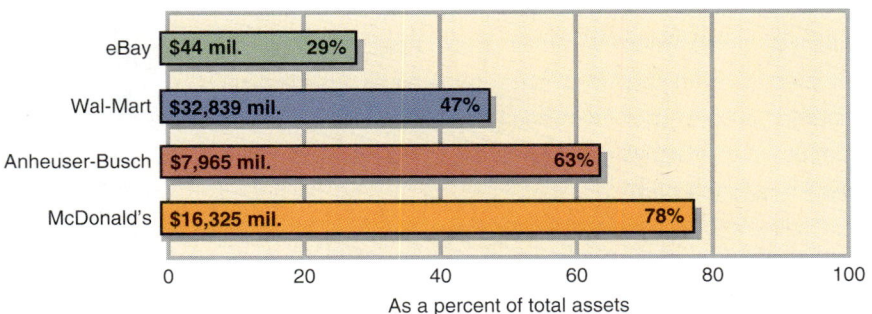

As a percent of total assets

Concept 11-1

Point: Amazon.Com's plant assets of $318 million make up 13% of its total assets, and Priceline.Com's plant assets of $28 million make up 6% of its total assets.

Plant assets are set apart from other assets by two important features. First, *plant assets are used in operations.* This makes them different from, for instance, inventory that is held for sale and not used in operations. The distinctive feature here is use, not type of asset. A company that purchases a computer for purposes of reselling it reports it on the balance sheet as inventory. If the same company purchases this computer to use in operations, however, it is a plant asset. Another example is a long-term investment such as land held for future expansion. However, if this land holds a factory used in operations, the land is part of plant assets. Another example is equipment held for use in the event of a breakdown or for peak periods of production. This equipment is reported in plant assets. If this same equipment is removed from use and held for sale, however, it is not reported in plant assets.

The second important feature is that *plant assets have useful lives extending over more than one accounting period.* This makes plant assets different from current assets such as supplies that are usually consumed in a short time after they are placed in use. The cost of current assets is assigned to that one period when they are used. Many prepaid expenses are distinguished from plant assets by the length of their useful lives.

Point: It often helps to view plant assets as prepaid expenses that benefit several future accounting periods.

The accounting for plant assets reflects these two important features. Since plant assets are used in operations, we try to match their costs against the revenues they generate. Also, since plant assets' useful lives extend over more than one period, our matching of costs and revenues must extend over several periods. We measure plant assets (balance sheet effect) and allocate assets' cost to periods benefiting from their use (income statement effect).

Exhibit 11.2 shows four main accounting issues with plant assets:

1. Compute the costs of plant assets.
2. Allocate the costs of plant assets (less any salvage amounts) against revenues for the periods they benefit.
3. Account for expenditures such as repairs and improvements to plant assets.
4. Record the disposal of plant assets.

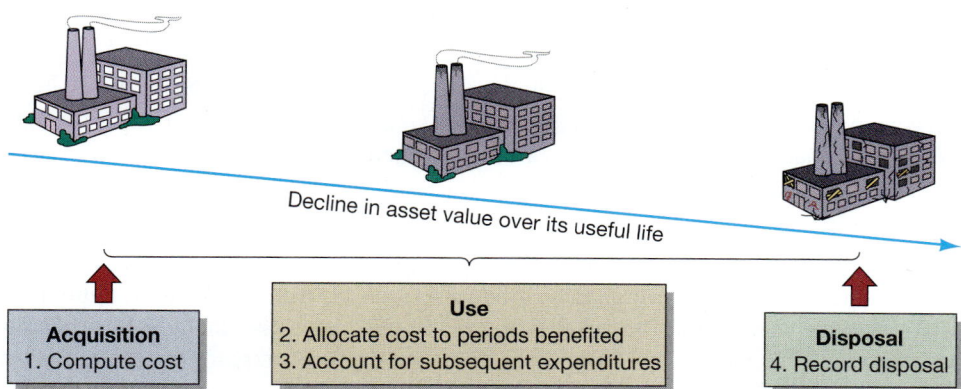

Exhibit 11.2

Issues in Accounting for Plant Assets

This chapter focuses on the decisions and factors surrounding each of these four important accounting issues.

Cost of Plant Assets

Plant assets are recorded at cost when purchased. This is consistent with the *cost principle.* **Cost** includes all normal and reasonable expenditures necessary to get the asset in place and ready for its intended use. The cost of a factory machine, for instance, includes its invoice price less any cash discount for early payment, plus any necessary freight, unpacking, and assembling costs. A plant asset's cost also includes any necessary costs to install and test it before placing it in use. Examples are the costs of building a base or foundation for a machine, providing electrical hook-ups, and adjusting the asset before using it in operations.

To be charged to and reported as part of the cost of a plant asset, an expenditure must be normal, reasonable, and necessary in preparing it for its intended use. If an asset is damaged during unpacking, the repairs are not added to its cost. Instead, they are charged to an expense account. Nor is a traffic fine paid for moving heavy machinery on city streets without a proper permit part of the machinery's cost, but payment for a proper permit is included in the cost of machinery. Charges in addition to the purchase price are sometimes incurred to modify or customize a new plant asset. These charges are added to the asset's cost. We explain in this section how to determine the cost of plant assets for each of the four major classes of plant assets.

P1 Apply the cost principle to compute the cost of plant assets.

Global: Many countries including Switzerland, Brazil, the Netherlands, and the United Kingdom permit asset revaluations under certain conditions. This is a deviation from the cost principle.

Land

When land is purchased for a building site, its cost includes the total amount paid for the land, including any real estate commissions. Its cost also includes fees for insuring the title, legal fees, and any accrued property taxes paid by the purchaser. Payments for surveying, clearing, grading, draining, and landscaping also are included in the cost of land. Other costs include local government assessments, whether incurred at the time of purchase or later, for items such as public roadways, sewers, and sidewalks. These assessments are included because they permanently add to the land's value.

Land purchased as a building site sometimes includes structures that must be removed. In such cases, the total purchase price is charged to the Land account along with the cost of removing the structures, less any amounts recovered through sale of salvaged materials. To illustrate, assume **Gap** paid $167,000 cash to acquire land for a retail store. This land contains an old service garage that is removed at a net cost of $13,000 ($15,000 in costs

Exhibit 11.3

Computing Cost of Land

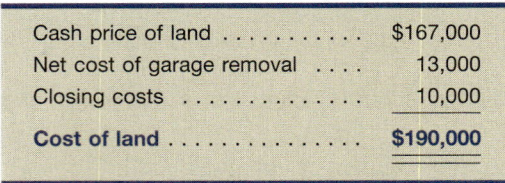

Cash price of land	$167,000
Net cost of garage removal	13,000
Closing costs	10,000
Cost of land	**$190,000**

less $2,000 proceeds from salvaged materials). Additional closing costs total $10,000, consisting of brokerage fees ($8,000), legal fees ($1,500), and title costs ($500). The cost of this land to Gap is $190,000 and is computed as shown in Exhibit 11.3.

Land Improvements

Because land has an unlimited life and is not usually used up over time, it is not subject to depreciation. **Land improvements** such as parking lot surfaces, driveways, fences, and lighting systems, however, have limited useful lives and are used up. While the costs of these improvements increase the usefulness of the land, they are charged to a separate Land Improvement account so their costs can be allocated to the periods they benefit.

Buildings

A Building account is charged for the costs of purchasing or constructing a building that is used in operations. When purchased, a building's costs usually include its purchase price, brokerage fees, taxes, title fees, and attorney costs. Its costs also include all expenditures to make it ready for its intended use, including any necessary repairs or renovations such as wiring, lighting, flooring, and wall coverings.

When a company constructs a building or any plant asset for its own use, its costs include materials and labor plus a reasonable amount of indirect overhead cost. Overhead includes the costs of items such as heat, lighting, power, and depreciation on machinery used to construct the asset. Costs of construction also include design fees, building permits, and insurance during construction. **Amazon.com** reports more than $83 million of construction in progress for its plant assets. However, costs such as insurance to cover the asset *after* it is placed in use are operating expenses.

Machinery and Equipment

The costs of machinery and equipment consist of all costs normal and necessary to purchase them and prepare them for their intended use. These include the purchase price, taxes, transportation charges, insurance while in transit, and installing, assembling, and testing machinery and equipment. **Sony**, for instance, disclosed in a recent annual report that: "capital expenditures [most of this for machinery and equipment] during the year under review increased . . . Sony intends to further increase its capital expenditures."

Example: If appraised values in Exhibit 11.4 are land, $24,000; land improvements, $12,000; and building, $84,000, what cost is assigned to the building? *Answer* (3 steps):.

(1) $24,000 + $12,000 + $84,000 = $120,000 (total appraisal)

(2) $84,000/$120,000 = 70% (building's percent of total)

(3) 70% × $90,000 = $63,000 (building's apportioned cost)

Lump-Sum Purchase

Plant assets sometimes are purchased as a group in a single transaction for a lump-sum price. This transaction is called a *lump-sum purchase,* or *group, bulk,* or *basket purchase.* When this occurs, we allocate the cost of the purchase among the different types of assets acquired based on their *relative market values.* Their market values can be estimated by appraisal or by using the tax-assessed valuations of the assets. To illustrate, Cola Company paid $90,000 cash to acquire a group of items consisting of land appraised at $30,000, land improvements appraised at $10,000, and a building appraised at $60,000. The $90,000 cost is allocated on the basis of appraised values as shown in Exhibit 11.4.

Exhibit 11.4

Computing Costs in a Lump-Sum Purchase

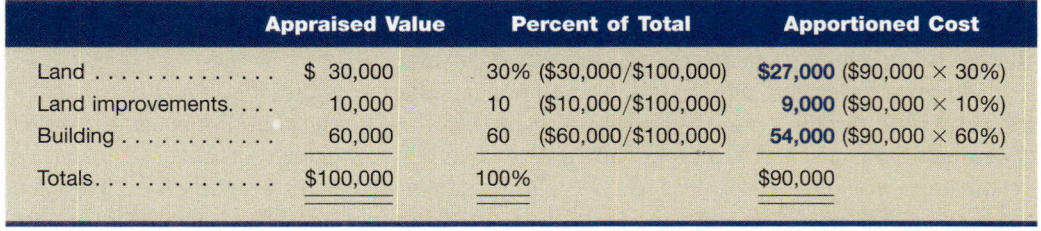

	Appraised Value	Percent of Total		Apportioned Cost
Land	$ 30,000	30%	($30,000/$100,000)	**$27,000** ($90,000 × 30%)
Land improvements. . . .	10,000	10	($10,000/$100,000)	**9,000** ($90,000 × 10%)
Building	60,000	60	($60,000/$100,000)	**54,000** ($90,000 × 60%)
Totals.	$100,000	100%		$90,000

Quick Check

1. Identify the asset category for each of the following: (a) office supplies, (b) office equipment, (c) merchandise, (d) land for future expansion, and (e) trucks used in operations.

2. Identify the account charged for each of the following: (a) purchase price of a vacant lot to be used in operations and (b) cost of paving that same vacant lot.

3. What amount is recorded as the cost of a new machine given the following payments related to its purchase: gross purchase price, $700,000; sales tax, $49,000; purchase discount taken, $21,000; freight to move machine to plant—terms FOB shipping point, $3,500; normal assembly costs, $3,000; cost of necessary foundation for machine, $2,500; cost of parts used in maintaining the machine, $4,200?

Answers—p. 464

Depreciation

We explained in the prior section that plant assets are tangible assets purchased to use in operations for more than one period. It is helpful to think of a plant asset as an amount of "usefulness" contributing to a company's operations throughout the asset's useful life. Because the lives of all plant assets other than land are limited, the amount of usefulness expires as an asset is used. This expiration of a plant asset's usefulness is called **depreciation,** which is the process of allocating the cost of a plant asset to expense in the accounting periods benefiting from its use. For instance, when a company buys a delivery truck to use as a plant asset, it acquires an amount of usefulness in the sense that it obtains a quantity of transportation. The total cost of this transportation is the cost of the truck less the proceeds expected to be received when the truck is sold or traded in at the end of its useful life. This net cost is allocated to the periods that benefit from the truck's use. This allocation of the truck's cost is depreciation.

Note that depreciation does not measure the decline in the truck's market value each period, nor does it measure the truck's physical deterioration. Depreciation is a process of allocating a plant asset's cost to expense over its useful life, nothing more. Because depreciation reflects the cost of using a plant asset, we do not begin recording depreciation charges until the asset is actually put into service. This section describes the factors we must consider in computing depreciation, the depreciation methods used, revisions in depreciation, and depreciation for partial periods.

C2 Explain depreciation and the factors affecting its computation.

Global: International accounting standards encourage use of the cost principle for plant assets. Plant asset revaluation is permitted provided it is consistently applied across periods.

Concept 11-2

Factors in Computing Depreciation

Three factors are relevant in determining depreciation: (1) cost, (2) salvage value, and (3) useful life.

Cost

The cost of a plant asset consists of all necessary and reasonable expenditures to acquire it and to prepare it for its intended use. We described the computation of cost earlier in this chapter.

Salvage Value

The total amount of depreciation to be charged off over an asset's benefit period equals the asset's cost minus its salvage value. **Salvage value,** also called *residual value* or *scrap value,* is an estimate of the asset's value at the end of its benefit period. This is the amount we expect to receive from disposing of the asset at the end of its benefit period. If we expect an asset to be traded in on a new asset, its salvage value is the expected trade-in value.

Point: If we expect additional costs in preparing a plant asset for disposal, the salvage value equals the expected amount from disposing of the asset less the disposal preparation costs.

Useful (Service) Life

The **useful life** of a plant asset is the length of time it is productively used in a company's operations. Useful life, also called **service life,** might not be as long as the asset's total productive life. For example, the productive life of a computer is often four to eight years

Point: Useful life and salvage value are estimates. Estimates require judgment based on consideration of all available information.

or more. Some companies, however, trade in old computers for new ones every two years. In this case, these computers have a two-year useful life, meaning the cost of these computers (less their expected trade-in values) is charged to depreciation expense over a two-year period.

Several variables often make the useful life of a plant asset difficult to predict. A major variable is the wear and tear from use in operations. Two other variables, inadequacy and obsolescence, also demand consideration. **Inadequacy** refers to the capacity of a company's plant assets that is unable to meet the company's growing productive demands. **Obsolescence** refers to a plant asset that is no longer useful in producing goods or services with a competitive advantage because of new inventions and improvements. Both inadequacy and obsolescence are difficult to predict because the timing of demand changes, new inventions, and improvements normally cannot be predicted. A company usually disposes of an inadequate or obsolete asset before it wears out.

A company is often able to better predict a new asset's useful life when it has past experience with a similar asset. When it has no such experience, a company relies on the experience of others or on engineering studies and judgment. In note 4 of its annual report, **Coca-Cola Bottling** reports the following useful lives:

> ### Did You Know?
>
> **Life Expectancy**   The life expectancy of plant assets is often in the eye of the beholder. For instance, both **Converse** and **Stride Rite** compete in the athletic shoe market, yet their buildings' life expectancies are quite different. Converse depreciates buildings over 5 to 10 years, but Stride Rite depreciates its buildings over 10 to 40 years. Such differences can dramatically impact financial statements.

The principal categories and estimated useful lives of property, plant and equipment were:	
Buildings	10–50 years
Machinery and equipment	5–20 years
Transportation equipment	4–10 years
Furniture and fixtures	7–10 years
Vending equipment	6–13 years

Depreciation Methods

P2 Compute and record depreciation using the straight-line, units-of-production, and declining-balance methods.

Many *depreciation methods* are used to allocate a plant asset's cost over the accounting periods in its useful life. The most frequently used method of depreciation is the straight-line method. Another common depreciation method is the units-of-production method. We explain both of these methods in this section. This section also describes accelerated depreciation methods, with a focus on the declining-balance method.

The computations in this section use information from an athletic shoe manufacturer. In particular, we look at a machine used for inspecting athletic shoes before packaging. Manufacturers such as **Converse**, **Reebok**, **Adidas**, and **Fila** use this machine. Data for its depreciation are in Exhibit 11.5.

Exhibit 11.5

Data for Athletic Shoe-Inspecting Machine

Cost	$10,000
Salvage value	1,000
Depreciable cost	$ 9,000
Useful life	
Accounting periods	5 years
Units inspected	36,000 shoes

Straight-Line Method

Straight-line depreciation charges the same amount of expense to each period of the asset's useful life. A two-step process is used. We first compute the *depreciable cost* of the asset; this amount is also called the *cost to be depreciated*. It is computed by subtracting the asset's salvage value from its total cost. Second, depreciable cost is divided by the number of accounting periods in the asset's useful life. The formula for straight-line depreciation, along with its computation for the inspection machine described above, are shown in Exhibit 11.6.

Exhibit 11.6

Straight-Line Depreciation Formula

$$\frac{\text{Cost} - \text{Salvage value}}{\text{Useful life in periods}} = \frac{\$10,000 - \$1,000}{5 \text{ years}} = \$1,800 \text{ per year}$$

If this machine is purchased on December 31, 2000, and used throughout its predicted useful life of five years, the straight-line method allocates an equal amount of depreciation to each of the years 2001 through 2005. We make the following adjusting entry at the end of each of the five years to record straight-line depreciation of this machine:

Dec. 31	Depreciation Expense	1,800	
	Accumulated Depreciation—Machinery . . .		1,800
	To record annual depreciation.		

Assets = Liabilities + Equity
−1,800   −1,800

The $1,800 Depreciation Expense is reported on the income statement among operating expenses. The $1,800 Accumulated Depreciation is a contra asset account to the Machinery account in the balance sheet.

The graph on the left in Exhibit 11.7 shows the $1,800 per year expense amount reported in each of the five years. The graph on the right shows the amounts reported on each of the six December 31 balance sheets while the company owns the asset.

Example: If salvage value of the machine is estimated to be $2,500, what is the annual depreciation expense? *Answer:* ($10,000 − $2,500)/5 years = $1,500.

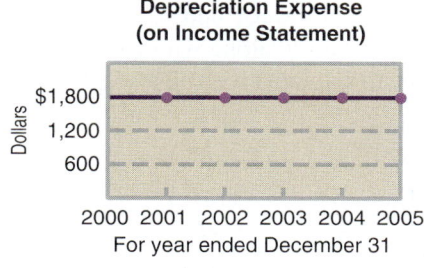

Depreciation Expense (on Income Statement)

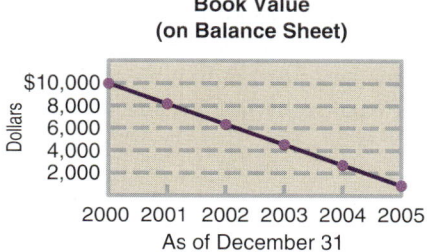

Book Value (on Balance Sheet)

Exhibit 11.7

Financial Statement Effects of Straight-Line Depreciation

The net balance sheet amount is the asset's **book value** and is computed as the asset's total cost less its accumulated depreciation. For example, at the end of year 2 (December 31, 2002), its book value is $6,400 and is reported in the balance sheet as follows:

| Machinery . . . . | $10,000 | |
| Less accumulated depreciation . . . . . | 3,600 | $6,400 |

The book value of this machine declines by $1,800 each year due to depreciation. From the graphs in Exhibit 11.7 we can see why this method is called straight line.

We also can compute the *straight-line depreciation rate,* defined as 100% divided by the number of periods in the asset's useful life. For the inspection machine, this rate is 20% (100% ÷ 5 years). We use this rate along with other information to compute the machine's *straight-line depreciation schedule* shown in Exhibit 11.8. Note three points in Exhibit 11.8. First, depreciation expense is the same each period. Second, accumulated depreciation is the

Exhibit 11.8

Straight-Line Depreciation Schedule

| | Depreciation for the Period | | | End of Period | |
Annual Period	Depreciable Cost*	Depreciation Rate	Depreciation Expense	Accumulated Depreciation	Book Value†
2000	—	—	—	—	$10,000
2001	$9,000	20%	**$1,800**	$1,800	8,200
2002	9,000	20	**1,800**	3,600	6,400
2003	9,000	20	**1,800**	5,400	4,600
2004	9,000	20	**1,800**	7,200	2,800
2005	9,000	20	**1,800**	9,000	**1,000**

* $10,000 − $1,000.   † Book value is cost minus accumulated depreciation.

Point: Depreciation requires estimates for salvage value and useful life. Decision ethics are relevant when managers might be tempted to choose estimates to achieve desired results on financial statements.

sum of current and prior periods' depreciation expense. Third, book value declines each period until it equals salvage value at the end of its useful life.

Units-of-Production Method

The straight-line method charges an equal share of an asset's cost to each period. If plant assets are used up in about equal amounts each accounting period, this method produces a reasonable matching of expenses with revenues. The use of some plant assets varies greatly, however, from one period to the next. A builder, for instance, might use a piece of construction equipment for a month and then not use it again for several months. When equipment use varies from period to period, the units-of-production depreciation method can better match expenses with revenues than can straight-line depreciation. **Units-of-production depreciation** charges a varying amount to expense for each period of an asset's useful life depending on its usage.

A two-step process is used to compute units-of-production depreciation. We first compute *depreciation per unit* by subtracting the asset's salvage value from its total cost and then dividing by the total number of units expected to be produced during its useful life. Units of production can be expressed in product or other units such as hours used or miles driven. The second step is to compute depreciation expense for the period by multiplying the units produced in the period by the depreciation per unit.

The formula for units-of-production depreciation, along with its computation for the machine described in Exhibit 11.5, are shown in Exhibit 11.9. (*Note:* 7,000 shoes are inspected and sold in its first year.)

Exhibit 11.9

Units-of-Production
Depreciation Formula

Step 1

$$\text{Depreciation per unit} = \frac{\text{Cost} - \text{Salvage value}}{\text{Total units of production}} = \frac{\$10,000 - \$1,000}{36,000 \text{ shoes}} = \$0.25 \text{ per shoe}$$

Step 2

$$\text{Depreciation expense} = \text{Depreciation per unit} \times \text{Units produced in period}$$

$$\$0.25 \text{ per shoe} \times 7,000 \text{ shoes} = \$1,750$$

Using actual data on the number of shoes inspected by the machine, we can compute the *units-of-production depreciation schedule* shown in Exhibit 11.10. For example, depreciation for the first year is $1,750 (7,000 shoes at $0.25 per shoe). Depreciation for the second year is $2,000 (8,000 shoes at $0.25 per shoe). The other years are similarly computed. Notice in Exhibit 11.10 that (1) depreciation expense depends on unit output, (2) accumulated depreciation is the sum of current and prior periods' depreciation expense, and (3) book value declines each period until it equals salvage value at the end of the asset's useful life.

Example: Refer to Exhibit 11.10. If the number of shoes inspected in 2005 is 5,500, what is depreciation expense for that year?
Answer: $1,250 (we never depreciate below salvage value)

Exhibit 11.10

Units-of-Production
Depreciation Schedule

	Depreciation for the Period			End of Period	
Annual Period	**Number of Units**	**Depreciation per Unit**	**Depreciation Expense**	**Accumulated Depreciation**	**Book Value**
2000	—	—	—	—	$10,000
2001	7,000	$0.25	**$1,750**	$1,750	8,250
2002	8,000	0.25	**2,000**	3,750	6,250
2003	9,000	0.25	**2,250**	6,000	4,000
2004	7,000	0.25	**1,750**	7,750	2,250
2005	5,000	0.25	**1,250**	9,000	**1,000**

Boise Cascade is one of many companies using the units-of-production depreciation method. It reports that "substantially all of the Company's paper and wood products manufacturing facilities determine depreciation by the units-of-production method."

Declining-Balance Method

An **accelerated depreciation method** yields larger depreciation expenses in the early years of an asset's life and smaller charges in later years. Of several accelerated methods, the most common is the **declining-balance method** of depreciation, which uses a depreciation rate of up to twice the straight-line rate and applies it to the asset's beginning-of-period book value. The amount of depreciation declines each period because book value *declines* each period.

A common depreciation rate for the declining balance method is double the straight-line rate. This is called the *double-declining-balance* or *DDB* method. This method is applied in three steps: (1) compute the asset's straight-line depreciation rate, (2) double the straight-line rate, and (3) compute depreciation expense by multiplying this rate by the asset's beginning-of-period book value.

To illustrate, let's return to the machine in Exhibit 11.5 and apply the double-declining-balance method to compute depreciation expense. Exhibit 11.11 shows the first year depreciation computation for the machine. The three-step process is to (1) divide 100% by five years to determine the straight-line rate of 20% per year, (2) double this 20% rate to get the declining-balance rate of 40% per year, and (3) compute depreciation expense as 40% multiplied by the beginning-of-period book value.

> **Global:** German accounting permits accelerated depreciation of up to three times the straight-line rate.

> **Point:** In the DDB method, *double* refers to the rate and *declining balance* refers to book value. The rate is applied to beginning book value each period.

Exhibit 11.11

Double-Declining-Balance Depreciation Formula

Step 1

Straight-line rate = 100% ÷ Useful life = 100% ÷ 5 years = 20%

Step 2

Double-declining-balance rate = 2 × Straight-line rate = 2 × 20% = 40%

Step 3

Depreciation expense = Double-declining-balance rate × Beginning-period book value

40% × $10,000 = $4,000 (for 2001)

The *double-declining-balance depreciation schedule* is shown in Exhibit 11.12. The schedule follows the formula except for year 2005, when depreciation expense is $296. This $296 is not equal to 40% × $1,296, or $518.40. If we had used the $518.40 for depreciation

> **Point:** Graph and describe the asset's book value over its useful life using the DDB method.

Exhibit 11.12

Double-Declining-Balance Depreciation Schedule

Annual Period	Depreciation for the Period			End of Period	
	Beginning of Period Book Value	Depreciation Rate	Depreciation Expense	Accumulated Depreciation	Book Value
2000	—	—	—	—	$10,000
2001	$10,000	40%	**$4,000**	$4,000	6,000
2002	6,000	40	**2,400**	6,400	3,600
2003	3,600	40	**1,440**	7,840	2,160
2004	2,160	40	**864**	8,704	1,296
2005	1,296	40	**296***	9,000	**1,000**

* Year 2005 depreciation is $1,296 − $1,000 = $296 (never depreciate book value below salvage value).

Example: What is DDB depreciation expense in year 2004 if the salvage value is $2,000? *Answer:* $2,160 − $2,000 = $160

expense in 2005, ending book value would equal $777.60, which is less than the $1,000 salvage value. Instead, the $296 is computed by subtracting the $1,000 salvage value from the $1,296 book value at the beginning of the fifth year (the year when DDB depreciation cuts into salvage value). This is done so that an asset is never depreciated below its salvage value.

A1 Compare and analyze depreciation for different methods.

Comparing Depreciation Methods

Exhibit 11.13 shows depreciation expense for the machine under each of the three depreciation methods.

Exhibit 11.13

Depreciation Expense for the Different Methods

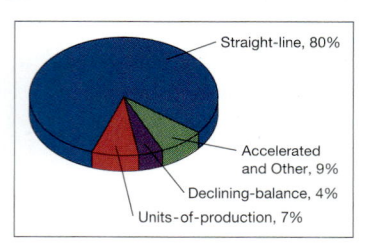

Period	Straight-Line	Units-of-Production	Double-Declining-Balance
2001	$1,800	$1,750	$4,000
2002	1,800	2,000	2,400
2003	1,800	2,250	1,440
2004	1,800	1,750	864
2005	1,800	1,250	296
Totals	$9,000	$9,000	$9,000

While the amount of depreciation expense per period differs for different methods, total depreciation expense is the same over the machine's useful life. Each method starts with a total cost of $10,000 and ends with a salvage value of $1,000. The difference is the pattern in depreciation expense over the useful life. The book value of the asset when using straight-line is always greater than the book value from using double-declining-balance, except at the beginning and end of the asset's useful life, when it is the same. Also, the straight-line method yields a steady pattern of depreciation expense while the units-of-production depreciation depends on the number of units produced. Each of these methods is acceptable because it allocates cost in a systematic and rational manner.

Did You Know?

Trends Approximately 80% of companies use straight-line depreciation for their plant assets, 7% use units-of-production, and 4% use declining balance. Another 9% use an unspecified accelerated method—most of these probably are declining balance.

Straight-line, 80%

Accelerated and Other, 9%

Declining-balance, 4%

Units-of-production, 7%

Global: Some Canadian companies are permitted to use an "increasing charge" depreciation (the opposite of accelerated depreciation).

Point: Differences between financial accounting and tax accounting records are normal and expected.

Point: Understanding depreciation for financial accounting will help in learning MACRS for tax accounting. Rules for MACRS are available from www.IRS.com.

Depreciation for Tax Reporting

The records a company keeps for financial accounting purposes are usually separate from the records it keeps for tax accounting purposes. This is so because financial accounting aims to report useful information on financial performance and position, whereas tax accounting reflects government objectives in raising revenues. Differences between these two accounting systems are normal and expected. Depreciation is a common example of how the records usually differ. For example, many companies use accelerated depreciation in computing taxable income. This reduces taxable income in the early years of an asset's life because higher depreciation expense is reported in these early years. On the other hand, the lower depreciation expense in later years means that taxable income is higher in later years. A company's goal here is to *postpone* its tax payments. This means a company can use these resources now to earn additional income before payment is due.

The U.S. federal income tax law has rules for depreciating assets. These rules include the **Modified Accelerated Cost Recovery System (MACRS).** MACRS allows straight-line depreciation for some assets, but it requires accelerated depreciation for most kinds of assets. MACRS separates depreciable assets into different classes and defines the depreciable life and rate for each class. MACRS is not acceptable for financial reporting because it often al-

Did You Know?

Depreciation. Technology Computer technology greatly simplifies depreciation computations and revisions. Many inexpensive, off-the-shelf software packages and business calculators allow a user to choose from a variety of depreciation methods for each asset entered. Depreciation schedules for both financial reporting and income tax reporting are quickly and accurately generated.

locates costs over an arbitrary period that is less than the asset's useful life. Details of MACRS are covered in tax accounting.

Partial Year Depreciation

Plant assets are purchased and disposed of at various times. When an asset is purchased (or disposed of) at a time other than the beginning or end of an accounting period, depreciation is recorded for part of a year. This is done so that the year of purchase or the year of disposal is charged with its share of the asset's depreciation.

To illustrate, let's return to the machine described in Exhibit 11.5. Assume that this machine is purchased and placed in service on October 8, 2000, and the annual accounting period ends on December 31. This machine costs $10,000, has a useful life of five years, and a salvage value of $1,000. Because this machine is purchased and used for nearly three months in 2000, the calendar-year income statement should report depreciation expense on the machine for that part of the year. Normally, the amount of depreciation is based on the assumption that the asset is purchased on the first day of the month nearest the actual date of purchase. In this case, since the purchase occurred on October 8, we assume an October 1 purchase date. This means that three months' depreciation is recorded in 2000. Using straight-line depreciation, we compute three months' depreciation of $450 as follows:

$$\frac{\$10,000 - \$1,000}{5 \text{ years}} \times \frac{3}{12} = \$450$$

A similar computation is necessary when an asset disposal occurs during a period. For example, let's suppose the machine is sold on June 24, 2005. Depreciation is recorded for the period January 1 through June 24 when it is disposed of. This partial year's depreciation, computed to the nearest whole month, is

$$\frac{\$10,000 - \$1,000}{5 \text{ years}} \times \frac{6}{12} = \$900$$

Revising Depreciation

Because depreciation is based on predictions of salvage value and useful life, depreciation expense is an estimate. During the useful life of an asset, new information may indicate that the original estimates are inaccurate. If our estimate of an asset's useful life and/or salvage value changes, what should we do? The answer is to use the new estimate to compute depreciation for current and future periods. This means we revise depreciation expense computation by spreading the cost yet to be depreciated over the useful life remaining. This approach is used for all depreciation methods.

Let's return to our machine described in Exhibit 11.8 using straight-line depreciation. At the beginning of this asset's third year, its book value is $6,400, computed as:

Cost	$10,000
Less two years' accumulated depreciation	3,600
Book value	$6,400

Assume that at the beginning of its third year, the estimated number of years remaining in its useful life changes from three to four years *and* its estimate of salvage value changes from $1,000 to $400. Straight-line depreciation for each of the four remaining years is computed as shown in Exhibit 11.14.

$$\frac{\text{Book value} - \text{Revised salvage value}}{\text{Revised remaining useful life}} = \frac{\$6,400 - \$400}{4 \text{ years}} = \$1,500 \text{ per year}$$

Exhibit 11.14

Computing Revised Straight-Line Depreciation

Global: Some countries require the depreciation method chosen for financial reporting to match the method chosen for tax reporting.

C3 Explain depreciation for partial years and changes in estimates.

Example: If the machine's salvage value is zero and purchase occurs on Oct. 8, 2000, how much depreciation is recorded at Dec. 31, 2000?
Answer: $10,000/5 × 3/12 = $500

Point: Remaining depreciable cost equals book value less revised salvage value at the point of revision.

Example: If at the beginning of its second year the machine's remaining useful life changes from four to three years and salvage value from $1,000 to $400, how much depreciation is recorded in the remaining years?
Answer: Revised depreciation = ($8,200 − $400)/3 = $2,600.

This means $1,500 of depreciation expense is recorded for the machine at the end of the third through sixth years of its remaining useful life. Since this asset was depreciated at $1,800 per year for the first two years, it is tempting to conclude that depreciation expense was overstated in the first two years. However, these expenses reflected the best information available at that time. We do not go back and restate prior years' financial statements for this type of new information. Instead, we adjust the current and future periods' statements to reflect this new information. Revising an estimate of the useful life or salvage value of a plant asset is referred to as a **change in an accounting estimate** and is reflected in current and future financial statements, not in prior statements.

Reporting Depreciation

Both the cost and accumulated depreciation of plant assets are reported on the balance sheet or in its notes. **Arctic Cat**, for instance, reports the following in its balance sheet:

Property and equipment ($ thousands):	
Machinery, equipment, and tooling	$71,936
Land, buildings, and improvements	16,861
	$88,797
Less accumulated depreciation	(52,411)
Total	$36,386

Many companies also show plant assets on one line with the net amount of cost less accumulated depreciation. When this is done, the amount of accumulated depreciation is disclosed in a note. **Nike** reports only the net amount of its property, plant, and equipment in its balance sheet in Appendix A. To satisfy the *full-disclosure principle,* Nike describes its depreciation methods in its Note 1 and the individual amounts comprising plant assets in its Note 3.

Point: A company usually keeps records for each asset showing its cost and depreciation to date. The combined records for individual assets are a type of subsidiary ledger.

Reporting both the cost and accumulated depreciation of plant assets helps users compare the assets of different companies. For example, a company holding assets costing $50,000 and accumulated depreciation of $40,000 is likely in a situation different from a company with new assets costing $10,000. While the net undepreciated cost of $10,000 is the same in both cases, the first company may have more productive capacity available but likely is facing the need to replace older assets. These insights are not provided if the two balance sheets report only the $10,000 book values.

Depreciation is a process of cost allocation. Plant assets are reported on a balance sheet at their undepreciated costs (book value), not at market values. This emphasis on costs rather than market values is based on the *going-concern principle* described in Chapter 2. This principle states that, unless there is evidence to the contrary, we assume that a company continues in business. This implies that plant assets are held and used long enough to recover their cost through the sale of products and services. Since plant assets are not for sale, their market values are not reported in financial statements. Instead, assets are reported on a balance sheet at cost less accumulated depreciation.

Accumulated depreciation is a contra asset account with a normal credit balance. It does not reflect funds accumulated to buy new assets when the assets currently owned are replaced. If a company has funds available to buy assets, the funds are shown on the balance sheet among liquid assets such as Cash or Investments.

You Make the Call—Ethics

Controller   You are the controller for Fascar, a struggling company. Fascar's operations require regular investments in equipment, and depreciation is its largest expense. Competitors also frequently replace equipment, which is typically depreciated over three years. Fascar's president instructs you to revise useful lives of equipment from three to six years and to use a six-year life on all new equipment. You suspect these instructions are motivated by a desire to improve reported income. What actions do you take?

Answer—p. 464

Quick Check

4. On January 1, 2002, a company pays $77,000 to purchase office furniture with a zero salvage value. The furniture's useful life is somewhere between 7 and 10 years. What is the year 2002 straight-line depreciation on the furniture using a (a) 7-year useful life and (b) 10-year useful life?

5. What does the term *depreciation* mean in accounting?

6. A company purchases a machine for $96,000 on January 1, 2003. Its useful life is five years or 100,000 units of product, and its salvage value is $8,000. During 2003, 10,000 units of product are produced. Compute the book value of this machine on December 31, 2003, assuming (a) straight-line depreciation and (b) units-of-production depreciation.

7. In early January 2002, a company acquires equipment for $3,800. The company estimates this equipment to have a useful life of three years and a salvage value of $200. Early in 2004, the company changes its estimates to a total four-year useful life and zero salvage value. Using straight-line, what is depreciation for the year ended 2004?

Answers—p. 464

Revenue and Capital Expenditures

P3 Distinguish between revenue and capital expenditures, and account for these expenditures.

Acquiring a plant asset and putting it into service often cause additional expenditures to operate, maintain, repair, and improve it. In recording these expenditures, we must decide whether to capitalize or expense them. To capitalize an expenditure is to debit the asset account. The issue is whether more useful information is provided by reporting these expenditures as current period expenses or by adding them to the plant asset's cost and depreciating them over its remaining useful life.

Revenue expenditures, also called *income statement expenditures,* are additional costs of plant assets that do not materially increase the asset's life or productive capabilities. They are recorded as expenses and deducted from revenues in the current period's income statement. Examples of revenue expenditures are cleaning, repainting, adjustments, and lubricants. **Capital expenditures,** also called *balance sheet expenditures,* are additional costs of plant assets that provide benefits extending beyond the current period. They are debited to asset accounts and reported on the balance sheet. Capital expenditures increase or improve the type or amount of service an asset provides. Examples are roofing replacement, plant expansion, and major overhauls of machinery and equipment.

Financial statements are affected for several years by the accounting choice of recording costs as either revenue expenditures or capital expenditures. Managers must be careful in classifying them. This classification decision is helped by identifying these expenditures as either ordinary repairs or as betterments and extraordinary repairs.

Point: If a manager's compensation is tied to net income, evidence suggests this can influence a manager's classification of expenditures.

Ordinary Repairs

Ordinary repairs are expenditures to keep the asset in normal, good operating condition. They are necessary if an asset is to perform to expectations over its useful life. Ordinary repairs do not extend an asset's useful life beyond its original estimate or increase its productivity beyond original expectations. Examples are normal costs of cleaning, lubricating, adjusting, and replacing (small) parts of a machine. Ordinary repairs are treated as *revenue expenditures.* This means their costs are reported as expenses on the current period income statement. Following this rule, **America West Airlines** reports "routine maintenance and repairs are charged to expense as incurred."

Few companies keep records for assets costing less than some minimum amount such as $500. Instead, these *low-cost plant assets* are treated as a revenue expenditure. This means their costs are charged to an expense account at the time of purchase. This practice is acceptable under the

Point: When an amount is said to be *capitalized* to an account, the amount is added to the account's normal balance.

Financial Statement Effect			
Treatment	**Accounting**	**Expense**	**Current Income**
Revenue expenditure	Income strnt. account debited	Currently recognized	Lower
Capital expenditure	Balance sheet account debited	Deferred to future	Higher

Point: Expenditures for both extraordinary repairs and betterments require revision of depreciation schedules.

Example: A company purchases a Web server. Identify each item as a revenue or capital expenditure: (1) purchase price, (2) necessary wiring, (3) platform for operation, (4) circuits to increase capacity, (5) cleaning after each three months use, (6) repair of a faulty connection, and (7) replaced a cooling fan. *Answer:* Capital expenditures: 1, 2, 3, 4; Revenue expenditures: 5, 6, 7.

Assets = Liabilities + Equity
+1,800
−1,800

materiality principle. Treating immaterial capital expenditures as revenue expenditures is unlikely to mislead users of financial statements. As an example, **Coca-Cola Bottling** capitalizes only major, or material, asset replacement: "minor replacements are charged to expense when incurred."

Betterments and Extraordinary Repairs

Betterments, also called *improvements,* are expenditures that make a plant asset more efficient or productive. A betterment often involves adding a component to an asset or replacing one of its old components with a better one. A betterment does not always increase an asset's useful life. An example is replacing manual controls on a machine with automatic controls to reduce labor costs. This machine will still wear out as fast as it would with manual controls. One special type of betterment is an *addition.* Examples are a new wing to a factory or a new dock to a warehouse.

Because a betterment benefits future periods, it is debited to the asset account as a capital expenditure. The new book value (less salvage value) is then depreciated over the asset's remaining useful life. To illustrate, suppose a company pays $8,000 for a machine with an eight-year useful life and no salvage value. After three years and $3,000 of depreciation, it adds an automated system to the machine at a cost of $1,800. This results in reduced labor costs when operating the machine in future periods. The cost of this betterment is added to the Machinery account with this entry:

Jan. 2	Machinery	1,800	
	Cash		1,800
	To record installation of automated system.		

After the betterment, the remaining cost to be depreciated is $6,800, computed as $8,000 − $3,000 + $1,800. Depreciation expense for the remaining five years is $1,360 per year, computed as $6,800/5 years.

Extraordinary repairs are expenditures extending the asset's useful life beyond its original estimate. Costs of extraordinary repairs are *capital expenditures* because they benefit future periods. As with betterments, they can be debited to the asset account. For example, **American West Airlines** reports: "the cost of major scheduled airframe, engine and certain component overhauls are capitalized (and expensed) . . . over the periods benefited." Extraordinary repairs also can be debited to the asset's accumulated depreciation account to reverse some effects of past depreciation—this approach is described in advanced courses.

You Make the Call

Entrepreneur Your start up Internet services company needs cash, and you are preparing financial statements to apply for a short-term loan. A friend suggests you treat as many expenses as possible as capital expenditures. What are the impacts on financial statements of this suggestion? What do you think is the aim of your friend's proposal?

Answer—p. 464

Disposals of Plant Assets

Plant assets are disposed of for several reasons. For example, many assets are eventually discarded because they wear out or become obsolete. Other assets are sold because of changing business plans, and sometimes an asset is exchanged for another asset. Regardless of the reason, disposals of plant assets occur in one of three basic ways: discarding, sale, or exchange. The general approach to accounting for each of these three types of disposals of plant assets is described in Exhibit 11.15.

Exhibit 11.15

Accounting for Disposals of Plant Assets

1. Record depreciation up to the date of disposal—this also updates Accumulated Depreciation.
2. Remove account balances of the disposed asset—including its Accumulated Depreciation.
3. Record any cash (and/or other assets) received or paid in the disposal.
4. Record any gain or loss—computed by comparing the disposed asset's book value with the market value of any assets received.*

* One exception to step 4 is the case of a gain on an asset exchange—it is described later in this section.

Discarding Plant Assets

P4 Account for asset disposal through discarding, selling, and exchanging an asset.

A plant asset is *discarded* when it is no longer useful to the company and it has no market value. To illustrate, assume that a machine costing $9,000 with accumulated depreciation of $9,000 is discarded. When accumulated depreciation equals the asset's cost, it is said to be *fully depreciated* (zero book value). The entry to record the discarding of this asset is

June 5	Accumulated Depreciation—Machinery	9,000	
	Machinery		9,000
	To discard fully depreciated machinery.		

Assets = Liabilities + Equity
+9,000
−9,000

This entry reflects all four steps of Exhibit 11.15. Step 1 is unnecessary since the machine is fully depreciated. Step 2 is reflected in the debit to Accumulated Depreciation and credit to Machinery. Since no other asset is involved, step 3 is irrelevant. Also, since book value is zero and no other asset is involved, no gain or loss is recorded in step 4.

How do we account for discarding an asset that is not fully depreciated? Or one whose depreciation is not up to date? To answer this, consider equipment costing $8,000 with accumulated depreciation of $6,000 on December 31 of the prior fiscal year-end. This equipment is being depreciated using straight line over eight years with zero salvage value. On July 1 it is discarded. Step 1 is to bring depreciation expense up to date:

Point: Recording depreciation expense up to date gives an up-to-date book value for determining gain or loss.

July 1	Depreciation Expense	500	
	Accumulated Depreciation—Equipment		500
	To record 6 months' depreciation ($1,000 × 6/12).		

Assets = Liabilities + Equity
−500   −500

Steps 2 through 4 of Exhibit 11.15 are reflected in the second (and final) entry:

July 1	Accumulated Depreciation—Equipment	6,500	
	Loss on Disposal of Equipment	1,500	
	Equipment		8,000
	To discard equipment with a $1,500 book value.		

Assets = Liabilities + Equity
+6,500   −1,500
−8,000

The loss is computed by comparing the equipment's $1,500 ($8,000 − $6,000 − $500) book value with the zero net cash proceeds. This loss is reported in the Other Expenses and Losses section of the income statement. Discarding an asset can sometimes require a cash payment that would increase the loss. More generally, the income statement reports any gain or loss from discarding the asset, and the balance sheet reports the changes in the asset and accumulated depreciation accounts.

Point: Gain or loss is determined by comparing "value given" (book value) to "value received."

Selling Plant Assets

Companies often sell plant assets when they restructure or downsize operations. To illustrate the accounting for selling plant assets, we consider BTO's March 31 sale of equipment that cost $16,000 and has accumulated depreciation of $12,000 at December 31 of the prior calendar year-end. Annual depreciation on this equipment is $4,000 computed using straight-line depreciation. Step 1 of this sale is to record depreciation expense and update accumulated depreciation to March 31 of the current year:

March 31	Depreciation Expense	1,000	
	Accumulated Depreciation—Equipment		1,000
	To record 3 months' depreciation ($4,000 × 3/12).		

Assets = Liabilities + Equity
−1,000   −1,000

Steps 2 through 4 of Exhibit 11.15 can be reflected in one entry that depends on the amount received from the asset's sale. We consider three different possibilities.

Sale at Book Value

If BTO receives $3,000, an amount equal to the equipment's book value as of March 31, no gain or loss occurs on disposal. The accounting in this case is

Assets = Liabilities + Equity
+3,000
+13,000
−16,000

March 31	Cash	3,000	
	Accumulated Depreciation—Equipment	13,000	
	Equipment		16,000
	To record sale of equipment for no gain or loss.		

Sale above Book Value

If BTO receives $7,000, an amount that is $4,000 above the equipment's book value as of March 31, a gain on disposal occurs. The entry is

Assets = Liabilities + Equity
+7,000   +4,000
+13,000
−16,000

March 31	Cash	7,000	
	Accumulated Depreciation—Equipment	13,000	
	Gain on Disposal of Equipment		4,000
	Equipment		16,000
	To record sale of equipment for a $4,000 gain.		

Sale below Book Value

If BTO receives $2,500, an amount that is $500 below the equipment's book value as of March 31, a loss on disposal occurs. The entry is

Assets = Liabilities + Equity
+2,500   −500
+13,000
−16,000

March 31	Cash	2,500	
	Loss on Disposal of Equipment	500	
	Accumulated Depreciation—Equipment	13,000	
	Equipment		16,000
	To record sale of equipment for a $500 loss.		

Exchanging Plant Assets

Many plant assets such as machinery, automobiles, and office equipment often are disposed of by exchanging them for newer assets. In a typical exchange of plant assets, a trade-in allowance is received on the old asset and the balance is paid in cash. Accounting for the exchange of assets is similar to any other disposal unless the old and the new assets are similar in the functions they perform. Trading an old truck for a new truck is an exchange of similar assets, whereas trading a truck for a machine is an exchange of dissimilar assets. This section describes the accounting for the exchange of similar assets. Similar asset exchanges are common, whereas dissimilar asset exchanges are not (the latter are discussed in advanced courses).

Accounting for exchanges of similar assets depends on whether the book value of the asset(s) given up is less or more than the market value of the asset(s) received. When the market value of the asset(s) received is less than the book value of the asset(s) given up, the difference is recognized as a loss. But when the value of the asset(s) received is more than the asset's book value given up, the gain is *not* recognized.

Receiving Less in Exchange: A Loss

Let's assume a company exchanges both old equipment and $33,000 in cash for new equipment. The old equipment originally cost $36,000 and has accumulated depreciation of $20,000 at the time of exchange. The new equipment has a market value of $42,000. These details are reflected in the middle ("Loss") columns of Exhibit 11.16.

Exhibit 11.16

Computing Gain or Loss on *Similar* Asset Exchange

Similar Plant Asset Exchange		Loss		Gain	
Market value of asset(s) received			$42,000		$52,000
Book value of asset(s) given up:					
Equipment ($36,000 − $20,000)	$16,000			$16,000	
Cash	33,000	49,000		33,000	49,000
Gain (loss) on exchange			$ (7,000)		$ 3,000

The entry to record this similar asset exchange is

Jan. 3	Equipment (**new**)	42,000	
	Loss on Exchange of Assets	7,000	
	Accumulated Depreciation—Equipment	20,000	
	Equipment (**old**)		36,000
	Cash		33,000
	To record exchange of old equipment and cash for new equipment.		

Assets = Liabilities + Equity
+42,000   −7,000
+20,000
−36,000
−33,000

The book value of the assets given up is $49,000. This includes the $33,000 cash and the $16,000 ($36,000 − $20,000) book value of the old equipment. The $49,000 book value of assets given up is compared to the market value of the new equipment received ($42,000). This yields a loss of $7,000 ($42,000 − $49,000).

Point: Parenthetical journal entry notes to "new" and "old" equipment are for illustration only. Both the debit and credit are to the same Equipment account in the general ledger.

Receiving More in Exchange: A Gain

Let's assume the same facts as in the preceding similar asset exchange *except* that the new equipment received has a market value of $52,000 instead of $42,000. The entry to record this similar asset exchange is

Jan. 3	Equipment (**new**)	49,000	
	Accumulated Depreciation—Equipment	20,000	
	Equipment (**old**)		36,000
	Cash		33,000
	To record exchange of old equipment and cash for new equipment.		

Assets = Liabilities + Equity
+49,000
+20,000
−36,000
−33,000

We show how to compute the gain from this exchange in the far right ("Gain") columns of Exhibit 11.16. This gain is *not* recognized in the entry because of a rule prohibiting recognizing a gain on similar asset exchanges.[1] The $49,000 recorded for the new equipment equals its cash price ($52,000) less the unrecognized gain ($3,000) on the exchange. The $49,000 cost recorded is called the *cost basis* of the new machine. This cost basis is the amount we use to compute depreciation and its book value. The cost basis of the new asset also can be computed by summing the book values of the assets given up as shown in Exhibit 11.17.

Point: No gain is recognized for similar asset exchanges.

Cost of old equipment	$36,000
Less accumulated depreciation ...	20,000
Book value of old equipment	$16,000
Cash paid in the exchange	33,000
Cost recorded for new equipment	**$49,000**

Exhibit 11.17

Cost Basis of New Asset when Gain Not Recognized

Example: Assume this old equipment is sold for $19,000 and, in a separate transaction, new equipment is purchased for $52,000. Record both transactions. *Answer:*
Cash 19,000
Accum. Depr—Eq. . 20,000
  Equipment (old) 36,000
  Gain on Sale of Eq. 3,000
Equipment (new) ... 52,000
  Cash 52,000

Quick Check

8. Early in the fifth year of a machine's 6-year useful life, it is overhauled, and its useful life is extended to nine years. This machine originally cost $108,000 and the overhaul cost is $12,000. Prepare the entry to record the overhaul cost.

9. Explain the difference between revenue expenditures and capital expenditures and how both are recorded.

10. What is a betterment? How is a betterment recorded?

[continued on next page]

[1] The reason a gain from a similar asset exchange is not recognized is that the earnings process is not considered complete for the exchanged asset. The decision to recognize a loss from a similar asset exchange is an application of *accounting conservatism* in measuring and recording asset values.

[continued from previous page]

11. A company acquires equipment on January 10, 2002, at a cost of $42,000. Straight-line depreciation is used with a five-year life and $7,000 salvage value. On June 27, 2003, the company sells this equipment for $32,000. Prepare the entry(ies) for June 27, 2003.

12. A company trades an old Web server for a new one. The cost of the old server is $30,000, and its accumulated depreciation at the time of the trade is $23,400. The new server has a cash price of $45,000. Prepare entries to record the trade under two different assumptions: the company receives a trade-in allowance of (a) $3,000 and (b) $7,000.

Answers—p. 465

Section 2— Natural Resources

P5 Account for natural resource assets and their depletion.

Natural resources are assets that are physically consumed when used. Examples are standing timber, mineral deposits, and oil and gas fields. Because they are consumed when used, they are often called *wasting assets*. These assets represent soon-to-be inventories of raw materials that will be converted into one or more products by cutting, mining, or pumping. Until that conversion takes place, they are noncurrent assets and are shown in a balance sheet using titles such as timberlands, mineral deposits, or oil reserves. Natural resources are reported under either plant assets or its own separate category. **Alcoa**, for instance, reports its natural resources under the balance sheet title *Properties, plants and equipment.* In a note to its financial statements, Alcoa reports a separate amount for *Land and land rights, including mines.* **Weyerhaeuser**, on the other hand, reports its huge timber holdings in a separate balance sheet category titled *Timber and timberlands.*

Acquisition Cost and Depletion

Natural resources are recorded at cost, which includes all expenditures necessary to acquire the resource and prepare it for its intended use. **Depletion** is the process of allocating the cost of a natural resource to the period when it is consumed, known as the resource's *useful life.* Natural resources are reported on the balance sheet at cost less *accumulated depletion.* The depletion expense per period is usually based on units extracted from cutting, mining, or pumping. This is similar to units-of-production depreciation. **Exxon Mobil** uses this approach to amortize the costs of discovering and operating its oil wells.

To illustrate depletion of natural resources, let's consider a mineral deposit with an estimated 500,000 tons of available ore. It is purchased for $500,000, and we expect zero salvage value. The depletion charge per ton of ore mined is $1, computed as $500,000 ÷ 500,000 tons. If 85,000 tons are mined and sold in the first year, the depletion charge for that year is $85,000. These computations are detailed in Exhibit 11.18.

Exhibit 11.18

Depletion Formula and Computations

Step 1

$$\text{Depletion per unit} = \frac{\text{Cost} - \text{Salvage value}}{\text{Total units of capacity}} = \frac{\$500,000 - \$0}{500,000 \text{ tons}} = \$1 \text{ per ton}$$

Step 2

$$\text{Depletion expense} = \text{Depletion per unit} \times \text{Units extracted in period}$$

$$= \$1 \times 85,000 = \$85,000$$

Depletion expense for the period is recorded as follows:

Assets = Liabilities + Equity
−85,000   −85,000

Dec. 31	Depletion Expense—Mineral Deposit	85,000	
	Accumulated Depletion—Mineral Deposit . .		85,000
	To record depletion of the mineral deposit.		

The period-end balance sheet reports the mineral deposit as shown in Exhibit 11.19.

Mineral deposit	$500,000	
Less accumulated depletion	**85,000**	$415,000

Exhibit 11.19

Balance Sheet Presentation of Natural Resources

Since all 85,000 tons of the mined ore are sold during the year, the entire $85,000 of depletion is reported on the income statement. If some of the ore remains unsold at year-end, however, the depletion related to the unsold ore is carried forward on the balance sheet and reported as Ore Inventory, a current asset.

Plant Assets Used in Extracting Resources

The conversion of natural resources by mining, cutting, or pumping usually requires machinery, equipment, and buildings. When the usefulness of these plant assets is directly related to the depletion of a natural resource, their costs are depreciated over the useful life of the natural resource in proportion to its depletion. This means depreciation is computed using the units-of-production method. For example, if a machine is permanently installed in a mine and 10% of the its ore is mined and sold in the period, then 10% of the machine's cost (less any salvage value) is allocated to depreciation expense. The same procedure is used when a machine is abandoned once resources are extracted. On the other hand, if a machine will be moved to and used at another site when extraction is complete, the machine is depreciated over its useful life.

Intangible assets are long-term rights, privileges, or competitive advantages that belong to the owner of such nonphysical assets used in operations. Examples are patents, copyrights, licenses, leaseholds, franchises, goodwill, and trademarks. Lack of physical substance is not sufficient for an asset to be an intangible. Notes and accounts receivable, for instance, lack physical substance, but they are not intangibles. This section identifies the more common types of intangible assets and explains the accounting for them.

Section 3—
Intangible Assets

P6   Account for intangible assets and their amortization.

Accounting for Intangible Assets

Accounting for intangible assets is similar to that for plant assets. An intangible asset is recorded at cost when purchased. Its cost must be systematically allocated to expense over its estimated useful life through the process of **amortization.** The amortization period for an intangible asset must be 40 years or less. The eventual disposal of an intangible asset involves removing its book value, recording any other asset(s) received or given up, and recognizing any gain or loss for the difference.

Point: The cost to acquire a Web site address is an intangible asset.

Amortization of intangible assets is similar to depreciation of plant assets and the depletion of natural resources in that it is a process of cost allocation. However, only the straight-line method is used for amortizing intangibles *unless* the company can show that another method is preferred. Another difference is that although the effects of depreciation and depletion are recorded in a contra account (Accumulated Depreciation or Accumulated Depletion), amortization is usually credited directly to the intangible asset account. This means the original cost of intangible assets is rarely reported on the balance sheet. Instead, only the net amount of unamortized cost (its book value) is reported.

Some intangibles have limited useful lives due to laws, contracts, or other asset characteristics. Examples are patents, copyrights, and leaseholds. Other intangibles such as goodwill, trademarks, and trade names have useful lives that cannot be easily determined. The cost of intangible assets is amortized over the periods expected to benefit by their use, but in no case can this period be longer than the asset's legal existence or longer than 40 years even when the life of an asset (for example, goodwill) can continue indefinitely into the future.

Intangible assets are often shown in a separate section of the balance sheet immediately after plant assets. **Callaway Golf**, for instance, follows this approach in reporting more than

Global: Japan permits recording the costs of both externally purchased and internally developed intangible assets.

$100 million of *intangible assets* in its recent balance sheet. Companies usually disclose the amortization periods they apply to intangibles. **Corning**'s annual report, for instance, says it amortizes intangible assets over a maximum of 15 years except for goodwill, which it amortizes over 40 years. The remainder of our discussion focuses on accounting for specific types of intangible assets.

Patents

The federal government grants patents to encourage the invention of new technology, mechanical devices, and production processes. A **patent** is an exclusive right granted to its owner to manufacture and sell a patented item, or to use a process for 17 years. When patent rights are purchased, the cost to acquire the rights is debited to an account called *Patents*. If the owner engages in lawsuits to successfully defend a patent, the cost of lawsuits is debited to the Patents account. However, the costs of research and development leading to a new patent are expensed when incurred.

A patent gives its owner exclusive rights to it for 17 years, but its cost is amortized over its estimated useful life (not to exceed 17 years). If we purchase a patent costing $25,000 with a useful life of 10 years, we make the following adjusting entry at the end of each of the 10 years to amortize one-tenth of its cost:

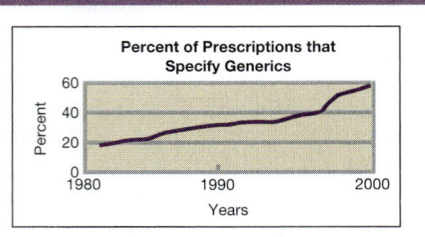

Percent of Prescriptions that Specify Generics

Assets = Liabilities + Equity
−2,500   −2,500

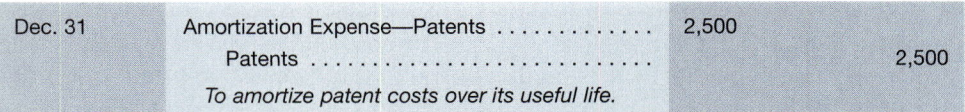

Dec. 31	Amortization Expense—Patents	2,500	
	Patents		2,500
	To amortize patent costs over its useful life.		

The $2,500 debit to Amortization Expense appears on the income statement as a cost of the product or service provided under protection of the patent. This entry uses the common practice of crediting the Patents account rather than using a contra account.

Copyrights

A **copyright** gives its owner the exclusive right to publish and sell a musical, literary, or artistic work during the life of the creator plus 50 years, although the useful life of most copyrights is much shorter. The costs of a copyright are amortized over its useful life. The only identifiable cost of many copyrights is the fee paid to the Copyright Office of the federal government or international agency granting the copyright. If this fee is immaterial, it is charged directly to an expense account, but if the identifiable costs of a copyright are material, they are capitalized (recorded in an asset account) and periodically amortized by debiting an account called *Amortization Expense—Copyrights*.

Leaseholds

Point: A leasehold implies existence of future benefits that the lessee controls because of a prepayment. It also meets the definition of an asset.

Property is rented under a contract called a **lease.** The property's owner, called the **lessor,** grants the lease. The one who secures the right to possess and use the property is called the **lessee.** A **leasehold** refers to the rights the lessor grant to the lessee under the terms of the lease. A leasehold is an intangible asset for the lessee.

Certain leases require no advance payment from the lessee but require monthly rent payments. In this case, we do not set up a Leasehold account. Instead, the monthly payments are debited to a Rent Expense account. If a long-term lease requires the lessee to pay the final period's rent in advance when the lease is signed, the lessee records this advance payment with a debit to a leasehold account. Because the advance payment is not used until the final period, the Leasehold account balance remains intact until that time. Then its balance is transferred to Rent Expense.[2]

A long-term lease can increase in value when current rental rates for similar property rise while the required payments under the lease remain constant. This increase in value of a lease is not reported on the lessee's balance sheet since no extra cost is incurred to acquire it. However, if the property is subleased and the new tenant makes a cash payment to the original lessee for the rights under the old lease, the new tenant debits this payment to a Leasehold account. The balance of this Leasehold account is amortized to Rent Expense of the new tenant over the remaining life of the lease.

Point: Capital leases are recorded by the lessee similar to a purchase; see Chapter 12.

To illustrate how the changing value of a lease can affect business decisions, consider **La Côte Basque**, a historic restaurant in New York. A few years ago, it sold the two years remaining on its lease to **Walt Disney Company**. La Côte Basque already knew it could not renew the lease when it expired because Disney had negotiated a long-term lease of the property with the building owner, **Coca-Cola Company**. La Côte Basque had been operating in this location for 36 years but could not compete with Disney's offer. The restaurant sold the remainder of its lease for a sizable amount and relocated earlier than required.

Leasehold Improvements

Long-term leases sometimes require the lessee to pay for alterations or improvements to the leased property such as partitions, painting, and storefronts. These alterations and improvements are called **leasehold improvements,** and their costs are debited to a *Leasehold Improvements* account. Since leasehold improvements become part of the property and revert to the lessor at the end of the lease, the lessee amortizes these costs over the life of the lease or the life of the improvements, whichever is shorter. The amortization entry debits Rent Expense and credits Leasehold Improvements.

> **Did You Know?**
>
> **Employee Assets**   Be nice to your employees says a recent study. Focusing on entrepreneurs who make accommodations to employees, the study confirms such employees are more productive and loyal and work to solve problems. One entrepreneur even lists employees' personal appointments on the company calendar so everyone can plan around those dates.

Franchises and Licenses

Franchises and **licenses** are rights that a company or government grants an entity to deliver a product or service under specified conditions. Many organizations, including **McDonald's**, **Pizza Hut**, **Major League Baseball**, and professional football and basketball, grant franchise and license rights. The costs of franchises and licenses are debited to a *Franchises and Licenses* asset account and are amortized over the lives of the agreements, not to exceed 40 years.

> **Did You Know?**
>
> **Logo Hold**   The **World Wrestling Federation** (WWF) licenses its mark and logo on thousands of retail products, including toys, video games, and apparel. Its licensing agreements yield it a percent of revenues; license revenues totaled more than $600 million this past year.

Goodwill

Goodwill has a specific meaning in accounting. **Goodwill** is the amount by which a company's value exceeds the value of its individual assets and liabilities. This usually implies that the company as a whole has certain valuable attributes not measured among its individual assets and liabilities. These can include superior management, skilled work force, good supplier or customer relations, quality products or services, good location, or other competitive advantages.

Point: IBM's balance sheet includes an item called *Investments and Sundry Assets*. A note to this item reports that it includes more than $1 billion of goodwill.

Point: Accounting for goodwill is different for financial accounting and tax accounting. The IRS requires the amortization of goodwill over a period not to exceed 15 years.

---

[2] Some long-term leases give the lessee essentially the same rights as a purchaser. This results in tangible assets and liabilities reported by the lessee. Chapter 12 describes these so-called *capital leases.*

Goodwill Illustration

Conceptually, a company has goodwill when its expected future income is greater than the normal income for its industry (competitors). To illustrate, consider the information in Exhibit 11.20 for two competing companies (Z2 and Burton) of roughly equal size in the snowboard industry.

Exhibit 11.20

Data for Goodwill Illustration

	Z2	Burton
Net assets* (excluding goodwill)	$190,000	$190,000
Normal return on net assets in the industry	10%	10%
Normal net income	$ 19,000	$ 19,000
Expected net income	24,000	19,000
Expected net income above normal	**$ 5,000**	**$ 0**

* Net assets (also called *equity*) equal total assets minus total liabilities.

The expected net income for Z2 is $24,000. This is $5,000 higher than the $19,000 industry norm based on the 10% return on net assets (equity) for its competitors. This implies that Z2 has goodwill that yields above normal net income. In contrast, Burton's expected income of $19,000 equals the norm for this industry. This implies zero goodwill for Burton. For Z2, it implies we are willing to pay more than just the value of its net assets—specifically, to acquire its goodwill asset.

In accounting, goodwill is usually recorded only when an entire company or business segment is purchased. The buyer and seller can estimate goodwill in more than one way. For instance, how do we value Z2's $5,000 per year above normal net income? One method is to value goodwill at some *multiple* of above normal net income. If we choose a multiple of 6, our goodwill estimate for Z2 is 6 times $5,000 (or $30,000). Another method is to assume the $5,000 above normal net income continues indefinitely (often called *capitalizing*). This is like an *annuity*. For example, if we assume a 16% discount (interest) rate, the goodwill estimate is $5,000/16%, or $31,250. Whatever method we choose, the value of goodwill is confirmed only by the price the seller is willing to accept and the buyer is willing to pay.

Global: In some countries, including the United Kingdom, the entire cost of goodwill can be charged against equity and, therefore, does not affect current or future earnings.

Accounting for Goodwill

To keep accounting information from being too subjective, goodwill is not recorded unless it is purchased. Purchased goodwill is measured by taking the purchase price of the company and subtracting the market value of its individual net assets (excluding goodwill). Goodwill is a major part of many company purchases. For instance, **Yahoo!** paid nearly $3.0 billion in stock and options to acquire **GeoCities**; where about $2.8 of the $3.0 billion was for goodwill and other intangibles.

Global: International accounting standards call for charging goodwill against income. The amortization period suggested is 5 or fewer years unless a longer period (up to 20 years) is justified.

Goodwill is amortized on a straight-line basis over its estimated useful life just as other intangible assets are. Since estimating the useful life of goodwill is difficult, estimates range widely. Exhibit 11.21 shows results from a recent survey on the goodwill amortization period. The most common amortization period is 40 years. If we assume that most companies that report "not exceeding 40" actually use 40 years, then nearly 60% of companies appear to choose the longest amortization period permitted. This is not surprising because it allows companies to spread goodwill costs over more years.

Exhibit 11.21

Goodwill Amortization Period

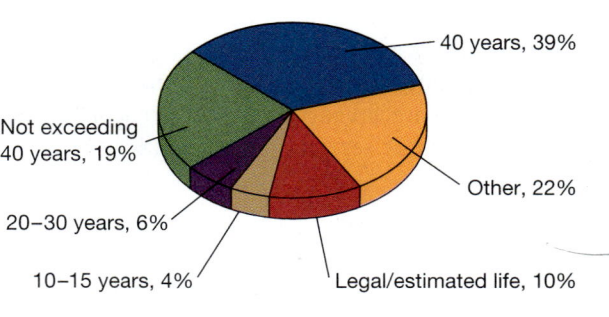

40 years, 39%
Not exceeding 40 years, 19%
20–30 years, 6%
10–15 years, 4%
Legal/estimated life, 10%
Other, 22%

Trademarks and Trade Names

Companies often adopt unique symbols or select unique names and brands in marketing their products. A **trademark** or **trade (brand) name** is a symbol, name, phrase, or jingle identified with a company, product, or service. Examples are Nike swoosh, Marlboro Man, Big Mac, Coca-Cola, and Corvette. Ownership and exclusive right to use a trademark or trade name is often established by showing that one company used it before another. Ownership is best established by registering a trademark or trade name with the government's Patent Office. The cost of developing, maintaining, or enhancing the value of a trademark or trade name (such as advertising) is charged to expense when incurred. If a trademark or trade name is purchased, however, its cost is debited to an asset account and then amortized.

Point: McDonald's "M" sign is one of the world's most valuable trademarks, yet this asset is not reported on McDonald's balance sheet.

Did You Know?

What's in a Name?   When it comes to branding, nobody does it better than **Nike**. Its swoosh is one of the world's best-known trademarks. It has helped Nike pump out sales and earnings growth exceeding its competitors. Equally impressive is the brand identity that the "**Intel Inside**" campaign created for a product that consumers never see and few understand.

Quick Check

Global: Some Australian and U.K. companies value brand names separately on their balance sheets.

13. Give an example of both a natural resource and an intangible asset.

14. A company pays $650,000 for an ore deposit. The deposit is estimated to have 325,000 tons of ore that will be mined over the next 10 years. During the first year, it mined, processed, and sold 91,000 tons. What is that year's depletion expense?

15. On January 6, 2002, a company pays $120,000 for a patent with a 17-year legal life to produce a toy expected to be marketable for three years. Prepare entries to record its acquisition and the December 31, 2002, adjustment.

Answers—p. 465

Most long-term asset acquisitions and disposals impact the statement of cash flows. Cash acquisitions of long-term assets are reported in the investing section of the statement of cash flows. Most acquisitions are an immediate *use* of cash, and the amount paid at acquisition is deducted in the statement. **Nike**, for instance, reports the following under investing activities in its statement of cash flows in Appendix A: "Additions to property, plant and equipment ($ millions) . . . $(419.9)."

Disposals of long-term assets usually create an immediate receipt of cash. When they do, they are reported as a *source* of cash (an addition) in the investing section of the statement of cash flows. Nike reports its disposals in Appendix A as follows: "Disposals of property, plant and equipment ($ millions) . . . $ 25.3." Note that a gain or loss from an asset disposal is the difference between an asset's book value and the value received. Neither reflects any cash flows. Depreciation and amortization also do *not* yield cash flows.

Cash Flow Impacts of Long-Term Assets

C4 Identify cash flow impacts of long-term asset transactions.

Total Asset Turnover

Using the Information

A company's assets are important in determining its ability to generate sales and earn income. Managers devote much attention to deciding what assets a company acquires, how much it invests in assets, and how to use assets most efficiently and effectively. One important measure of a company's ability to use its assets is **total asset turnover.** The formula for total asset turnover is in Exhibit 11.22.

A2 Compute total asset turnover and apply it to analyze a company's use of assets.

$$\text{Total asset turnover} = \frac{\text{Net sales}}{\text{Average total assets}}$$

Exhibit 11.22

Total Asset Turnover

Total asset turnover can be computed for any type of company, including manufacturing, merchandising, and service companies. The numerator, net sales, reflects amounts earned from the sale of products and services. The denominator, average total assets, reflects the total resources devoted to operating the company.

To illustrate, let's look at total asset turnover for two competing companies: **Coors** and **Anheuser-Busch**. Exhibit 11.23 reports total asset turnover for these two companies.

Exhibit 11.23

Analysis Using Total Asset Turnover

Company	($ in millions)	1999	1998	1997
Coors	Net sales	$ 2,057	$ 1,900	$ 1,821
	Total assets	$ 1,546	$ 1,461	$ 1,412
	Total asset turnover	**1.37**	**1.32**	**1.31**
Anheuser-Busch	Net sales	$11,704	$11,246	$11,066
	Total assets	$12,640	$12,484	$11,727
	Total asset turnover	**0.93**	**0.93**	**1.00**

To show how we compute and use total asset turnover, let's look at the numbers for Coors. We compute Coors's 1999 total asset turnover as follows: $2,057/[($1,546 + $1,461)/2] = 1.37$. We express Coors's use of assets in generating net sales by saying "it turned its assets over 1.37 times during the year." This means that each $1.00 of assets produced $1.37 of net sales for the year. Is a total asset turnover of 1.37 good or bad? It is safe to say that all companies desire a high total asset turnover. Like many ratio analyses, however, a company's total asset turnover must be interpreted in comparison with that of prior years and of its competitors. Interpreting the total asset turnover also requires an understanding of the company's operations. Some operations are capital intensive, meaning a relatively large amount is invested in assets to generate sales. This suggests a relatively lower total asset turnover. Other companies' operations are labor intensive, meaning they generate sales more by the efforts of people than the use of assets. In that case, we expect a higher total asset turnover.[3] Coors's turnover has been steady over the past three years and is superior to that for Anheuser-Busch. Total asset turnover for Coors's competitors, available in industry publications such as Dun & Bradstreet, is generally in the range of 1.0 to 1.1 over this same period. Overall, Coors appears to be competitive and doing slightly better than its competitors on total asset turnover.

You Make the Call

Environmentalist A paper manufacturer claims it cannot afford more environmental controls. It points to its low total asset turnover of 1.9 and argues that it cannot compete with companies whose total asset turnover is much higher. Examples cited are food stores (5.5) and auto dealers (3.8). How do you respond?

Answer—p. 464

Demonstration Problem

On July 14, 2002, Tulsa Company pays $600,000 to acquire a fully equipped factory. The purchase involves the following assets:

Asset	Appraised Value	Salvage Value	Useful Life	Depreciation Method
Land	$160,000			Not depreciated
Land improvements	80,000	$ 0	10 years	Straight-line
Building	320,000	100,000	10 years	Double-declining-balance
Machinery	240,000	20,000	10,000 units	Units-of-production*
Total	$800,000			

* The machinery is used to produce 700 units in 2002 and 1,800 units in 2003.

[3] There is a relation between total asset turnover and profit margin. Companies with low total asset turnover require higher profit margins (examples are hotels and real estate); companies with high total asset turnover can succeed with lower profit margins (examples are food stores and toy merchandisers).

Required

1. Allocate the total $600,000 purchase cost among the separate assets.

2. Compute the 2002 (six months) and 2003 depreciation expense for each asset and compute total depreciation expense for both years.

3. On the first day of 2004, Tulsa exchanged the machinery that was acquired on July 14, 2002, and $5,000 cash for similar machinery with a $210,000 market value. Journalize the exchange of these similar assets.

4. On the last day of calendar year 2004, Tulsa discarded machinery that had been on its books for five years. The machinery's original cost is $12,000 (estimated life of five years) and its salvage value is $2,000. No depreciation had been recorded for the fifth year when the disposal occurred. Journalize the fifth year of depreciation (straight-line method) and the asset's disposal.

5. At the beginning of year 2004, Tulsa purchased with cash a patent for $100,000. The company estimated the patent's useful life to be 10 years. Journalize the patent acquisition and its amortization for the year 2004.

6. Late in the year 2004, Tulsa acquired an ore deposit for $600,000 cash. It added roads and shafts for an additional cost of $80,000. Salvage value of the mine is estimated to be $20,000. The company estimated 330,000 tons of available ore. In year 2004, Tulsa mined and sold 10,000 tons of ore. Journalize the mine's acquisition and its first year's depletion.

Planning the Solution

- Complete a three-column schedule showing these amounts for each asset: appraised value, percent of total value, and apportioned cost.

- Using allocated costs, compute depreciation for 2002 (only one-half year) and 2003 (full year) for each asset. Summarize those computations in a table showing total depreciation for each year.

- Remember that gains on exchanges of similar assets are not recognized. Make a journal entry to add the acquired machinery to the books and to remove the old machinery, along with its accumulated depreciation, and the cash given in the exchange.

- Remember that depreciation must be recorded up to date before discarding an asset. Calculate and record depreciation expense for the fifth year using the straight-line method. Since salvage value is not received at the end of a discarded asset's life, the amount of any salvage value becomes a loss on disposal. Record the loss on the disposal as well as the removal of the discarded asset and its related accumulated depreciation.

- Record the patent (an intangible asset) at its purchase price. Use straight-line amortization over its useful life to calculate amortization expense. Remember that no accumulated amortization account is used. Instead, the intangible asset account is credited directly.

- Record the ore deposit (a natural resource asset) at its cost, including any added costs to ready the mine for use. Calculate depletion per ton using the depletion formula. Multiply the depletion per ton by the amount of tons mined and sold this year to calculate depletion expense for the year.

Solution to Demonstration Problem

1. Allocation of the total cost of $600,000 among the separate assets:

Asset	Appraised Value	Percent of Total Value	Apportioned Cost
Land	$160,000	20%	**$120,000** ($600,000 × 20%)
Land improvements	80,000	10	**60,000** ($600,000 × 10%)
Building	320,000	40	**240,000** ($600,000 × 40%)
Machinery	240,000	30	**180,000** ($600,000 × 30%)
Total	$800,000	100%	$600,000

2. Depreciation for each asset. (*Note:* Land is not depreciated.)

Land Improvements

Cost	$ 60,000
Salvage value	0
Depreciable cost	$ 60,000
Useful life	10 years
Annual depreciation expense ($60,000/10 years)	$ 6,000
2002 depreciation ($6,000 × 6/12)	**$ 3,000**
2003 depreciation	**$ 6,000**

Building

Straight-line rate = 100%/10 years = 10%
Double-declining-balance rate = 10% × 2 = 20%

2002 depreciation ($240,000 × 20% × 6/12)	**$ 24,000**
2003 depreciation [($240,000 − $24,000) × 20%]	**$ 43,200**

Machinery

Cost	$180,000
Salvage value	20,000
Depreciable cost	$160,000
Total expected units of production	10,000 units
Depreciation per unit ($160,000/10,000 units)	$ 16
2002 depreciation ($16 × 700 units)	**$ 11,200**
2003 depreciation ($16 × 1,800 units)	**$ 28,800**

Total depreciation expense:

	2002	2003
Land improvements	$ 3,000	$ 6,000
Building.	24,000	43,200
Machinery	11,200	28,800
Total	$38,200	$78,000

3. Record the exchange of similar assets (machinery) with a gain on the exchange: The book value on the exchange date is $180,000 (cost) − $40,000 (accumulated depreciation). The book value of the machinery given up in the exchange ($140,000) plus the $5,000 cash paid is less than the $210,000 value of the machine acquired. The entry to record this exchange of similar assets does not recognize the $65,000 gain on exchange:

Machinery (new)	145,000*	
Accumulated Depreciation—Machinery (old)	40,000	
Machinery (old)		180,000
Cash		5,000
To record exchange of similar assets.		

* Fair market value of acquired asset of $210,000 minus $65,000 gain.

4. Record the depreciation up to date on the discarded asset:

Depreciation Expense—Equipment	2,000	
Accumulated Depreciation—Equipment		2,000
To record depreciation of date of disposal: ($12,000 − $2,000)/5		

Record the removal of the discarded asset and its loss on disposal:

Accumulated Depreciation—Machinery	10,000	
Loss on Disposal of Machinery	2,000	
Machinery		12,000
To record the discarding of machinery with a $2,000 book value.		

5.

Patent	100,000	
Cash		100,000
To record patent acquisition.		

Amortization Expense—Patent	10,000	
Patent		10,000
To record amortization expense: $100,000/10 years = $10,000.		

6.

Ore Deposit	680,000	
Cash		680,000
To record ore deposit acquisition and its related costs.		

Depletion Expense—Ore Deposit	20,000	
Accumulated Depletion—Ore Deposit		20,000
To record depletion expense: ($680,000 − $20,000)/330,000 tons = $2 per ton. 10,000 tons mined and sold × $2 = $20,000 depletion.		

Summary

C1 **Describe plant assets and issues in accounting for them.** Plant assets are tangible assets used in the operations of a company that have a useful life of more than one accounting period. Plant assets are set apart from other tangible assets by two important features: use in operations and useful lives longer than one period. The four main accounting issues with plant assets are (1) computing their costs, (2) allocating their costs to the periods they benefit, (3) accounting for subsequent expenditures, and (4) recording their disposal.

C2 **Explain depreciation and the factors affecting its computation.** Depreciation is the process of allocating to expense the cost of a plant asset over the accounting periods that benefit from its use. Depreciation does not measure the decline in a plant asset's market value or its physical deterioration. Three factors determine depreciation: cost, salvage value, and useful life. Salvage value is an estimate of the asset's value at the end of its benefit period. Useful (service) life is the length of time an asset is productively used.

C3 **Explain depreciation for partial years and changes in estimates.** Partial year depreciation is often required because assets are bought and sold throughout the year. Depreciation is revised when changes in estimates such as salvage value and useful life occur. If the useful life of a plant asset changes, for instance, the remaining cost to be depreciated is spread over the remaining (revised) useful life of the asset.

C4 **Identify cash flow impacts of long-term asset transactions.** Acquisition and disposal of long-term assets for cash impact the investing section of the statement of cash flows. Acquisitions are a use of cash; disposals are a source of cash.

A1 **Compare and analyze depreciation for different methods.** The amount of depreciation expense per period is usually different for different methods, yet total depreciation expense over an asset's life is the same for all methods. Each method starts with the same total cost and ends with the same salvage value. The difference is in the pattern of depreciation expense over the asset's life. Common methods are straight-line, double-declining-balance, and units-of-production.

A2 **Compute total asset turnover and apply it to analyze a company's use of assets.** Total asset turnover measures a company's ability to use its assets to generate sales. Total asset turnover is defined as net sales divided by average total assets. While all companies desire a high total asset turnover, it must be interpreted in comparison with that for prior years and its competitors.

P1 **Apply the cost principle to compute the cost of plant assets.** Plant assets are recorded at cost when purchased. Cost includes all normal and reasonable expenditures necessary to get the asset in place and ready for its intended use. The cost of a lump-sum purchase is allocated among its individual assets.

P2 **Compute and record depreciation using the straight-line, units-of-production, and declining-balance methods.** The straight-line method divides cost less salvage value by the asset's useful life to determine depreciation expense per period. The units-of-production method divides cost less salvage value by the estimated number of units the asset will produce over its life to determine depreciation per unit. The declining-balance method multiplies the asset's book value by a factor that is usually double the straight-line rate.

P3 **Distinguish between revenue and capital expenditures, and account for these expenditures.** Revenue expenditures expire in the current period and are debited to expense accounts and matched with current revenues. Ordinary repairs are an example of revenue expenditures. Capital expenditures benefit future periods and are debited to asset accounts. Examples of capital expenditures are extraordinary repairs and betterments.

P4 **Account for asset disposal through discarding, selling, or exchanging an asset.** When a plant asset is discarded, sold, or exchanged, its cost and accumulated depreciation are removed from the accounts. Any cash proceeds from discarding or selling an asset are recorded and compared to the asset's book value to determine gain or loss. When similar assets are exchanged, losses are recognized but gains are not. When gains are not recognized, the new asset account is debited for the book value of the old asset plus any cash paid.

P5 **Account for natural resource assets and their depletion.** The cost of a natural resource is recorded in an asset account. Depletion of a natural resource is recorded by allocating its cost to depletion expense using the units-of-production method. Depletion is credited to an Accumulated Depletion account.

P6 **Account for intangible assets and their amortization.** An intangible asset is recorded at the cost incurred to purchase it. The cost of an intangible asset is allocated to expense using the straight-line method and is called *amortization*. Amortization is recorded with a credit directly to the asset account. Intangible assets include patents, copyrights, leaseholds, goodwill, and trademarks.

Guidance Answers to **You Make the Call**

Controller   You might tell the president of your concern that the longer estimate does not seem realistic in light of past experience. You might ask if the change implies a new replacement plan. Depending on the president's response, such a conversation might eliminate your concern. It is possible the president's instruction reflects an honest and reasonable prediction of the future. Since the company is struggling financially, the president may have concluded the normal pattern of replacing assets every three years cannot continue. Perhaps the strategy is to avoid costs of frequent replacements and stretch use of the equipment a few years longer until financial conditions improve. You should consider the possibility the president has a more complete understanding of the situation and honestly believes a six-year life is a good estimate. On the downside, you may be correct in suspecting the president is acting unethically. If you conclude the president's decision is unethical, you might confront the president with your opinion that it is unethical to change the estimate to increase income. Another possibility is to wait and see whether the auditor will insist on not changing the estimate. In either case, you should insist that the statements be based on reasonable estimates.

Entrepreneur   Treating an expense as a capital expenditure means reported expenses will be lower and income higher in the short run. This is so because a capital expenditure is not expensed immediately but is spread over the asset's useful life. Treating an expense as a capital expenditure also means asset and equity totals are reported at larger amounts in the short run. This continues until the asset is fully depreciated. Your friend is probably trying to help, but the suggestion hints at unethical behavior. Only an expenditure benefiting future periods is a capital expenditure.

Environmentalist   You must point out that the paper manufacturer's comparison of its total asset turnover with food stores and auto dealers is misdirected. Explain that these other industries' turnovers are higher because their profit margins are lower (about 2%). Profit margins for the paper industry are usually 3% to 3.5%. You need to collect data from competitors in the paper industry to show that a 1.9 total asset turnover is about right for this industry. You might also want to collect data on this company's revenues and expenses, along with compensation data for its high-ranking officers and employees.

Guidance Answers to **Quick Checks**

1. **a.** Office supplies—current assets
   b. Office equipment—plant assets
   c. Merchandise—current assets (inventory)
   d. Land for future expansion—long-term investments
   e. Trucks used in operations—plant assets
2. **a.** Land   **b.** Land Improvements
3. $700,000 + $49,000 − $21,000 + $3,500 + $3,000 + $2,500 = $737,000
4. **a.** Straight-line with 7-year life: ($77,000/7) = $11,000
   b. Straight-line with 10-year life: ($77,000/10) = $7,700

5. Depreciation is a process of allocating the cost of plant assets to the accounting periods that benefit from the assets' use.
6. **a.** Book value using straight-line depreciation:
   $96,000 − [($96,000 − $8,000)/5] = $78,400
   b. Book value using units of production:
   $96,000 − [($96,000 − $8,000) × (10,000/100,000)] = $87,200
7. ($3,800 − $200)/3 = $1,200 (original depreciation per year)
   $1,200 × 2 = $2,400 (accumulated depreciation)
   ($3,800 − $2,400)/2 = $700 (revised depreciation)

8.

Machinery	12,000	
Cash		12,000

9. A revenue expenditure benefits only the current period and should be charged to expense in the current period. A capital expenditure yields benefits that extend beyond the end of the current period and should be charged to an asset.

10. A betterment involves modifying an existing plant asset to make it more efficient, usually by replacing part of the asset with an improved or superior part. The cost of a betterment should be debited to the asset's account.

11.

Depreciation Expense	3,500	
Accumulated Depreciation		3,500
Cash	32,000	
Accumulated Depreciation	10,500	
Gain on Sale of Equipment		500
Equipment		42,000

12.

(a) Equipment	45,000	
Loss on Exchange of Assets	3,600	
Accumulated Depreciation, Equip. .	23,400	
Equipment		30,000
Cash ($45,000 − $3,000)		42,000

(b) Equipment (reflects $400 unrecog. gain)	44,600	
Accumulated Depreciation, Equip. .	23,400	
Equipment		30,000
Cash ($45,000 − $7,000)		38,000

13. Examples of intangibles are patents, copyrights, leaseholds, leasehold improvements, goodwill, trademarks, and licenses. Examples of natural resources are timberlands, mineral deposits, and oil reserves.

14. ($650,000/325,000 tons) × 91,000 tons = $182,000

15.

Jan. 6	Patents	120,000	
	Cash		120,000
Dec. 31	Amortization Expense	40,000*	
	Patents		40,000

* $120,000/3 years = $40,000.

Glossary

Accelerated depreciation method method that produces larger depreciation charges during the early years of an asset's life and smaller charges in its later years. (p. 445).

Amortization process of allocating the cost of an intangible asset to expense over its estimated useful life. (p. 455).

Betterment expenditure to make a plant asset more efficient or productive; also called *improvement*. (p. 450).

Book value total cost of an asset less its accumulated depreciation (or depletion, or amortization). (p. 443).

Capital expenditure additional costs of plant assets that provide material benefits extending beyond the current period; also called *balance sheet expenditure*. (p. 449).

Change in an accounting estimate change in an accounting estimate that results from new information, subsequent developments, better insight, or improved judgment. (p. 448).

Copyright right giving the owner the exclusive privilege to publish and sell musi-cal, literary, or artistic work during the creator's life plus 50 years. (p. 456).

Cost all normal and reasonable expenditures necessary to get a plant asset in place and ready for its intended use. (p. 439).

Declining-balance method method that determines depreciation charge for the period by multiplying a depreciation rate (up to twice the straight-line rate) by the asset's beginning-period book value. (p. 445).

Depletion process of allocating the cost of natural resources to periods when they are consumed. (p. 454).

Depreciation process of allocating the cost of a plant asset to expense in the periods benefiting from its use. (p. 441).

Extraordinary repairs major repairs that extend the useful life of a plant asset beyond prior expectations; treated as a capital expenditure. (p. 450).

Franchises, Licenses privileges granted by a company or government to sell a product or service under specified conditions. (p. 457).

Goodwill amount by which a company's value exceeds the value of its individual assets and liabilities. (p. 457).

Inadequacy condition in which the capacity of plant assets is too small to meet the company's productive demands. (p. 442).

Intangible assets long-term rights, privileges, or competitive advantages that belong to the owner of these nonphysical assets used in operations. (p. 455).

Land improvements assets that increase the benefits of land, have a limited useful life, and are depreciated. (p. 440).

Lease contract specifying the rental of property. (p. 456).

Leasehold rights the lessor grants to the lessee under the terms of a lease. (p. 456).

Leasehold improvements alterations or improvements to leased property such as partitions and storefronts. (p. 457).

Lessee party to a lease who secures the right to possess and use the property from another party (the lessor). (p. 456).

Lessor party to a lease who grants another party (the lessee) the right to possess and use property. (p. 456).

Modified Accelerated Cost Recovery System (MACRS) depreciation system required by federal income tax law. (p. 446).

Natural resources assets physically consumed when used; examples are timber, mineral deposits, and oil and gas fields; also called *wasting assets.* (p. 454).

Obsolescence condition in which, because of new inventions and improvements, a plant asset can no longer be used to produce goods or services with a competitive advantage. (p. 442).

Ordinary repairs repairs to keep a plant asset in normal, good operating condition; treated as a revenue expenditure. (p. 449).

Patent exclusive right granted to its owner to manufacture and sell an item or to use a process for 17 years. (p. 456).

Plant assets tangible assets used in a company's operations that have a useful life of more than one period. (p. 438).

Revenue expenditure expenditure reported on the current income statement as an expense because it does not provide benefits in future periods. (p. 449).

Salvage value estimate of amount to be recovered at the end of an asset's useful life; also called *residual,* or *scrap, value.* (p. 441).

Straight-line depreciation method that allocates an equal portion of the total depreciation for a plant asset (cost minus salvage) to each accounting period in its useful life. (p. 442).

Total asset turnover measure of a company's ability to use its assets to generate sales; computed by dividing net sales by average total assets. (p. 459).

Trademark or **trade (brand) name** symbol, name, phrase, or jingle identified with a company, product, or service. (p. 459).

Units-of-production depreciation method that charges a varying amount to depreciation expense for each period of an asset's useful life depending on its usage. (p. 444).

Useful (or service) life length of time an asset will be productively used in the operations of a business. (p. 441).

Questions

1. What is the general rule for costs included in a plant asset?
2. What characteristics of a plant asset make it different from other assets?
3. What is the balance sheet classification for land that is held for future expansion? Why is such land not classified as a plant asset?
4. What is different between land and land improvements?
5. Why is the Modified Accelerated Cost Recovery System not generally accepted for financial accounting purposes?
6. Does the balance in the Accumulated Depreciation—Machinery account represent funds to replace the machinery when it wears out? If not, what does it represent?
7. What accounting principle justifies charging low-cost plant asset purchases immediately to an expense account?
8. What is the difference between ordinary repairs and extraordinary repairs? How should each be recorded?
9. Identify events that might lead to disposal of a plant asset.
10. What is the process of allocating the cost of natural resources to expense as they are used?
11. What are the characteristics of an intangible asset?
12. Is the declining-balance method an acceptable way to compute depletion of natural resources?
13. What general procedures are followed in accounting for the acquisition and cost allocation of intangible assets?
14. When do we know a company has goodwill? When can goodwill appear in a company's balance sheet?
15. A company buys another business and pays for its goodwill. If the company plans to incur costs each year to maintain the value of the goodwill, must it also amortize goodwill?
16. How does accounting for long-term assets impact the statement of cash flows?
17. How is total asset turnover computed? Why would a financial statement user be interested in total asset turnover?
18. Refer to **Nike**'s balance sheet in Appendix A. What title does Nike use for its plant assets? What is its book value of plant assets as of May 31, 2000, and May 31, 1999?
19. Refer to **Reebok**'s balance sheet in Appendix A. How are Reebok's plant assets and intangibles reported (with amounts) on its 1999 balance sheet?
20. Refer to the January 29, 2000, balance sheet of **Gap** in Appendix A. What long-term assets discussed in this chapter are reported?

QUICK STUDY

QS 11-1

Cost of plant assets

U-Bowl installs automatic score-keeping equipment with an invoice price of $190,000. The electrical work required for the installation costs $20,000. Additional costs are $4,000 for delivery and $13,700 for sales tax. During the installation, a component of the equipment is carelessly left on a lane and hit by the automatic lane-cleaning machine. The cost of repairing the component is $1,850. What is the recorded cost of the automatic score-keeping equipment?

QS 11-2

Depreciation methods   **P2**

On January 2, 2002, Young Country acquires sound equipment for concert performances at a cost of $65,800. The band estimates it will use this equipment for four years, during which time it anticipates performing about 200 concerts. It estimates at that point it can sell the equipment for $2,000. During year 2002, the band performs 45 concerts. Compute the year 2002 depreciation using the (1) straight-line method and (2) units-of-production method.

Identify the main difference between (1) plant assets and current assets, (2) plant assets and inventory, and (3) plant assets and long-term investments.

QS 11-3
Defining assets

A fleet of refrigerated delivery trucks is acquired on January 5, 2002, at a cost of $830,000 with an estimated useful life of eight years and an estimated salvage value of $75,000. Compute the depreciation expense for the first three years using the double-declining-balance method.

QS 11-4
Double-declining-balance method

Refer to the facts in QS 11–2. Assume that Young Country chose straight-line depreciation but realizes early in the second year that due to concert bookings beyond expectations, this equipment will last only a total of three years. The salvage value remains unchanged. Compute the revised depreciation for both the second and third years.

QS 11-5
Computing revised depreciation

For each of the following investing activities, identify whether it is a source (A) or use (B) of cash.
A. Cash provided by investing activities.
B. Cash used by investing activities.
1. _____ Purchase of timberland for cash   **3.** _____ Cash purchase of machinery
2. _____ Cash sale of factory warehouse   **4.** _____ Sale of patents for cash

QS 11-6
Cash impacts from acquisitions and disposals

Fife Co. owns a machine that costs $42,400 with accumulated depreciation of $18,400. Fife exchanges the machine for a similar but newer model that has a market value of $52,000. Record the exchange assuming Fife also paid cash of (1) $30,000 and (2) $22,000.

QS 11-7
Similar asset exchange

---

1. Classify the following as either a revenue or a capital expenditure:
   a. Completed an addition to an office building for $225,000 cash.
   b. Monthly cost of replacement filters on an air conditioning system, $175.
   c. Cost of annual tune-ups for delivery trucks, $200 cash per truck.
   d. Replaced a compressor for a refrigeration system that extends its useful life by four years, $40,000 cash cost.
2. Prepare the journal entries to record items (a) and (d) of part (1).

QS 11-8
Revenue and capital expenditures

Outback Company acquires an ore mine at a cost of $1,400,000. It incurs additional costs of $400,000 to access the mine, which is estimated to hold 1,000,000 tons of ore. The estimated value of the land after the ore is removed is $200,000.
1. Prepare the entry to record the cost of the ore mine.
2. Prepare the year-end adjusting entry if 180,000 tons of ore are mined and sold the first year.

QS 11-9
Natural resources and depletion

Which of the following assets are reported on the balance sheet as intangible assets? Which are reported as natural resources? (a) Oil well, (b) Trademark, (c) Leasehold, (d) Gold mine, (e) Building.

QS 11-10
Classify assets

On January 4 of this year, Belair Boutique incurs a $105,000 cost to modernize its store. Improvements include new floors, ceilings, wiring, and wall coverings. These improvements are estimated to yield benefits for 10 years. Belair leases its store and has eight years remaining on the lease. Prepare the entry to record both the cost of modernization and the amortization at the end of this year.

QS 11-11
Intangible assets and amortization

Eastman Company reports the following: net sales of $14,880 million for 2003 and $13,990 million for 2002; end-of-year total assets of $15,869 million for 2003 and $17,819 million for 2002. Compute its total asset turnover for 2003.

QS 11-12
Computing total asset turnover

EXERCISES

Exercise 11-1
Recording costs of real estate

Ashgrove Manufacturing purchases a large lot on which an old building is located as part of its plans to build a new plant. The negotiated purchase price for this real estate is $280,000 for the lot plus $110,000 for the old building. The company pays $33,500 to tear down the old building and $47,000 to landscape the lot. It also pays a total of $1,540,000 in construction costs—this amount consists of the cost of the new building and $87,800 for lighting and paving a parking area next to the building. Prepare a single journal entry to record these costs incurred by Ashgrove, all of which are paid in cash.

Exercise 11-2
Cost of plant asset

Bottalico Co. purchases a machine for $12,500, terms 2/10, n/60, FOB shipping point. The seller prepaid the freight charges, $360, adding the amount to the invoice and bringing its total to $12,860. The machine requires special steel mounting and power connections costing $895. Another $475 is paid to assemble the machine and get it into operation. In moving the machine to its steel mounting, $180 in damages occurred. Later, $40 of materials is used in adjusting the machine to produce a satisfactory product. The adjustments are normal for this machine and are not the result of the damages. Compute the cost recorded for this machine. (Assume Bottalico pays for this machine within the cash discount period.)

Exercise 11-3
Lump-sum purchase of plant assets

Reese Company pays $375,280 for real estate plus $20,100 in closing costs. The real estate consists of land appraised at $156,820; land improvements appraised at $57,540; and a building appraised at $178,300. Allocate the total cost among the three purchased assets and prepare the journal entry to record the purchase.

Exercise 11-4
Depreciation methods

In early January 2002, LabOne purchases computer equipment for $154,000 to use in research and development activities for four years. It will then sell it at a $25,000 estimated salvage value. Prepare schedules showing the depreciation and book values for the four years assuming (1) straight-line and (2) double-declining-balance depreciation.

Exercise 11-5
Depreciation methods

Duce Company installs a computerized manufacturing machine in its factory at a cost of $43,500. The machine's useful life is estimated at 10 years, or 385,000 units of product, with a $5,000 salvage value. During its second year, the machine produces 32,500 units of product. Determine the machine's second-year depreciation under the (1) straight-line, (2) units-of-production, and (3) double-declining-balance methods.

Exercise 11-6
Depreciation methods; partial year depreciation

On April 1, 2002, Admiral's Backhoe Co. purchases a trencher for $280,000. The machine is expected to last five years and have a salvage value of $40,000. Compute depreciation expense for year 2003 using the (1) straight-line and (2) double-declining-balance methods.

Exercise 11-7
Revising depreciation

Top Notch Fitness Club uses straight-line depreciation for a machine costing $23,860, with an estimated four-year life and a $2,400 salvage value. After two years, Top Notch determines that the machine still has three more years of remaining useful life, after which it will have an estimated $2,000 salvage value. Compute (1) the machine's book value at the end of its second year and (2) the amount of depreciation for each of the final three years given the revised estimates.

Exercise 11-8
Income effects of depreciation methods

MES Enterprises pays $238,400 for equipment that will last five years and have a $43,600 salvage value. By using the machine in its operations for five years, the company expects to earn $88,500 annually, after deducting all expenses except depreciation. Prepare a schedule showing income before depreciation, depreciation expense, and net income for each year and the total five-year period, assuming (1) straight-line depreciation and (2) double-declining-balance depreciation.

Exercise 11-9
Extraordinary repairs; computations and entries

Mustang Company owns a building that appears on its prior year's balance sheet at its original $572,000 cost less $429,000 accumulated depreciation. The building is depreciated on a straight-line basis assuming a 20-year life and no salvage value. During the first week in January of the current year, major structural repairs are completed on the building at a $68,350 cost. The repairs extend its useful life for 7 years beyond the 20 years originally estimated.

1. Determine the building's age as of the end of the prior year.
2. Prepare the entry to record the cost of the structural repairs that are paid in cash.
3. Determine the book value of the building immediately after the repairs are recorded.
4. Prepare the entry to record the current year's depreciation.

Archer Company pays $264,000 for equipment expected to last four years and have a $25,000 salvage value. Prepare journal entries to record the following costs related to the equipment:

1. During the second year of the equipment's life, $22,000 cash is paid for a new component expected to increase the equipment's productivity by 10% a year.
2. During the third year, $6,250 cash is paid for normal repairs necessary to keep the equipment in good working order.
3. During the fourth year, $14,870 is paid for repairs expected to increase the useful life of the equipment from four to five years.

Exercise 11-10
Ordinary repairs, extraordinary repairs, and betterments

Blackbelt Construction trades in an old tractor for a new tractor, receiving a $29,000 trade-in allowance and paying the remaining $83,000 in cash. The old tractor cost $96,000, and straight-line accumulated depreciation of $52,500 had been recorded under the assumption that it would last eight years and have a $12,000 salvage value. Answer the following questions:

1. What is the book value of the old tractor at the time of exchange?
2. What is the loss on this similar asset exchange?
3. What amount should be recorded (debited) in the asset account for the new tractor?

Exercise 11-11
Exchanging similar assets

On January 2, 2002, Ritchfield Co. disposes of a machine costing $44,000 with accumulated depreciation of $24,625. Prepare the entries to record the disposal under each of the following separate assumptions:

a. Machine is sold for $18,250 cash.
b. Machine is traded in on a similar but newer machine having a $60,200 cash price. A $25,000 trade-in allowance is received, and the balance is paid in cash.
c. Machine is traded in on a similar but newer machine having a $60,200 cash price. A $15,000 trade-in allowance is received, and the balance is paid in cash.

Exercise 11-12
Recording plant asset disposals

Finesse Co. purchases and installs a machine on January 1, 2002, at a total cost of $105,000. Straight-line depreciation is taken each year for four years assuming a seven-year life and no salvage value. The machine is disposed of on July 1, 2006, during its fifth year of service. Prepare entries to record the partial year's depreciation on July 1, 2006, and to record the disposal under the following separate assumptions: (a) the machine is sold for $45,000 cash, and (b) Finesse receives an insurance settlement of $25,000 resulting from the total destruction of the machine in a fire.

Exercise 11-13
Partial year depreciation; disposal of plant asset
P4

On April 2, 2002, Cascade Mining Co. pays $3,736,250 for an ore deposit containing 1,525,000 tons. The company installs machinery in the mine costing $213,500, with an estimated seven-year life and no salvage value. The machinery will be abandoned when the ore is completely mined. Cascade began mining on May 1, 2002, and mined and sold 166,200 tons of ore during the remaining eight months of 2002. Prepare the December 31, 2002, entries to record both the ore deposit depletion and the mining machinery depreciation. Mining machinery depreciation should be in proportion to the mine's depletion.

Exercise 11-14
Depletion of natural resources
P5

Uptown Gallery purchases the copyright on an oil painting for $418,000 on January 1, 2002. The copyright legally protects its owner for 19 more years. However, the company plans to market and sell prints of the original for only 12 years. Prepare entries to record the purchase of the copyright on January 1, 2002, and its annual amortization on December 31, 2002.

Exercise 11-15
Amortization of intangible assets

Exercise 11-16
Goodwill estimation

Tracey Losh has devoted years to developing a profitable business that earns an attractive return. Losh is now considering selling the business and is attempting to estimate its goodwill. The value of the business's net assets (excluding goodwill) is $537,000, and in a typical year net income is about $90,000. Most businesses of this type are expected to earn a return of about 10% on their net assets. Estimate the value of this business's goodwill for the following separate cases assuming it is (a) equal to 10 times the amount that net income is above normal and (b) computed by capitalizing the amount that net income is above normal at a rate of 8%.

Exercise 11-17
Cash flows related to
plant assets

Refer to the statement of cash flows for **Gap** in Appendix A for the 52 week period ended January 29, 2000, to answer the following:

1. What amount of cash is used to purchase property and equipment?
2. How much depreciation and amortization are recorded?
3. What total amount of net cash is used in investing activities?
4. What amount of cash is used to acquire lease rights?

Exercise 11-18
Evaluating efficient
use of assets

Klink Co. reports net sales of $5,865,000 for 2002 and $8,689,000 for 2003. End-of-year balances for total assets are: 2001, $1,686,000; 2002, $1,800,000; and 2003, $1,982,000. Compute Klink's total asset turnover for 2002 and 2003 and comment on its efficiency in using assets.

PROBLEM SET A

Problem 11-1A
Plant asset costs;
depreciation methods

Check   (3) Depreciation, $9,624

Gunner Construction negotiates a lump-sum purchase of several assets from a company that is going out of business. The purchase is completed on January 1, 2002, at a total cash price of $802,000 for a building, land, land improvements, and six vehicles. The estimated market values of the assets are building, $506,000; land, $302,000; land improvements, $28,500; and six vehicles, $124,500. The company's fiscal year ends on December 31.

Required

Preparation Component

1. Prepare a table to allocate the lump-sum purchase price to the separate assets purchased. Prepare the journal entry to record the purchase.
2. Compute the depreciation expense for year 2002 on the building using the straight-line method, assuming a 15-year life and a $26,000 salvage value.
3. Compute the depreciation expense for year 2002 on the land improvements assuming a five-year life and double-declining-balance depreciation.

Analysis Component

4. Defend or refute this statement: Accelerated depreciation results in payment of less taxes over the asset's life.

Problem 11-2A
Real estate costs;
depreciation

In January 2002, Moonscapes pays $3,200,000 for a tract of land with two buildings on it. It plans to demolish Building 1 and build a new store in its place. Building 2 will be a company office; it is appraised at $645,000, with a useful life of 20 years and a $60,000 salvage value. A lighted parking lot near Building 1 has improvements (Land Improvements 1) valued at $420,000 and expected to last another 14 years with no salvage value. Without the buildings and improvements, the tract of land is valued at $1,785,000. Moonscapes also incurs the following additional costs:

Cost to demolish Building 1	$ 328,400
Cost of additional landscaping	175,400
Cost to construct new building (Building 3), having a useful life of 25 years and a $392,000 salvage value	2,202,000
Cost of new land improvements (Land Improvements 2) near Building 2 having a 20-year useful life and no salvage value	164,000

Required

1. Prepare a table with the following column headings: Land, Building 2, Building 3, Land Improvements 1, and Land Improvements 2. Allocate the costs incurred by Moonscapes to the appropriate columns and total each column.

2. Prepare a single journal entry to record all the incurred costs assuming they are paid in cash on January 1, 2002.

3. Using the straight-line method, prepare the December 31 adjusting entries to record depreciation for the 12 months of 2002 when these assets were in use.

Clampett Contractors completed the following transactions and events involving the purchase and operation of equipment in its business:

2002

Jan. 1 Paid $287,600 cash plus $11,504 in sales tax and $1,500 in transportation (FOB shipping point) for a new loader. The loader is estimated to have a four-year life and a $20,604 salvage value. Loader costs are recorded in the Equipment account.

Jan. 3 Paid $4,800 to enclose the cab and install air conditioning in the loader to enable operations under harsher conditions. This increased the estimated salvage value of the loader by another $1,396.

Dec. 31 Recorded annual straight-line depreciation on the loader.

2003

Jan. 1 Paid $5,400 to overhaul the loader's engine, which increased the loader's estimated useful life by two years.

Feb. 17 Paid $820 to repair the loader after the operator backs it into a tree.

Dec. 31 Recorded annual straight-line depreciation on the loader.

Required

Prepare journal entries to record these transactions and events.

Problem 11-3A

Computing and revising depreciation; revenue and capital expenditures

---

ACT Company completed the following transactions and events involving its delivery trucks:

2002

Jan. 1 Paid $20,515 cash plus $1,485 in sales tax for a new delivery truck estimated to have a five-year life and a $2,000 salvage value. Delivery truck costs are recorded in the Trucks account.

Dec. 31 Recorded annual straight-line depreciation on the truck.

2003

Dec. 31 Recorded annual straight-line depreciation on the truck. Due to new information obtained earlier in the year, the truck's estimated useful life was changed from five to four years, and the estimated salvage value was increased to $2,500.

2004

Dec. 31 Recorded annual straight-line depreciation on the truck.

Dec. 31 Sold the truck for $5,200 cash.

Required

Prepare journal entries to record these transactions and events.

Problem 11-4A

Computing and revising depreciation; selling plant assets

Part 1. A machine costing $257,500 with a four-year life and an estimated $20,000 salvage value is installed in Carlton Company's factory on January 1. The factory manager estimates the machine will produce 475,000 units of product during its life. It actually produces the following units: year 1, 220,000; year 2, 124,600; year 3, 121,800; and year 4, 15,200. The total number of units produced by the end of year 4 exceeds the original estimate—this difference was not predicted. (The machine must not be depreciated below its estimated salvage value.)

Required

Prepare a table with the following column headings:

Problem 11-5A

Depreciation methods; disposal of plant asset

Year	Straight-Line	Units-of-Production	Double-Declining-Balance

Compute depreciation for each year and the total depreciation of all years combined for the machine under each depreciation method.

Part 2. Casablanca purchases a used machine for $178,000 cash on January 2 and readies it for use the next day at a $2,840 cost. It is installed on a new platform costing $1,160. The company predicts the machine will be used for six years and have a $15,000 salvage value. Depreciation is to be charged on a straight-line basis. A full year's depreciation is charged on December 31, the end of the first year of the machine's use. On December 31 of its fifth year in use, it is disposed of.

Required

a. Prepare journal entries to record the machine purchase and cost to ready and install it. Cash is paid for all costs incurred.

b. Prepare journal entries to record depreciation of the machine at December 31 of its first year and at December 31 in the year of its disposal.

c. Prepare journal entries to record the machine's disposal under each of the following unrelated assumptions: (i) it is sold for $15,000 cash; (ii) it is sold for $50,000 cash; and (iii) it is destroyed in a fire and the insurance company pays $30,000 to settle the loss claim.

Problem 11-6A

Intangible assets and natural resources

Part 1. On July 1, 2002, Sweetman Company signs a contract to lease space in a building for 15 years. The lease contract calls for annual rental payments of $80,000 on each July 1 throughout the life of the lease, and that the lessee will pay for all additions and improvements to the leased property. On June 20, 2007, Sweetman decides to sublease the space to Kirk & Associates for the remaining 10 years of the lease—Kirk pays $200,000 to Sweetman for the right to sublease and it agrees to assume the obligation to pay the $80,000 annual rent to the building owner beginning July 1, 2007. After taking possession of the leased space, Kirk pays for improving the office portion of the leased space at a $130,000 cost. The improvements are paid for on July 5, 2007 and are estimated to have a useful life equal to the 16 years remaining in the life of the building.

Required

Prepare entries for Kirk to record (a) its payment to Sweetman for the right to sublease the building space, (b) its payment of the 2007 annual rent to the building owner, and (c) its payment for the office improvements. Prepare Kirk's year-end adjusting entries required at December 31, 2007, to (d) amortize the $200,000 cost of the sublease, (e) amortize the office improvements, and (f) record rent expense.

Part 2. On July 3 of the current year, Denver Mining Co. pays $4,725,000 for land estimated to contain 5,125 million tons of recoverable ore. It installs machinery costing $400,000 that has a 10-year life and no salvage value and is capable of mining the ore deposit in eight years. The machinery is paid for on July 25, seven days before mining operations begin. The company removes and sells 480,000 tons of ore during its first five months of operations. Depreciation of the machinery is in proportion to the mine's depletion as the machinery will be abandoned after the ore is mined.

Required

Preparation Component

Prepare entries to record (a) the purchase of the land, (b) the cost and installation of machinery, (c) the first five months' depletion assuming the land has a net salvage value of zero after the ore is mined, and (d) the first five months' depreciation on machinery.

Analysis Component

Describe both the similarities and differences in amortization, depletion, and depreciation.

Rent-A-Way, an equipment rental business, has the following balance sheet on December 31, 2002:

Problem 11-7A
Goodwill estimation
and amortization

Assets		
Cash		$ 87,800
Equipment	$725,300	
Accumulated depreciation—Equipment	303,500	421,800
Buildings	360,000	
Accumulated depreciation—Buildings	160,000	200,000
Land		102,000
Total assets		$811,600
Liabilities and Equity		
Accounts payable		$100,400
Long-term note payable		285,400
J. Reynolds, Capital		425,800
Total liabilities and equity		$811,600

In this industry, normal annual net income averages 20% of equity. Rent-A-Way regularly expects to earn $100,000 annually. The balance sheet amounts are reasonable estimates of market values for both assets (except goodwill) and liabilities. In negotiations to sell the business, Rent-A-Way proposes to measure goodwill by capitalizing the amount of above-normal net income at a rate of 15%. The potential buyer thinks that goodwill should be valued at five times the amount of above-normal net income.

Required

1. Compute the amount of goodwill as proposed by Rent-A-Way.

2. Compute the amount of goodwill as proposed by the potential buyer.

3. The buyer purchases the business for the net asset amount (assets less liabilities) reported on the December 31, 2002, balance sheet plus the amount proposed by Rent-A-Way for goodwill. What is the buyer's purchase price?

4. If the buyer earns $100,000 of net income *before* amortization of goodwill in its first year after acquiring the business under the terms in part (3), and goodwill is amortized over the longest permissible time period, what amount of net income is reported for the first year?

5. What rate of return does the buyer's investment earn for the first year given the facts in parts (3) and (4)?

Check   (1) $98,933 and
(2) $74,200

Asheville Company negotiates a lump-sum purchase of several assets from a contractor who is relocating. The purchase is completed on January 1, 2002, at a total cash price of $1,720,000 for a building, land, land improvements, and six trucks. The estimated market values of the assets are building, $895,400; land, $430,200; land improvements, $248,200; and six trucks, $203,900. The company's fiscal year ends on December 31.

PROBLEM SET B

Problem 11-1B
Plant asset costs;
depreciation methods

Required

Preparation Component

1. Prepare a table to allocate the lump-sum purchase price to the separate assets purchased. Prepare the journal entry to record the purchase.

2. Compute the depreciation expense for year 2002 on the building using the straight-line method, assuming a 12-year life and a $120,000 salvage value.

3. Compute the depreciation expense for year 2002 on the land improvements assuming a 10-year life and double-declining-balance depreciation.

Check   (3) Depreciation, $48,160

Analysis Component

4. Defend or refute this statement: Accelerated depreciation results in payment of more taxes over the assets life.

In January 2002, BuyTech pays $1,550,000 for a tract of land with two buildings. It plans to demolish Building A and build a new shop in its place. Building B will be a company office; it is appraised at a $489,900 value, with a useful life of 15 years and a $100,000 salvage value. A lighted parking lot near Building B has improvements (Land Improvements B) valued at $127,200 and expected to

Problem 11-2B
Real estate
costs; depreciation

last another six years with no salvage value. Without the buildings and improvements, the tract of land is valued at $802,549. BuyTech also incurs the following additional costs:

Cost to demolish Building A	$ 122,000
Cost of additional landscaping	174,500
Cost to construct new building (Building C), having a useful life of 20 years and a $258,000 salvage value	1,458,000
Cost of new land improvements (Land Improvements C) near building C, having a 10-year useful life and no salvage value	103,500

Required

1. Prepare a table with the following column headings: Land, Building B, Building C, Land Improvements B, and Land Improvements C. Allocate the costs incurred by BuyTech to the appropriate columns and total each column.

2. Prepare a single journal entry to record all incurred costs assuming they are paid in cash on January 1, 2002.

3. Using the straight-line method, prepare the December 31 adjusting entries to record depreciation for the 12 months of 2002 when these assets were in use.

Problem 11-3B

Computing and revising depreciation; revenue and capital expenditures

Pronto Delivery Service completed the following transactions and events involving the purchase and operation of its equipment for its business:

2002

Jan. 1   Paid $25,860 cash plus $1,810 in sales tax for a new delivery van that was estimated to have a five-year life and a $3,670 salvage value. Van costs are recorded in the Equipment account.

Jan. 3   Paid $1,850 to install sorting racks in the van for more accurate and quicker delivery of packages. This increases the estimated salvage value of the van by another $230.

Dec. 31   Recorded annual straight-line depreciation on the van.

2003

Jan. 1   Paid $2,080 to overhaul the van's engine, which increased the van's estimated useful life by two years.

May 10   Paid $800 to repair the van after the driver backed it into a loading dock.

Dec. 31   Record annual straight-line depreciation on the van.

Required

Prepare journal entries to record these transactions and events.

Problem 11-4B

Computing and revising depreciation; selling plant assets

Precision Instruments completed the following transactions and events involving its machinery:

2002

Jan. 1   Paid $107,800 cash plus $6,470 in sales tax for a new machine. The machine is estimated to have a six-year life and a $10,270 salvage value.

Dec. 31   Recorded annual straight-line depreciation on the machinery.

2003

Dec. 31   Recorded annual straight-line depreciation on the machine. Due to new information obtained earlier in the year, the machine's estimated useful life was changed from six to four years, and the estimated salvage value was increased to $14,100.

2004

Dec. 31   Recorded annual straight-line depreciation on the machine.

Dec. 31   Sold the machine for $25,240 cash.

Required

Prepare journal entries to record these transactions and events.

Part 1. On January 2, Brodie Co. purchases and installs a new machine costing $324,000 with a five-year life and an estimated $30,000 salvage value. Management estimates the machine will produce 1,470,000 units of product during its life. Actual production of units is as follows: year 1, 355,600; year 2, 320,400; year 3, 317,000; year 4, 342,600; and year 5, 138,500. The total number of units produced by the end of year 5 exceeds the original estimate—this difference was not predicted. (The machine must not be depreciated below its estimated salvage value.)

Problem 11-5B
Depreciation methods; disposal of plant assets

Required

Prepare a table with the following column headings:

Year	Straight-Line	Units-of-Production	Double-Declining-Balance

Compute depreciation for each year and total depreciation of all years combined for the machine under each depreciation method.

Check   DDB depreciation, Year 3, $46,656

Part 2. On January 1, Trek purchases a used machine for $150,000 and readies it for use the next day at a cost of $3,510. It is mounted on a new platform costing $4,600. Management estimates the machine will be used for seven years and have an $18,110 salvage value. Depreciation is to be charged on a straight-line basis. A full year's depreciation is charged on December 31 of the first through fifth years of the machine's use. On December 31 of its sixth year of use, the machine is disposed of.

Required

a. Prepare journal entries to record the machine purchase and the cost to ready and install it. Cash is paid for all costs incurred.

b. Prepare journal entries to record depreciation of the machine at December 31 of its first year and at December 31 in the year of its disposal.

c. Prepare journal entries to record the machine's disposal under each of the following unrelated assumptions: (i) it is sold for $28,000 cash; (ii) it is sold for $52,000 cash; and (iii) it is destroyed in a fire and the insurance company pays $25,000 to settle the loss claim.

Check   (iii) Dr. Loss from Fire, $13,110

Part 1. On January 1, 2002, Grandview Co. enters into a 12-year lease on a building. The lease contract requires: (1) annual rental payments of $36,000 each Jan. 1 throughout the life of the lease and (2) that the lessee will pay for all additions and improvements to the leased property. On January 1, 2009, Grandview decides to sublease the space to Moberly Co. for the remaining five years of the lease—Moberly pays $40,000 to Grandview for the right to sublease and agrees to assume the obligation to pay the $36,000 annual rent to the building owner beginning Jan. 1, 2009. After taking possession of the leased space, Moberly pays for improving the office portion of the leased space at a $20,000 cost. The improvements are paid for on Jan. 3, 2009, and are estimated to have a useful life equal to the 13 years remaining in the life of the building.

Problem 11-6B
Intangible assets and natural resources

Required

Prepare entries for Moberly to record (a) its payment to Grandview for the right to sublease the building space, (b) its payment of the 2009 annual rent to the building owner, and (c) its payment for the office improvements. Prepare Moberly's year-end adjusting entries required on December 31, 2009, to (d) amortize the $40,000 cost of the sublease, (e) amortize the office improvements, and (f) record rent expense.

Check   (e) Dr. Rent Expense, $4,000

Part 2. On February 19 of the current year, Rock Solid Co. pays $5,400,000 for land estimated to contain 4 million tons of recoverable ore. It installs machinery costing $400,000 that has a 16-year life and no salvage value and is capable of mining the ore deposit in 12 years. The machinery is paid for on March 21, 11 days before mining operations begin. The company removes and sells 254,000 tons of ore during its first nine months of operations. Depreciation of the machinery is in proportion to the mine's depletion as the machinery will be abandoned after the ore is mined.

Required

Preparation Component

Prepare entries to record (a) the purchase of the land, (b) the cost and installation of machinery, (c) the first nine months' depletion assuming the land has a net salvage value of zero after the ore is mined, and (d) the first nine months' depreciation on machinery.

Analysis Component

Describe both the similarities and differences in amortization, depletion, and depreciation.

Problem 11-7B

Goodwill estimation and amortization

P6

Tiki Casual Wear has the following balance sheet on December 31, 2003:

Assets		
Cash		$ 148,700
Merchandise inventory		608,950
Buildings	$ 452,800	
Accumulated depreciation—Buildings	212,800	240,000
Land		185,900
Total assets		$1,183,550
Liabilities and Equity		
Accounts payable		$ 108,520
Long-term note payable		415,975
M. Hepperly, Capital		659,055
Total liabilities and equity		$1,183,550

In this industry, normal annual net income averages 28% of equity. Tiki regularly expects to earn $200,000 annually. The balance sheet amounts are reasonable estimates of market values for both assets (except goodwill) and liabilities. In negotiations to sell the business, Tiki proposes to measure goodwill by capitalizing the amount of above-normal net income at a rate of 10%. The potential buyer believes that goodwill should be valued at eight times the amount of above-normal net income.

Required

1. Compute the amount of goodwill as proposed by Tiki.

2. Compute the amount of goodwill as proposed by the potential buyer.

3. The buyer purchases the business for the net asset amount (assets less liabilities) reported on the December 31, 2003, balance sheet plus the amount proposed by Tiki for goodwill. What is the buyer's purchase price?

4. If the buyer earns $200,000 of net income *before* amortization of goodwill in its first year after acquiring the business under the terms in part (3), and goodwill is amortized over the longest permissible time period, what amount of net income is reported for the first year?

5. What rate of return does the buyer's investment earn for the first year given the facts in parts (3) and (4)?

Beyond the Numbers

Reporting in Action

A1 **A2**

BTN 11-1   Refer to the financial statements for **Nike** in Appendix A to answer the following:

1. What percent of the original cost of Nike's property, plant, and equipment remains to be depreciated as of May 31, 2000, and May 31, 1999? Assume these assets have no salvage value.

2. Over what length(s) of time is Nike amortizing its intangible assets and goodwill?

3. What is the change in total property, plant, and equipment (before accumulated depreciation) for the year ended May 31, 2000? What is the amount of cash provided (used) by investing activities for property, plant, and equipment for the year ended May 31, 2000? What is one possible explanation for the difference between these two amounts?

4. Compute Nike's total asset turnover for the year ended May 31, 2000.

Swoosh Ahead

5. Access **Nike**'s annual report for fiscal years ending after May 31, 2000, at its Web site [**www.nike.com**] or the SEC's EDGAR database [**www.sec.gov**]. Recompute Nike's total asset turnover for the additional years' data you collect. Comment on any differences relative to the turnover computed in part (4).

BTN 11-2   Key comparative figures ($ in millions) for **Nike** and **Reebok** follow:

Comparative Analysis

A2

Key Figures	Nike			Reebok		
	Current Year	One Year Prior	Two Years Prior	Current Year	One Year Prior	Two Years Prior
Total assets	$5,856.9	$5,247.7	$5,397.4	$1,564.1	$1,684.6	$1,756.1
Net sales	8,995.1	8,776.9	9,553.1	2,899.9	3,224.6	3,643.6

Required

1. Compute total asset turnover for the most recent two years for both Nike and Reebok using the data shown.

2. Which company is more efficient in generating net sales given the total assets it employs?

BTN 11-3   Janice Griffin owns a small business and manages its accounting. Her company just finished a year in which a large amount of borrowed funds were invested in a new building addition as well as in equipment and fixture additions. Janice's banker requires her to submit semiannual financial statements so he can monitor the financial health of her business. He has warned her that if profit margins erode, he might raise the interest rate on the borrowed funds to reflect the increased loan risk from the bank's point of view. Janice knows profit margin is likely to decline this year. As she prepares year-end adjusting entries, she decides to apply the following depreciation rule: all asset additions are considered to be in use on the first day of the following month.

Ethics Challenge

C1 C2

Required

1. Identify decisions that managers like Janice must make in applying depreciation methods.

2. Is Janice's rule an ethical violation, or is it a legitimate decision in computing depreciation?

3. How will Janice's depreciation rule affect the profit margin of her business?

BTN 11-4   Teams are to select an industry, and each team member is to select a different company in that industry. Each team member is to acquire the annual report (form 10-K) of the company selected. Annual reports can be obtained at the company's Web site or the SEC's EDGAR database [**www.sec.gov**]. Use the annual report to compute total asset turnover. Communicate with teammates via a meeting, e-mail, or telephone to discuss the meaning of this ratio, how different companies compare to each other, and the industry norm. The team must prepare a one-page report that describes the ratios for each company and identifies the conclusions reached during the team's discussion.

Communicating in Practice

A2

BTN 11-5   Access **Adaptec**'s (ticker: ADPT) 10-K report filed on June 27, 2000, at <u>**www.edgar-online.com**</u> to answer the following.

Taking It to the Net

C1 P6

Required

1. Read the overview of Adaptec's business and briefly describe the types of products it produces.

2. On page 7 of the 10-K, what information is provided regarding the company's patents?

3. Does Adaptec show any patent-related revenue or expense on its consolidated statement of operations (income statement)?

4. How much goodwill did Adaptec amortize in year 2000 and year 1999?

Teamwork in Action

Point: This activity can follow an overview of each method. Step 1 allows for three areas of expertise. Larger teams will have some duplication of areas, but the straight-line choice should not be duplicated. The instructor should specify time allowed for each step. Expert teams can use the book and consult with the instructor.

BTN 11-6   Each team member is to become an expert on one depreciation method to facilitate teammates' understanding of that method. Follow these procedures:

a. Each team member is to select an area for expertise from one of the following depreciation methods: straight-line, units-of-production, and declining-balance.

b. Expert teams are to be formed from those who have selected the same area of expertise. The instructor will identify the location where each expert team meets.

c. Using the following data, expert teams are to collaborate and develop a presentation answering the requirements. Expert team members must write the presentation in a format they can show to their learning teams.

Presentation Data and Requirements

Data: On January 8, 2002, Whitewater Riders purchase a van to transport rafters back to the point of departure at the conclusion of the rafting adventures they operate. The cost of the van is $44,000. It has an estimated salvage value of $2,000 and is expected to be used for four years and driven 60,000 miles. The van is expected to be driven 12,000 miles in 2002, 18,000 miles in 2003, 21,000 in 2004, and 10,000 in 2005.

1. Compute annual depreciation expense for each year of the van's estimated useful life.
2. Explain when and how annual depreciation is recorded.
3. Explain the impact of this depreciation method versus others on income over the van's life.
4. Identify the van's book value for each year of its life and illustrate the reporting of this amount for any one year.

d. Reform original learning teams. In rotation, experts are to present to their teams the results from part (c). Experts are to encourage and respond to questions.

Business Week Activity

BTN 11-7   Read the commentary "Goodwill Accounting" in the August 30, 1999, issue of *Business Week*.

Required

1. Explain how goodwill is calculated in accounting terms?
2. Describe how goodwill was accounted for prior to 1970.
3. How is goodwill accounted for under existing accounting standards?
4. What proposal is the FASB seriously considering regarding the write-off period for goodwill?
5. What plan do the two accounting professors at Southern Methodist University propose in accounting for goodwill?

Entrepreneurial Decision

BTN 11-8   Jason Gannon is an entrepreneur and owner of **Game Haven**, which is a gameroom gallery providing high-tech action games aimed at teenagers and young adults. Game Haven consistently earns annual net sales of $350,000 on an average total asset investment of $100,000. To increase sales, Gannon proposes to expand the gameroom, which would increase average total assets by $50,000. This expansion is expected to increase net sales by $250,000.

Required

1. Compute this company's total asset turnover under (a) current conditions and (b) proposed conditions.
2. Evaluate and comment on the merits of Gannon's proposal given your analysis in part (1). Identify any concerns you would express about the proposal.

12

Current Liabilities

"Look for something missing in a given market."—Dennis Telfer

A Look Back

Chapter 11 focused on long-term assets including plant assets, natural resources, and intangibles. We showed how to record their costs, allocate their costs to periods benefiting from their use, and record their disposal.

A Look at This Chapter

This chapter emphasizes current liabilities and introduces long-term liabilities. We explain how to identify, compute, record, and report current liabilities in financial statements.

A Look Ahead

Chapter 13 explains the partnership form of organization. Important characteristics of this form of organization are described as are the accounting concepts and procedures for its basic transactions.

Learning Objectives

Conceptual

C1 Describe current and long-term liabilities and their characteristics.

C2 Identify and describe known current liabilities.

C3 Explain how to account for contingent liabilities.

C4 Describe accounting for long-term liabilities.

Analytical

A1 Compute the times interest earned ratio and use it to analyze liabilities.

Procedural

P1 Prepare entries to account for short-term notes payable.

P2 Compute and record *employee* payroll deductions and liabilities.

P3 Compute and record *employer* payroll expenses and liabilities.

P4 Account for estimated liabilities, including warranties and income taxes.

Carve and Slide

e LA JOLLA, CA—What do you get when you mix untamed ambition with a wild urge to carve, slide, and cross-step? The answer is **Sector 9** (**Sector9.com**), a skateboard manufacturer that traces its roots to three 20-something mavericks messing around in a backyard in La Jolla. Back then there wasn't anyone making long board skateboards. But Sector 9 changed all that when three skateboarding pals—Dennis Telfer, Dave Klimkiewicz, and Steve Lake—launched their skateboard manufacturing company. "It was something that was really different," says Telfer, describing how they did not focus on today's downscaled models but instead revived the long boards reminiscent of the 1970s. Skateboard manufacturers "pretty much laughed at us," recalls Telfer. But laugh no more. What started as a desire to skate more like one would surf or snowboard has developed into a craze for a growing number of skateboarders—and Sector 9 leads the way. Telfer says, "Our style of riding has opened up a totally new niche in the industry."

Still, it takes more than ideas and ambition to launch a company. The three worked hard testing different designs in Telfer's backyard before moving their fledgling skateboard craftsmanship to an indoor facility. Today, Sector 9, a company of 25 people, has a common goal of introducing the world to its style of skateboarding. Along the way, the friends learned to handle many aspects of business, including the crucial task of managing their liabilities, as well as obligations for payroll, skateboard materials, warranties, worker benefits, and taxes. Without effective management of liabilities, Sector 9 would not be where it is today. "It's pretty crazy," says Telfer, who recognizes that liability management continues to be crucial to the success of Sector 9. "As stressed as I am, though, I always love it." The three visionaries of Sector 9 continue to roll.

The market has embraced Sector 9 skateboards. Sector 9's annual sales projections are close to $5 million and its management of liabilities is first rate. Taking the skateboard path less traveled is proving rewarding for these three ardent skateboarders with humble beginnings. [Sources: *Sector 9 Web Site,* May 2001; *Entrepreneur,* November 12, 1998.]

Chapter Preview

Previous chapters introduced us to liabilities such as accounts payable, notes payable, wages payable, and unearned revenues. In this chapter, we learn more about these liabilities and additional ones such as warranties, taxes, payroll, vacation pay, and leases. We also describe contingent liabilities and look at some long-term liabilities. Our focus is on how to define, classify, measure, and analyze liabilities in order to report useful information about them to business decision makers.

Characteristics of Liabilities

This section discusses important characteristics of liabilities and how they are classified and reported.

Defining Liabilities

C1 Describe current and long-term liabilities and their characteristics.

A liability is a probable future payment of assets or services that a company is presently obligated to make as a result of past transactions or events. This definition includes three crucial factors:

- Due to a past transaction or event.
- Present obligation.
- Future payment of assets or services.

Exhibit 12.1

Characteristics of a Liability

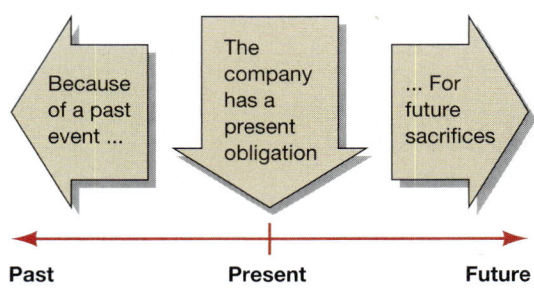

Past   Present   Future

These three important elements are portrayed visually in Exhibit 12.1. Liabilities do not include all expected future payments. For example, most companies expect to pay wages to their employees in upcoming months and years, but these future payments are not liabilities because no past event such as employee work resulted in a present obligation. Instead, the liabilities arise when employees perform their work and earn the wages.

Classifying Liabilities

Information about liabilities is more useful when the balance sheet identifies them as either current or long term. Decision makers need to know when obligations are due so they can plan for them and take appropriate action.

Current Liabilities

Current liabilities, also called *short-term liabilities,* are obligations due within one year or the company's operating cycle, whichever is longer. They are expected to be paid using current assets or by creating other current liabilities. Common examples of current liabilities are accounts payable, short-term notes payable, wages payable, warranty liabilities, lease liabilities, taxes payable, and unearned revenues.

Current liabilities are different across companies. A company's current liabilities depend on its type of operations. **Harley-Davidson,** for instance, recently included the following current accrued liabilities related to its motorcycle operations ($000s):

Warranty/recalls	$14,655
Dealer incentive programs	40,322

Univision, the leading Spanish-language television broadcaster, reports a much different set of current liabilities. For instance, it reports more than $140 million in current liabilities made up of items such as television programming and license fee liabilities.

Point: Improper classification of liabilities can distort key ratios used in financial statement analysis and decision making.

Global: In some countries such as France, the balance sheet does not separate current liabilities into their own category.

Long-Term Liabilities

A company's obligations not expected to be paid within the longer of one year or the company's operating cycle are reported as **long-term liabilities.** They can include long-term notes payable, warranty liabilities, lease liabilities, and bonds payable. They are sometimes reported on the balance sheet in a single long-term liabilities total or in multiple categories. **Domino's,** for instance, reports long-term liabilities in its recent balance sheet of ($ millions): long-term debt, $696; insurance reserves, $15; other, $22. They are reported after current liabilities. A single liability also can be divided between the current and noncurrent sections if a company expects to make payments toward it in both the short- and long-term. In the case of Domino's, it reports ($ millions) long-term debt, $696; and current portion of long-term debt, $21. The second item is reported in current liabilities. We sometimes see liabilities that do not have a fixed due date but are payable on the creditor's demand. These are reported as current liabilities because of the possibility of payment in the near-term. Exhibit 12.2 shows amounts of current and long-term liabilities for selected companies.

Point: The current ratio will be over-stated by a failure to classify the portion of long-term debt due next period as a current liability.

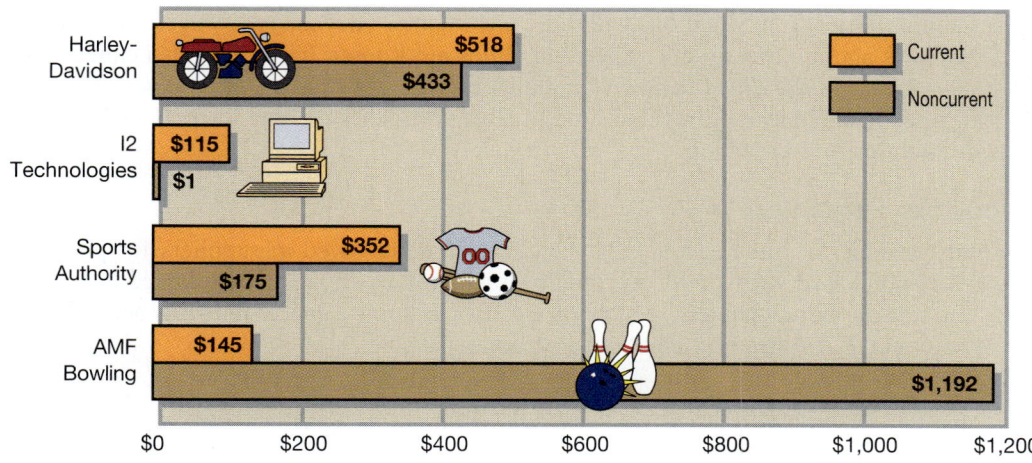

Exhibit 12.2

Current and Long-Term Liabilities ($ millions)

Uncertainty in Liabilities

Accounting for liabilities involves addressing three important questions: Whom to pay? When to pay? How much to pay? Answers to these questions are often decided when a liability is incurred. For example, if a company has a $100 account payable to a specific individual, payable on March 15, the answers are clear. The company knows whom to pay, when to pay, and how much to pay. However, the answers to one or more of these three questions are uncertain for some liabilities.

Uncertainty in Whom to Pay

Liabilities can involve uncertainty in whom to pay. For instance, a company can create a liability with a known amount when issuing a note that is payable to its holder. In this case, a specific amount is payable to the note's holder at a specified date, but the company does not know who the holder is until that date. Despite this uncertainty, the company reports this liability on its balance sheet.

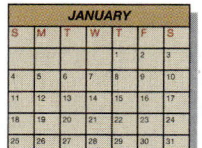

Uncertainty in When to Pay

A company can have an obligation of a known amount to a known creditor but not know when it must be paid. For example, a legal services firm can accept fees in advance from a client who plans to use the firm's services in the future. This means that the firm has a liability that it settles by providing services at an unknown future date. Although this uncertainty exists, the firm's balance sheet must report this liability. These types of obligations are reported as current liabilities because they are likely to be settled in the short term.

Uncertainty in How Much to Pay

A company can be aware of an obligation but not know how much will be required to settle it. For example, a company using electrical power is billed only after the meter has been read. This cost is incurred and the liability created before a bill is received. A liability to the power company is reported as an estimated amount if the balance sheet is prepared before a bill arrives.

Quick Check

1. What is a liability?
2. Is every expected future payment a liability?
3. If a liability is payable in 15 months, is it classified as current or long-term?

Answers—p. 509

Known (Determinable) Liabilities

 Identify and describe known current liabilities.

Most liabilities arise from situations with little uncertainty. They are set by agreements, contracts, or laws and are measurable. These liabilities are **known liabilities,** also called *definitely determinable liabilities.* Known liabilities include accounts payable, notes payable, payroll, sales taxes, unearned revenues, and leases. We describe how to account for these known liabilities in this section.

Accounts Payable

Accounts payable, or trade accounts payable, are amounts owed to suppliers for products or services purchased with credit. Accounting for accounts payable is explained and illustrated in several prior chapters. Much of our discussion of merchandising activities in Chapters 6 and 7, for instance, dealt with accounts payable.

Sales Taxes Payable

Nearly every state and many cities levy taxes on retail sales. Sales taxes are stated as a percent of selling prices. The retailer (seller) collects sales taxes from customers when sales occur and remits these collections (often monthly) to the proper government agency. Since retailers currently owe these collections to the government, this amount is a current liability for retailers. **Home Depot**, for instance, reports sales taxes payable of $269 million in its recent annual report. To illustrate, if Home Depot sells materials on August 31 worth $6,000 that are subject to a 5% sales tax, its entry is

Aug. 31	Cash	6,300	
	Sales		6,000
	Sales Taxes Payable ($6,000 × 0.05)		300
	To record cash sales and 5% sales tax.		

Assets = Liabilities + Equity
+6,300   +300   +6,000

Sales Taxes Payable is debited and Cash credited when it remits these collections to the government. Sales Taxes Payable is not an expense. It arises because laws require retailers to collect this cash from customers for the government.

Unearned Revenues

Unearned revenues (also called *deferred revenues, collections in advance,* and *prepayments*) are amounts received in advance from customers for future products or services. Advance ticket sales for sporting events or music concerts are examples. The **Boston Celtics**, for instance, reported "deferred game revenues" including advance ticket sales of $10.4 million in its recent balance sheet. When the Celtics sell $5 million of season tickets, its entry is

Point: To *defer* a revenue means to postpone recognition of a revenue collected in advance until it is earned. Sport teams must defer recognition of ticket sales until games are played.

June 30	Cash	5,000,000	
	Unearned Season Ticket Revenue		5,000,000
	To record sale of Celtic season tickets.		

Assets = Liabilities + Equity
+5,000,000   +5,000,000

When each game is played, the Celtics record revenue for the portion earned:

Oct. 31	Unearned Season Ticket Revenue	60,000	
	Season Ticket Revenue		60,000
	To record Celtic season ticket revenues earned.		

Assets = Liabilities + Equity
            −60,000   +60,000

Unearned Season Ticket Revenue is an unearned revenue account and is reported as a current liability. Unearned revenues also arise with airline ticket sales, magazine subscriptions, construction projects, hotel reservations, and custom orders.

Short-Term Notes Payable

A **short-term note payable** is a written promise to pay a specified amount on a definite future date within one year or the company's operating cycle, whichever is longer. These promissory notes are negotiable (as are checks), meaning they can be transferred from party to party by endorsement. The written documentation provided by notes is helpful in resolving disputes and for pursuing legal actions involving these liabilities. Most notes payable bear interest to compensate for use of the amount until payment is made. Short-term notes payable can arise from many transactions. A company that purchases merchandise on credit can sometimes extend the credit period by signing a note to replace an account payable. They also can arise when money is borrowed from a bank. We describe both of these cases in this section.

P1 Prepare entries to account for short-term notes payable.

Point: Required characteristics for negotiability of a note: (1) unconditional promise, (2) in writing, (3) specific amount, and (4) definite due date.

Note Given to Extend Credit Period

A company can replace an account payable with a note payable. A common example is a creditor that requires the substitution of an interest-bearing note for an overdue account payable that does not bear interest. A less common situation occurs when a debtor's weak financial condition motivates the creditor to obtain a note, sometimes for a lesser amount, and to close the account to ensure that this customer makes no additional credit purchases.

Illustration of note to extend credit period

To illustrate, let's assume that on August 23, Irwin asks to extend its past-due $600 account payable to McGraw. After some negotiations, McGraw agrees to accept $100 cash and a 60-day, 12%, $500 note payable to replace the account payable. Irwin records the transaction with this entry:

Aug. 23	Accounts Payable—McGraw	600	
	Cash		100
	Notes Payable		500
	Gave $100 cash and a 60-day, 12% note for		
	payment on account.		

Assets = Liabilities + Equity
−100   −600
             +500

Signing the note does not pay Irwin's debt. Instead, the form of debt is changed from an account payable to a note payable. McGraw prefers the note payable over the account payable because it earns interest and it is written documentation of the debt's existence, term, and amount. When the note comes due, Irwin pays the note and interest by giving McGraw a check for $510. This payment is recorded with this entry:

Point: Accounts payable are detailed in a subsidiary ledger, but notes payable are usually not. This means a creditor's name is not often necessary in an entry. A file with copies of notes often serves as a subsidiary ledger.

Oct. 22	Notes Payable	500	
	Interest Expense	10	
	Cash		510
	Paid note with interest ($500 × 12% × 60/360).		

Assets = Liabilities + Equity
−510   −500   −10

Point: Companies often compute interest using a 360-day year. This is known as the *banker's rule*.

Interest expense is computed by multiplying the principal of the note ($500) by the annual interest rate (12%) for the fraction of the year the note is outstanding (60 days/360 days).

Note Given to Borrow from Bank

Point: Cash received from long-term (short-term) borrowing is reported on the statement of cash flows as a source of financing (part of operating). Interest incurred on a note is reported on the income statement as an expense.

A bank nearly always requires a borrower to sign a promissory note when making a loan. When the note matures, the borrower repays the note with an amount larger than the amount borrowed. The difference between the amount borrowed and the amount repaid is *interest*. This section considers two types of notes. The first note type often states that the note's signer promises to pay *principal* (the amount borrowed) plus interest. In this case, the *face value* of the note equals principal. Face value is the value shown on the face (front) of the note. The second note type occurs when a bank has a borrower sign a note with a face value that includes both principal and interest. In this case, the note's signer receives *less* than the note's face value. The difference between the borrowed amount and the note's face value is interest. Since the borrowed amount is less than the note's face value, the difference is called **discount on note payable.** To illustrate these two types of notes, assume that a company needs $2,000 for a project and borrows this money from a bank at 12% annual interest. The loan is made on September 30, 2002, and is due in 60 days.

Point: If a company borrows money from a bank, the loan is reported as an asset (receivable) on the bank's balance sheet.

Face value equals amount borrowed

In many cases the borrowing company signs a note with its face value equal to the amount borrowed. The note includes a statement similar to this: *"I promise to pay $2,000 plus interest at 12% within 60 days after September 30."* This note is shown in Exhibit 12.3.

Exhibit 12.3

Note with Face Value Equal to Amount Borrowed

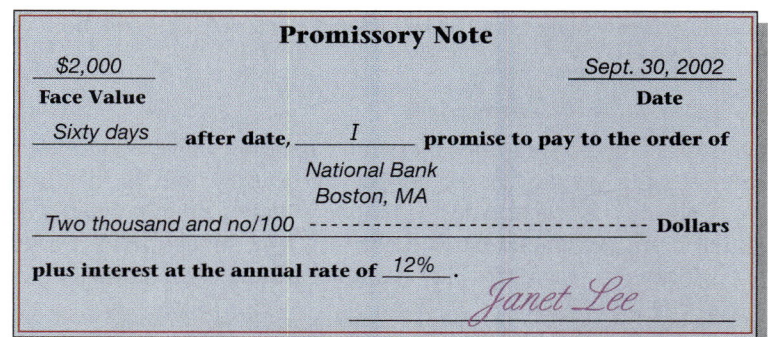

The borrower records its receipt of cash and the new liability with this entry:

Assets = Liabilities + Equity
+2,000   +2,000

Sept. 30	Cash	2,000	
	Notes Payable		2,000
	Borrowed $2,000 cash with a 60-day, 12%, $2,000 note.		

When principal and interest are paid, the borrower records payment with this entry:

Assets = Liabilities + Equity
−2,040   −2,000   −40

Nov. 29	Notes Payable	2,000	
	Interest Expense	40	
	Cash		2,040
	Paid note with interest ($2,000 × 12% × 60/360).		

Face value equals amount borrowed plus interest

Point: When interest is included in face value, the borrowing process is referred to as *discounting a note* since the borrower receives less than the face value, or a discounted amount.

In some cases the borrower signs a note with the interest included in its face value. This type of note includes a promise similar to this: *"I promise to pay $2,040 within 60 days after September 30."* This note is shown in Exhibit 12.4. The borrower receives $2,000 cash, and the note does not refer to the rate used to compute the $40 of interest included in the $2,040 face value. In other respects, this note is similar to the one in Exhibit 12.3. Since this note lacks a stated interest rate, it is sometimes called a **noninterest-bearing note,** which can be misleading since the note does bear interest that is included in the face value.

Promissory Note

$2,040	Sept. 30, 2002
Face Value	**Date**

___Sixty days___ after date, _____ I _____ promise to pay to the order of

National Bank
Boston, MA

Two thousand forty and no/100 -------------------------- **Dollars.**

Janet Lee

Exhibit 12.4

Note with Face Value Equal to Amount Borrowed plus Interest

When the face value of a note includes principal and interest, the borrower usually records this note with an entry to credit Notes Payable for its face value and to record the interest in a Discount on Notes Payable account as follows:

Point: Use of a contra liability account allows us to always enter face value when recording notes payable.

Sept. 30	Cash	2,000	
	Discount on Notes Payable	40	
	Notes Payable		2,040
	Borrowed $2,000 cash with a 60-day, $2,040 note.		

Assets = Liabilities + Equity
+2,000   +2,040
          −40

Discount on Notes Payable is a contra liability account to the Notes Payable account. If a balance sheet is prepared after this transaction on September 30, the $40 discount is subtracted from the $2,040 note to reflect the $2,000 net amount borrowed:[1]

Point: A discount reflects deferred interest expense. The matching principle supports regular recognition of this expense over time.

Notes payable	$2,040	
Less discount on notes payable	40	$2,000

When this note matures 60 days later on November 29, the entry to record the company's $2,040 payment to the bank is

Nov. 29	Notes Payable	2,040	
	Interest Expense	40	
	Cash		2,040
	Discount on Notes Payable		40
	Paid note with interest.		

Assets = Liabilities + Equity
−2,040   −2,040   −40
        +40

End-of-Period Adjustment to Notes

When the end of an accounting period falls between the signing of a note payable and its maturity date, the *matching principle* requires us to record the accrued but unpaid interest on the note. To illustrate, let's return to the earlier short-term note and assume the company borrows $2,000 cash on December 16, 2002, instead of September 30. This 60-day note

You Make the Call

Rock Band Your band needs $30,000 to upgrade equipment. You receive loan approvals for $30,000 cash at two banks. One bank's proposed loan contract reads: "Band promises to pay $30,000 plus interest at 14% within 6 months." The competing bank's loan contract reads: "Band promises to pay $32,000 within 6 months." Which loan do you prefer?

Answer—p. 509

[1] We can approximate the annual interest rate on a short-term loan as (**Interest paid** ÷ **Amount received**) × (**360 days** ÷ **Loan period in days**).

matures on February 14, 2003, and the company's fiscal year ends on December 31. Thus, we need to record interest expense for the final 15 days in December. The adjusting entry depends on the type of note.

Face value equals amount borrowed

When the note's face value equals the amount borrowed, any accrued interest is charged to expense and credited to an Interest Payable account. Specifically, we know that 15 days of the 60-day loan period for the $2,000, 12% note have elapsed by December 31. This means one-fourth (15 days/60 days) of the $40 total interest is an expense of year 2002. The borrower records this expense with the following adjusting entry:

Example: What is the annual interest rate for a (1) $2,000, 12%, 60-day note and (2) $2,000 noninterest-bearing, 60-day note with 12% interest included in its face? *Hint:* In the first case, the borrower receives $2,000; in the second, the borrower receives $1,960 ($2,000 less $40 interest). *Answer:*
Case 1 rate = $40/$2,000 = 2.0% for 60 days (or 12.0% annually).
Case 2 rate = $40/$1,960 = 2.041% for 60 days (or 12.245% annually).

Assets = Liabilities + Equity
+10   −10

2002			
Dec. 31	Interest Expense	10	
	Interest Payable		10
	To record accrued interest on note ($2,000 × 12% × 15/360).		

When this note matures on February 14, the borrower must recognize 45 days of interest expense for year 2003 and remove the balances of the two liability accounts:

Example: If this note is dated December 1 instead of December 16, how much expense is recorded on December 31? *Answer:*
$2,000 × 12% × 30/360 = $20

Assets = Liabilities + Equity
−2,040   −10   −30
          −2000

2003			
Feb. 14	Interest Expense*	30	
	Interest Payable	10	
	Notes Payable	2,000	
	Cash		2,040
	Paid note with interest. *($2,000 × 12% × 45/360)		

Did You Know?

Domi-Notes Many franchisors use notes to help entrepreneurs acquire their franchises. **Domino's** allows much of its franchise fee and store equipment to be paid with notes. Payments on these notes are usually collected monthly and are secured by the franchisees' assets.

Face value equals amount borrowed plus interest

When the face value of the note *includes* interest, any accrued interest is charged to Interest expense with an adjustment to the Discount on Notes Payable account. Specifically, for the $2,040 noninterest-bearing note entered into on December 16, the adjusting entry on December 31 needs to record the accrual for 15 days of interest. Accrued interest is recorded by reducing the balance of the contra liability account from $40 to $30. This adjustment increases the net liability to $2,010 ($2,040 note less $30 discount):

Assets = Liabilities + Equity
           +10   −10

2002			
Dec. 31	Interest Expense	10	
	Discount on Notes Payable		10
	To record accrued interest on note ($40 × 15/60).		

When this note matures, we need an entry both to accrue interest expense for its last 45 days and to record payment of both principal and interest:

Assets = Liabilities + Equity
−2,040   −2,040   −30
          +30

2003			
Feb. 14	Interest Expense*	30	
	Notes Payable	2,040	
	Discount on Notes Payable		30
	Cash		2,040
	Paid note with interest. *($40 × 45/60)		

Payroll Liabilities

An employer incurs several expenses and liabilities from having employees. These expenses and liabilities are often large and arise from salaries and wages earned, from employee benefits, and from payroll taxes levied on the employer. **Anheuser-Busch**, for instance, reports payroll-related current liabilities of more than $250 million from "accrued salaries, wages and benefits." We discuss payroll liabilities and related accounts in this section. The appendix to this chapter describes important details about payroll reports, records, and procedures.

P2 Compute and record *employee* payroll deductions and liabilities.

Employee Payroll Deductions

Gross pay is the total compensation an employee earns including wages, salaries, commissions, bonuses, and any compensation earned before deductions such as taxes.[2] **Net pay,** also called *take-home pay,* is gross pay less all deductions. **Payroll deductions,** commonly called *withholdings,* are amounts withheld from an employee's gross pay, either required or voluntary. Required deductions result from laws and include income taxes and Social Security taxes. Voluntary deductions, at an employee's option include pension and health contributions, union dues, and charitable giving. Exhibit 12.5 shows the typical payroll deductions of an employee. The employer withholds payroll

Did You Know?

Pay or Else Delay or failure to pay withholding taxes to government agencies has severe consequences. For example, a 100% penalty can be levied, with interest, on the unpaid balance. The government can even close the company, take its assets, and pursue legal actions against those involved.

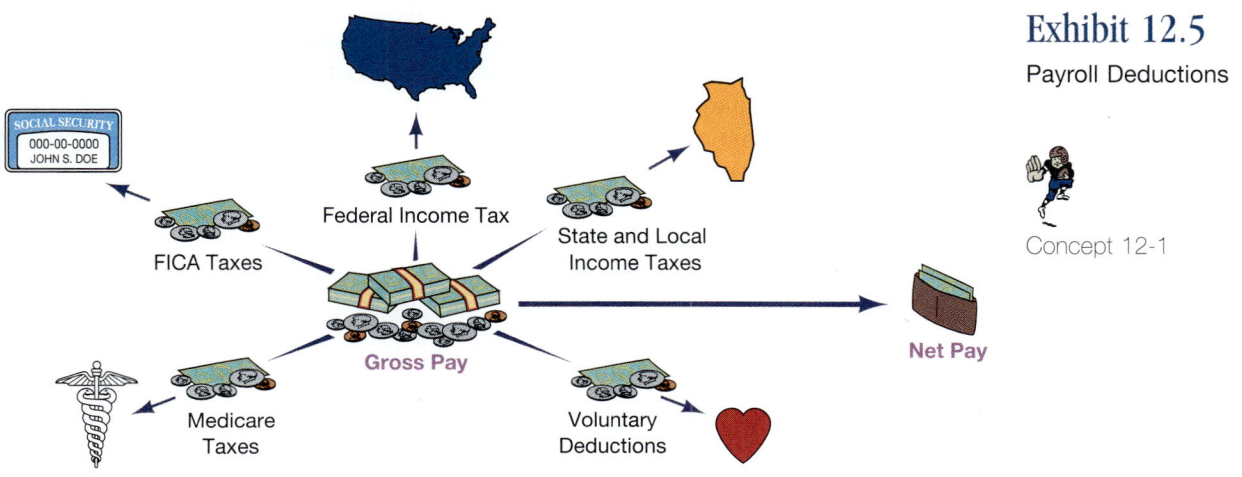

Exhibit 12.5
Payroll Deductions

Concept 12-1

---

[2] *Wages* usually refer to payments to employees at an hourly rate. *Salaries* usually refer to payments to employees at a monthly or yearly rate.

deductions from employees' pay and is obligated to transmit this money to the designated organization. The employer records payroll deductions as current liabilities until these amounts are transmitted. This section discusses the major payroll deductions.

Employee FICA taxes

The federal Social Security system provides retirement, disability, survivorship, and medical benefits to qualified workers. Laws *require* employers to withhold **Federal Insurance Contributions Act (FICA) taxes** from employees' pay to cover costs of the system. Employers usually separate FICA taxes into two groups: (1) retirement, disability, and survivorship and (2) medical. For the first group, the Social Security system provides monthly cash payments to qualified retired workers for the rest of their lives. These payments are often called *Social Security benefits.* Taxes related to this group are often called *Social Security taxes.* For the second group, the system provides monthly payments to deceased workers' surviving families and to disabled workers who qualify for assistance. These payments are commonly called *Medicare benefits,* which like those in the first group, are paid with *Medicare taxes* (part of FICA taxes).

Law requires employers to withhold FICA taxes from each employee's salary or wages on each payday. The taxes for Social Security and Medicare are computed separately. For example, for 2000, the amount withheld from each employee's pay for Social Security tax is 6.2% of the first $76,200 the employee earns in the calendar year, or a maximum of $4,724.40. The Medicare tax is 1.45% of *all* wages the employee earns. Medicare tax has no maximum amount because the government wants to maintain solvency of this program. For any changes in rates or with the maximum earnings level, check the IRS Web site at **www.IRS.USTreas.gov**.

Employers must pay withheld taxes to the Internal Revenue Service (IRS) on specific filing dates during the year. Employers who fail to send the withheld taxes to the IRS on time can be assessed substantial penalties. Until all the taxes are sent to the IRS, they are included in employers' current liabilities.

Employee income tax

Point: Part-time employees may claim "exempt from withholding" if they did not have any income tax liability in the prior year and do not expect any in the current year.

Point: IRS withholding tables are based on projecting weekly (or other period) pay into an annual figure.

Most employers are required to withhold federal income tax from each employee's paycheck. The amount withheld is computed using tables published by the IRS. The amount depends on the employee's annual earnings rate and the number of *withholding allowances* the employee claims. Allowances reduce the amount of taxes you owe the government. The more allowances you claim, the less tax your employer will withhold. Employees can claim allowances for themselves and their dependents. They also can claim additional allowances if they expect major declines in their taxable income for medical expenses. (An employee who claims more allowances than appropriate is subject to a fine.) Most states and many local governments require employers to withhold their income taxes from employees' pay and to remit them promptly to the proper government agency. Until they are paid, withholdings are reported as a current liability on the employer's balance sheet.

Employee voluntary deductions

Beyond Social Security, Medicare, and income taxes, employers often withhold other amounts from employees' earnings. These withholdings arise from employee requests, contracts, unions, or other agreements. They can include amounts for charitable giving, medical insurance premiums, pension contributions, and union dues. Until they are paid, these withholdings are employers' current liabilities.

Recording <u>Employee</u> Payroll Deductions

Employers must accrue payroll expenses and liabilities at the end of each pay period. To illustrate, assume that an employee earns a salary of $2,000 per month. At the end of January, the employer's entry to accrue payroll expenses and liabilities for this employee is

Jan. 31	Salaries Expense	2,000		Assets = Liabilities + Equity
	FICA—Social Security Taxes Payable (6.2%)		124	+124 −2,000
	FICA—Medicare Taxes Payable (1.45%) . . .		29	+29
	Employee Federal Income Taxes Payable* . .		213	+213
	Employee Medical Insurance Payable*		85	+85
	Employee Union Dues Payable*		25	+25
	Accrued Payroll Payable		1,524	+1,524
	To record payroll for January.			

* Amounts taken from employer's accounting records.

Salaries Expense (debit) shows the employee earns a gross salary of $2,000. The first five payables (credits) show liabilities the employer owes on behalf of this employee to cover FICA taxes, income taxes, medical insurance, and union dues. The Accrued Payroll Payable account (credit) records the $1,524 net pay the employee receives from the $2,000 gross pay earned. When the employee is paid, another entry (or a series of entries) is required to record the check written and distributed (or funds transferred). The entry to record cash payment to this employee is to debit Accrued Payroll Payable and credit Cash for $1,524.

Employer Payroll Taxes

Employers must pay payroll taxes in addition to those required of employees. These employer taxes include FICA and unemployment taxes.

Employer FICA tax

Employers must pay FICA taxes *equal in amount to* the FICA taxes withheld from their employees. An employer's tax is credited to the same FICA Taxes Payable accounts used to record the Social Security and Medicare taxes withheld from employees. (A self-employed person must pay both the employee and employer FICA taxes.)

Federal and state unemployment taxes

The federal government participates with states in a joint federal–state unemployment insurance program. Each state administers its own program. These programs provide unemployment benefits to qualified workers. The federal government approves state programs and pays a portion of their administrative expenses.

Federal Unemployment Taxes (FUTA). Employers are subject to a federal unemployment tax on wages and salaries paid to their employees. For 2000, an employer is required to pay FUTA taxes of as much as 6.2% of the first $7,000 earned by each employee. This federal tax can be reduced by a credit of up to 5.4% for taxes paid to a state program. As a result, the net federal unemployment tax is often only 0.8%.

State Unemployment Taxes (SUTA). All states support their unemployment insurance programs by placing a payroll tax on employers. (A few states require employees to make a contribution. In our assignments, we assume this tax is only on the employer.) In most states, the base rate for SUTA taxes is 5.4% of the first $7,000 paid each employee. This base rate is adjusted according to an employer's merit rating. The state assigns a **merit rating** that reflects a company's stability or instability in employing workers. A good rating reflects stability in employment and means an employer can pay less than the 5.4% base rate. A low

> **Did You Know?**
>
> **Payroll Control**   More than $600 million is lost annually to check schemes. Companies are fighting back with an internal control method called *positive pay*. Here's how it works: A company regularly (daily) sends the bank a "positive file" listing all checks written. When a check reaches the bank for payment, the bank compares the check against the positive file. This flags any forged checks, as well as authentic checks that have been altered. Discrepancies are reported to the company, which can stop payment.

P3   Compute and record *employer* payroll expenses and liabilities.

> **Did You Know?**
>
> **Tax Aid**   Technology helps reduce errors and increase speed in computing taxes as compared with manual use of tax tables. Tax tables can also be stored on computer or downloaded off the Web [**www.IRS.USTreas.gov**] and then used to accurately and quickly compute payroll taxes.

Web Designer   You take a summer job working for a family friend who runs a small IT service. When the time arrives for your first paycheck, the owner slaps you on the back, gives you full payment in cash, winks, and adds: "No need to pay those high taxes, eh." What action do you take?

Answer—p. 509

rating reflects high turnover or seasonal hirings and layoffs. A favorable merit rating translates into cash savings from lower taxes. To illustrate, an employer with 100 employees who each earn $7,000 or more per year saves $30,800 annually if it has a merit rating of 1.0% versus 5.4%. This is computed by comparing taxes of $37,800 at the 5.4% rate to only $7,000 at the 1.0% rate.

Recording <u>Employer</u> Payroll Taxes

Employer payroll taxes are an added expense beyond the wages and salaries earned by employees. These taxes are often recorded in an entry separate from the one recording payroll expenses and deductions. To illustrate, assume that the $2,000 recorded salaries expense on the previous page is earned by an employee whose earnings have not yet reached $5,000 for the year. Also assume that the federal unemployment tax rate is 0.8% and the state unemployment tax rate is 5.4%. The FICA portion of the employer's tax is $153, computed by multiplying both the 6.2% and 1.45% by the $2,000 gross pay. State unemployment (SUTA) taxes are $108 (5.4% of the $2,000 gross pay). Federal unemployment (FUTA) taxes are $16 (0.8% of $2,000). The entry to record the employer's payroll tax expense and related liabilities is

Example: If the employer's merit rating in this example reduces its SUTA rate to 2.9%, what is its SUTA liability? *Answer:* SUTA payable = $2,000 × 2.9% = $58

Assets = Liabilities + Equity
        +124   −277
        +29
        +108
        +16

Jan. 31	Payroll Taxes Expense	277	
	FICA—Social Security Taxes Payable (6.2%)		124
	FICA—Medicare Taxes Payable (1.45%) ..		29
	State Unemployment Taxes Payable		108
	Federal Unemployment Taxes Payable		16
	To record employer payroll taxes.		

Quick Check

6. A company pays its one employee $3,000 per month. This company's FUTA rate is 0.8% on the first $7,000 earned, its SUTA rate is 4.0% on the first $7,000, its Social Security tax rate is 6.2% of the first $76,200, and its Medicare tax rate is 1.45% of all amounts earned. The entry to record this company's March payroll includes what amount for total payroll taxes expense?

7. Identify whether the employer or employee or both pays each of the following: (a) FICA taxes; (b) FUTA taxes; (c) SUTA taxes; and (d) withheld income taxes.

Answers—p. 509

Estimated Liabilities

P4   Account for estimated liabilities, including warranties and income taxes.

An **estimated liability** is a known obligation of an uncertain amount, but one that can be reasonably estimated. Common examples are employee benefits such as pensions, health care and vacation pay, warranties offered by a seller, and income taxes. We discuss each of these in this section. Other examples of estimated liabilities include property taxes and certain contracts to provide future services.

Health and Pension Benefits

Many companies provide **employee benefits** beyond salaries and wages. An employer often pays all or part of medical, dental, life, and disability insurance. Many employers also contribute to *pension plans,* which are agreements by employers to provide benefits (payments) to employees after retirement. Many companies also provide medical care and insurance benefits to their retirees. When payroll taxes and charges for employee benefits are totaled, payroll cost often exceeds employees' gross earnings by 25% or more.

To illustrate, assume an employer agrees to (1) pay an amount for medical insurance equal to $8,000 and (2) contribute an additional 10% of employees' $120,000 gross salary to a retirement program. The entry to record these benefits is

> **Did You Know?**
>
> **Post Game Benefits**   Several ex-players are suing Major League Baseball over a pension system they say unfairly excludes them and fails to reward their contributions to the game. Gripes include failure to extend pensions to players whose careers ended before 1947, were interrupted by World War II, or were spent in the Negro League. A full pension is about $120,000 a year.

Jan. 31	Employee Benefits Expense.	20,000	
	Employee Medical Insurance Payable		8,000
	Employee Retirement Program Payable . . .		12,000
	To record costs of employee benefits.		

Assets = Liabilities + Equity
　　　　　+8,000　　−20,000
　　　　　+12,000

Vacation Pay

Many employers offer paid vacation benefits. For example, many employees earn 2 weeks' vacation by working 50 weeks. This benefit increases employers' payroll expenses because employees are paid for 52 weeks but work for only 50 weeks. Total annual salary is the same, but the cost per week worked is greater than the amount paid per week. To illustrate, if an employee is paid $20,800 for 52 weeks but works only 50 weeks, the weekly salary expense to the employer is $416 ($20,800/50 weeks) instead of the $400 paid weekly to the employee ($20,800/52 weeks). The $16 difference between these two amounts is recorded weekly to Salary Expense and Vacation Pay Liability. When the employee takes a vacation, the employer reduces the vacation pay liability but does not record any additional expense.

Global: Bonuses are considered part of salary expense in most countries. In Japan, bonuses to members of the board of directors and to external auditors are directly charged against equity rather than treated as an expense.

Bonus Plans

Many companies offer bonuses to employees, and many of the bonuses depend on net income. To illustrate, assume an employer offers a bonus to its employees equal to 5% of the company's annual net income (to be equally shared). The company's expected annual net income is $210,000. The year-end adjusting entry to record this benefit is

Dec. 31	Employee Bonus Expense*	10,000	
	Bonus Payable		10,000
	To record expected bonus costs.		

Assets = Liabilities + Equity
　　　　　+10,000　　−10,000

> * Bonus Expense is deducted in computing net income. This means it equals 5% of $210,000 *less the bonus*—computed as:
>
> $$B = 0.05\,(\$210{,}000 - B)$$
> $$B = \$10{,}500 - 0.05B$$
> $$1.05B = \$10{,}500$$
> $$\textbf{B} = \textbf{\$10{,}000}$$
>
> When the bonus is paid, Bonus Payable is debited and Cash is credited for $10,000.

Warranty Liabilities

A **warranty** is a seller's obligation to replace or correct a product (or service) that fails to perform as expected within a specified period. Most new cars, for instance, are sold with a warranty covering parts for a specified period of time. **Ford Motor Co.** reported more than $10 billion in "dealer and customer allowances and claims" in its recent annual report. To comply with the *full disclosure* and *matching principles,* the seller reports the expected warranty expense in the period when revenue from the sale of the product or service is reported.

Point: Zenith recently reported $32.1 million on its balance sheet for warranties.

The seller reports this warranty obligation as a liability, although the existence, amount, payee, and date of future sacrifices are uncertain. Still, such future sacrifices are probable, and the amount of this liability can be estimated using, for instance, past experience with warranties.

Illustration of Warranty Liabilities

To illustrate, consider a dealer who sells a used car for $16,000 on December 1, 2002, with a maximum of one-year or 12,000-mile warranty covering parts. This dealer's experience shows warranty expense averages about 4% of a car's selling price, or $640 in this case ($16,000 × 4%). The dealer records the estimated expense and liability related to this sale with this entry:

Assets = Liabilities + Equity
         +640   −640

2002			
Dec. 1	Warranty Expense	640	
	Estimated Warranty Liability		640
	To record estimated warranty expense.		

Point: Recognition of expected warranty liabilities is necessary to comply with the matching and full disclosure principles.

This entry alternatively could be made as part of end-of-period adjustments. Either way, the estimated warranty expense is reported on the 2002 income statement. It also results in a warranty liability on the balance sheet. To further extend this example, suppose the customer returns the car for warranty repairs on January 9, 2003. The dealer performs this work by replacing parts costing $200. The entry to record partial settlement of the estimated warranty liability is

Assets = Liabilities + Equity
−200   −200

2003			
Jan. 9	Estimated Warranty Liability.	200	
	Auto Parts Inventory.		200
	To record costs of warranty repairs.		

This entry reduces the balance of the estimated warranty liability. Warranty expense was previously recorded in 2002, the year the car was sold with the warranty. What happens if total warranty expenses are more or less than the estimated 4%, or $640? The answer is that management should monitor actual warranty expenses to see whether the 4% rate is accurate. If experience reveals a large difference from the estimate, the rate for current and future sales should be changed. Differences are expected, but they should be small.

Income Tax Liabilities

Financial statements of both proprietorships and partnerships do not include income taxes because these organizations do not directly pay income taxes. Instead, taxable income for these organizations is carried to the owners' personal tax return and taxed at that level. However, corporations are subject to income taxes and must estimate their income tax liability when preparing financial statements.

Illustration of Income Tax Liabilities

Income tax expense for a corporation creates a liability until payment is made to the government. Because this tax is created by earning income, a liability is incurred when income is earned. This tax must be paid quarterly under federal regulations. To illustrate, consider a corporation that prepares monthly financial statements. Based on its income in January 2002, this corporation estimates that it owes income taxes of $12,100. The following adjusting entry records this estimate:

Assets = Liabilities + Equity
         +12,100   −12,100

Jan. 31	Income Taxes Expense	12,100	
	Income Taxes Payable		12,100
	To accrue January income taxes.		

The tax liability is recorded each month until the first quarterly payment is made. If estimated taxes for this first quarter total $30,000, the entry to record its payment is

Apr. 10	Income Taxes Payable.	30,000	
	Cash		30,000
	Paid estimated quarterly income taxes based on first quarter income.		

Assets = Liabilities + Equity
−30,000   −30,000

This process of accruing and then paying estimated income taxes continues through the year. When annual financial statements are prepared at year-end, the corporation knows its actual total income and the actual amount of income taxes it must pay. This information allows it to properly record Income Taxes Expense for the quarter so that the total of the four quarters' expense amounts equals the taxes paid to the government.

Deferred Income Tax Liabilities

An income tax liability for corporations can arise when the amount of income before taxes that the corporation reports on its income statement is not the same as the amount of income reported on its income tax return. This difference occurs because income tax laws and GAAP measure income differently.[3]

Some differences between tax laws and GAAP are temporary. *Temporary differences* arise when the tax return and the income statement report a revenue or expense in different years. As an example, companies are often able to deduct higher amounts of depreciation in the early years of an asset's life and smaller amounts in later years for tax reporting in comparison to GAAP. This means in the early years, depreciation for tax reporting is often more than depreciation on the income statement. In later years, depreciation for tax reporting is often less than depreciation on the income statement. When temporary differences exist between taxable income on the tax return and the income before taxes on the income statement, corporations compute Income Taxes Expense based on the income reported on the income statement. The result is that Income Taxes Expense reported in the income statement is often different than the amount of Income Taxes Payable to the government. This difference is called *Deferred Income Tax*.

Illustration of Deferred Income Tax

To illustrate, assume that in recording its usual quarterly income tax payments, a corporation computes $25,000 of income taxes expense. It also determines that only $21,000 is currently due and $4,000 is deferred to future years (a timing difference). The entry to record this end-of-period adjustment is

Dec. 31	Income Taxes Expense	25,000	
	Income Taxes Payable		21,000
	Deferred Income Tax Liability.		4,000
	To record tax expense and deferred tax liability.		

Assets = Liabilities + Equity
         +21,000   −25,000
         +4,000

The credit to Income Taxes Payable reflects the amount currently due to be paid. The credit to **Deferred Income Tax Liability** reflects tax payments deferred until future years when the temporary difference reverses. **Coca-Cola Bottling**, for instance, reports deferred income taxes of $125 million among its liabilities on its recent balance sheet.

Temporary differences also can cause a company to pay income taxes *before* they are reported on the income statement as expense. If so, the company reports a *Deferred Income Tax Asset* on its balance sheet. **Dell**, for instance, reports deferred income taxes of $535 million as an asset in its recent balance sheet.

---

[3] Differences between tax laws and GAAP arise because Congress uses tax laws to generate receipts, stimulate the economy, and influence behavior, whereas GAAP are intended to provide financial information useful for decision making. Also, tax accounting often follows the cash basis, whereas GAAP follows the accrual basis.

Answers—p. 509

Contingent Liabilities

C3 Explain how to account for contingent liabilities.

	Probable	Reasonably Possible	Remote
Amount estimable	Record contingent liability	Disclose liability in notes	No action
Amount not estimable	Disclose liability in notes	Disclose liability in notes	No action

Point: Point out that a contingency is an *IF*. Namely, if a future event occurs, then financial consequences are likely for the entity.

A contingent liability is a potential obligation that depends on a future event arising from a past transaction or event. An example is a lawsuit pending in court. Here, a past transaction or event leads to a lawsuit whose result depends on the court's decision. Generally, future payment of a contingent liability depends on whether an uncertain future event occurs.

Accounting for Contingent Liabilities

Accounting for contingent liabilities depends on the likelihood that a future event will occur and the ability to estimate the future amount owed if this event occurs. Three categories are identified. (1) The future event is *probable* (likely) and the amount owed can be *reasonably estimated*. We record this amount as a liability. Examples are the estimated liabilities described earlier such as warranties, vacation pay, and income taxes. (2) The future event is *remote* (unlikely). We do not record or disclose information regarding these contingent liabilities. (3) Likelihood of the future event is between these two extremes. That is, if the future event is *reasonably possible* (could occur), we disclose information about the contingent liability in notes to the financial statements. The next section identifies contingent liabilities that often fall in the third category—when the future event is reasonably possible. Disclosing information about contingencies in the third category is motivated by the *full-disclosure principle,* which requires information relevant to decision makers be reported.

Reasonably Possible Contingent Liabilities

This section discusses common examples of reasonably possible contingent liabilities.

Potential Legal Claims. Many companies are sued or at risk of being sued. The accounting question is: whether the defendant should recognize a liability on its balance sheet or disclose a contingent liability in its notes while a lawsuit is outstanding and not yet settled. The answer is that a potential claim is recorded in the accounts *only* if payment for damages is probable and the amount can be reasonably estimated. If the potential claim cannot be reasonably estimated or is less than probable but reasonably possible, it is disclosed. **Ford Motor Company**, for example, includes the following note in its recent annual report: "Various legal actions, governmental investigations and proceedings and claims are pending . . . against the company . . . arising out of alleged defects in the company's products."

Point: A discounted note receivable is a contingent liability. It becomes a liability only if the original signer of the note fails to pay it at maturity.

Did You Know?

Boiling Mad   Remember the infamous lawsuit against **McDonald's** that awarded an 81-year-old New Mexico woman $2.9 million—later reduced to $640,000—after spilling hot coffee in her lap? Well, copycat litigation is booming. Fast-food chains are beset by suits over hot-drink and food spills. Companies from **Burger King** to **Starbucks** now print cautions on coffee cups, chili bowls, and so forth.

Debt Guarantees. Sometimes a company guarantees the payment of debt owed by a supplier, customer, or another company. The guarantor usually discloses the guarantee in its financial statement notes as a contingent liability. If it is probable that the debtor will default, the guarantor needs to record and report the guarantee in its financial statements as a liability. The **Boston Celtics** report a unique guarantee when it comes to coaches and players: "Certain of the contracts provide for guaranteed payments which must be paid even if the employee is injured or terminated."

Other Contingencies. Other examples of contingencies include environmental damages, possible tax assessments, insurance losses, and government investigations. **Sun,** for instance, reports "federal, state, local and foreign laws . . . result in loss contingencies . . . at Sun's refineries, service stations, terminals, pipelines and truck transportation facilities." Many of these contingencies require disclosure in notes to financial statements since they are reasonably possible. These contingencies can sometimes carry characteristics that cause them to be recorded as liabilities or, alternatively, omitted altogether.

Uncertainties. All organizations face uncertainties from future events such as natural disasters and the development of new competing products or services. If these events occur, they can damage a company's assets or drive it out of business. These uncertainties are not contingent liabilities because they are future events *not* arising from past transactions. Financial statements are not useful if they unduly speculate about the effects of possible future uncertainties such as these.

> ### Did You Know?
>
> **Eco Cops**   What's it worth to see from one side of the Grand Canyon to the other? What's the cost when beaches are closed due to pollution? One method to measure these environmental liabilities is called **contingent valuation** by which people are surveyed and asked to answer such questions. Regulators use their answers to levy fines, assess punitive damages, measure costs of clean-up, and assign penalties.

Point: Auditors and managers often have different views about whether a contingency is recorded, disclosed, or omitted.

Global: Accounting for contingencies varies across countries. Germany, for example, permits the recording of contingent liabilities that are reasonably possible.

Quick Check

11. A future payment is reported as a liability on the balance sheet if payment is contingent on a future event that (a) Is reasonably possible but the payment cannot be reasonably estimated; (b) Is probable and the payment can be reasonably estimated; or (c) Is not probable but the payment is known.

12. Under what circumstances is a future payment reported in the notes to the financial statements as a contingent liability?

Concept 12-2

Answers—p. 509

Long-Term Liabilities

Long-term liabilities are a company's obligations not requiring a payment within one year or its operating cycle, whichever is longer. Long-term liabilities often are identical to current liabilities except for the longer time interval until the obligation comes due. Long-term liabilities can arise from many different transactions and events. Probably their most common source is money borrowed from a bank in return for a note. They also occur when a company enters into a multiyear lease agreement similar to buying an asset. We explain long-term liabilities in the context of discussing known, estimated, and contingent long-term liabilities. The main discussion of accounting for long-term liabilities is in Chapter 15.

C4   Describe accounting for long-term liabilities.

Known Long-Term Liabilities

Many known or determinable liabilities are long term. These include most unearned revenues and notes payable. For example, if **Sports Illustrated** sells a five-year magazine subscription, it records amounts received for this subscription in an Unearned Subscription Revenues account. Amounts in this account are liabilities, but are they current or long term? They are *both*. The portion of the Unearned

> ### Did You Know?   *e*
>
> **Entrepreneurial Financing**   The Small Business Administration [www.sba.gov] publishes a yearly report of likely sources of small business loans by state. The report shows that small businesses number more than 25 million, employ 53% of the private work force, make 47% of all sales, create most new jobs, and produce 55% of innovations. It also shows that about 70% of small businesses with loans obtain this money from commercial banks.

Subscription Revenues account that will be fulfilled in the next year is reported as a current liability. The remaining portion is reported as a long-term liability.

The same analysis applies to notes payable. For example, a borrower reports a three-year note payable as a long-term liability in the first two years it is outstanding. In the third year, the borrower reclassifies this note as a current liability since it is due within one year or the operating cycle, whichever is longer. The **current portion of long-term debt** refers to that part of long-term debt due within one year or the operating cycle, whichever is longer. Long-term debt is reported under long-term liabilities, but the *current portion due* is reported under current liabilities. To illustrate, assume that a $7,500 debt is paid in installments of $1,500 per year for five years. The $1,500 due within the year is reported as a current liability. No journal entry is necessary. Instead, we simply classify the amounts for debt as either current or long term when the balance sheet is prepared.

Some known liabilities are rarely reported in long-term liabilities. These include accounts payable, sales taxes, and wages and salaries.

Estimated Long-Term Liabilities

Estimated liabilities are both current and long term. Examples include employee benefits and deferred income taxes. Pension liabilities to employees are long term to workers who will not retire within the next period. For employees who are retired or will retire within the next period, a portion of pension liabilities is current. The same analysis applies to employee health benefits, deferred income taxes payable for corporations, and warranties. For example, many warranties are for 30 or 60 days in length. Estimated costs under these warranties are properly reported in current liabilities, yet many automobile warranties are for three years or 36,000 miles. A portion of these warranties is reported as long-term.

Contingent Long-Term Liabilities

Contingent liabilities can be either, or both, current and long-term in nature. This extends to nearly every contingent liability, including litigation, debt guarantees, environmental clean-up, government investigations, and tax assessments.

| **Using the Information** | **Times Interest Earned** |

A1 Compute the times interest earned ratio and use it to analyze liabilities.

A company incurs interest expense on many of its current and long-term liabilities. Examples extend from its short-term notes and the current portion of long-term liabilities to its long-term notes and bonds. The amount of these liabilities is likely to remain in one form or another for a substantial period of time. Because of this, interest expense is often viewed as a *fixed expense*. This means the amount of interest is unlikely to fluctuate much from changes in sales or other operating activities. While fixed costs can be advantageous when a company is growing, they create risk. This risk stems from the possibility a company might be unable to pay fixed expenses if sales decline. To illustrate, consider **X-Caliber**'s results for year 2002 and two possible outcomes for year 2003 shown in Exhibit 12.6. X-Caliber manufactures water sports equipment and remains a family-owned operation.

Exhibit 12.6

X-Caliber's Actual and Projected Results

		Year 2003	
($ thousands)	Year 2002	Sales Increase	Sales Decrease
Sales	$600	$900	$300
Expenses (75% of sales)	450	675	225
Income before interest	150	225	75
Interest expense (fixed)	60	60	60
Net income	$ 90	$165	$ 15

Expenses excluding interest are at, and expected to remain at, 75% of sales. Expenses such as these that change with sales volume are called *variable expenses.* Interest expense is at, and expected to remain at, $60,000 per year due to its fixed nature.

The middle numerical column of Exhibit 12.6 shows that X-Caliber's income nearly doubles if sales increase by 50% to $900,000. The far right column shows that its profits fall sharply if sales decline by 50% to $300,000.

These results show that the amount of fixed interest expense it incurs each period affects a company's risk. The risk from fixed expenses is numerically reflected in the **times interest earned** ratio defined in Exhibit 12.7.

$$\text{Times interest earned} = \frac{\text{Income before interest expense}}{\text{Interest expense}}$$

Exhibit 12.7

Times Interest Earned

For 2002, X-Caliber's income before interest is $150,000. Its times interest earned is computed as $150,000/$60,000, or 2.5 times. This ratio suggests that X-Caliber faces low to moderate risk because its sales must decline sharply before it would be unable to cover its interest expenses.

We must use special care when computing the times interest earned ratio for a corporation. Since interest is deducted in determining taxable income for a corporation, the numerator for this ratio is *adjusted for a corporation* and expressed as

$$\begin{array}{c}\text{Times interest earned}\\\text{(corporation)}\end{array} = \frac{\text{Income before interest expense and income taxes}}{\text{Interest expense}}$$

Exhibit 12.8 shows **Circuit City**'s times interest earned ratio for 1998–2000. Its ratio ranged from 3.2 to 14.0. Most competitors' ratios ranged from 3.0 to 9.0 during this period. Experience shows when this ratio falls below 1.5 to 2.0 and remains at that level or lower for several periods, the default rate on liabilities increases sharply. This reflects increased risk for such companies and their creditors. We also must interpret the times interest earned ratio in light of information about the variability of a company's income before interest. If this amount is stable from year to year or if income is growing, the company can afford to take on added risk by borrowing. If its income before interest greatly varies from year to year, fixed interest expense can increase the risk that it will not earn a positive return and be unable to pay interest expense.

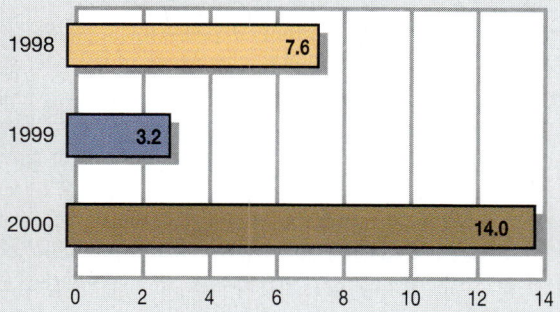

Exhibit 12.8

Circuit City's Times Interest Earned

Demonstration Problem

The following transactions and events took place at Kern Company during its recent calendar year reporting period (Kern does not use reversing entries):

a. In September 2002, Kern sold $140,000 of merchandise covered by a 180-day warranty. Prior experience shows that costs of the warranty equal 5% of sales. Compute September's warranty expense and prepare the adjusting journal entry for the warranty liability as recorded at September 30. Also prepare the journal entry on October 8 to record a $300 cash expenditure to provide warranty service on an item sold in September.

b. On October 12, 2002, Kern arranged with a supplier to replace Kern's overdue $10,000 account payable by paying $2,500 cash and signing a note for the remainder. The note matures in 90 days and has a 12% interest rate. Prepare the entries recorded on October 12, December 31, and January 10, 2003, related to this transaction.

c. In late December, Kern learns it is facing a product liability suit filed by an unhappy customer. Kern's lawyer advises that although it will probably suffer a loss from the lawsuit, it is not possible to estimate the amount of damages at this time.

d. Kern's net income for the year is $1,000,000. Its interest expense for the year is $275,000. Calculate Kern's times interest earned ratio.

e. Sally Kline works for Kern. For the pay period ended November 30, her gross earnings are $3,000. Sally has $800 deducted for federal income taxes and $200 for state income taxes from each paycheck. Additionally, a $35 premium for her health care insurance and a $10 donation for the United Way are deducted. Sally pays FICA Social Security taxes at a rate of 6.2% and FICA Medicare taxes at a rate of 1.45%. She has not earned enough this year to be exempt from FICA taxes. Journalize the payment of Sally's wages by Kern.

f. On November 1, Kern borrows $5,000 from a bank in return for a 60-day, 14%, $5,000 note. Record the note's issuance on November 1 and its repayment with interest on December 31.

g. On December 16, Kern issues a noninterest-bearing note promising to pay $2,050 within 60 days. Record the issuance of the note, the interest accrual on December 31, and the repayment of the note on February 14 ($50 of interest is included in the note's face value of $2,050).

h. (*Assume that Kern is a corporation for parts* h *and* i.) Kern has made and recorded its quarterly income tax payments. In reviewing its year-end tax adjustments, it identifies an additional $50,000 of income tax expense that should be recorded. A portion of this additional expense, $10,000, is deferrable to future years. Record this year-end income taxes expense adjusting entry.

i. Income taxes expense for the year is $225,000. Calculate Kern's time interest earned ratio.

Planning the Solution

- For *a,* compute the warranty expense for September and record it with an estimated liability. Record the October expenditure as a decrease in the liability.
- For *b,* eliminate the liability for the account payable and create the liability for the note payable. Compute interest expense for the 80 days that the note is outstanding in 2002 and record it as an additional liability. Record the payment of the note, being sure to include the interest for the 10 days in 2003.
- For *c,* decide whether the company's contingent liability needs to be disclosed or accrued (recorded) according to the two necessary criteria: probable loss and reasonably estimable.
- For *d,* calculate times interest earned according to the formula in the chapter.
- For *e,* set up payable accounts for all items in Sally's paycheck that require deductions. After deducting all necessary items, credit the remaining amount to Accrued Payroll Payable.
- For *f,* record the issuance of the note. Calculate 60 days' interest due using the 360-day convention in the interest formula.
- For *g,* record the note as a noninteresting-bearing note. Use the contra account Discount on Notes Payable for the interest portion of the proceeds upon issuance. Make the year-end adjustment for 15 days' interest to Interest Expense and Discount on Notes Payable. Record the repayment of the note, being sure to include the interest for the 45 days in 2003.
- For *h,* determine how much of the income taxes expense is payable in the current year and how much needs to be deferred.
- For *i,* apply and compute times interest earned.

Solution to Demonstration Problem

a. Warranty expense = 5% × $140,000 = $7,000

Sept. 30	Warranty Expense.	7,000	
	Estimated Warranty Liability.		7,000
	To record warranty expense for the month.		
Oct. 8	Estimated Warranty Liability	300	
	Cash		300
	To record the cost of the warranty service.		

b. Interest expense for 2002 = 12% × $7,500 × 80/360 = $200
Interest expense for 2003 = 12% × $7,500 × 10/360 = $25

Oct. 12	Accounts Payable.	10,000	
	Notes Payable		7,500
	Cash		2,500
	Paid $2,500 cash and gave a 90-day, 12% note to extend the due date on the account.		
Dec. 31	Interest Expense.	200	
	Interest Payable		200
	To accrue interest on note payable.		
Jan. 10	Interest Expense.	25	
	Interest Payable	200	
	Notes Payable	7,500	
	Cash		7,725
	Paid note with interest, including the accrued interest payable.		

c. Disclose the pending lawsuit in the financial statement notes. Although the loss is probable, no liability can be accrued since the loss cannot be reasonably estimated.

d. Times interest earned = $\dfrac{\text{Income before interest expense}}{\text{Interest expense}}$

$= \dfrac{\$1,000,000 + \$275,000}{\$275,000} = \underline{\underline{4.64 \text{ times}}}$

e.

Nov. 30	Salaries Expense	3,000.00	
	FICA—Social Security Taxes Payable (6.2%)		186.00
	FICA—Medicare Taxes Payable (1.45%) . .		43.50
	Employee Federal Income Taxes Payable . .		800.00
	Employee State Income Taxes Payable . . .		200.00
	Employee Medical Insurance Payable		35.00
	Employee United Way Payable		10.00
	Accrued Payroll Payable		1,725.50
	To record Kline's pay.		

f.

Nov. 1	Cash	5,000	
	Notes Payable		5,000
	Borrowed cash with a 60-day, 14% note.		

When the note and interest are paid 60 days later, Kern Company records this entry:

Dec. 31	Notes Payable	5,000.00	
	Interest Expense	116.67	
	Cash		5,116.67
	Paid note with interest ($5,000 × 14% × 60/360).		

g.

Dec. 16	Cash	2,000.00	
	Discount on Notes Payable	50.00	
	Notes Payable		2,050.00
	Borrowed cash with a 60-day note.		
Dec. 31	Interest Expense	12.50	
	Discount on Notes Payable		12.50
	To record accrued interest (15/60 days × $50).		

When the note matures on February 14, 2003, Kern records this entry:

Feb. 14	Interest Expense (45/60 days × $50)	37.50	
	Notes Payable	2,050.00	
	Cash		2,050.00
	Discount on Notes Payable		37.50
	Paid note with interest.		

h.

Dec. 31	Income Taxes Expense	50,000	
	Income Taxes Payable		40,000
	Deferred Income Tax Liability		10,000
	To record added income taxes expense and the deferred tax liability.		

i. $\text{Times interest earned} = \dfrac{\$1,000,000 + \$275,000 + \$225,000}{\$275,000} = \underline{\underline{5.45 \text{ times}}}$

12A Payroll Reports, Records and Procedures

Understanding payroll procedures and keeping adequate payroll reports and records is essential to a company's success. Many companies now use accounting software to maintain their payroll records. This appendix focuses on payroll accounting and its reports, records, and procedures.

Payroll Reports

Most employees and employers are required to pay local, state, and federal payroll taxes. Payroll expenses involve liabilities to individual employees, to federal and state governments, and to other organizations such as insurance companies. Beyond paying these liabilities, employers are required to prepare and submit reports explaining how they computed these payments.

Reporting FICA Taxes and Income Taxes

The Federal Insurance Contributions Act (FICA) requires each employer to file an Internal Revenue Service (IRS) **Form 941,** the *Employer's Quarterly Federal Tax Return,* within one month after the end of each calendar quarter. A form 941 is shown in Exhibit 12A.1 for Phoenix Sales & Service, a landscape design company. Accounting information and software are helpful in tracking payroll transactions and reporting the accumulated information on Form 941. Specifically, the employer reports total wages subject to income tax withholding on line 2 of Form 941. (For simplicity, this appendix uses *wages* to refer to both wages and salaries.) The income tax withheld is reported on lines 3 and 5. The combined amount of employees' and employer's FICA (Social Security) taxes for Phoenix Sales & Service is reported on line 6a (taxable Social Security wages, $36,599 × 12.4% = $4,538.28).

C5 Identify and describe payroll records.

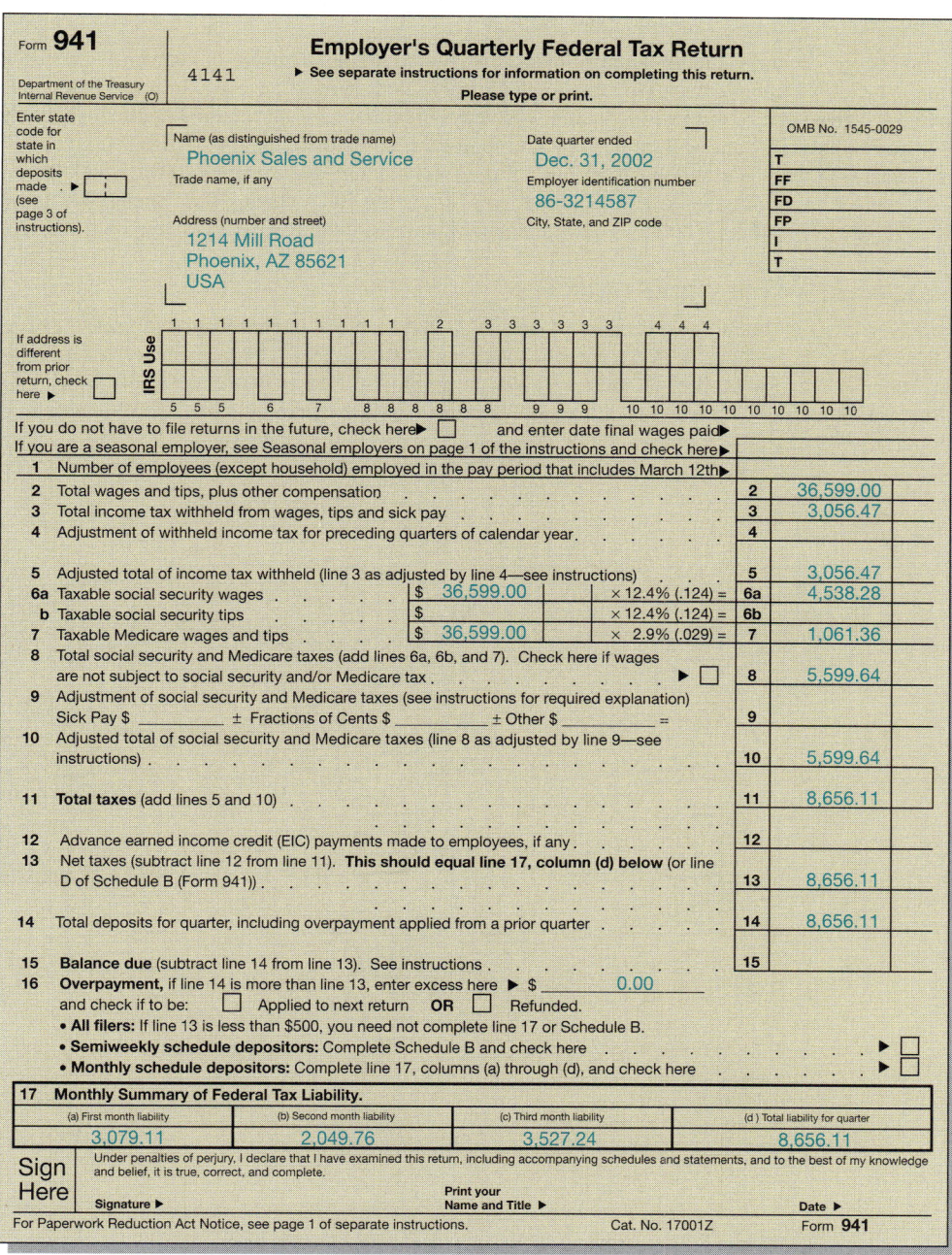

The 12.4% is the sum of the Social Security tax withheld, computed as 6.2% tax withheld from the employees' wages for the quarter plus the 6.2% tax levied on the employer. The combined amount of employees' Medicare wages is reported on line 7. The 2.9% is the sum of 1.45% withheld from employees' wages for the quarter plus 1.45% tax levied on the employer. Total FICA taxes are reported on lines 8 and 10 and are added to the total income taxes withheld of $3,056.47 to yield a total of $8,656.11. For this year, assume that income up to $76,200 is subject to Social Security tax. There is no income limit on amounts subject to Medicare tax. Congress sets annual limits on the amount owed for Social Security tax.

The total of amounts deposited in a **federal depository bank** is subtracted to determine whether a balance remains to be paid. Federal depository banks are authorized to accept deposits of amounts payable to the federal government. Deposit requirements depend on the amount of tax owed. For example, when the sum of FICA taxes plus the employees' income taxes is less than $500 for a quarter, the taxes can be paid when Form 941 is filed. Companies with large payrolls are often required to pay monthly or semiweekly. If taxes owed are $100,000 or more at the end of any day, they must be paid by the end of the next banking day.

Reporting FUTA Taxes and SUTA Taxes

An employer's federal unemployment taxes (FUTA) are reported on an annual basis by filing an *Annual Federal Unemployment Tax Return,* IRS **Form 940.** It must be mailed on or before January 31 following the end of each tax year. Ten more days are allowed if all required tax deposits are filed on a timely basis and the full amount of tax is paid on or before January 31. FUTA payments are made quarterly to a federal depository bank if the total amount due exceeds $100. If $100 or less is due, the taxes are remitted annually. Requirements for paying and reporting state unemployment taxes (SUTA) vary depending on the laws of each state. Most states require quarterly payments and reports.

Reporting Wages and Salaries

Employers are required to give each employee an annual report of his/her wages subject to FICA and federal income taxes along with the amounts of these taxes withheld. This report is called a *Wage and Tax Statement,* or **Form W-2.** It must be given to employees before January 31 following the year covered by the report. Exhibit 12A.2 shows Form W-2 for one of the employees at Phoenix Sales & Service.

Exhibit 12A.2

Form W-2

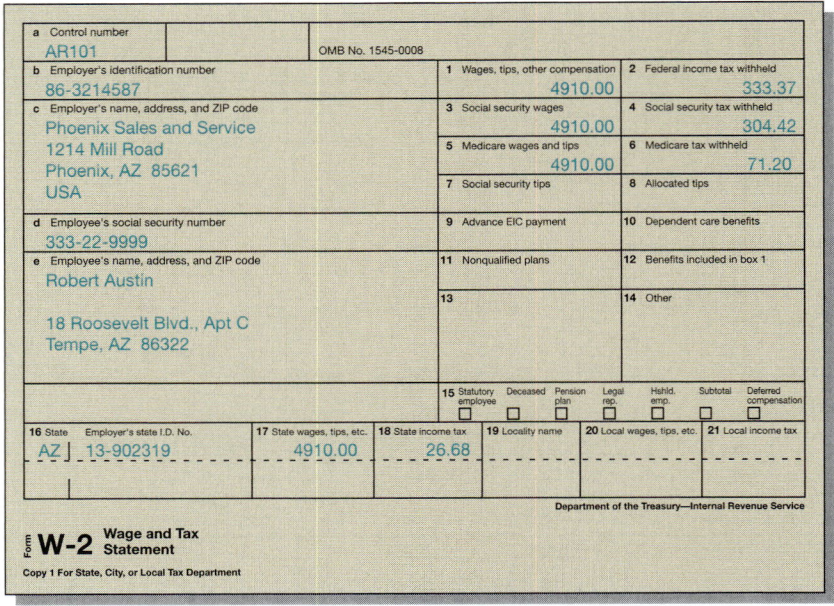

Copies of the W-2 Form must be sent to the Social Security Administration. There they post to each employee's Social Security account the amount of the employee's wages subject to FICA taxes and FICA taxes withheld. These posted amounts become the basis for determining an employee's retirement and survivors' benefits. The Social Security Administration also transmits to the IRS the amount of each employee's wages subject to federal income taxes and the amount of taxes withheld.

Payroll Records

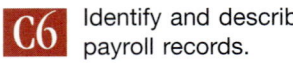

Identify and describe payroll records.

Employers must keep certain payroll records in addition to reporting and paying taxes. These records usually include a payroll register. Good records also require an individual earnings report for each employee.

Payroll Register

A **payroll register** shows the pay period dates, hours worked, gross pay, deductions, and net pay of each employee for each pay period. Exhibit 12A.3 shows a payroll register for Phoenix Sales &

Peachtree Accounting: Exhibit 12a-3									
File Edit Maintain Tasks Analysis Options Reports Window Help									

Phoenix Sales and Service
Payroll Register
For the Week Ending Oct. 8, 2002

Employee ID Employee SS No. Refer., Date	Pay Type	Pay Hours	Gross Pay	FIT	SIT	FICA-SS_EE	FICA-Med_EE	Net Pay
				FUTA	SUTA	FICA-SS_ER	FICA-Med_ER	
AR101 Robert Austin 333-22-9999 9001, 10/8/02	Regular Overtime	40.00	400.00 –	-28.99	-2.32	-24.80	-5.80	338.09
			400.00	-3.20	-10.80	-24.80	-5.80	
CJ102 Judy Cross 299-11-9201 9002, 10/8/02	Regular Overtime	40.00 1.00	560.00 21.00	-52.97	-4.24	-36.02	-8.42	479.35
			581.00	-4.65	-15.69	-36.02	-8.42	
DJ103 John Diaz 444-11-9090 9003, 10/8/02	Regular Overtime	40.00 2.00	560.00 42.00	-48.33	-3.87	-37.32	-8.73	503.75
			602.00	-4.82	-16.25	-37.32	-8.73	
KK104 Kay Keife 909-11-3344 9004, 10/8/02	Regular Overtime	40.00	560.00 –	-68.57	-5.49	-34.72	-8.12	443.10
			560.00	-4.48	-15.12	-34.72	-8.12	
ML105 Lee Miller 444-56-3211 9005, 10/8/02	Regular Overtime	40.00	560.00 –	-34.24	-2.74	-34.72	-8.12	480.18
			560.00	-4.48	-15.12	-34.72	-8.12	
SD106 Dale Sears 909-33-1234 9006, 10/8/02	Regular Overtime	40.00	560.00 –	-68.57	-5.49	-34.72	-8.12	443.10
			560.00	-4.48	-15.12	-34.72	-8.12	
Totals	Regular Overtime	240.00 3.00	3,200.00 63.00	-301.67	-24.15	-202.30	-47.31	2,687.57
			3,263.00	-26.11	-88.10	-202.30	-47.31	

Sales	Purchases	General Ledger	Payroll	Inventory	Company	Analysis

Exhibit 12A.3

Payroll Register

Service. It has a three-line heading and a four-line explanation of the information and data that make up this report. It is organized into nine columns:

Col. 1 Employee identification (ID); Employee name; Social Security number (SS No.); Reference (check number) and Date (date check issued)

Col. 2 Pay Type (regular and overtime)

Col. 3 Pay Hours (number of hours worked as regular and overtime)

Col. 4 Gross Pay (amount of gross pay)[4]

Col. 5 FIT (federal income taxes withheld); FUTA (federal unemployment taxes)

Col. 6 SIT (state income taxes withheld); SUTA (state unemployment taxes)

Col. 7 FICA-SS_EE (social security taxes withheld, employee); FICA-SS_ER (social security taxes, employer)

Col. 8 FICA-Med_EE (medicare tax withheld, employee); FICA-Med_ER (medicare tax, employer)

Col. 9 Net pay (Gross pay less amounts withheld from employees)

Net pay for each employee is computed as gross pay minus the items on the first line of columns 5–8. The employer's payroll tax for each employee is computed as the sum of items on the third line of columns 5–8. A payroll register includes all data necessary to record payroll in the general journal. In some software programs the entries to record payroll are made in a *payroll journal.*

Payroll Check

Payment of payroll is usually done by check or funds transfer. Exhibit 12A.4 shows a *payroll check* for a Phoenix employee. This check is accompanied with a detachable *statement of earnings* (at top) showing gross pay, deductions, and net pay.

---

[4] The Gross Pay column shows regular hours worked on the first line multiplied by the regular pay rate. This equals regular pay. Overtime hours multiplied by the overtime premium rate equals overtime premium pay reported on the second line. If employers are engaged in interstate commerce, federal law sets a minimum overtime rate of pay to employees. For this company, it is 50% of the regular rate for hours worked in excess of 40 per week. This means workers earn at least 150% of their regular rate for hours in excess of 40 per week.

Exhibit 12A.4

Check and Statement of
Earnings

EMPLOYEE NO.	EMPLOYEE NAME			SOCIAL SECURITY NO.	PAY PERIOD END	CHECK DATE
AR101	Robert Austin			333-22-9999	10/8/02	10/8/02

ITEM	RATE	HOURS	TOTAL	ITEM	THIS CHECK	YEAR TO DATE
Regular	10.00	40.00	400.00	Gross	400.00	400.00
Overtime	15.00			Fed. Income tax	-28.99	-28.99
				FICA-Soc. Sec.	-24.80	-24.80
				FICA-Medicare	-5.80	-5.80
				State Income tax	-2.32	-2.32

HOURS WORKED	GROSS THIS PERIOD	GROSS YEAR TO DATE	NET CHECK	CHECK No.
40.00	400.00	400.00	$338.09	9001

(Detach and retain for your records)

PHOENIX SALES AND SERVICE
1214 Mill Road
Phoenix, AZ 85621
602-555-8900

Pheonix Bank and Trust
Pheonix, AZ 85621
3312-87044

9001

CHECK NO.	DATE	AMOUNT
9001	Oct 8, 2002	**************$338.09*

Three Hundred Thirty–Eight and 9/100 Dollars

PAY TO THE ORDER OF

Robert Austin
18 Roosevelt Blvd., Apt C
Tempe, AZ 86322

Mary Wills
AUTHORIZED SIGNATURE

Employee Earnings Report

An **employee earnings report** is a cumulative record of an employee's hours worked, gross earnings, deductions, and net pay. Payroll information on this report is taken from the payroll register. The employee earnings report for R. Austin at Phoenix Sales & Service is shown in Exhibit 12A.5.

Exhibit 12A.5

Employee Earnings Report

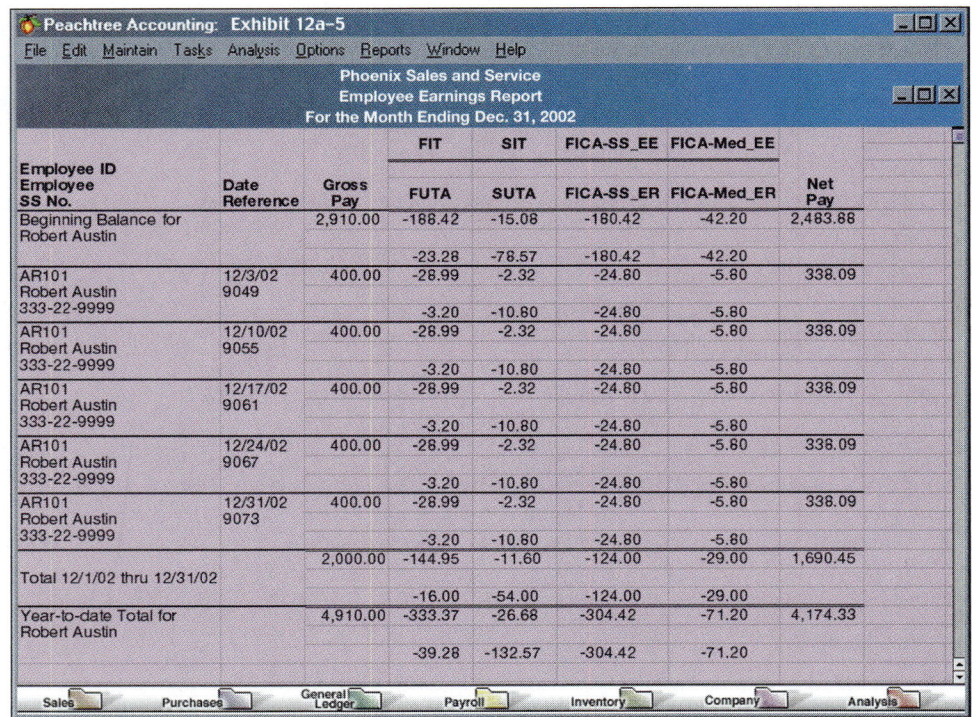

Employee ID Employee SS No.	Date Reference	Gross Pay	FIT	SIT	FICA-SS_EE	FICA-Med_EE	Net Pay
			FUTA	SUTA	FICA-SS_ER	FICA-Med_ER	
Beginning Balance for Robert Austin		2,910.00	-188.42	-15.08	-180.42	-42.20	2,483.88
			-23.28	-78.57	-180.42	-42.20	
AR101 Robert Austin 333-22-9999	12/3/02 9049	400.00	-28.99	-2.32	-24.80	-5.80	338.09
			-3.20	-10.80	-24.80	-5.80	
AR101 Robert Austin 333-22-9999	12/10/02 9055	400.00	-28.99	-2.32	-24.80	-5.80	338.09
			-3.20	-10.80	-24.80	-5.80	
AR101 Robert Austin 333-22-9999	12/17/02 9061	400.00	-28.99	-2.32	-24.80	-5.80	338.09
			-3.20	-10.80	-24.80	-5.80	
AR101 Robert Austin 333-22-9999	12/24/02 9067	400.00	-28.99	-2.32	-24.80	-5.80	338.09
			-3.20	-10.80	-24.80	-5.80	
AR101 Robert Austin 333-22-9999	12/31/02 9073	400.00	-28.99	-2.32	-24.80	-5.80	338.09
			-3.20	-10.80	-24.80	-5.80	
Total 12/1/02 thru 12/31/02		2,000.00	-144.95	-11.60	-124.00	-29.00	1,690.45
			-16.00	-54.00	-124.00	-29.00	
Year-to-date Total for Robert Austin		4,910.00	-333.37	-26.68	-304.42	-71.20	4,174.33
			-39.28	-132.57	-304.42	-71.20	

Did You Know?

High-Tech Reports   Computer technology is used to produce many payroll reports including the (1) payroll register, (2) payroll checks, and (3) employee earnings report. Many off-the-shelf and Web-based programs aid in producing these reports.

This employee earnings report accumulates information that can show when an employee's earnings reach the tax-exempt points for FICA, FUTA, and SUTA taxes. It also gives data employers need to prepare Form W-2.

Employers must be able to compute federal income tax for payroll purposes. This section explains how we compute this tax and how to use a payroll bank account.

Payroll Procedures

Computing Federal Income Taxes

To compute the amount of taxes withheld from each employee's wages, we need to determine both the employee's wages earned and the employee's number of *withholding allowances.* Each employee records the number of withholding allowances claimed on a withholding allowance certificate, **Form W-4,** filed with the employer. When the number of withholding allowances increases, the amount of income taxes withheld decreases.

Employers often use a **wage bracket withholding table** similar to the one shown in Exhibit 12A.6 to compute the federal income taxes withheld from each employee's gross pay. The table in Exhibit 12A.6 is for a single employee paid weekly. Tables are also provided for married employees and for biweekly, semimonthly, and monthly pay periods (most payroll software includes these tables). When using a wage bracket withholding table to compute federal income tax withheld from an employee's gross wages, we need to locate an employee's wage bracket within the first two columns of the table. We then find the amount withheld by looking in the withholding allowance column for that employee.

P5 Compute payroll taxes.

SINGLE Persons—**WEEKLY** Payroll Period
(For Wages Paid)

If the wages are –		And the number of withholding allowances claimed is —										
At least	But less than	0	1	2	3	4	5	6	7	8	9	10
		The amount of income tax to be withheld is —										
$600	$610	95	80	68	60	52	44	36	29	21	13	5
610	620	97	83	69	61	53	46	38	30	22	15	7
620	630	100	86	71	63	55	47	39	32	24	16	8
630	640	103	88	74	64	56	49	41	33	25	18	10
640	650	106	91	77	66	58	50	42	35	27	19	11
650	660	109	94	79	67	59	52	44	36	28	21	13
660	670	111	97	82	69	61	53	45	38	30	22	14
670	680	114	100	85	70	62	55	47	39	31	24	16
680	690	117	102	88	73	64	56	48	41	33	25	17
690	700	120	105	91	76	65	58	50	42	34	27	19
700	710	123	108	93	79	67	59	51	44	36	28	20
710	720	125	111	96	82	68	61	53	45	37	30	22
720	730	128	114	99	84	70	62	54	47	39	31	23
730	740	130	116	102	87	73	64	56	48	40	33	25
740	750	134	119	105	90	76	65	57	50	42	34	26

Exhibit 12A.6

Wage Bracket
Withholding Table

Payroll Bank Account

Companies with few employees often pay them with checks drawn on the company's regular bank account. Companies with many employees often use a special **payroll bank account** to pay employees. When this account is used, a company either (1) draws one check for total payroll on the regular bank account and deposits it in the payroll bank account or (2) executes an *electronic funds transfer* to the payroll bank account. The entry to record this transaction is

P6 Record payment of payroll.

Oct. 8	Accrued Payroll Payable	2,687.57	
	Cash		2,687.57
	To transfer cash to the payroll bank account.		

Assets = Liabilities + Equity
−2,687.57   −2,687.57

Individual payroll checks are then drawn on this payroll bank account. Because only one check for the total payroll is drawn on the regular bank account each payday, use of a special payroll bank account helps with internal control. It also helps in reconciling the regular bank account. When companies use a payroll bank account, they usually include check numbers in the payroll register. The payroll register in Exhibit 12A.3 shows check numbers in column 1. For instance, Check No. 9001 is issued to Robert Austin. With this information, the payroll register serves as a supplementary record of wages earned by and paid to employees.

Quick Check

13. What two items determine the amount deducted from an employee's wages for federal income taxes?

[continued on next page]

[continued from previous page]

---

14. What amount of income tax is withheld from the salary of an employee who is single with three withholding allowances and earnings of $675 in a week? (*Hint:* Use the wage bracket withholding table in Exhibit 12A.6.)

15. Which of the following steps are executed when a company draws one check for total payroll and deposits it in a special payroll bank account? (a) Write a check to the payroll bank account for the total payroll and record it with a debit to Accrued Payroll Payable and a credit to Cash. (b) Deposit a check (or transfer funds) for the total payroll in the payroll bank account. (c) Issue individual payroll checks drawn on the payroll bank account. (d) All of the above.

Answer—p. 509

Summary

C1 **Describe current and long-term liabilities and their characteristics.** Liabilities are probable future payments of assets or services that past transactions or events presently obligate an entity to make. Current liabilities are due within one year or the operating cycle, whichever is longer. All other liabilities are long term.

C2 **Identify and describe known current liabilities.** Known (determinable) current liabilities are set by agreements or laws and are measurable with little uncertainty. They include accounts payable, sales taxes payable, unearned revenues, notes payable, payroll liabilities, and the current portion of long-term debt.

C3 **Explain how to account for contingent liabilities.** If an uncertain future payment depends on a probable future event and the amount can be reasonably estimated, the payment is recorded as a liability. The uncertain future payment is reported as a contingent liability (in the notes) if (a) the future event is reasonably possible but not probable or (b) the event is probable but the payment amount cannot be reasonably estimated.

C4 **Describe accounting for long-term liabilities.** Long-term liabilities are obligations *not* requiring payment within one year or the operating cycle, whichever is longer. Long-term liabilities are similar to current liabilities except for the length of time until payment and the likely use of present value concepts.

C5 **Identify and describe payroll reporting.** Employers report FICA taxes and federal income tax withholdings using Form 941. FUTA taxes are reported on Form 940. Earnings and deductions are reported to each employee and the federal government on Form W-2.

C6 **Identify and describe payroll records.** An employer's payroll records include a payroll register for each pay period, payroll checks and statements of earnings, and individual employee earnings reports.

A1 **Compute the time interest earned ratio and use it to analyze liabilities.** Times interest earned is computed by dividing a company's net income before interest by the amount of fixed interest expenses. For a corporation, the numerator is net income before interest *and* taxes. Times interest earned ratio reflects a company's ability to pay fixed interest obligations.

P1 **Prepare entries to account for short-term notes payable.** Short-term notes payable are current liabilities; most bear interest. When a short-term note's face value equals the amount borrowed, it identifies a rate of interest to be paid at maturity. When a short-term note's face value equals the amount to be paid at maturity, its face value includes interest.

P2 **Compute and record *employee* payroll deductions and liabilities.** Employee payroll deductions include FICA taxes, income taxes, and voluntary deductions such as for pensions and charitable giving. They make up the difference between gross and net pay.

P3 **Compute and record *employer* payroll expenses and liabilities.** An employer's payroll expenses include employees' gross earnings, and benefits, and payroll taxes levied on the employer. Payroll liabilities include employees' net pay amounts withheld from their wages and benefits, and the employer's payroll taxes.

P4 **Account for estimated liabilities, including warranties and income taxes.** Liabilities for health and pension benefits, warranties, bonuses, and income taxes are recorded with estimated amounts. These items are recognized as expenses when incurred.

P5 **Compute payroll taxes.** Federal income tax deductions depend on the employee's earnings and the number of withholding allowances claimed. Wage bracket withholding tables are available for different pay periods and employee classes.

P6 **Record payment of payroll.** Employers with a large number of employees often use a separate payroll bank account. When this is done, the payment of employees is recorded with a transfer of cash from the regular bank account to the payroll bank account.

Guidance Answers to **You Make the Call**

Rock Band   Both banks agree to give the band $30,000 cash and require repayment in six months. Provided terms in these contracts are similar, the only potential difference is in the amount of interest the band must pay. The second bank's contract makes this clear—since $30,000 is borrowed and the band must pay $32,000, the interest charged is $2,000. For the first bank, we must compute interest on the contract. It is $2,100, computed as $30,000 × 14% × 6/12. The band prefers the contract requiring less interest, which is the one reading: "Band promises to pay $32,000 within 6 months."

Web Designer   You need to be concerned about being an accomplice to unlawful payroll activities. Not paying federal and state taxes on wages earned is illegal and unethical. Such payments also will not provide the employee with Social Security and some Medicare credits. The best course of action is to request payment by check. If this fails to change the owner's payment practices, you must consider quitting this job.

Entrepreneur   Risk is partly reflected by the times interest earned ratio. This ratio for the first franchise is 1.5 [($100,000 + $200,000)/$200,000], whereas the ratio for the second franchise is 3.5 [($100,000 + $40,000)/$40,000]. This analysis shows that the first franchise is more at risk of incurring a loss if its sales decline. The second question asks about variability of income before interest. If income before interest greatly varies, this increases the risk an owner will not earn sufficient income to cover interest. Since the first franchise has the greater variability, it is a riskier investment.

Guidance Answers to **Quick Checks**

1. A liability involves a probable future payment of assets or services that an entity is presently obligated to make as a result of past transactions or events.

2. No, an expected future payment is not a liability unless an existing obligation was created by a past event or transaction.

3. In most cases, a liability due in 15 months is classified as long term. It is classified as a current liability if the company's operating cycle is 15 months or longer.

4. A creditor prefers a note payable instead of an account payable so as to (a) charge interest and/or (b) have evidence of the debt and its terms for potential litigation or disputes.

5. The amount borrowed is $1,000 cash ($1,050 − $50). The rate of interest is 5% ($50/$1,000) for six months, which approximates an annual rate of 10%.

6. $1,000(.008) + $1,000(.04) + $3,000(.062) + $3,000(.0145) = $277.50

7. (a) FICA taxes are paid by both the employee and employer.
   (b) FUTA taxes are paid by the employer.

   (c) SUTA taxes are paid by the employer.
   (d) Withheld income taxes are paid by the employee.

8. (a)

9. (a) (Warranty expense was previously estimated.)

10. A corporation accrues an income tax liability for its quarterly financial statements because income tax expense is incurred when income is earned, not just at year-end.

11. (b)

12. A future payment is reported in the notes as a contingent liability if (a) the uncertain future event is probable but the amount of payment cannot be reasonably estimated or (b) the uncertain future event is not probable but has a reasonable possibility of occurring.

13. An employee's gross earnings and number of withholding allowances determine the deduction for federal income taxes.

14. $70

15. (d)

Glossary

Contingent liability potential liability that depends on a future event arising from a past transaction. (p. 496).

Current liability an obligation due within a year or the company's operating cycle, whichever is longer; paid using current assets or by creating other current liabilities, (p. 482).

Current portion of long-term debt portion of long-term debt due within one year or the operating cycle, whichever is longer; reported under current liabilities. (p. 498).

Deferred income tax liability corporation income taxes that are deferred until future years because of temporary differences between GAAP and tax rules. (p. 495).

Discount on note payable difference between the face value of a note payable and the amount borrowed; is interest to be paid on the note over its life. (p. 486).

Employee benefits additional compensation paid to or on behalf of employees, such as premiums for medical, dental, life, dis-

ability insurance, and contributions to pension plans. (p. 492).

Employee earnings report record of an employee's net pay, gross pay, deductions, and year-to-date information. (p. 506).

Estimated liability obligation of an uncertain amount that can be reasonably estimated. (p. 492).

Federal depository bank bank authorized to accept deposits of amounts payable to the federal government. (p. 503).

Federal Insurance Contributions Act (FICA) Taxes taxes assessed on both employers and employees; for Social Security and Medicare programs. (p. 490).

Federal Unemployment Taxes (FUTA) payroll taxes on employers assessed by the federal government to support the federal unemployment insurance program. (p. 491).

Form 940 IRS form used to report an employer's federal unemployment taxes (FUTA) on an annual filing basis. (p. 504).

Form 941 IRS form filed to report FICA taxes owed and remitted. (p. 502).

Form W-2 annual report by an employer to each employee showing the employee's wages subject to FICA and federal income taxes along with amounts withheld. (p. 504).

Form W-4 a withholding allowance certificate, filed with the employer, identifying the number of withholding allowances claimed. (p. 507).

Gross pay total compensation earned by an employee. (p. 489).

Known liabilities obligations of a company with little uncertainty; set by agreements, contracts, or laws; also called *definitely determinable liabilities*. (p. 484).

Long-term liability obligations *not* requiring payment within one year or the operating cycle, whichever is longer. (p. 483).

Merit rating rating assigned to an employer by a state based on the employer's record of employment. (p. 491).

Net pay gross pay less all deductions; also called *take-home pay.* (p. 489).

Noninterest-bearing note note with no stated rate of interest; interest is included in the face value of the note. (p. 487).

Payroll bank account bank account used solely for paying employees; each pay period an amount equal to the total employees' net pay is deposited in it and the employees' payroll checks are drawn on it. (p. 507).

Payroll deductions amounts withheld from an employee's gross pay; also called *withholdings.* (p. 489).

Payroll register record for a pay period that shows the pay period dates, regular and overtime hours worked, gross pay, net pay, and deductions. (p. 504).

Short-term note payable current obligation in the form of a written promissory note. (p. 485).

State Unemployment Taxes (SUTA) state payroll taxes on employers to support unemployment programs. (p. 491).

Times interest earned ratio of income before interest expense (and any income taxes) divided by interest expense; reflects risk of interest commitments when income varies. (p. 499).

Wage bracket withholding table table of the amounts of income tax withheld from employees' wages. (p. 507).

Warranty agreement that obligates the seller to correct or replace a product or service when it fails to perform properly within a specified period. (p. 493).

[Superscript letter ^A^ denotes assignments based on Appendix 12A.]

Questions

1. What are the three important questions concerning the uncertainty of liabilities?

2. What is the difference between a current and a long-term liability?

3. What is an estimated liability?

4. What is the combined amount (in percent) of the employees' and employer's Social Security tax rate?

5. What is the current Medicare tax rate?

6. What determines the amount deducted from an employee's wages for federal income taxes?

7. Which payroll taxes are the employee's responsibility and which are the employer's responsibility?

8. What is an employer's unemployment merit rating? How are these ratings assigned to employers?

9. Why are warranty liabilities usually recognized on the balance sheet as liabilities even when they are uncertain?

10. Suppose that a company has a facility located where disastrous weather conditions often occur. Should it report a probable loss from a future disaster as a liability on its balance sheet? Explain.

11.^A^ What is a wage bracket withholding table?

12.^A^ What amount of income tax is withheld from the salary of an employee who is single with two withholding allowances and earning $725 per week? What if the employee earned $625 and has no withholding allowances? (Use Exhibit 12A.6.)

13. Refer to **Nike**'s financial statements in Appendix A. Explain the change in current notes payable for 2000 with reference to a statement other than the balance sheet.

14. Refer to **Reebok**'s balance sheet in Appendix A. What accounts related to income taxes are on the balance sheet? Identify the meaning of each income tax account you identify.

15. Refer to **Gap**'s balance sheet in Appendix A. Which current liability account reports the payroll-related liabilities (if any) of Gap as of January 29, 2000?

Which of the following items are normally classified as a current liability for a company that has a 15-month operating cycle?

1. Bonds payable maturing in 2 years.

2. Note payable due in 11 months.

3. Portion of long-term note due in 15 months.

4. Salaries payable.

5. Note payable due in 18 months.

6. FICA taxes Payable.

Cube Computing sells $6,000 of merchandise for cash on September 30. The sales tax law requires Cube to collect 4% sales tax on every dollar of merchandise sold. Record the entry for the $6,000 sale and its applicable sales tax. Also record the entry that shows the remittance of the 4% tax on this sale to the state government on October 15.

Ticketmaster receives $5,000,000 in advance ticket sales for a four-date tour of the Rolling Stones. Record the advance ticket sales on October 31. Record the revenue earned for the first concert date of November 5 assuming it represents one-fourth of the advance ticket sales.

Regis Co. has five employees, each of whom earns $2,500 per month and has been employed since January 1. FICA Social Security taxes are 6.2% of gross pay and FICA Medicare taxes are 1.45% of gross pay. FUTA taxes are 0.8% and SUTA taxes are 2.8% of the first $7,000 paid to each employee. Prepare the March 31 journal entry to record March payroll taxes expense.

On November 7, 2002, Eager Company borrows $160,000 cash by signing a 90-day, 8% note payable with a face value of $160,000. (1) Compute the accrued interest payable on December 31, 2002, and (2) present the journal entry to record the payment of the note at maturity.

Hamm Company signs a noninterest-bearing note promising to pay $5,125 within 60 days after December 16. Record the signing of the note, the interest accrual on December 31, and the repayment of the note on February 14. (The note's face value of $5,125 includes $125 of interest.)

On September 11, 2002, Maxims sells a mower for $500 with a one-year warranty that covers parts. Warranty expense is estimated at 5% of sales. On July 24, 2003, the mower is brought in for repairs covered under the warranty requiring $55 in materials taken from the repair parts inventory. Prepare the July 24, 2003, entry to record the warranty repairs.

Ivanhoe Corporation has made and recorded its quarterly income tax payments. After a final review of taxes for the year, the company identifies an additional $40,000 of income tax expense that should be recorded. A portion of this additional expense, $6,000, is deferrable to future years. Record the year-end income tax expense adjusting entry for Ivanhoe.

The following legal claims exist for Kalamazoo Co. Identify the accounting treatment for each claim as either (a) a liability that is recorded or (b) an item described in notes to its financial statements.

1. Kalamazoo Company (defendant) estimates that a pending lawsuit could result in damages of $1,250,000; it is reasonably possible that the plaintiff will win the case.

2. Kalamazoo Company faces a probable loss on a pending lawsuit; the amount is not reasonably estimable.

3. Kalamazoo Company estimates damages in a case at $3,500,000 with a high probability of losing the case.

Fabrique Company offers an annual bonus to employees if it meets certain net income goals. Prepare the journal entry to record a $15,000 bonus owed to workers (to be shared equally) at year-end.

Compute the times interest earned for Sarafin Company, which reports income after interest expense of $1,675,500 and interest expense of $145,000. Sarafin Company is a proprietorship.

QUICK STUDY

QS 12-1
Identifying current and long-term liabilities

QS 12-2
Accounting for sales taxes

QS 12-3
Unearned revenue

QS 12-4
Record employer payroll taxes

QS 12-5
Interest-bearing note transactions

QS 12-6
Noninterest-bearing note transactions

QS 12-7
Recording warranty expenses

QS 12-8
Record deferred income tax liability

QS 12-9
Accounting for contingent liabilities

QS 12-10
Accounting for bonuses

QS 12-11
Times interest earned

EXERCISES

Exercise 12-1
Financial statement presentation—current liabilities

Rahid Company has the following selected accounts and balances after its adjusting entries:

Accounts payable	$ 60,000
Note payable, 6-month	5,000
Accumulated depreciation—Equipment	22,000
Accrued payroll payable	4,750
Estimated warranty liability	11,000
Discount on 6-month note payable	500
Payroll taxes expense	3,000
Long-term debt	105,000

Prepare the current liability section of Rahid Company's balance sheet, assuming $15,000 of the long-term debt is due within the next year.

Exercise 12-2
Classifying liabilities

The following items appear on the balance sheet of a company with a two-month operating cycle. Identify the proper classification of each item as follows: *C* if it is a current liability, *L* if it is a long-term liability, or *N* if it is not a liability.

_____ **1.** Notes payable (due in 6 to 12 months).
_____ **2.** Bonds payable (mature in five years).
_____ **3.** Mortgage payable (due in 12 months).
_____ **4.** Notes receivable (due in 30 days).
_____ **5.** Income taxes payable.
_____ **6.** Notes payable (due in 120 days).
_____ **7.** Mortgage payable (due after 13 months).
_____ **8.** Accounts receivable.
_____ **9.** Wages payable.
_____ **10.** Notes payable (due in 13 to 24 months).

Exercise 12-3
Warranty expense and liability

Yoko Co. sold a copier costing $4,800 with a two-year parts warranty to a customer on August 16, 2002, for $6,000 cash. Yoko uses the perpetual inventory system. Based on experience, Yoko expects to incur warranty costs equal to 4% of selling price. Warranty expense is recorded with an adjusting entry at the end of each year. On November 22, 2003, the copier requires on-site repairs that are completed the same day. The repairs cost $209 for materials taken from the parts inventory. These are the only repairs required in 2003 for this copier.

1. How much warranty expense does the company report in 2002 for this copier?
2. How much is the estimated warranty liability for this copier as of December 31, 2002?
3. How much warranty expense does the company report in 2003 for this copier?
4. How much is the estimated warranty liability for this copier as of December 31, 2003?
5. Prepare journal entries to record (a) the sale; (b) the adjustment on December 31, 2002, to recognize the warranty expense; and (c) the repairs that occur in November 2003.

Exercise 12-4
Accounting for income taxes

Caper Corporation prepares financial statements each month. As part of its accounting process, estimated income taxes are accrued each month for 30% of the current month's net income. The estimated income taxes are paid in the first month of each quarter for the amount accrued in the prior quarter. The following information is available for the last quarter of year 2002:

October net income	28,600
November net income	19,100
December net income	34,600

After all tax computations are completed in mid-January, Caper determines that the quarter's Income Taxes Payable account balance should be $28,300 on December 31.

Required

1. Determine the amount of the adjustment needed on December 31 to produce the proper ending balance in the Income Taxes Payable account.
2. Prepare journal entries to record (a) the December 31, 2002, adjustment to the Income Taxes Payable account and (b) the January 15, 2003, payment of the fourth-quarter taxes.

Peerless Systems borrows $104,000 cash on May 15, 2002, by signing a 60-day, 12% note.

1. On what date will this note mature?
2. How much interest expense results from this note? (Assume a 360-day year.)
3. Suppose the face value of the note equals $104,000, the principal of the loan. Prepare the journal entries to record issuance of the note and its payment at maturity.
4. Suppose the face value of the note is $106,080, which includes both the principal of the loan ($104,000) and the interest to be paid at maturity. Prepare the journal entries to record issuance of the note and its payment at maturity.

Exercise 12-5
Interest-bearing and noninterest-bearing notes payable

Excel Co. borrows $200,000 cash on November 1, 2002, by signing a 90-day, 9% note.

1. On what date will this note mature?
2. How much interest expense results from this note in 2002? (Assume a 360-day year.)
3. How much interest expense results from this note in 2003? (Assume a 360-day year.)
4. Suppose the face value of the note equals $200,000, the principal of the loan. Prepare journal entries to record issuance of the note, accrual of interest at the end of 2002, and payment of the note at maturity.
5. Suppose the face value of the note is $204,500, which includes both the principal of the loan ($200,000) and its interest ($4,500). Prepare journal entries to record issuance of the note, accrual of interest at the end of 2002, and payment of the note at maturity.

Exercise 12-6
Interest-bearing and noninterest-bearing short-term notes payable with year-end adjustments

---

TSI Co. has one employee. The employee and the company are subject to the following taxes:

Exercise 12-7
Computing payroll taxes

Tax	Rate	Applied To
FICA—Social Security	6.20%	First $76,200
FICA—Medicare	1.45	Gross pay
FUTA	0.80	First $7,000
SUTA	2.90	First $7,000

Compute TSI's amounts for these four taxes applied to the employee's gross earnings for September under each of three separate situations (a), (b), and (c):

	Gross Pay through August	Gross Pay for September
a.	$ 6,800	$ 900
b.	19,200	2,200
c.	71,200	8,000

Using the data in situation (a) of Exercise 12-7, prepare the employer's September 30 journal entries to record (1) salary expense and its related payroll liabilities for this employee and (2) the employer's payroll taxes expense and its related liabilities. The employee's federal income taxes withheld by the employer are $100.

Exercise 12-8
Payroll-related journal entries

Exercise 12-9

Adjusting entries for liabilities

Prepare any necessary adjusting entries at December 31, 2002, for Delta Company's year-end financial statements given the following information:

1. During December, Delta Company sold 4,000 units of a product that carries a 60-day warranty. December sales for this product total $150,000. The company expects 8% of the units to need repair under warranty, and it estimates the average repair cost per unit will be $17.

2. A disgruntled employee is suing Delta Company. Legal advisers believe that the company will probably have to pay damages, but the amount cannot be reasonably estimated.

3. Employees earn vacation pay at a rate of one day per month. During December, 20 employees qualify for vacation pay. Their average daily wage is $105 per employee.

4. Delta Company guarantees the $7,500 debt of a supplier. The supplier will probably not default on the debt.

5. Delta Company records an adjusting entry for $1,750,000 of previously unrecorded cash sales along with the sales taxes of 5%.

6. $75,000 of $100,000 previously received in advance for products is now earned.

Exercise 12-10

Computing and recording bonuses

For the year ended December 31, 2002, Warner Company has implemented an employee bonus program equal to 3% of Warner's net income that employees will share equally. Warner's net income is expected to be $500,000, and bonus expense is deducted in computing net income.

1. Compute the amount of the bonus payable to the employees at year-end (use the method described in the chapter and round to the nearest dollar).

2. Prepare the journal entry at December 31, 2002, to record the bonus due the employees.

3. Prepare the journal entry at January 19, 2003, to record payment of the bonus to employees.

Exercise 12-11

Computing and interpreting times interest earned

Use the following information from proprietorships (a) through (f) to compute times interest earned:

	Net Income (Loss)	Interest Expense
a.	$150,000	$44,000
b.	160,000	10,000
c.	170,000	12,000
d.	365,000	14,000
e.	89,000	14,000
f.	⟨5,000⟩	10,000

Which of the cases demonstrates the strongest ability to pay interest expenses as they come due?

Exercise 12-12ᴬ

Net pay computation

The payroll records of Classic Software show the following information about Trish Nyhart, an employee, for the weekly pay period ending September 30, 2002:

Total (gross) earnings for current pay period . . .	$ 725
Cumulative earnings previous pay periods	9,600

Trish is single and claims one allowance. Compute her Social Security tax (6.2%), Medicare tax (1.45%), federal income tax withholding, state income tax (0.5%), and net pay for the current pay period. The state income tax is 0.5 percent on $9,000 maximum. (Use the withholding table in Exhibit 12A.6.)

Exercise 12-13ᴬ

Gross and net pay computation

Wendy Geiger, an unmarried employee, works 48 hours in the week ended January 12. Her pay rate is $14 per hour, and her wages are subject to no deductions other than FICA—Social Security, FICA—Medicare, and federal income taxes. She claims two withholding allowances. Compute her regular pay, overtime pay (overtime premium is 50% of regular rate for hours in excess of 40 per week), and gross pay. Then compute her FICA tax deduction (use 6.2% for the Social Security portion and 1.45% for the Medicare portion), income tax deduction (use the wage bracket withholding table of Exhibit 12A.6), total deductions, and net pay.

Exercise 12-14ᴬ

Payroll entry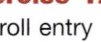

Using Exercise 12-13, prepare the journal entry to record the transfer of $573.30 cash to a payroll bank account.

Langholz Co. entered into the following transactions involving short-term liabilities in 2002 and 2003.

PROBLEM SET A

Problem 12-1A
Short-term notes payable
transactions and entries

G S

2002

Apr. 20	Purchased $40,250 of merchandise on credit from Fitz, terms are 1/10, n/30. Langholz uses the perpetual inventory system.
May 19	Replaced the account payable to Fitz with a 90-day, $35,000 note bearing 10% annual interest along with paying $5,250 in cash.
July 8	Borrowed $80,000 cash from Firstar Bank by signing a 120-day interest-bearing note for $80,000. The note's annual interest rate is 9%.
?	Paid the amount due on the note to Fitz at maturity.
?	Paid the amount due on the note to Firstar Bank at maturity.
Nov. 28	Borrowed $42,000 cash by signing a noninterest-bearing note with a face value of $42,560 to UMB Bank that matures in 60 days. The face value includes a principal amount of $42,000 and interest of $560.
Dec. 31	Recorded an adjusting entry for the accrual of interest on the note to UMB Bank.

2003

?	Paid the amount due on the note to UMB Bank at maturity.

Required

1. Determine the maturity dates for each of the three notes described.
2. Determine the interest due at maturity for the three notes. (Assume a 360-day year.)
3. Determine the interest to be recorded in the adjusting entry at the end of 2002.
4. Determine the interest to be recorded in 2003.
5. Prepare journal entries for all the preceding transactions and events for years 2002–2003.

Check (4) Year 2003 interest, $252

On October 29, 2002, Close Shave Products began operations by purchasing electric razors for resale at $75 each. Close Shave uses the perpetual inventory method. The razors are covered under a warranty that requires the company to replace any nonworking razor within 90 days. When a razor is returned, the company discards it and mails a new one from inventory to the customer. The company's cost for a new razor is $20 in both 2002 and 2003. The manufacturer has advised the company to expect warranty costs to equal 8% of dollar sales. The following transactions and events occurred in 2002 and 2003:

Problem 12-2A
Warranty expenses and
liabilities estimation

2002

Nov. 11	Sold 105 razors for $7,875 cash.
30	Recognized warranty expense for November with an adjusting entry.
Dec. 9	Replaced 15 razors that were returned under the warranty.
16	Sold 220 razors for $16,500 cash.
29	Replaced 30 razors that were returned under the warranty.
31	Recognized warranty expense for December with an adjusting entry.

2003

Jan. 5	Sold 150 razors for $11,250 cash.
17	Replaced 50 razors that were returned under the warranty.
31	Recognized warranty expense for January with an adjusting entry.

Required

1. Prepare journal entries to record these transactions and adjustments for 2002 and 2003.
2. How much warranty expense is reported for November 2002 and December 2002?
3. How much warranty expense is reported for January 2003?
4. What is the balance of the Estimated Warranty Liability account as of December 31, 2002?
5. What is the balance of the Estimated Warranty Liability account as of January 31, 2003?

Check (4) 12/31/02 Estim.
Warranty Liab. bal., $1,050 Cr.

Problem 12-3A
Computing and analyzing
times interest earned

Shown here are condensed income statements for two different proprietorships:

Acme Co.	
Sales	$1,000,000
Variable expenses (80%)	800,000
Income before interest	$ 200,000
Interest expense (fixed)	60,000
Net income	$ 140,000

Nadir Co.	
Sales	$1,000,000
Variable expenses (60%)	600,000
Income before interest	$ 400,000
Interest expense (fixed)	260,000
Net income	$ 140,000

Required

Preparation Component

1. Compute times interest earned for Acme Co.
2. Compute times interest earned for Nadir Co.

Check (3) Net income for Acme, $200,000 (43% increase)

3. What happens to each company's net income if sales increase by 30%?
4. What happens to each company's net income if sales increase by 50%?
5. What happens to each company's net income if sales increase by 80%?
6. What happens to each company's net income if sales decrease by 10%?
7. What happens to each company's net income if sales decrease by 20%?
8. What happens to each company's net income if sales decrease by 40%?

Analysis Component

9. Comment on what you observe in relation to the fixed cost strategies of the two companies and the ratio values you computed in parts (1) and (2).

Problem 12-4A
Payroll expenses,
withholdings, and taxes

Legal Eagles pays its employees every week. Employees' gross pay is subject to these taxes:

Tax	Rate	Applied To
FICA—Social Security	6.20%	First $76,200
FICA—Medicare	1.45	Gross pay
FUTA	0.80	First $7,000
SUTA	2.15	First $7,000

The company is preparing its payroll calculations for the week ended August 25. Payroll records show the following information for the company's four employees:

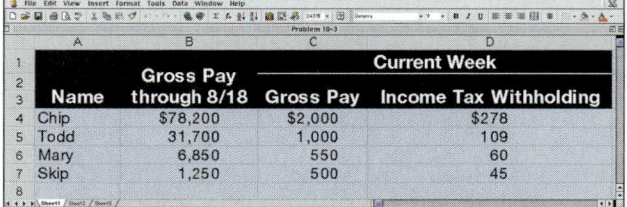

Name	Gross Pay through 8/18	Current Week Gross Pay	Current Week Income Tax Withholding
Chip	$78,200	$2,000	$278
Todd	31,700	1,000	109
Mary	6,850	550	60
Skip	1,250	500	45

In addition to gross pay, the company must pay one-half of the $34 per employee weekly health insurance; each employee pays the remaining one-half. The company also contributes an extra 8% of each employee's gross pay (at no cost to employees) to a pension fund.

Required

Compute the following for the week ended August 25 (round amounts to the nearest cent):

1. Each employee's FICA withholdings for Social Security.
2. Each employee's FICA withholdings for Medicare.

3. Employer's FICA taxes for Social Security.

4. Employer's FICA taxes for Medicare.

5. Employer's FUTA taxes.

6. Employer's SUTA taxes.

7. Each employee's net (take-home) pay.

Check   (7) Total net pay, $3,304.17

8. Employer's total payroll-related expense for each employee.

On January 8, the end of the first weekly pay period of the year, Kidwear Company's payroll register showed that its employees earned $22,760 of office salaries and $65,840 of sales salaries. Withholdings from the employees' salaries include FICA Social Security taxes at the rate of 6.2%, FICA Medicare taxes at the rate of 1.45%, $12,860 of federal income taxes, $1,340 of medical insurance deductions, and $840 of union dues. No employee earned more than $7,000 in this first period.

Required

1. Calculate FICA Social Security taxes payable and FICA Medicare taxes payable. Prepare the journal entry to record Kidwear Company's January 8 payroll expenses and liabilities.

2. Prepare the journal entry to record Kidwear's payroll taxes resulting from the January 8 payroll. Kidwear's merit rating reduces its state unemployment tax rate to 4.0% of the first $7,000 paid each employee. The federal unemployment tax rate is 0.8%.

3. Kidwear Company uses a payroll bank account and special payroll checks in paying its employees. Prepare the journal entry to transfer funds equal to the payroll from the regular bank account to the payroll bank account.

4. After the entry in part (3) is journalized and posted, are additional journal entries required to record the payroll checks and pay the employees?

Problem 12-5A[A]
Entries for payroll transactions

Check   (3) Dr. Accrued Payroll
Payable, $66,782.10

Friesen Company has 10 employees, each of whom earns $2,700 per month and is paid on the last day of each month. All 10 have been employed continuously at this amount since January 1. Friesen uses a payroll bank account and special payroll checks to pay its employees. On March 1, the following accounts and balances exist in its general ledger:

a. FICA—Social Security Taxes Payable, $3,348; FICA—Medicare Taxes Payable, $783 (The balances of these accounts represent total liabilities for *both* the employer's and employees' FICA taxes for the February payroll only.)

b. Employees' Federal Income Taxes Payable, $4,000 (liability for February only).

c. Federal Unemployment Taxes Payable, $432 (liability for January and February together).

d. State Unemployment Taxes Payable, $2,160 (liability for January and February together).

During March and April, the company had the following payroll transactions:

Mar. 15   Issued check payable to Fleet Bank, a federal depository bank authorized to accept employers' payments of FICA taxes and employee income tax withholdings. The $8,131 check is in payment of the February FICA and employee income taxes.

   31   Recorded the March payroll and transferred funds from the regular bank account to the payroll bank account. The payroll register shows the following summary totals for the March pay period:

Problem 12-6A[A]
Entries for payroll transactions

Salaries and Wages			FICA Taxes*	Federal Income Taxes	Net Pay
Office Salaries	Shop Wages	Gross Pay			
$10,800	$16,200	$27,000	$1,674.00	$4,000	$20,934.50
			$ 391.50		

* FICA taxes are Social Security and Medicare, respectively.

   31   Issued checks payable to each employee in payment of the March payroll.

   31   Recorded the employer's payroll taxes resulting from the March payroll. The company has a merit rating that reduces its state unemployment tax rate to 4.0% of the first $7,000 paid each employee. The federal rate is 0.8%.

Check   Dr. Payroll Taxes
Expenses, $2,833.50

Apr. 15   Issued check to Fleet Bank in payment of the March FICA and employee income taxes.

15   Issued check to the State Tax Commission for the January, February, and March state unemployment taxes. Mailed the check and the first quarter tax return to the Commission.

30   Issued check payable to Fleet Bank in payment of the employer's FUTA taxes for the first quarter of the year.

30   Mailed Form 941 to the IRS, reporting the FICA taxes and the employees' federal income tax withholdings for the first quarter.

Required

Prepare journal entries to record the transactions and events for both March and April.

PROBLEM SET B

Problem 12-1B
Short-term notes payable transactions and entries

Quinn Co. entered into the following transactions involving short-term liabilities in 2002 and 2003.

2002

Apr. 22   Purchased $5,000 of merchandise on credit from Cascade Products, terms are 1/10, n/30. Quinn uses the perpetual inventory system.

May 23   Replaced the account payable to Cascade Products with a 60-day, $4,600 note bearing 15% annual interest along with paying $400 in cash.

July 15   Borrowed $12,000 cash from Fall River Bank by signing a 120-day interest-bearing note for $12,000. The note's annual interest rate is 10%.

___?___   Paid the amount due on the note to Cascade Products at maturity.

___?___   Paid the amount due on the note to Fall River Bank at maturity.

Dec. 6   Borrowed $8,000 cash by signing a noninterest-bearing note with a face value of $8,090 to City Bank that matures in 45 days. The principal amount on the note is $8,000 and interest is $90.

31   Recorded an adjusting entry for the accrual of interest on the note to City Bank.

2003

___?___   Paid the amount due on the note to City Bank at maturity.

Required

1. Determine the maturity dates for each of the three notes described.

2. Determine the interest due at maturity for the three notes. (Assume a 360-day year.)

3. Determine the interest to be recorded in the adjusting entry at the end of 2002.

Check   (4) Year 2003 interest, $40

4. Determine the interest to be recorded in 2003.

5. Prepare journal entries for all the preceding transactions and events for years 2002–2003.

Problem 12-2B
Warranty expenses and liabilities estimation

On November 10, 2002, Maleta Co. began operations by purchasing electric coffee grinders for resale at $50 each. Maleta uses the perpetual inventory method. The grinders are covered under a warranty that requires the company to replace any nonworking grinder within 60 days. When a grinder is returned, the company discards it and mails a new one from inventory to the customer. The company's cost for a new grinder is $24 in both 2002 and 2003. The manufacturer has advised the company to expect warranty costs to equal 10% of dollar sales. The following transactions and events occurred in 2002 and 2003.

2002

Nov. 16   Sold 50 grinders for $2,500 cash.

30   Recognized warranty expense for November with an adjusting entry.

Dec. 12   Replaced six grinders that were returned under the warranty.

18   Sold 200 grinders for $10,000 cash.

28   Replaced 17 grinders that were returned under the warranty.

31   Recognized warranty expense for December with an adjusting entry.

2003

Jan. 7   Sold 40 grinders for $2,000 cash.

21   Replaced 38 grinders that were returned under the warranty.

31   Recognized warranty expense for January with an adjusting entry.

Required

1. Prepare journal entries to record these transactions and adjustments for 2002 and 2003.

2. How much warranty expense is reported for November 2002 and December 2002?

3. How much warranty expense is reported for January 2003?

4. What is the balance of the Estimated Warranty Liability account as of December 31, 2002?

5. What is the balance of the Estimated Warranty Liability account as of January 31, 2003?

Check   (4) 12/31/02 Estim. Warranty Liab. bal., $698 Cr.

Shown here are condensed income statements for two different proprietorships:

Problem 12-3B
Computing and analyzing times interest earned

Scorpio Co.	
Sales	$240,000
Variable expenses (50%)	120,000
Income before interest	$120,000
Interest expense (fixed)	90,000
Net income	$ 30,000

Gemini Co.	
Sales	$240,000
Variable expenses (75%)	180,000
Income before interest	$ 60,000
Interest expense (fixed)	30,000
Net income	$ 30,000

Required

Preparation Component

1. Compute times interest earned for Scorpio.

2. Compute times interest earned for Gemini.

3. What happens to each company's net income if sales increase by 10%?

4. What happens to each company's net income if sales increase by 40%?

5. What happens to each company's net income if sales increase by 90%?

6. What happens to each company's net income if sales decrease by 20%?

7. What happens to each company's net income if sales decrease by 50%?

8. What happens to each company's net income if sales decrease by 80%?

Check   (4) Net income of Scorpio, $78,000 (160% increase)

Analysis Component

9. Comment on what you observe in relation to the fixed cost strategies of the two companies and the ratio values you computed in parts (1) and (2).

Seahawk Company pays its employees every week. Employees' gross pay is subject to these taxes:

Problem 12-4B
Payroll expenses, withholdings, and taxes

Tax	Rate	Applied To
FICA—Social Security	6.20%	First $76,200
FICA—Medicare	1.45	Gross pay
FUTA	0.80	First $7,000
SUTA	1.75	First $7,000

The company is preparing its payroll calculations for the week ended September 30. Payroll records show the following information for the company's four employees:

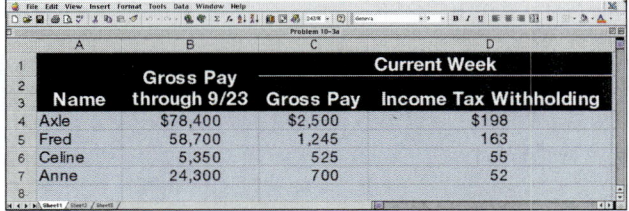

		Current Week	
Name	Gross Pay through 9/23	Gross Pay	Income Tax Withholding
Axle	$78,400	$2,500	$198
Fred	58,700	1,245	163
Celine	5,350	525	55
Anne	24,300	700	52

In addition to gross pay, the company must pay one-half of the $40 per employee weekly health insurance; each employee pays the remaining one-half. The company also contributes an extra 5% of each employee's gross pay (at no cost to employees) to a pension fund.

Required

Compute the following for the week ended September 30 (round amounts to the nearest cent):

1. Each employee's FICA withholdings for Social Security.
2. Each employee's FICA withholdings for Medicare.
3. Employer's FICA taxes for Social Security.
4. Employer's FICA taxes for Medicare.
5. Employer's FUTA taxes.
6. Employer's SUTA taxes.
7. Each employee's net (take-home) pay.
8. Employer's total payroll-related expense for each employee.

Check   (7) Total net pay, $4,196.80

Problem 12-5B[A]

Entries for payroll transactions

Genie Company's first weekly pay period of the year ends on January 8. On that date, the column totals in Genie's payroll register indicate its sales employees earned $34,745, its office employees earned $21,225, and its delivery employees earned $1,030. The employees are to have withheld from their wages FICA Social Security taxes at the rate of 6.2%, FICA Medicare taxes at the rate of 1.45%, $8,625 of federal income taxes, $1,160 of medical insurance deductions, and $138 of union dues. No employee earned more than $7,000 in the first pay period.

Required

1. Calculate FICA Social Security taxes payable and FICA Medicare taxes payable. Prepare the journal entry to record Genie Company's January 8 payroll expenses and liabilities.
2. Prepare the journal entry to record Genie's payroll taxes resulting from the January 8 payroll. Genie's merit rating reduces its state unemployment tax rate to 3.4% of the first $7,000 paid each employee. The federal unemployment tax rate is 0.8%.
3. Genie Company uses special payroll checks and a payroll bank account in paying its employees. Prepare the journal entry to transfer funds equal to the payroll from the regular bank account to the payroll bank account.
4. After the entry in part (3) is journalized and posted, are additional journal entries required to record the payroll checks and pay the employees?

Check   (3) Dr. Accrued Payroll Payable, $42,716.50

Problem 12-6B[A]

Entries for payroll transactions

CMI Company has five employees, each of whom earns $1,400 per month and is paid on the last day of each month. All five have been employed continuously at this amount since January 1. CMI uses a payroll bank account and special payroll checks to pay its employees. On June 1, the following accounts and balances exist in its general ledger:

a. FICA—Social Security Taxes Payable, $868; FICA—Medicare Taxes Payable, $203. (The balances of these accounts represent total liabilities for *both* the employer's and employees' FICA taxes for the May payroll only.)
b. Employees' Federal Income Taxes Payable, $1,050 (liability for May only).
c. Federal Unemployment Taxes Payable, $112 (liability for April and May together).
d. State Unemployment Taxes Payable, $560 (liability for April and May together).

During June and July, the company had the following payroll transactions:

June 15   Issued check payable to Security Bank, a federal depository bank authorized to accept employers' payments of FICA taxes and employee income tax withholdings. The $2,121 check is in payment of the May FICA and employee income taxes.

   30   Recorded the June payroll and transferred funds from the regular bank account to the payroll bank account. The payroll register shows the following summary totals for the June pay period:

| Salaries and Wages | | | | Federal | |
Office Salaries	Shop Wages	Gross Pay	FICA Taxes*	Income Taxes	Net Pay
$2,800	$4,200	$7,000	$434.00	$1,050	$5,414.50
			$101.50		

* FICA taxes are Social Security and Medicare, respectively.

30 Issued checks payable to each employee in payment of the June payroll.
30 Recorded the employer's payroll taxes resulting from the June payroll. The company has a merit rating that reduces its state unemployment tax rate to 4.0% of the first $7,000 paid each employee. The federal rate is 0.8%.
July 15 Issued check payable to Security Bank in payment of the June FICA and employee income taxes.
15 Issued check to the State Tax Commission for the April, May, and June state unemployment taxes. Mailed the check and the second quarter tax return to the State Tax Commission.
31 Issued check payable to Security Bank in payment of the employer's FUTA taxes for the second quarter of the year.
31 Mailed Form 941 to the IRS, reporting the FICA taxes and the employees' federal income tax withholdings for the second quarter.

Check Dr. Payroll Taxes Expenses, $535.50

Required

Prepare journal entries to record the transactions and events for both June and July.

BeGone Exterminators provides pest control services and also sells extermination products manufactured by other companies. The following six-column table contains the company's unadjusted trial balance as of December 31, 2002.

COMPREHENSIVE PROBLEM

BeGone Exterminators
(Review of Chapters 1–12)

 *Peach*Tree

BEGONE EXTERMINATORS December 31, 2002					
	Unadjusted Trial Balance		Adjustments	Adjusted Trial Balance	
Cash	$ 18,000				
Accounts receivable	5,000				
Allowance for doubtful accounts		$ 928			
Merchandise inventory	12,700				
Trucks	40,000				
Accum. depreciation—Trucks		0			
Equipment	55,000				
Accum. depreciation—Equip.		14,400			
Accounts payable		4,800			
Estimated warranty liability		1,400			
Unearned services revenue		0			
Long-term notes payable		15,000			
Discount on notes payable	3,974				
T. Bugg, Capital		62,600			
T. Bugg, Withdrawals	10,000				
Extermination services revenue		70,000			
Interest earned		872			
Sales		80,000			
Cost of goods sold	54,017				
Depreciation expense—Trucks	0				
Depreciation expense—Equip.	0				
Wages expense	32,500				
Interest expense	0				
Rent expense	10,000				
Bad debts expense	0				
Miscellaneous expense	1,338				
Repairs expense	671				
Utilities expense	6,800				
Warranty expense	0				
Totals	$250,000	$250,000			

The following information applies to the company at the end of the current year:

a. The bank reconciliation as of December 31, 2002, includes these facts:

Balance per bank	$16,100
Balance per books	18,000
Outstanding checks	1,800
Deposit in transit	1,450
Interest earned	52
Service charges (miscellaneous expense)	15

Included with the bank statement is a canceled check that the company failed to record. (Information from the bank reconciliation allows you to determine the amount of this check, which is a payment on account.)

b. An examination of customers' accounts shows that accounts totaling $779 should be written off as uncollectible. Using an aging of receivables, the company determines that the ending balance of the Allowance for Doubtful Accounts should be $800.

c. A truck is purchased and placed in service on January 1, 2002. Its cost is being depreciated with the straight-line method using these facts and estimates:

Original cost	$40,000
Expected salvage value	5,000
Useful life (years)	5

d. Two items of equipment (a sprayer and an injector) were purchased and put into service early in January 2000. They are being depreciated with the straight-line method using these facts and estimates:

	Sprayer	Injector
Original Cost	$35,000	$20,000
Expected salvage value	3,000	4,000
Useful life (years)	8	5

e. On August 1, 2002, the company is paid $7,680 in advance to provide monthly service for an apartment complex for one year. The company began providing the services in August. When the cash was received, the full amount was credited to the Extermination Services Revenue account.

f. The company offers a warranty for the services it sells. The expected cost of providing warranty service is 2.5% of sales. No warranty expense has been recorded for 2002. All costs of servicing warranties in 2002 were properly debited to the Estimated Warranty Liability account.

g. The $15,000 long-term note is a five-year, noninterest-bearing note that was issued to First National Bank on December 31, 2000. The market interest rate on the issuance of the loan was 8% and interest expense (not yet recorded) is $882 for year 2002.

h. The ending inventory of merchandise is counted and determined to have a cost of $12,700. BeGone uses a perpetual inventory system.

Required

1. Use the preceding information to determine amounts for the following items:

   a. Correct ending balance of Cash and the amount of the omitted check.

   b. Adjustment needed to obtain the correct ending balance of the Allowance for Doubtful Accounts.

   c. Depreciation expense for the truck acquired in January.

   d. Depreciation expense for the two items of equipment used during year 2002.

   e. Adjusted ending balances of the Extermination Services Revenue and Unearned Services Revenue accounts.

   f. Adjusted ending balances of the accounts for Warranty Expense and Estimated Warranty Liability.

   g. Adjusted ending balances of the accounts for Interest Expense and Discount on Notes Payable. (Round amounts to nearest whole dollar.)

Check   Adjustments Column
Totals, $25,294

2. Use the results of part (1) to complete the six-column table by first entering the appropriate adjustments for items (a) through (g) and then completing the adjusted trial balance columns. (*Hint*: Item (b) requires two adjustments.)

3. Present journal entries to record the adjustments entered on the six-column table. Assume BeGone's adjusted balance for Merchandise Inventory matches the year-end physical count.

4. Prepare a single-step income statement, a statement of changes in owner's equity, and a classified balance sheet.

Check   Net income, $23,370; Total assets, $98,271

Beyond the Numbers

BTN 12-1   Refer to the financial statements for **Nike** in Appendix A to respond to the following:

1. Compute times interest earned for the years ended May 31, 2000, 1999, and 1998. Comment on Nike's ability to cover its interest expense for this period.

2. What evidence can you identify for an indication that Nike has temporary differences between income reported on its income statement and income reported on its tax return?

Swoosh Ahead

3. Access Nike's annual report for fiscal years ending after May 31, 2000, at its Web site [**www.nike.com**] or the SEC's EDGAR database [**www.sec.gov**]. Compute Nike's times interest earned for years ending after May 31, 2000, that you have access to.

Reporting in Action

C3 A1

BTN 12-2   Key comparative figures ($ millions) for both **Nike** and **Reebok** follow:

Key Figures	NIKE			REEBOK		
	Current Year	One Year Prior	Two Years Prior	Current Year	One Year Prior	Two Years Prior
Net income	$579.1	$451.4	$399.6	$11.0	$23.9	$135.1
Income taxes . . .	340.1	294.7	253.4	10.1	11.9	12.5
Interest expense .	45.0	44.1	60.0	49.7	60.7	64.4

Comparative Analysis

A1

Required

1. Compute times interest earned for the three years' data shown for each company.

2. Comment on which company appears stronger in its ability to pay interest obligations if income should decline.

BTN 12-3   Mike Gates is a sales manager for an automobile dealership. He earns a bonus each year based on revenue from the number of autos sold in the year less related warranty expenses. Actual warranty expenses have varied over the prior 10 years from a low of 3% of an automobile's selling price to a high of 10%. In the past, Mike has tended to estimate warranty expenses on the high end to be conservative. He must work with the dealership's accountant at year-end to arrive at the warranty expense accrual for cars sold this year.

1. Does the warranty accrual decision create any ethical dilemma for Gates?

2. Since warranty expenses vary, what percent do you think Gates should choose for this year? Justify your response.

Ethics Challenge

P4

BTN 12-4   Matthew Stafford is the accounting and finance manager for a manufacturer. At year-end, he must determine how to account for the company's contingencies. His manager, John Harris, objects to Matthew's proposal to recognize an expense and a liability for warranty service on units of a new product introduced in the fourth quarter. John comments, "There's no way we can estimate this warranty cost. We don't owe anyone anything until a product breaks and is returned. Let's report an expense if and when we do repairs."

Communicating in Practice

C3

Required

Prepare a one-page memorandum for Matthew to send to John defending his proposal.

Taking It to the Net

BTN 12-5   Access the March 28, 2000, filing of the 10-K of **McDonald's Corporation** (Ticker: MCD), which is available from **www.edgar-online.com.**

Required

1. Identify the current liabilities on McDonald's balance sheet as of December 31, 1999.
2. What portion (in percent) of McDonald's long-term debt matures within the next 12 months?
3. Use the consolidated statement of income for the year ended December 31, 1999, to compute McDonald's times interest earned ratio.

Teamwork in Action

BTN 12-6   Your team is in business and you need to borrow $6,000 cash for short-term needs. You have been shopping banks for a loan, and you have the following two options:

A. Sign a $6,000, 90-day, 11% interest-bearing note dated June 1.

B. Sign a $6,172.50, 90-day, noninterest-bearing note dated June 1.

Required

1. Discuss these two options and determine the best choice. Ensure that all teammates concur with the decision and understand the rationale.
2. Each member of the team is to prepare *one* of the following journal entries:
   a. Option A—at date of issuance.
   b. Option B—at date of issuance.
   c. Option A—at maturity date.
   d. Option B—at maturity date.
3. In rotation, each member is to explain the entry he/she prepared in part (2) to the team. Ensure that all team members concur with and understand the entries.
4. Assume that the funds are borrowed on December 1 (instead of June 1) and your business operates on a calendar-year reporting period. Each member of the team is to prepare *one* of the following entries:
   a. Option A—the year-end adjustment.
   b. Option B—the year-end adjustment.
   c. Option A—at maturity date.
   d. Option B—at maturity date.
5. In rotation, each member is to explain the entry he/she prepared in part (4) to the team. Ensure that all team members concur with and understand the entries.

Business Week Activity

BTN 12-7   Read the article "The Second Income: Is It Worth It?" in the August 25, 1997, issue of *Business Week*.

Required

1. What assumptions does the article's analysis make regarding the couple's location, income, family members, mortgage, and 401(k) plans?
2. Based on the analysis in the table, what is the couple's take-home pay when the husband works and the wife stays home? What is the pretax value of the 401(k) savings in this first scenario?
3. Based on the analysis reported in the table, what is the couple's take-home pay when both the husband and the wife work? What is the pretax value of the 401(k) savings in this second scenario?
4. What conclusions can you draw from this one example of whether it pays for both members of this couple to work full-time?

BTN 12-8   Shania Swain is an entrepreneur and owner of **The Edge**, a manufacturer of skateboards and accesssories. The Edge is considering a major technological investment in its manufacturing process. This investment would cut variable costs from 60% of sales to 45% of sales. However, fixed interest expense would increase from $90,000 per year to $190,000 per year to fund the $800,000 plant asset investment (with zero salvage, 50-year life, and depreciated using straight-line). Its recent income statement follows:

Entrepreneurial Decision

THE EDGE Income Statement For Year Ended January 31, 2002	
Sales	$500,000
Depreciation	10,000
Variable expenses (60%)	300,000
Income before interest	$190,000
Interest expense (fixed)	90,000
Net income	$100,000

Required

1. Compute The Edge's times interest earned ratio at January 31, 2002.

2. If the Edge expects sales to remain at $500,000, what would net income equal if it makes the investment?

3. What would net income equal if sales increase to $600,000 and the investment is (a) not made and (b) made?

4. What would net income equal if sales increase to $773,333 and the investment is (a) not made and (b) made? (Round amounts to the nearest thousand dollar.)

5. What would net income equal if sales increase to $900,000 and the investment is (a) not made and (b) made?

6. Comment on the results from parts (1) through (5) and their relation to the times interest earned ratio.

13

Partnerships

"Work with something that you love." —Amy Nye Wolf

A Look Back

Chapter 12 primarily focused on current liabilities and secondarily on long-term liabilities. We explained how liabilities are identified, computed, recorded, and reported in financial statements.

A Look at This Chapter

This chapter explains the partnership form of organization. Important characteristics of this form of organization are described along with the accounting concepts and procedures for its most fundamental

A Look Ahead

Chapter 14 extends our discussion to the corporate form of organization. We describe the accounting for stock issuances, dividends, and other equity transactions. We also explain how income, earnings per share, and

Part Four

Learning Objectives

Conceptual

C1 Identify characteristics of partnerships and similar organizations.

Analytical

A1 Compute partner return on equity and use it to evaluate partnership performance.

Procedural

P1 Prepare entries for partnership formation.

P2 Allocate and record income and loss among partners.

P3 Account for the admission and withdrawal of partners.

P4 Prepare entries for partnership liquidation.

Carry-On Music

e NEW YORK—Amy Nye Wolf knows the value of a good idea and a partnership. Wolf was only 17 years old and hiking across Europe when she bought a cassette at a London airport musicstand. "Even though they were overpriced and it was a lousy selection, I bought one anyway," says Wolf. This experience planted the seeds of selling CDs to U.S. air travelers. A few years later, using her savings and a loan from her parents, Wolf set up a partnership called **AltiTUNES Partners LP** [**www.AltiTUNES.com**] to pursue her idea—selling CDs and portable electronic products from stands in airport terminals.

Wolf believes knowledge of financial analysis and partnerships is crucial to her business activities. "I don't think I could do what I'm doing today without having worked as an analyst. I mean, they [accounting professionals] teach you everything from cash flow analysis and literally how to put together an Excel spreadsheet, which is a key tool." Wolf also emphasizes the importance of partnership formation, agreements, and financial statements to stay afloat. "There's a lot of other things you can do in life rather than risk everything and start your own business. We were fortunate in that the business started to throw off cash pretty much in its first week."

After a few lean years, AltiTUNES is a hit with travelers. It currently operates music outlets in more than 25 airport locations as well as its first train station outlet in New York's Grand Central Terminal. This year's revenues are expected to exceed $10 million. With little competition, low overhead, captive buyers, and a nearly 40% gross margin, the ride ahead looks smooth for AltiTUNES. [Sources: *AltiTUNES Web site,* May 2001; *CNN Business Unusual,* November 1997; *Forbes.Com,* May 1999]

The three common types of business organizations are proprietorships, partnerships, and corporations. Partnerships are similar to proprietorships, except they have more than one owner. This chapter explains partnerships and looks at several variations of them. These variations include limited partnerships, limited liability partnerships, S corporations, and limited liability companies. Understanding the advantages and disadvantages of the partnership form of business organization is important for making informed business decisions. This chapter gives us information to make such decisions.

Partnership Form of Organization

A **partnership** is an unincorporated association of two or more people to pursue a business for profit as co-owners. Many businesses are organized as partnerships. They are especially common in small retail and service businesses. Many professional practitioners also organize their practices as partnerships, including physicians, lawyers, investors, and accountants.

Characteristics of Partnerships

C1 Identify characteristics of partnerships and similar organizations.

Partnerships are an important type of organization because they offer certain advantages with their unique characteristics. We describe these characteristics in this section.

Voluntary Association

A partnership is a voluntary association between partners. Joining a partnership increases the risk to one's personal financial position in a desire for financial or other rewards. Note that some courts have ruled that partnerships are created by the actions of individuals even when there is no expressed agreement to form one.

Partnership Agreement

Forming a partnership requires that two or more legally competent people (who are of age and of sound mental capacity) agree to be partners. Their agreement becomes a **partnership contract,** also called *articles of copartnership*. While it should be in writing, the contract is binding even if it is only expressed verbally. Partnership agreements normally include details of the partners' (1) names and contributions, (2) rights and duties, (3) sharing of income and losses, (4) withdrawal arrangement, (5) dispute procedures, (6) admission and withdrawal of partners, and (7) rights and duties in the event a partner dies.

Point: When a new partner is admitted, all parties usually must agree to the admission.

Limited Life

Point: The end of a partnership is referred to as its *dissolution*.

The life of a partnership is limited. Death, bankruptcy, or any event taking away the ability of a partner to enter into or fulfill a contract ends a partnership. Any one of the partners can also terminate a partnership at will.

Taxation

A partnership has the same tax status as a proprietorship and is not subject to taxes on its income. The income or loss of a partnership is allocated to the partners according to the partnership agreement, and it is included in determining the taxable income for each partner's tax return. Partnership income or loss is allocated each year whether or not cash is distributed to partners.

Point: Partners are taxed on their share of partnership income, not on their withdrawals.

Mutual Agency

Mutual agency implies that each partner is a fully authorized agent of the partnership. As its agent, a partner can commit or bind the partnership to any contract within the scope of the partnership business. For instance, a partner in a merchandising business can sign contracts binding the partnership to buy merchandise, lease a store building, borrow money, or hire employees. These activities are all within the scope of a merchandising firm. A partner in a law firm, acting alone, however, cannot bind the other partners to a contract to buy snowboards for resale or rent an apartment for parties. These actions are outside the normal scope of a law firm's business. Partners also can agree to limit the power of any one or more of the partners to negotiate contracts for the partnership. This agreement is binding on the partners and on outsiders who know it exists. It is not binding on outsiders who do not know it exists. Outsiders unaware of the agreement have the right to assume each partner has normal agency powers for the partnership. Mutual agency exposes partners to the risk of unwise actions by any one partner.

Point: The majority of states adhere to the Uniform Partnership Act for the basic rules of partnership formation, operation, and dissolution.

Unlimited Liability

Unlimited liability implies that each partner can be called on to pay a partnership's debts. When a partnership cannot pay its debts, creditors usually can apply their claims to partners' *personal* assets. If a partner does not have enough assets to meet his/her share of the partnership debt, the creditors can apply their claims to the assets of the other partners. Partnerships in which all partners have *mutual agency* and *unlimited liability* are called **general partnerships.** Mutual agency and unlimited liability are two main reasons that most general partnerships have only a few members.

Co-Ownership of Property

Partnership assets are owned jointly by all partners. Any investment by a partner becomes the joint property of all partners. Partners have a claim on partnership assets based on their capital account and the partnership contract.

Organizations with Partnership Characteristics

Organizations exist that combine certain characteristics of partnerships with other forms of organizations. We discuss several of these forms in this section.

Limited Partnerships

Some individuals who want to invest in a partnership are unwilling to accept the risk of unlimited liability. Their needs may be met with a **limited partnership.** This type of organization is identified in its name with the words "Limited Partnership," or "Ltd.," or "L.P."

A limited partnership has two classes of partners, general and limited. At least one partner must be a **general partner** who assumes management duties and unlimited liability for the debts of the partnership. The **limited partners** have no personal liability beyond the amounts they invest in the partnership. The general partner(s) manages a limited partnership. Limited partners have no active role except as specified in the partnership agreement. A limited partnership agreement often specifies unique procedures for allocating income and losses between general and limited partners. The accounting procedures are similar for both limited and general partnerships.

> **Did You Know?**
>
> **Celtic Partners**   The **Boston Celtics** is organized as a limited partnership. It owns and operates the Boston Celtics NBA team. The general partner of the Boston Celtics is Celtics, Inc., and Paul E. Gaston is chairman of the board of Celtics, Inc.
>
>

Limited Liability Partnerships

Most states allow individuals to form a **limited liability partnership.** This is identified in its name with the words "Limited Liability Partnership" or by "L.L.P." This type of partnership is designed to protect innocent partners from malpractice or negligence claims resulting from the acts of another partner. When a partner provides service resulting in a malpractice claim, that partner has personal liability for the claim. The remaining partners who were not responsible for the actions resulting in the claim are not personally liable for it. However, most states hold all partners personally liable for other partnership debts. Accounting for a limited liability partnership is the same as for a general partnership.

S Corporations

Certain corporations with 75 or fewer stockholders can elect to be treated as a partnership for income tax purposes. These corporations are called Sub-Chapter S or simply **S corporations.** This distinguishes them from other corporations, called Sub-Chapter C or simply **C corporations.** S corporations provide stockholders the same limited liability feature that C corporations do. The advantage of an S corporation is that it does not pay income taxes.

If stockholders work for an S corporation, their salaries are treated as expenses of the corporation. The remaining income or loss of the corporation is allocated to stockholders for inclusion on their personal tax returns. Except for C corporations having to account for income tax expenses and liabilities, the accounting procedures are the same for both S and C corporations.

Limited Liability Companies

Point: The majority of proprietorships and partnerships that are being organized today are being set up as an LLC.

A relatively new form of business organization is the **limited liability company.** The names of these businesses usually include the words "Limited Liability Company" or an abbreviation such as "L.L.C." or "L.C." This form of business has certain features similar to a corporation and others similar to a limited partnership. The owners, who are called *members,* are protected with the same limited liability feature as owners of corporations. While limited partners cannot actively participate in the management of a limited partnership, the members of a limited liability company can assume an active management role. A limited liability company usually has a limited life. For income tax purposes, a limited liability company is typically treated as a partnership. This treatment depends on factors such as whether the members' equity interests are freely transferable and whether the company has continuity of life. A limited liability company's accounting system is designed to help management comply with the dictates of the articles of organization and company regulations adopted by its members. The accounting system also must provide information to support the company's compliance with state and federal laws, including taxation.

Did You Know?

Tax Relief   A recent IRS rule lets individuals set themselves up as LLCs. Previously, an LLC needed to have at least two people. There is also a PLLC for professionals.

Point: Accounting for LLCs is similar to that for proprietorships and partnerships. One difference is that Owner (Partner), Capital is usually called Members, Capital for LLCs.

Choosing a Business Form

Choosing the proper business form is crucial. Many factors should be considered, including taxes, liability risk, tax and fiscal year-end, ownership structure, estate planning, business risks, and earnings and property distributions. The following table summarizes several important characteristics of business organizations:

	Proprietorship	Partnership	LLP	LLC	S Corp.	Corporation
Business entity	yes	yes	yes	yes	yes	yes
Legal entity	no	no	no	yes	yes	yes
Limited liability	no	no	limited*	yes	yes	yes
Business taxed	no	no	no	no	no	yes
One owner allowed	yes	no	no	yes	yes	yes

* A partner's personal liability for LLP debts is limited. Most LLPs carry insurance to protect against malpractice.

We must remember that this table is a summary, not a detailed list. Many details underlie each of these business forms, and several details differ across states. Also, state and federal laws change, and a body of law is still developing around LLCs. Business owners should look at these details and consider unique business arrangements such as organizing various parts of their businesses in different forms.

Quick Check

1. A partnership is terminated in the event (a) a partnership agreement is not in writing, (b) a partner dies, (c) a partner exercises mutual agency.

2. What does the term *unlimited liability* mean when applied to a general partnership?

3. Which of the following forms of organization do not provide limited liability to all of its owners: (a) S corporation, (b) limited liability company, (c) limited partnership?

Answers—p. 544

Accounting for a partnership is the same as accounting for a proprietorship with the exception for transactions directly affecting partners' equity. Because ownership rights in a partnership are divided among partners, partnership accounting

- Uses a capital account for each partner.
- Uses a withdrawals account for each partner.
- Allocates net income or loss to partners according to the partnership agreement.

This section describes partnership accounting for organizing a partnership, distributing income and loss, and preparing financial statements.

Basic Partnership Accounting

Organizing a Partnership

When partners invest in a partnership, their capital accounts are credited for the invested amounts. Partners can invest both assets and liabilities. Each partner's investment is recorded at an agreed-upon value, normally the market values of the contributed assets and liabilities at the date of contribution.

P1 Prepare entries for partnership formation.

To illustrate, Kate Steeley and David Breck organize a partnership called **BOARDS** that offers year-round facilities for skateboarding and snowboarding. Steeley's initial net investment in BOARDS is $30,000, made up of cash ($7,000), boarding facilities ($33,000), and a note payable reflecting a bank loan for the new business ($10,000). Breck's initial investment is cash of $10,000. These amounts are the values agreed upon by both partners. The entries to record these investments follow:

Steeley's Investment

Jan. 11	Cash	7,000	
	Boarding facilities	33,000	
	Note payable		10,000
	K. Steeley, Capital		30,000
	To record the investment of Steeley.		

Assets = Liabilities + Equity
+7,000   +10,000   +30,000
+33,000

Breck's Investment

Jan. 11	Cash	10,000	
	D. Breck, Capital		10,000
	To record the investment of Breck.		

Assets = Liabilities + Equity
+10,000   +10,000

Once a partnership is formed, accounting for its transactions is similar to accounting for those of a proprietorship. Chapters 2, 3, and 4 describe the basic accounting procedures for a proprietorship, and they apply here as well. Minor differences include the following:

Point: Both equity and cash are reduced when a partner withdraws cash from a partnership.

1. Partners' withdrawals are debited to their own separate withdrawals accounts.
2. Partners' capital accounts are credited (or debited) for their shares of net income (or net loss) when closing the accounts at the end of a period.
3. Each partner's withdrawals account is closed to that partner's capital account.

These procedures are similar to those used for a proprietorship, except that separate capital and withdrawals accounts are kept for each partner.

Did You Know?

Nutty Partners The Hawaii-based **ML Macadamia Orchards LP** is one of the world's largest growers of macadamia nuts. It reported the following partners' capital balances ($ thousands) in its recent balance sheet:

| General Partners . . . . | $ 613 |
| Limited Partners . . . . | $60,657 |

Dividing Income or Loss

P2   Allocate and record income and loss among partners.

Concept 13-1

Point: Partners can agree on one ratio to divide income and another ratio to divide a loss.

Partners are not employees of the partnership but are its owners. If partners devote their time and services to their partnership, they are understood to do so for profit, not for salary. This means there are no salaries to partners that are reported as expenses on the partnership income statement. However, when net income or loss of a partnership is allocated among partners, the partners can agree to allocate "salary allowances" reflecting the relative value of services provided. Partners also can agree to allocate "interest allowances" based on the amount invested. For instance, since Steeley contributes three times the investment of Breck, it is only fair that this be considered when allocating income between them. Like salary allowances, these interest allowances are not expenses on the income statement.

Partners can agree to any method of dividing income or loss. In the absence of an agreement, the law says that the partners share income or loss of a partnership equally. If partners agree on how to share income but say nothing about losses, they share losses the same way that income is shared. Several methods of sharing partnership income or loss are used. Three common methods to divide income or loss use (1) a stated fractional basis, (2) the ratio of capital investments, or (3) salary and interest allowances and any remainder according to a fixed ratio. We explain each of these methods in this section.

Allocation on Stated Ratios

Point: The fractional basis can be stated as a proportion, ratio, or percent. For example, a 3:2 basis is the same as ⅗ and ⅖, or 60% and 40%.

The *stated ratio* (also called the *income and loss ratio*, the *profit and loss ratio*, or the *P&L ratio*) method of allocating partnership income or loss gives each partner a fraction of the total. Partners must agree on the fractional share each receives. To illustrate, assume the partnership agreement of K. Steeley and D. Breck says Steeley receives two-thirds and Breck one-third of partnership income and loss. If their partnership's net income is $60,000, it is allocated to the partners when the Income Summary account is closed as follows:

Assets = Liabilities + Equity		
	−60,000	
	+40,000	
	+20,000	

Dec. 31	Income Summary	60,000	
	K. Steeley, Capital		40,000
	D. Breck, Capital		20,000
	To allocate income and close Income Summary.		

Allocation on Capital Balances

Point: To determine the percent of income received by each partner, divide an individual partner's share by total net income.

The *capital balances* method of allocating partnership income or loss assigns an amount based on the ratio of each partner's relative capital balance. If Steeley and Breck agree to share income and loss on the ratio of their beginning capital balances—Steeley's $30,000 and Breck's $10,000—Steeley receives three-fourths of any income or loss ($30,000/$40,000) and Breck receives one-fourth ($10,000/$40,000). The journal entry follows the same format as that using stated ratios.

Allocation on Services, Capital, and Stated Ratios

The *services, capital, and stated ratio* method of allocating partnership income or loss recognizes that service and capital contributions of partners often are not equal. Salary allowances can make up for differences in service contributions. Interest allowances can make up for unequal capital contributions. Also, the allocation of income and loss can include *both* salary and interest allowances. To illustrate, assume that the partnership agreement of K. Steeley and D. Breck reflects differences in service and capital contributions as follows:

1. Annual salary allowances of $36,000 to Steeley and $24,000 to Breck.
2. Annual interest allowances of 10% of a partner's beginning-year capital balance.
3. Any remaining balance of income or loss is shared equally.

These salaries and interest allowances are *not* reported as expenses on the income statement. They are simply a means of dividing partnership income or loss. The remainder of this section provides two illustrations using this 3-point allocation agreement.

	Steeley	Breck	Total
Net income			$70,000
Salary allowances			
Steeley	$36,000		
Breck		$24,000	
Interest allowances			
Steeley (10% × $30,000)	3,000		
Breck (10% × $10,000)		1,000	
Total salaries and interest	39,000	25,000	64,000
Balance of income			6,000
Balance allocated equally			
Steeley	3,000 ←		
Breck		3,000 ←	
Total allocated			6,000
Balance of income			$ 0
Income of each partner	**$42,000**	**$28,000**	

Handwritten annotations: 60,000 / 10,000 / − 4,000

Exhibit 13.1

Dividing Income When Income Exceeds Allowances

Illustration when income exceeds allowance

If BOARDS has first-year net income of $70,000, and Steeley and Breck apply the 3-point partnership agreement at the bottom of the prior page, then income is allocated as shown in Exhibit 13.1. Steeley gets $42,000 and Breck gets $28,000 of the $70,000 total.

Illustration when allowances exceed income

The sharing agreement between Steeley and Breck must be followed even if net income is less than the total of the allowances. For example, if BOARDS' first year net income is $50,000 instead of $70,000, it is allocated to the partners as shown in Exhibit 13.2. Computations for salaries and interest are identical to those in Exhibit 13.1. However, when we apply the total allowances against income, the balance of income is negative. This $(14,000) negative balance is allocated in the same manner as a positive balance.

Point: When allowances exceed income, the amount of this negative balance often is referred to as a *sharing agreement loss* or *deficit*.

	Steeley	Breck	Total
Net income			$50,000
Salary allowances			
Steeley	$36,000		
Breck		$24,000	
Interest allowances			
Steeley (10% × $30,000)	3,000		
Breck (10% × $10,000)		1,000	
Total salaries and interest	39,000	25,000	64,000
Balance of income			(14,000)
Balance allocated equally			
Steeley	(7,000) ←		
Breck		(7,000) ←	
Total allocated			14,000
Balance of income			$ 0
Income of each partner	**$32,000**	**$18,000**	

Exhibit 13.2

Dividing Income When Allowances Exceed Income

Point: Check to make sure the sum of the dollar amounts allocated to each partner equals net income or loss.

Point: When a loss occurs, it is possible for a specific partner's capital to increase (when closing income summary) if that partner's allowance is in excess of his or her share of the negative balance. This implies that decreases to the capital balances of other partners exceed the partnership's loss amount.

Accordingly, the equal sharing agreement for the remaining balance means a negative $(7,000) is allocated to each partner. In this case, Steeley ends up with $32,000 and Breck gets $18,000. If BOARDS had experienced a loss, Steeley and Breck would share it in the same manner as the $50,000 income. The only difference is that they would have begun with a negative amount because of the loss. Specifically, the partners would still have been allocated their salary and interest allowances, further adding to the negative balance of the loss. This *total* negative balance *after* salary and interest allowances would have been allocated equally between the partners. These allocations would have been applied against the positive numbers from any allowances to determine each partner's share of the loss.

Quick Check

4. Ben and Jerry form a partnership by contributing $70,000 and $35,000, respectively. They agree to an interest allowance equal to 10% of each partner's capital balance at the beginning of the year, with the remaining income shared equally. Allocate first-year income of $40,000 to each partner.

Answer—p. 544

Partnership Financial Statements

Partnership financial statements are very similar to those of a proprietorship. The **statement of changes in partners' equity,** also called *statement of partners' capital,* is one exception. It shows *each* partner's beginning capital balance, additional investments, allocated income or loss, withdrawals, and ending capital balance. To illustrate, Exhibit 13.3 shows the statement of changes in partners' equity for BOARDS prepared using the sharing agreement of Exhibit 13.1. Recall that BOARDS' income was $70,000 and that Steeley withdrew $20,000 and Breck $12,000 at year-end.

The equity section of the balance sheet of a partnership usually shows the separate capital account balance of each partner. In the case of BOARDS, both K. Steeley, Capital, and D. Breck, Capital, are listed in the owner's equity section along with their balances of $52,000 and $26,000, respectively.

Did You Know?

Hotel California   The **Casa Munras Hotel Partners LP** operates the Casa Munras Garden Hotel and several leased retail stores in Monterey, California. Its recent statement of changes in partners' equity reports that total partners' withdrawals (distributions) equal $270,000, of which $2,700 is distributed to general partners and the remainder of $267,300 to limited partners.

Exhibit 13.3

Statement of Changes in Partners' Equity

BOARDS Statement of Changes in Partners' Equity For Year Ended December 31, 2002		Steeley		Breck		Total
Beginning capital balances			$ 0		$ 0	$ 0
Plus						
Investments by owners			30,000		10,000	40,000
Net income						
Salary allowances	$36,000			$24,000		
Interest allowances	3,000			1,000		
Balance allocated	3,000			3,000		
Total net income			42,000		28,000	70,000
			72,000		38,000	110,000
Less partners' withdrawals			(20,000)		(12,000)	(32,000)
Ending capital balances			**$52,000**		**$26,000**	**$78,000**

A partnership is based on a contract between individuals. When a partner is admitted or withdraws, the present partnership ends. Still, the business can continue to operate as a new partnership consisting of the remaining partners. This section considers how to account for the admission and withdrawal of partners.

Admission of a Partner

A new partner is admitted in one of two ways: by purchasing an interest from one or more current partners, or by investing cash or other assets.

Purchase of Partnership Interest

The purchase of partnership interest is a *personal transaction between one or more current partners and the new partner*. To become a partner, the current partners must accept the purchaser. Accounting for the purchase of partnership interest involves reallocating current partners' capital to reflect the transaction. To illustrate, at the end of BOARDS' first year, D. Breck sells one-half of his partnership interest to Cris Davis for $18,000. This means Breck gives up a $13,000 recorded interest ($26,000 × 1/2) in the partnership (see the ending capital balance in Exhibit 13.3). The partnership records this as follows:

Jan. 4	D. Breck, Capital	13,000	
	C. Davis, Capital		13,000
	To record admission of Davis by purchase.		

After this entry is posted, BOARDS' equity shows K. Steeley, Capital; D. Breck, Capital; and C. Davis, Capital, and their respective balances of $52,000, $13,000, and $13,000.

Two aspects of this transaction are important. First, the partnership, does *not* record the $18,000 Davis paid Breck regardless of the amount Davis paid Breck. The partnership's assets, liabilities, and *total* equity are unaffected by this transaction among partners. Second, Steeley and Breck must agree if Davis is to become a partner. If they agree to accept Davis, a new partnership is formed and a new contract with a new income-and-loss-sharing agreement is prepared. If Steeley or Breck refuses to accept Davis as a partner, then (under the Uniform Partnership Act), Davis gets Breck's sold share of partnership income and loss. If the partnership is liquidated, Davis gets Breck's sold share of partnership assets. Davis gets no voice in managing the company unless he is admitted as a partner.

Investing Assets in a Partnership

Admitting a partner by accepting assets is a *transaction between the new partner and the partnership*. The invested assets become partnership property. To illustrate, if Steeley (with a $52,000 interest) and Breck (with a $26,000 interest) agree to accept Davis as a partner in BOARDS with her investment of $22,000 cash, this is recorded as

Jan. 4	Cash	22,000	
	C. Davis, Capital		22,000
	To record admission of Davis by investment.		

After this entry is posted, both assets (cash) and equity (C. Davis, Capital) increase by $22,000. Davis now has a 22% equity in the assets of the business, computed as $22,000 divided by the entire partnership equity ($52,000 + $26,000 + $22,000). She does not necessarily have a right to 22% of income. Dividing income and loss is a separate matter on which partners must agree.

Bonus to old partners

When the current value of a partnership is greater than the recorded amounts of equity, the partners usually require a new partner to pay a bonus for the privilege of joining. To illustrate, assume that Steeley and Breck agree to accept Davis as a partner with a 25% interest in BOARDS if she invests $42,000. Recall the partnership's accounting records show

Admission and Withdrawal of Partners

P3 Account for the admission and withdrawal of partners.

Concept 13-2

Assets = Liabilities + Equity
−13,000
+13,000

Point: Partners' withdrawals are not constrained by the partnership's annual income or loss.

Assets   = Liabilities + Equity
+22,000   +22,000

Steeley's recorded equity in the business is $52,000 and Breck's recorded equity is $26,000 (see Exhibit 13.3). Davis's equity is determined as follows:

Equities of existing partners ($52,000 + $26,000)	$ 78,000
Investment of new partner	42,000
Total partnership equity	$120,000
Equity of Davis (25% × $120,000)	$ 30,000

Although Davis invests $42,000, her equity in the new partnership is only $30,000. The $12,000 difference is called a *bonus* and is allocated to existing partners (Steeley and Breck) according to their income-and-loss-sharing agreement. A bonus is shared in this way because it is viewed as an increase in the value of the partnership that is not yet reflected in income. The entry to record this transaction follows:

Assets = Liabilities + Equity
+42,000   +30,000
              +6,000
              +6,000

Jan. 4	Cash	42,000	
	C. Davis, Capital		30,000
	K. Steeley, Capital ($12,000 × ½)		6,000
	D. Breck, Capital ($12,000 × ½)		6,000
	To record admission of Davis and bonus.		

Bonus to new partner

Alternatively, existing partners can grant a bonus to a new partner. This usually occurs when they need additional cash or the new partner has exceptional talents. The bonus to the new partner is in the form of a larger share of equity than the amount invested. To illustrate, assume Steeley and Breck agree to accept Davis as a partner with a 25% interest in the partnership, but they require Davis to invest only $18,000. Davis's equity is determined as follows:

Equities of existing partners ($52,000 + $26,000)	$78,000
Investment of new partner	18,000
Total partnership equity	$96,000
Equity of Davis (25% × $96,000)	$24,000

The old partners contribute the $6,000 bonus (computed as $24,000 minus $18,000) to Davis according to their income-and-loss-sharing ratio. Moreover, Davis's 25% equity does not necessarily entitle her to 25% of future income or loss. This is a separate matter for agreement by the partners. The entry to record the admission and investment of Davis is

Assets = Liabilities + Equity
+18,000   -3,000
               -3,000
              +24,000

Jan. 4	Cash	18,000	
	K. Steeley, Capital ($6,000 × ½)	3,000	
	D. Breck, Capital ($6,000 × ½)	3,000	
	C. Davis, Capital		24,000
	To record Davis's admission and bonus.		

Withdrawal of a Partner

A partner generally withdraws from a partnership in one of two ways. (1) First, the withdrawing partner can sell his/her interest to another person who pays for it in cash or other assets. For this, we need only debit the withdrawing partner's capital account and credit the new partner's capital account. (2) The second case is when cash or other assets of the partnership are distributed to the withdrawing partner in settlement of his/her interest. To illustrate these cases, assume that Breck withdraws from the partnership of BOARDS in some future period. Their partnership shows the following capital balances at the date of Breck's withdrawal: K. Steeley, $84,000; D. Breck, $38,000; and C. Davis, $38,000. The partners (Steeley, Breck, and Davis) share income and loss equally. Accounting for Breck's withdrawal depends on whether a bonus is paid. We describe three possibilities.

No Bonus

If Breck withdraws and takes cash equal to his capital balance, the entry is

Oct. 31	D. Breck, Capital	38,000	
	Cash............................		38,000
	To record withdrawal of Breck from partnership with no bonus.		

Assets = Liabilities + Equity
−38,000 −38,000

Breck can take any combination of assets to which the partners agree to settle his equity. Breck's withdrawal creates a new partnership between the remaining partners. A new partnership contract and a new income-and-loss-sharing agreement are required.

Bonus to Remaining Partners

A withdrawing partner is sometimes willing to take less than the recorded value of his/her equity to get out of the partnership or because the recorded value is overstated. Whatever the reason, when this occurs, the withdrawing partner in effect gives the remaining partners a bonus equal to the equity left behind. The remaining partners share this unwithdrawn equity in their income-and-loss-sharing ratio. To illustrate, if Breck withdraws and agrees to take $34,000 cash in settlement of his capital balance, the entry is

Oct. 31	D. Breck, Capital	38,000	
	Cash............................		34,000
	K. Steeley, Capital		2,000
	C. Davis, Capital		2,000
	To record withdrawal of Breck and bonus to remaining partners.		

Assets = Liabilities + Equity
−34,000 −38,000
+2,000
+2,000

Breck withdrew $4,000 less than his recorded equity of $38,000. This $4,000 is divided between Steeley and Davis according to their income-and-loss-sharing ratio.

Bonus to Withdrawing Partner

A withdrawing partner may be able to receive more than his/her recorded equity for at least two reasons. First, the recorded equity may be understated. Second, the remaining partners may agree to remove this partner by giving assets of greater value than this partner's recorded equity. In either case, the withdrawing partner receives a bonus. The remaining partners reduce their equity by the amount of this bonus according to their income-and-loss-sharing ratio. To illustrate, if Breck withdraws and receives $40,000 cash in settlement of his capital balance, the entry is

Assets = Liabilities + Equity
−40,000 −38,000
−1,000
−1,000

Oct. 31	D. Breck, Capital	38,000	
	K. Steeley, Capital.	1,000	
	C. Davis, Capital.	1,000	
	Cash.........................		40,000
	To record Breck's withdrawal from partnership with a bonus to Breck.		

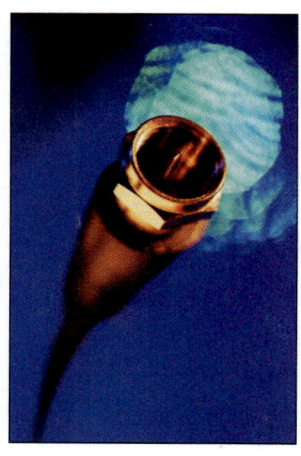

Falcon Communications LP has a partnership withdrawal agreement. Falcon owns and operates cable television systems in 25 states, and it has two managing general partners. The partnership agreement states that "at any time after September 30, 2005, either [partner] . . . can offer to sell to the other partner the offering partner's entire partnership interest . . . for a negotiated price. If the partner receiving such an offer rejects it, the offering partner may elect to cause [the partnership] . . . to be liquidated and dissolved."

You Make the Call—Ethics

Financial Planner   You are hired by the two remaining partners of a three-member partnership after the third partner's death. The partnership agreement states that a deceased partner's estate is entitled to a "share of partnership assets equal to the partner's relative equity balance" (partners' equity balances are equal). The estate argues it is entitled to one-third of the current value of partnership assets. The remaining partners say the distribution should use asset book values, which are 75% of current value. They also point to partnership liabilities, which equal 40% of total asset book value, and 30% of current value. How would you resolve this situation?

Answer—p. 543

Death of a Partner

A partner's death dissolves a partnership. A deceased partner's estate is entitled to receive his/her equity. The partnership contract should contain provisions for settlement in this case. These provisions usually require (1) closing the books to determine income or loss since the end of the previous period and (2) determining and recording current market values for both assets and liabilities. The remaining partners and the deceased partner's estate then must agree to a settlement of the deceased partner's equity. This can involve selling the equity to remaining partners or to an outsider, or it can involve withdrawing assets.

Liquidation of a Partnership

 Prepare entries for partnership liquidation.

When a partnership is liquidated, its business ends and four concluding steps are required:

1. Record the sale of noncash assets for cash and any gain or loss from their liquidation.
2. Allocate any gain or loss from liquidation of the assets in step (1) to the partners using their income-and-loss sharing ratio.
3. Pay or settle all partner liabilities.
4. Distribute any remaining cash to partners based on their capital balances.

Partnership liquidation usually falls into one of two cases as described in the following sections.

No Capital Deficiency

No capital deficiency means that all partners have a zero or credit balance in their capital accounts for final distribution of cash. To illustrate, assume that Steeley, Breck, and Davis operate their partnership in BOARDS for several years, sharing income and loss equally. The partners then decide to liquidate. On the liquidation date, the current period's income or loss is transferred to the partners' capital accounts according to the sharing agreement. After that transfer assume the partners' recorded equity balances (immediately prior to liquidation) are Steeley, $70,000; Breck, $66,000; and Davis, $62,000.

Next, assume that BOARDS sells its noncash assets for a net gain of $6,000. In a liquidation, gains or losses usually result from the sale of noncash assets, which are called *losses and gains from liquidation.* Partners share losses and gains from liquidation according to their income-and-loss-sharing agreement (equal for these partners) yielding the partners' revised equity balances of Steeley, $72,000; Breck, $68,000; and Davis, $64,000.[1] Then,

---

[1] The concepts behind these entries are not new. For example, assume BOARDS has two noncash assets recorded as boarding facilities, $15,000, and land, $25,000. The entry to sell these assets for $46,000 is

Jan. 15	Cash.	46,000	
	Boarding facilities		15,000
	Land		25,000
	Gain from Liquidation		6,000
	Sold noncash assets at a gain.		

We then record the allocation of any loss or gain (a gain in this case) from liquidation according to the partners' income-and-loss sharing agreement as follows:

Jan. 15	Gain from Liquidation	6,000	
	K. Steeley, Capital		2,000
	D. Breck, Capital		2,000
	C. Davis, Capital		2,000
	To allocate liquidation gain to partners.		

after partnership assets are sold and any gain or loss is allocated, the liabilities must be paid. After creditors are paid, any remaining cash is divided among the partners according to their capital account balances. BOARDS' only liability at liquidation is $20,000 in accounts payable. The entries to record the payment to creditors and the final distribution to partners are

Jan. 15	Accounts Payable.	20,000	
	Cash		20,000
	To pay claims of creditors.		
Jan. 15	K. Steeley, Capital.	72,000	
	D. Breck, Capital	68,000	
	C. Davis, Capital.	64,000	
	Cash		204,000
	To distribute remaining cash to partners.		

Assets = Liabilities + Equity
−20,000 −20,000

Assets = Liabilities + Equity
−204,000 −72,000
−68,000
−64,000

It is important to remember that the final cash payment is distributed to partners according to their capital account balances, whereas gains and losses from liquidation are allocated according to the income-and-loss-sharing ratio.

Capital Deficiency

Capital deficiency means that at least one partner has a debit balance in his/her capital account at the point of final cash distribution. This can arise from liquidation losses, excessive withdrawals before liquidation, or recurring losses in prior periods. A partner with a capital deficiency must, if possible, cover the deficit by paying cash into the partnership.

To illustrate, assume that Steeley, Breck, and Davis operate their partnership in BOARDS for several years, sharing income and losses equally. The partners then decide to liquidate. Immediately prior to the final distribution of cash, the partners' recorded capital balances are Steeley, $19,000; Breck, $8,000; and Davis, $(3,000). Davis's capital deficiency means she owes the partnership $3,000. Both Steeley and Breck have a legal claim against Davis's personal assets. The final distribution of cash in this case depends on how this capital deficiency is handled. Two possibilities exist.

Partner Pays Deficiency

Davis is obligated to pay $3,000 into the partnership to cover the deficiency. If she is willing and able to pay, the entry to record receipt of her payment is

Jan. 15	Cash	3,000	
	C. Davis, Capital		3,000
	To record payment of deficiency by Davis.		

Assets = Liabilities + Equity
+3,000 +3,000

After the $3,000 payment, the partners' capital balances are Steeley, $19,000; Breck, $8,000; and Davis, $0. The entry to record the final cash distributions to partners is

Jan. 15	K. Steeley, Capital.	19,000	
	D. Breck, Capital	8,000	
	Cash		27,000
	To distribute remaining cash to partners.		

Assets = Liabilities + Equity
−27,000 −19,000
−8,000

Partner Cannot Pay Deficiency

The remaining partners with credit balances absorb any partner's unpaid deficiency according to their income-and-loss-sharing ratio. To illustrate, if Davis is unable to pay the $3,000 deficiency, Steeley and Breck absorb it. Since they share equally, Steeley and Breck each absorb $1,500 of the deficiency. This is recorded as follows:

Assets = Liabilities + Equity
−1,500
−1,500
+3,000

Jan. 15	K. Steeley, Capital.	1,500	
	D. Breck, Capital	1,500	
	C. Davis, Capital		3,000
	To transfer Davis deficiency to Steeley and Breck.		

After Steeley and Breck absorb Davis's deficiency, the capital accounts of the partners are Steeley, $17,500; Breck, $6,500; and Davis, $0. The entry to record the final cash distributions to the partners is

Assets = Liabilities + Equity
−24,000
−17,500
−6,500

Jan. 15	K. Steeley, Capital.	17,500	
	D. Breck, Capital	6,500	
	Cash		24,000
	To distribute remaining cash to partners.		

Davis's inability to cover her deficiency does not relieve her of the liability. If she becomes able to pay at some future date, Steeley and Breck can each collect $1,500 from her.

Using the Information   Partner Return on Equity

A1 Compute partner return on equity and use it to evaluate partnership performances.

As with proprietorships, an important role of partnership financial statements is to aid current and potential partners in evaluating partnership success compared with other opportunities. One measure of this success is the **partner return on equity** ratio:

$$\text{Partner return on equity} = \frac{\text{Partner net income}}{\text{Average partner equity}}$$

This measure is separately computed for each partner. To illustrate, Exhibit 13.4 reports selected data from the **Boston Celtics LP** for 2000. The return on equity for the *total* partnership is computed as $452/[($1,188,074 + $1,144,780)/2] = 0.04\%$. However, return on equity can be quite different across partners. For example, the **Celtics LP** partner return on equity is computed as $43,491/[($223,298 + $266,789)/2] = 17.75\%$, whereas the **Boston Celtics Communications LP** partner return on equity is computed as $380/[($641,574 + $641,954)/2] = 0.06\%$. Partner return on equity provides each partner an assessment of its return on its equity invested in the partnership. A specific partner often uses this return to decide whether additional investment or withdrawal of resources is best for that partner. Exhibit 13.4 reveals that year 2000 produced poor returns for all partners except Celtics LP.

Exhibit 13.4

Selected Data from Boston Celtics LP

	Total	Boston Celtics LP I	Boston Celtics LP II	Celtics LP	Boston Celtics Communications LP
Balance at June 30, 1999	$1,188,074	$189,968	$133,234	$223,298	$641,574
Net income (loss) for year	452	(33,636)	(9,783)	43,491	380
Cash distribution	(43,746)	—	(43,746)	—	—
Balance at June 30, 2000	$1,144,780	$156,332	$ 79,705	$266,789	$641,954
Partner return on equity	0.04%	(19.43)%	(9.19)%	17.75%	0.06%

The following transactions and events affect the partners' capital accounts in several successive partnerships. Prepare a table with six columns, one for each of the five partners along with a total column to show the effects of the following events on the five partners' capital accounts.

Demonstration Problem

Part 1

4/13/2002   Ries and Bax create R&B Company. Each invests $10,000, and they agree to share profits equally.

12/31/2002   R&B Co. earns $15,000 in its first year. Ries withdraws $4,000 from the partnership, and Bax withdraws $7,000.

1/1/2003   Royce is made a partner in RB&R Company after contributing $12,000 cash. The partners agree that a 10% interest allowance will be given on each partner's beginning capital balance. In addition, Bax and Royce are to receive $5,000 salary allowances. The remainder of the income is to be divided evenly.

12/31/2003   The partnership's income for the year is $40,000, and withdrawals at year-end are Ries, $5,000; Bax, $12,500; and Royce, $11,000.

1/1/2004   Ries sells her interest for $20,000 to Murdock, whom Bax and Royce accept as a partner in the new BR&M Co. Income is to be shared equally after Bax and Royce each receive $25,000 salary allowances.

12/31/2004   The partnership's income for the year is $35,000, and year-end withdrawals are Bax, $2,500, and Royce, $2,000.

1/1/2005   Elway is admitted as a partner after investing $60,000 cash in the new Elway & Associates partnership. He is given a 50% interest in capital after the other partners transfer $3,000 to his account from each of theirs. A 20% interest allowance (on the beginning-of-year capital balances) will be used in sharing profits, there will be no salary allowances, and Elway will receive 40% of the remaining balance—the other three partners will each get 20%.

12/31/2005   Elway & Associates earns $127,600 for the year, and year-end withdrawals are Bax, $25,000; Royce, $27,000; Murdock, $15,000; and Elway, $40,000.

1/1/2006   Elway buys out Bax and Royce for the balances of their capital accounts after a revaluation of the partnership assets. The revaluation gain is $50,000, which is divided in the previous 1:1:1:2 ratio. Elway pays the others from personal funds. Murdock and Elway will share profits on a 1:9 ratio.

2/29/2006   The partnership earns $10,000 of income since the beginning of the year. Murdock retires and receives partnership cash equal to her capital balance. Elway takes possession of the partnership assets in his own name, and the company is dissolved.

Part 2

Journalize the events affecting the partnership for the year ended December 31, 2003.

Planning the Solution

- Evaluate each transaction's effects on the capital accounts of the partners.

- Each time a new partner is admitted or a partner withdraws, allocate any bonus based on the income-or-loss-sharing agreement.

- Each time a new partner is admitted or a partner withdraws, allocate subsequent net incomes or losses in accordance with the new partnership agreement.

- Prepare entries to (1) record Royce's initial investment; (2) record the allocation of interest, salaries, and remainder; (3) show the cash withdrawals from the partnership; and (4) close the withdrawal accounts on December 31, 2003.

Solution to Demonstration Problem

Part 1

Event	Ries	Bax	Royce	Murdock	Elway	Total
4/13/2002						
Initial Investment	$10,000	$10,000				$ 20,000
12/31/2002						
Income (equal)	7,500	7,500				15,000
Withdrawals	(4,000)	(7,000)				(11,000)
Ending balance	$13,500	$10,500				$ 24,000
1/1/2003						
New investment			$12,000			$ 12,000
12/31/2003						
10% interest	1,350	1,050	1,200			3,600
Salaries		5,000	5,000			10,000
Remainder (equal)	8,800	8,800	8,800			26,400
Withdrawals	(5,000)	(12,500)	(11,000)			(28,500)
Ending balance	$18,650	$12,850	$16,000			$ 47,500
1/1/2004						
Transfer interest	(18,650)			$18,650		$ 0
12/31/2004						
Salaries		25,000	25,000			50,000
Remainder (equal)		(5,000)	(5,000)	(5,000)		(15,000)
Withdrawals		(2,500)	(2,000)			(4,500)
Ending balance	$ 0	$30,350	$34,000	$13,650		$ 78,000
1/1/2005						
New investment					$ 60,000	60,000
Bonuses to Elway		(3,000)	(3,000)	(3,000)	9,000	0
Adjusted balance		$27,350	$31,000	$10,650	$ 69,000	$138,000
12/31/2005						
20% interest		5,470	6,200	2,130	13,800	27,600
Remainder (1:1:1:2) . . .		20,000	20,000	20,000	40,000	100,000
Withdrawals		(25,000)	(27,000)	(15,000)	(40,000)	(107,000)
Ending Balance		$27,820	$30,200	$17,780	$ 82,800	$158,600
1/1/2006						
Gain (1:1:1:2)		10,000	10,000	10,000	20,000	50,000
Adjusted balance		$37,820	$40,200	$27,780	$102,800	$208,600
Transfer interests		(37,820)	(40,200)		78,020	0
Adjusted balance		$ 0	$ 0	$27,780	$180,820	$208,600
2/29/2006						
Income (1:9)				1,000	9,000	10,000
Adjusted balance				$28,780	$189,820	$218,600
Settlements				(28,780)	(189,820)	(218,600)
Final balance				$ 0	$ 0	$ 0

Part 2

2003			
Jan. 1	Cash	12,000	
	Royce, Capital		12,000
	To record investment of Royce.		
Dec. 31	Income Summary	40,000	
	Ries, Capital		10,150
	Bax, Capital		14,850
	Royce, Capital		15,000
	To allocate interest, salaries, and remainders.		
Dec. 31	Ries, Withdrawals	5,000	
	Bax, Withdrawals	12,500	
	Royce, Withdrawals	11,000	
	Cash		28,500
	To record cash withdrawals by partners.		
Dec. 31	Ries, Capital	5,000	
	Bax, Capital	12,500	
	Royce, Capital	11,000	
	Ries, Withdrawals		5,000
	Bax, Withdrawals		12,500
	Royce, Withdrawals		11,000
	To close withdrawal accounts.		

Summary

C1 **Identify characteristics of partnerships and similar organizations.** Partnerships are voluntary associations, involve partnership agreements, have limited life, are not subject to income tax, include mutual agency, and have unlimited liability. Organizations that combine selected characteristics of partnerships and corporations include limited partnerships, limited liability partnerships, S corporations, and limited liability companies.

A1 **Compute partner return on equity and use it to evaluate partnership performance.** Partner return on equity provides each partner an assessment of his/her return on equity invested in the partnership.

P1 **Prepare entries for partnership formation.** A partner's initial investment is recorded at the fair market value of the assets contributed to the partnership.

P2 **Allocate and record income and loss among partners.** A partnership agreement should specify how to allocate partnership income or loss among partners. Allocation can be based on a stated ratio, capital balances, or salary and interest allowances to compensate partners for differences in their service and capital contributions.

P3 **Account for the admission and withdrawal of partners.** When a new partner buys a partnership interest directly from one or more existing partners, the amount of cash paid from one partner to another does not affect the partnership total recorded equity. When a new partner purchases equity by investing additional assets in the partnership, the new partner's investment can yield a bonus either to existing partners or to the new partner. The entry to record a withdrawal can involve payment from either (1) the existing partners' personal assets or (2) partnership assets. The latter can yield a bonus to either the withdrawing or remaining partners.

P4 **Prepare entries for partnership liquidation.** When a partnership is liquidated, losses and gains from selling partnership assets are allocated to the partners according to their income-and-loss-sharing ratio. If a partner's capital account has a deficiency that the partner cannot pay, the other partners share the deficit according to their relative income-and-loss-sharing ratio.

Guidance Answer to **You Make the Call**

Financial Planner   The partnership agreement apparently fails to mention liabilities or use the term *net assets*. To give the estate one-third of total assets is not fair to the remaining partners because if the partner had lived and the partners had decided to liquidate, the liabilities would need to be paid out of assets before any liquidation. Also, a settlement based on the deceased partner's recorded equity would fail to recognize excess of current value over book value. These value increases would be realized if the partnership were liquidated. A fair settlement would seem to be a payment to the estate for the balance of the deceased partner's equity based on the *current value of net assets*.

Guidance Answers to **Quick Checks**

1. (b)

2. Unlimited liability means that the creditors of a partnership require each partner to be personally responsible for all partnership debts.

3. (c)

4.

	Ben	Jerry	Total
Net Income			$40,000
Interest allowance (10%)	$ 7,000	$ 3,500	10,500
Balance of income			**$29,500**
Balance allocated equally ...	14,750	14,750	29,500
Balance of income			$ 0
Income of partners	**$21,750**	**$18,250**	

Glossary

C corporation corporation that does not qualify for and elect to be treated as a partnership for income tax purposes and therefore is subject to income taxes. (p. 529).

General partner partner who assumes unlimited liability for the debts of the partnership; responsible for partnership management. (p. 529).

General partnership partnership in which all partners have mutual agency and unlimited liability for partnership debts. (p. 529).

Limited liability company form of organization that combines corporation and limited partnership features, provides limited liability to its members (owners), and allows members to actively participate in management. (p. 530).

Limited liability partnership partnership in which a partner is not personally liable for malpractice or negligence unless that partner is responsible for providing the service that resulted in the claim. (p. 529).

Limited partners partners who have no personal liability for partnership debts beyond the amounts they invested in the partnership. (p. 529).

Limited partnership partnership that has two classes of partners, limited partners and general partners. (p. 529).

Mutual agency legal relationship among partners whereby each partner is an agent of the partnership and is able to bind the partnership to contracts within the scope of the partnership's business. (p. 528).

Partner return on equity partner net income divided by average partner equity. (p. 540).

Partnership unincorporated association of two or more persons to pursue a business for profit as co-owners. (p. 528).

Partnership contract agreement among partners that sets terms under which the affairs of the partnership are conducted. (p. 528).

Partnership liquidation dissolution of a partnership by (1) selling noncash assets and allocating any gain or loss according to partners' income-and-loss ratio, (2) paying liabilities, and (3) distributing any remaining cash according to partners' capital balances. (p. 538).

S corporation corporation that meets special tax qualifications so as to be treated like a partnership for income tax purposes. (p. 529).

Statement of changes in partners' equity financial statement that shows total capital balances at the beginning of the period, any additional investment by partners, the income or loss of the period, the partners' withdrawals, and the partners' ending capital balances; also called *statement of partners' capital.* (p. 534).

Unlimited liability legal relationship among general partners that makes each of them responsible for partnership debts if the other partners are unable to pay their shares. (p. 529).

Questions

1. If a partnership contract does not state the period of time the partnership is to exist, when does the partnership end?

2. What does the term *mutual agency* mean when applied to a partnership?

3. Can partners limit the right of a partner to commit their partnership to contracts? Would the agreement be binding (a) on the partners and (b) on outsiders?

4. Assume Amey and Lacey are partners. Lacey dies, and her son claims the right to take his mother's place in the partnership. Does he have this right? Why or why not?

5. Assume the Barnes and Ardmore partnership agreement provides for a two-thirds/one-third sharing of income but says nothing about losses. The first year of partnership operation resulted in a loss, and Barnes argues that the loss should be shared equally because the partnership agreement said nothing about sharing losses. Is Barnes correct? Explain.

6. Allocation of partnership income among the partners appears on what financial statement?

7. What does the term *unlimited liability* mean when it is applied to partnership members?

8. How does a general partnership differ from a limited partnership?

9. George, Burton, and Dillman have been partners for three years. The partnership is being dissolved. George is leaving the firm, but Burton and Dillman plan to carry on the business. In the final settlement, George places a $75,000 salary claim against the partnership. He contends that he has a claim for a salary of $25,000 for each year because he devoted all of his time for three years to the affairs of the partnership. Is his claim valid? Why or why not?

10. Kay, Kat, and Kim are partners. In a liquidation, Kay's share of partnership losses exceeds her capital account balance.

Moreover, she is unable to meet the deficit from her personal assets, and her partners shared the excess losses. Does this relieve Kay of liability?

11. After all partnership assets have been converted to cash and all liabilities paid, the remaining cash should equal the sum of the balances of the partners' capital accounts. Why?

12. Assume a partner withdraws from a partnership and receives assets of greater value than the book value of his equity. Should the remaining partners share the resulting reduction in their equities in the ratio of their relative capital balances or according to their income-and-loss-sharing ratio?

Jim and Jon are partners who agree that Jim will receive a $100,000 salary allowance after which any remaining income or loss will be shared equally. If Jon's capital account is credited $2,000 as his share of the net income in a given period, how much net income did the partnership earn?

QUICK STUDY

QS 13-1
Partnership income allocation

Ann Martin and Susie Meyer are partners in a business they started two years ago. The partnership agreement states that Ann should receive a salary allowance of $15,000 and that Susie should receive a $20,000 salary allowance. Any remaining income or loss is to be shared equally. Determine each partner's share of the current year's net income of $52,000.

QS 13-2
Partnership income allocation

Steve and Jack are partners in operating a store. Without consulting Steve, Jack enters into a contract to purchase merchandise for the store. Steve contends that he did not authorize the order and refuses to take delivery. The vendor sues the partners for the contract price of the merchandise. (*a*) Will the partnership have to pay? Why? (*b*) Does your answer differ if Steve and Jack are partners in a public accounting firm?

QS 13-3
Partnership liability

Lemm organized a limited partnership and is the only general partner. Moxie invested $20,000 in the partnership and was admitted as a limited partner with the understanding that he would receive 10% of the profits. After two unprofitable years, the partnership ceased doing business. At that point, partnership liabilities were $85,000 larger than partnership assets. How much money can the partnership's creditors obtain from Moxie's personal assets to satisfy the unpaid partnership debts?

QS 13-4
Liability in limited partnerships

Tomm agrees to pay Lennox and Bradley $10,000 each for a one-third (33⅓%) interest in the Lennox and Bradley partnership. When Tomm is admitted, each partner has a $30,000 capital balance. Make the journal entry to record Tomm's purchase of the partners' interest.

QS 13-5
Partner admission through purchase of interest

Chung and Choi are partners, each with $40,000 in their partnership capital accounts. Kwon is admitted to the partnership by investing $40,000 cash. Make the entry to show Kwon's admission to the partnership.

QS 13-6
Admission of a partner

Sig and Freed's company is organized as a partnership. At the prior year-end, partnership equity totals $150,000 ($100,000 from Sig and $50,000 from Freed). For the current year, partnership net income is $25,000 ($20,000 allocated to Sig and $5,000 allocated to Freed), and year-end total partnership equity is $200,000 ($140,000 from Sig and $60,000 from Freed). Compute the total partnership *and* individual partner return on equity ratios.

QS 13-7
Partner return on equity

EXERCISES

Exercise 13-1

Characteristics of partnerships

Next to the following list of eight characteristics of business organizations, write a brief description of how each characteristic applies to general partnerships.

Characteristic	Implication to General Partnerships
1. Life	
2. Owners' liability	
3. Legal status	
4. Tax status of income	
5. Owners' authority	
6. Ease of formation	
7. Transferability of ownership	
8. Ability to raise large amounts of capital	

Exercise 13-2

Forms of organization

For each of the following separate cases, recommend a form of business organization. With each recommendation, explain how business profits would be taxed if the owners adopt the form of organization recommended. Also list several advantages that the owners will enjoy from the form of business organization that you recommend.

1. Meg, Liz, and Chris are recent college graduates in computer science. They want to start a Web site development company. They all have college debts and currently do not own any substantial computer equipment needed to get the company started.

2. Dr. Fromm and Dr. Morris are recent graduates from medical residency programs. Both are family practice physicians and would like to open a clinic in an underserved rural area. Although neither has any funds to bring to the new venture, a banker has expressed interest in making a loan to provide start-up funds for their practice.

3. Phil has been out of school for about five years and has become quite knowledgeable about the commercial real estate market. He would like to organize a company that buys and sells real estate. Phil believes he has the expertise to manage the company but needs funds to invest in commercial property.

Exercise 13-3

Journalizing partnership transactions

On March 1, 2002, Favor and Alcox formed a partnership. Favor contributed $80,000 cash and Alcox contributed land valued at $60,000 and a building valued at $100,000. The partnership also assumed responsibility for Alcox's $80,000 long-term note payable associated with the land and building. The partners agreed to share profits as follows: Favor is to receive an annual salary allowance of $25,000, both are to receive an annual interest allowance of 10% of their beginning-year capital investment, and any remaining profit or loss is to be shared equally. On October 20, 2002, Favor withdrew cash of $34,000 and Alcox withdrew $20,000. After the adjusting and closing entries are made to the revenue and expense accounts at December 31, the Income Summary account had a credit balance of $90,000.

Required

1. Prepare journal entries to record the partners' initial capital investments, their cash withdrawals, and the December 31 closing of both the Withdrawals and Income Summary accounts.

2. Determine the balances of the partners' capital accounts as of December 31, 2002.

Exercise 13-4

Income allocation in a partnership

Cosmo and George began a partnership by investing $60,000 and $80,000, respectively. During its first year, the partnership earned $160,000. Prepare calculations showing how the $160,000 income should be allocated to the partners under each of the following three separate plans for sharing income and loss: (1) the partners failed to agree on a method to share income; (2) the partners agreed to share income and loss in proportion to their initial investments (round proportions to the nearest hundredth); and (3) the partners agreed to share income by granting a $50,000 per year salary allowance to Cosmo, a $40,000 per year salary allowance to George, 10% interest on their initial capital investments, and the remaining balance shared equally.

Assume that the partners of Exercise 13-4 agreed to share net income and loss by granting annual salary allowances of $50,000 to Cosmo and $40,000 to George, 10% interest allowances on their investments, and any remaining balance shared equally.

Exercise 13-5

Income allocation in a partnership

Required

1. Determine the partners' shares of Cosmo and George given a first-year net income of $98,800.

2. Determine the partners' shares of Cosmo and George given a first-year net loss of $16,800.

The partners in the Biz Partnership have agreed that partner Madonna may sell her $100,000 equity in the partnership to Streisand, for which Streisand will pay Madonna $85,000. Present the partnership's journal entry to record the sale of Madonna's interest to Streisand on September 30.

Exercise 13-6

Sale of partnership interest

The E-O Partnership has total partners' equity of $510,000, which is made up of Elm, Capital, $400,000, and Oak, Capital, $110,000. The partners share net income and loss in a ratio of 80% to Elm and 20% to Oak. On November 1, Ash is admitted to the partnership and given a 15% interest in equity and income and loss. Prepare the journal entry to record the admission of Ash under each of the following separate assumptions: Ash invests cash of (1) $90,000; (2) $120,000; and (3) $80,000.

Exercise 13-7

Admission of new partner

Holland, Flowers, and Wood have been partners sharing net income and loss in a 5:3:2 ratio. On January 31, the date Wood retires from the partnership, the equities of the partners are Holland, $150,000; Flowers, $90,000; and Wood, $60,000. Present journal entries to record Wood's retirement under each of the following separate assumptions: Wood is paid for his equity using partnership cash of (1) $60,000, (2) $80,000, (3) $30,000.

Exercise 13-8

Retirement of partner

The Red, White & Blue partnership was begun with investments by the partners as follows: Red, $180,000; White, $240,000; and Blue, $210,000. The operations did not go well, and the partners eventually decided to liquidate the partnership, sharing all losses equally. On August 31, after all assets were converted to cash and all creditors were paid, only $60,000 in partnership cash remained.

Exercise 13-9

Liquidation of partnership

Required

1. Compute the capital account balances of the partners after the liquidation of assets and the payment of creditors.

2. Any partner with a deficit agrees to pay cash to the partnership to cover the deficit. Present the journal entries on August 31 to record (*a*) the cash receipt from the deficient partner(s) and (*b*) the final disbursement of cash to the partners.

3. Assume that any partner with a deficit is not able to reimburse the partnership. Present journal entries (*a*) to transfer the deficit of any deficient partners to the other partners and (*b*) to record the final disbursement of cash to the partners.

Tuttle, Ritter, and Lee are partners who share income and loss in a 1:4:5 ratio. After lengthy disagreements among the partners and several unprofitable periods, the partners decided to liquidate the partnership. Before liquidation, the partnership balance sheet shows total assets, $126,000; total liabilities, $78,000; Tuttle, Capital, $2,500; Ritter, Capital, $14,000; and Lee, Capital, $31,500. The cash proceeds from selling the assets were sufficient to repay all but $28,000 to the creditors. Calculate the loss from selling the assets, allocate the loss to the partners, and determine how much of the remaining liability should be paid by each partner.

Exercise 13-10

Liquidation of partnership

Assume that the Tuttle, Ritter, and Lee partnership of Exercise 13-10 is a limited partnership. Tuttle and Ritter are general partners and Lee is a limited partner. How much of the remaining $28,000 liability should be paid by each partner?

Exercise 13-11

Liquidation of limited partnership

Hunt Sports Enterprises LP is organized as a limited partnership consisting of two individual partners: Soccer LP and Football LP. Both partners separately operate a minor league soccer team and a semipro football team. Compute partner return on equity for each limited partnership (and the total)

Exercise 13-12

Partner return on equity

for the year ended June 30, 2002, using the following selected data on partner capital balances from Hunt Sports Enterprises LP:

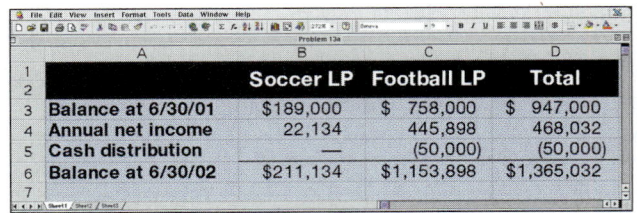

	Soccer LP	Football LP	Total
Balance at 6/30/01	$189,000	$ 758,000	$ 947,000
Annual net income	22,134	445,898	468,032
Cash distribution	—	(50,000)	(50,000)
Balance at 6/30/02	$211,134	$1,153,898	$1,365,032

PROBLEM SET A

Problem 13-1A

Allocating partnership income

Check (3) Simms, Capital, $97,800

Kim Ries, Tere Bax, and Kurt Simms invested $80,000, $112,000, and $128,000, respectively, in a partnership. During its first year, the firm earned $249,000.

Required

Prepare the entry to close the firm's Income Summary account as of its December 31 year-end and to allocate the $249,000 net income to the partners under each of the following separate assumptions: The partners (1) have no agreement on the method of sharing income and loss; (2) agreed to share income and loss in the ratio of their beginning capital investments; and (3) agreed to share income and loss by providing annual salary allowances of $66,000 to Ries, $56,000 to Bax, and $80,000 to Simms; granting 10% interest on the partners' beginning capital investments; and sharing the remainder equally.

Problem 13-2A

Allocating partnership income and loss; sequential years

Sid Braun and Ty Parnow are forming a partnership to which Braun will devote one-half time and Parnow will devote full time. They have discussed the following alternative plans for sharing income and loss: (a) in the ratio of their initial capital investments, which they have agreed will be $42,000 for Braun and $63,000 for Parnow; (b) in proportion to the time devoted to the business; (c) a salary allowance of $6,000 per month to Parnow and the balance in accordance with the ratio of their initial capital investments; or (d) a salary allowance of $6,000 per month to Parnow, 10% interest on their initial capital investments, and the balance shared equally. The partners expect the business to perform as follows: Year 1, $36,000 net loss; Year 2, $90,000 net income; and Year 3, $150,000 net income.

Required

Prepare three tables with the following column headings:

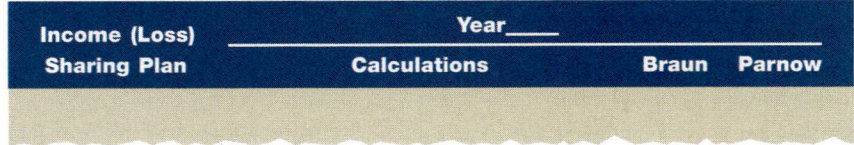

Income (Loss) Sharing Plan	Year____		
	Calculations	Braun	Parnow

Check Plan (d), Year 1, Parnow's share, $19,050

Complete the tables, one for each of the first three years, by showing how to allocate partnership income or loss to the partners under each of the four plans being considered. (Round answers to the nearest whole dollar.)

Problem 13-3A

Partnership income allocation, statement of changes in partners' equity, and closing entries

Trey Wiltse, Ron Buck, and Esther Ray formed the WBR Partnership by making capital contributions of $367,500, $262,500, and $420,000, respectively. They predict annual partnership net income of $450,000 and are considering the following alternative plans of sharing income and loss: (a) equally; (b) in the ratio of their initial capital investments; or (c) salary allowances of $80,000 to Wiltse, $60,000 to Buck, and $90,000 to Ray; interest allowances of 10% on their initial capital investments; and the balance shared equally.

Required

1. Prepare a table with the following column headings:

Income (Loss) Sharing Plan	Calculations	Wiltse	Buck	Ray	Total

Use the table to show how to distribute net income of $450,000 for the calendar year under each of the alternative plans being considered. (Round answers to the nearest whole dollar.)

2. Prepare a statement of changes in partners' equity showing the allocation of income to the partners assuming they agree to use plan (c), that income earned is $209,000, and that Wiltse, Buck, and Ray withdraw $34,000, $48,000, and $64,000, respectively, at year-end.

3. Prepare the December 31 journal entry to close Income Summary assuming they agree to use plan (c) and that net income is $209,000. Also close the withdrawals accounts.

Check (2) Ray, Ending Capital, $446,000

Part 1. Goering, Gore, and Schmit are partners with capital balances as follows: Goering, $168,000; Gore, $138,000; and Schmit, $294,000. The partners share income and loss in a 3:2:5 ratio. Gore decides to withdraw from the partnership, and the partners agree to not have the assets revalued upon his retirement. Prepare journal entries to record Gore's February 1 withdrawal from the partnership under each of the following separate assumptions: Gore (a) sells his interest to Getz for $160,000 after Goering and Schmit approve the entry of Getz as a partner; (b) gives his interest to a son-in-law, Swanson, and thereafter Goering and Schmit accept Swanson as a partner; (c) is paid $138,000 in partnership cash for his equity; (d) is paid $214,000 in partnership cash for his equity; and (e) is paid $30,000 in partnership cash plus equipment recorded on the partnership books at $70,000 less its accumulated depreciation of $23,200.

Problem 13-4A
Withdrawal of a partner

Check (e) Cr. Schmit, Capital, $38,250

Part 2. Assume that Gore does not retire from the partnership described in Part (1). Instead, Ford is admitted to the partnership on February 1 with a 25% equity. Prepare journal entries to record Ford's entry into the partnership under each of the following separate assumptions: Ford invests (a) $200,000; (b) $145,000; and (c) $262,000.

Quick, Drake, and Sage plan to liquidate their partnership. They share income and loss in a 3:2:1 ratio. On the day of liquidation their balance sheet appears as follows:

Problem 13-5A
Liquidation of a partnership

QUICK, DRAKE, AND SAGE Balance Sheet May 31			
Assets		**Liabilities and Equity**	
Cash	$180,800	Accounts payable	$245,500
Inventory	537,200	Quick, Capital	93,000
		Drake, Capital	212,500
		Sage, Capital	167,000
Total assets	$718,000	Total liabilities and equity	$718,000

Required

Prepare the journal entries for the sale of inventory, the allocation of its gain or loss, and the distribution of cash in each of the following separate cases: Inventory is sold for (1) $600,000; (2) $500,000; (3) $320,000 and any partners with capital deficits pay in the amount of their deficits; and (4) $250,000 and the partners have no assets other than those invested in the partnership.

Check (4) Cash distribution, Sage, $102,266.67

Kelli Cook, Ryan Moore, and Seth Davis invested $164,000, $98,400, and $65,600, respectively, in a partnership. During its first year, the firm earned $270,000.

PROBLEM SET B

Problem 13-1B
Allocating partnership income

Required

Prepare the entry to close the firm's Income Summary account as of its December 31 year-end and to allocate the $270,000 net income to the partners under each of the following separate assumptions. (Round answers to whole dollars.) The partners (1) have no agreement on the method of sharing income and loss; (2) agreed to share income and loss in the ratio of their beginning capital investments; and (3) agreed to share income and loss by providing annual salary allowances of $96,000 to Cook, $72,000 to Moore, and $50,000 to Davis; granting 10% interest on the partners' beginning capital investments; and sharing the remainder equally.

Check (3) Davis, Capital, $62,960

Problem 13-2B
Allocating partnership income and loss; sequential years

Maria Barto and J. R. Black are forming a partnership to which Barto will devote one-third time and Black will devote full time. They have discussed the following alternative plans for sharing income and loss: (a) in the ratio of their capital initial investments, which they have agreed will be $104,000 for Barto and $156,000 for Black; (b) in proportion to the time devoted to the business; (c) a salary allowance of $4,000 per month to Black and the balance in accordance with the ratio of their initial capital investments; or (d) a salary allowance of $4,000 per month to Black, 10% interest on their initial capital investments, and the balance shared equally. The partners expect the business to perform as follows: Year 1, $36,000 net loss; Year 2, $76,000 net income; and Year 3, $188,000 net income.

Required

Prepare three tables with the following column headings:

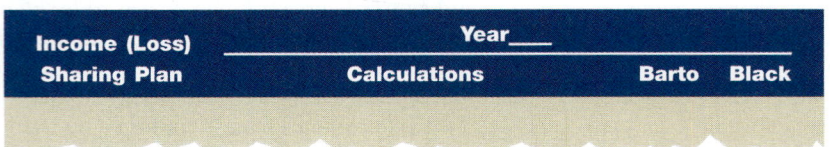

Check Plan (d), Year 1, Black's share, $8,600

Complete the tables, one for each of the first three years, by showing how to allocate partnership income or loss to the partners under each of the four plans being considered. (Round answers to the nearest whole dollar.)

Problem 13-3B
Partnership income allocation, statement of changes in partners' equity, and closing entries

Staci Long, Rachel Xi, and Ron Stack formed the LXS Partnership by making capital contributions of $144,000, $216,000, and $120,000, respectively. They predict annual partnership net income of $240,000 and are considering the following alternative plans of sharing income and loss: (a) equally; (b) in the ratio of their initial capital investments; or (c) salary allowances of $40,000 to Long, $30,000 to Xi, and $80,000 to Stack; interest allowances of 12% on their initial capital investments; and the balance shared equally.

Required

1. Prepare a table with the following column headings:

Use the table to show how to distribute net income of $240,000 for the calendar year under each of the alternative plans being considered. (Round answers to the nearest whole dollar.)

Check (2) Stack, Ending Capital, $150,400

2. Prepare a statement of changes in partners' equity showing the allocation of income to the partners assuming they agree to use plan (c), that income earned is $87,600, and that Long, Xi, and Stack withdraw $18,000, $38,000, and $24,000, respectively, at year-end.

3. Prepare the December 31 journal entry to close Income Summary assuming they agree to use plan (c) and that net income is $87,600. Also close the withdrawals accounts.

Problem 13-4B
Withdrawal of a partner

Part 1. Adams, Allen, and Aates are partners with capital balances as follows: Adams, $606,000; Allen, $148,000; and Aates, $446,000. The partners share income and loss in a 5:1:4 ratio. Adams decides to withdraw from the partnership, and the partners agree to not have the assets revalued upon her retirement. Prepare journal entries to record Adams's April 30 withdrawal from the partnership under each of the following separate assumptions: Adams (a) sells her interest to Adrian for $250,000 after Allen and Aates approve the entry of Adrian as a partner; (b) gives her interest to a daughter-in-law, Asp, and thereafter Allen and Aates accept Asp as a partner; (c) is paid $606,000 in partnership cash for her equity; (d) is paid $350,000 in partnership cash for her equity; and (e) is paid $200,000 in partnership cash plus manufacturing equipment recorded on the partnership books at $538,000 less its accumulated depreciation of $336,000.

Check (e) Cr. Aates, Capital, $163,200

Part 2. Assume that Adams does not retire from the partnership described in Part (1). Instead, Appier is admitted to the partnership on April 30 with a 20% equity. Prepare journal entries to record the entry of Appier under each of the following separate assumptions: Appier invests (a) $300,000; (b) $196,000; (c) $426,000.

Laman, Hinson, and Roney, who share income and loss in a 2:1:2 ratio, plan to liquidate their partnership. At liquidation, their balance sheet appears as follows:

Problem 13-5B
Liquidation of a partnership

LAMAN, HINSON, AND RONEY Balance Sheet January 18			
Assets		**Liabilities and Equity**	
Cash	$348,600	Accounts payable	$342,600
Equipment	617,200	Laman, Capital	300,400
		Hinson, Capital	195,800
		Roney, Capital	127,000
Total assets	$965,800	Total liabilities and equity	$965,800

Required

Prepare journal entries for the sale of equipment, the allocation of its gain or loss, and the distribution of cash in each of the following separate cases: Equipment is sold for (1) $650,000; (2) $530,000; (3) $200,000 and any partners with capital deficits pay in the amount of their deficits; and (4) $150,000, and the partners have no assets other than those invested in the partnership.

Check   (4) Cash distribution,
Laman, $73,600

Beyond the Numbers

BTN 13-1   Take a step back in time and imagine that **Nike** is in its infancy as a company. The year is 1965 and Nike is called BRS (Blue Ribbon Sports). BRS is organized as a partnership between two general partners, Bill Bowerman and Phil Knight.

Reporting in Action

Required

1. Refer to Nike's income statement in Appendix A. It varies in several key ways from what it would have shown for the BRS partnership. Explain how a corporate income statement differs from a partnership income statement.
2. Compare the Nike balance sheet in Appendix A to what the BRS partnership balance sheet would have shown in 1965. Identify and explain any differences you would anticipate.

BTN 13-2   Over the last 20 to 30 years, **Nike** and **Reebok** have evolved into large corporations. Today it is hard to imagine them as fledgling startups. Research Nike's history online. Numerous Web pages chronicle its beginnings. Also, research Reebok's history online.

Comparative Analysis

Required

1. Which company is older?
2. Which company was not started in the United States?
3. Which company started as a partnership between two men?
4. Which company was devised, in part, as a result of a classroom assignment?
5. Which company paid $35 to develop its logo?

BTN 13-3   Doctors Fair, Melchor, and Chandra have been in a group practice for several years. Fair and Melchor are family practice physicians, and Chandra is a general surgeon. Chandra receives many referrals for surgery from his family practice partners. Upon the partnership's original formation, the three doctors agreed to a two-part formula to share income. Every month each doctor receives a salary allowance of $4,000. Additional income is divided according to a percent of patient charges the doctors generate for the month. In the current month, Fair generated 10% of the billings, Melchor 30%,

Ethics Challenge
P2

and Chandra 60%. The group's income for this month is $60,000. Chandra has expressed dissatisfaction with the income-sharing formula and asks that income be split entirely on patient charge percents.

Required

1. Compute the income allocation for the current month using the original agreement.
2. Compute the income allocation for the current month using Chandra's proposed agreement.
3. Identify the ethical components of this partnership decision for the doctors.

Communicating in Practice

BTN 13-4   Assume that you are studying for an upcoming accounting exam with a good friend. Your friend says that she has a solid understanding of general partnerships but is less sure that she understands organizations that combine certain characteristics of partnerships with other forms of business organization. You offer to make some study notes for your friend to help her learn about limited partnerships, limited liability partnerships, S Corporations, and limited liability companies. Prepare a 2-page set of well-organized, complete study notes on these four forms of business organization.

Taking It to the Net

P1 **P2**

BTN 13-5   Access the September 15, 2000, 10-K filing of the **Boston Celtics Limited Partnership** at **www.edgar-online.com.**

Required

1. Locate the June 30, 2000, balance sheet for the Boston Celtics Limited Partnership. List the account titles used in the equity section of this balance sheet.
2. How many units of limited partnership interest are authorized, issued, and outstanding as of June 30, 2000?
3. What are the equity balances of the general partners and limited partners as of June 30, 2000?
4. What is the partnership's largest asset as of June 30, 2000?

Teamwork in Action

P2

BTN 13-6   This activity requires teamwork to reinforce understanding of accounting for partnerships.

Required

1. Assume that Baker, Warner, and Rice form the BWR Partnership by making capital contributions of $200,000, $300,000, and $500,000, respectively. BWR predicts annual partnership net income of $600,000. The partners are considering various plans for sharing income and loss. Assign a different team member to compute how the projected $600,000 income would be shared under each of the following separate plans:
   a. Shared equally.
   b. In the ratio of the partners' initial capital investments.
   c. Salary allowances of $50,000 to Baker, $60,000 to Warner, and $70,000 to Rice, with the remaining balance shared equally.
   d. Interest allowances of 10% on the partners' initial capital investments, with the remaining balance shared equally.
2. In sequence, each member is to present his/her income-sharing calculations with the team.
3. As a team, identify and discuss at least one other possible way that income could be shared.

Business Week Activity

C1

BTN 13-7   Read the article "I've Got the Horse Right Here" in the October 9, 2000, issue of *Business Week*.

Required

1. How does the article characterize the recent health of the horse racing industry?
2. What was the average price of a yearling in 2000 and in 1995?
3. The article states that investors may purchase shares of stallions through partnership interests. Explain what form these partnerships would likely take, general or limited.
4. If you were to invest in horses, which horses carry the least risk according to this article?

BTN 13-8   Ricky Dee wants to form a general partnership with his good friend Buddy Stanton to operate a Web programming and consulting service. Neither Ricky nor Buddy has organized a partnership business before.

Entrepreneurial Decision

Required

1. What details should Ricky and Buddy specify in their general partnership agreement?

2. What advantages should Ricky and Buddy be aware of with respect to organizing as a general partnership?

3. What disadvantages should Rick and Buddy be aware of with respect to organizing as a general partnership?

14

Equity Transactions and Corporate Reporting

"Somebody has to have the final word, and that's me."—Vince McMahon.

A Look Back

Chapter 13 focused on the partnership form of organization. We described crucial characteristics of partnerships and the accounting and reporting of their important transactions.

A Look at This Chapter

This chapter explains the corporate form of organization. Important characteristics of a corporation are described along with the accounting concepts and procedures for its equity transactions. We also explain how income, earnings per share, and retained earnings are reported.

A Look Ahead

Chapter 15 focuses on reporting and analyzing a company's cash flows. Special emphasis is directed to the statement of cash flows and its interpretation.

Blood, Sweat, and Corporations

e STAMFORD, CT—What's not unusual is that a company issued its stock to the public. What is unusual is that the company is the **World Wrestling Federation** [**WWF.com**], the brainchild of wrestling entrepreneur Vince McMahon. McMahon, who started as a wrestling commentator and script writer, has fought to turn a schlocky sport into mass entertainment with soap-opera scripts and enough cheeseball villains and heroes to make fans scream—and reach for their wallets. WWF's initial public offering (IPO) of its stock raised $179.3 million for more rock-'em, sock-'em action.

McMahon, a self-described juvenile delinquent who went to military school as a teenager to avoid a reformatory stint, is creating an entertainment empire that claims 35 million fans. Many are fervent in their devotion to pumped-up stars such as Stone Cold Steve Austin, The Rock, The Undertaker, Triple H, Chyna, and Kane and Kurt Angle. Such interest has helped annual sales slam ahead to $379 million, yielding earnings of nearly $60 million this past year. This performance has catapulted WWF to No. 3 on *Business Week*'s Hot Growth companies list—and has broadcasters salivating. Viacom and USA Networks are battling in court for the rights to WWF shows. NBC, meanwhile, just took a 3% stake in WWF for $30 million and will jointly own and broadcast the WWF's new XFL football league.

Recent controversies have dragged WWF stock down. Still, fans clearly do not share whatever worry stockholders may have. Advertising and sponsorship sales are up over $30 million; a CD featuring the theme songs of WWF stars rose to No. 2 on the music charts; and a biography by wrestler Mankind topped *The New York Times* best-seller list. McMahon says he's just beginning. Next up: an action adventure series, a late-night talk show featuring WWF talent, and international franchises in Australia, Britain, France, and Japan. Vince, who calls the WWF his mistress, boldly proclaims: "I don't mind people doubting us. We'll just have to prove them wrong." [Sources: *Business Week,* January 24, 2000, and October 30, 2000; *WWF Web Site,* May 2001.]

Learning Objectives

Conceptual

C1 Identify characteristics of corporations and their organization.

C2 Describe the components of stockholders' equity.

C3 Explain characteristics of common and preferred stock.

C4 Explain the form and content of a complete income statement.

C5 Explain the items reported in retained earnings.

Analytical

A1 Compute earnings per share and describe this ratio's use.

A2 Compute book value and explain its use in analysis.

A3 Compute dividend yield and explain its use in analysis.

A4 Compute price-earnings ratio and describe its use in analysis.

Procedural

P1 Record the issuance of corporate stock.

P2 Distribute dividends between common stock and preferred stock.

P3 Record transactions involving cash dividends.

P4 Account for stock dividends and stock splits.

P5 Record purchases and sales of treasury stock and the retirement of stock.

The three common types of business organizations are corporation, partnership, and proprietorship. This chapter focuses on corporations and accounting for them. Corporations are fewest in number of the three types of organization, but they transact more business than the other two forms combined. Understanding the advantages and disadvantages of a corporation is important to Vince McMahon of the **World Wrestling Federation**. The first part of this chapter describes the basics of the corporate form of organization; it explains accounting for common and preferred stock. We then focus on several special financing transactions, including cash and stock dividends, stock splits, and treasury stock. Next, we discuss the form and content of a complete income statement as well as earnings per share. The final section considers accounting for retained earnings, including prior period adjustments, retained earnings restrictions, and reporting guidelines.

Corporate Form of Organization

A **corporation** is an entity created by law and separate from its owners. It has most of the rights and privileges granted to individuals. Owners of corporations are called *stockholders* or *shareholders*. Corporations can be separated into privately held and publicly held corporations. A *privately held* (or *closely held*) corporation does not offer its stock for public sale and usually has few stockholders. A *publicly held* corporation offers its stock for public sale and can have thousands of stockholders. *Public sale* usually refers to issuance and trading on an organized stock market.

Characteristics of Corporations

C1 Identify characteristics of corporations and their organization.

Corporations represent an important type of organization because of the advantages offered by their unique characteristics. This section describes these characteristics.

Separate Legal Entity

As a separate legal entity, a corporation conducts its affairs with the same rights, duties, and responsibilities of a person. It takes actions through its agents, who are its officers and managers.

Limited Liability of Stockholders

A corporation is responsible for its own acts and its own debt because it is a separate legal entity. However, its stockholders are not liable for either. This limited liability is an important advantage of the corporate form from the stockholders' viewpoint.

Ownership Rights Are Transferable

Point: The *business entity principle* requires a corporation to be accounted for separately from its owners (shareholders).

Ownership of a corporation is by shares of stock that usually are easily bought and sold. The transfer of shares from one stockholder to another usually has no effect on the corporation or its operations. (A transfer of ownership can create significant effects if it causes a change in who controls or manages the corporation.) Millions of shares of many corporations are bought and sold daily in stock exchanges across the world.

Continuous Life

A corporation's life can continue indefinitely because it is not tied to the physical lives of its owners. Its life is sometimes initially limited by the laws of the state of its incorporation, but its charter can be renewed and its life extended when the stated time expires. Therefore, a corporation can have a perpetual life as long as it continues to be successful.

Stockholders Are Not Corporate Agents

A corporation acts through its agents, who are its officers and managers. Stockholders, who are not its officers or managers, do not have the power to bind the corporation to contracts. This is referred to as *lack of mutual agency*. Instead, stockholders impact the corporation's affairs by voting in stockholder meetings.

Ease of Capital Accumulation

Global: U.S., U.K., and Canadian corporations finance much of their operations with stock issuances, but companies in countries such as France, Germany, and Japan finance primarily with note and bond issuances.

Buying stock in a corporation often is attractive to investors because (1) stockholders are not liable for the corporation's actions and debts, (2) stock usually is transferred easily,

(3) the life of the corporation is unlimited, and (4) stockholders are not agents of the corporation. These advantages enable corporations to accumulate large amounts of capital from the combined investments of many stockholders. A corporation's capacity for raising capital is limited only by its ability to convince investors it can use their funds profitably relative to other investment opportunities.

Governmental Regulation

A corporation must meet requirements of a state's incorporation laws, which subject the corporation to state regulation and control. Proprietorships and partnerships escape many of the regulations and governmental reports required of corporations.

Corporate Taxation

Corporations are subject to the same property and payroll taxes as proprietorships and partnerships, but corporations are subject to *additional* taxes. The most burdensome of these are federal and state income taxes that together can take 40% or more of a corporation's pre-tax income. This results in the income of a corporation being taxed twice, first as income of the corporation and second as personal income to stockholders when cash is distributed to them as dividends. This is called *double taxation*. Proprietorships and partnerships are not subject to income taxes. Their income is taxed as the personal income of their owners. One exception is an S corporation that has the same tax status as a partnership. A corporation's tax situation is usually a disadvantage. It sometimes can be an advantage to stockholders because corporation and individual tax rates are progressive, which means that higher levels of income are taxed at higher rates and lower levels of income are taxed at lower rates. This suggests that taxes can be saved or at least delayed if a large amount of income is divided among two or more tax-paying entities. Also, by not paying dividends, the corporation's income is taxed only once at the lower corporate rate, at least temporarily until the stock is sold or dividends are paid.

Organizing and Managing a Corporation

This section describes the incorporation, costs, and management of corporate organizations.

Incorporation

A corporation is created by obtaining a charter from a state government. Charter requirements vary across states. A charter application usually must be signed by the prospective stockholders called *incorporators* or *promoters* and then filed with the proper state official. When the application process is complete and all fees have been paid, the charter is issued and the corporation is formed. Investors then purchase the corporation's stock, meet as stockholders, and elect a board of directors. Directors are responsible for overseeing a corporation's affairs.

Organization Costs

Organization costs are the costs to organize a corporation including legal fees, promoters' fees, and amounts paid to obtain a charter. The corporation records (debits) these costs to an asset account called *Organization Costs*. This intangible asset benefits the corporation throughout its life and its cost is amortized over a period no longer than 40 years. Income tax rules permit a corporation to record organization costs as a tax deduction over a minimum of five years. Therefore, many corporations use

---

Point: Double taxation is less severe when an owner-manager of a corporation collects a salary that is taxed only once as part of his/her personal income.

a five-year amortization period for financial reporting to ease recordkeeping. Since organization costs usually are small in amount, the *materiality principle* supports this arbitrary short amortization period.

Management of a Corporation

Corporations have different organizational structures, yet their ultimate control rests with stockholders. Stockholders control a corporation by electing its *board of directors,* or simply, *directors.* An individual stockholder's ability to affect management is limited to a vote in stockholder meetings; each stockholder usually has one vote for each share of stock owned. This control relation is shown in Exhibit 14.1. A corporation's board of directors is responsible for and has final authority for managing the corporation's activities. It can act only as a collective body. An individual director has no power to transact corporate business. Although the board has final authority, it usually limits its actions to establishing broad policy.

Exhibit 14.1

Corporation Authority Structure

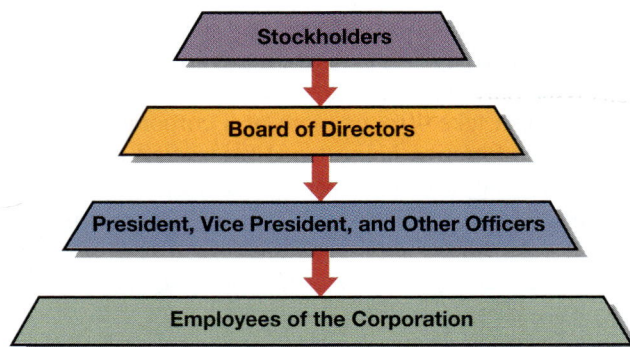

A corporation usually holds a stockholder meeting at least once a year to elect directors and transact business as required by its bylaws. A group of stockholders owning or controlling votes of more than a 50% share of a corporation's stock can elect the board and control the corporation. In many corporations, only a small percent of stockholders attend the annual meeting or participate in the voting process. Therefore, a smaller percent of stockholders is often able to dominate the election of board members. Still, stockholders who do not attend stockholders' meetings must have an opportunity to delegate their voting rights to an agent. A stockholder does this by signing a **proxy,** a document that gives a designated agent the right to vote the stock. Prior to a stockholders' meeting, a corporation's board of directors usually mails each stockholder an announcement of the meeting and a proxy listing the existing board chairperson as the voting agent of the stockholder. The announcement asks the stockholder to sign and return the proxy.

Day-to-day direction of corporate business is delegated to executive officers appointed by the board. A corporation's chief executive officer (CEO) is often its president. Several vice presidents, who report to the president, are commonly assigned specific areas of management responsibility such as finance, production, and marketing. The corporation secretary keeps minutes of stockholders' and directors' meetings and ensures that all legal responsibilities are met. In a small corporation, the secretary often is responsible for keeping a record of current stockholders and amounts of their stock interest. Another common corporate structure is the dual role of both the chairperson of the board of directors and the CEO. In this case, the president is usually designated the chief operating officer (COO).

Stock of a Corporation

This section explains stockholder rights, stock purchases and sales, and the role of registrar and transfer agents.

Rights of Stockholders

When investors buy stock, they acquire all *specific* rights the corporation's charter grants to stockholders. They also acquire *general* rights granted stockholders by the laws of the state in which the company is incorporated. When a corporation has only one class of stock, it is identified as **common stock,** which represents *residual equity,* meaning that creditors rank ahead of common stockholders if a corporation is liquidated. State laws vary, but common stockholders usually have the general right to

1. Vote at stockholders' meetings.

2. Sell or otherwise dispose of their stock.

3. Purchase their proportional share of any common stock later issued by the corporation. This right, called the **preemptive right,** protects stockholders' proportionate interest in the corporation. For example, a stockholder who owns 25% of a corporation's common stock has the first opportunity to buy 25% of any new common stock issued. This enables the stockholder to maintain a 25% interest if desired.

4. Share equally with other common stockholders in any dividends. This means each common share receives the same dividend.

5. Share equally in any assets remaining after creditors are paid when, and if, the corporation is liquidated. Therefore, each common share receives the same amount of remaining liquidated assets.

Stockholders also have the right to receive timely financial reports.

> **Global:** Stockholders' access to financial information varies across countries both in scope and by level of ownership. For instance, stockholders of Mexican companies holding small percent ownership often have difficulty obtaining quality financial information.

Stock Certificates and Transfer

When investors buy a corporation's stock, they sometimes receive a *stock certificate* as proof of share ownership. Many corporations issue only one certificate for each block of stock purchased. A certificate can be for any number of shares. Exhibit 14.2 shows an actual stock certificate of the **Green Bay Packers**.

A certificate shows the company name, stockholder name, number of shares, and other crucial information. (Issuance of certificates is becoming less common. Instead, many stockholders maintain accounts with the corporation or their stockbrokers and never receive actual certificates.)

When selling stock, a stockholder completes and signs a transfer endorsement on the back of the certificate and sends it to the corporation's secretary or transfer agent. The secretary or agent cancels and files the old certificate and issues a new certificate to the new stockholder if the company issues certificates. If the old certificate represents more shares than were sold, the corporation issues two new certificates, one to the new stockholder for the shares purchased and the other to the selling stockholder for the remaining unsold shares. When stockholders have their shares held in the name of their stock brokerage, the corporation's secretary or registrar records who owns the shares but does not send certificates to stockholders.

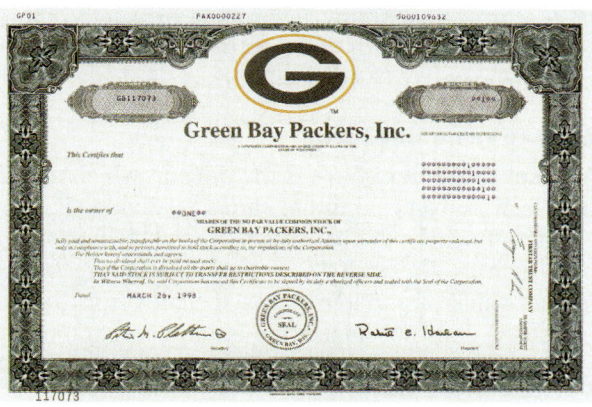

Exhibit 14.2
Stock Certificate

Registrar and Transfer Agents

If a corporation's stock is traded on a major stock exchange, the corporation must have a *registrar* and a *transfer agent*. A registrar keeps stockholder records and prepares official lists of stockholders for stockholder meetings and dividend payments. A transfer agent assists with purchases and sales of shares by receiving and issuing certificates as necessary. Registrars and transfer agents are usually large banks or trust companies having computer facilities and staff to do this work.

> **Did You Know?**
>
> **Online Trading**   Online brokerage service fees are as low as $5 to $10 per trade. These fees are a fraction of those charged by full-service firms. Online brokerage firms say technology has slashed their costs and eliminated most order-entry errors.

Basics of Capital Stock

Capital stock is a general term that refers to a corporation's stock used in obtaining its capital (owner financing). This section introduces capital stock terminology and some of the basics in accounting for capital stock.

> **C2**   Describe the components of stockholders' equity.

Authorized Stock

Global: Some countries, such as Switzerland, have no particular reporting standards for stockholders' equity.

Authorized stock is the total amount of stock that a corporation's charter authorizes it to sell. Most corporations authorize more stock than they anticipate selling either initially or in the near future. Therefore, the number of authorized shares usually exceeds the number of shares issued (and outstanding), often by a large amount. (*Outstanding stock* refers to issued stock held by stockholders. This distinction is important since corporations can buy back their issued stock, called *treasury stock*.) No formal journal entry is required for stock authorization. A corporation must apply to the state for a change in its charter if it wishes to issue more shares than previously authorized. A corporation discloses the number of shares authorized in the equity section of its balance sheet or notes. **Reebok**'s balance sheet in Appendix A reports 250 million shares authorized.

Did You Know?

Sizing Up an IPO A prospectus accompanies an initial public offering (IPO) of stock, giving financial information about the company issuing the stock. A prospectus should help answer these questions to price an IPO: (1) Is the underwriter reliable? (2) Is there growth in revenues, profits, and cash flows? (3) What is management's view of operations? (4) Are current owners selling? (5) What are the risks?

Selling Stock

A corporation can sell stock either directly or indirectly. To *sell directly*, it advertises its stock issuance to potential buyers. This type of issuance is most common with privately held corporations. To *sell indirectly*, a corporation pays a brokerage house (investment banker) to issue its stock. Some brokerage houses *underwrite* an indirect issuance of stock; they buy the stock from the corporation and take all gains or losses from its resale to stockholders.

Market Value of Stock

Market value per share is the price at which a stock is bought and sold. A variety of factors such as expected future earnings, dividends, growth, and other company and economic events influences market value. Traded stocks' market values are reported daily in newspapers such as *The Wall Street Journal* and are available online from the Web. The current market value of previously issued shares (for example, the price of stock in trades between investors) does not impact the issuing corporation's stockholders' equity.

Classes of Stock

Point: Managers are motivated to set a low par value when minimum legal capital and state issuance taxes are based on par value.

A corporation's charter authorizes it to issue a specified number of shares. If all authorized shares have the same rights and characteristics, the stock is called *common stock*. A corporation is sometimes authorized to issue more than one class of stock, including preferred stock and different classes of common stock. **American Greetings**, for instance, has two types of common stock outstanding: Class A stock has 1 vote per share and Class B stock has 10 votes per share.

Par Value Stock

Did You Know?

Stock Quotes The **Nike** stock quote shown is interpreted as (left to

52 Weeks				Yld		Vol				Net
Hi	Lo	Stock Sym	Div	%	PE	100s	Hi	Lo	Close	Chg
58^{50}	25^{81}	Nike B NKE	.48	1.3	18	6047	37^{75}	36^{44}	37^{06}	−1^{31}

right): **Hi,** highest price in past 52 weeks; **Lo,** lowest price in past 52 weeks; **Stock,** company; **Sym,** exchange symbol; **Div,** dividends paid per share in past year; **Yld %,** dividend divided by closing price; **PE,** stock price per share divided by earnings per share; **Vol 100s,** number of shares traded (in 100s); **Hi,** highest price for the day; **Lo,** lowest price for the day; **Close,** closing price for the day; **Net Chg,** change in closing price from the prior day.

Many stocks carry a **par value** established when they are authorized. **Par value stock** is a class of stock assigned a par value per share by the corporation in its charter. For example, **Novell**'s common stock has a par value of $0.10. Other commonly assigned par values are $25, $10, $5, $1 and $0.01. There is no restriction on the assigned par value. In many states, the par value of a stock establishes **minimum legal capital,** which refers to the least

Point: Minimum legal capital requirements often prohibit dividends if they would reduce equity below the minimum amount.

amount that the buyers of stock must contribute to the corporation or be subject to making up anything less at a future date. For example, if a corporation issues 1,000 shares of $10 par value stock, the minimum legal capital of the corporation in these states would be $10,000. Minimum legal capital is intended to protect a corporation's creditors. Since creditors cannot demand payment from the personal assets of stockholders, their claims are limited to the corporation's assets. Minimum legal capital limits a corporation's ability to distribute assets to stockholders. A corporation must maintain minimum legal capital until it is liquidated. At liquidation, all creditor claims are paid before any amounts are distributed to stockholders.

Point: Minimum legal capital was intended to protect creditors by requiring a minimum amount of net assets be kept in the corporation. However, such net assets can be lost by unprofitable operations.

No-Par Value Stock

No-par value stock, or simply *no-par stock,* is stock *not* assigned a value per share by the corporate charter. Nearly all states permit issuance of stock without par value. Its advantage is that it can be issued at any price without the possibility of a minimum legal capital deficiency. The entire proceeds from sale of no-par stock becomes minimum legal capital in some states.

Frequency of Par, No-Par, and Stated Value Common Stock

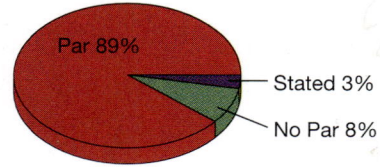

Par 89%
Stated 3%
No Par 8%

Stated Value Stock

Stated value stock is no-par stock to which the directors assign a "stated" value per share. Many states permit stated value stock. Stated value per share becomes the minimum legal capital per share in these cases. The directors can change stated value at any time.

Stockholder's Equity

A corporation's equity is known as **stockholders' equity,** also called *shareholders' equity* or *corporate capital.* Stockholders' equity consists of (1) contributed (or paid-in) capital and (2) retained earnings—see Exhibit 14.3 for an example. **Contributed capital** reflects the total amount of cash and other assets the corporation receives from its stockholders in exchange for common stock. **Retained earnings** is the cumulative net income (and loss) retained by a corporation. Exhibit 14.3 also compares the equity accounts for the three major forms of organizations. Details of shareholders' equity are described in the remainder of this chapter.

Point: Par, no-par, and stated value do *not* set the stock's market value.

Point: Contributed capital comes from stock-related transactions, whereas retained earnings comes from operations.

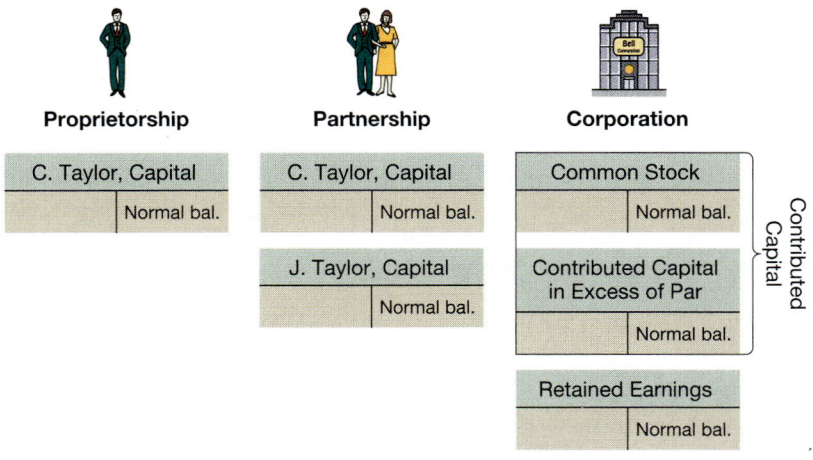

Exhibit 14.3
Equity Composition

Quick Check

1. Which of the following is *not* a characteristic of the corporate form of business? (a) Ease of capital accumulation, (b) stockholder responsibility for corporate debts, (c) easy transferability of ownership rights, (d) double taxation.

2. Why is a corporation's income said to be taxed twice?

3. What is a proxy?

Answers—p. 592

Common Stock

Record the issuance of corporate stock.

Concept 14-1

Accounting for the issuance of common stock affects only contributed capital accounts; no retained earnings accounts are affected.

Issuing Par Value Stock

Par value stock can be issued at par, at a premium, or at a discount. In each case, stock can be exchanged for either cash or noncash assets.

Issuing Par Value Stock at Par

When common stock is issued at par value, we record amounts for both the asset(s) received and the par value stock issued. Stock is most commonly issued in exchange for cash. To illustrate, the entry to record Dillon Snowboards' issuance of 30,000 shares of $10 par value stock for cash on June 5, 2002, is

June 5	Cash	300,000	
	Common Stock, $10 Par Value		300,000
	Issued 30,000 shares of $10 par value common stock at par.		

Assets   = Liabilities + Equity
+300,000   +300,000

Exhibit 14.4 shows the stockholders' equity of Dillon Snowboards at year-end 2002 (its first year of operations), after income of $65,000 and no dividend payments.

Exhibit 14.4

Stockholders' Equity for Stock Issued at Par

Stockholders' Equity	
Contributed capital	
Common Stock—$10 par value; 50,000 shares authorized;	
30,000 shares issued and outstanding	$300,000
Retained earnings	65,000
Total stockholders' equity	$365,000

Issuing Par Value Stock at a Premium

A **premium on stock** occurs when a corporation sells its stock for more than par value. To illustrate, if Dillon Snowboards issues its $10 par value common stock at $12 per share, this implies its stock is sold at a $2 per share premium. The premium is accounted for separately from par value in a ***Contributed Capital in Excess of Par Value*** account. This premium is reported as part of equity; it is not a revenue and is not listed on the income statement. The entry to record Dillon Snowboards' issuance of 30,000 shares of $10 par value stock for $12 per share on June 5, 2002, is

Point: The Contributed Capital in Excess of Par Value, Common Stock account is also called Premium on Common Stock.

June 5	Cash	360,000	
	Common Stock, $10 Par Value		300,000
	Contributed Capital in Excess of		
	Par Value, Common Stock		60,000
	Sold and issued 30,000 shares of $10 par value common stock at $12 per share.		

Assets   = Liabilities +   Equity
+360,000   +300,000
                        +60,000

Point: The *Contributed Capital* terminology is interchanged with *Paid-In Capital.*

The Contributed Capital in Excess of Par Value account is added to the par value of the stock in the equity section of the balance sheet as shown in Exhibit 14.5.

Issuing Par Value Stock at a Discount

A **discount on stock** occurs when a corporation sells its stocks for less than par value. Most states prohibit the issuance of stock at a discount because stockholders would be investing less than minimum legal capital. In states that allow stock issued at a discount, its purchasers usually become contingently liable to the corporation's creditors for the amount of the dis-

Stockholders' Equity		
Contributed capital		
Common Stock—$10 par value; 50,000 shares authorized;		
30,000 shares issued and outstanding	$300,000	
Contributed capital in excess of par value, common stock	**60,000**	
Total contributed capital		$360,000
Retained earnings		65,000
Total stockholders' equity		$425,000

Exhibit 14.5

Stockholders' Equity for Stock Issued at a Premium

count. If stock is issued at a discount, the amount by which issue price is less than par is debited to a *Discount on Common Stock* account, a contra to the common stock account, and its balance is subtracted from the par value of stock in the equity section of the balance sheet. This discount is not an expense and does not appear on the income statement.

Point: Retained earnings can be negative, reflecting accumulated losses. For example, Amazon.com had an accumulated deficit of $882 million at the start of 2000.

Issuing No-Par Value Stock

When no-par stock is issued and is not assigned a stated value, the amount the corporation receives becomes legal capital and is recorded as Common Stock. Thus, the entire proceeds are credited to a no-par stock account. To illustrate, if a corporation issues 1,000 shares of no-par stock for $40 per share, it is recorded as follows:

Oct. 20	Cash	40,000	
	Common Stock, No-Par Value		40,000
	Issued 1,000 shares of no-par value common stock at $40 per share.		

Assets = Liabilities + Equity
+40,000   +40,000

Issuing Stated Value Stock

When no-par stock is issued and assigned a stated value, its stated value becomes legal capital and is credited to a no-par stock account. Assuming that stated value stock is issued at an amount in excess of stated value, the excess is credited to Contributed Capital in Excess of Stated Value, Common Stock. To illustrate, if a corporation issues 1,000 shares of no-par common stock with stated value of $40 per share for cash of $50 per share, it is recorded as follows:

Oct. 20	Cash	50,000	
	Common Stock, $40 Stated Value		40,000
	Contributed Capital in Excess of Stated Value, Common Stock		10,000
	Issued 1,000 shares of $40 per share stated value stock at $50 per share.		

Assets = Liabilities + Equity
+50,000   +40,000
                 +10,000

The Contributed Capital in Excess of Stated Value, Common Stock account is reported in the contributed capital part of the stockholders' equity section.

Issuing Stock for Noncash Assets

A corporation can receive assets other than cash in exchange for its stock. (It can also assume liabilities on the assets received such as a mortgage on property received.) The corporation records the assets received at their market values as of the date of the transaction. The stock given in exchange is recorded at its par (or stated) value with any excess recorded in the Contributed Capital in Excess of Par (or Stated) Value account. (If no-par stock is exchanged, the stock is recorded at the assets' market value.) To illustrate, the entry to record receipt of land valued at $105,000 in return for issuance of 4,000 shares of $20 par value common stock is

Point: Par value (or stated value) of issued shares is recorded in the common stock account. Premium is the amount by which the issue price exceeds par (or stated) value and it is recorded in a separate equity account.

Stated Value
         or
market value.

June 10	Land	105,000	
	Common Stock, $20 Par Value		80,000
	Contributed Capital in Excess of Par Value,		
	Common Stock		25,000
	Exchanged 4,000 shares of $20 par value common stock for land.		

Assets = Liabilities + Equity
+105,000 +80,000
+25,000

Stock issued for noncash assets should be recorded at market value of either the stock or the noncash asset, whichever is clearly determinable.

Point: The matching principle supports capitalization (versus expensing) of organization costs.

As another example, a corporation sometimes gives shares of its stock to promoters in exchange for their services in organizing the corporation. The corporation receives the intangible asset of Organization Costs in exchange for this stock. The entry to record receipt of services valued at $12,000 in organizing the corporation in return for issuance of 600 shares of $15 par value common stock is

June 5	Organization Costs	12,000	
	Common Stock, $15 Par Value		9,000
	Contributed Capital in Excess of Par Value,		
	Common Stock		3,000
	Gave promoters 600 shares of $15 par value common stock in exchange for their services.		

Assets = Liabilities + Equity
+12,000 +9,000
+3,000

These noncash asset transactions used par value common stock, but any type of stock can be issued for noncash assets.[1]

Quick Check

4. A company issues 7,000 shares of its $10 par value common stock in exchange for equipment valued at $105,000. The entry to record this transaction includes a credit to (a) Contributed Capital in Excess of Par Value, Common Stock, for $35,000; (b) Retained Earnings for $35,000; (c) Common Stock, $10 Par Value, for $105,000.

5. What is a premium on stock?

6. Who is intended to be protected by minimum legal capital?

Answers—p. 592

Preferred Stock

C3 Explain characteristics of common and preferred stock.

Exhibit 14.6

Corporations and Preferred Stock

A corporation can issue two kinds of stock, common and preferred. **Preferred stock** has special rights that give it priority (or senior status) over common stock in one or more areas. Special rights typically include a preference for receiving dividends and for the distribution of assets if the corporation is liquidated. Preferred stock carries all rights of common stock unless the corporate charter nullified them. Most preferred stock, for instance, does not have the right to vote. **Nike** has preferred stock outstanding without general voting rights (see Appendix A, Note 7).[2] Exhibit 14.6 shows that preferred stock is issued by about one-fourth of large corporations. All corporations issue common stock.

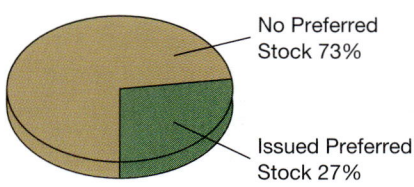

No Preferred Stock 73%

Issued Preferred Stock 27%

---

[1] Corporations sometimes issue stock through **stock subscriptions,** which involve sale of stock when the investor agrees to buy a certain number of shares at specified future dates and prices. The usual case occurs when a new corporation is formed and the organizers recognize both an immediate and a future need for financing.

[2] A corporation can also issue more than one class of stock. If it issues two classes of common stock, the primary difference between them usually involves voting rights. **Nike,** for instance, has Class A and Class B common stock. Its Class B stock has certain limitations in voting for directors (see its Form 10-K).

Issuing Preferred Stock

Preferred stock usually has a par value. Like common stock, it can be sold at a price different from par. Preferred stock is recorded in its own separate contributed capital accounts. To illustrate, if Dillon Snowboards issues 50 shares of $100 par value preferred stock for $6,000 cash on July 1, 2002, the entry is

July 1	Cash	6,000	
	Preferred Stock, $100 Par Value		5,000
	Contributed Capital in Excess of Par Value,		
	Preferred Stock		1,000
	Issued preferred stock for cash.		

Assets = Liabilities + Equity
+6,000   +5,000
                          +1,000

The preferred stock accounts are included as part of contributed capital. Also the equity section of the year-end balance sheet for Dillon Snowboards, including preferred stock, is shown in Exhibit 14.7.[3]

Stockholders' Equity

Contributed capital

   Common stock—$10 par value; 50,000 shares authorized;
     30,000 shares issued and outstanding $300,000

   Preferred stock—$100 par value; 1,000 shares authorized;
     50 shares issued and outstanding 5,000
   Contributed capital in excess of par value, preferred stock 1,000

Total contributed capital $306,000
Retained earnings 65,000

Total stockholders' equity $371,000

Exhibit 14.7

Stockholders' Equity with Common and Preferred Stock

Issuing no-par preferred stock is similar to issuing no-par common stock. Also, the entries for issuing preferred stock for noncash assets are similar to those for common stock.

Dividend Preference

Preferred stock usually carries a preference for dividends, meaning preferred stockholders are allocated their dividends before any dividends are allocated to common stockholders. The dividends allocated to preferred stockholders are usually expressed as a dollar amount per share or a percent applied to par value. A preference for dividends does *not* ensure dividends. If the directors do not declare a dividend, neither the preferred nor the common stockholders receive one.

P2 Distribute dividends between common stock and preferred stock.

Cumulative or Noncumulative Dividend

Most preferred stocks carry a cumulative dividend right. **Cumulative preferred stock** has a right to be paid both the current and all prior periods' unpaid dividends before any dividend is paid to common stockholders. When preferred stock is cumulative and the directors either do not declare a dividend to preferred stockholders or declare one that does not cover the total amount of cumulative dividend, the unpaid dividend amount is called **dividend in arrears.** Accumulation of dividends in arrears on cumulative preferred stock does not guarantee they will be paid. Also, **noncumulative preferred stock** has no right to prior periods' unpaid dividends if they were not declared in those prior periods.

Point: Dividend preference does not imply that preferred stockholders receive more dividends than common stockholders, nor does it guarantee a dividend.

---

[3] This exhibit assumes that the common stock was issued at par.

To illustrate the difference between cumulative and noncumulative preferred stock, assume that a corporation's outstanding stock includes (1) 1,000 shares of $100 par, 9% preferred stock and (2) 4,000 shares of $50 par common stock. During 2002, the first year of operations, the directors declare cash dividends of $5,000. In year 2003, they declare dividends of $42,000. Allocation of total dividends for these two years is shown in Exhibit 14.8. Note that allocation of year 2003 dividends depends on whether the preferred stock is noncumulative or cumulative. With noncumulative preferred, the preferred stockholders never receive the $4,000 skipped in 2002. If the preferred stock is cumulative, the $4,000 in arrears is paid in 2003 before any other dividends are paid.

Exhibit 14.8

Allocation of Dividends
(noncumulative vs. cumulative
preferred stock)

	Preferred	Common
If noncumulative preferred		
Year 2002	$ 5,000	$ 0
Year 2003		
Step 1: Current year's preferred dividend	$ 9,000	
Step 2: Remainder to common		$33,000
If cumulative preferred		
Year 2002	$ 5,000	$ 0
Year 2003		
Step 1: Dividend in arrears	$ 4,000	
Step 2: Current year's preferred dividend	9,000	
Step 3: Remainder to common		$29,000
Totals for year 2003	$13,000	$29,000

Example: What dividends do cumulative preferred stockholders receive in 2003 if the corporation paid only $2,000 of dividends in 2002? How does this affect dividends to common stockholders in 2003? *Answers:* $16,000 ($7,000 dividends in arrears, plus $9,000 current preferred dividends). Dividends to common stockholders decrease to $26,000.

A liability for a dividend does not exist until the directors declare a dividend. If a preferred dividend date passes and the corporation's board fails to declare the dividend on its cumulative preferred stock, the dividend in arrears is not a liability. The *full-disclosure principle* requires a corporation to report (usually in a note) the amount of preferred dividends in arrears as of the balance sheet date.

Participating or Nonparticipating Dividend

Nonparticipating preferred stock has a feature that limits dividends to a maximum amount each year. This maximum is often stated as a percent of the stock's par value or as a specific dollar amount per share. Once preferred stockholders receive this amount, the common stockholders receive any and all additional dividends. **Participating preferred stock** has a feature allowing preferred stockholders to share with common stockholders in any dividends paid in excess of the percent or dollar amount stated on the preferred stock. This participation feature does not apply until common stockholders receive dividends equal to the preferred stock's dividend percent. Many corporations are authorized to issue participating preferred stock but rarely do, and most managers never expect to issue it.[4]

---

[4] Participating preferred stock is usually authorized as a defense against a possible corporate *takeover* by an "unfriendly" investor (or a group of investors) who intends to buy enough voting common stock to gain control. Taking a term from spy novels, the financial world refers to this type of plan as a *poison pill* that a company swallows if enemy investors threaten its capture. A poison pill usually works as follows: A corporation's common stockholders on a given date are granted the right to purchase a large amount of participating preferred stock at a very low price. This right to purchase preferred shares is *not* transferable. If an unfriendly investor buys a large block of common shares (whose right to purchase participating preferred shares did *not* transfer to this buyer), the board can issue preferred shares at a low price to the remaining common shareholders who retained the right to purchase. Future dividends are then divided between the newly issued participating preferred shares and the common shares. This usually transfers value from common shares to preferred shares, causing the unfriendly investor's common stock to lose much of its value, and reducing the potential benefit of a hostile takeover.

Convertible Preferred Stock

Preferred stock is more attractive to investors if it carries a right to exchange preferred shares for a fixed number of common shares. **Convertible preferred stock** gives holders the option to exchange their preferred shares for common shares at a specified rate, a feature offering a higher potential return. When a company prospers and its common stock increases in value, convertible preferred stockholders can share in this success by converting their preferred stock into more valuable common stock. These holders also benefit from increases in the value of common stock without converting their preferred stock because the convertible preferred stock's market value is impacted by changes in common stock value.

Callable Preferred Stock

Callable preferred stock gives the issuing corporation the right to purchase (retire) this stock from its holders at specified future prices and dates. Many issues of preferred stock are callable. The amount paid to call and retire a preferred share is its **call price,** or *redemption value* and is set when the stock is issued. The call price normally includes the stock's par value plus a premium giving holders additional return on their investment. When the issuing corporation calls and retires a preferred stock, it usually must pay the call price *and* any dividends in arrears.

Point: The issuing corporation has the right, or option, to retire its callable preferred stock.

Motivation for Preferred Stock

Corporations issue preferred stock for several reasons. One is to raise capital without sacrificing control. For example, suppose a company's organizers have $100,000 cash to invest and wish to organize a corporation needing $200,000 of capital to start. If they sold $200,000 worth of common stock (with $100,000 to the organizers), they would have only 50% control and would need to negotiate extensively with other stockholders in making policy. However, if they issue $100,000 worth of common stock to themselves and sell outsiders $100,000 of 8%, cumulative preferred stock with no voting rights, they retain control.

A second reason to issue preferred stock is to boost the return earned by common stockholders. To illustrate, suppose a corporation's organizers expect their new company to earn an annual after-tax income of $24,000 on an investment of $200,000. If they sell and issue $200,000 worth of common stock, the $24,000 income produces a 12% return on the $200,000 of common stockholders' equity. However, if they issue $100,000 of 8% preferred stock to outsiders and $100,000 of common stock to themselves, their own return increases to 16% per year as shown in Exhibit 14.9.

Net (after-tax) income	$24,000
Less preferred dividends at 8%	(8,000)
Balance to common stockholders	$16,000
Return to common stockholders ($16,000/$100,000)	**16%**

Exhibit 14.9

Return to Common Stockholders When Preferred Stock Is Issued

Common stockholders earn 16% instead of 12% because assets contributed by preferred stockholders are invested to earn $12,000 while the preferred dividend is only $8,000. Use of preferred stock to increase return to common stockholders is an example of **financial leverage** (also called *trading on the equity*). As a general rule, when the dividend rate on preferred stock is less than the rate the corporation earns on its assets, the effect of issuing preferred stock is to increase (or *lever*) the rate earned by common stockholders. Financial leverage also occurs when debt is issued and the interest rate paid on it is less than the rate earned from using the assets the creditors lend the corporation.

You Make the Call

Concert Organizer You alter your business strategy from organizing concerts targeted at under 1,000 people to those targeted at between 5,000 to 20,000 people. You incorporate because of increased risk of lawsuits and a desire to issue stock for financing. It is important that you control the company for decisions on whom to schedule. What type of stock issuance do you offer?

Answer—p. 592

Point: Financial leverage is a main reason for borrowing. The borrower hopes to earn a return on borrowed funds in excess of the borrowing rate.

Other reasons for issuing preferred stock include its appeal to some investors who believe that the corporations' common stock is too risky or that the expected return on common stock is too low. Also, if a corporation's management wants to issue common stock but believes the current market price for common stock is too low, the corporation may issue preferred stock that is convertible into common stock. If and when the price of common stock increases, the preferred stockholders can convert their shares into common shares.

Quick Check

7. In what ways does preferred stock often have priority over common stock?

8. Increasing the return to common stockholders by issuing preferred stock is an example of (a) financial leverage; (b) cumulative earnings; (c) dividend in arrears.

9. A corporation has issued and outstanding (i) 9,000 shares of $50 par value, 10% cumulative, nonparticipating preferred stock and (ii) 27,000 shares of $10 par value common stock. No dividends have been declared for the past two years. During the current year, the corporation declares $288,000 in dividends. The amount paid to common shareholders is (a) $243,000; (b) $153,000; (c) $135,000.

Answers—p. 592

Dividends

P3 Record transactions involving cash dividends.

Dividends are normally paid out of retained earnings. A corporation's retained earnings ordinarily equal the total cumulative amount of reported net income less any net losses and dividends declared since the company started operating. This section describes dividend transactions involving both cash and stock.

Cash Dividends

Many state laws allow a corporation to pay cash dividends only if it has a sufficient amount of retained earnings. A corporation also must have cash in addition to retained earnings to pay a cash dividend. The decision to pay cash dividends rests with the board of directors and involves more than evaluating retained earnings and cash. The directors, for instance, may decide to keep the cash to invest in the corporation's growth, to meet emergencies, to take advantage of unexpected opportunities, or to pay off debt. Still, many corporations pay regular cash dividends to their stockholders at regular dates. These cash flows provide a return to investors and almost always affect the stock's market value.

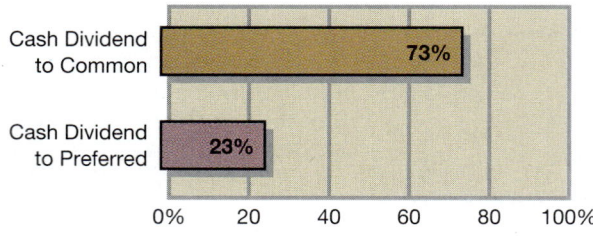

Dividend Types and Their Frequency

Cash Dividend to Common	73%
Cash Dividend to Preferred	23%

0%   20   40   60   80   100%

Entries for Cash Dividends

We sometimes assume for simplicity that dividends are declared and paid at the same time, but in practice their payment involves three important dates: declaration, record, and payment. **Date of declaration** is the date the directors vote to declare and pay a dividend. Stockholders receive a dividend only if the directors vote to declare one. Declaring a dividend creates a legal liability of the corporation to its stockholders. **Date of record** is the future date specified by the directors for identifying those stockholders listed in the corporation's records to receive dividends. The date of record usually follows the date of declaration by at least two weeks. Persons who own stock on the date of record receive dividends. **Date of payment** is the date when the corporation makes payment; it follows the date of record by enough time to allow the corporation to arrange checks or other means to pay its stockholders dividends.

To illustrate, the entry to record a January 9 declaration of a $1 per share dividend by the directors of Z-Tech, Inc., with 5,000 outstanding shares is[5]

Global: International accounting standards allow companies to reduce equity by an amount equal to any proposed dividends and prior to their date of declaration.

Point: A cash dividend reduces a company's assets (and its working capital).

Concept 14-2

---

[5] An alternative entry is to debit Dividends Declared instead of Retained Earnings. The balance in Dividends Declared is then closed to Retained Earnings at the end of the reporting period. Thus, the effect is the same: Retained Earnings is decreased and a Dividend Payable is increased. All assignments use the Retained Earnings account to record dividend declarations.

Date of Declaration

Jan. 9	Retained Earnings	5,000	
	Common Dividend Payable		5,000
	Declared $1 per common share cash dividend.		

Assets = Liabilities + Equity
　　　　　+5,000　　−5,000

Common Dividend Payable reflects the corporation's current liability to its stockholders. If a balance sheet is prepared between date of declaration and date of payment, the liability for this dividend is reported as a current liability. The date of record for the Z-Tech dividend is January 22. Those who own stock on this date will receive the dividend. *No journal entry is needed on the date of record.* The February 1 date of payment requires an entry to record distribution of the cash dividend. This entry records both the settlement of the liability and the reduction of the cash balance and is as follows:

Date of Payment

Feb. 1	Common Dividend Payable	5,000	
	Cash		5,000
	Paid $1 per common share cash dividend.		

Assets = Liabilities + Equity
−5,000　　−5,000

Deficits and Cash Dividends

A corporation with a debit (abnormal) balance for retained earnings is said to have a **retained earnings deficit,** which arises when a company incurs cumulative losses and/or pays more dividends than total earnings from current and prior years. A deficit is reported as a deduction on the balance sheet as shown in Exhibit 14.10.

Common stock, $10 par value, 5,000 shares authorized, issued, and outstanding	$50,000
Retained earnings deficit	**(6,000)**
Total stockholders' equity	$44,000

Exhibit 14.10

Stockholders' Equity with a Deficit

Point: The Retained Earnings Deficit account is also called Accumulated Deficit.

Point: The entry to close a net loss involves debiting (decreasing) Retained Earnings.

Most states prohibit a corporation with a deficit from paying a cash dividend to its stockholders. This legal restriction is designed to protect creditors by preventing distribution of assets to stockholders when the company may be in financial difficulty.

Some state laws allow cash dividends to be paid by returning a portion of the capital contributed by stockholders. This type of dividend is called a **liquidating cash dividend,** or simply *liquidating dividend,* because it returns a part of the original investment back to the stockholders. This requires a debit entry to one of the contributed capital accounts instead of Retained Earnings at the declaration date.

Did You Know?

Dividend Decline Cash dividends have declined as a percent of stock prices in U.S. markets. Cash dividends are increasingly viewed as an inefficient way to reward shareholders. Rates for dividend taxes, which are inescapable, can be nearly 40%. Companies are instead buying back shares, paying down debt, or expanding business.

Point: It is often said a dividend is a distribution of retained earnings, but it is more precise to describe a dividend as a distribution of assets to satisfy stockholder claims.

Quick Check

10. The Common Dividend Payable account is what type of an account?

11. What three crucial dates are involved in the process of paying a cash dividend?

12. When does a dividend become a company's legal obligation?

Answers—p. 592

P4 Account for stock dividends and stock splits.

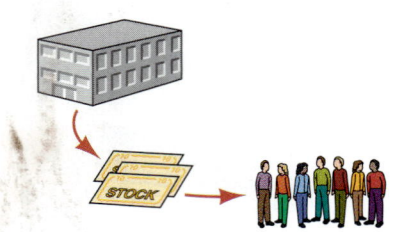

Stock Dividends

A **stock dividend** is a distribution of additional shares of the corporation's own stock to its stockholders without the receipt of any payment in return. Stock dividends and cash dividends are different. A stock dividend does not reduce a corporation's assets and equity, but a cash dividend does both. A stock dividend simply transfers a portion of equity from retained earnings to contributed capital. A stock dividend is declared by a corporation's directors.

Reasons for Stock Dividends

Stock dividends are declared and distributed for at least two reasons. First, directors are said to use stock dividends to keep the market price of the stock affordable. For example, if a corporation continues to earn income but does not distribute it to shareholders through cash dividends, the price of its common stock likely increases. The price of such a stock may become so high that it discourages some investors from buying the stock (especially in lots of 100 and 1,000). When a corporation declares a stock dividend, it increases the number of outstanding shares and lowers the per share price of its stock. Another reason for declaring a stock dividend is to provide evidence of management's confidence that the company is doing well and will continue to do well. The stock dividend can accomplish these goals without distributing needed cash.

Entries for Stock Dividends

A stock dividend does not affect assets or total equity, but it does affect the components of equity. It does this by transferring part of retained earnings to contributed capital accounts, sometimes described as *capitalizing* retained earnings.

Accounting for a stock dividend depends on whether it is a small or large stock dividend. A **small stock dividend** is a distribution of 25% or less of previously outstanding shares. It is recorded by capitalizing retained earnings for an amount equal to the market value of the shares to be distributed. A **large stock dividend** is a distribution of more than 25% of previously outstanding shares. It is likely to have a noticeable effect on the stock's market price. A large stock dividend is recorded by capitalizing retained earnings for the minimum amount required by state law governing the corporation. Most states require capitalizing retained earnings equal to the par or stated value of the stock.

To illustrate both small and large stock dividends, we use the equity section of X-Quest shown in Exhibit 14.11 just *before* its declaration of a stock dividend on December 31.

Exhibit 14.11

Stockholders' Equity **before** Declaring a Stock Dividend

Stockholders' Equity (before dividend)	
Common stock—$10 par value, 15,000 shares authorized, 10,000 shares issued and outstanding	$100,000
Contributed capital in excess of par value, common stock	8,000
Total contributed capital	$108,000
Retained earnings	35,000
Total stockholders' equity	$143,000

Recording a small stock dividend

Assume that X-Quest's directors declare a 10% stock dividend on December 31. This stock dividend of 1,000 shares, computed as 10% of its 10,000 issued and outstanding shares, is to be distributed on January 20 to the stockholders of record on January 15. Since the market price of X-Quest's stock on December 31 is $15 per share, this small stock dividend declaration is recorded as follows:

Date of Declaration

Dec. 31	Retained Earnings	15,000	
	Common Stock Dividend Distributable		10,000
	Contributed Capital in Excess of Par Value,		
	Common Stock		5,000
	Declared a 1,000-share (10%) stock dividend.		

Assets = Liabilities + Equity
                                  −15,000
                                  +10,000
                                   +5,000

The $10,000 credit in the declaration entry equals the par value of the dividend shares and is recorded in a contributed capital account called *Common Stock Dividend Distributable*. Its balance exists only until the shares are actually issued. The $5,000 credit equals the amount by which market value exceeds par value for the dividend shares. This amount increases the Contributed Capital in Excess of Par Value account in anticipation of the issue of shares. A stock dividend is never a liability on a balance sheet because it never reduces assets. Instead, any declared but undistributed stock dividend appears on the balance sheet as a part of contributed capital. In particular, a balance sheet changes in three ways when a company declares a stock dividend. First, the amount of equity attributed to common stock increases—from $100,000 to $110,000 for X-Quest for 1,000 additional declared shares. Second, contributed capital in excess of par increases by the excess of market value over par value for the declared shares. Third, retained earnings decreases, reflecting the transfer of amounts to both common stock and contributed capital in excess of par. The stockholders' equity of X-Quest is shown in Exhibit 14.12 *after* the 10% stock dividend is declared on December 31.

Point: The term *Distributable* (not *Payable*) is used for stock dividends.

Point: The credit to Contributed Capital in Excess of Par Value is recorded when the stock dividend is declared. This account is not affected when stock is later distributed.

Stockholders' Equity (after dividend)	
Common stock—$10 par value, 15,000 shares authorized,	
10,000 shares issued and outstanding	$100,000
Common stock dividend distributable—1,000 shares	**10,000**
Contributed capital in excess of par value, common stock	**13,000**
Total contributed capital	$123,000
Retained earnings	**20,000**
Total stockholders' equity	$143,000

Exhibit 14.12

Stockholders' Equity **after** Declaring a Stock Dividend

No entry is made on the date of record for a stock dividend. On January 20, the date of payment, X-Quest distributes the new shares to stockholders and records this entry:

Date of Payment

Jan. 20	Common Stock Dividend Distributable	10,000	
	Common Stock, $10 Par Value		10,000
	To record issuance of common stock dividend.		

Assets = Liabilities + Equity
                                  −10,000
                                  +10,000

The combined effect of these three stock dividend entries is to transfer (or capitalize) $15,000 of retained earnings to contributed capital accounts. The amount of capitalized retained earnings equals the market value of the 1,000 issued shares ($15 × 1,000 shares).

A stock dividend has no effect on the ownership percent of individual stockholders. To show this, assume that we own 200 shares of X-Quest's stock prior to the 10% stock dividend. When X-Quest sends each stockholder one new share for each 10 shares held, we receive 20 new shares (10% × 200 shares). Exhibit 14.13 shows no change in the book value of X-Quest and our shares from this dividend. Before the stock dividend, we owned 2% of X-Quest's stock, computed as 200 divided by 10,000 outstanding shares. After the dividend, we hold 220 shares, but our holding still equals 2% (220 divided by 11,000 shares now

Point: A small stock dividend does not affect a company's assets (or its working capital).

Exhibit 14.13

Financial Effects of
10% Stock Dividend

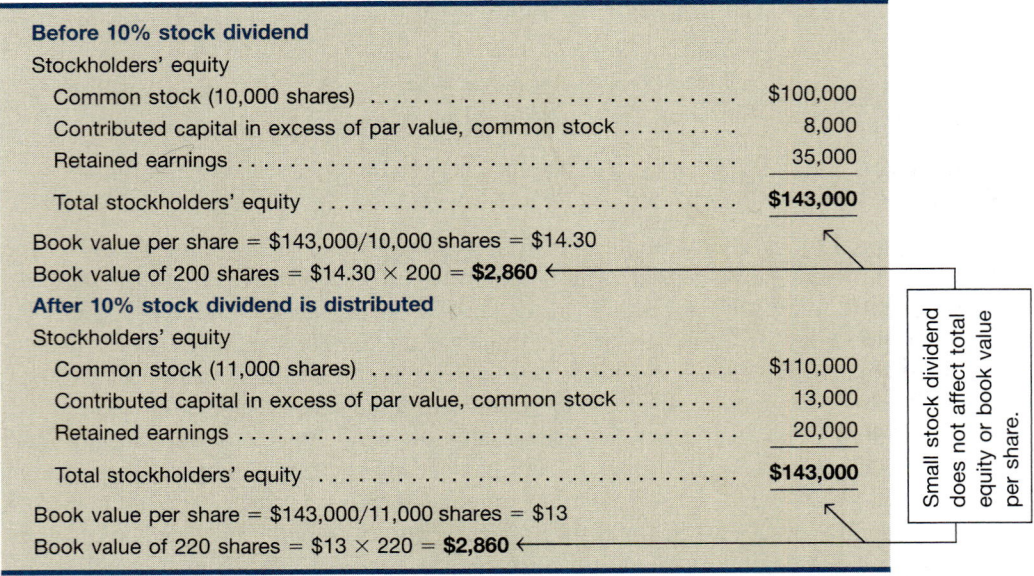

Before 10% stock dividend	
Stockholders' equity	
Common stock (10,000 shares)	$100,000
Contributed capital in excess of par value, common stock	8,000
Retained earnings	35,000
Total stockholders' equity	**$143,000**

Book value per share = $143,000/10,000 shares = $14.30
Book value of 200 shares = $14.30 × 200 = **$2,860**

After 10% stock dividend is distributed	
Stockholders' equity	
Common stock (11,000 shares)	$110,000
Contributed capital in excess of par value, common stock	13,000
Retained earnings	20,000
Total stockholders' equity	**$143,000**

Book value per share = $143,000/11,000 shares = $13
Book value of 220 shares = $13 × 220 = **$2,860**

Small stock dividend does not affect total equity or book value per share.

outstanding). Also, total book value of our holding remains at $2,860. Before the stock dividend, we owned 200 shares with a book value of $14.30 per share. After the dividend, we hold 220 shares with a book value of $13.00 per share. The only change in our 2% investment is that it is now divided among 220 shares instead of 200 shares. The only effect on equity is a transfer of $15,000 from retained earnings to contributed capital—total equity remains the same.

You Make the Call

Entrepreneur A company you co-founded and own stock in announces a 50% stock dividend. Has the value of your stock investment increased, decreased, or remained the same?

Answer—p. 592

Recording a large stock dividend

A corporation capitalizes retained earnings equal to the minimum amount required by state law for a large stock dividend. For most states, this amount is the par or stated value of the newly issued shares. To illustrate, suppose X-Quest's board declares a stock dividend of 30% instead of 10% on December 31. Because this dividend is more than 25%, it is treated as a large stock dividend. Thus, the par value of the 3,000 dividend shares is capitalized instead of the market value at the date of declaration with this entry:

Point: Large stock dividends are recorded at par or stated value.

Assets = Liabilities + Equity
                           −30,000
                           +30,000

Date of Declaration			
Dec. 31	Retained Earnings	30,000	
	Common Stock Dividend Distributable		30,000
	Declared a 3,000-share (30%) stock dividend.		

This transaction decreases retained earnings and increases contributed capital by $30,000. Subsequent entries related to a large stock dividend use the same accounts a small stock dividend uses. The effects from a large stock dividend on balance sheet accounts are similar to those for a small stock dividend except for the absence of any effect on contributed capital in excess of par.

Stock Splits

A **stock split** is the distribution of additional shares to stockholders according to their percent ownership. When a stock split occurs, the corporation "calls in" its outstanding shares and issues more than one new share in exchange for each old share. Splits can be done in any ratio, including 2-for-1, 3-for-1, or higher. Stock splits reduce the par or stated value per share.

To illustrate, CompTec has 100,000 outstanding shares of $20 par value common stock with a current market value of $88 per share. A 2-for-1 stock split cuts par value in half from $20 to $10 per share and replaces 100,000 shares of $20 par value stock with 200,000 shares of $10 par value stock. Also, market value is reduced from $88 per share to about $44 per share. The split does not affect either any equity amounts reported on the balance sheet or any individual stockholder's percent ownership. Both the Contributed Capital and Retained Earnings accounts are unchanged by a split, and *no journal entry is made*. The only effect on the accounts is a change in the stock account description. CompTec's 2-for-1 split on its $20 par value stock means that after the split, it changes its stock account title to Common Stock, $10 Par Value. This stock's description on the balance sheet also changes to reflect the additional authorized, issued, and outstanding shares and the new par value.

The difference between stock splits and large stock dividends is often blurred. Many companies report stock splits in their financial statements without calling in the original shares and changing their par value. This type of "split" is really a large stock dividend and results in additional shares issued to stockholders by capitalizing retained earnings or transferring other contributed capital to Common Stock. This approach avoids administrative costs of splitting the stock. **Harley-Davidson** recently declared a 2-for-1 stock split executed in the form of a 100% stock dividend.

Point: A **reverse stock split** is the opposite of a stock split. It increases both the market value per share and the par or stated value per share by specifying the split ratio to be less than 1-for-1, such as 1-for-2. A reverse stock split results in fewer shares.

Quick Check

13. How does a stock dividend impact assets and retained earnings?

14. What distinguishes a large stock dividend from a small stock dividend?

15. What amount of retained earnings is capitalized for a small stock dividend?

Answers—p. 592

Corporations acquire shares of their own stock for several reasons. First, they can use their shares to acquire another corporation. Second, they can repurchase shares to avoid a hostile takeover by an investor seeking to take control of the company. Third, they can buy shares and reissue them to employees as compensation. **Hewlett-Packard**, for example, has a stock repurchase program to compensate employees. Fourth, they can buy shares to maintain a strong or stable market for their stock. This is often done when a stock quickly and markedly declines in price. By buying shares, management shows its confidence in the price of its shares.

Treasury Stock

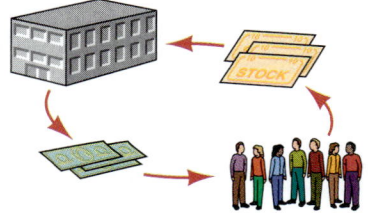

A corporation's reacquired shares are called **treasury stock,** which is similar to unissued stock in several ways. Neither treasury stock nor unissued stock is an asset. Neither receives cash dividends or stock dividends. Neither allows the exercise of voting rights. Still, treasury stock does differ from unissued stock in one major way. Specifically, the corporation can resell the stock at less than par without having the buyers incur a liability provided the treasury stock was originally issued at par value or higher. As shown in the margin, most large corporations have acquired some of their own stock.

Treasury stock purchases require management to exercise ethical sensitivity because corporate funds are being paid to specific stockholders instead of all stockholders. Managers must be sure the purchase is in the best interest of all stockholders. These concerns cause most companies to fully disclose treasury stock transactions.

Corporations and Treasury Stock

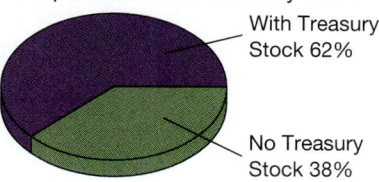

With Treasury Stock 62%

No Treasury Stock 38%

Purchasing Treasury Stock

Purchasing treasury stock reduces the corporation's assets and equity by equal amounts.[6] Exhibit 14.14 shows Cyber Corporation's account balances *before* any treasury stock purchase.

P5 Record purchases and sales of treasury stock and the retirement of stock.

---

[6] We describe the *cost method* of accounting for treasury stock, which is the most widely used method. The *par value* method is another method explained in advanced courses. Also, the term treasury stock is believed to arise from the fact that reacquired stock is held in a corporation's treasury.

Exhibit 14.14

Account Balances **before**
Purchasing Treasury Stock

Assets		Stockholders' Equity	
Cash	$ 30,000	Common stock—$10 par; 10,000 shares	
Other assets	95,000	authorized, issued, and outstanding	$100,000
		Retained earnings	25,000
Total assets	$125,000	Total stockholders' equity	$125,000

Global: Many countries, such as China, Japan, and Singapore, do not permit purchase of treasury stock.

Cyber then purchases 1,000 of its own shares for $11,500, which is recorded as follows:

Assets   = Liabilities + Equity
−11,500   −11,500

May 1	Treasury Stock, Common	11,500	
	Cash		11,500
	Purchased 1,000 treasury shares at $11.50 per share.		

This entry reduces equity from the debit to the Treasury Stock account, which is a contra equity account. Exhibit 14.15 shows account balances *after* this transaction.

Exhibit 14.15

Account Balances **after**
Purchasing Treasury Stock

Assets		Stockholders' Equity	
Cash	$ 18,500	Common stock—$10 par; 10,000 shares	
Other assets	95,000	authorized and issued; 1,000 shares in treasury	$100,000
		Retained earnings, $11,500 restricted by	
		treasury stock purchase	25,000
		Less cost of treasury stock	**(11,500)**
Total assets	$113,500	Total stockholders' equity	$113,500

Point: The Treasury Stock account is *not* an asset. This contra equity account is a subtraction in the equity section.

The treasury stock purchase reduces Cyber's cash, total assets, and total equity by $11,500 but does not reduce the balance of either the Common Stock or the Retained Earnings account. The equity reduction is reported by deducting the cost of treasury stock in the equity section. Two disclosures in this section describe the effects of the transaction. First, the stock description tells us 1,000 issued shares are in treasury, leaving only 9,000 shares outstanding. Second, the description for retained earnings tells us it is partly restricted.

Did You Know?

Buybacks Explode Buybacks, which refer to a company's purchase of its own stock, have exploded. Some believe buybacks explain the market's reduced dividend yield because shareholders' capital gains are taxed at more favorable rates than the more highly taxed cash dividends.

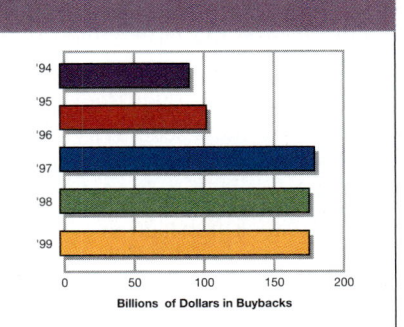

Billions of Dollars in Buybacks

Reissuing Treasury Stock

Treasury stock can be reissued by selling it at cost, above cost, or below cost. This section explains the accounting for reissuing treasury stock.

Selling Treasury Stock at Cost

If treasury stock is reissued at cost, the entry is the opposite of the entry made to record the purchase. For instance, if on May 21 Cyber reissues 100 of the treasury shares purchased on May 1 at the same $11.50 per share cost, the entry to record this sale is

Assets   = Liabilities + Equity
+1,150   +1,150

May 21	Cash	1,150	
	Treasury Stock, Common		1,150
	Received $11.50 per share for 100 treasury shares costing $11.50 per share.		

Exhibit 14.16

Income Statement for a Corporation

CompUS
Income Statement
For Year Ended December 31, 2002

Net sales		$8,478,000
Operating expenses		
Cost of goods sold	$5,950,000	
Depreciation expense	35,000	
Other selling, general, and administrative expenses	515,000	
Interest expense	20,000	
Total operating expenses		(6,520,000)
Other gains (losses)		
Loss on plant relocation		(45,000)
Gain on sale of surplus land		72,000
Income from continuing operations before taxes		1,985,000
Income taxes expense		(595,500)
Income from continuing operations		1,389,500
Discontinued segment		
Income from operating Division A (net of $180,000 taxes)	420,000	
Loss on disposal of Division A (net of $66,000 tax benefit)	(154,000)	266,000
Income before extraordinary items and cumulative effect of change in accounting principle		1,655,500
Extraordinary items		
Gain on sale of land taken by the state for development (net of $61,200 taxes)	142,800	
Loss from earthquake damage (net of $270,000 tax benefit)	(630,000)	(487,200)
Cumulative effect of a change in accounting principle		
Effect on prior years' income (through Dec. 31, 2001) of changing depreciation methods (net of $24,000 taxes)		56,000
Net income		$1,224,300
Earnings per common share (200,000 outstanding shares)		
Income from continuing operations		$ 6.95
Discontinued operations		1.33
Income before extraordinary items and cumulative effect of change in accounting principle		8.28
Extraordinary items		(2.44)
Cumulative effect of a change in accounting principle		0.28
Net income (basic earnings per share)		$ 6.12

Markers at left of statement: ① ② ③ ④ ⑤

---

extraordinary items in a separate category helps users predict future performance, absent the effects of extraordinary items. Few items qualify as extraordinary because they must be both *unusual* and *infrequent*. The following items are ***not*** considered extraordinary:

- Write-downs of inventories and write-offs of receivables.
- Gains and losses from disposing of segments.
- Financial effects of labor strikes.

Items that are usually considered extraordinary include these:

- Expropriation (taking away) of property by a foreign government.
- Condemning of property by a domestic government body.
- Prohibition against using an asset by a newly enacted law.
- Losses and gains from an unusual and infrequent calamity ("act of God").

Gains and losses that are neither unusual nor infrequent are reported as part of continuing operations. Gains and losses that are *either* unusual *or* infrequent, but *not* both, are reported as part of continuing operations *but* below the normal revenues, expenses, gains, and losses. Note that accounting standards require that certain items be reported as extraordinary to highlight their occurrence even when they do not meet the two criteria. One such item frequently encountered is a gain or loss from retiring debt.

> **You Make the Call**
>
> **Small Business Owner**   You own an orange grove near Jacksonville, Florida. A bad frost destroys about one-half of your oranges. You are currently preparing an income statement for a bank loan. Can you claim the loss of oranges as extraordinary?
>
> Answer—p. 592

Changes in Accounting Principles

The *consistency principle* requires that a company apply the same accounting principles once they are chosen. The phrase *accounting principles* in this context refers to accounting methods such as FIFO, LIFO, and straight-line depreciation. A company can change from one acceptable accounting principle to another as long as the change improves the usefulness of information in its financial statements. (Changes in accounting principles are sometimes required when new accounting standards are issued.)

Changes in accounting principles usually affect reported income in more than one way. To illustrate, CompUS purchased its only depreciable asset early in 1999 for $320,000. This asset has an eight-year life, a $40,000 salvage value, and is depreciated using the double-declining-balance method for the past three years. During 2002, CompUS decides its income statement would be more useful if depreciation is computed using the straight-line method instead of the double-declining-balance method.

Exhibit 14.17 compares the results of applying the two depreciation methods to the initial three years of this asset's life. The accelerated method yields $185,000 of depreciation from 1999 through 2001. If the straight-line method had been used from 1999 through 2001, only $105,000 of depreciation would have been reported. To adjust accounts to the balances they would be under the straight-line method, CompUS needs to decrease (debit) accumulated depreciation on this asset by $80,000. Also, since CompUS is subject to a 30% income tax, we offset this debit with credits of $24,000 (30% × $80,000) to deferred income taxes and $56,000 (remainder) to equity. Equity is increased because straight-line depreciation is less than that for double-declining balance for these earlier years.

Exhibit 14.17

Computing Cumulative Effect of a Change in Accounting Principle

	Double-Declining Depreciation	Straight-Line Depreciation	Pretax Difference	After-Tax Difference
Prior to change				
1999	$ 80,000	$ 35,000		
2000	60,000	35,000		
2001	45,000	35,000		
Totals	$185,000	$105,000	$80,000	$56,000*
Year of change				
2002	33,750	35,000†		
After change				
2003–2006		35,000		

* Reported on the year 2002 income statement as the cumulative adjustment for the differences in the three years prior to the change in 2002, net of $24,000 additional taxes to be paid (30% × $80,000).
† Reported on the year 2002 income statement as depreciation expense.

Reporting on Changes in Accounting Principles. The income statement in Exhibit 14.16 shows how to report a change in an accounting principle. First, section ① reports $35,000 of depreciation using the newly adopted straight-line method. This amount is taken from the Straight-Line Depreciation column in Exhibit 14.17. Straight-line depreciation also will be used in 2003 through 2006. Second, the income statement reports the $56,000 catch-up adjustment in section ④. This item is the cumulative effect of the change in accounting principle. Finally, a note should describe the accounting change and why it is an improvement over the prior principle. The note should also describe what the current year income would have been under the prior method. For CompUS, its note reports that 2002 depreciation of $33,750 would have been reported using double-declining balance instead of $35,000 under straight-line.

Quick Check

20. Which of the following is an extraordinary item? (a) A settlement paid to a customer injured while using the company's product; (b) a loss to a plant from damages caused by a meteorite; (c) a loss from selling old equipment.

21. Identify the five major sections of an income statement that are potentially reported.

22. A company using FIFO for the past 15 years decides to switch to LIFO. The effect of this event on past years' net income is (a) reported as a prior period adjustment to retained earnings; (b) ignored, because it is a change in an accounting estimate; (c) reported on the current year's income statement.

Answers—p. 592

Earnings per Share

The final section of the income statement in Exhibit 14.16 reports earnings per share results. Corporations must report earnings per share figures and usually report the amount of earnings per share for each of the four subcategories of income (continuing operations, discontinued segments, extraordinary items, and the effect of accounting principle changes) when they exist. **Earnings per share,** also called *net income per share,* is the amount of income earned per each share of a company's outstanding common stock. Investors find this ratio useful in their valuation of common shares, especially when compared with the market price per share discussed later in this chapter. The **basic earnings per share** formula is in Exhibit 14.18.

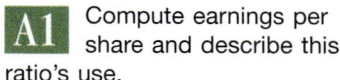 **A1** Compute earnings per share and describe this ratio's use.

$$\text{Basic earnings per share} = \frac{\text{Net income} - \text{Preferred dividends}}{\text{Weighted-average common shares outstanding}}$$

Exhibit 14.18

Basic Earnings per Share

This formula shows that the basic earnings per share (EPS) computation depends not only on net income but also on (1) any preferred dividends and (2) the weighted-average common shares outstanding. Our explanation of earnings per share begins by considering the simple case that has no changes in shares outstanding during the period. We then look at what happens when the number of common shares outstanding changes.

No Changes in Common Shares Outstanding. To illustrate, assume that Quantum Co. earns $40,000 net income in 2002 and declares dividends of $7,500 on its noncumulative preferred stock.[7] Quantum has 5,000 common shares outstanding during all of 2002. Its basic EPS is

Point: Earnings per share is often referred to as *EPS.*

Global: Some countries, such as Mexico, Spain, Switzerland, and Sweden, have no requirements to report earnings per share.

$$\text{Basic earnings per share} = \frac{\$40,000 - \$7,500}{5,000 \text{ shares}} = \$6.50$$

Changes in Common Shares Outstanding (Stock Sales and Purchases). When a company sells additional shares or purchases treasury shares during the period, the denominator of the basic EPS formula is adjusted to equal the weighted-average number of outstanding shares. The idea behind this computation is to compare earnings to the average number of shares outstanding during the period. To illustrate, assume that Quantum earns $40,000 in

---

[7] If preferred stock is *non*cumulative, the income available (numerator) is the period's net income less any preferred dividends *declared* in that same period. If preferred stock is cumulative, the income available is the period's net income less the preferred dividends whether declared or not.

2002 and declares preferred dividends of $7,500. Also assume that Quantum begins the year with 5,000 common shares outstanding, sells 4,000 additional shares on July 1, and purchases 3,000 treasury shares on November 1. Thus, 5,000 shares were outstanding for the first six months, 9,000 were outstanding for July through October (four months), and 6,000 were outstanding for the final two months. Exhibit 14.19 shows how to compute Quantum's weighted-average number of shares outstanding for 2002.

Exhibit 14.19

Computing Weighted-Average Number of Shares

Time Period	Outstanding Shares		Fraction of Year		Weighted Average
January–June	5,000	×	6/12	=	2,500
July–October	9,000	×	4/12	=	3,000
November–December	6,000	×	2/12	=	1,000
Weighted-average shares outstanding					**6,500**

Global: Some countries, such as France, Japan, and Australia, use the number of shares outstanding at the end of the period when computing EPS.

Quantum's basic EPS is

$$\text{Basic earnings per share} = \frac{\$40{,}000 - \$7{,}500}{6{,}500 \text{ shares}} = \$5$$

Changes in Common Shares Outstanding (Stock Splits and Dividends). Both a stock split and a stock dividend affect the computation of the weighted-average number of shares outstanding. We must restate the number of shares outstanding during the period to reflect a stock split or dividend *as if it occurred at the beginning of the period.* To illustrate, in addition to the facts above assume that Quantum executed a 2-for-1 stock split on December 1, 2002, that doubles the number of shares outstanding on December 1. In computing weighted-average shares outstanding we include an additional column reflecting the effect of the split as shown in Exhibit 14.20. Notice that the December outstanding shares already reflect the split and do not require any adjustment.

Did You Know?

EPS News A company's EPS is a major factor in determining its stock price. Even small changes in EPS estimates can affect stock price. For instance, after an analyst recently lowered **Citicorp**'s EPS forecast by 5%, its stock price fell 7 percent.

Exhibit 14.20

Computing Weighted-Average Number of Shares when Stock Splits (and Dividends) Occur

Time Period	Outstanding Shares		Effect of Split		Fraction of Year		Weighted Average
January–June	5,000	×	2	×	6/12	=	5,000
July–October	9,000	×	2	×	4/12	=	6,000
November	6,000	×	2	×	1/12	=	1,000
December	12,000	×	1	×	1/12	=	1,000
Weighted-average shares outstanding							**13,000**

Quantum's basic EPS under the 2-for-1 stock split is

$$\text{Basic earnings per share} = \frac{\$40{,}000 - \$7{,}500}{13{,}000 \text{ shares}} = \$2.50$$

We use the same computations when stock dividends occur. For instance, if the 2-for-1 stock split had been a 10% stock dividend, the outstanding shares prior to the dividend are multiplied by 1.1 instead of 2.0 because 110% (or 1.1) of the original number of shares are now outstanding, computed as 100% + 10%.[8]

Stock Options

The majority of corporations whose shares are publicly traded issue **stock options,** which are rights to purchase common stock at a fixed price over a specified period. As the stock's price rises above the fixed price, the option's value increases. Use of stock options is growing in popularity as a way to pay both managers and employees for performance. **Starbucks** and **Home Depot**, for instance, are leaders in offering stock options to both full- and part-time employees. Stock options are said to motivate managers and employees to (1) focus on company performance, (2) take a long-run perspective, and (3) remain with the company. A stock option is like having an investment with no risk (or "a carrot with no stick").

To illustrate, Quantum grants each of its employees the option to purchase 100 shares of its $1 par value common stock at its current market price of $50 per share any time within the next 10 years. If Quantum's stock price exceeds $50 per share, employees can exercise the option at a profit. For instance, if the stock price rises to $70 per share, an employee can exercise the option at a gain of $20 per share (acquire a $70 stock at the $50 option price). With 100 shares, a single employee would have a total gain of $2,000, computed as $20 × 100 shares.

Did You Know?

Future Fortunes   Some managers have fortunes to reap from stock options not yet exercised. Four of the larger treasure chests are:

Michael Eisner (Disney) . . . . . . $360 million
Wayne Calloway (PepsiCo) . . . . . 120 million
Stephen Case (America Online) . . 115 million
Eckhard Pfeiffer (Compaq) . . . . . 100 million

Protests of excessive stock options to managers are growing, often led by unions and religious organizations.

When options are granted, the difference between their estimated value and their exercise price is considered compensation expense and it is either recorded as compensation expense or, more commonly, reported in notes to the financial statements.

Quick Check

23. FDI reports 2002 net income of $250,000 and pays preferred dividends of $70,000. On January 1, 2002, FDI had 25,000 outstanding common shares; it purchased 5,000 treasury shares on July 1. Its 2002 basic EPS is (a) $8; (b) $9; (c) $10.

24. How are stock splits and stock dividends treated in computing the weighted-average number of outstanding common shares?

25. What EPS figures are reported for a complex capital structure company?

Answers—p. 592

Retained earnings generally consists of a company's cumulative net income less any net losses and dividends declared since its inception. Retained earnings is part of stockholders' claims on the company's net assets, but it does *not* imply that a certain amount of cash or other assets is available to pay stockholders. For example, **Harley-Davidson** has $1.1

Retained Earnings

C5 Explain the items reported in retained earnings.

---

[8] A corporation can be classified as having either a simple or complex capital structure. A **simple capital structure** refers to a company with only common stock and nonconvertible preferred stock outstanding. A **complex capital structure** refers to companies with dilutive securities. **Dilutive securities** include options, rights to purchase common stock, and any bonds or preferred stock that are convertible into common stock. A company with a complex capital structure must often report two EPS figures: basic and diluted. **Diluted earnings per share** is computed by adding all dilutive securities to the denominator of the basic EPS computation. It reflects the decrease in basic EPS *assuming* that all dilutive securities are converted into common shares. Since CompUS has a simple capital structure, it need report only basic EPS.

Global: Some countries, such as France, Germany, and Japan, require companies to set up reserves at specified rates for the protection of creditors.

Point: Retained earnings restrictions are different from retained earnings appropriations.

Point: If a year 2000 error is discovered in 2001, the company records the adjustment in 2001. But if the retained earnings statement includes 2000 and 2001 figures, the adjustment is not reported as a correction of 2001's beginning balance. Instead, the statement reports the correct amount of income for 2000, and a note describes the correction.

billion in retained earnings, but only $0.2 billion in cash. This section describes important events and transactions affecting retained earnings and how to report retained earnings in financial statements.

Restricted Retained Earnings

Restricted retained earnings refers to both statutory and contractual restrictions placed on corporate activities that depend on the amount of retained earnings. For instance, most states restrict the amount of treasury stock purchases to the amount of retained earnings. This is called a *statutory* (or legal) *restriction*. The balance sheet in Exhibit 14.15 identifies *restricted retained* earnings created by treasury stock purchases. Certain *contractual restrictions* such as loan agreements can also restrict retained earnings. They often include restrictions on paying dividends beyond a specified amount or percent of retained earnings. When important restrictions exist, they are usually described in the notes.

Appropriated Retained Earnings

Appropriated retained earnings refers to a voluntary transfer of amounts from Retained Earnings to Appropriated Retained Earnings to inform users of special activities that require funds. For example, a corporation's directors can voluntarily limit dividends to fund purchases of new facilities. Alternatively, management need not set up an Appropriated Retained Earnings account but can simply disclose in the letter to shareholders or other means of where funds are being directed.

Prior Period Adjustments

Prior period adjustments refer to corrections of material errors in prior periods' financial statements. These errors include making arithmetic mistakes, using unacceptable accounting principles, and ignoring relevant facts. Prior period adjustments are reported in the *statement of retained earnings* (or the statement of changes in stockholders' equity), net of any income tax effects. Prior period adjustments result in changing the beginning balance of retained earnings for events occurring prior to the earliest period reported in the current set of financial statements. To illustrate, assume that CompUS makes an error in a 2000 journal entry for the purchase of land by incorrectly debiting an expense account. When this is discovered in 2002, the statement of retained earnings includes a prior period adjustment as shown in Exhibit 14.21. This exhibit also shows the usual format of the statement of retained earnings.

Exhibit 14.21

Statement of Retained Earnings with a Prior Period Adjustment

CompUS Statement of Retained Earnings For Year Ended December 31, 2002	
Retained earnings, Dec. 31, 2001, as previously reported	$4,745,000
Prior period adjustment:	
Cost of land incorrectly expensed (net of $63,000 income taxes)	147,000
Retained earnings, Dec. 31, 2001, as adjusted	$4,892,000
Plus net income	1,224,300
Less cash dividends declared	(301,800)
Retained earnings, Dec. 31, 2002	$5,814,500

Changes in Accounting Estimates

Many items reported in financial statements are based on estimates. Future events are certain to reveal that some of these estimates were inaccurate even when based on the best data available at the time. These inaccuracies are *not* considered errors and are *not* reported as prior period adjustments. Instead, they are identified as **changes in accounting estimates** and are accounted for in current and future periods. To illustrate, we know depreciation is based on estimated useful lives and salvage values. As time passes and new information becomes available, we may need to change these estimates and the resulting depreciation expense. These types of changes in accounting estimates are applied in the current and future periods, and do not change prior period reports.

Point: Accounting for changes in accounting estimates is sometimes criticized as two wrongs to make a right. Consider a change in an asset's useful life. Neither the depreciation before the change nor the depreciation after the change is the amount computed if the revised estimate had been originally selected. Regulators chose this approach to avoid restating prior periods' numbers.

Statement of Changes in Stockholders' Equity

Few companies report a separate statement of retained earnings. Instead, they usually report a statement of changes in stockholders' equity that includes changes in retained earnings. A **statement of changes in stockholders' equity** lists the beginning and ending balances of each equity account and describes the changes that occur during the period. For instance, **Nike**, **Reebok**, and **Gap** report such a statement as shown in Appendix A. The usual format is to provide a column for each component of equity and use the rows to describe events occurring in the period. Exhibit 14.22 shows a condensed statement for **World Wrestling Federation**.

Exhibit 14.22

Statement of Changes in Stockholders' Equity

WORLD WRESTLING FEDERATION ENTERTAINMENT Statement of Changes in Stockholders' Equity					
($ thousands)	Common Stock	Contributed Capital in Excess of Par	Accumulated Other Comprehensive Income (Loss)	Retained Earnings	Total
Balance, April 30, 1999	$567	$ 1	$ (87)	$71,779	$ 72,260
Net (comprehensive) income	—	—	192	58,908	59,100
Initial public offering (net)	115	179,208	—	—	179,323
Stock option charges	—	15,330	—	—	15,330
Other	—	27,996	—	(95,472)	(67,476)
Balance, April 30, 2000	$682	$222,535	$105	$35,215	$258,537

Book Value per Share, Dividend Yield, and Price-Earnings Ratio | Using the Information

This section explains the computation of and analysis using book value per share, dividend yield, and the price-earnings ratio.

Book Value per Share

Common Stock (Only) Outstanding. Book value is the shareholders' recorded claim on a corporation's net assets (equity). **Book value per common share** is the recorded amount of stockholders' equity applicable to *common* shares on a per share basis and is defined in Exhibit 14.23.

A2 Compute book value and explain its use in analysis.

Exhibit 14.23

Book Value per Common Share

$$\text{Book value per common share} = \frac{\text{Stockholders' equity applicable to common shares}}{\text{Number of common shares outstanding}}$$

To illustrate, we compute the book value per common share for Dillon Snowboards at the end of year 2002 using data in Exhibit 14.4. Dillon has 30,000 outstanding common shares, and the stockholders' equity applicable to common shares is $365,000. Dillon's book value per common share is $12.17, computed as $365,000 divided by 30,000 shares.

Point: Book value per share is also referred to as the *stockholders' claim to assets on a per share basis.*

Common and Preferred Stock Outstanding. To compute book value when both common and preferred shares are outstanding, we must allocate total stockholders' equity between the two. The **book value per preferred share** is computed first, and its computation is shown in Exhibit 14.24.

Exhibit 14.24

Book Value per Preferred Share

$$\text{Book value per preferred share} = \frac{\text{Stockholders' equity applicable to preferred shares}}{\text{Number of preferred shares outstanding}}$$

The stockholders' equity applicable to preferred shares equals the preferred share's call price (or par value if the preferred is not callable) plus any cumulative dividends in arrears. The remaining stockholders' equity is the portion applicable to common shares. To illustrate, consider **MusicLive**'s stockholders' equity section in Exhibit 14.25. Its preferred stock is callable at $108 per share, and two years of cumulative preferred dividends are in arrears.

Exhibit 14.25

Stockholders' Equity with Preferred and Common Stock

Stockholders' Equity	
Preferred stock—$100 par value, 7% cumulative, 2,000 shares authorized, 1,000 shares issued and outstanding	$100,000
Common stock—$25 par value, 12,000 shares authorized, 10,000 shares issued and outstanding	250,000
Contributed capital in excess of par value, common stock	15,000
Retained earnings	82,000
Total stockholders' equity	$447,000

The book value of MusicLive preferred and common shares are computed in Exhibit 14.26. Note we must first allocate equity to preferred shares before we compute the book value of common shares.

Exhibit 14.26

Computing Book Value per Preferred and Common Share

Total stockholders' equity		$447,000
Less equity applicable to preferred shares		
Call price (1,000 shares × $108)	$108,000	
Dividends in arrears ($100,000 × 7% × 2 years)	14,000	(122,000)
Equity applicable to common shares		$325,000
Book value per preferred share ($122,000/1,000 shares)		$ 122.00
Book value per common share ($325,000/10,000 shares)		$ 32.50

Book value per share reflects the worth of each share if a company is liquidated at amounts reported on the balance sheet. Book value is also the starting point in many stock valuation models. Other uses include merger negotiations, price setting for public utilities, and loan contracts. The main limitation in using book value is the potential difference between recorded value and market value for both assets and liabilities. Investors often adjust their analysis for estimates of these differences.

Dividend Yield

Investors buy shares of a company's stock in anticipation of receiving a return from either or both cash dividends and stock price increases. Stocks that pay large dividends on a regular

You Make the Call

Investor You are considering investing in **Ride**, a leading manufacturer of snowboards. Its current book value per common share is $4, yet the stock exchange prices its common shares at $7 per share. From this information, are Ride's net assets priced higher or lower than its recorded values?

Answer—p. 592

basis, called *income stocks,* are attractive to investors who want recurring cash flows from their investments. In contrast, some stocks pay little or no dividends but are still attractive to investors because of their expected stock price increases. The stocks of companies that distribute little or no cash but use their cash to finance expansion are called *growth stocks.* One way to identify whether a stock is an income stock or a growth stock is to compute and analyze its dividend yield. **Dividend yield** shows the annual amount of cash dividends distributed to common shareholders relative to its market value and is defined in Exhibit 14.27.

A3 Compute dividend yield and explain its use in analysis.

$$\text{Dividend yield} = \frac{\textbf{Annual cash dividends per share}}{\textbf{Market value per share}}$$

Exhibit 14.27

Dividend Yield

Dividend yield can be computed for both current and prior periods using data on actual dividends and stock prices. It can also be computed for future periods using expected values. Exhibit 14.28 shows recent dividend and stock price data for **Microsoft** and **Philip Morris**. Dividend yields are also reported.

Company	Cash Dividends per Share	Market Value per share	Dividend Yield
Microsoft	$0.00	$70	0.0%
Philip Morris	1.92	30	6.4

Exhibit 14.28

Dividend and Stock Price Information

We can compare dividend yields to assess the importance of dividends relative to earnings reinvestment for companies' stock values. Dividend yield is zero for **Microsoft**. Its stock is classified in the growth stock category. An investor who purchases Microsoft would look for increases in stock prices (and eventual cash from the sale of stock). **Philip Morris** has a dividend yield of 6.4%. Its stock is classed as an income stock, implying that dividends are an important factor in assessing its value.

Price-Earnings Ratio

A stock's market value is determined by the expected future cash receipts of its stockholders. This means a stock's market value is affected by expected growth in earnings, dividends, and other items. A comparison of a company's EPS and its market value per share reveals information about these market expectations. This comparison is traditionally made using a **price-earnings** or **(PE) ratio,** expressed as *price earnings, price to earnings,* or *PE.* Some analysts interpret this ratio as what price the market is willing to pay for a company's current earnings. Price-earnings ratios can differ across companies that have the same earnings because of either higher or lower expectations of future earnings. The price-earnings ratio is defined in Exhibit 14.29.

A4 Compute price-earnings ratio and describe its use in analysis.

$$\text{Price-earnings ratio} = \frac{\textbf{Market value (price) per share}}{\textbf{Earnings per share}}$$

Exhibit 14.29

Price-Earnings Ratio

This ratio is often computed using EPS from the most recent period. However, many users compute this ratio using *expected* EPS for the next period. To illustrate, assume that a stock's market value is $100 per share and its next year's earnings are expected to be $8 per share. Its price-earnings ratio is 12.5, computed as $100 divided by $8.

Point: The average PE ratio for the 1950–2000 period is about 14. However, the PE ratio averages more than 16 when inflation is below 3.5%.

Some analysts apply the price-earnings ratio to search for over- or underpriced stocks. Such analysts view stocks with high PE ratios (say, higher than 20 to 25) as more likely to be overpriced and stocks with low PE ratios (say, less than 5 to 8) as more likely to be underpriced. These investors prefer to sell or avoid buying stocks with high PE ratios, and to buy or hold stocks with low PE ratios. However, investment decision making is rarely so simple as to rely on a single ratio. For instance, a stock with a high PE ratio may prove to be a good investment if its earnings continue to increase beyond current expectations. Similarly, a stock with a low PE ratio may prove to be a poor investment if its earnings decline below expectations. As with dividend yield, the price-earnings ratio is important in users' decisions but is only one piece of information.

Demonstration Problem 1

Barton Corporation began operations on January 1, 2002. The following transactions relating to stockholders' equity occurred in the first two years of the company's operations.

2002

Jan. 1   Authorized the issuance of 2 million shares of $5 par value common stock and 100,000 shares of $100 par value, 10% cumulative, preferred stock.

Jan. 2   Issued 200,000 shares of common stock for cash at $12 per share.

Jan. 3   Issued 100,000 shares of common stock in exchange for a building valued at $820,000 and merchandise inventory valued at $380,000.

Jan. 4   Paid cash to the company's founders for $100,000 of organization costs; these costs are to be amortized over 10 years.

Jan. 5   Issued 12,000 shares of preferred stock for cash at $110 per share.

2003

June 4   Issued 100,000 shares of common stock for cash at $15 per share.

Required

1. Prepare journal entries to record these transactions.

2. Prepare the stockholders' equity section of the balance sheet as of December 31, 2002, and December 31, 2003, based on these transactions.

3. Prepare a schedule showing dividend allocations and dividends per share for 2002 and 2003 assuming Barton declares the following cash dividends: 2002, $50,000; and 2003, $300,000.

4. Prepare the January 2, 2002, journal entry for Barton's issuance of 200,000 shares of common stock for cash at $12 per share assuming

   a. Common stock is no-par stock without a stated value.

   b. Common stock is no-par stock with a stated value of $10 per share.

Planning the Solution

- Record journal entries for the transactions for 2002 and 2003.
- Determine the balances for the 2002 and 2003 equity accounts for the balance sheet.
- Prepare the contributed capital portion of the 2002 and 2003 balance sheets.
- Prepare a schedule similar to Exhibit 14.8 showing dividend allocations for 2002 and 2003.
- Record the issuance of common stock under both specifications of no-par stock.

Solution to Demonstration Problem 1

1. Journal entries:

2002			
Jan. 2	Cash	2,400,000	
	Common Stock, $5 Par Value		1,000,000
	Contributed Capital in Excess of Par Value, Common Stock		1,400,000
	Issued 200,000 shares of common stock.		
Jan. 3	Building	820,000	
	Merchandise Inventory	380,000	
	Common Stock, $5 Par Value		500,000
	Contributed Capital in Excess of Par Value, Common Stock		700,000
	Issued 100,000 shares of common stock.		
Jan. 4	Organization Costs	100,000	
	Cash		100,000
	Paid founders for organization costs.		
Jan. 5	Cash	1,320,000	
	Preferred Stock, $100 Par Value		1,200,000
	Contributed Capital in Excess of Par Value, Preferred Stock		120,000
	Issued 12,000 shares of preferred stock.		
2003			
June 4	Cash	1,500,000	
	Common Stock, $5 Par Value		500,000
	Contributed Capital in Excess of Par Value, Common Stock		1,000,000
	Issued 100,000 shares of common stock.		

2. Balance sheet presentations:

	As of December 31	
	2002	**2003**
Stockholders' Equity		
Contributed capital:		
Preferred stock, $100 par value, 10% cumulative, 100,000 shares authorized, 12,000 shares issued and outstanding	$1,200,000	$1,200,000
Contributed capital in excess of par value, preferred stock	120,000	120,000
Total capital contributed by preferred stockholders	1,320,000	1,320,000
Common stock, $5 par value, 2,000,000 shares authorized, 300,000 shares issued and outstanding in 2002, and 400,000 shares issued and outstanding in 2003	1,500,000	2,000,000
Contributed capital in excess of par value, common stock	2,100,000	3,100,000
Total capital contributed by common stockholders	3,600,000	5,100,000
Total contributed capital	$4,920,000	$6,420,000

3. Dividend allocation schedule:

	Common	Preferred
2002 ($50,000)		
Preferred—current year (12,000 shares × $10 = $120,000)	$ 0	$ 50,000
Common—remainder (300,000 shares outstanding)	0	0
Total for the year	$ 0	$ 50,000
2003 ($300,000)		
Preferred—dividend in arrears from 2002 ($120,000 − $50,000)	$ 0	$ 70,000
Preferred—current year	0	120,000
Common—remainder (400,000 shares outstanding)	110,000	0
Total for the year	$110,000	$190,000
Dividends per share		
2002	$ 0.00	$ 4.17
2003	$ 0.28	$ 15.83

4. Journal entries:

   a. For 2002:

Jan. 2	Cash	2,400,000	
	Common Stock, No-Par Value		2,400,000
	Issued 200,000 shares of no-par common stock at $12 per share.		

   b. For 2002:

Jan. 2	Cash	2,400,000	
	Common Stock, $10 Stated Value		2,000,000
	Contributed Capital in Excess of		
	Stated Value, Common Stock		400,000
	Issued 200,000 shares of $10 stated value common stock at $12 per share.		

Demonstration Problem 2

Precision Company began year 2002 with the following balances in its stockholders' equity accounts:

Common stock—$10 par, 500,000 shares authorized, 200,000 shares issued and outstanding	$2,000,000
Contributed capital in excess of par, common stock	1,000,000
Retained earnings	5,000,000
Total	$8,000,000

All outstanding common stock was issued for $15 per share when the company was created.

Part 1

Prepare journal entries to account for the following transactions during year 2002:

Jan. 10	The board declared a $0.10 cash dividend per share to shareholders of record Jan. 28.
Feb. 15	Paid the cash dividend declared on January 10.
Mar. 31	Declared a 20% stock dividend. The market value of the stock is $18 per share.
May 1	Distributed the stock dividend declared on March 31.
July 1	Purchased 30,000 shares of treasury stock at $20 per share.
Sept. 1	Sold 20,000 treasury shares at $26 per share.
Dec. 1	Sold the remaining 10,000 shares of treasury stock at $7 per share.

Part 2

Use the following information to prepare a complete income statement for year 2002, including EPS results for each category of income for Precision (a technology consulting company).

Cumulative effect of a change in depreciation method (net of tax benefit)	$ (136,500)
Operating expenses related to continuing operations	(2,072,500)
Extraordinary gain on debt retirement (net of tax)	182,000
Gain on disposal of discontinued segment's assets (net of tax)	29,000
Gain on sale of long-term investments	400,000
Loss from operating discontinued segment (net of tax benefit)	(120,000)
Income taxes on income from continuing operations	(225,000)
Prior period adjustment for error (net of tax benefit)	(75,000)
Net sales	4,140,000
Loss on sale of equipment	(650,000)

Planning the Solution

- Calculate the total cash dividend to record by multiplying the cash dividend declared by the number of shares as of the date of record.
- Decide whether the stock dividend is a small or large dividend. Then analyze each event to determine the accounts affected and the appropriate amounts to be recorded.
- Based on shares of outstanding stock at the beginning of the year and the transactions during the year, compute the weighted-average number of outstanding shares for the year.
- Assign each listed item to an appropriate income statement category.
- Prepare an income statement similar to Exhibit 14.16, including EPS results.

Solution to Demonstration Problem 2

Part 1

Date	Account	Debit	Credit
Jan. 10	Retained Earnings	20,000	
	Common Dividend Payable		20,000
	Declared a $0.10 per share cash dividend.		
Feb. 15	Common Dividend Payable	20,000	
	Cash		20,000
	Paid $0.10 per share cash dividend.		
Mar. 31	Retained Earnings	720,000	
	Common Stock Dividend Distributable		400,000
	Contributed Capital in Excess of		
	Par Value, Common Stock		320,000
	Declared a small stock dividend of 20% or 40,000 shares; market value is $18 per share.		
May 1	Common Stock Dividend Distributable	400,000	
	Common Stock		400,000
	Distributed 40,000 shares of common stock.		
July 1	Treasury Stock, Common	600,000	
	Cash		600,000
	Purchased 30,000 common shares at $20 per share.		
Sept. 1	Cash	520,000	
	Treasury Stock, Common		400,000
	Contributed Capital, Treasury Stock		120,000
	Sold 20,000 treasury shares at $26 per share.		

Dec. 1	Cash	70,000	
	Contributed Capital, Treasury Stock	120,000	
	Retained Earnings	10,000	
	Treasury Stock, Common		200,000
	Sold 10,000 treasury shares at $7 per share.		

Part 2

Compute the weighted-average number of outstanding common shares:

Time Period	Outstanding Shares		Effect of Dividend		Fraction of Year		Weighted Average
January–April	200,000	×	1.2	×	4/12	=	80,000
May–June	240,000*	×	1	×	2/12	=	40,000
July–August	210,000	×	1	×	2/12	=	35,000
September–November	230,000	×	1	×	3/12	=	57,500
December	240,000	×	1	×	1/12	=	20,000
Weighted-average shares outstanding ...							**232,500**

* 200,000 shares × 1.2 = 240,000 shares.

PRECISION COMPANY
Income Statement
For Year Ended December 31, 2002

Net sales		$4,140,000
Operating expenses		(2,072,500)
Other gains (losses)		
Gain on sale of long-term investments		400,000
Loss on sale of equipment		(650,000)
Income from continuing operations before taxes		1,817,500
Income taxes expense		225,000
Income from continuing operations		1,592,500
Discontinued segment		
Loss from operating discontinued segment (net of tax benefit)	$(120,000)	
Gain on disposal of discontinued segment (net of tax)	29,000	(91,000)
Income before extraordinary item and cumulative effect of a		
change in accounting principle		1,501,500
Extraordinary item		
Extraordinary gain on debt retirement (net of tax)		182,000
Cumulative effect of a change in accounting principle		
Cumulative effect of change in deprec. method (net of tax benefit)		(136,500)
Net income		$1,547,000
Earnings per share (232,500 weighted-average shares):		
Income from continuing operations		$ 6.85
Discontinued operations		(0.39)
Income before extraordinary item and cumulative effect of		
change in accounting principle		6.46
Extraordinary item		0.78
Cumulative effect of change in accounting principle		(0.59)
Net income (basic earnings per share)		$ 6.65

Summary

C1 **Identify characteristics of corporations and their organization.** Corporations are legal entities whose stockholders are not liable for corporate debts. Stock is easily transferred and the life of a corporation does not end with the incapacity of a stockholder. A corporation acts through its agents, who are its officers and managers. Corporations are regulated and are subject to income taxes.

C2 **Describe the components of stockholders' equity.** Authorized stock is the amount of stock that a corporation's charter authorizes it to sell. Issued stock is the portion of authorized shares sold. Par value stock is a value per share assigned by the corporate charter. No-par value stock is stock *not* assigned a value per share by the charter. Stated value stock is no-par stock assigned a value per share by the directors. Stockholders' equity is made up of (1) contributed capital and (2) retained earnings. Contributed capital consists of funds raised by stock issuances. Retained earnings consists of cumulative earnings not distributed.

C3 **Explain characteristics of common and preferred stock.** Preferred stock has a priority (or senior status) relative to common stock in one or more areas. The usual areas include (1) dividends and (2) assets in case of liquidation. Preferred stock usually does not carry voting rights and can be convertible or callable. Convertibility permits the holder to convert preferred to common. Callability permits the issuer to buy back preferred under specified conditions.

C4 **Explain the form and content of a complete income statement.** Corporate income statements are similar to those for proprietorships and partnerships except for inclusion of income taxes and per share figures. An income statement has five *potential* sections: (1) continuing operations, (2) discontinued segments, (3) extraordinary items, (4) changes in accounting, and (5) earnings per share.

C5 **Explain the items reported in retained earnings.** Many companies face statutory and contractual restrictions on retained earnings. Corporations can voluntarily appropriate retained earnings to inform stockholders about its disposition. Prior period adjustments are corrections of errors in prior financial statements.

A1 **Compute earnings per share and describe this ratio's use.** A company with a simple capital structure computes basic EPS by dividing net income less any preferred dividends by the weighted-average number of outstanding common shares. A company with a complex capital structure must usually report both basic and diluted EPS.

A2 **Compute book value and explain its use in analysis.** Book value per common share is equity applicable to common shares divided by the number of outstanding common shares. Book value per preferred share is equity applicable to preferred shares divided by the number of outstanding preferred shares.

A3 **Compute dividend yield and explain its use in analysis.** Dividend yield is the ratio of a stock's annual cash dividends per share to its market value (price) per share. It gives the rate of return to stockholders from the company's cash dividends. Dividend yield can be compared with the yield of other companies to determine whether the stock is an income or growth stock.

A4 **Compute price-earnings ratio and describe its use in analysis.** A common stock's price-earnings (PE) ratio is computed by dividing the stock's market value (price) per share by its EPS. A stock's PE is based on expectations that may prove to be better or worse than eventual performance.

P1 **Record the issuance of corporate stock.** When stock is issued, its par or stated value is credited to the stock account and any excess is credited to a separate contributed capital account. If the stock has no par or stated value, the entire proceeds are credited to the stock account. Stockholders must contribute assets equal to minimum legal capital or be potentially liable for the deficiency.

P2 **Distribute dividends between common stock and preferred stock.** Preferred stockholders usually hold the right to dividend distributions before common stockholders. When preferred stock is cumulative and in arrears, the amount in arrears must be distributed to preferred before any dividends are distributed to common.

P3 **Record transactions involving cash dividends.** Three events involve cash dividends. On the date of declaration, the directors bind the company to pay the dividend. A dividend declaration reduces retained earnings and creates a current liability. On the date of record, recipients of the dividend are identified. On the date of payment, cash is paid to stockholders and the current liability is removed.

P4 **Account for stock dividends and stock splits.** Neither a stock dividend nor a stock split alter the fundamental value of the total company. However, the value of each share is less due to the distribution of additional shares. The distribution of additional shares is according to individual stockholders' ownership percent. Small stock dividends (≤25%) are recorded by capitalizing retained earnings equal to the market value of distributed shares. Large stock dividends (>25%) are recorded by capitalizing retained earnings equal to the par or stated value of distributed shares. Stock splits do not yield journal entries but do yield changes in the description of stock.

P5 **Record purchases and sales of treasury stock and the retirement of stock.** When a corporation purchases its own previously issued stock, it debits the cost of these shares to Treasury Stock. Treasury Stock is subtracted from equity in the balance sheet. If treasury stock is reissued, any proceeds in excess of cost are credited to Contributed Capital, Treasury Stock. If the proceeds are less than cost, they are debited to Contributed Capital, Treasury Stock to the extent a credit balance exists. Any remaining amount is debited to Retained Earnings. When stock is retired, all accounts related to the stock are removed.

Guidance Answers to **You Make the Call**

Concert Organizer   You have two basic options: (1) different classes of common stock or (2) common and preferred stock. Your objective is to issue stock to yourself that has all or a majority of the voting power. The other class of stock you issue would carry limited or no voting rights. In this way, you maintain control and are able to raise the necessary funds.

Entrepreneur   The 50% stock dividend provides you no direct income. A stock dividend often reveals management's optimistic expectations about the future and can improve a stock's marketability by making it affordable to more investors. Accordingly, a stock dividend usually reflects "good news" and because of this it likely increases the market value for your stock investment.

Small Business Owner   The frost loss is probably not extraordinary. Jacksonville experiences enough recurring frost damage to make it difficult to argue this event is both unusual and infrequent. Still, you want to highlight the frost loss and hope the bank views this uncommon event separately from continuing operations.

Director   This case deals with insider trading in a company's stock. The ethical conflict is between your responsibility to Intex's stockholders (and the public) and your interest in increasing personal wealth from the options. If information about the new con-

tract is kept private until after the option plan is approved and the options are priced, you are likely to make more money. (*Note:* Insider trading laws may make nondisclosure in this case a crime.) You should try to raise ethical and legal concerns to the board. You might also consider whether staying on the board of this company is proper since it appears there was some intent to deceive outsiders even if not implemented.

Investor   Book value reflects recorded values. Ride's book value is $4 per common share. Stock price reflects the market's expectation of net asset value (both tangible and intangible items). Ride's market value is about $7 per common share. Comparing these figures suggests Ride's market value of net assets is higher than its recorded values (by an amount of $7 versus $4 per share).

Manager   Since one company requires a payment of $19 for each $1 of earnings, and the other requires $25, you should purchase the stock with the PE of 19—it is a better deal given identical prospects. You should make sure these companies' earnings computations are roughly the same—for example, no extraordinary items, unusual events, and so forth. Also, your PE estimate for these companies does matter. If you are willing to pay $29 for each $1 of earnings for these companies, both are solid investments because you obviously expect both to exceed current market expectations.

Guidance Answers to **Quick Checks**

1. (b)

2. A corporation pays taxes on its income, and its stockholders pay personal income taxes on any cash dividends received from the corporation.

3. A proxy is a legal document used to transfer a stockholder's right to vote to another person.

4. (a)

5. A stock premium is an amount in excess of par (or stated) value paid by purchasers of newly issued stock.

6. Minimum legal capital intends to protect creditors of a corporation by constraining a corporation from excessive payments to stockholders.

7. Typically, preferred stock has a preference in receipt of dividends and distribution of assets.

8. (a)

9. (b)

Total dividend	$288,000
To preferred shareholders	135,000*
Remainder to common shareholders . . .	$153,000

*9,000 × $50 × 10% × 3 years = $135,000.

10. Common Dividend Payable is a current liability account.

11. The date of declaration, date of record, and date of payment.

12. A dividend is a legal liability at the date of declaration and it is also recorded as a liability on the date of declaration.

13. A stock dividend does not transfer assets to stockholders but it does require retained earnings be capitalized.

14. A small stock dividend is 25% or less of the previous outstanding shares. A large stock dividend is more than 25%.

15. Retained earnings equal to the distributable shares' market value should be capitalized for a small stock dividend.

16. (b)

17. No. The shares are an investment for Southern Inc. and are issued and outstanding shares for Northern Corp.

18. Treasury stock does not affect the number of authorized or issued shares, but it reduces the outstanding shares.

19. (a)

20. (b)

21. The five major sections are income from continuing operations, discontinued segments, extraordinary items, cumulative effects of changes in accounting principles, and earnings per share.

22. (c)

23. (a) Weighted-average shares: $(25,000 \times 6/12) + (20,000 \times 6/12) = 22,500$.

Earnings per share: $(\$250,000 - \$70,000)/22,500 = \$8$.

24. The number of shares previously outstanding is retroactively restated to reflect the stock split or stock dividend as if it occurred at the beginning of the period.

25. Basic EPS and diluted EPS.

Glossary

Appropriated retained earnings retained earnings reported separately to inform stockholders of funding needs. (p. 582).

Authorized stock total amount of stock that a corporation's charter authorizes it to sell. (p. 560).

Basic earnings per share net income less preferred dividends divided by weighted-average common shares outstanding. (p. 579).

Book value per common share recorded amount of equity applicable to common shares divided by the number of common shares outstanding. (p. 583).

Book value per preferred share equity applicable to preferred shares (equals the preferred share's call price [or par value if the preferred is not callable] plus any cumulative dividends in arrears) divided by the number of preferred shares outstanding. (p. 584).

Callable preferred stock preferred stock that the issuing corporation, at its option, may retire by paying the call price to preferred stockholders plus any dividends in arrears. (p. 567).

Call price amount that must be paid to call and retire a preferred share. (p. 567).

Capital stock general term referring to a corporation's stock used in obtaining capital (owner financing). (p. 559).

Changes in accounting estimates corrections to previous estimates of future events and outcomes; accounted for in current and future periods. (p. 583).

Common stock a corporation's basic stock; usually carries voting rights for controlling the corporation. (p. 558).

Complex capital structure capital structure that includes outstanding rights or options to purchase common stock or securities that are convertible into common stock. (p. 581).

Contributed capital total amount of cash and other assets received from stockholders in exchange for stock. (p. 561).

Convertible preferred stock preferred stock with an option to exchange it for common stock at a specified rate. (p. 567).

Contributed capital in excess of par value difference between the par value of stock and its issue price when issued at a price above par. (p. 562).

Corporation entity created by law and separate from its owners. (p. 556).

Cumulative preferred stock preferred stock on which undeclared dividends accumulate until paid; common stockholders cannot receive dividends until cumulative dividends are paid. (p. 565).

Date of declaration date the directors vote to pay a dividend. (p. 568).

Date of payment date the corporation makes the dividend payment. (p. 568).

Date of record date specified by directors for identifying stockholders to receive dividends. (p. 568).

Diluted earnings per share earnings per share calculation that requires dilutive securities be added to the denominator of the basic EPS calculation. (p. 581).

Dilutive securities securities having the potential to increase common shares outstanding; examples are options, rights, convertible bonds, and convertible preferred stock. (p. 581).

Discount on stock difference between the par value of stock and its issue price when issued at a price below par value. (p. 562).

Dividend in arrears unpaid dividend on cumulative preferred stock; must be paid before any regular dividends on preferred stock and before any dividends on common stock. (p. 565).

Dividend yield ratio of the annual amount of cash dividends distributed to common shareholders relative to the common stock's market value (price). (p. 585).

Earnings per share (EPS) amount of income earned by each share of a company's outstanding common stock; also called *net income per share*. (p. 579).

Extraordinary gain or loss gain or loss reported separately from continuing operations because it is both unusual and infrequent. (p. 576).

Financial leverage earning a higher return on common stock by paying dividends on preferred stock or interest on debt at a rate lower than the return earned with the assets from issuing preferred stock or debt. (p. 567).

Infrequent gain or loss gain or loss not expected to recur, given the operating environment of the business. (p. 576).

Large stock dividend stock dividend that is more than 25% of the previously outstanding shares. (p. 570).

Liquidating cash dividend distribution of assets that returns part of the original investment to stockholders; charged to contributed capital accounts. (p. 569).

Market value per share price at which stock is bought or sold. (p. 560).

Minimum legal capital amount of assets defined by law that stockholders must (potentially) invest in a corporation; usually defined as par value of the stock; intended to protect creditors. (p. 560).

Noncumulative preferred stock preferred stock on which the right to receive dividends is lost for any period when dividends are not declared. (p. 565).

Nonparticipating preferred stock preferred stock on which dividends are limited to a maximum amount each year. (p. 566).

No-par value stock stock class that has not been assigned a par value by the corporate charter. (p. 561).

Organization costs costs sush as legal fees and promoter fees to bring an entity into existence. (p. 557).

Participating preferred stock preferred stock that shares with common stockholders any dividends paid in excess of the percent stated on preferred stock. (p. 566).

Par value value assigned a share of stock by the corporate charter when the stock is authorized. (p. 560).

Par value stock class of stock assigned a par value by the corporate charter. (p. 560).

Preemptive right stockholders' right to maintain their proportionate interest in a corporation with any additional shares issued. (p. 559).

Preferred stock stock with a priority status over common stockholders in one or more ways, such as paying dividends or distributing assets. (p. 564).

Premium on stock see *contributed capital in excess of par*. (p. 562).

Price-earnings (P/E) ratio ratio of a company's current market value per share to its earnings per share. (p. 585).

Prior period adjustment correction of an error in a prior year that is reported in the statement of retained earnings (or statement of changes in stockholders' equity) net of any income tax effects. (p. 582).

Proxy legal document giving a stockholder's agent the power to exercise the stockholder's voting rights. (p. 558).

Restricted retained earnings retained earnings not available for dividends because of legal or contractual limitations. (p. 582).

Retained earnings cumulative income less cumulative losses and dividends. (p. 561).

Retained earnings deficit debit (abnormal) balance in Retained Earnings: occurs when cumulative losses and dividends exceed cumulative income. (p. 569).

Reverse stock split occurs when a corporation calls in its stock and replaces each share with less than one new share; increases both market value per share and any par or stated value per share. (p. 573).

Segment of a business part of operations that serves a line of business or class of customers and that has assets, liabilities, and operating results distinguishable from other parts. (p. 576).

Simple capital structure capital structure that consists of only common stock and nonconvertible preferred stock; consists of no dilutive securities. (p. 581).

Small stock dividend stock dividend that is 25% or less of a corporation's previously outstanding shares. (p. 570).

Stated value stock no-par stock assigned a stated value per share; this amount is recorded in the stock account when the stock is issued. (p. 561).

Statement of changes in stockholders' equity financial statement that lists the beginning and ending balances of each equity account and describes all changes in those accounts. (p. 583).

Stock dividend corporation's distribution of its own stock to its stockholders without the receipt of any payment. (p. 570).

Stockholders' equity a corporation's equity also called *shareholders' equity* or *corporate capital*. (p. 561).

Stock option right to purchase common stock at a fixed price over a specified period of time. (p. 581).

Stock split occurs when a corporation calls in its stock and replaces each share with more than one new share; decreases both the market value per share and any par or stated value per share. (p. 572).

Stock subscription investor's contractual commitment to purchase unissued shares at future dates and prices. (p. 564).

Treasury stock corporation's own stock that it reacquired and still holds. (p. 573).

Unusual gain or loss gain or loss that is abnormal or unrelated to the company's ordinary activities and environment. (p. 576).

Questions

1. What are organization costs? List examples.
2. How are organization costs classified on the balance sheet?
3. Who is responsible for directing a corporation's affairs?
4. What is the preemptive right of common stockholders?
5. List the general rights of common stockholders.
6. Why would an investor find convertible preferred stock attractive?
7. What is the difference between the par value and the call price of a share of stock?
8. Identify and explain the importance of the three dates relevant to corporate dividends.
9. Why is the term *liquidating dividend* used to describe cash dividends debited against contributed capital accounts?
10. How does declaring a stock dividend affect the corporation's assets, liabilities, and total stockholders' equity? What effects does the eventual distribution of the stock have?
11. What is the difference between a stock dividend and a stock split?
12. Courts have ruled that a stock dividend is not taxable income to stockholders. What justifies this decision?
13. How does the purchase of treasury stock affect the purchaser's assets and total stockholders' equity?
14. Why do state laws place limits on treasury stock purchases?
15. Where on the income statement does a company report an unusual gain not expected to occur more often than once every two years?

16. After taking five years of straight-line depreciation expense for an asset that was expected to have an eight-year useful life, a company decides that the asset will last six more years. Is this decision a change in accounting principle? How do the financial statements describe this change?
17. How are EPS results computed for a corporation with a simple capital structure?
18. Examine the balance sheet for **Nike** in Appendix A and determine the classes of stock that it has issued.
19. Refer to the financial statements for **Nike** in Appendix A. What cash amount is paid to purchase treasury stock for the year ended May 31, 2000? May 31, 1999?
20. Refer to the balance sheet for **Reebok** in Appendix A. What is the par value of its common stock? Suggest a rationale for the amount of par value it assigned.
21. Refer to the financial statements for **Reebok** in Appendix A. How many treasury stock shares does Reebok report as of December 31, 1999? Compute the average cost per treasury share.
22. Refer to the financial statements for **Gap** in Appendix A. Was Gap a net seller or net repurchaser of treasury stock for the fiscal year ended May 31, 2000? Explain.
23. What steps did Vince McMahon need to take to receive a corporate charter for **WWF**?

Of the following statements, which are true for the corporate form of organization?

1. It is a separate legal entity.

2. Ownership rights cannot be easily transferred.

3. Owners are not agents of the corporation.

4. Capital is more easily accumulated than with most other forms of organization.

5. It has a limited life.

6. Owners have unlimited liability for corporate debts.

7. Distributed income is usually taxed twice.

QUICK STUDY

QS 14-1
Characteristics of corporations

Each of these entries is recorded by a different corporation. Provide an explanation for the transaction described by each entry.

QS 14-2
Interpretation of journal entries for stock issuances

1. April 1	Cash	70,000	
	Common Stock, No-Par Value		70,000
2. April 1	Organization Costs	130,000	
	Common Stock, No-Par Value		86,000
	Contributed Capital in Excess of Stated Value, Common Stock		44,000
3. April 1	Merchandise Inventory	105,000	
	Machinery	145,000	
	Notes Payable		154,000
	Common Stock, $25 Par Value		50,000
	Contributed Capital in Excess of Par Value, Common Stock		46,000

On March 1, DVD Corporation issues 42,500 shares of $4 par value common stock for $297,500 cash. Prepare the entry to record this transaction.

QS 14-3
Issuance of common stock

Prepare journal entries to record the following transactions for Delta Corporation:

May 15   Declared a $54,000 cash dividend payable to common stockholders.
July 31   Paid the dividend declared on May 15.

QS 14-4
Accounting for cash dividends

Harmon Company's stockholders' equity includes (a) 80,000 shares of $5 par value, 8% cumulative preferred stock and (b) 250,000 shares of $1 par value common stock. Harmon did not declare any dividends during the prior year and now declares and pays a $110,000 cash dividend in the current year. Determine the amount distributed to each class of stockholders for this two-year-old company.

QS 14-5
Dividend allocation between classes of shareholders

The stockholders' equity section of Roanoke Company's balance sheet as of April 1 follows:

QS 14-6
Accounting for small stock dividend

Common stock—$5 par value, 375,000 shares authorized, 200,000 shares issued and outstanding	$1,000,000
Contributed capital in excess of par value, common stock	600,000
Total contributed capital	1,600,000
Retained earnings	833,000
Total stockholders' equity	$2,433,000

On April 2, Roanoke declares and distributes a 10% stock dividend. The stock's per share market value on April 2 is $20. Prepare the stockholders' equity section immediately after the stock dividend.

On May 3, Cypher Corporation purchased 4,000 shares of its own stock for $36,000. On November 4, Cypher reissued 850 shares of this treasury stock for $8,500. Prepare the November 4 journal entry to record Cypher's reissuance of treasury stock.

QS 14-7
Purchase and sale of treasury stock

QS 14-8
Accounting for estimate
changes and error
adjustments

Answer the following questions related to a company's activities for the year:

1. A review of the notes payable files discovers that last year the company reported the entire amount of a payment (principal and interest) on an installment note payable as interest expense. This mistake had a material effect on the amount of income in the prior year. How should the correction be reported in the current year financial statements?

2. After using an expected useful life of seven years and no salvage value to depreciate its office equipment over the preceding three years, the company decided early this year that the equipment will last only two more years. How should the effects of this decision be reported in the current financial statements?

QS 14-9
Basic earnings
per share

Chastain Company earned a net income of $900,000 this year. The number of common shares outstanding during the entire year was 400,000 and preferred shareholders received a cash dividend totaling $20,000. Compute Chastain Company's basic EPS.

QS 14-10
Weighted-average
shares outstanding

On January 1, Ventura Company had 200,000 shares of common stock outstanding. On February 1, it issued 40,000 additional shares of common stock. On June 1, it issued another 80,000 shares of common stock. Compute Ventura's weighted-average shares outstanding for the year.

QS 14-11
Weighted-average
shares outstanding

On January 1, Benton Company had 300,000 shares of common stock outstanding. On April 1, it purchased 24,000 treasury shares and on June 2, declared a 10% stock dividend. Compute Benton's weighted-average shares outstanding for the year.

QS 14-12
Book value per common share

The stockholders' equity section of Aurora Company's balance sheet follows:

Preferred stock, 5% cumulative, $10 par value, 20,000 shares authorized, issued and outstanding	$ 200,000
Common stock, $5 par value, 200,000 shares authorized, 150,000 shares issued and outstanding	750,000
Retained earnings	890,000
Total stockholders' equity	$1,840,000

The preferred stock's call price is $40. Determine the book value per share of the common stock.

QS 14-13
Price-earnings ratio

Compute Pax Company's price-earnings ratio if its common stock has a market value of $32.60 per share and its EPS is $3.95. Would an analyst reviewing this stock likely consider it over- or underpriced?

QS 14-14
Dividend yield

Fiva Company expects to pay a $2.30 per share cash dividend this year on its common stock. The current market value of Fiva stock is $32.50 per share. Compute the expected dividend yield on the Fiva stock. Would you classify the Fiva stock as growth or income stock?

EXERCISES

Exercise 14-1
Characteristics of
corporations

Briefly describe how each of the following eight characteristics of business organizations applies to corporations.

Characteristics	Application to Corporations
1. Owners' authority	
2. Ease of formation	
3. Transferability of ownership	
4. Ability to raise large amounts of capital	
5. Life	
6. Owners' liability	
7. Legal status	
8. Tax status of income	

HiLife Corporation issues 19,000 shares of its common stock for $152,000 cash on February 20. Prepare journal entries to record this event under each of the following separate situations:

1. The stock has neither par nor stated value.

2. The stock has a $2 par value.

3. The stock has a $5 stated value.

Exercise 14-2

Accounting for par and no-par stock issuances

Prepare journal entries to record the following four separate issuances of stock:

1. Two thousand shares of no-par common stock are issued to the corporation's promoters in exchange for their efforts, estimated to be worth $40,000. The stock has no stated value.

2. Two thousand shares of no-par common stock are issued to the corporation's promoters in exchange for their efforts, estimated to be worth $40,000. The stock has a $1 per share stated value.

3. Four thousand shares of $5 par value common stock are issued for $35,000 cash.

4. One thousand shares of $50 par value preferred stock are issued for $60,000 cash.

Exercise 14-3

Recording stock issuances

Match each description *1* through *6* with the characteristic of preferred stock that it best describes by writing the letter of the characteristic in the blank next to each description.

A. Callable   **B.** Convertible   **C.** Cumulative

D. Noncumulative   **E.** Nonparticipating   **F.** Participating

_____ **1.** Holders of the stock are not entitled to receive dividends in excess of the stated rate.

_____ **2.** Holders of the stock lose any dividends that are not declared.

_____ **3.** Holders of the stock are entitled to receive current and all past dividends before common stockholders receive any dividends.

_____ **4.** Holders of this stock can exchange it for shares of common stock.

_____ **5.** The issuing corporation can retire the stock by paying a prespecified price.

_____ **6.** Holders of the stock can receive dividends in excess of the stated rate under certain conditions.

Exercise 14-4

Identifying characteristics of preferred stock

Citishop's outstanding stock includes (a) 80,000 shares of noncumulative 7.5% preferred stock with a $5 par value and (b) 200,000 shares of common stock with a $1 par value. During its first four years of operation, the corporation declared and paid the following dividends:

2002	$ 20,000
2003	28,000
2004	200,000
2005	350,000

Determine the amount of dividends paid each year to each of the two classes of stockholders. Also compute the total dividends paid to each class for the four years combined.

Exercise 14-5

Dividends on common and noncumulative preferred stock

Use the data in Exercise 14-5 to determine the amount of dividends paid each year to each of the two classes of stockholders assuming that the preferred stock is cumulative. Also determine the total dividends paid to each class for the four years combined.

Exercise 14-6

Dividends on common and cumulative preferred stock

On June 30, 2002, American Corporation's common stock is priced at $62 per share before any stock dividend or split, and the stockholders' equity section of its balance sheet appears as follows:

Exercise 14-7

Stock dividends and splits

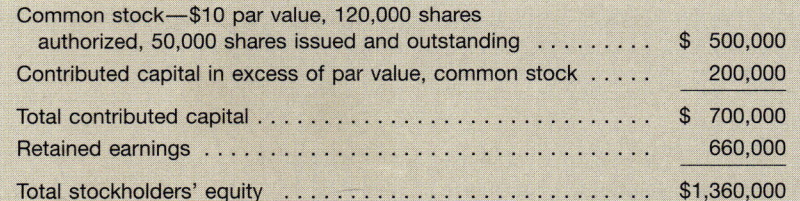

Common stock—$10 par value, 120,000 shares authorized, 50,000 shares issued and outstanding	$ 500,000
Contributed capital in excess of par value, common stock	200,000
Total contributed capital	$ 700,000
Retained earnings	660,000
Total stockholders' equity	$1,360,000

a. Assume that the company declares and immediately distributes a 50% stock dividend. This event is recorded by capitalizing retained earnings equal to the stock's par value. Answer these questions about stockholders' equity as it exists *after* issuing the new shares:

1. What is the retained earnings balance?
2. What is the amount of total stockholders' equity?
3. How many shares are outstanding?

b. Assume that the company implements a 3-for-2 stock split instead of the stock dividend in part *a*. Answer these questions about stockholders' equity as it exists *after* issuing the new shares:

1. What is the retained earnings balance?
2. What is the amount of total stockholders' equity?
3. How many shares are outstanding?

c. Explain the difference, if any, to a stockholder from receiving new shares distributed under a large stock dividend versus a stock split.

Exercise 14-8
Stock dividends and per share book values

The stockholders' equity of Biz.Com at the beginning of the day on February 5 follows:

Common stock—$10 par value, 150,000 shares authorized, 60,000 shares issued and outstanding	$ 600,000
Contributed capital in excess of par value, common stock	425,000
Total contributed capital	$1,025,000
Retained earnings	550,000
Total stockholders' equity	$1,575,000

The stock's market value is $40 per share on February 5 before any stock dividend. On that same date, the directors declare a 20% stock dividend distributable on February 28 to the February 15 stockholders of record. The stock's market value is $33.40 per share on February 28.

1. Prepare entries to record both the dividend declaration and its distribution.
2. One stockholder owned 800 shares on February 5 before the dividend. Compute the book value per share and total book value of this stockholder's shares immediately before and after the stock dividend of February 5.
3. Compute the total market value of the investor's shares in part (2) as of February 5 and February 28.

Exercise 14-9
Recording and reporting
treasury stock transactions

On October 10, the stockholders' equity of Perry Systems consists of the following:

Common stock—$10 par value, 72,000 shares authorized, issued, and outstanding	$ 720,000
Contributed capital in excess of par value, common stock	216,000
Total contributed capital	$ 936,000
Retained earnings	864,000
Total stockholders' equity	$1,800,000

1. Prepare journal entries to record the following transactions for Perry Systems:
   a. Purchased 5,000 shares of its own common stock at $25 per share on October 11.
   b. Sold 1,000 treasury shares on November 1 for $31 cash per share.
   c. Sold all remaining treasury shares on November 25 for $20 cash per share.
2. Explain how Perry's equity section changes after the October 11 treasury stock purchase.

Exercise 14-10
Income statement categories

In year 2002, Piazza Merchandise, Inc., sold its interest in a chain of wholesale outlets, taking the company completely out of the wholesaling business. The company still operates its retail outlets. Following is a list of the major sections of an income statement:

A. Income (loss) from continuing operations
B. Income (loss) from operating a discontinued segment

C. Gain (loss) on disposal of a discontinued segment

D. Extraordinary gain (loss)

E. Cumulative effect of a change in accounting principle

Indicate where each of the nine income-related items for this company appears on its 2002 income statement by writing the letter of the appropriate section in the blank beside each item.

Section	Item	Debit	Credit
_____	1. Net sales		$2,900,000
_____	2. Gain on state's condemnation of company property (net of tax)		230,000
_____	3. Cost of goods sold	$1,480,000	
_____	4. Effect of change from FIFO to LIFO (net of tax)		125,000
_____	5. Income taxes expense	217,000	
_____	6. Depreciation expense	232,500	
_____	7. Gain on sale of wholesale business segment (net of tax)		775,000
_____	8. Loss from operating wholesale business segment (net of tax)	444,000	
_____	9. Salaries expense	640,000	

Use the data for Piazza Merchandise, Inc., in Exercise 14-10 to prepare its income statement for 2002.

Exercise 14-11

Income statement presentation

Fast Tek put an asset costing $450,000 in service on January 1, 2002. Its predicted useful life is six years with an expected salvage value of $45,000. The company uses double-declining-balance depreciation and records $150,000 of depreciation in 2002 and $100,000 of depreciation in 2003. The scheduled depreciation expense for 2004 is $66,667. After consulting with the company's auditors, management decides to change to straight-line depreciation in 2004 without changing either the predicted useful life or salvage value. Under this new method, the annual depreciation expense for this asset is $67,500. This company has a 35% income tax rate.

1. Prepare a table like Exhibit 14.17 to analyze this change in accounting principle.

2. How much depreciation expense is reported on the company's income statement for this asset in 2004 and in each of the remaining years of its life?

3. What amount is reported on the company's 2004 income statement as the after-tax cumulative effect of the change in accounting principle?

Exercise 14-12

Reporting a change in accounting principle

CT Company reports $960,000 of net income for 2002 and declares $130,000 of dividends on preferred stock for 2002. At the beginning of 2002, the company had 100,000 outstanding shares of common stock. Three events change the number of outstanding common shares during year 2002.

June 1   Issued 60,000 common shares for cash.
Sept. 1   Purchased 26,000 shares of its own common stock.
Oct. 1   Completed a three-for-one stock split.

1. What amount of net income is available to common stockholders for 2002?

2. What is the weighted-average number of common shares outstanding for 2002?

3. What is the company's basic EPS for 2002?

Exercise 14-13

Weighted-average shares and earnings per share

TSR Company reports $2,700,000 of net income for 2002 and declares $390,000 of cash dividends on preferred stock for 2002. At the beginning of 2002, the company had 540,000 outstanding shares of common stock. Two events change the number of outstanding common shares during 2002:

May 1   Issued 360,000 common shares for cash.
Nov. 1   Purchased 216,000 shares of its own common stock.

1. What amount of net income is available to common stockholders for 2002?

2. What is the weighted-average number of common shares outstanding for 2002?

3. What is the company's basic EPS for 2002?

Exercise 14-14

Weighted-average shares and earnings per share

Exercise 14-15
Book value per share

The equity section of Tabak Corporation's balance sheet shows the following:

Preferred stock, 6% cumulative, $25 par value, $30 call price, 10,000 shares issued and outstanding	$ 250,000
Common stock, $10 par value, 80,000 shares issued and outstanding	800,000
Retained earnings	535,000
Total stockholders' equity	$1,585,000

Determine the book value per share of the preferred and common stock under two separate situations:

1. No preferred dividends are in arrears.

2. Three years of preferred dividends are in arrears.

Exercise 14-16
Dividend yield computation
and interpretation

Compute the dividend yield for each of these four separate companies:

Company	Annual Cash Dividend per Share	Market Value per Share
1	$16.00	$220.00
2	14.00	136.00
3	4.00	72.00
4	1.00	80.00

Which company's stock would probably *not* be classified as an income stock?

Exercise 14-17
Price-earnings ratio
computation and interpretation

Compute the price-earnings ratio for each of these four separate companies:

Company	Earnings per Share	Market Value per Share
1	$12.00	$176.00
2	10.00	96.00
3	7.50	94.00
4	50.00	250.00

Which stock might an analyst investigate as being undervalued by the market?

PROBLEM SET A

Problem 14-1A
Stockholders' equity
transactions

Context Products is incorporated at the beginning of this year and engages in a number of transactions. The following journal entries impacted its stockholders' equity during its first year of operations:

a.	Cash	300,000	
	Common Stock, $25 Par Value		250,000
	Contributed Capital in Excess of Par Value, Common Stock		50,000
b.	Organization Costs	150,000	
	Common Stock, $25 Par Value		125,000
	Contributed Capital in Excess of Par Value, Common Stock		25,000

c.	Cash	43,000	
	Accounts Receivable	15,000	
	Building	81,500	
	Notes Payable		59,500
	Common Stock, $25 Par Value		50,000
	Contributed Capital in Excess of		
	Par Value, Common Stock		30,000
d.	Cash	120,000	
	Common Stock, $25 Par Value		75,000
	Contributed Capital in Excess of		
	Par Value, Common Stock		45,000

Required

1. Explain each journal entry *a* through *d*.

2. How many shares of common stock are outstanding at year-end?

3. What is the amount of minimum legal capital (based on par value) at year-end?

4. What is the total contributed capital at year-end?

5. What is the book value per share of the common stock at year-end if contributed capital plus retained earnings equals $695,000?

Check   (4) Contributed capital, $650,000

Tetrix Corporation reports the following components of stockholders' equity on December 31, 2001:

Problem 14-2A

Cash dividends, treasury stock, and statement of retained earnings

Common stock—$10 par value, 100,000 shares authorized, 40,000 shares issued and outstanding	$400,000
Contributed capital in excess of par value, common stock	60,000
Retained earnings	270,000
Total stockholders' equity	$730,000

In year 2002, the following transactions affect its stockholders' equity accounts:

Jan. 1   Purchased 4,000 shares of its own stock at $20 per share.

Jan. 5   Directors declared a $2 per share cash dividend payable on Feb. 28 to the Feb. 5 stockholders of record.

Feb. 28   Paid the dividend declared on January 5.

July 6   Sold 1,500 of the treasury shares at $24 per share.

Aug. 22   Sold 2,500 of the treasury shares at $17 per share.

Sept. 5   Directors declared a $2 per share cash dividend payable on October 28 to the September 25 stockholders of record.

Oct. 28   Paid the dividend declared on September 5.

Dec. 31   Closed the $388,000 credit balance (from net income) in the Income Summary account to Retained Earnings.

Required

1. Prepare journal entries to record the transactions and closings for 2002.

2. Prepare a statement of retained earnings for the year ended December 31, 2002.

3. Prepare the stockholders' equity section of the company's balance sheet as of December 31, 2002.

Check   Retained earnings, Dec. 31, 2002, $504,500.

At September 30, the end of Navstar Company's third quarter, the following stockholders' equity accounts appear:

Problem 14-3A

Description of equity changes with journal entries and account balances

Common stock, $12 par value	$360,000
Contributed capital in excess of par value, common stock	90,000
Retained earnings	320,000

In the fourth quarter, the following entries related to its equity accounts are recorded:

Oct. 2	Retained Earnings	60,000	
	Common Dividend Payable		60,000
Oct. 25	Common Dividend Payable	60,000	
	Cash		60,000
Oct. 31	Retained Earnings	75,000	
	Common Stock Dividend Distributable		36,000
	Contributed Capital in Excess of Par Value, Common Stock		39,000
Nov. 5	Common Stock Dividend Distributable	36,000	
	Common Stock, $12 Par Value		36,000
Dec. 1	Memo—Change the title of the common stock account to reflect the new par value of $4.		
Dec. 31	Income Summary	210,000	
	Retained Earnings		210,000

Required

1. Explain each journal entry.

2. Complete the following table showing the balances of the company's equity accounts at each indicated date:

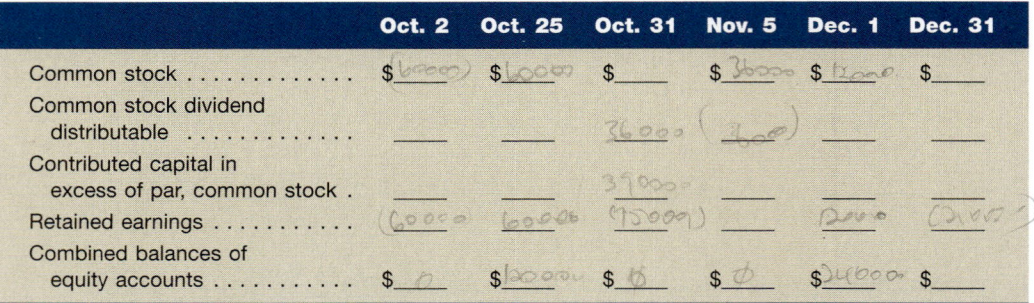

	Oct. 2	Oct. 25	Oct. 31	Nov. 5	Dec. 1	Dec. 31
Common stock	$_____	$_____	$_____	$_____	$_____	$_____
Common stock dividend distributable	_____	_____	_____	_____	_____	_____
Contributed capital in excess of par, common stock .	_____	_____	_____	_____	_____	_____
Retained earnings	_____	_____	_____	_____	_____	_____
Combined balances of equity accounts	$_____	$_____	$_____	$_____	$_____	$_____

Check Total equity, Dec. 31, $920,000

Problem 14-4A

Analysis of changes in stockholders' equity accounts

The equity sections from EOG Group's 2002 and 2003 balance sheets follow:

Stockholders' Equity (December 31, 2002)

Common stock—$4 par value, 100,000 shares authorized, 40,000 shares issued and outstanding	$160,000
Contributed capital in excess of par value, common stock	120,000
Total contributed capital	$280,000
Retained earnings	320,000
Total stockholders' equity	$600,000

Stockholders' Equity (December 31, 2003)

Common stock—$4 par value, 100,000 shares authorized, 47,400 shares issued, 3,000 in the treasury	$189,600
Contributed capital in excess of par value, common stock	179,200
Total contributed capital	$368,800
Retained earnings ($30,000 restricted)	400,000
	$768,800
Less cost of treasury stock	(30,000)
Total stockholders' equity	$738,800

The following transactions and events affect its equity accounts during year 2003:

Jan. 5   Declared a $0.50 per share cash dividend, date of record January 10.
Mar. 20   Purchased treasury stock.
Apr. 5   Declared a $0.50 per share cash dividend, date of record April 10.
July 5   Declared a $0.50 per share cash dividend, date of record July 10.
July 31   Declared a 20% stock dividend when the stock's market value is $12 per share.
Aug. 14   Issued stock dividend.
Oct. 5   Declared a $0.50 per share cash dividend, date of record October 10.

Required

1. How many common shares are outstanding on each cash dividend date?
2. What is the dollar amount for each of the four cash dividends?
3. What is the amount of the capitalization of retained earnings for the stock dividend?
4. What is the per share cost of the treasury stock purchased?
5. How much net income did the company earn during year 2003?

Check   Net income, $248,000

Selected account balances from the adjusted trial balance for Emulox Corporation as of December 31, 2002, follow:

Problem 14-5A
Income statement presentation

	Debit	Credit
a. Interest earned		$ 14,000
b. Depreciation expense—Equipment	$ 34,000	
c. Loss on sale of equipment	25,850	
d. Accounts payable		44,000
e. Other operating expenses	106,400	
f. Accumulated depreciation—Equipment		71,600
g. Gain from settlement of lawsuit		40,000
h. Cumulative effect of change in accounting principle (pretax)	61,000	
i. Accumulated depreciation—Buildings		174,500
j. Loss from operating a discontinued segment (pretax)	18,250	
k. Gain on retirement of debt (pretax)		29,125
l. Net sales		998,500
m. Depreciation expense—Buildings	52,000	
n. Correction of overstatement of prior year's sales (pretax)	16,000	
o. Gain on sale of discontinued segment's assets (pretax)		34,000
p. Loss from settlement of lawsuit	23,750	
q. Income taxes expense	?	
r. Cost of goods sold	482,500	

Required

Answer each of the following questions by providing supporting computations:

1. Assuming the company's income tax rate is 30% for all items, identify the tax effects and after-tax measures of the items labeled pretax.
2. What is the amount of the company's income from continuing operations before income taxes? What is the amount of the company's income taxes expense? What is the amount of the company's income from continuing operations?
3. What is the total amount of after-tax income (loss) associated with the discontinued segment?
4. What is the amount of income (loss) before both any extraordinary items and any cumulative effect of changes in accounting principle?
5. What is the amount of net income for the year?

Check   Net income, $218,312

On January 1, 2002, Alliance, Inc., purchases equipment costing $300,000 with an expected salvage value of $15,000 at the end of its five-year useful life. Depreciation is allocated to 2002, 2003, and 2004 with the double-declining-balance method. Early in 2005, the company decides to change to the

Problem 14-6A
Change in accounting principle (depreciation) and its disclosure

straight-line method to produce more useful financial statements and to be consistent with other firms in the industry.

Required

Preparation Component

1. Do generally accepted accounting principles allow Alliance to change depreciation methods in 2005?

2. Prepare a table to show the amount of depreciation expense allocated to 2002 through 2004 using the double-declining-balance method.

3. Prepare a table to show the amount of depreciation expense that would have been allocated to 2002 through 2004 using the straight-line method.

Check After-tax cumulative effect, $44,940

4. Organize your answers from parts (2) and (3) into a table like Exhibit 14.17 and compute the before- and after-tax cumulative effects of the accounting change. The company's income tax rate is 30%. (Round to the nearest dollar.)

5. How should the cumulative effect of the change in accounting principle be reported? Does the cumulative effect increase or decrease net income?

6. How much depreciation expense is reported on the company's income statement for 2005?

Analysis Component

7. Assume that Alliance mistakenly treats the change in depreciation methods as a change in accounting estimate. Using your answers from parts (2), (3), and (4), describe the effect of this error on the 2005 financial statements.

Problem 14-7A
Earnings per share calculation and presentation

The income statements for Crestline, Inc., as reported when they were initially published in 2002, 2003, and 2004 follow:

	2002	2003	2004
Net sales	$740,000	$850,000	$825,000
Operating expenses	465,000	520,000	491,000
Income from continuing operations	$275,000	$330,000	$334,000
Loss on discontinued segment	(105,000)	—	—
Income before extraordinary items	$170,000	$330,000	$334,000
Extraordinary gain (loss)	—	66,000	(140,000)
Net income	$170,000	$396,000	$194,000

The company also experienced changes in the number of outstanding shares from the following events:

Outstanding shares on December 31, 2001	80,000
2002	
Treasury stock purchase on April 1	− 8,000
Issuance of new shares on June 30	+ 24,000
10% stock dividend on October 1	+ 9,600
Outstanding shares on December 31, 2002	105,600
2003	
Issuance of new shares on July 1	+ 32,000
Treasury stock purchase on November 1	− 9,600
Outstanding shares on December 31, 2003	128,000
2004	
Issuance of new shares on August 1	+ 40,000
Treasury stock purchase on September 1	− 8,000
3-for-1 stock split on October 1	+320,000
Outstanding shares on December 31, 2004	480,000

Required

Preparation Component

1. Compute the weighted average of the common shares outstanding for year 2002.

2. Compute the EPS component amounts to report with the year 2002 income statement for income from continuing operations, loss on discontinued segment, and net income.

3. Compute the weighted average of the common shares outstanding for year 2003.

4. Compute the EPS component amounts to report with the year 2003 income statement for income from continuing operations, the extraordinary gain, and net income.

Check   2003 earnings per share (net income), $3.30

5. Compute the weighted average of the common shares outstanding for year 2004.

6. Compute the EPS component amounts to report with the year 2004 income statement for income from continuing operations, the extraordinary loss, and net income.

Analysis Component

7. Explain how you would use the EPS data from part (6) to predict EPS for 2005.

Reliant Corporation's common stock is currently selling on a stock exchange at $85 per share, and its current balance sheet shows the following stockholders' equity section:

Problem 14-8A

Computation of book values and dividend allocations

Preferred stock, 5% cumulative $___ par value, 1,000 shares authorized, issued, and outstanding	$ 50,000
Common stock, $___ par value, 4,000 shares authorized, issued, and outstanding	80,000
Retained earnings	150,000
Total stockholders' equity	$280,000

Required

Preparation Component

1. What is the current market value (price) of this corporation's common stock?

2. What are the par values of the corporation's preferred stock and its common stock?

3. If no dividends are in arrears, what are the book values per share of the preferred stock and the common stock?

4. If two years' preferred dividends are in arrears, what are the book values per share of the preferred stock and the common stock?

Check   (4) Book value of common, $56.25

5. If two years' preferred dividends are in arrears and the preferred stock is callable at $55 per share, what are the book values per share of the preferred stock and the common stock?

6. If two years' preferred dividends are in arrears and the board of directors declares dividends of $11,500, what total amount will be paid to the preferred and to the common shareholders? What is the amount of dividends per share for the common stock?

Analysis Component

7. What are some factors that can contribute to a difference between the book value of common stock and its market value (price)?

Knight Rider Company is incorporated at the beginning of this year and engages in a number of transactions. The following journal entries impacted its stockholders' equity during its first year of operations:

PROBLEM SET B

Problem 14-1B

Stockholders' equity transactions

a.	Cash	120,000	
	Common Stock, $1 Par Value		3,000
	Contributed Capital in Excess of Par Value, Common Stock		117,000
b.	Organization Costs	40,000	
	Common Stock, $1 Par Value		1,000
	Contributed Capital in Excess of Par Value, Common Stock		39,000

c.	Cash	13,300	
	Accounts Receivable	8,000	
	Building	37,000	
	Notes Payable		18,300
	Common Stock, $1 Par Value		800
	Contributed Capital in Excess of Par Value, Common Stock		39,200
d.	Cash	60,000	
	Common Stock, $1 Par Value		1,200
	Contributed Capital in Excess of Par Value, Common Stock		58,800

Required

1. Explain each journal entry *a* through *d*.

2. How many shares of common stock are outstanding at year-end?

3. What is the amount of minimum legal capital (based on par value) at year-end?

4. What is the total contributed capital at year-end?

5. What is the book value per share of the common stock at year-end if contributed capital plus retained earnings equals $283,000?

Check　(4) Contributed capital, $260,000

Problem 14-2B

Cash dividends, treasury stock, and statement of retained earnings

Unocol Corp. reports the following components of stockholders' equity on December 31, 2001:

Common stock—$1 par value, 320,000 shares authorized, 200,000 shares issued and outstanding	$ 200,000
Contributed capital in excess of par value, common stock	1,400,000
Retained earnings	2,160,000
Total stockholders' equity	$3,760,000

It completes the following transactions related to stockholders' equity in year 2002:

Jan. 10　Purchased 40,000 shares of its own stock at $12 per share.

Mar. 2　Directors declared a $1.50 per share cash dividend payable on March 31 to the March 15 stockholders of record.

Mar. 31　Paid the dividend declared on March 2.

Nov. 11　Sold 24,000 of the treasury shares at $13 per share.

Nov. 25　Sold 16,000 of the treasury shares at $9.50 per share.

Dec. 1　Directors declared a $2.50 per share cash dividend payable on January 2, 2003, to the December 10 stockholders of record.

Dec. 31　Closed the $1,072,000 credit balance (from net income) in the Income Summary account to Retained Earnings.

Required

1. Prepare journal entries to record the transactions and closings for 2002.

2. Prepare a statement of retained earnings for the year ended December 31, 2002.

3. Prepare the stockholders' equity section of the company's balance sheet as of December 31, 2002.

Check　Retained earnings, Dec. 31, 2002, $2,476,000

Problem 14-3B

Description of equity changes with journal entries and account balances

At December 31, the end of Open Channel Communication's third quarter, the following stockholders' equity accounts appear:

Common stock, $10 par value	$ 960,000
Contributed capital in excess of par value, common stock	384,000
Retained earnings	1,600,000

In the fourth quarter, the following entries related to its equity accounts are recorded:

Jan. 17	Retained Earnings	96,000	
	Common Dividend Payable		96,000
Feb. 5	Common Dividend Payable	96,000	
	Cash		96,000
Feb. 28	Retained Earnings	252,000	
	Common Stock Dividend Distributable		120,000
	Contributed Capital in Excess of Par Value, Common Stock		132,000
Mar. 14	Common Stock Dividend Distributable	120,000	
	Common Stock, $10 Par Value		120,000
Mar. 25	Memo—Change the title of the common stock account to reflect the new par value of $5.		
Mar. 31	Income Summary	720,000	
	Retained Earnings		720,000

Required

1. Explain each journal entry.

2. Complete the following table showing the balances of the company's equity accounts at each indicated date:

	Jan. 17	Feb. 5	Feb. 28	Mar. 14	Mar. 25	Mar. 31
Common stock	$____	$____	$____	$____	$____	$____
Common stock dividend distributable	____	____	____	____	____	____
Contributed capital in excess of par, common stock	____	____	____	____	____	____
Retained earnings	____	____	____	____	____	____
Combined balances of equity accounts	$____	$____	$____	$____	$____	$____

Check   Total equity, Mar. 31, $3,568,000

The equity sections from Scanat Corporation's 2002 and 2003 balance sheets follow:

Problem 14-4B

Analysis of changes in stockholders' equity accounts

Stockholders' Equity (December 31, 2002)	
Common stock—$20 par value, 30,000 shares authorized, 17,000 shares issued and outstanding	$340,000
Contributed capital in excess of par value, common stock	60,000
Total contributed capital	$400,000
Retained earnings	270,000
Total stockholders' equity	$670,000

Stockholders' Equity (December 31, 2003)	
Common stock—$20 par value, 30,000 shares authorized, 19,000 shares issued, 1,000 in the treasury	$380,000
Contributed capital in excess of par value, common stock	104,000
Total contributed capital	$484,000
Retained earnings ($40,000 restricted)	295,200
	$779,200
Less cost of treasury stock	(40,000)
Total stockholders' equity	$739,200

The following transactions and events affect its equity accounts during year 2003:

Feb. 15	Declared a $0.40 per share cash dividend, date of record five days later.
Mar. 2	Purchased treasury stock.
May 15	Declared a $0.40 per share cash dividend, date of record five days later.
Aug. 15	Declared a $0.40 per share cash dividend, date of record five days later.
Oct. 4	Declared a 12.5% stock dividend when the stock's market value is $42 per share.
Oct. 20	Issued stock dividend.
Nov. 15	Declared a $0.40 per share cash dividend, date of record five days later.

Required

1. How many common shares are outstanding on each cash dividend date?

2. What is the dollar amount for each of the four cash dividends?

3. What is the amount of the capitalization of retained earnings for the stock dividend?

4. What is the cost per share of the treasury stock purchased?

Check Net income, $136,000

5. How much net income did the company earn during year 2003?

Problem 14-5B
Income statement
presentation

Selected account balances from the adjusted trial balance for PXG Corp. as of December 31, 2002, follow:

	Debit	Credit
a. Accumulated depreciation—Buildings		$ 400,000
b. Interest earned		20,000
c. Cumulative effect of change in accounting principle (pretax)		92,000
d. Net sales		2,640,000
e. Income taxes expense	$?	
f. Loss on retirement of debt (pretax)	64,000	
g. Accumulated depreciation—Equipment		220,000
h. Other operating expenses	328,000	
i. Depreciation expense—Equipment	100,000	
j. Loss from settlement of lawsuit	36,000	
k. Gain from settlement of lawsuit		68,000
l. Loss on sale of equipment	24,000	
m. Loss from operating a discontinued segment (pretax)	120,000	
n. Depreciation expense—Buildings	156,000	
o. Correction of overstatement of prior year's expense (pretax)		48,000
p. Cost of goods sold	1,040,000	
q. Loss on sale of discontinued segment's assets (pretax)	180,000	
r. Accounts payable		132,000

Required

Answer each of the following questions by providing supporting computations:

1. Assuming the company's income tax rate is 25% for all items, identify the tax effects and after-tax measures of the items labeled pretax.

2. What is the amount of the company's income from continuing operations before income taxes? What is the amount of the company's income taxes expense? What is the amount of the company's income from continuing operations?

3. What is the total amount of after-tax income (loss) associated with the discontinued segment?

4. What is the amount of income (loss) before both any extraordinary items and any cumulative effect of changes in accounting principle?

Check Net income, $579,000

5. What is the amount of net income for the year?

Problem 14-6B
Change in accounting
principle (depreciation)
and its disclosure

On January 1, 2002, Couric Corp. purchases equipment costing $400,000 with an expected salvage value of zero at the end of its five-year useful life. Depreciation is allocated to 2002, 2003, and 2004 with the double-declining-balance method. Early in 2005, the company decides to change to the straight-line method to produce more useful financial statements and to be consistent with other firms in the industry.

Required

Preparation Component

1. Do generally accepted accounting principles allow Couric to change depreciation methods in 2005?

2. Prepare a table to show the amount of depreciation expense allocated to 2002 through 2004 using the double-declining-balance method.

3. Prepare a table to show the amount of depreciation expense that would have been allocated to 2002 through 2004 using the straight-line method.

4. Organize your answers from parts (2) and (3) into a table like Exhibit 14.17 and compute the before- and after-tax cumulative effect of the change. The company's income tax rate is 25%.

5. How should the cumulative effect of the change in accounting principle be reported? Does the cumulative effect increase or decrease net income?

6. How much depreciation expense is reported on the company's income statement for 2005?

Analysis Component

7. Assume that Couric mistakenly treats the change in depreciation methods as a change in accounting estimate. Using your answers from parts (2), (3), and (4), describe the effect of this error on the 2005 financial statements.

Check   After-tax cumulative effect, $55,200

The income statements for Bix, Inc., as reported when they were initially published in 2002, 2003, and 2004 follow:

Problem 14-7B
Earnings per share calculation and presentation

	2002	2003	2004
Net sales	$500,000	$600,000	$800,000
Operating expenses	320,000	430,000	540,000
Income from continuing operations	$180,000	$170,000	$260,000
Loss on discontinued segment	(52,290)	—	—
Income before extraordinary items	$127,710	$170,000	$260,000
Extraordinary gain (loss)	—	28,200	(74,250)
Net income	$127,710	$198,200	$185,750

The company also experienced changes in the number of outstanding shares from the following events:

Outstanding shares on December 31, 2001	20,000
2002	
Treasury stock purchase on July 1	− 2,000
Issuance of new shares on September 30	+ 7,000
20% stock dividend on December 1	+ 5,000
Outstanding shares on December 31, 2002	30,000
2003	
Issuance of new shares on March 31	+ 8,000
Treasury stock purchase on October 1	− 3,000
Outstanding shares on December 31, 2003	35,000
2004	
Issuance of new shares on July 1	+ 6,000
Treasury stock purchase on October 1	− 3,500
2-for-1 stock split on November 1	+37,500
Outstanding shares on December 31, 2004	75,000

Required

Preparation Component

1. Compute the weighted-average of the common shares oustanding for year 2002.
2. Compute the EPS component amounts to report with the year 2002 income statement for income from continuing operations, loss on discontinued segment, and net income.
3. Compute the weighted-average of the common shares outstanding for year 2003.
4. Compute the EPS component amounts to report with the year 2003 income statement for income from continuing operations, the extraordinary gain, and net income.
5. Compute the weighted-average of the common shares outstanding for year 2004.
6. Compute the EPS component amounts to report with the year 2004 income statement for income from continuing operations, the extraordinary loss, and net income.

Analysis Component

7. Explain how you would use the EPS data from part (6) to predict EPS for 2005.

Problem 14-8B
Computation of book values and dividend allocations

Big Hat, Inc.'s common stock is currently selling on a stock exchange at $90 per share, and its current balance sheet shows the following stockholders' equity section:

Preferred stock, 8% cumulative, $___ par value, 1,500 shares authorized, issued, and outstanding	$ 375,000
Common stock, $___ par value, 18,000 shares authorized, issued, and outstanding	900,000
Retained earnings	1,125,000
Total stockholders' equity	$2,400,000

Required

Preparation Component

1. What is the current market value (price) of this corporation's common stock?
2. What are the par values of the corporation's preferred stock and its common stock?
3. If no dividends are in arrears, what are the book values per share of the preferred stock and the common stock?
4. If two years' preferred dividends are in arrears, what are the book values per share of the preferred stock and the common stock?
5. It two years' preferred dividends are in arrears and the preferred stock is callable at $280 per share, what are the book values per share of the preferred stock and the common stock?
6. If two years' preferred dividends are in arrears and the board of directors declares dividends of $100,000, what total amount will be paid to the preferred and to the common shareholders? What is the amount of dividends per share for the common stock?

Analysis Component

7. Discuss why the book value of common stock may not always be a good estimate of its market value.

Beyond the Numbers

Reporting in Action

BTN 14-1 Refer to **Nike**'s financial statements in Appendix A to answer the following questions:

1. Has Nike issued any preferred stock? If so, what are its features?
2. How many shares of both class A and class B common stock are outstanding at the end of fiscal years 2000 and 1999? How do these numbers compare with the weighted-average common shares outstanding at the end of fiscal years 2000 and 1999?
3. What is the book value of its entire common stock at May 31, 2000?

4. What is its cash dividend declared per common share for fiscal years 2000 and 1999? What is the total amount of cash dividends paid to common and preferred stockholders for fiscal years 2000 and 1998?

5. Indicate and compare basic EPS share amounts across years 2000, 1999, and 1998. Identify and comment on any significant changes.

6. Does Nike hold any treasury stock as of May 31, 2000, or May 31, 1999?

7. Does Nike report any changes in accounting principles or the occurrence of extraordinary items for fiscal years ended May 31, 2000 or 1999? Are there gains or losses on disposal of a business segment for fiscal years 2000 or 1999?

Swoosh Ahead

8. Access Nike's annual reports for fiscal years ending after May 31, 2000, from either its Web site [**www.nike.com**] or the SEC's EDGAR database [**www.sec.gov**]. Is the redeemable preferred stock still outstanding? Has the number of common shares outstanding increased since May 31, 2000? Has Nike increased the total amount of cash dividends paid compared to fiscal year 2000?

BTN 14-2   Key comparative figures for both **Nike** and **Reebok** follow:

Key Figures	Nike	Reebok
Net income (in millions)	$ 579.1	$ 11.0
Cash dividends declared per common share	$ 0.48	$ 0.00
Common shares outstanding (in millions)	269.6	56.3
Market value (price) per share	$ 42.88	$ 8.19
Equity applicable to common shares (in mil.)	$3,135.7	$528.8

Comparative Analysis

A1   A2   A3   A4

NIKE   Reebok

Required

1. Compute the book value per common share for each company using these data.

2. Compute the basic EPS for each company using these data.

3. Compute the dividend yield for each company using these data. Does the dividend yield of either company characterize it as an income or growth stock? Explain.

4. Compute, compare, and interpret the price-earnings ratio for each company using these data.

BTN 14-3   This chapter describes CompUS's change in accounting principle from the double-declining-balance method of depreciation to the straight-line method. CompUS argues that its income statement now is more useful when depreciation is computed using the straight-line method. This change in accounting principle adds $56,000 to net income for year 2002. As this company's auditor, you must review the decision to change the accounting principle. You review the equipment in question and learn that it is a piece of high-tech equipment, whose risk of obsolescence in the near future is high. You also are aware that management receives year-end bonuses based on net income.

Required   As the auditor, would you support the change in depreciation method or ask management to continue using the double-declining-balance method? Justify your response.

Ethics Challenge

C4

BTN 14-4   Teams are to select an industry, and each team member is to select a different company in that industry. Next, each team member is to acquire the selected company's annual report (or Form 10-K). Annual reports can be obtained in many ways, including accessing the SEC EDGAR site [**www.sec.gov**]. Use the annual report to determine basic EPS. Use the financial press (or **quote.yahoo.com**) to determine the market price of this stock, and then compute the price-earnings ratio. Communicate with teammates via a meeting, e-mail, or telephone to discuss the meaning of this ratio, how companies compare, and the industry norm. The team must prepare a single memorandum reporting the ratio for each company and identifying the team conclusions or consensus of opinion. The memorandum is to be duplicated and distributed to the instructor and teammates.

Communicating in Practice

A1   A4

Hint: Make a transparency of each team's memo for a class discussion.

Taking It to the Net

BTN 14-5 Access the March 21, 2000, 10-K report of Quaker Oats Company (ticker OAT) from **www.edgar-online.com.**

Required

1. How many classes of stock has the Quaker Oats Company issued?
2. What are the par values of the classes of stock you identified in part (1)?
3. How much capital did Quaker Oats raise in 1999 from issuing stock?
4. What total amount did Quaker Oats pay in 1999 to repurchase stock?
5. What amount did Quaker Oats pay out in cash dividends for 1999?

Teamwork in Action

P5

Hint: Instructor should be sure each team completes part 1 accurately before proceeding.

BTN 14-6 This activity requires teamwork to reinforce understanding of accounting for treasury stock.

1. Write a brief team statement (a) generalizing what happens to a corporation's financial position when it engages in a stock "buyback" and (b) identifying reasons that a corporation would engage in this activity.
2. Assume that an entity acquires 100 shares of its $100 par value common stock at a cost of $134 per share. Discuss the entry to record this acquisition. Next, assign *each* team member to prepare *one* of the following entries (assume each entry applies to all shares):
   a. Reissue treasury shares at cost.
   b. Reissue treasury shares at $150 per share.
   c. Reissue treasury shares at $120 per share—assume the contributed capital account from treasury shares has a $1,500 balance.
   d. Reissue treasury shares at $120 per share—assume the contributed account from treasury shares has a $1,000 balance.
   e. Reissue treasury shares at $120 per share—assume the contributed capital account from treasury shares has a zero balance.
3. In sequence, each member is to present his/her entry to the team and explain the *similarities* and *differences* between that entry and the previous entry. Encourage team members to ask questions, and be sure concepts are understood before proceeding.

Business Week Activity

P5

BTN 14-7 Read the article "Paul Harris Aims to Get Spruced Up" from the October 26, 1998, issue of *Business Week*.

Required

1. What type of stores are the **Paul Harris** stores?
2. How did the price of the Paul Harris stock behave in 1998?
3. In September 1998, what action did Paul Harris management take in response to its stock price?
4. Access Paul Harris's stock prices for 1998, 1999, and 2000 at **quote.yahoo.com.** Obtain a printout of its stock price history for these years. Comment on any trends.
5. In retrospect, did management take the correct action in September 1998? Explain.

Entrepreneurial Decision

BTN 14-8 An entrepreneur planning to start a new business needs $312,500 of start-up capital. This person will contribute $250,000 of personal assets in return for 5,000 shares of common stock but needs to raise another $62,500 in cash. There are two alternative plans for raising the additional cash. Plan A is to sell 1,250 shares of common stock to one or more investors for $62,500 cash. Plan B is to sell 625 shares of cumulative preferred stock to one or more investors for $62,500 cash (this preferred stock would have a $100 par value, an annual 8% dividend rate, and be issued at par).

1. If the business is expected to earn $45,000 of after-tax net income in the first year, what rate of return on beginning equity will this entrepreneur personally earn under each alternative? Which plan will provide the higher expected return to the entrepreneur?
2. If the business is expected to earn $10,500 of after-tax net income in the first year, what rate of return on beginning equity will the entrepreneur personally earn under each alternative? Which plan will provide the higher expected return to the entrepreneur?
3. Analyze and interpret the differences between the results for parts (1) and (2).

15

Long-Term Liabilities

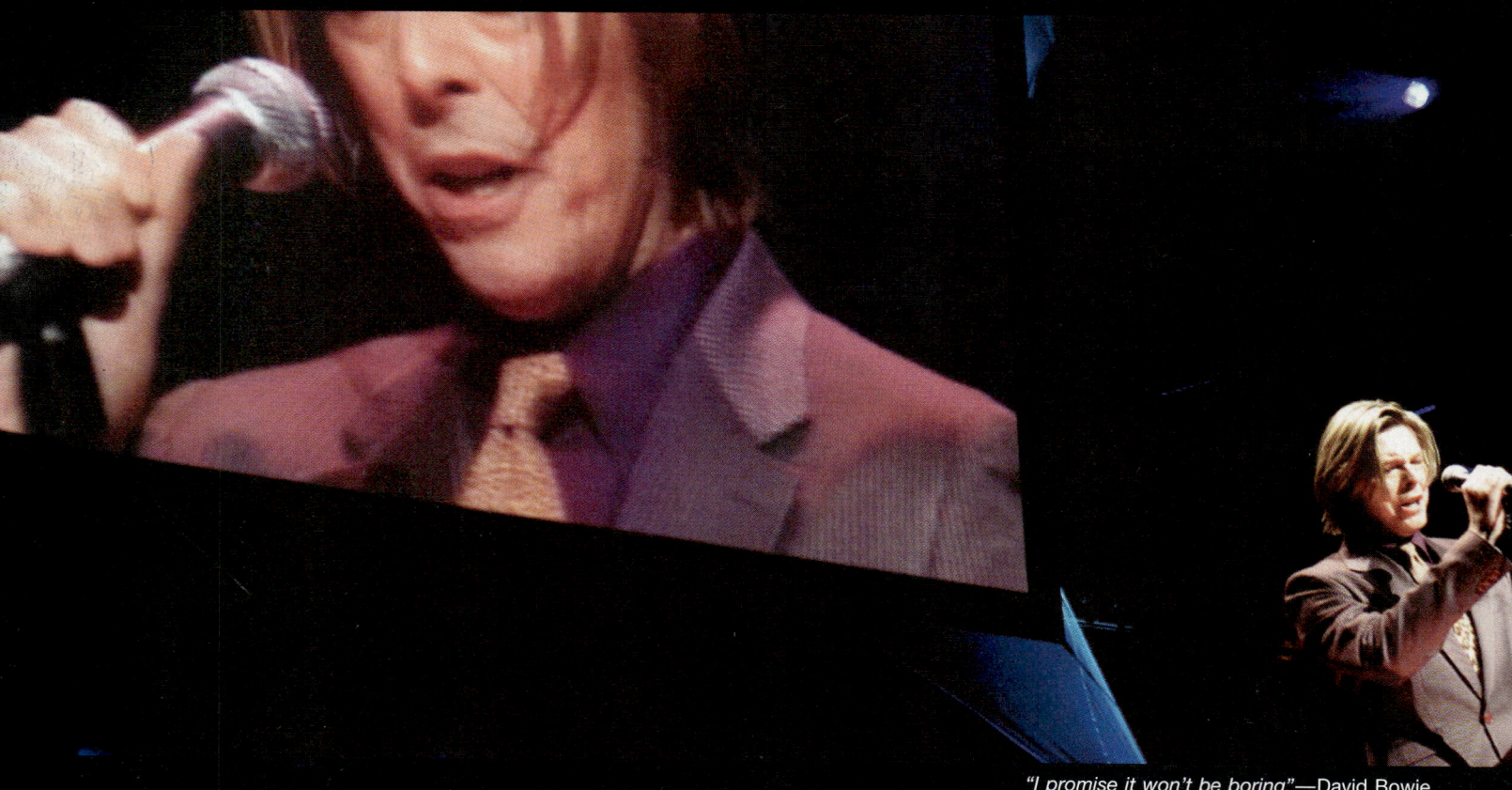

"I promise it won't be boring"—David Bowie

A Look Back

Chapter 14 focused on the corporate form of organization. We described its characteristics and its important transactions. We also explained corporate accounting and the reporting of income, earnings per share, and retained earnings.

A Look at This Chapter

This chapter describes the accounting for bonds and notes. We explain their characteristics, payment patterns, interest computations, retirement, and reporting requirements. An appendix to this chapter explains accounting for leases and pensions.

A Look Ahead

Chapter 16 focuses on long-term investments in securities. We explain how to identify, account for, and report long-term investments in both debt and equity securities. We also introduce foreign exchange rates and describe accounting for transactions listed in a foreign currency.

Learning Objectives

Conceptual

C1 Explain the types of bonds and the procedures for issuing them.

C2 Explain the types and payment patterns of notes.

Analytical

A1 Compare bond financing with stock financing.

A2 Explain collateral agreements and their effects on loan risk.

A3 Compute the ratio of pledged assets to secured liabilities and explain its use.

Procedural

P1 Prepare entries to record bond issuance and bond interest expense.

P2 Compute and record amortization of bond discount.

P3 Compute and record amortization of bond premium.

P4 Record the retirement of bonds.

P5 Prepare entries to account for notes.

Bowie Bonds

NEW YORK—David Bowie continues to jam in the information age. Well known for his unique musical style and innovations in the world of music, he's now rocking Wall Street with the introduction of "Bowie bonds." Bowie, the godfather of "glam rock," created and issued bonds backed by his greatest hits. The bond issue generated millions for Bowie and enabled him to pursue some of his other passions, including his online Internet services at **DavidBowie.com**.

The Bowie bonds are called *secured bonds,* meaning they are backed by other assets. Secured bonds are common in business and are backed by assets such as land, homes, and automobiles. Secured bonds are less risky because bondholders can potentially demand that assets be sold to cover interest and principal. This lower risk has led to an asset-backed bond market that exceeds $200 billion, yet Bowie's secured bonds are unique—the assets backing them are his expected future royalties from 25 of his past albums. These include *Ziggy Stardust, Thin White Duke,* and *Let's Dance.*

Such securities are normally considered risky and, thus, shunned by Wall Street—especially one backed by future royalties of a rock star, but Moody's Investors Service gave the Bowie bonds the highest investment-grade rating (AAA). Moreover, Prudential Insurance Company dove in, snatching up all Bowie bonds for a cool $55 million. Prudential will earn a 7.9% return over the 10-year life of the bonds. The success of the bond issue has intrigued other musical artists wanting to raise cash to fund ambitious projects. These artists include Rod Stewart, Michael Jackson, and Crosby, Stills and Nash.

So what's next for Bowie? Derivatives? Options? Nobody knows for sure. The only thing certain is that he remains on the cutting edge. Says Bowie, "I don't know where I'm going from here, but I promise it won't be boring." Wall Street is certainly not underestimating him. He might just ch-ch-ch-change everything! [*Sources: CNN's Web Site,* September 29, 1998; *DavidBowie Web Site,* May 2001; *Fortune,* June 8, 1998]

Individuals, companies, and governments issue bonds to finance their activities. In return for financing, bonds promise to repay the lender with interest. This chapter explains the basics of bonds and the accounting for their issuance and retirement. The chapter also describes long-term notes as another financing source, including interest-bearing, noninterest-bearing, and installment notes. We explain how present value concepts impact both the accounting for and reporting of bonds and notes. An appendix to this chapter discusses present value concepts applicable to liabilities and the accounting for leases and pensions. Understanding how bonds, notes, and other liabilities are used to a company's advantage is an important goal of this chapter.

Basics of Bonds

Many companies finance operations and borrow money by issuing bonds. This section explains the basics of bonds and a company's motivation for issuing them.

Bond Financing

A1 Compare bond financing with stock financing.

Companies can finance their business activities in several ways, including issuing notes, leasing assets, and using owner investments. Projects that demand large amounts of money often are funded from bond issuances.[1] A **bond** is its issuer's written promise to pay an amount identified as the par value of the bond along with interest. The **par value of a bond,** also called the *face amount* or *face value,* is paid at a specified future date known as the bond's *maturity date.* Most bonds also require the issuer to make semiannual interest payments. The amount of interest paid each year is determined by multiplying the par value of the bond by the bond's contract rate of interest. This section explains both advantages and disadvantages of bond financing.

Advantages of Bonds

These are the three main advantages of bond financing:

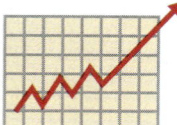

1. *Bonds can increase return on equity.* A company earning a higher return with the borrowed funds than it pays in interest, increases its return on equity. This process is called *financial leverage* or *trading on the equity.*

2. *Bonds do not affect owner control.* Equity financing reflects ownership in a company, whereas bond financing does not. A person who contributes $1,000 of a company's $10,000 equity financing typically controls one-tenth of all owners' decisions. A person who owns a $1,000, 11%, 20-year bond has no ownership right. This person, or bondholder, has a receivable from the bond issuer. The bondholder's right is to receive 11% interest, or $110, each year the bond is outstanding and $1,000 when it matures in 20 years.

3. *Interest on bonds is tax deductible.* Bond interest payments are tax deductible, but equity payments (distributions) to owners are not. This feature is important for corporations. For example, assume that a corporation with no bond financing earns $15,000 in income *before* paying taxes at a 40% tax rate. This corporation would owe $6,000 ($15,000 × 40%) in taxes. If a portion of its financing is in bonds, however, the resulting bond interest is deducted in computing taxable income. That is, if bond interest expense is $10,000, the taxes owed would be $2,000 ([$15,000 − $10,000] × 40%), which is much less than the $6,000 owed with no bond financing.

Point: Financial leverage can be achieved by issuing either common or preferred stock.

Before proceeding let's illustrate the impact of bond financing for return on equity. Consider Magnum Co., which has $1 million in equity and is planning a $500,000 expansion to meet increasing demand for its product. Magnum predicts the $500,000 expansion will yield $125,000 in additional income before paying any interest. Magnum currently earns $100,000 per year and has no interest expense. Magnum is considering three plans. Plan A

---

[1] Bonds are issued by both for-profit and nonprofit companies, as well as the federal government and other governmental units, such as cities, states, and school districts. Although the examples in this chapter deal with business situations, all issuers use similar practices to account for bonds.

is not to expand. Plan B is to expand and raise $500,000 from equity financing. Plan C is to expand and issue $500,000 of bonds that pay 10% annual interest ($50,000). Exhibit 15.1 shows how these three plans affect Magnum's net income, equity, and return on equity (net income/equity).

	Plan A Do not Expand	Plan B Equity Financing	Plan C Bond Financing
Income before interest expense	$ 100,000	$ 225,000	$ 225,000
Interest expense	—	—	(50,000)
Net Income	**$ 100,000**	**$ 225,000**	**$ 175,000**
Equity	$1,000,000	$1,500,000	$1,000,000
Return on equity	**10.0%**	**15.0%**	**17.5%**

Exhibit 15.1

Financing with Bonds or Equity

Analysis of these plans shows the owner(s) will earn a higher return on equity if expansion occurs. Moreover, the preferred expansion plan is to issue bonds. Projected net income under Plan C ($175,000) is smaller than under Plan B ($225,000), but the return on equity is larger because of less equity investment. This illustration reflects a general rule: *Return on equity increases when the expected rate of return from the new assets is greater than the rate of interest expense on the bonds.*

Example: Compute return on equity for all three plans if Magnum currently earns $150,000 instead of $100,000. *Answer* ($ in 000s):
Plan A = 15%   ($150/$1,000)
Plan B = 18.3%   ($275/$1,500)
Plan C = 22.5%   ($225/$1,000)

Disadvantages of Bonds

The two main disadvantages of bond financing are:

1. *Bonds can decrease return on equity.* When a company earns a lower return with the borrowed funds than it pays in interest, it decreases its return on equity. This is the downside risk of financial leverage; it is more likely to arise when a company has periods of low income or net losses.

2. *Bonds require payment of both periodic interest and the par value at maturity.* Bond payments can be especially burdensome when income and cash flow are low. Equity financing, on the other hand, does not require any payments because cash withdrawals (and dividends) are paid at the discretion of the owner (or board).

A company must weigh the risks and returns of the disadvantages and advantages of bond financing when deciding whether to issue bonds to finance operations.

Types of Bonds

We describe the more common types of bonds and their characteristics in this section.

C1 Explain the types of bonds and the procedures for issuing them.

Secured and Unsecured Bonds

Secured bonds have specific assets of the issuer pledged (or *mortgaged*) as collateral. This arrangement gives bondholders added protection against the issuer's default. If the issuer fails to pay interest or par value, the secured bondholders can demand the collateral be sold and the proceeds used to pay the bond obligation. **Unsecured bonds,** also called *debentures,* are backed by the issuer's general credit standing. Unsecured bonds are riskier than secured bonds. An issuer generally must be financially strong to successfully issue debentures at a favorable interest rate. *Subordinated debentures* refer to creditors whose claims on the issuer's assets are second to those of other unsecured liabilities. In a liquidation, subordinated debentures are not repaid until the claims of the more senior, unsecured liabilities have been settled.

Secured Bond   **Unsecured Bond**

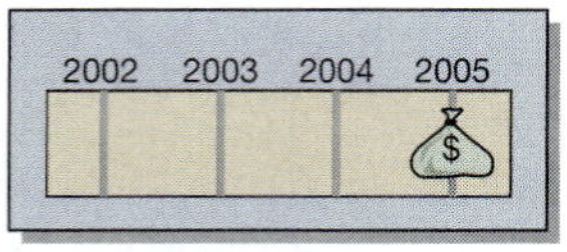

Term Bond

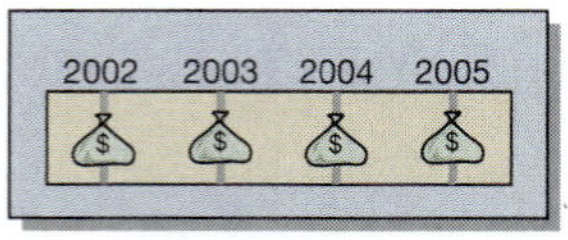

Serial Bond

Term and Serial Bonds

Term bonds are scheduled for maturity at a single specified date. **Serial bonds** mature at several different dates (in series) and thus are repaid over a number of periods. For instance, $1 million of serial bonds might mature at the rate of $100,000 each year from 6 to 15 years after they are issued. This involves 10 groups (or series) of bonds of $100,000 each with one series maturing after six years, another after seven years, and another each successive year until the final series is repaid. Many bonds are also **sinking fund bonds.** To reduce the holder's risk, sinking fund bonds require the issuer to create a *sinking fund* of assets set aside at specified amounts and dates to repay the bonds at maturity.

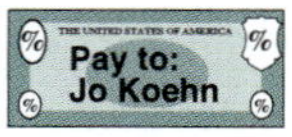

Registered Bond

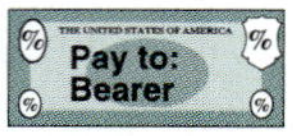

Bearer Bond

Registered Bonds and Bearer Bonds

Bonds issued in the names and addresses of their holders are **registered bonds.** The issuer makes bond payments by sending checks (or cash transfers) to these registered holders. When a registered holder sells a bond to another holder, the issuer must be notified of the change. Registered bonds offer the issuer the practical advantage of not having to actually issue bond certificates. This arrangement protects holders against loss or theft of bonds.

Bonds payable to whoever holds them (the *bearer*) are called **bearer bonds,** or *unregistered bonds*. Since sales or exchanges might not be recorded, the holder of a bearer bond is presumed to be its rightful owner. As a result, lost or stolen bearer bonds are difficult to replace. Many bearer bonds are also **coupon bonds.** This term reflects interest coupons that are attached to these bonds. Each coupon matures on a specific interest payment date. The holder detaches each coupon when it matures and presents it to a bank or broker for collection. At maturity, the holder follows the same process and presents the bond certificate for collection. Income tax law discourages companies from issuing coupon bonds because there is no readily available record of who actually receives the interest.

Did You Know?

Munis There are more than a million municipal bonds, or "munis," to choose from, and many are exempt from taxes. Munis are issued by all types of government agencies such as states, cities, towns, and counties to pay for a variety of public projects including schools, roads, bridges, and stadiums.

Tax-Exempt Bonds Representative prices for several active tax-exempt revenue and refunding bonds, based on institutional trades. Changes rounded to the nearest one-eighth. Yield is to maturity. Source: The Bond Buyer.

Issue	Coupon	Maturity	Price	Chg	Yld
MD Hlth & Hgr Ed Au	5.000	07-01-27	96⅞	−⅜	5.21
Miami-Dade FL Ser 97B	5.000	10-01-37	95½	−⅜	5.27
Mich St Hsp Fin Auth	5.000	05-15-28	95⅝	−½	5.31
Mo Hlth & Ed Fac	5.000	11-15-37	95½	−½	5.27
Nashville-Davidson Co	4.875	11-01-28	93⅝	−½	5.29

Convertible and Callable Bonds

Convertible bonds can be exchanged for a fixed number of shares of the issuing corporation's common stock. Convertible bonds offer bondholders the potential to participate in future increases in a stock's market value. Bondholders receive periodic interest while the bonds are held and will receive the par value if the bond is held to maturity. In most cases, it is the bondholders who decide whether and when to convert the bonds to stock. **Callable bonds** have an option exercisable by the issuer to retire them at a stated dollar amount prior to maturity.

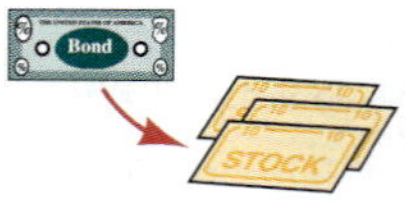

Convertible Bond

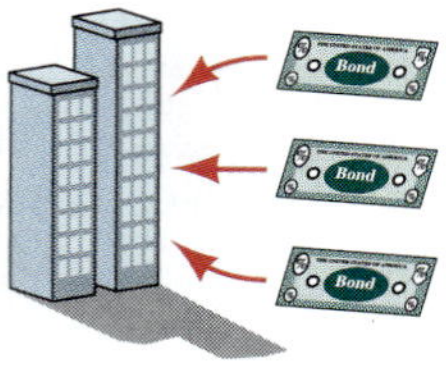

Callable Bond

Did You Know?

Quotes The CompUSA bond quote shown here is interpreted as (left to right):

Bonds	Rate	Mat	Yld	Vol	Close	Chg
CompUSA	9½	10	9.2	145	103½	+⅛

Bonds, issuer name; **Rate,** contract interest rate (9½%) for this bond; **Mat,** matures in year 2010 when bond principal is paid; **Yld,** yield rate (9.2%) of bond at current price; **Vol,** daily dollar worth ($145,000) of bonds traded in 1,000s; **Close,** closing price ($1,035) for the day as percent of par value; **Chg,** change ($0.125) in closing price from the prior day's closing price.

Bond Trading

Bonds are securities that can be readily bought and sold. A large number of bonds trade on both the New York Exchange and the American Exchange. A bond issue consists of a large number of bonds, usually in denominations of $1,000 or $5,000, and is sold to many different lenders. After bonds are issued, they often are bought and sold by investors, meaning that any particular bond probably has a number of owners before it matures. Because bonds are exchanged (bought and sold) in the market, they have a market value (price). For convenience, bond market values are expressed as a percent of their par (face) value. For example, a company's bonds might be trading at 103½, meaning they can be bought or sold for 103.5% of their par value. Bonds can also trade below par value. For instance, if a company's bonds are trading at 95, they can be bought or sold at 95% of their par value.

Bond-Issuing Procedures

State and federal laws govern bond issuances. Bond issuers also want to ensure that they do not violate any of their existing contractual agreements. Authorization of bond issuances includes the number of bonds authorized, their par value, and the contract interest rate. The legal document identifying the rights and obligations of both the bondholders and the issuer is called the **bond indenture,** which acts as the legal contract between the issuer and the bondholders. A bondholder may also receive a bond certificate as evidence of the company's debt. A **bond certificate,** such as shown in Exhibit 15.2, includes specifics such as the issuer's name, the bond's par value, the contract interest rate, and the maturity date. Many companies reduce costs by not issuing certificates to bondholders.

The issuing company normally sells its bonds to an investment firm called an *underwriter,* which then resells them to the public. An issuing company can also sell bonds directly to investors. When an underwriter sells bonds to a large number of investors, a *trustee* represents and protects the bondholders' interests. The trustee monitors the issuer to ensure that it complies with the obligations in the bond indenture. Most trustees are large banks or trust companies. The trustee writes and accepts the terms of a bond indenture before it is issued. When bonds are offered to the public, called *floating an issue,* they must be registered with the Securities and Exchange Commission (SEC). SEC registration requires the issuer to file certain financial information. Most company bonds are issued in par value units of $1,000 or $5,000. A *baby bond* is a bond with a par value of less than $1,000, such as $100.

Point: Issuers of coupon bonds cannot deduct the related interest expense for taxable income. This is to prevent abuse by taxpayers who own coupon bonds but fail to report interest income on their tax returns.

Point: Note that *indenture* refers to a bond's legal contract, whereas *debenture* refers to an unsecured bond.

Exhibit 15.2
Bond Certificate

Point: The *spread* between what buyers pay and the dealer's cost can be huge. Dealers are said to earn more than $25 billion in annual spread revenue. A tight oligopoly of Wall Street brokers and dealers continues to control bond prices.

Global: In the United Kingdom, government bonds are called *GILTS*—short for gilt-edged investments.

This section explains accounting for bond issuances at par, below par (discount), and above par (premium). We also describe the amortization of a discount or premium and how to record bonds issued between interest payment dates.

Issuing Bonds at Par

To illustrate an issuance of bonds at par value, suppose a company receives authorization to issue $800,000 of 9%, 20-year bonds dated January 1, 2002, that mature on December 31, 2021. They pay interest semiannually on each June 30 and December 31. After the trustee accepts the bond indenture on behalf of the bondholders, all or a portion of the bonds can be sold to an underwriter. If all bonds are sold at par value, the issuer records the sale:

2002			
Jan. 1	Cash	800,000	
	Bonds Payable		800,000
	Sold bonds at par.		

This entry reflects increases in both the issuer's cash and its long-term liabilities.

Bond Issuances

P1 Prepare entries to record bond issuance and bond interest expense.

Assets = Liabilities + Equity
+800,000 +800,000

Concept 15-1

The issuer records the first semiannual interest payment as follows:

Assets = Liabilities + Equity
−36,000   −36,000

2002			
June 30	Bond Interest Expense	36,000	
	Cash		36,000
	Paid semiannual interest (9% × $800,000 ×		
	½ year).		

The issuer pays and records its semiannual interest obligation every six months until the bonds mature. When they mature, the issuer records its payment of principal:

Assets = Liabilities + Equity
−800,000   −800,000

2021			
Dec. 31	Bonds Payable	800,000	
	Cash		800,000
	Paid bonds at maturity.		

Did You Know?

Ratings Game   Many bond buyers rely on rating services to assess bond risk. The best known are **Standard and Poor's** and **Moody's**. These services focus on the issuer's financial statements in setting ratings. Standard and Poor's ratings, from best quality to default, are AAA, AA, A, BBB, BB, B, CCC, CC, C, and D. Ratings can include a plus (+) or minus (−) to show relative standing within a category.

Point: Business acquisitions are sometimes financed by issuing "junk bonds" that carry high market rates of interest but offer little security. Bondholders can suffer huge losses when the acquired companies do not generate adequate cash flows to pay interest and principal.

Bond Discount or Premium

The bond issuer pays the interest rate specified in the indenture, which is called the **contract rate.** The contract rate is also referred to as the *coupon rate, stated rate,* or *nominal rate.* The annual interest paid is determined by multiplying the bond par value by the contract rate. The contract rate is usually stated on an annual basis, even if interest is paid semiannually. For example, if a company issues a $1,000, 8% bond paying interest semiannually, its annual interest of $80 (8% × $1,000) is paid in two semiannual payments of $40 each.

The contract rate sets the amount of interest the issuer pays in *cash,* which is not necessarily the *bond interest expense* actually incurred by the issuer. Bond interest expense depends on the bond's market value at issuance, which is determined by market expectations of the risk of lending to the issuer. The bond's market rate of interest reflects this expected risk, as does the supply of and demand for bonds. The **market rate** is the rate that borrowers are willing to pay and lenders are willing to accept for a particular bond and its risk level. As the risk level increases, the rate increases. The increased market rate compensates purchasers for the bonds' increased risk. Also, the market rate is generally higher when the time period until the bond matures is longer. This is so because many events can occur with a company over a longer period of time.

Many bond issuers try to set a contract rate of interest equal to the market rate they expect as of the bond issuance date. When the contract rate and market rate are equal, a bond sells at par value, but when they are not equal, a bond does not sell at par value. Instead, it is sold at a *premium* above par value or at a *discount* below par value. Exhibit 15.3 shows the relation between the contract rate, market rate, and a bond's issue price.

Exhibit 15.3

Relation between Bond Issue Price, Contract Rate, and Market Rate

Contract Rate Is		Bond Sells
Above market rate	➡	At a premium
Equal to market rate	➡	At par value
Below market rate	➡	At a discount

Quick Check

1. Unsecured bonds backed only by the issuer's general credit standing are called (a) serial bonds, (b) debentures, (c) registered bonds, (d) convertible bonds, or (e) bearer bonds.
2. How do you compute the amount of interest a bond issuer pays in cash each year?
3. When the contract rate is above the market rate, do bonds sell at a premium or a discount? Do purchasers pay more or less than the par value of the bonds?

Answers—p. 647

Issuing Bonds at a Discount

A **discount on bonds payable** occurs when a company issues bonds with a contract rate less than the market rate. This means the issue price is less than par value. To illustrate, assume that **Fila** announces an offer to issue bonds with a $100,000 par value, an 8% annual contract rate (paid semiannually), and a five-year life. The market rate for Fila's bonds is 10%, meaning the bonds will sell at a discount since the contract rate is less than the market rate. The exact issue price for these bonds is 92.277 (or 92.277% of par value). We show how to compute this issue price later in the chapter. These bonds obligate the issuer to pay two separate types of future cash flows:

1. Par value of $100,000 at the end of the bonds' five-year life.
2. Cash interest payments of $4,000 (4% × $100,000) at the end of each semiannual period during the bonds' five-year life.

The pattern of cash flows for the Fila's bonds is shown in Exhibit 15.4.

Exhibit 15.4

Cash Flows for Fila Bonds

When Fila accepts $92,277 cash for its bonds on the issue date of December 31, 2002, it records the sale as follows:

Dec. 31			
	Cash	92,277	
	Discount on Bonds Payable	7,723	
	Bonds Payable		100,000
	Sold bonds at a discount on their issue date.		

These bonds are reported in the long-term liability section of the issuer's December 31, 2002, balance sheet as shown in Exhibit 15.5.

Long-term liabilities		
Bonds payable, 8%, due December 31, 2007	$100,000	
Less discount on bonds payable	**7,723**	$92,277

Exhibit 15.5

Balance Sheet Presentation of Bond Discount

A discount is deducted from the par value of bonds to yield the **carrying (book) value** of the bonds payable. Discount on Bonds Payable is a contra liability account.

Amortizing a Bond Discount

The issuer (Fila) receives $92,277 for its bonds, but it must pay bondholders $100,000 after five years (plus semiannual interest payments). Notice the $7,723 discount is paid to bondholders at maturity and is part of the cost of using the $92,277 for five years. The upper portion of Exhibit 15.6 shows that total bond interest expense of $47,723 is the difference between the total amount repaid to bondholders ($140,000) and the amount borrowed from bondholders ($92,277). Alternatively, we can compute total bond interest expense as the sum of the 10 interest payments and the bond discount. This alternative computation is shown in the lower portion of Exhibit 15.6.

P2 Compute and record amortization of bond discount.

Point: The difference between the contract rate and market rate of interest on a new bond issue is usually a fraction of a percent. We use a difference of 2% to emphasize the effects.

Assets = Liabilities + Equity
+92,277 +100,000
−7,723

Point: Book value at issuance always equals the cash amount borrowed.

You Make the Call

Bond Rater You must assign a rating to a bond that reflects its risk to bondholders. Identify factors you consider in assessing bond risk. For the factors you identify, indicate their likely levels (relative to the norm) for a bond that sells at a discount.

Answer—p. 647

Point: *Zero-coupon bonds* do not pay periodic interest (contract rate is zero). These bonds always sell at a discount because their 0% contract rate is always below the market rate.

Exhibit 15.6

Total Interest Expense for
Bonds Issued at a Discount

Concept 15-2

Amount repaid to bondholders		
Ten interest payments of $4,000		$ 40,000
Par value at maturity		100,000
Total repaid to bondholders		$140,000
Less amount borrowed from bondholders		(92,277)
Total bond interest expense		**$ 47,723**
Alternative Computation		
Ten payments of $4,000		$ 40,000
Plus discount		7,723
Total bond interest expense		**$ 47,723**

Did You Know?

Junk Bonds Junk bonds are company bonds with low credit ratings. Issuers of junk bonds are more likely than average to default on repayment. On the upside, the high risk of junk bonds can yield high returns to junk bondholders if the issuer survives and repays its debt. Junk bond issuances are now running at over $100 billion a year. The percent of junk bond issuances in default fell from 33% to 9% in the past decade.

The total $47,723 bond interest expense must be allocated across the 10 semiannual periods in the bonds' life, and the carrying value of the bonds must be updated at each balance sheet date. Two alternative methods accomplish these steps: the straight-line and the effective interest methods. Both methods systematically reduce the discount on the bonds to zero over their five-year life. This process is called *amortizing the bond discount*.

Straight-Line Method

Global: Some countries such as Italy report bonds and notes at their par (face) value, and not at book value.

Point: The straight-line method was more widely used before development of inexpensive computers.

The **straight-line method** is the simpler of the two methods to amortize a bond discount. It allocates an equal portion of the total bond interest expense to each of the 10 semiannual interest periods. To apply the straight-line method to Fila's bonds, we divide the total bond interest expense of $47,723 by 10 (the number of semiannual periods in the bonds' life). This gives us a bond interest expense of $4,772 per period (all computations, including those for assignments, are rounded to the nearest whole dollar). Alternatively, we can find this number by dividing the $7,723 original discount by 10. The resulting $772 is the amount of discount to be amortized in each interest period. When the $772 of amortized discount is added to the $4,000 cash payment, the bond interest expense for each semiannual period is $4,772. In either case, the issuer records bond interest expense and updates the balance of the bond liability account for *each* semiannual period (June 30, 2003, through Dec. 31, 2007):

Assets = Liabilities + Equity
−4,000   +772   −4,772

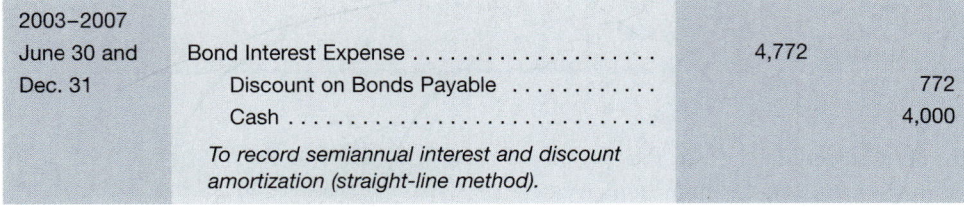

2003–2007			
June 30 and	Bond Interest Expense	4,772	
Dec. 31	Discount on Bonds Payable		772
	Cash		4,000
	To record semiannual interest and discount amortization (straight-line method).		

Global: Accounting for a discount and premium varies across countries. In some countries such as Belgium, Sweden, and Japan, a discount and premium can be immediately written off.

This entry is made at the end of each of the 10 semiannual interest periods. The $772 credit to the Discount on Bonds Payable account *increases* the bonds' carrying value. This increase occurs because a credit *decreases* the debit balance of the Discount on Bonds Payable (contra) account, which is subtracted from the Bonds Payable account. Exhibit 15.7 shows this pattern of decreases in the Discount on Bonds Payable account, along with the increase in the bonds' carrying value. The following points summarize straight-line amortization of the Fila discount bonds:

1. The $92,277 cash received from issued bonds equals the $100,000 par value less the initial $7,723 discount from issuing the bonds at less than par.

2. Semiannual bond interest expense of $4,772 equals total bond interest expense of $47,723 divided by the 10 semiannual periods (alternatively computed as the $4,000 cash paid

plus the periodic discount amortization of $772).

3. The semiannual credit to the Discount on Bonds Payable account equals the total $7,723 discount divided by 10 semiannual periods.

4. Semiannual $4,000 interest payment equals the bonds' $100,000 par value multiplied by the 4% semiannual contract rate.

5. Carrying (or book) value of bonds continues to increase each period by the $772 discount amortization until it equals par value when the bonds mature.

Semiannual Period-End	Unamortized Discount*	Carrying Value†
12/31/2002	$7,723	$ 92,277
6/30/2003	6,951	93,049
12/31/2003	6,179	93,821
6/30/2004	5,407	94,593
12/31/2004	4,635	95,365
6/30/2005	3,863	96,137
12/31/2005	3,091	96,909
6/30/2006	2,319	97,681
12/31/2006	1,547	98,453
6/30/2007	775	99,225
12/31/2007	**0‡**	**100,000**

Exhibit 15.7

Straight-Line Amortization of Bond Discount

* Total bond discount ($7,723) less accumulated periodic amortization ($772 per semiannual period).

† Bond par value less unamortized discount.

‡ Adjusted for rounding.

Notice that Fila incurs a $4,772 bond interest expense each period but pays only $4,000 cash. The $772 unpaid portion of this expense is added to the book balance (carrying value) of the liability by decreasing the Discount on Bonds Payable account balance. (The $7,723 unamortized discount is "paid" when the bonds mature—namely, $100,000 is paid at maturity when only $92,277 was received at issuance.)

Effective Interest Method

The straight-line method yields changes in the bonds' carrying value (see Exhibit 15.7) while the amount for bond interest expense remains constant (always equal to $4,772 for Fila bonds). This gives the impression of a changing interest rate when users divide a constant bond interest expense over a changing carrying value. As a result, accounting standards allow use of straight line only when its results do not differ materially from those obtained using the effective interest method. The **effective interest method,** or simply *interest method,* allocates total bond interest expense over the life of the bonds in a way that yields a constant rate of interest. This constant rate of interest is the market rate at the issue date. Bond interest expense for a period is then computed by multiplying the carrying value of the bond at the beginning of that period by the market rate when issued.

An *amortization table* can help track interest allocation and the balances of bond related accounts. Exhibit 15.8 shows an effective interest amortization table for the Fila bonds. The key difference between the effective interest and straight-line methods lies in computing bond interest expense. Instead of assigning an equal amount of bond interest expense to each period, the effective interest method assigns a bond interest expense amount that increases over the bonds' life. Both methods allocate the *same* $47,723 of total bond interest expense to the bonds' life, but in different patterns. Specifically, as with the straight-line method, the amortization table in Exhibit 15.8 shows that the balance of the discount (column D) is amortized by the effective interest method until it reaches zero. Also, the bonds' carrying value (column E) changes each period until it equals par value at maturity. Compare columns D and E to the columns in Exhibit 15.7. Moreover, total bond interest expense is $47,723, composed of $40,000 of semiannual cash payments and $7,723 of the original discount below par value—the same for both methods.

Except for differences in amounts, journal entries recording the expense and updating the liability balance are the same under the effective interest method and the straight-line method. For instance, we record the interest payment at the end of the first semiannual period:

Global: The U.S. generally requires use of the effective interest method, but some countries prefer straight-line amortization, and Brazil requires it.

Point: The effective interest method consistently computes bond interest expense using the market rate at issuance. This rate is applied to a changing carrying value.

2003			
June 30	Bond Interest Expense	4,614	
	Discount on Bonds Payable		614
	Cash		4,000
	To record semiannual interest and discount amortization (effective interest method).		

Assets = Liabilities + Equity
−4,000   +614   −4,614

Exhibit 15.8

Effective Interest Amortization
of Bond Discount

	Bonds: $100,000 Par Value, Semiannual Interest Payments, Five-Year Life, 4% Semiannual Contract Rate, 5% Semiannual Market Rate				
Semiannual Interest Period-End	**(A) Cash Interest Paid**	**(B) Bond Interest Expense**	**(C) Discount Amortization**	**(D) Unamortized Discount**	**(E) Carrying Value**
12/31/2002				$7,723	$ 92,277
6/30/2003	$ 4,000	$ 4,614	$ 614	7,109	92,891
12/31/2003	4,000	4,645	645	6,464	93,536
6/30/2004	4,000	4,677	677	5,787	94,213
12/31/2004	4,000	4,711	711	5,076	94,924
6/30/2005	4,000	4,746	746	4,330	95,670
12/31/2005	4,000	4,784	784	3,546	96,454
6/30/2006	4,000	4,823	823	2,723	97,277
12/31/2006	4,000	4,864	864	1,859	98,141
6/30/2007	4,000	4,907	907	952	99,048
12/31/2007	4,000	4,952	952	0	100,000
	$40,000	$47,723	$7,723		

Column (**A**) is par value ($100,000) multiplied by the semiannual contract rate (4%).

Column (**B**) is prior period's carrying value multiplied by the semiannual market rate (5%).

Column (**C**) is the difference between interest paid and bond interest expense, or $[(B) - (A)]$.

Column (**D**) is the prior period's unamortized discount less the current period's discount amortization.

Column (**E**) is par value less unamortized discount, or $[\$100,000 - (D)]$.

We can use the numbers in Exhibit 15.8 to record each semiannual entry throughout the five-year life of the bonds (June 30, 2003, through December 31, 2007).

Quick Check

Five-year, 6% bonds with a $100,000 par value are issued at a price of $91,893. Interest is paid semiannually, and the bonds' market rate is 8% on the issue date. Use this information to answer the following questions:

4. Are these bonds issued at a discount or premium? Explain why.

5. What is the issuer's journal entry to record the issuance of these bonds?

6. What is the amount of bond interest expense recorded at the first semiannual period using the (a) straight-line method and (b) effective interest method?

Answers—p. 647

Issuing Bonds at a Premium

P3　Compute and record amortization of bond premium.

When bonds have a contract rate higher than the market rate, they sell at a price higher than par value. The amount by which the bond price exceeds par value is the **premium on bonds.** To illustrate, assume that **Adidas** issues bonds with a $100,000 par value, a 12% annual contract rate, semiannual interest payments, and a five-year life. The market rate for Adidas's bonds is 10% on the issue date, meaning the bonds will sell at a premium because the contract rate is higher than the market rate. The exact issue price for these bonds is 107.72 (or 107.72% of par value). We show how to compute this issue price later in the chapter. These bonds obligate the issuer to pay out two separate future cash flows:

1. Par value of $100,000 at the end of the bonds' five-year life.

2. Cash interest payments of $6,000 (6% × $100,000) at the end of each semiannual period during the bonds' five-year life.

The pattern of cash flows for the Adidas's bonds is shown in Exhibit 15.9.

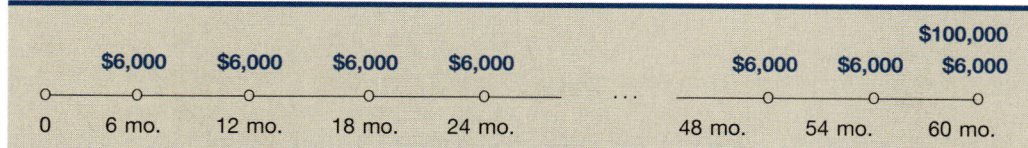

Exhibit 15.9

Cash Flows for Adidas Bonds

When Adidas accepts $107,720 cash for its bonds on the issue date of December 31, 2002, it records this transaction as follows:

Dec. 31	Cash	107,720	
	Premium on Bonds Payable		7,720
	Bonds Payable		100,000
	Sold bonds at a premium on their issue date.		

Assets = Liabilities + Equity
+107,720 +100,000
        +7,720

These bonds are reported in the long-term liability section of the issuer's December 31, 2002, balance sheet as shown in Exhibit 15.10.

Long-term liabilities		
Bonds payable, 12%, due December 31, 2007	$100,000	
Plus premium on bonds payable	**7,720**	$107,720

Exhibit 15.10

Balance Sheet Presentation of Bond Premium

A premium is added to par value to yield the carrying (book) value of bonds payable. Premium on Bonds Payable is an adjunct (also called *accretion*) liability account.

Amortizing a Bond Premium

The issuer (Adidas) receives $107,720 for its bonds, but it will pay bondholders only $100,000 after five years (plus semiannual interest payments). This $7,720 premium not re-paid to bondholders at maturity goes to reduce the expense of using the $107,720 for five years. The upper portion of Exhibit 15.11 shows that total bond interest expense of $52,280 is the difference between the total amount repaid to bondholders ($160,000) and the amount borrowed from bondholders ($107,720). Alternatively, we can compute total bond interest expense as the sum of the 10 interest payments less the bond premium. The premium is sub-tracted because it will not be paid to bondholders when the bonds mature—see the lower portion of Exhibit 15.11. Total bond interest expense must be allocated over the 10 semi-annual periods using either the straight-line or the effective interest method.

Amount repaid to bondholders	
Ten interest payments of $6,000	$ 60,000
Par value at maturity	100,000
Total repaid to bondholders	$160,000
Less amount borrowed from bondholders	(107,720)
Total bond interest expense	**$ 52,280**
Alternative Computation	
Ten payments of $6,000	$ 60,000
Less premium	(7,720)
Total bond interest expense	**$ 52,280**

Exhibit 15.11

Total Interest Expense for Bonds Issued at a Premium

Straight-Line Method

We explained earlier how the straight-line method allocates an equal portion of total bond interest expense to each of the bonds' semiannual interest periods. To apply the straight-line method to Adidas's bonds, we divide the five years' total bond interest expense of $52,280 by 10 (the number of semiannual periods in the bonds' life). This gives a total bond interest expense of $5,228 per period. The issuer records bond interest expense and updates the balance of the bond liability account for *each* semiannual period (June 30, 2003, through Dec. 31, 2007) as follows:

Point: Notice that a premium decreases Bond Interest Expense while a discount increases it.

Assets = Liabilities + Equity
−6,000   −772   −5,228

2003–2007 June 30 and Dec. 31	Bond Interest Expense	5,228	
	Premium on Bonds Payable	772	
	Cash		6,000
	To record semiannual interest and premium amortization (straight-line method).		

This entry is made at the end of each of the 10 semiannual interest periods. The $772 debit to the Premium on Bonds Payable account *decreases* the bonds' carrying value. Exhibit 15.12 shows this decrease in the unamortized premium for the five-year bond life.

Exhibit 15.12

Straight-Line Amortization of Bond Premium

Semiannual Period-End	Unamortized Premium*	Carrying Value†
12/31/2002	$7,720	$107,720
6/30/2003	6,948	106,948
12/31/2003	6,176	106,176
6/30/2004	5,404	105,404
12/31/2004	4,632	104,632
6/30/2005	3,860	103,860
12/31/2005	3,088	103,088
6/30/2006	2,316	102,316
12/31/2006	1,544	101,544
6/30/2007	772	100,772
12/31/2007	0	100,000

* Total bond premium ($7,720) less accumulated periodic amortization ($772 per semiannual period).

† Bond par value plus unamortized premium.

Effective Interest Method

Exhibit 15.13 shows the amortization table using the effective interest method for Adidas's bonds. Column A lists the semiannual cash payments. Column B shows the amount of bond interest expense, computed as the 5% market rate at issuance multiplied by the beginning-of-period carrying value. The amount of cash paid in column A is larger than the bond interest expense because the cash payment is based on the higher 6% contract rate. The excess cash payment over the interest expense reduces the principal. These amounts are shown in column C. Column E shows the carrying value after deducting the amortized premium in column C from the prior period's carrying value. Column D shows how the premium is reduced by periodic amortization. When the issuer makes the first semiannual interest payment, the effect of premium amortization on bond interest expense and bond liability is recorded as:

Assets = Liabilities + Equity
−6,000   −614   −5,386

2003 June 30	Bond Interest Expense	5,386	
	Premium on Bonds Payable	614	
	Cash		6,000
	To record semiannual interest and premium amortization (effective interest method).		

Similar entries with different amounts are recorded at each payment date until the bond matures at the end of 2007. The effective interest method yields decreasing amounts of bond interest expense and increasing amounts of premium amortization over the bonds' life.

Bonds: $100,000 Par Value, Semiannual Interest Payments, Five-Year Life, 6% Semiannual Contract Rate, 5% Semiannual Market Rate					
Semiannual Interest Period-End	(A) Cash Interest Paid	(B) Bond Interest Expense	(C) Premium Amortization	(D) Unamortized Premium	(E) Carrying Value
12/31/2002				$7,720	$107,720
6/30/2003	$ 6,000	$ 5,386	$ 614	7,106	107,106
12/31/2003	6,000	5,355	645	6,461	106,461
6/30/2004	6,000	5,323	677	5,784	105,784
12/31/2004	6,000	5,289	711	5,073	105,073
6/30/2005	6,000	5,254	746	4,327	104,327
12/31/2005	6,000	5,216	784	3,543	103,543
6/30/2006	6,000	5,177	823	2,720	102,720
12/31/2006	6,000	5,136	864	1,856	101,856
6/30/2007	6,000	5,093	907	949	100,949
12/31/2007	6,000	5,051*	949	0	100,000
	$60,000	$52,280	$7,720		

Exhibit 15.13

Effective Interest Amortization of Bond Premium

Column (A) is par value ($100,000) multiplied by the semiannual contract rate (6%).

Column (B) is prior period's carrying value multiplied by the semiannual market rate (5%).

Column (C) is the difference between interest paid and bond interest expense, or [(A) − (B)].

Column (D) is the prior period's unamortized premium less the current period's premium amortization.

Column (E) is par value plus unamortized premium, or [$100,000 + (D)].

* Adjusted for rounding.

Issuing Bonds between Interest Dates

An issuer can sell bonds at a date other than an interest payment date. When this occurs, the buyers normally pay the issuer the purchase price plus any interest accrued since the prior interest payment date. This accrued interest is then repaid to these buyers on the next interest payment date. To illustrate, suppose **Avia** sells $100,000 of its 9% bonds at par on March 1, 2002, two months after the stated issue date. The interest on Avia's bonds is payable semiannually on each June 30 and December 31. Because two months have passed, the issuer collects two months' interest from the buyers at the time of issuance. This amount is $1,500 ($100,000 × 9% × 2/12 year). This case is reflected in Exhibit 15.14.

> **Did You Know?**
>
> **Excel Amortization** Spreadsheet and accounting software such as **Excel** and **PeachTree** make amortization tables easy. We need only enter the bonds' par value, selling price, contract rate, and life to get a complete amortization table.

Exhibit 15.14

Accruing Interest between Interest Payment Dates

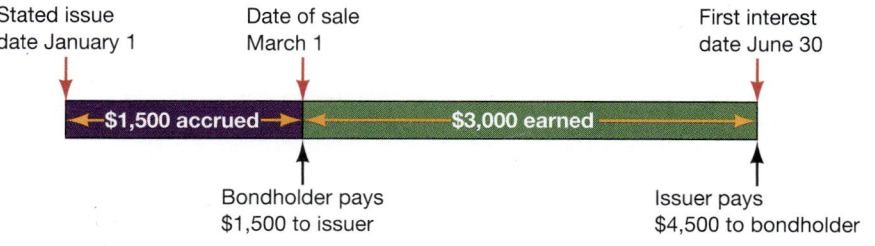

Avia records the issuance of these bonds on March 1, 2002, as follows:

Mar. 1	Cash	101,500	
	Interest Payable		1,500
	Bonds Payable		100,000
	Sold bonds at par with accrued interest.		

Assets = Liabilities + Equity
+101,500 +100,000
          +1,500

Example: How much interest is collected from a buyer of $50,000 of Avia bonds sold at par on June 1, 2002? *Answer:* $1,875 (computed as $50,000 × 9% × $\frac{2}{12}$ year)

Note that liabilities for interest payable and bonds payable are recorded in separate accounts. When the June 30, 2002, semiannual interest date arrives, Avia pays a full six months' interest of $4,500 ($100,000 × 9% × ½ year) to the bondholders. This payment includes the four months' interest of $3,000 earned by the bondholders from March 1 to June 30 *plus* the repayment of two months' accrued interest collected by Avia when the bonds were sold. Avia records this first semiannual interest payment as follows:

Assets = Liabilities + Equity
−4,500   −1,500   −3,000

June 30	Interest Payable	1,500	
	Bond Interest Expense	3,000	
	Cash		4,500
	Paid semiannual interest on the bonds.		

The practice of collecting and then repaying accrued interest with the next interest payment is to simplify the issuer's administrative efforts. To explain, suppose an issuer sells bonds on 15 or 20 different dates between the stated issue date and the first interest payment date. If the issuer did not collect accrued interest from buyers, it would need to pay different amounts of cash to each of them according to the time that had passed since they purchased the bonds. The issuer would need to keep detailed records of buyers and the dates they bought bonds. Issuers avoid this recordkeeping by having each buyer pay accrued interest at the time of purchase. Issuers then pay a full six months' interest to all buyers, regardless of when they bought bonds.

Global: In some countries such as Kuwait, Saudi Arabia, and Iran, charging explicit interest for use of money is rare due to Islamic Law.

Accruing Bond Interest Expense

If a bond's interest period does not coincide with the issuer's accounting period, an adjusting entry is necessary to recognize bond interest expense accrued since the most recent interest payment. To illustrate, assume the Adidas bonds described in Exhibit 15.13 are issued on a stated issue date of September 1, 2002, instead of December 31, 2002. As a result, four months' interest (and premium amortization) accrue before the end of the 2002 calendar year. Interest for these four months equals $3,591, which is $\frac{4}{6}$ of the first six months' interest of $5,386. The premium amortization is $409, which is $\frac{4}{6}$ of the first six months' amortization of $614. The sum of the bond interest expense and the amortization is $4,000 ($3,591 + $409), which equals $\frac{4}{6}$ of the $6,000 cash payment due on February 28, 2003. Adidas records these effects with an adjusting entry at December 31, 2002:

Assets = Liabilities + Equity
          −409   −3,591
         +4,000

Dec. 31	Bond Interest Expense	3,591	
	Premium on Bonds Payable	409	
	Interest Payable		4,000
	To record four months' accrued interest and premium amortization.		

Similar entries with different amounts are made on each December 31 throughout the five-year life of the bonds. When the $6,000 cash payment occurs on each February 28 interest payment date, Adidas must recognize bond interest expense and amortization for January and February. It must also eliminate the interest payable liability created by the December 31 adjusting entry. For example, Adidas records payment on February 28, 2003, as:

Assets = Liabilities + Equity
−6,000   −4,000   −1,795
        −205

Feb. 28	Interest Payable	4,000	
	Bond Interest Expense ($5,386 × $\frac{2}{6}$)	1,795	
	Premium on Bonds Payable ($614 × $\frac{2}{6}$)	205	
	Cash		6,000
	To record two months' interest and amortization and eliminate accrued interest liability.		

The interest payments made each August 31 are recorded as usual because the entire six-month interest period is included within this company's calendar year reporting period.

Bond Pricing

Prices for bonds traded on an organized exchange are often published in newspapers and available through online services. This information normally includes the bond price (called *quote*), its contract rate, and its current market (called *yield*) rate. However, only a fraction of bonds are traded on organized exchanges. To compute the price of a bond, we apply present value concepts. This section explains how we use *present value concepts* to price the Fila discount bond and the Adidas premium bond described earlier.

Point: Access BondOnline.com for information on investing in bonds.

Present Value of a Discount Bond

The issue price of bonds is found by computing the present value of the bonds' cash payments, discounted at the bonds' market rate. When computing the present value of the Fila bonds, we work with *semiannual* compounding periods because this is the time between interest payments; the annual market rate of 10% is considered as a semiannual rate of 5%. Also, the five-year bond life is viewed as 10 semiannual periods. The computation is twofold: (1) find the present value of the $100,000 par value paid at maturity and (2) find the present value of the series of 10 payments of $4,000 each; see Exhibit 15.4. These present values can be found by using present value tables. Appendix B at the end of this book shows present value tables and describes their use. Table B.1 in Appendix B is used for the single $100,000 maturity payment, and Table B.3 in Appendix B is used for the $4,000 series of interest payments. Specifically, we go to Table B.1, row 10, and across to the 5% column to identify the present value factor of 0.6139 for the maturity payment. Next, we go to Table B.3, row 10, and across to the 5% column, where the present value factor is 7.7217 for the series of interest payments. Then, we compute bond price by multiplying the cash flow payments by their corresponding present value factors and adding them together—see Exhibit 15.15.

Point: A bond's market value (issue price) at issuance equals the present value of all its future cash payments (where the interest rate equals the bond's market rate).

Point: Many calculators provide present value functions for computation of bond prices.

Cash Flow	Table	Present Value Factor		Amount		Present Value
$100,000 par (maturity) value	B.1	0.6139	×	$100,000	=	$61,390
$4,000 interest payments	B.3	7.7217	×	4,000	=	30,887
Price of bond						$92,277

Exhibit 15.15

Computing Issue Price for Fila Bonds

Present Value of a Premium Bond

We get the issue price of the Adidas bonds by using the market rate to compute the present value of its future cash flows. When computing the present value of these bonds, we again work with *semiannual* compounding periods because this is the time between interest payments. The annual 10% market rate is applied as a semiannual rate of 5%, and the five-year bond life is viewed as 10 semiannual periods. The computation is twofold: (1) find the present value of the $100,000 par value paid at maturity and (2) find the present value of the series of 10 payments of $6,000 each; see Exhibit 15.9. These present values can be found by using present value tables. First, go to Table B.1, row 10, and across to the 5% column where the present value factor is 0.6139 for the maturity payment. Second, go to Table B.3, row 10, and across to the 5% column, where the present value factor is 7.7217 for the series of interest payments. The bonds' price is computed by multiplying the cash flow payments by their corresponding present value factors and adding them together—see Exhibit 15.16.

Point: Access InvestingInBonds.com for use as a bond research and learning source.

Point: There are nearly 5 million individual U.S. bond issues—ranging from huge treasuries to tiny municipalities. This compares to about 12,000 individual U.S. stocks that are traded.

Cash Flow	Table	Present Value Factor		Amount		Present Value
$100,000 par (maturity) value	B.1	0.6139	×	$100,000	=	$61,390
$6,000 interest payments	B.3	7.7217	×	6,000	=	46,330
Price of bond						$107,720

Exhibit 15.16

Computing Issue Price for Adidas Bonds

Quick Check

On December 31, 2001, a company issues 16%, 10-year bonds with a par value of $100,000. Interest is paid on June 30 and December 31. The bonds are sold to yield a 14% annual market rate at an issue price of $110,592. Use this information to answer questions 7 through 9:

7. Are these bonds issued at a discount or premium? Explain.

8. Using the effective interest method to allocate bond interest expense, the issuer records the second interest payment (on December 31, 2002) with a debit to Premium on Bonds Payable in the amount of (a) $7,470, (b) $7,741, (c) $259, (d) $530, or (e) $277.

9. How are these bonds reported in the long-term liability section of the issuer's balance sheet as of December 31, 2002?

10. On May 1, a company sells 9% bonds with a $500,000 par value that pays semiannual interest on each January 1 and July 1. The bonds are sold at par value plus interest accrued since January 1. The issuer records the first semiannual interest payment on July 1 with (a) a debit to Interest Payable for $15,000, (b) a debit to Bond Interest Expense for $22,500, or (c) a credit to Interest Payable for $7,500.

Answers—p. 647

Bond Retirement

P4 Record the retirement of bonds.

This section describes the retirement of bonds (1) at maturity, (2) before maturity, and (3) by converting them to stock.

Bond Retirement at Maturity

The carrying value of bonds at maturity always equals par value. For example, both Exhibits 15.8 (a discount) and 15.13 (a premium) show that the carrying value of these bonds at the end of their five-year life equals par value ($100,000). To record retirement of these bonds at maturity, assuming interest is already paid and entered, is recorded as follows:

Assets = Liabilities + Equity
−100,000   −100,000

2007			
Dec. 31	Bonds Payable	100,000	
	Cash		100,000
	To record retirement of bonds at maturity.		

Bond Retirement before Maturity

Point: Bond retirement is also referred to as *bond redemption*.

Global: Some countries such as Spain, Germany, and Korea offer no specific accounting guidelines for retirement of bonds or debt.

Issuers sometimes wish to retire some or all of their bonds prior to maturity. For instance, if interest rates decline significantly, an issuer may wish to replace high-interest-paying bonds with new low-interest bonds. Two common ways to retire bonds before maturity are to (1) exercise a call option or (2) purchase them on the open market. In the first instance, an issuer can reserve the right to retire bonds early by issuing callable bonds. The bond indenture can give the issuer an option to *call* the bonds before they mature by paying the par value plus a *call premium* to bondholders. In the second case, the issuer retires bonds by repurchasing them on the open market at their current price. Whether bonds are called or repurchased, the issuer is unlikely to pay a price that exactly equals their carrying value. When a difference exists between the bonds' carrying value and the amount paid, the issuer records a gain or loss equal to the difference. (Gains and losses from retiring bonds or other debt must be reported on the issuer's income statement as an extraordinary item.)

To illustrate the accounting for retiring callable bonds, assume that a company issued callable bonds with a par value of $100,000. The call option requires the issuer to pay a call premium of $3,000 to bondholders in addition to the par value. Next, assume that after the June 30, 2002, interest payment, the bonds have a carrying value of $104,500. Then on

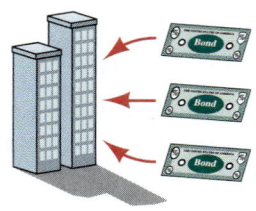
Callable Bond

July 1, 2002, the issuer calls these bonds and pays $103,000 to bondholders. The issuer recognizes a $1,500 gain from the difference between the bonds' carrying value of $104,500 and the retirement price of $103,000. The issuer records this bond retirement as:

July 1	Bonds Payable	100,000	
	Premium on Bonds Payable	4,500	
	Gain on Bond Retirement (extraordinary)		1,500
	Cash		103,000
	To record retirement of bonds before maturity.		

Assets = Liabilities + Equity
−103,000 −100,000 +1,500
−4,500

An issuer usually must call all bonds when it exercises a call option. However, to retire as many or as few bonds as it desires, an issuer can purchase them on the open market. If it retires less than the entire class of bonds, it recognizes a gain or loss for the difference between the carrying value of those bonds retired and the amount paid to acquire them.

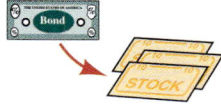

Convertible Bond

Bond Retirement by Conversion

We described convertible bonds earlier in the chapter and explained how these bondholders have the right to convert their bonds to stock. When conversion occurs, the bonds' carrying value is transferred to capital accounts and no gain or loss is recorded (the market prices of the bonds and stock are not relevant to the entry for conversion). Knowledge of the material in Chapter 14 is helpful in understanding this transaction. To illustrate, assume that on January 1 the $100,000 par value bonds of **Converse**, with a carrying value of $100,000, are converted to 15,000 shares of $2 par value common stock. The entry to record this conversion is:

Did You Know?

Cruis'n Convertibles Over the past decade, convertible bonds have delivered about 80% of the returns of diversified stock funds but with only 66% of the price volatility. Convertibles protect holders

Bonds	Return
Convertible Bonds	17.8%
L-T Gov. Bonds	12.1
L-T Corp. Bonds	11.3
L-T Munis	9.9
International Bonds	9.9
All Bond Funds	9.4

against stock price declines, yet they give holders the chance to make more money if stock prices increase by converting bonds to stock.

Jan. 1	Bonds Payable	100,000	
	Common Stock		30,000
	Contributed Capital in Excess of Par Value		70,000
	To record retirement of bonds by conversion.		

Assets = Liabilities + Equity
−100,000 +30,000
+70,000

Quick Check

11. Six years ago, a company issued $500,000 of 6%, eight-year bonds at a price of 95. The current carrying value is $493,750. The company decides to retire 50% of these bonds by buying them on the open market at a price of 102½. What is the amount of gain or loss on retirement of these bonds?

Answer—p. 647

Like bonds, notes are issued to obtain assets such as cash. Unlike bonds, notes are typically transacted with a *single* lender such as a bank. An issuer initially records a note at its selling price—the note's face value minus any discount or plus any premium. Over the note's life, the amount of interest expense allocated to each period is computed by multiplying the market rate (at issuance of the note) by the beginning-of-period balance of the note. The note's carrying (book) value at any point in time equals its face value minus any unamortized discount or plus any unamortized premium—carrying value is computed as the present value of all remaining future payments, discounted using the market rate at the time of issuance.

Long-Term Notes Payable

 C2 Explain the types and payment patterns of notes.

Interest-Bearing Notes

Assume that a company buys Web server equipment on January 2, 2002, with a market value of $45,000 by issuing an 8%, three-year note with a face value of $45,000 to the seller. The note pays its accumulated interest *at maturity,* and the market rate applied to the note at the time of issuance is 8%. The company records this purchase as follows:

Assets = Liabilities + Equity
+45,000   +45,000

Jan. 2	Equipment	45,000	
	Notes Payable		45,000
	Issued a note payable for equipment.		

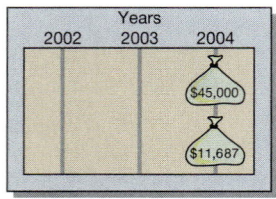

The issuer's annual interest expense is computed by multiplying each year's beginning balance by the 8% market rate at issuance. Interest is then added to the note's beginning balance to yield its year-end balance. A period's ending balance then becomes next period's beginning balance. Exhibit 15.17 shows annual interest expense computations and the yearly balances of the note. The amount of annual interest expense increases over the life of the note because the balance grows from compounding. The final ending balance of $56,687 equals the original $45,000 borrowed plus accumulated interest of $11,687. A note such as this that delays interest payments is usually issued by low-risk companies that wish to defer their cash payments. This type of note is often backed with assets as collateral. The annual interest is accrued at each year-end. For example, at December 31, 2002, the company debits Interest Expense and credits Interest Payable for $3,600. The company records the payment of both accrued interest ($3,600 + $3,888 + $4,199) and principal ($45,000) at January 2, 2005, as follows:

You Make the Call

Entrepreneur   You are an electronics retailer planning a holiday sale on a custom stereo system that requires no payments for two years. At the end of two years, buyers must pay the full amount. The system's suggested retail price is $4,100, but you are willing to sell it today for $3,000 cash. What is your holiday sale price if payment will not occur for two years and the market interest rate is 10%?

Answer—p. 647

Assets = Liabilities + Equity
−56,687   −11,687
         −45,000

Jan. 2	Interest Payable	11,687	
	Notes Payable	45,000	
	Cash		56,687
	Paid interest-bearing note at maturity.		

Exhibit 15.17

Interest-Bearing Note with Interest Paid at Maturity

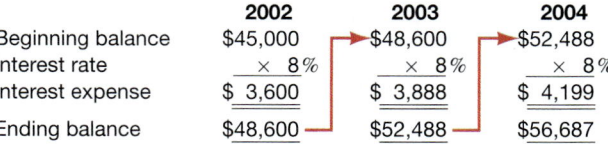

	2002	**2003**	**2004**
Beginning balance	$45,000	$48,600	$52,488
Interest rate	× 8%	× 8%	× 8%
Interest expense	$ 3,600	$ 3,888	$ 4,199
Ending balance	$48,600	$52,488	$56,687

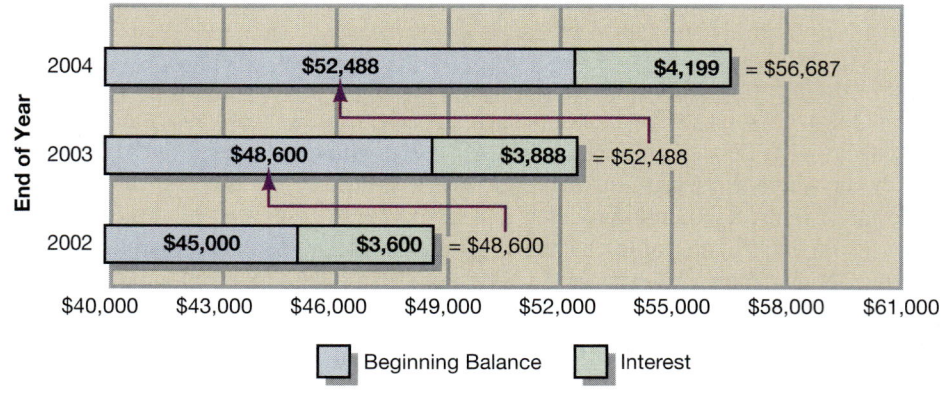

Noninterest-Bearing Notes

A *noninterest-bearing note* includes interest in its face (maturity) value. When a noninterest-bearing note is used to acquire an asset such as cash, the note's face value (because it includes interest) is higher than the asset's market value. Both the note and the asset are recorded at the market value of either the note or the asset, whichever is more determinable. A note's market value, like that of a bond, is computed using the market rate when it is issued. An asset's market value is determined by current market transactions.

To illustrate, assume that a company buys machinery on January 2, 2001, by issuing a noninterest-bearing, five-year, $10,000 note payable. Exhibit 15.18 shows this note's cash flows. This company decides its estimate of the machinery's

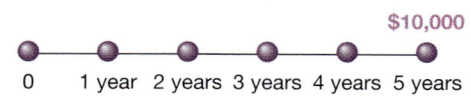

Exhibit 15.18

Cash Flows for Noninterest-Bearing Note

market value is less reliable than using the current 10% market rate to value the note. The note's market value when issued, using a 10% rate, is $6,209.[2] (This amount is the implied market value of the machinery.) This purchase is recorded as follows:

Jan. 2	Machinery	6,209	
	Discount on Notes Payable	3,791	
	Notes Payable		10,000
	Exchanged a five-year note for machinery.		

Assets	=	Liabilities	+	Equity
+6,209		−3,791		
		+10,000		

The $3,791 debit to Discount on Notes Payable is the *total interest expense* to be allocated among the five years of the note's life. Exhibit 15.19 shows each year's interest, the allocation of the discount, and the note's balance for its five-year life. The note's *net* balance increases over the five years until it reaches its $10,000 face value at the end of five years. The Discount on Notes Payable balance decreases from $3,791 at January 2, 2001, to $0 after five years. This pattern reflects the *amortizing of the discount*. The process of computing each year's interest is the same as in the previous example of the interest-bearing

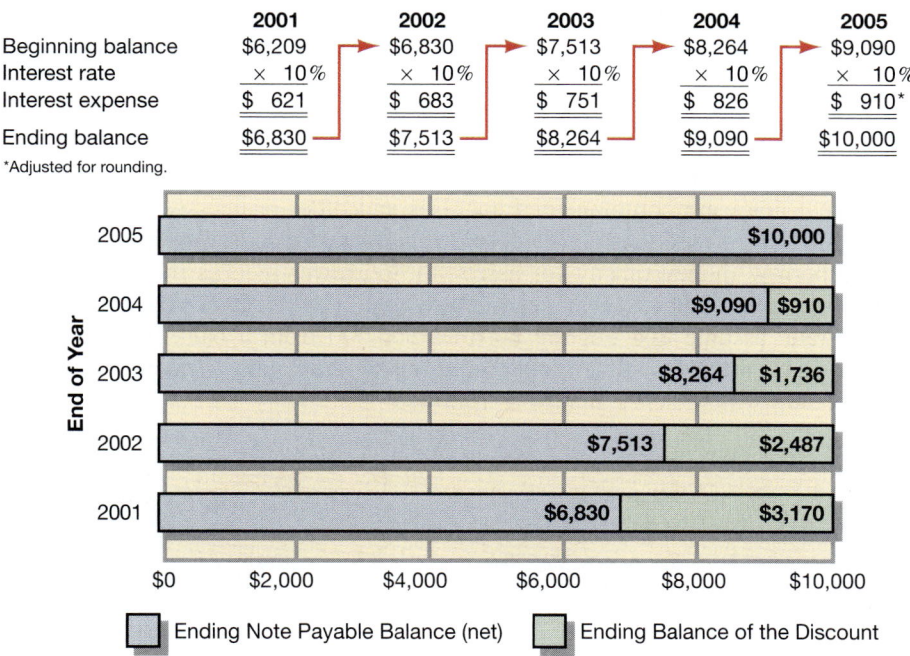

Exhibit 15.19

Noninterest-Bearing Note

---

[2] The note's market value is computed as the present value of the $10,000 payment due after five years discounted at the 10% market rate. Table B.1 in Appendix B shows the present value of 1 discounted at 10% for five years is 0.6209. The present (market) value of the note is $6,209, computed as $10,000 × 0.6209.

Point: The Discount on Notes Payable account can be viewed as "deferred interest expense."

note. In particular, the note's net balance at the beginning of each year is multiplied by the 10% market rate from the time of the note's issuance to determine interest for that year. The first year's interest expense and discount amortization ($6,209 × 10%) are recorded when we make year-end adjusting entries for that first year as follows:

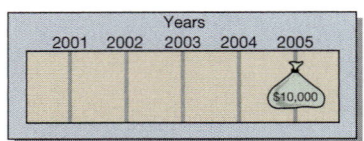

2001			
Dec. 31	Interest Expense	621	
	Discount on Notes Payable		621
	To record first year's interest expense on note.		

Assets = Liabilities + Equity
+621   −621

Similar entries with different amounts are recorded at each year-end until the balance of the discount account equals $0 and the note payable net balance equals $10,000. When the note payable matures on January 2, 2006, the issuer records its payment as follows:

2006			
Jan. 2	Notes Payable	10,000	
	Cash		10,000
	Paid noninterest-bearing note at maturity.		

Assets = Liabilities + Equity
−10,000   −10,000

Quick Check

12. On January 1, 2002, a company signs a $6,000 three-year note payable bearing 6% annual interest. The principal and all three years' interest (compounded annually) are paid on December 31, 2004. How much interest expense is allocated to year 2003? (a) $0, (b) $360, (c) $381.60, (d) $404.50.

13. A company promises to pay a lender $4,000 at the end of four years. The annual market interest rate is 8% and interest is included in the $4,000 payment. This means the note's current (present) value is $2,940. Record this note's issuance.

Answers—p. 648

Installment Notes

P5 Prepare entries to account for notes.

An **installment note** is an obligation requiring a series of periodic payments to the lender. Installment notes are common for franchises and other businesses when lenders and borrowers agree to spread these large costs over several periods. When an installment note is used to borrow money or pay for assets, the borrower records the note with an increase (debit) to cash or other assets and an increase (credit) to the Notes Payable liability account. To illustrate, assume that Foghog borrows $60,000 from a bank to purchase equipment. Foghog signs an 8% installment note requiring six annual payments of principal plus interest and records the note's issuance as follows:

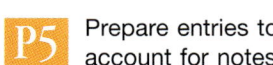

Dec. 31	Cash	60,000	
	Notes Payable		60,000
	Borrowed $60,000 by signing an 8%, six-year installment note.		

Assets = Liabilities + Equity
+60,000   +60,000

Alternatively, Foghog could issue a note directly to the seller of the equipment. In this case, it records the equipment received instead of cash.

Payments on an installment note normally include the interest expense accruing to the date of the payment plus a portion of the amount borrowed (the *principal*). Generally, we can identify two payment pattern types: (1) accrued interest plus equal principal payments and (2) equal payments. This section describes these two patterns and how we account for them.

Accrued Interest plus Equal Principal Payments

One common payment pattern for an installment note is accrued interest plus equal amounts of principal. This pattern creates cash flows that decrease in size over the note's life. This decrease occurs because each principal payment reduces the note's principal balance, yielding less accrued interest expense for the next period.

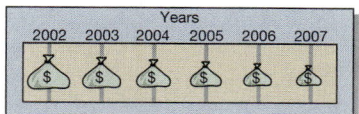

To illustrate, assume that Foghog's $60,000, 8% note requires it to make a payment at the end of each of six years equal to *accrued interest plus $10,000 of principal*. Exhibit 15.20 shows these payments and the changes in the balance of this note. Column A lists the note's annual beginning balance. Columns B, C, and D list each annual cash payment and its division between interest and principal. Column B shows interest expense for each year at 8% of the beginning balance. Column C shows that each principal payment reduces the Notes Payable account balance by $10,000. Column D is the total annual payment. Column E shows the note's ending balance, which equals the beginning balance in column A minus the principal payment in column C. We include *debit* or *credit* in column headings to show the accounting effects. Note that the sum of debits to both interest expense and notes payable equals the credit to Cash. Also notice that total interest expense is $16,800 and total principal is $60,000, which means cash payments for the five years total $76,800. The graph in

Exhibit 15.20

Installment Note:
Accrued Interest plus
Equal Principal Payments

Period Ending Date	(A) Beginning Balance	(B) Debit Interest Expense 8% × (A)	+	(C) Debit Notes Payable $60,000/6	=	(D) Credit Cash (B) + (C)	(E) Ending Balance (A) − (C)
12/31/2002	$60,000	$ 4,800		$10,000		$14,800	$50,000
12/31/2003	50,000	4,000		10,000		14,000	40,000
12/31/2004	40,000	3,200		10,000		13,200	30,000
12/31/2005	30,000	2,400		10,000		12,400	20,000
12/31/2006	20,000	1,600		10,000		11,600	10,000
12/31/2007	10,000	800		10,000		10,800	0
		$16,800		$60,000		$76,800	

Legend: □ Principal ■ Interest

Equal Principal Payments — Decreasing Accrued Interest — Decreasing Total Payments

End of Year	Cash Payment Pattern
2007	$10,000	$800
2006	$10,000	$1,600
2005	$10,000	$2,400
2004	$10,000	$3,200
2003	$10,000	$4,000
2002	$10,000	$4,800

0    $2,500 $5,000 $7,500 $10,000 $12,500 $15,000

Cash Payment Pattern

the lower portion of Exhibit 15.20 shows the decreasing pattern in total payments made up of decreasing accrued interest and constant principal payments. Foghog records its first two payments (for years 2002 and 2003) as follows:

Assets = Liabilities + Equity
−14,800   −10,000   −4,800

Dec. 31	Interest Expense	4,800	
	Notes Payable	10,000	
	Cash		14,800
	To record first installment payment.		

Assets = Liabilities + Equity
−14,000   −10,000   −4,000

Dec. 31	Interest Expense	4,000	
	Notes Payable	10,000	
	Cash		14,000
	To record second installment payment.		

After all six payments are recorded, the balance of the Notes Payable account is zero.

Equal Total Payments

A common type of installment note requires the borrower to make a series of equal payments that consist of changing amounts of both interest and principal. To illustrate, assume that Foghog borrows $60,000 by signing a $60,000 note that requires six *equal payments* of $12,979 at the end of each year. (The present value of an annuity of six annual payments of $12,979, discounted at 8%, equals $60,000—we show this computation later in the section.) The $12,979 includes both interest and principal, the amounts of which change with each payment. Exhibit 15.21 shows the pattern of equal total payments and its two parts, interest and principal. Column A shows the note's beginning balance. Column B shows accrued interest for each year at 8% of the beginning note balance. Column C shows the change in the note's principal, which equals the difference between the total payment in column D and the interest expense in column B. Column E shows the note's annual ending balance.

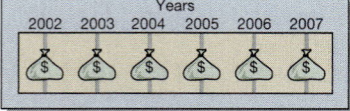
Years
2002 2003 2004 2005 2006 2007

Although the six cash payments are equal, accrued interest decreases each year because the principal balance of the note declines. As the amount of interest decreases each year, the portion of each payment applied to principal increases. This pattern is graphed in the lower part of Exhibit 15.21. Foghog uses the amounts in Exhibit 15.21 to record its first two payments (for years 2002 and 2003) as follows:

Point: Most consumer notes are installment notes that require equal total payments.

Assets = Liabilities + Equity
−12,979   −8,179   −4,800

Dec. 31	Interest Expense	4,800	
	Notes Payable	8,179	
	Cash		12,979
	To record first installment payment.		

Assets = Liabilities + Equity
−12,979   −8,833   −4,146

Dec. 31	Interest Expense	4,146	
	Notes Payable	8,833	
	Cash		12,979
	To record second installment payment.		

Foghog records similar entries but with different amounts for each of the remaining four payments. After six years, the Notes Payable account balance is zero.

It is useful to compare the two payment patterns in Exhibits 15.20 and 15.21. The series of equal total payments yields more interest expense over the life of the note because the first

Period Ending Date	(A) Beginning Balance	Payments			(E) Ending Balance (A) − (C)
		(B) Debit Interest Expense 8% × (A) +	**(C) Debit Notes Payable (D) − (B)** =	**(D) Credit Cash (computed)**	
12/31/2002	$60,000	$ 4,800	$ 8,179	$12,979	$51,821
12/31/2003	51,821	4,146	8,833	12,979	42,988
12/31/2004	42,988	3,439	9,540	12,979	33,448
12/31/2005	33,448	2,676	10,303	12,979	23,145
12/31/2006	23,145	1,852	11,127	12,979	12,018
12/31/2007	12,018	961	12,018	12,979	0
		$17,874	$60,000	$77,874	

Exhibit 15.21

Installment Note: Equal Total Payments

Cash Payment Pattern

three payments in Exhibit 15.21 are smaller and do not reduce the principal as quickly as the first three payments in Exhibit 15.20.[3]

Mortgage Notes

A **mortgage** is a legal agreement that helps protect a lender if a borrower fails to make required payments on bonds or notes. A mortgage gives the lender a right to be paid from the cash proceeds of the sale of a borrower's assets identified in the mortgage. A legal document, called a *mortgage contract,* describes the mortgage terms.

Example: Suppose the $60,000 installment loan has an 8% interest rate with eight equal annual payments. What is the annual payment? *Answer:* (Using Table B.3) $60,000/5.7466 = $10,441

---

[3] Table B.3 in Appendix B is used to compute the dollar amount of the six payments equivalent to the initial note balance of $60,000 at 8% interest. We go to Table B.3, row 6, and across to the 8% column, where the value is 4.6229. The payment amount is then computed by solving this relation:

Table	Present Value Factor		Amount		Present Value
B.3 ...	4.6229	×	?	=	60,000

We solve for the payment amount by dividing $60,000 by 4.6229, yielding $12,979.

Point: The Truth-in-Lending Act requires lenders to provide consumers information about the cost of their loans. This includes finance charges and the annual interest rate.

Mortgage notes carry a mortgage contract pledging title to specific assets as security for the note. While less common, *mortgage bonds* backed by the issuer's assets also exist. A mortgage contract is given to the lender who accepts a mortgage note or to the trustee of mortgage bonds. This contract usually requires the issuer (borrower) to pay all property taxes on the mortgaged assets, to maintain them properly, and to carry adequate insurance against fire and other types of losses. These requirements are designed to keep the property from losing value and avoid diminishing the lender's security. Mortgage notes are especially popular in the purchase of homes and the acquisition of plant assets.

Accounting for mortgage notes and bonds is essentially the same as accounting for unsecured notes and bonds. The primary difference is that the mortgage agreement needs to be disclosed to users of financial statements. For instance, more than 10% of **MusicLand**'s long-term liabilities are in mortgage notes. MusicLand reports that its "mortgage note payable is collateralized by land, buildings and certain fixtures of three of the Company's Media Play stores." MusicLand's note carries a variable interest rate, also called a *floating rate*.

Global: Countries vary in the preference given to debtholders vs. stockholders when a company is in financial distress. Some countries such as Germany, France, and Japan give preference to stockholders over the interests of debtholders.

Most mortgage contracts grant the lender the right to *foreclose* on the property if the borrower fails to pay in accordance with the terms of the agreement. If foreclosure occurs, a court either orders the property to be sold or simply grants legal title for the mortgaged property to the lender. If the property is sold, the proceeds are first applied to court costs and then to the mortgage holder's claims. The borrower receives any additional proceeds subject to claims from its other creditors.

Quick Check

14. Which of the following is true for an installment note requiring a series of equal total cash payments? (a) Payments consist of increasing interest and decreasing principal; (b) Payments consist of changing amounts of principal but constant interest; or (c) Payments consist of decreasing interest and increasing principal.

15. How is the interest portion of an installment note payment computed?

16. When a borrower records an interest payment on an installment note, how are the balance sheet and income statement affected?

Answers—p. 648

Using the Information

Pledged Assets to Secured Liabilities

This section explains how lenders can reduce their risk of loss and how borrowers can achieve more favorable terms by entering into collateral agreements. We also describe an important measure of this risk.

Collateral Agreements

A2 Explain collateral agreements and their effects on loan risk.

Collateral agreements can reduce the risk of loss for both bonds and notes. Unsecured bonds and notes are riskier because the issuer's obligation to pay interest and principal has the same priority as all other unsecured liabilities in the event of bankruptcy. If a company is unable to pay its debts in full, the unsecured creditors (including the holders of debentures) lose all or a proportion of their balances.

A company's ability to borrow money with or without collateral agreements depends on its credit rating. In some cases, debt financing is unavailable unless the borrower can provide security to creditors with a collateral agreement. Even if unsecured loans are available, the creditors are likely to charge a higher rate of interest to compensate for the added risk. To borrow funds at a more favorable rate, many bonds and notes are secured by collateral agreements in the form of mortgages. Information about a company's security agreements with its lenders is important to users. Notes to financial statements sometimes describe the amounts of assets pledged as security against liabilities. The next section describes a ratio used to assess a borrower's situation with respect to its security agreements.

Ratio of Pledged Assets to Secured Liabilities

Buyers (investors) of a company's secured debt obligations need to determine whether the debtor's pledged assets provide adequate security. One method to evaluate this is to compute the ratio of **pledged assets to secured liabilities.** This is computed by dividing the book value of the company's assets pledged as collateral by the book value of liabilities secured by these collateral agreements as shown in Exhibit 15.22.

$$\text{Pledged assets to secured liabilities} = \frac{\text{Book value of pledged assets}}{\text{Book value of secured liabilities}}$$

A3 Compute the ratio of pledged assets to secured liabilities and explain its use.

Exhibit 15.22

Pledged Assets to Secured Liabilities

To illustrate, assume that a company owns assets with a book value of $230,000 pledged against loans with a balance of $100,000. The pledged assets to secured liabilities ratio is 2.3 (often expressed as 2.3 to 1) and is computed as $230,000/$100,000. There are no exact guidelines for interpreting the values for this ratio, but a 2.3 value is sufficiently high to provide secured creditors with some comfort that their loans are covered by the borrower's assets. As another example, the recent annual report of **Chock Full O'Nuts** reveals that "borrowings under the Loan Agreements . . . are collateralized by . . . accounts receivable and inventories, and substantially all of the machinery and equipment and real estate." We can use this information to compute its pledged assets to secured liabilities ratio of 20.6 ($206 million/$10 million). This ratio implies that more than $20 of collateral exists for each $1 of secured liabilities. This huge collateral commitment likely accounts for the low 8.5% interest that Chock Full O'Nuts pays on these secured liabilities.

Pledging assets for the benefit of secured creditors also affects unsecured creditors. When a larger portion of assets is pledged, the unsecured creditors are at greater risk for two reasons. Namely, secured creditors often demand a high ratio when they perceive that (1) the values of the assets in liquidation are low and (2) the likelihood that the company will meet its obligations from operating cash flows is not high. Consequently, unsecured creditors also gain information from the ratio of pledged assets to secured liabilities.

When using this ratio, we must be aware that reported book values of a company's assets are unlikely to exactly reflect market values. This ratio is improved if we can determine the assets' market values and then use them in the ratio instead of book values. A company's lenders can sometimes obtain this information directly by asking the borrower to provide recent appraisals. Using the ratio also requires knowledge about secured liabilities and pledged assets— how they are both measured and reported. This requires analysis of information in both the financial statements and their notes.

You Make the Call

Bond Investor You plan to purchase debenture bonds from one of two companies in the same industry that are similar in size and performance. The first company has $350,000 of unsecured liabilities, $575,000 of secured liabilities, and $1,265,000 in book value of pledged assets. The second company has $1,200,000 of unsecured liabilities, $800,000 of secured liabilities, and $2,000,000 in book value of pledged assets. Which company's debenture bonds are less risky based on the ratio of pledged assets to secured liabilities?

Answer—p. 647

Water Sports Company (WSC) patented and successfully test-marketed a new product. To expand its ability to produce and market the new product, WSC needs to raise $800,000 of financing. On January 1, 2002, the company obtains the money in two ways:

a. WSC signs a $400,000, 10% installment note to be repaid with five equal annual installments. The payments will be made on December 31 of 2002 through 2006.

b. WSC issues five-year bonds with a par value of $400,000. The bonds have a 12% annual contract rate and pay interest on June 30 and December 31. The annual market rate for the bonds is 10% as of January 1, 2002.

Demonstration Problem

Required

1. For the installment note, (a) compute the size of each annual payment, (b) prepare an amortization table such as Exhibit 15.21, and (c) prepare the journal entry for the first payment.

2. For the bonds, (a) compute their issue price; (b) prepare the January 1, 2002, journal entry to record their issuance; (c) prepare an amortization table using the effective interest method; (d) prepare the June 30, 2002, journal entry to record the first interest payment; and (e) prepare a journal entry to record retiring the bonds at a $416,000 call price on January 1, 2004.

Planning the Solution

- For the installment note, divide the borrowed amount by the annuity factor (from Table B.3) using the 10% rate and five payments. Prepare a table similar to Exhibit 15.21 and use the numbers in the table's first line for the journal entry.

- For the bonds, compute the issue price by using the market rate to find the present value of the bonds' cash flows (use tables found in Appendix B). Then use this result to record the bonds' issue. Next, prepare an amortization table like Exhibit 15.13 and use it to get the numbers needed for the journal entry. Also use the table to find the carrying value as of the date of the bonds' retirement that you need for the journal entry.

Solution to Demonstration Problem

Part 1: Installment Note

a. Annual payment = Note balance/Annuity factor = $400,000/3.7908 = $105,519 (Note: Annuity factor is for five payments and a rate of 10%.)

b. Amortization table:

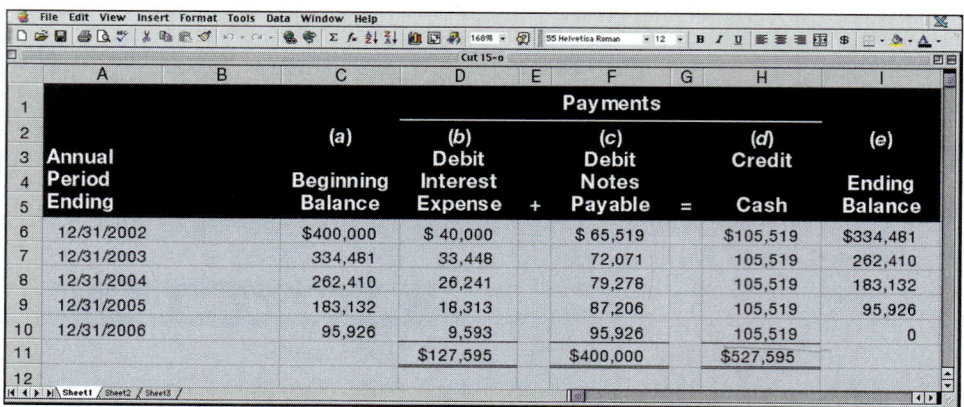

Annual Period Ending	(a) Beginning Balance	(b) Debit Interest Expense	+	(c) Debit Notes Payable	=	(d) Credit Cash	(e) Ending Balance
12/31/2002	$400,000	$ 40,000		$ 65,519		$105,519	$334,481
12/31/2003	334,481	33,448		72,071		105,519	262,410
12/31/2004	262,410	26,241		79,278		105,519	183,132
12/31/2005	183,132	18,313		87,206		105,519	95,926
12/31/2006	95,926	9,593		95,926		105,519	0
		$127,595		$400,000		$527,595	

c. Journal entry for December 31, 2002, payment:

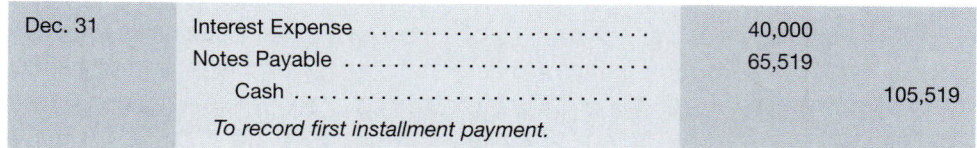

Dec. 31	Interest Expense	40,000	
	Notes Payable	65,519	
	Cash		105,519
	To record first installment payment.		

Part 2: Bonds

a. Compute the bonds' issue price:

Cash Flow	Table	Present Value Factor*		Amount		Present Value
Par (maturity) value	B.1 in App. B (PV of 1)	0.6139	×	400,000	=	$245,560
Interest payments	B.3 in App. B (PV of annuity)	7.7217	×	24,000	=	185,321
Price of bond						$430,881

* Present value factors are for 10 payments using an interest rate of 5%.

b. Journal entry for January 1, 2002, issuance:

Jan. 1	Cash	430,881	
	Premium on Bonds Payable		30,881
	Bonds Payable		400,000
	Sold bonds at a premium.		

c. Amortization table:

	A	B	C	D	E	F
1		(A) Cash	(B) Interest	(C) Premium	(D) Unamortized	(E) Carrying
2	Semiannual					
3	Interest	Interest Paid	Expense	Amortization	Premium	Value
4	Period	6% × $400,000	5% × Prior (E)	(A) − (B)	Prior (D) − (C)	$400,000 + (D)
5	1/1/2002				$30,881	$430,881
6	6/30/2002	$ 24,000	$ 21,544	$ 2,456	28,425	428,425
7	12/31/2002	24,000	21,421	2,579	25,846	425,846
8	6/30/2003	24,000	21,292	2,708	23,138	423,138
9	12/31/2003	24,000	21,157	2,843	20,295	420,295
10	6/30/2004	24,000	21,015	2,985	17,310	417,310
11	12/31/2004	24,000	20,866	3,134	14,176	414,176
12	6/30/2005	24,000	20,709	3,291	10,885	410,885
13	12/31/2005	24,000	20,544	3,456	7,429	407,429
14	6/30/2006	24,000	20,371	3,629	3,800	403,800
15	12/31/2006	24,000	20,200*	3,800	0	400,000
16		$240,000	$209,119	$30,881		

* Adjusted for rounding.

d. Journal entry for June 30, 2002, payment:

June 30	Bond Interest Expense	21,544	
	Premium on Bonds Payable	2,456	
	Cash		24,000
	Paid semiannual interest on bonds.		

e. Journal entry for January 1, 2004, bond retirement:

Jan. 1	Bonds Payable	400,000	
	Premium on Bonds Payable	20,295	
	Cash		416,000
	Gain on Retirement Bonds		4,295
	To record retirement of bonds (carrying value determined as of December 31, 2003).		

APPENDIX

Present Values of Bonds and Notes

15A

Accounting for long-term liabilities such as bonds and notes presents challenges because of the extended time period until these obligations are settled. This appendix explains how to apply present value techniques both to measure a long-term liability when it is created and to assign interest expense to the periods until it is settled. Appendix B near the end of the book provides additional discussion of present value concepts.

Explain and compute the present value of an amount to be paid at a future date.

Present Value Concepts

Accounting for long-term liabilities requires some understanding of present value concepts. The basic present value concept is the idea that cash paid (or received) in the future has less value now than the same amount of cash paid (or received) today. To illustrate, if we must pay $1 one year from now, its present value is less than $1. To see this, assume that we borrow $0.9259 today that must be paid back in one year with 8% interest. Our interest expense for this loan is computed as $0.9259 × 8%, or $0.0741. When the $0.0741 interest is added to the $0.9259 borrowed, we get the $1 payment necessary to repay our loan with interest. This is formally computed in Exhibit 15A.1. The $0.9259 borrowed is the present value of the $1 future payment. More generally, an amount borrowed equals the present value of the future payment. (This same interpretation applies to an investment. If $0.9259 is invested at 8%, it yields $0.0741 in revenue after one year. This amounts to $1, made up of principal and interest.)

Exhibit 15A.1

Components of a One-Year Loan

Amount borrowed	$0.9259
Interest for one year at 8%	0.0741
Amount owed after 1 year	$1.0000

Point: Benjamin Franklin is said to have described compounding as "the money, money makes, makes more money."

To extend this example, assume that we owe $1 two years from now instead of one year, and the 8% interest is compounded annually. *Compounded* means that interest during the second period is based on the total of the amount borrowed plus the interest accrued from the first period. The second period's interest is then computed as 8% multiplied by the sum of the amount borrowed plus interest earned in the first period. Exhibit 15A.2 shows how we compute the present value of $1 to be paid in two years. This amount is $0.8573. The first year's interest of $0.0686 is added to the principal so that the second year's interest is based on $0.9259. Total interest for this two-year period is $0.1427, computed as $0.0686 plus $0.0741.

Exhibit 15A.2

Components of a Two-Year Loan

Amount borrowed	$0.8573
Interest for first year ($0.8573 × 8%)	0.0686
Amount owed after 1 year	$0.9259
Interest for second year ($0.9259 × 8%)	0.0741
Amount owed after 2 years	$1.0000

Present Value Tables

The present value of $1 that we must repay at some future date can be computed by using this formula: $1/(1 + i)^n$. The symbol i in the formula is the interest rate per period and n is the number of periods until the future payment must be made. Applying this formula to our two-year loan, we get $1/(1.08)^2$, or $0.8573. This is the same value shown in Exhibit 15A.2. We can use this formula to find any present value. However, a simpler method is to use a *present value table,* which lists present values computed with this formula for various interest rates and time periods. Many people find it helpful in learning present value concepts to first work with the table and then move to using a calculator.

Example: If interest in this example is 6% instead of 8%, what amount does the borrower receive for a promise to pay $1 in 1 year? How much is interest?
Answer: Amount borrowed: $1/1.06 = $0.9434. Interest for 1 year: 6% × $0.9434 = $0.0566

Exhibit 15A.3

Present Value of 1

Periods	Rate		
	6%	8%	10%
1	0.9434	0.9259	0.9091
2	0.8900	0.8573	0.8264
3	0.8396	0.7938	0.7513
4	0.7921	0.7350	0.6830
5	0.7473	0.6806	0.6209
6	0.7050	0.6302	0.5645
7	0.6651	0.5835	0.5132
8	0.6274	0.5403	0.4665
9	0.5919	0.5002	0.4241
10	0.5584	0.4632	0.3855

Exhibit 15A.3 shows a present value table for a future payment of 1 for up to 10 periods at three different interest rates. Present values in this table are rounded to four decimal places. This table is drawn from the larger and more complete Table B.1 in Appendix B near the end of the book. Notice that the first value in the 8% column is 0.9259, the value we computed earlier for the present value of a $1 loan for one year at 8% (see Exhibit 15A.1). Go to the second row in the same 8% column and find the present value of 1 discounted at 8% for two years, or 0.8573. This $0.8573 is the present value of our obligation to repay $1 after two periods at 8% interest (see Exhibit 15A.2).

Example: Use Exhibit 15A.3 to find the present value of $1 discounted for 2 years at 6%.
Answer: Present value = $0.8900

Applying a Present Value Table

To illustrate how to measure a liability using a present value table, assume that a company plans to borrow cash and repay it as follows:

Payment after 1 year	$ 2,000
Payment after 2 years	3,000
Payment after 3 years	5,000
Total payments	$10,000

How much does this company receive today if the interest rate is 10% on this loan? For the answer, we need to compute the present value of the three future payments, discounted at 10%. This computation is shown in Exhibit 15A.4 using present values from Exhibit 15A.3. The company can borrow $8,054 today at 10% interest in exchange for its promise to make these three payments at the scheduled dates.

Periods	Payments	Present Value of 1 at 10%	Present Value of Payments
1	$2,000	0.9091	$1,818
2	3,000	0.8264	2,479
3	5,000	0.7513	3,757
Present value of all payments			$8,054

Exhibit 15A.4

Present Value of a Series of Unequal Payments

Present Value of an Annuity

The $8,054 present value for the loan in Exhibit 15A.4 equals the sum of the present values of the three payments. When payments are not equal, their combined present value is best computed by adding the individual present values as shown in Exhibit 15A.4. Sometimes payments follow an **annuity,** which is a series of *equal* payments at equal time intervals. The present value of an annuity is readily computed.

To illustrate, assume that a company must repay a 6% loan with a $5,000 payment at each year-end for the next four years. This loan amount equals the present value of the four payments discounted at 6%. Exhibit 15A.5 shows how to compute this loan's present value of $17,326 by multiplying each payment by its matching present value factor taken from Exhibit 15A.3. Since the series of $5,000 payments is an annuity, we can compute its present value with either of two shortcuts. First, the third column of Exhibit 15A.5 shows that the sum of the present values of 1 at 6% for periods 1 through 4 equals 3.4651. One shortcut is to multiply this total of 3.4651 by the $5,000 annual payment to get the combined present value of $17,326. It requires one multiplication instead of four.

The second shortcut uses an *annuity table* such as the one shown in Exhibit 15A.6, which is drawn from the more complete Table B.3 in Appendix B. We go directly to the annuity table to get the present value factor for a specific number of payments and interest rate. We then multiply this factor by the amount of the payment to find the present value of the annuity. Specifically, find the row for four periods and go across to 6% column, where the factor is 3.4651. This factor equals the present value of an annuity with four payments of 1, discounted at 6%. We then multiply 3.4651 by $5,000 to get the $17,326 present value of the annuity.

C4 Explain and compute the present value of a series of equal amounts to be paid at future dates.

Periods	Payments	Present Value of 1 at 6%	Present Value of Payments
1	$5,000	0.9434	$ 4,717
2	5,000	0.8900	4,450
3	5,000	0.8396	4,198
4	5,000	0.7921	3,961
Present value of all payments		3.4651	$17,326

Exhibit 15A.5

Present Value of a Series of Equal Payments (Annuity) by Discounting Each Payment

	Rate		
Periods	6%	8%	10%
1	0.9434	0.9259	0.9091
2	1.8334	1.7833	1.7355
3	2.6730	2.5771	2.4869
4	**3.4651**	3.3121	3.1699
5	4.2124	3.9927	3.7908
6	4.9173	4.6229	4.3553
7	5.5824	5.2064	4.8684
8	6.2098	5.7466	5.3349
9	6.8017	6.2469	5.7590
10	7.3601	6.7101	6.1446

Exhibit 15A.6

Present Value of an Annuity of 1

Example: Use Exhibit 15A.6 to find the present value of an annuity of eight $15,000 payments with an 8% interest rate.
Answer: Present value = $15,000 × 5.7466 = $86,199

Compounding Periods Shorter than a Year

Our present value examples all involved periods of a year. In many situations, however, interest is compounded over shorter periods. For example, the interest rate on bonds is usually stated as an annual rate but interest is often paid every six months (semiannually). This means the present value of interest payments from such bonds must be computed using interest periods of six months.

Assume that a borrower wants to know the present value of a series of ten $4,000 *semiannual payments* made over five years at an *annual interest rate* of 12%. The interest rate is stated as an annual rate of 12%, but it is actually a rate of 6% per semiannual interest period. To compute the present value of this series of $4,000 payments, go to row 10 of Exhibit 15A.6 and across to the 6% column to find the factor 7.3601. The present value of this annuity is $29,440 (7.3601 × $4,000).

We recommend reading Appendix B to learn more about present value concepts. It also includes more complete present value tables and additional assignments.

Example: If this borrower makes five semiannual payments of $8,000, what is the present value of this annuity at a 12% annual rate?
Answer: 4.2124 × $8,000 = $33,699

Quick Check

17. A company enters into an agreement to make four annual year-end payments of $1,000 each, starting one year from now. The annual interest rate is 8%. The present value of these four payments is (a) $2,923, (b) $2,940, (c) $3,312, (d) $4,000, or (e) $6,733.

18. Suppose a company has an option to pay either (a) $10,000 after one year or (b) $5,000 after six months and another $5,000 after one year. Which choice has the lower present value?

Answers—p. 648

APPENDIX

15B Leases and Pensions

This appendix explains the accounting and analysis for both leases and pensions.

Lease Liabilities

C5 Describe the accounting for leases and pensions.

A **lease** is a contractual agreement between a *lessor* (asset owner) and a *lessee* (asset renter or tenant) that grants the lessee the right to use the asset for a period of time in return for cash (rent) payments. Some estimates suggest that up to one-fourth of all equipment purchases is financed with leases. The advantages of lease financing include the lack of an immediate large cash payment and the potential to deduct rental payments in computing taxable income. From an accounting perspective leases can be classified as either operating or capital leases.

Operating Leases

Operating leases are short-term (or cancelable) leases in which the lessor retains the risks and rewards of ownership. Examples include most car and apartment rental agreements. The lessee records lease payments as expenses; the lessor records them as revenue. To illustrate, if an employee of Amazon leases a car for $300 at an airport while on company business, Amazon (lessee) records this cost:

Assets = Liabilities + Equity
−300   −300

Rental Expense	300	
Cash		300
To record lease rental payment.		

Also, the lessee does not report the leased item as its asset or its liability (it is the lessor's asset).

Capital Leases

Capital leases are long-term (or noncancelable) leases in which the lessor transfers substantially all risks and rewards of ownership to the lessee.[4] Examples include most leases of airplanes and department store buildings. The lessee records the leased item as its own asset along with a lease liability at the start of the lease term; the amount recorded equals the present value of all lease payments. To illustrate, assume that K2 Co. enters into a six-year lease of a building in which it will sell sporting equipment. The lease transfers all the risks and rewards of building ownership to K2 (the present value of its $12,979 annual lease payments is $60,000). K2 records this transaction as follows:

Leased Asset—Building	60,000	
Lease Liability		60,000
To record leased asset and lease liability.		

Point: Home Depot's recent annual report indicates that its rental expenses from operating leases total more than $250 million.

Assets = Liabilities + Equity
+60,000 +60,000

K2 reports the leased asset as a plant asset. The lease liability is reported as a long-term liability. However, the portion of the lease liability expected to be paid in the next year is reported as a current liability.[5] At each year-end, K2 records depreciation on the leased asset (assume straight-line depreciation, six-year lease term, and no salvage value) as follows:

Depreciation Expense—Building	10,000	
Accumulated Depreciation—Building		10,000
To record depreciation on leased asset.		

Assets = Liabilities + Equity
−10,000   −10,000

K2 also accrues interest on the lease liability at each year-end. Interest expense is computed by multiplying the remaining lease liability by the interest rate on the lease. Specifically, K2 records its annual interest expense as part of its annual lease payment ($12,979) as follows (for its first year):

Interest Expense	4,800	
Lease Liability	8,179	
Cash		12,979
*To record first annual lease payment.**		

Assets = Liabilities + Equity
−12,979 −8,179   −4,800

* These numbers are computed from a *lease payment schedule*. For simplicity, we use the same numbers from Exhibit 15.21 for this lease payment schedule—with different headings as follows:

| | (A) | (B) | | (C) | | (D) | (E) |
| | | *Debit* | | *Debit* | | *Credit* | |
Period Ending Date	Beginning Balance of Lease	Interest on Lease Liability 8% × (A)	+	Lease Liability (D) − (B)	=	Cash Lease Payment	Ending Balance of Lease (A) − (C)
12/31/2002	$60,000	$ 4,800		$ 8,179		$12,979	$51,821
12/31/2003	51,821	4,146		8,833		12,979	42,988
12/31/2004	42,988	3,439		9,540		12,979	33,448
12/31/2005	33,448	2,676		10,303		12,979	23,145
12/31/2006	23,145	1,852		11,127		12,979	12,018
12/31/2007	12,018	961		12,018		12,979	0
		$17,874		$60,000		$77,874	

Point: Home Depot reports *"certain retail locations are leased under capital leases."* The net present value of its capital lease liabilities is about $150 million.

[4] A capital lease is one that meets any one or more of four criteria: (1) transfers title of leased asset to lessee, (2) contains a bargain purchase option, (3) has a lease term that is 75% or more of the leased asset's useful life, or (4) has a present value of lease payments that is 90% or more of the leased asset's market value.

[5] Most lessees try to keep leased assets and lease liabilities off their balance sheets by failing to meet one of the four criteria of a capital lease because a lease liability increases a company's total liabilities, making it more difficult to obtain additional financing. The acquisition of assets with liabilities not reported on the balance sheet is called **off-balance-sheet financing.**

Point: Fringe benefits are often 40% or more of salaries and wages, and pension benefits make up nearly 15% of fringe benefits.

Point: The two types of pension plans are (1) *defined benefit plan*—where the retirement benefit is defined and the employer estimates the contribution necessary to pay these benefits, and (2) *defined contribution plan*—where the pension contribution is defined and the employer and/or employee contributes amounts specified in the pension agreement.

Pension Liabilities

A **pension plan** is a contractual agreement between an employer and its employees for the employer to provide benefits (payments) to employees after they retire. Most employers pay the full cost of the pension, but sometimes employees pay part of the cost. An employer records its payment into a pension plan with a debit to Pension Expense and a credit to Cash. A *plan administrator* receives payments from the employer, invests them in pension assets, and makes benefit payments to *pension recipients* (retired employees). Insurance and trust companies often serve as pension plan administrators.

Many pensions are known as *defined benefit plans* that set future benefits, where the employer's contributions vary, depending on assumptions about future pension assets and liabilities. Several disclosures are necessary in this case. Specifically, a pension liability is reported when the accumulated benefit obligation is *more than* the plan assets, a so-called *underfunded plan.* The accumulated benefit obligation is the present value of promised future pension payments to retirees. *Plan assets* refer to the market value of assets the plan administrator holds. On the other hand, a pension asset is reported when the accumulated benefit obligation is *less than* the plan assets, a so-called *overfunded plan.* Also, an employer reports pension expense when it receives the benefits from the employees' services, which is sometimes decades before it pays pension benefits to employees. (*Other Postretirement Benefits* refer to nonpension benefits such as health care and life insurance benefits. Similar to a pension, costs of these benefits are estimated and liabilities accrued when the employees earn them.)

Summary

C1   **Explain the types of bonds and the procedures for issuing them.** Certain bonds are secured by the issuer's assets; other bonds, called *debentures,* are unsecured. Serial bonds mature at different points in time; term bonds mature at one time. Registered bonds have each bondholder's name and address recorded by the issuer; bearer bonds are payable to the holder. Convertible bonds are exchangeable for shares of the issuer's stock. Callable bonds can be retired by the issuer at a set price. Bonds are often issued by an underwriter.

C2   **Explain the types and payment patterns of notes.** Notes are either interest bearing or noninterest bearing. Notes can require repayment of principal and interest (1) at the end of a period or (2) gradually over a period in either equal or unequal amounts. Notes repaid over a period of time are called *installment notes* and usually follow one of two payment patterns: (1) decreasing payments of interest plus equal amounts of principal or (2) equal total payments.

C3   **Explain and compute the present value of an amount to be paid at a future date.** The basic concept of present value is that an amount of cash to be paid or received in the future is worth less than the same amount of cash to be paid or received today. Another important present value concept is that interest is compounded, meaning interest is added to the balance and used to determine interest for succeeding periods.

C4   **Explain and compute the present value of a series of equal amounts to be paid at future dates.** An annuity is a series of equal payments occurring at equal time intervals. An annuity's present value can be computed as the sum of individual present values for each payment. The alternative and preferred approach is to compute the present value of the entire series using the present value table for an annuity (or a calculator).

C5   **Describe the accounting for leases and pensions.** A lease is a rental agreement between the lessor and the lessee. When the lessor retains the risks and rewards of asset ownership (called an *operating lease*), the lessee debits Rent Expense and

credits Cash for its lease payments. When the lessor substantially transfers the risks and rewards of asset ownership to the lessee (called a *capital lease*), the lessee capitalizes the leased asset and records a lease liability. Pension agreements can result in either pension assets or pension liabilities.

A1   **Compare bond financing with stock financing.** Bond financing is used to fund business activities. Advantages of bond financing versus stock include (1) no effect on owner control, (2) tax savings, and (3) increased earnings due to financial leverage. Disadvantages include (1) interest and principal payments and (2) amplification of poor performance.

A2   **Explain collateral agreements and their effects on loan risk.** Collateral agreements alter the risk of loss for creditors. Unsecured bonds and notes are riskier because the issuer's obligation to pay interest and principal has the same priority as all other unsecured liabilities in the event of bankruptcy. To borrow funds at a more favorable rate, many bonds and notes are secured by collateral agreements called *mortgages.*

A3   **Compute the ratio of pledged assets to secured liabilities and explain its use.** Both secured and unsecured creditors are concerned about the relation between the amounts of assets the debtor owns and the amounts of secured liabilities. Secured creditors are at less risk when the ratio of pledged assets to secured liabilities is larger, but the risks of unsecured creditors are often increased when this ratio is high because their claims to assets are secondary to secured creditors.

P1   **Prepare entries to record bond issuance and bond interest expense.** When bonds are issued at par, Cash is debited and Bonds Payable is credited for the bonds' par value. At bond interest payment dates, Bond Interest Expense is debited and Cash credited for an amount equal to the bond par value multiplied by the appropriate bond contract rate (usually semiannual).

P2   **Compute and record amortization of bond discount.** Bonds are issued at a discount when the contract rate is less than the market rate, making the issue (selling) price less than par. When this occurs, the issuer records a credit to Bonds Payable (at par) and debits both Discount on Bonds Payable and Cash. The amount of bond interest expense assigned to each period is computed using either the straight-line or effective interest method. Straight line can be used only if the results are not materially different from the effective interest method.

P3 **Compute and record amortization of bond premium.** Bonds are issued at a premium when the contract rate is higher than the market rate, making the issue (selling) price greater than par. When this occurs, the issuer records a debit to Cash and credits both Premium on Bonds Payable and Bonds Payable (at par). The amount of bond interest expense assigned to each period is computed using either the straight-line or effective interest method. The Premium on Bonds Payable is allocated to reduce bond interest expense over the life of the bonds.

P4 **Record the retirement of bonds.** Bonds are retired at maturity with a debit to Bonds Payable and a credit to Cash at par value. The issuer can retire the bonds early by exercising a call option or by purchasing on the open market. Bondholders can also retire bonds early by exercising a conversion feature on convertible bonds. The issuer recognizes a gain or loss for the difference between the amount paid and the bond carrying value.

P5 **Prepare entries to account for notes.** Interest is allocated to each period in a note's life by multiplying its beginning-period carrying value by its market rate at issuance. If a note is repaid with equal payments, the payment amount is computed by dividing the borrowed amount by the present value of an annuity factor (taken from a present value table) using the market rate and the number of payments.

Guidance Answers to **You Make the Call**

Bond Rater Bonds that have longer repayment periods and smaller interest payments over their life have higher risk. Also, bonds issued by companies in financial difficulties or facing higher than normal uncertainties have higher risk. Moreover, companies with higher than normal debt and with large fluctuations in earnings are considered of higher risk.

Entrepreneur This is a "present value" question. The market interest rate (10%) and present value ($3,000) are known, but the payment required two years later is unknown. This amount ($3,630) can be computed as $3,000 × 1.10 × 1.10. (This is similar to the computations in Exhibit 15.17.) This means the sale price is $3,630 when no payments are received for two years. Note that the $3,630 received two years from today is equivalent to $3,000 cash today.

Bond Investor The ratio of pledged assets to secured liabilities for the first company is 2.2 ($1,265,000/$575,000) and for the second company is 2.5 ($2,000,000/$800,000), suggesting that the second company's secured creditors are at less risk than secured creditors of the first company. But *debenture bonds are unsecured.* Therefore, since the first company has fewer secured liabilities, it is of lower risk for unsecured debenture bonds. The first company also has fewer liabilities and, since the companies are of equal size, the first company's liabilities make up a smaller portion of total assets. Consequently, as a buyer of unsecured debenture bonds, you prefer the first company.

Guidance Answers to **Quick Checks**

1. (b)

2. Multiply the bond's par value by its contract rate of interest.

3. Bonds sell at a premium when the contract rate exceeds the market rate and the purchasers pay more than their par value.

4. The bonds are issued at a discount, meaning issue price is less than par value. A discount occurs because the bond contract rate (6%) is less than the market rate (8%).

5.

Cash	91,893
Discount on Bonds Payable	8,107
Bonds Payable	100,000

6. (a) $3,811 (Total bond interest expense of $38,107 divided by 10 periods, or the $30,000 cash paid plus the $8,107 discount divided by 10 periods.)

   (b) $3,676 (Beginning carrying value of $91,893 multiplied by the 4% market rate at issuance.)

7. The bonds are issued at a premium, meaning issue price is higher than par value. A premium occurs because the bonds' contract rate (16%) is higher than the market rate (14%).

8. (e) On 6/30/2002: $110,592 × 7% = $7,741 bond interest expense; $8,000 − $7,741 = $259 premium amortization; $110,592 − $259 = $110,333 bond payable carrying value. On 12/31/2002: $110,333 × 7% = $7,723 bond interest expense; $8,000 − $7,723 = $277 premium amortization.

9.

Bonds payable, 16%, due 12/31/2011 .	$100,000
Plus premium on bonds payable	10,056* $110,056

* Original premium balance of $10,592 less $259 and $277 amortized on 6/30/2002 and 12/31/2002, respectively.

10. (a) Reflects payment of accrued interest recorded back on May 1.

11. $9,375 loss. Computed as the difference between the repurchase price of $256,250 [50% of ($500,000 × 102.5%)] and the carrying value of $246,875 (50% of $493,750).

12. (c) $[\$6,000 + (\$6,000 \times 0.06)] \times 0.06 = \$381.60$

13.

Cash	2,940	
Discount on Notes Payable	1,060	
Notes Payable		4,000
Exchanged a noninterest-bearing note for cash.		

14. (c)

15. The interest portion of an installment payment equals the period's beginning loan balance multiplied by the market interest rate at the time of issuance.

16. On the balance sheet, the account balances of the related liability (note payable) and asset (cash) accounts are decreased. On the income statement, interest expense is recorded.

17. (c) Computed as $3.3121 \times \$1,000 = \$3,312$.

18. The option of paying $10,000 after one year has a lower present value. It postpones paying the first $5,000 by six months. More generally, the present value of a further delayed payment is always lower than a less delayed payment.

Glossary

Annuity series of equal payments at equal intervals. (p. 643).

Bearer bonds bonds made payable to whoever holds them (the *bearer*); also called *unregistered bonds*. (p. 618).

Bond written promise to pay the bond's par (or face) value and interest at a stated contract rate; often issued in denominations of $1,000. (p. 616).

Bond certificate document containing bond specifics such as issuer's name, bond par value, contract interest rate, and maturity date. (p. 619).

Bond indenture contract between the bond issuer and the bondholders; identifies the parties' rights and obligations. (p. 619).

Callable bonds bonds that give the issuer an option to retire them at a stated amount prior to maturity. (p. 618).

Capital leases long-term leases in which the lessor transfers substantially all risk and rewards of ownership to the lessee. (p. 645).

Carrying (book) value of bonds net amount at which bonds are reported on the balance sheet; equals the par value of the bonds less any unamortized discount or plus any unamortized premium; also called *carrying amount*. (p. 621).

Contract rate interest rate specified in a bond indenture; multiplied by the bonds' par value to determine the interest paid each period; also called *coupon rate, stated rate,* or *nominal rate*. (p. 620).

Convertible bonds bonds that bondholders can exchange for a set number of the issuer's shares. (p. 618).

Coupon bonds bonds with interest coupons attached to their certificates; bondholders detach coupons when they mature and present them to a bank or broker for collection. (p. 618).

Discount on bonds payable difference between a bond's par value and its lower issue price or carrying value; occurs when the contract rate is less than the market rate. (p. 621).

Effective interest method allocates interest expense over the bond life to yield a constant rate of interest; interest expense for a period is found by multiplying the balance of the liability at the beginning of the period by the bond market rate at issuance; also called *interest method*. (p. 623).

Installment note liability requiring a series of periodic payments to the lender. (p. 634).

Lease contractual agreement between *lessor* and *lessee* that grants a lessee the right to use an asset for a period of time in return for cash payments. (p. 644).

Market rate interest rate borrowers are willing to pay and lenders are willing to accept for a specific debt agreement at its risk level. (p. 620).

Mortgage legal agreement that protects a lender by giving the lender the right to be paid from the cash proceeds from the sale of a borrower's assets identified in the mortgage. (p. 637).

Off-balance-sheet financing acquisition of assets by agreeing to liabilities not reported on the balance sheet. (p. 645).

Operating leases short-term (or cancelable) leases in which lessor retains risks and rewards of ownership. (p. 644).

Par value of a bond amount the bond issuer agrees to pay at maturity and the amount on which interest payments are based; also called *face amount* or *face value*. (p. 616).

Pension plan contractual agreement between an employer and its employees for the employer to provide benefits to employees after they retire. (p. 646).

Pledged assets to secured liabilities ratio of the book value of a company's pledged assets to the book value of its secured liabilities. (p. 639).

Premium on bonds difference between a bond's par value and its higher issue price or carrying value; occurs when the contract rate is higher than the market rate. (p. 624).

Registered bonds bonds owned by investors whose names and addresses are recorded by the issuer; interest payments are made to the registered owners. (p. 618).

Secured bonds bonds that have specific assets of the issuer pledged as collateral. (p. 617).

Serial bonds bonds consisting of separate amounts that mature at different dates. (p. 618).

Sinking fund bonds bonds that require the issuer to make deposits to a separate account; bondholders are repaid at maturity from that account. (p. 618).

Straight-line method method allocating an equal amount of interest expense to each period in the life of bonds. (p. 622).

Term bonds bonds scheduled for payment (mature) at a single specified date. (p. 618).

Unsecured bonds bonds backed only by the issuer's credit standing; almost always riskier than secured bonds; also called *debentures*. (p. 617).

[The superscript ᴮ denotes assignments based on Appendix 15B.]

Questions

1. What is the main difference between a bond and a share of stock?

2. What is the main difference between notes payable and bonds payable?

3. What are the duties of a trustee for bondholders?

4. What is the advantage of issuing bonds instead of obtaining financing from the company's owners?

5. What is a bond indenture? What provisions are usually included in an indenture?

6. What are the *contract* and *market* rates for bonds?

7. What factors affect the market rates for bonds?

8. Does the straight-line or effective interest method produce an allocation of interest expense that yields a constant rate of interest over a bond's life? Explain.

9. Why does a company that issues bonds between interest dates collect accrued interest from the bonds' purchasers?

10. If you know the par value of bonds, the contract rate, and the market rate, how do you compute the bonds' price?

11. What is the issue price of a $2,000 bond sold at 98¼? What is the issue price of a $6,000 bond sold at 101½?

12. Describe two common alternative payment patterns for installment notes.

13. Explain why unsecured creditors are concerned when the pledged assets to secured liabilities ratio for a borrower increases.

14. Refer to **Nike**'s annual report in Appendix A. Is there any indication that Nike has issued bonds?

15. Refer to the statement of cash flows for **Reebok** in Appendix A. For the year ended December 31, 1999, what is Reebok's "Net borrowings (payments) of notes payable to banks"?

16. Refer to the annual report for **Gap** in Appendix A. For the 52 weeks ended January 29, 2000, did Gap raise more cash by issuing stock or debt?

17. What obligation does an entrepreneur have to investors that purchase bonds to finance the business?

18.ᴮ When can a lease create both an asset and a liability for the lessee?

19.ᴮ Compare and contrast an operating lease with a capital lease.

20.ᴮ Describe the two basic types of pension plans.

Gore Company issues 8%, 10-year bonds with a par value of $250,000 and semiannual interest payments. On the issue date, the annual market rate for these bonds is 10%, which implies a selling price of 87½. The straight-line method is used to allocate interest expense.

1. What are the issuer's cash proceeds from issuance of these bonds?

2. What total amount of bond interest expense will be recognized over these life of these bonds?

3. What is the amount of bond interest expense recorded on the first interest payment date?

QUICK STUDY

QS 15-1
Bond interest computation—straight-line

Top Tier issues 10%, 15-year bonds with a par value of $240,000 and semiannual interest payments. On the issue date, the annual market rate for these bonds is 8%, which implies a selling price of 117¼. The effective interest method is used to allocate interest expense.

1. What are the issuer's cash proceeds from issuance of these bonds?

2. What total amount of bond interest expense will be recognized over the life of these bonds?

3. What is the amount of bond interest expense recorded on the first interest payment date?

QS 15-2
Bond interest computation—effective interest

Prepare the journal entry for the issuance of the bonds in both QS 15-1 and QS 15-2. Assume that both bonds are issued on January 1, 2002.

QS 15-3
Journalize bond issuance

Using the bond details in both QS 15-1 and QS 15-2, confirm that the bonds' selling prices given in each problem are approximately correct. Use the present value tables B.1 and B.3 in Appendix B.

QS 15-4
Computing bond price

Lafrentz Company issues 8% bonds on January 1, 2002, with a par value of $4,000,000. The company sells $3,600,000 of the bonds on the stated issue date. The remaining $400,000 sell at par on March 1, 2002. The bonds pay interest semiannually as of June 30 and December 31. Record the entry for the March 1 sale of bonds.

QS 15-5
Issuing bonds between interest dates

QS 15-6
Bond terminology

Enter the letter of the description *A* through *H* that best fits each term in the blank next to that term.

A. Records and tracks the bondholders' names and addresses.
B. Is unsecured; backed only by the issuer's credit standing.
C. Has varying maturity dates for amounts owed.
D. Identifies rights and responsibilities of the issuer and the bondholders.
E. Can be exchanged for shares of the issuer's stock.
F. Is unregistered; interest is paid to whoever possesses them.
G. Maintains a separate asset account from which bondholders are paid at maturity.
H. Pledges specific assets of the issuer as collateral.

1. __D__ Bond indenture   **5.** __E__ Convertible bonds
2. __B__ Debentures   **6.** __G__ Sinking fund bonds
3. __F__ Bearer bonds   **7.** __C__ Serial bonds
4. __A__ Registered bonds   **8.** __H__ Secured bonds

QS 15-7
Bond retirement by
stock conversion

On January 1, 2002, the $2,000,000 par value bonds of Lott Company with a carrying value of $2,000,000 are converted to 1,000,000 shares of $1.00 par value common stock. Record the entry for the conversion of the bonds.

QS 15-8
Bond retirement by call option

On July 1, 2002, Hamm Company exercises an $8,000 call option (plus par value) on its outstanding bonds that have a carrying value of $416,000 and par value of $400,000. The company exercises the call option after the semiannual interest is paid on June 30, 2002. Record the entry to retire the bonds.

QS 15-9
Computing equal payments
for an installment note

Sydney Company borrows $340,000 cash from a bank and in return it signs an installment note that calls for five annual payments of equal size, with the first payment due one year after the note is signed. Use Table B.3 in Appendix B to compute the amount of the annual payment for each of the following annual market rates: (a) 4%, (b) 8%, and (c) 12%.

QS 15-10
Computing amount
due on interest-bearing
note

On January 1, 2002, Thorpe Company borrows $150,000 cash in exchange for an interest-bearing note. The note plus compounded interest at an annual market rate of 8% is due on December 31, 2004. Determine the amount that Thorpe must pay on the note's due date. (Round to the nearest dollar.)

QS 15-11
Interpretation of collateral
agreements

Note 2 of **Collins Industries** annual report states: "The credit facility [line] is collateralized by receivables, inventories, equipment and certain real property. Under the terms of the Agreement, the Company is required to maintain certain financial ratios and other financial conditions. The Agreement also prohibits the Company from incurring certain additional indebtedness, limits certain investments, advances or loans and restricts substantial asset sales, capital expenditures and cash dividends." What restrictions are placed on Collins Industries by the bank that has granted the credit?

QS 15-12
Ratio of pledged assets to
secured liabilities

Compute the ratio of pledged assets to secured liabilities for these two companies:

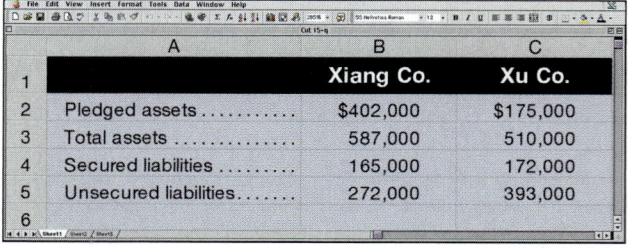

	Xiang Co.	Xu Co.
Pledged assets	$402,000	$175,000
Total assets	587,000	510,000
Secured liabilities	165,000	172,000
Unsecured liabilities	272,000	393,000

Which company appears to have the riskier secured liabilities?

Sarah Morris, an employee of ETrain.com, leases a car when she arrives at O'Hare airport for a 3-day business trip. The cost of the rental is $250. Prepare the entry by ETrain.com to record Sarah's short-term car lease cost.

QS 15-13^B

Recording operating leases

Bazooka, Inc., signs a five year lease for office equipment with Office Interiors. The present value of the lease payments is $15,499. Prepare the journal entry that Bazooka will record at the inception of this capital lease.

QS 15-14^B

Recording capital leases

Round dollar amounts to the nearest whole dollar. Assume no reversing entries are used.

EXERCISES

On January 1, 2002, Cruise Enterprises issues bonds that have a $3,400,000 par value, mature in 20 years, and pay 9% interest semiannually on June 30 and December 31. The bonds are sold at par.

1. How much interest will Cruise pay to the bondholders every six months?
2. Show the journal entries to record (a) the issuance of bonds on January 1, 2002; (b) the first interest payment on June 30, 2002; and (c) the second interest payment on December 31, 2002.
3. Record the journal entry for issuance assuming the bonds are issued at (a) 98 and (b) 102.

Exercise 15-1

Journal entries for bond issuance and interest

Couric Company issues bonds with a par value of $800,000 on their stated issue date. The bonds mature in 10 years and pay 6% annual interest in semiannual payments. On the issue date, the annual market rate for the bonds is 8%.

1. What is the amount of each semiannual interest payment for these bonds?
2. How many semiannual interest payments will be made on these bonds over their life?
3. Use the interest rates given to determine whether the bonds are issued at par, at a discount, or at a premium.
4. Compute the price of the bonds as of their issue date.
5. Prepare the journal entry to record the bonds' issuance.

Exercise 15-2

Computing bond interest and price, and recording its issuance

---

Tyler, Inc., issues bonds with a par value of $150,000 on their stated issue date. The bonds mature in five years and pay 10% annual interest in semiannual payments. On the issue date, the annual market rate for the bonds is 8%.

1. What is the amount of each semiannual interest payment for these bonds?
2. How many semiannual interest payments will be made on these bonds over their life?
3. Use the interest rates given to determine whether the bonds are issued at par, at a discount, or at a premium.
4. Compute the price of the bonds as of their issue date.
5. Prepare the journal entry to record the bonds' issuance.

Exercise 15-3

Computing bond interest and price, and recording its issuance

---

TMP issues bonds with a par value of $180,000 on January 1, 2002. The annual contract rate on the bonds is 8%, and interest is paid semiannually on June 30 and December 31. The bonds mature in three years. The annual market rate at the date of issuance is 10%, and the bonds are sold for $170,862.

1. What is the amount of the discount on these bonds at issuance?
2. How much total bond interest expense will be recognized over the life of these bonds?
3. Prepare an amortization table like Exhibit 15.7 for these bonds; use the straight-line method to amortize the discount.

Exercise 15-4

Straight-line amortization of bond discount

On January 1, 2002, Stryker issues $700,000 of 10%, 15-year bonds at a price of 97¾. Six years later, on January 1, 2008, Stryker retires 20% of these bonds by buying them on the open market at 104½. All interest is accounted for and paid through December 31, 2007, the day before the purchase. The straight-line method is used to amortize any bond discount.

1. How much does the company receive when it issues the bonds on January 1, 2002?
2. What is the amount of the discount on the bonds at January 1, 2002?
3. How much amortization of the discount is recorded on the bonds for the entire period from January 1, 2002, through December 31, 2007?

Exercise 15-5

Bond computations, straight-line amortization, and retirement

4. What is the carrying (book) value of the bonds as of the close of business on December 31, 2007? What is the carrying value of the 20% soon-to-be-retired bonds on this same date?

5. How much did the company pay on January 1, 2008, to purchase the bonds that it retired?

6. What is the amount of the recorded gain or loss from retiring the bonds?

7. Prepare the journal entry to record the bond retirement at January 1, 2008.

Exercise 15-6

Journal entries for bond issuance with accrued interest

On May 1, 2002, Cruise Enterprises issues bonds dated January 1, 2002, that have a $3,400,000 par value, mature in 20 years, and pay 9% interest semiannually on June 30 and December 31. The bonds are sold at par plus four months' accrued interest.

1. How much accrued interest is paid to Cruise by the purchasers of its bonds on May 1, 2002?

2. Show the journal entries to record (a) the issuance of bonds on May 1, 2002; (b) the first interest payment on June 30, 2002; and (c) the second interest payment on December 31, 2002.

Exercise 15-7

Straight-line amortization and accrued bond interest expense

Simon issues bonds with a par value of $100,000 and a four-year life on June 1, 2002. The annual contract rate is 7%, and interest is paid semiannually on November 30 and May 31. The bonds are issued at a price of $95,948.

1. Prepare an amortization table like Exhibit 15.7 for these bonds. Use the straight-line method of interest amortization.

2. Show the journal entries to record the first two interest payments and to accrue interest as of December 31, 2002.

Exercise 15-8

Effective interest amortization of bond discount

Shapiro Company issues bonds with a par value of $500,000 on January 1, 2002. The annual contract rate on the bonds is 9%, and interest is paid semiannually on June 30 and December 31. The bonds mature in three years. The annual market rate at the date of issuance is 12%, and the bonds are sold for $463,140.

1. What is the amount of the discount on these bonds at issuance?

2. How much total bond interest expense will be recognized over the life of these bonds?

3. Prepare an amortization table like Exhibit 15.8 for these bonds; use the effective interest method to amortize the discount.

Exercise 15-9

Effective interest amortization of bond premium

Mountain View Company issues bonds with a par value of $400,000 on January 1, 2002. The annual contract rate is 13%, and interest is paid semiannually on June 30 and December 31. The bonds mature in three years. The annual market rate at the date of issuance is 12%, and the bonds are sold for $409,850.

1. What is the amount of the premium on these bonds at issuance?

2. How much total bond interest expense will be recognized over the life of these bonds?

3. Prepare an amortization table like Exhibit 15.13 for these bonds; use the effective interest method to amortize the premium.

Exercise 15-10

Entries for noninterest-bearing note

Cape Company acquires a machine on December 1, 2002, by giving a $120,000 noninterest-bearing note due in one year. The market rate of interest for this note is 10%. Prepare journal entries to record the note's (a) issuance on December 1, 2002, (b) accrued interest as of December 31, 2002, and (c) payment on December 1, 2003.

Exercise 15-11

Installment note with equal principal payments

On December 31, 2002, JET borrows $50,000 cash by signing a four-year, 7% installment note that requires annual payments of accrued interest and equal amounts of principal on December 31 of each year from 2003 through 2006.

1. How much principal is included in each of the four annual payments?

2. Prepare an amortization table for this installment note like the one in Exhibit 15.20.

Exercise 15-12

Installment note entries

Use the information in Exercise 15-11 to prepare the journal entries for JET to record the loan on December 31, 2002, and the four payments from December 31, 2003, through December 31, 2006.

On December 31, 2002, Tucker borrows $100,000 cash by signing a four-year, 7% installment note. The note requires four equal total payments of accrued interest and principal on December 31 of each year from 2003 through 2006.

1. Compute the amount of each of the four equal total payments.

2. Prepare an amortization table for this installment note like the one in Exhibit 15.21.

Exercise 15-13
Installment note with equal total payments

Use the information in Exercise 15-13 to prepare the journal entries for Tucker to record the loan on December 31, 2002, and the four payments from December 31, 2003, through December 31, 2006.

Exercise 15-14
Installment note entries

An unsecured creditor of Telnet Co. has been monitoring the company's financing activities. Two years ago, its ratio of pledged assets to secured liabilities was 1.9. One year ago, the ratio climbed to 2.5, and the most recent financial report shows the ratio is now 3.3. Describe what this trend likely indicates about the company's activities, specifically from the point of view of this unsecured creditor.

Exercise 15-15
Pledged assets to secured liabilities

Lessee Dextech signs a 5-year capital lease requiring a $10,000 annual lease payment. The present value of the five annual lease payments is $41,000, based on an interest rate with the lease of 7%.

1. What journal entry will Dextech record at inception of the lease?

2. If the leased asset has a 5-year useful life with no salvage value, what journal entry will Dextech record each year to recognize depreciation expense related to the leased asset?

Exercise 15-16[B]
Accounting for capital lease

For each separate case, indicate whether the company has entered into an operating lease or a capital lease.

1. The lessor retains title to the asset and the lease term is 3 years on an asset that has a 5-year useful life.

2. The title is transferred to the lessee, the lessee can purchase the asset for $1 at the end of the lease, and the lease term is 5 years. The leased asset has an expected useful life of 6 years.

3. The present value of the lease payments is 95% of the leased asset's market value, and the lease term is 70% of the leased asset's useful life.

Exercise 15-17[B]
Identifying capital and operating leases

GM ran an advertisement offering three alternatives for a 25-month lease on a new Blazer. The three alternatives are (1) zero dollars down and a lease payment of $590 per month for 25 months, (2) $2,000 down and $498 per month for 25 months, or (3) $12,975 down and no payments for 25 months. Use the present value Table B.3 in the Appendix B to determine which is the best alternative (assume you have enough cash to accept any of the three alternatives and the interest rate is 12% [annual] return compounded monthly).

Exercise 15-18[B]
Identifying capital and operating leases

Round dollar amounts to the nearest whole dollar. Assume no reversing entries are used.

PROBLEM SET A

KC Research issues bonds on January 1, 2003, that pay interest semiannually on June 30 and December 31. The bonds have a $40,000 par value, the annual contract rate is 10%, and the bonds mature in 10 years.

Problem 15-1A
Computing bond price and recording issuance

Required

For each of the following three separate situations, (a) determine the bonds' issue price and (b) show the journal entry to record their issuance.

1. Market rate at the date of issuance is 8%.

2. Market rate at the date of issuance is 10%.

3. Market rate at the date of issuance is 12%.

Check (1) Bond premium, $5,437

Problem 15-2A
Straight-line amortization of both bond discount and bond premium.

Check   (3) Total bond interest expense, $4,143,552

On January 1, 2002, Harrigan issues $4,000,000 of 6%, 15-year bonds that pay interest semiannually on June 30 and December 31. The bonds are issued at a price of $3,456,448.

Required

1. Prepare the journal entry to record the bonds' issuance.
2. For each semiannual period, compute (a) the cash payment, (b) the straight-line discount amortization, and (c) the bond interest expense.
3. Determine the total bond interest expense that will be recognized over the life of these bonds.
4. Prepare the first two years of an amortization table like Exhibit 15.7 using the straight-line method.
5. Prepare the journal entries in which Harrigan would record the first two interest payments.
6. Assume that the bonds are issued at a price of $4,895,980. Repeat parts (1–5).

Problem 15-3A
Effective interest amortization of bond premium and computing bond price

Check   (2) Bond carrying value at 6/30/2004, $252,865

GM Products issues 6.5%, five-year bonds with a par value of $250,000 on January 1, 2002. The bonds pay interest on June 30 and December 31 and are issued at a price of $255,333. The market rate is 6% on the issue date.

Required

1. Calculate the total bond interest expense over the life of the bonds.
2. Prepare an effective interest amortization table like Exhibit 15.13 covering the life of these bonds.
3. Prepare the journal entries in which GM Products would record the first two interest payments.
4. Use the market rate at issuance to compute the present value of the remaining cash flows for these bonds as of December 31, 2004. Compare your answer with the amount shown on the amortization table as the balance for that date and explain your findings.

Problem 15-4A
Effective interest amortization of bond discount

Check   (2) Total bond interest expense, $97,819

On January 1, 2002, Sweetman issues $325,000 of 5%, four-year bonds that pay interest semiannually on June 30 and December 31. The bonds are issued at a price of $292,181. The market rate is 8% at the issue date.

Required

Preparation Component

1. Prepare the journal entry to record the bonds' issuance.
2. Determine the total bond interest expense that will be recognized over the life of these bonds.
3. Prepare the first two years of an amortization table like Exhibit 15.8 using the effective interest method.
4. Prepare the journal entries in which Sweetman would record the first two interest payments.

Analysis Component

5. Assume the market rate on January 1, 2002, is 4% instead of 8%. Without providing numbers, describe how this change would affect the amounts presented on Sweetman's financial statements.

Problem 15-5A
Effective interest amortization of bond premium; retiring bonds

Check   (3) Bond interest expense for period ending 6/30/2003, $9,159

On January 1, 2002, McNeil Company issues $180,000 of 11%, three-year bonds that pay interest semiannually on June 30 and December 31. The bonds are issued at a price of $184,566. The market rate is 10% at the issue date.

Required

Preparation Component

1. Prepare the journal entry to record the bonds' issuance.
2. Determine the total bond interest expense that will be recognized over the life of these bonds.
3. Prepare the first two years of an amortization table like Exhibit 15.13 using the effective interest method.
4. Prepare the journal entries in which McNeil would record the first two interest payments.
5. Prepare the journal entry to record the retirement of these bonds on December 31, 2003, at a price of 98.

Analysis Component

6. Assume that the market rate on January 1, 2002, is 12% instead of 10%. Without presenting numbers, describe how this change would affect the amounts presented on McNeil's financial statements.

On October 31, 2002, Cook Ltd. borrows $200,000 from a bank by signing a five-year installment note bearing 8% interest. Terms of the note require equal total payments each year on October 31.

Required

1. Compute the total amount of each installment payment.

2. Complete an amortization table for this installment note similar to Exhibit 15.21.

3. Prepare the journal entries in which Cook would record accrued interest as of December 31, 2002 (the end of its annual reporting period), and the first annual payment on the note.

4. Assume that the note does not require equal payments but requires five payments of accrued interest and equal amounts of principal. Complete an amortization table for this note similar to Exhibit 15.20. Prepare the journal entries to record accrued interest as of December 31, 2002 (the end of its annual reporting period), and the first annual payment on the note.

Problem 15-6A
Installment notes

Check   (2) Interest expense for period ending 10/31/2006, $7,146

On January 1, 2002, Badger Company issues at par its 11%, four-year bonds with a $270,000 par value. They are secured by a mortgage that specifies assets totaling $360,000 as collateral. Also on January 1, 2002, Spartan Company issues at par its 11%, four-year bonds with a par value of $120,000. Spartan secures its bonds with a mortgage that includes $250,000 of pledged assets. The December 31, 2001, balance sheet information for both companies follows:

Problem 15-7A
Ratio of pledged assets to secured liabilities

	Badger Co.	Spartan Co.
Total assets	$1,000,000*	$550,000†
Liabilities		
Secured	$ 260,000	$100,000
Unsecured	200,000	240,000
Equity	540,000	210,000
Total liabilities and equity	$1,000,000	$550,000

* 43% are pledged. † 55% are pledged.

Required

Preparation Component

1. Compute the ratio of pledged assets to secured liabilities for each company at January 1, 2002.

Check   Badger, 1.49 to 1

Analysis Component

2. Which company's bonds appear less risky? What other information might help to evaluate the risks of these companies' bonds?

Gould Company signs a long-term 5-year capital lease for office equipment with Frazier Company. The annual lease payment is $10,000, and the interest rate is 8%.

Required

1. Compute the present value of the lease payments for Gould Company.

2. Prepare the journal entry to record the capital lease for Gould at the inception of the lease.

3. Complete a lease payment schedule with the following headings for the 5-years of the lease. Assume the beginning balance of the lease liability (present value of lease payments) is $39,927. To find the amount allocated to interest in year one, multiply the interest rate by the beginning-of-year lease liability. The amount of the annual lease payment not allocated to interest will be allocated to principal. Reduce the lease liability by the amount allocated to principal to update the lease liability at each year-end.

Problem 15-8A[B]
Capital lease accounting

Period Ending Date	Beginning Balance of Lease Liability	Interest on Lease Liability	Reduction of Lease Liability	Ending Balance of Lease Liability

4. Use straight-line depreciation and prepare the journal entry to depreciate the leased asset at the end of year 1. Assume zero salvage value for the office equipment.

PROBLEM SET B

Problem 15-1B

Computing bond price and recording issuance

Check (1) Bond premium, $6,948

Synergy Systems issues bonds on January 1, 2003, that pay interest semiannually on June 30 and December 31. The bonds have a $90,000 par value, the annual contract rate is 12%, and the bonds mature in five years.

Required

For each of the following three separate situations, (a) determine the bonds' issue price and (b) show the journal entry to record their issuance.

1. Market rate at the date of issuance is 10%.
2. Market rate at the date of issuance is 12%.
3. Market rate at the date of issuance is 14%.

Problem 15-2B

Straight-line amortization of both bond discount and bond premium

Check (3) Total bond interest expense, $3,790,000

On January 1, 2002, ParView issues $3,400,000 of 10%, 10-year bonds that pay interest semiannually on June 30 and December 31. The bonds are issued at a price of $3,010,000.

Required

1. Prepare the journal entry to record the bonds' issuance.
2. For each semiannual period, compute (a) the cash payment, (b) the straight-line discount amortization, and (c) the bond interest expense.
3. Determine the total bond interest expense that will be recognized over the life of these bonds.
4. Prepare the first two years of an amortization table like Exhibit 15.7 using the straight-line method.
5. Prepare the journal entries in which ParView would record the first two interest payments.
6. Assume that the bonds are issued at a price of $4,192,932. Repeat requirements (1–5).

Problem 15-3B

Effective interest amortization of bond premium and computation of bond price

Check (2) Bond carrying value at 6/30/2004, $327,136

Tiger Company issues 9%, five-year bonds with a par value of $320,000 on January 1, 2002. The bonds pay interest on June 30 and December 31 and are issued at a price of $332,988. The market rate is 8% on the issue date.

Required

1. Calculate the total bond interest expense over the life of the bonds.
2. Prepare an effective interest amortization table like Exhibit 15.13 covering the life of these bonds.
3. Prepare the journal entries in which Tiger would record the first two interest payments.
4. Use the market rate at issuance to compute the present value of the remaining cash flows for these bonds as of December 31, 2004. Compare your answer with the amount shown on the amortization table as the balance for that date and explain your findings.

Problem 15-4B

Effective interest amortization of bond discount

Check (2) Total bond interest expense, $257,506

On January 1, 2002, Morris Manufacturing issues $240,000 of 6%, 15-year bonds that pay interest semiannually on June 30 and December 31. The bonds are issued at a price of $198,494. The market rate is 8% at the issue date.

Required

1. Prepare the journal entry to record the bonds' issuance.
2. Determine the total bond interest expense that will be recognized over the life of these bonds.
3. Prepare the first two years of an amortization table like Exhibit 15.8 using the effective interest method.
4. Prepare the journal entries in which Morris would record the first two interest payments.

Problem 15-5B

Effective interest amortization of bond premium; retiring bonds

Check (3) Bond interest expense for period ending 6/30/2003, $24,212

On January 1, 2002, Hamm Brothers issues $450,000 of 13%, four-year bonds that pay interest semiannually on June 30 and December 31. The bonds are issued at a price of $493,608. The market rate is 10% at the issue date.

Required

Preparation Component

1. Prepare the journal entry to record the bonds' issuance.
2. Determine the total bond interest expense that will be recognized over the life of these bonds.
3. Prepare the first two years of an amortization table like Exhibit 15.13 using the effective interest method.

4. Prepare the journal entries in which Hamm Brothers would record the first two interest payments.

5. Prepare the journal entry to record the retirement of these bonds on December 31, 2003, at a price of 106.

Analysis Component

6. Assume that the market rate on January 1, 2002, is 14% instead of 10%. Without presenting numbers, describe how this change would affect the amounts presented on Hamm's financial statements.

On September 30, 2002, Venice Enterprises borrows $150,000 cash from a bank by signing a three-year installment note bearing 10% interest. Terms of the note require equal total payments each year on September 30.

Required

1. Compute the total amount of each installment payment.

2. Complete an amortization table for this installment note similar to Exhibit 15.21.

3. Prepare the journal entries in which Venice would record accrued interest as of December 31, 2002 (the end of its annual reporting period) and the first annual payment on the note.

4. Assume that the note does not require equal payments but requires three payments of accrued interest and equal amounts of principal. Complete an amortization table for this note similar to Exhibit 15.20. Prepare the journal entries to record accrued interest as of December 31, 2002 (the end of its annual reporting period) and the first annual payment on the note.

Problem 15-6B
Installment notes

Check   (2) Interest expense for period ending 9/30/2004, $10,468

On January 1, 2003, Pine Company issues $50,000 of its 12%, 10-year bonds at par that are secured by a mortgage that specifies assets totaling $125,000 as collateral. Also on January 1, 2003, Maple Company issues its 12%, 10-year bonds at their par value of $160,000. Maple secures its bonds by a mortgage that includes $235,000 of pledged assets. The December 31, 2002, balance sheet information for both companies follows:

Problem 15-7B
Ratio of pledged assets to secured liabilities

	Pine Co.	Maple Co.
Total assets	$185,000*	$755,000†
Liabilities		
Secured	$ 41,000	$ 59,000
Unsecured	43,000	507,500
Equity	101,000	188,500
Total liabilities and equity	$185,000	$755,000

* 59% are pledged. † 10% are pledged.

Required

Preparation Component

1. Compute the ratio of pledged assets to secured liabilities for each company at January 1, 2003.

Check   Pine, 2.57 to 1

Analysis Component

2. Which company's bonds appear less risky? What other information might help to evaluate the risks of these companies' bonds?

Parker Company signs a long-term 5-year capital lease for office equipment with Starbuck Company. The annual lease payment is $20,000, and the interest rate is 10%.

Problem 15-8B[B]
Capital lease accounting

Required

1. Compute the present value of the lease payments for Parker Company.

2. Prepare the journal entry to record the capital lease for Parker at the inception of the lease.

3. Complete a lease payment schedule with the following headings for the 5 years of the lease. Assume the beginning balance of the lease liability (present value of lease payments) is $75,816. To find the amount allocated to interest in year one, multiply the interest rate by the beginning-of-year lease liability. The amount of the annual lease payment not allocated to interest will be allocated to principal. Reduce the lease liability by the amount allocated to principal to update the lease liability at each year-end.

Period Ending Date	Beginning Balance of Lease Liability	Interest on Lease Liability	Reduction of Lease Liability	Ending Balance of Lease Liability

4. Use straight-line depreciation and prepare the journal entry to depreciate the leased asset at the end of year 1. Assume zero salvage value for the office equipment.

Beyond the Numbers

Reporting in Action

BTN 15-1   Refer to **Nike**'s financial statements in Appendix A to answer the following questions:

1. Does Nike have any bonds or long-term notes payable that are issued and outstanding?

2. How much cash is paid to reduce long-term debt for the year ended May 31, 2000?

3. Did Nike have any additions to long-term debt for the year ended May 31, 2000?

Swoosh Ahead

4. Access Nike's annual report for a year ending after May 31, 2000, from its Web site [**www.nike.com**] or the SEC's EDGAR database [**www.sec.gov**]. Has Nike issued additional long-term debt since the year ended May 31, 2000?

Comparative Analysis

BTN 15-2   Key comparative figures ($ millions) for both **Nike** and **Reebok** follow:

Key Figures	Nike		Reebok	
	Current Year	Prior Year	Current Year	Prior Year
Accounts receivable, net	$1,567.2	$1,540.1	$417.4	$517.8
Inventory	1,446.0	1,170.6	414.6	535.2
Property and equipment, net	1,583.4	1,265.8	178.1	172.6
Long-term debt (includes current portion)	520.4	387.1	555.5	641.1

Required

1. Assume that both Nike and Reebok have pledged substantially all of their accounts receivable, inventory, and property and equipment to collateralize their long-term debt. Compute the ratio of pledged assets to secured liabilities for both companies.

2. Use the ratio you computed in part (1) to determine which company's long-term debt is less risky.

Ethics Challenge

BTN 15-3   Brevard County needs a new building for its county government that would cost $24 million. The politicians feel that voters are unlikely to approve a municipal bond issue to fund the building since it would increase taxes. They opt for a different approach. They have a state bank issue $24 million of tax-exempt securities to pay for the building construction. The county then will make yearly lease payments (of principal and interest) to repay the obligation. Unlike conventional municipal bonds, the lease payments are not binding obligations on the county and therefore, no voter approval is required.

Required

1. Do you think the actions of the politicians and the bankers are ethical in this situation?

2. How do the tax-exempt securities used to pay for the building compare in risk to a conventional municipal bond issued by Brevard County?

Communicating in Practice

P3

BTN 15-4   Your business associate mentions that he is considering investing in corporate bonds currently selling at a premium. He says that since the bonds are selling at a premium, they are highly valued and his investment will yield more than the going rate of return for the risk involved. Reply with a memorandum to confirm or correct your associate's interpretation of premium bonds.

BTN 15-5   Access the March 9, 2000, filing of the 1999 calendar-year 10-K report of **Coca-Cola Co.** (Ticker KO) from **www.edgar-online.com.** Refer to Coca-Cola's statement of cash flows for the year ended December 31, 1999, to answer the following questions.

Taking It to the Net

C1

Required

1. Did the company issue any new debt in 1999?
2. Did the company repay any of its debt in 1999?
3. Did the company raise more new capital in 1999 from issuing debt or from issuing stock?
4. The company's 10-K report shows three years of cash flow data. Is the company showing a trend of issuing more or less debt over this three-year period?

BTN 15-6   Break into teams and complete the following requirements.

Teamwork in Action

P2   P3

1. Each team member is to independently prepare a blank table with proper headings for amortization of a bond premium. When all have finished, compare tables and ensure all are in agreement.

Parts 2 and 3 require use of these facts: On January 1, 2002, BC issues $100,000, 9%, five-year bonds at 104.1. The market rate at issuance is 8%. BC pays interest semiannually on June 30 and December 31.

2. In rotation, *each* team member must explain how to complete *one* line of the bond amortization table, including all computations for his/her line. (Round amounts to the nearest dollar.) All members are to fill in their tables during this process. You need not finish the table; stop after all members have explained a line.
3. In rotation, *each* team member is to identify a separate column of the table and indicate what the final number in that column will be and explain the reasoning.
4. Reach a team consensus as to what the total bond interest expense on this bond issue will be if the bond is not retired before maturity.
5. As a team, prepare a list of similarities and differences between the amortization table just prepared and the amortization table if the bond had been issued at a discount.

Hint: At conclusion, rotate teams to report on parts (4) and (5). Consider requiring entries for issuance and interest payments.

BTN 15-7   Read the article "The Debt That's Dragging Nissan Downhill" from the April 5, 1999, issue of *Business Week*.

Business Week Activity

C1

Required

1. In the fourth paragraph of the article, the sentence begins, "Nissan's big losses make it tougher for the company to service its own debt . . ." What does the phrase *to service its debt* mean?
2. How much does Nissan Motor Company pay in interest each year on its debt?
3. What new accounting rule that took effect in April 2000 impacts how Nissan reports its debt on its balance sheet?
4. What steps has Nissan taken to repay its debt?

BTN 15-8   Andrew Hamill is the young entrepreneur and owner of WebWorks, a provider of Internet services and Web site development. WebWorks has $250,000 in equity and is considering a $100,000 expansion to meet increased demand. The $100,000 expansion will yield $16,000 in additional annual income before interest expense. WebWorks currently earns $40,000 annual income before interest expense of $10,000, yielding a return on equity of 12% ($30,000/$250,000). To fund the expansion, WebWorks is considering the issuance of a 10-year, $100,000 note with annual interest payments and with the principal amount due at the end of 10 years.

Entrepreneurial Decision

Required

1. Using return on equity as the decision criterion, show computations to support or reject WebWorks' expansion if interest on the $100,000 note is (a) 10%, (b) 15%, (c) 16%, (d) 17%, and (e) 20%.
2. What general rule do the results in part (1) illustrate?

16

Long-Term Investments and International Transactions

"If you can make a huge profit and make a difference, that's nice."—Rory Stear.

A Look Back

Chapter 15 focused on long-term liabilities. We explained how these liabilities are valued, recorded, amortized, and reported in financial statements. We also described the accounting for leases and pensions.

A Look at This Chapter

This chapter focuses on long-term investments in securities. We explain how to identify, account for, and report long-term investments in both debt and equity securities. We also introduce foreign exchange rates and describe accounting for transactions listed in a foreign currency.

A Look Ahead

Chapter 17 focuses on reporting and analyzing a company's cash flows. Special emphasis is directed at the statement of cash flows—reported under the direct and indirect methods.

Freeplay's Fast Track

e CAPE TOWN, SA—Not every hot entrepreneur these days comes from the high-tech world. Take Rory Stear and Chris Staines, co-founders of **Freeplay** [**Freeplay.net**]. This duo has built a fast-growing business—and stayed true to a belief in social justice—selling wind-up radios that don't need batteries or electricity. Winding for 30 seconds produces up to an hour of play-ing time on a radio. To help educate people about preventing AIDS, they dis-tribute them through agencies in the developing world. Recently, they've begun to sell the radios to campers and boaters at Radio Shack, Sharper Image, and Sports Authority.

"We're not just in the radio business," insists Stear. "We're creating a whole new industry that can improve peoples' lives, whether they're in Los Angeles or Lagos." Adds Staines, "We want to see self-powered products in every village and every city in the world." In addition to radios and lanterns, Freeplay is feverishly developing self-powered products such as water purifiers, global-positioning systems, laptop computers, and cellular phones.

Freeplay's co-founders are social activists with a grounding in business. Staines, for instance, has a background in accounting. He quips, "I suppose I'm an accountant with a vision." With these skills, they quickly obtained fi-nancing and launched their business. They also carried out international trans-actions, struck up investment relationships, and set up an accounting system to effectively report and monitor company performance. Admits Stear, "We all want to make startling good profits." To do that, they must continue to expand internationally and pursue additional investment opportunities. They currently operate two factories with 270 employees. "We're like the dog that catches the bus," jokes Stear. "What do we do with it now?" What they have done is build a company in five years—where this year's sales should hit $50 million. "Even if you're a billionaire" says Stear, "you'll need some kind of self-powered device when the lights go out." [Sources: *Business Week,* January 10, 2000; *Fast Company Magazine,* 1999; *Freeplay Web site,* May 2001.]

Learning Objectives

Conceptual

C1 Distinguish long-term investments from short-term investments.

C2 Identify classes of securities in long-term investments.

C3 Describe how to report equity securities with controlling influence.

C4 Explain foreign exchange rates between currencies.

Analytical

A1 Compute and analyze the components of return on total assets.

Procedural

P1 Account for held-to-maturity securities.

P2 Account for available-for-sale securities.

P3 Account for equity securities with significant influence.

P4 Record transactions listed in a foreign currency.

Chapter Preview

This chapter's main focus is long-term investments. Many companies have long-term investments, and many of these are in the form of debt and equity securities issued by other companies. We describe long-term investments in these securities and how they are accounted for. An increasing number of companies also invest in international operations. The financial statement effects of these investments are often far reaching. We explain how international transactions listed in foreign currencies are accounted for and reported. Understanding the topics in this chapter is important for effectively reading and interpreting financial statements.

Classifying Investments

C1 Distinguish long-term investments from short-term investments.

Concept 16-1

C2 Identify classes of securities in long-term investments.

In this section, we first describe the distinction between short- and long-term investments and then describe the different classifications of long-term investments.

Short-Term versus Long-Term Investments

We explained in Chapter 10 how to account for short-term investments in debt and equity securities. *Short-term investments* are current assets that must meet two requirements. First, they are expected to be converted into cash within one year or the current operating cycle, whichever is longer. Second, they are readily convertible to cash. Short-term investments are usually held as an investment of cash for use in current operations. (It is helpful to review short-term investments in Chapter 10 and the basics of bonds and stocks in Chapters 14 and 15.)

Long-term investments are investments in debt and equity securities that are not readily convertible to cash or are not intended to be converted into cash in the short term. Long-term investments also include funds earmarked for a special purpose, such as bond sinking funds and investments in land or other assets not used in the company's operations. Long-term investments are reported in the noncurrent section of the balance sheet, often in its own separate section titled *Long-Term Investments*.

Classes of Long-Term Investments

Accounting for long-term investments depends on two factors. The first factor is whether the securities can be classified as (1) debt securities *held-to-maturity* or (2) debt and equity securities *available-for-sale*. These two classes of investments are either long term or short term depending on what the company intends to do with them. (Note that investments in trading securities always are short-term investments.) The second factor applies to equity securities and depends on the company's (investor's) percent ownership in the other company's (investee's) shares. Exhibit 16.1 classifies long-term securities on the basis of these two factors and describes the accounting required. The four classifications shown are (1) debt securities *held-to-maturity,* (2) debt and equity securities *available-for-sale,* (3) equity securities with a significant influence over an investee, and (4) equity securities with control over an investee. We describe each of these four classes of securities and how to account for them.

Exhibit 16.1

Accounting for Long-Term Investments in Securities

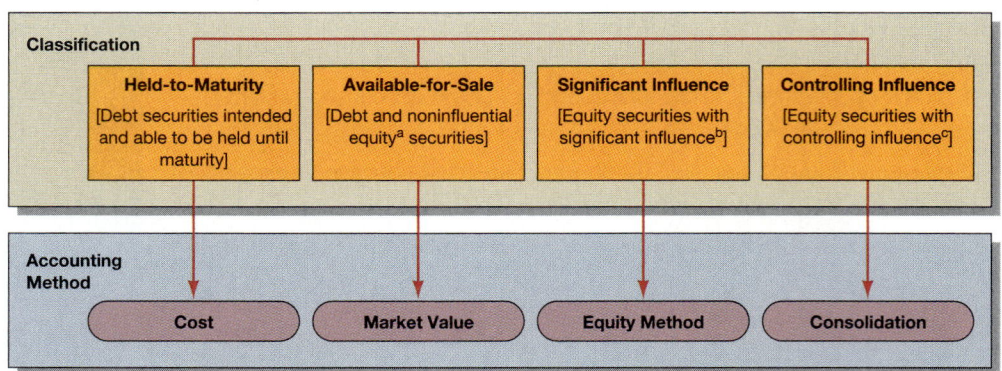

a Holding less than 20% of voting stock (equity securities only). b Holding 20% or more, but not more than 50%, of voting stock.
c Holding more than 50% of voting stock

Similar to the accounting for short-term investments, a long-term investment is recorded at cost when purchased. *Cost* is defined as all necessary expenditures to acquire the investment, including any commissions or brokerage fees paid. After the purchase, the accounting treatment for long-term investments depends on its classification.

Held-to-Maturity Securities

Held-to-maturity securities are *debt* securities a company intends and is able to hold until maturity. Debt securities held to maturity are classified as long-term investments when their maturity dates extend beyond one year or the operating cycle, whichever is longer. They are recorded at cost when purchased. Interest revenue for long-term investments in held-to-maturity debt securities must be recorded as it accrues.

The cost of an investment in a held-to-maturity debt security can be either higher or lower than the maturity value of the debt security. When the investment is long term, the difference between cost and maturity value is amortized over the remaining life of the security. Chapter 15 explains how we amortize such a premium or discount. Here we assume for ease of computations that the cost of a debt security equals its maturity value.

Illustration: Held-to-Maturity debt security

Music City paid $29,500 plus a $500 brokerage fee on August 31, 2002, to buy Improv's 7%, two-year bonds payable with a $30,000 par value. The bonds pay interest semiannually on August 31 and February 28. The amount of each interest payment is $1,050, computed as $30,000 par value × 7% interest × 6/12 year. Music City intends to hold the bonds until they mature on August 31, 2004. The entry to record this purchase is

2002			
Aug. 31	Long-Term Investments	30,000	
	Cash		30,000
	Purchased bonds to be held to maturity.		

Assets = Liabilities + Equity
+30,000
−30,000

On December 31, 2002, at the end of its accounting period, Music City accrues interest receivable as follows:

Dec. 31	Interest Receivable	700	
	Interest Earned		700
	Accrue interest earned ($30,000 × 7% × ⁴⁄₁₂).		

Assets = Liabilities + Equity
+700   +700

The $700 reflects 4/6 of the semiannual cash receipt of interest. This is the portion Music City earned as of December 31. Relevant sections of Music City's financial statements at December 31, 2002, are shown in Exhibit 16.2.

On the income statement for year 2002:	
Interest earned	$ 700
On the December 31, 2002, balance sheet:	
Long-term investments—Held-to-maturity securities (at amortized cost)	$30,000

On February 28, 2003, Music City records receipt of semiannual interest:

Feb. 28	Cash	1,050	
	Interest Receivable		700
	Interest Earned		350
	Received 6 months' interest on Improv bonds.		

Assets = Liabilities + Equity
+1,050   +350
−700

Exhibit 16.2

Financial Statement Effects of Held-to-Maturity Securities

When the bonds mature, their proceeds are recorded as follows:

Assets = Liabilities + Equity
+30,000
−30,000

2004			
Aug. 31	Cash	30,000	
	Long-Term Investments.		30,000
	Received cash from matured bonds.		

This illustration reflects what is called the *cost method* of accounting for long-term investments in held-to-maturity debt securities. This method is required.

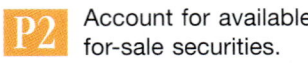

Account for available-for-sale securities.

Available-for-Sale Securities

Available-for-sale securities are held with the intent to sell them in the future. If the intent is to hold them at least through the next year or operating cycle, they are classified as long-term investments. Exhibit 16.1 shows that long-term investments in available-for-sale securities can include both debt securities and noninfluential equity securities. This section describes the accounting for both of these available-for-sale securities.

You Make the Call

Money Manager   You expect interest rates to sharply fall within a few weeks and remain at this lower rate. What is your strategy for investments in fixed-rate bonds and notes?

Answer—p. 676

Available-for-Sale Debt Securities

Accounting for **available-for-sale debt securities** is similar to accounting for held-to-maturity debt securities. First, debt securities are recorded at cost when purchased. Second, while debt securities are held, interest is recorded as it accrues. The difference in accounting for held-to-maturity debt securities versus available-for-sale debt securities is the amount reported on the balance sheet. Held-to-maturity debt securities are reported at cost, adjusted for the amortized amount of any difference between cost and maturity value. Available-for-sale debt securities are reported at (fair) market value.

Did You Know?

Trading Secrets   Trading records for mutual fund companies are kept secret for many reasons, including regulatory requirements and potential lawsuits. But a mystery arose when trading records for the multi-billion-dollar **Fidelity Magellan** fund appeared in the *Washington Post*. Since then, Fidelity's fund managers have been barred from talking about individual stocks with the press, and it has stopped internal circulation of daily trading activities.

Illustration: Available-for-Sale debt security

To illustrate the accounting for an available-for-sale debt security, assume that Music City does not intend to hold the Improv bonds to maturity (see the prior case). The Improv bonds are then classified as available-for-sale securities. The entries in the prior section to record the purchase of the Improv bonds on August 31, the accrual of interest on December 31, 2002, and the receipt of interest on February 28, 2003, remain the same provided the bonds are not yet sold. If Music City were to sell the bonds as planned (before they mature), any gain or loss on this sale is reported in the income statement. Also, (1) there is no amortization of any discount or premium and (2) any unrealized gain or loss from adjusting these securities to market value is reported in the equity section of the balance sheet.

Available-for-Sale Equity Securities

The accounting is similar for short-term and long-term investments in **available-for-sale equity securities.** First, these investments are recorded at cost. Second, cash dividends received are credited to Dividend Revenue and reported in the income statement. Third, when the shares are sold, proceeds from the sale are compared with the cost of the investment, and any gain or loss on the sale is reported in the income statement. However, if a long-term investment in an equity security gives the investor significant influence over the investee, it cannot be classified as available-for-sale. Significant influence usually exists if the investor owns 20% or more of the investee company's voting stock.

Point: Some users of financial statements are concerned that certain managers hold AFS securities that have incurred losses, while selling those that incur gains (which increases income).

Illustration: Available-for-Sale equity security

Music City purchases 1,000 shares of Intex common stock at par value for $86,000 on October 10, 2002, and it records this purchase as follows:

Oct. 10	Long-Term Investments	86,000	
	Cash		86,000
	Purchased 1,000 shares of Intex.		

Assets = Liabilities + Equity
+86,000
−86,000

On November 2, Music City receives a $1,720 quarterly cash dividend on the Intex shares, which it records as follows:

Nov. 2	Cash	1,720	
	Dividend Revenue		1,720
	Received dividend of $1.72 per share.		

Assets = Liabilities + Equity
+1,720   +1,720

On December 20, Music City sells 500 of the Intex shares for $45,000 and records this sale:

Dec. 20	Cash	45,000	
	Long-Term Investments		43,000
	Gain on Sale of Long-Term Investments ...		2,000
	Sold 500 Intex shares ($86,000 × 500/1,000).		

Assets = Liabilities + Equity
+45,000   +2,000
−43,000

Example: What is the entry if Music City sells 500 Intex shares for $41,000? *Answer:*
Cash 41,000
Loss on Sale of
  L-T Invest. ... 2,000
    L-T Investments 43,000

Reporting Market Value of Available-for-Sale Securities

Long-term investments in available-for-sale (both debt and equity) securities are reported at (fair) market value on the balance sheet. Any unrealized holding gain or loss on these securities is not reported on the standard income statement. Instead, it bypasses the income statement and is directly reported in equity (as part of *comprehensive income*). All changes in equity for a period, except those from investments by and distributions to owners, make up *comprehensive income*. The items making up comprehensive income (beyond the standard income statement items) are typically reported in the equity section of the balance sheet and as part of the statement of changes in equity. (Two other options are to report these items in a separate comprehensive income statement or in a combined statement of comprehensive income. These options are left for advanced courses.)

Illustration: Reporting on available-for-sale securities

Assume that Music City had no prior investments in available-for-sale securities other than the bonds purchased on August 31 and the stock purchased on October 10. Exhibit 16.3 shows both the book value and market value of these investments on December 31, 2002.

Point: Unrealized Loss—Equity and Unrealized Gain—Equity are *permanent* (balance sheet) *accounts*.

	Book Value	Market Value
Improv bonds	$30,000	$29,050
Intex common stock, 500 shares	43,000	45,500
Total	$73,000	$74,550

Exhibit 16.3

Book and Market Value of Available-for-Sale Securities

The entry to record the market value of these investments follows:

Dec. 31	Market Adjustment—Available for Sale	1,550	
	Unrealized Gain—Equity		1,550
	To record adjustment to market value of available-for-sale securities.		

Assets = Liabilities + Equity
+1,550   +1,550

Example: If market value in Exhibit 16.3 is $70,000 (instead of $74,550), what entry is made? *Answer:*
Unreal. Loss—Equity . . . 3,000
  Market Adj.   3,000

Exhibit 16.4

Balance Sheet Presentation of Available-for-Sale Securities

It is common to combine the cost of investments with the balance in the Market Adjustment account and report the net as a single amount. Exhibit 16.4 shows this reporting approach for Music City's December 31, 2002, balance sheet.

Long-Term investments—Available-for-sale at market (cost is $73,000)	$74,550
Equity:	
. . . *usual equity and capital accounts* . . .	
Add: Unrealized gain on available-for-sale securities*	$ 1,550

* Often included under the caption Accumulated Other Comprehensive Income.

Assume that at the end of its next calendar year (December 31, 2003), Music City's available-for-sale securities have an $81,000 book (cost) value and an $82,000 market value. It must record the adjustment to market value as follows:

Assets = Liabilities + Equity
−550   −550

Dec. 31	Unrealized Gain—Equity	550	
	Market Adjustment—Available-for-Sale . . .		550
	To record adjustment to market value of available-for-sale securities.		

Example: If book value is $83,000 and market is $82,000 at Dec. 31, 2003, Music City records the adjustment:
Unreal. Gain—Eq. . . . 1,550
Unreal. Loss—Eq. . . . 1,000
  Mkt. Adj.—AFS . .   2,550

The effects of year 2002 and 2003 securities transactions are reflected in the following T-accounts:

Market Adjustment — Available-for-Sale (LT)				**Unrealized Gain — Equity**			
Bal. 12/31/02	1,550	Adj. 12/31/03	550	Adj. 12/31/03	550	Bal. 12/31/02	1,550
Bal. 12/31/03	**1,000**					**Bal. 12/31/03**	**1,000**

Amounts reconcile.

Quick Check

1. Give at least two examples of assets classified as long-term investments.
2. What are the requirements for an equity security to be listed as a long-term investment?
3. Identify similarities and differences in accounting for long-term investments in debt securities that are held-to-maturity versus those available-for-sale.

Answer—p. 677

P3 Account for equity securities with significant influence.

Investment in Equity Securities with Significant Influence

A long-term investment classified in **equity securities with significant influence** implies that the investor can exert significant influence over the investee. An investor that owns 20% or more (but not more than 50%) of a company's voting stock is usually presumed to have a significant influence over the investee. In some cases, however, the 20% test of significant influence is overruled by other, more persuasive, evidence. This evidence can either lower the 20% requirement or increase it. The **equity method** of accounting and reporting is used for long-term investments in equity securities with significant influence.

Did You Know?

Mob on Wall Street   The stock market confronts a small but vexing problem: organized crime. The Mob's activities seem confined to stocks traded in the OTC "bulletin board" and NASDAQ small-cap markets. Its chief means of activity is ripping off investors by driving share prices up—and dumping them on an unsuspecting public.

Illustration: Investment in equity securities with significant influence

Long-term investments in equity securities with significant influence are recorded at cost when acquired. To illustrate, Micron Co. records the purchase of 3,000 shares (30%) of JVT common stock at a total cost of $70,650 on January 1, 2002:

Jan. 1	Long-Term Investments	70,650	
	Cash		70,650
	To record purchase of 3,000 JVT shares.		

Assets = Liabilities + Equity
+70,650
−70,650

Under the equity method, earnings of the investee (JVT) increase both the investee's net assets and the investor's (Micron) claims on the investee's net assets. Thus, when the investee reports its earnings, the investor records its share of those earnings in its investment account. To illustrate, assume that JVT reports net income of $20,000 for 2002. Micron then records its 30% share of those earnings as follows:

You can influence, but NOT control me!

Dec. 31	Long-Term Investments	6,000	
	Earnings from Long-Term Investment		6,000
	To record 30% equity in investee earnings.		

Assets = Liabilities + Equity
+6,000   +6,000

The debit reflects the increase in Micron's equity in JVT. The credit reflects 30% of JVT's net income that appears on Micron's income statement. If the investee incurs a net loss instead of a net income, the investor records its share of the loss and reduces (credits) its investment account. The investor closes this earnings or loss account to Income Summary.

The receipt of cash dividends is not recorded as revenue under the equity method because the investor has already recorded its share of the earnings reported by the investee. Instead, cash dividends received by an investor from an investee are viewed as a conversion of one asset to another. Dividends thus reduce the balance of the investor's investment account but increase cash. To illustrate, JVT declares and pays $10,000 in cash dividends on its common stock. Micron records its 30% share of these dividends received on January 9, 2003:

Point: *Insider trading* usually refers to officers and employees of a corporation who buy or sell shares in their corporation based on information not yet released to the public. Generally, insider trading is illegal in the U.S., but some countries permit it.

Jan. 9	Cash	3,000	
	Long-Term Investments		3,000
	To record share of dividend paid by JVT.		

Assets = Liabilities + Equity
+3,000
−3,000

The book value of an investment under the equity method equals the cost of the investment plus (minus) the investor's equity in the *undistributed* (*distributed*) earnings of the investee. Once we record these transactions for Micron, its investment account appears as shown in Exhibit 16.5.

Date	Explanation	Debit	Credit	Balance
2002				
Jan. 1	Investment acquisition	70,650		70,650
Dec. 31	Share of earnings	6,000		76,650
2003				
Jan. 9	Share of dividend		3,000	73,650

Exhibit 16.5

Investment in JVT Common Stock (Ledger Account)

Micron's account balance on January 9, 2003, for its investment in JVT is $73,650. This is the investment's cost *plus* Micron's equity in JVT's earnings since its purchase *less* Micron's equity in JVT's cash dividends since its purchase. When an investment in equity securities is sold, the gain or loss is computed by comparing proceeds from the sale with the book value of the investment on the date of sale. If Micron sells its JVT stock for $80,000 on January 10, 2003, it records the sale as:

$Assets = Liabilities + Equity$
$+80,000 \qquad\qquad +6,350$
$-73,650$

Jan. 10	Cash	80,000	
	Long-Term Investments		73,650
	Gain on Sale of Investment		6,350
	Sold 3,000 shares of stock for $80,000.		

Investment in Equity Securities with Controlling Influence

C3   Describe how to report equity securities with controlling influence.

A long-term investment classified in **equity securities with controlling influence** implies that the investor can exert a controlling influence over the investee. An investor who owns more than 50% of a company's voting stock has control over the investee. This investor can dominate all other shareholders in electing the corporation's board of directors and has control over the investee's management. In some cases, controlling influence can extend to situations of less than 50% ownership.

The equity method is used to account for long-term investments in equity securities with controlling influence. The investor reports *consolidated financial statements* when owning such securities. Exhibit 16.6 summarizes the accounting for investments in equity securities based on an investor's ownership in the stock.

Did You Know?

Tinseltown Securities Did you ever wish you could share in the profits of Hollywood films like *Independence Day, The Lost World, Titanic,* or *Speed?* Well, you can now. Both **Fox** and **Universal Studios** are selling equity shares in their upcoming movies to outside investors.

Exhibit 16.6

Accounting for Equity Investments by Percent of Ownership

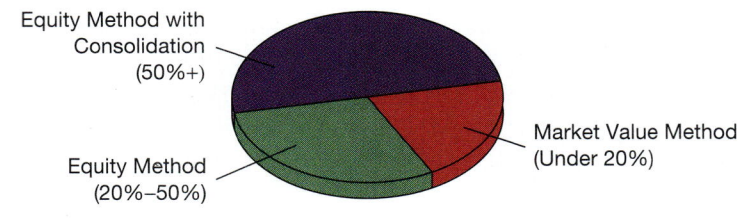

Equity Method with Consolidation (50%+)

Equity Method (20%–50%)

Market Value Method (Under 20%)

Illustration: Equity security with controlling influence

The controlling investor is called the **parent** and the investee is called the **subsidiary.** Many companies are parents with subsidiaries. Examples are (1) **McGraw-Hill**, the parent of *Business Week,* Standard and Poor's, and Compustat; (2) **GAP**, the parent of Gap, Old Navy, and Banana Republic; and (3) **Brunswick**, the parent of Mercury Marine, Sea Ray, and U.S. Marine. A company owning all the outstanding stock of a subsidiary can, if it desires, take over the subsidiary's assets, retire the subsidiary's stock, and merge the subsidiary into the parent. However, there often are financial, legal, and tax advantages if a business operates as a parent controlling one or more subsidiaries. When a company operates as a parent with subsidiaries, each entity maintains separate accounting records. From a legal viewpoint, the parent and each subsidiary are separate entities with all rights, duties, and responsibilities of individual companies.

Consolidated financial statements show the financial position, results of operations, and cash flows of all entities under the parent's control, including all subsidiaries. These statements are prepared as if the business were organized as one entity. The parent uses the equity method in its accounts, but the investment account is *not* reported on the parent's financial statements. Instead, the individual assets and liabilities of the parent and its subsidiaries are combined on one balance sheet. Their revenues and expenses also are combined on one income statement and their cash flows are combined on one statement of cash flows. The detailed procedures for preparing consolidated financial statements are included in advanced courses.

Quick Check

4. What are the three classes of long-term equity investments? Describe the criteria for each class and the method used to account for each.

Answer—p. 677

Accounting Summary for Investments in Securities

Exhibit 16.7 summarizes the accounting for investments in securities. Recall that many investment securities can be classified as either short term or long term depending on management's intent and ability to convert them in the future. Understanding the accounting for these investments enables us to draw better conclusions from financial statements in making business decisions.

Class of Investment Securities	Accounting Method
Short-term investment in securities	
Held-to-maturity (debt) securities	Cost (without any discount or premium amortization)
Trading (debt and equity) securities	Market value (with market adjustment to income)
Available-for-sale (debt and equity) securities	Market value (with market adjustment to equity)
Long-term investment in securities	
Held-to-maturity (debt) securities	Cost (with any discount or premium amortization)
Available-for-sale (debt and equity) securities	Market value (with market adjustment to equity)
Equity securities with significant influence	Equity method
Equity securities with controlling influence	Equity method (with consolidation)

Exhibit 16.7

Accounting for Investments in Securities

Investments in International Operations

Many entities from small entrepreneurs to large corporations conduct business internationally. The operations of some entities occur in so many different countries that they are called **multinationals.** Many of us, for example, think of **Coca-Cola** and **McDonald's** as primarily U.S. companies, but both earn most of their sales from outside the United States. Exhibit 16.8 shows the percent of international sales and income for selected U.S. companies. Managing and accounting for companies with international operations present new challenges. This section describes some of these challenges and how we account for and report these activities.

Two major accounting challenges arise when companies have international operations. Both relate to transactions that occur using more than one currency. The two challenges can be described as (1) accounting for sales and purchases listed in a foreign currency and (2) preparing consolidated financial statements with international subsidiaries. For ease in this discussion, we use companies with a base of operations in the U.S. and with a need to prepare financial statements in U.S. dollars. This means the *reporting currency* of these companies is the U.S. dollar.

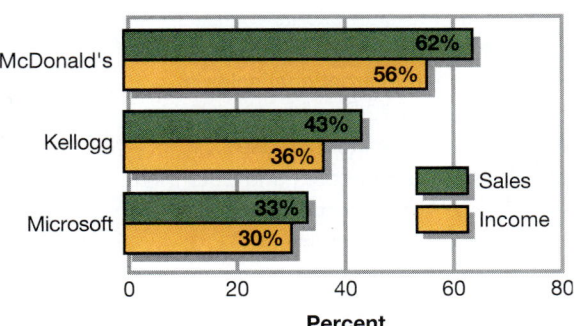

Exhibit 16.8

International Sales and Income as a Percent of Their Totals

Concept 16-2

Point: Transactions *listed or stated* in a foreign currency are said to be *denominated* in that currency.

Exchange Rates between Currencies

Markets for the purchase and sale of foreign currencies exist all over the world. In these markets, U.S. dollars can be exchanged for Canadian dollars, British pounds, French francs, Japanese yen, or any other legal currencies. The

C4 Explain foreign exchange rates between currencies.

price of one currency stated in terms of another currency is called a **foreign exchange rate.** Exhibit 16.9 lists recent exchange rates for selected currencies. The exchange rate for British pounds and U.S. dollars is $1.6152, meaning 1 British pound can be purchased for $1.6152. On that same day, the exchange rate between German marks and U.S. dollars is $0.5446, or 1 German mark can be purchased for $0.5446.

Exchange rates fluctuate due to changing economic and political conditions, including the supply and demand for currencies and expectations about future events.

Exhibit 16.9

Foreign Exchange Rates for Selected Currencies*

Source (unit)	Price in $U.S.	Source (unit)	Price in $U.S.
Britain (pound)	$1.6152	Canada (dollar)	$0.6720
Germany (mark)	0.5446	France (franc)	0.1624
Mexico (peso)	0.1063	Japan (yen)	0.0085
Taiwan (dollar)	0.0305	Europe (Euro)	1.0651

* Rates will vary over time based on economic and political changes.

Sales and Purchases Listed in a Foreign Currency

P4 Record transactions listed in a foreign currency.

When a U.S. company makes a credit sale to an international customer, accounting for the sale and the account receivable is straightforward if sales terms require the international customer's payment in U.S. dollars. If sale terms require (or allow) payment in a foreign currency, however, the U.S. company must account for the sale and the account receivable in a certain way.

To illustrate, consider the case of the U.S.-based manufacturer Boston Company, which makes credit sales to London Outfitters, a British retail company. A sale occurs on December 12, 2002, for a price of £10,000 with payment due on February 10, 2003. Boston Company keeps its accounting records in U.S. dollars. To record the sale, Boston Company must translate the sales price from pounds to dollars. This is done using the exchange rate on the date of the sale. Assuming the exchange rate on December 12, 2002, is $1.80, Boston records this sale as follows:

Assets = Liabilities + Equity
+18,000   +18,000

Dec. 12	Accounts Receivable—London Outfitters	18,000	
	Sales (£10,000 × $1.80)		18,000
	To record a sale at £10,000, when the exchange rate equals $1.80.		

Global: The creation and implementation of the European Union (EU) facilitate both European and global transactions.

When Boston Company prepares its annual financial statements on December 31, 2002, the current exchange rate is $1.84. Thus, the current dollar value of Boston Company's receivable is $18,400 (10,000 × $1.84). This amount is $400 higher than the amount recorded on December 12. Accounting principles require a receivable to be reported in the balance sheet at its current dollar value. Thus, Boston Company must make the following entry to record the increase in the dollar value of this receivable at year-end:

Dec. 31	Accounts Receivable—London Outfitters	400	
	Foreign Exchange Gain		400
	To record the increased value of the British pound for the receivable.		

Assets = Liabilities + Equity
+400   +400

On February 10, 2003, Boston Company receives London Outfitters' payment of £10,000. It immediately exchanges the pounds for U.S. dollars. On this date, the exchange rate for pounds is $1.78. Thus, Boston Company receives only $17,800 (£10,000 × $1.78). It records the cash receipt and the loss associated with the decline in the exchange rate as follows:

Point: Foreign exchange gains are credits and foreign exchange losses are debits.

Feb. 10	Cash	17,800	
	Foreign Exchange Loss	600	
	Accounts Receivable—London Outfitters . .		18,400
	Received foreign currency payment of an account and converted it into dollars.		

Assets = Liabilities + Equity
+17,800   −600
−18,400

Gains and losses from foreign exchange transactions are accumulated in the Foreign Exchange Gain (or Loss) account. After year-end adjustments, the balance in the Foreign Exchange Gain (or Loss) account is reported on the income statement and closed to the Income Summary account.

Accounting for credit purchases from an international seller is similar to the case of a credit sale to an international customer. In particular, if the U.S. company is required to make payment in a foreign currency, the account payable must be translated into dollars before the U.S. company can record it. If the exchange rate is different when preparing financial statements and when paying for the purchase, the U.S. company must recognize a foreign exchange gain or loss at those dates.

Example: Assume that a U.S. company makes a credit purchase from a British company for £10,000 when the exchange rate is $1.62. At the balance sheet date, this rate is $1.72. Does this imply a gain or loss for the U.S. company? *Answer:* A loss.

Consolidated Statements with International Subsidiaries

A second challenge in accounting for international operations involves preparing consolidated financial statements when the parent company has one or more international subsidiaries. Consider the U.S.-based company, **Classic Winery**, which owns a controlling interest in a French subsidiary. The reporting currency of the U.S. parent is the dollar. The French subsidiary maintains its financial records in francs. Before preparing consolidated statements, the parent must translate financial statements of the French company into U.S. dollars. After this translation is complete, it prepares consolidated statements the same as for domestic subsidiaries.[1] Procedures for translating an international subsidiary's account balances depend on the nature of the subsidiary's operations. The process requires the parent company to select appropriate foreign exchange rates and to apply those rates to the foreign subsidiary's account balances. This is described in advanced courses.

> ### You Make the Call
>
> **Entrepreneur**   You are a U.S. home builder that purchases lumber from mills in both the U.S. and Canada. The price of the Canadian dollar in terms of the U.S. dollar jumps from US$0.70 to US$0.80. Are you now more or less likely to buy lumber from Canadian or U.S mills?
>
> Answer—p. 676

Global: A weaker U.S. dollar often increases global sales for U.S. companies.

Comprehensive Income

Comprehensive income refers to all changes in equity for a period except those due to investments and distributions to owners. This means that it includes (1) the revenues, gains, expenses, and losses reported in net income, *and* (2) the gains and losses that bypass net income but affect equity. An example of an item that bypasses net income is unrealized gains and losses on available-for-sale securities. These items make up *other comprehensive income*

---

[1] The problem is more challenging when accounts of the French subsidiary are maintained in accordance with French GAAP. The French statements then must be converted to U.S. GAAP before consolidation.

and are usually reported as a part of the statement of changes in stockholders' equity.[2] Most often this simply requires one additional column for Other Comprehensive Income in the usual columnar form of the statement of changes in equity (the details of this are left for advanced courses). The FASB encourages, but does *not* require, other comprehensive income items to be grouped under the caption *Accumulated Other Comprehensive Income* in the equity section of the balance sheet, which would include unrealized gains and losses on available-for-sale securities. For instructional benefits, we use actual account titles for these items in the equity section instead of this general, less precise caption.

Using the Information   Components of Return on Total Assets

A1   Compute and analyze the components of return on total assets.

Chapter 1 described a company's **return on total assets** (or simply *return on assets*) and explained its importance in assessing financial performance. The return on total assets can be separated into two components to help analyze financial statements. The two components are profit margin and total asset turnover. Profit margin, or net profit margin, is explained in Chapter 4, and total asset turnover in Chapter 11. Exhibit 16.10 shows how these two components determine return on total assets.

Exhibit 16.10

Components of Return on Total Assets

$$\text{Return on total assets} = \text{Profit margin} \times \text{Total asset turnover}$$

$$\frac{\text{Net income}}{\text{Average total assets}} = \frac{\text{Net income}}{\text{Net sales}} \times \frac{\text{Net sales}}{\text{Average total assets}}$$

Profit margin (net income ÷ net sales) is the first component and reflects the percent of net income in each dollar of net sales. Total asset turnover (net sales ÷ average total assets) is the second component and reflects a company's ability to produce net sales from total assets. All companies desire a high return on total assets. By considering these two components, we can often discover strengths and weaknesses not revealed by return on total assets alone. This improves our ability to assess future performance and company strategy.

Consider return on total assets and its components for **Reebok** and **Nike**. Reebok's return on total assets and its components are shown in Exhibit 16.11.

Exhibit 16.11

Reebok's Components of Return on Total Assets

Year	Return on Total Assets	=	Profit Margin	×	Total Asset Turnover
1999	0.7%	=	0.4%	×	1.78
1998	1.4%*	=	0.7%	×	1.86
1997	7.6%	=	3.7%	×	2.06

* Minor rounding differences.

At least three findings emerge. First, Reebok's return on total assets declined from 1997 through 1999. Second, total asset turnover also declined but not markedly. Third, Reebok's profit margin sharply fell between 1997 and 1999. These components also reveal the dual role of profit margin and total asset turnover. They show that the cause of Reebok's decline is not total asset turnover but profit margin. Reebok's costs and expenses have increased as a percent of sales, and cost management is necessary.

More generally, if a company is to maintain its return on total assets, it must meet a decline in either profit margin or total asset turnover with an increase in the other. If not, return on assets will decline. Companies consider these components in planning future strategies. A component analysis can also reveal where a company is weak and where changes are needed, especially in a competitor analysis. If asset turnover is lower than the industry

[2] Two other options are (1) as a second separate income statement or (2) as a combined income statement of comprehensive income. These less common options are described in advanced courses.

norm, for instance, a company should focus on raising asset turnover at least to the norm. The same applies to profit margin. Exhibit 16.12 shows Nike's components for its fiscal year ending May 31, 2000.

Fiscal Year	Return on Total Assets	=	Profit Margin	×	Total Asset Turnover
2000	10.4%	=	6.4%	×	1.62

Exhibit 16.12

Nike's Components of Return on Total Assets

Nike's return on total assets is better than Reebok's. However, component analysis shows Reebok is slightly better than Nike on total asset turnover. This analysis also highlights Reebok's sharp decline in profit margin in recent years. One potential cause is Reebok's increased cost of goods sold and increased selling, general and administrative expenses as a percent of net sales (see its income statement in Appendix A). Reebok should focus on reducing these expenditures as a percent of sales.

You Make the Call

Retailer   You are an entrepreneur and owner of a retail sporting goods store. The store's recent annual performance reveals (industry norms in parentheses): return on total assets = 11% (11.2%); profit margin = 4.4% (3.5%); and total asset turnover = 2.5 (3.2). What does your analysis of these figures suggest?

Answer—p. 676

The following transactions relate to Brown Company's long-term investment activities during 2002 and 2003. Brown did not own any long-term investments prior to 2002. Show (1) the appropriate journal entries and (2) the portions of each year's balance sheet and income statement that describe these transactions for both 2002 and 2003.

Demonstration Problem

2002

Sept. 9   Purchased 1,000 shares of Packard, Inc., common stock for $80,000 cash. These shares represent 30% of Packard's outstanding shares.

Oct. 2   Purchased 2,000 shares of AT&T common stock for $60,000 cash. These shares represent less than a 1% ownership in AT&T.

      17   Purchased as a long-term investment 1,000 shares of Apple Computer common stock for $40,000 cash. These shares are less than 1% of Apple's outstanding shares.

Nov. 1   Received $5,000 cash dividend from Packard.

      30   Received $3,000 cash dividend from AT&T.

Dec. 15   Received $1,400 cash dividend from Apple.

      31   Packard's 2002 net income is $70,000.

      31   Market values for the investments in equity securities are Packard, $84,000; AT&T, $48,000; and Apple Computer, $45,000.

      31   After closing the accounts, select account balances on Brown Company's books are Common Stock, $500,000, and Retained Earnings, $350,000.

2003

Jan. 1   Sold Packard, Inc., shares for $108,000 cash when it is taken over by other investors.

May 30   Received $3,100 cash dividend from AT&T.

June 15   Received $1,600 cash dividend from Apple.

Aug. 17   Sold the AT&T stock for $52,000 cash.

      19   Purchased 2,000 shares of Coca-Cola common stock for $50,000 cash as a long-term investment. The stock represents less than a 5% ownership in Coca-Cola.

Dec. 15   Received $1,800 cash dividend from Apple.

      31   Market values of the investments in equity securities are Apple, $39,000, and Coca-Cola, $48,000.

      31   After closing the accounts, select account balances on Brown Company's books are Common Stock, $500,000, and Retained Earnings, $410,000.

Planning the Solution

- Account for the investment in Packard under the equity method.
- Account for the investments in AT&T, Apple, and Coca-Cola as long-term investments in securities available for sale.
- Prepare the information for the two years' balance sheets by including the appropriate asset and stockholders' equity accounts.

Solution to Demonstration Problem

1. Journal entries for 2002:

Sept. 9	Long-Term Investments (Packard)	80,000	
	Cash		80,000
	Acquired 1,000 shares, representing a 30% equity in Packard.		
Oct. 2	Long-Term Investments (AT&T)	60,000	
	Cash		60,000
	Acquired 2,000 shares as a long-term investment in available-for-sale securities.		
Oct. 17	Long-Term Investments (Apple)	40,000	
	Cash		40,000
	Acquired 1,000 shares as a long-term investment in available-for-sale securities.		
Nov. 1	Cash	5,000	
	Long-Term Investments (Packard)		5,000
	Received dividend from Packard.		
Nov. 30	Cash	3,000	
	Dividend Revenue		3,000
	Received dividend from AT&T.		
Dec. 15	Cash	1,400	
	Dividend Revenue		1,400
	Received dividend from Apple.		
Dec. 31	Long-Term Investments (Packard)	21,000	
	Earnings from Investment (Packard)		21,000
	To record 30% share of Packard's annual earnings of $70,000.		
Dec. 31	Unrealized Loss—Equity	7,000	
	Market Adjustment—Available-for-Sale* . . .		7,000
	To record change in market value of long-term available-for-sale securities.		

* Market adjustment computations:

	Cost	Market Value
AT&T	$ 60,000	$48,000
Apple	40,000	45,000
Total	$100,000	$93,000

Required credit balance of Market Adjustment
—Available-for-Sale (LT) account:

($100,000 − $93,000)	$7,000
Existing balance	0
Necessary credit adjustment	$7,000

2. The December 31, 2002, balance sheet items appear as follows:

Assets
Long-term investments:

Available-for-Sale securities (at market value)	$93,000
Investment in significant equity securities	96,000
Total long-term investments	$189,000

(continued from previous page)

Stockholders' Equity	
Common stock	500,000
Retained earnings	350,000
Unrealized loss	(7,000)

The income statement items for the year ended December 31, 2002 appear as follows:

Dividend revenue	$ 4,400
Earnings from investment	21,000

1. Journal entries for 2003:

Jan. 1	Cash	108,000	
	Long-Term Investments (Packard)		96,000
	Gain on Sale of Investments		12,000
	Sold 1,000 shares for cash.		
May 30	Cash	3,100	
	Dividend Revenue		3,100
	Received dividend from AT&T.		
June 15	Cash	1,600	
	Dividend Revenue		1,600
	Received dividend from Apple.		
Aug. 17	Cash	52,000	
	Loss on Sale of Investments	8,000	
	Long-Term Investments (AT&T)		60,000
	Sold 2,000 shares for cash.		
Aug. 19	Long-Term Investments (Coca-Cola)	50,000	
	Cash		50,000
	Acquired 2,000 shares as a long-term investment in available-for-sale securities.		
Dec. 15	Cash	1,800	
	Dividend Revenue		1,800
	Received dividend from Apple.		
Dec. 31	Market Adjustment—Available-for-Sale*.	4,000	
	Unrealized Loss—Equity		4,000
	To record change in market value of long-term available-for-sale securities.		

* Market adjustment computations:

	Cost	Market Value
Apple	$40,000	$39,000
Coca Cola	50,000	48,000
Total	$90,000	$87,000

Required credit balance of Market Adjustment —Available-for-Sale (LT) account:	
($90,000 − $87,000)	$3,000
Existing credit balance	7,000
Necessary debit adjustment	$4,000

2. The December 31, 2003, balance sheet items appear as follows:

Assets	
Long-term investments:	
Available-for-Sale securities (at market value)	$ 87,000
Stockholders' Equity	
Common stock	500,000
Retained earnings	410,000
Unrealized loss	(3,000)

The income statement items for the year ended December 31, 2003, appear as follows:

Dividend revenue	$ 6,500
Gain on sale of investments	12,000
Loss on sale of investments	(8,000)

Summary

C1 | **Distinguish long-term investments from short-term investments.** Short-term investments in securities are current assets that meet two criteria. First, they are expected to be converted into cash within one year or the current operating cycle of the business, whichever is longer. Second, they are readily convertible to cash, or *marketable*. All other investments in securities are long-term investments. Long-term investments also include assets not used in operations and those held for special purposes, such as land for expansion.

C2 | **Identify classes of securities in long-term investments.** Long-term investments in securities are classified into one of four groups: (1) debt securities held-to-maturity, (2) debt and equity securities available-for-sale, (3) equity securities in which an investor has a significant influence over the investee, and (4) equity securities in which an investor has a controlling influence over the investee.

C3 | **Describe how to report equity securities with controlling influence.** If an investor owns more than 50% of another company's voting stock and controls the investee, the investor's financial reports are prepared on a consolidated basis. These reports are prepared as if the company were organized as one entity.

C4 | **Explain foreign exchange rates between currencies.** A foreign exchange rate is the price of one currency stated in terms of another. An entity with transactions in a foreign currency when the exchange rate changes between the transaction dates and their settlement will experience exchange gains or losses.

A1 | **Compute and analyze the components of return on total assets.** Return on total assets has two components: profit margin and total asset turnover. A decline in one component must be met with an increase in another if return on assets is

to be maintained. Component analysis is helpful in assessing company performance compared to that of competitors.

P1 | **Account for held-to-maturity securities.** Debt securities held-to-maturity are reported at cost when purchased. Interest revenue is recorded as it accrues. The cost of held-to-maturity securities is adjusted for the amortization of any difference between cost and maturity value.

P2 | **Account for available-for-sale securities.** Debt and equity securities available-for-sale are recorded at cost when purchased. Available-for-sale securities are reported at their market values with unrealized gains or losses shown in the equity section of the balance sheet. Gains and losses realized on the sale of these investments are reported in the income statement.

P3 | **Account for equity securities with significant influence.** The equity method is used when an investor has a significant influence over an investee. This usually exists when an investor owns 20% or more of the investee's voting stock but not more than 50%. The equity method means an investor records its share of investee earnings with a debit to the investment account and a credit to a revenue account. Dividends received satisfy the investor's equity claims and reduce the investment account balance.

P4 | **Record transactions listed in a foreign currency.** When a company makes a credit sale to a foreign customer and sales terms call for payment in a foreign currency, the company must translate the foreign currency into dollars to record the receivable. If the exchange rate changes before payment is received, exchange gains or losses are recognized in the year they occur. The same treatment is used when a company makes a credit purchase from a foreign supplier and is required to make payment in a foreign currency.

Guidance Answers to You Make the Call

Money Manager If you have investments in fixed-rate bonds and notes when interest rates fall, the value of your investments increases. This is so because the bonds and notes you hold continue to pay the same (high) rate while the market is demanding a new lower interest rate. Your strategy is to continue holding your investments in bonds and notes, and, potentially, to increase these holdings through additional purchases.

Entrepreneur You are now less likely to buy Canadian lumber because it takes more U.S. money to buy a Canadian dollar (and lumber). For instance, the purchase of lumber from a Canadian mill with a $1,000 (Canadian dollars) price cost the U.S. builder $700 (U.S. dollars, computed as C$1,000 × US$0.70) before the rate change, and $800 (US dollars, computed as C$1,000 × US$0.80) after the rate change.

Retailer Your store's return on assets is 11%, which is similar to the industry norm of 11.2%. However, disaggregation of return on assets reveals that your store's profit margin of 4.4% is much higher than the norm of 3.5%, but your total asset turnover of 2.5 is much lower than the norm of 3.2. These results suggest that, as compared with competitors, you are less efficient in using assets. You need to focus on increasing sales or reducing assets. You might consider reducing prices to increase sales, provided such a strategy does not reduce your return on assets. For instance, you could reduce your profit margin to 4% to increase sales. If total asset turnover increases to more than 2.75 when profit margin is lowered to 4%, your overall return on assets is improved.

Guidance Answers to **Quick Checks**

1. Long-term investments include (1) funds earmarked for a special purpose, (2) debt and equity securities that do not meet the requirements of a current asset, and (3) assets not used in the regular operations of the business.

2. An equity investment is classified as a long-term investment if it is not marketable or, if marketable, it is not held as an available source of cash to meet the needs of current operations.

3. Debt securities held-to-maturity and debt securities available-for-sale are both recorded at cost. Also, interest on both is accrued as earned. However, only securities held-to-maturity

require amortization of the difference between cost and maturity value. In addition, only securities available-for-sale require a period-end adjustment to market value.

4. Long-term equity investments are placed in one of three categories and accounted for as follows: (a) **available-for-sale** (noninfluential, less than 20% of outstanding stock)—market value; (b) **significant influence** (20% to 50% of outstanding stock)—equity method; and (c) **controlling influence** (holding more than 50% of outstanding stock)—equity method with consolidation.

Glossary

Available-for-sale debt securities long-term investments in debt securities held with the intent to sell them in the future. (p. 664).

Available-for-sale equity securities long-term investments in noninfluential equity securities held with the intent to sell them in the future. (p. 664).

Comprehensive income net change in equity for a period, excluding owner investments and distributions. (p. 671).

Consolidated financial statements financial statements that show all (combined) activities under the parent's control, including those of any subsidiaries. (p. 668).

Equity method accounting method used for long-term investments when the investor has "significant influence" over the investee. (p. 666).

Equity securities with controlling influence long-term investment when the investor is able to exert controlling influence over the investee; investors owning 50% or more of voting stock are presumed to exert controlling influence. (p. 668).

Equity securities with significant influence long-term investment when the investor is able to exert significant influence over the investee; investors owning 20% or more (but less than 50%) of voting stock are presumed to exert significant influence. (p. 666).

Foreign exchange rate price of one currency stated in terms of another currency. (p. 670).

Held-to-maturity securities debt securities that the company has the intent and ability to hold until they mature. (p. 663).

Long-term investments investments in equity and debt securities that are not marketable or, if marketable, are not intended to be converted into cash in the short term; also special-purpose funds and assets not used in operations. (p. 662).

Multinational company that operates in several countries. (p. 669).

Parent company that owns a controlling interest in a corporation (requires more than 50% of voting stock). (p. 668).

Return on total assets measure of operating efficiency, computed as net income divided by average total assets. (p. 672).

Subsidiary entity controlled by another entity (parent) in which the parent owns more than 50% of the subsidiary's voting stock. (p. 668).

Questions

1. Identify the four main classes of long-term investments in securities.

2. Under what conditions should investments be classified as current assets? As long-term assets?

3. If a company purchases its only long-term investments in available-for-sale debt securities this period and their market value is below cost at the balance sheet date, what entry is required to recognize this unrealized loss?

4. On a balance sheet, what valuation must be reported for long-term debt securities classified as available-for-sale?

5. Under what circumstances are long-term investments in debt securities reported at cost including an adjustment for amortization of any difference between cost and maturity value?

6. For long-term investments in available-for-sale securities, how are unrealized (holding) gains and losses reported?

7. In accounting for investments in common stock, when should the equity method be used?

8. Under what circumstances does a company prepare consolidated financial statements?

9. What are two major challenges in accounting for international operations?

10. Assume a U.S. company makes a credit sale to a foreign customer who is required to make payment in its foreign currency. In the current period, the exchange rate is $1.40 on the date of the sale and is $1.30 on the date the customer pays the receivable. Will the U.S. company record an exchange gain or loss?

11. If a U.S. company makes a credit sale to a foreign customer who is required to make payment in U.S. dollars, can the U.S. company have an exchange gain or loss as a result of this sale?

12. What amount does **Nike** report as Accumulated Other Comprehensive Income on its balance sheet as of May 31, 2000, and May 31, 1999?

13. Refer to the balance sheet of **Reebok** in Appendix A. How can you tell that Reebok uses the consolidated method of accounting?

14. Refer to the financial statements of **Gap** in Appendix A. Compute its return on total assets for the year ended January 24, 2000.

QUICK STUDY

QS 16-1

Identifying long-term investments

Which of the following are true of long-term investments?

a. They may include investments in trading securities.

b. They are always easily sold and therefore qualify as being marketable.

c. They may include debt and equity securities available-for-sale.

d. They are held as an investment of cash available for current operations.

e. They may include debt securities held-to-maturity.

f. They may include bonds and stocks not intended to serve as a ready source of cash.

g. They may include funds earmarked for a special purpose, such as bond sinking funds.

QS 16-2

Describing investments in securities

Complete the following descriptions by filling in the blanks.

1. Accrual of interest on bonds held as long-term investments requires a credit to _Interest Payable._

2. The controlling investor (more than 50% ownership) is called the _____ _____ and the investee company is called the _____.

3. Trading securities are classified as _____ assets.

4. Equity securities giving an investor significant influence are accounted for using the _____ _____.

5. Available-for-sale debt securities are reported on the balance sheet at _____ _____.

QS 16-3

Recording equity securities

On May 20, 2002, Cornwell Co. paid $1,000,000 to acquire 25,000 shares (10%) of JVM Corp.'s outstanding common shares as a long-term investment. On August 5, 2004, Cornwell sold half of these shares for $625,000. What method should be used to account for this stock investment? Prepare entries to record both the acquisition of these shares and their sale.

QS 16-4

Equity method transactions

Assume the same facts as in QS 16-3 except that the stock acquired represents 40% of JVM Corp.'s outstanding stock. Also assume that JVM Corp. paid a $100,000 dividend on November 1, 2002, and reported a net income of $700,000 for 2002. Prepare the entry to record the receipt of the dividend and the December 31, 2002, year-end adjustment required for the investment account.

QS 16-5

Debt securities transactions

On February 1, 2002, Bob Dejonge purchased 6% bonds issued by Cross Utilities at a cost of $40,000, which equals their par value. The bonds pay interest semiannually on July 31 and January 31. Prepare the entries to record the July 31 receipt of interest and the December 31 year-end interest accrual.

QS 16-6

Recording market adjustment for securities

During the current year, Ross Consulting Group acquires long-term investment securities at a $70,000 cost. These securities are classified as available-for-sale. At December 31 year-end, these securities had a market value of $58,000. The consulting group owns no other long-term investments.

1. Prepare the necessary year-end adjustment related to these securities.

2. Explain how each account used in part (1) is reported in the financial statements.

QS 16-7

Foreign currency transactions

A U.S. company sells a British company a product with the transaction listed in British pounds. On the date of the sale, the transaction of $14,500 is billed as £10,000, reflecting an exchange rate of 1.45 (that is, $1.45 per pound). Show the entry to record (1) the sale and (2) the receipt of the payment in pounds when the exchange rate is 1.35.

QS 16-8

Foreign currency transactions

On March 1, 2002, a U.S. company made a credit sale requiring payment in 30 days from a German company, Taschen Corp., in 20,000 German marks. Assuming the exchange rate between German marks and U.S. dollars is $0.4538 on March 1 and $0.4899 on March 31, prepare the entries to record the sale on March 1 and the cash receipt on March 31.

QS 16-9

Return on total assets

How is return on total assets computed? What does this ratio reflect?

Write the formula to separate the return on total assets into its components. Explain how components of the return on total assets are useful to users of financial statements.

QS 16-10
Component return on total assets
 A1

On December 31, 2002, Stillwater Co. held the following long-term available-for-sale securities:

	Cost	Market Value
Nintendo Co. common stock	$44,450	$48,900
Atlantic Richfield Co. bonds payable ...	49,000	47,000
Kellogg Co. notes payable	25,000	23,200
McDonald's Corp. common stock	46,300	44,800

164 750   163 900

Stillwater had no long-term securities investments prior to the current period. Prepare the December 31 year-end adjusting entry to record the change in market value for these investments.

EXERCISES

Exercise 16-1
Recording market values of long-term investments

P2

Columbian Co. began operations in 2001. At calendar year-end 2002, it held the following long-term investments in available-for-sale securities:

	Cost	Market Value
Long-term investments in available-for-sale securities		
On December 31, 2001	$87,855	$80,293
On December 31, 2002	89,980	88,980

7572
1000.

177 835   169 272   = 8562

Prepare Columbian's December 31, 2002, adjusting entry to record market values of these investments.

Exercise 16-2
Recording market values of long-term investments in securities

 P2

MutualMass Company's investments in securities, with their December 31, 2002, market values, are as follows:

a. Beeman Company bonds: $420,500 cost, $457,000 market value. MutualMass intends to hold these bonds until they mature in 2005.

b. Baybridge common stock: 29,500 shares; $362,450 cost; $391,375 market value. MutualMass owns 32% of Baybridge's voting stock and it has a significant influence over Baybridge.

c. Carrollton common stock: 12,000 shares; $165,500 cost, $179,000 market value. The goal of this investment, which amounts to 3% of Carrollton's outstanding shares, is to earn dividends over the next few years.

d. Newtech common stock: 3,500 shares; $90,300 cost; $88,625 market value. The goal of this investment is to reap an increase in market value of the stock over the next three to five years. Newtech has 30,000 total common shares outstanding.

e. Flockhart common stock: 16,300 shares; $100,860 cost; $111,210 market value. This stock is marketable and is held as an investment of cash available for operations.

State whether each of these investments should be classified as a current asset or a long-term investment. For each long-term item, indicate in which of the four types of long-term investment classifications the item should be placed. Prepare a journal entry dated December 31, 2002, to record the market value adjustment of the long-term investments in available-for-sale securities. MutualMass had no long-term investments prior to year 2002.

Exercise 16-3
Classifying investments in securities; recording market values

P2

Prepare journal entries to record the following transactions involving both the short- and long-term investments of Cascade Corp., all of which occurred during calendar year 2002. Use the account Short-Term Investments for any transactions that you determine are short term.

a. On February 15, paid $160,000 cash to purchase American General's 90-day short-term notes at par, which are dated February 15 and pay 10% interest.

b. On March 22, bought 700 shares of Franklin Industries common stock at $51 per share plus a $150 brokerage fee.

Exercise 16-4
Transactions in short- and long-term investments

 C1   P1   P2

c. On May 16, received a check from American General in payment of the principal and 90 days' interest on the notes purchased in transaction *a*.

d. On July 30, paid $100,000 cash to purchase MP3 Electronics' 8% notes at par, dated July 30, 2002, and maturing on January 30, 2003.

e. On September 1, received a $1 per share cash dividend on the Franklin Industries common stock purchased in transaction *b*.

f. On October 8, sold 350 shares of Franklin Industries common stock for $64 per share, less a $125 brokerage fee.

g. On October 30, received a check from MP3 Electronics for three months' interest on the notes purchased in transaction *d*.

Exercise 16-5

Securities transactions; equity method

Prepare journal entries to record the following transactions and events of Kinney Company:

2002

Jan. 2   Purchased 30,000 shares of Montex Co. common stock for $408,000 cash plus a broker's fee of $3,000 cash. Montex has 90,000 shares of common stock outstanding and admits its policies will be significantly influenced by Kinney.

Sept. 1   Montex declared and paid a cash dividend of $1.50 per share.

Dec. 31   Montex announced that net income for the year is $486,900.

2003

June 1   Montex declared and paid a cash dividend of $2.10 per share.

Dec. 31   Montex announced that net income for the year is $702,750.

Dec. 31   Kinney sold 10,000 shares of Montex for $320,000 cash.

Exercise 16-6

Market value adjustments for available-for-sale securities

Big Board Services began operations in 2002 and regularly makes long-term investments in available-for-sale securities. Annual total cost and market value for these investments follow:

	Cost	Market Value
On December 31, 2002	$372,000	$360,860
On December 31, 2003	428,500	455,800
On December 31, 2004	600,200	700,500
On December 31, 2005	876,900	780,200

Prepare journal entries to record the market adjustment of its investments at each year-end.

Exercise 16-7

Foreign currency transactions

Rainboy of New York sells its products to customers in the United States and the United Kingdom. On December 16, 2002, Rainboy sold merchandise on credit to Bronson Ltd. of London at a price of 17,000 pounds. The exchange rate on that day for £1 was $1.4583. On December 31, 2002, when Rainboy prepared its financial statements, the rate was £1 for $1.4382. Bronson paid its bill in full on January 15, 2003, at which time the exchange rate was £1 for $1.4482. Rainboy immediately exchanged the 17,000 pounds for U.S. dollars. Prepare journal entries on December 16, December 31, and January 15 for Rainboy.

Exercise 16-8

Computing foreign exchange gains and losses on receivables

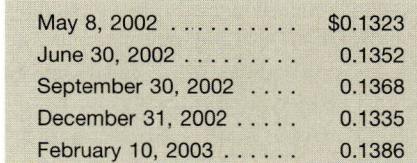

On May 8, 2002, Jett Company (a U.S. company) made a credit sale to DeNeuve (a French company). The terms of the sale required DeNeuve to pay 800,000 francs on February 10, 2003. Jett prepares quarterly financial statements on March 31, June 30, September 30, and December 31. The exchange rates for francs during the time the receivable is outstanding follow:

May 8, 2002	$0.1323
June 30, 2002	0.1352
September 30, 2002	0.1368
December 31, 2002	0.1335
February 10, 2003	0.1386

Compute the foreign exchange gain or loss that Jett should report on each of its quarterly income statements for the last three quarters of 2002 and the first quarter of 2003. Also compute the amount reported on Jett's balance sheets at the end of each of its last three quarters of 2002.

The following information is available from the financial statements of Ripon Industries:

Exercise 16-9
Return on total assets

File Edit View Insert Format Tools Data Window Help			
		Cut 16-c	
A	**B**	**C**	**D**
1	**2001**	**2002**	**2003**
2 Total assets, December 31	$210,000	$340,000	$770,000
3 Net income	30,200	38,400	60,300
4			

Compute Ripon's return on total assets for 2002 and 2003. (Round percentages to one decimal place.) Comment on the company's efficiency in using its assets in 2002 and 2003.

Kobe Security invests in long-term available-for-sale securities. Following is a series of transactions and events relevant to its long-term investment activity:

PROBLEM SET A

Problem 16-1A
Transactions and market adjustments for long-term investments

2002

Jan. 20	Purchased 1,000 shares of Johnson & Johnson at $20.50 per share plus a $240 commission.
Feb. 9	Purchased 1,200 shares of Sony at $46.20 per share plus a $225 commission.
June 12	Purchased 1,500 shares of Mattel at $27.80 per share plus a $195 commission.
Dec. 31	Per share market values for stocks in the portfolio are Johnson & Johnson, $21.50; Mattel, $30.90; Sony, $38.00.

2003

Apr. 15	Sold 1,000 shares of Johnson & Johnson at $23.50 per share less a $525 commission.
July 5	Sold 1,500 shares of Mattel at $23.90 per share less a $235 commission.
July 22	Purchased 600 shares of Sara Lee at $22.50 per share plus a $480 commission.
Aug. 19	Purchased 900 shares of Eastman Kodak at $17.00 per share plus a $198 commission.
Dec. 31	Per share market values for stocks in the portfolio are Kodak, $19.25; Sara Lee, $20.00; Sony, $35.00

2004

Feb. 27	Purchased 2,400 shares of Microsoft at $67.00 per share plus a $525 commission.
June 21	Sold 1,200 shares of Sony at $48.00 per share less an $880 commission.
June 30	Purchased 1,400 shares of Black & Decker at $36.00 per share plus a $725 commission.
Aug. 3	Sold 600 shares of Sara Lee at $16.25 per share less a $435 commission.
Nov. 1	Sold 900 shares of Eastman Kodak at $22.75 per share less a $625 commission.
Dec. 31	Per share market values for stocks in the portfolio are Black & Decker, $39.00; Microsoft, $69.00.

Required

1. Prepare journal entries to record these transactions and events and any year-end adjustments needed to record the market values of the long-term investments.

2. Prepare a table that shows the total cost, total market value adjustment, and total market value of the long-term investments at each year-end.

3. For each year, prepare a table that shows the realized gains and losses included in earnings and the total unrealized gains or losses at each year-end.

Check   Unrealized Gain for 2004, $7,750

Problem 16-2A

Long-term investment transactions; unrealized and realized gains and losses

Ryan Co.'s long-term investment portfolio at December 31, 2001, consists of the following:

Available-for-Sale Securities	Cost	Market Value
40,000 shares of Company A common stock	$535,300	$490,000
7,000 shares of Company B common stock	159,375	154,000
17,500 shares of Company C common stock	662,750	640,938

Ryan enters into the following long-term investment transactions during year 2002.

Jan. 29   Sold 3,500 shares of Company B common stock for $79,188 less a brokerage fee of $1,500.

Apr. 17   Purchased 10,000 shares of Company W common stock for $197,500 plus a brokerage fee of $2,400. The shares represent a 30% ownership in Company W.

July 6   Purchased 4,500 shares of Company X common stock for $126,562 plus a brokerage fee of $1,750. The shares represent a 10% ownership in Company X.

Aug. 22   Purchased 50,000 shares of Company Y common stock for $375,000 plus a brokerage fee of $1,200. The shares represent a 51% ownership in Company Y.

Nov. 13   Purchased 8,500 shares of Company Z common stock for $266,900 plus a brokerage fee of $3,450. The shares represent a 5% ownership in Company Z.

Dec. 9   Sold 40,000 shares of Company A common stock for $515,000 less a brokerage fee of $4,100.

The market values of Ryan's investments at December 31, 2002, are: B, $81,375; C, $610,312; W, $191,250; X, $118,125; Y, $531,250; Z, $278,800.

Required

1. Determine what amount Ryan should report on its December 31, 2002, balance sheet for its long-term investments in available-for-sale equity securities.

Check (2) Cr. Unrealized Gain—Equity, $19,999.50

2. Prepare a December 31, 2002, adjusting entry, if necessary, to record the market value adjustment for the long-term investments in available-for-sale equity securities.

3. What amount of gains or losses on transactions relating to long-term investments in available-for-sale equity securities should Ryan report on its December 31, 2002, income statement?

Problem 16-3A

Accounting for stock investments

Case Steel Works is organized on January 4, 2002. The following investment transactions and events subsequently occurred:

2002

Jan. 5   Case purchased 60,000 shares (20%) of Kildaire's common stock for $1,560,000.

Oct. 23   Kildaire declared and paid a cash dividend of $3.20 per share.

Dec. 31   Kildaire's net income for 2002 is $1,164,000, and the market value of its stock is $30.00 per share.

2003

Oct. 15   Kildaire declared and paid a cash dividend of $2.60 per share.

Dec. 31   Kildaire's net income for 2003 is $1,476,000, and the market value of its stock is $32.00 per share.

2004

Jan. 2   Case sold all of its investment in Kildaire for $1,894,000 cash.

Part 1

Assume that Case has a significant influence over Kildaire with its 20% share.

Required

1. Prepare entries to record the preceding transactions and events for Case.

Check (2) Carrying value per share, $29.00

2. Compute the carrying (book) value per share of Case's investment in Kildaire common stock as reflected in the investment account on January 1, 2004.

3. Compute the change in Case's equity from January 5, 2002, through January 2, 2004, resulting from its investment in Kildaire.

Part 2

Assume that although Case owns 20% of Kildaire's outstanding stock, circumstances indicate that it does not have a significant influence over the investee.

Required

1. Prepare entries to record the preceding transactions and events for Case. Prepare an entry dated January 2, 2004, to remove any balance related to the market value adjustment.

2. Compute the cost per share of Case's investment in Kildaire common stock as reflected in the investment account on January 1, 2004.

3. Compute the change in Case's equity from January 5, 2002, through January 2, 2004, resulting from its investment in Kildaire.

Point: Ask student teams to review their solutions to parts (1) and (2) and discuss any differences. Why is accounting for an investment when the investor has a significant influence not the same as for an investment when the investor does not have significant influence?

Check   (3) Net increase, $682,000

Rockytop Co. is a U.S. corporation with customers in several foreign countries. Following are its selected transactions for 2002 and 2003:

Problem 16-4A
Foreign currency transactions

P4

2002

Apr. 8   Sold merchandise to Salinas & Sons of Mexico for $5,938 cash. The exchange rate for pesos is $0.1043 on this day.

July 21   Sold merchandise on credit to Sumitomo Corp. in Japan. The price of 1.5 million yen is to be paid 120 days from the date of sale. The exchange rate for yen is $0.0094 on this day.

Oct. 14   Sold merchandise for 19,000 pounds to Smithers Ltd. of Great Britain, payment in full to be received in 90 days. The exchange rate for pounds is $1.4566 on this day.

Nov. 18   Received Sumitomo's payment in yen for its July 21 purchase and immediately exchanged the yen for dollars. The exchange rate for yen is $0.0092 on this day.

Dec. 20   Sold merchandise for 17,000 marks to Schmidt Haus of Germany, payment in full to be received in 30 days. On this day, the exchange rate for marks is $0.4501.

Dec. 31   Prepared adjusting entries to recognize exchange gains or losses on Rockytop's annual financial statements. Rates for exchanging foreign currencies on this day follow:

Pesos (Mexico)	$0.1055
Yen (Japan)	0.0093
Pounds (Britain)	1.4620
Marks (Germany)	0.4456

2003

Jan. 12   Received full payment in pounds from Smithers for the October 14 sale and immediately exchanged the pounds for dollars. The exchange rate for pounds is $1.4699 on this day.

Jan. 19   Received Schmidt Haus's full payment in marks for the December 20 sale and immediately exchanged the marks for dollars. The exchange rate for marks is $0.4420 on this day.

Required

Preparation Component

1. Prepare journal entries for these transactions for Rockytop (round amounts to the penny).

2. Compute the foreign exchange gain or loss to be reported on Rockytop's 2002 income statement.

Check   2002 total foreign exchange loss, $273.90

Analysis Component

3. What actions might Rockytop consider to reduce its risk of foreign exchange gains or losses?

Berlin Enterprises invests in long-term available-for-sale securities. Following is a series of transactions and events relevant to its long-term investment activity:

PROBLEM SET B

Problem 16-1B
Transactions and market adjustments for long-term investments

2002

Mar. 10   Purchased 1,200 shares of Apple Computer at $25.50 per share plus $800 commission.

Apr. 7   Purchased 2,500 shares of Ford at $22.50 per share plus $1,033 commission.

Sept. 1   Purchased 600 shares of Polaroid at $47.00 per share plus $890 commission.

Dec. 31   Per share market values for stocks in the portfolio are Apple, $27.50; Ford, $21.00; Polaroid, $49.00.

2003

Apr. 26	Sold 2,500 shares of Ford at $20.50 per share less $1,207 commission.
June 2	Purchased 1,800 shares of Duracell at $19.25 per share plus $1,050 commission.
June 14	Purchased 1,200 shares of Sears at $21.00 per share plus $280 commission.
Nov. 27	Sold 600 shares of Polaroid at $51 per share less $845 commission.
Dec. 31	Per share market values for stocks in the portfolio are Apple, $29.00; Duracell, $18.00; Sears, $23.00.

2004

Jan. 28	Purchased 1,000 shares of Coca-Cola Co. at $40 per share plus $1,480 commission.
Aug. 22	Sold 1,200 shares of Apple at $21.50 per share less $1,850 commission.
Sept. 3	Purchased 3,000 shares of Motorola at $28.00 per share plus $780 commission.
Oct. 9	Sold 1,200 shares of Sears at $24.00 per share less $599 commission.
Oct. 31	Sold 1,800 shares of Duracell at $15.00 per share less $898 commission.
Dec. 31	Per share market values for stocks in the portfolio are Coca-Cola, $48.00; Motorola, $24.00.

Required

1. Prepare journal entries to record these transactions and events and any year-end adjustments needed to record the market values of the long-term investments.

2. Prepare a table that shows the total cost, total market value adjustment, and total market value of the long-term investments at each year-end.

Check   Unrealized loss for 2004, $6,260

3. For each year, prepare a table that shows the realized gains and losses included in earnings and the total unrealized gains or losses at each year-end.

Problem 16-2B
Long-term investment transactions; unrealized and realized gains and losses

Dynegy's long-term investment portfolio at December 31, 2001, consists of the following:

Available-for-Sale Securities	Cost	Market Value
27,500 shares of Company R common stock	$559,125	$599,063
8,500 shares of Company S common stock	308,380	293,250
11,000 shares of Company T common stock	147,235	151,800

Dynegy enters into the following long-term investment transactions during year 2002:

Jan. 13	Sold 2,125 shares of Company S common stock for $72,250 less a brokerage fee of $1,195.
Mar. 24	Purchased 15,500 shares of Company U common stock for $282,875 plus a brokerage fee of $1,980. The shares represent a 62% ownership in Company U.
Apr. 5	Purchased 42,500 shares of Company V common stock for $133,875 plus a brokerage fee of $1,125. The shares represent a 10% ownership in Company V.
Sept. 2	Sold 11,000 shares of Company T common stock for $156,750 less a brokerage fee of $2,700.
Sept. 27	Purchased 2,500 shares of Company W common stock for $50,500 plus a brokerage fee of $1,050. The shares represent a 25% ownership in Company W.
Oct. 30	Purchased 5,000 shares of Company X common stock for $48,750 plus a brokerage fee of $1,170. The shares represent a 13% ownership in Company X.

The market values of Dynegy's investments at December 31, 2002, are: R, $568,125; S, $210,375; U, $272,800; V, $134,938; W, $54,689; X, $45,625.

Required

1. Determine what amount Dynegy should report on its December 31, 2002, balance sheet for its long-term investments in available-for-sale equity securities.

Check   (2) Dr. Unrealized Loss—Equity, $16,267; Cr. Market Adjustment, $45,640

2. Prepare a December 31, 2002, adjusting entry, if necessary, to record the market value adjustment of the long-term investments in available-for-sale equity securities.

3. What amount of gains or losses on transactions relating to long-term investments in available-for-sale equity securities should Dynegy report on its December 31, 2002, income statement?

Backstreet Company is organized on January 3, 2002. The following investment transactions and events subsequently occurred:

Problem 16-3B
Accounting for stock investments

2002

Jan. 5   Backstreet purchased 20,000 shares (25%) of Bloch's common stock for $200,500.
Aug. 1   Bloch declared and paid a cash dividend of $1.05 per share.
Dec. 31   Bloch's net income for 2002 is $82,000, and the market value of its stock is $11.90 per share.

2003

Aug. 1   Bloch declared and paid a cash dividend of $1.35 per share.
Dec. 31   Bloch's net income for 2003 is $78,000, and the market value of its stock is $13.65 per share.

2004

Jan. 8   Backstreet sold all of its investment in Bloch for $275,000 cash.

Part 1

Assume that Backstreet has a significant influence over Bloch with its 25% share.

Required

1. Prepare entries to record the preceding transactions and events for Backstreet.

2. Compute the carrying (book) value per share of Backstreet's investment in Bloch common stock as reflected in the investment account on January 7, 2004.

Check   (2) Carrying value per share, $9.63

3. Compute the change in Backstreet's equity from January 5, 2002, through January 8, 2004, resulting from its investment in Bloch.

Part 2

Assume that although Backstreet owns 25% of Bloch's outstanding stock, circumstances indicate that it does not have a significant influence over the investee.

Required

1. Prepare entries to record the preceding transactions and events for Backstreet. Prepare an entry dated January 8, 2004, to remove any balance related to the market value adjustment.

2. Compute the cost per share of Backstreet's investment in Bloch common stock as reflected in the investment account on January 7, 2004.

3. Compute the change in Backstreet's equity from January 5, 2002, through January 8, 2004, resulting from its investment in Bloch.

Check   (3) Net increase, $122,500

Informix is a U.S. corporation with customers in several foreign countries. Following are its selected transactions for 2002 and 2003:

Problem 16-4B
Foreign currency transactions

P4

2002

May 26   Sold merchandise for 5.5 million yen to Fuji Company of Japan, payment in full to be received in 60 days. On this day, the exchange rate for yen is $0.0093.
June 1   Sold merchandise to Fordham Ltd. of Great Britain for $64,800 cash. The exchange rate for pounds is $1.4498, on this day.
July 25   Received Fuji's payment in yen for its May 26 purchase and immediately exchanged the yen for dollars. The exchange rate for yen is $0.0092 on this day.
Oct. 15   Sold merchandise on credit to Martinez Brothers of Mexico. The price of 378,000 pesos is to be paid 90 days from the date of sale. On this day, the exchange rate for pesos is $0.1020.
Dec. 6   Sold merchandise for 250,000 francs to LeFevre Company of France, payment in full to be received in 30 days. The exchange rate for francs is $0.1439 on this day.
Dec. 31   Prepared adjusting entries to recognize exchange gains or losses on Informix's annual financial statements. Rates of exchanging foreign currencies on this day follow:

Yen (Japan)	$0.0094
Pounds (Britain)	1.4580
Pesos (Mexico)	0.1060
Francs (France)	0.1450

2003

Jan. 5　Received LeFevre's full payment in francs for the December 6 sale and immediately exchanged the francs for dollars. The exchange rate for francs is $0.1580 on this day.

Jan. 13　Received full payment in pesos from Martinez for the October 15 sale and immediately exchanged the pesos for dollars. The exchange rate for pesos is $0.1039 on this day.

Required

Preparation Component

1. Prepare journal entries for these transactions for Informix (round amounts to the penny).

2. Compute the foreign exchange gain or loss to be reported on Informix's 2002 income statement.

Analysis Component

3. What actions might Informix consider to reduce its risk of foreign exchange gains or losses?

Check　2002 total foreign exchange gain, $1,237

Beyond the Numbers

Reporting in Action

BTN 16-1　Refer to **Nike**'s financial statements in Appendix A to answer the following:

1. Are Nike's financial statements consolidated? How can you tell?

2. What is Nike's *comprehensive income* for the year ended May 31, 2000?

3. Does Nike have any foreign operations? How can you tell?

4. Is there a foreign exchange gain or loss on its income statement? Describe what you find or do not find.

5. Compute Nike's return on total assets for the year ended May 31, 2000.

Swoosh Ahead

6. Access Nike's annual report for a fiscal year ending after May 31, 2000, from either its Web site [**www.nike.com**] or the SEC's EDGAR database [**www.sec.gov**]. Recompute Nike's return on total assets for the years subsequent to May 31, 2000.

Comparative Analysis

BTN 16-2　Key comparative figures ($ millions) for both **Nike** and **Reebok** follow:

Key Figures	Nike			Reebok		
	Current Year	1 year Prior	2 years Prior	Current Year	1 year Prior	2 years Prior
Net income	$ 579	$ 451	$ 400	$ 11	$ 24	$ 135
Net sales	8,995	8,777	9,553	2,900	3,225	3,644
Total assets	5,857	5,248	5,397	1,564	1,685	1,756

Required

1. Compute return on total assets for both Nike and Reebok for the two most recent years.

2. Break down the return on total assets computed in part (1) into its components for both companies and both years according to the formula in Exhibit 16.10.

3. Which company has the higher total return on assets? The higher profit margin? The higher total asset turnover? Compare your findings to the chapter's discussion of return on total assets that compared Nike and Reebok.

Ethics Challenge

BTN 16-3　Kendra Stone is the controller for Jayhawk Company, which has numerous long-term investments in debt securities. During the past year, the company had investments in 10-year bonds. Kendra is preparing the year-end financial statements. In accounting for long-term investments, she knows she must designate each long-term investment as a held-to-maturity or an available-for-sale security. Since the bonds were purchased, interest rates have risen sharply, meaning their market value has declined. The company does not necessarily intend to hold the bonds for the entire 10 years. Also, Kendra earns a bonus each year, which is computed as a percent of net income.

Required

1. Will Kendra's bonus depend in any way on the classification of the debt securities?

2. What criteria must Kendra use to classify the securities as held-to-maturity or available-for-sale?

3. Is there likely any company oversight of Kendra's classification of the securities?

BTN 16-4   You are Jackson Company's accountant. The company owner, Abel Terrio, has reviewed the financial statements you prepared for 2003 and questions the $6,000 loss reported on the sale of its investment in Blackhawk Co. common stock. Jackson acquired 50,000 shares of Blackhawk's common stock on December 31, 2001, at a cost of $500,000. This stock purchase represented a 40% interest in Blackhawk. The 2002 income statement reported that earnings from all investments were $126,000. On January 3, 2003, Jackson Company sold the Blackhawk stock for $575,000. Blackhawk did not pay any dividends during 2002 but reported a net income of $202,500 for that year. Terrio believes that because the Blackhawk stock purchase price was $500,000 and it was sold for $575,000, the 2003 income statement should report a $75,000 gain on the sale.

Communicating in Practice

Required

Draft a one-half page memorandum to Terrio explaining why the $6,000 loss on sale of Blackhawk stock is correctly reported.

BTN 16-5   Access the March 28, 2000, filing date of the 10-K report of **Harley-Davidson**, Inc. (ticker HDI) from **www.edgar-online.com.**

Taking It to the Net

C4

Required

1. Prepare a table (in thousands) that shows total assets, net sales, and net income for Harley-Davidson for the years 1999 and 1998. Also insert a 1997 column and list Harley-Davidson's total assets for 1997 as $1,598,901.

2. Compute the return on total assets for Harley-Davidson for the years 1999 and 1998.

3. Show the disaggregated return on total assets for the years 1999 and 1998 (see Exhibit 16.10).

4. Which component of the disaggregation is driving the return on total assets? (Refer to your analysis for part *3*.)

BTN 16-6   Each team member is to become an expert on a specific classification of long-term investments. This expertise will be used to facilitate other teammates' understanding of the concepts and procedures relevent to the classification chosen.

Teamwork in Action

1. Each team member must select an area for expertise by choosing one of the following classifications of long-term investments.

   a. Held-to-maturity debt securities

   b. Available-for-sale debt and equity securities

   c. Equity securities with significant influence

   d. Equity securities with controlling influence

2. Learning teams are to disburse and expert teams are to be formed. Expert teams are made up of those who select the same area of expertise. The instructor will identify the location where each expert team will meet.

3. Expert teams will collaborate to develop a presentation based on the following requirements. Students must write the presentation in a format they can show to their learning teams in part (4).

Requirements for Expert Presentation

   a. Write a transaction for the acquisition of this type of investment security. The transaction description is to include all necessary data to reflect the chosen classification.

      b. Prepare the journal entry to record the acquisition.
[*Note:* The expert team on equity securities with controlling influence will substitute requirements *d* and *e* with a discussion of the reporting of these investments.]

      c. Identify information necessary to complete the end-of-period adjustment for this investment.

      d. Assuming that this is the only investment owned, prepare any necessary year-end entries.

      e. Present the relevant balance sheet section(s).

4. Re-form learning teams. In rotation, experts are to present to their teams the presentations they developed in part (3). Experts are to encourage and respond to questions.

Business Week Activity

BTN 16-7   Read the article "A Vise Is Tightening around Profits" in the December 13, 1999, issue of *Business Week*.

Required

1. How have U.S. profit margins for nonfinancial businesses changed, on average, over the past three years?

2. Use the profit margins reported in the article for nonfinancial businesses to compute the average return on assets for nonfinancial businesses for the past three years. (Assume that businesses, on average, have an asset turnover of 2.0.)

3. For each 1% change in profit margin, how much will return on total assets change?

Entrepreneurial Decision

BTN 16-8   Jeb Turner operates a successful company that generates a regular cash flow. He usually deposits funds not needed for operations in the form of bank certificates of deposit that have paid, at best, 6% for 24-month terms. Jeb would like to consider other options for his company's excess cash and is thinking of making some long-term stock investments. However, he does not understand the difference between an unrealized loss (gain) and a realized loss (gain). Jeb also does not understand how unrealized gains or losses would be reported in his financial statements at year-end.

Required

1. Would Jeb's business benefit from investing in long-term stock investments rather than CDs? Are there any disadvantages?

2. Explain to Jeb the difference between an unrealized and a realized gain or loss.

3. If Jeb purchases available-for-sale equity securities, will any unrealized gains or losses on those securities affect his company's income statement? Explain.

17

Reporting and Analyzing Cash Flows

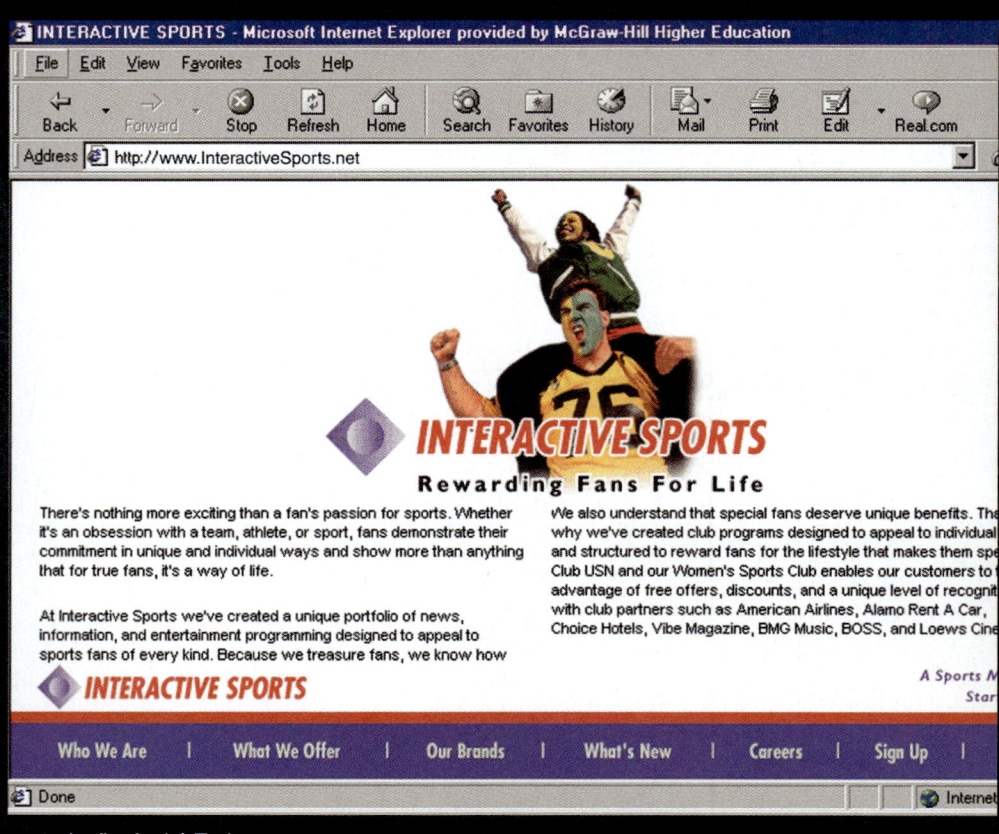

"The less money you have, the more creative you have to be."—André Taylor

A Look Back

Chapter 16 focused on long-term investments in securities. We explained how to identify, account for, and report them. We also described accounting for transactions listed in a foreign currency.

A Look at This Chapter

This chapter focuses on reporting and analyzing cash inflows and cash outflows. We emphasize how to prepare and interpret the statement of cash flows.

A Look Ahead

Chapter 18 focuses on tools to help us analyze financial statements. We describe comparative analysis and the application of ratios for financial analysis.

Part Five

Learning Objectives

Conceptual

C1 Explain the purpose and importance of cash flow information.

C2 Distinguish among operating, investing, and financing activities.

C3 Identify and disclose noncash investing and financing activities.

C4 Describe the format of the statement of cash flows.

Analytical

A1 Analyze the statement of cash flows.

A2 Compute and apply the cash flow on total assets ratio.

Procedural

P1 Prepare a statement of cash flows.

P2 Compute cash flows from operating activities using the direct method.

P3 Compute cash flows from operating activities using the indirect method.

P4 Determine cash flows from both investing and financing activities.

Show Me the Money!

e NEW YORK—Like many entrepreneurs, André Taylor had a promising business plan but little cash (just $1,000) to make it happen. Taylor wished to create a sports media company to provide cutting-edge news, analysis, and other programming aimed at women and the urban sports fan. The new company would also provide state-of-the-art services for sports teams to help them analyze their own performance and that of their competitors. Taylor's plans eventually led to the launch of **Interactive Sports** (**www.InteractiveSports.net**).

To get his fledgling company off the ground, Taylor needed cash—and lots of it! After all, survival of his type of technology-based company depends on developing costly software and other services that usually require large cash outflows—an especially difficult burden on start-ups. In addition, once open for business, Taylor knew he would have to manage cash carefully and monitor cash inflows and outflows. But Interactive Sports had a problem. "Because we didn't have money, we didn't have the ability to develop the software," Taylor recalls.

Taylor had a unique response. He came up with an alternative to making cash payments to suppliers of software and programming services—the centuries-old process of barter. "We knocked on the doors of technology companies and invited them to participate based on the potential rewards on royalties rather than equity in the company." Taylor's creativity in cash management paid off. In one barter arrangement, Interactive Sports gets access to the technology team of Sprint. In return, Interactive Sports promotes Sprint's product through its programming outlets. Both companies obtain valuable services—without the need for cash outflows.

Interactive Sports is a success, and the number of subscribers to its services (Urban Sports Network, Women's Sports Channel, and ISWire) continues to increase. Moreover, over three-fourths of teams in the NBA, NFL, NHL, and MLB subscribe to one or more of its services. At a time when sports seems to be driven by a "show me the money" attitude, Interactive Sports is thriving with a "less is more" cash strategy. [Sources: *ISWire News,* March 10, 1999; *Interactive Sports Web Site,* May 2001; *Entrepreneur, November 12, 1998*]

Chapter Preview

Profitability is a primary goal of most managers, but not the only goal. A company cannot achieve or maintain profits without carefully managing cash. Managers and other users of information pay close attention to a company's cash position and the events and transactions affecting cash. Information about these events and transactions is reported in the statement of cash flows. This chapter explains how we prepare, analyze, and interpret a statement of cash flows. It also discusses the importance of cash flow information for predicting future performance and making managerial decisions. More generally, effectively using the statement of cash flows is crucial for managing and analyzing the operating, investing, and financing activities of businesses.

Basics of Cash Flow Reporting

C1 Explain the purpose and importance of cash flow information.

This section describes the basics of cash flow reporting, including its purpose, measurement, classification, format, and preparation.

Purpose of the Statement of Cash Flows

The purpose of the **statement of cash flows** is to report all major cash receipts (inflows) and cash payments (outflows) during a period. This includes separately identifying the cash flows related to operating, investing, and financing activities. The statement of cash flows does more than simply report changes in cash. It is the detailed disclosure of individual cash flows that makes this statement useful to users. Information in this statement helps users answer questions such as these:

- How does a company obtain its cash?
- Where does a company spend its cash?
- What explains the change in the cash balance?

The statement of cash flows addresses these important questions by summarizing, classifying, and reporting a company's cash inflows and outflows for each period.

Importance of Cash Flows

Point: An income statement reports revenues, gains, expenses, and losses on an accrual basis. The statement of cash flows reports cash received and cash paid for operating, financing, and investing activities.

Information about cash flows and its sources and uses can influence decision makers in important ways. For instance, we look more favorably at a company that is financing its expenditures with cash from operations than one that does it by selling its assets. Information about cash flows also helps users decide whether a company has enough cash to pay its existing debts as they mature. It is also relied upon to evaluate a company's ability to meet unexpected obligations and pursue unexpected opportunities. External information users especially want to assess a company's ability to take advantage of new business opportunities. Internal users such as managers use cash flow information to plan day-to-day operating activities and make long-term investment decisions.

Macy's striking turnaround is an example of how careful analysis and management of cash flows can lead to improved financial stability. A few years ago, Macy's obtained temporary protection from bankruptcy, at which time it desperately needed to improve its cash flows. It did so by engaging in aggressive cost-cutting measures. As a result of this effort, Macy's annual cash inflow rose to $210 million—up from a negative cash flow of $38.9 million in the prior year. Macy's eventually met its financial obligations and then successfully merged with **Federated Department Stores**.

The case of **W. T. Grant Co.** is a classic example of the importance of cash flow information in predicting a company's future performance and financial strength. Grant reported net income of more than $40 million per year for three consecutive years. At that same time,

Did You Know?

Cash Valuation   Some experts who value private companies do so on the basis of a multiple of operating cash flow. For example, medium-sized private companies usually sell for five to seven times operating cash flows. Larger companies can command somewhat higher multiples.

it was experiencing an alarming decrease in cash provided by operations. For instance, net cash outflow was more than $90 million by the end of that three-year period. Grant soon went bankrupt. Users who relied solely on Grant's income numbers were unpleasantly surprised. This reminds us that cash flows as well as income statement and balance sheet information are crucial in making business decisions.

Measuring Cash Flows

Cash flows are defined to include both *cash* and *cash equivalents* in the statement of cash flows; the statement explains the difference between the beginning and ending balances of cash and cash equivalents. We continue to use the phrases *cash flows* and the *statement of cash flows,* but we must remember that both phrases refer to cash and cash equivalents. As we discussed in Chapter 9, a cash equivalent must satisfy two criteria: (1) be readily convertible to a known amount of cash and (2) be sufficiently close to its maturity so its market value is unaffected by interest rate changes. In most cases, a security must be within three months of its maturity to satisfy these criteria. Classifying short-term, highly liquid investments as cash equivalents is based on the idea that companies make these investments to earn a return on idle cash balances.

Items meeting the criteria of cash equivalents are sometimes not held as short-term investments of idle cash. For instance, an investment company that specializes in the purchase and sale of securities often buys cash equivalents as part of its investing strategy. Companies in this situation are allowed to exclude these securities from the cash equivalents account, but these companies must follow a clear policy for determining the items to include and not include. These policies are disclosed in notes to their financial statements and must be followed consistently from period to period. **American Express**, for example, defines its cash equivalents as "time deposits with original maturities of 90 days or less, excluding those that are restricted by law or regulation."

Cash and Cash Equivalents

Global: International accounting standards define cash flows as *net monetary assets*—meaning cash, demand deposits, and highly liquid investments minus short-term loans.

Point: Internal users rely on the statement of cash flows to make investing and financing decisions. External users rely on this statement to assess the amount and timing of a company's cash flows.

> ### Did You Know?
>
> **Cash Analysis** "A lender must have a complete understanding of a borrower's cash flows to assess both the borrowing needs and repayment sources. This requires information about the major types of cash inflows and outflows. I have seen many companies, whose financial statements indicate good profitability, experience severe financial problems because the owners or managers lacked a good understanding of the companies' cash flows."—Mary E. Garza, **NationsBank of Texas**.

Classifying Cash Flows

Since we treat cash and cash equivalents as a single item on the statement of cash flows, the statement does not report transactions between cash and cash equivalents such as cash paid to purchase cash equivalents and cash received from selling cash equivalents. However, all other cash receipts and cash payments are classified and reported on the statement as operating, investing, or financing activities. Individual cash receipts and payments for each of these three categories are labeled to identify their source transactions or events. Cash receipts and payments are then summarized for each category by netting them against each other. A net cash inflow (source) occurs when the receipts in a category exceed the payments. A net cash outflow (use) occurs when the payments in a category exceed the receipts.

C2 Distinguish among operating, investing, and financing activities.

Concept 17-1

Global: Several countries such as Saudi Arabia and Italy do not require the statement of cash flows.

Point: Common errors include misclassification of *cash dividends received* and *cash interest received* as investing activities and *cash interest paid* as financing. The FASB requires these cash flows be reported as operating activities.

Operating Activities

Operating activities include those transactions and events that determine net income. Examples are the production and purchase of merchandise, the sale of goods and services to customers, and the expenditures toward administering the business. Not all items in income, such as unusual gains and losses, are operating activities (we discuss these exceptions later in the chapter). Exhibit 17.1 lists the more common cash inflows and outflows from operating activities.

Investing Activities

Investing activities generally include those transactions and events that affect long-term assets—namely, the purchase and sale of long-term assets. However, they also include the (1) purchase and sale of short-term investments other than cash equivalents, and (2) lending

Exhibit 17.1

Cash Flows from
Operating Activities

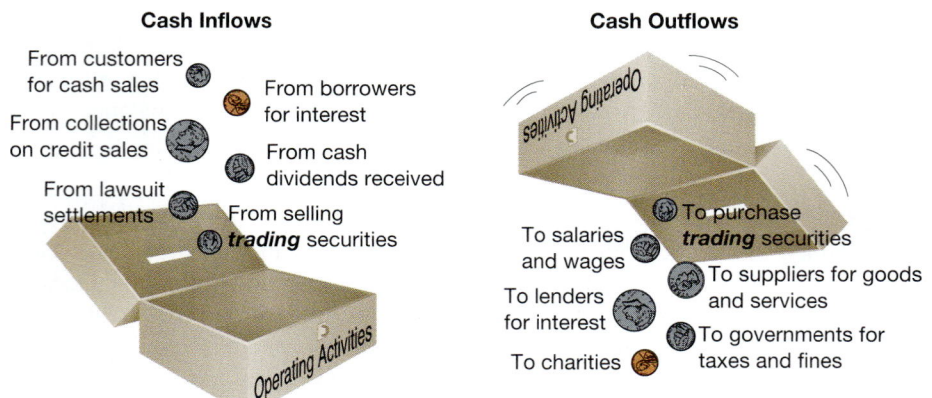

Point: Investing activities exclude transactions in trading securities.

and collecting money for notes receivable. Exhibit 17.2 lists examples of cash flows from investing activities. Proceeds from collecting the principal amounts of notes deserve special mention. If the note results from sales to customers, its cash receipts are classed as operating activities whether short term or long term. If the note results from a loan to another party apart from sales, however, the cash receipts from collecting the principal of the note are classed as an investing activity. The FASB requires the collection of interest on loans be reported as an operating activity.

Exhibit 17.2

Cash Flows from
Investing Activities

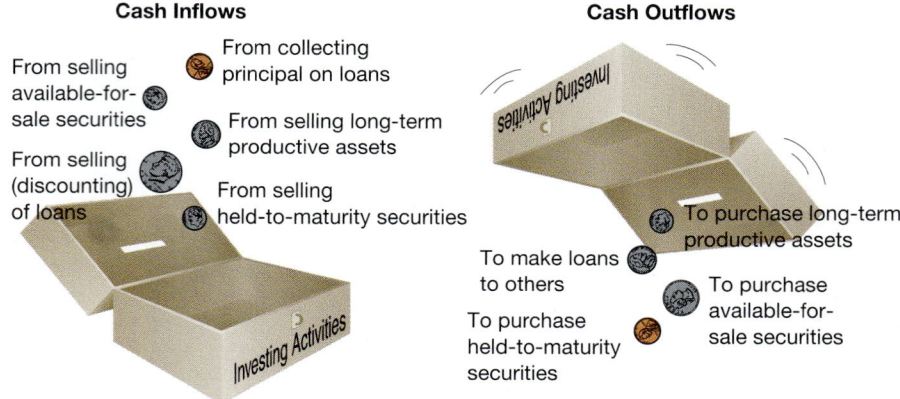

Financing Activities

Point: Interest payments on a loan are classified as operating activities, but payments of loan principal are financing activities.

Financing activities include those transactions and events that affect long-term liabilities and equity. Examples are (1) obtaining cash from issuing debt and repaying the amounts borrowed and (2) cash from or distributed to owners. These activities all involve transactions with a company's owners and creditors. They also often involve borrowing and repaying principal amounts relating to both short- and long-term debt. Note that payments of interest expense are classified as operating activities. Also, cash payments to settle credit purchases of merchandise, whether on account or by note, are operating activities. Exhibit 17.3 lists examples of cash flows from financing activities.

Noncash Investing and Financing

C3   Identify and disclose noncash investing and financing activities.

Some important investing and financing activities do not affect cash receipts or payments. Important noncash investing and financing activities are disclosed at the bottom of the statement of cash flows or in a note to the statement because of their importance and the *full-disclosure principle*. One example of such a transaction is the purchase of long-term assets by giving a long-term note payable. This transaction involves both investing and financing activities, but it does not affect any cash inflow or outflow and is not reported in any of the

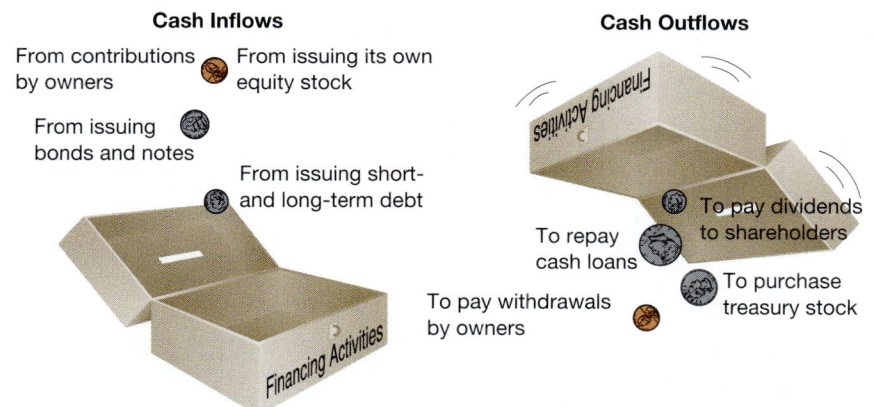

Cash Inflows

From contributions by owners

From issuing its own equity stock

From issuing bonds and notes

From issuing short- and long-term debt

Financing Activities

Cash Outflows

Financing Activities

To repay cash loans

To pay dividends to shareholders

To pay withdrawals by owners

To purchase treasury stock

Exhibit 17.3

Cash Flows from Financing Activities

three sections of the statement of cash flows. Other examples are investing and financing activities involving cash receipts or payments for only part of the transaction.

To illustrate, assume that Goorin purchases machinery for $12,000 by paying $5,000 cash and trading in old equipment with a $7,000 market value. The investing section of the statement of cash flows reports only the $5,000 cash outflow for equipment purchase. The $12,000 investing transaction is only partially described in the body of the statement of cash flows, yet this information is potentially important to users because it changes the makeup of assets. Companies must use one of two ways to disclose important noncash investing and financing activities not reported in the body of the statement of cash flows: (1) a note or (2) a separate schedule attached to the statement. Goorin could either describe the transaction in a note or include a small schedule at the bottom of its statement that lists the $12,000 asset investment along with the financing of $5,000 and a $7,000 trade-in of old equipment.

We consider two cases to show the application in practice. **Seagate Technology** discloses its noncash investing and financing activity in a note as follows: "receipt of note receivable for sale of building, $5,000,000." **Union Camp** discloses its noncash investing and financing activity in a separate schedule ($ in thousands) as follows:

Fair value of assets acquired	$8,345
Less: Cash paid	7,115
Liabilities incurred or assumed	$1,230

This schedule describes an exchange of assets involving both cash and noncash aspects. Union Camp reports the $7,115 cash payment in the statement of cash flows as an investing activity. Moreover, the asset purchase involves a noncash aspect: a liability to pay in the future. Exhibit 17.4 lists some transactions disclosed as noncash investing and financing activities.

> **You Make the Call**
>
> **Entrepreneur**   You are considering acquiring a manufacturing shop. The manufacturer reported a recent $110,000 annual net loss and a $225,000 positive annual net cash flow. How are these results possible?
>
> Answer—p. 724

Point: A stock dividend transaction involving a transfer from retained earnings to common stock, or a credit to contributed capital, is *not* considered a noncash investing and financing activity because the company receives no consideration (asset) for shares issued.

- Retirement of debt by issuing equity stock.
- Conversion of preferred stock to common stock.
- Lease of assets in a capital lease transaction.
- Purchase of long-term asset by issuing a note or bond.
- Exchange of noncash assets for other noncash assets.
- Purchase of noncash assets by issuing equity or debt.

Exhibit 17.4

Examples of Noncash Investing and Financing Activities

Format of the Statement of Cash Flows

C4 Describe the format of the statement of cash flows.

Accounting standards require companies to include a statement of cash flows in a complete set of financial statements. This statement must report information about a company's cash receipts and cash payments during the period. Exhibit 17.5 shows the usual format of the statement of cash flows. A company must report cash flows from three activities: operating, investing, and financing. Detailed cash inflows and cash outflows are reported for each category. The statement explains how transactions and events impact the beginning-of-period cash (and cash equivalents) balance to produce its end-of-period balance.

Exhibit 17.5

Format of the Statement of Cash Flows

COMPANY NAME
Statement of Cash Flows
For *period* Ended *date*

Cash flows from operating activities
  [List of individual inflows and outflows]
  Net cash provided (used) by operating activities . . . . $ #
Cash flows from investing activities
  [List of individual inflows and outflows]
  Net cash provided (used) by investing activities . . . .   #
Cash flows from financing activities
  [List of individual inflows and outflows]
  Net cash provided (used) by financing activities . . . .   #

Net increase (decrease) in cash . . . . $ #
Cash (and equivalents) balance at beginning of period . . . .   #
Cash (and equivalents) balance at end of period . . . . $ #

Global: International accounting standards require a statement of cash flows separated into operating, investing, and financing activities.

Note: Separate schedule or note disclosure of any "noncash investing and financing transactions" is required.

Quick Check

1. Does a statement of cash flows disclose cash payments to purchase cash equivalents? Does it disclose cash receipts from selling cash equivalents?

2. Identify the categories of cash flows reported separately on the statement of cash flows.

3. Identify the activity category for each transaction: (a) purchase equipment for cash, (b) payment of wages, (c) sale of common stock for cash, (d) receipt of cash dividends from stock investment, (e) cash collection from customers, (f) bonds issuance for cash.

Answers—p. 724

Preparing the Statement of Cash Flows

P1 Prepare a statement of cash flows.

Preparation of a statement of cash flows involves five steps: (1) compute the net increase or decrease in cash; (2) compute and report net cash provided (used) by operating activities (using either the direct or indirect method—both are explained in this chapter); (3) compute and report net cash provided (used) by investing activities; (4) compute and report net cash provided (used) by financing activities; and (5) compute net cash flow by combining net cash provided (used) by operating, investing, and financing activities and then *prove it* by adding it to the beginning cash balance to show that it equals the ending cash balance. All important noncash investing and financing activities are disclosed in either a note or a separate schedule to the statement.

Step 1 in preparing the statement—computing the net increase or net decrease in cash—is a simple but crucial computation. It equals the current period's cash balance minus the prior period's cash balance. This is the *bottom line* figure for the statement of cash flows and is a helpful check on the accuracy of one's work.

The information we need to prepare a statement of cash flows comes from a variety of sources including comparative balance sheets at the beginning and end of the period, and an income statement for the period—essentially an analysis of noncash accounts. Alternatively, because cash inflows and cash outflows are captured in the accounting system, we can examine the transactions that affect the Cash account. This section briefly describes these two alternative approaches to preparing the statement: (1) analyzing the Cash account and (2) analyzing noncash accounts.

Analyzing the Cash Account

A company's cash receipts and cash payments are recorded in the Cash account in the general ledger. The Cash account is therefore a natural place to look for information about cash flows from operating, investing, and financing activities. To illustrate, review the summarized Cash T-account of Genesis, Inc., in Exhibit 17.6. Individual cash transactions are summarized in this Cash account according to the major types of cash receipts and cash payments. For instance, only the total of cash receipts from all customers is listed. Individual cash transactions underlying these totals can number in the thousands. Accounting software programs are available to provide summarized cash accounts similar to the one illustrated.

Preparing a statement of cash flows from Exhibit 17.6 requires us to determine whether an individual cash inflow or outflow is an operating, investing, or financing activity, and then to list each by activity. This yields the statement shown in Exhibit 17.7. However, preparing the statement of cash flows from an analysis of the summarized Cash account has two limitations. First, most companies have many individual cash receipts and payments, making it difficult to review them all. Accounting software greatly minimizes this burden, but it is still a task requiring professional judgment for many transactions. Second, the Cash account does not usually carry an adequate description of each cash transaction, making assignment of all cash transactions according to activity difficult.

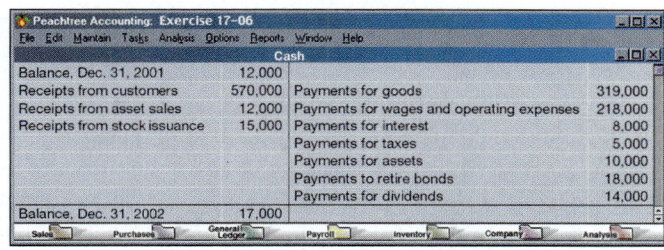

Step 1: Compute net increase or decrease in cash

Step 2: Compute net cash from operating activities

Step 3: Compute net cash from investing activities

Step 4: Compute net cash from financing activities

Step 5: Prove and report beginning and ending cash balances

Exhibit 17.6
Summarized Cash Account

Point: View the change in cash as a *TARGET* number that you will fully explain and prove in the statement of cash flows.

Analyzing Noncash Accounts

A second approach to preparing the statement of cash flows is based on analyzing noncash accounts. This approach uses the fact that when a company records cash inflows and outflows with debits and credits to the Cash account (as reflected in the prior section), it also records credits and debits in other noncash accounts (reflecting double-entry accounting). Many of these noncash accounts are balance sheet accounts, for instance, the sale of land for cash. Others are revenue and expense accounts that are closed to equity—either a capital account or Retained Earnings. For instance, the sale of services for cash yields a credit to Services Revenue that is closed to Retained Earnings for a corporation. In sum, *all cash transactions eventually affect noncash balance sheet accounts*. Thus, we can determine cash inflows and cash outflows by analyzing changes in noncash balance sheet accounts. We are not limited to analyzing the Cash account.

Exhibit 17.8 uses the accounting equation to show the important relation between the Cash account and the noncash balance sheet accounts. This exhibit starts with the familiar accounting equation at the top. We then expand it in line (2) to separate cash from noncash asset accounts. Next, we move noncash asset accounts to the right-hand side of the equality in line (3) where they are subtracted. This shows that cash equals the sum of the liability and equity accounts *minus* the noncash asset accounts. Line (4) points out that *changes*

Global: Some countries require a statement of funds flow instead of a statement of cash flows, which often defines *funds* as *working capital* (current assets minus current liabilities).

Exhibit 17.7

Statement of Cash Flows—
Direct Method

GENESIS Statement of Cash Flows For Year Ended December 31, 2002		
Cash flows from operating activities		
Cash received from customers	$570,000	
Cash paid for merchandise	(319,000)	
Cash paid for wages and other operating expenses	(218,000)	
Cash paid for interest	(8,000)	
Cash paid for taxes	(5,000)	
Net cash provided by operating activities		$20,000
Cash flows from investing activities		
Cash received from sale of plant assets	12,000	
Cash paid for purchase of plant assets	(10,000)	
Net cash provided by investing activities		2,000
Cash flows from financing activities		
Cash received from issuing stock	15,000	
Cash paid to retire bonds	(18,000)	
Cash paid for dividends	(14,000)	
Net cash used in financing activities		(17,000)
Net increase in cash		$ 5,000
Cash balance at beginning of year		12,000
Cash balance at end of year		$17,000

in one side of the accounting equation equal *changes* on the other side. It also shows that we can explain changes in cash by analyzing changes in the noncash accounts consisting of liability accounts, equity accounts, and noncash assets accounts. By analyzing all noncash balance sheet accounts and any related income statement accounts, we have the information for preparing a statement of cash flows.

Information to Prepare the Statement

Information to prepare the statement of cash flows usually comes from three sources: (1) comparative balance sheets, (2) current income statement, and (3) additional information.

Did You Know?

E-Cash   Every credit transaction on the Net leaves a trail that a hacker, an aggressive marketer, or the government  can pick up. Enter e-cash. E-cash is the electronic equivalent of cash —digital money that can be used as freely and anonymously as cash. With e-cash, the encryption not only protects your money from snoops and thieves but also obscures your identity. When you spend e-cash, it cannot be traced back to you—not even by the issuing bank.

Exhibit 17.8

Relation between Cash and
Noncash Accounts

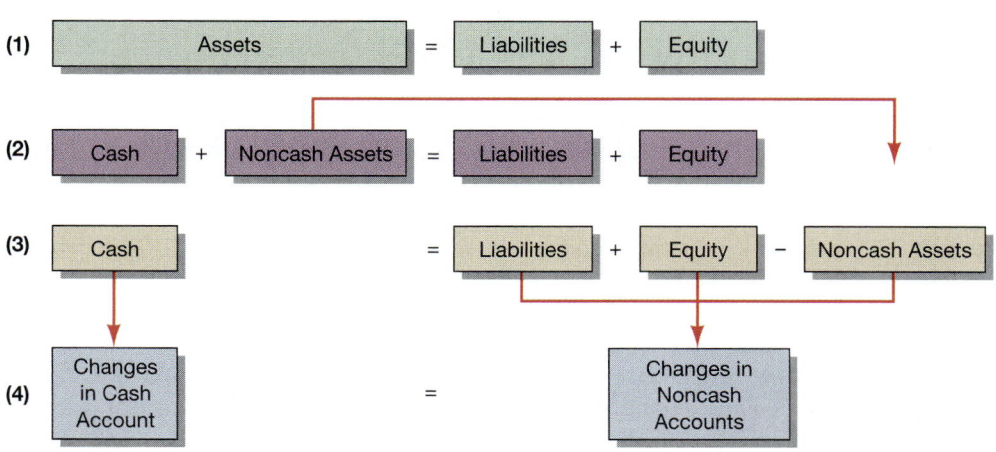

Comparative balance sheets are used to compute changes in noncash accounts from the beginning to the end of the period. The current income statement is used to help compute cash flows from operating activities. Additional information often includes details on transactions and events that help explain both the cash flows and noncash investing and financing activities.

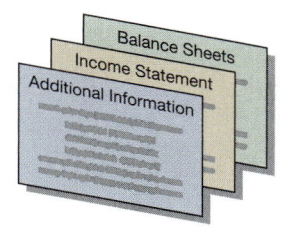

Cash Flows from Operating

This section describes the reporting of cash flows from operating activities using the direct method and the indirect method. *These two different methods apply only to the operating activities section.*

Reporting Operating Cash Flows

The net cash flows provided (used) by operating activities can be reported in one of two ways: the *direct method* or the *indirect method*. The **direct method** separately lists each major item of operating cash receipts (such as cash received from customers) and each major item of operating cash payments (such as cash paid for merchandise). The cash payments are subtracted from cash receipts to determine the net cash provided (used) by operating activities. The operating activities section of Exhibit 17.7 is an example of the direct method of reporting operating cash flows.

The **indirect method** reports net income and then adjusts it for items necessary to obtain net cash provided (used) by operating activities. It does *not* report individual items of cash inflows and cash outflows from operating activities. Instead, the indirect method reports the necessary adjustments to reconcile net income to net cash provided (used) by operating activities. The operating activities section prepared under the indirect method is shown in Exhibit 17.9.

Point: Operating activities are generally related to activities that determine income, which are often reflected in changes in current assets and current liabilities.

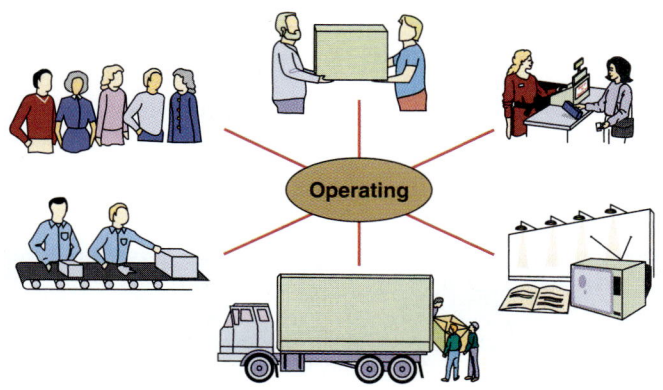

Cash flows from operating activities	
Net income	$38,000
Adjustments to reconcile net income to net	
cash provided by operating activities	
Increase in accounts receivable	(20,000)
Increase in merchandise inventory	(14,000)
Increase in prepaid expenses	(2,000)
Decrease in accounts payable	(5,000)
Decrease in interest payable	(1,000)
Increase in income taxes payable	10,000
Depreciation expense	24,000
Loss on sale of plant assets	6,000
Gain on retirement of bonds	(16,000)
Net cash provided by operating activities	**$20,000**

Exhibit 17.9

Operating Activities Section— Indirect Method

Note that the amount of net cash provided by operating activities is *identical* under both the direct and indirect methods. This equality always exists. The difference in these methods is with the computation and presentation of this amount.

The indirect method of reporting operating cash flows does not provide as much detail about the sources and uses of cash as does the direct method. The FASB recommends the direct method, but since it is not required and the indirect method is arguably easier to compute, most companies report operating cash flows using the indirect method. We describe both methods in this chapter.

Concept 17-2

Point: To better understand the direct and indirect methods of reporting operating cash flows, identify the similarities and differences between Exhibits 17.7 and 17.17.

Since the direct method is presented like the income statement, many people find the direct method easier to understand when first learning about cash flow reporting. It also reports the amount of revenues and expenses actually received and paid in cash, and it follows the format of the income statement. Many internal users such as managers and budget officers use the direct method to predict future cash requirements and availability.

To illustrate both methods, we prepare the operating activities section of the statement of cash flows for **Genesis, Inc**. Exhibit 17.10 shows the December 31, 2001, and 2002, balance sheets of Genesis along with its year 2002 income statement. We use this information to prepare a statement of cash flows to explain the $5,000 increase in cash for year 2002 as reported in its balance sheets. This $5,000 is computed as Cash of $17,000 at the end of 2002 minus Cash of $12,000 at the end of 2001. Genesis discloses additional information about year 2002 transactions:

a. Accounts payable balances result from merchandise inventory purchases.

b. Plant assets costing $70,000 are purchased by paying $10,000 cash and issuing $60,000 of bonds payable.

c. Plant assets with an original cost of $30,000 and accumulated depreciation of $12,000 are sold for $12,000 cash. This yields a $6,000 loss.

d. Cash received from issuing 3,000 shares of common stock is $15,000.

e. Paid $18,000 to retire bonds with a book value of $34,000. This yields a $16,000 gain.

f. Cash dividends of $14,000 are declared and paid.

Exhibit 17.10

Financial Statements

GENESIS — Balance Sheet — December 31, 2002 and 2001

	2002	2001
Assets		
Current assets		
Cash	$ 17,000	$ 12,000
Accounts receivable	60,000	40,000
Merchandise inventory	84,000	70,000
Prepaid expenses	6,000	4,000
Total current assets	$167,000	$126,000
Long-term assets		
Plant assets	250,000	210,000
Accumulated depreciation	(60,000)	(48,000)
Total assets	$357,000	$288,000
Liabilities		
Current liabilities		
Accounts payable	$ 35,000	$ 40,000
Interest payable	3,000	4,000
Income taxes payable	22,000	12,000
Total current liabilities	$ 60,000	$ 56,000
Long-term liabilities		
Bonds payable	90,000	64,000
Total liabilities	$150,000	$120,000
Equity		
Common stock, $5 par	$ 95,000	$ 80,000
Retained earnings	112,000	88,000
Total equity	$207,000	$168,000
Total liabilities and equity	$357,000	$288,000

GENESIS — Income Statement — For Year Ended December 31, 2002

Sales		$590,000
Cost of goods sold	$300,000	
Wages & other operating expenses	216,000	
Interest expense	7,000	
Depreciation expense	24,000	(547,000)
Other gains (losses)		
Loss on sale of plant assets		(6,000)
Income before taxes		$ 37,000
Income taxes expense*		(15,000)
Income from continuing operations		$ 22,000
Extraordinary item		
Gain on retirement of debt*		16,000
Net income		$ 38,000

* Income Taxes Expense is restated to include the taxes related to the extraordinary gain. This means the $16,000 extraordinary gain is at its gross amount, not net of tax. This restatement is made prior to preparing the statement of cash flows because the FASB requires *all income taxes paid be classified as operating cash outflows.*

The next section describes the direct method. The section following that one describes the indirect method (see p. 706). An instructor may choose to cover either one or both methods for preparing a statement of cash flows. Neither section depends on the other.

Direct Method of Reporting

We compute cash flows from operating activities under the direct method by adjusting accrual-based income statement items to the cash basis. The usual approach is to adjust income statement accounts related to operating activities for changes in their related balance sheet accounts as follows:

P2   Compute cash flows from operating activities using the direct method.

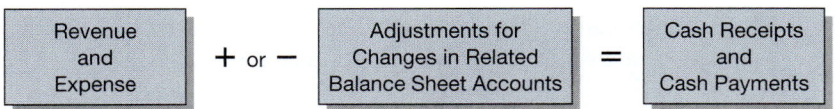

The framework for reporting the major classes of cash receipts and cash payments is shown in Exhibit 17.11. This framework is for the operating section of the cash flow statement under the direct method. In preparing the operating section, we consider cash receipts first and then cash payments.

Global: Some countries such as Australia require the direct method of reporting.

Exhibit 17.11

Major Classes of Operating Cash Flows

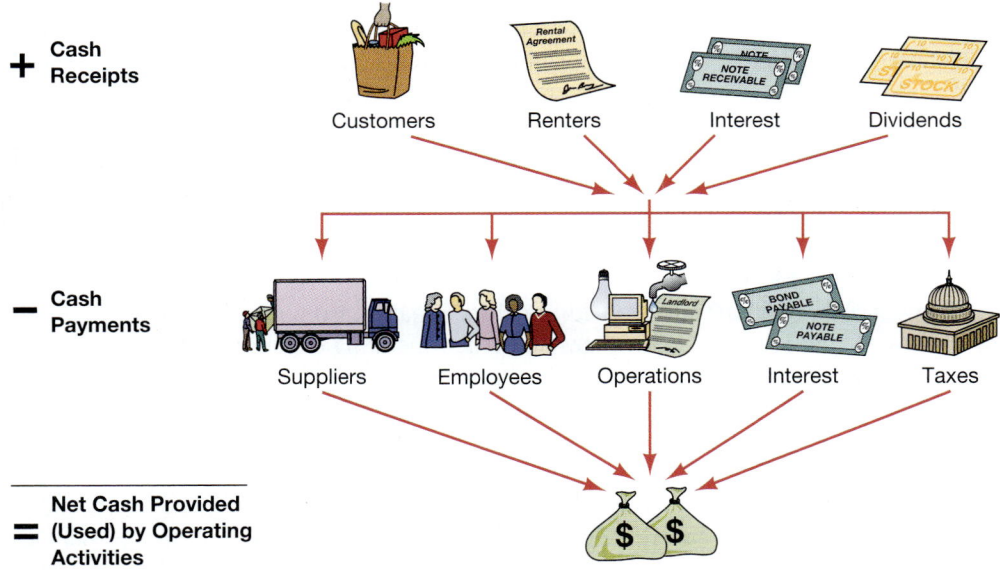

Operating Cash Receipts

A review of Exhibit 17.10 and the additional information reported by Genesis suggests only one potential cash receipt—sales to customers. This section, therefore, starts with sales to customers as reported on the income statement and then adjusts it as necessary to obtain cash received from customers to report on the statement of cash flows.

Cash received from customers

If all sales are for cash, the amount of cash received from customers equals sales reported on the income statement. When some or all sales are on account, however, we must adjust the amount of sales revenue for the change in Accounts Receivable. It is often helpful to use *account analysis* for this purpose. This usually involves setting up a T-account and reconstructing its major entries, with emphasis on cash receipts and payments. To illustrate, we set up a T-account that includes accounts receivable balances for Genesis on December 31, 2001 and 2002. The beginning balance is $40,000 and the ending balance is $60,000. Next, the income statement shows sales of $590,000, which we enter on the debit side of this account. We now can reconstruct the Accounts Receivable account to determine the amount of cash received from customers as follows:

Point: An accounts receivable increase implies cash received from customers is less than sales (the converse is also true).

Accounts Receivable			
Bal., Dec. 31, 2001	40,000		
Sales	590,000	Cash receipts =	570,000
Bal., Dec. 31, 2002	60,000		

This T-account shows that the Accounts Receivable balance begins at $40,000 and increases to $630,000 from sales of $590,000, yet its ending balance is only $60,000. This implies that cash receipts from customers are $570,000, computed as $40,000 + $590,000 − [?] = $60,000. This computation can be rearranged to express cash received as equal to sales of $590,000 minus a $20,000 increase in accounts receivable. This computation is summarized in Exhibit 17.12. The statement of cash flows in Exhibit 17.7 reports the $570,000 cash received from customers as a cash inflow from operating activities.

Exhibit 17.12

Formula to Compute Cash Received from Customers— Direct Method

$$\text{Cash received from customers} = \text{Sales} - \begin{cases} + \text{ Decrease in accounts receivable} \\ \text{or} \\ - \text{ Increase in accounts receivable} \end{cases}$$

Other cash receipts

While Genesis's cash receipts are limited to collections from customers, we often see other types of cash receipts. The most common are cash receipts involving rent, interest, and dividends. We compute cash received from these items by subtracting an increase in their respective receivable or adding a decrease. For instance, if rent receivable increases in the period, cash received from renters is less than rent revenue reported on the income statement. If rent receivable decreases, cash received is more than reported rent revenue. The same logic applies to interest and dividends. The formulas for these computations are summarized in Exhibit 17.16 later in this section.

Operating Cash Payments

A review of Exhibit 17.10 and the additional information from Genesis shows four operating expenses: cost of goods sold, wages and other operating expenses, interest expense, and taxes expense. We analyze each of these expenses to compute their cash amounts for the statement of cash flows. (We then examine depreciation and the other losses and gains.)

Cash paid for merchandise

We compute cash paid for merchandise by analyzing both cost of goods sold and merchandise inventory. If all merchandise purchases are for cash and the ending balance of Merchandise Inventory is unchanged from the beginning balance, the amount of cash paid for merchandise equals cost of goods sold—an uncommon situation. We usually see some change in the Merchandise Inventory balance in a period. Also, some or all merchandise purchases are often made on credit, and this yields changes in the Accounts Payable balance. When the balances of Merchandise Inventory and Accounts Payable change, we must adjust the cost of goods sold for changes in both accounts to compute cash paid for merchandise. This is a two-step adjustment.

First, we use the change in the account balance of Merchandise Inventory and the cost of goods sold amount to compute cost of purchases for the period. An increase in merchandise inventory implies that we bought more than we sold, and we add this inventory increase to cost of goods sold to compute cost of purchases. A decrease in merchandise inventory implies that we bought less than we sold, and we subtract the inventory decrease from cost of goods sold to compute purchases.

The second step uses the change in the balance of Accounts Payable and the amount of cost of purchases to compute cash paid for merchandise. A decrease in accounts payable implies that we paid for more goods than we acquired this period, and we then add the accounts payable decrease to cost of purchases to compute cash paid for merchandise. An increase in accounts payable implies that we paid for less than the amount of goods acquired, and we subtract the accounts payable increase from purchases to compute cash paid for merchandise.

We illustrate this two-step process for Genesis. The *first step* is to use account analysis of Merchandise Inventory to compute cost of purchases. We do this by reconstructing the Merchandise Inventory account:

Merchandise Inventory			
Bal., Dec. 31, 2001	70,000		
Purchases =	**314,000**	Cost of goods sold	300,000
Bal., Dec. 31, 2002	84,000		

The beginning balance is $70,000, and the ending balance is $84,000. The income statement shows that cost of goods sold is $300,000, which we enter on the credit side of this account. With this information, we determine the amount for cost of purchases to be $314,000. This computation can be rearranged to express cost of purchases as equal to cost of goods sold of $300,000 plus the $14,000 increase in inventory.

The *second step* is to compute cash paid for merchandise by adjusting purchases for the change in accounts payable. This is done by reconstructing the Accounts Payable account:

Accounts Payable			
		Bal., Dec. 31, 2001	40,000
Cash payments =	**319,000**	Purchases	314,000
		Bal., Dec. 31, 2002	35,000

This account shows that its beginning balance of $40,000 plus purchases of $314,000 minus an ending balance of $35,000 yields cash paid of $319,000 (or $40,000 + $314,000 − [?]= $35,000). Alternatively, we can express cash paid for merchandise as equal to purchases of $314,000 plus the $5,000 decrease in accounts payable. Exhibit 17.7 shows that the $319,000 cash paid for merchandise is reported on the statement of cash flows as a cash outflow under operating activities. We summarize this two-step adjustment to cost of goods sold to compute cash paid for merchandise inventory in Exhibit 17.13.

Example: If the ending balances of Inventory and Accounts Payable are $60,000 and $50,000, respectively (instead of $84,000 and $35,000), what is cash paid for merchandise? *Answer:* $280,000

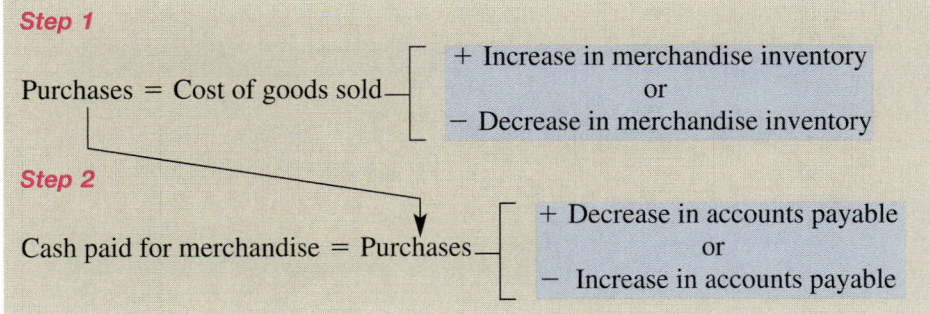

Exhibit 17.13

Two Steps to Compute Cash Paid for Merchandise—Direct Method

Cash paid for wages and operating expenses (excluding depreciation)

The income statement of Genesis shows wages and other operating expenses of $216,000 (see Exhibit 17.10). To compute cash paid for wages and other operating expenses, we adjust this amount for any changes in their related balance sheet accounts. We begin by looking for any prepaid expenses and accrued liabilities related to wages and other operating expenses in the balance sheets of Genesis in Exhibit 17.10. The balance sheets show prepaid expenses but no accrued liabilities, meaning adjustment is limited to the change in prepaid expenses. The amount of adjustment is computed by assuming that all cash paid for wages and other operating expenses is initially debited to Prepaid Expenses. This assumption allows us to reconstruct the Prepaid Expenses account:

Prepaid Expenses			
Bal., Dec. 31, 2001	4,000		
Cash payments =	**218,000**	Wages and other operating exp.	216,000
Bal., Dec. 31, 2002	6,000		

Prepaid Expenses increases by $2,000 in the period, meaning cash paid for wages and other operating expenses exceeds the reported expense by $2,000. Alternatively, we can express cash paid for wages and other operating expenses as equal to its reported expenses of $216,000 plus the $2,000 increase in prepaid expenses.[1]

Exhibit 17.14 summarizes the adjustments to wages (including salaries) and other operating expenses. While the Genesis balance sheet did not report accrued liabilities, we would add them to explain the adjustment to cash when they do exist. A decrease in accrued liabilities implies that we paid cash for more goods or services than received this period, and we must add the decrease in accrued liabilities to the expense amount to obtain cash paid for these goods or services. An increase in accrued liabilities implies that we paid cash for less than what was acquired, and we must subtract this increase in accrued liabilities from the expense amount to get cash paid.

Exhibit 17.14

Formula to Compute Cash Paid for Wages and Operating Expenses—Direct Method

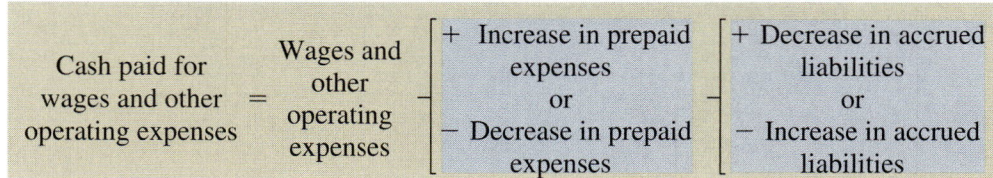

Cash paid for interest and income taxes

Computing operating cash flows for interest and taxes is similar to that for operating expenses. Both require adjustments to their amounts reported on the income statement for changes in their related balance sheet accounts. We begin with the Genesis income statement showing interest expense of $7,000 and income taxes expense of $15,000. To compute the cash paid, we adjust interest expense for the change in interest payable and income taxes expense for the change in income taxes payable. These computations involve reconstructing both liability accounts:

Interest Payable			
		Bal., Dec. 31, 2001	4,000
Cash paid for interest =	**8,000**	Interest expense	7,000
		Bal., Dec. 31, 2002	3,000

Income Taxes Payable			
		Bal., Dec. 31, 2001	12,000
Cash paid for taxes =	**5,000**	Income taxes expense	15,000
		Bal., Dec. 31, 2002	22,000

These accounts reveal cash paid for interest of $8,000 and cash paid for income taxes of $5,000. The formulas to compute these amounts are shown in Exhibit 17.15. Both of these cash payments are reported as operating cash outflows on the statement of cash flows in Exhibit 17.7.

---

[1] The assumption that all cash payments for wages and operating expenses are initially debited to Prepaid Expenses is not necessary for our analysis to hold. If cash payments are debited directly to the expense account, the total amount of cash paid for wages and other operating expenses still equals the $216,000 expense plus the $2,000 increase in Prepaid Expenses (which arise from end-of-period adjusting entries).

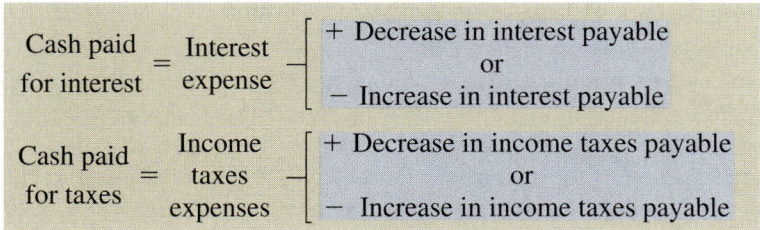

Exhibit 17.15

Formulas to Compute Cash
Paid for Both Interest and
Taxes—Direct Method

Analysis of additional expenses, gains, and losses

Genesis has three additional items reported on its income statement: depreciation, loss on sale of assets, and gain on retirement of debt. We also must consider each of these for their potential cash effects.

Depreciation expense   Depreciation expense is $24,000. It is known as a *noncash expense* because there are no cash flows from depreciation. Depreciation expense is an allocation of the depreciable cost of an asset. The cash outflow with a plant asset is reported as part of investing activities when it is paid for. This means that depreciation expense is *never* reported on a statement of cash flows using the direct method. Depletion and amortization expenses are treated similarly.

Loss on sale of assets   Sales of assets frequently result in gains and losses reported as part of net income, but the amount of recorded gain or loss does *not* reflect any cash flows in these transactions. Asset sales result in cash inflow equal to the cash amount received, regardless of whether the asset was sold at a gain or a loss. This cash inflow is reported under investing activities, meaning that the loss or gain on a sale of assets is *never* reported on a statement of cash flows using the direct method.

Gain on retirement of debt   A retirement of debt usually yields a gain or loss reported as part of net income, but that gain or loss does *not* reflect cash flow in this transaction. Debt retirement results in cash outflow equal to the cash paid to settle the debt, regardless of whether the debt is retired at a gain or loss. This cash outflow is reported under financing activities, meaning the loss or gain from retirement of debt is *never* reported on a statement of cash flows using the direct method.

Summary of Adjustments for Direct Method

Exhibit 17.16 summarizes common adjustments for items making up net income to yield net cash provided (used) by operating activities under the direct method.

Exhibit 17.16

Summary of Selected
Adjustments for Direct Method

Item	From Income Statement	Adjustments to Obtain Cash Flow Numbers	
Receipts			
From sales	Sales Revenue	+ Decrease in Accounts Receivable − Increase in Accounts Receivable	
From rent	Rent Revenue	+ Decrease in Rent Receivable − Increase in Rent Receivable	
From interest	Interest Revenue	+ Decrease in Interest Receivable − Increase in Interest Receivable	
From dividends	Dividend Revenue	+ Decrease in Dividends Receivable − Increase in Dividends Receivable	
Payments			
To suppliers	Cost of Goods Sold	+ Increase in Inventory − Decrease in Inventory	+ Decrease in Accounts Payable − Increase in Accounts Payable
For operations	Operating Expense	+ Increase in Prepaids − Decrease in Prepaids	+ Decrease in Accrued Liabilities − Increase in Accrued Liabilities
To employees	Wages (Salaries) Expense	+ Decrease in Wages (Salaries) Payable − Increase in Wages (Salaries) Payable	
For interest	Interest Expense	+ Decrease in Interest Payable − Increase in Interest Payable	
For taxes	Income Tax Expense	+ Decrease in Income Tax Payable − Increase in Income Tax Payable	

Direct Method Format of Operating Activities Section

Exhibit 17.7 shows the Genesis statement of cash flows using the direct method. Major items of cash inflows and cash outflows are listed separately in the operating activities section. The format requires that operating cash outflows be subtracted from operating cash inflows to get net cash provided (used) by operating activities. The FASB recommends that the operating activities section of the statement of cash flows be reported using the direct method, which is considered more useful to financial statement users. *However, the FASB requires a reconciliation of net income to net cash provided (used) by operating activities when the direct method is used.* This reconciliation is similar to preparing the operating activities section of the statement of cash flows using the indirect method. The next section describes this indirect method.

Point: Some preparers argue that it is easier to prepare a statement of cash flows using the indirect method. This likely explains its greater frequency.

Did You Know?

Win, Loss, and Cash The NBA's **Boston Celtics** report operating cash flows using the direct method. Its operating activities section from its recent annual statement of cash flows is shown here ($ in 000s). For this same period, its operating income is $9,011 (in 000s).

Basketball regular season receipts:	
Ticket sales	$37,851
Television and radio broadcast fees	28,074
Other, principally advertising	8,308
Costs and expenses:	
Basketball regular season expenditures	(49,559)
General and administrative expenses	(5,048)
Selling and promotional expenses	(4,059)
Other expenses and income	(4,065)
Net cash flows from operations	$11,502

Quick Check

4. Is the direct or indirect method of reporting operating cash flows more informative? Explain. Which method is more common in practice?

5. Net sales in a period are $590,000, beginning accounts receivable are $120,000, and ending accounts receivable are $90,000. What amount is collected from customers in the period?

6. The Merchandise Inventory account balance decreases in the period from a beginning balance of $32,000 to an ending balance of $28,000. Cost of goods sold for the period is $168,000. If the Accounts Payable balance increases $2,400 in the period, what is the amount of cash paid for merchandise inventory?

7. Wages and other operating expenses incurred total $112,000. Beginning-of-period prepaid expenses totaled $1,200, and its ending balance is $4,200. The end-of-period wages payable equal $5,600, whereas there were no accrued liabilities at period-end. How much cash is paid for wages and other operating expenses?

Answers—p. 724

Indirect Method of Reporting

P3 Compute cash flows from operating activities using the indirect method.

Net income is computed using accrual accounting, which recognizes revenues when earned and expenses when incurred. Revenues and expenses do not necessarily reflect the receipt and payment of cash. The indirect method of computing and reporting net cash flows from operating activities involves adjusting the net income figure to obtain the net cash provided (used) by operating activities. This includes subtracting noncash increases (credits) from net income and adding noncash charges (debits) back to net income.

We use the Genesis statements in Exhibit 17.10 to illustrate the indirect method. The indirect method begins with Genesis net income of $38,000 and adjusts it to obtain net cash provided (used) by operating activities. Exhibit 17.17 shows the results of the indirect method of reporting operating cash flows for Genesis. The net cash provided by operating activities is $20,000. This amount is the same as that for the direct method of reporting operating cash flows (see Exhibit 17.7). *The two methods always yield the same net cash flow provided (used) by operating activities*. Only the computations and presentation are different.

The indirect method does not report individual operating cash inflows or cash outflows. Instead, it adjusts net income for three types of adjustments as identified in Exhibit 17.17. There are adjustments ① to reflect changes in noncash current assets and current liabilities relating to operating activities, ② to income statement items involving operating activities that do not affect cash inflows or outflows in the period, and ③ to eliminate gains and losses resulting from investing and financing activities (not part of operating activities). This section describes each of these three types of adjustments.

Point: Noncash *credits* refer to *revenue amounts* reported on the income statement that are *not collected in cash* this period. Noncash *charges* refer to *expense amounts* reported on the income statement that are *not paid* this period.

Global: Some countries such as Spain require the indirect method of reporting.

Exhibit 17.17

Statement of Cash Flows—Indirect Method

GENESIS — Statement of Cash Flows — For Year Ended December 31, 2002		
Cash flows from operating activities		
Net income	$38,000	
Adjustments to reconcile net income to net cash provided by operating activities:		
① Increase in accounts receivable	(20,000)	
Increase in merchandise inventory	(14,000)	
Increase in prepaid expenses	(2,000)	
Decrease in accounts payable	(5,000)	
Decrease in interest payable	(1,000)	
Increase in income taxes payable	10,000	
② Depreciation expense	24,000	
③ Loss on sale of plant assets	6,000	
Gain on retirement of bonds	(16,000)	
Net cash provided by operating activities		$20,000
Cash flows from investing activities		
Cash received from sale of plant assets	12,000	
Cash paid for purchase of plant assets	(10,000)	
Net cash provided by investing activities		2,000
Cash flows from financing activities		
Cash received from issuing stock	15,000	
Cash paid to retire bonds	(18,000)	
Cash paid for dividends	(14,000)	
Net cash used in financing activities		(17,000)
Net increase in cash		$ 5,000
Cash balance at beginning of year		12,000
Cash balance at end of year		$17,000

① Adjustments for Changes in Current Assets and Current Liabilities

This section describes adjustments for changes in noncash current assets and current liabilities for determining operating cash flows using the indirect method.

Adjustments for changes in noncash current assets

Changes in noncash current assets are normally the result of operating activities. Examples are sales affecting accounts receivable and rented asset usage affecting prepaid rent expense. Thus, adjustments to net income in computing operating cash flows under the indirect method reflect decreases in noncash current assets as follows:

Decreases in noncash current assets are added to net income.

To see the logic for this adjustment, consider that a decrease in a noncash current asset such as accounts receivable suggests more available cash at the end of the period compared to the beginning of the period. This is so because a decrease in accounts receivable implies higher cash receipts. We add these higher cash receipts (from decreases in noncash current assets) to net income when computing net cash flow from operations.

In contrast, an increase in noncash current assets such as accounts receivable implies decreased cash receipts. For instance, an increase in prepaid rent expense suggests more cash is paid for rent than is deducted as rent expense. We therefore subtract this increase in prepaid rent from net income in computing the amount of cash flow from operations. This yields the following adjustment to reflect increases in noncash current assets under the indirect method of reporting operating cash flows:

Increases in noncash current assets are subtracted from net income.

We apply these adjustments to the Genesis noncash current assets in Exhibit 17.10.

Accounts receivable   Accounts Receivable *increases* $20,000 in the period, from a beginning balance of $40,000 to an ending balance of $60,000. This increase implies that Genesis collects less cash than its reported sales for the period. It also means that some of these sales are in the form of accounts receivable, leaving accounts receivable with an increase. The lower amount of cash receipts compared to sales is reflected in the Accounts Receivable T-account:

Accounts Receivable			
Bal., Dec. 31, 2001	40,000		
Sales	590,000	**Cash receipts =**	**570,000**
Bal., Dec. 31, 2002	60,000		

Accordingly, the $20,000 increase in Accounts Receivable is subtracted from net income as part of the adjustments to obtain net cash provided by operating activities. Subtracting it adjusts sales to the cash receipts amount.

Merchandise inventory   Merchandise inventory *increases* $14,000 in the period, from a $70,000 beginning balance to an $84,000 ending balance. This increase implies that Genesis had a larger amount of cash purchases than cost of goods sold this period. This larger amount of cash purchases is in the form of inventory, resulting in an increase in the Merchandise Inventory account:

Merchandise Inventory			
Bal., Dec. 31, 2001	70,000		
Purchases =	**314,000**	Cost of goods sold	300,000
Bal., Dec. 31, 2002	84,000		

The $14,000 increase in Merchandise Inventory is subtracted from net income as part of the adjustments to determine net cash provided by operating activities.

Prepaid expenses   Prepaid expenses *increase* $2,000 in the period, from a $4,000 beginning balance to a $6,000 ending balance. This increase implies that Genesis's cash payments exceed its operating expenses incurred this period. These higher cash payments increase the amount of Prepaid Expenses as reflected in its T-account:

Prepaid Expenses			
Bal., Dec. 31, 2001	4,000		
Cash payments =	**218,000**	Wages and other operating exp.	216,000
Bal., Dec. 31, 2002	6,000		

The $2,000 increase in Prepaid Expenses is subtracted from net income as part of the adjustments to determine net cash provided by operating activities. Subtracting it adjusts operating expenses to a cash payments amount.

Adjustments for changes in current liabilities

Changes in current liabilities are normally the result of operating activities. An example is a purchase that affects accounts payable. Adjustments to net income in computing operating cash flows under the indirect method reflect increases in current liabilities as follows:

Increases in current liabilities are added to net income.

To see the logic for this adjustment, consider that an increase in the Accounts Payable account suggests that cash payments are less than the related (cost of sales) expense. As another example, an increase in wages payable implies that wages expense exceed cash paid for the period. Because more is deducted as an expense than is paid in cash, we add the increase in wages payable to net income when computing net cash flow from operations.

Conversely, when current liabilities decrease in the period, the indirect method for reporting operating cash flows requires the following adjustment:

Decreases in current liabilities are subtracted from net income.

We apply these adjustments to the current liabilities in Exhibit 17.10.

Accounts payable Accounts Payable *decreases* $5,000 in the period, from a beginning balance of $40,000 to an ending balance of $35,000. This decrease implies that its cash payments exceed its merchandise purchases by $5,000 for the period. This higher amount for cash payments compared to purchases is reflected in the Accounts Payable T-account:

Accounts Payable			
		Bal., Dec. 31, 2001	40,000
Cash payments =	319,000	Purchases	314,000
		Bal., Dec. 31, 2002	35,000

The $5,000 decrease in Accounts Payable is subtracted from net income as part of the adjustments to determine net cash provided by operating activities.

Interest payable Interest Payable *decreases* $1,000 in the period, from a $4,000 beginning balance to a $3,000 ending balance. This decrease indicates that cash paid for interest exceeds interest expense for the period by $1,000. This larger cash payment compared to reported interest expense is reflected in the Interest Payable T-account:

Interest Payable			
		Bal., Dec. 31, 2001	4,000
Cash paid for interest =	8,000	Interest expense	7,000
		Bal., Dec. 31, 2002	3,000

The $1,000 decrease in Interest Payable is subtracted from net income as part of the adjustments to get net cash provided by operating activities.

Income taxes payable Income Taxes Payable *increases* $10,000 in the period, from a $12,000 beginning balance to a $22,000 ending balance. This increase implies that income taxes incurred exceed the cash paid for them by $10,000. This smaller cash payment compared to taxes incurred is reflected in the Income Taxes Payable T-account:

Income Taxes Payable			
		Bal., Dec. 31, 2001	12,000
Cash paid for taxes =	5,000	Income taxes expense	15,000
		Bal., Dec. 31, 2002	22,000

The $10,000 increase in Income Taxes Payable is added to net income as part of the adjustments to determine net cash provided by operating activities.

② Adjustments for Operating Items Not Providing or Using Cash

The income statement usually includes expenses that do not reflect cash outflows in the period. Examples are depreciation, amortization of intangibles, depletion of natural resources, and bad debts expense. The indirect method for reporting operating cash flows requires that

Expenses with no cash outflows are added back to net income.

To see the logic of this adjustment, recall that items such as depreciation, amortization, depletion, and bad debts originate from debits to expense accounts and credits to noncash accounts. These entries have *no* cash effect, and we need to add them back to net income when computing net cash flows from operations. Adding them back cancels their deductions.

Similarly, when net income includes revenues that do not reflect cash inflows in the period, the indirect method for reporting operating cash flows requires that

Revenues with no cash inflows are subtracted from net income.

We apply these adjustments to the Genesis operating items that do not provide or use cash.

Depreciation

Depreciation expense is the only Genesis operating item that does not affect cash flows in the period. We must add back the $24,000 depreciation expense to net income to obtain net cash provided by operating activities. (Later in the chapter, we explain that the cash outflow to acquire a plant asset is reported as an investing activity.)

③ Adjustments for Nonoperating Items

Net income often includes losses that are not part of operating activities but are classified as either investing or financing activities. Examples are a loss from sale of a plant asset and a loss from retirement of a bond payable. Under the indirect method for reporting operating cash flows

Nonoperating losses are added back to net income.

To see the logic, consider that items such as a plant asset sale and a bond retirement are normally recorded by recognizing the cash, removing all plant asset or bond accounts, and recognizing any loss or gain. The cash received or paid is not part of operating activities but is recorded under either investing or financing activities. *No* operating cash flow effect occurs. However, since the nonoperating loss is a deduction in computing net income, we need to add it back to net income when computing the net cash flow from operations. Adding it back cancels the deduction.

Similarly, when net income includes gains not part of operating activities, the indirect method for reporting operating cash flows requires

Nonoperating gains are subtracted from net income.

These net income adjustments are part of computations to determine net cash provided by operating activities. We now look at the Genesis individual nonoperating items.

Loss on sale of plant assets

Genesis reports a $6,000 loss on sale of plant assets as part of net income. This loss is a proper deduction in computing income, but it is *not part of operating activities*. Instead, a sale of plant assets is part of investing activities. The $6,000 nonoperating loss is added back to net income as part of our adjustments to determine cash provided by operating activities. Adding it back cancels the loss. Later we explain how to report the cash inflow from the asset sale in investing activities.

Gain on retirement of debt

A $16,000 gain on retirement of debt is reported in net income. This gain is properly included in net income, but it is *not part of operating activities*. The $16,000 nonoperating gain is subtracted from net income as part of our adjustments to obtain net cash provided by operating activities. Subtracting it cancels the recorded gain. Later we describe how to report the cash outflow to retire debt in financing activities.

Summary of Adjustments for Indirect Method

Exhibit 17.18 summarizes common adjustments to net income when computing net cash provided (used) by operating activities under the indirect method.

Did You Know?

Cash or Income The difference between net income and operating cash flows can be large. The bar chart to the side shows net income and operating cash flows for four well-known companies. Note that operating cash flows can be either higher or lower than net income. The difference between net income and operating cash flows is a focus of many analysts.

Exhibit 17.18

Summary of Selected Adjustments for Indirect Method

Net Income

+ Decrease in noncash current asset
− Increase in noncash current asset
+ Increase in current liability*
− Decrease in current liability*

⟩ ① Adjustments for changes in current assets and current liabilities

+ Depreciation, depletion, and amortization
+ Accrued expenses
− Accrued revenues

⟩ ② Adjustments for operating items not providing or using cash

+ Loss on disposal of long-term asset
+ Loss on retirement of debt
− Gain on disposal of long-term asset
− Gain on retirement of debt

⟩ ③ Adjustments for nonoperating items

Net cash provided (used) by operating activities

* Excludes current portion of long-term debt and any short-term notes payable if unrelated to sales—both are considered financing activities.

The computations in determining net cash provided (used) by operating activities are different for the direct and indirect methods, but the result is identical. Both methods yield the same $20,000 figure for net cash provided (used) by operating activities for Genesis—see Exhibits 17.7 and 17.17.

Quick Check

8. Determine net cash provided (used) by operating activities using the following data: net income, $74,900; decrease in accounts receivable, $4,600; increase in inventory, $11,700; decrease in accounts payable, $1,000; loss on sale of equipment, $3,400; payment of cash dividends, $21,500.

9. Why are expenses such as depreciation and amortization added to net income when cash flow from operating activities is computed by the indirect method?

10. A company reports net income of $15,000 that includes a $3,000 gain on the sale of plant assets. Why is this gain subtracted from net income in computing cash flow from operating activities using the indirect method?

Answers—p. 724

Cash Flows from Investing

Point: Investing activities include (1) purchasing and selling long-term assets, (2) lending and collecting on notes receivable, and (3) purchasing and selling short-term investments other than cash equivalents and trading securities.

P4 Determine cash flows from both investing and financing activities.

Point: Financing and investing info is available in ledger accounts to help explain changes in comparative balance sheets. Post references lead us to relevant entries and explanations.

The third major step in preparing the statement of cash flows is to compute and report net cash flows from investing activities. We normally do this by identifying changes in (1) all noncurrent asset accounts and (2) the current accounts for both notes receivable and investments in securities (excluding trading securities). We then analyze changes in these accounts using available information to determine their effect, if any, on cash. Results of this analysis are reported in the investing activities section of the statement of cash flows. *Reporting of investing activities is identical under the direct method and the indirect method.*

Information to compute cash flows from investing activities is usually taken from beginning and ending balance sheets and the income statement. We use a three-step process to determine net cash provided (used) by investing activities: (1) identify changes in investing-related accounts, (2) explain these changes using reconstruction analysis, and (3) report their cash flow effects.

Analysis of Noncurrent Assets

Information provided earlier in the chapter about the Genesis transactions reveals that it both purchased and sold plant assets during the period. Both transactions are investing activities and are analyzed for their cash flow effects in this section.

Plant Asset Purchase

The first step in analyzing the plant asset account and its related accumulated depreciation is to identify any changes in these accounts from comparative balance sheet information in Exhibit 17.10. This analysis reveals a $40,000 increase in plant assets from $210,000 to $250,000 and a $12,000 increase in accumulated depreciation from $48,000 to $60,000. The second step is to explain these changes. Items *b* and *c* of the additional information reported for Genesis (page 700) are relevant in this case. Recall that the Plant Assets account is affected by both its purchases and sales, while its Accumulated Depreciation account is normally increased from depreciation and decreased from the removal of accumulated depreciation from asset sales. To explain changes in these accounts and to identify their cash flow effects, we prepare *reconstructed entries,* which are recreations of entries from prior transactions; *they are not the actual entries by the preparer.* Item *b* reports that Genesis purchases plant assets of $70,000 by issuing $60,000 in bonds payable to the seller and paying $10,000 in cash. The reconstructed entry for analysis of item *b* follows:

Assets = Liabilities + Equity
+70,000   +60,000
−10,000

Reconstruction	Plant Assets	70,000	
	Bonds Payable		60,000
	Cash		**10,000**

This entry reveals a $10,000 cash outflow for plant assets, and a $60,000 noncash investing and financing transaction involving bonds exchanged for plant assets.

Plant Asset Sale

Item *c* reports that Genesis sells plant assets costing $30,000 (with $12,000 of accumulated depreciation) for cash of $12,000, resulting in a loss of $6,000. The reconstructed entry for analysis of item *c* follows:

Assets = Liabilities + Equity
+12,000   −6,000
−30,000
+12,000

Reconstruction	**Cash**	**12,000**	
	Accumulated Depreciation	12,000	
	Loss on Sale of Plant Assets	6,000	
	Plant Assets		30,000

This entry reveals a $12,000 cash inflow from assets sold. The $6,000 loss is computed by comparing the asset book value to the cash received and does not reflect any cash inflow or outflow. In addition, we also reconstruct the entry for Depreciation Expense using information from the income statement:

Reconstruction	Depreciation Expense	24,000	
	Accumulated Depreciation		24,000

Assets = Liabilities + Equity
−24,000   −24,000

This entry shows that Depreciation Expense results in no cash flow effects. These reconstructed entries are reflected in the following accounts.

Plant Assets			
Bal., Dec. 31, 2001	210,000		
Purchase	70,000	Sale	30,000
Bal., Dec. 31, 2002	250,000		

Accumulated Depreciation, Plant Assets			
		Bal., Dec. 31, 2001	48,000
Sale	12,000	Depr. expense	24,000
		Bal., Dec. 31, 2002	60,000

Preparers of the statement of cash flows have the entire ledger and additional information at their disposal. For brevity reasons, we are given only the additional information needed for reconstructing accounts and verifying that our analysis of the investing-related accounts is complete.

The final step in analyzing investing activities is to make the necessary disclosures on the statement of cash flows. Disclosure of the two cash flow effects in the investing section of the statement appears as follows (also see Exhibit 17.7 or 17.17):

> **Cash flows from investing activities**
> Cash received from sale of plant assets $12,000
> Cash paid for purchase of plant assets . . . . (10,000)

Example: If a plant asset costing $40,000 with $37,000 of accumulated depreciation is sold at a $1,000 loss, what is the cash flow? What is the cash flow if this asset is sold at a gain of $3,000? *Answers:* +$2,000; +$6,000.

The $60,000 portion of the purchase described in item *b* and financed by issuing the bonds is a noncash investing and financing activity. It can be reported in a note or in a separate schedule to the statement as follows:

> **Noncash investing and financing activity**
> Purchased plant assets with issuance of bonds $60,000

We have now reconstructed plant asset accounts by explaining how the beginning balances of these accounts are affected by purchases, sales, and depreciation in yielding their ending balances. The change in plant assets from $210,000 to $250,000 is fully explained by the $70,000 purchase and the $30,000 sale. Also, the change in accumulated depreciation from $48,000 to $60,000 is fully explained by the sale of assets (with $12,000 of accumulated depreciation) and depreciation expense of $24,000.

Analysis of Other Assets

Many other asset transactions (including those involving current notes receivable and investments in securities) are considered investing activities and can affect a company's cash flows. Since Genesis did not enter into other investing activities impacting assets, we do not need to extend our analysis to these other assets. If such transactions did exist, we would analyze them using the same three-step process illustrated for plant assets.

Point: Equity and debt investments usually refer to investments in stocks and bonds, respectively.

Quick Check

11. Equipment costing $80,000 with accumulated depreciation of $30,000 is sold at a loss of $10,000. What is the cash receipt from this sale? In what section of the statement of cash flows is it reported?

Answer—p. 724

Cash Flows from Financing

Point: Financing activities generally refer to changes in the noncurrent liability and the equity accounts. Examples are (1) receiving cash from issuing debt or repaying amounts borrowed and (2) receiving cash from or distributing cash to owners.

The fourth major step in preparing the statement of cash flows is to compute and report net cash flows from financing activities. We normally do this by identifying changes in all non-current liability accounts (including the current portion of any notes and bonds) and equity accounts. These accounts include long-term debt, notes payable, bonds payable, owner's capital, common stock, and retained earnings. Changes in these accounts are then analyzed using available information to determine their effect, if any, on cash. Results of this analysis are reported in the financing activities section of the statement. *Reporting of financing activities is identical under the direct method and indirect method.*

We again use a three-step process to determine net cash provided (used) by financing activities: (1) identify changes in financing-related accounts, (2) explain these changes using reconstruction analysis, and (3) report their cash flow effects.

Analysis of Noncurrent Liabilities

Information provided earlier about Genesis reveals two transactions involving noncurrent liabilities. We have analyzed one of those—the $60,000 issuance of bonds payable to purchase plant assets. This transaction is reported as a significant noncash investing and financing activity in a note or a separate schedule to the statement of cash flows. The other remaining transaction involving noncurrent liabilities is the cash retirement of bonds payable. We analyze it in this section.

Bonds Payable Retirement

The first step in analysis of bonds is to review comparative balance sheet information from Exhibit 17.10 for bonds payable, which reveals an increase in bonds payable from $64,000 to $90,000. The second step is to explain this change. Item *e* of the additional information for Genesis (page 700) reports that bonds with a carrying value of $34,000 are retired for $18,000 cash, resulting in a $16,000 gain. The reconstructed entry for analysis of item *e* follows:

Assets = Liabilities + Equity
−18,000   −34,000   +16,000

Reconstruction	Bonds Payable	34,000	
	Gain on retirement of debt		16,000
	Cash		**18,000**

This entry reveals an $18,000 cash outflow for retirement of bonds and a $16,000 gain from comparing the bonds payable carrying value to the cash received. This gain does not reflect any cash inflow or outflow. In addition, item *b* of the additional information reports that Genesis purchased plant assets costing $70,000 by issuing $60,000 in bonds payable to the seller and paying $10,000 in cash. We reconstructed this entry for analysis of investing activities. Recall that it increases bonds payable by $60,000 and is reported as a noncash investing and financing transaction. The Bonds Payable account reflects (and is fully explained by) these reconstructed entries:

Bonds Payable			
		Bal., Dec. 31, 2001	64,000
Retired bonds	**34,000**	**Issued bonds**	**60,000**
		Bal., Dec. 31, 2002	90,000

The third step is to disclose the cash flow effect of the bond retirement in the financing section of the statement as follows (also see Exhibit 17.7 or 17.17):

Cash flows from financing activities	
Cash paid to retire bonds	$(18,000)

We have now reconstructed the Bonds Payable account by showing how the change in bonds payable from $64,000 to $90,000 is explained by the $34,000 retirement and the $60,000 issuance.

Analysis of Equity

The Genesis information reveals two transactions involving equity accounts. The first is the issuance of common stock for cash. The second is the declaration and payment of cash dividends. We analyze both transactions in this section.

Did You Know?
Free Cash Flow *Free cash flow* refers to operating cash flows available after allowing for investing and financing requirements. Free cash flow is often defined as operating cash flows minus capital expenditures and cash dividends. Growth and financial flexibility depend on adequate free cash flow.

Common Stock Issuance

The first step in analyzing common stock is to review comparative balance sheet information from Exhibit 17.10, which reveals an increase in common stock from $80,000 to $95,000. The second step is to explain this change. Item *d* of the Genesis additional information reports that it issued 3,000 shares of common stock at par for $5 per share. The reconstructed entry for analysis of item *d* follows:

Reconstruction	**Cash**	**15,000**		Assets	= Liabilities + Equity
	Common Stock		15,000	+15,000	+15,000

This entry reveals a $15,000 cash inflow from stock issuance and is reflected in (and explains) the Common Stock account as follows:

Common Stock		
	Bal., Dec. 31, 2001	80,000
	Issued stock	**15,000**
	Bal., Dec. 31, 2002	95,000

The third step is to disclose the cash flow effect from stock issuance in the financing section of the statement as follows (also see Exhibit 17.7 or 17.17):

Cash flows from financing activities	
Cash received from issuing stock	$15,000

The $15,000 stock issuance fully explains the change in the Common Stock account.

Cash Dividend Payment

The first step in analyzing the Retained Earnings account is to review comparative balance sheet information from Exhibit 17.10. This reveals an increase in retained earnings from $88,000 to $112,000. The second step is to explain this change. Item *f* of the additional information for Genesis reports that it paid dividends of $14,000. The reconstructed entry for analysis of item *f* follows:

Reconstruction	Retained Earnings	14,000		Assets	= Liabilities + Equity
	Cash		**14,000**	−14,000	−14,000

This entry reveals a $14,000 cash outflow for cash dividends. Retained earnings is also impacted by net income of $38,000. (Net income was analyzed under the operating section of the statement of cash flows.) Our reconstruction analysis is reflected in (and explains) the Retained Earnings account:

Retained Earnings			
		Bal., Dec. 31, 2001	88,000
Cash dividend	14,000	**Net income**	**38,000**
		Bal., Dec. 31, 2002	112,000

Point: Financing activities not affecting cash flow include *declaration* of a cash dividend, *declaration* of a stock dividend, payment of a stock dividend, and a stock split.

Global: There are no requirements to separate domestic and international cash flows, leading some users to ask "where in the world is cash flow?"

The third step is to disclose the cash flow effect from the cash dividend in the financing section of the statement as follows (also see Exhibit 17.7 or 17.17):

Cash flows from financing activities	
Cash paid for dividends	$(14,000)

The $14,000 dividend payment and the $38,000 of net income explain the change in Retained Earnings.

We now have identified and explained all of the Genesis cash inflows and cash outflows along with one noncash investing and financing transaction. Specifically, our analysis has reconciled changes in all noncash balance sheet accounts.

Proving Cash Balances

The fifth and final step in preparing the statement is to report the beginning and ending cash balances and prove that the *net change in cash* is explained by operating, investing, and financing net cash flows. This step is shown here for Genesis. This table shows that the

Net cash provided by operating activities	$20,000
Net cash provided by investing activities	2,000
Net cash used in financing activities	(17,000)
Net increase in cash	**$ 5,000**
Cash balance at beginning of 2002	12,000
Cash balance at end of 2002	$17,000

You Make the Call

Reporter   As a reporter covering a workers' strike, management grants you an interview and highlights recent losses and negative cash flows. Financial statements reveal a recent $600,000 net loss including a $930,000 extraordinary loss and a total net cash outflow of $550,000 (which includes net cash outflows of $850,000 for investing activities and $350,000 for financing activities). What is your assessment?

Answer—p. 724

$5,000 net increase in cash, from $12,000 at the beginning of the period to $17,000 at the end, is reconciled by net cash flows from operating ($20,000 inflow), investing ($2,000 inflow), and financing ($17,000 outflow) activities. This is formally reported at the bottom of the statement of cash flows as shown in both Exhibit 17.7 and 17.17.

Using the Information   Cash Flow Analysis

This section explains analysis of the statement of cash flows and describes the usefulness of the cash flow on total assets ratio.

Analyzing Cash Sources and Uses

A1   Analyze the statement of cash flows.

Most managers stress the importance of understanding and predicting cash flows for many business decisions. In addition, creditors evaluate a company's ability to generate cash before deciding whether to lend money. Investors also assess cash inflows and outflows before buying and selling stock. Information in the statement of cash flows helps address these and other questions such as (1) How much cash is generated from or used in operations? (2) What expenditures are made with cash from operations? (3) What is the source of cash for debt payments? (4) What is the source of cash for distributions to owners? (5) How is the increase in investing activities financed? (6) What is the source of cash for new plant assets? (7) Why is cash flow from operations different from income? (8) How is cash from financing used? Cash flows from investing and financing activities are important in these decisions, but we pay special attention to operating cash flows. A statement of cash flows helps by separating investing, financing, and operating activities.

To illustrate the importance of separately analyzing cash flows by activities, consider data from three different companies in Exhibit 17.19. These companies operate in the same industry and have been in business for several years.

($ in thousands)	Fisher	Sprint	Tektron
Cash provided (used) by operating activities	$90,000	$40,000	$(24,000)
Cash provided (used) by investing activities			
Proceeds from sale of plant assets			26,000
Purchase of plant assets	(48,000)	(25,000)	
Cash provided (used) by financing activities			
Proceeds from issuance of debt			13,000
Repayment of debt	(27,000)		
Net increase (decrease) in cash	$15,000	$15,000	$ 15,000

Exhibit 17.19

Cash Flows of Competitors

Each company generates an identical $15,000 net increase in cash flows, but their sources and uses of cash flows are very different. Fisher's operating activities provide net cash flows of $90,000, allowing it to purchase additional plant assets for $48,000 and repay $27,000 of its debt. Sprint's operating activities provide $40,000 of cash flows, limiting its purchase of plant assets to $25,000. Tektron's net cash increase is due to selling plant assets and incurring additional debt. Its operating activities yield a net cash outflow of $24,000. Overall, analysis of these cash flows reveals that Fisher is more capable of generating cash to meet its future obligations than is Sprint or Tektron. Also, Fisher's strong operating cash flows bode well for future performance, while Tektron's operating outlook is poor. This evaluation is, of course, tentative and must be supported by other information, including data from the balance sheet and income statement.

Cash Flow on Total Assets

Cash flow accounting recognizes cash inflows when received (not necessarily earned) and cash outflows when paid (not necessarily incurred). Cash flow information has limitations, but it can help us measure a company's ability to meet its obligations, pay dividends, expand operations, and obtain financing. Because of the importance of cash flows, users often consider a cash-based ratio called *cash flow on total assets*. It is similar to return on total assets except that its numerator is net cash flows from operating activities (not net income). The **cash flow on total assets** ratio is defined in Exhibit 17.20.

A2 Compute and apply the cash flow on total assets ratio.

$$\text{Cash flow on total assets} = \frac{\text{Operating cash flows}}{\text{Average total assets}}$$

Exhibit 17.20

Cash Flow on Total Assets

The cash flow on total assets ratio reflects actual cash flows and is not affected by the accounting constraints of income recognition and measurement. It can also help business decision makers estimate the amount and timing of cash flows when planning and analyzing operating activities.

To illustrate, consider the cash flow on total assets ratio for **Nike** at May 31, 2000. It is computed as follows ($ in millions): $759.9/[($5,856.9 + $5,247.7)/2] = 13.7\%$. Is a 13.7% cash flow on total assets ratio good or bad for Nike? To help answer this question, we can compare this ratio with the ratios of prior years, its competitors, and the market. For example, we show Nike's cash flow on total assets ratio for its most recent five years in the second column of Exhibit 17.21. Its return on total assets is provided for comparison purposes.

Exhibit 17.21

Nike's Cash Flow on
Total Assets

Year	Cash Flow on Total Assets	Return on Total Assets
2000	13.7%	10.4%
1999	18.1	8.5
1998	9.6	7.4
1997	6.9	17.1
1996	9.6	15.6

Nike's cash flow on total assets has increased in the past two years. Moreover, the ratio exceeds its return on total assets for the period 1998–2000, leading some analysts to infer that Nike's *earnings quality* is high for this period. These analysts presume higher earnings quality when more earnings are realized in the form of cash.

In sum, the statement of cash flows is an important bridge between the income statement and balance sheet and is valuable in financial analysis. The cash flow on total assets ratio is a useful part of this analysis and can be an indicator of earnings quality.

Demonstration Problem

Umlauf's comparative balance sheets, income statement, and additional information follow.

UMLAUF COMPANY
Income Statement
For Year Ended December 31, 2002

Sales		$446,100
Cost of goods sold	$222,300	
Other operating expenses	120,300	
Depreciation expense	25,500	(368,100)
Other gains (losses)		
Loss on sale of equipment		(3,300)
Income before taxes		$ 74,700
Income taxes expense*		(13,725)
Income from continuing oper.		$ 60,975
Extraordinary item		
Loss on retirement of bonds*		(825)
Net income		$ 60,150

UMLAUF COMPANY
Balance Sheet
December 31, 2002 and 2001

	2002	2001
Assets		
Cash.	$ 43,050	$ 23,925
Accounts receivable.	34,125	39,825
Merchandise inventory	156,000	146,475
Prepaid expenses	3,600	1,650
Equipment.	135,825	146,700
Accum. depreciation—Equip.	(61,950)	(47,550)
Total assets.	$310,650	$311,025
Liabilities and Equity		
Accounts payable	$ 28,800	$ 33,750
Income taxes payable	5,100	4,425
Dividends payable	0	4,500
Bonds payable.	0	37,500
Common stock, $10 par.	168,750	168,750
Retained earnings	108,000	62,100
Total liabilities and equity	$310,650	$311,025

* Income Taxes Expense is restated to include the tax effects from the extraordinary loss. This means that the $825 extraordinary loss is at its gross amount, not net of tax.

Additional Information

a. All sales are made on credit.

b. All merchandise inventory purchases are on credit.

c. Accounts Payable balances result from merchandise inventory purchases.

d. Prepaid expenses relate to "other operating expenses."

e. Equipment costing $21,375 with accumulated depreciation of $11,100 is sold for cash.

f. Equipment purchases are for cash.

g. Accumulated Depreciation account is affected by depreciation expense and the sale of equipment.

h. The balance of Retained Earnings is affected by dividend declarations and net income.

Required

1. Prepare a statement of cash flows using the direct method for year 2002.

2. Prepare a statement of cash flows using the indirect method for year 2002.

Planning the Solution

- Prepare two blank statements of cash flows with sections for operating, investing, and financing activities using the (1) direct method format and (2) indirect method format.
- Compute cash received from customers, cash paid for merchandise, cash paid for other operating expenses, and cash paid for taxes as illustrated in the chapter.
- Compute the cash paid for equipment and the cash received from the sale of equipment using the additional information provided along with the amount for depreciation expense and the change in the balances of equipment and accumulated depreciation. Use T-accounts to help chart the effects of the sale and purchase of equipment on the balances of the Equipment account and the Accumulated Depreciation account.
- Calculate the effect of net income on the change in the Retained Earnings account balance. Assign the difference between the change in retained earnings and the amount of net income to dividends declared. Adjust the dividends declared amount for the change in the Dividends Payable balance.
- Enter the cash effects of reconstruction entries to the appropriate section(s) of the statement.
- Total each section of the statement, determine the total net change in cash, and add it to the beginning balance to get the ending balance of cash.

Solution to Demonstration Problem

Supporting computations for cash receipts and cash payments:

(1) Sales		$446,100
	Add decrease in accounts receivable	5,700
	Cash received from customers	**$451,800**
(2) Cost of goods sold		$222,300
	Plus increase in merchandise inventory	9,525
	Purchases	$231,825
	Plus decrease in accounts payable	4,950
	Cash paid for merchandise	**$236,775**
(3) Other operating expenses		$120,300
	Plus increase in prepaid expenses	1,950
	Cash paid for other operating expenses	**$122,250**
(4) Income taxes expense		$ 13,725
	Less increase in income taxes payable	(675)
	Cash paid for income taxes	**$ 13,050**
(5) Cost of equipment sold		$ 21,375
	Accumulated depreciation of equipment sold	(11,100)
	Book value of equipment sold	$ 10,275
	Loss on sale of equipment	(3,300)
	Cash received from sale of equipment	**$ 6,975**
	Cost of equipment sold	$ 21,375
	Less decrease in the equipment account balance	(10,875)
	Cash paid for new equipment	**$ 10,500**

Supporting T-account analysis for part (5) above:

Equipment			
Bal., Dec. 31, 2001	146,700		
Cash purchase	10,500	Sale	21,375
Bal., Dec. 31, 2002	135,825		

Accumulated Depreciation—Equipment			
		Bal., Dec. 31, 2001	47,550
Sale	11,100	Depr. expense	25,500
		Bal., Dec. 31, 2002	61,950

(6) Loss on retirement of bonds	$	825
Carrying value of bonds retired		37,500
Cash paid to retire bonds		**$ 38,325**
(7) Net income		$ 60,150
Less increase in retained earnings		45,900
Dividends declared		$ 14,250
Plus decrease in dividends payable		4,500
Cash paid for dividends		**$ 18,750**

UMLAUF COMPANY
Statement of Cash Flows (Direct Method)
For Year Ended December 31, 2002

Cash flows from operating activities		
Cash received from customers	**$451,800**	
Cash paid for merchandise	**(236,775)**	
Cash paid for other operating expenses	**(122,250)**	
Cash paid for income taxes	**(13,050)**	
Net cash provided by operating activities		$79,725
Cash flows from investing activities		
Cash received from sale of equipment	6,975	
Cash paid for equipment	(10,500)	
Net cash used in investing activities		(3,525)
Cash flows from financing activities		
Cash paid to retire bonds payable	(38,325)	
Cash paid for dividends	(18,750)	
Net cash used in financing activities		(57,075)
Net increase in cash		$19,125
Cash balance at beginning of year		23,925
Cash balance at end of year		$43,050

UMLAUF COMPANY
Statement of Cash Flows (Indirect Method)
For Year Ended December 31, 2002

Cash flows from operating activities	
Cash flows from operating activities:	
Net income	**$60,150**
Adjustments to reconcile net income to net cash provided by operating activities	
Decrease in accounts receivable	**5,700**

[continued on next page]

[continued from previous page]

UMLAUF COMPANY
Statement of Cash Flows (Indirect Method)
For Year Ended December 31, 2002

Increase in merchandise inventory	(9,525)	
Increase in prepaid expenses	(1,950)	
Decrease in accounts payable	(4,950)	
Increase in income taxes payable	675	
Depreciation expense	25,500	
Loss on sale of plant assets	3,300	
Loss on retirement of bonds	825	
Net cash provided by operating activities		$79,725
Cash flows from investing activities		
Cash received from sale of equipment	6,975	
Cash paid for equipment	(10,500)	
Net cash used in investing activities		(3,525)
Cash flows from financing activities		
Cash paid to retire bonds payable	(38,325)	
Cash paid for dividends	(18,750)	
Net cash used in financing activities		(57,075)
Net increase in cash		$19,125
Cash balance at beginning of year		23,925
Cash balance at end of year		$43,050

APPENDIX

Spreadsheet Preparation of the Statement of Cash Flows

17A

This appendix explains how to use a spreadsheet to prepare the statement of cash flows under the indirect method.

Preparing the Indirect Method Spreadsheet

Analyzing noncash accounts can be challenging when a company has a large number of accounts and many operating, investing, and financing transactions. A *spreadsheet,* also called *work sheet* or *working paper,* can help us organize the information needed to prepare a statement of cash flows. A spreadsheet also makes it easier to check the accuracy of our work. To illustrate, we return to the comparative balance sheets and income statement shown in Exhibit 17.10. Information needed for the spreadsheet in preparing the statement of cash flows along with identifying letters follow:

P5 Illustrate spreadsheet use in preparing a statement of cash flows.

a. Net income is $38,000.

b. Accounts receivable increase by $20,000.

c. Merchandise inventory increases by $14,000.

d. Prepaid expenses increase by $2,000.

e. Accounts payable decrease by $5,000.

f. Interest payable decreases by $1,000.

g. Income taxes payable increase by $10,000.

h. Depreciation expense is $24,000.

i. Plant assets costing $30,000 with accumulated depreciation of $12,000 are sold for $12,000 cash. This yields a loss on sale of assets of $6,000.

j. Bonds with a book value of $34,000 are retired with a cash payment of $18,000. Gain on retirement of bonds is $16,000.

k. Plant assets costing $70,000 are purchased with a cash payment of $10,000 and an issuance of bonds payable for $60,000.

l. Issued 3,000 shares of common stock for $15,000 cash.

m. Paid cash dividends of $14,000.

Exhibit 17A.1 shows the indirect method spreadsheet for Genesis. We enter both beginning and ending balance sheet amounts on the spreadsheet. We also enter information in the Analysis of Changes columns (keyed to the additional information items *a* through *m*) to explain changes in the accounts and determine the cash flows for operating, investing, and financing activities. Information about noncash investing and financing activities is reported near the bottom. The spreadsheet for the statement of cash flows begins with net income and then adjusts it as necessary to compute the amount of cash flows from operating activities.

Exhibit 17.A1

Spreadsheet for Preparing Statement of Cash Flows—Indirect Method

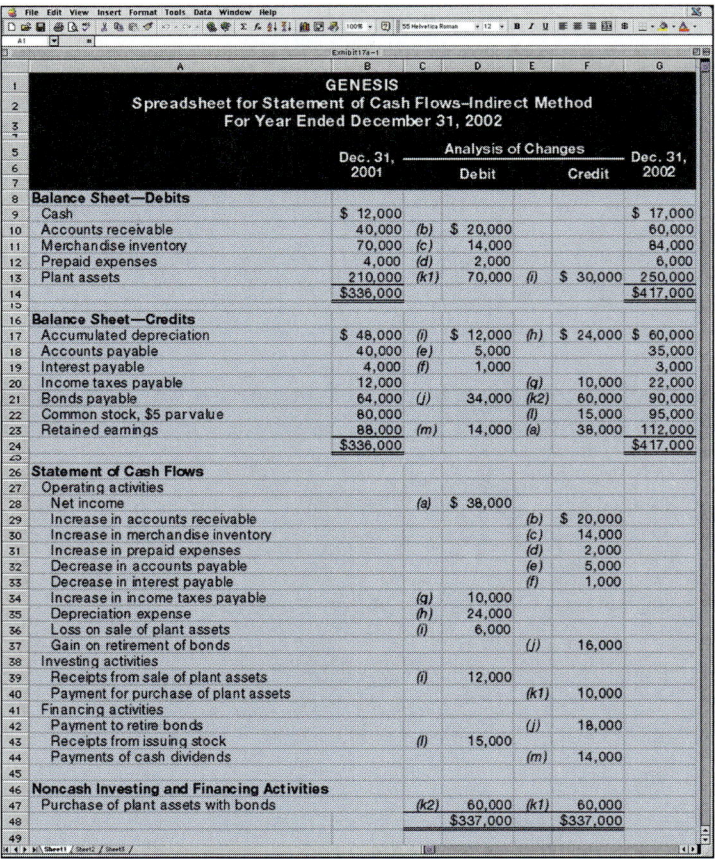

Entering the Analysis of Changes on the Spreadsheet

The following sequence of procedures is used to complete the spreadsheet after the balance sheet accounts are entered:

① Enter net income as the first item for computing operating cash inflow (debit) and as a credit to Retained Earnings.

② In the Statement of Cash Flows section, adjustments to net income are entered as debits if they increase cash flows and as credits if they decrease cash flows. Applying this same rule, adjust net income for the change in each noncash current asset and current liability account related to operating activities. For each adjustment to net income, the offsetting debit or credit must help reconcile the beginning and ending balances of a current asset or current liability account.

③ Enter adjustments to net income for income statement items not providing or using cash in the period. For each adjustment, the offsetting debit or credit must help reconcile a noncash balance sheet account.

④ Adjust net income to eliminate any gains or losses from investing and financing activities. Because the cash from a gain must be excluded from operating activities, the gain is entered as a credit in the operating activities section. Losses are entered as debits. For each adjustment, the related debit and/or credit must help reconcile balance sheet accounts and involve reconstructed entries to show the cash flow from investing or financing activities.

⑤ After reviewing any unreconciled balance sheet accounts and related information, enter the remaining reconciling entries for investing and financing activities. Examples are purchases of plant assets, issuances of long-term debt, sales of stock, and dividend payments. Some of these may require entries in the noncash investing and financing activities section of the spreadsheet (reconciled).

⑥ Check accuracy by totaling the Analysis of Changes columns and by determining that the change in each balance sheet account has been explained (reconciled).

Point: Analysis of the changes on the spreadsheet can be summarized as follows:

1. Cash flows from operating activities generally affect net income, current assets, and current liabilities.
2. Cash flows from investing activities generally affect noncurrent asset accounts.
3. Cash flows from financing activities generally affect noncurrent liability and equity accounts.

We illustrate these steps in Exhibit 17A.1 for Genesis:

Step	Entries
①.	(a)
②.	(b) through (g)
③.	(h)
④.	(i) through (j)
⑤.	(k) through (m)

Because adjustments *i, j,* and *k* are more challenging, we show them in the following debit and credit format. These entries are for purposes of our understanding—they are *not* the entries actually made in the journals. Changes in the Cash account are identified as sources or uses of cash.

i.	Loss from sale of plant assets	6,000	
	Accumulated depreciation	12,000	
	Receipt from sale of plant assets (source of cash)	12,000	
	Plant assets		30,000
	To describe sale of plant assets.		
j.	Bonds payable	34,000	
	Payments to retire bonds (use of cash)		18,000
	Gain on retirement of bonds		16,000
	To describe retirement of bonds.		
k1.	Plant assets	70,000	
	Payment to purchase plant assets (use of cash)		10,000
	Purchase of plant assets financed by bonds		60,000
	To describe purchase of plant assets.		
k2.	Purchase of plant assets financed by bonds	60,000	
	Bonds payable		60,000
	To issue bonds for purchase of assets.		

Summary

C1 **Explain the purpose and importance of cash flow information.** The main purpose of the statement of cash flows is to report the major cash receipts and cash payments for a period. This includes identifying cash flows as relating to either operating, investing, or financing activities. Most business decisions involve evaluating activities that provide or use cash.

C2 **Distinguish among operating, investing, and financing activities.** Operating activities include transactions and events that determine net income. Investing activities include transactions and events that mainly affect long-term assets. Financing activities include transactions and events that mainly affect long-term liabilities and equity.

C3 **Identify and disclose noncash investing and financing activities.** Noncash investing and financing activities must be disclosed in either a note or in a separate schedule attached to the statement of cash flows. Examples are the retirement of debt by issuing equity and the exchange of a note payable for plant assets.

C4 **Describe the format of the statement of cash flows.** The statement of cash flows separates cash receipts and payments into operating, investing, or financing activities.

A1 **Analyze the statement of cash flows.** To understand and predict cash flows, users stress identification of the sources and uses of cash flows by operating, investing, and financing activities. Emphasis is on operating cash flows since they derive from continuing operations.

A2 **Compute and apply the cash flow on total assets ratio.** The cash flow on total assets ratio is defined as operating cash flows divided by average total assets. Analysis of current and past cash flow on total assets ratios reflects a company's ability to yield regular and positive cash flows. It is also viewed as a measure of earnings quality.

P1 **Prepare a statement of cash flows.** Preparation of a statement of cash flows involves five steps: (1) Compute the net increase or decrease in cash; (2) compute net cash provided (used) by operating activities (*using either the direct or indirect method*); (3) compute net cash provided (used) by investing activities; (4) compute net cash provided (used) by financing activities; and (5) report the beginning and ending cash balance and prove that it is explained by net cash flows. Noncash investing and financing activities are disclosed in a note or a separate schedule.

P2 **Compute cash flows from operating activities using the direct method.** The direct method for reporting net cash provided (used) by operating activities lists major operating cash inflows less cash outflows to yield net cash inflow or outflow from operations. The FASB recommends the direct method.

P3 **Compute cash flows from operating activities using the indirect method.** The indirect method for reporting net cash provided (used) by operating activities starts with net income and then adjusts it for three items: (1) changes in noncash current assets and current liabilities related to operating activities, (2) revenues and expenses not providing (using) cash, and (3) gains and losses from investing and financing activities.

P4 **Determine cash flows from both investing and financing activities.** Cash flows from both investing and financing activities are determined by identifying the cash flow effects of transactions and events affecting each balance sheet account related to these activities. All cash flows from these activities are identified when we can explain changes in these accounts from the beginning to the end of the period.

P5 **Illustrate spreadsheet use in preparing a statement of cash flows.** A spreadsheet is a useful tool in preparing a statement of cash flows. Six key steps (described in the appendix) are applied when using the spreadsheet to prepare a statement of cash flows.

Guidance Answers to **You Make the Call**

Entrepreneur   Several factors might explain an increase in net cash flows when a net loss is reported, including (1) early recognition of expenses relative to revenues generated (such as research and development), (2) advances on long-term sales contracts not yet recognized in income, (3) issuances of debt or equity to finance expansion, (4) selling of assets, (5) delay of cash payments, and (6) prepayment on sales. Analysis needs to focus on the components of both the net loss and the net cash flows and their implications for future performance.

Reporter   Your initial action is to verify management's claim about poor performance. A $600,000 loss with a $550,000 decrease in net cash flows seemingly supports its claim. However, closer scrutiny reveals a different picture. Cash flow from operating activities is $650,000, computed as [?] − $850,000 − $350,000 = ($550,000). You also note net income *before* the extraordinary loss is $330,000, computed as [?] − $930,000 = ($600,000). This is powerful information that reveals a more positive picture of this company's performance.

Guidance Answers to **Quick Checks**

1. No to both. The statement of cash flows reports changes in the sum of cash plus cash equivalents. It does not report transfers between cash and cash equivalents.

2. The three categories of cash inflows and outflows are operating activities, investing activities, and financing activities.

3. a. Investing   c. Financing   e. Operating
   b. Operating   d. Operating   f. Financing

4. The direct method is probably most informative because it separately lists each major item of operating cash receipts and each major item of operating cash payments. However, the indirect method is most often reported.

5. $590,000 + ($120,000 − $90,000) = $620,000

6. $168,000 − ($32,000 − $28,000) − $2,400 = $161,600

7. $112,000 + ($4,200 − $1,200) − $5,600 = $109,400

8. $74,900 + $4,600 − $11,700 − $1,000 + $3,400 = $70,200

9. Expenses such as depreciation and amortization do not require current cash outflows. Therefore, adding these expenses back to net income eliminates noncash items from the net income number, converting it to a cash basis.

10. A gain on the sale of plant assets is subtracted from net income because a sale of plant assets is not an operating activity; it is an investing activity. Also, such a gain yields no cash effects (instead, it is the cash received from its sale).

11. $80,000 − $30,000 − $10,000 = $40,000 cash receipt. The $40,000 cash receipt is reported as an investing activity.

Glossary

Cash flow on total assets ratio of operating cash flows to average total assets; not affected by income recognition and measurement; reflects earnings quality. (p. 717).

Direct method presentation of net cash from operating activities that lists major operating cash receipts less major operating cash payments. (p. 699).

Financing activities transactions with owners and creditors that include obtaining cash from issuing debt, repaying amounts borrowed, and obtaining cash from or distributing cash to owners. (p. 694).

Indirect method presentation that reports net income and then adjusts it by adding and subtracting items to yield net cash from operating activities. (p. 699).

Investing activities transactions that involve purchasing and selling of long-term assets, including making and collecting notes receivable and investments in other than cash equivalents. (p. 693).

Operating activities activities that involve the production or purchase of merchandise and the sale of goods or services to customers, including expenditures related to administering the business. (p. 693).

Statement of cash flows financial statement that reports cash inflows and cash outflows for an accounting period and classifies them as operating, investing, or financing activities. (p. 692).

[The superscript ᴬ denotes assignments based on Appendix 17A.]

Questions

1. When a statement of cash flows is prepared by the direct method, what are some cash flows from operating activities?

2. What is the direct method to report cash flows from operating activities?

3. What is the indirect method to report cash flows from operating activities?

4. What are some investing activities reported on the statement of cash flows?

5. What are some financing activities reported on the statement of cash flows?

6. Where on the statement of cash flows is the payment of cash dividends reported?

7. Assume that a company purchases land for $100,000, paying $20,000 cash and borrowing the remainder with a long-term note payable. How should this transaction be reported on a statement of cash flows?

8. On June 3, a company borrows $50,000 cash by giving its bank a 160-day, interest-bearing note. On the statement of cash flows, where should this be reported?

9. If a company reports positive net income for the year, is it possible for the company to show a net cash outflow from operating activities? Explain.

10. Is depreciation a source of cash flow?

11. Refer to **Nike**'s statement of cash flows in  Appendix A. (a) Which method is used to compute net cash provided by operating activities? (b) While its balance sheet shows an increase in receivables from fiscal years 1999 to 2000, why is this increase in receivables subtracted when computing net cash provided by operating activities for fiscal year 2000?

12. Refer to **Reebok**'s statement of cash flows in Appendix A. What are its cash flows from financing activities for 1999?

13. Refer to **Gap**'s statement of cash flows in Appendix A. What investing activities result in cash outflows for the year ended January 29, 2000?

Describe the contents and presentation of a statement of cash flows, including its three separate sections.

QUICK STUDY

QS 17-1
Statement of cash flows **C1**

List at least three transactions classified as investing activities in a statement of cash flows.

QS 17-2
Transaction classification **C2**

List at least three transactions classified as financing activities in a statement of cash flows.

QS 17-3
Transaction classification **C2**

QS 17-4

Transaction classification by activity

Classify the following cash flows as operating, investing, or financing activities:

1. Cash from sale of long-term investments.

2. Received cash payments from customers.

3. Paid wages and salaries.

4. Purchased inventories for cash.

5. Paid cash dividends.

6. Issued common stock for cash.

7. Received interest on a note.

8. Paid interest on outstanding bonds.

9. Cash from sale of land at a loss.

10. Paid property taxes on building.

QS 17-5

Noncash transaction identification

List at least three transactions classified as significant noncash financing and investing activities in the statement of cash flows.

QS 17-6

Computing cash received from customers

Use the following balance sheet and income statement to answer QS 17-6 through QS 17-11.

ORWELL, INC.
Income Statement
For Year Ended December 31, 2002

Sales		$488,000
Cost of goods sold		(314,000)
Gross profit		$174,000
Operating expenses		
Depreciation expense	$37,600	
Other expenses	89,100	(126,700)
Income before taxes		$ 47,300
Income taxes		(17,300)
Net income		$ 30,000

ORWELL, INC.
Comparative Balance Sheet
December 31, 2002

	2002	2001
Assets		
Cash	$ 94,800	$ 24,000
Accounts receivable (net)	41,000	51,000
Inventory	85,800	95,800
Prepaid expenses	5,400	4,200
Furniture	109,000	119,000
Accum. depreciation—Furniture	(17,000)	(9,000)
Total assets	$319,000	$285,000
Liabilities and Equity		
Accounts payable	$ 15,000	$ 21,000
Wages payable	9,000	5,000
Income taxes payable	1,400	2,600
Notes payable (long-term)	29,000	69,000
Common stock, $5 par value	229,000	179,000
Retained earnings	35,600	8,400
Total liabilities and equity	$319,000	$285,000

How much cash is received from sales to customers for year 2002?

QS 17-7

Computing cash paid for inventory

Refer to the data in QS 17-6. How much cash is paid to acquire merchandise inventory during year 2002?

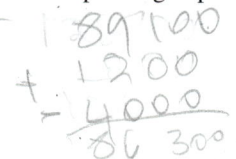

QS 17-8

Computing cash paid for expenses   P2

Refer to the data in QS 17-6. How much cash is paid for operating expenses during year 2002?

Refer to the data in QS 17-6. Furniture costing $55,000 is sold at its book value in 2002. Acquisitions of furniture total $45,000 cash, on which no depreciation is necessary since it is acquired at year-end. What is the cash inflow related to the sale of furniture?

QS 17-9
Computing cash from asset sales

Refer to the data in QS 17-6. All common stock is issued for cash. What amount of cash dividends is paid during 2002?

QS 17-10
Computing cash paid for dividends

Refer to the data in QS 17-6. Using the indirect method, prepare the cash provided (used) from operating activities section only of the statement of cash flows.

QS 17-11
Computing cash from operations (indirect)

Refer to the data in QS 17-6. Using the direct method, prepare the cash provided (used) from operating activities section only of the statement of cash flows.

QS 17-12
Computing cash from operations (direct)

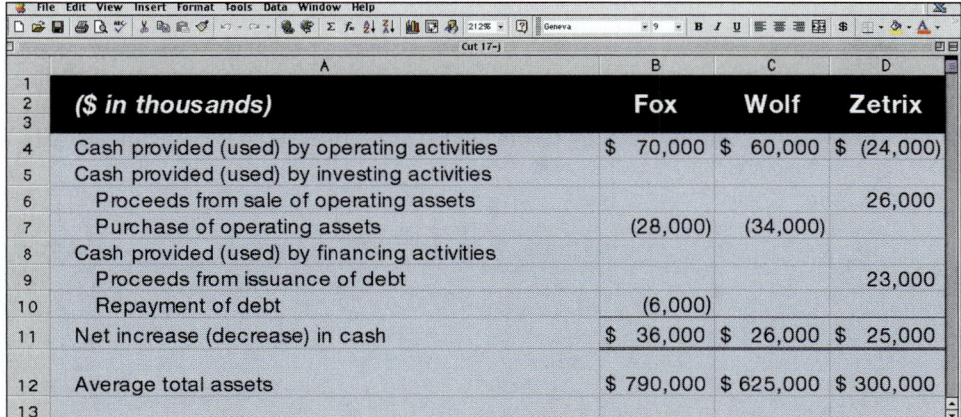

QS 17-13
Analyses of sources and uses of cash

($ in thousands)	Fox	Wolf	Zetrix
Cash provided (used) by operating activities	$ 70,000	$ 60,000	$ (24,000)
Cash provided (used) by investing activities			
Proceeds from sale of operating assets			26,000
Purchase of operating assets	(28,000)	(34,000)	
Cash provided (used) by financing activities			
Proceeds from issuance of debt			23,000
Repayment of debt	(6,000)		
Net increase (decrease) in cash	$ 36,000	$ 26,000	$ 25,000
Average total assets	$ 790,000	$ 625,000	$ 300,000

1. Which of the three competitors is in the strongest position as shown by their cash flow statements?
2. Compare the strength of Fox's cash flow on total assets ratio to that of Wolf.

When a spreadsheet for a statement of cash flows is prepared, all changes in noncash balance sheet accounts are fully explained on the spreadsheet. Explain how we use noncash balance sheet accounts to fully account for cash flows on a spreadsheet.

QS 17-14[A]
Noncash accounts on a spreadsheet

For each of the following three separate cases, use the information provided about the calendar year 2002 operations of Meadowbrook Company to compute the required cash flow information:

EXERCISES

Exercise 17-1
Computation of cash flows

Case A: Compute cash paid for salaries:

Salaries expense	$ 52,000
Salaries payable, January 1	3,850
Salaries payable, December 31	3,950

Case B: Compute cash received from customers:

Sales	$515,000
Accounts receivable, January 1	27,200
Accounts receivable, December 31	33,600

Case C: Compute cash paid for insurance:

Insurance expense	$ 65,400
Prepaid insurance, January 1	12,400
Prepaid insurance, December 31	16,100

Exercise 17-2

Computation of cash flows

For each of the following three separate cases, use the information provided about the calendar year 2002 operations of Riley Company to compute the required cash flow information:

Case A: Compute cash received as interest:	
Interest revenue	$132,000
Interest receivable, January 1	4,000
Interest receivable, December 31	4,600
Case B: Compute cash paid for rent:	
Rent expense	$139,800
Rent payable, January 1	7,800
Rent payable, December 31	6,200
Case C: Compute cash paid for merchandise:	
Cost of goods sold	$525,000
Merchandise inventory, January 1	158,600
Accounts payable, January 1	66,700
Merchandise inventory, December 31	130,400
Accounts payable, December 31	82,000

Exercise 17-3

Transaction classification on statement of cash flows (direct)

The following transactions and events occurred during the year. Assuming that this company uses the direct method to report cash provided by operating activities, indicate the accounting classification for each item on the statement of cash flows by placing an *x* in the appropriate column.

	Operating Activities	Investing Activities	Financing Activities	Noncash Investing and Financing Activities	Not Reported on Statement or in Note
a. Long-term bonds payable retired by issuing common stock.	___	___	___	___	___
b. Depreciation expense recorded.	___	___	___	___	___
c. Cash dividend declared in a prior period is paid this period.	___	___	___	___	___
d. Inventory sold for cash.	___	___	___	___	___
e. Borrowed cash from bank by signing a 9-month note payable.	___	___	___	___	___
f. Paid cash to purchase patent.	___	___	___	___	___
g. 6-month note receivable accepted in exchange for plant assets.	___	___	___	___	___

The heading for this table reads: Statement of Cash Flows (spanning Operating Activities, Investing Activities, Financing Activities).

Exercise 17-4

Transaction classification on statement of cash flows (indirect)

The following transactions and events occurred during the year. Assuming that this company uses the indirect method to report cash provided by operating activities, indicate the accounting classification for each item on its statement of cash flows by placing an *x* in the appropriate column.

	Operating Activities	Investing Activities	Financing Activities	Noncash Investing and Financing Activities	Not Reported on Statement or in Note
a. Paid cash to purchase inventory.	___	___	___	___	___
b. Purchased land by issuing common stock.	___	___	___	___	___
c. Accounts receivable decreased in the year. . . .	___	___	___	___	___
d. Sold equipment at a loss.	___	___	___	___	___
e. Recorded depreciation expense.	___	___	___	___	___
f. Income taxes payable increased in the year. . .	___	___	___	___	___
g. Declared and paid a cash dividend.	___	___	___	___	___

The heading for this table reads: Statement of Cash Flows (spanning Operating Activities, Investing Activities, Financing Activities).

Use the following information about the cash flows of Sanuk Company to prepare a statement of cash flows (direct method) for the year ended December 31, 2002. Use a note disclosure for any noncash investing and financing activities.

Cash and cash equivalents balance, December 31, 2001	$ 40,000
Cash and cash equivalents balance, December 31, 2002	148,000
Cash received as interest	3,500
Cash paid for salaries	76,500
Bonds payable retired by issuing common stock (no gain or loss on retirement)	185,500
Cash paid to retire long-term notes payable	100,000
Cash received from sale of equipment	60,250
Cash received in exchange for six-month note payable	35,000
Land purchased by issuing long-term note payable	105,250
Cash paid for store equipment	24,750
Cash dividends paid	10,000
Cash paid for other expenses	20,000
Cash received from customers	495,000
Cash paid for merchandise	254,500

Exercise 17-5
Preparation of statement of cash flows (direct) and supporting note

Use the following income statement and information about changes in noncash current assets and current liabilities to prepare the cash flows from operating activities section only of the statement of cash flows using the direct method:

Exercise 17-6
Cash flows from operating activities (direct)

P2

BRADHAM COMPANY Income Statement For Year Ended December 31, 2002		
Sales		$1,828,000
Cost of goods sold		(991,000)
Gross profit		$ 837,000
Operating expenses		
Salaries expense	$245,535	
Depreciation expense	44,200	
Rent expense	49,600	
Amortization expenses—Patents	4,200	
Utilities expense	18,125	(361,660)
Gain on sale of equipment		6,200
Net income		$ 481,540

Changes in current asset and current liability accounts for the year that relate to operations follow:

Accounts receivable	$30,500 increase	Accounts payable	$12,500 decrease
Merchandise inventory	25,000 increase	Salaries payable	3,500 decrease

Refer to the information about Bradham Company in Exercise 17-6. Use the indirect method to prepare the cash provided (used) by operating activities section only of the statement of cash flows.

Exercise 17-7
Cash flows from operating activities (indirect)

P3

Exercise 17-8
Cash flows from operating activities (indirect)

Mandela Company's calendar year 2002 income statement shows the following: Net Income, $374,000; Depreciation Expense, $44,000; Amortization Expense, $7,200; Gain on Sale of Plant Assets, $6,000. An examination of the company's current assets and current liabilities reveals the following changes (all from operating activities): Accounts Receivable decrease, $17,100; Merchandise Inventory decrease, $42,000; Prepaid Expenses increase, $4,700; Accounts Payable decrease, $8,200; Other Payables increase, $1,200. Use the indirect method to compute cash flow from operating activities.

Exercise 17-9
Preparation of statement of cash flows (direct)

Part 1

Use the financial statements and additional information shown to prepare a statement of cash flows for the year ended June 30, 2002, using the direct method.

PASSAT INC.
Income Statement
For Year Ended June 30, 2002

Sales		$678,000
Cost of goods sold		(411,000)
Gross profit		$267,000
Operating expenses		
Depreciation expense	$58,600	
Other expenses	67,000	
Total operating expenses		(125,600)
Other gains (losses)		
Gain on sale of equipment		2,000
Income before taxes		$143,400
Income taxes		(43,890)
Net income		$ 99,510

PASSAT INC.
Comparative Balance Sheet
June 30, 2002

	2002	2001
Assets		
Cash	$ 86,500	$ 44,000
Accounts receivable (net)	65,000	51,000
Inventory	63,800	86,500
Prepaid expenses	4,400	5,400
Equipment	125,000	115,000
Accum. depreciation—Equip.	(27,000)	(9,000)
Total assets	$317,700	$292,900
Liabilities and Equity		
Accounts payable	$ 25,000	$ 30,000
Wages payable	6,000	15,000
Income taxes payable	3,400	3,800
Notes payable (long term)	30,000	60,000
Common stock, $5 par value	220,000	160,000
Retained earnings	33,300	24,100
Total liabilities and equity	$317,700	$292,900

Additional Information

a. A $30,000 note payable is retired at its carrying (book) value.
b. The only changes affecting retained earnings are net income and cash dividends paid.
c. New equipment is acquired for $58,600 cash.
d. Received cash for the sale of equipment that cost $48,600, yielding a $2,000 gain.
e. Prepaid Expenses and Wages Payable relate to Other Expenses on the income statement.
f. All sales and purchases of merchandise inventory are on credit.

Part 2

Compute the cash flow on total assets ratio for Passat, Inc., for its fiscal year 2002.

Exercise 17-10
Preparation of statement of cash flows (direct) from journal information

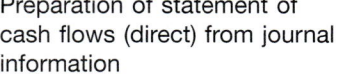

The following summarized journal entries reflect the total debits and total credits to the Cash account of Triangle Corporation for calendar year 2002.

Part 1

Use this information to prepare a statement of cash flows for year 2002. The cash provided (used) by operating activities should be reported using the direct method. In the statement of cash flows, identify the entry supporting each cash flow item. The beginning balance of cash is $135,200.

a.	Cash	1,540,000	
	Common Stock, $10 Par Value		410,000
	Contributed Capital in Excess of Par, Common Stock		1,130,000
	Issued common stock for cash.		
b.	Cash	2,600,000	
	Notes Payable		2,600,000
	Borrowed cash with a note payable.		
c.	Merchandise Inventory	490,000	
	Cash		490,000
	Purchased merchandise for cash.		
d.	Accounts Payable	1,100,000	
	Cash		1,100,000
	Paid for credit purchases of merchandise.		
e.	Wages Expense	550,000	
	Cash		550,000
	Paid wages to employees.		
f.	Rent Expense	320,000	
	Cash		320,000
	Paid rent for buildings.		
g.	Cash	4,000,000	
	Sales		4,000,000
	Made cash sales to customers.		
h.	Cash	2,000,000	
	Accounts Receivable		2,000,000
	Collected accounts from credit customers.		
i.	Machinery	2,236,000	
	Cash		2,236,000
	Purchased machinery for cash.		
j.	Investments—Available-for-Sale	2,260,000	
	Cash		2,260,000
	Purchased investments for cash.		
k.	Interest Expense	218,000	
	Notes Payable	386,000	
	Cash		604,000
	Paid notes and accrued interest.		
l.	Cash	208,400	
	Dividends Revenue		208,400
	Collected dividends from investments.		
m.	Cash	220,000	
	Loss on Sale of Investments	30,000	
	Investments—Available-for-Sale		250,000
	Sold investments for cash.		
n.	Cash	710,000	
	Accumulated Depreciation—Machinery	410,000	
	Machinery		950,000
	Gain on Sale of Machinery		170,000
	Sold machinery for cash.		

[continued on next page]

[continued from previous page]

o.	Common Dividend Payable	500,000	
	Cash		500,000
	Paid cash dividends to stockholders.		
p.	Income Taxes Payable	450,000	
	Cash		450,000
	Paid income taxes owed for the year.		
q.	Treasury Stock, Common	218,000	
	Cash		218,000
	Acquired treasury stock for cash.		

Part 2

Refer to the statement of cash flows you prepared for part (1) to answer the following questions:

1. Which section—operating, investing, or financing—shows the largest cash (a) inflow and (b) outflow?

2. What is the largest individual item among the investing cash outflows?

3. Are the cash proceeds larger from issuing notes or issuing stock?

4. Does the company have a net cash inflow or outflow from borrowing activities?

PROBLEM SET A

Problem 17-1A
Statement of cash flows
(direct method)

Bushtex Company, a merchandiser, recently completed its year 2002 operations. For the year, (1) all sales are credit sales, (2) all credits to accounts receivable reflect cash receipts from customers, (3) purchases of inventory are on credit, (4) all debits to accounts payable reflect cash payments for inventory, and (5) other expenses are paid in advance and are initially debited to Prepaid Expenses. Bushtex's balance sheet and income statement follow:

BUSHTEX COMPANY
Comparative Balance Sheet
December 31, 2002

	2002	2001
Assets		
Cash	$ 49,800	$ 73,500
Accounts receivable	65,810	50,625
Merchandise inventory	275,656	251,800
Prepaid expenses	1,250	1,875
Equipment	157,500	108,000
Accum. depreciation—Equip.	(36,625)	(46,000)
Total assets	$513,391	$439,800
Liabilities and Equity		
Accounts payable	$ 53,141	$114,675
Short-term notes payable	10,000	6,000
Long-term notes payable	65,000	48,750
Common stock, $5 par value	162,750	150,250
Contributed capital in excess		
of par, common stock	37,500	0
Retained earnings	185,000	120,125
Total liabilities and equity	$513,391	$439,800

BUSHTEX COMPANY
Income Statement
For Year Ended December 31, 2002

Sales		$582,500
Cost of goods sold		(285,000)
Gross profit		297,500
Operating expenses		
Depreciation expense	$ 20,750	
Other expenses	132,400	(153,150)
Other gains (losses)		
Loss on sale of equipment		(5,125)
Income before taxes		$139,225
Income taxes		(24,250)
Net income		$114,975

Additional Information on Year 2002 Transactions

a. The loss on cash sale of equipment is $5,125 (details in *b*).

b. Sold equipment costing $46,875, with accumulated depreciation of $30,125, for $11,625 cash.

c. Purchased equipment costing $96,375 by paying cash of $30,000 and signing a long-term note payable for the balance.

d. Borrowed $4,000 cash by signing a short-term note payable.

e. Paid $50,125 cash to reduce the long-term notes payable.

f. Issued 2,500 shares of common stock for cash at $20 per share.

g. Declared and paid cash dividends of $50,100.

Required

Preparation Component

1. Prepare a complete statement of cash flows; report its operating activities using the direct method. Disclose any noncash investing and financing activities in a note.

Check Cash from operating activities, $40,900

Analysis Component

2. Analyze and discuss the cash flow information in your answer to part (1), giving special attention to the wisdom of the cash dividend payment.

Refer to Bushtex Company's financial statements and related information in Problem 17-1A.

Required

Prepare a complete statement of cash flows; report its operating activities according to the indirect method. Disclose any noncash investing and financing activities in a note.

Problem 17-2A
Statement of cash flows (indirect method)

Check Cash used in financing activities, $(46,225)

Refer to the information reported about Bushtex Company in Problem 17-1A.

Required

Prepare a statement of cash flows using a spreadsheet as in Exhibit 17A.1 under the indirect method of reporting cash flows from operating activities. Identify the debits and credits in the Analysis of Changes columns with letters that correspond to the following list of transactions and events:

a. Net income is $114,975.

b. Accounts receivable increased.

c. Merchandise inventory increased.

d. Prepaid expenses decreased.

e. Accounts payable decreased.

f. Depreciation expense is $20,750.

g. Sold equipment costing $46,875, with accumulated depreciation of $30,125, for $11,625 cash. This yielded a loss of $5,125.

h. Purchased equipment costing $96,375 by paying $30,000 cash and **(i.)** by signing a long-term note payable for the balance.

j. Borrowed $4,000 cash by signing a short-term note payable.

k. Paid $50,125 cash to reduce the long-term notes payable.

l. Issued 2,500 shares of common stock for cash at $20 per share.

m. Declared and paid cash dividends of $50,100.

Problem 17-3A[A]
Cash flows spreadsheet (indirect method)

Check Analysis of Changes column totals, $600,775

Pierpont Corporation, a merchandiser, recently completed its 2002 operations. For the year, (1) all sales are credit sales, (2) all credits to accounts receivable reflect cash receipts from customers, (3) all purchases of inventory are on credit, (4) all debits to accounts payable reflect cash payments for inventory, (5) other operating expenses are cash expenses, and (6) any change in income taxes payable reflects the accrual and cash payment of taxes. Pierpont's balance sheet and income statement follow:

Problem 17-4A
Statement of cash flows (direct method)

PIERPONT CORPORATION
Income Statement
For Year Ended December 31, 2002

Sales		$1,792,000
Cost of goods sold		(1,086,000)
Gross profit		$ 706,000
Operating expenses		
Depreciation expense	$ 54,000	
Other expenses	494,000	(548,000)
Income before taxes		$ 158,000
Income taxes		(22,000)
Net income		$ 136,000

PIERPONT CORPORATION
Comparative Balance Sheet
December 31, 2002

	2002	2001
Assets		
Cash	$ 164,000	$107,000
Accounts receivable	83,000	71,000
Merchandise inventory	601,000	526,000
Equipment	335,000	299,000
Accum. depreciation—Equip.	(158,000)	(104,000)
Total assets	$1,025,000	$899,000
Liabilities and Equity		
Accounts payable	$ 87,000	$ 71,000
Income taxes payable	28,000	25,000
Common stock, $2 par value	592,000	568,000
Contributed capital in excess of par value, common stock	196,000	160,000
Retained earnings	122,000	75,000
Total liabilities and equity	$1,025,000	$899,000

Additional Information on Year 2002 Transactions

a. Purchased equipment for $36,000 cash.

b. Issued 12,000 shares of common stock for cash at $5 per share.

c. Declared and paid $89,000 of cash dividends.

Required

Check Cash from operating activities, $122,000

Prepare a complete statement of cash flows (report its cash inflows and cash outflows from operating activities according to the direct method).

Problem 17-5A
Statement of cash flows (indirect method)

Check Cash used in financing activities, $(29,000)

Refer to Pierpont Corporation's financial statements and related information in Problem 17-4A.

Required

Prepare a complete statement of cash flows (report its cash flows from operating activities according to the indirect method).

Problem 17-6A[A]
Cash flows spreadsheet (indirect method)

Check Analysis of Changes column totals, $481,000

Refer to the information reported about Pierpont Corporation in Problem 17-4A.

Required

Prepare a statement of cash flows using a spreadsheet as in Exhibit 17A.1 under the indirect method of reporting cash flows from operating activities. Identify the debits and credits in the Analysis of Changes columns with letters that correspond to the following list of transactions and events:

a. Net income is $136,000.

b. Accounts receivable increased.

c. Merchandise inventory increased.

d. Accounts payable increased.

e. Income taxes payable increased.

f. Depreciation expense is $54,000.

g. Purchased equipment for $36,000 cash.

h. Issued 12,000 shares at $5 per share.

i. Declared and paid $89,000 of cash dividends.

Keller Corporation, a merchandiser, recently completed its year 2002 operations. For the year, (1) all sales are credit sales, (2) all credits to accounts receivable reflect cash receipts from customers, (3) purchases of inventory are on credit, (4) all debits to accounts payable reflect cash payments for inventory, and (5) other expenses are paid in advance and are initially debited to Prepaid Expenses. Keller's balance sheet and income statement follow:

PROBLEM SET B

Problem 17-1B
Statement of cash flows
(direct method)

KELLER CORPORATION
Comparative Balance Sheet
December 31, 2002

	2002	2001
Assets		
Cash	$123,450	$ 61,550
Accounts receivable	77,100	80,750
Merchandise inventory	240,600	250,700
Prepaid expenses	15,100	17,000
Equipment	262,250	200,000
Accum. depreciation—Equip.	(110,750)	(95,000)
Total assets	$607,750	$515,000
Liabilities and Equity		
Accounts payable	$ 17,750	$ 102,000
Short-term notes payable	15,000	10,000
Long-term notes payable	100,000	77,500
Common stock, $5 par	215,000	200,000
Contributed capital in excess of par, common stock	30,000	0
Retained earnings	230,000	125,500
Total liabilities and equity	$607,750	$515,000

KELLER CORPORATION
Income Statement
For Year Ended December 31, 2002

Sales		$1,185,000
Cost of goods sold		(595,000)
Gross profit		$ 590,000
Operating expenses		
Depreciation expense	$ 38,600	
Other expenses	362,850	
Total operating expenses		(401,450)
Other gains (losses)		
Loss on sale of equipment		(2,100)
Income before taxes		$ 186,450
Income taxes		(28,350)
Net income		$ 158,100

Additional Information on Year 2002 Transactions

a. The loss on cash sale of equipment is $2,100 (details in *b*).

b. Sold equipment costing $51,000, with accumulated depreciation of $22,850, for $26,050 cash.

c. Purchased equipment costing $113,250 by paying cash of $43,250 and signing a long-term note payable for the balance.

d. Borrowed $5,000 cash by signing a short-term note payable.

e. Paid $47,500 cash to reduce the long-term notes payable.

f. Issued 3,000 shares of common stock for cash at $15 per share.

g. Declared and paid cash dividends of $53,600.

Required

Preparation Component

1. Prepare a complete statement of cash flows; report its operating activities using the direct method. Disclose any noncash investing and financing activities in a note.

Analysis Component

2. Analyze and discuss the cash flow information in your answer to part (1), giving special attention to the wisdom of the cash dividend payment.

Check Cash from operating activities, $130,200

Refer to Keller Corporation's financial statements and related information in Problem 17-1B.

Required

Prepare a complete statement of cash flows; report its operating activities according to the indirect method. Disclose any noncash investing and financing activities in a note.

Problem 17-2B
Statement of cash flows
(indirect method)

Check Cash used in financing activities, $(51,100)

Problem 17-3B^A

Cash flows spreadsheet
(indirect method)

Refer to the information reported about Keller Corporation in Problem 17-1B.

Required

Prepare a statement of cash flows using a spreadsheet as in Exhibit 17A.1 under the indirect method of reporting cash flows from operating activities. Identify the debits and credits in the Analysis of Changes columns with letters that correspond to the following list of transactions and events:

a. Net income is $158,100.

b. Accounts receivable decreased.

c. Merchandise inventory decreased.

d. Prepaid expenses decreased.

e. Accounts payable decreased.

f. Depreciation expense is $38,600.

g. Sold equipment costing $51,000, with accumulated depreciation of $22,850, for $26,050 cash. This yielded a loss of $2,100.

h. Purchased equipment costing $113,250 by paying $43,250 cash and **(i.)** by signing a long-term note payable for the balance.

j. Borrowed $5,000 cash by signing a short-term note payable.

k. Paid $47,500 cash to reduce the long-term notes payable.

l. Issued 3,000 shares of common stock for cash at $15 per share.

m. Declared and paid cash dividends of $53,600.

Problem 17-4B

Statement of cash flows
(direct method)

Takisha Company, a merchandiser, recently completed its 2002 operations. For the year, (1) all sales are credit sales, (2) all credits to accounts receivable reflect cash receipts from customers, (3) all purchases of inventory are on credit, (4) all debits to accounts payable reflect cash payments for inventory, (5) other operating expenses are cash expenses, and (6) any change in income taxes payable reflects the accrual and cash payment of taxes. Takisha's balance sheet and income statement follow:

TAKISHA COMPANY
Comparative Balance Sheet
December 31, 2002

	2002	2001
Assets		
Cash	$ 58,750	$ 28,400
Accounts receivable	20,222	25,860
Merchandise inventory	165,667	140,320
Equipment	107,750	77,500
Accum. depreciation—Equip.	(46,700)	(31,000)
Total assets	$305,689	$241,080
Liabilities and Equity		
Accounts payable	$ 20,372	$157,530
Income taxes payable	2,100	6,100
Common stock, $5 par	40,000	25,000
Contributed capital in excess		
of par, common stock	68,000	20,000
Retained earnings	175,217	32,450
Total liabilities and equity	$305,689	$241,080

TAKISHA COMPANY
Income Statement
For Year Ended December 31, 2002

Sales		$750,800
Cost of goods sold		(269,200)
Gross profit		$481,600
Operating expenses		
Depreciation expense	$ 15,700	
Other expenses	173,933	(189,633)
Income before taxes		$291,967
Income taxes		(89,200)
Net income		$202,767

Additional Information on Year 2002 Transactions

a. Purchased equipment for $30,250 cash.

b. Issued 3,000 shares of common stock for cash at $21 per share.

c. Declared and paid $60,000 of cash dividends.

Required

Prepare a complete statement of cash flows (report its cash inflows and cash outflows from operating activities according to the direct method).

Check   Cash from operating activities, $57,600

Refer to Takisha Company's financial statements and related information in Problem 17-4B.

Required

Prepare a complete statement of cash flows (report its cash flows from operating activities according to the indirect method).

Problem 17-5B
Statement of cash flows (indirect method)

Check   Cash from financing activities, $3,000

Refer to the information reported about Takisha Company in Problem 17-4B.

Required

Prepare a statement of cash flows using a spreadsheet as in Exhibit 17A.1 under the indirect method of reporting cash flows from operating activities. Identify the debits and credits in the Analysis of Changes columns with letters that correspond to the following list of transactions and events:

a. Net income is $202,767.

b. Accounts receivable decreased.

c. Merchandise inventory increased.

d. Accounts payable decreased.

e. Income taxes payable decreased.

f. Depreciation expense is $15,700.

g. Purchased equipment for $30,250 cash.

h. Issued 3,000 shares at $21 per share.

i. Declared and paid $60,000 of cash dividends.

Problem 17-6B^A
Cash flows spreadsheet (indirect method)

Check   Analysis of Changes column totals, $543,860

Beyond the Numbers

BTN 17-1   Refer to **Nike**'s financial statements in Appendix A to answer the following questions:

1. Is Nike's statement of cash flows prepared under the direct method or the indirect method?

2. For each of the fiscal years 2000, 1999, and 1998, is the amount of cash provided by operating activities more or less than the cash paid for dividends?

3. What is the largest amount in reconciling the difference between net income and cash flow from operating activities in 2000? In 1999? In 1998?

4. Identify the major cash flows for investing and for financing activities in 2000 and 1999.

Reporting in Action

Swoosh Ahead

5. Obtain Nike's annual report information for a fiscal year ending after May 31, 2000, from either its Web site **[www.nike.com]** or the SEC's EDGAR database **[www.sec.gov]**. Since May 31, 2000, what are Nike's largest cash outflows and inflows in the investing and in the financing sections of its cash flow statement?

BTN 17-2   Key comparative figures ($ millions) for both **Nike** and **Reebok** follow:

Comparative Analysis

	Nike			Reebok		
Key Figures	**Current Year**	**1 year Prior**	**2 years Prior**	**Current Year**	**1 year Prior**	**2 years Prior**
Operating cash flows	$ 759.9	$ 961.0	$ 517.5	$ 281.6	$ 151.8	$ 127.0
Total assets	5,856.9	5,247.7	5,397.4	1,564.1	1,684.6	1,756.1

Required

1. Compute the recent two years' cash flow on total assets ratios for both Nike and Reebok.

2. What does the cash flow on total assets ratio measure?

3. Which company has the higher cash flow on total assets ratio?

4. Does the cash flow on total assets ratio reflect on the quality of earnings? Explain.

Ethics Challenge

BTN 17-3 Julie Vignery is preparing for a meeting with her banker. Her business is finishing its fourth year of operations. In the first year, it had negative cash flows from operations. In the second and third years, cash flows from operations turned positive. However, inventory costs rose significantly in year 4, and cash flows from operations will probably be down 25%. Julie wants to secure a line of credit from her banker as a financing buffer. From experience, she knows a focus of the meeting will be cash flows from operations. The banker will scrutinize cash flows for years 1 through 4 and will want a projected number for year 5. Julie knows that a steady progression upward in cash flows for years 1 through 4 will help her case. She decides to use her discretion as owner and considers several business actions that will turn her cash flow in year 4 from a decrease to an increase over year 3.

Required

1. Identify two business actions Julie might take to improve cash flows from operations.

2. Comment on the ethics and possible consequences of Julie's decision to pursue these actions.

Communicating in Practice

BTN 17-4   Your friend, Jenny Hunter, recently completed the second year of her business and just received annual financial statements from her accountant. Jenny finds the income statement and balance sheet informative, but she does not understand the statement of cash flows. She says the first section is especially confusing because it contains a lot of additions and subtractions that do not make sense to her. Jenny adds, "The income statement tells me the business is more profitable than last year and that's most important. If I want to know how cash changes, I can look at comparative balance sheets."

Required

Write a one-half page memorandum to your friend explaining the purpose of the statement of cash flows. Speculate as to why the first section is so confusing and how it might be rectified.

Taking It to the Net

BTN 17-5   Access the April 25, 2000, filing date of the 10-K report of **J. Crew Group, Inc.**, at **www.edgar-online.com.**

Required

1. Does J. Crew use the direct or indirect method to construct the consolidated statement of cash flows?

2. For the fiscal year ended January 29, 2000, what is the largest item recorded in reconciling the net loss to cash flow provided by operations?

3. Over the past three years, J. Crew has recorded a net loss. Has the company been more successful in generating operating cash flows over this time period than in generating net income?

4. In the year ended January 29, 2000, what was the largest cash outflow for the investing and for the financing sections?

5. What items does J. Crew present as supplementary cash flow information?

6. Does J. Crew show any noncash financing activities?

Teamwork in Action

BTN 17-6   Team members are to coordinate and independently answer one question within each of the following three sections. Team members should then report to the team and confirm or correct teammates' answers.

1. Answer *one* of the following questions about the statement of cash flows:
   a. What is this statement's reporting objectives?
   b. What two methods are used to prepare it? Identify similarities and differences between them.
   c. What steps are followed to prepare the statement?
   d. What types of analyses are often made from this statement's information?

2. Identify and explain the formula for computing cash flows from operating activities using the direct method for *one* of the following items:
   a. Cash receipts from sales to customers.
   b. Cash paid for merchandise inventory.

   c. Cash paid for wages and operating expenses.

   d. Cash paid for interest and taxes.

3. Identify and explain the adjustment from net income to cash flows from operating activities using the indirect method for **one** of the following items:

   a. Noncash operating revenues and expenses.

   b. Nonoperating gains and losses.

   c. Increases and decreases in current assets.

   d. Increases and decreases in current liabilities.

Note: For teams of more than four, some pairing within teams is necessary. Use as an in-class activity or as an assignment. If used in class, specify a time limit on each part. Conclude with reports to the entire class, using team rotation. Each team can prepare responses on a transparency.

BTN 17-7   Read the article "Making Sure the Price Is Right" in the March 29, 1999, issue of *Business Week*.

Business Week **Activity**

A1

Required

1. Why is it important for a business owner to know the value of the business?

2. In the article, how did the professional business appraiser calculate the value of VTE?

3. How is *free cash flow* defined?

4. How much would it probably cost for an outside appraisal of a business with about $1 million in annual sales?

5. In today's business environment, which businesses might be easiest to sell?

BTN 17-8   Jenna and Matt Wilder are completing their second year of operating **Mountain High**, a downhill ski area and resort. Mountain High reports a net loss of $(10,000) this year, which includes an $85,000 extraordinary loss from fire. This past year also involved major purchases of plant assets for renovation and expansion, yielding a year-end total asset amount of $800,000. Mountain High's net cash outflow for this year is $(5,000); a summarized version of its statement of cash flows follows:

Entrepreneurial Decision

A1 A2 C2

e

Net cash flow provided by operating activities	$295,000
Net cash flow used by investing activities	(310,000)
Net cash flow provided by financing activities	10,000

Required

Write a one-page memorandum to the Wilders evaluating Mountain High's current performance and assessing its future. Give special emphasis to cash flow data and their interpretation.

Analysis of Financial Statements

k Back

17 focused on reporting and
cash inflows and cash
We explained how to
and interpret the statement
lows.

k at This Chapter

oter emphasizes the analysis
pretation of financial
t information. We learn to
rizontal, vertical, and ratio
to better understand
performance and financial
.

k Ahead

19 introduces us to
al accounting. We discuss
ses, concepts, and roles in
nanagers gather and
information for decision
We also explain management
.

*mean to mislead
Carnell Korsmeyer
vn Ladies)

Cookin' the Books

BEARDSTOWN, IL.—Is nothing sacred? The **Beardstown Ladies** [**Beardstown.org/ladies.htm**], those home-spun, grandmotherly investors whose supposed success created a mini-industry, are being called frauds. The ladies fudged the figures.

With several books to their name, the Beardstown Ladies are a fixture on the lecture circuit, riding a bull market in homespun advice. But their best advice might have been "know your accounting." The ladies' *Common-Sense Investment Guide* claims an annual return of 23.4% over the decade covered in the book, but this return is computed by averaging the ladies' two best years—1991 and 1992—and ignoring the other eight years.

Oops, that's not the way it's done. This would mean their total returns were nowhere as great as claimed. The accounting firm PricewaterhouseCoopers, which did an audit of the ladies' books, says the actual return over the period covered is 9.1%. This figure is well below the 23.4% claimed by the ladies and less than the 15% return of the overall stock market for the same period.

Experts in accounting and analysis are not surprised. The ladies' investment strategy was simple and not fundamentally sound. They pooled their money and bought shares of big, low-risk companies, and then watched as the stock rose with the general increase in the stock market. An index fund would have returned about double that of the ladies' return over the same period.

Still, their apparent success and their folksiness made them popular guests on television shows and brought some work as money management experts. Their first book sold more than 800,000 copies. Senior partner Betty Sinnock says she is "just sick" about what's happened. A piece of homespun advice they didn't give: if it looks too good to be true, it probably is. [*Sources: Fortune Web* site, March 30, 1998; CNN Web, *Moneyline,* March 17, 1998; *Beardstown Ladies Web* site, May 2001.]

Learning Objectives

Conceptual

C1 Explain the purpose of analysis.

C2 Identify the building blocks of analysis.

C3 Describe standards for comparisons in analysis.

C4 Identify the tools of analysis.

Analytical

A1 Summarize and report results of analysis.

Procedural

P1 Explain and apply methods of horizontal analysis.

P2 Describe and apply methods of vertical analysis.

P3 Define and apply ratio analysis.

This chapter shows us how to use information in financial statements to further evaluate a company's financial performance and condition. We describe the purpose of financial statement analysis, its basic building blocks, the information available, standards for comparisons, and tools of analysis. Three major analysis tools are emphasized: horizontal analysis, vertical analysis, and ratio analysis. We illustrate the application of each of these tools using **Nike**'s financial statements. We also introduce comparative analysis using **Reebok**'s financial statements. Moreover, this chapter expands and organizes the ratio analyses introduced at the end of each chapter. Understanding financial statement analysis is crucial to effective business decision making, and its proper application avoids reliance on sources such as the ladies from Beardstown.

Basics of Analysis

Financial statement analysis applies analytical tools to general-purpose financial statements and related data for making business decisions. It involves transforming accounting data into useful information. Financial statement analysis reduces our reliance on hunches, guesses, and intuition. It also reduces our uncertainty in decision making. It does not lessen the need for expert judgment, however; instead, it provides us an effective and systematic basis for making business decisions. This section describes the purpose of financial statement analysis, its information sources, the use of comparisons, and some issues in computations.

Purpose of Analysis

C1 Explain the purpose of analysis.

The purpose of financial statement analysis is to help users make better business decisions. These users include decision makers both internal and external to the company.

Internal users of accounting information are the individuals involved in managing and operating the company. They include managers, officers, internal auditors, consultants, budget officers, and market researchers. Internal users make a company's strategic and operating decisions. The purpose of financial statement analysis for these users is to provide information helpful in improving the company's efficiency and effectiveness in providing products and services.

Point: Financial statement analysis tools are also used for personal financial investment decisions.

External users of accounting information are *not* directly involved in running the company. They include shareholders, lenders, directors, customers, suppliers, regulators, lawyers, brokers, and the press. These users are affected by, and sometimes affect, the company's activities. External users rely on financial statement analysis to make better and more informed decisions in pursuing their own goals.

Point: Financial statement analysis is an important topic on the CPA, CMA, CIA, and CFA exams.

We can identify many examples of the use of financial statement analysis. Shareholders and creditors assess future company prospects for investing and lending decisions. A board of directors analyzes financial statements in monitoring management's decisions. Employees and unions use the information in financial statements in labor negotiations. Suppliers use financial statement information in establishing credit terms. Customers analyze financial statements in deciding whether to establish supply relationships. Public utilities set customer rates by analyzing financial statements. Auditors use financial statements in assessing the "fair presentation" of their clients' financial statement numbers. Analyst services such as **Dun & Bradstreet**, **Moody's**, and **Standard & Poor's** use financial statements in making buy-sell recommendations and setting credit ratings. The common goal of all of these users is to evaluate company performance and financial condition. This includes evaluating (1) past and current performance, (2) current financial position, and (3) future performance and risk.

Building Blocks of Analysis

C2 Identify the building blocks of analysis.

Financial statement analysis focuses on one or more elements of a company's financial condition or performance. Our analysis emphasizes four areas of inquiry—with varying degrees of importance. These four areas are described and illustrated in this chapter and are considered the *building blocks* of financial statement analysis:

■ **Liquidity** and **Efficiency**—ability to meet short-term obligations and to efficiently generate revenues.

- **Solvency**—ability to generate future revenues and meet long-term obligations.
- **Profitability**—ability to provide financial rewards sufficient to attract and retain financing.
- **Market Prospects**—ability to generate positive market expectations.

Applying the building blocks of financial statement analysis involves determining (1) the objectives of analysis and (2) the relative emphasis among the building blocks. For instance, when evaluating the investment merit of a common stock, an investor often emphasizes profitability, efficiency, and market prospects. Serious analysis requires an investor to assess other building blocks as well with perhaps less emphasis. Attention to these other areas is necessary to assess risk exposure, which usually involves some analysis of liquidity and solvency. Further analysis can reveal important risks that outweigh earning power and can lead to new directions in the financial statement analysis of a company.

We distinguish among these four building blocks to emphasize the different aspects of a company's financial condition or performance, yet we must remember that these areas of analysis are interrelated. For instance, a company's operating performance is affected by the availability of financing and short-term liquidity conditions. Similarly, a company's credit standing is not limited to satisfactory short-term liquidity but depends also on its profitability and efficiency in using assets. Early in our analysis, we need to determine the relative emphasis of each building block and the order of their analysis given our objectives. Emphasis and analysis can later change as a result of evidence collected.

> **Did You Know?**
>
> **Chips and Brokers**   The term *blue chips* is used to refer to stock of big, profitable companies. The term comes from poker—where the most valuable chips are the blue ones. *Brokers* execute orders to buy or sell stock. The term comes from wine retailers—individuals who broach (break) wine casks.

Information for Analysis

We explained how decision makers such as managers, employees, directors, customers, suppliers, current and potential owners, current and potential lenders, brokers, regulatory authorities, lawyers, economists, labor unions, analysts, and consultants need to analyze financial statements. Some of these people, such as managers and a few regulatory agencies, are able to receive special financial reports prepared to meet their needs. However, most users must rely on general-purpose financial statements that companies periodically release. **General-purpose financial statements** include the (1) income statement, (2) balance sheet, (3) statement of changes in equity (or statement of retained earnings), (4) statement of cash flows, and (5) notes to these statements.

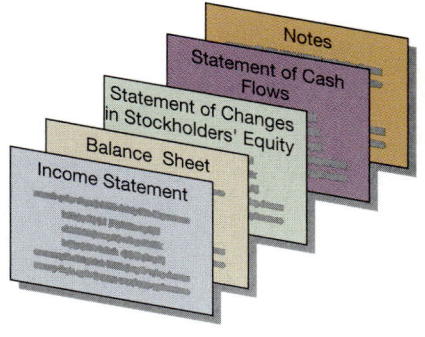

General-purpose financial statements are part of financial reporting. **Financial reporting** refers to the communication of relevant financial information to decision makers. It includes not only financial statements but also information from 10-K or other filings with the Securities and Exchange Commission, news releases, shareholders' meetings, forecasts, management letters, auditors' reports, and analyses published in annual reports. Financial reporting broadly refers to information useful for making investment, credit, and other business decisions. It helps users assess the amounts, timing, and uncertainty of future cash inflows and outflows.

Point: Decision makers rely on financial statement analysis to help them better understand the financial position and profitability of a business. Auditors use financial statement analysis to assess the reasonableness of amounts presented in those statements.

One example of useful information outside the traditional financial statements is the Management Discussion and Analysis (MD&A). **Nike**'s MD&A, for example, includes several parts (available at **NikeBiz.com**). It begins with a list of four highlights: net income, revenues, gross margins, and expenses. It then proceeds to compare operating activities for 2000 with 1999, and 1999 with 1998. This analysis includes a breakdown of Nike's revenues between footwear and apparel and between domestic and international activities. The

> **Did You Know?**
>
> **Analysis Online**   Many Web sites offer free access and screening of companies by key financial numbers such as earnings and sales. For instance, **Standard & Poor's** has information for more than 10,000 stocks [**www.standardpoor.com**].

third part of its analysis examines liquidity and capital resources—roughly equivalent to investing and financing activities. The fourth and final part explains Nike's market risk—including its exposure to currency changes, interest rates, and derivatives. The MD&A is an excellent starting point in understanding the business activities of a company.

Standards for Comparisons

C3 Describe standards for comparisons in analysis.

When computing and interpreting analysis measures as part of a financial statement analysis, we need to decide whether these measures suggest good, bad, or average performance. To make these judgments, we need standards (benchmarks) for comparisons. Standards for comparisons can include these:

■ *Intracompany*—The company under analysis provides standards for comparisons based on prior performance and relations between its financial items. **Nike**'s current net income, for instance, can be compared with prior years' net income and in relation to its revenues or total assets.

■ *Competitor*—One or more direct competitors of the company being analyzed can provide standards for comparisons. **Coca-Cola**'s profit margin, for instance, can be compared with **PepsiCo**'s profit margin.

■ *Industry*—Industry statistics can provide standards of comparisons. Published industry statistics are available from several services such as Dun & Bradstreet, Standard & Poor's, and Moody's.

Point: Each chapter's *Reporting in Action* problems engage students in *intracompany* analysis, whereas *Comparative Analysis* problems require analyzing information relative to a competitor (Nike vs. Reebok).

■ *Guidelines (rules of thumb)*—General standards of comparisons can develop from past experiences. Examples are the 2:1 level for the current ratio or 1:1 level for the acid-test ratio. These guidelines, or rules of thumb, must be carefully applied since their context is often crucial.

All of these standards of comparisons are useful when properly applied, yet analysis measures taken from a selected competitor or group of competitors are often the best. Intracompany and industry measures are also important parts of all analyses. Guidelines or rules of thumb should be applied with care, and then only if they seem reasonable in light of past experience and industry norms.

Quick Check

1. Who are the intended users of general-purpose financial statements?
2. General-purpose financial statements consist of what information?
3. Which of the following is *least* useful as a basis for comparison when analyzing ratios? (a) company results from a different economy, (b) subjective standards from past experience, (c) rule-of-thumb standards, (d) industry averages.
4. What is the preferred basis of comparison for ratio analysis?

Answers—p. 768

C4 Identify the tools of analysis.

Did You Know?

Ticker Prices *Ticker prices* refer to a band of moving data on a monitor carrying up-to-the-minute stock prices. The term comes from *ticker tape*—a 1-inch wide strip of paper spewing stock prices from a printer that ticked as it ran. Most of today's investors have never seen actual ticker tape, but the term survives.

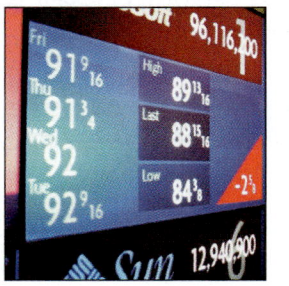

Tools of Analysis

Three of the most common tools of financial statement analysis are:

1. **Horizontal analysis**—Comparison of a company's financial condition and performance across time.
2. **Vertical analysis**—Comparison of a company's financial condition and performance to a base amount.
3. **Ratio analysis**—Measurement of key relations between financial statement items.

The remainder of this chapter describes these tools of analysis and how to apply them.

Analysis of any single financial number is of limited value. Instead, financial analysis must use the important relations that exist between items and across time. Much of financial statement analysis involves identifying and describing relations between numbers, groups of numbers, and changes in those numbers. Horizontal analysis is a tool to evaluate changes in financial statement data *across time*.[1]

Horizontal Analysis

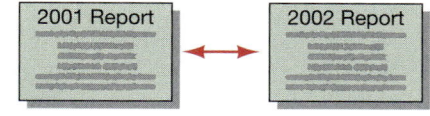

Comparative Statements

Comparing amounts for two or more successive periods often helps in analyzing financial statement data. **Comparative financial statements** facilitate this comparison by showing financial amounts in side-by-side columns on a single statement. Each financial statement is presented in a *comparative format*. For instance, **Nike**'s *Financial History* report in Appendix A is a comparative statement based on 6 years of financial performance. Using figures from Nike's financial statements, this section explains how to compute dollar changes and percent changes for comparative statements.

 P1 Explain and apply methods of horizontal analysis.

Concept 18-1

Computation of Dollar Changes and Percent Changes

Comparing financial statements over relatively short time periods—two to three years—is often done by analyzing changes in line items. A change analysis usually includes analysis of absolute dollar amount changes as well as percent changes. Both analyses are relevant since dollar changes can yield large percent changes inconsistent with their importance. For instance, a 50% change from a base figure of $100 is less important than the same percent change from a base amount of $100,000 in the same statement. Reference to dollar amounts is necessary to retain a proper perspective and to assess the importance of changes. We compute the *dollar change* for a financial statement item as follows:

> **Dollar change = Analysis period amount − Base period amount**

where *analysis period* is the point or period of time for the financial statements under analysis, and *base period* is the point or period of time for the financial statements used for comparison purposes. The prior year is commonly used as a base period. We compute the *percent change* by dividing the dollar change by the base period amount and then multiplying this quantity by 100 as follows:

$$\text{Percent change } (\%) = \frac{\text{Analysis period amount} - \text{Base period amount}}{\text{Base period amount}} \times 100$$

We can always compute a dollar change, but we must be aware of a few rules in working with percent changes. To illustrate, look at four separate cases in this chart:

Case	Analysis Period	Base Period	Change Analysis Dollar	Change Analysis Percent
A	$ 1,500	$(4,500)	$6,000	—
B	(1,000)	2,000	(3,000)	—
C	8,000	—	8,000	—
D	0	10,000	(10,000)	(100%)

When a negative amount appears in the base period and a positive amount in the analysis period (or vice versa), we cannot compute a meaningful percent change—see cases A and B. Also, when no value is in the base period, no percent change is computable—see case C. Finally, when an item has a value in the base period and zero in the analysis period, the decrease is 100 percent—see case D.

---

[1] The term *horizontal analysis* arises from the left-to-right (or right-to-left) movement of our eyes as we review comparative financial statements across time.

It is common when using horizontal analysis to compare amounts to either average or median values from prior periods.[2] Comparing changes to average or median values computed from more than one prior period highlights unusual happenings because average and median values smooth out erratic or unusual fluctuations. We also commonly round per-

Exhibit 18.1

Comparative Balance Sheet

NIKE **Comparative Balance Sheet** **May 31, 2000 and 1999**				
(in millions)	2000	1999	Dollar Change	Percent* Change
Assets				
Current assets				
Cash and equivalents	$ 254.3	$ 198.1	$ 56.2	28.4%
Accounts receivable, less allowance for doubtful accounts of $71.4 and $57.2	1,567.2	1,540.1	27.1	1.8
Inventories	1,446.0	1,170.6	275.4	23.5
Deferred income taxes	111.5	120.6	(9.1)	(7.5)
Income taxes receivable	2.2	15.9	(13.7)	(86.2)
Prepaid expenses	215.2	219.6	(4.4)	(2.0)
Total current assets	$3,596.4	$3,264.9	$ 331.5	10.2%
Property, plant and equipment, net	1,583.4	1,265.8	317.6	25.1
Identifiable intangible assets and goodwill	410.9	426.6	(15.7)	(3.7)
Deferred income taxes and other assets	266.2	290.4	(24.2)	(8.3)
Total assets	$5,856.9	$5,247.7	$ 609.2	11.6%
Liabilities and Equity				
Current liabilities				
Current portion of long-term debt	$ 50.1	$ 1.0	$ 49.1	4,910.0%
Notes payable	924.2	419.1	505.1	120.5
Accounts payable	543.8	473.6	70.2	14.8
Accrued liabilities	621.9	553.2	68.7	12.4
Total current liabilities	$2,140.0	$1,446.9	$ 693.1	47.9%
Long-term debt	470.3	386.1	84.2	21.8
Deferred income taxes and other liabilities	110.3	79.8	30.5	38.2
Commitments and contingencies	—	—		
Redeemable preferred stock	0.3	0.3	0.0	0.0
Shareholders' equity				
Common stock at stated value				
Class A convertible—99.2 and 100.7 shares outstanding	0.2	0.2	0.0	0.0
Class B—170.4 and 181.6 shares outstanding	2.6	2.7	(0.1)	(3.7)
Capital in excess of stated value	369.0	334.1	34.9	10.4
Unearned stock compensation	(11.7)	—	(11.7)	—
Accumulated other comprehensive income . . .	(111.1)	(68.9)	(42.2)	(61.2)
Retained earnings	2,887.0	3,066.5	(179.5)	(5.9)
Total shareholders' equity	$3,136.0	$3,334.6	$(198.6)	(6.0)%
Total liabilities and equity	$5,856.9	$5,247.7	$ 609.2	11.6%

* Percents are rounded to the first decimal point.

---

[2] *Median* is the middle value in a group of numbers. For instance, if five prior years' incomes are (in 000s) $15, $19, $18, $20, and $22, the median value is $19. When there are two middle numbers, we can take their average. For instance, if four prior years' sales are (in 000s) $84, $91, $96, and $93, the median is $92 (computed as the average of $91 and $93).

cents and ratios to one or two decimal places, but practice on this matter is not uniform. Computations are as detailed as necessary, which is judged by whether or not rounding potentially affects users' decisions. Computations should not be so excessively detailed that important relations are lost among a mountain of decimal points.

Comparative Balance Sheet

One of the most useful comparative statements is the comparative balance sheet. It consists of amounts from two or more balance sheet dates arranged side by side. The usefulness of comparative financial statements is often improved by showing each item's dollar change and percent change. This type of presentation highlights large dollar and percent changes for decision makers. Exhibit 18.1 shows a comparative balance sheet for Nike.

Analysis of comparative financial statements begins by focusing on items that show large dollar or percent changes. We then try to identify the reasons for these changes and, if possible, determine whether they are favorable or unfavorable. We also follow up on items with small changes when we expected the changes to be large.

With Nike's comparative balance sheet in Exhibit 18.1, a few items stand out. Among current assets, Cash and Equivalents, with a $56.2 million increase (28.4%), and Inventories, with a $275.4 million increase (23.5%), are notable. The statement of cash flows in Appendix A reveals that a substantial portion of the increase in cash is due to cash flows from financing activities, mainly cash from issuance of notes payable. Moreover, the notes reveal that much of the increase in inventories is due to finished goods inventory. The comparative analysis also shows that Nike's total current liabilities increased by $693.1 million with most of this attributed to notes payable. Further analysis also reveals a large increase ($317.6 million) in property, plant and equipment. This increase is larger in magnitude than that in any other asset account. We need to monitor this increase in productive assets to be certain that such expansion is the best use of available resources. Finally, we see a general increase in debt (liability) financing and a decrease in equity financing.

Example: If cash and equivalents increased in 2000 by an additional $100 million, what is the percent change in cash and equivalents? *Answer:* ($254.3 + $100.0 − $198.1)/$198.1 = 78.8%

Comparative Income Statement

A comparative income statement is prepared similarly to the comparative balance sheet. Amounts for two or more periods are placed side by side, with additional columns for dollar and percent changes. Exhibit 18.2 shows Nike's comparative income statement.

Point: Business consultants use comparative statement analysis to provide management advice.

Exhibit 18.2

Comparative Income Statement

NIKE **Comparative Income Statement** **For Years Ended May 31, 2000 and 1999**				
(in millions, except per share data)	2000	1999	**Dollar** **Change**	**Percent*** **Change**
Revenues	$8,995.1	$8,776.9	**$218.2**	2.5%
Costs and expenses				
Costs of sales	5,403.8	5,493.5	**(89.7)**	**(1.6)**
Selling and administrative	2,606.4	2,426.6	**179.8**	**7.4**
Interest expense	45.0	44.1	**0.9**	**2.0**
Other income and expense, net	23.2	21.5	**1.7**	**7.9**
Restructuring charge, net	(2.5)	45.1	**(47.6)**	**(105.5)**
Total costs and expenses	$8,075.9	$8,030.8	**$ 45.1**	**0.6**
Income before income taxes	919.2	746.1	**173.1**	**23.2**
Income taxes	340.1	294.7	**45.4**	**15.4**
Net income	$ 579.1	$ 451.4	**$127.7**	**28.3**
Basic earnings per common share	$ 2.10	$ 1.59	**$ 0.51**	**32.1**
Average common shares outstanding	275.7	283.3		

* Percents are rounded to the first decimal point.

Point: We can also compute percent changes by dividing the current period by the prior period and subtracting 1.0. For example, the 2.5% revenue increase of Exhibit 18.2 is computed as: ($8,995.1/$8,776.9) − 1.

Nike's growth in revenues in 2000 was small as shown by its 2.5% revenues increase in Exhibit 18.2. Because Nike is a consumer products company, its revenues depend heavily on consumer tastes. Changes in consumer tastes were not especially favorable for Nike in 2000. This might partly explain the increase in finished goods inventory evidenced in Exhibit 18.1. To counter the slow revenue growth, Nike spent $179.8 million more on selling and administrative activities. Nike is not currently reaping adequate benefits from the increase in these expenses.

Exhibit 18.2 shows an increase in gross margin (revenues − cost of sales). This is evident from the 2.5% revenue increase coupled with the 1.6% decrease in cost of sales. The result is that the gross margin ratio rises to 39.9% of revenues in 2000, compared to 37.4% in 1999.

Did You Know?

Analysis Tech   Spreadsheet programs can produce horizontal, vertical, and ratio analyses, including graphical depictions of financial relations. The key is using this information properly and effectively for business decision making.

Trend Analysis

Trend analysis, also called *trend percent analysis* or *index number trend analysis,* can reveal patterns in data across successive periods. It involves computing trend percents for a series of financial numbers. This analysis method is a variation on the use of percent changes for horizontal analysis. The difference is that trend analysis does not subtract the base period amount in the numerator. To compute trend percents, we do the following:

1. Select a *base period* and assign each item in the base period a weight of 100%.
2. Express financial numbers as a percent of their base period number.

A *trend percent,* also called an *index number,* is the amount in the analysis period divided by the amount of the same item from the base period, multiplied by 100 to get the percent form as follows:

Point: *Index* refers to the comparison of the analysis period to the base period. Percents determined for each period are called *index numbers.*

$$\text{Trend percent (\%)} = \frac{\text{Analysis period amount}}{\text{Base period amount}} \times 100$$

To illustrate trend analysis, we use selected Nike data as reported in Exhibit 18.3.

Exhibit 18.3

Revenues and Expenses

($ in millions)	2000	1999	1998	1997	1996	1995
Revenues	$8,995.1	$8,776.9	$9,553.1	$9,186.5	$6,470.6	$4,760.8
Costs of sales	5,403.8	5,493.5	6,065.5	5,503.0	3,906.7	2,865.3
Selling and administrative . .	2,606.4	2,426.6	2,623.8	2,303.7	1,588.6	1,209.8

Point: In trend analysis, the first period in a series of periods is usually chosen as the base period.

These data are from Nike's financial history in Appendix A and its prior statements.

We select 1995 as the base period and compute the trend percent in each subsequent year by dividing each year's amount by its 1995 amount. For instance, the revenue trend percent for 2000 is 188.9%, computed as $8,995.1/$4,760.8. The trend percents for the data from Exhibit 18.3 are shown in Exhibit 18.4.

Exhibit 18.4

Trend Percents of Revenues and Expenses

(in percents)	2000	1999	1998	1997	1996	1995
Revenues	188.9%	184.4%	200.7%	193.0%	135.9%	100%
Costs of sales	188.6	191.7	211.7	192.1	136.3	100
Selling and administrative	215.4	200.6	216.9	190.4	131.3	100

Point: Trend analysis expresses a percent of base, not a percent of change.

Graphical depictions often aid analysis of trend percents. Exhibit 18.5 shows the trend percents from Exhibit 18.4 in a *line graph,* which can help us identify trends and detect changes in direction or magnitude. It reveals that through 1997, costs of sales increased at a rate almost identical to the increase in revenues. In particular, at no time did the revenues and costs of sales lines deviate by more than 1%. However, in 1998, cost of sales jumped 11.0% above revenues (211.7% vs. 200.7%). By 2000, Nike appears to have cost of sales back in line with earlier relations (revenues [green line] at 188.9% vs. cost of sales [red line] at 188.6%). It also reveals that both revenues and costs of sales markedly increased from 1995–1998, but flatten out in 1999–2000.

The line graph in Exhibit 18.5 also shows that the increase in selling and administrative expenses exceeded the increase in both revenues and costs of sales in 1998–2000. Its trend line rises to 215.4% in 2000 compared to 100% in 1995. As suggested from Exhibit 18.2, we should continue to monitor these expenses.

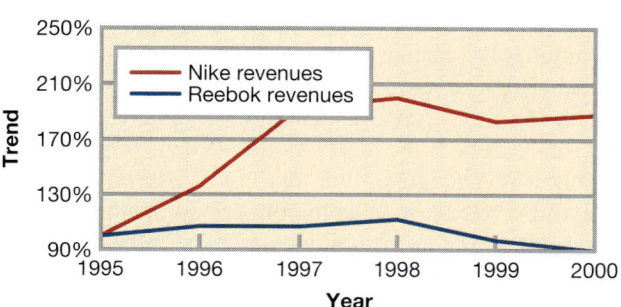

Exhibit 18.5
Trend Percent Lines for Revenues and Expenses

Exhibit 18.6 compares **Nike**'s revenue trend line to that of **Reebok** for this recent six-year period. Nike's revenues sharply increased in 1996–1997, while those of Reebok did not. Both companies' revenues declined in 1999. However, Nike's revenues for 2000 increased, but Reebok's did not.

Exhibit 18.6
Trend Percent Lines— Nike vs. Reebok

Trend analysis of financial statement items also can include comparisons of relations between items on different financial statements. For instance, Exhibit 18.7 is a comparison of Nike's revenues and total assets. The rate of increase in total assets (186.4%) is slightly less than the increase in revenues (188.9%). Is this result favorable or not? It suggests that Nike was slightly more efficient in using its assets in 2000 than in earlier years. Overall we must remember that an important part of financial statement analysis is identifying questions and areas of interest, which often direct us to important factors bearing on the company's future. Accordingly, financial statement analysis should be seen as a continuous process of refining our understanding and expectations of company performance and financial condition.

You Make the Call

Auditor Your tests reveal a 3% increase in sales from $200,000 to $206,000 and a 4% decrease in expenses from $190,000 to $182,400. Both changes are within your "reasonableness" criterion of ±5% and, thus, you don't pursue additional tests. The audit partner in charge questions your lack of follow-up and mentions the *joint relation* between sales and expenses. To what is the partner referring?

Answer—p. 768

	2000	1995	Trend Percent (2000 vs 1995)
Revenues	$8,995.1	$4,760.8	188.9%
Total assets	5,856.9	3,142.7	186.4

Exhibit 18.7
Revenues and Total Assets Data for Nike

Vertical Analysis

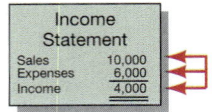

P2 Describe and apply methods of vertical analysis.

Vertical analysis is a tool to evaluate individual financial statement items or a group of items in terms of a specific base amount. We usually define a key aggregate figure as the base, and the base amount is commonly defined as 100%. For instance, an income statement's base is usually revenue and a balance sheet's base is usually total assets. Since the sum of individual items in vertical analysis is 100%, this analysis is also called *common-size analysis*. This section explains vertical analysis and applies it to Nike.[3]

Common-Size Statements

The comparative statements in Exhibits 18.1 and 18.2 show the change in each item over time, but they do not emphasize the relative importance of each item. We use **common-size financial statements** to reveal changes in the relative importance of each financial statement item. All individual amounts in common-size statements are redefined in terms of common-size percents. A *common-size percent* is measured by dividing each individual financial statement amount under analysis by its base amount:

$$\text{Common-size percent } (\%) = \frac{\text{Analysis amount}}{\text{Base amount}} \times 100$$

Common-Size Balance Sheet

Common-size statements express each item as a percent of a *base amount,* which for a common-size balance sheet is usually total assets. It is assigned a value of 100%. This implies that the total amount of liabilities plus equity equals 100% since this amount equals total assets. We then compute a common-size percent for each asset, liability, and equity item using total assets as the base amount. When we present a company's successive balance sheets in this way, changes in the mixture of assets, liabilities, and equity are apparent.

Exhibit 18.8 shows a common-size comparative balance sheet for Nike. Some relations that stand out on both a magnitude and percent basis include (1) an increase in inventory (22.3% to 24.7%), (2) an increase in property, plant and equipment (24.1% to 27.0%), and (3) an increase in notes payable (8.0% to 15.8%). None of these happenings is necessarily favorable to Nike. In particular, the increasing inventory warrants special attention due to risk of excess and slow-moving products. Also, its increase in property, plant and equipment must be offset with increased net income in current and/or future periods to support such asset acquisitions.

Common-Size Income Statement

Our analysis also benefits from examining a common-size income statement. The amount of revenues is usually the base amount, which is assigned a value of 100%. Each common-size income statement item appears as a percent of revenues. If we think of the 100% revenues amount as representing one sales dollar, the remaining items show how each revenue dollar is distributed among costs, expenses, and income.

Exhibit 18.9 shows the comparative income statement for each dollar of Nike's revenues. The exhibit shows that Nike's costs and expenses, as a percent of revenues, have decreased from 1999 (91.5%) to 2000 (89.8%). The largest change is a decrease in costs of sales, from 62.6 cents on the dollar to 60.1 cents. This favorable change overcomes the unfavorable increase in selling and administrative expenses from 27.7% to 29.0%.

One advantage of computing common-size percents for successive income statements is that it helps uncover potentially important changes in a company's expenses. Evidence of no changes, especially when changes are expected, is also valuable information for analysis purposes.

Common-Size Graphics

Two of the most common tools of common-size analysis are trend analysis of common-size statements and graphical analysis. The trend analysis of common-size statements is similar

---

[3] The term *vertical analysis* arises from the up-down (or down-up) movement of our eyes as we review common-size financial statements.

Exhibit 18.8

Common-Size Comparative
Balance Sheet

NIKE Common-Size Comparative Balance Sheet May 31, 2000 and 1999			Common-Size Percents*	
(in millions)	2000	1999	2000	1999
Assets				
Current assets				
Cash and equivalents	$ 254.3	$198.1	4.3%	3.8%
Accounts receivable, less allowance for doubtful accounts of $65.4 and $73.2	1,567.2	1,540.1	26.8	29.3
Inventories	1,446.0	1,170.6	24.7	22.3
Deferred income taxes	111.5	120.6	1.9	2.3
Income taxes receivable	2.2	15.9	0.0	0.3
Prepaid expenses	215.2	219.6	3.7	4.2
Total current assets	$3,596.4	$3,264.9	61.4%	62.2%
Property, plant and equipment, net	1,583.4	1,265.8	27.0	24.1
Intangible assets and goodwill	410.9	426.6	7.0	8.1
Deferred taxes and other assets	266.2	290.4	4.6	5.6
Total assets	$5,856.9	$5,247.7	100.0%	100.0%
Liabilities and Shareholders' Equity				
Current liabilities				
Current portion of long-term debt	$ 50.1	$ 1.0	0.8%	0.0%
Notes payable	924.2	419.1	15.8	8.0
Accounts payable	543.8	473.6	9.3	9.0
Accrued liabilities	621.9	553.2	10.6	10.5
Total current liabilities	$2,140.0	$1,446.9	36.5%	27.5%
Long-term debt	470.3	386.1	8.0	7.4
Deferred taxes and other liabilities	110.3	79.8	1.9	1.5
Commitments and contingencies	—	—		
Redeemable preferred stock	0.3	0.3	0.0	0.0
Shareholders' equity:				
Common stock at stated value				
Class A convertible—99.2 and 100.7 shares outstanding	0.2	0.2	0.0	0.0
Class B—170.4 and 181.6 shares outstanding	2.6	2.7	0.1	0.1
Capital in excess of stated value	369.0	334.1	6.3	6.4
Unearned stock compensation	(11.7)	—	(0.2)	—
Accumulated other comprehensive income	(111.1)	(68.9)	(1.9)	(1.3)
Retained earnings	2,887.0	3,066.5	49.3	58.4
Total shareholders' equity	$3,136.0	$3,334.6	53.5%	63.5%
Total liabilities and equity	$5,856.9	$5,247.7	100.0%	100.0%

* Percents are rounded to the first decimal point.

to that of comparative statements discussed under vertical analysis. It is not illustrated here because the only difference is the substitution of common-size percents for percent changes. Instead, this section discusses graphical analysis of common-size statements.

An income statement readily lends itself to common-size graphical analysis. This is so because revenues affect nearly every item in an income statement. Exhibit 18.10 shows Nike's 2000 common-size income statement in graphical form. This pie chart highlights the contribution of each component of revenues.

Exhibit 18.9

Common-Size Comparative
Income Statement

NIKE Common-Size Comparative Income Statement For Years Ended May 31, 2000 and 1999			Common-Size Percents*	
(in millions, except per share data)	2000	1999	2000	1999
Revenues	$8,995.1	$8,776.9	100.0%	100.0%
Costs and expenses				
Costs of sales	5,403.8	5,493.5	60.1	62.6
Selling and administrative	2,606.4	2,426.6	29.0	27.7
Interest expense	45.0	44.1	0.5	0.5
Other income and expense, net	23.2	21.5	0.2	0.2
Restructuring charge, net	(2.5)	45.1	(0.0)	0.5
Total costs and expenses	$8,075.9	$8,030.8	89.8%	91.5%
Income before income taxes	919.2	746.1	10.2	8.5
Income taxes	340.1	294.7	3.8	3.4
Net income	$ 579.1	$ 451.4	6.4%	5.1%
Basic earnings per common share	$ 2.10	$ 1.59		
Average common shares outstanding	275.7	283.3		

* Percents are rounded to the first decimal point.

Exhibit 18.10

Common-Size Graphic of
Nike Income Statement

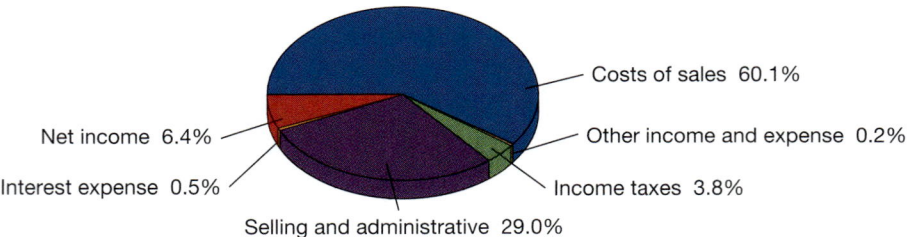

Exhibits 18.11 and 18.12 give a preview of more complex graphical analyses available and the insights they provide. The data for these graphs are taken from **Nike**'s MD&A. The bar chart in Exhibit 18.11 shows a graphical breakdown of 2000 versus 1998 by apparel and footwear for both U.S. and non–U.S. revenues. It is immediately apparent from this chart that each segment's revenues remained about the same or decreased from 1998 to 2000.

Exhibit 18.11

Nike Revenue Breakdown
in Dollars

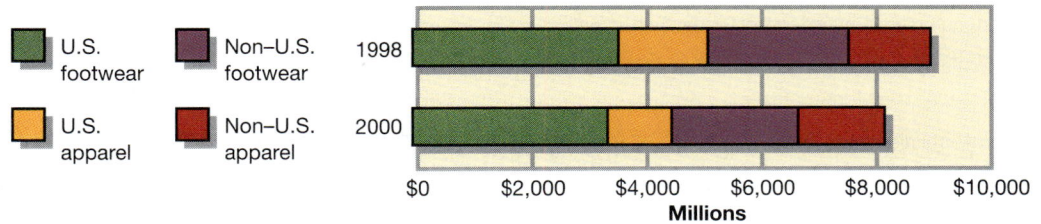

Exhibit 18.12

Nike Revenue Breakdown
as Percent of Total

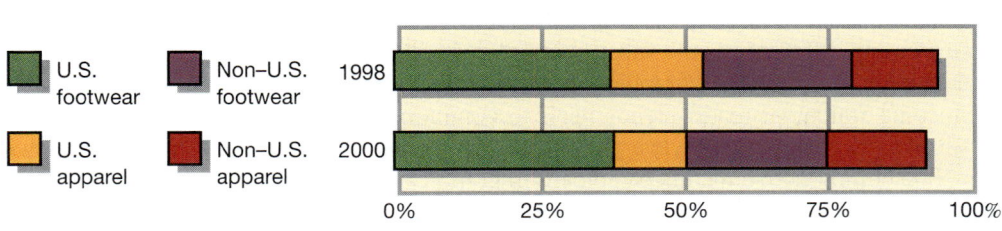

Exhibit 18.12 shows a bar chart measuring each segment's revenues as a percent of its annual revenues. This presentation highlights the decline in magnitude of U.S. apparel revenues for Nike's total operations. In particular, its U.S. apparel revenues made up 15.2% of its total revenues in 1998, but by 2000 it declined to 12.8% of total revenues. In contrast, non–U.S. revenues increased (as a percent of the total) for both footwear and apparel. This raises Nike's risk exposure to changes in the global economy. Graphical analysis is also useful in evaluating a balance sheet. It is especially helpful in identifying (1) sources of financing including the distribution among current liabilities, noncurrent liabilities, and equity capital and (2) types of investing activities including the distribution among current and noncurrent assets.

Common-size balance sheet analysis is often extended to examine the composition of subgroups. For instance, in assessing liquidity of current assets, knowing what proportion of current assets consists of inventories is often important, and not simply what proportion inventories are of total assets. Exhibit 18.13 shows a common-size graphical display of Nike's assets.

Common-size financial statements are also useful in comparing different companies. Exhibit 18.14 shows common-size graphics of both Nike and **Reebok** on financing sources. This graphic highlights the much larger percent of debt financing for Reebok compared to that for Nike. However, common-size statements fail to reflect the relative sizes of companies. Comparison of a company's common-size statements with competitors' or industry common-size statistics alerts our attention to differences in the structure or distribution of its financial statements, but not to their dollar magnitude.

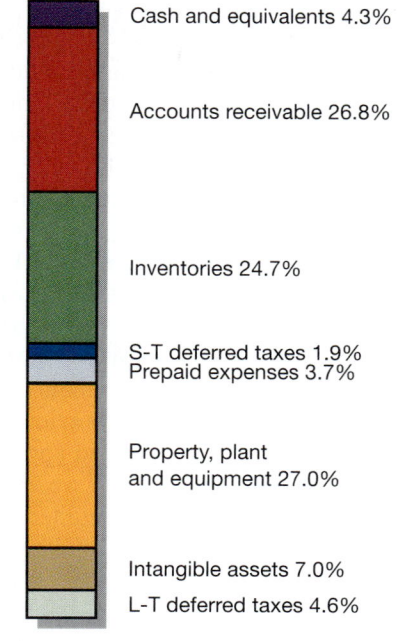

Cash and equivalents 4.3%

Accounts receivable 26.8%

Inventories 24.7%

S-T deferred taxes 1.9%
Prepaid expenses 3.7%

Property, plant and equipment 27.0%

Intangible assets 7.0%

L-T deferred taxes 4.6%

Exhibit 18.13

Common-Size Graphic of Nike Asset Components

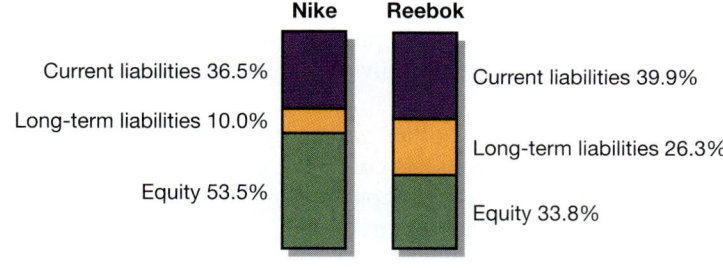

Nike   Reebok

Current liabilities 36.5%

Long-term liabilities 10.0%

Equity 53.5%

Current liabilities 39.9%

Long-term liabilities 26.3%

Equity 33.8%

Exhibit 18.14

Common-Size Graphic of Financing Sources— Competitor Analysis

Quick Check

5. Which of the following is true for common-size comparative statements? (a) Each item is expressed as a percent of a base amount. (b) Total assets often are assigned a value of 100%. (c) Amounts from successive periods are placed side by side. (d) All are true.

6. What is the difference between the percents shown on a comparative income statement and those shown on a common-size comparative income statement?

7. Trend percents are (a) shown on comparative income statements and balance sheets, (b) shown on common-size comparative statements, or (c) also called *index numbers*.

Answers—p. 768

Ratio Analysis

P3 Define and apply ratio analysis.

Concept 18-2

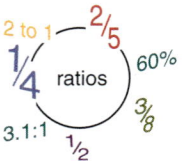

Point: Some sources for industry norms are *Annual Statement Studies* by Robert Morris Associates, *Industry Norms & Key Business Ratios* by Dun & Bradstreet, *Standard and Poor's Industry Surveys,* and **www.MarketGuide.com.**

Ratios are among the more popular and widely used tools of financial analysis. They provide clues to and symptoms of underlying conditions. Ratios, properly interpreted, identify areas requiring further investigation. A ratio can help us uncover conditions and trends difficult to detect by inspecting individual components making up the ratio. Ratios, like other analysis tools, are usually future oriented; they are often adjusted for their probable future trend and magnitude. Usefulness of ratios depends on our skillful interpretation of them.

A ratio expresses a mathematical relation between two quantities. It can be expressed as a percent, rate, or proportion. For instance, a change in an account balance from $100 to $250 can be expressed as (1) 150%, (2) 2.5 times, or (3) 2.5 to 1 (or 2.5:1). Computation of a ratio is a simple arithmetic operation, but its interpretation is not. To be meaningful, a ratio must refer to an economically important relation. For example, a direct and crucial relation exists between an item's sales price and its cost. Accordingly, the ratio of cost of goods sold to sales is significant. In contrast, no obvious relation exists between freight costs and the balance of long-term investments.

This section describes an important set of financial ratios and shows how to apply them. The selected ratios are organized into the four building blocks of financial statement analysis: (1) liquidity and efficiency, (2) solvency, (3) profitability, and (4) market prospects. All of these ratios have been previously explained at relevant points in prior chapters. The purpose here is to organize and apply them under a summary framework.

As we discussed earlier, we use four common standards for comparisons: intracompany, competitor, industry, and guidelines. Our analysis of **Nike** uses three of the four standards in varying degrees: intracompany, competitor (**Reebok**), and guideline comparisons. Since no obvious industry comparison is available for Nike, we do not use industry standards as we normally would. For instance, constructing industry standards using Reebok, Adidas, and Fila might be useful, but since Adidas and Fila are non–U.S. companies and do not publish statements readily comparable to those of Nike, this is not done.

Liquidity and Efficiency

Liquidity refers to the availability of resources to meet short-term cash requirements. A company's short-term liquidity is affected by the timing of cash inflows and outflows along with its prospects for future performance. Our analysis of liquidity is aimed at a company's capital requirements. *Efficiency* refers to how productive a company is in using its assets. Efficiency is usually measured relative to how much revenue is generated from a certain level of assets.

Both liquidity and efficiency are important and complementary in our analysis. If a company fails to meet its current obligations, its continued existence is doubtful. Viewed in this light, all other measures of analysis are of secondary importance. Although accounting measurements assume the company's continued existence, our analysis must always assess the validity of this assumption using liquidity measures. Efficiency indicates how well a company uses its assets; inefficient use can cause liquidity problems.

A lack of liquidity often precedes lower profitability and fewer opportunities. It can foretell a loss of owner control or loss of investment. When a company's owners possess unlimited liability (as with proprietorships and certain partnerships), a lack of liquidity can endanger their personal assets. To a company's creditors, lack of liquidity can yield delays in collecting interest and principal payments or the loss of amounts due them. A company's customers and suppliers of goods and services are affected by short-term liquidity problems. Implications include a company's inability to execute contracts and potential damage to important customer and supplier relationships. This section describes and illustrates key ratios relevant to accessing liquidity and efficiency.

Point: Amazon's stock price decline corresponded with its decline in working capital (WC):

Date	Price	WC	(mil.)
Mar.	00	$67.000	$704
June	00	36.313	559
Sept.	00	38.438	504
Dec.	00	15.563	386

Working Capital and Current Ratio

The amount of current assets less current liabilities is called **working capital,** or *net working capital.* A company needs an adequate amount of working capital to meet current debts, carry sufficient inventories, and take advantage of cash discounts. A company that runs low on working capital is less likely to meet current obligations or continue operating. When evaluating a company's working capital, we must look beyond the dollar amount of current assets less current liabilities. We also must consider the relation between the amounts of current assets and current liabilities. Recall from Chapter 5 that the *current ratio* reflects a company's ability to pay its short-term obligations and is defined as follows:

$$\text{Current ratio} = \frac{\text{Current assets}}{\text{Current liabilities}}$$

Example: Refer to Reebok's financial statements in Appendix A. What is its working capital on Dec. 31, 1999? *Answer (in mil.):*

Current assets	$1,243.118
Current liabilities	(623.903)
Working capital	$ 619.215

Drawing on information in Exhibit 18.1, **Nike**'s working capital and current ratio for both 2000 and 1999 are shown in Exhibit 18.15. Reebok's current ratio of 1.99 is shown in the margin. It is higher than Nike's current ratio (1.68), but neither company appears in danger of defaulting on loan payments. A high current ratio suggests a strong liquidity position and a company's ability to meet its current obligations. A company can also have a current ratio that is too high. An excessively high ratio means that the company has invested too much in current assets compared to its current obligations. Since current assets normally generate a low return on investment (compared with long-term assets), an excessive investment in current assets is not an efficient use of funds.

($ in millions)	2000	1999
Current assets	$3,596.4	$3,264.9
Current liabilities	2,140.0	1,446.9
Working capital	**$1,456.4**	**$1,818.0**
Current ratio		
$3,596.4/$2,140.0	1.68 to 1	
$3,264.9/$1,446.9		2.26 to 1

Exhibit 18.15

Nike's Working Capital and Current Ratio

Reebok
Current ratio = 1.99

Many users apply a guideline of 2:1 for the current ratio in helping evaluate a company's debt-paying ability. A company with a 2:1 or higher current ratio is generally thought to be a good credit risk in the short run. Such a guideline must recognize at least three additional factors: (1) type of business, (2) composition of current assets, and (3) turnover rate of current asset components.

Type of Business. The type of business a company operates affects an assessment of its current ratio. A service company that grants little or no credit and carries no inventories other than supplies can probably operate on a current ratio of less than 1:1 if its revenues generate enough cash to pay its current liabilities on time. On the other hand, a company selling high-priced clothing or furniture requires a higher ratio because of difficulties in judging customer demand and other factors. For instance, if demand falls, this company's inventory may not generate as much cash as expected. Accordingly, analysis of the current ratio should include a comparison with ratios from successful companies in the same industry and from prior periods. We must also recognize that a company's accounting methods, especially choice of inventory method, affect the current ratio. For instance, a company using LIFO tends to report a smaller amount of current assets than if it uses FIFO when costs are rising. These factors should be considered before we decide whether a given current ratio is adequate.

Point: When a firm uses LIFO in a period of rising prices, the standard for an adequate current ratio usually is lower than if it used FIFO.

Composition of Current Assets. The composition of a company's current assets is important to an evaluation of short-term liquidity. For instance, cash, cash equivalents, and short-term investments are more liquid than accounts and notes receivable. Also, short-term receivables normally are more liquid than merchandise inventory. We know cash can be used to immediately pay current debts. Items such as accounts receivable and merchandise inventory, however normally must be converted into cash before payments can be made. An excessive amount of receivables and inventory weakens a company's ability to pay current liabilities. One way to understand the composition of current assets is to evaluate the acid-test ratio. We discuss this in the next section.

You Make the Call

Banker You are a banker, and a company calls on you for a 1-year, $200,000 loan to finance expansion. This company's current ratio is 4:1, with current assets of $160,000. Key competitors carry a current ratio of about 1.9:1. Using this information, do you approve the loan application? Does your decision change if the application is for a 10-year loan?

Answer—p. 768

Global: Ratio analysis helps overcome most currency translation problems, but it does *not* overcome differences in accounting principles.

Turnover Rate of Assets. Asset turnover measures a company's efficiency in using its assets. One relevant measure of asset efficiency is the revenue generated. The measure of total asset turnover is revenues divided by total assets, but evaluation of turnover for individual assets is also useful in our analysis. We discuss total asset turnover with both receivables turnover and inventory turnover in the next section.

Acid-Test Ratio

Chapter 6 introduced us to the *acid-test ratio,* also called *quick ratio,* which focuses on current asset composition. Quick assets are cash, short-term investments, accounts receivable, and current notes receivable. These are the most liquid types of current assets. We compute the acid-test ratio as:

$$\text{Acid-test ratio} = \frac{\text{Cash} + \text{Short-term investments} + \text{Current receivables}}{\text{Current liabilities}}$$

Using information in Exhibit 18.1, we compute **Nike**'s acid-test ratio in Exhibit 18.16.

Exhibit 18.16

Nike Acid-Test Ratio

Reebok
Acid-test ratio = 1.12

($ in millions)	2000	1999
Cash and equivalents	$ 254.3	$ 198.1
Accounts receivable, less allowance	1,567.2	1,540.1
Total quick assets	$1,821.5	$1,738.2
Current liabilities	$2,140.0	$1,446.9
Acid-test ratio		
$1,821.5/$2,140.0	0.85 to 1	
$1,738.2/$1,446.9		1.20 to 1

Nike's 2000 acid-test ratio (0.85) is less than both **Reebok**'s (1.12) and the common guideline for an acceptable acid-test ratio of 1:1, but it appears adequate. Similar to our analysis of the current ratio, we need to consider other factors. For instance, the frequency with which a company converts its current assets into cash affects its working capital requirements. This implies that our analysis of short-term liquidity should also include an analysis of receivables and inventories. We next consider these analyses.

Accounts Receivable Turnover

We can measure how frequently a company converts its receivables into cash by computing *accounts receivable turnover.* As explained in Chapter 10, it is computed as follows:

$$\text{Accounts receivable turnover} = \frac{\text{Net sales}}{\text{Average accounts receivable}}$$

This ratio is called *accounts receivable turnover,* but short-term receivables from customers are normally included in the denominator along with accounts receivable. Also, accounts receivable turnover is more precise if credit sales are used for the numerator, but external users generally use net sales (or net revenues) because information about credit sales is typically not reported. Nike's 2000 accounts receivable turnover is computed as follows ($ millions):

Reebok
Accounts receivable turnover = 6.2

$$\frac{\$8,995.1}{(\$1,567.2 + \$1,540.1)/2} = 5.8 \text{ times}$$

Nike's value of 5.8 is slightly lower than **Reebok**'s 6.2. If accounts receivable are collected quickly, the accounts receivable turnover is high. A high turnover is favorable because it means the company need not commit large amounts of capital to accounts receivable. An accounts receivable turnover can be too high, however; this can occur when credit terms are so restrictive that they negatively affect sales volume. Note, that ending accounts receivable is sometimes substituted for the average balance in computing accounts receivable turnover. This is acceptable if the difference between ending and average receivables is insignificant. Also, some users prefer using gross accounts receivable (before subtracting the allowance for doubtful accounts) to avoid the influence of a manager's bad debts estimates.

Point: Average collection period is estimated by dividing 365 by the accounts receivable turnover ratio. For example, 365 divided by an accounts reveivable turnover of 6.1 indicates a 60-day average collection period.

Inventory Turnover

How long a company holds inventory before selling it affects working capital requirements. One measure of this effect is the *inventory turnover,* also called *merchandise turnover* or *merchandise inventory turnover.* Inventory turnover is defined in Chapter 7:

$$\text{Inventory turnover} = \frac{\text{Cost of goods sold}}{\text{Average inventory}}$$

Using costs of sales (**Nike**'s term for cost of goods sold) and inventories information from Exhibits 18.1 and 18.2, we compute Nike's inventory turnover for 2000:

$$\frac{\$5,403.8}{(\$1,446.0 + \$1,170.6)/2} = 4.1 \text{ times}$$

Reebok
Inventory turnover = 3.8

Average inventory is estimated by averaging the beginning and the ending inventories for 2000. If the beginning and ending inventories do not represent the amount normally available, an average of quarterly or monthly inventories can be used. Nike's inventory turnover is 4.1 and is slightly higher than **Reebok**'s 3.8. A company with a high turnover requires a smaller investment in inventory than one producing the same sales with a lower turnover. Inventory turnover can be too high, however, if the inventory a company keeps is so small that it restricts sales volume.

Days' Sales Uncollected

We already described the use of accounts receivable turnover to evaluate how frequently a company collects its accounts. Another measure of this activity is *days' sales uncollected,* defined in Chapter 9 as:

$$\text{Days' sales uncollected} = \frac{\text{Accounts receivable}}{\text{Net sales}} \times 365$$

Any short-term notes receivable from customers are normally included in the numerator. We illustrate this ratio's application by using Nike's information from Exhibits 18.1 and 18.2. The days' sales uncollected on May 31, 2000, is as follows:

$$\frac{\$1,567.2}{\$8,995.1} \times 365 = 63.6 \text{ days}$$

Reebok
Day's sales uncollected = 52.5

Nike's days' sales uncollected of 63.6 days is longer than the 52.5 days for Reebok. Days' sales uncollected is more meaningful if we know Nike's and Reebok's credit terms. A rough guideline states that days' sales uncollected should not exceed one and one-third times the days in its (1) credit period, if discounts are not offered or (2) discount period, if favorable discounts are offered.

Days' Sales in Inventory

Chapter 7 explained how *days' sales in inventory* is a useful measure in evaluating inventory liquidity. Days' sales in inventory is linked to inventory in a way that days' sales uncollected is linked to receivables. We compute days' sales in inventory as:

$$\text{Days' sales in inventory} = \frac{\text{Ending inventory}}{\text{Cost of goods sold}} \times 365$$

We compute Nike's days' sales in inventory for 2000 as follows:

$$\frac{\$1,446.0}{\$5,403.8} \times 365 = 97.7 \text{ days}$$

If the products in Nike's inventory are in demand by customers, this formula estimates that its inventory will be converted into receivables (or cash) in 97.7 days. If all of Nike's sales are credit sales, the conversion of inventory to receivables in 97.7 days *plus* the conversion of receivables to cash in 63.6 days implies that inventory will be converted to cash in about 161.3 days (97.7 + 63.6).

Total Asset Turnover

Total asset turnover describes a company's ability to use its assets to generate sales. We explained in Chapter 11 the computation of this ratio as:

$$\textbf{Total asset turnover} = \frac{\textbf{Net sales}}{\textbf{Average total assets}}$$

In computing **Nike**'s total asset turnover for 2000, we follow the usual practice of averaging total assets at the beginning and the end of the year. Taking the information from Exhibits 18.1 and 18.2, this computation is

$$\frac{\$8,995.1}{(\$5,856.9 + \$5,247.7)/2} = 1.62 \text{ times}$$

Total asset turnover is an important part of operating efficiency. Nike's performance on this factor is not as strong as **Reebok**'s.

Quick Check

8. This information is from Paff Co. at Dec. 31, 2002: cash, $820,000; accounts receivable, $240,000; inventories, $470,000; plant assets, $910,000; accounts payable, $350,000; and income taxes payable, $180,000. Compute its (a) current ratio and (b) acid-test ratio.

9. On Dec. 31, 2001, Paff Company (question 8) had accounts receivable of $290,000 and inventories of $530,000. During 2002, net sales amounted to $2,500,000 and cost of goods sold was $750,000. Compute (a) accounts receivable turnover, (b) days' sales uncollected, (c) inventory turnover, and (d) days' sales in inventory.

Answers—p. 768

Solvency

Solvency refers to a company's long-run financial viability and its ability to cover long-term obligations. All business activities of a company—financing, investing, and operating—affect its solvency. Analysis of solvency is long term and uses less precise but more encompassing measures as compared to liquidity. One of the most important components of solvency analysis is the composition of a company's capital structure. *Capital structure* refers to a company's sources of financing. It ranges from relatively permanent equity capital to riskier or more temporary short-term financing. Assets represent security for financiers ranging from loans secured by specific assets to the assets available as general security to unsecured creditors.

This section describes the tools of solvency analysis. Our analysis focuses on a company's ability to both meet its obligations and provide security to its creditors *over the long run*. Indicators of this ability include *debt* and *equity* ratios, the relation between *pledged assets and secured liabilities,* and the company's capacity to earn sufficient income to *pay fixed interest charges.*

Debt and Equity Ratios

One element of solvency analysis is to assess the portion of a company's assets contributed by its owners and the portion contributed by creditors. This relation is reflected in the debt ratio described in Chapter 3. Recall that the *debt ratio* expresses total liabilities as a percent of total assets. The **equity ratio** provides complementary information by expressing total equity as a percent of total assets. **Nike**'s debt and equity ratios are computed here:

Point: Bank examiners from the FDIC and other regulatory agencies use debt and equity ratios to monitor compliance with regulatory capital requirements imposed on banks and S&Ls.

($ in millions)	2000	Ratios	
Total liabilities	$2,720.9	46.5%	[Debt ratio]
Total equity	3,136.0	53.5	[Equity ratio]
Total liabilities and equity	5,856.9	100.0%	

Reebok
Debt ratio = 66.2%
Equity ratio = 33.8%

Nike's financial statements reflect less debt than equity. Also, its debt mainly consists of current liabilities—comprising nearly 80% of its total liabilities, computed as $2,140/$2,720.9. A company is considered less risky if its capital structure (equity and long-term debt) contains more equity. One risk factor is the required payment for interest and principal when debt is outstanding. Another factor is the amount of financing provided by stockholders (owners). The greater is stockholder financing, the more losses a company can absorb through equity before the assets become inadequate to satisfy creditors' claims.

From the stockholders' point of view, including debt in a company's capital structure is desirable so long as risk is not too great. If a company earns a return on borrowed capital that is higher than the cost of borrowing, the difference represents increased income to stockholders. Because debt can have the effect of increasing the return to stockholders, the inclusion of debt is described as *financial leverage*. Companies are said to be highly leveraged if a large portion of their assets is financed by debt.

Pledged Assets to Secured Liabilities

We explained in Chapter 15 how we use the ratio of pledged assets to secured liabilities to evaluate the risk of nonpayment faced by secured creditors. This ratio also is relevant to unsecured creditors because of what it implies about the remaining assets available. We compute the ratio as:

$$\text{Pledged assets to secured liabilities} = \frac{\text{Book value of pledged assets}}{\text{Book value of secured liabilities}}$$

The information needed to compute this ratio is seldom reported in financial statements. This means that the ratio is used primarily by persons who have the ability to obtain information directly from the company, such as bankers and lenders. A generally agreed minimum value for this ratio is about 2:1 (from a secured creditor perspective), but the ratio needs careful interpretation because it is based on the *book value* of pledged assets. Book values are not necessarily intended to reflect amounts to be received from assets in event of liquidation. Also, a company's long-run earning ability can be more important than the value of its pledged assets. Creditors prefer that a debtor be able to pay with cash generated by operating activities rather than with cash obtained by liquidating assets.

Times Interest Earned

Chapter 12 explained the *times interest earned* ratio. Its purpose is to reflect the risk of repayments with interest to creditors. The amount of income before the deductions for interest expense and income taxes is the amount available to pay interest expense. We compute this ratio as:

Point: The times interest earned ratio and the debt and equity ratios are of special interest to bank lending officers.

$$\text{Times interest earned} = \frac{\text{Income before interest expense and income taxes}}{\text{Interest expense}}$$

Reebok
Times interest earned = 1.4

The larger this ratio, the less risky is the company for lenders. A guideline for this ratio says that creditors are reasonably safe if the company earns its fixed interest expense by two or more times each year. Exhibit 18.2 shows Nike's interest expense of $45.0 million. Its times interest earned ratio is computed as follows:

$$\frac{\$579.1 + \$340.1 + \$45.0}{\$45.0} = 21.4$$

The value of this ratio suggests that Nike's creditors have little risk of repayment.

Profitability

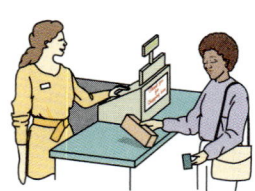

We are especially interested in a company's ability to use its assets efficiently to produce profits (and positive cash flows). *Profitability* refers to a company's ability to generate an adequate return on invested capital. Return is judged by assessing earnings relative to the level and sources of financing. Profitability is also relevant to solvency. This section describes key profitability measures and their importance to financial statement analysis. We also explain variations in return measures and their interpretation. We analyze the components of return on invested capital for additional insights.

Profit Margin

A company's operating efficiency and profitability can be expressed in two components. The first is its *profit margin.* We explained in Chapter 4 that profit margin reflects a company's ability to earn a net income from sales. It is measured by expressing net income as a percent of sales (*sales* and *revenues* are similar terms). We use the information in Exhibit 18.2 to compute **Nike**'s 2000 profit margin:

Reebok
Profit margin = 0.4%

$$\text{Profit margin} = \frac{\text{Net income}}{\text{Net sales}} = \frac{\$579.1}{\$8,995.1} = 6.4\%$$

To evaluate profit margin, we must consider the industry. For instance, a publishing company might be expected to have a profit margin between 10% and 15%; a retail supermarket might expect a normal profit margin of 1% or 2%.

   The second component of operating efficiency is *total asset turnover.* We described this ratio earlier in this section. Both profit margin and total asset turnover make up the two basic components of operating efficiency. These ratios also reflect management performance since managers are ultimately responsible for operating efficiency. The next section explains how we use both measures to analyze return on total assets.

Return on Total Assets

The two components of operating efficiency, profit margin and total asset turnover, are used to compute a summary measure. This summary measure is the *return on total assets* we described in Chapter 1. It is computed as follows:

$$\text{Return on total assets} = \frac{\text{Net income}}{\text{Average total assets}}$$

Nike's return on total assets for 2000 is:

Reebok
Return on total assets = 0.7%

$$\frac{\$579.1}{(\$5,856.9 + \$5,247.7)/2} = 10.4\%$$

Nike's 10.4% return on total assets is lower than that for many businesses but is higher than Reebok's return of 0.7%. We need comparisons with other competitors and alternative investment opportunities, however, before drawing reliable conclusions. We also should evaluate any trend in the rate of return. The following computation shows the important relation between profit margin, total asset turnover, and return on total assets:

$$\textbf{Profit margin} \times \textbf{Total asset turnover} = \textbf{Return on total assets}$$

or

$$\frac{\textbf{Net income}}{\textbf{Net sales}} \times \frac{\textbf{Net sales}}{\textbf{Average total assets}} = \frac{\textbf{Net income}}{\textbf{Average total assets}}$$

Notice that both profit margin and total asset turnover contribute to overall operating efficiency, as measured by return on total assets. If we apply this formula to Nike, we get

$$6.4\% \times 1.62 = 10.4\%$$

Reebok: 0.4% × 1.79 = 0.7%

This analysis shows that while Nike has a less favorable total asset turnover compared to that for Reebok, it has both a higher profit margin and a higher return on assets.

Return on Common Stockholders' Equity

Perhaps the most important goal in operating a company is to earn net income for its owner(s). The *return on common stockholders' equity* measures a company's success in reaching this goal. We explained in Chapter 2 how we compute return on equity. This return measure is slightly modified for a corporation as follows:

$$\textbf{Return on common stockholders' equity} = \frac{\textbf{Net income} - \textbf{Preferred dividends}}{\textbf{Average common stockholders' equity}}$$

Nike's *Note 7* reports that it has $0.03 million in dividends on redeemable preferred stock in 2000. From this information and data in its statements, we compute Nike's 2000 return on common stockholders' equity as:

$$\frac{\$579.1 - \$0.03}{(\$3,136.0 + \$3,334.6)/2} = 17.9\%$$

Reebok
Return on common stockholders' equity = 2.1%

The denominator in this computation is the book value of common equity. In the numerator, the dividends on Nike's cumulative preferred stock are subtracted whether they are declared or are in arrears. If preferred stock is not cumulative, its dividends are subtracted only if declared.

Did You Know?

Wall Street   *Wall Street* is synonymous with financial markets and capitalism. Its name comes from the street location of the original New York Stock Exchange. Interestingly, the street's name derives from stockades built by early settlers to protect New York from pirate attacks.

Market Prospects

Market measures are useful for analyzing corporations with publicly traded stock. In their computation, these market measures use stock price, which reflects the market's (public's) expectations for the company. This includes both a company's return and risk characteristics as the market perceives it.

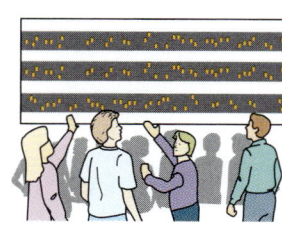

Price-Earnings Ratio

We explained in Chapter 14 the computation of the *price-earnings ratio* as follows:

$$\textbf{Price-earnings ratio} = \frac{\textbf{Market price per share}}{\textbf{Earnings per share}}$$

Point: The PE ratio can be viewed as an indicator of the market's expected growth and risk for a stock. A high level of expected risk suggests a low PE ratio. A high growth rate suggests a high PE ratio.

We also noted that the predicted earnings per share for the next period is often used in the denominator of this computation. Reported earnings per share for the most recent period is also commonly used. In both cases, the ratio is used as an indicator of the future growth of and risk related to a company's earnings as perceived by the stock's buyers and sellers.

The market price of Nike's common stock during fiscal 2000 ranged from a low of $26.563 to a high of $64.125, with a year-end price of $42.875 at May 31, 2000. Using Nike's $2.10 basic earnings per share reported in Exhibit 18.2, we compute its price-earnings ratio as follows (some analysts compute this ratio at both the low and high stock price):

$$\frac{\$42.875}{\$2.10} = 20.4$$

Reebok
PE (year-end) = 40.9

Nike's price-earnings ratio is higher than many companies' ratios. (Reebok's ratio is high due to abnormally low earnings.) Nike's high ratio reflects investors' expectation that the company will continue to grow at a rate faster than the typical company. Alternatively, some might suggest that its stock is priced quite high given its earnings per share level.

Point: Some investors avoid stocks with high price-earnings ratios under the belief they are "overpriced." Alternatively, some investors *sell these stocks short*—hoping for price declines.

Dividend Yield

We explained in Chapter 14 how to use *dividend yield* to compare the dividend-paying performance of different investment alternatives. We compute dividend yield as:

$$\text{Dividend yield} = \frac{\textbf{Annual cash dividends per share}}{\textbf{Market price per share}}$$

Nike's dividend yield, based on its fiscal year-end market price per share of $42.875 and its $0.48 dividends per share from its financial history section, is computed as:

$$\frac{\$0.48}{\$42.875} = 1.1\%$$

Reebok
Dividend yield = 0.0%

Point: Corporate PE ratios and dividend yields are found in daily stock market quotations listed in *The Wall Street Journal, Investor's Business Daily,* or other business publications and Web sites.

Some companies decide not to declare and pay dividends because they prefer to reinvest their cash. **Microsoft**, for instance, does not pay cash dividends on its common stock.

Summary of Ratios

Exhibit 18.17 summarizes the major financial statement analysis ratios illustrated in this chapter and throughout the book. This summary includes each ratio's title, its formula, and the purpose for which it is commonly used.

Quick Check

10. Which ratio best reflects a company's ability to meet immediate interest payments? (a) debt ratio, (b) equity ratio, (c) times interest earned, (d) pledged assets to secured liabilities.

11. Which ratio best measures a company's success in earning net income for its owner(s)? (a) profit margin, (b) return on common stockholders' equity, (c) price-earnings ratio, (d) dividend yield.

12. If a company has net sales of $8,500,000, net income of $945,000, and total asset turnover of 1.8 times, what is its return on total assets?

Exhibit 18.17

Financial Statement
Analysis Ratios

Ratio	Formula	Measure of
Liquidity and Efficiency		
Current ratio	$= \dfrac{\text{Current assets}}{\text{Current liabilities}}$	Short-term debt-paying ability
Acid-test ratio	$= \dfrac{\text{Cash} + \text{Short-term investments} + \text{Current receivables}}{\text{Current liabilities}}$	Immediate short-term debt-paying ability
Accounts receivable turnover	$= \dfrac{\text{Net sales}}{\text{Average accounts receivable}}$	Efficiency of collection
Inventory turnover	$= \dfrac{\text{Cost of goods sold}}{\text{Average inventory}}$	Efficiency of inventory management
Days' sales uncollected	$= \dfrac{\text{Accounts receivable}}{\text{Net sales}} \times 365$	Liquidity of receivables
Days' sales in inventory	$= \dfrac{\text{Ending inventory}}{\text{Cost of goods sold}} \times 365$	Liquidity of inventory
Total asset turnover	$= \dfrac{\text{Net sales}}{\text{Average total assets}}$	Efficiency of assets in producing sales
Solvency		
Debt ratio	$= \dfrac{\text{Total liabilities}}{\text{Total assets}}$	Creditor financing and leverage
Equity ratio	$= \dfrac{\text{Total equity}}{\text{Total assets}}$	Owner financing
Pledged assets to secured liabilities	$= \dfrac{\text{Book value of pledged assets}}{\text{Book value of secured liabilities}}$	Protection to secured creditors
Times interest earned	$= \dfrac{\text{Income before interest expense and income taxes}}{\text{Interest expense}}$	Protection in meeting interest payments
Profitability		
Profit margin ratio	$= \dfrac{\text{Net income}}{\text{Net sales}}$	Net income in each sales dollar
Gross margin ratio	$= \dfrac{\text{Net sales} - \text{Cost of goods sold}}{\text{Net sales}}$	Gross margin in each sales dollar
Return on total assets	$= \dfrac{\text{Net income}}{\text{Average total assets}}$	Overall profitability of assets
Return on common stockholders' equity	$= \dfrac{\text{Net income} - \text{Preferred dividends}}{\text{Average common stockholders' equity}}$	Profitability of owner's investment
Book value per common share	$= \dfrac{\text{Shareholders' equity applicable to common shares}}{\text{Number of common shares outstanding}}$	Liquidation at reported amounts
Basic earnings per share	$= \dfrac{\text{Net income} - \text{Preferred dividends}}{\text{Weighted-average common shares outstanding}}$	Net income on each common share
Market Prospects		
Price-earnings ratio	$= \dfrac{\text{Market price per common share}}{\text{Earnings per share}}$	Market value relative to earnings
Dividends yield	$= \dfrac{\text{Annual cash dividends per share}}{\text{Market price per share}}$	Cash return to each common share

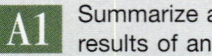 Summarize and report results of analysis.

Understanding the purpose of financial statement analysis is crucial to the usefulness of the analysis. This understanding leads to efficiency of effort, effectiveness in application, and relevance in focus. The purpose of most financial statement analyses is to reduce uncertainty through a rigorous and sound evaluation. A *financial statement analysis report* helps by directly addressing the building blocks of analysis and by identifying weaknesses in inference by requiring explanation—it forces us to organize our reasoning and to verify the flow and logic of analysis. A report also serves as a communication link with readers, and the writing process reinforces our judgments and vice versa. Finally, the report helps us to (re)evaluate evidence and refine conclusions on key building blocks.

A good report separates interpretations and conclusions of analysis from the information underlying them. This separation enables readers to see our process and rationale of analysis and to draw personal conclusions and make modifications as appropriate. A good analysis report usually consists of six sections:

1. **Executive summary**—Brief focus on important analysis results and conclusions.
2. **Analysis overview**—Background material on the company, its industry, and its economic environment.
3. **Evidential matter**—Financial statements and information used in the analysis, including ratios, trends, comparisons, statistics, and all analytical measures assembled. Often organized under the building blocks of analysis.
4. **Assumptions**—Identification of important assumptions regarding a company's industry and economic environment, and other important assumptions for estimates.
5. **Key factors**—List of important favorable and unfavorable factors, both quantitative and qualitative, for company performance—usually by areas of analysis.
6. **Inferences**—Forecasts, estimates, interpretations, and conclusions drawing on all sections of the report.

We must remember that the user dictates relevance, meaning that our analysis report should include a brief table of contents to help readers focus on those areas most relevant to their decisions. All irrelevant matter must be eliminated. For example, decades-old details of obscure transactions and detailed miscues of our analysis are irrelevant. Ambiguities and qualifications to avoid responsibility or hedging inferences should be eliminated. Finally, writing is important. Mistakes in grammar and errors of fact compromise the credibility of our analysis.

Did You Know?

Short Selling   *Short selling* refers to selling stock before you buy it. Here's an an example of how it works: You borrow 100 shares of Nike stock, sell them in the market at $40 each, and receive money from their sale. You then wait. Your hope is that Nike's stock price falls to, say, $35 each and you can replace the borrowed stock for less money than you sold it for—reaping a profit of $5 each less any transaction fees.

Demonstration Problem

Use the following financial statements of Precision Co. to complete these requirements:

1. Prepare a comparative income statement showing the percent increase or decrease for year 2002 in comparison to year 2001.
2. Prepare a common-size comparative balance sheet for years 2002 and 2001.
3. Compute the following ratios as of December 31, 2002, or for the year ended December 31, 2002, and identify its building block category for financial statement analysis:

   a. Current ratio
   b. Acid-test ratio
   c. Accounts receivable turnover
   d. Days' sales uncollected
   e. Inventory turnover
   f. Debt ratio
   g. Pledged assets to secured liabilities
   h. Times interest earned
   i. Profit margin
   j. Total asset turnover
   k. Return on total assets
   l. Return on common stockholders' equity

PRECISION COMPANY Comparative Income Statement For Years Ended December 31, 2002 and 2001		
	2002	2001
Sales	$2,486,000	$2,075,000
Cost of goods sold	1,523,000	1,222,000
Gross profit	$ 963,000	$ 853,000
Operating expenses		
Advertising expense	145,000	100,000
Sales salaries expense	240,000	280,000
Office salaries expense	165,000	200,000
Insurance expense	100,000	45,000
Supplies expense	26,000	35,000
Depreciation expense	85,000	75,000
Miscellaneous expenses	17,000	15,000
Total operating expenses	$ 778,000	$ 750,000
Operating income	$ 185,000	$ 103,000
Less interest expense	44,000	46,000
Income before taxes	$ 141,000	$ 57,000
Income taxes	47,000	19,000
Net income	$ 94,000	$ 38,000
Earnings per share	$ 0.99	$ 0.40

PRECISION COMPANY Comparative Balance Sheet December 31, 2002 and 2001		
	2002	2001
Assets		
Current assets		
Cash	$ 79,000	$ 42,000
Short-term investments	65,000	96,000
Accounts receivable (net)	120,000	100,000
Merchandise inventory	250,000	265,000
Total current assets	$ 514,000	$ 503,000
Plant assets		
Store equipment (net)	400,000	350,000
Office equipment (net)	45,000	50,000
Buildings (net)	625,000	675,000
Land	100,000	100,000
Total plant assets	$1,170,000	$1,175,000
Total assets	$1,684,000	$1,678,000
Liabilities		
Current liabilities		
Accounts payable	$ 164,000	$ 190,000
Short-term notes payable	75,000	90,000
Taxes payable	26,000	12,000
Total current liabilities	$ 265,000	$ 292,000
Long-term liabilities		
Notes payable (secured by mortgage on buildings & land)	400,000	420,000
Total liabilities	$ 665,000	$ 712,000
Stockholders' Equity		
Common stock, $5 par value	$ 475,000	$ 475,000
Retained earnings	544,000	491,000
Total stockholders' equity	$1,019,000	$ 966,000
Total liabilities and equity	$1,684,000	$1,678,000

Planning the Solution

• Set up a four-column income statement; enter the year 2002 and year 2001 amounts in the first two columns and then enter the dollar change in the third column and the percent change from 2001 in the fourth column.

• Set up a four-column balance sheet; enter the 2002 and 2001 year-end amounts in the first two columns and then compute and enter the amount of each item as a percent of total assets.

• Compute the required ratios using the data provided. Use the average of beginning and ending amounts when appropriate (see Exhibit 18.17 for definitions).

Solution to Demonstration Problem

1.

PRECISION COMPANY Comparative Income Statement For Years Ended December 31, 2002 and 2001			Increase (Decrease) in 2002	
	2002	2001	Amount	Percent
Sales	$2,486,000	$2,075,000	$411,000	19.8%
Cost of goods sold	1,523,000	1,222,000	301,000	24.6%
Gross profit	$ 963,000	$ 853,000	$110,000	12.9
Operating expenses				
Advertising expense	145,000	100,000	45,000	45.0
Sales salaries expense	240,000	280,000	(40,000)	(14.3)
Office salaries expense	165,000	200,000	(35,000)	(17.5)
Insurance expense	100,000	45,000	55,000	122.2
Supplies expense	26,000	35,000	(9,000)	(25.7)
Depreciation expense	85,000	75,000	10,000	13.3
Miscellaneous expenses	17,000	15,000	2,000	13.3
Total operating expenses	$ 778,000	$ 750,000	$ 28,000	3.7
Operating income	$ 185,000	$ 103,000	$ 82,000	79.6
Less interest expense	44,000	46,000	(2,000)	(4.3)
Income before taxes	$ 141,000	$ 57,000	$ 84,000	147.4
Income taxes	47,000	19,000	28,000	147.4
Net income	$ 94,000	$ 38,000	$ 56,000	147.4
Earnings per share	$ 0.99	$ 0.40	$ 0.59	147.5

2.

PRECISION COMPANY Common-Size Comparative Balance Sheet December 31, 2002 and 2001	December 31		Common-Size Percents	
	2002	2001*	2002	2001*
Assets				
Current assets				
Cash	$ 79,000	$ 42,000	4.7%	2.5%
Short-term investments	65,000	96,000	3.9	5.7
Accounts receivable (net)	120,000	100,000	7.1	6.0
Merchandise inventory	250,000	265,000	14.8	15.8
Total current assets	$ 514,000	$ 503,000	30.5	30.0
Plant assets				
Store equipment (net)	400,000	350,000	23.8	20.9
Office equipment (net)	45,000	50,000	2.7	3.0
Buildings (net)	625,000	675,000	37.1	40.2
Land	100,000	100,000	5.9	6.0
Total plant assets	$1,170,000	$1,175,000	69.5	70.0
Total assets	$1,684,000	$1,678,000	100.0	100.0

[continued on next page]

PRECISION COMPANY Common-Size Comparative Balance Sheet December 31, 2002 and 2001				
	December 31		**Common-Size Percents**	
	2002	**2001***	**2002**	**2001***
Liabilities				
Current liabilities				
Accounts payable	$ 164,000	$ 190,000	9.7%	11.3%
Short-term notes payable	75,000	90,000	4.5	5.4
Taxes payable	26,000	12,000	1.5	0.7
Total current liabilities	$ 265,000	$ 292,000	15.7	17.4
Long-term liabilities				
Notes payable (secured by mortgage on buildings & land)	400,000	420,000	23.8	25.0
Total liabilities	$ 665,000	$ 712,000	39.5	42.4
Stockholders' Equity				
Common stock, $5 par value	$ 475,000	$ 475,000	28.2	28.3
Retained earnings	544,000	491,000	32.3	29.3
Total stockholders' equity	$1,019,000	$ 966,000	60.5	57.6
Total liabilities and equity	$1,684,000	$1,678,000	100.0	100.0

* Columns do not always add to 100 due to rounding.

3. Ratios for year 2002:

a. Current ratio: $514,000/$265,000 = 1.9:1 (liquidity and efficiency)

b. Acid-test ratio: ($79,000 + $65,000 + $120,000)/$265,000 = 1.0:1 (liquidity and efficiency)

c. Average receivables: ($120,000 + $100,000)/2 = $110,000
Accounts receivable turnover: $2,486,000/$110,000 = 22.6 times (liquidity and efficiency)

d. Days' sales uncollected: ($120,000/$2,486,000) × 365 = 17.6 days (liquidity and efficiency)

e. Average inventory: ($250,000 + $265,000)/2 = $257,500
Inventory turnover: $1,523,000/$257,500 = 5.9 times (liquidity and efficiency)

f. Debt ratio: $665,000/$1,684,000 = 39.5% (solvency)

g. Pledged assets to secured liabilities: ($625,000 + $100,000)/$400,000 = 1.8:1 (solvency)

h. Times interest earned: $185,000/$44,000 = 4.2 times (solvency)

i. Profit margin: $94,000/$2,486,000 = 3.8% (profitability)

j. Average total assets: ($1,684,000 + $1,678,000)/2 = $1,681,000
Total asset turnover: $2,486,000/$1,681,000 = 1.48 times (liquidity and efficiency)

k. Return on total assets: $94,000/$1,681,000 = 5.6% or 3.8% × 1.48 = 5.6% (profitability)

l. Average total common equity: ($1,019,000 + $966,000)/2 = $992,500
Return on common stockholders' equity: $94,000/$992,500 = 9.5% (profitability)

Summary

C1 **Explain the purpose of analysis.** The purpose of financial statement analysis is to help users make better business decisions. Internal users want information to improve company efficiency or effectiveness in providing products and services. External users want information to make better and more informed decisions in pursuing their goals. The common goals of all users are to evaluate a company's (1) past and current performance, (2) current financial position, and (3) future performance and risk.

C2 **Identify the building blocks of analysis.** Financial statement analysis mainly focuses on four "building blocks" of analysis: (1) liquidity and efficiency—ability to meet short-term obligations and to efficiently generate revenues; (2) solvency—ability to generate future revenues and meet long-term obligations, (3) profitability—ability to provide financial rewards sufficient to attract and retain financing; and (4) market prospects—ability to generate positive market expectations.

C3 **Describe standards for comparisons in analysis.** Standards for comparisons include (1) intracompany—prior performance and relations between financial items for the company under analysis; (2) competitor—one or more direct competitors of the company under analysis; (3) industry—industry statistics; and (4) guidelines (rules of thumb)—general standards developed from past experiences and personal judgments.

C4 **Identify the tools of analysis.** The three most common tools of financial statement analysis are (1) horizontal analysis—comparing a company's financial condition and performance across time; (2) vertical analysis—comparing a company's financial condition and performance to a base amount such as revenues or total assets; and (3) ratio analysis—using and quantifying key relations among financial statement items.

A1 **Summarize and report results of analysis.** A financial statement analysis report is often organized around the building blocks of analysis. A good report separates interpretations and conclusions of analysis from the information underlying them. This separation enables readers to see the process and rationale of analysis. It also enables the reader to draw personal conclusions and make modifications as appropriate. An analysis report often consists of six sections: (1) executive summary; (2) analysis overview; (3) evidential matter; (4) assumptions; (5) key factors; and (6) inferences.

P1 **Explain and apply methods of horizontal analysis.** Horizontal analysis is a tool to evaluate changes in data across time. Two important tools of horizontal analysis are comparative statements and trend analysis. Comparative statements show amounts for two or more successive periods, often with changes disclosed in both absolute and percent terms. Trend analysis is used to reveal important changes occurring from one period to the next.

P2 **Describe and apply methods of vertical analysis.** Vertical analysis is a tool to evaluate each financial statement item or group of items in terms of a base amount. This base amount is commonly set at 100%. Two tools of vertical analysis are common-size statements and graphical analyses. Each item in common-size statements is expressed as a percent of a base amount. For the balance sheet, the base amount is usually total assets, and for the income statement, it is usually sales.

P3 **Define and apply ratio analysis.** Ratio analysis provides clues and symptoms of underlying conditions. Ratios, properly interpreted, identify areas requiring further investigation. A ratio expresses a mathematical relation between two quantities such as a percent, rate, or proportion. Ratios can be organized into the building blocks of analysis: (1) liquidity and efficiency, (2) solvency, (3) profitability, and (4) market prospects.

Guidance Answers to **You Make the Call**

Auditor The *joint relation* referred to is the combined increase in sales and the decrease in expenses yielding more than a 5% increase in income. In particular, both *individual* accounts (sales and expenses) yield percent changes within the ±5% acceptable range. However, a joint analysis suggests a different picture. For example, consider a joint analysis using the profit margin ratio (net income/sales). The client's profit margin is 11.46% ($206,000 − $182,400/$206,000) for the current year compared with 5.0% ($200,000 − $190,000/$200,000) for the prior year—a 129% increase in profit margin! This is what concerns the partner, and it suggests expanding audit tests to verify or refute the client's figures.

Banker Your decision on the loan application is positive for at least two reasons. First, the current ratio suggests a strong ability to meet short-term obligations. Second, current assets of $160,000 and a current ratio of 4:1 imply current liabilities of $40,000 (one-fourth of current assets) and a working capital excess of $120,000. This working capital excess is 60% of the loan amount. However, if the application is for a 10-year loan, our decision is less optimistic. The current ratio and working capital suggest a good safety margin, but there are indications of inefficiency in operations. In particular, a 4:1 current ratio is more than double its key competitors' ratio. This is characteristic of inefficient asset use.

Guidance Answers to **Quick Checks**

1. General-purpose financial statements are intended for a variety of users interested in a company's financial condition and performance but without the power to require it to prepare specialized financial reports to meet their specific needs.

2. General-purpose financial statements include the income statement, balance sheet, statement of changes in stockholders' (owner's) equity, and statement of cash flows, plus the notes related to these statements.

3. (a)

4. Data from one or more direct competitors are usually preferred for comparative purposes.

5. (d)

6. Percents on a comparative income statement show the increase or decrease in each item from one period to the next. On a common-size comparative income statement, each item is shown as a percent of net sales for that period.

7. (c)

8. (a); ($820,000 + $240,000 + $470,000)/ ($350,000 + $180,000) = 2.9 to 1.
   (b); ($820,000 + $240,000)/($350,000 + $180,000) = 2:1.

9. (a); $2,500,000/[($290,000 + $240,000)/2] = 9.43 times.
   (b); ($240,000/$2,500,000) × 365 = 35 days.
   (c); $750,000/[($530,000 + $470,000)/2] = 1.5 times.
   (d); ($470,000/$750,000) × 365 = 228.7 days.

10. (c)

11. (b)

12. Profit margin × $\frac{\text{Total asset}}{\text{turnover}}$ = $\frac{\text{Return on}}{\text{total assets}}$

   $\dfrac{\$945,000}{\$8,500,000}$ × 1.8 = 20%

Glossary

Common-size financial statement statement that expresses each amount as a percent of a base amount. In the balance sheet, total assets is usually the base amount and is expressed as 100%. In the income statement, net sales is usually the base amount. (p. 750).

Comparative financial statement statement with data for two or more successive periods placed in side-by-side columns, often with changes shown in dollar amounts and percents. (p. 745).

Efficiency company's productivity in using its assets; usually measured relative to how much revenue a certain level of assets generates. (p. 742).

Equity ratio portion of total assets provided by equity, computed as total equity divided by total assets. (p. 759).

Financial reporting process of communicating information relevant to investors, creditors, and others in making investment, credit, and other decisions. (p. 743).

Financial statement analysis application of analytical tools to general-purpose financial statements and related data for making business decisions. (p. 742).

General-purpose financial statements statements published periodically for use by a variety of interested parties; includes the income statement, balance sheet, statement of changes in equity (or statement of retained earnings), statement of cash flows, and notes to these statements. (p. 743).

Horizontal analysis comparison of a company's financial condition and performance across time. (p. 744).

Liquidity availability of resources to meet short-term cash requirements. (p. 742).

Market prospects expectations (both good and bad) about a company's future performance as assessed by users and other interested parties. (p. 743).

Profitability company's ability to generate an adequate return on invested capital. (p. 743).

Ratio analysis determination of key relations between financial statement items. (p. 744).

Solvency company's long-run financial viability and its ability to cover long-term obligations. (p. 743).

Vertical analysis evaluation of each financial statement item or group of items in terms of a specific base amount. (p. 744).

Working capital current assets minus current liabilities. (p. 754).

Questions

1. What is the difference between comparative financial statements and common-size comparative statements?

2. Which items are usually assigned a 100% value on (a) a common-size comparative balance sheet and (b) a common-size comparative income statement?

3. Explain the difference between financial reporting and financial statements.

4. What three factors would influence your decision as to whether a company's current ratio is good or bad?

5. Suggest several reasons that a 2:1 current ratio may not be adequate for a particular company.

6. Why is working capital given special attention in the process of analyzing balance sheets?

7. What does the number of days' sales uncollected indicate?

8. What does a relatively high accounts receivable turnover indicate about a company's short-term liquidity?

9. Why is a company's capital structure, as measured by debt and equity ratios, important to financial statement users?

10. How does inventory turnover provide information about a company's short-term liquidity?

11. What ratios would you compute to evaluate management performance?

12. Why must the ratio of pledged assets to secured liabilities be interpreted with caution?

13. Why would a company's return on total assets be different from its return on common stockholders' equity?

14. Using **Nike**'s financial statements in Appendix A, compute its return on total assets for the years ended May 31, 2000 and 1999. Total assets at May 31, 1998, are $5,397.4 million.

15. Refer to **Reebok**'s financial statements in Appendix A. Compute its equity ratio as of December 31, 1999 and 1998.

16. Refer to **Gap**'s financial statements in Appendix A. Compute its profit margin for the fiscal year ended January 29, 2000.

17. Refer to the chapter's opening article about the **Beardstown Ladies**. Identify at least two factors that impact the return computation for a group (portfolio) of stocks and that might have contributed to the error Betty Sinnock made.

---

1. Which term describes the difference between current assets and current liabilities?

2. Which two ratios are the components in measuring a company's operating efficiency? Which ratio summarizes these two components?

3. Which two short-term liquidity ratios measure how frequently a company collects its accounts?

QUICK STUDY

QS 18-1

Identification of ratios

QS 18-2

Ratio comparision

What are four possible standards of comparisons used to analyze financial statement ratios? Which of these is generally considered to be the most useful? Which one is least likely to provide a good basis for comparison?

QS 18-3

Financial reporting

Which of the following items (1) through (6) are part of financial reporting but are not included within general-purpose financial statements? (1) stock price information and analysis, (2) statements of cash flows, (3) management discussion and analysis of financial performance, (4) income statements, (5) company news releases, (6) balance sheets.

QS 18-4

Common-size and trend percents

Use the following information for Neef Corporation to determine (1) the common-size percents for gross profit and (2) the trend percents for net sales, using 2001 as the base year.

	2002	2001
Net sales	$202,800	$116,200
Cost of goods sold	110,600	61,400

QS 18-5

Ratio interpretation

For each ratio listed, identify whether the change in ratio value from 2001 to 2002 is generally regarded as favorable or unfavorable.

Ratio	2002	2001	Ratio	2002	2001
1. Profit margin	9%	8%	5. Accounts receivable turnover	5.5	6.7
2. Debt ratio	47%	42%	6. Basic earnings per share	$1.25	$1.10
3. Gross margin	34%	46%	7. Inventory turnover	3.6	3.4
4. Acid-test ratio	1.00	1.15	8. Dividend yield	2%	1.2%

QS 18-6

Building blocks of analysis

Match the ratio to the building block of financial statement analysis to which it best relates.

A. Liquidity and efficiency   **C.** Profitability
B. Solvency   **D.** Market prospects

1. _____ Gross margin
2. _____ Acid-test ratio
3. _____ Equity ratio
4. _____ Return on total assets
5. _____ Dividend yield

6. _____ Book value per common share
7. _____ Days' sales in inventory
8. _____ Accounts receivable turnover
9. _____ Pledged assets to secured liabilities
10. _____ Times interest earned

EXERCISES

Exercise 18-1

Computation of percent changes

Compute the dollar changes and the percent changes for each of the following account balances:

	2002	2001
Short-term investments	$220,000	$160,000
Accounts receivable	38,000	44,000
Notes payable	60,000	0

Express the following income statement in common-size percents and assess whether or not this company's situation has improved.

Exercise 18-2
Common-size percent
computation and interpretation

GERALDO CORPORATION Comparative Income Statement For Years Ended December 31, 2002 and 2001		
	2002	**2001**
Sales	$740,000	$625,000
Cost of goods sold	560,300	290,800
Gross profit	$179,700	$334,200
Operating expenses	128,200	218,500
Net income	$ 51,500	$115,700

Compute trend percents for the following items, using 2000 as the base year. State whether the situation as revealed by the trends appears to be favorable or unfavorable.

Exercise 18-3
Computation and analysis of
trend percents

P1

	2004	**2003**	**2002**	**2001**	**2000**
Sales	$282,880	$270,800	$252,600	$234,560	$150,000
Cost of goods sold	128,200	122,080	115,280	106,440	67,000
Accounts receivable	18,100	17,300	16,400	15,200	9,000

Common-size and trend percents for TLC Company's sales, cost of goods sold, and expenses follow:

Exercise 18-4
Determination of income
effects from common-size and
trend percents

	Common-Size Percents			**Trend Percents**		
	2003	**2002**	**2001**	**2003**	**2002**	**2001**
Sales	100.0%	100.0%	100.0%	105.4%	104.2%	100.0%
Cost of goods sold	63.4	61.9	59.1	103.0	101.1	100.0
Expenses	15.3	14.8	15.1	95.0	91.0	100.0

Determine whether net income increased, decreased, or remained unchanged in this three-year period.

The following information is available for Tuff Company and Tesa Company, similar firms operating in the same industry:

Exercise 18-5
Analysis of short-term financial
condition

	Tuff			Tesa		
	2003	2002	2001	2003	2002	2001
Current ratio	1.7	1.8	2.1	3.2	2.7	1.9
Acid-test ratio	1.0	1.1	1.2	2.8	2.5	1.6
Accounts receivable turnover	30.5	25.2	29.2	16.4	15.2	16.0
Merchandise inventory turnover	24.2	21.9	17.1	14.5	13.0	12.6
Working capital	$70,000	$58,000	$52,000	$131,000	$103,000	$78,000

Team Project: Assume that the
two companies apply for a one-year
loan from the team. Identify
additional information the companies
must provide before the team can
make a loan decision.

Write a one-half page report comparing Tuff and Tesa using the available information. Your discussion should include their ability to meet current obligations and to use current assets efficiently.

Exercise 18-6

Analysis of efficiency and financial leverage

Rison Company and Kearse Company are similar firms that operate in the same industry. Kearse began operations in 2002 and Rison in 1999. In 2004, both companies pay 7% interest on their debt to creditors. The following additional information is available:

	Rison Company			Kearse Company		
	2004	**2003**	**2002**	**2004**	**2003**	**2002**
Total asset turnover	3.1	2.8	3.0	1.7	1.5	1.2
Return on total assets	9.0%	9.6%	8.8%	5.9%	5.6%	5.3%
Profit margin	2.4%	2.5%	2.3%	2.8%	3.0%	2.9%
Sales	$410,000	$380,000	$396,000	$210,000	$170,000	$110,000

Write a one-half page report comparing Rison and Kearse using the available information. Your analysis should include their ability to use assets efficiently to produce profits. Also comment on their success in employing financial leverage in 2004.

Exercise 18-7

Short-term liquidity analysis

Dixon Company's year-end balance sheets show the following:

	2003	**2002**	**2001**
Cash	$ 31,800	$ 35,625	$ 37,800
Accounts receivable, net	89,500	62,500	50,200
Merchandise inventory	112,500	82,500	54,000
Prepaid expenses	10,700	9,375	5,000
Plant assets, net	278,500	255,000	230,500
Total assets	$523,000	$445,000	$377,500
Accounts payable	$129,900	$ 75,250	$ 51,250
Long-term notes payable secured by mortgages on plant assets	98,500	101,500	83,500
Common stock, $10 par value	163,500	163,500	163,500
Retained earnings	131,100	104,750	79,250
Total liabilities and equity	$523,000	$445,000	$377,500

Analyze the year-end short-term liquidity position of this company at the end of 2003, 2002, and 2001 by computing the (1) current ratio and (2) acid-test ratio. Comment on the ratio results.

Exercise 18-8

Common-size percents   P2

Refer to Dixon Company's balance sheets in Exercise 18-7. Express the balance sheets in common-size percents. Round amounts to the nearest one-tenth of a percent.

Exercise 18-9

Short-term liquidity analysis

Refer to the information in Exercise 18-7 about Dixon Company. The company's income statements for the years ended December 31, 2003 and 2002, show the following:

	2003		**2002**	
Sales		$673,500		$532,000
Cost of goods sold	$411,225		$345,500	
Other operating expenses	209,550		134,980	
Interest expense	12,100		13,300	
Income taxes	9,525		8,845	
Total costs and expenses		(642,400)		(502,625)
Net income		$ 31,100		$ 29,375
Earnings per share		$ 1.90		$ 1.80

For the years ended December 31, 2003 and 2002, assume that all sales are on credit and then compute the following: (1) days' sales uncollected, (2) accounts receivable turnover, (3) merchandise inventory turnover, and (4) days' sales in inventory. Comment on the changes in the ratios from 2002 to 2003.

Refer to the information in Exercises 18-7 and 18-9 about Dixon Company. Compare the company's long-term risk and capital structure positions at the end of 2003 and 2002 by computing these ratios: (1) debt and equity ratios, (2) pledged assets to secured liabilities, and (3) times interest earned. Comment on these ratio results.

Exercise 18-10
Risk and capital
structure evaluation

Refer to Dixon Company's financial statements in Exercises 18-7 and 18-9. Evaluate the company's efficiency and profitability by computing the following: (1) profit margin, (2) total asset turnover, and (3) return on total assets. Comment on these ratio results.

Exercise 18-11
Efficiency and
profitability evaluation

Refer to Dixon Company's financial statements in Exercises 18-7 and 18-9. The following is additional information about the company:

Exercise 18-12
Profitability evaluation

Common stock market price, December 31, 2003 . . .	$30.00
Common stock market price, December 31, 2002 . . .	$28.00
Annual cash dividends per share in 2003	0.29
Annual cash dividends per share in 2002	0.24

To help evaluate the company's profitability, compute the following for 2003 and 2002: (1) return on common stockholders' equity, (2) price-earnings ratio on December 31, and (3) dividend yield.

Peak Corporation began the month of May with $700,000 of current assets, a current ratio of 2.5:1, and an acid-test ratio of 1.1:1. During the month, it completed the following transactions (the company uses a perpetual inventory system):

May 2   Purchased $50,000 of merchandise on credit.
   8   Sold merchandise that cost $55,000 for $110,000 cash.
   10   Collected a $20,000 account receivable.
   15   Paid a $22,000 account payable.
   17   Wrote off a $5,000 bad debt against the Allowance for Doubtful Accounts account.
   22   Declared a $1 per share cash dividend on the 50,000 shares of outstanding common stock.
   26   Paid the dividend declared on May 22.
   27   Borrowed $100,000 cash by giving the bank a 30-day, 10% note.
   28   Borrowed $80,000 cash by signing a long-term secured note.
   29   Used the $180,000 cash proceeds from the notes to buy new machinery.

PROBLEM SET A

Problem 18-1A
Transactions, working capital,
and liquidity ratios

Check   May 29, Current ratio, 1.80;
Working capital, $325,000

Required

Prepare a table showing Peak's (1) current ratio, (2) acid-test ratio, and (3) working capital after each transaction. Round ratios to two decimal places.

Selected comparative financial statements of Bartiromo Company follow:

Problem 18-2A
Ratios, common-size
statements, and trend percents

BARTIROMO COMPANY Comparative Income Statement For Years Ended December 31, 2003, 2002, and 2001			
	2003	**2002**	**2001**
Sales	$555,000	$340,000	$278,000
Cost of goods sold	283,500	212,500	153,900
Gross profit	$271,500	$127,500	$124,100
Selling expenses	102,900	46,920	50,800
Administrative expenses	50,668	29,920	22,800
Total expenses	$153,568	$ 76,840	$ 73,600
Income before taxes	$117,932	$ 50,660	$ 50,500
Income taxes	40,800	10,370	15,670
Net income	$ 77,132	$ 40,290	$ 34,830

BARTIROMO COMPANY Comparative Balance Sheet December 31, 2003, 2002, and 2001			
	2003	**2002**	**2001**
Assets			
Current assets	$ 52,390	$ 37,924	$ 51,748
Long-term investments	0	500	3,950
Plant assets, net	100,000	96,000	60,000
Total assets	$152,390	$134,424	$115,698
Liabilities and Equity			
Current liabilities	$ 22,800	$ 19,960	$ 20,300
Common stock	72,000	72,000	60,000
Other contributed capital	9,000	9,000	6,000
Retained earnings	48,590	33,464	29,398
Total liabilities and equity	$152,390	$134,424	$115,698

Required

Preparation Component

1. Compute each year's current ratio.

2. Express the income statement data in common-size percents.

Check 2003, Total assets trend, 131.71%

3. Express the balance sheet data in trend percents with 2001 as the base year.

Analysis Component

4. Comment on any significant relations revealed by the ratios and percents computed.

Problem 18-3A

Calculation and analysis of trend percents

Selected comparative financial statements of Lazar Company follow:

LAZAR COMPANY Comparative Income Statement ($000) For Years Ended December 31, 2007–2001							
	2007	**2006**	**2005**	**2004**	**2003**	**2002**	**2001**
Sales	$1,694	$1,496	$1,370	$1,264	$1,186	$1,110	$928
Cost of goods sold	1,246	1,032	902	802	752	710	586
Gross profit	$ 448	$ 464	$ 468	$ 462	$ 434	$ 400	$342
Operating expenses	330	256	234	170	146	144	118
Net income	$ 118	$ 208	$ 234	$ 292	$ 288	$ 256	$224

LAZAR COMPANY Comparative Balance Sheet ($000) December 31, 2007–2001							
	2007	**2006**	**2005**	**2004**	**2003**	**2002**	**2001**
Assets							
Cash	$ 58	$ 78	$ 82	$ 84	$ 88	$ 86	$ 89
Accounts receivable, net	490	514	466	360	318	302	216
Merchandise inventory	1,838	1,364	1,204	1,032	936	810	615
Other current assets	36	32	14	34	28	28	9
Long-term investments	0	0	0	146	146	146	146
Plant assets, net	2,020	2,014	1,752	944	978	860	725
Total assets	$4,442	$4,002	$3,518	$2,600	$2,494	$2,232	$1,800

[continued on next page]

LAZAR COMPANY Comparative Balance Sheet ($000) December 31, 2007–2001							
	2007	2006	2005	2004	2003	2002	2001
Liabilities and Equity							
Current liabilities	$1,220	$1,042	$ 718	$ 614	$ 546	$ 522	$ 282
Long-term liabilities	1,294	1,140	1,112	570	580	620	400
Common stock	1,000	1,000	1,000	850	850	650	650
Other contributed capital	250	250	250	170	170	150	150
Retained earnings	678	570	438	396	348	290	318
Total liabilities and equity . . .	$4,442	$4,002	$3,518	$2,600	$2,494	$2,232	$1,800

Required

Preparation Component

1. Compute trend percents for the components of both statements using 2001 as the base year.

Check 2007, Total assets trend, 246.8%

Analysis Component

2. Analyze and comment on the financial statements and trend percents from part (1).

Selected year-end financial statements of McCune Corporation follow:

Problem 18-4A
Calculation of financial statement ratios

McCUNE CORPORATION Income Statement For Year Ended December 31, 2002	
Sales	$ 448,600
Cost of goods sold	297,250
Gross profit	$151,350
Operating expenses	98,600
Interest expense	4,100
Income before taxes	$ 48,650
Income taxes	19,598
Net income	$ 29,052

McCUNE CORPORATION Balance Sheet December 31, 2002			
Assets		**Liabilities and Equity**	
Cash	$ 10,000	Accounts payable	$ 17,500
Short-term investments	8,400	Accrued wages payable	3,200
Accounts receivable, net	29,200	Income taxes payable	3,300
Notes receivable (trade)*	4,500	Long-term note payable, secured	
Merchandise inventory	32,150	by mortgage on plant assets . . .	63,400
Prepaid expenses	2,650	Common stock, $1 par value	90,000
Plant assets, net	153,300	Retained earnings	62,800
Total assets	$240,200	Total liabilities and equity	$240,200

* Short-term notes receivable arising from customer sales.

Assume that all sales are on credit. Selected balance sheet amounts at December 31, 2001, were total assets, $189,400; common stock, $90,000; and retained earnings, $22,748.

Required

Check   Acid-test ratio, 2.2 to 1

Compute the following: (1) current ratio, (2) acid-test ratio, (3) days' sales uncollected, (4) merchandise inventory turnover, (5) days' sales in inventory, (6) ratio of pledged assets to secured liabilities, (7) times interest earned, (8) profit margin, (9) total asset turnover, (10) return on total assets, and (11) return on common stockholders' equity.

Problem 18-5A
Comparative analysis
using
ratios

Two companies competing in the same industry are being evaluated by a bank that can lend money to only one of them. Summary information from the financial statements of the two companies follows:

	Rowland Company	Pierce Company		Rowland Company	Pierce Company
Data from the current year-end balance sheets:			**Data from the current year's income statement:**		
Assets			Sales	$770,000	$880,200
Cash	$ 19,500	$ 34,000	Cost of goods sold	585,100	632,500
Accounts receivable, net	37,400	57,400	Interest expense	7,900	13,000
Current notes receivable (trade)	9,100	7,200	Income tax expense	14,800	24,300
Merchandise inventory	84,440	132,500	Net income	162,200	210,400
Prepaid expenses	5,000	6,950	Basic earnings per share	4.51	5.11
Plant assets, net	290,000	304,400			
Total assets	$445,440	$542,450			
			Beginning-of-year balance sheet data:		
Liabilities and Equity			Accounts receivable, net	$ 29,800	$ 54,200
Current liabilities	$ 61,340	$ 93,300	Current notes receivable (trade)	0	0
Long-term notes payable	80,800	101,000	Merchandise inventory	55,600	107,400
Common stock, $5 par value	180,000	206,000	Total assets	398,000	382,500
Retained earnings	123,300	142,150	Common stock, $5 par value	180,000	206,000
Total liabilities and equity	$445,440	$542,450	Retained earnings	98,300	93,600

Required

Check   Accounts receivable
turnover, Pierce 14.8

1. For both companies compute the (a) current ratio, (b) acid-test ratio, (c) accounts (including notes) receivable turnover, (d) merchandise inventory turnover, (e) days' sales in inventory, and (f) days' sales uncollected. Identify the company you consider to be the better short-term credit risk and explain why.

2. For both companies compute the (a) profit margin, (b) total asset turnover, (c) return on total assets, and (d) return on common stockholders' equity. Assuming that each company paid cash dividends of $3.80 per share and each company's stock can be purchased at $75 per share, compute their (e) price-earnings ratios and (f) dividend yields. Identify which company's stock you would recommend as the better investment and explain why.

PROBLEM SET B

Problem 18-1B
Transactions, working capital,
and liquidity ratios

Ready Corporation began the month of June with $300,000 of current assets, a current ratio of 2.5:1, and an acid-test ratio of 1.4:1. During the month, it completed the following transactions (the company uses a perpetual inventory system):

June 1   Sold merchandise that cost $75,000 for $120,000 cash.
    3   Collected an $88,000 account receivable.
    5   Purchased $150,000 of merchandise on credit.
    7   Borrowed $100,000 cash by giving the bank a 60-day, 10% note.
    10   Borrowed $120,000 cash by signing a long-term secured note.
    12   Purchased machinery for $275,000 cash.

15   Declared a $1 per share cash dividend on the 80,000 shares of outstanding common stock.
19   Wrote off a $5,000 bad debt against Allowance for Doubtful Accounts.
22   Paid a $12,000 account payable.
30   Paid the dividend declared on June 15.

Check   June 30, Working capital, $(10,000); Current ratio, 0.97

Required

Prepare a table showing the company's (1) current ratio, (2) acid-test ratio, and (3) working capital after each transaction. Round ratios to two decimal places.

Selected comparative financial statements of Terradyne Corporation follow:

Problem 18-2B
Ratios, common-size statements, and trend percents

TERRADYNE CORPORATION Comparative Income Statement For Years Ended December 31, 2003, 2002, and 2001			
	2003	2002	2001
Sales	$198,800	$166,000	$143,800
Cost of goods sold	108,890	86,175	66,200
Gross profit	$ 89,910	$ 79,825	$ 77,600
Selling expenses	22,680	19,790	18,000
Administrative expenses	16,760	14,610	15,700
Total expenses	$ 39,440	$ 34,400	$ 33,700
Income before taxes	$ 50,470	$ 45,425	$ 43,900
Income taxes	6,050	5,910	5,300
Net income	$ 44,420	$ 39,515	$ 38,600

TERRADYNE CORPORATION Comparative Balance Sheet December 31, 2003, 2002, and 2001			
	2003	2002	2001
Assets			
Current assets	$ 54,860	$ 32,660	$ 36,300
Long-term investments	0	1,700	10,600
Plant assets, net	112,810	113,660	79,000
Total assets	$167,670	$148,020	$125,900
Liabilities and Equity			
Current liabilities	$ 22,370	$ 19,180	$ 16,500
Common stock	46,500	46,500	37,000
Other contributed capital	13,850	13,850	11,300
Retained earnings	84,950	68,490	61,100
Total liabilities and equity	$167,670	$148,020	$125,900

Required

Preparation Component

1. Compute each year's current ratio.

2. Express the income statement data in common-size percents.

3. Express the balance sheet data in trend percents with 2001 as the base year.

Check   2003, Total assets trend, 133.18%

Analysis Component

4. Comment on any significant relations revealed by the ratios and percents computed.

Problem 18-3B

Calculation and analysis of trend percents

Selected comparative financial statements of Chao Company follow:

CHAO COMPANY Comparative Income Statement ($000) For Years Ended December 31, 2007–2001							
	2007	**2006**	**2005**	**2004**	**2003**	**2002**	**2001**
Sales	$560	$610	$630	$680	$740	$770	$860
Cost of goods sold	276	290	294	314	340	350	380
Gross profit	$284	$320	$336	$366	$400	$420	$480
Operating expenses	84	104	112	126	140	144	150
Net income	$200	$216	$224	$240	$260	$276	$330

CHAO COMPANY Comparative Balance Sheet ($000) December 31, 2007–2001							
	2007	**2006**	**2005**	**2004**	**2003**	**2002**	**2001**
Assets							
Cash	$ 44	$ 46	$ 52	$ 54	$ 60	$ 62	$ 68
Accounts receivable, net	130	136	140	144	150	154	160
Merchandise inventory	166	172	178	180	186	190	208
Other current assets	34	34	36	38	38	40	40
Long-term investments	36	30	26	110	110	110	110
Plant assets, net	510	514	520	412	420	428	454
Total assets	$920	$932	$952	$938	$964	$984	$1,040
Liabilities and Equity							
Current liabilities	$148	$156	$186	$190	$210	$260	$ 280
Long-term liabilities	92	120	142	148	194	214	260
Common stock	160	160	160	160	160	160	160
Other contributed capital	70	70	70	70	70	70	70
Retained earnings	450	426	394	370	330	280	270
Total liabilities and equity	$920	$932	$952	$938	$964	$984	$1,040

Required

Preparation Component

1. Compute trend percents for the components of both statements using 2001 as the base year.

Analysis Component

2. Analyze and comment on the financial statements and trend percents from part (1).

Check 2007, Total assets trend, 88.5%

Selected year-end financial statements of Upland Corporation follow:

Problem 18-4B
Calculation of financial
statement ratios

UPLAND CORPORATION Income Statement For Year Ended December 31, 2002	
Sales	$315,500
Cost of goods sold	236,100
Gross profit	$ 79,400
Operating expenses	49,200
Interest expense	2,200
Income before taxes	$ 28,000
Income taxes	4,200
Net income	$ 23,800

UPLAND CORPORATION Balance Sheet December 31, 2002			
Assets		**Liabilities and Equity**	
Cash	$ 6,100	Accounts payable	$ 11,500
Short-term investments	6,900	Accrued wages payable	3,300
Accounts receivable, net	12,100	Income taxes payable	2,600
Notes receivable (trade)*	3,000	Long-term note payable, secured	
Merchandise inventory	13,500	by mortgage on plant assets	30,000
Prepaid expenses	2,000	Common stock, $5 par value	35,000
Plant assets, net	73,900	Retained earnings	35,100
Total assets	$117,500	Total liabilities and equity	$117,500

* Short-term notes receivable arising from customer sales.

Assume that all sales are on credit. Selected balance sheet amounts at December 31, 2001, were total assets, $94,900; common stock, $35,500; and retained earnings, $18,800.

Required

Compute the following: (1) current ratio, (2) acid-test ratio, (3) days' sales uncollected, (4) merchandise inventory turnover, (5) days' sales in inventory, (6) ratio of pledged assets to secured liabilities, (7) times interest earned, (8) profit margin, (9) total asset turnover, (10) return on total assets, and (11) return on common stockholders' equity.

Check Acid-test ratio, 1.6 to 1

Two companies competing in the same industry are being evaluated by a bank that can lend money to only one of them. Summary information from the financial statements of the two companies follows:

Problem 18-5B
Comparative analysis
using ratios

	Lincoln Company	Mertz Company		Lincoln Company	Mertz Company
Data from the current year-end balance sheet:			**Data from the current year's income statement:**		
Assets			Sales	$393,600	$667,500
Cash	$ 20,000	$ 36,500	Cost of goods sold	290,600	480,000
Accounts receivable, net	77,100	70,500	Interest expense	5,900	10,400
Current notes receivable (trade)	11,600	9,000	Income tax expense	5,700	12,300
Merchandise inventory	86,800	82,000	Net income	33,850	61,700
Prepaid expenses	9,700	10,100	Basic earnings per share	1.27	2.19
Plant assets, net	176,900	252,300			
Total assets	$382,100	$460,400			

[continued on next page]

	Lincoln Company	Mertz Company		Lincoln Company	Mertz Company
Data from the current year-end balance sheet:			**Beginning-of-year balance sheet data:**		
Liabilities and Equity			Accounts receivable, net	$ 72,200	$ 73,300
Current liabilities	$ 90,500	$ 97,000	Current notes receivable (trade)	0	0
Long-term notes payable	93,000	93,300	Merchandise inventory	105,100	80,500
Common stock, $5 par value	133,000	141,000	Total assets	383,400	443,000
Retained earnings	65,600	129,100	Common stock, $5 par value	133,000	141,000
Total liabilities and equity	$382,100	$460,400	Retained earnings	49,100	109,700

Required

Check Accounts receivable turnover, Lincoln, 4.9

1. For both companies compute the (a) current ratio, (b) acid-test ratio, (c) accounts (including notes) receivable turnover, (d) merchandise inventory turnover, (e) days' sales in inventory, and (f) days' sales uncollected. Identify the company you consider to be the better short-term credit risk and explain why.

2. For both companies compute the (a) profit margin, (b) total asset turnover, (c) return on total assets, and (d) return on common stockholders' equity. Assuming that each company paid cash dividends of $1.50 per share and each company's stock can be purchased at $25 per share, compute their (e) price-earnings ratios and (f) dividend yields. Identify which company's stock you would recommend as the better investment and explain why.

Beyond the Numbers

Reporting in Action

BTN 18-1   Refer to **Nike**'s financial statements in Appendix A to answer the following questions:

1. Using 1998 as the base year, compute trend percents for 1998, 1999, and 2000 for revenues, cost of sales, selling and administrative expenses, income taxes, and net income. (Round to the nearest whole percent.)

2. Compute common-size percents for 2000 and 1999 for the following categories of assets: (a) total current assets, (b) property, plant and equipment—net, (c) identifiable intangible assets and goodwill, and (d) deferred income taxes and other assets. (Round to the nearest tenth percent.)

3. Comment on any significant changes across the years for the income statement trends computed in part (1) and the balance sheet percents computed in part (2).

Swoosh Ahead

4. Access Nike's annual report for fiscal years ending after May 31, 2000, through Nike's Web site [**www.nike.com**] or the SEC database [**www.sec.gov**]. Update your work for parts (1), (2), and (3) using the new information accessed.

Comparative Analysis

BTN 18-2   Key comparative figures ($ millions) for both **Nike** and **Reebok** follow:

Key Figures	Nike	Reebok	Key Figures	Nike	Reebok
Cash and equivalents . . .	$ 254.3	$ 281.7	Income taxes	$ 340.1	$ 10.1
Accounts receivable	1,567.2	417.4	Revenues (Nike)	8,995.1	—
Inventories	1,446.0	414.6	Net sales (Reebok) . . .	—	2,899.9
Retained earnings	2,887.0	1,170.9	Total assets	5,856.9	1,564.1
Costs of sales	5,403.8	1,783.9			

Required

1. Compute common-size percents for both companies using the data provided.

2. Which company incurs a higher percent of its revenues (net sales) in income taxes?

3. Which company retains a higher portion of cumulative net income in the company?

4. Which company has a higher gross margin ratio on sales?

5. Which company holds a higher percent of its total assets as inventory?

BTN 18-3   As controller of Boxer Company, you are responsible for keeping the board of directors informed about the company's financial activities. At the board meeting, you present the following data:

	2003	2002	2001
Sales trend percent	147.0%	135.0%	100.0%
Selling expenses to net sales	10.1%	14.0%	15.6%
Sales to plant assets	3.8 to 1	3.6 to 1	3.3 to 1
Current ratio	2.9 to 1	2.7 to 1	2.4 to 1
Acid-test ratio	1.1 to 1	1.4 to 1	1.5 to 1
Merchandise inventory turnover	7.8 times	9.0 times	10.2 times
Accounts receivable turnover	7.0 times	7.7 times	8.5 times
Total asset turnover	2.9 times	2.9 times	3.3 times
Return on total assets	9.1%	9.7%	10.4%
Return on stockholders' equity	9.75%	11.50%	12.25%
Profit margin	3.6%	3.8%	4.0%

After the meeting, the company's CEO holds a press conference with analysts in which she mentions the following ratios:

	2003	2002	2001
Sales trend percent	147.0%	135.0%	100.0%
Selling expenses to net sales	10.1%	14.0%	15.6%
Sales to plant assets	3.8 to 1	3.6 to 1	3.3 to 1
Current ratio	2.9 to 1	2.7 to 1	2.4 to 1

Required

1. Why do you think the CEO decided to report 4 ratios instead of the 11 that you prepared?

2. Comment on the possible consequences of the CEO's reporting decision.

BTN 18-4   Each team is to select a different industry, and each team member is to select a different company in that industry and acquire its annual report. Use the annual report to analyze the company, using at least one ratio from each of the four building blocks of analysis. When necessary, use the financial press to determine the market price of its stock. Communicate with teammates via a meeting, e-mail, or telephone to discuss how different companies compare to each other and to industry norms. The team is to prepare a single one-page memorandum reporting on its analysis and the conclusions reached.

Communicating in Practice

Hint: Make a transparency of each team's memo to use in a class discussion.

BTN 18-5   Access the March 30, 2000, filing of the 10-K report of **Yahoo! Inc.** (ticker YHOO) at **www.edgaronline.com.** The profitability of Yahoo! and other Internet companies is becoming an increasingly important issue in the stock market.

Required

Compute or locate the following profitability ratios for Yahoo! for the fiscal years ending December 31, 1999 and 1998.

1. Profit margin

2. Gross profit ratio

3. Return on total assets (Note: 1997 total assets were $143,512,000.)

4. Return on common stockholders' equity (Note: 1997 total shareholders' equity was $118,358,000.)

5. Basic earnings per share

Teamwork in Action

Hint: Pairing within teams may be necessary for (2). Use as an in-class activity or as assignment. Consider presentations to the entire class using team rotation with transparencies.

BTN 18-6   A team approach to analyzing information in financial statements is often useful.

Required

1. The team should discuss the company and then write a description of horizontal and vertical analysis that all team members agree with and understand. Illustrate each description with an example.
2. **Each** member of the team is to select **one** of the following categories of ratio analysis. Explain what the ratios in that category measure. Choose one ratio from the category selected, present its formula, and explain what it measures.

   a. Liquidity and efficiency   **c.** Profitability
   b. Solvency   **d.** Market prospects

3. Each team member is to present his or her notes from part (2) to the other teammates. Team members are to confirm or correct other teammates' presentation.

Business Week Activity

BTN 18-7   Read the article "Research Firm Off the Record Is on the Mark" in the December 6, 1999, issue of *Business Week*.

Required

1. What is the name of the research firm highlighted in the article?
2. How does OTR conduct research?
3. How does OTR's research interface with traditional financial statement analysis?
4. What incentive does OTR offer its survey respondents?
5. As an individual, you cannot access OTR's research. What can you learn, however, from the firm's methods?

Entrepreneurial Decision

BTN 18-8   Jose Sanchez owns and operates **Western Gear**, a small merchandiser in outdoor recreational equipment. You have been hired to review the three most recent years of operations for Western Gear. Your financial statement analysis reveals the following results:

	2002	2001	2000
Sales trend	137.0%	125.0%	100.0%
Selling expenses to net sales	9.8%	13.7%	15.3%
Sales to plant assets	3.5 to 1	3.3 to 1	3.0 to 1
Current ratio	2.6 to 1	2.4 to 1	2.1 to 1
Acid-test ratio	0.8 to 1	1.1 to 1	1.2 to 1
Merchandise inventory turnover	7.5 times	8.7 times	9.9 times
Accounts receivable turnover	6.7 times	7.4 times	8.2 times
Total asset turnover	2.6 times	2.6 times	3.0 times
Return on total assets	8.8%	9.4%	10.1%
Return on owner's equity	9.75%	11.50%	12.25%
Profit margin	3.3%	3.5%	3.7%

Required

Use these data to answer each of the following questions with explanations:

1. Is it becoming easier for the company to meet its current debts on time and to take advantage of cash discounts?
2. Is the company collecting its accounts receivable more rapidly?
3. Is the company's investment in accounts receivable decreasing?
4. Are dollars invested in inventory increasing?
5. Is the company's investment in plant assets increasing?
6. Is the owner's investment becoming more profitable?
7. Is the company using its assets efficiently?
8. Did the dollar amount of selling expenses decrease during the three-year period?

19

Managerial Accounting Concepts and Principles

"I'm selling 3D paper glasses to the world and I can't stop"—John Jerit.

A Look Back

Chapter 18 described the analysis and interpretation of financial statement information. We applied horizontal, vertical, and ratio analyses to better understand company performance and financial condition.

A Look at This Chapter

We begin our study of managerial accounting by explaining its purpose and describing its major characteristics. We also discuss cost concepts and describe how they help managers to gather and organize information they need for making decisions. The reporting of manufacturing activities is also discussed.

A Look Ahead

Chapters 20 through 26 discuss information that managers need to make informed decisions and how they obtain that information. We explain the types of decisions managers must make and how managerial accounting helps with these decisions. The first of these chapters, Chapter 20, considers how we measure costs assigned to certain types of processes.

Part Six

3D Business

e BARTLETT, TN—While working summers to pay for school, John Jerit sold fireworks and 3D glasses to enhance viewing of fireworks. "We sold 7,000 pairs of glasses at Memphis In May and the next day sold 12,000 glasses at the River Fest in Little Rock," says Jerit. "We took in $20,000 in one weekend with a minimal investment. So I took this show on the road." That road led to the launch of **American Paper Optics** (**APO**) [**www.3DGlassesOnline.com**], a company Jerit founded to manufacture and market 3D glasses. However, the harsh realities of business soon followed. "It was tough," he says. "Things were getting tight and I started questioning what I had done."

Jerit responded with a customer orientation. He began by hawking his products carnie-style at fireworks shows and had groups like the Kiwanis and the Boys Club of America do it for a cut. Jerit's biggest move was to envision demand for 3D glasses beyond fireworks, including television, video, lasers, theme park rides, concerts, and Web sites. His customer orientation and application of sound manufacturing principles got him over the hump. Still, because a pair of glasses sells for pennies, he had to effectively classify, monitor, and control costs and manufacturing activities to turn a profit. He has now sold more than 500 million 3D glasses and expects annual revenues of nearly $10 million—that's a lot of pennies.

Jerit says he must continue to monitor customer needs and control manufacturing costs. "It is still hard to convince the public why they need one of these," says Jerit. With large orders from accounts such as the KISS concert tour, National Geographic, and Walt Disney World, and sales for events such as eclipses and holiday parties, he hopes to continue his success. "I've got to continue to try to find a way to make a product that will be a legitimate retail item for the consumer that will be profitable for us," says Jerit. That requires application of sound managerial accounting concepts and principles. [Sources: *APO Web site,* May 2001; *Memphis Business Journal,* April 1998; *Entrepreneur,* November 1999]

Learning Objectives

Conceptual

C1 Explain the purpose of managerial accounting.

C2 Describe major characteristics of managerial accounting.

C3 Describe the lean business model.

C4 Describe accounting concepts useful in classifying costs.

C5 Define product and period costs and explain how they impact financial statements.

C6 Explain how the balance sheets for manufacturing and merchandising companies differ.

C7 Explain how income statements for manufacturing and merchandising companies differ.

C8 Explain manufacturing activities and the flow of manufacturing costs.

Analytical

A1 Compute unit contribution margin and describe what it reveals about a company's cost structure.

Procedural

P1 Compute cost of goods sold for a manufacturer.

P2 Prepare a manufacturing statement and explain its purpose and links to financial statements.

Managerial accounting, like financial accounting, provides information to help users make better decisions. However, managerial accounting and financial accounting differ in important ways, differences which we explain. We also compare the accounting and reporting practices used by manufacturing and merchandising companies. Both types of companies earn revenues by selling products.[1] A merchandising company sells products without changing their condition. A manufacturing company buys raw materials and turns them into finished products for sale to customers. We conclude the chapter by explaining the flow of manufacturing activities and preparing the manufacturing statement.

Introduction to Managerial Accounting

The previous chapters explained a financial accounting system whose main purpose is to prepare general-purpose financial statements. However, this information is incomplete for internal decision makers who manage organizations. For this purpose, a managerial accounting system (also called a *management accounting system*) is required. **Managerial accounting** (also called **management accounting**) is an activity that provides financial and nonfinancial information to managers and other internal decision makers of an organization. This section explains the purpose of managerial accounting and compares it with financial accounting.

Purpose of Managerial Accounting

C1 Explain the purpose of managerial accounting.

Both managerial accounting and financial accounting share the common purpose of providing useful information to decision makers. They do this by collecting, managing, and reporting information in a manner desired by users of accounting data. Both areas of accounting also share the common practice of reporting monetary information.[2] They even report some of the same information. For instance, a company's financial statements contain information useful for both its managers (insiders) and other persons interested in the company (outsiders).

The remainder of this book looks carefully at managerial accounting information, how accounting professionals gather it, and how managers use it. We consider the concepts and procedures used to determine the costs of products and services as well as topics such as budgeting, break-even analysis, product costing, profit planning, and cost analysis. Information about the costs of products and services is important for many decisions that managers make. These decisions include predicting the future costs of a product or service. Predicted costs are used in product pricing, profitability analysis, and in deciding whether to make or buy a product or component. More generally, much of managerial accounting involves gathering information about costs for planning and control decisions.

Planning is the process of setting goals and making plans to achieve them. Companies formulate long-term strategic plans that usually span a 5- to 10-year horizon and then refine them with medium-term and short-term plans. Strategic plans usually set a firm's long-term direction by developing a road map for the future based on potential opportunities such as new products, new markets, and capital investments. The goals and objectives of a strategic plan are often broadly defined given its long-term orientation. Medium- and short-term plans are more operational in nature. They translate the strategic plan into actions. These plans are more concrete and consist of objectives and goals that are better defined. A short-term plan often covers a one-year period that, when translated in monetary terms, is known as a budget (see Chapter 24).

Control is the process of monitoring planning decisions and evaluating an organization's activities and employees. Control includes measurement and evaluation of actions, processes, and outcomes. The feedback provided by the control function allows managers to revise their plans. The measurement of actions and processes also allows managers to take cor-

Point: Costs are important to managers because they impact both the financial position and profitability of a business. Managerial accounting assists in analysis, planning, and control of costs.

---

[1] A service company is another type of company. It earns revenues by providing services rather than products. The skills, tools, and techniques developed for measuring a manufacturing company's activities apply to service companies as well.

[2] Managerial accounting includes reporting nonmonetary information in additon to monetary information.

rective actions to avoid undesirable outcomes. For example, managers periodically compare actual results with planned results using a process called variance analysis (see Chapter 25). Exhibit 19.1 portrays the important management functions of planning and control.

Managers also use information to plan and control business activities. Information about costs helps managers identify problems that require corrective actions. In later chapters, we explain more about how managers use cost information in controlling and planning business activities. This includes directing business activities and improving business operations.

Exhibit 19.1

Planning and Control

Nature of Managerial Accounting

Managerial accounting has its own special characteristics. To understand these characteristics, we compare managerial accounting to financial accounting; they differ in at least seven important ways. These differences are summarized in Exhibit 19.2.

C2 Describe major characteristics of managerial accounting.

Exhibit 19.2

Major Differences between Managerial Accounting and Financial Accounting

	Financial Accounting	Managerial Accounting
1. Users and decision makers	Investors, creditors, and other users external to the organization	Managers, employees, and decision makers internal to the organization
2. Purpose of information	Assist external users in making investment, credit, and other decisions	Assist managers in making planning and control decisions
3. Flexibility of practice	Structured and often controlled by GAAP	Relatively flexible (no GAAP)
4. Timeliness of information	Often available only after an audit is complete	Available quickly without the need to wait for an audit
5. Time dimension	Historical information with some predictions	Many projections and estimates; historical information also presented
6. Focus of information	Emphasis on whole organization	Emphasis on an organization's projects, processes, and subdivisions
7. Nature of information	Monetary information	Mostly monetary; but also nonmonetary information

Users and Decision Makers

Companies accumulate, process, and report financial accounting and managerial accounting information for different groups of decision makers. Financial accounting information is primarily provided to external users including investors, creditors, analysts, and regulators. External users rarely have a major role in managing a company's daily activities. Managerial accounting information is primarily provided to internal users who are responsible for making and implementing decisions about a company's business activities.

Point: It is desirable to accumulate information for management reports in a database separate from financial accounting records.

Purpose of Information

Investors, creditors, and other external users of financial accounting information must often decide whether to invest in or lend to a company. If they have already done so, they must decide whether to continue owning the company or carrying the loan. Internal decision makers must plan a company's future. They seek to take advantage of opportunities or to overcome obstacles. They also try to control activities and ensure their effective and efficient implementation. Managerial accounting information helps these internal users make both planning and control decisions.

Flexibility of Practice

Point: The *Institute of Management Accountants* issues statements that govern the practice of managerial accounting. Accountants who pass a qualifying exam are awarded the CMA.

External users make comparisons between companies by using financial reports and need protection against false or misleading information. Accordingly, financial accounting relies on accepted principles that are enforced through an extensive set of rules and guidelines, or GAAP. Internal users need managerial accounting information for planning and controlling their company's activities rather than for external comparisons. They require different types of information depending on the activity. This makes standardizing managerial accounting systems across companies difficult. Instead, managerial accounting systems are flexible. Also, since managers have access to most company data, they require less protection against false or misleading information compared to external users. Accordingly, the design of a company's managerial accounting system largely depends on the nature of the business and the arrangement of the company's internal operations. Managers can decide for themselves what information they want and how they want it reported. Even within a single company, different managers often design their own systems to meet their special needs. This flexibility allows managers to modify their systems quickly in response to changes in the environment. The important question a manager must ask is whether the information being collected and reported is useful for planning, decision-making, and control purposes.

Timeliness of Information

Point: Financial statements are usually issued several weeks after the fiscal year-end. GAAP requires the reporting of important events that occur while the statements are being prepared. These events are called *subsequent events*.

Point: Independent auditors test the integrity of managerial accounting records when they are used in preparing financial statements.

Formal financial statements reporting past transactions and events are not immediately available to outside parties. Independent certified public accountants often must audit a company's financial statements before it provides them to external users. Since audits often take one to several weeks to complete, annual financial reports to outsiders usually are not available until well after the year-end. However, managerial accounting information can be quickly forwarded to managers. External auditors need not review it. Estimates and projections are acceptable. To get information quickly, managers often accept less precision in reports. As an example, an early internal report to management prepared right after the year-end might report net income for the year between $4.2 and $4.8 million. An audited income statement might later show net income for the year at $4.6 million. The internal report is not precise, but its information can be more useful because it is available earlier.

Internal auditing plays an important role in managerial accounting. Internal auditors evaluate the flow of information not only inside the company but also outside it. Managers are responsible for preventing and detecting fraudulent activities in their companies.

Time Dimension

To protect external users from false expectations, financial reports deal primarily with results of both past activities and current conditions. While some predictions such as service lives and salvage values of plant assets are necessary, financial accounting avoids predictions whenever possible. Managerial accounting regularly includes predictions of conditions and events. As an example, one

You Make the Call—Ethics

Production Supervisor You invite three friends to a restaurant. When the dinner check arrives, David, a self-employed entrepreneur, picks it up saying, "Here, let me pay. I'll deduct it as a business expense on my tax return. It won't cost me as much." Denise, a salesperson, takes the check from David's hand and says, "I'll put this on my company's credit card. It won't cost us anything." Derek, a factory manager for a company, laughs and says, "Neither of you understands. I'll put this on my company's credit card and call it overhead on a cost-plus contract my company has with the government." (*A cost-plus contract means the company receives its costs plus a percent of those costs.*) Adds Derek, "That way, my company pays for dinner *and* makes a profit too." Who should pay the bill?

Answer—p. 808

important managerial accounting report is a budget, which predicts revenues, expenses, and other items. If managerial accounting reports were restricted to the past and present, managers would be less able to plan activities and less effective in managing and evaluating current activities.

Focus of Information

Companies often organize into divisions and departments, but investors rarely can buy shares in one division or department. Nor do creditors lend money to a company's single division or department. Instead, they own shares in or make loans to the whole company. Since external users need information about the whole company, financial accounting focuses primarily on a company as a whole as depicted in Exhibit 19.3. The focus of managerial accounting is different. While top-level managers are responsible for managing the whole company, most other managers are responsible for much smaller sets of activities. These middle-level and lower-level managers need managerial accounting reports dealing with specific activities, projects, and subdivisions for which they are responsible. For instance, division sales managers are directly responsible only for the results achieved in their divisions. While they often want to see results for all divisions, they usually do not need a companywide report. Division sales managers need information about results achieved in their own divisions to improve their performance. This information includes the level of success achieved by each individual or department in each division as depicted by the many pieces in Exhibit 19.4.

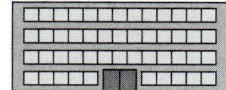

Exhibit 19.3

Focus of External Reports

Exhibit 19.4

Focus of Internal Reports

Nature of Information

Both financial and managerial accounting systems report monetary information. However, managerial accounting systems also report considerable nonmonetary information. While monetary information is an important part of managerial decisions, nonmonetary information plays a crucial role. This is especially so when monetary effects are difficult to measure. Common examples of nonmonetary information are the quality and delivery criteria of purchasing decisions.

Point: To apply these concepts, work QS 19-2.

> **You Make the Call**
>
> **Division Manager**   At a recent managers meeting, you are asked to explore manufacturing a component that your division has been purchasing from an outside supplier for several years. What information do you collect to evaluate these two alternative sources?
>
> Answer—p. 808

Decision-Making Focus

The previous section emphasized differences between financial and managerial accounting, but they are not entirely separate. Similar information is useful to both external and internal users. For instance, information about costs of manufacturing products is useful to all users in making decisions. Also, both financial and managerial accounting can affect peoples' actions. Important managerial decisions are often related to each other and to people's behavior. For example, **Harley-Davidson**'s design of a sales compensation plan affects the behavior of its salesforce. It also must estimate the dual effects of promotion and sales compensation plans on buying patterns of customers. These estimates impact the equipment purchase decisions for manufacturing and can affect the supplier selection criteria established by purchasing. This example shows that financial and managerial accounting systems do more than measure; they affect people's decisions and actions.

Increased Relevance of Managerial Accounting

We have explained the importance of managerial accounting for internal decision making. Although the analytical tools and techniques of managerial accounting have always been useful, their relevance and importance have greatly increased in the past decade. This is so because of changes in the business environment. This section describes some of these changes and their impact on managerial accounting.

 Describe the lean business model.

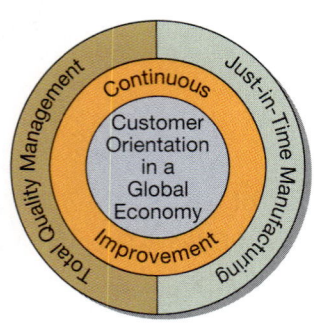

Lean Business Model

Two important factors have encouraged companies to be more effective and efficient in running their operations. First, there is an increased emphasis on *customers* as the most important constituent of a business. Customers expect to derive a certain value for the money they spend to buy products and services. Specifically, they expect that their suppliers will offer them the right service (or product) at the right time and the right price. This implies that companies accept the notion of **customer orientation,** which means that employees understand the changing needs and wants of their customers and align their management and operating practices accordingly.

Second, our *global economy* expands competitive boundaries, thereby providing customers with more choices. The global economy also produces changes in business activities. One notable case that reflects these changes in customer demand and global competition is auto manufacturing. The top three Japanese auto manufacturers (**Honda**, **Nissan**, and **Toyota**) once controlled more than 40% of the U.S. auto market. Customers perceived that Japanese auto manufacturers provide value not available from other manufacturers. Many of the European and North American auto manufacturers responded to this challenge and regained much of the lost market share.

Point: Many industries, in addition to the automobile industry, can benefit from a JIT system.

Companies must be alert to these and other factors. Many companies have responded by adopting the **lean business model,** whose goal is to *eliminate waste* while "satisfying the customer" and "providing a positive return" to the company.

Lean Practices

Point: Goals of a TQM process include reduced waste, better control of inventory, fewer defects, and continuous improvement. Just-in-time concepts have similar goals.

Continuous improvement rejects the notions of "good enough" or "acceptable" and challenges employees and managers to continuously experiment with new and improved business practices. This has led companies to adopt practices such as total quality management (TQM) and just-in-time (JIT) manufacturing. The philosophy underlying both practices is continuous improvement; the difference is in the focus.

Total quality management focuses on quality improvement and applies this standard to all aspects of business activities. In doing so, managers and employees seek to uncover waste in business activities including accounting activities such as payroll and disbursements. To encourage an emphasis on quality, the U.S. Congress established the Malcolm Baldridge National Quality Award (MBQNA). Entrants must conduct a thorough analysis and evaluation of their business using guidelines from the Baldridge committee. **Ritz Carlton Hotel Company, L.L.C** is a recent recipient of the Baldridge award in the service category. The company applies a core set of values, collectively called *The Gold Standards,* to improve customer service.

Point: The time between buying raw materials and selling the finished goods is called *throughput time.*

Just-in-time manufacturing is a system that acquires inventory and produces only when needed. An important aspect of JIT is that companies manufacture products only after they receive an order (a *demand-pull* system) and then deliver the customer's requirements on time. This means that processes must be aligned to eliminate any delays and inefficiencies including inferior inputs and outputs. Companies must also establish good relations and communications with their suppliers. On the downside, JIT is more susceptible to disruption than traditional systems. As one recent example, several **General Motors** plants were temporarily shut down due to a strike at an assembly division—the plants supplied components *just in time* to the assembly division.

Implications for Managerial Accounting

Adopting the lean business model can be challenging because all systems and procedures that a company follows must be realigned to foster its implementation. Managerial accounting has an important role to play by providing accurate cost and performance in-

formation. Companies must understand the nature and sources of cost and must develop systems that capture costs accurately. Developing such a system is important to measuring the "value" provided to customers. The price that customers pay for acquiring goods and services is an important determinant of value. In turn, the costs a company incurs are key determinants of price. All else being equal, the better a company is at controlling its costs, the better its performance.

Did You Know?

Balanced Scorecard   The *balanced scorecard* aids continuous improvement by augmenting financial measures with information on the "drivers" (indicators) of future financial performance along four dimensions: (1) *financial*—profitability and risk, (2) *customer*—value creation and product and service differentiation, (3) *internal business processes*—businesses activities that create customer and owner satisfaction, and (4) *learning and growth*—organizational change, innovation, and growth.

Quick Check

1. Managerial accounting produces information (a) to meet internal users' needs, (b) to meet a user's specific needs, (c) often focusing on the future, or (d) all of these.

2. What is the difference between the intended users of financial and managerial accounting?

3. Do generally accepted accounting principles (GAAP) control and dictate managerial accounting?

4. What is the basic objective for a company practicing total quality management?

Answers—p. 809

An organization incurs many different types of costs that are classified differently, depending on the needs of management (different costs for different purposes). Specifically, we can classify costs on the basis of their (1) behavior, (2) traceability, (3) controllability, (4) relevance, and (5) function. This section explains each concept for assigning costs to products and services.

Cost Accounting Concepts

C5   Describe accounting concepts useful in classifying costs.

Concept 19-1

Classification by Behavior

At a basic level, a cost can be classified as fixed or variable. A **fixed cost** does not change with changes in the volume of activity (within a range of activity known as an activity's *relevant range*). For example, straight-line depreciation on equipment is a fixed cost. A **variable cost** changes in proportion to changes in the volume of activity. Sales commissions computed as a percent of sales revenue are variable costs. Additional examples of fixed and variable costs are provided in Exhibit 19.5 for a bike manufacturer. When cost items are combined, total cost can be fixed, variable, or mixed. *Mixed* means that it is a combination of fixed and variable costs. Equipment rental often includes a fixed cost for some minimum amount and a variable cost based on amount of usage. Classification of costs by behavior is helpful in cost-volume-profit analyses and short-term decision making. We discuss these in Chapters 23 and 26.

Exhibit 19.5

Fixed and Variable Costs

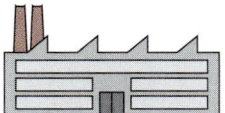

Fixed Cost: Rent for Rocky Mountain Bikes' building is $22,000, and doesn't change with the number of bikes produced.

Variable Cost: Cost of bicycle tires is variable with the number of bikes produced—this cost is $15 per pair.

Classification by Traceability

A cost is often traced to a **cost object,** which is a product, process, department, or customer to which costs are assigned. When a cost is traceable to a cost object, it is classified as a direct cost. **Direct costs** are incurred for the benefit of one specific cost object. For example, if

Exhibit 19.6
Direct and Indirect Costs

Direct Costs
- Salaries of maintenance department employees
- Equipment purchased by maintenance department
- Materials purchased by maintenance department
- Maintenance department equipment depreciation

Indirect Costs
- Factory accounting
- Factory administration
- Factory rent
- Factory managers' salary
- Factory light and heat
- Factory internal audit
- Factory intranet

a product is a cost object, then material and labor costs are usually directly traceable. **Indirect costs** are incurred for the benefit of more than one cost object. An example of an indirect traceable cost is a maintenance plan that benefits two or more departments. Exhibit 19.6 identifies examples of both direct and indirect costs for the maintenance department in a manufacturing plant. Classification of costs by traceability is useful for cost allocation. This is discussed in Chapter 22.

You Make the Call   *e*

Entrepreneur You wish to trace as many of your assembly department's direct costs as possible. You can trace 90% of them in an economical manner. To trace the other 10%, you need sophisticated and costly accounting software. Do you purchase this software?

Answer—p. 809

Exhibit 19.7
Controllability of Costs

Senior Manager
Controls costs of investment in land, buildings, and equipment.

Supervisor
Controls daily expenses such as supplies, maintenance, and overtime.

Point: Opportunity costs are not recorded by the accounting system.

Classification by Controllability

A cost can be defined as **controllable** or **not controllable.** Whether a cost is controllable or not depends on the employee's responsibilities, as shown in Exhibit 19.7. This is referred to as *hierarchical levels* in management, or *pecking order.* For example, investments in machinery are controllable by upper-level managers but not lower-level managers. Many daily operating expenses such as overtime often are controllable by lower-level managers. Classification of costs by controllability is especially useful for assigning responsibility to and evaluating managers.

Classification by Relevance

A cost can be classified by relevance by identifying it as either a sunk cost or an out-of-pocket cost. A **sunk cost** has already been incurred and cannot be avoided or changed. It is irrelevant to future decisions. One example is the cost of office equipment previously purchased by a company. An **out-of-pocket cost** requires a future outlay of cash and is relevant for decision making. Future purchases of equipment involve out-of-pocket costs.

A discussion of relevant costs must also consider opportunity costs. An **opportunity cost** is the potential benefit lost by choosing a specific action from two or more alternatives. One example is a student giving up wages from a job to attend summer school. Consideration of opportunity cost is important when, for example, an insurance company must decide whether to outsource its payroll function or maintain it internally. This is discussed in Chapter 26.

You Make the Call

Purchase Manager You are evaluating two potential suppliers of seats for the manufacturing of motorcycles. One supplier (A) quotes a price of $145 per seat and ensures 100% quality standards and on-time delivery. The second supplier (B) quotes a price of $115 per seat but does not give any written assurances on quality or delivery. You decide to contract with the second supplier (B), saving $30 per seat. Does this decision have opportunity costs?

Answer—p. 809

C5 Define product and period costs and explain how they impact financial statements.

Classification by Function

Another classification of costs (for manufacturers) is one of capitalization as inventory or to expense as incurred. Costs capitalized as inventory are called **product costs,** which refer to expenditures that are necessary and integral to finished products. They include direct materials, direct labor, and overhead costs. Product costs pertain to activities carried out to manufacture the product. Costs expensed are called **period costs,** which refer to expenditures identified more with a time period than with finished products. They include selling and general administrative expenses. Period costs pertain to activities that are not part of the manufacturing process. A distinction between product and period costs is important because period costs are expensed in the income statement and product costs are assigned to inventory on the balance sheet. An ability to understand and identify product costs and period costs is crucial to using and interpreting a *manufacturing statement* described later in this chapter. Exhibit 19.8 shows the different effects of product and period costs. Period costs flow directly to the current income statement as expenses. They are not reported as assets. Product costs are first assigned to inventory. Their final treatment depends on when inventory is sold or disposed of. Product costs assigned to finished goods that are sold in year 2002 are reported on the 2002 income statement as part of cost of goods sold. Product costs assigned to unsold inventory are carried forward on the balance sheet at the end of year 2002. If this inventory is sold in year 2003, product costs assigned to it are reported as part of cost of goods sold in that year's income statement.

Point: Only costs of production and purchases are classed as product costs.

Point: Product costs are either in the income statement as part of cost of goods sold or in the balance sheet as inventory. Period costs appear only on the income statement under operating expenses. See Exhibit 19.8.

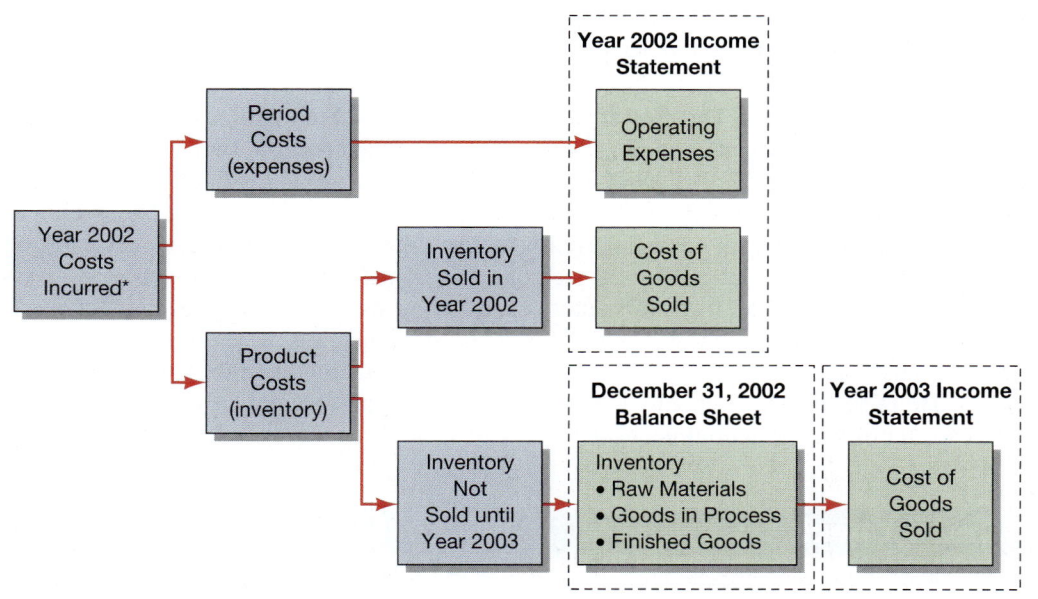

* This diagram excludes costs to acquire assets other than inventory.

Exhibit 19.8

Period and Product Costs in Financial Statements

The difference between period and product costs explains why the year 2002 income statement does not report under operating expenses either factory workers' wages or depreciation on factory buildings and equipment. Instead, both costs are combined with the cost of raw materials to compute the product cost of finished goods. A portion of these manufacturing costs (reflecting the goods sold) is reported in the year 2002 income statement as part of Cost of Goods Sold. The other portion is reported on the balance sheet at the end of that year as part of the cost of inventory. The portion assigned to inventory could be included in any or all of raw materials, goods in process, or finished goods inventories.

Point: For a team approach to identifying period and product costs, see *Teamwork in Action* in the *Beyond the Numbers* section.

Point: To apply these concepts, work Exercise 19-6.

Identifying Cost Classification

It is important to understand that a cost can be classified using any one (or combination) of the five different means described here. However, to do this we must understand costs and operations. Specifically, for the five classifications, we must be able to identify the *activity* for behavior, *cost object* for traceability, *management hierarchical level* for controllability, *opportunity cost* for relevance, and *benefit period* for function. Factory rent, for instance, can be classified as a product cost, it is fixed with respect to number of units produced, it is indirect with respect to the product, and it is not controllable by a production supervisor. Potential multiple classifications are shown in Exhibit 19.9 using different cost items incurred in manufacturing mountain bikes. The finished bike is the cost object.

Point: All expenses of service companies are period costs because service companies do not have inventory.

Exhibit 19.9

Examples of Multiple Cost Classifications

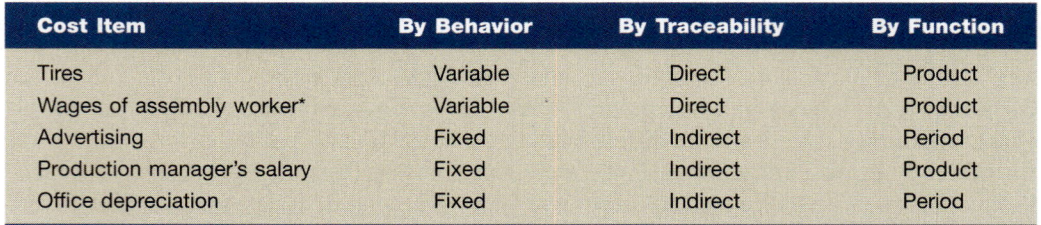

Cost Item	By Behavior	By Traceability	By Function
Tires	Variable	Direct	Product
Wages of assembly worker*	Variable	Direct	Product
Advertising	Fixed	Indirect	Period
Production manager's salary	Fixed	Indirect	Product
Office depreciation	Fixed	Indirect	Period

* Although an assembly worker's wages are classified as variable costs, their actual behavior depends on how workers are paid and whether their wages are based on a union contract (such as piece rate or monthly wages).

Proper allocation of these costs and managerial decisions based on cost data depend on a correct cost classification.

Cost Concepts for Service Companies

The cost concepts just described are generally applicable to service organizations. For example, consider **Delta Air Lines**. Its cost of food for passengers is a variable cost based on the number of passengers. The cost of leasing an aircraft is fixed with respect to the number of passengers. We can also trace a flight crew's salary to a specific flight whereas wages for the ground crew are unlikely traceable to a specific flight. Classification by function (such as product versus period costs) is not relevant to service companies because services are not inventoried. Instead, costs incurred by a service firm are expensed in the reporting period when incurred. Managers in service companies must understand and apply cost concepts. They must seek and rely on accurate estimates of costs for many decisions. For example, an airline manager must often decide between canceling or rerouting flights. The manager must also be able to estimate costs saved by canceling a flight versus rerouting. Knowledge of fixed costs is equally important. We explain more about the cost requirements for these and other managerial decisions in Chapter 26.

Service Costs

- Food and beverages
- Cleaning fees
- Pilots' salaries
- Attendants' salaries
- Fuel costs
- Travel agents' fees
- Ground crew's salaries

Quick Check

5. Which type of cost behavior increases total costs when volume of activity increases?

6. How might traceability of costs improve managerial decisions?

Answers—p. 809

Reporting Manufacturing Activities

Companies with manufacturing activities are different from both merchandising and service companies. The main difference between merchandising and manufacturing companies is that merchandisers buy goods ready for sale while manufacturers produce goods from materials and labor. **Payless** is an example of a merchandising company. It buys and sells shoes without physically changing them. **Nike** is primarily a manufacturer of shoes and apparel. It purchases materials such as leather, cloth, dye, plastic, rubber, glue, and laces and then uses employees' labor to convert these materials to products. **Delta Air Lines** is a service company that transports people and items.

Much of our focus in this book has been on the business activities of merchandising and service companies. We described their activities and how to account for them. Manufacturing activities differ from both selling merchandise and providing services. Also, the financial statements for manufacturing companies are slightly different. This section looks at some of these differences and compares them to accounting for a merchandising company.

Manufacturer's Balance Sheet

Manufacturers carry several unique assets and usually have three inventories instead of the single inventory that merchandisers carry. Exhibit 19.10 shows three different inventories in

C6 Explain how the balance sheets for manufacturing and merchandising companies differ.

Exhibit 19.10

Balance Sheet for a
Manufacturer

ROCKY MOUNTAIN BIKES
Balance Sheet
December 31, 2002

Assets			Liabilities and Equity		
Current assets			Current liabilities		
Cash		$ 11,000	Accounts payable		$ 14,000
Accounts receivable	$32,000		Wages payable		540
Allowance for doubtful accounts	(1,850)	30,150	Interest payable		2,000
			Income taxes payable		32,600
Raw materials inventory		**9,000**			
Goods in process inventory		**7,500**	Total current liabilities		$ 49,140
Finished goods inventory		**10,300**	Long-term liabilities		
Factory supplies		350	Long-term notes payable		50,000
Prepaid insurance		300	Total liabilities		$ 99,140
Total current assets		$ 68,600			
Plant assets			Stockholders' equity		
Small tools		1,100	Common stock, $5 par		100,000
Delivery equipment, net		5,000	Retained earnings		49,760
Office equipment, net		1,300	Total stockholders' equity		$149,760
Factory machinery, net		65,500	Total liabilities and equity		$248,900
Factory building, net		86,700			
Land		9,500			
Total plant assets		$169,100			
Intangible assets (patents)		11,200			
Total assets		$248,900			

the current asset section of the balance sheet for **Rocky Mountain Bikes**, a manufacturer. The three inventories are raw materials, goods in process, and finished goods.

Raw Materials Inventory

Raw materials inventory refers to the goods a company acquires to use in making products. It uses raw materials in two ways: directly and indirectly. Most raw materials physically become part of a product and are identified with specific units or batches of a product. Raw materials used directly in a product are called direct materials. Other materials used to support production processes are sometimes not as clearly identified with specific units or batches of product. These materials are called **indirect materials** because they are not clearly identified with specific units or batches of product. Items used as indirect materials often appear on a balance sheet as factory supplies or are included in raw materials. Some direct materials are classified as indirect materials when their costs are low (insignificant). Examples include screws and nuts used in assembling mountain bikes and staples and glue used in manufacturing shoes. Using the materiality principle, individually tracing the costs of each of these materials and classifying them separately as direct materials does not make much economic sense. For instance, keeping detailed records of the amount of glue used to manufacture one shoe is not cost beneficial.

Point: Reducing the size of inventories saves storage costs and frees money for other uses.

Inventories of Rocky Mountain Bikes

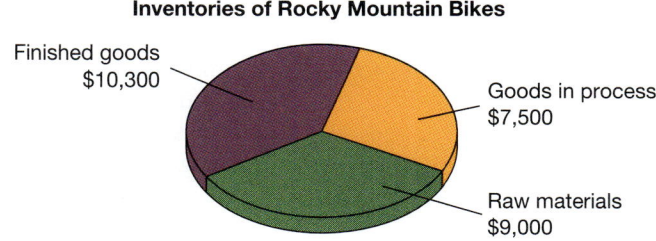

Finished goods
$10,300

Goods in process
$7,500

Raw materials
$9,000

Goods in Process Inventory

Another inventory held by manufacturers is **goods in process inventory,** also called *work in process inventory*. It consists of products in the process of being manufactured but not yet complete. The amount of goods in process inventory depends on the type of production process. If the time required to produce a unit of product is short, the goods in process inventory is likely small, but if weeks or months are needed to produce a unit, the goods in process inventory is usually larger.

Finished Goods Inventory

A third inventory owned by a manufacturer is **finished goods inventory,** which consists of completed products ready for sale. This inventory is similar to merchandise inventory owned by a merchandising company. Manufacturers also often own unique plant assets such as small tools, factory buildings, factory equipment, and patents to manufacture products. The balance sheet in Exhibit 19.10 shows that Rocky Mountain Bikes owns all of these assets. Some manufacturers invest millions or even billions of dollars in production facilities and patents. **Caterpillar**'s recent balance sheet shows a $5.2 billion net investment in land, buildings, machinery and equipment, much of which involves production facilities.

Manufacturer's Income Statement

C7 Explain how income statements for manufacturing and merchandising companies differ.

The main difference between the income statement of a manufacturer and that of a merchandiser involves the items making up cost of goods sold. Exhibit 19.11 compares the components of cost of goods sold for a manufacturer and a merchandiser. A merchandiser adds its cost of goods purchased to beginning merchandise inventory and then subtracts ending merchandise inventory to get cost of goods sold. A manufacturer adds its cost of goods manufactured to beginning finished goods inventory and then subtracts ending finished goods inventory to get cost of goods sold.

Exhibit 19.11

Cost of Goods Sold Computation

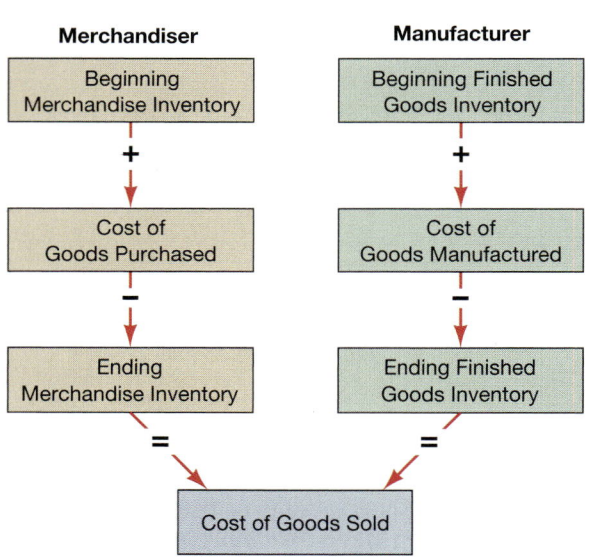

A merchandiser often uses the term *merchandise* inventory; a manufacturer often uses the term *finished goods* inventory. A manufacturer's inventories of raw materials and goods in process are not included in finished goods because they are not available for sale. A manufacturer also shows cost of goods *manufactured* instead of cost of goods *purchased*. This difference occurs because a manufacturer produces its goods instead of purchasing them

P1 Compute cost of goods sold for a manufacturer.

ready for sale. We show later in this chapter how to derive cost of goods manufactured from the manufacturing statement.

The Cost of Goods Sold section for both a merchandiser (Tele-Mart) and a manufacturer (Rocky Mountain Bikes) is shown in Exhibit 19.12 to highlight these differences. The remaining income statement sections are similar.

Except for these differences, the cost of goods sold computations are the same. However, the numbers in these computations reflect different activities. A merchandiser's cost of goods purchased is the cost of buying products to be sold. A manufacturer's cost of goods manufactured is the sum of direct materials, direct labor, and factory overhead costs incurred in producing products. The remainder of this section further explains these three manufacturing costs and describes prime and conversion costs.

Concept 19-2

Exhibit 19.12

Cost of Goods Sold for a
Merchandiser and Manufacturer

Merchandising Company		Manufacturing Company	
Cost of goods sold:		Cost of goods sold:	
Beginning *merchandise* inventory	$ 14,200	Beginning *finished goods* inventory	$ 11,200
Cost of merchandise *purchased*	234,150	Cost of goods *manufactured**	170,500
Goods available for sale	$248,350	Goods available for sale	$181,700
Ending *merchandise* inventory	(12,100)	Ending *finished goods* inventory	(10,300)
Cost of goods sold	$236,250	Cost of goods sold	$171,400

* Cost of goods manufactured is reported in the income statement of Exhibit 19.14.

Direct Materials

Direct materials are tangible components of a finished product. **Direct material costs** are the expenditures for direct materials that are separately and readily traced through the manufacturing process to finished goods. Examples of direct materials in manufacturing a mountain bike include its tires, seat, frame, pedals, brakes, cables, gears, and handlebars. The chart in the margin shows that direct materials generally make up about 45% of manufacturing costs in today's products, but this amount varies across industries and companies.

Typical Manufacturing Costs in Today's Products

Direct materials 45%

Factory overhead 40%

Direct labor 15%

Direct Labor

Direct labor refers to the efforts of employees who physically convert materials to finished product. **Direct labor costs** are the wages and salaries for direct labor that are separately and readily traced through the manufacturing process to finished goods. Examples of direct labor in manufacturing a mountain bike include operators directly involved in converting raw materials into finished products (welding, painting, forming) and assembly workers who attach materials such as tires, seats, pedals, and brakes to the bike frames. Costs of other workers on the assembly line who assist direct laborers are classified as **indirect labor costs.** Efforts of indirect laborers are not linked to specific units or batches of the product.

Point: Indirect labor costs are part of factory overhead.

Factory Overhead

Factory overhead involves components or activities that support the manufacturing process but are not direct materials or direct labor. **Factory overhead costs** are the expenditures for factory overhead that cannot be separately or readily traced to finished goods. These costs include indirect materials and indirect labor, costs not directly traceable to the product. Overtime paid to direct laborers is also included in overhead because overtime is due to delays, interruptions, or constraints not necessarily identifiable to a specific product or batches of product. Factory overhead costs also include maintenance of the mountain bike factory, supervision of its employees, repairing manufacturing equipment, factory utilities (water, gas, electricity), production manager's salary, factory rent, depreciation on factory buildings and equipment, factory insurance, property taxes on factory buildings and equipment, and factory accounting and legal services. Factory overhead does *not* include selling and administrative expenses because they are not incurred in manufacturing products. These expenses are called *period costs* and are recorded as expenses on the income statement when incurred.

Point: Factory overhead is also called *manufacturing overhead.*

Prime and Conversion Costs

Direct material costs and direct labor costs are also called **prime costs**—expenditures directly associated with the manufacture of finished goods. Direct labor costs and overhead costs are called **conversion costs**—expenditures incurred in the process of converting raw materials to finished goods. Note that direct labor costs are considered both prime costs and conversion costs. Exhibit 19.13 conveys the relation between prime and conversion costs and their components of direct material, direct labor, and factory overhead.

Exhibit 19.13

Prime and Conversion Costs and Their Components

Point: Prime costs = Direct materials + Direct labor. Conversion costs = Direct labor + Factory overhead.

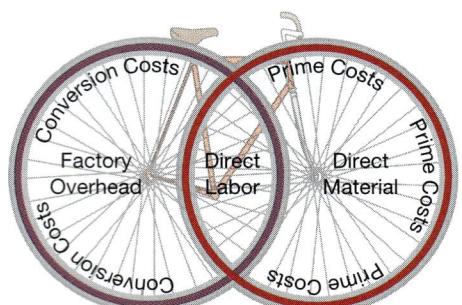

Reporting Performance

Exhibit 19.14 shows the income statement for Rocky Mountain Bikes.

Exhibit 19.14

Income Statement for a Manufacturer

ROCKY MOUNTAIN BIKES Income Statement For Year Ended December 31, 2002		
Sales		$310,000
Cost of goods sold		
Finished goods inventory, Dec. 31, 2001	$ 11,200	
Cost of goods manufactured	**170,500**	
Goods available for sale	181,700	
Finished goods inventory, Dec. 31, 2002	(10,300)	
Cost of goods sold		171,400
Gross profit		$138,600
Operating expenses		
Selling expenses		
Sales salaries expense	18,000	
Advertising expense	5,500	
Delivery wages expense	12,000	
Shipping supplies expense	250	
Insurance expense—Delivery equipment	300	
Depreciation expense—Delivery equipment	2,100	
Total selling expenses		$ 38,150
General and administrative expenses		
Office salaries expense	15,700	
Miscellaneous expense	200	
Bad debts expense	1,550	
Office supplies expense	100	
Depreciation expense—Office equipment	200	
Interest expense	4,000	
Total general and administrative expenses		$ 21,750
Total operating expenses		59,900
Income before income taxes		$ 78,700
Less income taxes expense		(32,600)
Net income		$ 46,100
Net income per common share (20,000 shares)		$ 2.31

The operating expenses in Exhibit 19.14 include sales salaries, office salaries, and depreciation of delivery and office equipment. Operating expenses do not include manufacturing costs such as factory workers' wages and depreciation of production equipment and the factory buildings. These manufacturing costs are reported as part of cost of goods manufactured and included in cost of goods sold. We explained why and how this is done in the section Classification by Function.

Point: Manufacturers treat costs such as depreciation and rent as product costs if they are related to manufacturing.

Quick Check

7. What are the three types of inventory on a manufacturing company's balance sheet?

8. How does cost of goods sold differ for merchandising versus manufacturing companies?

Answers—p. 809

Flow of Manufacturing Activities

To understand manufacturing and its reports, we must first understand the flow of manufacturing activities and costs. Exhibit 19.15 shows the flow of manufacturing activities for a manufacturer. This exhibit has three important sections: *materials activity, production activity,* and *sales activity.* We explain each activity in this section.

C8 Explain manufacturing activities and the flow of manufacturing costs.

Materials Activity

The far left side of Exhibit 19.15 shows the flow of raw materials. Most manufacturers usually start a period with some beginning raw materials inventory. This is shown as carried over from the previous period. During the current period, the company acquires additional

Exhibit 19.15

Activities and Cost Flows in Manufacturing

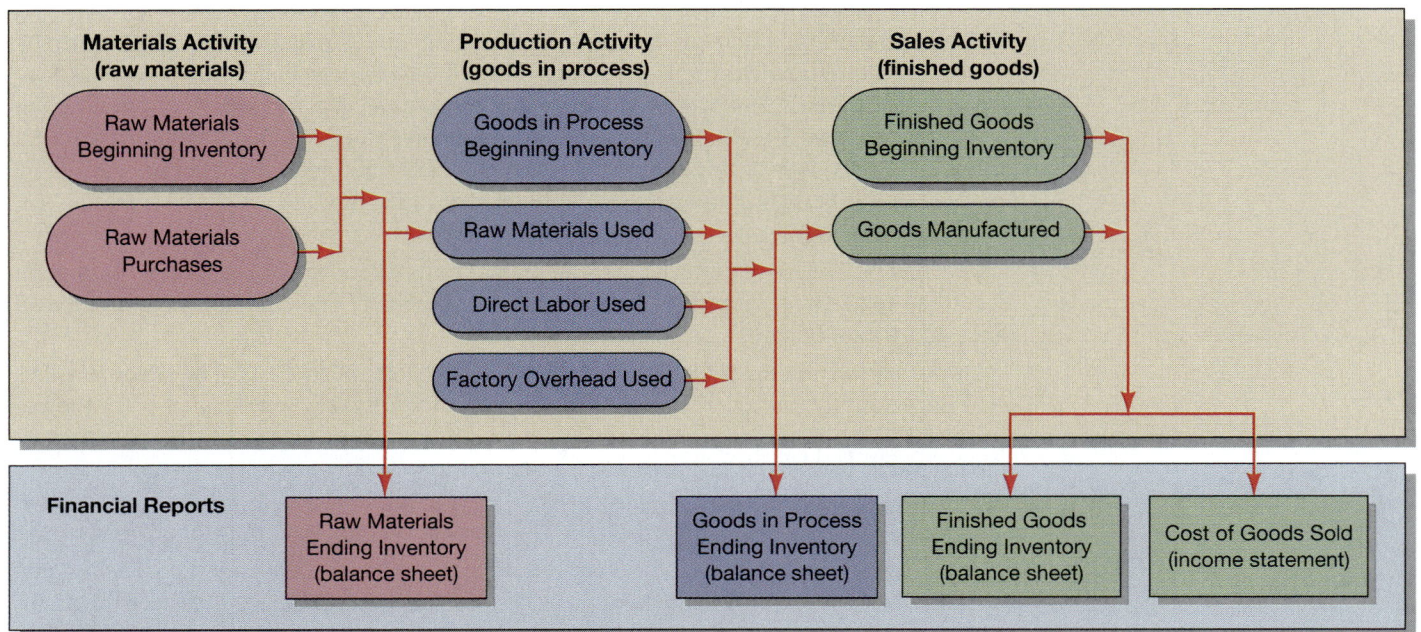

raw materials. When these purchases are added to beginning inventory, we have total raw materials available for use in production. These raw materials are then either used in production in the current period or remain in inventory at the end of the period for use in future periods.

Production Activity

The middle section of Exhibit 19.15 describes production activity. Four factors come together in production: beginning goods in process inventory, direct materials, direct labor, and overhead. Beginning goods in process inventory consists of partly assembled products from the previous period. Production activity results in products that are either finished or remain unfinished. The cost of finished products makes up the cost of goods manufactured for the current period. Unfinished products are identified as ending goods in process inventory. The cost of unfinished products consists of direct materials, direct labor, and factory overhead. This cost is reported on the current period's balance sheet. The costs of both finished goods manufactured and goods in process are *product costs*.

Sales Activity

The company's sales activity is portrayed in the far right side of Exhibit 19.15. Newly completed units are combined with beginning finished goods inventory to make up total finished goods available for sale in the current period. The cost of finished products sold is reported on the income statement as cost of goods sold. The cost of products not sold is reported on the current period's balance sheet as ending finished goods inventory.

Manufacturing Statement

A company's manufacturing activities are described in a special financial report called the **manufacturing statement,** also called the *schedule of manufacturing activities* or the *schedule of cost of goods manufactured.* The manufacturing statement summarizes the types and amounts of costs incurred in a company's manufacturing process. Exhibit 19.16 shows the manufacturing statement for Rocky Mountain Bikes. The statement is divided into four parts: *direct materials, direct labor, overhead,* and *computation of cost of goods manufactured.* We describe each of these parts in this section.

① The manufacturing statement begins by computing direct materials used. We start by adding beginning raw materials inventory of $8,000 to the current period's purchases of $86,500. This yields $94,500 of total raw materials available for use. A physical count of inventory shows $9,000 of ending raw materials inventory. We then compute total cost of raw materials used during the period as $85,500 ($94,500 total raw materials available for use − $9,000 ending inventory). (Note that all raw materials are direct materials for Rocky Mountain Bikes.)

② The second part of the manufacturing statement reports direct labor costs. Rocky Mountain Bikes had total direct labor cost of $60,000 for the period. This amount includes payroll taxes and fringe benefits.

③ The third part of the manufacturing statement reports overhead costs. The statement lists each important factory overhead item and its cost. Total factory overhead cost for the period is $30,000. Some companies report only *total* factory overhead on the manufacturing statement and attach a separate schedule listing individual overhead costs.

④ The final section of the manufacturing statement computes and reports the *cost of goods manufactured.* (Total manufacturing costs for the period are $175,500 ($85,500 + $60,000 + $30,000). This is the sum of direct materials used and direct labor and overhead costs incurred). This amount is first added to beginning goods in process inventory. This gives the total goods in process inventory of $178,000 ($175,500 + $2,500).

Exhibit 19.16

Manufacturing Statement

ROCKY MOUNTAIN BIKES
Manufacturing Statement
For Year Ended December 31, 2002

Direct materials		
Raw materials inventory, Dec. 31, 2001	$ 8,000	
Raw materials purchases	86,500	
Raw materials available for use	94,500	
Raw materials inventory, Dec. 31, 2002	(9,000)	
Direct materials used		$ 85,500
Direct labor		$ 60,000
Factory overhead		
Indirect labor	9,000	
Factory supervision	6,000	
Factory utilities	2,600	
Repairs—Factory equipment	2,500	
Property taxes—Factory building	1,900	
Factory supplies used	600	
Factory insurance expired	1,100	
Small tools written off	200	
Depreciation—Factory equipment	3,500	
Depreciation—Factory building	1,800	
Amortization—patents	800	
Total factory overhead costs		$ 30,000
Total manufacturing costs		$175,500
Add goods in process inventory, Dec. 31, 2001		2,500
Total cost of goods in process		$178,000
Deduct goods in process inventory, Dec. 31, 2002		(7,500)
Cost of goods manufactured		$170,500

We then compute the current period's cost of goods manufactured of $170,500 by taking the $178,000 total goods in process and subtracting the $7,500 cost of ending goods in process inventory. The $7,500 amount assigned to the ending goods in process inventory consists of direct materials, direct labor, and factory overhead. The cost of goods manufactured amount is also called *net cost of goods manufactured* or *cost of goods completed*. Exhibit 19.14 shows that this item and amount are listed in the Cost of Goods Sold section of Rocky Mountain Bikes' income statement.

Since Rocky Mountain Bikes includes a detailed list of overhead costs in its manufacturing statement, we show the alternative use of a supporting schedule in Exhibit 19.17. Note that the manufacturing statement includes total factory overhead in its computation of cost of goods manufactured. Cost of goods manufactured is then carried to the income statement and shown as part of cost of goods sold.

Management uses information in the manufacturing statement to plan and control the company's manufacturing activities. To provide timely information for decision making, the statement is often prepared monthly, weekly, or even daily. The manufacturing statement contains information useful to external users, but it is not a general-purpose financial statement. Most companies view this information as proprietary and potentially harmful to the company if released to competitors. As a result, companies rarely publish the manufacturing statement.

Point: Manufacturers sometimes report variable and fixed overhead separately in the manufacturing statement to provide more information to managers about cost behavior.

Point: To apply these concepts, work Exercise 19-11.

Exhibit 19.17

Overhead Cost Flows across
Accounting Reports

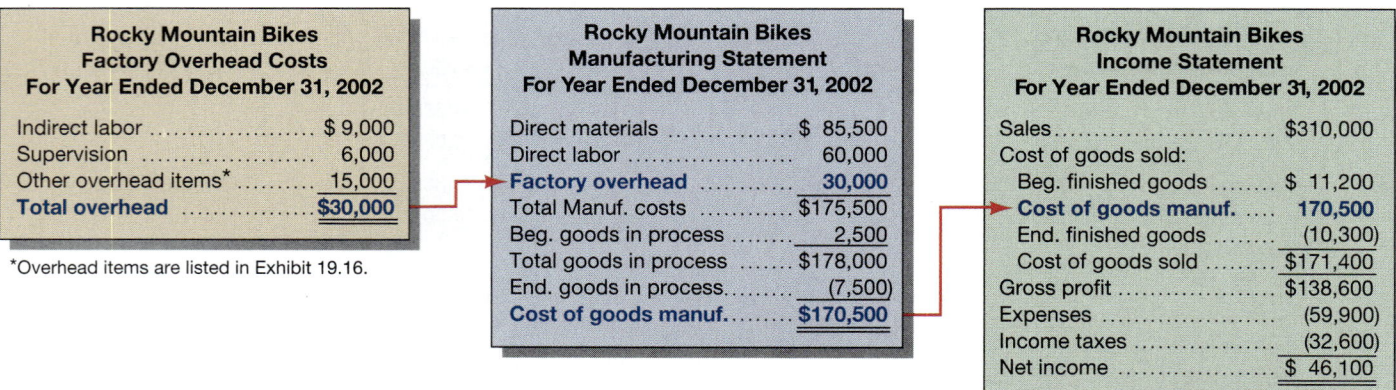

Rocky Mountain Bikes Factory Overhead Costs For Year Ended December 31, 2002	
Indirect labor	$ 9,000
Supervision	6,000
Other overhead items*	15,000
Total overhead	**$30,000**

*Overhead items are listed in Exhibit 19.16.

Rocky Mountain Bikes Manufacturing Statement For Year Ended December 31, 2002	
Direct materials	$ 85,500
Direct labor	60,000
Factory overhead	**30,000**
Total Manuf. costs	$175,500
Beg. goods in process	2,500
Total goods in process	$178,000
End. goods in process	(7,500)
Cost of goods manuf.	**$170,500**

Rocky Mountain Bikes Income Statement For Year Ended December 31, 2002	
Sales	$310,000
Cost of goods sold:	
Beg. finished goods	$ 11,200
Cost of goods manuf.	**170,500**
End. finished goods	(10,300)
Cost of goods sold	$171,400
Gross profit	$138,600
Expenses	(59,900)
Income taxes	(32,600)
Net income	$ 46,100

Quick Check

9. A manufacturing statement (a) computes cost of goods manufactured for the period, (b) computes cost of goods sold for the period, or (c) reports operating expenses incurred for the period.

10. Are companies required to report a manufacturing statement?

11. How are both beginning and ending goods in process inventories reported on a manufacturing statement?

Answers—p. 809

Using the Information   **Unit Contribution Margin**

A1 Compute unit contribution margin and describe what it reveals about a company's cost structure.

We explained in this chapter how managers classify costs by behavior. This usually refers to costs as being fixed or variable with respect to volume of activity. In manufacturing companies, volume of activity usually refers to the number of units produced. We then classify a cost as either fixed or variable, depending on whether total cost changes as the number of units produced changes. Once we separate costs by behavior, we can then compute a product's contribution margin. **Unit contribution margin,** or *contribution margin per unit,* is the amount a product's unit selling price exceeds its total unit variable cost. This excess amount contributes to covering fixed costs and generating profits on a per unit basis. Exhibit 19.18 shows the unit contribution margin formula.

Exhibit 19.18

Unit Contribution Margin

Unit contribution margin = Sales price per unit − Total variable cost per unit

Users often use contribution margin in the form of a **contribution margin ratio,** which is the percent of a unit's selling price that exceeds total unit variable cost. It can be interpreted as the percent of each sales dollar that remains after deducting total unit variable cost. Exhibit 19.19 shows the formula for the contribution margin ratio, defined as contribution margin divided by sales price.

Exhibit 19.19

Contribution Margin Ratio

$$\text{Contribution margin ratio} = \frac{\text{Unit contribution margin}}{\text{Sales price per unit}}$$

We use Rocky Mountain Bikes' Tracker® product to show the usefulness of these measures. The selling price of a Tracker mountain bike is $450, and the variable costs of its manufacturing and marketing are $200. The contribution margin per bike is computed as $250 ($450 − $200). This measure is useful to managers in determining the money contributed by the sale of each Tracker bike to both (1) fixed costs and (2) net income. Specifically, each sale of a Tracker bike yields a $250 contribution margin to cover fixed costs of Rocky Mountain Bikes. Once fixed costs are covered, net income is left.

We also compute the contribution margin ratio of the Tracker mountain bike as 55.55% ($250/$450). This information is useful to managers when working with estimates of sales in dollars. Specifically, approximately 56¢ (or 55.55%) of each sales dollar is available as contribution to fixed costs and profits. The contribution margin ratio is also useful in cost-volume-profit (CVP) analysis, a method we use to assess the volume of activity necessary to achieve different performance levels (including income, loss, and break-even points). We explain CVP analysis in Chapter 23.

Contribution Margin	Variable Costs
56¢	44¢

You Make the Call

Sales Manager You are evaluating orders from two customers, but you can accept only one of these orders because of your company's limited capacity. The first order is for 100 units of a product with a contribution margin ratio of 60% and a selling price of $1,000. The second order is for 500 units of a product with a contribution margin ratio of 20% and a selling price of $800. The incremental fixed costs are the same for both orders. Which order do you accept?

Answer—p. 809

Demonstration Problem 1—Cost Behavior

Understanding the classification and assignment of costs is important. Consider the following company, **Chip Making Systems (CMS),** that manufactures computer chips. CMS incurs the following costs in manufacturing chips and in operating the company:

1. Plastic board used to mount the chip, $3.50 each.
2. Assembly worker pay of $15 per hour to attach chips to plastic board.
3. Salary for factory maintenance workers who maintain factory equipment.
4. Factory supervisor pay of $55,000 per year to supervise employees.
5. Real estate taxes paid on the factory, $14,500.
6. Real estate taxes paid on the company office, $6,000.
7. Depreciation costs on machinery used by workers, $30,000.
8. Salary paid to the chief financial officer, $95,000.
9. Advertising costs of $7,800 paid to promote products.
10. Salespersons' commissions of $0.50 for each assembled chip sold.
11. CMS could rent the manufacturing plant to store medical records for six local hospitals instead of producing and assembling chips.

Classify each cost in the following table according to the categories listed across the top of the chart. A cost can be classified under more than one category. The plastic board used to mount chips, for instance, is classified as a direct material product cost and as a direct unit cost.

Cost	Period Costs	Product Costs			Unit Cost Classification		Sunk Cost	Opportunity Cost
	Selling and Administrative	Direct Material (prime cost)	Direct Labor (prime and conversion)	Factory Overhead (conversion cost)	Direct	Indirect		
1. Plastic board used to mount the chip, $3.50 each		✔			✔			

Solution to Demonstration Problem 1

| Cost* | Period Costs | Product Costs | | | Unit Cost Classification | | Sunk Cost | Opportunity Cost |
	Selling and Administrative	Direct Material (prime cost)	Direct Labor (prime and conversion)	Factory Overhead (conversion cost)	Direct	Indirect		
1.		✔			✔			
2.			✔		✔			
3.				✔		✔		
4.				✔		✔		
5.				✔		✔		
6.	✔							
7.				✔		✔	✔	
8.	✔							
9.	✔							
10.	✔							
11.								✔

* Costs 1–11 match the 11 cost items described at the beginning of the problem.

Demonstration Problem 2— Reporting for Manufacturers

The balance sheet and income statement for a manufacturing company are different than those for a merchandising or service company.

Required

1. Fill in the [**BLANKS**] on the partial balance sheets for both the manufacturing company and the merchandising company. Explain why a different presentation is required.

Manufacturing Company

CHIP MAKING SYSTEMS
Partial Balance Sheet
December 31, 2002

Current assets:	
Cash	$10,000
[BLANK]	8,000
[BLANK]	5,000
[BLANK]	7,000
Supplies	500
Prepaid insurance	500
Total current assets	$31,000

Merchandising Company

PAYLESS SHOE OUTLET
Partial Balance Sheet
December 31, 2002

Current assets:	
Cash	$ 5,000
[BLANK]	12,000
Supplies	500
Prepaid insurance	500
Total current assets	$18,000

2. Fill in the [**BLANKS**] on the income statements for the manufacturing company and the merchandising company. Explain why a different presentation is required.

Manufacturing Company

CHIP MAKING SYSTEMS Partial Income Statement For Year Ended December 31, 2002		
Sales		$200,000
Cost of goods sold		
Finished goods inventory, Dec. 31, 2001	$ 10,000	
[BLANK]	120,000	
Goods available for sale	$130,000	
Finished goods inventory, Dec. 31, 2002	(7,000)	
Cost of goods sold	123,000	
Gross profit		$ 77,000

Merchandising Company

PAYLESS SHOE OUTLET Partial Income Statement For Year Ended December 31, 2002		
Sales		$190,000
Cost of goods sold		
Merchandise inventory, Dec. 31, 2001	$ 8,000	
[BLANK]	108,000	
Net purchases	$116,000	
Merchandise inventory, Dec. 31, 2002	(12,000)	
Cost of goods sold	104,000	
Gross profit		$ 86,000

3. The manufacturer's cost of good manufactured is the sum of (a) _____, (b) _____, and (c) _____ costs incurred in producing the product.

Solution to Demonstration Problem 2

1. Inventories for a manufacturer and for a merchandiser.

Manufacturing Company

CHIP MAKING SYSTEMS Partial Balance Sheet December 31, 2002	
Current assets:	
Cash	$10,000
Raw materials inventory	8,000
Goods in process inventory	5,000
Finished goods inventory	7,000
Supplies	500
Prepaid insurance	500
Total current assets	$31,000

Merchandising Company

PAYLESS SHOE OUTLET Partial Balance Sheet December 31, 2002	
Current assets:	
Cash	$ 5,000
Merchandise inventory	12,000
Supplies	500
Prepaid insurance	500
Total current assets	$18,000

Explanation: A manufacturing company must control and measure three types of inventories: raw materials, goods in process, and finished goods. In the sequence of making a product, the raw materials move into production—called *goods in process inventory*—and then to finished goods. All raw materials and goods in process inventory at the end of each accounting period are considered current assets. All unsold finished inventory is considered a current asset at the end of each accounting period. The merchandising company must control and measure only one type of inventory, purchased goods.

2. Cost of goods sold for a manufacturer and for a merchandiser.

Manufacturing Company

CHIP MAKING SYSTEMS Partial Income Statement For Year Ended December 31, 2002		
Sales		$200,000
Cost of goods sold		
Finished goods inventory, Dec. 31, 2001	$ 10,000	
Cost of goods manufactured	**120,000**	
Goods available for sale	$130,000	
Finished goods inventory, Dec. 31, 2002	(7,000)	
Cost of goods sold		123,000
Gross profit		$ 77,000

Merchandising Company

PAYLESS SHOE OUTLET Partial Income Statement For Year Ended December 31, 2002		
Sales		$190,000
Cost of goods sold		
Merchandise inventory, Dec. 31, 2001	$ 8,000	
Cost of purchases	**108,000**	
Net purchases	$116,000	
Merchandise inventory, Dec. 31, 2002	(12,000)	
Cost of goods sold		104,000
Gross profit		$ 86,000

Explanation: Manufacturing and merchandising companies use different reporting terms. In particular, the terms *finished goods* and *cost of goods manufactured* are used to reflect the production of goods, yet the concepts and techniques of reporting cost of goods sold for a manufacturing company and merchandising company are similar.

3. A manufacturer's cost of goods manufactured is the sum of (a) **direct material,** (b) **direct labor,** and (c) **factory overhead** costs incurred in producing the product.

Demonstration Problem 3— Manufacturing Statement

The following account balances and other information are from the accounting records of SUNN Corporation for the year ended December 31, 2002. Use this information to prepare (1) a table listing of factory overhead costs, (2) a manufacturing statement (show only the total factory overhead cost), and (3) an income statement.

Advertising expense	$ 85,000	Goods in process inventory, Dec. 31, 2001	$ 8,000
Amortization of patents	16,000	Goods in process inventory, Dec. 31, 2002	9,000
Bad debts expense	28,000	Income taxes	53,400
Depreciation expense—Office equipment	37,000	Indirect labor	26,000
Depreciation—Factory building	133,000	Interest expense	25,000
Depreciation—Factory equipment	78,000	Miscellaneous expense	55,000
Direct labor	250,000	Property taxes on factory equipment	14,000
Factory insurance expired	62,000	Raw materials inventory, Dec. 31, 2001	60,000
Factory supervision	74,000	Raw materials inventory, Dec. 31, 2002	78,000
Factory supplies used	21,000	Raw materials purchases	313,000
Factory utilities	115,000	Repairs on factory equipment	31,000
Finished goods inventory, Dec. 31, 2001	15,000	Salaries expense	150,000
Finished goods inventory, Dec. 31, 2002	12,500	Sales	1,630,000

Planning the Solution

- Analyze the account balances and select those that are part of factory overhead costs.
- Arrange these costs in a table that lists factory overhead costs for the year.
- Analyze the remaining costs and select those related to production activity for the year; selected costs should include the materials and goods in process inventories and direct labor.
- Prepare a manufacturing statement for the year showing the calculation of the cost of materials used in production, the cost of direct labor, and the total factory overhead cost. When presenting overhead cost on this statement, report only total overhead cost from the table of overhead costs for the

year. Show the costs of beginning and ending goods in process inventory to determine cost of goods manufactured.

- Organize the remaining revenue and expense items into the income statement for the year. Combine cost of goods manufactured from the manufacturing statement with the finished goods inventory amounts to compute cost of goods sold for the year.

Solution to Demonstration Problem

SUNN CORPORATION
Factory Overhead Costs
For Year Ended December 31, 2002

Amortization of patents	$ 16,000
Depreciation—Factory building	133,000
Depreciation—Factory equipment	78,000
Factory insurance expired	62,000
Factory supervision	74,000
Factory supplies used	21,000
Factory utilities	115,000
Indirect labor	26,000
Property taxes on factory equipment	14,000
Repairs on factory equipment	31,000
Total factory overhead	$570,000

SUNN CORPORATION
Manufacturing Statement
For Year Ended December 31, 2002

Direct materials		
Raw materials inventory, Dec. 31, 2001	$ 60,000	
Raw materials purchase	313,000	
Raw materials available for use	373,000	
Raw materials inventory, Dec. 31, 2002	(78,000)	
Direct materials used		$ 295,000
Direct labor		250,000
Factory overhead		570,000
Total manufacturing costs		$1,115,000
Goods in process inventory, Dec. 31, 2001		8,000
Total cost of goods in process		$1,123,000
Goods in process inventory, Dec. 31, 2002		(9,000)
Cost of goods manufactured		$1,114,000

SUNN CORPORATION
Income Statement
For Year Ended December 31, 2002

Sales		$1,630,000
Cost of goods sold		
Finished goods inventory, Dec. 31, 2001	$ 15,000	
Cost of goods manufactured	1,114,000	
Goods available for sale	1,129,000	
Finished goods inventory, Dec. 31, 2002	(12,500)	
Cost of goods sold		(1,116,500)
Gross profit		$ 513,500
Operating expenses		
Advertising expense	85,000	
Bad debts expense	28,000	
Depreciation expense—Office equip.	37,000	
Interest expense	25,000	
Miscellaneous expense	55,000	
Salaries expense	150,000	
Total operating expenses		(380,000)
Income before income taxes		$ 133,500
Income taxes		(53,400)
Net income		$ 80,100

Summary

C1 **Explain the purpose of managerial accounting.** The purpose of managerial accounting is to provide useful information to management and other internal decision makers. It does this by collecting, managing, and reporting both monetary and nonmonetary information in a manner useful to internal users.

C2 **Describe major characteristics of managerial accounting.** Major characteristics of managerial accounting include (1) focus on internal decision makers, (2) emphasis on planning and control, (3) flexibility, (4) timeliness, (5) reliance on forecasts and estimates, (6) focus on segments and projects, and (7) reporting both monetary and nonmonetary information.

C3 **Describe the lean business model.** The main purpose of the lean business model is the elimination of waste. Concepts such as total quality management and just-in-time production often aid in effective application of the model.

C4 **Describe accounting concepts useful in classifying costs.** We can classify costs on the basis of their (1) behavior—fixed vs. variable, (2) traceability—direct vs. indirect, (3) controllability—controllable vs. uncontrollable, (4) relevance—sunk vs. out of pocket, and (5) function—product vs. period. A cost can be classified in more than one way, depending on the purpose for which the cost is being determined. These classifications help to understand cost patterns, analyze performance, and plan operations.

C5 **Define product and period costs and explain how they impact financial statements.** Costs that are capitalized because they are expected to have future value are called *product costs*; costs that are expensed are called *period costs*. This classification is important because it affects the amount of costs expensed in the income statement and the amount of costs assigned to inventory on the balance sheet. Product costs are commonly made up of direct materials, direct labor, and overhead. Period costs include selling and administrative expenses.

C6 **Explain how the balance sheets for manufacturing and merchandising companies differ.** The main difference is that manufacturers usually carry three inventories instead of one inventory that merchandisers carry. The three inventories are raw materials, goods in process, and finished goods.

C7 **Explain how income statements for manufacturing and merchandising companies differ.** The main difference between income statements of manufacturers and merchandisers is the items making up cost of goods sold. A merchandiser adds beginning merchandise inventory to cost of goods purchased and then subtracts ending merchandise inventory to get cost of goods sold. A manufacturer adds beginning finished goods inventory to cost of goods manufactured and then subtracts ending finished goods inventory to get cost of goods sold.

C8 **Explain manufacturing activities and the flow of manufacturing costs.** Manufacturing activities consist of materials, production, and sales activities. The materials activity consists of the purchase and issuance of materials to production. The production activity consists of converting materials into finished goods. At this stage in the process, the materials, labor, and overhead costs have been incurred and the manufacturing statement is prepared. The sales activity consists of selling some or all of finished goods available for sale. At this stage in the process, the cost of goods sold is determined.

A1 **Compute unit contribution margin and describe what it reveals about a company's cost structure.** Unit contribution margin is a product's sales price less its total variable costs. Contribution margin ratio is a product's unit contribution margin divided by its sales price. Unit contribution margin is the amount received from each sale that contributes to fixed costs and income. The contribution margin ratio reveals what portion of each sales dollar is available as contribution to fixed costs and income.

P1 **Compute cost of goods sold for a manufacturer.** A manufacturer adds beginning finished goods inventory to cost of goods manufactured and then subtracts ending finished goods inventory to get cost of goods sold.

P2 **Prepare a manufacturing statement and explain its purpose and links to financial statements.** The manufacturing statement reports computation of cost of goods manufactured for the period. It begins by showing the period's costs for direct materials, direct labor, and overhead and then adjusts these numbers for the beginning and ending inventories of the goods in process to yield cost of goods manufactured.

Guidance Answers to You Make the Call

Production Supervisor It appears that all three friends want to pay the bill with someone else's money. David is using money belonging to the tax authorities, Denise is taking money from her company, and Derek is defrauding the government. To prevent such practices, companies have internal audit mechanisms. Many companies also adopt ethical codes of conduct to help guide employees in such decisions. We must recognize that some entertainment expenses are justifiable and even encouraged. For example, the tax law allows certain deductions for entertainment that have a business purpose. Corporate policies also sometimes allow and encourage reimbursable spending for social activities, and government contracts can include entertainment as allowable costs. Nevertheless,

without further details, payment for this bill should be made from personal accounts.

Division Manager You need information pertaining to the costs of making it in-house: direct materials, direct labor, and overhead. You also need information about investments in machinery required to make the component. Regarding the possibility of continuing to buy from the outside, you need information about the costs of outside purchase: price of components, costs to place the order, and costs to receive and store components. You must also consider nonfinancial factors such as quality of components currently supplied and the quality of in-house production.

Entrepreneur   Tracing all costs directly to cost objects is always desirable, but you need to be able to do so in an economically feasible manner. In this case, you are able to trace 90% of the assembly department's direct costs. It may not be economical to spend more money on a new software to trace the final 10% of costs. You need to make a cost-benefit trade-off. If the software offers benefits beyond tracing the remaining 10% of the assembly department's costs, your decision should consider this.

Purchase Manager   Opportunity costs relate to the potential quality and delivery benefits given up by not choosing supplier (A) as the supplier. Selecting supplier (B) might involve future costs of poor-quality seats (inspection, repairs, and returns) Also, because of potential delivery delays, work might be interrupted and manufacturing costs increased. Your company might also incur sales losses if the product quality of supplier (B) is low. As purchase manager, you are responsible for these costs and must consider them in making your decision.

Sales Manager   The contribution margin for the first order is $600 per unit (60% of $1,000); the contribution margin per unit for the second order is $160 (20% of $800). You are likely tempted to accept the first order based on its high contribution margin per unit, but you must compute total contribution margin based on the number of units sold for each order. Total contribution margin is $60,000 ($600 per unit × 100 units) and $80,000 ($160 per unit × 500 units) for the two orders, respectively. The second order provides the largest return in absolute dollars and is the order you would accept. Another factor to consider in your selection is the potential for a long-term relationship with these customers including repeat sales.

Guidance Answers to **Quick Checks**

1. (d)
2. Financial accounting information is intended for users external to an organization such as investors, creditors, and government authorities. Managerial accounting, on the other hand, focuses on providing information to managers, officers, and other decision makers within the organization.
3. No, GAAP do not control the practice of managerial accounting. Unlike external users, the internal users need managerial accounting information for planning and controlling business activities rather than for external comparison. Different types of information are required, depending on the activity. Therefore it is difficult to standardize managerial accounting.
4. Under TQM, all managers and employees should strive toward higher standards in their work and in the products and services they offer to customers.
5. Variable costs increase when volume of activity increases.
6. By being able to trace costs to cost objects (say, to products and departments), managers have a better understanding of the total costs associated with a cost object. This is useful when managers consider making changes to the cost object (e.g., dropping the product or expanding the department).
7. The three different types of inventory on a manufacturing company's balance sheet are raw materials inventory, goods in process inventory, and finished goods inventory.
8. The cost of goods sold for merchandising companies includes all costs of acquiring the merchandise; the cost of goods sold for manufacturing companies includes the three costs of manufacturing—direct materials, direct labor, and overhead.
9. (a)
10. No
11. Beginning goods in process inventory is added to total manufacturing costs to yield total goods in process. Ending goods in process inventory is subtracted from total goods in process to yield cost of goods manufactured for the period.

Glossary

Continuous improvement concept requiring every manager and employee continually to look to improve operations. (p. 790).

Contribution margin product's sale price less its total variable costs. (p. 802).

Contribution margin ratio product's contribution margin divided by its sale price. (p. 802).

Control process of monitoring planning decisions and evaluating the organization's activities and employees. (p. 786).

Controllable or not controllable cost cost depending on the manager's responsibilities and whether or not he/she is in a position to make decisions that impact this cost. (p. 792).

Conversion costs expenditures incurred in the process of converting raw materials to finished goods—includes direct labor costs and factory overhead costs. (p. 798).

Cost object Product, process, department, or customer to which costs are assigned. (p. 791).

Customer orientation company's managers and employees are in tune with the changing wants and needs of consumers. (p. 790).

Direct costs costs incurred for the benefit of one specific cost object. (p. 791).

Direct labor efforts of employees who physically convert materials to finished product. (p. 797).

Direct labor costs wages and salaries for direct labor that are separately and readily traced through the manufacturing process to finished goods. (p. 797).

Direct material raw material that physically becomes part of the product and is clearly identified with specific products or batches of product. (p. 797).

Direct material costs expenditures for direct material that are separately and readily traced through the manufacturing process to finished goods. (p. 797).

Factory overhead factory activities supporting the manufacturing process that are not direct material or direct labor; also called *overhead* and *manufacturing overhead*. (p. 797).

Factory overhead costs expenditures for factory overhead that cannot be separately or readily traced to finished goods. (p. 797).

Finished goods inventory products that have completed the manufacturing process and are ready for sale. (p. 796).

Fixed cost cost that does not change with changes in the volume of activity. (p. 791).

Goods in process inventory products in the process of being manufactured but are not yet complete; also called *work in process inventory*. (p. 796).

Indirect costs costs incurred for the benefit of more than one cost object. (p. 792).

Indirect labor efforts of manufacturing employees who do not work specifically on converting direct materials into finished products and who are not clearly identified with specific units or batches of product. (p. 797).

Indirect material material used to support the production process but not clearly identified with products or batches of product. (p. 795).

Just-in-time (JIT) manufacturing Process of acquiring or producing inventory only when needed. (p. 790).

Lean business model Practice of eliminating waste while meeting customer needs

and yielding positive company returns. (p. 790).

Managerial accounting area of accounting that serves the decision making needs of internal users (also called *management accounting*). (p. 786).

Manufacturing statement report that summarizes the types and amounts of costs incurred in a company's manufacturing process for a period; also called *cost of goods manufacturing statement*. (p. 800).

Opportunity cost potential benefit lost by choosing a specific action from two or more alternatives. (p. 792).

Out-of-pocket cost cost requiring a future outlay of cash; relevant to current and future decisions. (p. 792).

Period costs expenditures identified more with a time period than with finished products costs; includes selling and general administrative expenses. (p. 792).

Planning process of setting goals and preparing to achieve them. (p. 786).

Prime costs expenditures directly identified with the manufacturing of finished goods—include direct material costs and direct labor costs. (p. 798).

Product costs costs that are capitalized as inventory because they produce benefits expected to have future value; include direct materials, direct labor, and factory overhead. (p. 792).

Raw materials inventory goods a company acquires to use to make products. (p. 795).

Sunk cost cost already incurred and cannot be avoided or changed. (p. 792).

Total quality management (TQM) concept calling for all managers and employees at all stages of operations to strive toward higher standards and a reduced number of defects. (p. 790).

Variable cost cost that changes in proportion to changes in the activity volume. (p. 791).

Questions

1. Discuss the managerial accountant's role in business planning, control, and decision making.
2. Distinguish between managerial and financial accounting on
   a. Users and decision makers   d. Time dimension
   b. Purpose of information   e. Focus of information
   c. Flexibility of practice
3. Identify changes a company must make when it adopts a customer orientation.
4. Distinguish between direct material and indirect material.
5. Distinguish between direct labor and indirect labor.
6. Distinguish between factory overhead and selling and administrative overhead.
7. What product cost is listed as both a prime cost and a conversion cost?
8. Assume that you tour **Reebok**'s factory where it  makes basketball shoes for WNBA teams. List three direct costs and three indirect costs you are likely to see.
9. Should we evaluate a manager's performance on the basis of controllable or noncontrollable costs? Why?
10. Explain why knowledge of cost behavior is useful in product performance evaluation.
11. Explain why product costs are capitalized but period costs are expensed in the current accounting period.
12. Explain how business activities and inventories for a manufacturing company, a merchandising company, and a service company differ.
13. Why does managerial accounting often involve working with numerous predictions and estimates?
14. How do an income statement and a balance sheet for a manufacturing company and a merchandising company differ?

15. Refer to Appendix A and identify **Nike**'s three  inventory components (see its note 2) and reconcile this total to the amount reported on its balance sheet.
16. Besides inventories, what other assets often appear on manufacturers' balance sheets but not on merchandisers' balance sheets?
17. Why does a manufacturing company require three different inventory categories?
18. Manufacturing activities of a company are described in a special report called the _____. This statement summarizes the types and amounts of costs incurred in a company's manufacturing _____.
19. What are the three categories of manufacturing costs?
20. List several examples of factory overhead.
21. What is the difference between factory overhead and selling and administrative overhead?
22. List the four components of a manufacturing 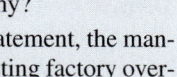 statement and provide specific examples of each for **Reebok**.
23. Prepare a proper title for the annual "manufacturing" statement of **Gap**. Does the date match the balance sheet or income statement? Why?
24. Describe the relations among the income statement, the manufacturing statement, and a detailed table listing factory overhead costs.
25. Define and describe unit contribution margin.
26. Define and explain the contribution margin ratio.
27. Describe the contribution margin ratio in layperson's terms.
28. Why is the contribution margin ratio a useful measure for **Nike** in deciding what shoes to manufacture?

Managerial accounting (choose one):
1. Must follow generally accepted accounting principles.
2. Provides information to aid management in planning and controlling business activities.
3. Is directed at reporting aggregate data on the company as a whole.
4. Provides information that is widely available to all interested parties.

Identify whether each description most likely applies to managerial or financial accounting:
1. _____ Its primary focus is on the organization as a whole.
2. _____ Its principles and practices are very flexible.
3. _____ It is directed at external users in making investment, credit, and other decisions.
4. _____ Its primary users are company managers.
5. _____ Its information is often available only after an audit is complete.

QS 19-2
Managerial accounting versus financial accounting

C2

Match each lean business concept with its best description by entering its letter in the blank:
1. _____ Customer orientation
2. _____ Total quality management
3. _____ Just-in-time manufacturing
4. _____ Continuous improvements

A. Inventory is acquired or produced only as needed.
B. Flexible product designs can be modified to accommodate customer choices.
C. Every manager and employee constantly looks for ways to improve company operations.
D. Focuses on quality throughout the production process.

QS 19-3
Lean business concepts

C3

Which of these statements is true regarding fixed and variable costs?
1. Fixed costs increase and variable costs decrease in total as activity volume decreases.
2. Fixed costs stay the same and variable costs increase in total as activity volume increases.
3. Both fixed and variable costs increase as activity volume increases.
4. Both fixed and variable costs stay the same in total as activity volume increases.

QS 19-4
Fixed and variable costs

C4

Which of these statements is true regarding product and period costs?
1. Sales commission is a product cost and factory rent is a period cost.
2. Factory wages is a product cost and direct material is a period cost.
3. Factory maintenance is a product cost and sales commission is a period cost.
4. Sales commission is a product cost and depreciation on factory equipment is a product cost.

QS 19-5
Product and period costs

C5

Three inventory categories are reported on a manufacturing company's balance sheet: (a) raw materials, (b) goods in process, and (c) finished goods. Identify the usual order in which these inventory items are reported on a balance sheet.
1. (a)(b)(c)   **2.** (b)(a)(c)   **3.** (b)(c)(a)   **4.** (c)(b)(a)

QS 19-6
Inventory reporting for manufacturers

A company has year-end cost of goods manufactured of $4,000, beginning finished goods inventory of $500, and ending finished goods inventory of $750. Its cost of goods sold is
1. $4,250   **2.** $4,000   **3.** $3,750   **4.** $3,900

QS 19-7
Cost of goods sold

Identify the usual sequence of manufacturing activities by filling in the blank (1, 2, or 3) corresponding to its order: _____ Production activities; _____ Sales activities; _____ Materials activities.

QS 19-8
Manufacturing flows identified

QS 19-9
Cost of goods manufactured

Determine the cost of goods manufactured for Net-It Company using this information:

Direct materials	$190,500
Direct labor	63,150
Factory overhead costs	24,000
Goods in process, Dec. 31, 2001	157,600
Goods in process, Dec. 31, 2002	142,750

QS 19-10
Contribution margin ratio

Compute and interpret the contribution margin ratio using the following data: sales, $5,000; total variable cost, $3,000.

QS 19-11
Cost of goods sold

Compute cost of goods sold for year 2002 using the following information:

Finished goods inventory, Dec. 31, 2001	$345,000
Goods in process inventory, Dec. 31, 2001	83,500
Goods in process inventory, Dec. 31, 2002	72,300
Cost of goods manufactured, year 2002	918,700
Finished goods inventory, Dec. 31, 2002	283,600

EXERCISES

Exercise 19-1
Sources of accounting information

Both managerial accounting and financial accounting provide useful information to decision makers. Indicate in this chart the most likely source of information for each business decision (a decision can require major input from both sources):

Business Decision	Primary Information Source	
	Managerial	**Financial**
Estimate product cost for a new line of basketball shoes	____	____
Plan the budget for next quarter	____	____
Report financial performance to the board of directors	____	____
Measure profitability of all individual stores	____	____
Prepare financial reports according to GAAP	____	____
Determine amount of dividends to pay common stockholders	____	____
Determine location and size for a new plant	____	____
Evaluate a purchasing department's performance	____	____

Exercise 19-2
Planning and control descriptions

Complete the following statements by filling in the blanks:

1. _____ is the process of setting goals and making plans to achieve them.

2. _____ _____ usually covers a period of 5 to 10 years.

3. _____ _____ usually covers a period of one year.

4. _____ is the process of monitoring planning decisions and evaluating an organization's activities and employees.

Exercise 19-3
Characteristics of financial accounting and managerial accounting

In the following chart, compare financial accounting and managerial accounting by describing how each differs for the items listed. Be specific in your responses.

	Financial Accounting	Managerial Accounting
1. Users and decision makers	____	____
2. Purpose of information	____	____
3. Flexibility of practice	____	____
4. Timeliness of information	____	____
5. Time dimension	____	____
6. Focus of information	____	____
7. Nature of information	____	____

Customer orientation means that a company's managers and employees respond to changing wants and needs of consumers. You are to stop at a restaurant, hotel, or other local business in your area and pick up a customer response card. (1) On the right hand side of a sheet of paper, write the usual competitive forces: time, quality, cost, and flexibility of service. Attach the customer response card to the left side of the sheet. Draw arrows linking questions on the customer response card to the competitive forces. (2) Identify how the response card provides information to management and employees to better meet competitive forces. Be prepared to form small groups to compare and contrast customer response cards across the types of businesses.

Exercise 19-4
Customer orientation in practice

The following lists three separate events affecting the managerial accounting systems for different companies. Match the management concept(s) that the company is likely to adopt for the event identified. There is some overlap in the meaning of customer orientation and total quality management and, therefore, some responses can include more than one concept.

Exercise 19-5
Management concepts

Event	Manufacturing Management Principle
_____ 1. The company starts measuring inventory turnover and discontinues elaborate inventory records. Its new focus is to pull inventory through the system.	a. Total quality management (TQM)
_____ 2. The company starts reporting measures on customer complaints and product returns from customers.	b. Just-in-time (JIT) c. Continuous improvement (CI)
_____ 3. The company starts reporting measures such as the percent of defective products and the number of units scrapped.	d. Customer orientation (CO)

Procter & Gamble, a manufacturing company, incurs the costs shown below. (1) Classify each cost as either a product or a period cost. If a product cost, identify it as a prime and/or conversion cost. (2) Classify each cost as either a direct cost or an indirect cost using the product as the cost object.

Exercise 19-6
Cost analysis and identification

Cost	Product Costs Prime	Product Costs Conversion	Period Cost	Direct Cost	Indirect Cost
Direct materials used	____	____	____	____	____
State and federal income taxes	____	____	____	____	____
Payroll taxes for production supervisor	____	____	____	____	____
Amortization of patents on factory machine	____	____	____	____	____
Accident insurance on factory workers	____	____	____	____	____
Wages to assembly workers	____	____	____	____	____
Factory utilities	____	____	____	____	____
Small tools used	____	____	____	____	____
Bad debts expense	____	____	____	____	____
Depreciation—Factory building	____	____	____	____	____
Advertising			____		
Office supplies used	____	____	____	____	____

Identify each of the five cost classifications discussed in the chapter. Explain the purposes of identifying these separate cost accounting concepts.

Exercise 19-7
Cost classifications

Exercise 19-8
Cost analysis and classification

Listed here are product costs for the production of 1,000 soccer balls. (1) Classify each cost (a) as either fixed or variable and (b) as either direct or indirect. (2) What pattern do you see regarding the relation between costs classified by behavior and costs classified by traceability?

Product Cost	Cost by Behavior		Cost by Traceability	
	Variable	Fixed	Direct	Indirect
Leather cover for soccer balls	____	____	____	____
Lace to hold leather together	____	____	____	____
Wages of assembly workers	____	____	____	____
Taxes on factory	____	____	____	____
Annual flat fee paid to an office security company	____	____	____	____
Coolants for machinery	____	____	____	____
Machinery depreciation	____	____	____	____

Exercise 19-9
Balance sheet identification and preparation

Current assets for two different companies at calendar year-end 2002 are listed here. One is a manufacturer, Roller Blades Mfg., and the other, Wholesale Foods, is a grocery distribution company. (1) Identify which set of numbers relates to the manufacturer and which to the merchandiser. (2) Prepare the current asset section for each company from this information. Discuss why the current asset section for these two companies is different.

Account	Company 1	Company 2
Cash	$ 7,000	$ 5,000
Raw materials inventory	—	42,000
Merchandise inventory	45,000	—
Goods in process inventory	—	30,000
Finished goods inventory	—	50,000
Accounts receivable	62,000	75,000
Prepaid expenses	1,500	900

Exercise 19-10
Cost of goods sold computation

Compute cost of goods sold for each of these two companies for the year ended December 31, 2002:

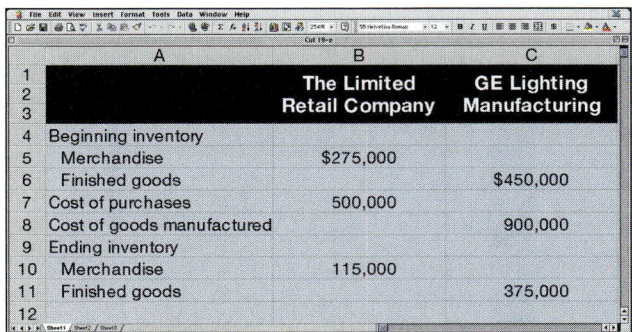

Using the following data, compute (1) the cost of goods manufactured and (2) the cost of goods sold for both Poke Company and Mon Company.

Exercise 19-11
Cost of goods manufactured and cost of goods sold computation

	Poke Company	Mon Company
Beginning finished goods inventory	$12,000	$16,450
Beginning goods in process inventory	14,500	19,950
Beginning raw materials inventory	7,250	9,000
Lease on factory equipment	27,000	22,750
Direct labor	19,000	35,000
Ending finished goods inventory	17,650	13,300
Ending goods in process inventory	22,000	16,000
Ending raw materials inventory	5,300	7,200
Factory utilities	9,000	12,000
Factory supplies used	8,200	3,200
General and administrative expenses	21,000	43,000
Indirect labor	1,250	7,660
Repairs—Factory equipment	4,780	1,500
Raw materials purchases	33,000	52,000
Sales salaries	50,000	46,000

For each of the following account balances for a manufacturing company, place a ✔ in the appropriate column indicating that it appears on the balance sheet, the income statement, the manufacturing statement, and/or a detailed listing of factory overhead costs. Assume that the income statement shows the calculation of cost of goods sold and the manufacturing statement shows only the total amount of factory overhead. (*An account balance may appear on more than one report.*)

Exercise 19-12
Components of financial statements

Account	Balance Sheet	Income Statement	Manufacturing Statement	Overhead Report
Accounts receivable				
Computer supplies used in office				
Beginning finished goods inventory				
Beginning goods in process inventory				
Beginning raw materials inventory				
Cash				
Depreciation expense—Factory building				
Depreciation expense—Factory equipment				
Depreciation expense—Office building				
Depreciation expense—Office equipment				
Direct labor				
Ending finished goods inventory				
Ending goods in process inventory				
Ending raw materials inventory				
Factory maintenance wages				
Computer supplies used in factory				
Income taxes				
Insurance on factory building				
Rent on office building				
Office supplies used				
Property taxes on factory building				
Raw materials purchases				
Sales				

Exercise 19-13
Manufacturing statement
preparation

Given the selected account balances of Sherman Corp. shown here, prepare its manufacturing statement in proper form for the year ended on December 31, 2002. Include a listing of the individual overhead account balances in this statement.

Sales	$1,250,000
Raw materials inventory, Dec. 31, 2001	37,000
Goods in process inventory, Dec. 31, 2001	53,900
Finished goods inventory, Dec. 31, 2001	62,750
Raw materials purchases	175,600
Direct labor	225,000
Factory computer supplies used	17,840
Indirect labor	47,000
Repairs—Factory equipment	5,250
Rent on factory building	57,000
Advertising expenses	94,000
General and administrative expenses	129,300
Raw materials inventory, Dec. 31, 2002	42,700
Goods in process inventory, Dec. 31, 2002	41,500
Finished goods inventory, Dec. 31, 2002	67,300

Exercise 19-14
Income statement
preparation

Use the information in Exercise 19-13 to prepare an income statement for Sherman Corporation (a manufacturer). Assume that its cost of goods manufactured is $534,390.

Exercise 19-15
Cost flows in manufacturing

The following chart shows how costs flow through a business as a product is manufactured. Some boxes in the flowchart show cost amount. Other boxes contain question marks, and for these, you are to compute the cost amounts.

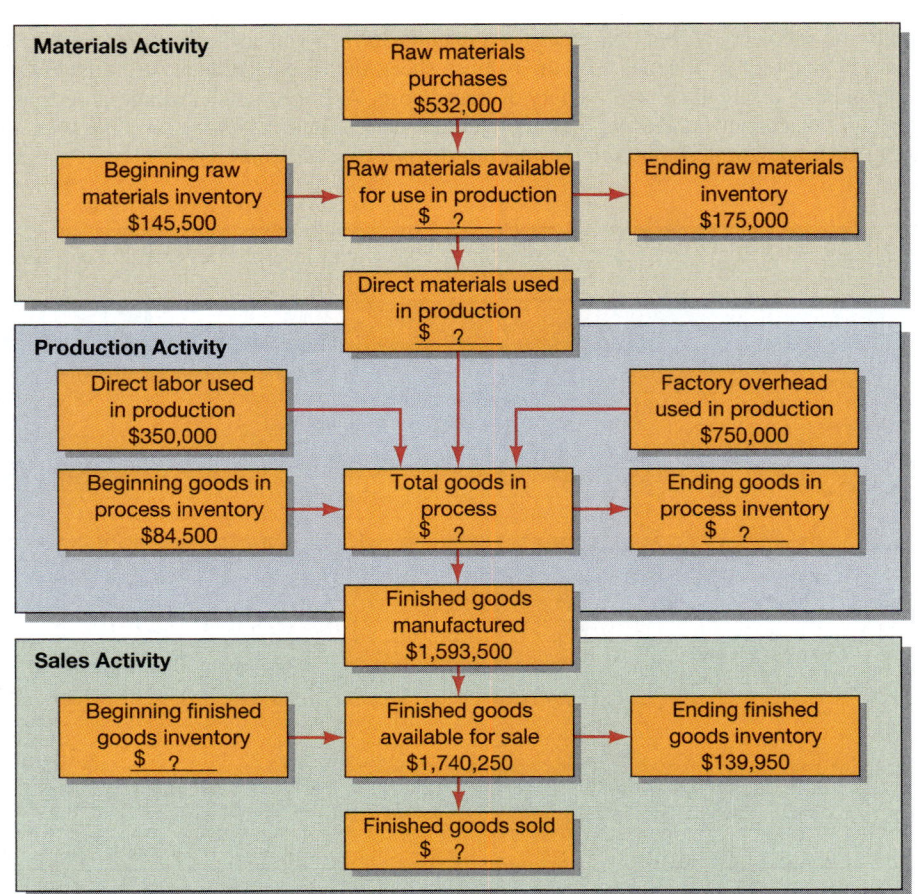

This chapter discusses the purposes of managerial accounting and the current business environment. You are to look through the *automobile* section of your local newspaper; the Sunday paper is often best. Review advertisements of sport utility vehicles and note how many manufacturers offer these products and what factors they compete on.

Required

Discuss the potential contributions and responsibilities of the managerial accounting professional in helping an automobile manufacturer succeed. (*Hint:* Think about information and estimates that a managerial accountant might provide new entrants into the sports utility market.)

Problem Set A

Problem 19-1A
Managerial accountant's role

A trip through a drive-up window of any leading fast-food restaurant is useful in understanding concepts such as total quality management (TQM), just-in-time (JIT), and continuous improvement (CI). Each restaurant can be viewed as a small manufacturing center. List two fast-food restaurants you are familiar with in the first column of the following table (e.g., McDonald's, Taco Bell, Burger King, and KFC). Record in the table how each company is putting each of these lean business concepts into action, both favorably and unfavorably.

Problem 19-2A
Lean business concepts

Restaurant	TQM	JIT	CI

Listed here are the total costs associated with the production of 1,000 drum sets manufactured by DrumLand. The drum sets sell for $500 each.

Problem 19-3A
Cost computation, classification, and analysis

Costs	Cost by Behavior		Cost by Function	
	Variable	Fixed	Product	Period
Plastic for casing—$17,000	$17,000		$17,000	
Wages of assembly workers—$82,000				
Taxes on factory—$5,000				
Accounting staff salaries—$35,000				
Drum stands (1,000 stands outsourced)—$26,000				
Lease of equipment for sales staff—$10,000				
Upper management salaries—$125,000				
Annual flat fee for maintenance service—$10,000				
Sales commissions—$15 per unit				
Machinery depreciation—$40,000				

Required

Preparation Component

1. Classify each cost and its amount as (a) either fixed or variable and (b) either product or period (the first cost is completed as an example).
2. Compute the (a) contribution margin and (b) contribution margin ratio by filling in the boxes in this table:

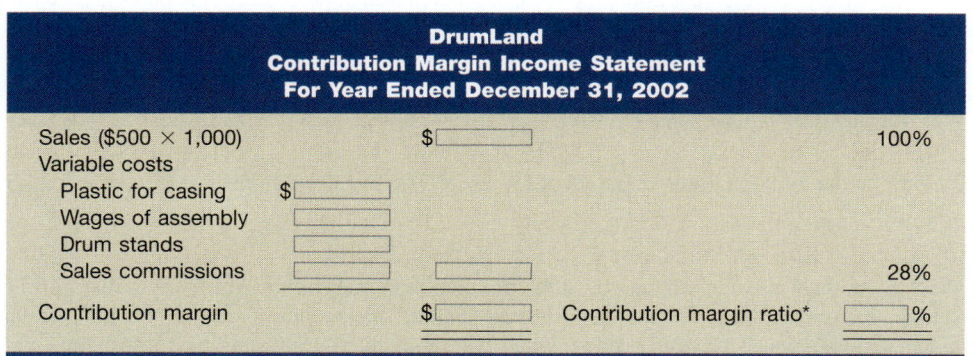

Check Total variable cost, $140,000

* Contribution margin ratio = Contribution margin/Sales.

Analysis Component

3. Interpret the contribution margin and the contribution margin ratio.

Problem 19-4A
Cost classification and explanation

You must make a presentation to the marketing staff explaining the difference between product and period costs. Your supervisor tells you the marketing staff would also like clarification regarding prime and conversion costs and an explanation of how these terms fit with product and period cost. You are told that many on the staff are unable to identify these terms in their merchandising activities.

Required

Prepare a one-page memorandum to your supervisor outlining your presentation to the marketing staff.

Problem 19-5A
Opportunity cost estimation and application

Refer to *You Make the Call,* **Purchase Manager,** in this chapter. Assume that you are the motorcycle manufacturer's managerial accountant. The purchasing manager asks you about preparing an estimate of the related costs for buying motorcycle seats from supplier (B). She tells you this estimate is needed because unless dollar estimates are attached to nonfinancial factors, such as lost production time, her supervisor will not give it full attention. The purchasing manager also shows you this information:

• Production output is 1,000 motorcycles per year based on 250 production days a year.
• Production time per day is 8 hours at a cost of $2,000 per hour to run the production line.
• Lost production time due to poor quality is 1%.
• Satisfied customers purchase, on average, three motorcycles during a lifetime.
• Satisfied customers recommend the product, on average, to five other people.
• Marketing estimates that using seat (B) will result in five lost customers per year from repeat business and referrals.
• Average contribution margin per motorcycle is $3,000.

Required

Estimate the costs (including opportunity costs) of buying motorcycle seats from supplier (B). This problem requires you to think creatively and make reasonable estimates and, therefore, there could be more than one correct answer. [*Hint:* Reread the answer to *You Make the Call* and compare the cost savings for buying from supplier (B) to the sum of lost customer revenue from repeat business and referrals and the cost of lost production time.]

Check Cost of lost production time, $40,000

Problem 19-6A
Ending inventory computation and evaluation

Western Boot Company makes specialty boots for the rodeo circuit. On December 31, 2001, the company had (a) 300 boots in finished goods inventory and (b) 1,200 heels at a cost of $8 each in raw materials inventory. During year 2002, the company purchased 35,000 additional heels at $8 each and manufactured 33,200 boots.

Required

Preparation Component

Check Ending (heel) inventory, $24,000 (3,000 units)

1. Determine the unit and dollar amounts of raw materials inventory in heels at December 31, 2002.

Analysis Component

2. Write a one-half page memorandum to the production manager explaining why a just-in-time inventory system for heels should be considered. Include the amount of working capital that can be reduced at December 31, 2002, if the ending heel raw material inventory is cut in half.

Shown here are the annual financial data at December 31, 2002, taken from two different companies.

	World Sport Retail	Sno-Board Manufacturing
Beginning inventory		
Merchandise	$200,000	
Finished goods		$500,000
Cost of purchases	300,000	
Cost of goods manufactured		875,000
Ending inventory		
Merchandise	175,000	
Finished goods		225,000

Problem 19-7A
Inventory computation and reporting

Required

1. Compute the cost of goods sold section of the income statement at December 31, 2002, for each company. Include proper title and format in the solution.

2. Write a half-page memorandum to your instructor (a) identifying the inventory accounts and (b) describing where each is reported on the income statement and balance sheet for both companies.

Check Sno-Board's cost of goods sold, $1,150,000

The following information is taken from the December 31, 2002, adjusted trial balance and other records of Patio Company before the calendar year-end closing entries are recorded:

Problem 19-8A
Manufacturing and income statements; inventory analysis **P2**

Advertising expense	$ 28,750		Direct labor	675,480
Depreciation expense—Office equipment	7,250		Income taxes expense	233,725
Depreciation expense—Selling equipment	8,600		Indirect labor	56,875
Depreciation expense—Factory equipment	33,550		Miscellaneous production costs	8,425
Factory supervision	102,600		Office salaries expense	63,000
Factory supplies used	7,350		Raw materials purchases	925,000
Factory utilities	33,000		Rent expense—Office space	22,000
Inventories			Rent expense—Selling space	26,100
Raw materials, December 31, 2001	166,850		Rent expense—Factory building	76,800
Raw materials, December 31, 2002	182,000		Maintenance—Factory equipment	35,400
Goods in process, December 31, 2001	15,700		Sales	4,525,000
Goods in process, December 31, 2002	19,380		Sales discounts	62,500
Finished goods, December 31, 2001	167,350		Sales salaries expense	392,560
Finished goods, December 31, 2002	136,490			

Required

Preparation Component

1. Prepare the 2002 manufacturing statement for the company.

2. Prepare the 2002 income statement for the company that reports separate categories for (a) selling expenses and (b) general and administrative expenses.

Check Cost of goods manufactured, $1,935,650

Analysis Component

3. Compute the (a) inventory turnover and (b) days' sales in inventory for both its raw materials inventory and its finished goods inventory (see Chapter 7). Discuss some possible reasons for differences between these ratios for the two types of inventories.

Woodruff grocery chain, a market leader, wants to increase sales to its existing customers by creating a customer orientation to better meet buyer needs and wants. Assume that Woodruff hires you as a consultant to analyze its operations and suggest improvements. Woodruff's goal is to increase its contribution margin by $40,000.

Problem 19-9A
Sales and costs estimation; contribution margin analysis

Required

1. To increase Woodruff's sales and contribution margin from existing customers, offer three improvements that you have observed in other stores and believe would be successful here.

2. What level of increase in sales is necessary for Woodruff to increase contribution margin by $40,000? (Hint: With each suggestion in part [1], identify the expected sales dollars and the contribution margin ratio to meet the $40,000 increase in contribution margin.)

Problem Set B

Problem 19-1B
Managerial accountant's role

This chapter discusses the purposes of managerial accounting and the current business environment. You are to look through the *home electronics* section of your local newspaper; the Sunday paper is often best. Review advertisements of home electronics and note how many manufacturers offer these products and what factors they compete on.

Required

Discuss the potential contributions and responsibilities of the managerial accounting professional in helping a home electronics manufacturer succeed. (*Hint:* Think about information and estimates that a managerial accountant might provide new entrants into the home electronics market.)

Problem 19-2B
Lean business concepts

A trip to the photography store is useful in understanding concepts such as total quality management (TQM), just-in-time (JIT), and continuous improvement (CI). List two photography stores you are familiar with in the first column of the following table. Record in the table how each store is putting each of these lean business concepts into action, both favorably and unfavorably. (*Hint:* To prepare a response to this question, you may want to watch how film is processed and prints prepared within 1 hour.)

Photography Store	TQM	JIT	CI

Problem 19-3B
Cost computation, classification, and analysis

Listed here are the total costs associated with the production of 12,000 CDs manufactured by CD land. The CDs sell for $18 each.

	Cost by Behavior		Cost by Function	
Costs	**Variable**	**Fixed**	**Product**	**Period**
Plastic for CDs—$1,500	$1,500		$1,500	
Wages of assembly workers—$30,000				
Rent on factory—$6,750				
Systems staff salaries—$15,000				
Labeling (12,000 outsourced)—$3,750				
Lease of office equipment—$1,050				
Upper management salaries—$120,000				
Annual fixed fee for cleaning service—$4,520				
Sales commissions—$0.50 per CD				
Machinery depreciation—$20,000				

Required

Preparation Component

1. Classify each cost and its amount as (a) either fixed or variable and (b) either product or period.

2. Compute the (a) contribution margin and (b) contribution margin ratio by filling in the boxes in this table:

CD LAND			
Contribution Margin Income Statement			
For Year Ended December 31, 2002			
Sales ($18 × 12,000)	$ ☐		100%
Variable costs			
Plastic for CDs	$ ☐		
Wages of assembly	☐		
Labels outsourced	☐		
Sales commissions	☐	☐	19%
Contribution margin	$ ☐	Contribution margin ratio* ☐ %	

* Contribution margin ratio = Contribution margin/Sales.

Check   Total variable cost, $41,250

Analysis Component

3. Interpret the contribution margin and the contribution margin ratio.

You must make a presentation to a client explaining the difference between prime and conversion costs. The client makes and sells bread for 200,000 customers per week. The client tells you that her sales staff also would like a clarification regarding product and period costs. She tells you that many on the staff have financial accounting training but lack training in managerial accounting.

Problem 19-4B
Cost classification and explanation

Required

Prepare a one-page memorandum to your client outlining your planned presentation to her sales staff.

Refer to *You Make the Call,* **Purchase Manager,** in this chapter. Assume that you are the motorcycle manufacturer's managerial accountant. The purchasing manager asks you about preparing an estimate of the related costs for buying motorcycle seats from supplier (B). She tells you this estimate is needed because unless dollar estimates are attached to nonfinancial factors such as lost production time, her supervisor will not give it full attention. The purchasing manager also shows you this information:

- Production output is 1,000 motorcycles per year based on 250 production days a year.
- Production time per day is 8 hours at a cost of $500 per hour to run the production line.
- Lost production time due to poor quality is 1%.
- Satisfied customers purchase, on average, three motorcycles during a lifetime.
- Satisfied customers recommend the product, on average, to four other people.
- Marketing estimates that using seat (B) will result in four lost customers per year from repeat business and referrals.
- Average contribution margin per motorcycle is $4,000.

Problem 19-5B
Opportunity cost estimation and application

Required

Estimate the costs (including opportunity costs) of buying motorcycle seats from supplier (B). This problem requires you to think creatively and make reasonable estimates and, therefore, there could be more than one correct answer. [*Hint:* Reread the answer to *You Make the Call,* and compare the cost savings for buying from supplier (B) to the sum of lost customer revenue from repeat business and referrals and the cost of lost production time.]

Check   Cost of lost production time, $10,000

Candle Skate, Inc., makes specialty skates for the ice skating circuit. On December 31, 2001, the company had (a) 1,500 skates in finished goods inventory and (b) 2,500 blades at a cost of $20 each in raw materials inventory. During year 2002, Candle Skate purchased 45,000 additional blades at $20 each and manufactured 41,500 skates.

Problem 19-6B
Ending inventory computation and evaluation

Required

Preparation Component

1. Determine the unit and dollar amounts of raw materials inventory in blades at December 31, 2002.

Check   Ending (blade) inventory, $120,000 (6,000 units)

Analysis Component

2. Write a one-half page memorandum to the production manager explaining why a just-in-time inventory system for blades should be considered. Include the amount of working capital that can be reduced at December 31, 2002, if the ending blade raw material inventory is cut in half.

Problem 19-7B
Inventory computation and reporting

Shown here are the annual financial data at December 31, 2002, taken from two different companies.

	Cardinal CD Retail	Van Conversion Inc. Manufacturing
Beginning inventory		
Merchandise	$100,000	
Finished goods		$300,000
Cost of purchases	250,000	
Cost of goods manufactured		586,000
Ending inventory		
Merchandise	150,000	
Finished goods		200,000

Required

Check Cardinal CD cost of goods sold, $200,000

1. Compute the cost of goods sold section of the income statement at December 31, 2002, for each company. Include proper title and format in the solution.
2. Write a half-page memorandum to your instructor (a) identifying the inventory accounts and (b) identifying where each is reported on the income statement and balance sheet for both companies.

Problem 19-8B
Manufacturing and income statements; analysis of inventories

The following information is taken from the December 31, 2002, adjusted trial balance and other records of Fine Furniture, Inc., before the calendar year-end closing entries are recorded:

Advertising expense	$ 20,250		Direct labor	562,500
Depreciation expense—Office equipment	8,440		Income taxes expense	136,700
Depreciation expense—Selling equipment	10,125		Indirect labor	59,000
Depreciation expense—Factory equipment	35,400		Miscellaneous production costs	8,440
Factory supervision	121,500		Office salaries expense	70,875
Factory supplies used	6,060		Raw materials purchases	894,375
Factory utilities	37,500		Rent expense—Office space	23,625
Inventories			Rent expense—Selling space	27,000
Raw materials, December 31, 2001	40,375		Rent expense—Factory building	93,500
Raw materials, December 31, 2002	70,430		Maintenance—Factory equipment	30,375
Goods in process, December 31, 2001	12,500		Sales	5,000,000
Goods in process, December 31, 2002	14,100		Sales discounts	57,375
Finished goods, December 31, 2001	177,200		Sales salaries expense	295,300
Finished goods, December 31, 2002	141,750			

Required

Preparation Component

Check Cost of goods manufactured, $1,816,995

1. Prepare the 2002 manufacturing statement for the company.
2. Prepare the 2002 income statement for the company that reports separate categories for (a) selling expenses and (b) general and administrative expenses.

Analysis Component

3. Compute the (a) inventory turnover and (b) days' sales in inventory for both its raw materials inventory and its finished goods inventory (see Chapter 7). Discuss some possible reasons for differences between these ratios for the two types of inventories.

American Bagel Store chain, a market leader, wishes to increase sales to its existing customers by creating a customer orientation to better meet buyer needs and wants. Assume that American Bagel hires you as a consultant to analyze its operations and suggest improvements. American Bagel's goal is to increase its contribution margin by $10,000.

Problem 19-9B

Sales and costs estimation; contribution margin analysis

Required

1. To increase American Bagle's sales and contribution margin from existing customers, offer three improvements that you have observed in other stores and believe would be successful here.
2. What level of increase in sales is necessary for American Bagel to increase contribution margin by $10,000? (*Hint:* With each suggestion in part [1], identify the expected sales dollars and contribution margin ratio to meet the $10,000 increase in contribution margin.)

Beyond the Numbers

BTN 19-1   Managerial accounting is more than recording, maintaining, and reporting financial results. Managerial accountants must provide managers with both financial and nonfinancial information including estimates, projections, and forecasts. Looking into the future involves risk, however. **Nike**'s managers, including its managerial accountants, must notify shareholders of this risk.

Reporting in Action

Required

1. Access and read Nike's Management Discussion and Analysis (MD&A) section in either its annual report or its 10-K for the year ended May 31, 2000 [**www.nike.com**]. What risks do Nike's shareholders face as management and employees work to position the company for long-term success?
2. What are the managerial accountants' responsibilities in evaluating risk?

Swoosh Ahead

3. Access Nike's annual report for a fiscal year ending after May 31, 2000, from either its Web site [**www.nike.com**] or the SEC's EDGAR database [**www.sec.gov**]. Answer the questions in parts (1) and (2) after reading the MD&A section. Identify any major changes.

BTN 19-2   **Nike** and **Reebok** are primarily manufacturing companies. Answer the following questions using their financial information reported in Appendix A.

Comparative Analysis

Required

1. Review each company's balance sheet and then identify and record clues indicating that each is a manufacturer.
2. Search the notes to Nike's financial statements for evidence that it is a manufacturer. Record your evidence.
3. Compute inventory turnover (using ending inventory in the denominator) and days' sales in inventory for the most recent two years reported for each company. Interpret both ratios.
4. What likely impact would a just-in-time inventory system have on the turnover values in part (3)?

BTN 19-3   You are the managerial accountant at Adtec, Inc., a manufacturer of hard drives, CDs, and diskettes. Its financial reporting year-end is December 31. The chief financial officer is concerned about having enough cash to pay the expected corporate tax bill because of poor cash flow management. On November 15, the purchasing department purchased excess inventory of CD raw materials in anticipation of rapid growth of this product beginning in January. To decrease the company's tax liability, the chief financial officer tells you to record the purchase of this inventory as part of supplies and expense it in the current year—this would decrease the company's tax liability by increasing expenses.

Ethics Challenge

Required

1. In which account should the purchase of CD raw materials be recorded?
2. How should you respond to this request by the chief financial officer?

Communicating in Practice

BTN 19-4   Write a one-page memorandum to a prospective college student about salary expectations for graduates in business. Compare and contrast the expected salaries for accounting (including different subfields such as public, corporate, tax, audit, and so forth), marketing, management, and finance majors. Prepare a graph showing average starting salaries (and those for experienced professionals in those fields if available). To get this information, stop by your school's career services office; libraries also have this information. The Web site **http://jobsmart.org** (click on *Salary Info*) can get you started.

Taking It to the Net
C1 C2

BTN 19-5   Managerial accounting professionals follow a code of ethics. As a member of the Institute of Management Accountants, the managerial accountant must comply with Standards of Ethical Conduct. Identify, print, and read the *Ethical Standards* posted at the following Web site: **www.IMAnet.org.** (Search using "ethical standards.")

Teamwork in Action
C8 P2

BTN 19-6   The following information is taken from the December 31, 2002, adjusted trial balance and other records of Dawls Company before the year-end closing entries are recorded:

Advertising expense	$ 19,125	Direct labor	650,750
Depreciation expense—Office equipment	8,750	Indirect labor	60,000
Depreciation expense—Selling equipment	10,000	Miscellaneous production costs	8,500
Depreciation expense—Factory equipment	32,500	Office salaries expense	100,875
Factory supervision	122,500	Raw materials purchases	872,500
Factory supplies used	15,750	Rent expense—Office space	21,125
Factory utilities	36,250	Rent expense—Selling space	25,750
Inventories		Rent expense—Factory building	79,750
Raw materials, December 31, 2001	177,500	Maintenance—Factory equipment	27,875
Raw materials, December 31, 2002	168,125	Sales	3,275,000
Goods in process, December 31, 2001	15,875	Sales discounts	57,500
Goods in process, December 31, 2002	14,000	Sales salaries expense	286,250
Finished goods, December 31, 2001	164,375		
Finished goods, December 31, 2002	129,000		

Required

1. *Each* team member is to be responsible for computing **one** of the following amounts. You are not to duplicate your teammates' work. Get any necessary amounts from teammates. Each member is to explain the computation to the team in preparation for reporting to class.
   a. Materials used.
   d. Total cost of goods in process.
   b. Factory overhead.
   e. Cost of goods manufactured.
   c. Total manufacturing costs.
2. Check your cost of goods manufactured with the instructor. If it is correct, proceed to part (3).
3. *Each* team member is to be responsible for computing **one** of the following amounts. You are not to duplicate your teammates' work. Get any necessary amounts from teammates. Each member is to explain the computation to the team in preparation for reporting to class.
   a. Net sales.
   d. Total operating expenses.
   b. Cost of goods sold.
   e. Net income or loss before taxes.
   c. Gross profit.

Point: Provide teams with transparencies and markers for presentation purposes.

BTN 19-7 The success or failure of many companies depends on the income earned between October 15 and December 24 of each year. Read the article "Why Win98's Delay Is O.K." in the September 29, 1997, issue of *Business Week*.

Required

1. Why were businesses—manufacturing, distribution, and retail—concerned about the release of an operating system by **Microsoft**? Does the managerial accounting professional need to know about the release of products and customer reactions to any products other than the ones his/her company sells?

2. Assume that you make keyboards for **Dell Computer**. Write a one-page memorandum to your company's management outlining the possible impact on your product from Microsoft's delay of the release of a future operating system upgrade.

BTN 19-8 Liana Lindsay, a computer science major, is considering starting a company. The company would either focus on developing Internet-based software for children (developed by herself) or sell such computer software developed by others. You are her only friend with knowledge of management accounting, and she comes to you for advice. (Note: She is a full-time student and can devote at most 30 hours per week toward this start-up company.)

Required

Which alternative do you recommend? What factors must she consider in this decision? Prepare your response to these questions in a one-half page memorandum to Liana Lindsay. (*Hint*: In answering the question, think about the resources required and the types of costs she will incur.)

20

Job Order
Cost Accounting

"We're growing at an incredibly rapid pace."—Brad Aronson.

A Look Back

Chapter 19 introduced us to managerial accounting. We compared it to financial accounting and explained basic cost concepts. We also described the lean business model and the reporting of manufacturing activities, including the manufacturing statement preparation.

A Look at This Chapter

We begin this chapter by describing a general accounting system and a cost accounting system. We then explain the procedures used to determine costs using a job order costing system. We conclude with a discussion of over- and underapplied overhead.

A Look Ahead

Chapter 21 considers how we measure costs in process production industries. We explain process production in detail, describe how to assign costs to processes, and compute and analyze the cost per equivalent unit.

Learning Objectives

Conceptual

C1 Explain the periodic and perpetual inventory systems.

C2 Describe important features of job order manufacturing.

C3 Explain job cost sheets and how they are used in job order cost accounting.

Analytical

A1 Apply job order costing in pricing services.

Procedural

P1 Describe and record the flow of materials costs in job order cost accounting.

P2 Describe and record the flow of labor costs in job order cost accounting.

P3 Describe and record the flow of overhead costs in job order cost accounting.

P4 Determine adjustments for overapplied and underapplied factory overhead.

Costing e-Ads for Profits

e PHILADELPHIA—Four years ago, 24-year-old Brad Aronson was working as a resident staffer in a group home for underprivileged kids when he started his online advertising services firm with only a computer in his bedroom. Today, Aronson's firm, **i-FRONTIER** (**www.i-FRONTIER.com**), has a staff of nearly 100, billings approaching $90 million, and revenues of almost $10 million. "I learned it all myself. I bought every book [and] subscribed to every magazine," says Aronson.

Aronson's success depends on cost controls and an emphasis on quality services. "We stick to our core business. We don't talk to clients and say we offer everything." A focus on quality work on each job has enabled Aronson to land lucrative clients such as Coppertone, Claritin, StarMedia Network, and Discovery Channel. He effectively monitors and controls labor and overhead costs; he also charges more than many competitors. Says Aronson, "By charging more, we're making a clear statement about our value."

This strategy has helped i-FRONTIER avoid the pitfalls of many online ventures that failed to use cost accounting systems to manage runaway costs. Much of its client list is buttoned-down, old-economy, and heavyweight. "We have a lot of bricks-and-mortar clients," says Aronson. "It's not the market that could trip us up. It's ourselves." Still, Aronson admits that i-FRONTIER must consistently deliver "quality innovative work and return on investment for our clients and their brands," with emphasis on cost measurement and controls.

Oh, about his social-work gig—Aronson still volunteers time at the group home. "There are issues more important than the decisions that come with owning a business," says Aronson. With such solid footing along with cost management, Brad Aronson should be around for a long time to come. [Sources: *i-FRONTIER Web site,* May 2001; *Philadelphia Business Journal,* September 2000; *dbusiness.com,* June 2000; *Entrepreneur,* November 1999.]

This chapter introduces two different systems for assigning costs to the flow of goods through a production process: the periodic and perpetual inventory systems. We then describe in detail a *job order cost accounting system*. Job order costing is frequently used by manufacturers of custom products or providers of custom services. Manufacturers who use job order costing typically base it on a perpetual inventory system, which provides a continuous record of materials, goods in process, and finished goods inventories.

Inventory System and Accounting for Costs

C1 Explain the periodic and perpetual inventory systems.

This section explains the accounting methods used to compile the costs reported in the manufacturing statement (see Exhibit 19.16). We begin with a brief discussion of accounting for manufacturing activities using a general accounting system. Our main emphasis, however, is describing accounting for manufacturing activities using a cost accounting system.

General Accounting System

A **general accounting system** records manufacturing activities using a *periodic* inventory system. A periodic inventory system measures costs of raw materials, goods in process, and finished goods from physical counts of quantities available at the end of each period. This information is used to compute amounts of the product used, finished, and sold during a period. Some companies still use a general accounting system, but its frequency of use is declining. Competitive forces and customer demands have increased pressures on companies to better manage inventories. Also, an increasing number of companies need more timely and precise information on inventories than what a general accounting system provides. (For those interested, the closing process for a manufacturer using a general accounting system is described in Appendix 20A, located on this book's Web site.)

Cost Accounting System

Point: Cost accounting systems accumulate costs and then assign them to products or services.

Point: Many professional examinations require knowledge of job order and process cost accounting. These include the CPA and CMA exams.

An ever-increasing number of companies use a cost accounting system to generate timely and accurate inventory information. A **cost accounting system** records manufacturing activities using a *perpetual* inventory system, which continuously updates records for costs of materials, goods in process, and finished goods inventories. A cost accounting system also provides timely information about inventories and about manufacturing costs per unit of product. This is especially helpful for managers' efforts to control costs and determine selling prices. The two basic types of cost accounting systems are *job order cost accounting* and *process cost accounting*. We describe the first type, job order cost accounting, in this chapter. The second type, process cost accounting, is explained in Chapter 21.

Job Order Cost Accounting

C2 Describe important features of job order manufacturing.

Concept 20-1

Point: To apply these concepts, work QS 20-2.

This section describes a job order manufacturing and cost accounting system. Understanding a job order manufacturing system and its activities is important before we can understand how to account for them. We explain that system and its activities in this section.

Job Order Manufacturing

Many companies manufacture products individually designed to meet the needs of a specific customer. Each customized product is manufactured separately and its production is called **job order manufacturing** (also called *customized production,* which is the production of products in response to special orders). Examples are special machines, a building, custom-made jewelry, and artwork. The production activities for a customized product represent a **job.** Although we use the term *job order manufacturing,* the principle of customization is equally applicable to both manufacturing *and* service companies. Most service companies meet customers' needs by performing a custom service for a specific customer. Examples of such services include an accountant auditing a client's financial statements, an interior designer remodeling an office, a wedding consultant planning and supervising a reception, and a lawyer defending a client. Whether the setting is manufacturing or services, job order operations involve meeting the needs of customers by producing or performing custom jobs. This type of system is likely to be flexible in the number of different products and services it offers.

McDonnell Douglas's aerospace division is one example of a job order manufacturing system. Its primary business is twofold: (1) design, develop, and integrate space carriers and (2) systems engineering and integration of Department of Defense (DoD) systems. Most orders are customized.

When a job involves producing more than one unit of a special product, it is often called a **job lot.** Products produced as job lots might include benches for a church, imprinted T-shirts for a 10K race or company picnic, or advertising signs for a chain of stores. Although these orders involve more than one unit, the volume of production is typically low, such as 50 benches, 200 T-shirts, or 100 signs. Another feature of job order manufacturing is the diversity, often called *heterogeneity,* of the products manufactured. Namely, each customer order is likely to be different from another in some important respect. These variations can be minor or major.

Events in Job Order Manufacturing

The initial event in a normal job order manufacturing operation is the receipt of a customer order for a custom product. This causes the manufacturer to begin work on a job. A less common case occurs when management decides to begin work on a job before it has a signed contract. This is referred to as *jobs manufactured on speculation.*

The first step in both cases is to predict the cost to complete the job. This cost depends on the product design prepared by either the customer or the manufacturer. The second step is to negotiate a sales price and decide whether to pursue the job. Some jobs are priced on a *cost-plus basis;* meaning the customer pays the manufacturer for costs incurred on the job plus a negotiated amount or rate of profit. The third step is for the manufacturer to schedule production of the job to meet the customer's needs and to fit within its own production constraints. Preparation of this work schedule should consider workplace facilities including equipment, personnel, and supplies. Once this schedule is complete, the manufacturer can place orders for raw materials. Production occurs as materials and labor are applied to the job.

An overview of job order production activity is shown in Exhibit 20.1. This exhibit shows the March production activity of **Road Warriors**, which manufactures security-equipped cars and trucks. The company converts any vehicle by giving it a diversity of security items such as alarms, reinforced exterior, bulletproof glass, and bomb detectors. The company began by catering to high-profile celebrities, but it has grown and now caters to anyone who desires added security in a vehicle.

Job order manufacturing for Road Warriors requires materials, labor, and overhead costs. Recall that direct materials are goods used in manufacturing that are clearly identified with a particular job. Similarly, direct labor is effort devoted to a particular job. Overhead costs support production of more than one job. Common overhead items are depreciation on factory buildings and equipment, factory supplies, supervision, maintenance, cleaning, and utilities.

Did You Know?

Build-to-Order   A Copernican revolution of sorts is underway. Managers used to imagine their companies as the center of a solar system orbited by suppliers and customers. Now the customer is becoming the center of the business universe. Companies such as **Dell Computer** encourage consumers to customize products. **General Motors** and **Ford** will soon join **Toyota** in giving this power to car buyers. The manager of GM's online division, dubbed e-GM, declares that the customer will be able to configure the vehicle over the Internet and climb behind the wheel within a few days. To fill orders in Internet time, the mass-production model must be revamped—and perhaps scrapped. Where carmakers go, other manufacturers are sure to follow. Soon consumers may be able to personalize almost any product, from cellular phones to appliances.

Did You Know?

Job Order Education   With more companies investing in their employees, the demand for executive education is on the rise. Annual spending on U.S. corporate training and education recently rose to $16.5 billion. Moreover, annual revenues for 63 providers of executive education recently surveyed by *Business Week* averaged $11.9 million, with 43% of revenues coming from custom programs designed for one or a group of companies.

You Make the Call

Management Consultant One of your tasks is to control and manage costs for a consulting company. At the end of a recent month, you find that three consulting jobs have been completed and two are 60% complete. Each unfinished job is estimated to cost $10,000 and to earn a revenue of $12,000. You are unsure how to recognize goods in process inventory and record costs and revenues. Do you recognize any inventory? If so, how much? Also, how much revenue is recorded for the unfinished jobs in this month?

Answer—p. 845

Exhibit 20.1 shows that materials, labor, and overhead are added to Job Numbers B5, B6, B7, B8, and B9 during March. Road Warriors completed Jobs B5, B6, and B7 in March and delivered Jobs B5 and B6 to customers. At the end of March, Jobs B8 and B9 remain in goods in process inventory and Job B7 is in finished goods inventory. Labor and materials are also divided into their direct and indirect components. Their indirect amounts are added to overhead. Total overhead cost is then allocated to the various jobs.

Exhibit 20.1

Job Order Manufacturing
Activities

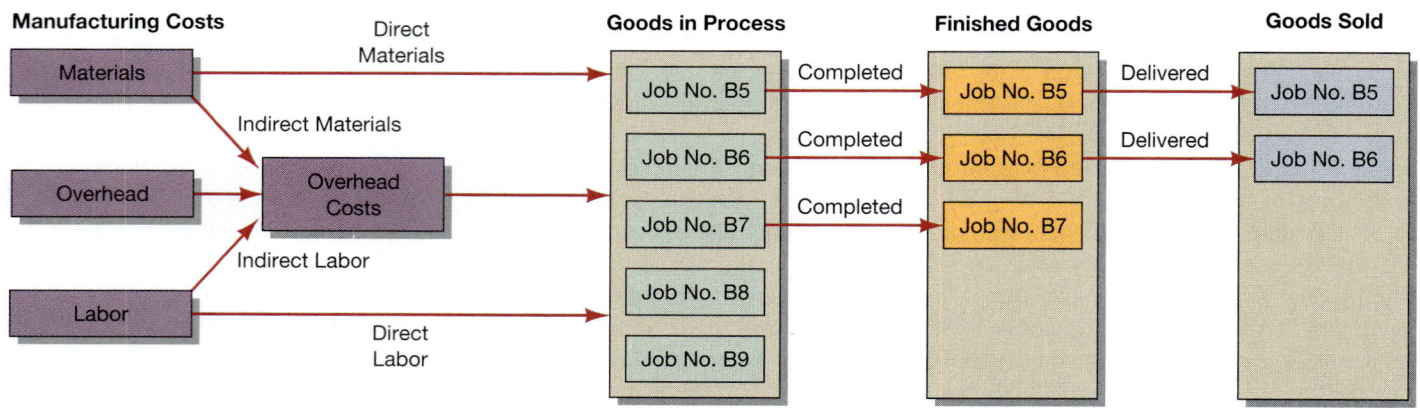

Job Cost Sheet

C3 Explain job cost sheets and how they are used in job order cost accounting.

General ledger accounts usually do not provide the accounting information that managers of job order cost operations need to plan and control production activities. This is so because the needed information often involves detailed data. Instead, such data are usually stored in subsidiary records controlled by general ledger accounts. Subsidiary records store information about raw materials, overhead costs, jobs in process, finished goods, and other items. This section describes the use of these records within job order cost accounting.

A major aim of a **job order cost accounting system** is to determine the cost of producing each job or job lot. In the case of a job lot, it also aims to compute the cost per unit. The accounting system must include separate records for each job to accomplish this, and it must capture information about costs incurred and charge these costs to each job.

A **job cost sheet** is a separate record maintained for each job. Exhibit 20.2 shows a job cost sheet for an alarm system that Road Warriors produced for a customer. This job cost sheet identifies the customer, the number assigned to the job, the product, and key dates. Costs incurred on the job are immediately recorded on this sheet. When each job is complete, the supervisor enters the date of completion, records any remarks, and signs the sheet. The job cost sheet in Exhibit 20.2 classifies costs as direct materials, direct labor, or overhead. It shows that a total of $600 in direct materials is added to Job B15 on four different dates. It also shows seven entries for direct labor costs that total $1,000. Road Warriors *allocates* (also termed applies, assigns, or charges) factory overhead costs of $1,600 to this job using an allocation rate of 160% of direct labor cost (160% × $1,000)—we discuss overhead allocation later in this chapter.

Point: Factory overhead consists of costs (other than direct materials and direct labor) to ensure production activity is carried out.

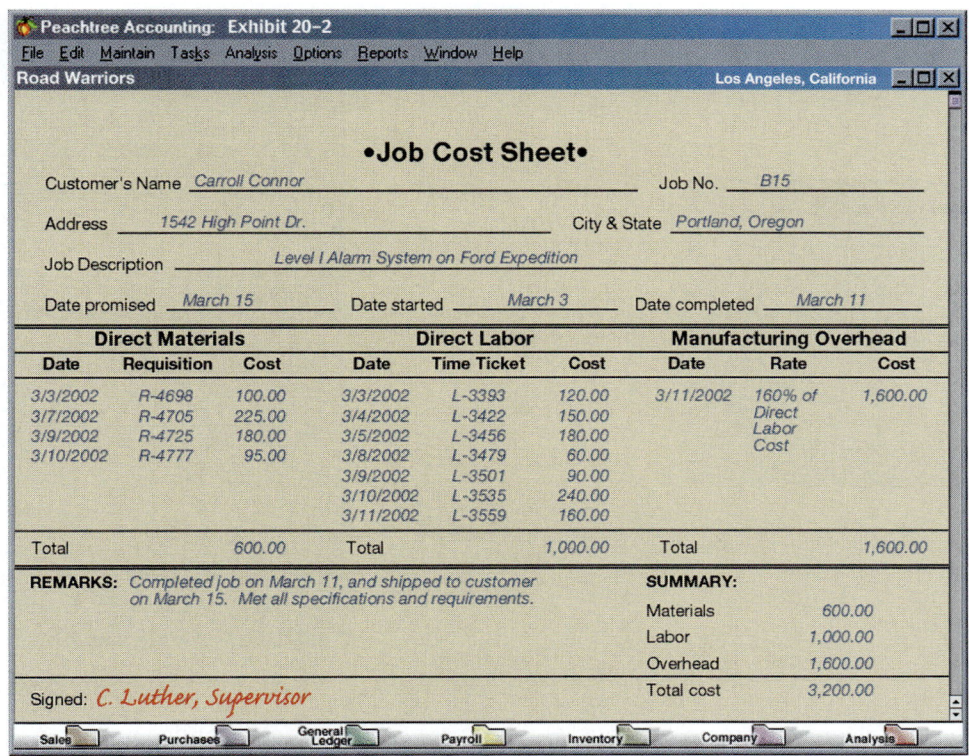

Exhibit 20.2

Job Cost Sheet

While a job is being manufactured, its accumulated costs are kept in **Goods in Process Inventory.** The collection of job cost sheets for all jobs in process makes up a subsidiary ledger controlled by the Goods in Process Inventory account in the general ledger. Managers use job cost sheets to monitor costs incurred to date and to predict and control costs for each job.

When a job is finished, its job cost sheet is completed and moved from the jobs in process file to the finished jobs file. This latter file acts as a subsidiary ledger controlled by the **Finished Goods Inventory** account. When a finished job is delivered to a customer, the job cost sheet is moved to a permanent file supporting the total cost of goods sold. This permanent file contains records from both current and prior periods.

Point: To apply these concepts, work QS 20-3.

Point: Documents are crucial in a job order system and the job cost sheet is a cornerstone. Understanding it aids in grasping concepts of capitalizing product costs and product cost flow.

Quick Check

1. Which of these products is likely to involve job order manufacturing? (a) inexpensive watches, (b) racing bikes, or (c) bottled soft drinks.

2. What is the difference between a job and a job lot?

3. Which of these statements is correct? (a) The collection of job cost sheets for unfinished jobs makes up a subsidiary ledger controlled by the Goods in Process account, (b) Job cost sheets are financial statements provided to investors, or (c) A separate job cost sheet is maintained in the general ledger for each job in process.

4. What three costs are normally accumulated on job cost sheets?

Answers—p. 845

Materials Cost Flows and Documents

This section focuses on the flow of materials costs and the related documents in a job order cost accounting system. We begin analysis of the flow of materials cost by discussing Exhibit 20.3. When materials are first received from suppliers, the employees count and inspect them. They record the quantity and cost of items on a receiving

Materials

P1 Describe and record the flow of materials costs in job order cost accounting.

Exhibit 20.3

Materials Cost Flows through
Subsidiary Records

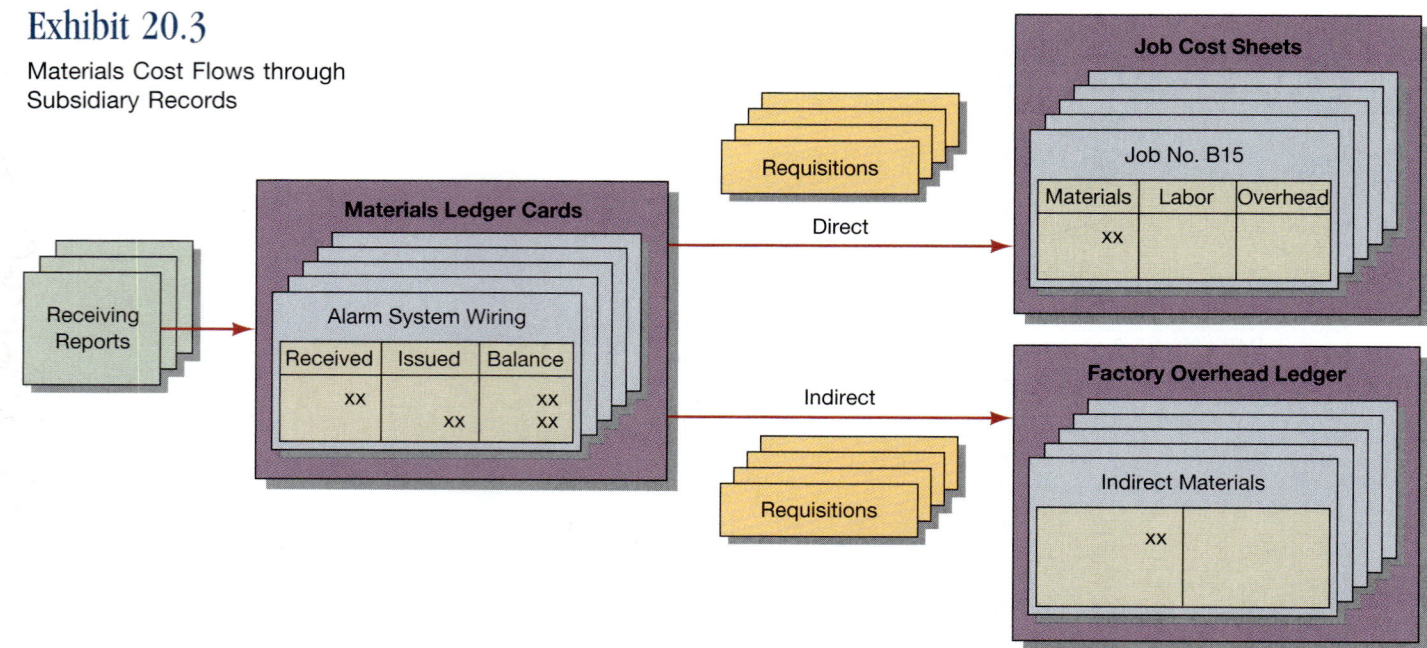

report. The receiving report serves as the *source document* for recording materials received in both a materials ledger card and in the general ledger. In nearly all job order cost systems, **materials ledger cards** (or files) are perpetual records that are updated each time units are purchased and each time units are issued for use in production.

Exhibit 20.3 shows that materials can be requisitioned for use either on a specific job (direct materials) or as overhead (indirect materials). Cost of direct materials flows from the materials ledger card to the job cost sheet. The cost of indirect materials flows from the materials ledger card to the Indirect Materials account in the factory overhead ledger. The factory overhead ledger is a subsidiary ledger controlled by the Factory Overhead account in the general ledger.

Exhibit 20.4 shows a materials ledger card for material received and issued by Road Warriors. The card identifies the item as alarm system wiring and shows the item's stock number, its location in the storeroom, information about the maximum and minimum quantities that should be available, and the reorder quantity. For example, note that alarm system wiring is issued and recorded on March 7, 2002. The job cost sheet in Exhibit 20.2 showed that Job No. B15 used this wiring.

When materials are needed in production, a production manager prepares a **materials requisition** and sends it to the materials manager. The requisition shows the job number,

Point: Some companies certify certain suppliers for the quality of their materials. Goods received from these suppliers are not always inspected by the purchaser to save costs.

Point: Requisitions are often accumulated and recorded in one entry. The frequency of entries depends on the job, the industry, and management procedures.

Exhibit 20.4

Materials Ledger Card

Road Warriors

Item __Alarm system wiring__   Stock No. __M–347__   Location in Storeroom __Bin 137__

Maximum quantity __5 units__   Minimum quantity __1 unit__   Quantity to reorder __2 units__

	Received				Issued				Balance		
Date	Receiving Report Number	Units	Unit Price	Total Price	Requisition Number	Units	Unit Price	Total Price	Units	Unit Price	Total Price
									1	225.00	225.00
3/ 4/2002	C-7117	2	225.00	450.00					3	225.00	675.00
3/ 7/2002					R–4705	1	225.00	225.00	2	225.00	450.00

the type of material, the quantity needed, and the signature of the manager authorized to make the requisition. Exhibit 20.5 shows the materials requisition for alarm system wiring for Job No. B15. To see how this requisition ties to the flow of costs, compare the information on the requisition with the March 7, 2002, data in Exhibits 20.2 and 20.4.

Road Warriors
MATERIALS REQUISITION NUMBER R–4705

Job No. _____ B15 _____   Date _____ 3/7/2002 _____

Material Stock No. _____ M–347 _____   Material Description _____ Alarm system wiring _____

Quantity Requested _____ 1 _____   Requested By _____ C. Luther _____

==

Quantity Provided _____ 1 _____   Date Provided _____ 3/7/2002 _____

Filled By _____ M. Bateman _____   Material Received By _____ C. Luther _____

Remarks _____

Exhibit 20.5
Materials Requisition

The use of alarm system wiring on Job No. B15 yields the following entry (locate this cost item in the job cost sheet shown in Exhibit 20.2):

Mar. 7	Goods in Process Inventory—Job No. B15	225	
	Raw Materials Inventory—M-347		225
	To record use of material on Job No. B15.		

Assets = Liabilities + Equity
+225
−225

This entry is posted both to its general ledger accounts and to subsidiary records. Posting to subsidiary records includes a debit to a job cost sheet and a credit to a materials ledger card. (Note: An entry to record use of indirect materials is the same as that for direct materials *except* the debit is to Factory Overhead. In the subsidiary factory overhead ledger, this entry is posted to Indirect Materials.)

Labor Cost Flows and Documents

Exhibit 20.6 shows the flow of labor costs from clock cards and the Factory Payroll account to subsidiary records of the job order cost accounting system. Recall that costs in subsidiary records give detailed information needed to manage and control operations.

Factory Labor

P2 Describe and record the flow of labor costs in job order cost accounting.

The flow of costs in Exhibit 20.6 begins with **clock cards.** Employees commonly use these cards to record the number of hours worked, and they serve as source documents for entries to record labor costs. Clock card data on the number of hours worked is used at the end of each pay period to determine total labor cost. This amount is then debited to the Factory Payroll account, a temporary account containing the total payroll cost (both direct and indirect). Payroll cost is later allocated to both specific jobs and overhead.

To assign labor costs to specific jobs and to overhead, we must know how each employee's time is used and how much it costs. Source documents called **time tickets** usually capture these data. Employees regularly fill out time tickets to report how much time they spent on each job. An employee who works on several jobs during a day completes a separate time ticket for each job. Tickets are also prepared for time that is charged to overhead as indirect labor. A supervisor signs an employee's time ticket to confirm its accuracy.

Exhibit 20.7 shows a time ticket reporting the time a Road Warrior employee spent working on Job No. B15. The employee's supervisor signed the ticket to confirm its accuracy. The hourly rate and total labor cost are computed after the time ticket is turned in. To see the effect of this time ticket on the job cost sheet, look at the entry dated March 8, 2002, in Exhibit 20.2.

Point: Indirect materials are included in overhead on the job cost sheet. Assigning overhead costs to products is described in the next section.

Exhibit 20.6

Labor Cost Flows through
Subsidiary Records

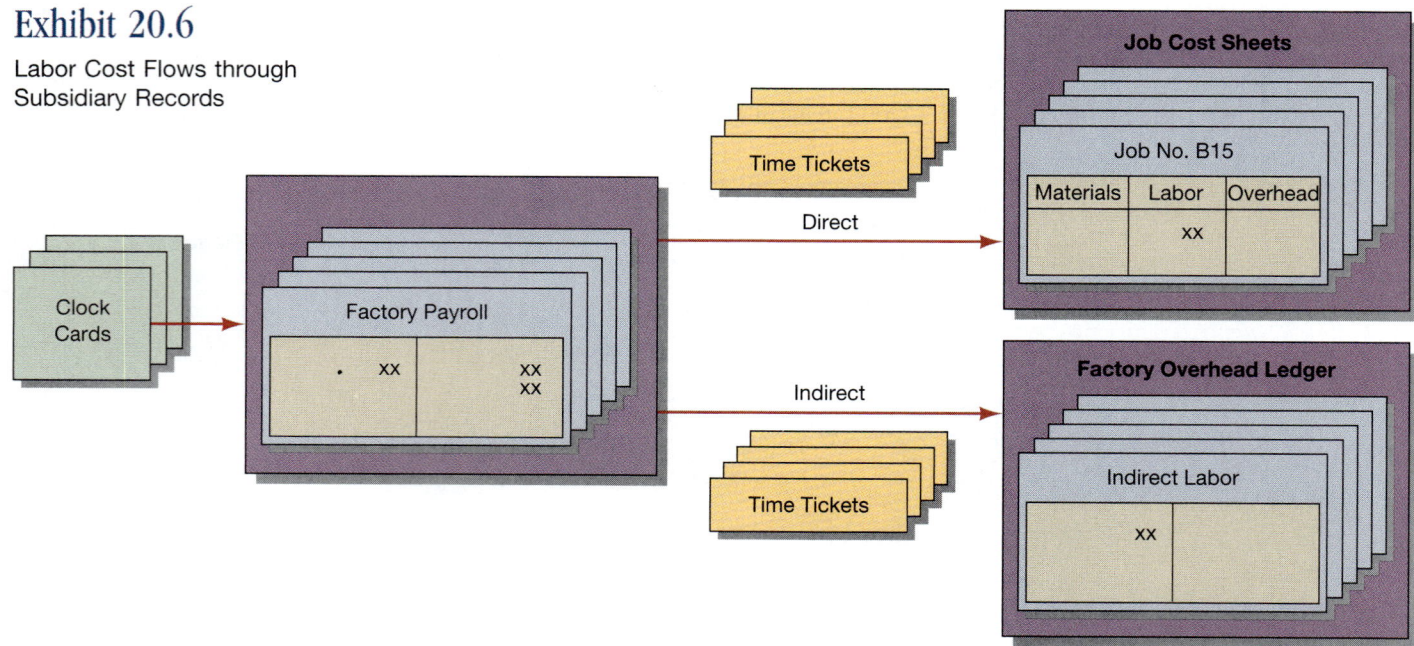

Exhibit 20.7

Time Ticket

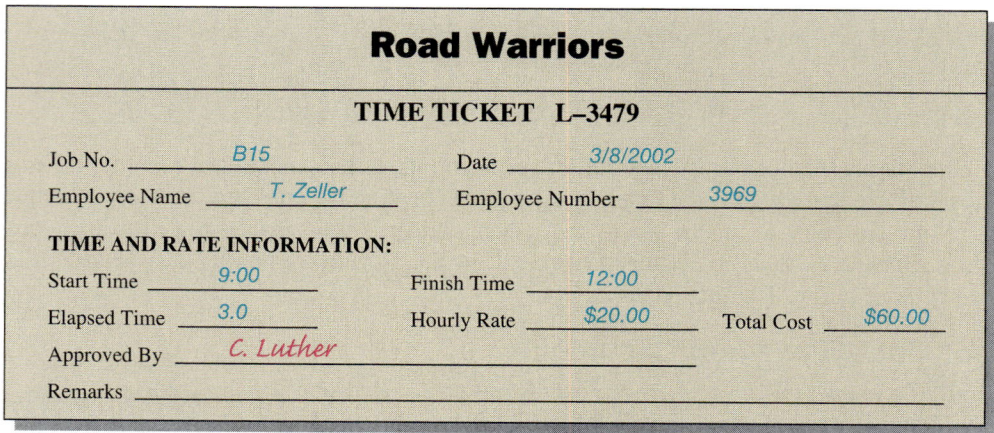

When time tickets report labor used on a specific job, this cost is recorded as direct labor. The following entry records the data from the time ticket in Exhibit 20.7:

Assets = Liabilities + Equity
+60   +60[1]

Mar. 8	Goods in Process Inventory—Job. No. B15	60	
	Factory Payroll		60
	To record direct labor used on Job No. B15.		

The debit in this entry is posted both to the general ledger account and to the appropriate job cost sheet. (Note: An entry to record indirect labor is the same as for direct labor *except* that it debits Factory Overhead and credits Factory Payroll. In the subsidiary factory overhead ledger, the debit in this entry is posted to the Indirect Labor account.)

------

[1] In the accounting equation, we treat accounts such as Factory Overhead and Factory Payroll as temporary accounts, which hold various expenses until they are allocated to balance sheet or income statement accounts.

Overhead Cost Flows and Documents

Factory overhead (or simply overhead) cost flows are shown in Exhibit 20.8. Factory overhead includes all manufacturing costs other than direct materials and direct labor. Two sources of overhead costs are indirect materials and indirect labor. These costs are recorded from requisitions for indirect materials and time tickets for indirect labor. Two other sources of overhead are (1) vouchers authorizing payments for items such as supplies or utilities and (2) adjusting entries for costs such as depreciation.

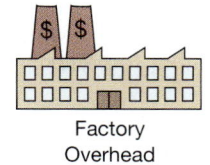

Factory Overhead

P3 Describe and record the flow of overhead costs in job order cost accounting.

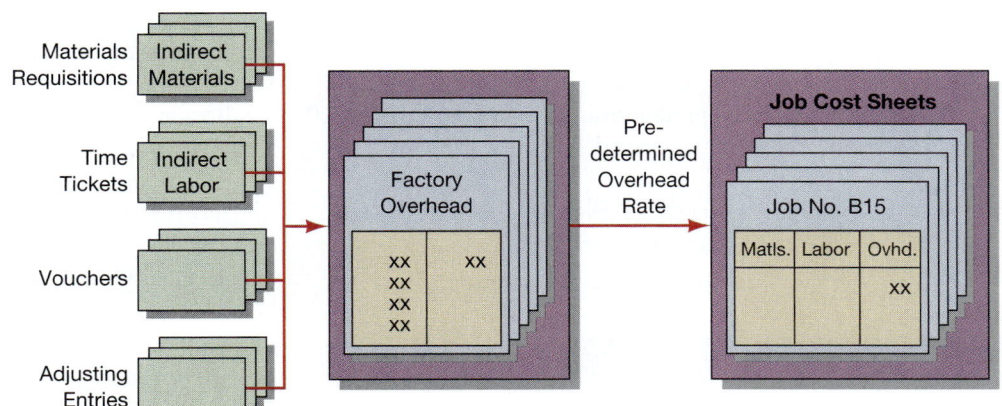

Exhibit 20.8

Overhead Cost Flows through Subsidiary Records

Factory overhead usually includes many different costs and, thus, a separate account for each is often maintained in a subsidiary factory overhead ledger. This ledger is controlled by the Factory Overhead account in the general ledger. Factory Overhead is a temporary account that accumulates costs until they are allocated to jobs.

Concept 20-2

Recall that overhead costs are recorded with debits to the Factory Overhead account and with credits to other accounts such as Cash, Accounts Payable, and Accumulated Depreciation—Equipment. In the subsidiary factory overhead ledger, the debits are posted to their respective accounts such as Depreciation—Factory Equipment, Insurance on Factory Equipment, or Amortization—Patents.

Exhibit 20.8 shows that overhead costs flow from the Factory Overhead account to job cost sheets. Since overhead is made up of costs not directly associated with specific jobs or job lots, we cannot determine the dollar amount incurred on a specific job. We know, however, that overhead costs represent a necessary part of business activities. If a job cost is to include all costs needed to complete the job, some amount of overhead must be included. Given the difficulty in determining the overhead amount for a specific job, however, we allocate (or assign) overhead to individual jobs in some reasonable manner.

We generally allocate overhead by linking it to another factor used in production, such as direct labor or machine hours. The factor to which overhead costs are linked is known as the *allocation base*. A manager must think carefully about how many and which allocation bases to use. This managerial decision influences the accuracy with which overhead costs are allocated to individual jobs. In Exhibit 20.2, overhead is expressed as 160% of direct labor. We then allocated overhead by multiplying 160% by the estimated amount of direct labor on the jobs.

Since we use perpetual inventory records as part of the job order costing system (demanding immediate and up-to-date costs), we cannot wait until the end of a period to allocate overhead to jobs. Instead, we must predict overhead in advance and assign it to jobs so that a job's total costs can be estimated prior to its completion. This estimated cost is useful for managers in many decisions including setting prices. Being able to estimate overhead in advance requires us to compute a **predetermined overhead allocation rate,** or simply *predetermined overhead rate*. This rate requires us to estimate total overhead cost and an allocation factor such as total direct labor cost before the start of the period. Exhibit 20.9 shows

Example: If management predicts total direct labor costs of $100,000 and total overhead costs of $200,000, what is its predetermined overhead rate? *Answer:* 200% of direct labor cost.

Point: Predetermined overhead rates can be estimated using mathematical equations, statistical analysis, or professional experience.

Point: To apply these concepts, work QS 20-6 and Exercise 20-3.

Exhibit 20.9

Predetermined Overhead Allocation Rate Formula

Point: The predetermined overhead rate is computed at the start of the period and is used throughout the period to allocate overhead to jobs.

Assets = Liabilities + Equity
+1,600   +1,600

the usual formula for computing a predetermined overhead allocation rate (where estimates are commonly based on annual amounts). This rate is used during the period to allocate overhead to jobs. It is common for companies to use multiple allocation factors (bases) and multiple predetermined overhead rates for different types of products and services.

$$\text{Predetermined overhead allocation rate} = \frac{\text{Estimated overhead costs}}{} \div \frac{\text{Estimated factor costs}}{}$$

To illustrate, Road Warriors allocates overhead by linking it to direct labor. At the start of the current period, management predicts total direct labor costs of $125,000 and total overhead costs of $200,000. Using these estimates, management computes its predetermined overhead rate as 160% of direct labor cost ($200,000 ÷ $125,000). Specifically, reviewing the job order cost sheet in Exhibit 20.2, we see that $1,000 of direct labor went into Job No. B15. We then use the predetermined overhead rate of 160% to allocate $1,600 of overhead to this job. The entry to record this allocation is

Mar. 11	Goods in Process Inventory—Job. No. B15	1,600	
	Factory Overhead		1,600
	To assign overhead to Job No. B15.		

You Make the Call—Ethics

Web Consultant You are working on seven client engagements. Two clients reimburse your firm for actual costs plus a 10% markup. The other five pay a fixed fee for services. Your firm's costs include overhead allocated at $47 per labor hour. The partner of your firm instructs you to record as many labor hours as possible to the two markup engagements by transferring labor hours from the other five. What do you do?

Answer—p. 845

Since the allocation rate for overhead is estimated at the start of a period, the total amount assigned to jobs during a period rarely equals the amount actually incurred. We explain how this difference is treated later in this chapter.

Summary of Manufacturing Cost Flows

We showed journal entries for charging Goods in Process Inventory (Job No. B15) with the cost of (1) direct materials requisitions, (2) direct labor time tickets, and (3) factory overhead. We made separate entries for each of these costs, but they are usually recorded in one entry. Specifically, materials requisitions are often collected for a day or a week and recorded with a single entry summarizing them. The same is done with labor time tickets. When summary entries are made, supporting schedules of the jobs charged and the types of materials used provide the basis for postings to subsidiary records.

Point: Study the flow of manufacturing costs through general ledger accounts and job cost sheets. Use Exhibit 20.11 as reinforcement.

Point: To apply these concepts, work Exercises 20-2 and 20-5.

To show all manufacturing cost flows for a period and their related entries, we again look at Road Warriors' activities. Exhibit 20.10 shows costs linked to all of Road Warriors' manufacturing activities for March. Road Warriors did not have any jobs in process at the beginning of March, but it did apply materials, labor, and overhead costs to five new jobs in March. Job Nos. B15 and B16 are completed and delivered to customers in March, Job No. B17 is completed but not delivered, and Job Nos. B18 and B19 are still in process. Exhibit 20.10 also shows purchases of raw materials for $2,750, labor costs incurred for $5,300, and overhead costs of $6,720.

You Make the Call

Entrepreneur Your division's product is facing increasing competition; competitors' prices are often lower than your own. Of the total product cost used in setting prices, 53% is factory overhead allocated using direct labor hours. You believe that product costs are distorted, and you wonder whether there is a better way to allocate factory overhead and to set product price. What do you suggest?

Answer—p. 845

The upper part of Exhibit 20.11 shows the flow of these costs through general ledger accounts and the end-of-month balances in key subsidiary records. Arrow lines are numbered to show the flows of costs for March. Each numbered cost flow reflects several entries made in March. The lower part of Exhibit 20.11 shows summarized job cost sheets and their status at the end of March. The sum of costs assigned to the jobs in process ($1,970 + $1,870)

equals the $3,780 balance in Goods in Process Inventory shown in Exhibit 20.10. Also, costs assigned to Job No. B17 equal the $3,360 balance in Finished Goods Inventory. The sum

Exhibit 20.10

Job Order Costs of All
Manufacturing Activities

ROAD WARRIORS
Job Order Manufacturing Costs
For Month Ended March 31, 2002

Explanation	Materials	Labor	Overhead Incurred	Overhead Assigned	Goods in Process	Finished Goods	Cost of Goods Sold
Job B15	$ 600	$1,000		$1,600			$3,200
Job B16	300	800		1,280			2,380
Job B17	500	1,100		1,760		$3,360	
Job B18	150	700		1,120	$1,970		
Job B19	250	600		960	1,810		
Total job costs	$1,800	$4,200		$6,720	$3,780	$3,360	$5,580
Indirect materials	550		$ 550				
Indirect labor		1,100	1,100				
Other overhead			5,070				
Total costs used in production	$2,350	$5,300	$6,720				
Ending materials inventory	1,400						
Materials available	$3,750						
Less beginning materials inventory	(1,000)						
Materials purchased	$2,750						

Exhibit 20.11

Job Order Cost Flows and
Ending Job Cost Sheets

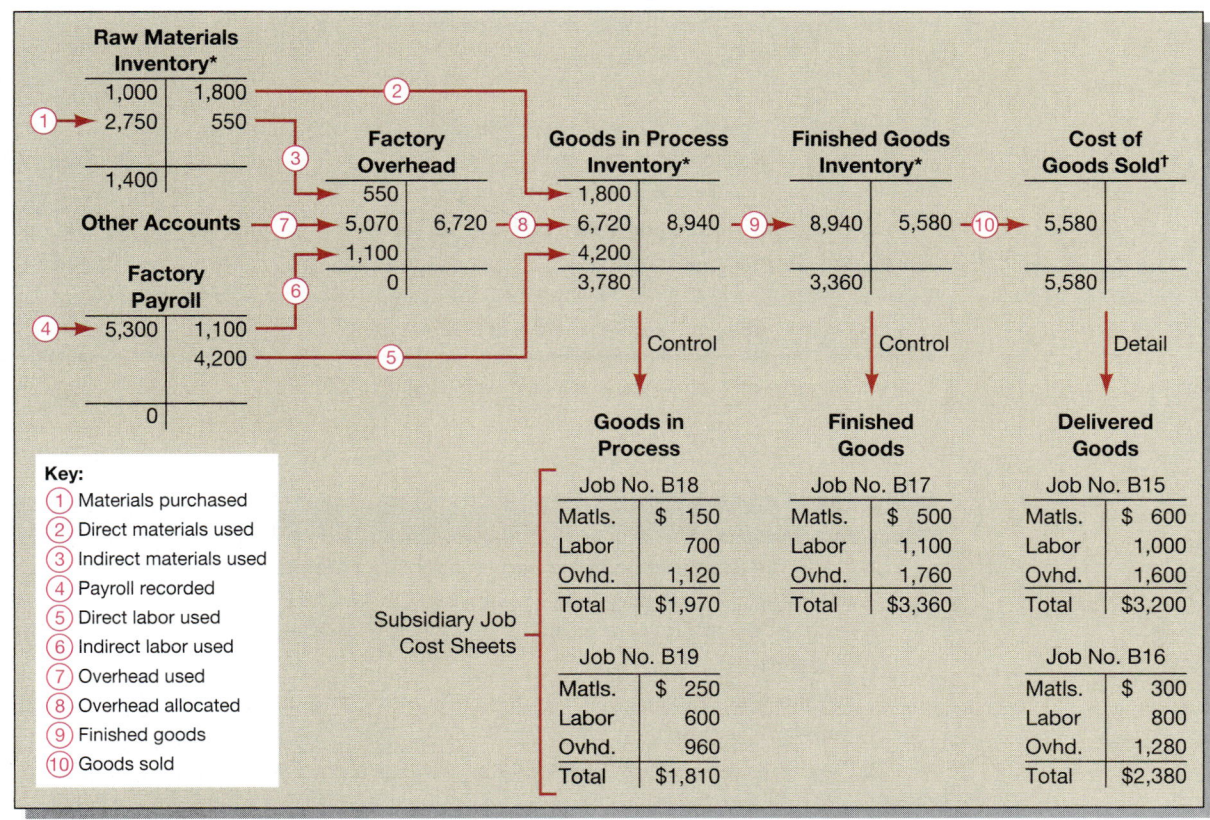

* The ending balances in the inventory accounts are carried to the balance sheet.
†The Cost of Goods Sold balance is carried to the income statement.

of costs assigned to Job Nos. B15 and B16 ($3,200 + $2,380) equals the $5,580 balance in Cost of Goods Sold.

Exhibit 20.12 shows each cost flow with a single entry summarizing the actual individual entries made in March. Each entry is numbered to link with the arrow lines in Exhibit 20.11.

Exhibit 20.12

Entries for Job Order Manufacturing Costs*

①	Raw Materials Inventory	2,750	
	Accounts Payable		2,750
	Acquired materials on credit for factory use.		
②	Goods in Process Inventory	1,800	
	Raw Materials Inventory		1,800
	To assign costs of direct materials used.		
③	Factory Overhead	550	
	Raw Materials Inventory		550
	To record use of indirect materials.		
④	Factory Payroll	5,300	
	Cash (and other accounts)		5,300
	To record salaries and wages of factory workers (including various payroll liabilities).		
⑤	Goods in Process Inventory	4,200	
	Factory Payroll		4,200
	To assign costs of direct labor used.		
⑥	Factory Overhead	1,100	
	Factory Payroll		1,100
	To record indirect labor costs as overhead.		
⑦	Factory Overhead	5,070	
	Cash (and other accounts)		5,070
	To record factory overhead costs such as insurance, utilities, rent, and depreciation.		
⑧	Goods in process Inventory	6,720	
	Factory Overhead		6,720
	To apply overhead at 160% of direct labor.		
⑨	Finished Goods Inventory	8,940	
	Goods in Process Inventory		8,940
	To record completion of B15, B16, and B17.		
⑩	Cost of Goods Sold	5,580	
	Finished Goods Inventory		5,580
	To record sale of Job Nos. B15 and B16.		

Point: Actual overhead is debited to Factory Overhead. Allocated overhead is credited to Factory Overhead.

* Transactions are numbered to be consistent with arrow lines in Exhibit 20.11.

Quick Check

5. In job order cost accounting, which account is debited in recording a raw materials requisition? (a) Raw Materials Inventory, (b) Raw Materials Purchases, (c) Goods in Process Inventory if for a job, or (d) Goods in Process Inventory if they are indirect materials.

6. What are four sources of information for recording costs in the Factory Overhead account?

7. Why does job order cost accounting require a predetermined overhead rate?

8. What events result in a debit to Factory Payroll? What events result in a credit?

Refer to the debits in the Factory Overhead account in Exhibit 20.11 (or Exhibit 20.10). The total cost of factory overhead incurred during March is $6,720 ($550 + $5,070 + $1,100). The $6,720 exactly equals, the amount assigned to goods in process inventory (see arrow line ⑧). Therefore, the overhead incurred equals the overhead applied in March. The amount of overhead incurred rarely equals the amount of overhead applied, however, because a job order cost accounting system uses a predetermined overhead rate in applying factory overhead costs to jobs. This rate is determined using estimated amounts before the period begins, and estimates rarely equal the exact amounts actually incurred. This section explains what we do when too much or too little overhead is applied to jobs.

Adjusting Overapplied and Underapplied Overhead

Underapplied Overhead

When less overhead is applied than is actually incurred, the remaining debit balance in the Factory Overhead account at the end of the period is called **underapplied overhead.** To illustrate, assume that Road Warriors actually incurred *other overhead costs* of $5,550 instead of the $5,070 shown in Exhibit 20.11. This yields an actual total overhead cost of $7,200 in March. Since the amount of overhead applied was only $6,720, the Factory Overhead account is left with a $480 debit balance as shown in the ledger account in Exhibit 20.13.

P4 Determine adjustments for overapplied and underapplied factory overhead.

Factory Overhead				Acct. No. 540
Date	Explanation	Debit	Credit	Balance
2002				
Mar. 31	Indirect materials cost	550		550 Dr.
31	Indirect labor cost	1,100		1,650 Dr.
31	Other overhead cost	5,550		7,200 Dr.
31	Overhead costs applied to jobs		6,720	480 Dr.

Exhibit 20.13

Underapplied Overhead in the Factory Overhead Ledger Account

The $480 debit balance reflects manufacturing costs not assigned to jobs. This means that the balances in Goods in Process Inventory, Finished Goods Inventory, and Cost of Goods Sold do not include all manufacturing costs incurred. When the underapplied overhead amount is immaterial, it is allocated (closed) to the Cost of Goods Sold account with the following adjusting entry:[2]

Example: If we do not adjust for underapplied overhead, will net income be overstated or understated? *Answer:* Overstated.

Mar. 31	Cost of Goods Sold	480	
	Factory Overhead		480
	To adjust for underapplied overhead costs.		

Assets = Liabilities + Equity
            −480
            +480

The $480 debit (increase) to Cost of Goods Sold reduces income by $480.

---

[2] When the underapplied (or overapplied) overhead is significant, the amount is normally allocated to the Cost of Goods Sold, Finished Goods Inventory, and Goods in Process Inventory accounts. The preferred method of allocating underapplied (or overapplied) overhead in this case is one consistent with the allocation method used in the period. For Road Warriors, underapplied overhead is allocated to jobs based on direct labor. Jobs B15 and B16, which are sold, account for 42.8% of the total direct labor cost in March. Also, 26.2% of direct labor was consumed by B17, which is in Finished Goods inventory, and the remaining 31% was consumed by jobs B18 and B19, which are in Goods in Process inventory. These percents are multiplied by $480 to compute the amount of underapplied overhead allocated to each account (for example, 42.8% of $480, or $205, is allocated to the Cost of Goods Sold account). An adjusting entry records this allocation:

Mar. 31	Goods in Process Inventory	149	
	Finished Goods Inventory	126	
	Cost of Goods Sold	205	
	Factory Overhead		480
	To adjust for underapplied overhead costs.		

Overapplied Overhead

When the overhead applied in a period exceeds the overhead incurred, the resulting credit balance in the Factory Overhead account is called **overapplied overhead.** We treat overapplied overhead at the end of the period in the same way we treat underapplied overhead, except that we debit Factory Overhead and credit Cost of Good Sold.

Quick Check

9. In a job order cost accounting system, why does the Factory Overhead account usually have an overapplied or underapplied balance at the period-end?

10. When the Factory Overhead account has a debit balance at period-end, does this reflect overapplied or underapplied overhead?

Answers—p. 845

Using the Information	Pricing for Services

 A1 Apply job order costing in pricing services.

The chapter described job order costing using mainly a manufacturing setting. However, these concepts and procedures are applicable to a service setting. Consider AdWorld, an advertising agency that develops Web-based ads for small firms. Each of its customers has unique requirements, so costs for each individual job must be tracked separately.

AdWorld uses two types of labor: Web designers ($65 per hour) and computer staff ($50 per hour). AdWorld also incurs overhead costs that it assigns using two different predetermined overhead allocation rates: $125 per designer hour and $96 per staff hour. For each job, AdWorld must estimate the number of designer and staff hours needed. Then total costs pertaining to each job are determined using the procedures in the chapter. (Note: Most service firms will have neither the category of materials cost nor inventory.)

To illustrate, RedGolf, a manufacturer of golf balls requested a quote from AdWorld for an advertising engagement. AdWorld estimates that this job will require 43 designer hours and 61 staff hours, with the total estimated cost for this job as follows:

Direct Labor	
Designers (43 hours × $65)	$ 2,795
Staff (61 hours × $50)	3,050
Total direct labor	$ 5,845
Overhead	
Designer related (43 hours × $125) .	$ 5,375
Staff related (61 hours × $96)	5,856
Total overhead	$11,231
Total estimated job cost	$17,076

AdWorld can use this cost information to help determine the price quote for the job (see *You Make the Call*, **Sales Manager**). Another source of information that AdWorld must consider is the market—that is, how much competitors will quote for this job. Competitor information is often unavailable; therefore, AdWorld's managers must use estimates based on their assessment of the competitive environment.

You Make the Call

Sales Manager   As AdWorld's sales manager, assume that you estimate the costs pertaining to the RedGolf job to be $17,000. Your company's normal pricing policy is to apply a markup of 18% from total costs. Your assessment of the competition suggests that three other agencies are likely to bid for the same job, and that their quotes will range from $16,500 to $22,000. What price should you quote? What factors other than cost must you consider?

Answer—p. 845

The following information reflects Peak Manufacturing Company's job order manufacturing activities for May:

Raw materials purchases	$16,000
Factory payroll cost	15,400
Overhead costs incurred	
Indirect materials	5,000
Indirect labor	3,500
Other factory overhead	9,500

The predetermined overhead rate is 150% of direct labor cost. These costs are allocated to the three jobs worked on during May as follows:

	Job 401	Job 402	Job 403
Balances on April 30			
Direct materials	$3,600		
Direct labor	1,700		
Applied overhead	2,550		
Costs during May			
Direct materials	3,550	$3,500	$1,400
Direct labor	5,100	6,000	800
Applied overhead	?	?	?
Status on May 31	Finished (sold)	Finished (unsold)	In process

Required

1. Determine the total cost of:
   a. The April 30 inventory of jobs in process.
   b. Materials used during May.
   c. Labor used during May.
   d. Factory overhead incurred and applied during May and the amount of any over- or underapplied overhead on May 31.
   e. Each job as of May 31, the May 31 inventories of goods in process and finished goods, and the goods sold during May.

2. Prepare summarized journal entries for the month to record:
   a. Materials purchases (on credit), the factory payroll (paid with cash), indirect materials, indirect labor, and the other factory overhead (paid with cash).
   b. Assignment of direct materials, direct labor, and overhead costs to the Goods in Process Inventory account. (Use separate debit entries for each job.)
   c. Transfer of each completed job to the Finished Goods Inventory account.
   d. Cost of goods sold.
   e. Removal of any underapplied or overapplied overhead from the Factory Overhead account. (Assume the amount is not material.)

3. Prepare a manufacturing statement for May.

Planning the Solution

• Determine the cost of the April 30 goods in process inventory by totaling the materials, labor, and applied overhead costs for Job 401.

• Compute the cost of materials used and labor by totaling the amounts assigned to jobs and to overhead.

• Compute the total overhead incurred by totaling the amounts of the three components. Compute the amount of applied overhead by multiplying the total direct labor cost by the predetermined overhead rate. Compute the underapplied or overapplied amount as the difference between the actual cost and the applied cost.

- Determine the total cost charged to each job by adding the costs incurred in April (if any) to the materials, labor, and overhead applied during May.
- Group the costs of the jobs according to their completion status.
- Record the direct materials costs assigned to the three jobs, using a separate Goods in Process Inventory account for each job; do the same for the direct labor and the applied overhead.
- Transfer costs of Jobs 401 and 402 from Goods in Process Inventory to Finished Goods.
- Record the costs of Job 401 as cost of goods sold.
- Record the transfer of underapplied overhead from the Factory Overhead account to the Cost of Goods Sold account.
- On the manufacturing statement, remember to include the beginning and ending goods in process inventories and to deduct the underapplied overhead.

Solution to Demonstration Problem

1. Total cost of

a. April 30 inventory of jobs in process (Job 401):

Direct materials	$3,600
Direct labor	1,700
Applied overhead	2,550
Total cost	$7,850

b. Materials used during May:

Direct materials		
Job 401		$ 3,550
Job 402		3,500
Job 403		1,400
Total direct materials		8,450
Indirect materials		5,000
Total materials used		$13,450

c. Labor used during May:

Direct labor		
Job 401		$ 5,100
Job 402		6,000
Job 403		800
Total direct labor		11,900
Indirect labor		3,500
Total labor used		$15,400

d. Factory overhead incurred in May:

Actual overhead		
Indirect materials		$ 5,000
Indirect labor		3,500
Other factory overhead		9,500
Total actual overhead		18,000
Overhead applied (150% × $11,900) . .		17,850
Underapplied overhead		$ 150

e. Total cost of each job:

	401	402	403
From April			
Direct materials	$ 3,600		
Direct labor	1,700		
Applied overhead*	2,550		
From May			
Direct materials	3,550	$ 3,500	$1,400
Direct labor	5,100	6,000	800
Applied overhead*	7,650	9,000	1,200
Total costs	$24,150	$18,500	$3,400

* Equals 150% of the direct labor cost.

Total cost of the May 31 inventory of goods in process (Job 403) = $3,400

Total cost of the May 31 inventory of finished goods (Job 402) = $18,500

Total cost of goods sold during May (Job 401) = $24,150

2. Journal entries:

a.

Raw Materials Inventory	16,000	
Accounts Payable		16,000
To record materials purchases.		
Factory Payroll	15,400	
Cash		15,400
To record factory payroll.		
Factory Overhead	5,000	
Raw Materials Inventory		5,000
To record indirect materials.		
Factory Overhead	3,500	
Factory Payroll		3,500
To record indirect labor.		
Factory Overhead	9,500	
Cash		9,500
To record other factory overhead.		

b. Assignment of costs to Goods in Process Inventory:

Goods in Process Inventory (Job 401)	3,550	
Goods in Process Inventory (Job 402)	3,500	
Goods in Process Inventory (Job 403)	1,400	
Raw Materials Inventory		8,450
To assign direct materials to jobs.		
Goods in Process Inventory (Job 401)	5,100	
Goods in Process Inventory (Job 402)	6,000	
Goods in Process Inventory (Job 403)	800	
Factory Payroll		11,900
To assign direct labor to jobs.		
Goods in Process Inventory (Job 401)	7,650	
Goods in Process Inventory (Job 402)	9,000	
Goods in Process Inventory (Job 403)	1,200	
Factory Overhead		17,850
To apply overhead to jobs.		

c. Transfer of completed job to Finished Goods Inventory:

Finished Goods Inventory	42,650	
Goods in Process Inventory (Job 401)		24,150
Goods in Process Inventory (Job 402)		18,500
To record completion of jobs.		

d.

Cost of Goods Sold	24,150	
Finished Goods Inventory		24,150
To record sale of job 401.		

e.

Cost of Goods Sold	150	
Factory Overhead		150
To assign underapplied overhead.		

3.

PEAK MANUFACTURING COMPANY
Manufacturing Statement
For Month Ended May 31

Direct materials		$ 8,450
Direct labor		11,900
Factory overhead		
Indirect materials	$5,000	
Indirect labor	3,500	
Other factory overhead	9,500	18,000
Total manufacturing costs		$38,350
Add goods in process, April 30		7,850
Total cost of goods in process		$46,200
Deduct goods in process, May 31		(3,400)
Deduct underapplied overhead		(150)
Cost of goods manufactured		$42,650

Note how underapplied (and overapplied) overhead is reported.

Summary

C1 **Explain the periodic and perpetual inventory systems.** A *periodic* inventory system measures costs of inventories based on physical counts of quantities available at the end of each period. The *perpetual* inventory system continuously updates records for transactions and events that affect inventory costs.

C2 **Describe important features of job order manufacturing.** Certain manufacturers called *job order manufacturers* produce custom-made products for customers. These customized or special products are manufactured in response to a customer's orders. A job order manufacturer produces products that usually are different and, typically, manufactured in low volumes. The manufacturing systems of job order companies are flexible and are not highly standardized.

C3 **Explain job cost sheets and how they are used in job order cost accounting.** In a job order cost accounting system, the costs of producing each job are accumulated on a separate job cost sheet. Costs of direct materials, direct labor, and manufacturing overhead are accumulated separately on the job cost sheet and then added to determine the total cost of a job. Job cost sheets for jobs in process, finished jobs, and jobs sold make up subsidiary records controlled by general ledger accounts.

A1 **Apply job order costing in pricing services.** Job order costing can usefully be applied to a service setting. The resulting job cost estimate can then be used to help determine a price for services.

P1 **Describe and record the flow of materials costs in job order cost accounting.** Costs of materials flow from receiving reports to materials ledger cards and then to either job cost sheets or the Indirect Materials account in the factory overhead ledger.

P2 **Describe and record the flow of labor costs in job order cost accounting.** Costs of labor flow from clock cards to the Factory Payroll account and then to either job cost sheets or the Indirect Labor account in the factory overhead ledger.

P3 **Describe and record the flow of overhead costs in job order cost accounting.** Overhead costs are accumulated in the Factory Overhead account that controls the subsidiary factory overhead ledger. Then, using a predetermined overhead application rate, overhead costs are charged to jobs.

P4 **Determine adjustments for overapplied and underapplied factory overhead.** At the end of each period, the Factory Overhead account usually has a residual debit or credit balance. A debit balance reflects underapplied overhead; a credit balance reflects overapplied overhead. If the balance is not material, it is transferred to Cost of Goods Sold, but if it is material, it is allocated to Goods in Process Inventory, Finished Goods Inventory, and Cost of Goods Sold.

Guidance Answers to **You Make the Call**

Management Consultant   Service companies (such as this consulting firm) do not recognize goods in process inventory or finished goods inventory—an important difference between service and manufacturing companies. For the two jobs that are 60% complete, you could recognize revenues and costs at 60% of the total expected amounts. This means you could recognize revenue of $7,200 (0.60 × $12,000) and costs of $6,000 (0.60 × $10,000), yielding net income of $1,200 from each job.

Web Consultant   The partner has a monetary incentive to *manage* the numbers and assign more costs to the two cost-plus engagements. This also would reduce costs on the fixed-price engagements. To act in such a manner is unethical. As a professional and an honest person, it is your responsibility to engage in ethical behavior. You must not comply with the partner's instructions. If the partner insists you act in an unethical manner, you should report the matter to a higher authority in the organization.

Entrepreneur   An inadequate cost system can distort product costs. You should review overhead costs in detail. Once you know

the different cost elements in overhead, you can classify them into groups such as material related, labor related, or machine related. Other groups can also be formed (we discuss this in Chapter 22). Once you have classified overhead items into groups, you can better establish overhead allocation bases and use them to compute predetermined overhead rates. These multiple rates and bases can then be used to assign overhead costs to products. This will likely improve product pricing.

Sales Manager   The price based on AdWorld's normal pricing policy is $20,060 ($17,000 × 1.18), which is within the price range offered by competitors. One option is to apply normal pricing policy and quote a price of $20,060. On the other hand, assessing the competition, particularly in terms of their service quality and other benefits they might offer, would be useful. Although price is an input customers use to select suppliers, factors such as quality and timeliness (responsiveness) of suppliers are important. Accordingly, your price can reflect such factors.

Guidance Answers to **Quick Checks**

1. (b)

2. A job is a special order for a custom product. A job lot consists of a quantity of identical, special-order items.

3. (a)

4. Three costs normally accumulated on a job cost sheet are direct materials, direct labor, and factory overhead.

5. (c)

6. Four sources of factory overhead are materials requisitions, time tickets, vouchers, and adjusting entries.

7. Since a job order cost accounting system uses perpetual inventory records, overhead costs must be assigned to jobs be-

fore the end of a period. This requires the use of a predetermined overhead application rate.

8. Debits are recorded when wages and salaries of factory employees are paid or accrued. Credits are recorded when direct labor costs are assigned to jobs and when indirect labor costs are transferred to the Factory Overhead account.

9. Overapplied or underapplied overhead usually exists at the end of a period because application of overhead is based on estimates of overhead and another variable such as direct labor. Estimates rarely equal actual amounts incurred.

10. A debit balance reflects underapplied factory overhead.

Glossary

Clock card a source document used to record the number of hours an employee works and to determine the total labor cost for each pay period. (p. 833).

Cost accounting system accounting system for manufacturing activities based on the perpetual inventory system. (p. 828).

Finished goods inventory completed products that are ready for sale by the manufacturer. (p. 831).

General accounting system accounting system for manufacturing activities based on the *periodic* inventory system. (p. 828).

Goods in process inventory products in the process of being manufactured but not yet complete. (p. 831).

Job production of a customized product or service. (p. 828).

Job cost sheet separate record maintained for each job. (p. 830).

Job lot production of more than one unit of a customized product or service. (p. 829).

Job order cost accounting system cost accounting system to determine the cost of producing each job or job lot. (p. 830).

Job order manufacturing production of special-order products; also called *customized production*. (p. 828).

Materials ledger card perpetual record updated each time units are purchased or issued for production use. (p. 832).

Materials requisition source document that production managers use to request materials for manufacturing and that is used to assign materials costs to specific jobs or overhead. (p. 832).

Overapplied overhead amount by which the overhead applied to jobs in a period with the predetermined overhead allocation rate exceeds the overhead incurred in a period. (p. 840).

Predetermined overhead allocation rate rate established prior to the beginning of a period that relates estimated overhead to another variable, such as estimated direct labor, and is used to assign overhead cost to jobs. (p. 835).

Time ticket source document used to report the time an employee spent working on a job or on overhead activities and then to determine the amount of direct labor to charge to the job or the amount of indirect labor to charge to overhead. (p. 833).

Underapplied overhead amount by which overhead incurred in a period exceeds the overhead applied to jobs with the predetermined overhead allocation rate. (p. 839).

Questions

1. Refer to **Nike**'s financial statements and notes in Appendix A. What are the major components and amounts of Nike's inventory for 2000? **NIKE**

2. Why must a company estimate the amount of factory overhead assigned to individual jobs or job lots?

3. The chapter used a percent of labor cost to assign factory overhead to jobs. Identify another factor (or base) a company might reasonably use to assign overhead costs.

4. What information is recorded on a job cost sheet? How do management and employees use job cost sheets?

5. In a job order cost accounting system, what records serve as a subsidiary ledger for Goods in Process Inventory? For Finished Goods Inventory?

6. What journal entry is recorded when a materials manager receives a materials requisition and then issues materials (both direct and indirect) for use in the factory?

7. How does the materials requisition help safeguard the company's assets?

8. What is the difference between a clock card and a time ticket?

9. What events cause debits to be recorded in the Factory Overhead account? What events cause credits to be recorded in the Factory Overhead account?

10. What account(s) is used to eliminate overapplied or underapplied overhead from the Factory Overhead account, assuming the amount is not material?

11. **Reebok** produced a batch of 300 football shoes, colored green and gold, for an NFL team. Does it account for this as 300 individual jobs or as a job lot? Explain (consider costs and benefits). **Reebok**

12. Why must a company prepare a predetermined factory overhead rate when using job order cost accounting?

13. How would a hospital apply job order costing? Explain.

QUICK STUDY

QS 20-1
Factory overhead rates

FasTrack Company incurred the following manufacturing costs this period: direct labor, $468,000; direct materials, $354,500; and factory overhead, $117,000. Compute overhead cost as a percent of (1) direct labor and (2) direct materials.

QS 20-2
Jobs and job lots

Determine which products are most likely to be manufactured as a job and which as a job lot:
1. A hand-crafted table.
2. A 90-foot motor yacht.
3. Wedding dresses for a chain of stores.
4. A custom-designed home.
5. Hats imprinted with company logo.
6. Little League trophies.

QS 20-3
Job cost computation

The following information is from the materials requisitions and time tickets for Job 9-1005 completed by Bayliner Boats for Redfish Rentals. The requisitions are identified by code numbers starting with the letter Q and the time tickets start with W:

Date	Document	Amount
7/1/2002	Q-4698	$1,250
7/1/2002	W-3393	600
7/5/2002	Q-4725	1,000
7/5/2002	W-3479	450
7/10/2002	W-3559	300

At the start of the year, management estimated that overhead cost would equal 110% of direct labor cost for each job. Determine the total cost on the job cost sheet for Job 9-1005.

During the current month, a company that uses a job order cost accounting system purchases raw materials for $50,000 cash. It then uses $12,000 of raw materials indirectly as factory supplies and uses $32,000 of raw materials as direct materials. Prepare entries to record these three transactions.

QS 20-4
Direct materials journal entries

During the current month, a company that uses a job order cost accounting system incurred a monthly factory payroll of $80,000, paid in cash. Of this amount, $40,000 is classified as indirect labor and the remainder as direct. Prepare entries to record these transactions.

QS 20-5
Direct labor journal entries

During the current month, a company that uses a job order cost accounting system incurred a monthly factory payroll of $120,000, paid in cash. Of this amount, $30,000 is classified as indirect labor and the remainder as direct for the production of a job lot. Factory overhead is applied at 90% of direct labor. Prepare the entry to apply factory overhead to this job lot.

QS 20-6
Factory overhead journal entries

Relay Company allocates overhead at a rate of 150% of direct labor cost. Actual overhead cost for the current period is $950,000, and direct labor cost is $600,000. Prepare the entry to close over- or underapplied overhead to cost of goods sold.

QS 20-7
Entry for over- or underapplied overhead

The left column lists the titles of documents used in job order cost accounting. The right column presents short descriptions of the purposes of the documents. Match each document in the left column to its numbered description in the right column.

EXERCISES

Exercise 20-1
Documents in job order cost accounting

A. Factory Payroll account
B. Materials ledger card
C. Time ticket
D. Voucher
E. Materials requisition
F. Factory Overhead account
G. Clock card

_____ **1.** Communicates the need for materials to complete a job.
_____ **2.** Shows only total time an employee works each day.
_____ **3.** Shows amount approved for payment of an overhead cost.
_____ **4.** Shows amount of time an employee works on a job.
_____ **5.** Temporarily accumulates the cost of incurred overhead until the cost is assigned to specific jobs.
_____ **6.** Temporarily accumulates incurred labor costs until they are assigned to specific jobs or to overhead.
_____ **7.** Perpetual inventory record of raw materials received, used, and available for use.

As of the end of June, the job cost sheets at Skateboards-For-You, Inc., show the following total costs accumulated on three custom jobs:

Exercise 20-2
Analysis of cost flows

	Job 102	Job 103	Job 104
Direct materials	$16,500	$32,000	$19,000
Direct labor	9,000	14,500	10,000
Overhead	4,500	7,250	5,000

Job 102 was started in production in May and the following costs were assigned to it in May: direct materials, $5,000; direct labor, $2,000; and overhead, $1,000. Jobs 103 and 104 are started in June. Overhead cost is applied with a predetermined rate based on direct labor cost. Jobs 102 and 103 are finished in June, and Job 104 is expected to be finished in July. No raw materials are used indirectly in June. Using this information, answer the following questions:

1. What is the cost of the raw materials requisitioned in June for each of the three jobs?
2. How much direct labor cost is incurred during June for each of the three jobs?
3. What predetermined overhead application rate is used during June?
4. How much total cost is transferred to finished goods during June?

Exercise 20-3

Overhead application rate; costs assigned to jobs

In December 2001, Amazon Computer's management establishes the year 2002 overhead application rate based on direct labor cost. The information used in setting this rate includes the accountant's estimates that the company will incur $747,500 of overhead costs and $575,000 of direct labor cost in year 2002. During March 2002, Amazon began and completed Job No. 13-56.

1. Compute the overhead application rate for year 2002.

2. Use the information on the following job cost sheet to determine the total cost of the job:

JOB COST SHEET

Customer's Name	Keiser Co.					Job No.	13-56
Job Description		5 color monitors—21 inch					

	Direct Materials			Direct Labor		Overhead Costs Applied	
Date	Requisition No.	Amount		Time-Ticket No.	Amount	Rate	Amount
Mar. 8	4-129	$5,000		T-306	$ 700		
Mar. 11	4-142	7,020		T-432	1,250		
Mar. 18	4-167	3,330		T-456	1,250		
Totals							

Exercise 20-4

Analysis of costs assigned to goods in process

Andiron Company uses a job order cost accounting system that charges overhead to jobs on the basis of direct material. At year-end, the Goods in Process Inventory account shows the following:

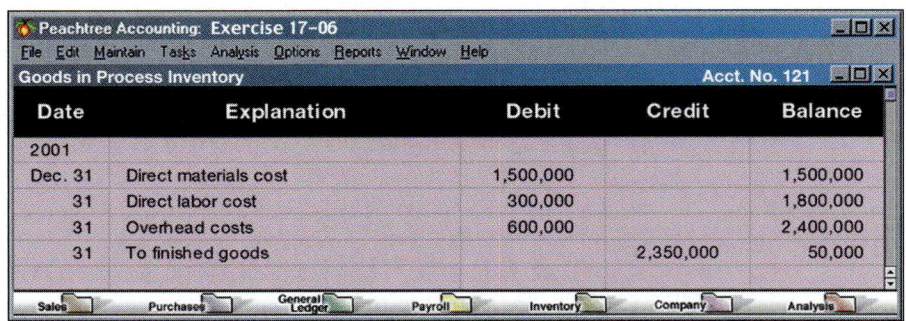

Date	Explanation	Debit	Credit	Balance
2001				
Dec. 31	Direct materials cost	1,500,000		1,500,000
31	Direct labor cost	300,000		1,800,000
31	Overhead costs	600,000		2,400,000
31	To finished goods		2,350,000	50,000

1. Determine the overhead application rate (based on direct material cost) used.

2. Only one job remained in the goods in process inventory at December 31, 2002. Its direct materials cost is $30,000. How much direct labor cost and overhead cost are assigned to it?

Exercise 20-5

Cost flows in a job order cost system

The following information is available for B-Safe Company, which produces special-order security products and uses a job order cost accounting system:

	April 30	May 31
Inventories		
Raw materials	$43,000	$ 52,000
Goods in process	10,200	21,300
Finished goods	63,000	35,600
Activities and information for May		
Raw materials purchases (paid with cash)		210,000
Factory payroll (paid with cash)		345,000
Factory overhead		
Indirect materials		15,000
Indirect labor		80,000
Other overhead costs		120,000
Sales (received in cash)		1,400,000
Predetermined overhead rate based on direct labor cost		70%

Compute the following amounts for the month of May:

1. Cost of direct materials used.   **4.** Cost of goods sold.

2. Cost of direct labor used.   **5.** Gross profit.

3. Cost of goods manufactured.   **6.** Overapplied or underapplied overhead.

Use information in Exercise 20-5 to prepare journal entries for the following events in May:

1. Raw materials purchases.

2. Direct materials usage.

3. Indirect materials usage.

4. Factory payroll costs.

5. Direct labor usage.

6. Indirect labor usage.

7. Factory overhead other than indirect materials and indirect labor (record credit to Other Accounts).

8. Application of overhead to goods in process.

9. Transfer of finished jobs to the finished goods inventory.

10. Sale and delivery of finished goods to customers for cash.

11. Allocation (closing) of overapplied or underapplied overhead to Cost of Goods Sold.

Exercise 20-6

Journal entries for a job order cost accounting system

In December 2001, Entertainment Inc. established its predetermined overhead application rate for movies produced during year 2002 by using the following cost predictions: overhead costs, $1,680,000, and direct labor costs, $480,000. At year end 2002, the company's records show that actual overhead costs for the year are $1,652,000. Actual direct labor cost had been assigned to jobs as follows:

Movies completed and released	$425,000
Movies still in production	50,000
Total actual direct labor cost	$475,000

1. Compute the predetermined overhead application rate for year 2002.

2. Set up a T-account for overhead and enter the overhead costs incurred and the amounts applied to movies during the year using the predetermined overhead rate.

3. Determine whether overhead is overapplied or underapplied (and the amount) during the year.

4. Prepare the adjusting entry to allocate any over- or underapplied overhead to Cost of Goods Sold.

Exercise 20-7

Factory overhead computed, applied, and adjusted

In December 2001, Fosby Company established its predetermined overhead application rate for jobs produced during year 2002 by using the following cost predictions: overhead costs, $750,000, and direct labor costs, $625,000. At year end 2002, the company's records show that actual overhead costs for the year are $830,000. Actual direct labor cost had been assigned to jobs as follows:

Jobs completed and sold	$513,750
Jobs in finished goods inventory	102,750
Jobs in goods in process inventory	68,500
Total actual direct labor cost	$685,000

1. Compute the predetermined overhead application rate for year 2002.

2. Set up a T-account for Factory Overhead and enter the overhead costs incurred and the amounts applied to jobs during the year using the predetermined overhead rate.

3. Determine whether overhead is overapplied or underapplied (and the amount) during the year.

4. Prepare the adjusting entry to allocate any over- or underapplied overhead to cost of goods sold.

5. Prepare the adjusting entry to allocate any over- or underapplied overhead to Cost of Goods Sold and the various inventories.

Exercise 20-8

Factory overhead computed, applied, and adjusted

Exercise 20-9
Overhead rate calculation
and analysis

Colby Company uses the relation between factory overhead and direct labor costs to assign factory overhead to its inventories of goods in process and finished goods. The company incurred the following costs during 2002: direct materials used, $650,000; direct labor costs, $3,000,000; and factory overhead costs, $1,800,000.

1. Estimate the company's overhead allocation rate for year 2002.

2. Assuming that the company's $71,000 ending Goods in Process Inventory account for year 2002 had $20,000 of direct labor costs, determine the inventory's direct material costs.

3. Assuming that the company's $490,000 ending Finished Goods Inventory account for year 2002 had $250,000 of direct material costs, determine the inventory's direct labor cost and its overhead costs.

Exercise 20-10
Costs allocated to ending
inventories

Royal Company's ending Goods in Process Inventory account consists of 5,000 units of partially completed product, and its Finished Goods Inventory account consists of 12,000 units of product. The factory manager determines that Goods in Process Inventory includes direct materials cost of $10 per unit and direct labor cost of $7 per unit. The company established the predicted overhead rate for jobs produced by using the following predictions: estimated direct labor cost, $300,000, and estimated factory overhead, $375,000. Finished goods are estimated to have $12 of direct materials cost per unit and $9 of direct labor cost per unit. During the period, the company incurred these costs: direct materials, $535,000; direct labor, $290,000; and factory overhead, $365,000. The company allocates factory overhead to its goods in process and finished goods inventories by relating overhead to direct labor cost.

1. Compute the overhead allocation rate.

2. Compute the total cost of the two ending inventories.

3. Compute cost of goods sold for the year (assume no beginning inventories).

Exercise 20-11
Cost-based pricing

Multimega Corporation has requested bids from several architects to design its new corporate headquarters. Artec Architects is one of the firms bidding on the job. Artec estimates that the job will require the following direct labor:

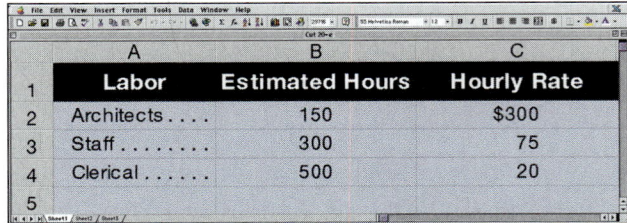

	A	B	C
1	**Labor**	**Estimated Hours**	**Hourly Rate**
2	Architects	150	$300
3	Staff	300	75
4	Clerical	500	20
5			

Artec applies overhead to jobs at 175% of direct labor cost. Artec would like to earn at least $80,000 profit on the building. Based on past experience and market research, it estimates that the competition will bid between $285,000 and $350,000 for the job.

1. What is Artec's estimated cost to design the building?

2. What bid would you suggest that Artec submit?

PROBLEM SET A

Problem 20-1A
Manufacturing costs
computed and recorded;
reports prepared

LTD Co.'s March 31 inventory of raw materials is $80,000. Raw materials purchases in April are $500,000. Factory payroll cost in April is $363,000. Overhead costs incurred in April are indirect materials, $50,000; indirect labor, $23,000; factory rent; $32,000; factory utilities, $19,000; and factory equipment depreciation, $51,000. The predetermined overhead rate is 50% of direct labor cost. Job 306 is sold for $635,000 cash in April. Costs of the three jobs worked on in April follow:

	Job 306	**Job 307**	**Job 308**
Balances on March 31			
Direct materials	$ 29,000	$ 35,000	
Direct labor	20,000	18,000	
Applied overhead	10,000	9,000	
Costs during April			
Direct materials	135,000	220,000	$100,000
Direct labor	85,000	150,000	105,000
Applied overhead	?	?	?
Status on April 30	Finished (sold)	Finished (unsold)	In process

Required

Preparation Component

1. Determine the total of each manufacturing cost incurred for April (direct labor, direct materials, allocated overhead), and the total cost assigned to each job (including the balances from March 31).

2. Prepare journal entries for the month to record
   a. Materials purchases (on credit), factory payroll (paid in cash), and actual overhead costs including indirect materials and indirect labor. (Factory rent and utilities are paid in cash.)
   b. Assignment of direct materials, direct labor, and applied overhead costs to the Goods in Process Inventory.
   c. Transfer of Jobs 306 and 307 to the Finished Goods Inventory.
   d. Cost of goods sold for Job 306. ~~two in ceord~~
   e. Revenue from the sale of Job 306.
   f. Assignment of any underapplied or overapplied overhead to the Cost of Goods Sold account. (The amount is not material.)

3. Prepare a manufacturing statement for April (use a single line presentation for direct materials and show the details of overhead cost).

Check   Cost of goods manufactured, $828,500

4. Calculate gross profit for April. Show how to present the inventories on the April 30 balance sheet.

Analysis Component

5. When the over- or underapplied overhead adjustment is made, we close Factory Overhead to Cost of Goods Sold. Discuss how this adjustment impacts business decision making regarding individual jobs or batches of jobs.

Tokyo Bay's computer system generated the following trial balance on the afternoon of December 31, 2002. The company's manager knows something is wrong with the trial balance because it does not show any balance for Goods in Process Inventory but does show balances for the Factory Payroll and Factory Overhead accounts.

Problem 20-2A
Source documents, journal entries, overhead, and financial reports

	Debit	Credit
Cash	$102,000	
Accounts receivable	75,000	
Raw materials inventory	80,000	
Goods in process inventory	0	
Finished goods inventory	15,000	
Prepaid rent	3,000	
Accounts payable		$ 17,000
Notes payable		25,000
Common stock		50,000
Retained earnings		271,000
Sales		373,000
Cost of goods sold	218,000	
Factory payroll	68,000	
Factory overhead	115,000	
Operating expenses	60,000	
Totals	$736,000	$736,000

After searching various files, the manager finds six source documents that need to be processed to bring the accounting records up to date:

Materials requisition 21-3010:	$10,200 direct materials to Job 402
Materials requisition 21-3011:	$18,600 direct materials to Job 404
Materials requisition 21-3012:	$ 5,600 indirect materials
Labor time ticket 6052:	$36,000 direct labor to Job 402
Labor time ticket 6053:	$23,800 direct labor to Job 404
Labor time ticket 6054:	$ 8,200 indirect labor

Jobs 402 and 404 are the only units in process at year-end. The predetermined overhead application rate is 200% of direct labor cost.

Required

Preparation Component

1. Use the information on the six source documents to prepare journal entries to assign the following costs:
    a. Direct material costs to Goods in Process Inventory.
    b. Direct labor costs to Goods in Process Inventory.
    c. Overhead costs to Goods in Process Inventory.
    d. Indirect material costs to the Factory Overhead account.
    e. Indirect labor costs to the Factory Overhead account.
2. Determine the revised balance of the Factory Overhead account after making the entries in part (1). Determine whether there is any under- or overapplied overhead for the year. Prepare the adjusting entry to allocate any over- or underapplied overhead to Cost of Goods Sold, assuming the amount is not material.
3. Prepare a revised trial balance.

Check Net income, $85,800

4. Prepare an income statement for year 2002 and a balance sheet as of December 31, 2002.

Analysis Component

5. Assume that the $5,600 on materials requisition 21-3012 should have been direct materials charged to Job 404. Without providing specific calculations, describe the impact of this error on the income statement for 2002 and the balance sheet at Dec. 31, 2002.

Problem 20-3A

Source documents, journal entries, and accounts in job order cost accounting

Skidoo Watercraft Co.'s predetermined overhead application rate for year 2002 is 200% of direct labor. The company's activities related to manufacturing during May 2002 follow:

a. Purchased raw materials on credit, $200,000.
b. Paid $126,000 cash for factory wages.
c. Paid $15,000 cash to a computer consultant to reprogram factory equipment.
d. Materials requisitions record use of the following materials for the month:

Job 136	$ 48,000
Job 137	32,000
Job 138	19,200
Job 139	22,400
Job 140	6,400
Total direct materials	$128,000
Indirect materials	19,500
Total materials used	$147,500

e. Time tickets record use of the following labor for the month:

Job 136	$ 12,000
Job 137	10,500
Job 138	37,500
Job 139	39,000
Job 140	3,000
Total direct labor	$102,000
Indirect labor	24,000
Total	$126,000

f. Applied overhead to Jobs 136, 138, and 139.

g. Transferred Jobs 136, 138, and 139 to Finished Goods.

h. Sold Jobs 136 and 138 on credit at a total price of $525,000.

i. Incurred the following overhead costs during the month (credit Prepaid Insurance for expired factory insurance):

Depreciation of factory building	$66,000
Depreciation of factory equipment . . .	36,500
Expired factory insurance	10,000
Accrued property taxes payable	35,000

j. Applied overhead at month-end to the Goods in Process (Jobs 137 and 140) using the predetermined rate of 200% of direct labor cost.

Required

1. Prepare a job cost sheet for each job worked on during the month. Use the following simplified form:

Job No. _____	
Materials	$
Labor	
Overhead	
Total cost	$

2. Prepare journal entries to record the events and transactions *a* through *j*.

3. Set up T-accounts for each of the following general ledger accounts, each of which started the month with a zero balance: Raw Materials Inventory; Goods in Process Inventory; Finished Goods Inventory; Factory Payroll; Factory Overhead; Cost of Goods Sold. Then post the journal entries to these T-accounts and determine the balance of each account.

4. Prepare a report showing the total cost of each job in process and prove that the sum of their costs equals the Goods in Process Inventory account balance. Prepare similar reports for Finished Goods Inventory and Cost of Goods Sold.

Check Finished Goods Inventory, $139,400

Problem 20-4A
Overhead allocation
and adjustment using a
predetermined overhead rate

In December 2001, Cantu Company's manager estimated next year's total direct labor cost using 50 persons working an average of 2,000 hours each at an average wage rate of $25 per hour. The manager also estimated the following manufacturing overhead costs for year 2002:

Indirect labor	$ 319,200
Factory supervision	240,000
Rent on factory building	140,000
Factory utilities	88,000
Factory insurance expired	68,000
Depreciation—Factory equipment	480,000
Repairs—Factory equipment	60,000
Factory supplies used	68,800
Miscellaneous production costs	36,000
Total estimated overhead costs	$1,500,000

At the end of 2002, records show the company incurred $1,520,000 of actual overhead costs. It completed and sold five jobs with the following direct labor costs: Job 201, $604,000; Job 202, $563,000; Job 203, $298,000; Job 204, $716,000; and Job 205, $314,000. In addition, Job 206 is in process at the end of 2002 and had been charged $17,000 for direct labor. No jobs were in process at the end of 2001. The company's predetermined overhead allocation rate is based on direct labor cost.

Required

1. Determine the following:

    a. Predetermined overhead allocation rate for year 2002.

    b. Total overhead cost applied to each of the six jobs during year 2002.

    c. Over- or underapplied overhead at year-end.

Check   Cr. Factory Overhead
$12,800

2. Assuming that any over- or underapplied overhead is not material, prepare the adjusting entry to allocate any over- or underapplied overhead to Cost of Goods Sold at the end of year 2002.

Problem 20-5A
Manufacturing transactions;
subsidiary records; source
documents

If the working papers that accompany this book are not available, do not attempt to solve this problem.
Kaplan Company manufactures variations of its product, a technopress, in response to special orders from its customers. On May 1, the company had no inventories of goods in process or finished goods but held the following raw materials:

Material M . . .	200 units @ $250 =		$50,000
Material R	95 units @	180 =	17,100
Paint	55 units @	75 =	4,125
Total cost			$71,225

On May 4, the company began working on two technopresses: Job 102 for Grobe Company and Job 103 for Reynco Company.

Required

Follow the instructions in this list of activities and complete the materials provided in the working papers:

a. Purchased raw materials on credit and recorded the following information from receiving reports and invoices:

> Receiving Report No. 426, Material M, 250 units at $250 each.
> Receiving Report No. 427, Material R, 90 units at $180 each.

Instructions: Record these purchases with a single journal entry and post it to general ledger T-accounts, using the transaction letter *a* to identify the entry. Enter the receiving report information on the materials ledger cards.

b. Requisitioned the following raw materials for production:

> Requisition No. 35, for Job 102, 135 units of Material M.
> Requisition No. 36, for Job 102, 72 units of Material R.
> Requisition No. 37, for Job 103, 70 units of Material M.
> Requisition No. 38, for Job 103, 38 units of Material R.
> Requisition No. 39, for 15 units of paint.

Instructions: Enter amounts for direct materials requisitions on the materials ledger cards and the job cost sheets. Enter the indirect material amount on the materials ledger card and record a debit to the Indirect Materials account in the subsidiary factory overhead ledger. Do not record a journal entry at this time.

c. Received the following employee time tickets for work in May:

> Time tickets Nos. 1 to 10 for direct labor on Job 102, $90,000.
> Time tickets Nos. 11 to 30 for direct labor on Job 103, $65,000.
> Time tickets Nos. 31 to 36 for equipment repairs, $19,250

Instructions: Record direct labor from the time tickets on the job cost sheets and then debit indirect labor to the Indirect Labor account in the subsidiary factory overhead ledger. Do not record a journal entry at this time.

d. Paid cash for the following items during the month: factory payroll, $174,250, and miscellaneous overhead items, $102,000.
Instructions: Record these payments with journal entries and then post them to the general ledger accounts. Also record a debit in the Miscellaneous Overhead account in the subsidiary factory overhead ledger.

e. Finished Job 102 and transferred it to the warehouse. The company assigns overhead to each job with a predetermined overhead allocation rate equal to 80% of direct labor cost.
Instructions: Enter the allocated overhead on the cost sheet for Job 102, fill in the cost summary section of the cost sheet, and then mark the cost sheet "Finished." Prepare a journal entry to record the job's completion and its transfer to Finished Goods and then post it to the general ledger accounts.

f. Delivered Job 102 and accepted the customer's promise to pay $400,000 within 30 days.
Instructions: Prepare journal entries to record the sale of Job 102 and the cost of goods sold. Post them to the general ledger accounts.

g. Applied overhead to Job 103 based on the job's direct labor to date.
Instructions: Enter overhead on the job cost sheet but do not make a journal entry at this time.

h. Recorded the total direct and indirect materials costs as reported on all the requisitions for the month.
Instructions: Prepare a journal entry to record these costs and post it to general ledger accounts.

i. Recorded the total direct and indirect labor costs as reported on all time tickets for the month.
Instructions: Prepare a journal entry to record these costs and post it to general ledger accounts.

j. Recorded the total overhead costs applied to jobs.
Instructions: Prepare a journal entry to record the allocation of these overhead costs and post it to general ledger accounts.

Check Balance in Factory Overhead, $1,625 Cr., overapplied

PROBLEM SET B

Problem 20-1B
Manufacturing costs
computed and recorded;
reports prepared

Alliance Co.'s August 31 inventory of raw materials is $150,000. Raw materials purchases in September are $400,000. Factory payroll cost in September is $220,000. Overhead costs incurred in September are indirect materials, $30,000; indirect labor, $14,000; factory rent, $20,000; factory utilities, $12,000; and factory equipment depreciation, $30,000. The predetermined overhead rate is 50% of direct labor cost. Job 114 is sold for $380,000 cash in September. Costs for the three jobs worked on in September follow:

	Job 114	Job 115	Job 116
Balances on August 31			
Direct materials	$ 14,000	$ 18,000	
Direct labor	18,000	16,000	
Applied overhead	9,000	8,000	
Costs during September			
Direct materials	100,000	170,000	$ 80,000
Direct labor	30,000	68,000	120,000
Applied overhead	?	?	?
Status on September 30 ..	Finished (sold)	Finished (unsold)	In process

Required

Preparation Component

1. Determine the total of each manufacturing cost incurred for September (direct labor, direct materials, allocated overhead), and the total cost assigned to each job (including the balances from August 31).

2. Prepare journal entries for the month to record
   a. Materials purchases (on credit), factory payroll (paid in cash), and actual overhead costs including indirect materials and indirect labor. (Factory rent and utilities are paid in cash.)
   b. Assignment of direct materials, direct labor, and applied overhead costs to Goods in Process Inventory.
   c. Transfer of Jobs 114 and 115 to the Finished Goods Inventory.
   d. Cost of Job 114 in the Cost of Goods Sold account.
   e. Revenue from the sale of Job 114.
   f. Assignment of any underapplied or overapplied overhead to the Cost of Goods Sold account. (The amount is not material.)

Check   Cost of goods
manufactured, $500,000

3. Prepare a manufacturing statement for September (use a single line presentation for direct materials and show the details of overhead cost).

4. Calculate gross profit for September. Show how to present the inventories on the September 30 balance sheet.

Analysis Component

5. When the over- or underapplied overhead adjustment is made, we close Factory Overhead to Cost of Goods Sold. Discuss how this adjustment impacts business decision making regarding individual jobs or batches of jobs.

Problem 20-2B
Source documents, journal
entries, overhead, and
financial reports

Da Kine's computer system generated the following trial balance on the afternoon of December 31, 2002. The company's manager knows that it is wrong because the trial balance does not show any balance for Goods in Process Inventory but does show balances for the Factory Payroll and Factory Overhead accounts.

	Debit	Credit
Cash	$ 48,000	
Accounts receivable	42,000	
Raw materials inventory	26,000	
Goods in process inventory	0	
Finished goods inventory	9,000	
Prepaid rent	3,000	
Accounts payable		$ 10,500
Notes payable		13,500
Common stock		30,000
Retained earnings		87,000
Sales		180,000
Cost of goods sold	105,000	
Factory payroll	16,000	
Factory overhead	27,000	
Operating expenses	45,000	
Totals	$321,000	$321,000

After searching various files, the manager finds six source documents that need to be processed to bring the accounting records up to date:

Materials requisition 94-231:	$4,600 direct materials to Job 603
Materials requisition 94-232:	$7,600 direct materials to Job 604
Materials requisition 94-233:	$2,100 indirect materials
Labor time ticket 765:	$5,000 direct labor to Job 603
Labor time ticket 766:	$8,000 direct labor to Job 604
Labor time ticket 777:	$3,000 indirect labor

Jobs 603 and 604 are the only units in process at year-end. The predetermined overhead application rate is 200% of direct labor cost.

Required

Preparation Component

1. Use the information on the six source documents to prepare journal entries to assign the following costs:
  a. Direct materials costs to Goods in Process Inventory.
  b. Direct labor costs to Goods in Process Inventory.
  c. Overhead costs to Goods in Process Inventory.
  d. Indirect materials costs to the Factory Overhead account.
  e. Indirect labor costs to the Factory Overhead account.
2. Determine the revised balance of the Factory Overhead account after making the entries in part (1). Determine whether there is under- or overapplied overhead for the year. Prepare the adjusting entry to allocate any over- or underapplied overhead to Cost of Goods Sold, assuming the amount is not material.
3. Prepare a revised trial balance.
4. Prepare an income statement for year 2002 and a balance sheet as of December 31, 2002.

Check   Net income, $23,900

Analysis Component

5. Assume that the $2,100 indirect materials on materials requisition 94-233 should have been direct materials charged to Job 604. Without providing specific calculations, describe the impact of this error on the income statement for 2002 and the balance sheet at Dec. 31, 2002.

Problem 20-3B

Source documents, journal
entries, and accounts in job
order cost accounting

SuperFly Company's predetermined overhead application rate is 200% of direct labor. The company's
activities related to manufacturing during September 2002 follow:

a. Purchased raw materials on credit, $125,000.

b. Paid $84,000 cash for factory wages.

c. Paid $11,000 cash for miscellaneous factory overhead costs.

d. Materials requisitions record use of the following materials for the month:

Job 487	$30,000
Job 488	20,000
Job 489	12,000
Job 490	14,000
Job 491	4,000
Total direct materials	$80,000
Indirect materials	12,000
Total materials used	$92,000

e. Time tickets record use of the following labor for the month:

Job 487	$ 8,000
Job 488	7,000
Job 489	25,000
Job 490	26,000
Job 491	2,000
Total direct labor	$68,000
Indirect labor	16,000
Total	$84,000

f. Allocated overhead to Jobs 487, 489, and 490.

g. Transferred Jobs 487, 489, and 490 to Finished Goods.

h. Sold Jobs 487 and 489 on credit for a total price of $340,000.

i. Incurred the following overhead costs during the month (credit Prepaid Insurance for expired
factory insurance):

Depreciation of factory building	$37,000
Depreciation of factory equipment . . .	21,000
Expired factory insurance	7,000
Accrued property taxes payable	31,000

j. Applied overhead at month-end to the Goods in Process (Jobs 488 and 491) using the predetermined rate of 200% of direct labor cost.

Required

1. Prepare a job cost sheet for each job worked on during the month. Use the following simplified
form:

Job No. _____	
Materials	$
Labor	
Overhead	
Total cost	$

2. Prepare journal entries to record the events and transactions *a* through *j*.

3. Set up T-accounts for each of the following general ledger accounts, each of which started the month with a zero balance: Raw Materials Inventory, Goods in Process Inventory, Finished Goods Inventory, Factory Payroll, Factory Overhead, Cost of Goods Sold. Then post the journal entries to these T-accounts and determine the balance of each account.

4. Prepare a report showing the total cost of each job in process and prove that the sum of their costs equals the Goods in Process Inventory account balance. Prepare similar reports for Finished Goods Inventory and Cost of Goods Sold.

Check Finished goods inventory, $92,000

In December 2001, Watson Company's manager estimated next year's total direct labor cost using 50 persons working an average of 2,000 hours each at an average wage rate of $15 per hour. The manager also estimated the following manufacturing overhead costs for year 2002.

Indirect labor	$159,600
Factory supervision	120,000
Rent on factory building	70,000
Factory utilities	44,000
Factory insurance expired	34,000
Depreciation—Factory equipment	240,000
Repairs—Factory equipment	30,000
Factory supplies used	34,400
Miscellaneous production costs	18,000
Total estimated overhead costs	$750,000

Problem 20-4B
Overhead allocation and adjustment using a predetermined overhead rate

At the end of 2002, records show the company incurred $725,000 of actual overhead costs. It completed and sold five jobs with the following direct labor costs: Job 625, $354,000; Job 626, $330,000; Job 627, $175,000; Job 628, $420,000; and Job 629, $184,000. In addition, Job 630 is in process at the end of 2002 and had been charged $10,000 for direct labor. No jobs were in process at the end of 2001. The company's predetermined overhead allocation rate is based on direct labor cost.

Required

1. Determine the following:

  a. Predetermined overhead allocation rate for year 2002.

  b. Total overhead cost applied to each of the six jobs during year 2002.

  c. Over- or underapplied overhead at year-end.

2. Assuming that any over- or underapplied overhead is not material, prepare the adjusting entry to allocate any over- or underapplied overhead to Cost of Goods Sold at the end of year 2002.

Check Dr. Factory Overhead, $11,500

If the working papers that accompany this book are not available, do not attempt to solve this problem. Natkin Company manufactures variations of its product, a megatron, in response to special orders from its customers. On June 1, the company had no inventories of goods in process or finished goods but held the following raw materials:

Problem 20-5B
Manufacturing transactions; subsidiary records; source documents

Material M ...	120 units @ $200 =	$24,000
Material R	80 units @ 160 =	12,800
Paint	44 units @ 72 =	3,168
Total cost		$39,968

On June 3, the company began working on two megatrons: Job 450 for Ancira Company and Job 451 for Montero, Inc.

Required

Follow instructions in this list of activities and complete the materials provided in the working papers.

a. Purchased raw materials on credit and recorded the following information from receiving reports and invoices:

> Receiving Report No. 20, Material M, 150 units at $200 each.
> Receiving Report No. 21, Material R,   70 units at $160 each.

Instructions: Record these purchases with a single journal entry and post it to general ledger T-accounts, using the transaction letter *a* to identify the entry. Enter the receiving report information on the materials ledger cards.

b. Requisitioned the following raw materials for production:

> Requisition No. 223, for Job 450, 80 units of Material M.
> Requisition No. 224, for Job 450, 60 units of Material R.
> Requisition No. 225, for Job 451, 40 units of Material M.
> Requisition No. 226, for Job 451, 30 units of Material R.
> Requisition No. 227, for 12 units of paint.

Instructions: Enter amounts for direct materials requisitions on the materials ledger cards and the job cost sheets. Enter the indirect material amount on the materials ledger card and record a debit to the Indirect Materials account in the subsidiary factory overhead ledger. Do not record a journal entry at this time.

c. Received the following employee time tickets for work in June:

> Time tickets Nos. 1 to 10 for direct labor on Job 450, $40,000.
> Time tickets Nos. 11 to 20 for direct labor on Job 451, $32,000.
> Time tickets Nos. 21 to 24 for equipment repairs, $12,000.

Instructions: Record direct labor from the time tickets on the job cost sheets and then debit indirect labor to the Indirect Labor account in the subsidiary factory overhead ledger. Do not record a journal entry at this time.

d. Paid cash for the following items during the month: factory payroll, $84,000, and miscellaneous overhead items, $36,000.
Instructions: Record these payments with journal entries and post them to the general ledger accounts. Also record a debit in the Miscellaneous Overhead account in the subsidiary factory overhead ledger.

e. Finished Job 450 and transferred it to the warehouse. The company assigns overhead to each job with a predetermined overhead allocation rate equal to 70% of direct labor cost.
Instructions: Enter the allocated overhead on the cost sheet for Job 450, fill in the cost summary section of the cost sheet, and then mark the cost sheet "Finished." Prepare a journal entry to record the job's completion and its transfer to Finished Goods and then post it to the general ledger accounts.

f. Delivered Job 450 and accepted the customer's promise to pay $290,000 within 30 days.
Instructions: Prepare journal entries to record the sale of Job 450 and the cost of goods sold. Post them to the general ledger accounts.

g. Applied overhead cost to Job 451 based on the job's direct labor used to date.
Instructions: Enter overhead on the job cost sheet but do not make a journal entry at this time.

h. Recorded the total direct and indirect materials costs as reported on all the requisitions for the month.
Instructions: Prepare a journal entry to record these costs and post it to general ledger accounts.

i. Recorded the total direct and indirect labor costs as reported on all time tickets for the month.
Instructions: Prepare a journal entry to record these costs and post it to general ledger accounts.

j. Recorded the total overhead costs applied to jobs.
Instructions: Prepare a journal entry to record the allocation of these overhead costs and post it to general ledger accounts.

Check   Balance in Factory Overhead, $1,536 Cr., overapplied

Beyond the Numbers

BTN 20-1   **Nike**'s annual report in Appendix A indicates growth potential from international sales.

Required

1. Identify at least two types of costs that will predictably increase as a percent of sales with growth in international sales.
2. Explain why you believe the types of costs identified for part (1) will increase, and describe how you might assess Nike's success with these costs. (*Hint:* You might consider the gross margin ratio.)

Swoosh Ahead

3. Obtain Nike's annual report for a fiscal year ending after May 31, 2000, from its Web site [**www.nike.com**] or the SEC's EDGAR database [**www.sec.gov**]. Review Nike's growth in international sales along with its cost and income levels (including its gross margin ratio).

Reporting in Action

BTN 20-2   Both **Nike** and **Reebok** want to know the impact of a just-in-time inventory system for their operating cash flows. Review each company's statement of cash flows in Appendix A and answer the following:

Required

1. Identify the impact on operating cash flows (increase or decrease) for changes in inventory levels (increase or decrease) for both companies for each of the three most recent years.
2. What impact would a JIT inventory system have on both Nike's and Reebok's level of raw materials and their operating cash flows? Link the answer to your response for part (1).
3. Would the move to a JIT system have a one-time or recurring impact on operating cash flow?

Comparative Analysis

BTN 20-3   An accounting professional requires at least two skill sets. The first is to be technically competent. Knowing how to capture, manage, and report information is a necessary skill. Second, the ability to estimate managers' and employees' actions and biases from accounting analysis is another skill. For instance, knowing how a person is compensated helps anticipate information biases. Draw on these skills and write a one-half page memo to the financial officer on the practice of allocating overhead in the following company:

Background: The company sells portable housing to general contractors and the government. It sells jobs to contractors on a bid basis. A contractor asks for three bids from different manufacturers. The combination of low bid and high quality wins the job. Jobs sold to the government are bid on a cost-plus basis. This means price is determined by adding all costs plus a profit based on cost at a specified percent, such as 10%. You observe that the amount of overhead allocated to government jobs is higher than that allocated to contract jobs. These allocations concern you and motivate your memo.

Ethics Challenge

Point: Students could compare responses and discuss differences in concerns with allocating overhead.

BTN 20-4   You are preparing for a second interview with a manufacturing company. The company is impressed with your credentials but has indicated that it has several qualified applicants. You anticipate that in this second interview, you need to show how you can offer something special over other candidates. You learn the company currently uses a periodic inventory system and is not satisfied with the timeliness of its information and its inventory management. The company manufactures special-order holiday decorations and display items. To show your ability to improve the operation, you plan to recommend that it use a cost accounting system.

Communicating in Practice

Required

In preparation for the interview, prepare notes outlining the following:
1. Your cost accounting system recommendation and why it is suitable for this company.
2. A general description of the documents that the cost accounting system requires.
3. How the documents in part *2* facilitate the operation of the cost accounting system.

Point: Have students present a mock interview, one assuming the role of the president of the company and the other the applicant.

Taking It to the Net

C2

BTN 20-5   Most architects and contractors work on custom jobs that usually require a job order costing system.

Required

Access the Web site **www.aec.geac.com** and click on *Job Cost Accounting*. Prepare a one-page memorandum for the CEO of a construction company providing information about the job order costing software this company offers. Would you recommend that the company purchase this software?

Teamwork in Action

C2

BTN 20-6   Consider the activities undertaken by a medical clinic in your area.

Required

1. Do you consider a job order cost accounting system appropriate for the clinic?

2. Identify as many factors as possible that would lead you to conclude that it uses a job order system.

Business Week Activity

C1 **C2**

BTN 20-7   Managing materials in the production process is a challenging and crucial task for a company. Read the article "Porsche Is Back—And Then Some" in the September 15, 1997, issue of *Business Week*.

Required

1. Explain how Wendelin Wiedeking used supply management to revive Porsche.

2. Discuss what Wiedeking achieved in comparison to what we see in a successful grocery store.

Entrepreneurial Decision

C2

BTN 20-8   Mikey Bladsworth is a manager in One-For-All Computers. Sales have recently declined because customers are demanding computers to better fit their needs. Bladsworth is planning to start his own company, Build-Your-Own Computers, to satisfy this demand for customized computers. As an entrepreneur, he must decide the extent of customization he wishes to provide (for example, will he supply "neon-green" computers?). He is especially concerned about how he will record and track the costs of potentially thousands of custom computers.

Required

1. What unique and identifiable characteristics can a computer system possess?

2. How concerned should Bladsworth be regarding the cost tracking system? What type of costing system should he use?

3. Do you recommend that Bladsworth pursue the proposed business? Explain.

21

Process Cost Accounting

"Just ignore negativity"—Stephanie Hirsch

A Look Back

Chapter 19 introduced managerial accounting and described cost concepts and the reporting of manufacturing activities. Chapter 20 explained job order costing—an important cost accounting system for customized products and services.

A Look at This Chapter

This chapter focuses on how we measure and account for costs in process operations. We explain process production, describe how to assign costs to processes, and compute cost per equivalent unit for a process.

A Look Ahead

Chapter 22 describes managerial accounting reports useful in directing a company's activities. We explain how to allocate factory overhead costs to different products and describe the activity-based costing method of overhead allocation.

Inca Inspiration

NEW YORK—After college, Stephanie Hirsch worked as a waitress and stylist-assistant while searching for a career. "I never felt right in any job," says Hirsch. "It sucked the soul out of me." She needed a change and drifted to South America, where she found herself pondering life while perusing street markets. Later, while hiking the Inca Trail, Hirsch had an epiphany—she would launch a company to design and create handbags inspired by the colors and materials of her travels, hence **INCA** [**www.INCABag.com**].

With limited resources, Hirsch began operating out of her home and later expanded to a shipping loft and added sales reps. Her unique styles, colors, and designs quickly caught the attention of the fashion crowd, and press copy in *Vogue* and *Marie Claire* quickly followed. In a short time, Hirsch had a collection of Inca-inspired handbags, but cost controls were crucial to continued success. She carefully monitored and controlled the costs of INCA's manufacturing processes. This included her oversight of materials, labor, and overhead while maintaining the special qualities of INCA products.

At the ripe old age of 28, Hirsch is a veteran of entrepreneurial activity. She has expanded her handbag line to an entire lifestyle collection that includes bikinis, mini skirts, and sarongs. INCA products have been spotted on the likes of Courtney Cox, Liz Hurley, Kate Capshaw, and Cindy Crawford. *Sports Illustrated* even featured an INCA swimsuit in its swimsuit issue. Her plastic bamboo beach mat is a phenomenon unto itself with skyrocketing sales and popularity. INCA's total sales for this year are expected to exceed $3 million. Still, sufficient net income and return on equity depend on cost controls . . . and inspiration. For the latter, Hirsch continues to travel and look for old-world cultural styles to blend with innovative designs. Says Hirsch, "Just making a living is not enough." [Sources: *INCA Web site*, May 2001; *Business Start-Ups*, April 2000.]

Learning Objectives

Conceptual

C1 Explain process operations and the way they differ from job order operations.

C2 Define equivalent units and explain their use in process cost accounting.

C3 Explain the four steps in accounting for production activity in a period.

C4 Define a process cost summary and describe its purposes.

C5 Explain a hybrid costing system.

Analytical

A1 Compare process cost accounting and job order cost accounting.

Procedural

P1 Record the flow of direct materials costs in process cost accounting.

P2 Record the flow of direct labor costs in process cost accounting.

P3 Record the flow of factory overhead costs in process cost accounting.

P4 Compute equivalent units produced in a period.

P5 Prepare a process cost summary.

P6 Record the transfer of goods between departments.

P7 Record the transfer of completed goods to Finished Goods Inventory and Cost of Goods Sold.

Chapter Preview

The type of product or service a company offers determines its cost accounting system. We focused on job order costing in Chapter 20. Companies use it to account for a job that consists of one unit (or a group of units) that is custom designed to meet the requirements of a particular customer. Not all products are manufactured in this way; many carry standard designs where one unit is no different than any other unit. This system often produces large numbers of units on a continuous basis, all of which pass through similar manufacturing steps or processes. This chapter describes how to use a process cost accounting system to account for these types of products. We explain how manufacturing costs are accumulated for each process and then assigned to units passing through those processes. This information helps to understand and estimate the cost of each process as well as find ways to reduce costs and improve processes.

Process Operations

C1 Explain process operations and the way they differ from job order operations.

Process manufacturing, also called *process operations* or *process production,* is the mass production of products in a continuous flow of steps. This means that products pass through

a series of sequential processes. Petroleum refining is a common example of process operations. Crude oil passes through a series of steps before it is processed into different grades of petroleum. The assembly line at the **Ford** Mustang plant in Michigan reflects a process operation. An important characteristic of process operations is the high level of standardization necessary if the system is to produce large volumes of products. Process operations also extend to services. Examples include mail sorting in large post offices and order processing in large mail-order firms such as **L.L. Bean** and **Lands' End**. The common feature in these service organizations is that operations are performed in a sequential manner using a series of standardized processes.

Each of these examples of products and services involves operations having a series of *processes,* or steps. Each process involves a different set of activities. A manufacturing operation that processes chemicals, for instance, might include the four steps shown in Exhibit 21.1. Understanding these processes is important for measuring their costs.

Exhibit 21.1

Process Manufacturing Operations: Chemicals

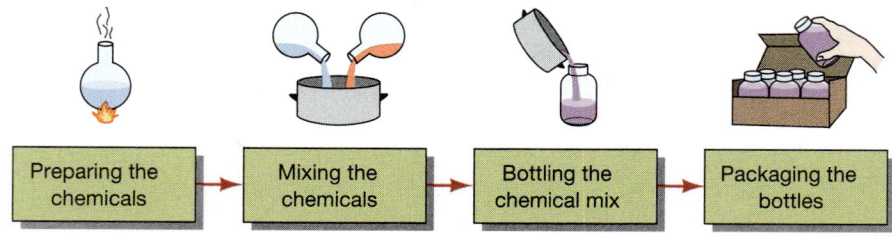

Comparing Job Order and Process Operations

A1 Compare process cost accounting and job order cost accounting.

Job order and process operations can be considered as two ends of a continuum. Important features of both systems are shown in Exhibit 21.2. While we often describe job order and process operations with manufacturing examples, they both apply to service companies. In a job order costing system, the measurement focus is on the individual job or batch. In a process costing system, the measurement focus is on the process itself and the standardized units produced.

Exhibit 21.2

Comparing Job Order and Process Operations

Job Order Systems	Process Systems
• Custom orders	• Repetitive operations
• Heterogeneous products	• Homogeneous products
• Low production volume	• High production volume
• High product flexibility	• Low product flexibility
• Low to medium standardization	• High standardization

Organization of Process Operations

In a process manufacturing operation, each process is identified as a separate *production department, workstation,* or *work center.* With the exception of the first process or department, each receives the output from the prior department as a partially processed product. Depending on the nature of the process, a company applies direct labor, overhead, and, perhaps, additional direct materials to move the product toward completion. Only the final process or department in the series produces finished goods ready for sale to customers.

Exhibit 21.3 shows an operation in which components of a final product are manufactured in three parallel processes (shown in horizontal layout) and then combined at different stages of production. In addition to parallel processes, many manufacturing operations involve numerous components and related production processes.

Did You Know?

Full Service Accounting Many service companies use process departments to perform specific tasks for consumers. Hospitals, for instance, have radiology and physical therapy facilities with special equipment and trained employees. When patients need services, they are processed through departments to receive prescribed care. In a different setting, **AT&T** uses a system similar to process cost accounting to accumulate costs for services such as directory assistance. Service companies need process cost accounting information as much as manufacturers to estimate costs of providing services, to plan future operations, to control costs, and to determine charges to customers.

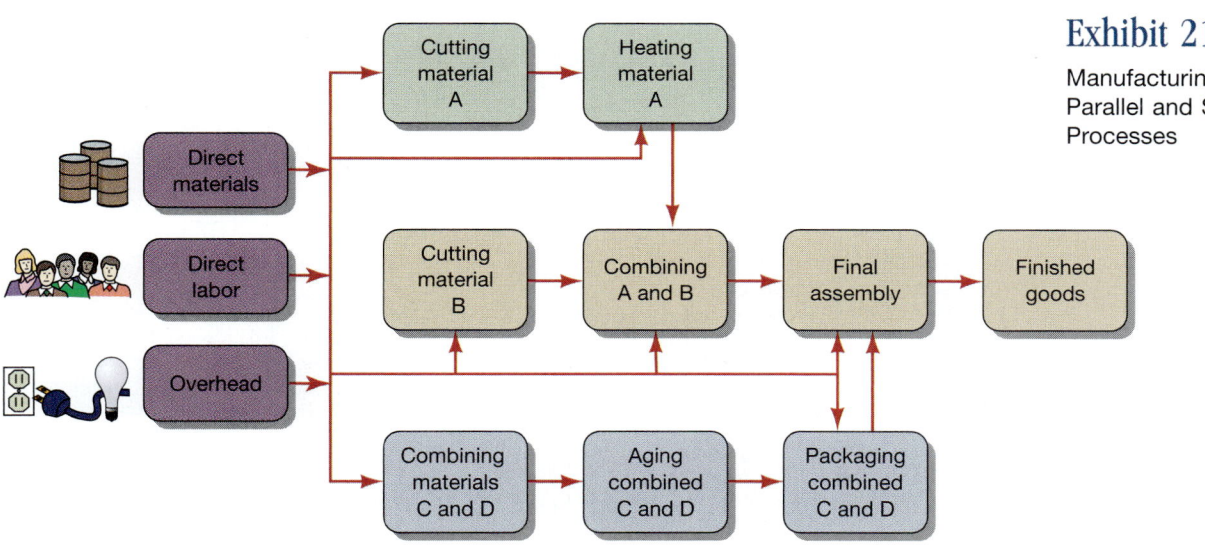

Exhibit 21.3

Manufacturing Operations with Parallel and Sequential Processes

GenX Company—An Illustration

The **GenX Company** illustrates process operations. It produces Profen®, an over-the-counter pain reliever for athletes. GenX sells Profen to wholesale distributors who in turn sell it to retailers. Profen is produced in two steps. Step 1 uses a grinding process to pulverize blocks of its active ingredient, Profelene. Step 2 mixes the resulting powder with flavorings and preservatives, molds it into Profen tablets, and packages the tablets. Exhibit 21.4 shows a summary floor plan of the GenX factory, which has five areas:

1. *Storeroom*—materials are received and then distributed when requisitioned.
2. *Production support offices*—used by administrative and maintenance employees who support manufacturing operations.
3. *Locker rooms*—workers change from street clothes into sanitized uniforms before working in the factory.
4. *Production floor*—areas divided between the grinding and mixing departments.
5. *Warehouse*—finished products are stored before being shipped to wholesalers.

Point: Robots, computers, and online information are common in today's factory.

Exhibit 21.4

Floor Plan of GenX's Factory

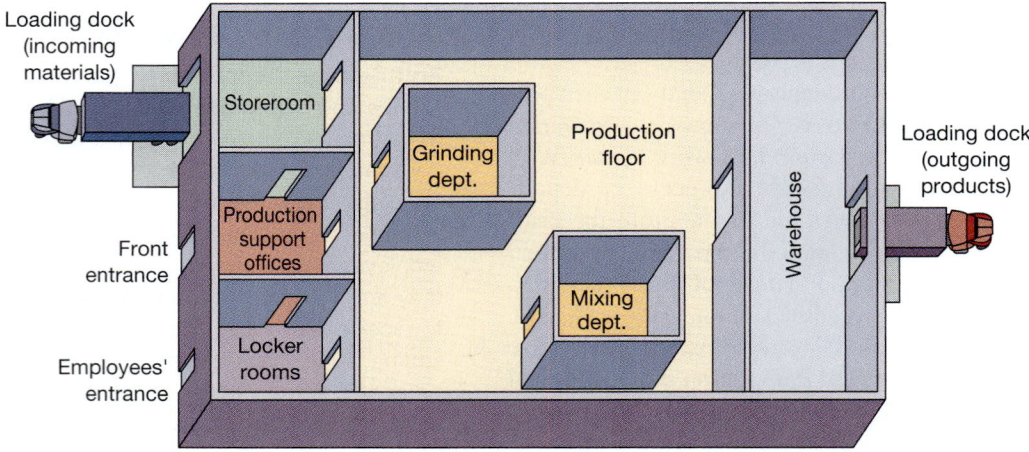

The first step in process manufacturing is the decision to produce a product. Management must determine the types and quantities of materials and labor needed and then schedule the work for departments. Based on these plans, production begins. The flowchart in Exhibit 21.5 shows the production steps for GenX. The table below the flowchart in this exhibit summarizes GenX's cost of its manufacturing processes for April. This includes costs at the beginning of April, the costs incurred in April, and the application of these costs to the grinding and mixing departments. The following sections explain how GenX uses a process cost accounting system to compute these costs. Many of the explanations refer back to this exhibit and its numbered cost flows.

Exhibit 21.5

Process Manufacturing Operations and Costs: GenX

A. Process Manufacturing Operations

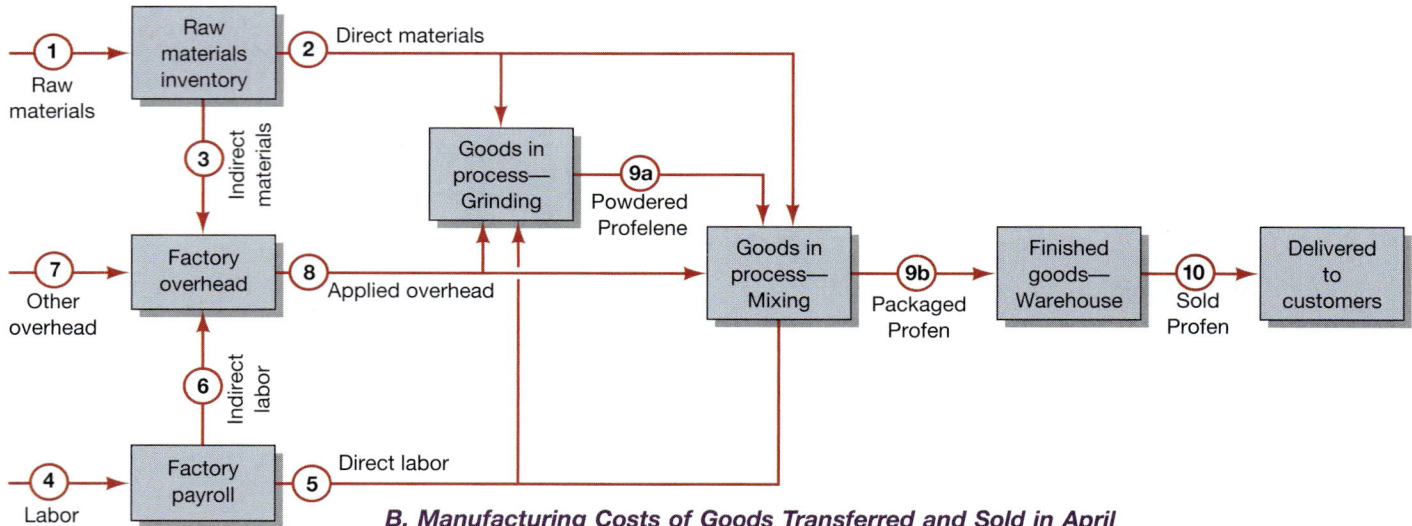

B. Manufacturing Costs of Goods Transferred and Sold in April

	Grinding Department	Mixing Department	Finished Goods
Beginning inventory	$ 4,250	$ 3,520	$ 6,440
Direct materials	9,900	2,040	
Direct labor	5,700	5,100	
Overhead applied*	4,275	1,020	
Total costs—Grinding	24,125		
Less ending inventory—Grinding	(2,725)		
Transferred to Mixing	$21,400 ⟶	21,400	
Total costs—Mixing		33,080	
Less ending inventory—Mixing		(3,610)	
Transferred to finished goods		$29,470 ⟶	29,470
Less ending inventory—Finished goods			(5,251)
Cost of goods sold			$30,659

* Overhead is applied to the two production departments using predetermined overhead allocation rates based on direct labor dollars. Actual overhead incurred: Indirect materials, $1,195; indirect labor, $3,220; other overhead purchases and costs, $880.

Process and job order manufacturing operations are similar in that they both combine materials, labor, and overhead in the process of producing products. They differ in how they are organized and managed. The measurement focus in a job order costing system is on the individual job or batch, whereas in a process costing system, it is on the individual process. Regardless of the measurement focus, we are ultimately interested in determining the cost per unit of product (or service) resulting from either system.

Specifically, the **job order cost accounting system** assigns direct materials, direct labor, and overhead to jobs. The total job cost is then divided by the number of units to compute a cost per unit for that job. The **process cost accounting system** assigns direct materials, direct labor, and overhead to specific processes. The total costs associated with each process are then divided by the number of units passing through that process to determine the cost per equivalent unit (defined later in the chapter) for that process. The cost per equivalent unit for each process is summed for all processes to determine the total cost per unit of a product. The differences in the way these two systems apply materials, labor, and overhead costs are highlighted in Exhibit 21.6.

Point: The cost object in a job order system is the specific job whereas the cost object in a process costing system is the process.

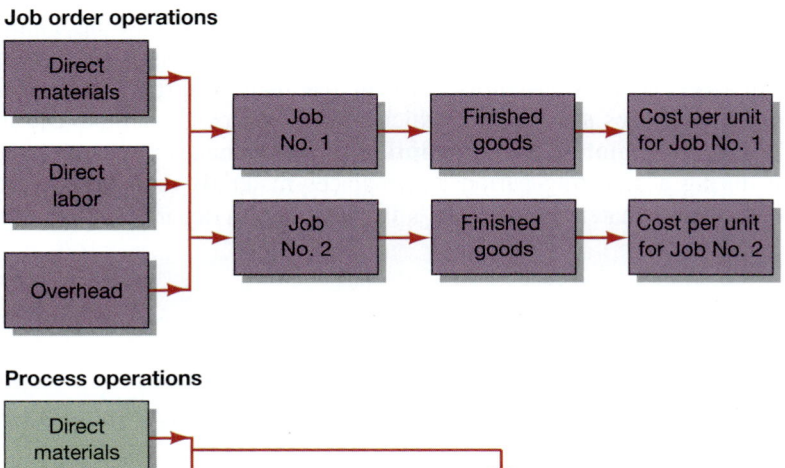

Exhibit 21.6

Comparing Job Order and Process Cost Accounting Systems

Direct and Indirect Costs

Chapter 20 explained how materials and labor used on jobs (in job order costing) are charged to the jobs as direct costs. Materials and labor that contribute to manufacturing but that are not linked with specific jobs are indirect costs and are allocated to jobs as overhead. Process cost accounting systems also use the concepts of direct and indirect costs. Materials and labor that are clearly linked with specific processes are assigned to those processes as direct costs. Materials and labor not clearly linked with a specific process are indirect costs and are assigned to overhead. Some costs classified as overhead in a job order system may be classified as direct costs in process cost accounting. For example, depreciation of a machine used entirely by one process is a direct cost of that process. The next three subsections explain the accounting for materials, labor, and overhead in a process cost accounting system.

Point: If a cost can be directly linked to the cost object, it is direct; if it cannot, it is indirect.

Point: Manufacturing companies typically use a perpetual inventory system for materials.

Did You Know?

JIT Boon to Process Operations Companies that adopt JIT manufacturing often organize their production system as a series of sequential processes. One survey found 60% of companies that converted to JIT used process operations; this compares to only 20% before converting to JIT.

Accounting for Materials Costs

P1 Record the flow of direct materials costs in process cost accounting.

In Exhibit 21.5, arrow line ① reflects the arrival of materials at GenX's factory. These materials include Profelene, flavorings, preservatives, and packaging. They also include supplies for the production support office. GenX uses a perpetual inventory system and makes all purchases on credit. The summary entry for receipts of raw materials in April is as follows (dates in journal entries numbered ② through ⑩ are omitted because they are summary entries, often reflecting two or more transactions or events):

Assets = Liabilities + Equity
+14,135   +14,135

①	Raw Materials Inventory	14,135	
	Accounts Payable		14,135
	Acquired materials on credit for factory use.		

Arrow line ② in Exhibit 21.5 reflects the flow of direct materials to the grinding and mixing departments, where they are used to produce Profen. Most direct materials are physically combined into the finished product. Direct materials can also include supplies used in a specific process when those supplies can be clearly linked with that process. The manager of a process usually obtains materials to use in the process by submitting a *materials requisition* to the materials storeroom manager. In some situations, materials move continuously from raw materials inventory through the manufacturing process. **Coca-Cola Bottling**, for instance, uses a process in which inventory moves continuously through the system. In these cases, a **materials consumption report** summarizes the materials used by a department during a reporting period and replaces materials requisitions. The entry to record the use of direct materials by GenX's two production departments in April follows:

Assets = Liabilities + Equity
+9,900
+2,040
−11,940

②	Goods in Process Inventory—Grinding	9,900	
	Goods in Process Inventory—Mixing	2,040	
	Raw Materials Inventory		11,940
	To assign costs of direct materials used in the grinding and mixing departments.		

Use of two Goods in Process Inventory accounts allows the costs incurred by each process to be separately accumulated. Also, this entry does not increase or decrease total assets but merely transfers costs from one asset account to two other asset accounts.

In Exhibit 21.5, the arrow line ③ reflects the flow of indirect materials from the storeroom to factory overhead. These materials are not clearly linked with either the grinding or the mixing departments but are used to support overall production activity. This entry records the cost of indirect materials used by GenX in April:

Example: What types of materials might the flow of arrow line ③ in Exhibit 21.5 reflect? *Answer:* Goggles, gloves, protective clothing, recordkeeping supplies, and cleaning supplies.

Assets = Liabilities + Equity
−1,195   −1,195

③	Factory Overhead	1,195	
	Raw Materials Inventory		1,195
	To record indirect materials used in April.		

After the entries for both direct and indirect materials are posted, the Raw Materials Inventory account appears as shown in Exhibit 21.7. The April 30 balance sheet reports the $5,000 Raw Materials Inventory account as a current asset.

Exhibit 21.7

Raw Materials Inventory Ledger Account

Raw Materials Inventory				Acct. No. 132		
Date		Explanation	Debit	Credit	Balance
2002					
Mar.	31	Balance			4,000
Apr.	30	Materials purchases	14,135		18,135
	30	Direct materials usage		11,940	6,195
	30	Indirect materials usage		1,195	5,000

Accounting for Labor Costs

Exhibit 21.5 shows factory payroll costs of GenX as reflected in arrow line ④. Total labor costs of $14,020 are paid in cash and are recorded in the Factory Payroll account with this entry:

P2 Record the flow of direct labor costs in process cost accounting.

④	Factory Payroll	14,020	
	Cash		14,020
	To record factory wages for April.		

Assets = Liabilities + Equity
−14,020   −14,020

This entry is triggered by time reports from the two production departments and the production support office. (For simplicity, we do not separately identify withholdings and additional payroll taxes for employees.) In a process operation, the direct labor of a production department (such as mixing) includes all labor used exclusively by that department. This is the case even if the labor is not applied to the product itself. If a production department in a process operation, for instance, has a full-time manager and a full-time maintenance worker, their salaries are direct labor costs of a process, not factory overhead.

Arrow line ⑤ in Exhibit 21.5 shows GenX's use of direct labor in the grinding and mixing departments. This entry transfers April's direct labor costs from the Factory Payroll account to the two Goods in Process Inventory accounts:

⑤	Goods in Process Inventory—Grinding	5,700	
	Goods in Process Inventory—Mixing	5,100	
	Factory Payroll		10,800
	To assign costs of direct labor used in the grinding and mixing departments.		

Assets = Liabilities + Equity
+5,700   +10,800
+5,100

Arrow line ⑥ in Exhibit 21.5 reflects GenX's indirect labor costs. These employees provide clerical, maintenance, and other services that help both the grinding *and* mixing departments produce Profen more efficiently. For example, they order materials, deliver them to the factory floor, repair equipment, operate and program computers used in production, keep payroll and other production records, clean up, and move the finished goods to the warehouse. This entry charges these indirect labor costs to factory overhead:

Point: A department's indirect labor cost might include an allocated portion of the salary of a manager who supervises two departments. Allocation of costs between departments is discussed in Chapter 22.

⑥	Factory Overhead	3,220	
	Factory Payroll		3,220
	To record indirect labor as overhead.		

Assets = Liabilities + Equity
                                  −3,220
                                  +3,220

After these entries for both direct and indirect labor are posted, the Factory Payroll account appears as shown in Exhibit 21.8. The Factory Payroll account is now closed and ready to receive entries for May.

Factory Payroll				Acct. No. 530	
Date		**Explanation**	**Debit**	**Credit**	**Balance**
2002					
Mar.	31	Balance			0
Apr.	30	Total payroll for April	14,020		14,020
	30	Direct labor costs		10,800	3,220
	30	Indirect labor costs		3,220	0

Exhibit 21.8

Factory Payroll Ledger Account

Accounting for Factory Overhead

Overhead costs other than indirect materials and indirect labor are reflected by arrow line ⑦ in Exhibit 21.5. These overhead items include the costs of insuring manufacturing assets,

P3 Record the flow of factory overhead costs in process cost accounting.

renting the factory building, using factory utilities, and depreciating equipment not directly related to a specific process. This entry records overhead costs for April:

⑦	Factory Overhead	880	
	Prepaid Insurance		80
	Utilities Payable		200
	Cash		250
	Accumulated Depreciation—Factory Equipment		350
	To record overhead items incurred in April.		

After this entry is posted, the Factory Overhead account balance is $5,295, comprising indirect materials of $1,195, indirect labor of $3,220, and $880 of other overhead.

Arrow line ⑧ in Exhibit 21.5 reflects the application of factory overhead to the two production departments. Recall from Chapters 19 and 20 that factory overhead is applied to products or jobs by relating overhead cost to another variable such as direct labor hours or machine hours used in production. Process cost systems use a similar procedure along with predetermined rates. In many situations, a single allocation basis such as direct labor hours (or a single rate for the entire plant) fails to provide useful allocations. As a result, management may use different rates for different production departments. Based on an analysis of each department's operations, GenX applies its April overhead on the basis of direct labor cost but with different rates, as shown in Exhibit 21.9.

Point: The time it takes to process (cycle) products through a process can also be used to allocate costs.

Exhibit 21.9

Applying Factory Overhead

Production Department	Direct Labor Cost	Predetermined Rate*	Overhead Applied
Grinding	$5,700	75%	$4,275
Mixing	5,100	20	1,020
Total			$5,295

* Predetermined overhead allocation rates:
Grinding department . . . .   75% of direct labor cost
Mixing department . . . . .   20% of direct labor cost

Example: If grinding uses a 70% rate (instead of 75%), what balance remains in the factory overhead account after overhead is applied to both departments? *Answer:*

Overhead costs	$5,295
Overhead applied	5,010
Underapplied overhead	$ 285

GenX records its applied overhead with the following entry:

⑧	Goods in Process Inventory—Grinding	4,275	
	Goods in Process Inventory—Mixing	1,020	
	Factory Overhead		5,295
	Allocated overhead costs to grinding department at 75% of direct labor cost and to mixing department at 20% of direct labor cost.		

After posting this entry, the Factory Overhead account appears as shown in Exhibit 21.10. For GenX, the amount of overhead applied equals the actual overhead incurred during April. In most cases, using a predetermined overhead allocation rate leaves an overapplied or underapplied balance in the Factory Overhead account. At the end of the period, this overapplied or underapplied balance should be either closed to the Cost of Goods Sold account or allocated among the Cost of Goods Sold, the Goods in Process Inventory, and the Finished Goods Inventory. Procedures for this allocation are the same as that described in Chapter 20 for job order cost accounting systems.

You Make the Call — Ethics

Budget Officer   You are working to identify the direct and indirect costs of a new processing department that has several machines. This department's manager instructs you to classify a majority of the costs as indirect to take advantage of the direct labor–based overhead allocation method so as it will be charged a lower amount of overhead (owing to its small direct labor cost). This would penalize other departments that would be hit with higher allocations. It also will cause the performance ratings of managers in these other departments to suffer. What action(s) do you take?

Answer—p. 890

Factory Overhead			Acct. No. 540		
Date	Explanation	Debit	Credit	Balance
2002				
Mar. 31	Balance			0
Apr. 30	Indirect materials usage	1,195		1,195
30	Indirect labor costs	3,220		4,415
30	Other overhead costs	880		5,295
30	Applied to production departments		5,295	0

Exhibit 21.10

Factory Overhead
Ledger Account

Example: If applied overhead results in a $5,400 credit to the factory overhead account, does it yield an over- or underapplied overhead amount?
Answer: $105 overapplied

Quick Check

1. A process manufacturing operation (a) is another name for a job order operation, (b) does not use the concepts of direct materials or direct labor, (c) typically produces large quantities of homogenous products.

2. Under what conditions is a process cost accounting system more suitable for measuring manufacturing costs than a job order cost accounting system?

3. When direct materials are assigned and used in both Department X and Department Y, the entry to record their use includes (a) a credit to Goods in Process Inventory—Department X, (b) a debit to Goods in Process Inventory—Department Y, or (c) a credit to Goods in Process Inventory—Department Y.

4. What are the three cost categories incurred by both job order and process operations?

5. How many Goods in Process Inventory accounts are needed in a process cost system?

Answers—p. 890

We explained how materials, labor, and overhead costs for a period are accumulated in separate Goods in Process Inventory accounts for each manufacturing process, but we have not explained the arrow lines labeled ⑨ₐ, ⑨ᵦ and ⑩ in Exhibit 21.5. These lines reflect the transfer of products from the grinding department to the mixing department, from the mixing department to finished goods inventory, and from finished goods inventory to cost of goods sold. To determine the costs recorded for these flows, we must first determine the cost per unit of product and then apply this result to the number of units transferred.

Equivalent Units of Production

C2 Define equivalent units and explain their use in process cost accounting.

Concept 21-1

Accounting for Goods in Process

If a manufacturing process has *no beginning and no ending goods in process inventory,* the unit cost of goods transferred out of a process is defined as follows:

> **Total cost assigned to the process (direct materials, direct labor, and overhead)**
> **Total number of units started and finished in the period**

If a process has a beginning or ending inventory of partially processed units (or both), however, the total cost assigned to the process must be allocated to all completed and uncompleted units worked on during the period. Therefore, the denominator must measure the entire production activity of the process for the period—called **equivalent units of production** (or **EUP**), a term that refers to the number of units that would be completed if all effort during a period had been applied to only those units started in that period. This measure is then used to compute the cost per equivalent unit and to assign costs to finished goods and goods in process inventory (explained later in the chapter).

To illustrate, assume that GenX adds (or introduces) 100 units into the grinding process during a period. Suppose at the end of that period, the production supervisor determines that those 100 units are 60% processed. Therefore, equivalent units of production for that period total 60 units (100 units × 60%). This means that if we had introduced 60 units into the process, we would have completely processed these 60 units.

Differences between Equivalent Units for Materials and for Labor and Overhead

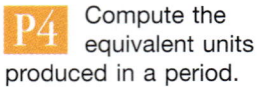

P4 Compute the equivalent units produced in a period.

In many manufacturing processes, the equivalent units of production for materials are not the same as for labor and overhead. To illustrate, consider the process operation shown in Exhibit 21.11.

Exhibit 21.11

Process Manufacturing: An Example

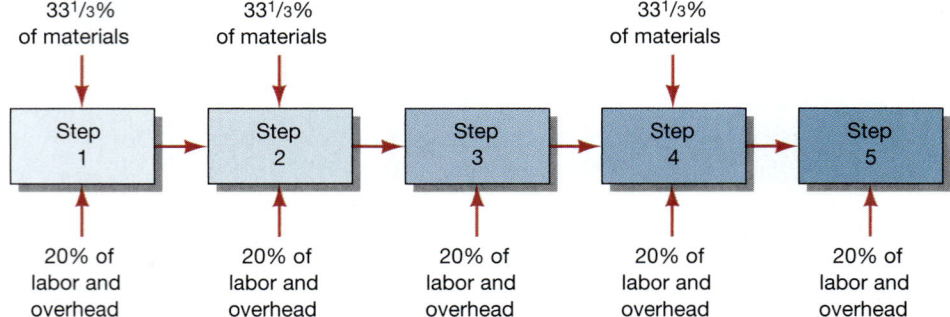

This exhibit shows a single production process consisting of five steps. One-third of the direct material cost is added at each of three steps: 1, 2, and 4. One-fifth of the direct labor cost is added at each of the five steps. Since overhead is applied as a percent of direct labor for this company, one-fifth of the overhead also is added at each step.

When units finish step 1, they are one-third complete with respect to materials but only one-fifth complete with respect to labor and overhead. When they finish step 2, they are two-thirds complete with respect to materials but only two-fifths complete with respect to labor and overhead. When they finish step 3, they remain two-thirds complete with respect to materials but are now three-fifths complete with respect to labor and overhead. When they finish step 4, they are 100% complete with respect to materials (all materials have been added) but only four-fifths complete with respect to labor and overhead.

To further illustrate, if 300 units of product are started and processed through step 1 of Exhibit 21.11, they are said to be one-third complete *with respect to materials*. Expressed in terms of equivalent finished units, the processing of these 300 units is equal to finishing 100 units (300 units × $33\frac{1}{3}$%). On the other hand, only one-fifth of direct labor and overhead has been applied to the 300 units at the end of step 1. This means that the equivalent units of production *with respect to direct labor and overhead* total 60 units (300 units × 20%).

Accounting for First (Grinding) Department

This section applies the concepts and procedures of process costing to GenX's grinding department. Exhibit 21.12 shows selected information from the grinding department for the month of April.

Beginning inventory (March 31)	
Units of product	30,000
Percentage of completion—direct materials	100%
Percentage of completion—direct labor	33⅓%
Direct materials costs	$ 2,780
Direct labor costs	$ 700
Factory overhead costs	$ 770
Activities during the current period	
Units started this period (April)	90,000
Units transferred to mixing (during April)	100,000
Direct materials costs	$ 9,900
Direct labor costs	$ 5,700
Factory overhead costs	$ 4,275
Ending inventory (April 30)	
Units of product	20,000
Percentage of completion—direct materials	100%
Percentage of completion—direct labor	25%

Exhibit 21.12

Production Data—Grinding Department

In computing equivalent units, we assume that each of GenX's production departments processes units on a first-in, first-out basis.[1] Accounting for a department's activity for a period includes four steps involving analysis of (1) physical flow, (2) equivalent units, (3) cost per equivalent unit, and (4) cost reconciliation. The next sections describe each step.

C3 Explain the four steps in accounting for production activity in a period.

Physical Flow of Units

Physical flow is a reconciliation of (1) the physical units started in a period with (2) the physical units completed in that period. A physical flow reconciliation for GenX is shown in Exhibit 21.13 for April.

Units to Account For		Units Accounted For	
Beginning inventory	30,000 units	Units transferred from grinding to mixing	100,000 units
Units started (in April)	90,000 units	Ending inventory	20,000 units
Total number of units	**120,000 units**	Total number of units	**120,000 units**

reconciled

Exhibit 21.13

Physical Flow Reconciliation— Grinding Department

The 100,000 units transferred from grinding to mixing during April include the 30,000 units from the beginning goods in process inventory (or simply beginning inventory). The remaining 70,000 units transferred out are from units started in April. A total of 90,000 units is started in April. Because 70,000 of these 90,000 units are completed, only 20,000 units remain unfinished at the end of the period.

Equivalent Units of Production

The second step is to compute *equivalent units of production* in the grinding department for direct materials, direct labor, and factory overhead for April. Overhead is applied using

---

[1] We assume a FIFO flow for all computations and assignments in this chapter—unless explicitly stated differently. Weighted average and LIFO also can be used, but they are less useful for measuring how effectively costs are controlled during a period. When using a just-in-time inventory system, the different inventory methods yield similar results because inventories are immaterial.

direct labor as the allocation base. This means that the equivalent units are the same for both labor and overhead for GenX.

Equivalent Units—Direct Materials

Direct materials (the Profelene blocks) are added at the *beginning* of the process. A unit of product is 100% complete with respect to materials as soon as it is started. This means that beginning goods in process inventory for April received all its materials in March and is not assigned any additional materials. The 70,000 units started and completed in April and the 20,000 units in ending goods in process inventory on April 30 (or simply ending inventory) received all of their materials in April. The grinding department's equivalent units of production for materials are computed in Exhibit 21.14.

Exhibit 21.14

Equivalent Units of Production (Direct Materials)—Grinding Department

	Units of Product		Percent Added This Period		Equivalent Units
Beginning goods in process	30,000	×	0%	=	0
Goods started and completed	70,000	×	100	=	70,000
Ending goods in process	20,000	×	100	=	20,000
Total units	120,000				90,000

Equivalent Units—Direct Labor and Factory Overhead

Direct labor and factory overhead, both considered conversion costs, are assigned uniformly throughout the GenX process. Recall that beginning inventory of 30,000 units is partially completed in March. In April, additional labor and overhead are assigned to these units to complete them. Based on percent of completion (see Exhibit 21.12), $33\frac{1}{3}\%$ of labor and overhead was assigned in March. The remaining $66\frac{2}{3}\%$ is assigned in April. The 70,000 units started and completed in April are assigned 100% of labor and overhead. The 20,000 partly completed units in ending inventory are assigned only 25% of labor at the end of April. Exhibit 21.15 shows these computations.

Point: To apply these concepts, work QS 21-3.

Exhibit 21.15

Equivalent Units of Production (Direct Labor and Overhead)— Grinding Department

	Units of Product		Percent Added This Period		Equivalent Units
Beginning goods in process	30,000	×	$66\frac{2}{3}\%$	=	20,000
Goods started and completed	70,000	×	100	=	70,000
Ending goods in process	20,000	×	25	=	5,000
Total units	120,000				95,000

Example: If ending goods in process are 20% complete, what are total equivalent units for labor and overhead for April? *Answer:* 94,000 units

A summary of April's equivalent units of production for the grinding department is shown in Exhibit 21.16.[2]

---

[2] Under the *weighted-average method,* the 100,000 units transferred out during April are *not* separated into its two components of 30,000 from beginning inventory and 70,000 started and completed during the month. This means that the equivalent units for direct materials amount to 120,000 $[(100,000 \times 100\%) + (20,000 \times 100\%)]$. The equivalent units for direct labor and overhead amount to 105,000 $[(100,000 \times 100\%) + (20,000 \times 25\%)]$.

	Equivalent Units of Production		
	Direct Materials	Direct Labor*	Factory Overhead*
Beginning goods in process	0	20,000	20,000
Goods started and completed in current period	70,000	70,000	70,000
Ending goods in process	20,000	5,000	5,000
Equivalent units of production for period	90,000	95,000	95,000

Exhibit 21.16

Equivalent Units of Production (Summary)—Grinding Department*

* The columns for direct labor and factory overhead are sometimes combined and termed *conversion costs*—when this is done, these columns in all other reports should be similarly combined.

Cost per Equivalent Unit

The third step is to compute the *cost per equivalent unit* for direct materials, direct labor, and factory overhead as shown in Exhibit 21.17. Specifically, the $9,900 direct materials costs for April (from Exhibit 21.5) are assigned to the 90,000 equivalent units for materials, yielding a cost per equivalent unit of $0.11. The $5,700 direct labor costs and the $4,275 factory overhead costs for April (from Exhibit 21.5) are assigned to 95,000 equivalent units for direct labor and factory overhead, yielding costs per equivalent unit of $0.06 and $0.045, respectively. Total cost per equivalent unit for the grinding department amounts to $0.215 ($0.11 + $0.06 + $0.045).[3]

Activities during April	Direct Materials	Direct Labor	Factory Overhead
Costs assigned to grinding in current period	$ 9,900	$ 5,700	$ 4,275
Equivalent units of production in current period	90,000	95,000	95,000
Cost per equivalent unit for period	$ 0.11	$ 0.06	$ 0.045

Exhibit 21.17

Cost per Equivalent Unit—Grinding Department

Cost Reconciliation

The fourth and final step in this process is to reconcile the *costs to account for* with the *costs accounted for* in the period. We do this by identifying the costs to (1) process beginning inventory, (2) start and complete units transferred from grinding to mixing, and (3) process ending inventory. Exhibit 21.18 shows this cost reconciliation.

The total *costs to account for* must equal the total *costs accounted for* in a cost reconciliation (minor differences can exist due to rounding). Also, the cost of each unit trans-

Concept 21-2

---

[3] The cost per equivalent units computation is slightly different under the *weighted-average method* because we add the costs of beginning inventory to the costs incurred during the current period. This means the cost of direct materials is $12,680 ($9,900 + $2,780), and the cost per equivalent unit for direct materials is $0.106 ($12,680/120,000 equivalent units). Similarly, the costs of direct labor and factory overhead are $6,400 ($5,700 + $700) and $5,045 ($4,275 + $770), respectively. Then the costs per equivalent unit for direct labor and factory overhead are $0.061 ($6,400/105,000 equivalent units) and $0.048 ($5,045/105,000 equivalent units), respectively. The total cost per equivalent unit is $0.215, which is the same as in the FIFO method. Note that the costs per equivalent unit for direct materials and direct labor under the weighted-average method are lower than those under FIFO; the reverse is the case for factory overhead. This implies that costs incurred for direct materials and direct labor in the prior period were lower than those incurred in the current period but were higher for factory overhead. When end-of-period inventories are large and costs fluctuate, FIFO is the superior method for controlling and monitoring costs because it focuses on the activities and costs for the current period.

Exhibit 21.18

Cost Reconciliation (April)—
Grinding Department

Costs to Account for		
From beginning inventory		$ 4,250
Assigned in period (direct materials, direct labor, and overhead)		19,875
Total costs		**$24,125** ◄
Costs Accounted for		
Beginning inventory completed in period (April)		
Costs from prior period	$4,250	
Costs assigned in current period		
Direct materials (0 units × $0.11)	0	
Direct labor (20,000 units × $0.06)	1,200	
Factory overhead (20,000 units × $0.045)	900	
Costs to process beginning inventory in period (April)		$ 6,350
Cost of units started and completed in period (April) (70,000 × $0.215)		15,050
Ending inventory for period (April)		
Direct materials (20,000 units × $0.11)	2,200	
Direct labor (5,000 units × $0.06)	300	
Factory overhead (5,000 units × $0.045)	225	
Costs of ending inventory for period (April)		2,725
Total costs		**$24,125** ◄

ferred out of the department must include the cost of completing beginning inventory in the current period ($6,350) and the cost of units started and completed in the current period ($15,050)—yielding $21,400 for 100,000 units transferred out, or $0.214 per unit. This leaves ending inventory at $2,725, which is carried over to the next period.[4]

Exhibit 21.17 showed that total cost per equivalent unit for April is $0.215, but the cost per unit for the units transferred out is $0.214. The difference of $0.001 exists because the total cost per equivalent unit is different for March—recall that $4,250 of the $21,400 is carried forward from March. As we explained earlier, the FIFO method uses only current period's costs and activities to compute the cost per equivalent unit for that period.

Process Cost Summary

C4 Define a process cost summary and describe its purposes.

An important managerial accounting report for a process cost accounting system is the **process cost summary** prepared separately for each process or production department. Three purposes of the summary are to (1) help department managers control and monitor their departments, (2) help factory managers evaluate department managers' performances, and (3) provide cost information for financial statements. A process cost summary achieves these purposes by describing the costs charged to each department, computing the equivalent units of production achieved by each department, and determining the costs assigned to each de-

---

[4] Using the *weighted-average method,* the *costs to account for* are $24,125—the same as with FIFO—but the *costs accounted for* are computed differently (note a $40 difference from rounding):

Costs of units transferred during period (April) (100,000 units × $0.215)		$21,500
Ending inventory for period (April)		
Direct materials (20,000 units × $0.106)	$2,120	
Direct labor (5,000 units × $0.061)	305	
Factory overhead (5,000 units × $0.048)	240	
Costs of ending inventory for period (April)		2,665
Total costs		$24,165

partment's output. For our purposes, it is prepared using a combination of Exhibits 21.13,
21.16, 21.17, and 21.18.

The process cost summary for GenX is
shown in Exhibit 21.19. The summary is divided into three sections. Section 1 lists the total costs charged to the department, including
direct materials, direct labor, and overhead
costs incurred, as well as the cost of the be-
ginning goods in process inventory. Section 2 describes the equivalent units of production
for the department. Equivalent units for materials, labor, and overhead are often in separate
columns. GenX reports equivalent units for labor and overhead in one column because it
applies overhead using labor as the allocation base. It also reports direct materials, direct
labor, and overhead costs per equivalent unit. Section 3 allocates total costs among units
worked on in the period. Costs of completing beginning inventory units are computed and
added to the cost carried forward from March to get total processing cost of $6,350 for
beginning inventory units. Also, costs of processing 70,000 units from start to finish are
computed and added to get their total processing cost of $15,050. The $21,400
($6,350 + $15,050) is the total cost of goods transferred out of the department. The final
part of section 3 computes the $2,725 cost of partially processed ending inventory units.
The assigned costs are then added to show that the total $24,125 cost charged to the de-
partment in section 1 is now assigned to the units in section 3.

P5 Prepare a process cost
summary.

Point: To apply these concepts,
work Exercise 21-9.

Transfers between Departments

Arrow line ⑨ in Exhibit 21.5 reflects the transfer of units (powdered Profelene) from the
grinding department to the mixing department. The $21,400 cost of this transfer, as com-
puted in Section 3 of the process cost summary of Exhibit 21.19, is recorded with the following entry:

P6 Record the transfer of
goods between
departments.

⑨ₐ	Goods in Process Inventory—Mixing	21,400	
	Goods in Process Inventory—Grinding		21,400
	To record transfer of partially completed goods from the grinding department to the mixing department.		

Assets   = Liabilities + Equity
+21,400
−21,400

Exhibit 21.19

Process Cost Summary—
Grinding Department

GENX COMPANY
Process Cost Summary—(Grinding Department)
For Month Ended April 30, 2002

Costs Charged to Department

Direct materials requisitioned	$ 9,900
Direct labor charged	5,700
Overhead allocated (at predetermined rate)	4,275
Total processing costs for the period	$19,875
Goods in process at the beginning of the period	4,250
Total costs to be accounted for	**$24,125**

① for the Costs Charged to Department section.

Equivalent Unit Processing Costs	Units of Product	Equivalent Units Direct Materials	Labor and Overhead
Units processed			
Beginning goods in process	30,000	0	20,000
Units started and completed	70,000	70,000	70,000
Ending goods in process	20,000	20,000	5,000
Total	120,000	90,000	95,000

Total direct materials cost for the period	$9,900
Direct materials cost per equivalent unit ($9,900/90,000 units)	$0.110
Total direct labor cost for the period	$5,700
Direct labor cost per equivalent unit ($5,700/95,000 units)	$0.060
Total overhead cost for the period	$4,275
Overhead cost per equivalent unit ($4,275/95,000 units)	$0.045

② for the Equivalent Unit Processing Costs section.

Assignment of Costs to Output of Department	Equivalent Units	Cost per Unit	Total Cost
Goods in process, March 31, 2002, and completed in the period			
Costs from prior period			$ 4,250
Direct materials added			0
Direct labor added	20,000	$0.060	1,200
Overhead applied	20,000	0.045	900
Total costs to process			$ 6,350
Goods started and completed in the period			
Direct materials added	70,000	$0.110	$ 7,700
Direct labor added	70,000	0.060	4,200
Overhead applied	70,000	0.045	3,150
Total costs to process			$15,050
Total costs transferred to next department (unit cost = $21,400/100,000 units = $0.214)			$21,400
Goods in process, April 30, 2002			
Direct materials added	20,000	$0.110	$ 2,200
Direct labor added	5,000	0.060	300
Overhead applied	5,000	0.045	225
Total costs to process			$ 2,725
Total costs accounted for ($21,400 + $2,725)			**$24,125**

③ for the Assignment of Costs to Output of Department section.

After this entry is posted, the Goods in Process Inventory—Grinding account appears as shown in Exhibit 21.20. The $2,725 ending balance in this account equals the cost assigned to partially completed units as shown in section 3 of the process cost summary.

Point: The balance in the general ledger Goods in Process Inventory account at the end of an accounting period is equal to the balance shown on the process cost summary.

Goods in Process Inventory — Grinding			Acct. No. 133		
Date		Explanation	Debit	Credit	Balance
2002					
Mar.	31	Balance			4,250
Apr.	30	Direct materials usage	9,900		14,150
	30	Direct labor costs	5,700		19,850
	30	Applied overhead	4,275		24,125
	30	Transfer to mixing department		21,400	2,725

Exhibit 21.20

Goods in Process Inventory— (Grinding) Ledger Account

Accounting for Second (Mixing) Department

The mixing department begins work on Profelene when it is received from the grinding department. Most of its costs are in the form of labor for specialists mixing the compounds and laborers packaging the product. Direct labor and overhead are added at the same rate as direct materials for this department.

Equivalent Units of Production

The mixing department requires only one computation of equivalent units of production because direct materials, direct labor, and overhead are used at the same rate. Exhibit 21.21 provides the data needed to compute equivalent units of production for the mixing department for April.

Beginning inventory (March 31)	
Units of product	16,000
Percentage of completion—direct materials, direct labor, and overhead	25%
Units received from grinding (in April)	100,000
Units transferred to finished goods (in April)	101,000
Ending inventory (April 30)	
Units of product	15,000
Percentage of completion—direct materials, direct labor, and overhead	33⅓%

Exhibit 21.21

Production Data—Mixing Department

We see that a total of 101,000 units is transferred from the mixing department to finished goods in the period. Based on a first-in, first-out assumption, 16,000 of these units are from beginning goods in process inventory and another 85,000 are received and completed in the current period. Since 100,000 units are received from the grinding department this period and only 85,000 of these units are completed, this leaves 15,000 units in the ending goods in process inventory.

Exhibit 21.22 computes the mixing department's equivalent units of production for direct materials, direct labor, and overhead for the month of April. (Recall that since materials, labor, and overhead are added at the same rate, we need only one report.)

	Units of Product		Percent Added This Period		Equivalent Units
Beginning goods in process	16,000	×	75%	=	12,000
Goods started and completed	85,000	×	100	=	85,000
Ending goods in process	15,000	×	33⅓	=	5,000
Total units	116,000				102,000

Exhibit 21.22

Equivalent Units of Production (Materials, Labor, and Overhead)—Mixing Department

Exhibit 21.23

Process Cost Summary—
Mixing Department

GENX COMPANY Process Cost Summary—(Mixing Department) For Month Ended April 30, 2002			
Costs Charged to Department			
Direct materials requisitioned			$ 2,040
Direct labor charged			5,100
Overhead allocated (at predetermined rate)			1,020
Total processing costs for the period			$ 8,160
Goods in process at the beginning of the period			3,520
Costs transferred in from grinding department (100,000 units at $0.214 each)			21,400
Total costs to be accounted for			**$33,080**

Equivalent Unit Processing Costs	Units of Product	Equivalent Units of Production	
Units processed			
Beginning goods in process	16,000	12,000	
Units received and completed	85,000	85,000	
Ending goods in process	15,000	5,000	
Total	116,000	102,000	
Total direct materials cost for the period			$2,040
Direct materials cost per equivalent unit ($2,040/102,000 units)			$0.020
Total direct labor cost for the period			$5,100
Direct labor cost per equivalent unit ($5,100/102,000 units)			$0.050
Total overhead cost for the period			$1,020
Overhead cost per equivalent unit ($1,020/102,000 units)			$0.010

Assignment of Costs to Output of Department	Equivalent Units	Cost per Unit	Total Cost
Goods in process, March 31, 2002, and completed in the period			
Costs from prior period			$ 3,520
Direct materials added	12,000	$0.020	240
Direct labor added	12,000	0.050	600
Overhead applied	12,000	0.010	120
Total costs to process			$ 4,480
Goods received and completed in the period			
Costs transferred in (85,000 × $0.214)			$18,190
Direct materials added	85,000	$0.020	1,700
Direct labor added	85,000	0.050	4,250
Overhead applied	85,000	0.010	850
Total costs to process			$24,990
Total costs transferred to finished goods			
(unit cost = $29,470/101,000 units = $0.2918)			$29,470
Goods in process, April 30, 2002			
Costs transferred in (15,000 × $0.214)			$ 3,210
Direct materials added	5,000	$0.020	100
Direct labor added	5,000	0.050	250
Overhead applied	5,000	0.010	50
Total costs to process			$ 3,610
Total costs accounted for ($29,470 + $3,610)			**$33,080**

Process Cost Summary

Exhibit 21.23 shows the mixing department's process cost summary. The costs charged to the department in section 1 include $21,400 transferred in from the grinding department. Section 2 shows the equivalent units of production for the direct materials, direct labor, and overhead for the mixing department. Section 2 also computes the costs per equivalent unit. Section 3 shows how costs charged to the department are assigned to its output. The $29,470 cost of the 101,000 units transferred to finished goods is computed as the combined cost of the 16,000 beginning units in process and the 85,000 units received and completed in the period. Also, none of the Profelene transferred in during April is used to complete the beginning inventory because the beginning goods in process inventory is 100% complete with respect to Profelene. Instead, the $21,400 cost transferred in during April relates to the 100,000 units that the mixing department received in April. Section 3 shows that $18,190 of this $21,400 is assigned to the 85,000 units received and completed in April (85,000 × $0.214), while the remaining $3,210 is assigned to the 15,000 units remaining in ending inventory (15,000 × $0.214).

Quick Check

10. What effect does the transfer of a partially completed product from one production department to another have on the company's total assets?

11. A ski manufacturer's total processing costs are $262,500 for its waxing department in December. To complete beginning goods in process, this department added 20,000 equivalent units of materials, labor, and overhead and started and completed 70,000 units during the month. It had 15,000 equivalent units remaining in process at month-end. Costs transferred in from the sanding department for December total $300,000, of which 25% relates to units the waxing department had not finished by month-end. What does the waxing department's process cost summary show as the total costs to process goods received and completed?

Answers—p. 890

Arrow line ⑨b in Exhibit 21.5 reflects the transfer of completed products from the mixing department to finished goods inventory. The process cost summary for the mixing department shows that the 101,000 units of finished Profen are assigned a cost of $29,470. The entry to record this transfer is:

⑨b			
	Finished Goods Inventory	29,470	
	Goods in Process Inventory— Mixing		29,470
	To record transfer of completed units.		

After this entry is posted, the Goods in Process Inventory—Mixing account appears as shown in Exhibit 21.24. The ending balance of this account equals the cost assigned to the partially completed units in section 3 of Exhibit 21.23.

Transfers to Finished Goods Inventory and Cost of Goods Sold

Assets = Liabilities + Equity
+29,470
−29,470

Goods in Process Inventory—Mixing			Acct. No. 134		
Date		Explanation	Debit	Credit	Balance
2002					
Mar.	31	Balance			3,520
Apr.	30	Direct materials usage	2,040		5,560
	30	Direct labor costs	5,100		10,660
	30	Applied overhead	1,020		11,680
	30	Transfer in from grinding department	21,400		33,080
	30	Transfer to warehouse		29,470	3,610

Exhibit 21.24

Goods in Process Inventory (Mixing) Ledger Account

P7   Record the transfer of completed goods to Finished Goods Inventory and Cost of Goods Sold.

Arrow line ⑩ in Exhibit 21.5 reflects the sale of finished goods. GenX sold 106,000 units of Profen in April. The beginning inventory of finished goods consists of 23,000 units with a cost of $6,440. All 23,000 units are sold in April. The remaining 83,000 units sold are from the 101,000 units completed in April. Ending finished goods inventory equals the 18,000 units remaining. Section 3 of Exhibit 21.23 shows that total cost per unit of finished goods in April is $0.2918 ($29,470/101,000 units). Using this information, we can compute cost of goods sold for April as shown in Exhibit 21.25.

Exhibit 21.25

Cost of Goods Sold

23,000 units from beginning inventory*	$ 6,440
83,000 units processed in period (83,000 × $0.2918)	24,219
Total cost of goods sold	$30,659

* Computations assume a FIFO inventory system.

The summary entry to record cost of goods sold for April is:

Assets = Liabilities + Equity
−30,659   −30,659

⑩	Cost of Goods Sold	30,659	
	Finished Goods Inventory		30,659
	To record cost of goods sold for April.		

The Finished Goods Inventory account now appears as shown in Exhibit 21.26.

Exhibit 21.26

Finished Goods Inventory Ledger Account

\multicolumn{3}{} Finished Goods Inventory				Acct. No. 135		
Date		**Explanation**	**Debit**	**Credit**	**Balance**
2002					
Mar.	31	Balance			6,440
Apr.	30	Transfer in from mixing department	29,470		35,910
	30	Cost of goods sold		30,659	5,251

Summary of Cost Flows

Exhibit 21.27 shows GenX's manufacturing cost flows for April. Each of these cost flows and the entries to record them have been explained. The flow of costs through the accounts reflects the flow of manufacturing activities and products.

Lean Business Model and Process Operations

Did You Know?

Gadgets at Work   Attention to customer orientation has led to improved processes for companies. A manufacturer of control devices improved quality and reduced production time by forming teams to study processes and suggest improvements. Another company set up project groups and a steering committee to evaluate all of its manufacturing processes. Still another company uses statistical process control to identify problem areas and implement corrective actions.

We described several lean business practices in Chapter 19. Adopting these practices yields changes in some process operations. Management concerns with throughput and just-in-time manufacturing, for instance, cause boundary lines between departments to become less distinct. In some cases, higher quality and better efficiency are obtained by entirely reorganizing production processes. For example, instead of producing different types of **Reebok** shoes in a series of departments, a separate work center for each shoe can be established in one department. When this rearrangement occurs, the

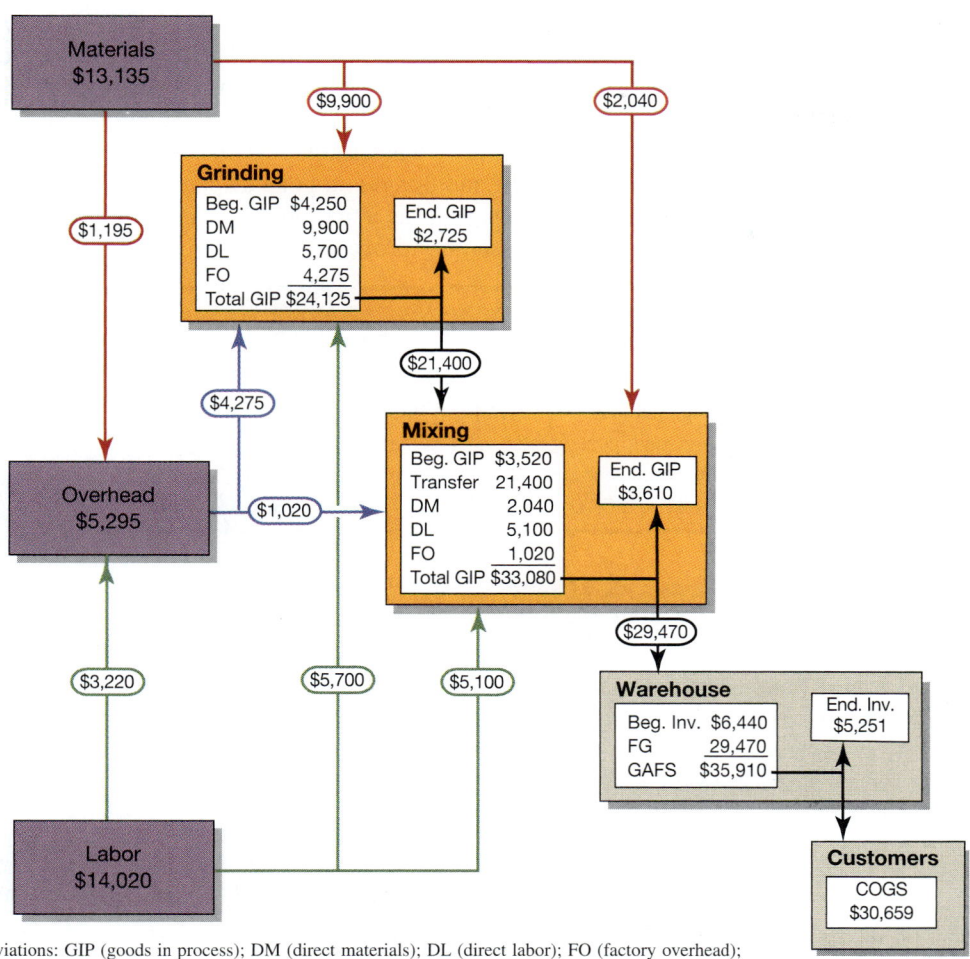

Exhibit 21.27*

Cost Flows through GenX

*Abbreviations: GIP (goods in process); DM (direct materials); DL (direct labor); FO (factory overhead); FG (finished goods); GAFS (goods available for sale); COGS (cost of goods sold).

process cost accounting system is changed to account for each work center's costs.

When a company adopts a just-in-time inventory system, the inventories described in this chapter can almost disappear. For example, if raw materials are not ordered or received until needed, a Raw Materials Inventory account may be unnecessary. Instead, materials cost is immediately debited to the Goods in Process Inventory account. Similarly, a Finished Goods Inventory account may not be needed. Instead, cost of finished goods can be immediately debited to the Cost of Goods Sold account.

Hybrid Costing System

Using the Information

This chapter explained the process costing system and contrasted it with the job order costing system described in Chapter 20. Although we explained the two systems separately, many organizations use a *hybrid system* that contains features of both job order and process operations. A recent survey of manufacturers revealed that a majority use hybrid systems. To illustrate, consider a car manufacturer's assembly line. On one hand, the line resembles a process operation in that the assembly steps for each car are nearly identical. On the other hand, the specifications of most cars have several important differences. At the **Ford** Mustang plant in Michigan, each car assembled on a given day can be different from the previous car and the next car. This means that the costs of materials (subassemblies or components)

C5 Explain a hybrid costing system.

for each car can differ. Accordingly, while the conversion costs (direct labor and overhead) can be accounted for using a process costing system, the component costs (direct materials) are accounted for using a job order system (separately for each car or type of car).

A hybrid system of processes requires a *hybrid costing system* to properly cost products or services. In the Ford assembly plant case, the assembly costs per car are readily determined using process costing. The costs of additional components can then be added to the assembly costs to determine each car's total cost (as in job order costing). To illustrate, consider the following information for the assembly process at Ford for a recent day:

Assembly process costs	
Direct materials	$5,800,000
Direct labor	$2,900,000
Factory overhead	$3,100,000
Number of cars assembled	1,000
Costs of three different types of steering wheels	$120, $165, $240
Costs of three different types of seats	$310, $420, $680

The assembly process costs $11,800 per car. Depending on the type of steering wheel and seats the customer requests, the cost of a car can range from $12,230 to $12,720 (a $490 difference).

Today companies are increasingly trying to standardize processes while attempting to meet individual customer needs. To the extent that differences among individual customers' requests are large, understanding the costs to satisfy those requests is important. Moreover, monitoring and controlling process costs are equally important.

Demonstration Problem

Pennsylvania Company produces a product that passes through a molding process and then through an assembly process. Information related to its manufacturing activities for July follows:

Raw Materials

Beginning inventory	$100,000
Raw materials purchased on credit	300,000
Direct materials—molding	(190,000)
Direct materials—assembly	(88,600)
Indirect materials used	(51,400)
Ending inventory	$ 70,000

Factory Payroll

Direct labor—molding	$ 42,000
Direct labor—assembly	55,375
Indirect labor used	50,625
Total payroll cost (paid in cash)	$148,000

Factory Overhead

Indirect materials used	$ 51,400
Indirect labor used	50,625
Other overhead costs	71,725
Total factory overhead incurred	$173,750

Factory Overhead Applied

Molding (150% of direct labor)	$ 63,000
Assembly (200% of direct labor)	110,750
Total factory overhead applied	$173,750

Molding Department

Beginning goods in process inventory (units)	5,000
Percentage completed—materials	100%
Percentage completed—labor and overhead	60%
Units started and completed	17,000
Ending goods in process inventory (units)	8,000
Percentage completed—materials	100%
Percentage completed—labor and overhead	25%
Costs:	
Beginning goods in process inventory	$ 53,000
Direct materials added	190,000
Direct labor added	42,000
Overhead applied (150% of direct labor)	63,000
Total costs	$348,000

Assembly Department

Beginning goods in process inventory	$154,800
Ending goods in process inventory	108,325

Finished Goods Inventory

Beginning inventory	$ 96,400
Cost transferred in from assembly	578,400
Cost of goods sold	(506,100)
Ending Inventory	$168,700

Required

1. Compute the equivalent units of production for the molding department for July and determine the costs per equivalent unit for direct materials, direct labor, and factory overhead.

2. Compute the cost of the units transferred from molding to assembly in July and the cost of the ending goods in process inventory for the molding department.

3. Prepare summary journal entries to record the transactions and events of July for (a) raw materials purchases, (b) direct materials usage, (c) indirect materials usage, (d) factory payroll costs, (e) direct labor usage, (f) indirect labor usage, (g) other overhead costs (credit Other Accounts), (h) application of overhead to the two departments, (i) transfer of partially completed goods from molding to assembly, (j) transfer of finished goods out of assembly, and (k) the cost of goods sold.

Planning the Solution

- Compute the molding department's equivalent units of production and cost per unit with respect to direct materials.

- Compute the molding department's equivalent units of production with respect to direct labor and overhead and determine the cost per unit for each.

- Compute the total cost of the goods transferred to the assembly department by using the equivalent units and unit costs to determine (a) the cost of the beginning in-process inventory, (b) the materials, labor, and overhead costs added to the beginning in-process inventory, and (c) the materials, labor, and overhead costs added to the units started and completed in the month.

- Use the information to record the summary journal entries for July.

Solution to Demonstration Problem

1. Equivalent units of production—direct materials:

	Units of Product		Percent Added This Period		Equivalent Units
Beginning goods in process	5,000	×	0%	=	0
Goods started and completed	17,000	×	100	=	17,000
Ending goods in process	8,000	×	100	=	8,000
Total units	30,000				**25,000**

The direct materials used in molding total $190,000. Therefore,

Materials cost per equivalent unit = $190,000/25,000 units = $7.60 per unit

Equivalent units of production—direct labor and overhead:

	Units of Product		Percent Added This Period		Equivalent Units
Beginning goods in process	5,000	×	40%	=	2,000
Goods started and completed	17,000	×	100	=	17,000
Ending goods in process	8,000	×	25	=	2,000
Total units	30,000				**21,000**

The direct labor used in molding totals $42,000. Therefore,

Labor cost per equivalent unit = $42,000/21,000 units = $2 per unit

The overhead applied in molding totals 150% of direct labor cost. Therefore,

Overhead cost per equivalent unit = $63,000/21,000 units = $3 per unit

2. Cost of units transferred from molding to assembly in July:

	Equivalent Units	Cost per Unit	Total Cost
Beginning goods in process			
Costs from prior month			$ 53,000
Direct materials added	0	$7.60	0
Direct labor added	2,000	2.00	4,000
Overhead applied	2,000	3.00	6,000
Total cost to process			$ 63,000
Goods started and completed			
Direct materials added	17,000	$7.60	$129,200
Direct labor added	17,000	2.00	34,000
Overhead applied	17,000	3.00	51,000
Total cost to process			$214,200
Cost of transferred units			**$277,200**

Cost of the July ending goods in process inventory for the molding department:

	Equivalent Units	Cost per Unit	Total Cost
Direct materials added	8,000	$7.60	$60,800
Direct labor added	2,000	2.00	4,000
Overhead applied	2,000	3.00	6,000
Cost of ending good in process inventory			**$70,800**

3. Summary journal entries for the transactions and events in July:

a.	Raw Materials Inventory	300,000	
	Accounts Payable		300,000
	To record raw materials purchases.		
b.	Goods in Process Inventory—Molding	190,000	
	Goods in Process Inventory—Assembly	88,600	
	Raw Materials Inventory		278,600
	To record direct materials usage.		
c.	Factory Overhead	51,400	
	Raw Materials Inventory		51,400
	To record indirect materials usage.		
d.	Factory Payroll	148,000	
	Cash		148,000
	To record factory payroll costs.		
e.	Goods in Process Inventory—Molding	42,000	
	Goods in Process Inventory—Assembly	55,375	
	Factory Payroll		97,375
	To record direct labor usage.		
f.	Factory Overhead	50,625	
	Factory Payroll		50,625
	To record indirect labor usage.		
g.	Factory Overhead	71,725	
	Other Accounts		71,725
	To record other overhead costs.		

[continued on next page]

[continued from previous page]

h.	Goods in Process Inventory—Molding	63,000	
	Goods in Process Inventory—Assembly	110,750	
	Factory Overhead		173,750
	To record application of overhead.		
i.	Goods in Process Inventory—Assembly	277,200	
	Goods in Process Inventory—Molding		277,200
	To record transfer of partially completed goods from molding to assembly.		
j.	Finished Goods Inventory	578,400	
	Goods in Process Inventory—Assembly . . .		578,400
	To record transfer of finished goods out of assembly.		
k.	Cost of Goods Sold	506,100	
	Finished Goods Inventory		506,100
	To record cost of goods sold.		

Summary

C1 **Explain process operations and the way they differ from job order operations.** Process operations produce large quantities of similar products or services by passing them through a series of processes, or steps, in production. Like job order operations, they combine direct materials, direct labor, and overhead in the operations. Unlike job order operations that assign the responsibility for each job to a manager, process operations assign the responsibility for each *process* to a manager.

C2 **Define equivalent units and explain their use in process cost accounting.** Equivalent units of production measure the activity of a process as the number of units that would be completed in a period if all effort had been applied to units that were started and finished. This measure of production activity is used to compute the cost per equivalent unit and to assign costs to finished goods and goods in process inventory.

C3 **Explain the four steps in accounting for production activity in a period.** The four steps involved in accounting for production activity in a period are (1) recording the physical flow of units, (2) computing the equivalent units of production, (3) computing the cost per equivalent unit of production, and (4) reconciling costs. The last step involves assigning costs to finished goods and goods in process inventory for the period.

C4 **Define a process cost summary and describe its purposes.** A process cost summary reports on the activities of a production process or department for a period. It describes the costs charged to the department, the equivalent units of production for the department, and the costs assigned to the output. The report aims to (1) help managers control their departments, (2) help factory managers evaluate department managers' performances, and (3) provide cost information for financial statements.

C5 **Explain a hybrid costing system.** A hybrid costing system contains features of both job order and process costing systems. Generally, certain direct materials are accounted for by individual products as in job order costing, but direct labor and overhead costs are accounted for similar to process costing.

A1 **Compare process cost accounting and job order cost accounting.** Process and job order manufacturing operations are similar in that they both combine materials, labor, and factory overhead to produce products or services. They differ in the way they are organized and managed. In job order operations, the job order cost accounting system assigns materials, labor, and overhead to specific jobs. In process operations, the process cost accounting system assigns materials, labor, and overhead to specific processes. The total costs associated with each process are then divided by the number of units passing through that process to get cost per equivalent unit. The costs per equivalent unit for all processes are added to determine the total cost per unit of a product or service.

P1 **Record the flow of direct materials costs in process cost accounting.** Materials purchased are debited to a Raw Materials Inventory account. As direct materials are issued to processes, they are separately accumulated in a Goods in Process Inventory account for that process.

P2 **Record the flow of direct labor costs in process cost accounting.** Direct labor costs are initially debited to the Factory Payroll account. The total amount in it is then assigned to the goods in process inventory account pertaining to each process.

P3 **Record the flow of factory overhead costs in process cost accounting.** The different factory overhead items are first accumulated in the Factory Overhead account and are then allocated, using a predetermined overhead rate, to the different processes. The allocated amount is debited to the goods in process inventory account pertaining to each process.

P4 **Compute equivalent units produced in a period.** To compute equivalent units, determine the number of units that would have been finished if all materials (or labor or overhead) had been used to produce units that were started and completed during the period. The costs incurred by a process are divided by its equivalent units to yield cost per unit.

P5 **Prepare a process cost summary.** A process cost summary includes the physical flow of units, equivalent units of production, costs per equivalent unit, and a cost reconciliation. It reports the units and costs to account for during the period and how they were accounted for during the period. In terms of units, the summary includes the beginning goods in process inventory and the units started during the month. These units are accounted for in terms of the goods completed and transferred out, and the ending goods in process inventory. With respect to costs, the summary includes materials, labor, and overhead costs assigned to the process during the period. It shows how these costs are assigned to goods completed and transferred out, and to ending goods in process inventory.

P6 **Record the transfer of completed goods to Finished Goods Inventory and Cost of Goods Sold.** As units complete the final process and are eventually sold, their accumulated cost is transferred to Finished Goods Inventory and finally to Cost of Goods Sold.

P7 **Record the transfer of goods between departments.** As units of product are transferred from one process to the next, the accumulated cost of those units is transferred from one goods in process account to the next. Once the goods are completed in the preceding process, they are transferred out to the next process in the sequence. Costs associated with goods completed in the preceding process are then debited to the goods in process inventory of the next process.

Guidance Answers to **You Make the Call**

Budget Officer   By instructing you to classify a majority of costs as indirect, the manager is passing some of his department's costs to a common overhead pool that other departments will partially absorb. Since overhead costs are allocated on the basis of direct labor for this company and the new department has a relatively low direct labor cost, the new department will be assigned less overhead. Such action suggests unethical behavior by this manager. You must object to such reclassification. If this manager refuses to comply, you must inform someone in a more senior position.

Cost Manager   Differences between the FIFO and weighted-average methods are greatest when large work in process inventories exist and when costs fluctuate. The method used if inventories are eliminated does not matter; both produce identical costs (although weighted-average is arguably easier to apply). However,

the cost manager should not immediately switch to the weighted-average method until inventories have actually been eliminated and he/she is confident that inventories will not later accumulate.

Entrepreneur   By spreading the added quality-related costs across three customers, the entrepreneur is probably trying to remain competitive with respect to the customer that demands the 100% quality inspection. Moreover, the entrepreneur is partly covering the added costs by recovering 2/3 of them from the other two customers who are paying 110% of total costs. This act likely breaches the trust placed by the two customers in this entrepreneur's application of its costing system. The costing system should be changed, and the entrepreneur should consider renegotiating the pricing and/or quality-test agreement with this one customer (at the risk of losing this currently loss-producing customer).

Guidance Answers to **Quick Checks**

1. (c)

2. When a company produces large quantities of similar products/services, a process cost system is often more suitable.

3. (b)

4. The costs are direct materials, direct labor, and overhead.

5. A goods in process inventory account is needed for *each* production department.

6. (a)

7. Equivalent units with respect to direct labor are the number of units that would have been produced if all labor had been used on units that were started and finished during the period.

8.

	Units of Product		Percent Added		Equivalent Units
Beginning Inventory	8,000	×	75%	=	6,000
Units started and finished ..	50,000	×	100	=	50,000
Ending inventory	6,000	×	33⅓	=	2,000
Equivalent units					58,000

9. The first section shows the costs charged to the department. The second section describes the equivalent units produced by the department. The third section shows the assignment of total costs to units worked on during the period.

10. The transfer decreases one Goods in Process Inventory account and increases another. This has no effect on total assets.

11. Equivalent unit processing cost: $262,500/(20,000 + 70,000 + 15,000) units = $2.50. Costs to process goods received and completed are

Costs transferred in	$225,000
Total costs added (70,000 × $2.50) ...	175,000
Total costs to process	$400,000

Glossary

Equivalent units of production (EUP) number of units that would be completed if all effort during a period had been applied to units that were started and finished. (p. 873).

Job order cost accounting system cost system designed to determine the cost to produce each job or job lot. (p. 869).

Materials consumption report document that summarizes the materials a department uses during a reporting period; replaces materials requisitions. (p. 870).

Process cost accounting system system of assigning direct materials, direct labor, and overhead to specific processes. The total costs associated with each process are then divided by the number of units passing through that process to determine the cost per equivalent unit. (p. 869).

Process cost summary report of costs charged to a department, its equivalent units of production achieved, and the costs assigned to its output. (p. 878).

Process manufacturing processing of products in a continuous (sequential) flow of steps (also called *process operations* or *process production*). (p. 866).

Assume FIFO inventory method is used for all assignments unless stated differently.

Questions

1. Can services be delivered by means of process operations? Support your answer with an example.

2. What is the main factor for a company in selecting between the job order costing and process costing accounting systems? Give two likely applications of each system.

3. Identify the control document for materials flow when a materials requisition slip is not used.

4. The focus in a job order costing system is the job or batch. Identify the main focus in process costing.

5. Are the journal entries that match cost flows to product flows in process costing primarily the same or much different than those in job order costing? Explain.

6. Explain in simple terms the notion of equivalent units of production (EUP). Why is it necessary to use EUP in process costing?

7. What are the two main inventory methods used in process costing? What are the differences between these methods?

8. Why is it possible for direct labor in process operations to include the labor of employees who do not work directly on products or services?

9. Assume that a company produces a single product by processing it first through a mixing department and next through a cutting department. Direct labor costs flow through what accounts in this company's process cost system?

10. After all labor costs for a period are allocated, what balance should remain in the Factory Payroll account?

11. Is it possible to have underapplied or overapplied overhead costs in a process cost accounting system?

12. Explain why equivalent units of production for both direct labor and overhead can be the same as, and why they can be different from, equivalent units for direct materials.

13. List the four steps in accounting for production activity in a period (for process operations).

14. What purposes are served by a process cost summary?

15. Assume that **Nike** takes a special order to produce shoes for all employees of **The Walt Disney Company**. Chart Nike's production process assuming three production departments: (1) cutting, (2) Disney design set to the material, and (3) assembly. Begin the flowchart with delivery of raw materials and finish with the shipment of goods (see Exhibit 21.5 for guidance).

16. **Reebok** produces shirts with a multiple process production line. Starting with cutting the fabric, list some of its shirt manufacturing processes.

For each of the following products and services, indicate whether it is most likely produced in a process operation or in a job order operation:

1. Grand pianos
2. Wall clocks
3. Sport shirts
4. Bolts and nuts
5. Folding chairs
6. Door hinges
7. Cut flower arrangements
8. House paints
9. Concrete swimming pools
10. Custom tailored suits

QUICK STUDY

QS 21-1
Matching of product to cost accounting system

C1

Cool Jeans Co. manufactures a product requiring two processes, cutting and sewing. During August, partially completed units with a cost of $297,500 are transferred from cutting to sewing. The sewing department requisitions $58,200 of direct materials and incurs direct labor of $96,000. Overhead is applied to the sewing department at 115% of direct labor. Finally, units with a cost of $108,400 are completed and transferred from sewing to finished goods. Prepare entries to record these August activities of the sewing department: (1) goods transferred from cutting to sewing, (2) direct materials used, (3) direct labor used, (4) overhead applied, and (5) goods transferred from sewing to finished goods.

QS 21-2
Identifying and recording cost flows

QS 21-3

Computing equivalent units of production—FIFO

This information refers to units processed in Lowe Printing's binding department in March:

	Units of Product	Percent of Labor Added
Beginning goods in process	150,000	60%
Goods started and completed	340,000	100
Ending goods in process	120,000	25

Compute the total equivalent units of production with respect to labor for March using the FIFO inventory method.

QS 21-4

Computing equivalent units—weighted average

Refer to QS 21-3 and compute the total equivalent units of production with respect to labor for March using the weighted-average inventory method.

QS 21-5

Computing EUP cost

The cost of beginning inventory plus the costs added during the period should equal the cost of units _____ plus the cost of _____.

EXERCISES

Exercise 21-1

Terminology in process cost accounting

Match each of the following items A through H with the best description of its purpose:

A. Materials consumption report
B. Process cost summary
C. Equivalent units of production
D. Goods in Process Inventory—Dept. A
E. Raw Materials Inventory account
F. Materials requisition
G. Finished Goods Inventory account
H. Factory Overhead account

_____ **1.** Notifies the materials manager to send materials to a production department.
_____ **2.** Holds costs of indirect materials, indirect labor, and similar costs until assigned to production.
_____ **3.** Holds costs of direct materials, direct labor, and applied overhead until products are transferred from Department A.
_____ **4.** Describes the direct materials used in a production department.
_____ **5.** Standardizes partially completed units into completed units.
_____ **6.** Holds costs of finished products until sold to customers.
_____ **7.** Describes the activity and output of a production department for a period.
_____ **8.** Holds costs of materials until they are used in production or as factory overhead.

Exercise 21-2

Journal entries in process cost accounting

Holloway Toy Company manufactures products with two processes: sanding and painting. Prepare entries to record its following manufacturing activities for January:

1. Purchased $80,000 of raw materials on credit.
2. Used $30,000 of direct materials in the sanding department and $12,000 in the painting department.
3. Used $22,500 of indirect materials.
4. Incurred total labor cost of $95,000, which is paid in cash.
5. Used $50,000 of direct labor in the sanding department and $25,000 in the painting department.
6. Used $20,000 of indirect labor.
7. Incurred other overhead costs of $38,750 (paid in cash).
8. Applied overhead at 125% of direct labor in the sanding department and at 75% of direct labor in the painting department.
9. Transferred partially completed products with a cost of $119,500 from the sanding department to the painting department.
10. Transferred completed products with a cost of $135,600 from the painting department to the finished goods inventory.
11. Sold $315,000 of products on credit. Their accumulated cost is $175,000.

The following journal entries are recorded in Limited Co.'s process cost accounting system. Limited produces clothing items by passing them through a cutting department and an assembly department. Overhead is applied to production departments based on direct labor cost for the period. Prepare a brief explanation for each journal entry *a* through *k*.

Exercise 21-3
Interpretation of journal entries in process cost accounting

a.	Raw Materials Inventory	52,000	
	Accounts Payable		52,000
b.	Goods in Process Inventory—Cutting	24,000	
	Goods in Process Inventory—Assembly	18,000	
	Raw Materials Inventory		42,000
c.	Goods in Process Inventory—Cutting	16,000	
	Goods in Process Inventory—Assembly	10,000	
	Factory Payroll		26,000
d.	Factory Payroll	32,000	
	Cash		32,000
e.	Factory Overhead	10,000	
	Other Accounts		10,000
f.	Factory Overhead	10,000	
	Raw Materials Inventory		10,000
g.	Factory Overhead	6,000	
	Factory Payroll		6,000
h.	Goods in Process Inventory—Cutting	12,000	
	Goods in Process Inventory—Assembly	14,000	
	Factory Overhead		26,000
i.	Goods in Process Inventory—Assembly	60,000	
	Goods in Process Inventory—Cutting		60,000
j.	Finished Goods Inventory	88,000	
	Goods in Process Inventory—Assembly ...		88,000
k.	Accounts Receivable	250,000	
	Sales		250,000
	Cost of Goods Sold	100,000	
	Finished Goods Inventory		100,000

Wetherby Lumber produces shredded bark using a two-step process. The system begins by processing bark chips through the shredding department and then through the bagging department. The following information describes manufacturing operations for October.

Exercise 21-4
Recording cost flows in a process cost system

	A	B	C
		Shredding Department	**Bagging Department**
3	Direct materials used	$ 22,000	$ 500,000
4	Direct labor used	$ 70,000	$ 60,000
5	Predetermined overhead allocation rate (based on direct labor)	120%	200%
6	Goods transferred from shredding to bagging	$(190,000)	
7	Goods transferred from bagging to finished goods		$(595,000)

Revenue for the month totaled $950,000 from credit sales, and its cost of goods sold for the month is $540,000. Prepare summary journal entries to record the October manufacturing activities for: (1) direct material usage, (2) direct labor usage, (3) overhead allocation, (4) goods transfer from shredding to bagging, (5) goods transfer from bagging to finished goods, and (6) sales.

Exercise 21-5

Computing equivalent units of production—FIFO

During April, the production department of a process manufacturing system completed a number of units of a product and transferred them to finished goods. Of these transferred units, 60,000 were in process in the department at the beginning of April and 240,000 were started and completed in April. April's beginning inventory units were 60% complete with respect to materials and 40% complete with respect to labor. At the end of April, 82,000 additional units were in process in the department and were 80% complete with respect to materials and 30% complete with respect to labor. Compute (1) the number of units transferred to finished goods and (2) the number of equivalent units with respect to both materials used and labor produced in the department for April using the FIFO method.

Exercise 21-6

Computing equivalent units of production—weighted-average

Refer to the information in Exercise 21-5 to compute the number of equivalent units with respect to both materials used and labor produced in the department for April using the weighted-average method.

Exercise 21-7

Costs assigned to inventories—FIFO

The production department described in Exercise 21-5 had $850,000 of direct materials and $650,000 of direct labor cost charged to it during April. Also, its beginning inventory included $90,000 of direct materials cost and $40,000 of direct labor. (1) Compute the direct materials cost and the direct labor cost per equivalent unit for the department (see Exhibit 21.17 for guidance). (2) Assign costs to the department's output; specifically, its beginning and ending goods in process inventories and the goods started and completed during April using the FIFO method (see section 3 of Exhibit 21.19 for guidance).

Exercise 21-8

Costs assigned to inventories—weighted-average

Refer to the information in Exercise 21-7 and complete its parts (1) and (2) using the weighted-average method.

Exercise 21-9

Equivalent units computed

The production department in a process manufacturing system completed 80,000 units of product and transferred them to finished goods during a recent period. Of these units, 24,000 were in process at the beginning of the period. The other 56,000 units were started and completed during the period. At the end of the period, 16,000 units were in process. Compute the department's equivalent units of production with respect to direct materials under each of the following three separate assumptions: (1) All direct materials are added to products when processing begins. (2) Direct materials are added to products evenly throughout the process. Beginning goods in process inventory was 40% complete, and ending goods in process inventory was 75% complete. (3) One-half of direct materials is added to products when the process begins and the other half is added when the process is 75% complete as to direct labor. Beginning goods in process inventory is 40% complete as to direct labor and ending goods in process inventory is 60% complete as to direct labor.

Exercise 21-10

Flowchart of costs for a process operation

The flowchart on the opposite page shows the production activity of the punching and bending departments of the Cardboard Box Company for August. Use the amounts shown on the flowchart to compute the missing numbers identified by question marks.

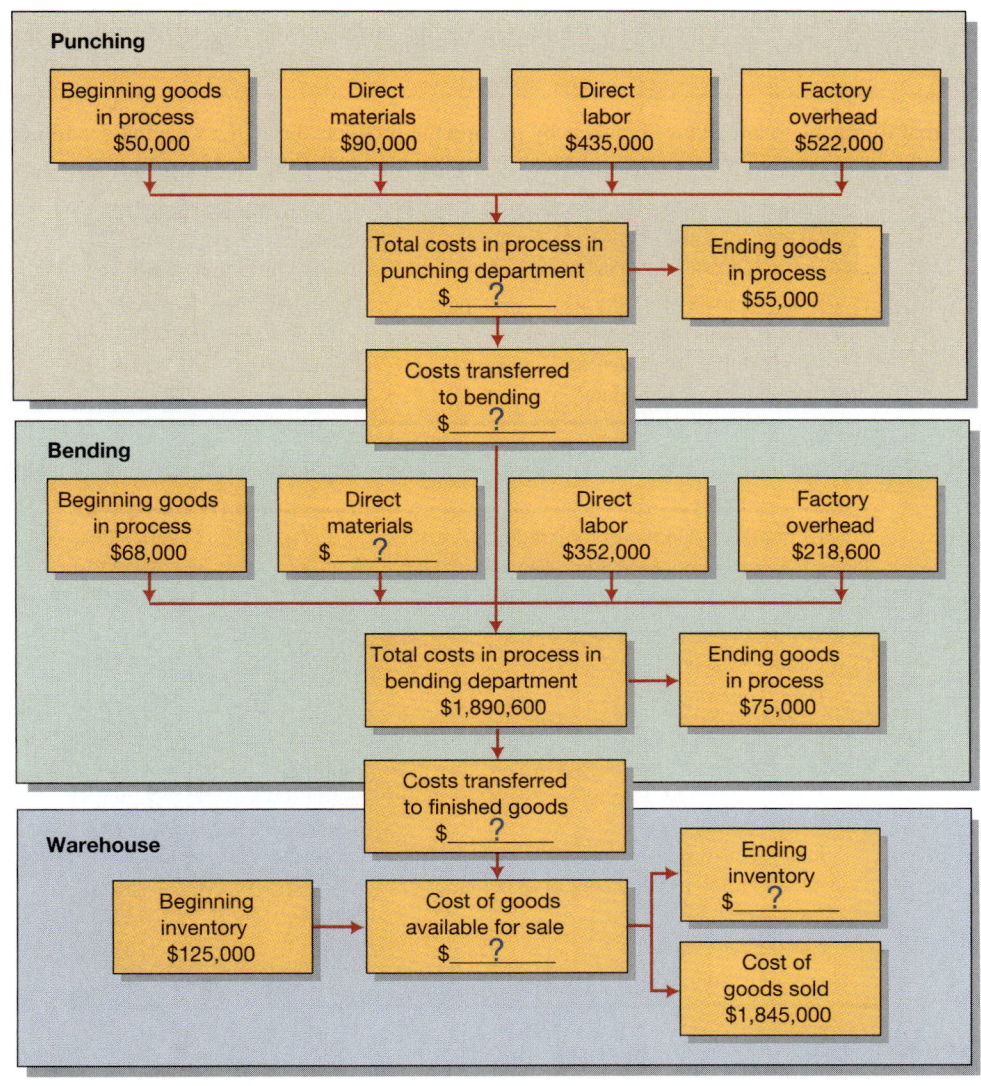

The following partially completed process cost summary describes the July activities of Serranos Company's slicing department. The slicing department's output is sent to the canning department, which sends the finished goods to the warehouse for shipping.

Exercise 21-11
Completing a process cost summary

Costs Charged to the Department			
Direct materials requisitioned			$357,500
Direct labor charged			62,890
Overhead allocated (at 200% of direct labor)			125,780
Total processing costs for the month			546,170
Goods in process at the beginning of the month			22,000
Total costs to be accounted for			$568,170

		Equivalent Units	
Equivalent Unit Processing Costs	Units of Product	Direct Materials	Labor and Overhead
Units processed			
Beginning goods in process	2,000	0	1,600
Units started and completed	30,000	30,000	30,000
Ending goods in process	2,500	2,500	1,500
Total	34,500	32,500	33,100

Prepare the process cost summary for the slicing department by completing both (1) the *Equivalent Unit Processing Costs* section and (2) the *Assignment of Costs to Output of Department* sections.

PROBLEM SET A

Problem 21-1A
Production cost flow and measurement; journal entries prepared

Thermal Company manufactures blankets by passing the products through a weaving department and a sewing department. The following information is available regarding its May inventories:

	Beginning Inventory	Ending Inventory
Raw materials inventory	$ 60,000	$ 50,000
Goods in process inventory—weaving	150,000	165,000
Goods in process inventory—sewing	285,000	350,000
Finished goods inventory	633,000	605,000

The following additional information describes the company's manufacturing activities for May:

Raw materials purchases (on credit)	$ 250,000
Factory payroll cost (paid in cash)	1,530,000
Other overhead cost (credited Other Accounts)	78,000
Materials used	
Direct—weaving	$ 120,000
Direct—sewing	37,500
Indirect	60,000
Labor used	
Direct—weaving	$ 600,000
Direct—sewing	180,000
Indirect	750,000
Overhead rates as a percent of direct labor	
Weaving	75%
Sewing	120%
Sales (on credit)	$2,000,000

Check Cost of goods sold $1,551,500

Required

1. Compute (a) the cost of products transferred from weaving to sewing, (b) the cost of products transferred from sewing to finished goods, and (c) the cost of goods sold. (*Hint:* Follow the cost flows and computations in Exhibit 21.5).

2. Prepare summary journal entries to record the following manufacturing activities during May: (a) raw materials purchases, (b) direct materials usage, (c) indirect materials usage, (d) payroll costs, (e) direct labor costs, (f) indirect labor costs, (g) other overhead costs, (h) overhead applied, (i) goods transferred from weaving to sewing, (j) goods transferred from sewing to finished goods, and (k) sale of finished goods.

Problem 21-2A
Cost per equivalent unit; costs assigned to products

Carver Company passes its product through several departments, the last of which is the carving department where direct labor is added evenly throughout the process. Also, one-fourth of direct materials is added at the beginning of the carving process and the remaining three-fourths is added when the process is 50% complete with respect to direct labor. During November, the carving department transferred 700,000 units of product to finished goods. Of these units, 150,000 were 40% complete with respect to labor at the beginning of the period and 550,000 were started and completed during the period. At the end of November, the goods in process inventory consists of 180,000 units that are 30% complete with respect to labor. The carving department's direct labor cost for November is $2,220,800, and its direct materials cost is $3,254,500.

Required

Preparation Component

1. Determine the carving department's equivalent units of production with respect to (a) direct labor and (b) direct materials.

2. Compute both the direct labor cost and the direct materials cost per equivalent unit (see Exhibit 21.17 for guidance).

3. Compute both direct labor cost and direct materials cost assigned to the (a) beginning goods in process inventory, (b) units started and completed, and (c) ending goods in process inventory (see section 3 of Exhibit 21.19 for guidance).

Check   Direct labor cost per equivalent unit, $3.20

Analysis Component

4. Carver sells and ships all units to customers as soon as they are completed. Assume that an error is made in determining the percentage of completion for units in ending inventory. Instead of being 30% complete with respect to labor, they are actually 60% complete. Write a one-page memo to the plant manager describing how this error affects its November financial statements.

Walden Company produces large quantities of a product that pass through two processes, spinning and cutting. The following information is available on its manufacturing activities for March:

Problem 21-3A

Journalizing in process cost accounting; equivalent units and costs

Raw materials	
Beginning inventory	$ 16,000
Raw materials purchased (on credit)	250,000
Direct materials—spinning	(100,000)
Direct materials—cutting	(68,000)
Indirect materials used	(70,000)
Ending inventory	$ 28,000
Factory payroll	
Direct labor—spinning	$ 52,650
Direct labor—cutting	147,200
Indirect labor used	45,000
Total payroll cost (paid in cash)	$244,850
Factory overhead incurred	
Indirect materials used	$ 70,000
Indirect labor used	45,000
Other overhead costs	168,980
Total factory overhead incurred	$283,980
Factory overhead applied	
Spinning (120% of direct labor)	$ 63,180
Cutting (150% of direct labor)	220,800
Total factory overhead applied	$283,980

Information about the inventory in the *spinning department* follows:

Units		**Costs**	
Beginning in process inventory	2,000	Beginning in process inventory	$ 15,000
Started and completed	15,000	Direct materials added	100,000
Ending in process inventory	5,000	Direct labor added	52,650
Beginning in process inventory		Overhead applied (120% of	
Materials—percent complete	100%	direct labor)	63,180
Labor and overhead—percent complete	35%	Total costs	$230,830
Ending in process inventory		Transferred goods from spinning	
Materials—percent complete	100%	to cutting department	(197,580)
Labor and overhead—percent complete	25%	Ending in process inventory	$ 33,250

Information about the goods in process inventories for the *cutting department* follows: beginning in process inventory, $156,000; and ending in process inventory, $120,000. Also, information regarding finished goods follows:

Beginning finished goods inventory . . .	$150,000
Cost transferred in from cutting	570,000
Cost of goods sold	(590,000)
Ending finished goods inventory	$130,000

During March, 10,000 units of finished goods are sold for cash for $120 each.

Required

Preparation Component

1. Prepare journal entries to record the following March activities: (a) raw materials purchases, (b) direct materials usage, (c) indirect materials usage, (d) payroll costs, (e) direct labor costs, (f) indirect labor costs, (g) other overhead costs, (h) overhead applied, (i) goods transferred from spinning to cutting, (j) goods transferred from cutting to finished goods, (k) sale of finished goods.

Check Cost per equivalent unit: materials, $5.00; labor, $3.00; overhead, $3.60

2. Compute the spinning department's equivalent units of production and its cost per equivalent unit for direct materials, direct labor, and overhead for March.

3. Compute the cost of the ending goods in process inventory for the spinning department.

Analysis Component

4. Walden provides incentives to managers of its departments by paying monthly bonuses based on their success in controlling costs per equivalent unit of production. Assume that the spinning department underestimates the percentage of completion for units in ending inventory with the result that its equivalent units of production in ending inventory for March are understated. What impact does this error have on the March bonuses paid to the managers of the spinning department and the cutting department? What impact, if any, does this error have on April bonuses?

Problem 21-4A
Process cost summary; equivalent units

PraxAir Co. produces its product through a single processing department. Direct materials, direct labor, and overhead are added to the product evenly throughout the process. The company uses monthly reporting periods for its process cost accounting system. The Goods in Process Inventory account appears as follows after posting entries for direct materials, direct labor, and overhead costs for October:

Goods in Process Inventory					**Acct. No. 133**
Date		**Explanation**	**Debit**	**Credit**	**Balance**
Oct.	1	Balance			40,800
	31	Direct materials	102,050		142,850
	31	Direct labor	408,200		551,050
	31	Applied overhead	125,600		676,650

During October, the company finished and transferred 150,000 units of its product to finished goods. Of these units, 30,000 were in process at the beginning of the month and 120,000 were started and completed during the month. The beginning goods in process inventory was 30% complete. At the end of the month, the goods in process inventory consisted of 20,000 units that were 80% complete.

Required

1. Compute the number of equivalent units of production for October.

Check Total cost transferred to finished goods, $611,850

2. Prepare the department's process cost summary for October.

3. Prepare the journal entry to transfer the cost of the completed units to finished goods inventory.

Xiang Co. manufactures a single product in one department. All direct materials are added at the beginning of the manufacturing process. Direct labor and overhead are added evenly throughout the process. Xiang uses monthly reporting periods for its process cost accounting system. During May, the company completed and transferred 22,200 units of product to finished goods inventory. The beginning goods in process inventory consisted of 3,000 units that were 100% complete with respect to direct materials and 40% complete with respect to direct labor and overhead. The other 19,200 completed units were started during the month. Also, 2,400 units (100% complete with respect to direct materials and 80% complete with respect to direct labor and overhead) are in process at the end of the month. After posting entries to record direct materials, direct labor, and overhead for May, the company's Goods in Process Inventory account appears as follows:

Problem 21-5A
Process cost summary;
equivalent units

Goods in Process Inventory		Acct. No. 133			
Date		Explanation	Debit	Credit	Balance
May	1	Balance			181,260
	31	Direct materials	496,800		678,060
	31	Direct labor	1,203,300		1,881,360
	31	Applied overhead	962,640		2,844,000

Required

1. Compute the equivalent units of production in May for direct materials and for direct labor and overhead.

2. Prepare the department's process cost summary for May.

3. Prepare the journal entry to transfer the cost of completed units to finished goods inventory.

Check   Cost transferred to finished goods, $2,607,360

Analysis Components

4. The cost accounting process depends on numerous estimates.

   a. Identify two major estimates that determine the cost per equivalent unit.

   b. In what direction might you anticipate a bias from management for each estimate in part (a) (assume that management compensation is based on maintaining low inventory amounts)? Explain.

Tots Toys Company manufactures dolls by passing the products through a molding department and an assembly department. The following information is available regarding its June inventories:

PROBLEM SET B

Problem 21-1B
Production cost flow and
measurement; journal entries
prepared

	Beginning Inventory	Ending Inventory
Raw materials inventory	$ 72,000	$ 40,000
Goods in process inventory—molding	24,000	42,000
Goods in process inventory—assembly	132,000	108,000
Finished goods inventory	156,000	198,000

The following additional information describes the company's manufacturing activities for June:

Raw materials purchases (on credit)	$ 200,000
Factory payroll cost (paid in cash)	400,000
Other overhead cost (credited Other Accounts)	100,000
Materials used	
Direct—molding	$ 12,000
Direct—assembly	108,000
Indirect	42,000
Labor used	
Direct—molding	$ 200,000
Direct—assembly	150,000
Indirect	50,000
Overhead rates as a percent of direct labor	
Molding	75%
Assembly	80%
Sales (on credit)	$1,000,000

Required

1. Compute (a) the cost of products transferred from molding to assembly, (b) the cost of products transferred from assembly to finished goods, and (c) the cost of goods sold. (*Hint:* Follow the cost flows and computations in Exhibit 21.5.)
2. Prepare journal entries to record the following manufacturing activities during June: (a) raw materials purchases, (b) direct materials usage, (c) indirect materials usage, (d) payroll costs, (e) direct labor costs, (f) indirect labor costs, (g) other overhead costs, (h) overhead applied, (i) goods transferred from molding to assembly, (j) goods transferred from assembly to finished goods, and (k) sale of finished goods.

Problem 21-2B
Cost per equivalent unit; assignment of costs to products

Penbrook Company passes its product through several departments, the last of which is the bagging department where direct materials are added evenly throughout the process. Also, one-half of the direct labor is added at the beginning of the bagging process and the other half is added when the process is 50% complete with respect to materials. During September, the bagging department transferred 80,000 units of product to finished goods. Of these units, 18,000 were 60% complete with respect to materials at the beginning of the period and 62,000 were started and completed during the period. At the end of September, the goods in process inventory consists of 8,000 units that are 25% complete with respect to materials. The bagging department's direct materials cost for September is $712,000, and its direct labor cost is $1,980,000.

Required

Preparation Component

1. Determine the bagging department's equivalent units of production with respect to (a) direct labor and (b) direct materials.

2. Compute both the direct labor cost and the direct materials cost per equivalent unit (see Exhibit 21.17 for guidance).
3. Compute both direct labor cost and direct materials cost assigned to the (a) beginning goods in process inventory, (b) units started and completed, and (c) ending goods in process inventory (see section 3 of Exhibit 21.19 for guidance).

Analysis Component

4. Penbrook sells and ships all units to customers as soon as they are completed. Assume that an error is made in determining the percentage of completion for units in ending inventory. Instead of being 25% complete with respect to materials, they are actually 75% complete. Write a one-page memo to the plant manager describing how this error affects Penbrook's September financial statements.

Problem 21-3B
Journalizing in process cost accounting; equivalent units and costs

Holden Company produces large quantities of a product that pass through two processes, tooling and machining. The following information is available on its manufacturing activities for May:

Raw materials		Factory overhead incurred	
Beginning inventory	$ 32,000	Indirect materials used	$ 40,560
Raw materials purchased (on credit)	221,120	Indirect labor used	36,320
Direct materials—tooling	(160,000)	Other overhead costs	91,640
Direct materials—machining	(37,120)		
Indirect materials used	(40,560)	Total factory overhead incurred	$168,520
Ending inventory	$ 15,440	**Factory overhead applied**	
		Tooling (125% of direct labor)	$ 85,000
Factory payroll		Machining (150% of direct labor)	83,520
Direct labor—tooling	$ 68,000		
Direct labor—machining	55,680	Total factory overhead applied	$168,520
Indirect labor used	36,320		
Total payroll cost (paid in cash)	$160,000		

Information about the inventory in the *tooling department* follows:

Units		Costs	
Beginning in process inventory	4,000	Beginning in process inventory ..	$ 41,000
Started and completed	12,000	Direct materials added	160,000
Ending in process inventory	8,000	Direct labor added	68,000
Beginning in process inventory		Overhead applied (125% of	
Materials—percent complete	100%	direct labor)	85,000
Labor and overhead—percent complete ..	25%	Total costs	$354,000
Ending in process inventory		Transferred goods from tooling to	
Materials—percent complete	100%	machining department	(272,000)
Labor and overhead—percent complete ..	25%	Ending in process inventory	$ 82,000

Information about the goods in process inventories for the *machining department* follows: beginning in process inventory, $174,000, and ending in process inventory, $177,120. Also, information regarding finished goods follows:

Beginning finished goods inventory	$ 148,400
Cost transferred in from machining	445,200
Cost of goods sold	(530,000)
Ending finished goods inventory	$ 63,600

During May, 10,000 units of finished goods are sold for cash for $120 each.

Required

Preparation Component

1. Prepare journal entries to record the following May activities: (a) raw materials purchases, (b) direct materials usage, (c) indirect materials usage, (d) payroll costs, (e) direct labor costs, (f) indirect labor costs, (g) other overhead costs, (h) overhead applied, (i) goods transferred from tooling to machining, (j) goods transferred from machining to finished goods, (k) sale of finished goods.

2. Compute the tooling department's equivalent units of production and its cost per equivalent unit for direct materials, direct labor, and overhead for May, assuming that all product costs are added evenly throughout the process.

3. Compute the cost of the ending goods in process inventory for the tooling department.

Check   Cost per equivalent unit: materials, $8; labor, $4; overhead, $5

Analysis Component

4. Holden provides incentives to managers of its departments by paying monthly bonuses based on their success in controlling costs per equivalent unit of production. Assume that the tooling department overestimates the percentage of completion for units in ending inventory with the result that its equivalent units of production in ending inventory for May are overstated. What impact does this error have on bonuses paid to the managers of the tooling department and the machining department? What impact, if any, does this error have on these managers' June bonuses?

Osiris Company produces its product through a single processing department. Direct materials, direct labor, and overhead are added to the product evenly throughout the process. The company uses monthly reporting periods for its process cost accounting system. The Goods in Process Inventory account appears as follows after posting entries for direct materials, direct labor, and overhead costs for November:

Problem 21-4B
Process cost summary; equivalent units

Goods in Process Inventory			Acct. No. 133		
Date		Explanation	Debit	Credit	Balance
Nov.	1	Balance			70,000
	30	Direct materials	116,400		186,400
	30	Direct labor	426,800		613,200
	30	Applied overhead	640,200		1,253,400

During November, the company finished and transferred 100,000 units of its product to finished goods. Of these units, 7,500 were in process at the beginning of the month, and 92,500 were started and completed during the month. The beginning goods in process inventory was 80% complete. At the end of the month, the goods in process inventory consisted of 12,000 units that were 25% completed.

Required

1. Compute the number of equivalent units of production for November.
2. Prepare the department's process cost summary for November.
3. Prepare the journal entry to transfer the cost of the completed units to finished goods inventory.

Check   Cost of goods transferred to finished goods, $1,216,800

Problem 21-5B
Process cost summary; equivalent units

Jiffy Manufacturing Co. manufactures a single product in one department. Direct labor and overhead are added evenly throughout the process. Direct materials are added as needed. The company uses monthly reporting periods for its process cost accounting system. During January, Jiffy completed and transferred 220,000 units of product to finished goods inventory. The beginning goods in process inventory consisted of 20,000 units (75% complete with respect to direct materials and 60% complete with respect to direct labor and overhead). The other 200,000 completed units were started during the month. Also, 40,000 units (50% complete with respect to direct materials and 30% complete with respect to direct labor and overhead) are in process at the end of the month. After posting entries for direct materials, direct labor, and overhead for January, the company's Goods in Process Inventory account appears as follows:

Goods in Process Inventory				Acct. No. 133	
Date		Explanation	Debit	Credit	Balance
Jan.	1	Balance			41,100
	31	Direct materials	112,500		153,600
	31	Direct labor	176,000		329,600
	31	Applied overhead	440,000		769,600

Required

1. Compute the equivalent units of production for direct materials and for direct labor and overhead.
2. Prepare the department's process cost summary for January.
3. Prepare the journal entry to transfer the cost of completed units to finished goods inventory.

Check   Cost of goods transferred to finished goods, $726,000

Analysis Components

4. The cost accounting process depends on several estimates.
   a. Identify two major estimates that affect the cost per equivalent unit.
   b. In what direction might you anticipate a bias from management for each estimate in part (a) (assume that management compensation is based on maintaining low inventory amounts)? Explain.

COMPREHENSIVE PROBLEM

Corked Bat Company
(Review of Chapters 3, 6, 19, 21)

Corked Bat Company manufactures baseball bats. The bats go through two processes: one cuts the wood into bats and drills a hole for the cork (department 1), and the other fills the hole with cork and stamps the company's logo on the bat (department 2). All of department 1's output is transferred to department 2. In addition to the goods in process inventories in departments 1 and 2, Corked Bat maintains inventories of raw materials and finished goods. The company uses raw materials as direct materials in both departments and also as indirect materials. Its factory payroll costs include direct labor for each department and indirect labor. All materials are added at the beginning of the process in each department, and direct labor and factory overhead are applied uniformly throughout each department's process.

Required

You are to maintain records and produce measures of inventories to reflect the July events of this company. All computations of unit costs are rounded to the nearest penny and all other dollar amounts to the nearest whole dollar. Set up the following general ledger accounts and enter their June 30 balances: Raw Materials Inventory, $50,000; Goods in Process Inventory—Department 1, $130,000; Goods in Process Inventory—Department 2, $50,000; Finished Goods Inventory, $220,000; Sales, $0; Cost of Goods Sold, $0; Factory Payroll, $0; and Factory Overhead, $0.

1. Prepare journal entries to record the following July transactions and events:

   a. Purchased raw materials for $250,000 cash (it uses a perpetual inventory system).

   b. Used raw materials as follows: department 1, $60,000; department 2, $44,880; and indirect materials, $20,000.

   c. Incurred factory payroll cost of $454,500 paid in cash (ignore taxes).

   d. Assigned factory payroll costs as follows: department 1, $270,000; department 2, $134,500; and indirect labor, $50,000.

   e. Incurred additional factory overhead costs of $160,000 paid in cash.

   f. Allocated factory overhead to departments 1 and 2 at 50% of direct labor costs.

2. Information about the July inventories for the two departments follows:

	Department 1	Department 2
Units		
Beginning inventory	500 units	1,000 units
Started and finished	2,000 units	1,800 units
Ending inventory	1,000 units	1,600 units
Beginning inventory		
Materials—percent complete	100%	100%
Labor and overhead—percent complete	20%	75%
Ending inventory		
Materials—percent complete	100%	100%
Labor and overhead—percent complete	30%	40%

Use this information with that from part (1) to compute the following:

   a. Department 1's equivalent units of production and its per unit costs for labor, materials, and overhead.

   b. Department 2's equivalent units of production and its per unit costs for labor, materials, and overhead.

3. Using results from part (2) and the available information, make computations and prepare journal entries to record the following:

   a. Total costs transferred from department 1 to department 2 for July (label entry *g*).

   b. Total costs transferred from department 2 to finished goods for July (label entry *h*).

   c. Sale of finished goods costing $531,400 for $1,250,000 in cash (label entry *i*).

4. Post entries from parts (1) and (3) to the ledger accounts set up at the beginning of the problem.

5. Compute the amount of gross profit from the sales in July.

Check   (3a) $530,000
(3b) $757,510

Beyond the Numbers

BTN 21-1   A company must consider the costs and benefits to reporting externally precise estimates of the percentage complete for goods in process inventory. It must also consider whether reasonable estimates are acceptable. Review **Nike**'s inventory (Note 2 in Appendix A) and assume that its work-in-process inventory value for 2000 is overstated by 10% and for 1999 is understated by 15% due to estimation errors.

Reporting in Action

Required

1. Compute the dollar amount that work-in-process inventory is (a) overstated for 2000 and (b) understated for 1999. Compute the impact on net income for each year (assume a 40% tax rate).

2. Compute the amount (in percent) that Nike's net income increased or decreased for 2000 and for 1999 due to the estimation errors. (Hint: Work a simple example to see how an error in inventory impacts income.)

3. Are amounts in part (2) material? Explain in reference to costs and benefits of decision makers.

Swoosh Ahead

4. Access Nike's annual report for fiscal years ending after May 31, 2000, from its Web site [**www.nike.com**] or the SEC's EDGAR database [**www.sec.gov**]. Identify Nike's current period work-in-process inventory value and assume a 10% understatement and a 40% tax rate. Recompute answers for parts (1) through (3) using this current information.

Comparative Analysis

C1

BTN 21-2   Leading process manufacturers such as **Nike** and **Reebok** usually work to maintain a high-quality and low-cost operation. One ratio routinely computed for this assessment is the cost of goods sold divided by total expenses. A decline in this ratio can mean that the company is spending too much on selling and administrative activities but not enough on production. An increase in this ratio beyond a reasonable level can mean that the company is spending too much on production or not enough on selling activities. (Assume for this analysis that total expenses equal cost of goods sold plus selling and administrative expenses.)

Required

1. For both Nike and Reebok, refer to Appendix A and compute the ratio of cost of goods sold to total expenses for their two most recent fiscal years.

2. Comment on the similarities or differences in the ratio results across years and companies.

Ethics Challenge

C1   **C3**

BTN 21-3   Many accounting and accounting-related professionals are skilled in financial analysis, but most are not skilled in manufacturing. This is especially the case for process manufacturing environments (for example, a bottling plant or chemical factory). To provide professional accounting and financial services, one must understand the industry, product, and processes. We have an ethical responsibility to develop this understanding before offering services to clients in these areas.

Required

Write a one-page action plan, in memorandum format, on how you would obtain an understanding of key business processes of a company that hires you to provide financial services. The memorandum should specify an industry, product, and one selected process and should draw on at least one reference, such as a professional journal or industry magazine.

Communicating in Practice

A1   **C1**   **P1**   **P2**

BTN 21-4   You hire a new assistant production manager whose prior experience is with a company that produced goods to order. Your company engages in continuous production of homogeneous products that go through various manufacturing processes. Your new assistant sends you an e-mail questioning some cost classifications on an internal report, specifically, questioning why the costs of some materials that do not actually become part of the finished product, including some labor costs not directly associated with producing the product, are classified as direct costs. Respond to this concern via memorandum.

Taking It to the Net

C1   **C3**

BTN 21-5   Teamwork is essential for business success and for the effective application of accounting software. Software products must work together to be useful in providing information in support of decision making. Check the following Web site for **QPR Management Software** [**www.QPR.fi/pgmetho.html**] and answer the following questions:

Required

1. Give examples of common business processes.

2. Click on *QPR Management Software.* Go through the details of "QPR Procen Guide" and explain how such software is helpful to business.

Teamwork in Action

C1   **P1**   **P2**   **P3**

P6   **P7**

BTN 21-6   The purpose of this team activity is to ensure that each team member understands process operations and the related accounting entries. Find the activities and flows identified in Exhibit 21.5 with numbers ①–⑩. Pick a member of the team to start by describing activity number ① in this exhibit, then verbalizing the related journal entry, and describing how the amounts in the entry are computed. The other members of the team are to agree or disagree; discussion is to continue until all express understanding. Rotate to the next numbered activity and next team member until all activities and entries have been discussed. If at any point a team member is uncertain about an answer, the team member may pass and get back in the rotation when he/she can contribute to the team's discussion.

BTN 21-7   Does a change in company strategy result in changes to the process costing system? Read the article "Microprocessors Are for Wimps" in the December 15, 1997, issue of *Business Week* and answer the following questions in a one-page memorandum to your instructor.

1. Identify and describe the shift in **Motorola**'s market focus for microprocessor production.

2. What changes can you suggest in the process costing system to support the new market focus?

Business Week
Activity

Entrepreneurial Decision

BTN 21-8   Many businesses are outsourcing selected parts of their processes (for example, payroll) to outside firms. As an entrepreneur, how would you evaluate which process to retain and which to outsource?

22

Cost Allocation and Performance Measurement

Kate Spade—from temp agency employee to handbag millionaire.

A Look Back

Chapter 21 focused on how to measure and account for costs in process operations. It explained process production, described how to assign costs to processes, and computed cost per equivalent unit for a process.

A Look at This Chapter

This chapter describes cost allocation and activity-based costing. It identifies managerial reports useful in directing a company's activities. It also describes responsibility accounting, measuring departmental performance, and allocating

A Look Ahead

Chapter 23 looks at cost behavior and explains how its identification is useful to managers in performing cost-volume-profit analyses. It also describes break-even analysis and how to apply cost-volume-profit analysis for managerial

Ace of Spade

e NEW YORK—Most women put their money in their handbags—that's where trendy designer Kate Spade is making hers. Spade's lines of elegant and whimsical bags, which range from pink herringbone carryalls and velvet tiger-print shoppers to simple nylon totes, are among fashion's hottest must-haves. Spade and her husband, Andy, started **Kate Spade** [**KateSpade.com**] seven years ago from a New York City loft apartment with $35,000 of his savings. Kansas City native "Katie" has scored big by making handbags fashionable as well as functional. Last year, sales doubled to more than $50 million.

While her designs yield bags of money, business is her focus. "It was less about wanting to be a designer and more wanting to start a business," says Spade. Since she "loved handbags," Spade quit her job and stayed at home to cut shapes out of construction paper and glued them together to get the bags' proportions just right. "I wanted simple little shapes," says Spade. Simplicity and product differentiation enable her business to thrive. Then she checked out manufacturers in Brooklyn.

Cost management and quality control were key to Spade's success. As Spade's business expands, she continues to monitor and control the quality and costs of products within each of her departments. This is especially crucial now as she branches out into stationery, shoes, and a line of men's bags. Such expansion requires cost allocations and departmental and responsibility accounting. Spade proves that cost management and entrepreneurial creativity can win out. "Luckily, I haven't had to go and get my old job back." [Sources: *Kate Spade Web site*, May 2001; *Urban Desires*, 1996; *Business Week*, January 10, 2000.]

Learning Objectives

Conceptual

C1 Explain departmentalization and the role of departmental accounting.

C2 Distinguish between direct and indirect expenses.

C3 Identify bases for allocating indirect expenses to departments.

C4 Explain controllable costs and responsibility accounting.

C5 Describe allocation of joint costs across products.

Analytical

A1 Analyze investment centers using return on total assets.

Procedural

P1 Assign overhead costs using two-stage cost allocation.

P2 Assign overhead costs using activity-based costing.

P3 Prepare departmental income statements.

P4 Prepare departmental contribution reports.

The three prior chapters focused on measuring the costs of products and services, including the reporting and analysis of those costs in managerial reports. This chapter discusses the issue of cost allocation. It describes how to allocate costs shared by more than one product across these different products and how to allocate indirect costs of shared items such as utilities, advertising, and rent. The chapter also describes activity-based costing and how it traces the costs of individual activities. This knowledge helps us better understand how costs are assigned and performance assessed. The chapter introduces additional managerial accounting reports useful in managing a company's activities and explains how and why management divides companies into departments.

Overhead Cost Allocation Methods

Point: Use of a single overhead allocation rate is known as using a *plant-wide rate*.

P1 Assign overhead costs using two-stage cost allocation.

Point: Use of a separate overhead allocation rate for each department is known as using *departmental rates*.

We previously explained how to assign overhead costs to jobs (and processes) by using a predetermined overhead allocation rate per unit of an allocation base such as direct labor cost. When a single overhead allocation rate is used on a companywide basis, all overhead is lumped together and a predetermined overhead allocation rate per unit of an allocation base is computed and used to assign overhead to jobs (and processes). The use of a single predetermined overhead allocation rate suggests that this allocation process is simple. In reality, it can be complicated. This chapter explains the traditional two-stage cost allocation procedure and then introduces the activity-based cost allocation procedure.

Two-Stage Cost Allocation

Overhead costs are incurred in many activities of an organization. These activities can be identified with various departments, which can be broadly classified as either *operating* or *service* departments. *Operating departments* are those areas of an organization that perform its main functions. For example, an accounting firm's main functions usually include auditing, tax, and advisory services. Similarly, the production and selling departments of a manufacturing firm perform its main functions and serve as operating departments. *Service departments* are those areas of an organization that provide support to operating departments. Examples of service departments are payroll, human resource management, accounting, and executive management. Service departments do not engage in activities that generate revenues, yet their support is crucial for the success of operating departments. In this section, we apply a two-stage cost allocation procedure to assign (1) service department costs to operating departments and (2) operating department costs, including those assigned from service departments, to the organization's output.

Illustration of Two-Stage Cost Allocation

We use Exhibit 22.1 to explain the two-stage cost allocation procedure. This exhibit illustrates cost allocations for **AutoGrand**, a custom automobile manufacturer. AutoGrand has five manufacturing-related departments: janitorial, maintenance, factory accounting, machining, and assembly. Expenses incurred by each of these departments of AutoGrand are considered product costs. Its three service departments (janitorial, maintenance, and factory accounting) incur expenses of $10,000, $15,000 and $8,000, respectively. As shown in Exhibit 22.1, the first stage of the two-stage procedure involves allocating the costs of the three service departments to the two operating departments (machining and assembly). The two operating departments use the resources of these service departments.

To illustrate the first stage of cost allocation, look at the janitorial department. Its costs are allocated to machining and assembly in the ratio 60 : 40. This means that 60%, or $6,000, of janitorial costs are assigned to the machining department and 40%, or $4,000, to the assembly department. Similarly, the expenses incurred by the maintenance and factory accounting departments are assigned to machining and assembly. We then add the expenses directly incurred by each operating department to these assigned costs to determine the total expenses for each operating department. This yields total costs of $25,000 for machining and $36,000 for assembly.

In the second stage, we compute predetermined overhead rates for each operating department. For machining we use machine hours as the allocation base and for assembly we use labor hours as the allocation base. The predetermined overhead rate is $2.50 per machine hour for the machining department and $1.80 per labor hour for the assembly department. These predetermined overhead rates are then used to assign overhead to output.

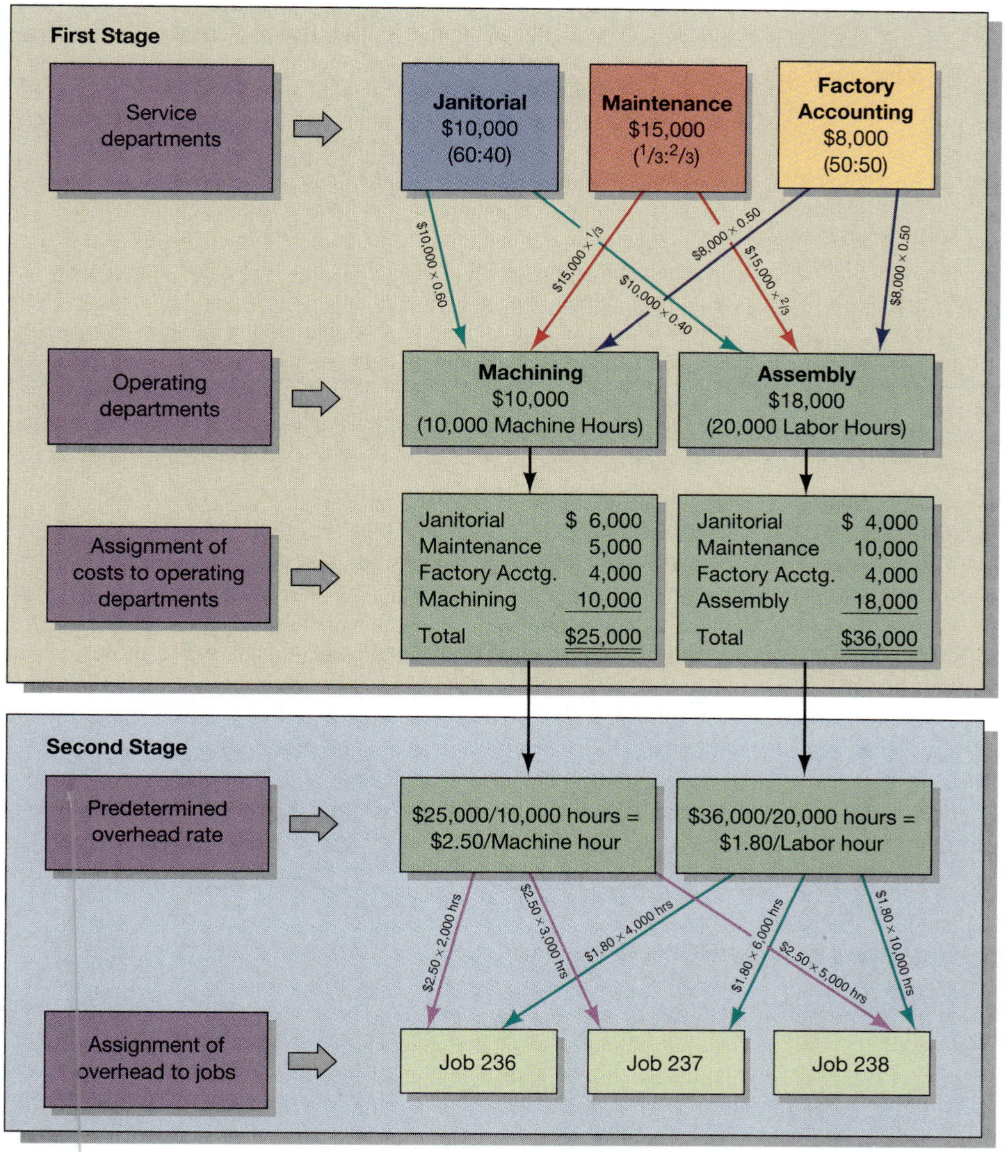

Exhibit 22.1

Two-Stage Cost Allocation

First Stage

| Service departments | | Janitorial $10,000 (60:40) | Maintenance $15,000 ($^1/_3$:$^2/_3$) | Factory Accounting $8,000 (50:50) |

Allocation of service department costs to operating departments.

$10,000 × 0.60
$15,000 × $^1/_3$
$8,000 × 0.50
$15,000 × $^2/_3$
$10,000 × 0.40
$8,000 × 0.50

| Operating departments | | Machining $10,000 (10,000 Machine Hours) | Assembly $18,000 (20,000 Labor Hours) |

| Assignment of costs to operating departments | | | |

	Machining		Assembly	
Janitorial	$ 6,000	Janitorial	$ 4,000
Maintenance	5,000	Maintenance	10,000
Factory Acctg.	4,000	Factory Acctg.	4,000
Machining	10,000	Assembly	18,000
Total	$25,000	Total	$36,000

Second Stage

| Predetermined overhead rate | | $25,000/10,000 hours = $2.50/Machine hour | $36,000/20,000 hours = $1.80/Labor hour |

Allocation of overhead costs to output.

$2.50 × 2,000 hrs
$2.50 × 3,000 hrs
$1.80 × 4,000 hrs
$1.80 × 6,000 hrs
$2.50 × 5,000 hrs
$1.80 × 10,000 hrs

| Assignment of overhead to jobs | | Job 236 | Job 237 | Job 238 |

To illustrate, three jobs were started and finished in a recent month. These jobs consumed resources as follows: Job 236—2,000 machine hours in machining and 4,000 labor hours in assembly; Job 237—3,000 machine hours and 6,000 labor hours; Job 238—5,000 machine hours and 10,000 labor hours. The overhead assigned to these three jobs is shown with the arrow lines in the bottom row of Exhibit 22.1. Exhibit 22.2 summarizes these allocations. Total overhead allocated to Jobs 236, 237, and 238, is $12,200, $18,300, and $30,500, respectively. These allocated costs sum to $61,000, which is the total amount of overhead we started with.

Point: Direct labor is less than 5% of total product costs for some manufacturers.

Activity-Based Cost Allocation

Overhead costs are usually too complex to be explained by one factor such as direct labor. Also, because of technological advances, direct labor costs have declined as a percent of total cost. In some companies, direct labor cost is such a small part of total cost that it is treated as overhead. Computing multiple overhead rates, as in the

Did You Know?

Misled by Overhead **Futura Computer** recently outsourced 2 million units of a "money-losing" product to a Korean firm for manufacturing. Its own manufacturing facility was retooled to produce extra units of a "more profitable" product. Profits did not materialize, and losses grew to more than $20 million! What went wrong? It turns out the better product was a loser, while the losing product was a winner. Futura's management was misled by poor overhead allocations.

Exhibit 22.2

Assignment of Overhead
Costs to Output

	Job 236	Job 237	Job 238
Machining			
$2.50 × 2,000 hours	$ 5,000		
$2.50 × 3,000 hours		$ 7,500	
$2.50 × 5,000 hours			$12,500
Assembly			
$1.80 × 4,000 hours	7,200		
$1.80 × 6,000 hours		10,800	
$1.80 × 10,000 hours			18,000
Total overhead assigned	$12,200	$18,300	$30,500

P2 Assign overhead costs using activity-based costing.

Concept 22-1

Point: A recent survey found that most respondents believe that activity-based costing is worth the investment because of improved management decisions.

Exhibit 22.3

Activity-Based Cost Allocation

two-stage cost allocation, is an improvement over a single allocation rate based on direct labor. However, because the allocation bases used in the second stage of two-stage allocation are still volume based (such as machine hours), they fail to reflect many overhead cost items not driven by the volume of production or services. Unfortunately, inappropriate allocations can distort unit costs. Moreover, when the number of jobs, products, or departments increases, the possibility of improperly assigning costs increases. This can lead managers to make poor decisions and to the eventual failure of a company.

Activity-based costing (ABC) attempts to better allocate costs to the proper users of overhead by focusing on *activities*. Costs are traced to individual activities and then allocated to cost objects. Exhibit 22.3 shows the (two-stage) activity-based cost allocation method. The first stage identifies the activities involved in processing jobs 236, 237, and 238 and then forms activity cost *pools* by combining these activities into sets. The second stage involves computing predetermined overhead cost allocation rates for each cost pool and then assigning costs to jobs.

First Stage

Sets of Activities	Activity 1 Activity 2 • • •	Activity 1 Activity 2 • • •	Activity 1 Activity 2 • • •	Activity 1 Activity 2 • • •	Activity 1 Activity 2 • • •

Activity Cost Pools (Cost Drivers)	**Janitorial** $10,000 (10,000 Square feet)	**Maintenance** $15,000 (5,000 Maintenance Hours)	**Factory Accounting** $8,000 (2,000 Transactions)	**Machining** $10,000 (10,000 Machine Hours)	**Assembly** $18,000 (20,000 Labor Hours)

Second Stage

Predetermined Overhead Rate	$10,000/10,000 = $1/Square Foot	$15,000/5,000 = $3/Maint. Hour	$8,000/2,000 = $4/ Transaction	$10,000/10,000 = $1/Machine Hour	$18,000/20,000 = $0.90/Labor Hour

Assignment of Overhead to Jobs	Job 236	Job 237	Job 238

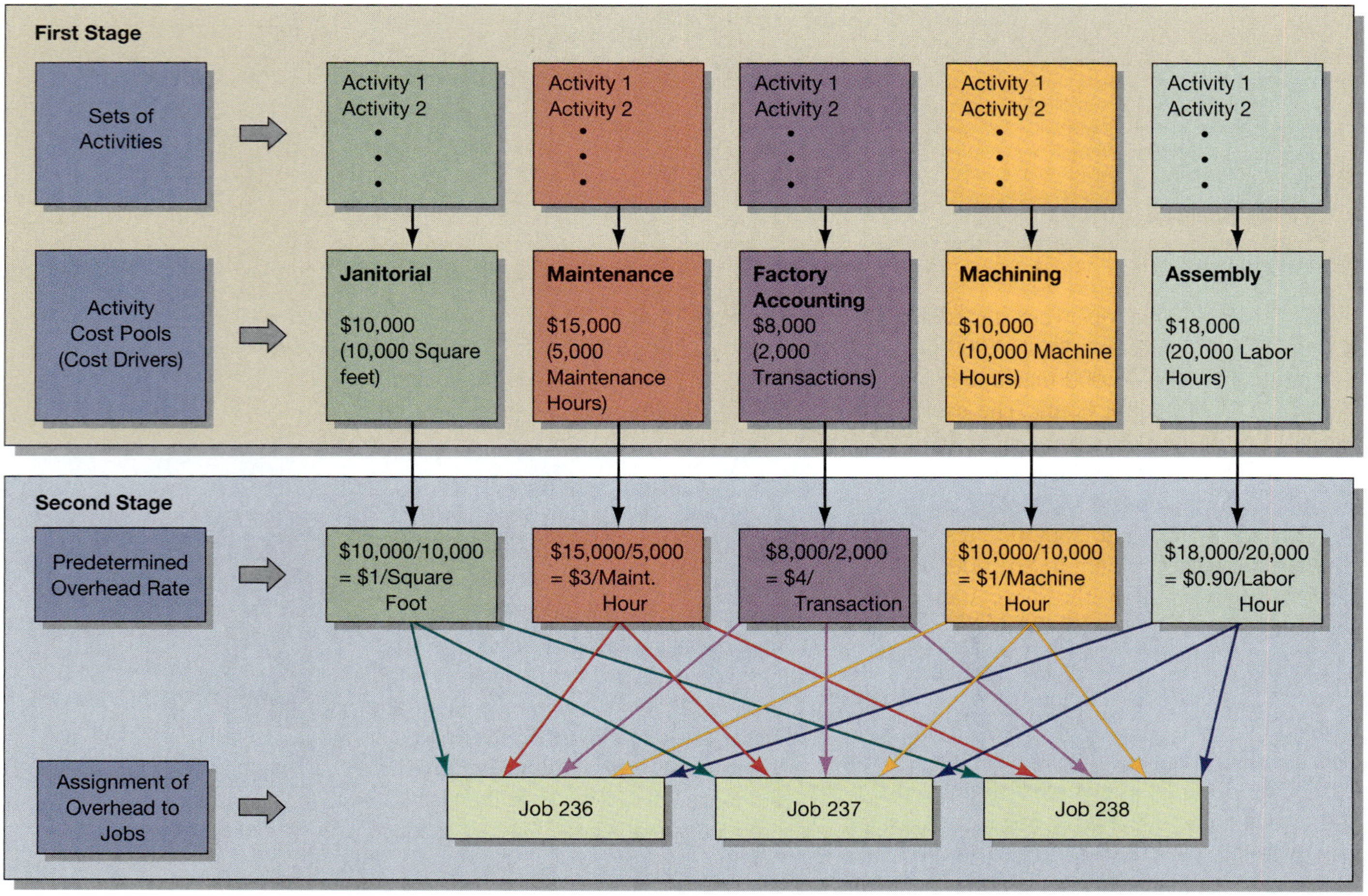

We begin our explanation at the top of Exhibit 22.3. The first stage identifies individual activities, which are then pooled in a logical manner into homogenous groups, or *cost pools*. A homogenous cost pool consists of activities that belong to the same process and/or are caused by the same **cost driver.** A cost driver is a factor that causes the cost of an activity to go up or down. For example, preparing an invoice, checking it, and dispatching it are activities of the "invoicing" process and can therefore be grouped in a single cost pool. Moreover, the number of invoices processed likely drives the costs of these activities.

An **activity cost pool** is a temporary account accumulating the costs a company incurs to support an identified set of activities. Costs accumulated in an activity cost pool include the variable and fixed costs of the activities included in the pool. Variable costs pertain to resources acquired as needed (such as materials), whereas fixed costs pertain to resources acquired in advance (such as equipment). An activity cost pool account is handled like a factory overhead account. In the second stage, after all activity costs have been accumulated in an activity cost pool account, costs are allocated to cost objects (users) based on cost drivers (allocation bases).

Point: A cost driver is different from an allocation base. An allocation base is used as a basis for assigning overhead but need not have a cause-effect relation with the costs assigned. However, a cost driver has a cause-effect relation with the cost assigned.

Illustration of Activity-Based Costing

To illustrate, let's return to AutoGrand's three jobs. Assume that resources are used to complete Jobs 236, 237, and 238 as shown in Exhibit 22.4.

Resources Used	Job 236	Job 237	Job 238
Square feet of space	5,000	3,000	2,000
Maintenance hours	2,500	1,500	1,000
Number of transactions	500	700	800
Machine hours	2,000	3,000	5,000
Direct labor hours	4,000	6,000	10,000

Exhibit 22.4

Activity Resource Use

The $61,000 of total overhead costs are assigned to these three jobs using activity-based costing as shown in Exhibit 22.5 (overhead rates are taken from the second stage of Exhibit 22.3).

	Job 236	Job 237	Job 238
Janitorial			
$1.00 × 5,000 sq. ft.	$ 5,000		
$1.00 × 3,000 sq. ft.		$ 3,000	
$1.00 × 2,000 sq. ft.			$ 2,000
Maintenance			
$3.00 × 2,500 maint. hrs.	7,500		
$3.00 × 1,500 maint. hrs.		4,500	
$3.00 × 1,000 maint. hrs.			3,000
Factory Accounting			
$4.00 × 500 transactions	2,000		
$4.00 × 700 transactions		2,800	
$4.00 × 800 transactions			3,200
Machining			
$1.00 × 2,000 machine hrs.	2,000		
$1.00 × 3,000 machine hrs.		3,000	
$1.00 × 5,000 machine hrs.			5,000
Assembly			
$0.90 × 4,000 labor hrs.	3,600		
$0.90 × 6,000 labor hrs.		5,400	
$0.90 × 10,000 labor hrs.			9,000
Total overhead assigned	$20,100	$18,700	$22,200

Exhibit 22.5

Activity-Based Assignment of Overhead to Output

Comparing Exhibits 22.2 and 22.5, we see that the overhead amounts assigned to the three jobs vary markedly depending on whether two-stage cost allocation or activity-based costing is used. Overhead assigned to Job 236 goes from $12,200 using two-stage cost allocation to $20,100 under activity-based costing. Overhead assigned to Job 238 declines from $30,500 to $22,200. These differences in amounts assigned result from more accurately tracing overhead costs to each job under activity-based costing because it uses allocation bases reflecting actual cost drivers.

Comparing Two-Stage and Activity-Based Cost Allocation Methods

Traditional cost systems capture overhead costs by individual department (or function) and accumulate these costs in one or a small number of overhead accounts. Companies then assign these overhead costs using a single allocation base such as direct labor or multiple allocation bases. Unfortunately, traditional cost systems have tended to use allocation bases that are often not closely related to the way these costs are actually incurred.

In contrast, activity-based cost systems capture costs by individual activity. These activities and their costs are then accumulated into activity cost pools. A company selects a cost driver (allocation base) for each activity pool. It uses this cost driver to assign the accumulated activity costs to cost objects (such as jobs or products) benefiting from the activity.

An activity-based costing system commonly consists of more allocation bases as compared to a traditional cost system. For example, a Chicago-based manufacturer currently uses nearly 20 different activity cost drivers to assign overhead costs to its products. Also, an activity-based cost system was recently set up at **Perkin-Elmer**, a maker of analytical instruments. The company's controller reports that at first they tried to analyze too many cost drivers. Eventually, they set up cross-functional teams able to identify the important cost drivers for each pool. Exhibit 22.6 lists examples of overhead cost pools and their cost drivers.

Exhibit 22.6

Cost Pools and Cost Drivers in Activity-Based Costing

Activity Cost Pool	Cost Driver
Materials purchasing	Number of purchase orders
Materials handling	Number of materials requisitions
Personnel processing	Number of employees hired or laid off
Equipment depreciation	Number of products produced or hours of use
Quality inspection	Number of units inspected
Indirect labor in setting up equipment	Number of setups required
Engineering costs for product modifications	Number of modifications (engineering change orders)

Activity-based costing is especially effective when the same department or departments produce many different types of products. For instance, more complex products likely require more help from service departments such as engineering, maintenance, and materials handling. If the same amount of direct labor is applied to the complex and simple products, a traditional overhead allocation system assigns the same overhead cost to both. With activity-based costing, however, the complex products are assigned a larger portion of over-

Point: To apply these concepts, work QS 22-3.

head. The difference in overhead assigned can affect product pricing, make-or-buy, and other managerial decisions. Activity-based costing allows production managers to focus on managing activities that drive overhead cost instead of reducing allocated overhead by reducing direct labor cost.

Activity-based costing causes managers to pay closer attention to all activities. If overhead costs are accumulated in one account, attention is less likely to be directed at controlling any individual item. Activity-based costing requires managers to look at each item and encourages

> ## You Make the Call — Ethics
>
> **Accounting Officer**   You work for a company that produces expensive garments, the production of which involves many complex and specialized activities. The company's general manager recently learned about activity-based costing (ABC) and requests your opinion. However, your supervisor does not want to disturb the existing cost system and instructs you to prepare a report stating that "implementation of ABC is a complicated process involving too many steps and not worth the effort." You actually believe ABC will help the company to identify sources of costs and control them. What action do you take?
>
> Answer—p. 929

them to manage each cost to increase the benefit from each dollar spent. It also encourages managers to cooperate because it shows how their efforts are interrelated. This results in *activity-based management.*

> ## Quick Check
>
> 1. What is a cost driver?
> 2. When activity-based costing is used rather than traditional allocation methods:
>   (a) managers must identify cost drivers for various items of overhead cost,
>   (b) individual cost items in service departments are allocated directly to products or services, (c) managers can direct their attention to the activities that drive overhead cost, or (d) all of the above.
>
> Answers—p. 930

Departmental Accounting

Companies are divided into *departments,* also called *subunits,* when they are too large to be managed effectively as a single unit. Managerial accounting for departments has two main goals. The first is to set up a **departmental accounting system** to provide information for managers to use to evaluate the profitability or cost effectiveness of each department's activities. The second goal is to set up a **responsibility accounting system** to control costs and expenses and evaluate managers' performances by assigning costs and expenses to the managers responsible for controlling them. Departmental and responsibility accounting systems are related and share much information. We discuss departmental accounting in this and the next section. Then, responsibility accounting is described.

Motivation for Departmentalization

Many companies are sufficiently large and complex, and are broken into separate divisions for efficiency and/or effectiveness purposes. Furthermore, divisions are usually organized into separate departments. When a company is departmentalized, each department is often placed under the direction of a manager. As a company grows, management often divides departments into new departments so that responsibilities for a department's activities do not overwhelm the manager's ability to oversee and control them. A company also creates departments to take advantage of the skills of individual managers. As mentioned earlier in this chapter, departments are broadly classified as either operating or service departments.

C1 Explain departmentalization and the role of departmental accounting.

Point: To improve profitability, **Sears, Roebuck & Co.** eliminated several departments, including its catalog division.

Concept 22-2

Point: Selling departments are often treated as *revenue centers;* managers of revenue centers are responsible for maximizing sales revenues.

Departmental Evaluation

When a company is divided into departments, managers need to know how each department is performing. The accounting system must supply information about resources used and outputs achieved by each department. This requires a system to measure and accumulate revenue and expense information for each department whenever possible.

Departmental information is rarely distributed publicly because of its potential usefulness to competitors. Information about departments is prepared for internal managers to help control operations, appraise performance, allocate resources, and plan strategy. If a department is highly profitable, management may decide to expand its operations, or if a department is performing poorly, information about revenues and expenses can suggest useful changes.

More companies are emphasizing customer satisfaction as a main responsibility of many departments. (However, some departments have only "internal customers.") This has led to changes in the measures reported in responsibility accounting systems. Increasingly, financial measurements are being supplemented with quality and customer satisfaction indexes. **Motorola**, for instance, uses two key measures: the number of defective parts per million parts produced and the percent of orders delivered on time to customers.

Financial information used to evaluate a department depends on whether it is evaluated as a profit center or a cost center. A **profit center** incurs costs and generates revenues; selling departments are often evaluated as profit centers. A **cost center** incurs costs without directly generating revenues. Manufacturing departments of a manufacturer and its service departments such as accounting, advertising, and purchasing, are all cost centers. Evaluating managers' performance depends on whether they are responsible for profit centers or cost centers. Managers of profit centers are judged on their ability to generate revenues in excess of the department's costs. They are assumed to influence both revenue generation and cost incurrence. Managers of cost centers are judged on their ability to control costs by keeping them within a satisfactory range under an assumption they only influence costs.

Point: Some retailers use a point-of-sales system capturing sales data and creating documents to release inventory from the warehouse and order additional merchandise. **Wal-Mart**'s sales system not only collects data for internal use, but also is used by **Procter & Gamble** to plan its production and delivery schedule of products sold to **Wal-Mart.**

Point: Link Wood Products, a manufacturer of lawn and garden products, records each sale by department on a spreadsheet. Daily totals are accumulated in another spreadsheet to obtain monthly totals by department.

Point: Computer spreadsheets are useful for performing a departmental spreadsheet analysis. These programs are also useful for allocating expenses.

Departmental Reporting and Analysis

Companies use a variety of measurements (financial and nonfinancial) and reporting formats to evaluate their departments. The type and form of information depend on management's focus and philosophy. **Hewlett Packard**'s statement of corporate objectives, for instance, indicates that its goal is to satisfy customer needs. Its challenge is to set up managerial accounting systems to provide relevant feedback for evaluating performance in terms of its stated objectives. Also, the means used to obtain information about departments depend on how extensively a company uses computer and information technology.

When accounts are not maintained separately in the general ledger by department, a company can create departmental information by using a *departmental spreadsheet analysis*. For example, after recording sales in its usual manner, a company can compute daily total sales by department and enter these totals on a sales spreadsheet. At period-end, column totals of the spreadsheet show sales by department. The combined total of all columns equals the balance of the Sales account. A merchandiser that uses a spreadsheet analysis of department sales often uses separate spreadsheets to accumulate sales, sales returns, purchases, and purchases returns by department. If each department keeps a count of its inventory, it can also compute its gross profit (assuming it's a profit center).

Quick Check

3. What is the difference between a departmental accounting system and a responsibility accounting system?

4. Service (support) departments (a) manufacture products, (b) make sales directly to customers, (c) produce revenues, (d) assist operating departments.

5. Explain the difference between a cost center and a profit center. Cite an example of each.

Answers—p. 930

When a company computes departmental profits, it confronts some accounting challenges that involve allocating its expenses across its operating departments.

Direct and Indirect Expenses

Direct expenses are costs that are readily traced to a department because they are incurred for the sole benefit of that department. They require no allocation across departments. For example, the salary of an employee who works in only one department is a direct expense of that one department.

Indirect expenses are costs that are incurred for the joint benefit of more than one department and cannot be readily traced to only one department. For example, if two or more departments share a single building, all enjoy the benefits of the expenses for rent, heat, and light. Indirect expenses are allocated across departments benefiting from them when we need information about departmental profits. Ideally, we allocate indirect expenses by using a cause-effect relation. When we cannot identify cause-effect relations, each indirect expense is allocated on a basis approximating the relative benefit each department receives. Measuring the benefit for each department from an indirect expense can be difficult or sometimes impossible. Even when a reasonable allocation basis is chosen, considerable doubt can exist regarding the amount charged to each department.

Illustration of Indirect Expense Allocation

To illustrate how to allocate an indirect expense, we consider a retail store that purchases janitorial services from an outside company. Management allocates this cost across the store's three departments according to the floor space each occupies. Costs of janitorial services for a recent month are $300. Exhibit 22.7 shows the square feet of floor space each department occupies. The store computes the percent of total square feet allotted to each department and uses it to allocate the $300 cost.

Departmental Expense Allocation

C2 Distinguish between direct and indirect expenses.

Point: Utility expense has elements of both direct and indirect expenses.

Department	Square Feet	Percent of Total	Allocated Cost
Jewelry	2,400	60%	$180
Watch repair	600	15	45
China and silver	1,000	25	75
Totals	4,000	100%	$300

Exhibit 22.7
Indirect Expense Allocation

Specifically, because the jewelry department occupies 60% of the floor space, 60% of the total $300 cost is assigned to it. The same procedure is applied to the other departments. When the allocation process is complete, these and other allocated costs are deducted from the gross profit for each department to determine net income for each. One consideration in allocating costs is to motivate managers and employees to behave as desired. As a result, a cost incurred in one department might be best allocated to other departments when one of the other departments caused the cost and can potentially influence it.

Allocation of Indirect Expenses

This section describes how to identify the bases used to allocate indirect expenses across departments. No standard rule identifies what basis is best because expense allocation involves several factors, and the relative importance of these factors varies across departments and organizations. Judgment is required, and people do not always agree. In our discussion, note the parallels between activity-based costing and the departmental expense allocation procedures described here.

Point: Expense allocations cannot always avoid some arbitrariness.

Wages and Salaries

Employee wages and salaries can be either direct or indirect expenses. If their time is spent entirely in one department, their wages are direct expenses of that department. However, if employees work for the benefit of more than one department, their wages are indirect expenses and must be allocated across the departments benefited. An employee's contribution to a department usually depends on the number of hours worked in contributing to that department. Thus, a reasonable basis for allocating employee wages and salaries is the *relative amount of time spent in each department.* In the case of a supervisor who manages more than one department, recording the time spent in each department may not always be practical. Instead, a company can allocate supervisory salaries to departments on the basis of the number of employees in each department—a reasonable basis if a supervisor's main task is managing people. Another basis of allocation is on sales across departments, also a reasonable basis if a supervisor's job reflects on departmental sales.

Point: Some companies ask supervisors to estimate time spent supervising specific departments for purposes of expense allocation.

Rent and Related Expenses

Rent expense for a building is reasonably allocated to departments on the basis of floor space occupied by each department. Some floor space is often more valuable than other space because of location. Thus, the allocation method can charge departments that occupy more valuable space a higher expense per square foot. Ground floor retail space, for instance, is often more valuable than basement or upper-floor space because all customers pass departments near the entrance while fewer go beyond the first floor. When no precise measures of floor space values exist, basing allocations on data such as customer traffic and real estate assessments are helpful. When a company owns its building, its expenses for depreciation, taxes, insurance, and other related building expenses are allocated like rent expense.

Advertising Expenses

Point: To apply these concepts, work QS 22-2.

Effective advertising of a department's products increases its sales and customer traffic. Since customers also often buy unadvertised products, advertising products for some departments usually helps sales of all departments. Therefore, many stores treat advertising as an indirect expense that is often allocated on the basis of each department's proportion of total sales. For example, a department with 10% of a store's total sales is assigned 10% of advertising expense. Another method is to analyze each advertisement to compute the Web/newspaper space or TV/radio time devoted to the products of a department. That department is then charged for the proportional costs of advertisements. Management must consider whether this more detailed and costly method is justified.

Equipment and Machinery Depreciation

Point: Employee morale suffers when allocations are perceived as unfair. It is important to carefully design and explain the allocation of service department costs.

Depreciation on equipment and machinery used only in one department is a direct expense of that department. Depreciation on equipment and machinery used by more than one department is an indirect expense to be allocated across departments. Accounting for each department's depreciation expense requires a company to keep records showing which departments use specific assets. The number of hours that a department uses equipment and machinery is a reasonable basis for allocating depreciation.

Utilities Expenses

Utilities expenses such as heating and lighting are usually allocated on the basis of floor space occupied by departments. This practice assumes their use is uniform across departments. When this is not so, a more involved allocation can be necessary, although there is often a trade-off between the usefulness of more precise allocations and the effort to compute them.

Service Department Expenses

To generate revenues, operating departments require support services provided by departments such as personnel, payroll, advertising, and purchasing. Such service departments are typically evaluated as cost centers because they do not produce revenues. (Evaluating them as profit centers requires the use of a system that "charges" user departments a price that then serves as the "revenue" generated by service departments.) A departmental accounting system can accumulate and report costs incurred directly by each service department for this purpose. The system then allocates a service department's indirect expenses to operating departments benefiting from them. This is often done, for example, using traditional two-stage cost allocation (see Exhibit 22.1). Exhibit 22.8 shows some commonly used bases for allocating service department expenses to operating departments.

Point: Manufacturers often allocate electricity cost to departments on the basis of the horsepower of equipment located in each department.

Point: When a service department "charges" its user departments within a company, a *transfer pricing system* must be set up to determine the "revenue" from its services provided.

Service Department	Common Allocation Bases
Office expenses	Number of employees or sales in each department
Personnel expenses	Number of employees in each department
Payroll expenses	Number of employees in each department
Advertising expenses	Sales or amount of advertising charged directly to each department
Purchasing costs	Dollar amounts of purchases or number of purchase orders processed
Cleaning expenses	Square feet of floor space occupied
Maintenance expenses	Square feet of floor space occupied

Exhibit 22.8

Bases for Allocating Service Department Expenses

Departmental Income Statements

An income statement can be prepared for each operating department once its relevant expenses have been assigned to it. Its expenses include both direct expenses and its share of indirect expenses. For this purpose, compiling all expenses incurred in service departments before assigning them to operating departments is often useful. We illustrate the steps to prepare departmental income statements using **A-1 Hardware** and its five departments. Two of them (office and purchasing) are service departments and the other three (hardware, housewares, and appliances) are operating (selling) departments. Allocating costs to operating departments and preparing departmental income statements involves four steps.

P3 Prepare departmental income statements.

Step 1

Step 1 is to accumulate direct expenses for each service and operating department as shown in Exhibit 22.9. Direct expenses include salaries, wages, and other expenses that each department incurs but does not share with any other department. This information is accumulated in departmental expense accounts.

Direct Expenses	Direct Expenses	Direct Expenses	Direct Expenses	Direct Expenses
 General office	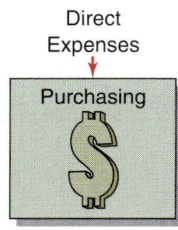 Purchasing	 Hardware	 Housewares	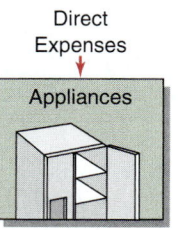 Appliances

Exhibit 22.9

Step 1: Direct Expense Accumulation

Exhibit 22.10

Step 2: Indirect Expense Allocation

Point: We sometimes allocate service department costs across other service departments before allocating them to operating departments. This "step-wise" process is in advanced courses.

Exhibit 22.11

Step 3: Service Department Expense Allocation

Point: To apply these concepts, work Exercise 22-1.

Exhibit 22.12

Departmental Expense Allocation Spreadsheet

Step 2

Step 2 allocates indirect expenses across all departments using the allocation base identified for each expense as shown in Exhibit 22.10. Indirect expenses can include items such as depreciation, rent, advertising, and any other expenses that cannot be directly assigned to a department. Indirect expenses are recorded in expense accounts, and costs are allocated using a *departmental expense allocation spreadsheet* described in step 3.

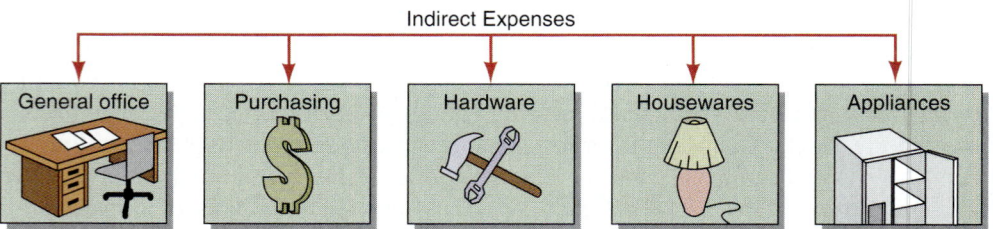

Step 3

Step 3 allocates expenses of the service departments (office and purchasing) to the operating departments. Exhibit 22.11 reflects the allocation of service department expenses using the allocation base(s).

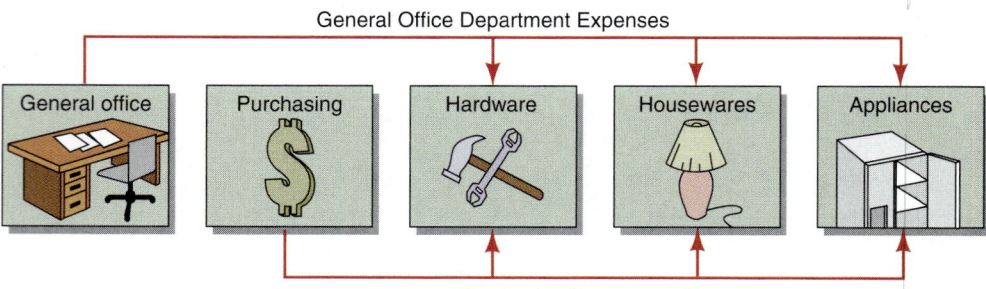

Computations for both steps 2 and 3 are commonly made using a departmental expense allocation spreadsheet as shown in Exhibit 22.12.[1] The first two sections of the spreadsheet in Exhibit 22.12 list direct expenses and indirect expenses by department. The third section lists the service department expenses and their allocations to operating departments. The

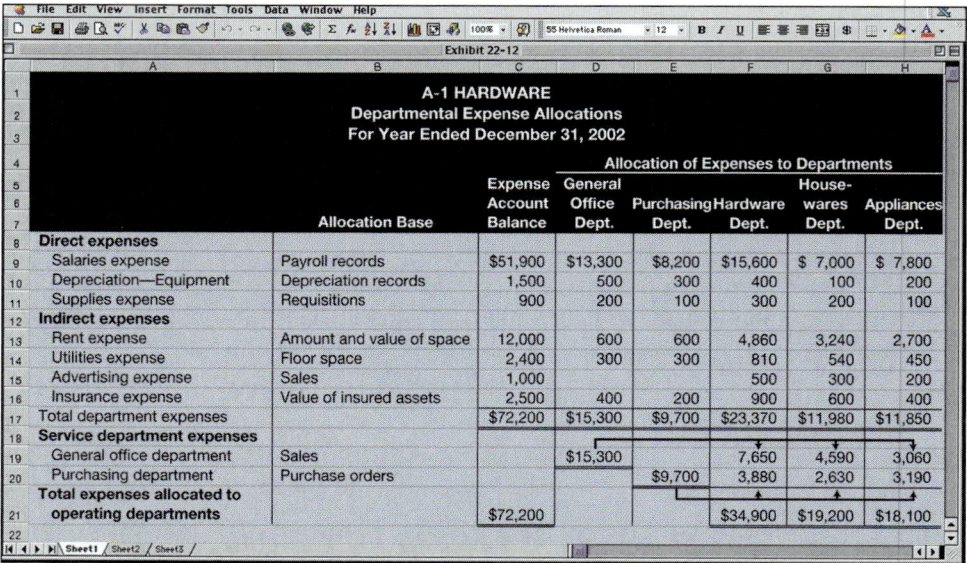

A-1 HARDWARE
Departmental Expense Allocations
For Year Ended December 31, 2002

	Allocation Base	Expense Account Balance	General Office Dept.	Purchasing Dept.	Hardware Dept.	House-wares Dept.	Appliances Dept.
Direct expenses							
Salaries expense	Payroll records	$51,900	$13,300	$8,200	$15,600	$ 7,000	$ 7,800
Depreciation—Equipment	Depreciation records	1,500	500	300	400	100	200
Supplies expense	Requisitions	900	200	100	300	200	100
Indirect expenses							
Rent expense	Amount and value of space	12,000	600	600	4,860	3,240	2,700
Utilities expense	Floor space	2,400	300	300	810	540	450
Advertising expense	Sales	1,000			500	300	200
Insurance expense	Value of insured assets	2,500	400	200	900	600	400
Total department expenses		$72,200	$15,300	$9,700	$23,370	$11,980	$11,850
Service department expenses							
General office department	Sales		$15,300		7,650	4,590	3,060
Purchasing department	Purchase orders			$9,700	3,880	2,630	3,190
Total expenses allocated to operating departments		$72,200			$34,900	$19,200	$18,100

---

[1] In some cases we allocate expenses of a service department to other service departments when they use its services. For example, expenses of a payroll office benefit all service and operating departments and can be assigned to all departments. Nearly all examples and assignment materials in this book allocate service expenses only to operating departments for simplicity.

allocation bases are identified in the second column, and total expense amounts are reported in the third column.

Specifically, the departmental expense allocation spreadsheet is useful in implementing the first three steps. First (step 1), the three direct expenses of salaries, depreciation, and supplies are accumulated in each of the five departments.

Second (step 2), the four indirect expenses of rent, utilities, advertising, and insurance are allocated to all departments using the allocation bases identified. To illustrate step 2, we focus on rent allocation. Exhibit 22.13 lists the five departments' square footage of space occupied. The two service departments (office and purchasing) occupy 25% of the total space (3,000 sq. feet/12,000 sq. feet). However, they are located near the back of the building, which is of lower value than space near the front that is occupied by operating departments. Management estimates that space near the back accounts for $1,200

General office	1,500 sq. ft.
Purchasing	1,500 sq. ft.
Hardware	4,050 sq. ft.
Housewares	2,700 sq. ft.
Appliances	2,250 sq. ft.
Total	12,000 sq. ft.

Exhibit 22.13

Departments' Square Footages

of the total rent expense of $12,000. Exhibit 22.14 shows how we allocate the $1,200 rent expense between these two service departments in proportion to their square footage. We then

Department	Square Feet	Percent of Total	Allocated Cost
General office	1,500	50.0%	$ 600
Purchasing	1,500	50.0	600
Totals	3,000	100.0%	$1,200

Exhibit 22.14

Allocating Indirect (Rent) Expense to Service Departments

allocate the remaining $10,800 of rent expense to the three operating departments as shown in Exhibit 22.15. We continue step 2 by allocating the $2,400 of utilities expense to all de-

Department	Square Feet	Percent of Total	Allocated Cost
Hardware	4,050	45.0%	$ 4,860
Housewares	2,700	30.0	3,240
Appliances	2,250	25.0	2,700
Totals	9,000	100.0%	$10,800

Exhibit 22.15

Allocating Indirect (Rent) Expense to Operating Departments

partments based on the square footage occupied as shown in Exhibit 22.16. The rows in Exhibit 22.12 for rent and utilities expenses show the amounts from Exhibits 22.14, 22.15, and 22.16. The allocations of the two other indirect expenses of advertising and insurance are similarly computed. Note that since advertising expense is allocated on the basis of sales and since service departments do not have sales, it is allocated only to the three operating departments.

Department	Square Feet	Percent of Total	Allocated Cost
General office	1,500	12.50%	$ 300
Purchasing	1,500	12.50	300
Hardware	4,050	33.75	810
Housewares	2,700	22.50	540
Appliances	2,250	18.75	450
Totals	12,000	100.00%	$2,400

Exhibit 22.16

Allocating Indirect (Utilities) Expense to All Departments

Third (step 3), we allocate total expenses of the two service departments to the three operating departments using the allocation bases shown in the final three rows of Exhibit 22.12.

Exhibit 22.17

Departmental Income Statements

Step 4

When the departmental expense spreadsheet is complete, the amounts in the operating department columns are used to prepare departmental income statements as shown in Exhibit 22.17. This exhibit uses the spreadsheet for its operating expenses; information on sales and cost of goods sold comes from departmental records.

	A-1 HARDWARE Departmental Income Statements For Year Ended December 31, 2002			
	Hardware Department	**Housewares Department**	**Appliances Department**	**Combined**
Sales	$119,500	$71,700	$47,800	$239,000
Cost of goods sold	73,800	43,800	30,200	147,800
Gross profit	$ 45,700	$27,900	$17,600	$ 91,200
Operating expenses				
Salaries expense	15,600	7,000	7,800	30,400
Depreciation expense—Equip.	400	100	200	700
Supplies expense	300	200	100	600
Rent expense	4,860	3,240	2,700	10,800
Utilities expense	810	540	450	1,800
Advertising expense	500	300	200	1,000
Insurance expense	900	600	400	1,900
Share of general office expenses	7,650	4,590	3,060	15,300
Share of purchasing expenses	3,880	2,630	3,190	9,700
Total operating expenses	$ 34,900	$19,200	$18,100	$ 72,200
Net income (loss)	**$ 10,800**	**$ 8,700**	**$ (500)**	**$ 19,000**
Partial analysis				
Gross profit as percent of sales	38.2%	38.9%	36.8%	38.2%

Departmental Contribution to Overhead

Data from departmental income statements are not always best for evaluating each department's performance, especially when indirect expenses are a large portion of total expenses and when weaknesses in assumptions and decisions in allocating indirect expenses can markedly affect net income. In these and other cases, we might evaluate department performance using departmental contributions to overhead. The **departmental contribution to overhead** is a report of the amount of revenues less *direct* expenses.[2]

The upper half of Exhibit 22.18 shows a departmental contribution to overhead as part of an expanded income statement. This format is common when reporting departmental contributions to overhead. Using the information in Exhibits 22.17 and 22.18, we can evaluate the profitability of the three operating departments. For instance, let's compare the performance of the appliances department as described in these two exhibits. Exhibit 22.17 shows a $500 net loss resulting from this department's operations; but Exhibit 22.18 shows a $9,500 positive contribution to overhead, which is 19.9% of sales. The contribution of the appliances department is not as large as that of the other selling departments, but a $9,500 contribution to overhead is better than a $500 loss. This tells us that the appliances department is not a money loser. On the contrary, it is contributing $9,500 toward defraying total indirect expenses of $40,500.

---

[2] A department's contribution is said to be "to overhead" because of the practice of considering all indirect expenses as overhead. Thus, the excess of a department's revenues over direct expenses is a contribution toward at least a portion of its total overhead.

Exhibit 22.18

Departmental Contribution
to Overhead

A-1 HARDWARE Income Statement Showing Departmental Contributions to Overhead For Year Ended December 31, 2002				
	Hardware Department	Housewares Department	Appliances Department	Combined
Sales	$119,500	$71,700	$47,800	$239,000
Cost of goods sold	73,800	43,800	30,200	147,800
Gross profit	$ 45,700	$27,900	$17,600	$ 91,200
Direct expenses				
Salaries expense	15,600	7,000	7,800	30,400
Depreciation expense—Equipment	400	100	200	700
Supplies expense	300	200	100	600
Total direct expenses	$ 16,300	$ 7,300	$ 8,100	$ 31,700
Departmental contributions to overhead	**$ 29,400**	**$20,600**	**$ 9,500**	**$ 59,500**
Indirect expenses				
Rent expense				10,800
Utilities expense				1,800
Advertising expense				1,000
Insurance expense				1,900
General office department expense				15,300
Purchasing department expense				9,700
Total indirect expenses				$ 40,500
Net income				$ 19,000
Contribution as percent of sales	24.6%	28.7%	19.9%	24.9%

Quick Check

6. If a company has two operating (selling) departments (shoes and hats) and two service departments (payroll and advertising), which of the following statements is correct? (a) Wages incurred in the payroll department are direct expenses of the shoe department, (b) Wages incurred in the payroll department are indirect expenses of the operating departments, or (c) Advertising department expenses are allocated to the other three departments.

7. Which of the following bases can be used to allocate salaries of supervisors across operating departments? (a) Hours spent in each department, (b) number of employees in each department, (c) sales achieved in each department, or (d) any of the above, depending on which information is most relevant and accessible.

8. What three steps are used to allocate expenses to operating departments?

9. On an income statement showing the departmental and combined contribution to overhead, (a) indirect expenses are subtracted from each department's revenues, (b) only direct expenses are subtracted from each department's revenues, or (c) net income is shown for each department.

Answers—p. 930

Departmental accounting reports often provide data used to evaluate a department's performance, but are they useful in assessing how well a department *manager* performs? Neither departmental income nor its contribution to overhead may be useful because many expenses can be outside a manager's control. Instead, we often evaluate a manager's performance

Responsibility Accounting

C4 Explain controllable costs and responsibility accounting.

using responsibility accounting reports that describe a department's activities in terms of **controllable costs.**[3] Chapter 19 explained that a cost is controllable if a manager has the power to determine or at least strongly affect the amounts incurred. **Uncontrollable costs** are not within the manager's control or influence.

Controllable versus Direct Costs

Controllable costs are not always the same as direct costs. Direct costs are readily traced to a department, but the department manager might or might not control their amounts. For example, department managers often have little or no control over depreciation expense because they cannot affect the amount of equipment assigned to their departments. Also, these managers rarely control their own salaries. However, they can control or influence items such as the cost of goods sold and the supplies used in the department. When evaluating managers' performances, we should use data reflecting their departments' outputs along with their controllable costs and expenses. A manager's performance is thus often judged by comparing current period's results with both its planned levels and those of prior periods.

Distinguishing between controllable and uncontrollable costs depends on the particular manager and time period under analysis. For example, the cost of property insurance is usually not controllable at the department manager's level, but it is controllable by the executive responsible for obtaining the company's insurance coverage. Likewise, this executive might not control costs resulting from insurance policies already in force. However, when a policy expires, this executive can renegotiate a replacement policy and then controls these costs. Therefore, all costs are controllable at some management level if the time period is sufficiently long. We must use good judgment in identifying controllable costs.

Point: To apply these concepts, work Exercise 22-8.

Responsibility Accounting System

A *responsibility accounting system* uses the concept of controllable costs to assign managers the responsibility for costs and expenses under their control. Prior to each reporting period, a company prepares plans that identify costs and expenses under each manager's control. These plans are called **responsibility accounting budgets.** To ensure the cooperation of managers and the reasonableness of budgets, managers should be involved in preparing their budgets.

A responsibility accounting system also involves performance reports. A **responsibility accounting performance report** accumulates and reports costs and expenses that a manager is responsible for and their budgeted amounts. Management analyzes differences between budgeted amounts and actual costs and expenses, which often results in corrective or strategic managerial actions. Upper-level management uses performance reports to evaluate the effectiveness of lower-level managers in controlling costs and expenses and keeping them within budgeted amounts. Chapter 25 further explains the nature and use of performance reports.

A responsibility accounting system recognizes that control over costs and expenses belongs to several levels of management. We illustrate this by considering the organization chart in Exhibit 22.19. The

Exhibit 22.19

Organizational Responsibility Chart

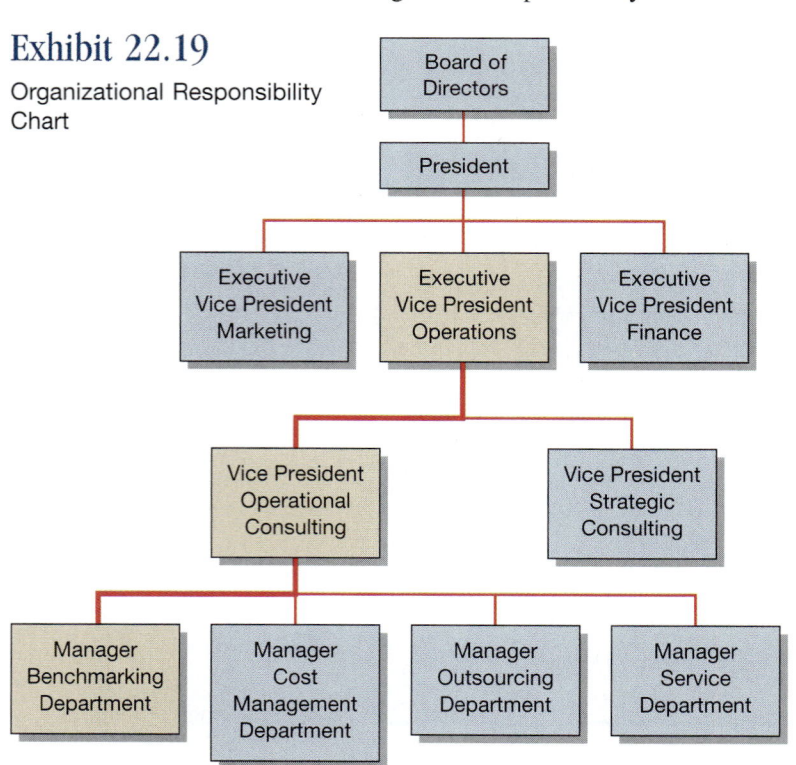

---

[3] The terms *cost* and *expense* are often used interchangeably in managerial accounting, but they are not necessarily the same. *Cost* often refers to the monetary outlay to acquire some resource that can have present and future benefit. *Expense* usually refers to an expired cost. That is, as the benefit of a resource expires, a portion of its cost is written off as an expense.

lines in this chart connecting the managerial positions reflect channels of authority. For example, the four department managers of this consulting firm (benchmarking, cost management, outsourcing, and service) are responsible for controllable costs and expenses incurred in their departments, but these same costs are subject to the overall control of the vice president (VP) for operational consulting. Similarly, this VP's costs are subject to the control of the executive vice president (EVP) for operations, the president, and, ultimately, the board of directors.

At lower levels, managers have limited responsibility and relatively little control over costs and expenses. Performance reports for low-level management typically cover few controllable costs. Responsibility and control broaden for higher-level managers; therefore, their reports span a wider range of costs. However, reports to higher-level managers seldom contain the details reported to their subordinates but are summarized for two reasons: (1) lower-level managers are often responsible for these detailed costs and (2) detailed reports can obscure broader, more important issues facing a company.

Exhibit 22.20 shows summarized performance reports for the three management levels identified in Exhibit 22.19. Exhibit 22.20 shows that costs under the control of the benchmarking department manager are totaled and included among controllable costs of the VP for operational consulting. Also, costs under the control of the VP are totaled and included among controllable costs of the EVP for operations. In this way, a responsibility accounting system provides relevant information for each management level.

Point: Responsibility accounting does not place blame. Instead, responsibility accounting is used to identify opportunities for improving performance.

Point: A responsibility accounting system usually divides a company into subunits called *responsibility centers*. The manager of each center is evaluated on how well the center performs, as reported in responsibility accounting reports.

Exhibit 22.20

Responsibility Accounting Performance Reports

Executive Vice President, Operations — For July

Controllable Costs	Budgeted Amount	Actual Amount	Over (Under) Budget
Salaries, VPs	$ 80,000	$ 80,000	$ 0
Quality control costs	21,000	22,400	1,400
Office costs	29,500	28,800	(700)
Operational Consulting	**276,700**	**279,500**	**2,800** ◄
Strategic Consulting	390,000	380,600	(9,400)
Totals	$797,200	$791,300	$(5,900)

Vice President, Operational Consulting — For July

Controllable Costs	Budgeted Amount	Actual Amount	Over (Under) Budget
Salaries, Department managers	$ 75,000	$ 78,000	$3,000
Depreciation	10,600	10,600	0
Insurance	6,800	6,300	(500)
► **Benchmarking department**	**79,600**	**79,900**	**300**
Cost Management department	61,500	60,200	(1,300)
Outsourcing department	24,300	24,700	400
Service department	18,900	19,800	900
Totals	**$276,700**	**$279,500**	**$2,800**

Manager, Benchmarking Department — For July

Controllable Costs	Budgeted Amount	Actual Amount	Over (Under) Budget
Salaries	$51,600	$52,500	$ 900
Supplies	8,000	7,800	(200)
Other controllable costs	20,000	19,600	(400)
Totals	**$79,600**	**$79,900**	**$ 300**

Technological advances increase our ability to produce vast amounts of information that often exceeds our ability to use it. Good managers select relevant data for planning and controlling the areas under their responsibility. A good responsibility accounting system makes every effort to provide relevant information to the right person (the one who controls the cost) at the right time (before a cost is out of control).

Quick Check

10. Are the reports of departmental net income and the departmental contribution to overhead useful in assessing a department manager's performance? Explain.

11. Performance reports to evaluate managers should (a) include data about controllable expenses, (b) compare actual results with budgeted levels, or (c) both (a) and (b).

Joint Costs

C5 Describe allocation of joint costs across products.

Most manufacturing processes involve **joint costs,** which refer to costs incurred to produce or purchase two or more products at the same time. A joint cost is like an indirect expense in the sense that more than one cost object share it. For example, a petroleum refining company incurs a joint cost when it buys crude oil that it separates into gasoline, lubricating oil, kerosene, paraffin, and ethylene as shown in Exhibit 22.21. The joint cost includes the crude oil (raw material) and its refining (conversion). Likewise, a sawmill incurs joint costs when it buys a log and cuts it into boards classified as Clear, Select, No. 1 Common, No. 2 Common, No. 3 Common, and other types of lumber and by-products.

When a joint cost is incurred, a question arises as to whether it should be allocated to different products produced from it. The answer is that when management wishes to estimate the total cost of individual products, joint costs are included in the computation and must be allocated to these joint products. However, when management needs information to help decide whether to sell a product at a certain point in the production process or to process it further, the joint costs are ignored.

Exhibit 22.21

Joint Products from Petroleum Refining

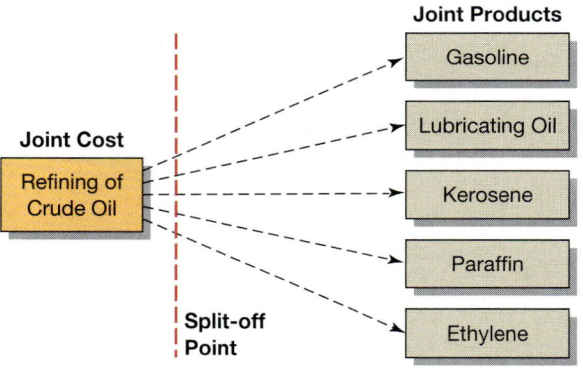

Financial statements prepared according to GAAP must assign joint costs to products. To do this, management must decide how to allocate joint costs across products benefiting from these costs. If some products are sold and others remain in inventory, allocating joint costs involves assigning costs to both cost of goods sold and ending inventory.

The two usual methods to allocate joint costs are the (1) *physical basis* and (2) the *value basis*. The physical basis typically involves allocating joint cost using physical characteristics such as the ratio of pounds, cubic feet, or gallons of each joint product to the total pounds, cubic feet, or gallons of all joint products flowing from the cost. This method is not commonly applied because the resulting cost allocations do not reflect the relative market values the joint cost generates. The preferred approach is the value basis, which allocates joint cost in proportion to the sales value of the output produced by the process at the "split-off point"—see Exhibit 22.21.

Physical Basis Allocation of Joint Cost

To illustrate the physical basis of allocating a joint cost, we consider a sawmill that bought logs for $30,000. When cut, these logs produce 100,000 board feet of lumber in the grades and amounts shown in Exhibit 22.22. The logs produce 20,000 board feet of No. 3 Common lumber, which is 20% of the total. With physical allocation, the No. 3 Common lumber is assigned 20% of the $30,000 cost of the logs, or $6,000 ($30,000 × 20%). Because this low-grade lumber sells for $4,000, this allocation gives a $2,000 loss from its production and sale. The physical basis for allocating joint costs does not reflect the extra value flowing into some products or the inferior value flowing into others. That is, the portion of a log that produces structural grade lumber is worth more than the portion used to produce the three grades of common lumber, but the physical basis fails to reflect this.

Exhibit 22.22

Allocating Joint Costs on a Physical Basis

Grade of Lumber	Board Feet Produced	Percent of Total	Allocated Cost	Sales Value	Gross Profit
Structural	10,000	10.0%	$ 3,000	$12,000	$ 9,000
No. 1 Common	30,000	30.0	9,000	18,000	9,000
No. 2 Common	40,000	40.0	12,000	16,000	4,000
No. 3 Common	20,000	20.0	6,000	4,000	(2,000)
Totals	100,000	100.0%	$30,000	$50,000	$20,000

Value Basis Allocation of Joint Cost

Exhibit 22.23 illustrates the value basis method of allocation. It determines the percents of the total costs allocated to each grade by the ratio of each grade's sales value to the total sales value of $50,000 (sales value is the unit selling price multiplied by the number of units produced). The structural grade lumber receives 24% of the total cost ($12,000/$50,000) instead of the 10% portion using a physical basis. The No. 3 Common lumber receives only 8% of the total cost, or $2,400, which is much less than the $6,000 assigned to it using the physical basis.

Exhibit 22.23

Allocating Joint Costs on a Value Basis

Grade of Lumber	Sales Value	Percent of Total	Allocated Cost	Gross Profit
Structural	$12,000	24.0%	$ 7,200	$ 4,800
No. 1 Common	18,000	36.0	10,800	7,200
No. 2 Common	16,000	32.0	9,600	6,400
No. 3 Common	4,000	8.0	2,400	1,600
Totals	$50,000	100.0%	$30,000	$20,000

Example: Refer to Exhibit 22.23. If the sales value of Structural lumber is changed to $10,000, what is the revised ratio of the market value of No. 1 Common to the total? *Answer:* $18,000/$48,000 = 37.5%

An outcome of value basis allocation is that *each* grade produces exactly the same 40% gross profit at the split-off point. This 40% rate equals the gross profit rate from selling all the lumber made from the $30,000 logs for a combined price of $50,000.

Quick Check

12. A company produces three products, B1, B2, and B3. The joint cost incurred for the current month for these products is $180,000. The following data relate to this month's production:

Product	Units Produced	Unit Sales Value
B1	96,000	$3.00
B2	64,000	6.00
B3	32,000	9.00

The amount of joint cost allocated to product B3 using the value basis allocation is (a) $30,000, (b) $54,000, or (c) $90,000.

Answer—p. 930

Using the Information | Return on Total Assets by Investment Centers

A1 Analyze investment centers using return on total assets.

Concept 22-2

We discussed the classification of departments (and/or divisions) as profit centers or cost centers. Another way is to classify (and evaluate) a department as an **investment center.** The manager of an investment center is responsible for wisely using the center's assets for purposes of generating income for the center. A measure often used to evaluate the performance of an investment center manager is the **investment center return on total assets,** also called *return on investment.* This measure is computed as a center's net income divided by the center's average total assets. To illustrate, if a center with an average investment of $1 million yields a net income of $210,000, its return on total assets is 21%.

A center's return on total assets can be used by top management to assess how well a center manager has utilized the center's assets to generate returns for the company. Top management can also compare performance across departments and/or divisions using this measure. Many companies establish a center's target return on total assets and reward managers based on whether the targets are met. In addition, center managers often use the center's return on total assets to decide whether they want to invest additional resources in the center.

You Make the Call

Center Manager Your center's usual return on total assets is 19%. You are considering two new investing opportunities for your center. The first requires a $250,000 average investment and is expected to yield annual net income of $50,000. The second requires a $1 million average investment with an expected annual net income of $175,000. Do you pursue either opportunity?

Answer—p. 929

Demonstration Problem

We must prepare departmental income statements for Hacker's Haven, a computer store that has five departments. Three are operating departments (hardware, software, and repairs) and two are service departments (general office and purchasing).

	General Office	Purchasing	Hardware	Software	Repairs
Sales	—	—	$960,000	$600,000	$840,000
Cost of goods sold	—	—	500,000	300,000	200,000
Direct expenses					
Payroll	$60,000	$45,000	80,000	25,000	325,000
Depreciation	6,000	7,200	33,000	4,200	9,600
Supplies	15,000	10,000	10,000	2,000	25,000

The departments incur several indirect expenses. To prepare departmental income statements, the indirect expenses must be allocated across the five departments. Then the expenses of the two service departments must be allocated to the three operating departments. Total cost amounts and the allocation bases for each indirect expense are as follows:

Indirect Expense	Total Cost	Allocation Basis
Rent	$150,000	Square footage occupied
Utilities	50,000	Square footage occupied
Advertising	125,000	Dollars of sales
Insurance	30,000	Value of assets insured
Service departments		
General office	?	Number of employees
Purchasing	?	Dollars of cost of goods sold

The following additional information is needed for indirect expense allocations:

Department	Square Feet	Sales	Insured Assets	Employees	Cost of Goods Sold
General office	500		$ 60,000		
Purchasing	500		72,000		
Hardware	4,000	$ 960,000	330,000	5	$ 500,000
Software	3,000	600,000	42,000	5	300,000
Repairs	2,000	840,000	96,000	10	200,000
Totals	10,000	$2,400,000	$600,000	20	$1,000,000

Required

1. Prepare a departmental expense allocation spreadsheet for Hacker's Haven.
2. Prepare a departmental income statement reporting net income for each operating department and for all operating departments combined.

Planning the Solution

- Set up and complete four tables to allocate the indirect expenses—one each for rent, utilities, advertising, and insurance.
- Allocate the departments' indirect expenses using a spreadsheet like the one in Exhibit 22.12. Enter the given amounts of the direct expenses for each department. Then enter the allocated amounts of the indirect expenses that you computed.
- Complete two tables for allocating the general office and purchasing department costs to the three operating departments. Enter these amounts on the spreadsheet and determine the total expenses allocated to the three operating departments.
- Prepare departmental income statements like the one in Exhibit 22.17. Show sales, cost of goods sold, gross profit, individual direct and indirect expenses, and net income for each of the three operating departments and for the combined company.

Solution to Demonstration Problem

Allocations of the four indirect expenses across the five departments:

Rent	Square Feet	Percent of Total	Allocated Cost
General office	500	5.0%	$ 7,500
Purchasing	500	5.0	7,500
Hardware	4,000	40.0	60,000
Software	3,000	30.0	45,000
Repairs	2,000	20.0	30,000
Totals	10,000	100.0%	$150,000

Utilities	Square Feet	Percent of Total	Allocated Cost
General office	500	5.0%	$ 2,500
Purchasing	500	5.0	2,500
Hardware	4,000	40.0	20,000
Software	3,000	30.0	15,000
Repairs	2,000	20.0	10,000
Totals	10,000	100.0%	$50,000

Advertising	Sales Dollars	Percent of Total	Allocated Cost
Hardware	$ 960,000	40.0%	$ 50,000
Software	600,000	25.0	31,250
Repairs	840,000	35.0	43,750
Totals	$2,400,000	100.0%	$125,000

Insurance	Assets Insured	Percent of Total	Allocated Cost
General office	$ 60,000	10.0%	$ 3,000
Purchasing	72,000	12.0	3,600
Hardware	330,000	55.0	16,500
Software	42,000	7.0	2,100
Repairs	96,000	16.0	4,800
Totals	$600,000	100.0%	$30,000

1. Allocations of service department expenses to the three operating departments:

General Office Allocations to	Employees	Percent of Total	Allocated Cost
Hardware	5	25.0%	$23,500
Software	5	25.0	23,500
Repairs	10	50.0	47,000
Totals	20	100.0%	$94,000

Purchasing Allocations to	Cost of Goods Sold	Percent of Total	Allocated Cost
Hardware	$ 500,000	50.0%	$37,900
Software	300,000	30.0	22,740
Repairs	200,000	20.0	15,160
Totals	$1,000,000	100.0%	$75,800

HACKER'S HAVEN
Departmental Expense Allocations
For Year Ended December 31, 2002

	Allocation Base	Expense Account Balance	General Office Dept.	Purchasing Dept.	Hardware Dept.	Software Dept.	Repairs Dept.
Direct Expenses							
Payroll		$ 535,000	$60,000	$45,000	$ 80,000	$ 25,000	$325,000
Depreciation		60,000	6,000	7,200	33,000	4,200	9,600
Supplies		62,000	15,000	10,000	10,000	2,000	25,000
Indirect Expenses							
Rent	Square ft.	150,000	7,500	7,500	60,000	45,000	30,000
Utilities	Square ft.	50,000	2,500	2,500	20,000	15,000	10,000
Advertising	Sales	125,000	—	—	50,000	31,250	43,750
Insurance	Assets	30,000	3,000	3,600	16,500	2,100	4,800
Total expenses		$1,012,000	$94,000	$75,800	$269,500	$124,550	$448,150
Service Department Expenses							
General office	Employees		$94,000		23,500	23,500	47,000
Purchasing	Goods sold			$75,800	37,900	22,740	15,160
Total expenses allocated to operating departments		$1,012,000			$330,900	$170,790	$510,310

2. Departmental income statements for Hacker's Haven:

HACKER'S HAVEN
Departmental Income Statements
For Year Ended December 31, 2002

	Hardware	Software	Repairs	Combined
Sales	$960,000	$600,000	$840,000	$2,400,000
Cost of goods sold	500,000	300,000	200,000	1,000,000
Gross profit	$460,000	$300,000	$640,000	$1,400,000
Expenses				
Payroll	80,000	25,000	325,000	430,000
Depreciation	33,000	4,200	9,600	46,800
Supplies	10,000	2,000	25,000	37,000
Rent	60,000	45,000	30,000	135,000
Utilities	20,000	15,000	10,000	45,000
Advertising	50,000	31,250	43,750	125,000
Insurance	16,500	2,100	4,800	23,400
Share of general office	23,500	23,500	47,000	94,000
Share of purchasing	37,900	22,740	15,160	75,800
Total expenses	$330,900	$170,790	$510,310	$1,012,000
Net income	**$129,100**	**$129,210**	**$129,690**	**$ 388,000**

Summary

C1 **Explain departmentalization and the role of departmental accounting.** Companies are divided into departments when they are too large to be effectively managed as a single unit. Operating departments carry out the main functions of an organization. Service departments support the activities of operating departments. Departmental accounting systems provide information for evaluating departmental performance.

C2 **Distinguish between direct and indirect expenses.** Direct expenses are traced to a specific department and are incurred for the sole benefit of that department. Indirect expenses benefit more than one department. Indirect expenses are allocated to departments when computing departmental net income.

C3 **Identify bases for allocating indirect expenses to departments.** Ideally, we allocate indirect expenses by using a cause-effect relation for the allocation base. When a cause-effect relation is not identifiable, each indirect expense is allocated on a basis reflecting the relative benefit received by each department.

C4 **Explain controllable costs and responsibility accounting.** A controllable cost is one that is influenced by a specific level of management. The total expenses of operating a department often include some items a department manager does not control. Responsibility accounting systems provide information for evaluating the performance of department managers. Performance reports from a responsibility accounting system for evaluating department managers should include only the expenses (and revenues) that each manager controls.

C5 **Describe allocation of joint costs across products.** A joint cost refers to costs incurred to produce or purchase two or more products at the same time. When income statements are prepared, joint costs are usually allocated to the resulting joint products using either a physical or value basis.

A1 **Analyze investment centers using return on total assets.** A measure often used to evaluate an investment center manager is the *investment center return on total assets,* also called return on investment. This measure is computed as the center's net income divided by the center's average total assets.

P1 **Assign overhead costs using two-stage cost allocation.** In the traditional two-stage cost allocation procedure, service department costs are first assigned to operating departments. Then, in the second stage, a predetermined overhead allocation rate is computed for each operating department and is used to assign overhead to output.

P2 **Assign overhead costs using activity-based costing.** In activity-based costing, the costs of related activities are collected and then pooled in some logical manner into activity cost pools. After all activity costs have been accumulated in an activity cost pool account, users of the activity, termed *cost objects,* are assigned a portion of the total activity cost using a cost driver (allocation base).

P3 **Prepare departmental income statements.** Each profit center (department) is assigned its expenses to yield its own income statement. These costs include its direct expenses and its share of indirect expenses. The departmental income statement lists its revenues and costs of goods sold to determine gross profit. Its operating expenses (direct expenses and its indirect expenses allocated to the department) are deducted from gross profit to yield departmental net income.

P4 **Prepare departmental contribution reports.** The departmental contribution report is similar to the departmental income statement in terms of computing the gross profit for each department. Then the direct operating expenses for each department are deducted from gross profit to determine the contribution generated by each department. Indirect operating expenses are deducted *in total* from the combined contribution of the company.

Guidance Answers to You Make the Call

Director of Operations   You should collect details on overhead items and review them to see whether direct labor does indeed drive these costs. If it does not, overhead might be improperly assigned to departments. The situation also provides an opportunity to consider other overhead allocation bases, including the use of activity-based costing.

Accounting Officer   You should not author a report that you disagree with. You are responsible for ascertaining all the facts of ABC (implementation procedures, advantages and disadvantages, and costs). You should then approach your supervisor with these facts and suggest that you would like to modify the report to request, for example, a pilot implementation. The pilot test will allow you to further assess the suitability of ABC. Your suggestion might be rejected, at which time you may wish to speak with a more senior-level manager.

Center Manager   We must first realize that the two investment opportunities are not comparable on the basis of absolute dollars of income or on assets. For instance, the second investment provides a higher income in absolute dollars but requires a higher investment. Accordingly, we need to compute return on total assets for each alternative: (1) $50,000 \div $250,000 = 20\%$, and (2) $175,000 \div $1 million = 17.5\%$. Alternative 1 has the higher return and is preferred over alternative 2. Do you pursue one, both, or neither? Given that alternative 1's return is higher than the center's usual return of 19%, it should be pursued, assuming its risks are acceptable. Also, since alternative 1 requires a small investment, top management is likely to be more agreeable to pursuing it. Alternative 2's return is lower than the usual 19% and is not likely to be acceptable.

Guidance Answers to **Quick Checks**

1. Cost drivers are the factors that have a cause-effect relation with costs (or activities that pertain to costs).

2. (d)

3. A departmental accounting system provides information used to evaluate the performance of *departments*. A responsibility accounting system provides information used to evaluate the performance of *department managers*.

4. (d)

5. A cost center, such as a service department, incurs costs without directly generating revenues. A profit center, such as a product division, incurs costs but also generates revenues.

6. (b)

7. (d)

8. 1) Assign the direct expenses to each department. 2) Allocate indirect expenses to all departments. 3) Allocate the service department expenses to the operating departments.

9. (b)

10. No, because many expenses that enter into these calculations are beyond the manager's control, and managers should not be evaluated using costs they do not control.

11. (c)

12. (b) $180,000 \times ([32,000 \times \$9]/[96,000 \times \$3 + 64,000 \times \$6 + 32,000 \times \$9]) = \underline{\underline{\$54,000}}$.

Glossary

Activity-based costing (ABC) cost allocation method that focuses on activities performed; costs are traced to activities and then assigned to cost objects. (p. 910).

Activity cost pool temporary account that accumulates costs a company incurs to support an activity. (p. 911).

Controllable costs costs that a manager has the power to control or at least strongly influence. (p. 922).

Cost center department that incurs costs (but generates no revenues), such as the accounting or legal department. (p. 914).

Cost driver variable that causes an activity's cost to go up or down; a causal factor. (p. 911).

Departmental accounting system accounting system that provides information

useful in evaluating the profitability or cost effectiveness of a department. (p. 913).

Departmental contribution to overhead amount by which a department's revenues exceed its direct expenses. (p. 920).

Direct expenses expenses traced to a specific department that are incurred for the sole benefit of that department. (p. 915).

Indirect expenses expenses incurred for the joint benefit of more than one department. (p. 915).

Investment center center in which a manager is responsible for revenues, costs, and asset investments. (p. 926).

Investment center return on total assets center net income divided by average total assets for the center. (p. 926).

Joint cost cost incurred to produce or pur-

chase two or more products at the same time. (p. 924).

Profit center business unit that incurs costs and generates revenues. (p. 914).

Responsibility accounting budget report of expected costs and expenses under a manager's control. (p. 922).

Responsibility accounting performance report responsibility report that compares actual costs and expenses for a department with budgeted amounts. (p. 922).

Responsibility accounting system system that provides information that management can use to evaluate the performance of a department's manager. (p. 913).

Uncontrollable costs costs that a manager does not have the power to determine or strongly influence. (p. 922).

Questions

1. Why are many companies divided into departments?

2. Complete the following for a traditional two-stage allocation system: In the first stage, service department costs are assigned to _____ departments. In the second stage, a predetermined overhead allocation rate is computed for each operating department and used to assign overhead to _____.

3. What is the difference between operating departments and service departments?

4. What is activity-based costing?

5. Identify at least four common cost pools for activity-based costing in most organizations.

6. In activity-based costing, costs in a cost pool are allocated to _____ using predetermined overhead rates.

7. What company circumstances especially encourage use of activity-based costing?

8. What are two main goals in managerial accounting for departments?

9. Is it possible to evaluate a cost center's profitability? Explain.

10. What is the difference between direct and indirect expenses?

11. Suggest a reasonable basis for allocating each of the following indirect expenses to departments: (a) salary of a supervisor who manages several departments, (b) rent, (c) heat, (d) electricity for lighting, (e) janitorial services, (f) advertising, (g) expired insurance on equipment, and (h) property taxes on equipment.

12. How is a department's contribution to overhead measured?

13. What are controllable costs?

14. Controllable and uncontrollable costs must be identified with a particular _____ and a definite _____ period.

15. Why should managers be closely involved in preparing their responsibility accounting budgets?

16. In responsibility accounting, who receives timely cost reports and specific cost information? Explain.

17. What is a joint cost? How are joint costs usually allocated among the products produced from them?

18. Give two examples of products with joint costs.

19. **Nike** receives orders for merchandise from different types of stores, such as sporting goods super stores and specialty running shoe stores. Why is it useful to (a) collect information for each particular store category and (b) treat each category as a profit center?

20. **Reebok** delivers its products to locations around the world. List three controllable and three uncontrollable costs for Reebok's delivery department.

In each blank next to the following terms, place the identifying letter of its best description.

1. _____ Cost center
2. _____ Investment center
3. _____ Departmental accounting system
4. _____ Operating department
5. _____ Profit center
6. _____ Responsibility accounting system
7. _____ Service department

A. Incurs costs without directly yielding revenues.
B. Provides information used to evaluate the performance of a department manager.
C. Holds manager responsible for revenues, costs, and investments.
D. Engages directly in manufacturing or in making sales directly to customers.
E. Does not directly manufacture products but contributes to profitability of the entire company.
F. Incurs costs and also generates revenues.
G. Provides information used to evaluate the performance of a department.

QUICK STUDY

QS 22-1

Allocation and measurement terms

For each of the following types of indirect expenses and service department expenses, identify one possible allocation basis that could be used to distribute it to the departments indicated:

1. Computer services expenses for scheduling of factory production to factory departments.
2. Electric utility expenses to all departments.
3. Maintenance department expenses to the operating departments.
4. General office department expenses to the operating departments.

QS 22-2

Basis for cost allocation

C3

The following is taken from Fost Co.'s internal records of its factory with two operating departments:

	Direct Labor	Hours of Machine Use
Operating Department 1	$ 9,400	1,200
Operating Department 2	6,600	2,000
Totals	$16,000	3,200
Factory overhead		
Rent and utilities	$ 6,100	
Indirect labor	2,700	
General office expense	1,700	
Depreciation—Equipment	1,500	
Supplies	900	
Total factory overhead	$12,900	

QS 22-3

Activity-based costing and overhead allocation

P2

The cost driver for indirect labor and supplies is direct labor costs, and the cost driver for the remaining overhead items is number of hours of machine use. Compute the total amount of overhead cost allocated to Operating Department 1 using activity-based costing.

QS 22-4

Joint cost allocation

A company purchases a 10,020 square foot commercial building for $325,000 and spends an additional $50,000 to divide the space into two separate rental units and get it ready to rent. Unit A, which has the desirable location on the corner and contains 3,340 square feet, will be rented for $1.00 per square foot. Unit B contains 6,680 square feet and will be rented for $0.75 per square foot. How much of the joint cost should be assigned to Unit B using the value basis of allocation?

QS 22-5

Departmental contribution to overhead

Use the information in the following table to compute each department's contribution to overhead (both in dollars and as a percent). Which department contributes the highest dollar amount to total overhead? Which contributes the highest percent?

	Dept. A	Dept. B	Dept. C
Sales	$53,000	$180,000	$84,000
Cost of goods sold	34,185	103,700	49,560
Gross profit	$18,815	$ 76,300	$34,440
Total direct expenses	3,660	37,060	7,386
Contribution to overhead	$	$	$
Contribution percent	%	%	%

QS 22-6

Investment center analysis

Compute return on assets for each of these Reebok shoe divisions (each is an investment center). Comment on the relative performance of each investment center.

Division	Net Income	Average Assets	Return on Assets
Basketball	$4,500,000	$20,000,000	_____
Soccer	1,500,000	12,500,000	_____
Cross-trainer	800,000	10,000,000	_____

EXERCISES

Exercise 22-1

Departmental expense allocations

Comvia Co. has four departments: materials, personnel, manufacturing, and packaging. In a recent month, the four departments incurred three shared indirect expenses. The amounts of these indirect expenses and the bases used to allocate them follow:

Indirect Expense	Cost	Allocation Base
Supervision	$ 82,500	Number of employees
Utilities	50,000	Square feet occupied
Insurance	22,500	Value of assets in use
Total	$155,000	

Departmental data for the company's recent reporting period follow:

Department	Employees	Square Feet	Asset Values
Materials	27	25,000	$ 6,000
Personnel	9	5,000	1,200
Manufacturing	63	55,000	37,800
Packaging	51	15,000	15,000
Total	150	100,000	$60,000

Use this information to allocate each of the three indirect expenses across the four departments. Then prepare a summary table that reports total indirect expenses assigned to the four departments.

Clear-as-Glass Company manufactures two types of glass shelving, rounded edge and squared edge, on the same production line. For the current period, the company reports the following data:

Exercise 22-2
Activity-based costing of overhead

	Rounded Edge	Squared Edge	Total
Direct materials	$ 9,500	$21,600	$ 31,100
Direct labor	6,100	11,900	18,000
Overhead (300% of direct labor cost)	18,300	35,700	54,000
Total cost	$33,900	$69,200	$103,100
Quantity produced	10,500 ft.	14,100 ft.	
Average cost per ft.	$ 3.23	$ 4.91	

The controller of Clear-as-Glass Company wishes to apply activity-based costing (ABC) to the $54,000 of overhead costs incurred by the two product lines to see whether cost per foot would change significantly from that recorded above. She has collected the following information:

Overhead Cost Category (Activity Cost Pool)	Cost
Supervision	$ 2,700
Depreciation of machinery........................	28,300
Assembly line preparation........................	23,000
Total overhead	$54,000

She has also collected the following information about the cost drivers for each category (cost pool) and the amount of each driver used by the two product lines:

		Usage		
Category (Cost Pool)	Driver	Rounded Edge	Squared Edge	Total
Supervision	Direct labor cost($)	$8,100	$9,900	$18,000
Depreciation of machinery .	Machine hours	250 hours	750 hours	1,000 hours
Assembly line preparation .	Setups (number)	20 times	105 times	125 times

Use this information to (1) assign these three overhead cost pools to each of the two products using ABC, (2) determine average cost per foot for each of the two products using ABC, and (3) compare the average cost per foot under ABC with the average cost per foot under the current method for each product. Explain why a difference between the two cost allocation methods exists.

Check   (2) Rounded edge, $2.63; Squared edge, $5.36

Auto Accessories, Inc., pays $130,000 rent each year for its two-story building. The space in this building is occupied by five departments as specified here:

Exercise 22-3
Rent expense allocated to departments

P1 C3

Paint department	1,440 square feet of first-floor space
Engine department	3,360 square feet of first-floor space
Window department	2,016 square feet of second-floor space
Electrical department	960 square feet of second-floor space
Accessory department	1,824 square feet of second-floor space

The company allocates 65% of total rent expense to the first floor and 35% to the second floor and then allocates rent expense for each floor to the departments occupying that floor on the basis of space occupied. Determine the rent expense to be allocated to each department. (Round percents to the nearest one-tenth and dollar amounts to the nearest whole dollar.)

Check   Paint dept., $25,350

Exercise 22-4

Departmental expense allocation spreadsheet

Continuous Cycle Shop has two service departments (advertising and administration) and two operating departments (cycles and clothing). During 2002, the departments had the following direct expenses and occupied the following amount of floor space:

Department	Direct Expenses	Square Feet
Advertising	$ 18,000	1,120
Administrative	25,000	1,400
Cycles	103,000	7,140
Clothing	15,000	4,340

The advertising department developed and distributed 120 advertisements during the year. Of these, 90 promoted cycles and 30 promoted clothing. The store sold $350,000 of merchandise during the year. Of this amount, $273,000 is from the cycles department, and $77,000 is from the clothing department. The utilities expense of $64,000 is an indirect expense to all departments. Prepare a departmental expense allocation spreadsheet for the Continuous Cycle Shop. The spreadsheet should assign (a) direct expenses to each of the four departments, (b) the $64,000 of utilities expense to the four departments on the basis of floor space occupied, (c) the advertising department's expenses to the operating departments on the basis of the number of ads placed that promoted a department's products, and (d) the administrative department's expenses to the operating departments based on the amount of sales. Provide supporting computations for the expense allocations.

Check Total expenses allocated to Cycles, $177,472

Exercise 22-5

Service department expenses allocated to operating departments

The following is a partially completed lower section of a departmental expense allocation spreadsheet for Bookworm Bookstore. It reports the total amounts of direct and indirect expenses allocated to the five departments:

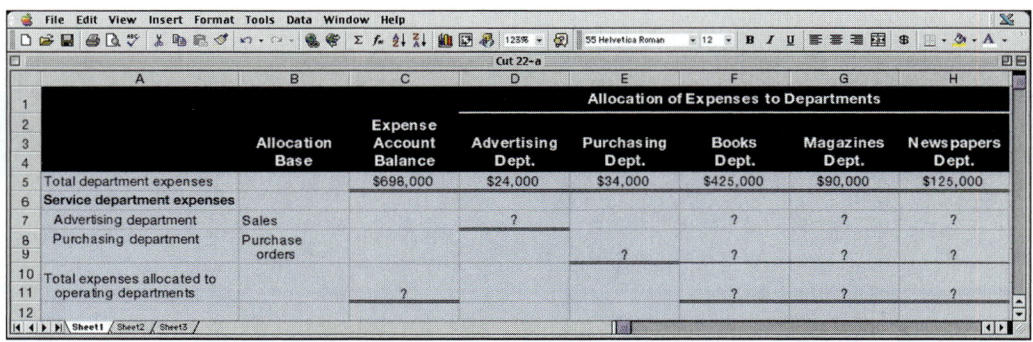

Check Total expenses allocated to Books, $452,820

Complete the spreadsheet by allocating the expenses of the two service departments (advertising and purchasing) to the three operating departments. Information about the allocation bases for the three operating departments follows:

Department	Sales	Purchase Orders
Books	$495,000	516
Magazines	198,000	360
Newspapers . . .	207,000	324
Total	$900,000	1,200

Exercise 22-6

Indirect payroll expense allocated to departments

Jenna Nagy works in both the jewelry department and the hosiery department of a retail store. Nagy assists customers in both departments and arranges and stocks merchandise in both departments. The store allocates Nagy's $30,000 annual wages between the two departments based on a sample of the time worked in the two departments. The sample is obtained from a diary of hours worked that Nagy kept in a randomly chosen two-week period. The diary showed the following hours and activities spent in the two departments:

Selling in jewelry department	51 hours
Arranging and stocking merchandise in jewelry department	6 hours
Selling in hosiery department	12 hours
Arranging and stocking merchandise in hosiery department	7 hours
Idle time spent waiting for a customer to enter one of the selling departments	4 hours

Allocate Nagy's annual wages between the two departments.

Skipper's Seafood Company purchases lobsters and processes them into tails and flakes. It then sells the lobster tails for $21 per pound and the flakes for $14 per pound. On average, 100 pounds of lobster are processed into 52 pounds of tails and 22 pounds of flakes, with 26 pounds of waste. Assume that Skipper's purchased 2,400 pounds of lobster for $4.50 per pound. The lobsters are then processed with an additional labor cost of $1,800. No materials or labor costs are assigned to the waste. If 1,096 pounds of tails and 324 pounds of flakes are sold, what is the allocated cost of the sold items and the allocated cost of the ending inventory? Skipper allocates joint costs on a value basis. (Round the dollar cost per pound to the nearest thousandth.)

Exercise 22-7
Joint product costs assigned

Check   Inventory cost, $2,268

Cathy Long manages the auto service department of an auto dealership. The recent month's income statement for her department follows:

Exercise 22-8
Managerial performance evaluation

Revenues		
Sales of parts	$ 72,000	
Sales of services	105,000	$177,000
Costs and expenses		
Cost of parts sold	30,000	
Building depreciation	9,300	
Income taxes allocated to department	8,700	
Interest on long-term debt	7,500	
Manager's salary	12,000	
Payroll taxes	8,100	
Supplies	15,900	
Utilities	4,400	
Wages (hourly)	16,000	
Total costs and expenses		111,900
Departmental net income		$ 65,100

Analyze the items on the income statement and identify those that definitely should be included on a performance report used to evaluate Cathy's performance. List them and explain why you chose them. Then list and explain the items that should definitely be excluded. Finally, list the items that are not definitely included or excluded and explain why they fall into that category.

HomeFront Properties is developing a subdivision that includes 600 home lots. The 450 lots in the Canyon section are below a ridge and do not have views of the neighboring canyons and hills; the 150 lots in the Hilltop section offer unobstructed views. The expected selling price for each Canyon lot is $55,000 and for each Hilltop lot is $110,000. The developer acquired the land for $4,000,000 and spent another $3,500,000 on street and utilities improvements. Assign the joint land and improvement costs to the lots using the value basis of allocation and determine the average cost per lot.

Exercise 22-9
Joint real estate costs assigned

You must prepare a return on investment analysis for the regional manager of Fast Burgers. This growing chain is trying to decide which outlet among two alternatives to open. The first location (A) requires a $1,000,000 investment and is expected to yield annual net income of $160,000. The second location (B) requires a $600,000 investment and is expected to yield annual net income of $108,000. Compute the return on investment for each Fast Burgers alternative and then make your recommendation in a one-half page memorandum to the regional manager.

Exercise 22-10
Investment center analysis

PROBLEM SET A

Problem 22-1A
Allocation of building
occupancy costs to
departments

Appliance City Co. has several departments that occupy both floors of a two-story building. The departmental accounting system has a single account, Building Occupancy Cost, in the ledger. The types and amounts of occupancy costs recorded in this account for the current period follow:

Depreciation—Building	$18,000
Interest—Building mortgage	27,000
Taxes—Building and land	9,000
Gas (heating) expense	3,000
Lighting expense	3,000
Maintenance expense	6,000
Total	$66,000

The building has 4,000 square feet on each floor. In prior periods, the accounting manager merely divided the $66,000 occupancy cost by 8,000 square feet to find an average cost of $8.25 per square foot and then charged each department a building occupancy cost equal to this rate times the number of square feet that it occupied.

Juan Diaz manages a first-floor department that occupies 1,000 square feet, and Perry Leonard manages a second-floor department that occupies 1,800 square feet of floor space. In discussing the departmental reports, they question whether using the same rate per square foot for all departments makes sense because the first-floor space is more valuable. The two managers also check a recent real estate study of average local rental costs for similar space that shows that first-floor space is worth $30 per square foot and second-floor space is worth $20 per square foot (these rental values exclude costs for heating, lighting, and maintenance).

Required

Preparation Component

1. Allocate all occupancy costs to the Diaz and Leonard departments using the current allocation method.

Check (2) Total occupancy cost to
Diaz, $9,600

2. Allocate the depreciation, interest, and taxes occupancy costs to the Diaz and Leonard departments in proportion to the relative market values of the floor space. Allocate the heating, lighting, and maintenance costs to the Diaz and Leonard departments in proportion to the square feet occupied (ignoring floor space market values).

Analysis Component

3. Which allocation method would you prefer if you were a manager of a second-floor department? Explain.

Problem 22-2A
Activity-based costing

Patient Care is an outpatient surgical center that was profitable for many years, but Medicare recently cut its reimbursements by as much as 50%. As a result, the center wants to better understand its costs. It decides to prepare an activity-based cost analysis, including an estimate of the average cost of both general surgery and orthopedic surgery. The company's three cost centers and their cost drivers follow:

Cost Center	Cost	Cost Driver	Driver Quantity
Professional salaries	$2,000,000	Professional hours	10,000
Patient services and supplies..	37,500	Number of patients	500
Building cost	300,000	Square feet	2,000

The two main surgical units and their related data follow:

Service	Hours	Square Feet*	Patients
General surgery	2,500	720	400
Orthopedic surgery	7,500	1,280	100

* Orthopedic surgery requires more space for patients, supplies, and equipment.

Required

Preparation Component

1. Compute the cost per cost driver for each of the three cost centers.

2. Use the results from part *1* to allocate costs from each of the three cost centers to both the general surgery and the orthopedic surgery units. Compute total cost and average cost per patient for both the general surgery and the orthopedic surgery units.

Check Average cost of general (orthopedic) surgery, $1,595 ($16,995) per patient

Analysis Component

3. Without providing computations, would the average cost of general surgery be higher or lower if all center costs were allocated based on the number of patients? Explain.

Bogart Co. began operations in January 2002 with two operating (selling) departments and one service (office) department. Its departmental income statements follow:

Problem 22-3A
Departmental income statements; forecasts

BOGART Co. Departmental Income Statements For Year Ended December 31, 2002			
	Clock	**Mirror**	**Combined**
Sales	$130,000	$55,000	$185,000
Cost of goods sold	63,700	34,100	97,800
Gross profit	$ 66,300	$20,900	$ 87,200
Direct expenses			
Sales salaries	20,000	7,000	27,000
Advertising	1,200	500	1,700
Store supplies used	900	400	1,300
Depreciation—Equipment	1,500	300	1,800
Total direct expenses	$ 23,600	$ 8,200	$ 31,800
Allocated expenses			
Rent expense	7,020	3,780	10,800
Utilities expense	2,600	1,400	4,000
Share of office department expenses	10,500	4,500	15,000
Total allocated expenses	$ 20,120	$ 9,680	$ 29,800
Total expenses	$ 43,720	$17,880	61,600
Net income	$ 22,580	$ 3,020	$ 25,600

Bogart plans to open a third department in January 2003 that will sell paintings. Management predicts that the new department will generate $50,000 in sales with a 55% gross profit margin and will require the following direct expenses: sales salaries, $8,000; advertising, $800; store supplies, $500; and equipment depreciation, $200. The company currently rents space in a building. It will fit the new department into the current space by taking some square footage from the other two departments. When the new painting department is opened, it will fill one-fifth of the space presently used by the clock department and one-fourth used by the mirror department. Management does not predict any increase in utilities costs, which are allocated to the departments in proportion to occupied space (or rent expense). The company allocates office department expenses to the operating departments in proportion to their sales. It expects the painting department to increase total office department expenses by $7,000. Since the painting department will bring new customers into the store, management expects sales in both the clock and mirror departments to increase by 8%. No changes for those departments' gross profit percents or their direct expenses are expected, except for store supplies used, which will increase in proportion to sales.

Required

Prepare departmental income statements that show the company's predicted results of operations for calendar year 2003 for the three operating (selling) departments and their combined totals. (Round percents to the nearest one-tenth and dollar amounts to the nearest whole dollar.)

Check 2003 forecasted combined net income (sales), $43,472 ($249,800)

Problem 22-4A

Responsibility accounting
performance reports;
controllable and budgeted
costs

Sally Kelley, the plant manager of Travel Trailer's Indiana plant, is responsible for all of that plant's costs other than her own salary. The plant has two operating departments and one service department. The camper and trailer operating departments manufacture different products and have their own managers. The office department, which Kelley also manages, provides services equally to the two operating departments. A budget is prepared for each operating department and the office department. The company's responsibility accounting system must assemble information to present budgeted and actual costs in performance reports for each operating department manager and the plant manager. Each performance report includes only those costs that a particular operating department manager can control: raw materials, wages, supplies used, and equipment depreciation. The plant manager is responsible for the department managers' salaries, utilities, building rent, office salaries other than her own, and other office costs plus all costs controlled by the two operating department managers. The annual departmental budgets and actual costs for the two operating departments follow:

	Budget			Actual		
	Campers	**Trailers**	**Combined**	**Campers**	**Trailers**	**Combined**
Raw materials	$195,000	$275,000	$ 470,000	$194,200	$273,200	$ 467,400
Employee wages	104,000	205,000	309,000	106,600	206,400	313,000
Dept. manager salary	43,000	52,000	95,000	44,000	53,500	97,500
Supplies used	33,000	90,000	123,000	31,700	91,600	123,300
Depreciation—Equip.	60,000	125,000	185,000	60,000	125,000	185,000
Utilities	3,600	5,400	9,000	3,300	5,000	8,300
Building rent	5,700	9,300	15,000	5,300	8,700	14,000
Office department costs . .	68,750	68,750	137,500	67,550	67,550	135,100
Totals	$513,050	$830,450	$1,343,500	$512,650	$830,950	$1,343,600

The office department's annual budget and its actual costs follow:

	Budget	Actual
Plant manager salary	$ 80,000	$ 82,000
Other office salaries	32,500	30,100
Other office costs	25,000	23,000
Totals	$137,500	$135,100

Required

Preparation Component

1. Prepare responsibility accounting performance reports like those in Exhibit 22.20 that list costs controlled by the following:

   a. Manager of the camper department.

   b. Manager of the trailer department.

   c. Manager of the Indiana plant.

In each report, include the budgeted and actual costs and show the amount that each actual cost is over or under the budgeted amount.

Analysis Component

2. Did the plant manager or the operating department managers better manage costs? Explain.

Check   (c) Indiana plant
controllable costs, $1,900 under
budget

SunRipe Orchards produced a good crop of peaches this year. After preparing its following income statement, SunRipe believes it should have given its No. 3 peaches to charity and saved its efforts.

Problem 22-5A
Allocation of joint costs

SUNRIPE ORCHARDS Income Statement For Year Ended December 31, 2002				
	No. 1	No. 2	No. 3	Combined
Sales (by grade)				
No. 1: 300,000 lbs. @ $1.50/lb	$450,000			
No. 2: 300,000 lbs. @ $1.00/lb		$300,000		
No. 3: 750,000 lbs. @ $0.25/lb			$ 187,500	
Total sales				$937,500
Costs				
Tree pruning and care @ $0.30/lb	90,000	90,000	225,000	405,000
Picking, sorting, and grading @ $0.15/lb	45,000	45,000	112,500	202,500
Delivery costs @ $0.05/lb	15,000	15,000	37,500	67,500
Total costs	$150,000	$150,000	$ 375,000	$675,000
Net income (loss)	$300,000	$150,000	$(187,500)	$262,500

In preparing this statement, SunRipe allocated joint costs among the grades on a physical basis as an equal amount per pound. Also, its records on delivery costs show that $30,000 of the $67,500 relates to crating the No. 1 and No. 2 peaches and hauling them to the buyer. The remaining $37,500 of delivery costs is for crating the No. 3 peaches and hauling them to the cannery where they are used to make preserves.

Required

Preparation Component

1. Prepare reports showing cost allocations on a sales value basis to the three grades of peaches. Separate the delivery costs into the amounts directly identifiable with each grade. Then allocate any shared delivery costs on the basis of the relative sales value of each grade. (Round percents to the nearest one-tenth and dollar amounts to the nearest whole dollar.)

2. Using your answers to part (1), prepare an income statement using the joint costs allocated on a sales value basis.

Check   (2) Net income from No. 1
(No. 2) peaches, $140,400 ($93,600)

Analysis Component

3. Do you think delivery costs fit the definition of a joint cost? Explain.

DePere's has several departments that occupy all floors of a two-story building that includes a basement floor. DePere rented this building under a long-term lease negotiated when rental rates were lower. The departmental accounting system has a single account, Building Occupancy Cost, in the ledger. The types and amounts of occupancy costs recorded in this account for the current period follow:

PROBLEM SET B
Problem 22-1B
Allocation of building
occupancy costs to
departments

Building rent	$400,000
Lighting expense	25,000
Cleaning expense	40,000
Total	$465,000

The building has 7,500 square feet on each of the upper two floors but only 5,000 square feet in the basement. In prior periods, the accounting manager merely divided the $465,000 occupancy cost by 20,000 square feet to find an average cost of $23.25 per square foot and then charged each department a building occupancy cost equal to this rate times the number of square feet that it occupies.

Mel Dawson manages a department that occupies 2,000 square feet of floor space in the basement. In discussing the departmental reports with other managers, he questions whether using the same rate per square foot for all departments makes sense because different floor space has different values. Dawson checked a recent real estate report of average local rental costs for similar space that shows that first-floor space is worth $40 per square foot, second-floor space is worth $20 per square foot, and basement space is worth $10 per square foot (these rental values exclude costs for lighting and cleaning).

Required

Preparation Component

1. Allocate all occupancy costs to Dawson's department using the current allocation method.

Check (2) Total costs allocated to Dawson, $22,500

2. Allocate the building rent occupancy cost to Dawson's department in proportion to the relative market value of the floor space. Allocate the lighting and heating costs to Dawson's department in proportion to the square feet occupied (ignoring floor space market values).

Analysis Component

3. Which allocation method would you prefer if you were a manager of a basement department?

Problem 22-2B

Activity-based costing

Greenscape Landscaping has enjoyed profits for many years, but new competition has cut service revenue by as much as 30%. As a result, the company wants to better understand its costs. It decides to prepare an activity-based cost analysis, including an estimate of the average cost of both general landscaping services and custom design landscaping services. The company's three cost centers and their cost drivers follow:

Cost Center	Cost	Cost Driver	Driver Quantity
Professional salaries	$600,000	Professional hours	10,000
Customer supplies	150,000	Number of customers	800
Building cost	240,000	Square feet	2,500

The two main landscaping units and their related data follow:

Service	Hours	Square Feet*	Customers
General landscaping	2,500	1,000	600
Custom design landscaping	7,500	1,500	200

* Custom design landscaping requires more space for equipment, supplies, and planning.

Required

Preparation Component

1. Compute the cost per cost driver for each of the three cost centers.

Check Average cost of general (custom) landscaping, $597.5 ($3,157.5) per customer

2. Use the results from part *1* to allocate costs from each of the three cost centers to both the general landscaping and the custom design landscaping units. Compute total cost and average cost per customer for both the general landscaping and the custom design landscaping units.

Analysis Component

3. Without providing computations, would the average cost of general landscaping be higher or lower if all center costs were allocated based on the number of customers? Explain.

Electronic Entertainment began operations in January 2002 with two operating (selling) departments and one service (office) department. Its departmental income statements follow:

Problem 22-3B
Departmental income
statements; forecasts

P3

ELECTRONIC ENTERTAINMENT **Departmental Income Statements** **For Year Ended December 31, 2002**	Movies	Video Games	Combined
Sales	$600,000	$200,000	$800,000
Cost of goods sold	420,000	154,000	574,000
Gross profit	$180,000	$ 46,000	$226,000
Direct expenses			
Sales salaries	37,000	15,000	52,000
Advertising	12,500	6,000	18,500
Store supplies used	4,000	1,000	5,000
Depreciation—Equipment	4,500	3,000	7,500
Total direct expenses	$ 58,000	$ 25,000	$ 83,000
Allocated expenses			
Rent expense	41,000	9,000	50,000
Utilities expense	7,380	1,620	9,000
Share of office department expenses	56,250	18,750	75,000
Total allocated expenses	$104,630	$ 29,370	$134,000
Total expenses	$162,630	$ 54,370	$217,000
Net income (loss)	$ 17,370	$ (8,370)	$ 9,000

Electronic Entertainment plans to open a third department in January 2003 that will sell compact discs. Management predicts that the new department will generate $300,000 in sales with a 35% gross profit margin and will require the following direct expenses: sales salaries, $18,000; advertising, $10,000; store supplies, $2,000; and equipment depreciation, $1,200. The company currently rents space in a building. It will fit the new department into the current space by taking some square footage from the other two departments. When the new compact disc department is opened, it will fill one-fourth of the space presently used by the movie department and one-third of the space used by the video game department. Management does not predict any increase in utilities costs, which are allocated to the departments in proportion to occupied space (or rent expense). The company allocates office department expenses to the operating departments in proportion to their sales. It expects the compact disc department to increase total office department expenses by $10,000. Since the compact disc department will bring new customers into the store, management expects sales in both the movie and video game departments to increase by 8%. No changes for those departments' gross profit percents or for their direct expenses are expected, except for store supplies used, which will increase in proportion to sales.

Required

Prepare departmental income statements that show the company's predicted results of operations for calendar year 2003 for the three operating (selling) departments and their combined totals. (Round percents to the nearest one-tenth and dollar amounts to the nearest whole dollar.)

Check   2003 forecasted movies
net income (sales), $52,450
($648,000)

Ann Polson, the plant manager of AMP Co.'s Chicago plant, is responsible for all of that plant's costs other than her own salary. The plant has two operating departments and one service department. The refrigerator and dishwasher operating departments manufacture different products and have their own managers. The office department, which Polson also manages, provides services equally to the two operating departments. A monthly budget is prepared for each operating department and the office department. The company's responsibility accounting system must assemble information to present budgeted and actual costs in performance reports for each operating department manager and the plant manager. Each performance report includes only those costs that a particular operating department manager can control: raw materials, wages, supplies used, and equipment depreciation. The plant manager is responsible for the department managers' salaries, utilities, building rent, office salaries other than her own, and other office costs plus all costs controlled by the two operating department managers. The April departmental budgets and actual costs for the two operating departments follow:

Problem 22-4B
Responsibility accounting
performance reports;
controllable and budgeted
costs

	Budget			Actual		
	Refrigerators	Dishwashers	Combined	Refrigerators	Dishwashers	Combined
Raw materials	$400,000	$200,000	$ 600,000	$385,000	$202,000	$ 587,000
Employee wages	170,000	80,000	250,000	174,700	81,500	256,200
Dept. manager salary	55,000	49,000	104,000	55,000	46,500	101,500
Supplies used	15,000	9,000	24,000	14,000	9,700	23,700
Depreciation—Equip.	53,000	37,000	90,000	53,000	37,000	90,000
Utilities	30,000	18,000	48,000	34,500	20,700	55,200
Building rent	63,000	17,000	80,000	65,800	16,500	82,300
Office department costs ..	70,500	70,500	141,000	75,000	75,000	150,000
Totals	$856,500	$480,500	$1,337,000	$857,000	$488,900	$1,345,900

The office department's budget and its actual costs for April follow:

	Budget	Actual
Plant manager salary	$ 80,000	$ 85,000
Other office salaries	40,000	35,200
Other office costs	21,000	29,800
Totals	$141,000	$150,000

Required

Preparation Component

1. Prepare responsibility accounting performance reports like those in Exhibit 22.20 that list costs controlled by the following:

    a. Manager of the refrigerator department.

    b. Manager of the dishwasher department.

    c. Manager of the Chicago plant.

Check (c) Chicago plant controllable costs, $3,900 over budget

In each report, include the budgeted and actual costs for the month and show the amount by which each actual cost is over or under the budgeted amount.

Analysis Component

2. Did the plant manager or the operating department managers better manage costs? Explain.

Problem 22-5B
Allocation of joint costs

Kathy and Ken Vine own and operate a tomato grove. After preparing the following income statement, Kathy believes they should have offered the No. 3 tomatoes to the public for free and saved themselves time and money.

KATHY AND KEN VINE
Income Statement
For Year Ended December 31, 2002

	No. 1	No. 2	No. 3	Combined
Sales (by grade)				
No. 1: 500,000 lbs. @ $1.80/lb	$900,000			
No. 2: 400,000 lbs. @ $1.25/lb		$500,000		
No. 3: 100,000 lbs. @ $0.40/lb			$ 40,000	
Total sales				$1,440,000
Costs				
Land preparation, seeding, and cultivating @ $0.70/lb ..	350,000	280,000	70,000	700,000
Harvesting, sorting, and grading @ $0.04/lb	20,000	16,000	4,000	40,000
Delivery costs @ $0.02/lb	10,000	8,000	2,000	20,000
Total costs	$380,000	$304,000	$ 76,000	$ 760,000
Net income (loss)	$520,000	$196,000	$(36,000)	$ 680,000

In preparing this statement, Kathy and Ken allocated joint costs among the grades on a physical basis as an equal amount per pound. Also, their records on delivery costs show that $17,000 of the $20,000 relates to crating the No. 1 and No. 2 tomatoes and hauling them to the buyer. The remaining $3,000 of delivery costs is for crating the No. 3 tomatoes and hauling them to the cannery where they are stewed and canned.

Required

Preparation Component

1. Prepare reports showing cost allocations on a sales value basis to the three grades of tomatoes. Separate the delivery costs into the amounts directly identifiable with each grade. Then allocate any shared delivery costs on the basis of the relative sales value of each grade. (Round percents to the nearest one-tenth and dollar amounts to the nearest whole dollar.)

2. Using your answers to part (1), prepare an income statement using the joint costs allocated on a sales value basis.

Check   (2) Net income from No. 1 (No. 2) tomatoes, $426,569 ($237,151)

Analysis Component

3. Do you think delivery costs fit the definition of a joint cost? Explain.

Beyond the Numbers

BTN 22-1   A careful review of **Nike**'s financial statements in Appendix A offers clues to its growth in global revenues. In particular, you should read Nike's *Financial History* section.

Required

1. Compute the growth (in percent) for Nike's revenues using 1998 as the base for 1999 and 1999 as the base for 2000. Do this for each of the four geographic areas listed in its note.

2. What geographic area in part (1) is growing the fastest for Nike?

3. How can Nike's managers use this information?

Swoosh Ahead

4. Access Nike's annual report for a fiscal year ending after May 31, 2000, from its Web site [www.nike.com] or the SEC's EDGAR database [www.sec.gov]. Compute its growth in revenues by geographic areas for the most recent reporting period(s). Compare results to those from part (1). What growth patterns, if any, do you observe?

Reporting in Action

NIKE

BTN 22-2   **Reebok** and **Nike** compete in several sporting goods markets. The most common competitive markets for these two companies are sports footwear and apparel.

Required

1. Design a three-tier responsibility accounting organizational chart assuming that you have available internal information for both companies. Use Exhibit 22.19 as an example. The goal of this assignment is to design a reporting framework for the companies; numbers are not required. Limit your reporting framework to sales activity only.

2. Explain why it is important to have similar performance reports when comparing performance within a company and across different companies. Be specific in your response.

Comparative Analysis

BTN 22-3   Creative Services (CS) offers a range of security services for senior citizens. Each type of service is considered within a separate department. Carl Stone, the overall manager, is compensated partly on the basis of departmental performance by staying within the quarterly cost budget. He often revises operations to make sure departments stay within budget. Says Carl, "I will not go over budget even if it means slightly compromising the level and quality of service. These are minor compromises that don't significantly affect my clients, at least in the short term."

Ethics Challenge

Required

1. Is there an ethical concern in this situation? If so, which parties are affected?
2. Can Carl Stone take action to eliminate or reduce any ethical concerns?
3. What is Creative Services ethical responsibility in offering professional services?

Communicating in Practice

C4 C5 P3

BTN 22-4 Home Improvements is a national home improvement chain with more than 100 stores throughout the country. The manager of each store receives a salary plus a bonus equal to a percent of the store's net income for the reporting period. The following net income calculation is on the Denver store manager's performance report for the recent monthly period:

Sales	$2,500,000
Cost of goods sold	800,000
Wages expense	500,000
Utilities expense	200,000
Home office expense	75,000
Net income	$ 925,000
Manager's bonus (0.5%)	$ 4,625

In previous periods, the bonus had also been 0.5%, but the performance report had not included any charges for the home office expense, which is now assigned to each store as a percent of its sales.

Required

Assume that you are the national office manager. Write a one-half page memorandum to your store managers explaining why home office expense is in the new performance report.

Taking It to the Net

A1

BTN 22-5 This chapter described and used spreadsheets to prepare various managerial reports (see Exhibit 22-12). You can download from Web sites' various tutorials showing how spreadsheets are used in managerial accounting and other business applications.

Required

1. Check out the Web site **www.lacher.com**. Open its table of contents (TOC). Select "Business Solutions" under "Tutorials" and identify three tutorials for review.
2. Describe in a one-half page memorandum to your instructor how the applications described in each tutorial are helpful in business and managerial decision making.

Teamwork in Action

C1 C2

BTN 22-6 Activity-based costing (ABC) is increasingly popular as a useful managerial tool to (1) measure the cost of resources consumed and (2) assign cost to products and services. This managerial tool has been available to accounting and business decision makers for more than 25 years.

Required

Break into teams and identify at least three likely reasons that activity-based costing has gained popularity in recent years. Be prepared to present your answers in a class discussion. (*Hint:* What changes have occurred in products and services over the past 25 years?)

Business Week Activity

C4

BTN 22-7 Assume that you manage the truck division of a Ford dealership in Seattle, Washington. The dealership's owner asks you to read "AUTO—Prognosis 1998" in the January 12, 1998, issue of *Business Week*, pp. 102–103, and make any necessary revisions to the dealership's 2002 budget prepared in late 2001 assuming that this prognosis is applicable to the current budget period.

Required

The following table lists the controllable items in the 2002 budget. Identify whether you plan to increase, decrease, or make no change in modifying this budget given the auto industry prognosis described in *Business Week*. Explain. Be prepared to present your answers in a class discussion.

Description	Amount	I = increase; D = decrease; NC = no change
Sales	$10,000,000	
Commissions	500,000	
Advertising	2,500,000	
Training	750,000	
Heat and lights	1,000,000	
Maintenance	500,000	
Projected income	$ 4,750,000	

BTN 22-8   Valerie Mason has just opened a small resort offering several recreational activities including skiing, exercising, and spa baths. Although the business is currently small, it is very popular. Mason knows that she must expand in the very near future to meet the growing demand. After reading several business management books and attending a few seminars, Mason has decided to create separate departments for each of the different recreational activities. However, she is not sure how to determine the costs associated with each department's activity, particularly because several costs are common across the entire business.

Entrepreneurial Decision

Required

1. As a consultant to Valerie Mason, how would you suggest she address the cost allocation issue?

2. What type of costing system would you implement to monitor the performance of the individual departments?

23

Cost-Volume-Profit Analysis

"I will not accept 'no' just because it's the standard"—Walter Latham.

A Look Back

Chapter 22 focused on cost allocation, activity-based costing, and performance measurement. We identified several managerial reports useful in measuring and analyzing the activities of a company, its departments, and its managers.

A Look at This Chapter

This chapter shows how information on both costs and sales behavior is useful to managers in performing cost-volume-profit analysis. This analysis is an important part of successful management and sound business decisions.

A Look Ahead

Chapter 24 introduces and describes the budgeting process and its importance to management. It also explains the master budget and its usefulness to the planning of future company activities.

Part Seven

Learning Objectives

Conceptual

C1 Describe different types of cost behavior in relation to production and sales volume.

C2 Identify assumptions in cost-volume-profit analysis and explain their impact.

C3 Describe several applications of cost-volume-profit analysis.

Analytical

A1 Compare the scatter diagram, high-low, and regression methods of estimating costs.

A2 Analyze changes in sales using the degree of operating leverage.

Procedural

P1 Determine cost estimates using three different methods.

P2 Compute the break-even point for a single product company.

P3 Graph costs and sales for a single product company.

P4 Compute break-even point for a multiproduct company.

Behind the Throne

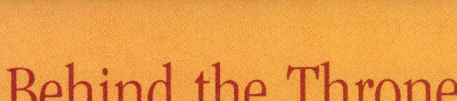 GREENSBORO, NC—Walter Latham says perseverance is his entrepreneurial ammo. At 29, he's an entertainment mogul, heading **Latham Entertainment**, the largest urban comedy promotion company in the U.S. Many promoters are content to wait for the phone to ring, but Latham makes calls and generates ideas. His "Kings of Comedy" tour has taken audiences by storm. The troupe consists of four African-American comics hand-picked by Latham: Cedric the Entertainer, Steve Harvey, Bernie Mac, and D.L. Hughley. They are hardly household names, yet to date they've played more than 100 venues, sold out 20,000-seat arenas across the U.S., and earned more than $40 million in ticket sales. It is the highest-grossing comedy tour in history. "I always ask myself, 'Why didn't anybody else try this?'" says Latham. "I found out that just because no one has ever done it doesn't mean it can't be done."

It was not an easy road to riches. Latham was raised by a single mother in Brooklyn, New York. He had an aunt in North Carolina and eventually made his way there. After a stint as a customer sales rep for American Express and a try at the Air Force, he turned to promoting. With just $5,000 from his family to start, Latham transformed himself from small-time promoter to multimedia giant. "This is all bigger than me," says Latham. "I was blessed to be in this position so early, to come from my background."

Still, don't be fooled. Latham is market savvy and business smart. Who else figured 4,000 people would pay $40 to $50 per ticket to see Steve Harvey? Or to see Bernie Mac, D.L. Hughley, or Cedric the Entertainer? Indeed, who thought that 20,000 plus would show up? Latham did, or hoped they would. He estimated costs, predicted sales, and hoped for profits. Moreover, controlling fixed costs and monitoring variable costs were crucial to his success—and he's done better than break-even. Through it all, Latham has kept a level head. "I like what I do, but I like other things more," says Latham. "I like family."

[Sources: *New York Daily News,* August 30, 2000; *Entrepreneur,* November 1999; *Business Journal of the Greater Triad Area,* December 6, 1999.]

This chapter describes different types of costs and shows how changes in a company's operating volume affect these costs. The chapter also analyzes a company's costs and sales to understand how different operating strategies affect profit or loss. Managers use this type of analysis to forecast what will happen if changes are made to costs, sales volume, selling prices, or product mix. They then use these forecasts to select the best business strategy for the company.

Identifying Cost Behavior

Point: *Profit* is another term for *income*.

Planning a company's future activities and events is a crucial phase in successful management. One of the first steps in planning is to predict the volume of activity, the costs to be incurred, sales to be made, and profit to be received. An important tool to help managers carry out this step is **cost-volume-profit (CVP) analysis,** which helps managers predict how changes in costs and sales levels affect income. In its basic form, CVP analysis involves computing the sales level at which a company neither earns an income nor incurs a loss, called the *break-even point*. For this reason, this basic form of cost-volume-profit analysis is often called *break-even analysis*. Managers use variations of CVP analysis to answer questions such as these:

Did You Know?

Thinking Outside the PC Hardly a week goes by without a wild-eyed start-up announcing some scheme to give away free PCs to potential customers. Following the footsteps of other companies, New York–based **Gobi** announced that it will give away free PCs to cunsumers who sign up for 3 years of Internet service. How can Gobi break-even, let alone earn profits? Its CEO says it will break-even because Gobi buys PCs directly from a manufacturer and charges a premium for Internet service.

- What sales volume is needed to earn a target income?
- What is the change in income if selling prices decline and sales volume increases?
- How much does income increase if we install a new machine to reduce labor costs?
- What is the income effect if we change the sales mix of our products or services?

Consequently, the phrase *cost-volume-profit analysis* better describes the potential applications of this tool to aid a wide range of business decisions.

Conventional cost-volume-profit analysis requires management to classify all costs as either *fixed* or *variable* with respect to production or sales volume. We introduced different cost behaviors in Chapter 19, including the concepts of fixed and variable costs. The remainder of this section extends that discussion of cost behavior as it relates to CVP analysis.

Concept 23-1

Fixed Costs

C1 Describe different types of cost behavior in relation to production and sales volume.

Point: Fixed costs do not change when volume changes, but the per-unit cost declines as volume increases.

A **fixed cost** is one that remains unchanged in amount when volume of activity varies from period to period within a relevant range. For example, $5,000 in monthly rent paid for a factory building remains the same whether the factory operates with a single eight-hour shift or around the clock with three shifts. This means that rent cost is the same each month at any level of output from zero to the plant's full productive capacity. Notice that while *total* fixed cost does not change as the level of production changes, the fixed cost *per unit* of output decreases as volume increases. For instance, if 20 units are produced when monthly rent is $5,000, the average rent cost per unit is $250 (computed as $5,000/20 units). When production increases to 100 units per month, the average cost per unit decreases to $50 (computed as $5,000/100 units). The average cost decreases to $10 per unit if production increases to 500 units per month. Common examples of fixed costs include depreciation, property taxes, office salaries, and many service department costs.

When production volume and costs are graphed, units of product are usually plotted on the *horizontal axis* and dollars of cost are plotted on the *vertical axis*. Fixed costs then are rep-

Did You Know?

Fixed Costs Deals Fixed costs were a driving force behind the **Daimler-Benz** and **Chrysler** merger. The auto business has huge fixed costs, mainly in plant and equipment. This means that with higher sales volume, fixed costs can be spread over more units. This yields lower fixed costs (and price) per auto.

resented as a horizontal line because they remain constant at all levels of production. To illustrate, the graph in Exhibit 23.1 shows that fixed costs remain at $32,000 at all production levels up to the company's monthly capacity of 2,000 units of output. The *relevant range* for fixed costs in Exhibit 23.1 is 0 to 2,000 units. If the relevant range changes (that is, production capacity extends beyond this range), the amount of fixed costs will likely change.

Example: If the fixed cost line in Exhibit 23.1 is shifted upward, does the total cost line shift up, down, or remain in the same place? *Answer:* It shifts up by the same amount.

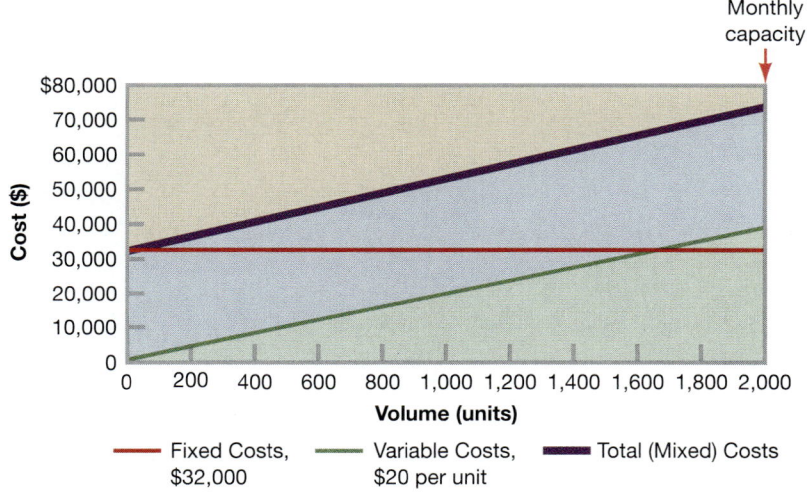

Exhibit 23.1

Relations of Fixed and Variable Costs to Volume

Variable Costs

A **variable cost** is one that changes in proportion to changes in volume of activity. The direct material cost of a product is one example of a variable cost. If one unit of product requires material costing $20, total material costs are $200 when 10 units of product are manufactured, $400 for 20 units, $600 for 30 units, and so on. Notice that variable cost *per unit* remains constant while the *total* amount of variable cost changes with the level of production. Besides direct material, common variable costs include direct labor (if employees are paid per unit), sales commissions, shipping costs, and some overhead costs.

When variable costs are plotted on a graph of cost and volume, they appear as a straight line starting at the zero cost level. This straight line is upward (positive) sloping. The line rises as volume of activity increases. The variable cost line using a $20 per unit cost is graphed in Exhibit 23.1.

Point: Fixed costs are constant in total, but vary (decline) per unit as more units are produced. Variable costs vary in total, but are fixed per unit.

Mixed Costs

A **mixed cost** is one that includes both fixed and variable cost components. For example, compensation for sales representatives often includes a fixed monthly salary and a variable commission based on sales. The total cost line in Exhibit 23.1 is a mixed cost. Like a fixed cost, it is greater than zero when volume is zero, but unlike a fixed cost, it increases steadily in proportion to increases in volume. The mixed cost line in Exhibit 23.1 starts on the vertical axis at the $32,000 fixed cost point. Thus, at the zero volume level, total cost equals the fixed costs. As the activity level increases, the mixed cost line increases at an amount equal to the variable cost per unit. This line is highest when volume of activity is at 2,000 units (the end point of the relevant range). In CVP analysis, mixed costs are often separated into fixed and variable components. The fixed component is added to other fixed costs, and the variable component is added to other variable costs.

Example: If the level of fixed costs in Exhibit 23.1 changes, does the slope of the total cost line change? *Answer:* No, the slope doesn't change. The total cost line is simply shifted upward or downward.

Step-Wise Costs

A **step-wise cost** is one that reflects a step pattern in costs. Salaries of production supervisors often behave in a step-wise manner in that their salaries are fixed within a *relevant range* of the current production volume. However, if production volume expands significantly (for example, with the addition of another shift), additional supervisors must be hired. This means that the total cost for supervisory salaries goes up by a lump-sum amount. Similarly, if volume takes another significant step up, supervisory salaries will increase by another lump sum. This behavior reflects a step-wise cost, also known as *stair-step costs.* A step-wise cost is graphed in Exhibit 23.2. See how it is flat within ranges (steps). Then, when volume significantly changes, it shifts to another level for that range (step).

Exhibit 23.2

Step-Wise and Curvilinear Costs

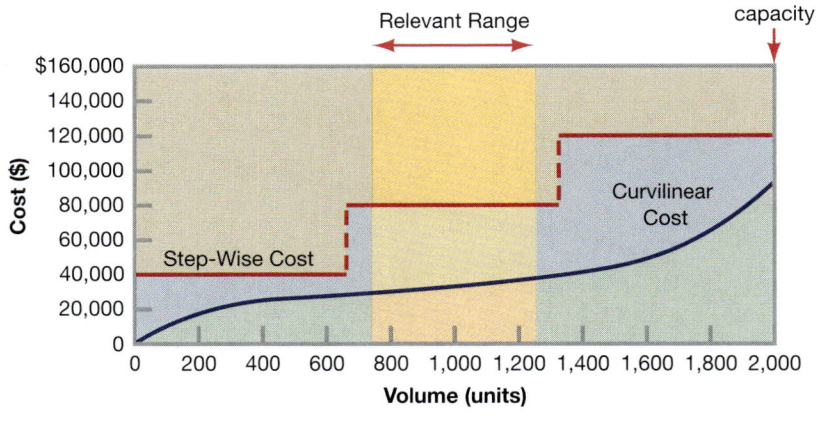

In a conventional CVP analysis, a step-wise cost is usually treated as either a fixed cost or a variable cost. This treatment involves judgment on the manager's part and depends on the width of the range and the expected volume. To illustrate, suppose after the production of every 25 snowboards, an operator lubricates the finishing machine. The cost of this lubricant reflects a step-wise pattern. Also, suppose that after the production of every 1,000 units, the snowboard cutting tool is replaced. Again, this is a step-wise cost. Note that the range of 25 snowboards is much narrower than the range of 1,000 snowboards. Some managers might treat the lubricant cost as a variable cost and the cost of the cutting tool as a fixed cost.

Point: Computer spreadsheets are important and effective tools for CVP analysis and for analyzing alternative strategies.

Point: To apply these concepts, work QS 23-1 and QS 23-2.

Point: Cost-volume-profit analysis helped Rod Canion, Jim Harris, and Bill Murto raise start-up capital of $20 million to launch **Compaq Computer.** They showed that break-even volumes were attainable within the first year.

Curvilinear Costs

A variable cost, as explained earlier, is a *linear* cost, meaning that it increases at a constant rate as volume of activity increases. A **curvilinear cost,** also called *nonlinear cost,* is one that increases at a nonconstant rate as volume increases. When graphed, curvilinear costs appear as a curved line. Exhibit 23.2 shows a curvilinear cost beginning at zero when production is zero and then increasing at different rates. Cost is highest when sales volume reaches the maximum for the period.

An example of a curvilinear cost is total direct labor cost when workers are paid by the hour. At low to medium levels of production, adding more employees allows each of them to specialize by doing certain tasks repeatedly instead of doing several different tasks. This often yields additional units of output at lower costs. A point is eventually reached at which adding more employees creates inefficiencies. For instance, a large crew demands more time and effort in communicating and coordinating their efforts. While adding employees in this case increases output, the labor cost per unit increases, and the total labor cost goes up at a steeper slope. This pattern is seen in Exhibit 23.2 where the curvilinear cost curve starts at zero, rises, flattens out, and then increases at a faster rate as output nears the maximum.

Quick Check

1. Which of the following statements is typically true? (a) Variable cost per unit increases as volume increases, (b) fixed cost per unit decreases as volume increases, or (c) a curvilinear cost includes both fixed and variable elements.
2. Describe the behavior of a fixed cost.
3. If cost per unit of activity remains constant (fixed), why is it called a variable cost?

Answers—p. 965

Identifying and measuring cost behavior requires careful analysis and judgment. An important part of this process is to identify costs that can be classified as either fixed or variable, which often requires analysis of past cost behavior. Three methods are commonly used to analyze past costs: scatter diagrams, high-low method, and least-squares regression. Each method is discussed in this section using the sales and cost data shown in Exhibit 23.3, which is taken from a start-up company. It uses sales volume (in dollars) as the activity base in estimating cost behavior.

Measuring Cost Behavior

P1 Determine cost estimates using three different methods.

Scatter Diagrams

Scatter diagrams display past cost data in graphical form. In preparing a scatter diagram, sales volume ($) is plotted on the horizontal axis and cost is plotted on the vertical axis. Each individual point on a scatter diagram reflects the cost and sales levels for a prior period. In Exhibit 23.4, the prior 12 months' cost and sales figures are graphed. Each point reflects total costs incurred and sales volume for one of those months. For instance, the point labeled March had sales of $25,000 and costs of $25,000.

Exhibit 23.3

Data for Estimating Cost Behavior

Month	Sales Volume ($)	Total Cost ($)
January	$17,500	$20,500
February	27,500	21,500
March	25,000	25,000
April	35,000	21,500
May	47,500	25,500
June	22,500	18,500
July	30,000	23,500
August	52,500	28,500
September ..	37,500	26,000
October	57,500	26,000
November ...	62,500	31,000
December ...	67,500	29,000

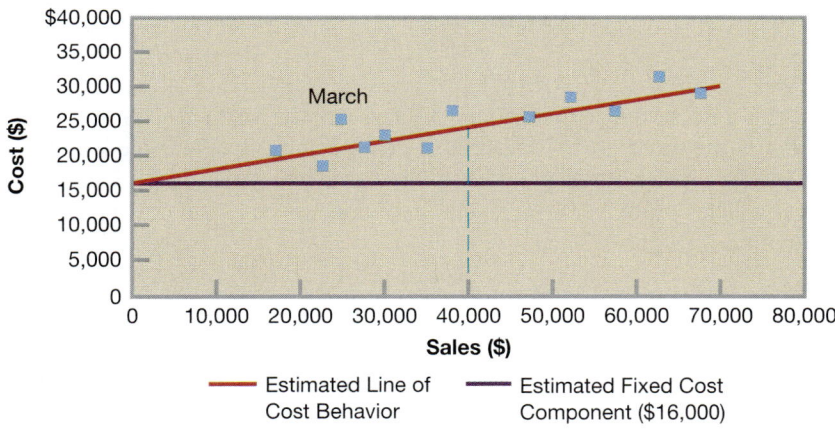

Exhibit 23.4

Scatter Diagram

The **estimated line of cost behavior** is drawn on a scatter diagram to reflect the relation between cost and sales volume. This line best "fits" visually the points in a scatter diagram. Fitting this line demands judgment. The line drawn in Exhibit 23.4 intersects the vertical axis at approximately $16,000, which reflects fixed cost. To compute variable cost per unit, or the slope, we perform three steps. First, we select any two points on the horizontal axis (sales), say $0 and $40,000. Second, we draw a vertical line from each of these points to intersect the estimated line of cost behavior. The point on the vertical axis (cost) corresponding to the $40,000 sales point that intersects the estimated line is roughly $24,000. Similarly, the cost corresponding to zero sales is $16,000 (the fixed cost point). Third, we compute the slope of the line, or variable cost, as the change in cost divided by the change in sales. Exhibit 23.5 shows this computation.

Point: To apply these concepts, work QS 23-3.

$$\frac{\text{Change in cost}}{\text{Change in sales}} = \frac{\$24,000 - \$16,000}{\$40,000 - \$0} = \frac{\$8,000}{\$40,000} = \$0.20 \text{ per sales dollar}$$

Exhibit 23.5

Variable Cost per Unit (Scatter Diagram)

Variable cost is $0.20 per sales dollar. The cost equation used by management to estimate costs for different sales levels is **$16,000 plus $0.20 per sales dollar**.

High-Low Method

The **high-low method** is a means to estimate the cost equation by graphically connecting the two cost amounts at the highest and lowest sales volumes. In our case, the lowest sales volume is $17,500, and the highest is $67,500. The costs corresponding to these sales volumes are $20,500 and $29,000, respectively (see data in Exhibit 23.3). The estimated line of cost behavior for the high-low method is then drawn by connecting these two points on the scatter diagram corresponding to the lowest and highest sales volumes as follows:

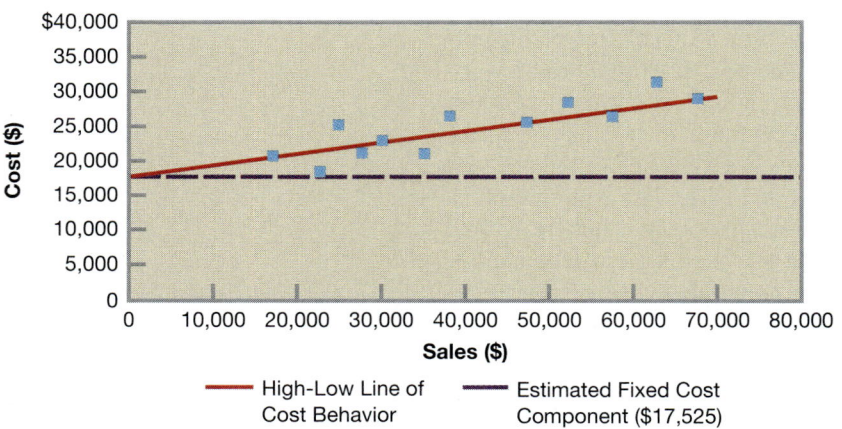

If we extend this line to the vertical axis, it intersects the vertical axis at a cost of about $17,525, which is the fixed cost. The variable cost per unit is determined as the change in cost divided by the change in sales and uses the data from Exhibit 23.3 corresponding to the high and low sales volumes. This results in a slope, or variable cost per sales dollar, of $0.17 as computed in Exhibit 23.6.

Exhibit 23.6

Variable Cost per Unit
(High-Low Method)

$$\frac{\text{Change in cost}}{\text{Change in sales}} = \frac{\$29,000 - \$20,500}{\$67,500 - \$17,500} = \frac{\$8,500}{\$50,000} = \$0.17 \text{ per sales dollar}$$

The cost equation used to estimate costs at different sales levels is **$17,525 plus $0.17 per sales dollar**. This cost equation is slightly different from that used to determine the cost with the scatter diagram method. A deficiency of the high-low method is that it ignores all sales points except the highest and lowest. The result is less precision because the high-low method uses the most extreme points rather than the more usual conditions that are likely to occur in future periods.

Least-Squares Regression

Least-squares regression is a statistical method for identifying cost behavior. For our purposes, we use the cost equation estimated from this method but leave the details of the process for more advanced courses. The computations for least-squares regression are readily done using most spreadsheet programs and calculators.

The regression cost equation for the data presented in Exhibit 23.3 is **$16,947 plus $0.19 per sales dollar**; that is, fixed cost is estimated as $16,947 and variable cost at $0.19 per sales dollar. Both costs are reflected in the following graph:

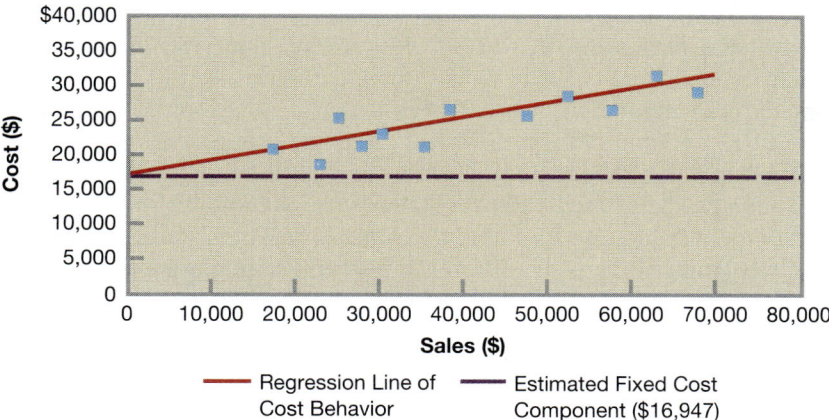

Regression Line of Cost Behavior — Estimated Fixed Cost Component ($16,947)

Comparing Cost Estimation Methods

The three cost estimation methods result in slightly different estimates of fixed and variable costs as summarized in Exhibit 23.7. Estimates from the scatter diagram are based on a visual fit of the cost line and are subject to interpretation. Estimates from the high-low method use only two sets of values corresponding to the lowest and highest sales volumes. Estimates from least-squares regression use a statistical technique and all available data points.

A1 Compare the scatter diagram, high-low, and regression methods of estimating costs.

Estimation Method	Fixed Cost	Variable Cost
Scatter diagram	$16,000	$0.20 per sales dollar
High-low method	17,525	0.17 per sales dollar
Least-squares regression	16,947	0.19 per sales dollar

Exhibit 23.7

Comparison of Cost Estimation Methods

We must remember that all three methods use *past data.* Thus, cost estimates resulting from these methods are only as good as the data used for estimation. Managers must establish that the data are reliable in deriving cost estimates for future costs.

Quick Check

4. Which of the following methods is likely to yield the most precise estimated line of cost behavior? (a) high-low, (b) least-squares regression, or (c) scatter diagram.

5. What is the primary weakness of the high-low method?

6. Using conventional CVP analysis, a mixed cost should be (a) disregarded, (b) treated as a fixed cost, or (c) separated into fixed and variable components.

Answers—p. 965

Break-even analysis is a special case of cost-volume-profit analysis. This section describes break-even analysis including computation of the break-even point and preparing a CVP (or break-even) chart.

Break-Even Analysis

Computing Break-Even Point

The **break-even point** is the sales level at which a company neither earns a profit nor incurs a loss. The concept of break-even is applicable to nearly all organizations, activities,

P2 Compute break-even point for a single product company.

Point: While a company may operate at a level in excess of its break-even point, management may decide to stop operating because it is not earning a reasonable return on investment.

and events. One of the most important items of information when launching a project is whether it will break even—that is, whether sales will at least cover total costs. The break-even point can be expressed either in units or dollars of sales.

To illustrate the computation of break-even analysis, let's look at **Rydell**, which sells footballs for $100 per unit and incurs $70 of variable costs per unit sold. Its fixed costs are $24,000 per month with monthly capacity of 1,800 units (footballs). Rydell breaks even for the month when it sells 800 footballs (sales volume of $80,000). We compute this break-even point using the formula in Exhibit 23.8. This formula uses the **contribution margin per unit,** which is the difference between selling price per unit and variable cost per unit (see Chapter 19). For Rydell, the contribution margin per unit is $30 ($100 − $70). From this we can compute break-even sales volume as $24,000/$30, or 800 units per month.

Exhibit 23.8

Formula for Computing Break-Even Sales (in units)[1]

$$\text{Break-even point in units} = \frac{\text{Fixed costs}}{\text{Contribution margin per unit}}$$

Concept 23-2

At a price of $100 per unit, monthly sales of 800 units yields sales dollars of $80,000 (called *break-even sales dollars*). This break-even sales of $80,000 can be computed directly using the formula in Exhibit 23.9. The **contribution margin ratio** is the *proportion* of a unit's selling price that exceeds its unit variable cost, which is defined as contribution margin per unit divided by unit selling price.

Exhibit 23.9

Formula for Computing Break-Even Sales (in dollars)[2]

$$\text{Break-even point in dollars} = \frac{\text{Fixed costs}}{\text{Contribution margin ratio}}$$

Point: The break-even point is where total expenses equal total sales and the profit is zero.

For Rydell, the contribution margin ratio is 30%, computed as $30/$100. Break-even sales dollars are then computed as $24,000/0.30, or $80,000 of monthly sales. To verify that Rydell's break-even point equals $80,000 (or 800 units), we prepare a simplified income statement in Exhibit 23.10. It shows that the $80,000 revenue from sales of 800 units exactly equals the sum of variable and fixed costs.

---

[1] To obtain this formula, we define S = Sales in units; R = Revenue per unit; F = Fixed costs per period; V = Variable cost per unit; $S \times R$ = Dollar sales; $S \times V$ = Total variable cost; and contribution margin per unit = $R - V$. At break-even, net income is zero, so therefore,

$$\text{Sales} = \text{Fixed costs} + \text{Variable costs}$$
$$(S \times R) = F + (S \times V)$$
$$(S \times R) - (S \times V) = F$$
$$S \times (R - V) = F$$
$$S = F/(R - V)$$
$$S = F/\text{Contribution margin per unit}$$

[2] To obtain this formula, recall that: Contribution margin ratio = $(R - V)/R$. Then, at break-even,

$$S = F/(R - V) \,[\text{from footnote 1}]$$
$$S \times R = (F \times R)/(R - V)$$
$$S \times R = F \times [R/(R - V)]$$
$$S \times R = F/[(R - V)/R]$$
$$S \times R = F/\text{Contribution margin ratio}$$

The statement in Exhibit 23.10 is called a *contribution margin income statement*. It differs in format from a conventional income statement in two ways. First, it separately classifies costs and expenses as variable or fixed. Second, it reports contribution margin, which is sales less variable costs and expenses.

RYDELL COMPANY Contribution Margin Income Statement (at Break-Even)	
Sales (800 units @ $100 each)	$80,000
Variable costs (800 units @ $70 each)	56,000
Contribution margin	$24,000
Fixed costs	24,000
Net income	$ 0

Exhibit 23.10

Contribution Margin Income Statement for Break-Even Sales

Point: A *contribution margin income statement* groups variable and fixed expenses separately, and reports the contribution margin.

The contribution margin income statement format is used in this chapter's assignment materials because of its usefulness in CVP analysis.

Preparing a Cost-Volume-Profit Chart

Exhibit 23.11 is a graph of the cost-volume-profit relations for Rydell. This graph is called a **cost-volume-profit (CVP) chart,** or a *break-even chart* or *break-even graph.* The horizontal axis is the number of units sold and the vertical axis is dollars of sales and costs. The lines in the chart depict both sales and costs at different output levels.

P3 Graph costs and sales for a single product company.

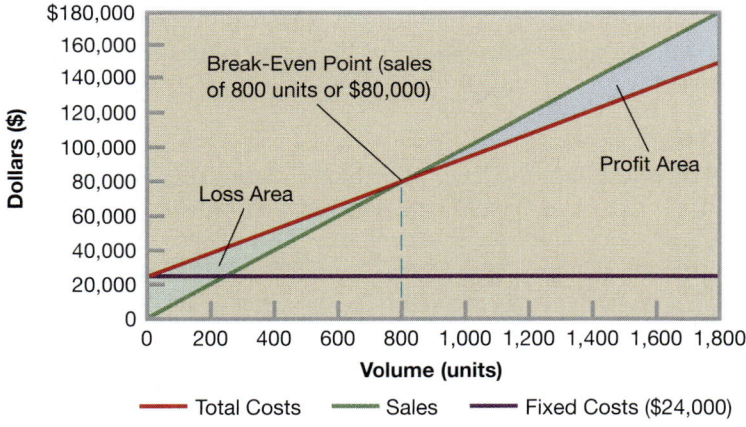

Exhibit 23.11

Cost-Volume-Profit Chart

To prepare a CVP chart, we follow three steps (the chart can also be drawn with computer programs that convert numeric data to graphs):

1. Plot fixed costs on the vertical axis ($24,000 for Rydell). Draw a horizontal line at this level to show that fixed costs remain unchanged regardless of sales volume (drawing this fixed cost line is not essential to the chart).
2. Draw the total costs (variable costs plus fixed costs) line for a relevant range of sales levels. This line starts at the fixed costs level on the vertical axis because total costs equal fixed costs at zero sales. The slope of the total cost line equals the variable cost per unit ($70). To draw the line, compute the total costs for any sales level, and connect this point with the vertical axis intercept ($24,000). Do not draw this line beyond the productive capacity for the planning period (1,800 units for Rydell).
3. Draw the sales line. Start at the origin (zero units and zero dollars of sales) and make the slope of this line equal to the selling price per unit ($100). To sketch the line, compute dollar sales for any sales level and connect this point with the origin. Do not extend this line beyond the productive capacity. Total sales will be at the highest level at maximum capacity.

Point: A contribution margin income statement is also referred to as a *variable costing income statement.* This type of statement differs from the traditional *absorption costing* approach where product costs are assigned to units sold and to units in ending inventory. This is different from variable costing where all product costs are expensed. Thus, income for the two approaches differs depending on the level of finished goods inventory. When an inventory system such as JIT minimizes finished goods inventory, income under the two approaches is similar.

Point: Selling prices and variable costs are usually expressed in per-unit amounts. Fixed costs are usually expressed in total amounts.

Example: In Exhibit 23.11, the sales line intersects the total cost line at 800 units. At what point would the two lines intersect if selling price is increased by 20% to $120 per unit? *Answer:* $24,000/ ($120 − $70) = 480 units

You Make the Call e

Operations Manager As a start-up manufacturer, one of your tasks is to identify the behavior of manufacturing costs to develop a production cost budget. You know three methods can be used to identify cost behavior from past data, but past data are not available because this is a start-up. What do you do?

Answer—p. 964

C2 Identify assumptions in cost-volume-profit analysis and explain their impact.

The total costs line and the sales line intersect at 800 units in Exhibit 23.11. This intersection is the break-even point, the point where total dollar sales of $80,000 equals the sum of both fixed and variable costs ($80,000).

On either side of the break-even point, the vertical distance between the sales line and the total costs line at any specific volume measures the profit or loss expected at that point. At volume levels to the left of the break-even point, this vertical distance is the amount of the expected loss because the total costs line is above the total sales line. At volume levels to the right of the break-even point, the vertical distance represents the expected profit because the total sales line is above the total costs line.

Assumptions of Cost-Volume-Profit Analysis

Cost-volume-profit analysis assumes that relations can normally be expressed as simple lines similar to those in Exhibits 23.1 and 23.11. This assumption allows users of CVP to classify all costs as either fixed or variable with respect to sales volume. CVP analysis also treats sales as variable, with all units of a product being sold at the same unit price. These assumptions allow users to answer several important questions, but the usefulness of the answers depends on the validity of three assumptions: (1) selling price per unit is constant, (2) variable costs per unit are constant, and (3) total fixed costs are constant. These assumptions are not always realistic, but they do not necessarily limit the usefulness of CVP analysis as a way to better understand costs and sales. This section discusses these assumptions and other issues for CVP analysis.

Output Measures

Point: CVP analysis can be very useful for business decision making even when its assumptions are not strictly met.

CVP analysis usually describes the level of activity in terms of *sales volume,* which can be expressed in terms of either units sold or dollar sales. However, other measures of output exist. For instance, with a manufacturer, the number of units produced can be a measure of output. Also, to simplify analysis, we often assume that production level is the same as the sales level. That is, inventory levels are ignored. This often is justified by arguing that CVP analysis provides only approximations.

Working with Assumptions

The behavior of individual costs and sales often is not perfectly consistent with CVP assumptions. If the expected costs and sales behavior differ from the assumptions, the results of CVP analysis can be limited. Still, we can perform useful analyses in spite of limitations with these assumptions for several reasons.

Summing costs can offset individual deviations. Deviations from assumptions with individual costs are often minor when these costs are summed. That is, individual variable cost items may not be perfectly variable, but when we sum these variable costs, their individual deviations can offset each other. This means the assumption of variable cost behavior can be proper for total variable costs. Similarly, an assumption that total fixed costs are constant can be proper even when individual fixed cost items are not exactly constant.

CVP is applied to a relevant range of operations. Sales, variable costs, and fixed costs often are reasonably reflected in straight lines on a graph when the assumptions are applied over a relevant range. The **relevant range of operations** is the normal operating range for a business. Except for unusually difficult or prosperous times, management typically plans for operations within a range of volume neither close to zero nor at maximum capacity. The relevant range excludes extremely high and low operating levels that are unlikely to occur. The validity of assuming that a specific cost is fixed or variable is more acceptable when operations are within the relevant range. As shown in Exhibit 23.2, a curvilinear cost can

Point: To apply these concepts, work QS 23-7.

be treated as variable and linear if the relevant range covers volumes where it has a near constant slope. Management must plan according to the normal relevant range of activity. If the normal range of activity changes, some costs might need reclassification.

CVP analysis yields estimates. CVP analysis yields approximate answers to questions about costs, volumes, and profits. These answers do not have to be precise because the analysis makes rough estimates about the future. As long as managers understand that CVP analysis gives estimates, it can be a useful tool for starting the planning process. Other qualitative factors also must be considered.

Point: Activity-based costing challenges the classification of costs as fixed or variable on the basis of sales volume and, thus, complicates CVP analysis.

Example: If selling price declines, what happens to the break-even point? *Answer:* It increases.

Quick Check

7. Fixed cost divided by the contribution margin ratio yields the (a) break-even point in dollars, (b) contribution margin per unit, or (c) break-even point in units.

8. A company sells a product for $90 per unit with variable costs of $54 per unit. What is the contribution margin ratio?

9. Refer to Quick Check (8). If fixed costs for the period are $90,000, what is the break-even point in dollars?

10. What three basic assumptions are used in CVP analysis?

Answers—p. 965

Managers consider a variety of strategies in planning business operations. These strategies often affect costs and sales for the company. Cost-volume-profit analysis is useful in helping managers evaluate the likely effects of these strategies. This section explains several applications of cost-volume-profit analysis.

Computing Income from Sales and Costs

An important question managers often need an answer to is "What is the predicted income from a predicted level of sales?" To answer this, we look at four variables in CVP analysis. These variables and their relations to income (pretax) are shown in Exhibit 23.12. We use these relations to compute expected income from predicted sales and cost levels.

$$\text{Income (pretax)} = \text{Sales} - \text{Variable costs} - \text{Fixed costs}$$

To illustrate, let's assume that Rydell's management expects to sell 1,500 units this month. What is the amount of income if this sales level is achieved? At this level, sales are $150,000 (1,500 units × $100). Also, Rydell's fixed costs are $24,000 per month, its variable costs per unit are $70, and its total variable costs for 1,500 units are $105,000 (1,500 units × $70). Following Exhibit 23.12, we compute Rydell's expected income in Exhibit 23.13.

$$\text{Income (pretax)} = [1{,}500 \text{ units} \times \$100] - [1{,}500 \text{ units} \times \$70] - \$24{,}000$$
$$= \$21{,}000$$

The $21,000 income does not include the effects of income taxes, which corporations must pay. To find the amount of *after-tax* income from selling 1,500 units, management must

Applying Cost-Volume-Profit Analysis

C3 Describe several applications of cost-volume-profit analysis.

Exhibit 23.12

Income Relations in CVP Analysis

Exhibit 23.13

Computing Expected Income from Expected Sales

"How many units must I sell to earn $50,000?"

apply the proper tax rate to the $21,000. If the tax rate is 25%, income tax is $5,250 and net income is $15,750. Management then assesses whether this net income is an adequate return on assets invested. Management should also consider whether sales and income can be increased by raising or lowering prices. CVP analysis is a good tool for addressing these kinds of "what-if" questions.

Computing Sales for a Target Income

Many companies' annual plans are based on certain income targets (sometimes called budgets). Rydell's income target for this year is to increase income by 10% over the prior year. When prior year income is known, Rydell easily computes its target income. CVP analysis helps to determine the sales level needed to achieve the target income. Computing this sales level is important because planning for the year is then based on this level. We use the formula shown in Exhibit 23.14 to compute sales for a target *after-tax* income.

Exhibit 23.14

Computing Sales (dollars) for a Target After-Tax Income[3]

$$\text{Dollar sales at target after-tax income} = \frac{\text{Fixed costs} + \text{Target after-tax income} + \text{Income taxes}}{\text{Contribution margin ratio}} \quad or = \frac{\text{Fixed costs} + \text{Target pretax income}}{\text{Contribution margin ratio}}$$

Example: If variable costs decline, what happens to the break-even point? *Answer:* It decreases.

To illustrate, we return to Rydell, which has monthly fixed costs of $24,000 and a 30% contribution margin ratio. Assume that it sets a target monthly after-tax income of $9,000 when the tax rate is 25%. This means the pretax income is targeted at $12,000 $[\$9,000/(1 - 0.25)]$ with a tax expense of $3,000. Using the formula in Exhibit 23.14, we find that $120,000 of sales is needed to produce a $9,000 after-tax income. We show this computation in Exhibit 23.15.

Exhibit 23.15

Rydell's Dollar Sales for a Target Income

$$\text{Dollar sales at target after-tax income} = \frac{\$24,000 + \$9,000 + \$3,000}{30\%} = \$120,000$$

We can alternatively compute *unit sales* instead of dollar sales. To do this, we substitute *contribution margin per unit* for the contribution margin ratio in the denominator. This gives us the number of units needed to be sold to reach the target after-tax income. Exhibit 23.16 illustrates this for Rydell. The two computations in Exhibits 23.15 and 23.16 are equivalent because sales of 1,200 units at $100 per unit equals $120,000 of sales.

Exhibit 23.16

Computing Sales (units) for a Target After-Tax Income

$$\text{Unit sales at target after-tax income} = \frac{\text{Fixed costs} + \text{Target after-tax income} + \text{Income taxes}}{\text{Contribution margin per unit}} \quad or = \frac{\text{Fixed costs} + \text{Target pretax income}}{\text{Contribution margin per unit}}$$

$$= \frac{\$24,000 + \$9,000 + \$3,000}{\$30} = 1,200 \text{ units}$$

Point: If a company is not subject to taxes, we substitute *pretax income* for *after-tax income* and delete *income taxes* in both Exhibits 23.14 and 23.16.

---

[3] To obtain this formula, we define S = Sales in units; R = Revenue per unit; F = Fixed costs per period; V = Variable cost per unit; N = Target net income; T = Income taxes; $S \times R$ = Dollar sales; $S \times V$ = Total variable cost; and the Contribution margin ratio = $(R - V)/R$. The after-tax target net income is then defined as:

$$(S \times R) - F - (S \times V) - T = N$$
$$(S \times R) - (S \times V) = F + N + T$$
$$S \times (R - V) = F + N + T$$
$$S = (F + N + T)/(R - V)$$
$$S \times R = [(F + N + T) \times R]/(R - V)$$
$$S \times R = (F + N + T) \times [R/(R - V)]$$
$$S \times R = (F + N + T)/[(R - V)/R]$$
$$S \times R = (F + N + T)/\text{Contribution margin ratio}$$

Computing the Margin of Safety

All companies wish to sell more than the break-even number of units to earn income. The excess of expected sales over the break-even sales level is called a company's **margin of safety,** which is the amount that sales can drop before the company incurs a loss. It can be expressed in units, dollars, or even as a percent of the predicted level of sales. To illustrate, if Rydell's expected sales are $100,000, the margin of safety is $20,000, above break-even sales of $80,000. As a percent, the margin of safety is 20% of expected sales as shown in Exhibit 23.17.

You Make the Call — Ethics

Supervisor   You are part of a team debating a new product. You see a range of income levels from different sales projections. One member suggests picking numbers yielding favorable income because any estimate is "as good as any other." Also, fixed and variable costs are being estimated from a scatter diagram of 20 months' production on a comparable product. A team member asks whether unfavorable data points can be dropped to see if this improves the cost picture. Your task is to conduct a cost-volume-profit analysis to reflect these suggestions. What do you do?

Answer—p. 965

$$\text{Margin of safety (in percent)} = \frac{\text{Expected sales} - \text{Break-even sales}}{\text{Expected sales}}$$

$$= \frac{\$100,000 - \$80,000}{\$100,000} = 20\%$$

Exhibit 23.17

Computing Margin of Safety (in percent)

Management must assess whether the margin of safety is adequate in light of factors such as sales variability, competition, consumer tastes, and economic conditions.

Sensitivity Analysis

Knowing the effects of changing some estimates used in CVP analysis is often useful because they are *estimates,* not actual values. For instance, we might want to know what happens if we reduce a product's selling price to increase sales. Or we might want to know what happens to income if we automate a currently manual process. We can use CVP analysis to predict income if we can describe how these changes affect a company's fixed costs, variable costs, selling price, and volume.

To illustrate, let's assume that Rydell Company is looking into buying a new machine that would increase monthly fixed costs from $24,000 to $30,000 but decrease variable costs from $70 per unit to $60 per unit. The machine is used to produce output whose selling price will remain unchanged at $100. This results in increases in both the unit contribution margin and the contribution margin ratio. The revised contribution margin per unit is $40 ($100 − $60), and the revised contribution margin ratio is 40% of selling price ($40/$100). A manager would want to know what the break-even point is if this machine is bought. We use CVP analysis to help answer that question. If Rydell buys the machine, its revised break-even point in dollars would be $75,000 as computed in Exhibit 23.18.

Did You Know?

Eco-Cars   Honda Insight, Toyota Prius, and Ford Escape are hybrid cars powered by a small gas engine and an electric motor. Both the Insight and Prius promise to save owners $500 a year in fuel costs relative to comparable cars. These cars also generate less carbon dioxide and other greenhouse gases. Are these cars economically feasible? Analysts estimate that **Honda** loses $8,000 on each Insight that it sells, but it expects to break even in 2 years. Similarly, **Ford** claims that its Escape can reach breakeven when a $3,000 premium is paid over comparable gas-based models.

Example: If fixed costs decline, what happens to the break-even point? *Answer:* It decreases.

$$\text{Revised break-even point in dollars} = \frac{\text{Revised fixed costs}}{\text{Revised contribution margin ratio}} = \frac{\$30,000}{40\%} = \$75,000$$

Exhibit 23.18

Revising Break-Even When Changes Occur

Point: Price competition led paging companies to give business to resellers—companies that lease services at a discount and then resell to subscribers. **Paging Network** charged some resellers under $1 per month, less than a third of what is needed to break even. Its CEO now admits the low-price strategy was flawed.

The revised fixed costs and the revised contribution margin ratio can also be used to address other issues including computation of (1) expected income for a given sales level and (2) the sales level needed to earn a target income. Another use of sensitivity analysis is to generate three different sets of revenue and cost estimates that are *optimistic, pessimistic,* and *most likely.* Different CVP analyses based on these estimates provide different scenarios that management can analyze and use in planning business strategy.

Quick Check

11. A firm has fixed costs of $50,000 and a 25% contribution margin ratio. What dollar sales are necessary to achieve an after-tax net income of $120,000 if the tax rate is 20%? (a) $800,000, (b) $680,000, or (c) $600,000.

12. If the contribution margin ratio decreases from 50% to 25%, what can be said about unit sales needed to achieve the same target income level?

13. What is a company's margin of safety?

Answers—p. 965

Computing Multiproduct Break-Even Point

P4 Compute break-even point for a multiproduct company.

To this point, we have looked only at cases where the company sells a single product or service. This was to keep the basic CVP analysis simple. However, many companies sell multiple products or services, and we can modify the CVP analysis for use in these cases. An important assumption in a multiproduct setting is that the sales mix of different products is known and remains constant during the planning period. **Sales mix** is the ratio (proportion) of the sales volumes for the various products. For instance, if a company normally sells 10,000 footballs, 5,000 baseballs, and 4,000 basketballs per month, its sales mix can be expressed as 10:5:4 for footballs, baseballs, and basketballs.

To apply multiproduct CVP analysis, we need to estimate the break-even point by using a **composite unit,** which consists of a specific number of units of each product in proportion to their expected sales mix. Multiproduct CVP analysis treats this composite unit as a single product. To illustrate, let's look at **Hair-Today**, a styling salon that offers three cuts: basic, ultra, and budget in the ratio of 4 units of basic to 2 units of ultra to 1 unit of budget (expressed as 4:2:1). Management wants to estimate its break-even point for next year. Unit selling prices for these three cuts are basic, $10; ultra, $16; and budget, $8. Using the 4:2:1 sales mix, the selling price of a composite unit of the three products is computed as follows:

4 units of basic @ $10 per unit	$40
2 units of ultra @ $16 per unit	32
1 unit of budget @ $8 per unit	8
Selling price of a composite unit	**$80**

Hair-Today's fixed costs are $96,000 per year, and its variable costs of the three products are basic, $6.50; ultra, $9.00; and budget, $4.00. Variable costs for a composite unit of these products follow:

4 units of basic @ $6.50 per unit	$26
2 units of ultra @ $9.00 per unit	18
1 unit of budget @ $4.00 per unit	4
Variable costs of a composite unit . . .	**$48**

Once we determine the variable costs and the selling price of a composite unit of the company's products, we can compute Hair-Today's contribution margin for a composite unit. This is computed as $32 by subtracting the variable costs ($48) of a composite unit from its selling price ($80). We then can use the $32 contribution margin to determine Hair-Today's break-even point in composite units as shown in Exhibit 23.19.

Point: To apply these concepts, work QS 23-9.

$$\text{Break-even point in composite units} = \frac{\text{Fixed costs}}{\text{Contribution margin per composite unit}}$$

$$= \frac{\$96,000}{\$32} = 3,000 \text{ composite units}$$

Exhibit 23.19

Break-Even Point in Composite Units

This computation implies that Hair-Today breaks even when it sells 3,000 composite units. To determine how many units of each product it must sell to break even, we multiply the number of units of each product in the composite by 3,000:

Point: The break-even point in dollars for Exhibit 23.19 is: $96,000/($32/$80) = $240,000.

Basic:	4 × 3,000	12,000 units
Ultra:	2 × 3,000	6,000 units
Budget:	1 × 3,000	3,000 units

The schedule in Exhibit 23.20 verifies these results by showing Hair-Today's sales and costs at this break-even point using a contribution margin income statement.

HAIR-TODAY
Forecasted Contribution Margin Income Statement (at Break-Even)

	Basic	Ultra	Budget	Combined
Sales				
Basic (12,000 @ $10)	$120,000			
Ultra (6,000 @ $16)		$96,000		
Budget (3,000 @ $8)			$24,000	
Total sales				$240,000
Variable costs				
Basic (12,000 @ $6.50)	78,000			
Ultra (6,000 @ $9)		54,000		
Budget (3,000 @ $4)			12,000	
Total variable costs				144,000
Contribution margin	$ 42,000	$42,000	$12,000	$ 96,000
Fixed costs				96,000
Net income				$ 0

Exhibit 23.20

Multiproduct Break-Even Income Statement

A CVP analysis using composite units can be used to answer a variety of planning questions. Once a product mix is set, all answers are based on the assumption that the mix remains constant at all relevant sales levels as other factors in the analysis do. We also can vary the sales mix to see what happens under alternative strategies.

You Make the Call   *e*

Entrepreneur   A CVP analysis indicates that your start-up, which markets electronic products, will just break even with the current sales mix and price levels. You have a target income in mind. What analysis might you perform to assess likelihood for achieving this income?

Answer—p. 965

Quick Check

14. The sales mix of a company's two products, X and Y, is 2:1. Unit variable costs for both products are $2, and unit sales price is $5 for X and $4 for Y. What is the contribution margin per composite unit? (a) $5, (b) $10, or (c) $8.

15. What additional assumption about sales mix must be made in doing a conventional CVP analysis for a company that produces and sells more than one product?

Using the Information   Operating Leverage

A2 Analyze changes in sales levels using the degree of operating leverage.

CVP analysis is especially useful when management begins the planning process and wishes to predict outcomes of alternative strategies. These strategies can involve changes in selling prices, fixed costs, variable costs, sales volume, and product mix. Managers are interested in seeing the effects of changes in some or all of these factors.

One goal of all managers is to get maximum benefits from their fixed costs. Managers would like to use 100% of their output capacity so that fixed costs are spread over the largest number of units. This would decrease fixed cost per unit and increase income. The extent, or relative size, of fixed costs in the total cost structure is known as **operating leverage.** Companies having a higher proportion of fixed costs in their total cost structure are said to have higher operating leverage. An example of this is a company that chooses to automate its processes instead of using direct labor, increasing its fixed costs and lowering its variable costs. A useful managerial measure to help assess the effect on income of changes in the level of sales is the **degree of operating leverage (DOL)** defined as:

> **Total contribution margin (in dollars)/Pretax income.**

To illustrate, let's return to Rydell Company. At a sales level of 1,200 units, the total contribution margin for Rydell is $36,000 (1,200 units × $30 contribution margin per unit). Its pretax income, after subtracting fixed costs of $24,000, is $12,000 (computed as $36,000 minus $24,000). The degree of operating leverage for Rydell at this sales level is 3.0, computed as contribution margin divided by pretax income (or $36,000/$12,000). We can use DOL to measure the effect of changes in the level of sales for pretax income. For instance, suppose Rydell expects sales to increase by 10%. If this increase is within the relevant range of operations, we can expect this 10% increase in sales to result in a 30% increase in pretax income computed as DOL multiplied by the increase in sales (3.0 × 10%). Similar analyses can be done for expected decreases in sales.

Demonstration Problem

Sport Caps Co. manufactures and sells caps for different sporting events. The fixed costs of operating the company are $150,000 per month, and the variable costs for caps are $5 per unit. The caps are sold for $8 per unit. The fixed costs provide a production capacity of up to 100,000 caps per month.

Required

1. Use the formulas in the chapter to compute the following:
   a. Contribution margin per cap.
   b. Break-even point in terms of the number of caps produced and sold.
   c. Amount of net income at 30,000 caps sold per month (ignore taxes).
   d. Amount of net income at 85,000 caps sold per month (ignore taxes).
   e. Number of caps to be produced and sold to provide $45,000 of after-tax income, assuming an income tax rate of 25%.

2. Draw a CVP chart for the company, showing cap output on the horizontal axis. Identify the break-even point and the amount of pretax income when the level of cap production is 70,000. (Omit the fixed cost line.)

3. Use the formulas in the chapter to compute the

  a. Contribution margin ratio.

  b. Break-even point in terms of sales dollars.

  c. Amount of net income at $250,000 of sales per month (ignore taxes).

  d. Amount of net income at $600,000 of sales per month (ignore taxes).

  e. Dollars of sales needed to provide $45,000 of after-tax income, assuming an income tax rate of 25%.

Planning the Solution

- Identify the formulas in the chapter for the required items expressed in units and solve them using the data given in the problem.
- Draw a CVP chart that reflects the facts in the problem. The horizontal axis should plot the volume in units up to 100,000, and the vertical axis should plot the total dollars up to $800,000. Plot the total cost line as upward sloping, starting at the fixed cost level ($150,000) on the vertical axis and increasing until it reaches $650,000 at the maximum volume of 100,000 units. Verify that the break-even point (where the two lines cross) equals the amount you computed in part (1).
- Identify the formulas in the chapter for the required items expressed in dollars and solve them using the data given in the problem.

Solution to Demonstration Problem

1. a. Contribution margin per cap
$$= \text{Selling price per unit} - \text{Variable cost per unit}$$
$$= \$8 - \$5 = \underline{\underline{\$3}}$$

  b. Break-even point in caps
$$= \frac{\text{Fixed costs}}{\text{Contribution margin per cap}} = \frac{\$150,000}{\$3} = \underline{\underline{50,000 \text{ caps}}}$$

  c. Net income at 30,000 caps sold
$$= (\text{Units} \times \text{Contribution margin per unit}) - \text{Fixed costs}$$
$$= (30,000 \times \$3) - \$150,000 = \underline{\underline{\$(60,000) \text{ loss}}}$$

  d. Net income at 85,000 caps sold
$$= (\text{Units} \times \text{Contribution margin per unit}) - \text{Fixed costs}$$
$$= (85,000 \times \$3) - \$150,000 = \underline{\underline{\$105,000 \text{ profit}}}$$

  e. Pretax income $= \$45,000/(1 - 0.25) = \$60,000$

    Income taxes $= \$60,000 \times 25\% = \$15,000$

    Units needed for $45,000 income
$$= \frac{\text{Fixed costs} + \text{Target income} + \text{Income taxes}}{\text{Contribution margin per cap}}$$
$$= \frac{\$150,000 + \$45,000 + \$15,000}{\$3} = \underline{\underline{70,000 \text{ caps}}}$$

2. CVP chart:

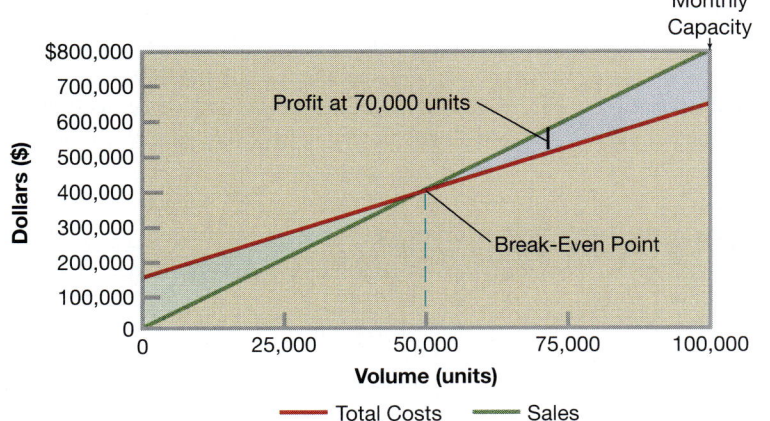

3. a. Contribution margin ratio $= \dfrac{\text{Contribution margin per unit}}{\text{Selling price per unit}} = \dfrac{\$3}{\$8} = \underline{\underline{0.375, \text{ or } 37.5\%}}$

b. Break-even point in dollars $= \dfrac{\text{Fixed costs}}{\text{Contribution margin ratio}} = \dfrac{\$150,000}{37.5\%} = \underline{\underline{\$400,000}}$

c. Net income at sales of $250,000 $= (\text{Sales} \times \text{Contribution margin ratio}) - \text{Fixed costs}$
$= (\$250,000 \times 37.5\%) - \$150,000 = \underline{\underline{\$(56,250) \text{ loss}}}$

d. Net income at sales of $600,000 $= (\text{Sales} \times \text{Contribution margin ratio}) - \text{Fixed costs}$
$= (\$600,000 \times 37.5\%) - \$150,000 = \underline{\underline{\$75,000 \text{ income}}}$

e. Dollars of sales to yield $45,000 income $= \dfrac{\text{Fixed costs} + \text{Target income} + \text{Income taxes}}{\text{Contribution margin ratio}}$
$= \dfrac{\$150,000 + \$45,000 + \$15,000}{37.5\%} = \underline{\underline{\$560,000}}$

Summary

C1 **Describe different types of cost behavior in relation to production and sales volume.** Cost behavior is described in terms of how its amount changes in relation to volume of activity changes within a relevant range. Fixed costs remain constant to changes in volume. Total variable costs change in direct proportion to volume changes. Mixed costs display the effects of both fixed and variable components. Step-wise costs remain constant over a small volume range, then change by a lump sum and remain constant over another volume range, and so on. Curvilinear costs change in a nonlinear relation to volume changes.

C2 **Identify assumptions in cost-volume-profit analysis and explain their impact.** Conventional cost-volume-profit analysis is based on assumptions that the product's selling price remains constant and that variable and fixed costs behave in a manner consistent with their variable and fixed classifications.

C3 **Describe several applications of cost-volume-profit analysis.** Cost-volume-profit analysis can be used to predict what can happen under alternative strategies concerning sales volume, selling prices, variable costs, or fixed costs. Applications include "what-if" analysis, computing sales for a target income, and break-even analysis.

A1 **Compare the scatter diagram, high-low method, and regression cost estimates.** Cost estimates from a scatter diagram are based on a visual fit of the cost line. Estimates from the high-low method are based only on costs corresponding to the lowest and highest sales. The least-squares regression method is a statistical technique and uses all data points.

A2 **Analyze changes in sales using the degree of operating leverage.** The extent, or relative size, of fixed costs in a company's total cost structure is known as *operating leverage.* One tool useful in assessing the effect of changes in sales on income is the degree of operating leverage, or DOL. DOL is the ratio of the contribution margin divided by pretax income. This ratio can be used to determine the expected percent change in income given a percent change in sales.

P1 **Determine cost estimates using three different methods.** Three different methods used to estimate costs are the scatter diagram, the high-low method, and least-squares regression. All three methods use past data to estimate costs.

P2 **Compute break-even point for a single product company.** A company's break-even point for a period is the sales volume at which total revenues equal total costs. To compute a break-even point in terms of sales units, we divide total fixed costs by the contribution margin per unit. To compute a break-even point in terms of sales dollars, divide total fixed costs by the contribution margin ratio.

P3 **Graph costs and sales for a single product company.** The costs and sales for a company can be graphically illustrated using a CVP chart. In this chart, the horizontal axis represents the number of units sold and the vertical axis represents dollars of sales or costs. Straight lines are used to depict both costs and sales on the CVP chart.

P4 **Compute break-even point for a multiproduct company.** CVP analysis can be applied to a multiproduct company by expressing sales volume in terms of composite units. A composite unit consists of a specific number of units of each product in proportion to their expected sales mix. Multiproduct CVP analysis treats this composite unit as a single product.

Guidance Answers to You Make the Call

Operations Manager Without the availability of past data, none of the three methods described in the chapter can be used to measure cost behavior. Instead, the manager must investigate whether he/she can get access to data from similar manufacturers. This is likely difficult due to the sensitive nature of such data. In the absence of data, the manager should develop a list of the different production inputs and identify input-output relations. This provides guidance to the manager in measuring cost behavior. After several months, actual cost data will be available for analysis.

Entrepreneur   You must first compute the level of sales required to achieve the desired net income. Then you must conduct sensitivity analysis by varying the price, sales mix, and cost estimates. Results from the sensitivity analysis provide information you can use to assess the possibility of reaching the target sales level. For instance, you might have to pursue aggressive marketing strategies to push the high-margin products, or you might have to cut prices to increase sales and profits, or another strategy might emerge.

Supervisor   Your dilemma is whether to go along with the suggestions to "manage" the numbers to make the project look like it will achieve sufficient profits. You should not succumb to these suggestions. Many people will likely be affected negatively if you manage the predicted numbers and the project eventually is unprofitable. Moreover, if it does fail, an investigation would likely reveal that data in the proposal were "fixed" to make it look good. Probably the only benefit from managing the numbers is the short-term payoff of pleasing those who proposed the product. One way to deal with this dilemma is to prepare several analyses showing results under different assumptions and then let senior management make the decision.

Guidance Answers to **Quick Checks**

1. (b)

2. A fixed cost remains unchanged in total amount regardless of output levels. (However, fixed cost *per unit* declines with increased output.)

3. Such a cost is considered variable because the total cost changes in proportion to volume changes.

4. (b)

5. The high-low method ignores all costs and sales (activity-base) volume data points except the costs corresponding to the highest and lowest (most extreme) sales (activity-base) volume.

6. (c)

7. (a)

8. $(\$90 - \$54)/\$90 = 40\%$

9. $\$90,000/40\% = \$225,000$

10. Three basic CVP assumptions are that (1) selling price per unit is constant, (2) variable costs per unit are constant, and (3) total fixed costs are constant.

11. (a). Two steps are required for explanation:
(1) Pretax income $= \$120,000/(1 - 0.20) = \$150,000$

(2) $\dfrac{\$50,000 + \$120,000 + (\$150,000 \times 20\%)}{25\%} = \$800,000$

12. If the contribution margin ratio decreases from 50% to 25%, unit sales would have to double.

13. A company's margin of safety is the excess of the predicted sales level over its break-even sales level.

14. (c). Selling price of a composite unit follows:

2 units of X @ $5 per unit	$10
1 unit of Y @ $4 per unit	4
Selling price of a composite unit	$14

Variable costs of a composite unit follows:

2 units of X @ $2 per unit	$4
1 unit of Y @ $2 per unit	2
Variable costs of a composite unit	$6

Therefore, contribution margin per composite unit is $8.

15. It must be assumed that the sales mix remains unchanged at all sales levels in the relevant range.

Glossary

Break-even point output level where sales equals fixed plus variable costs. (p. 953).

Composite unit consists of a specific number of units of each product in proportion to their expected sales mix. (p. 960).

Contribution margin per unit amount that the sale of one unit contributes toward recovering fixed costs and earning profit. (p. 954).

Contribution margin ratio contribution margin per unit expressed as a percent of the product's selling price. (p. 954).

Cost-volume-profit (CVP) analysis planning method that includes predicting the volume of activity, the costs incurred, sales earned, and profits received. (p. 948).

Curvilinear cost cost that changes with volume but not at a constant rate. (p. 950).

CVP chart graphic representation of cost-volume-profit relations. (p. 955).

Degree of operating leverage (DOL) ratio of contribution margin divided by pretax income; used to assess the effect on income of changes in sales. (p. 962).

Estimated line of cost behavior line drawn on a graph to visually fit the relation between cost and sales. (p. 951).

Fixed cost cost that remains unchanged in total amount even when volume varies. (p. 948).

High-low method yields an estimated line of cost behavior by connecting costs associated with the highest and lowest sales volume. (p. 952).

Least-squares regression statistical method for deriving an estimated line of cost behavior that is more precise than the high-low method and a scatter diagram. (p. 952).

Margin of safety excess of expected sales over the level of break-even sales. (p. 959).

Mixed cost cost that behaves like a combination of fixed and variable costs. (p. 949).

Operating leverage extent, or relative size, of fixed costs in the total cost structure. (p. 962).

Relevant range of operations company's normal operating range; excludes extremely high and low volumes not likely to occur. (p. 956).

Sales mix ratio of sales volumes for the various products sold by a company. (p. 960).

Scatter diagram graph used to display data about past cost behavior and sales volumes as points on a diagram. (p. 951).

Step-wise cost cost that remains fixed over limited ranges of volumes but changes by

a lump sum when volume changes occur outside these limited ranges. (p. 949).

Variable cost cost that changes in proportion to changes in output volume. (p. 949).

Questions

1. How is cost-volume-profit analysis useful?
2. What is a variable cost? Identify two variable costs.
3. When output volume increases, do variable costs per unit increase, decrease, or stay the same within the relevant range of activity? Explain.
4. When output volume increases, do fixed costs per unit increase, decrease, or stay the same within the relevant range of activity? Explain.
5. How do step-wise costs and curvilinear costs differ?
6. In performing CVP analysis for a manufacturing company, what simplifying assumption is usually made about the volume of production and the volume of sales?
7. What two arguments tend to justify classifying all costs as either fixed or variable even though individual costs might not behave perfectly consistently with these classifications?
8. How does assuming that operating activity occurs within a relevant range affect cost-volume-profit analysis?
9. List three methods to measure cost behavior.
10. How is a scatter diagram used to identify and measure the behavior of a company's costs?
11. In cost-volume-profit analysis, what is the estimated profit at the break-even point?

12. A straight line on a CVP chart intersects the vertical axis at the level of fixed costs and has a positive slope that rises with each additional unit of volume by the amount of the variable costs per unit. What does this line represent?
13. Why are fixed costs depicted as a horizontal line on a CVP chart?
14. Each of two similar companies has sales of $20,000 and total costs of $15,000 for a month. Company A's total costs include $10,000 of variable costs and $5,000 of fixed costs. If Company B's total costs include $4,000 of variable costs and $11,000 of fixed costs, which company will enjoy more profit if sales double?
15. _____ of _____ reflects expected sales in excess of the level of break-even sales.
16. **Nike** manufactured commemorative hats sold  during the Olympic games. Identify some of the variable and fixed product costs associated with that production. [*Hint:* Limit costs to product costs.]
17. **Gap** is thinking of expanding sales of its most popular women's jeans by 65%. Do you expect its variable and fixed costs to stay within the relevant range? Explain.

QUICK STUDY

QS 23-1

Cost behavior identification

Determine whether each of the following is best described as a fixed, variable, or mixed cost with respect to product units:

1. Maintenance of factory machinery.
2. Packaging expense.
3. Wages of an assembly-line worker paid on the basis of acceptable units produced.
4. Factory supervisor's salary.
5. Taxes on factory building.
6. Rubber used to manufacture athletic shoes.

QS 23-2

Cost behavior identification

Listed here are four series of separate costs measured at various volume levels. Examine each series and identify whether it is best described as a fixed, variable, step-wise, or curvilinear cost.

Volume (Units)	Series 1	Series 2	Series 3	Series 4
0	$ 0	$450	$ 800	$100
100	800	450	800	105
200	1,600	450	800	120
300	2,400	450	1,600	145
400	3,200	450	1,600	190
500	4,000	450	2,400	250
600	4,800	450	2,400	320

This scatter diagram reflects past maintenance hours and their corresponding maintenance costs:

QS 23-3
Cost behavior estimation

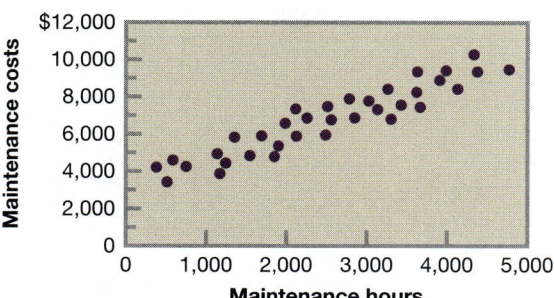

1. Draw an estimated line of cost behavior.
2. Estimate the fixed and variable components of maintenance costs.

ATI Phone Company sells its cordless phone for $90 per unit. Fixed costs total $150,000, and variable costs are $40 per unit. Determine (1) contribution margin per unit and (2) break-even point in units.

QS 23-4
Contribution margin per unit and break-even units

Refer to QS 23-4. Determine (1) contribution margin ratio and (2) break-even point in dollars.

QS 23-5
Contribution margin ratio and break-even dollars
P2

Refer to QS 23-4. Assume that ATI Phone Co. is subject to an income tax rate of 30%. Compute the units of product that must be sold to earn after-tax income of $140,000.

QS 23-6
CVP analysis and target income

Which one of the following is an assumption that underlies cost-volume-profit analysis?
1. Selling price per unit must change in proportion to the number of units sold in the planning period.
2. All costs have approximately the same relevant range.
3. For costs classified as variable, the costs per unit of output must change constantly.
4. For costs classified as fixed, the costs per unit of output must remain constant.

QS 23-7
CVP assumptions
C2

A high proportion of Company A's total costs are variable with respect to units sold; a high proportion of Company B's total costs are fixed with respect to units sold. Which company is likely to have a higher degree of operating leverage (DOL)? Explain.

QS 23-8
Operating leverage analysis
A2

Beeper Company manufactures and sells two products, green beepers and gold beepers, in the ratio of 5:3. Fixed costs are $85,000, and the contribution margin per composite unit is $119. What number of both green and gold beepers is sold at the break-even point?

QS 23-9
Multiproduct break-even

EXERCISES

Exercise 23-1

Cost behavior in graphs

Following are five graphs representing various cost behaviors.

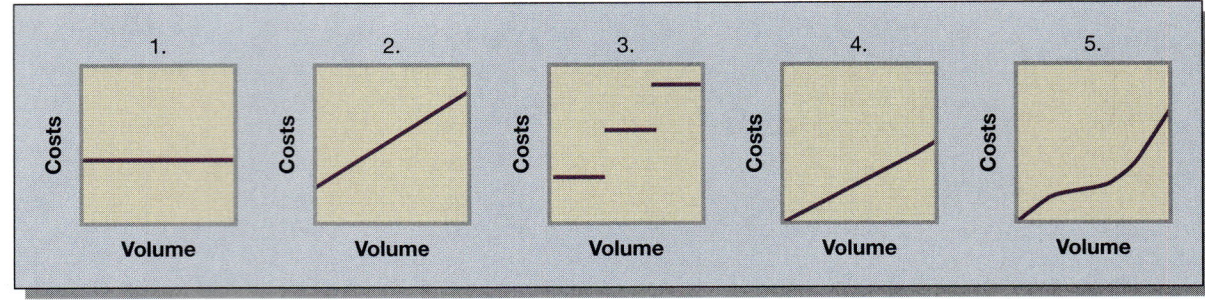

Identify whether the cost behavior in each graph is mixed, step-wise, fixed, variable, or curvilinear. Next, identify the graph (by number) that best illustrates each cost behavior: (a) Factory policy requires one supervisor for every 30 factory workers; (b) real estate taxes on factory; (c) electricity charge that includes the standard monthly charge plus a charge for each kilowatt hour; (d) commissions to salespersons; and (e) costs of hourly paid workers that provide substantial gains in efficiency when a few workers are added but gradually smaller gains in efficiency when more workers are added.

Exercise 23-2

Cost behavior defined

The left column lists several categories of costs. The right column presents short definitions of those costs. In the blank space beside each of the numbers in the right column, write the letter of the cost best described by the definition.

A. Total cost

B. Mixed cost

C. Variable cost

D. Curvilinear cost

E. Step-wise cost

F. Fixed cost

_____ **1.** This cost remains constant over a limited range of volume; when it reaches the end of its limited range, it changes by a lump sum and remains at that level until it exceeds another limited range.

_____ **2.** This cost has a component that remains the same over all volume levels and another component that increases in direct proportion to increases in volume.

_____ **3.** This cost increases when volume increases, but the increase is not constant for each unit produced.

_____ **4.** This cost remains constant over all volume levels within the productive capacity for the planning period.

_____ **5.** This cost increases in direct proportion to increases in volume; its amount is constant for each unit produced.

_____ **6.** This cost is the combined amount of all the other costs.

Exercise 23-3

Cost behavior identification

Following are five series of costs A through E measured at various volume levels. Examine each series and identify which is fixed, variable, mixed, step-wise, or curvilinear.

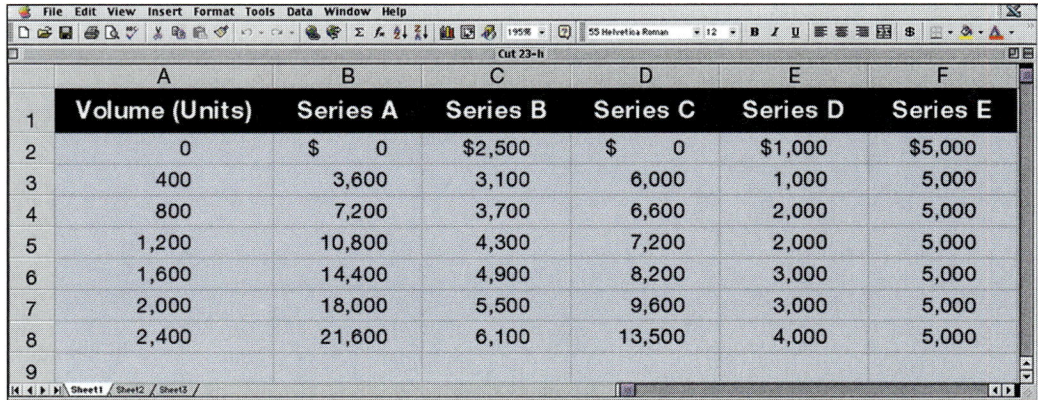

Volume (Units)	Series A	Series B	Series C	Series D	Series E
0	$ 0	$2,500	$ 0	$1,000	$5,000
400	3,600	3,100	6,000	1,000	5,000
800	7,200	3,700	6,600	2,000	5,000
1,200	10,800	4,300	7,200	2,000	5,000
1,600	14,400	4,900	8,200	3,000	5,000
2,000	18,000	5,500	9,600	3,000	5,000
2,400	21,600	6,100	13,500	4,000	5,000

Use the following information about sales volume and its costs to prepare a scatter diagram. Draw a cost line that reflects the behavior displayed by this cost. Determine whether the cost is variable, step-wise, fixed, mixed, or curvilinear.

Exercise 23-4

Scatter diagram and measurement of cost behavior

Period	Sales	Cost	Period	Sales	Cost
1	$760	$590	9	$580	$390
2	800	560	10	320	240
3	200	230	11	240	230
4	400	400	12	720	550
5	480	390	13	280	260
6	620	550	14	440	410
7	680	590	15	380	260
8	540	430			

A company reports the following information about its sales and its cost of sales. Each unit of its product sells for $500.

Exercise 23-5

Measurement of cost behavior using a scatter diagram

Period	Sales	Cost
1	$22,500	$15,150
2	17,250	11,250
3	15,750	10,500
4	11,250	8,250
5	13,500	9,000
6	18,750	14,250

Use these data to prepare a scatter diagram. Draw an estimated line of cost behavior and determine whether the cost appears to be variable, fixed, or mixed.

The management of Phoenix Company predicts that it will incur fixed costs of $160,000 and earn pretax income of $164,000 in the next period. Its expected contribution margin ratio is 25%. Use this information to compute the amounts of (1) total dollar sales and (2) total variable costs.

Exercise 23-6

Predicting sales and variable costs using contribution margin

Caper Company manufactures a single product that sells for $180 per unit, and whose total variable costs are $135 per unit. The company's annual fixed costs are $562,500. (1) Use this information to compute the company's (a) contribution margin, (b) contribution margin ratio, (c) break-even point in units, and (d) break-even point in dollars of sales. (2) Draw a CVP chart for the company.

Exercise 23-7

Contribution margin, break-even, and CVP chart

Refer to Exercise 23-7 and prepare a contribution margin income statement for Caper Company showing sales, variable costs, and fixed costs at the break-even point. If Caper's fixed costs increase by $135,000, what amount of sales (in dollars) would be needed to break even?

Exercise 23-8

Income reporting and break-even analysis

The management of Caper Company (in Exercise 23-7) targets an annual after-tax income of $810,000. The company is subject to an income tax rate of 20%. Assume that fixed costs remain at $562,500. Compute the (1) unit sales to earn the target after-tax net income and (2) dollar sales to earn the target after-tax net income.

Exercise 23-9

Computing sales to achieve target income

The sales manager of Caper Company (in Exercise 23-7) predicts that annual sales of the company's product will soon reach 40,000 units and its price will increase to $200 per unit. According to the production manager, the variable costs are expected to increase to $140 per unit but fixed costs will remain at $562,500. The income tax rate is 20%. What amounts of pretax and after-tax income can the company expect to earn from these predicted changes? (*Hint:* Prepare a forecasted contribution margin income statement as in Exhibit 23.20.)

Exercise 23-10

Forecasted income statement

Exercise 23-11

Predicting unit and dollar sales

The management of Legrand Company predicts $390,000 of variable costs, $430,000 of fixed costs, and a pretax income of $155,000 in the next period. Management also predicts that the contribution margin per unit will be $9. Use this information to compute the (1) total expected dollar sales for the period and (2) number of units expected to be sold in the period.

Exercise 23-12

Computation of variable and fixed costs; CVP chart

Rodriguez Company expects to sell 200,000 units of its product next year, which would generate total sales of $17 million. Management predicts that pretax net income for next year will be $1,250,000 and that the contribution margin per unit will be $25. (1) Use this information to compute next year's total expected (a) variable costs and (b) fixed costs. (2) Prepare a CVP chart from this information.

Exercise 23-13

Operating leverage computed and applied

Company A is a manufacturer with current sales of $3,000,000 and a 60% contribution margin. Its fixed costs equal $1,300,000. Company B is a consulting firm with current service revenues of $3,000,000 and a 25% contribution margin. Its fixed costs equal $250,000. Compute the degree of operating leverage (DOL) for each company. Identify which company benefits more from a 20% increase in sales and explain why.

Exercise 23-14

CVP analysis using composite units

Home Builders sells windows and doors in the ratio of 8:2 (8 windows for every 2 doors). The selling price of each window is $200 and the selling price of each door is $500. The variable cost of a window is $125 and of a door is $350. Next period's fixed costs are expected to be $900,000. Use this information to determine the (1) selling price per composite unit, (2) variable costs per composite unit, (3) break-even point in composite units, and (4) number of units of each product that will be sold at the break-even point.

PROBLEM SET A

Problem 23-1A

Scatter diagram and cost behavior estimation

Harris Co.'s monthly sales and cost data for its operating activities of the past year are shown below. Management wants to use these data to predict future fixed and variable costs.

Period	Sales	Total Cost
1	$320,000	$160,000
2	160,000	100,000
3	280,000	220,000
4	200,000	100,000
5	300,000	230,000
6	200,000	120,000
7	340,000	220,000
8	280,000	160,000
9	80,000	60,000
10	160,000	140,000
11	100,000	100,000
12	110,000	80,000

Required

1. Prepare a scatter diagram for these data with sales volume (in $) plotted on the horizontal axis and total cost plotted on the vertical axis.

2. Estimate the line of cost behavior by a visual inspection and draw it on the scatter diagram. (Assume a linear relation, which means that you should draw a straight cost line on the graph.)

3. Using the estimated line of cost behavior from part 2 and the assumption that the future will be like the past, predict the monthly fixed costs. Also predict variable costs *per sales dollar*.

4. Use the estimated line of cost behavior and results from part 3 to predict future total costs when sales volume is (a) $200,000 and (b) $300,000.

Sports Equipment Co. manufactures and markets a number of rope products. Management is considering the future of Product XT, a special rope for hang gliding, that has not been as profitable as planned. Since this product is manufactured and marketed independently of the other products, its total costs can be precisely measured. Next year's plans call for a selling price of $190 per 100 yards of XT rope. Its fixed costs for the year are expected to be $250,000, up to a maximum capacity of 700,000 yards. Forecasted variable costs are $140 per 100 yards of XT rope.

Problem 23-2A

CVP analysis and charting

Required

1. Estimate the break-even point for Product XT in terms of (a) sales units and (b) sales dollars.

2. Prepare a CVP chart for Product XT like that in Exhibit 23.11. Use 700,000 yards as the maximum number of sales units on the horizontal axis of the graph, and $1,400,000 as the maximum dollar amount on the vertical axis.

3. Prepare a contribution margin income statement showing sales, variable costs, and fixed costs for Product XT at the break-even point.

Check (1) Break-even sales, 5,000 units or $950,000

Juanita Co. sold 20,000 units of its only product and incurred a $50,000 loss (ignoring taxes) for the current year as shown:

Problem 23-3A

Break-even analysis; income targeting and forecasting

C3

JUANITA COMPANY Contribution Margin Income Statement For Year Ended December 31, 2002	
Sales	$1,000,000
Variable costs	800,000
Contribution margin	$ 200,000
Fixed costs	250,000
Net loss	$ (50,000)

During a planning session for year 2003's activities, the production manager notes that variable costs can be reduced 50% by installing a machine that automates several operations. To obtain these savings, the company must increase its annual fixed costs by $200,000. The maximum output capacity of the company is 40,000 units per year.

Required

1. Compute the break-even point in dollar sales for year 2002.

2. Compute the break-even point in dollar sales for year 2003 assuming the machine is installed and there is no change in unit sales price.

3. Prepare a forecasted contribution margin income statement for 2003 that shows the expected results with the machine installed. Assume that the unit sales price and the number of units sold will not change. Assume no income taxes.

4. Compute the sales level required in both dollars and units to earn $140,000 of after-tax income in 2003 with the machine installed and no change in unit sales price. The income tax rate is 30%. (*Hint:* Use procedures in Exhibits 23.14 and 23.16.)

5. Prepare a forecasted contribution margin income statement that shows the results at the sales level computed in part (4). Assume an income tax rate of 30%.

Check (3) Net income, $150,000

Check (4) Required sales, $1,083,333 or 21,667 units

Check (5) Net income, $140,000

Beach Co. produces and sells two products, T and O. It manufactures these products in separate factories and markets them through different channels. They have no shared costs. This year, Beach sold 50,000 units of each product. Sales and costs for each product are reflected in the following financial results:

Problem 23-4A

Break-even analysis, different cost structures, and income calculations

C3

	Product T	Product O
Sales	$2,000,000	$2,000,000
Variable costs	1,600,000	250,000
Contribution margin	$ 400,000	$1,750,000
Fixed costs	125,000	1,475,000
Income before taxes	$ 275,000	$ 275,000
Income taxes (32% rate)	88,000	88,000
Net income	$ 187,000	$ 187,000

Required

Preparation Component

1. Compute the break-even point in dollar sales for each product.

2. Assume that the company expects sales of each product to decline to 30,000 units next year with no change in unit sales price. Prepare forecasted financial results for next year following the format of the contribution margin income statement at the bottom of page 971 with columns for each of the two products (assume a 32% tax rate). Also, assume that any loss before taxes yields a 32% tax savings.

3. Assume that the company expects sales of each product to increase to 60,000 units next year with no change in unit sales price. Prepare forecasted financial results for next year following the format of the contribution margin income statement at the bottom of page 971 with columns for each of the two products (assume a 32% tax rate).

Analysis Component

4. If sales greatly decrease, which product would experience a greater loss? Explain.

5. Describe some factors that might have created the different cost structures for these two products.

Problem 23-5A

Analysis of price, costs, and volume changes on contribution margin and net income

This year Clark Company sold 40,000 units of its only product for $25 per unit. Manufacturing and selling the product required $200,000 of fixed manufacturing costs and $325,000 of fixed selling and administrative costs. Its per unit variable costs were as follows:

Material	$8.00
Direct labor (paid on the basis of completed units)	5.00
Variable overhead costs	1.00
Variable selling and administrative costs	0.50

Next year the company will use new material that is easier to work with than the old material. The new material will reduce material costs by 50% and direct labor costs by 60%, and the new material will not affect product quality or marketability. Since the factory's output is nearing its annual output capacity of 45,000 units, management is considering an increase in the unit sales price to reduce the number of units sold. Two plans are being considered. Under plan 1, the company will keep the price at the current level and sell the same volume as last year. This plan will increase income because of the reduced costs from using the new material. Under plan 2, the company will increase price by 20%. This plan will decrease unit sales volume by 10%. Under both plans 1 and 2, the total fixed costs and the variable costs per unit for overhead and for selling and administrative costs will remain the same.

Required

1. Compute the break-even point in dollar sales for both (a) plan 1 and (b) plan 2.

2. Prepare a forecasted contribution margin income statement with two columns showing the expected results of plan 1 and plan 2. The statements should report sales, total variable costs, contribution margin, total fixed costs, income before taxes, income taxes (30% rate), and net income.

Problem 23-6A

Break-even analysis with composite units

Peabody Co. manufactures and sells three products: red, white, and blue. Their unit sales prices are red, $20 per unit; white, $35 per unit; and blue, $65 per unit. The per unit variable costs to manufacture and sell these products are red, $12; white, $22; and blue, $50. Their sales mix is reflected in a ratio of 5:4:2 (red:white:blue). Annual fixed costs shared by all three products are $250,000. One type of raw material is used to manufacture all three products. The company has developed a new material that is of equal quality for less cost. However, the new material would reduce variable costs per unit as follows: red, by $6; white, by $12; and blue, by $10. However, the new material requires new equipment, which will increase annual fixed costs by $50,000. (Round answers to whole composite unit.)

Required

1. If it continues to use the old material, determine the company's break-even point in both sales units and sales dollars of each individual product.

2. If it uses the new material, determine the company's new break-even point in both sales units and sales dollars of each individual product.

Analysis Component

3. What insight does this analysis offer management for long-term planning?

Fredrickson Co.'s monthly sales and costs data for its operating activities of the past year are shown at the side. Management wants to use these data to predict future fixed and variable costs.

Period	Sales	Total Costs
1	$195	$ 97
2	125	87
3	105	73
4	155	89
5	95	81
6	215	110
7	145	93
8	185	105
9	135	85
10.	85	65
11	175	95
12	115	79

PROBLEM SET B

Problem 23-1B
Scatter diagram and cost behavior estimation

Required

1. Prepare a scatter diagram for these data with sales volume (in $) plotted on the horizontal axis and total costs plotted on the vertical axis.

2. Estimate the line of cost behavior by a visual inspection and draw it on the scatter diagram. (Assume a linear relation, which means that you should draw a straight cost line on the graph.)

3. Use the estimated line of cost behavior from part 2 and the assumption that the future will be like the past, predict the monthly fixed costs. Also predict variable costs *per sales dollar*.

4. Use the estimated line of cost behavior and results from part 3 to predict future total costs when sales volume is (a) $100 and (b) $170.

Check (3) Variable costs, $0.30 per sales dollar; Fixed costs, $45

Musical Arts Co. manufactures and markets a number of products. Management is considering the future of one product, electronic keyboards, that has not been as profitable as planned. Since this product is manufactured and marketed independently of the other products, its total costs can be precisely measured. Next year's plans call for a selling price of $350 per unit. The fixed costs for the year are expected to be $42,000, up to a maximum capacity of 700 units. Forecasted variable costs are $210 per unit.

Problem 23-2B
CVP analysis and charting

Required

1. Estimate the break-even point for keyboards in terms of (a) sales units and (b) sales dollars.

2. Prepare a CVP chart for keyboards like that in Exhibit 23.11. Use 700 keyboards as the maximum number of sales units on the horizontal axis of the graph, and $200,000 as the maximum dollar amount on the vertical axis.

3. Prepare a contribution margin income statement showing sales, variable costs, and fixed costs for keyboards at the break-even point.

Check (1) Break-even sales, 300 units or $105,000

Capital Co. sold 20,000 units of its only product and incurred a $50,000 loss (ignoring taxes) for the current year as shown:

Problem 23-3B
Break-even analysis; income targeting and forecasting

CAPITAL COMPANY
Contribution Margin Income Statement
For Year Ended December 31, 2002

Sales	$750,000
Variable costs	600,000
Contribution margin	$150,000
Fixed costs	200,000
Net loss	$ (50,000)

During a planning session for year 2003's activities, the production manager notes that variable costs can be reduced 50% by installing a machine that automates several operations. To obtain these savings, the company must increase its annual fixed costs by $150,000. The maximum output capacity of the company is 40,000 units per year.

Required

1. Compute the break-even point in dollar sales for year 2002.

2. Compute the break-even point in dollar sales for year 2003 assuming the machine is installed and there is no change in unit sales price. (Round the change in variable costs to a whole number.)

Check   (3) Net income, $100,000

3. Prepare a forecasted contribution margin income statement for 2003 that shows the expected results with the machine installed. Assume that the unit sales price and the number of units sold will not change. Assume no income taxes.

Check   (4) Required sales,
$916,667 or 24,445 units

4. Compute the sales level required in both dollars and units to earn $140,000 of after-tax income in 2003 with the machine installed and no change in unit sales price. The income tax rate is 30%. (*Hint:* Use procedures in Exhibits 23.14 and 23.16.)

Check   (5) Net income, $140,000

5. Prepare a forecasted contribution margin income statement that shows the results at the sales level computed in part (4). Assume an income tax rate of 30%.

Problem 23-4B
Break-even analysis, different
cost structures,
and income calculations

Model Co. produces and sells two products, BB and TT. It manufactures these products in separate factories and markets them through different channels. They have no shared costs. This year, Model Co. sold 50,000 units of each product. Sales and costs for each product are reflected in the following financial results:

	Product BB	Product TT
Sales	$800,000	$800,000
Variable costs	560,000	100,000
Contribution margin	$240,000	$700,000
Fixed costs	100,000	560,000
Income before taxes	$140,000	$140,000
Income taxes (32% rate)	44,800	44,800
Net income	$ 95,200	$ 95,200

Required

Preparation Component

1. Compute the break-even point in dollar sales for each product.

Check   (2) After-tax income: BB,
$39,712; TT, $(66,640)

2. Assume that the company expects sales of each product to decline to 33,000 units next year with no change in unit sales price. Prepare forecasted financial results for next year following the format of the contribution margin income statement as shown above with columns for each of the two products (assume a 32% tax rate).

Check   (3) After-tax income: BB,
$140,896; TT, $228,480

3. Assume that the company expects sales of each product to increase to 64,000 units next year with no change in unit sales price. Prepare forecasted financial results for next year following the format of the contribution margin income statement as shown above with columns for each of the two products (assume a 32% tax rate).

Analysis Component

4. If sales greatly increase, which product would experience a greater increase in profit? Explain.

5. Describe some factors that might have created the different cost structures for these two products.

Problem 23-5B
Analysis of price, costs,
and volume changes on
contribution margin and
net income

This year Novelty Company earned a disappointing 4.5% after-tax return on sales from marketing 100,000 units of its only product. The company buys its product in bulk and repackages it for resale at the price of $20 per unit. Novelty incurred the following costs this year:

Total variable unit costs	$800,000
Total variable packaging costs	$100,000
Fixed costs	$950,000
Income tax rate	25%

The marketing manager claims that next year's results will be the same as this year's unless some changes are made. The manager predicts the company can increase the number of units sold by 80% if it reduces the selling price by 20% and upgrades the packaging. This change would increase variable packaging costs by 20%. Increased sales would allow the company to take advantage of a 25% quantity purchase discount on the cost of the bulk product price. Neither the packaging change nor the volume discount would affect fixed costs, which provide an annual output capacity of 200,000 units.

Required

1. Compute the break-even point in dollar sales under the (a) existing business strategy and (b) new strategy that alters both unit sales price and variable costs.

2. Prepare a forecasted contribution margin income statement with two columns showing the expected results of (a) the existing strategy and (b) changing to the new strategy. The statements should report sales, total variable costs (unit and packaging), contribution margin, fixed costs, income before taxes, income taxes, and net income. Also determine the after-tax return on sales for these two strategies.

Check (1) Break-even for both strategies, $1,727,273

Check (2) Net income: Existing strategy, $112,500; New strategy, $475,500

Triad Co. manufactures and sells three products: product 1, product 2, and product 3. Their unit sales prices are product 1, $40; product 2, $30; and product 3, $20. The per unit variable costs to manufacture and sell these products are product 1, $30; product 2, $15; and product 3, $8. Their sales mix is reflected in a ratio of 6:4:2. Annual fixed costs shared by all three products are $270,000. One type of raw material is used to manufacture products 1 and 2. The company has developed a new material that is of equal quality for less cost. The new material would reduce variable costs per unit as follows: product 1 by $10, and product 2, by $5. However, the new material requires new equipment, which will increase annual fixed costs by $50,000.

Problem 23-6B
Break-even analysis with composite units

Required

1. If it continues to use the old material, determine the company's break-even point in both sales units and sales dollars of each individual product.

2. If it uses the new material, determine the company's new break-even point in both sales units and sales dollars of each individual product.

Check Old plan break-even, 1,875 composite units

Check New plan break-even, 1,429 composite units

Analysis Component

3. What insight does this analysis offer management for long-term planning?

Beyond the Numbers

BTN 23-1 Nike expanded its product line from running shoes to a full assortment of athletic footwear and apparel in the past decade. You are assigned to head Nike's new product, snowboards, to be sold through its sporting goods distribution channels. You are given permission to use all existing resources in getting the product to market, such as Nike's purchasing department, legal department, and buildings and equipment.

Reporting in Action

Required

1. What costs, variable or fixed, are your most immediate concern? Explain.

2. Identify the direct costs of snowboards and where they are primarily reflected in financial reports.

3. Assume that the contribution margin per snowboard is 60% and you anticipate snowboard sales of $5 million this year. Explain why gross margin on the income statement will not fully reflect your success. (*Hint:* Consider the difference between gross margin and contribution margin.)

BTN 23-2 Both Nike and Reebok make basketball shoes, but one company is usually more profitable than the other with its shoes. We know that each company makes decisions about purchasing plant assets to produce basketball shoes and that the fixed costs along with the variable costs of manufacturing and selling determine the break-even point and profitability of these companies.

Comparative Analysis

Required

1. Using the following data, compute the total cost per each pair (or unit) of basketball shoes for Nike and Reebok. (Assume that sales volume equals production volume.)

	Nike	Reebok
Estimated sales units and price	10,000 units @ $60/unit	10,000 units @ $60/unit
Direct material per unit	$10/unit	$10/unit
Direct labor per unit	$30/unit	$34/unit
Factory rent per month	$30,000	$10,000
Factory equipment (depreciation)	$50,000	$60,000

2. Compare Nike and Reebok using the results from your analysis of part (1) to explain why one company is more profitable than the other.

3. If sales decline to very low levels, which company will yield the higher net income (computations are unnecessary)?

Ethics Challenge

BTN 23-3 Labor costs of an auto repair mechanic are usually not based on actual hours worked. Instead, the amount paid a mechanic is based on an industry average amount of time estimated to complete a repair job. The repair shop bills the customer for the industry average amount of time at the repair center's billable cost per hour. This means that a customer can pay, for example, $120 for two hours of work on a car when the actual time worked may be only one hour. Many experienced mechanics can complete repair jobs well under the industry average. The average data are compiled by engineering studies and surveys conducted in the auto repair business. Assume that you are asked to complete such a survey for a repair center. The survey calls for objective input, and many questions require detailed cost data and analysis. The mechanics and owners know you have the survey and are encouraging you to complete it in a way that increases the average billable cost per hour for repair work.

Required

Write a one-page memorandum to the mechanics and owners that describes the direct labor analysis you will undertake in completing this survey.

Communicating in Practice

BTN 23-4 Several important assumptions underlie CVP analysis. Assumptions often help simplify and focus our analysis of sales and costs. A common application of CVP analysis is as a tool to forecast sales, costs, and income.

Required

Assume that you are actively searching for a job. Prepare a one-half page report identifying three assumptions relating to your expected revenue (salary) and three assumptions relating to your expected costs for the first year of your new job. Be prepared to discuss your assumptions in class.

Taking It to the Net

BTN 23-5 Access and review the entrepreneurial information at **Business Owner's Toolkit** [**www.Toolkit.cch.com**]. If available, access and review its *Initial Cash Requirements Worksheet* for a business start-up [**www.Toolkit.cch.com/text/P01_2200.asp**] or similar worksheets related to controls of cash and costs.

Required

Write a one-half page report that describes the information and resources available at the Business Owner's Toolkit to help the owner of a start-up business to control and monitor its costs.

Teamwork in Action

BTN 23-6 The owner of a local movie theater explains to you that ticket sales on weekends and evenings are strong, but attendance during the weekdays, Monday through Thursday, is poor. The owner proposes to offer a contract to the local grade school to show educational materials at the theater for a set charge per student during school hours. The owner asks your help to prepare a CVP analysis listing the cost and sales projections for the proposal. The owner must propose to the school's administration a charge per child. At a minimum, the charge per child needs to be sufficient for the theater to break even.

Required

Your team is to prepare two separate lists of questions that enable you to complete a reliable CVP analysis of this situation. One list is to be answered by the school's administration, the other by the owner of the movie theater.

BTN 23-7   We normally applaud deflation in the prices we pay for products and services, but is deflation good news for the business world? Read "The Zero Inflation Economy" in the January 19, 1998, issue of *Business Week* and think about the impact of deflation on a company when managers make decisions about cost behavior and CVP analysis.

Required

1. Define price stability.

2. List advantages of price stability in predicting sales and cost behavior within the relevant range.

3. Explain why deflation negatively impacted the metal industry discussed in this article.

4. What impact does deflation have on companies in the metal industry when preparing a CVP analysis?

BTN 23-8   Mary Jensen is an entrepreneur and owner of Innovations, a cable provider. She is considering a special "bundled product" offer combining phone, fax, Internet, and TV cable to consumers. Jensen's immediate concern is how to price this bundled product to attract sufficient customers and still be profitable. Another concern is how costs might change when customers of individual products become customers of bundled products.

Required

What information do you recommend that Jensen collect to help answer her concerns? What managerial accounting tool(s) might be especially useful to her in this situation?

24

Master Budgets and Planning

Tony Hawk—*Plays to win at sports . . . and business.*

A Look Back

Chapter 23 looked at cost behavior and described its relevance for managers in performing cost-volume-profit analysis. That chapter also explained and illustrated the application

A Look at This Chapter

This chapter explains the importance of budgeting and describes the master budget and its preparation. It also discusses the value of the master budget to the planning of future

A Look Ahead

Chapter 25 focuses on flexible budgets, standard costs, and variance reporting. It explains the usefulness of these procedures and reports for business decisions.

Hawking Boards

e HUNTINGTON BEACH, CA—Tony Hawk is not your typical entrepreneur. For one thing, he executed the first-ever 900-degree trick performed on a skateboard in X-Games competition. Second, his start-up company **Birdhouse Projects** [**www.b-house.com**] manufactures skateboards, which is risky even in the high-risk entrepreneurial world. Hawk and fellow pro skater Per Welinder launched Birdhouse with $80,000 in combined savings. By marketing their brand in specialty sports shops and using slick advertising and promotions with the Birdhouse skate team, Hawk and Welinder have built a skateboard, clothing, and accessories company well respected by their discerning customers.

Just as Hawk does with his tricks on the board, he and Welinder painstakingly plan Birdhouse's business activities to help ensure success. They listen to the kids and teams they sponsor and then react with products geared to those needs. "We really listen to our team because they're on the pulse of what's happening," says Hawk. "They're living it, and they know what kids think is legitimate and what's not." Birdhouse then creates master budgets and plans in response to that feedback, and it continues to monitor and control its merchandising and manufacturing processes. This hands-on policy extends from sales and expense budgets all the way through budgeted financial statements. Hawk's advice is to get your hands dirty with the financials because without it, he says, "I've seen [plans and budgets] that fail over and over again."

Hawk expects Birdhouse to bring in $12 million in sales this year. He's also adamant that Birdhouse stay in touch with its customer base. Budgets and plans are crucial to the bottom line, but quality and affordable products drive sales. Says Hawk, "Kids are the first ones to know it's contrived." [Sources: *Birdhouse Web site,* May 2001; *Entrepreneur,* November 1999.]

Learning Objectives

Conceptual

C1 Describe the importance and benefits of budgeting.

C2 Explain the process of budget administration.

C3 Describe a master budget and the process of preparing it.

Analytical

A1 Analyze expense planning using activity-based budgeting.

Procedural

P1 Prepare each component of a master budget and link each to the budgeting process.

P2 Link both operating and capital expenditure budgets to budgeted financial statements.

After management applies cost-volume-profit analysis or other techniques in devising a strategy for future periods, it then seeks to turn this strategy into action plans. These action plans include financial details that are compiled in a master budget. The budgeting process serves several purposes, including motivating employees and effectively communicating with them. The budget process also helps coordinate a company's activities toward common goals and is useful in evaluating actual results and management performance. In this chapter, we explain how to prepare a master budget and use it as a formal plan of a company's future activities. The ability to prepare this type of formal plan is of enormous help in starting and operating a company. Such planning gives us a glimpse into the future, and it can help us translate plans into actions.

Budgeting Process

We explained in Chapter 19 that most companies prepare long-term strategic plans spanning 5 to 10 years. These are then fine tuned in preparing medium-term and short-term plans. Strategic plans usually set a company's long-term direction. They provide a road map for the future about potential opportunities such as new products, markets, and investments. The strategic plan can be inexact, given its long-term focus. Medium- and short-term plans are more operational and translate strategic plans into actions. These action plans are fairly concrete and consist of defined objectives and goals.

C1 Describe the importance and benefits of budgeting.

Short-term plans are usually called *budgets* and typically cover a one-year period. A **budget** is a formal statement of a company's future plans. It is usually expressed in monetary terms because the economic or financial aspects of the business are the primary factors driving management's decisions. All managers should be involved in **budgeting,** which is the process of planning future business actions and expressing them as formal plans. Managers who plan carefully and formalize plans in a budgeting process increase the likelihood of both personal and company success. (Although most firms prepare annual budgets, it is not unusual for organizations to prepare three-year and five-year budgets that are revised at least annually.)

Analysis and Future Focus

The relevant focus of a budgetary analysis is the future. Management must focus on future transactions and events and the opportunities available. A focus on the future is important because the pressures of daily operating problems often divert management's attention and take precedence over planning. A good budgeting system counteracts this tendency by formalizing the planning process and demanding relevant input. Budgeting makes planning an explicit management responsibility.

Basis for Evaluation

The control function requires management to evaluate (benchmark) business operations against some norm. Evaluation involves comparing actual results against one of two usual alternatives: (1) past performance or (2) expected performance. An evaluation assists management in identifying problems and taking corrective actions if necessary. Evaluation using expected, or budgeted, performance is potentially superior to using past performance to decide whether actual results trigger a need for corrective actions. This is so because past performance is often an inferior standard for evaluation as it fails to consider several changes that can affect current and future activities. Changes in economic conditions, shifts in competitive advantages within the industry, new product developments, increased or decreased advertising, and other factors reduce the usefulness of comparisons with past results. In hi-tech industries, for instance, increasing competition, technological advances, and other innovations often reduce the usefulness of performance comparisons across years. Budgeted performance is computed after careful analysis and research that attempts to anticipate and adjust for changes in important company, industry, and economic factors. Therefore, budgets usually provide management with an effective control and monitoring system.

Point: Managers can evaluate performance by preparing reports that compare actual results to budgeted plans. Performance reports are described in Chapter 25.

Employee Motivation

Budgeting provides standards for evaluating performance and can affect the attitudes of employees who are evaluated by them. It can be used to create a positive effect on employees' attitudes, but it can also create negative effects if not properly applied. Budgeted levels of performance, for instance, must be realistic to avoid discouraging employees. Personnel who will be evaluated should be consulted and involved in preparing the budget to increase their commitment to meeting it. Evaluations of performance must allow the affected employees to explain the reasons for apparent performance deficiencies. More generally, there are three important guidelines in the budgeting process: (1) Employees affected by a budget should be consulted when it is prepared (*participatory budgeting*), (2) goals reflected in a budget should be attainable, and (3) evaluations should be made carefully with opportunities to explain any failures. Budgeting can be a positive motivating force when these guidelines are followed. Budgeted performance levels can provide goals for employees to attain or even exceed as they carry out their responsibilities. This is especially important in organizations that consider the annual budget a "sacred" document.

Point: The practice of involving employees in the budgeting process is known as *participatory budgeting*.

> ### Did You Know?
>
> **Going Public with Budgets** In the world of e-commerce, **Saisu Technologies** [**www.saisutech.com**] enables organizations to make better use of their information by blending Saisu's Web-based shell products around clients' existing applications. With products (applications) such as *Metals R Us*, Saisu aims to enhance clients' supply-chain relationships. Saisu recently went public, which meant that management had to develop specific future plans. For this purpose, it developed a detailed six-month budget and less-detailed budgets spanning 30 and 60 months.

Coordination of Activities

An important management objective in large companies is to ensure that activities of all departments contribute to meeting the company's overall goals. This requires coordination. Budgeting provides a way to achieve this coordination. We describe later in this chapter that a company's budget, or operating plan, is based on its objectives. This operating plan starts with the sales budget, which drives all other budgets including production, materials, labor, and overhead. The budgeting process coordinates the activities of these various departments to meet the company's overall goals.

Communication of Plans

A manager of small companies can adequately explain business plans directly to employees through conversations and other informal communications. However, conversations can create uncertainty and confusion if not supported by clear documentation of the plans. A written budget is preferred and can inform employees

> ### You Make the Call—Ethics
>
> **Budget Staffer** You learn that your company's earnings for the current period will be far below the budgeted amount reported in the press. You also know that one of your superiors, who is also aware of the earnings shortfall, has accepted a management position with a competitor. This superior is selling her shares of the company. Does this situation present ethical concerns for you?
>
> Answer—p. 1001

in all types of organizations about management's plans. The budget can also communicate management's specific action plans for the employees in the budget period.

Budgeting is an important and detailed activity that must be properly administered. This section explains the details of budget administration.

Budget Administration

Budget Committee

C2 Explain the process of budget administration.

The task of preparing a budget should not be the sole responsibility of any one department. Similarly, the budget should not be simply handed down as top management's final word. Instead, budget figures and budget estimates developed through a *bottom-up* process usually are more useful. This includes, for instance, involving the sales department in preparing sales estimates. Likewise, the production department should have initial responsibility for preparing its own expense budget. Without active employee involvement in preparing budget figures, there is a risk these employees will feel that the numbers fail to reflect their special problems and needs.

Most budgets should be developed by a bottom-up process, but the budgeting system requires central guidance. This guidance is supplied by a budget committee of department heads and other executives responsible for seeing that budgeted amounts are realistic and coordinated. If a department submits initial budget figures not reflecting efficient performance, the budget

Point: In a large company, developing a budget through a bottom-up process can involve hundreds of employees and take many weeks to complete.

committee should return them with explanatory comments on how to improve them. Then the originating department must either adjust its proposals or explain why they are acceptable. Communication between the originating department and the budget committee should continue as needed to ensure that both parties accept the budget as reasonable, attainable, and desirable.

The concept of continuous improvement applies to budgeting as well as production. **BP Amoco** recently streamlined its monthly budget report from a one-inch-thick stack of monthly control reports to a tidy, two-page flash report on monthly earnings and key production statistics. The key to this efficiency gain was the integration of new budgeting and cost allocation processes with its strategic planning process. BP Amoco's controller explained the new role of the finance department with respect to the budgetary control process as follows: "there's less of an attitude that finance's job is to control. People really have come to see that our job is to help attain business objectives."

Budget Reporting

The budget period usually coincides with the accounting period. Most companies prepare at least an annual budget, which reflects the objectives for the next year. To provide specific guidance, the annual budget usually is separated into quarterly or monthly budgets. These short-term budgets allow management to periodically evaluate performance and take needed corrective action. Managers can compare actual results to budgeted amounts in a report such as that shown in Exhibit 24.1. This report shows actual amounts, budgeted amounts, and their differences. A difference is called a *variance,* which we discuss in detail in Chapter 25. Management examines variances to identify areas for improvement and corrective action.

Exhibit 24.1

Comparing Actual Performance with Budgeted Performance

ECCENTRIC MUSIC Income Statement with Variations from Budget For Month Ended April 30, 2002	Actual	Budget	Variance
Sales	$63,500	$60,000	$+3,500
Less: Sales returns and allowances	1,800	1,700	+100
Sales discounts	1,200	1,150	+50
Net sales	$60,500	$57,150	$+3,350
Cost of goods sold	41,350	39,100	+2,250
Gross profit	$19,150	$18,050	$+1,100
Operating expenses			
Selling expenses			
Sales salaries	6,250	6,000	+250
Advertising	900	800	+100
Store supplies	550	500	+50
Depreciation—Store equipment	1,600	1,600	
Total selling expenses	$ 9,300	$ 8,900	$ +400
General and administrative expenses			
Office salaries	2,000	2,000	
Office supplies used	165	150	+15
Rent	1,100	1,100	
Insurance	200	200	
Depreciation—Office equipment	100	100	
Total general and admin. expenses	$ 3,565	$ 3,550	$ +15
Total operating expenses	$12,865	$12,450	$ +415
Net income	$ 6,285	$ 5,600	$ +685

Example: Assume that you must explain variances to top management. Which variances in Exhibit 24.1 would you research and why? *Answer:* Sales and cost of goods sold—due to their large variances.

Budget Timing

The time period required for the annual budgeting process can considerably vary. For example, budgeting for 2003 can begin as early as January 2002 or as late as December 2002. Larger, more complex organizations usually require a longer time to prepare their budgets than do smaller organizations. This is so because considerable effort is required to coordinate the different units (departments) within large organizations.

Many companies apply **continuous budgeting** by preparing **rolling budgets.** As each monthly or quarterly budget period goes by, these companies revise their entire set of budgets for the months or quarters remaining and add new monthly or quarterly budgets to replace the ones that have lapsed. At any point in time, monthly or quarterly budgets are available for the next 12 months or four quarters. Exhibit 24.2 shows rolling budgets prepared

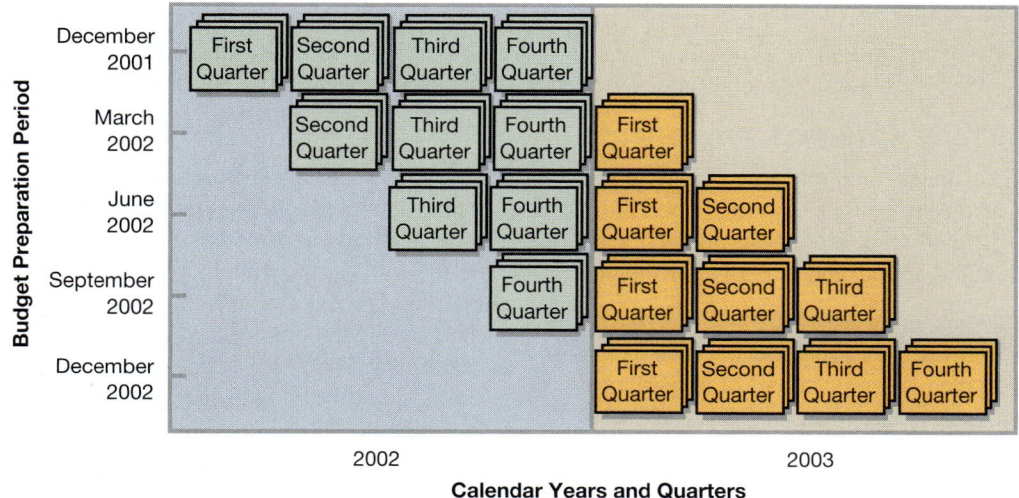

Exhibit 24.2

Rolling Budgets

at the end of five consecutive periods. The first set is prepared in December 2001 and covers the four calendar quarters of the year 2002. In March 2002, the company prepares another rolling budget for the next four quarters through March 2003. This same process is repeated every three months. As a result, management is continuously planning ahead.

Did You Know?

Budget Calendar   Penn Fuel Gas (PFG), a public utility, uses long-range operating budgets. Three groups influence its budgets: bankers, directors, and management. All three are interested in future cash flows and earnings. PFG's budget process begins six months before the budget is due to the board of directors. Its budget calendar, shown here, provides insight into the budget process during this period. [Source: R.N. West and A.M. Snyder, "How to Set Up a Budgeting and Planning System," *Management Accounting,* January 1997.]

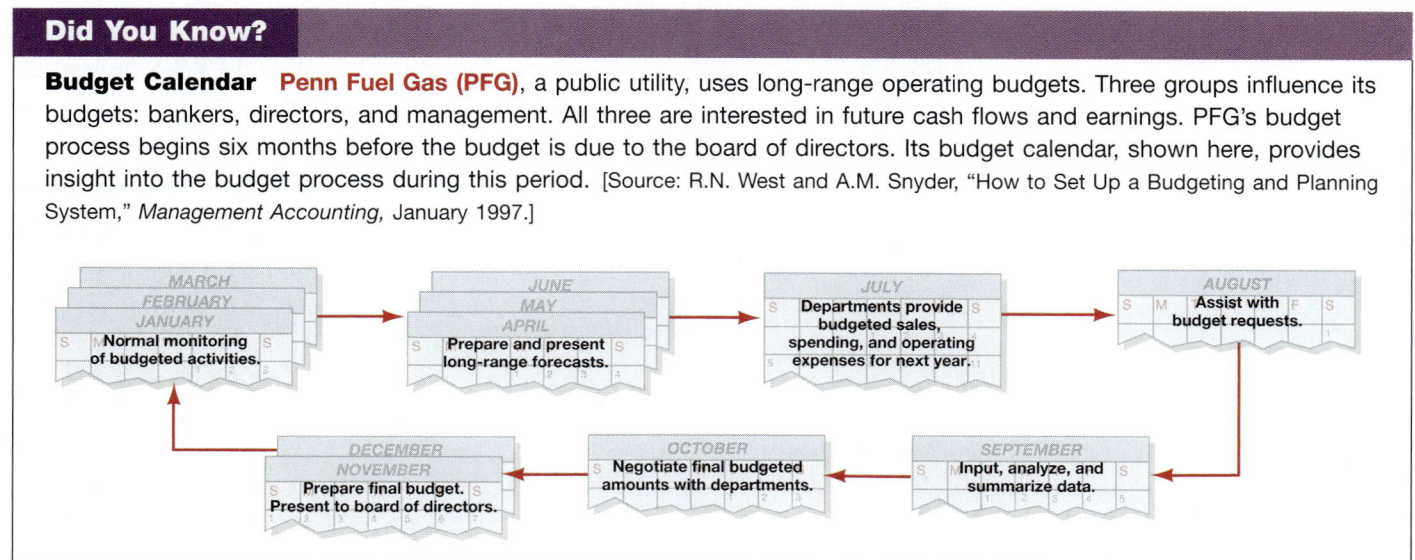

Exhibit 24.2 reflects an annual budget composed of four quarters prepared four times per year using the most recent information available. For example, the budget for the fourth quarter of 2002 is prepared in December 2001 and revised in March, June, and September of 2002. When continuous budgeting is not used, the fourth-quarter budget is nine months old and perhaps out of date when applied.

Quick Check

1. What are the major benefits of budgeting?
2. What is the main responsibility of the budget committee?
3. What is the usual time period covered by a budget?
4. What are rolling budgets?

Answers—p. 1002

Master Budget

A **master budget** is a formal, comprehensive plan for the future of a company. It contains several individual budgets that are linked with each other to form a coordinated plan.

C3 Describe a master budget and the process of preparing it.

Master Budget Components

The master budget typically includes individual budgets for sales, purchases, production, various expenses, capital expenditures, and cash. Managers often express the expected financial results of these planned activities with both a budgeted income statement for the budget period and a budgeted balance sheet for the end of the budget period. The usual number and types of budgets included in a master budget depend on the size and complexity of the company. A master budget should include, at a minimum, the budgets listed in Exhibit 24.3. In addition to these individual budgets, managers often include supporting calculations and additional tables with the master budget.

Did You Know?

Budgeting Acquisitions Budgeting is a crucial part of acquisitions analysis at **Koch Industries**. Analysis begins by projecting annual sales volume and prices. It then estimates cost of sales and selling, general, and administrative expenses. These are combined to form a potential acquisition's projected income for the next several years. By computing the present value of this projected income stream, Koch determines the price to offer.

Some budgets require the input of other budgets. For example, the merchandise purchases budget cannot be prepared until the sales budget has been prepared because the number of units to be purchased depends on how many units are expected to be sold. As a result, we must often sequentially prepare budgets within the master budget. A typical sequence for a quarterly budget consists of the five steps in Exhibit 24.4. Any stage in this budgeting process might reveal undesirable outcomes, so changes often must be made to prior budgets by repeating the previous steps. For instance, an early version of the cash budget might show an insufficient amount of cash unless cash outlays are reduced. This might yield a reduction in planned equipment purchases. A preliminary budgeted balance sheet might also reveal too much debt from an ambitious capital expenditures budget. Findings such as these often result in revised plans and budgets.

Concept 24-1

Exhibit 24.3

Basic Components of a Master Budget

- ■ **Operating budgets**
  - • *Sales budget*
  - • For merchandisers add: *Merchandise purchases budget* (specifying units to be purchased)
  - • For manufacturers add: *Production budget* (specifying units to be produced)
    Manufacturing budget (specifying manufacturing costs)
  - • *Selling expense budget*
  - • *General and administrative expense budget*
- ■ **Capital expenditures budget** (specifying expenditures for plant assets)
- ■ **Financial budgets**
  - • *Cash budget* (specifying cash receipts and disbursements)
  - • *Budgeted income statement*
  - • *Budgeted balance sheet*

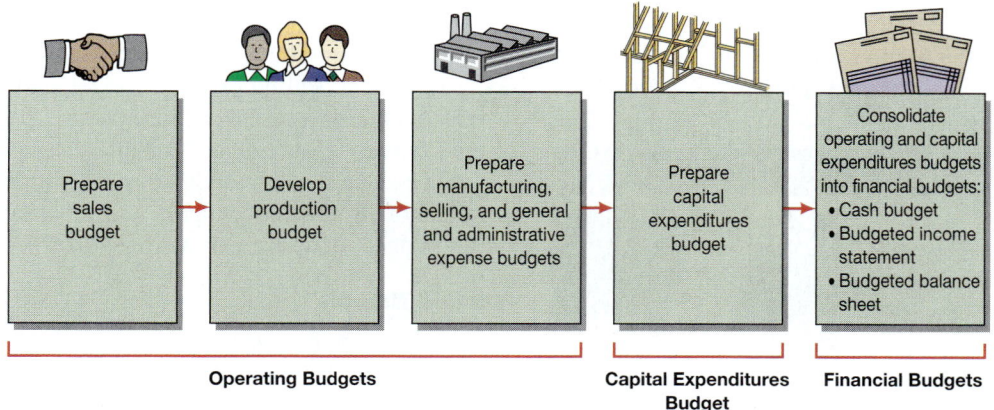

Exhibit 24.4
Master Budget Sequence

The remainder of this section explains how Hockey Den (HD), a retailer of youth hockey sticks, prepares its master budget. Its master budget includes operating, capital expenditures, and cash budgets for each month in each quarter. It also includes a budgeted income statement for each quarter and a budgeted balance sheet as of the last day of each quarter. We will show how HD prepares budgets for October, November, and December 2002. Exhibit 24.5 presents HD's balance sheet at the start of this budgeting period, which we will often refer to as we prepare the component budgets.

Exhibit 24.5
Balance Sheet Prior to the Budgeting Periods

HOCKEY DEN
Balance Sheet
September 30, 2002

Assets

Cash		$ 20,000
Accounts receivable		42,000
Inventory (900 units @ $60)		54,000
Equipment*	$200,000	
Less accumulated depreciation	(36,000)	164,000
Total assets		$280,000

Liabilities and Equity

Liabilities		
Accounts payable	$ 58,200	
Income taxes payable (due 10/31/2002)	20,000	
Note payable to bank	10,000	$ 88,200
Stockholders' equity		
Common stock	150,000	
Retained earnings	41,800	191,800
Total liabilities and equity		$280,000

*Equipment is depreciated on a straight-line basis over 10 years (salvage value is $20,000).

Example: Refer to Exhibit 24.5. Which budgets are affected by changing the salvage value for equipment? Which budgets are affected by changing the cash balance at September 30, 2002? *Answer:* Budgeted balance sheet, budgeted income statement, and cash budget.

Quick Check

5. What is a master budget?

6. A master budget (a) always includes a manufacturing budget specifying the units to be produced, (b) is prepared with a process starting with the operating budgets and continues with the capital expenditures budget, and then financial budgets, or (c) is prepared with a process ending with the sales budget.

7. What are the three primary categories of budgets in the master budget?

Answers—p. 1002

P1 Prepare each component of a master budget and link each to the budgeting process.

Operating Budgets

This section explains Hockey Den's preparation of operating budgets. Its operating budgets consist of the sales budget, merchandise purchases budget, selling expense budget, and general and administrative expense budget. It does not prepare production and manufacturing budgets because it is a merchandiser. (The preparation of production budgets and manufacturing budgets is described in Appendix 24A.)

Did You Know?

No Business Like Snow

Business   Costs of manmade snow to ski resorts are in the tens of millions of dollars for snowmaking equipment alone. Snowmaking involves spraying droplets of water into the air, causing them to freeze and come down as snow. Making snow can cost up to $2,000 an hour. Snowmaking accounts for 40 to 50 percent of the operating budgets for many ski resorts.

Sales Budget

The first step in preparing the master budget is planning the **sales budget.** This budget shows the planned sales units and the expected dollars from these sales. The sales budget is the starting point in the budgeting process because plans for most departments are linked to sales. The sales budget should emerge from a careful analysis of forecasted economic and market conditions, business capacity, proposed selling expenses (such as advertising), and predictions of unit sales. Because people normally feel a greater commitment to goals they helped set, a company's sales personnel are usually asked to develop predictions of sales for each territory and department. Another advantage of using this participatory budgeting approach is that it draws on knowledge and experience of people involved in the activity.

Point: A sales budget can be used as a what-if tool. By using CVP analysis (Chapter 23), income can be predicted for various levels of sales.

Example: Assume a company's sales force receives a bonus when sales exceed the budgeted amount. How would this arrangement affect the bottom-up process of sales forecasts? *Answer:* Sales reps may understate their budgeted sales.

To illustrate, in September 2002, Hockey Den sold 700 hockey sticks at $100 per unit. After considering sales predictions and market conditions, Hockey Den prepares its sales budget for the next quarter (three months) plus one extra month (see Exhibit 24.6). The sales budget includes January 2003 because the purchasing department relies on estimated January sales to decide on December 2002 inventory purchases.

Exhibit 24.6

Sales Budget Showing Planned Unit and Dollar Sales

Concept 24-2

HOCKEY DEN Monthly Sales Budget October 2002–January 2003			
	Budgeted Unit Sales	Budgeted Unit Price	Budgeted Total Sales
September 2002 (actual)	700	$100	$ 70,000
October 2002	1,000	$100	$100,000
November 2002	800	100	80,000
December 2002	1,400	100	140,000
Total for the quarter	3,200	$100	$320,000
January 2003	900	$100	$ 90,000

The sales budget in Exhibit 24.6 includes forecasts of both unit sales and unit prices. Some sales budgets are expressed only in total sales dollars, but most are more detailed. Management finds it useful to know budgeted units and unit prices for many different products, regions, departments, and sales representatives.

You Make the Call

Entrepreneur   You run a start-up that manufacturers designer clothes. Business is seasonal, and fashions and designs quickly change. How do you prepare reliable annual sales budgets?

Answer—p. 1001

Merchandise Purchases Budget

Companies use various methods to help managers make inventory purchasing decisions. These methods recognize that the number of units added to inventory depends on budgeted sales volume. Whether a company manufactures or purchases the product it sells, budgeted future sales volume is the primary factor in most inventory management decisions. A company must also consider its inventory system and other factors that we discuss below.

Just-in-time inventory systems Managers of *just-in-time* (JIT) inventory systems use sales budgets for short periods (often as few as one or two days) to order just enough merchandise or materials to satisfy the immediate sales demand. As a result, the amount of inventory is held to a minimum (or zero in an ideal situation). A just-in-time system minimizes the costs of maintaining inventory, but it is practical only if customers are content to order in advance or if managers can accurately determine short-term sales demand. Also, suppliers must be able and willing to ship small quantities regularly and promptly.

Point Accurate estimates of future sales are crucial in a JIT system.

Safety stock inventory systems Market conditions and manufacturing processes for some products do not allow a just-in-time system to be used. Companies in these cases maintain sufficient inventory to reduce the risk and cost of running short. This practice requires enough purchases to satisfy the budgeted sales amounts and to maintain a safety stock. A **safety stock** is a quantity of inventory that provides protection against lost sales caused by unfulfilled demands from customers or delays in shipments from suppliers.

Merchandise purchases budget preparation A merchandiser usually expresses a **merchandise purchases budget** in both units and dollars. Exhibit 24.7 shows the general layout for this budget in equation form. If this formula is expressed in units and only one product is involved, we can compute the number of dollars of inventory to be purchased for the budget by multiplying the units to be purchased by the cost per unit.

Exhibit 24.7

Formula for a Merchandise Purchases Budget

To illustrate, after assessing the cost of keeping inventory along with the risk and cost of inventory shortages, Hockey Den decided that the number of units in its inventory at each month-end should equal 90% of next month's predicted sales. For example, inventory at the end of October should equal 90% of budgeted November sales, and the November ending inventory should equal 90% of budgeted December sales, and so on. Also, Hockey Den's suppliers expect the September 2002 per unit cost of $60 to remain unchanged through January 2003. This information along with knowledge of 900 units in inventory at September 30 (see Exhibit 24.5) allow the company to prepare the merchandise purchases budget shown in Exhibit 24.8.

Example: Assume Hockey Den adopts a JIT system in purchasing merchandise. How will its sales budget be different from its merchandise purchases budget? *Answer:* The two budgets will be similar because future inventory should be near zero.

Exhibit 24.8

Merchandise Purchases Budget

HOCKEY DEN Merchandise Purchases Budget October 2002–December 2002	October	November	December
Next month's budgeted sales (units)	800	1,400	900
Ratio of inventory to future sales	× 90%	× 90%	× 90%
Budgeted ending inventory (units)	720	1,260	810
Add budgeted sales (units)	1,000	800	1,400
Required units of available merchandise	1,720	2,060	2,210
Deduct beginning inventory (units)	(900)	(720)	(1,260)
Units to be purchased	820	1,340	950
Budgeted cost per unit	$ 60	$ 60	$ 60
Budgeted cost of merchandise purchases	$49,200	$80,400	$57,000

Example: If ending inventory in Exhibit 24.8 is required to equal 80% of next month's predicted sales, how many units must be purchased each month? *Answer:* Budgeted ending inventory: Oct. = 640 units; Nov. = 1,120 units; Dec.= 720 units. Required purchases: Oct. = 740 units; Nov. = 1,280 units; Dec. = 1,000 units.

Point: To apply these concepts, work QS 24-4.

The first three lines of Hockey Den's merchandise purchases budget determine the required ending inventories (in units). Budgeted unit sales are then added to the desired ending inventory to give us the required units of available merchandise. We then subtract beginning inventory to determine the budgeted number of units to be purchased. The last line is the budgeted cost of the purchases, computed by multiplying the number of units to be purchased by the predicted cost per unit.

We already indicated that some budgeting systems describe only the total dollars of budgeted sales. Likewise, a system can express a merchandise purchases budget only in terms of the total cost of merchandise to be purchased, omitting the number of units to be purchased. This method assumes a constant relation between sales and cost of goods sold. Hockey Den, for instance, might assume the expected cost of goods sold to be 60% of sales, computed from the budgeted unit cost of $60 and the budgeted sales price of $100. However, it still must consider the effects of changes in beginning and ending inventories in determining the amounts to be purchased.

Selling Expense Budget

The **selling expense budget** is a plan listing the types and amounts of selling expenses expected during the budget period. Its initial responsibility usually rests with the vice president of marketing or an equivalent sales manager. The selling expense budget is normally created to provide sufficient selling expenses to meet sales goals reflected in the sales budget. Predicted selling expenses are based on both the sales budget and the experience of previous periods. After some or all of the master budget is prepared, management might decide that projected sales volume is inadequate. If so, subsequent adjustments in the sales budget can require corresponding adjustments in the selling expense budget.

To illustrate, Hockey Den's selling expense budget is in Exhibit 24.9. The firm's selling expenses consist of commissions paid to sales personnel and a $2,000 monthly salary paid to the sales manager. Sales commissions equal 10% of total sales and are paid in the month sales occur. Sales commissions are variable with respect to sales volume, but the sales manager's salary is fixed. No advertising expenses are budgeted for this particular quarter.

Exhibit 24.9

Selling Expense Budget

	HOCKEY DEN **Selling Expense Budget** **October 2002–December 2002**			
	October	**November**	**December**	**Total**
Budgeted sales	$100,000	$80,000	$140,000	$320,000
Sales commission percent	× 10%	× 10%	× 10%	× 10%
Sales commissions	$ 10,000	$ 8,000	$ 14,000	$ 32,000
Salary for sales manager	2,000	2,000	2,000	6,000
Total selling expenses	$ 12,000	$10,000	$ 16,000	$ 38,000

Example: If sales commissions in Exhibit 24.9 are increased, which budgets are affected? *Answer:* Selling expenses budget, cash budget, and budgeted income statement.

General and Administrative Expense Budget

The **general and administrative expense budget** plans the predicted operating expenses not included in the selling expenses budget. General and administrative expenses can be either variable or fixed with respect to sales volume. The office manager responsible for general administration often is responsible for preparing the initial general and administrative expense budget.

While interest expense and income tax expense are often classified as general and administrative expenses in published income statements, they normally cannot be planned at this stage of the budgeting process. The prediction of interest expense follows the preparation of the cash budget and the decisions regarding debt. The predicted income tax expense depends on the budgeted amount of pretax income. Both interest and income taxes are usually beyond the control of the office manager. As a result, they are not used in comparison to the budget to evaluate that person's performance. Exhibit 24.10 shows Hockey Den's general and administrative expense budget. It includes salaries of $54,000 per year, or $4,500 per month (paid each month when they are earned). Using information in Exhibit 24.5, the depreciation on equipment is computed as $18,000 per year [($200,000 − $20,000)/10 years], or $1,500 per month ($18,000/12 months).

Example: In Exhibit 24.10, how would a rental agreement of $5,000 per month plus 1% of sales affect the general and administrative expense budget? (Budgeted sales are in Exhibit 24.6.) *Answer: Rent expense:* Oct. = $6,000; Nov. = $5,800; Dec. = $6,400; Total = $18,200. *Revised total general and administrative expenses:* Oct. = $12,000; Nov. = $11,800; Dec. = $12,400; Total = $36,200.

Exhibit 24.10

General and Administrative Expense Budget

HOCKEY DEN General and Administrative Expense Budget October 2002–December 2002				
	October	**November**	**December**	**Total**
Administrative salaries	$4,500	$4,500	$4,500	$13,500
Depreciation of equipment	1,500	1,500	1,500	4,500
Total general and admin. expenses	$6,000	$6,000	$6,000	$18,000

Quick Check

8. In preparing monthly budgets for the third quarter, a company budgeted sales of 120 units for July and 140 units for August. Management wants each month's ending inventory to be 60% of next month's sales. The June 30 finished goods inventory consists of 50 units. How many units of product for July acquisition should the merchandise purchases budget specify for the third quarter? (a) 84, (b) 120, (c) 154, or (d) 204.

9. How do the operating budgets for merchandisers and manufacturers differ?

10. How does a just-in-time inventory system differ from a safety stock system?

Answers—p. 1002

Capital Expenditures Budget

The **capital expenditures budget** lists dollar amounts to be both received from plant and equipment disposals and spent to purchase additional plant and equipment to carry out the budgeted business activities. It is usually prepared after the operating budgets. Since a company's plant and equipment determine its productive capacity, this budget is usually affected by long-range plans for the business instead of short-term sales budgets for the next year or quarter. The process of preparing a sales or purchases budget can reveal that the company requires more (or less) capacity and additional equipment.

Capital budgeting is the process of evaluating and planning for capital (plant and equipment) expenditures. This is an important management task because these expenditures often involve long-run commitments of large amounts. Capital expenditures often have a major effect on predicted cash flows and the company's need for debt or equity financing. This means that the capital expenditures budget is often linked with management's evaluation of the company's ability to take on more debt. We discuss capital budgeting in detail in Chapter 26.

In the case of Hockey Den, it does not anticipate any disposal of equipment through December 2002, but it does plan to acquire additional equipment for $25,000 cash near the end of December 2002. This is the only budgeted capital expenditure from October 2002 through January 2003. Thus, no separate budget is shown. The cash budget in Exhibit 24.11 reflects this $25,000 planned expenditure.

Financial Budgets

P2 Link both operating and capital expenditure budgets to budgeted financial statements.

After preparing the operating and capital expenditures budgets, a company uses information from these budgets to prepare at least three financial budgets: the cash budget, budgeted income statement, and budgeted balance sheet.

Cash Budget

After developing budgets for sales, merchandise purchases, expenses, and capital expenditures, the next step is to prepare the cash budget. The **cash budget** shows expected cash inflows and outflows during the budget period. It is especially important to maintain a cash balance necessary to meet ongoing obligations. By preparing a cash budget, management can prearrange loans to cover anticipated cash shortages before they are needed. A cash budget also helps management avoid a cash balance that is too large. Too much cash is undesirable because it earns a relatively low (if any) return.

When preparing a cash budget, we add expected cash receipts to the beginning cash balance and deduct expected cash disbursements. If the expected ending cash balance is inadequate, additional cash requirements appear in the budget as planned increases from short-term loans. If the expected ending cash balance exceeds the desired balance, the excess is used to repay loans or to acquire short-term investments. Information for preparing the cash budget is mainly taken from the operating and capital expenditures budgets.

To illustrate, Exhibit 24.11 presents Hockey Den's cash budget. The beginning cash balance for October is taken from the September 30, 2002, balance sheet in Exhibit 24.5. The remainder of this section describes the computations in the cash budget.

Exhibit 24.11

Cash Budget

HOCKEY DEN Cash Budget October 2002–December 2002	October	November	December
Beginning cash balance	$ 20,000	$ 20,000	$ 22,272
Cash receipts from customers (Exhibit 24.12)	82,000	92,000	104,000
Total cash available	$102,000	$112,000	$126,272
Cash disbursements			
Payments for merchandise (Exhibit 24.13)	58,200	49,200	80,400
Sales commissions (Exhibit 24.9)	10,000	8,000	14,000
Salaries			
Sales (Exhibit 24.9)	2,000	2,000	2,000
Administrative (Exhibit 24.10)	4,500	4,500	4,500
Income taxes payable (Exhibit 24.5)	20,000		
Dividends ($150,000 × 2%)		3,000	
Interest on bank loan			
October ($10,000 × 1%)	100		
November ($22,800 × 1%)		228	
Purchase of equipment			25,000
Total cash disbursements	$ 94,800	$ 66,928	$125,900
Preliminary cash balance	$ 7,200	$ 45,072	$ 372
Additional loan from bank	12,800		19,628
Repayment of loan to bank		(22,800)	
Ending cash balance	$ 20,000	$ 22,272	$ 20,000
Loan balance, end of month	$ 22,800	$ 0	$ 19,628

We begin with reference to the budgeted sales of Hockey Den (Exhibit 24.6). Analysis of past sales indicates that 40% of the firm's sales are for cash. The remaining 60% are credit sales, these customers are expected to pay in full in the month following the sales. We now can compute the budgeted cash receipts from customers as shown in Exhibit 24.12. October's budgeted cash receipts consist of $40,000 from expected cash sales ($100,000 × 40%) plus the anticipated collection of $42,000 of accounts receivable from the end of September. Each month's cash receipts from customers are transferred to the second line of Exhibit 24.11.

Exhibit 24.12

Computing Budgeted
Cash Receipts

	September	October	November	December
Sales	$70,000	$100,000	$80,000	$140,000
Ending accounts receivable (60%)	42,000	60,000	48,000	84,000
Cash receipts from				
Cash sales (40% of sales)		$ 40,000	$32,000	$ 56,000
Collections of prior month's receivables ..		42,000	60,000	48,000
Total cash receipts		$ 82,000	$92,000	$104,000

Next, we note that Hockey Den's purchases of merchandise are entirely on account. It then makes full payments during the month following the purchases. Therefore, cash disbursements for purchases can be computed from the September 30, 2002, balance sheet (Exhibit 24.5) and the merchandise purchases budget (Exhibit 24.8). This computation is shown in Exhibit 24.13.

Exhibit 24.13

Computing Cash
Disbursements for Purchases

October payments (September 30 balance)	$58,200
November payments (October purchases)	49,200
December payments (November purchases)	80,400

The monthly budgeted cash disbursements for sales commissions and salaries are taken from the selling expense budget (Exhibit 24.9) and the general and administrative expense budget (Exhibit 24.10). The cash budget is unaffected by depreciation as reported in the general and administrative expenses budget.

Income taxes are due and payable in October as shown in the September 30, 2002, balance sheet (Exhibit 24.5). The cash budget in Exhibit 24.11 shows this $20,000 expected payment in October. Predicted income tax expense for the quarter ending December 31 is 40% of net income and is due in January 2003. It is therefore not reported in the October–December 2002 cash budget but in the budgeted income statement as income tax expense and on the budgeted balance sheet as income tax liability.

Hockey Den also pays a cash dividend equal to 2% of the par value of common stock in the second month of each quarter. The cash budget in Exhibit 24.11 shows a November payment of $3,000 for this purpose (2% of $150,000; see Exhibit 24.5).

Hockey Den has an agreement with its bank that promises additional loans at the end of each month, if necessary, to keep a minimum cash balance of $20,000. If the cash balance exceeds $20,000 at the end of a month, the company uses the excess to repay loans. Interest is paid at each month-end at the rate of 1% of the beginning balance of these loans. For October, this payment is 1% of the $10,000 amount reported in the balance sheet of Exhibit 24.5. For November, the company expects to pay interest of $228, computed as 1% of the $22,800 expected loan balance at October 31. No interest is budgeted for December because the company expects to repay the loans in full at the end of November. Exhibit 24.11 shows

Example: If the minimum ending cash balance in Exhibit 24.11 is changed to $25,000 for each month, what is the projected loan balance at Dec. 31, 2002? *Answer:*

Loan balance, Oct. 31	$27,800
November interest	278
November payment	25,022
Loan balance, Nov. 30	2,778
December interest	28
Additional loan in Dec.	21,928
Loan balance, Dec. 31	24,706

Example: Give one reason for maintaining a minimum cash balance when the budget shows extra cash is not needed. *Answer:* For unexpected events.

Point: To apply these concepts, work Exercises 24-2 and 24-3.

that the October 31 cash balance declines to $7,200 (before any loan-related activity). This amount is less than the $20,000 minimum. Hockey Den will bring this balance up to the minimum by borrowing $12,800 with a short-term note. At the end of November, the budget shows an expected cash balance of $45,072 before any loan activity. This means that the company expects to repay $22,800 of debt. The equipment purchase budgeted for December reduces the expected cash balance to $372, far below the $20,000 minimum. The company expects to borrow $19,628 in that month to reach the minimum desired ending balance.

Did You Know?

Managing Cash   **Harley-Davidson**'s net cash outflows for investing activities were $300 million this past year. Part of this was due to a $165 million outflow for capital expenditures.

Budgeted Income Statement

One of the final steps in preparing the master budget is to summarize the income effects. The **budgeted income statement** is a managerial accounting report showing predicted amounts of sales and expenses for the budget period. Information needed for preparing a budgeted income statement is primarily taken from already prepared budgets. The volume of information summarized in the budgeted income statement is so large for some companies that they often use spreadsheets to accumulate the budgeted transactions and classify them by their effects on income. We condense the budgeted income statement for Hockey Den and show it in Exhibit 24.14. All information in this exhibit is taken from earlier budgets. Also, we now can predict the amount of income tax expense for the quarter, computed as 40% of the budgeted pretax income. This amount is included in the cash budget and/or the budgeted balance sheet as necessary.

Did You Know?

Mission Plans   Most companies allocate dollars based on budgets submitted by department managers. These managers ensure that the numbers are correct and then monitor the budget during the period for discrepancies. Managers must remember, however, that a budget is judged by its success in helping achieve the organization's mission. One analogy is that a pilot must know the destination to plan a flight and then must monitor flight performance.

Exhibit 24.14

Budgeted Income Statement

HOCKEY DEN Budgeted Income Statement For Three Months Ended December 31, 2002		
Sales (Exhibit 24.6, 3,200 units @ $100)		$320,000
Cost of goods sold (3,200 units @ $60)		192,000
Gross profit		$128,000
Operating expenses		
Sales commissions (Exhibit 24.9)	$32,000	
Sales salaries (Exhibit 24.9)	6,000	
Administrative salaries (Exhibit 24.10)	13,500	
Depreciation on equipment (Exhibit 24.10)	4,500	
Interest expense (Exhibit 24.11)	328	(56,328)
Income before income taxes		$ 71,672
Income tax expense ($71,672 × 40%)		(28,669)
Net income		$ 43,003

Point: Lending institutions often require potential borrowers to provide cash budgets, budgeted income statements, and budgeted balance sheets, as well as data on past performance.

Budgeted Balance Sheet

The final step in preparing the master budget is summarizing the company's financial position. The **budgeted balance sheet** shows predicted amounts for the company's assets, liabilities, and equity as of the end of the budget period. Hockey Den's budgeted balance sheet in Exhibit 24.15 is prepared using information from the other budgets. The sources of amounts are reported in the notes to the budgeted balance sheet.[1]

Point: To apply these concepts, work Exercise 24-4.

Exhibit 24.15
Budgeted Balance Sheet

HOCKEY DEN
Budgeted Balance Sheet
December 31, 2002

Assets

Cash[a]		$ 20,000
Accounts receivable[b]		84,000
Inventory (810 unit @ $60)[c]		48,600
Equipment[d]	$225,000	
Less accumulated depreciation[e]	(40,500)	184,500
Total assets		$ 337,100

Liabilities and Equity

Liabilities		
Accounts payable[f]	$ 57,000	
Income taxes payable[g]	28,669	
Bank loan payable[h]	19,628	$ 105,297
Stockholders' equity		
Common stock[i]	150,000	
Retained earnings[j]	81,803	231,803
Total liabilities and equity		$337,100

[a] Ending balance for December from the cash budget in Exhibit 24.11.

[b] 60% of $140,000 sales budgeted for December from the sales budget in Exhibit 24.6.

[c] 810 units in budgeted December ending inventory at the budgeted cost of $60 per unit (from the purchases budget in Exhibit 24.8).

[d] September 30 balance of $200,000 from the beginning balance sheet in Exhibit 24.5 plus $25,000 cost of new equipment from the cash budget in Exhibit 24.11.

[e] September 30 balance of $36,000 from the beginning balance sheet in Exhibit 24.5 plus $4,500 expense from the general and administrative expense budget in Exhibit 24.10.

[f] Budgeted cost of purchases for December from the purchases budget in Exhibit 24.8.

[g] Income tax expense from the budgeted income statement for the fourth quarter in Exhibit 24.14.

[h] Budgeted December 31 balance from the cash budget in Exhibit 24.11.

[i] Unchanged from the beginning balance sheet in Exhibit 24.5.

[j] September 30 balance of $41,800 from the beginning balance sheet in Exhibit 24.5 plus budgeted net income of $43,003 from the budgeted income statement in Exhibit 24.14 minus budgeted cash dividends of $3,000 from the cash budget in Exhibit 24.11.

Quick Check

11. In preparing a budgeted balance sheet, (a) plant assets are determined by analyzing the capital expenditures budget and the balance sheet from the beginning of the budget period, (b) liabilities are determined by analyzing the general and administrative expense budget, or (c) retained earnings are determined from information contained in the cash budget and the balance sheet from the beginning of the budget period.

12. What sequence is followed in preparing the budgets that constitute the master budget?

Answers—p. 1002

[1] An eight-column spreadsheet, or work sheet, can be used to prepare a budgeted balance sheet (and income statement). The first two columns show the post-closing trial balance as of the last day of the period prior to the budget period. The budgeted transactions and adjustments are entered in the third and fourth columns in the same manner as end-of-period adjustments are entered on an ordinary work sheet. After all budgeted transactions and adjustments have been entered, the post-closing trial balance amounts in the first two columns are combined with the budget amounts in the third and fourth columns and sorted to the proper Income Statement (fifth and sixth columns) and Balance Sheet columns (seventh and eighth columns). Balances in these columns are used to prepare the budgeted income statement and balance sheet.

Using the Information

Activity-Based Budgeting

A1 Analyze expense planning using activity-based budgeting.

Activity-based budgeting (ABB) is a budget system based on expected activities. Knowledge of expected activities and their levels for the budget period enables management to plan for resources required to perform the activities. To illustrate, we consider the budget of an organization's accounting department. Traditional budgeting systems list items such as salaries, supplies, equipment, and utilities. Such an itemized budget informs management of the use of the funds budgeted (for example, salaries), but management cannot assess the basis for increases or decreases in budgeted amounts as compared to prior periods. Accordingly, management often makes across-the-board cuts or increases. In contrast, ABB would require management to list activities performed by, say, the accounting department such as auditing, tax reporting, financial reporting, and cost accounting. Exhibit 24.16 contrasts a traditional budget

Exhibit 24.16

Activity-Based Budgeting versus Traditional Budgeting

Activity-Based Budget		Traditional Budget	
Auditing	$ 58,000	Salaries	$152,000
Tax reporting	71,000	Supplies	22,000
Financial reporting	63,000	Depreciation	36,000
Cost accounting	32,000	Utilities	14,000
Total	$224,000	Total	$224,000

with an activity-based budget for a company's accounting department. An understanding of the resources required to perform the activities, the costs associated with these resources, and the

You Make the Call

Environmental Manager You are the new manager responsible for a chemical company's environmental control. This is a new position within the company. You are asked to develop a budget for your job and identify job responsibilities. How do you proceed?

Answer—p. 1001

way resource use changes with changes in activity levels allow management to better assess how much expenses must increase to accommodate increases in activity levels. Moreover, by knowing the relation between activities and costs, management can attempt to reduce costs by eliminating nonvalue-added activities.

Demonstration Problem

Wild Wood Co's management asks you to prepare its master budget using the following information. The budget is to cover the months of April, May, and June 2002.

WILD WOOD COMPANY Balance Sheet March 31, 2002				
Assets			**Liabilities and Equity**	
Cash		$ 50,000	Accounts payable	$156,000
Accounts receivable		175,000	Short-term notes payable	12,000
Inventory		126,000	Total current liabilities	$168,000
Total current assets		$351,000	Long-term note payable	200,000
Equipment	$480,000		Total liabilities	$368,000
Accumulated depreciation	(90,000)	390,000	Common stock	235,000
			Retained earnings	138,000
			Total stockholders' equity	$373,000
Total assets		$741,000	Total liabilities and equity	$741,000

Additional Information

a. Sales for March total 10,000 units. Each month's sales are expected to exceed the prior month's results by 5%. The product's selling price is $25 per unit.

b. Company policy calls for ending inventory of a given month to equal 80% of next month's expected unit sales. The March 31 inventory is 8,400 units, which is in compliance with the policy. The purchase price is $15 per unit.

c. Sales representatives' commissions are 12.5% and are paid in the month of the sales. The sales manager's salary will be $3,500 in April and $4,000 thereafter.

d. General and administrative expenses include administrative salaries of $8,000 per month, depreciation of $5,000 per month, and 0.9% monthly interest on the long-term note payable.

e. The company expects 30% of sales to be for cash and the remaining 70% on credit. Receivables are collected in full in the month following the sale (none is collected in the month of the sale).

f. All merchandise purchases are on credit, and no payables arise from any other transactions. One month's purchases are fully paid in the next month.

g. The minimum ending cash balance for all months is $50,000. If necessary, the company will borrow enough cash to reach the minimum. The resulting short-term note will require an interest payment of 1% at the end of each month. If the ending cash balance exceeds the minimum, the excess will be applied to repaying the short-term notes payable balance.

h. Dividends of $100,000 are to be declared and paid in May.

i. No cash payments for income taxes are to be made during the second calendar quarter. Income taxes will be assessed at 35% in the quarter.

j. Equipment purchases of $55,000 are scheduled for June.

Required

Prepare the following budgets and other financial information as required:

1. Sales budget, including sales for July.
2. Purchases budget, the budgeted cost of goods sold for each month and quarter, and the cost of the June 30 budgeted inventory.
3. Selling expense budget.
4. General and administrative expense budget.
5. Expected cash receipts from customers and the expected June 30 balance of accounts receivable.
6. Expected cash payments for purchases and the expected June 30 balance of accounts payable.
7. Cash budget.
8. Budgeted income statement.
9. Budgeted statement of retained earnings.
10. Budgeted balance sheet.

Planning the Solution

- The sales budget shows expected sales for each month in the quarter. Start by multiplying March sales by 105% and then do the same for the remaining months. July's sales are needed for the purchases budget. To complete the budget, multiply the expected unit sales by the selling price of $25 per unit.

- Use these results and the 80% inventory policy to budget the size of ending inventory for April, May, and June. Add the budgeted sales to these numbers and subtract the actual or expected beginning inventory for each month. The result is the number of units to be purchased each month. Multiply these numbers by the per unit cost of $15. Find the budgeted cost of goods sold by multiplying the unit sales in each month by the $15 cost per unit. Compute the cost of the June 30 ending inventory by multiplying the expected units available at that date by the $15 cost per unit.

- The selling expense budget has only two items. Find the amount of the sales representatives' commissions by multiplying the expected dollar sales in each month by the 12.5% commission rate. Then include the sales manager's salary of $3,500 in April and $4,000 in May and June.

- The general and administrative expense budget should show three items. Administrative salaries are fixed at $8,000 per month, and depreciation is $5,000 per month. Budget the monthly interest expense on the long-term note by multiplying its $200,000 balance by the 0.9% monthly interest rate.

- Determine the amounts of cash sales in each month by multiplying the budgeted sales by 30%. Add to this amount the credit sales of the prior month (computed as 70% of prior month's sales). April's cash receipts from collecting receivables equals the March 31 balance of $175,000. The expected June 30 accounts receivable balance equals 70% of June's total budgeted sales.

- Determine expected cash payments on accounts payable for each month by making them equal to the merchandise purchases in the prior month. The payments for April equal the March 31 balance of accounts payable shown on the beginning balance sheet. The June 30 balance of accounts payable equals merchandise purchases for June.

- Prepare the cash budget by combining the given information and the amounts of cash receipts and cash payments on account that you computed. Complete the cash budget for each month by either borrowing enough to raise the preliminary balance to the minimum or paying off short-term debt as much as the balance allows without falling below the minimum. Show the ending balance of the short-term note in the budget.
- Prepare the budgeted income statement by combining the budgeted items for all three months. Determine the income before income taxes and multiply it by the 35% rate to find the quarter's income tax expense.
- The budgeted statement of retained earnings should show the March 31 balance plus the quarter's net income minus the quarter's dividends.
- The budgeted balance sheet includes updated balances for all items that appear in the beginning balance sheet and an additional liability for unpaid income taxes. Amounts for all asset, liability, and equity accounts can be found either in the budgets, other calculations, or by adding amounts found there to the beginning balances.

Solution to Demonstration Problem

1. Sales budget

	April	May	June	July
Prior month's sales	10,000	10,500	11,025	11,576
Plus 5% growth	500	525	551	579
Projected unit	10,500	11,025	11,576	12,155

	April	May	June	Quarter
Projected unit sales	10,500	11,025	11,576	
Selling price per unit	× $25	× $25	× $25	
Projected sales	$262,500	$275,625	$289,400	$827,525

2. Purchases budget:

	April	May	June	Quarter
Next month's unit sales (*part 1*)	11,025	11,576	12,155	
Ending inventory percent	× 80%	× 80%	× 80%	
Desired ending inventory	8,820	9,261	9,724	
This month's unit sales (*part 1*)	10,500	11,025	11,576	
Units to be available	19,320	20,286	21,300	
Beginning inventory	(8,400)	(8,820)	(9,261)	
Units to be purchased	10,920	11,466	12,039	
Budgeted cost per unit	× $15	× $15	× $15	
Projected purchases	$163,800	$171,990	$180,585	$516,375

Budgeted cost of goods sold:

	April	May	June	Quarter
This month's unit sales (*part 1*)	10,500	11,025	11,576	
Budgeted cost per unit	× $15	× $15	× $15	
Projected cost of goods sold	$157,500	$165,375	$173,640	$496,515

Budgeted inventory for June 30:

Units (*part 1*)	9,724
Cost per unit	× $15
Total	$145,860

3. Selling expense budget:

	April	May	June	Quarter
Budgeted sales (*part 1*)	$262,500	$275,625	$289,400	$827,525
Commission percent	× 12.5%	× 12.5%	× 12.5%	× 12.5%
Sales commissions	$ 32,813	$ 34,453	$ 36,175	$103,441
Manager's salary	3,500	4,000	4,000	11,500
Projected selling expenses	$ 36,313	$ 38,453	$ 40,175	$114,941

4. General and administrative expense budget:

	April	May	June	Quarter
Administrative salaries	$ 8,000	$ 8,000	$ 8,000	$24,000
Depreciation	5,000	5,000	5,000	15,000
Interest on long-term note payable (0.9% × $200,000)	1,800	1,800	1,800	5,400
Projected expenses	$14,800	$14,800	$14,800	$44,400

5. Expected cash receipts from customers:

	April	May	June	Quarter
Budgeted sales (*part 1*)	$262,500	$275,625	$289,400	
Ending accounts receivable (70%)	$183,750	$192,938	$202,580	
Cash receipts				
Cash sales (30%)	$ 78,750	$ 82,687	$ 86,820	$248,257
Collections of prior month's receivables ...	175,000	183,750	192,938	551,688
Total cash to be collected	$253,750	$266,437	$279,758	$799,945

6. Expected cash payments to suppliers:

	April	May	June	Quarter
Cash payments (equal to prior month's purchases)	$156,000	$163,800	$171,990	$491,790
Expected June 30 balance of accounts payable (June purchases)			$180,585	

7. Cash budget:

	April	May	June
Beginning cash balance	$ 50,000	$ 89,517	$ 50,000
Cash receipts (*part 5*)	253,750	266,437	279,758
Total cash available	$303,750	$355,954	$329,758
Cash payments			
Payments for merchandise (*part 6*)	156,000	163,800	171,990
Sales commissions (*part 3*)	32,813	34,453	36,175

[continued on next page]

[continued from previous page]

	April	May	June
Salaries			
Sales (*part 3*)	3,500	4,000	4,000
Administrative (*part 4*)	8,000	8,000	8,000
Interest on long-term note (*part 5*)	1,800	1,800	1,800
Dividends		100,000	
Equipment purchase			55,000
Interest on short-term notes			
April ($12,000 × 1.0%)	120		
June ($6,099 × 1.0%)			61
Total cash payments	$202,233	$312,053	$277,026
Preliminary balance	$101,517	$ 43,901	$ 52,732
Additional loan		6,099	
Loan repayment	(12,000)		(2,732)
Ending cash balance	$ 89,517	$ 50,000	$ 50,000
Ending short-term notes	$ 0	$ 6,099	$ 3,367

8.

WILD WOOD COMPANY
Budgeted Income Statement
For Quarter Ended June 30, 2002

Sales (*part 1*)		$827,525
Cost of goods sold (*part 2*)		(496,515)
Gross profit		$331,010
Operating expenses		
Sales commissions (*part 3*)	$103,441	
Sales salaries (*part 3*)	11,500	
Administrative salaries (*part 4*)	24,000	
Depreciation (*part 4*)	15,000	
Interest on long-term note (*part 4*)	5,400	
Interest on short-term notes (*part 7*)	181	
Total operating expenses		(159,522)
Income before income taxes		$171,488
Income taxes (35%)		(60,021)
Net income		$111,467

9.

WILD WOOD COMPANY
Budgeted Statement of Retained Earnings
For Quarter Ended June 30, 2002

Beginning retained earnings (*given*)	$138,000
Net income (*part 8*)	111,467
	$249,467
Dividends (*given*)	(100,000)
Ending retained earnings	$149,467

10.

WILD WOOD COMPANY Budgeted Balance Sheet June 30, 2002		
Assets		
Cash (*part 7*)		$ 50,000
Accounts receivable (*part 5*)		202,580
Inventory (*part 2*)		145,860
Total current assets		$398,440
Equipment (*given plus purchase*)	$535,000	
Accumulated depreciation (*given plus expense*)	(105,000)	430,000
Total assets		$828,440
Liabilities and Equity		
Accounts payable (*part 6*)		$180,585
Short-term notes payable (*part 7*)		3,367
Income taxes payable (*part 8*)		60,021
Total current liabilities		$243,973
Long-term note payable (*given*)		200,000
Total liabilities		$443,973
Common stock (*given*)		235,000
Retained earnings (*part 9*)		149,467
Total stockholders' equity		$384,467
Total liabilities and equity		$828,440

Production and Manufacturing Budgets

24

Unlike a merchandising company, a manufacturer must prepare a **production budget** instead of a merchandise purchases budget. A production budget, which shows the number of units to be produced each month, is similar to merchandise purchases budgets except that the number of units to be purchased each month (as shown in Exhibit 24.8) is replaced by the number of units to be manufactured each month. A production budget does not show costs—it is *always expressed in units of product*. Exhibit 24A.1 shows the production budget for **Toronto Sticks Company** (**TSC**), a manufacturer of hockey sticks. TSC is an exclusive supplier of hockey sticks to Hockey Den, meaning that TSC uses Hockey Den's budgeted sales figures (Exhibit 24.6) to determine its production and manufacturing budgets.

P3 Prepare production and manufacturing budgets.

Exhibit 24A.1
Production Budget

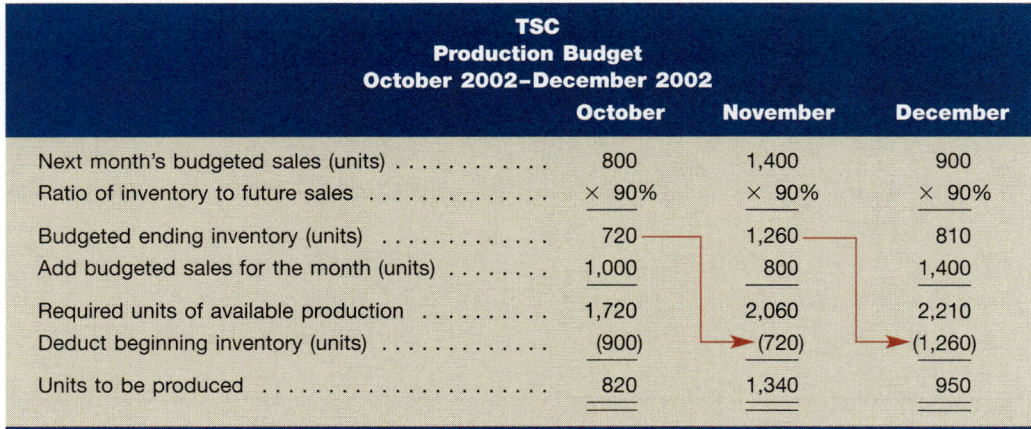

TSC Production Budget October 2002–December 2002	October	November	December
Next month's budgeted sales (units)	800	1,400	900
Ratio of inventory to future sales	× 90%	× 90%	× 90%
Budgeted ending inventory (units)	720	1,260	810
Add budgeted sales for the month (units)	1,000	800	1,400
Required units of available production	1,720	2,060	2,210
Deduct beginning inventory (units)	(900)	(720)	(1,260)
Units to be produced	820	1,340	950

A **manufacturing budget** shows the budgeted costs for direct materials, direct labor, and overhead. It is based on the budgeted production volume from the production budget. The manufacturing budget for most companies consists of three individual budgets: direct materials budget, direct labor budget, and overhead budget. Exhibits 24A.2–24A.4 show these three manufacturing budgets for TSC. These budgets yield the total expected cost of goods to be manufactured in the budget period.

The *direct materials budget* is driven by the budgeted materials needed to satisfy each month's production requirement. To this we must add the desired ending inventory requirements. The desired ending inventory of direct materials as shown in Exhibit 24A.2 is 50% of next month's budgeted materials requirements of wood. For instance, in October 2002, an ending inventory of 335 units of material is desired (50% of November's 670 units). The desired ending inventory for December 2002 is 225 units, computed from the direct material requirement of 450 units for a production level of 900 units in January 2003. The total materials requirements are computed by adding the desired ending inventory figures to that month's budgeted production material requirements. For October 2002, the total materials requirement is 745 units (335 + 410). From the total materials requirement, we then subtract the units of materials available in beginning inventory. For October 2002, the materials available from September 2002 are computed as 50% of October's materials requirements to satisfy production, or 205 units (50% of 410). Therefore, direct materials purchases in October 2002 are budgeted at 540 units (745 − 205). See Exhibit 24A.2.

Exhibit 24A.2

Direct Materials Budget

TSC Direct Materials Budget October 2002–December 2002	October	November	December
Budget production (units)	820	1,340	950
Materials requirements per unit	× 0.5	× 0.5	× 0.5
Materials needed for production (units)	410	670	475
Add budgeted ending inventory (units)	335	237.5	225
Total materials requirements (units)	745	907.5	700
Deduct beginning inventory (units)	(205)	(335)	(237.5)
Materials to be purchased (units)	540	572.5	462.5
Material price per unit	$ 20	$ 20	$ 20
Total cost of direct materials purchases	$10,800	$11,450	$9,250

The *direct labor budget* for TSC is shown in Exhibit 24A.3. About 15 minutes of labor time is required to produce one unit. Labor is paid at the rate of $12 per hour. Budgeted labor hours are computed by multiplying the budgeted production level for each month by one quarter (0.25) of an hour. Direct labor cost is then computed by multiplying budgeted labor hours by the labor rate of $12 per hour.

Exhibit 24A.3

Direct Labor Budget

TSC Direct Labor Budget October 2002–December 2002	October	November	December
Budgeted production (units)	820	1,340	950
Labor requirements per unit (hours)	× 0.25	× 0.25	× 0.25
Total labor hours needed	205	335	237.5
Labor rate (per hour)	$ 12	$ 12	$ 12
Labor dollars	$2,460	$4,020	$2,850

The *factory overhead budget* for TSC is shown in Exhibit 24A.4. The variable portion of overhead is assigned at the rate of $2.50 per unit of production. The fixed portion stays constant at $1,500 per month. The budget in Exhibit 24A.4 is in condensed form; most overhead budgets are more detailed, listing each overhead cost item.

TSC Factory Overhead Budget October 2002–December 2002	October	November	December
Budgeted production (units)	820	1,340	950
Variable factory overhead rate	× $2.50	× $2.50	× $2.50
Budgeted variable overhead	$2,050	$3,350	$2,375
Budgeted fixed overhead	1,500	1,500	1,500
Budgeted total overhead	$3,550	$4,850	$3,875

Exhibit 24A.4

Factory Overhead Budget

Summary

C1 Describe the importance and benefits of budgeting.
Planning is a management responsibility of crucial importance to business success. Budgeting is the process management uses to formalize its plans. Budgeting promotes analysis by management and focuses its attention on the future. Budgeting also provides a basis for evaluating performance, serves as a source of motivation, is a means of coordinating activities, and communicates management's plans and instructions to employees.

C2 Explain the process of budget administration.
Budgeting is a detailed activity that requires administration. At least three aspects are important: budget committee, budget reporting, and budget timing. A budget committee oversees the budget preparation. The budget period pertains to the time period for which the budget is prepared such as a year or month.

C3 Describe a master budget and the process of preparing it. A master budget is a formal overall plan for a company. It consists of plans for business operations and capital expenditures, plus the financial results of those activities. The budgeting process begins with a sales budget. Based on expected sales volume, companies can budget purchases, selling expenses, and administrative expenses. Next, the capital expenditures budget is prepared, followed by the cash budget and budgeted financial

statements. Manufacturers also must budget production quantities, materials purchases, labor costs, and overhead.

A1 Analyze expense planning using activity-based budgeting. Activity-based budgeting requires management to identify activities performed by departments, plan necessary activity levels, identify resources required to perform these activities, and budget the resources.

P1 Prepare each component of a master budget and link each to the budgeting process. The term *master budget* refers to a collection of individual component budgets. Each component budget is designed to guide persons responsible for activities covered by that component. A master budget must reflect the components of a company and their interaction in pursuit of company goals.

P2 Link both operating and capital expenditures budgets to budgeted financial statements. The operating budgets, capital expenditures budget, and cash budget contain much of the information to prepare a budgeted income statement for the budget period and a budgeted balance sheet at the end of the budget period. Budgeted financial statements show the expected financial consequences of the planned activities described in the budgets.

Guidance Answers to You Make the Call

Budget Staffer—Ethics Your superior's actions appear unethical because she is using private information for personal gain. As a budget staffer, you are low in the company's hierarchical structure and probably unable to confront this superior directly. You should inform an individual with a position of authority within the organization about your concerns.

Entrepreneur You must deal with two issues. First, because fashions and designs frequently change, you cannot heavily rely on previous budgets. As a result, you must carefully analyze the market to understand what designs are in vogue. This will help you plan the product mix and estimate demand. The second issue is the budget-

ing period. Since tastes can quickly change, an annual sales budget may be unreliable. Your best bet might be to prepare monthly and quarterly sales budgets that you continuously monitor and revise.

Environmental Manager As a new position, you are unlikely to have data to draw on in preparing your budget. In this situation, you can use activity-based budgeting. This requires you to develop a list of activities you plan to conduct, the resources required to perform these activities, and the expenses associated with these resources. You should challenge yourself to be absolutely certain that the listed activities are necessary and that the listed resources are required.

Guidance Answers to **Quick Checks**

1. Major benefits include (a) promoting a focus on the future; (b) providing a basis for evaluating performance; (c) providing a source of motivation; (d) coordinating the departments of a business; and (e) communicating plans and instructions.

2. The budget committee's responsibility is to provide guidance to ensure that budget figures are realistic and coordinated.

3. Budget periods usually coincide with accounting periods and therefore cover a month, quarter, or a year. Budgets can also be prepared for longer time periods, such as five years.

4. Rolling budgets are budgets that are periodically revised in the ongoing process of continuous budgeting.

5. A master budget is a comprehensive or overall plan for the company that is generally expressed in monetary terms.

6. (b)

7. The master budget includes operating budgets, the capital expenditures budget, and financial budgets.

8. (c); Computed as $(60\% \times 140) + 120 - 50 = 154$.

9. Merchandisers prepare merchandise purchases budgets; manufacturers prepare production and manufacturing budgets.

10. A just-in-time system keeps the level of inventory to a minimum and orders merchandise or materials to meet immediate sales demand. A safety stock system maintains an inventory that is large enough to meet sales demands plus an amount to satisfy unexpected sales demands and an amount to cover delayed shipments from suppliers.

11. (a)

12. (a) Sales budget (and any other operating budgets), (b) capital expenditures budget, (c) financial budgets: cash budget, budgeted income statement, and budgeted balance sheet.

Glossary

Activity-based budgeting (ABB) budget system based on expected activities. (p. 994).

Budget formal statement of future plans, usually expressed in monetary terms. (p. 980).

Budgeted balance sheet accounting report that presents predicted amounts of the company's assets, liabilities, and equity balances as of the end of the budget period. (p. 992).

Budgeted income statement accounting report that presents predicted amounts of the company's revenues and expenses for the budget period. (p. 992).

Budgeting process of planning future business actions and expressing them as formal plans. (p. 980).

Capital expenditures budget plan that lists dollar amounts to be both received from disposal of plant assets and spent to purchase plant assets. (p. 989).

Cash budget plan that shows expected cash inflows and outflows during the budget period, including receipts from loans needed to maintain a minimum cash balance and repayments of such loans. (p. 990).

Continuous budgeting practice of preparing budgets for a selected number of future periods and revising those budgets as each period is completed. (p. 983).

General and administrative expense budget plan that shows predicted operating expenses not included in the selling expenses budget. (p. 988).

Manufacturing budget plan that shows the predicted costs for direct materials, direct labor, and overhead costs to be incurred in manufacturing units in the production budget. (p. 1000).

Master budget comprehensive business plan that includes specific plans for expected sales, product units to be produced, merchandise (or materials) to be purchased, expenses to be incurred, plant assets to be purchased, and amounts of cash to be borrowed or loans to be repaid, as well as a budgeted income statement and balance sheet. (p. 984).

Merchandise purchases budget plan that shows the units or costs of merchandise to be purchased by a merchandising company during the budget period. (p. 987).

Production budget plan that shows the units to be produced each period. (p. 999).

Rolling budgets new set of budgets a firm adds for the next period (with revisions) to replace the ones that have lapsed. (p. 983).

Safety stock quantity of inventory or materials over the minimum needed to satisfy budgeted demand. (p. 987).

Sales budget plan showing the units of goods to be sold or services to be earned; the starting point in the budgeting process for most departments. (p. 986).

Selling expense budget plan that lists the types and amounts of selling expenses expected in the budget period. (p. 988).

[The superscript letter ^A denotes assignment material based on Appendix 24A.]

Questions

1. Identify at least three roles that budgeting plays in helping managers control and monitor a business.

2. What two common benchmarks can be used to evaluate actual performance? Which of the two is generally more useful?

3. What is the benefit of continuous budgeting?

4. Identify three usual time horizons for short-term planning and budgets.

5. Why should each department participate in preparing its own budget?

6. How does budgeting help management coordinate and plan business activities?

7. Why is the sales budget so important to the budgeting process?

8. What is a selling expense budget? What is a capital expenditures budget?

9. Budgeting promotes good decision making by requiring managers to conduct _____ and by focusing their attention on the _____.

10. What is a cash budget? Why must operating budgets and the capital expenditures budget be prepared before the cash budget?

11. Assume that **Nike**'s athletic apparel division is charged with preparing a master budget. Identify the participants—for example, the sales manager for the sales budget—and describe the information each person provides in preparing the master budget.

12. Does the manager of a local **GAP** retail outlet participate in long-term budgeting?

13ᴬ. What is the difference between a production budget and a manufacturing budget?

Which of the following items are components of the master budget?

1. Sales budget, operating budgets, and historical financial budgets.

2. Operating budgets, historical income statement, and budgeted balance sheet.

3. Operating budgets, financial budgets, and capital expenditures budget.

4. Prior sales reports, capital expenditures budget, and financial budgets.

QUICK STUDY

QS 24-1
Components of a master budget

Identify three guidelines that should be followed by organizations if budgeting is to serve effectively as a source of motivation for employees?

QS 24-2
Budget motivation

Explain why the bottom-up approach to budgeting is considered a more successful management technique than a top-down approach. Provide an example.

QS 24-3
Budgeting process

Fogdog Company's July sales budget calls for sales of $600,000. The store expects to begin July with $50,000 of inventory and to end the month with $40,000 of inventory. Gross margin is typically 40% of sales. Determine the budgeted cost of purchases for July.

QS 24-4
Purchases budget

Light Company anticipates total sales for June and July of $420,000 and $398,000, respectively. Cash sales are normally 60% of total sales. Of the credit sales, 20% are collected in the same month as the sale, 70% are collected during the first month after the sale, and the remaining 10% are collected in the second month. Determine the amount of accounts receivable reported on Light's budgeted balance sheet as of July 31.

QS 24-5
Computing budgeted accounts receivable

Use the following information to prepare a cash budget for the month ended on March 31 for MC Company. The budget should show expected cash receipts and cash disbursements for the month of March and the balance expected on March 31.

a. Beginning cash balance on March 1, $72,000.

b. Cash receipts from sales, $300,000.

c. Budgeted cash disbursements for purchases, $140,000.

d. Budgeted cash disbursements for salaries, $80,000.

e. Other budgeted cash expenses, $45,000.

f. Cash repayment of bank loan, $20,000.

QS 24-6
Cash budget

Describe activity-based budgeting, and explain its preparation of budgets. How does activity-based budgeting differ from traditional budgeting?

QS 24-7
Activity-based budgeting

Time Company manufactures watches and has a JIT policy that ending inventory must equal 10% of the next month's sales. Time estimates that October's actual ending inventory will consist of 45,000 watches. November and December sales are estimated to be 400,000 and 350,000 watches, respectively. Calculate the number of watches to be produced that would appear on Time's production budget for the month of November.

QS 24-8ᴬ
Production budget

EXERCISES

Exercise 24-1

Preparation of merchandise purchases budgets
(for three periods)

Check July budgeted purchases, $200,250

In-Line Skates Company prepares monthly budgets. The current budget plans for a September ending inventory of 30,000 units. The company has a policy to end each month with merchandise inventory equal to a specified percent of budgeted sales for the following month. Budgeted sales and merchandise purchases for the three most recent months follow:

	Sales (Units)	Purchases (Units)
July	180,000	200,250
August	315,000	308,250
September	270,000	259,500

(1) Prepare the merchandise purchases budget for the months of July, August, and September. (2) Compute the ratio of ending inventory to the next month's sales for each of the budgets prepared in part (1). (3) How many units are budgeted for sale in October?

Exercise 24-2

Preparation of cash budgets
(for three periods)

Check January ending cash balance, $30,000

Kelley Co. budgeted the following cash receipts and cash disbursements for the first three months of next year:

	Cash Receipts	Cash Disbursements
January	$525,000	$475,000
February	400,000	350,000
March	450,000	525,000

According to a credit agreement with the company's bank, Kelley promises to have a minimum cash balance of $30,000 at the end of each month. In return, the bank has agreed that the company can borrow up to $150,000 at an annual interest rate of 12%, paid on the last day of each month. The interest is computed based on the beginning balance of the loan for the month. The company has a cash balance of $30,000 and a loan balance of $60,000 of January 1. Prepare monthly cash budgets for each of the first three months of next year.

Exercise 24-3

Preparation of a cash budget

Check Ending cash balance, $122,400

Use the following information to prepare the July cash budget for Multimedia, Inc. It should show expected cash receipts and cash disbursements for the month and the cash balance expected on July 31.

a. Beginning cash balance on July 1: $50,000.

b. Cash receipts from sales: 30% is collected in the month of sale, 50% in the next month, and 20% in the second month after sale (uncollectible accounts are negligible and can be ignored). Sales amounts are: May (actual), $1,720,000; June (actual), $1,200,000; and July (budgeted), $1,400,000.

c. Payments on merchandise purchases: 60% in the month of purchase and 40% in the month following purchase. Purchases amounts are: June (actual), $700,000; and July (budgeted), $750,000.

d. Budgeted cash disbursements for salaries in July: $275,000.

e. Budgeted depreciation expense for July: $36,000.

f. Other cash expenses budgeted for July: $200,000.

g. Accrued income taxes due in July: $80,000.

h. Bank loan interest due in July: $6,600.

Exercise 24-4

Preparing a budgeted income statement and balance sheet

Check Net income, $71,680; Total assets, $2,686,400

Use the information in Exercise 24-3 and the following additional information to prepare a budgeted income statement for the month of July and a budgeted balance sheet for July 31:

a. Cost of goods sold is 55% of sales.

b. Inventory at the end of June is $80,000 and at the end of July is $60,000.

c. Salaries payable on June 30 are $50,000 and are expected to be $60,000 on July 31.

d. The equipment account balance is $1,600,000 on July 31. On June 30, the accumulated depreciation on equipment is $280,000.

e. The $6,600 cash payment of interest represents the 1% monthly expense on a bank loan of $660,000.

f. Income taxes payable on July 31 are $30,720, and the income tax rate applicable to the company is 30%.

g. The only other balance sheet accounts are: Common Stock, with a balance of $600,000 on June 30; and Retained Earnings, with a balance of $964,000 on June 30.

Handle Company's cost of goods sold is consistently 60% of sales. The company plans to carry ending merchandise inventory for each month equal to 20% of the next month's budgeted cost of goods sold. All merchandise is purchased on credit, and 50% of the purchases made during a month is paid for in that month. Another 35% is paid for during the first month after purchase, and the remaining 15% is paid for during the second month after purchase. Expected sales are: August (actual), $325,000; September (actual), $320,000; October (estimated), $250,000; November (estimated), $310,000. Use this information to determine October's expected cash payments for purchases. (*Hint:* Use the layout of Exhibit 24.8, but revised for the facts given here.)

Exercise 24-5
Computing budgeted cash payments for purchases

Camping World Company purchases all of its merchandise on credit. It has recently budgeted the following month-end accounts payable balances and merchandise inventory balances:

	Accounts Payable	Merchandise Inventory
May 31	$150,000	$250,000
June 30	200,000	400,000
July 31	235,000	300,000
August 31	195,000	330,000

Cash payments on accounts payable during each month are expected to be: May, $1,600,000; June, $1,490,000; July, $1,425,000; and August, $1,495,000. Use the available information to (a) compute the budgeted amounts of merchandise purchases for June, July, and August, and (b) compute the budgeted amounts of cost of goods sold for June, July, and August.

Exercise 24-6
Computing budgeted purchases and costs of goods sold

Check June purchases, $1,540,000; June cost of goods sold, $1,390,000

Sound Galaxy, a merchandising company specializing in home computer speakers, budgets its monthly cost of goods sold to equal 70% of sales. Its inventory policy calls for ending inventory in each month to equal 20% of the next month's budgeted cost of goods sold. All purchases are on credit, and 25% of the purchases in a month is paid for in the same month. Another 60% is paid for during the first month after purchase, and the remaining 15% is paid for in the second month after purchase. The following sales budgets are set: July, $350,000; August, $290,000; September, $320,000; October, $275,000; and November, $265,000. Compute the following: (a) budgeted merchandise purchases for July, August, September, and October; (b) budgeted payments on accounts payable for September and October; and (c) budgeted ending balances of accounts payable for September and October.

Exercise 24-7
Computing budgeted accounts payable and purchases

Check July purchases, $236,600; Sept. payments on accts. pay., $214,235

UVW Company manufactures an innovative automobile transmission for electric cars. Management predicts that ending inventory for the first quarter will be 75,000 units. The following unit sales of the transmissions are expected during the rest of the year: second quarter, 450,000 units; third quarter, 525,000 units; and fourth quarter, 475,000 units. Management's policy calls for the ending inventory of a quarter to equal 20% of the next quarter's budgeted sales. Prepare a production budget for both the second and third quarters that shows the number of transmissions that should be manufactured.

Exercise 24-8[A]
Preparing production budgets (for two periods)

Check Second quarter prod., 480,000

Bowler's Supply is a merchandiser that sells three different products. The company's February 28 inventories are footwear, 20,000 units; sports equipment, 80,000 units; and apparel, 50,000 units. Management believes that excessive inventories have accumulated for all three products. As a result, a new policy dictates that ending inventory in any month should equal 30% of the expected unit sales for the following month. Expected sales in units for March, April, May, and June follow:

PROBLEM SET A
Problem 24-1A
Preparation and analysis of merchandise purchases budgets

Budgeted Sales in Units			
	March	April	May	June
Footwear	15,000	25,000	32,000	35,000
Sports equipment	70,000	90,000	95,000	92,000
Apparel	40,000	38,000	37,000	25,000

Required

Preparation Component

1. Prepare a merchandise purchases budget (in units) for each product for each of the months of March, April, and May.

Analysis Component

2. The purchases budgets in part (1) should reflect fewer purchases of all three products in March compared to those in April and May. What factor caused fewer purchases to be planned? Suggest business conditions that would cause this factor to both occur and impact this company in this way.

Problem 24-2A
Preparation and analysis of cash budgets with supporting inventory and purchases budgets

Cal-Towne Company sells its product for $180 per unit. Its actual and projected sales follow:

	Units	Dollars
April (actual)	4,000	$ 720,000
May (actual)	2,000	360,000
June (budgeted)	6,000	1,080,000
July (budgeted)	5,000	900,000
August (budgeted)	3,800	684,000

All sales are on credit. Recent experience shows that 20% of credit sales is collected in the month of the sale, 50% in the month after the sale, 28% in the second month after the sale, and 2% proves to be uncollectible. The purchase price of the product is $110 per unit. All purchases are payable within 12 days. Thus, 60% of purchases made in a month is paid in that month and the other 40% is paid in the next month. Cal-Towne's management has a policy to maintain an ending monthly inventory of 20% of the next month's unit sales plus a safety stock of 100 units. The April 30 and May 31 actual inventory levels are consistent with this policy. Selling and administrative expenses for the year are $1,320,000 and are paid evenly throughout the year in cash. The company's minimum cash balance for the end of a month is $100,000. This minimum is maintained, if necessary, by borrowing cash from the bank. If the balance exceeds $100,000, the company repays as much of the loan as it can without going below the minimum. This type of loan carries an annual 12% interest rate. On May 31, the balance of the loan is $25,000, and the company's cash balance is $100,000.

Required

Preparation Component

1. Prepare a table that shows the computation of cash collections of its credit sales (accounts receivable) in each of the months of June and July.

2. Prepare a table that shows the computation of budgeted ending inventories (in units) for April, May, June, and July.

3. Prepare the merchandise purchases budget for May, June, and July. Present calculations in units and then show the dollar amount of purchases for each month.

4. Prepare a table showing the computation of cash payments on product purchases for June and July.

5. Prepare a cash budget for June and July, including any loan activity and interest expense. Compute the loan balance at the end of each month.

Analysis Component

6. Refer to your answer to part (5). Cal-Towne's cash budget indicates the company will need to borrow more than $18,000 in June and will be able to pay it back in July. Suggest some reasons that knowing this information in May would be helpful to management.

Problem 24-3A
Preparation of cash budgets (for three periods)

During the last week of August, the owner of Electronic Arts Company approaches the bank for a $100,000 loan to be made on September 2 and repaid on November 30 with annual interest of 12%, for an interest cost of $3,000. The owner plans to increase the store's inventory by $80,000 during September and needs the loan to pay for inventory acquisitions. The bank's loan officer needs more information about Electronic Arts' ability to repay the loan and asks the owner to forecast the store's

November 30 cash position. On September 1, Electronic Arts is expected to have a $5,000 cash balance, $148,000 of accounts receivable, and $125,000 of accounts payable. Its budgeted sales, merchandise purchases, and various cash disbursements for the next three months follow:

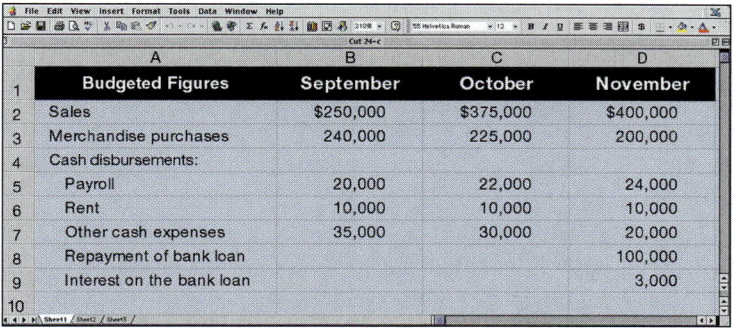

Budgeted Figures	September	October	November
Sales	$250,000	$375,000	$400,000
Merchandise purchases	240,000	225,000	200,000
Cash disbursements:			
Payroll	20,000	22,000	24,000
Rent	10,000	10,000	10,000
Other cash expenses	35,000	30,000	20,000
Repayment of bank loan			100,000
Interest on the bank loan			3,000

The budgeted September merchandise purchases include the inventory increase. All sales are on account. Company experience shows that 25% of credit sales is collected in the month of the sale, 45% in the month following the sale, 20% in the second month, 9% in the third, and the remainder is uncollectible. Applying these percents to the September 1 accounts receivable balance, for example, shows that $95,000 of the $148,000 will be collected in September, $40,000 in October, and $12,000 in November. All merchandise is purchased on credit; eighty percent of the balance is paid in the month following a purchase, and the remaining 20% is paid in the second month. For example, of the $125,000 of accounts payable at the end of August, $100,000 will be paid in September and $25,000 in October.

Required

Prepare a cash budget for September, October, and November for Electronic Arts Company. Show supplemental calculations as needed.

Check Budgeted cash balance: September, $97,500; October, $64,750; November, $10,500

Halbert, a one-product mail-order firm, buys its product for $75 per unit and sells it for $150 per unit. The sales staff receives a 10% commission on the sale of each unit. Its December income statement follows:

Problem 24-4A
Preparation and analysis of budgeted income statements

HALBERT COMPANY
Income Statement
For Month Ended December 31, 2002

Sales	$2,250,000
Cost of goods sold	1,125,000
Gross profit	$1,125,000
Expenses	
Sales commissions (10%)	225,000
Advertising	250,000
Store rent	30,000
Administrative salaries	45,000
Depreciation	50,000
Other expenses	10,000
Total expenses	$ 610,000
Net income	$ 515,000

The company's management expects December's results to be repeated in January, February, and March of 2003 without any changes in strategy. Management, however, has an alternative plan. It believes that unit sales will increase at a rate of 10% *each* month for the next three months (beginning with January) if the item's selling price is reduced to $125 per unit and advertising expenses are increased by 15% and remain at that level for all three months. The cost of its product will remain at $75 per unit, the sales staff will continue to earn a 10% commission, and the remaining expenses will stay the same.

Required

Preparation Component

1. Using a three-column format (one column for each month), prepare a budgeted income statement for each of the months of January, February, and March that show the expected results from implementing the proposed changes.

Analysis Component

2. Use the budgeted income statement to recommend whether management should implement the proposed changes.

Check   Budgeted net income: January, $196,250; February, $258,125; March, $326,187

Problem 24-5A

Preparation of a complete master budget

Near the end of 2002, the management of Cool Sports Co., a merchandising company, prepared the following estimated balance sheet for December 31, 2002:

COOL SPORTS COMPANY		
Estimated Balance Sheet		
December 31, 2002		
Assets		
Cash		$ 36,000
Accounts receivable		525,000
Inventory		150,000
Total current assets		$ 711,000
Equipment	$540,000	
Less accumulated depreciation	67,500	472,500
Total assets		$1,183,500
Liabilities and Equity		
Accounts payable	$360,000	
Bank loan payable	15,000	
Taxes payable (due 3/15/2003)	90,000	
Total liabilities		$ 465,000
Common stock	472,500	
Retained earnings	246,000	
Total stockholders' equity		718,500
Total liabilities and equity		$1,183,500

To prepare a master budget for January, February, and March of 2003, management gathers the following information:

a. Cool Sport's single product is purchased for $30 per unit and resold for $55 per unit. The expected inventory level of 5,000 units on December 31, 2002, is more than management's desired level for 2003, which is 20% of the next month's expected sales (in units). Expected sales are: January, 7,000 units; February, 9,000 units; March, 11,000 units; and April, 10,000 units.

b. Cash sales and credit sales represent 25% and 75%, respectively, of total sales. Of the credit sales, 60% is collected in the first month after the sale and 40% in the second month after the sale. For the December 31, 2002, accounts receivable balance, $125,000 will be collected in January and the remaining $400,000 will be collected in February.

c. Merchandise purchases are paid for as follows: 20% in the month after purchase and 80% in the second month after purchase. For the December 31, 2002, accounts payable balance, $80,000 will be paid in January and the remaining $280,000 will be paid in February.

d. Sales commissions equal to 20% of sales are paid each month. Sales salaries (excluding commissions) are $60,000 per year.

e. General and administrative salaries are $144,000 per year. Maintenance expense equals $2,000 per month and is paid in cash.

f. Equipment reported in the December 31, 2002, balance sheet was purchased in January 2002. It is being depreciated over eight years under the straight-line method with no salvage value. The following amounts for new equipment purchases are planned in the coming quarter: January, $36,000; February, $96,000; and March, $28,800. This equipment will be depreciated under the straight-line method over eight years with no salvage value. A full month's depreciation is taken for the month in which equipment is purchased.

g. The company plans to acquire land at the end of March at a cost of $150,000, which will be paid with cash on the last day of the month.

h. Cool Sports has a working arrangement with its bank to obtain additional loans as needed. The interest rate is 12% per year, and the interest is paid at the end of each month based on the beginning balance. Partial or full payments on these loans can be made on the last day of the month. The company has agreed to maintain a minimum ending cash balance of $25,000 in each month.

i. The income tax rate for the company is 40%. Income taxes on the first quarter's income will not be paid until April 15.

Required

Prepare a master budget for each of the first three months of 2003; include the following component budgets (show supporting calculations as needed, and round amounts to the nearest dollar):

1. Monthly sales budgets (showing both budgeted unit sales and dollar sales).

2. Monthly merchandise purchases budgets.

3. Monthly selling expense budgets.

4. Monthly general and administrative expense budgets.

5. Monthly capital expenditures budgets.

6. Monthly cash budgets.

7. Budgeted income statement for the entire first quarter (not for each month).

8. Budgeted balance sheet as of March 31, 2003.

Check   (2) Budgeted purchases: January, $114,000; February, $282,000; (3) Budgeted selling expenses: January, $82,000; February, $104,000

Check   (6) Ending cash bal.: January, $30,100; February, $210,300

Check   (8) Budgeted total assets at March 31, $1,568,650

Mountain Sports Company produces snow skis. Each ski requires two pounds of carbon fiber. The company's management predicts that 5,000 skis and 6,000 pounds of carbon fiber will be in inventory on June 30 of the current year and that 150,000 skis will be sold during the next (third) quarter. Management wants to end the third quarter with 3,500 skis and 4,000 pounds of carbon fiber in inventory. Carbon fiber can be purchased for $15 per pound.

Problem 24-6A[A]
Preparing production and direct materials budgets

Required

1. Prepare the third-quarter production budget for skis.

2. Prepare the third-quarter direct materials (carbon fiber) budget (include the dollar cost of purchases).

Check   (1) Units manuf., 148,500; (2) Cost of carbon fiber purchases, $4,425,000

Water Sports Corp. is a merchandiser that sells three different products. The company's March 31 inventories are water skis, 40,000 units; tow ropes, 90,000 units; and life jackets, 150,000 units. Management believes that excessive inventories have accumulated for all three products. As a result, a new policy dictates that ending inventory in any month should equal 10% of the expected unit sales for the following month. Expected sales in units for April, May, June, and July follow:

PROBLEM SET B
Problem 24-1B
Preparation and analysis of merchandise purchases budgets

	Budgeted Sales in Units			
	April	**May**	**June**	**July**
Water skis	70,000	90,000	130,000	100,000
Tow ropes	100,000	90,000	110,000	100,000
Life jackets	160,000	190,000	200,000	120,000

Required

Preparation Component

1. Prepare a merchandise purchases budget (in units) for each product for each of the months of April, May, and June.

Analysis Component

2. The purchases budgets in part (1) should reflect fewer purchases of all three products in April compared to those in May and June. What factor caused fewer purchases to be planned? Suggest business conditions that would cause this factor to both occur and affect the company as it has.

Check   April budgeted purchases: Water skis, 39,000; Tow ropes, 19,000; Life jackets, 29,000

Problem 24-2B

Preparation and analysis of cash budgets with supporting inventory and purchases budgets

Universal Company sells its product for $22 per unit. Its actual and projected sales follow:

	Units	Dollars
January (actual)	18,000	$396,000
February (actual)	22,500	495,000
March (budgeted)	19,000	418,000
April (budgeted)	18,750	412,500
May (budgeted)	21,000	462,000

All sales are on credit. Recent experience shows that 40% of credit sales is collected in the month of the sale, 35% in the month after the sale, 23% in the second month after the sale, and 2% proves to be uncollectible. The purchase price of the product is $12 per unit. All purchases are payable within 21 days. Thus, 30% of purchases made in a month is paid in that month and the other 70% is paid in the next month. Universal Co.'s management has a policy to maintain an ending monthly inventory of 20% of the next month's unit sales plus a safety stock of 100 units. The January 31 and February 28 actual inventory levels are consistent with this policy. Selling and administrative expenses for the year are $1,920,000 and are paid evenly throughout the year in cash. The company's minimum cash balance for the end of a month is $50,000. This minimum is maintained, if necessary, by borrowing cash from the bank. If the balance exceeds $50,000, the company repays as much of the loan as it can without going below the minimum. This type of loan carries an annual 12% interest rate. At February 28, the balance of the loan is $12,000, and the company's cash balance is $50,000.

Required

Preparation Component

Check (1) Cash collections: March, $431,530; April, $425,150

1. Prepare a table that shows the computation of cash collections of its credit sales (accounts receivable) in each of the months of March and April.

2. Prepare a table showing the computations of budgeted ending inventories (units) for January, February, March, and April.

Check (3) Budgeted purchases: February, $261,600; March, $227,400

3. Prepare the merchandise purchases budget for February, March, and April. Present calculations in units and then show the dollar amount of purchases for each month.

4. Prepare a table showing the computation of cash payments on product purchases for March and April.

Check (5) Ending cash balance: March, $58,070, April, $94,920

5. Prepare a cash budget for March and April, including any loan activity and interest expense. Compute the loan balance at the end of each month.

Analysis Component

6. Refer to your answer to part (5). Universal's cash budget indicates the company will be able to pay off $12,000 of the loan at the end of March. Suggest some reasons that knowing this information in February would be helpful to management.

Problem 24-3B

Preparation of cash budgets (for three periods)

During the last week of March, the owner of Sound Buy Stereo approaches the bank for an $80,000 loan to be made on April 1 and repaid on June 30 with annual interest of 12%, for an interest cost of $2,400. The owner plans to increase the store's inventory by $60,000 in April and needs the loan to pay for inventory acquisitions. The bank's loan officer needs more information about Sound Buy Stereo's ability to repay the loan and asks the owner to forecast the store's June 30 cash position. On April 1, Sound Buy Stereo is expected to have a $3,000 cash balance, $120,000 of accounts receivable, and $100,000 of accounts payable. Its budgeted sales, merchandise purchases, and various cash disbursements for the next three months follow:

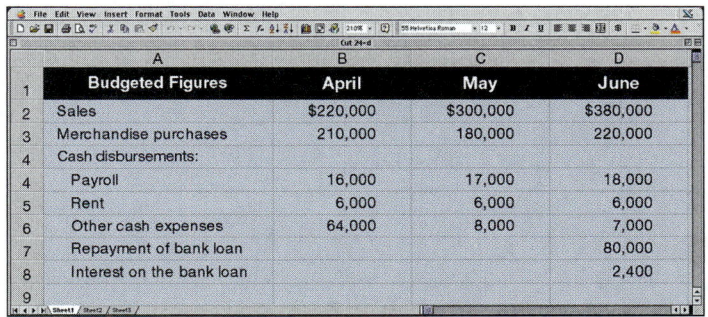

Budgeted Figures	April	May	June
Sales	$220,000	$300,000	$380,000
Merchandise purchases	210,000	180,000	220,000
Cash disbursements:			
Payroll	16,000	17,000	18,000
Rent	6,000	6,000	6,000
Other cash expenses	64,000	8,000	7,000
Repayment of bank loan			80,000
Interest on the bank loan			2,400

The budgeted April merchandise purchases include the inventory increase. All sales are on account. Company experience shows that 25% of credit sales is collected in the month of the sale, 45% in the month following the sale, 20% in the second month, 9% in the third, and the remainder is uncollectible. Applying these percents to the April 1 accounts receivable balance, for example, shows that $81,000 of the $120,000 will be collected in April, $36,000 in May, and $3,000 in June. All merchandise is purchased on credit; eighty percent of the balance is paid in the month following a purchase and the remaining 20% is paid in the second month. For example, of the $100,000 of accounts payable at the end of March, $80,000 will be paid in April and $20,000 in May.

Required

Prepare a cash budget for April, May, and June for Sound Buy Stereo. Show supporting calculations as needed.

Check   Budgeted cash balance: April, $53,000; May, $44,000; June, $21,600

Compu-Graph buys its product for $60 and sells it for $130 per unit. The sales staff receives a 10% commission on the sale of each unit. Its June income statement follows:

Problem 24-4B
Preparation and analysis of budgeted income statements

COMPU-GRAPH COMPANY Income Statement For Month Ended June 30, 2002	
Sales	$1,300,000
Cost of goods sold	600,000
Gross profit	$ 700,000
Expenses	
Sales commissions (10%)	130,000
Advertising	200,000
Store rent	24,000
Administrative salaries	40,000
Depreciation	50,000
Other expenses	12,000
Total expenses	$ 456,000
Net income	$ 244,000

The company's management expects June's results to be repeated in July, August, and September without any changes in strategy. Management, however, has another plan. It believes that unit sales will increase at a rate of 10% *each* month for the next three months (beginning with June) if the item's selling price is reduced to $115 per unit and advertising expenses are increased by 25% and remain at that level for all three months. The cost of its product will remain at $60 per unit, the sales staff will continue to earn a 10% commission, and the remaining expenses will stay the same.

Required

Preparation Component

1. Using a three-column format (one column for each month), prepare a budgeted income statement for each of the months of July, August, and September that show the expected results from implementing the proposed changes.

Check   Budgeted net income: July, $102,500; August, $150,350; September, $202,985

Analysis Component

2. Use the budgeted income statement to recommend whether management should implement the proposed plan.

Problem 24-5B

Preparation of a complete master budget

Near the end of 2002, the management of Holmes Corp., a merchandising company, prepared the following estimated balance sheet for December 31, 2002:

HOLMES CORPORATION Estimated Balance Sheet December 31, 2002		
Assets		
Cash		$ 36,000
Accounts receivable		525,000
Inventory		150,000
Total current assets		$ 711,000
Equipment	$540,000	
Less accumulated depreciation . .	67,500	472,500
Total assets		$1,183,500
Liabilities and Equity		
Accounts payable	$360,000	
Bank loan payable	15,000	
Taxes payable (due 3/15/2003) . .	90,000	
Total liabilities		$ 465,000
Common stock	472,500	
Retained earnings	246,000	
Total stockholders' equity		718,500
Total liabilities and equity		$1,183,500

To prepare a master budget for January, February, and March of 2003, management gathers the following information:

a. Holmes Corporation's single product is purchased for $30 per unit and resold for $45 per unit. The expected inventory level of 5,000 units on December 31, 2002, is more than management's desired level for 2003, which is 25% of the next month's expected sales (in units). Expected sales are: January, 6,000 units; February, 8,000 units; March, 10,000 units; and April, 9,000 units.

b. Cash sales and credit sales represent 25% and 75%, respectively, of total sales. Of the credit sales, 60% is collected in the first month after the sale and 40% in the second month after the sale. For example, 60% of the December 31, 2002, balance of accounts receivable will be collected in January and 40% will be collected in February.

c. Merchandise purchases are paid for as follows: 20% in the month after purchase and 80% in the second month after purchase. For example, 20% of the accounts payable balance on December 31, 2002, will be paid in January, and 80% will be paid in February.

d. Sales commissions equal to 20% of sales are paid each month. Sales salaries (excluding commissions) are $90,000 per year.

e. General and administrative salaries are $144,000 per year. Maintenance expense equals $3,000 per month and is paid in cash.

f. Equipment reported in the December 31, 2002, balance sheet was purchased in January 2002. It is being depreciated over eight years under the straight-line method with no salvage value. The following amounts for new equipment purchases are planned in the coming quarter: January, $72,000; February, $96,000; and March, $28,800. This equipment will be depreciated using the straight-line method over eight years with no salvage value. A full month's depreciation is taken for the month in which equipment is purchased.

g. The company plans to acquire land at the end of March at a cost of $150,000, which will be paid with cash on the last day of the month.

h. Holmes Corporation has a working arrangement with its bank to obtain additional loans as needed. The interest rate is 12% per year, and the interest is paid at the end of each month based on the beginning balance. Partial or full payments on these loans can be made on the last day of the month. Holmes Corporation has agreed to maintain a minimum ending cash balance of $36,000 in each month.

i. The income tax rate for the company is 40%. Income taxes on the first quarter's income will not be paid until April 15.

Required

Prepare a master budget for each of the first three months of 2003; include the following component budgets (show supporting calculations as needed, and round amounts to the nearest dollar):

1. Monthly sales budgets (showing both budgeted unit sales and dollar sales).

2. Monthly merchandise purchases budgets.

3. Monthly selling expense budgets.

4. Monthly general and administrative expense budgets.

5. Monthly capital expenditures budgets.

6. Monthly cash budgets.

7. Budgeted income statement for the entire first quarter (not for each month).

8. Budgeted balance sheet as of March 31, 2003.

Check (2) Budgeted purchases: January, $90,000; February, $255,000; (3) Budgeted selling expenses: January, $61,500; February, $79,500

Check (6) Ending cash bal.: January, $182,850; February, $107,850

Check (8) Budgeted total assets at March 31, $1,346,875

Millenium Company produces baseball bats. Each bat requires three pounds of aluminum alloy. The company's management predicts that 8,000 bats and 15,000 pounds of aluminum alloy will be in inventory on March 31 of the current year and that 250,000 bats will be sold during this year's second quarter. Management wants to end the second quarter with 6,000 finished bats and 12,000 pounds of aluminum alloy in inventory. Aluminum alloy can be purchased for $4 per pound.

Problem 24-6B[A]
Preparing production and direct materials budgets

Required

1. Prepare the second-quarter production budget for bats.

2. Prepare the second-quarter direct materials (aluminum alloy) budget (include the dollar cost of purchases).

Check (1) Units manuf., 248,000; (2) Cost of aluminum purchases, $2,964,000

Beyond the Numbers

BTN 24-1 Financial statements often serve as a starting point for information in formulating the upcoming budget. You are assigned to review **Nike**'s financial statements to determine its cash paid for dividends in the current year and the budgeted cash needed to pay its next year's dividend.

Reporting in Action

Required

1. Which financial statement(s) reports the amount of (a) cash dividends paid and (b) annual cash dividends declared? Explain where on the statement(s) this information is reported.

2. Indicate the amount of cash dividends (a) paid in the year ended May 31, 2000, and (b) to be paid (budgeted for) next year under the assumption that annual cash dividends equal 25% of the prior year's net income.

Swoosh Ahead

3. Access Nike's annual financial statements for a fiscal year ending after May 31, 2000, from either its Web site [**www.nike.com**] or the SEC's EDGAR database [**www.sec.gov**]. Compare your answer for part (2) with actual cash dividends paid for the year ended May 31, 2001. Compute the error, if any, in your estimate. Speculate as to why dividends were higher or lower than budgeted.

BTN 24-2 One source of cash savings for a company is improved management of ending inventory. To illustrate, assume that **Nike** and **Reebok** both have $2,000,000 per month in footwear sales in the Virginia area, and both forecast this level of sales per month for the next 24 months. Also assume that both Nike and Reebok have a 20% contribution margin and equal fixed costs and that cost per shoe is the only variable cost. Assume the main difference between Nike and Reebok is the footwear distribution system. Nike has a well-established distribution system and requires an ending inventory of only 10% of next month's sales in inventory at the end of each month. However, Reebok is building a new distribution system and requires 40% of next month's sales in inventory at the end of each month.

Comparative Analysis

Required

1. Compute the amount by which Reebok can reduce its inventory level if it can match Nike's system of maintaining an inventory equal to 10% of next month's sales. (*Hint:* Focus on the facts given and only on the Virginia area.)
2. Explain how the analysis in part (1) that shows ending inventory levels for both the 40% and 10% required inventory policies can help justify a just-in-time inventory system. You can assume a 15% interest cost for resources that are tied up in ending inventory.

Ethics Challenge

BTN 24-3   Both the budget process and the budgets themselves can impact management actions—both positively and negatively. For instance, a common practice among not-for-profit organizations and government agencies is for management to spend any amounts remaining in a budget at the end of the budget period. This practice is often called "use it or lose it." The view is that if a department manager does not spend the budgeted amount, top management reduces next year's budget by the amount not spent. To avoid losing budget dollars, department managers often spend all budgeted amounts regardless of the value added to products or services. All of us pay for the costs associated with this budget system.

Required

Write a one-half page report to a local not-for-profit organization or government agency offering a solution to the "use it or lose it" budgeting problem.

Communicating in Practice

BTN 24-4   The sales budget is usually the first and most crucial of the component budgets in a master budget because all other budgets usually rely on it for planning purposes.

Required

Assume that your company's sales staff provides information on expected sales and selling prices for items making up the sales budget. Prepare a one-page memorandum to your supervisor outlining concerns with the sales staff's input in the sales budget when its compensation is at least partly tied to these budgets. More generally, explain the importance of assessing any potential bias in information provided to the budget process.

Taking It to the Net

BTN 24-5   Access the **e-budgets** Web site [**www.ebudgets.com**]. Review the information at this site; if it is available, click on the link *cfo tour* and examine the information provided.

Required

Assume the role of a senior manager in a large, multidivision company.
1. What are the benefits of using e-budgets?
2. As a senior manager, what concerns do you have with the concept and application of e-budgets?

Teamwork in Action

BTN 24-6   Your team is to prepare a budget report outlining the costs of attending college (full-time) for the next two semesters (30 hours) or three quarters (45 hours). The focus of this budget is solely on attending college; do not include personal items in the team's budget. Your budget must include tuition, books, supplies, club fees, food, housing, and all costs associated with travel to and from college. This budgeting exercise is similar to the initial phase in activity-based budgeting. Include a list of any assumptions you use in completing the budget. Be prepared to present your budget in class.

Business Week Activity

BTN 24-7   Read the article "Dell's Second Web Revolution" in the September 18, 2000, issue of *Business Week*.

Required

1. Assume the role of the budget manager of one of Dell's main suppliers. What are the advantages of having access to Dell's order information as a supplier?
2. Could Dell's system have any disadvantages? Explain.

BTN 24-8   Stacey Green, a part-time college student, volunteered to help senior citizens shop and run errands. Her reliable and courteous services to seniors led to numerous for-pay services to non-seniors. Stacey soon was unable to fulfill the growing demands of her business by herself. She needed more resources (a van, answering service, and distribution and accounting systems) and an employee or two. Stacey called on a financial institution for backing and was asked for a detailed business plan and budgets.

Entrepreneurial Decision
C1 *e*

Required

1. What should Stacey's business plan include?

2. How can budgeting help Stacey develop and effectively operate her business?

25

Flexible Budgets and Standard Costs

"We've got a look the rest of the world really wants"—Richard Allred.

A Look Back

Chapter 24 explained the importance of budgeting. It also described the master budget and its component budgets as well as their usefulness for planning and monitoring company activities.

A Look at This Chapter

This chapter describes flexible budgets, variance analysis, and standard costs. It explains how each is used for purposes of better controlling and monitoring business activities.

A Look Ahead

Chapter 26 focuses on capital budgeting decisions. It explains and illustrates several procedures used in evaluating many short-term managerial decisions.

Standards for Toes and Nose

COSTA MESA, CA—Success for clothing and accessory companies usually depends on the current fad. **Toes on the Nose** [**www.ToesOnTheNose.com**] rejects that notion and focuses instead on timeless fashions. "It's really based on the classic surf clothing and lifestyle," say Toes founder Richard Allred. Toes' designs reflect the easygoing lifestyle of the islands with contemporary styles.

To launch his start-up, Allred collected $100,000 from family and savings and began manufacturing classic Hawaiian-print clothing. Motivated by early success, he expanded into additional surf-inspired clothing and accessories for men, women, and children—targeted at surf shops. More recently, Allred branched out into home furnishings. "Surfing in general is hot," he says, "and we've got a look the rest of the world really wants."

Toes' success, however, depends on analysis and control of costs while maintaining product quality. "The way we've made ourselves different is by staying totally true to what we make," says Allred. With that in mind, Toes is expanding into more mainstream markets with an aggressive marketing campaign aimed at nonsurf-related magazines, including *Teen* and *Jump*. "We may have more items and offer more variety, but our look is exactly the same," says Allred. To help ensure success, Toes uses budgets, standard costs, and cost variance analysis. The payback for these tools is in the numbers: Toes expects sales to exceed $10 million this year. Keys for future success include continued cost and quality control along with product differentiation. Says Allred, "If people want a classic surf look, if they want the best Hawaiian prints, they come to Toes on the Nose." [Sources: *Toes on the Nose Web site,* May 2001; *Entrepreneur,* November 1999; *Business Start-Ups,* May 2000.]

Learning Objectives

Conceptual

C1 Define standard costs and explain their computation and uses.

C2 Describe variances and what they reveal about performance.

C3 Explain how standard cost information is useful for management by exception.

Analytical

A1 Compare fixed and flexible budgets.

A2 Analyze changes in sales from expected amounts.

Procedural

P1 Prepare a flexible budget and interpret a flexible budget performance report.

P2 Compute materials and labor variances.

P3 Compute overhead variances.

P4 Prepare journal entries for standard costs and account for price and quantity variances.

Chapter Preview

In Chapter 24, we explained how budgeting helps organize and formalize management's planning activities. We also explained how budgets provide a basis for evaluating actual performance. This chapter extends that discussion to look more closely at the use of budgets to evaluate performance. Evaluations are important for controlling and monitoring business activities. We also describe and illustrate the use of standard costs and variance analyses. These managerial tools are useful for both evaluating and controlling organizations and for the planning of future activities.

Section 1—Flexible Budgets

Section 1 begins by introducing fixed budgets and fixed budget performance reports. It then introduces flexible budgets and flexible budget performance reports. The advantages of flexible budgets and performance reports are illustrated with comparisons to fixed budgets and reports.

Budgetary Process

A master budget reflects management's planned objectives for a future period. In Chapter 24, we explained the preparation of a master budget based on a predicted level of activity such as sales volume for the budget period. This section discusses the effects on the usefulness of budget reports when the actual level of activity differs from the predicted level.

Budgetary Control and Reporting

Budgetary control is the use of budgets by management to monitor and control a company's operations. This includes the use of budgets to see that planned objectives are met. **Budget reports** contain relevant information that compares actual results to planned activities. This comparison is motivated by a need to both monitor performance and control activities. Budget reports are sometimes viewed as progress reports, or *report cards,* on management's performance in achieving planned objectives. These reports can be prepared at any time and for any period. Three common periods for a budget report are a month, quarter, and year.

Point: Budget reports are often used as a base to determine bonuses of managers.

The process of budgetary control involves at least four steps: (1) develop the budget from planned objectives, (2) compare actual results to budgeted amounts and analyze any differences, (3) take corrective and strategic actions, and (4) establish new planned objectives and prepare a new budget. Exhibit 25.1 shows this continual process of budgetary control. Budget reports and related documents are effective tools for managers to obtain the greatest benefits from this budgetary process.

Exhibit 25.1

Process of Budgetary Control

Develop Budget → Compare Actual to Budget → Take Action → Set New Plans

Fixed Budget Performance Report

In a fixed budgetary control system, the master budget is based on a single prediction for sales volume or other activity level. The budgeted amount for each cost essentially assumes that a specific (or *fixed*) amount of sales will occur. A **fixed budget,** also called *static budget,* is based on a single predicted amount of sales or other measure of activity.

We explained in Chapter 24 that one benefit of a budget is its usefulness in comparing actual results with planned activities. Information useful for analysis is often presented for comparison in a performance report. A **fixed budget performance report** is shown in Exhibit 25.2. This report compares Optel's actual results for January 2002 with the results expected under its fixed budget that predicted 10,000 (composite) units of sales. Optel manufactures inexpensive eyeglasses, frames, contact lens, and related supplies. For this report, its production volume equals sales volume (its inventory level did not change).

Exhibit 25.2

Fixed Budget
Performance Report

OPTEL Fixed Budget Performance Report For Month Ended January 31, 2002	Fixed Budget	Actual Results	Variances*
Sales (in units)	10,000	12,000	
Sales (in dollars)	$100,000	$125,000	$25,000 F
Cost of goods sold			
Direct materials	10,000	13,000	3,000 U
Direct labor	15,000	20,000	5,000 U
Overhead			
Factory supplies	2,000	2,100	100 U
Utilities	3,000	4,000	1,000 U
Depreciation—Machinery	8,000	8,000	0
Supervisory salaries	11,000	11,000	0
Selling expenses			
Sales commissions	9,000	10,800	1,800 U
Shipping expenses	4,000	4,300	300 U
General and administrative expenses			
Office supplies	5,000	5,200	200 U
Insurance expenses	1,000	1,200	200 U
Depreciation—Office equipment	7,000	7,000	0
Administrative salaries	13,000	13,000	0
Total expenses	$ 88,000	$ 99,600	$11,600 U
Income from operations	$ 12,000	$ 25,400	$13,400 F

* F = Favorable variance; and U = Unfavorable variance.

This type of performance report designates differences between budgeted and actual results as variances. We see the letters *F* and *U* located beside the numbers in the third number column of this report. Their meanings are as follows:

F = **Favorable variance**   When compared to budget, the actual cost or revenue contributes to a *higher* income. That is, actual revenue is higher than budgeted revenue, or actual cost is lower than budgeted cost.

U = **Unfavorable variance**   When compared to budget, the actual cost or revenue contributes to a *lower* income; actual revenue is lower than budgeted revenue, or actual cost is higher than budgeted cost.

This convention is common in practice and is used throughout this chapter.

Budget Reports for Evaluation

One of the primary uses of budget reports is for management to monitor and control operations. In Optel's case, management's evaluation is likely to focus on a variety of questions that might include these:

Example: How is it that the favorable sales variance in Exhibit 25.2 is linked with so many unfavorable cost and expense variances? *Answer:* Costs have increased with the increase in sales.

■ Why is actual income from operations $13,400 higher than budgeted?

■ Are amounts paid for each expense item too high?

■ Is manufacturing using too much direct material?

■ Is manufacturing using too much direct labor?

The performance report in Exhibit 25.2 provides little help in answering these questions because actual sales volume is 2,000 units higher than budgeted. A manager does not know if this higher level of sales activity is the cause of variations in total dollar sales and expenses or if other factors have influenced these amounts. This inability of fixed budget reports to adjust for changes in activity levels is a major limitation of a fixed budget performance report. That is, it fails to show whether actual costs are out of line due to a change in actual sales volume or some other factor.

Flexible Budget Reports

 A1 Compare fixed and flexible budgets.

Concept 25-1

This section explains the purposes of both a flexible budget and a flexible budget performance report and describes their preparation.

Purpose of Flexible Budgets

To help management address limitations with the fixed budget performance report, particularly from the effects of changes in sales volume, we look to a flexible budget. A **flexible budget,** also called a *variable budget,* is a report based on predicted amounts of revenues and expenses corresponding to the actual level of output. Unlike fixed budgets, a flexible budget is prepared after a period's activities are complete. A flexible budget can be viewed as a fixed budget prepared at the activity level corresponding to the actual level of activity. Many companies prepare and use flexible budgets.

The primary purpose of a flexible budget is to help managers evaluate past performance. It is especially useful for such an evaluation because it reflects budgeted revenues and costs based on the actual level of activity. Thus, comparisons of actual results with budgeted performance are more likely to identify the causes of any differences. This can help managers focus attention on real problem areas and implement corrective actions. This is in contrast to a fixed budget, whose primary purpose is to assist managers in planning future activities and whose numbers are based on a single predicted amount of budgeted sales or production.

Preparing Flexible Budgets

P1 Prepare a flexible budget and interpret a flexible budget performance report.

A flexible budget is designed to reveal the effects from volume of activity on revenues and costs. To prepare a flexible budget, management relies on the distinctions between fixed and variable costs, which are described under cost-volume-profit analysis in Chapter 23 and in Chapter 19. Recall that the cost per unit of activity remains constant for variable costs. This means that the total amount of a variable cost changes in direct proportion to a change in level of activity. For fixed costs, the total amount of cost remains unchanged regardless of changes in the level of activity within a relevant (normal) operating range. (We assume that costs can be reasonably classified as variable or fixed within a relevant range.)

When we create the numbers constituting a flexible budget, we need to express each variable cost as either a constant amount per unit of sales or as a percent of a sales dollar. In the case of a fixed cost, we need to express its budgeted amount as the total amount expected to occur at any sales volume within the relevant range.

Exhibit 25.3 shows a set of flexible budgets for Optel in January 2002. Seven of its expenses are classified as variable costs. Its remaining five expenses are fixed costs. These classifications result from management's investigation of each of the company's expenses

Point: Usefulness of a flexible budget depends on valid classification of variable and fixed costs. Some costs are mixed and must be analyzed to determine their variable and fixed portions.

using the cost estimation methods from Chapter 23. Variable and fixed expense categories are *not* the same for every company, and we must avoid drawing conclusions from specific cases. For example, depending on the nature of a company's operations, office supplies expense can be either fixed or variable with respect to sales.

Point: To apply these concepts, work Exercise 25-2.

Exhibit 25.3

Flexible Budgets

OPTEL Flexible Budgets For Month Ended January 31, 2002	Flexible Budget Variable Amount per Unit	Flexible Budget Total Fixed Cost	Flexible Budget for Unit Sales of 10,000	Flexible Budget for Unit Sales of 12,000	Flexible Budget for Unit Sales of 14,000
Sales	$10.00		$100,000	$120,000	$140,000
Variable costs					
Direct materials	1.00		10,000	12,000	14,000
Direct labor	1.50		15,000	18,000	21,000
Factory supplies	0.20		2,000	2,400	2,800
Utilities	0.30		3,000	3,600	4,200
Sales commissions	0.90		9,000	10,800	12,600
Shipping expenses	0.40		4,000	4,800	5,600
Office supplies	0.50		5,000	6,000	7,000
Total variable costs	$ 4.80		$ 48,000	$ 57,600	$ 67,200
Contribution margin	$ 5.20		$ 52,000	$ 62,400	$ 72,800
Fixed costs					
Depreciation—Machinery		$ 8,000	8,000	8,000	8,000
Supervisory salaries		11,000	11,000	11,000	11,000
Insurance expense		1,000	1,000	1,000	1,000
Depreciation—Office equipment . . .		7,000	7,000	7,000	7,000
Administrative salaries		13,000	13,000	13,000	13,000
Total fixed costs		$40,000	$ 40,000	$ 40,000	$ 40,000
Income from operations			$ 12,000	$ 22,400	$ 32,800

The layout for the flexible budgets in Exhibit 25.3 begins with sales followed by variable costs and then fixed costs. Both individual and total variable costs are reported and then subtracted from sales. As we explained in Chapter 23, the difference between sales and variable costs equals contribution margin. The expected amounts of fixed costs are listed next, followed by the expected income from operations before taxes.

The first and second number columns of Exhibit 25.3 show the flexible budget amounts for variable costs per unit and each fixed cost for any volume of sales in the relevant range. The third, fourth, and fifth columns show the flexible budget amounts computed for three different sales volumes. For instance, the third column's flexible budget is based on 10,000 units. These numbers are the same as those in the fixed budget of Exhibit 25.2 because the expected volumes are the same for these two budgets.

Recall that Optel's actual sales volume for January is 12,000 units. This sales volume is 2,000 units more than the 10,000 units originally predicted in the master budget. When differences between actual and predicted volume arise, the usefulness of a flexible budget is apparent. For instance, compare the flexible budget for 10,000 units in the third column (which is the same as the fixed budget in Exhibit 25.2) with the flexible budget for 12,000 units in the fourth column. The higher levels for both sales and variable costs reflect

Example: Using Exhibit 25.3, what is the budgeted income from operations for unit sales of (a) 11,000 and (b) 13,000? *Answers:* $17,200 for unit sales of 11,000. $27,600 for unit sales of 13,000.

Point: Flexible budgeting allows a budget to be prepared at the *actual* level of output. Performance reports are then prepared comparing the flexible budget to actual revenues and costs. Performance reports were first discussed in Chapter 22.

Point: A flexible budget yields an "apples to apples" comparison because budgeted activity levels are the same as the actual.

nothing more than the increase in sales activity. Any budget analysis comparing actual with planned results that ignores this information is less useful to management.

To illustrate, when we evaluate Optel's performance, we need to prepare a flexible budget showing actual and budgeted values at 12,000 units. As part of a complete profitability analysis, managers could compare the actual income of $25,400 (from Exhibit 25.2) with the $22,400 income expected at the actual sales volume of 12,000 units (from Exhibit 25.3). This results in a total income variance of $3,000 needing to be explained and interpreted. This variance is markedly different from the $13,400 variance identified in Exhibit 25.2 using a fixed budget. After receiving the flexible budget based on January's actual volume, management's task is to determine what caused this $3,000 difference. The next section describes a flexible budget performance report that provides guidance in this analysis.

Flexible Budget Performance Report

Point: To apply these concepts, work QS 25-1.

A **flexible budget performance report** lists differences between actual performance and budgeted performance based on actual sales volume or other level of activity. This report helps direct management's attention to those costs or revenues that differ substantially from budgeted amounts. Exhibit 25.4 shows Optel's flexible budget performance report for January. We prepare this report after the actual volume is known to be 12,000 units. This report shows a $5,000 favorable variance in total dollar sales. Since actual and budgeted volumes are both 12,000 units, the $5,000 sales variance must have resulted from a selling price that was higher than expected. Further analysis of the facts surrounding this $5,000 sales variance reveals a favorable sales variance per unit of nearly $0.42 as shown here:

Actual average price per unit (rounded to cents)	$125,000/12,000 = $10.42
Budgeted price per unit	$120,000/12,000 = 10.00
Favorable sales variance per unit	$5,000/12,000 = $ 0.42

The other variances in Exhibit 25.4 also direct management's attention to areas where corrective actions can help control Optel's operations. Each expense variance is analyzed as the sales variance was. We can think of each expense as the joint result of using a given number of units and paying a specific price per unit.

More generally, each variance in Exhibit 25.4 is due in part to a difference between *actual price* per unit of input and *budgeted price* per unit of input. This is a **price variance.** A variance also can be due in part to a difference between *actual quantity* of input used and *budgeted quantity* of input. This is a **quantity variance.** We explain more about this breakdown, known as **variance analysis,** later in the chapter in the section on standard costs.

You Make the Call

Entrepreneur The heads of both strategic consulting and tax consulting divisions of your financial services firm complain to you about the unfavorable variances on their performance reports. "We worked on more consulting assignments than planned. It's not surprising our costs are higher than expected. To top it off, this report characterizes our work as *poor!*" How do you respond?

Answer—p. 1042

Quick Check

1. A flexible budget (a) shows fixed costs as constant amounts of cost per unit of activity, (b) shows variable costs as constant amounts of cost per unit of activity, or (c) is prepared based on one expected amount of budgeted sales or production.

2. What is the initial step in preparing a flexible budget?

3. What is the main difference between a fixed and a flexible budget?

4. What is contribution margin?

Answers—p. 1043

OPTEL Flexible Budget Performance Report For Month Ended January 31, 2002	Flexible Budget	Actual Results	Variances*
Sales (12,000 units)	$120,000	$125,000	**$5,000 F**
Variable costs			
Direct materials	12,000	13,000	**1,000 U**
Direct labor	18,000	20,000	**2,000 U**
Factory supplies	2,400	2,100	**300 F**
Utilities	3,600	4,000	**400 U**
Sales commissions	10,800	10,800	**0**
Shipping expenses	4,800	4,300	**500 F**
Office supplies	6,000	5,200	**800 F**
Total variable costs	$ 57,600	$ 59,400	**$1,800 U**
Contribution margin	$ 62,400	$ 65,600	**$3,200 F**
Fixed costs			
Depreciation—Machinery	8,000	8,000	**0**
Supervisory salaries	11,000	11,000	**0**
Insurance expense	1,000	1,200	**200 U**
Depreciation—Office equipment	7,000	7,000	**0**
Administrative salaries	13,000	13,000	**0**
Total fixed costs	$ 40,000	$ 40,200	**$ 200 U**
Income from operations	$ 22,400	$ 25,400	**$3,000 F**

Exhibit 25.4

Flexible Budget Performance Report

* F = Favorable variance; and U = Unfavorable variance.

Section 2—Standard Costs

We described job order and process cost accounting systems in Chapters 20 and 21. The costs described in those chapters are historical costs. Historical (actual) costs are the dollar amounts a company paid in past transactions and are useful for many analyses. To decide whether these historical costs are reasonable or excessive, management needs a measure of comparison. Standard costs offer one basis for comparison. **Standard costs** are preset costs for delivering a product or service under normal conditions. These costs are established through personnel, engineering, and accounting studies using past experiences and data. Management uses them to assess the reasonableness of actual costs incurred for producing the product or service. When actual costs vary from standard costs, management follows up to identify potential problems and take corrective actions.

Standard costs are often used in preparing budgets because they are the anticipated cost incurred under normal conditions. Terms such as *standard materials cost, standard labor cost,* and *standard overhead cost* are often used to refer to amounts budgeted for direct materials, direct labor, and overhead.

C1 Define standard costs and explain their computation and uses.

Point: Because standard costs are often budgeted costs, they can be used to prepare both fixed budgets and flexible budgets.

Materials and Labor Standards

This section explains how we set materials and labor standards. It also shows how to prepare a standard cost card.

Identifying Standard Costs

Managerial accountants, engineers, personnel administrators, and other managers combine their efforts to set standard costs. To identify standards for direct labor costs, we can conduct time and motion studies for each labor operation in the process of providing a product

Point: Business practice often uses the word *budget* when speaking of total values and *standard* when discussing per unit values.

or service. From these studies, management can learn the best way to perform the operation and then sets the standard labor time required for the operation under normal conditions. In a similar way, standards for materials are set by studying the quantity, grade, and cost of each material used. Standards for overhead costs are explained later in the chapter.

Regardless of the care used in setting standard costs and in revising them as conditions change, actual costs frequently differ from standard costs, often as a result of more than one factor. For instance, the actual quantity of material used can differ from the standard, or the price paid per unit of material can differ from the standard. Quantity and price differences from standard amounts can also occur for labor. That is, the actual labor time and actual labor rate can vary from what was expected. The same analysis applies to overhead costs.

Did You Know?

Cruis'n Standards   The sleek **Chrysler** convertible consists of hundreds of parts for which engineers establish standards. Various types of labor are also involved in its production, including machining, assembly, painting, and welding, and standards are established for them. At periodic points, actual results are compared with standards to assess production performance.

Setting Standard Costs

Example: What factors might be considered when deciding whether to revise standard costs? *Answer:* Look for changes in the processes and/or resources needed to carry out the processes.

Point: Companies promoting continuous improvement strive to achieve ideal standards by eliminating inefficiencies and waste.

To illustrate the setting of a standard cost, we consider the case of a professional league baseball bat manufactured by ProBat. Its engineers have determined that manufacturing one bat requires 0.90 kgs. of high-grade wood. They also expect some loss of material as part of the process because of inefficiencies and waste. This results in adding an *allowance* of 0.10 kgs. This means the standard requirement is 1.0 kg. of wood for each bat.

The 0.90 kgs. portion is called an *ideal standard;* it is the quantity of material required if the process is 100% efficient without any loss or waste. Reality suggests that some loss of material usually occurs with any process. The standard of 1.0 kg. is known as the *practical standard,* the quantity of material required under normal application of the process.

High-grade wood can be purchased at a standard price of $25 per kg. This is the price the purchasing department sets as the expected price for the budget period. To determine this price, the purchasing department considers factors such as the quality of materials, future economic conditions, supply factors (shortages and excesses), and any available discounts. The engineers also decide that two hours of labor time (after including allowances) are re-

Exhibit 25.5

Standard Cost Card

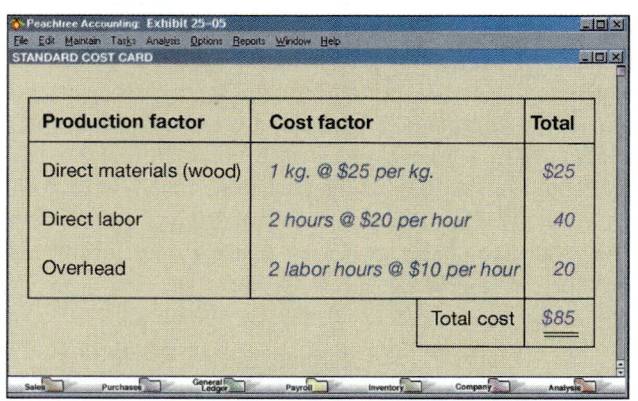

quired to manufacture a bat. The wage rate is $20 per hour (better than average skilled labor is required). ProBat assigns all overhead at the rate of $10 per labor hour. The standard costs of direct materials, direct labor, and overhead for one bat are as shown in Exhibit 25.5 in what is called a *standard cost card.* These cost amounts are then used to prepare manufacturing budgets for a budgeted level of production.

Cost Variances

C2 Describe variances and what they reveal about performance.

A **cost variance,** also simply called a *variance,* is the difference between actual and standard costs. A cost variance can be favorable or unfavorable. A variance from standard cost is considered favorable if actual cost is less than standard cost. It is considered unfavorable if actual cost is more than standard cost.[1] This section discusses variance analysis and its application.

---

[1] Short-term favorable variances can sometimes lead to long-term unfavorable variances. For instance, if management spends less than the budgeted amount on maintenance or insurance, the performance report would show a favorable variance. Cutting these expenses can lead to major losses in the long run if machinery wears out prematurely or insurance coverage proves inadequate.

Cost Variance Analysis

Variances are usually identified in performance reports. When a variance occurs, management wants to determine the factors causing it. This often involves analysis, evaluation, and explanation. The results of these efforts should enable management to assign responsibility for the variance and then to take actions to correct the situation.

To illustrate, Optel's standard materials cost for producing 12,000 units of its product is $12,000. Its actual materials cost for January proved to be $13,000. The $1,000 unfavorable variance raises questions that call for answers that, in turn, can lead to changes to correct the situation and eliminate this variance in the next period. A performance report often identifies the existence of a problem, but we must follow up with further investigation to see what can be done to improve future performance.

Exhibit 25.6 shows the flow of events in the effective management of variance analysis. It shows four steps: (1) preparation of a standard cost performance report, (2) computation and analysis of variances, (3) identification of questions and their explanations, and (4) corrective and strategic actions. These variance analysis steps are interrelated and are frequently applied in good organizations.

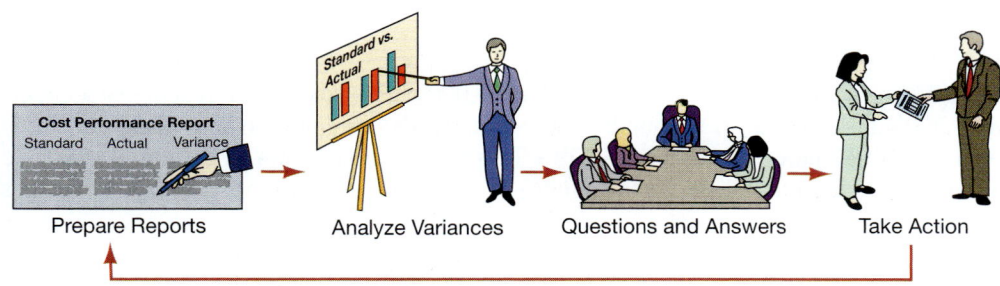

Exhibit 25.6

Variance Analysis

Computing Cost Variances

Management needs information about the factors causing a cost variance, but first it must properly compute the variance. In its most simple form, a cost variance (CV) is computed as the difference between actual cost (AC) and standard cost (SC) as shown in Exhibit 25.7.

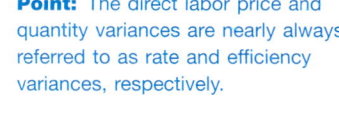

> **Cost Variance** (CV) = **Actual Cost** (AC) − **Standard Cost** (SC)
>
> where:
>
> **Actual Cost** (AC) = **Actual Quantity** (AQ) × **Actual Price** (AP)
> **Standard Cost** (SC) = **Standard Quantity** (SQ) × **Standard Price** (SP)

Exhibit 25.7

Cost Variance Formulas

A cost variance is further defined by its components. Actual quantity (AQ) is the input (material or labor) used to manufacture the quantity of output. Standard quantity (SQ) is the expected input for the quantity of output. Actual price (AP) is the amount paid to acquire the input (material or labor), and standard price (SP) is the expected price.

Two main factors cause a cost variance: (1) the difference between actual price and standard price results in a *price* (or rate) *variance,* and (2) the difference between actual quantity and standard quantity results in a *quantity* (or usage or efficiency) *variance*. To assess the impacts of these two factors on a cost variance, we use the formula in Exhibit 25.8.

Point: The direct labor price and quantity variances are nearly always referred to as rate and efficiency variances, respectively.

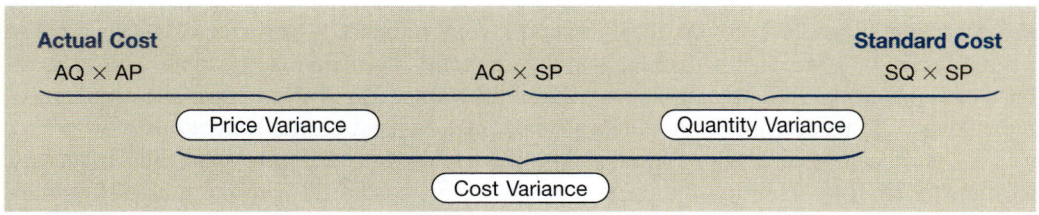

Exhibit 25.8

Price Variance and Quantity Variance Formulas

These formulas identify the sources of the cost variance. Managers sometimes find it useful to apply an alternative (but equivalent) computation for the price and quantity variances as shown in Exhibit 25.9.

Exhibit 25.9

Alternative Price Variance and Quantity Variance Formulas

> **Price Variance (PV) = [Actual Price (AP) − Standard Price (SP)] × Actual Quantity (AQ)**
>
> **Quantity Variance (QV) = [Actual Quantity (AQ) − Standard Quantity (SQ)] × Standard Price (SP)**

The results from applying the formulas in Exhibits 25.8 and 25.9 are identical.

Materials and Labor Variances

P2 Compute materials and labor variances.

We illustrate the computation of the materials and labor cost variances using data from **G-Max,** a company that makes specialty golf equipment and accessories for individual customers. This company has set the following standard quantities and prices for materials and labor per unit for one of its hand-crafted golf clubheads:

Direct materials (1 lb. per unit at $1 per lb.)	$1.00
Direct labor (1 hr. per unit at $8 per hr.)	8.00
Total standard direct cost per unit	$9.00

Materials Cost Variances

During May 2002, G-Max budgeted to produce 4,000 clubheads (units). It actually produced only 3,500 units. It used 3,600 pounds of direct materials (titanium) costing $1.05 per pound, meaning its total materials cost was $3,780. This information allows us to compute both actual and standard direct materials costs for G-Max's 3,500 units and its direct materials cost variance:

Concept 25-2

Actual cost	3,600 lbs. @ $1.05 per lb.	= $3,780
Standard cost	3,500 lbs. @ $1.00 per lb.	= 3,500
Direct materials cost variance (unfavorable)		= $ 280

The materials price and quantity variances for these G-Max clubheads are computed and shown in Exhibit 25.10.

Exhibit 25.10

Materials Price and Quantity Variances

Actual Cost		**Standard Cost**
AQ × AP	AQ × SP	SQ × SP
3,600 lbs. × $1.05	3,600 lbs. × $1.00	3,500 lbs. × $1.00
$3,780	$3,600	$3,500

$180 U — Price Variance

$100 U — Quantity Variance

$280 U — Total Direct Materials Variance

Example: Identify at least two factors that might have caused the $100 unfavorable quantity variance and the $180 unfavorable price variance in Exhibit 25.10. *Answer:* Poor quality materials or untrained workers for the former; Poor price negotiation or higher quality materials for the latter.

Example: Give an example of a manufacturing situation in which a favorable price variance for material might be the cause of an unfavorable quantity variance. *Answer:* Buying cheap materials.

The unfavorable price variance of $180 results from paying 5 cents more than the standard price, computed as 3,600 lbs × $0.05. The unfavorable quantity variance of $100 is due to using 100 lbs more materials than the standard quantity, computed as 100 lbs × $1. The total direct materials variance is $280 and is unfavorable. This information allows management to ask the responsible individuals for explanations and corrective actions.

The purchasing department is usually responsible for the price paid for materials. Responsibility for explaining the price variance in this case rests with the purchasing manager if a price higher than standard caused the variance. The production department is usually responsible for the amount of material used and in this case is responsible for explaining why the process used more than the standard amount of materials.

Variance analysis presents challenges. For instance, the production department could have used more than the standard amount of material because its quality did not meet specifications and led to excessive waste. In this case, the purchasing manager is responsible for explaining why inferior materials were acquired. However, the production manager is responsible for explaining what happened if analysis shows that waste was due to inefficiencies, not poor-quality material.

In evaluating price variances, managers must recognize that a favorable price variance can indicate a problem with poor product quality. **Redhook Ale**, a micro brewery in the Pacific Northwest, can probably save 10% to 15% in material prices by buying six-row barley malt instead of the better two-row from Washington's Yakima valley. Attention to quality, however, has helped Redhook Ale become the only craft brewer to be "kosher" certified. Redhook's purchasing activities are judged on both the quality of the materials and the purchase price variance. This stand on quality has helped Redhook report increases in both sales and gross margin.

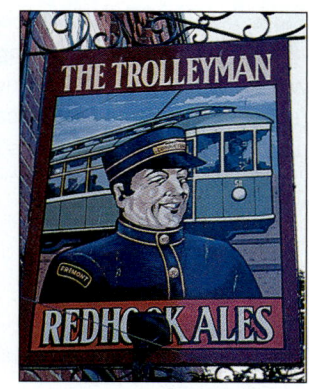

Labor Cost Variances

Labor cost for a specific product or service depends on the number of hours worked (quantity) and the wage rate paid to employees (price). When actual amounts for a task differ from standard, the labor cost variance can be divided into a rate (price) variance and an efficiency (quantity) variance.

To illustrate, G-Max's direct labor standard for 3,500 units of its hand-crafted clubheads is one hour per unit, or 3,500 hours at $8 per hour. Since only 3,400 hours at $8.30 per hour were actually used to complete the units, the actual and standard labor costs are

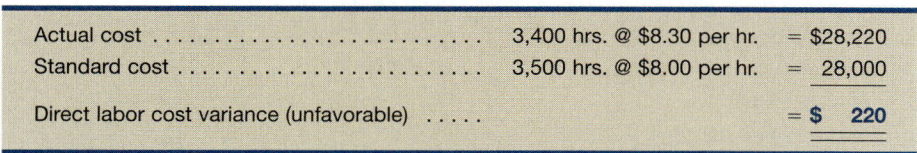

Actual cost	3,400 hrs. @ $8.30 per hr.	= $28,220
Standard cost	3,500 hrs. @ $8.00 per hr.	= 28,000
Direct labor cost variance (unfavorable)		= $ 220

This analysis shows that actual cost is merely $220 over the standard and suggests no immediate concern. Computing both the labor rate and efficiency variances reveals a different picture, however, as shown in Exhibit 25.11.

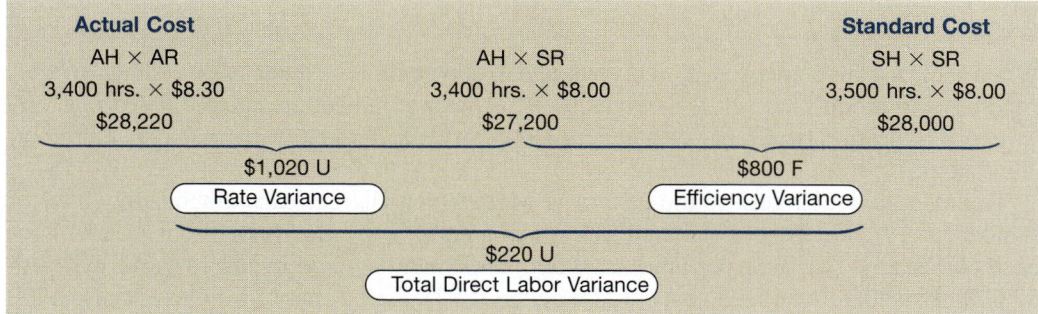

Actual Cost		**Standard Cost**
AH × AR	AH × SR	SH × SR
3,400 hrs. × $8.30	3,400 hrs. × $8.00	3,500 hrs. × $8.00
$28,220	$27,200	$28,000

$1,020 U — Rate Variance

$800 F — Efficiency Variance

$220 U — Total Direct Labor Variance

Exhibit 25.11
Labor Rate and Efficiency Variances*

* AH is actual direct labor hours; AR is actual wage rate; SH is standard direct labor hours allowed for actual output; SR is standard wage rate.

The analysis in Exhibit 25.11 shows that the favorable efficiency variance of $800 results from using 100 fewer direct labor hours than standard for the units produced, but this favorable variance is more than offset by a wage rate that is $0.30 higher than standard. The personnel administrator, or possibly the production manager, needs to explain why the wage rate is higher than expected. The production manager should also explain how the labor hours were reduced. If this experience can be repeated and transferred to other departments, more savings are possible.

Example: Compute the rate variance and the efficiency variance for Exhibit 25.11 if 3,700 actual hours are used at an actual price of $7.50 per hour. *Answer:* $1,850 favorable labor rate variance and $1,600 unfavorable labor efficiency variance.

Point: To apply these concepts, work Exercise 25-5.

One possible explanation of these labor rate and efficiency variances is the use of workers with different skill levels. If this is the reason, the company must discuss the implications with the production manager as this manager has the responsibility to assign workers to tasks with the appropriate skill level. In this case, an investigation might show that higher skilled workers were used to produce 3,500 units of handcrafted clubheads. As a result, fewer labor hours might be required for the work, but the wage rate paid to such workers is higher than standard because of their greater skills. In G-Max's situation, the effect of this strategy would be a higher than standard total cost, which would require actions to remedy the situation or adjust the standard.

You Make the Call

Human Resource Manager You receive the manufacturing variance report for June and discover a large unfavorable labor efficiency (quantity) variance. What factors do you investigate to identify its possible causes?

Answer—p. 1042

Quick Check

5. A standard cost: (a) changes in direct proportion to changes in the level of activity, (b) is an amount incurred at the actual level of production for the period, or (c) is an amount incurred under normal conditions to provide a product or service.

6. What is a cost variance?

7. The following information is available for York Co.:

Actual direct labor hours per unit	2.5 hours
Standard direct labor hours per unit	2.0 hours
Actual production (units)	2,500 units
Budgeted production (units)	3,000 units
Actual rate per hour	$3.10
Standard rate per hour	$3.00

The labor efficiency variance is: (a) $3,750 U, (b) $3,750 F, or (c) $3,875 U.

8. Refer to Quick Check 7; the labor rate variance is (a) $625 F or (b) $625 U.

9. If a material quantity variance is favorable and a material price variance is unfavorable, can the total material cost variance be favorable?

Answers—p. 1043

Overhead Standards and Variances

When standard costs are used, a predetermined overhead rate is used to assign standard overhead costs to products or services produced. This predetermined rate is often based on some overhead allocation base (such as standard labor cost, standard labor hours, or standard machine hours).

To illustrate, let's return to the case of G-Max, which charges each clubhead with $2 of standard overhead cost per standard direct labor hour. Since the direct labor standard for each clubhead is one hour per unit, the 3,500 units manufactured in May are charged with $7,000 of standard overhead costs (3,500 hours × $2). Recall that G-Max used only 3,400 actual direct labor hours to produce 3,500 clubheads, yet overhead costs are assigned to units on the basis of standard labor hours, not on the basis of actual labor hours. Standard labor hours are used because the total amount of overhead charged to all units produced should equal the total flexible budget overhead cost for the period. This is true for variable overhead, but the fixed overhead assigned will equal the budget only when actual production equals expected production. A difference between actual and expected production yields a *fixed overhead volume variance,* which we discuss later in the chapter.

Setting Overhead Standards

Standard overhead costs are the amounts expected to occur at a certain level of activity. Unlike direct materials and direct labor, overhead includes fixed costs and variable costs.

This results in the average overhead cost per unit changing as the predicted volume changes. Since standard costs are also budgeted costs, they must be established before the reporting period begins. Standard overhead costs are therefore average per unit costs based on the predicted level of activity.

To establish the standard overhead cost rate, management uses the same cost structure that it used to construct a flexible budget at the end of a period. This cost structure identifies the different overhead cost components and classifies them as variable or fixed. To get the standard overhead rate, management selects a level of activity (volume) and predicts total overhead cost. It then divides this total by the allocation base to get the standard rate. Standard direct labor hours expected to be used to produce the predicted volume is a common allocation base and is used in this section.

Exhibit 25.12 shows the overhead cost structure used to develop G-Max's flexible overhead budgets for May 2002. It sets the predetermined standard overhead rate for May before the month begins. The first two number columns lists the per unit amounts of variable costs and the monthly amounts of fixed costs. The right-most four columns show the costs expected to occur at four different levels of activity. The predetermined overhead rate per labor hour is smaller as volume of activity increases because fixed costs remain constant.

Point: Managers consider the types of overhead costs when choosing the basis for assigning overhead costs to products. Predetermined overhead rates are explained in Chapter 20.

Exhibit 25.12

Flexible Overhead Budgets

G-MAX Flexible Overhead Budgets For Month Ended May 31, 2002						
	Flexible Budget		Flexible Budget at 70% Capacity	Flexible Budget at 80% Capacity	Flexible Budget at 90% Capacity	Flexible Budget at 100% Capacity
	Variable Amount per Unit	Total Fixed Cost				
Production (in units)	1 unit		3,500	4,000	4,500	5,000
Factory overhead						
Variable costs						
Indirect labor	$0.40/unit		$1,400	$1,600	$1,800	$2,000
Indirect materials	0.30/unit		1,050	1,200	1,350	1,500
Power and lights	0.20/unit		700	800	900	1,000
Maintenance	0.10/unit		350	400	450	500
Total variable overhead costs	$1.00/unit		$3,500	$4,000	$4,500	$5,000
Fixed costs (per month)						
Building rent		$1,000	1,000	1,000	1,000	1,000
Depreciation—Machinery		1,200	1,200	1,200	1,200	1,200
Supervisory salaries		1,800	1,800	1,800	1,800	1,800
Total fixed overhead costs		$4,000	$4,000	$4,000	$4,000	$4,000
Total factory overhead			$7,500	$8,000	$8,500	$9,000
Standard direct labor hours	1 hr./unit		3,500 hrs.	4,000 hrs.	4,500 hrs.	5,000 hrs.
Predetermined overhead rate per standard direct labor hour			$2.14	$2.00	$1.89	$ 1.80

In setting the standard overhead budget for May, G-Max managers predicted an 80% activity level, or a production volume of 4,000 clubheads. At this volume, they budget $8,000 as the total overhead for May. This choice implies a $2 per unit (labor hour) average

Point: Chapter 23 explained how variable costs per unit remain constant but fixed costs per unit decline with increases in volume. This means the average total overhead cost per unit declines with increases in volume.

overhead cost ($8,000/4,000 units). Since G-Max has a standard of one direct labor hour for each unit, the predetermined standard overhead application rate for May is $2 per standard direct labor hour. The variable overhead rate remains constant at $1 per direct labor hour regardless of the budgeted production level. The fixed overhead rate changes according to the budgeted production volume. For instance, for the predicted level of 4,000 units of production, the fixed rate is $1 per hour ($4,000 fixed costs/4,000 units). For a production level of 5,000 units, however, the fixed rate is $0.80 per hour.

When choosing the predicted activity level for a company, management considers many factors. The level can be set as high as 100% of capacity, but this is rare. Factors causing the activity level to be less than full capacity include difficulties in scheduling work, equipment under repair or maintenance, and insufficient product demand. Good long-run management practices often call for some plant capacity in excess of current operating needs to allow for special opportunities and demand changes.

Did You Know?

Measuring Up In the spirit of continuous improvement, companies are setting new standards (benchmarks) for performance. Competitors are comparing their processes and performance standards against benchmarks established by industry leaders. This implies continuous revision of standards in all areas of an organization to improve productivity. Corporate giants such as **Xerox**, **Motorola**, and **AT&T** use benchmarking.

Overhead Cost Variance Analysis

P3 Compute overhead variances.

When standard costs are used, the cost accounting system applies overhead to the good units produced using the predetermined standard overhead rate. At the end of the period, the difference between the total overhead cost applied to products and the total overhead cost actually incurred is called an **overhead cost variance,** which is defined in Exhibit 25.13.

Exhibit 25.13

Overhead Cost Variance

> **Overhead cost variance (OCV) = Actual overhead incurred (AOI) − Standard overhead applied (SOA)**

To help management identify factors causing the overhead cost variance, we analyze this variance separately for variable and fixed overhead. The results provide information useful to management for taking strategic actions to improve company performance. Similar to our analysis of direct materials and direct labor variances, both the variable and fixed overhead variances can be separated into useful components as shown in Exhibit 25.14.

Exhibit 25.14

Variable and Fixed Overhead Variances

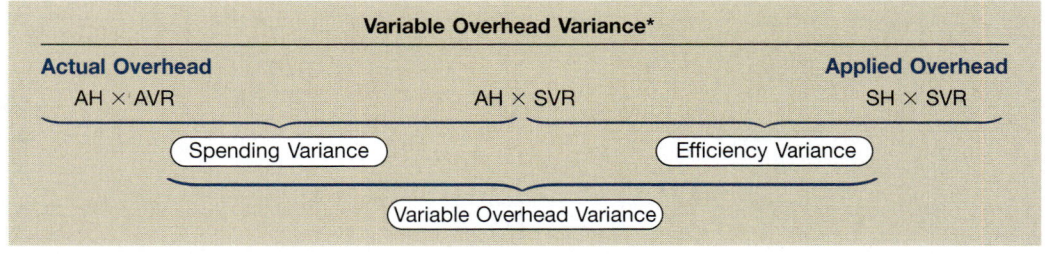

* AH = actual direct labor hours; AVR = actual variable overhead rate; SH = standard direct labor hours; SVR = standard variable overhead rate.

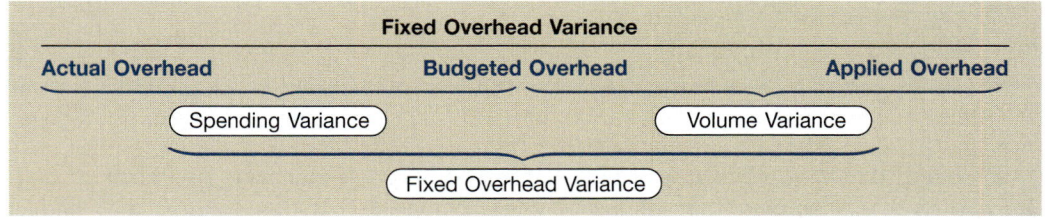

A **spending variance** occurs when management pays an amount different than the standard price to acquire an item. For instance, the actual wage rate paid to indirect labor might be higher than the standard rate. Similarly, actual supervisory salaries might be different than expected. Spending variances such as these cause management to investigate the reasons that the amount paid differs from the standard. Both variable and fixed overhead costs can yield their own spending variances. The analysis of variable overhead includes computing an efficiency variance. An **efficiency variance** occurs when standard direct labor hours (the allocation base) expected for actual production differ from the actual direct labor hours used. This efficiency variance is unrelated to whether variable overhead is used efficiently. Instead, this variance results from whether the overhead allocation base (such as direct labor) is used efficiently.

A **volume variance** occurs when a difference occurs between the actual volume of production and the standard volume of production. The budgeted fixed overhead amount is the same regardless of the volume of production (within the relevant range). This budgeted amount is computed based on standard direct labor hours that the budgeted production volume allows. The applied overhead is based, however, on the standard direct labor hours allowed for the actual volume of production. If there is a difference between budgeted and actual production volumes, there is a difference in the standard direct labor hours allowed for these two production levels. This situation yields a volume variance different from zero.

We can combine the variable overhead spending variance, the fixed overhead spending variance, and the variable overhead efficiency variance to get **controllable variance;** see Exhibit 25.15. The controllable variance is so named because it refers to activities usually under management control.

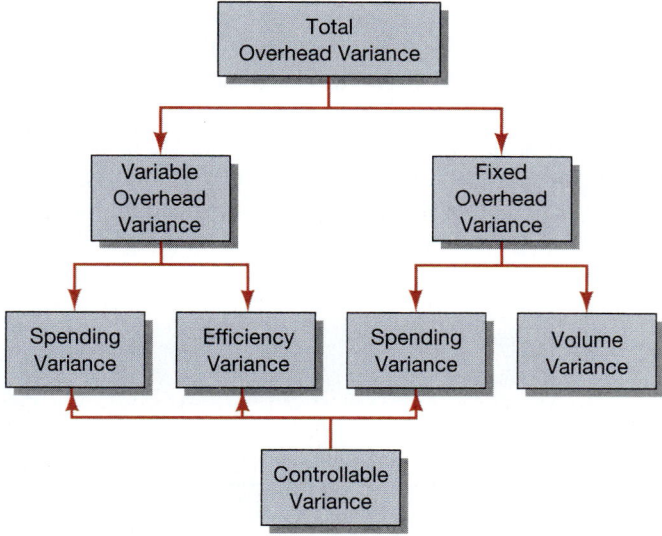

Exhibit 25.15

Framework for Understanding Total Overhead Variance

Computing Overhead Cost Variances

To illustrate how we compute overhead cost variances, we return to the data from G-Max. We know that it actually produced 3,500 units but 4,000 units were budgeted. Additional data from G-Max show that actual overhead cost incurred is $7,650 (variable portion of $3,650; fixed portion of $4,000). Using this information, we can compute overhead variances for both variable and fixed overhead.

Variable Overhead Cost Variances

Recall that G-Max applies overhead based on direct labor hours as the allocation base. We know that 3,400 direct labor hours are used to produce 3,500 units. This compares favorably to the standard requirement of 3,500 direct labor hours at one labor hour per unit. We compute and separate G-Max's variable overhead cost variances as shown in Exhibit 25.16.

Exhibit 25.16

Computing Variable Overhead Cost Variances

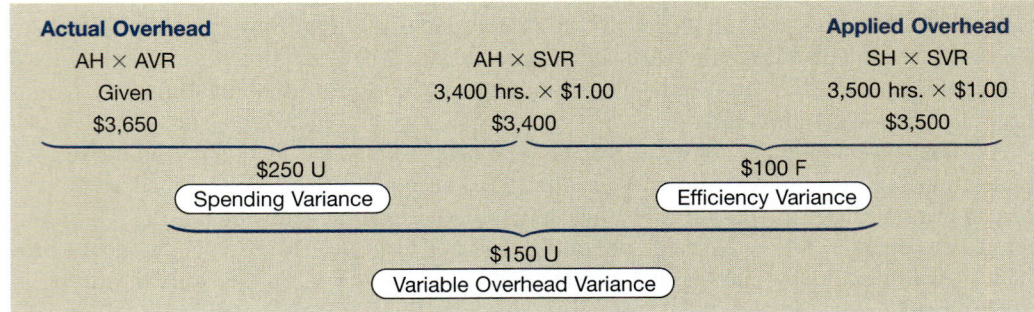

The actual variable overhead amount of $3,650 is available from G-Max's cost records. We use this amount to compute the actual variable overhead rate of $1.07 per direct labor hour ($3,650/3,400 direct labor hours approximately). This reveals that, on average, G-Max incurred $0.07 more per direct labor hour in variable overhead than the standard rate. The middle column of Exhibit 25.16 is computed by multiplying the actual direct labor hours (3,400) by the standard rate of $1 per direct labor hour. The right-hand side is the applied overhead, it is computed by multiplying the standard hours allowed for actual production (3,500) by the standard rate of $1 per direct labor hour.

Fixed Overhead Cost Variances

G-Max reports that it incurred $4,000 in actual fixed overhead; this amount equals the budgeted fixed overhead for May (see Exhibit 25.12). G-Max's budgeted fixed overhead application rate is $1 per hour ($4,000/4,000 direct labor hours), but the actual production level is only 3,500 units. Using this information, we can compute the fixed overhead cost variances shown in Exhibit 25.17. The applied fixed overhead is computed by multiplying standard hours allowed for the actual production (3,500) by the fixed overhead allocation rate ($1). Exhibit 25.17 reveals that the fixed overhead spending variance is zero and the volume variance is $500. The volume variance occurs because 500 fewer units are produced than budgeted because 80% of the manufacturing capacity is budgeted but only 70% is used.

Exhibit 25.17

Computing Fixed Overhead Cost Variances

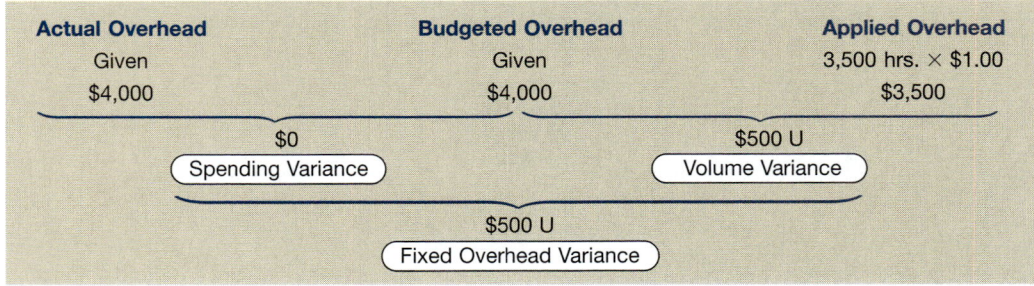

We show this volume variance graphically in Exhibit 25.18. The upward-sloping line reflects the amount of fixed overhead costs applied to the units produced in May using the predetermined fixed overhead rate. The uppermost horizontal line reflects the $4,000 of total fixed costs budgeted for May. These two lines cross at the planned operating volume of 4,000 units. When unit volume is 3,500 units, the overhead-costs-applied line falls $500 below the budgeted fixed overhead line. This shortfall is the volume variance.

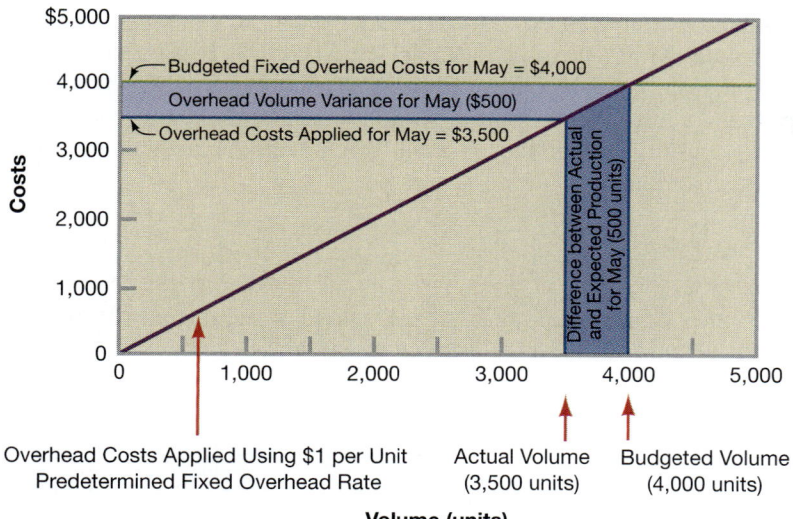

Exhibit 25.18

Fixed Overhead
Volume Variance

An unfavorable volume variance implies that the company did not reach its predicted operating level. Of course, management would already know this result. More important, it needs to know why the actual level of performance differs from the expected level. The main purpose of the volume variance is to identify what portion of the total variance is caused by failing to meet the expected volume level. This information permits management to focus on the controllable variance.

A complete overhead variance report provides managers information about specific overhead costs and how they differ from budgeted amounts. Exhibit 25.19 shows G-Max's overhead variance report for May. It reveals that (1) fixed costs and maintenance cost were incurred as expected, (2) costs for indirect labor and power and lights were higher than expected, and (3) indirect materials cost was less than expected.

Exhibit 25.19

Overhead Variance Report

G-MAX
Overhead Variance Report
For Month Ended May 31, 2002

Volume Variance

Expected production level	80% of capacity
Production level achieved	70% of capacity
Volume variance	$500 (unfavorable)

Controllable Variance	Flexible Budget	Actual Results	Variances*
Variable overhead costs			
Indirect labor	$1,400	$1,525	$125 U
Indirect materials	1,050	1,025	25 F
Power and lights	700	750	50 U
Maintenance	350	350	0
Total variable overhead costs	$3,500	$3,650	$150 U†
Fixed overhead costs			
Building rent	$1,000	$1,000	$ 0
Depreciation—Machinery	1,200	1,200	0
Supervisory salaries	1,800	1,800	0
Total fixed overhead costs	$4,000	$4,000	$ 0‡
Total overhead costs	$7,500	$7,650	$150 U

*F = Favorable variance; and U = Unfavorable variance.
†Total variable overhead (spending and efficiency) variance.
‡Fixed overhead spending variance.

Using information from Exhibits 25.16 and 25.17, we can compute the total controllable overhead variance as $150 unfavorable ($250 U + $100 F + $0). This amount is also readily available from Exhibit 25.19. The overhead variance report shows the total volume variance as $500 unfavorable (shown at the top) and the $150 unfavorable controllable variance. The sum of the controllable variance and the volume variance equals the total (fixed and variable) overhead variance of $650 unfavorable.

Extending Standard Costs

This section extends the application of standard costs for use in control systems, for use by service companies, and for use in the accounting system.

Standard Costs for Control

C3 Explain how standard cost information is useful for management by exception.

To control business activities, top management must be able to affect the actions of lower-level managers responsible for the company's revenues and costs. After preparing a budget and establishing standard costs, management should take actions to gain control when actual costs differ from the standard or budgeted amounts.

Reports such as the ones illustrated in this chapter call management's attention to variances from business plans and other standards. When managers use these reports to focus on problem areas, the budgeting process contributes to the control function. In using budgeted performance reports, practice of management by exception is often useful. **Management by exception** means that managers focus attention on the most significant variances and give less attention to areas where performance is reasonably close to the standard. This practice leads management to concentrate on the exceptional or irregular situations and to defer any serious analysis of areas showing actual results that are reasonably close to the plan. Management by exception is especially useful when directed at controllable items.

Standard Costs for Services

Many managers use standard costs and variance analysis to investigate manufacturing costs. Many managers also recognize that standard costs and variances can help them control *non*-manufacturing costs. Companies providing services to customers instead of products can especially benefit from the use of standard costs. Application of standard costs and variances can be readily adapted to these nonmanufacturing situations. To illustrate, many service providers use standard costs to help control expenses. First, they use standard costs as a basis for budgeting all services. Second, they use periodic performance reports to compare actual results to standards. Third, they use these reports to identify significant variances within specific areas of responsibility. Fourth, they implement the appropriate control procedures.

Standard Cost Accounting System

P4 Prepare journal entries for standard costs and account for price and quantity variances.

We have shown how companies use standard costs in management reports. Most standard cost systems also record these costs and variances in the accounts. This practice simplifies recordkeeping and helps in preparing reports. Although we do not need knowledge of standard cost accounting practices to understand standard costs and how they are used, we must know how to interpret the accounts in which standard costs and variances are recorded. The entries in this section briefly illustrate the important aspects of this process for G-Max's standard costs and variances for May.

The first of these entries records standard materials cost incurred in May in the Goods in Process Inventory account. This part of the entry is similar to the usual accounting entry, but the amount of the debit equals the standard cost ($3,500) instead of the actual cost ($3,780). This entry credits Raw Materials Inventory for actual cost. The difference between standard and actual costs is recorded with debits to two separate materials variance accounts (recall Exhibit 25.10). Both the materials price and quantity variances are recorded as debits because they reflect additional costs higher than the standard cost (if actual costs were less than the standard, they are recorded as credits). This treatment (debit) reflects their unfavorable effect because they represent higher costs and lower income.

May 31	Goods in Process Inventory	3,500	
	Direct Materials Price Variance*	100	
	Direct Materials Quantity Variance	180	
	Raw Materials Inventory		3,780
	To charge production for standard quantity of materials used (3,500 lbs.) at the standard price ($1 per lb.), and to record material price and material quantity variances.		

Assets	= Liabilities +	Equity
+3,500		−100
−3,780		−180

* Many companies record the materials price variance when materials are purchased. For simplicity, we record both the materials price and quantity variances when materials are issued to production.

The second entry debits Goods in Process Inventory for the standard labor cost of the goods manufactured during May ($28,000). Actual labor cost ($28,220) is recorded with a credit to the Factory Payroll account. The difference between standard and actual labor costs is explained by two variances (see Exhibit 25.11). The direct labor rate variance is unfavorable and is debited to that account. The direct labor efficiency variance is favorable and is credited. The direct labor efficiency variance is favorable because it represents a lower cost and a higher net income.

May 31	Goods in Process Inventory	28,000	
	Direct Labor Rate Variance	1,020	
	Direct Labor Efficiency Variance		800
	Factory Payroll		28,220
	To charge production with 3,500 standard hours of direct labor at the standard $8 per hour rate, and to record the labor rate and efficiency variances.		

Assets	= Liabilities +	Equity
+28,000		+28,220
		− 1,020
		+ 800

The entry to assign standard predetermined overhead to the cost of goods manufactured must debit the predetermined amount ($7,000) to the Goods in Process Inventory account. The actual overhead costs of $7,650 are debited to the Factory Overhead account. Thus, when Factory Overhead is applied to Goods in Process Inventory, the amount applied is debited to the Goods in Process Inventory account and credited to the Factory Overhead account. To account for the difference between actual and standard costs, the entry includes a debit of $250 to the Variable Overhead Spending Variance, a credit of $100 to the Variable Overhead Efficiency Variance, and a debit of $500 to the Volume Variance (recall Exhibits 25.16 and 25.17). An alternative (simpler) approach, which we show here, is to record the difference with a debit of $150 to the Controllable Variance account and a debit of $500 to the Volume Variance account (recall from Exhibit 25.15 that controllable variance is the sum of both variable overhead variances and the fixed overhead spending variance).

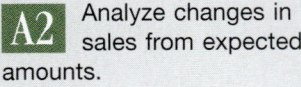

Assets = Liabilities + Equity
+7,000   +7,650
                           −   150
                           −   500

May 31	Goods in Process Inventory	7,000	
	Controllable Variance	**150**	
	Volume Variance	**500**	
	Factory Overhead		7,650
	To apply overhead at the standard rate of $2 per standard direct labor hour (3,500 hours), and to record overhead variances.		

The balances of these six different variance accounts accumulate until the end of the accounting period. As a result the unfavorable variances of some months offset the favorable variances of others.

   These variance account balances, which reflect results of various transactions and events in the period, are closed at the end of the period. If the variances are *material*, they are added to or subtracted from the balances of the Goods in Process Inventory, the Finished Goods Inventory, and the Cost of Goods Sold accounts. If the amounts are *immaterial*, they are added to or subtracted from the balance of the Cost of Goods Sold account. This process is similar to that shown in Chapter 20 for eliminating an underapplied or over-applied balance in the Factory Overhead account. (*Note:* Since these variance balances represent differences between actual and standard costs, they must be added to or subtracted from the materials, labor, and overhead costs recorded in the period. In this way, the recorded costs equal the actual costs incurred in the period—a company must use actual costs in external financial statements prepared in accordance with generally accepted accounting principles.)

Point: To apply these concepts, work Exercise 25-8.

Answers—p. 1043

Quick Check

10. Under what conditions is an overhead volume variance considered favorable?

11. To use management by exception with standard costs, a company (a) must record standard costs in its accounting, (b) should compute variances from flexible budget amounts to allow management to focus its attention on significant differences between actual and budgeted results, or (c) should analyze only variances for direct materials and direct labor.

12. A company uses a standard cost accounting system. Prepare the journal entry to record these direct materials variances:

Direct materials cost actually incurred	$73,200
Direct materials quantity variance (favorable)	3,800
Direct materials price variance (unfavorable)	1,300

13. If standard costs are recorded in the manufacturing accounts, how are recorded variances treated at the end of an accounting period?

Using the Information   Sales Variances

A2 Analyze changes in sales from expected amounts.

This chapter explained the computation and analysis of cost variances. A similar variance analysis can be applied to sales. To illustrate, consider the following sales data from G-Max for two of its golf products, fluorescent Excel balls and Big Bert® drivers.

	Budgeted	Actual
Sales of Excel golf balls (units)	1,000	1,100
Sales price per Excel golf ball	$ 10	$ 10.50
Sales of Big Bert® drivers (units)	150	140
Sales price per Big Bert® driver	$ 200	$ 190

Using this information, we compute both the *sales price variance* and the *sales volume variance* as shown in Exhibit 25.20. The total sales price variance is $850 unfavorable, and the total sales volume variance is $1,000 unfavorable. Neither variance implies anything positive about these two products. Further analysis of these total sales variances reveals that both the sales price and sales volume variances for Excel golf balls are favorable, meaning that both the unfavorable total sales price variance and the unfavorable total sales volume variance are due to the Big Bert driver.

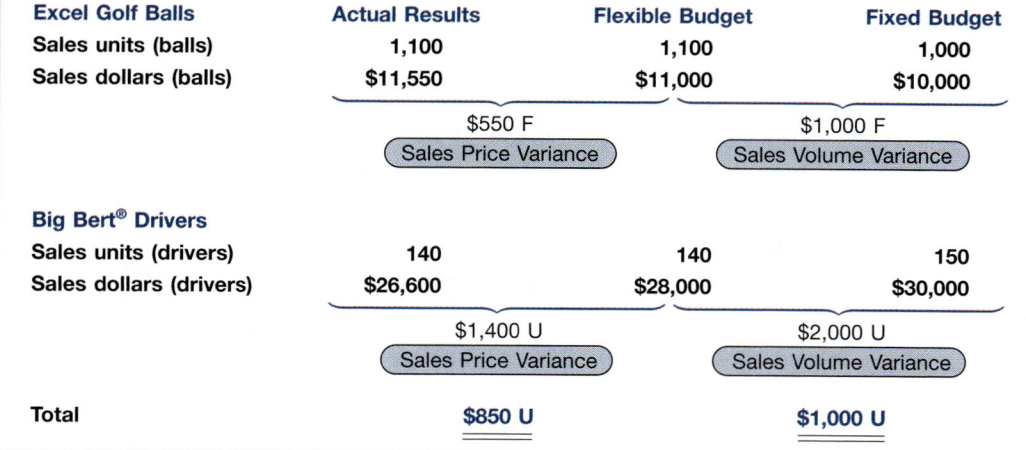

Exhibit 25.20

Computing Sales Variances

Managers use sales variances for planning and control purposes. With respect to planning, the sales variance information is used to plan future actions to avoid unfavorable variances. G-Max sold a total of 90 combined units (both balls and drivers) more than planned, but these 90 units were not sold in the proportion budgeted. G-Max sold fewer than the budgeted quantity of the higher margin driver, which contributed to the unfavorable total sales variances. Managers use this detail to ask questions about what caused the company to sell more golf balls and fewer drivers. With respect to control, managers use this information to evaluate and even reward their salespeople. Extra compensation is paid to salespeople who contribute to a higher profit margin. Finally, with multiple products, the sales volume variance can be separated into a *sales mix variance* and a *sales quantity variance*. The sales mix variance is the difference between the actual and budgeted sales mix of the products. The sales quantity variance is the difference between the total actual and total budgeted quantity of units sold.

You Make the Call

Sales Manager   The current performance report reveals a large favorable sales volume variance but an unfavorable sales price variance. You are confused because you didn't expect to see a large increase in sales volume. What steps do you take to further analyze this situation?

Answer—p. 1042

Demonstration Problem

Pacific Company provides the following information about its budgeted and actual results for June 2002. Although the expected volume for June was 25,000 units produced and sold, the company actually produced and sold 27,000 units as detailed here:

	Budget (25,000 units)	Actual (27,000 units)
Selling price	$5.00 per unit	$5.23 per unit
Variable costs (per unit)		
Direct materials	1.24 per unit	1.12 per unit
Direct labor	1.50 per unit	1.40 per unit
Factory supplies*	0.25 per unit	0.37 per unit
Utilities*	0.50 per unit	0.60 per unit
Selling costs	0.40 per unit	0.34 per unit
Fixed costs (per month)		
Depreciation—Machinery*	$3,750	$3,710
Depreciation—Building*	2,500	2,500
General liability insurance	1,200	1,250
Property taxes on office equipment ..	500	485
Other administrative expense	750	900

* Indicates factory overhead item; $0.75 per unit or $3 per direct labor hour for variable overhead, and $0.25 per unit or $1 per direct labor hour for fixed overhead.

Standard costs based on expected output of 25,000 units:

	Per Unit of Output	Quantity to Be Used	Total Cost
Direct materials, 4 oz. @ $0.31/oz.	$1.24/unit	100,000 oz.	$31,000
Direct labor, 0.25 hrs. @ $6.00/hr.	1.50/unit	6,250 hrs.	37,500
Overhead	1.00/unit		25,000

Actual costs incurred to produce 27,000 units:

	Per Unit of Output	Quantity Used	Total Cost
Direct materials, 4 oz. @ $0.28/oz.	$1.12/unit	108,000 oz.	$30,240
Direct labor, 0.20 hrs. @ $7.00/hr.	1.40/unit	5,400 hrs.	37,800
Overhead	1.20/unit		32,400

Standard costs based on expected output of 27,000 units:

	Per Unit of Output	Quantity to Be Used	Total Cost
Direct materials, 4 oz. @ $0.31/oz.	$1.24/unit	108,000 oz.	$33,480
Direct labor, 0.25 hrs. @ $6.00/hr.	1.50/unit	6,750 hrs.	40,500
Overhead			26,500

Required

1. Prepare flexible budgets for June showing expected sales, costs, and net income under assumptions of 20,000, 25,000, and 30,000 units of output produced and sold.
2. Prepare a flexible budget performance report that compares actual results with the amounts budgeted if the actual volume had been expected.
3. Apply variance analysis for direct materials, for direct labor, and for overhead.

Planning the Solution

- Prepare a table showing the expected results at the three specified levels of output. Compute the variable costs by multiplying the per unit variable costs by the expected volumes. Include fixed costs at the given amounts. Combine the amounts in the table to show total variable costs, contribution margin, total fixed costs, and income from operations.

- Prepare a table showing the actual results and the amounts that should be incurred at 27,000 units. Show any differences in the third column and label them with either an *F* for favorable if they increase income or a *U* for unfavorable if they decrease income.

- Using the variance format from the chapter, compute these total variances and the individual variances requested:

  - Total materials variance (including the direct materials quantity variance and the direct materials price variance).

  - Total direct labor variance (including the direct labor efficiency variance and the direct labor rate variance).

  - Total overhead variance (including both variable and fixed overhead variances and their component variances).

Solution to Demonstration Problem

1.

PACIFIC COMPANY
Flexible Budgets
For Month Ended June 30, 2002

	Flexible Budget Variable Amount per Unit	Flexible Budget Total Fixed Cost	Flexible Budget for Unit Sales of 20,000	Flexible Budget for Unit Sales of 25,000	Flexible Budget for Unit Sales of 30,000
Sales	$5.00		$100,000	$125,000	$150,000
Variable costs					
Direct materials	1.24		24,800	31,000	37,200
Direct labor	1.50		30,000	37,500	45,000
Factory supplies	0.25		5,000	6,250	7,500
Utilities	0.50		10,000	12,500	15,000
Selling costs	0.40		8,000	10,000	12,000
Total variable costs	$3.89		$ 77,800	$ 97,250	$116,700
Contribution margin	$1.11		$ 22,200	$ 27,750	$ 33,300
Fixed costs					
Depreciation—Machinery		$3,750	3,750	3,750	3,750
Depreciation—Building		2,500	2,500	2,500	2,500
General liability insurance		1,200	1,200	1,200	1,200
Property taxes on office equip.		500	500	500	500
Other administrative expense		750	750	750	750
Total fixed costs		$8,700	$ 8,700	$ 8,700	$ 8,700
Income from operations			$ 13,500	$ 19,050	$ 24,600

2.

PACIFIC COMPANY Flexible Budget Performance Report For Month Ended June 30, 2002	Flexible Budget	Actual Results	Variance*
Sales (27,000 units)	$135,000	$141,210	$6,210 F
Variable costs			
Direct materials	33,480	30,240	3,240 F
Direct labor	40,500	37,800	2,700 F
Factory supplies	6,750	9,990	3,240 U
Utilities	13,500	16,200	2,700 U
Selling costs	10,800	9,180	1,620 F
Total variable costs	$105,030	$103,410	$1,620 F
Contribution margin	$ 29,970	$ 37,800	$7,830 F
Fixed costs			
Depreciation—Machinery	3,750	3,710	40 F
Depreciation—Building	2,500	2,500	0
General liability insurance	1,200	1,250	50 U
Property taxes on office equipment	500	485	15 F
Other administrative expense	750	900	150 U
Total fixed costs	$ 8,700	$ 8,845	$ 145 U
Income from operations	$ 21,270	$ 28,955	$7,685 F

* F = Favorable variance; and U = Unfavorable variance.

3. Variance analysis of materials, labor, and overhead costs:

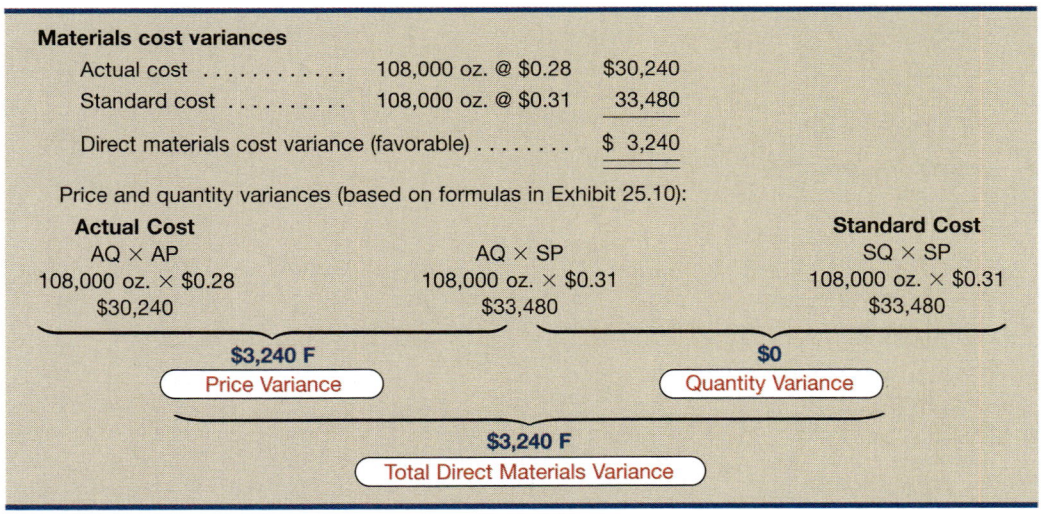

Labor cost variances

Actual cost	5,400 hrs. @ $7.00	$37,800
Standard cost	6,750 hrs. @ $6.00	40,500
Direct labor cost variance (favorable)		$ 2,700

Rate and efficiency variances (based on formulas in Exhibit 25.11):

Actual Cost		**Standard Cost**
AH × AR	AH × SR	SH × SR
5,400 hrs. × $7	5,400 hrs. × $6	6,750 hrs. × $6
$37,800	$32,400	$40,500

$5,400 U
Rate Variance

$8,100 F
Efficiency Variance

$2,700 F
Total Direct Labor Variance

Overhead cost variances

Total overhead cost incurred	27,000 units @ $1.20	$32,400
Total overhead applied	27,000 units @ $1.00	27,000
Overhead cost variance (unfavorable)		$ 5,400

Variable overhead variance (factory supplies and utilities)

Variable overhead cost incurred	(given)	$26,190
Variable overhead cost applied	6,750 hrs. @ $3/hr.	20,250
Variable overhead cost variance (unfavorable)		$ 5,940

Spending and efficiency variances (based on formulas in Exhibit 25.14):

Actual Overhead		**Applied Overhead**
AH × AVR	AH × SVR	SH × SVR
	5,400 × $3	6,750 × $3
$26,190	$16,200	$20,250

$9,990 U
Spending Variance

$4,050 F
Efficiency Variance

$5,940 U
Total Variable Overhead Variance

Fixed overhead (depreciation on machinery and building)

Fixed overhead cost incurred	(given)	$6,210
Fixed overhead cost applied	6,750 hrs. @ $1/hr.	6,750
Fixed overhead cost variance (favorable)		$ 540

Spending and volume variances (based on formulas in Exhibit 25.14):

Actual Overhead	**Budgeted Overhead**	**Applied Overhead**
		6,750 × $1
$6,210	$6,250	$6,750

$40 F
Spending Variance

$500 F
Volume Variance

$540 F
Total Fixed Overhead Variance

We can also compute

Controllable variance:	$5,900 U (both spending variances plus efficiency variance)
Volume variance:	500 F (identified as above)

Summary

C1 **Define standard costs and explain their computation and uses.** Standard costs are the normal costs that should be incurred to produce a product or perform a service. They should be based on a careful examination of the processes used to produce a product or perform a service as well as the quantities and prices that should be incurred in carrying out those processes. On a performance report, standard costs (which are flexible budget amounts) are compared to actual costs, and the differences are presented as variances.

C2 **Describe variances and what they reveal about performance.** Management can use variances to monitor and control activities. Total cost variances can be broken into price and quantity variances to direct management's attention to those responsible for quantities used and prices paid.

C3 **Explain how standard cost information is useful for management by exception.** Standard cost accounting provides management information about costs that differ from budgeted (expected) amounts. Performance reports disclose the costs or areas of operations that have significant variances from budgeted amounts. This allows managers to focus attention on the exceptions and less attention on areas proceeding normally.

A1 **Compare fixed and flexible budgets.** A fixed budget shows the revenues and costs expected to occur at a specified volume level. If actual volume is at some other level, the amounts in the fixed budget do not provide a reasonable basis for evaluating actual performance. A flexible budget expresses variable costs in per unit terms so that it can be used to develop budgeted amounts for any volume level within the relevant range. Thus, managers compute budgeted amounts after a period for the volume that actually occurred.

A2 **Analyze changes in sales from expected amounts.** Actual sales can differ from budgeted sales, and managers can investigate this difference by computing both the sales price and sales volume variances. The *sales price variance* refers to that portion of total variance resulting from a difference between actual and budgeted selling prices. The *sales volume variance* refers to that portion of total variance resulting from a difference between actual and budgeted sales quantities.

P1 **Prepare a flexible budget and interpret a flexible budget performance report.** To prepare a flexible budget, we express each variable cost as a constant amount per unit of sales (or as a percent of sales dollar). In contrast, the budgeted amount of each fixed cost is expressed as a total amount expected to occur at any sales volume within the relevant range. The flexible budget is then determined using these computations and amounts for fixed and variable costs at the expected sales volume.

P2 **Compute materials and labor variances.** Materials and labor variances are due to differences between the actual costs incurred and the budgeted costs. The price (or rate) variance is computed by comparing the actual cost with the flexible budget amount that should have been incurred to acquire the actual quantity of resources. The quantity (or efficiency) variance is computed by comparing the flexible budget amount that should have been incurred to acquire the actual quantity of resources with the flexible budget amount that should have been incurred to acquire the standard quantity of resources.

P3 **Compute overhead variances.** Overhead variances are due to differences between the actual overhead costs incurred and the overhead applied to production. An overhead spending variance arises when the actual amount incurred differs from the budgeted amount of overhead. An overhead efficiency (or volume) variance arises when the flexible overhead budget amount differs from the overhead applied to production. It is important to realize that overhead is assigned using an overhead allocation base, meaning that an efficiency variance (in the case of variable overhead) is a result of the overhead application base being used more or less efficiently than planned.

P4 **Prepare journal entries for standard costs and account for price and quantity variances.** When a company records standard costs in its accounts, the standard costs of materials, labor, and overhead are debited to the Goods in Process Inventory account. Based on an analysis of the material, labor, and overhead costs, each quantity variance, price variance, volume variance, and controllable variance is recorded in a separate account. At the end of the period, if the variances are material, they are allocated among the balances of the Goods in Process Inventory, Finished Goods Inventory, and Cost of Goods Sold accounts. If they are not material, they are simply debited or credited to the Cost of Goods Sold account.

Guidance Answers to **You Make the Call**

Entrepreneur From the complaints, this performance report appears to compares actual results with a fixed budget. This comparison is useful in determining whether the amount of work actually performed was more or less than what was planned, but it is not useful in determining whether the divisions were more or less efficient than planned. If the two consulting divisions worked on more assignments than expected, some costs will certainly increase. Therefore, you should prepare a flexible budget using the actual number of consulting assignments and then compare actual performance to the flexible budget.

Human Resource Manager As HR manager, you may not be directly responsible for a labor efficiency variance. However, you

should still investigate the causes for any labor-related variances. An unfavorable labor efficiency variance occurs because more labor hours than standard were used during the period. There are at least three possible reasons for this: (1) materials quality could be poor, resulting in more labor consumption due to rework, (2) unplanned interruptions (strike, breakdowns, accidents), could have occurred during the period, and (3) the production manager could have used a different labor mix to expedite orders. This new labor mix could have consisted of a larger proportion of untrained labor, which resulted in more labor hours.

Sales Manager The unfavorable sales price variance suggests that actual prices were lower than budgeted prices. As the sales manager, you want to know the reasons for a lower than expected price.

Perhaps your salespersons lowered the price of certain products by offering quantity discounts. You then might want to know what prompted them to offer the quantity discounts (perhaps competitors were offering discounts). You want to break the sales volume variance into both the sales mix and sales quantity variances. You could find that although the sales quantity variance is favorable, the sales mix variance is not. Then you need to investigate why actual sales mix differs from budgeted sales mix.

Internal Auditor Although the managers' actions might not be unethical, this action is undesirable. The internal auditor should report this behavior. The auditor might recommend that for the purchase of such discretionary items, the manager must provide budgetary requests using an activity-based budgeting process. The internal auditor would then be given full authority to verify this budget request.

Guidance Answers to **Quick Checks**

1. (b)

2. The first step is classifying each cost as variable or fixed.

3. A fixed budget is prepared using an expected volume of sales or production. A flexible budget is prepared using the actual volume of activity.

4. Contribution margin equals sales less variable costs.

5. (c)

6. It is the difference between actual cost and standard cost.

7. (a): Total actual hours: $2,500 \times 2.5 = 6,250$

Total standard hours: $2,500 \times 2.0 = 5,000$

Efficiency variance $= (6,250 - 5,000) \times \$3.00$
$= \$3,750$ U

8. (b): Rate variance $= (\$3.10 - \$3.00) \times 6,250 = \$625$ U

9. Yes, this will occur when the materials quantity variance is more than the materials price variance.

10. The overhead volume variance is favorable when the actual operating level is higher than the expected level.

11. (b)

12.

Goods in Process Inventory	75,700	
Direct Materials Price Variance	1,300	
Direct Materials Quantity Variance ..		3,800
Raw Materials Inventory		73,200

13. If the variances are material, they should be prorated among the Goods in Process Inventory, Finished Goods Inventory, and Cost of Goods Sold accounts. If they are not material, they can be closed to Cost of Goods Sold.

Glossary

Budgetary control management use of budgets to monitor and control company operations. (p. 1018).

Budget report report comparing actual results to planned objectives; sometimes used as a progress report. (p. 1018).

Controllable variance combination of both overhead spending variances (variable and fixed) and the variable overhead efficiency variance. (p. 1031).

Cost variance difference between the actual incurred cost and the standard cost. (p. 1024).

Efficiency variance difference between the actual quantity of an input and the standard quantity of that input. (p. 1031).

Favorable variance difference in revenues or costs, when the actual value compared to the budgeted value contributes to a higher income. (p. 1019).

Fixed budget planning budget based on a single predicted amount of volume; unsuitable for evaluations if the actual volume differs from predicted volume. (p. 1018).

Fixed budget performance report report that compares actual revenues and costs

with fixed budgeted amounts and identifies the differences as favorable or unfavorable variances. (p. 1019).

Flexible budget budget prepared (using actual volume) after a period is complete that helps managers evaluate past performance; uses fixed and variable costs in determining total costs. (p. 1020).

Flexible budget performance report report that compares actual revenues and costs with their variable budgeted amounts based on actual sales volume (or other level of activity) and identifies the differences as variances. (p. 1022).

Management by exception management process to focus on significant variances and give less attention to areas where performance is close to the standard. (p. 1034).

Overhead cost variance difference between the total overhead cost applied to products and the total overhead cost actually incurred. (p. 1030).

Price variance difference between actual and budgeted revenue or cost caused by the difference between the actual price per unit and the budgeted price per unit. (p. 1022).

Quantity variance difference between actual and budgeted revenue or cost caused by the difference between the actual number of units and the budgeted number of units. (p. 1022).

Spending variance difference between the actual price of an item and its standard price. (p. 1031).

Standard costs costs that should be incurred under normal conditions to produce a product or component or to perform a service. (p. 1023).

Unfavorable variance difference in revenues or costs, when the actual value is compared to the budgeted value, that contributes to a lower income. (p. 1019).

Variance analysis process of examining differences between actual and budgeted revenues or costs and describing them in terms of the amounts that resulted from price and quantity differences. (p. 1022).

Volume variance difference between two dollar amounts of fixed overhead cost. One amount is the total budgeted overhead cost; the other is the overhead cost allocated to products using the predetermined fixed overhead rate. (p. 1031).

Questions

1. What limits the usefulness of fixed budget performance reports?

2. Identify the primary purpose of a flexible budget.

3. Prepare a flexible budget performance report title (in proper form) for Spalding Company for the calendar year 2002. Why is a proper title important for this or any report?

4. What type of analysis does a flexible budget performance report help management conduct?

5. In what sense can a variable cost be considered constant?

6. What department is usually responsible for a direct labor rate variance? What department is usually responsible for a direct labor efficiency variance? Explain.

7. What is a price variance? What is a quantity variance?

8. What is the purpose of using standard costs?

9. In an analysis of fixed overhead cost variances, what is the volume variance?

10. What is the predetermined standard overhead rate? How is it computed?

11. In general, variance analysis is said to provide information about _____ and _____ variances.

12. In an analysis of overhead cost variances, what is the controllable variance and what causes it?

13. Assume that **Gap** is budgeted to operate at 80% of capacity but actually operates at 75% of capacity. What effect will the 5% deviation have on the controllable variance? The volume variance?

14. **Nike** has a standard cost for a special line of women's running shoes. List several factors that might cause the actual cost incurred to vary from the standard cost.

15. Assume that **Reebok**'s overhead costs consist only of variable costs and its actual sales volume is 10% higher than its budgeted sales volume, what type of volume variance would it experience?

16. What is the relation among standard costs, flexible budgets, variance analysis, and management by exception?

QUICK STUDY

Milestone Company reports the following selected financial results for May:

QS 25-1
Flexible budget
performance report

Sales (150,000 units)	$1,275,000
Variable costs	712,500
Fixed costs	300,000

For the level of production achieved in May, sales were budgeted at $1,300,000, variable costs at $750,000, and fixed costs at $300,000. Prepare a flexible budget performance report for May.

QS 25-2
Labor cost variances

Neely Company's output for the current period results in an unfavorable direct labor rate variance of $20,000 and an unfavorable direct labor efficiency variance of $10,000. The products produced for this same period involved a standard direct labor cost of $400,000. What is the actual total direct labor cost incurred for this period?

QS 25-3
Materials cost variances

Clawson Company's output for the current period involved a standard direct materials cost of $150,000. For this same period, the direct materials variances included a favorable price variance of $12,000 and a favorable quantity variance of $2,000. What is the actual total direct materials cost for this period?

QS 25-4
Materials cost
variances

For the current period, Holloway Company's manufacturing operations yield an unfavorable price variance of $4,000 on its direct materials usage. The actual price per pound of material is $78; the standard price is $77.50. How many pounds of material are used in the current period?

QS 25-5
Management
by exception

Describe the concept of management by exception. Explain how standard costs help managers apply this concept to monitor and control costs.

QS 25-6
Overhead cost
variances

Trek Company's output for the current period yields a favorable overhead volume variance of $20,000 and an unfavorable overhead controllable variance of $60,400. Standard overhead charged to production for the period amounts to $225,000. What is the actual total overhead cost incurred for the period?

Refer to the information in QS 25-6. Trek records standard costs in its accounts. Prepare the journal entry to charge overhead costs to the Goods in Process Inventory account and to record any variances.

QS 25-7
Preparing overhead entries

Minivans, Inc., specializes in selling used minivans. During the first six months of 2002, the dealership sold 50 minivans at an average price of $9,000 each. The budget for the first six months of 2002 was to sell 45 minivans at an average price of $9,500 each. Compute the dealership's sales price variance and sales volume variance for the first six months of 2002.

QS 25-8
Computing sales price and volume variances

EXERCISES

Maxine Company's fixed budget for the first quarter of calendar year 2002 reveals the following:

Exercise 25-1
Preparation of flexible budgets

Sales (7,000 units)		$2,800,000
Cost of goods sold		
Direct materials	$280,000	
Direct labor	490,000	
Production supplies	175,000	
Plant manager salary	65,000	1,010,000
Gross profit		$1,790,000
Selling expenses		
Sales commissions	140,000	
Packaging	154,000	
Advertising	125,000	419,000
Administrative expenses		
Administrative salaries	85,000	
Depreciation—Office equip.	35,000	
Insurance	20,000	
Office rent	36,000	176,000
Income from operations		$1,195,000

Following the format of Exhibit 25.3, prepare flexible budgets that show variable costs per unit, fixed costs, and three different flexible budgets for sales volumes of 6,000, 7,000, and 8,000 units.

Check   Income (at 6,000 units), $972,000

TKD Company manufactures and sells mountain bikes. It normally operates eight hours a day, five days a week. Using this information, classify each of the following costs as fixed or variable. If additional information would affect your decision, describe the information.

Exercise 25-2
Classification of costs as fixed or variable

a. Bike frames
b. Direct labor
c. Screws for assembly
d. Repair expense for tools
e. Management salaries
f. Incoming shipping expenses
g. Office supplies
h. Depreciation on tools
i. Taxes on property
j. Pension cost
k. Gas used for heating

Barnes Company's fixed budget performance report for June shows this information:

Exercise 25-3
Preparation of a flexible budget performance report

	Fixed Budget	Actual Results	Variances
Sales (in units)	8,400	10,800	
Sales (in dollars)	$420,000	$540,000	$120,000 F
Total expenses	315,000	378,000	63,000 U
Income from operations	$105,000	$162,000	$ 57,000 F

Check   Income variance, $21,000 F   The budgeted expenses of $315,000 include $294,000 of variable expenses and $21,000 of fixed expenses. The actual expenses include $27,000 of fixed expenses. Prepare a flexible budget performance report that shows any variances between budgeted results and actual results. List fixed and variable expenses separately.

Exercise 25-4
Preparation of a flexible budget performance report

Lexington Company's fixed budget performance report for July shows this information:

	Fixed Budget	Actual Results	Variances
Sales (in units)	7,500	7,200	
Sales (in dollars)	$750,000	$737,000	$13,000 U
Total expenses	647,500	641,000	6,500 F
Income from operations	$102,500	$ 96,000	$ 6,500 U

Check   Income variance, $4,000 F   The budgeted expenses of $647,500 include $487,500 of variable expenses and $160,000 of fixed expenses. The actual expenses include $158,000 of fixed expenses. Prepare a flexible budget performance report that shows any variances between budgeted results and actual results. List fixed and variable expenses separately.

Exercise 25-5
Computation and interpretation of labor variances

After evaluating Zero Company's manufacturing process, management decides to establish standards of 3 hours of direct labor per unit of product and $15 per hour for the labor rate. During October, the company uses 16,250 hours of direct labor at a total cost of $247,813 to produce 5,600 units of product. In November, the company uses 22,000 hours of direct labor at a total cost of $335,500 to produce 6,000 units of product. (1) Compute the rate variance, the efficiency variance, and the total direct labor cost variance for each of these two months. (2) Interpret the October direct labor variances.

Exercise 25-6
Computation and interpretation of overhead variances

Shallow Company set the following standard costs for one unit of its product for 2002:

Direct material (20 lbs. @ $2.50 per lb.)	$ 50.00
Direct labor (10 hrs. @ $8.00 per hr.)	80.00
Factory variable overhead (10 hrs. @ $4.00 per hr.) . . .	40.00
Factory fixed overhead (10 hrs. @ $1.60 per hr.)	16.00
Standard cost	$186.00

The $5.60 ($4.00 + $1.60) total overhead rate per direct labor hour is based on an expected operating level equal to 75% of the factory's capacity of 50,000 units per month. The following monthly flexible budget information is also available:

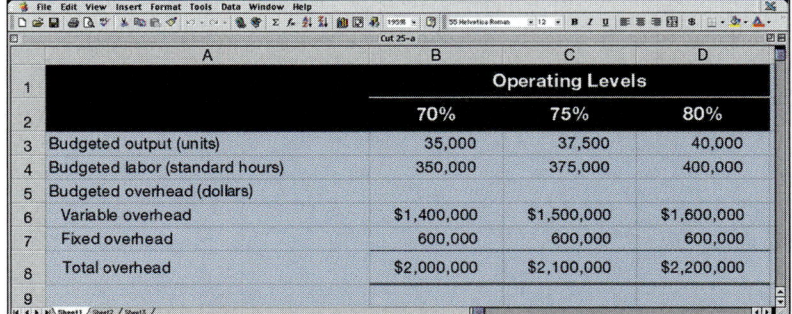

A	Operating Levels		
	70%	75%	80%
Budgeted output (units)	35,000	37,500	40,000
Budgeted labor (standard hours)	350,000	375,000	400,000
Budgeted overhead (dollars)			
Variable overhead	$1,400,000	$1,500,000	$1,600,000
Fixed overhead	600,000	600,000	600,000
Total overhead	$2,000,000	$2,100,000	$2,200,000

During the current month, the company operated at 70% of capacity, employees worked 340,000 hours, and the following actual overhead costs are incurred:

Variable overhead costs	$1,375,000
Fixed overhead costs	628,600
Total overhead costs	$2,003,600

(1) Show how the company computed its predetermined overhead application rate per hour for total overhead, variable overhead, and fixed overhead. (2) Compute and interpret the variable overhead spending and efficiency variances. (3) Compute and interpret the fixed overhead spending and volume variances.

Check Variable overhead: Spending, $15,000 U; Efficiency, $40,000 F

AMP Company made 3,000 bookshelves using 22,000 board feet of wood costing $266,200. The company's direct materials standards for one bookshelf are 8 board feet of wood at $12 per board foot. (1) Compute the direct materials variances incurred in manufacturing these bookshelves. (2) Interpret the direct materials variances.

Exercise 25-7
Computation and interpretation of materials variances

Refer to Exercise 25-7. AMP Company records standard costs in its accounts. It also records its material variances in separate accounts when it assigns materials costs to the Goods in Process Inventory account. (1) Show the journal entry that both charges the direct materials costs to the Goods in Process Inventory account and records the materials variances in their proper accounts. (2) Assume that AMP's material variances are the only variances accumulated in the accounting period and that they are considered immaterial. Prepare the adjusting journal entry to close the variance accounts at the end of the period. (3) Identify the variance that should be investigated according to the management by exception concept. Explain.

Exercise 25-8
Materials variances recorded and closed

Earth Company expected to operate last month at 80% of its productive capacity of 40,000 units per month. At this planned level, the company expected to use 25,000 standard hours of direct labor. Overhead is allocated to products using a predetermined standard rate based on direct labor hours. At the 80% capacity level, the total budgeted cost includes $50,000 of fixed overhead cost and $275,000 of variable overhead cost. In the current month, the company incurred $305,000 of actual overhead and 22,000 actual labor hours while producing 35,000 units. Compute the (1) total overhead variance, (2) overhead volume variance, and (3) overhead controllable variance.

Exercise 25-9
Computation of volume and controllable overhead variances

Computer Outlet, Inc., specializes in selling computers. During May 2002, the company sold 350 computers at an average price of $1,200 each. The budget for May 2002 included sales of 365 computers at an average price of $1,100 each. Compute the sales price variance and the sales volume variance for May 2002. Interpret the findings.

Exercise 25-10
Computing and interpreting sales variances

Penn Company's master budget for 2002 included the following fixed budget performance report. It is based on expected production and sales volume of 15,000 units.

PROBLEM SET A

Problem 25-1A
Preparation and analysis of a flexible budget

PENN COMPANY Fixed Budget Performance Report For Year Ended December 31, 2002		
Sales		$3,000,000
Cost of goods sold		
Direct materials	$975,000	
Direct labor	225,000	
Machinery repairs (variable cost)	60,000	
Depreciation—Plant equipment	300,000	
Utilities ($45,000 is variable)	195,000	
Plant management salaries	200,000	1,955,000
Gross profit		$1,045,000
Selling expenses		
Packaging	75,000	
Shipping	105,000	
Sales salary (fixed annual amount)	250,000	430,000
General and administrative expenses		
Advertising expense	125,000	
Salaries	241,000	
Entertainment expense	90,000	456,000
Income from operations		$ 159,000

Required

1. Classify all items listed in the fixed budget as either variable or fixed. Also determine their amounts per unit or their amounts for the year, as appropriate.

Check   (2) Budgeted income at 16,000 units, $260,000

2. Prepare flexible budgets (see Exhibit 25.3) for the company at sales volumes of 14,000 and 16,000 units.

3. The company's business conditions are improving, and one possible result is a sales volume of approximately 18,000 units. The company president is confident that this volume is within the relevant range of existing capacity. How much would operating income increase over the 2002 budgeted amount of $159,000 if this level is reached without increasing capacity?

Check   (4) Potential operating loss, $(144,000)

4. An unfavorable change in business is remotely possible; in this case, production and sales volume for 2002 could fall to 12,000 units. How much income (or loss) from operations would occur if sales volume falls to this level?

Problem 25-2A
Preparation and analysis of a flexible budget performance report

Refer to information in Problem 25-1A. Penn Company's actual income statement for 2002 follows:

PENN COMPANY		
Statement of Income from Operations		
For Year Ended December 31, 2002		
Sales (18,000 units)		$3,648,000
Cost of goods sold		
Direct materials	$1,185,000	
Direct labor	278,000	
Machinery repairs (variable cost)	63,000	
Depreciation—Plant equipment	300,000	
Utilities (fixed cost is $147,500)	200,500	
Plant management salaries	210,000	2,236,500
Gross profit		$1,411,500
Selling expenses		
Packaging	87,500	
Shipping	118,500	
Sales salary (annual)	268,000	474,000
General and administrative expenses		
Advertising expense	132,000	
Salaries	241,000	
Entertainment expense	93,500	466,500
Income from operations		$ 471,000

Required

Preparation Component

1. Prepare a flexible budget performance report for 2002.

Check   (1) Variances: Fixed costs, $36,000 U; Income, $9,000 F

Analysis Component

2. Analyze and interpret both the (a) sales variance and (b) direct materials variance.

Problem 25-3A
Flexible budget preparation; computation of materials, labor, and overhead variances; and overhead variance report

Hard Drive Company has set the following standard costs for one unit of its product:

Direct material (6 lbs. @ $5 per lb.)	$ 30.00
Direct labor (2 hrs. @ $17 per hr.)	34.00
Overhead (2 hrs. @ $18.50 per hr.)	37.00
Total standard cost	$101.00

The predetermined overhead rate ($18.50 per direct labor hour) is based on an expected volume of 75% of the factory's capacity of 20,000 units per month. Following are the company's budgeted overhead costs per month at the 75% level:

Overhead Budget (75% capacity)		
Variable overhead costs		
Indirect materials	$ 45,000	
Indirect labor	180,000	
Power	45,000	
Repairs and maintenance	90,000	
Total variable overhead costs		$360,000
Fixed overhead costs		
Depreciation—Building	24,000	
Depreciation—Machinery	80,000	
Taxes and insurance	12,000	
Supervision	79,000	
Total fixed overhead costs		195,000
Total overhead costs		$555,000

The company incurred the following actual costs when it operated at 75% of capacity in October:

Direct materials (91,000 lbs. @ $5.10 per lb.)		$ 464,100
Direct labor (30,500 hrs. @ $17.25 per hr.)		526,125
Overhead costs		
Indirect materials	$ 44,250	
Indirect labor	177,750	
Power	43,000	
Repairs and maintenance	96,000	
Depreciation—Building	24,000	
Depreciation—Machinery	75,000	
Taxes and insurance	11,500	
Supervision	89,000	560,500
Total costs		$1,550,725

Required

1. Classify all items in the overhead budget as either variable or fixed. Also determine their amounts per unit or for the month, as appropriate.

2. Prepare flexible overhead budgets (as in Exhibit 25.12) for October showing the amounts of each variable and fixed cost at the 65%, 75%, and 85% capacity levels.

3. Compute the direct materials cost variance, including its price and quantity variances.

4. Compute the direct labor cost variance, including its rate and efficiency variances.

5. Compute the (a) variable overhead spending and efficiency variances, (b) fixed overhead spending and volume variances, and (c) total overhead controllable variance.

6. Prepare a detailed overhead variance report (as in Exhibit 25.19) that shows the variances for individual items of overhead.

Check (2) Budgeted total overhead at 13,000 units, $507,000. (3) Materials variances: Price, $9,100 U; Quantity, $5,000 U. (4) Labor variances: Rate, $7,625 U; Efficiency, $8,500 U

Peach Company has set the following standard costs per unit for the product it manufactures:

Direct material (15 lbs. @ $4 per lb.)	$ 60.00
Direct labor (3 hrs. @ $15 per hr.)	45.00
Overhead (3 hrs. @ $3.50 per hr.)	10.50
Total standard cost	$115.50

Problem 25-4A

Materials, labor, and overhead variances; and overhead variance report

The predetermined overhead rate is based on a planned operating volume of 100% of the productive capacity of 10,000 units per month. The following flexible budget information is available:

	Operating Levels		
	70%	**80%**	**90%**
Production in units	7,000	8,000	9,000
Standard direct labor hours	21,000	24,000	27,000
Budgeted overhead			
Variable overhead costs			
Indirect materials	$13,125	$15,000	$16,875
Indirect labor	21,000	24,000	27,000
Power	5,250	6,000	6,750
Maintenance	2,625	3,000	3,375
Total variable costs	$42,000	$48,000	$54,000
Fixed overhead costs			
Rent of factory building	$15,000	$15,000	$15,000
Depreciation—Machinery	10,000	10,000	10,000
Supervisory salaries	20,000	20,000	20,000
Total fixed costs	$45,000	$45,000	$45,000
Total overhead costs	$87,000	$93,000	$99,000

During May of this year, the company operated at 90% of capacity and produced 9,000 units, incurring the following actual costs:

Direct materials (138,000 lbs. @ $3.75 per lb.)		$ 517,500
Direct labor (31,000 hrs. @ $15.10 per hr.)		468,100
Overhead costs		
Indirect materials	$15,000	
Indirect labor	26,500	
Power	6,750	
Maintenance	4,000	
Rent of factory building	15,000	
Depreciation—Machinery	10,000	
Supervisory salaries	22,000	99,250
Total costs		$1,084,850

Required

Check (1) Materials variances: Price, $34,500 F; Quantity, $12,000 U. (2) Labor variances: Rate, $3,100 U; Efficiency, $60,000 U.

1. Compute the direct materials variance, including its price and quantity variances.
2. Compute the direct labor variance, including its rate and efficiency variances.
3. Compute (a) the variable overhead spending and efficiency variances, (b) the fixed overhead spending and volume variances, and (c) the total overhead controllable variance.
4. Prepare a detailed overhead variance report (as in Exhibit 25.19) that shows the variances for individual items of overhead.

Problem 25-5A
Computation of materials, labor, and overhead variances

Tuna Company set the following standard unit costs for its single product:

Direct material (30 lbs. @ $4 per lb.)	$120.00
Direct labor (5 hrs. @ $14 per hr.)	70.00
Factory overhead—Variable (5 hrs. @ $8 per hr.)	40.00
Factory overhead—Fixed (5 hrs. @ $10 per hr.)	50.00
Total standard cost	$280.00

The predetermined overhead rate is based on a planned operating volume of 80% of the productive capacity of 60,000 units per quarter. The following flexible budget information is available:

	Operating Levels		
	70%	**80%**	**90%**
Production in units	42,000	48,000	54,000
Standard direct labor hours	210,000	240,000	270,000
Budgeted overhead			
Fixed factory overhead	$2,400,000	$2,400,000	$2,400,000
Variable factory overhead	$1,680,000	$1,920,000	$2,160,000

During the current quarter, the company operated at 90% of capacity and produced 54,000 units of product; actual direct labor totaled 265,000 hours. Units produced are assigned the following standard costs:

Direct materials (1,620,000 lbs. @ $4 per lb.)	$ 6,480,000
Direct labor (270,000 hrs. @ $14 per hr.)	3,780,000
Factory overhead (270,000 hrs. @ $18 per hr.)	4,860,000
Total standard cost	$15,120,000

Actual costs incurred during the current quarter follow:

Direct materials (1,615,000 lbs. @ $4.10)	$ 6,621,500
Direct labor (265,000 hrs. @ $13.75)	3,643,750
Fixed factory overhead costs	2,350,000
Variable factory overhead costs	2,200,000
Total actual costs	$14,815,250

Required

1. Compute the direct materials cost variance, including its price and quantity variances.
2. Compute the direct labor variance, including its rate and efficiency variances.
3. Compute (a) the variable overhead spending and efficiency variances, (b) the fixed overhead spending and volume variances, and (c) the total overhead controllable variance.

Check   (1) Materials variance: Price, $161,500 U; Quantity, $20,000 F. (2) Labor variances: Rate, $66,250 F; Efficiency, $70,000 F

Best Company's standard cost accounting system recorded the following information from its operations for December:

Problem 25-6A

Materials, labor, and overhead variances recorded and analyzed

Standard direct materials cost	$100,000
Direct materials quantity variance (unfavorable) ...	3,000
Direct materials price variance (favorable)	500
Actual direct labor cost	90,000
Direct labor efficiency variance (unfavorable)	7,000
Direct labor rate variance (favorable)	1,200
Actual overhead cost	375,000
Volume variance (favorable)	12,000
Controllable variance (unfavorable)	9,000

Required

Preparation Component

1. Prepare December 30 journal entries to record the company's costs and variances for the month.

Check   Dr. Goods in Process Inventory (for overhead), $378,000

Analysis Component

2. Identify the areas that would attract the attention of a manager who uses management by exception. Explain what action(s) the manager should consider.

PROBLEM SET B

Problem 25-1B
Preparation and analysis of a flexible budget

Ranch Company's master budget for 2002 included the following fixed budget performance report. It is based on expected production and sales volume of 20,000 units.

RANCH COMPANY Fixed Budget Performance Report For Year Ended December 31, 2002		
Sales		$3,000,000
Cost of goods sold		
Direct materials	$1,200,000	
Direct labor	260,000	
Machinery repairs (variable cost)	57,000	
Depreciation—Machinery	250,000	
Utilities (25% is variable cost)	200,000	
Plant manager salaries	140,000	2,107,000
Gross profit		$ 893,000
Selling expenses		
Packaging	80,000	
Shipping	116,000	
Sales salary (fixed annual amount)	160,000	356,000
General and administrative expenses		
Advertising	81,000	
Salaries	241,000	
Entertainment expense	90,000	412,000
Income from operations		$ 125,000

Required

1. Classify all items listed in the fixed budget as either variable or fixed. Also determine their amounts per unit or their amounts for the year, as appropriate.

Check (2) Budgeted income at 24,000 units, $372,400

2. Prepare flexible budgets (see Exhibit 25.3) for the company at sales volumes of 18,000 and 24,000 units.

3. The company's business conditions are improving, and one possible result is a sales volume of approximately 28,000 units. The company president is confident that this volume is within the relevant range of existing capacity. How much would operating income increase over the 2002 budgeted amount of $125,000 if this level is reached without increasing capacity?

Check (4) Potential operating loss, $(246,100)

4. An unfavorable change in business is remotely possible; in this case, production and sales volume for 2002 could fall to 14,000 units. How much income (or loss) from operations would occur if sales volume falls to this level?

Problem 25-2B
Preparation and analysis of a flexible budget performance report

Refer to information in Problem 25-1B. Ranch Company's actual income statement for 2002 follows:

RANCH COMPANY Statement of Income from Operations For Year Ended December 31, 2002		
Sales (24,000 units)		$3,648,000
Cost of goods sold		
Direct materials	$1,400,000	
Direct labor	360,000	
Machinery repairs (variable cost)	60,000	

[continued on next page]

[continued from previous page]

Depreciation—Machinery	250,000	
Utilities (fixed cost is $154,000)	218,000	
Plant manager salaries	155,000	2,443,000
Gross profit		$1,205,000
Selling expenses		
Packaging	90,000	
Shipping	124,000	
Sales salary (annual)	162,000	376,000
General and administrative expenses		
Advertising expense	104,000	
Salaries	232,000	
Entertainment expense	100,000	436,000
Income from operations		$ 393,000

Required

Preparation Component

1. Prepare a flexible budget performance report for 2002.

Check (1) Variances: Fixed costs, $45,000 U; Income, $20,600 F

Analysis Component

2. Analyze and interpret both the (a) sales variance and (b) direct materials variance.

Tropical Company has set the following standard costs for one unit of its product:

Direct material (4.5 lb. @ $6 per lb.)	$27.00
Direct labor (1.5 hrs. @ $12 per hr.)	18.00
Overhead (1.5 hrs. @ $16.00 per hr.)	24.00
Total standard cost	$69.00

Problem 25-3B
Flexible budget preparation;
computation of materials,
labor, and overhead variances;
and overhead variance report

The predetermined overhead rate ($16 per direct labor hour) is based on an expected volume of 75% of the factory's capacity of 20,000 units per month. Following are the company's budgeted overhead costs per month at the 75% level:

Overhead Budget (75% capacity)		
Variable overhead costs		
Indirect materials	$22,500	
Indirect labor	90,000	
Power	22,500	
Repairs and maintenance	45,000	
Total variable overhead costs		$180,000
Fixed overhead costs		
Depreciation—Building	24,000	
Depreciation—Machinery	72,000	
Taxes and insurance	18,000	
Supervision	66,000	
Total fixed overhead costs		180,000
Total overhead costs		$360,000

The company incurred the following actual costs when it operated at 75% of capacity in December:

Direct materials (69,000 lbs. @ $6.10) ...		$ 420,900
Direct labor (22,800 hrs. @ $12.30)		280,440
Overhead costs		
Indirect materials	$21,600	
Indirect labor	82,260	
Power	23,100	
Repairs and maintenance	46,800	
Depreciation—Building	24,000	
Depreciation—Machinery	75,000	
Taxes and insurance	16,500	
Supervision	66,000	355,260
Total costs		$1,056,600

Required

Check (2) Budgeted total overhead at 13,000 units, $336,000; (3) Materials variances: Price, $6,900 U; Quantity, $9,000 U (4) Labor variances: Rate, $6,840 U; Efficiency, $3,600 U

1. Classify all items in the overhead budget as either variable or fixed. Also determine their amounts per unit or for the month, as appropriate.
2. Prepare flexible overhead budgets (as in Exhibit 25.12) for December showing the amounts of each variable and fixed cost at the 65%, 75%, and 85% capacity levels.
3. Compute the direct materials cost variance, including its price and quantity variances.
4. Compute the direct labor cost variance, including its rate and efficiency variances.
5. Compute the (a) variable overhead spending and efficiency variances, (b) fixed overhead spending and volume variances, and (c) total overhead controllable variance.
6. Prepare a detailed overhead variance report (as in Exhibit 25.19) that shows the variances for individual items of overhead.

Problem 25-4B

Materials, labor, and overhead variances; and overhead variance report

Challenger Company has set the following standard costs per unit for the product it manufactures:

Direct material (10 lb. @ $3.00 per lb.)	$30.00
Direct labor (4 hr. @ $6 per hr.)	24.00
Overhead (4 hr. @ $2.50 per hr.)	10.00
Total standard cost	$64.00

The predetermined overhead rate is based on a planned operating volume of 80% of the productive capacity of 10,000 units per month. The following flexible budget information is available:

	Operating Levels		
	70%	**80%**	**90%**
Production in units	7,000	8,000	9,000
Standard direct labor hours	28,000	32,000	36,000
Budgeted overhead			
Variable overhead costs			
Indirect materials	$ 8,750	$10,000	$11,250
Indirect labor	14,000	16,000	18,000
Power	3,500	4,000	4,500
Maintenance	1,750	2,000	2,250
Total variable costs	$28,000	$32,000	$36,000
Fixed overhead costs			
Rent of factory building	12,000	12,000	12,000
Depreciation—Machinery	20,000	20,000	20,000
Taxes and insurance	2,400	2,400	2,400
Supervisory salaries	13,600	13,600	13,600
Total fixed costs	$48,000	$48,000	$48,000
Total overhead costs	$76,000	$80,000	$84,000

During March of this year, the company operated at 90% of capacity and produced 9,000 units, incurring the following actual costs:

Direct materials (92,000 lbs. @ $2.95 per lb.)		$271,400
Direct labor (37,600 hrs. @ $6.05 per hr.)		227,480
Overhead costs		
Indirect materials	$10,000	
Indirect labor	16,000	
Power	4,500	
Maintenance	3,000	
Rent of factory building	12,000	
Depreciation—Machinery	19,200	
Taxes and insurance	3,000	
Supervisory salaries	14,000	81,700
Total costs		$580,580

Required

1. Compute the direct materials cost variance, including its price and quantity variances.
2. Compute the direct labor variance, including its rate and efficiency variances.
3. Compute (a) the variable overhead spending and efficiency variances, (b) the fixed overhead spending and volume variances, and (c) the total overhead controllable variance.
4. Prepare a detailed overhead variance report (as in Exhibit 25.19) that shows the variances for individual items of overhead.

Check   (1) Materials variances:
Price, $4,600 F; Quantity, $6,000 U.
(2) Labor variances: Rate, $1,880 U;
Efficiency, $9,600 U.

Titletown Company set the following standard unit costs for its single product:

Problem 25-5B
Computation of materials,
labor, and overhead variances

Direct material (25 lbs. @ $4 per lb.)	$100.00
Direct labor (6 hrs. @ $8 per hr.)	48.00
Factory overhead—Variable (6 hrs. @ $5 per hr.)	30.00
Factory overhead—Fixed (6 hrs. @ $7 per hr.)	42.00
Total standard cost	$220.00

The predetermined overhead rate is based on a planned operating volume of 80% of the productive capacity of 60,000 units per quarter. The following flexible budget information is available:

	Operating Levels		
	70%	**80%**	**90%**
Production in units	42,000	48,000	54,000
Standard direct labor hours	252,000	288,000	324,000
Budgeted overhead			
Fixed factory overhead	$2,016,000	$2,016,000	$2,016,000
Variable factory overhead	1,260,000	1,440,000	1,620,000

During the current quarter, the company operated at 70% of capacity and produced 42,000 units of product; direct labor hours worked were 250,000. Units produced are assigned the following standard costs:

Direct materials (1,050,000 lbs. @ $4 per lb.)	$4,200,000
Direct labor (252,000 hrs. @ $8 per hr.)	2,016,000
Factory overhead (252,000 hrs. @ $12.00 per hr.) ...	3,024,000
Total standard cost	$9,240,000

Actual costs incurred during the current quarter follow:

Direct materials (1,000,000 lbs. @ $4.25)	$4,250,000
Direct labor (250,000 hrs. @ $7.75)	1,937,500
Fixed factory overhead costs	1,960,000
Variable factory overhead costs	1,200,000
Total actual costs	$9,347,500

Required

1. Compute the direct materials cost variance, including its price and quantity variances.
2. Compute the direct labor variance, including its rate and efficiency variances.
3. Compute (a) the variable overhead spending and efficiency variances, (b) the fixed overhead spending and volume variances, and (c) the total overhead controllable variance.

Problem 25-6B

Materials, labor, and overhead
variances recorded and
analyzed

Kraft Company's standard cost accounting system recorded the following information from its operations for June:

Standard direct materials cost	$130,000
Direct materials quantity variance (unfavorable) . . .	5,000
Direct materials price variance (favorable)	1,500
Actual direct labor cost	65,000
Direct labor efficiency variance (favorable)	7,000
Direct labor rate variance (unfavorable)	500
Actual overhead cost	250,000
Volume variance (unfavorable)	12,000
Controllable variance (unfavorable)	8,000

Required

Preparation Component

1. Prepare journal entries dated June 30 to record the company's costs and variances for the month.

Analysis Component

2. Identify the areas that would attract the attention of a manager who uses management by exception. Describe what action(s) the manager should consider.

Beyond the Numbers

**Reporting in
Action**

C1

BTN 25-1 Analysis of flexible budgets and standard costs emphasizes that the unit of measure must be the same to make meaningful comparisons and evaluations. When **Nike** compiles its financial reports in compliance with GAAP, it applies the same unit of measurement, U.S. dollars, for most measures of business operations. Without this practice, comparisons with other companies and across time are meaningless. One issue for Nike is how best to adjust account values for its subsidiaries that compile financial reports in currencies other than the U.S. dollar.

Required

1. Read Nike's Note 1 in Appendix A and identify the financial statement where Nike reports its foreign currency translation.
2. Record the annual amount of Nike's foreign currency translation adjustment and its ending balance for the three fiscal years 1998–2000.

Swoosh Ahead

3. Access Nike's financial statement information for a fiscal year ending after May 31, 2000, from either its Web site [**www.nike.com**] or the SEC's EDGAR database [**www.sec.gov**]. (a) Identify the May 31, 2001, foreign currency translation adjustment. (b) Does this adjustment increase or decrease net income? Explain.

BTN 25-2   The usefulness of budgets, variances, and subsequent related analyses often depends on the accuracy of management's estimates of future sales activity.

Comparative Analysis

Required

1. Identify and record the prior three years' sales (in dollars) for both **Nike** and **Reebok** using their financial statements in Appendix A.
2. Using the data in part (1), predict both companies' sales activity for the next two to three years. (If possible, compare your predictions to actual sales figures for these years.)

BTN 25-3   Setting materials, labor, and overhead standards is challenging. If standards are set too low, companies might purchase inferior products and employees might not work to their full potential. If standards are set too high, companies could be unable to offer a quality product at a profitable rate and employees could be overworked. The ethical challenge is to set a high standard that is reasonable. Assume that you are a manager and you are asked to set the standard materials price and quantity for the new 1,000 CKB Mega-Max chip. This is a technically advanced product. To properly set the price and quantity standards, you assemble a team of specialists to provide input.

Ethics Challenge

C1

Required

Identify four types of specialists that you would assemble to provide information to help set the materials price and quantity standards. Briefly explain why you chose each individual type.

BTN 25-4   The reason we use the words *favorable* and *unfavorable* when evaluating variances is made clear when we look at the closing of accounts. To see this, consider that (1) all variance accounts are closed at the end of each period (temporary accounts), (2) a favorable variance is always a credit balance, and (3) an unfavorable variance is always a debit balance. (Assume that variance accounts are closed to Cost of Goods Sold.) Write a one-half page memorandum to your instructor with three parts that answer these three questions.

Communicating in Practice

Required

1. Does Cost of Goods Sold increase or decrease when closing a favorable variance? Does gross margin increase or decrease when a favorable variance is closed to Cost of Goods Sold? Explain.
2. Does Cost of Goods Sold increase or decrease when closing an unfavorable variance? Does gross margin increase or decrease when an unfavorable variance is closed to Cost of Goods Sold? Explain.
3. Explain the meaning of a favorable variance and an unfavorable variance.

BTN 25-5   Access **Hoover's Online** Web site [**www.hoovers.com**] and click on in sequence (1) *Business Links,* (2) *Corporate Functions & Operations,* (3) *Management,* and (4) *Benchmarking & Best Practices.* Click on and read *S.M. Thacker & Associates: An Introduction to Benchmarking.*

Taking It to the Net

C1

Required

1. Write a one-paragraph explanation (in layperson's terms) of benchmarking.
2. How does standard costing relate to benchmarking?

BTN 25-6   Many service industries link labor rate and time (quantity) standards with their processes. One example is the standard time to board an aircraft. The reason time plays such an important role in the service industry is that it is viewed as a competitive advantage: best service in the

Teamwork in Action   **C2**

shortest amount of time. Although the labor rate component is difficult to observe, the time component of a service delivery standard is often readily apparent, for example, "Lunch will be served in less than five minutes, or it is free."

Required

Break into teams and select two service industries for your analysis. Identify and describe all the time elements each industry uses to create a competitive advantage.

Business Week Activity

BTN 25-7   In Germany, labor unions are influential in setting both the wage rate and the standard amount of hours worked in a week. This influence impacts the German economy. Read "The German Worker Is Making a Sacrifice" in the July 28, 1997, issue of **Business Week** and answer the following questions.

Required

1. Identify the concerns linked to labor unions in terms of the health of the German economy.
2. Identify how German labor unions are supporting the country's economic recovery in setting wage rates and hours worked. Identify three companies and their unions as examples.

Entrepreneurial Decision

BTN 25-8   Britney Baxter is in the first year of her start-up consulting business aimed at Web services and control. She is frustrated because each of her first seven major engagements required different levels of resources although she believed the jobs were reasonably similar in nature.

Required

How should Baxter go about establishing standards for her consulting work? Explain.

26

Capital Budgeting and Managerial Decisions

"Pick something, learn it, and then do it better"—Mike Manclark.

A Look Back

Chapter 25 discussed flexible budgets, variance analysis, and standard costs. It explained how management uses each to control and monitor business activities.

A Look at This Chapter

This chapter focuses on evaluating capital budgeting decisions. It also explains several tools and procedures used in making and evaluating short-term managerial decisions.

Learning Objectives

Flying High

e SANTA ANA, CA—Mike Manclark knew he had it in him. While he fueled and moved airplanes at Orange County's airport to earn a living, he watched as various companies serviced airplanes, providing painting and internal reconfigurations, maintenance, and fuel cell repair. Manclark realized he could provide these services, only better. Manclark, then 19, borrowed $3,000 from his dad and launched **Leading Edge Aviation Services** [**LeadingEdgeCorp.com**]. Says Manclark, "Everyone, and I mean everyone, thought I was crazy."

Manclark started by detailing jets, including those of Frank Sinatra and Bob Hope. The company quickly grew as he applied three personal mandates: (1) never say no; (2) perform above expectations; and (3) hire the best employees you can. He quickly built a stellar reputation in the industry based on quality and dependable services. This past year, Leading Edge reported $26 million in sales, and it is now the leading provider of aircraft painting services.

Manclark admits, however, that the profitability of projects is often difficult to judge. He applies several capital budgeting procedures to assess the attractiveness of projects. Some projects, but not all, yield sufficient payback and adequate returns. The key is being able to distinguish the profitable projects from those that are not. Manclark also makes managerial decisions that require difficult calls on what to scrap or not, what to make or buy, and what to pass on or process. In spite of these tough capital budgeting and managerial decisions, Manclark loves where he is. "I don't do this for the money," he says. "I do it for the love of airplanes." The money is not bad either; Manclark hopes to grow Leading Edge's equity to $100 million within the next four years. For that amount, many people would learn to love airplanes. [Sources: *Leading Edge Web site,* May 2001; *Entrepreneur,* November 1999; *Brandweek,* March 1998.]

Business decisions involve choosing between alternative courses of action. Many factors affect business decisions, yet analysis typically focuses on finding the alternative that offers the highest return on investment or the greatest reduction in costs. Some decisions are based on little more than an intuitive understanding of the situation because available information is too limited to allow a more systematic analysis. In other cases, intangible factors such as convenience, prestige, and environmental considerations are more important than strictly quantitative factors. In all situations, we can reach a sounder decision if we identify the consequences of alternative choices in financial terms. This chapter explains several methods of analysis that can help managers make business decisions.

Section 1—Capital Budgeting

C1 Explain the importance of capital budgeting.

We described the capital expenditures budget in Chapter 24. It is management's plan for acquiring and selling plant assets. **Capital budgeting** is the process of analyzing alternative long-term investments and deciding which assets to acquire or sell. These decisions can involve developing a new product or process, buying a new machine or a new building, or acquiring an entire company. An objective for all of these decisions is to earn a satisfactory return on investment.

Capital budgeting decisions require careful analysis because they are usually the most difficult and risky decisions that managers make. These decisions are difficult because they require predictions of events that will not occur until well into the future. Many of these predictions are tentative and potentially unreliable. Specifically, a capital budgeting decision is risky because (1) the outcome is uncertain, (2) large amounts of money are usually involved, (3) the investment involves a long-term commitment, and (4) the decision could be difficult or impossible to reverse, no matter how poor it turns out to be. Risk is especially high for investments in technology due to innovations and uncertainty.

Point: The nature of capital spending has changed with the business environment. Budgets for information technology have increased from about 25% of corporate capital spending 20 years ago to an estimated 35% today.

Managers use several methods to evaluate capital budgeting decisions. Nearly all of these methods involve predicting cash inflows and cash outflows of proposed investments, assessing the risk of and returns on those flows, and then choosing the investments to be made. Given that the cash flows are generated in the future, management often restates future cash flows in terms of their present value. This approach applies the time value of money: A dollar today is worth more than a dollar tomorrow. Similarly, a dollar tomorrow is worth less than a dollar today. The process of restating future cash flows in terms of their present value is called *discounting*. Consideration of the time value of money is important when evaluating capital investments, but managers sometimes apply evaluation methods that do not explicitly consider it. This chapter describes four methods for comparing alternative investments.

Methods Not Using Time Value of Money

All investments, whether they involve the purchase of a machine or another long-term asset, are expected to produce net cash flows. *Net cash flow* is cash inflows minus cash outflows for a period. Some management methods perform simple analyses of the financial feasibility of an investment's net cash flow without using the time value of money. This section explains two of the most common methods in this category: (1) payback period and (2) accounting rate of return.

Payback Period

P1 Compute payback period and describe its use.

An investment's **payback period (PBP)** is the expected time period to recover the initial investment amount. Managers prefer investing in assets with shorter payback periods to reduce the risk of an unprofitable investment over the long run. Acquiring assets with short payback periods reduces a company's risk from potentially inaccurate long-term predictions of future cash flows.

Computing Payback Period with Even Cash Flows

To illustrate use of the payback period for an investment with even cash flows,[1] we look at data from FasTrac, a manufacturer of exercise equipment and supplies. FasTrac is considering several different capital investments, one of which is the purchase of a machine to use in manufacturing a new product. This machine costs $16,000 and is expected to have an eight-year life with no salvage value. Management predicts this machine will produce 1,000 units of product each year and that the new product will be sold for $30 per unit. Exhibit 26.1 shows the expected annual net cash flows for this asset over its life as well as the expected annual revenues and expenses (including depreciation and income taxes) from investing in the machine.

FASTRAC Cash Flow Analysis — New Machinery January 15, 2002	Expected Net Accrual Figures	Expected Net Cash Flows
Annual sales of new product	$30,000	$30,000
Deduct annual expenses		
Cost of materials, labor, and overhead (except depr.)	(15,500)	(15,500)
Depreciation—Machinery	(2,000)	
Additional selling and administrative expenses	(9,500)	(9,500)
Annual pretax accrual income	$ 3,000	
Income taxes (30%)	(900)	(900)
Annual net income	$ 2,100	
Annual net cash flow		**$ 4,100**

Exhibit 26.1

Cash Flow Analysis

The amount of net cash flow from the machinery is computed by subtracting expected cash outflows from expected cash inflows. The cash flows column of Exhibit 26.1 excludes all noncash revenues and expenses. For FasTrac, depreciation is the only noncash item. Alternatively, some managers adjust the projected net income for revenue and expense items that do not affect cash flows. In the case of FasTrac, this means taking the net income of $2,100 and adding back the $2,000 depreciation.

The formula for computing the payback period of an investment that yields even net cash flows is in Exhibit 26.2.

Point: Note that annual net cash flow in Exhibit 26.1 is equal to net income plus depreciation (a noncash expense).

$$\text{Payback period} = \frac{\text{Cost of investment}}{\text{Annual net cash flow}}$$

Exhibit 26.2

Payback Period Formula with Even Cash Flows

The payback period reflects the amount of time for the investment to generate enough net cash flow to return (or pay back) the cash initially invested to purchase it. In FasTrac's case, the payback period for this machine is just under four years:

$$\text{Payback period} = \frac{\$16,000}{\$4,100} = 3.9 \text{ years}$$

Example: If an alternative machine (with different technology) yields a payback period of 3.5 years, which one do you choose? *Answer:* The alternative (3.5 is less than 3.9).

---

[1] *Even cash flows* refers to cash flows that are the same each cand every year. *Uneven cash flows* refers to cash flows that are not all equal in amount.

Point: To apply these concepts, work Exercise 26-1.

The initial investment is fully recovered in 3.9 years, or just before we reach the halfway point of this machine's useful life of eight years.

Computing Payback Period with Uneven Cash Flows

Computation of the payback period in the prior section assumes even net cash flows. What happens if the net cash flows are uneven? In this case, the payback period is computed using the *cumulative total of net cash flows*. Cumulative refers to the addition of each period's net cash flows as we progress through time. To illustrate, let's look at data for another potential investment that FasTrac is considering. This machine is predicted to generate uneven net cash flows over the next eight years. The relevant data along with computation of the payback period are shown in Exhibit 26.3.

Exhibit 26.3

Payback Period Calculation with Uneven Cash Flows

Period*	Expected Net Cash Flows	Cumulative Net Cash Flows
Year 0	$(16,000)	$(16,000)
Year 1	3,000	(13,000)
Year 2	4,000	(9,000)
Year 3	4,000	(5,000)
Year 4	4,000	(1,000)
Year 5	5,000	4,000
Year 6	3,000	7,000
Year 7	2,000	9,000
Year 8	2,000	11,000
		Payback period = 4.2 years

* All cash inflows and outflows occur uniformly during the year.

Example: Find the payback period in Exhibit 26.3 if net cash flows for the first 4 years are:
Year 1 = $6,000; Year 2 = $5,000;
Year 3 = $4,000; Year 4 = $3,000.
Answer: 3.33 years

Year 0 refers to the period of initial investment in which the $16,000 cash outflow occurs at the end of year 0 to acquire the machinery. By the end of year 1, the cumulative net cash flow is reduced to $(13,000), computed as the $(16,000) initial cash outflow plus year 1's $3,000 cash inflow. This process continues throughout the asset's life. The cumulative net cash flow amount changes from negative to positive in year 5. Specifically, at the end of year 4, the cumulative net cash flow is $(1,000). As soon as FasTrac receives net cash inflow of $1,000 during the fifth year, it would have fully recovered the investment. If we assume that cash flows are received uniformly *within* each year, then receipt of the $1,000 occurs about one-fifth of the way through the year. This is computed as $1,000 divided by year 5's total net cash flow of $5,000, or 0.20. This yields a payback period of 4.2 years, computed as 4 years plus 0.20 of year 5.

Point: To apply these concepts, work Exercise 26-2.

Using the Payback Period

Companies desire a short payback period to increase return and reduce risk. The more quickly a company receives cash, the sooner it is available for other uses, and the less time it is at risk of loss. A shorter payback period also improves the company's ability to respond to unanticipated changes and lowers its risk of having to keep an unprofitable investment.

Payback period should never be the only consideration in evaluating investments. This is so because it ignores at least two important factors. First, it fails to reflect differences in the timing of net cash flows within the payback period. In Exhibit 26.3, FasTrac's net cash flows in the first five years were $3,000, $4,000, $4,000, $4,000, and $5,000. If another investment had predicted cash flows of $9,000, $3,000, $2,000, $1,800, and $1,000 in these five years, its payback period would also be 4.2 years, but this second alternative could be more desirable because it provides cash more quickly. The second important factor is that the payback period ignores *all* cash flows after the point where its costs are fully recovered. For example, one investment might pay back its cost in 3 years but stop producing cash after 4 years. A second investment might require 5 years to pay back its cost yet continue to produce net cash flows for another 15 years. A focus on only the payback period would mistakenly lead management to choose the first investment over the second.

Point: The time value of money is described in Appendix B of this book and is also discussed later in this chapter.

Point: To apply these concepts, work QS 26-1.

Quick Check

1. Capital budgeting is (a) concerned with analyzing alternative sources of capital, including debt and equity, (b) an important activity for companies when considering what assets to acquire or sell, or (c) best done by intuitive assessments of the value of assets and their usefulness.

2. Why are capital budgeting decisions often difficult?

3. A company is considering the purchase of equipment costing $75,000. Future annual net cash flows from this equipment are $30,000, $25,000, $15,000, $10,000, and $5,000. The payback period is (a) 4 years, (b) 3.5 years, or (c) 3 years.

4. If depreciation is an expense, why is it added back to an investment's net income to compute the net cash flow from that investment?

5. If two investments have the same payback period, are they equally desirable? Explain.

Answers—p. 1085

Accounting Rate of Return

The **accounting rate of return,** also called *return on average investment,* is computed by dividing a project's after-tax net income by the average amount invested in it. To illustrate, let's return to the $16,000 machinery investment by FasTrac described in Exhibit 26.1. Our first step is to compute (1) the after-tax net income and then (2) the average amount invested. The after-tax net income of $2,100 is already available from Exhibit 26.1. To compute the average amount invested we assume that net cash flows are received evenly throughout each year. Thus, the average investment for each year is computed as the average of its beginning and ending book values. If FasTrac's $16,000 machine is depreciated $2,000 each year, the average amount invested in the machine for each year is computed as shown in Exhibit 26.4. The average for any year is the average of the beginning and ending book values.

P2 Compute accounting rate of return and explain its use.

	Beginning Book Value	Annual Depreciation	Ending Book Value	Average Book Value
Year 1	$16,000	$2,000	$14,000	$15,000
Year 2	14,000	2,000	12,000	13,000
Year 3	12,000	2,000	10,000	11,000
Year 4	10,000	2,000	8,000	9,000
Year 5	8,000	2,000	6,000	7,000
Year 6	6,000	2,000	4,000	5,000
Year 7	4,000	2,000	2,000	3,000
Year 8	2,000	2,000	0	1,000
				$ 8,000

Exhibit 26.4

Computing Average Amount Invested

Next we need the average book value for the asset's entire life. This amount is computed by taking the average of the individual yearly averages. This average equals $8,000, computed as $64,000 (the sum of the individual years' averages) divided by eight years (see last column of Exhibit 26.4).

Note that if a company uses straight-line depreciation, we can find the average amount invested by using the formula in Exhibit 26.5. Since FasTrac uses straight-line depreciation, its average amount invested for the eight years equals the sum of the book value at the beginning of the asset's investment period and the book value at the end of its investment period, divided by 2, as shown in Exhibit 26.5.

Point: General formula for *annual average investment* is the sum of individual year's average book values divided by the number of years of the planned investment.

$$\text{Annual average investment} = \frac{\text{Beginning book value} + \text{Ending book value}}{2}$$
(straight-line case only)
$$= \frac{\$16,000 + \$0}{2} = \$8,000$$

Exhibit 26.5

Computing Average Amount Invested under Straight-Line Depreciation

Note that if an investment carries a salvage value, the average amount invested when using straight-line depreciation is computed as (Beginning book value + Salvage value)/2.

Once we determine the after-tax net income and the average amount invested, the accounting rate of return on the investment can be computed by dividing the annual after-tax net income by the average amount invested as shown in Exhibit 26.6.

Exhibit 26.6

Accounting Rate of
Return Formula

$$\text{Accounting rate of return} = \frac{\text{Annual after-tax net income}}{\text{Annual average investment}}$$

This yields an accounting rate of return for FasTrac of 26.25% ($2,100/$8,000). Management must decide whether accounting rate of return of 26% is a satisfactory rate of return. To make this decision, we must factor in the investment's risk. For instance, we cannot say an investment with a 26% return is preferred over one with a lower return unless we recognize any differences in risk. Thus, an investment's return is satisfactory or unsatisfactory only when it is related to returns from other investments with similar lives and risk.

When accounting rate of return is used to choose among capital investments, the one with the least risk, the shortest payback period, and the highest return for the longest time period is often identified as the best. However, use of accounting rate of return in evaluating investment opportunities is limited because it bases the amount invested on book values (and not predicted market values) for future periods. Accounting rate of return is also limited when an asset's net incomes are expected to vary from year to year. This requires that the rate be computed using *average* annual net incomes, yet this accounting rate of return fails to distinguish between two investments that have the same average annual net income but different amounts of income in early years versus later years or different levels of income variability.

Point: To apply these concepts, work QS 26-4 and Exercise 26-4.

Quick Check

6. The following data relate to a company's decision whether to purchase a machine:

Cost	$180,000
Salvage value	15,000
Annual after-tax net income	40,000

The machine's accounting rate of return, assuming even receipt of its net cash flows during the year and use of straight-line depreciation is: (a) 22%, (b) 41%, or (c) 21%.

7. Is a 15% accounting rate of return for a machine a good rate?

Answers—p. 1085

Methods Using Time Value of Money

This section describes methods that help managers with capital budgeting decisions and that use the time value of money. The two methods described are (1) net present value and (2) internal rate of return. *(To apply these methods, we need a basic understanding of the concept of present value. An expanded explanation of present value concepts is in Appendix B near the end of the book. We can use the present value tables at the end of Appendix B to solve many of this chapter's assignments that use the time value of money.)*

Net Present Value

P3 Compute net present value and describe its use.

Concept 26-1

A net present value analysis uses the time value of money applied to future cash inflows and cash outflows so that management can evaluate a project's benefits and costs at one point in time.

Specifically, **net present value (NPV)** is computed by discounting the future net cash flows from the investment at the project's required rate of return and then subtracting the initial amount invested. To illustrate, let's return to the proposed machinery purchase by

FasTrac described in Exhibit 26.1. Does this machine provide a satisfactory return while recovering the amount invested? Recall that this machine requires a $16,000 investment and is expected to provide annual net cash inflows of $4,100 for the next eight years. If we assume that net cash flows from this machine are received at the end of each year and that FasTrac requires a 12% annual return, net present value can be computed as shown in Exhibit 26.7.

Point: The assumption of end-of-year cash flows simplifies computations and is common in practice.

	Net Cash Flows†	Present Value of 1 at 12%*	Present Value of Net Cash Flows
Year 1	$ 4,100	0.8929	$ 3,661
Year 2	4,100	0.7972	3,269
Year 3	4,100	0.7118	2,918
Year 4	4,100	0.6355	2,606
Year 5	4,100	0.5674	2,326
Year 6	4,100	0.5066	2,077
Year 7	4,100	0.4523	1,854
Year 8	4,100	0.4039	1,656
Totals	$32,800		$20,367
Amount invested			(16,000)
Net present value			$ 4,367

Exhibit 26.7

Net Present Value Calculation with Equal Cash Flows

* Present value of 1 factors are taken from Table B.1 in Appendix B.
† Cash flows occur at the end of each year.

The first number column of Exhibit 26.7 shows the annual net cash flows. Present value of 1 factors, also called *discount factors,* are shown in the second column. Taken from Table B.1 in Appendix B, they assume that net cash flows are received at the end of each year. *(To simplify present value computations and for assignment material at the end of this chapter, we assume that net cash flows are received at the end of each year.)* Annual net cash flows from the first column of Exhibit 26.7 are multiplied by the discount factors in the second column to give present values shown in the third column. The last three lines of this exhibit show the final NPV computations. The asset's $16,000 initial cost is deducted from the $20,367 total present value of all future net cash flows to give us this asset's NPV of $4,367. The machine is therefore expected to (1) recover its cost, (2) provide a 12% compounded return, and (3) generate $4,367 above cost. We summarize this analysis by saying the present value of this machine's future net cash flows to FasTrac exceeds the $16,000 investment by $4,367.

Point: The amount invested includes all costs that must be incurred to get the asset in its proper location and ready for use (see Chapter 11).

Example: What is the net present value in Exhibit 26.7 if a 10% return is applied? *Answer:* $5,873

Net Present Value Decision Rule

The decision rule in applying NPV is as follows: When the expected cash flows from an asset are discounted at the required rate and yield a *positive* net present value, the asset should be acquired. This decision rule is reflected in the chart at the right. When comparing several investment opportunities of about the same cost and the same risk, we prefer the one with the highest positive net present value.

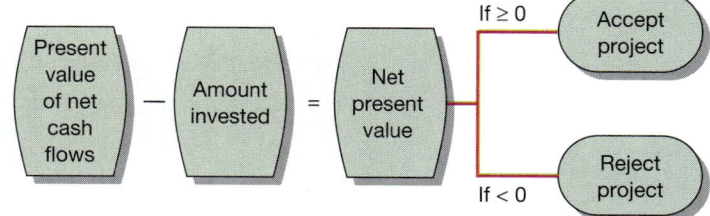

Simplifying Computations

The computations in Exhibit 26.7 use separate present value of 1 factors for each of the eight years. Each year's net cash flow is multiplied by its present value of 1 factor to determine its present value. The individual present values for each of the eight net cash flows are added to give the asset's total present value. This computation can be simplified in two ways if annual net cash flows are equal in amount. One simplification is to add the eight

Example: Why does the net present value of an investment increase when a lower discount rate is used? *Answer:* Time value of money.

annual present value of 1 factors for a total of 4.9676 and multiply this amount by the annual net cash flow of $4,100 to get the $20,367 total present value of net cash flows.[2] A second simplification is to use a calculator with compound interest functions or a spreadsheet program. Whatever procedure is chosen, it is important that we understand the concepts behind these computations. The actual procedure we use does not matter so long as we apply it properly.

Uneven Cash Flows

Point: To apply these concepts, work Exercise 26-7.

Net present value analysis can also be applied when net cash flows are uneven (unequal). To illustrate, assume that FasTrac can choose only one capital investment from among projects A, B, and C. Each project requires the same $12,000 initial investment. Future net cash flows for each project are shown in the first three number columns of Exhibit 26.8.

Exhibit 26.8

Net Present Value Calculation with Uneven Cash Flows

	Net Cash Flows			Present Value of	Present Value of Net Cash Flows		
	A	**B**	**C**	**1 at 10%**	**A**	**B**	**C**
Year 1	$ 5,000	$ 8,000	$ 1,000	0.9091	$ 4,546	$ 7,273	$ 909
Year 2	5,000	5,000	5,000	0.8264	4,132	4,132	4,132
Year 3	5,000	2,000	9,000	0.7513	3,757	1,503	6,762
Totals	$15,000	$15,000	$15,000		$12,435	$12,908	$11,803
Amount invested					(12,000)	(12,000)	(12,000)
Net present value . .					$ 435	$ 908	$ (197)

Example: If 12% is the required return in Exhibit 26.8, which project is preferred? *Answer:* Project B. Net present values are: A = $10; B = $553; C = $(715).

Example: Will the rankings of Projects A, B, and C change with the use of different discount rates, assuming the same rate is used for all projects? *Answer:* No; only the NPV amounts will change.

Point: Projects with higher cash flows in earlier years generally yield higher net present values.

The three projects in Exhibit 26.8 have the same expected total net cash flows of $15,000. Project A is expected to produce equal amounts of $5,000 each year. Project B is expected to produce a larger amount in the first year. Project C is expected to produce a larger amount in the third year. The fourth column of Exhibit 26.8 shows the present value of 1 factors from Table B.1. Since the patterns of net cash flows are different, we expect these projects to yield different net present values.

Computations in the right-most columns show that Project A has a $435 positive NPV. Project B has the largest NPV of $908 because it brings in cash more quickly. Project C has a $(197) *negative* NPV because its larger cash inflows are delayed. If FasTrac requires a 10% return, then it should reject Project C because its NPV implies a return *under* 10%. If only one project can be accepted, project B appears best because it yields the highest NPV.

Salvage Value and Accelerated Depreciation

FasTrac predicted the $16,000 machine to have zero salvage value at the end of its useful life (recall Exhibit 26.1). In many cases, assets are expected to have salvage values. If so, this amount is an additional net cash inflow received at the end of the final year of the asset's life. All other computations remain the same.

---

[2] We can simplify this computation even further using Table B.3, which gives the present value of 1 to be received periodically for a number of periods. To determine the present value of these eight annual receipts discounted at 12%, go down the 12% column of Table B.3 to the factor on the eighth line. This cumulative discount factor, also known as an *annuity* factor, is 4.9676. We then compute the $20,367 present value for these eight annual $4,100 receipts, computed as 4.9676 × $4,100.

Depreciation computations also affect net present value analysis. FasTrac computes depreciation using the straight-line method. Accelerated depreciation is also commonly used, especially for income tax reports. Accelerated depreciation produces larger depreciation deductions in the early years of an asset's life and smaller deductions in later years. This pattern results in smaller income tax payments in early years and larger payments in later years. Accelerated depreciation does not change the basics of a present value analysis, but it can change the result. Using accelerated depreciation for tax reporting affects the NPV of an asset's cash flows because it produces larger net cash inflows in the early years of the asset's life and smaller ones in later years. Being able to use accelerated depreciation for tax reporting always makes an investment more desirable, because early cash flows are more valuable than later ones.

Use of Net Present Value

In deciding whether to proceed with a capital investment project, we approve the proposal if the NPV is positive but reject it if the NPV is negative. When considering several projects of similar investment amounts and risk levels, we can compare the NPV of the different projects and rank them on the basis of their NPVs. However, if the amount invested differs substantially across projects, the NPV is of limited value for comparison purposes. To illustrate, suppose that Project X requires an investment of $1 million and provides an NPV of $100,000. Project Y requires an investment of only $100,000 and returns an NPV of $75,000. Ranking on the basis of NPV puts Project X ahead of Y, yet X's NPV is only 10% of the initial investment whereas Y's NPV is 75% of its investment. We must also remember that when reviewing projects with different risks, the NPVs of individual projects are computed using different discount rates. The higher the risk, the higher the discount rate.

Internal Rate of Return

Another means to evaluate capital investments is to use the internal rate of return. The **internal rate of return (IRR)** is a rate used to evaluate an investment's acceptability. It equals the rate that yields an NPV of zero for an investment. This means that if we compute the total present value of a project's net cash flows using the IRR as the discount rate and then subtract the initial investment from this total present value, we get a zero NPV.

To illustrate, we use the data for Project A of FasTrac from Exhibit 26.8 to compute its IRR. Exhibit 26.9 shows the two-step process in computing IRR.

Example: When is it appropriate to use different discount rates for different projects? *Answer:* When risk levels are different.

Point: Chapter 11 on plant assets describes depreciation for tax reporting.

P4 Compute internal rate of return and explain its use.

Exhibit 26.9

Computing Internal Rate of Return (with even cash flows)

Step 1: Compute present value factor for FasTrac's three-year project:

$$\text{Present value factor} = \frac{\text{Amount invested}}{\text{Net cash flows}} = \frac{\$12,000}{\$5,000} = 2.4000$$

Step 2: Identify the discount rate (IRR) yielding the present value factor

Search Table B.3 for a present value factor of 2.4000 in the three-year row. The 12% discount rate yields a present value factor of 2.4018. This implies that the IRR is approximately 12%.*

---

* Since the present value factor of 2.4000 is not exactly equal to the 12% factor of 2.4018, we can more precisely estimate the IRR as follows:

Discount rate	Present value factor from Table B.3
12%	2.4018
15%	2.2832
	0.1186 = difference

$$\text{Then, IRR} = 12\% + \left[(15\% - 12\%) \times \frac{2.4018 - 2.4000}{0.1186} \right] = 12.05\%$$

When cash flows are equal, as with Project A, we compute the present value factor (as shown in Exhibit 26.9) by dividing the initial investment by its annual net cash flows. We then use an annuity table to determine the discount rate equal to this present value factor. For FasTrac's

Project A, we look across the three-period row of Table B.3 and find that the discount rate corresponding to the present value factor of 2.4000 roughly equals the 2.4018 value for the 12% rate. This row is reproduced here:

Present Value of an Annuity of 1 for Three Periods

			Rate		
Periods	1%	5%	10%	12%	15%
3	2.9410	2.7232	2.4869	2.4018	2.2832

The 12% rate is the Project's IRR. A more precise estimate of the IRR can be computed following the procedure shown in the note to Exhibit 26.9. Spreadsheet software and calculators can also compute this IRR.

Uneven Cash Flows

If net cash flows are uneven, we must use trial and error to compute the IRR. We do this by selecting any reasonable discount rate and computing the NPV. If the amount is positive (negative), we recompute the NPV using a higher (lower) discount rate. We continue these steps until we reach a point where two consecutive computations result in NPVs having different signs (positive and negative). Since the NPV is zero using IRR, we know that the IRR lies between these two discount rates. We can then estimate its value. Spreadsheet programs and calculators can do these computations for us.

Use of Internal Rate of Return

C2 Describe the selection of a hurdle rate for an investment.

When we use the IRR to evaluate a project, we compare it to a predetermined **hurdle rate,** which is a minimum acceptable rate of return and is applied as follows:

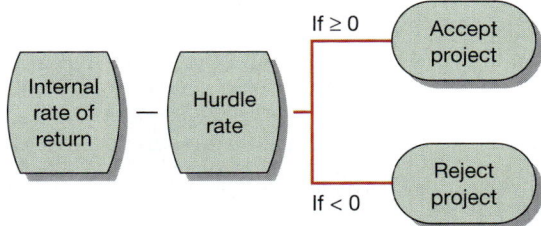

Top management selects the rate to use as the hurdle in evaluating capital investments. Financial formulas aid in this selection, but the choice of a minimum rate is subjective and left to management. For projects financed from borrowed funds, the hurdle rate must exceed the interest rate paid on these funds. The return on an investment must cover its interest and provide an additional profit to reward the company for its risk. For instance, if money is borrowed at 10%, a required after-tax return of 15% (or 5% above the borrowing rate) is often required by the management of companies with average risk. We must remember that lower-risk investments require a lower rate of return compared with higher-risk investments.

If the project is internally financed, the hurdle rate is often based on actual returns from comparable projects. If the IRR is higher than the hurdle rate, the project is accepted. Multiple projects are often ranked by the extent to which their IRR exceeds the hurdle rate. The hurdle rate for individual projects is often different, depending on the risk involved. IRR is not subject to the limitations of NPV when comparing projects with different amounts invested because the IRR is expressed as a percent rather than as an absolute dollar value in NPV.

Example: How can management evaluate the risk of an investment? _Answer:_ It must assess the uncertainty of future cash flows.

Point: To apply these concepts, work Exercise 26-7.

You Make the Call

Entrepreneur For a new product being developed, you use a 12% discount rate to compute its NPV. Your banker, with whom you share your analysis, expresses concern that your discount rate is too low. How do you respond?

Answer—p. 1084

Comparing Capital Budgeting Methods

We explained four methods that managers use to evaluate capital investment projects. How do these methods compare with each other? This section addresses that question.

Neither the payback period nor the accounting rate of return considers the time value of money. On the other hand, both the net present value and the internal rate of return do. Exhibit 26.10 identifies this and other differences.

Exhibit 26.10

Comparing Capital Budgeting Methods

	Payback Period	Accounting Rate of Return	Net Present Value	Internal Rate of Return
Measurement basis	• Cash flows	• Accrual income	• Cash flows • Profitability	• Cash flows • Profitability
Measurement unit	• Years	• Percent	• Dollars	• Percent
Strengths	• Easy to understand	• Easy to understand	• Reflects time value of money	• Reflects time value of money
	• Allows comparison of projects	• Allows comparison of projects	• Reflects varying risks over project's life	• Allows comparisons of dissimilar projects
Limitations	• Ignores time value of money	• Ignores time value of money	• Difficult to compare dissimilar projects	• Ignores varying risks over life of project
	• Ignores cash flows after payback period	• Ignores annual rates over life of project		

The payback period is probably the simplest method. It gives managers an estimate of how soon they will recover their initial investment. Managers sometimes use this method when they have limited cash to invest and a number of projects to choose from. The accounting rate of return yields a percent measure computed using accrual income instead of cash flows. The accounting rate of return is an average rate for the entire investment period. Net present value considers all estimated net cash flows for the project's expected life. It can be applied to even and uneven cash flows and can reflect changes in the level of risk over a project's life. Since it yields a dollar measure, a comparison of projects of unequal sizes is more difficult. The internal rate of return considers all cash flows from a project. It is readily computed when the cash flows are even but requires some trial and error estimation when cash flows are uneven. Since the IRR is a percent measure, it is readily used to compare projects with different investment amounts. However, changes in risk over a project's life are not reflected in the IRR.

Did You Know?

And the Winner Is. . .

How do we choose among the methods for evaluating capital investments? Management surveys consistently show the internal rate of return (IRR) as the most popular method. It is followed by the payback period and net present value (NPV). Few companies use the accounting rate of return (ARR), but nearly all use more than one of these methods.

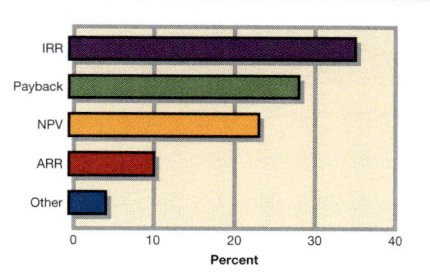

Quick Check

8. A company can invest in only one of two projects, A or B. Each project requires a $20,000 investment and is expected to generate end-of-period, annual cash flows as follows:

	Year 1	Year 2	Year 3	Total
Project A	$12,000	$8,500	$4,000	$24,500
Project B	4,500	8,500	13,000	26,000

Assuming a discount rate of 10%, which project has the higher net present value?

9. Two investment alternatives are expected to generate annual cash flows with the same net present value (assuming the same discount rate applied to each). Using this information, can you conclude that the two alternatives are equally desirable?

10. When two investment alternatives have the same total expected cash flows but differ in the timing of those flows, which method of evaluating those investments is superior, (a) accounting rate of return or (b) net present value?

Answers—p. 1085

Section 2—Managerial Decisions

This section focuses on the use of accounting information for several important managerial decisions. The emphasis is on the use of quantitative measures to help managers make business decisions. Most of these involve short-term decisions. Methods for long-term managerial decisions are described in the first section of this chapter and in several other chapters of this book. Thus, a primary goal of this section is to explain what costs and other financial factors are most relevant to short-term business decisions.

Decisions and Information

This section explains how managers make decisions and the information relevant to these decisions.

Decision Making

Managerial decision making involves five steps: (1) define the decision task, (2) identify alternative courses of action, (3) collect relevant information to evaluate each alternative, (4) select the preferred course of action, and (5) analyze and assess decisions made. These five steps are illustrated in Exhibit 26.11.

Exhibit 26.11

Managerial Decision Making

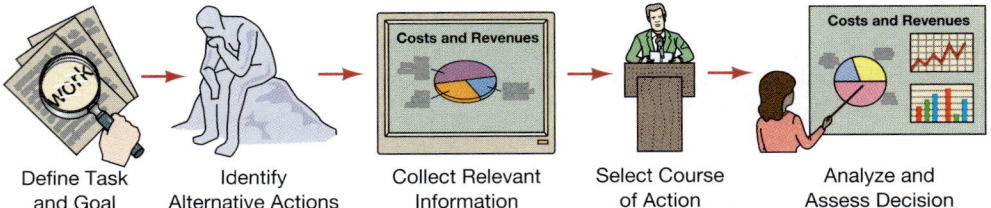

| Define Task and Goal | Identify Alternative Actions | Collect Relevant Information | Select Course of Action | Analyze and Assess Decision |

Both managerial and financial accounting information play an important role in most management decisions. The accounting system is expected to provide primarily *financial* information such as performance reports and budget analyses for decision making. *Nonfinancial* information is also relevant, however; it includes information on environmental effects, political sensitivities, and social responsibility.

Relevant Costs

C3 Describe the importance of relevant costs for short-term decisions.

Most financial measures of revenues and costs from cost accounting systems are based on historical costs. Although historical costs are important and useful for many tasks such as product pricing and the control and monitoring of business activities, we sometimes find that an analysis of *relevant costs,* or *avoidable costs,* is especially useful for certain managerial decisions. Three types of costs were identified in Chapter 19 that are pertinent to our discussion of relevant costs: sunk costs, out-of-pocket costs, and opportunity costs.

A **sunk cost** arises from a past decision and cannot be avoided or changed; it is irrelevant to future decisions. An example is the cost of computer equipment previously purchased by a company. Most of a company's allocated costs, including fixed overhead items such as depreciation and administrative expenses, are sunk costs.

An **out-of-pocket cost** requires a future outlay of cash and is relevant for current and future decision making. These costs are usually the direct result of management's decisions. For instance, future purchases of computer equipment involve out-of-pocket costs.

An **opportunity cost** is the potential benefit lost by taking a specific action when two or more alternative choices are available. An example is a student giving up wages from a job to attend summer school. Companies continually must choose from alternative courses of action. For instance, a company making standardized products might be approached by a customer to supply a special (nonstandard) product. A decision to accept or reject the special order must consider not only the profit to be made from the special order but also the profit given up by devoting time and resources to this order instead of pursuing an alternative project. The profit given up is an opportunity cost. Consideration of opportunity costs is important. The implications extend to internal resource allocation decisions. For instance, a computer manufacturer must decide between internally manufacturing a chip versus buying it externally. In another case, management of a multidivisional company must decide whether to continue operating or close a particular division.

Besides relevant costs, management must also consider the relevant benefits associated with a decision. **Relevant benefits** refer to the additional or *incremental* revenue generated by selecting a particular course of action over another. For instance, a student must decide the relevant benefits of taking one course over another. In sum, both relevant costs and relevant benefits are crucial to managerial decision making.

Example: Depreciation and amortization are allocations of the original cost of plant and intangible assets. Are they out-of-pocket costs? *Answer:* No; they are sunk costs.

Point: Opportunity costs are not entered in accounting records. This does not reduce their relevance for managerial decisions.

Managers confront many different types of tasks that require analyzing alternative actions and making a decision. We describe several different types of decision tasks in this section. We set these tasks in the context of FasTrac, the exercise supplies and equipment manufacturer introduced earlier. *We treat each of these decision tasks as separate from another.*

Managerial Decision Tasks

Additional Business

FasTrac is operating at its normal level of 80% of full capacity. At this level, it produces and sells approximately 100,000 units of product annually. FasTrac's per unit and annual total costs are shown in Exhibit 26.12.

A1 Evaluate short-term managerial decisions using relevant costs.

	Per Unit	Annual Total
Sales (100,000 units)	$10.00	$1,000,000
Direct materials	(3.50)	(350,000)
Direct labor	(2.20)	(220,000)
Overhead	(1.10)	(110,000)
Selling expenses	(1.40)	(140,000)
Administrative expenses	(0.80)	(80,000)
Total costs and expenses	$ (9.00)	$ (900,000)
Operating income	$ 1.00	$ 100,000

Exhibit 26.12

Selected Operating Income Data

A current buyer of FasTrac's products wants to purchase additional units of its product and export them to another country. This buyer offers to buy 10,000 units of the product at $8.50 per unit, or $1.50 less than the current price. The offer price is low, but FasTrac is considering the proposal because this sale would be several times larger than any single previous sale made by the company. Also, the units will be exported, meaning this new business will not affect its current sales.

To determine whether to accept or reject this order, management needs to know whether acceptance of the offer will increase net income. The analysis in Exhibit 26.13 shows that if management relies on per unit historical costs, it would reject the sale because it yields a loss. However, historical costs are *not* relevant to this decision. Instead, the relevant costs are the additional costs called incremental costs. **Incremental costs,** also called *differential costs,* are the additional costs incurred if a company pursues a certain course of action. FasTrac's incremental costs are those related to the added volume that this new order would bring.

Exhibit 26.13

Analysis of Additional
Business Using
Historical Costs

	Per Unit	Total
Sales (10,000 additional units)	$ 8.50	$85,000
Direct materials	(3.50)	(35,000)
Direct labor	(2.20)	(22,000)
Overhead	(1.10)	(11,000)
Selling expenses	(1.40)	(14,000)
Administrative expenses	(0.80)	(8,000)
Total costs and expenses	$(9.00)	$(90,000)
Operating loss	$(0.50)	$ (5,000)

To make its decision, FasTrac must analyze the costs of this new business in a different manner. The following information regarding the order is available:

■ Manufacturing 10,000 additional units requires direct materials of $3.50 per unit and direct labor of $2.20 per unit (same as for all other units).

■ Manufacturing 10,000 additional units adds $5,000 of incremental overhead costs for power, packaging, and indirect labor (all variable costs).

■ Incremental commissions and selling expenses from this sale of 10,000 additional units would be $2,000 (all variable costs).

■ Incremental administrative expenses of $1,000 for clerical efforts are needed (all fixed costs) with the sale of 10,000 additional units.

We use this information, as shown in Exhibit 26.14, to assess how accepting this new business will affect FasTrac's income.

Exhibit 26.14

Analysis of Additional
Business Using
Relevant Costs

	Current Business	Additional Business	Combined
Sales	$1,000,000	$ 85,000	$1,085,000
Direct materials	(350,000)	(35,000)	(385,000)
Direct labor	(220,000)	(22,000)	(242,000)
Overhead	(110,000)	(5,000)	(115,000)
Selling expenses	(140,000)	(2,000)	(142,000)
Administrative expense	(80,000)	(1,000)	(81,000)
Total costs and expenses	$ (900,000)	$(65,000)	$ (965,000)
Operating income	$ 100,000	$ 20,000	$ 120,000

Example: Exhibit 26.14 uses quantitative information. Suggest some qualitative factors to be considered when deciding whether to accept this project. *Answer:* (1) Impact on relationships with other customers, and (2) Improved relationship with customer buying additional units.

The analysis of relevant costs in Exhibit 26.14 suggests that the additional business be accepted. It would provide $85,000 of added revenue while incurring only $65,000 of added costs. This would yield $20,000 of additional pretax income, or a pretax profit margin of 23.5%. More generally, FasTrac would increase its income with any price that exceeded $6.50 per unit ($65,000 incremental cost/10,000 additional units).

An analysis of the incremental costs pertaining to the additional volume is always relevant for this type of decision. We must proceed cautiously, however, when the additional volume approaches or exceeds the factory's existing available capacity. If the additional volume requires the company to expand its capacity by obtaining more equipment, more space, or more personnel, the incremental costs could quickly exceed the incremental revenue. Another cautionary note is the effect on existing sales. All new units of the extra business will be sold outside FasTrac's normal domestic sales channels. If accepting additional business would cause existing sales to decline, this information must be included in our analysis. The contribution margin lost from a decline in sales is an opportunity cost. If future cash flows over several time periods are affected, their net present value also must be computed and used in this analysis.

The key point is that management must not blindly use historical costs, especially allocated overhead costs. Instead, the accounting system needs to provide information about the incremental costs to be incurred if the additional business is accepted.

Make or Buy

The managerial decision to make or buy a component for one of its current products is commonplace and must rely on incremental costs. To illustrate, FasTrac has excess productive capacity that it can use to manufacture Part 417, a component of the main product it sells. The component is currently purchased and delivered to the plant at a cost of $1.20 per unit. FasTrac estimates that making Part 417 would cost $0.45 for direct materials, $0.50 for direct labor, and an undetermined amount for overhead. Our task is to determine how much overhead to add to these costs so we can decide whether to make or buy Part 417. If FasTrac's normal predetermined overhead application rate is 100% of direct labor cost, we might be tempted to conclude that overhead cost is $0.50 per unit, computed as 100% of the $0.50 direct labor cost. We would then mistakenly conclude that total cost is $1.45 ($0.45 of materials + $0.50 of labor + $0.50 of overhead). A wrong decision in this case would be to conclude that the company is better off buying the part at $1.20 each than making it for $1.45 each.

Instead, as we explained earlier, only incremental overhead costs are relevant in this situation. We must compute an *incremental overhead rate*. Incremental overhead costs might include, for example, additional power for operating machines, extra supplies, added cleanup costs, materials handling, and quality control. We can prepare a per unit analysis in this case as shown in Exhibit 26.15.

We can see that if incremental overhead costs are less than $0.25 per unit, the total cost of making the component is less than the purchase price of $1.20 and FasTrac should make the part. FasTrac's decision rule in this case is that any amount of overhead less than $0.25 per unit yields a total cost for Part 417 that is less than the $1.20 purchase price. FasTrac must consider several factors in the make or buy decision, including product quality, timeliness of delivery (especially in a just-in-time setting), reactions of customers and suppliers, and other intangibles such as employee morale and workload. It must also consider whether making the part requires incremental fixed costs to expand plant capacity. When these added factors are considered, small cost differences may not matter. A key point is that historical costs provided by the accounting system are not always the most relevant to a make or buy decision. Incremental costs are most relevant in this case.

Scrap or Rework

Managers often must make a decision on whether to scrap or rework products in process. In this regard, we must remember that costs already incurred in manufacturing the units of a product that do not meet quality standards are

You Make the Call

Partner You are a partner in a small accounting firm that specializes in keeping the books and preparing taxes for clients such as doctors and lawyers. A local restaurant is interested in obtaining these services from your firm. Your manager has asked you to provide her advice that might be relevant in deciding whether to accept the assignment. What type of advice do you provide?

Answer—p. 1084

Concept 26-2

Point: To apply these concepts, work Exercise 26-8.

Exhibit 26.15
Make or Buy Analysis

	Make	Buy
Direct materials	$0.45	—
Direct labor	0.50	—
Overhead costs	**[?]**	—
Purchase price	—	$1.20
Total incremental costs . .	**$0.95 + [?]**	**$1.20**

Point: To apply these concepts, work QS 26-6.

Did You Know?

Make or Buy Services Just as companies apply make or buy decisions to manufacturing, they can apply them to services as well. **Marine & Restaurant Fabricators (MRF)** in San Diego now outsources its payroll activities to **Paychex**, a payroll service, after finding itself at the wrong end of an IRS notice. The price paid for the service is close to what it costs MRF to do it, but the absence of headaches is worth it, says MRF's office manager.

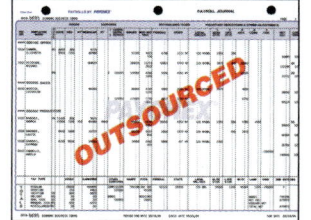

sunk costs—costs that have been incurred and cannot be changed. Sunk costs are irrelevant in any decision on whether to sell the substandard units as scrap or to rework them so they meet quality standards.

To illustrate, let's assume that FasTrac has 10,000 defective units of a product that have already cost $1 per unit to manufacture. These units can be sold as is (as scrap) for $0.40 each, or they can be reworked for $0.80 per unit and then sold for their full price of $1.50 each. Should FasTrac sell the units as scrap or rework them?

To make this decision, management must recognize that the already incurred manufacturing costs of $1 per unit are sunk (unavoidable). These costs are *entirely irrelevant* to the decision. In addition, we must be certain that all costs of reworking defects, including interfering with normal operations, are accounted for in our analysis. For instance, reworking the defects means that FasTrac is unable to manufacture 10,000 *new* units with an incremental cost of $1 per unit and a selling price of $1.50 per unit, meaning it incurs an opportunity cost equal to the lost $5,000 net return from making and selling 10,000 new units. This opportunity cost is the difference between the $15,000 revenue (10,000 units $\times$ $1.50) from selling these new units and their $10,000 manufacturing costs (10,000 units $\times$ $1). Our analysis of this entire situation is reflected in Exhibit 26.16.

Exhibit 26.16

Scrap or Rework Analysis

	Scrap	Rework
Sale of scrapped/reworked units	$4,000	$15,000
Less costs to rework defects		(8,000)
Less opportunity cost of not making new units		**(5,000)**
Incremental net income	$4,000	$ 2,000

The analysis yields a $2,000 difference in favor of scrapping the defects, yielding a total incremental net income of $4,000. If we had failed to include the opportunity costs of $5,000, the rework option would have shown an income of $7,000 instead of $2,000. This would have mistakenly made reworking appear more favorable than scrapping.

Quick Check

11. A company receives a special order for 200 units. This order requires the buyer's name be stamped on each unit, yielding an additional fixed cost of $400 to its normal costs. Without the order, the company is operating at 75% of capacity and produces 7,500 units of product at the following costs:

Direct materials	$37,500
Direct labor	60,000
Overhead (30% variable)	20,000
Selling expenses (60% variable)	25,000

The special order will not affect normal unit sales and will not increase fixed overhead and selling expenses. Variable selling expenses on the special order are reduced to one-half the normal amount. The price per unit necessary to earn $1,000 on this order is (a) $14.80, (b) $15.80, (c) $19.80, (d) $20.80, or (e) $21.80.

12. What are the incremental costs of accepting additional business?

Answers—p. 1085

Sell or Process

The managerial decision to sell partially completed products as is or to process them further for sale depends importantly on relevant costs. To illustrate, suppose that FasTrac has

40,000 units of partially finished Product Q. It has already spent $0.75 per unit to manufacture these 40,000 units at a total cost of $30,000. FasTrac can sell the 40,000 units to another manufacturer as raw material for $50,000. Alternatively, it can process them further and produce finished products X, Y, and Z at an incremental cost of $2 per unit. The added processing yields the products and revenues shown in Exhibit 26.17. FasTrac must decide whether the added revenues from selling finished products X, Y, and Z exceed the costs of finishing them.

Exhibit 26.17

Revenues from Processing Further

Product	Price	Units	Revenues
Product X	$4.00	10,000	$ 40,000
Product Y	6.00	22,000	132,000
Product Z	8.00	6,000	48,000
Spoilage	—	2,000	0
Totals		40,000	$220,000

Point: To apply these concepts, work Exercise 26-10.

Exhibit 26.18 shows the two-step analysis for this decision. First, FasTrac computes its incremental revenue from further processing Q into products X, Y, and Z. This amount is the difference between the $220,000 revenue from the further processed products and the $50,000 FasTrac will give up by not selling Q as is (a $50,000 opportunity cost). Second, FasTrac computes its incremental costs from further processing Q into X, Y, and Z. This amount is $80,000 (40,000 units × $2 incremental cost). The analysis shows that FasTrac can earn incremental net income of $90,000 from a decision to further process Q. (Notice that the earlier incurred $30,000 manufacturing cost for the 40,000 units of Product Q does not appear in Exhibit 26.18 because it is a sunk cost and as such is irrelevant to the decision.)

Exhibit 26.18

Sell or Process Analysis

Revenue if processed	$220,000
Revenue if sold as is	(50,000)
Incremental revenue	$170,000
Cost if processed	(80,000)
Incremental net income	**$ 90,000**

Example: Does the decision change if incremental costs in Exhibit 26.18 increase to $4 per unit and the opportunity cost increases to $95,000? *Answer:* Yes. There is now an incremental net loss of $35,000.

Quick Check

13. Assume that a company has already incurred a cost of $1,000 in partially producing its four products. Selling prices for these products when partially and fully processed follow along with additional costs necessary to finish these partially processed units:

Product	Unfinished Selling Price	Finished Selling Price	Further Processing Costs
Alpha	$300	$600	$150
Beta	450	900	300
Gamma	275	425	125
Delta	150	210	75

Which product(s) should *not* be processed further, (a) Alpha, (b) Beta, (c) Gamma, or (d) Delta?

14. Under what conditions is a sunk cost relevant to decision making?

Answers—p. 1085

Selecting Sales Mix

When a company sells a mix of products, some are likely to be more profitable than others. Management is often wise to concentrate sales efforts on more profitable products. If production facilities or other factors are limited, an increase in the production and sale of one product usually requires a company to reduce the production and sale of others. In this case, management must identify the most profitable combination, or *sales mix* of products. To identify the best sales mix, management must know the contribution margin of each product, the facilities required to produce these products, any constraints on these facilities, and the markets for these products.

Point: Contribution margin concepts were described in Chapter 23.

To illustrate, assume that FasTrac makes and sells two products, A and B. The same machines are used to produce both products. A and B have the following selling prices and variable costs per unit:

	Product A	Product B
Selling price per unit	$5.00	$7.50
Variable costs per unit	3.50	5.50
Contribution margin per unit	$1.50	$2.00

The variable costs are included in the analysis because they are the incremental costs of producing these products within the existing capacity of 100,000 machine hours per month. We consider three separate cases.

Case 1: Assume that (1) each product requires 1 machine hour per unit for production and (2) the markets for these products are unlimited. Under these conditions, FasTrac should produce as much of Product B as it can because of its larger contribution margin of $2 per unit. At full capacity, FasTrac would produce $200,000 of total contribution margin per month, computed as $2 per unit times 100,000 machine hours.

Case 2: Assume that (1) Product A requires 1 machine hour per unit, (2) Product B requires 2 machine hours per unit, and (3) the markets for these products are unlimited. Under these conditions, FasTrac should produce as much of Product A as it can because it has a contribution margin of $1.50 per machine hour compared with only $1 per machine hour for Product B. Exhibit 26.19 shows the relevant analysis.

Exhibit 26.19

Sales Mix Analysis

	Product A	Product B
Selling price per unit	$5.00	$7.50
Variable costs per unit	3.50	5.50
Contribution margin per unit	$1.50	$2.00
Machine hours per unit	1.0	2.0
Contribution margin per machine hour	**$1.50**	**$1.00**

Example: For Case 2, if Product B's variable costs per unit increase to $6, Product A's variable costs per unit decrease to $3, and the same machine hours per unit are used, which product should FasTrac produce? *Answer:* Product A. Its contribution margin of $2 per machine hour is higher than B's $.75 per machine hour.

Point: To apply these concepts, work QS 26-5.

At its full capacity of 100,000 machine hours, FasTrac would produce 100,000 units of Product A, yielding $150,000 of total contribution margin per month. In contrast, if it uses all 100,000 hours to produce Product B, only 50,000 units would be produced yielding a contribution margin of $100,000. These results suggest that when a company faces excess demand and limited capacity, only the most profitable product per input should be manufactured.

Case 3: The need for a mix of different products arises when market demand is not sufficient to allow a company to sell all that it produces. For instance, assume that (1) Product A requires 1 machine hour per unit, (2) Product B requires 2 machine hours per unit, and (3) the market for Product A is limited to 80,000 units. Under these conditions, FasTrac should produce no more than 80,000 units of Product A. This would leave another 20,000 machine hours of capacity for making Product B. FasTrac should use this spare capacity to produce 10,000 units of Product B. This sales mix would maximize FasTrac's total contribution margin per month at an amount of $140,000.

Eliminating a Segment

Point: A method called *linear programming* is useful for finding the optimal sales mix for several products subject to many market and production constraints. This method is described in advanced courses.

When a segment such as a department or division is performing poorly, management must consider eliminating it. Segment information on either net income (loss) or its contribution to overhead is not sufficient for this decision. Instead, we must look at the segment's avoidable expenses and unavoidable expenses. **Avoidable expenses,** also called *escapable expenses,* are amounts the company would not incur if it eliminated the segment. **Unavoidable expenses,** also called *inescapable expenses,* are amounts that would continue even if the segment is eliminated.

To illustrate, FasTrac is considering eliminating its treadmill division because its total expenses of $48,300 are higher than its sales of $47,800. Classification of this division's operating expenses into avoidable or unavoidable expenses is shown in Exhibit 26.20.

	Total	Avoidable Expenses	Unavoidable Expenses
Cost of goods sold	$30,000	$30,000	—
Direct expenses			
Salaries expense	7,900	7,900	—
Depreciation expense—Equipment	200	—	$ 200
Indirect expenses			
Rent and utilities expense	3,150	—	3,150
Advertising expense	400	400	—
Insurance expense	400	300	100
Service department costs			
Share of office department expenses	3,060	2,200	860
Share of purchasing expenses	3,190	1,000	2,190
Total	**$48,300**	**$41,800**	**$6,500**

Exhibit 26.20

Classification of Segment Operating Expenses for Analysis

FasTrac's analysis shows that it can avoid expenses of $41,800 if it eliminates the treadmill division. Since this division's sales are $47,800, eliminating it will cause FasTrac to lose $6,000 of income. *Our decision rule is that a segment is a candidate for elimination if its revenues are less than its avoidable expenses.* Avoidable expenses can be viewed as the costs to generate this segment's revenues.

When considering elimination of a segment, we must assess its impact on other segments. A segment could be unprofitable on its own, but it might still contribute to other segment's revenues and profits. It is possible then to continue a segment even when its revenues are less than its avoidable expenses. Similarly, a profitable segment might be discontinued if its space, assets, or staff can be more profitably used by expanding existing segments or by creating new ones. Our decision to keep or eliminate a segment requires a more complex analysis than simply looking at a segment's performance report. Such reports provide useful information, but they do not provide all the information necessary for this decision.

Example: How can insurance be classified as either avoidable or unavoidable? *Answer:* Depends on whether the assets insured can be removed and the premiums canceled.

Example: Give an example of a segment that might be profitably used by a company to attract customers even though it might incur a loss. *Answer:* Warranty and post-sales services.

Point: To apply these concepts, work Exercise 26-11.

Quick Check

15. What is the difference between avoidable and unavoidable expenses?

16. A segment is a candidate for elimination if (a) its revenues are less than its avoidable expenses, (b) it has a net loss, (c) its unavoidable expenses are higher than its revenues.

Answers—p. 1085

Qualitative Decision Factors

Managers must consider qualitative factors in making managerial decisions. Consider a make or buy decision to buy a component from an outside supplier or continue to make it. Several qualitative decision factors must be considered. For example, the quality, delivery, and reputation of the proposed supplier are important. The effects from deciding not to make the component can include potential layoffs and impaired worker morale. Consider another situation in which a company is considering a one-time sale to a new customer at a special low price. Qualitative factors to consider in this situation include the effects of a low price on the company's image and the threat that regular customers might demand a similar price. The company must also consider whether this customer is really a one-time customer. If not, can it continue to offer this low price in the long run? Clearly, management cannot rely solely on financial data to make decisions.

A2 Analyze a capital investment project using break-even time.

The first section of this chapter explained several methods used to evaluate capital investments. Break-even time of an investment project is a variation of the payback period method that overcomes the limitation of not using the time value of money. **Break-even time (BET)** is a time-based measure used to evaluate the acceptability of a capital investment. Its computation yields a measure of expected time, reflecting the time period until the *present value* of the net cash flows from an investment equals the initial cost of the investment. In basic terms, break-even time is computed by restating future cash flows in terms of present values and then determining the payback period using these present values.

To illustrate, let's return to the FasTrac case described in Exhibit 26.1 involving a $16,000 investment in machinery. The annual net cash flows from this investment are projected at $4,100 for eight years. Exhibit 26.21 shows the computation of break-even time for this investment decision.

Exhibit 26.21

Break-Even Time Analysis*

Year	Cash Flows	Present Value of 1 at 10%	Present Value of Cash Flows	Cumulative Present Value of Cash Flows
0	$(16,000)	1.0000	$(16,000)	$(16,000)
1	4,100	0.9091	3,727	(12,273)
2	4,100	0.8264	3,388	(8,885)
3	4,100	0.7513	3,080	(5,805)
4	4,100	0.6830	2,800	(3,005)
5	4,100	0.6209	2,546	(459)
6	4,100	0.5645	2,314	1,855
7	4,100	0.5132	2,104	3,959
8	4,100	0.4665	1,913	5,872

*The time of analysis is the start of year 1 (same as end of year 0). All cash flows occur at the end of each year.

The right-most column of this exhibit shows that break-even time is between 5 and 6 years, or about 5.2 years. This is the time it takes for the project to break even after considering the time value of money (recall that the payback period computed without considering the time value of money was 4.2 years). We interpret this as cash flows earned after 5.2 years contribute to a positive net present value that, in this case, eventually amounts to $5,872.

Break-even time is a useful measure for managers because it identifies the point in time when they can expect the cash flows to begin to yield net positive returns. Managers expect a positive net present value from an investment if break-even time is less than the investment's estimated life. The method allows managers to compare and rank alternative investments, giving the project with the shortest break-even time the highest rank.

You Make the Call

Investment Manager As the investment manager, management asks you to evaluate three alternative investments. Investment recovery time is crucial because cash is scarce. The time value of money is also important. Which capital budgeting method(s) do you choose to evaluate the investments?

Answers—p. 1084

Determine the appropriate action in each of the following managerial decision situations:

1. Packer Company is operating at 80% of its manufacturing capacity of 100,000 product units per year. A chain store has offered to buy an additional 10,000 units at $22 each and sell them to customers so as not to compete with Packer Co. The following data are available:

Costs at 80% Capacity	Per Unit	Total
Direct materials	$ 8.00	$ 640,000
Direct labor	7.00	560,000
Overhead (fixed and variable)	12.50	1,000,000
Totals	$27.50	$2,200,000

In producing 10,000 additional units, fixed overhead costs would remain at their current level but incremental variable overhead costs of $3 per unit would be incurred. Should the company accept or reject this order?

2. Green Company uses Part JR3 in manufacturing its products. It has always purchased this part from a supplier for $40 each. It recently upgraded its own manufacturing capabilities and has enough excess capacity (including trained workers) to begin manufacturing Part JR3 instead of buying it. The accountant has prepared the following cost projections of making the part, assuming that overhead is allocated to the part at the normal predetermined rate of 200% of direct labor cost.

Direct materials	$11
Direct labor	15
Overhead (fixed and variable) (200% of direct labor) ...	30
Total	$56

The required volume of output to produce the part will not require any incremental fixed overhead. Incremental variable overhead cost will be $17 per unit. Should the company make or buy this part?

3. Gold Company's manufacturing process causes a relatively large number of defective parts to be produced. The defective parts can be (a) sold for scrap, (b) melted to recover the recycled metal for reuse, or (c) reworked to be good units. Reworking defective parts reduces the output of other good units because no excess capacity exists. Each unit reworked means that one new unit cannot be produced. The following information reflects 500 defective parts currently available:

Proceeds of selling as scrap	$2,500
Additional cost of melting down defective parts	$ 400
Cost of purchases avoided by using recycled metal from defects	$4,800
Cost to rework 500 defective parts	
Direct materials	$ 0
Direct labor	1,500
Incremental overhead	1,750
Cost to produce 500 new parts	
Direct materials	$6,000
Direct labor	5,000
Incremental overhead	3,200
Selling price per good unit	$ 40

Should the company melt the parts, sell them as scrap, or rework them?

4. White Company can invest in one of two projects, TD1 or TD2. Each project requires an initial investment of $100,000 and produces the year-end cash inflows shown in the following table. Use

net present values to determine which project, if any, should be chosen. Assume that the company requires a 10% return from its investments.

| | Net Cash Flows | |
	TD1	TD2
Year 1	$ 20,000	$ 40,000
Year 2	30,000	40,000
Year 3	70,000	40,000
Totals	$120,000	$120,000

Planning the Solution

• Determine whether the Packer Company should accept the additional business by finding the incremental costs of materials, labor, and overhead that will be incurred if the order is accepted. Omit fixed costs that the order will not increase. If the incremental revenue exceeds the incremental cost, accept the order.

• Determine whether Green Company should make or buy the component by finding the incremental cost of making each unit. If the incremental cost exceeds the purchase price, the component should be purchased. If the incremental cost is less than the purchase price, make the component.

• Determine whether the Gold Company should sell the defective parts, melt them down and recycle the metal, or rework them. To compare the three choices, examine all costs incurred and benefits received from the alternatives in working with the 500 defective units versus the production of 500 new units. For the scrapping alternative, include the costs of producing 500 new units and subtract the $2,500 proceeds from selling the old ones. For the melting alternative, include the costs of melting the defective units, add the net cost of new materials in excess over those obtained from recycling, and add the direct labor and overhead costs. For the reworking alternative, add the costs of direct labor and incremental overhead. Select the alternative that has the lowest cost. The cost assigned to the 500 defective units is sunk and not relevant in choosing among the three alternatives.

• For White Co., compute the net present value of each investment using a 10% discount rate.

Solution to Demonstration Problem

1. This decision concerns accepting additional business or not. Since current unit costs are $27.50, it appears initially as if the offer to sell for $22 should be rejected, but the $27.50 cost includes fixed costs. When the analysis includes only *incremental* costs, the per unit cost is as shown in the table below. The offer should be accepted because it will produce $4 of additional profit per unit (computed as $22 price less $18 incremental cost), which yields a total profit of $40,000 for the 10,000 additional units.

Direct materials	$ 8.00
Direct labor	7.00
Variable overhead (given)	3.00
Total incremental cost	$18.00

2. For this make or buy decision, the analysis must not include the nonincremental overhead of $13 per unit ($30 − $17). When only the incremental overhead of $17 is included, the relevant unit cost of manufacturing the part is shown in the table below. It would be better to continue buying the part for $40 instead of making it for $43.

Direct materials	$11.00
Direct labor	15.00
Variable overhead	17.00
Total incremental cost	$43.00

3. The goal of this scrap or rework decision is to identify the alternative that produces the greatest net benefit to the company. To compare the alternatives, we determine the net cost of obtaining 500 marketable units as follows:

Incremental Cost to Produce 500 Marketable Units	Sell as Is	Melt and Recycle	Rework Units
Direct materials			
New materials	$ 6,000	$6,000	
Recycled (metal) materials		(4,800)	
Net materials cost		$1,200	
Melting costs		400	
Total direct materials cost	$ 6,000	$1,600	
Direct labor	5,000	5,000	$1,500
Incremental overhead	3,200	3,200	1,750
Cost to produce 500 marketable units	$14,200	$9,800	$3,250
Less proceeds of selling defects as scrap	(2,500)		
Opportunity costs*			$5,800
Net cost	$11,700	$9,800	$9,050

* The opportunity cost of $5,800 is the lost contribution margin from not being able to produce and sell 500 units because of reworking, computed as ($40 − $28.40) × 500 units.

The incremental cost of 500 marketable parts is smallest if the defects are reworked.

4. TD1:

	Net Cash Flows	Present Value of 1 at 10%	Present Value of Net Cash Flows
Year 1	$ 20,000	0.9091	$ 18,182
Year 2	30,000	0.8264	24,792
Year 3	70,000	0.7513	52,591
Totals	$120,000		$ 95,565
Amount invested			(100,000)
Net present value			$ (4,435)

TD2:

	Net Cash Flows	Present Value of 1 at 10%	Present Value of Net Cash Flows
Year 1	$ 40,000	0.9091	$ 36,364
Year 2	40,000	0.8264	33,056
Year 3	40,000	0.7513	30,052
Totals	$120,000		$ 99,472
Amount invested			(100,000)
Net present value			$ (528)

White Co. should not invest in either project. Both are expected to yield a negative net present value, and it should invest only in positive net present value projects.

Summary

C1 Explain the importance of capital budgeting. Capital budgeting is the process of analyzing alternative investments and deciding which assets to acquire or sell. It involves predicting the cash flows to be received from the alternatives, evaluating their merits, and then choosing which ones to pursue.

C2 Describe the selection of a hurdle rate for an investment. Top management should select the hurdle (discount) rate to use in evaluating capital investments. The required hurdle rate should be at least higher than the interest rate on money borrowed because the return on an investment must cover the interest and provide an additional profit to reward the company for risk.

C3 Describe the importance of relevant costs for short-term decisions. A company must rely on relevant costs pertaining to alternative courses of action rather than historical costs. Out-of-pocket expenses and opportunity costs are relevant because these are avoidable, whereas sunk costs are irrelevant because they result from past decisions and are therefore unavoidable. Managers must also consider the relevant benefits associated with alternative decisions.

A1 Evaluate short-term managerial decisions using relevant costs. Relevant costs are useful in making decisions such as accepting additional business, make or buy, and sell as is or process further. For example, in deciding whether to produce and sell additional units of product, the relevant factors are the incremental costs and incremental revenues from the additional volume.

A2 Analyze a capital investment project using break-even time. Break-even time (BET) is a method for evaluating capital investments by restating future cash flows in terms of their present values (discounting the cash flows) and then calculating the payback period using these present values of cash flows.

P1 Compute payback period and describe its use. One way to compare potential investments is to compute and compare their payback periods. The payback period is an estimate of the expected time before the cumulative net cash inflow from the investment equals its initial cost. A payback period analysis fails to reflect risk of the cash flows, differences in the timing of cash flows within the payback period, and cash flows that occur after the payback period.

P2 Compute accounting rate of return and explain its use. A project's accounting rate of return is computed by dividing the expected annual after-tax net income by the average amount of investment in the project. When the net cash flows are received evenly throughout each period and straight-line depreciation is used, the average investment is computed as the average of the investment's initial book value and its salvage value.

P3 Compute net present value and describe its use. An investment's net present value is determined by predicting the future cash flows that it is expected to generate, discounting them at a rate that represents an acceptable return and then by subtracting the initial cost of the investment from the sum of the present values. This technique can deal with any pattern of expected cash flows and applies a superior concept of return on investment.

P4 Compute internal rate of return and explain its use. The internal rate of return (IRR) is the discount rate that results in a zero net present value. When the cash flows are equal, we can compute the present value factor corresponding to the IRR by dividing the initial investment by the annual cash flows. We then use the annuity tables to determine the discount rate corresponding to this present value factor.

Guidance Answers to You Make the Call

Systems Manager Your dilemma is whether to abide by rules designed to prevent abuse or to bend those rules to acquire an investment that you believe will benefit the firm. You should not pursue this action because breaking up the order into small components is dishonest and there are consequences of being caught at a later stage. You should develop a proposal for the entire package and then do all you can to expedite its processing, particularly by pointing out its benefits. When faced with controls that are not working, there is rarely a reason to overcome its shortcomings by dishonesty. A direct assault on those limitations is more sensible and ethical.

Entrepreneur The banker is probably concerned that new products are risky and should therefore be evaluated using a higher rate of return. You should conduct a thorough technical analysis and obtain detailed market data and information about any similar products available in the market. These factors might provide sufficient information to support the use of a lower return. You must convince yourself that the risk level is consistent with the discount rate used.

You should also be confident that your company has the capacity and the resources to handle the new product.

Partner You should identify the differences between existing clients and this potential client. One key difference is that the restaurant business has additional components of inventory (groceries, vegetables, meats, etc.) and is likely to have a higher proportion of depreciable assets. These differences imply that the partner in charge of this client must spend more hours auditing the records and understanding the business, regulations and standards that pertain to the restaurant business. Such differences suggest that the partner must use a different "formula" for quoting a price to this potential client vis-a-vis current clients.

Investment Manager Since both the time value of money and recovery time are important, you should probably focus on either the payback period or break-even time. The latter method is superior because it accounts for the time value of money, which is an important consideration in this decision.

Guidance Answers to **Quick Checks**

1. (b)

2. A capital budgeting decision is difficult because (1) the outcome is uncertain, (2) large amounts of money are usually involved, (3) a long-term commitment is required and (4) the decision could be difficult or impossible to reverse.

3. (b)

4. Depreciation expense is subtracted from revenues in computing net income but does not use cash and should be added back to net income to compute net cash flows.

5. Not necessarily. One investment can continue to generate cash flows beyond the payback period for a longer time period than the other. The timing of their cash flows within the payback period also can differ.

6. (b): Annual average investment = ($180,000 + $15,000)/2
= $97,500
Accounting rate of return = $40,000/$97,500 = 41%

7. For this determination, we need to compare it to the returns expected from alternative investments with similar risk.

8. Project A has the higher net present value as shown:

		Project A		Project B	
Year	Present Value of 1 at 10%	Net Cash Flows	Present Value of Net Cash Flows	Net Cash Flows	Present Value of Net Cash Flows
1	0.9091	$12,000	$10,909	$ 4,500	$ 4,091
2	0.8264	8,500	7,024	8,500	7,024
3	0.7513	4,000	3,005	13,000	9,767
Totals		$24,500	$20,938	$26,000	$20,882
Amount invested			(20,000)		(20,000)
Net present value			**$ 938**		**$ 882**

9. No, the information is too limited to draw that conclusion. For example, one investment could have more risk than the other, or one could require a substantially larger initial investment.

10. (b) net present value.

11. (e): Variable costs per unit for this order of 200 units follow:

Direct materials ($37,500/7,500)	$ 5.00
Direct labor ($60,000/7,500)	8.00
Variable overhead [(0.30 × $20,000)/7,500]	0.80
Variable selling expenses [(0.60 × $25,000 × 0.5)/7,500]	1.00
Total variable costs per unit	$14.80

Cost to produce special order: (200 × $14.80) + $400
= $3,360.
Price per unit to earn $1,000: ($3,360 + $1,000)/200 = 21.80.

12. They are the additional (new) costs of accepting new business.

13. (d)

	Incremental benefits		Incremental costs
Alpha	$300 ($600 − $300)	>	$150 (given)
Beta	$450 ($900 − $450)	>	$300 (given)
Gamma	$150 ($425 − $275)	>	$125 (given)
Delta	$ 60 ($210 − $150)	<	$ 75 (given)

14. A sunk cost is *never* relevant because it results from a past decision and is already incurred.

15. Avoidable expenses are those that a company will not incur by eliminating a segment, whereas unavoidable expenses will continue even after a segment is eliminated.

16. (a)

Glossary

Accounting rate of return rate used to evaluate the acceptability of an investment; equals the after-tax periodic income from a project divided by the average investment in the asset; also called *rate of return on average investment*. (p. 1065).

Avoidable expense expense (or cost) that is relevant for decision making; expense that is not incurred if a department, product, or service is eliminated. (p. 1078).

Break-even time (BET) time-based measurement used to evaluate the acceptability of an investment; equals the time expected to pass before the present value of the net cash flows from an investment equals its initial cost. (p. 1080).

Capital budgeting process of analyzing alternative investments and deciding which assets to acquire or sell. (p. 1062).

Hurdle rate minimum acceptable rate of return (set by management) for an investment. (p. 1070).

Incremental cost additional cost incurred only if a company pursues a specific course of action. (p. 1073).

Internal rate of return (IRR) rate used to evaluate the acceptability of an investment; equals the rate that yields a net present value of zero for an investment. (p. 1069).

Net present value (NPV) dollar estimate of an asset's value to the company that is used to evaluate the acceptability of an investment; computed by discounting future cash flows from the investment at a satisfactory rate and then subtracting the initial cost of the investment. (p. 1067).

Opportunity cost cost that represents the potential benefits lost by choosing an alternative course of action. (p. 1072).

Out-of-pocket cost cost incurred or avoided as a result of management's decisions. (p. 1072).

Payback period (PBP) time-based measurement used to evaluate the acceptability of an investment; equals the time expected to pass before an investment's net cash flows equal its initial cost. (p. 1062).

Relevant benefits additional or incremental revenue generated by selecting a particular course of action over another. (p. 1073).

Sunk cost cost that cannot be avoided or changed because it arises from a past decision; irrelevant to current and future decisions. (p. 1072).

Unavoidable expense expense (or cost) that is not relevant for business decisions; an expense that would continue even if a department, product, or service is eliminated. (p. 1079).

Questions

1. What is capital budgeting?

2. Identify four reasons why capital budgeting decisions are risky.

3. Capital budgeting decisions require careful analysis because they are generally the _____ _____ and _____ decisions that management faces.

4. Identify two disadvantages of using the payback period for comparing investments.

5. Why is an investment more attractive if it has a shorter payback period?

6. What is the average amount invested in a machine during its predicted five-year life if it costs $200,000 and has a $20,000 salvage value? Assume that net income is received evenly throughout each year and straight-line depreciation is used.

7. If the present value of the expected net cash flows from a machine, discounted at 10%, exceeds the amount to be invested, what can you say about the expected rate of return on the investment? What can you say about the expected rate of return if the present value of the net cash flows, discounted at 10%, is less than the amount of the investment?

8. Why is the present value of $100 that you expect to receive one year from today worth less than $100 received today? What is the present value of $100 that you expect to receive one year from today, discounted at 12%?

9. Why should the required rate of return always be set higher than the rate at which money can be borrowed when making a typical capital budgeting decision?

10. Why does the use of the accelerated depreciation method (instead of straight line) for income tax reporting increase an investment's value?

11. What is an out-of-pocket cost? What is an opportunity cost? Are opportunity costs recorded in the accounting records?

12. Assume that **Gap** manufactures and sells 500,000 units of product at $30 per unit in domestic markets. The product costs $20 per unit to manufacture ($13 variable cost per unit, $7 fixed cost per unit). Can you describe a situation under which the company is willing to sell an additional 25,000 units of the product in an international market at $15 per unit?

13. Identify the incremental costs incurred by **Nike** for shipping one additional pair of running shoes to a retail sporting goods store along with the store's normal order of 1,000 pairs of running shoes.

14. Why are sunk costs irrelevant in deciding whether to sell a product in its present condition or to make it into a new product through additional processing?

QUICK STUDY

QS 26-1

Analyzing payback periods

Freeman Company is considering two alternative investments. The payback period is 3.5 years for Investment A and 4 years for Investment B. Why might Freeman's analysis of these two alternatives lead to the selection of B over A?

QS 26-2

Payback period

Brooks Company is considering an investment that requires immediate payment of $27,000 and provides expected cash inflows of $9,000 annually for four years. What is the investment's payback period?

QS 26-3

Computation of net present value

If Fox Company invests $50,000 today, it can expect to receive $10,000 at the end of each year for the next seven years plus an extra $6,000 at the end of the seventh year. What is the net present value of this investment assuming a required 10% return on investments?

QS 26-4

Computation of accounting rate of return

Pad Company is considering an investment that is expected to generate an average net income after taxes of $1,950 for three years. The investment costs $45,000 and has an estimated $6,000 salvage value. Compute the accounting rate of return for this investment.

Byte Company can sell all the units of computer memory X and Y that it can produce, but it has limited production capacity. It can produce two units of X per hour *or* three units of Y per hour, and it has 4,000 production hours available. Contribution margin is $5 for Product X and $4 for Product Y. What is the most profitable sales mix for Byte Company?

QS 26-5

Selection of sales mix

Marker Company incurs a $9 per unit cost for Product A, which it currently manufactures and sells for $13.50 per unit. Instead of manufacturing and selling this product, Marker can purchase Product B for $5 per unit and sell it for $12 per unit. If it does so, unit sales would remain unchanged and $5 of the $9 per unit costs assigned to Product A would be eliminated. Should Marker continue to manufacture Product A or purchase Product B for resale?

QS 26-6

Analysis of incremental costs

Cut-To-Fit, a shoe manufacturer, is evaluating the costs and benefits of new equipment that would custom fit each pair of athletic shoes. The customer would have his/her foot scanned by digital computer equipment; this information would be used to cut the raw materials to provide the customer a perfect fit. The new equipment costs $150,000 and is expected to generate an additional $52,500 in cash flows for five years. A bank will make a $150,000 loan to Cut-To-Fit at a 10% interest rate for this equipment's purchase. Use the following table to determine the break-even time for this equipment.

QS 26-7

Computation of break-even time

Year	Cash Flows*	Present Value of 1 at 10%	Present Value of Cash Flows	Cumulative Present Value of Cash Flows
0	$(150,000)	1.0000		
1	52,500	0.9091		
2	52,500	0.8264		
3	52,500	0.7513		
4	52,500	0.6830		
5	52,500	0.6209		

* All cash flows occur at year-end.

Compute the payback period for each of these two separate investments:

a. A new control system for an existing machine is expected to cost $520,000 and have a useful life of six years. The system yields an incremental after-tax income of $150,000 each year after deducting its straight-line depreciation. The predicted salvage value of the system is $10,000.

b. A machine costs $380,000, has a $20,000 salvage value, is expected to last eight years, and will generate an after-tax income of $60,000 per year after straight-line depreciation.

EXERCISES

Exercise 26-1
Payback period computation; even cash flows

Weyer Company is considering the purchase of an asset for $180,000. The asset is expected to produce the following net cash flows:

	Year 1	Year 2	Year 3	Year 4	Year 5	Total
Net cash flows	$60,000	$40,000	$70,000	$120,000	$38,000	$328,000

The cash flows occur evenly throughout each year. Compute the payback period for this investment.

Exercise 26-2
Payback period computation; uneven cash flows

Check   3.083 years

A machine can be purchased for $150,000 and used for 5 years, yielding the following net incomes:

	Year 1	Year 2	Year 3	Year 4	Year 5
Net incomes	$10,000	$25,000	$50,000	$37,500	$100,000

In projecting net incomes, double-declining balance depreciation is deducted, using a 5-year life and a zero salvage value. Compute the machine's payback period. Ignore taxes.

Exercise 26-3
Payback period computation; declining-balance depreciation

Check   2.265 years

Exercise 26-4
Accounting rate of
return

A machine costs $700,000 and is expected to yield an after-tax net income of $52,000 each year. Management predicts this machine has a 10-year service life and a $100,000 salvage value. Compute the accounting rate of return for this machine.

Exercise 26-5
Payback period and
accounting rate of return
on investment

Lee Co. is considering the purchase of equipment that would allow the company to add a new product to its line. The equipment is expected to cost $360,000 with a six-year life and no salvage value. It will be depreciated on a straight-line basis. The company expects to sell 144,000 units of the equipment's product each year. The expected annual income related to this equipment follows:

Sales	$225,000
Costs	
Materials, labor, and overhead (except depreciation) . . .	120,000
Depreciation on new equipment	30,000
Selling and administrative expenses	22,500
Total costs and expenses	$172,500
Pretax income	$ 52,500
Income taxes (30%)	15,750
Net income	$ 36,750

Check (a) 5.39 years (b) 20.42%

Compute the (a) payback period and (b) accounting rate of return for this equipment.

Exercise 26-6
Computing net present
value

After evaluating the risk of the investment described in Exercise 26-5, the Lee Co. concludes that it must earn at least an 8% return on this investment. Compute the net present value of this investment.

Exercise 26-7
Computation and
interpretation of net present
value and internal rate of
return

Badger Company can invest in each of three cheese-making projects: C1, C2, and C3. Each project requires an initial investment of $228,000 and would yield the following annual cash flows:

	C1	C2	C3
Year 1	$ 12,000	$ 96,000	$180,000
Year 2	108,000	96,000	60,000
Year 3	168,000	96,000	48,000
Totals	$288,000	$288,000	$288,000

(1) Assuming that the company requires a 12% return from its investments, use net present value to determine which projects, if any, should be acquired. (2) Using the answer from (1), explain whether the internal rate of return is higher or lower than 12% for project C2? (3) Compute the internal rate of return for project C2.

Check (3) IRR = 13%

Exercise 26-8
Decision to accept additional
business or not

Farnsworth Co. expects to sell 150,000 units of its product in the next period with the following results:

Sales (150,000 units)	$2,250,000
Costs and expenses	
Direct materials	300,000
Direct labor	600,000
Overhead	150,000
Selling expenses	225,000
Administrative expenses	385,500
Total costs and expenses	$1,660,500
Net income	$ 589,500

The company has an opportunity to sell 15,000 additional units at a price of $12 per unit. The additional sales would not affect the expected sales. Direct materials and labor costs would be the same for the additional units as they are for the regular units. However, the additional volume would create the following incremental costs: (1) total overhead would increase by 15% and (2) administrative expenses would increase by $64,500. Prepare an analysis to determine whether the company should accept or reject the offer to sell additional units at the reduced price of $12 per unit.

Check   Income increase, $3,000

Michaels Company currently manufactures one of its crucial parts at a cost of $4.45 per unit. This cost is based on a normal production rate of 65,000 units per year. Variable costs are $1.95 per unit, fixed costs related to making this part are $65,000 per year, and allocated fixed costs are $58,500 per year. Allocated fixed costs are unavoidable whether the company makes or buys the part. Michaels is considering buying the part from a supplier that has quoted a price of $3.50 per unit guaranteed for a three-year period. Should the company continue to manufacture the part, or should it buy the part from the outside supplier? Support your answer with analyses.

Exercise 26-9
Make or buy decision

Check $35,750 increased costs to buy

Kim Company has already manufactured 28,000 units of Product A at a cost of $28 per unit. The 28,000 units can be sold at this stage for $700,000. Alternatively, they can be further processed at a total additional cost of $420,000 and be converted into 5,600 units of Product B and 11,200 units of Product C. Selling price for Product B is $105 per unit and for Product C is $70 per unit. Prepare an analysis that shows whether the 28,000 units of Product A should be processed further or not.

Exercise 26-10
Sell or process decision

Suresh Co. expects its five departments to yield the following income for next year:

Exercise 26-11
Analysis of income effects from eliminating departments

	A	B	C	D	E	F
1						
2		**Dept. M**	**Dept. N**	**Dept. O**	**Dept. P**	**Dept. T**
3	Sales	$63,000	$ 35,000	$56,000	$42,000	$ 28,000
4	Expenses:					
5	Avoidable	9,800	36,400	22,400	14,000	37,800
6	Unavoidable	51,800	12,600	4,200	29,400	9,800
7	Total expenses	$61,600	$ 49,000	$26,600	$43,400	$ 47,600
8	Net income (loss)	$ 1,400	$(14,000)	$29,400	$ (1,400)	$(19,600)
9						

Recompute and prepare the departmental income statements (including a combined total column) for the company under each of the following separate scenarios: Management (1) does not eliminate any department, (2) eliminates departments with expected net losses, and (3) eliminates departments with sales dollars that are less than avoidable expenses. Explain your answers to parts (2) and (3).

Check   Total income (loss):
(2) $(21,000), (3) $7,000

Dual Company owns a machine that can produce two specialized products. Production time for Product TLX is two units per hour and for Product MTV is five units per hour. The capacity of the machine is 2,750 hours per year. Both products are sold to a single customer who has agreed to buy all of the company's output up to a maximum of 4,700 units of Product TLX and 2,500 units of Product MTV. Selling prices and variable costs per unit to produce the products follow:

Exercise 26-12
Sales mix determination and analysis

	Product TLX	Product MTV
Selling price per unit	$15.00	$9.50
Variable costs per unit	4.80	5.50

Determine (a) the most profitable sales mix for the company and (b) the contribution margin that results from that sales mix.

Check   (b) $55,940

This chapter explained two methods to evaluate investments using recovery time, the payback period and break-even time (BET). Refer to QS 26-7 and (1) compute the recovery time for both the payback period and break-even time, (2) discuss the advantage(s) of break-even time over the payback period, and (3) list two conditions under which payback period and break-even time are similar.

Exercise 26-13
Comparison of payback and BET

Problem Set A

Problem 26-1A

Computation of payback period, accounting rate of return, and net present value

Emerson Company is planning to add a new product to its line. To manufacture this product, the company needs to buy a new machine at a cost of $480,000. This machine is expected to have a four-year life and a $20,000 salvage value. All sales are for cash, and all costs are out of pocket except for depreciation on the new machine. Additional information includes the following:

Expected annual sales of new product	$1,840,000
Expected annual costs of new product	
Direct materials	480,000
Direct labor	672,000
Overhead excluding straight-line depreciation on new machine	336,000
Selling and administrative expenses	160,000
Income taxes	30%

Required

1. Compute straight-line depreciation for each year of this new machine's life.
2. Determine expected net income and net cash flow for each year of this machine's life.
3. Compute the payback period for this machine, assuming that cash flows occur evenly throughout each year.

Check (4) 21.56%

4. Compute the accounting rate of return for this machine, assuming that income is earned evenly throughout each year.

Check (5) $107,356

5. Compute the net present value for this machine using a discount rate of 7% and assuming that cash flows occur at each year-end. (*Hint:* Salvage value is a cash inflow at the end of the asset's life.)

Problem 26-2A

Analysis and computation of payback period, accounting rate of return, and net present value

Pleasant Company has an opportunity to invest in one of two new projects. Project Y requires an investment of $350,000 for new machinery having a four-year life and no salvage value. Project Z requires an investment of $350,000 for new machinery having a three-year life and no salvage value. The two projects yield the following predicted annual results:

	Project Y	Project Z
Sales	$350,000	$280,000
Expenses		
Direct materials	49,000	35,000
Direct labor	70,000	42,000
Overhead including depreciation	126,000	126,000
Selling and administrative expenses	25,000	25,000
Total expenses	$270,000	$228,000
Pretax income	$ 80,000	$ 52,000
Income taxes (30%)	24,000	15,600
Net income	$ 56,000	$ 36,400

The company uses straight-line depreciation, and cash flows occur evenly throughout each year.

Required

Preparation Component

1. Compute the annual expected net cash flows for each project.
2. Determine the payback period for each project.

Check For Project Y: (2) 2.44 years, (3) 32%, (4) $125,286

3. Compute the accounting rate of return for each project.
4. Determine the net present value for each project using 8% as the discount rate. For part (4) only, assume that cash flows occur at each year-end.

Analysis Component

5. Identify the project you would recommend to management and explain your choice.

Flight Corporation is considering a new project requiring a $90,000 investment in special test equipment with no salvage value. The project would produce $66,000 of pretax income before depreciation at the end of each of the next six years. The company's income tax rate is 40%. In compiling its tax return and computing its income tax payments, the company can choose between the two alternative depreciation schedules shown in the table.

Problem 26-3A
Computation of cash flows and net present values with alternative depreciation methods

	Straight-Line Depreciation	MACRS Depreciation*
Year 1	$ 9,000	$18,000
Year 2	18,000	28,800
Year 3	18,000	17,280
Year 4	18,000	10,368
Year 5	18,000	10,368
Year 6	9,000	5,184
Totals	$90,000	$90,000

* The modified accelerated cost recovery system (MACRS) for depreciation is discussed in Chapter 11.

Required

Preparation Component

1. Prepare a five-column table that reports amounts (assuming use of straight-line depreciation) for each of the following items for each of the six years: (a) pretax income before depreciation, (b) straight-line depreciation expense, (c) taxable income, (d) income taxes, and (e) net cash flow. Net cash flow equals the amount of income before depreciation minus the income taxes.

2. Prepare a five-column table that reports amounts (assuming use of MACRS depreciation) for each of the following items for each of the six years: (a) pretax income before depreciation, (b) MACRS depreciation expense, (c) taxable income, (d) income taxes, and (e) net cash flow. Net cash flow equals the amount of income before depreciation minus the income taxes.

3. Compute the net present value of the investment if straight-line depreciation is used. Use 10% as the discount rate.

4. Compute the net present value of the investment if MACRS depreciation is used. Use 10% as the discount rate.

Check Net present value: (3) $108,518, (4) $110,303

Analysis Component

5. Explain why the MACRS depreciation method increases this project's net present value.

Design Products manufactures underwater markers that it sells to wholesalers at $6 per package. The company manufactures and sells approximately 400,000 packages of markers each year to deep-sea treasure hunting teams. Annual costs for the production and sale of this quantity are shown in the table.

Problem 26-4A
Analysis of income effects of additional business

Direct materials	$ 576,000
Direct labor	144,000
Overhead	320,000
Selling expenses	150,000
Administrative expenses	100,000
Total costs and expenses	$1,290,000

A new wholesaler has offered to buy 50,000 packages for $5.20 each. These markers would be marketed under the wholesaler's name and would not affect Design Products' sales through its normal channels. A study of the costs of this additional business reveals the following:

- Direct materials costs are 100% variable.

- Per unit direct labor costs for the additional units would be 50% higher than normal because their production would require overtime pay at one-and-one-half times the usual labor rate.

- One-fourth of the normal annual overhead costs are fixed at any production level from 350,000 to 500,000 units. The remaining three-fourths of the annual overhead cost is variable with volume.

- Accepting the new business would involve no additional selling expenses.
- Accepting the new business would increase administrative expenses by a fixed amount of $5,000.

Required

Prepare a three-column comparative income statement that shows the following:

1. Annual operating income without the special order (column 1).
2. Annual operating income received from the new business only (column 2).
3. Combined annual operating income from normal business and the new business (column 3).

Check Operating income: (1) $1,110,000, (2) $126,000

Problem 26-5A

Analysis of sales mix strategies

Packer Company is capable of producing two products, G and B, with the same machine in its factory. The following per unit information is known:

	Product G	Product B
Selling price per unit	$120	$160
Variable costs per unit	40	90
Contribution margin per unit	$ 80	$ 70
Machine hours to produce 1 unit	0.4 hours	1.0 hours
Maximum unit sales per month	600 units	200 units

The company presently operates the machine for a single eight-hour shift for 22 working days each month. Management is thinking about operating the machine for two shifts, which will increase the machine's availability by another eight hours per day for 22 days per month. This change would require additional fixed costs of $15,000 per month.

Required

1. Determine the contribution margin per machine hour that each product generates.
2. How many units of G and B should the company produce if it continues to operate with only one shift? How much total contribution margin is produced each month with this mix?
3. If the company adds another shift, how many units of G and B should it produce? How much total contribution margin would this mix produce each month? Should the company add the new shift?
4. Suppose that the company determines that it can increase the maximum sales of Product G to 700 units per month by spending $12,000 per month in marketing efforts. Should the company pursue this strategy and the double shift?

Check Units of G: (2) 440, (3) 600, (4) 700

Problem 26-6A

Analysis of possible elimination of a department

Home Appliance Company's management is trying to decide whether to eliminate Department 200, which has produced losses or low profits for several years. The company's 2002 departmental income statement shows the following:

HOME APPLIANCE COMPANY Departmental Income Statement For Year Ended December 31, 2002	Dept. 100	Dept. 200	Combined
Sales	$436,000	$290,000	$726,000
Cost of goods sold	262,000	207,000	469,000
Gross profit	$174,000	$ 83,000	$257,000
Operating expenses			
Direct expenses			
Advertising	17,000	12,000	29,000
Store supplies used	4,000	3,800	7,800
Depreciation—Store equipment	5,000	3,300	8,300
Total direct expenses	$ 26,000	$ 19,100	$ 45,100

[continued on next page]

[continued from previous page]

HOME APPLIANCE COMPANY Departmental Income Statement For Year Ended December 31, 2002			
Allocated expenses			
Sales salaries	65,000	39,000	104,000
Rent expense	9,440	4,720	14,160
Bad debts expense	9,900	8,100	18,000
Office salary	18,720	12,480	31,200
Insurance expense	2,000	1,100	3,100
Miscellaneous office expenses	2,400	1,600	4,000
Total allocated expenses	$107,460	$ 67,000	$174,460
Total expenses	$133,460	$ 86,100	$219,560
Net income (loss)	$ 40,540	$ (3,100)	$ 37,440

In analyzing whether to eliminate Department 200, management considers the following items:

a. The company has one office worker who earns $600 per week, or $31,200 per year, and four sales-clerks who each earn $500 per week, or $26,000 per year.

b. The full salaries of two sales clerks are charged to Department 100. The full salary of one sales clerk is charged to Department 200. The fourth clerk works half-time in both departments, and her salary is divided evenly between the two departments.

c. Eliminating Department 200 would avoid the sales salaries and the office salary currently allocated to it. However, management prefers another plan. Two sales clerks have indicated that they will be quitting soon. Management thinks that their work can be done by the other two clerks if the one office worker works in sales half-time. Eliminating Department 200 will allow this shift of duties. If this change is implemented, half the office worker's salary would be reported as sales salaries and half would be reported as office salary.

d. The store building is rented under a long-term lease that cannot be changed. Therefore, Department 100 will use the space and equipment currently used by Department 200.

e. Closing Department 200 will eliminate: its expenses for advertising, bad debts, and store supplies; 70% of the insurance expense allocated to it to cover its merchandise inventory; and 25% of the miscellaneous office expenses presently allocated to it.

Required

Preparation Component

1. Prepare a three-column report that lists items and amounts for (a) the company's total expenses (including cost of goods sold)—column 1, (b) the expenses that would be eliminated by closing Department 200—column 2, and (c) the expenses that will continue—column 3.

Check (1) Total expenses: (a) $688,560, (b) $284,070

2. Prepare a forecasted annual income statement for the company reflecting the elimination of Department 200 assuming that it will not affect Department 100's sales and gross profit. The statement should reflect the reassignment of the office worker to one-half time as a salesclerk.

Check (2) Forecasted net income without Department 200, $31,510

Analysis Component

3. Reconcile the company's combined net income with the forecasted net income assuming that Department 200 is eliminated (list both items and amounts). Analyze the reconciliation and explain why you think the department should or should not be eliminated.

Problem Set B

Problem 26-1B

Computation of payback period, accounting rate of return, and net present value

Continental Company is planning to add a new product to its line. To manufacture this product, the company needs to buy a new machine at a cost of $300,000. This machine is expected to have a four-year life and a $20,000 salvage value. All sales are for cash and all costs are out-of-pocket, except for depreciation on the new machine. Additional information includes the following:

Expected annual sales of new product	$1,150,000
Expected annual costs of new product	
Direct materials	300,000
Direct labor	420,000
Overhead excluding straight-line depreciation on new machine . .	210,000
Selling and administrative expenses	100,000
Income taxes	30%

Required

1. Compute straight-line depreciation for each year of this new machine's life.
2. Determine expected net income and net cash flow for each year of this machine's life.
3. Compute the payback period for this machine, assuming that cash flows occur evenly throughout each year.

Check (4) 21.88%

4. Compute the accounting rate of return for this machine, assuming that income is earned evenly throughout each year.

Check (5) $70,915

5. Compute the net present value for this machine using a discount rate of 7% and assuming that cash flows occur at each year-end. (*Hint:* Salvage value is a cash inflow at the end of the asset's life.)

Problem 26-2B

Analysis and computation of payback period, accounting rate of return, and net present value

Green Company has an opportunity to invest in one of two projects. Project A requires an investment of $240,000 for new machinery having a four-year life and no salvage value. Project B also requires an investment of $240,000 for new machinery having a three-year life and no salvage value. The two projects yield the following predicted annual results:

	Project A	Project B
Sales	$250,000	$200,000
Expenses		
Direct materials	35,000	25,000
Direct labor	50,000	30,000
Overhead including depreciation	90,000	90,000
Selling and administrative expenses	18,000	18,000
Total expenses	$193,000	$163,000
Pretax income	57,000	$ 37,000
Income taxes (30%)	17,100	11,100
Net income	$ 39,900	$ 25,900

The company uses straight-line depreciation, and cash flows occur evenly throughout each year.

Required

Preparation Component

1. Compute the annual expected net cash flows for each project.
2. Determine the payback period for each project.
3. Compute the accounting rate of return for each project.

Check For Project A: (2) 2.40 years, (3) 33.25%, (4) $90,879

4. Determine the net present value for each project using 8% as the discount rate. For part (4) only, assume that cash flows occur at each year-end.

Analysis Component

5. Identify the project you would recommend to management and explain your choice.

Grill Corporation is considering a new project requiring a $30,000 investment in an asset having no salvage value. The project would produce $12,000 of pretax income before depreciation at the end of each of the next six years. The company's income tax rate is 40%. In compiling its tax return and computing its income tax payments, the company can choose between two alternative depreciation schedules as shown.

Problem 26-3B
Computation of cash flows and net present values with alternative depreciation methods   **P3**

Required

Preparation Component

1. Prepare a five-column table that reports amounts (assuming use of straight-line depreciation) for each of the following items for each of the six years: (a) pretax income before depreciation, (b) straight-line depreciation expense, (c) taxable income, (d) income taxes, and (e) net cash flow. Net cash flow equals the amount of income before depreciation minus the income taxes.

	Straight-Line Depreciation	MACRS Depreciation*
Year 1	$ 3,000	$ 6,000
Year 2	6,000	9,600
Year 3	6,000	5,760
Year 4	6,000	3,456
Year 5	6,000	3,456
Year 6	3,000	1,728
Totals	$30,000	$30,000

* The modified accelerated cost recovery system (MACRS) for depreciation is discussed in Chapter 11.

2. Prepare a five-column table that reports amounts (assuming use of MACRS depreciation) for each of the following items for each of the six years: (a) income before depreciation, (b) MACRS depreciation expense, (c) taxable income, (d) income taxes, and (e) net cash flow. Net cash flow equals the amount of income before depreciation minus the income taxes.

3. Compute the net present value of the investment if straight-line depreciation is used. Use 10% as the discount rate.

4. Compute the net present value of the investment if MACRS depreciation is used. Use 10% as the discount rate.

Check   Net present value:
(3) $10,041, (4) $10,635

Analysis Component

5. Explain why the MACRS depreciation method increases the net present value of this project.

Wire Company manufactures parts that it sells to wholesalers in the local area at $4 per unit. The company manufactures and sells approximately 300,000 units each month. Monthly costs for the production and sale of this quantity follow:

Problem 26-4B
Analysis of income effects of additional business

Direct materials	$384,000
Direct labor	96,000
Overhead	288,000
Selling expenses	120,000
Administrative expenses	80,000
Total costs and expenses	$968,000

A new out-of-state distributor has offered to buy 50,000 units next month for $3.44 each. These units would be marketed in other states and would not affect Wire's sales through its normal channels. A study of the costs of this new business reveals the following:

• Direct materials costs are 100% variable.

• Per unit direct labor costs for the additional units would be 50% higher than normal because their production would require time-and-a-half overtime pay to meet the distributor's deadline.

• One-fourth of the normal annual overhead costs are fixed at any production level from 250,000 to 400,000 units. The remaining three-fourths is variable with volume.

• Accepting the new business would involve no additional selling expenses.

• Accepting the new business would increase administrative expenses by a fixed amount of $4,000.

Required

Prepare a three-column comparative income statement that shows the following:

1. Monthly operating income without the special order (column 1).

2. Monthly operating income received from the new business only (column 2).

3. Combined monthly operating income from normal business and the new business (column 3).

Check   Operating income:
(1) $232,000, (2) $44,000

Problem 26-5B

Analysis of sales mix strategies

Branck Company is capable of producing two products, Product 23 and Product 47, with the same machine in its factory. The following per unit information is known:

	Product G	Product B
Selling price per unit	$ 60	$ 80
Variable costs per unit	20	45
Contribution margin per unit	$ 40	$ 35
Machine hours to produce 1 unit	0.4 hours	1.0 hours
Maximum unit sales per month	550 units	175 units

The company presently operates the machine for a single eight-hour shift for 22 working days each month. Management is thinking about operating the machine for two shifts, which will increase the machine's availability by another eight hours per day for 22 days per month. This change would require additional fixed costs of $3,250 per month.

Required

1. Determine the contribution margin per machine hour that each product generates.

2. How many units of Product 23 and Product 47 should the company produce if it continues to operate with only one shift? How much total contribution margin is produced each month with this mix?

Check Units of Product 23:
(2) 440, (3) 550, (4) 675

3. If the company adds another shift, how many units of Product 23 and Product 47 should it produce? How much total contribution margin would this mix produce each month? Should the company add the new shift? Explain.

4. Suppose that the company determines that it can increase the maximum sales of Product 23 to 675 units per month by spending $4,500 per month in marketing efforts. Should the company pursue this strategy and the double shift? Explain.

Problem 26-6B

Analysis of possible elimination of a department

TeeTime Company's management is trying to decide whether to eliminate Department Z, which has produced low profits or losses for several years. The company's 2002 departmental income statement shows the following:

TEETIME COMPANY Departmental Income Statement For Year Ended December 31, 2002	Dept. A	Dept. Z	Combined
Sales	$700,000	$175,000	$875,000
Cost of goods sold	461,300	125,100	586,400
Gross profit	$238,700	$ 49,900	$288,600
Operating expenses			
Direct expenses			
Advertising	27,000	3,000	30,000
Store supplies used	5,600	1,400	7,000
Depreciation—Store equipment	14,000	7,000	21,000
Total direct expenses	$ 46,600	$ 11,400	$ 58,000
Allocated expenses			
Sales salaries	70,200	23,400	93,600
Rent expense	22,080	5,520	27,600
Bad debts expense	21,000	4,000	25,000
Office salary	20,800	5,200	26,000
Insurance expense	4,200	1,400	5,600
Miscellaneous office expenses	1,700	2,500	4,200
Total allocated expenses	$139,980	$ 42,020	$182,000
Total expenses	$186,580	$ 53,420	$240,000
Net income (loss)	$ 52,120	$ (3,520)	$ 48,600

In analyzing whether to eliminate Department Z, management considers the following items:

a. The company has one office worker who earns $500 per week or $26,000 per year and four sales-clerks who each earn $450 per week or $23,400 per year.

b. The full salaries of three salesclerks are charged to Department A. The full salary of one sales-clerk is charged to Department Z.

c. Eliminating Department Z would avoid the sales salaries and the office salary currently allocated to it. However, management prefers another plan. Two salesclerks have indicated that they will be quitting soon. Management thinks that their work can be done by the two remaining clerks if the one office worker works in sales half time. Eliminating Department Z will allow this shift of du-ties. If this change is implemented, half the office worker's salary would be reported as sales salaries and half would be reported as office salary.

d. The store building is rented under a long-term lease that cannot be changed. Therefore, Department A will use the space and equipment currently used by Department Z.

e. Closing Department Z will eliminate: its expenses for advertising, bad debts, and store supplies; 65% of the insurance expense allocated to it to cover its merchandise inventory; and 30% of the miscellaneous office expenses presently allocated to it.

Required

Preparation Component

1. Prepare a three-column report that lists items and amounts for (a) the company's total expenses (including cost of goods sold)—column 1, (b) the expenses that would be eliminated by closing Department Z—column 2, and (c) the expenses that will continue—column 3.

2. Prepare a forecasted annual income statement for the company reflecting the elimination of Department Z assuming that it will not affect Department A's sales and gross profit. The state-ment should reflect the reassignment of the office worker to one-half time as a salesclerk.

Analysis Component

3. Reconcile the company's combined net income with the forecasted net income assuming that Department Z is eliminated (list both items and amounts). Analyze the reconciliation and explain why you think the department should or should not be eliminated.

Check (1) Total expenses:
(a) $826,400, (b) $181,960

Check (2) Forecasted net income
without Department Z, $55,560

Beyond the Numbers

BTN 26-1 Locate the notes for **Nike**'s annual report in Appendix A and answer the following.

Reporting in Action

Required

1. Locate note 1 and identify the depreciation methods Nike used for property, plant, and equipment.

2. Locate the note that reports the percent of gross property, plant, and equipment that consists of machinery and equipment for May 2000 and 1999. Report these amounts.

3. Using your answers to parts (1) and (2), why do you think that Nike uses its chosen depreciation method for its machinery and equipment when this method reduces Nike's reported earnings in the early years of the investment period? (Hint: Consider taxes and cash flows.)

C1 A1 P3

NIKE

Swoosh Ahead

4. Access Nike's annual report information for a fiscal year ending after May 31, 2000, from either its Web site [**www.nike.com**] or the SEC's EDGAR database [**www.sec.gov**]. If the tax laws do not change for depreciation, do you expect Nike to follow the same depreciation method in sub-sequent years for machinery and equipment? Check your response with Nike's current statements.

BTN 26-2 **Reebok** and **Nike** sell several different products; some are profitable but others are not. Teams of employees in each company make advertising, investment, and product mix decisions. A certain portion of advertising for both companies is on a local basis to a target audience.

Comparative Analysis

C3

Required

1. Find one major advertisement of a product or group of products for each company in your local newspaper. Contact the newspaper and ask the approximate cost of this ad space (for example, cost of one page or one-half page of advertising).
2. Estimate how many products must be sold from this advertisement to justify its cost. Begin by taking the selling price of the product advertised for each company and assume a 20% contribution margin.
3. Prepare a one-half page memorandum explaining the importance of effective advertising when making a product mix decision. Be prepared to present your ideas in class.

Ethics Challenge

BTN 26-3   A consultant commented that "too often the numbers look good but feel bad." This comment stems from estimation error commonly found in capital budgeting proposals relating to the number of years that a project is assumed to generate cash flows. This error often has three reasons. First, reliably predicting cash flows several years into the future is very difficult. Second, the present value of cash flows many years into the future (say, beyond 10 years) is often very small. Third, it is difficult for personal biases and expectations not to unduly influence present value computations.

Required

1. Compute the present value of $100 to be received in 10 years assuming a 12% discount rate.
2. Why is understanding the three reasons mentioned for estimation errors important when evaluating investment projects? Link this response to your answer for part (1).

Communicating in Practice

BTN 26-4   Payback period, accounting rate of return, net present value, and internal rate of return are common techniques used to evaluate capital investment opportunities. Assume that your manager asks you to identify the type of measurement basis each perspective offers and to list the advantages and disadvantages of each. Present your response in memorandum format of less than one page.

Taking It to the Net

BTN 26-5   Capital budgeting is an important issue for every organization, particularly as it relates to an organization's future. The U.S. set up a commission to study capital budgeting at the federal government level. Access the commission's report from the following Web site: http://www.whitehouse.gov/pcscb/.

Required

1. Does the commission's notion of *capital* for federal government differ from that used by the private sector?
2. Are the investment analysis techniques explained in the chapter relevant to the government?

Teamwork in Action

BTN 26-6   Break into teams and identify four reasons that an international airline such as United, Delta, or American would invest in a project when its direct analysis using both payback period and net present value indicate it to be a poor investment. (Hint: Think about qualitative factors.) Provide an example of an investment project supporting your answer.

Business Week Activity

BTN 26-7   Outsourcing is common practice for many firms. Given the changes in the business environment, both firms that outsource portions of their operations and those that provide these services must identify their relevant costs. Read "The Web of Quality" in *Business Week*, June 26, 2000.

Required

1. Why is product/service quality important for effective management decision making?
2. How does quality affect business costs?

BTN 26-8   Paula Ali and her husband Michael Richards are business partners. Their company offers business services including preparing business plans, offering accounting and legal advice, and consulting on marketing and sales strategies. Ali and Richards believe that their company has expanded into too many services and they are considering eliminating some.

Entrepreneurial Decision

Required

1. Why might Ali and Richards want to restrict themselves to a smaller set of services?

2. How should they go about deciding which services to eliminate?

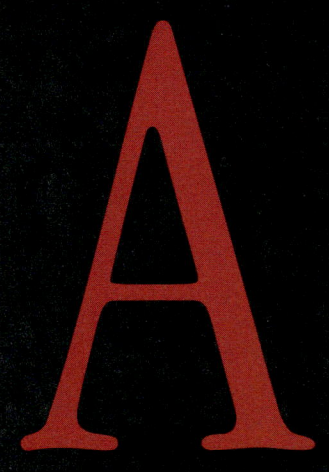

Financial Statement Information

This appendix includes financial information for (1) Nike, (2) Reebok, and (3) Gap. This information is taken from their annual reports. An **annual report** is a summary of a company's financial results for the year, along with its current financial condition and future plans. This report is directed to external users of financial information, but it also affects the actions and decisions of internal users.

A company uses an annual report to showcase itself and its products. Many annual reports include attractive photos, diagrams, and illustrations related to the company. The primary objective of annual reports, however, is the *financial section,* which communicates much information about a company, with most data drawn from the accounting information system. The layout of an annual report's financial section is fairly established and typically includes the following:

- Letter to Shareholders
- Financial History and Highlights
- Management Discussion and Analysis
- Management's Report
- Report of Independent Accountants (Auditor's Report)
- Financial Statements
- Notes to Financial Statements
- List of Directors and Officers

This appendix provides the financial statements for Nike (plus selected notes), Reebok, and Gap. The appendix is organized as follows:

- Nike   A-2 through A-10
- Reebok   A-11 through A-14
- Gap   A-15 through A-18

Many assignments at the end of each chapter refer to information in this appendix. We encourage readers to spend time with these assignments; they are especially useful in showing the relevance and diversity of financial accounting and reporting.

Special note: The SEC maintains the EDGAR (**E**lectronic **D**ata **G**athering, **A**nalysis, and **R**etrieval) database at **www.sec.gov.** The **Form 10-K** is the annual report form for most companies. It provides electronically accessible information. The **Form 10-KSB** is the annual report form filed by "small businesses." It requires slightly less information than the Form 10-K. Both forms must be filed within 90 days after the company's fiscal year-end. (Forms 10-K405, 10-KT, 10-KT405, and 10-KSB405 are slight variations of the usual form due to certain regulations or rules.)

NIKE

Financial History

(in millions, except per share data, financial ratios and number of shareholders)

YEAR ENDED MAY 31,	2000	1999	1998	1997	1996	1995
Revenues	$8,995.1	$8,776.9	$9,553.1	$9,186.5	$6,470.6	$4,760.8
Gross margin	3,591.3	3,283.4	3,487.6	3,683.5	2,563.9	1,895.6
Gross margin %	39.9%	37.4%	36.5%	40.1%	39.6%	39.8%
Restructuring charge	(2.5)	45.1	129.9	—	—	—
Net income	579.1	451.4	399.6	795.8	553.2	399.7
Basic earnings per common share	2.10	1.59	1.38	2.76	1.93	1.38
Diluted earnings per common share	2.07	1.57	1.35	2.68	1.88	1.36
Average common shares outstanding	275.7	283.3	288.7	288.4	286.6	289.6
Diluted average common shares outstanding	279.4	288.3	295.0	297.0	293.6	294.0
Cash dividends declared						
per common share	0.48	0.48	0.46	0.38	0.29	0.24
Cash flow from operations	759.9	961.0	517.5	323.1	339.7	254.9
Price range of common stock						
High	64.125	65.500	64.125	76.375	52.063	20.156
Low	26.563	31.750	37.750	47.875	19.531	14.063

MAY 31,						
Cash and equivalents	$ 254.3	$ 198.1	$ 108.6	$ 445.4	$ 262.1	$ 216.1
Inventories	1,446.0	1,170.6	1,396.6	1,338.6	931.2	629.7
Working capital	1,456.4	1,818.0	1,828.8	1,964.0	1,259.9	938.4
Total assets	5,856.9	5,247.7	5,397.4	5,361.2	3,951.6	3,142.7
Long-term debt	470.3	386.1	379.4	296.0	9.6	10.6
Redeemable Preferred Stock	0.3	0.3	0.3	0.3	0.3	0.3
Shareholders' equity	3,136.0	3,334.6	3,261.6	3,155.9	2,431.4	1,964.7
Year-end stock price	42.875	60.938	46.000	57.500	50.188	19.719
Market capitalization	11,559.1	17,202.2	13,201.1	16,633.0	14,416.8	5,635.2

FINANCIAL RATIOS						
Return on equity	17.9%	13.7%	12.5%	28.5%	25.2%	21.6%
Return on assets	10.4%	8.5%	7.4%	17.1%	15.6%	14.5%
Inventory turns	4.1	4.3	4.4	4.8	5.0	5.2
Current ratio at May 31	1.7	2.3	2.1	2.1	1.9	1.8
Price/Earnings ratio at May 31 (diluted)	20.7	38.8	34.1	21.5	26.6	14.5

GEOGRAPHIC REVENUES						
United States	$5,017.4	$5,042.6	$5,460.0	$5,538.2	$3,964.7	$2,997.9
Europe	2,350.9	2,255.8	2,096.1	1,789.8	1,334.3	980.4
Asia Pacific	955.1	844.5	1,253.9	1,241.9	735.1	515.6
Americas (exclusive of United States)	671.7	634.0	743.1	616.6	436.5	266.9
Total Revenues	$8,995.1	$8,776.9	$9,553.1	$9,186.5	$6,470.6	$4,760.8

All per common share data has been adjusted to reflect the 2-for-1 stock splits paid October 23, 1996, October 30, 1995 and October 5, 1990. The Company's Class B Common Stock is listed on the New York and Pacific Exchanges and trades under the symbol NKE. At May 31, 2000, there were approximately 153,000 shareholders of Class A and Class B common stock.

NIKE

Nike, Inc. Consolidated Statement of Income

(in millions, except per share data)

YEAR ENDED MAY 31,	2000	1999	1998
Revenues	$8,995.1	$8,776.9	$9,553.1
Costs and expenses:			
Cost of sales	5,403.8	5,493.5	6,065.5
Selling and administrative	2,606.4	2,426.6	2,623.8
Interest expense (Notes 4 and 5)	45.0	44.1	60.0
Other income/expense, net (Notes 1, 10 and 11)	23.2	21.5	20.9
Restructuring charge, net (Note 13)	(2.5)	45.1	129.9
Total costs and expenses	8,075.9	8,030.8	8,900.1
Income before income taxes	919.2	746.1	653.0
Income taxes (Note 6)	340.1	294.7	253.4
Net income	$ 579.1	$ 451.4	$ 399.6
Basic earnings per common share (Notes 1 and 9)	$ 2.10	$ 1.59	$ 1.38
Diluted earnings per common share (Notes 1 and 9)	$ 2.07	$ 1.57	$ 1.35

NIKE

Nike, Inc. Consolidated Balance Sheet

(in millions)

MAY 31,	2000	1999
ASSETS		
Current Assets:		
Cash and equivalents	$ 254.3	$ 198.1
Accounts receivable, less allowance for doubtful accounts of $65.4 and $73.2	1,567.2	1,540.1
Inventories (Note 2)	1,446.0	1,170.6
Deferred income taxes (Notes 1 and 6)	111.5	120.6
Income taxes receivable	2.2	15.9
Prepaid expenses (Note 1)	215.2	219.6
Total current assets	3,596.4	3,264.9
Property, plant and equipment, net (Note 3)	1,583.4	1,265.8
Identifiable intangible assets and goodwill (Note 1)	410.9	426.6
Deferred income taxes and other assets (Notes 1 and 6)	266.2	290.4
Total assets	$5,856.9	$5,247.7
LIABILITIES AND SHAREHOLDERS' EQUITY		
Current Liabilities:		
Current portion of long-term debt (Note 5)	$ 50.1	$ 1.0
Notes payable (Note 4)	924.2	419.1
Accounts payable (Note 4)	543.8	473.6
Accrued liabilities	621.9	553.2
Total current liabilities	2,140.0	1,446.9
Long-term debt (Notes 5 and 14)	470.3	386.1
Deferred income taxes and other liabilities (Notes 1 and 6)	110.3	79.8
Commitments and contingencies (Notes 12 and 15)	—	—
Redeemable Preferred Stock (Note 7)	0.3	0.3
Shareholders' Equity :		
Common stock at stated value (Note 8):		
Class A convertible – 99.2 and 100.7 shares outstanding	0.2	0.2
Class B – 170.4 and 181.6 shares outstanding	2.6	2.7
Capital in excess of stated value	369.0	334.1
Unearned stock compensation	(11.7)	—
Accumulated other comprehensive income	(111.1)	(68.9)
Retained earnings	2,887.0	3,066.5
Total shareholders' equity	3,136.0	3,334.6
Total liabilities and shareholders' equity	$5,856.9	$5,247.7

Nike, Inc. Consolidated Statement of Cash Flows

(in millions)

YEAR ENDED MAY 31,	2000	1999	1998
Cash provided (used) by operations:			
Net income	$579.1	$451.4	$399.6
Income charges (credits) not affecting cash:			
Depreciation	188.0	198.2	184.5
Non-cash portion of restructuring charge	—	28.0	59.3
Deferred income taxes	36.8	37.9	(113.9)
Amortization and other	35.6	30.6	49.0
Changes in certain working capital components:			
(Increase) decrease in inventories	(275.4)	226.0	(58.0)
(Increase) decrease in accounts receivable	(27.1)	134.3	79.7
Decrease (increase) in other current assets and income taxes receivable	65.6	25.0	(12.6)
Increase (decrease) in accounts payable, accrued liabilities and income taxes payable	157.3	(170.4)	(70.1)
Cash provided by operations	759.9	961.0	517.5
Cash provided (used) by investing activities:			
Additions to property, plant and equipment	(419.9)	(384.1)	(505.9)
Disposals of property, plant and equipment	25.3	27.2	16.8
Increase in other assets	(51.3)	(60.8)	(87.4)
Increase (decrease) in other liabilities	5.9	1.2	(18.5)
Cash used by investing activities	(440.0)	(416.5)	(595.0)
Cash provided (used) by financing activities:			
Additions to long-term debt	0.1	—	101.5
Reductions in long-term debt including current portion	(1.8)	(1.5)	(2.5)
Increase (decrease) in notes payable	505.1	(61.0)	(73.0)
Proceeds from exercise of options	23.9	54.4	32.2
Repurchase of stock	(646.3)	(299.8)	(202.3)
Dividends – common and preferred	(133.1)	(136.2)	(127.3)
Cash used by financing activities	(252.1)	(444.1)	(271.4)
Effect of exchange rate changes on cash	(11.6)	(10.9)	12.1
Net increase (decrease) in cash and equivalents	56.2	89.5	(336.8)
Cash and equivalents, beginning of year	198.1	108.6	445.4
Cash and equivalents, end of year	$254.3	$198.1	$108.6
Supplemental disclosure of cash flow information:			
Cash paid during the year for:			
Interest	$ 45.0	$ 47.1	$ 52.2
Income taxes	221.1	231.9	360.5
Non-cash investing and financing activity:			
Assumption of long-term debt to acquire property, plant, and equipment	$108.9	—	—

Nike, Inc. Consolidated Statement of Shareholders' Equity
(in millions)

| | COMMON STOCK | | | | CAPITAL IN EXCESS OF STATED VALUE | UNEARNED STOCK COMPENSATION | ACCUMULATED OTHER COMPREHENSIVE INCOME | RETAINED EARNINGS | TOTAL |
| | CLASS A | | CLASS B | | | | | | |
	SHARES	AMOUNT	SHARES	AMOUNT					
BALANCE AT MAY 31, 1997	101.7	$0.2	187.6	$2.7	$210.6	$ —	$ (31.3)	$2,973.7	$3,155.9
Stock options exercised			2.1		57.2				57.2
Conversion to Class B Common Stock	(0.2)		0.2						
Repurchase of Class B Common Stock			(4.4)		(5.3)			(197.0)	(202.3)
Dividends on common stock								(132.9)	(132.9)
Comprehensive income:									
Net income								399.6	399.6
Foreign currency translation (net of tax benefit of $3.7)							(15.9)		(15.9)
Comprehensive income							(15.9)	399.6	383.7
BALANCE AT MAY 31, 1998	101.5	0.2	185.5	2.7	262.5	—	(47.2)	3,043.4	3,261.6
Stock options exercised			2.7		80.5				80.5
Conversion to Class B Common Stock	(0.8)		0.8						
Repurchase of Class B Common Stock			(7.4)		(8.9)			(292.7)	(301.6)
Dividends on common stock								(135.6)	(135.6)
Comprehensive income:									
Net income								451.4	451.4
Foreign currency translation (net of tax benefit of $12.5)							(21.7)		(21.7)
Comprehensive income							(21.7)	451.4	429.7
BALANCE AT MAY 31, 1999	100.7	0.2	181.6	2.7	334.1	—	(68.9)	3,066.5	3,334.6
Stock options exercised			1.3		38.7				38.7
Conversion to Class B Common Stock	(1.5)		1.5						
Repurchase of Class B Common Stock			(14.5)	(0.1)	(17.3)			(627.1)	(644.5)
Dividends on common stock								(131.5)	(131.5)
Issuance of shares to employees			0.5		13.5	(13.5)			—
Amortization of unearned compensation						1.8			1.8
Comprehensive income:									
Net income								579.1	579.1
Foreign currency translation (net of tax benefit of $9.3)							(42.2)		(42.2)
Comprehensive income							(42.2)	579.1	536.9
BALANCE AT MAY 31, 2000	99.2	$0.2	170.4	$2.6	$369.0	$ (11.7)	$(111.1)	$2,887.0	$3,136.0

Nike, Inc. Notes to Consolidated Financial Statements

NOTE 1—SUMMARY OF SIGNIFICANT ACCOUNTING POLICIES:

Basis of consolidation: The consolidated financial statements include the accounts of NIKE, Inc. and its subsidiaries (the Company). All significant intercompany transactions and balances have been eliminated.

Recognition of revenues: Revenues recognized include sales and fees earned on sales by licensees. Revenues are recognized when title passes based on the terms of the sale, which are generally upon shipment.

Advertising and promotion: Advertising production costs are expensed the first time the advertisement is run. Media (TV and print) placement costs are expensed in the month the advertising appears. Accounting for endorsement contracts, the majority of the Company's promotional expenses, is based upon specific contract provisions. Generally, endorsement payments are expensed uniformly over the term of the contract after giving recognition to periodic performance compliance provisions of the contracts. Contracts requiring prepayments are included in prepaid expenses or other assets depending on the length of the contract. Total advertising and promotion expenses were $978.2 million, $978.6 million and $1,129.1 million for the years ended May 31, 2000, 1999 and 1998, respectively. Included in prepaid expenses and other assets was $158.7 million and $180.9 million at May 31, 2000 and 1999, respectively, relating to prepaid advertising and promotion expenses.

Cash and equivalents: Cash and equivalents represent cash and short-term, highly liquid investments with original maturities of three months or less.

Inventory valuation: Inventories are stated at the lower of cost or market. Inventories are valued on a first-in, first-out (FIFO) basis. In the fourth quarter of fiscal year 1999, the Company changed its method of determining cost for substantially all of its U.S. inventories from last-in, first-out (LIFO) to FIFO. See Note 11.

Property, plant and equipment and depreciation: Property, plant and equipment are recorded at cost. Depreciation for financial reporting purposes is determined on a straight-line basis for buildings and leasehold improvements over 2 to 30 years and principally on a declining balance basis for machinery and equipment over 2 to 8 years. Computer software is depreciated on a straight-line basis over 3 to 7 years.

Identifiable intangible assets and goodwill: At May 31, 2000 and 1999, the Company had patents, trademarks and other identifiable intangible assets with a value of $215.2 million and $213.0 million, respectively. The Company's excess of purchase cost over the fair value of net assets of businesses acquired (goodwill) was $323.5 million and $324.8 million at May 31, 2000 and 1999, respectively.

Identifiable intangible assets and goodwill are being amortized over their estimated useful lives on a straight-line basis over five to forty years. Accumulated amortization was $127.8 million and $111.2 million at May 31, 2000 and 1999, respectively. Amortization expense, which is included in other income/expense, was $18.5 million, $19.4 million and $19.8 million for the years ended May 31, 2000, 1999 and 1998, respectively. Intangible assets are periodically reviewed by the Company for impairments to assess if the fair value is less than the carrying value.

Foreign currency translation: Adjustments resulting from translating foreign functional currency financial statements into U.S. dollars are included in the currency translation adjustment, a component of accumulated other comprehensive income in shareholders' equity.

Derivatives: The Company enters into foreign currency contracts in order to reduce the impact of certain foreign currency fluctuations. Firmly committed transactions and the related receivables and payables may be hedged with forward exchange contracts or purchased options. Anticipated, but not yet firmly committed, transactions may be hedged through the use of purchased options. Premiums paid on purchased options and any realized gains are included in prepaid expenses or accrued liabilities and are recognized in earnings when the transaction being hedged is recognized. Gains and losses arising from foreign currency forward and option contracts, and cross-currency swap transactions are recognized in income or expense as offsets of gains and losses resulting from the underlying hedged transactions. Hedge effectiveness is determined by evaluating whether gains and losses on hedges will offset gains and losses on the underlying exposures. This evaluation is performed at inception of the hedge and periodically over the life of the hedge. Occasionally, hedges may cease to be effective and are thus terminated prior to recognition of the underlying transaction. Gains and losses on these hedges are deferred until the point in time ineffectiveness is determined and will be included in the basis of the underlying transaction. Hedges will also be terminated if the underlying transaction is no longer expected to occur. When this occurs all related deferral gains and losses are recognized in earnings immediately. Cash flows from risk management activities are classified in the same category as the cash flows from the related investment, borrowing or foreign exchange activity. See Note 15 for further discussion.

Income taxes: Income taxes are provided currently on financial statement earnings of non-U.S. subsidiaries expected to be repatriated. The Company intends to determine annually the amount of undistributed non-U.S. earnings to invest indefinitely in its non-U.S. operations. The Company accounts for income taxes using the asset and liability method. This approach requires the recognition of deferred tax assets and liabilities for the expected future tax consequences of temporary differences between the carrying amounts and the tax bases of other assets and liabilities. See Note 6 for further discussion.

Earnings per share: Basic earnings per common share is calculated by dividing net income by the average number of common shares outstanding during the year. Diluted earnings per common share is calculated by adjusting outstanding shares, assuming conversion of all potentially dilutive stock options and awards. See Note 9 for further discussion.

Management estimates: The preparation of financial statements in conformity with generally accepted accounting principles requires management to make estimates, including estimates relating to assumptions that affect the reported amounts of assets and liabilities and disclosure of contingent assets and liabilities at the date of financial statements and the reported amounts of revenues and expenses during the reporting period. Actual results could differ from these estimates.

Reclassifications: Certain prior year amounts have been reclassified to conform to fiscal year 2000 presentation. These changes had no impact on previously reported results of operations or shareholders' equity.

NOTE 2 – INVENTORIES:

Inventories by major classification are as follows:

(in millions)

MAY 31,	2000	1999
Finished goods	$1,416.6	$1,127.6
Work-in-progress	17.3	21.2
Raw materials	12.1	21.8
	$1,446.0	$1,170.6

As stated in Note 1, the Company changed its inventory valuation method for substantially all U.S. inventories in fiscal year 1999.

NOTE 3 – PROPERTY, PLANT AND EQUIPMENT:

Property, plant and equipment includes the following:

(in millions)

MAY 31,	2000	1999
Land	$ 180.6	$ 99.6
Buildings	503.4	374.2
Machinery and equipment	981.9	923.3
Leasehold improvements	279.6	273.4
Construction in process	448.3	330.8
	2,393.8	2,001.3
Less accumulated depreciation	810.4	735.5
	$1,583.4	$1,265.8

Capitalized interest expense incurred was $4.8 million, $6.9 million and $6.5 million for the fiscal years ended May 31, 2000, 1999 and 1998, respectively.

NOTE 7 – REDEEMABLE PREFERRED STOCK:

NIAC is the sole owner of the Company's authorized Redeemable Preferred Stock, $1 par value, which is redeemable at the option of NIAC at par value aggregating $0.3 million. A cumulative dividend of $0.10 per share is payable annually on May 31 and no dividends may be declared or paid on the common stock of the Company unless dividends on the Redeemable Preferred Stock have been declared and paid in full. There have been no changes in the Redeemable Preferred Stock in the three years ended May 31, 2000. As the holder of the Redeemable Preferred Stock, NIAC does not have general voting rights but does have the right to vote as a separate class on the sale of all or substantially all of the assets of the Company and its subsidiaries, on merger, consolidation, liquidation or dissolution of the Company or on the sale or assignment of the NIKE trademark for athletic footwear sold in the United States.

NOTE 9 – EARNINGS PER SHARE:

The following represents a reconciliation from basic earnings per share to diluted earnings per share. Options to purchase 9.7 million and 3.3 million shares of common stock were outstanding at May 31, 2000 and May 31, 1998, respectively, but were not included in the computation of diluted earnings per share because the options' exercise prices were greater than the average market price of the common shares and, therefore, the effect would be antidilutive. No such antidilutive options were outstanding at May 31, 1999.

(in millions, except per share data)

YEAR ENDED MAY 31,	2000	1999	1998
Determination of shares:			
Average common shares outstanding	275.7	283.3	288.7
Assumed conversion of dilutive stock options and awards	3.7	5.0	6.3
Diluted average common shares outstanding	279.4	288.3	295.0
Basic earnings per common share	$ 2.10	$ 1.59	$ 1.38
Diluted earnings per common share	$ 2.07	$ 1.57	$ 1.35

NOTE 10 – BENEFIT PLANS:

The Company has a profit sharing plan available to substantially all employees. The terms of the plan call for annual contributions by the Company as determined by the Board of Directors. Contributions of $15.7 million, $12.8 million and $11.2 million to the plan are included in other expense in the consolidated financial statements for the years ended May 31, 2000, 1999 and 1998, respectively. The Company has a voluntary 401(k) employee savings plan. The Company matches a portion of employee contributions with common stock, vesting that portion over 5 years. Company contributions to the savings plan were $6.7 million, $7.4 million and $8.1 million for the years ended May 31, 2000, 1999 and 1998, respectively, and are included in selling and administrative expenses.

NOTE 11 – OTHER INCOME/EXPENSE, NET:

Included in other income/expense for the years ended May 31, 2000, 1999, and 1998, was interest income of $13.6 million, $13.0 million and $16.5 million, respectively. In addition, included in other income/expense in fiscal 1999 was income of $15.0 million related to the change in accounting for inventories in the U.S. from the LIFO to the FIFO method. The change was effected in the fourth quarter of fiscal 1999 and was not considered significant to show the cumulative effect or to restate comparable income statements as dictated by Accounting Principles Board Opinion No. 20.

NIKE

NOTE 12 – COMMITMENTS AND CONTINGENCIES:

The Company leases space for its offices, warehouses and retail stores under leases expiring from one to seventeen years after May 31, 2000. Rent expense aggregated $145.5 million, $129.5 million and $129.6 million for the years ended May 31, 2000, 1999 and 1998, respectively. Amounts of minimum future annual rental commitments under non-cancelable operating leases in each of the five fiscal years 2001 through 2005 are $121.1 million, $107.3 million, $89.0 million, $69.9 million, $59.3 million, respectively, and $299.5 million in later years.

At May 31, 2000, the Company had letters of credit outstanding totaling $678.2 million. These letters of credit were issued for the purchase of inventory.

Lawsuits arise during the normal course of business. In the opinion of management, none of the pending lawsuits will result in a significant impact on the consolidated results of operations or financial position.

NOTE 16 – OPERATING SEGMENTS AND RELATED INFORMATION:

Revenues by Major Product Lines: Revenues to external customers for NIKE Brand products are attributable to sales of Footwear, Apparel, and Equipment & Other NIKE Brand. Revenues to external customers for Other Brands include external sales by the non-NIKE brand subsidiaries.

(in millions)

YEAR ENDED MAY 31,	2000	1999	1998
Footwear	$5,561.5	$5,218.4	$5,959.0
Apparel	2,698.6	2,822.9	2,885.7
Equipment	328.2	316.8	277.4
Other brands	406.8	418.8	431.0
	$8,995.1	$8,776.9	$9,553.1

Report of Independent Accountants

Portland, Oregon
June 29, 2000
To the Board of Directors and
Shareholders of NIKE, Inc.

In our opinion, the accompanying consolidated balance sheet and the related consolidated statements of income, of cash flows and of shareholders' equity present fairly, in all material respects, the financial position of NIKE, Inc. and its subsidiaries at May 31, 2000 and 1999, and the results of their operations and their cash flows for each of the three years in the period ended May 31, 2000 in conformity with accounting principles generally accepted in the United States. These financial statements are the responsibility of the Company's management; our responsibility is to express an opinion on these financial statements based on our audits. We conducted our audits of these statements in accordance with auditing standards generally accepted in the United States, which require that we plan and perform the audit to obtain reasonable assurance about whether the financial statements are free of material misstatement. An audit includes examining, on a test basis, evidence supporting the amounts and disclosures in the financial statements, assessing the accounting principles used and significant estimates made by management, and evaluating the overall financial statement presentation. We believe that our audits provide a reasonable basis for the opinion expressed above.

PricewaterhouseCoopers LLP

REEBOK INTERNATIONAL LTD.

CONSOLIDATED STATEMENTS OF INCOME

	Year Ended December 31		
	1999	1998	1997
	(Amounts in thousands, except per share data)		
Net sales	$2,899,872	$3,224,592	$3,643,599
Other income (expense)	(8,635)	(19,167)	(6,158)
	2,891,237	3,205,425	3,637,441
Costs and expenses:			
Cost of sales	1,783,914	2,037,465	2,294,049
Selling, general and administrative expenses	971,945	1,043,199	1,069,433
Special charges	61,625	35,000	58,161
Amortization of intangibles	5,183	3,432	4,157
Interest expense	49,691	60,671	64,366
Interest income	(9,159)	(11,372)	(10,810)
	2,863,199	3,168,395	3,479,356
Income before income taxes and minority interest	28,038	37,030	158,085
Income taxes	10,093	11,925	12,490
Income before minority interest	17,945	25,105	145,595
Minority interest	6,900	1,178	10,476
Net income	$ 11,045	$ 23,927	$ 135,119
Basic earnings per share	$ .20	$ .42	$ 2.41
Diluted earnings per share	$ .20	$ .42	$ 2.32

Reebok

REEBOK INTERNATIONAL LTD.
CONSOLIDATED BALANCE SHEETS

	December 31	
	1999	**1998**
	(Amounts in thousands, except share data)	
Assets		
Current assets:		
Cash and cash equivalents	$ 281,744	$ 180,070
Accounts receivable, net of allowance for doubtful accounts (1999, $46,217; 1998, $47,383)	417,404	517,830
Inventory	414,616	535,168
Deferred income taxes	88,127	79,484
Prepaid expenses and other current assets	41,227	50,309
Total current assets	1,243,118	1,362,861
Property and equipment, net	178,111	172,585
Other non-current assets:		
Intangibles, net of amortization	68,892	68,648
Deferred income taxes	43,868	43,147
Other	30,139	37,383
	142,899	149,178
Total Assets	$1,564,128	$1,684,624
Liabilities and Stockholders' Equity		
Current liabilities:		
Notes payable to banks	$ 27,614	$ 48,070
Current portion of long-term debt	185,167	86,640
Accounts payable	153,998	203,144
Accrued expenses	248,822	177,133
Income taxes payable	8,302	27,597
Total current liabilities	623,903	542,584
Long-term debt, net of current portion	370,302	554,432
Minority interest and other long-term liabilities	41,107	46,672
Commitments and contingencies		
Outstanding redemption value of equity put options		16,559
Stockholders' equity:		
Common stock, par value $.01; authorized 250,000,000 shares; issued shares 92,985,737 in 1999; 93,306,642 shares in 1998	930	933
Retained earnings	1,170,885	1,156,739
Less 36,716,227 shares in treasury at cost	(617,620)	(617,620)
Unearned compensation		(26)
Accumulated other comprehensive income (expense)	(25,379)	(15,649)
	528,816	524,377
Total Liabilities and Stockholders' Equity	$1,564,128	$1,684,624

REEBOK INTERNATIONAL LTD.
CONSOLIDATED STATEMENTS OF STOCKHOLDERS' EQUITY

	Shares	Total	Common Stock (Par Value $.01)	Retained Earnings	Treasury Stock	Unearned Compensation	Accumulated Other Comprehensive Income (Expense)
			(Dollar amounts in thousands)				
Balance, December 31, 1996	92,556,295	$381,234	$926	$ 992,563	$(617,620)	$(283)	$ 5,648
Comprehensive income:							
Net income		135,119		135,119			
Adjustment for foreign currency translation		(26,933)					(26,933)
Comprehensive income		108,186					
Issuance of shares to certain employees	9,532			431		(431)	
Amortization of unearned compensation		566				566	
Shares repurchased and retired	(313)	8				8	
Shares issued under employee stock purchase plans	151,210	4,363	1	4,362			
Shares issued upon exercise of stock options	399,111	10,044	4	10,040			
Income tax reductions relating to exercise of stock options		2,756		2,756			
Balance, December 31, 1997	93,115,835	507,157	931	1,145,271	(617,620)	(140)	(21,285)
Comprehensive income:							
Net income		23,927		23,927			
Adjustment for foreign currency translation		5,636					5,636
Comprehensive income		29,563					
Issuance of shares to certain employees	14,704			458		(458)	
Amortization of unearned compensation		387				387	
Shares repurchased and retired	(114,920)	(3,181)	(1)	(3,365)		185	
Shares issued under employee stock purchase plans	223,583	3,821	2	3,819			
Shares issued upon exercise of stock options	67,440	1,187	1	1,186			
Put option contracts outstanding		(16,559)		(16,559)			
Premium received from unexercised equity put options		2,002		2,002			
Balance, December 31, 1998	93,306,642	524,377	933	1,156,739	(617,620)	(26)	(15,649)
Comprehensive income:							
Net income		11,045		11,045			
Adjustment for foreign currency translation		(9,730)					(9,730)
Comprehensive income		1,315					
Issuance of shares to certain employees	4,449			116		(116)	
Amortization of unearned compensation		142				142	
Shares repurchased pursuant to equity put options	(625,000)	0	(6)	6			
Shares issued under employee stock purchase plans	292,432	2,885	3	2,882			
Shares issued upon exercise of stock options	7,214	97		97			
Balance, December 31, 1999	92,985,737	$528,816	$930	$1,170,885	$(617,620)	$ (0)	$(25,379)

REEBOK INTERNATIONAL LTD.

CONSOLIDATED STATEMENTS OF CASH FLOWS

	Year Ended December 31		
	1999	**1998**	**1997**
	(Amounts in thousands)		
Cash flows from operating activities:			
Net income	$ 11,045	$ 23,927	$ 135,119
Adjustments to reconcile net income to net cash provided by operating activities:			
Depreciation and amortization	48,643	48,017	47,423
Minority interest	6,900	1,178	10,476
Deferred income taxes	(9,364)	(28,074)	(17,285)
Special charges	61,625	35,000	58,161
Changes in operating assets and liabilities:			
Accounts receivable	85,698	63,951	(13,915)
Inventory	109,381	39,134	(47,937)
Prepaid expenses and other	5,986	8,626	(4,155)
Accounts payable and accrued expenses	(18,338)	(65,616)	18,295
Income taxes payable	(19,951)	25,634	(59,257)
Total adjustments	270,580	127,850	(8,194)
Net cash provided by operating activities:	281,625	151,777	126,925
Cash flows from investing activity:			
Payments to acquire property and equipment	(51,197)	(53,616)	(23,910)
Net cash used for investing activity	(51,197)	(53,616)	(23,910)
Cash flows from financing activities:			
Net borrowings (repayments) of notes payable to banks	(22,269)	2,048	27,296
Repayments of long-term debt	(85,020)	(121,016)	(156,966)
Proceeds from issuance of common stock to employees	2,982	5,008	17,163
Proceeds from premium on equity put options		2,002	
Dividends to minority shareholders	(17,966)	(6,649)	(3,900)
Repurchases of common stock	(16,559)	(3,366)	
Net cash used for financing activities	(138,832)	(121,973)	(116,407)
Effect of exchange rate changes on cash	10,078	(5,884)	(9,207)
Net increase (decrease) in cash and cash equivalents	101,674	(29,696)	(22,599)
Cash and cash equivalents at beginning of year	180,070	209,766	232,365
Cash and cash equivalents at end of year	$ 281,744	$ 180,070	$ 209,766
Supplemental disclosures of cash flow information:			
Interest paid	$ 43,620	$ 58,224	$ 59,683
Income taxes paid	35,147	26,068	115,985

Reebok

GAP, Inc.

CONSOLIDATED STATEMENTS OF EARNINGS

($000 except per share amounts)	52 Weeks Ended Jan. 29, 2000	Percentage to Sales	52 Weeks Ended Jan. 30, 1999	Percentage to Sales	52 Weeks Ended Jan. 31, 1998	Percentage to Sales
Net sales	$11,635,398	100.0%	$ 9,054,462	100.0%	$ 6,507,825	100.0%
Costs and expenses						
Cost of goods sold and occupancy expenses	6,775,262	58.2	5,318,218	58.7	4,021,541	61.8
Operating expenses	3,043,432	26.2	2,403,365	26.5	1,635,017	25.1
Net interest expense (income)	31,755	0.3	13,617	0.2	(2,975)	0.0
Earnings before income taxes	1,784,949	15.3	1,319,262	14.6	854,242	13.1
Income taxes	657,884	5.6	494,723	5.5	320,341	4.9
Net earnings	$ 1,127,065	9.7%	$ 824,539	9.1%	$ 533,901	8.2%
Weighted-average number of shares–basic	853,804,924		864,062,060		891,404,945	
Weighted-average number of shares–diluted	895,029,176		904,374,383		922,951,706	
Earnings per share–basic	$ 1.32		$ 0.95		$ 0.60	
Earnings per share–diluted	1.26		0.91		0.58	

See Notes to Consolidated Financial Statements.

GAP

GAP, Inc.

CONSOLIDATED BALANCE SHEETS

($000 except par value)	Jan. 29, 2000	Jan. 30, 1999
Assets		
Current Assets		
Cash and equivalents	$ 450,352	$ 565,253
Merchandise inventory	1,462,045	1,056,444
Other current assets	285,393	250,127
Total current assets	2,197,790	1,871,824
Property and Equipment		
Leasehold improvements	1,426,537	1,040,959
Furniture and equipment	2,083,604	1,601,572
Land and buildings	278,422	160,776
Construction-in-progress	414,725	245,020
	4,203,288	3,048,327
Accumulated depreciation and amortization	(1,487,973)	(1,171,957)
Property and equipment, net	2,715,315	1,876,370
Lease rights and other assets	275,651	215,725
Total assets	$5,188,756	$3,963,919
Liabilities and Shareholders' Equity		
Current Liabilities		
Notes payable	$ 168,961	$ 90,690
Accounts payable	805,945	684,130
Accrued expenses and other current liabilities	751,710	655,770
Income taxes payable	26,263	122,513
Total current liabilities	1,752,879	1,553,103
Long-Term Liabilities		
Long-term debt	784,925	496,455
Deferred lease credits and other liabilities	417,907	340,682
Total long-term liabilities	1,202,832	837,137
Shareholders' Equity		
Common stock $.05 par value		
Authorized 2,300,000,000 shares; issued 1,007,356,790 and 997,496,214 shares; outstanding 850,498,941 and 857,960,032 shares	50,368	49,875
Additional paid-in capital	669,490	349,037
Retained earnings	4,172,796	3,121,360
Accumulated other comprehensive loss	(6,759)	(12,518)
Deferred compensation	(23,150)	(31,675)
Treasury stock, at cost	(2,629,700)	(1,902,400)
Total shareholders' equity	2,233,045	1,573,679
Total liabilities and shareholders' equity	$5,188,756	$3,963,919

See Notes to Consolidated Financial Statements.

GAP, Inc.

CONSOLIDATED STATEMENTS OF CASH FLOWS

($000)	52 Weeks Ended Jan. 29, 2000	52 Weeks Ended Jan. 30, 1999	52 Weeks Ended Jan. 31, 1998
Cash Flows from Operating Activities			
Net earnings	$1,127,065	$ 824,539	$ 533,901
Adjustments to reconcile net earnings to net cash provided by operating activities:			
Depreciation and amortization	436,184	326,447	269,706
Tax benefit from exercise of stock options and vesting of restricted stock	211,891	79,808	23,682
Deferred income taxes	2,444	(34,766)	(13,706)
Change in operating assets and liabilities:			
Merchandise inventory	(404,211)	(322,287)	(156,091)
Prepaid expenses and other	(55,519)	(77,292)	(44,736)
Accounts payable	118,121	265,296	63,532
Accrued expenses	89,071	231,178	107,365
Income taxes payable	(94,893)	38,805	(8,214)
Deferred lease credits and other long-term liabilities	47,775	62,433	69,212
Net cash provided by operating activities	1,477,928	1,394,161	844,651
Cash Flows from Investing Activities			
Net purchase of property and equipment	(1,238,722)	(797,592)	(465,843)
Acquisition of lease rights and other assets	(39,839)	(28,815)	(19,779)
Net maturity of short-term investments	—	—	174,709
Net purchase of long-term investments	—	—	(2,939)
Net cash used for investing activities	(1,278,561)	(826,407)	(313,852)
Cash Flows from Financing Activities			
Net increase in notes payable	84,778	1,357	44,462
Net issuance of long-term debt	311,839	—	495,890
Issuance of common stock	76,211	36,655	23,309
Net purchase of treasury stock	(707,125)	(879,383)	(585,798)
Cash dividends paid	(75,795)	(76,888)	(79,503)
Net cash used for financing activities	(310,092)	(918,259)	(101,640)
Effect of exchange rate fluctuations on cash	(4,176)	2,589	(1,634)
Net (decrease) increase in cash and equivalents	(114,901)	(347,916)	427,525
Cash and equivalents at beginning of year	565,253	913,169	485,644
Cash and equivalents at end of year	$ 450,352	$ 565,253	$ 913,169

See Notes to Consolidated Financial Statements.

CONSOLIDATED STATEMENTS OF SHAREHOLDERS' EQUITY

GAP, Inc.

($000 except share and per share amounts)	Common Stock Shares	Common Stock Amount	Additional Paid-in Capital	Retained Earnings	Accumulated Other Comprehensive Loss	Deferred Compensation	Treasury Stock Shares	Treasury Stock Amount	Total	Comprehensive Earnings
Balance at January 31, 1998	989,826,394	$ 49,491	$ 205,393	$2,392,750	$ (15,230)	$ (38,167)	(105,277,081)	$(1,010,251)	$1,583,986	$ 523,858
Issuance of common stock pursuant to stock option plans	7,575,195	380	46,709			(10,351)			36,738	
Net issuance of common stock pursuant to management incentive restricted stock plans	94,625	4	4,361			(3,873)			492	
Tax benefit from exercise of stock options by employees and from vesting of restricted stock			79,808						79,808	
Adjustments for foreign currency translation ($1,893) and fluctuations in fair market value of financial instruments ($819)					2,712				2,712	2,712
Amortization of restricted stock and discounted stock options						20,716			20,716	
Purchase of treasury stock							(35,714,475)	(910,387)	(910,387)	
Reissuance of treasury stock			12,766				1,455,374	18,238	31,004	
Net earnings				824,539					824,539	824,539
Cash dividends ($.11 per share)				(95,929)					(95,929)	
Balance at January 30, 1999	997,496,214	$ 49,875	$ 349,037	$3,121,360	$ (12,518)	$ (31,675)	(139,536,182)	$(1,902,400)	$1,573,679	$ 827,251
Issuance of common stock pursuant to stock option plans	9,933,713	497	81,456			(9,186)			72,767	
Net cancellations of common stock pursuant to management incentive restricted stock plans	(73,137)	(4)	2,583			(3,411)			(832)	
Tax benefit from exercise of stock options by employees and from vesting of restricted stock			211,891						211,891	
Adjustments for foreign currency translation ($3,305) and fluctuations in fair market value of financial instruments ($2,454)					5,759				5,759	5,759
Amortization of restricted stock and discounted stock options			72			21,122			21,194	
Purchase of treasury stock			4,276				(18,500,000)	(745,056)	(740,780)	
Reissuance of treasury stock			20,175				1,178,333	17,756	37,931	
Net earnings				1,127,065					1,127,065	1,127,065
Cash dividends ($.09 per share)				(75,629)					(75,629)	
Balance at January 29, 2000	1,007,356,790	$ 50,368	$ 669,490	$4,172,796	$ (6,759)	$ (23,150)	(156,857,849)	$(2,629,700)	$2,233,045	$1,132,824

See Notes to Consolidated Financial Statements.

B

Present and Future Values

Learning Objectives

Conceptual

C1 Describe the earning of interest and the concepts of present and future values.

Procedural

P1 Apply present value concepts to a single amount by using interest tables.

P2 Apply future value concepts to a single amount by using interest tables.

P3 Apply present value concepts to an annuity by using interest tables.

P4 Apply future value concepts to an annuity by using interest tables.

Appendix Preview

The concepts of present and future values are important to modern business activity. The purpose of this appendix is to explain, illustrate, and compute present and future values. We apply these concepts to both business and everyday activities.

Present and Future Value Concepts

C1 Describe the earning of interest and the concepts of present and future values.

There's an old saying, *"Time is money."* This saying reflects the notion that as time passes, the value of our assets and liabilities changes. This change is due to *interest,* which is the payment to the owner of an asset for its use by a borrower. The most common example of interest is a savings account asset. As we keep a balance of cash in the account, it earns interest that the financial institution pays us. An example of a liability is a car loan. As we carry the balance of the loan, we accumulate interest costs on it. We must ultimately repay this loan with interest.

Present and future value computations enable us to measure or estimate the interest component of holding assets or liabilities over time. The present value computation is important when we want to know the value of future-day assets *today.* The future value computation is important when we want to know the value of present-day assets *at a future date.* The first section focuses on the present value of a single amount. The second section focuses on the future value of a single amount. Then both the present and future values of a series of amounts (called an *annuity*) are defined and explained.

Present Value of a Single Amount

We graphically express the present value, called p, of a single future amount, called f, that is received or paid at a future date in Exhibit B.1.

Exhibit B.1

Present Value of a Single Amount Diagram

$$
\begin{array}{ccc}
 & f & \\
\bullet & \longrightarrow & \bullet \quad \rightarrow \text{Time} \\
p & & \\
\uparrow & & \uparrow \\
\text{Today} & & \text{Future}
\end{array}
$$

The formula to compute the present value of a single amount is shown in Exhibit B.2 where p = present value; f = future value; i = rate of interest per period; and n = number of periods. (Interest is also called the *discount,* and an interest rate is also called the *discount rate.*)

Exhibit B.2

Present Value of a Single Amount Formula

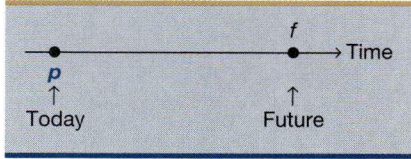

$$p = \frac{f}{(1 + i)^n}$$

To illustrate present value concepts, assume we need $220 one period from today. We want to know how much we must invest now, for one period, at an interest rate of 10% to provide for this $220. For this illustration, the p, or present value, is the unknown amount—the specifics are shown graphically as follows:

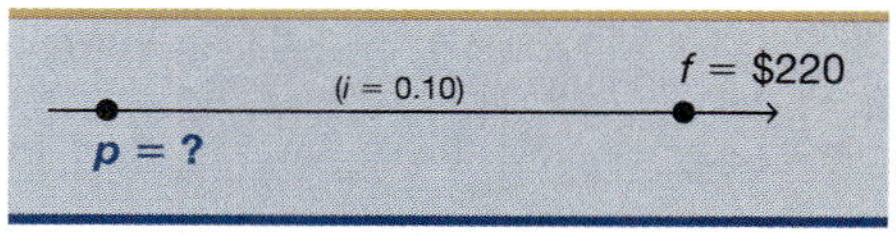

$$
\begin{array}{ccc}
 & (i = 0.10) & f = \$220 \\
\bullet & \longrightarrow & \bullet \\
p = ? & &
\end{array}
$$

Conceptually, we know p must be less than $220. This is obvious from the answer to this question: Would we rather have $220 today or $220 at some future date? If we had $220 today, we could invest it and see it grow to something more than $220 in the future. Therefore, we would prefer the $220 today. This means if we were promised $220 in the future, we would take less than $220 today. But how much less? To answer that question, we compute an estimate of the present value of the $220 to be received one period from now using the formula in Exhibit B.2 as follows:

$$p = \frac{f}{(1 + i)^n} = \frac{\$220}{(1 + 0.10)^1} = \$200$$

We interpret this result to say that given an interest rate of 10%, we are indifferent between $200 today or $220 at the end of one period.

We can also use this formula to compute the present value for *any number of periods.* To illustrate, consider a payment of $242 at the end of two periods at 10% interest. The present value of this $242 to be received two periods from now is computed as follows:

$$p = \frac{f}{(1 + i)^n} = \frac{\$242}{(1 + 0.10)^2} = \$200$$

Together, these results tell us we are indifferent between $200 today, or $220 one period from today, or $242 two periods from today given a 10% interest rate per period.

The number of periods (n) in the present value formula does not have to be expressed in years. Any period of time such as a day, a month, a quarter, or a year can be used. Whatever period is used, the interest rate (i) must be compounded for the same period. This means if a situation expresses n in months and i equals 12% per year, then i is transformed into interest earned per month (or 1%). In this case, interest is said to be *compounded monthly.*

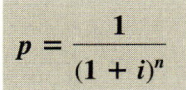

I will pay your allowance at the end of the month. Do you want to wait or receive its present value today?

A present value table helps us with present value computations. It gives us present values (factors) for a variety of both interest rates (i) and periods (n). Each present value in a present value table assumes the future value (f) equals 1. When the future value (f) is different from 1, we need simply multiply the present value (p) from the table by that future value to give us the estimate. The formula used to construct a table of present values for a single future amount of 1 is shown in Exhibit B.3.

P1   Apply present value concepts to a single amount by using interest tables.

$$p = \frac{1}{(1 + i)^n}$$

Exhibit B.3

Present Value of 1 Formula

This formula is identical to that in Exhibit B.2 except that f equals 1. Table B.1 at the end of this appendix is such a present value table. It is often called a **present value of 1 table**. A present value table involves three factors: p, i, and n. Knowing two of these three factors allows us to compute the third. (A fourth is f, but as already explained, we need only multiply the 1 used in the formula by f.) To illustrate the use of a present value table, consider three cases.

Case 1 (solve for p when knowing i and n). To show how we use a present value table, let's again look at how we estimate the present value of $220 (the f value) at the end of one period ($n = 1$) where the interest rate (i) is 10%. To solve this case, we go to the present value table (Table B.1) and look in the row for 1 period and in the column for 10% interest. Here we find a present value (p) of 0.9091 based on a future value of 1. This means, for instance, that $1 to be received 1 period from today at 10% interest is worth $0.9091 today. Since the future value in this case is not $1 but $220, we multiply the 0.9091 by $220 to get an answer of $200.

Case 2 (solve for n when knowing p and i). To illustrate, assume a $100,000 future value ($f$) that is worth $13,000 today ($p$) using an interest rate of 12% (i) but where n is unknown. In particular, we want to know how many periods (n) there are between the present value

and the future value. To put this in context, it would fit a situation in which we want to retire with $100,000 but currently have only $13,000 that is earning a 12% return. How long
will it be before we can retire? To answer this, we go to Table B.1 and look in the 12% interest column. Here we find a column of present values (p) based on a future value of 1.
To use the present value table for this solution, we must divide $13,000 ($p$) by $100,000
(f), which equals 0.1300. This is necessary because *a present value table defines f equal to
1, and p as a fraction of 1*. We look for a value nearest to 0.1300 (p), which we find in the
row for 18 periods (n). This means the present value of $100,000 at the end of 18 periods
at 12% interest is $13,000 or, alternatively stated, we must work 18 more years.

Case 3 (solve for i when knowing p and n). In this case, we have, say, a $120,000 fu-
ture value (f) that is worth $60,000 today ($p$) when there are nine periods (n) between the
present and future values but the interest rate is unknown. As an example, suppose we want
to retire with $120,000, but we have only $60,000 and hope to retire in nine years. What
interest rate must we earn to retire with $120,000 in nine years? To answer this, we go to
the present value table (Table B.1) and look in the row for nine periods. To use the present
value table, we must divide $60,000 ($p$) by $120,000 ($f$), which equals 0.5000. Recall that
this step is necessary because a present value table defines f equal to 1, and p as a fraction
of 1. We look for a value in the row for nine periods that is nearest to 0.5000 (p), which
we find in the column for 8% interest (i). This means the present value of $120,000 at the
end of nine periods at 8% interest is $60,000 or, in our example, we must earn 8% annual
interest to retire in nine years.

Quick Check

1. A company is considering an investment expected to yield $70,000 after six years.
   If this company demands an 8% return, how much is it willing to pay for this
   investment?

Answer—p. B-8

Future Value of a Single Amount

Exhibit B.4

Future Value of a Single
Amount Formula

We must modify the formula for the present value of a single amount to obtain the formula
for the future value of a single amount. In particular, we multiply both sides of the equation in Exhibit B.2 by $(1 + i)^n$ to get the result shown in Exhibit B.4.

$$f = p \times (1 + i)^n$$

The future value (f) is defined in terms of p, i, and n. We can use this formula to determine
that $200 ($p$) invested for 1 ($n$) period at an interest rate of 10% (i) yields a future value of
$220 as follows:

$$
\begin{aligned}
f &= p \times (1 + i)^n \\
  &= \$200 \times (1 + 0.10)^1 \\
  &= \$220
\end{aligned}
$$

This formula can also be used to compute the future value of an amount for *any number of
periods* into the future. To illustrate, assume that $200 is invested for three periods at 10%.
The future value of this $200 is $266.20, computed as follows:

$$
\begin{aligned}
f &= p \times (1 + i)^n \\
  &= \$200 \times (1 + 0.10)^3 \\
  &= \$266.20
\end{aligned}
$$

A future value table makes it easier for us to compute future values (f) for many different combinations of interest rates (i) and time periods (n). Each future value in a future value table assumes the present value (p) is 1. As with a present value table, if the future amount is something other than 1, we simply multiply our answer by that amount. The formula used to construct a table of future values (factors) for a single amount of 1 is in Exhibit B.5.

P2 Apply future value concepts to a single amount by using interest tables.

$$f = (1 + i)^n$$

Exhibit B.5

Future Value of 1 Formula

Table B.2 at the end of this appendix shows a table of future values for a current amount of 1. This type of table is called a **future value of 1 table**.

There are some important relations between Tables B.1 and B.2. In Table B.2, for the row where $n = 0$, the future value is 1 for each interest rate. This is so because no interest is earned when time does not pass. Also notice that Tables B.1 and B.2 report the same information but in a different manner. In particular, one table is simply the *inverse* of the other. To illustrate this inverse relation, let's say we invest $100 annually for a period of five years at 12% per year. How much do we expect to have after five years? We can answer this question using Table B.2 by finding the future value (f) of 1, for five periods from now, compounded at 12%. From that table we find $f = 1.7623$. If we start with $100, the amount it accumulates to after five years is $176.23 ($100 × 1.7623). We can alternatively use Table B.1. Here we find that the present value (p) of 1, discounted five periods at 12%, is 0.5674. Recall the inverse relation between present value and future value. This means $p = 1/f$ (or equivalently, $f = 1/p$). This means we can compute the future value of $100 invested for five periods at 12% as follows: $f = $100 × (1/0.5674) = 176.24.

A future value table involves three factors: f, i, and n. Knowing two of these three factors allows us to compute the third. To illustrate, consider these three possible cases.

Case 1 (solve for f when knowing i and n). Our preceding example fits this case in which we need to solve for f when knowing i and n. We found that $100 invested for five periods at 12% interest accumulates to $176.24.

Case 2 (solve for n when knowing f and i). In this case, we have, say, $2,000 ($p$) and we want to know how many periods (n) it will take to accumulate to $3,000 ($f$) at 7% ($i$) interest. To answer this, we go to the future value table (Table B.2) and look in the 7% interest column. Here we find a column of future values (f) based on a present value of 1. To use a future value table, we must divide $3,000 ($f$) by $2,000 ($p$), which equals 1.500. This is necessary because *a future value table defines p equal to 1, and f as a multiple of 1*. We look for a value nearest to 1.50 (f), which we find in the row for six periods (n). This means that $2,000 invested for six periods at 7% interest accumulates to $3,000.

Case 3 (solve for i when knowing f and n). In this case, we have, say, $2,001 ($p$) and in nine years ($n$), we want to have $4,000 ($f$). What rate of interest must we earn to accomplish this? To answer that, we go to Table B.2 and search in the row for nine periods. To use a future value table, we must divide $4,000 ($f$) by $2,001 ($p$), which equals 1.9990. Recall that this is necessary because a future value table defines p equal to 1 and f as a multiple of 1. We look for a value nearest to 1.9990 (f), which we find in the column for 8% interest (i). This means that $2,001 invested for nine periods at 8% interest accumulates to $4,000.

Quick Check

2. Assume that you win a $150,000 cash sweepstakes. You decide to deposit this cash in an account earning 8% annual interest, and you plan to quit your job when the account equals $555,000. How many years will it be before you can quit working?

Answer—p. B-8

Present Value of an Annuity

An annuity is a series of equal payments occurring at equal intervals. One example is a series of three annual payments of $100 each. An *ordinary annuity* is defined as equal end-of-period payments at equal intervals. An ordinary annuity of $100 for 3 periods and its present value (*p*) are illustrated in Exhibit B.6.

Exhibit B.6

Present Value of an Ordinary Annuity Diagram

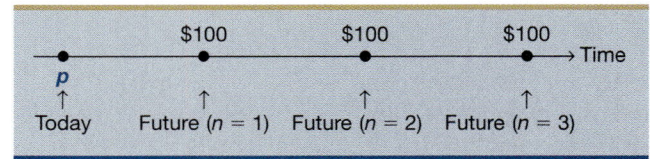

	$100	$100	$100
p			→ Time
↑	↑	↑	↑
Today	Future (*n* = 1)	Future (*n* = 2)	Future (*n* = 3)

P3 Apply present value concepts to an annuity by using interest tables.

One way for us to compute the present value of an ordinary annuity is to find the present value of each payment using our present value formula from Exhibit B.3. We then add each of the three present values. To illustrate, let's look at three $100 payments at the end of each of the next three periods with an interest rate of 15%. Our present value computations are

$$p = \frac{\$100}{(1 + 0.15)^1} + \frac{\$100}{(1 + 0.15)^2} + \frac{\$100}{(1 + 0.15)^3} = \$228.32$$

This computation is identical to computing the present value of each payment (from Table B.1) and taking their sum or, alternatively, adding the values from Table B.1 for each of the three payments and multiplying their sum by the $100 annuity payment.

A more direct way is to use a present value of annuity table. Table B.3 at the end of this appendix is one such table. This table is called a **present value of an annuity of 1 table**. If we look at Table B.3 where *n* = 3 and *i* = 15%, we see the present value is 2.2832. This means the present value of an annuity of 1 for three periods, with a 15% interest rate, equals 2.2832.

A present value of an annuity formula is used to construct Table B.3. It can also be constructed by adding the amounts in a present value of 1 table. To illustrate, we use Table B.1 and B.3 to confirm this relation for the prior example:

From Table B.1		From Table B.3	
i = 15%, *n* = 1	0.8696		
i = 15%, *n* = 2	0.7561		
i = 15%, *n* = 3	0.6575		
Total.	2.2832	*i* = 15%, *n* = 3	2.2832

We can also use business calculators or spreadsheet programs to find the present value of an annuity.

Future Value of an Annuity

The future value of an *ordinary annuity* is the accumulated value of each annuity payment with interest as of the date of the final payment. To illustrate, let's consider the earlier annuity of three annual payments of $100. Exhibit B.7 shows the point in time for the future value (f). The first payment is made two periods prior to the point when future value is determined, and the final payment occurs on the future value date.

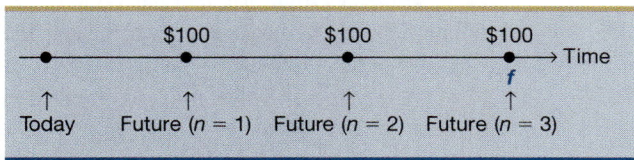

Exhibit B.7

Future Value of an Ordinary Annuity Diagram

One way to compute the future value of an annuity is to use the formula to find the future value of *each* payment and add them. If we assume an interest rate of 15%, our calculation is

$$f = \$100 \times (1 + 0.15)^2 + \$100 \times (1 + 0.15)^1 + \$100 \times (1 + 0.15)^0 = \$347.25$$

This is identical to using Table B.2 and summing the future values of each payment, or by adding the future values of the three payments of 1 and multiplying the sum by $100.

A more direct way is to use a table showing future values of annuities. Such a table is called a **future value of an annuity of 1 table**. Table B.4 at the end of this appendix is one such table. Note that in Table B.4 when $n = 1$, the future values equal 1 ($f = 1$) for all rates of interest. This is so because such an annuity consists of only one payment and the future value is determined on the date of that payment—no time passes between the payment and its future value. The future value of an annuity formula is used to construct Table B.4. We can also construct it by adding the amounts from a future value of 1 table. To illustrate, we use Tables B.2 and B.4 to confirm this relation for the prior example:

P4 Apply future value concepts to an annuity by using interest tables.

From Table B.2		From Table B.4	
$i = 15\%, n = 0$.....	1.0000		
$i = 15\%, n = 1$.....	1.1500		
$i = 15\%, n = 2$.....	1.3225		
Total............	3.4725	$i = 15\%, n = 3$	3.4725

Note that the future value in Table B.2 is 1.0000 when $n = 0$, but the future value in Table B.4 is 1.0000 when $n = 1$. Is this a contradiction? No. When $n = 0$ in Table B.2, the future value is determined on the date when a single payment occurs. This means that no interest is earned, since no time has passed, and the future value equals the payment. Table B.4 describes annuities with equal payments occurring at the end of each period. When $n = 1$, the annuity has one payment, and its future value equals 1 on the date of its final and only payment. Again, no time passes from the payment and its future value date.

Quick Check

4. A company invests $45,000 per year for five years at 12% annual interest. Compute the value of this annuity investment at the end of five years.

Answer—p. B-8

Summary

C1 **Describe the earning of interest and the concepts of present and future values.** Interest is payment by a borrower to the owner of an asset for its use. Present and future value computations are a way for us to estimate the interest component of holding assets or liabilities over a period of time.

P1 **Apply present value concepts to a single amount by using interest tables.** The present value of a single amount received at a future date is the amount that can be invested now at the specified interest rate to yield that future value.

P2 **Apply future value concepts to a single amount by using interest tables.** The future value of a single amount

invested at a specified rate of interest is the amount that would accumulate by the future date.

P3 **Apply present value concepts to an annuity by using interest tables.** The present value of an annuity is the amount that can be invested now at the specified interest rate to yield that series of equal periodic payments.

P4 **Apply future value concepts to an annuity by using interest tables.** The future value of an annuity invested at a specific rate of interest is the amount that would accumulate by the date of the final payment.

Guidance Answers to Quick Checks

1. $70,000 × 0.6302 = $44,144 (use Table B.1, $i = 8\%$, $n = 6$).

2. $555,000/$150,000 = 3.7000; Table B.2 shows this value is not achieved until after 17 years at 8% interest.

3. $10,000 × 5.2421 = $52,421 (use Table B.3, $i = 4\%$, $n = 6$).

4. $45,000 × 6.3528 = $285,876 (use Table B.4, $i = 12\%$, $n = 5$).

QUICK STUDY

QS B-1

Identifying interest rates in tables

You must make future value estimates using the *future value of 1 table* (Table B.2). Which interest rate column do you use when working with the following rates?

1. 8% compounded quarterly

2. 12% compounded annually

3. 6% compounded semiannually

4. 12% compounded monthly

QS B-2

Interest rate on an investment

Ken Francis is offered the possibility of investing $2,745 today and then in return receiving $10,000 after 15 years. What is the annual rate of interest for this investment? (Use Table B.1.)

QS B-3

Number of periods of an investment

Megan Brink is offered the possibility of investing $6,651 today at 6% interest per year in a desire to have $10,000. How many years must Brink wait to accumulate $10,000? (Use Table B.1.)

QS B-4

Present value of an amount

Flaherty is considering an investment which, if paid for immediately, is expected to return $140,000 five years from now. If Flaherty demands a 9% return, how much is she willing to pay for this investment?

CII, Inc., invests $630,000 in a project expected to earn a 12% annual rate of return. The earnings will be reinvested in the project each year until the entire investment is liquidated 10 years later. What will the cash proceeds be when the project is liquidated?

QS B-5
Future value of an amount **P2**

Beene Distributing is considering a project that will return $150,000 annually at the end of each year for six years. If Beene demands an annual return of 7% and pays for the project immediately, how much is it willing to pay?

QS B-6
Present value of an annuity **P3**

Claire Fitch is planning to begin an individual retirement program in which she will invest $1,500 annually at the end of each year. Fitch plans to retire after making 30 annual investments in the program earning a return of 10%. What is the value of the program on the date of the last payment?

QS B-7
Future value of an annuity **P4**

Bill Thompson expects to invest $10,000 at 12% and, at the end of a certain period, receive $96,463. How many years will it be before Thompson receives the payment? (Use Table B.2.)

EXERCISES

Exercise B-1
Number of periods of an investment **P2**

Ed Summers expects to invest $10,000 for 25 years, after which he wants to receive $108,347. What rate of interest must Summers earn? (Use Table B.2.)

Exercise B-2
Interest rate on an investment **P2**

Jones expects an immediate investment of $57,466 to return $10,000 annually for eight years, with the first payment to be received one year from now. What rate of interest must Jones earn? (Use Table B.3.)

Exercise B-3
Interest rate on an investment **P3**

Keith Riggins expects an investment of $82,014 to return $10,000 annually for several years. If Keith earns a return of 10%, how many annual payments will he receive? (Use Table B.3.)

Exercise B-4
Number of periods of an investment **P3**

Algoe expects to invest $1,000 annually for 40 years to yield an accumulated value of $154,762 on the date of the last investment. For this to occur, what rate of interest must Algoe earn? (Use Table B.4.)

Exercise B-5
Interest rate on an investment **P4**

Kate Beckwith expects to invest $10,000 annually that will earn 8%. How many annual investments must Kate make to accumulate $303,243 on the date of the last investment? (Use Table B.4.)

Exercise B-6
Number of periods of an investment **P4**

Sam Weber finances a new automobile by paying $6,500 cash and agreeing to make 40 monthly payments of $500 each, the first payment to be made one month after the purchase. The loan bears interest at an annual rate of 12%. What is the cost of the automobile?

Exercise B-7
Present value of an annuity **P3**

Spiller Corp. plans to issue 10%, 15-year, $500,000 par value bonds payable that pay interest semiannually on June 30 and December 31. The bonds are dated December 31, 2002, and are issued on that date. If the market rate of interest for the bonds is 8% on the date of issue, what will be the total cash proceeds from the bond issue?

Exercise B-8
Present value of bonds **P1** **P3**

McAdams Company expects to earn 10% per year on an investment that will pay $606,773 six years from now. Use Table B.1 to compute the present value of this investment.

Exercise B-9
Present value of an amount **P1**

Exercise B-10
Present value of
an amount and
an annuity

Compute the amount that can be borrowed under each of the following circumstances:

1. A promise to pay $90,000 in seven years hence at an interest rate of 6%.
2. An agreement made on February 1, 2002, to make three separate payments of $20,000 on February 1 of 2003, 2004, and 2005. The annual interest rate is 10%.

Exercise B-11
Present value
of an amount

On January 1, 2002, a company agrees to pay $20,000 in three years. If the annual interest rate is 10%, determine how much cash the company can borrow with this agreement.

Exercise B-12
Present value
of an amount

Find the amount of money that can be borrowed today with each of the following separate debt agreements *a* through *f*:

Case	Single Future Payment	Number of Periods	Interest Rate
a.	$40,000	3	4%
b.	75,000	7	8
c.	52,000	9	10
d.	18,000	2	4
e.	63,000	8	6
f.	89,000	5	2

Exercise B-13
Present values of annuities

C&H Ski Club recently borrowed money and agrees to pay it back with a series of six annual payments of $5,000 each. C&H subsequently borrows more money and agrees to pay it back with a series of four annual payments of $7,500 each. The annual interest rate for both loans is 6%.

1. Use Table B.1 to find the present value of these two separate annuities. (Round amounts to the nearest dollar.)
2. Use Table B.3 to find the present value of these two separate annuities.

Exercise B-14
Present value with semiannual
compounding

Otto Co. borrows money on April 30, 2002, by promising to make four payments of $13,000 each on November 1, 2002, May 1, 2003, November 1, 2003, and May 1, 2004.

1. How much money is Otto able to borrow if the interest rate is 8%, compounded semiannually?
2. How much money is Otto able to borrow if the interest rate is 12%, compounded semiannually?
3. How much money is Otto able to borrow if the interest rate is 16%, compounded semiannually?

Exercise B-15
Future value
of an amount

Mark Welsch deposits $7,200 in an account that earns interest at an annual rate of 8%, compounded quarterly. The $7,200 plus earned interest must remain in the account 10 years before it can be withdrawn. How much money will be in the account at the end of 10 years?

Exercise B-16
Future value
of an annuity

Kelly Malone plans to have $50 withheld from her monthly paycheck and deposited in a savings account that earns 12% annually, compounded monthly. If Kelly continues with her plan for two and one half years, how much will be accumulated in the account on the date of the last deposit?

Exercise B-17
Future value of
an amount plus
an annuity

Starr Company decides to establish a fund that it will use 10 years from now to replace an aging production facility. The company will make an initial contribution of $100,000 to the fund and plans to make quarterly contributions of $50,000 beginning in three months. The fund earns 12%, compounded quarterly. What will be the value of the fund 10 years from now?

Exercise B-18
Future value of
an amount

Catten, Inc., invests $163,170 today earning 7% per year for nine years. Use Table B.2 to compute the future value of the investment nine years from now.

For each of the following situations, identify (1) it as either a (a) present or future value and (b) single amount or annuity case, (2) the table you would use in your computations (but do not solve the problem), and (3) the interest rate and time periods you would use.

a. You need to accumulate $10,000 for a trip you wish to take in four years. You are able to earn 8% compounded semiannually on your savings. You plan to make only one deposit and let the money accumulate for four years. How would you determine the amount of the one-time deposit?

b. Assume the same facts as in part (a) except you will make semiannual deposits to your savings account.

c. You want to retire after working 40 years with savings in excess of $1,000,000. You expect to save $4,000 a year for 40 years and earn an annual rate of interest of 8%. Will you be able to retire with more than $1,000,000 in 40 years?

d. A sweepstakes agency names you a grand prize winner. You can take $225,000 immediately or elect to receive annual installments of $30,000 for 20 years. You can earn 10% annually on any investments you make. Which prize do you choose to receive?

Exercise B-19
Using present and future value tables

Table B.1

Present Value of 1

$$p = 1/(1 + i)^n$$

Periods	1%	2%	3%	4%	5%	6%	7%	8%	9%	10%	12%	15%
1	0.9901	0.9804	0.9709	0.9615	0.9524	0.9434	0.9346	0.9259	0.9174	0.9091	0.8929	0.8696
2	0.9803	0.9612	0.9426	0.9246	0.9070	0.8900	0.8734	0.8573	0.8417	0.8264	0.7972	0.7561
3	0.9706	0.9423	0.9151	0.8890	0.8638	0.8396	0.8163	0.7938	0.7722	0.7513	0.7118	0.6575
4	0.9610	0.9238	0.8885	0.8548	0.8227	0.7921	0.7629	0.7350	0.7084	0.6830	0.6355	0.5718
5	0.9515	0.9057	0.8626	0.8219	0.7835	0.7473	0.7130	0.6806	0.6499	0.6209	0.5674	0.4972
6	0.9420	0.8880	0.8375	0.7903	0.7462	0.7050	0.6663	0.6302	0.5963	0.5645	0.5066	0.4323
7	0.9327	0.8706	0.8131	0.7599	0.7107	0.6651	0.6227	0.5835	0.5470	0.5132	0.4523	0.3759
8	0.9235	0.8535	0.7894	0.7307	0.6768	0.6274	0.5820	0.5403	0.5019	0.4665	0.4039	0.3269
9	0.9143	0.8368	0.7664	0.7026	0.6446	0.5919	0.5439	0.5002	0.4604	0.4241	0.3606	0.2843
10	0.9053	0.8203	0.7441	0.6756	0.6139	0.5584	0.5083	0.4632	0.4224	0.3855	0.3220	0.2472
11	0.8963	0.8043	0.7224	0.6496	0.5847	0.5268	0.4751	0.4289	0.3875	0.3505	0.2875	0.2149
12	0.8874	0.7885	0.7014	0.6246	0.5568	0.4970	0.4440	0.3971	0.3555	0.3186	0.2567	0.1869
13	0.8787	0.7730	0.6810	0.6006	0.5303	0.4688	0.4150	0.3677	0.3262	0.2897	0.2292	0.1625
14	0.8700	0.7579	0.6611	0.5775	0.5051	0.4423	0.3878	0.3405	0.2992	0.2633	0.2046	0.1413
15	0.8613	0.7430	0.6419	0.5553	0.4810	0.4173	0.3624	0.3152	0.2745	0.2394	0.1827	0.1229
16	0.8528	0.7284	0.6232	0.5339	0.4581	0.3936	0.3387	0.2919	0.2519	0.2176	0.1631	0.1069
17	0.8444	0.7142	0.6050	0.5134	0.4363	0.3714	0.3166	0.2703	0.2311	0.1978	0.1456	0.0929
18	0.8360	0.7002	0.5874	0.4936	0.4155	0.3503	0.2959	0.2502	0.2120	0.1799	0.1300	0.0808
19	0.8277	0.6864	0.5703	0.4746	0.3957	0.3305	0.2765	0.2317	0.1945	0.1635	0.1161	0.0703
20	0.8195	0.6730	0.5537	0.4564	0.3769	0.3118	0.2584	0.2145	0.1784	0.1486	0.1037	0.0611
25	0.7798	0.6095	0.4776	0.3751	0.2953	0.2330	0.1842	0.1460	0.1160	0.0923	0.0588	0.0304
30	0.7419	0.5521	0.4120	0.3083	0.2314	0.1741	0.1314	0.0994	0.0754	0.0573	0.0334	0.0151
35	0.7059	0.5000	0.3554	0.2534	0.1813	0.1301	0.0937	0.0676	0.0490	0.0356	0.0189	0.0075
40	0.6717	0.4529	0.3066	0.2083	0.1420	0.0972	0.0668	0.0460	0.0318	0.0221	0.0107	0.0037

Table B.2

Future Value of 1

$$f = (1 + i)^n$$

Periods	1%	2%	3%	4%	5%	6%	7%	8%	9%	10%	12%	15%
0	1.0000	1.0000	1.0000	1.0000	1.0000	1.0000	1.0000	1.0000	1.0000	1.0000	1.0000	1.0000
1	1.0100	1.0200	1.0300	1.0400	1.0500	1.0600	1.0700	1.0800	1.0900	1.1000	1.1200	1.1500
2	1.0201	1.0404	1.0609	1.0816	1.1025	1.1236	1.1449	1.1664	1.1811	1.2100	1.2544	1.3225
3	1.0303	1.0612	1.0927	1.1249	1.1576	1.1910	1.2250	1.2597	1.2950	1.3310	1.4049	1.5209
4	1.0406	1.0824	1.1255	1.1699	1.2155	1.2625	1.3108	1.3605	1.4116	1.4641	1.5735	1.7490
5	1.0510	1.1041	1.1593	1.2167	1.2763	1.3382	1.4026	1.4693	1.5386	1.6105	1.7623	2.0114
6	1.0615	1.1262	1.1941	1.2653	1.3401	1.4185	1.5007	1.5869	1.6771	1.7716	1.9738	2.3131
7	1.0721	1.1487	1.2299	1.3159	1.4071	1.5036	1.6058	1.7138	1.8280	1.9487	2.2107	2.6600
8	1.0829	1.1717	1.2668	1.3686	1.4775	1.5938	1.7182	1.8509	1.9926	2.1436	2.4760	3.0590
9	1.0937	1.1951	1.3048	1.4233	1.5513	1.6895	1.8385	1.9990	2.1719	2.3579	2.7731	3.5179
10	1.1046	1.2190	1.3439	1.4802	1.6289	1.7908	1.9672	2.1589	2.3674	2.5937	3.1058	4.0456
11	1.1157	1.2434	1.3842	1.5395	1.7103	1.8983	2.1049	2.3316	2.5804	2.8531	3.4785	4.6524
12	1.1268	1.2682	1.4258	1.6010	1.7959	2.0122	2.2522	2.5182	2.8127	3.1384	3.8960	5.3503
13	1.1381	1.2936	1.4685	1.6651	1.8856	2.1329	2.4098	2.7196	3.0658	3.4523	4.3635	6.1528
14	1.1495	1.3195	1.5126	1.7317	1.9799	2.2609	2.5785	2.9372	3.3417	3.7975	4.8871	7.0757
15	1.1610	1.3459	1.5580	1.8009	2.0789	2.3966	2.7590	3.1722	3.6425	4.1772	5.4736	8.1371
16	1.1726	1.3728	1.6047	1.8730	2.1829	2.5404	2.9522	3.4259	3.9703	4.5950	6.1304	9.3576
17	1.1843	1.4002	1.6528	1.9479	2.2920	2.6928	3.1588	3.7000	4.3276	5.0545	6.8660	10.7613
18	1.1961	1.4282	1.7024	2.0258	2.4066	2.8543	3.3799	3.9960	4.7171	5.5599	7.6900	12.3755
19	1.2081	1.4568	1.7535	2.1068	2.5270	3.0256	3.6165	4.3157	5.1417	6.1159	8.6128	14.2318
20	1.2202	1.4859	1.8061	2.1911	2.6533	3.2071	3.8697	4.6610	5.6044	6.7275	9.6463	16.3665
25	1.2824	1.6406	2.0938	2.6658	3.3864	4.2919	5.4274	6.8485	8.6231	10.8347	17.0001	32.9190
30	1.3478	1.8114	2.4273	3.2434	4.3219	5.7435	7.6123	10.0627	13.2677	17.4494	29.9599	66.2118
35	1.4166	1.9999	2.8139	3.9461	5.5160	7.6861	10.6766	14.7853	20.4140	28.1024	52.7996	133.176
40	1.4889	2.2080	3.2620	4.8010	7.0400	10.2857	14.9745	21.7245	31.4094	45.2593	93.0510	267.864

$$p = \left[1 - \frac{1}{(1 + i)^n}\right]/i$$

Table B.3

Present Value of an Annuity of 1

Periods	1%	2%	3%	4%	5%	6%	7%	8%	9%	10%	12%	15%
1	0.9901	0.9804	0.9709	0.9615	0.9524	0.9434	0.9346	0.9259	0.9174	0.9091	0.8929	0.8696
2	1.9704	1.9416	1.9135	1.8861	1.8594	1.8334	1.8080	1.7833	1.7591	1.7355	1.6901	1.6257
3	2.9410	2.8839	2.8286	2.7751	2.7232	2.6730	2.6243	2.5771	2.5313	2.4869	2.4018	2.2832
4	3.9020	3.8077	3.7171	3.6299	3.5460	3.4651	3.3872	3.3121	3.2397	3.1699	3.0373	2.8550
5	4.8534	4.7135	4.5797	4.4518	4.3295	4.2124	4.1002	3.9927	3.8897	3.7908	3.6048	3.3522
6	5.7955	5.6014	5.4172	5.2421	5.0757	4.9173	4.7665	4.6229	4.4859	4.3553	4.1114	3.7845
7	6.7282	6.4720	6.2303	6.0021	5.7864	5.5824	5.3893	5.2064	5.0330	4.8684	4.5638	4.1604
8	7.6517	7.3255	7.0197	6.7327	6.4632	6.2098	5.9713	5.7466	5.5348	5.3349	4.9676	4.4873
9	8.5660	8.1622	7.7861	7.4353	7.1078	6.8017	6.5152	6.2469	5.9952	5.7950	5.3282	4.7716
10	9.4713	8.9826	8.5302	8.1109	7.7217	7.3601	7.0236	6.7101	6.4177	6.1446	5.6502	5.0188
11	10.3676	9.7868	9.2526	8.7605	8.3064	7.8869	7.4987	7.1390	6.8052	6.4951	5.9377	5.2337
12	11.2551	10.5753	9.9540	9.3851	8.8633	8.3838	7.9427	7.5361	7.1607	6.8137	6.1944	5.4206
13	12.1337	11.3484	10.6350	9.9856	9.3936	8.8527	8.3577	7.9038	7.4869	7.1034	6.4235	5.5831
14	13.0037	12.1062	11.2961	10.5631	9.8986	9.2950	8.7455	8.2442	7.7862	7.3667	6.6282	5.7245
15	13.8651	12.8493	11.9379	11.1184	10.3797	9.7122	9.1079	8.5595	8.0607	7.6061	6.8109	5.8474
16	14.7179	13.5777	12.5611	11.6523	10.8378	10.1059	9.4466	8.8514	8.3126	7.8237	6.9740	5.9542
17	15.5623	14.2919	13.1661	12.1657	11.2741	10.4773	9.7632	9.1216	8.5436	8.0216	7.1196	6.0472
18	16.3983	14.9920	13.7535	12.6593	11.6896	10.8276	10.0591	9.3719	8.7556	8.2014	7.2497	6.1280
19	17.2260	15.6785	14.3238	13.1339	12.0853	11.1581	10.3356	9.6036	8.9501	8.3649	7.3658	6.1982
20	18.0456	16.3514	14.8775	13.5903	12.4622	11.4699	10.5940	9.8181	9.1285	8.5136	7.4694	6.2593
25	22.0232	19.5235	17.4131	15.6221	14.0939	12.7834	11.6536	10.6748	9.8226	9.0770	7.8431	6.4641
30	25.8077	22.3965	19.6004	17.2920	15.3725	13.7648	12.4090	11.2578	10.2737	9.4269	8.0552	6.5660
35	29.4086	24.9986	21.4872	18.6646	16.3742	14.4982	12.9477	11.6546	10.5668	9.6442	8.1755	6.6166
40	32.8347	27.3555	23.1148	19.7928	17.1591	15.0463	13.3317	11.9246	10.7574	9.7791	8.2438	6.6418

$$f = [(1 + i)^n - 1]/i$$

Table B.4

Future Value of an Annuity of 1

Periods	1%	2%	3%	4%	5%	6%	7%	8%	9%	10%	12%	15%
1	1.0000	1.0000	1.0000	1.0000	1.0000	1.0000	1.0000	1.0000	1.0000	1.0000	1.0000	1.0000
2	2.0100	2.0200	2.0300	2.0400	2.0500	2.0600	2.0700	2.0800	2.0900	2.1000	2.1200	2.1500
3	3.0301	3.0604	3.0909	3.1216	3.1525	3.1836	3.2149	3.2464	3.2781	3.3100	3.3744	3.4725
4	4.0604	4.1216	4.1836	4.2465	4.3101	4.3746	4.4399	4.5061	4.5731	4.6410	4.7793	4.9934
5	5.1010	5.2040	5.3091	5.4163	5.5256	5.6371	5.7507	5.8666	5.9847	6.1051	6.3528	6.7424
6	6.1520	6.3081	6.4684	6.6330	6.8019	6.9753	7.1533	7.3359	7.5233	7.7156	8.1152	8.7537
7	7.2135	7.4343	7.6625	7.8983	8.1420	8.3938	8.6540	8.9228	9.2004	9.4872	10.0890	11.0668
8	8.2857	8.5830	8.8923	9.2142	9.5491	9.8975	10.2598	10.6366	11.0285	11.4359	12.2997	13.7268
9	9.3685	9.7546	10.1591	10.5828	11.0266	11.4913	11.9780	12.4876	13.0210	13.5795	14.7757	16.7858
10	10.4622	10.9497	11.4639	12.0061	12.5779	13.1808	13.8164	14.4866	15.1929	15.9374	17.5487	20.3037
11	11.5668	12.1687	12.8078	13.4864	14.2068	14.9716	15.7835	16.6455	17.5603	18.5312	20.6546	24.3493
12	12.6825	13.4121	14.1920	15.0258	15.9171	16.8699	17.8885	18.9771	20.1407	21.3843	24.1331	29.0017
13	13.8093	14.6803	15.6178	16.6268	17.7130	18.8821	20.1406	21.4953	22.9534	24.5227	28.0291	34.3519
14	14.9474	15.9739	17.0863	18.2919	19.5986	21.0151	22.5505	24.2149	26.0192	27.9750	32.3926	40.5047
15	16.0969	17.2934	18.5989	20.0236	21.5786	23.2760	25.1290	27.1521	29.3609	31.7725	37.2797	47.5804
16	17.2579	18.6393	20.1569	21.8245	23.6575	25.6725	27.8881	30.3243	33.0034	35.9497	42.7533	55.7175
17	18.4304	20.012	21.7616	23.6975	25.8404	28.2129	30.8402	33.7502	36.9737	40.5447	48.8837	65.0751
18	19.6147	21.4123	23.4144	25.6454	28.1324	30.9057	33.9990	37.4502	41.3013	45.5992	55.7497	75.8364
19	20.8109	22.8406	25.1169	27.6712	30.5390	33.7600	37.3790	41.4463	46.0185	41.1591	63.4397	88.2118
20	22.0190	24.2974	26.8704	29.7781	33.0660	36.7856	40.9955	45.7620	51.1601	57.2750	72.0524	102.444
25	28.2432	32.0303	36.4593	41.6459	47.7271	54.8645	63.2490	73.1059	84.7009	98.3471	133.334	212.793
30	34.7849	40.5681	47.5754	56.0849	66.4388	79.0582	94.4608	113.283	136.308	164.494	241.333	434.745
35	41.6603	49.9945	60.4621	73.6522	90.3203	111.435	138.237	172.317	215.711	271.024	431.663	881.170
40	48.8864	60.4020	75.4013	95.0255	120.800	154.762	199.635	259.057	337.882	442.593	767.091	1,779.09

Credits

Page 2 Courtesy JobDirect
Page 4 © The McGraw-Hill Companies, Inc.
Page 9 © Lands' End, Inc. Used with permission
Page 17 Courtesy of Standard & Poor

Page 34 © Steve Hix/FPG International
Page 42 © AFP/CORBIS
Page 43 © Caroline Penn/CORBIS
Page 44 © Steve Cole/PhotoDisc, Inc.
Page 49 AP Photo/Beth A. Keiser
Page 49 AP Photo/General Motors, Blake J. Discher
Page 55 Courtesy of Amazon.com, Inc.

Page 78 Courtesy Creative Assets
Page 82 AP Photo/George Widman
Page 84 Courtesy of Cleveland Indians
Page 85 Courtesy of Boston Celtics
Page 90 © Ken Fisher/Stone
Page 101 Courtesy of Converse, Inc.

Page 124 Photo courtesy of CrossWorlds
Page 127 Courtesy FUBU
Page 128 Photofest/Walt Disney Pictures
Page 133 AP Photo/Kathy Willens

Page 168 Courtesy Red Hat, Inc.
Page 173 Photofest
Page 181 AP Photo/Sun Microsystems, Court Mast
Page 183 © Jess Stock/Stone

Page 212 Courtesy Wooden Ships
Page 217 © Phil Degginger/Stone
Page 222 Courtesy of WMS Industries
Page 225 © Bill Aron/PhotoEdit
Page 232 © Lowell Georgia/CORBIS

Page 260 Courtesy FUBU
Page 268 AP Photo/Christof Stache
Page 271 © Spencer Grant/PhotoEdit
Page 277 Courtesy of Dell Computer Corporation

Page 300 Courtesy Netledger
Page 303 AP Photo/Stephen J. Carrera
Page 304 Courtesy of Netledger
Page 307 © John Acurso/CORBIS
Page 318 © 1997–1998 Federal Express Corporation. All Rights Reserved.

Page 352 AP Photo/Randi Lynn Beach
Page 355 © James L. Amos/CORBIS
Page 356 Courtesy Viisage Technology
Page 357 © Spike/PhotoDisc, Inc.
Page 360 AP Photo/Chris O'Meara

Page 394 Courtesy Tarina Tarantino Designs
Page 398 AP Photo/MasterCard International, HO
Page 405 © Shaun Egan/Stone
Page 407 © Patrick Ward/CORBIS
Page 411 AP Photo/Paul Sakuma

Page 436 Courtesy Papa John's International, Inc.
Page 440 ©AP Photo/Barry Sweet
Page 442 © Paul Chesley/Stone
Page 448 © Dennis O'Clair/Stone
Page 449 Courtesy of America West
Page 455 © John Henley/The Stock Market

Page 480 Courtesy Sector 9 Skateboards
Page 484 © AP Photo/Paul Sakuma
Page 488 © Michael Newman/PhotoEdit
Page 493 © Bettmann/CORBIS

Page 526 © Courtesy of AliTunes
Page 529 © PhotoDisc, Inc.
Page 531 © James L. Amos/CORBIS
Page 534 © Craig Lovell/CORBIS
Page 537 © D. Boone/CORBIS

Page 554 © Mark Solomon/CORBIS
Page 557 © Thomas Del Brase/Stone
Page 559 Courtesy of Green Bay Packers, Inc.
Page 560 Courtesy of American Greetings
Page 581 AP Photo/Nick Ut

Page 614 © Reuters NewMedia Inc./CORBIS

Page 660 © Louise Gubb/SABA
Page 663 © Susan Van Etten: PhotoEdit
Page 668 Photofest
Page 668 Courtesy of New York Stock Exchange
Page 669 © Michael Simpson/FPG International

Page 690 Courtesy Interactive Sports. Photography by Nina Barnett.
Page 690 Courtesy Interactive Sports
Page 692 © A. Ramey/PhotoEdit
Page 698 Courtesy of E-Cash
Page 706 AP Photo/Gretchen Ertl

Page 740 © Bulcao/Liaison Agency
Page 743 © James Mejuto
Page 744 © AFP/CORBIS
Page 757 © Steve Rubin/The Image Works
Page 761 © Vic Bider/PhotoEdit

Page 784 Courtesy American Paper Optics, Inc.
Page 789 © Michael Newman/PhotoEdit

Page 790 AP Photo/Sherwin Crasto
Page 794 AP Photo/Ric Feld
Page 796 © Karl Weatherly/Stone

Page 826 © 2001 Bradley Clark Bower/Mercury Pictures
Page 829 Courtesy of the National Aeronautics and Space Administration
Page 829 © Roger Ressmeyer/CORBIS
Page 829 © Stewart Cohen/Stone

Page 864 Courtesy INCA
Page 864 Courtesy INCA
Page 867 PRNewsFoto/Lands' End
Page 870 © Phil Matt
Page 884 © Charles Gupton/The Stock Market

Page 906 © 2000 Marc Bryan-Brown
Page 909 © R. Ian Lloyd/CORBIS
Page 912 © Michael Newman/PhotoEdit
Page 914 AP Photo/Greg Baker
Page 920 AP Photo/Tom Gannam

Page 946 AP Photo/Kevork Djansezian
Page 948 © Michael Newman/PhotoEdit
Page 954 PhotoLink/PhotoDisc, Inc.
Page 959 AP Photo/Carlos Osorio, File

Page 978 © Grant Brittain 2000
Page 982 AP Photo
Page 986 © 2001 CORBIS. All rights reserved.
Page 988 © Jack Affleck
Page 992 PhotoLink/PhotoDisc, Inc.

Page 1016 Courtesy Toes on the Nose
Page 1024 © AFP/CORBIS
Page 1026 AP Photo/Mark Lennihan
Page 1027 © Bruce Ayres/Stone
Page 1027 Courtesy of the Redhook Ale Brewery

Page 1060 Courtesy Leading Edge Aviation Services
Page 1063 © AFP/CORBIS

Page B–6 AP Photo

Reebok logo Courtesy of Reebok International Ltd.

Index

A

Abercrombie and Fitch, 17, 396
Abnormal balance, 90
Abnormal credit balance, 190
Absorption costing, 955
Accelerated depreciation method, 445
Access, computer control and, 354
Account, 81
Account balance, 86
Account form balance sheet, 141
Accounting, 4
Accounting activities, 6
Accounting books, 80
Accounting careers, 18–20
  accounting specialization, 19
  budgeting, 19
  cost accounting, 19
  financial accounting, 18
  general accounting, 18
  internal auditing, 18
  management consulting, 19
  managerial accounting, 19
  outlook/compensation, 20
  tax accounting, 19
Accounting changes, 578, 579
Accounting cycle, 181, 182
Accounting distribution, 378
Accounting equation, 11, 46
Accounting equation analysis, 96
Accounting equation and transactions, 46–52, 92–95
  accounting equation analysis, 96
  facilities rendered for credit, 49, 50
  investment by owner, 46, 92
  payment of accounts payable, 50, 94
  payment of cash for future insurance coverage, 94
  payment of expenses in cash, 48, 93, 95
  purchase equipment for cash, 47, 92
  purchase equipment on credit, 47
  purchase supplies for cash, 46, 47, 92, 95
  purchase supplies on credit, 47, 92
  receipt of cash for future services, 94
  receipt of cash on account, 50, 93
  rental rendered for credit, 93
  services rendered for cash, 47, 48, 93

services rendered for credit, 49, 50
withdrawal of cash by owner, 51, 94
Accounting estimates, 583
Accounting ethics, 16, 17
Accounting information
  users of, 13–16
    creditors, 13
    customers, 14
    distribution, 15
    employees, 14
    external, 13, 14
    external auditors, 14
    human resources, 15
    internal, 14, 15
    lenders, 13
    marketing, 15
    production, 15
    purchasing, 15
    regulators, 14
    research and development, 15
    servicing, 15
    suppliers, 14
Accounting information systems, 300–350, 302
information processor, 304
information storage, 304
input devices, 303, 304
output devices, 304, 305
source documents, 303
system principles, 302, 303
technology-based systems, 316–318
Accounting period, 126
Accounting principles
  business entity principle, 44
  conservatism principle, 274
  consistency principle, 268
  cost principle, 44
  full disclosure principle, 412
  general principles, 43
  going-concern principle, 45
  international, 43
  matching principle, 127, 400
  materiality principle, 401
  monetary unit principle, 45
  objectivity principle, 44
  revenue recognition principle, 49
  setting, 42, 43
  specific principles, 43
Accounting salaries, 20
Accounting software, 317
Accounting specialists, 19
Accounting techies, 357
Accounting year, 36, 126
Accounts payable, 39, 83, 484

Accounts payable ledger, 306
Accounts payable subsidiary ledger, 306
Accounting rate of return, 1064, 1065
Accounts receivable, 396–407
  aging of accounts receivable method, 405, 406
  allowance method, 401–403
  bad debt expense, 400–403
  credit card sales, 398, 399
  credit sales, 396, 397
  direct write-off method, 400, 401
  estimating uncollectibles, 403–406
  installment, 407
  percent of accounts receivable method, 404, 405
  percent of sales method, 403, 404
  pledging, 411
  selling, 411
  valuing, 399–403
Accounts receivable ledger, 306, 396
Accounts receivable subsidiary ledger, 306
Accounts receivable turnover, 416, 417, 756, 757
Accrual basis accounting, 128
Accrual reversals in future periods, 138–140
Accrued expenses, 134, 135, 139
Accrued interest expense, 135, 136
Accrued interest revenue, 136
Accrued liabilities, 84
Accrued revenues, 136, 137, 139, 140
Accrued salaries expense, 134, 135
Accrued services revenue, 136
Accumulated deficit, 569
Accumulated depletion, 454
Accumulated depreciation, 132, 448
Accumulated other comprehensive income, 672
Acid-test ratio, 233, 756
Activity-based budgeting (ABB), 994
Activity-based costing (ABC), 909–913, **910**
Activity-based management, 913
Activity cost pool, 911
Additional business, accept/reject, 1073–1075
Adidas, 624

Adjusted trial balance, 138, 139
Adjusting entries, 129
  accrued expenses, 134, 135
  accrued interest expense, 135, 136
  accrued interest revenue, 136
  accrued revenues, 135, 136
  accrued salaries expense, 134, 135
  accrued services revenue, 136
  bank reconciliation, 371–373
  depreciation, 131–133
  framework for adjustments, 129
  journalizing, 138
  links to financial statements, 137
  merchandising companies, 227, 228
  prepaid expenses, 130, 131
  prepaid insurance 130, 131, 144, 145
  prepaid rent, 131
  purpose of adjusting, 127
  summary (chart) 137
  supplies, 130, 131
  unearned revenues, 133, 134, 145, 146
Adjusting entry method, 242
Admission of a partner; see Partnerships
Aging of accounts receivable, 405
Aging of accounts receivable method, 405, 406
Alcoa, 127, 454
Alfred, Richard, 1016, 1017
Allocation base, 835
Allowance for doubtful accounts, 401
Allowance method, 401–403
  in financial statements, 401, 402
  recording bad debt expense, 401
  writing off bad debts, 402
AltiTUNES Partners, 527
Amazon.com, 5, 438, 440
America Online, 569
American Express, 405
American Greetings, 560
American Paper Optics (APO), 785
American West Airlines, 449, 450
Amortization, 455
  accounting/spreadsheet software, 627
  bond discount, 621–624
  bond premium, 625–627
  noninterest-bearing note, 633

Amortization table, 623, 624, 627
Amortizing the bond discount, 622
Amortizing the discount, 633
Analysis of financial statements; *see* Financial statement analysis
Analysis report; *see* Financial statement analysis report
Analyzing and recording transactions, 78–123
  accounting equation analysis, 96
  analyzing transactions, 92–95
    investment by owner, 92
    partial payment of account payable, 94
    payment of cash for future insurance coverage, 94
    payment of expenses in cash, 93, 95
    provide services for cash, 93
    provide services on credit, 93
    purchase equipment for cash, 92
    purchase supplies for cash, 92, 95
    purchase supplies on credit, 92
    receipt of cash for future services, 94
    receipt of cash on account, 93
    withdrawal by owner, 94
  documents, and, 80, 81
  events, and, 80
  financial statement links, 97
  source documents, and, 80, 81
  trial balance; *see* Trial balance
Andreessen, Marc, 557
Anheuser-Busch, 438, 460, 489
Annual financial statements, 126
Annual report, A–1
Annual Statement Studies, 22, 754
Annuity, 643
Annuity table, 643
Apple Computer, 417
Appropriated retained earnings, 582
Arctic Cat, 448
Aronson, Brad, 826, 827
Articles of copartnership, 528
ASB, 43
Asset accounts, 82, 83
  accounts receivable, 396–407
  buildings, 83
  cash, 82
  equipment, 83
  insurance, prepaid, 83
  land, 83
  notes receivable, 82, 407–410
  office supplies, 83
  prepaid expenses, 82, 83, 130, 131, 144, 145
  store supplies, 83
Asset management, 11
Assets, 39
AT&T, 30, 867, 1030
Audit, 18

Auditing Standards Board (ASB), 43
Auditor, 378
Authorized stock, 560
Available-for-sale debt securities, 664
Available-for-sale equity securities, 664, 665
Available-for-sale securities, 415, 416, 664–666
Average, 746n
Average collection period, 757
Average cost, 265
Avia, 627
Avoidable cost, 1072
Avoidable expenses, 1078

B

Baby bond, 619
Bad debt expense, 400–403
Bad debts, 399–407
  allowance method; *see* Allowance method
  direct write-off method, 400, 401
  estimating, 403–407
    accounts receivable methods, 404
    aging of accounts receivable, 405, 406
    percent of accounts receivable, 404, 405
    percent of sales, 403, 404
  matching principle for, 400
  materiality principle for, 401
  recording expense, 400
Baker's rule, 408
Balance column account, 89, 90
Balance per bank, 372
Balance per book, 372
Balance sheet, 38, 39
  account form, 141
  adjusted trial balance, and, 141
  allowance for bad debts, 402
  budgeted, 992, 993
  classified, 182–185
  common-size, 750, 751
  comparative, 746, 747
  inventory errors, 270
  manufacturing company, 795, 796
  natural resources, 455
  preparation, 53, 54
  report form, 140
  short-term investments, 416
Balance sheet equation, 46
Balance sheet expenditures, 449
Balanced scorecard, 791, 914
Baldridge award, 790
Bank account, 366
Bank check, 367
Bank deposit, 366
Bank examiners (FDIC), 759
Bank lending officers, 759
Bank One, 404
Bank reconciliation, 369–373
  additions for collections, 370
  additions for interest, 370
  adjusting entries from, 371–373
  check printing charges, 372

  collection of note, 372
  deductions for services, 370
  deductions for uncollectible items, 370
  deposits in transit, 369
  errors, 370
  illustration of, 371
  interest earned, 372
  NSF checks, 370
  outstanding checks, 369
  outstanding deposits, 369
  purpose of, 369
  steps in, 371
Bank statement, 367–369
Banking activities as controls, 366–373
  bank account, 366
  bank check, 367
  bank deposit, 366
  bank reconciliation, 369–373
  bank statement, 367–369
  EFT, 367
Bar chart, 753
Bar code readers, 271, 304
Basic earnings per share, 579, 580, 763
Basket purchase, 440
Batch processing, 317
Bear market, 760
Beardstown Ladies, 741
Bearer, 618
Bearer bonds, 618
Bell, Rachel, 3
Ben & Jerry's, 16, 142, 185, 186
Benchmarking, 1030
Best Buy, 273
BET, 1080
Betterments, 450
Big Five accounting firms, 42
Birdhouse Projects, 979
Blue chip stocks, 743
Board of directors, 558
Boise Cascade, 445
Bond certificate, 619
Bond indenture, 619
Bond-issuing procedures, 619
Bond pricing, 629
Bond ratings, 620
Bond redemption, 630
Bond retirement, 630, 631
Bond trading, 618, 619
Bonded employees, 355
Bonds, 6, 616–631
  advantages, 616
  bearer, 618
  callable, 618
  collateral agreements, 638
  convertible, 618
  coupon, 618
  defined, 616
  disadvantages, 617
  issuances, 619–629; *see also* Issuance of bonds
  junk, 620, 622
  Liberty, 619
  mortgage, 638
  municipal, 618
  present value concepts, 629, 641–644
  pricing, 629

  rating agencies, 620
  registered, 618
  retirement of, 630, 631
  secured, 617
  serial, 618
  sinking fund, 618
  tax-exempt, 618
  term, 618
  trading, 618, 619
  types, 617, 618
  unregistered, 618
  unsecured, 617
  zero-coupon, 620
Bonus
  current liability, as, 494, 495
  to new partners, 536
  to old partners, 535, 536
  to remaining partners, 537
  to withdrawing partners, 537
Book of original entry, 89
Book value, 133, 621
Book value per common share, 583, 763
Book value per preferred share, 584
Book value per share, 583, 584
Book's Web site, 4
Bookkeeping, 6
Books, 80, 81
Boston Celtics, 85, 133, 484, 497, 529, 706
Boston Celtics Limited Partnership (BCLP), 8, 540
Boston Company, 670
Bowerman, Bill, 9
Bowie, David, 614, 615
Bowie bonds, 615
BP Amoco, 982
Brand name, 459
Break-even analysis, 953–957
  break-even point, 953, 954
  contribution margin income statement, 955
  CVP chart, 955, 956
  multiproduct break-even point, 960, 961
Break-even chart, 955
Break-even graph, 955
Break-even point, 953, 954
Break-even sales dollars, 954
Break-even time (BET), 1080
Brokers, 743
Brunswick, 668
Budget, 980
Budget administration, 981–984
Budget committee, 981, 982
Budget reporting, 981
Budget reports, 1018
Budget timing, 981
Budgetary control, 1018
Budgetary process, 978–1015, 1018–1020
  activity-based budgeting, 994
  budget committee, 981, 982
  budget reporting, 982
  budget reports for evaluation, 1019, 1020
  budget timing, 983
  budgetary control and reporting, 1018

budgeted balance sheet, 992, 993

budgeted income statement, 992

capital expenditures budget, 989

cash budget, 990–992

communication of plans, and, 981

continuous improvement, 982

coordination of activities, and, 981

direct labor budget, 1000

direct materials budget, 1000

employee motivation, and, 980

financial budgets, 990–993

fixed budget, 1018

fixed budget performance report, 1018, 1019

flexible budget performance report, 1022

flexible budget reports, 1020–1023

general and administrative expense budget, 988, 989

manufacturing budget, 1000

manufacturing overhead budget, 1001

master budget components, 984

master budget sequence, 985

merchandise purchases budget, 986–988

operating budgets, 986–989

participative budgeting, 981

production budget, 999

rolling budgets, 983

sales budget, 986

selling expense budget, 988

Budgeted balance sheet, 992, 993

Budgeted income statement, 992

Budgeting, 19, 980

Buendia, Paola, 213

Building blocks of analysis, 742, 743

Buildings, 440

Bulk purchase, 440

Bull market, 760

Business, 5

Business and investment
business defined, 5
business profit, 5
return and risk, 5

Business entity principle, 44

Business form; see Forms of organization

Business income, 5

Business organizations, 7–9

Business Owner's Toolkit, 976

Business papers, 80

Business segment, 319

Business transaction, 46

C

C corporations, 529

Cadbury's, 45

Call premium, 630

Call price, 567

Callable bonds, 618

Callable preferred stock, 567

Callaway Golf, 455

Calendar-year companies, 36

Canceled checks, 368

Canion, Rod, 949

Cannondale, 165

Capital, 39

Capital balances method of allocating partnership income, 532

Capital budgeting, 1062–1071
accounting rate of return, 1064, 1065
break-even time, 1080
comparing methods, 1071
defined, 1062
internal rate of return (IRR), 1069, 1070
net percent value (NPV) analysis, 1066–1069
payback period, 1062–1064

Capital deficiency, 539

Capital expenditures, 449, 450
betterments, 450
extraordinary repairs, 450
ordinary repairs, 449, 450

Capital expenditures budget, 989

Capital leases, 645

Capital stock, 9, 559
authorized stock, 560
classes of stock, 560
issuance of, 562–564; see also Issuance of stock
market value of stock, 560
no-par value stock, 561
par value stock, 560, 561
selling stock, 560
stated value stock, 561
stockholder's equity, 561

Capital structure, 758

Capshaw, Kate, 865

Career opportunities in accounting practice, 18–20
accounting specialization, 19
budgeting, 19
cost accounting, 19
financial accounting, 18
general accounting, 19
internal auditing, 19
management consulting, 19
managerial accounting, 19
outlook/compensation, 20
tax accounting, 19

Carrying amount, 621, 648

Carrying (book) value, 621

Casa Munras Hotel Partners LP, 534

Cash, 359; see also Control of cash

Cash accounts, 82

Cash and cash equivalents, 183

Cash basis accounting, 128

Cash budget, 990–992

Cash disbursements journal, 315, 316, 326

Cash discount, 219

Cash dividends, 568, 569

Cash equivalents, 359

Cash flow analysis, 716–718

Cash flow on total assets, 717, 718

Cash flow statement; see Statement of cash flows

Cash flows, 692

Cash over and short, 360

Cash payments journal, 315

Cash receipt journal, 311–313, 325
cash from credit customers, 312
cash from other sources, 312
cash sales, 312
crossfooting, 312
footing, 312
journalizing, 313
posting, 313, 314

Cash register, 356

Cashiers, 360

Casio, 354

Catalina Supermarkets, 225

Catalog price, 218

Caterpillar, 670, 796

CB, 20

CDUniverse, 302

Celebrity investment, 5

Centennial Technology, 127, 362

CEO, 558

Certificate in management accounting (CMA), 19

Certified bookkeeper (CB), 20

Certified internal auditor (CIA), 19

Certified payroll professional (CPP), 20

Certified public accountants (CPAs), 19

CFA, 20

Change analysis, 745–747

Change in an accounting estimate, 448, 583

Charles Schwab, 575

Chart of accounts, 86, C–1, C–2

Charter, 557

Chartered financial analyst (CFA), 20

Check, 367, 368

Check authorization, 377

Check protector, 356

Check register, 316

Chief executive officer (CEO), 558

Chief operating officer (COO), 558

Chiquita, 577

Chock Full O'Nuts, 639

Chrysler/Daimler-Benz merger, 948

CIA, 19

CIT Group, 411

Classic Winery, 671

Classified balance sheet, 182–185
current assets, 183
current liabilities, 185
intangible assets, 184, 185
long-term investments, 183
long-term liabilities, 185
owner's equity, 185
plant assets, 184

Classifying costs
by behavior, 791
by controllability, 792
by function, 792, 793
by relevance, 792
by traceability, 791, 792

Cleveland Indians, 84

Clock card, 833

Closely held corporation, 556

Closing entries, 170–173, 228

Closing entry method, 239, 240, 242

Closing process, 170–174
closing entries, 170–173
income summary, 170–172
nominal accounts, 170
permanent accounts, 170
post-closing trial balance, 174
real accounts, 170
source of closing entry information, 173
temporary accounts, 170

CMA, 19

Coca-Cola, 17, 28, 43, 669, 744

Coca-Cola Bottling, 450, 492, 495, 870

Codes of ethics, 17

Collateral, 617

Collateral agreements, 638

Collections in advance, 484

College tuition fees, 82

Collins Industries, 650

Collusion, 355

Columnar journal, 307

Common dividend payable, 569

Common stock, 9, 558
classes, 560
issuance of, 562–564; see also Issuance of stock

Common-Sense Investment Guide (Beardstown Ladies), 741

Common-size analysis, 750; see also Vertical analysis

Common-size balance sheet, 750, 751

Common-size balance sheet analysis, 750, 751, 753

Common-size graphics, 750–753

Common-size income statement, 750, 752

Common-size percent, 750

Common-size statements, 750

Common stock dividend distributable, 571

Compaq Computer, 222, 949

Comparable information, 41

Comparative balance sheet, 746, 747

Comparative financial statements, 745–748

Comparative income statement, 747, 748

Compatibility principle, 302

Complex capital structure, 581n

Composite unit, 960

Compound journal entry, 93

Compounded, 642

Comprehensive income, 671, 672

CompUSA, 576, 582, 618

Computer hardware, 317

Computer networks, 318

Computer software, 317
Computer technology, 317; *see also* Technology
Conservatism principle, 274
Consignee, 271
Consignment, 271
Consignor, 271
Consistency principle, 268
Consolidated financial statements, 668
Contingent liability, 412, 496, 497
Contingent long-term liabilities, 498
Contingent valuation, 497
Continuous budgeting, 983
Continuous improvement, 790
Contra account, 132
Contra equity account, 85
Contract rate, 620
Contractual restriction, 582
Contributed capital, 40, 561
Contributed capital in excess of par value, 562, 593
Contribution margin income statement, 955
Contribution margin per unit, 802, 803, **954**
Contribution margin ratio, 802, 803, **954**
Control, 786
Control of cash, 358–366
  cash disbursements, 361
  cash over and short, 360
  guidelines, 358
  mail receipts, 360, 361
  over-the-counter cash receipts, 359, 360
  petty cash system, 362–365
  purchase discounts, 365, 366
  voucher system
    document flow, 362, 375–378
    invoice, 377
    invoice approval, 377
    nature of, 361, 362
    purchase order, 377
    purchase requisition, 377
    receiving report, 377
    voucher, 361, 362
Control principle, 302
Controllability of costs, 792
Controllable costs, 792, 922
Controllable variance, 1031
Controller, 19
Controlling account, 306
Controlling influence, equity securities with, 668
Convenience financial statements, 748
Converse, 16, 442, 631
Conversion costs, 798
Convertible bonds, 618
Convertible funds, 631
Convertible preferred stock, 567
COO, 558
Coors, 460
Copyright, 456
Corning, 456
Corporate capital, 561

Corporate taxation, 557
Corporate training and education, 829
Corporation authority structure, 558
Corporations, 9, 556
  capital stock, 559–561
  characteristics
    capital accumulation, ease of, 556, 557
    continuous life, 556
    government regulation, 557
    limited liability, 556
    ownership rights, transferability, 556
    separate legal entity, 556
    stockholders, not corporate agents, 556
    taxation, 557
  common stock; *see* Common stock
  incorporation, 557
  management of, 558
  organization costs, 557
  preferred stock, 564–568; *see also* Preferred stock
  stockholder rights, 558, 559
Correcting entry, 100
Cost(s), 439, 922n
  avoidable, 1078
  classification, 791–793
  controllable/not controllable, 792, 922
  conversion, 798
  curvilinear, 950
  differential, 1073
  direct, 791, 792
  direct labor, 797
  direct material, 797
  expense, contrasted, 922n
  factory overhead, 797
  fixed, 791, 948, 949
  incremental, 1073
  indirect, 792
  indirect labor, 797
  joint, 924, 925
  linear, 950
  mixed, 949
  nonlinear, 950
  opportunity, 792, 1072
  out-of-pocket, 792, 1072
  period, 792, 793
  prime, 798
  product, 792, 793
  relevant, 1072
  service, 794
  stair-step, 950
  standard; *see* Standard costs
  step-wise, 949, 950
  sunk, 792, 1072
  uncontrollable, 922
  variable, 791, 949
Cost accounting, 19
Cost accounting system, 828
Cost allocation and performance measurement, 906–945
  activity-based costing, 909–913
  departmental accounting, 913–921; *see also* Departmental accounting

  responsibility accounting, 921–925
  two-stage cost allocation, 908, 909
Cost-benefit principle, 303
Cost center, 914
Cost driver, 911
Cost estimation methods, 951–953
  high-low method, 952
  least-squares regression, 952
  scatter diagram, 951
Cost object, 791
Cost of goods manufactured, 796
Cost of goods sold, 216
Cost of plant assets, 439, 440
  buildings, 440
  land, 439, 440
  land improvements, 440
  lump-sum purchase, 440
  machinery/equipment, 440
Cost of sales, inventory and, 260–299
  inventory analysis and effect, 266–270
    balance sheet effects, errors from, 270
    consistency in reporting, 268
    errors in reporting inventory, 268–270
    financial reporting, 266, 267
    income statement effects, errors from, 268–270
    tax reporting, 267, 268
  inventory costing, 262–266
    conservatism principle, 274
    estimating physical inventory at cost, 275
    estimating physical inventory shortage at cost, 275
    first-in, first-out (FIFO), 264, 284
    gross profit method, 275, 276
    last-in, first-out (LIFO), 265, 284
    lower of cost or market (LCM), 273, 274
    periodic system; *see* Periodic inventory system
    retail inventory method, 274, 275
    specific identification method, 263, 264, 284
    subsidiary inventory records, 272
    technology, and, 265, 266
    weighted-average method, 265, 284, 285
  inventory items and costs
    goods damaged and obsolete, 271
    goods in consignment, 271
    goods in transit, 270
    physical count of merchandise inventory, 271, 272
Cost-plus basis, 829
Cost-plus contract, 788
Cost principle, 44

Cost-to-benefit constraint, 271
Cost variance, 1024; *see also* Variance analysis
Cost variance formulas, 1025
Cost-volume-profit (CVP) analysis, 946–977, 948
  applications of, 957–962
  assumptions, 956
  break-even analysis, 953–957
  composite units, 960, 961
  computing income from sales, 957, 958
  computing sales for target income, 958
  curvilinear costs, 950
  fixed costs, 949
  high-low method, 952
  least-squares regression, 952
  margin of safety, 959
  measuring cost behavior, 951–953
  mixed costs, 949
  multiproduct break-even point, 960, 961
  output measures, 956
  relevant range of operations, 956, 957
  scatter diagram, 951
  sensitivity analysis, 959, 960
  step-wise costs, 949, 950
  summing costs, 956
  variable costs, 949
  what-if questions, 958
Cost-volume-profit (CVP) chart, 955
Costa Rica, 17
Coupon bonds, 618
Coupon rate, 620
Cox, Courtney, 865
CPAs, 19
CPP, 20
Crawford, Cindy, 865
Creative Assets, 79
Credit, 86–88
Credit balance, 86
Credit memorandum, 226
Credit period, 218
Credit rating, 638
Credit standing, 743
Credit terms, 218, 219
Creditor financing, 10
Creditors, 13, 39
Creditors ledger, 306
Crosby, Stills and Nash, 615
CrossWorlds, 125
Cumulative preferred stock, 565, 566
Current assets, 183
Current liabilities, 185, 482, 484–492
Current portion of long-term debt, 498
Current ratio, 185, 186, 755, 756
  composition of current assets, 755
  formula, 755
  guidelines, 755
  turnover rate of assets, 756
  types of business, 755
Curvilinear cost, 950

Customer orientation, **790**
Customers, 14
Customers ledger, 306
Customized production, 828
CVP analysis; *see* Cost-volume-profit (CVP) analysis
CVP chart, 955
Cyberfashion, 304
Cybersleuthing, 359

D

Daimler-Benz/Chrysler merger, 948
Dairy Queen, 414
Damaged goods, 271
Database management programs, 317
Data processing, 317
Date of declaration, 568
Date of payment, 568
Date of record, 568
Days' sales in inventory, 277, 757, 758
Days' sales in receivables, 373
Days' sales uncollected, 373, 757
Days' stock on hand, 277
Dayton Hudson, 215
DDB method, 445, 446
Debentures, 617
Debit, 86–88
Debit balance, 86
Debit memorandum, 220
Debt guarantees, 496
Debt ratio, 101, 759
Debt securities, 413
Debtors, 39
Decision making, 1072; *see also* Managerial decisions
Declining-balance method, 445
Deferred income tax liabilities, 495
Deferred revenues, 133, 484
Deficit, 569
Defined benefit plan, 646
Defined contribution plan, 646
Definitely determinable liabilities, 484
Degree of operating leverage (DOL), 962
Delivery expense, 221
Dell, Michael, 266
Dell Computer, 21, 266, 417, 495, 825, 829
Delta Air Lines, 794
Demand deposits, 359
Demand-pull system, 790
Departmental accounting, 913–921
departmental contribution to overhead, 920, 921
departmental evaluation, 914
departmental expense allocation, 915–921
departmental income statements, 917–920
departmental reporting and analysis, 914
equipment/machinery depreciation, 916

indirect expense allocation, 915–917
motivation for departmentalization, 913
rent/related expenses, 916
services, 917
utilities, 916, 917
wages/salaries, 916
Departmental accounting system, 913
Departmental contribution to overhead, 920, 921
Departmental expense allocation, 915–921
Departmental income statements, 917–920
Departmental spreadsheet analysis, 914
Departments, 913
Depletion, 454
Deposit ticket, 366, 367
Deposits in transit, 369
Depreciation, 131–133, **441**–448
accumulated, 448
declining-balance method, 445, 446
factors in computing, 441, 442
cost, 441
salvage value, 441
service life, 441, 442
useful life, 441, 442
partial year, 447
reporting, 448
revising, 447, 448
straight-line method, 442–444
tax reporting, 446, 447
units-of-production method, 444, 445
Deteriorated goods, 271
Differential costs, 1073
Diluted earnings per share, 581n
Dilutive securities, 581n
Direct costs, 791, 792
Direct expenses, 915
Direct labor, 797
Direct labor budget, 1000
Direct labor cost variance, 1027
Direct labor costs, 797
Direct labor efficiency variance, 1027
Direct labor rate variance, 1027
Direct material costs, 797
Direct materials, 797
Direct materials budget, 1000
Direct materials variance, 1026
Direct method, 274, 699
cash paid for interest and income taxes, 704, 705
cash paid for merchandise, 702, 703
cash paid for wages/operating expenses, 703, 704
cash received from customers, 701, 702
depreciation expense, 705
FASB recommended, 699
format, 698, 706
gain on retirement of debt, 705
loss on sale of assets, 705

operating cash payments, 702–705
operating cash receipts, 701, 702
summary of adjustments, 705
user friendly, 700
Direct method (LCM), 274
Direct posting of sales invoices, 310
Direct write-off method, 400, 401
Directors, 558
Discontinued segments, 576
Discount lost, 366
Discount on bonds payable, 621
Discount on common stock, 563
Discount on note payable, 486–488, 634
Discount on stock, 562
Discount period, 219
Discounting, 1062
Discounting notes receivable, 411, 412
Discounting process, 486
Dishonored note, 409, 410
Disney Company, 37, 128
Distribution, 15
Dividend in arrears, 565
Dividend yield, 585, 762
Dividends, 41
cash, 568, 569
date of declaration, 568
date of payment, 568
date of record, 568
in arrears, 565
liquidating, 569
stock, 570–572
yield, 584, 585
DOL, 962
Dollar, U.S., 670
Dollar changes, 745–747
Dollar signs, 100
Domini Social Index, 17
Domino's, 483, 488
Donovan, Mark, 212, 213
Double-declining-balance (DDB) method, 445, 446
Double-entry accounting, 87
Double taxation, 9, 557
Dun & Bradstreet, 22, 742, 754

E

E-budgets, 1014
E-cash, 698
Earnings, 5
Earnings per share, 579–581
eBay, 353, 438
Eco-cars, 959
Effective interest method, 623, 624, 626, 627
Efficiency, 742, 754
Efficiency measures; *see* Liquidity analysis
Efficiency variance, 1025, 1026, 1031
Electronic funds transfer (EFT), 305, **367**
Eliminating a segment, 1078, 1079

Employee benefits, 492
Employee earnings report, 506
Employee FICA taxes, 490
Employee fraud, 354–356
Employee income tax, 490
Employee payroll deductions, 489, 490
Employee voluntary deductions, 490
Employees
bonding of, 355
demand for, 357
employee benefits, 492
employee earnings report, 506
external information users, as, 14
Employeescreen.com, 355
Employer FICA tax, 491
Employer payroll taxes, 491
Enterprise resource planning (ERP) software, 318
Entrepreneur incubators, 232
Entrepreneur wish list, 83
Entrepreneurial financing, 497
Entrepreneurial giving, 267
Entrepreneurship, 9
Environmental budgeting, 1020
Environmental Protection Agency (EPA), 1020
EOM, 218
EPA, 1020
EPS, 579–581
Equipment, 83
Equity, 39
Equity accounts, 84, 85
owner's capital, 85
owner's withdrawals, 85
revenues and expenses, 85
Equity method, 666, 667
Equity ratio, 759
Equity securities, 413
Equity securities with controlling influence, 668
Equity securities with significant influence, 666–668
Equivalent units of production (EUP), 873, 874
Ernst & Young, 20
ERP software, 318
Errors
bank, 370
bank reconciliation, and, 370
correcting, 100
depositor, 370
human, 358
inventory, 268–270
processing, 357
searching for, 98
self-correcting, 269
transposition, 98n, 99n
Escapable expenses, 1078
Estimated liabilities, 492–495
Estimated line of cost behavior, 951
Estimated long-term liabilities, 498
Estimates, 583
Estimating bad debts expense, 403–406

accounts receivable methods, 404–406
  aging of accounts receivable, 405, 406
  percent of accounts receivable method, 404, 405
  percent of sales method, 403, 404
  spreadsheet software, 406
  summary of principles, 406
Ethics, 16
  accounting, 16, 17
  codes of, 17
  ethics defined, 16
  guidelines for making ethical decisions, 16
  organizational, 16
Ethics codes, 17
EU, 670
EUP, 873, 874
European Union (EU), 670
Evaluation, 980
Events, 80
Excel, 317, 627
Exchange rates, 45, 669–671
Exchanging plant assets, 452–454
  dissimilar assets, 452
  gains, 453, 454
  losses, 452, 453
  similar assets, 452
Executive management, 10
Expanded accounting equation, 84
Expense, 922n; *see also* Cost(s)
Expense accounts, 85
Expenses, 5, 37
External auditors, 14
External transactions, 80
External users of accounting information, 13, 14
  contributors to nonprofit organizations, 14
  creditors, 13
  customers, 14
  employees, 14
  external auditors, 14
  lenders, 13
  owners, 13, 14
  regulators, 14
  shareholders, 13, 14
  suppliers, 14
  voters/legislators/elected officials, 14
Extraordinary gains and losses, 576
Extraordinary items, 576–578
Extraordinary repairs, 450
Exxon Mobil, 454

F

Face amount, 616
Face-recognition program, 356
Face value, 616
Factor, 411
Factoring fee, 411
Factors in computing depreciation, 441, 442
  cost, 441
  salvage value, 441
  service life, 441, 442
  useful life, 441, 442

Factory overhead, 797
Factory overhead costs, 797
Factory overhead ledger account, 873
Factory payroll ledger account, 871
Falcon Communications LP, 537
FASB, 7, 42
Favorable variance, 1019
FDIC, bank examiners, 759
Federal depository bank, 503
Federal Express, 318
Federal Insurance Contribution Act (FICA) taxes, 490, 491
Federal unemployment taxes (FUTA), 491
Federated Department Stores, 692
FICA taxes
  employee, 490
  employer, 490
Fidelity Magellan, 664
FIFO, 264, 284
Fila, 621
Financial accounting, 13, 18, 787
Financial Accounting Standards Board (FASB), 7, 42
Financial budgets
  budgeted balance sheet, 992, 993
  budgeted income statement, 992
  cash budget, 990–992
Financial leverage, 101, 567, 568, 759
Financial management, 10
Financial ratios; *see* Ratio analysis
Financial reporting, 743
Financial statement analysis, 740–782
  building blocks of analysis, 742, 743
  common-size analysis, 749–753
  comparative statements, 745–748
  external users of accounting information, 742
  guidelines, 744
  horizontal analysis, 745–749
  information for analysis, 743, 744
  internal users of accounting information, 742
  liquidity/efficiency, 754–758
  market prospects, 761, 762
  profitability measures, 760, 761
  purpose of analysis, 742
  ratio analysis, 754–763; *see also* Ratio analysis
  report, 764
  rules of thumb, 744
  solvency analysis, 758–760
  standards for comparisons, 744
  tools of analysis, 744
  trend analysis, 748, 749
  vertical analysis, 749–753
Financial statement analysis report
  analysis overview, 764
  assumptions, 764

evidential matter, 764
  executive summary, 764
  inferences, 764
  key factors, 764
Financial statements
  adjusting entries, and, 137
  annual, 126
  balance sheet; *see* Balance sheet
  cash flow statement; *see* Statement of cash flow
  common-size, 750
  comparative, 745–747
  Gap, The, A–15 to A–18
  general-purpose, 13, 743
  income statement; *see* Income statement
  interim, 126
  links, 54, 97
  Nike, A–2 to A–10
  owner's equity; *see* Statement of changes in owner's equity
  partnership, 534
  presentation issues, 100
  Reebok, A–11 to A–14
Financing activities, 10, 55, **694**
Finished goods inventory, 796, 831
First-in, first-out (FIFO), 264, 284
Fiscal year, 126
Fixed assets; *see* Plant assets
Fixed budget, 1018
Fixed budget performance report, 1019
Fixed cost, 791, 948, 949
Fixed overhead, 800
Fixed overhead variance, 1030, 1032, 1033
Fixed overhead volume variance, 1032, 1033
Flexibility principle, 302, 303
Flexible budget, 1020–1022
Flexible budget performance report, 1022, 1023
Flexible budget reports, 1020–1023
Floating an issue, 619
Floating rate, 638
Florida Panthers, 82
Flow of manufacturing activities, 799, 800
FOB, 221
FOB destination, 222
FOB factory, 222
FOB shipping point, 222
Ford Motor Company, 493, 496, 866, 885, 959
Foreclosure, 638
Foreign exchange rate, 669–671, **670**
Form 10-K, A–1
Form 10-KSB, A–1
Form 940, 504
Form 941, 502
Form W-2, 504
Form W-4, 507
Forms of organization
  choosing a business form, 530
  corporation, 9
  nonbusiness organization, 9, 10

partnership; *see* Partnerships
  sole proprietorship, 8
Fox, 668
France Telecom, 988
Franchises, 457
Fraud, 358
Free cash flow, 715
Freeplay, 661
Freight-in, 221
Freight-out, 221
Fringe benefits, 646
FUBU, 261
Full disclosure principle, 412
FUTA, 491
Futura Computer, 909
Future value; *see* Time value of money
Future value of 1 table, B–5, B–12
Future value of an annuity of 1 table, B–7, B–13

G

GAAP, 7, 41, 44
GAAS, 41
Gap, Inc., 126, 166, A–15 to A–18, 583, 668
Garbage in, garbage out, 303
Garnett, Katrina, 124, 125
Gaston, Paul E., 529
General accounting, 19
General accounting system, 828
General and administrative expense budget, 988, 989
General and administrative expenses, 230
General journal, 89, 316
General Motors, 49, 790, 829
General partner, 529
General partnership, 529
General principles, 43
General-purpose financial statements, 13, 743
Generally accepted accounting principles (GAAP), 7, 41, 44
Generally accepting auditing standards (GAAS), 41
GenX Company, 867–885
GeoCities, 458
GILTS, 619
Going-concern principle, 45
Gold Standard, The, 790
Goldberg, Evan, 300, 301
Goods in process inventory, 796, 831
Goods in transit, 270
Goods on consignment, 271
Goodwill, 457, 458
Government accountants, 19
Governmental regulation, 557
Green Bay Packers, 559
Griffey, Ken, Jr., 271
Gross margin, 214
Gross margin ratio, 233, 234, 763
Gross method, 365
Gross pay, 489
Gross profit, 214
Gross profit method, 275, 276

Group purchase, 440
Growth stocks, 585
GTE, 30

H

Harley-Davidson, 84, 268, 319,
    320, 407, 482, 573, 581,
    687, 789, 992
Harris, Jim, 949
Hasbro, 373, 374
Hawk, Tony, 978, 979
Health and pension benefits, 492,
    493
Held-to-maturity debt securities,
    663, 664
**Held-to-maturity securities, 414,
    663,** 664
Heterogeneity, 829
Hewlett-Packard, 573, 914
Hierarchical levels, 792
High-low method, 952
Hirsch, Stephanie, 864, 865
Historical cost principle, 44
Hogan, Mark T., 829
Home Depot, 274, 484, 581, 645
Honda, 790, 959
Hoover's Online, 1057
Horizontal analysis, 744–749
    comparative balance sheet, 746,
        747
    comparative income statement,
        747, 748
    defined, 744
    dollar changes, 745–747
    percent changes, 745–747
    spreadsheet programs, 748
    trend analysis, 748, 749
Hostile takeover, 566n
House of GAAP, 44
Human error, 358
Human fraud, 358
Human resources, 15
Hurley, Liz, 865
Hybrid costing system, 885, 886

I

i-FRONTIER, 827
IASC, 43
IBM, 16, 455, 576
Ideal standard, 1024
Improvements, 450
Inadequacy, 442
INCA, 865
Income, 5
Income smoothing, 127
Income statement, 37
    adjusted trial balance, and, 140
    budgeted, 992
    common-size, 750, 752
    comparative, 747, 748
    continuing operations, 576
    contribution margin, 955
    departmental, 917–920
    discontinued segments, 576
    extraordinary items, 576–578
    inventory errors, 268–270
    manufacturing company, 796–
        799
    multi-step, 230, 231

multiproduct break-even, 961
    preparation, 52, 53
    single-step, 230, 231
Income statement expenditures,
    449
Income stocks, 585
Income summary, 170–172
Income tax liabilities, 494, 495
Incorporation, 557
Incorporators, 557
Incremental costs, 1073
Incremental overhead rate, 1075
Independent auditors, 14
Indenture, 619
Index number, 748
Index number trend analysis, 748
Indirect costs, 792
Indirect expense allocation, 915–
    917
Indirect expenses, 915
Indirect labor costs, 797
Indirect method, 699, 706–711
    accounts payable, 709
    accounts receivable, 708
    adjustments for changes in
        current liabilities, 709
    adjustments for changes in
        noncash current assets, 707–
        709
    adjustments for noncash items,
        710
    adjustments for nonoperating
        items, 710
    depreciation, 710
    format, 707
    gain on retirement of debt, 711
    income taxes payable, 709
    interest payable, 709
    loss on sale of plant assets, 710
    merchandise inventory, 708
    prepaid expenses, 708
    spreadsheet, 721–723
    summary of adjustments, 711
    working paper, 721–723
Industry norms, 754
Industry Norms and Key Ratios,
    22, 754
Industry statistics, 744
Inescapable expenses, 1079
Information age, 4
Information for analysis, 743, 744
Information processor, 304
Information storage, 304
Information superhighway, 4
Informix, 127
Infrequent gain or loss, 576
Initial public offering (IPO), 560
Input devices, 303, 304
Installment accounts receivable,
    407
Installment note, 634–637
Institute of Management
    Accountants, 788
Insurance, 83
Intangible assets, 455–459
    amortization, 455
    copyrights, 456
    franchises/licenses, 457
    goodwill, 457, 458
    leasehold improvements, 457
    leaseholds, 456, 457

patents, 456
    trademarks/trade names, 459
Integrated computer-based
    accounting system, 317
Intel, 411, 459
Interactive Sports, 691
Interest, 408
Interest-bearing notes, 632
Interest expense, 135
Interest method, 623
Interest revenue, 137
Interim financial statements, 126
Internal auditing, 19, 788
Internal control system, 352–
    392, **354**
    banking activities, 366–373;
        see also Banking activities as
        controls
    cash, 358–366; *see also*
        Control of cash
    human error, 358
    human fraud, 358
    limitations, 357, 358
    principles, 354–356
        bond key employees, 355
        establish responsibilities, 355
        insure assets, 355
        maintain adequate records,
            255
        reviews, regular and
            independent, 356
        separate
            recordkeeping/custody of
            assets, 355
        separation of duties, 356
        technological controls, 356
    purpose, 354
    technology, 356, 357
Internal controls, 302
Internal operating functions, 15
**Internal rate of return (IRR),
    1069,** 1070
Internal Revenue Service (IRS),
    14, 267, 268
Internal transactions, 80
Internal users of accounting
    information, 14, 15
    distribution, 15
    human resources, 15
    marketing, 15
    production, 15
    purchasing, 15
    research and development, 15
    servicing, 15
International accounting
    principles, 43
**International Accounting
    Standards Committee
    (IASC), 43**
International operations, 669–671
International Organization of
    Securities Commission
    (IOSCO), 7
Internet fraud, 356
Inventory, 216; *see also*
    Merchandise inventory
Inventory analysis and effects,
    266–270
    consistency in reporting, 268
    errors in reporting inventory,
        268–270

financial reporting, 266, 267
    tax reporting, 267, 268
Inventory costing
    FIFO, 264, 284
    LIFO, 265, 284
    periodic system, 283–285
    perpetual system, 262–266
    specific identification, 263, 284
    technology, and, 265, 266
    weighted average, 265, 284,
        285
Inventory errors
    balance sheet effects, 370
    income statement effects, 268–
        270
Inventory items and costs
    goods damaged or obsolete,
        271
    goods in transit, 270
    goods on consignment, 271
Inventory records, real-time, 317
Inventory ticket, 271, 272
Inventory turnover, 277, 757
Investing activities, 10, 11, 55,
    712, **725**
Investments
    classifying, 662
    foreign exchange rates, 669–
        671
    international operations, 669–
        671
    long-term; *see* Long-term
        investments
    securities, 669
    short-term; *see* Short-term
        investments
Investor's Business Daily, 762
Invoice, 217, 218, **377**
Invoice approval, 377
Invoice date, 218
IOSCO, 7
IPO, 560
IRR, 1069, 1070
IRS, 14, 267, 268
Islamic law, 628
Issuance of bonds, 619–629
    at discount, 621–624
    at par, 619, 620
    at premium, 624–627
    between interest dates, 627,
        628
Issuance of stock
    no-par value stock, 563
    par value stock at discount,
        562, 563
    par value stock at par, 562
    par value stock at premium,
        562
    preferred stock, 565
    stated value stock, 563
    stock for noncash assets, 563,
        564
Itex Corp, 44

J

J.C. Penney, 223, 224, 398
Jackson, Michael, 615
Japanese auto manufacturers, 790
Jerit, John, 784, 785
JIT inventory systems, 987

JIT manufacturing, 790
Job, 828
Job cost sheet, 830, 831
Job lot, 829
**Job order cost accounting
    system,** 826–862, **830**
    clock card, 833
    job cost sheet, 830, 831
    job order manufacturing, 828–
        830
    labor costs flows and
        documents, 833, 834
    materials cost flows and
        documents, 831–833
    materials ledger card, 832
    materials requisition, 832, 833
    overapplied overhead, 840
    overhead cost flows and
        documents, 835, 836
    predetermined overhead
        allocation rate, 835, 836
    process systems, compared, 866
    summary of manufacturing cost
        flows, 836–838
    time ticket, 833, 834
    underapplied overhead, 839
Job order manufacturing, 828
JobDirect, 3, 5
Jobs manufactured on speculation,
    829
John, Daymond, 260, 261
Johnson, Clark, 173
Joint costs, 924, 925
Joint relation, 749, 768
Journal, 88
Journal entry explanations, 100
Journalizing, 89
Junk bonds, 620, 622
Just-in-time (JIT) inventory
    systems, 233, 987
**Just-in-time (JIT)
    manufacturing, 790**

K

Kate Spade, 907
Kellogg, 669
Kimkiewicg, Dave, 481
Kmart, 267
Knight, Kristin, 78, 79
Knight, Philip, 9
Known liabilities, 484
    accounts payable, 484
    sales taxes payable, 484
    short-term notes payable, 485–
        488
    unearned revenues, 484, 485
KnowX.com, 355
Koch Industries, 984
Korsmeyer, Carnell, 740
Kroger, 216

L

L.L. Bean, 866
La Côte Basque, 457
Labor cost flows and documents,
    833, 834
Labor cost variances, 1027, 1028
Labor efficiency variance, 1027

Labor rate variance, 1027
Lack of liquidity, 754
Lack of mutual agency, 556
Lake, Steve, 481
LAN, 318
Land, 439, 440
Land improvements, 440
Land's End, 866
Large stock dividend, 570
Last-in, first-out (LIFO), 265, 284
Latham, Walter, 946, 947
Latham Entertainment, 947
Leading Edge Aviation Services,
    1061
Lean business model, 790
Lean practices, 790
Lease, 456, 457, **644,** 645
Leasehold, 456, 457
Leasehold improvements, 457
Least-squares regression, 952
Ledger, 81, 85
Legal claims, 496
Legal restriction, 582
Lenders, 13
Lessee, 456, 644
Lessor, 456, 644
Leverage
    financial, 101, 567, 568, 759
    operating, 962
Liabilities, 39, 482–497
    contingent, 496, 497
    current, 482, 484–492
    deferred income tax, 495
    defined, 482
    estimated, 492–495
    income tax, 494, 495
    known, 484–492
    long-term, 483, 497, 498
    payroll, 489–492
    uncertainty in, 483, 484
    warranty, 493, 494
Liability accounts, 83, 84
    accounts payable, 83
    accrued liabilities, 84
    note payable, 83, 84
    unearned revenue, 84
Liberty Bonds, 619
Licenses, 457
LIFO, 265, 284
Limited, The, 215
**Limited liability company
    (LLC), 530**
Limited liability of stockholders,
    556
**Limited liability partnership
    (LLP), 529**
Limited partners, 529
Limited partnership (LP), 529
Line graph, 748, 749
Linear cost, 950
Link Wood Products, 914
Liquid assets, 359
Liquidating cash dividend, 569
Liquidating dividend, 569
Liquidation of partnership
    capital deficiency
        partner cannot pay, 539
        partner pays, 539
    no capital deficiency, 538, 539
Liquidity, 359, 742, 754

Liquidity analysis, 754–758
    accounts receivable turnover,
        756, 757
    acid-test ratio, 756
    average collection period, 757
    current ratio, 755, 756
    days' sales in inventory, 757,
        758
    days' sales uncollected, 757
    inventory turnover, 757
    quick ratio, 756
    summary of ratios, 763
    total asset turnover, 758
    working capital, 754, 755
List price, 218
LLC, 530
LLP, 529
Local area network (LAN), 318
London Outfitters, 670
Long-term investments, 183, 662
    available-for-sale debt
        securities, 664
    available-for-sale equity
        securities, 664, 665
    available-for-sale securities,
        664–666
    classes, 662
    cost method of accounting, 664
    equity method of accounting,
        664
    equity securities with
        controlling influence, 668
    equity securities with
        significant influence, 666–
        668
    held-to-maturity securities, 663,
        664
Long-term liabilities, 185, 483,
    497, 498
    bond financing; *see* Bonds
    collateral agreements, 638
    installment note, 634–637
    interest-bearing notes, 632
    leases, 644, 645
    mortgage notes, 637, 638
    noninterest-bearing notes, 633,
        634
    pensions, 646
    present value concepts, 641–644
Long-term payable, 631–638
    collateral agreements, 638
    installment note, 634–637
    interest-bearing notes, 632
    mortgage notes, 637, 638
    noninterest-bearing notes, 633,
        634
    present-value concepts, 641–
        644
Loss, 5
Losses and gains for liquidation,
    539
**Lower of cost or market
    (LCM), 273,** 274
LP, 529
Lump-sum purchase, 440

M

Macy's, 692
McDonald's, 16, 438, 496, 669

McDonnell Douglas, 829
McGraw-Hill, 668
Machinery and equipment, 440
McMahon, Vince, 554, 555
MACRS, 446, 447
Mail receipts, 360, 361
Make-or-buy decision, 1075
Maker of a note, 408
Malcolm Baldridge National
    Quality Award (MBQNA),
    790
Management accounting, 786;
    see also Managerial
    accounting
Management accounting system,
    786
Management by exception, 1034
Management consulting, 19
Management discussion and
    analysis (MD&A), 10, 743,
    744
Managerial accounting, 14, 19,
    786
    decision-making focus, 789
    financial accounting, compared,
        787
    flexibility of practice, 788
    focus of information, 789
    lean business model, 790
    nature of information, 789
    purpose of information, 788
    relevance, 789
    time dimension, 788, 789
    timeliness of information, 788
    users/decision makers, 787
Managerial decisions, 1072–1080
    additional business, 1073–1075
    decision-making process, 1072
    eliminating a segment, 1078,
        1079
    make-or-buy decision, 1075
    qualitative decision factors,
        1079, 1080
    relevant costs, 1072, 1073
    sales mix, 1077, 1078
    scrap-or-rework decision, 1075,
        1076
    sell-or-process decision, 1076,
        1077
Manclark, Mike, 1060, 1061
Mandatory vacation policy, 355
Manufacturing budget, 1000
    direct labor budget, 1000
    direct materials budget, 1000
    manufacturing overhead budget,
        1001
Manufacturing company
    balance sheet, 795, 796
    contribution margin ratio, 802,
        803
    conversion costs, 798
    cost of goods manufactured, 796
    cost of goods sold, 796, 797
    defined, 786
    direct labor, 797
    direct materials, 797
    factory overhead, 797
    finished goods inventory, 796
    flow of activities, 798, 800
    goods in process inventory, 796

income statement, 796–799
manufacturing statement, 800, 801
overhead cost flows, 802
prime costs, 798
raw materials inventory, 795
unit contribution margin, 802, 803
Manufacturing overhead, 797
Manufacturing overhead budget, 1001
Manufacturing statement, 800, 801
Margin of safety, 959
Marine & Restaurant Fabricators (MRF), 1075
Market prospects, 743
defined, 743
dividend yield, 762
PE ratio, 761, 762
Market rate, 620
Market value per share, 560
Marketable securities, 413–416
accounting treatment, 413
available-for-sale securities, 415, 416
balance sheet presentation, 416
held-to-maturity securities, 414
trading securities, 414, 415
Marketing, 15
Marriott, 16, 214n
Master budget, 984; *see also* Budgetary process
Matching principle, 127, 400
Material cost variances, 1026, 1027
Material price variance, 1026
Material quantity variance, 1026
Materiality principle, 271, 401
Materials consumption report, 870
Materials cost flows and documents, 831–833
Materials ledger card, 832
Materials requisition, 832, 833
Mattel, 359, 373, 374
Maturity date, 616
Maturity date of a note, 408
MCI, 581
MD&A, 743, 744
Mechanical change and currency counters, 356
Median, 746n
Medicare benefits, 490
Medicare taxes, 490
Members, 530
Merchandise inventory, 215, 260–299
assigning costs to inventory, 262–266
consistency in reporting, 268
costs of, 271
errors in reporting, 268–270
FIFO, 264, 284
financial reporting, 266, 267
gross profit method, 275, 276
items in, 270, 271
LIFO, 265, 284
lower of cost or market (LCM), 273, 274

physical count, 271, 272
retail inventory method, 274, 275
specific identification, 263, 284
subsidiary records, 272
tax reporting, 267, 268
weighted average, 265, 284, 285
Merchandise inventory account, 218
Merchandise inventory turnover, 277, 757
Merchandise purchases, 217–223
discounts and returns, 221
managing discounts, 219, 220
purchase discounts, 218, 219
purchase returns and allowances, 220, 221
recording purchases information, 222, 223
trade discounts, 218
transfer of ownership, 221, 222
transportation costs, 221
Merchandise purchases budget, 986–988, **987**
Merchandise sales, 223–226
sales discounts, 224, 225
sales returns and allowances, 225, 226
sales transactions, 223, 224
Merchandise turnover, 757
Merchandiser, 214
Merchandising activities, 214–217
Merchandising cash flows, 231, 232
Merchandising companies, 212–299
adjusting entries, 227, 228
cash flows, 231, 232
closing entries, 228
cost flows/cost accounts, 229
cost/price adjustments, 226
inventory; *see* Merchandise inventory
inventory systems, 216, 217; *see also* Inventory systems
operating cycle, 215, 216
purchases, 217–223
reporting financial condition, 215
reporting financial performance, 214
sales, 223–226
work sheet, 241, 242
Merchandising cost accounts, 229
Merchandising cost flows, 229
Merchandising operating cycle, 215, 216
Merit rating, 491
Microsoft, 585, 669
Microvision, 304
Middleware, 317
Midway Games, 37, 222
Minimum legal capital, 560, 561, 593
MIT's Media Laboratory, 304
Mixed cost, 949
ML Macadamia Orchards LP, 531
Mobil, 267

Modified accelerated cost recovery system (MACRS), 446, 447
Modified profit margin, 142
Modified return on equity, 56
Modified return on investment, 21
Monetary unit principle, 45
Monetary units, 45
Monsanto, 318
Moody's, 620, 742
Mortgage, 637
Mortgage bonds, 638
Mortgage contract, 637
Mortgage notes, 637, 638
Motorola, 271, 304, 904, 1030
Mott's, 318
Multinational, 669
Multiple-step income statement, 230, 231
Multiproduct break-even income statement, 961
Multiproduct CVP analysis, 960, 961
Municipal bonds (munis), 618
Murto, Bill, 949
MusicLand, 638
MusicLive, 584
Mutual agency, 528
n/10 EOM, 218

N

National Venture Capital Association, 557
Natural business year, 127
Natural resources, 454, 455
Net assets, 39
Net cash flow, 1062
Net income, 37
Net income per share, 579
Net loss, 37
Net method, 365
Net pay, 489
Net present value, 1067
Net present value (NPV) analysis, 1066–1069
Net present value decision rule, 1067
Net realizable value, 271
Net working capital, 754
NetLedger, 301
Netscape, 557
New York Times, 133
Newman, Paul, 18
Nike, 5, 9, 10, 12, 14, 17, 21, 23, 31, 32, 36, 75, 82, 100, 141, 165, 319, 390, 448, 459, A–2 to A–10, 564, 564n, 583, 611, 657, 672, 673, 686, 717, 718, 737, 743–762, 780, 794, 823, 976, 1056, 1097
Nintendo, 45
Nissan, 790
No capital deficiency, 538, 539
No-par stock, 561
No-par value stock, 561
Nominal accounts, 170
Nominal rate, 620
Non-calendar year companies, 36

Non-sufficient funds (NSF) check, 370
Nonbusiness organizations, 9, 10
Noncash investing and financing, 694, 695
Noncumulative preferred stock, 565, 566
Noninterest-bearing notes, 633, 634
Nonlinear cost, 950
Nonowner financing, 10
Nonparticipating preferred stock, 566
Normal balance, 90
Not controllable costs, 792, 922
Notes payable, 39, 83, 84, 485–488; *see also* Long-term payable
Notes receivable, 82, 407–410
accounts, 82
computations for, 408, 409
converting to cash before maturity, 411
discounting, 411, 412
dishonored note, 409, 410
end-of-period interest adjustment, 410
honored note, 409
interest, 408
interest adjustment, end-of-period, 410, 411
interest computation, 408
maker of note, 408
maturity date/period, 408
payee of note, 408
principal of note, 408
promissory note, 407
receipt of note, 409
recording dishonored note, 409
recording honored note, 409
NPV analysis, 1066–1069
NSF check, 370

O

Objectivity principle, 44
Obsolescence, 442
Obsolete goods, 271
Off-balance-sheet financing, 645n
Office equipment, 83
Office supplies, 83
Off-the-shelf accounting programs, 317
Omidyar, Pierre, 352, 353
On-line processing, 317
Online brokerage firms, 559
Operating activities, 11, 55, 699, **725**
Operating budgets
general and administrative expense budget, 988, 989
merchandise purchases budget, 986–988
sales budget, 986
selling expense budget, 988
Operating cycle, 182, 183, 215, 216
Operating departments, 908
Operating efficiency, 760

Operating expenses, 214
Operating leases, 644
Operating leverage, 962
Operating performance, 743
Opinion, 18, 19
Opportunities in accounting
     practice, 18–20
   accounting specialization, 19
   budgeting, 19
   cost accounting, 19
   financial accounting, 18
   general accounting, 19
   internal auditing, 19
   management consulting, 19
   managerial accounting, 19
   outlook/compensation, 20
   tax accounting, 19
Opportunity cost, 792, 1072, 1073
Oracle, 318
Ordinary repairs, 449, 450
Organization costs, 557
Organization plan, 10
Organizational ethics, 16
Organizational responsibility, 922
Organizations
   activities in, 10, 11
     financing, 10, 55
     investing, 10, 11, 55
     operating, 11, 55
     planning, 10
   forms of
     choosing a business form,
        530
     corporation, 9
     nonbusiness organization, 9,
        10
     partnership; *see* Partnerships
     sole proprietorship, 8
Organized crime, 666
Other comprehensive income,
     671, 672
Other postretirement benefits, 646
Outboard Marine, 185, 396
Out-of-pocket cost, 792, 1072
Output devices, 304, 305
Outstanding checks, 369
Outstanding deposits, 369
Outstanding stock, 560
Over-the-counter cash receipts,
     359
Overapplied overhead, 840
Overfunded plan, 646
Overhead cost flows, 802
Overhead cost flows and
     documents, 835, 836
Overhead cost variance, 1030
Overhead cost variance analysis,
     1030–1034
Overhead standards, 1028–1030
Overhead volume report, 1033
Overpriced stocks, 762
Owner financing, 10
Owner's capital, 85
Owner's equity, 11, 39, 185
Owner's withdrawal, 85

P

Pacioli, Luca, 87
Packard Bell, 411

Paging Network, 958
Paid-in capital, 40, 562
Paper shredder, 357
Pappa John's, 437
Par value, 560
Par value of a bond, 616
Par value stock, 560
Parent, 668
Parker Hannifin, 670
Partial year depreciation, 447
Participating preferred stock,
     566
Participatory budgeting, 981
Partnership contract, 528
Partnership liquidation, 538–
     540
   capital deficiency
     partner cannot pay, 539
     partner pays, 539
   no capital deficiency, 538, 539
Partnership return on equity,
     540
Partnerships, 526–553, 528
   admission of partner, 535, 536
     bonus to new partner, 536
     bonus to old partner, 535,
        536
     investing assets in
        partnership, 535
     purchase of partnership
        interest, 535
   capital balances method of
     allocation, 532
   characteristics of
     articles of copartnership, 528
     co-ownership of property,
        529
     limited life, 528
     mutual agency, 528, 529
     taxation, 538
     unlimited liability, 529
     voluntary association, 528
   death of partner, 538
   defined, 528
   dividing income/loss, 532–534
   financial statements, 534
   general, 529
   limited, 529
   liquidation, 538–540
   LLP, 529
   organizing, 531
   return on equity, 540
   services, capital, and stated
     ratio method of allocation,
        532
   stated ratio method of
     allocation, 532
   withdrawal of partner, 536, 537
     bonus to remaining partners,
        537
     bonus to withdrawing
        partner, 537
     no bonus, 537
Patent, 456
Payback period (PBP), 1062–
     1064
Paychex, 1075
Payee of a note, 408
Paying accrued expenses, 139
Payless, 794

PayPal, 398
Payroll bank account, 507
Payroll check, 505, 506
Payroll deductions, 489
   FICA taxes, 490
   income tax, 490
   recording, 490, 491
   voluntary, 490
Payroll journal, 505
Payroll liabilities, 489–492
Payroll procedures, 507
Payroll records, 504–506
Payroll register, 504, 505
Payroll reports, 502–504
PBP, 1062–1064
PE ratio, 585, 586, 761, 762
PeachTree, 317, 627
Pecking order, 792
Penn Fuel Gas (PFG), 983
Pension plans, 493
Pension recipients, 646
Pentagon, 277
PepsiCo, 28, 581, 744
Percent changes, 745–747
Percent of accounts receivable
     method, 404, 405
Percent of sales method, 403, 404
Period costs, 792, 793
Periodic inventory system, 216,
     217, 828
   adjusted trial balance, 239
   adjusting entries, 238–240
   adjusting entry method, 242
   assigning costs to inventory,
     283–285
   closing entries, 239–241
   perpetual system, compared,
     237–241
   purchases, 237, 238
   sales, 238
   special journals, 324–326
Periodicity principle, 126
Perkin-Elmer, 912
Permanent accounts, 170
Perpetual inventory system, 217
   adjusted trial balance, 239
   adjusting entries, 238–240
   assigning costs to inventory,
     262–266
   benefits, 266
   merchandise purchases, 217–
     223, 237, 238
   merchandise sales, 223–226,
     238
   periodic system, compared,
     237–241
   special journals, 305–316
Personal financial specialist
     (PFS), 20
Personal identification scanners,
     356
Petroleum refining, 866
Petty cash custodian, 363
Petty cash disbursements, 362
Petty cash payments report, 364
Petty cash receipt, 363
Petty cash system, 362–365
   cash over and short, 365
   illustration of petty cash fund,
     363, 364

increasing/decreasing fund, 364
   operating a fund, 363
Petty cash ticket, 363
Petty cashbox, 363
Petty cashier, 363
Pfizer, 396
PFS, 20
Philip Morris, 585
Photo credits, CR–1
Physical basis allocation of joint
     cost, 924, 925
Physical count of inventory, 216,
     271, 272
Pie chart analysis, 53
Plan administrator, 646
Planning, 10, 786
Plant assets, 438–453
   cost, 439, 440
   depreciation, 441–448; *see also*
     Depreciation
   discarding, 451
   disposal of, 450–453
   exchanging, 452, 453
   repairs and maintenance, 449,
     450
   selling, 451, 452
Pledging assets, 638, 639
Pledged assets to secured
     liabilities, 639, 759
Pledging accounts receivable, 411
Poison pill, 566n
Polaris, 307
Post-closing trial balance, 174
Posting, 89
Posting process, 90, 91
Posting reference (PR) column,
     89
PP&E; *see* Plant assets
Practical standard, 1024
Predetermined overhead
     allocation rate, 835, 836
Predetermined overhead rate, 835
Predetermined standard overhead
     rate, 1029
Preemptive right, 559
Preferred stock, 564
   callable, 567
   convertible, 567
   cumulative, 565, 566
   issuance of, 565
   motivation for, 567, 568
   noncumulative, 565, 566
   nonparticipating, 566
   participating, 566
Premium on bonds, 624
Premium on bonds payable, 625
Premium on common stock, 562
Premium on stock, 562
Prepaid expenses, 130
   adjusting entries, 130, 131
   alternate accounting treatment,
     144, 145
   insurance, 83, 130
   nature of, 82
   rent, 131
   supplies, 130, 131
Prepaid insurance, 82, 82, 130
Prepaid rent, 131
Prepayments, 484
Preprinted forms, 355

Present value, 641–644; *see also* Time value of money
  annuity, 643
  compounding periods shorter than year, 644
  discount bond, 629
  premium bond, 629
Present value of 1 table, B–3, B–12
Present value of annuity, 643
Present value of an annuity of 1 table, B–6, B–13
Present value tables, 642, 643
Presentation issues, 100
Price-earnings ratio, 585, 586, 761, 762
Price variance, 1022, 1025, 1026
Priceline.com, 438
Pricewaterhouse-Coopers LLP, 14
Prime costs, 798
Principal of a note, 408
Principle of internal control, 354–356
Principles of accounting; *see* Accounting principles
Principles of internal control, 354–356
  bond key employees, 355
  establish responsibilities, 355
  insure assets, 355
  maintain adequate records, 255
  reviews, regular and independent, 356
  separate recordkeeping/custody of assets, 355
  separation of duties, 356
  technological controls, 356
Prior period adjustments, 582
Private accounting, 19
Privately held corporation, 556
Pro forma statements, 180
Process cost accounting system, 864–904, **869**
  direct/indirect costs, 869
  equivalent units of production, 873, 874
  factory overhead, 871–873
  first (grinding) department, 874–881
    cost per equivalent unit, 877
    cost reconciliation, 877, 878
    equivalent units of production, 875–877
    physical flow of units, 875
    process cost summary, 878, 879
    transfers between departments, 879, 881
  goods in process, 873
  job order systems, compared, 866
  labor costs, 871
  material costs, 870
  materials consumption report, 870
  organization of process operations, 867
  process cost summary, 878–880, 882, 883

second (mixing) department, 881–883
  transfers to finished goods inventory/cost of goods sold, 883, 884
Process cost summary, 878–880, 882, 883
Process manufacturing, 866
Process operations, 866
Process production, 866
Processes, 866
Processing transaction, 88–91
Procter & Gamble, 914
Product costs, 792, 793
Product warranties, 84
Production, 15
Production budget, 999
Profen, 867
Professional designations, 19, 20
Professional opinion, 18, 19
Profit, 5
Profit center, 914
Profit margin, 142, 760
Profitability, 743, 760
Profitability analysis, 760–762
  basic earnings per share, 763
  book value per common share, 763
  gross margin ratio, 763
  profit margin, 760
  return on common stockholders' equity, 762
  return on total assets, 760, 761
  summary of ratios, 763
Progress reports, 1018
Promissory note, 82, 407, 486
Promoters, 557
Property, plant, and equipment; *see* Plant assets
Proprietorship, 8
Prospectus, 560
Proxy, 558
Prudential Insurance Company, 615
Public accounting, 19
Public sale, 556
Publicly held corporation, 556
Purchase allowance, 220
Purchase discount, 219
Purchase order, 376, 377
Purchase requisition, 376
Purchase returns, 220
Purchases, 237, 238
  of equipment for cash, 47
  of equipment on credit, 47
  of merchandise; *see* Merchandise purchases
  of supplies for cash, 46
Purchases journal, 313, 314, 325, 326
Purchasing, 15

Q

QPR Management Software, 904
Quantity variance, 1022, 1025, 1026
Quick assets, 233
Quick ratio, 233, 756
QuickBooks, 317

R

Rate variance, 1025, 1026
Ratio, 754
Ratio analysis, 744, 754–763
  accounts receivable turnover, 756, 757
  acid-test ratio, 756
  average collection period, 757
  basic earnings per share, 763
  book value per common share, 763
  current ratio, 755, 756
  days' sales in inventory, 757, 758
  days' sales uncollected, 757
  debt ratio, 759
  defined, 744
  dividend yield, 762
  equity ratio, 759
  gross margin ratio, 763
  inventory turnover, 757
  liquidity/efficiency, 754–758
  market prospects, 761, 762
  PE ratio, 761, 762
  pledged assets to secured liabilities, 759
  profit margin, 760
  profitability, 760–762
  quick ratio, 756
  return on common stockholders' equity, 761
  return on total assets, 760, 761
  solvency, 758–760
  spreadsheet programs, 748
  summary of ratios, 763
  times interest earned, 759, 760
  total asset turnover, 758
  working capital, 754, 755
Raw materials inventory, 795
Raw materials inventory ledger account, 870
Real accounts, 170
Real-time inventory reports, 317
Realizable value, 401
Reasonably possible contingent liabilities, 496, 497
Receivables; *see* Accounts receivable; Notes receivable
Receiving accrual revenues, 139, 140
Receiving report, 377
Recordkeeping, 6, 355
Red Hot, 169
Redemption value, 567
Redhook Ale, 1027
Reebok, 17, 21, 32, 75, 165, 230, 390, A–11 to A–14, 560, 583, 611, 657, 672, 686, 737, 749, 753–762, 780
Registered bonds, 618
Registrar, 559
Regulators, 14
Relevance principle, 302
Relevant benefits, 1073
Relevant cost, 1072
Relevant information, 41
Relevant range, 791
Relevant range of operations, 956, 957

Reliable information, 41
Remittance advice, 367, 368
Repairs and maintenance, 449, 450
Report cards, 1018
Report form balance sheet, 140
Reporting income information, 576–581
  changes in accounting principles, 578, 579
  continuing operations, 576
  discontinuing segments, 576
  earnings per share, 579–581
  extraordinary items, 576–578
  stock options, 581
Research and development, 15
Residual value, 441
Responsibility accounting, 921–925
  controllable vs. direct costs, 922
  joint costs, 924, 925
  physical basis allocation of joint cost, 924, 925
  responsibility accounting system, 922–924
  value basis allocation of joint cost, 925
Responsibility accounting budget, 922
Responsibility accounting performance report, 922, 923
Responsibility accounting system, 913, 922–924
Responsibility center, 923
Restricted retained earnings, 582
Retail inventory method, 274, 275
Retailer, 214
Retained earnings, 40, 561, 581–583
  appropriated, 582
  changes in accounting estimates, 583
  prior period adjustments, 582
  restricted, 582
  statement of, 582
  statement of changes in stockholders' equity, 583
Retained earnings deficit, 569
Return, 5
Return on assets (ROA), 21, 672
Return on average investment, 1065
Return on common stockholders' equity, 761
Return on equity, 56
Return on investment, 5, 21
Return on sales, 142
Return on total assets, 672, 760, 761
Revaluation capital, 569
Revenue accounts, 85
Revenue expenditures, 449
Revenue recognition principle, 49
Revenues, 5, 37
Reverse stock split, 573

Reversing entries, 188–190
Ride, 584
Risk, 5
Risk-return tradeoff, 5
Ritz Carlton Hotel Company,
     L.L.C., 790
ROA, 21
Robert Morris Associates, 22, 754
ROI, 5, 21
Rolling budgets, 983
Rounding, 747
Russ, M. D., 277

S

S corporations, 9, 529, 530
S&P 500, 17
Safety stock, 987
Safety stock inventory systems,
     987
Safeway, 216
Saisu Technologies, 981
Salaries, 93, 489n
Salaries expense, 134, 135
Sales, 5; *see also* Merchandise
     sales
Sales allowances, 225
Sales budget, 986
Sales discounts, 219, 224, 225
Sales journal, 307–310
   direct posting of sales invoices,
     310
   journalizing, 307, 308
   periodic inventory system, 324,
     325
   positing, 308, 309
   proving the ledger, 309
   sales returns and allowances,
     310
   sales taxes, 309, 310
Sales mix, 960, 1077, 1078
Sales mix variance, 1037
Sales price variance, 1037
Sales quantity variance, 1037
Sales returns and allowances, 225,
     310
Sales slips, 355
Sales taxes, 309, 310
Sales taxes payable, 484
Sales variances, 1036, 1037
Sales volume variance, 1037
Salvage value, 441
SAP, 318
SBA, 636
Scanned sales data, 266
Scanners, 304
Scatter diagram, 951
**Schedule of accounts payable,
     314**
**Schedule of accounts receivable,
     309**
Schedule of cost of goods
     manufactured, 800, 801
Schedule of manufacturing
     activities, 800, 801
Schnatter, John, 436, 437
Score Board, 271
Scrap-or-rework decision, 1075,
     1076
Scrap value, 441

Seagate Technology, 695
Sears, Roebuck & Co., 85, 398,
     914
SEC, 7, 42
Sector 9, 481
Secured bonds, 615, 617
**Securities and Exchange
     Commission (SEC), 7,** 42
**Segment contribution matrix,
     319,** 320
Segment of a business, 576
Sell-or-process decision, 1076,
     1077
Selling accounts receivable, 411
Selling expense budget, 988
Selling expenses, 230
Selling short, 762, 764
Sensitivity analysis, 959, 960
Separation of duties
   computer systems, 357
   divide responsibility for related
     transactions, 356
   separate recordkeeping/custody
     of assets, 355
Serial bonds, 618
Service company, 786n, 794
Service departments, 908
Service life, 441
Services, capital, and stated ratio
     method of allocating
     partnership income, 532
Services revenue, 136
Servicing, 15
SFAS, 42
Shareholder rights, 558, 559
Shareholders, 9, 13, 14, 556
Shareholders' equity, 561
Shares, 9
Shoplifting, 227
Short selling, 762, 764
Short-term investments, 413–
     416
   available-for-sale securities,
     415, 416
   debt securities, 413
   equity securities, 413
   held-to-maturity securities, 414
   statement presentation, 416
   trading securities, 414, 415
Short-term liabilities, 482
Short-term note payable, 485–
     488
Shrinking, 227
Sierra Systems, 121
Signature card, 366
Significant influence, equity
     securities with, 666–668
Simple capital structure, 581n
**Single-step income statement,
     230,** 231
Sinking fund bonds, 618
Sinnock, Betty, 741
Sketchers, 396
Small Business Administration
     (SBA), 636
Small stock dividend, 570
Snyder, A. M., 983
Social programs, 17, 18
Social responsibility, 17, 18
Social Security benefits, 490

Social Security taxes, 490
Sole proprietorship, 8
Solvency, 743, 758
Solvency analysis, 758–760
   debt ratio, 759
   equity ratio, 759
   pledged assets to secured
     liabilities, 759
   summary of ratios, 763
   times interest earned, 759, 760
Sony, 440
Source documents, 80, 81, 303,
     832
Spade, Kate, 906, 907
Special journals, 305–316
   cash disbursements journal,
     315, 316, 326
   cash receipts journal, 311–313,
     325
   purchase journal, 313, 314,
     325, 326
   sales journal, 307–310, 324,
     325
Specific identification, 263, 264,
     284
Specific invoice inventory pricing,
     283
Specific principles, 43
Spending variance, 1031
Sports Illustrated, 497
Spreadsheet, 721
Spreadsheet programs, 317, 748
Sprint, 404
Staines, Chris, 661
Stair-step costs, 950
Standard & Poor's, 620, 742, 743
*Standard and Poor's Industry
     Surveys,* 754
Standard cost accounting system,
     1034–1036
Standard cost card, 1024
Standard costs, 1023–1034
   control, and, 1034
   cost variances; *see* Variance
     analysis
   defined, 1023
   ideal/practical standards, 1024
   identifying, 1023, 1024
   management by exception, 1034
   overhead standards, 1028–1030
   services, and, 1034
   setting, 1024
Standard labor cost, 1023
Standard materials cost, 1023
Standard overhead costs, 1023,
     1028, 1029
Standards for comparisons
   competitor, 744
   guidelines (rule of thumb), 744
   industry, 744
   intracompany, 744
Standards of ethical conduct for
     management accountants,
     824
Starbucks, 581
**State unemployment taxes
     (SUTA), 491**
Stated rate, 620
Stated ratio method of allocating
     partnership income, 532

Stated value stock, 561
Statement of cash flows, 39, 40,
     180, 181, 690–739, **692**
   analysis of equity, 715
   analysis of noncurrent assets,
     713, 714
   analysis of noncurrent
     liabilities, 714
   analyze cash account, 697
   analyze noncash accounts, 697,
     698
   analyzing cash sources/uses,
     716, 717
   bonds payable retirement, 714
   cash dividend payment, 715,
     716
   cash flow on total assets, 717,
     718
   cash flows from financing,
     713–716
   cash flows from investing, 712,
     713
   common stock issuance, 715
   direct method, 699; *see also*
     Direct method
   FASB recommendations, 699,
     706
   financing activities, 55, 694
   importance of cash flows, 692,
     693
   indirect method, 699; *see also*
     Direct method
   information to prepare
     statement, 698, 699
   international accounting
     standards, 696
   investing activities, 55
   noncash investing and
     financing, 694, 695
   operating activities, 55
   plant asset purchase, 712
   plant asset sale, 712, 713
   preparation, 53–55
   providing cash balances, 716
   purpose, 692
   reporting operating cash flows,
     699–711
   spreadsheet preparation, 721–
     723
   steps in preparation, 696, 697
**Statement of changes in owner's
     equity, 37,** 38
   adjusted trial balance, and, 140
   preparation, 53, 54
**Statement of changes in
     partners' equity, 534**
**Statement of changes in
     stockholders' equity, 583**
Statement of earnings, 505, 506
Statement of financial position;
   see Balance sheet
Statement of funds flow, 697
Statement of partners' capital, 534
Statement of retained earnings,
     582
**Statements of financial
     accounting standards
     (SFAS), 42**
Static budget, 1018
Statutory restriction, 582

Stear, Rory, 660, 661
Step-wise cost, 949, 950
Stewart, Rod, 615
Stock, 9
  capital; *see* Capital stock
  common; *see* Common stock
  preferred, 564–568; *see also*
    Preferred stock
  treasury, 573–575
Stock Certificate, 559
Stock dividends, 570–572
  cash flows, and, 695
  large, 570, 572
  reasons for, 570
  small, 570–572
Stock options, 581
Stock split, 572, 573
Stock subscriptions, 564n
Stockbrokers, 743
Stockholder meeting, 558
Stockholder rights, 558, 559
Stockholder's equity, 561
Stockholders, 9, 556
Store equipment, 83
Store supplies, 83
Straight-line depreciation, 132,
  442–444
Straight-line method, 622, 623,
  626
Strategic management, 11
Stride Rite, 101, 442
Subordinated debentures, 617
Subsequent events, 788
Subsidiary, 668
Subsidiary inventory records, 272
Subsidiary ledger, 306, 307
Subunits, 913
Sun Microsystems, 181
Sundaram Brake Linings (SBL),
  790
Sunk cost, 792, 1072
Supplemental records, 223
Supplementary records, 223
Suppliers, 14
Supplies, 130, 131
SUTA, 491
Sutton, Sara, 3

T

T-account, 86, 87
Take-home pay, 489
Takeover, 566n
Taking an inventory, 271
Tarantino, Tarina, 394, 395
Target, 287
Tarina Tarantino Designs, 395
Tax accounting, 19
Tax-exempt bonds, 618
Taylor, André, 690, 691
Technology
  accounting, and, 7
  database management
    programs, 317
  evidence of processing, 357
  extensive testing of records,
    357
  internal control, and, 356, 357
  inventory costing, 265, 266
  middleware, 317

off-the-shelf accounting
    programs, 317
real-time inventory reports, 317
reduced processing errors, 357
scanned sales data, 266
separation of duties, 357
spreadsheet programs, 317
word processing programs, 317
Technology-based accounting
  information systems, 316–
  318
Telfer, Dennis, 480, 481
Temporary accounts, 170
Temporary differences, 495
Temporary investments, 413–416
Term bonds, 618
The Gap; *see* Gap, Inc.
The Limited, 215
3Com, 304
Throughput time, 790
Ticker prices, 744
Ticker tape, 744
Time clock, 356
Time deposits, 359
Time period principle, 126
Time ticket, 833, 834
Time value of money
  future value of annuity, B–7,
    B–8
  future value of single amount,
    B–4, B–5
  future value tables, B–12, B–
    13
  present value of annuity, B–6
  present value of single amount,
    B–2 to B–4
  present value tables, B–12, B–
    13
Times interest earned, 499, 759,
  760
Toes on the Nose, 1017
Tools of analysis
  horizontal analysis, 745–749
  ratio analysis, 754–763
  vertical analysis, 749–753
Total asset turnover, 459, 460,
  758, 760
**Total quality management
  (TQM), 790**
Totes, 220
Toyota, 790
Toys "R" Us, 278
TQM, 790
Traceability of costs, 791, 792
Tracer Detection Technology, 355
Trade accounts payable, 484
Trade (brand) name, 459
Trade discount, 218
Trade payables, 83
Trademark, 459
Trading on the equity, 567
Trading securities, 414, 415
Transactions, 80
Transactions and the accounting
  equation, 46–52, 92–95
  accounting equation analysis,
    96
  facilities rendered for credit,
    49, 50
  investment by owner, 46, 92

payment of accounts payable,
  50, 94
payment of cash for future
  insurance coverage, 94
payment of expenses in cash,
  48, 93, 95
purchase equipment for cash,
  47, 92
purchase equipment on credit,
  47
purchase supplies for cash, 46,
  47, 92, 95
purchase supplies on credit, 47,
  92
receipt of cash for future
  services, 94
receipt of cash on account, 50,
  93
rental rendered for credit, 93
services rendered for cash, 47,
  48, 93
services rendered for credit, 49,
  50
withdrawal of cash by owner,
  51, 94
Transfer agent, 559
Transfer of ownership, 221, 222
Transfer pricing, 917
Transportation costs, 221
Transportation-in, 221
Transportation-out, 221
Transposition error, 98n, 99n
Treasury stock, 573–575
  purchasing, 573, 574
  reissuing, 574, 575
  retiring, 575
  selling above cost, 575
  selling at cost, 574
  selling bellow cost, 575
Trend analysis, 748, 749
Trend percent, 748
Trend percent analysis, 748
Trend percent lines, 749
Tri Star, 271
Trial balance, 97
  adjusted, 138, 139
  correcting errors, 100
  post–closing, 174
  preparing, 97
  presentation issues, 100
  searching for errors, 98
  unadjusted, 138, 139
  using, 97
Trustee, 619
Truth-in-Lending Act, 637
Two-stage cost allocation, 908, 909
2/10, n/60, 219
Tyco, 412

U

U.S. dollar, 670
Unadjusted trial balance, 138,
  139
Unavoidable expenses, 1079
Uncertainties, 497
Uncollectible accounts, 399; *see
  also* Bad debts
Uncollectible accounts expense,
  401

Uncontrollable costs, 922
Underapplied overhead, 839
Underfunded plan, 646
Underwriter, 619
Unearned revenues, 84, 133
  adjusting entries, 133, 134
  alternative accounting
    treatment, 145, 146
  known liabilities, as, 484, 485
  nature of, 84
Unemployment taxes, 491
Unfavorable variance, 1019
Union Camp, 695
Unit contribution margin, 802,
  803
**Units-of-production
  depreciation, 444**
Universal Studios, 668
Univision, 482
Unlimited liability, 529
Unregistered bonds, 618
Unsecured bonds, 617
Unusual gain or loss, 576
Upper Deck, 271
Upjohn, 670
Usage variance, 1025, 1026
Useful life, 441
Users of accounting information,
  13–16
  creditors, 13
  customers, 14
  distribution, 15
  employees, 14
  external users, 13, 14
  external auditors, 14
  human resources, 15
  internal users, 14, 15
  lenders, 13
  marketing, 15
  production, 15
  purchasing, 15
  regulators, 14
  research and development, 15
  servicing, 15
  suppliers, 14

V

Vacation pay, 493
Value basis allocation of joint
  cost, 925
Value chain, 800
Variable budget, 1020
Variable cost, 791, 800, 949
Variable costing, 955
Variable overhead, 800
Variable overhead variance, 1030,
  1032
Variance, 1024
Variance analysis, 1022–1034
  cost variance formulas, 1025
  defined, 1043
  labor cost variances, 1027, 1028
  material cost variances, 1026,
    1027
  overhead cost variances, 1030–
    1034
  price variance, 1025, 1026
  quantity variance, 1025, 1026
  sales variances, 1036, 1037

Vendee, 377
Vendor, 376
Vertical analysis, 744, 749–753
  common-size balance sheet,
    750
  common-size graphics, 750–
    753
  common-size income statement,
    750
  defined, 744
  spreadsheet programs, 748
Viisage Technology, 356
Virtual retinal display (VRD), 304
Volume variance, 1031
Voucher system, 361, 362, 375–
    378
  document flow, 362, 375–378
  invoice, 377
  invoice approval, 377
  nature of, 361, 362
  purchase order, 377
  purchase requisition, 377

  receiving report, 377
  voucher, 361, 362
VRD, 304

W

W.T. Grant Co., 692
**Wage bracket withholding table,
    507**
Wages, 93, 489n
Wal-Mart, 318, 360, 438, 914
Wall Street Journal, 762
Walt Disney, 128
Warranties, 84, **493**
Warranty liabilities, 493, 494
Wasting assets, 454
Weighted average, 265, 284, 285
Welinder, Per, 979
West, R. N., 983
Western Merchandisers, 217
Weyerhauser, 454
Wholesaler, 214

With recourse, 412
Withdrawals, 41
Withholding allowance, 507
Withholdings, 489
Without recourse, 412
Wolf, Amy Nye, 526, 527
Wooden Ships of Hoboken, 213
Woods, Tiger, 271
Word, 317
Word processing programs, 317
WordPerfect, 317
Work in process inventory,
    796
Work sheet, 174–180, 721
  application/analysis, 180
  benefits, 176
  merchandising company, 241,
    242
  steps in process, 177
  using, 176–180
Working capital, 754, 755
Working papers, 174, 721

World Wrestling Federation
    (WWF), 15, 457, 555, 583
Wrigley Company, 575

X

X-Caliber, 498
Xerox, 17, 1030

Y

Yahoo!, 458, 781
Young, Bob, 168, 169

Z

Zenith, 411, 493
Zero balance, 86, 90
Zero-coupon bonds, 620

Chart of Accounts

Assets

Current Assets

101 Cash
102 Petty cash
103 Cash equivalents
104 Short-term investments
105 Market adjustment, _____ securities (S-T)
106 Accounts receivable
107 Allowance for doubtful accounts
108 Legal fees receivable
109 Interest receivable
110 Rent receivable
111 Notes receivable
115 Subscriptions receivable, Common stock
116 Subscriptions receivable, Preferred stock
119 Merchandise inventory
120 _____ inventory
121 _____ inventory
124 Office supplies
125 Store supplies
126 _____ supplies
128 Prepaid insurance
129 Prepaid interest
131 Prepaid rent
132 Raw materials inventory
133 Goods in process inventory, _____
134 Goods in process inventory, _____
135 Finished goods inventory

Long-Term Investments

141 Long-term investments
142 Market adjustment, _____ securities (L-T)
144 Investment in _____
145 Bond sinking fund

Plant Assets

151 Automobiles
152 Accumulated depreciation, Automobiles
153 Trucks
154 Accumulated depreciation, Trucks
155 Boats
156 Accumulated depreciation, Boats
157 Professional library
158 Accumulated depreciation, Professional library
159 Law library
160 Accumulated depreciation, Law library
161 Furniture
162 Accumulated depreciation, Furniture
163 Office equipment
164 Accumulated depreciation, Office equipment
165 Store equipment
166 Accumulated depreciation, Store equipment
167 _____ equipment
168 Accumulated depreciation, _____ equipment
169 Machinery
170 Accumulated depreciation, Machinery
173 Building _____
174 Accumulated depreciation, Building _____
175 Building _____
176 Accumulated depreciation, Building _____
179 Land improvements _____
180 Accumulated depreciation, Land improvements _____
181 Land improvements _____
182 Accumulated depreciation, Land improvements _____
183 Land

Natural Resources

185 Mineral deposit
186 Accumulated depletion, Mineral deposit

Intangible Assets

191 Patents
192 Leasehold
193 Franchise
194 Copyrights
195 Leasehold improvements
196 Organization costs

Liabilities

Current Liabilities

201 Accounts payable
202 Insurance payable
203 Interest payable
204 Legal fees payable
207 Office salaries payable
208 Rent payable
209 Salaries payable
210 Wages payable
211 Accrued payroll payable
214 Estimated warranty liability
215 Income taxes payable
216 Common dividend payable
217 Preferred dividend payable
218 State unemployment taxes payable
219 Employee federal income taxes payable
221 Employee medical insurance payable
222 Employee retirement program payable
223 Employee union dues payable
224 Federal unemployment taxes payable
225 FICA taxes payable
226 Estimated vacation pay liability

Unearned Revenues

230 Unearned consulting fees
231 Unearned legal fees
232 Unearned property management fees
233 Unearned _____ fees
234 Unearned _____ fees
235 Unearned janitorial revenue
236 Unearned _____ revenue
238 Unearned rent

Notes Payable

240 Short-term notes payable
241 Discount on short-term notes payable
245 Notes payable
251 Long-term notes payable
252 Discount on long-term notes payable

Long-Term Liabilities

253 Long-term lease liability
255 Bonds payable
256 Discount on bonds payable
257 Premium on bonds payable
258 Deferred income tax liability

Equity

Owner's Equity

301 _____, Capital
302 _____, Withdrawals
303 _____, Capital
304 _____, Withdrawals
305 _____, Capital
306 _____, Withdrawals

Contributed Capital

307 Common stock, $ _____ par value
308 Common stock, no par
309 Common stock subscribed
310 Common stock dividend distributable
311 Contributed capital in excess of par value, Common stock
312 Contributed capital in excess of stated value, No-par common stock
313 Contributed capital from retirement of common stock
314 Contributed capital, Treasury stock
315 Preferred stock
316 Contributed capital in excess of par value, Preferred stock
317 Preferred stock subscribed

Retained Earnings

318 Retained earnings
319 Cash dividends declared
320 Stock dividends declared

Other Equity Accounts

321 Treasury stock, Common
322 Unrealized gain—Equity
323 Unrealized loss—Equity

Revenues

401 _____ fees earned
402 _____ fees earned
403 _____ services revenue
404 _____ services revenue
405 Commissions earned
406 Rent earned
407 Dividends earned
408 Earnings from investment in _____
409 Interest revenue (or Interest earned)
410 Sinking fund earnings
413 Sales
414 Sales returns and allowances
415 Sales discounts

Cost of Sales

Cost of Goods Sold

502 Cost of goods sold
505 Purchases
506 Purchases returns and allowances
507 Purchases discounts
508 Transportation-in

Manufacturing

520 Raw materials purchases
521 Freight-in on raw materials
530 Factory payroll
531 Direct labor
540 Factory overhead
541 Indirect materials
542 Indirect labor
543 Factory insurance expired
544 Factory supervision
545 Factory supplies used
546 Factory utilities
547 Miscellaneous production costs
548 Property taxes on factory building
549 Property taxes on factory equipment
550 Rent on factory building
551 Repairs, factory equipment
552 Small tools written off
560 Depreciation of factory equipment
561 Depreciation of factory building

Standard Cost Variance

580 Direct material quantity variance
581 Direct material price variance
582 Direct labor quantity variance
583 Direct labor price variance
584 Factory overhead volume variance
585 Factory overhead controllable variance

Expenses

Amortization, Depletion, and Depreciation

601 Amortization expense, _____
602 Amortization expense, _____
603 Depletion expense, _____
604 Depreciation expense, Boats
605 Depreciation expense, Automobiles
606 Depreciation expense, Building _____
607 Depreciation expense, Building _____
608 Depreciation expense, Land improvements _____
609 Depreciation expense, Land improvements _____
610 Depreciation expense, Law library
611 Depreciation expense, Trucks
612 Depreciation expense, _____ equipment
613 Depreciation expense, _____ equipment
614 Depreciation expense, _____
615 Depreciation expense, _____

Employee-Related Expenses

620 Office salaries expense
621 Sales salaries expense
622 Salaries expense
623 _____ wages expense
624 Employees' benefits expense
625 Payroll taxes expense

Financial Expenses

630 Cash over and short
631 Discounts lost
632 Factoring fee expense
633 Interest expense

Insurance Expenses

635 Insurance expense, Delivery equipment
636 Insurance expense, Office equipment
637 Insurance expense, _____

Rental Expenses

640 Rent expense
641 Rent expense, Office space
642 Rent expense, Selling space
643 Press rental expense
644 Truck rental expense
645 _____ rental expense

Supplies Expenses

650 Office supplies expense
651 Store supplies expense
652 _____ supplies expense
653 _____ supplies expense

Miscellaneous Expenses

655 Advertising expense
656 Bad debts expense
657 Blueprinting expense
658 Boat expense
659 Collection expense
661 Concessions expense
662 Credit card expense
663 Delivery expense
664 Dumping expense
667 Equipment expense
668 Food and drinks expense
669 Gas, oil, and repairs expense
671 Gas and oil expense
672 General and administrative expense
673 Janitorial expense
674 Legal fees expense
676 Mileage expense
677 Miscellaneous expenses
678 Mower and tools expense
679 Operating expense
681 Permits expense
682 Postage expense
683 Property taxes expense
684 Repairs expense, _____
685 Repairs expense, _____
687 Selling expense
688 Telephone expense
689 Travel and entertainment expense
690 Utilities expense
691 Warranty expense
695 Income taxes expense

Gains and Losses

701 Gain on retirement of bonds
702 Gain on sale of machinery
703 Gain on sale of short-term investments
704 Gain on sale of trucks
705 Gain on _____
706 Foreign exchange gain or loss
801 Loss on disposal of machinery
802 Loss on exchange of equipment
803 Loss on exchange of _____
804 Loss on sale of notes
805 Loss on retirement of bonds
806 Loss on sale of investments
807 Loss on sale of machinery
808 Loss on _____
809 Unrealized gain—Income
810 Unrealized loss—Income

Clearing Accounts

901 Income summary
902 Manufacturing summary